TLA Film & Video Guide

1998–1999

TLA FILM
AND
VIDEO
GUIDE

THE DISCERNING
FILM LOVER'S GUIDE
1998–1999

DAVID BLEILER
EDITOR

ST. MARTIN'S GRIFFIN
New York

Designed by TLA Publications®
1520 Locust Street
Suite 200
Philadelphia, PA. 19102

TLA Publications® is a registered trademark of TLA Entertainment Group, Inc.

ISBN 0–312–17053–X

First St. Martin's Griffin Edition: October 1997

10 9 8 7 6 5 4 3 2 1

TLA Film & Video Guide
The Discerning Film Lover's Guide
1998-1999

Edited by David Bleiler

MANAGING EDITOR/DESIGNER
Eric Moore

ASSOCIATE EDITORS
Marc Walkow
Ann M. Yarabinee

CONTRIBUTING EDITOR
S. Damien Segal

CONTRIBUTING ARTISTS
Robert Dieters
Kathleen Ziegler

CONTRIBUTING WRITERS
Dean C. Galanis
David Greenberg
Byl Holte
Claire Brown Kohler
Gary Kramer
John Libson
Jay Medley
Raymond Murray
Irv Slifkin
Geo. Stewart
Richard P. Mulhearn
Rachel Tubman

CONTENTS

INTRODUCTION

With the proliferation of movie and video books that has flooded the market these past few years, one might ask, "Do I really need another film/video guide?" My immediate response would be "Yes," if what you are looking for is an insightful, well-written and strongly opinionated publication that will assist you in choosing (and avoiding) films to rent (or watch on TV). The TLA Film and Video Guide does just that, and places an emphasis on international and independent cinema at no expense to mainstream movies. While "Leonard Maltin's Movie & Video Guide" and "Mick Martin & Marsha Porter's Video Movie Guide" are excellent reference sources, our reviews are more comprehensive in their critical analysis than the standard blurb found in these and other similarly themed books. This enables us to better explore a film's merits and shortcomings. And possibly more important, our critical eye for film allows the reader to discover many rewarding and possibly heretofore unknown movie gems which may have bypassed the traditional theatrical markets (just take a look at "TLA Favorites"). In other words, you'll find more eye-opening oddities and cinematic finds and less of the made-for-TV/made-for-cable/made-for-video/made-for-the-Quick Buck dreck that often fill the stacks of the typical video store.

The book is presented in an easy-to-read A-Z listing with over 8,500 titles reviewed. All films listed are obviously on video and are available for rental at TLA Video stores as well as better stocked stores throughout the United States and Canada. Most titles are available for sale and those that are not have not been given prices. Films have a star ratings system (from one to four) for easy review, and there is an exhaustive index and cross-reference system which highlights country of origin; film genres; director and star filmographies; and hundreds of themes (ranging from Adoption to Zombies and including writers and composers).

The history of TLA is important in understanding our commitment and enthusiasm to film and video. TLA Video was established in 1985 as a subsidiary of The Theatre of the Living Arts, a repertory cinema with a long history of presenting hundreds of films each year. The Theatre of the Living Arts was founded in the 1960s as a live performance house for alternative theatre, and featured a fledgling acting troupe that included Danny DeVito, Ron Liebman, Sally Kirkland and Judd Hirsch, under the direction of Andre Gregory. In the 1970s, the theatre reverted to its cinematic origins, and continued in that venue until its closing in 1987. That is when we concentrated our energies on home video while still being able to retain our commitment to the programming which made The Theatre of the Living Arts one of the nation's leading cinema houses — the same type of dedication which has now made TLA Video one of the most recognized and respected video businesses in the country.

Whether to steer you away from celluloid's worst (*Striptease, Speed 2*), offer suggestions on the overlooked and underappreciated (*Mars Attacks!, Brassed Off*), take a different approach to films you would ordinarily avoid (*Showgirls*), or simply highlight the best that cinema has to offer (*Fargo* and *Secrets and Lies* for example), it is my hope that the TLA Film & Video Guide will help in removing some of the promotional hype and its ensuing guess work out of your viewing decisions but without eliminating the exhilaration of the moviegoing experience.

—David Bleiler

ABOUT THE EDITOR:

David Bleiler has been involved in the film and video industry since the 1970s. He has worked in theatrical exhibition as manager and programmer for the Philadelphia art cinema Roxy Screening Rooms; in publishing as Senior Editor of *Home Viewer Magazine* and *Video Extra*, Managing Editor of the *New York Metro Herald*, Editor of "Images in the Dark," and has worked as a freelance film reviewer; and on radio (as a guest host on numerous film shows). He is currently Editor of *Rewind*, TLA Video's bimonthly entertainment magazine.

EXPLANATION OF TEXT

Alphabetization:

The guide is alphabetized in word order, not letter order, therefore *All That Jazz* would come before *Alligator*. Also, foreign titles adhere to the English rule concerning A, An and The beginning a sentence: whereas *The Godfather* would be listed under G; *La Cage aux Folles* would be listed under C, *Das Boot* under B, etc.

Foreign articles include:
French: *La, Le, Les, Un, Une*
German: *Das, Die*
Italian: *I, Il, La, Le*
Spanish: *El, La*
(American films beginning with *El* are listed under E)

With the exception of *Mrs.*, abbreviations are alphabetized under the word's full spelling:
Mr. Smith Goes to Washington is under *Mister*;
Dr. Strangelove is under *Doctor*;
The St. Valentine's Day Massacre is under *Saint*.

Pricing:

Prices listed are as of publication date. Many full price videos (in the $79.99-$99.99 range) are reduced six to nine months after their initial video release, so please call for updated information.

Certain titles are listed even though they were not available or announced as of publication date. In these instances, they were assumed to be full price.

In a case when a title has no price, that video was unavailable for sale at publication date; but it's possible it could be reissued later. Please call for updated information.

Index Listings:

There are several instances in which a film can be found in the indexes but lack a corresponding review. This is to make the indexes more complete and therefore more useful. However, only films on video have been mentioned.

Ordering:

To order any title listed in the TLA Film & Video Guide, use the handy order form located in the back of the book, or call the TLA Video 800 number listed on the form. TLA offers special rates to institutions and individuals placing large orders.

À la Mode

(1994, 90 min, France, Rémy Duchemin) Can you say "French fluff"? In some regards, this is too soft a term for this mildly enjoyable but ultimately wispy comedy. In keeping with the genre of "Sex and the French Teenager," *À la Mode* follows the ever eventful life of young Fausto – from the bicycle accident that leaves him orphaned to his apprenticeship with a Jewish tailor in Paris. It is not an exaggeration to say that practically nothing by way of significant story or character development comes Fausto's way, but he does, almost magically, find himself becoming a prestigious fashion designer – overnight! The standard stuff is on display here: the coy redhead with whom he gets his first lay, the good-hearted best friend with a talent for farting the tunes of Beethoven...beginning to get the picture? Still, the film is amiable, gooey fun and for those in search of hollow entertainment, this will be just the ticket. (French with English subtitles) ★★½ $19.99

À Nos Amours (To Our Lovers)

(1984, 102 min, France, Maurice Pialat) A beautifully rendered portrait of a sexually explosive young girl and her tumultuous home life. Sixteen-year-old Suzanne faces the wrath of a neurotic mother, a withdrawn father and an abusive brother because of her casually nubile air and promiscuous wanderings. This fascinating study of a smoldering family climate features Sandrine Bonnaire (*Vagabond*) who charges the role of the troubled teenager with a powerfully erotic presence. (French with English subtitles) ★★★½ $19.99

À Nous la Liberté

(1931, 97 min, France, René Clair) A surreal and satirical attack on automation and industrialization, this intoxicating, brilliantly executed romp follows the exploits of a bum who becomes a millionaire only to realize that he was happier poor. The central character and many comic scenes provided the inspiration for Charlie Chaplin's *Modern Times*. (French with English subtitles) ★★★★ $29.99

AMG — The Fantasy Factory/ Revisited/A Third Visit

(60 min, US) Pre-dating modern male pornography, the Los Angeles-based Athletic Model Guild, guided by Bob Mizer from the years 1956 thru 1969, produced thousands of nudie flicks that were for the most part the only sexually suggestive images available for gay men of that period. The films were not the feature-length hard-core videos of today, but almost chaste displays of male beauty (mainly the "boy next door" type) based around scenes of models posing, wrestling, and enactments of playful fantasies and male iconography (cops, Roman gladiators, prisoners, bikers, body-builders). Featuring men either scantily clad in posing straps or, in later films, flaccidly naked, these vidoes, narrated by Steve Malis, are compilations of many of these short (running two to nine minutes), black-and-white films that take the viewer nostalgically back to a more discreet time in male erotica. (*A Third Visit* sells for $39.99) $49.99

Aardman Animations

(1992, 60 min, US) An anthology of short films that is a must-see for anyone interested in clay animation. In addition to the several brilliant works featured in this collection, there is also a documentary about the Aardmans' unique style of animation. Their process of "lip-synching" original situations to pre-existing soundtracks results in astonishingly rich films that are both funny and haunting. Includes Nick Parks' Academy Award-winning *Creature Comforts.* ★★★ $29.99

Abbott and Costello Meet Dr. Jekyll and Mr. Hyde

(1953, 77 min, US, Charles Lamont) After much success meeting Frankenstein and Captain Kidd, Abbott and Costello set their sights on Robert Louis Stevenson's famous doc and his alter ego. In Victorian London, Bud & Lou are policemen on the trail of Jekyll, or is it Hyde? Some good laughs though the film is not as consistently funny as their earlier efforts. ★★½ $14.99

Abbott and Costello Meet Frankenstein

(1949, 83 min, US, Charles Barton) Bud and Lou found great success in this very funny horror spoof. The boys get involved with Frankenstein, Dracula and the Wolf Man (even the Invisible Man makes an "appearance"). There are plenty of snappy one-liners and silly shenanigans, and Bud and Lou's enjoyment is clearly infectious. The creatures are played by Glenn Strange, Bela Lugosi and Lon Chaney, Jr. ★★★½ $14.99

The Abduction from the Seraglio

(1980, 145 min, GB, Dave Heather) This extravagant, opulent production of Mozart's opera, staged by the Glyndebourne Festival Opera, features imaginative set design and costuming and joyful, engaging performances propelled by crystalline, mellifluous voices. Belmonte (Ryland Davies) seeks to rescue his fiancée Constanze (Valerie Masterson), who was captured by pirates and sold to the harem of the Turkish Pasha (Joachim Bissmeier). A frothy, pleasantly enjoyable variation on Mozart's recurring theme of tribulations com-

passionately resolved by a wise and merciful father figure. Also in good voice are Willard White, James Hoback and Lillian Watson, performing with the London Philharmonic Orchestra and the Glyndebourne Festival Chorus. ★★★½ $29.99

Abigail's Party

(1977, 105 min, GB, Mike Leigh) Allison Steadman stars as an overwrought hostess of a small get-together with the neighbors. Clearly adapted from the stage, the action is filmed on video and never leaves the claustrophobic confines of her living room. As she and her guests top off with gin and tonic after gin and tonic, the sparks begin to fly and her highly strung husband becomes all the more agitated. While the piece is filled with several hilarious moments, the overall tenor becomes more and more nerve-wracking due to Steadman's almost fascistic insistence that her guests "drink up." ★★½ $29.99

The Abominable Dr. Phibes

(1971, 94 min, GB, Robert Fuest) Vincent Price camps it up in one of the few horror films which successfully marries laughs and shivers. Joseph Cotten and Terry-Thomas are just two of the victims on whom Price seeks vengeance for his disfigurement and his wife's death. The Art Deco sets give the film a stylish look. ★★★ $9.99

About Last Night...

(1986, 113 min, US, Edward Zwick) David Mamet's play "Sexual Perversity in Chicago" comes to the screen in the form of this sluggish adaptation which fails to fully capture the play's hard edge. Rob Lowe and Demi Moore play Chicago singles who begin an affair, but their relationship suffers from Lowe's lack of commitment. Ditto the film. James Belushi and Elizabeth Perkins co-star in far more interesting roles as the leads' respective best friends. ★★ $14.99

Above Suspicion

(1943, 90 min, US, Richard Thorpe) Joan Crawford takes on the Nazis in this standard but nevertheless compelling spy thriller set in 1939. Crawford and Fred MacMurray are newlyweds on a European honeymoon who are

À la Mode

asked to do their part for British intelligence. Up against Joan, who had the benefit of those shoulders, the Germans never had a chance. ★★★ $19.99

Above the Law

(1988, 99 min, US, Andrew Davis) The fact that martial arts macho guy Steven Seagal was allowed to make more movies after this, his debut, must be proof of his being above the laws of common sense. Seagal's performance is robotic and difficult to watch and the story that he gets partial credit for is conventional, convoluted and, at times, preachy. On top of all that, the fight scenes here are surprisingly tame. Considering Seagal's much-hyped martial arts pedigree, one might expect at least some flashy moves, but our hero seems almost tentative here, mostly just pushing the cartoonish bad guys to the ground. Director Davis had previously made the half-decent Chuck Norris film *Code of Silence* and would go on to make *The Package* and *The Fugitive*, but here his talents seem to be in hibernation; there are few action sequences of note. ★★ $14.99

Absence of Malice

(1981, 116 min, US, Sydney Pollack) Paul Newman and Sally Field's first-rate performances distinguish this absorbing social drama about Newman's efforts to clear his name after reporter Field is duped into printing an article falsely implicating him in the murder of a union leader. Melinda Dillon gives a touching performance as Newman's girlfriend also affected by the story. Screenwriter Kurt Luedtke (a former reporter) has fashioned an insightful and penetrating treatise on the responsibility of the press and of the manipulation of truth and the media. Also with Bob Balaban and Wilford Brimley, who nearly steals the show as a no-nonsense prosecutor. ★★★ $14.99

Absolute Beginners

(1986, 107 min, GB, Julien Temple) Temple's rousing musical is a journey into the heart of the swinging teenage scene of London in the late 1950s and the brutal racism which still afflicts that city today. Eddie O'Connell stars as a young photographer drawn into the music and fashion worlds; Patsy Kensit is the designer he's in love with. David Bowie makes a neat cameo as a slick associate of the nefarious James Fox, and he sings the title tune, too. The music, as orchestrated by jazz giant Gil Evans, is unbeatable and includes a truly seductive number by Sade. ★★★½ $14.99

Absolute Power

(1997, 120 min, US, Clint Eastwood) There's more to worry about than campaign finances and Congressional mistrust in President Alan Richmond's White House; the Secret Service has just murdered his girlfriend, and hampering a cover-up is the witness who was hiding in the next room. In Eastwood's sleek, competent thriller, efficiently adapted by William Goldman (based on David Baldacci's novel), politics does indeed breed strange bedfellows. Giving a particularly effacing, witty performance, Eastwood plays Luther Whitney, a thief who is now on the run after witnessing the handywork of President Richmond (played

with great vigor and venom by Gene Hackman) and his staff. All of Washington, D.C. becomes a board game of cat and mouse as Whitney tries to elude government agents, the police (led by a no-nonsense Ed Harris) and questions from his estranged daughter (Laura Linney). That this works at all is testament to director Eastwood — he sets up many scenes with the clarity of Hitchcock even if some of the story isn't always plausible. But it's always in focus, and *Absolute Power* is a wild ride up and down the Beltway all the same. ★★★ $102.99

Absolutely Fabulous

(1991-96, 90 min each, GB) Edina Monsoon (Jennifer Saunders), actively recuperating from her psychedelic teen years, has never met a fad she didn't like. Patsy Stone (Joanna Lumley), Eddie's best friend, confidante and leech, consumes drink and drugs as others breathe, and will hump anything with a pulse. They are selfish, manipulative, shameless, contemptuous and completely without any trace of redeeming value save this: They are hysterically funny. They utterly exploit family, friends, employees and indigent nations in their ceaseless quest to acquire things. *Anythings*. Their escapades are punctuated with flashbacks to their youth, when they first became allies against a world burdened with rules, expectations and dress codes. Eddie's daughter Saffron has devised the ultimate rebellion: utter normalcy. Eddie is also at war with her two ex-husbands and her dotty British mum, while Patsy rails at the ghost of her bohemian mother. Is their frenetic obsession for consumer products driven by the void of existential despair? Are they never satisfied because their real, unrecognized needs are spiritual, not material? Who cares? Pour yourself a glass of wine, darling, and indulge in rude, wickedly funny and extremely witty excess. Just don't look in any mirrors for a while afterwards. ★★★½ $19.99 each

Series 1, Part 1: Edina and Patsy discover "Fashion" when they organize a show; Is Edina getting "Fat"? It's time to exercise, or liposuction; The girls are bound for "France" but this vacation isn't exactly what they had in mind.

Series 1, Part 2: Eddie's daughter is graduating, and she's stuck in an "Iso Tank"; It's Eddie's "Birthday," and life isn't beginning very well at 40; In "Magazine," Eddie has a new boyfriend, and it's not fair that Patsy doesn't have one.

Series 2, Part 1: Patsy has to look 35 for a magazine article, so is it a trip to the "Hospital" to do it?; In "Death," Eddie's father dies, but is it art?; Eddie and Patsy take a trip to "Morocco" on a fashion shoot.

Series 2, Part 2: "New Best Friend" finds old friends coming to visit; Will Eddie be "Poor" when her two ex-husbands cut her off?; Eddie thinks Saffron's ready to give "Birth" when she discovers the teen may have a boyfriend.

Series 3, Part 1: Will Edina fly all the way to New York just to purchase a "Doorhandle"?; It's all for fun and fun for all as Eddie and Patsy have a "Happy New Year"; The girls have "sex" on the brain when they plan an orgy to get in touch with their inner selves.

Series 3, Part 2: Model Naomi Campbell appears as Eddie gets "Jealous"; "Fear" is all that's left when Patsy threatens to move to New York; It's "The End" when Eddie searches for Patsy in New York.

"The Last Shout": The very final episode of "Absolutely Fabulous." Edina's near-death experience on the Alpine slopes coupled with daughter Saffron's impending marriage bring out Eddie's own inimitable brand of mother love and caretaking. Another frenetic, high-octane ride through the pop cultural morass of the late 20th century. The two-episode tape runs 100 minutes.

Absolution

(1978, 105 min, GB, Anthony Page) Another wicked thriller from Anthony Shaffer, the author of *Sleuth*. Richard Burton stars as a "holier-than-thou" priest whose teaching efforts at a Catholic boarding school are mocked by his mischievous star pupil, with tragic results. Though made in 1978, the film was not released in this country until 1988, four years after Burton's death. ★★★ $9.99

Abuse

(1983, 85 min, US, Arthur Bressan, Jr.) This daring, powerful yet sensitive account of a battered adolescent's coming to grips with his abusive parents and his awakening homosexuality caused quite a stir in the gay community with its positive approach to man/boy love. While filming a documentary on child abuse for his master's thesis, 35-year-old Larry (Richard Ryder) meets 14-year-old Thomas (Raphael Sbarge), the victim of abuse from his violent mother and father. The two become close, with Thomas beginning a healing process with the help of the older filmmaker. Their nurturing relationship, spurred by the advances of Thomas, eventually turns to love. Faced with certain breakup and, for Thomas, more beatings, they flee together to San Francisco. A controversial film which isn't quite as incendiary as it may appear. ★★★ $79.99

The Abyss

(1989, 145 min, US, James Cameron) Outstanding special effects and production design highlight this suspenseful underwater science-fiction adventure. Though Cameron combines the same excitement and tension he created in *Aliens* and *The Terminator*, he shifts the pace halfway through the film, and the result is a heart-pounding thriller which gradually becomes an under-the-sea *E.T.* Ed Harris stars as the commander of an oil rigging outfit who makes contact with an alien being. Forget the similarly themed *Deep Star Six* and the silly *Leviathan* which came before it, for this is far superior entertainment. (Letterboxed version of the director's cut is available for $19.99) ★★★ $9.99

Accattone!

(1961, 120 min, Italy, Pier Paolo Pasolini) Pasolini's first feature film is a harrowing, realistic and unsentimental look inside the slums of Rome, where its denizens — the prostitutes, hustlers and petty thieves — attempt to eke out an existence any way they can. Within this underworld of corruption is Accattone (Franco Citti), a young pimp who is torn

Ace Ventura When Nature Calls

between the easy pickings on the street and his efforts, motivated by love, to go straight. A brutal slice-of-life film which documents Pasolini's lifelong obsession with the outcasts of society, an obsession which eventually led to his death in 1975 at the hands of a man not unlike Accattone. Pasolini was assisted on the film by a young Bernardo Bertolucci. (Italian with English subtitles) ★★★½ $29.99

Accident

(1967, 105 min, GB, Joseph Losey) Harold Pinter wrote the screenplay adaptation for this penetrating and thought-provoking examination of a love affair between a professor (Dirk Bogarde) and his student (Jacqueline Sassard). Bogarde and Michael York both deliver sterling performances in this complex psychological drama. ★★★½

The Accidental Tourist

(1988, 121 min, US, Lawrence Kasdan) William Hurt stars in this Oscar-nominated adaptation of Anne Tyler's whimsical best-seller as an emotionally numb travel guide writer who must begin life anew after the death of his young son and separation from his wife (Kathleen Turner). As he sets out into the world, he becomes involved, almost unwittingly, with an eccentric dog trainer (Geena Davis) who slowly reawakens his long-dormant feelings. The film, like its hero, is leisurely and a bit distant but also enormously endearing, thanks mostly to a refreshingly open and enchanting performance by Oscar-winner Davis. ★★★ $14.99

The Accompanist

(1992, 111 min, France, Claude Miller) Sophie, a naive, unworldly 20-year-old pianist in Nazi-occupied France, is hired as accompanist to a concert vocalist, a beautiful and talented woman who, with her industrialist husband, is viewed as a collaborator. As the young Sophie, Romane Bohringer's subdued, con-

trolled performance is in marked contrast to her frenzied portrayal in *Savage Nights*. Sophie is an accompanist not only in concerts and practice sessions: She views it as her life's role, and not even the devastation and upheaval of war shakes her position of observer and accomplice. The film's denouement is curiously anticlimactic, yet is an unnerving reflection of Sophie's suppressed affect and despondency. In the end, a disturbing character study of an isolated individual adrift in a world of turmoil. Also with Elena Safonova and Richard Bohringer. (French with English subtitles) ★★★ $19.99

The Accused

(1988, 110 min, US, Jonathan Kaplan) Jodie Foster and Kelly McGillis star in this harrowing and hard-hitting look at the emotional and moral consequences of rape. Foster won an Oscar for her stunning and gritty portrayal of a back room gang rape victim who struggles to regain her self-respect while battling an insensitive legal system. McGillis is compelling as the prosecuting attorney who becomes entangled in her own moral sense of right and wrong. Based on an actual and highly publicized incident, this superbly acted and tightly focused film expertly examines the pain endured by the victims of rape long after the crime has been committed. ★★★ $14.99

Ace Ventura: Pet Detective

(1994, 85 min, US, Tom Shadyac) This nauseating comedy stars "In Living Color"'s Jim Carrey and became a surprise box-office success, sending Carrey to the unlikely ranks of stardom. To be fair, Carrey is an outstanding physical comedian, but his schtick needs the support of an intelligent script and that is what's most lacking here. The story follows the exploits of Carrey's Ace Ventura, who retrieves lost or stolen pets for their heartbroken owners. Hired by the Miami Dolphins to locate their kidnapped mascot, he finds himself

doing battle with Miami's police chief, played by Sean Young, who yawns her way through the film with the excitement of a tranquilized basset hound. ★½ $14.99

Ace Ventura When Nature Calls

(1995, 92 min, US, Steve Oedekerk) Jim Carrey returns in this annoying hit comedy sequel as the incompetent pet detective Ace Ventura. With a motto of "If they loved stupid in the first film, give 'em more of it," this second film starts off with a couple of funny and silly laughs with a way over-the-top Carrey shamelessy mugging and making idiotic faces. A couple good sight gags (and a William Shatner imitation) seem to get the film rolling. However, the ridiculous and boring plot takes over – about Ace tracking down the sacred bat of an African village – and no matter how much Carrey wiggles his ears, screams, dances or says "All righty," *Ace Ventura When Nature Calls* is a poor excuse for comedy and enough to insult the very memory of those broadly played Jerry Lewis comedies of the 1960s – for which Carrey obviously has an affection. No one expects high-brow from Ace, but Carrey is such a talented comedian we all have a right to expect better. ★½ $14.99

Aclá

(1992, 86 min, Italy, Aurelio Grimaldi) The inordinately harsh life of Sicilian peasant miners – and one blond, 11-year-old boy in particular – in 1930s Italy is the subject of this unrelentingly grim drama. Young Aclá, a handsome youth with a streak of independence, comes of age to accompany his father and two older brothers to the underground sulfur mines where they work six days a week for little pay and food. He is sold off as an indentured worker, a virtual slave and must endure horrible conditions made worse by the casual brutality inflicted on him. Only his dreams of the sea and escape enable Aclá to struggle against the surrounding inhumanity. Using poetic (pederastic?) license, the director displays all of the workers in the excessively hot mines laboring only in loincloths, and casual homosexual acts between the mostly heterosexual workers is depicted. (Italian with English subtitles) ★★½ $69.99

Acqua e Sapone

(1983, 100 min, Italy, Carlo Verdone) A high-spirited comedy that follows the adventures of a world-famous young fashion model let loose upon the city of Rome. Complications arise when her strict tutor, who was hired to accompany the model by her overprotective mother, is impersonated by a randy janitor. (Italian with English subtitles) ★★★ $19.99

Across 110th Street

(1972, 102 min, US, Barry Shear) Three black men hit a Mafia cash drop in Harlem for $300,000, killing family members, associates and two policemen, precipitating an intensive manhunt – one conducted by the police, the other by the mob with their Harlem business partners. Racism is the permeating undercurrent, defining the tensions between the Mafia and their Harlem counterparts, and mirrored in the relationship between white, old-guard captain Anthony Quinn and black lieutenant

Katharine Hepburn (r.), Judy Holliday (c.) and Spencer Tracy star in *Adam's Rib* (1949)

Yaphet Kotto, who's placed in charge of the investigation. The hunt is made easier by the free-wheeling spending of one of the hit men (Antonio Fargas), whose tell-tale behavior compromises his accomplices. The film is harsh, rough-hewn and uncompromising, filled with raw anger and seething violence, and bolstered by on-target performances from the entire cast, which also includes Anthony Franciosa, Richard Ward and Paul Benjamin. ★★★ $14.99

Across the Pacific

(1942, 97 min, US, John Huston) Director Huston and his *Maltese Falcon* stars Humphrey Bogart, Mary Astor and Sydney Greenstreet reteamed for this involving spy thriller. Bogey goes undercover and sets sail for the Orient to get the goods on agent Greenstreet. Astor is the mysterious passenger romanced by Bogart. Suspenseful action, more humor than would be expected, and solid performances by all make this a winner. ★★★ $19.99

Acting on Impulse

(1993, 93 min, US, Sam Irvin) Made for cable, this comic thriller has its tongue planted firmly in cheek, as with director Irvin's previous outing *Guilty as Charged*. The ravishing Linda Fiorentino plays a "scream queen" goddess of B-horror films. After a fatal argument in which her producer is found dead, Fiorentino sets out for a little R&R, where she is stalked by "adoring" fans. Then the body count starts piling up. Featuring a little lesbian teasing between a playful Fiorentino and Nancy Allen, and a steamy Fiorentino-C. Thomas Howell sex scene, the film is leisurely paced, offers a few well-placed jabs at the horror film industry, and has an eclectic supporting line-up, including Dick Sargent, Paul Bartel, Adam Ant, Isaac Hayes, Zelda Rubinstein and Mary Woronov. ★★½ $89.99

Action in the North Atlantic

(1943, 127 min, US, Lloyd Bacon) Humphrey Bogart heads a good cast in this stirring WWII actioner with Bogey and Raymond Massey as Merchant Marine officers leading their men in action against the Nazis in the North Atlantic. Also with Alan Hale and Ruth Gordon. ★★★ $19.99

Action Jackson

(1988, 95 min, US, Craig R. Baxley) Carl Weathers stars as the title character in this

stiffly acted but ultimately satisfying panoply of car chases, explosions and fist fights. Weathers' Jackson is an ex-cop who is determined to uncover the evil doings of an unscrupulous businessman (Craig T. Nelson) who had been the instrument of Jackson's fall from grace. Vanity is the token dame who accompanies Weathers on his vengeful rampage. Bill Duke and Sharon Stone also appear in support in this pyrotechnical juggernaut that is short on script and short on ideas, but so what. It's enjoyable, combustible fun nonetheless. ★★½ $14.99

An Actor's Revenge

(1963, 113 min, Japan, Kon Ichikawa) With magnificently stylized sets, vibrant color and a spectacular performance by Kabuki actor Kazuo Hasegawa, this tale of revenge and murder ranks as one of Japan's greatest films. Set in the early part of the 19th century, Hasegawa, an *onnagata* (female impersonator) of the Kabuki theatre, discovers the identity of the three nobles who forced the suicide of his parents many years before. In an elaborate scheme of revenge, our hero/heroine exacts a plot that does not have him simply kill them, but rather have the men turn against themselves or die at their own hands. A complex period melodrama that concerns itself with opposites: love/hate, illusion/reality, masculinity/femininity. (Japanese with English subtitles) ★★★★ $29.99

Adam Had Four Sons

(1941, 81 min, US, Gregory Ratoff) Ingrid Bergman is in Bette Davis/*All This and Heaven, Too* territory as a governess looking after four children after their mother dies. Warner Baxter is the father, and a young Susan Hayward plays the "bad" girl who pits the family against each other. Warm dramatics and a pleasing performance by Bergman more than compensate for the sometimes predictable direction of the story line. ★★★ $59.99

Adam's Rib

(1949, 101 min, US, George Cukor) In their sixth film together, Katharine Hepburn and Spencer Tracy demonstrate such a magnificent rapport on-screen that they make (with exception to *Woman of the Year*) their prior film appearances together look like blind dates by comparison. Kate and Spence play lawyers handling opposite sides of a murder case. He's the prosecutor, she's the defense attorney. In her first major role, Judy Holliday is the defendant accused of trying to murder her philandering husband (Tom Ewell). Garson Kanin and Ruth Gordon's wonderfully funny screenplay is full of sublime observations on romantic expectations and the roles men and women play (or are expected to play), and director Cukor deftly brings together slapstick, sophistication and romance to create a classic battle-of-the-sexes comedy. ★★★★ $19.99

Adam's Rib

(1992, 77 min, USSR, Vyacheslav Krishtofovich) Based on the novel "House of Young Women" by Anatole Kourtchatkine,

Adam's Rib is a wonderfully endearing story revolving around three generations of Russian women (a grandmother, mother, and her two daughters) all sharing the same apartment. The film slips in elements of coming-of-age and parental disputes with social commentary on the new elements of capitalism in Russia. Lida, the older daughter, is having an affair with a married man while the younger daughter is a rebel and a savvy businessperson. Mother is trying to make ends meet, take care of her ailing mother and she just happens to be picked up by a farmer at her job. A poignant and quite remarkable film. (Russian with English subtitles) ★★★★ $19.99

The Addams Family

(1991, 102 min, US, Barry Sonnenfeld) First-time director Sonnenfeld's (former cinematographer for the Coen brothers) hilarious revival of the cult-TV series may be thin on plot, but don't let that dissaude you from renting it, for the action flies furiously and the laughs are abundant. Raul Julia and Anjelica Huston deliver inspired, passionately macabre performances as Gomez and Morticia, the bizzare patriarch and matriarch of Charles Addams' ghoulish family (thankfully, they do justice to the characters created by John Astin and Carolyn Jones). Christopher Lloyd feasts on the role of Uncle Fester and young Christina Ricci is devilishly coy as the younger Addams, Wednesday, with a penchant for girl scout cookies made from *real* girl scouts. Followed by an equally enjoyable sequel, *Addams Family Values*. ★★★ $14.99

Addams Family Values

(1993, 87 min, US, Barry Sonnenfeld) Dripping with deliciously mordant one-liners, this outlandish sequel to *The Addams Family* is a possibly funnier outing than the original. Morticia (the unearthly and serene Anjelica Huston) has a baby, Pubert, much to the delight of Gomez (Raul Julia) and most of the family. The children, Pugsly (Jimmy Workman) and Wednesday (Christina Ricci), however, see the little nipper as nothing more than an usurper and respond to his arrival with murderous zeal. The kids are soon dragged off to summer camp by the baby's new nanny (Joan Cusack), a gold-digging black widow with designs on Fester (Christopher Lloyd). This broad plot outline is ripe with hilariously morbid jokes and is a sly fable on the revenge of the outcasts. Ricci is especially good as the death-obsessed, pale-faced Wednesday, who supplies the film with its best retorts. ★★★ $9.99

Addicted to Love

(1997, 100 min, US, Griffin Dunne) If love is a game for fools, then in Dunne's sometimes very funny but unrealized black comedy on obsessive love, it's not how you play the game, but whether you win or lose. When his fiancée Linda leaves him for handsome Frenchman Anton, astronomer Sam (Matthew Broderick) begins spying on her. The sparks of retaliation begin to fly when Maggie (Meg Ryan), Anton's former girlfriend, joins Sam in his *Rear Window* vigil from the abandoned building across the street. Maggie and Sam soon engage in a revenge scheme which begins as a series of set-ups and which eventually escalates into often hilarious bits of malicious "ex"-bashings. Though nasty as it wants to be, *Addicted to Love*'s shortcoming is that it aims for the jugular but often settles for the aorta, and for this type of venom to work, the mean-spiritedness must be consistent. When *Love* loses its edge, it becomes just another dopey, insufficient romantic comedy. Ryan and Broderick, both of whom can be cloyingly cute, have a wonderful chemistry and seem to really enjoy the progeny of their nefarious shenanigans. ★★½ $102.99

The Addiction

(1995, 84 min, US, Abel Ferrara) Needlessly dense, pretentious, and shot so amateurishly as to sometimes look like a student film, *The Addiction* is Ferrara's take on the vampire mythos, equating vampirism with a physical drug addiction and setting its latest telling among the angst-ridden, *tres existentielle* intellectual elite of New York City's graduate student culture. Lili Taylor plays a philosophy doctoral student who is bitten by a vampire (Annabella Sciorra). She spends the rest of the film trying to come to terms with her new existence as a nocturnal predator. Light on narrative, the film's characters spend most of their time in philosophical discussions, which works completely against the purposes of the film. Not even the presence of real-life vampire Christopher Walken can enliven the film. His unfortunately short scene is the best. He begins as a potential victim of Taylor's, but turns out to be another vampire. While the premise of the film is intriguing and a few sequences shine through as something unique to the genre, *The Addiction* is ultimately a horror film without any scares, a philosophical meditation without any good ideas, and a vampire film without any blood. ★½ $96.99

L'Addition (The Patsy)

(1984, 93 min, France, Denis Amar) This incisive and compelling prison drama stars Richard Berry as an out-of-work actor who gets himself imprisoned when he goes to the aid of a woman accused of shoplifting. From there it is an ever-deepening descent into hell as he becomes the twisted obsession of a sadistic prison guard who follows the rules only as a means to pervert them. (aka: *The Caged Heart*) (Dubbed) ★★★

The Adjuster

(1992, 102 min, Canada, Atom Egoyan) With his earlier efforts *Speaking Parts* and *Family Viewing*, director Egoyan firmly established himself as one of the most original, and bizarre, filmmakers, and he certainly doesn't disappoint here. Egoyan's twisted tale follows Noah Render (Elias Koteas), a predatory insurance adjuster who shows up at house fires to comfort the victims and process their claims. He keeps all of his clients in a run-down motel, where he visits them daily, often engaging them in sex (male and female alike). Meanwhile, his wife (played by Egoyan's real-life spouse Arsinee Khanjian) is secretly videotaping the graphic sex she watches as part of her job as a government censor. Into the picture comes Bubba (Maury Chaykin), an off-the-wall con artist who convinces the Renders that he wants to use their house (a lonely model unit in an as-of-yet unbuilt develop-

ment) to make a film. Egoyan uses this odd conglomeration of circumstances to plumb the depths of his characters' existential loneliness and to voyeuristically expose their sexual proclivities. ★★★½ $19.99

Adoption

(1975, 89 min, Hungary, Márta Mészáros) The winner of the Best Film award at the Berlin Film Festival. Kati wants a child, but her married lover is insensitive to her desire. So it is up to Anna, her newfound friend, to help her fulfill her dream of motherhood and learn about love and survival. A warm and intimate drama exploring a love and friendship between two women. (Hungarian with English subtitles) ★★★ $69.99

Adult Animation

(1976-1988, US) While not as "dirty" as some of the films in our X-rated cartoon collection, this compilation of eight shorts attempts a little more by focusing on the humor, smut, loneliness and sadness inherent in sex and love. Initiating the series is *The Censor*, a very funny spoof on the prurient tastes of a censorship board. Other highlights include *Night on the Town*, a Brothers Quay-influenced urban nightmare; the gruesomely surreal *Malice in Wonderland*; and a fun short of local interest, *Wild Times in the Wildwoods*. ★★★ $29.99

Adventures in Babysitting

(1987, 99 min, US, Chris Columbus) There's charm to spare in this entertaining teen comedy with Elisabeth Shue (long before her *Leaving Las Vegas* triumph) a delight as a babysitter whose journey into Chicago with her three charges turns into a comic nightmare. Directorial debut for writer Columbus, who would go on to helm such hits as *Home Alone* and *Mrs. Doubtfire*. ★★★ $9.99

The Adventures of Baron Munchausen

(1989, 126 min, GB, Terry Gilliam) The third and final entry in director Gilliam's fantasy trilogy (*Time Bandits* and *Brazil* were before it) is a whimsical, outlandishly funny and visually

stunning adventure film chronicling the amazing exploits of the infamous adventurer/explorer/soldier and man-about-town, Baron Munchausen. Set during the late 18th century, the film follows the odyssey taken by a now-older Baron who travels to the Moon, Heaven and numerous exotic locations in-between, to help save a small city under siege. ★★★ $14.99

The Adventures of Buckaroo Banzai

(1984, 103 min, US, W.D. Richter) Renowned neurosurgeon, respected physicist and charismatic rock star...he's Buckaroo Banzai — savior of the universe and star of this gonzo sci-fi fantasy. Don't even bother to follow the pretzel-like plot twists; just remember: red Lectroids dislike black Lectroids, Rastafarians in silver lamé sports coats are on our side, Lord John Whorfin (alias Emilio Lizardo) is a dastardly sort and no matter where you go...there you are. Peter Weller as Buckaroo is joined by John Lithgow, Ellen Barkin, Jeff Goldblum and Christopher Lloyd. ★★★

Adventures of Don Juan

(1948, 110 min, US, Vincent Sherman) Errol Flynn is in swashbuckling good form in this opulent costumer. Flynn stars as the legendary Spanish lover who battles the evil Duke de Lorca and protects the royal crown. Much of the mood is tongue-in-cheek, and Flynn, though a decade past his great '30s epics, and resembling Ronald Colman, still cuts a fine figure. Max Steiner's score and the outstanding sets and costumes help immeasurably. ★★★ $19.99

The Adventures of Eliza Fraser

(1976, 114 min, Australia, Tim Burstall) In the mood for an Australian burlesque period romp starring British actress Susannah York? If that doesn't scare you off, read on... Reminiscent of the American West, 1830s Australia was a lawless and untamed land and definitely not a place for a beautiful, cultured woman. Eliza Fraser not only survived but flourished despite the chains of a jealous husband, being pursued and lusted after by penal

Arsinee Khanjian bootlegs the graphic sex she's paid to censor in *The Adjuster*

A

5

colony escapees, being involved in a shipwreck, captured by aboriginal savages and even hounded by the police. This is her *Indiana Jones*-like tale of courage and rollicking adventures. ★★½ $14.99

The Adventures of Ford Fairlane

(1990, 96 min, US, Renny Harlin) Forget the controversy surrounding comic Andrew Dice Clay and his treatment of women and minorities; his starring debut is just a bad film. Clay's arrogant, chauvinistic persona, here in the form of a detective, is the center of an unfunny comedy which is poorly scripted and directed, and whose rambling plot will keep one and all scratching their head in disbelief and confusion. ★ $19.99

The Adventures of Huck Finn

(1993, 106 min, US, Stephen Sommers) Disney's version of the Mark Twain classic is a highly entertaining adaptation which should more than entrance children of most ages, effortlessly transporting them to another time and place. Sparked by two engaging performances from young Elijah Wood as the mischievous Huck, and Courtney B. Vance, with a slightly modernized but appropriate interpretation of runaway slave Jim, the film is actually better than most screen versions — though the best is probably still the 1939 film with Mickey Rooney. Jason Robards and Robbie Coltrane, both enjoying themselves overplaying their parts as greedy con men, add to the film's level of high-spiritedness and rustic charm, as does a good evocation of 19th-century America. ★★★ $9.99

The Adventures of Huckleberry Finn

(1939, 90 min, US, Richard Thorpe) Faithful film version of Mark Twain's family classic about the misadventures of Mississippi youths Huck Finn and Tom Sawyer, and of Huck's relationship with Jim, a runaway slave. Starring Mickey Rooney, Walter Connelly, Rex Ingram and William Frawley. Of all the many screen versions, this may well be the best. ★★★ $19.99

The Adventures of Mark Twain

(1986, 90 min, US, Will Vinton) Outstanding claymation highlights this average children's film about Twain characters Huck Finn, Tom Sawyer and Becky Thatcher accompanying their literary creator on a balloon ride to Halley's Comet. ★★½ $14.99

The Adventures of Milo and Otis

(1986, 76 min, Japan, Masanori Hata) Sort of like "Wild Kingdom" for the pet set, this lushly photographed nature story about the friendship and adventures of a kitten and dog has shown remarkable appeal with children. It's harmless, corny and just the change of pace from old "Lassie" reruns. This version, longer than the original Japanese film, is narrated by Dudley Moore. ★★ $14.99

Adventures of Picasso

(1978, 88 min, Sweden, Tage Danielsson) The wacky life of Pablo Picasso is imaginatively recounted in this mad farce that promises to reveal "1,000 loving lies" about his mythical life and times. Actually, the film — similar in style and veracity to *Young Einstein* — bears

absolutely no relation to the famous man, but uses his biography as a springboard to those crazy times and even crazier people who inhabited the bohemian art world in Europe at the early part of the 20th century. Spoken in many languages but only using simple words, grunts or noises, the film is a funny if not labored attempt at tickling the international funny bone. ★★½

The Adventures of Priscilla, Queen of the Desert

(1994, 102 min, Australia, Stephan Elliott) 1960s international sex symbol Terence Stamp is a transgendered marvel as the mature, demure but tough transsexual Bernadette who teams up with two transvestites on a cross-country trip through Australia's Outback in this rousingly fun cross-dressing musical comedy. Muscular Felicia (Guy Pearce), sad-sack Mitzi (Hugo Weaving) and the wisecracking Bernadette leave the safe confines of Sydney in a ramshackle tour bus (named Priscilla) to travel nearly a thousand miles away to play a four-week casino engagement. Along the way, the fabulously attired threesome encounter more than their fair share of problems but through it all keep their spirits high, their feathers and sequins unruffled and their gravity-defying wigs straight (so to speak). There are moments of seriousness when homophobia, potentially violent culture clashes and regret of roads not taken confront them, but they readily conquer all in this buoyant and infectiously good-natured tale. ★★★½ $19.99

The Adventures of Robin Hood

(1938, 106 min, US, Michael Curtiz) The quintessential swashbuckler with Errol Flynn as a devilishly dashing Robin Hood, Olivia deHavilland as Maid Marion, Claude Rains as a particularly villainous Prince John, and the great Basil Rathbone, master swordsman and scene stealer, as Sir Guy. The film sports great action scenes, tongue-in-cheek humor, the very

The Adventures of Priscilla, Queen of the Desert

best in swordplay and glorious Technicolor cinematography. ★★★★ $14.99

The Adventures of Sherlock Holmes

(1939, 85 min, US, Alfred L. Werker) One of the definitive Sherlock Holmes pictures, this exciting and atmospheric piece stars Basil Rathbone and Nigel Bruce as the famous sleuth and his companion Dr. Watson. Holmes' archenemy, the evil Professor Moriarty, attempts to commit the "crime of the century" right beneath the detective's nose. ★★★ $19.99

Advise and Consent

(1962, 139 min, US, Otto Preminger) A finely interwoven plot and exceptional ensemble acting highlight Preminger's treatment of the Allen Drury novel. The machinations of government, on the floor of the Senate and behind the scenes, are examined with an eye to formal procedure and individual idiosyncracy in this story of a controversial presidential nomination. Don Murray is full of idealistic vigor as the chairman of a House sub-committee investigating the Secretary of State nominee (played by Henry Fonda). However, when he refuses to endorse Fonda, he is blackmailed for a homosexual encounter while in the service. In his final film, Charles Laughton offers an excellent performance as a slick Southern senator. Mammoth in scope and engrossing in detail, this makes an interesting companion piece to *The Best Man*. (Letterboxed version) ★★★½ $14.99

The Advocate

(1994, 101 min, GB, Leslie Megahey) Writer-director Megahey has taken what has to be a virtually unknown medieval law and with it fashioned a scintillating black comedy masquerading as a murder mystery. Colin Firth plays a 15th-century Parisian lawyer who escapes the rigors and hardships of the city for a simpler life in the country. But a peaceful landscape and gentle countryfolk are not what he finds when he immediately becomes embroiled in the murder trial of a young boy — and his defendant is a pig! It seems at the time animals could be tried and put to death with all the pomp befitting any human. As Firth tries to uncover the facts, he comes face to face with political corruption, religious bureaucracy and a bevy of beautiful women all trying to bed him. The situation is ripe with satiric possibilities, and Megahey has wondrously exploited them with a light touch and marvelous wit. Firth is quite good as the befuddled advocate, and Ian Holm and Donald Pleasence offer fine support as the town's religious and municipal leaders. ★★★½ $19.99

Aelita: Queen of Mars

(1924, 113 min, USSR, Yakov Protazanov) Definitely not your typical silent Soviet film, *Aelita* is a big-budget science-fiction spectacle boasting enormous, Cubist-inspired futuristic sets and wildly designed costumes. A Russian engineer, a soldier and a detective all travel to Mars where they become embroiled in a Martian proletarian uprising. Their situation gets even more complicated when the engineer falls madly in love with Queen Aelita. A huge popular success in its time, the film is an interesting precursor to Fritz Lang's similarly themed *Metropolis*. (Silent with piano accompaniment) ★★★ $29.99

An Affair to Remember

(1957, 115 min, US, Leo McCarey) Based on the 1939 classic *Love Affair*, this sentimental soap opera features Cary Grant and Deborah Kerr in very appealing performances as two lovers separated by fate. Artist Grant and engaged Kerr enjoy a shipboard romance. In a famous cinematic rendezvous, they vow to meet six months later at the Empire State Building. One of them doesn't make it. Though the film is awash in hokey drama (especially the subplot of Kerr involved with a children's association), the chemistry of the two stars, Grant's expert comic timing and a touching romance make this a semi-classic and fan fave. ★★★ $9.99

Afraid of the Dark

(1992, 91 min, US, Mark Peploe) Academy Award-winning screenwriter Peploe (*The Last Emperor*) turns his hand to directing with this psychological thriller in which nothing is as it seems. James Fox stars as the father of a precocious kid who decides to track down a psychopath preying on the blind. To say more would be detrimental to the plot's essential twist, but the patient viewer will be rewarded. Also starring Fanny Ardant, Paul McGann, and Ben Keyworth as little Lucas. ★★½ $14.99

An African Dream

(1990, 94 min, GB, John Smallcombe) When a young schoolteacher moves to colonial South Africa with her husband, she is appalled by the racial hatred which pervades her new home. She develops a relationship with an educated African who is teaching at a small school in the black area and is involuntarily sucked into the fray. John Kani, a longtime collaborator with South African playwright Athol Fugard, and Kitty Aldridge star. ★★★ $89.99

The African Queen

(1951, 106 min, US, John Huston) One of the all-time greats, *The African Queen* stars Humphrey Bogart (in his Oscar-winning role) and Katharine Hepburn as unlikely lovebirds who encounter the dangers of the rapids, the Germans and each other. In a quintessential performance, Hepburn plays Rose Sawyer, a missionary serving in the Congo. She is paired with boozy captain Charlie Alnut (Bogey in a wonderfully endearing performance) when she must flee her village from the enemy army via Bogey's dilapidated boat. Aided by two veteran performers at the peak of their talents and an excellent screenplay, director Huston has crafted a thrilling adventure both comic and exciting. ★★★★ $14.99

After Dark, My Sweet

(1990, 114 min, US, James Foley) 1990 was a good year for gritty adaptations of the books of Jim Thompson. In addition to *The Grifters*, this disturbing yet highly entertaining melodrama represented a miniature revival for the novelist. Jason Patric stars as Collie, a literally punch-drunk ex-boxer who is on the run from a mental institution. Dazed, Collie wanders

into the seedier side of Palm Springs and becomes tragically entangled with an alcoholic widow (Rachel Ward) and a local con man (Bruce Dern) who are hatching a scheme to pick up some quick bucks. Patric's performance is strikingly complex and intense. Rachel Ward is equally good, and Bruce Dern has found his best role in years. *After Dark, My Sweet* is an excellent and claustrophobic study of three social misfits caught in a dangerous *pas de trois*. ★★★½ $14.99

After Hours

(1985, 97 min, US, Martin Scorsese) Ever had one of those days? Paul Hackett (Griffin Dunne) is about to have one of those nights. What begins as an innocent date with a kooky girl he meets at a coffee shop escalates into a night befitting a "Twilight Zone" episode. This exhilarating Scorsese black comedy follows Paul's misadventures in Greenwich Village (and vicinity) where each character confronted is crazier and more unpredictable than the one before. A great supporting cast includes Rosanna Arquette, Teri Garr, John Heard and Linda Fiorentino. ★★★★ $19.99

Cary Grant and Deborah Kerr engage in *An Affair to Remember*

After Pilkington

(1987, 100 min, GB, Christopher Morahan) An Oxford professor's quiet academic lifestyle becomes imperiled when a childhood sweetheart, whom he hasn't seen in years, suddenly resurfaces and begs him to help her dispose of a corpse. Miranda Richardson and Bob Peck star in this offbeat tale of obsession and murder. ★★½ $19.99

After the Fox

(1966, 103 min, GB, Vittorio De Sica) Who would imagine De Sica directing Peter Sellers in a film scripted by Neil Simon? Well, here it is – and not an unworthy effort, at that. Sellers is an ingenious convict who produces a film in order to cover up a big caper. As the movie star Sellers convinces to star in the "movie,"

Victor Mature gets the most laughs just for being himself. Also starring Britt Ekland. ★★★ $14.99

After the Rehearsal

(1984, 72 min, Sweden, Ingmar Bergman) A provocative probing of the thoughts and fears of a renowned stage director (Erland Josephson) poised between love and solitude, ambition and resignation, bitterness and longing. On the verge of a production, he is confronted by two actresses, who in distinctly different fashions, force him into a position of self-examination. Along with *Wild Strawberries*, this is one of Bergman's most personal reflections on the demands and delusions of the artist. (Swedish with English subtitles) ★★★½ $19.99

After the Thin Man

See: The Thin Man Series

Afterburn

(1992, 100 min, US, Robert Markowitz) Laura Dern is arresting as a fighter pilot's widow who takes on the U.S. military when her husband's crash in an F-16 in Korea is attributed to pilot error. Knowing that her husband (Vincent Spano) was one of the most highly rated pilots, her doubts and suspicions regarding the official story escalate in the face of increasing evidence of a cover-up. Robert Loggia delivers a strong performance as Dern's lawyer. A compelling HBO treatment of a real-life incident. ★★★½ $19.99

Against All Odds

(1984, 128 min, US, Taylor Hackford) An interesting if not totally successful updating of the noir classic *Out of the Past*. Jeff Bridges stars as a down-and-out ex-football player who is hired by an ex-teammate-turned-gangster (James Woods) to locate the woman (Rachel Ward) who he says tried to kill him. Hackford's remake relies on solid performances, star chemistry and a few plot twists to puff up what could have been a rather shopworn premise, and the film also benefits from an over-the-top performance by Woods. Jane Greer, who plays Ward's mother, starred as the missing femme fatale in the original film, and Richard Widmark also stars. ★★½ $9.99

Against the Wall

(1993, 111 min, US, John Frankenheimer) This made-for-HBO docudrama chronicles the events that took place during the violent uprising at the Attica State Penitentiary in the early '70s. Kyle MacLachlan stars as the rookie guard who gets stuck in the middle and becomes a hostage for the inmates. Samuel L. Jackson gives a fine performance as the Islamic inmate who unofficially becomes the go-between for the media and the prisoners. This exciting, heart-pounding film is one of the finest ever to come from HBO. ★★★★ $19.99

Agatha

(1978, 98 min, GB/US, Michael Apted) Director Apted (*Coal Miner's Daughter*, *Gorillas in the Mist*) weaves this fictional account of the 1926 11-day disappearance of famed mystery writer Agatha Christie. Vanessa Redgrave's sensitive portrayal lends touching insight into "the price of fame," while helping to offset Dustin Hoffman's grating turn as the

Aguirre, the Wrath of God

American reporter who ultimately tracks her down. Also with Timothy Dalton as Christie's estranged husband. ★★½ $14.99

L'Âge d'Or
(1930, 60 min, France, **Luis Buñuel**) Following the success of their first collaboration, *Un Chien Andalou*, Buñuel and Salvador Dali further antagonized the Right, the Church and the powers that be with this wickedly funny, bizarre and scandalous masterpiece. Buñuel has said that this dreamlike tale of mad love unconsummated is "a romantic film performed in full surrealist frenzy." (French with English subtitles) ★★★½

The Age of Innocence
(1993, 133 min, US, **Martin Scorsese**) Scorsese ventured into the virgin territory (for him) of period drama with this visually dazzling and sumptuously produced, but ultimately disappointing adaptation of Edith Wharton's novel. Set in 1870s New York City, the film stars Daniel Day-Lewis as Newland Archer, a young lawyer and rising member of the ruling elite. Smitten by the Countess Olenska (Michelle Pfeiffer), a former member of polite society who has returned home surrounded by gossip over her intent to divorce her husband, Archer furthers the scandal by falling in love with her despite his betrothal to Olenska's cousin (Winona Ryder). The acting by all three principals is superbly nuanced and first-rate; special mention goes to Miriam Margolyes as a matronly aunt. While the film aptly captures the sense of social suffocation that Wharton no doubt intended, it lacks a much-needed passion. ★★½ $14.99

Agnes of God
(1985, 98 min, US, **Norman Jewison**) A trio of solid performances highlight this intriguing mystery based on the Broadway hit. Jane Fonda plays a court-appointed psychiatrist who must determine the sanity of a novice accused of murdering her newborn baby. Oscar nominations went to Anne Bancroft as the convent's worldly Mother Superior, and Meg Tilly as the troubled young woman. ★★★ $9.99

The Agony and the Ecstasy
(1965, 140 min, US, **Carol Reed**) Not considered a Reed classic, this historical account follows Michelangelo's aesthetic battles with Pope Julius II as he toiled on the Sistine Chapel. Charlton Heston and Rex Harrison provide worthy performances, but the film's slightly overblown production values and its considerable length overshadow their efforts. ★★½ $19.99

Aguirre, the Wrath of God
(1972, 94 min, West Germany, **Werner Herzog**) A mesmerizing, adventurous tale of a Spanish expedition's search for El Dorado, the lost city of gold. Along the way, a power-hungry conquistador, Aguirre, takes control and leads them on an insane journey into the Amazon and the heart of darkness. Although Herzog's hyper-realistic style of direction makes for a few slow sequences, Klaus Kinski's intense performance as the traitorous title character is riveting. A compelling portrait of a mad and brilliant leader. (German with English subtitles) ★★★½ $29.99

Ah, Wilderness!
(1935, 98 min, US, **Clarence Brown**) A very able cast brings Eugene O'Neill's stage comedy about a 1906 New England family merrily to life. The film's success is painting a heartwarming portrait of early 20th-century Americana while avoiding the bathetic trappings of so many films of the '30s – the *Andy Hardy* series, for example. Heading a fine ensemble is Lionel Barrymore as the patriarch of the Miller clan. Barrymore is often given the film's best lines, and he makes the most of them. Wallace Beery gives a showy portrayal as an uncle prone to drink; and Spring Byington sparkles as the family's mother. ★★★½ $19.99

Aileen Wuornos — The Selling of a Serial Killer
(1993, 87 min, GB, **Nick Broomfield**) A chilling crime and justice documentary that would make the events in *The Thin Blue Line* seem like a paragon of legal competence, this mesmerizing and tenacious investigative film attempts to gather the facts in the case against convicted serial killer Aileen Wuornos. Wuornos, a lesbian and prostitute, was convicted of brutally killing seven men. Director Broomfield digs beyond the seemingly open-and-shut case and uncovers an elaborate web of deception and profiteering both on the part of law enforcement officers, her "friends" and her lover. Wuornos appears to be a thoughtful and rather intelligent woman who, while probably guilty, did not receive an ounce of justice as she was railroaded to several convictions and a date with the electric chair. The lasting effect of the film is not only a document of the gross miscarriage by the judicial system, but a look at a personal tragedy as well. ★★★★ $19.99

Ailey Dances
(1982, 85 min, US, **James Lipton**) A remarkable presentation given by one of the nation's most acclaimed dance companies, the Alvin Ailey American Dance Theatre. This dynamic and graceful performance was recorded live at New York's City Center Theater during a 1982 tour and consists of four of the company's best-known pieces including "The Lark Ascending" and the rousing spiritual "Revelations." Narration and an introduction to each performance is provided by former Ailey star Judith Jamison. ★★★½ $39.99

Air America
(1990, 112 min, US, **Roger Spottiswoode**) Lumbering political satire with Mel Gibson and Robert Downey, Jr. as off-the-wall pilots working for a covert government airline in Laos during the years of the Vietnam War. The film can't decide what it wants to be – left-wing, right-wing, comic romp, anti-war – and suffers as a result. The appealing chemistry of the two stars is wasted on this nonsense. ★ $14.99

Air Force
(1943, 124 min, US, **Howard Hawks**) After five years of solid support and second leads, John Garfield takes center stage in this crisp WWII actioner about the aerial adventures of a B-17 bomber crew, both before and after Pearl Harbor. Hawks directs with his usual keen eye for adventure. Garfield is a com-

manding presence, and the supporting cast includes Gig Young, Arthur Kennedy and (what Warner film would be complete without) George Tobias. ★★★ $19.99

The Air Up There

(1994, 88 min, US, Paul M. Glaser) Kevin Bacon stars as an assistant college basketball coach who travels all the way to Kenya to recruit a nearly seven-foot tribesman (an engaging Charles Gitonga Maina) for his team. While there, he suffers culture shock, befriends the natives, and helps right the village's wrongs. The locale provides a nice travelogue backdrop, and the finale's basketball game is rather exciting despite its obvious outcome; but this formulaic sports film is only for those who think Hollywood doesn't make enough basketball flicks. Bacon has an easygoing, natural charm which all the more makes one wish the film was as noteworthy as its star. ★★ $9.99

Airheads

(1994, 91 min, US, Michael Lehmann) Lehmann's self-consciously hip, one-joke comedy is about a rock band — The Lone Rangers — who hold a radio station hostage in order to get their demo played. The one joke? That a rock band holds a radio station hostage in order to get their demo played. As repetitious as it sounds, the film isn't helped by a tired script and one-dimensional performances by Brendan Fraser and Steve Buscemi as two of the sympathetic Rangers, Michael McKean as a typical movie yuppie-scum, and Joe Mantegna as a hapless D.J. However, Adam Sandler saves the day with a truly amusing portrayal of the band's dim-witted drummer. ★½ $96.89

Airplane!

(1980, 86 min, US, Jim Abrahams, David Zucker & Jerry Zucker) A dash of Marx Brothers, a taste of Chaplin, a whole lot of Three Stooges slapstick, and puns, puns and more puns are the ingredients for this send-up of every airplane disaster film from *Zero Hour* to *Airport*. This non-stop laugh fest relentlessly hits us over the head with jokes. There are so many jokes, in fact, that blinking is not advised. Besides the million or so laughs, this is the film which first introduced Leslie Nielsen as a comic actor — let's give thanks for that, too. Also with Robert Hays, Julie Hagerty, Robert Stack, Lloyd Bridges, "Beaver"'s mom Barbara Billingsley and Ethel Merman. ★★★★ $9.99

Airplane II: The Sequel

(1982, 85 min, US, Ken Finkleman) This sequel to the hit *Airplane!* doesn't pack the stomach-wrenching humor as did the first. Handed over to first-time director Finkleman, the film just can't match the pace of its predecessor. This time around, retired pilot Robert Hays becomes the only man available to fly a Space Shuttle-like craft. Although the plot is predictable, there are still enough funny moments to satisfy fans of the first. ★★½ $14.99

Akermania Vol. 1

(1968-84, 89 min, Belgium, Chantal Akerman) Three short subjects from independent feminist filmmaker Akerman. *I'm*

Hungry, I'm Cold (1984): Two young girls run away to Paris from their native Brussels and learn very direct, immediate approaches to getting their needs met. *Blow Up My Town* (1968): A young woman in a small flat with too much unchanneled energy races through the mundane activities of daily life until she's caught in the vortex of their execution. This can be seen as a precursor to Akerman's *Jeanne Dielman*. *Hotel Monterey* (1974): Without sound, the camera wanders through the lobby, into the elevator, hallways, various rooms and out to the roof of the hotel. This process eventually creates a portrait of impersonal space, and the people captured in it seem transient, impermanent, ephemeral. An eerie and disquieting experience. ★★★ $19.99

Akira

(1989, 102 min, Japan, Katsuhiro Otomo) A sometimes grim but entertaining look into a not-too-distant future. Taking place in neo-Tokyo, complete with bike gangs, mutants and corrupt government officials, this film pushes the boundaries of animation into a truly adult realm. Visually striking, *Akira* will especially appeal to those who grew up on a diet of "8th Man," "Astro Boy" and "Speed Racer" cartoons. A groundbreaking state-of-the-art Japanese animation classic which makes some earlier efforts (like *Laputa*) look like stick-figure drawings. (Dubbed) (A letterboxed edition is available for $29.99; a subtitled and letterboxed version is available for $39.99) ★★★★ $19.99

Akira Kurosawa's Dreams

(1990, 120 min, Japan, Akira Kurosawa) In his most personal film, Kurosawa takes time to reflect on his innermost hopes, fears and joys. Through a series of eight vignettes, or "dreams," Kurosawa takes us through his childhood terrors, his horror at the state of the environment and the use of nuclear power, his love of art and, finally, his peaceful vision of a world where people live harmoniously with nature. Filmed in vivid, sometimes explosive colors, *Dreams* represents a thoughtful summing to the impressive filmography of this cinematic giant. (Japanese with English subtitles) ★★★★ $92.99

Akira Production Report

(1989, 52 min, Japan, Katsuhiro Otomo) Fans of *Akira*, the boldly imaginative post-apocalyptic sci-fi feature, can get a behind-the-scenes look in this interesting documentary. Mixing clips from the film with interviews with Katsuhiro Otomo, the author and director of the immensely popular novel series "Akira," the film takes a look into the state-of-the-art production processes which help make the movie an unforgettable animation classic. ★★½ $24.99

Aladdin

(1992, 87 min, US, John Musker & Ron Clements) A consistently entertaining and gloriously funny achievement, *Aladdin* features a nice musical score by Alan Menken, Tim Rice and Howard Ashman; delightful animation; and wonderful laugh-out-loud jokes. This alone makes the film first-class. But it also has Robin Williams. As the voice of the genie whose iconoclastic references will split any side,

Williams catapults the film to unimaginable comic heights — and the Disney artists have matched his vocal escapades with inspired drawings. A marriage made in cartoon heaven, this is Williams and Disney at their best. The third and possibly strongest of the Disney-Menken-Ashman trilogy, which also includes *The Little Mermaid* and *Beauty and the Beast*. A film adults will love even more than children. (Followed by *Return of Jafar*) ★★★★ $59.99

Aladdin and the King of Thieves

(1996, 83 min, US) The third entry in Disney's popular *Aladdin* series marks the return of Robin Williams as the voice of the Genie, and his contribution can't be underestimated or overappreciated as he brings a wealth of humor to this enjoyable animated tale. Aladdin and Princess Jasmine are about to be married when their service is interrupted by the 40 Thieves. They were searching for the magical Hand of Midas — which can turn anything it touches to gold. When an oracle reveals Aladdin's father is still alive, the wedding is put on hold — again — as he sets out to find his father. The story offers little complexity for the little ones, and as long as Genie is on screen, which is about half of the time, it's laugh-out-loud funny. ★★★ $24.99

The Alamo

(1960, 161 min, US, John Wayne) Wayne's dream project (he served as writer, producer and director as well as starred in it) is an epic of Texas-sized proportions. The story, of course, has to do with the heroic last stand made by Texas patriots in the face of the overwhelming Mexican army. Wayne stars as a larger-than-life Davy Crockett, Richard Widmark plays Jim Bowie, and Laurence Harvey is Will Travis. The battle scenes are impressive and include great cavalry charges, artillery bombardments and hundreds upon hundreds of extras. The first half of the film is slow going, but Wayne creates an effective sense of impending doom throughout. The remastered, restored full-length version. (Letterboxed) ★★★ $24.99

Alamo Bay

(1985, 98 min, US, Louis Malle) Ed Harris stars as a fisherman and Vietnam vet who, like most of his small Texas community, feels a sense of resentment towards the Asian refugees who have settled in their town. Paradoxical complexity arrives when these ex-soldiers, who once fought to defend the Vietnamese, must now fight them for jobs and a way of life. Though the film retains a certain power, Malle creates little tension in this precarious moral dilemma, letting the conflict speak for itself instead of adding dimension for the camera. Also with Amy Madigan and Ho Nguyen. ★★ $79.99

Alan and Naomi

(1992, 95 min, US, Sterling VanWagenen) Young Lukas Haas' sincere, heartfelt performance dominates this slowly paced but nevertheless touching WWII drama. Haas brings unexpected depth to the role of a 14-year-old Brooklyn youth who is forced by his family to befriend a traumatized French girl, whose father was murdered by Nazis right before her eyes. At first reluctant to associate with the neighborhood "crazy," Haas slowly develops a relationship with the girl, allowing the tormented youngster to escape her protective shell, and present a glimmer of hope for recovery. Michael Gross (TV's "Family Ties") co-stars as Haas' father, and Vanessa Zaoui ably plays the young girl. Good evocation of wartime America. ★★½ $89.99

Alaska

(1996, 104 min, US, Fraser C. Heston) This above-average family film has it all: the brooding adolescent who matures into a thoughtful teen; the traumatic family experience that brings out the best in everyone; villains you love to hate; a gorgeous landscape; and a polar bear who steals the show. Dirk Benedict plays the pilot dad who moves his two kids (Thora Birch and Vincent Kartheiser) to Alaska after the death of their mom. When the father's plane crashes and he is given up for dead, the son overcomes his anger about the move and sets off with his sister to find him in the wilderness. Along the way, they are befriended by the polar bear who is being pursued by a poacher, played with great humor and depravity by director Fraser's dad Charlton. Excellent acting, a terrific score and breathtaking scenery all work together to create a wonderful family feature. ★★★½ $21.99

Alberto Express

(1992, 90 min, Italy/France, Arthur Joffe) With a wickedly farcical premise and the presence, however brief, of Italian funny man Nino Manfredi, this frantic family comedy should be more entertaining than it is. Alberto, a frumpy 40-year-old man about to be a first-time father, is summoned to his father's attic for a meeting. Pop, observing a family tradition, calmly begins calculating every expense incurred in raising Alberto and presents him with a bill that must be repaid before his wife delivers his child. From this, Alberto schemes and connives his way through the continent, in hopes of somehow coming up with the money. While his antics are at times quite hilarious, Sergio Castellitto as Alberto is somehow not quite right for the part — too much of a forlorn sad-sack with not enough comic inventiveness to carry a comedy of this type. But despite the griping, the film has enough yuks. (Italian with English subtitles) ★★½ $19.99

Albino Alligator

(1997, 105 min, US, Kevin Spacey) Having won a well-deserved Oscar for his riveting performance in the seminal noir thriller *The Usual Suspects*, it would only make sense that Spacey would return to the genre for his directorial debut. Demonstrating moments of great understanding of the gangster film, Spacey's first film has terrific scenes but doesn't quite come together as a whole. Borrowing a little from *The Petrified Forest*, the story concerns small-time New Orleans hoods Matt Dillon, Gary Sinise and William Fichtner who, after bungling a burglary and having the police on their trail, hole up in a seedy bar. Taking customers and employees hostage, the little remaining remnants of rational thought these men have dissipate, eventually causing a crisis of morality for all concerned. Dillon ably

walks the fine line between mug and thug, Faye Dunaway is smashing as a bartender unafraid to talk back, and Fichtner makes a great impression as the hoodlums' loose cannon. Joe Mantegna doesn't fare as well in the clichéd role of a police inspector. In this promising debut, Spacey captures the mood, but the screenplay lacks some of the necessary grit. ★★½ $102.99

The Alchemist

(1985, 84 min, US, Charles Band) This rural horror film is set in 1955 in which a century-old curse has Robert Ginty living as an animal. It takes the lovely Lucinda Dooling to break the wretched curse in this gender-reversed "Sleeping Beauty" rip-off. Nothing much to scream about in this clichéd film except for how poor it is. Filmed in 1981, but released four years later. ★ $79.99

Alex in Wonderland

(1970, 109 min, US, Paul Mazursky) What do you do when your filmmaking debut is a huge box-office success? Mazursky's response is this meandering trifle which poses the very same question — following, as it did, on the heels of his surprise hit *Bob & Carol & Ted & Alice*. Donald Sutherland offers a nice portrayal of Mazursky's alter ego Alex, a hippie-dippie director whose initial triumph makes him a hot property at the studio, but whose conscience bristles at the thought of becoming another Hollywood lapdog. Mazursky's loosely scattered narrative, along with a cameo by Federico Fellini, makes it clear that he yearns for the freedoms enjoyed by European directors. The result, sadly, is a jumble (many Americans of the era tried to imitate the European style with little success), but the subject is of enough interest to film enthusiasts to be worth a look. Ellen Burstyn is excellent as Sutherland's wife, and Jeanne Moreau appears in a cameo. ★★½ $19.99

Alexander Nevsky

(1938, 105 min, USSR, Sergei Eisenstein) Eisenstein's first sound film is a grand epic of Prince Nevsky's heroic defense of Russia against the invading Teutonic Knights in 1242. The final battle sequence on the ice of Lake Piepus is magnificent in its visual splendor and in the use of a stirring Prokofiev score instead of natural sound. (Russian with English subtitles) ★★★★ $19.99

Alfie

(1966, 114 min, GB, Lewis Gilbert) Michael Caine is flawless as an unscrupulous Cockney womanizer who can't decide whether his lustful life is really worth the effort. It's a quirky film which strips bare all the lecherous qualities nurtured within the male mystique. An excellent supporting cast includes Vivien Merchant, Shelley Winters and Denholm Elliott. This was the film that catapulted Caine into the realm of international stardom. ★★★★ $14.99

Alfred Hitchcock Presents

(1962, 120 min, US, Alfred Hitchcock) If you are craving suspense, twist endings and dark humor, look no further than this collection of episodes from Alfred Hitchcock's classic tele-

vision series. The master himself directs, and he delivers the goods in one segment after another (especially in the now-famous "Lamb to the Slaughter"). Also preserved in this anthology are Hitchcock's droll introductions and running commentary. *Hitchcock Presents* will leave you wondering why nobody makes TV mysteries this good anymore. ★★★ $14.99

Algiers

(1938, 95 min, US, John Cromwell) A svelte and darkly handsome Charles Boyer exudes sinister charm as Pepe le Moko, the crown prince of thieves in the Casbah, a labyrinthine complex of dens and warrens in the heart of Algiers, whose inhabitants are dedicated to the procurement of ill-gotten gains. A police inspector newly arrived from France intends to capture the nefarious Pepe, much to the amusement of the local constabulary. While the pace is somewhat laborious by contemporary standards, the film evokes an inticing aura of menace. The well-cast players also include Sigrid Gurie, Hedy Lamarr, Joseph Calleia (an Oscar nominee), Alan Hale and Gene Lockhart. ★★★ $12.99

Ali: Fear Eats the Soul

(1973, 94 min, West Germany, Rainer Werner Fassbinder) Fassbinder's bittersweet love story about the affair between a lonely 60-year old German cleaning woman and a reticent Moroccan auto mechanic half her age is a raw, intense look at racial attitudes and unconventional relationships. Brigitte Mira and El Hedi Ben Salem star as the two lovers who find brief solace with each other in spite of family objections, social rejection and racial prejudice. Fassbinder's first film to play theatrically in the U.S., *Ali* is startling in its examination of xenophobia, and is an unflinching study of the passion between "societal misfits," one of the director's favorite themes. (German with English subtitles) ★★★½ $29.99

Alice

(1987, 86 min, Czechoslovakia, Jan Svankmajer) Animator Svankmajer has taken Lewis Carroll's "Alice in Wonderland" and created a distinctly original and personal interpretation of the classic children's story. Utilizing live-action with his trademark stop-motion animation, Svankmajer's *Alice* owes more to the surrealist techniques of Buñuel and Dali than to Disney. While the narration of the familiar tale unfolds, the filmmaker's interest lies less with the story's odd and fanciful characters and more with the underlying cruel, erotic and amoral ideas of an innocent girl lost during a wickedly bizarre journey. Not for children, obviously, and not even for many adults, this extraordinary work will amaze, baffle and delight fans of the surreal. (Dubbed in English) ★★★★ $59.99

Alice

(1991, 106 min, US, Woody Allen) This is Allen's delightful paean to Lewis Carrol's "Alice in Wonderland" and Federico Fellini's *Juliet of the Spirits*. Mia Farrow stars as Alice, a woman who has been married for 16 years to highly successful businessman William Hurt. Theirs is the lifestyle of $100 lunches and shopping sprees at Bergdorf Goodman's, but something is missing for Alice; she has a calling, she's just not sure what. With the help of a strange herbalist/acupuncturist, and through the fantasy of having an affair with divorcé Joe Mantegna, she experiences a series of a whimsical, supernatural and often hilarious events which help guide her toward inner happiness. Farrow is superb as she presents the perfect female embodiment of Allen's nebbish, and Mantegna delivers his usual offbeat charm. Veteran actor Keye Luke steals the film as the beguiling and mysterious doctor. A series of wonderful cameos come from Alec Baldwin, Blythe Danner, Judy Davis, Bernadette Peters and Gwen Verdon. ★★★½ $14.99

Alice Adams

(1935, 99 min, US, George Stevens) Katharine Hepburn, in one of her best roles, is a girl of the bourgeoisie trying to compete with the swells for the attentions of extremely eligible and quite well-heeled Fred MacMurray in Stevens' adaptation of the Boothe Tarkington novel. Throw in a little corporate skullduggery and some strikingly visualized evidences of class distinctions. ★★★★ $19.99

Alice Doesn't Live Here Anymore

(1974, 113 min, US, Martin Scorsese) Ellen Burstyn won an Oscar for her bravura performance in this touching, sometimes humorous and sensitive character study of one woman's personal liberation. After her husband dies and leaves her penniless, Alice, with her young son Tommy, moves to Phoenix, Arizona, where she attempts to survive on her own, both emotionally and financially. Wonderful supporting roles include Diane Ladd as Flo, Jodie Foster as Tommy's young friend, and Vic Tayback as Mel. Kris Kristofferson is at his best as Alice's love interest. ★★★★ $14.99

Alice in the Cities

(1973, 110 min, West Germany, Wim Wenders) Wenders' German-made films usually share several recurring themes: man's alienation and his ensuing search for meaning in life, American cultural imperialism in Germany, and the exploration of personal relationships. In *Alice in the Cities*, a brooding, remarkable examination of the director's favorite themes, we follow a 31-year-old journalist who, when traveling in the United States, suddenly finds himself with a precocious nine-year-old girl abandoned by her mother. The two return to Germany in search of the girl's grandmother. (German with English subtitles) ★★★

Alice in Wonderland

(1950, 83 min, GB, Lou Bunin) Released a year before Disney's version of the story, this mixture of animation and live action virtually disappeared in the U.S. after threats of reprisal from the Disney studio. Closer to Lewis Carroll's original work in satirical tone than Disney's, this *Alice* is equally enjoyable by both adults and children, although aimed at the latter. The story begins at Oxford, where lonely lecturer Charles Dodgson spins fantastic tales for Alice Liddel and her two sisters. It then shifts to Wonderland, where the familiar characters of the White Rabbit, Cheshire Cat,

Mad Hatter and the Queen of Hearts are brought vividly to life through stop-motion animation. The animation is impressively intercut with the live Alice, creating a fantasy world of giant talking caterpillars, gryphons and mock turtles. ★★★ $24.99

Alice in Wonderland

(1951, 75 min, US, Clyde Geronimi, Hamilton Luske & Wilfred Jackson) Disney's adaptation of Lewis Carroll's classic is a colorful, tune-filled excursion through Wonderland. More eccentric and slightly more surreal than Disney's usual fare (with exception, of course, to *Fantasia*), the film follows the familiar journey taken by Alice as she enters a wondrous dimension populated by the White Rabbit, talking caterpillars and where she's likely to be any size from one moment to the next. Of the songs, "I'm Late" is the most well-known, though "A Very Merry Un-Birthday" is kinda cute, too. Some of this may be a little over the head of the wee ones. ★★★½ $24.99

Alice to Nowhere

(1986, 210 min, Australia, John Power) Rosey Jones and the Australian John Waters star in this exceedingly long but at times rousing adventure yarn made for Aussie television. A woman, who doesn't know that in her possession is a cache of priceless jewels, finds herself pursued by thieves and just regular bad guys. Her adventures take her and her two guides through many perilous, grueling outback regions in this *Indiana Jones*-like epic. ★★★ $59.99

Alice's Restaurant

(1969, 111 min, US, Arthur Penn) Penn's follow-up to *Bonnie and Clyde* was a film version of Arlo Guthrie's communal sing-along which accurately captures the cultural upheaval going on at the end of the 1960s. Quirky and entertaining, the film features a surprisingly downbeat ending proving to be more prophetic than the hyperbole of *Easy Rider*. ★★★ $14.99

Alien

(1979, 117 min, US, Ridley Scott) Terror lurks in every corner in this frightening story of a completely hostile and virtually indestructible creature which sneaks aboard the spaceship *Nostromo*, via John Hurt's navel, and brings an absolute nightmare to its crew: Sigourney Weaver, Tom Skerritt, Harry Dean Stanton, Yaphet Kotto, Veronica Cartwright and Ian Holm. Director Scott masterfully blends pulse-pounding suspense and some gory, amazing F/X, and the film is greatly benefitted by H.R. Giger's outstanding production design. ★★★½ $14.99

Alien 3

(1992, 115 min, US, David Fincher) The third chapter in the *Alien* series from first-time director Fincher follows two classics in the horror/sci-fi genre. Fincher had his work cut out for him – and though his film delivers some of the goods, there's no comparison to the first two films. Sigourney Weaver, with shaved head, returns at Lt. Ripley, now the sole survivor of the escape made at the end of *Aliens*. And it seems she's brought an old friend along. Ripley

has crash landed at a maximum security prison on some distant bleak planet. And there's not much for her to do but balance her time between the hostile inmates and one angry alien who's come a-lookin' for one final confrontation. Like the music videos Fincher cut his teeth on, *Alien 3* has a great look but very little substance. (Followed in 1997 by *Alien Resurrection*, starring Weaver and Winona Ryder.) ★★½ $14.99

Alien Nation

(1988, 94 min, US, Graham Baker) James Caan is well cast as a tough Los Angeles cop who is partnered with an alien – from outer space. It seems in the not-so-distant future, an alien race will arrive on Earth after the destruction of their own planet, though they are welcomed with not-so-opened arms. The first half of the film is an intriguing sci-fi adventure, but the story disintegrates into a routine buddy film. Mandy Patinkin is oddly affecting as Caan's man-from-outer space partner. ★★½ $9.99

Aliens

(1986, 137 min, US, James Cameron) The blockbuster sequel to *Alien* does the original one better; dazzling special effects and nerve-racking suspense make this definitely not for the weak of heart. Sigourney Weaver reprises her role as Warrant Officer Ripley in an Oscar-nominated performance. Ripley is convinced to return to the planet where the deadly aliens were initially found when an Earth colony loses contact with its home base. Director Cameron assaults the senses in a unrelenting barrage of terror, and just when you thought it couldn't get any more suspenseful – it does! For those with Hi-Fi stereo VCRs, *Aliens* boasts amazing stereo sound. ★★★★ $14.99

Alive

(1993, 125 min, US, Frank Marshall) Despite containing some truly trite Hollywood contrivances, this high-altitude action film offers excellent thrills and a lot of food for thought. Recounting the harrowing two-month ordeal suffered by the surviving passengers of an Uruguayan airliner which crashed in the Chilean Andes, the film begins with a bang with an extremely well-staged crash sequence which achieves an unparalleled sense of realism. Most of the passengers were members of an Uruguayan rugby team and their captain (Vincent Spano) quickly takes charge of the situation. But when they learn that the search for survivors has been called off, his leadership fails and falls into the hands of the firebrand, Ethan Hawke. The film bogs down a little towards the middle, occasionally straying into the haze of religious piety. Overall, however, the film is an exciting testament to the power of the human spirit to survive in absolutely untenable conditions. ★★★ $9.99

All About Eve

(1950, 138 min, US, Joseph L. Mankiewicz) *The* Bette Davis classic, which still remains the definitive Hollywood movie about theatre life. Bette, in what is possibly the quintessential Davis role, stars as Margo Channing, a first lady of the theatre whose professional and personal life is changed forever when a seemingly starstruck young woman (Anne Baxter) enters her life. A brilliantly scathing, enormously witty look behind the masks of the players who strut and fret their hour upon the stage. Celeste Holm, George Sanders and Thelma Ritter are all superb in supporting roles. ★★★★ $19.99

All Dogs Go to Heaven

(1989, 85 min, US, Don Bluth) Charming animated tale about a roguish German Shepherd who becomes the unlikely guardian to an orphaned girl named Anne Marie. Beautiful visuals from Don Bluth and company (*An American Tail*). Featuring the vocal talents of Burt Reynolds, Loni Anderson, Dom DeLuise, Melba Moore, Vic Tayback, Charles Nelson Reilly and Judith Barsi. ★★★ $14.99

All Dogs Go to Heaven 2

(1996, 82 min, US) Most children, if they believe in Heaven, think of it as a great place to be. They may have second thoughts after seeing this film. Reprieved from the original film, Charlie (now vocalized by Charlie Sheen) is bored by Heaven and longs to leave. He gets his chance when Gabriel's horn accidentally falls to Earth and must be rescued, since its absence leaves all the new angelic canines stranded at Heaven's Gate. Reunited with his old friend Itchy (Dom DeLuise), the two return to Earth where a devilish cat bestows them with earthly bodies. While there, Charlie falls for a sexy Irish Setter (Sheena Easton) who has befriended a runaway young boy. In a rather half-hearted plot, all of these elements are entwined into a resolution that provides Charlie with some sort of newfound ethics. The passable animation and questionable story line create a lackluster movie. ★★ $22.99

All Fall Down

(1962, 110 min, US, John Frankenheimer) Adapted for the screen by William Inge, *All Fall Down* centers on a dysfunctional Cleveland family headed by alcoholic father Karl Malden and domineering mother Angela Lansbury. Warren Beatty, looking impossibly young and handsome, is the eldest son Berry-berry, a louse of a drifter who returns home at the insistence of his idolizing brother Brandon deWilde. Eva Marie Saint rounds out a first-rate cast as a family friend who, unfortunately, becomes involved with Beatty. Director Frankenheimer concentrates on the dark side of the American family, exploring a bruised familial psyche with numerous open wounds. And thanks to its perceptive direction and script, the film cuts deeper than the usual Gothic drama. It's Lansbury who walks away with the acting honors, though Barbara Baxley is fine in a small but potent role as one of Beatty's pick-ups. ★★★½ $19.99

All Night Long

(1981, 88 min, US, Jean-Claude Tramont) An offbeat and marvelous comic romp with Gene Hackman in great form as an all-night drugstore manager who begins an affair with his sexually frustrated neighbor's wife, Barbra Streisand. She, in turn, is involved with Hackman's teenage son, Dennis Quaid. A small gem, and vastly underrated. ★★★½

All of Me

(1984, 93 min, US, Carl Reiner) Reincarnation, the hereafter, gurus and modern romance are all equally spoofed in director Reiner's splendidly funny romp which offered Steve Martin his first real chance to prove his immense comic abilities. Lily Tomlin co-stars as a dying, rich invalid whose belief in returning from the dead prompts some hasty legal maneuvering. This sends lawyer Martin to her side. But in a strange turn of events, Tomlin's soul has now been transported into the body of Martin, who only wants her out. As the inspired silliness continues, Martin engages in a battle of young German soldiers with his spiritual houseguest. Though the premise and its execution are engaging, it is really Martin's virtuoso performance which distinguishes the film. Martin literally gets in touch with both his masculine and feminine sides as he fights Tomlin for control of his body, sending him on a hilarious, slapstick search for inner tranquility. ★★★½ $14.99

All Quiet on the Western Front

(1930, 130 min, US, Lewis Milestone) Milestone won an Oscar as Best Director for this classic anti-war film based on the Erich Maria Remarque novel about the experiences of a group of young German soldiers in battle during WWI. The film won an Oscar for Best Picture, and Lew Ayres became a star with his haunting portrayal of the young infantryman. In supporting roles, Slim Summerville and especially Louis Wolheim are terrific as Ayres' fellow soldiers. A made-for-TV version was made in 1979 with Richard Thomas and Ernest Borgnine. ★★★★ $19.99

All Screwed Up

(1973, 105 min, Italy, Lina Wertmüller) Two young men, orphans from the countryside, come to the big city (here Milan) looking for fame and fortune. Upon their arrival, they get arrested, swindled and fall in love, eventually living in a commune with three women while all their romantic and professional aspirations experience ups and downs. Wertmüller's social comedy — made before her more well-known and accomplished works — has its appealing moments, especially when the director allows her camera to sit still and concentrate on the characters' interpersonal relationships. But much of the film is static, and in an effort to demonstrate the frenzy of city life, the story becomes victim to what it is satirizing. The video release is badly dubbed, which doesn't help the film's coherency. ★★

All That Jazz

(1979, 119 min, US, Bob Fosse) Fosse's dynamic and semiautobiographical tribute to the rigors and razzle-dazzle of showbiz. Roy Scheider portrays Fosse's self-absorbed alter ego whose creativity is well matched by his destructive excesses. Ben Vereen, Ann Reinking and Jessica Lange co-star. Film includes some brilliant, unparalleled dance sequences. ★★★½ $9.99

All the King's Men

(1949, 109 min, US, Robert Rossen) A Best Picture Oscar went to this searing adaptation of Robert Penn Warren's Pulitzer Prize-winning novel about the rise and fall of a Huey Long-like politician. Academy Award winner Broderick Crawford gives the performance of a lifetime as the power-crazed senator. Mercedes McCambridge also won an Oscar for her rich portrayal of his devoted secretary. ★★★★ $19.99

All the Mornings of the World (Tous les Matins du Monde)

(1991, 114 min, France, Alain Corneau) Elaborately costumed and acted yet filmed in an almost serene fashion, this story of creativity, passion and betrayal between two composers in 17th-century France should prove to be of interest to serious film lovers and of greater appeal to lovers of classical music. Marin Marais (Gérard Depardieu), a successful composer at the Court of Versailles, painfully looks back into his youth and his volatile relationship with his taciturn music teacher. Told in flashbacks with Depardieu's son, Guillaume, playing the younger Marais, the story explores the contentious relationship between the prodigious student and his gifted teacher Sainte Colombe. Studied and intense, the film's greatest moments occur in the stirring chords of its passionate Baroque music. (French with English subtitles) ★★★½ $19.99

All the President's Men

(1976, 138 min, US, Alan J. Pakula) The film that successfully captures the heady paranoia of the Watergate years. Journalism departments' enrollments skyrocketed after the Woodward-Bernstein team, who broke the Watergate story in *The Washington Post*, were portrayed in this film by Robert Redford and Dustin Hoffman. Superlative support (Oscar-winner Jason Robards, Jack Warden, Martin

All Quiet on the Western Front

All the Vermeers in New York

Balsam, Hal Holbrook, Ned Beatty and others), an Oscar-winning script by William Goldman and taut, incisive direction by Pakula are weaved together to produce an intelligent, blistering account of political chicanery and investigative prowess. Yes, this is the first time you asked the question, "What did the President know and when did he know it?" ★★★★ $19.99

All the Right Moves

(1983, 91 min, US, Michael Chapman) An earnest Tom Cruise plays a Pennsylvania high school football star who sees an athletic scholarship as a way out of his small mining town. Craig T. Nelson also stars as his hot-tempered coach himself looking for a ticket out. Predictable, uneventful but slickly directed and performed. ★★ $9.99

All the Vermeers in New York

(1990, 97 min, US, Jon Jost) Radical independent filmmaker Jost presents an austere, amusing jab at wealthy New Yorkers and the commodification of art in this story of a lonely stockbroker (Stephen Lack) who becomes obsessed with a wispy, emotionally reserved French actress (Emmanuelle Chaulet of *Boyfriends and Girlfriends*) after he meets her in the Vermeer Room of the Metropolitan Museum. With an almost cinema verité starkness, the film uncovers the hollow lives of Manhattan's power brokers and effectively unmasks their haughty pretenses. In a clear juxaposition, Jost cuts from Lack at his brokerage job to a spirited conversation between a gallery owner (Gracie Mansion) and a struggling artist (Gordon Joseph Weiss) who is begging her for a $10,000 advance — it's a marvelously subversive interplay of images. Exquisitely shot, the film features an excellent jazz score by The Bay Area Jazz Composers Orchestra. ★★★ $24.99

All This, and Heaven Too

(1940, 143 min, US, Anatole Litvak) Handsomely produced tearjerker starring Bette Davis and Charles Boyer as a 19th-century Paris aristocrat who murders his wife after falling in love with his children's governess (Davis). Great performances by the two leads. ★★★ $19.99

All Through the Night

(1942, 107 min, US, Vincent Sherman) Before he tangled with Nazis in *Casablanca*, Humphrey Bogart took on German spies right here in the USA. Bogey plays Gloves Donahue, a hotshot Manhattan gambler whose investigation into the murder of an old family friend leads him hot on the trail of a Nazi spy ring. With its Runyon-esque characters, sparkling dialogue, snappy one-liners and detestable villains, this comic espionage thriller is a supremely enjoyable lark. Bogey is in great form, and is given first-rate support by the likes of William Demarest, Frank McHugh, Conrad Veidt, Peter Lorre, Judith Anderson and, in two early roles, Phil Silvers and Jackie Gleason. ★★★½ $19.99

Allegro Non Troppo

(1976, 75 min, Italy, Bruno Bozzetto) Italian animation artist Bozzetto offers his own answer to Walt Disney's *Fantasia*. This delightfully whimsical work features a variety of bizarre creatures cavorting to the music of Debussy, Dvorak, Ravel, Sibelius, Vivaldi and Stravinsky. ★★★½ $29.99

Alligator

(1980, 94 min, US, Lewis Teague) John Sayles wrote the screenplay for this tongue-in-cheek, very entertaining horror film about a giant alligator terrorizing the populace of Chicago. With Robert Forster, Robin Riker and Henry Silva. (Those stories about gators being flushed down the toilet are obviously true.) ★★★

Alligator Eyes

(1990, 101 min, US, John Feldman) A trio of friends hit the road to try and get away from it all but wind up deep in the middle of something else when they pick up a mysterious, sexy hitchhiker. Tensions between the four well-conceived characters mount as their relationships are tested and secrets revealed. Though the film has an intriguing premise that never fully delivers on its potential, the engaging performances by a cast of unknowns and the film's good use of settings along the Outer Banks of North Carolina make it a trip worth taking. ★★★ $89.99

Allonsanfan

(1974, 100 min, Italy, Paolo & Vittorio Taviani) The year 1816 finds Europe settling into a conservative period after the upheavals of the Napoleonic era. This unusual time is the setting for the Taviani brothers' lavish yet intelligent political costume drama. Marcello Mastroianni is Giulio, a petite bourgeois who returns to the new European order after spending time in prison. Disillusioned by what he sees, he becomes torn between his comfortable upbringing and his revolutionary ideals. Mastroianni excels as the spineless aristocrat who must decide between loyalty to his old radical compatriots or betrayal of them for personal gain. (Italian with English subtitles) ★★★½ $29.99

Almonds and Raisins

(1984, 85 min, US, Russ Karel) Orson Welles narrates this delightful account of the history of a once-flourishing segment of American movie making: the Yiddish cinema. From 1927 through 1939, some 300 Yiddish films — including musicals, gangster films, screwball comedies and even a Yiddish western — were produced for the teeming New York Jewish immigrants. Few of these films exist in their entirety, but through film clips and interviews with surviving actors, directors and producers, filmmaker Karel has fashioned an enthralling image of this lost industry and culture. ★★★½ $79.99

Almost You

(1984, 96 min, US, Adam Brooks) Josh Mostel's wonderful supporting turn nearly makes this mediocre romantic comedy worth watching. Too bad stars Brooke Adams, Griffin Dunne and Karen Young can't accomplish as much. Dunne plays a New York executive who begins an affair with his injured wife's nurse. ★★ $79.99

Alphaville

(1965, 95 min, France/Italy, Jean-Luc Godard) This is quintessential Godard, complete with fragmented musical score, existential reflections, jump cuts, hyperbolic expostulation, disjointed conversations and unexpected silences. Positing the notion that a fabricated legend can communicate complex realities, Godard creates Lemmy Caution (Eddie Constantine), a chiseled-face man with a gun who's not hesitant to use it. He says he's been assigned by his newspaper (*Figaro-Pravda*) to Alphaville, a sterile, joyless urban complex, where day is as dark as night and language has no meaning, where magnificent paranoia is the correct response to abject dehumanization and routinized violence. Anna Karina is Caution's official government tour guide, a woman of ethereal beauty and mechanical compliance, who becomes both savior and saved. It's Godard: You'll find the film to be either monumental gibberish or a stimulating exercise in philosophical exposition and filmic device. ★★★½ $29.99

Alpine Fire

(1985, 117 min, Switzerland, Fredi M. Murer) Visually stunning and scrupulously detailed, this sublime drama is about the life and traumas of a family of four who live in near isolation in a remote area of the Alps. The film focuses on the teenage son, a mildly retarded deaf-mute whose pangs of adolescent sexual and emotional turmoil are comforted by his understanding older sister — a close bind which inevitably leads to incest. (Available dubbed and in German with English subtitles) ★★★ $79.99

Alsino and the Condor

(1982, 90 min, Nicaragua, Miguel Littin) The recipient of the Best Feature awards at the L.A. Filmex and the Moscow International Film Festival, this remarkably moving drama concerns the abrupt abduction of a young boy in a battle-scarred Nicaraguan village. Chilean director Littin strikes a rueful, poetic tone and the expressive face of Alan Esquivel (as Alsino) captures the searing pain of a stolen childhood. Also with Dean Stockwell. (Spanish with English subtitles) ★★★½

Altered States

(1980, 120 min, US, Ken Russell) This fantastic assault on the senses is one of Russell's best films. In his first starring role, William Hurt portrays an inquisitive scientist who experiments with powerful mind-altering drugs in a quest for his primal self. Gradually, he undergoes a series of mental and physical transformations and experiences some spine-chilling hallucinations. Paddy Chayefsky's novel is brought to life with the help of some shocking, state-of-the-art special effects. And though Chayefsky disowned the film, and had his name removed, this is nevertheless an unforgettable film experience. Blair Brown co-stars as Hurt's long-suffering but compassionate wife, and Charles Haid is terrific as one of Hurt's disbelieving colleagues. ★★★★ $14.99

Always

(1985, 105 min, US, Henry Jaglom) One of director Jaglom's most accomplished and accessible works, this funny, semiautobiographical comedy examines the interaction of three couples spending the July 4th holiday together. As usual, Jaglom unflinchingly bares his soul in front of the camera to present a discourse on the modern relationship. Jaglom's ex-wife Patrice Townsend plays his separated spouse. ★★★ $79.99

Always

(1989, 121 min, US, Steven Spielberg) A glossy, over-produced, technically superior remake of the 1943 Spencer Tracy/Irene Dunne favorite, *A Guy Named Joe*. Richard Dreyfuss, in the Tracy role, stars as a dedicated Montana forest firefighter who dies in the line of duty, only to return to guide (spiritually) an apprentice firefighter – who happens to be romantically involved with the woman (Holly Hunter) he left behind. Though the story lapses into sappy sentimentality, the strength of this Spielberg film is the conviction which a mostly talented cast brings to it. John Goodman and Audrey Hepburn also star. ★★½ $19.99

Always for Pleasure

(1978, 58 min, US, Les Blank) New Orleans has a gut-level mythic quality. *Always for*

Melissa Leo (r.) Henry Jaglom (c.) and Patrice Townsend in Jaglom's *Always*

Pleasure is an in-depth insider's look at the Mardi Gras Festival and the numerous musical traditions and celebrations which support the working-class neighborhoods in that truly unique American city. ★★★ $49.99

Amadeus

(1984, 158 min, US, Milos Forman) Forman's masterful adaptation of Peter Shaffer's Broadway smash is a literate, humorous and visually stunning examination of the rivalry (albeit a fictional one) between musical genius Wolfgang Amadeus Mozart and court composer Antonio Salieri in 18th-century Vienna. F. Murray Abraham is brilliant as the tortured Salieri, and Tom Hulce is equally commanding as the childish Mozart. Winner of eight Academy Awards including Picture, Director and Actor (Abraham). ★★★★ $14.99

Amarcord

(1974, 127 min, Italy, Federico Fellini) Fellini uses a gentle mixture of dreamlike fantasy and bittersweet cynicism in this autobiographical examination of a small Italian town. Young Bruno Zanin (the director's alter ego) hangs out with his friends, gets in trouble, obsesses over women, and attempts to figure out his life. On the surface, the film is a funny and warm coming-of-age story (Fellini's recollection of facing a father confessor as an adolescent boy is alone worth the price of rental). But the specter of impending fascism that looms throughout the picture raises complex and challenging questions. One of Fellini's most accessible and compelling films. (Italian with English subtitles) ★★★★ $39.99

Amateur

(1995, 105 min, US, Hal Hartley) French film star Isabelle Huppert crosses the channel to star in this black comedy of errors about a wannabe-nymphomaniacal ex-nun who discovers an amnesiac (Martin Donovan) left for dead on the streets of New York City. She becomes determined to unlock the mystery of his identity. Along the way, the two encounter such urban denizens as a vengeance-seeking porn star (Elina Lowensohn), a pair of corporate assassins, and an accountant on the verge of a nervous breakdown – each holding a piece of the puzzle. Hartley's deliberately kinky examination of sex, love, identity and intimacy is more plot-driven than his earlier works *Simple Men* and *The Unbelievable Truth*, but still relies too much on having the characters speak their thoughts rather than emoting them, rendering the film somewhat stage-bound. However, the performances are uniformly good and the story line is quirky and appealing. ★★★ $96.89

The Amazing Colossal Man

(1957, 80 min, US, Bert I. Gordon) This above-average 1950s sci-fi schlockfest features better than usual F/X and employs documentary footage. Cold war nuclear paranoia combines with a cynicism uncharacteristic of the era to give us

scenes such as the one in which a Bible shrinks to unreadable size in the hands of the title character. A perfect companion piece to *Attack of the 50 Ft. Woman*. ★★½ $9.99

Amazing Grace (Hessed Mufla)

(1992, 95 min, Israel, Amos Gutman) Set in Tel Aviv, this intense, melancholy drama focuses on Jonathan, a gangly and romantic gay teenager who faces an early-life crisis when he finds himself abandoned by his lover. The youth's passions are rekindled after he befriends Thomas, the handsome, HIV-positive older son of his upstairs neighbor. Their budding yet tentative relationship provides the backdrop for this ambitious, thought-provoking social and sexual drama which touches upon such issues as AIDS, death, drug abuse, the gay milieu of Tel Aviv and family dysfunctionalism. ★★★ $79.99

Amazing Grace and Chuck

(1987, 115 min, US, Mike Newell) Engaging Capra-esque drama about a 12-year-old little league champ who trades the athletic field for the political arena when he refuses to play in protest of nuclear arms. Soon, other athletes the world over follow his lead. With Jamie Lee Curtis, Gregory Peck and Alex English. ★★½ $14.99

The Amazing Panda Adventure

(1995, 90 min, US, Christopher Cain) Set against the magnificent backdrop of the Chinese countryside, this story of the rescue of a Panda cub by an American father and son has sensational scenery, lots of action and plenty of Pandas (both real and animatronic), but both the acting and the screenplay are lackluster. A young boy (Ryan Slater) is sent to China to visit his father (Stephen Lang), a Panda protectionist who is consumed by his work. Upon his arrival, they are both off in pursuit of poachers who have kidnapped a baby Panda. The boy and the translator, a young Chinese girl, are separated along with the cub and struggle to find their way back to civilization. Their developing relationship is the one of the more interesting aspects of the film as they struggle against cultural and gender related differences to become friends. Kids will probably enjoy the action and animals in spite of the film's many weaknesses. ★★ $19.99

Amazon Women on the Moon

(1986, 127 min, US, John Landis) Inconsistent series of vignettes is meant to evoke the feeling of channel surfing through 57 channels of TV schlock. While some sequences are genuinely hysterical and feature interesting cameos (Russ Meyer as a video store clerk), the central joke of a hokey sci-fi movie drags on way too long. You'll be reaching for the fast-forward button. The cast includes Rosanna Arquette, Griffin Dunne, Paul Bartel, Michelle Pfeiffer, Arsenio Hall and David Alan Grier. ★★ $14.99

The Ambulance

(1990, 95 min, US, Larry Cohen) Eric Roberts stars as a police sketch artist who finds himself at the center of a bizarre conspiracy in which people begin disappearing off the streets of New York. While this film boldly borrows from

Elina Lowensohn in *Amateur*

the shockers *Coma* and *The Car*, the lifeless acting and equally dull screenplay can only make one hope that the participants in this lame exercise in tedium (including James Earl Jones) can find a nearby cemetery to hide in, since that's the only place where there are worse plots. ★ $19.99

American Avant-Garde Films

While the musical accompaniment and print quality of some of these shorts leave something to be desired, this fascinating compilation of early experimental shorts provides a startling overview of early collaborations between film and the fine arts, especially the surrealist, expressionist and cubist movements. *Dream of a Rarebit Fiend* (1906, 6 min, Edwin S. Porter) displays the magical possibilities of film in this surrealist story of a man who overeats and drinks and then dreams of flying. *Salomé* (1922, 30 min, Alla Nazimova) is an extravagant version of Oscar Wilde's play, with set and costumes by Valentino's wife Natasha Rambova. Sensual and wildly stylized, the story of Herod's vixen stepdaughter is an outrageous tale. *The Fall of the House of Usher* (1928, 12 min, James Watson & Melville Webber) is based on the Edgar Alan Poe classic. *Lot in Sodom* (1933, 28 min, James Watson & Melville Webber) is an avant-garde interpretation of the Old Testament story. The film features homoerotic imagery, sensual dances and distorted multiple images in telling its tale of a good man haunted by a sexually charged band of homosexual Sodomites. ★★★ $29.99

American Boyfriends

(1990, 90 min, Canada, Sandy Wilson) Margaret Langrick and John Wildman star in this heartwarming though ordinary sequel to the successful *My American Cousin*. Set in 1965, this coming-of-age film opens with three Canadian teenyboppers searching for American adventure, good times, and boys boys boys! What our three young thrill-seekers end up with is an unforgettable lesson about the meaning of friendship, love and understanding. Featuring an upbeat soundtrack of classic 1960s tunes. ★★½ $79.99

American Buffalo

(1996, 88 min, US, Michael Corrente) David Mamet's 1975 play finally makes it to the screen with mixed results courtesy of director Corrente (*Federal Hill*). Dennis Franz plays Don, a pawn shop owner who enlists the aid of a troubled teen (Sean Nelson) to help him steal from a scam-artist customer. Teach (Dustin Hoffman playing the role Al Pacino created on stage), Don's loser friend, convinces him to let him in on the deal. As is often the case with Mamet, loyalties shift, tempers flare, regrets are voiced and recriminations are answered during the course of events until the inevitable conclusion. In fact, all of Mamet's stylistic trademarks are here as well: profane, hyper-real dialogue, ugly situations, desperate characters and — also as is often the case in Mamet screen adaptations — terrific acting. Franz gives a superb, subtle performance, and Hoffman hasn't been this good in quite some time. More than holding his own with these two vets, Nelson proves his excellent performance in *Fresh* was no fluke. The acting more than compensates for Corrente's static direction, which lacks imagination and can't overcome an uncinematic, filmed-play feel. ★★½ $99.99

American Dream

(1989, 100 min, US, Barbara Kopple) Let this stunning documentary serve as a warning to all those who feel emboldened in the post-Reagan/Bush world that the wounds inflicted by management on labor over the last decade will have far-reaching consequences. Kopple brilliantly chronicles the long and bitter strike at the Hormel Meat Packing plant in Austin, Minnesota. As is her style, Kopple — whose *Harlan County, U.S.A.* won numerous awards, including an Oscar — spent a period of several months living with the townspeople, letting her camera roll until it almost faded into the background. Consequently, she is able to capture some incredibly poignant and uncensored moments in the lives of the people affected by the strike. She shows how the Union Local steered its members in the wrong direction, much to the consternation of the International, in pushing their demands beyond the breaking point. But of course, she doesn't let industry off the hook, either, as she documents the steady lifestyle decline of the American worker under laissez faire policies which put the bottom line and greed above people and community. ★★★★ $19.99

American Dreamer

(1984, 105 min, US, Rick Rosenthal) JoBeth Williams stars in this endearing action-comedy about a bored housewife who wins a trip to Paris via a creative writing contest — thanks to the adventures of a female superspy, "Rebecca Ryan." Once there, she's mugged, develops amnesia and begins to think she *is* Rebecca Ryan. Cutish romance and intrigue follow. Also with Giancarlo Giannini and Tom Conti. Call this one *Romancing the Clone*. ★★½ $19.99

American Fabulous

(1992, 105 min, US, Reno Dakota) A gay white trash Spalding Gray, bitchy motor-mouth Jeffrey Strouth dominates the screen in this amusingly campy one-man performance piece.

Shot primarily in the back seat of a '57 Cadillac as it cruises across the country, Jeffrey, like a mincing Tallulah Bankhead, extemporaneously pontificates on any subject that enters his mind, elaborately weaving tales culled from his past, with wild imagination; stories that are at once unbelievable, hilarious and semi-tragic. With a razor-sharp wit, the thirtyish Southerner recounts significant moments from his life while the filmmaker simply lets the camera roll, offering free reign to the catty and amusingly acerbic storyteller. There are a few problems with the film — visually it is numbingly static and a bit too long — and while Jeffrey's an entertaining host, a better night might be with some of your more animated and tackier gay friends. ★★ $29.99

American Flyers

(1985, 113 min, US, John Badham) Steve Tisch (*Breaking Away*) wrote the screenplay for this involving story about two estranged brothers, each coming to terms with the death of their father, who enter a grueling three-day bicycle race in the Colorado Rockies. Kevin Costner, in one of his first starring roles, appears as one of the brothers. Also with David Grant and Rae Dawn Chong. ★★½ $14.99

The American Friend

(1977, 127 min, US/France/West Germany, Wim Wenders) Complexities abound when a mysterious American go-between (Dennis Hopper) lures a dying man (Bruno Ganz) into a cunning game of murder and revenge. Director Wenders illustrates his favorite themes of anomie, mortality and cultural infiltration. (In English and German with English subtitles) ★★★ $29.99

American Gigolo

(1980, 117 min, US, Paul Schrader) Richard Gere plays Julian Kaye, a shallow, narcissistic, high-priced prostitute who becomes involved with a senator's wife (Lauren Hutton). As their affair gets steamy and serious, Gere is framed for the murder of one of his clients. And the only person who could help him — Hutton — can't. Writer-director Schrader seems to particularly enjoy wallowing in the sleaze of Los Angeles' underbelly of pimps, addicts and whores; though he unsuccessfully tries to masquerade his tale with a pretentious and artsy examination of one man's failure to find himself. Stylish and empty, *American Gigolo* is more enjoyable as a trashy romantic melodrama than as an overheated sexual thriller. Hector Elizondo hits just the right note as a determined detective on Gere's case. ★★ $14.99

American Graffiti

(1973, 110 min, US, George Lucas) This film turns back the clock to a summer night in 1962 — wait! This film isn't like the rest; it's the first and best of its kind. In this classic comedy, we spend the evening with a couple of teens who are getting together before leaving for college in the fall. Most of the cast is famous now — Richard Dreyfuss, Paul LeMat, Ron Howard, Charles Martin Smith, Cindy Williams, Harrison Ford, Mackenzie Phillips, not to mention the director, George Lucas. Great performances, a great score and a great feel to it. ★★★★ $14.99

A

American Heart

(1993, 117 min, US, Martin Bell) Director Bell picks up where *Streetwise*, his gripping 1984 documentary about Seattle street kids, left off with this hard-edged, brutally honest depiction of an ex-convict father and his teenage son scrapping for both a living and reconciliation. In a startling performance, a long-haired and muscularly lithe Jeff Bridges plays a recently paroled jewel thief who is reunited with his estranged son (Edward Furlong). The two move into a sleazy Seattle apartment building living amongst the city's underbelly and forgotten classes. As Bridges attempts to go straight and, however improbably, act as head of this fragile family unit, Furlong takes up with a youthful street clique, slowly entangling him in a life of petty crime. *American Heart* is unflinching in its realistic portrayal of life on the edge, and only misses the mark at the very end with an unsatisfactory finale. Delivering one of his best performances, Bridges' stinging portrayal is smartly complemented by Furlong's anguished dreamer. ★★★½ $19.99

An American in Paris

(1951, 102 min, US, Vincente Minnelli) The glorious music of George and Ira Gershwin and the incomparable dancing/choreography of Gene Kelly combine to make this one of the most accomplished musicals of all time. Gene plays an artist living in post-WWII Paris who is torn between waif Leslie Caron and patron Nina Foch. Academy Award for Best Picture. ★★★★ $14.99

American Me

(1992, 125 min, US, Edward James Olmos) Edward James Olmos makes a skilled directorial debut with this good-looking if heavily dramatic and clichéd prison/gang drama. Olmos stars as Santana Montoya, a Mexican youth who is incarcerated, and from his lengthy stay behind bars becomes the leader of the Mexican Mafia of Folsom Prison. With the aid of his two childhood buddies (William Forsythe and Pepe Serna), Montoya rules with an iron fist. On his release, however, he finds his time on the outside as difficult as it was on the inside. Trying to go straight, Montoya becomes another victim to injustice as he is unable to escape his murderous past. Though supposedly incorporating an anti-gang theme, Olmos seems to relish in the violence he is protesting. A brutal, dark work that, at least, has something to say. ★★½ $19.99

The American President

(1995, 112 min, US, Rob Reiner) "I'm trying to savor the Capra-esque quality" Annette Bening's enthusiastic lobbyist says as she enters the White House. "Capra-esque" also ably describes Reiner's sweet-natured romantic comedy set against the drama of Washington, D.C.'s behind-the-scenes deals and presidential procedure. In his most likable performance, Michael Douglas plays a Democratic President up for re-election. An idealistic widower, he meets Bening when she lashes out against his policies — and in true Capra fashion love is on the horizon. Reiner balances the film with equal parts joyful romantic comedy and bristling political observations. And though *The American President* wears its heart on its "left" sleeve (Richard Dreyfuss, looking and acting like Phil Gramm, is Douglas' dastardly Republican opponent), its partisan slant is all the more appreciated having been made during the height of Newt's revolution. Martin Sheen and Michael J. Fox are compelling in support, and as this American president notices, Bening is simply irresistible. (Available letterboxed and pan & scan) ★★★ $19.99

American Sexual Revolution

(1970, 66 min, US, John Williams) The proliferation of sex in America (through peep shows, porno movies and X-rated magazines) is exposed in this campily awkward, "behind-the-scenes" documentary. The narrator takes a sympathetic, even enthusiastic stance as the camera travels to several different American cities to visit various people who make their living in the new industry. At one point we are taken to a film set and watch a porno film, initially involving two blonde women and a young man, being made. Also included are some early stag films from the 1920s, a sex photo shoot, shots of a gay pride parade and interviews with various people on the street and their reactions to the proliferation of graphic sex. Fun and educational, an X-rated film that will bring misty-eyed nostalgia to many fans of that flesh-obsessed era. ★★

The American Soldier

(1970, 80 min, West Germany, Rainer Werner Fassbinder) Fassbinder pays homage to American film noir and the milieu of Samuel Fuller, Humphrey Bogart and Lemmy Caution in this atmospheric gangster pic. The story concerns the fatalistic prowlings of Rickey, a professional killer hired to bump off a few problem crooks (and then some) for the German police. (German with English subtitles) ★★★ $29.99

American Taboo

(1982, 94 min, US) Winner of the Academy Award for Best Student Film, this impressive first feature seems more like a bonafide independent production rather than a simple student work. The story, sort of a poor man's *Something Wild*, follows the budding romance between a shy, awkward 30-year-old photographer and a beautiful teenage girl. The man, an introvert who lives life voyeuristically and vicariously through his photography, soon finds his ordered, neurotically secure life transformed by his romantic involvement with his sexy, fun-loving nymphette neighbor. Filmed with assurance and a strong sense of narrative, the effort is marred only by an inconsistent script. ★★★ $69.99

An American Tail

(1986, 80 min, US, Don Bluth) A charming animated feature produced by Steven Spielberg about a young immigrant mouse who becomes separated from his family upon arrival in America, then finds all sorts of adventures with his new friends. The cute story, which is easy for little ones to follow, draws upon some serious subjects without heavy-handedness, and the animation is well done. ★★★

An American Tail: Fievel Goes West

(1991, 75 min, US, Don Bluth) Don Bluth once again charms kids of all ages with this second installment of the Mouskovitz family epic, which finds them leaving the cat-infested and crime-laden big city behind for the wild frontier, unwittingly led by a deceitful feline (the mischievous voice of John Cleese). The excellent animation and musical score are first-rate. ★★★ $19.99

An American Werewolf in London

(1981, 98 min, US, John Landis) Two typical American lads (David Naughton and Griffin Dunne) on holiday in Europe find more adventure than they bargained for in this chilling and gloriously entertaining mirth-filled terror fest. Director Landis (arguably at his best) combines a great rock score, excellent F/X, an erotic love story and moments of inspired humor to tell the tale of a vacationing college student, David (Naughton), who is attacked by a werewolf on the moors of the English countryside. As his friend Jack (Dunne), who died in the same attack, haunts him from the grave in a gruesome series of deteriorating visits, a hallucinating David begins to doubt his own sanity until he eventually terrorizes London under the glow of the silvery full moon. Jenny Agutter also stars as a nurse who takes a liking to David. Rick Baker was the first recipient (and deservedly so) for the newly created Oscar category of Makeup. ★★★½ $9.99

The Americanization of Emily

(1964, 117 min, US, Arthur Hiller) Biting military satire with James Garner in top form as an American naval officer who is the unwitting dupe in an admiral's plan to turn a Normandy invasion casualty into a publicity stunt. Julie Andrews (in her first film after *Mary Poppins*) plays a British war widow who falls in love with Garner. Exceptional script

Jeff Bridges in *American Heart*

by Paddy Chayefsky (based on William Bradford Huie's novel). ★★★½

The Amityville Horror

(1979, 117 min, US, Stuart Rosenberg) Mediocre film version of Jay Anson's popular novel detailing the supposedly true-life events which led the Lutz family to leave their Long Island dream home. James Brolin and Margot Kidder star in this ghost story about demonic poltergeists scaring our hapless heroes out of their wits (and into a national best-seller). ★½

Amityville II: The Possession

(1982, 104 min, US, Damiano Damiani) An awful Freudian prequel to the 1979 haunted house shocker, this time focusing on the original tenants, an "average American family" whose run-of-the-mill existence is ripped asunder by demonic possession. Senseless and curiously lethargic. With Burt Young, Rutanya Alda and Moses Gunn. ★ $9.99

Among the Cinders

(1983, 109 min, Australia, Rolf Haedrich) A 16-year-old boy, deeply disturbed by the death of his best friend, is sent to live with his grandmother. There he meets a woman whose anger matches his grief. A moving drama of a boy's passage into manhood. ★★½ $14.99

Amongst Friends

(1993, 88 min, US, Rob Weiss) Tightly structured, swiftly moving and surprisingly effective, this film from director Weiss begs comparison to Scorsese's gritty classics. Strong performances and a hyperkinetic script (by Weiss) highlight this story about the lives of three youths on the deceptively mean streets of Long Island. Childhood loyalties fall prey to the harsh realities of the adult world as young men with everything look for the one thing that can never be given but only earned — respect. The director appears as the thug at the post-holdup party who explains why he had to shoot that security guard in the ass. ★★★½ $14.99

Amor Bandido

(1980, 90 min, Brazil, Bruno Barreto) Told with melodramatic gusto and imbued with loads of nudity, this torrid and violent story of doomed love is played out amidst the backdrop of an alternately seedy, and yet beautiful, Rio de Janeiro. Thrown out by her detective father, a 17-year-old girl becomes an erotic dancer and hooker at a club in the tough Copacabana. It is here that Sandra meets Tony, a baby-faced teenager and cold-blooded killer. Fueled by loneliness and lust, the two fall passionately in love — all the while unaware that the noose of retribution is tightening around their necks. (Portuguese with English subtitles) ★★★ $19.99

El Amor Brujo

(1986, 100 min, Spain, Carlos Saura) Manuel de Falla's electrifying and passionate gypsy ballet is brought to the screen by the incomparable team of choreographer Antonio Gades and director Saura. Exuberant flamenco dance punctuates this steamy tale of a young widow who is tormented by her late husband's ghost. The strikingly handsome Antonio Gades plays her suitor, who desperately seeks to break the spell. Also starring the undeniably sensual Laura del Sol. (Spanish with English subtitles) ★★★ $29.99

Amos & Andrew

(1993, 95 min, US, E. Max Frye) When Andrew Sterling (Samuel L. Jackson), Pulitzer Prize-winning playwright and wealthy black man, arrives at his new home on an island in New England, his neighbors mistake him for a burglar and call in the local police and set in motion what was surely intended to be a comical farce, poking fun at racial attitudes. Instead, the result is non-stop inanity and annoying stereotypes. Local police chief Dabney Coleman attempts to cover his tracks by setting loose petty thief Nicolas Cage (who plays Amos) on the unsuspecting Jackson. Cage and Jackson seem to sleepwalk their way through the anemic screenplay, Coleman suffers his usual indignities and Giancarlo Esposito submits a truly bilious caricature of the Rev. Al Sharpton. ★ $14.99

Amsterdamned

(1988, 114 min, The Netherlands, Dick Maas) The city of Amsterdam becomes an unwitting accomplice to a series of grisly murders when a sadistic killer uses the city's canals to amphibiously stalk his prey. This "Amsterdam Vice" police thriller proves that Hollywood does not have a lock on great action films. The story follows the frantic efforts of a good-looking detective with a five-day beard (shades of you-know-who) who is assigned to seek out the underwater killer. Great locales, wonderful camera work and a heart-throbbing chase scene through the canals help make this a memorable action drama. (Dutch with English subtitles) ★★★ $9.99

Anaconda

(1997, 100 min, US, Luis Llosa) It's hard to argue with a good monster movie, and this one is more than adequate. Basically this story of a bunch of people lost in the jungle and who are chased and killed off by a giant snake (as if you couldn't guess) succeeds at being suspenseful and fun at the same time. Where it doesn't succeed is in originality and in successful execution of its special effects. The computer-generated anaconda looks terrible, but fortunately is onscreen so little (until the end) and moves so quickly, that its artificiality can be overlooked by an extra-generous suspension of disbelief. Jennifer Lopez is appealing in her first action role, Ice Cube's character's fate is not what one would expect, and Jon Voight spends the movie doing a bad impression of Al Pacino in *Scarface*. It may be as brainless as its title character, but *Anaconda* manages to consistently entertain. ★★½ $99.99

Anastasia

(1956, 105 min, US, Anatole Litvak) In 1956, Ingrid Bergman appeared in her first American production in six years since being exiled to Europe for her affair with the director Roberto Rossellini. Shot on location in Paris, *Anastasia* heralded her triumphant return, and she was justly rewarded an Oscar for her excellent performance. Bergman stars as a woman who, while in an asylum, claimed to be the youngest daughter of assassinated Russian Czar Nicholas. Yul Brynner is an ex-Russian military leader searching for a lookalike of the princess to set up a swindle. When they cross paths, Brynner plays Higgins to Bergman's Dolittle. But as he coaches her, it becomes apparent she may be who she claims to be. Based on the hit play, the film is a captivating story of identity and remembrance, made all the more appealing by the virtuoso portrayal by Bergman. Her reunion scene with Helen Hayes, playing the Dowager Empress, is extremely moving. ★★★½ $19.99

Anatomy of a Murder

(1959, 160 min, US, Otto Preminger) This riveting courtroom drama, a groundbreaker when released, maintains its punch and relevance today. The tension-filled, complex plot — about small-town lawyer James Stewart defending soldier Ben Gazzara who murdered a bartender who allegedly raped his wife Lee Remick — is sustained by tour de force ensemble acting from the star-studded cast; highlighted by Stewart's portrayal of the deceptively easy-going defense attorney. Strong direction by Preminger is punctuated by the throbbing Duke Ellington score. Outstanding in support are George C. Scott, Arthur O'Connell, Eve Arden and real-life Army-McCarthy hearings lawyer Joseph Welch. ★★★★ $19.99

Anchors Aweigh

(1945, 140 min, US, George Sidney) Gene Kelly and Frank Sinatra's first musical together is a sentimental though fun romp about two sailors on leave (a theme which would re-occur in *On the Town* and even indirectly in *It's Always Fair Weather*) in Tinseltown. This is the one where Gene dances with Jerry the Mouse. ★★½ $19.99

And a Nightingale Sang

(1989, 90 min, GB, Robert Knights) Made for Masterpiece Theatre, this delightfully charm-

Michael Douglas and Annette Bening in *The American President*

ing little comedy-drama tells the tale of a working-class British family during WWII. The story revolves around Helen, the family's eldest daughter, a 31-year-old spinster who at long last finds love with a young soldier. Filled with mirth and a smattering of social commentary, the film exhibits the same kind of tenderness for the misbegotten which makes Mike Leigh's films so thoroughly enjoyable. Joan Plowright co-stars as the family's fervently Catholic matriarch. ★★★ $19.99

And God Created Woman

(1957, 92 min, France, Roger Vadim) BB Mania (Brigitte Bardot that is) pulsated after the release of this sex comedy, which by today's standards is chastefully harmless. Bardot is a man-teasing 18-year-old whose lustful encounters with the irresistible opposite sex are enacted out amid the sun and splendor of St. Tropez. (Dubbed) ★★½

And God Created Woman

(1987, 98 min, US, Roger Vadim) Vadim's tepid remake of his own 1957 cause célèbre stars Rebecca DeMornay in the Brigitte Bardot role. The story's about a prison escapee who just wants to play rock 'n' roll. Vincent Spano also stars as the carpenter wrapped around her thumb, and Frank Langella is her sexual plaything. ★½ $14.99

And Hope to Die

(1972, 95 min, France/Canada, René Clément) From the director of such intriguing films as Forbidden Games, Joy House and Rider on the Rain comes this stylish but disappointing thriller made in Canada. Robert Ryan, Aldo Ray and Jean-Louis Trintignant star as criminals who plan and execute an elaborate plot to kidnap the moll of an underworld chief and hold her for a million dollar ransom. (Filmed in English) ★★

...And Justice for All

(1979, 117 min, US, Norman Jewison) Al Pacino received an Oscar nomination for his impassioned portrayal of an idealistic lawyer defending a judge accused of rape. Though dramatically uneven in its sometimes satirical portrait of the legal system, a good cast more than compensate for the occasional heavy-handedness — including Jack Warden, Lee Strasberg and Christine Lahti. ★★½ $9.99

And Nothing But the Truth

(1982, 90 min, GB, Karl Francis) This earnest examination of the roles and responsibilities of the media stars Glenda Jackson and Jon Finch as a documentary filmmaker and reporter. While covering a story, they find themselves passionately split on how to investigate the issue at hand. The film offers an intriguing look at how television news is selected, edited and finally seen by the viewer. ★★★

And Now for Something Completely Different

(1972, 80 min, GB, Ian McNaughton) Supreme silliness prevails in this, Monty Python's first movie. Essentially it's a collection of the best of their BBC television program and features dead parrots, transvestite lumberjacks, a killer joke, upper-class twits,

and a lesson on how to defend yourself against a person who is armed with fresh fruit. Wink's as good as a nod to a blind bat, eh? Say no more... ★★★ $19.99

And Now My Love

(1974, 121 min, France, Claude Lelouch) With the theme that one must go back generations to understand the participants in a love story, director Lelouch has fashioned an intoxicating romantic fable with the twist that the lovers don't meet until the film's final seconds. The story begins during WWI, tracing the lives of three generations of Jewish women to introduce the story's young heroine, Sara, an heiress with Marxist leanings who is waiting for the right man. That man is Simon, a petty crook who after his imprisonment becomes a filmmaker despite his idealistic beliefs. Lelouch mixes romance, politics, religion and many of the 20th-century's most momentous occasions in his masterful blender to serve a humorous, energetic and always fascinating discourse on human emotions. It's a wonderful salute to life and love in our time and a thoughtful look at the role of fate and passion in our lives. An engaging cast includes Marthe Keller (playing daughter, mother and grandmother) and André Dussollier as Simon. (Dubbed) ★★★½ $19.99

And the Band Played On

(1993, 144 min, US, Roger Spottiswoode) Based on Randy Shilts' controversial book, this star-studded film adaptation is structured as an investigative medical thriller, and as such has an almost insurmountable problem in that the villain is a virus, its discoveries bring no joy, and there is no happy ending. Historically and scientifically comprehensive, the story centers on a government virologist, Don Francis (Matthew Modine), who almost single-handedly works on solving the mystery that was (is) HIV. The high-profile cast includes Lily Tomlin as a health official, Richard Gere as a Michael Bennett-like director, Phil Collins as a bathhouse owner, Ian McKellen as a gay activist, B.D. Wong as his lover, and Alan Alda, who savors his role as Dr. Robert Gallo. The film indicts nearly everyone involved; and while powerful and engrossing, it does suffer in the depiction of gay characters and in the perception that straight men and women came to the rescue of the gay community. ★★★★ $19.99

And the Ship Sails On

(1983, 138 min, Italy, Federico Fellini) Continuing to eschew traditional narrative methods, Fellini presents a deliberately artificial yet graceful spectacle aboard a luxury ocean liner in 1914. In his serious moments, Fellini concerns himself with the creative force of artistic expression and also portrays a world about to lose its innocence and plunge into WWI. The film's greatest rewards lie in its sweeping images, boldly stylized scenery, impromptu operatic turns and the usual circus of Fellini oddities. (Italian with English subtitles) ★★★ $59.99

The Anderson Platoon

(1967, 65 min, France, Pierre Schoendoerffer) With English narration by director Schoendoerffer (Le Crabe Tambour, The 317th Platoon) himself, this harrowing doc-

umentary follows the very real battle conditions endured by a group of American soldiers stationed in Vietnam. Returning to a land where he himself was stationed for 13 years with the French Army, and fascinated by America's rationale for its participation but claiming to be "on the side of the soldier," the director joined for six weeks an integrated platoon headed by a black West Point graduate, Lt. Joseph B. Anderson. We follow the soldiers' patrols in the Viet Cong-rife jungle and their involvement in actual combat in scenes that create real danger and fear. A fascinating film that finally produces an overwhelming sadness for the embattled young men. Please note that the quality of the tape transfer is below average. Winner of the Academy Award for Best Documentary. ★★★½ $19.99

The Anderson Tapes

(1972, 98 min, US, Sidney Lumet) Sean Connery stars as the mastermind of an elaborate scheme to rob every apartment in a large complex. Little does he know that, for one reason or another, each vault is under surveillance. The tension, along with the irony, is high in this entertaining action film from director Lumet. Also starring Dyan Cannon, Alan King, Martin Balsam (in an offensive gay caricature) and, in his film debut, Christopher Walken. ★★★ $19.99

Andersonville

(1995, 168 min, US, John Frankenheimer) The most notorious Confederate prisoner of war camp during the Civil War was Andersonville, located in Georgia; the commandant was the only soldier tried for crimes against humanity after that conflict. Its squalor and misery are unflinchingly presented in this compelling made-for-cable drama, a follow-up to Gettysburg from Turner. Andersonville begins when a small group of Union soldiers are captured and imprisoned. They are greeted by disease, brutality and death. A cesspool serves as both a toilet and bathing/drinking source, and rapacious fellow inmates rule the confines and prey on new arrivals. At its best, which is much of the time, Andersonville conveys in a sometimes repulsive though gripping manner the hardships endured, and a tense sequence captures the inmates' longing for civility as they form a tribunal and punish the criminals in their midst. An often moving, rarely maudlin testament to the moral heights — and depths — man can attain. ★★★ $49.99

Andre

(1994, 94 min, US, George Miller) Andre generated some bad press upon its opening for miscasting the main character, an East Coast seal, using instead a West Coast sea lion. That's only the beginning of its problems. A harbor master (Keith Carradine) and his family befriend an orphaned seal and alienate many of the human inhabitants of their Maine fishing village. The father's eldest daughter and the fishermen are angered by the amount of time he spends with the seal and his youngest daughter (played by Corrina, Corrina's Tina Majorino). Although this is based on a true story, the manipulative plot and overly dramatic ending will limit its appeal to fans of animal stories or, at most, seal lovers. ★★ $14.99

Andrei Rublev

(1965, 185 min, USSR, Andrei Tarkovsky) The life, times and art of early 15th-century icon painter Andrei Rublev are explored in this brilliant and visionary work. Told in eight imaginary episodes, the film follows the painter's journeys through Russia where the artist, numbed by the horrors he sees, gradually loses his faith in God, his ability to speak and his drive to create art. A powerful, slow and dense epic that probes into the role of the artist in society. (Russian with English subtitles) ★★★★ $19.99

Androcles and the Lion

(1952, 98 min, US, Chester Erskine) George Bernard Shaw's delicious satire makes a pleasant film comedy for this story about a young tailor in Imperial Rome who saves his fellow Christians in a lion he once befriended. Good cast includes Jean Simmons, Victor Mature, Alan Young (yes, from TV's "Mr. Ed") and Maurice Evans. ★★★ $29.99

Android

(1982, 80 min, US, Aaron Lipstadt) A fun-filled futuristic adventure set on an isolated space station. Max 404 (Don Opper) is a capable, somewhat waifish android – with a penchant for Jimmy Stewart movies and rock 'n' roll – whose job is to assist his creator, a renegade scientist (Klaus Kinski). Unknown to Max, the good doctor is working on a female and prototype android, destined to replace him. Further complicating matters is the intrusion of three intergalactic criminals, who may be the answer Max needs to fulfill his ambition of voyaging to Earth. Part *Metropolis*, part *Frankenstein* and part *2001*, *Android* is genuinely inspired and thoroughly entertaining. ★★★ $69.99

The Andromeda Strain

(1971, 130 min, US, Robert Wise) The first screen adaptation of a Michael Crichton novel is a pulse-pounding, extremely intelligent sci-fi thriller expertly directed by Wise, who summons both the suspense and style of his *The Haunting* and the imagination and enterprise of his *The Day the Earth Stood Still*. Crichton, who studied to be a doctor, makes efficient use of medical vocabulary and possibility to tell the story of a group of scientists investigating a space virus which has devastated a small New Mexico town. Arthur Hill, James Olson, David Wayne and the great Kate Reid are the doctors racing against the clock whose only clues are two survivors: a screaming baby and an alcoholic. ★★★½ $9.99

Andy Warhol: Superstar

(1990, 87 min, US, Chuck Workman) Focusing on the exceptional life of Andy Warhol, one of the leading (and most photographed) figures in the American Pop Art world, this idolatrous, entertaining documentary probes not only into his phenomenally successful career as a conceptual artist, filmmaker and publisher, but also takes a gossipy peek into his Studio 54/Beautiful People clubbing scenes. From his childhood upbringing in Pittsburgh and his schooling at Carnegie Institute of Technology, through his Factory days and finally to his unusual position as pop icon, the film is well-researched and features interviews with such diverse characters as his farmer brother and aunts, to Dennis Hopper, Sally Kirkland, Liza Minnelli and Viva. A celebration of an enigmatic man and artist whose fascination with fame, beauty and soup cans earned him a remarkable place in 20th-century art. ★★★ $14.99

Andy Warhol's Bad

(1976, 100 min, US, Jed Johnson) Andy Warhol lent his name to this slick, sick and subversive *Pink Flamingos*-like black comedy of extremely bad taste by former Warhol soundman and editor Johnson. A slumming-for-dollars Carroll Baker stars as the tough, nefarious head of a female kill-for-hire organization based in Queens which specializes in especially difficult cases (e.g. a neighbor's pesky dog or a mother's screaming baby). All is going well for her and her immoral ingenues until a stranger (Perry King) enters the scene. *Bad* is gross, highly offensive and disgustingly enjoyable, though the infamous "baby splatter scene" has been edited out. ★★★

Andy Warhol's Dracula

(1974, 93 min, Italy/France, Paul Morrissey) Spawned by the commercial succes of *Flesh for Frankenstein*, this campy treatment of the well-worn Transylvanian tale features Udo Kier as Dracula, the creepy vampire in search of ripe, succulent throats and virginal blood. Leaving Hungary for the purer pastures offered in Catholic Italy, the Count's toothy appetite for a fix of virgins proves elusive as the strapping Joe Dallesandro makes sure that the Count's intended victims are no virgins – even if it means deflowering a 14-year-old. (aka: *Blood for Dracula*) ★★ $14.99

Andy Warhol's Frankenstein

(1974, 94 min, Italy/West Germany/France, Paul Morrissey) B-movie dialogue, over-the-top performances and buckets of gore abound in this campy retelling of the classic horror story, served up with a weird sexual twist. Udo Kier is the mad baron who feverishly works on piecing together body parts from the recently dead to create a pair of perfect creatures – a beautiful female and a sex-crazed male. Joe Dallesandro plays the horny stud to the baron's wife/sister. Originally shown in 3-D, and rated a tantalizing "X." As the baron says, "You haven't known life till you've fucked it in the gall bladder." When asked by a reporter what his actual involvement with the filmmaking process was, Andy Warhol replied, "I go to all the parties." (aka: *Flesh for Frankenstein*) ★★ $14.99

Andy Warhol's Heat

(1972, 100 min, US, Paul Morrissey) Kinky and funny, this many times vulgar takeoff of *Sunset Boulevard* stars Sylvia Miles as the shrillish Sally Todd, a fading movie star (actually a has-been chorus girl) who shares her dreary home with her lesbian daughter and the latter's sadistic girlfriend. Their lives are briefly stimulated when Joe Dallesandro enters the scene. All have the hots for Little Joe — prompting mom to complain her daughter "can't even make a good dyke." An insightful tale of unsatisfactory sex, elusive love and ever-present alienation masked as delightful camp. (aka: *Heat*) ★★★

An Angel at My Table

(1990, 150 min, New Zealand, Jane Campion) The story of New Zealand novelist and poet Janet Frame is lovingly rendered and subtly moving without ever employing cheap sentimental devices. Frame published various successful works while hospitalized for schizophrenia, but that's only one part of this sprawling portrait of self-discovery from *Sweetie* director Campion. A remarkable performance by Kerry Fox as the adult Frame. ★★★ $9.99

Angel Dust

(1994, 116 min, Japan, Sogo [Toshihiro] Ishii) This ambitious effort falls short of the mark due to an unnecessarily dense script which seems to be complex but is really only substituting convolutedness for substance. Relentlessly stylish, particularly during its excellent first half hour, the story centers around

Andrei Rublev

Setsuko, a police psychologist who has the bizarre ability to place herself into the mind of a killer. She begins investigating a series of murders which have been occurring at 6 p.m. each Monday on a particular line of the Tokyo subway. Each of the victims is a young woman killed by an injection of poison while in the middle of a large crowd. As the investigation progresses, Setsuko finds that she is much closer to the killer than she had originally imagined. Multiple viewings are probably required to pick up all of the film's clues and red herrings, but unfortunately the story is not involving enough to support such scrutiny. As pretty as *The Usual Suspects*, but lacking its witty script and original, compelling story. (Japanese with English subtitles) ★★½ $89.99

Angel Heart

(1986, 112 min, US, Alan Parker) Yes, the film with the controversial nude scene with Lisa Bonet. That's all most people seem to remember from this story about a private eye (Mickey Rourke) and a case he is given by Mr. Louis Cypher (Robert De Niro). Parker combines film noir and his penchant for stark, brutal realism to create a creepy, atmospheric film. Not for all tastes, due to its gore. This is the uncut version. ★★★ $9.99

Angela

(1977, 91 min, Canada, Boris Segal) Sophia Loren stars in this curiously uninvolving drama as an older woman who begins an affair with a handsome young man (Steve Railsback) who, unbeknownst to either of them, is her son — separated when he was a child. The stars ignite few sparks between them, and even the film's controversial story line is boring. ★½

Angèle

(1934, 130 min, France, Marcel Pagnol) Acknowledged by De Sica and Rossellini as a great inspiration in their careers, this innovative neorealist melodrama about a girl's seduction, betrayal and eventual redemption is considered by many to be Pagnol's finest work. In the naturalist setting of Provence, a naive peasant girl (Orane Demazis) has a child. Abandoned by her lover and bullied by her domineering father (Fernandel, in his first dramatic role), she runs off to Marseilles where she is soon forced into prostitution. Her father, a simple-minded farmer, driven by love for his daughter, goes to the city to find Angèle and return her home. (French with English subtitles) ★★★★ $59.99

The Angelic Conversation

(1985, 78 min, GB, Derek Jarman) Eschewing narrative form, with the only dialogue being Judi Dench's offscreen reading of twelve Shakespeare sonnets, this cryptic assemblage of stop-action photography can be slow-going; but for those who persist, this allegorical mood piece can be a hypnotically beautiful film. Featuring several Bruce Weber beauties, Jarman, on a soul-searching mission, celebrates life and captures the sensual grace of male youth as well as his feelings on premature death caused by AIDS. With original music by Coil, the film remains an affirmation of life as well as an original and daring work by one of England's greatest film artists. ★★★ $29.99

Angelo, My Love

(1983, 115 min, US, Robert Duvall) Duvall wrote and directed this charming tale about an 11-year-old Gypsy boy in his quest to find a stolen ancestral ring. Angelo Evans plays himself in this loosely structured and somewhat improvisational film, full of wit, energy and passion. ★★★ $59.99

Angels and Insects

(1995, 117 min, US/GB, Philip Haas) Amidst the tidal wave of Jane Austen-mania of 1995 comes this marvelously twisted, psycho-sexual period piece that examines not only the class inequities, but the repressed sexual mores of Victorian society — try to imagine *Sense and Sensibility* updated by 60 years and interpreted by Peter Greenaway. The story (based on A.S. Byatt's novella "Morpho Eugenia") revolves around William Adamson (Mark Rylance), a low-born entomologist who specializes in rare tropical butterflies and moths. Adamson lands a position at the manor of Sir Harold Alabaster (Jeremy Kemp) where he catalogs his employer's collection of zoological specimens as well as tutors his children. He falls in love with Alabaster's emotionally reserved daughter Eugenia (Patsy Kensit) despite the obvious attraction between him and the family's outgoing and well-educated niece Matty (an engaging Kristin Scott Thomas). Dark family secrets lurk in the background, however, giving everything in the film an overriding sense of dread. As Adamson, Rylance is a well of quiet, proletarian moral courage in the face of the cruel indifference of the monied class. Second-time director Haas (*The Music of Chance*) avoids the sophomore blues with a visually striking and emotionally haunting narrative that effectively uses its protagonist's fascination with insects as a metaphor for human interaction. ★★★½ $19.99

Angels Die Hard

(1970, 86 min, US, Richard Compton) It's the Angels vs. militant townspeople as cyclists honor the memory of a comrade run down after being released from the local jail. Bikers turn out to be the "good guys" in this enjoyably familiar biker film starring Tom Baker (star of Warhol's *I, a Man*) and William Smith. ★★½ $9.99

Angels in the Outfield

(1951, 99 min, US, Clarence Brown) The always delightfully gruff Paul Douglas stars in this funny, semi-classic baseball fantasy. Douglas plays the manager of the Pittsburgh Pirates, whose season makes the 1994 San Diego Padres look like champions. With the help of a young orphan and some heavenly spirits, the team turns around and makes a drive towards the pennant. There's plenty of surprise cameos, and a very young Janet Leigh also stars. Remade in 1994 with Danny Glover and Christopher Lloyd. ★★★½ $14.99

Angels in the Outfield

(1994, 105 min, US, William Dear) Disney's remake of the wonderfully sweet 1951 baseball fantasy has been updated both in story and technically without capturing the charm and cheerfulness of the original. The only clever aspect of the screenplay is changing teams to the California Angels (who weren't around in the 1950s). Otherwise, this is a by-the-books revision. Danny Glover plays the manager of the team, a bunch of screw-ups and has-beens. They're soon aided by angel Christopher Lloyd and some heavenly friends, whom only a foster child can see. Whereas in the original the angels couldn't be seen, here the angels are F/X creations, and disappointing ones at that. While some of the baseball footage is genuinely amusing, it's surrounded by sappy, even depressing dramatics. ★★ $19.99

Chico and Harpo duke it out while Groucho and Margaret Dumont observe in *Animal Crackers*

Angels over Broadway

(1940, 80 min, US, Ben Hecht) One of the most offbeat and original film projects of the 1940s, *Angels over Broadway*, written and directed by noted author Hecht (in his only directing job), is a puzzling though irresistible black comedy set in the theatrical confines of New York City. A suicidal embezzler (John Qualen) has his final act rewritten for him by three of life's lost souls: a failing, boozy playwright (Thomas Mitchell in a scintillating performance), a con man determined to do good (Douglas Fairbanks, Jr.) and a call girl (the beautiful Rita Hayworth in one of her first starring roles). ★★★ $19.99

Angels with Dirty Faces

(1938, 97 min, US, Michael Curtiz) This is the classic with James Cagney and Pat O'Brien as childhood friends; the former becoming a gangster, the latter a priest. When Jimmy returns to his old neighborhood, O'Brien has his hands full when the street kids "doing time" at the local parish come to idolize the criminal. *Angels* is fast-paced and well-acted, and who could forget Cagney's walk to the chair? Humphrey Bogart appears as a vicious hood; Ann Sheridan and The Dead End Kids also star. ★★★½ $19.99

Angie

(1994, 108 min, US, Martha Coolidge) A poor woman's *Moonstruck*, *Angie*, based on Avra Wing's novel "Angie, I Says," stars Geena Davis as a Bensonhurst secretary who reexamines her life. Engaged to a likable, macho plumber, Angie learns she is pregnant. But instead of marrying the father, she dumps him and begins an affair with an affected Manhattan artist (Stephen Rea). The film begins on a congenial level – introducing affable characters and playful moments of schtick. Half-way through, however, the story takes a distressing turn and disintegrates into a depressing, yawn-producing soap opera. Davis gives an earnest performance, considering the material, but – like the film – she never captures the character's spirit. ★★ $9.99

Angry Harvest

(1985, 102 min, Germany, Agnieszka Holland) Holland, a former assistant to Andrzej Wajda, has delivered a powerful, sometimes brutal and always gripping view of the Holocaust. Rosa, a Viennese matron, jumps the transport to Auschwitz; Leon, a sexually repressed farmer, reluctantly shelters and then guiltily lusts after her. Armin Mueller-Stahl brilliantly portrays Leon, a bundle of contradictions: coarse and complicated, prissy and sadistic. He becomes infatuated with Rosa's helplessness and his own sense of control. *Angry Harvest* might be called a psychological action film in which the characters are inexorably drawn together by the forces of war. (German with English subtitles) ★★★½

The Angry Red Planet

(1959, 83 min, US, Ib Melchior) It's cheesy. It's silly. It's wonderful. This is an extremely schlocky tale of an expedition to Mars (the angry red planet) where astronauts encounter giant spider-like creatures and killer plants. The acting is stiff and the dialogue is so bad it's funny. Hilarious use of bogus scientific theories to explain what is going on is the staple in these B-flicks and you get plenty of it in this one. A bright red filter is used for any scenes that take place on Mars to further push the angry red planet theme. A perfect Saturday matinee film. ★★

Angus

(1995, 90 min, US, Patrick Read Johnson) Unfortunately, the box art says it all. Angus (Charlie Talbert) is not nearly as unattractive as the cover photo makes him look and this tale of teen angst is so extreme that it makes "My So Called Life" look like a romp in the park. Overweight and overly bright, Angus is the sworn enemy of his high school's most popular student, who makes his life a living hell. The story is taken to such lengths that it is literally painful to watch. The saving grace comes at the end in a stirring and inspired speech from Angus about being different – it should comfort many outcasts. A good cast (with George C. Scott as the youth's grandfather) and soundtrack help distract from the very heavy-handedness of the plot. ★★ $14.99

Anima Mundi

(1992, 30 min, US, Godfrey Reggio) From the team of director Reggio and composer Philip Glass (*Koyanisqaatsi* and *Powaqaatsi*) comes this somewhat aimless yet nevertheless visually exciting paean to the diversity of life on Earth. Produced by the World Wildlife Fund, the film is a dazzling 30-minute montage of the various fauna which inhabit the globe, all set to Glass' pulsating score. The film will probably be of interest mostly to wildlife enthusiasts and possibly children, but the final seven-minute collage of several animals at full gallop in slow motion should delight just about everyone. ★★½ $19.99

Animal Behavior

(1989, 88 min, US, H. Anne Riley) A good cast (Karen Allen, Armande Assante and Holly Hunter) is wasted in this mindless romantic comedy about a music teacher (Assante) who meets a psychologist (Allen) and her "subject": a chimp named Michael. ★ $19.99

Animal Crackers

(1930, 98 min, US, Victor Heerman) The Marx Brothers' second film finds them still struggling to get a footing in their new medium. With blocking that exposes its stage origins, *Animal Crackers* finds the farcical foursome crashing a society party being held by Margaret Dumont (who else?). Groucho makes his grand entrance as the noted African explorer Jeffrey T. Spaulding ("The 'T' stands for Edgar") while Harpo follows close behind blowing chocolate smoke bubbles. Ultimately, Chico and Harpo get roped into stealing a painting, which leads to one of their classic routines. Despite its flaws, though, the film is at times a riotous skewering of the upper class that will leave one resting assured that in "Alabama the tusks are loosa'." ★★½ $14.99

Animal Farm

(1955, 75 min, GB, John Halas & Joy Batchelor) George Orwell's famous satire on totalitarianism and fascism tells the story of a group of farm animals who band together to oust their oppressive farmer only to find that their chosen leader, the pig, is a ruthless dictator. A simplistic translation, *Animal Farm*'s animation is perfunctory, and though Orwell's allegory is a striking one, there's an overall haziness to the production. This is one animated feature that's not for kids. ★★ $29.99

Animal Instinct

(1992, 94 min, US, Gregory Hippolyte) A "B-movie" lover's dream cast heavy-breathes life into this fact-based exercise in political incorrectness taken straight from "tabloid TV." Maxwell Caulfield stars as a sexually dysfunctional cop who gives new meaning to the term "coming attractions" when he begins videotaping the rampant sexual exploits of his beautiful but bored wife (Shannon Whirry) for his own voyeuristic pleasures. Also with Jan-Michael Vincent, John Saxon, David Carradine, Mitch Gaylord and soft-core starlet Delia Sheppard. ★★ $89.99

Animals Are Beautiful People Too

(1974, 92 min, South Africa, Jamie Uys) This documentary by director Uys (*The Gods Must Be Crazy*) humorously explores the animal world, from hedgehogs and hyenas to a lovesick rhinoceros and a baboon with a hangover. ★★★ $19.99

Animation for Fallen Catholics

(60 min, US) Surprisingly, and disappointingly, not as blasphemous as its title suggests, this compilation of shorts avoids cheap shots at the Church and instead feeds on memories of Catholic upbringing and its "wonderfully" dogmatic principles. Included in the series is Daina Krumins' surrealistically religious *Divine Miracle*; Maria Elena Rodriguez' hilarious remembrances of parochial school and those mysteriously habited nuns, *Regina Coeli*; and an innovative short on a seriously disturbed priest in *Landscape with the Fall of Icarus* by Christopher Sullivan. So grab your Baltimore Catechism, say a quick act of contrition and enjoy! ★★½ $24.99

Animation in the Netherlands

(30 min, The Netherlands) A strong introduction to a country more noted for tulips than animation. The highlight is a rare look at George Pal's work before he left for America and Paramount to do his Puppetoons and sci-fi films. The behind-the-scenes footage of the different studios and animators at work elevates this program beyond being just another collection of excerpts. ★★★ $29.99

Animation of the Apocalypse

(60 min, US) Definitely not for the kids, this ambitious and thought-provoking series of eight shorts all deal with visions of doom, urban decay, moral decline and the end of the world! Included in this series is John Schnall's *The Fall of the House of Usher*; Lynn Tomlinson's clay-on-glass *I Heard a Fly Buzz When I Died*; and Christopher Sullivan's *Master of Ceremonies*, about skeletal Death going about his business wreaking havoc on mankind. ★★★ $29.99

A

Anita: Dances of Vice

(1987, 82 min, Germany, Rosa von Praunheim) Lotti Huber stars as an old woman who thinks that she is the reincarnation of Anita Berber, the infamous nude dancer in Weimar Berlin who flaunted her bisexuality, acknowledged taking drugs and generally scandalized the nation with her notorious behavior. Von Praunheim's splashy, provocative film intercuts black-and-white footage of the ragged old woman spouting her outrageous claims with colorful re-creations of the old woman living the life of her alter ego. (German with English subtitles) ★★★ $59.99

Anna

(1987, 100 min, US, Yurek Bogayevicz) Sally Kirkland's riveting Oscar-nominated performance highlights this involving, offbeat version of *All About Eve*, about a middle-aged, once-famous Czech film actress, now struggling in New York, and the young immigrant who befriends her to learn the craft. ★★★

Anna and the King of Siam

(1946, 128 min, US, John Cromwell) The inspiration for the musical *The King and I*, this usually overlooked classic is a perfect blend of Hollywood schmaltz and heart-tugging drama. In an effervescent performance, Irene Dunne is Anna, a mid-19th-century English schoolteacher who travels to Bangkok to instruct the children of the King (an excellent Rex Harrison). As the strong-willed teacher comes in conflict with the equally determined ruler, they fall in love, all the while aware neither is able to act on their feelings. ★★★½ $19.99

Anna Christie

(1930, 89 min, US, Clarence Brown) "Gimme a whiskey, ginger ale on the side. And don't be stingy, baby." With these words, the immortal Greta Garbo spoke her first words on film, evolving from silent star to full-fledged screen legend. Based on Eugene O'Neill's classic play, Garbo plays Anna, the disillusioned prostitute who returns home after 15 years to her sea captain father. Marie Dressler is outstanding as Garbo's alcoholic confidant and drinking buddy, and a youthful Charles Bickford portrays the gruff sailor who falls in love with and then rejects the embittered woman. Though the pace may be slow and the production less than technically savvy, O'Neill's earthy prose and Garbo's radiant performance contribute to make this a rewarding film experience. ★★★ $19.99

Anna Karenina

(1935, 95 min, US, Clarence Brown) Tolstoy's tragic love story is immortalized by the outstanding performance of Greta Garbo in the title role. Her fusion with the character of the doomed heroine is so complete that one might think that Tolstoy had her in mind when he penned the tale. The film also stars Basil Rathbone (who is superb as Karenin), Freddie Bartholomew and Fredric March as her lover. ★★★½ $19.99

Anne Frank Remembered

(1995, 122 min, GB/US, Jon Blair) With 26 million copies of her diary sold around the world, and having been the subject of an award-winning play and an award-winning film based on that play, there's not much more one could possibly think there would be to know about Anne Frank. Such is the beauty and artistry of *Anne Frank Remembered*, an illuminating documentary which not only presents heretofore unknown and fascinating information on the courageous Jewish teen killed during WWII, but also pays tribute to Miep Gies, the heroic woman who hid the Frank family in Nazi-occupied Amsterdam for two years. Though its subject matter may be somber, the film comes alive with an urgency that cannot be ignored. All of the traditional components of the documentary are here, but director Blair and the film's participants make it seem so fresh. Wisely, Blair doesn't go for the easy tear, but instead works on the mind while touching the heart. ★★★½ $19.99

Anne of Avonlea

(1987, 224 min, Canada, Kevin Sullivan) The adventures of Anne continue in this surprisingly enjoyable and captivating sequel to *Anne of Green Gables*. Now eighteen, Anne gets a job as a schoolteacher; and being the feisty, determined redhead that she is, she believes she is ready to try her hand at romance. Colleen Dewhurst returns as her stepmother and there is a special appearance by Wendy Hiller. A humorous, heartwarming tale. ★★★ $29.99

Anne of Green Gables

(1985, 197 min, Canada, Kevin Sullivan) Based on the best-seller by L.M. Montgomery, this enchanting story of the adventures and growing maturity of a teenage girl proves to be a captivating film experience suitable for the entire family. Anne (Megan Follows), a dreamy orphan, is sent to beautiful Prince Edward Island to live with a stern but loving woman (Colleen Dewhurst) and her kindly brother (Richard Farnsworth). This award-winning epic, produced originally for Canadian Television, chronicles our charming heroine as she struggles with the obstacles of adolescence and young adulthood. ★★★½ $29.99

Anne of the 1,000 Days

(1969, 145 min, US, Charles Jarrott) Henry VIII is at it again as he courts, weds and later beheads Anne Boleyn. Richard Burton gives a larger-than-life performance befitting the monarch, and Genevieve Bujold is excellent in her first starring role as the doomed queen. Terrific production values (art direction, costumes, cinematography, editing, etc.) and Bujold's lovely portrayal combine to make this a commendable historical epic. ★★★ $19.99

L'Année des Meduses

(1986, 110 min, France, Christopher Frank) Skin...French skin...Valerie Kaprisky's skin. Fans of soft-core foreign "art" films have their hands full in this erotic tale set mostly on the topless beaches of St. Tropez. Kaprisky can barely keep her makeup on, let alone her clothes, as she plays an 18-year-old nymphet whose only desire is to win over her mother's lover (ambitious she's not). This *Pauline at the Beach* sans moral dilemmas is a delightful soufflé that should please people who want nothing more demanding than viewing a bevy of beautiful bodies. (French with English subtitles) ★★

Les Années 80 (The Eighties)

(1983, 82 min, Belgium/France, Chantal Akerman) The creative genesis of art and the filmmaking process is examined and deconstructed in this unusually fascinating and pleasurable film. Unlike director Akerman's previous somber films, this is a giddy work: a musical set in a suburban shopping mall, and nothing like the Hollywood musicals of the past. The first part of the film features a series of confusingly repetitive and jumbled scenes of a group of women singing, talking, discussing and arguing. Pushing the viewer's tolerance, the film changes direction completely in the second half to reveal the end result of all this confusion — a deliriously fun and lively musical extravaganza. A witty, tongue-in-cheek film that can be frustrating but proves to be well worth the wait. (French with English subtitles) ★★★

Annie

(1982, 128 min, US, John Huston) One of the most popular and admittedly annoying songs ever to come from a Broadway musical, "Tomorrow," is given the red-carpet, zillion-piece orchestra, sing-it-till-you-drop treatment in this over-produced adaptation from director Huston (of all people to direct a musical!). Little Aileen Quinn stars as the title character, who is whisked from her orphanage to spend time with Daddy Warbucks (Albert Finney), the richest man in the world. Carol Burnett, who gives the film's most spirited performance, is the head of the orphanage who sees a way to "Easy Street" thanks to Annie's rich, new pal. The Tony Award-winning stage production had charm in abundance; this *Annie* is cloying, abrasive and frivolous. Also with Tim Curry, Bernadette Peters and Ann Reinking. ★★ $14.99

Annie Hall

(1977, 94 min, US, Woody Allen) Allen's masterpiece is still perhaps his sharpest and wittiest work to date (though some would argue that belongs to *Manhattan*). In this ultimate of crowd pleasers, Allen adroitly puts his finger on the social milieu of the '70s as he explores the ups and downs of modern relationships. Oscar winner Diane Keaton is at her best as Woody's star-crossed lover. A delightful blend of uproarious one-liners, delicious comic schtick, intuitive dialogue, smart performances and penetrating observations on today's mores, *Annie Hall* is pure enchantment. Also with Tony Roberts, Paul Simon, Christopher Walken, Colleen Dewhurst, Carol Kane and Shelley Duvall. ★★★★ $14.99

Annie Oakley

(1935, 88 min, US, George Stevens) Barbara Stanwyck stars as that rootin'-tootin' markswoman Annie Oakley in this episodic but amiable western which follows her rise to fame in Buffalo Bill's Wild West Show in the 1880s. Giving a rather subdued portrayal considering the flamboyant characteristics usually associated with Oakley, Stanwyck plays Annie as a naive and rather feminine romantic who gets all gooey-eyed at the sight of an egocentric sharpshooter (Preston Foster). With a thing or two to say about showmanship, fame and Indian affairs, the film is a little rough around the edges, though certain scenes — especially the re-creations of Bill's show — are well-staged and entertaining. Melvyn Douglas also stars as the show's manager, and Moroni Olsen is a larger-than-life Buffalo Bill. ★★★ $14.99

Annie Oakley

(1985, 53 min, US, Michael Lindsay-Hogg) Jamie Lee Curtis stars as Annie Oakley, that legendary cowgirl of the Wild Wild West. The film follows her story as a young girl mastering the art of shooting, through her marriage to marksman Frank Butler (Cliff DeYoung) and finally features her as a star performer in Buffalo Bill's (Brian Dennehy) Wild West Show. From Shelley Duvall's "Tall Tales and Legends." ★★★ $9.99

The Annunciation

(1990, 101 min, Hungary, András Jeles) Defying placement in any simple category, *The Annunciation* is a strange, poetic and almost surreal feature which — with a cast composed entirely of children from ages eight thru 12 — enacts nothing less than mankind's tragic and tumultuous tale of life on earth. A self-satisfied Satan, in the guise of a pretty blond cherub boy, decides to take Adam and Eve through time, to both witness and partake in the violence, sadness and struggle brought on by their disobedience to God's will. From ancient Greek mythology to the French Revolution and eventually to a plague-stricken 19th-century London, they witness firsthand man's fruitless struggle for liberty and love while drowning in a sea of misery, oppression, death and deception. In what could have been a simple gimmick film, similar to what *Bugsy Malone* was to gangster flicks, *The Annunciation* soon develops into a hypnotic journey through history infused with melancholic religious and existential themes. The acting is uniformly good, with the children's faces suggesting a knowledge and world-weariness well beyond their years. An ambitious, sensual and eerie drama which should engross adventurous videophiles. (Hungarian with English subtitles) ★★★½ $69.99

Another 48 HRS.

(1990, 98 min, US, Walter Hill) Eddie Murphy's career continued its pre-*Nutty Professor* descent with this sequel — let's call it a Xerox — of his 1982 debut. Director Hill, who should know better, keeps the action moving at a brisk enough pace and the villains have been suitably modernized for the '90s, but it's all been done before and it was much better the first time. Nick Nolte also returns and, like everything else, he's a carbon copy of his former self. ★★ $14.99

Another Country

(1984, 90 min, GB, Marek Kanievska) This marvelously acted and elegantly photographed film version of Julien Mitchell's hit London play speculates on the public school days of real-life traitor/defector Guy Burgess. Rupert Everett is the languid "innocent," denied entry to the school's ruling elite because of an indiscreet homosexual affair. Cary Elwes is Everett's handsome lover. ★★★½

Another Stakeout

(1993, 109 min, US, John Badham) Six years after the release of the highly enjoyable

Stakeout comes this inferior sequel, ill-timed and only sporadically entertaining. Richard Dreyfuss and Emilio Estevez, neither looking the worse for wear, repeat their roles as Seattle surveillance cops. Their new assignment is to lay in waiting for a government witness who has flown the coop. They are joined by Assistant D.A. Rosie O'Donnell, whose lack of both training and tact causes an immediate personality clash with our laid-back jokesters. Only a mistaken identity subplot elevates the film, as the policework is virtually nonexistent and the comedy hit-and-miss. ★★ $9.99

Another Thin Man

See: The Thin Man Series

Another Time, Another Place

(1958, 98 min, US, Lewis Allen) Lana Turner chews the scenery in this ordinary soap opera with Turner as a correspondent based in England during WWII who suffers a nervous breakdown when her lover dies. Also with Barry Sullivan and a young Sean Connery. ★★ $14.99

Another Time, Another Place

(1984, 104 min, GB, Michael Radford) This poignant drama observes the effects of a group of Italian POWs on a remote Scottish village in 1944. Three of the Italians are housed next to Janie (Phyllis Logan), who lives a tedious life with her taciturn husband. As they try to relieve each other's loneliness, a sexual attraction develops between Janie and one of the POWs which both frightens and entices her. An extremely impressive debut for both Logan and writer-director Radford. ★★★ $24.99

Another Way

(1982, 102 min, Hungary, Karoly Makk) This courageous and intelligent lesbian love story is set in Hungary immediately after the 1956 uprising and concerns the mutual attraction and budding relationship between two female journalists. Livia, married to an army officer, shyly begins accepting the advances of Eva, an outspoken reporter with whom she shares an office. Director Makk (*Love*) juxtaposes this tender but doomed love affair with the high hopes and bitter suppression of the Budapest Spring. An impassioned plea for tolerance in a land long bereft of it. (Hungarian with English subtitles) ★★★ $69.99

Another Woman

(1988, 81 min, US, Woody Allen) After the disaster of *September*, Allen turns yet again to Ingmar Bergman territory with this complex examination of a woman (Gena Rowlands) whose life-long resistance to her passions is shattered when she accidentally overhears the confessions of a therapy patient (Mia Farrow). Though not as subtle as *Interiors*, the film is a complete success thanks to Rowlands' remarkable performance, and the efforts of a powerhouse cast which includes Gene Hackman, Blythe Danner, Ian Holm, John Houseman and Sandy Dennis. ★★★ $14.99

Ansel Adams: Photographer

(1981, 60 min, US, John Huszar) Ansel Adams, one of the greatest photographers of the 20th century, demonstrates his legendary techniques and talks about his life in this

warmhearted, absorbing and sumptuously photographed documentary. ★★★ $24.99

Antarctica

(1985, 112 min, Japan, Koreyoshi Kurahara) A harrowing adventure story about survival and companionship set in the harshest climate on earth. Based on a true incident, the film features breathtaking cinematography by Akira Shizaka and a haunting score by Vangelis. ★★★ $59.99

Anthony Adverse

(1936, 137 min, US, Mervyn LeRoy) An intermittently interesting adaptation of Hervey Allen's epic novel set during the Napoleonic era. Fredric March ably plays the title character, whose life is covered from his youthful world travels to his rise to power and his marriage to an opera star from poor beginnings. Also starring Olivia deHavilland, Claude Rains, Edmund Gwenn and Oscar-winner Gale Sondergaard ★★ $19.99

Antigone

(1962, 93 min, Greece, George Tzavellas) Sophocle's poetic parable is successfully translated to the screen in this eloquent drama. Maria Callas gives a magnificent performance as Antigone, daughter of Oedipus who, following the dictates of her own conscience, is condemned to death for defying King Creon and burying her two dead brothers. Director Tzavellas, aware of the difficulties of filming Greek tragedies, substitutes the traditional chorus with an unobtrusive offscreen narrator and, coupled with Callas' excellent portrayal, brings this ancient tale to life. (Greek with English subtitles) ★★★ $59.99

Antonia and Jane

(1991, 75 min, GB, Beeban Kidron) This delightfully funny low-budget gem, an Anglicized, feminist homage to Woody Allen, explores the loving and tempestuous relationship between two decidedly different women. Antonia, the plain-looking, insecure but adventurous one narrates the film's opening, giving details of her hilarious obsession with Jane, her pretty, married and seemingly well-balanced childhood friend whom she is about to meet for their annual lunch. Midway through the film, Jane takes over the narration duties and gives us her side of the story. Pleasantly amusing and deceptively simple, *Antonia and Jane* is highly recommended. ★★★½ $89.99

Antonia's Line

(1995, 93 min, The Netherlands, Marleen Gorris) A celebration of the love, unity and strength of women, this wonderfully endearing and touching family chronicle/fable centering on four generations of women playfully alternates between dramatic realism and magical realism (and might very well have been what the film version of Isabelle Allende's *The House of the Spirits* should have been). As written by Gorris, *Antonia's Line* is muted in its anti-male attitude as compared with her previous diatribe-filled dramas. (That's not to say that the men get off easy — for they are seen as boorish and oppressive, a necessary evil in some cases, acceptable mates in others). The story, set in a small Dutch village, spans decades — from the devastation of the post-war period to the present – and follows the fiercely independent-minded Antonia (Willeke van Ammelrooy), who returns to her childhood farmhouse to till the soil and raise a family; all without the aid of the misogynist townsfolk, a hypocritical church and the often violence-prone men. Antonia is aided by her lesbian daughter, a granddaughter and great-granddaughter and a group of social rejects who flock to her. This Oscar-winning Best Foreign Film is masterful storytelling that enthralls. (Dutch with English subtitles) ★★★★ $19.99

Antonio das Mortes

(1969, 95 min, Brazil, Glauber Rocha) Brazilian filmmaker Rocha, winner of the Best Director Award at Cannes in 1969, was forced into exile after the release of this impassioned protest against the oppression of workers by the landowning class. Set in the arid northeast of Brazil, the film, mixing suspenseful storytelling with the area's rich legacy of cultural mysticism and native folk art, follows the violent uprising of a group of peasants who draw strength and inspiration when the "warrior saint," Santo Antonio, aids their rebellion. A powerful drama as well as a stirring political allegory. (Portuguese with English subtitles) ★★★½ $59.99

Any Wednesday

(1966, 109 min, US, Robert Ellis Miller) Jane Fonda sparkles in this saucy bedroom farce based on the hit Broadway comedy about a married executive (Jason Robards) who uses his mistress' (Fonda) apartment to entertain clients. ★★★ $19.99

Anzio

(1968, 117 min, US, Edward Dmytryk) A few distinguished battle scenes add little to this all-star WWII actioner about the Allied invasion of Anzio. Starring Robert Mitchum, Peter Falk, Robert Ryan, Arthur Kennedy and Earl Holliman. ★★ $9.99

Aparajito

(1956, 113 min, India, Satyajit Ray) Ray's second installment of the Apu Trilogy portrays Apu's life from the age of 10, when his father moves the family to the holy city of Benares, to his entrance to college years later. The family's struggles, including the father's death and Apu's efforts to win a scholarship, are vividly chronicled in this unbearably poignant, beautifully filmed cinematic treasure. (Bengali with English subtitles) ★★★★ $19.99

Apart from Hugh

(1994, 87 min, US, Jon FitzGerald) This low-budget film from the Pacific Northwest, while sincere and affectionately gay, fails both dramatically and technically as either a gay romance or character study. For the drama about two young men's struggle to maintain their individual independence and their commitment to each other is handed deadly blows with its laborious plot, slow-as-Bergman pacing, less-than-professional acting and a heavy-handed somberness that drags both the film and its viewers into a near catatonic stupor. Living in rural domesticity, 20ish Collin (David Merwin) and the slightly older Hugh (Steve Arnold) find their seemingly happy and stable relationship undergoing a potential crisis when the vaguely discontented Collin contemplates leaving. *Apart from Hugh* is a gentle slice-of-life story, filmed in black and white, that stresses the complexities and nuances of the relationship at the expense of any audience-involving drama. ★½ $39.99

The Apartment

(1960, 125 min, US, Billy Wilder) This Oscar-winning Best Picture stars Jack Lemmon and Shirley MacLaine in what may be their best screen performances. Lemmon plays a young executive on the go who gets more than he bargains for when he allows superiors to use his apartment for extra-marital encounters and falls in love with his boss' mistress (MacLaine). Writer-director Wilder offers his customary sardonic wit and stinging commentary to lay bare the hypocrisies of the corporate world and the imperfections of love. A scintillating comedy-drama. Fred MacMurray, Jack Kruschen and Ray Walston offer fine support. (Available letterboxed and pan & scan) ★★★★ $19.99

Apartment Zero

(1989, 114 min, GB, Martin Donovan) A multi-layered, stylish thriller which never fails to elicit a strong emotional response, *Apartment Zero* creates an atmosphere of wicked sexual tension through the subtle use of suggestion and innuendo. Set in an English-speaking community in Buenos Aires, the film stars Colin Firth as a sexually repressed cinephile with a penchant for the classics who takes in a swaggering, handsome American boarder (Hart Bochner) with many skeletons in his "closet." Suspicions abound as gruesome political murders haunt the Argentine city upon the arrival of Firth's new roommate. Firth and Bochner shine in their roles, each bringing a subtle suggestion of sexual manipulation and dormant passion to an already explosive scenario. Donovan uses stylish camerawork and extreme close-ups to seduce the viewer into his world of intrigue. ★★★ $19.99

Aphrodite

(1984, 90 min, France, Robert Fuest) The meltingly beautiful Valerie Kaprisky (*Breathless* with Richard Gere) stars in this sensuous staging of Pierre Louys' masterpiece of erotic literature. Set in the Greek islands in 1914, the story is a sensual journey into a world of licentiousness, debauchery and unleashed sexual splendor. In other words, it's not *Mary Poppins*! The complete, unrated and unedited version. (Dubbed) ★★

Apocalypse Now

(1979, 150 min, US, Francis Ford Coppola) A masterpiece of modern cinema, Coppola's epic reworking of Joseph Conrad's "Heart of Darkness" is a mind-blowing, semi-hallucinatory examination of not only the insanity of the Vietnam War, but of war itself. Martin Sheen gives a career performance as a military assassin sent on a mission deep into enemy territory to hunt down a renegade colonel (Marlon Brando). Frederic Forrest, Sam Bottoms and Laurence Fishburne are the unfortunates who must accompany him on his suicide trip up river. Robert Duvall, as an air cavalry commander, gets to utter the classic line, "I love the smell of napalm in the morning," and Dennis Hopper is positively nutty as a devoted follower of Brando. Coppola, cast and crew made a real-life, two-year sojourn into the Philippine jungle to make the film. Along the way Sheen suffered a heart attack, sets were destroyed by typhoons, and the script was rewritten daily. (The making of *Apocalypse* is expertly chronicled in the documentary *Hearts of Darkness*.) If ever there was a foray into experimental improvisation on a big-budget film, this is it. The result, which could have easily been disastrous, is instead a remarkably coherent, superbly acted peek into human cruelty and frailty. (Available letterboxed and pan & scan) ★★★★ $29.99

Antonia's Line

Apollo 13

(1995, 135 min, US, Ron Howard) Though comparisons to *The Right Stuff* – Philip Kaufman's 1983 brilliant tale about the infancy of our space program – are inevitable, director Howard's epic *Apollo 13* is an impressive, suspenseful telling of the near-disastrous 1970 attempted lunar landing which, while lacking *The Right Stuff*'s determined style and hard edge, is nevertheless a well-crafted story of heroism in the face of insurmountable odds. History tells us of the flight of Apollo 13, whose mission to the moon was thwarted by a tank explosion and whose uncertain return home kept Americans spellbound for nearly a week. What Howard has created in his fascinating, straightforward adventure film – aided by excellent effects and a knowing mood of the times – is a hypnotic tale which follows almost to the letter the actual events. The cast is almost secondary to the action, but led by Tom Hanks (as Jim Lovell), Kevin Bacon and Bill Paxton as the astronauts, and Ed Harris and Gary Sinise are ground-control managers, the entire ensemble lends credibility and conviction to their roles. (Available letterboxed and pan & scan) ★★★★ $22.99

The Appaloosa

(1966, 99 min, US, Sidney J. Furie) A lushly photographed though sluggish western with Marlon Brando as a horse breeder who embarks on a south-of-the-border trek to retrieve his prized stallion, stolen by a Mexican outlaw. John Saxon is the ruthless bandit; Anjanette Comer also stars. ★★ $14.99

Appleseed

(1988, 70 min, Japan, Kazuyoshi Katayama) This explosive, cyberpunk Japanese animated tale is set in the utopian mega-city Olympus after World War III. Bioroids (artifical humanoids) and humans coexist peacefully. But the tranquility is shattered when an anti-bioroid terrorist group begins to wreak havoc throughout the city. Original story by Masamune Shirow. (Japanese with English subtitles) ★★★ $34.99

Appointment with Death

(1988, 108 min, US, Michael Winner) Peter Ustinov returns as Agatha Christie's Belgian detective Hercule Poirot, here investigating the murder of greedy widow Lauren Bacall. Could have been Carrie Fisher, John Gielgud, Piper Laurie or Hayley Mills, among others. Disappointing thriller will leave you caring little about who done it. ★★ $14.99

Apprentice to Murder

(1988, 94 min, US, R.L. Thomas) In the late 1920s in rural Pennsylvania, a 16-year-old farm boy befriends a "powwow" doctor (a combination of a religious faith healer and an herbalist) who may or may not be crazy and a murderer. Chad Lowe is the innocent teenager who comes under the influence of the creepy Donald Sutherland; the two setting out to undermine a suspected demonic neighbor. Based on a true story. Note: The cover art on the box is very misleading. It is not the spooky, satanic horror film it suggests. Rather, the film is a slowly paced mystery about manipulation and religious hysteria. ★★ $9.99

The Apprenticeship of Duddy Kravitz

(1974, 121 min, Canada, Ted Kotcheff) In a career-defining role, Richard Dreyfuss stars as Duddy Kravitz, a likable young man from Montreal's Jewish ghetto who stops at nothing and for no one in his ambitious drive for success. Set in 1948, this serio-comedic film features many enjoyable scenes and characters with the highlight being Denholm Elliott's hilarious performance as a drunken English film director hired by Duddy to "tastefully" film a Bar Mitzvah. ★★★½ $14.99

April Fool's Day

(1986, 88 min, US, Fred Walton) *Friday the 13th* horror and teen comedy don't mix in this attempted spoof about a group of teens staying at a friend's mansion, being bumped off one by one. ★½ $19.99

Arabesque

(1966, 105 min, US, Stanley Donen) Director Donen (*Charade*) is in familiar Hitchcock territory with this effective spy thriller about a college professor (Gregory Peck) who unwittingly becomes involved in a plot to assassinate an Arab prime minister. Though this doesn't deliver the thrills to the degree *Charade* did, Peck and co-star Sophia Loren and a rather complex story compensate. ★★★ $14.99

Arabian Nights

(1974, 130 min, Italy, Pier Paolo Pasolini) Pasolini's final film in his "Trilogy of Life" series – which includes *The Decameron* and *The Canterbury Tales* – is a bawdy and visually opulent fable of idyllic sexuality based on the classic Arabian tales. Told in dreamlike vignettes, the stories derive from three cultures – Persia, Egypt and India – and range from the ninth century to the Renaissance. A celebration of joyous sensuality rarely found in our present industrialized Western culture. (Italian and Arabic with English subtitles) ★★★½ $79.99

Arachnophobia

(1990, 109 min, US, Frank Marshall) Marshall, a product of the Spielberg farm system, made his directorial debut with this entertaining horror-laced comedy. A highly poisonous spider from the Amazon hitches a ride stateside and takes up residence in the home of a relocated big-city doctor (Jeff Daniels); it mates with a domestic female and thereby creates a whole new breed of creepy-crawlers. John Goodman steals the show as a know-it-all, G.I. Joe exterminator. But, of course, the real stars are the spiders themselves, who provide many a non-offensive scare. ★★★ $9.99

Archer's Adventure

(1985, 120 min, Australia, Denny Lawrence) Dave Powers, a horse trainer's apprentice, volunteers to ride race horse Archer across 600 miles of Australia's roughest terrain to the Melbourne Cup. He overcomes staggering odds to make horse racing history. This compelling drama is based on a true story. ★★½ $9.99

Are You Being Served?, Vols. 1-2

(89 min, GB, Bernard Thompson) Made popular by its successful showing on PBS, this irreverent and very funny British comedy series follows the merry exploits of a group of salespeople in a London department store, Grace Brothers. When the men's and women's department are consolidated due to budget cut-backs, it's a continual battle of the sexes peppered by outrageous schemes of one-upmanship to grab the customers' attention. Inevitably, all get their comeuppance. The staff includes Mrs. Slocombe (Molly Sugden), the indomitable head clerk who's always bragging about her pussy(cat); Mr. Humphries (John Inman), a gay salesman with a penchant for disguises, costumes and stories; Miss Brahams (Wendy Richard), a pretty sales clerk; and Mr. Peacock (Frank Thornton), the floor's pompous manager. Sexual innuendo, impersonations and social disorder is the order of the day. $14.99 each

Vol. 1: *Big Brother* – Three episodes include "His and Hers," in which a sexy saleslady proves to be too much competition; "Cold Comfort" is what the staff gets when the heat is turned off; and in "Big Brother," a surveillance camera catches a lot more than just suspected burglars.

Vol. 2: *Dear Sexy Knickers* – Love letters find themselves in all the wrong pockets in the first episode; when "Our Figures Are Slipping," the staff is under pressure to increase sales – any way they can; and in "Camping In," a rail strike forces the staff to stay over night at the store, but the sleeping arrangements aren't what (and who) they expected.

L'Argent

(1983, 90 min, France/Switzerland, Robert Bresson) The corrupting power of money, the cancerous spread of evil resulting from its use, and man's eventual redemption from its sins are the themes in director Bresson's thoughtful Marxist fable. Based on a short story by Tolstoy, the film – shot in Bresson's unique style of ascetic narrative – follows the tragic course of Yvon, a young truck driver accused of counterfeiting. Fired from his job as a result of a set-up, he is eventually sent to prison, where he is incarcerated for years. Losing his wife and child, Yvon finally rebels and purges himself of his rage. ★★★ $79.99

Aria

(1987, 100 min, GB, Various) A sensual explosion of sight and sound, *Aria* is a bold and adventurous collage of vignettes inspired by the greatest opera arias of all time. Ten of the finest and most innovative contemporary filmmakers (including Robert Altman, Bruce Beresford, Jean-Luc Godard, Derek Jarman, Nicolas Roeg, Ken Russell, Julien Temple) were asked to choose their favorite operatic arias and create a short interpretation of the music, independent of the original libretto. The result is a series of mini-masterpieces filled with tantalizing imagery exposing the raw emotional power and deeply erotic nature of opera. Starring Theresa Russell, Tilda Swinton, Bridget Fonda and Beverly D'Angelo. ★★★ $9.99

Ariel

(1988, 74 min, Finland, Aki Kaurismaki) Voted Best Foreign Film of 1990 by the National Society of Film Critics, *Ariel* is from director Kaurismaki (*Leningrad Cowboys Go*

America). Kaurismaki probes in his films the gritty, near-hopeless condition of his characters with a near dead-pan cinematic style graced with both insight and biting satire. This black-and-white comedy-drama of forgotten hopes and resilient love follows an alienated, down-on-his-heels drifter who, in his huge Cadillac convertible, embarks on a journey from Lapland to Helsinki that soon involves him in crime, a murder, a jailbreak, a marriage and eventually a chance to escape all his problems. An invigorating black comedy that will remind one of a European Jim Jarmusch or a quirkier Wim Wenders. (Finnish with English subtitles) ★★★ $79.99

Arise! The Church of the Subgenius
(1991, 80 min, US) Warning early on that, "For the unworthy, the viewing of this tape can be a one-way ticket down a bottomless mental trap from which there can be no escape," this amusing oddity proselytizes the Gospel According to Bob. Bob, a pipe-smoking '50s dad with a mischievous grin, is the deity from which springs forth a "religion" based on "slack." Culled from footage from old TV shows and movies, and spliced with hilarious verbal calisthenics, this insubordinate flick makes a great party tape. More importantly, however, if you are unfulfilled by Catholicism, Judaism or the other mainstream religions, you could do worse than to try Bob. ★★ $29.99

The Aristocats
(1970, 78 min, US, Wolfgang Reitherman) This Disney animated feature isn't in the same league as some of their "classics" but is charming nevertheless. Duchess (*purr*fectly voiced by Gabor) and her three kittens belong to a wealthy old lady who has willed her fortune to the felines to the dismay of the butler. He kidnaps them in an attempt to get the inheritance for himself and, knowing that as city cats they will be in danger in the country, leaves them to fend for themselves. Enter the charming Thomas O'Malley, Alley Cat (Harris), who rescues them and returns them to their rightful home with plenty of adventures and romance along the way. The usual high Disney quality in addition to some adorable songs will make repeat viewings a pleasure. ★★★½ $29.99

Arizona Dream
(1994, 119 min, US, Emir Kusturica) Director Kusturica (*Time of the Gypsies*) seamlessly blends together reality, fantasy and dreams to create this emotionally complex vision of a young man's journey into adulthood. Johnny Depp stars as a lyrical N.Y.C. government employee who travels to Arizona to attend the wedding of his car salesman uncle (a somewhat schticky Jerry Lewis). Both Faye Dunaway and Lili Taylor give appropriately bizarre but grounded performances as a mother and daughter who take turns seducing/torturing Depp with their weird and dangerous charms. Not for everyone and somewhat psychedelic in mood, *Arizona Dream* is precisely what it says it is: a dream. It's not exactly clear in its meaning but is filled with intriguing ideas and imagery that last long after the movie has ended. ★★★ $19.99

Armed and Dangerous
(1986, 113 min, US, Mark L. Lester) This bungling John Candy comedy stars the big guy

as an ex-policeman who becomes a security guard and, through no skill of his own, exposes a crooked union official. Candy's ex-"S.C.T.V." mate Eugene Levy also stars. ★½ $9.99

Armistead Maupin's Tales of the City
See: Tales of the City

Army of Darkness
(1993, 85 min, US, Sam Raimi) This wildly stylish and deliriously imaginative sequel to the cult classics *Evil Dead* and *Evil Dead 2* continues the misadventures of the reluctant hero, Ash (Bruce Campbell), as he, along with a chainsaw, sawed-off shotgun and a 1970s Oldsmobile, are mysteriously sent back to medieval times to retrieve "The Book of the Dead," battle netherworld demons and more. Laced with director Raimi's trademark seizure-inducing camerawork, hysterically gruesome special effects and black-humored violence, the film succeeds on all levels as we follow Ash's exploits as he attempts to get back to modern times and his job at S-Mart ("Shop smart – shop S-mart"). Trivia buffs will also enjoy the many cinematic homages liberally sprinkled throughout the film including nods to: *Gulliver's Travels*, *The 7th Voyage of Sinbad*, *Monty Python's Holy Grail*, "The Three Stooges" and many more. ★★★½ $14.99

Around the World in 80 Days
(1956, 167 min, US, Michael Anderson) A mammoth and vastly entertaining version of Jules Verne's novel. David Niven stars as Phineas Fogg, the globe-trotting British gentleman whose bet that he can circle the world in 80 days leads him and Cantiflas on a succession of adventures, including meeting up with princess Shirley MacLaine. The film features 44 cameos and the location shootings are remarkable. Winner of five Oscars, including Best Picture. ★★★★ $29.99

Around the World in Eighty Ways
(1986, 90 min, Australia, Stephen MacLean) While it would help to have a Sydney audience cue an American in on the cultural humor and inside jokes, this energetically wacky Aussie comedy is still entertaining in an easy-going, non-demanding way. Philip Quast is Wally, a resourceful and cash-poor tour guide who comes up with the zaniest of schemes: take dear old, senile dad on an improvised and very fake tour around the world – staged in a neighbor's tacky suburban home – and pocket the money that would have paid for a real trip. Quickly paced and manic, the film has a sweet, gentle heart. Quast gives a fast, funny performance – impersonating everyone from Hawaiian hula dancers to Elvis to the Pope – in this infectious, spirited comedy. ★★★ $19.99

The Arrival
(1996, 109 min, US, David Twohy) Charlie Sheen, clearly cast against type, stars as a radio astronomer and all-around good guy who uncovers a secret government plot and intergalactic conspiracy in this directorial debut from screenwriter Twohy (*The Fugitive*, *Waterworld*). When he records a radio frequency spike from outer space and delivers the news to his boss (Ron Silver), he is promptly demoted and his discovery is covered up and

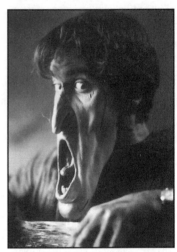

Bruce Campbell in *Army of Darkness*

destroyed, and all those who know about it are quickly disappearing. Sheen soon follows a trail to Mexico where uncovers the truth: the temperature of the Earth is increasing, making it habitable for alien life – but deadly for humans! Pleasantly surprising, this medium-budgeted sci-fi thriller, though not entirely original (it is reminiscent of *They Live*), it is consistently engaging, with a variety of special effects which – while done on the cheap – are very convincing. ★★★ $19.99

Arrowsmith
(1931, 101 min, US, John Ford) Ronald Colman's stirring performance as a dedicated medical researcher highlights this sincere, classy adaptation of the Sinclair Lewis novel. Helen Hayes as Colman's first wife and Myrna Loy also star. ★★★★ $19.99

Arsenic and Old Lace
(1944, 118 min, US, Frank Capra) This Capra gem takes place in Brooklyn on Halloween. The skeletons aren't in the closet, they're in the basement. Cary Grant's brother thinks he's Teddy Roosevelt, and his poison-happy aunts think of themselves as sane. Cary's other brother (played with panache by Raymond Massey) bears a striking resemblance to Boris Karloff, and hangs out with Peter Lorre. And the viewer has as much fun watching all this as the cast obviously had in making it. ★★★★ $19.99

The Art of Touch
(1992, 45 min, US, Craig Cooper) Not confining itself solely to massage, this video demonstrates the therapeutic and pleasurable effects simple but "time tested" touching techniques can offer a gay couple. Six attractive male models engage in various forms of touch, caress and massage exercises while a narrator describes every move and New Age music drones in the background. The demonstrations should be of help to many couples interested in increased intimacy and physical exploration, although its sappy approach ("get lost in the embrace," "If you come in contact with the genitals, slowly graze them and move on") distracts from its real intent. ★★ $24.99

The Art of Touch II — A Taoist Erotic Massage

(1993, 50 min, GB, Mike Esser) Notwithstanding its gimmicky but undeniably fun 3-D effects (one receives 2 pairs of glasses with the tape), this instructional massage video demonstrates the tender, relaxing and erotic possibilities offered in the Oriental massage technique called Taoist Erotic Massage. With six unbelievably hunky instructors (nude and occasionally enjoying the massage a little *too* much), the video is ideal for gay couples who want to go beyond simple sexual intimacy. But what can be spiritual for some will be tantilizing and titillating for others as the beautifully sculpted men pull, stroke, caress and touch each other. Be sure to keep handy both body oils and Dramamine as in an effort to heighten the 3-D look, the camera is constantly revolving around the massage bed, creating a potentially dizzying effect. ★★½ $24.99

Arthur

(1981, 97 min, US, Steve Gordon) Recalling the very best of the screwball comedies, first-time director Gordon's hilariously sweet tale is rich in both near-convulsive one-liners and high spirits. In a role which brought him an Oscar nomination and reminds us of the true star potential he once demonstrated, Dudley Moore is perfection as the title character, a drunken poor little rich man (net worth: $700 million) who risks it all to woo the personable (but penniless) Liza Minnelli. Moore's endearing clown is one of the screen's great comedic inebriates, but even he is upstaged by John Gielgud, who won a much-deserved Oscar as Arthur's acerbic valet and confidant. Sadly, writer-director Gordon died shortly after the release of *Arthur*, leaving only speculation as to what joys would have followed his wonderful debut. ★★★★ $9.99

Arthur 2: On the Rocks

(1988, 110 min, US, Bud Yorkin) The presence of the original's writer-director, Steve Gordon, is sorely missed in this uninspired sequel. Dudley Moore can probably do this bit in his sleep, and he manages to produce a few laughs despite the absence of a substantial script; but for the most part, this is tough going. Liza Minnelli returns, as do Geraldine Fitzgerald and John Gielgud. You wanna see lovable Dudley and Liza again, rent the original. ★½ $9.99

Arthur C. Clarke's Mysterious World: Vol. 1 — UFOs

(1980, 60 min, US) See remarkable photos and film of innumerable UFOs observed around the world. Gaze into the heavens and contemplate the star of Bethlehem, a lost planet, the intriguing canals of Mars and the making of a massive moon crater. Scientific revelation or total rubbish: you decide. ★★½ $14.99

Article 99

(1992, 99 min, US, Howard Deutch) Ray Liotta and Kiefer Sutherland star in this compelling if familiar comedy-drama in the *M*A*S*H* vein about a group of dedicated doctors working for the Veterans Administration. Liotta plays the chief surgeon who, along with new-cutter-on-the-block Sutherland, leads the fight against bureaucratic red tape and administrative corruption. An impressive and accomplished supporting cast includes Forest Whitaker, Lea Thompson, John Mahoney, Eli Wallach, John C. McGinley, Keith David and Kathy Baker. ★★½ $14.99

Artists and Models

(1955, 109 min, US, Frank Tashlin) A crazy Dean Martin-Jerry Lewis romp with artist Martin and writer Lewis trying to get ahead. Dean ultimately uses Jerry's nightly dreams as inspiration for a comic book. Shirley MacLaine plays Jerry's kooky, astrology-reading girlfriend (an image she'd have to begin living down some 25 years later). Jerry's antics are particularly funny. ★★★ $14.99

As If It Were Yesterday

(1980, 85 min, France/US, Myriam Abramowicz & Ether Hoffenberg) Made by two women — one American and the other French — *As If It Were Yesterday* documents the little known heroism of the Belgian people who, during the Nazi occupation, hid, placed or helped over 4,000 Jewish children escape deportation and extermination. Through interviews with grown-up survivors and with Belgians who hid Jewish children, a deeply moving story unfolds. An exhilarating celebration of unsung heroes and heroines. (French with English subtitles) ★★★½

As Is

(1986, 86 min, US, Michael Lindsay-Hogg) Based on the acclaimed Broadway production, this powerful, opened-up play stars Robert Carradine and Jonathan Hadary as ex-lovers who are brought together when the former is stricken with AIDS. Often humorous and never morose, author William Hoffman doesn't pull his punches with either his portrayal of a gay lifestyle or of the emotional toll the disease takes. ★★★ $19.99

As Summers Die

(1986, 88 min, US, Jean-Claude Tramont) A small Southern town's richest family makes an attempt to take away farm land from an elderly black woman, believing that the land is rich with oil in this tale of greed, racism and justice circa 1950. A pleasant if slender made-for-TV drama that stars Scott Glenn, Jamie Lee Curtis, Beah Richards and Bette Davis. ★★½

As You Desire Me

(1932, 71 min, US, George Fitzmaurice) Greta Garbo gives an earnest performance in this fair adaptation of Pirandello's play. Garbo stars as an amnesiac who is reunited with husband Melvyn Douglas, only she doesn't remember him. Erich von Stroheim is appropriately slimy as an ex-lover who has other ideas about her true identity. Garbo and Douglas would reunite in 1939 for the classic *Ninotchka*. ★★ $19.99

As Young as You Feel

(1951, 77 min, US, Harmon Jones) Monty Woolley gives a spirited performance in this fetching comedy (based on a Paddy Chayefsky story) which takes a playful swipe at big business. Woolley plays an employee who is retired upon turning 65. In response, he impersonates the president of his firm's parent company to reverse the retirement policy. Things get out of hand when he is forced to continue the charade. Thelma Ritter appears as Woolley's exasperated daughter-in-law, and David Wayne and Marilyn Monroe co-star. ★★★ $19.99

Ashes and Diamonds

(1958, 104 min, Poland, Andrzej Wajda) Wajda, initiator of the Polish Film Renaissance, creates a penetrating account of a young WWII Resistance fighter whose loyalty to his comrades conflicts with his internal desires. Zbigniew Cybulski ("the Polish Brando") is the ambivalent youth lost in the chaos of the post-war days. A serious, insightful and brilliantly structured examination of both wartime and peacetime allegiances and turmoil. Wajda's

Arsenic and Old Lace

Zbigniew Cybulski gets roughed up in *Ashes and Diamonds*

final film in his acclaimed "War Trilogy" which includes *A Generation* and *Kanal*. (Polish with English subtitles) ★★★★ $24.99

Ashik Kerib

(1988, 75 min, USSR, Sergei Paradjanov) Dedicated to the memory of Andrei Tarkovsky, Paradjanov's final film is an exotic and ebullient Georgian folk tale based on a story by Mikhail Lermontov. Although pregnant with symbolism and oblique nationalistic references to Georgia's ancient culture, the film remains accessible and even quite enjoyable because of its age-old story of love conquering all. A handsome but poor minstrel must travel through the countryside to earn enough money to marry his young love, the beautiful daughter of a rich Turkish merchant. His fantastic adventures are spectacularly filmed in poetic, almost fantastic images. There is little dialogue, with the episodic story infused with striking visuals and hypnotic traditional music and dances. Often obscure, but always riveting. (Georgian with English subtitles) ★★★ $59.99

Ask Any Girl

(1959, 101 min, US, Charles Walters) Shirley MacLaine has one of her best early-career roles in this effervescent gender-gap comedy. MacLaine plays a small-town girl who moves to the big city, thus beginning an enchanting and laugh-filled sex farce. The story follows MacLaine's romantic trials and tribulations as she searches for the perfect mate. After a few false starts, MacLaine is employed by brothers David Niven and Gig Young. Thinking Young "the one," she cajoles Niven to help her trap his brother; which they do in a most outrageous fashion. MacLaine absolutely beguiles: she's sassy, daffy and smart. Niven is as debonair as ever. And Young is a good comic foil. Also good in support is Rod Taylor as one of MacLaine's first beaus. One of the best of that era's sexual comedies. ★★★½ $19.99

The Asphalt Jungle

(1950, 112 min, US, John Huston) One of Huston's most memorable efforts, this taut drama is a brilliantly stylized crime story about a group of hoods plotting a major heist. Led

by a curious, almost mystical German expatriate, the gang woos the local establishment for backing. An insightful tale of moral corruption, the film is a classic example of superb ensemble acting featuring flawless characterizations by Sterling Hayden, James Whitmore, Sam Jaffe, Louis Calhearn and Marilyn Monroe. Filmed in a striking and moody black and white. ★★★★ $19.99

The Asphyx

(1972, 99 min, GB, Peter Newbrook) Intriguing, highly original horror film about a 19th-century British scientist (Robert Stephens) who uncovers one of the secrets of death and uses it to become immortal. Also starring Jane Lapotaire and Robert Powell. ★★★

The Assassination Bureau

(1969, 110 min, GB, Basil Dearden) Fans of the old "Avengers" series won't want to miss this lustrous black pearl of a comedy from the director of *Dead of Night* and *League of Gentlemen*. The ex-"Mrs. Peel," Diana Rigg, stars as a turn-of-the-century journalist who goes up against a secret society of self-appointed assassins charged with ridding the world of undesirables. Based on a story by Robert Louis Stevenson, the film recalls such cinematic treasures as *The Abominable Doctor Phibes* and *The Wrong Box*. Also with Oliver Reed, Telly Savalas, Curt Jurgens and Clive Revill. ★★★ $9.99

The Assassination of Trotsky

(1972, 103 min, GB/France, Joseph Losey) Losey's uneven and unhistorical account of the last days of the exiled Trotsky is buoyed by an outstanding performance from Richard Burton. Alain Delon is effectively enigmatic as the Stalinist assassin sent to Mexico to hunt him down. Also with Romy Schneider. ★★ $19.99

Assassins

(1995, 132 min, US, Richard Donner) Playing an aging professional killer, Sylvester Stallone looks as though he can't wait to get to the phone to fire his agent. But it's too little, too late. In this brainless actioner, Sly finds himself dogged and pursued by new hit man-on-the-block Antonio Banderas. The young upstart means to prove himself by killing

Stallone, the best in his field. Banderas is also after Julianne Moore — a good actress but a most unlikely electronic thief (was Sandra Bullock busy?) — whom Sly originally had to silence but now finds himself drawn to in a protective father sort of way. The inevitable chase begins, ending in a dusty Mexican town which gives way to too many clichés. Director Donner seems to be copying John Woo, down to slow-motion shots and protagonists leaping through the air, pistols blazing. What he produces, however, is a boring and confusing movie. Banderas overacts and is given to heavy breathing and hissing; Stallone, in comparison, comes off best — that should be warning enough. ★½ $19.99

The Assault

(1986, 150 min, The Netherlands, Fons Rademakers) The moving and emotional story of a boy's traumatic wartime experiences and its after-effects on him as an adult, won the 1986 Academy Award for Best Foreign-Language Film, yet oddly was released on video only in the dubbed version. The film is set in two time periods: a small town during World War II, where a young boy's family is killed by the Nazis; and in the adult years of the boy, as he struggles to reconcile his parents' death and to begin a new life. (Dubbed) ★★★½ $79.99

Assault at West Point

(1993, 98 min, US, Harry Moses) Told in flashback and with a lighter-in-skin-tone Al Freeman, Jr., this real-life tale of racism focuses on a young African-American West Point cadet (Seth Gilliam) who is accused and finally court-martialed for faking his own attack. With Sam Waterston and Samuel L. Jackson starring as the defendant's lawyers, the film features zombie-esque performances, and this combined with Gilliam's even less-impressive thesping, help to reduce what should have been a thought-provoking, intense experience to a disappointment. ★½ $9.99

Assault of the Killer Bimbos

(1988, 85 min, US, Anita Rosenberg) Sophomoric hijinks as three buxom beauties, planning their careers in the movie biz, head for Mexico. But not before they take on over-sexed surfers, jealous boyfriends and the police. ★½ $14.99

Assault on Precinct 13

(1976, 90 min, US, John Carpenter) A novice Carpenter directed this intense, immensely satisfying thriller, a harbinger of things to come from the young filmmaker. A Los Angeles gang seizes control of an almost deserted police station, forcing the officers and civilians trapped inside to fight for their lives. Suggested by Howard Hawks' *Rio Bravo*. ★★★½ $14.99

The Associate

(1996, 114 min, US, Donald Petrie) 1996 was not the kindest year to Whoopi Goldberg. *T-Rex*, *Bogus* and *Eddie*, all released in '96 were box office and artistic disappointments. So when a fourth film was released, it was bunched with the other three. That's a shame, because *The Associate*, besides being the best of them, is a genuinely enjoyable satire of Wall Street. Sort of a low-keyed *Jerry Maguire* meets *Tootsie*, *The Associate* casts Whoopi as a talented financial analyst who is passed over for a promotion at her Wall Street firm clearly for reasons of gender. Deciding to start her own agency, she discovers not being part of the old boys' network is bad for business — that is until she invents a ficticious male partner. With the help of savvy secretary Dianne Wiest, Whoopi takes Wall Street by storm — even if it means a little male drag. *The Associate* doesn't go as far as it could have, and isn't as consistently funny as one would wish. But it does have good-natured barbs (which actually have something to say), humorous characterizations, and Whoopi in good form. ★★★ $19.99

Asylum

(1972, 92 min, GB, Roy Ward Baker) A young psychiatrist arrives at his new job and must hear the personal stories of four inmates in this horror anthology film from England's Amicus Studios. Written by Robert Bloch (the creator of *Psycho*), the film is very interesting and effectively scary; some characters are better than others, but most films of this type are similarly uneven. The fine cast includes Peter Cushing, Herbert Lom and Charlotte Rampling; Rampling's story is the weakest, probably because it is concerned more with psychology than with the supernatural. The first story in the quartet is the most frightening, involving the bizarre form a murdered wife's revenge takes. And just when you think the whole thing is over, one final terror awaits the unwary viewer. The 1960s and '70s were a time of magnificent revitalization of the horror genre, particularly in England. This film, while perhaps not as famous as its Hammer cousins, is fun, frightening and solidly enjoyable. ★★★ $79.99

At Close Range

(1986, 115 min, US, James Foley) This intense drama examines the brittle relationship between a teenager and his estranged father, a small-time hood who introduces the youth to petty crime and murder. Christopher Walken and Sean Penn offer stunning performances. The good cast includes Mary Stuart Masterson, Christopher Penn and Crispin Glover. Based on a true story. ★★★½

At Home with the Webbers

(1993, 109 min, US, Brad Marlowe) Could you imagine having your family broadcast live on television during its most intimate moments? The Webbers are chosen to be the stars of a new 24-hour cable show. They are moved into a house equipped with video cameras in almost every corner. Jennifer Tilly plays the sex-hungry daughter who is willing to do anything to get plaster casts of male body parts. David Arquette is the morbid, suicidal son who becomes the heartthrob for thousands of pimple-faced, teenaged girls. ★★½ $92.99

At Play in the Fields of the Lord

(1992, 186 min, US, Hector Babenco) Babenco (*Kiss of the Spider Woman*, *Pixote*) directs this ambitious and sweeping epic about a group of fundamentalist missionaries who come in conflict with a tribe of Amazonian Indians. Tom Berenger stars as a half-breed Native American who believes he's returned to his spiritual source. Those familiar with Peter Matthiessen's richly textured parable on faith and the soul might be disappointed by the film's lack of cohesive direction. However, the finely detailed work of the ensemble cast (including Berenger, John Lithgow, Kathy Bates, Aidan Quinn, Daryl Hannah and Tom Waits), coupled with the beautiful cinematography of the lush South American jungle, will carry the viewer easily through the three-hour and six-minute running time. ★★★ $19.99

At the Circus

(1939, 87 min, US, Edward Buzzell) Lydia, oh Lydia, say, have you met Lydia... Groucho Marx walks on the ceiling with Eve Arden; it's all in the line of duty, of course. He's after the $10,000 stolen from the disinherited nephew of Newport heiress Margaret Dumont, which is needed to keep the circus from being taken over by the nefarious scalliwag who stole the money. Got that? Chico and Harpo are there to assist. Though not among the handful of Marx Brothers' classics, there are quite a few funny scenes to be had. ★★½ $19.99

L'Atalante

(1934, 89 min, France, Jean Vigo) This lyrical, cinematic poem follows a honeymooning couple (German actress Dita Parlo and Jean Dasté) as they blissfully float down the Seine on a barge accompanied by their first mate, the crusty Michel Simon (*Boudo Saved from Drowning*). Long considered one of the greatest romance stories in film history, *L'Atalante* was one of only two films made by director Vigo before his untimely death at age 29 from septicemia, but this classic of French cinema was surrounded by controversy and innuendo from its inception. Having just recently finished *Zero for Conduct* (which had been banned in France immediately upon its making), Vigo was a contentious choice to direct *L'Atalante* and indeed his original cut was rejected by the movie theatre owners and ultimately re-edited. Tragically, Vigo died just weeks after the film's unsuccessful run at the box office and a year later, the film was once again amended. This unhappy saga at long last came to an end in 1989 when archivists went into the vaults and resurrected Vigo's original version of the film, now available in a remastered print. (French with English subtitles) ★★★★ $69.99

Athens, Georgia — Inside/Out

(1986, 82 min, US, Tony Gayton) This dynamic documentary chronicles the remarkable music scene that emanated from Athens, Georgia, home of R.E.M. and The B-52's. Packed full of the earnest and energetic sounds of the town's many locally born bands, the film depicts Athens as the cultural Mecca of an artistically suppressed region. Far from your standard refugee fare, however, these bright-eyed Southern youth have exploded onto the national music scene with a vengeance. Spectacular concert footage of R.E.M. and The B-52's is augmented by the intimate "small club" footage of up-and-coming bands. ★★★ $29.99

Atlantic City

(1981, 104 min, Canada, Louis Malle) In this fascinating, intelligent character study, director Malle captures the Atlantic City of the '80s, a city living with its faded past and a fragile optimism for the future. Burt Lancaster, in what may be the performance of his career, brilliantly plays a small-time numbers runner with notions of grandeur who gets a chance at the big score when he crosses paths with casino employee Susan Sarandon and her ex-husband and drug pusher Robert Joy. The simplicity of the characters' lives and dreams belies the tumultuous events which follow when all are eventually tempted by the attainable usually just beyond their grasp. Kate Reid is especially good as a former beauty contest winner living with the ghost of her gangster husband, and Sarandon, whose first great performance this was, demonstrates the eroticism of lemons in an unforgettable scene. Arguably Malle at his very best. ★★★★ $14.99

The Atomic Cafe

(1982, 90 min, US, Kevin Rafferty) A nervously funny juxtaposition of atomic propaganda films. The footage includes testament to the beauty of the blast, reassurances of the minimal cause for worry and other testing examples of governmental lunacy. ★★★ $29.99

Attack Force Z

(1981, 84 min, Australia, Tim Burstall) A young Mel Gibson stars in this competent WWII adventure film about an elite group of commandos who are assigned to rescue a defecting Japanese official from an enemy-held island in the Pacific. Awaiting the men are unbearable heat, an uncharted jungle and thousands of Japanese soldiers. John Phillip Law and Sam Neill also star. ★★½ $24.99

Attack of the 5'2" Women

(1994, 83 min, US, Julie Brown & Richard Wenk) Savage parodist Brown takes pot-shots at tacky tabloid queens Tonya Harding and Lorena Bobbitt in this made-for-cable double feature that easily merits the "John Waters Seal of Approval" for tasteless humor. In the first part, Brown is Tonya Hardly, the big-butt, white trash Olympic wannabe who schemes to have her husband put the competition out of the running. Next, she's the castrating spitfire Lenora Babbitt, who cuts off her husband's manhood when he fails to give her an orgasm. Brown's sophomore effort is sophomoric at best, suffering in comparison to her earlier spoof of Madonna, *Medusa – Dare to Be Truthful*. But this is to be expected: her subjects here are their own self-parodies. ★★ $91.99

Attack of the Fifty-Foot Woman

(1958, 66 min, US, Nathan Juran) The title is no more outlandish than the story, the acting and especially the special effects in this sci-fi tale that only Ed Wood could have loved. When she goes on the prowl for her (normal sized) philandering husband, the big gal leaves no building unturned in her search. ★ $14.99

Attack of the Killer Tomatoes

(1980, 87 min, US, John DeBello) Unbelievably silly horror spoof about some ravenous, rampaging tomatoes ravaging San

Diego and its poor, defenseless citizens. Is there no one but the San Diego chicken to help? Will the Secret Service outwit these gruesome garnishments from a chef's salad? Will Nixon end the war? ★★ $12.99

Attila 74: The Rape of Cyprus

(1975, 103 min, Greece, Michael Cacoyannis) Filmmaker Cacoyannis (*Zorba the Greek*) was in London at the time of the Turkish invasion of Cyprus in 1974. Returning immediately to his besieged homeland, he began making this part-documentary, part-personal journal. A deeply passionate and devastatingly powerful film that bears witness to the horrors of the invasion and mounts strong evidence on its accusations against the Turks, the Greek puppet leaders and international indifference. (Greek with English subtitles) ★★★½ $59.99

Au Revoir les Enfants

(1987, 103 min, France, Louis Malle) Director Malle's acclaimed autobiographical tale of his early school days is a poignant reminiscence of childhood camaraderie, social responsibility and the human tragedy of war. Set in occupied France during WWII, the story centers on the friendship which blossoms between two young, gifted schoolboys — one Catholic and one Jewish — when the latter hides out in a private boarding school to escape the Nazis. The beauty and mastery of Malle's film lies in his precise eye for period detail, well-structured character development, and an insightful and accurate portrayal of adolescent behavior. (French with English subtitles) ★★★★ $19.99

Austin Powers: International Man of Mystery

Audrey Rose

(1977, 114 min, US, Robert Wise) This over-long, plodding thriller about reincarnation tries to be both scary and meaningful, but fails in both departments. Ivy is a precocious young girl living with her well-to-do parents in New York City. A mysterious stranger (Anthony Hopkins) soon begins following the family around the city while at the same time a recurring nightmare Ivy has been having increases in both intensity and frequency. The stranger eventually approaches the family with an unbelievable tale about how his daughter, Audrey Rose, killed in an auto accident, has been reincarnated as Ivy. Marsha Mason also stars as Ivy's distraught mother, who initially refuses to believe the story. The actors try their best with the material, but are hampered by a weak script which makes the film, alternately, a ghost story, a courtroom drama and a diatribe on Eastern religion. ★½ $14.99

Auntie Lee's Meat Pies

(1992, 100 min, US, Joseph F. Robertson) This hilarious grade-B send-up of *Eating Raoul* and *Parents* stars Karen Black as a Julia Child-from-Hell who sends her four nymphete nieces, led by adult film starlet Teri Weigel, to hunt for the secret ingredient in her tasty meat pies — young men! Campy entertainment for the easy bake oven set. ★★★ $79.99

Auntie Mame

(1958, 143 min, US, Morton Da Costa) Rosalind Russell shines in a career-topping performance as everybody's favorite relative: Auntie Mame. Based on the hit play by Patrick Dennis, this gloriously funny adaptation follows the comic antics of an orphaned nephew who moves in with his eccentric aunt. A classic instance in which role and performer were destined for each other. Auntie Mame's best lesson: "Life is a banquet and most poor suckers are starving to death." ★★★★ $19.99

Austin Powers: International Man of Mystery

(1997, 95 min, US, Jay Roach) A hilariously goofy, off-the-wall and dead-on-target spoof of James Bond and other '60s spy movies, *Austin Powers* finds Mike Myers back in terrific comedic form after the disaster of *So I Married an Axe Murderer*. Myers sports a set of crooked dentures, thick horn-rimmed glasses, an unsightly swath of artificial chest hair and gets decked-out in velvety '60s garb as Austin Powers, a "swingin'" 1960s English superspy. Myers also plays Powers' nemesis, the nefarious but insecure Dr. Evil. Both Powers and Dr. Evil are cryogencially frozen and thawed out in 1997, and they awake to a world that has long

since surpassed them. The key to the film's side-splittingly funny humor is the loving attention to detail and its no-holds-barred, un-PC naughtiness (instead of Pussy Galore, we get a luscious femme fatale named Alotta Fagina!). A few of the jokes fall flat, and some references will be lost on all but devoted 007 fans, but *Austin Powers* nevertheless is witty, inspired lunacy from start to finish. Topped off with a fab soundtrack, this is "shag-a-delic" fun. Just watch out for those alluring Fembots. And beware of mutated, ill-tempered sea bass. ★★★½ $99.99

Author! Author!

(1982, 110 min, US, Arthur Hiller) Al Pacino stars in this heartwarming comedy as a struggling playwright who must contend with raising his children when his flaky wife leaves him. Hiller directs a fine cast who deliver endearing performances across the board. The well-written script comes from playwright Israel Horovitz. ★★½ $14.99

Autobiography of a Princess

(1975, 59 min, GB, James Ivory) Produced by Ismail Merchant with a screenplay by Ruth Prawer Jhabvala, this delicate character study stars James Mason and Merchant Ivory favorite Madhur Jaffrey. An imperious princess, self-exiled in London and long-divorced, invites her father's ex-tutor to a yearly tea to reminisce about a "happier" past only to find that their memories of the Royal India differ. ★★★ $29.99

An Autumn Afternoon

(1962, 115 min, Japan, Yasujiro Ozu) Master Japanese filmmaker Ozu's final film is a deceptively simple, contemplative and lyrical family drama. Continuing his theme from *Late Summer*, the story follows an aging widower who, against his wishes, arranges for a marriage for his only daughter; a move that leaves him lonely, with only his old drinking cronies for company. (Japanese with English subtitles) ★★★½ $69.99

Autumn Marathon

(1979, 100 min, USSR, Georgy Panelia) Mid-life crisis is the theme of this poignant and at times funny drama. Georgy, a mild-mannered Leningrad professor, finds himself dissatisfied and unfulfilled by his seemingly successful life. He becomes increasingly muddled in his relationships with his loving wife, his attractive but demanding mistress, his students and colleagues and even his jogging-buddy neighbor. (Russian with English subtitles) ★★★ $59.99

Autumn Sonata

(1978, 97 min, Sweden, Ingmar Bergman) For the first time, Bergman's emotionally shattering drama about the frail yet indestructible bond between a mother (Ingrid Bergman) and her daughter (Liv Ullmann) is available in its original Swedish language (with English subtitles). ★★★★ $39.99

Avalon

(1990, 127 min, US, Barry Levinson) Director Levinson continues his acclaimed Baltimore stories (*Diner* and *Tin Men*) with this heartfelt reminiscence — spanning five decades — about three generations of a Jewish immigrant fami-

The Awful Truth

ly. Armin Mueller-Stahl gives a towering performance as the Krichinsky family's proud patriarch, whose haunting stories of emigration to "a place called Avalon" are constantly echoing from his memory. Aidan Quinn ably plays his son, a salesman with Wanamaker-sized dreams of department store splendor. Also with Elizabeth Perkins and Joan Plowright. A superb evocation of post-war life, *Avalon* is a remarkable achievement: an intimate memory piece rich in atmosphere and flowing with good humor. Levinson's most personal film, and one of his best. ★★★★ $19.99

L'Avventura (The Adventure)

(1960, 145 min, Italy, Michelangelo Antonioni) Antonioni established his international reputation with this perceptive study of the alienation, ennui and despair suffered by a group of vacationing friends when faced with the disappearance of a young woman from the party. (Italian with English subtitles) ★★★ $29.99

Awakenings

(1990, 121 min, US, Penny Marshall) Based on Oliver Sachs' true story, this extremely moving and accomplished film stars Robin Williams as a neurologist whose experiments in a 1960s Brooklyn hospital "awaken" patients who have been victims of a decades-long "sleeping sickness." Robert De Niro gives an astonishing performance as Leonard, Williams' first patient to undergo the medical treatment. The story centers on the doctor's fight to use the experimental medicine, and the recovering and orienting process facing all the patients. Williams nicely underplays his part as the introverted physician; he and De Niro make a remarkable team. Terrific support from Julie Kavner and particularly Ruth Nelson as De Niro's mother. ★★★½ $9.99

The Awful Truth

(1937, 94 min, US, Leo McCarey) McCarey won a well-deserved Best Director Oscar for this hilarious screwball classic starring Cary Grant and Irene Dunne, both at the peak of their comic abilities. Grant and Dunne play a divorcing couple waiting out their 90-day interlocutory period (and fighting a custody battle for their pet terrier). When they begin dating other people, each goes to great lengths to disrupt the other's newfound romance; each scheme being more outrageous than the one before it. *The Awful Truth* is screwball comedy at its best and, in addition to Grant's *Bringing Up Baby*, is the epitome of the genre. ★★★★ $19.99

An Awfully Big Adventure

(1994, 113 min, GB, Mike Newell) A dingy 1947 Liverpool is the setting for this very British comedy-drama on life within a repertory theatre troupe. Fifteen-year-old orphan Stella (Georgina Cates) finds a family and many life lessons when she is hired as a starry-eyed apprentice and part-time actress. The troupe is headed by Meredith Potter (Hugh Grant), a maniacally egotistical gay director with a taste for using and abusing the younger male workers. Grant's Meredith is a wonderful creation — a pale, nervous, obviously vain chain-smoker with looks that suggest a prissy, upper-class Clark Kent. A chubby Peter Firth plays Bunny, the stage manager who quietly loves the philandering Meredith but is often at the receiving end of the director's bitchy verbal wrath. Alan Rickman is splendid as the troupe's aging leading man. At its best, *Adventure* is an entertaining glimpse behind the curtain, but the film suffers from a disjointed story line and a menagerie of perpetually pitiful characters. ★★½ $19.99

Ay, Carmela!

(1990, 107 min, Spain, Carlos Saura) Carmen Maura, the perky star of so many Pedro Almodóvar films, teams with director Saura in this stirring look at the Spanish Civil War. Carmela (Maura) and Paulino (Andres Pajares) are Republican entertainers who contribute to the war effort by putting on shows for the troops. The film follows them as they travel to various war-torn areas of Spain, always fearful of being apprehended by the Fascists. Maura, in her first major role outside of the Almodóvar camp, delivers a sparkling, heartfelt performance as the vivacious vaudevillain whose political passions and love for the troops lead her to place her own life in danger. *Ay, Carmela!*, while clearly Republican in its sentiment, offers an evenhanded and humanistic view of Spain's bloody past. (Spanish with English subtitles) ★★★ $89.99

B

Babe

(1995, 91 min, Australia, Chris Noonan) It's hard to believe, but it would take a while to find another children's film as thoroughly irresistible as this one about a talking pig. Forget Arnold and Gordy. In fact, forget Francis, Mr. Ed and the rest of their pals, for *Babe* brings home the bacon. The story follows the misadventures of Babe, a piglet who is won by the kindly farmer Hoggett (James Cromwell). On this farm, Hoggett's animals are able to communicate with each other, though each must obey the social structure the animals have set for themselves. That is until Babe works his magic and brings all the animals together. This is a wondrous world where a duck wants to be a rooster, Brechtian mice act as a Greek chorus, and Babe thinks himself to be a sheepdog. And as Babe proves, you can be anything you want. The film ingeniously interacts the animals and humans, and its clever screenplay and a splendid use of ground-level cinematography bring all the animals (some real, some Henson creations) to life. An Oscar nominee for Best Picture. ★★★★ $22.99

The Babe

(1992, 115 min, US, Arthur Hiller) As old fashioned as the period costumes its large cast wears, *The Babe* is a brash, sentimental and entertaining look at the life of baseball legend Babe Ruth. Sticking to the facts more consistently than the pretty bad 1948 biopic *The Babe Ruth Story*, the film benefits from a larger-than-life characterization from big guy John Goodman. Weighed down by some heavily dramatic scenes, the story follows Ruth's meteoric rise in the 1920s where, first as a Red Sox and then as a New York Yankee, he would make baseball history. Fans of the sport should

find *The Babe* endearing; though non-fans may be at a loss as the film almost canonizes the Bambino. ★★½ $9.99

Babes in Arms

(1939, 91 min, US, Busby Berkeley) Trimmed-down but delightfully entertaining version of the Rodgers and Hart Broadway musical. Judy Garland and Mickey Rooney are terrific together as the children of vaudevillians who decide to "put on a show" to help their struggling parents. Though '30s schmaltz all the way, this is probably the best of the Judy-Mickey "Let's put on a show" musicals. ★★★ $19.99

Babette's Feast

(1987, 102 min, Denmark, Gabriel Axel) Director Axel's Oscar-winning adaptation of Isak Dinesen's ("Out of Africa") poignant novella is an inspired celebration of the triumph of art over puritanical zeal. Set in a tiny and bleak 19th-century Scandinavian village, the story follows the lives of two devoutly religious sisters who have retreated into the desolate, but safe, enclave of their pious upbringings. Into their lives comes Babette (Stéphane Audran) — a maid who was forced to flee her native France and unbeknownst to the two women, was once a renowned and celebrated gourmet chef. After years of service, Babette one day receives word that she has won the lottery, and decides to lavish the household — to repay the sisters' kindness — with the most extravagant dinner ever to be seen (or tasted) on the entire Jutland peninsula; a feast which kindles the fire of humanity in the deadened souls of the tiny hamlet. (Danish and French with English subtitles) ★★★★ $19.99

Baby Boom

(1987, 103 min, US, Charles Shyer) One of the more enjoyable baby comedies which proliferated in the late 1980s. Diane Keaton gives

a charming performance as a successful executive whose life is turned upside-down when she becomes guardian to a deceased relative's infant. Harold Ramis does the aggressive yuppie thing again, and Sam Shepard does the nice-guy thing again. ★★★ $9.99

Baby Cakes

(1989, 100 min, US, Paul Schneider) *Baby Cakes* is a Cinderella story of sorts. Our heroine isn't a naive waif physically and mentally abused by her wicked stepmother, she's an overweight and unhappy mortician's assistant (Ricki Lake) who is ignored by just about everyone. Her prince is a handsome young subway car driver (Craig Sheffer) who is stuck in an essentially loveless relationship. This is your standard made-for-TV fare, with well-meaning but bumbling fathers, insensitive stepmoms and doomsday-obsessed best friends. Worth noting is Lake, who with innuendo in her throaty voice and a twinkle in her eye, is able to wrench a sense of mischievous sexuality out of otherwise flacid dialogue. But the best thing about *Baby Cakes* is that it may lead viewers back to the German film on which it is based, *Sugarbaby*, a disturbing yet tender portrait of a lonely woman in search of love. ★½ $89.99

Baby Doll

(1956, 114 min, US, Elia Kazan) The first motion picture from a major American studio ever to be publicly condemned by the Legion of Decency, this twisted piece of Southern Gothic is still quite effective some four decades after its initial release. Tennessee Williams wrote and Kazan directed this tale of "Baby Doll," a child-bride who sleeps in a crib and endures the ever-lurking (and sexual pressures) of her "adult" husband, an over-the-top Karl Malden. The film features excellent supporting performances, most notably from a bitchy Eli Wallach as Malden's revenge-seeking boss, and eerie black-and-white cinematography. But the film belongs to Carroll Baker as Baby Doll; she is the embodiment of adolescent sexuality and manipulation. A decadent delight. ★★★½ $19.99

Baby Face

(1933, 70 min, US, Alfred E. Green) Barbara Stanwyck shines in a "bad girl" role in this provocative pre-Production Code melodrama. Stanwyck literally sleeps her way to the top when she leaves her Erie speakeasy to conquer a New York banking company, using and discarding men at her whim. A must see for Stanwyck fans, students of 1930s cinema, or anyone interested in an exorbitantly good time. Also with George Brent and a young John Wayne (as one of Stanwyck's conquests). ★★★ $19.99

The Baby-Sitter's Club

(1995, 92 min, US, Melanie Mayron) There are so few films for teen girls that this is a welcome addition to that arena. Although too fluffy at times and in too many directions, the enjoyable cast and engaging premise should win over its intended adolescent audience. Taken from the very popular series of the same name, the story takes place over summer vacation when the baby-sitters club, a tight-knit group of girls aged

Babe

11 to 13, decide to open a summer day camp for their clients. The president of the club, wonderfully played by Schuyler Fisk, faces a dilemma when her long-lost dad returns, demanding that she tell no one of his presence. The strain of secrecy and her mixed feelings about his reappearance take their toll before being resolved in the reaffirming climax. There a many subplots which alternately enhance and distract from the plot. ★★★ $19.99

Baby's Day Out

(1994, 90 min, US, Patrick Read Johnson) This is for all those who loved *Home Alone*. Just add one more villain, reduce the age of the child, add a ransom note, and you have the latest variation of a theme. The baby is adorable and the bad guys (led by Joe Mantegna) are strangely likable, but Baby Bink crawling alone across a busy Manhattan street stretches the formula pretty thin. However, the special effects are clever, with the baby fitting seamlessly into ever wilder situations; and the acting is as good as the material will allow. Lara Flynn Boyle turns in a particularly affecting performance as the worried mother. ★★½ $14.99

Baby, It's You

(1983, 105 min, US, John Sayles) One of the most popular films ever to play at TLA, this is Sayles' endearing ode to adolescent yearning and awakening maturity. Rosanna Arquette stars in a remarkably textured performance as a young woman whose horizons expand beyond the grasp of her volatile high school beau (Vincent Spano). A warm comic remembrance of faded affections, bygone youth and the golden age of rock 'n' roll. The supporting cast includes then-unknowns Matthew Modine and Robert Downey, Jr. ★★★½ $79.99

Babyfever

(1994, 110 min, US, Henry Jaglom) Sometimes called the "West Coast Woody Allen," director Jaglom crafts films around topics of neurotic obsession and lets his actors run with it through a loosely structured narrative. This time around, the topic of white, middle-aged angst is reproduction: As biological clocks tick away, a collection of female friends explore their options from turkey basters to men more interested in having children than they are. The various protagonists balance the instinct to procreate with the many entanglements and obligations inherent in late 20th-century America. Often self-indulgent and sometimes unexpectedly touching, *Babyfever* — like the director's other films — is an acquired taste which may not be palatable for all. But if your own clock is ticking, or if you fantasize about father-son softball games, this might suit your fancy. ★★½ $19.99

Bach and Broccoli

(1986, 96 min, France, Andre Melançon) A tender family film about a small orphan girl who leaves her sick grandmother to live with her bachelor uncle. Though he protests, young Fanny moves in, along with her pet snake, Broccoli. As Uncle John practices for his upcoming Bach organ competition, Fanny adds stray animals to her ever-increasing collection. Though not demonstrative in his feelings for the girl, it's not until the authorities

threaten to take her away that the uncle shows his love, and begins a fight to keep his niece. (Dubbed) ★★★ $14.99

The Bachelor

(1991, 105 min, Italy/Hungary/GB, Roberto Faenza) Miranda Richardson stars in a dual role in this sumptuous though somewhat confusing period piece about a turn-of-the-century doctor (Keith Carradine) who is unexpectedly given a second chance at life and love when his spinster sister (Richardson) commits suicide. While cut from the same cloth as *Howards End* and *A Room with a View*, the unusual tale of a man's sexual awakening lacks the skillful tailoring of either and at times works better as a travelogue than as the character study it was meant to be. Also stars Kristin Scott Thomas and Max von Sydow. ★★ $89.99

The Bachelor and the Bobbysoxer

(1947, 95 min, US, Irving Reis) The usually dapper Cary Grant gets a chance to let down his well-ordered hair by acting like a teenager in this delightful Oscar-winning comedy, one of Grant's biggest box-office hits. When "bobbysoxer" Shirley Temple becomes infatuated with playboy/artist Grant, little Shirley's sister, judge Myrna Loy, orders the bemused bachelor to date the adolescent adulator in the hopes she soon gets over him. In no time, Myrna and the born-again teenager are falling in love. Academy Award for Best Original Screenplay. ★★★½ $19.99

Bachelor Mother

(1939, 81 min, US, Garson Kanin) A charming romantic comedy with Ginger Rogers as a single working girl who finds an abandoned baby; everyone around her presumes it's hers, including boss David Niven, who has a romantic interest in her. Directed with style by Kanin, this is one of the better screwball romances popular at the time. ★★★ $19.99

Bachelor Party

(1984, 106 min, US, Neal Israel) In his first box-office hit, Tom Hanks demonstrates little of the comic presence which would be tapped that same year in *Splash*. This goonish comedy casts Hanks as a groom-to-be celebrating his upcoming wedding. Predictable shenanigans happen as the party gets out of hand. Harmless but very silly. ★★ $9.99

Back in the USSR

(1991, 88 min, US, Deran Sarafian) Frank Whaley stars in this Hitchcockian suspenser as an American student abroad who accidentally steps into a web of intrigue involving a stolen religious artifact and Soviet spies. Russian actors Natalya Negoda and Ravil Issayanov, along with Roman Polanski's portrayal of a shrewd and heartless villain, and the fabulous Russian scenery, propel this otherwise average thriller. ★★ $19.99

Back Street

(1961, 107 min, US, David Miller) Ross Hunter produced this third screen adaptation of Fannie Hurst's novel, giving it the same glossy treatment as his other late-1950s melodramas (*Imitation of Life, Magnificent Obsession*, etc). Susan Hayward stars as the young woman entangled in a hopeless love affair with a mar-

ried man (John Gavin). Though the earlier two versions are dramatically superior, this is nevertheless an effective (if campily fantastic) soaper. ★★½ $14.99

Back to Ararat

(1990, 100 min, US/Armenia, Pea Holmquist) The 1915 death march, the eventual genocide of 1.5 million Armenians and the ensuing annexation of parts of Armenia by Turkish forces are explored in this startling documentary. In addition to recounting the horrors of the genocide, the film focuses on three generations of Armenians scattered throughout the world, all of whom dream of the day when it will be possible to return to the lands surrounding the holy mountain of Ararat. ★★★ $49.99

Back to School

(1986, 96 min, US, Alan Metter) Rodney Dangerfield had a big hit with this funny campus comedy. The Man-of-No-Respect shines as a crass but lovable millionaire who enrolls in his son's college, both getting an unexpected education. Keith Gordon plays his son, and Robert Downey, Jr. is a fellow student. Good one-liners. ★★★ $14.99

Back to the Beach

(1987, 92 min, US, Lyndall Hobbs) Frankie Avalon and Annette Funicello are back together again in this forced piece of baby boomer nostalgia. The sweethearts of the '60s, now parents living in the Midwest, travel to California to visit their daughter, and keep running into various '60s TV stars. Connie Stevens looking great as ever, is there, as well as cameos by Bob Denver, Alan Hale, Jr., Jerry Mathers, Tony Dow and Don Adams. ★★ $14.99

Back to the Future

(1985, 116 min, US, Robert Zemeckis) Classic time-travel comedy with Michael J. Fox as a teenager who travels back in time to 1955. There he interferes with the meeting of his parents, and is forced to play Cupid to his beautiful mom and nerdish dad. Christopher Lloyd is terrific as Fox's "crazy scientist" pal, and Crispin Glover and Lea Thompson are his parents. An inventive, very funny and well-structured screenplay, nice special effects and a genuinely charismatic cast all contribute to the enjoyment level of this box-office smash. ★★★★

Back to the Future, Part II

(1989, 107 min, US, Robert Zemeckis) Picking up where the original left off, Doc Brown whisks Marty and girlfriend Jennifer to the year 2015. In the future, however, the time machine is stolen by Biff, who uses it to alter the past. Doc and Marty must return to the past to save the present. If it sounds a bit confusing, it is. Michael J. Fox and Christopher Lloyd return, and both are in fine form, though the screenwriters don't give either actor the opportunity for a comic tour de force as in the original. Director Zemeckis, who encores from the first film, engages some truly impressive split-screen special effects, but the story is rambling and only occasionally funny. The parallel future looks more like Pottersville in *It's a Wonderful Life*, making Fox an unlikely

George Bailey. This *Future* is decidedly dark and inferior to its predecessor. ★★½ $19.99

Back to the Future, Part III

(1990, 119 min, US, Robert Zemeckis) The exciting finale to Zemeckis' trilogy finds our hero Marty McFly (Michael J. Fox) scrambling back in time to the Old West to track down his friend Dr. Emmett Brown (Christopher Lloyd). Unlike the second film, which jumped back and forth between eons and even took a hitch into an alternative dimension, the main part of the narrative here stays with the frontier setting and to great effect. Lloyd and Fox are both in their element as they get to ham up their respective roles and Mary Steenburgen is a pleasing addition as a Victorian schoolteacher who romances Dr. Brown. ★★★ $19.99

Backbeat

(1994, 100 min, GB, Iain Softley) With the high-octane energy of a Beatles song, *Backbeat* is the exhilarating story of artist and musician Stu Sutcliffe, who flirted with fame as the "fifth Beatle." It's 1960, and the struggling Beatles have accepted a gig at a dive bar in Hamburg. The story focuses on the friendship of best mates Sutcliffe (Stephen Dorff) and John Lennon (Ian Hart), whose close relationship is put to the test when Sutcliffe falls in love with a bohemian German woman, Astrid (Sheryl Lee in a captivating performance). As Stu and Astrid initiate their relationship, Stu abandons the band to pursue Astrid and art school. Though the many musical sequences are thrilling and have a life of their own, they are only a small part of the film's success, and these scenes are smartly complemented by bristling characterizations and finely tuned dramatics. Hart gives an extraordinary portrayal which goes beyond mimicry in bringing Lennon's wit, sarcasm and genius to the surface, and Dorff is equally compelling as Stu. ★★★★ $19.99

Backdraft

(1991, 135 min, US, Ron Howard) An impressively mounted if dramatically awkward homage to the bravery of our nation's firefighters. Kurt Russell and William Baldwin stars as brothers and firemen, whose volatile relationship is as explosive as the fires they fight. The fine cast also includes the splendid Robert De Niro as a fire inspector investigating a series of arsons, and Scott Glenn as Russell's seasoned co-worker. But the real star of the film is the spectacular fire-fighting scenes — director Howard has captured some awe-inspiring footage of firefighting in action. (Available letterboxed and pan & scan) ★★★ $19.99

Backfire

(1987, 92 min, US/Canada, Gilbert Cates) Karen Allen stars as yet another duplicitous housewife whose plans to drive her wealthy shell-shocked husband (Jeff Fahey) to suicide and collect his fortune backfire when he is left an invalid in her care. Also with Keith Carradine, Bernie Casey and Dean Paul Martin. Some nice twists punctuate this noirish thriller, which is short on development but contains some stylish flourishes. ★★½ $29.99

Background to Danger

(1943, 80 min, US, Raoul Walsh) As a poor man's Humphrey Bogart, George Raft finds himself up against the Nazis in this WWII espionage thriller which, while cheesy, is not without its fair share of twists and intrigue. Raft plays an American salesman traveling through Turkey who becomes involved with German, Russian and Turkish agents when he stumbles upon a Nazi plot trying to force the hand of Turkey to rescind its neutrality and side with Germany. Sydney Greenstreet is the iniquitous Nazi agent behind the set-up, and Peter Lorre also stars as a spy who may or may not be a Russian agent, but who definitely likes his Vodka. ★★★ $19.99

Backstage at the Kirov

(1984, 80 min, US, Derek Hart) Only one dance company has given the world Balanchine, Nureyev, Markova and Baryshnikov: the Kirov. This absorbing documentary captures the magic and drama of this outstanding company, both onstage and in the wings — a must for dance lovers. ★★★ $14.99

The Bad and the Beautiful

(1952, 118 min, US, Vincente Minnelli) The film Minnelli directed in between his glorious technicolor musicals *An American in Paris* and *The Band Wagon* is black-and-white melodrama of the highest studio order. It's a quintessential Hollywood story with Kirk Douglas as an ambitious (ruthless?) producer and his effect on an actress (Lana Turner), a writer (Dick Powell) and a director (Barry Sullivan). Winner of five Oscars including Best Screenplay (Charles Schnee) and Best Supporting Actress (Gloria Graham). ★★★★ $19.99

Bad Behavior

(1992, 103 min, GB, Les Blair) Stephen Rea and Sinead Cusack star in this mostly improvised domestic comedy which skillfully hits its mark. Rea and Cusack are Gerry and Ellie McAllister: middle-aged, the parents of two sons, and owners of a North London row home in need of repairs. While he trudges off to work every day to the town planning commission, she plays host to a parade of locals who stop in to share their worries over a cup of tea. In the tradition of Mike Leigh, director Blair has molded a film where not much happens, but we are nonetheless drawn into the characters' lives on a wonderfully intimate and enjoyable level. Rea and Cusack, both consummate actors, ably anchor the cast which includes Phil Daniels (in a dual role) and Philip Jackson (as a shady real estate huckster). ★★★½ $94.99

Bad Boys

(1983, 123 min, US, Rick Rosenthal) Sparks fly in this intense drama as Sean Penn and Esai Morales square off as adversaries in a juvenile prison. Tough and violent, the film packs quite a wallop in its presentation of youthful lives behind bars. ★★★ $14.99

Bad Boys

(1995, 118 min, US, Michael Bay) TV stars Martin Lawrence and Will Smith trade off their sitcom personalities to good effect in this otherwise formulaic buddy movie/police

actioner. As partners in crime-solving, Lawrence plays the faithful husband to Smith's single playboy — and they're such an incessantly bickering couple that they make Glover and Gibson seem like the Brady kids. The story begins when a friend is killed investigating murderous drug dealers. Teaming with an eyewitness (Téa Leoni), they try to track down the killers while protecting their charge at the same time. Balancing comedy and action, the film is much more appealing when the two stars are snapping the one-liners rather than blasting the bullets. There are only two action sequences of note, but both are well-paced and very exciting though the subplot involving Lawrence's wife wears thin rather quickly. ★★½ $19.99

Bad Company

(1972, 93 min, US, Robert Benton) This lyrical, haunting western from director Benton (*Kramer vs. Kramer*, *Places in the Heart*) stars Jeff Bridges and Barry Brown as two drifters robbing their way West during the Civil War. Benton and David Newman, who worked together on *Bonnie and Clyde*, wrote the insightful and unexpectedly humorous screenplay, and the film is enhanced by beautiful cinematography (Gordon Willis). ★★★½ $9.99

Bad Company

(1995, 108 min, US, Damian Harris) Laurence Fishburne stars in this simplistic yet thought-provoking spy thriller which gives a sardonic clue as to what some soldiers may do once the war is over. In a role not unlike his excellent turn in *Deep Cover*, Fishburne plays a blacklisted ex-CIA agent enlisted by Ellen Barkin and Frank Langella to join a mysterious company whose stock-in-trade is translating post-Cold War tactics (blackmail, bribery, murder) to the world of big business and high finance. This intriguing premise turns stale, however, as in high order Barkin lures Fishburne first into bed and then into a deadly hostile takeover. As sincere as the two leads are, the peripheral characters carry much more depth: including Spalding Gray as a whiny industrialist on the verge of ruin, David Ogden Stiers as a soft-hearted judge with a fatal weakness for gambling, and Michael Beach as an ex-operative being blackballed for being gay. ★★½ $14.99

Bad Day at Black Rock

(1955, 81 min, US, John Sturges) Spencer Tracy heads a first-rate cast in this suspenseful modern-day western with Tracy in a commanding performance as a one-armed visitor to a small town who unwittingly uncovers a local secret, which puts him in imminent danger. Director Sturges maintains high tension throughout, and the story is an invigorating study of mob mentality and the bravery to stand against it. Also starring Robert Ryan, Walter Brennan, Ernest Borgnine, Lee Marvin and Dean Jagger. ★★★★ $19.99

Bad Dreams

(1988, 84 min, US, Andrew Fleming) Sickly, gory horror film about a young woman, waking up after a long coma — which she went into after escaping from a mass suicide — who is haunted by those who died those many years before. ★ $89.99

Bad Girls

(1994, 100 min, US, Jonathan Kaplan) Andie MacDowell, Drew Barrymore and Mary Stuart Masterson save fellow honky tonk harlot Madeleine Stowe from the hangman's noose. The four newly minted outlaws hit the road, with hired Pinkerton detectives on their trail. This revisionist, feminist western, combining elements of *Young Guns* with *The Ballad of Little Jo*, is actually better than the bullets and bustiers, girls-with-guns expectations it generates. Although certainly not perfect, with an often meandering script and many hackneyed contrivances, it's hard not to appreciate women who shoot to kill when sufficiently provoked. Also appreciated is one particularly memorable line: "If your laws don't include me, then they just don't apply to me, either." Amen, sister. ★★½ $9.99

Bad Guys

(1979, 93 min, Hungary, Gyorgy Szomjas) This curiosity, a "Goulash western" so to speak, is set in Hungary in the 1860s and recounts the saga of a band of outlaws who begin a reign of terror on the populace of several villages. In territory not unlike the Old West, the townspeople organize a posse and set off on the trail of the desperado and his henchmen. (Hungarian with English subtitles) ★★½ $69.99

Bad Influence

(1990, 99 min, US, Curtis Hanson) This pulsating, gritty thriller stars James Spader as a successful businessman who is befriended by mysterious ne'er-do-well Rob Lowe. Taking the passive yuppie under his wing, Lowe introduces Spader to the seedier side of Los Angeles life. With hints of *Strangers on a Train* and writer David Koepp's own *Apartment Zero*, their seemingly innocent friendship becomes twisted and lethal, leading to blackmail and murder. Lowe gives a well-textured portrait of

Harvey Keitel in *The Bad Lieutenant*

deceit and malevolence, and Spader again proves that he is one of the leading actors of his generation. It is ironic, however, that the actors, one on- and one off-screen, have found some notoriety videotaping sexual acts, which is an important plot device in this slick, suspenseful film. ★★★ $14.99

Bad Lieutenant

(1992, 96 min, US, Abel Ferrara) Erupting from the bowels of Hell comes this highly original, raw and shocking slice of life. Beginning with a corrupt, money-stealing, gambling addicted cop (Harvey Keitel) snorting coke off his dashboard after dropping his two sons off at school, we soon begin a slow, painful journey into a swirling abyss of heroin shooting, crack smoking, hooker humping and countless acts of self-degradation. Looking for redemption, our bad seed of a cop takes on a brutal rape case involving a nun, sending him further into a self-destructive Hades. The vividly realistic screenplay (co-written by *Ms. 45* starlet Zoe Tamerlis) and the gutsy, riveting performance of Keitel combine to make this one of the sleaziest films ever made. It's not for all tastes, but is nonetheless an important film. ★★★½ $19.99

Bad Moon

(1996, 79 min, US, Eric Red) It's dog versus werewolf in this poorly written attempt to teach an old genre some new tricks. Unfortunately, all *Bad Moon* can do is roll over and play dead. Michael Paré is some sort of adventurer who is bitten by a werewolf. He survives and, of course, we all know what that means. He relocates to the Pacific Northwest (the movie includes some fantastic scenery) to stay with his sister (Muriel Hemingway) and her child; they can't understand all the animal attacks which are plaguing the region. Lucky for them, the smartest member of the family is Thor the German shepherd, who immediately starts marking his territory and giving suspicious glances to the new dog in town. A test of wills ensues, but instead of an innovative examination of Paré's "beast within," we get a cliché-ridden, lame-brained child-in-peril movie. The werewolf effects, at least, are admirable, but terribly overlit. ★½ $99.99

The Bad News Bears

(1976, 102 min, US, Michael Ritchie) Though two pallid sequels have soured the memory of the original, this is quite a delightful and funny baseball comedy. Walter Matthau is especially good as a beer-guzzling, slobbish coach to a team of misfit little leaguers. Tatum O'Neal is charming as the team's last hope — a pitcher with a wicked fast ball. Followed by two sequels: *The Bad News Bears in Breaking Training* and *The Bad News Bears Go to Japan*. ★★★ $14.99

The Bad Seed

(1956, 129 min, US, Mervyn LeRoy) This unsettling version of the Broadway hit about a psychopathic little girl is so effective it prompted the studio upon its release to add a closing introduction to the featured players — perhaps the birth of the tagline, "Remember, it's only a movie." Patty McCormack and Nancy Kelly recreate their stage roles as, respectively, the

amoral title character and her disbelieving mother. ★★★½ $14.99

The Bad Sleep Well

(1960, 135 min, Japan, Akira Kurosawa) This chilling tale of corruption in the modern Japanese corporate world stars director Kurosawa's mainstay, Toshiro Mifune, as an embittered, grieving son and rising executive whose father supposedly committed suicide. Not believing the official version of his death, and convinced that a large corporation and its officials were somehow involved, Mifune plots revenge. This stylish crime thriller, based on an Ed McBain story, provides a fascinating commentary on the twisted self-interests of big business. (Japanese with English subtitles) ★★★

Bad Taste

(1987, 90 min, New Zealand, Peter Jackson) This hysterical horror spoof from first-time director Jackson, who would go on to make the gorefest *Dead Alive* and the critical success *Heavenly Creatures*, is about a group of paramilitary investigators who are the first line of defense against an attempted alien invasion of the Earth. The members of the team, including Jackson himself, must thwart an attempt by these "intergalactic wankers" to harvest the latest universal fast-food sensation: human flesh. Many horror and action clichés are sent up in the meantime and the body count and amount of gore make the film live up to its title in every way. It is also as funny as it is gross and the amateur cast members (who also wrote and performed the music, edited the film, provided the locations, etc.) perform admirably amidst the carnage. Sure to please fans of the genre, *Bad Taste* is essential viewing for anyone with a strong stomach and a rowdy sense of humor. ★★★

Badlands

(1973, 95 min, US, Terrence Malick) As legend has it, Terrence Malick just decided that he wanted to give filmmaking a whirl. That whirl yielded a classic — a haunting, touching and often humorous piece of work. Based on the story of 1950s killer Charles Starkweather, *Badlands* boasts a richly textured screenplay, exquisite cinematography, wonderful use of music and, above all else, astonishing performances by Martin Sheen and Sissy Spacek as young lovers on the run. In a film full of moody, funny, breathtaking sequences, the all-too-brief scene where Sheen and Spacek, hiding out in the woods, dance around while their radio plays Mickey and Sylvia singing "Love Is Strange" is a standout, a priceless moment of cinematic art. Malick, after reaping much critical praise, reportedly decided to retire from filmmaking following his auspicious debut. However, he returned to make the outstanding *Days of Heaven* in 1978. He has not made a film since then. ★★★★ $19.99

Bagdad Cafe

(1988, 91 min, West Germany, Percy Adlon) This enchanting and affectionate fable unveils, in a series of wonderful vignettes, the developing friendship between several oddball characters. Marianne Sagebrecht is a corpulent Bavarian tourist who, stranded somewhere in the Mojave Desert, arrives one day at the near-comatose Bagdad Cafe, a dusty road-side cafe run by an irascible black woman (CCH Pounder). Director Adlon takes his time in showing their differences, as well as their blossoming friendship. A wonderful comedy-drama about misfits in tune with the world which features a show-stealing performance by Jack Palance as an eccentric but charming painter. ★★★½ $14.99

Bail Jumper
(1989, 95 min, US, Christian Faber) Unnatural natural calamities befall two Southern thieves in love in this strange, wacky comedy. Joe and Elaine, both petty criminals, decide to leave their home in Murky Springs, Missouri, for the more promising shores of Long Island. But along the way, they are visited by a swarm of locusts, hit with a tornado and, in their new home, greeted with a tidal wave. ★★½ $89.99

The Baker's Wife
(1938, 124 min, France, Marcel Pagnol) The wonderfully enchanting comedic actor Raimu shines as a lovesick and inconsolable baker who goes on a baking strike after he discovers that his flighty wife has run off with a handsome shepherd. The breadless villagers, desperate to get life back to normal, take the situation in their own hands in an effort to get the two back together again. Infused with humor and casting a sympathetic eye towards the villagers and provincial life, Pagnol's charming tale is successful in dealing with the natural pleasures and sufferings of life. (French with English subtitles) ★★★★ $59.99

Le Bal
(1982, 110 min, Italy/France, Ettore Scola) Within the setting of a Parisian dance hall, director Scola ingeniously presents 50 years of European social and political history through a series of vignettes. With no dialogue, just the musical accompaniment of Charles Aznavour, Irving Berlin, Charele Trene and others, *Le Bal* sweeps us through the turbulent 20th century in a highly stylized yet poignant and absorbing way. ★★★ $79.99

La Balance
(1982, 102 min, France, Bob Swaim) This gangster sensation swept the French César Awards and took the Best Feature, Actor and Actress honors. Nathalie Baye stars as a tough, high-class hooker caught in a cat-and-mouse struggle between her boyfriend/pimp and a determined detective. A kind of Gallic *Dirty Harry*, *La Balance* is a taut and jolting journey through the Parisian underworld. (Dubbed) ★★★

The Balcony
(1963, 83 min, US/GB, Joseph Strick) Jean Genet's allegorical play set in a brothel comes to life in this vivid and boisterous low-budget film. Shelley Winters is the beleaguered lesbian madam of the bustling bordello. This "house of illusion," where people play out their dreams, is left undisturbed despite a ravaging rebellion outside its doors. An interesting and at times surreal find which also stars Peter Falk, Ruby Dee, Lee Grant (who plays Winters' lover) and Leonard Nimoy. ★★★ $29.99

Balkan Express
(1984, 102 min, Yugoslavia, Branko Baletic) This offbeat and tragic comedy follows the manic adventures of the Balkan Express Band, a troupe of roving musicians whose music is just a cover for their real work: con men and thieves. Their easy and wild living is interrupted during the Nazi occupation as this motley group discover that they must overcome their petty self-interests and work to overcome the oppression. Outrageously madcap and full of dramatic twists set against the dark horror of war. (Dubbed) ★★★ $9.99

Ball of Fire
(1941, 111 min, US, Howard Hawks) Gary Cooper stars as a professor of English researching slang for an encyclopedia — he's shy but he's a real solid sender anyway. Barbara Stanwyck is Sugarpuss O'Shea, a gangster's moll on the lam — now she's definitely rockin' with a solid eight. When Coop and his seven associates unwittingly give shelter to this killer diller, she turns their lives topsy-turvy, and when Cooper and Stanwyck hit the giggles, oh boy, it's hot toi toi: root, zoot, cute, and solid to boot. This delightful, whimsical comedy was directed by the great Howard Hawks (*His Girl Friday*), and gave Stanwyck her second Oscar nomination. (Give a ring on the Ameche if you liked it.) ★★★½ $19.99

Ballad in Blue
(1966, 89 min, GB, Paul Henreid) Ray Charles found the perfect showcase for his talents in this restrained melodrama about an American jazz musician who befriends a young blind boy. The story is overly maudlin and not too substantial, but the film provides ample footage of Charles at his piano belting out his favorites including "I Got a Woman," "What'd I Say?" and "Cry." A pleasure for even the mildest of fans. ★★½

Ballad of a Soldier
(1959, 89 min, USSR, Grigori Chukhrai) A sensitive and romantic story about a 19-year-old soldier in WWII who sets out on leave to visit his mother. The trip is punctuated with scenes of the horrors of war but is highlighted by the hero falling in love with a beautiful young girl. A moving experience, this tender love story will soften even the hardest of hearts. (Russian with English subtitles) ★★★½ $29.99

The Ballad of Cable Hogue
(1970, 121 min, US, Sam Peckinpah) Peckinpah is in a notably lighter mood with this vigorously entertaining western. Though the Old West is still dusty and dangerous as in any of his other more volatile works, the wild in this Wild West is for unpredictable and strange antics. Jason Robards heads a good cast as an eccentric prospector whose dream of an oasis in the middle of the desert may not be as crazy as everyone thinks. In her best screen role, Stella Stevens is sharp as a needle as the good-hearted, feisty prostitute who takes up with Robards. As the remaining player in this quest, David Warner is splendid as an unusually loony preacher. ★★★½ $14.99

Ballad of a Soldier

The Ballad of Gregorio Cortez
(1982, 99 min, US, Robert M. Young) Sincere telling of one of the most unsettling manhunts in Texas history is a gritty and unsettling examination of bigotry. Edward James Olmos stars as a young Mexican who, in a miscommunication of language, kills a U.S. sheriff and becomes the object of a state-wide hunt. ★★★ $29.99

The Ballad of Little Jo
(1993, 120 min, US, Maggie Greenwald) Part of 1993's parade of cross-dressing titles (*Farewell My Concubine*, *Orlando*, etc.), this profound little odyssey examines feminine oppression in the tale of a young woman who finds herself wandering the countryside at the end of the Civil War. Constantly at peril of being raped by marauding ex-soldiers, she decides to head west where she masquerades as a man in a shithole mining town. Based on a true story lifted from a newspaper headline of the day, Greenwald's film delivers a wonderfully satisfying, gritty look at the Old West which rivals *Unforgiven*. Suzy Amis, in the lead role, creates an excellent portrait of rugged and determined survival. Ian McKellen gives great support as a grizzly miner, portrayed initially as a decent man but who eventually shows his true misogynist colors. ★★★★ $14.99

The Ballad of Narayama
(1983, 130 min, Japan, Shohei Imamura) This exquisitely photographed film paints a sublime portrait of the harsh life endured in a secluded, 19th-century village high in the mountains of northern Japan. Reacting to their raw existence, the people have adopted several unusual customs, including one which dictates that the elderly, upon reaching the age of 70, are escorted to the top of Narayama Mountain to die in solitude. Director Imamura depicts a cruel and sometimes shocking world to the viewer but one which is based on simple survival. (Japanese with English subtitles) ★★★★ $29.99

The Ballad of the Sad Cafe
(1991, 108 min, US, Simon Callow) The Deep South has played host to many a curious tale, but none more strange or bewildering than this wildly uneven but nevertheless hypnotic adaptation of the Edward Albee play, itself based on the Carson McCullers novella. Never a stranger to risk-taking, Vanessa Redgrave gives a bold, mesmerizing performance as Miss Amelia, the masculine town tycoon whose crew-cut and gangly walk send fear into the local residents. All except Lymon (Cork

Hubbard), a hunchback dwarf who arrives one day claiming to be Miss Amelia's cousin. A ne'er-do-well, Lymon convinces her to open a cafe, which becomes the pulse of the tiny town. However, things change drastically when Miss Amelia's estranged husband, Marvin (Keith Carradine), returns from prison. As Lymon turns his loyalties to Marvin, the stage is set for a battle-of-the-sexes showdown which culminates in an unbelieveable fist-fight finale. Not for all tastes, but for the more adventurous viewer. ★★½ $89.99

Ballot Measure 9

(1995, 72 min, US, Heather MacDonald) In contrast to its dry, didactic sounding title, this documentary about the events leading up to the vote on the 1992 Colorado and Oregon anti-gay ballot initiatives is in fact both thought-provoking and exhilarating. Written and directed by MacDonald, the film examines the hysteria and hatred generated by those against "special rights for gays and lesbians" especially by members of the Christian Right. While the film strives for balance, the greater emphasis is on those who galvanized themselves into organizations to defeat the proposals — laws that would have denied homosexuals legal recourse against discrimination in housing and employment and have prevented cities from enacting their own gay/lesbian civil rights legislation. MacDonald uses a low-key approach to the contentious issue, and because of it, gained access to interviews with many of the measure's more virulent proponents. Engrossing and a significant document in the history of the lesbian and gay civil rights movement. ★★★ $29.99

Balto

(1995, 78 min, US, Simon Wells) This charming piece of animation has a strong plot (based on a true story), good vocals, and high production values; had it been produced by Disney instead of Amblin Entertainment, name recognition would have made it much more popular than it was. Another example that there really is quality children's films being made outside of the land of Disney. Balto is half-wolf, half-dog, and lives in Nome, Alaska, in the mid-1920s. Spurned by dog and man alike for his mixed heritage, he steps in to save the day when a diphtheria epidemic

threatens the lives of the town's children. He leads a rag-tag team through Arctic blizzards to deliver the much-needed medicine. *Balto* is an appealing package that offers an exciting story, some valuable lessons about tolerance and bravery, and a few rather sophisticated innuendos that will should keep adults interested as well. ★★★ $14.99

Bambi

(1942, 72 min, US) One of the few films which can be said to have affected generations that have seen it, Walt Disney's classic animated feature follows the adventures of a forest deer, Bambi, and his little forest friends, including the lovable Thumper the rabbit. The animation is brilliant, and the story will captivate viewers of all ages. (Remastered in THX) ★★★½ $29.99

Bananas

(1971, 81 min, US, Woody Allen) After the very funny escapades of *Take the Money and Run*, Allen sharpened both his comic skills and his filmmaking techniques to tell the riotous story of Fielding Melish, a meek and mild products tester in New York who finds himself the rebel leader of a group of South American guerrillas. The film is a non-stop barrage of sight gags and one-liners, most of which hit the bulls-eye. ★★★½ $14.99

Band of Outsiders

(1964, 97 min, France, Jean-Luc Godard) Godard's fresh approach to the gangster musical follows the antics of three highly spirited but ineffectual crooks. Interesting aspect of the film is the inserts of Godard's personal philosophical observations and his thoughts on the action in the story. One of Godard's most interesting and accessible films. (French with English subtitles) ★★★½ $59.99

The Band Wagon

(1953, 112 min, US, Vincente Minnelli) One of Fred Astaire's most captivating musicals, this glorious comedic look at the making of a Broadway show has Fred as a Hollywood actor who is persuaded to star on the Great White Way with a renowned ballerina (the beautiful Cyd Charisse). Also with Nanette Fabray, Oscar Levant and Jack Buchanan. A fine score, sensational dance numbers and charming per-

formances by all combine to make this a classic of the musical genre. ★★★★ $19.99

Bandit Queen

(1994, 119 min, India/GB, Shekhar Kapur) This film adaptation of the harrowing yet ultimately triumphant life of Indian folkhero Phoolan Devi is a blistering attack on her culture's horrifying treatment of women and its crushing caste system. Based on her prison diaries, the film opens with a lowborn 11-year-old Phoolan being married to a man 20 years her senior. After being raped by her new husband, she escapes and returns to her home village only to be branded a whore, attacked by young ruling-caste "Thakur" boys and banished by the village elders. Kidnapped and brutally humiliated by a gang of bandits, she eventually rises within their ranks to become the leader of her own gang. Her bitter and ruthless quest for vengeance against not only those men who stole her honor but Thakurs in general leads her to become regarded as a savior by throngs of lowborn Indians. With an unrelentingly hard-core depiction of Indian society, the film offers a fascinating peek into the intricate and complex social machinations of India's highly organized bandit armies. Definitely not for the weak of heart, the film is well-paced and emotionally arousing as both action-adventure story and scathing social critique. ★★★½ $19.99

Bandits

(1987, 98 min, France, Claude Lelouch) Director Lelouch (*A Man and a Woman*) has fashioned a real gem (no pun intended) about the relationship between an imprisoned jewel thief and his daughter. Jean Yanne (*Le Boucher*) is charming as the father who hides his young daughter in a Swiss boarding school after a jewel heist ends in his wife's murder and his arrest. This is a near-perfect film with a great script, first-rate acting and plenty of plot twists. (French with English subtitles) ★★★★ $19.99

Bandolero

(1968, 106 min, US, Andrew V. McLaglen) James Stewart and Dean Martin play sibling outlaws who escape to Mexico with Raquel Welch as a hostage. Stewart and Martin are riding in familiar western territory here, though they play well together. ★★½ $19.99

Bang the Drum Slowly

(1973, 97 min, US, John Hancock) Two standout performances by Michael Moriarty and Robert De Niro highlight this stirring drama, based on a 1956 TV drama (which starred a young Paul Newman) about the relationship between two big-league ball players: a star pitcher (Moriarty) and his catcher (De Niro), dying of Hodgkin's Disease. Vincent Gardenia is priceless as their colorful manager. ★★★½ $14.99

The Bank Dick

(1940, 74 min, US, Eddie Cline) Inept, bungling W.C. Fields gets a job as a guard in a bank, forcing him to deal with the stress of employment as well as the encumberment of wife and family. But forget the plot. This is one of the true comedy classics. The only problem is, it's too short. ★★★½ $14.99

The Ballad of Narayama

Bank Robber

(1993, 94 min, US, Nick Mead) Writer-director Mead combines the typical heist film with a story line inspired by Ionesco's Theatre of the Absurd to produce this entertainingly bizarre and challenging film. A pumped-up Patrick Dempsey plays a nice-guy bank robber who is forced to hide out in a creepy L.A. hotel until the heat blows over. His nightmare begins, however, as he is visited by a succession of characters who know his identity and exploit him at every turn. These include the pizza delivery boy, the hotel clerk and a gay motorcycle cop into S/M. An engaging cast includes Lisa Bonet as a hooker, and Forest Whitaker and Judge Reinhold as two inept cops on his trail. ★★★ $92.99

Bar Girls

(1995, 95 min, US, Marita Giovanni) The mating rites and the accompanying mind games of L.A. lesbians are uncovered in this knowing romantic comedy. Lauran Hoffman's script (based on her autobiographical play) centers most of the action at the West Hollywood Girl Bar where "love" comes easy and often for its denizens and where warm flesh can sometimes be only a tequila away. Loretta (Nancy Allison Wolfe), a writer and one of the bar's bed-hopping regulars, meets and all-too-quickly falls for the self-assured Rachel (Liza D'Agnostino), a bewitching aspiring actress. Their union is threatened, however, when J.R. (Camilla Riggs), an attractively butch cop, enters the scene. The sex-induced theatrics of these and other characters are detailed in both a humorous and dramatic fashion and, unlike the buoyantly chipper *Go Fish*, the women in *Bar Girls* are not entirely likable. While the acting is unremarkable, the staging uninspired and the production values minimal, the film nevertheless is endowed with spunky charm which ultimately wins the viewer over. ★★★ $19.99

Baraka

(1992, 96 min, US, Ron Fricke) "Baraka" is an ancient Sufi word meaning a blessing or the breath or essence of life from which the evolutionary process unfolds. An examination of the diversity of the world's life is the subject of the film, shot in 24 countries in Todd-AO 70mm format. Like the similar *Koyaanisqatsi*, it has no dialogue or narration and combines images and music to enlighten and entertain. The subjects and areas *Baraka* explores include religion, the forces of weather and nature, tribal practices, chicken factories, and the beauty of natural formations and phenomena. Always an incredibly beautiful film, *Baraka* is unfortunately confusing, feeling sometimes like a harmless travelogue and other times like a manipulative, self-conscious political treatise, especially when images of Desert Storm begin to interrupt peaceful visions of nature. Social agenda notwithstanding, *Baraka* is terrific viewing, though its music, taken from a variety of sources, lacks the minimalist power of Philip Glass' magnificent compositions for *Koyaanisqatsi* and *Powaqqatsi*; nor does it mesh with the images the way Glass' work did in the two earlier films. ★★★ $29.99

Barb Wire

(1996, 90 min, US, David Hogan) Imagine a futuristic *Casablanca*, but with a silicone-enhanced Bogart packing automatic weapons, and you have, in a C-cup, the plot of this camp showcase for TV sex symbol Pamela Anderson Lee. In this adaptation of the comic, she plays a former soldier-now-nightclub proprietess who's content to wait out the ongoing Second American Civil War. Her peace is shattered when an ex (Temuera Morrison) walks in, on the run because of his association with a freedom fighter. He enlists her aid to help them escape. On a certain level – as a piece of kitsch – *Barb Wire* is somewhat enjoyable, but it's all just rather flat (the only thing not flat is...never mind). Adding to the camp value is Lee's nonexistent acting ability; in fact, she's surrounded by several equally bad actors not to make her stand out as much. The production values are of the "always raining because it looked cool in *Blade Runner*" variety, and the action scenes are competently done. ★★ $19.99

Barbarella

(1967, 98 min, France, Roger Vadim) There's something for everyone in this imaginative, sexually charged sci-fi camp classic. Featuring a young Jane Fonda – before Vietnam, exercise videos, two Oscars and rich Southern media moguls – as a fetching, pre-liberated sex goddess, this wacky film shows off all of her best bodily talents. As the sexy 40th-century space traveler, Fonda, when not fighting off demonic, razor-teethed dolls or killer canaries, displays a wonderful assortment of the latest in revealing intergalactic fashion. ★★★ $14.99

Barbarians at the Gate

(1993, 122 min, US, Glenn Jordan) It's the 1980s and it's morning in America. Entire companies are bought, sold and discarded faster than pantyhose. Multi-million dollar leveraged buyouts are routinely handled before lunch; the billion dollar deals take a little more time. Sweeping across this frenetic landscape is one rich former Canadian who, in a fast-paced tap dance through the boardrooms of the country, concocts a plan to purchase the leading baking corporation in the land. Fantastic parody, right? The truly fantastic element is that it's all true – well, not true in the sense of This Dialogue Guaranteed Verbatim; but all the major events are documented and have been entered in the annals of United States business history. James Garner is mesmerizing as F. Ross Johnson, CEO of RJR Nabisco, whose attempts to buy out the company are set forth in this humorous and extremely entertaining HBO production. The superlative supporting cast includes Jonathan Pryce, Peter Riegert and Joanna Cassidy. ★★★½ $19.99

Barbarosa

(1981, 90 min, Australia, Fred Schepisi) A thrilling western yarn that combines the charismatic acting of Willie Nelson and the spectacular photography and sharp, tightly controlled direction of Schepisi. A farm boy (Gary Busey) on the lam is rescued from the ravages of the desert by the outlaw Barbarosa (Nelson). A strong alliance and friendship develops as they roam the West battling

Bar Girls

thieves, the elements and angry in-laws. ★★★ $9.99

Barbary Coast

(1935, 90 min, US, Howard Hawks) Hawks distinguished himself as a director par excellence in two film genres: the screwball comedy and the action-flavored drama. This story of 19th-century San Francisco during the California Gold Rush days falls into the latter category. Edward G. Robinson is perfectly cast as a gangster nightclub owner, Miriam Hopkins is the club's star attraction, and Joel McCrea is the Easterner who comes between them. ★★★ $19.99

Barcelona

(1994, 101 min, US, Whit Stillman) The sophomore curse strikes again as Stillman's follow-up to his acclaimed *Metropolitan* fails to totally capture the freshness and ingenuity of his first film. Set in Spain during the last days of the Cold War, the story follows the romantic exploits of two Americans living in Barcelona. Taylor Nichols, sort of a low-rent Hugh Grant, plays a dweeby salesman whose cousin (Chris Eigeman), a Navy attaché, arrives unexpectedly. This gives way to the two aimlessly musing about life, death, romance, politics, and whatever else randomly enters their minds. Like the two principals, the film is a little too chatty for its own good, but Stillman's script occasionally offers amusing and accurate observations on the machinations of the modern relationship. This would have been much more enjoyable, though, if the supporting characters (as in *Metropolitan*) were as well-defined as the leads – especially the women's roles, which are nothing more than window dressing. ★★½ $19.99

The Barefoot Contessa

(1954, 128 min, US, Joseph L. Mankiewicz) Another slick, savvy "showbiz of the '50s" fairy tale from the pen of writer-director Mankiewicz. Ava Gardner is radiant in the title role, a "Cinderella" who refuses to wear the Hollywood glass slipper, while Humphrey Bogart dons the mantle of world-weary cynic (a staple in Mankiewicz's screenplays) all too well and willingly. Also with Rossano Brazzi as the "Prince Charming" type, and Edmond O'Brien, whose performance as a press agent earned him a well-deserved Oscar. Not as potent of a biting exposé as the director's earlier triumph, *All About Eve*; but nevertheless, it manages some well-aimed shots. ★★★ $19.99

Barefoot in the Park

(1967, 105 min, US, Gene Saks) Frothy Neil Simon comedy, based on his hit Broadway play, with Robert Redford and Jane Fonda as newlyweds living on top of a five-floor walk-up in New York City, experiencing big city life and marital woes. Though not one of Simon's classics, there's more than enough to entertain, and a good supporting cast (Charles Boyer, Mildred Natwick and Herb Edelman) adds sparkle. ★★★ $14.99

Barfly

(1987, 97 min, US, Barbet Schroeder) Director Schroeder has perfectly captured the spirit of Charles Bukowski's autobiography about the resilience of the creative force. Mickey Rourke, in possibly his best performance, plays the alcoholic writer who begins an affair with fellow inebriate Faye Dunaway (remarkable in a non-typecast role); the two enjoying the seedy Los Angeles bar scene in search of libation and unorthodox fulfillment. A brilliantly conceived and hilariously funny character study. ★★★½ $19.99

The Barkleys of Broadway

(1949, 109 min, US, Charles Walters) The last Fred Astaire and Ginger Rogers musical (made after a 10-year separation) is charming fluff about a theatrical couple who split when one wants to abandon the act for "serious" drama. Screenplay by Betty Comden-Adolphe Green (*Singin' in the Rain*). ★★★ $19.99

Barnum

(1986, 113 min, GB, Terry Hughes) The London theatrical production of the smash musical extravaganza is brought to video in this rousing musical starring a leaping, spinning and singing Michael Crawford ("Phantom of the Opera"). With music by Cy Coleman ("Sweet Charity," "City of Angels") and lyrics by Michael Stewart, the story follows the famed showman's career from his beginnings as a sideshow promoter to his co-founding of the Barnum & Bailey Circus, "The Greatest Show on Earth!" ★★★ $29.99

Barocco

(1976, 102 min, France, André Téchiné) Gérard Depardieu and Isabelle Adjani star in this frustrating noir tale of blackmail and murder. Adjani plays a young woman who convinces her ex-boxer boyfriend (Depardieu) to accept a bribe to discredit a local politician. Then the boyfriend is murdered by a hit man (also played by Depardieu). Adjani, who witnesses the murder, remembers every detail about the killer with the exception that he's a look-alike of the deceased, a fact which escapes the police, as well. It's the old, annoying Superman/Clark Kent story. Eventually and predictably, the woman reinvents the hit man as her boyfriend and they escape together. If you can get past the forced plot device of iden-

tity, *Barocco* is an acceptable thriller, but Depardieu has certainly done better. (French with English subtitles) ★★ $69.99

Barry Lyndon

(1975, 184 min, GB, Stanley Kubrick) Almost all of Kubrick's films are masterpieces, and this is no exception to that rule. In *Barry Lyndon*, Kubrick goes beyond the bounds of normal cinematography and uses the camera as a paintbrush and the screen as a canvas with which to tell his story through still lifes and landscapes. Adapted from Thackeray's novel, the film follows Barry Lyndon on his search for success in 18th-century England. Starring Ryan O'Neal, Marisa Berenson, John Alcott and Patrick Magee. ★★★★ $29.99

Barry Mackenzie Holds His Own

(1974, 93 min, Australia, Bruce Beresford) This zany Aussie comedy is filled with Down Under in-jokes, raunchy humor and an always unpredictable plot. Australia's Everyman (before the advent of "Crocodile" Dundee), Barry Mackenzie (Barry Crocker), with his Aunt Edna (drag superstar Barry Humphries), gets into all sorts of adventures, including being kidnapped to Transylvania. Fans of low-brow, off-the-wall humor will appreciate this romp. ★★★ $19.99

Barton Fink

(1991, 112 min, US, Joel Coen) The Coen brothers have manufactured a mesmerizing parable on the death of innocence and the perversion of artistic integrity in the face of gross crudity and greed. John Turturro is terrific as the title character, Barton Fink, an acclaimed, socially conscious New York playwright (styled after Clifford Odets) who is lured by Hollywood's false hope. While being reduced to another cog in the studio machine, he develops a strained camaraderie with John Goodman, the next-door neighbor in his steam-bath hotel — it's a relationship which comes to define his California experience. Turturro and Goodman bring total credibility to otherwise fantastical characters in an exaggerated, surreal world of peeling wallpaper and oddly threatening drainpipes. Judy Davis and Michael Lerner (an Oscar nominee) give excellent support. ★★★½ $19.99

Baryshnikov by Tharp

(60 min, US, Don Mischer) Three ballets highlight a brilliant choreographer's vision of a great dancer, and of dance itself. Twyla Tharp and Mikhail Baryshnikov join forces and present "The Little Ballet," "Sinatra Suite" and "Push Comes to Shove." Featuring members of the American Ballet Theatre. ★★★½ $39.99

Basic Instinct

(1992, 127 min, US, Paul Verhoeven) When it opened at movie theatres, this ultra-chic, sexually explicit thriller was surrounded by controversy. Picketed in several cities, the film raised a red flag for gays, lesbians and feminists with its shockingly "retro" stereotypes of man-hating lesbians and a "basic instinct" for murder. Basically an adolescent sex fantasy disguised as a murder mystery, the film follows Michael Douglas as a burned-out cop who inadvisedly falls in "lust" with the prime suspect in a series

of brutal icepick murders, lasciviously portrayed by Sharon Stone. Verhoeven, as always, directs with a sense of style and atmosphere which elevates it above the average action/thriller, but at the heart of the film is Joe Eszterhas' multi-million dollar screenplay which, while particularly hateful of women, is misanthropic on the whole. Worthy of controversy? Perhaps, but basically this is just another thriller which really doesn't cover any new ground. Also starring George Dzundza, Jeanne Tripplehorn and Dorothy Malone. ★★ $14.99

Basic Instinct: Director's Cut

(1992, 154 min, US, Paul Verhoeven) *Do not let the running time fool you.* The MPAA made director Verhoeven tone down some of the scenes. A shot or two in the beginning and primarily a major erotic scene between Michael Douglas and Sharon Stone are the most notable. All in all, it's the same film with an estimated 40 seconds added on. Most of the additional footage is taken up by interviews, including Michael Douglas, Sharon Stone, Jeanne Tripplehorne and Verhoeven. All of the analysis sort of takes away from some of the impact. Now what they should've done is have screenwriter Joe Ezsterhas give his interpretation to a film that has become even more convoluted with discussion. ★★ $24.99

Basileus Quartet

(1982, 118 min, Italy, Fabio Capri) When one of the elderly members of a staid classical quartet dies, he is replaced by a handsome young man. His effervescent approach to life and music proves to be both a tonic and a curse as he affects each member. A stylized drama of artistic expression, the film is sabotaged by an irresponsible portrayal of a gay quartet member. (Available both dubbed and in Italian with English subtitles) ★★½ $29.99

Basket Case

(1982, 91 min, US, Frank Henenlotter) If John Waters ever makes a splatter movie, it won't be any better than this. Country bumpkin tries to make it in New York City while saddled with his mutant brother that he carries around Times Square in a wicker basket. Few serious filmmakers have captured the seamier side of the city better than this little gross-out gem. ★★★

Basket Case II

(1990, 90 min, US, Frank Henenlotter) Belial's back and he's sharing his basket with a babe at Aunt Ruth's private clinic. Just as outlandish as the first, with an ending that left grind house patrons cheering in disbelief. ★★★

Basket Case 3

(1991, 90 min, US, Frank Henenlotter) Director Henenlotter's *Basket Case* series continues its downward spiral in this cheap and uninspired installment. Filled with amateur acting and saddled by a script that's mostly filler, gore fans are advised to rent Henenlotter's earlier *Brain Damage* — a gripping, imaginative little splatterfest that triumphs where this one fails. ★ $19.99

The Basketball Diaries

(1995, 102 min, US, Scott Kalvert) Jim Carroll's underground, autobiographical novel depicting his young adult years as a drug addict makes for powerful moments of anguish and alienation, and gives Leonardo DiCaprio solid ground to construct an impressive portrayal, but this screen adaptation falls short in its dramatic foundation. Whereas Carroll's book took place in the mid-1960s and defined a generational mindset, the story has been ill-advisedly updated to the 1990s where counterculture ritual and spirit are at odds with MTV sensibilities. However, the strength of the film lies in the simplicity of the intimate relationships it develops between Carroll and his mates as they each chart their self-destructive routes. As one of them, Mark Wahlberg is especially good as an abused teen who crosses the line. In examining the lives of streetwise teens living on the mean streets of New York, *The Basketball Diaries* covers little new ground; but DiCaprio's startling transformations and Carroll's vivid perspective on camaraderie and his harrowing search for redemption are at the heart of a film whose voice is muted but aware. ★★½ $19.99

Michelle Pfeiffer laps up her role like a bowl of warm milk in *Batman Returns*

Basquiat

(1996, 108 min, US, Julian Schnabel) Jeffrey Wright is mesmerizing as Jean-Michael Basquiat, a poor Haitian-American graffiti artist who rapidly ascends New York's rarified art world only to lose it all to heroin addiction and an early death. While the premise of blind ambition and the price that is to be paid has been used in films many times before (was *Citizen Kane* the first?), this story is unusual in the depiction of the title character. For instead of a headstrong, "success or bust" personality, we see an innocent and emotionally fragile artist lured, seduced and used by others — to the point where self-destruction seems the only escape. The result is an indelible portrait of an artist as a doomed young man. In addition to the heartbreaking performance by Wright, there are several interesting supporting turns, including Gary Oldman as a thinly disguised version of the director, and David Bowie, who makes a humorous, interpretive incarnation of Andy Warhol. ★★★½ $102.99

Bastard Out of Carolina

(1996, 101 min, US, Anjelica Huston) Huston delivers a solid directorial debut with *Bastard Out of Carolina*. Making optimum use of a uniformly talented cast, her well-paced, fluid camera moves with authority and authenticity through a story line that easily could have surrendered to bathos. Jena Malone is a wonder as the illegitimate daughter of an illegitimate daughter growing up in 1950s South Carolina. Her fortunes rise and fall with her mother's (Jennifer Jason Leigh, who deftly executes a complex role) choice of men, illustrating economic inequities and the hardships of societal condemnation. From the casual cruelty of other children and uncaring bureaucracies to physical and sexual abuse at the hands of adults, the film delineates the financial and emotional dependence of single mothers struggling to support their families. Malone's character maintains a vibrant autonomy with the aid of a strong extended family and an unyielding if sometimes tragically misguided mother's love. The supporting cast each contributes on-target performances. Huston seems to have inherited her father's facility for

revealing base human weaknesses as well as those occasional moments of triumph which elevate mundane existence and daily toil. An engrossing and involving film. ★★★ $99.99

Bat 21

(1988, 105 min, US, Peter Markle) America's awakening to the horrors of the Vietnam War is the theme of this rather routine action film elevated to prominence by Gene Hackman's performance. Hackman stars as a desk officer, far removed from the war, who is literally plunged into a Viet Cong-infested jungle — and forced to fend for himself. Danny Glover costars as the copter pilot assigned to rescue him. ★★½ $9.99

Batman

(1989, 126 min, US, Tim Burton) What can we say about this megahit? Well, we could go out on a limb and say that several of us at TLA felt that the movie fell short of its potential; that Michael Keaton's understated portrayal of the Caped Crusader — while challenging and daringly offbeat — was somehow flat; that Kim Basinger's Vicky Vale plays far too great a role; that we couldn't understand why Billy Dee Williams was all but written out of the picture; and finally that the film's finale appears to have been scraped together in the midst of the writers' strike. We could say all that, but you probably wouldn't believe us anyway. Jack Nicholson's Joker is astounding: Jack, we love ya, and you deserve every penny — it's your movie, babe. ★★½ $14.99

Batman and Robin

(1997, 125 min, US, Joel Schumacher) George Clooney becomes the third actor to don the mask and cape in this star-filled, flashy, megabudget testament to Hollywood gloss. This time, Batman and his Boy Wonder Robin (Chris O'Donnell) are up against a truly titanic villain: the blue-faced Mr. Freeze (Arnold Schwarzenegger), who has had a grudge against the world since his wife contracted a disease which his medical skills were insufficient to defeat. Uma Thurman also headlines as Poison Ivy, a nebbishy chemist transformed

into a maniacal supervillain through a scientific accident. While more substantial dramatically than its predecessor (Mr. Freeze's longing for his lost wife and the encroaching illness of Alfred the butler are high points), it nevertheless succumbs to a problem that has plagued all the sequels: it focuses too little on its hero. Clooney is relegated to under ten minutes of screen time as Bruce Wayne, and his scenes as Batman almost all involve him playing second fiddle to the villains or to Robin and their new partner Batgirl (the unimpressive Alicia Silverstone). The introduction of a growing rift between the Caped Crusaders is mildly interesting, but who notices such things when the extravagant sets and shiny costumes look so good? ★★½ $24.99

Batman Forever

(1995, 121 min, US, Joel Schumacher) Long live Val Kilmer! The third installment of the Caped Crusader's recent foray into moviedom finds Kilmer replacing Michael Keaton in the title role, and he breathes some depth of character into a role made far too enigmatic by his predecessor. As in the previous two episodes, the plot is mostly incidental filler (wacko badguys have it out for Batman...again!) that sets up outrageous pyrotechnical action sequences. But hey, the name of the game here is Gothic atmosphere, special effects and action, action and more action; and in this arena *Batman Forever* does not disappoint. Chris O'Donnell is an excellent foil as a circus performer who, finding himself orphaned and hellbent for vengeance, transforms himself into Robin (a long-overdue and welcome addition to the lineup). As for the villains, Jim Carrey offers a spectacularly rubber-faced and over-the-top interpretation of The Riddler which overshadows Tommy Lee Jones' Two-Face. Nicole Kidman has a throwaway role as a criminal psychologist who tries to probe the depths of Bruce Wayne's psyche — as well as some parts of his anatomy. ★★★ $19.99

Batman Returns

(1992, 126 min, US, Tim Burton) Burton's follow-up to 1989's box-office mega-hit is a vastly superior and far more entertaining foray into the shadowy world of Gotham City and the Caped Crusader. As in the original film, Michael Keaton's brooding and gloomy Batman/Bruce Wayne character takes a back seat to the story's vivacious villains — here Michelle Pfeiffer as Catwoman and Danny DeVito as The Penguin. Pfeiffer shines as the furtive feline anti-hero, lapping up her role like a warm bowl of milk; and DeVito ably fills the shoes of Burgess Meredith with his demented Dickensian take on the grotesquely deformed Penguin. The screenplay, penned by *Heathers* writer Daniel Waters, provides a far more interesting spin than the original through its parable of urban decay and political corruption. And in a nod to early German cinema, Christopher Walken plays the city's evil industrialist overlord, Max Schreck, the name of the actor who played the vampire in F.W. Murnau's *Nosferatu*. ★★★ $14.99

Batman: The Movie

(1966, 105 min, US, Leslie Martinson) Before Keaton and Nicholson came on the scene, there was Adam West and Burt Ward as the crime-fighting Dynamic Duo (you only get one crime-fighter with Keaton). All-out camp. The Joker, the Penguin, Catwoman and the Riddler battle the caped crusader and the boy wonder. ★★½ $14.99

Batman: Mask of the Phantasm

(1993, 77 min, US, Bruce Timm & Eric Radomski) This enthralling animated action-adventure is inspired by the popular Fox-TV series. The Dark Knight (aka Batman) is labeled a vigilante when members of Gotham City's mob begin to turn up dead. Paranoid about his own possible "rub out," underworld kingpin Sal Valestra hires The Joker to "hit" Batman first. Bat-fans and novices will love the fast-paced action and mature themes explored in this highly entertaining film that clearly proves that cartoons aren't just for kids. Voices include Kevin Conroy, Mark Hamill, Abe Vigoda and Dana Delany. ★★★ $19.99

Batmania: From Comics to Screen

(1989, 45 min, US) The fully documented story of Batman — his genesis, his development and his overall entertainment value. Told with dramatic insight, this action-filled documentary will satisfy every fan who ever delighted in Batmania. ★★★ $9.99

Baton Rouge

(1988, 94 min, Spain, Rafael Moleon) As was the case with Rutger Hauer before him, now that Antonio Banderas has hit the big time in the United States, all of his earlier European efforts are crawling out of the video woodwork. In this smarmy psychological thriller, a late-night encounter between prowling gigolo Banderas and monied neurotic Victoria Abril leads to double cross and murder. The socialite's recurring nightmares of rape by an unknown assailant lead her to seek help from psychologist Carmen Maura. Maura's ensuing involvement with Banderas and the lure of Abril's supposed wealth are the catalysts for plot and counterplot, along with Banderas' desire to take his younger brother — mute since their mother's death — on a road trip to the States, to Baton Rouge. Hooker with a heart of gold? No wonder he gets along so well with Melanie. (Spanish with English subtitles) ★★ $89.99

Battle Angel

(1993, 70 min, Japan, Hiroshi Fukutomi) Based on the long-running *manga* (Japanese comic book) by writer/illustrator Yukito Kishiro, this OAV (original animated video) is a faithful adaptation of the artist's original work. Known as *Gunnm* in Japan, *Battle Angel* is actually two short episodic films: "Gunnm — Rusty Angel" and "Gunnm — Tears Sign." Tersely directed by Fukutomi, the story line follows the exploits of a female bounty hunter cyborg, Gally, and her numerous battles with the violent denizens of the futuristic Scrap Iron City. Fluid animation, memorable character designs, and an exciting science-fiction setting make this essential viewing for anime fans. *Note:* Production was supervised by the legendary Rin Taro (director of *Harmageddon* and *The Dagger of Kamui*), and also includes a video production art portfolio segment. (Japanese with English subtitles) ★★★½ $34.99

Battle Beyond the Stars

(1980, 102 min, US, Jimmy T. Murakami) John Sayles wrote the script for this entertaining sci-fi quickie produced by Roger Corman about intergalactic soldiers of fortune coming to the rescue to save the planet Akira. Starring Richard Thomas, John Saxon and Robert Vaughn. ★★★

Battle for the Planet of the Apes

(1973, 96 min, US, J. Lee Thompson) The fifth and final entry in the *Planet of the Apes* series finds the apes and man warring for control of the planet. The series long lost its charm, and this last episode is for die-hard fans only. Starring Roddy McDowall, Paul Williams and John Huston. ★★ $19.99

The Battle of Algiers

(1965, 123 min, Algeria, Gillo Pontecorvo) Director Pontecorvo brilliantly re-creates the street riots and other events that led up to Algeria's independence from France in this astonishingly realistic movie masterpiece. Pontecorvo's triumph includes his sympathetic handling of both sides of the agonizing, brutal struggle for independence. The cast of superbly used non-professional actors and the director's technical ability to create newsreel-like authenticity combine to make this a legendary film. (French with English subtitles) ★★★★ $24.99

The Battle of Austerlitz

(1960, 175 min, France/Italy, Abel Gance) This is a recently restored, full-length version of Gance's grand re-creation of Napoleon's most important battle. An epic, lavish production that features an international cast: Orson Welles, Claudia Cardinale, Vittorio de Sica, Jean-Louis Trintignant and dozens more. Unbelievably, the film was originally shown in a 73-minute version. (French with English subtitles) ★★★½

Battle of Britain

(1969, 132 min, GB, Guy Hamilton) One of those WWII epics that probably cost more than the actual war effort. The action follows a stalwart group of RAF pilots who battle an invading Nazi air unit. There's lots of air battles, and the film has a cast of thousands — well, hundreds and hundreds — headed up by half the known thespians in England; among them Michael Caine, Laurence Olivier, Trevor Howard, Christopher Plummer, Michael Redgrave, Ralph Richardson, Robert Shaw and Harry Andrews. You get the idea. There's good special effects and extremely well-staged battle sequences, but the story treads on familiar war-movie ground. ★★ $14.99

Battleship Potemkin

(1925, 74 min, USSR, Sergei Eisenstein) This gripping account of the revolt by the crew of the Potemkin and their part in the Revolution of 1905 is a landmark film for its ground-breaking use of editing and montage. The rebellion, the support for it by the people of Odessa and the ensuing attack by Cossack troops still excite and overwhelm audiences today. (Silent with a musical soundtrack) ★★★★ $19.99

The Bawdy Adventures of Tom Jones

(1976, 94 min, GB, Cliff Owen) Based on the London stage musical, this mildly amusing version of Henry Fielding's tale has its moments, but it can't hold a candle to Tony Richardson's classic. Trevor Howard, Joan Collins and Terry-Thomas lend their talents, but fail to elevate the film above its mediocre status. ★★ $59.99

Baxter

(1991, 85 min, France, Jerome Boivin) This maliciously dark French comedy is told primarily from the point of view of a misanthropic bull terrier who gets bounced around to a series of different masters. Starting in the kennel, he is originally given as a present to the dowdy old mother of the pound owner's wife. But fate (or is it?) intervenes and he winds up with the sex obsessed couple next door, whose prowess he has already witnessed from the bedroom window. Eventually, he falls into the hands of a sadistic young boy who has romantic delusions about Hitler and Eva Braun. Peppered with wry narration from the twisted mind of this pesky canine, the film points to the vicious behavior of humans and pets alike in this dog-eat-dog world. (French with English subtitles) ★★★ $19.99

The Bay Boy

(1985, 107 min, Canada, Daniel Petrie) Kiefer Sutherland, in a pre-Brat Pack role, stars in this well-meaning but predictable coming-of-age drama set in 1930s Nova Scotia. He plays an awkward 16-year-old who is eager to be initiated into the rites of manhood, although opportunities are limited in the dismal mining town in which he and his mother (Liv Ullmann) live. Attractively photographed, the film falls flat when dealing with the well-trodded theme of adolescent angst. ★★ $79.99

Beach Blanket Bingo

(1965, 96 min, US, William Asher) Though not exactly Preston Sturges or Billy Wilder, this playful '60s beach movie is probably the best of the series. Frankie Avalon and Annette Funicello and the rest of the gang get involved with mermaids and kidnappers; not to mention Paul Lynde and Don Rickles. ★★½

Beaches

(1988, 123 min, US, Garry Marshall) Bette Midler and Barbara Hershey star in this effective though familiar tearjerker which follows the friendship – and its ups and downs – of two women through the years. Midler is dynamic, giving one of her patented larger-than-life performances as a singer/actress determined to make it in show business. Hershey, new lips and all, is slightly eclipsed in Midler's shadow, but nicely essays the role of an upper-class attorney beset by personal misfortunes. Get out the hankies for this one. ★★½ $9.99

The Bear

(1989, 95 min, France, Jean-Jacques Annaud) Some people steered clear of this wildlife adventure story about an orphaned bear cub on the assumption that it would be "too cute." On a certain level, they would have been right, but what a shame to miss this spectacularly photographed and brilliantly directed tale about the cruelty and the compassion of nature and man. Filmed in the dazzling peaks of the Dolomite Mountain range (a part of the Alps which stretches from Austria to northern Italy), the film tells the story of a young cub who, upon being orphaned, wanders aimlessly until one day he meets up with a massive male grizzly. Together they flee the sights of a group of tenacious hunters who have it out for the big bear. ★★★½ $14.99

The Beast

(1988, 109 min, US, Kevin Reynolds) Set in Afghanistan during the Soviet Occupation, this suspenseful war adventure follows a Russian tank crew's fight for survival when a group of Afghan civilians seek vengeance for their small village's brutal destruction. As the citizens are able to demobilize the monster tank, its crew must battle their sadistic commander as well as the Afghans, while struggling with the moral dilemma of war. Jason Patric plays an idealistic soldier, and George Dzundza is very effective as the maniacal chief. ★★★½ $89.99

The Beast from 20,000 Fathoms

(1953, 80 min, US, Eugene Lourie) Based on a short story by Ray Bradbury, this sci-fi favorite features nifty special effects by F/X master Ray Harryhausen. One of the first films to warn of the dangers of Atomic Bomb testings (the '50s tell us they would unleash some horrible monster or another), a giant beast (a prehistoric rhedosauras to be exact) goes for a swim after its atomic wake-up call and decides to munch on the Big Apple. The Coney Island rollercoaster proves to be too much for it, however. ★★★ $14.99

The Beast with Five Fingers

(1947, 89 min, US, Robert Florey) Robert Alda and Peter Lorre star in this heavily atmospheric chiller about the severed hand of a dead pianist which may be murdering the pianist's squabbling inheritors during their stay at his shadowy old mansion in Italy. Despite its lurid title, the film is actually a reasonably intelligent exploration of madness and superstition with smart performances from Alda, Lorre and J. Carrol Naish. Fine special effects and a good musical score contribute to the film's success, but its real highlight is Florey's use of the camera. He is constantly surprising the viewer with inventive ways to photograph the two or three sets used throughout the entire film, particularly the grand entry hall of the mansion. Light and shadow are used very well, turning what is supposed to be a relatively modern story into a neo-Gothic thriller. The only major problem with the film is a goofy coda tacked onto its end, which effectively ridicules any supernatural element it may have contained. ★★★ $19.99

The Beast Within

(1982, 90 min, US, Philippe Mora) A woman is raped by a large demon-like creature with very hairy legs and gives birth to – you guessed it – a Jekyll and Hyde-like boy who transforms himself when he gets upset. This Hulk-like tale goes absolutely nowhere. Some interesting gore effects, including a spurting decapitation scene, won't even satisfy die-hard slasher film fans. ★ $14.99

Beat Girl

(1960, 90 min, US, Edward T. Greville) Bad girls, strip tease and murder amongst a low-budget production. Look for Christopher Lee as "a grubby nightclub owner out for one thing...a good time with a great body." ★ $24.99

Beat the Devil

(1954, 92 min, US, John Huston) This offbeat black comedy left audiences in a daze when first released. Reportedly, the filming began without a finished script, forcing Huston and a young Truman Capote to collaborate daily before shooting and allowing the actors to ad-lib many scenes. The result is a zany spoof of spy thrillers dealing with a gang of international crooks concocting a uranium swindle. The peculiar cast includes Humphrey Bogart, Gina Lollobrigida, Jennifer Jones (blond-wigged and brilliant as a compulsive liar), Peter Lorre and Robert Morley. Not to be missed. ★★★½ $19.99

Beatrice

(1987, 132 min, France, Bertrand Tavernier) Tavernier's somber exploration of medieval life abandons many of the traditional myths (e.g. the romances of King Arthur) and instead concentrates on the dark side of human nature: infidelity, jealousy, humiliation, hatred, incest and murder. François, as a child, killed his mother's lover. He returns from war 25 years later, tormented by his hatred of women, to be greeted at his castle by his loving and beautiful daughter, Beatrice. Having faithfully awaited her father's return, her love turns to defiance and repulsion as her increasingly demented father turns to incest. A compelling mood piece. (French with English subtitles) (aka: *The Passion of Beatrice*) ★★★ $79.99

Beau Geste

(1939, 114 min, US, William Wellman) Part of the 1939 wave of some of the greatest films in American history, this sweeping – and superlative – version of P.C. Wren's romantic novel is every bit as exciting and moving as you would think. A strong and courageous Gary Cooper stars as the title character, with an Oscar-nominated Brian Donlevy as the sadistic sergeant. In essence the story of a missing gem, a debt of honor and of savagery in the Foreign Legion, this beautifully shot epic, with a great performance from a sartorially correct Cooper, still stirs the soul. Also with Robert Preston and Ray Milland. Remake of the Ronald Colman 1926 silent classic; an inferior version followed in 1966. ★★★½ $14.99

Le Beau Marriage

(1982, 100 min, France, Eric Rohmer) Rohmer continues his series of "Comedies and Proverbs" with this witty and engaging story of a young student's attempts to snare the perfect man and a "good marriage." An insightful comedy of logic and love in modern Paris. (French with English subtitles) ★★★

Le Beau Serge

(1958, 110 min, France, Claude Chabrol) Chabrol's first feature film is about a young man who leaves the city to go back to the village of his youth in an attempt to rehabilitate a childhood friend, now a drunkard living in squalor. A deeply felt drama that explores male friendship and commitment. (French with English subtitles) ★★★

The Beautiful Blonde From Bashful Bend

(1949, 77 min, US, Preston Sturges) Old West dance-hall chanteuse and eagle-eye sharpshooter Betty Grable skips town after shooting a federal judge – Twice! Accidentally! – and poses as a schoolmarm. Cesar Romero and Rudy Vallee join in on the fun in this minor though entertaining Sturges spoof. ★★½ $19.99

Beautiful Dreamers

(1990, 108 min, Canada, John Harrison) Rip Torn stars as Walt Whitman in this touching drama in which he befriends the superintendent of a Canadian insane asylum (played by Colm Feore of *32 Short Films About Glenn Gould*). Their friendship results in the young doctor challenging the beliefs and practices of his profession as he tries to put a more human face on the psychiatry of the late 1800s. The film portrays the conflict between the Christian-based hierarchy of the day and the nascent humanism represented by Whitman – it's a struggle which, it could be argued, is still with us. Torn puts in another strong performance as the free-thinking poet. Whitman's homosexuality is strangely never mentioned, although it is alluded to when someone wonders why he never married. ★★★ $14.99

Beautiful Girls

(1996, 113 min, US, Ted Demme) A great team of young Hollywood veterans (Timothy Hutton, Matt Dillon) and rising stars (Mira Sorvino, Michael Rapaport, Natalie Portman) gives it their best shot in this rambling comedy-drama about young adults coming dangerously close to settling into the grooves that could carry them through the rest of their lives. The problem here is that, despite a rich portrayal of life in a small, blue-collar town, screenwriter Scott Rosenberg (author of the witty *Things to Do in Denver When You're Dead*)

Beavis and Butt-head Do America, heh heh heh...

soundtrack. Menken and Ashman's music would be equally remarkable for a live-action film. A total delight for all ages, *Beauty* is not to be missed. ★★★★ $59.99

Beavis and Butt-head Do America

(1996, 80 min, US, Mike Judge) MTV's lame-brained bad boys Beavis and Butt-head get the Hollywood feature film treatment — and civilization will never be the same again. There's good news and bad news, here. The good news is creator Mike Judge's nasty wit is undiluted; the bad news is Judge is unable to maintain the laugh-a-minute pace of the TV show for a feature-length film — even at this abbreviated running time. The film begins — à la *Pee-wee's Big Adventure* — with the boys' most valuable possession (their TV, of course) being stolen. This leads them on a cross-country search, and their ever-present mission to "score." Much of the film is laugh-out-loud funny (much as you may try to stifle a giggle), with Cornholio, a dig at Congress and the terrific opening credits sequence among the highlights. While the movie is watchable, it's never quite as funny as you want it to be; the TV show's most familiar gimmick, that of B&B sittin' around bustin' MTV, is completely absent. It also gets a wee *too* mean-spirited. Still, any film which ends with Englebert Humperdink singing "Lesbian Seagull" can't be all bad. ★★½ $99.99

Bebe's Kids

(1992, 74 min, US, Bruce Smith) This adult-oriented, street-hip animated feature is based on popular characters created by the late comedian Robin Harris (*House Party*). His cartoon alter-ego is smitten with the beautiful Jamika. On their first date, she greets him with her soft-spoken son, Leon, and homegirl Bebe's hellraising spawn, who turn the couple's date at a theme park into a nightmare. Also included is the highly entertaining seven-minute animated short *Itsy Bitsy Spider*, featuring the voice of Jim Carrey as a *Terminator*-inspired exterminator trying to rid a home of a pest problem. ★★★ $14.99

Becket

(1964, 148 min, GB, Peter Glenville) Richard Burton and Peter O'Toole deliver magnificent performances in this gritty adaptation of the Jean Anouilh play. Burton is the stoic and indomitable Thomas Becket, Archbishop of Canterbury, whose longstanding friendship with King Henry II (O'Toole) becomes irrevocably frayed as they stray down opposite political paths. A gripping and powerful historical exploration of the inhuman burdens of power. O'Toole would play Henry II once more in *The Lion in Winter*. ★★★★ $59.99

Beckett Directs

Samuel Beckett, one of the greatest dramatists and novelists of the 20th century, is best known for a relatively small amount of his overall output with "Waiting for Godot," "Endgame" and "Happy Days" considered his most celebrated. His plays and novels all share themes on a despairing human condition with the soul of man alienated by modern society and his incomprehensible existence. Born in Ireland in 1906, Beckett eventually moved to Paris in the 1920s and began writing in French

has no compelling narrative to offer. The film is a collection of subplots which feature a smattering of great moments (the near romance of thirtysomething Hutton and 13-year-old Portman — who gives the film's best performance) and speeches (Rosie O'Donnell's "anatomy of a supermodel" speech, Rapaport's "Philosophy of Beautiful Girls") that are, for the most part, totally out of place in the movie (and out-of-synch with the characters). Rather than the *Diner*-for-the-'90s that it could have been, it settles for *St. Elmo's Fire* set in small-town Americana. ★★ $19.99

Beautiful Mystery

(1993, 60 min, Japan, Nakamura Genji) Another in the independently made soft-core art films from Japan grouped under the title "Pink Films," *Beautiful Mystery* is a pleasant surprise because it is both funny and erotic. There is an adolescent protagonist who joins a bodybuilding and paramilitary clique run by a Mishima-like man who builds a private army around himself. Within this all-male domain, a routine develops — strenuous exercise by day and plenty of homo sex at night. The youth falls in love, and he and his lover leave the compound only to become drag queens and eventually prostitutes. Some good jokes are the result of a rigid censorship that forbids the presentation of male genitalia, and absurd camera angles are chosen and strange objects are placed in front of the lens to obscure private parts. A visually striking satire that also depicts male bonding in the most homoerotic light. (Japanese with English subtitles) ★★★ $39.99

Beautiful Thing

(1996, 90 min, GB, Hettie Macdonald) This affectionate story of two teenagers' sexual coming out in a working-class development in London is an inspiring, tender, emotional tale that is sure to enthrall. Jamie (Glen Berry) is a reserved 16-year-old, close to his pub manager

mum (Linda Henry), and who prefers old Hollywood musicals to sports. His friendship with neighbor Ste (Scott Neal), a fellow student who suffers through a troubled family life, soon develops into a sexual and eventually a loving relationship. How the two boys tentatively handle their nascent sexual drives and how it affects their family and friends is handled in both a fresh and surprisingly upbeat fashion. Standouts include next-door neighbor Leah (Tameka Empson), a Jamaican-British teen who is obsessed with Mama Cass, and Jamie's mom, a tough but warmhearted single mother trying to juggle a career, a love life and raise a son. A wonderful comedy-drama and possibly the best gay coming-out film of the decade. ★★★½ $98.39

Beauty and the Beast

(1946, 90 min, France, Jean Cocteau) This enchanting interpretation of the famous fairy tale is a sumptuous and beguiling adventure in surrealist cinema. Jean Marais gives a moving performance as the love-stricken Beast and Josette Day is the beautiful object of his amour. (French with English subtitles) ★★★★ $24.99

Beauty and the Beast

(1991, 85 min, US, Gary Trousdale & Kirk Wise) On the heels of *The Little Mermaid*, one of Disney's finest animated features, comes an even more impressive achievement, the first animated film to be nominated for an Academy Award as Best Picture. Based on the classic fairy tale, Disney animators have created a masterpiece of color and scope, complete with refreshingly good humor and a captivating text. But what makes *Beauty* soar is the outstanding musical score by *Mermaid* and *Little Shop of Horrors* team Alan Menken and Howard Ashman. Including the Oscar-winning title ballad and the exuberant "Be Our Guest," the score has the style and brilliance of a classic Broadway musical rather than, what most musicals are today, a promo for a best-selling after WWII. Famous for his lifelong reluctance to discuss or analyze his work, Beckett did take an active interest in the production of his plays, being present at rehearsals (but never present on opening nights) and relying on certain favorite actors and directors. The productions which follow are all based on Beckett's original mise-en-scene with Beckett himself supervising the work and the San Quentin Drama Workshop presenting the productions. Beckett has said that, "This is my last word on the subject of these three plays."

Krapp's Last Tape (1988, 89 min, US, **Walter D. Asmus**) On a dark stage, barren save for a table, some bananas and a tape recorder, a wizened 69-year-old man (Beckett favorite Rich Cluchey), clothed in pajamas and a bathrobe, tries to make sense of his life through various tapes that he recorded 30 years past. A demanding, oblique film on memory and the pain of the past and sadness of the present. ★★★ $29.99

Endgame (1988, 96 min, US, **Robert Bilheimer**) Beckett's deeply disturbing post-Apocalypse masterpiece is a chilling allegory for the interdependence of family and the death of parents. Set in a dingy basement after some unnamed holocaust, the play revolves around a hunched-over, shuffling middle-aged man (the son), an older blind man (the father) and the two limbless grandparents who live in a pair of garbage cans at the side of the stage. As in many of Beckett's plays, the action and dialogue are sparse and brimming with nuance, sharp wit and an overriding nihilistic existentialism. As performed here, the plot takes on a highly theatrical and stilted quality which Beckett no doubt intended. It is an absorbing and important piece of theatre; however, it is recommended viewing for "high brow" audiences only. ★★★½ $39.99

Waiting for Godot (1985, 128 min, US, **Walter D. Asmus**) In this, one of the classics of modern theatre, Beckett presents a story of two tramps, Vladimir and Estragon, who, while waiting for someone they do not know and are not even sure that is indeed his name, argue,

debate and bicker on a wide range of subjects all set in a sort of vaudeville comedy routine. Entering into the picture at certian points is Pozzo and his servant/slave Lucky and a young boy. Whether the play is an allegory on the German Occupation of France (as has been postulated) or man waiting for the future while lost in a meaningless void, this profound and beguiling play is a must for all serious lovers of film and theatre. ★★★½ $39.99

Becky Sharp

(1935, 67 min, US, **Rouben Mamoulian**) The first Technicolor (three-strip) film is a witty though stagey adaptation of Thackeray's "Vanity Fair" with Miriam Hopkins giving a notable Oscar-nominated performance as the social-climbing title character. (Note: This copy is in black and white, and runs 67 minutes as opposed to its original 83 minutes. It is, unfortunately, the only version available on video.) ★★★

Becoming Colette

(1992, 97 min, US/France, **Danny Huston**) While never quite overcoming its pedestrian handling of a potentially illuminating subject, this steamy drama, sort of a poor man's *Henry and June*, replete with female frontal nudity and "shocking" lesbian love scenes, is filmed in a lush, bombastic and romantic style. The story concerns the early years in the life of Sidone-Gabrielle Colette, one of France's greatest and most popular writers of the 20th century. Young Gabrielle (Mathilda May) meets sweet-talking bon vivant Willy (Klaus Maria Brandauer) and quickly sweeps him off his feet. They move to Paris to begin a carefree life of society living. But when Gabrielle shows him some of her writing, he publishes the work as his own and becomes the talk of the town. Frustrated at being merely cash-producing chattel for her now-philandering husband, the young woman begins a lesbain relationship with a friend, and with her assistance and support, the increasingly sophisticated Gabrielle starts on her road to self-determination. Despite director Huston's heavy handling, the

film is entertaining in telling the story of one woman's growth, maturation and success, all accomplished on her own terms. ★★★ $89.99

Bed of Roses

(1996, 87 min, US, **Michael Goldenberg**) A pleasing if uneventful romantic comedy-drama, *Bed of Roses* casts Christian Slater in another shy-boy role and Mary Stuart Masterson as yet another neurotic romantic: call this *Untamed Benny & Joon*. Seeing her crying through her apartment window one night, Slater anonymously sends Masterson a bouquet of flowers. She soon learns Slater's identity, and balks at establishing a relationship with such a "perfect" man. She moves in with him, anyway, though unable to fully commit. And though Slater may be the most considerate lover since Alan Bates in *An Unmarried Woman*, Masterson spends the rest of the film whining about her past and inability to love. (Though she does whine rather attractively.) The film sets a genuinely sweet tone as the two court and fall in love, though once they move in together and meet the folks (a distracting, sappy episode), the film has no where to go and idles till its inevitable climax. Pamela Segall as Masterson's best friend supplies much-needed humor and punch. ★★½ $14.99

Bedazzled

(1967, 107 min, GB, **Stanley Donen**) This hysterical adaptation of the Faust legend stars Peter Cook as a mischievous Mephistopheles who grants the nebbishy Dudley Moore seven wishes in exchange for his soul. All of his wishes end in disaster for Moore who only wants his Whimpy Burger co-worker (Eleanor Bron) to love him. The humor is hurled about so unrelentingly and with such outrageous and inventive abandon that only the most mordant of viewers won't find some cause for laughter. The screenplay by Cook provides an even better vehicle for himself and Moore than *The Wrong Box*. Raquel Welch appears as "Lust." ★★★★

The Bedford Incident

(1965, 102 min, US, **James B. Harris**) Richard Widmark and Sidney Poitier give compelling performances in this exciting Cold War thriller. Widmark is a ship's captain and Poitier is a newspaper reporter who are at odds with each other when a Russian ship is discovered off the coast of Greenland. ★★★ $14.99

Bedknobs and Broomsticks

(1971, 112 min, US, **Robert Stevenson**) Charming live-action and animated musical fantasy from Disney. An apprentice witch (Angela Lansbury), with the help of three children, repels Nazi invaders from her British countryside home. Music is by Richard and Robert Sherman (*Mary Poppins*), and an Oscar was won for Special Effects. ★★★ $19.99

The Bedroom Window

(1987, 112 min, US, **Curtis Hanson**) Hitchcockian thriller, with more than a nod to *Rear Window*, stars Steve Guttenberg as a young exec who admits to seeing an attempted murder to protect his mistress, who actually saw the crime. In doing so, he becomes the prime suspect. Clever plot twists and engaging

Becky Sharp

Before Sunrise

performances by Guttenberg, Elizabeth McGovern and Isabelle Huppert elevate the sometimes obvious scenario. ★★½ $9.99

Bedtime for Bonzo

(1951, 83 min, US, Frederick de Cordova) Ronald Reagan, later to be the leader of the Free World, plays daddy to a chimp in the interests of science. Is this where George Bush got the idea for a kinder, gentler nation? Did Ron think he was really once a scientist? We don't know. The film's kinda cute, though. ★★½ $12.99

Bedtime Story

(1964, 99 min, US, Ralph Levy) It's a race to the finish as con men Marlon Brando and David Niven are out to outdo each other in their efforts to swindle American heiress Shirley Jones. Some good laughs, though the recent remake, *Dirty Rotten Scoundrels*, is funnier. ★★½ $14.99

Beethoven

(1936, 116 min, France, Abel Gance) One of the pioneering masters of early French cinema, Gance had an unusually long filmmaking career which stretched over almost 60 years. His epic productions (*J'Accuse, Napoleon*) featured innovative techniques of editing and montage as well as the experimental use of music. In this symphonic epic, Harry Baur portrays the towering musical genius as a successful but lonely and heartsick man. Restored to its full length, this melodramatic look at the life of one of history's little understood masters has been given a facelift and had its soundtrack restored. (French with English subtitles) ★★★ $19.99

Beethoven

(1992, 87 min, US, Brian Levant) This congenial shaggy dog comedy holds few surprises to anyone who has seen the theatrical trailer, which contains the film's best scenes. A runaway St. Bernard takes up residence at the middle-class home of Charles Grodin and family. It's a comedy of errors as the big-as-life mutt creates havoc for Grodin and proves to

be a canine Mary Poppins for the rest of the family. An unrecognizable Dean Jones co-stars as a villainous vet, who looks suspiciously like a dastardly doc from *Marathon Man*. Pre-adolescent children should be entertained, though non-animal lovers should probably avoid it. ★★½ $14.99

Beethoven's 2nd

(1993, 87 min, US, Rod Daniel) Those who enjoyed the canine antics which made *Beethoven* a surprise box-office hit should be equally pleased by its amiable sequel. Though the accent here is more on cute than slapstick, there's enough good-natured comedy to satisfy both child and parent. That monstrous St. Bernard is now a daddy, and borrowing just a touch of treachery from *101 Dalmations*, the adorable little puppies fall prey to a nasty villainess. Charles Grodin returns as the head of the Newton household, and, as in the original, his slow burns, tirades and pie-in-the-face humiliations make him a most wonderful foil. ★★★ $14.99

Beethoven's Nephew

(1985, 103 min, France/West Germany, Paul Morrissey) Independent filmmaker Morrissey sheds his well-deserved reputation as a sensationalistic chronicler of life on the fringe in this thoughtful and opulent story of the destructively possessive relationship between Ludwig Von Beethoven and his handsome nephew. In a rewrite of history, Morrissey shows Beethoven in his later years as a furious and demanding "superstar" who, after winning a vicious court battle for the custody of his sister's son, becomes consumed with an insanely jealous love for the boy. With surprising control in its examination of the composer's obsession, the film elicits a deep sympathy for his torment without compromising the severity of his tyrannical grip on the boy's life. ★★★ $9.99

Beetlejuice

(1988, 92 min, US, Tim Burton) Dick Cavett's acting is just one of the lesser surprises in Burton's breakthrough comedy about a dead

couple (Geena Davis and Alec Baldwin) learning how to haunt their house by mad ghoul Michael Keaton. Similar in tone to his *Pee-wee's Big Adventure*, Burton's film sports a more comprehensive story, more outlandish special effects, another great score by Danny Elfman, plus a winning performance by Winona Ryder. ★★★½ $14.99

Before and After

(1996, 108 min, US, Barbet Schroeder) There's a fine sense of mystery to the opening moments of *Before and After*, an awkward drama which solemnly attempts to explore the boundaries of love and law. Parents Meryl Streep and Liam Neeson are visited by police officers when their son's girlfriend is found murdered and he was the last one to be seen with her. As the father attempts to "cover up" the evidence he discovers in the garage, his mother puts her faith in her son and legal procedure. But as the story unfolds, the narrative becomes unfocused, undecided whether to be a hard-hitting exposé of community ostracism or a sappy drama of parents coming to terms with the possibility that their child has taken a life. And though the latter offers far more dramatic possibilities, it is the former from which the film finds its strengths. ★★½ $19.99

Before Stonewall

(1985, 87 min, US, Greta Schiller) This extraordinary recollection/documentary traces the evolution of the gay movement in the U.S. from the 1920s to the '60s and touches on the major milestones in the development of gay-lesbian consciousness. Narrated by Rita Mae Brown and aided by archival footage and memorable interviews, *Before Stonewall* vividly paints a picture of what it was like to be "in the life" during this period of repression. The pioneers of the liberation recall their experiences – from the lesbian bars in 1920s Harlem to the gay soldier's experiences in WWII to what it was like for gay blacks and Native Americans. The unwritten history of the fight for gay rights comes alive in this entertaining tribute to the forces that shaped a fledgling community. ★★★½ $29.99

Before Sunrise

(1995, 101 min, US, Richard Linklater) After the laid-back indulgence of *Slacker* and *Dazed and Confused*, director Linklater applies a little more polish to this pleasant surprise about a chance encounter between two students traveling through Europe. This encounter develops into that rarest of occurrences – an enchanted commingling of mind and spirit, a gift of pure happenstance. Engaging characterizations by Ethan Hawke and Julie Delpy and an intelligent, whimsical script (co-written by Linklater and Kim Krizan) capture that time of young adulthood when possibilities are unlimited and time retains the fluidity of childhood. The director makes good use of silence and empty spaces to explore how people get to know one another and, through that, themselves. Linklater has managed to create a confection which is sweet but not cloying, winsome but not silly, idealized but not artificial. ★★★ $19.99

Peter Sellers in *Being There*

Before the Rain

(1994, 112 min, Macedonia, Milchio Manchevski) Three interwoven stories about choices, fate and the inevitability of violence form a circle which "is not round" in this Oscar nominee for Best Foreign-Language Film. The stories also touch upon the growing danger of a Bosnia-type ethnic war erupting in nearby Macedonia. The particular subjects for the three stories are about a young monk's relationship with an Albanian refugee; an Englishwoman's decision whether to leave her husband for a Macedonian photographer; and that photographer's return to his home village after 16 years. All of the stories converge, more or less, at the film's end, and drive home the belabored lesson that all violence — ethnic or otherwise — is futile though inescapable. The final story, the best of the three, works on a deeper level because in it we watch the approaching storm of conflict in Macedonia through the eyes of an estranged native. Featuring gorgeous camerawork, *Before the Rain* is an interesting if obvious tale about our inability to prevent ancient habits from being carried into modern times and how brutal humanity will continue to be. (Macedonian with English subtitles) ★★½ $19.99

Before the Revolution

(1964, 112 min, Italy, Bernardo Bertolucci) Long regarded as one of the grand masters of cinema, Bertolucci was just 22 years old when he directed this absorbing polemic about European politics and Marxism. A young man flirts with Communism and incestuously lusts after his aunt. This potentially volatile mix of youthful idealism and unbridled desire leads him to a crisis of faith over his political ideals. (Italian with English subtitles) ★★★½ $29.99

Begotten

(1989, 78 min, US, Edmund E. Merhige) The box art for this experimental avant-garde feature boasts that it makes *Eraserhead* look like a sunny day in the park, and indeed, that it does. But to what end? This disgusting nightmare vision of life as a wriggling, oozing, pus-encrusted torment is without a doubt for adventurous viewers only! The film's opening scene portrays a man (later identified as God) disemboweling himself in a river of blood; out of his corpse crawls a young maiden (later identified as Mother Earth) who proceeds to stroke the still-erect penis of the eviscerated deity and impregnate herself with his posthumous cum — get the picture? Filmed in high-contrast, grainy black and white reminiscent of the German Expressionist period, and without a scintilla of dialogue, the film is at the same time visually interesting and infuriatingly obscure. Its visceral thrills are akin to taking a peek at life in a leper colony. ★½ $24.99

The Beguiled

(1971, 109 min, US, Don Siegel) Very effective and complex psychosexual Gothic chiller with Clint Eastwood as a wounded Union soldier who is taken in by the women of a Southern girls' school, awakening the dormant sexual emotions of head mistress Geraldine Page and teacher Elizabeth Hartman. An unusual though exceptional study of passion and jealousy, with Eastwood giving one of his best performances. ★★★½ $14.99

Behind the Veil — Nuns

(1984, 130 min, Canada, Margaret Wescott) This fascinating documentary explores the secretive and widely misunderstood world of the Catholic religious orders for women. Using thoroughly researched historical information for background, the film takes an in-depth look at the many different lifestyles of nuns — from the cloistered to the teachers and activists — and includes their individual reflections. The film also brings to light the politics within the orders as well as the continual misogyny of the male-dominated Catholic Church hierarchy. ★★★ $29.99

Being at Home with Claude

(1991, 90 min, Canada, Jean Beaudin) Queer criminality meets romantic love in this riveting and unconventional murder mystery. Set in Montreal, this adaptation of Rene-Daniel Dubois' taut, claustrophobic play opens up the action and heightens its original dramatic force. Relying less on the whodunit angle and more on "why-did-he-do-it," the film opens with an erotic, hyperkenetic sequence focusing on a steamy sex scene which ends with a brutal murder. Three days later, Yves, a sexy male prostitute, summons the police to a judge's chamber and admits to the apparently senseless crime. Unapologetically gay and not the killer type, Yves, the lover of the deceased Claude, soon becomes embroiled in a harrowing interrogation which lays bare his tortured soul to the tough but strangely sympathetic cop. A fine drama that works both as a suspense thriller and an absorbing tale of gay passions and desperate love. (French with English subtitles) ★★★½ $39.99

Being Human

(1994, 118 min, GB, Bill Forsyth) Robin Williams plays a series of characters set in time periods ranging from the stone age to the new age and proves that no matter what age you live in, your life can be deathly boring — at least to those watching it on the screen. As Williams struggles dryly with daily dilemmas related to being a homo sapien, the film's unbelievably slow pace and unimaginative and poorly constructed episodes will give any viewer a struggle to stay awake. ★ $19.99

Being There

(1979, 130 min, US, Hal Ashby) A sublime satire of the TV age and American myth-making, *Being There* stars Peter Sellers in a tour de force performance as Chance, a dim-witted gardener whose homelessness sets him on the road to the presidency. Wandering the streets of Washington, D.C., Sellers is struck by the limo of dying millionaire/power player Melvyn Douglas (in a sterling Oscar-winning performance). When he's given shelter by the influential businessman, Chance's naiveté is mistaken for insight and wisdom, ultimately making him a media darling and political prospect. Shirley MacLaine also stars as Douglas' companion, and Richard Dysart is appropriately befuddled as a physician aware of Chance's identity. Jerzy Kosinski's literate and biting adaptation of his own story has been wonderfully complemented by director Ashby's marvelous pacing and his keen observations of cultural attitudes. ★★★★ $19.99

Beirut: The Last Home Movie

(1988, 90 min, US, Jennifer Fox) This unusual documentary, set in present-day, war-torn Beirut, eschews the typical politics one would expect and instead focuses on one wealthy (and atypical) family who decide to remain in the battle-scarred city, despite their ability to leave. Residing in an opulent 200-year-old palace, the Bustros family consist of three sisters, a brother and their mother. Seemingly oblivious to the dangers and destruction all around, this Greek Orthodox Christian family continues their normal life undisturbed. Fiercely insular, their personal feelings, relationships and motivations in staying home become the focus of the film, the result being a humanistic approach to a subject all too accustomed to inhuman violence. Academy Award winner for Best Documentary. ★★★½

The Believers

(1987, 114 min, US, John Schlesinger) Suspenseful occult thriller starring Martin Sheen as a New York therapist whose counseling of a disturbed policeman leads him into a series of bizarre and gory ritual slayings. Director Schlesinger creates a chilling atmosphere as he juxtaposes a menacing New York City with the tribal rituals of the voodoo ceremony Santeria. ★★★ $14.99

Bell, Book and Candle

(1958, 108 min, US, Richard Quine) A lively cast brightens up this fun-filled adaptation of John Van Druten's Broadway comedy about an engaged publisher (James Stewart) who becomes entangled with a coven of Greenwich Village witches — and lovely (and bewitching)

Kim Novak, in particular. Great support from Jack Lemmon as a bongo-playing warlock, Hermione Gingold as a high priestess, and the wonderful Ernie Kovacs as a skeptical author. ★★★ $19.99

Belle de Jour

(1967, 100 min, France/Italy, Luis Buñuel) Buñuel's kinky skewering of bourgeois pretensions stars a luminous Catherine Deneuve as a terminally bored doctor's wife who escapes her ennui in bizarre, masochistic sexual daydreams. These fantasies turn to reality when she lands an afternoon shift at a high-class Parisian brothel where she is given the alias "Belle de Jour." Like most of Buñuel's work of the period, *Belle de Jour* is a mostly cerebral but masterful and at times giddy dialectic on sexual repression, the Church and the meaningless, philistine lives of the upper classes. As usual, Buñuel mixes fantasy, reality and flashback to the point where the viewer is pressed to wonder which is real. Deneuve is hypnotic as the wistful Belle, whose desire for sexual humiliation seems to be her only avenue for rebellion against the constraints of her social position. Genevieve Page is in fine form as the Belle's madam, a lesbian who fancies the icy beauty of her newest protégé. By today's loose standards, the film is tame, but its content is nonetheless delightfully radical. (French with English subtitles) ★★★½ $19.99

Belle Epoque

(1993, 108 min, Spain, Fernando Trueba) The winner of the 1993 Academy Award for Best Foreign-Language Film, *Belle Epoque* is a disarmingly gentle and comic tale of female seduction set in the Civil War-ravaged Spain of 1931. AWOL soldier Fernando (Jorge Sanz of *Lovers*), a handsome rogue-wannabe, finds brief solace, love, sex and emotional turmoil in the home of an elderly gentleman who has four beautiful and flirtatious daughters. Each woman, with a different reason for doing so, seduces the confused but eagerly accomodating young man, all under the blind eye of Papa. The sexual shenanigans continue when Mama, a traveling cabaret performer, returns with her lover in tow and, à la *Smiles of a Summer Night*, all the characters are thrown into romantic confusion. (Available dubbed and in Spanish with English subtitles) ★★★ $19.99

La Belle Epoque 1890-1914

(1983, 60 min, US, Suzanne Bauman & Jim Burroughs) Douglas Fairbanks, Jr. hosts this absorbing overview of "The Beautiful Era," a time when the rich and famous of the Western world gave themselves over to a life of elegance and grace, ignoring the rising storm of social and political unrest. ★★★ $39.99

La Belle Noiseuse

(1991, 240 min, France, Jacques Rivette) At a running time of four hours, this Grand Prize winner at the Cannes Film Festival is quite an undertaking. The film tells the story of a renowned painter whose ten-year hiatus comes to an end after becoming inspired by a young artist, and in particular the young artist's lover (Emmanuelle Beart), who becomes the model for his return to the canvas. It's a slow, methodical exploration into the artistic

process and the ensuing obsessions it brings for both artist and model. Rivette's brilliant direction makes this film a rich and rewarding experience. (French with English subtitles) ★★★½ $89.99

The Belle of Amherst

(1976, 90 min, US, Charles S. Dubin) In 1976, Julie Harris won a Tony Award for Best Actress for her tour de force performance as writer Emily Dickinson. This one-woman play on film captures the brilliance of Harris' portrayal and the lovely prose of the 19th-century poet. Set in two acts, the story covers through both imaginary conversation and bittersweet recollections the life of Dickinson who lived in the small town of Amherst, Massachusetts, all her life. Author William Luce magically incorporates Dickinson's writings into Emily's monologue to illustrate how her work commented on her life. Witty and touching, the show is an example of one of America's greatest stage actresses at work, and Harris standing center stage and alone for 90 minutes is simply exhilarating. ★★★½ $59.99

The Belle of New York

(1952, 82 min, US, Charles Walters) Good dance sequences highlight this otherwise ordinary Fred Astaire musical with Fred as a Gay '90s playboy who courts Salvation Army girl Vera-Ellen. Also with Marjorie Main, Keenan Wynn and Alice Pearce. ★★½ $19.99

Belle of the Nineties

(1934, 73 min, US, Leo McCarey) Only somewhat restricted by the Production Code, Mae West is her usual bouncy, naughty self in this effervescent comedy. Set in the Gay '90s, West, who also wrote the snappy screenplay, stars as an entertainer involved with an up-and-coming boxer (Roger Pryor). As with most West comedies, there's treachery and deceit on the course of true love, and the boxer falls victim to a set-up. He leaves her, which sends her packing to New Orleans to work for a new, shady employer. But as luck has it, Pryor comes to town, but he's being set up again, unknown to Mae who is out for revenge — Mae West style. West gets to sing a couple songs, and her witty one-liners still manage to titillate. Duke Ellington and His Orchestra are featured, and wait till you see West dressed up as the Statue of Liberty. ★★★ $14.99

Bellissima

(1951, 108 min, Italy, Luchino Visconti) With the fury of a hurricane, the magnificent Anna Magnani sweeps into the filmmaking process as a mother determined to get her seven-year-old daughter into the movies. When a casting call is announced for an unknown girl, hundreds of stage mothers storm the Cinecittà Studios in Rome. None, however, with the determination of the blustery Maddalena Cecconi (Magnani), a working-class wife from the tenements. When her daughter Maria (the wide-eyed Tina Apicella) is chosen for a second

call, Maddalena involves herself with a variety of show business hangers-on and con artists all in the hopes of getting an edge. Visconti's neo-realist glimpse into the absurdities of movie making is an intoxicating blend of observational comedy and human drama which bears the hallmarks of both Sturges and Wilder. But it's all brought together by Magnani's ferocious portrayal of a mother whose unrelenting pursuit for her daughter's success is only outweighed by the love for her child. (Italian with English subtitles) ★★★½

Bellissimo

(1987, 110 min, Italy, Gianfranco Mingozzi) This ambitious documentary sets out to encapsulate the important events, movements, stars and directors of Italy's filmmaking history during the past 40 years. Interspersing footage from many of the classics of Italian cinema (*Open City, Divorce Italian Style, 8½, Seven Beauties*) with interviews from both behind and in front of the camera, the film attempts to reconstruct a detailed history of one of the world's great filmmaking centers. Some of the interviewees include directors Federico Fellini, Bernardo Bertolucci, Pier Paolo Pasolini and Lina Wertmüller, and such leading actors as Sophia Loren, Giancarlo Giannini and Monica Vitti. An invaluable aid to all students and fans of Italian filmmaking. (Italian with English subtitles) ★★★ $29.99

Bellman and True

(1988, 112 min, GB, Richard Loncraine) An outstanding crime thriller which masterfully combines the exciting tale of a computer engineer caught up in an elaborate bank heist scheme and the very human drama of that man's battle for both the safety of his kidnapped son and his own personal redemption. Bernard Hill plays Hiller, who is coerced by a ruthless gang to plan and execute a daring robbery of one of England's largest banks. Director Loncraine (*The Missionary, Brimstone and Treacle*) weaves a hypnotic and rewarding tale rich in style, atmosphere and suspense. ★★★½ $14.99

Bells Are Ringing

(1960, 127 min, US, Vincente Minnelli) A good-natured adaptation of Betty Comden and Adolph Green's hit Broadway musical with Judy Holliday re-creating her acclaimed stage role as an answering service operator

Belle de Jour

who falls in love with one of her clients (Dean Martin). Judy is a delight in her final screen appearance. Songs include "The Party's Over" and "Just in Time." ★★★ $19.99

The Belly of an Architect

(1987, 118 min, GB, Peter Greenaway) Brian Dennehy stars as a rotund American architect who travels to Rome with wife Chloe Webb to oversee the mounting of a show honoring 18th-century French designer Boulée. As Dennehy becomes more and more obsessed with the project, his life begins to mirror that of the ill-fated Boulée, who died of a mysterious stomach ailment. For Greenaway's part, he's obsessed with Dennehy's portly midsection. The stocky actor puts in what can only be called an immense performance as Greenaway's camera explores his tummy from all angles. While visually stunning, the film is one of Greenaway's less-successful efforts. ★★½ $19.99

Ben Hur

(1926, 148 min, US, Fred Niblo) One of the great spectaculars of all times, with all the pluses and minuses inherent in the genre. The chariot race and the sea battle have rarely been equaled for sheer edge-of-your-seat excitement. A Brownlow & Gill reconstruction, with the original tinting and toning, plus the two-strip Technicolor sequence and another fabulous score by Carl Davis. ★★★½ $29.99

Ben-Hur

(1959, 212 min, US, William Wyler) A biblical epic on a scale even the Caesars could appreciate. This tale of two friends (Charlton Heston, Stephen Boyd) who become enemies during the time of Jesus is bathed in sincerity and brimming with spectacle. Director Wyler uses all his skill with actors to even bring a human element to the production. Sure it's not as much flat-out fun as DeMille's *The Ten Commandments*, but this winner of 11 Oscars is better — and less corny — than anyone would have a right to expect. The famed chariot race remains a knockout. (Available in a deluxe 35th anniversary edition for $39.99) (Available letterboxed and pan & scan) ★★★½ $24.99

Bend of the River

(1952, 91 min, US, Anthony Mann) Robust western adventure with James Stewart and Arthur Kennedy squaring off against each other during a wagon train's journey to Oregon in the mid-1800s. Also starring Rock Hudson, in one of his earliest roles, as a gambler. ★★★ $14.99

Beneath the Planet of the Apes

(1970, 95 min, US, Ted Post) The first sequel to *Planet of the Apes* pits astronaut James Franciscus against the simian inhabitants of a futuristic Earth in his search for Charlton Heston and crew. Not as satisfying as the original, but not without its entertaining moments. Heston, Kim Hunter and Maurice Evans all repeat their roles. ★★½ $19.99

Beneath the Valley of the Ultravixens

(1979, 93 min, US, Russ Meyer) Meyer's last theatrical release once again features the hyperkinetic editing and absurdly large breasts

Mary Stuart Masterson (l.), Johnny Depp (c.) and Aidan Quinn in *Benny & Joon*

that have been the trademarks of his singular vision. The plot, which concerns faith healing and sexual misadventures in a small California town, is really just an excuse for an endless parade of naked bodies and bad dialogue. The film is complete schlock, of course, but Meyer is in on the joke. Perverse fun. ★★½ $79.99

Benjamin Britten's Death in Venice

(1988, 138 min, GB, Robin Lough) Benjamin Britten's final opera, based on the Thomas Mann novella, is a haunting and atmospheric work performed by the Glyndebourne Touring Opera conducted by Graeme Jenkins. Tenor Robert Tear is Gustav von Aschenbach, an acclaimed but tortured writer who, on a visit to Venice, sees perfection in the person of a beautiful teenage boy and soon becomes fatally obsessed with him. Combining words, music and dance with austere, stylized sets and some erotically charged beach scenes, the opera plays out Aschenbach's pursuit of love and beauty. Alan Opie is especially effective in a multitude of roles, all menacing and foreboding. Directed for the stage by Stephen Lawless and Martha Clarke and for this video by Lough. Sung in English. ★★★ $39.99

Benny & Joon

(1993, 109 min, US, Jeremiah Chechik) Not since *Harold and Maude* have two crazies endeared themselves so winningly as Johnny Depp and Mary Stuart Masterson in *Benny & Joon*, a hilarious, offbeat charmer if ever there was one. Aidan Quinn is Benny, a thoughtful garage mechanic who gallantly looks after his mentally ill sister Joon (Masterson). Into their lives steps Sam (Depp), a Buster Keaton clone whom Benny wins in a card game. Soon, Sam and Joon bring new definition to "crazy in love," forcing an emotional showdown for all three characters. Writer Barry Berman's script works on many levels: as comedy, romantic fable, hip character study, and even homage to the great silent clowns. What's more, this is a sentimental romantic comedy specifically for those who detest sentimentality. As Sam, Depp is a marvel: his silent comedy schtick is uncanny, and his soulful eyes and puppy-dog face punctuate an appealing romantic idol. Masterson ably captures the right mixture of waif and firebrand, and Quinn is excellent. ★★★½ $9.99

Berenice Abbott — A View of the 20th Century

(1993, 60 min, US, Kay Weaver & Martha Wheelock) For most people the name Berenice Abbott brings no recognition, but this pioneering woman who died at age 93 in 1990 is considered one of the most important photographers of the 20th century. Her work includes wonderful portrait photography, vivid documentary photos and trailblazing scientific work that she began while in her sixties. Informative and stirring, this documentary — much of it narrated by Abbott herself — vividly presents her prodigious professional life. The young Abbott went to France in 1920 and began her work photographing most of the artists that flocked to the city including Jean Cocteau, Djuna Barnes, Edna St. Vincent Millay, Andre Gide and James Joyce. Her return to the States brought about spectacular work with the most celebrated being her photos of the people and architecture of New York City. The viewer will be amazed by the courage, perseverance and insight of this downright eccentric artist. This film will both educate and delight. ★★★½ $49.99

The Berlin Affair

(1986, 101 min, Italy/West Germany, Liliana Cavani) A searing and provocative tale of sexual obsession and domination set in 1938 where the dangerously seductive charms of a beautiful Japanese woman entraps three willing victims and takes them into the netherworld of blackmail, drugs and forbidden love. From the director of *The Night Porter* and starring Gudrun Landgrebe (*A Woman in Flames*). (Dubbed) ★★★ $79.99

Berlin Alexanderplatz

(1980, 930 min, West Germany, Rainer Werner Fassbinder) Fassbinder's stunning 15 ½-hour epic is set in post-WWI Germany and continues through the birth and growth of Nazism. Simply told, it's the story of a slow-witted Berlin transit worker who, after accidentally killing his girlfriend and serving time, unwittingly becomes involved in the Berlin underworld. Originally produced for German TV, Fassbinder's masterpiece is one of the few films in our collection that probably works better on home video rather than at a theatre. (German with English subtitles) ★★★★

Berlin Express

(1948, 86 min, US, Jacques Tourneur) Authentic locations (filmed in the war-torn cities of Frankfurt and Berlin) heighten the realism of this taut and suspenseful spy thriller. Four train passengers, a cross-section of the Allied forces, band together with secretary Merle Oberon to search for a German statesman — a key figure for German unification — who has been kidnapped by a Nazi underground. Robert Ryan represents the Americans. ★★★½ $19.99

Berserk

(1967, 96 min, GB, Jim O'Connolly) Joan Crawford leads a cast of characters in this twisted, plodding shocker. Crawford is the owner of a British circus which is being haunted by brutal murders. Once the public gets wind of the performers' deaths, ticket sales begin to skyrocket. The police begin to investigate the strange circumstances and Crawford herself. Crawford is typically overwrought in this late role. ★★ $19.99

Bert Rigby, You're a Fool

(1989, 94 min, US, Carl Reiner) For those who have ever uttered those infamous nine words, "They sure don't make 'em like they used to," comes this entertaining, sweetly old-fashioned though plodding musical comedy which is a 94-minute tribute to the musicals of the '50s, and to Gene Kelly in particular. Tony Award winner Robert Lindsay ("Me and My Girl") gives an effervescent performance as an English coal miner who dreams of stardom, and through a series of odd twists, arrives in Hollywood for a chance at the brass ring. Sure, the film is too sentimental, and some scenes creak along, but it's Lindsay's performance which is the attraction here. ★★½ $14.99

Best Boy

(1979, 111 min, US, Ira Wohl) This Academy Award winner follows the director's 52-year-old retarded cousin Philly as he comes to grips with his father's death, his mother's failing health and subsequent efforts to better integrate him into society. Moving yet unsentimental, Wohl has captured moments of epiphany for Philly as he realizes untapped skills and new joys such as a backstage duet with Zero Mostel singing "If I Were a Rich Man." ★★★★ $29.99

The Best Intentions

(1992, 182 min, Sweden, Billie August) Ingmar Bergman wrote the screenplay for this moving epic about the lives of his parents. And if the thought of 182 minutes of angst-ridden Swedish self-reflection is terrifying, not to worry. Director August, with the help of Bergman's script, has fashioned a heartwarming love story which is sprinkled throughout with humor and is anything but tedious. The story begins when a young Henrik Bergman, a poor seminarian, falls for Anna, a somewhat spoiled rich girl. Despite her mother's best efforts to derail their affections, the young lovers persist and eventually wed. Their class differences become apparent immediately, but

in the end, their devotion is true and the film follows their life together for 20 years, right up to Ingmar's birth. Winner of the Palme D'Or at Cannes, the film's charm is augmented by winning performances from Samuel Froler and Pernilla August in the lead roles. (Swedish with English subtitles) ★★★ $29.99

The Best Little Whorehouse in Texas

(1982, 114 min, US, Colin Higgins) Burt Reynolds and Dolly Parton bring a degree of charm to this glossy but uneven adaptation of the hit Broadway musical (which was directed by Tommy Tune) about a Texas bordello — called the Chicken Ranch — run by Parton and under attack by a local televangelist. Burt is the sheriff caught in the middle. Charles Durning received an Oscar nomination for his scene-stealing bit as the Governor. ★★½ $9.99

The Best Man

(1964, 102 min, US, Franklin J. Schaffner) Outstanding adaptation of Gore Vidal's vitriolic play centering on two politicians campaigning for the presidential nomination and trying to woo support of the party and the ailing ex-president. Cliff Robertson stars as a ruthless conservative nominee running against the idealistic Henry Fonda. Through the course of their politicking, betrayal, blackmail and political chicanery will rear their ugly heads as Vidal rips open (years before it became fashionable) the sometimes corrupt facade of politics. Also with Edie Adams, Margaret Leighton, Shelley Berman and Lee Tracy (excellent as the former chief). ★★★½ $19.99

The Best of Betty Boop, Vols 1 & 2

(1930s, 85 each min, US) The Max Fleischer Studios captured the essence of Big City Jazz in the Thirties not so much from the music they incorporated (though they had the best — from Louis Armstrong to Cab Calloway), but in the free-wheeling improvisational quality of the animation. No one — no thing — is ever at rest in a Betty Boop cartoon: everything pulses to a universal beat. A field day for you Freudians, one cartoon has Betty being chased with her dog Bimbo by a string of hot dogs through the forest, he (Bimbo) being initiated into her "secret" society. These two tapes are a must for anyone who thinks that Walt Disney was/is the final word in animation. ★★★½ $14.99

Best of Blank

(1967-1987, 85 min, US, Les Blank) Renowned documentary filmmaker Blank has fashioned a rich portrait of our "lower states" in this collection of musical interludes excerpted from some of his most famous works (In Heaven There Is No Beer, Gap-Toothed Women, The Blues According to Lightnin' Hopkins, and others). ★★★ $29.99

The Best of Broadway Musicals

(1994, 56 min, US) During his long-running "Ed Sullivan Show," the showman presented numerous production numbers from Broadway musicals. This one-hour compilation is a sample of those scenes, and though a veritable history of the American musical theatre, only a few songs make this of interest to non-fans. These standouts — which highlight original costumes, scenery and stars — are

excellent, and include "West Side Story," "My Fair Lady," "Camelot" and the stirring "Sweet Charity." Gwen Verdon's performance in the latter leaves little doubt as to her legendary theatrical status. ★★★ $19.99

The Best of Spike Jones, Vol. 1

(1950s, 70 min, US) John Cage has nothing on this guy, who mixed gunshots with his glissamos, belches with his forte. Spike's TV show was every bit as funny as his music, with lots of low slapstick humor, funny suits and people running around a lot. $29.99

Best of the Fests — 1988

(1988, 90 min, US) Short films, usually made by independents and students attempting to make a filmic calling card, are an almost forgotten art form. Rarely shown on TV or in the theatres, these interesting and many times hugely entertaining featurettes can usually be seen only in film festivals. But now with this series of film compilations, many of the best and most creative films have been culled on an annual basis and are now available on video. This, the first of the series, includes nine different shorts ranging from comedy, drama, experimental, documentary and animation with the highlight being A Slice of Life, a black comedy involving a fat man, a young woman and her baby son — and a hot pizza. $29.99

Best of the Fests — 1989

(1989, 90 min, US) Expanding on the concept that has made the International Tournees of Animation such long-running successes, this compilation film of 10 shorts gives a wonderfully diverse overview of what is happening in the American short film arena and includes live-action films as well as documentaries and animation. Included in this package of award-winning shorts from various American film festivals are That Grip, a five-minute parody of Marlo Thomas' "That Girl"; Feed the Dog, by J. Stephen Leeper; and Suelto!, a documentary on the festivities at the Pamplona bull runs. $29.99

Best of the Fests — 1990

(1990, 90 min, US) This series of award-winning short subjects includes the comedy Dr. Ded Bug, about a chef battling a cockroach in a restaurant; Macha's Curse, an animated Irish tale painted directly on 35mm film; and the experimental film Spartacus Rex, a 16-minute sensory overload meditation on what it means and what it takes to be "cool." $29.99

Best of the Fests — 1991

(1991, 90 min, US) An entertaining collection of award-winning short films gathered from several festivals throughout the country. The eclectic mix of animated, experimental and narrative works ranges in quality from the haunting and original Wanting for Bridge to the just plain mediocre Man Descending. Overall, however, this is an excellent introduction to the world of independent filmmaking. $29.99

Best of the Fest for Kids

(50 min, US) This mini film festival features eight vastly different shorts that have won awards in various film festivals around the United States. Both live-action and animation, highlights include Skip It, about kids in the

Skip It International Rope-jumping tournament; the cartoon *Fanarond*; *Charlie's Boogie Woogie*, where squiggly magic-marker people hop and bop to boogie-woogie piano music; and *Travels of a Dollar Bill*, a five-minute short of an old dollar bill who tells his life story to his grandchildren — a nickel and a penny. $19.99

The Best of the Two Ronnies

(1980s, 60 min, GB) The wildly funny comedic talents of British comedians Ronnie Corbett and Ronnie Barker are in full evidence in this 60-minute compilation of some of their best sketches from their BBC-TV shows. Sort of a thinking man's Benny Hill, the Two Ronnies' eccentric comedy makes great use of the English language as well as all the British hold sacred in creating their own almost surreal brand of comedy. Fans of Monty Python, Dame Edith Everage and "The Goon Show" should really enjoy the inspired antics of two of England's favorite comedians. $14.99

The Best of Times

(1986, 104 min, US, Roger Spottiswoode) This disappointing comedy manages a few smiles but considering the talent involved, there should have been more. Robin Williams stars as a former high school football player who dropped the winning pass in a championship game, and stages a rematch 20 years later. Kurt Russell plays his former teammate and friend. ★★ $14.99

The Best of W.C. Fields

(1930s, 61 min, US) To make certain that he would enter sound films on his own terms, W.C. Fields did a series of shorts for Sennett and RKO where he refined and perfected his persona. From his vaudeville skit *The Golf Specialist* (1930) to the ribald roughhousing of *The Dentist* (1932) (censored at the time), to the Brechtian distancing devices found in *The Fatal Glass of Beer* (1933), this collection captures an artist just on the cusp of his mature work. $19.99

Best Seller

(1987, 110 min, US, John Flynn) James Woods stars as a retired hit man whose offer to collaborate with a cop-turned-author (Brian Dennehy) on a tell-all autobiography ruffles the feathers of his wealthy ex-employer (Paul Shenar). Powerhouse performances by Woods and Dennehy distinguish this intriguing and tightly focused thriller. Also with Victoria Tennant. ★★★ $14.99

The Best Way

(1976, 85 min, France, Claude Miller) A summer camp for boys is the setting for this absorbing study of the tensions and sexual attraction of two male counselors. Marc, the overly masculine sports director, discovers Philippe, the music teacher, dressed in women's clothing. His inability to deal with his repressed feeling causes him to humiliate and persecute Philippe to the point were he must deal with the truth of his actions. A fine drama on sexual identity and male friendships. (French with English subtitles) ★★★ $49.99

The Best Years of Our Lives

(1946, 172 min, US, William Wyler) A landmark war film, and immensely popular in its day, this Oscar-winning drama is a masterful examination into the lives of three WWII veterans returning home. Fredric March won the second of his two Oscars for his rich portrayal of a family man having difficulty reorienting himself to civilian life. A great cast includes Myrna Loy as his wife, Teresa Wright, Dana Andrews (his best screen performance as a pilot haunted by his experiences), Virginia Mayo and Harold Russell, a real-life amputee who also won an Oscar as a young soldier adjusting to life without hands. ★★★★ $19.99

La Bête Humaine

(1938, 99 min, France, Jean Renoir) This atmospheric thriller follows the actions of a psychotic train engineer who falls for a married woman and plots to kill her husband. A dark, intense work from one of the masters of the French cinema. Starring Jean Gabin and Simone Simon. (French with English subtitles) ★★★½ $39.99

Betrayal

(1988, 95 min, GB, David Jones) Harold Pinter, in adapting his acclaimed stage production, has crafted a marvelous study of entwined lives, conflicting loyalties and emotional ambiguity which is both wickedly funny and endlessly intriguing. Ben Kingsley and Jeremy Irons are bound by their literary pursuits, their enduring friendship and their mutual involvement with Kingsley's wife (Patricia Hodge). Director Jones and writer Pinter effectively use the author's theatrical device of presenting the story's many acts backwards — thus beginning with the outcome of the characters' infidelity and then tracing the steps leading to that point. The three leads are uniformly good, and the film is exceptionally mounted and thoroughly engaging. ★★★★

Betrayed

(1988, 127 min, US, Constantin Costa-Gavras) Director Costa-Gavras turns his eyes on racial intolerance in this powerful but ultimately contrived thriller. Debra Winger stars as an FBI agent who goes undercover to expose a white supremacist group responsible for a series of racially motivated murders. While its scenes of racial prejudice are all-too real and emotionally devastating, the film itself is betrayed by an unbelievable romantic subplot between the agent and her prime suspect, a farmer played with chilling intensity by Tom Berenger. ★★½ $9.99

The Betsy

(1978, 125 min, US, Daniel Petrie) An all-star cast, headed by a slumming Laurence Olivier, gives varying degrees of over-the-top performances in this overwrought potboiler adapted from Harold Robbins' best-seller. With only occasional moments of interest, this heavy-handed melodrama charts the course of an auto manufacturing dynasty. Olivier plays the patriarch, and Robert Duvall is the grandson now running the company. About as subtle as a...well, Harold Robbins novel, this is the usual cacophony of lurid melodramatic loves and familial treachery. ★★ $19.99

Betsy's Wedding

(1990, 94 min, US, Alan Alda) Alda is in *Father of the Bride* territory with this sitcomish tale of a family preparing their daughter's wedding. Molly Ringwald is the bride-to-be, and surprise! — the wedding plans go awry. Though Alda does create some amusing scenarios for his characters, the story is remarkably familiar and the film's pacing is either too meandering or too over-the-top to achieve a comedic consistency. The cast includes Madeline Kahn, Joe Pesci, Ally Sheedy and Catherine O'Hara, but it's Anthony LaPaglia who steals the show as a mobster with a touch of class. ★★ $9.99

The Bette Midler Show

(1976, 84 min, US, Tom Tirbouch) The Divine Miss M offers comic skits and outlandish interpretations of "Boogie Woogie Bugle Boy," "Friends" and many others in this immensely entertaining "live from Cleveland" concert. ★★★½

Bette Midler: Art or Bust

(1984, 82 min, US, Thomas Schlamme) "Art or Bust" exhibits both in ample quantities as Ms. Midler and her wheelchair-bound mermaids cavort through this HBO special augmented with 20 additional minutes of songs and shenanigans. Not as lively as *The Bette Midler Show*, but nevertheless enjoyable for Midler fans. ★★★

Better Off Dead

(1985, 97 min, US, Savage Steve Holland) This wacky and hilarious — if underrated — comedy stars John Cusack as a teenager who loses the girl of his dreams and thinks himself *Better Off Dead*. Not a satire on suicide (à la *Heathers*), but rather a collection of crazy sketches, the majority of which hit the comedic bulls-eye. ★★★ $79.99

A Better Tomorrow, Pts. 1 & 2

(1986/1987, 120 min each, Hong Kong, John Woo) These are the two breakaway films that established Woo as a masterful action director; and both star Chow Yun-Fat (*The Killer*), Ti Lung and Leslie Cheung. Both films chronicle the story of two friends working in the counterfeiting trade and what lengths they go to in the name of friendship. The amazing amounts of action are played out in epic fashion showing the strong influence of Sam Peckinpah and Sergio Leone, with Woo's camerawork giving us an incredibly violent view of extreme gunplay. These two Egg Foo Yung westerns also feature a major subplot involving the Ti Lung character, Ho, and his brother Kit, who is a young cop, in which both brothers work to nail a crime boss, but from opposing sides. Part I — $14.99; Part II — $92.99 ★★★½

Betty

(1993, 103 min, France, Claude Chabrol) Director Chabrol delivers another existential look at a French woman trying to find her place in life. Told in flashbacks, the film tells the story of Betty (Marie Trintignant), a young alcoholic woman cast aside by her husband and desperately trying to keep her emotions and sanity in check. Betty is befriended by an older woman (Stéphane Audran), and as the story unfolds, the viewer learns more about these two women's lives and how they got to where they are. *Betty* is highly emotional, tragic and ultimately satisfying. (French with English subtitles) ★★★★ $89.99

Betty Blue

(1986, 110 min, France, Jean-Jacques Beineix) Beineix, director of the trendsetting *Diva* as well as the stilted *Moon in the Gutter*, has fashioned this humorous and engrossing tale of *amour fou*. The story follows the passionate and at times tempestuous relationship between Betty (Beatrice Dalle), a vulnerable young beauty, and her boyfriend Zog (Jean-Hugues Anglade), a young man hopelessly captivated by her enigmatic but beguiling charm. Wonderfully scripted and acted, this charmer should not be missed. (French with English subtitles) ★★★½ $79.99

Betty Dodson: Self-Loving

(1991, 60 min, US) Betty Dodson, artist, author and unusual sex instructor, has been a leading public advocate of women's sexual liberation for over 20 years. With a mantra-like philosophy that "masturbation is the ongoing love affair with ourselves," Dodson leads a two-day, ten-woman workshop aimed at getting to better know and love one's body and enhance sexual pleasure. This graphic yet never exploitative video, featuring mostly heterosexual women from 28 to 60 years of age, begins with simple breathing exercises. The women go on to explore each other's genitals, experiment with the use of vaginal bar bells, and eventually achieve obviously satisfying orgasms. It's a fascinating hour of sexual exploration which would seem impossible for a group of similarly heterosexual men to participate in. ★★★ $39.99

Betty Page Bondage Loops

(1950s, 100 min, US, Irving Klaw) See a bevy of buxom babes performing a variety of rope tricks, spanking and other related activities in this fine collection of short 8mm films made by king of backroom smut peddling Irving Klaw. Many of these films feature legendary pin-up princess Betty Page. A must-see for fans of vintage kink. $24.99

Betty Page Strip Loops

(1950s, 100 min, US, Irvin Klaw) Betty Page, America's favorite trailer-park Barbie, returns in this great collection of classic 8mm loop films featuring her stripping to some newly added 1970s tunes. A must see for fans of vintage burlesque.

Between Heaven and Earth

(1992, 80 min, France, Marion Hansel) Truly a bizarre French twist on *Look Who's Talking*, this odd little film stars Spanish leading lady Carmen Maura as a Parisian TV reporter whose developing fetus talks to her from in utero. As an epidemic of overdue babies and stillbirths occupy the headlines, Maura's talking zygote explains that the fetuses are essentially on strike and refuse to be born into such a miserable world. It's a slight premise on which to build a feature-length film, but certainly more could have been made of it. Maura, for her part, is always a pleasure, and performs

in French with what looks to be relative ease. (French with English subtitles) ★★ $79.99

Between Heaven and Hell

(1956, 93 min, US, Richard Fleischer) An interesting if talky war drama with Robert Wagner in his semi-successful bid to become a full-fledged movie star. Wagner plays an unscrupulous Southern landowner whose experiences in the Pacific during WWII help him recover his lost compassion and humanity. Broderick Crawford is the maniacal commanding officer at odds with the young soldier. Also with Terry Moore and Buddy Ebsen. ★★½ $14.99

Between the Lines

(1977, 101 min, US, Joan Micklin Silver) The trials and tribulations of the staff of a Boston underground newspaper during the 1960s is at the heart of director Silver's quirky and highly spirited low-budget charmer. Full of counter-culture sentiments and refreshingly original humor, the film boasts an endearing cast of eccentrics fighting the system and fulfilling their journalistic aspirations — until faced with the fateful decision to "sell out." A solid ensemble of then-unknowns (Michael J. Pollard was probably the most recognizable name) are all first-rate in bringing the convictions and passions of a generation to life — including Jeff Goldblum, John Heard, Jill Eikenberry, Stephen Collins, Marilu Henner, Lindsay Crouse, Joe Morton and Bruno Kirby. ★★★½

The Beverly Hillbillies

(1993, 93 min, US, Penelope Spheeris) It's bad news for a comedy when its funniest moments stem from surprise "star" cameos and out-takes during the end credits. Such is the case for *The Beverly Hillbillies*, a sappy, big-screen rendition of the popular 1960s TV series. In an A to B plot line, Arkansas hillbilly patriarch Jed Clampett strikes it rich, moves to Beverly (Hills, that is), and becomes the target for con artists. The comedy is played even broader than the TV series, which seems subtle by comparison. Of the film's cast, Lily Tomlin as Miss Hathaway, and the woefully underused Cloris Leachman as Granny will suffer the least ill-effect for their appearances here. ★★ $9.99

Beverly Hills Cop

(1984, 105 min, US, Martin Brest) Eddie Murphy is Axel Foley, a Detroit cop who travels to Beverly Hills to avenge a friend's death...and make the biggest grossing comedy of the decade. Not nearly as memorable as *48 Hrs.*, but entertaining if you don't think about it too much. Judge Reinhold steals the show as Rosewood, an unorthodox cop who helps the displaced detective. Good soundtrack, and a slam-bang opening scene. ★★★ $9.99

Beverly Hills Cop 2

(1987, 103 min, US, Tony Scott) This extremely disappointing sequel has none of the ingredients which made the first film the popular success it was. Eddie Murphy tries his best, but how many times can we watch him con his way into ritzy Beverly Hills establishments? There's some slick, polished direction by Scott, but it

can't hide the formulaic script and forced performances. For die-hard Murphy fans only. ★★ $14.99

Beverly Hills Cop III

(1994, 103 min, US, John Landis) Eddie Murphy dusts off the gun and jacket of Axel Foley for this third (and probably last) installment. Featuring uninspired direction by Landis, this occasionally amusing but incredibly formulaic film has Axel returning to California to investigate a lead in a carjack ring/murder case. The trail leads to a Disneyland-type park, which serves as a cover for the bag guys. Murphy gives an earnest try, though he's been through all this before, and it shows. However, *III* does provide more pleasure than *B.H.C. II*, and Judge Reinhold returns once more as Rosewood. ★★½ $14.99

Beware, My Lovely

(1952, 77 min, US, Harry Horner) This thrilling study of insanity and terror stars Robert Ryan as a deranged handyman who holds captive his widowed employer, Ida Lupino, inside her home. Haunted by the murder of his previous employer (whom he may or may not have killed), Ryan alternates between being a gentle if slightly dazed man and an angry, potentially violent loony. ★★★ $19.99

Beware of a Holy Whore

(1970, 103 min, West Germany, Rainer Werner Fassbinder) An autobiographical meditation on the turbulent interactions and shifting power relationships which make up the filmmaking process, this is RFW's *8½*, *Day for Night* and *Contempt*. Based in part on Fassbinder's own experiences making *Whity*, *Beware a Holy Whore* follows a film crew and a group of actors who anxiously lounge around an opulent Spanish hotel arguing, drinking and becoming involved in destructive sex and power games as they endlessly wait for the film's star (Eddie Constantine), production money and especially the director (played by Fassbinder) to bring them to life. This was RFW's last collaboration with the collective Anti-Teater (Fassbinder's repertory company). Also with Lou Castel, Hanna Schygulla and Ulli Lommel. (German with English subtitles) ★★★ $19.99

Beyond a Reasonable Doubt

(1956, 80 min, US, Fritz Lang) An anti-capital punishment newspaper publisher implicates himself in a murder by using circumstantial evidence, hoping to expose the weakness of the system. However, things go wrong when he plays it too convincingly, is found guilty and then sent to prison. Dana Andrews and Joan Fontaine star in this, Lang's final American film, that while far-fetched, is an undeniably grim and gripping melodrama. ★★★

Beyond Rangoon

(1995, 100 min, US, John Boorman) Patricia Arquette stars as an American tourist visiting Burma who becomes involved in that country's bloody struggle for democracy in this gripping and moving political drama. After the murder of her husband and young son, doctor Laura Bowman (Arquette) attempts to find solace in the supposedly peaceful landscapes of the Far East. After witnessing in Rangoon a people's demonstration against the military dictator-

B

ship, she sets out with an "unofficial" tour guide, U Aung Ko, to see the country beyond the city. However, a military crackdown forces both Bowman and U Aung Ko to flee for their lives in an attempt to reach the border. Suggested by an actual incident, *Beyond Rangoon* at its best recalls *The Killing Fields* as a strong narrative and taut direction combine to tell a harrowing tale of political oppression and heroism. Arquette gives a competent performance, but she fails to bring an edge to the role. First-time actor and expatriate professor U Aung Ko, playing himself, gives a nurtured performance which evokes the urgency of the widespread massacre which went unnoticed throughout the world. ★★★½ $96.89

Beyond Reasonable Doubt

(1980, 117 min, New Zealand, John Laing) A jolting, true-life drama that documents the stilted investigation and legislative practices responsible for the incarceration of a mild-mannered New Zealand farmer. David Hemmings gives a powerful performance as the corrupt police inspector who makes it a personal quest to seal the fate of the accused man, a baffled witness to his own demise. This Hitchcockian tale of questionable guilt and justice is a fascinating and thoroughly engrossing motion picture. ★★★ $29.98

Beyond the Forest

(1949, 96 min, US, King Vidor) Bette Davis misses her mark as a murderous crack shot in this tepid melodrama about a woman who'll stop at nothing to rise above her life as the wife of a country doctor (Joseph Cotten). Notable for Davis' immortal line, "What a dump." Also starring Ruth Roman. ★★ $19.99

Beyond the Mind's Eye

(1992, 45 min, US, Michael Boydstun) Computer animation extraordinaire! Computer whiz Boydstun has compiled some of the most astonishing computer-generated shorts from around the globe — many are award-winners. Featuring a hypnotic score by Jan Hammer ("Miami Vice"), this collection will have your head spinning and your jaw dropping in no time. ★★★ $19.99

Beyond the Valley of the Dolls

(1970, 109 min, US, Russ Meyer) A classic late-nite cult title, this brilliantly raunchy, in-name-only sequel to *Valley of the Dolls* tells the torrid tale of a female rock band, The Carrie Nations, and their deliriously funny struggle to get to the top. Featuring director Meyer's trademark wit and camerawork, this ahead-of-its-time exploitation favorite remains one of the best of the genre. Co-scripted by film critic Roger Ebert. ★★★★ $19.99

Beyond the Walls

(1984, 103 min, Israel, Uri Barbash) Inside the walls of an Israeli prison, Jews and Arabs are confined in a society which mirrors the pressures and tensions on the outside. Cruelty is commonplace and loyalty is fleeting. This already volatile situation is further exacerbated by the arrival of an Israeli army officer who is jailed for attempting to speak to the PLO. As the inmates struggle with ideological hatreds on the inside, they attempt to maintain contact with their families and communities on the

outside, with decreasing effectiveness and increasing frustration. The cast delivers uniformly authentic portrayals, conveyed with raw intensity and unflinching emotion. Especially arresting are Arnon Zadok as a Jewish cell block leader and Muhamad Bakri as a PLO insurgent. A powerful experience, a film that in the midst of centuries-old animosities manages to find some common ground and a faint hope of peace. (Hebrew with English subtitles) ★★★ $79.99

Beyond Therapy

(1987, 93 min, US, Robert Altman) Christopher Durang co-adapted his own hit off-Broadway play for the screen in this Altman comedy about the frantic goings-on of a group of sex-obsessed neurotics and their equally unbalanced psychologists. Jeff Goldblum is the bisexual Bruce, who lives with semi-swishy Bob (Christopher Guest), but who takes a liking to hopelessly frazzled Prudence (Julie Hagerty). Tom Conti and Glenda Jackson play two crazy therapists whose advice only makes everyone more crazy. Unpredictable, loony and wildly uneven, *Beyond Therapy* can also be quite charming in-between the out-of-control shenanigans. Though set in New York, Altman filmed in Paris. ★★½ $9.99

The Bicycle Thief

Bhaji on the Beach

(1994, 100 min, GB, Gurinder Chadha) This well-intentioned and somewhat lighthearted look at the lives of a group of Anglo-Indian/Pakistani women has its moments, but ultimately fails to captivate. The film follows three generations of women on an outing to the British seaside resort of Blackpool. Led by the self-assured feminist Simi, they land on the beach with a variety of issues at hand. The twentysomething Ginder has drawn the wrath of her entire community for having left her abusive husband while her counterpart, Hashida, has just discovered she's pregnant — worse news for her family, her boyfriend is black. The two teenagers on the trip, Ladhu and Madhu, have no trouble integrating themselves into Blackpool's shmaltziness while flirting with a couple of hotdog vendors. The group's elders Puspha and Bina are a couple of sari-clad worriers who long for a return to traditional values. All of these threads are loosely pulled together through Asha, a middle-aged housewife who drifts into daydreams about Lord Raman and struggles between her

sense of duty and dignity. Individually, all of the stories are interesting enough and the acting is strong throughout, but as the film wanders among its characters, it becomes diluted and ultimately comes off like a protracted episode of "EastEnders." ★★½ $96.89

The Bible

(1966, 174 min, US, John Huston) Dino De Laurentiis produced this megalithic and completely blundering attempt to bring the "number one best-seller" to the screen. Some projects are better left alone. Why Huston agreed to helm this ill-begotten ship is a mystery. Perhaps only so he himself could portray Noah in the film's only redeeming chapter. Also starring: Richard Harris, George C. Scott, Ava Gardner, Peter O'Toole and Franco Nero. If you're really interested, read the book. ★½ $19.99

Les Biches

(1968, 104 min, France/Italy, Claude Chabrol) Stéphane Audran has never looked more elegantly decadent than in this twisted bisexual drama of sexual domination, obsession, despair and revenge, filmed in Chabrol's trademark cool, detached style. Audran is Frederique, a glamorous woman of lesbian leaning who, on a trip to Paris, meets then seduces a poor, enigmatic young woman named Why. She soon whisks her new love off to her home in St. Tropez to continue their affair, but the balance is changed when a man (Jean-Louis Trintignant) enters the picture and, after a brief attraction to Why, takes up permanently with Frederique. The centerpiece of this explosive love triangle is Audran's wanton sexual appeal, a power that eventually leads to bitter consequences. Letterboxed format. (French with English subtitles) ★★★½ $79.99

The Bicycle Thief

(1948, 90 min, Italy, Vittorio De Sica) One of the undisputed neorealist classics, *The Bicycle Thief* adeptly uses the postwar devastation of Italy as harsh backdrop for this poignant story of a marginal man whose simple existence depends on his bicycle, which he needs to earn his living. He is devastated by the bicycle's theft; his family's well-being is jeopardized and the police are indifferent. He is left to his own devices to scour the city with his young son, a victim without aid or support, alienated and isolated. Filmed with great caring and compassion, and yet without sympathetic gloss, by director De Sica, who can use a single human face to speak volumes about the human condition. ★★★★ $29.99

Il Bidone (The Swindlers)

(1955, 92 min, Italy, Federico Fellini) Broderick Crawford is memorable as the selfish ringleader of a trio of con men who impersonate priests in an elaborate scam that preys on the avarice of ignorant peasants. A satire that begins as a light comedy and concludes with tragedy, this pre-flamboyant Fellini forms part two of his trilogy (which includes *La Strada* and *Nights of Cabiria*) of outsiders eking out an existence on the road. Co-starring Giulietta Masina and Richard Basehart. (Italian with English subtitles) ★★★ $69.99

B

Big

(1988, 102 min, US, Penny Marshall) Tom Hanks gives a brilliantly complex and funny performance as the end result of a 12-year-old boy's wish to be "big." When his wish comes true, he is thrust into an adult world of big business, office politics and romance, all the while maintaining his refreshing child's-eye view of the world. Gary Ross' delightful script takes aim at corporate rivalry, consumerism and alienation while bringing a fresh perspective to the "fish out of water" scenario. Director Marshall exhibits a playful knack for comedy both physical and verbal, though she does somewhat bask in the sentimental. Also starring Elizabeth Perkins, Robert Loggia, John Heard and Mercedes Ruehl. ★★★½ $9.99

The Big Bang

(1989, 81 min, US, James Toback) Beginning with his theory that the creation of the universe was the result of an "orgasmic explosion of God," director Toback (*Fingers*, *The Pick-Up Artist*) leaves the world of fiction to explore various other thoughts on existence in this rambling yet entertaining documentary. Interviewing a series of people from diverse backgrounds (basketball player Darryl Dawkins, filmmaker Don Simpson, violinist Eugene Fodor, Auschwitz survivor Barbara Traub), Toback elicits their divergent thoughts on life, death, creativity, sex, love and the existence of God. A funny, touching and even a little enlightening 81 minutes. ★★★ $19.99

The Big Blue

(1988, 119 min, France, Luc Besson) Only Besson's most ardent fans, or those of you who fantasize about things aquatic, will be swayed by the stunning underwater photography in this waterlogged story about the rivalry between two deep-sea free divers (Jean Reno and Jean-Marc Barr). Rosanna Arquette co-stars as a ditzy New York insurance salesperson who falls in love with one of them only to be rejected for a dolphin. (Filmed in English and French with subtitles) ★★ $19.99

The Big Brawl

(1980, 95 min, US, Robert Clouse) Jackie Chan stars in his first and only lead in an American-made film. This gangster film set in 1930s Chicago is more or less a showcase for the incredibly talented Chan. Lots of comedy and fighting keep the film interesting, but this is far from being one of Chan's best. Not much here for non-Jackie fans. ★★½

Big Business

(1988, 97 min, US, Jim Abrahams) Lightning doesn't strike twice as *Ruthless People* star Bette Midler and director Abrahams reunite in this rather tame though genial comedy. Midler and Lily Tomlin star as two sets of twins switched at birth who run across each other's paths in the Big Apple. A good premise, a nice turn from the Divine Miss M and some nifty special effects can't save this lightweight comedy; though it does manage a few laughs, it is a disappointment considering the talent involved. ★★ $9.99

The Big Chill

(1983, 103 min, US, Lawrence Kasdan) Borrowing liberally from John Sayles' wonderful *Return of the Secaucus Seven*, director and co-author Kasdan has fashioned an equally entertaining and smartly written ode to the lasting power of friendship. Utilizing a talented all-star cast, Kasdan's comedy-drama focuses on the reunion of a group of college friends from the '60s who have come together in the '80s for the funeral for one of their own. Kevin Kline and Glenn Close are a married couple who play host to their clique, which includes TV star Tom Berenger, *People* magazine writer Jeff Goldblum (in a particularly sharp portrayal), injured Vietnam vet William Hurt, housewife JoBeth Williams and career woman Mary Kay Place. What distinguishes Kasdan's story are the personable characters and the remarkable relationships between them. With a golden oldies soundtrack which emphasizes the infectious good times, *The Big Chill* is as comfortable as a longtime friend. That's Kevin Costner as the deceased (his flashback scenes were cut from the final release). ★★★½ $9.99

The Big Country

(1958, 166 min, US, William Wyler) Epic western adventure starring Gregory Peck as an exsea captain who returns home to marry and start a ranch, becoming caught in a feud over water rights. This mammoth production also stars Charlton Heston, Jean Simmons, Carroll Baker and Burl Ives in an Oscar-winning performance as the patriarch of one of the feuding families. ★★★ $29.99

Big Deal on Madonna Street

(1956, 91 min, Italy, Mario Monticelli) The wild misadventures of a group of bungling would-be crooks who attempt to rob a pawn shop and who make a complete mess of it is a classic example of *commedia all'italiana*. A hilarious parody of American caper films that many think to be one of the funniest Italian films to come out of the era. Louis Malle remade the film, but with much less success, as *Crackers*. (Italian with English subtitles) ★★★½ $29.99

The Big Dis

(1988, 88 min, US, Gordon Eriksen & John O'Brien) This charming, black-and-white low-budget comedy-drama will remind one of Spike Lee's *She's Gotta Have It* in its often hilarious theme about the sexual attitudes and posturing of young middle-class blacks. J.D., a handsome but thoroughly sexist black soldier, returns to his family's suburban home on a weekend leave; his overwhelming ambition: to get laid. But everything seems to go wrong as he comes ever so close but never grabs the ring. ★★½ $59.99

The Big Doll House

(1971, 93 min, US, Jack Hill) Valley girls and Hollywood starlets trapped in a hellhole Filipino prison! One of the earliest and most commercially succesful of the "women-in-prison" films which were so popular in the 1970s, this is almost chaste compared to its cheesier successors. Filmed in a breezy, comedic fashion, the film features the requisite S&M beating, shower and claws-out fighting sequences to tell its tale of prisoners who revolt against their ruthless warden. Starring Pam Grier and Judy Brown. ★★½ $19.99

The Big Easy

(1987, 101 min, US, Jim McBride) A glorious blend of screwball comedy and detective story, this scintillating thriller stars Dennis Quaid as a New Orleans detective who becomes involved with sexy district attorney Ellen Barkin, who is investigating local police corruption. Quaid and Barkin are about the most attractive duo on the screen in years, and their love scenes are among the steamiest, also. Great supporting cast includes Ned Beatty, John Goodman, Ebbe Roe Smith and Charles Ludlam in a stand-out role as a Tennessee Williams-ish lawyer. ★★★½ $14.99

The Big Fix

(1978, 108 min, US, Jeremy Paul Kagan) Roger L. Simon adapted his own novel about private eye Moses Wine, a former '60s campus radical, who is hired by an old college girlfriend to help locate a fugitive from their Berkeley days. An entertaining comedy-mystery with Richard Dreyfuss in good form as Wine. Supporting cast includes Bonnie Bedelia, Susan Anspach, John Lithgow and F. Murray Abraham. ★★★ $59.99

Big Girls Don't Cry...They Get Even

(1992, 90 min, US, Joan Micklin Silver) If you are post-pubescent, you might feel slightly silly watching this tale of the ultimate dysfunctional family. However, *Big Girls Don't Cry...They Get Even* is actually entertaining once you get over the embarrassment of watching something with such an inane title. Hilary Wolf stars as Lauren (a 14-year-old with a ready cannister of one-liners), who runs away after she decides that her mother, stepfather and various step-siblings just don't care about her. The ensuing search to bring her home unites the various and eccentric members of her family. Special mention should go to Adrienne Shelly who gives a lovely, understated performance as Lauren's real father's artsy, very young and pregnant girlfriend. ★★½ $9.99

The Big Grab (Melodie en sous-sol)

(1963, 118 min, France, Henri Verneuil) A young Alain Delon is the punk assistant to master thief Jean Gabin in this taut cops and robbers flick. Their attempt to pull off "the crime of the century" is intricately detailed as their plans become more and more complicated. A good, well-told story in the tradition of *Bob le Flambeur*. (French with English subtitles) ★★★ $19.99

The Big Green

(1995, 100 min, US, Holly Goldberg Sloan) While certainly not the best of this genre of films that chronicles the transformation of a team of kids from losers to winners, there's enough here to satisfy most young viewers. The fact that this time soccer is the sport will broaden its appeal. A young exchange teacher from England (d'Abo) decides to teach the game to her students, a group of kids from a very small and depressed Texas town, in an attempt to get them motivated and more confident. Guttenberg is the local sheriff who, despite his dislike of kids, ends up as her assistant coach in order to encourage a relationship between him and d'Abo. Among the team of fairly likable kids is the inevitable ringer, a Mexican youth whose mother is reluctant to let him play because she is an illegal alien. This problem and several others are satisfactorily resolved in the championship play-off for a heartwarming ending. ★★½ $14.99

A Big Hand for the Little Lady

(1966, 95 min, US, Fielder Cook) Henry Fonda and Joanne Woodward are in fine form in this sly western comedy. Fonda plays an ex-gambler who arrives with his wife (Woodward) in the town of Laredo just as the big card tournament begins. He enters the game, and gets the hand of a lifetime. Only before he can finish the hand, he suffers a heart attack. When his wife takes his place, the now-penniless woman has some fancy talking to do to stay in the game. A good supporting cast includes Jason Robards, Burgess Meredith, Paul Ford and Kevin McCarthy. And ya gotta love that surprise ending. ★★★ $19.99

The Big Heat

(1953, 90 min, US, Fritz Lang) Although the story of mob operations and political corruption is pale compared to today's headlines, Lang's direction and some potent performances lose none of their impact. Especially effective are Glenn Ford as the honest cop, Lee Marvin as the psychotic hood and an amazing Gloria Grahame as the gangster's moll. Yes, this is the one with the coffee-throwing scene. ★★★½ $59.99

Big Night

(1996, 107 min, US, Stanley Tucci & Campbell Scott) Adding yet another chapter to the annals of grand cinematic feasts, this charming little indie feature tells the tale of two Italian immigrant brothers who make a go at the American Dream. One part comedy and two parts drama and set in the 1950s on the North Jersey shore, the story centers around Primo (Tony Shalhoub) and Secondo's (Stanley Tucci) desperate attempt to kickstart their failing bistro. While Primo and Secondo go out of their way to present authentic and upscale Italian fare, their competitor down the street (Ian Holm) is clobbering them with his low-brow, "Americanized" fare. Ultimately, they gear up for one big splash as they anticipate a visit from Italo-American bandleader Louis Prima. The ensuing feast is worthy of its long list of cinematic antecedants (*Babette's Feast*, *Like Water for Chocolate* and *Eat Drink Man Woman*) and will send any viewer with so much as a twinge of epicureanism rushing to their local trattoria begging for timpano. Superbly acted, the film's cast is rounded out by Scott (who co-directed with Tucci) as an affable car salesman, Minnie Driver as Secondo's girlfriend and Isabella Rossellini as Holm's lover. ★★★½ $19.99

The Big Parade

(1925, 126 min, US, King Vidor) Vidor's stunning anti-war film is one of the classics of silent cinema. Containing realistic, remarkably staged battle sequences and moments of rare powerful dramatics, *The Big Parade* follows the enlistment of an American soldier (silent

Stanley Tucci (l.) and Tony Shalhoub in *Big Night*

screen great John Gilbert) who fights in France during WWI. Though made at the infancy of American filmmaking, Vidor has a superior command of the medium, creating scenes as achingly intimate and disturbing as they are brilliantly constructed. This epic may have influenced Stanley Kubrick's *Paths of Glory*. ★★★★ $29.99

The Big Picture

(1989, 99 min, US, Christopher Guest) Hollywood, and the movie industry in particular, take it on the chin in this biting and funny satire. Reminiscent of *S.O.B.* and *This Is Spinal Tap*, *The Big Picture* pokes some good-natured and wacky, on-target jabs at the Hollywood establishment in its story of a student filmmaker who tries to direct his first feature film. Kevin Bacon stars as the talented newcomer who "goes Hollywood." While a couple of jokes may be too "in" for some, most of this material is accessible to all. Co-starring Emily Longstreth, Michael McKean, the delightful Jennifer Jason Leigh, and Martin Short as a highly outrageous agent. ★★★ $19.99

The Big Red One

(1980, 113 min, US, Samuel Fuller) Lee Marvin is the sergeant, the archetypal soldier, in Fuller's *The Big Red One*, a war story from the foot soldiers' point of view. It opens at the end of WWI with the sergeant's creation of the First Infantry insignia: the big red one. The film jumps a quarter century to North Africa, and follows Marvin and his squad, among them Mark Hamill, David Carradine and Bobby DiCicco, as they trek across a thousand miles fighting for their lives. Based on his own war experiences, the film was written and directed by Fuller, who is unequalled in revealing in intimate detail the individual's struggle against the panorama of monumental cataclysm. Deliberately paced, methodically structured and finely detailed – a quintessential war film, made with compassion but not sentiment, affection but not pathos. The film's closing sequences offer unassailable testimony that there are moments in history when the horrors of war must be borne in defiance of

pure evil. And, at some time, the war is finally over. ★★★½ $14.99

The Big Sleep

(1946, 114 min, US, Howard Hawks) Humphrey Bogart is Philip Marlowe, who's not very tall but tries to be. A classic film noir, slightly seedy and heavy on atmosphere. There's lots of tough guys and guys who would be tough, lots of fast women and loose talk, cigarette smoke you could cut with a knife, and guns, lots of guns. The plot, which has something to do with Bogey being hired to protect a young, wild heiress, is so convoluted that the guy who wrote the book (Raymond Chandler) didn't know who committed one of the murders. William Faulkner was one of the scriptwriters. Lauren Bacall co-stars. ★★★★ $19.99

The Big Squeeze

(1996, 100 min, US, Marcus De Leon) If Quentin Tarantino directed an Afterschool Special, the result might be something like *The Big Squeeze*. It's an amiable, sunny noir (a contradiction that works) about an unhappy wife and a scam artist who team to sting her born-again husband out of $130,000. In light of the hyperviolence and cruelty of recent crime films, *The Big Squeeze* is refreshingly upbeat, so that even its double-crossing and infidelities seem good-natured. There's also an unexpected (though successful) religious miracle theme. Unfortunately, the character intros are irritatingly cutesy, and the film as a whole tends to be too sitcomish. But the appealing performances (especially Lara Flynn Boyle and Danny Nucci) and light pace certainly compensate. ★★½ $97.99

The Big Steal

(1949, 71 min, US, Don Siegel) Siegel's third feature film is his only true film noir, an exciting and well-paced thriller of a heist gone wrong. Robert Mitchum gives a sturdy, three-dimensional performance of a man trying to capture the real culprits of the crime of which he has been accused. The film has witty dialogue, lots of action and numerous, unexpected plot twists. Watch for a great car chase scene early on that would become the prototype for action films. Also starring the luminous Jane Greer. ★★★★ $19.99

The Big Store

(1941, 80 min, US, Charles Riesner) This Marx Brothers romp isn't really in the same caliber of *Duck Soup* or *Horsefeathers*, but it does produce a few laughs. Detective Groucho goes undercover at Margaret Dumont's department store, and finds Chico and Harpo and crooks. ★★½ $19.99

Big Time

(1988, 87 min, US, Chris Blum) This concert film, taken from a performance at L.A.'s Wiltern Theatre, allows us to get a taste of some of Tom Waits' multiple personalities. The raspy-voiced singer goes from character to character while singing classic songs from "Frank's Wild Years," "Rain Dogs," and other early Waits albums. This is as close as you'll get to Tom Waits without seeing him live. ★★★

Big Top Pee-wee

(1988, 90 min, US, Randal Kleiser) Pee-wee's heart takes flight when he meets the new trapeze artist whose circus is staying at his farm. Youngsters should like this second outing for Paul Reubens' alter ego almost as much as the first: it's got kids and animals and Danny Elfman's great score. With Susan Tyrrell, Penelope Ann Miller, Kris Kristofferson and Valeria Golino. ★★½ $14.99

Big Trouble

(1985, 93 min, US, John Cassavetes) *Double Indemnity* meets *Ruthless People* in this plot-twisted comedy about an underpaid insurance agent (Alan Arkin) who falls in with a fickle femme fatale (Beverly D'Angelo) and her plot to kill her wealthy husband (Peter Falk). Director Cassavetes shows little flair for the comedic moment, but zany situations and characterizations make this an enjoyable entry. ★★★ $19.99

Big Trouble in Little China

(1986, 99 min, US, John Carpenter) Kurt Russell does his best John Wayne imitation in this amiable, light-hearted adventure spoof as a tough truck driver who (sort of) helps rescue his best friend's girlfriend. It seems she was kidnapped by a 2000-year-old magician who rules a secret underground society beneath San Francisco's Chinatown. Director Carpenter crams a lot of action into the 99-minute running time, and if some of the production is overblown, there's quite a few good sequences which make it easy to like. ★★★ $9.99

A Bigger Splash

(1974, 90 min, GB, David Hockney) Controversial British painter Hockney stars as himself in this penetrating, semi-fictitious portrait of his personal and artistic life. Centered around the actual breakup of Hockney and his lover/model, Peter Schlessinger, this witty and revealing work meditates on the relationship of art to life. Vignettes of Hockney with friends, lovers and ex-lovers create an impressionistic study of the swirling influences in one artist's world. ★★★

Bilitis

(1982, 93 min, GB, David Hamilton) Well-known as a photographer of young female erotic art, Hamilton makes his first venture into the world of film with this account of a 16-year-old girl's sexual awakening. The softly focused photography works well with the plot, making for a very moving and sensual experience. ★★★

Bill & Ted's Excellent Adventure

(1989, 90 min, US, Stephen Herer) Feeling overwhelmed by the world today? Thank goodness there's still every American's inalienable right of – stupidity. This film is a case in point. Bill and Ted are a couple of airheads who just wanna have fun. But when they're in danger of being shipped off to military school for failing history, what do they do? They resort to the best special effects Industrial Light and Magic can drum up. George Carlin, playing an equally mindless muck from the future, comes to the Valley with a time machine for our homeboys to experience history firsthand. ★★½ $14.99

Bill & Ted's Bogus Journey

(1991, 98 min, US, Peter Hewitt) That most awesome and excellent duo, Bill and Ted, are back in this bit of lunacy with Keanu Reeves and Alex Winter repeating their roles as the 1990s' most endearing party-on dudes. With a nod to *The Terminator*, Bill and Ted are pursued by evil look-alike robots from the future who are out to kill them. The bad guys almost succeed, which causes the good guys to meet Death. In one of the most inspired scenes, Bill and Ted (in another filmic nod, this time to *The Seventh Seal*) challenge Death to a game of...Twister! It's just as silly as the first film, and Reeves and Winter clearly are having fun, though some of the comic mileage is starting to wear thin. ★★½ $9.99

A Bill of Divorcement

(1932, 69 min, US, George Cukor) The film which both introduced the ravishing Katharine Hepburn and started her illustrious association with director Cukor. John Barrymore gives a fine performance as a veteran who returns home after a long stay at a mental hospital, trying to establish a relationship with his daughter Kate. Billie Burke superbly plays Barrymore's wife, whose plans of remarriage significantly alter his hopes of a happy homecoming. The caliber of acting from these three performers make this a must-see. ★★★½ $39.99

Billy Bathgate

(1991, 106 min, US, Robert Benton) Benton (*Kramer vs. Kramer*) directed this fast-paced and tense adaptation of E.L. Doctorow's novel, recounting the fall of mobster Dutch Schultz (Dustin Hoffman) as seen through the eyes of an ambitious teenager, Billy Bathgate (Loren Dean). Though slightly miscast, Hoffman excels as the moody gangster. Able support is provided by Nicole Kidman as the femme fatale and Steven Hill as Bathgate's toady Otto Berman. Nestor Almendros' eerie cinematography imbues the film with a grim and destructive mood. ★★★ $9.99

Billy Budd

(1962, 112 min, GB, Peter Ustinov) In 1797, under the Rights of War Act, an English warship, the Avenger, conscripts a young, good-natured innocent (Terence Stamp) from the Rights of Man, a merchant ship at sea. The Avenger's master at arms (Robert Ryan) is particularly sadistic, even by the standards of the British Navy at the time, whose officers had life and death control over their crews. Outstanding performances from the entire cast are supported by solid direction from Ustinov, who also produced and co-scripted, as well as plays the ship's captain. A strong, straightforward story of morality and honor, based on the novella by Herman Melville. ★★★½ $59.99

Billy Jack

(1971, 114 min, US, T.C. Frank [Tom Laughlin]) If *Rambo: First Blood Part II* was the socio-political sensation of the 1980s, then this pacifist action-adventure is the 1970s' equivalent. Tom Laughlin plays the title character, a Native American karate expert who is pushed too far by the authorities. He fights back and becomes a folk hero in the process. Immensely popular, though not in its original theatrical run, but later in 1974 in a major re-release. ★★½ $9.99

Billy Liar

(1963, 96 min, GB, John Schlesinger) One of the benchmark films in the British "kitchen sink" school of filmmaking, Schlesinger's early effort is an outstanding examination of middle-class life. Tom Courtenay is sparkling as a young daydreamer who is stuck in the mundanity of his boorish life. In her film debut, Julie Christie is a wonderful young mod woman who offers Courtenay an escape into a world of fantasy. ★★★½ $9.99

Billy Madison

(1995, 89 min, US, Tamra Davis) Which is more annoying? The rash of idiotic films from former "SNL" regulars, or complaining about the rash of idiotic films from "SNL" regulars? Either way, they've done it again. Adam Sandler, who was one of the lesser gifted comics on the show, plays a moronic heir to a $600 million throne. His dad (Darren McGavin) isn't sure whether to leave the business to his idiot son, so said idiot son goes back to school (grades 1-12) to prove he's not an idiot. What follows is a series of scatological and juvenile jokes and pranks that only Beavis and Butt-head would find funny ("Heh-heh. He said 'shit'"). It's unclear who this was intended for (pre-adolescents, teens, young adults), but save for one or two funny scenes (and a saving grace cameo from Steve Buscemi), *Billy Madison* is one big loser. ★ $14.99

Biloxi Blues

(1988, 106 min, US, Mike Nichols) The second in Neil Simon's acclaimed autobiographical trilogy (including *Brighton Beach Memoirs* and *Broadway Bound*). Matthew Broderick is the perfect reincarnation of young Simon, who here is sent to Biloxi, Mississippi, for ten weeks of boot camp. Simon's dialogue is refreshing and funny, and his work is seasoned with both poignancy and insight. Christopher

Walken is at his best as the company's possibly unstable sergeant. ★★★½ $9.99

The Bingo Long Traveling All-Stars & Motor Kings

(1976, 110 min, US, John Badham) A winning screenplay, great period design, a glorious performance by James Earl Jones and terrific supporting turns by Richard Pryor and Stan Shaw all contribute to make this high-spirited baseball comedy one of the 1970s' most underrated and enjoyable films. Billy Dee Williams stars as the manager of a black barnstorming team in the late 1930s whose group of highly irregulars becomes the main attraction in the independent league circuit. ★★★½ $9.99

Bird

(1988, 161 min, US, Clint Eastwood) Though he had many credits as director to his name before this remarkable musical biography of jazz great Charlie Parker, Eastwood for the first time demonstrated complete control of the medium and a distinctive storytelling ability. In a most challenging role, Forest Whitaker gives a sensitive though commanding performance as the jazz man who was considered to be the greatest saxophonist of his time. In a series of flashbacks (which sometimes border on the confusing), *Bird* recalls Parker's meteoric rise in the jazz world, his troublesome homelife, and the drug addiction which ultimately led to his death at the early age of 34. Diane Verona is excellent as Parker's wife. Featuring an outstanding musical soundtrack, *Bird* is most definitely a labor of love from Clint Eastwood. ★★★½ $19.99

Bird on a Wire

(1990, 110 min, US, John Badham) In *Tequila Sunrise*, Mel Gibson teamed with Kurt Russell. Now, he bares his buns for Russell's significant other, Goldie Hawn, in a far-fetched chase film/love story. This is commercial high-concept filmmaking at its most cynical – the whole thing is a big cut and paste job. Mel plays an on-the-run witness protectee who teams for some not-very-exciting misadventures with ex-girlfriend Hawn. ★½ $14.99

The Bird with the Crystal Plumage

(1970, 98 min, Italy, Dario Argento) Italian maestro of the macabre Argento's directorial debut, *Bird* is a stylish murder mystery starring Tony Musante as an American author who, after witnessing an attempted homicide, becomes obsessed with solving the case himself. A string of murders are linked to this latest crime, so Musante becomes a valuable asset to a major investigation. With the blessing of the local police captain, he tries to reconstruct what he witnessed, unearthing from his memory some missing pieces of information which leads him to suspect that the crime was not exactly what it seemed to be on the surface. The killer soon targets Musante and the writer comes to find himself to be both hunter and hunted. This film has all the trademarks of later Argento films: the bizarre and violent set-piece murders; the red herrings; the unusual camera angles and setups; and the inquisitive outsider who holds the key to solving the mystery. One important difference, however, is Argento's use of an atmospheric Ennio

Morricone score instead of his later reliance upon loud, pounding synth-rock soundtracks. An impressive beginning to a career which has gotten even better, *Bird* is a good introduction to a distinctive, European style of horror filmmaking. ★★★

The Birdcage

(1996, 100 min, US, Mike Nichols) An often hilariously funny and successfully Americanized, upliftingly pro-gay remake of the French farce *La Cage aux Folles*. The setting is Miami Beach's hip South Beach where Armand Goldman (Robin Williams) runs an extravagant drag revue called The Birdcage. His longtime lover Albert (Nathan Lane) is the star attraction, billed as Starina. The two men live in an uninhibited, gloriously tacky apartment tended by Agador (a very funny Hank Azaria), their Guatemalan houseboy (think Lucy on steroids). The story remains the same: Armand's son wants to bring his fiancée and her right-wing parents over to meet the family, forcing the men to put on a "family values" show for the unsuspecting future in-laws. Gene Hackman and Dianne Wiest wonderfully underplay their roles as an arch-conservative U.S. Senator and his doting wife. As Armand, Williams is subtly fey and delivers the film's best lines, and Lane steals the show as the theatrically swishy diva "mom" with an ear-piercing squeal. Possibly too contemporary (will its *au courant* political jokes work in a few years?), the comedy is meant to be "non-offensive" to all, as the most intimate the lovers get is holding hands. ★★★ $19.99

Birdman of Alcatraz

(1962, 143 min, US, John Frankenheimer) Giving one of his most memorable performances, Burt Lancaster beautifully assumes the real-life role of Robert "Robby" Stroud, a hard-as-nails, world-hating convict sentenced to life who becomes an authority on birds during his incarceration. Though mainly set in Stroud's prison cell, the film is devoid of claustrophobia and is compelling throughout. Also starring Karl Malden, Thelma Ritter and Oscar-nominee Telly Savalas. Deftly directed by Frankenheimer. ★★★½ $19.99

The Birds

(1963, 120 min, US, Alfred Hitchcock) After his great success with *Psycho*, Hitchcock further pushed the boundaries of suspense and his own cinematic techniques with this harrowing nature-gone-awry tale. Tippi Hedren made her film debut as a carefree socialite whose initiation of a practical joke leads her to the small coastal town of Bodega Bay. Rod Taylor is the stoic object of her prank. But nature soon has a joke of its own when our fine feathered friends begin attacking the townspeople with no apparent motive. Hitchcock takes his time in building the tension – which by film's end is overwhelming – with a series of spectacularly staged attacks (and all this without benefit of a musical score which is so important in creating suspense). The birthday party, the classroom scene and the finale have all assumed legendary status in both the horror genre and the director's body of work. Suzanne Pleshette, a young Veronica Cartwright and Jessica Tandy also star. ★★★★ $14.99

Birdy

(1984, 120 min, US, Alan Parker) Parker's adventurous adaptation of the William Wharton best-seller poses a young man's erotic avian obsession as a logical option in a bird-brained world. Filmed largely in Philadelphia, *Birdy* features Matthew Modine as the pigeon fancier who goes to seed after a wartime trauma; Nicolas Cage is his buddy, trying desperately to help his friend. ★★★½ $19.99

Birgitt Haas Must Be Killed

(1981, 105 min, France, Laurent Heynemann) A former left-wing terrorist (Lisa Kreuzer) is targeted to be assassinated and it is an unscrupulous police officer (Philippe Noiret) who plots a romantic fling as bait to snare her. An engrossing and complex police thriller. (Dubbed) ★★★

Birth of a Nation

(1915, 159 min, US, D.W. Griffith) Griffith was a Hollywood pioneer and his *Birth of a Nation* was Hollywood's first epic. Hailed for its groundbreaking technical advances and mounted on an unprecedented scale, this rousing saga of two families thrown into turmoil by the Civil War features an early performance by the legendary Lillian Gish. Although marred by undeniable racist sentiments (the Ku Klux Klan are depicted as the heroes!), it remains a landmark, a movie by which all others would be measured for many years. ★★★★ $39.99

The Bishop's Wife

(1947, 109 min, US, Henry Koster) An enchanted comedy with an unusually reserved Cary Grant as an angel and David Niven as an overwhelmed bishop in need of some heavenly assistance. When raising money for a new church becomes too taxing for the young clergyman, emissary Grant is sent to Earth to help; but instead is caught in the middle of a romantic triangle when bishop's wife Loretta Young becomes enamored with the handsome spirit. Supporting cast includes Monty Woolley, Gladys Cooper and Elsa Lanchester. (Remade in 1996 as *The Preacher's Wife*) ★★★½ $19.99

Bite the Bullet

(1975, 131 min, US, Richard Brooks) A grand, epic-sized comic western with Gene Hackman and James Coburn in good form (when is Hackman *not* in good form?) as contestants in a 600-mile horse race, set during the turn-of-the-century. Also with Candice Bergen, Ben Johnson, Jan-Michael Vincent and Ian Bannen. ★★★ $9.99

Bitter Moon

(1993, 135 min, France/GB, Roman Polanski) This trashy but bizarrely entertaining psychosexual drama (comedy?) is about a humorously uptight British couple (Hugh Grant and Kristen Scott-Thomas) who meet up with the wheelchair-bound American expatriate Oscar (Peter Coyote) and his voluptuously sexy wife Mimi (Emmanuelle Seigner) on a Mediterranean cruise. Much to his frustration, Grant's Nigel becomes transfixed with Oscar's near pornographic accounts of his and Mimi's tumultuous relationship – one that includes obsessive love, excessive sex, playful sadomasochism, water sports, betrayal, bitter hatred and sick revenge (it's a long cruise). The fun really begins when it's time for the obligatory sexual games and swapping. ★★ $19.99

The Bitter Tears of Petra Von Kant

(1972, 124 min, West Germany, Rainer Werner Fassbinder) A lurid and stylized account of the mangled web of domination, sadomasochism and jealousy among three lesbians. One of Fassbinder's most controversial (and entertaining) works, the film takes place in a single setting — fashion designer Petra's (Margit Carstensen) opulently appointed apartment — amid the music of Verdi and The Platters. The story focuses on the increasingly destructive power games between the mistress of the house and the object of her passion, the model Karin (Hanna Schygulla). Petra's maid also becomes involved in the mental mind games, which are played out to the hilt. (German with English subtitles) ★★★ $29.99

Bizarre, Bizarre

(1937, 109 min, France, Marcel Carné) Carné and Jacques Prévert fashioned this exuberant farce/burlesque/mystery with an all-French staff playing a group of Victorian Englishmen, enmeshed in a web of disguises, lies, murder and romance. An acute, humorous examination of how the French thought of their channel-mates, the British. (French with English subtitles) ★★★ $29.99

Bizarre Rituals: Dances Sacred and Profane

(1987, 83 min, US, Mark & Dan Jury) Far from being a seamy exploitation flick, this fascinating documentary is likely to alter the way you view such taboo behavior as sadomasochistic sex. The film focuses on the research of anthropologist Charles Gatewood, who explores alternative cultures within our society from bondage clubs to the rituals of modern primitives like Fakir Musafar. Startling not just for its unique footage, but also for the enlightening interviews and analysis it provides. ★★★

Bizarre Rituals II: Voodoo in Haiti

(1989, 50 min, US, Andrea Leland & Bob Richards) This unworthy follow-up to *Dances Sacred and Profane* documents Haitian voodoo ceremonies but, whereas the original delved into its subject thoroughly, this one barely manages to skim the surface. ★½

Black Adder

(GB) British comedian Rowan Atkinson headlines this side-splitting BBC comedy show that was produced as four separate series. The first, "The Black Adder I," is set in the darkest days of the Dark Ages and finds Atkinson as Prince Edmund, a weasly little Richard III-type coniver who's always looking for an angle to be next in line for daddy's (a hilariously over-the-top Brian Blessed) throne. "The Black Adder II" jumps forward to a quasi-Elizabethan era with Atkinson's character upgraded to Lord Edmund Blackadder. Also starring in the series are Miranda Richardson and Stephen Fry. "The Blackadder III" makes yet another historical leap to the court of King George III (yes, the one who went loony!) and Edmund now playing butler to the dim-witted Prince of

Wales (Hugh Laurie). The final installment brings the proceedings into the 20th century with Capt. Edmund Blackadder creating hilarious disorder on the battlefields of WWI. ★★★★ $14.99 each

The Black Adder I: Part One (1986, 100 min, Martin Shardlow): Peter Cook appears as the ghost of Richard III in "The Foretelling," which introduces the hapless Prince Blackadder; A visiting Scotsman thinks he's "Born to Be King"; Edmund is next in line to be "The Archbishop."

The Black Adder I: Part Two (1986, 96 min, Martin Shardlow): Edmund pursues an eligible princess (Miriam Margolyes) in "The Queen of Spain's Red Beard"; The "Witchsmeller Pursuivant" tries to expell a curse of the king; Rik Mayall guest stars in "The Black Seal," in which Edmund plots to dethrone the king.

Black Adder II: Parte the Firste (1986, 88 min, Mandie Fletcher): "Bells" introduces the great, great grandson of Edmund Blackadder, Edmund; Edmund has been appointed Minister of Religious Genocide and Lord High Executioner and promptly cuts off the "Head" of Lord Farrow; In "Potato," Edmund sets on a quest for new potatoes.

Black Adder II: Parte the Seconde (1986, 89 min, Mandie Fletcher): Edmund tangles with a Bishop in "Money"; In "Beer," a puritanical aunt sends the Blackadder household into a frenzy; Edmund is in "Chains" thanks to a crazed Spanish interrogator.

Black Adder III: Part 1 (1989, 89 min, Mandie Fletcher): Wily servant Blackadder tries to save his master from bankruptcy in "Dish and Dishonesty"; In "Ink and Incapability," a writer tries to get Prince George to approve a new dictionary; Black Adder is imprisoned in "Nob and Nobility."

Black Adder III: Part 2 (1989, 89 min, Mandie Fletcher): Prince George hires two actors to help him rehearse a speech in "Sense and Senility"; In "Amy and Amiability," the Prince is dead broke and looking for a rich wife; The Prince of Wales and the Duke of Wellington duel it out in "Duel and Duality."

Black Adder Goes Forth: Part I (1989, 89 min, Richard Boden): Captain Blackadder is introduced in "Captain Cook"; Cannibalism and war plans are featured in "Corporal Punishmnet"; Baldrick becomes a "Major Star" after a Chaplin impersonation.

Black Adder Goes Forth: Part II (1989, 89 min, Richard Boden): Rik Mayall guest stars in "Private Plane" as Blackadder is trapped between the Germans and a firing squad; Miranda Richardson guest stars as a nurse in "General Hospital"; Blackadder bids "Goodbyee" in the final episode.

Black Adder's A Christmas Carol (1991, 43 min, Richard Boden): Dickens' classic is given the Black Adder treatment as Robbie Coltrane, Miranda Richardson, Hugh Laurie, Stephen Fry, Miriam Margolyes and Jim Broadbent co-star.

Black and White in Color

(1976, 90 min, Ivory Coast, Jean-Jacques Annaud) This powerful Academy Award

Winner (Best Foreign Film) explores the horror and absurdity of war as French and German factions conflict in colonial West Africa before the first World War. (French with English subtitles) $39.99

Black Beauty

(1994, 87 min, GB, Caroline Thompson) While the equestrian acting is outstanding, the re-creation of 19th-century England is flawless and the story line is loyal to Anna Sewell's classic book, the trials and tribulations of Black Beauty will be a bit much for most small children. The retelling of what must be one of the first animal rights stories is moving and absorbing, and the horses are unbelievably human in their responses. Adapted and directed by Thompson (who wrote *Edward Scissorhands* and *The Secret Garden*), starring Sean Bean and David Thewlis and with music by Danny Elfman, this is an excellent, if somber family film. ★★★ $14.99

The Black Bird

(1975, 98 min, US, David Giler) This spoof of *The Maltese Falcon* has George Segal as Sam Spade, Jr. in search of the famous statue, once again. Though Elisha Cook, Jr. and Lee Patrick repeat their roles from John Huston's classic, this is minimally entertaining. ★★ $9.99

The Black Cat

(1934, 66 min, US, Edgar G. Ulmer) Boris Karloff and Bela Lugosi star as archenemies who use a young couple as pawns in a sinister game of chess in this atmospheric and striking suspense classic. Karloff plays a fascistic officer whose war crimes haunt Lugosi, a kind-hearted doctor. One stormy night, Lugosi travels to Karloff's ultramodern home in the wilderness, built on the tombs of the war dead, to have his final reckoning with the evil man. A road accident brings into the game a young engaged couple, who realize too late what is unfolding in their overnight home. *The Black Cat* was made shortly after Lugosi and Karloff made *Dracula* and *Frankenstein*, respectively, and it gives both actors ample opportunity to show off their talents at playing something other than monsters. Karloff is reserved and menacing as the almost-robotic host, while Lugosi begins the film as a trusted friend only to have his madness erupt as the game wears on. With its heavily shadowed "nouveau" sets (as opposed to the castle walls one might expect in such a film) and its wonderful, emotional musical score, *The Black Cat* is one of the best Universal horror films of the 1930s and a landmark in the careers of both its stars. ★★★½ $14.99

Black Christmas

(1975, 98 min, Canada, Bob Clark) A truly mean-spirited holiday psycho/slasher flick with a sorority house setting, obscene phone calls, plastic dry cleaning bags (didn't anyone read the warning label? This is not a toy!) and a fine cast including Margot Kidder, Olivia Hussey and Andrea Martin. Director Clark would go on to direct *Porky's*. (aka: *Silent Night, Evil Night*) ★★ $14.99

Black God & White Devil

(1964, 102 min, Brazil, Glauber Rocha) Set in arid northeast Brazil, Rocha's first major film deals with Manuel, a worker who, after killing his boss in self-defense, finds himself on the run from the law. Enlightened to the horrendous conditions of the peasants by the rich landowners, he becomes a bandit of honor, a self-styled black saint, preaching bloodshed and the return of the land to the people. A violent yet lyrical political drama that utilizes an intoxicating mixture of social realism, symbolism, myths and references to Brazilian history and culture. (Portuguese with English subtitles) ★★★½ $59.99

The Black Hole

(1979, 97 min, US, Gary Nelson) Disney's nod to *Star Wars* is a cheesy sci-fi adventure about a space expedition which comes in conflict with a "mad" scientist about to explore a black hole. Nice special effects and a fine score by John Barry. With Maximilian Schell, Anthony Perkins and Yvette Mimieux. ★★½

Black Like Me

(1964, 107 min, US, Carl Lerner) In the late 1950s, a white journalist took drugs which darkened his skin color enough to allow him to "pass" for black. Based on his book, this is an emotional, well-produced and empathic adaptation recounting his experiences with racial prejudice. James Whitmore, who stars as the reporter, used the same drugs in preparation for the role. The story is not as dated as it should be. ★★★ $19.99

Black Lizard

(1968, 86 min, Japan, Kinji Fukasaku) Mix elements of *What's Up, Tiger Lily?* with *Beyond the Valley of the Dolls*, throw in lurid color schemes and weird camera angles by a seemingly drug-imbued cinematographer and you'll have some idea of the make-up of this wildly campy detective yarn. Japan's most famous female impersonator, Akihiri Maruyama, stars as the villainous jewel thief, The Black Lizard — a fatally seductive temptress who'll stop at nothing to get her dainty hands on the fabulous Star of Egypt diamond. Yukio Mishima, who adapted the original novel for the stage, is featured in this entertaining curiosity as a naked human statue in the glamorous chanteuse's demented private museum. She's so evil! Letterboxed format. (Japanese with English subtitles) ★★★ $79.99

Black Magic M-66

(1987, 48 min, Japan, Masamune Shirow) Cross *The Terminator* with *Blade Runner*, add a hint of comedy, and you have the basic plot for this superb anime OAV (original animated video) from master *magna* artist Shirow (*Appleseed, Dominion Tank Police*). Based on a story from Shirow's comic book, this animated science-fiction thriller follows the exploits of Sybel, a video journalist investigating a failed military experiment involving android assassins. When she finds herself one step ahead of the government task force tracking down the rogue androids, Sybel goes from covering the story to becoming a player in the all-too-real drama. Shirow blends edge-of-your-seat action sequences, comedy, suspense and unforget-

table characters into 48 minutes of sheer anime excitement. The climactic confrontation with the remaining android on a rapidly collapsing skyscraper is a must-see for all anime fans. (Japanese with English subtitles) ★★★½ $34.99

Black Magic Woman

(1990, 91 min, US, Deryn Warren) Mark Hamill, Amanda Wyss and Apollonia form the corners of the tedious triangle at the center of this unnecessary rehash of *Fatal Attraction*. Hamill and Wyss are business partners and lovers whose relationship takes a turn for the worse when voodoo vixen Apollonia enters the picture. A few good chills (and Santana's theme tune) can't elevate this above the made-for-cable level. ★½ $89.99

Black Moon Rising

(1986, 100 min, US, Harley Cokliss) A government agent hides secret information in a high-powered auto. When the car is stolen, he must battle not only the gang that stole the auto, but the hoodlums who are out to get the info back. Tommy Lee Jones, Linda Hamilton and Robert Vaughn star in this vigorous, better-than-average action-adventure. ★★★ $14.99

Black Narcissus

(1946, 99 min, GB, Michael Powell & Emeric Pressburger) This visually sumptuous tale of a group of nuns who establish a mission in a remote Himalayan outpost was once considered one of the most breathtaking color films ever made. Deborah Kerr and Jean Simmons star in this dramatically charged saga of physical and emotional turmoil. ★★★★ $14.99

The Black Orchid

(1959, 96 min, US, Martin Ritt) The ever-glamorous Sophia Loren "dresses down" in this high-strung melodrama from the director of *Hud* and *Norma Rae*, about a lonely businessman (Anthony Quinn) whose courtship of a gangster's widow meets with resistance from his mentally unbalanced daughter. A minor league film from a major league director. ★½ $14.99

Black Orpheus

(1958, 98 min, Brazil, Marcel Camus) This extravagant explosion of colorful sights and sounds is a modern reenactment of Orpheus and Eurydice's tragic tale set against the splendid backdrop of Carnival in Rio. Virtually non-stop visual and musical excitement. Winner of the Academy Award for Best Foreign Film. (Portuguese with English subtitles) ★★★★ $29.99

Black Rain

(1989, 120 min, US, Ridley Scott) Scott's overblown, relentlessly grim and humorless police thriller set in modern-day Tokyo is a routine action film under the guise of an examination of a Japanese and American culture clash in police techniques. Michael Douglas stars as a tough, world-weary cop (is there any other kind?) who is assigned with partner Andy Garcia to escort a New York-based hit man for the Japanese mob back to Japan. When the assassin escapes, Douglas tears apart the city of Tokyo looking for him,

coming into conflict with the local police force and the mob; not to mention expatriate hostess Kate Capshaw. ★½ $14.99

Black Rain

(1990, 123 min, Japan, Shohei Imamura) August 6, 1945 — a date that has long been etched into the Japanese psyche, for this is when the atomic bomb was dropped on Hiroshima. Having suppressed the consequences of this national tragedy, director Imamura has, in a grimly realistic, unrelenting fashion, exposed the national wounds by dealing with both the actual bombing of the city and its terrible aftereffects. In a determinedly non-sentimental and almost documentary approach, this haunting drama follows one family who were near Hiroshima at the time of the explosion. The family — grandmother, husband, wife and daughter — attempt to rebuild their shattered lives. But within five years all grow terribly ill due to radiation. A powerful and chilling film that explores not only the ignorance, fear, frustrations and pain inflicted by radiation but the national shame caused by the people who viewed its victims with suspicion and as outcasts. A stunningly photographed modern masterpiece. (Japanese with English subtitles) ★★★★ $19.99

Black Rainbow

(1991, 103 min, US, Dick Hodges) Rosanna Arquette stars as a carnival clairvoyant whose questionable abilities take a suddenly strange turn when she begins receiving psychic transmissions from people who aren't dead — yet. Jason Robards co-stars as her cynical, alchoholic father, and Tom Hulce plays a hounding reporter who's hot for her story. A well-crafted and engaging thriller from the director of *A Prayer for the Dying*. ★★★ $9.99

Black Robe

(1991, 100 min, Canada, Bruce Beresford) Beresford's impassioned examination of the cruelty and oppression intentionally and unintentionally imposed by the European settlers as they brought their "civilization" and Christian beliefs to the native peoples of the New World. While the story breaks little new ground, *Black Robe* is saved from familiarity by its strikingly beautiful Canadian landscapes and its absorbing and emotional drama of faith and the will to survive. Lothaire Bluteau (*Jesus of Montreal*) plays a 17th-century French Jesuit missionary whose religious zeal compels him to risk martyrdom in order to bring Catholicism to the Hurons of Canada. Along with a native chief, his daughter and a young French settler, he embarks on a harrowing journey up the St. Lawrence River — a symbolic canoe ride that begins in an explosively colorful autumn and ends during a torturously inhospitable winter. This striking epic bears a resemblance, but is superior in many ways, to *Dances with Wolves*. ★★★½ $14.99

The Black Room

(1935, 67 min, US, Roy William Neill) Boris Karloff has a field day in this Gothic tale of twin brothers (one good, one evil, both Karloff) whose destinies are overshadowed by a family curse. ★★½ $9.99

Black Shadows on a Silver Screen: The Black Film Industry from 1915-1950

(1986, 52 min, US) Ossie Davis narrates this exhaustive and eye-opening documentary about the contributions to the cinema made by Afro-Americans. Includes rare film clips and performances from Paul Robeson, Cab Calloway, Duke Ellington and many others. ★★★ $19.99

Black Sheep

(1996, 87 min, US, Penelope Spheeris) After the spirited hijinks of their funny *Tommy Boy*, Chris Farley and David Spade – the Laurel and Hardy for the '90s – regurgitate the same plot but with considerably less successful results. Once again, Farley is a screw-up who must be baby-sitted by sarcastic little twit Spade. Unfortunately, Farley is less likable, Spade is not so sarcastic, and most of their routines aren't that funny. The plot has to do with big brother Tim Matheson running for governor; Farley is his younger sibling who's "Roger Clinton, Billy Carter and every Reagan family member rolled into one." If only he were that interesting. Director Spheeris tries to infuse some life to a tired screenplay, but she's as sabotaged as Matheson's campaign. The only few laughs that do occur are courtesy of Farley and Spade's mugging. ★★ $14.99

The Black Stallion

(1979, 118 min, US, Carroll Ballard) A heart-warming tale of a young boy and his devoted stallion as they share both adventures on an isolated island and a quest for a racing championship. There's ravishing cinematography, with an Oscar-nominated performance by Mickey Rooney as a seasoned horse trainer. ★★★½ $14.99

The Black Stallion Returns

(1983, 105 min, US, Robert Dalva) Adequate sequel to the 1979 family favorite. Kelly Reno is back as Alec, who finds himself in the exotic Sahara in hot pursuit of his beloved horse Black, who's been kidnapped by his original owner – desert chieftain Abu Ben Ishak (Ferdinand Mayne). Teri Garr, Vincent

Spano, Allen Goorwitz and Woody Strode also star. Produced by Francis Ford Coppola. ★★½ $14.99

Black Sunday

(1961, 83 min, Italy, Mario Bava) This horror classic is Bava's masterpiece. Barbara Steele stars as a condemned witch who rises from the dead to seek vengeance on the descendents of those who executed her. This Gothic tale is full of atmosphere and chilling black-and-white cinematography. As with most Italian horror films, the plot is weak and sometimes silly, but the visuals are lush and creepy. A must-see for Argento fans and classic horror buffs. ★★★½ $29.99

Black Sunday

(1977, 143 min, US, John Frankenheimer) From the director of *The Manchurian Candidate* comes this gripping adaptation of the Thomas Harris best-seller about a terrorist plot to blow up the Super Bowl, with a little bit of help from a demented ex-POW (Bruce Dern at his maniacal best). Robert Shaw is the government expert on the case. Also starring Marthe Keller and Fritz Weaver. ★★★ $14.99

Black Tights

(1960, 120 min, France, Terence Young) Exquisite ballet film featuring four classic ballet performnces. With Cyd Charisse, Moira Shearer, Zizi Jeanmarie, Dick Sanders and Roland Petit. ★★★ $49.99

Black Water

(1992, 105 min, US, Nicolas Gessner) Julian Sands is an uptight British tax attorney and Stacy Dash is the street urchin/femme fatale he plucks off the highway in this unimaginative thriller set in the Tennessee hills. After witnessing what he thinks is a murder, Sands finds he is being tailed on his way to an innocent fishing trip. The not-so-innocent Dash offers him help, but is she playing both sides of the fence? Who knows, and more importantly, who cares? ★ $92.99

Black Widow

(1987, 101 min, US, Bob Rafelson) Debra Winger and Theresa Russell square off in this

spine-tingling suspense story. Russell is a jet-setting sophisticate whose husbands have a habit of dying shortly after their wedding day. Winger is the FBI agent who catches on to Russell's shenanigans and sets out to uncover her deadly scheme. Instead, the two become locked in a heated tête-à-tête (or more appropriately *coeur-a-coeur*) which sizzles with underlying sexual tension. ★★★ $9.99

Blackbeard's Ghost

(1968, 107 min, US, Robert Stevenson) Fluffy Disney comedy with Peter Ustinov as the ghost of the infamous pirate Blackbeard who helps Dean Jones, Suzanne Pleshette and Elsa Lanchester fight off the bad guys. ★★½

The Blackboard Jungle

(1955, 101 min, US, Richard Brooks) Glenn Ford stars in this harrowing adaptation of Evan Hunter's novel about a New York teacher who is schooled in the ways of the streets by his students. In comparison to the Uzi-toting, crack addicted youth of today's Hollywood high schools, these mid-'50s punks seem relatively harmless. But the drama here is tense and excellent performances are registered by Sidney Poitier and Vic Morrow. ★★★½ $19.99

Blackmail

(1929, 78 min, GB, Alfred Hitchcock) In his first talkie (which initially started as a silent), Hitchcock demonstrates some of the cunning cinematic trickery which he would later define and master. Starting unusually slow for a Hitchcock film, the story picks up considerable speed once the plot is in motion. It has to do with a flirtatious shopgirl who murders her attempted rapist and is blackmailed by a sleazy eyewitness. Though awkwardly paced, the film nevertheless maintains suspense throughout, and contains several scenes which could only be described as pure Hitchcock. This includes a terrific sequence in which the girl only hears snippets of conversation: the word "knife" over and over. ★★★ $12.99

Blade Runner

(1982, 114 min, US, Ridley Scott) Harrison Ford stars in this jagged, futuristic thriller as an authorized exterminator of androids gone awry. Rutger Hauer and Daryl Hannah star as a pair of renegade robots whose physical prowess forces Ford out of the role of hunter and into the role of hunted. Scott's space-age L.A. is a smoky, neon-drenched landscape seething with danger and decay. A stunning film adaptation of Philip K. Dick's "Do Androids Dream of Electric Sheep?" (The director's cut presented in letterboxed format) ★★★★ $19.99

Blame It on Rio

(1984, 100 min, US, Stanley Donen) This Americanized version of the French sex farce *One Wild Moment* is a surprisingly entertaining, albeit TV sitcomish, comedy about the sexual philandering between a group of friends and their ensuing bed-hopping, all under the seductive rays of Rio de Janeiro. Michael Caine is the befuddled husband who becomes the object of desire of the nymphette daughter of his best friend, Joseph Bologna. Caine valiantly attempts to hold off her advances,

Harrison Ford stalks renegade androids through the streets of a futuristic L.A. in *Blade Runner*

B

and when that fails, his efforts to keep the affair from his friend is one of the film's high points. ★★½

Blame It on the Bellboy

(1992, 78 min, GB, Mark Herman) A bumbling bellboy mixes the schedules of three travelers and serves up a comedy of errors. Dudley Moore, Bryan Brown and Richard Griffiths are three visitors to Venice, and they are all staying at the same hotel. It is there that bellboy Bronson Pinchot sends each man on one of the other's business. This includes assassinating a crime boss, buying a villa, and escaping for a "pleasure" weekend. Though this comedy never hits the inspired heights of another 1992 farce, *Noises Off*, there are a few (if silly) laughs awaiting the patient viewer. ★★ $9.99

Blank Check

(1994, 90 min, US, Rupert Wainwright) This *Home Alone* clone from Disney tries to do the Macaulay Culkin hit one better: What if he's home alone — but he has a million dollars at his disposal? Such is the case when misunderstood Preston (Brian Bonsall) has his bike run over and is given a blank check by the bad guy (Miguel Ferrer) who did it. Preston buys a neat home down the street and lives every kid's ultimate fantasy life — until the bad-guy and his associates come looking for him. Even with a little morality lesson thrown in, pre-adolescents may enjoy Preston's carefree, adult-bashing antics. The film, however, is processed junk food. ★★ $9.99

Blankman

(1994, 96 min, US, Mike Binder) *Blankman* is a charming comic satire featuring "In Living Color"'s Damon Wayans and David Alan Grier as a pair of vigilantes. With more than a few nods to the 1960s TV series "Batman," this mindlessly entertaining film follows the pair's wild adventures fighting evil while clad in bulletproof underwear and Grandma's housecoat. Spiced with crazy comic book action and fun supporting performances by "Seinfeld"'s Jason Alexander and Robin Givens, this outrageous laff-fest is sure to please those who like their comedy with a superhuman dose of satire. ★★★ $19.99

Blast 'Em

(1992, 103 min, US, Joseph Blasioli) This is a highly entertaining documentary about the competition among the paparazzi which focuses on acid-tongued imp Victor Malafronte, who pursues his celebrity prey with the precision of a trained assassin. Follow Malafronte and other photographers' exploits, including the pathetic Twinkie-addicted Queerdonna, as they stalk several stars, such as Robert De Niro, Sigourney Weaver, Michael J. Fox, John F. Kennedy, Jr. and a very funny and revealing Sally Kirkland. A must-see for star gazers everywhere. ★★★ $89.99

Blaze

(1989, 108 min, US, Ron Shelton) Shelton, who authored the terrific *Bull Durham*, makes a rousing directorial debut in this sexy and funny story based on Blaze Starr's autobiographical novel about the famous stripper's "scandalous" affair with Louisiana

Governor Earl Long. The film tells the entertaining story of how country girl Blaze moved to the big city (New Orleans) and became mistress to the powerful "Guv'nor" Long. Shelton has a keen ear for romantic repartee, and *Blaze* is at its glorious best in these scenes between Long and Starr. Paul Newman gives a full-blooded, larger-than-life characterization as Long and newcomer Lolita Davidovich is well-cast physically but lacks the spark to set her rising Starr apart from other film ecdysiasts. ★★★ $9.99

Blazing Saddles

(1974, 93 min, US, Mel Brooks) Brooks' uproarious comedy did wonders for making racism, sexism and bodily functions laughing matters. Richard Pryor helped script this scathing spoof of the Wild West. Gene Wilder, Cleavon Little, Madeline Kahn and Harvey Korman are just some of the comic lunatics on hand. ★★★½ $14.99

Bleak House

(1987, 391 min, GB, Ross Devenish) Charles Dickens' scathing look at the Byzantine judicial process of 19th-century England is brought to the small screen with the usual aplomb associated with BBC television. Diana Rigg and Denholm Elliott deliver fine performances in this classic tale which follows the plight of the Jarndyce family, whose legal problems have been dragged through the courts for generations and devastated the lives of many. For lovers of English drama, the running time of more than six hours shouldn't be a hindrance. ★★★★ $39.99

Blessed Event

(1932, 78 min, US, Roy Del Ruth) Lee Tracy (who created the Hildy Johnson role for the original Broadway show "The Front Page") stars as Alvin Roberts, a very ambitious Broadway gossip columnist who makes a name for himself through his scandal-mongering. Unfortunately, he makes a lot of enemies along the way. Fast-paced dialogue highlights this Depression-era film dealing with moral and ethical dilemmas. ★★½ $19.99

Blind Date

(1987, 93 min, US, Blake Edwards) Though not top-notch Edwards, there are enough laughs to keep one mildly entertained. Bruce Willis is the exec who desperately needs a date for a business dinner; Kim Basinger is the answer to his prayers — or is she? It seems once she drinks, she's uncontrollably manic, sort of like this comedy. ★★½ $11.99

Blind Fury

(1990, 85 min, US, Phillip Noyce) Australian director Noyce (*Dead Calm*) has liberally culled ideas from the "Zatoichi" Japanese swordsman film series and added fine comic action-adventure footage. The incomparable Rutger Hauer stars as a Vietnam vet who, after being blinded in the jungle, is befriended by local villagers and taught the sacred art of swinging the sword. Back in the U.S., our blind, blond samurai hero battles the bad guys at every turn. With its tongue-in-cheek humor, fast-paced fight sequences and the mesmerizing

screen presence of Hauer, this is a film any action fan should not miss. ★★★ $14.99

Blind Side

(1992, 90 min, US, Geoff Murphy) Rebecca DeMornay and Ron Silver star as a couple on a business trip to Mexico who accidentally kill a policeman and then are tormented upon their return home by a menacing Rutger Hauer. This film may sound good on paper, but it doesn't play well on the screen. DeMornay and Silver consistently overact and Hauer, here a cross between Marlon Brando and Mr. Rogers, provides excellent comic relief. If you have a couple of friends who enjoy laughing at bad movies, this is the one to watch. ★ $14.99

Blind Trust (Pouvoir Intime)

(1987, 86 min, Canada, Yves Simoneau) This riveting suspense thriller chronicles the planning, execution and bloody aftermath of a failed armed robbery attempt in Montreal. Successfully balancing its sympathy for both the criminals as well as a guard held captive in the armored truck, this taut crime caper should keep the viewer enthralled throughout. A small interesting note is that the guard who decides to fight back is gay. (French with English subtitles) ★★★½

Blink

(1994, 106 min, US, Michael Apted) Madeleine Stowe gives a revelatory performance as a gutsy but vulnerable folk musician, blind since childhood, who regains her vision just in time to witness a murderer fleeing the scene of the crime. Aidan Quinn is the hardboiled detective who, not blind to her considerable charms, sets out to find the killer before he finds her. Under the direction of Apted, what might have been just another *Wait Until Dark* rip-off is redeemed through its excellent use of visual effects and an attention to detail and character usually missing in the thriller genre. Granted, the mystery's resolution is a little slapdash with its "watch me pull a killer out of my hat" routine, but nevertheless *Blink* is a refreshingly eye-opening chiller. ★★★ $9.99

Bliss

(1985, 112 min, Australia, Ray Lawrence) This outrageous and daring film stars Barry Otto as Harry Joy, a wistful Sydney advertising man whose near-fatal (or was it fatal?) heart attack launches him into a surrealistic, mind-expanding and satirical adventure. A nightmarish examination of life, death and the eternal search for happiness. ★★★½ $9.99

The Bliss of Mrs. Blossom

(1968, 93 min, GB, Joe McGrath) Here's a fun-filled piece of '60s oddball British kitsch. Shirley MacLaine stars as the wife of a brassiere manufacturer (Richard Attenborough) who keeps a man in her attic for five years! While perhaps not on the level of other British comedies of the era (*The Magic Christian, Bedazzled*), it's still an interesting period piece with a lot of funny moments. Look for miniscule appearances by John Cleese and Barry Humphries. ★★★ $14.99

The Blob

(1958, 80 min, US, Irvin S. Yeaworth) This '50s sci-fi minor classic is a camp favorite. A very young Steve McQueen stars as a teenager who tries to warn everyone in his small town that an intergalactic goo is on a path of destruction. Foolish adults – they never listen! (Remade in 1988) ★★½

The Blob

(1988, 92 min, US, Chuck Russell) Entertaining and imaginative remake of the Steve McQueen cult classic – owing more to John Carpenter's *The Thing* than to the '50s original. A gelatinous goo falls from the sky to wreak havoc on an unsuspecting small town, gobbling all in its path. Kevin Dillon and Shawnee Smith are two teenagers out to stop the plasmic menace. ★★★ $14.99

Blonde in Black Leather

(1966, 88 min, Italy, Carlo DiPalma) This entertaining and "far out" adventure film stars Claudia Cardinale as a bored housewife who is taken on a series of hilarious escapades by the leather-clad, motorcycle-driving Monica Vitti. Not to be confused with *L'Avventura*! (Dubbed) ★★

Blonde Venus

(1932, 97 min, US, Josef von Sternberg) The ever radiant Marlene Dietrich is nothing less than stunning as a woman who leaves her husband when she becomes convinced that she is no good for him. The true highlight of the film comes when Dietrich sings "Hot Voodoo" in a gorilla suit. The film also stars a very young Cary Grant and Herbert Marshall. ★★½ $14.99

Blood and Concrete

(1990, 97 min, US, Jeffrey Reiner) Billy Zane delivers a delicious performance in this contemporary film noir about a larcenously hip and dissolute Everyman. When he literally stumbles over a suicidal Jennifer Beals, he finds himself drawn into a convoluted maze of conflicted loyalties amid an amazing assortment of L.A. low-lifes. Deftly directed by Reiner, who co-wrote the nifty script with producer Richard LaBrie, the film pays homage to its roots with acknowledgements to Samuel Fuller, John Boorman, Richard Widmark and Lee Marvin in the closing credits. Darren McGavin and Harry Shearer co-star. Beals' first musical number is a treat. ★★★ $89.99

Blood and Roses

(1961, 74 min, Italy, Roger Vadim) Featuring Mel Ferrer and Elsa Martinelli, this atmospheric and slightly erotic film centers around a young girl's obsession with her family tree, which includes vampires. Based on Sheridan le Fanu's "Carmilla" and later remade as *The Vampire Lovers*. ★★½ $9.99

Blood and Sand

(1922, 80 min, US, Fred Niblo) Matador Rudolph Valentino can't decide between the good girl or the vamp, so he takes it out on the bull. While the acting style in this hyperbolic classic is humorously bug-eyed and stilted when viewed today, this proved to be one of Valentino's most popular films. ★★★ $29.99

Blood & Wine

(1997, 101 min, US, Bob Rafelson) Treacherous waters run deep in this moody

thriller which reunites Jack Nicholson and director Rafelson for a fifth time. Though not completely successful in its storytelling, *Blood & Wine* moves at a fast clip; and its characters are always up to something – part of its noir appeal is figuring what. Nicholson is a Miami wine merchant whose position with the city's wealthier clientel gives him access to their property – which helps when he and slimy associate Michael Caine decide to empty their safes. When Nicholson's wife Judy Davis decides to leave her husband and unknowingly walks off with a stolen necklace, she and son Stephen Dorff become targets of the maniacal Caine with Nicholson stuck in the middle. Rafelson gives the film a good look, and there's a terrific car chase scene, but there's also nothing new to the genre here, and Dorff's romantic involvement and devotion to his stepfather's mistress (Jennifer Lopez) is flimsy at best. ★★½ $102.99

Blood Feast

(1963, 70 min, US, Hershell Gordon Lewis) The first of the "Sue" films from the "master of splatter" Lewis. *Blood Feast* is the gruesome tale of Fuad Ramses, Egyptian caterer and limping psychopath. With notably bad performances from HGL regulars Tom Wood and ex-Playmate Connie Mason. Music, photography and gore-F/X (filmed in "Blood Color") by HGL. ★ $19.99

Blood Feud

(1979, 112 min, Italy, Lina Wertmüller) For the fans of Wertmüller comes this pleasant, although not exceptional, sex comedy about a Sicilian widow in the 1920s (Sophia Loren) who receives the lustful advances of both a lawyer (Marcello Mastroianni) and a shady gangster (Giancarlo Giannini). Not on the same artistic level as *Swept Away...* or *Seven Beauties*, it is still an enjoyable little movie filled with many of the Wertmüller touches. (Dubbed) ★★½

Blood in the Face

(1991, 78 min, US, Anne Bohlen, Kevin Rafferty & James Ridgeway) Directors Bohlen, Rafferty and Ridgeway, with Michael Moore (*Roger and Me*), interview participants at a Nazi rally in Michigan. We enter a world where "Ronald Reagan works for the Jews," the Holocaust is a hoax and only whites have a conscience because they can blush (show blood in the face). Interspersed is footage of George Lincoln Rockwell likening Hitler to the second coming of Christ and (pre-plastic surgery) David Duke in Klan garb and Nazi uniform. Numerological theory and the appearance of Halley's Comet are used to explain the coming racial conflict. It's tempting to chuckle as if this were a right-wing *Reefer Madness*, but pay attention to the soft-spoken housewife. When you find out who her husband is, you won't be laughing. Based on Ridgeway's reportage and his book of the same name. ★★★ $29.99

Blood of a Poet

(1930, 58 min, France, Jean Cocteau) Considered one of the most influential avantgarde films of all-time, *Blood of a Poet* explores the plight of the artist and the forces of cre-

ative thought. Constructed as a collage of dreamlike situations, autobiographical revelations and enigmatic images, the film is an odyssey into the poet's imagination. Freud described the film as being "like looking through a keyhole at a man undressing." (French with English subtitles) ★★★★ $29.99

Blood of Beasts (Le Sang des Bêtes)

(1949, 22 min, France, Georges Franju) This landmark documentary, and first film by Franju, begins by lulling the viewer with scenes of a tranquil Parisian suburb. But tranquility is far from the theme of this film, for the camera soon enters an abattoir and begins to unflinchingly chronicle a day in the life of a slaughterhouse. Disturbing in its methodical violence, we witness the actual slaughtering of cows, sheep, calves and even horses – all done by placid workers who systematically kill, skin and disembowel the animals, and transform their flesh into "meat" – all in an atmosphere of blood, violence and suffering. Not for the faint-of-heart. Please note that the subtitles for this film are quite poor. (French with English subtitles) ★★★ $29.99

The Blood of Heroes

(1990, 97 min, US, David Peoples) Set in a post-apocalyptic future, this intelligent, suspenseful action film stars Rutger Hauer as the leader of sort of a minor league nomadic sports team which travels from village to village to compete against locals in a torturous, savage game called jugging, which is part football, part hockey and part bloodbath. Joan Chen also stars as a woman so adept at the game that she joins the team in hopes of making it to "the majors" – where coveted players enjoy the good life in the confines of an underground city. ★★★ $14.99

The Blood of Others

(1984, 130 min, France/Canada, Claude Chabrol) A great international cast (Jodie Foster, Michael Ontkean, Sam Neill, Stéphane Audran, Lambert Wilson) cannot save this made-for-cable romance ineptly adapted from Simone de Beauvoir's 1946 novel. Set in Paris during the Second World War, the film stars Foster as a fashion designer who falls in love with an imprisoned French resistance fighter. In a successful attempt to get him released, she begins an affair with an influential German commander, only to be accused of collusion by her fellow countrymen. Cut 40 minutes from the original broadcast running time, this misfire from Chabrol is a sadly convoluted and uninvolving mess. (Filmed in English) ★ $79.99

Blood on the Moon

(1948, 88 min, US, Robert Wise) This solid western tale boasts a good cast, including Robert Mitchum, Barbara Bel Geddes and Robert Preston, to tell the story of drifter Mitchum involved in shady goings-on out West. Preston is memorable as the villain. ★★★ $14.99

Blood Relatives

(1977, 107 min, France/Canada, Claude Chabrol) Adapted from an Ed McBain novel, this pedestrian police thriller can not be considered one of Chabrol's best works. The film features Donald Sutherland as a Montreal detective assigned to a particularly savage murder case. A young girl is gruesomely killed in a back alley and the only witness, her 15-year-old cousin, implicates her brother in the case. Told in a straightforward way, Sutherland investigates, attempting to piece together the puzzle of this potentially passion-driven murder. Fans of good murder mysteries can safely pass this one up; for while the film starts off promisingly, it is too one-dimensional and concludes with a decidely anticlimactic denouement. Stéphane Audran, Donald Pleasence and David Hemmings are featured and underutilized in supporting roles. (English language) ★★ $79.99

Blood Simple

(1984, 97 min, US, Joel Coen) This extremely well-crafted first feature from the Coen Brothers pays tribute to classic film noir. The story revolves around a crazy, jealous husband who hires a shady hit man to take out his wife. Although the film was done on a shoestring budget, the Coen Brothers manage to create a technically dazzling film which boasts a gleefully ghoulish sense of humor, dazzling camera acrobatics and a plot with more loops than the L.A. Freeway. Corruption and distrust ooze from every frame of this torrid tale of tangled passions in a dusty Texas town. ★★★★ $14.99

The Blood Spattered Bride (La Novia Ensangrentada)

(1972, 84 min, Spain, Vincente Aranda) Sexy lesbian vampires are on the prowl once again in this erotic, bloody and creepy Spanish production. Horrified by the violence and domination of her husband's sexual advances, a young bride is haunted by visions of knife-wielding beauties and castrated husbands. Her life is "saved" when Carmila, a mysterious and elegant stranger, arrives. Carmila, a centuries-old vampiress, and the innocent bride are immediately attracted to each other and seal their relationship with a memorable kiss filled with blood and sexual ecstasy. Now united, the two lovers plot the death of the bride's hated hubby who "Pierced my flesh to humiliate me. Spat inside me to enslave me." A shocking and violently bloody finale will keep the viewer engrossed as this kinky horror film brings new meaning (and warning) to the problems of marital life. Take that, Mr. Man! Based on Sheridan le Fanu's "Carmilla."(Spanish with English subtitles) ★★½ $59.99

Blood Wedding

(1981, 72 min, Spain, Carlos Saura) The first of three collaborations between director Saura and dancer/choreographer Antonio Gades (the other two are Carmen and El Amor Brujo), this stunning flamenco adaptation of Federico Garcia Lorca's tragic play, "La Boda de Sangre," is an exquisitely realized study of the theatrical process. The camera follows Gades and his cast through the process of putting on makeup, warming up and finally a full-dress run through of Gades' interpretation of the Lorca classic. Saura's camera lovingly examines the rehearsal in precise detail giving the viewer an intimate and exciting peek into this exquisite art form. A must for lovers of theatre, dance, Flamenco or Spanish culture. ★★★½ $24.99

Bloodhounds of Broadway

(1989, 101 min, US, Howard Brookner) An impressive, though rather restrained cast, is the highlight of Brookner's alternately charming and forced comic mystery based on four Damon Runyon short stories. Set on New Year's Eve on Broadway in 1928, the story revolves around a group of gamblers, showgirls and aristocrats whose lives intersect after a local gangster is nearly slain. The colorful cast of characters include Matt Dillon as the worst gambler in New York, Jennifer Grey and Madonna as showgirls, and Randy Quaid (who best captures the spirit of Runyon) as a dimwitted high roller in love with Madonna (that's a twosome!). ★★½

Bloodline

(1979, 116 min, US, Terence Young) Embarrassing screen version of Sidney Sheldon's best-seller with Audrey Hepburn as the heiress to a pharmaceutical company who takes over the business when her father dies under mysterious circumstances. Ben Gazzara, James Mason, Michelle Phillips and Omar Sharif also star. ★ $14.99

Bloodsucking Freaks

(1978, 89 min, US, Joel M. Reed) Universally reviled blood and guts show, with the highpoint (or lowpoint, depending on your tastes) being the scene in which a woman's brain is sucked out with a straw by one of the thirsty lunatics. ★ $19.99

Bloody Mama

(1970, 90 min, US, Roger Corman) Shelley Winters stars as the infamous Ma Barker, the matriarch of mayhem during the Depression. Unlike Bonnie and Clyde, whose characters were remotely sympathetic, this film has criminals who are totally unlikable. The film's primary assets are its players (particularly a very young Robert De Niro as one of her sons, a junkie) and its action scenes. Corman directed this curiosity piece that's not for the squeamish. ★★½

Blossoms in the Dust

(1941, 100 min, US, Mervyn LeRoy) Greer Garson and Walter Pidgeon's first film together is a touching soap opera about a woman who loses her husband and child in an accident, inspiring her to found an orphanage. Features a good performance by Garson. ★★½ $19.99

Blow Out

(1981, 107 min, US, Brian De Palma) De Palma serves up this interesting rehash of Antonioni's Blow-Up. Movie sound engineer John Travolta inadvertently records a car accident that turns out to be no accident. Nancy Allen co-stars as the accident's survivor who knows more than she should. John Lithgow, in a chilling performance, is the psycho on her trail. De Palma makes good use of various Philadelphia locations. ★★★

Blow-Up

(1966, 108 min, Italy/GB, Michelangelo Antonioni) Antonioni's hypnotic and provocative film stars David Hemmings as a fashion photographer in swinging 1960s London who possibly sees a murder within one of his photographs. The film's lasting power lies in the way the images begin to reveal the mystery, all without the use of dialogue or sound. (Filmed in English) ★★★★ $19.99

Blown Away

(1994, 120 min, US, Stephen Hopkins) In contrast to Speed, another 1994 action film about a mad bomber, Blown Away is much more concerned with plot and character, and mixing action with a developed narrative is what gives the film both its slight edge and many weaknesses. The always reliable Jeff Bridges plays a Boston bomb squad specialist who goes one on one with a former IRA bomber, played by the underused Tommy Lee Jones. As Jones targets members of Bridges' force, the race is on to locate and stop the madman from blowing up half the city. For an

Marlene Dietrich in The Blue Angel

action film, there are surprisingly few scenes of carnage and mayhem (after all, this *is* about a psychotic bomber), although there are two sequences which are riveting. ★★½ $19.99

Blue

(1993, 76 min, GB, Derek Jarman) Jarman, who died of AIDS in February 1994, had been battling the disease for six years at the time of making the film. With impaired eyesight and deteriorating health, Jarman created a startling experimental film in which he invites his audience into his sight-deprived world creating a womb-like meditative state by employing a completely blue screen throughout the film. A cast including Tilda Swinton and Nigel Terry reads from Jarman's often poetic journals, recounting the director's medical complexities, thoughts on the loss of loved ones, and reflections on his own life and art. Amazingly devoid of anger and neither sermonizing nor self-pitying, *Blue* is a fitting closure to an eventful career. ★★★ $24.99

Blue

(1993, 98 min, France, Krzysztof Kieslowski) A haunting and visually stunning film, *Blue* is the first in director Kieslowski's "color" trilogy, which would be followed by *White* and *Red*. Juliette Binoche (*Damage*) is compelling as a grieving widow who withdraws from life after the sudden loss of her husband and daughter. Despite her efforts to remain detached from her past and present, she slowly regains her emotional balance when she uncovers her husband's secret life. The film boasts wonderful acting and beautiful cinematography, but at times gets bogged down in its overladen visual symbolism. Winner of Best Actress and Best Picture at the Venice Film Festival. (French with English subtitles) ★★★ $19.99

The Blue Angel

(1930, 90 min, Germany, Josef von Sternberg) Emil Jannings seems a paragon of order and control, a diligent and respected schoolteacher who commands attention and obedience. But behind this facade is a repressed man, a man so needy for simple human contact that he falls prey to the almost violent sensuality of Lola-Lola (Marlene Dietrich, in the role which brought her international recognition), the earthy cabaret singer who performs with a troupe of traveling players. He exchanges his security for the illusion of warmth and caring, and pays for his obsession with every shred of dignity and purpose he'd ever attained. Jannings is devastating, Dietrich is mesmerizing and von Sternberg guides the performers through Expressionistic set designs with a sure hand and an unerring eye for human foibles. A film worthy of its classic status. ★★★★ $24.99

Blue Chips

(1994, 108 min, US, William Friedkin) Nick Nolte is a grumpy old basketball coach in this authentic sports story that's about more than just whether the home team will win before the final buzzer sounds. When Nolte's college team experiences a slump, he takes to the road to recruit players who expect new cars, bags of cash and even tractors in return for their premium services, all of which is, of course, illegal. With rousing basketball scenes, the film

debut of NBA superstar Shaquille O'Neal, a good performance by Nolte and a moving ethical dilemma, *Blue Chips* lacks a cast of interesting supporting characters to round out the story. This is surprising since it was written by Ron Shelton, who penned two delightful sports related films, *Bull Durham* and *White Men Can't Jump*. ★★½ $19.99

Blue Collar

(1978, 114 min, US, Paul Schrader) A searing drama with Richard Pryor and Harvey Keitel as auto workers up against their corporate bosses, and their own union, in a losing battle. Pryor and Keitel are both outstanding in what may be their best screen performances. As a fellow worker also caught up in their ill-fated fight, Yaphet Kotto gives a mesmerizing performance. ★★★ $14.99

Blue Country

(1978, 104 min, France, Jean-Charles Tacchella) Following his success with *Cousin, Cousine*, Tacchella directed this enchanting romantic comedy about two free souls who leave the troubles of city living behind to renew their love and begin a new life amidst the idyllic French countryside. (French with English subtitles) ★★★

Blue Desert

(1991, 98 min, US, Bradley Battersby) Courtney Cox stars as a New York City comic book artist who finds herself hitting the road after being victimized by crime one time too many. Unfortunately, life in the small Southwestern town where she ends up proves no friendlier than the big city when Cox attracts the attentions of a troubled ex-con (Craig Scheffer) and a local cop (D.B. Sweeney). Director Battersby creates an ominous, uneasy tone from start to finish. This above-average thriller is uniformly well-acted and provides a good look into the psychology of a victim while also making a statement about the position of an attractive single woman in a world where men call the shots. ★★★ $89.99

Blue Fin

(1977, 93 min, Australia, Carl Schultz) A father and son, not on the best of terms, sail on a small boat to fish for tuna off Australia's southern coast. Disaster strikes when a storm at sea disables the boat and the young boy is the only one capable of saving the lives of his father and the crew. A scenic adventure for the whole family. ★★★

Blue Hawaii

(1961, 101 min, US, Norman Taurog) Pleasant Elvis Presley musical with Elvis as a returning soldier who bypasses the family business to work for a local tourist agency. Joan Blackman is the love interest, and Angela Lansbury adds a touch of class as Presley's mom. Elvis sings "Can't Help Falling in Love" and the title tune. ★★½ $19.99

The Blue Hour

(1992, 88 min, Germany, Marcel Gisler) The vulnerability and loneliness of a pretty "rent boy" and a flighty salesgirl is the theme of this absorbing drama. Theo is a Berlin hustler, a handsome young man who, despite selling his

Jessica Lange won an Oscar for *Blue Sky*

body, retains an amazingly sweet and trusting nature. Despite living the "good life," Theo begins feeling a little old, tired and alienated. His sadness is relieved a bit when he strikes up an uneasy relationship with his next door neighbor, Marie. She's a punkishly outlandish French woman who's just broken up with her boyfriend and is also looking for something better. Their friendship is not the stuff of high drama, but it is a simple, surprisingly touching tale of an unlikely love between two social outcasts. (German with English subtitles) ★★★ $39.99

Blue Ice

(1993, 96 min, GB, Russell Mulcahy) An underrated espionage drama from the director of *Highlander* starring the ubiquitous Michael Caine as a spy who came in from the cold, only to find himself frost-bitten when his oldest friends start turning up dead — with the only link being the beautiful femme fatale (Sean Young) who recently entered his life. Caine's faithful performance harkens back to his old "Harry Palmer" days in *The Ipcress File* and *Funeral in Berlin*. Worth the price of a rental for the mental torture sequence alone, the film also sports strong support from Ian Holm and (an uncredited) Bob Hoskins. ★★★ $19.99

Blue in the Face

(1995, 90 min, US, Wayne Wang & Paul Auster) Not really a sequel, the ingratiating *Blue in the Face* is a new collection of stories which concentrate on the customers of a Brooklyn smoke shop which was first featured in *Smoke*. Harvey Keitel returns as Auggie, the gregarious sales clerk who acts as both father confessor and camp counselor to a fresh crop of playmates. Told in a semidocumentary and more fragmented style than the previous film, *Blue in the Face*, as with *Smoke*, revels in the diversity of its Park Slope neighborhood, here through the many talking-heads interviews, anecdotes, monologues and fictionalized stories which populate this funny film. An eclectic, engaging cast weaves its way through the skimpy narrative, the best of them including a very amusing Lou Reed who rattles on about his home town, Lily Tomlin in an extended cameo as a homeless man, an almost unrecognizable Michael J. Fox as a survey taker, and Mel Gorham, Giancarlo Esposito and Victor Argo who also return from *Smoke*. Though not totally as successful or in-depth as the first film, this outing's goals are simpler but nevertheless appealingly met. ★★★½ $19.99

Blue Jeans

(1981, 101 min, France, Hugues Burin des Roziers) This interesting curiosity follows the first loves of a 13-year-old boy who is sent to England one summer to study English. His first tentative advances with a young girl are charming. However, she is soon lured away from him by another, older boy which leaves our hero alone. The strange twist is that he also becomes attached to the other boy and develops a crush on the unresponsive young man. A touching and sensitive look at the heartache of first love. (French with English subtitles) ★★★ $59.99

The Blue Kite

(1993, 138 min, China, Tian Zhuangzhuang) This harrowing tale of a family's struggle to survive in revolutionary China is told from the perspective of a young boy, Tietou, who witnesses firsthand the cruelty of class struggle. Banned by the Chinese authorities and ultimately resulting in the exile of filmmaker Tian, the film received favorable reviews in its limited release here in the U.S., but sadly lacks the emotive power of the films of Zhang Yimou and Chen Kaige. The film is strikingly similar to Zhang's *To Live*, in that it tells the story of one family from the Great Leap Forward through the Cultural Revolution. But where *To Live* succeeded in drawing the viewer into the intimate lives of a small family, *The Blue Kite* introduces too many players and it is hard to keep them all straight. The result is a dispassionate distancing from the characters as their lives fall victim to unwarranted punishments. Still, a must see for those Sino enthusiasts out there. (Mandarin with English subtitles) ★★½ $79.99

The Blue Max

(1966, 156 min, US, John Guillermin) Believe it or not, George Peppard actually had a career before "The A Team" and in this high-flying romance/adventure story he does an able job portraying a German WWI pilot who has a steamy love affair with Ursula Andress. Excellent aerial photography punctuates the dogfight scenes. ★★★ $19.99

Blue Sky

(1994, 101 min, US, Tony Richardson) Shot in 1990 and on the shelf for four years, Richardson's final film is an affecting melodrama of a family in crisis which is further enhanced by two exceptional performances by Jessica Lange and Tommy Lee Jones. Set in the early 1960s, the story concerns military nuclear engineer Jones, wife Lange and their family who move to a new Army base where infidelity, betrayal and conspiracy await them. A flirtatious Southern belle in the Blanche DuBois/Scarlett O'Hara mold, Lange's Oscar-winning portrayal of Carly is a revelation of sexuality and naiveté, and as Carly is the heart of the story, Lange's smoldering portrait is very much the centerpiece of the film. As her

understanding but perplexed idealistic husband, Jones gives a subtle portrayal of a man at odds with his conscience. Powers Boothe, Carrie Snodgress and Chris O'Donnell also star. ★★★ $14.99

Blue Steel

(1990, 95 min, US, Kathryn Bigelow) Jamie Lee Curtis delivers a cooly understated performance in this atmospheric police thriller as a rookie cop who empties her gun into an armed robber, and is promptly suspended when the dead man's gun cannot be found. Unbeknownst to her, the witness who stole the weapon is the same man she has just started dating — the man responsible for a series of killings using bullets with her name on them. Ron Silver is effective as the serial killer. Director Bigelow suffuses the film with the noir glow that permeated her acclaimed vampire saga, *Near Dark*. ★★½ $9.99

Blue Thunder

(1983, 108 min, US, John Badham) Fascism was never so much fun as in this movie with grown-up little boys playing with their war toys. Roy Scheider is the Vietnam vet who, after a particularly bad psychotic episode, steals the government's surveillance helicopter. Malcolm McDowell is the unhappy government rep out for Scheider's blood. Amazing aerial chases over Los Angeles heighten the suspense of this otherwise silly thriller. ★★ $9.99

Blue Velvet

(1986, 120 min, US, David Lynch) Director Lynch unleashes his demented imagination with all its perversely poetic force. Both witty and luridly beautiful, the film is part mystery, part surrealist dream. Lynch uses the postcard perfect town of Lumberton to plunge into an all-embracing ritual of sinful crime, sadism and redemption. Kyle MacLachlan innocently discovers a human ear in his backyard one day and is quickly drawn into the sordid, masochistic world of a nightclub singer (Isabella Rossellini). Dennis Hopper is at his lunatic best as the all-powerful psychotic drug thug Frank Booth. *Blue Velvet* is a piece of primal pop art, an erotic parable with trance-like power. ★★★★

The Blues According to Lightnin' Hopkins

(1968, 31 min, US, Les Blank) A compelling look at blues master Lightnin' Hopkins. Includes musical performances and down-home scenes. ★★★ $49.99

The Blues Brothers

(1980, 132 min, US, John Landis) The most, and possibly only successful example of a "Saturday Night Live" sketch turned into a feature-length movie, stars John Belushi and Dan Aykroyd as Jake and Elwood Blues, good-hearted petty criminals and dedicated bluesmen. The story about a quest to find the money to save an orphanage and the possible consequences of running a red light, is really just an excuse to string together as many hilarious episodes as the filmmakers can. This movie has it all: monumental car chases (and car crashes), a mysterious killer stalking the duo, a

mission from God, raucous concert scenes and cameos by everyone from John Candy to Steven Spielberg, but also full musical performances by Aretha Franklin, Ray Charles, James Brown, Cab Calloway and John Lee Hooker. The movie is briskly paced, filled equally with action and musical scenes, tremendously funny and is a virtual tour of the city of Chicago, birthplace of the urban blues. This "soul, rhythm and blues, and blues revue" is a lasting tribute both to the artists who created that sound and to John Belushi's genius. ★★★½ $19.99

Blume in Love

(1973, 117 min, US, Paul Mazursky) Mazursky's perceptive and engaging comedy-drama about love and rejection stars George Segal as a divorce lawyer whose life is turned upside-down when his wife (Susan Anspach) walks out on him. Kris Kristofferson, Marsha Mason and Shelley Winters also star. ★★★ $14.99

Blunt: The Fourth Man

(1992, 86 min, GB, John McGlasham) Anthony Hopkins is a delight as Guy Burgess, the British government official who fled England before the discovery that he and several others were spies for the Soviets. Knowledge of this story is beneficial for the film presents its story with the assumption that the viewer is well aware of the much-publicized scandal. At the center of the tale is Burgess' fellow spy, Anthony Blunt (wonderfully played by Ian Richardson), who recruited Burgess while attending Cambridge in the 1930s. Set in the early 1960s, the film shows Blunt as a well-respected art historian. When his well-ordered life is threatened, Blunt begins an elaborate cover-up and damage control campaign. His biggest challenge is protecting Burgess, his former lover and close friend. An inviting and well-produced tale whose characters can also be seen in *Another Country* and *An Englishman Abroad*. ★★★ $19.99

The Boat

See: Boot, Das

The Boat Is Full

(1981, 104 min, Switzerland, Markus Imhoof) A haunting account of a group of Jewish refugees who attempt to seek asylum in Switzerland, despite that country's strict and subtly prejudiced immigration laws. Their struggle for freedom and life provides the emotional center to this film that is both horrifying in the depiction of a peoples' racial attitudes and heartrending in another's efforts to overcome them. (German with English subtitles) ★★★½ $59.99

Bob & Carol & Ted & Alice

(1969, 104 min, US, Paul Mazursky) Mazursky's breakthrough directorial debut is a somewhat dated but nevertheless enjoyable treatise on marriage and sex (but not necessarily in that order). Robert Culp and Natalie Wood are a married couple who try to convince friends Elliott Gould and Dyan Cannon to express themselves sexually — by wife-swapping. Both Gould and Cannon received Oscar nominations for their delightful performances. ★★★ $9.99

Bob le Flambeur

(1955, 102 min, France, Jean-Pierre Melville) Melville, the Father of the French New Wave, has made a quirky, highly stylized film which revolves around Bob, an aging but elegant gangster who plans a daring robbery of the Deauville Casino. The tension builds as Bob recruits his Montmarte co-horts, plans the break-in and attempts to execute "the biggest heist of the century." An entertaining comedy of manners as well as an exciting drama. (French with English subtitles) ★★★½

Bob Roberts

(1992, 103 min, US, Tim Robbins) 1992 was a banner year for Tim Robbins. In addition to starring in Robert Altman's *The Player*, he wrote, directed and starred in this scathingly brilliant political satire about the senatorial campaign of a right-wing candidate. Told in a mockumentary style, reminiscent of *This Is Spinal Tap*, the film often recalls *The Player*, introducing a gallery of characters who weave in and out of the story, many of whom are portrayed by terrific celebrity cameos. But Robbins, as an actor, writer and director, has an instinctive and incisive wit which gives the film a definition all its own. As the country music-singing, neo-fascist, *laissez faire*-invoking Roberts, Robbins gives a priceless performance; there are few of his generation who can handle comedy with such finese. Standouts from a most impressive cast include Giancarlo Esposito as a radical left-wing reporter, Lynne Thigpin as an adversarial anchorwoman, James Spader, Alan Rickman, Ray Wise and Gore Vidal. ★★★★ $19.99

Bobby Deerfield

(1977, 124 min, US, Sydney Pollack) Al Pacino makes a valiant effort to breathe some life into this turgid romantic drama, but even his talents can't save this story of a race car driver who falls in love with socialite Marthe Keller, who's suffering from "Ali MacGraw's Disease." (And Al, next time, leave the impressions to Rich Little.) ★ $14.99

La Boca del Lobo

(1988, 111 min, Peru, Francisco J. Lombardi) The human tragedy of the Peruvian Civil War is explored in this intense drama. Set in a poor Indian village in the Andes, the bucolic calm of the town is disturbed when a small army patrol is sent to investigate possible insurgent activity. The soldiers, like the American forces in Vietnam, soon become entrenched in a bloody, morally ambivalent and increasingly frustrating guerrilla war of attrition. The desperate situation explodes after a newly appointed lieutenant declares the entire village guilty of treason and leads his forces toward a horrible atrocity. A young soldier in the group must choose between blind obedience of his superior or follow the dictates of his conscience and oppose him. (Spanish with English subtitles) ★★★ $79.99

Bodies, Rest & Motion

(1993, 93 min, US, Michael Steinberg) Steinberg, who co-directed *The Waterdance* with Neal Jiminez, goes solo for his second effort, a loosely structured drama about four disillusioned twentysomethings looking for themselves. Bridget Fonda plays a young woman who finds herself in a dilemma when her estranged boyfriend (Tim Roth) just takes off one day. Eric Stoltz (the film's co-producer) is a house painter, quite content with life in the nowhere Arizona town where the film takes place, who meets and falls in love with stressed-out Fonda. Phoebe Cates rounds out this solid ensemble cast as Fonda's best friend and Roth's ex. Far less formulaic and a bit more insightful than *Singles*, Steinberg lets things unfold simply and slowly, which is much to the film's benefit. ★★★ $19.99

Body and Soul

(1947, 104 min, US, Robert Rossen) John Garfield gives a career performance in this hard-hitting, sometimes brutal but always mesmerizing boxing drama. Garfield plays Charlie Davis, a tough, ambitious kid from the poor part of town who makes a name for himself in the boxing world. As his career takes off, he loses sight of his dreams and honor and succumbs to the easy money supplied by his gangster manager. Lilli Palmer plays Peg, his fiancée who stands beside him while hopelessly witnessing his descent; though Palmer is an attractive performer, the part begs for the likes of Ida Lupino who would have given the character more dimension. In support, Anne Revere and Canada Lee, as Davis' mother and opponent-turned-trainer, respectively, are excellent. With a taut and polished screenplay by Abraham Polonsky, *Body and Soul* is an uncompromising tale of greed, corruption and redemption, brilliantly realized by director Rossen. One of the greatest of all boxing films. ★★★★ $14.99

Body Bags

(1993, 95 min, US, John Carpenter & Tobe Hooper) This fun horror anthology is hosted by John Carpenter and features buckets of gore and bizarre humor. Highlights include "The Gas Station," a grim slasher tale and the incredibly funny "Hair" starring Stacy Keach as a middle-aged balding man with an overwhelming desire for a full head of hair. Some fright fans may be turned off by the sometimes heavy-handed attempts at comedy, but inventive casting, which includes Mark Hamill, Deborah Harry, Sheena Easton and Twiggy, combines with good brisk pacing to provide for plenty of shocks and yucks. ★★½ $94.99

Body Double

(1984, 109 min, US, Brian De Palma) De Palma's acclaimed sleazy thriller about a voyeuristic actor (Craig Wasson) whose penchant for peeping involves him in the grisly murder of a woman (Deborah Shelton, looking positively luminescent) on whom he's been spying. A pre-stardom Melanie Griffith also stars as a porn star. De Palma borrows from Hitchcock (here *Rear Window*) once again, with successful results. ★★ $9.99

Body Heat

(1981, 113 min, US, Lawrence Kasdan) Simmering passions and deadly schemes are ignited under the hot Florida sun in Kasdan's remarkable, sensuous thriller which almost single-handedly brought noir back to vogue. With nods to *Double Indemnity* and *The Postman Always Rings Twice*, Kasdan's riveting tale stars William Hurt as a second-rate lawyer who begins an affair with sultry and very married Kathleen Turner (her memorable debut). Only her husband (Richard Crenna) stands in the way of their happiness. Kasdan takes the traditional femme fatale tale and spices it up with sexy lovemaking scenes, crackling dialogue and twist upon twist. In their first appearance together, Hurt and Turner are simply dynamite. ★★★★ $14.99

Body Melt

(1993, 82 min, Australia, Philip Brophy) A scientific experiment turns an Australian community into melting zombies. The plot is weak. The acting is weaker. The special effects are truly disgusting and the film boasts a shameless group of backwoods *Deliverance*-type hicks who are more repulsive than any melting zombies. *Body Melt* tries to ride on the coattails of Peter Jackson's successful *Dead Alive*, but misses the mark by a mile. Not for kids or the squeamish. ★ $89.99

Body of Evidence

(1992, 99 min, US, Uli Edel) Madonna and Willem Dafoe star in this lethargic psycho-sexual mystery that makes *Basic Instinct* look like the *Citizen Kane* of the whodunit-in-the-sack thrillers. The "body" in question is Madonna's over-exposed corpus; the evidence shows that said body was the lethal weapon in a classic case of come-and-gone lovemaking. Dafoe is Frank Delaney, the morally dubious lawyer who must prove that while S&M hellcat Madonna is a "killer" in bed (wielding handcuffs, candles and mega-developed inner thighs), she's not actually a murderer. But can he maintain professional distance and resist the pint-sized dynamo who "does it like animals do it"? Sure, Madonna's acting doesn't amount to much more than eyelash batting, hip-swivel-

Bob le Flambeur

ing and lip-licking, but (and this is the sad part) she still out-acts Dafoe who gives the worst performance of his career. As the prosecuting attorney, Joe Mantegna can barely conceal his disdain for the entire affair. ★ $14.99

Body Parts

(1991, 88 min, US, Eric Red) Jeff Fahey loses an arm in an auto accident and his distraught wife approves emergency surgical replacement with a donated limb. The surgery is a success, but the donor — an executed murderer — wants his arm back! While the movie occasionally slips into hackneyed horror contrivance, it is often surprisingly effective in its treatment of Fahey's bizarre predicament. Where does consciousness reside? In the mind? In the soul? Or in individual body parts? Director and co-writer Red also scripted *Near Dark* and *The Hitcher*. Brad Dourif co-stars. ★★½ $14.99

The Body Snatcher

(1945, 77 min, US, Robert Wise) Wise's second film for producer Val Lewton (the first being *Curse of the Cat People*) is an exceptionally atmospheric thriller about a 19th-century medical school professor in league with a grave robber. Based on a Robert Louis Stevenson story. Starring Boris Karloff, Henry Daniell and Bela Lugosi. ★★★ $19.99

Body Snatchers

(1993, 96 min, US, Abel Ferrara) From the director of such hard-hitting hits as *Bad Lieutenant* and *King of New York* comes this eerie but redundant second remake of the 1956 sci-fi classic *Invasion of the Body Snatchers* about soul-stealing seed pods from space. Gabrielle Anwar (*Scent of a Woman*) toplines as a divorce-brat whose unsuspecting father accepts a job assignment relocating him to a military base now being used as an alien stronghold. As director Philip Kaufman proved with his remake in 1978, some updatings are improved by big-budget effects; and while this glossy retread is no exception to that rule, it is also not exceptional. Also with Billy Wirth, Forest Whitaker and Meg Tilly. ★★½ $19.99

The Bodyguard

(1992, 129 min, US, Mick Jackson) Kevin Costner plays the title character to Whitney Houston's big, big movie star in this idiotic romantic thriller which despite itself manages to create some entertaining moments. When she is plagued by death threats, Houston's manager signs on rambling man Costner, tops in his profession, but who never stays in one place too long (he's probably in constant search for a good barber). At odds from the beginning, Costner and Houston become enraptured with each other, leading to an inevitable fling. This, of course, puts their employee-employer relationship at risk, while a killer closes in. It won't take long to figure out who hired the hit man, probably the thinnest of the numerous ill-conceived plot lines. There's a good lake-side sequence, but nothing else in the film nears the level of its short-lived excitement. In her film debut, Houston is in her element vocally, but her acting — as with the movie — while not all bad, is simply nothing out of the ordinary. ★★ $19.99

Boeing, Boeing

(1965, 102 min, US, John Rich) Tony Curtis and Jerry Lewis team in this frantic sex farce which — even for the '60s — is particularly anti-feminist. Curtis hams it up royally as a journalist who literally has his hands full juggling the simultaneous relationships with three live-in fiancées, all stewardesses and strangers to each other. Enter fellow reporter Lewis, who is forced to help Curtis in keeping the three women from meeting when all unexpectedly arrive at the same time. Thelma Ritter proves to be a saving grace, providing most of the laughs as Curtis' exasperated housekeeper. A film to win the heart of any member of the Spur Posse. ★★ $14.99

Gérard Depardieu is Haley Joel Osment's imaginary friend in *Bogus*

Bogus

(1996, 111 min, US, Norman Jewison) Disarming despite its own shortcomings, *Bogus* is a children's fantasy which tells children the world is not always a nice place — so that's why there are such things as invisible childhood friends. Bogus is one such presence. He appears to Albert (Haley Joel Osment), a seven-year-old boy whose mother has been killed in a car accident. With no family, the youngster is sent to live with his mother's foster sister, Harriet (Whoopi Goldberg), a career-minded woman with no time for a kid. The story concentrates on their efforts to learn to love each other, with a little help from Bogus. The scenes between Bogus and Albert are the film's most appealing moments, and, as Bogus, Gérard Depardieu has rarely demonstrated such a light side — especially in his English-language films. More demanding, Albert and Harriet's scenes are more difficult to watch, and they underscore the story's sparseness. ★★½ $99.99

La Bohème

(1967, 104 min, Italy, Franco Zeffirelli) Herbert von Karajan leads the La Scala Chorus and Orchestra in this rousing production of Puccini's classic opera. Soloists include Mirella Freni, Ruggeri Raimondi, Martino and Panerai. (Italian with English subtitles) $24.99

Boiling Point

(1993, 93 min, US, James B. Harris) Wesley Snipes heads an eclectic cast as a treasury agent out to avenge his partner's death (how original) at the hands of a shifty grifter (Dennis Hopper) and his trigger-happy henchman (Viggo Mortensen). While the film garnered many favorable reviews for its focus on character rather than gunplay, it is by no means the *Lethal Weapon* derivative it might have been. As a result, the movie simmers when it should have boiled. Also in the soup are Valerie Perrine as Hopper's past-prime paramour, and Lolita Davidovich as Snipe's nurturing call-girl friend. ★★½ $14.99

Bolero

(1984, 104 min, US, John Derek) Bo Derek takes her clothes off in the quest to lose her virginity. Surely there must have been one immediate taker so we wouldn't have had to suffer for 104 minutes. ★

Bombay Talkie

(1970, 108 min, India, James Ivory) Lucia, an American novelist, arrives in India in a desperate search for new sensations and experiences which will help her forget her approaching middle age. She soon meets and begins an affair with Vikram, a dazzling movie actor. Vikram eventually leaves his wife and family and destroys his life and career in a futile pursuit of an image that does not exist. Director Ivory and writer Ruth Prawer Jhabvala present an interesting look at culture clash, but the romantic dramatics are very much in the range of the familiar. ★★½ $19.99

Bombshell

(1933, 95 min, US, Victor Fleming) This fast-paced, early satire on Hollywood hasn't lost a bit of its bite over the years. Jean Harlow stars as the used and abused Hollywood starlet whose face and name are plastered across the country. And now she wants to change her image. The snappy dialogue keeps this film rolling along. Harlow, who could have been playing herself, gives one of her best performances in this hysterical film. ★★★½ $19.99

Bon Voyage & Aventure Malgache

(1944, 26/31 min, France, Alfred Hitchcock) During World War II, Alfred Hitchcock made these two shorts in an effort to boost morale, particularly that of the French Resistance. *Bon Voyage* is classic Hitchcock, a taut spy story about an RAF pilot who escapes from a POW camp that grows more and more intense with each plot twist. *Aventure Malgache* tells the story about the Resistance fighting a corrupt government in Madagascar. Though it is not as suspenseful as the first film, it is especially intriguing because it is based on a true story. Both films showcase many of the director's stylish and thematic trademarks and should not be missed by die-hard fans of the Master of Suspense. (French with English subtitles) ★★★ $39.99

The Bonfire of the Vanities

(1990, 125 min, US, Brian De Palma) Based on Tom Wolfe's runaway best-seller, this absurdly uneven film adaptation by De Palma was one of the most anticipated releases of

1990, and created one of that year's loudest thuds. This satire on greed and justice, though not totally abysmal, is a disappointment on numerous levels. In one of the many ill-advised changes from the book, the miscast Tom Hanks plays a basically likable Sherman McCoy, the Wall Street wizard who is thrust into the media spotlight when he and his mistress (Melanie Griffith) are involved in the hit-and-run of a black man. Bruce Willis makes an earnest stab at the now-American author Peter Fallow, the down-on-his-heels journalist who lucks into the story of the year. ★½ $19.99

Bongo Man

(1982, 89 min, Jamaica/West Germany, Stefan Paul) The normally peaceful island of Jamaica, rocked with dissention and bloodied by riots during the presidential elections of the early 1980s, provides the dramatic backdrop to this Reggae Sunsplash-styled concert film featuring Jimmy Cliff. The potentially explosive situation is intercut with the Rasta and reggae music of Cliff and Bob Marley and the Wailers in an effort to promote the idea that "politicians divide, musicians unite." ★★★

Bonjour Tristesse

(1958, 94 min, US, Otto Preminger) The French Riviera is the setting of this skillful adaptation of Francoise Sagan's novella about a young girl (Jean Seberg) who drives a wedge between her rake father (David Niven) and his mistress (Deborah Kerr). Exceptional performances from both Niven and Kerr. ★★★ $69.99

Bonnie and Clyde

(1967, 111 min, US, Arthur Penn) *Bonnie and Clyde* marked the arrival of the New Hollywood in the late Sixties with a burst of creative energy. An exceptional script by David Newman and Robert Benton, stylish direction by Penn, Dede Allen's brilliant editing and great performances from the entire cast (including Warren Beatty and Faye Dunaway as the title characters) combine to make this one of the most daring and successful of all mainstream American productions. Based on the exploits of the real-life pair who went on a crime spree through the Midwest, the movie is by turns humorous, thrilling, romantic and shocking. The climactic sequence is a tour de force of visceral filmmaking impossible to dismiss. ★★★★ $19.99

The Boogeyman

(1980, 86 min, US, Ulli Lommel) This boring and pointless low-budget production begins as a pair of siblings murder their mother's abusive boyfriend. Shift forward twenty years (the first, but not the last horror-film cliché employed in this movie) to the brother and sister, now grown but still suffering the psychological consequences of that terrible night. In an attempt to overcome her fears, the sister returns to the scene of the crime, only to find that a mirror on the bedroom wall (remarkably still in place after twenty years and a succession of other homeowners) has captured the soul of the understandably pissed-off but nevertheless dead boyfriend. The mirror breaks, his vengeful spirit is released, and you can guess the rest. Everything about this film — from the acting, lighting and camerawork to

the makeup effects and scare tactics — is amateurish and routine. ★

Boomerang

(1992, 118 min, US, Reginald Hudlin) Eddie Murphy stars in this entertaining comedy about a way smooth, way charming advertising man in search of the ideal woman. But his cavalier use of sex to avoid communicating and his overemphasis on a woman's appearance come back at him when he meets his new boss, Robin Givens. The film's amiable "buppy" characters and romantic sentiment put its heart in the right place, but the level of the humor rarely rises above the belt. A solid supporting cast includes David Allen Grier, Grace Jones, Eartha Kitt, Geoffrey Holder, Martin Lawrence and, most notably, Halle Berry. ★★½ $14.99

The Boost

(1988, 95 min, US, Harold Becker) James Woods and Sean Young star in this totally mishandled "say no to drugs" treatise about a hotshot salesman and his wife whose fresh new start in L.A. becomes a cocaine nightmare. Of value only as the film that sparked the real-life "fatal attraction" skirmish between stars Young and Woods. ★★ $14.99

Das Boot (The Boat)

(1981, 145 min, West Germany, Wolfgang Petersen) Few films convey the horror of war as powerfully as Petersen's claustrophobic account of a German U-boat's passage through hostile waters. Dispelling traditional film images of war heroism, *Das Boot* substitutes a truer vision of the waste and inhumanity inherent in battle. (Available letterboxed and pan & scan) (The three-and-a-half-hour, letterboxed director's cut is available for $24.99) (German with English subtitles) ★★★★ $19.99

Boots, Biceps and Bulges — The Life & Works of Tom of Finland

(1988, 30 min, US, James Williams) Not to be confused with the film *Daddy and the Muscle Academy*, this fascinating film treads similar ground in documenting the life and unique erotic art of Tom of Finland. Tom, who died in 1992 at age 72, developed over the years a strong underground following for his fanciful and sexually graphic depictions of gay men from around the world. Exaggerating their features and equipment, his homoerotic drawings of super-masculine, ruggedly handsome men, many times in various uniforms or leather, have become gay icons. The film intersperses an interview with Tom in 1988 with shots of hundreds of his drawings. A mesmerizing look into the thoughts and works of a genuine gay folk artist. ★★★ $39.99

Bopha!

(1993, 120 min, US, Morgan Freeman) Actor Freeman makes his directorial debut with this solemn and powerful anti-Apartheid drama based on the play by Percy Mtwa. Danny Glover stars as a black South African police sergeant whose position requires him to unwittingly enforce the country's racist laws. Labeled a traitor by his community, his world further deteriorates when he comes in conflict with his student rebel son (Marius Weyers),

who helps open his eyes to the injustices around them. As a study of racism, *Bopha!* doesn't instill anger but rather succinctly explores the ways this practice tears apart the fabric of black families. Slowly paced at times, the performances of Glover, Alfre Woodard (as his wife), the understated Weyers and an icy Malcolm McDowell help bring to light the reality of South Africa. ★★★ $19.99

Bordello of Blood

(1996, 87 min, US, Gilbert Adler) Producer Robert Zemeckis and the other slumming talent behind the "Tales from the Crypt" series have given us another bloodless vampire movie, starring Angie Everhart as the legendary Queen of the Undead. Accidentally resurrected, she sets up residence in a mortuary, playing madam to a group of undead ladies of the night. When a young Christian crusader (Erika Eleniak) loses her brother (Corey Feldman) to the vampiric legions, she enlists the aid of a private detective (Dennis Miller) to help find him. Throw into the mix a rock 'n' roll preacher (Chris Sarandon) and you've got the kind of mess only a cadre of seasoned Hollywood screenwriters can create. The gore scenes are lame and bloodless (unlike those in the first "Crypt" movie *Demon Knight*) and much of the script is reminiscent of *From Dusk Till Dawn*. Even the usually funny Miller seems embarrassed — he's just playing himself. ★½ $19.99

The Border

(1982, 107 min, US, Tony Richardson) Jack Nicholson stars as a U.S. Border Guard who gets caught up in the business of transporting illegal aliens to pay for the materialistic lifestyle his wife craves. His morals come to haunt him in the form of a young Mexican mother and her child, whom he comes to care about. An engrossing film with excellent performances from Nicholson, Valerie Perrine and Harvey Keitel. ★★★ $14.99

Border Radio

(1987, 88 min, US, Allison Anders) Set against the alternative music scene of Los Angeles, the story follows a rock star who is on the run when he "steals" money owed to him by a sleazy club owner. Meanwhile, his wife searches for the musician, unraveling both a mystery and the emotional ties which hold their relationship together. Includes John Doe of X, Chris D. of Divine Horsemen and Dave Alvin of the Blasters. ★★

Boris and Natasha

(1991, 88 min, US, Charles Martin Smith) When we last left our evil villains, Boris Badenov and Natasha Fatale, they were two-dimensional characters drawn on paper — and still they had more depth than these live-action blow-ups made flesh by Dave Thomas (of "SCTV" fame) and Sally Kellerman (who also produced). True, Kellerman puts in a nice turn as the old-fashioned Pottsylvanian moll who comes to America and becomes a "woman of the '90s," and the script does retain some of the original cartoon nuttiness, but the plot...the animated Boris came up with better ideas. The theme song sums it up: "It's good to be bad" — but it's bad to be mediocre. ★★ $89.99

B

B

Born on the Fourth of July

(1989, 144 min, US, Oliver Stone) Stone won a much-deserved Oscar as Best Director for this brilliant, gut-wrenching adaptation of Vietnam vet Ron Kovic's autobiography. Tom Cruise gives a remarkable performance as the initially gung-ho soldier, whose life is covered in various, almost-episodic scenes, from his tour of duty and injury to the horrendous healing process to Kovic's gradual political awakening and activism. Although Stone's *Platoon* is generally acknowledged as a landmark in the myriad of war movies, *Born* is the definitive Vietnam film to date: for Kovic, like our country itself, began the war with undying faith, and endured a painful crippling and anguishing soul-searching which ultimately suggested we hadn't done the right thing. ★★★★ $19.99

Born to Be Wild

(1995, 99 min, US, John Gray) While a boy and his gorilla is an innovative twist on the clichéd boy and his dog, this slow-moving family film could have used some imagination. Rick, a troubled teenager (Wil Horneff), befriends a 400-pound gorilla named Katie who has learned to communicate via sign language in an experiment headed by Rick's mom. When Katie is forced to become an attraction at the local flea market, Rick helps her escape and they both embark on a unique road adventure heading towards freedom in Canada. The touching and unexpected ending helps to revive a maudlin and sluggish story line. ★★½ $19.99

Born to Dance

(1936, 105 min, US, Roy Del Ruth) That national treasure from the 1930s, Eleanor Powell, stars with James Stewart in this Cole Porter musical. The story, concerning a sailor in love, is routine; but Powell's musical numbers are sensational. Score includes "Easy to Love" and "I've Got You Under My Skin." ★★½ $19.99

Born to Kill

(1947, 97 min, US, Robert Wise) *Born to Kill* is a tough and gritty film noir, directed by Wise early in his career when he was just beginning to explore the possibilities of the genre. This hard-boiled melodrama probes the dark side

of human nature and shows the results of giving in to those urges. Lawrence Tierney is harrowing as a murderer who will do anything to get what he wants — and what he wants is his wife's sister, played by an alluring Claire Trevor. ★★★ $19.99

Born Yesterday

(1950, 103 min, US, George Cukor) Though director Cukor's staging is more stage-bound than most of his stage-to-screen adaptations, *Born Yesterday* is nonetheless a thoroughly delightful comedy which earned Judy Holliday an Oscar for her first starring role. Re-creating the part of Billie Dawn which she played on stage, Judy gives one of the classic "dumb blonde" portrayals as a gangster's moll who comes under the tutelage of "cultured" writer William Holden. Broderick Crawford is her slobbish boyfriend negotiating unsavory political connections in the nation's capitol. It was a remarkable win for Holliday, besting that year both Bette Davis (*All About Eve*) and Gloria Swanson (*Sunset Boulevard*). Garson Kanin adapted his own stage hit. ★★★½ $19.99

Born Yesterday

(1993, 101 min, US, Luis Mandoki) More appropriately titled *Born Again Yesterday*, this by-the-book remake of the 1950 Judy Holliday vehicle casts squeakbox Melanie Griffith as the airhead consort of a loutish tycoon (John Goodman). When she goes along with Goodman's plans to smarten her up, she falls for the teacher: yummy Washington columnist Don Johnson. The updated screenplay doesn't stray too much from the original text, which accounts for the film's many laughs. But Griffith gives a superficial performance, and Johnson only goes through the motions. Goodman, however, captures the spirit of the crooked businessman, though in this version he's made to be a bit more sympathetic. ★★½ $9.99

The Borrower

(1991, 97 min, US, John McNaughton) Director McNaughton follows up his *Henry: Portrait of a Serial Killer* with this gory revamping of 1987's *The Hidden*, wherein an alien psycho-killer is sent to Earth for a lifelong prison sentence. This time, our other-worldly friend survives by tearing off and borrowing the heads of his victims, thereby acquiring personalities and memories as a side effect. The film stars Rae Dawn Chong as a hard-boiled feminist detective and Antonio Fargas appears as a homeless person. ★★½ $14.99

The Boston Strangler

(1968, 120 min, US, Richard Fleischer) Tony Curtis' gripping performance as the infamous psychopath dominates this intense story — told in quasi-documentary style — of his insidious campaign of fear and subsequent capture and trial. Henry Fonda also stars as the police detective on the case. ★★★ $19.99

The Bostonians

(1984, 122 min, GB, James Ivory) An exceptionally strong performance by Vanessa Redgrave and a commendable portrayal from Christopher Reeve highlight this Merchant Ivory adaptation of Henry James' novel. Set in

19th-century New England, the story concerns a love triangle in which Redgrave, an early feminist heroine, and Reeve, a reactionary Southern lawyer, battle for the love (and political soul) of a young girl. Ruth Prawer Jhabvala (who has scripted most Merchant Ivory productions) gleaned the emotional core out of James' work and her screenplay unearths the story's underlying passion. ★★★½ $19.99

Bottle Rocket

(1996, 91 min, US, Wes Anderson) In a world of diminished expectations, three disaffected misfits tackle Goal #1 of the master plan of the trio's least stable member. Too old for adolescent rebellion but with no clue of adulthood, they embark on a multi-decade program for a life of crime. This dark comedy employs engaging performances from a cast of mostly unknowns in a well-paced, quirky and surprisingly poignant tale of modern-day rites of passage. Director Anderson's fluid camera and effective use of his performers informs a bittersweet tale of unfocused desires and misspent energy, creating an oddly affecting and ingratiating parable about the dangers of self-delusion and misplaced trust. James Caan has an extended cameo as a consummate con artist, the ill-chosen guru of the master plan's author. ★★★ $19.99

Le Boucher

(1969, 94 min, France, Claude Chabrol) The countryside in and around a small French village is the deceivingly bucolic setting for this well-paced and compelling Hitchcockian murder thriller. The stunning Stéphane Audran stars as Hélène, a sophisticated schoolteacher. Emotionally scarred by a spurned love affair, she befriends a shy butcher who is tortured by his experiences in the Indochina war. Tensions mount and tragedy strikes after Hélène begins to suspect that the man is responsible for a series of sadistic killings of young women. Chabrol at his best. (French with English subtitles) ★★★½ $79.99

Boudu Saved from Drowning

(1932, 87 min, France, Jean Renoir) A humane book seller saves the life of a tramp (the wonderful Michel Simon) who tries to commit suicide in the Seine. Disastrous results are his thanks when the uninhibited Simon moves into the man's home and proceeds to seduce his wife and maid. Unlike the 1986 remake, *Down and Out in Beverly Hills*, Renoir's tramp evades encroaching "respectability" and stays true to his anarchistic ways. (French with English subtitles) ★★★½ $59.99

Boulevard

(1994, 96 min, US/Canada, Penelope Buttenhuis) The plot for this not uninteresting drama couldn't be more familiar: a battered teen leaves her small town for the rough 'n' tumble streets of the big city. A frail, bruised but still beautiful Jennifer runs off to Toronto in an effort to escape from her abusive white-trash boyfriend. Penniless and friendless, she is clutched from the city's mean streets by Ola (Rae Dawn Chong), a tough-talking prostitute (yes, with a heart of gold). The tired plot features an over-acting Lou Diamond Phillips as the bad pimp, a seen-it-all cop (Lance

Henriksen) and a bevy of stereotypical whores. The film takes a Sapphic turn when the two women realize that men are shits (and the male characters in the film sanction this point-of-view) and that they love each other. But love proves to be fleeting as violence rears its head. ★★½ $92.99

Boulevard of Broken Dreams

(1993, 95 min, Australia, Pino Amenta) Experiencing a mid-life crisis, Tom Garfield (played by actor John Waters) returns to his native Australia after a ten-year absence. Having found great success in New York and Hollywood as a writer, he's back home to try to pick up the pieces of his scattered life – including reconciling with his estranged wife and daughter. Filmed at a snail's pace, *Boulevard of Broken Dreams* does offer a mildly interesting glimpse into the private and personal life of an artist. However, the film unfolds so slowly that it's rough going to get to the story's touching, second-half revelation. ★★ $92.99

La Boum

(1981, 100 min, France, Claude Pinoteau) This charming French farce stars Sophie Marceau as a 13-year-old girl who auspiciously encounters the rites of teendom and the rituals of adulthood. An ingenious and graceful depiction of adolescent growth and familial affairs. (French with English subtitles) ★★★

Bound

(1996, 108 min, US, Larry Wachowski & Andy Wachowski) In this stunning debut feature, the brothers Wachowski have accomplished a remarkable feat: They've taken a tried-and-true cinematic formula (film noirish plans, scams and betrayal) and added a very '90s sensibility to it, not to mention a major lesbian plot angle, without losing any of the thrill, intrigue, or snappy dialogue which characterized its '40s counterparts. Gina Gershon and Jennifer Tilly star as neighbors who become lovers first, then partners in crime. Or as Gershon says, "I can fuck somebody when I've just met them; but to steal with them, I have to know them better than myself." The question for the rest of the film then becomes who will betray whom. The intelligent script avoids every cliché it approaches and is constantly taking the viewer into new angles of the familiar story line. *Bound* is an unexpected accomplishment, stylishly shot and edge-of-your-seat tense, and both actresses give their best performances to date. Joe Pantoliano is also great as Tilly's mob-connected boyfriend, bringing a sympathetic shading to the character which is rarely seen in "genre" films. ★★★★ $99.99

Bound and Gagged: A Love Story

(1993, 96 min, US, Daniel Appleby) This frantic "My girlfriend's left me, but I'm gonna get her back" lesbian comedy is an amazingly self-assured independent feature by Appleby. Cliff (Chris Denton) is a hetero slacker who is thrown into a suicidal funk by his wife's gleeful, vindictive departure. His best friend is Elizabeth (Elizabeth Saltarrelli), a fun-loving but irrational bisexual who sleeps with men but is hopelessly in love with Leslie (former

porn queen Ginger Lynn Allen), a young woman stuck in a marriage with an abusive husband (Chris Mulkey). When Leslie's hubby demands that the two stop seeing each other, Elizabeth, with a befuddled Cliff in tow, abducts Leslie and goes on the road, roaming the Midwest in a queer *Thelma and Louise* fashion. A snappily bizarre romp filled with weird, zany, and not always likable characters which mischievously explores the mysteries of obsessive but elusive love. ★★★ $89.99

Bound for Glory

(1976, 149 min, US, Hal Ashby) A Best Picture nomination went to this acclaimed biography of the great singer-composer Woody Guthrie. David Carradine gives an exceptional performance as Guthrie, whose travels across the country during the Depression would inspire his legendary folk songs. The fine supporting cast includes Melinda Dillon, Ronny Cox, Gail Strickland and Randy Quaid. Superb cinematography by Haskell Wexler. ★★★½ $19.99

The Bounty

(1984, 130 min, Australia, Roger Donaldson) Donaldson's lavish and sensual production presents a decidedly different and allegedly more authentic version of the infamous nautical mutiny. Anthony Hopkins as Captain Bligh is not the tyrannical madman of previous interpretations, but rather a puritanically moral and unflinchingly formal seaman. Mel Gibson is Fletcher Christian, former friend of the captain, who becomes a reluctant figurehead in the takeover. ★★★

Boxcar Bertha

(1972, 97 min, US, Martin Scorsese) Scorsese's first feature-length film is not what you'd expect from a Roger Corman production with a title like this. Barbara Hershey gives a fine performance as a Depression-era orphan whose life is radicalized through association with renegade Keith Carradine. Well worth checking out, especially for Scorsese aficionados. ★★★

The Boxer and Death

(1962, 107 min, Czechoslovakia, Peter Solan) A Polish amateur boxer, imprisoned in a German concentration camp, is forced to literally fight for his life after the camp's burly commandant, a boxer himself, spares him from death, but forces him into pummeling fighting matches. Initially stunned when he begins to receive special treatment while the commandant "fattens" him up for the kill, the prisoner faces not only the resentment of his fellow prisoners, but must decide whether to continue playing the patsy or risk his life by beating the egocentric commandant. Holding little back in depicting the wretched conditions of the death camps, the film is an unforgettably harrowing tale of bitter survival. (Czech and German with English subtitles) ★★★ $79.99

Boxing Helena

(1993, 95 min, US, Jennifer Lynch) Only a child of the '80s, who was raised on "Dallas" and MTV, could think it acceptable to resolve a dramatic conflict with an "it was all a dream" sequence disguised as a music video. And

twentysomething director Lynch shows her age in this immature study of love and image. Though the leads (Julian Sands and Sherilyn Fenn) are undoubtedly physically attractive, Sands' twitchy, insecure performance makes the film extremely difficult to watch, even before the "dismember the one you love" theme comes to bear. ★½ $19.99

A Boy and His Dog

(1975, 87 min, US, L.Q. Jones) A quirky, sci-fi comedy that envisions a future of roving scavengers and secluded townspeople. A very young Don Johnson, accompanied by his highly intelligent talking dog, enters a surreal world of Americana only to be faced with imprisonment and the spectre of becoming a semen-producing machine for the women of the town. A cult favorite based on Harlan Ellison's WWIII novel. ★★★ $29.99

A Boy Named Charlie Brown

(1969, 85 min, US, Bill Melendez) Good grief, Charlie Brown in his own animated feature. The entire Peanuts gang is on hand in this engaging children's romp. ★★★ $14.99

The Boy Who Left Home to Find Out About the Shivers

(1983, 60 min, US, Graeme Clifford) Vincent Price narrates this charming tale of a boy who knows no fear – be it ghost or dragon or monster – until faced with the prospect of marriage. With Peter MacNichol, Dana Hill, Christopher Lee, David Warner and Frank Zappa. From Shelley Duvall's Faerie Tale Theatre. ★★★

The Boy with Green Hair

(1948, 82 min, US, Joseph Losey) An involving WWII drama about a young war orphan who becomes a social outcast when overnight his hair turns green. A very young Dean Stockwell, who had one of his best child roles here, stars as the youth who is passed around from relative to relative, and ultimately becomes a symbol of the futility of war. ★★★ $19.99

The Boyfriend

(1971, 140 min, GB, Ken Russell) All-out musical numbers and spectacle abound in this lavishly entertaining musical – a glamorous tribute to Busby Berkeley – starring Twiggy, Tommy Tune and Christopher Gable. In a cameo appearance, Glenda Jackson is the star who, before opening night of the "big show," breaks her leg, forcing her mousy understudy (Twiggy) into the spotlight and onto the road to superstardom. The film was recently restored with additional footage. ★★★ $19.99

Boyfriends and Girlfriends (L'Ami de Mon Amie)

(1987, 103 min, France, Eric Rohmer) This, Rohmer's sixth in his series of "Comedies & Proverbs," comes dangerously close to being a parody of his best work. Intellectually lightweight with only a wisp of a plot, the film, which concerns itself with the questions of friendship, fidelity, compassion and betrayal, revolves around a group of young, attractive and rich friends who, when not being shallow and self-centered, are on the prowl for sex.

Blanche, a shy, lonely civil servant (and Dr. Joyce Brothers look-alike) befriends the carefree Lea, who attempts to find her a lover only to see it backfire when Blanche becomes involved with Fabian, her boyfriend. Set in the beautifully designed but emotionally cold new city of Cergy outside of Paris, Rohmer observes these people's love follies with his usual detached amusement. (French with English subtitles) ★★ $19.99

Boys

(1996, 87 min, US, Stacy Cochran) As *Boys* illustrates through rather clichéd dramatics: Left to their own devices, boys will be boys. This film also illustrates: A contrived script left underdeveloped will soon be forgotten. *Boys* is based on a short story by James Salter, and the premise would stretch the limits of a 20-minute short film let alone a feature-length one. An extremely talented child actor who has less luck with his first "grown-up" role, Lukas Haas plays a high school senior at a boys' academy who shelters injured Winona Ryder, who's avoiding the authorities; though why is a mystery. As the school becomes abuzz about a girl on campus, the young teen falls for the hard-partying, "older" woman. Scenes are dragged on too long, as if padding the 87-minute running time. And it takes forever to get to the puzzle of what happened – by then you just won't care. Director Cochran, however, displays a sure hand in several scenes; she could make an impression with the right material. ★½ $19.99

The Boys from Brazil

(1978, 123 min, US, Franklin J. Schaffner) Laurence Olivier stars in this high-tension political thriller as a Nazi-hunter who uncovers the existence of a war criminal (Gregory Peck) and his plans to resurrect the Third Reich by cloning Adolph Hitler. Based on the novel by Ira Levin, the film co-stars James Mason, Uta Hagen, Lilli Palmer, Steve Guttenberg and Denholm Elliott. ★★★ $9.99

Boys in Love

(83 min) A collection of four gay-themed shorts by various directors. *Death in Venice, CA* (1994, 30 min, David Ebersole) is a wry sexual drama, surprisingly professional and a pleasurable tale on the perils of romantic love. The story (suggested by Mann's novella) centers on the relationship between an older English writer and a muscular youth he meets at the California beach town. Also included are: *Achilles* (1995, 11 min, GB, Barry JC Purves), an 11-minute short about Achilles and his lover Petroclus imaginatively told through puppets; *My Polish Waiter* (1994, 12 min, US, Gary Terracino), a charming short about a man who falls for a silent and inscrutable waiter; and *Miguel My Love* (1995, 29 min, US, George Camarda), which follows the story of Miguel, an HIV-positive man who is dumped by his protective lover, and who learns self-reliance, strength and discovers the ability to love. ★★★ $29.99

The Boys in the Band

(1970, 118 min, US, William Friedkin) Historically and politically significant despite (or because of) the pervading self-loathing and wallowing self-pity of its gay characters, *The Boys in the Band* is a stage-bound, hyperventilating comedy-drama about eight friends who get together for a simple birthday party. What ensues during the course of the evening is enough emotion, acid-laced barbs and self-analysis to last a lifetime. Michael (Kenneth Nelson), a guilt-ridden Catholic with a drinking problem, is the host of the party. Harold (marvelously played by Leonard Frey) is the birthday boy. And the guests include a bickering couple, a hustler (a present for Harold), and a limp-wristed, lisping interior designer (immortally played by Cliff Gorman). With a screenplay peppered with many memorable lines, *The Boys in the Band* is a pre-liberation classic which is dated but hilarious and at times surprisingly offensive to '90s gay sensibility. It's also an important step in the depiction of gays in film. ★★★ $59.99

Boys Life

(90 min) A collection of three gay-themed short films. *Pool Days* (1993, 29 min, US, Brian Sloan) is a wryly humorous, sexy and sensitive coming-out story set in a gym where handsome 17-year-old Justin gets a summer job as a lifeguard/attendant. Still confused about his sexuality, the gay world comes to him as steam room sex, naked male bodies and one particularly enticing swimmer cloud his head with sex, sex, and more sex. Also included are *A Friend of Dorothy* (directed by Raoul O'Connell) and *The Disco Years* (directed by Robert Lee King). ★★★ $59.99

The Boys Next Door

(1985, 91 min, US, Penelope Spheeris) Charlie Sheen and Maxwell Caulfield are Bo and Roy, respectively, two California high school grads who vent their frustrations by going on a killing spree. In a hard-hitting, semidocumentary-like style, the film examines the damaged psyches of these two killers as they wend their way throughout Los Angeles randomly choosing and then murdering their victims. The murder scenes are especially brutal, but don't border on the gratuitous as they serve to illustrate the duo's twisted minds. There's a subplot of gay bashing (one of the film's most disturbing sequences) which brings to light Roy's closeted homosexual feelings; Caulfield's sexually repressed teen is a terrifying, but unfortunately, all-too-real characterization. ★★★ $14.99

Boys of Cell Block Q

(1992, 90 min, US, Alan Daniels) Teetering between being an enjoyably cheesy C&A "boys in prison" spoof and actual drama, this poor man's *Fortune and Men's Eyes* works best for those seeking humor and skin (but alas, no sex!). The setting is Sunnyvale Labor Farm for wayward boys – a veritable hotbed of homosexuality, pumped-up pecs, sadistic guards, lecherous priests, and a coterie of pretty boys who seem to be at all times in various stages of undress. The story focuses on one cell of boys: Tim, the innocent "virgin" with a murderous past; Beef, the hunky chieftain and self-proclaimed "Top Cock"; and Lana, the acid-tongued queen. Adapted from a John C. Wall play and filled with campy lines such as, "He thought that it would be bad to be a homosexual in love with a minor who kills people" and "Put that in your crockpot and simmer it," the film won't be confused with Shakespeare, but then again, what was the last Shakespeare play with studs entangled in a steamy, naked brawl in the showers? ★★ $29.99

The Boys of St. Vincent

(1992, 184 min, Canada, John N. Smith) This compelling two-part drama of physical and sexual abuse at a Canadian boys' orphanage unravels like a wrenching sexual horror film and makes for a riveting, if uncomfortable, viewing. Part One, set in a Newfoundland school in 1975, centers on a withdrawn ten-year-old boy who is the sexual pet of Brother Lavin, the dictatorial and devil-like principal. It takes a sympathetic janitor to call the police, but Church complicity and police reluctance to interfere conspire to cover up the problem in a veil of secrecy. Part Two, set 15 years later, finds the boys, now emotionally scarred men, successfully initiating charges against the brothers involved. The story, based on true events, is quite disturbing, and the scenes of physical and sexual abuse are almost too painful to watch. ★★★ $89.99

Whoopi Goldberg (l.), Mary-Louise Parker (c.) and Drew Barrymore in *Boys on the Side*

Boys on the Side

(1995, 117 min, US, Herbert Ross) Singer-musician Joan (Whoopi Goldberg), reeling from the break-up of her latest band, takes a ride-share to L.A. with Robin (Mary-Louise Parker), a seemingly pristine yuppie who bemoans the crash of the real estate market. En route, they stop to visit Joan's friend Holly (Drew Barrymore), interrupting her savage beating at the hands of her drug-dealing, scummy boyfriend. The swiftly moving odyssey which follows is punctuated by strong characterizations by the three leads and seamless support by an ensemble including James Remar, Matthew McConaughey and Estelle Parsons. Fine cinematography indulges the glowing desert vistas of Tucson, a pit stop which extends to include birth and death. The film flirts with mawkishness during the last half-hour, only momentarily crossing the line. While comparisons to *Thelma and Louise* are to be made, the film's more about survival than allegory. And that's its gritty strength. Goldberg's portrayal of Joan is among her best, though her lesbian character is the only lead not offered a romantic involvement. ★★★ $19.99

Boys' Shorts

(1990-91, 119 min) A compilation of six short films dealing with gay issues. *Resonance* (1991, 11 min, Australia, Stephen Cummins) is a visually impressive, abstract story about a queer-bashing. *R.S.V.P.* (1991, 23 min, Canada, Laurie Lynd) centers on a group of students remembering their teacher who has died of AIDS. *Anthem* (1990, 9 min, US, Marlon Riggs) is a poetic rap exploration of love and desire as it relates to gay African-Americans. *Relax* (1991, 25 min, GB, Christopher Newby) is a humorous, imaginative take on one man's decision to take an HIV test. *Billy Turner's Secret* (1990, 26 min, US, Michael Mayson) is the entertaining story of a man coming out to his none-too-enlightened roommate. *The Dead Boys' Club* (1992, 25 min, US, Mark Christopher) is the best of the bunch. A pair of shoes magically transport a shy and closeted man to the carefree, boisterous days of the 1970s. ★★★ $39.99

Boys Town

(1938, 96 min, US, Norman Taurog) Fine sentimental drama with Spencer Tracy winning an Oscar for his poignant portrayal of Father Flanagan, the founder of a school for troubled youths. Also with Mickey Rooney as a street-wise delinquent. ★★★ $19.99

Boyz N the Hood

(1991, 107 min, US, John Singleton) Singleton's powerful directorial debut is a brilliant examination of the crises facing young black men in the '90s, as well as a searing indictment of the culture of violence which holds sway in American ghettoes today. Set in the rough-and-tumble of South Central Los Angeles, the film tells the story of three black teens who face the unrelenting, and often deadly, realities of urban life. Singleton successfully avoids stereotyping his three heroes as inner-city misfits and instead portrays them as average American youth caught in an untenable situation. The acting is superb, especially

on the part of the young leads: Cuba Gooding, Jr., Ice Cube and Morris Chestnut. Laurence Fishburne gives solid support as Gooding's morally upright dad. ★★★★ $14.99

The Brady Bunch Movie

(1995, 89 min, US, Betty Thomas) The millions who loved — or hated — "The Brady Bunch," that heavenly family from hell who invaded our collective living rooms from 1969 to 1974, have reason to rejoice in this hilarious polyester and plaid restoration that asks the question, "What would happen if America's favorite family of the '70s ever collided with the naughty '90s?" In true sitcom fashion, this week's episode finds the Bradys on the verge of losing their groovy pad unless they can raise the $20,000 they owe in back taxes. And to add to the stew, Jan's sibling rivalry with "Marcia! Marcia! Marcia!" reaches fever pitch; Marcia's best friend at school has a lesbian crush on her; and the high school guidance counselor is a transvestite (RuPaul)! Shelley Long and Gary Cole appear as parents Carol & Mike, but it's Christine Taylor and especially Jennifer Elise Cox who shine as Marcia and Jan, respectively. Chock full of in-jokes and cameos by original cast members, this double-knitted comedy strikes a nostalgic chord even as it hits the funny bone. (Followed by a 1996 sequel, *A Very Brady Sequel*) ★★★ $14.99

Brain Damage

(1988, 94 min, US, Frank Henenlotter) If you loved *Frankenhooker* or *Basket Case*, then this offbeat gem is for you. In a sharp parable about drug addiction, Rick Herbst must cater to his talking parasite's every whim, or be deprived of its euphoria-inducing excreta. Horror show host Zacherley (in Philly he was known as Roland) supplies the voice for the wise-cracking slug. ★★★ $14.99

Brain Dead

(1989, 85 min, US, Adam Simon) Well-intentioned psychological thriller that asks the question, "Are we the dreamer, or the dream?" Bill Pullman stars as a scientist whose brain research leads to the recesses of his own mind. To say more would be to give the show away, but suffice to say that the film is highly original and well-staged. Also with Bill Paxton and Bud Cort. ★★★ $79.99

Brain Donors

(1992, 79 min, US, Dennis Dugan) Anyone who has been blown away by the intensity of John Turturro must also have been impressed by the actor's versatility. From modern-day mafia butcher in *Men of Respect*; to a snivelling traitor in *Miller's Crossing*; to a self-important playwright with nothing to say in *Barton Fink*, Turturro's cutting-edge performances invariably leave one asking, "What does he do for an encore?" Well, try this for size, as he takes on the ambitious role of Groucho Marx. Updated and restaged to the world of ballet, this well-meaning remake of the Marx Brothers' classic *A Night at the Opera* benefits from Turturro's frenetic turn as an ambulance-chasing shyster masquerading as an impresario of the dance. Nancy Marchand pays ample tribute to Margaret Dumont in her role as a beleaguered

society matron. Bob Nelson and Mel Smith are on hand as Harpo and Chico. ★★½ $14.99

The Brain from Planet Arous

(1958, 70 min, US, Nathan Juran) In this precursor to *The Hidden*, a lascivious criminal brain from another galaxy commandeers the body of nuclear scientist John Agar for its own nefarious purposes. Another brain from Arous, this one benevolent, comes to Earth and enlists the help of Agar's girlfriend, her father and her dog (which it inhabits), in an attempt to foil the plans of the evil brain, named Gor. Throughout the course of the movie, through Agar's body, Gor blows up two airplanes by looking at them, tries to date-rape Agar's girlfriend, and makes a serious attempt to conquer and enslave the Earth. Agar makes an appropriately insane, if overacting, villain when he is being controlled by Gor, and the brisk movie is engaging in a campy way, but overall it is 1950s horror schlock, complete with cheesy special effects and one-dimensional plot and characters. It is, however, fun to watch, especially at the end, when Agar, having escaped the clutches of Gor, goes head-to-head with him in the form of a big rubber prop brain. ★★ $9.99

The Brain That Wouldn't Die

(1963, 81 min, US, Joseph Green) A scientist wants to graft the body of a hooker onto the decapitated head of his girlfriend. The seven-foot tall mutant in the closet doesn't think that's such a good idea. With occasional moments of gore, this is so bad, it's...well, bad. It's also cheesy, late-nite fun. ★½ $9.99

Brainscan

(1994, 96 min, US, John Flynn) This high-tech horror yawn fest shamelessly borrows from the *Nightmare on Elm Street* films. A teenage video game addict (Edward Furlong) orders a new interactive game which penetrates his subconscious. When friends and neighbors start turning up dead, he becomes the center of an investigation headed by a homicide detective (Frank Langella), while at the same time he's coaxed by a CD-ROM spawned villain named The Trickster (T. Ryder Smith). Long on dazzling special effects but lacking in plot, this tired retread will leave the viewer in need of a brainscan. ★★ $19.99

Brainstorm

(1983, 106 min, US, Douglas Trumbull) Forever to be remembered chiefly as Natalie Wood's last film (a double was used to finish some scenes), this energetic, highly original sci-fi yarn covers a lot of the same ground as *Flatliners*, but with better special effects (director Trumbull did the magic for *2001: A Space Odyssey*, after all). Louise Fletcher is a knock-out as a scientist grappling with the moral repercussions of a euphoria-making sensory device. ★★★ $14.99

Bram Stoker's Dracula

(1992, 127 min, US, Francis Ford Coppola) Coppola's extravagant adaptation of the literary classic delivers the goods with visceral, almost apocalyptic images of carnage juxtaposed with lush, Gothic visuals befitting an Anne Rice novel. These elements coupled with

Keanu Reeves is the Beauty to Gary Oldman's Beast in *Bram Stoker's Dracula*

a truly seductive performance by Gary Oldman as the bloodsucking anti-hero makes for a riveting journey through time. The film opens in the 14th century where Vlad the Impaler (sometimes thought to be Stoker's inspiration for his novel) renounces God in favor of evil following his beloved's premature death. The film then jumps to 19th-century England where Vlad, now known as Count Dracul, finds his eternal love reincarnated as a young beauty, portrayed by Winona Ryder. The film is augmented by an eclectic supporting cast, with an over-the-top Anthony Hopkins as Professor Van Helsing, Keanu Reeves as Jonathan Harker, and Tom Waits as Renfield, all of whom bring new texture to familiar characters. A boldly original and satisfying interpretation of vampire lore. (Available letterboxed or pan & scan) ★★★½ $19.99

Branford Marsalis: The Music Tells You

(1992, 60 min, US, D.A. Pennebaker & Chris Hegedus) Pennebaker and Hegedus take their camera and follow premiere jazz musician Branford Marsalis on tour, working in the studio and relaxing off-hours in this enthralling musical documentary. Appearing with Branford and his trio members, Jeff "Tain" Watts and Robert Hurst, are Sting and Jerry Garcia. ★★★½ $19.99

Brassed Off

(1997, 107 min, GB, Mark Herman) In the wonderful tradition of "small" British social comedies from everything from Ealing Studios gems to *Local Hero* to *The Englishman Who Went Up a Mountain...* comes this unexpected pleasure with one of the most unlikely topics for a ravishing and delectable comedy: a brass band competition. In the small northern England mining town of Grimley, miners have proudly played in the town's brass band for over a century. But the imminent closing of the mines threatens not only the livelihood of an entire town, but the band as well. Under the direction of Pete Postlethwaite (whose solid performance anchors the film), the band tries to persevere as the championship and an uncertain future lie ahead. Writer-director

Herman has created an absolute joy — its humor is sharp, its political observations sharper, and the film is peopled with most appealing and nicely defined characters. These include Ewan McGregor's youthful realist, Tara Fitzgerald as a new band member who's more than she's saying, and, in a brilliant portrayal of comic verve and touching desperation, Stephen Tompkinson as Postlethwaite's devoted son. ★★★½ $99.99

The Brave Little Toaster

(1987, 90 min, US, Jerry Rees) Cute animated musical adventure of a dejected toaster who rounds up the other household appliances — the vacuum cleaner, electric blanket, bedside lamp and radio — and leaves their country cottage for the big city in search of their beloved owner. Featuring the voices of Jon Lovitz and Phil Hartman. ★★★ $22.99

Braveheart

(1995, 179 min, US, Mel Gibson) Gibson's second feature film as director is an accomplished, realistically staged historical epic about 13th-century Scottish patriot and freedom fighter William Wallace. Written by Randall Wallace, reportedly a descendant of the hero himself, it shows us William's youth, courtship of his wife, his reluctant entry into "the Troubles" with the English King Edward the Longshanks (Patrick McGoohan), and his eventual embrace of the military leadership of his country. The script parallels Wallace and Robert the Bruce, the nominal political leader of the Scots, and shows how power can slowly corrupt even the most high-minded and well-intentioned person. Three hours in length, *Braveheart* is remarkably never dull — a credit to Gibson's direction since the script must juggle several story lines. The most amazing thing about the film, however, is its savagely authentic battle scenes, two of which are of an epic scale not seen in film since *Spartacus*. But Wallace's psychological transition from revenge to revolution and his courage in the face of death lift the film above the limitations of an action/adventure movie. Beautifully photographed, *Braveheart* succeeds on many levels: as a rousing adventure film, a heartbreaking

tale of romantic loss, and as a moving tribute to courage, loyalty and conviction. (Available letterboxed and pan & scan) ★★★½ $24.99

Brazil

(1985, 131 min, US, Terry Gilliam) The second in Gilliam's "trilogy" about the realm of fantasy intruding into everyday life (the first being *Time Bandits*, the last *The Adventures of Baron Munchausen*), this darkly comic film is the best of the three. It stars Jonathan Pryce as a bureaucrat stuck in a chaotic government styled in equal parts after *Metropolis*, *1984* and Chaplin's *Modern Times*. He accidentally discovers a mistake made by an authoritarian wing of the government where a man was tortured to death because of a clerical error. His struggle with both his conscience and with the authorities who are now after him is interwoven with his increasingly frequent flights of fancy involving a mysterious stranger he loves and a huge samurai-like demon he must defeat to save her. Robert De Niro also appears as a plumber working for the underground resistance, who takes Pryce into his confidence. Bob Hoskins has a hilarious cameo as another plumber, this one working for the government. Gilliam's vision is perfectly realized here; his futuristic society is a black, towering megalith of ductwork, fascist architecture and machinery crammed into every possible space. A towering achievement for Gilliam, especially considering the struggle he reportedly had to have the film released in its original form — a struggle with a mindless bureaucracy not unlike the one experienced by Pryce in this work of "fiction." ★★★★ $14.99

Break of Hearts

(1935, 80 min, US, Philip Moeller) Katharine Hepburn and Charles Boyer offer good performances in this gentle romantic drama about a young composer (Kate) and her love affair with a famous conductor (Boyer). ★★½ $19.99

Breakdown

(1997, 93 min, US, Jonathan Moslow) Somewhere in the Texas desert, a husband and wife (Kurt Russell and Kathleen Quinlan) are "taking the scenic route" on their way to San Diego and a new life. The financial worry they share is nothing compared to the trouble which lay ahead when she disappears in this tension-filled thriller. Stranded in the middle of nowhere, Quinlan accepts a ride from a friendly trucker (J.T. Walsh) while Russell stays with the car. But when Russell meets up with

Braveheart

Walsh, he insists they've never met and knows nothing about his wife. Recalling *Duel* and Polanski's *Frantic* but with a tempo all its own, the story follows Russell as he desperately tries to piece the puzzle together and locate his wife. Director Moslow creates quite a lot of suspense from the simple premise, and manages to do so with only barren landscape and narrative thrift. Russell's compelling Everyman performance helps, too. *Breakdown* won't do much for Texas tourism, but it certainly will get the pulse racing. ★★★ $99.99

Breaker Morant

(1979, 107 min, Australia, Bruce Beresford) "Breaker" Morant, a cavalry officer serving in South Africa's Boer War, was tried for war crimes, brutality and murder along with two other Australian soldiers. They were defended by an inexperienced but spirited military defense attorney who valiantly tried to expose the political nature of the trial. This fact-based drama stars Edward Woodward, in a sterling performance, as Morant, a heroic soldier who also happened to be a sensitive poet and sometime philosopher. Contrasted with him are the other two soldiers on trial: one a rowdy ne'er-do-well (Bryan Brown) and the other an inexperienced introvert who still believes in the fairness of the British military system. Beautifully filmed, *Breaker Morant* incorporates exciting flashbacks as the facts are presented in the courtroom. It's also profoundly moving, a riveting exposition of a series of events open to many interpretations which lead to a definite conception of what truth is — a conception tragically not shared by judges and the powers that be. ★★★★ $19.99

Breakfast at Tiffany's

(1961, 114 min, US, Blake Edwards) Based on a Truman Capote story, this winning romantic comedy stars Audrey Hepburn as small-town Texas girl Holly Golightly, who leaves home to conquer the Manhattan party scene. There's zesty direction by Edwards and a fanciful Henry Mancini score including the Oscar-winning "Moon River." ★★★½ $14.99

The Breakfast Club

(1985, 92 min, US, John Hughes) Perceptive and entertaining teen drama written and directed by Hughes. Five high school students spend a Saturday detention at the school library. Each of the students comes to learn a little about themselves, as well as their newly acquainted classmates. As the students, Emilio Estevez, Anthony Michael Hall, Judd Nelson, Molly Ringwald and Ally Sheedy have rarely been better. ★★★ $14.99

Breaking Away

(1979, 100 min, US, Peter Yates) A funny, exhilarating ode to growing up. Four recent high school graduates compete against insecurity, frustration and an Italian bicycle racing team. Sensitively directed by Yates. With Dennis Christopher, Daniel Stern and a young Dennis Quaid. ★★★★ $59.99

Breaking Glass

(1980, 104 min, GB, Brian Gibson) The rise to stardom is old fodder for the story mill and this unexceptional punk/new wave success

story does nothing to give it new life. This is a fairly predictable tale of the exploits of Hazel O'Connor as she works her way out of the dingy clubs of London to become a punk superstar. Only exceptional performances by O'Connor, Phil Daniels (of *Quadrophenia* fame), and Jonathan Pryce save this film from complete mediocrity. ★★ $49.99

Breaking In

(1989, 91 min, US, Bill Forsyth) This heist comedy by Forsyth was anticipated by many in the film community with great relish. Couple Forsyth's knack for putting together charming, off-kilter comedies and the screenwriting genius of John Sayles; add to the mix the inimitable talents of Burt Reynolds and the youthful energy of newcomer Casey Siemaszko (*Three O'Clock High*) and it's easy to see why so many people were expecting so much from this story about an aging safecracker (Reynolds) and his overly enthusiastic apprentice (Siemaszko). The result, however, is a somewhat mild, not overly ambitious comedy-of-errors which, while not overtly uninteresting, only occasionally captivates. ★★½ $14.99

Breaking the Code

(1986, 90 min, GB, Herbert Wise) Re-creating his Tony Award-winning performance for this exceptional play-on-film, Derek Jacobi is outstanding as mathematician and WWII hero Alan Turing, who was naively open about his homosexuality in an intolerant society. A mathematical genius, Turing was responsible for single-handedly breaking the impenetrable Nazi Enigma code, a breakthrough which virtually guaranteed an Allied victory against the German navy. Hugh Whitemore's intelligent screenplay, based on his own play (which was based on Andrew Hodges' novel "Alan Turing: The Enigma"), traces Turing's life as a university student, his time working for British intelligence, and his post-war years as a government researcher in crystal-clear flashbacks. Complex, often humorous and intellectually satisfying, Whitemore's story, while paying tribute to Turing, is a stinging indictment of homophobia and its often high cost. Society's loss has rarely been more apparent. As the stuttering, nail-biting, completely candid Turing, Jacobi mesmerizes with a stunning portrayal rich in subtle shadings, honest emotions and profound compassion. ★★★★ $19.99

Breaking the Rules

(1992, 100 min, US, Neal Israel) Attempting to fill the market niche somewhere between the inane teen comedy and the serious adult drama, this tedious tale of three young men who reunite a few years after college to confront their past and their futures sadly breaks no rules and blazes no new trails. In all fairness, the three young leads, Jonathan Silverman, C. Thomas Howell and Jason Bateman, do their best with a lethal script which follows the trio as they set off on a cross-country road trip after Bateman reveals to them that he is dying of cancer. Annie Potts enlivens things as a small-town waitress who joins them on their trail of tears. (Filmed in 1989 but released three years later.) ★½ $14.99

Emily Watson in *Breaking the Waves*

Breaking the Waves

(1996, 156 min, GB/Scotland, Lars von Trier) Danish director von Trier, who has established himself as a world class cinema experimenter with his earlier films (*Zentropa*, *The Kingdom*), has managed to tightrope his way toward straight narrative while at the same time making a thoroughly unconventional movie. And it must be said at the outset that this 156-minute marathon is definitely not for all tastes. But for those who are not put off by a claustrophobic, hand-held, ultra-intimate character study of the pitiful lives of a few hardy souls in an inhospitable Scottish hamlet on the North Sea coast, the result is a riveting and thought-provoking examination of obsessive love and one's relationship to God. Bess (Emily Watson) is an emotionally unstable young woman who breaks the village taboo by marrying an outsider, Jan (Stellan Skarsgard). Jan, a big bear of an oil rig worker with a heart of gold, seems bent on seeing her passions flower beyond her strict religious background. But on the fateful day that he must return to his rig, she breaks apart mentally and thus begins her slide into all-out obsession. Watson won a Best Actress nomination as Bess, who regularly throughout the film holds intimate two-way conversations with God — as hokey as they could have been, Watson miraculously pulls them off. Ultimately the film seems as confused about faith as its characters are, but that by no means diminishes its effectiveness as a philosophical puzzler. ★★★★ $102.99

A Breath of Scandal

(1960, 98 min, US, Michael Curtiz) The ghost of Ernst Lubitsch was vainly resurrected for this uneven adaptation of the Ferenc Molnar play. Sophia Loren gives a gallant attempt to be sexy and funny, playing an Austrian princess. Unfortunately, she's cast opposite the monotonous John Gavin as an American businessman who enters her life and with whom she falls in love. Gavin is miscast — the part begs for the sophisticated charm of a Cary Grant or a Rock Hudson — and Gavin is neither. Director Curtiz, not known for a light touch, evokes a small degree of playfulness, but misses many comic opportunities. However, former Lubitsch leading man

Maurice Chevalier appears as Loren's father, and he elevates every scene in which he appears. ★★ $9.99

Breathless (À Bout de Souffle)

(1959, 89 min, France, Jean-Luc Godard) Godard shook the film world with his dynamic style of editing, sound usage, character development and plot progression in this, his first feature film. Jean-Paul Belmondo is the two-bit, existential hood engaged in a fateful affair with Jean Seberg. (French with English subtitles) ★★★★ $29.99

A Breed Apart

(1984, 101 min, US, Philippe Mora) Millionaire egg collector Donald Pleasence wants two rare Bald Eagle eggs, even if it means extinguishing the species. He offers $150,000 to world-famous mountain climber Powers Boothe to scale the rock face on which the nest sits, on an island owned by Vietnam vet turned back-to-nature survivalist Rutger Hauer. Kathleen Turner is the requisite love interest. An idiosyncratic little film saved from its shortcomings by the performances of its cast. ★★½ $9.99

Brenda Starr

(1992, 87 min, US, Robert Ellis Miller) It took four painstaking years to bring Dale Messick's popular comic strip character straight to home video, and this is so bad it's easy to see why it was never released theatrically. Brooke Shields headlines as the star reporter for The Flash who, along with her dashing mystery man Basil St. John (Timothy Dalton), is hot on the trail of the scoop of the century: a new, secret formula created by an ex-Nazi scientist which could open the door to star travel. Dalton fought to have his name removed from the credits. It has to be seen to be disbelieved. ★ $19.99

Brewster McCloud

(1970, 101 min, US, Robert Altman) A quirky oddity that, although seemingly dated today, still should please fans of fantasy as well as devotees of director Altman. Bud Cort stars as the misunderstood young man who lives within the catacombs of Houston's Astrodome and dreams of flying on his own. Sally Kellerman is his fairy godmother who helps make it happen, and the delightful Shelley Duvall plays a Dome tour guide who befriends him. A funny fable about man's lofty ambitions as well as the forces of self-destruction. ★★★ $19.99

Brewster's Millions

(1985, 101 min, US, Walter Hill) Though Richard Pryor and John Candy are appealing performers, and work rather well together, there's not much to recommend in this oft-told tale. Pryor plays a baseball player who stands to collect $300 million — but only if he can spend $30 million in exactly one month. ★★ $19.99

Brian's Song

(1970, 73 min, US, Buzz Kulik) Well-made and moving TV drama about Chicago Bears player Brian Piccolo, and his special friendship with teammate Gale Sayers when the former is diagnosed with cancer. James Caan as Piccolo and Billy Dee Williams as Sayers bring remarkable heartfelt conviction to their roles. ★★★ $9.99

The Bride

(1985, 118 min, US, Franc Roddam) Rock star Sting plays Dr. Frankenstein whose monster (Clancy Brown) runs away from the lab after being rejected by Jennifer Beals, his newly created bride-to-be. On the road, the goodhearted but muddled monster is befriended by a conniving midget (David Rappaport). The friendship that develops is both funny and touching and makes the film worth watching despite the inane activities going on back at Frankenstein's castle. ★★½ $9.99

The Bride Came C.O.D.

(1941, 92 min, US, William Keighley) Though neither was known specifically for comedy, Bette Davis and James Cagney bring a lot of life to this zesty 1940s romp about flier Cagney kidnapping bride-to-be Davis at her millionaire father's request. The fireworks start when they crash land in the desert. ★★★ $19.99

The Bride of Frankenstein

(1935, 75 min, US, James Whale) Dr. Frankenstein (Colin Clive) makes a bride for his creature (Boris Karloff), and all hell breaks loose. Arguably better than its predecessor — both emotionally and stylistically — Whale's moody sequel to his 1931 classic Frankenstein best illustrates the director's macabre sense of humor and filmmaking talent. Elsa Lanchester plays a dual role as "the bride" and as author Mary Shelley. Whale personally designed Lanchester's spiffy hair-do. ★★★★ $14.99

Bride of Re-Animator

(1990, 99 min, US, Brian Yuzna) This sequel to the horror cult classic Re-Animator carries on the tradition of presenting graphic bloodshed so outrageous it's goofy. Jeffrey Combs reprises his role as Herbert West, a young, brilliant and thoroughly demented medical student who is obsessed with reanimating dead tissue — especially dead human tissue. Here, Herbert launches a new project at med school. Filled with hilarious one-liners and ludicrous scenarios only possible in films like this, Bride of Re-Animator is silly and entertaining, equal parts comedy and horror. ★★½ $9.99

The Bride with White Hair

(1993, 111 min, Hong Kong, Ronny Yu) Set in a fantasy world which sometimes resembles feudal China and sometimes looks like Rudyard Kipling on acid, this expensive Hong Kong film is about a young warrior (Leslie Cheung Kwok-Wing), the successor to the leadership of the clan Wu Tang, who falls in love with a powerful warrior/witch (Brigitte Lin Ching-Hsia) who is the bound slave of a pair of evil siblings whose intent is to destroy Wu Tang and rule the world. These star-crossed lovers make a pact to run away together, but things naturally go awry and betrayal rears its ugly head, leaving bloodshed in its wake. Filled with the usual Hong Kong action setpieces, Bride is distinguished by its adult tone and heartfelt love story. Every frame of the film has been designed for maximum visual and emotional impact. Lin (Chungking Express) is absolutely stunning as the Bride of the title and Cheung (Farewell My Concubine) proves that he can handle his action sequences as well as his dramatic ones. Easily one of the best films to come out of Hong Kong in the last ten years. (In Cantonese with English subtitles) ★★★★ $79.99

The Bride with White Hair 2

(1993, 80 min, Hong Kong, David Wu) Made right on the heels of Bride part one, this dull and pointless sequel picks up ten years after the events of the original. Ni-chang (Brigitte Lin Ching-Hsia), the white-haired witch, is now inexplicably the leader of a man-hating cult populated by women who have been cheated on or betrayed by their lovers and confidants. Seeking to destroy the remnants of the Wu Tang clan, Lin kidnaps the bride of the nephew of Cho Yi-hang (Leslie Cheung Kwok-Wing), the man who originally betrayed her. The nephew, of course, must rally his forces and storm the fortress of the evil cult to rescue his beloved, who has unfortunately been brainwashed to hate and murder him. Tepid, lackluster and sorely missing the style, emotions and grandeur of the first production (except when it flashes back to scenes from the original), Bride 2 only becomes worthwhile during its last ten minutes, when Lin and Cheung are finally (and inevitably) reunited. Unfortunately, it's too long to wait. (In Cantonese with English subtitles) ★½ $79.99

The Bride Wore Black

(1967, 107 min, France, François Truffaut) Jeanne Moreau stars as the inscrutable femme fatale with a murderous mission in Truffaut's haunting, suspense-filled homage to Hitchcock. Widowed on her wedding day, Moreau vows vengeance on her husband's killers. Stylish and extremely satisfying with a score by Bernard Herrmann. (French with English subtitles) ★★★½ $19.99

The Bride Wore Red

(1937, 103 min, US, Dorothy Arzner) In a nod to "Pygmalion" and with a touch of "Cinderella," an eccentric count, trying to prove his theory about class difference, sends nightclub singer Joan Crawford off to a posh Austrian resort. There she poses as royalty, meets postman Franchot Tone and rich playboy Robert Young. Echoing many themes from "Pygmalion," director Arzner isn't afforded the luxury of a classic screenplay, but manages to infuse a degree of high spirits into her social comedy. Crawford is well cast and looks great. ★★★ $19.99

Brides of Dracula

(1960, 85 min, GB, Terence Fisher) Dracula's back and this time he's a blond! David Peel stars in this quasi-Freudian take on the vampire legend as a bloodthirsty count whose dining-out privileges are revoked by his mother, who keeps him locked in the castle tower. Who says blonds have more fun? Peter Cushing reprises his role as the fearless vampire hunter, Professor Van Helsing. ★★★ $14.99

Brideshead Revisited

(1980, 581 min, GB, Charles Sturridge/Michael Lindsay-Hogg) A brilliant and haunting adaptation of Evelyn Waugh's best-loved novel. Don't be put off by the length of this miniseries as it is divided into six easily viewed and totally captivating episodes which chronicle a young man's enigmatic and obsessive relationship with a rich, aristocratic British family. Jeremy Irons heads an all-star cast, including Anthony Andrews, Claire Bloom, Diana Quick and special guest stars Laurence Olivier and John Gielgud. Spanning three decades from the early 1920s to the end of WWII, the story begins as a disenchanted British army captain, Charles Ryder (Irons), looks back on his earlier life, in happier days. It was then he first encountered Sebastian Flyte — the dazzling ill-starred son of Lord and Lady Marchmain. Sebastian brings Charles to the family home of Brideshead, beginning Charles' compulsive love affair with this strange, doomed family. Irons is outstanding in what may be the finest miniseries on video. (Six volumes are also available at $19.99 each) ★★★★ $119.99

The Bridge

(1959, 102 min, West Germany, Bernhard Wicki) Based on the autobiography of one of the participants, *The Bridge* is set during the final days of World War II, when Allied armies were triumphantly advancing across the German countryside and the Nazi war machine was grinding to a halt. In desperation, Hitler and his generals tapped the last resource available to defend their homeland: German children. The film tells the story of a group of boys, friends in school, who enthusiastically take up rifles and don uniforms to defend their hometown when the call is given. Due to an unfortunate set of coincidences, their adult commander is accidentally killed and they are left, leaderless, to guard the bridge leading into their town. After the rest of the nearby German army retreats past them, they remain at their posts to face the approaching Americans, without a wiser, guiding force to tell them when to retreat or surrender. Extremely powerful but unremittingly bleak, *The Bridge* is a strongly anti-war film which paradoxically contains some remarkable battle sequences. You won't soon forget its harsh picture of children forced to die like men. (German with English subtitles) ★★★½ $29.99

The Bridge on the River Kwai

(1957, 161 min, GB, David Lean) This magnificent wartime drama won seven Academy Awards and stands out as one of the greatest and most powerful films ever made about war and its degenerative effect on the minds of men. Filled with high-powered action sequences and intense psychological torture, the film stars Oscar-winner Alec Guinness, William Holden and Jack Hawkins. (Available letterboxed and pan & scan) ★★★★ $19.99

Bridge to Nowhere

(1986, 82 min, Australia, Ian Mune) Bruno Lawrence (*The Quiet Earth*) stars in this tense action-adventure film about five teenagers who, on an outdoor camping trip, cross paths with a psychotic hermit. Their struggle for survival reminds one of an Aussie *Deliverance*. ★★★ $19.99

A Bridge Too Far

(1977, 175 min, GB, Richard Attenborough) Though most will regard this as "a film too long," Attenborough's adaptation of Cornelius Ryan's book about a disastrous raid behind German lines in WWII Holland does offer a meticulous examination of the ill-fated mission. An all-star cast includes Dirk Bogarde, James Caan, Sean Connery, Robert Redford, Gene Hackman, Anthony Hopkins, Laurence Olivier and Liv Ullmann. (Available letterboxed and pan & scan) ★★★ $24.99

The Bridges at Toko-Ri

(1954, 103 min, US, Mark Robson) William Holden stars in this powerful Korean War drama based on James Michener's novel about a civilian lawyer recalled to military duty overseas. Grace Kelly also stars as his wife who patiently waits at home. Holden and Kelly give fine performances, as do Fredric March, as a world-weary admiral, and Mickey Rooney, as a fellow pilot. ★★★½ $14.99

The Bridges of Madison County

(1995, 135 min, US, Clint Eastwood) Robert James Walker's best-selling novel makes for a grand love story, beautifully evoking the romanticism of the novel and further illustrating the lyricism and range of director Eastwood. Meryl Streep plays Francesca Johnson, an Iowa housewife and Italian émigré whose children, upon her death, discover their seemingly staid mother was involved in an extramarital affair. As the film flashbacks to the mid-1960s, the story focuses on the four-day romance between Francesca and a photojournalist, Robert Kincaid (Eastwood), who is photographing local bridges for *National Geographic*. Director Eastwood changes gears from what's usually expected of him and has produced a truly romantic, knowing drama which is as intimate as two lovers. Only one or two slowly paced scenes which interrupt the movement of the story keep this from being the romantic masterwork it very nearly is. Streep, donning yet another accent to give yet another remarkably subtle characterization, has a rapport with Eastwood like no other actress with whom he's appeared. And he is commendable in a role which seems to have the Robert Redford stamp all over it. ★★★½ $19.99

Brief Encounter

(1946, 86 min, GB, David Lean) A masterpiece from Britain's post-war cinema, this extraordinary romantic drama stars Trevor Howard and Celia Johnson, both giving impeccable performances, as two ordinary, middle-aged people involved in a short but compassionate extramarital affair. Subtle, masterful direction from Lean. Based on Noël Coward's one-act play, "Still Life." ★★★★ $14.99

A Brief History of Time

(1992, 80 min, US, Errol Morris) This fascinating, intellectually demanding documentary examines the life of British theoretical physicist Stephen Hawking, based on his own best-selling book. Interweaving biographical and academic information, the film balances its time between insightful glimpses into Hawking's past and colleagues expounding on his scientific theories. And though the scholarly topics, such as the Big Bang, black holes and the origin of the universe, may not be easy to comprehend for many, it is to director Morris' credit that these cerebral exercises are not completely over the head of the average viewer. A victim of ALS (Lou Gehrig's disease), Hawking is completely paralyzed and confined to a wheelchair, but his amazing inner strength and incredible intellect shine through, making his ideas and the film itself all the more mesmerizing. It's the most stimulating Advanced Physics class you'll never attend. ★★★½ $19.99

The Brig

(1964, 55 min, US, Jonas Mekas) A Living Theatre production that, interestingly, was furiously filmed in five hours in a theatre that was closed for tax reasons. This searing drama depicts a hellish Marine Corps prison where humiliation, degradation and brutality are the norm. An impassioned, unrelentingly powerful drama. ★★★½ $29.99

Brigadoon

(1954, 109 min, US, Vincente Minnelli) Gene Kelly and Van Johnson play two American hunters who stumble upon a magical 18th-cen-

Meryl Streep and Clint Eastwood flirt in *The Bridges of Madison County*

tury village in the Scottish Highlands — a village that comes alive only once every 100 years. Cyd Charisse also stars in this enchanting adaptation of the Broadway musical. ★★★ $14.99

Bright Eyes

(1934, 83 min, US, David Butler) Shirley Temple sings "On the Good Ship Lollipop." Who could ask for anything more? The story has to do with a custody battle over little Shirley. ★★★ $19.99

Bright Lights, Big City

(1988, 110 min, US, James Bridges) Uptown boy Michael J. Fox doesn't realize that he should just say "No" in this fair adaptation of Jay McInerney's best-seller. Fox gives an earnest performance as the young magazine editor whose life becomes entrapped by an endless cycle of work, drugs and decadent nightlife. Kiefer Sutherland is well-cast as Fox's sleazy bar pal, Tad. ★★½ $9.99

Brighton Beach Memoirs

(1986, 108 min, US, Gene Saks) The first of playwright Neil Simon's autobiographical trilogy on his coming-of-age. The story focuses on the Jeromes, a tight-knit Jewish family living in a poor Brooklyn neighborhood in the late 1930s. Jonathan Silverman makes a personable young Simon, and Blythe Danner has some good moments as his mother. Not as successful as the second film, *Biloxi Blues*, but entertaining all the same. ★★★ $19.99

Brighton Rock

(1947, 87 min, GB, John Boulting) A very young and eerily menacing Richard Attenborough stars in this tense drama, based on the novel by Graham Greene, examining the criminal underworld in Brighton. Attenborough is Pinky, an inexperienced but ambitious thug who, with his rag-tag gang of hooligans, begins to stake out his turf on the bustling streets of Brighton. Carol Marsh is the innocent waitress who tragically falls in love with the soulless, immoral killer; Hermione Baddeley is the woman determined to defeat him. ★★★½ $39.99

Brimstone and Treacle

(1982, 85 min, GB, Richard Loncraine) A satanic young man (Sting) methodically forces his way into the lives of a middle-class suburban family by claiming to be the suitor of their mute and immobilized daughter. This unusual and malevolent thriller is not for the faint of heart, but will pay off for those with a need for something out-of-the-ordinary. Also starring Denholm Elliott. ★★★ $14.99

Bring Me the Head of Alfredo Garcia

(1974, 112 min, US, Sam Peckinpah) Warren Oates is a piano player who becomes a bounty hunter when the title command is proclaimed by a rich Mexican landowner. Oates sets off across the dirty, dusty modern landscape to find and deliver that head, which belongs to the father of the landowner's daughter's child. Oates is helped by Isela Vega, his sometimes lover who knows Garcia's last whereabouts. They plan to deliver the head, accept the bounty and make a better life for themselves together. As is not uncommon in Peckinpah's films, this happy, nonviolent outcome is unlikely.

Bringing up Baby

Their journey and search fills most of the film, as they fight both each other and other bounty hunters and killers. Every character is sweaty, miserable and unattractive, double-crossing and betraying each other constantly — only at the very end does Oates perform an act of kindness which redeems him and sets him apart from nearly everyone else in the film. An uncharacteristic film for Peckinpah — it harkens back to his earlier *Ride the High Country* — *Alfredo Garcia* is somber and rather downbeat, but it will please those who are willing to take a brief interest in the struggling lives of its unhappy characters. ★★★ $14.99

Bringing Up Baby

(1938, 102 min, US, Howard Hawks) The definitive screwball comedy, and one of the funniest films ever made. Cary Grant gives his best comic performance as a hilariously befuddled, bespectacled anthropologist who becomes mixed up with daffy but determined heiress Katharine Hepburn (also in one of her funniest performances). Together, they tear apart the Connecticut countryside searching for leopards, pet terriers and an intercostal clavicle; all the while being mistaken for the notorious "Leopard Gang," big game hunters and nuts from Brazil. Grant and Hepburn's flawless comic timing and Hawks' inspired direction combine to make this a timeless and much-adored classic. ★★★★ $19.99

Brink of Life

(1958, 82 min, Sweden, Ingmar Bergman) A simple direct drama by Bergman with a great "Bergman cast" of Eva Dahlbeck, Ingrid Thulin, Bibi Andersson and Max von Sydow. The film focuses on three women facing childbirth during a 24-hour period in a maternity ward. Bergman won the Best Director prize at Cannes for this effort. (Swedish with English subtitles) ★★½ $29.99

The Brinks Job

(1978, 103 min, US, William Friedkin) One of director Friedkin's most entertaining films, this splendid caper comedy re-creates the famous heist which rocked Boston in 1950. Peter Falk is the gang leader, and Peter Boyle, Allen Garfield, Gena Rowlands, Warren Oates and Paul Sorvino round out the cast. ★★★ $12.99

Britannia Hospital

(1982, 115 min, GB, Lindsay Anderson) This scathingly funny and winningly absurd black comedy sums up the ailing state of the once mighty British Empire. Preparations for a visit by the Queen Mother to a floundering medical institution are set against the backdrop of violent protests against the specialized care given to a ruthless African dictator. In the midst of the melee, every possible (and impossible) catastrophe arises until Graham Crowden (as the inimitably insane Dr. Millar) eloquently sums up the meaning of human existence. ★★★½ $9.99

Broadcast News

(1987, 131 min, US, James L. Brooks) An extraordinary study of the ethical proprieties of television journalism, this is a surgically fine and remarkably funny dissection of the daily goings-on of a TV newsroom. Holly Hunter is nothing short of brilliant as the slightly neurotic but talented producer who is saddled with undisciplined newcomer William Hurt, a superficial neophyte with whom she begins an affair. As Hunter's co-worker and pal, Albert Brooks gives one of the great comic performances of recent years. James L. Brooks has written a superbly detailed and intelligent screenplay, and his direction is equally as commanding. ★★★★ $9.99

Broadway Danny Rose

(1984, 83 min, US, Woody Allen) Allen stars as a hopelessly inept talent agent in this charming comedy, doggedly plugging his fourth-rate clients on the borscht circuit. Nick Apollo Forte, as a beefy lounge crooner, is his prize attraction, and Mia Farrow is a gum-chewing moll in distress. ★★★½ $14.99

Broadway Melody

(1929, 104 min, US, Harry Beaumont) The first musical to win a Best Picture Oscar, this backstage tuner shows its age. The story is about two sisters trying to make it on Broadway. Bessie Love and Anita Page play the starstruck siblings, and there's a pleasant score. Billed as "The First All-Talking, All-

Singing, All-Dancing Musical" — and it was. ★★½ $19.99

Broadway Melody of 1940

(1940, 102 min, US, Norman Taurog) Sparkling backstage musical starring Fred Astaire, George Murphy and the great Eleanor Powell. Excellent dance numbers, and a lovely Cole Porter score including "Begin the Beguine" and "I've Got My Eyes on You" set the tone. ★★★ $19.99

Broken Arrow

(1950, 93 min, US, Delmar Daves) After his great success in *Winchester 73*, James Stewart jumped back in the saddle for this acclaimed "pro-Indian" saga with Stewart as an ex-military officer acting as mediator between the Army and Apache chief Cochise (well-played by Jeff Chandler). One of the first of those great '50s westerns to sympathetically portray Native Americans. ★★★ $14.99

Broken Arrow

(1996, 110 min, US, John Woo) Woo's second American film is a moderately successful, big-budget action adventure, but it will be a letdown to the director's fans who have followed his transition from Hong Kong (*The Killer*) to the United States. John Travolta and Christian Slater star as Air Force pilots and steadfast buddies who fly a test run of a new B3 bomber. With nuclear weapons aboard the plane, Travolta ejects them and then himself leaving his friend aboard the plummeting aircraft. Slater survives and teams up with a park ranger (Samantha Mathis), together going after Travolta who is in league with terrorists who plan to sell the weapons back to the government. While the plot is pure Woo — two honorable men of action, former friends, fighting to the death — the film's execution does not live up to his earlier reputation. Much of *Broken Arrow* is undermined by an inane script which eventually throws logic out the window to facilitate its major action

The Brother from Another Planet

sequences. While it may be somewhat (if brainlessly) entertaining, the film is indistinguishable from any other garden-variety, over-produced American action flick. (Available letterboxed and pan & scan) ★★½ $19.99

Broken Blossoms

(1919, 95 min, US, D.W. Griffith) Griffith directed this silent classic of a self-appointed Asian emissary of peace (Richard Barthelmess) and his efforts to protect a young girl (Lillian Gish) from exploitation and abuse by her London thug father (Donald Crisp). This sepia and blue-tinted video contains a short introduction by Ms. Gish. The original musical score strongly supports the film's dramatic undercurrents. ★★★½ $24.99

Broken Lance

(1954, 96 min, US, Edward Dmytryk) This remake of *House of Strangers* has been transferred out West, and bears more than a little resemblance to "King Lear." Spencer Tracy is dynamic as the patriarch of a cattle dynasty whose three sons become at odds with their father and each other. Also with Robert Wagner, Jean Peters, Richard Widmark and Hugh O'Brian. ★★★ $14.99

Broken Noses

(1987, 75 min, US, Bruce Weber) The provocative photographer famed for his salacious Calvin Klein underwear ads, Weber has produced, in this low-budget short feature, a surprisingly touching and strikingly provocative documentary on Golden Gloves Champion Andy Minsker and the pre-pubescent and teenage boys of the Mount Scott Boxing Club. Weber takes his camera into Andy's home where we watch and listen to his family and friends as well as Andy's own thoughts on the rigors of professional boxing and his obvious role as another "Great White Hope." The camera captures the romantic and sensual machismo of the young boxers and the film features the music of Julie London, Chet Baker and Gerry Mulligan. ★★★ $29.99

Broken Vows

(1986, 95 min, Canada, Jud Taylor) Made for television, this atrocious religious drama stars Tommy Lee Jones as a priest who undergoes a spiritual conflict when he falls in love. His troubles begin when he becomes obsessed with finding a killer. He befriends the deceased man's girlfriend (Annette O'Toole), and while trying to piece together the puzzle, they fall in love. Jones must have needed rent money, for he walks through his role with little conviction. He's not given much help, however, as the direction is sluggish and the script astonishingly bad. ★ $19.99

Bronco Billy

(1980, 119 min, US, Clint Eastwood) One of Eastwood's most underrated films, this endearing western fable follows the adventures of a traveling Old West show run by cowboy Clint. His crazy posse includes Sondra Locke, Geoffrey Lewis and Scatman Crothers. ★★★ $14.99

A Bronx Tale

(1993, 122 min, US, Robert De Niro) In his directorial debut, De Niro recalls the films of

his longtime director Martin Scorsese with this beautifully shot and eloquent crime drama based on the play by Chazz Palminteri. Set in the early 1960s, the story traces the relationship between a Bronx youth, Calogero, and a local gangster, Sonny (effectively played by Palminteri), whom the boy refused to identify in a gangland slaying. As "Cee" grows up, he forms a bond with Sonny much to the dismay of his ethical father (De Niro in a subtle performance). Against the backdrop of petty crime, camaraderie, murder and good times, Cee must decide which path to take, which "father" to emulate. Francis Capra and Lillo Brancato as the child and teenaged Cee, respectively, both create memorable characterizations. ★★★½ $14.99

The Brood

(1979, 90 min, Canada, David Cronenberg) The shape of rage is the subject of Cronenberg's fourth visceral medical horror feature — and also the title of the book written by Oliver Reed's character, a renowned but controversial psychiatrist whose "psychoplasmics" method of therapy encourages patients to give physical form to their emotions and fears. Samantha Eggar, Reed's star patient, is undergoing intensive treatment at his new age-type colony in the woods. It is there she gives life to a bizarre group of mutant children who murder her enemies. *The Brood* has the framework of an ordinary horror film, but it is distinguished by an intelligent exploration of the darkest pathologies of the human psyche. Highlighted by a growing sense of unease throughout, the film is one of Cronenberg's best early works — both terrifying and thought-provoking. ★★★

The Brother from Another Planet

(1984, 110 min, US, John Sayles) After his spaceship plummets into New York harbor, a mute black alien (Joe Morton) stumbles into Harlem and learns the earthly ropes. Sayles' comic version of a stranger in a strange land is slyer than *Starman*, earthier than *E.T.* and a potent commentary on the everyday alienation of urban inhabitants. ★★★½

Brother Sun, Sister Moon

(1973, 110 min, GB/Italy, Franco Zeffirelli) Sappy, meandering, hippie-esque (in the bad sense of the word) and plagued by a soundtrack by Donovan, Zeffirelli's romantic story of 13th-century St. Francis of Assisi is quite enjoyable nonetheless. A young man from a wealthy family has a burning quest for spiritual fulfillment which causes him to abandon all worldly possessions and pleasures and live a simple life among nature and the poor. Spectacularly beautiful scenery and sumptuous costumes highlight the tale, which stars an attractive Graham Faulkner in the lead role. ★★½ $14.99

Brother's Keeper

(1992, 105 min, US, Joe Berlinger & Bruce Sinofsky) The quiet, nearly impoverished farming community of Munnville, New York, became the center of a media barrage in 1990 when semi-illiterate farmer Delbert Ward was arrested for killing his 60-year-old brother while their two brothers slept nearby. Having been arrested and signed a confession under duress, Delbert was subsequently released on bail with the support of the local townspeople who believed in his innocence. This award-winning documentary, while scrutinizing the particulars of the case, becomes a fascinating probe into the mindset of rural America. Interviewing Delbert's siblings, their neighbors, relatives and the prosecutors, the filmmakers try to uncover the truth. It becomes painfully obvious that Delbert was a disoriented victim railroaded into a plainly false confession, which is the one very minor drawback of the film as it lacks none of the dramatic tension of *The Thin Blue Line*. However, as an examination of the chasm between rural and urban cultures, *Brother's Keeper* excels. It's a mesmerizing sociological and legal look at an almost forgotten piece of the American pie. ★★★★ $19.99

The Brothers Karamazov

(1958, 146 min, US, Richard Brooks) Epic adaptation of Fyodor Dostoyevsky's novel set in 19th-century Russia. Four brothers of disparate temperament react to the death of their tyrannical father. A psychological study well-scripted by director Brooks and competently acted by its cast, including Yul Brynner, Lee J. Cobb, William Shatner and Maria Schell. ★★★ $24.99

The Brothers McMullen

(1995, 97 min, US, Edward Burns) Burns' directorial debut is an unaffected, refreshing and surprisingly involving look at three Irish-American brothers. As they bury their abusive, alcoholic father, they are advised by their mom not to make the same mistakes she did. She leaves from the cemetery to catch a plane to Ireland to be with the man she's always loved. Commitment is struggle for the three siblings — one married, one engaged, one adamantly unattached — a struggle made no easier by their mother's revelation after their lifelong witness to the pain of an unhappy union. Jack Mulcahy, Mike McGlone and Burns, while physically dissimilar, somehow convey the relaxed familiarity of brothers — their subtle and natural performances supporting the free-flowing and often acerbic dialogue. While the women in their lives don't get as much screen time, their presence rings as affably true as the men's. This small, pleasant, bemusing comedy opens a window on life's foibles, offering a view both engaging and endearing. ★★★ $19.99

Brother of Sleep

(1996, 127 min, Austria, Joseph Vilsmaier) A hypnotic tale set in a remote Alpine village, *Brother of Sleep* is a strange combination of religious parable and tragic love story. Writer-director-cinematographer Joseph Vilsmaier has succeeded admirably in capturing the film's palpable atmosphere, but the magnificent visuals are sadly diminished on video. Screenwriter Robert Schneider adapted his own novel depicting the jealousies and prejudices of the residents of Eschberg, a hateful little hamlet that is blessed — or cursed — with the bastard birth of Elias Alder (Andre Eisermann). Elias possesses exceptional hearing and he soon becomes the town's celebrat-

ed church organist. In the film's most ecstatic scenes, the soundtrack magnifies ominously as he communes with nature. Complicating Elias' natural gift is his love for his half-sister, Elsbeth (Dana Vavrova), and the bitter rivalry of his friend Peter (Ben Becker) for his affection. Although the film is slow going at times, the unerring performances keep the film focused when the action sags. Eisermann, in particular, seems to be remarkably entranced. (German with English subtitles) ★★★ $98.99

The Brothers Quay

(1980s, 50 min, GB) The grotesquely inspired and totally original puppet animation by the Academy of Fine Art's alumni twins is featured in this compilation of three of their shorts. The delightfully bizarre offerings include *Epic of Gilgamesh*, *Rehearsals for Extinct Anatomies* and *Nocturna Artificialia*. $49.99

Brothers Quay: Street of Crocodiles/The Cabinet of Jan Svankmajer

(1986/1984, 21/14 min, GB) *Street of Crocodiles* (1986, 21 Min), *The Cabinet of Jan Svankmajer* (1984, 14 Min). The artistic possibilities of puppet animation take a great leap forward in these two surrealistic and visionary shorts made by former Philadelphia art students, the Quay Brothers. These identical twins, whose works are heavily influenced by the works of Franz Kafka and the animation masters of Eastern Europe, propel us into an eerily beautiful miniaturized world where common objects and primitive machines take on their own nightmarish life. Providing only glimpses into their imaginatively weird minds, these shorts create powerful and disturbing images that one cannot easily forget. $39.99

The Browning Version

(1951, 93 min, GB, Anthony Asquith) Michael Redgrave gives a stirring performance in this outstanding drama about a stodgy English boarding schoolteacher who finds himself being forced out of his teaching position and discovers his wife's infidelity. He finds redemption in an unexpected act of kindness when one of his young students gives him a copy of "The Browning Version" of Aeschylus' "Agamemnon," a play which he has translated. Terence Rattigan scripted this adaptation of his own play, and his poignant screenplay, Redgrave's classic portrayal and a splendid supporting cast make this must-viewing. ★★★★ $19.99

The Browning Version

(1994, 97 min, US, Mike Figgis) This elegantly produced and deliberately paced film explores the sterile isolation of a profoundly unhappy professor at what appears to be the anticlimactic end of his career. Albert Finney is a marvel of nuance and understatement as the tightly controlled and rigidly repressed teacher. World War II has ended, and Finney is the victim of modernization — he's being transferred to another school. His departure marks a loss of prestige and place, mirrored with intense disdain in the eyes of his embittered, spiteful wife (Greta Scacchi). These most basic human emotions are played out against the seemingly idyllic ivied halls. A

chance gift from an appreciative student serves as catharsis for the beleaguered scholar, precipitating a reevaluation of a life hitherto defined by unspoken recriminations and calcified regrets. ★★★ $19.99

Brubaker

(1980, 132 min, US, Stuart Rosenberg) Based on a true story, Robert Redford stars as a newly appointed warden of an Arkansas prison whose humane reforms uncover a web of corruption and murder. Slightly overlong, this is nevertheless compelling drama with earnest performances by Redford, Jane Alexander, Yaphet Kotto and Morgan Freeman. ★★★ $9.99

Bruce Lee in Green Hornet/Fury of the Dragon

(1974/1975, 84/93 min, US, William Beaudine, Darrel Hallenbeck, Norman Foster) Kung Fu legend Bruce Lee stars as Kato in these rarely seen full-length features compiled from episodes of the short-lived, 1966 TV series. In the first film, the Green Hornet (Van Williams) and his affirmative-action sidekick, Kato, battle rich game hunters, phony aliens with a bomb, and a masked Asian street gang that beats up shopkeepers for protection money. The second film highlights laser-wielding criminals, political assassinations, kidnappers, bloodletting racketeers and, of course, some martial arts mayhem from Mr. Lee. Great nostalgic fun and highly recommended for those in search of campy hard-boiled action. ★★½ $89.99

Bruno Bozzetto, Animator Pt. 1

(58 min, Italy) Here, in one sitting, is an opportunity to examine the animation works of this wunderkind. When barely out of his teens, he began working with John Halas in London. Shortly after, he returned to Milan to open his own studio. After completing a series of successful shorts, he tackled full-length animated features with *West and Soda*, *Vip, Mio Fra Tello Superuomo* and his most popular film *Allegro Non Troppo*, a devastating sendup of Disney's *Fantasia*. This collection of some of his award-winning shorts is a good overview of the many different styles, concerns and techniques Bozzetto uses. $29.99

Brussels-Transit

(1980, 90 min, Belgium, Samy Szlingerbaum) With blurry images of a cold, impersonal subway station and tram cars slowly moving through the fog of a northern European city, a woman's voice begins to sing a heartfelt poem in Yiddish. So begins this fascinating "art" film that delves into one Jewish family's life when they leave Lodz, Poland, after WWII. Narrated by the director's mother, the film uses her reminiscences of her family's life as she, her tailor husband and their two small children eventually settle in Brussels and attempt to eke out an existence despite a devastated Europe and ignorance of the language and customs. Spanning the years 1947 through the early 1950s, the director's approach to his story is enigmatic. He begins with static images and his mother's stories in the first part and then settles into a more conventional filmmaking technique in the second part. Overall, an unusual, somber yet touching document of one family's determination to survive. (Yiddish with English subtitles) ★★★ $69.99

El Bruto (The Brute)

(1952, 83 min, Mexico, Luis Buñuel) This is the ironic tale of a not-too-bright but tender-hearted brute who is hired by a rich landlord to evict a group of striking tenants. He does his job only too well, resulting in the death of an elderly man. The young wife of the landlord, like a moth to flame, is fatally attracted to this "primeval man" and in quick succession seduces the hulking worker, abandons her husband and runs off with her lover. The price for her infidelity is increasing sexual torment and a descent into madness. A passionate exploration of the mechanisms of desire and the potential consequences of its fulfillment. (Spanish with English subtitles) ★★★ $24.99

Bubbe's Boarding House

(1989, 41 min, US) Likable and humorous puppet characters celebrate Chanukah at Bubbe's (grandma's) boarding house. Watch and you'll surely enjoy Bubbe's lively retelling of the story of Chanukah: the clash of the Maccabees and the Greeks; the oil that miraculously burned for eight days; and the importance of just being yourself. ★★★½ $19.99

Buck Privates

(1941, 84 min, US, Arthur Lubin) One of Abbott and Costello's funniest comedies. The Andrews Sisters also star. Bud and Lou join the Army, with predictable comedic results; Patty, Maxine and Laverne sing. ★★★ $14.99

A Bucket of Blood

(1959, 66 min, US, Roger Corman) With exception to *Little Shop of Horrors*, this sly horror parody is director Corman's best work from his early and extremely low-budget days. That great character actor Dick Miller is center stage as a beatnik coffeehouse waiter whose newly found prominence as a sculptor is helped greatly by the dead bodies underneath his clay. ★★★ $9.99

The Buddha of Suburbia

(1993, 220 min, GB, Roger Michell) Hanif Kureishi's (*My Beautiful Laundrette*) serio-comic novel of life among the bohemians and bohemian-wannabes in 1970s London is the basis for this accomplished BBC miniseries. The story focuses on handsome Karim (Naveen Andrews), a bisexual teenager of an unconventional English mother (Brenda Blethyn) and a surprisingly eccentric Indian father (Roshen Seth) who longs to escape the confines of suburban Bromley and experience life. Karim finally gets his wish — and the film comes into its own — and moves to a frenetic, punk-filled London when his father becomes a guru in the '70s Buddhist scene. Sort of an English *Tales from the City*, this sprawling slice-of-life story created some controversy when it first aired in Britain, prompting London's *Sun* to decry the film's sex orgies, nudity and homosexuality. Music by David Bowie. ★★★ $29.99

Buddy, Buddy

(1981, 96 min, US, Billy Wilder) This American version of the French film *A Pain in the A–* is a low-key black comedy highlighted by the pairing of Jack Lemmon and Walter Matthau. Lemmon plays a hit man whose job is interrupted by an obnoxious hotel neighbor played by Matthau. The magic between them makes up for the fair script, though this is a must for fans of the two actors. Wilder directed and wrote the script along with I.A.L. Diamond. ★★★ $19.99

The Buddy Holly Story

(1978, 113 min, US, Steve Rash) The life of Buddy Holly, the legendary rockabilly king, is brought to the screen with Gary Busey in the title role. In an amazing metamorphosis, Busey transforms himself into the rock 'n' roll pioneer; not only in looks, but also with his singing. Songs include "That'll Be the Day," "Peggy Sue," "Rave On," "Maybe Baby" and more. ★★★½ $9.99

The Buddy System

(1984, 110 min, US, Glenn Jordan) Wil Wheaton plays matchmaker for his mom (Susan Sarandon) and his school security guard (Richard Dreyfuss). The couple experience hate at first sight but, of course, one thing leads to another and they fall in love. The story here is obviously nothing new, but the performances are the main attraction. ★★½ $59.99

Buffalo Bill and the Indians

(1976, 135 min, US, Robert Altman) The wild, wild West — Robert Altman style. Based on the off-Broadway hit "Indians" by Arthur Kopit, Paul Newman stars as the legendary Buffalo Bill, who is now a carnival attraction reliving the mythic adventures of his youthful Indian-fighting days, and believing it's all true. A cynical examination of heroes, legends and show business. Also with Burt Lancaster, Geraldine Chaplin and Joel Grey. ★★★ $19.99

Buffet Froid (Cold Cuts)

(1979, 102 min, France, Bertrand Blier) A surrealist urban landscape is the setting for this absurdist comedy of despair in which violence is a way of life and everyone is either a murderer or his victim. Gérard Depardieu stars as a drifter who is obsessed with death. After stabbing a man whom he had just met, he runs home to his wife and confesses the crime. Unperturbed, she simply throws the knife into the dishwasher. But before the machine completes its last cycle, she, in turn, is killed by an intruder. In the bewildering course of events that follow, Depardieu meets and befriends both an amoral police chief as well as his wife's killer. Blier maliciously blends elements of urban terror gone berserk with a Kafkaesque sense of an individual trapped in a world of desensitized and twisted logic. (French with English subtitles) ★★★ $59.99

Buffy the Vampire Slayer

(1992, 86 min, US, Fran Rubel Kuzui) A potentially amusing horror spoof which unfortunately gets mired in an internal confusion over whether to be *Bill & Ted* meets *The Lost Boys* or *Heathers* meets *Dracula*, *Buffy* is a vampire saga in search of some bite. Buffy (Kristy Swanson) is an average airhead California cheerleader before Donald Sutherland shows up to inform her that it is her destiny to rid the earth of the evil bloodsucking undead. Joining Buffy in her quest is Hunk-of-the-Month Luke Perry, who plays drifter/'90s-man Pike, the kind of guy whose masculinity isn't threatened when Buffy rescues him from the clutches of a leather-jacketed vampire, gleefully played by Paul Reubens. *Buffy* is about as stimulating as a weekend at the mall, though at least it has the good sense to visit the nicer clothing stores. ★★ $9.99

Bugsy

(1991, 135 min, US, Barry Levinson) Though *Bugsy* boasts an intelligent screenplay, outstanding production values and strong direction, it's Warren Beatty's fascinating and remarkably complex performance which dominates and distinguishes Levinson's taut, colorful gangster saga. Beatty is "Bugsy" Siegel, a New York crime lord who was sent by the mob to Hollywood in the 1940s, eventually helping to found Las Vegas and its first casino, the Flamingo. Annette Bening (whose offscreen romance with Beatty was highly publicized) is terrific as Virginia Hill, an aspiring actress who becomes involved with Bugsy and whose vitriolic demeanor is more than a match for the egotistical, psychotic gangster. The film evenly — and quite successfully — divides its time between the volatile relationship between Bugsy and Virginia, and Bugsy's near-obsessive quest to build his desert resort. Excellent in support are Oscar nominees Ben Kingsley (as Meyer Lansky) and Harvey Keitel (as Mickey Cohen). ★★★½ $9.99

Bugsy Malone

(1976, 93 min, GB, Alan Parker) Doing a mean Joan Blondell imitation, Jodie Foster steals the show in this charming children's musical which features an all-child cast. With not an adult in sight, this parody of 1930s gangster flicks pits two crime bosses against each other for control of the town. Scott Baio is the likable hero who falls in with the wrong crowd. Foster plays a nightclub headliner who can zing a one-liner with the best of them. Paul Williams wrote the unmemorable score. And parents, don't worry — there are no bullets, only whipped cream. ★★★ $14.99

Bull Durham

(1988, 108 min, US, Ron Shelton) Kevin Costner stars in this entertaining, literate and very sexy comedy as a veteran catcher who joins the minor league Durham Bulls and is relegated to playing babysitter to a hotshot pitcher (Tim Robbins). Both become involved with the town's leading baseball authority/groupie, the ever-incredible Susan Sarandon. A major achievement from first-time director Shelton. ★★★½ $9.99

Bulldog Drummond

(1929, 85 min, US, F. Richard Jones) In his first sound film, Ronald Colman's splendid performance illustrates why he was one of the most popular actors of his time. Colman is the ever-glib and suave Capt. "Bulldog" Drummond, the ex-British Army officer looking for excitement. He finds it when he places an ad offering his services to anyone for anything. It's a very young Joan Bennett who answers, involving Drummond in a kidnapping, blackmail and murder scheme, as her uncle is being held against his will. The film holds up surprisingly well, and features a nifty plot, good humor and fun characters. Oh, besides his acting ability, there's another reason Colman survived the talkies: that beautiful, resonant voice of his. ★★★½ $19.99

Bullet in the Head

(1990, 118 min, Hong Kong, John Woo) Woo's dark, grim, brutally violent tale of three friends in 1967 Hong Kong, whose exploits include smuggling, gang-turf wars, gold theft, greed-induced betrayal and more. With the Vietnam War, political unrest, cold-blooded assassinations and merciless executions serving as a backdrop, this must-see departure from Woo's "spaghetti Eastern" style of filmmaking leaves one drained, emotionally and physically. (Chinese with English subtitles) ★★★½ $59.99

Bulletproof Heart

(1995, 96 min, US, Mark Malone) Anthony LaPaglia and Mimi Rogers dance a lethal *pas de deux* in this sly if formulaic thriller about a coldhearted hit man hired to kill a gorgeous socialite/dominatrix who, for mysterious reasons, is quite ready and willing to die. Intrigued by his latest "client," he sets out to unlock the secret of her past and ends up in a torrid affair that leads to a twist ending. With a script driven more by character than by plot, Malone's film is a worthy addition to the so-called "cinema of amorality" heralded by such films as *The Last Seduction* and *Red Rock West*. ★★½ $9.99

Bullets over Broadway

(1994, 99 min, US, Woody Allen) Set in 1920s New York City, one of Allen's brightest and funniest films blends his own comic sensibilities with a touch of Damon Runyon to tell the tale of a political idealist and playwright (John Cusack) desperate to get his play on Broadway. His only source of funding is a mobster who insists that his moll (a perfectly cast Jennifer Tilly) star in the show. Pride tossed aside, he begins rehearsals only to find his leading lady accompanied by a nettlesome and opinionated bodyguard (Chazz Palminteri). His oddball cast is rounded out by a wifty stage legend (Dianne Wiest, who won a much-deserved Oscar) and an overeating leading man (Jim Broadbent). While Wiest received the Academy's recognition, kudos must also go to Palminteri who dominates his interactions with Cusack and gives the film a solid narrative anchor. Hilarious throughout, the film would make an interesting double feature with, as well as mirthful antidote to, the less humorful but similarly themed *Barton Fink*. ★★★★ $14.99

Bullitt

(1968, 113 min, US, Peter Yates) Yates' exceptionally exciting police thriller redefined the chase sequence for years to come. Steve McQueen is a tough San Francisco detective on the trail of a witness' killers. Though the film is noted for the classic car chase scene, there's much more to recommend here. ★★★ $14.99

Buona Sera, Mrs. Campbell

(1968, 113 min, US, Melvin Frank) The premise reeks of '60s dreck: Gina Lollabrigida plays an Italian mother who has been accepting child support for 20 years from three American WWII vets — who each thinks her daughter is his — and now they are all returning for a reunion to her small village. But this one-joke comedy is a lot funnier than it has a right to be, for it is a constant source of well-earned laughs. Lollabrigida has probably never been funnier on screen, and she has the good fortune to play off the considerable comedic skills of, as the returning G.I.s, Telly Savalas, Peter Lawford and the ever-funny Phil Silvers; and Shelley Winters and Lee Grant as two of their wives. Co-written and directed by Frank (*A Touch of Class*). ★★★ $19.99

The 'burbs

(1989, 103 min, US, Joe Dante) This sometimes humorous, shallow comedy plays like "Leave It to Beaver" meets "The Munsters" rather than the dark, crazy romp it could have been. Tom Hanks plays the suburban Everyman whose voice of sanity amongst the insanity around him is soon stifled when he and his neighbors begin to suspect that the new and very strange family which just moved in are cannibalistic murderers. Are they or aren't they? Surely you'll have it figured out before the cast of characters. ★★ $9.99

Burden of Dreams

(1982, 94 min, US, Les Blank) Blank's revealing documentary of Werner Herzog's inexorable pursuit in filming *Fitzcarraldo* is a gripping portrait of artistic obsession and the creative process. Captured in this absorbing film are the moments of frustration and boredom, elation and prophecy which seized Herzog's crew (and himself) during their stay in the South American wilderness. ★★★ $59.99

Burglar

(1987, 102 min, US, Hugh Wilson) Though Whoopi Goldberg tries her best with this mediocre material, and Bobcat Goldthwait is a very appealing supporting character, there's not much to recommend in this comic mystery with Whoopi as a second-rate burglar who witnesses a murder and, being the number one suspect, tries to solve it herself. ★★ $14.99

The Burglar

(1987, 83 min, USSR, Valery Ogorodnikov) Soviet rock star Konstantin Kinchev stars as a Western-influenced rocker determined to make it big at any cost. His ambition gets him in trouble after he steals a synthesizer for his group. The situation gets even more complicated after Senka, his "good brother," tries to take the heat by claiming that he stole the instrument. An unusual post-*glasnost* slice-of-life drama. (Russian with English subtitles) ★★★ $59.99

Burke and Wills

(1987, 140 min, Australia, Graeme Clifford) This may not be the film that you'll want to watch on a hot summer's day — an epic retelling of an expedition into the searing heat of the Australian Outback. Jack Thompson and Nigel Havers star as the 19th-century explorers whose ambition it is to cut a path through uncharted South Australian territory — distancing over 1,000 miles. Both actors give bravura performances as a pair of men determined to chart the uncharted no matter what the cost. The film's dazzling Cinemascope images may be lost on video, but the taut drama and heroic vision will not. The film also stars the luminous Greta Scacchi as Thompson's girlfriend. ★★★½ $19.99

BurLEZk Live!

(1987, 90 min, US, Nan Kineey & Debi Sundahl) Adding new meaning to "girls' night out," this sexually tantalizing peek at a women's-only striptease club was taped live at a San Francisco nightclub, where women strip and dance for the enjoyment of other women. The types of the dances run the gamut of styles to produce safe but sleazy lesbian fun. $29.99

BurLEZk II Live!

(1988, 60 min, US, Nan Kinney & Debi Sundahl) The steamy eroticism heated up by the gyrations and teasing dances of female stripping in front of a lesbian audience continues in this entertaining exhibition. Artistic pretensions meet raunchy sensuality as Fanny Fatale performs a dance to safe sex and other women dance up a sexy storm. It may not be politically correct, but it's all harmless fun. $29.99

Dianne Wiest implores John Cusack, "don't speak," in *Bullets over Broadway*

The Burmese Harp

(1956, 98 min, Japan, Kon Ichikawa) A magnificent, poetic piece of filmmaking. The action takes place during the closing stages of the war in Burma. A young Japanese soldier, a musician and mystic, hears a call to remain behind with his harp to minister to the dead, both friend and foe alike. (aka: *Harp of Burma*) (Japanese with English subtitles) ★★★½ $29.99

Burn! (Queimada)

(1969, 112 min, Italy/France, Gillo Pontecorvo) Marlon Brando is brilliant as the Machiavellian Sir William Walker, a soldier-of-fortune sent by a British company to investigate a slave uprising on a sugar-producing Caribbean Island governed by repressive Portuguese colonials during the mid-1800s. After witnessing the brutal exploitation of the peasants and feeling that he can offer a better deal, Walker helps instigate a successful native rebellion. But when the revolt turns financially sour for the British, he switches sides and battles the leaders of the fledgling nation. A complex, anti-colonial political drama; the viewer alternately admires and hates the morally corrupt Sir William. ★★★ $19.99

The Burning Season

(1994, 100 min, US, John Frankenheimer) The late and sorely missed Raul Julia delivers his final performance, giving a pristine portrayal of Chico Mendes, the Brazilian union leader murdered while trying to preserve the rain forest and, with it, his way of life. The HBO docudrama opens with Mendes as a young boy getting his first lesson in exploitation by watching his father be grossly underpaid for a rubber delivery. In later years, the conflict between the rubber harvesters and the land barons is delineated in the larger stories of international investments and ecological issues; but the focus never strays too far from one man's passion to protect and serve his community. An impassioned, successful piece of filmmaking which features a superb supporting cast including Edward James Olmos, Sonia Braga and Esai Morales. Julia won a posthumous Best Actor Emmy for his work here. ★★★½ $19.99

Burning Secret

(1988, 110 min, GB, Andrew Birkin) Faye Dunaway and Klaus Maria Brandauer give affecting performances in this beautifully filmed period piece set in 1919 Vienna about the love affair between the repressed wife of an American diplomat (Dunaway) and a war-battered Austrian nobleman (Brandauer). Most remarkable is David Eberts as Dunaway's young, asthmatic son, who introduces the two lovers and becomes an unlikely protagonist in a most unusual triangle. ★★★ $9.99

The Burns and Allen Show, Vol. 1

(1952-1953, 60 min, US) Gracie lives in a parallel universe with its own internal logic. Fred Clark, Bea Benadera and Harry Vonzel are the journeyman actors trying to do a traditional sitcom. And George is the bemused ringmaster who lives by the paradigm "The play's the thing." Jack Benny shows up for no good reason (but to good effect). Complete with the

original commercials, one of which is for an asbestos kitchen floor covering. ★★★ $14.99

Burnt by the Sun

(1994, 134 min, Russia, Nikita Mikhalkov) The simplicity of a family outing on a tranquil Sunday afternoon is a potent and deceiving backdrop for betrayal and corruption in Mikhalkov's powerful yet lyrical Oscar-winning drama. An allegory for Stalin's clandestine reign of terror which engulfed the Russian landscape in the mid-1930s, the Chekhovian *Burnt by the Sun* tells the story of a Russian civil war hero (played with gusto by the director), his wife and child (Mikhalkov's real-life daughter and she's a real charmer). Set during one summer's day, the action takes place at the family's dacha where the wife's former lover (the appealing Oleg Manchikov) has returned. A clownish, beguiling man, Manchikov's presence is greeted with delight by all, and as he reminisces and charms, it soon becomes clear he has a sinister, ulterior motive. Director Mikhalkov's success lies in both his leisurely pacing (a Russian Merchant Ivory?) which is cunning and his sharp, subtle portrait of malevolence which is unexpected. (Russian with English subtitles) ★★★½ $19.99

Burnt Offerings

(1976, 115 min, US, Dan Curtis) A chilling haunted house film from the director of "Dark Shadows." A family moves into a luxurious country estate, where one by one they succumb to the unknown force surrounding the house. Starring Karen Black, Oliver Reed, Burgess Meredith, Lee Montgomery, and, in one of her best late-career performances, Bette Davis. ★★★ $14.99

Burroughs

(1983, 87 min, US, Howard Brookner) Celebrated novelist William S. Burroughs is vividly profiled in this informative and fascinating study of his life and work. The author of "Junkie," "Naked Lunch" and "Nova Express" recounts with several of his friends the momentous episodes of a wildly eventful existence. A splendid glimpse into the mind of a true literary maverick. ★★★½ $59.99

Bus Stop

(1956, 96 min, US, Joshua Logan) Marilyn Monroe displays her usual sex appeal as well as surprising pathos in this delightful adaptation of the William Inge comedy. MM stars as a torchy cafe singer who becomes the object of affection — and obsession — of young naive cowpoke Don Murray (who received an Oscar nomination for his sensationally wild performance). Great support from Eileen Heckart as Marilyn's waitress confidant and Arthur O'Connell as Murray's seasoned manager. ★★★½

The Bushido Blade

(1979, 104 min, Japan, Tom Kotani) In his final performance, Richard Boone is exceptionally hammy as the leader of a group of Shogun warriors. Their mission is to search for a coveted sword through 19th-century Japan. James Earl Jones also stars in this pretty but not very satisfying kung-fu action tale. Lots of beheadings keep you from falling asleep. Filmed in English. ★½ $69.99

Bushwhacked

(1995, 90 min, US, Greg Beeman) As the bad guy in *Home Alone* and the voice of the boy in "The Wonder Years," Daniel Stern had appropriate supporting or vocal roles. As the lead in *Bushwhacked*, an inferior, terribly conceived family comedy, his wild-eyed antics and bumbling, slapstick acting style wear thin quickly. He plays Max Grebelski, a package delivery man who is framed for murder and chased by the FBI. He sets off for Devil's Peak, a remote mountaintop, upon learning that proof of his innocence may be there. Along the way, he is mistaken for a top-notch scout leader and forced to lead four boys and a girl on an overnight hike. Of course, he is completely incompetent. Of course, he overcomes his fears to rescue the kids from the bad guys. Of course, he proves his innocence. It's recommended that you steer a course away from the film. ★½ $19.99

Business as Usual

(1987, 89 min, GB, Lezli-An Barrett) Glenda Jackson delivers a typically strong performance in this interesting but somewhat preachy discourse on sexual harassment in the workplace. Jackson plays a Liverpool boutique manager who is fired after she files a complaint against her boss on behalf of a co-worker (Cathy Tyson). Based on a true story which became a *cause-célèbre* in England. ★★ $19.99

Buster

(1988, 102 min, GB, David Green) Phil Collins makes his film debut as Buster Edwards, the only conspirator in the Great Train Robbery (the biggest heist in British history) who managed to elude police. Collins delivers a strong performance and Julie Walters is excellent, as always, as his devoted but neglected wife. ★★½ $19.99

Bustin' Loose

(1981, 94 min, US, Oz Scott) Richard Pryor is in splendid comic form as an ex-con who drives teacher Cicely Tyson and a busload of orphaned and problem children cross-country. Pryor and Tyson make an appealing team. ★★★ $14.99

Busting

(1973, 89 min, US, Peter Hyams) Patently offensive to gays, lesbians, blacks and other members of the disenfranchised, this standard police comedy-drama doesn't pit cops against robbers, but rather cops against the "socially and sexually deviant." Quite despicable and at times painful in its violent racism and homophobia, the film stars Elliott Gould (remember when he "starred" in movies?) and Robert Blake as two out-of-control vice cops, rampaging through the underworld of prostitution and gay bars undeterred by the Bill of Rights and basic justice. One gay sequence – in which the two cops "disguise" themselves as fags and raid a "fruit bar" – turns violent after the queers (depicted as limp-wristed queens), sick of another police incursion (aka Stonewall) refuse to go quietly and begin a riot, fighting off the two until overcome by additional police. Though this was probably intended to be more of a social comedy "exposing" the misdirection of a corrupt police force, anti-gay

Bye Bye Brazil

slurs abound, and over time its noxious depiction of gays is what one remembers. ★ $14.99

Butch Cassidy and the Sundance Kid

(1969, 110 min, US, George Roy Hill) Classic western (and box-office smash) with Paul Newman and Robert Redford as outlaws on the run from a relentless posse. Told with great humor and infinite style. Winner of four Academy Awards, including William Goldman's screenplay, Score and Song ("Raindrops Keep Falling on My Head"). ★★★★ $9.99

The Butcher's Wife

(1991, 107 min, US, Terry Hughes) Demi Moore has the title role in this whimsical romantic comedy as a Southern clairvoyant who impulsively marries a doughy butcher (George Dzundza) from Greenwich Village. In her new surroundings, she sets off a farcical chain reaction of sexual trysts through her predictions of love to a neighborhood starving for it. She also finds romance with neighbor/psychiatrist Jeff Daniels. Moore is actually quite appealing here, and an engaging cast — which also includes Mary Steenburgen, Frances McDormand and Max Perlich — makes the most of the material. ★★★ $14.99

Butterfield 8

(1960, 109 min, US, Daniel Mann) Elizabeth Taylor won an Oscar (though many say it was because of her nearly dying of pneumonia) for her sultry portrayal of an expensive call girl who lives with her mom and doesn't think she's a prostitute. The film features great histrionics and a swell supporting cast, especially a charmingly slimy Laurence Harvey. A

good, old-fashioned soaper with some fine, campy dialogue. ★★½ $19.99

By Dawn's Early Light

(1990, 100 min, US, Jack Sholder) This made-for-cable nuclear drama is a classy, edge-of-your-seat thriller combining elements of *Fail Safe* and *The Hunt for Red October*. Powers Boothe and Rebecca De Mornay star as romantically involved pilots who face a moral and personal dilemma when they are assigned to drop the bomb against the "enemy" when Washington D.C. is devastated in an accidental attack. Martin Landau also stars as the cautious and concerned President of the U.S. whose presumed death brings the country to the brink of nuclear catastrophe. ★★★½ $14.99

By Design

(1981, 88 min, Canada, Claude Jutra) The sexual revolution travels north in this quirky comedy directed by Quebecer Jutra. Patty Duke Astin (Helen) and Sara Botsford (Angel) star as two fashion designers, business partners and lovers who decide they want to have a baby. Rejected by the adoption agency and finding artificial insemination "gross," the frustrated pair decide that a stud is needed. After slapstick encounters cruising the straight discos, bars and construction sites of Vancouver, Helen and Angel choose Terry, an oafish photographer who eagerly accepts the mission. The deft handling of the relationship between the trio makes this an offbeat and touching comedy. ★★½ $59.99

Bye, Bye Birdie

(1963, 112 min, US, George Sidney) It's like an episode of "Dobie Gillis" with songs in this

rather benign satire on the foibles of rock 'n' roll. Before reporting for his military service, an Elvis-like character makes a visit to a small Midwestern town. And wouldn't you know it, those darn teenagers just get all silly. Dick Van Dyke repeats his star-making Broadway role, and is helped by pleasant performances from Ann-Margret and Paul Lynde. Enjoyable tunes like "Put on a Happy Face" and "Kids" enliven this ever-so-amusing confection. (Remade for TV in 1996 with Jason Alexander and Vanessa Williams) ★★★ $14.99

Bye Bye Blues

(1990, 110 min, US, Anne Wheeler) A provocative romantic drama set during WWII. The wife of a military doctor captured by the Japanese, in an effort to make ends meet, takes a job with a local swing band and falls in love with the lead singer. Starring Rebecca Jenkins, Luke Reilly, Stuart Margolin, Michael Ontkean and Kate Reid. A stylish and tuneful exploration of one woman's liberation. ★★★ $29.99

Bye Bye Brazil

(1979, 110 min, Brazil, Carlos Diegues) Diegues' lyrical journey across Brazil is part road movie, part travelogue sprinkled with hints of political message and a touch of magical realism. José Wilker stars as Lord Gypsy, the leader of a troupe of traveling performers known as Caravana Rolidei. The film follows this group in a quasi-documentary style on a revelatory trip across the Trans-Amazon highway and beyond. Betty Faria co-stars as Salome, Queen of the Rumba and Fabio Junior is along for the ride as a naive young accordionist. Diegues and his cast and crew actually embarked on a 9,000-mile journey to make the film letting much of the material come to them along the way. The resulting "journal" of their experiences is not always successful, but is at times mesmerizing and offers a unique look at the rapidly changing face of Brazil. ★★★ $19.99

Bye Bye, Love

(1995, 107 min, US, Sam Weisman) From the director of *D2: The Mighty Ducks* comes this story of three divorced dads...that would usually be enough to warrant skipping ahead to the next title. But thanks to three very appealing performances by Matthew Modine, Paul Reiser and Randy Quaid; a director with enough sense to allow them room to work; and an involving screenplay both comic and aware, *Bye Bye, Love* is a most pleasant surprise. Three divorced fathers meet regularly at McDonald's for the exchange of children with the ex-wives. In the course of a weekend, the story follows them as they toss one-liners, date, commiserate and fulfill their parental duties. To its credit, the film never trivializes divorce, only finding comic and sometimes touching fallout from it; though to its discredit, the wives' parts are sketchily written. Quaid is extremely funny, and his scenes with blind date Janeane Garofalo, herself hilarious, are among the film's best. ★★★ $19.99

Cabaret

C (1972, 124 min, US, Bob Fosse) Fosse's savory depiction of Christopher Isherwood's '30s Berlin stars an effervescent Liza Minnelli as nightclub singer and carefree bohemian Sally Bowles and Michael York as Isherwood's alter ego Brian Roberts. The short-lived decadent world of pre-Hitler Berlin as well as the rising nationalistic tide of Fascism are effectively captured in this trendsetting musical. Helmut Griem also stars as a wealthy and debonair baron who sweeps both Sally and Brian off their feet. The musical numbers performed at the Kit Kat Klub are just some of the film's rousing highlights, a collection of great songs belted by both Minnelli and Academy Award winner Joel Grey as the devilishly cynical Master of Ceremonies. ★★★★ $19.99

Cabeza de Vaca

(1992, 108 min, Mexico, Nicholas Echevarria) In 1528, a Spanish expedition shipwrecks off the coast of Florida – 600 of the men aboard die. One survivor roams the countryside searching for his comrades, but instead finds the Iguase, an ancient Indian tribe. Over the next eight years, the survivor, Cabeza de Vaca, learns their alien culture, becoming a healer and a leader. But he soon has to confront his past when newly arriving conquistadors seek to enslave the Indians. A vividly entertaining, large-scale film with stunning visuals and a sometimes surrealistic story which at times drifts into territory blazed by films such as *El Topo* and *A Man Called Horse*. (Spanish with English subtitles) ★★★½ $24.99

Cabin Boy

(1994, 81 min, US, Adam Resnick) A television skit stretched to a barely feature-length 81 minutes, this initially funny but ultimately tedious comedy stars Chris Elliott as an obnoxious rich boy (forget the fact that he's balding and in his thirties) who mistakenly embarks on an "it's gonna make you a man" high-seas adventure. Playing the self-centered, moronic innocent character to the hilt, Elliott brings some antic humor to the otherwise disappointing tale. But don't expect it to be highbrow wit or subtle humor for the film relishes in its insipid cartoonish comedy. David Letterman has some fun in an early cameo (you get to see him before slumber sets in) and Ann Magnuson is featured as a vampish, six-armed creature from the sea. ★½ $19.99

The Cabin in the Cotton

(1932, 77 min, US, Michael Curtiz) Okay trivia buffs, one of Bette Davis' most repeated lines is: "Ah'd love to kiss ya but I just washed my hay-uh." And it's said in this period melodrama, an important step in Davis' rise to stardom. In a supporting part, Davis had her first "bad girl" role as a Southern vixen out to set honest sharecropper's son Richard Barthelmess (a silent screen actor whose star was fading) on the road to ruin. Bette is terrific in this otherwise routine drama, and it's easy to see why this led to her being signed for her career-making *Of Human Bondage*. ★★ $19.99

Cabin in the Sky

(1943, 99 min, US, Vincente Minnelli) A stellar black cast (Lena Horne, Louis Armstrong, Ethel Waters, Duke Ellington) is featured in Minnelli's musical fable about the forces of good and evil vying for the soul of Little Joe (Eddie Anderson). ★★★ $19.99

The Cabinet of Dr. Caligari

(1919, 69 min, Germany, Robert Wiene) Setting in motion the wave of German Expressionism, director Wiene created this nightmarish universe which lies beneath the facade of order and reason. This horror classic employs dazzling use of art direction, lighting and cubist set design to tell its chilling tale of a carnival hypnotist using a somnambulist for the former's evil purposes. (Silent with musical accompaniment) ★★★½ $29.99

Cabiria

(1914, 123 min, Italy, Giovanni Pastrone) The most ambitious and spectacular of the historical epics for which Italy was famous before World War I, *Cabiria* set the standard for big-budget feature-length movies and opened the way for D.W. Griffith and Cecil B. DeMille. During the war between Carthage and Rome, a girl – Cabiria – is separated from her parents. In her odyssey through the world of ancient Rome, she encounters an erupting volcano, the barbaric splendor of Carthage, human sacrifice and Hannibal crossing the Alps. Mastered from a 35mm archive print using variable speed projection to match the hand-cranked camera, *Cabiria* features a newly recorded soundtrack from the original 1914 score. ★★★ $39.99

The Cable Guy

(1996, 91 min, US, Ben Stiller) You have to give Jim Carrey credit for trying something different. After doing strictly stupid, light schtick in the profitable *Ace Ventura* films and *Dumb and Dumber*, the $20 million comedian attempts the difficult genre of black comedy stamped with his own unique brand of humor. However, humor is not what you get with *The Cable Guy*, an unfunny, undisciplined comedy in the *What about Bob?* vein. Carrey plays an obnoxious cableman whose present of free cable to customer Matthew Broderick turns the latter's life upside-down. As Carrey latches on to – even stalks – the protesting Broderick, his family and friends only see one swell guy. The scenario can lend itself to many humorous situations, as *Bob* proves; however, the result here is mean-spirited – its malice underscored by a deficiency of laughs – and lacking in ironic counterpoint (*The War of the Roses* is a successful example of that). What *The Cable Guy* does accomplish is prove that Carrey can sustain characterization – a gift which will be fully appreciated when he lands better scripts. ★½ $19.99

Cactus

(1986, 96 min, Australia, Paul Cox) Isabelle Huppert stars as a young French woman visiting Australia who begins to lose her sight after a car accident. Her acceptance of the possibility of total blindness is difficult until she meets Robert, a wise and witty young man who was born blind. They fall in love and they both help each other accept their limitations and handicaps. While not totally successful, this film does feature a hypnotic score and many affecting scenes between the lovers. ★★½

Cactus Flower

(1969, 103 min, US, Gene Saks) The enchanting performances of Walter Matthau, Ingrid Bergman and especially Goldie Hawn make this lackluster screen version of Abe Burrows' Broadway hit tolerable. Walter plays a dentist secretly in love with his nurse Ingrid, though he's having an affair with Goldie. Hawn won the Oscar for her delightful screen debut. ★★½ $11.99

Liza Minnelli and Joel Grey in *Cabaret*

Caddie

(1976, 107 min, Australia, Donald Crombie) An affectionate account of a determined woman struggling for independence in Sydney during the 1920s and `30s. Helen Morse excels as the strong-willed heroine. ★★★ $59.99

The Caddy

(1953, 95 min, US, Norman Taurog) Jerry Lewis supplies most of the laughs in this minor Lewis and Martin comedy. Jerry is the son of a golf pro who's afraid of crowds. Dino sings "That's Amore." ★★½ $14.99

Caddyshack

(1980, 98 min, US, Harold Ramis) Depending on your comedic tastes, this wacky comedy will either cause moments of silly hysteria or pains of anguish. Either way, good taste is thrown by the wayside. Chevy Chase and Rodney Dangerfield (in a terrifically funny performance) are just two of the crazy members of an exclusive country club. Bill Murray chases gophers a lot, and Michael O'Keefe determines his future by playing golf. ★★½ $14.99

Caddyshack II

(1988, 93 min, US, Allan Arkush) As in the original *Caddyshack*, a seasoned comedian (Rodney Dangerfield in the first, Jackie Mason in the sequel) is the only reason to even consider this otherwise sophomoric comedy. For the likes of Chevy Chase, Dan Aykroyd, Dyan Cannon and Robert Stack, it's merely career low-points (on second thought, not for Chase or Aykroyd). ★½ $14.99

Cadillac Man

(1990, 97 min, US, Roger Donaldson) Robin Williams is a fast-talking, womanizing car salesman and Tim Robbins is the gun-toting jealous husband who decides to take Williams and his dealership hostage. Williams has to do all his usual schtick to keep the picture afloat and he usually manages, but this one should have been better. ★★½ $9.99

Caesar and Cleopatra

(1946, 127 min, GB, Gabriel Pascal) No this isn't Shakespeare, this is Shaw. Claude Rains and Vivien Leigh star in this sluggish rendition of George Bernard Shaw's play about the aging Roman conqueror and the beautiful, soft-headed Queen of the Nile. Great performances capture some of Shaw's unique wit, but the plot has a tendency to drag. ★★½ $14.99

Café au Lait

(1993, 94 min, France, Mathieu Kassovitz) Attempting to become his country's Jewish Spike Lee, director/star Kassovitz has put together a racially charged, but ultimately tame little film about an interracial ménage-à-trois. The film's impressive opening credits take place over a lightning-paced bicycle-wheel's-eye ride through Paris that leads to the collision of Felix (Kassovitz), a gawky Jewish bicycle messenger, and Jamal (Hubert Kounde), the handsome, well-groomed son of an African ambassador. Unbeknownst to either, they have shared the affections of Lola (Julie Mauduech), a light-skinned beauty of Carribean descent. The two men wind up on her doorstep together, whereupon she informs them that she is pregnant and doesn't know, much less care who the father is. In her mind, they can all live as one big happy family. Needless to say, for the rest of the film, the men joust over race and ego, tossing epithets at each other with little reserve. As a director, Kassovitz is clearly concerned with race (he made the somewhat controversial *Hate*). *Café au Lait's* problem is that while it tries to be lighthearted comedy, the slurs are laid on a little too thick. What makes Lee's films work (when they do) is that he takes on serious issues and *injects* humor into them. Here, Kassovitz has attempted to turn comedy serious, and it just isn't the same. (French with English subtitles) ★★ $89.99

Cafe Express

(1981, 89 min, Italy, Nanni Loy) Nino Manfredi, star of the now legendary *Bread and Chocolate*, stars in this top-notch Italian comedy about a charming flim-flam man's attempts to aid his ailing son, outwitting the dim-witted police in the process. A lovable, compassionate portrait by Italy's most inventive comedy director, Loy. (Italian with English subtitles) ★★★

Cafe Flesh

(1984, 80 min, US, Rinse Dream) "Post-nuke thrill freaks looking for a kick!" Decadent hardly suffices in describing this concoction of tongue-in-cheek punk pornography. In the post-apocalyptic future, those capable of engaging in sex (positives) are employed to perform for the vast majority of impotent onlookers (negatives), who succumb to nausea at the very outbreak of foreplay. Demented, you say? You'll never take sex for granted again. ★★ $19.99

La Cage aux Folles

(1978, 91 min, France/Italy, Edouard Molinaro) This frolicsome farce that finally made drag respectable stars Ugo Tognazzi and Michel Serrault as gay lovers who must, amid mounting complications, pose as mom and dad for the sake of a prospective daughter-in-law and her straight-laced parents. The laughs are plentiful, and Serrault creates an endearing, even resilient characterization of the drag queen Alban. Followed by two sequels, an American remake (*The Birdcage*), and adapted into a popular Broadway musical. (Available both dubbed and in French with English subtitles) ★★★½ $14.99

La Cage aux Folles II

(1980, 101 min, France, Edouard Molinaro) This sequel to the popular comedy reunited the original stars (Ugo Tognazzi & Michel Serrault) who, as gay lovers Alban and Renato, become involved with spies and are forced to flee the country. Alban's valiant attempts to masquerade as a Sicilian peasant woman is one of the hilarious highlights to this otherwise uneven sequel. (Available both dubbed and in French with English subtitles) ★★½ $14.99

La Cage aux Folles III: The Wedding

(1985, 88 min, France, Georges Lautner) Who saw this film when it came out theatrically? Judging from the box office receipts, not many. Gay cabaret star Alban learns he is to inherit a fortune — but only on the condition that he marry and provide an heir in 18 months. The magic is gone, though Ugo Tognazzi and Michel Serrault are still a joy to watch. (Dubbed) ★½ $19.99

Caged Heat

(1974, 84 min, US, Jonathan Demme) This ain't no party, this ain't no disco, this ain't no *Stop Making Sense*. Demme's first-time directorial touch raises this women-behind-bars low-budget potboiler above the norm. Surprisingly competent performances in this semi-skin-flick morality tale. Remember: It is unlawful to transport weapons or narcotics into a federal penal institute. ★★½

The Caine Mutiny

(1954, 125 min, US, Edward Dmytryk) In his last great role, Humphrey Bogart stars as the neurotic Captain Queeg in this sensational screen version of Herman Wouk's Pulitzer Prize-winning novel. During a fierce typhoon, the men of the USS Caine relieve their captain of command when he suffers a breakdown, leading to a court-martial of the executive officers behind the "mutiny." Fred MacMurray, Van Johnson and Jose Ferrer offer excellent support. ★★★★ $19.99

The Caine Mutiny Court-Martial

(1988, 100 min, US, Robert Altman) Altman's made-for-TV movie is a solid translation of the Herman Wouk play. Altman briskly takes us through 100 minutes' worth of interrogation all the while building and never losing the dramatic tension. Featuring some trademark Altman touches including, of course, multi-layered dialogue, the film includes a number of powerful performances. Brad Davis plays the infamous Lt. Commander Queeg, Jeff Daniels is the lieutenant on trial for mutiny, Peter Gallagher is the young prosecuting attorney and Eric Bogosian puts in a brilliant performance as the complex, first-time defense lawyer. ★★★½

Cal

(1984, 94 min, Ireland, Pat O'Connor) A Catholic youth (John Lynch) who lives in a predominantly Protestant section of Ulster becomes romantically involved with the widow of a Protestant policeman. His political belief structure is severely tried when he realizes that he was a participant in her husband's death. This powerful, gut-wrenching drama stars Helen Mirren (who won the award for Best

Helen Mirren in *Cal*

Actress at Cannes for her work in the film) and features a score by Mark Knopfler of Dire Straits fame. ★★★½ $19.99

Calamity Jane

(1953, 101 min, US, David Butler) Doris Day gives one of her most appealing performances in this entertaining musical western as the legendary Calamity Jane, the tomboyish sharpshooter who changes her ways when she falls for Wild Bill Hickok (Howard Keel). Musical score includes the Oscar-winning "Secret Love." ★★★ $19.99

Caligula

(1979, 156 min, US, Tinto Brass) No, this isn't an ersatz PBS documentary. Despite its prestigious cast, including Malcolm McDowell, Peter O'Toole and John Gielgud, this controversial production manages to steer clear of most socially accepted standards of decency. But for those chagrined at having missed the decadence and excess of the Roman Empire, this X-rated epic is as satisfying as a day of debauchery. ★

Call Northside 777

(1948, 111 min, US, Henry Hathaway) This true story stars James Stewart as a 1940s Chicago newspaperman whose investigation into an 11-year-old crime helps set free an innocent man. Directed in fascinating semi-documentary style by Hathaway (he also filmed the equally riveting *The House on 92nd Street* in the same manner), the film traces the route taken by Stewart as he slowly uncovers evidence of police corruption and conspiracy. Lee J. Cobb is very good as Stewart's editor, and Richard Conte is the unjustly convicted prisoner. Hathaway creates a tension throughout even though the outcome is obvious. ★★★½ $19.99

Came a Hot Friday

(1985, 101 min, New Zealand, Ian Muneli) A rollicking comic adventure about two con men who roam through the New Zealand countryside, cheating bookmakers and hustling the locals. As their fortunes turn bad, they form an alliance with an insane eccentric with a pronounced Zorro fetish. A silly and mirth-filled examination of the underbelly of the capitalistic urge. ★★★ $19.99

Camelot

(1967, 174 min, GB, Joshua Logan) This big-budget film version of the Lerner and Loewe Broadway hit is tragically short on excitement and none of those in the cast can really sing. Richard Harris (who would go on to perform the role in a successful revival in the '80s) is a capable King Arthur, who recounts his story of chivalry, romance and betrayal. Vanessa Redgrave, though miscast, is a lovely Guinevere, Arthur's betrothed and future queen. Franco Nero is a handsome Lancelot, David Hemmings plays Mordred, and Lionel Jeffries is an almost amusing Merlin. (Available letterboxed and pan & scan) ★★ $24.99

The Cameraman

(1927, 70 min, US, Edward Sedgwick) In his first film under the constricting dictates of the M-G-M front office (read: Mayer, Thalberg), Buster Keaton still manages many fine

Isabelle Adjani in *Camille Claudel*

moments of comedic poetry as an inept newsreel photographer who gets mixed up with gangsters. ★★★ $29.99

The Cameraman's Revenge & Other Fantastic Tales...

(1912-1958, 80 min, Russia/France, Ladislaw Starewicz) A treat for everyone in the family, this is truly a treasure-trove of animation. There is much to be said for Starewicz's art, the influence of which is evident in the work of Tim Burton, the Brothers Quay and other surrealist animators. Each piece in this collection shows a growing understanding of manipulating the media, culminating in true mastery of the craft in works like *Mascot* and *Voice of the Nightingale*. The musical accompaniment of the earlier works is sloppy and undistinguished, but with the advent of sound in the later works, the true richness of music fully compliments his work. It is interesting to note that in Starewicz's "relocation" to Paris in the early '20s, he changed his name and became much more commercial and made his allegories less striking. (Russian with English subtitles) ★★★★ $59.99

Camila

(1984, 105 min, Argentina, Maria Luisa Bemberg) Taken from a true story that was one of Argentina's most notorious scandals, *Camila* tells the haunting tale of a doomed and forbidden love. Set in 1847, Camila, the daughter of a wealthy politican, falls in love with a Jesuit priest. Unable to suppress their desire, the couple are forced to flee. However, the government, her family and the Church, outraged by their "sacrilege," unite in an effort to hunt them down. A gripping, elegant and erotic love story. (Spanish with English subtitles) ★★★ $59.99

Camilla

(1994, 90 min, Canada, Deepa Mehta) If it's not exactly the most fitting end to an extraordinary acting career, *Camilla*, the last theatrical film of the great Jessica Tandy, is nevertheless an appealing road movie with the actress in wonderful form. Tandy plays the title character, a retired concert violinist who lives in a past of accolade and romance. Slightly scandalous and given to exaggeration more than not, she begins a cross-country trip from her Georgia home to Toronto with Bridget Fonda, a fellow if untalented musician with an uncertain future. On the way, they meet a select group of eccentrics and try to come to terms with their individual concerns. Both actresses are delightful, and it's to their credit that each is able to overcome the generic dialogue and predictable dramatics. Hume Cronyn also appears as Tandy's old flame, and their scenes together — especially in the knowledge that these would be their last — are poignant beyond words. ★★½ $19.99

Camille

(1936, 110 min, US, George Cukor) Classic 1930s tear-jerker with Greta Garbo in one of her best roles (most Garbo-ites feel this is her definitive portrayal) as Alexander Dumas' doomed courtesan. One of the better examples of those opulent M-G-M productions which the studio either excelled at (as in this instance) or overproduced and ultimately butchered. They could have found a better Armand than Robert Taylor, but Henry Daniell is sensational as the villainous Baron de Varville. ★★★½ $19.99

Camille 2000

(1969, 115 min, Italy, Radley Metzger) File this cheesy Italian soap opera under campy sexploitation! Poor Dumas' classic tale gets trashed in this "naughty" exposé of heated passions, duplicitous lovers, cheating wives, horny but handsome men and sexually overcharged women and, last but not least, true love. The poor acting actually helps in giving this trash some camp value, but fans of Italian erotica and art had better steer clear. (Dubbed) ★

Camille Claudel

(1988, 149 min, France, Bruno Nuytten) The twin titans of French cinema, Isabelle Adjani and Gérard Depardieu, star in this stirring look at the troubled life of the young sculptress Camille Claudel and her fateful relationship with Auguste Rodin. The movie examines the young artist and the creative fire which burned in her soul and eventually thrust her to the perilous heights of the male-dominated and very misogynist Parisian art world. Her romantic obsession with her mentor and lover, Rodin, eventually plunged her into a world of loneliness and madness. A haunting love story featuring a mesmerizing performance by Adjani. ★★★ $19.99

Camp Nowhere

(1994, 96 min, US, Jonathan Prince) *Camp Nowhere* is a zany and surprisingly funny romp which borrows just a little from the semi-classic British comedy *The Happiest Days of Your Life*. A group of adolescents, who are all being shipped off to various theme camps for the summer (military, diet, computer, etc.), unite their resources and rent a run-down location all their own. This is done with the help of flaky drama teacher Christopher Lloyd. The kids enjoy their adult-free vacation until the moms and dads decide to visit, prompting a wacky, complicated ruse. As the camp's token adult, Lloyd is quite good, combining his unique brand of kookiness with some amusing impersonations. Add to that an enjoyable premise, silly shenanigans and a deft directorial touch, and this *Camp* is one summer spot most will want to attend. ★★★ $9.99

Can She Bake a Cherry Pie?

(1983, 90 min, US, Henry Jaglom) As quirky comedies go, this one takes the cake, so to speak. Independent filmmaker Jaglom delivers an eccentric love story among a group of decidedly peculiar New York neurotics. Karen Black is Zee, an emotional wreck, frazzled by her recent break-up with her husband and starved for affection. She meets Eli (Michael Emil), a balding, opinionated, health-obsessed rationalist, who goes so far as to measure his pulse during sex to gauge the strength of his orgasms. Pure emotion meets pure logic and the result is an oddly charming couple. ★★★ $39.99

Can't Buy Me Love

(1987, 94 min, US, Steve Rash) Patrick Dempsey amd Amanda Peterson make for an attractive twosome in this well-played though slight teen comedy with Dempsey as a high school nerd paying school beauty Peterson to pretend to be his girlfriend. ★★½ $9.99

Can-Can

(1960, 131 min, US, Walter Lang) The powerhouse cast of Frank Sinatra, Shirley MacLaine, Louis Jordan and Maurice Chevalier isn't enough to offset the many lethargic moments in this only occasionally entertaining Cole Porter musical. Shirley wants to dance the "shameful" title dance; the police say no, lawyer Frank says she can-can. Songs include "I Love Paris" and a few not in the original stage production. ★★½ $9.99

Canadian Animation

Since its inception in 1941, the animation division of the National Film Board of Canada has sponsored and produced hundreds of animated shorts including seven Oscar winners and 46 Oscar nominees. Working with the Board, young independent filmmakers have gotten

the encouragement and financial assistance to help create an excitingly diverse range of animation — from the hilariously weird to the boldly experimental. $29.99

The Candidate

(1972, 109 min, US, Michael Ritchie) Potent and vastly entertaining political satire and exposé. Robert Redford stars as an idealistic, dark-horse senatorial candidate running against a powerful, conservative incumbent. The extremely authentic flavor to the behind-the-scenes meetings and pow-wows, and an incisive screenplay by Oscar-winner Jeremy Larner add greatly to the success of the film. Great supporting cast includes Peter Boyle, Allen Garfield, Don Porter (as Redford's rival) and Melvyn Douglas as the young candidate's father. ★★★½ $19.99

Candide

(1991, 147 min, US/GB, Humphrey Burton) Performed in 1989 at London's Barbican Centre, Leonard Bernstein's rousing musical — first performed on Broadway in 1956 — is based on Voltaire's satiric book. With a youthfully animated Bernstein conducting, this production stars Jerry Hadley-Land as Candide and June Anderson as Cunegonde. With lyrics by Lillian Hellman, Dorothy Parker and Stephen Sondheim, the show follows the adventures that befall Candide in his search for "The Best of All Possible Worlds." ★★★ $34.99

Candy Mountain

(1988, 91 min, US, Robert Frank & Ruth Wurlitzer) Infused with a '50s Beat mentality, *Candy Mountain* is an engagingly charming and funny road movie. Kevin J. O'Connor plays an impassive, down-on-his-heels rocker who hits the road in search of the mythical master guitar maker Elmore Silk. His travels are punctuated with a bevy of oddball, on-the-fringe characters variously played by such musicians as Tom Waits, David Johansen, Joe Strummer and Leon Redbone. A quirky, decidedly American low budgeter reminiscent of such road sagas as *Easy Rider* and *Stranger Than Paradise*. ★★★ $14.99

Candyman

(1992, 101 min, US, Bernard Rose) British director Rose follows up his 1988 film *Paperhouse*, a psychologically astute horror film which stood out from that year's selections, with this solid adaptation of goremeister Clive Barker's short story, "The Forbidden." Virginia Madsen gives a gutsy performance as a graduate student whose research into contemporary myths and legends summons the vengeful hook-handed spirit of a slave (Tony Todd) who was murdered for daring to love a white woman. In what has been called the first horror movie with an interracial love theme, Rose sacrifices cheesy special effects in favor of interesting characterizations and bizarre set designs, making this an enduring horror movie for the art-house set. ★★★ $14.99

Candyman 2: Farewell to the Flesh

(1995, 95 min, US, Bill Condon) When a young woman (Kelly Rowan) loses both her father and husband to The Candyman (Tony Todd), she comes to realize that maybe the two

are bound by more than just coincidence. Clive Barker's hook-handed menace returns in this savage sequel that explains (through flashback and in graphic detail) how the urban legend came to be. Taking place as though the original never happened, Condon's film more directly tackles the topic of racial harmony and intolerance, though it relies less on mysticism than on sheer blood and guts horror — a combination that may or may not please the original audience. Philip Glass' mesmerizing and passionate score adds just the right note of poetic justice to this tragic tale. Also with Veronica Cartwright. ★★½ $19.99

Cane Toads

(1987, 47 min, US, Mark Lewis) Sardonic wit and imaginative direction elevate this unusual documentary above the level of mere agricultural travelogue. The film details the introduction of cane toads from Hawaii to North Queensland, Australia, in 1935 to combat a cane grub infestation that was ravaging the sugar industry. Prolific breeders who lacked natural enemies in their new home, the toads quickly overwhelmed over 40% of Queensland and, at the time of filming, were expanding down the coast, rapidly adapting to new environments and killing off natural wildlife. Idolized by some and cursed by others, these insectivorous amphibians have become a staple of the local mythology. This film is a fascinating look at a man-made catastrophe, a magnificently bungled attempt to alter the natural order. ★★★ $89.99

Cannery Row

(1982, 120 min, US, David S. Ward) Nick Nolte and Debra Winger are well-matched in this appealing, if unusual romantic comedy-drama based on the John Steinbeck stories, "Cannery Row" and "Sweet Tuesday." Nolte is a former baseball player-turned-biologist who is thrown together with feisty good-time girl Winger, thanks to the denizens of Cannery Row. Directorial debut for writer Ward (*The Sting*). ★★★ $19.99

A Canterbury Tale

(1944, 124 min, GB, Michael Powell & Emeric Pressburger) One of the most original films to come out of wartime Britain, this Powell/Pressburger tale bears no relation to the Chaucer story. It is, instead, an offbeat tale about a young woman, a British officer and an American sergeant who arrive in the small village in Kent, befriend each other and become involved in an effort to apprehend the "glue man" — a mysterious individual who has been pouring glue on the heads of young ladies escorting soldiers. Filled with interesting commentary on the effects of war on a small community, this film is a very entertaining and thought-provoking WWII classic. ★★★½ $39.99

The Canterbury Tales

(1971, 109 min, Italy, Pier Paolo Pasolini) Pasolini's second film in his "Trilogy of Pleasure" adopts six of the ribald stories contained in Chaucer's classic. Set in England and featuring the director as Chaucer himself, the film seeks out the raciest, most exotic and controversial aspects of life in the Middle Ages.

Rumor has it that Pasolini, long known for working with non-professionals in his films, even used hitchhikers he picked up during his travels in England for major roles in the film. (Italian with English subtitles) ★★★ $79.99

The Canterville Ghost

(1944, 96 min, US, Jules Dassin) He may be a hambone, but what great fun when Charles Laughton is on the screen as the haunter of a 17th-century castle. He can't leave until descendant Robert Young does one heroic act — besides not murdering Una O'Connor to stop her incessant screeching. ★★★ $19.99

Cape Fear

(1962, 105 min, US, J. Lee Thompson) One of the most nerve-wracking and suspenseful films of all time, this thriller is set in the seemingly tranquil Louisiana bayous. The story centers around Gregory Peck, an upstanding criminal prosecutor whose family falls under the terror of a man whom Peck sent to jail years earlier — the menacing Robert Mitchum. Through a series of chilling yet all-too-believable scare tactics, Mitchum enacts his revenge on Peck's family with such determination and cool-headedness that the film at times becomes almost too intense to watch. Brilliant cinematography, a terrific score and outstanding performances elevate this often-imitated thriller to an almost unbearable level of tension. Martin Scorsese directed Robert De Niro in a 1991 remake. ★★★½ $14.99

Cape Fear

(1991, 130 min, US, Martin Scorsese) Director Scorsese's masterful updating of the 1962 thriller. Upon his release from a 14-year prison term, Max Cady (Robert De Niro) travels to the hometown of his former defense attorney, Sam Bowden (Nick Nolte). Because of the atrocious nature of the crime, Bowden suppressed information and lost the case. And now Cady has come to instruct his counselor on the meaning of loss. As the sociopath Cady, De Niro, with his patented ability to convey tightly controlled rage, delivers an intense, breathtaking portrait of evil. As the family he terrorizes with half-truths and innuendo, Nolte, Jessica Lange (as his wife) and Juliette Lewis (as their daughter) are uniformly fine. Lewis and De Niro's scene set in a school auditorium is a mesmerizing exercise in corruption. Though Cape Fear boasts virtuoso production values, some of the visual potency may be lost on the small screen; but the searing characterizations maintain full strength. This can be added to Scorsese's list of classics. ★★★½ $14.99

Captain Blood

(1935, 99 min, US, Michael Curtiz) The first of the many Curtiz-Errol Flynn-Olivia deHavilland swashbucklers; and an immensely entertaining film. Flynn stars as an Irish doctor who is sentenced to life-long servitude in the Americas after treating a wounded rebel. He later escapes to captain a pirate ship. Contains one of the best sword fight scenes in the movies: Flynn and Basil Rathbone dueling it out on a rocky beach. ★★★½ $19.99

Captain Horatio Hornblower

(1951, 117 min, GB, Raoul Walsh) Gregory Peck is appropriately gallant in the title role as Britain's dashing naval hero in this lively adaptation of the C.S. Forester novels. It's the Napoleonic Wars, and England is at a crisis. Not to worry, though, for Capt. Hornblower is at the helm. The good captain takes on the French, a Spanish rebel, and almost single-handedly saves the day. Things really get explosive when he rescues her ladyship Virginia Mayo who's adrift at sea. There's a couple of nifty battle scenes and even a romantic subplot doesn't drag the action. Hornblower looks good in his early 19th-century costumes; he's got a funny name, though. ★★★ $19.99

Captains Courageous

Captain January

(1936, 75 min, US, David Butler) Little Shirley Temple lets the tears flow in this sentimental tale of a young orphan being taken away from her adoptive father (Guy Kibbee). Shirley sings "The Codfish Ball." ★★½ $14.99

Captain Newman M.D.

(1963, 126 min, US, David Miller) Compelling comedy-drama starring Gregory Peck as a dedicated military doctor treating mentally disturbed soldiers stateside during WWII. Also starring Tony Curtis, Angie Dickinson and Oscar-nominee Bobby Darin. ★★★ $14.99

Captain Ron

(1992, 99 min, US, Thom Eberhardt) In this amiable variation of *What About Bob?*, *Captain Ron* stars Martin Short as a mild-mannered family man who inherits a boatload of trouble when he takes his family sailing with the help of lovable, ne'er-do-well Captain Ron (Kurt Russell). Like Richard Dreyfuss' psychiatrist, Short's exasperated father is the only one to notice a bumbler's shortcomings which the rest of the family is blind to. Short's comic instincts are still on the mark (though he lacks the freedom of his "SCTV" years), but it is Russell's surprising flair for comedy which makes these hijinks seaworthy. ★★½ $9.99

The Captain's Paradise

(1953, 80 min, GB, Anthony Kimmins) Alec Guinness is true to form in this romping farce about a ferry boat captain who gives life to the saying "a woman in every port." Thinking he

has conquered life's ills, he shuttles merrily back and forth between his betrothed, one in Tangier and one in Gibraltar. But the comedy heats up when his scheme begins to unravel. Yvonne De Carlo and Celia Johnson provide fine support as the victims of Guinness' chicanery. ★★★½ $19.99

The Captain's Table

(1958, 90 min, GB, Jack Lee) This fluffy British comedy follows the exploits of Captain Epps who, after serving 30 years as skipper of a run-down cargo vessel, is suddenly transferred to the luxurious SS Queen Adelane. More adept at hauling cargo than people, the captain becomes a fish out of water with occasional hilarious results. ★★★ $19.99

Captains Courageous

(1937, 116 min, US, Victor Fleming) Well-produced, exciting adaptation of Rudyard Kipling's adventure story. A rich, pampered youth falls off a ship and is rescued by a Portuguese fisherman, teaching the boy his love for the sea. Spencer Tracy won the first of his two Oscars as the fisherman, Freddie Bartholomew is well-cast as the youth, and Mickey Rooney, Lionel Barrymore and Melvyn Douglas also star. ★★★½ $19.99

Captives

(1996, 99 min, GB, Angela Pope) When she accepts a part-time position as dentist at a maximum security prison in London, a newly divorced woman begins a hesitant affair with a prisoner and is thrust into perilous circumstances. *Captives* may not feature the most original plot line, but thanks to extremely appealing performances from its two leads, and a thoughtful, well-versed screenplay, this romantic drama/thriller is consistently engaging. Julia Ormand is understated and totally captivating as a woman caught off guard, whose act of kindness leads her to a road she never anticipated. Tim Roth plays her lover with smoldering intensity, a victim to his surroundings and loneliness as much as the woman he falls in love with. *Captives* never relies on the obvious, instead creating a believable and sensual relationship between the two characters while pitting them against outside forces. Their eventual strength and loyalty only makes them and the film all the more winning. ★★★ $19.99

Car Trouble

(1985, 93 min, GB, David Green) Vicious *War of the Roses*-style comedy about a harried air-traffic controller and his long-suffering wife of nine years (Ian Charleson, Julie Walters) whose lives become a nightmare when he takes on a mistress — a jazzy red sports car! A caustic comedy of the blackest sort, marred only by its implausible ending. ★★½

Caravaggio

(1986, 93 min, GB, Derek Jarman) Michelangelo Merisi Caravaggio (1573-1610) was the last, perhaps the greatest, and certainly the most controversial painter of the Italian Renaissance. This stylish, adventurous tribute to the outlandish artist is directed by Jarman and is further proof of his ability to stretch artistic invention. The temperaments of Jarman and Caravaggio are well-suited; the

C

result is a bold and quirky film with contemporary touches, spectacular camera work and an impressionistic feel. ★★★ $79.99

The Caravaggio Conspiracy

(1984, 60 min, GB, Nigel Finch) This is the true story of London Times journalist Peter Watson, who goes undercover disguised as a wealthy art dealer, interested in buying stolen masterpieces. What art he recovers, and what he learns about the international art market, makes for an intriguing hour. ★★★ $39.99

Career Opportunities

(1991, 85 min, US, Bryan Gordon) John Hughes wrote the screenplay for this far-fetched, underdeveloped comedy, sort of an adult *Home Alone*. Frank Whaley plays a night janitor at a discount store who comes across rich kid Jennifer Connelly, who got locked in. Together they defend the store against two burglars who are about to clean the place out. ★½ $19.99

Carefree

(1938, 80 min, US, Mark Sandrich) Though this Fred Astaire-Ginger Rogers musical's dance sequences can't compare to some of their 1930s contemporaries, *Carefree* boasts one of the duo's strongest screenplays. A lively screwball outing, the story deals with radio star Ginger falling for psychiatrist Fred, even though she's engaged to his best friend (perennial best friend Ralph Bellamy). Ginger, probably because she's the romantic aggressor for once, is at her most spirited as she lets her subconscious roam wild to remain a patient. Irving Berlin's score is pleasant but not among his best, though two dance numbers, including "Dancing in the Dark" and an elaborately choreographed tour through a country club, are sublime. ★★★ $19.99

Careful

(1992, 100 min, Canada, Guy Maddin) A culture of repression and paranoid caution inhabits a small mountain valley community living in stringently enforced guilt, guarding against the threat of avalanche. This alternate world is described by director Madden (*Tales of Gimli*

Carmen Jones

Hospital) in saturated colors and stark imagery coupled with kitschy detail, creating a hyper-reality of repressed passions; a rigidly organized hotbed of Freudian conflicts where dead fathers try to caution Oedipal sons, and daughters vie for fathers' affections. The landscape itself is another character, and strange tricks of sound convey secret communications to unintended ears. Visually sumptuous, witty and truly unique, *Careful* can be described as "David Lynch meets German Expressionism" via dream therapy. It's both stimulating and adventurous. ★★★ $79.99

Careful, He Might Hear You

(1983, 116 min, Australia, Carl Schultz) This poignant and emotionally charged drama digs deep to expose the underlying spitefulness of a quietly waged battle between two sisters (Wendy Hughes and Robyn Nevin) vying for the custody of their displaced nephew. Directed by Schultz with epicurean zeal, the film benefits from brilliant performances by the ensemble. ★★★

Carlito's Way

(1993, 141 min, US, Brian De Palma) *Scarface* star Al Pacino and director De Palma reunite to create another Hispanic gangster drama. But unlike that film's Tony Montana, Carlito Brigante (Pacino) is a man defined by romanticism and simplicity. After serving five years in prison, Carlito simply wants to go to the Bahamas to start a car-rental agency. However, loyalties to his friend David Kleinfeld (stunningly portrayed by Sean Penn), a corrupt and double-dealing lawyer, threaten to drag him down. Pacino delivers a solid performance, as does Penelope Ann Miller as his girlfriend, and there's amazing camerawork; though one can only feel that this territory has already been heavily traveled. ★★½ $14.99

Carlton-Browne of the F.O.

(1959, 88 min, GB, Jeffrey Dell & Roy Boulting) A hilarious screwball farce about the Island of Gallardia — a British protectorate which was somehow forgotten for 50 years. When this embarrassing circumstance is uncovered, the blundering Terry-Thomas is sent to lead the Foreign Office. This scathing satire on diplomacy also stars Peter Sellers. ★★★

Carmen

(1984, 130 min, Italy/France, Francesco Rosi) In a season of several Carmens, Rosi's stirring version is certainly truest to the Bizet opera. As the gypsy heroine, Julia-Migenes Johnson is a lusty fireball of unkempt urges. Placido Domingo brings his robust tenor to the role of the soldier broken by her powerful allure. (French with English subtitles) ★★★ $19.99

Carmen Jones

(1954, 105 min, US, Otto Preminger) Directed by Preminger (who also directed *Porgy and Bess*) and scored by Oscar Hammerstein, Bizet's famous opera is transformed into an all-black musical starring Dorothy Dandridge as a flirtatious party girl who causes soldier Harry Belafonte to go off the deep end because of his passion for her. Laced with many fine performances, including Pearl Bailey, Brock Peters and Diahann Carroll, this highly entertaining songfest also

made Dandridge the first black performer nominated for an Oscar in a leading role. ★★★ $19.99

Carnal Knowledge

(1971, 97 min, US, Mike Nichols) Director Nichols collaborated with Jules Feiffer to create this brutally honest and surprisingly perceptive examination of American sexual politics, seen over the course of two decades through the eyes of two college buddies and their relationships with various women. The camera is unflinching and revelatory, capturing the most ephemeral of moments: the awkward tentativeness of youthful encounters, the exploitative cynicism of middle-aged desperation, the self-deceptive smug assuredness which accompanies the acquisition of a new partner — nothing is glossed over or ameliorated. Jack Nicholson is brutally honest in his depiction of a man for whom women are at best a pleasure and at worst an alimony payment. Art Garfunkel is the best friend who likes to think of himself as more highly evolved. Candice Bergen and Ann-Margret are two of the women who pass through their lives. All give superior performances in a remarkable piece of work. ★★★★

Carnival of Souls

(1962, 80 min, US, Herk Harvey) This eerily chilling and angst-ridden cult classic follows Mary Henry (icily portrayed by Candace Hilligoss), a taciturn organist who miraculously survives a near-fatal car accident. Shaken, she decides to start life anew, and sets out for new pastures. No sooner has she hit the road than she is haunted by a ghoul who is invisible to all but her. Filmed in shadowy black and white, the film's visual power — which set precedent for such chillers as *Night of the Living Dead*, etc. — evokes an undeniably menacing and twisted tone. *Carnival of Souls* takes us back to an era when the horror genre probed the supernatural with an eye to the psyche and spirit rather than indulging in the gut-bucket gore which assaults moviegoers today. ★★★ $12.99

Carnival Rock

(1958, 80 min, US, Roger Corman) Thrill-seeking kids, grimy gangsters and psychopathic teens clash in a rockabilly, rhythm 'n' blues, rock 'n' roll nightclub. With Susan Cabit, Dick Miller and The Platters. ★★ $9.99

Carnosaur

(1993, 83 min, US, Adam Simon) Diane Ladd stars in this Roger Corman-produced shocker as a genetic engineer working for a food corporation who develops a virus that can turn a mild-mannered chicken embryo into a bloodthirsty Tyrannosaurus Rex. Fueled by the amphetamine-overdrive performance of Ladd, well-paced snatches of humor, cheesy special effects that can only be rivaled by the children's show "Land of the Lost," and jabs at *Jurassic Park*, this entertaining schlock-fest is sure to appeal to those who like heavy doses of vitamin "B" in their viewing diet. ★★½ $14.99

Carnosaur 2

(1994, 83 min, US, Louis Morneau) This dreadfully misconceived sequel to the charmingly cheap and fun *Carnosaur* is a humorless excursion into the usually enjoyable trailer-park sub-genius of Roger Corman's brand of grade-B schlock. Little more than an attempt to clone *Aliens*, *C2* follows the exploits of an irreverent group of wise-cracking mercenaries enlisted by a corrupt bureaucrat to do battle with the mutant chicken dino beasts from *C1*. With great potential for more rib-tickling and gore-soaked madness, *C2* instead relies on an untalented cast, awful dialogue and a rip-off ending, making this foray into late-night cheese-o-rama all the more disappointing. ★ $14.99

Carny

(1980, 107 min, US, Robert Kaylor) A quirky, moody drama about life on the road with a carnival. Gary Busey and Robbie Robertson are carnival hustlers, or "carnys," whose lives are interrupted when they take in teenage runaway Jodie Foster. Unusual and offbeat, though very satisfying. ★★★ $19.99

Caro Diario

(1994, 142 min, Italy, Nanni Moretti) An endearing and delightful odyssey in three parts based on director Moretti's personal diaries which he literally transposes in staged reenactments, *Caro Diario* ("Dear Diary") is an amusing, insightful and illuminating journey. In the first segment, "On My Vespa," Moretti zooms around Rome and its adjoining neighborhoods making wry commentary on the architectual styles, inhabitants and social trends. "Islands" finds Moretti and a friend traveling to Italy's Lipari Islands in search of a relaxing place to work only to be put off by the increasing eccentricities of each successive archipelago. In the final tale, "Doctors," Moretti comes face to face with the medical profession in an attempt to root out the cause of a mysterious skin ailment — any who have suffered at the hands of "specialists" will find this particularly humorous. (Italian with English subtitles) ★★★½ $19.99

Carol Burnett — My Personal Best, Vols. 1 & 2

(1987, 60 min, US) Carol Burnett selects some of her favorite skits from her award-winning variety series, including "Mama's Family," the Shirley Temple take-offs and the hilarious *Gone with the Wind* spoof. $29.99

Carousel

(1956, 128 min, US, Henry King) Invigorating screen version of the Rodgers and Hammerstein musical (based on Molnar's "Liliom") about a roguish carnival barker (Gordon MacRae) who tries to change his ways when he falls for Shirley Jones. Songs include "Soliloquy (My Boy Bill)," "June Is Busting Out All Over" and "You'll Never Walk Alone." ★★★ $19.99

Carpool

(1996, 90 min, US, Arthur Hiller) This icky "family comedy" equates reckless driving and the mass destruction it causes with getting in touch with your inner child. Or that may be, at least, one subtext to think about to keep yourself awake while watching this almost laughless, frequently annoying mess. Giving an almost likable performance, Tom Arnold plays a would-be thief who takes ad exec David

Carrington

Paymer and the five kids in his carpool hostage after a botched robbery. But of course he's a friendly criminal, and everybody ends up smiling in one of those warm and fuzzy, artificial endings that's actually quite depressing. Along the way, there are potshots aimed at the media, the police and ad agencies; at least Rhea Perlman and Rod Steiger have amusing cameos. ★½ $19.99

Carreras, Domingo, Pavarotti

(1990, 86 min, GB, Brian Large) Three of opera's great tenors — Jose Carreras, Placido Domingo and Luciano Pavarotti — take the stage for an evening of arias from the world's greatest composers. Conducted by Zubin Mehta. Filmed in Rome at the Ferme di Caracalla. $24.99

Carrie

(1952, 118 min, US, William Wyler) Jennifer Jones plays the title role, a turn-of-the-century country girl who comes to Chicago to pursue a life on the stage. There she becomes involved with wealthy and married Laurence Olivier, whose relationship with the actress leads to his downfall. Based on Theodore Dreiser's ("An American Tragedy") satirical novel. Olivier is simply brilliant, and Jones gives one of her most accomplished performances. ★★★ $19.99

Carrie

(1976, 97 min, US, Brian De Palma) De Palma's chilling adaptation of the Stephen King novel tells the story of a mousy high school girl taunted by classmates. What her tormentors don't know is that Carrie posseses frightening telekinetic powers, eliciting film's most famous temper tantrum. Perhaps the worst mother-daughter relationship since Joan and Christina, Sissy Spacek and Piper Laurie, as Carrie and her bible-thumping mother, respectively, were both nominated for Oscars and deservedly so. ★★★½ $14.99

Carried Away

(1996, 105 min, US, Bruno Barreto) A low-key but quite involving romance based on the novel "Farmer" by Jim Harrison. Dennis

Hopper plays a small-town farmer and school-teacher who can't quite commit to marrying longtime girlfriend Rosealee (Amy Irving). When a young, sexy student (Amy Locane) enters his classroom, his life changes irrevocably. What sounds like a *Fatal Attraction* ripoff (especially considering the cast and the advertising) is actually an understated, quietly powerful sleeper about a man's midlife crisis, handled with sensitivity and a minimum of clichés. The ensemble is uniformly good, with uncharacteristic yet effective portrayals by Gary Busey and Hopper, both of whom leave behind their manic schtick — Hopper's heartfelt, wholly believable performance is his best in years. *Carried Away* unfolds with the tempo of a rich novella — it's not epic in scope but nevertheless creates moments of unexpected joy. ★★★ $19.99

Carrington

(1995, 123 min, GB, Christopher Hampton) Based on the book "Lytton Strachey" by Michael Holyroyd, *Carrington* is the story of the relationship and attraction between artist Dora Carrington (Emma Thompson) and gay Bloomsbury Group writer Lytton Strachey (Jonathan Pryce). Their unconventional but enduring friendship and love story begins when Strachey, a somewhat flamboyant "bachelor," becomes attracted to what he thinks is a boy. He is embarrassed to find out the "boy" is actually Dora Carrington. A tentative kiss by Strachey does not lead to sexual relations, but Carrington does fall in love with him despite being told by a fellow art student that Lytton is a "bugger." They eventually move in together and sleep together and even find themselves attracted to the same men, including Carrington's future husband (Steven Waddington). Bearded, painfully thin and always ready with the satiric quip, Pryce's Strachey is a revelation; it's a memorable depiction of a gay man. Director Hampton has fashioned a fine, sometimes dark period piece, complete with lush surroundings and it is well-served by an intelligent screenplay. ★★★½ $19.99

Carry Me Back

(1982, 93 min, Australia, John Reid) This Aussie black comedy is about two brothers and their cantankerous father who venture from their family farm to watch a rugby match hundreds of miles from home. During the match the old codger dies in the hotel room. Problems arise when the brothers discover that in order to inherit the family estate, the father must die on the family's property. What ensues is a series of funny complications as the two attempt to smuggle old dad home without anyone knowing he's a stiff! ★★½

Carry on Cleo

(1968, 92 min, GB, Gerald Thomas) One of the best of the "Carry On" series. This is admittedly a qualified endorsement which can only be taken with so much seriousness, but this witty reworking of ancient history features lots of silly hijinks, along with Cleopatra, Caesar, Marc Antony and lots of vestal virgins. ★★½

Carry on Cruising

(1962, 89 min, GB, Gerald Thomas) The zany, pre-Python "Carry On" gang unleash themselves on a Mediterranean cruise ship. Though not a serious thesis on the state of human existence, the film has lots of slapstick gags and lowbrow humor, which in most cases will suffice. ★★½

Carry on Doctor

(1968, 95 min, GB, Gerald Thomas) More hijinks from the "Carry On" crew with their sights set this time on the medical profession. This romping farce is set at an English hospital filled with crazy doctors, crazier patients and a bevy of sex-starved nurses. ★★

The Cars That Ate Paris

(1974, 92 min, Australia, Peter Weir) A bizarre horror tale of a mutated town struggling to survive by cannibalizing the vehicles of unsuspecting travelers and leaving the inhabitants either dead or "veggies" for medical experimentation. A tongue-in-cheek shot at automotive madness. Original full-length version. (aka: *The Cars That Eat People*) ★★★ $19.99

Cartoons for Big Kids

(1989, 44 min, US) Scathing satirical shorts with Bugs Bunny, Daffy Duck, Screwy Squirrel and others filled with put-downs and caricatures of contemporary heads of state, movie idols and studio chiefs, originally deemed too controversial for kids. Includes Red Hot Riding Hood, "the girl they banned from television." Hosted by Leonard Maltin. $19.99

Cartouche

(1961, 115 min, France, Philippe de Broca) He robs from the rich and gives to the poor. Sound familiar? Director de Broca (*King of Hearts*) presents his variation of the Robin Hood legend with the always suave Jean-Paul Belmondo as Cartouche, the once-petty thief turned avenger of the poor. This slapstick adventure has Belmondo fighting the foes with a quick sword and a witty tongue and romancing the women with pretty much the same. Though the film is occasionally slow and slightly dated, it's fairly enjoyable nevertheless. ★★ $29.99

Casablanca

(1942, 102 min, US, Michael Curtiz) As time goes by, no film equals the popularity of this indisputable classic. In quintessential roles, Humphrey Bogart and Ingrid Bergman are former lovers reunited in wartorn Casablanca. Bogey is the cynical cafe owner who lives by his own moral code and sticks his neck out for "no one." Bergman, as the beautiful wife of Resistance leader Paul Henried, finds herself torn between two lovers when she reenters Bogey's life. The film's great success lies in the inimitable pairing of its two stars, a thoroughly romantic story line, terrific humor and numerous moments of suspense. Of course, that great ending helps, too. Studio filmmaking from the 1940s doesn't come better than this, and director Curtiz masterfully handles the action, comedy and romance. Nearly stealing the film is Claude Rains as a "poor, corrupt official" who as a Nazi puppet soon discovers the beginning of a beautiful friendship. Academy Award winner for Best Picture. ★★★★ $19.99

Casablanca

Casanova's Big Night

(1954, 86 min, US, Norman Z. McLeod) The laughs are plentiful in this engaging Bob Hope spoof with Bob mistaken as the legendary ladies' man and doing nothing to correct the error. No one can play ham like Hope. ★★★ $14.99

Casino

(1995, 177 min, US, Martin Scorsese) A gangster who lives by his own moral code; a hotheaded hit man with a hair-trigger temper; a fascinating peek into the inner-workings of underworld crime; meticulous production values: these are all familiar trappings of director Scorsese's best-known works. And in *Casino*, his ambitious examination of a mob-controlled Las Vegas, these familiarities both enhance and hinder the director's epic story of love among the slots. Robert De Niro plays a crafty casino manager whose life is intruded upon by two opposing forces – a volatile mob associate (Joe Pesci) who invades his business and a gorgeous ex-prostitute (Sharon Stone) who captures his heart. A prisoner to the honorable dictates of loyalty and love and to the emotions of jealousy and power, De Niro's life soon spirals out of control. *Casino* is at its best during the first half, introducing its gallery of players and detailing the daily operation of the casino. However, once Stone's character experiences her own descent, the film appears to somewhat lose its balance and momentum. Stone is terrific in a breakthrough role, though, truthfully, we've seen De Niro and Pesci do all this before. (Available letterboxed and pan & scan) ★★★ $19.99

Casino Royale

(1967, 130 min, GB, John Huston, Ken Hughes, Robert Parrish, Joseph McGrath, Val Guest) Peter Sellers, David Niven, Ursula Andress, Woody Allen, Orson Welles and an endless array of others star in this grand spoof of the James Bond genre. Often muddled, perhaps by the multitude of talents more than anything else, the film is nonetheless filled with hilarious moments and is guaranteed to please comedy buffs. ★★½ $9.99

Casper

(1995, 95 min, US, Brad Silberling) Children of all ages should delight in this special effects charmer based on the popular comic and cartoon. Filled with spiffy cameos, amazing ghostly creatures and a dash of mischief, *Casper* casts Bill Pullman and Christina Ricci as a ghostbusting father and his unconventional daughter who move into a haunted house to rid it of prankish poltergeists. Though the screenplay is very much on a sitcomish level, the film exhibits truly spectacular effects as Casper and his three devilish uncles haunt, eat, fight, drink and fly about. The film's other feather is the creation of Casper: Not a simpy do-gooder as in the old cartoons, he's a "fleshed"-out kid with humor and spunk. As Casper's human friend, Ricci is adorable (though she's not given the wondrous zingers like in the *Addams Family* films), and Pullman is amiable as her father. ★★★ $14.99

Cass

(1981, 90 min, Australia, Chris Noonan) This wrenching drama deals with a young female filmmaker whose life is thrown in crisis after making a film about a primitive, tribal society. Fascinated by their matriarchal rituals, the woman returns to "civilized society" and her husband. She soon realizes, however, that she is a changed person with new values and eventually becomes isolated from her husband, ridiculed by her boss and finds herself falling in love with another woman. The film focuses on her attempts to resolve her newly discovered inner conflicts. ★

Cass Timberlane

(1947, 119 min, US, George Sidney) Spencer Tracy stars as the titular character of this very standard 1940s romantic drama based on Sinclair Lewis' novel of class distinction and self-discovery. Set in a small Midwestern town, the film features Tracy as a middle-aged, widowed judge who is charmed by young artist Lana Turner, who's from the wrong side of the tracks. The story focuses on their May-December romance, as Turner vies for acceptance from her husband's snobbish country club set and is tempted by Tracy's pal Zachary Scott. Tracy and Turner are a compatible couple, but neither is helped by clichéd situations and characters. ★★ $19.99

Cast a Deadly Spell

(1991, 92 min, US, Martin Campbell) Fred Ward is a delight as H. Philip Lovecraft, the only private eye in 1948 Los Angeles who does *not* use magic in his daily life. Renting his office from licensed witch and certified dance instructor Mrs. Kropotkin, Lovecraft is hired by David Warner (who has come to wear sinister as a favorite suit) to retrieve a pilfered book...a large, ornate book containing the secrets of ultimate power and world domination. Warner's daughter, when not hunting unicorns on the estate grounds, complicates Lovecraft's quest for the tempting tome and alters the fate of mankind. There's also a femme fatale chanteuse, some wise guy cops, really spiffy clothes, great noirish dialogue and enticing special effects. Made for cable with tongue in cheek, *Cast a Deadly Spell* pays loving homage to the horror and supernatural genre. ★★★½ $89.99

The Castle

(1968, 89 min, West Germany, Rudolf Noelte) A stylized, if somewhat indistinct version of Franz Kafka's novel. Maximilian Schell stars as a stranger known as "K" who arrives at a small village claiming he is the new land surveyor for a nearby castle. However, in true Kafkaesque fashion, K, confronted with a sinisterly bureaucratic and regimented populace, cannot gain admittance to the fortress. (Filmed in English) ★★½

Casual Sex?

(1988, 97 min, US, Genevieve Robert) Harmless, diverting sex comedy with Lea Thompson and Victoria Jackson as single women in search of more than a one-night stand in the age of AIDS. Andrew Dice Clay plays a sexist creep (what a casting inspiration) who turns out to be Mr. Nice Guy. ★★½ $9.99

Casualties of War

(1989, 113 min, US, Brian de Palma) Set in 1966 Vietnam, this harrowing, fact-based story is about a Vietnamese woman who is kidnapped, raped and murdered by four soldiers. Michael J. Fox stars as a newly arrived private who is forced to participate; Sean Penn is the near-maniacal platoon sergeant who heads the assault. Superbly directed by De Palma, the film divides its running time between the horrific act and its aftereffect; on Fox in particular, who, though passively resistant during the ordeal, ultimately brings the men to trial. Thuy Thu Le is heartbreaking as the murdered woman. ★★★½ $9.99

Cat and Mouse

(1975, 107 min, France, Claude Lelouch) This mesmerizing and ingenious Parisian murder mystery is full of unexpected twists and humorous turns as an unorthodox detective delves into the death of a millionaire. The murder, thinly disguised as suicide, leads the detective to a variety of suspects and many baffling questions. (French with English subtitles) ★★★½

The Cat and the Canary

(1927, 70 min, Germany, Paul Leni) This delightfully eerie thriller is a classic of the horror genre and set the style for the famous Universal horror films of the 1930s. A group of relatives gather at midnight in an abandoned mansion to read the will of an old man. The dead man's niece is the heiress, but only if she spends the night in the house. During the course of the spooky night, she encounters clutching hands, sliding panels, revolving bookcases and a cat-like apparition. (Silent with musical accompaniment) ★★★ $29.99

Cat Ballou

(1965, 96 min, US, Elliot Silverstein) Jane Fonda sparkles in the lead role in this wonderful western spoof as a schoolteacher who turns outlaw to avenge her father's murder. But it's Lee Marvin who walked away with an Oscar for his performance in dual roles – he plays both the film's villain and the washed-up, alcoholic gunman who is forced out of retirement to hunt him down. Nat King Cole and Stubby Kaye spice up the film with intermittent musical numbers as a pair of wandering minstrels. A breezy, comedic homage to the classic western take on the conflict between good and evil. ★★★½ $14.99

The Cat from Outer Space

(1978, 104 min, US, Norman Tokar) More Disney fluff about an alien kitty stranded on Earth who needs help to get back home (though it may sound like an *E.T.* ripoff, this actually came first). With Sandy Duncan and Ken Berry. ★★½

The Cat O'Nine Tails

(1971, 89 min, Italy, Dario Argento) Karl Malden and James Franciscus star in Argento's second neo-Hitchcockian thriller, a confusing murder mystery involving industrial espionage in the world of experimental genetics. Malden is a blind ex-newspaper reporter who may hold some important information about the mysterious accidental death of a scientist. He contacts Franciscus, himself a reporter, and the two of them begin an investigation which leads them closer to the truth and into a deadly race with the killer. Malden and Franciscus are both good and Malden in particular lends his role a credibility seldom seen in Argento's films, but the story is needlessly confusing and not very engaging even when it is clarified at the end. This, however, is hardly surprising, as the U.S. video release of *Cat* is missing nearly 22 minutes from the original edit. Only one scene, involving a grave robbery and violent struggle in a mausoleum, is truly chilling. (Filmed in English) ★★ $12.99

Cat on a Hot Tin Roof

(1958, 108 min, US, Richard Brooks) Everyone has a skeleton in their closet in Tennessee Williams' Pulitzer Prize-winning drama. Elizabeth Taylor sinks her claws into the role of Maggie the Cat, the tormented, sexually frustrated wife of guilt-ridden ex-jock Brick (Paul Newman). The prototypic tale of family conflict and confrontation. ★★★★ $19.99

Cat on a Hot Tin Roof

(1984, 122 min, US, Jack Hofsiss) An excellent made-for-TV adaptation of the Tennessee Williams play, with particularly strong performances from Jessica Lange as Maggie the Cat; Rip Torn as Big Daddy; and Tommy Lee Jones as Brick, Big Daddy's favorite son, an alcoholic ex-jock with a burden from his past that he cannot resolve. Good support from Kim Stanley, David Dukes and Penny Fuller as other members of the conflicted Southern family. ★★★½

Cat People

(1942, 70 min, US, Jacques Tourneur) Of the eight horror films Val Lewton produced for RKO Pictures in the 1940s, this moody and suspenseful thriller — awash in stark shades of black and white — is his classic. Simone Simon stars as a mysterious woman who refuses to consummate her marriage to architect Kent

Robert De Niro (l.) and Joe Pesci are consummate goodfellas in *Casino*

Smith on the belief that she is descended from a race of cat people and if sexually aroused, she will transform into a panther. Remade in 1982. ★★★½ $19.99

Cat People

(1982, 118 min, US, Paul Schrader) Schrader's gory remake of Val Lewton's 1942 classic chiller is shameless fun, even more so with the director's psychological baggage to laugh at. Malcolm McDowell and Nastassja Kinski play kissin' cousins who can't get down from their family tree. The whole production exudes an all-pervasive air of fetid evil, perversity and eroticism — much like the city in which it is set: New Orleans. ★★½ $14.99

Cat's Eye

(1985, 94 min, US, Lewis Teague) Stephen King's horror trilogy. Drew Barrymore, James Woods, Alan King, Robert Hays and James Naughton appear in three King stories about a clinic which helps smokers quit; a mobster who gets even with his wife's lover; and (the best sequence) a cat who protects a young girl from a deadly troll. ★★½ $14.99

Cat's Play

(1974, 115 min, Hungary, Karoly Makk) From the director of *Another Way* comes this contemplative drama about rekindled passion, love, friendship and growing old. Two sisters, living in different regions of the country, continue to communicate through letters and phone calls. The correspondence, usually centering on earlier, happier times, turns darker when one of them falls desperately in love with her old flame, an elderly opera singer. Despite her sister's imploring, the normally sedate woman becomes girlish in her efforts to restart the affair, and despondent and self-destructive when it fails. Told in the form of an epistolary novel and utilizing vivid images to convey the character's innermost thoughts, the film is a serious, stylistically daring and deeply involving drama. (Hungarian with English subtitles) ★★★½ $59.99

Catamount Killing

(1974, 93 min, West Germany, Krzystof Zannusi) Polish director Zannusi (*A Year of the Quiet Sun*) tries his hand at film noir in this English-speaking thriller set in a bucolic Vermont town. Horst Bucholz stars as a newly arrived bank manager who seduces an older woman and then involves her in the faking of a robbery at his bank. Their plans go awry, however, resulting in murderous cover-ups. Bucholz is great as the psychotic young manager who is slowly tormented to the point of a violent crack-up. ★★½ $89.99

Catch-22

(1970, 121 min, US, Mike Nichols) Brilliant screen adaptation of Joseph Heller's best-selling anti-war novel. Alan Arkin heads a first-rate all-star cast as a WWII Army pilot caught up in the absurdities of military life. Get this cast: Jon Voight, Martin Sheen, Orson Welles, Art Garfunkle (fine in his film debut), Richard Benjamin, Paula Prentiss, Bob Newhart, Anthony Perkins, Jack Gilford and Buck Henry. A powerful and subversively funny black comedy. ★★★★ $14.99

The Catered Affair

(1956, 93 min, US, Richard Brooks) Good performances distinguish this absorbing family drama. Bette Davis is in fine form as the wife of Bronx cabbie Ernest Borgnine whose determination to give daughter Debbie Reynolds an elegant wedding far exceeds the family's income. ★★★ $19.99

Caught

(1949, 88 min, US, Max Ophûls) Intriguing film noir psychodrama with Barbara Bel Geddes as a mistreated wife caught between her villainous millionaire husband (Robert Ryan) and a caring doctor (James Mason). ★★★ $19.99

Caught

(1996, 109 min, US, Robert M. Young) Nick (Arie Verveen), a "mysterious drifter," is taken in by Joe (Edward James Olmos), a fish shop owner, and his wife Betty (Maria Conchita Alonso). He's given a job and the bedroom of their son, who's in Hollywood trying to break into movies. Things are rosy until Betty and Nick start having an affair, and things get really tense when son Danny pays a surprise visit. While the scenario and conclusion fit neatly into the glib "adultery-never-pays" agenda of most erotic thrillers, *Caught* is far more believable and involving than one would expect, with good performances and a deliberate pace that allows scenes to unfold naturally, without ever going slack. Alonso's feelings about her husband could have been fleshed out more, and the message is too conventional to carry weight. But *Caught* is nevertheless a good, solid drama. ★★★ $99.99

Caught in the Draft

(1941, 82 min, US, David Butler) Bob Hope gets *Caught in the Draft* and the service will never be the same. Congress has just legalized the draft, and movie star Hope schemes to avoid both induction into the Army and marriage to colonel's daughter Dorothy Lamour. Of course, it all backfires, and Hope, who faints at the sound of a gun shot, is thrust on an unsuspecting military. This winning comedy is an arsenal of one-liners and sight gags, and its screenplay adheres to a much tighter structure than the standard Hope comedy. Lamour isn't given much to do but react to Hope, but she looks great; Eddie Bracken (who would star in the decade's greatest service comedy, *Hail the Conquering Hero*) and Lynne Overman are tops in support as Hope's henchmen. ★★★ $14.99

Caught Looking/North of Vortex

(1991, 24/58 min, GB, Constantine Giannaris) Two short films from British director Giannaris. *Caught Looking*, winner of the Best Gay Short at the 1992 Berlin Film Festival, is witty, sexy and highly inventive. A man uses an interactive virtual reality machine to fulfill his sexual fantasies, bringing to vivid life different sexual scenarios. *North of Vortex* is a lyrical, leisurely paced black-and-white road movie set in the American West. Traveling in his convertible, a gay poet picks up a bisexual sailor and a waitress. The film explores the shifting emotional relationship between them. ★★★½ $39.99

Cavalcade

(1933, 110 min, US, Frank Lloyd) Noël Coward's 1930s stage hit is given superior treatment in this Oscar-winning adaptation. Clive Brook and Diana Wynyard head an upper-class British family at the turn-of-the-century. The film follows their lives through the first World War and into the 1930s. Though she was nominated for a Best Actress Oscar, Wynyard's performance seems exaggerated and dated, but the film does not. First-rate production values and an engrossing story make this one of the classics from its era. ★★★½ $19.99

CB4

(1993, 83 min, US, Tamra Davis) "Saturday Night Live"'s Chris Rock stars in this hip-hop, gangsta rap parody, which he co-wrote with former music critic and author Nelson George. The film, which starts out as a hysterically funny pseudo-documentary, strays from its course by turning into a narrative tale and morality play. The film is filled with hilarious moments that are sharp-witted comments on African-American, B-Boys stereotypes, but all of that is lost in a weak story. ★★½ $19.99

Céleste

(1981, 107 min, West Germany, Percy Adlon) With no plot to speak of, this subtle yet involving and ultimately inspiring love story chronicles the daily routine of an uneducated peasant girl (the wonderful Eva Mattes) who is hired as the housekeeper for the ailing author, Marcel Proust. The film's power lies in the evolving relationship between the intellectual Proust and the simple, caring woman who in the course of nine years not only tends to his house but becomes his companion, secretary, friend and surrogate mother. Set in 1913, this moving drama is based on the memoirs of the real Céleste Albaret. (German with English subtitles) ★★★ $29.99

Celestial Clockwork (Mécanicas Célestes)

(1994, 86 min, France/Venezuela/Spain/Belgium, Fina Torres) Exuberant, fanciful and infused with magical realism, this "Alice in Wonderland/Cinderella"-like comedy is a delightful celebration of the pursuit of individual happiness and sexual open-mindedness. In dusty Caracas, the lovely Ana suddenly comes to her senses on the altar and flees, leaving her stunned husband-to-be and her former life behind. She jumps aboard the next Paris-bound plane and takes up residence in a funky crash pad with her old friend Alma. The apartment is right out of Almódovar, populated by a bevy of Latina exiles aggressively excercising their free will and indulging in outrageous Parisianne chic. Ana sets out to pursue her career as an operatic soloist, but along the way runs afoul of the immigration authorities and discovers her budding lesbiansim, falling desperately in love with an attractive high-tech psychoanalyst who interviews all her patients remotely by video. It's touches like this that give *Celestial Clockwork* its joie-de-vivre, brimming with oddball characters and loopy plot twists, the film is a highly entertaining ride with Ana on her picaresque journey to self-fulfillment. (Spanish and French with English subtitles) ★★★★ $99.99

Celine and Julie Go Boating

Celine and Julie Go Boating

(1974, 193 min, France, Jacques Rivette) A truly magical cinematic journey if ever there was one, this 1970s art-house classic is "Alice in Wonderland" meets Cocteau. Celine (Juliet Berto) is a magician who becomes fast friends with librarian Julie (Dominique Labourier) after they meet at the steps of Montmarte. Forming an uncanny, symbiotic bond, they move into the same flat and begin sharing completely of each others' lives: bed, clothes, boyfriend, etc. Ultimately, they begin sharing the same alternate reality when they partake of a magic candy that transports them into an imaginary (or is it) haunted house, where they become involved in the drama of its inhabitants. Just as this reaches a climax, the hallucination ends and Celine and Julie must begin again. Rivette commits a huge cinematic risk by presenting this scene again and again as each time it inches closer to its conclusion (hence the 193-minute run time) and voila! It pays off. As delightful and engaging as its two main characters, this is one of those favorite films that has long been awaited by serious lovers of cinema. (French with English subtitles) ★★★★ $89.99

The Celluloid Closet

(1995, 102 min, US, Rob Epstein & Jeffrey Friedman) Inspired by the late Vito Russo's seminal book on the depiction of homosexuality in Hollywood cinema, this funny, informative and occasionally moving documentary offers — through interviews and a vast assortment of film clips — a candid mini-history of gays and lesbians on-screen. *The Celluloid Closet* takes a chronological approach to the subject, offering clips from the turn of the century (*The Gay Brothers*) thru the silents to the effeminate caricatures of the 1930s (*Broadway Melody*), the pitiful homosexual of the 1950s and '60s, the violently deviant homosexual of the '70s and '80s, and concluding with the squeaky clean image of recent times. While encompassing in scope, the film is too simplistic and suffers from the lack of critical analysis and a central point-of-view. And, there are too many straight actors who offer nothing other than having played a gay/lesbian — only Tony Curtis and Susan Sarandon offer insight into the queer roles they have played. With that said, however, *The Celluloid Closet* is more than recommended (and should be required viewing for those interested in the subject), but for something deeper, it is best to read Russo's book. ★★★ $19.99

Celtic Pride

(1996, 91 min, US, Tom De Cerchio) Horrible, obnoxious and unfunny, *Celtic Pride* casts an irritating Dan Aykroyd and a killable Daniel Stern as two pathetic Boston Celtic fans who kidnap the opposing team's star player (a bored Damon Wayans) to ensure their beloved team's victory. What should have been a vicious, wicked satire on professional sports and their more obsessive fans instead is a grueling debut by a film student-like director who has little knowledge of direction, sports or comic timing. Every potentially interesting exchange or insight is diverted to a cheap insult or unnecessary pratfall. Every camera set-up or movement seems designed to kill laughs in the womb. Even reliable veterans such as Aykroyd and Stern are wasted. However, their fans should rejoice — for future performances couldn't possibly be as bad as what's on the screen here. ★ $19.99

The Cement Garden

(1996, 108 min, GB, Andrew Birkin) Based on a novel by Ian McEwan ("The Comfort of Strangers"), this bizarre and twisted little tale of adolescence run amok is at once fascinating and seductively repulsive. The film is set at the extreme fringe of society — a barren wasteland on the edge of some unidentified British city where there stands a lone remaining house. Its four young occupants suddenly find themselves orphaned. Julie (Charlotte Gainsbourg) is the eldest survivor at 16 and becomes the defacto leader of the clan. All the while, she toys with the sexual attentions of her brother Jack (Andrew Robertson), who, when his head's not lost in a sci-fi fantasy novel, is usually masturbating. Completing the family circle are Tom (Ned Birkin), an 8-year-old cross-dresser, and Sue (Alice Coultard), a 13-something conformist. They decide to dispose of mum's body and avoid the orphanages and thus begins a summer of complete descent into childish fantasy that's a pointed allegory — à la "Lord of the Flies" — about the decay of social behavior in a crumbling industrial society. With a haunting soundtrack by Edward Shearmer, the film teases the viewer with snippets of coherency only to settle back into an infuriatingly alluring moral ambiguity. It will certainly not be for all tastes, but it is undeniably interesting. ★★★ $89.99

The Cemetery Club

(1992, 106 min, US, Bill Duke) Two Academy Award winners (Ellen Burstyn and Olympia Dukakis) and two Academy Award nominees (Diane Ladd and Danny Aiello) come together and attempt to breathe life into this sappy adaptation of the failed Broadway comedy. Sadly, despite their considerable talents, this meandering saga of three middle-aged widows who gather at the cemetery to toss one-liners at their husbands' graves falls well wide of its mark — straddling the line between comedy and drama, but failing to be either funny or dramatic. Burstyn gives the most charming performance of the film as the one widow who picks up a romantic interest in the form of Aiello (who is at the cemetery crying over *his* wife's grave). ★★ $9.99

Cemetery Man

(1994, 100 min, Italy/US, Michele Soavi) Dario Argento's protégé Soavi comes wholly into his own with this highly original adaptation of a novel by Italian pop writer Titiano Sclavi. Rupert Everett stars as Francesco Dellamorte, caretaker of both the Buffalore Cemetery and his semi-human assistant, Gnaghi (Francois Hadji-Lazaro). What would seem a quiet job has recently become quite a problem, however, as the dead have been returning to life soon after burial, and it is up to Dellamorte and Gnaghi to put them permanently back into their graves (by either a gunshot or blow to the head). Soon Dellamorte is killing the living in order to keep them from rising from the dead and he can no longer distinguish between fantasy and reality, life and death. Though the film is somewhat convoluted and definitely unreal, Soavi's camera rarely stops moving. Most good films are content with one or two visually arresting moments — *Cemetery Man* is full of them. Entertaining and enticing, the film is not for the casual viewer, but those who visit the graveyard several times a week will find rewards in store. (Filmed in English) ★★★ $96.89

La Cérémonie

(1996, 111 min, France, Claude Chabrol) Director Chabrol casts a sideways glance at class warfare in this somewhat off-center thriller that examines the tentative relationship between the modern aristocracy and their domestics. Sandrine Bonnaire stars as the newly appointed maid for Jacqueline Bisset and her industrialist husband Jean-Pierre Cassel. She seems a perfect new hire — fastidious cleaner, excellent cook and appropriately subservient. But what seems like coy respect for her new employers slowly gives way under the strain of bitter secrets and a spotted past. Into the picture walks Isabelle Huppert (radiant as ever... does this woman ever age?), as a smart-ass postal worker with a rocky past of her own who holds some sort of dialectical grudge against Bisset and family. The atmosphere is tense throughout as Bonnaire's perfect veneer begins to crack and the family becomes increasingly intolerant of her rebelliousness and her budding friendship with Huppert. Chabrol explores this territory with characteristic understatement and a "classical" panache that makes the film feel more "arty" than it really is, but his intricate study of character makes this captivating viewing nonetheless. ★★★½ $102.99

César

(1936, 117 min, France, Marcel Pagnol) Emboldened by the success of *Marius* and *Fanny*, Pagnol decided to direct the final installment of his stage trilogy himself. Once again Raimu steals the film as Marius' father, but this time the film bares his name so it's all right. Short on plot but long on everything else (especially running time), *César*, like all of the films to come out of Pagnol's studio, is full of people whose company one enjoys, all of whom inhab-

C

it a little village in which one would have loved to have lived. The plot concerns Fanny's young son who discovers that Marius is his real father. Through his efforts, they are reunited after 20 years. (French with English subtitles) ★★★ $39.99

César and Rosalie

(1972, 110 min, France, Claude Sautet) Yves Montand and Romy Schneider give compelling performances in this charming comedy, a bittersweet tale of friendship and love. Schneider plays a divorcée living with tycoon Montand who becomes involved with young artist Sami Frey. Quite unexpectedly, however, the two men, who at first see each other as nothing more than rivals, become friends; laying the framework for an unusual and caring relationship between the three lovers. (French with English subtitles) ★★★½

Chain Lightning

(1950, 95 min, US, Stuart Heisler) Actual war and aerial footage highlight this routine aviation adventure, with Humphrey Bogart hitting the skies as a former WWII bomber pilot who tests the new jets. Raymond Massey is the multibillionaire with a fascination for airplanes who funds the tests, and Eleanor Parker looks ravishing as Bogey's long-lost love. ★★½ $19.99

Chain of Desire

(1992, 105 min, US, Temistocles Lopez) From the director of the intriguing *Exquisite Corpses* comes this stylistically inventive and wittily droll observation and AIDS allegory on sexual yearning and unrequited love in the age of AIDS. Linda Fiorentino is Alma, a singer in a slick New York nightclub who sleeps with Jesus, a married, Hispanic worker. This successful coupling begins a humorous but sexually frustrating daisy chain of purely sexual encounters with a succession of New York characters. Malcolm McDowell is featured as a cheesy closeted journalist with a taste for street urchins and Seymour Cassel plays a philandering artist who catches his previously chaste wife humping a startled canvas stretcher. A titillating highlight (and the most sexually satisfying for the film's characters) is a three-way, voyeuristically charged masturbation scene (both gay and straight) between three people in three different curtain-less high-rise apartments. An erotic updating of *La Ronde* exploring sexual desire. ★★★ $9.99

Chain Reaction

(1996, 100 min, US, Andrew Davis) Keanu Reeves takes his turn as the unjustly accused pawn in a game of industrial intrigue in Davis' attempted reworking of his megahit *The Fugitive.* Reeves stars as a young machinist working on a university physics project attempting to find a new, cheap, clean source of energy. Once the team makes its groundbreaking discovery, dark forces take over and the lab is blown to smithereens, with the team members either killed or missing, leaving only Reeves and a young associate of his holding the secret to the discovery. Framed for the murders, they must run for their lives, both from the police and from the nefarious forces behind the set-up. Even casual moviegoers have seen this story before, and done much

better. Tedious, overlong and full of gaping plot holes, it contains nothing to recommend it except Morgan Freeman's usual stalwart performance, this time as a corporate supporter who may or may not be on Reeves' side. ★ $14.99

Chained

(1934, 76 min, US, Clarence Brown) Clark Gable and Joan Crawford enjoy a brief encounter aboard a cruise ship in this familiar romantic drama. Gable pursues Crawford until she gives in, but when she returns to New York and lover Otto Kruger, she becomes torn between the two men. Lots of chemistry between the two stars, who were, briefly, lovers offscreen. ★★ $19.99

Chained Heat

(1983, 97 min, US, Paul Nicholas) Sex, violence, showers, sex, drugs, prostitution, white slavery, sex, corruption (did we mention sex?) from the producer of *The Concrete Jungle.* One of the great treats (meaning sleaziest) in the women-in-prison genre, this violent and sexually explicit exploitation film stars the genre's reigning queens: Linda Blair and Sybil Danning. Blair plays the innocent who's sent to jail for involuntary vehicular homicide. She's in for a quick and brutal education, as the prison is run by a drug-dealing wretch of a warden, controlled by a sadistic chief guard, and populated with hard-as-nails, knife-wielding peroxide babes. If Blair thought being possessed by the Devil was tough, she's never spent time in a women's prison. ★★½

Chained Heat 2

(1993, 98 min, US, Lloyd Simani) An exploitative lesbian *Midnight Express,* this women-in-prison actioner is politically incorrect fun. All hope seems lost for pretty strawberry blonde Alex when she is falsely imprisoned in a hellish all-female Czechoslovakian prison for drug smuggling. The hell-hole is head by Magda Kassar, a suit-and-tie attired warden (played by Brigitte Nielsen) who, aided by her knife-wielding, cigar-chomping, Lotte Lenya wannabe henchwoman Rosa, rules her roost. Will our heroine ever escape? Will any of the actresses ever attend acting classes? Filmed in an actual Prague prison, the film is laughably bad, featuring the requisite bevy of beauties, plenty of gratuitous flesh and several lesbian lovemaking scenes. How would you like your exploitation? With cheese, please. ★½ $14.99

The Chalk Garden

(1964, 106 min, GB, Ronald Neame) Deborah Kerr gives a beautiful performance as a governess who helps a troubled youngster coming of age. Hayley Mills is affecting as the young girl; her father John Mills and Edith Evans offer solid support. ★★★ $19.99

The Challengers

(1993, 97 min, Canada, Eric Till) Winner of five International Film Awards, this story of an 11-year-old girl who has lost her father and moved to a small town from the big city

Chan Is Missing

addresses pre-teen alienation and development with sympathy and humor. Mackie Daniels (Gema Zamprogna) wants to be a "Challenger" and play in their band but this boys' group excludes girls. She decides to masquerade as a boy and quickly becomes good friends under the guise of "Mack." The strain of being both boy and girl finally takes its toll, but the resolution is both heartwarming and satisfactory. ★★★ $89.99

The Chamber

(1996, 110 min, US, James Foley) In *A Time to Kill,* a particularly good John Grisham adaptation also released in 1996, race relations is the focal point to a complex and involving tale. In this Grisham adaptation, race relations once again plays a major role in the story, but it's watered down and merely a plot device to a uneventful drama. Chris O'Donnell sleepwalks through his role as a young lawyer who attempts to get a stay of execution for his grandfather (Gene Hackman), a racist KKK member and convicted murderer sentenced to death. As he races against the clock, he tries to get to know a man he never knew who is unwilling to either defend himself or reconcile. Not a lot happens — O'Donnell rushes here and there, and Hackman breaks into choruses of epithets every other scene. The moral of the tale may be commendable, and (as usual) Hackman offers a terrific performance, but whatever there is to like about *The Chamber* is offset by flat character development and a plodding pace. ★★ $19.99

Chameleon Street

(1988, 98 min, US, Wendell B. Harris, Jr.) One of the merits of video is that it allows such overlooked gems as this to finally have their day in the sun. Fledgling filmmaker Harris wrote, directed and stars in this hip comedy (based on a true story) about a man who attempts to beat the system by impersonating various upstanding members of society — and getting away with it! Harris' witty, world-weary narration adds just the right touch, imbuing the film with a '90s attitude offset by '70s sensibilities. ★★★ $19.99

Champion

(1949, 90 min, US, Mark Robson) Hard-nosed boxing tale without *Rocky* schmaltz about a nasty fighter (Kirk Douglas) who sacrifices everything as he punches his way to the top. With Marilyn Maxwell, Arthur Kennedy and Ruth Roman. Douglas gives an exceptional performance as the would-be champ. ★★★½ $14.99

Chan Is Missing

(1982, 80 min, US, Wayne Wang) Wang's first feature film was also the first ever exclusively produced, directed and acted by Asian-Americans. Shot in Wang's hometown of San Francisco for a mere $20,000, the film follows the wanderings of a middle-aged cab driver and his wise-cracking nephew as they search all over Chinatown for Chan — who has mysteriously disappeared with the $2,000 meant to buy their taxi permit. A sophisticated statement about the trials and tribulations of ethnic assimilation. ★★★½ $79.99

Chances Are

(1989, 108 min, US, Emile Ardolino) From the director of *Dirty Dancing* comes this routine "switch" comedy saved by Robert Downey, Jr.'s charming performance. The spirit of Cybill Shepherd's deceased husband turns up in her daughter's boyfriend (Downey). With Mary Stuart Masterson and Ryan O'Neal as the confused partners of Downey and Shepherd. ★★ $9.99

Chanel Solitaire

(1981, 120 min, France, George Kaczender) This melodramatic biopic stars Marie-France Pisier as Coco Chanel, the famous couturiere who overcame a poor childhood to conquer Paris and the world with her fabulous designs. Co-starring Karen Black, Rutger Hauer and Timothy Dalton. (Filmed in English) ★★ $19.99

Chang

(1927, 67 min, US/Siam, Merian C. Cooper & Ernest B. Schoedsack) Remastered from an original negative, this entertaining and exciting documentary/fiction film was shot entirely in the jungles of Siam. The story follows a native family who live in a tree house on the edge of the dark, potentially dangerous jungle. The film depicts their everyday routine of farming, hunting and family life, until disaster strikes when a spectacularly filmed elephant stampede overruns their village. A tender tale of survival that features a new musical score by composer Bruce Gaston and performed by Fong Naam, Thailand's renowned traditional music ensemble. ★★★ $39.99

The Changeling

(1979, 109 min, Canada, Peter Medak) Creepy and very effective ghost story/murder mystery about a composer (George C. Scott) whose recent loss of wife and daughter make him receptive to the hauntings of a murdered child. You would never think a wheelchair could be so frightening. Also with Trish Van Devere and Melvyn Douglas. ★★★ $14.99

Changing Face

(1993, 103 min, US, Robert Tate & Robert Roznowski) An earnest independent production which presents in a conventional soap opera structure the inconsequential life of a stable gay couple. Filmmakers Tate and Roznowski star as Tom and Dan, two ordinary men as bland as their names. Monogamous, twentysomething yuppies given to petty squabbles, they're suffering from mid-life crisis. Providing some semblance of life in their lives are a familiar collection of wacky New York friends. The filmmakers mistakenly use the couple's heightened bickering as the story's only dramatic tension, which only accentuates the lack of a plot. ★★ $19.99

Chaplin

(1992, 140 min, GB/US, Richard Attenborough) Director Attenborough's biopic of Charlie Chaplin aspires towards the sweep of his many epics and, while it's fine for the bigger scenes, it leaves the smaller, more personal moments in the film lacking emotion. Part of the problem may be with Robert Downey Jr., who dons astonishingly accurate Chaplinesque movements, gestures and expressions (and earned an Oscar nomination for it), but never really gets into Chaplin's mind or soul. The story covers Chaplin's poor childhood in England to his arrival in America and eventual stardom through his many ups and downs throughout his career. Though the screenplay is, for the most part, extremely witty, so much screen time is given to Chaplin's numerous love affairs and ongoing feud with J. Edgar Hoover, one has to wonder when the immortal tramp ever had time to devote to his own brilliant films. An excellent supporting cast includes Kevin Kline as Douglas Fairbanks, Diane Lane as Paulette Goddard, and Geraldine Chaplin, playing her own grandmother, as Charlie's mentally unstable mom. ★★½ $9.99

Charade

(1963, 114 min, US, Stanley Donen) The ever radiant Audrey Hepburn and the dapper Cary Grant star in this delightfully comic ode to Hitchcock. The recently widowed Hepburn finds herself terrorized by the gang of her late husband's ex-associates all bent on finding his missing fortune. Not knowing where to turn, she seeks safety with Grant, but is he all he's cracked up to be? James Coburn, Walter Matthau and George Kennedy also star in this twisting tale of intrigue. ★★★½ $19.99

The Charge of the Light Brigade

(1936, 116 min, US, Michael Curtiz) Rousing Errol Flynn adventure inspired by Tennyson's poem about the famous British infantrymen fighting to the death in 19th-century India. Olivia deHavilland (who else?) plays Flynn's love interest. ★★★ $19.99

Chariots of Fire

(1981, 123 min, GB, Hugh Hudson) This occasionally heavy-handed portrait of the passionate careers of British track stars Eric Liddell and Harold Abrahams is nonetheless an elegant and poignant drama about religious and social differences in the England of 1924. The stories of Lidell, a deeply religious Scotsman, and Abrahams, one of the first Jews to attend Cambridge, unfold with a depth and grace which made this film a rousing international success. Academy Award winner for Best Picture. ★★★½ $19.99

Charleen/Backyard

(1978/1976, 59/40 min, US, Ross McElwee) Die hard fans of director McElwee (*Sherman's March*) should appreciate these two early documentaries focusing on his friends and family in North Carolina. *Charleen* (1978) is a personal portrait of a chatty, opinionated and, at times, remarkable woman who teaches poetry to poor children and who had befriended Ezra Pound as well as e.e. cummings. *Backyard* (1976) chronicles the minidramas of McElwee's friends, family and their (indentured?) household staff back in Charlotte, North Carolina. Mildly interesting stuff, although the *Boston Globe* has called *Charlene* "A cinematic poem...inspirational in a way we've forgotten films can be." ★★ $49.99

The Charles Bukowski Tapes

(1987, 240 min, US, Barbet Schroeder) Charles Bukowski, the grizzled, drunken Beat poet whose writings ("Barfly," "Tales of Ordinary Madness") as well as his own life reflect the tragic beauty and painful loneliness of the "defeated, demented and damned," is profiled in this stimulating documentary/interview. Broken up in numerous segments, the film lets Bukowski ramble on, usually tanked up on beer or wine, about everything: his travels throughout the seedy terrain of American cities, the forces behind creativity, sleazy sex, even the pleasures of pollution. Whether in his run-down L.A. home, in a car reminiscing of the bars and strip shows of old or in his old childhood home, Bukowski proves to be both a pontificating drunk and chronicler of the losers as well as a fascinating if self-indulgent philosopher — an American original. ★★★★ $99.99

Charles et Lucie

(1979, 96 min, France, Nelly Kaplan) This Gallic comedy is the rags-to-riches-to-rags story of a poor Parisian couple who find that they have inherited a beautiful mansion on the Riviera. The only catch is that they must sell all their furniture in order to pay the lawyer fees. But sell they do, as they go driving off to the Riviera with their dreams of riches. The couple confront a series of adventures that rekindle their love and taste for living. A delightfully refreshing love story. (French with English subtitles) ★★★½

Charlie Chaplin, the Early Years

(1916-1917, US, Charles Chaplin) It was during the period of 1916-1917 that Charles Chaplin began to evolve his character from "The Tramp" to "The Little Man," even though from all outward appearances nothing had changed. In these rare works from his year at Mutual Studios, his control of the narrative advanced in sophistication as gags naturally progressed as opposed to the vaudeville free-for-alls common to the times. Contains *The Immigrant*, *The Count* and others. ★★★ $19.99

Charlie Chaplin, the Keystone Years

(1914, US, Charles Chaplin) It was Mack Sennett who discovered Charles Chaplin, but it was Chaplin who discovered "The Little

Ben Affleck falls for lesbian Joey Lauren Adams in *Chasing Amy*

Tramp," a character that in its time was the most recognized figure in the world. These films from Sennett's Keystone Studios find Chaplin struggling to insert any little bit of characterization he can between Sennett's demand for wall-to-wall laughter. ★★★ $19.99

The Charlie Chaplin Film Festival

(1916-1917, 80 min, US, Charles Chaplin) Four shorts from Charles Chaplin's Mutual days. *The Cure* finds the Tramp taking the waters at a toney health spa. Chaplin's on the lam from the cops in *The Adventurer* while *The Immigrant* finds the actor expanding his palette as a director, deftly balancing social commentary, pathos and laughs. And *Easy Street* proves itself to be anything but. ★★★

Charlotte

(1974, 110 min, France, Roger Vadim) The twisted mixture of sex and death make for a shocking 110 minutes in this Vadim excursion into excess. Entering into William Burroughs-land, Vadim shows a woman strangled at the point of orgasm while having her eyeballs removed. Smelling the perfect ingredients of a steamy novel, a curious writer begins to investigate the killing. Vadim's films are not for all; but for his fans, this one will certainly fascinate. (Dubbed) ★★½

Charlotte's Web

(1973, 85 min, US, Charles A. Nichols) Captivating animated feature based on the writings of E.B. White centering on the friendship of a spider and a pig. Voices of Debbie Reynolds, Henry Gibson, Paul Lynde and Charles Nelson Reilly. ★★★ $14.99

Charly

(1968, 103 min, US, Ralph Nelson) Cliff Robertson won an Oscar for his poignant performance as a retarded man who undergoes scientific experiments and becomes super-intelligent. Claire Bloom lovingly plays his caseworker. Based on "Flowers for Algernon" by Daniel Keyes. ★★★ $14.99

The Chase

(1966, 135 min, US, Arthur Penn) Robert Redford is an escaped prisoner who returns to his small Texas town, stirring up both trouble and passions. Marlon Brando is the sheriff, and Jane Fonda the old girlfriend. Screenplay by Lillian Hellman, based on Horton Foote's novel. Though there's a lot of talent involved here, this notoriously troubled production suffers from too-many-chiefs (producer Sam Spiegal's constant interference); however, there are some interesting moments. ★★½ $9.99

The Chase

(1994, 87 min, US, Adam Rifkin) From Rifkin, the director of the gratuitously weird *Dark Backwards*, comes – when not dwelling on the sappy romance at its core – a film that is remarkable in its savage skewering of the feeding frenzy network news has become. Charlie Sheen stars as a wrongly accused fugitive who accidentally takes the daughter of a Donald Trump-style millionaire (Ray Wise) hostage, thereby setting off a high-speed run for the border – with full media circus in tow. Rifkin's deft satire mixes hip, self-assured MTV-style photography with dead-on lampoons of media-ocrity to create a smart comedy. Interestingly, this extended, real-time car chase is in many ways a carbon copy of *Speed*. Who says there's no more insider trading? ★★½ $9.99

Chasers

(1994, 102 min, US, Dennis Hopper) William McNamara plays a wise-cracking naval officer who gets paired up with a tough sergeant (Tom Berenger) in order to escort a "sexy and sassy" prisoner (Erika Eleniak) in this *Last Detail* rip-off. If you used your imagination to predict wild and wacky misadventures for the three to encounter, you'd be doing more than the screenwriters. With a cast including Gary Busey, Dean Stockwell, Crispin Glover, Marilu Henner and director Hopper himself, you'd think there would be something of interest here. This film does prove one positive thing:

Dennis Hopper must have a lot of devoted friends. ★ $14.99

Chasing Amy

(1997, 105 min, US, Kevin Smith) Making a hyperspace jump from his previous two efforts, writer-director Smith has fashioned a very funny, but also mature, insightful and painfully honest romantic comedy for the '90s. Ben Affleck plays a popular comic book artist who meets a kindred spirit (Joey Lauren Adams), seemingly his soul mate, at a comic book convention. After a few fun, platonic dates, the truth comes out: she's a lesbian. Their friendship develops, but he finally breaks down and confesses his love for her. At first angry, she soon declares her similar feelings and they begin a relationship. That is, until he discovers her sordid, straight past, which he can't stop obsessing over. Some remarkably mature observations about love and relationships are made by Smith, particularly in his recurring role as "Silent Bob," who ironically gives a rather momentous speech this time around. Gone are the bathroom jokes and farcical nonsense which ruined *Mallrats* and prevented *Clerks* from becoming more than an entertaining first film. Instead, we have an accomplished, enjoyable movie which accurately pokes fun at a variety of modern relationships (straight, gay and bi) and even manages a few honestly tear-jerking sequences. Jason Lee has also come a long way from *Mallrats*, bringing humor and texture to the role of the "other man." ★★★½ $99.99

Le Chat (The Cat)

(1970, 88 min, France, Pierre Granier Deferre) Simone Signoret and Jean Gabin are an elderly married couple of 25 years whose early love has turned into a silent hate. Set in a decaying and soon-to-be-demolished apartment house, the film explores the relationship of the two, who have no one else and who refuse to talk to each other. The probing of the reasons for the embittered separation are acted out in this sad yet unforgettable drama. Brilliantly acted by two of the great stars of the French cinema. (Available both dubbed and in French with English subtitles) ★★★

Chattahoochee

(1990, 98 min, US, Mick Jackson) When a Korean War veteran (Gary Oldman) disrupts life in his sleepy, small Florida town by firing off a barrage of ammunition in a clumsy attempt to get himself killed, he's promptly shipped off to an asylum that makes *The Snake Pit* look like a politician's prison. Oldman is remarkable as the incarcerated vet who rediscovers himself as he opposes the insanity of the institution that confines him. The strong supporting cast is highlighted by Dennis Hopper, Frances McDormand and Pamela Reed. ★★★ $19.99

The Cheap Detective

(1978, 92 min, US, Robert Moore) There are lots of laughs in Neil Simon's follow-up to *Murder by Death*. Peter Falk stars in this private-eye parody, *The Maltese Falcon* in particular, ably assisted by Eileen Brennan ("If it's something cheap you're looking for"), Ann-Margret, Dom DeLuise, Stockard Channing, James

Coco, Madeline Kahn, Sid Caesar and Phil Silvers. Who cares if some of the jokes are forced; the film is in good humor and what a cast! ★★★ $9.99

The Cheat

(1915, 59 min, US, Cecil B. DeMille) Racist — racy — deMille at his best, before his bombast interfered with his pandering to his middle-class clientele. A vivacious socialite becomes the Occidental tourist when she loses the community chest fund in a bad stock deal. Salvation comes in the form of a wily, Asian gentleman who prefers to take his interest out in trade, branding her — literally — a scarlet woman. Sessue Hayakawa gives a wonderfully modulated performance, his Zen-like calm evoking still waters against the raging torrents of stock company histrionics exhibited by the rest of the ensemble. (★★★½) Also included is an abridged version of *A Girl's Folly* (1917, 30 min, US, Maurice Tourneur), a behind-the-scenes look at the day-by-day workings of a film studio. A gentle satire of a nascent industry, the film is alive with warmth and it is that which survives the intervening decades. ★★★½ $29.99

Cherry 2000

(1988, 93 min, US, Steve DeJarnatt) Futuristic, post-apocalyptic adventure with Melanie Griffith (just before she became a *Working Girl*) as a mercenary who helps a husband looking for the prototype of his robot-wife — stored in a factory located in a forbidden zone. An enjoyable sci-fi outing which wants to please, and for the most part succeeds. ★★½ $9.99

Cherry, Harry and Raquel

(1969, 71 min, US, Russ Meyer) Set in a dusty Arizona border town, *Cherry, Harry and Raquel* depicts double-crossing drug smugglers involved in power struggles, interspersed with various sexual encounters both lesbian and heterosexual. Meyer's last film before working for 20th Century Fox, where he would make one of his best films, *Beyond the Valley of the Dolls*. ★★ $79.99

Le Chèvre (The Goat)

(1981, 91 min, France, Francis Véber) Pierre Richard and Gérard Depardieu, the hilarious sleuthing duo of *Les Compares*, are reunited in this "prequel" by Francis Véber, screenwriter of *La Cage aux Folles* and *The Tall Blond Man with One Black Shoe*. Private-eye Depardieu

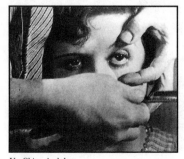

Un Chien Andalou

reluctantly teams up with the bungling Richard as they travel to Mexico to find a missing woman. What follows is a series of misadventures of epic proportions. The stone-faced Depardieu is surprisingly delightful as the straight man to Richard's never-ending encounters with slamming doors, crashing planes and even lethal drinking straws in this comedy for all ages. (French with English subtitles) ★★★

Cheyenne Autumn

(1964, 158 min, US, John Ford) Ford's last western is a sprawling account of the Cheyenne Nation's 1,500-mile journey from the arid Southwest to their northern homeland. Ford depicts multiple aspects of the story: the influence of land speculators in Washington, sensationalization by the press, the varying attitudes of Army personnel, and the overwhelming hardships of the Cheyenne. Fine performances throughout, especially by Richard Widmark, Carroll Baker and Edward G. Robinson. Shot in 70mm, the visual impact of the landscapes is retained on the small screen. Note: The Dodge City sequence, with a very funny James Stewart, was cut after first release; it's restored on video. ★★★ $19.99

The Cheyenne Social Club

(1970, 103 min, US, Gene Kelly) Henry Fonda and James Stewart dusted off their spurs to team together in this appealing though formula western comedy with the two Hollywood legends playing aging cowpokes who hang their hats at a new home — Stewart's newly acquired bordello. Shirley Jones runs the place. ★★½ $14.99

Chicken Hawk

(1994, 60 min, US, Adi Sideman) Uncomfortably sleazy even for many normally tolerant viewers, this documentary eschews the tenets of offering a balanced approach as it takes a sympathetic view of pedophilia. Downplaying the moral, legal and psychological issues of child abuse, the filmmaker interviews several middle-aged and older men who put their faces to the camera and proclaim their desire for prepubescent and teenaged boys. Of poor technical quality, the film allows these men a forum to pontificate lines such as teenage boys are "like a flower in bloom." There is even one interview with a teen who claims he was involved with an older man at age ten, and in control of the relationship. Allen Ginsberg appears briefly, as do other members of NAMBLA (North American Man-Boy Love Association). A troubling point of view that will upset and infuriate, especially most gay men. ★

Chicken Ranch

(1983, 90 min, US, Nick Broomfield & Sandi Sissel) Capitalism thrives at this legendary Nevadan pleasure palace that inspired the musical *Best Little Whorehouse in Texas*. A legalized sex stockade, complete with V.I.P. rooms, jacuzzis and package tour accomodations. The Ranch and its glamorous "girls" are amusingly observed in this intimate documentary. ★★½

Un Chien Andalou/ Land without Bread

(1928/1932, 17/45 min, France/Spain, Luis Buñuel) Beginning with a pristine copy of *Un Chien Andalou*, this video of two of Buñuel's earliest film work also includes his documentary on the unbelievably impoverished Spanish region of Hurdanos. Told with English narration, this moving and sad account of these stoic people is an unusual departure for Buñuel, for he forsakes his trademark humor and surrealism and instead takes the job of a social realist as he photographs the parched, mountainous area and films the people in their medieval-like towns, virtually untouched by the wealth and conveniences offered in the 20th century. An unrelenting and somber portrait of a people and one that was immediately banned by the Franco government. $29.99

La Chienne

(1931, 100 min, France, Jean Renoir) This somber, naturalistic melodrama, whose surprisingly modern theme of sexual obsession and violence created tremendous controversy when first released in France, did not receive its American premiere until 1976. Realistically filmed on the noisy streets of Montmartre, this story of uncontrolled passion is about an unhappily married clerk (Michel Simon) who falls in love with a prostitute, steals for her, then, in a fit of rage, murders her and keeps quiet while her pimp goes to the guillotine. Unsentimental, this amoral story, whose film translation is *The Bitch*, was remade by Fritz Lang in *Scarlet Street* (1945). Reportedly, the film's producer, after seeing the rough cut, banned Renoir from the studio and vainly attempted to re-edit and make it more palatable; but in the end, Renoir regained control and the film was edited the way he wanted. (French with English subtitles) ★★★½ $59.99

A Child Is Waiting

(1962, 102 min, US, John Cassavetes) Judy Garland is splendid in this poignant tale of a sympathetic woman's relationship with a mentally retarded boy. Featuring actual retarded children, *A Child Is Waiting* pulls no punches in portraying the inadequacy and frustration teachers feel in trying to reach the youngsters, and the guilt parents bear in surrendering their children to mental hospitals. Most touching of all, though, are the performances of the children; they are joyous and innocent, and truly in the heart of everyone they touch. Also starring Burt Lancaster and Gena Rowlands. ★★★ $19.99

Child's Play

(1988, 87 min, US, Tom Holland) Chucky is a popular talking doll, sweet as peaches and cream (and a complexion to match). That is until one of the dolls is possessed by the spirit of a murderer; then little Chucky is spewing forth naughty words and hacking people to death. Unchallenging, silly and slickly-made, it does manage to produce a few chills. ★★½ $14.99

Child's Play 2

(1990, 85 min, US, John Lafia) Chucky's back and this time he's powered by an even more insidious force: capitalism! Chucky tries to take possession of young Andy's body, once again, lest he remain in the valley of the dolls forever. Enter Grace Zabriskie as a child welfare worker who won't believe Andy's "boy who cried doll" stories, and Jenny Agutter and Gerrit Graham as the adoptive parents who make the mistake of coming between a doll and his boy in the *Fatal Attraction* for the preschool set. ★ $19.99

The Children Are Watching Us (I Bambini Ci Guardano)

(1942, 89 min, Italy, Vittorio De Sica) One of De Sica's most heartrending films as well as an unusually critical look at Mussolini's Italy. The story focuses on the effects that a marital breakup and a suicide have on a lonely and unwanted four-year-old boy. A sad and touching story from the master of Italian neorealism. (Italian with English subtitles) ★★★½ $29.99

Children of a Lesser God

(1986, 119 min, US, Randa Haines) Marlee Matlin won an Oscar for her immensely moving portrait of an embittered deaf woman reluctant to commit herself to a relationship. William Hurt is equally as compelling as the idealist special education teacher who falls in love with her. ★★★ $14.99

Children of Nature

(1991, 85 min, Iceland, Fridrik Thor Fridriksson) Nominated for a Best Foreign Film Oscar, this lushly photographed and deliberately paced film follows the odyssey of a man nearing the end of his life. After an uncomfortable attempt at living with his daughter and her family, he enters a nursing home, where he meets a woman he knew in his youth. Her fiesty exuberance compliments his stoic strength; their shared desire for independence unites them in a journey of adventure and discovery. These two protagonists are portrayed with warmth and gentle vigor in a film peppered with telling moments of quiet revelation. Set against the breathtaking vistas of Iceland's landscapes, *Children of Nature* is a lyrical meditation on humankind's relationship with nature and society. (Icelandic with English subtitles) ★★★ $19.99

Children of Paradise (Les Enfants du Paradis)

(1945, 188 min, France, Marcel Carné) Considered by many to be one of the greatest films ever made, this intensely romantic melodrama wonderfully re-creates the teeming excitement of the early 1800s — both for the French theatre as well as Paris' *Boulevard du Crime*. In a complicated series of events, the film follows the interlocking fates of four central characters: Frederick (Pierre Brasseau), a haughty actor who communicates through words; Baptiste (Jean-Louis Barrault), a sensitive pantomimist; Garance (Arletty), an elusive, glamorous woman of easy virtue who stands between them and the fourth character, a murderous thief. All four speed toward material success, only to find that once they attain it, it means nothing without love. Using the theatre as a metaphor for life, the Jacques Prévert-scripted story is a richly entertaining, immense masterpiece of postwar cinema. (French with English subtitles) ★★★★ $39.99

Children of the Revolution

(1997, 102 min, Australia, Peter Duncan) Judy Davis stars in this boisterous political farce/satire that supposes what might become of Joseph Stalin's illegitimate son if he were raised by an ardent communist mom in middle-class Australia. Davis is in top form as Joan Fraser, a vociferous 1950s era proponent of the "dictatorship of the proletariat" whose ideological fervor leads her to write love letters to "Uncle Joe." The aging and lonely Stalin (F. Murray Abraham) catches wind of her ardor and invites her to the Kremlin for a bit of a dialectical frolic. The rest, as they say, is history. Davis returns to Oz pregnant, but is the child Stalin's or that of Australian double agent spy Sam Neill? Needless to say, the fun is just getting started as the film follows little Joe through childhood to his adult years through a series of nicely strung together vignettes. Writer-director Duncan takes his narrative over the top with conviction and gusto making *Children of the Revolution* a capricious and thoroughly agreeable romp through a mock history as seen through a shattered mirror (or perhaps that should be a fun house mirror). Richard Roxburgh is a delight as the adult "little Joe" and Rachel Griffiths makes a nice showing as the S&M obsessed cop he falls in love with. ★★★½ $99.99

Children of the Corn

(1984, 93 min, US, Fritz Kiersch) Silly Stephen King horror story about a young couple who arrive in a small Iowa town controlled by demonic children. ★ $14.99

Children of the Corn II — The Final Sacrifice

(1993, 93 min, US, David F. Price) Joining the ranks of unnecessary horror sequels (*Amityville Horror, The Howling*, etc.), this high-fiber exercise in tedium begins with a tabloid reporter's investigation into the strange deaths of 50 people in a small Nebraska town. Teaming up with his estranged son, the reporter soon encounters other deaths: A man who bleeds to death

inexplicably, a doctor murdered by his own instruments and others. ★ $14.99

Children of the Night

(1991, 92 min, US, Tony Randel) From the director of *Hellbound: Hellraiser 2* comes this procession of nightmarish set pieces that succeed in being both atmospheric and chilling. With a story that centers around a small town, vampires and teenage girls, and starring Karen Black, Peter DeLuise and Garrett Morris, this does inject new life into an overworked genre. Two fangs up! ★★★ $14.99

Children of Theatre Street

(1978, 92 min, US, Robert Dornhelm) Acclaimed, Oscar-nominated documentary examining the daily training and recreation of students at the famed Kirov School, Russia's premier ballet school (which has produced the likes of Nijinsky, Pavlova, Nureyev and Baryshnikov). ★★★★ $19.99

Children Shouldn't Play with Dead Things

(1972, 85 min, US, Benjamin [Bob] Clark) Cheapie horror film (from the director of *Porky's*, no less) about young film students making a movie in a graveyard and resurrecting the dead. Eeek. ★½ $59.99

The Children's Hour

(1961, 107 min, US, William Wyler) Wyler's compelling though stagey second treatment of Lillian Hellman's play (1936's *These Three* was the first) tells of the devastating effects of gossip and scandalous rumors about two women. Audrey Hepburn and Shirley MacLaine are teachers at an all-girls' boarding school. When a vindictive little girl accuses the two of having an affair, their lives (and their careers) are ruined after a self-righteous community believes the unsubstantiated allegations (shades of McCarthyism!). However, the rumor also forces MacLaine to come to terms with her closeted lesbian feelings. Attempting to right the wrong of his original film which was not allowed to discuss the theme of lesbianism, Wyler rather flimsily addresses it

Children of the Revolution

here. The performances by Hepburn and MacLaine are competent, and James Garner and Miriam Hopkins also star. ★★½ $19.99

Chilly Scenes of Winter

(1982, 99 min, US, Joan Micklin Silver) Silver's bittersweet comedy on the trials and triumphs of love. John Heard portrays the quirky but amiable civil servant whose desperate passion confuses the reluctant object of his adoration, Mary Beth Hurt. A warm, beguiling film on the fragile bliss of romance. ★★★½ $19.99

China Girl

(1987, 88 min, US, Abel Ferrara) Absorbing, gritty update of "Romeo and Juliet" set in New York's Little Italy and Chinatown, with Italian James Russo and Chinese Sari Chang falling in love against a gangland backdrop. ★★★ $9.99

China Moon

(1994, 99 min, US, John Bailey) Q): What do you get when you mix a rich husband, a beautiful wife and a tough guy who should know better? A): This umpteenth steamy, hard-boiled film noir *Body Heat* rip-off. Ed Harris stars as a savvy police detective who becomes involved with rich banker's wife Madeleine Stowe. When her husband (Charles Dance) turns up dead, Harris must help her erase any clues to the crime. But is he being set up as patsy? After 50 years, it takes a lot to give film noir a fresh spin (see the recent *The Last Seduction* for that), and though *China Moon* has its moments, this is mostly run of the mill material. ★★ $14.99

China, My Sorrow

(1989, 86 min, China, Dai Sijie) A wonderful story of imprisoned men in a mountain camp for noncompliant citizens under Chairman Mao. The story follows young "Four-eyes" as he is sent to the re-education center for playing music unsuitable to a young comrade (oddly enough, the song sounds much like the patriotic tune from *Yellow Earth*). "Four-eyes" and the other undesirables are put through grueling days of hard labor and dehumanizing treatment in hopes of turning them into "good workers." The film was shot in France to avoid Chinese censorship. The story line is deeply spiritual and the photography rivals Zhang Yimou's works. (Mandarin and Shanghaiese with English subtitles) ★★★ $79.99

China Seas

(1935, 88 min, US, Tay Garnett) A good cast highlights this box-office hit with Clark Gable as a steamship captain — transporting a secret cargo to China — who becomes romantically involved with passengers Jean Harlow and Rosalind Russell. Also with Wallace Beery, Lewis Stone and Hattie McDaniel. ★★★ $19.99

The China Syndrome

(1979, 123 min, US, James Bridges) Though this nuclear thriller greatly benefitted from the timely publicity from the Three Mile Island accident, this outstanding drama would have succeeded without it. Jane Fonda is excellent as a television reporter who inadvertently films an accident at a nuclear power plant, involving her in political intrigue. Jack

Lemmon gives a superlative portrayal of a loyal plant supervisor whose search for the truth leads to tragedy. Michael Douglas is well-cast as Fonda's radical cameraman who helps in the investigation. A tension-filled examination of corporate cover-up which is both cautionary and unrelentingly suspenseful. Special mention goes to Wilford Brimley for his first-rate turn as Lemmon's long-time co-worker. ★★★★ $9.99

Chinatown

(1974, 131 min, US, Roman Polanski) A superb, Oscar-winning script and consistently outstanding performances are supported by meticulous production values to deliver a classic tale of intrigue, conflicted loyalties, overwhelming greed and the futility of honor in a corrupt world. Jack Nicholson plays Jake Gittes, a Los Angeles private eye called into what at first appears to be a simple case of marital infidelity. Faye Dunaway arrives at his offices to declare that she is the real wife of the man Gittes has been paid to follow, and she has no desire to see her husband tailed. Gittes, with more curiosity than forethought, delves even deeper into the mystery; the governmental malfeasance he uncovers is child's play compared to the murky family secrets lying even deeper below. Especially arresting is John Huston's portrayal as Dunaway's father, a man who accepts no limits to his power and position, whether in business or in his home-life. A contemporary American film classic featuring one of Nicholson's best performances. Followed by a sequel, *The Two Jakes*. ★★★★ $19.99

Chinese Boxes

(1984, 87 min, GB, Chris Petit) Will Patton stars in this unusual though compelling thriller as an American tourist caught up in international intrigue in West Berlin after the death of a drug pusher. ★★½ $69.99

A Chinese Ghost Story

(1987, 95 min, Hong Kong, Ching Siu-Tung) Moving from his commercially successful martial arts flicks, director Ching has gone the way of *Ghost* and *Truly, Madly, Deeply* with this entertaining and atmospheric supernatural love story with surprisingly impressive special effects. Set during the Ming Dynasty, the story features a wandering scholar who, while visiting a haunted temple, meets and falls in love with a glamorous female ghost. But their love is never tranquil as he soon finds that he must do battle with a hoard of hellish creatures out to end their relationship. (Cantonese with English subtitles) ★★★ $39.99

Chinese Roulette

(1976, 86 min, West Germany, Rainer Werner Fassbinder) Anna Karina stars in this elegant Gothic thriller. Set during a weekend retreat in a castle, a crippled girl organizes a bizarre and fiendish truth game in order to psychological-

Jack Nicholson in *Chinatown*

ly attack her philandering parents and their respective lovers. With sweeping camera movement, lush scenery and music, this cruelly humorous melodrama is pure Fassbinder. (German with English subtitles) ★★★ $29.99

Chitty Chitty Bang Bang

(1968, 143 min, US, Ken Hughes) Dick Van Dyke stars as a slightly crackpot scientist who turns an old racing car into a magical flying machine. Unmemorable songs dampen the amiable spirits of this otherwise genial children's musical, which should entertain those in the pre-teen years. ★★½ $14.99

Chloë in the Afternoon

(1972, 97 min, France, Eric Rohmer) Rohmer's final entry in his series of "Moral Tales" continues with the theme of temptation met and mastered in this fascinating story of a happily married suburban man who struggles to stay faithful after he meets an unstable woman out of his past. Although constantly harboring lecherous tendencies, our chaste Don Juan must decide between fidelity and the rueful charms of Chloë, a young, attractive free spirit intent on seducing him. An elegant comedy of sexual mores. (French with English subtitles) ★★★★ $19.99

Chocolat

(1988, 105 min, France, Claire Denis) This surprisingly assured and quietly emotional film is a most impressive debut for director Denis. The story centers around a young white woman who returns to Cameroon, recalling her life there as a child of the French colonial governor. Her reminiscences — that of a young girl isolated in an exotic but foreign land — evoke the repression of the people, but focus primarily on the special relationship she had with the family's black houseboy. (French with English subtitles) ★★★ $19.99

The Chocolate War

(1988, 106 min, US, Keith Gordon) First-time director Gordon has fashioned a somber but thoughtful version of the "high school hell" film. Set in an oppressive Catholic school, young Jerry (Ilan Mitchell-Smith) refuses to conform with his classmates by declining to participate in the school's annual fund-raising effort — the chocolate bar sale. In response, the entire student body bombards him with both physical and emotional retribution. At first glance, *The Chocolate War* appears to be a simple us-against-them film, but on a deeper level, it is a scathing comment on fascism and authoritarian rule. ★★★

Choice of Arms

(1983, 117 min, France, Alain Corneau) Reminiscent of the best works of Claude Chabrol and Jean-Pierre Melville, this classy gangster film adroitly explores the complex and often-times violent relationship between a reformed underworld chieftain (Yves Montand) and his recently paroled crony: a wonderfully bestial and explosive Gérard Depardieu. Co-starring Catherine Deneuve, this modern film noir gem is a must for those who enjoy taut, psychologically charged thrillers. (French with English subtitles) ★★★½

Choke Canyon

(1986, 96 min, US, Chuck Bail) Nifty chase scenes highlight this thriller about a scientist (Stephen Collins) who comes into conflict with the owners of a nuclear power plant and the assassin they hired to kill him. ★★½

Choose Me

(1984, 114 min, US, Alan Rudolph) Rudolph looks at the mate-swapping, bed-hopping antics of L.A. singles looking for love under all the wrong sheets. Keith Carradine is the sinuous Lothario pursuing Lesley Ann Warren, Genevieve Bujold and Rae Dawn Chong with amorous abandon. ★★★½ $14.99

A Chorus Line

(1985, 113 min, US, Richard Attenborough) Those who did not see the Broadway production of this Pulitzer Prize and Tony Award-winning musical may appreciate Attenborough's lifeless adaptation. All others will long for the energy, class and integrity of the original. The story, of course, is about a group of dancers auditioning for the chorus of a Broadway musical. The show's famous song, "What I Did for Love" (the song, a dancer's anthem, has been changed from "What if I couldn't dance anymore" to a whiny lovers' lament), is thrown away by Attenborough's over-the-shoulder, off-handed nonchalance; and the classic finale "One" is considerably less than show-stopping. ★★

A Chorus of Disapproval

(1989, 92 min, GB, Michael Winner) Alan Ayckbourn's award-winning play about the comic transformation of a timid widower into a heart-breaking Lothario is brought to the screen in this humorous, engaging and finely acted farce. Jeremy Irons plays Guy Jones, a reserved and recently widowed young man who moves into a new town in northern England and, in an effort to "have fun and meet friends," joins the local amateur acting company's production of "The Beggar's Opera." The heads (and pelvises) of the ladies in the troupe are all turned on young Guy as he sheds his shyness and becomes entangled in a love nest involving the middle-aged wife (Prunella Scales) of the play's director and the

company's sexually insatiable bombshell (Jenny Seagrove). Anthony Hopkins is wonderful as the play's blustering and tempestuous director. ★★★ $19.99

The Chosen

(1981, 108 min, US, Jeremy Paul Kagan) An extraordinarily tender and moving screen version of Chaim Potok's novel about the friendship and conflicting loyalties of two Jewish teenagers: Hasidic Robby Benson and liberalized Barry Miller. The film is a loving re-creation of 1940s Brooklyn, and the stellar cast includes Rod Steiger (a stand-out as Benson's rabbi father) and Maximilian Schell. ★★★½ $59.99

Les Choses de la Vie (The Things of Life)

(1969, 90 min, France, Claude Sautet) This appealing romantic comedy centers on an architect who, after suffering a near fatal auto accident, takes the time to reflect on his life and loves. The always capable, ubiquitous Michel Picoli stars as a sensitive man torn between his love for his estranged wife (Lea Massari) and his mistress (Romy Schneider). A nicely observed tragi-comedy that builds to a moving examination of the fragility of life and relationships. (French with English subtitles) ★★★ $79.99

Christ Stopped at Eboli

(1979, 118 min, Italy, Francesco Rosi) Rosi's award-winning adaptation of Carlo Levi's classic is a rich, resonant film about a writer/artist and political exile, who is banned to a village in southern Italy by Mussolini in 1935. The exile's experiences in this world of poverty and quiet despair open his eyes to the unshakable values of the resolute villagers. A film full of faith in human values, stunningly directed. (Italian with English subtitles) ★★★½ $59.99

Christabel

(1989, 148 min, GB, Adrian Shergold) This outstanding BBC production tells the true-life story of Christabel Bielenberg, an aristocratic English woman who marries a German lawyer and finds herself plunged into the nightmare of Nazi Germany. Having joined the Resistance, her husband is arrested and sent to the notorious Ravensbruck concentration camp. Based on her autobiography, the film follows Bielenberg as she travels across war-ravaged Germany and takes on the Nazi beauracracy and the Gestapo in an effort to free her husband. ★★★½ $19.99

Christiane F.

(1981, 124 min, West Germany, Ulrich Edel) The spine-tingling account of a young German girl lost in the dark abyss of drug dependency and prostitution. Based on a true story, the film has a striking authenticity acquired through the use of actual locales (Berlin's seamiest junkie havens) and a pallid complexioned cast. David Bowie makes a guest appearance and provides the soundtrack music. (Dubbed) ★★★

Christine

(1983, 111 min, US, John Carpenter) Horror mavens Carpenter and Stephen King joined forces for this stylish though basic adaptation

of King's novel with Keith Gordon making the most of a shy teenager who is under the spell of a demonic '58 Plymouth. ★★ $14.99

A Christmas Carol

(1951, 86 min, GB, Brian Desmond Hurst) A wonderful, heartwarming rendition of Charles Dickens' classic tale, featuring a terrific performance by the delightful Alastair Sim as Scrooge. A hardy perennial that has become a well-loved part of the Christmas experience. ★★★★ $14.99

Christmas in Connecticut

(1945, 101 min, US, Peter Godfrey) Barbara Stanwyck stars in this breezy if lightweight comedy of mistaken identity. Stanwyck plays a successful writer for a women's housekeeping magazine who contrary to her image can neither cook, clean, lives in the country nor is married. When a war hero (Dennis Morgan) is invited by the magazine's publisher (Sydney Greenstreet) to stay on "her" farm for the weekend, Stanwyck is forced to impersonate the woman her readers (and publisher) think she is. Of course, love blossoms between Stanwyck and Morgan, even though he thinks she is really married (an unusual comedic swipe at adultery for the '40s). This role was probably routine for Stanwyck at this stage of her career, but she's funny and effortlessly charming. Morgan doesn't make much of a presence, though Greenstreet and the delightful S.Z. Sakall supply good support. The laughs aren't consistent but it's fun nonetheless. ★★½ $14.99

Christmas in July

(1940, 67 min, US, Preston Sturges) A practical joke escalates into a frenzy of consumerism and wish-fulfillment in this whimsical Sturges look at the American Dream. Dick Powell thinks he's won $25,000 in a slogan contest; but does money really buy happiness? Or, as the boss said to Jimmy, "Now that you're a capitalist, I don't know how you feel about working for a living..." ★★★½ $14.99

A Christmas Story

(1983, 98 min, US, Bob Clark) It's hard to believe this absolutely charming adaptation of Jean Shepherd's short story was directed by the same man who gave us *Porky's*. A delight for both children and adults, this endearing reminiscence of the holiday season circa 1940 captures the everyday life of the era, as young Peter Billingsley hopes (anguishes is more accurate) for a Red Ryder BB gun. Darren McGavin and Melinda Dillon are simply wonderful as his somewhat unconventional parents. ★★★½ $14.99

Christo's Valley Curtain

(1984, 28 min, US, Maysles Brothers) A perfect companion piece to *Islands*, the film documenting nature-artist Christo's "wrapping" of the islands in Biscayne Bay, Florida, this short film directed by the Maysles Brothers documents Christo and his equally fervent "visualization" crew as they set out to literally construct a curtain across a canyon. Set against the backdrop of the desert Southwest, and, amusingly, a golf course scattered with disbelieving onlookers, the film takes us on a journey from the inception of his vision, done as three-dimensional drawings, to his eventual tension-filled execution of his dream. Another fascinating and dream-driven work from two of the most eclectic (as far as subject matter goes) filmmakers working today. ★★★ $39.99

Christopher Columbus: The Discovery

(1992, 121 min, US, John Glen) From the production team that brought us *Superman* (Alexander and Ilya Salkind) comes this equally mythological depiction of the seafaring Genoan of American folklore, Cristóbal Colón. Brimming with lots of overblown production values, the film sets sail into the murky waters of historical narrative with its compass askew and its rigging tangled. Despite these failings, however, the film will still be satisfying viewing to lovers of melodramatic adventure on the high seas. George Corraface, who made a good showing in Peter Brooks' *The Mahabarata*, performs ably in the title role, making the best of a bad script. The "all-star" cast is rounded out by Rachel Ward, Tom Selleck, Marlon Brando, Nigel Terry and Robert Davi. ★★ $19.99

Christopher Strong

(1933, 77 min, US, Dorothy Arzner) One of the few female directors of her time, Arzner brings an enchanting perspective to this capable romantic drama with Katharine Hepburn in her element as an aviatrix in romantic and professional conflict. Colin Clive is one of the reasons for both. Billie Burke, who portrayed Hepburn's mother in *A Bill of Divorcement*, also stars. ★★★ $19.99

C.H.U.D.

(1984, 88 min, US, Douglas Cheek) If you're a fan of spoofy-played-for-straight horror films, then this *C.H.U.D.*'s for you. All others, however, may not enjoy this tale of street people becoming Cannibalistic Humanoid Underground Dwellers when they become exposed to radioactive gunk and begin murderous rampage. ★★ $14.99

C.H.U.D. II: Bud the Chud

(1989, 84 min, US, David Irving) The Cannibalistic Humanoid Underground Dwellers are back with less intelligence, less chills, less wit...you get the picture. With Brian Robbins, Gerrit Graham, Robert Vaughn, Bianca Jagger and June Lockhart. ★ $14.99

Chungking Express

(1994, 103 min, Hong Kong, Wong Kar-Wai) The stories of two Hong Kong police officers who are dumped by their girlfriends are interwoven in this brilliant, engrossing, yet low-budget pastiche from the latest hot export from the colony, writer and director Wong. Made while working in postproduction on his angst-ridden swordsman movie *Ashes of Time*, *Chungking*'s swift genesis and execution shows. It is vibrant, immediate and exudes a truthfulness and poignancy which can be attributed to its lack of rewrites and production tinkering. Parts of it seem to have been improvised and the entire production was filmed on only two locations. Comparisons to Godard's work have been made regarding Wong's style, but he is truly a complete origi-

nal. Slow motion, jump cuts, pixellated movement and the recurrent use of a handful of pop tunes all combine to make the film very different from its Hong Kong brethren yet set firmly within that diverse genre. There is also at least a kernel of truth for most people in this film about romantic relationships and how we adapt to their beginnings as well as their ends. (Cantonese with English subtitles) ★★★★ $99.99

The Church

(1990, 110 min, US/Italy, Michele Soavi) Italian shockmaestro Dario Argento (*Suspiria*, *Inferno*) produced this so-so chiller about a group of people trapped in a church built on top of a satanic burial ground. Director Soavi, an acknowledged protégé of Argento as well as the director of the documentary *Dario Argento's World of Horror*, delivers all the style of the master, but few of the shocks. This is the unrated version. ★★ $89.99

Ciao! Federico!

(1970, 62 min, US, Gideon Bachmann) This absorbing look at the great Italian filmmaker Federico Fellini is recorded during the making of *Fellini's Satyricon*. Includes interviews with the director and scenes from the classic film. (Italian with English subtitles) ★★★

Ciao! Manhattan

(1965-1971, 84 min, US, John Palmer & David Weisman) This kaleidoscopic journey through the life of Warhol superstar Edie Sedgwick is both a searing psychodrama of burn-out syndrome and a dynamic potpourri of Sixties cultural paraphernalia. From Edie's rise to the throne of the pop underground to her tragic plummet into drug abuse and mental illness, *Ciao!* manages to be comical, perplexing and poignant. Filming began in 1965, capturing the orgiastic frenzy of the Warhol Factory's heyday. Work resumed years later with a crumbling Edie living at the bottom of a swimming pool on the West Coast. Only months after the completion of filming, Edie died of a barbiturate overdose. She was 28 years old. ★★★½

Ciao, Professore!

(1994, 99 min, Italy, Lina Wertmüller) A flip soundbite for this breezy comedy-drama would be to call it a pubescent spaghetti *To Sir with Love*. A portly middle-aged teacher (Paolo Villaggio) from northern Italy is accidentally sent to a poverty stricken seaside town near Naples. What he finds when he arrives is a beleaguered school and a class full of truant third graders. His formidable task is to round up the group of streetwise kids, gain their trust and begin to teach them. Wertmüller overcomes the hackneyed and predictable plot through the inspired casting of the children — all of them tough but cute mini-adults, each with a personality that would soften the most curmudgeonly heart. A decidedly different but equally accomplished film from the director of such '70s masterpieces as *Seven Beauties* and *Swept Away*. (Italian with English subtitles) ★★★ $19.99

The Cigarette Girl of Mosselprom

(1924, 78 min, USSR, Yuri Zhelyabuzhsky) A delightful and boisterous comedy satirizing Soviet life and filmmaking in the 1920s. The story follows the exploits of a young woman who is tossed from street vending into the movies when she is cast in a romantic melodrama. (Silent with orchestral accompaniment) ★★★ $29.99

Cimarron

(1931, 124 min, US, Wesley Ruggles) The first western to win an Oscar for Best Picture is a severely dated and rather lumbering period piece based on an Edna Ferber story about American pioneers in the Old West. Richard Dix gives the kind of performance which is subject to parody, though Irene Dunne's solid portrait certainly elevates the production. For film and western buffs. ★★ $19.99

Cinderella

(1950, 74 min, US, Wilfred Jackson) Walt Disney's classic animated feature is a remarkable achievement, and one of his best loved. The story, of course, follows "poor Cinderella" from abused step-sister to princess of the ball. It is the combination of the superb animation, the enchanting songs and a wonderful gallery of characters which makes *Cinderella* a timeless masterpiece. ★★★★

Cinderella

(1964, 77 min, US) Rodgers and Hammerstein wrote the score for this enchanting musical based on the fairy tale classic, and it's ideal for younger viewers. Lesley Ann Warren sweetly plays the title character. ★★★ $14.99

Cinderella Liberty

(1973, 117 min, US, Mark Rydell) Two strong performances from James Caan and Oscar-nominee Marsha Mason highlight this touching drama about a sailor who becomes involved with a prostitute and her illegitimate black son. Caan has never been better, here playing the good-natured seaman who falls for the hard-bitten Mason. The film effectively combines the gritty realism of the surroundings and the classic elements of the star-crossed romantic melodrama. ★★★ $59.99

Cinema Paradiso

(1990, 123 min, Italy, Giuseppe Tornatore) Italian filmmaking, in a decline for most of the 1980s, received a resuscitating shot in the cin-

Ciao! Manhattan

ematic arm with this wonderfully endearing and emotionally satisfying story of remembrance and love. The story is about the developing relationship and love between a precocious fatherless boy of eight, Toto (engagingly played by Salvatore Cascio), and a crusty old projectionist, Alfredo (a perfectly cast Philippe Noiret). Set mostly in a movie theater in a dusty Sicilian town after WWII, these two characters, seemingly so different, are drawn together and soon develop an unusual attachment. The movie is told in a series of flashbacks when Toto, now a successful film director in Rome, prepares to return to his boyhood village for the funeral of Alfredo. His loving memories of early childhood and adolescence provide the emotional core. For all but the most jaded, *Cinema Paradiso* will prove to be a rare, tender and unforgettable film. (Available dubbed and in Italian with English subtitles) ★★★★ $19.99

Circle of Friends

(1995, 114 min, Ireland, Pat O'Connor) Director O'Connor, known more for his intense dramas (*Cal, A Month in the Country*), is in a sweetly romantic mood and creates a picturesque atmosphere for an improbable love story with this beguiling adaptation of Maeve Binchy's novel. Benny (Minnie Driver) could probably be called the "ugly duckling" among her group of childhood friends, and growing up in a small Irish town in the late 1950s hasn't exactly given her the opportunity for romantic or social encounters. But that's all about to change when Benny enters university and falls under the spell of the soccer team's handsome star player (Chris O'Donnell). From *Georgy Girl* to *Muriel's Wedding*, "plain Jane" Cinderellas have found their Prince Charmings, and while *Circle of Friends* follows that formula, it's done so with a refreshing voice and a very grounded view of the world. Driver is wonderful as Benny, imbuing her character with sensibility and spirit. O'Donnell is believable as heartthrob, lover and Irishman. ★★★½ $14.99

Circle of Iron

(1979, 102 min, US, Richard Moore) Offbeat martial arts adventure (filmed in Israel and started by Bruce Lee before his death) about a young karate master in search of spiritual perfection and a sacred book of knowledge. With David Carradine, Jeff Cooper, Roddy McDowall and Eli Wallach. ★★½

Circuitry Man

(1989, 85 min, US, Steven Loy) Cheap sci-fi actioner about a post-apocalyptic age where the Earth's oxygen has been depleted, everybody lives underground, and the last remaining frontier is the human mind. Starring Vernon Wells as "Plughead." ★½ $19.99

The Circus/A Day's Pleasure

(1928/1919, 80 min, US, Charles Chaplin) Two Charlie Chaplin classics on one tape. *The Circus* has the Little Tramp as a member of the greatest show on Earth. This rarely seen gem features fantastic sight gags and lots of Chaplin's trademark physical humor. *A Day's Pleasure* is an early short which follows the mishaps of a family on a picnic. ★★★★

Circus Angel

(1965, 80 min, France, Albert Lamorisse) From the director of *The Red Balloon* comes this whimsical children's tale about a man who is mistaken for an angel by his small community. (Dubbed) ★★★

Cirque du Soleil

(1991, 60 min, Canada) An entertaining hour with the amazing Quebecois circus group, Cirque du Soleil. While the basic elements of circus remain unchanged, the presentation is not and the acts (including a contortionist, acrobats, tightrope walkers, bicycle tricks and a hilarious spoof on classical music conducting) are top-notch. Fun for the whole family. ★★★ $19.99

The Cisco Kid

(1993, 95 min, US, Luis Valdez) Mildly entertaining action-comedy which tells the story of the famous south of the border bandit with about as much accuracy as a counterfeit Rolex. The suave Jimmy Smits stars as the Cisco Kid, who teams up with Pancho (Cheech Marin) as he tries to save Mexico from corrupt politicians, double-crossing gun runners and nefarious Frenchmen. Spiced with many stunts and ill-placed jokes for lack of a real story. ★★ $14.99

The Citadel

(1938, 112 min, US/GB, King Vidor) An extraordinary retelling of A.J. Cronin's novel featuring superior performances by Robert Donat and Rosalind Russell. Donat stars as an idealistic and hard-working London doctor whose flirtation with the rich (and an easier case load) leads him to ignore his principles and his wife (Russell). Ralph Richardson is terrific in support as an old family friend, and a young Rex Harrison also appears. ★★★★ $24.99

Citizen Barnes, an American Dream

(1993, 57 min, France, Alain Jaubert & Philippe Pilard) This French documentary lauds the collection of paintings, sculptures and commissioned works collected by Albert Barnes. This film pays homage to Barnes' inspired sense of philanthropy and fiercely competitive nature. Interviews include artists and Barnes Foundation members, all praising his appreciation for visual arts and his passion for spreading his perspective on art education throughout the art world. There are some meditations on the design of the Foundation building, including the history of the Matisse mural, but overall there is little said on the controversial tour of the collection which began in 1993. ★★½ $29.99

Citizen Cohn

(1992, 112 min, US, Frank Pierson) Based on the novel by Nicholas von Hoffman, this engrossing biographical and political drama on the life of Roy Cohn — Communist headhunter, ruthless lawyer and closeted homosexual who died of AIDS in 1986 — is great explosive fun. Using his trademark hyper-energy coupled with his on-edge, often grating on-screen personality to unforgettable use, a seemingly possessed James Woods stars as the charismatic, but at times demonic Cohn. Made for HBO, the film is structured in a series of flashbacks, as the now disbarred Cohn lies semi-conscious in a hospital bed, dying of AIDS and hallucinating on many of the contentious incidents from his life — a past full of grievances, perceived slights and a relentless blood-thirsty quest for glory. Pulling no punches, the story chronicles Cohn's early triumphs as the prosecutor at the Rosenbergs' trial, his work as henchman/conciliator to Joe McCarthy during the Communist witch-hunts as well as his later years as an arrogant lawyer and power broker. ★★★½ $19.99

Citizen Kane

(1941, 119 min, US, Orson Welles) This masterful union of form and content stretched the boundaries of cinema with its ingeniously crafted narrative and stunning shot construction. The tale of Charles Foster Kane contains all the

Chris O'Donnell and Minnie Driver in *Circle of Friends*

Citizen Kane

vital elements of epic tragedy: greed, jealousy, scandal and failure. A devastating critique of the American Dream and an unmatched singular tour de force by producer, director, star and co-author Welles. ★★★★ $19.99

Citizen Ruth

(1996, 104 min, US, Alexander Payne) Laura Dern stars in this scathingly funny satire that dares to take on the super-charged issue of abortion. Dern is Ruth Stoops, a hard-core skid-row regular whose passion in life is inhaling solvents she steals from the local hardware store. Pregnant for the fifth time, she's hauled before a local magistrate for vagrancy and ordered by the court to have an abortion. Just like that — wham! — she finds herself at the center of a mushrooming controversy. The first to "adopt" her are local pro-lifers Mary Kay Place and Kurtwood Smith, who take her into their home and attempt to make a good Christian of her. Eventually, the other side catches wind and she's stolen away by a couple of radical lesbians (Swoosie Kurtz and Kelly Preston). With both sides wanting to make her their respective "abortion poster child," Ruth smells opportunity — especially when "Baby Savers" president (Burt Reynolds) offers a cash reward for her *not* to have an abortion. Though writer-director Payne seems to express a mildly pro-choice point of view, he leaves no one unscathed as he lampoons both sides for their unyielding zealotry with hilarious results — yes, a comedy about abortion, and it's actually funny to boot. ★★★½ $99.99

Citizen X

(1995, 103 min, US, Chris Gerolmo) Made for HBO, *Citizen X* is a tense, carefully detailed thriller about Russia's most horrific serial killer and the years-long search for him. Shot in Hungary, the film stars a somber Stephen Rea as a forensics expert and amateur detective who, upon the discovery of several bodies in a secluded wooded area, is assigned to head the investigation to track the killer. His task is made all the more difficult by an uncooperative Russian bureaucracy, uncaring associates and antiquated investigatory procedures. Donald Sutherland is well-cast as Rea's superior who may or may not be on his side, and Max von Sydow has a small but important role as the psychiatrist who helps crack the case. Adult in nature, the story doesn't flinch from the realities of its subject, and writer-director Gerolmo casts an eerie, ominous spell. ★★★½ $19.99

Citizen's Band

(1977, 98 min, US, Jonathan Demme) A delightful slice of Americana, this satire on the CB craze interweaves several stories revolving around an odd and lovable assortment of characters, all obsessed with their short wave radios. A good cast includes Paul Le Mat, Candy Clark, Ann Wedgeworth and Marcia Rodd. A quirky original from director Demme. (aka: *Handle with Care*.) ★★★½ $59.99

City Hall

(1996, 110 min, US, Harold Becker) The story of a small-town boy who gets an ugly lesson in life through his adventures in the big city gets another telling in this occasionally gritty political drama which is far less provocative than it thinks it is. John Cusack plays the Deputy Mayor of New York City, an idealistic, loyal foot soldier to Al Pacino's gregarious and often charming mayor. When a young child is killed during a gangland/police shootout, the administration gets into high gear investigating the murder and playing damage control. As Cusack digs deeper, he discovers a trail of cover-ups and widespread corruption — but how high does it go? With his Southern accent and stories of a more innocent life in Louisiana, Cusack ably conveys the turmoil of a naive politico suddenly learning not only the meaning of hard ball but how to play it as well. Pacino is able to carve emotion from a rather one-dimensional character, and he's given to less theatrical outbursts. *City Hall* presents an intriguing view of a machine at work, it's just so indifferent about it all it's hard to get really excited. ★★½ $19.99

City Heat

(1984, 98 min, US, Richard Benjamin) The combined talents of Clint Eastwood, Burt Reynolds, Jane Alexander and Madeline Kahn is, sadly, not enough to elevate the enjoyment level of this disappointing '30s-style gangster take-off. ★★ $14.99

City Lights

(1931, 90 min, US, Charles Chaplin) Chaplin's final silent film is one of the screen's true masterworks. Charlie plays the Little Tramp, who falls in love with a blind flower girl and vows to obtain the money needed for an operation to restore her sight. Filled with great humor and overwhelming emotional poignancy. ★★★★

City Limits

(1985, 85 min, US, Aaron Lipstadt) It's another post-apocalyptic thriller with gangs of youths roving barren cities on motorcycles.

This second feature from the team which produced *Android*, while not as successful as their earlier effort, still manages to rise slightly above its overworked premise thanks, in part, to performances from Rae Dawn Chong, Kim Cattrall, Robby Benson and James Earl Jones. ★★ $79.99

City Lovers/Country Lovers

(1982, 105 min, South Africa, Barney Simon/Mamie van Rensberg) Two works by South African dramatist Nadine Gordimer. In *City Lovers*, a middle-aged white geologist begins an affair with a black cashier; in the latter story, the son of a wealthy white farmer and the daughter of a black farmhand, who have grown up together, are secret lovers. The unifying theme in both of Gordimer's works is that the lovers must suffer the consequences of their relationships from the strict, oppressive South African government, which has banned interracial romances. ★★★ $69.99

City of Hope

(1991, 129 min, US, John Sayles) Sayles' take on the decline of the American city during the Reagan-Bush years is a masterfully layered exposé of corruption, greed, political favoritism, street crime and neighborhood vigilantism. Vincent Spano stars as the disillusioned son of a corrupt city contractor who, fed up with graft, quits his "ghost job" on a high-rise construction project only to find himself at the center of a swirling web of local political intrigue. Sayles manages to tinge his story with just about every major news item of the early '90s and then some. Spano, who also starred in Sayles' *Baby It's You*, is well-cast as the enlightened thug, and Joe Morton (who was Sayles' *Brother from Another Planet*) puts in a fine turn as an idealistic City Councilman who struggles with the more radical elements in his community. Another Sayles veteran, David Strathairn, is terrific as a street person witness to it all. ★★★½ $19.99

City of Joy

(1992, 134 min, GB, Roland Joffé) An aimless and disillusioned American surgeon (Patrick Swayze) attempts to lose himself in the back streets of Calcutta. Against his will, he's drawn into the operations of a health clinic run by a nurse (Pauline Collins of *Shirley Valentine*), who's committed to the clinic's survival with pragmatic optimism and iron will. Together, they battle against the overwhelming need and abject poverty of their patients, and confront a brutal and exploitive local boss. Some engaging performances and arresting location shooting elevate the film above its predictable story line. Director Joffé's experience in documentary work is much in evidence. ★★½ $19.99

City of Lost Children

(1995, 112 min, France, Marc Caro & Jean-Pierre Jeunet) The second film of the dazzlingly brilliant yet undeniably bizarre directing team of former animators Jeunet and Caro, *City of Lost Children* is a fascinating, engrossing and disturbing fractured fairy tale. Set in and around an eerie, oddly futuristic yet late 19th-century waterfront (it's a setting seemingly inspired by Samuel Beckett and Fritz Lang), the film follows a hulking but pea-brained circus strongman (Ron Perlman) known only as "One" who is on a desperate search to find his ward, Little Brother, who was abducted by a freakish, quasi-religious group of cyclopes. Along the way, he joins forces with a group of street urchins who steal for a Fagin-esque Siamese twin. The search ultimately leads to a sea-platform/laboratory where Krank, the genetically created orphan of a mad scientist, lords over his siblings (six identical clones, a female dwarf and a talking brain in a box) and conducts diabolical dream experiments. Though not as seamless as their previous *Delicatessen*, the directors have crafted a truly unique tale that is complemented by good performances, mind-blowing imagery and superb special effects. (Available dubbed and in French with English subtitles) ★★★½ $96.89

City of Women

(1981, 139 min, Italy, Federico Fellini) Marcello Mastroianni stars as the bruised, baffled and bedazzled man who stumbles into a feminist convention, which sets off a series of wild, surrealistic fantasies. Fellini continues his eternal search into his psyche with an eloquent flourish. (Italian with English subtitles) ★★★ $79.99

City Slickers

(1991, 108 min, US, Ron Underwood) Billy Crystal, Daniel Stern and Bruno Kirby star in this hilarious and often heartwarming farce about three adventure-seeking Manhattanite buddies who sign up for an "authentic" Western cattle drive. Along the way, they confront their fears and unfulfilled childhood fantasies, along with various other aspects of their respective mid-life crises. This may sound like a recipe for cheap sentimentality, but thanks to solid performances and razor-sharp, quick-witted dialogue, the film is a fun-filled, action-packed and poignant examination of the disillusionment of middle-age. Excellent supporting work comes from Patricia Wettig, Helen Slater, Josh Mostel and, especially, Jack Palance as the real-life cowboy who leads the round-up. ★★★½ $14.99

City of Women

City Slickers II: The Legend of Curly's Gold

(1994, 105 min, US, Paul Weiland) Billy Crystal, Jack Palance and Daniel Stern are back in the saddle again in this genial sequel which is less a continuation and more a carbon copy of the original. Crystal learns that Curly (the Palance character who died in the first film) may have left behind a fortune in gold. He, Stern and brother Jon Lovitz head west to search for it. On the way, Curly's twin brother shows up (allowing Oscar winner Palance to return) and all face the same series of western misadventures as in the first film. Though there's no lack of funny lines, and Crystal is a delight to watch, the sorry subplot of Lovitz and Crystal's strained relationship and an overwhelming feeling of *deja vu* make this only intermittently entertaining. ★★½ $14.99

La Ciudad y los Perros (The City and the Dogs)

(1987, 135 min, Peru, Francisco J. Lombardi) Although very few of its films reach the United States, this powerful drama of personal honor amidst rampant terror proves that Peruvian cinema is quite vibrant. The story is set in a boy's military academy outside Lima. Within the confines of the repressive structure, four angry cadets form a private circle that begins to victimize and dominate the other cadets. It is only after a theft escalates into possible murder that a brave young man confronts the group. A hard-hitting and absorbing drama from Mario Vargas Llosa's classic novel. (Spanish with English subtitles) ★★★

Civilization

(1916, 86 min, US, Raymond B. West) Contemporary with Griffith's *Intolerance*, producer Thomas Ince proved himself every bit the director's equal with this impressive silent exhibiting strong plot construction and narrative economy. The film is a cautionary tale of a nation on the brink due to unsatiable expansionist desires. Set in the mythical kingdom of Teutonic, the story depicts that country's plunge into the surreal madness of war. Only when Christ himself returns to take the sovereign on an amazing journey to see the resulting carnage is the country saved. *Civilization* was both a commercial and critical success upon its release in 1916, and was not only used to help reelect President Wilson but also was a rallying cry against America's entry into WWI. The film became frightfully out of fashion when America entered the war. ★★★ $29.99

Civilization

(1969, 650 min, GB, Michael Gill, Peter Montagnon & Ann Turner) Produced by the BBC, this fascinating 13-part series is the brainchild of Lord Kenneth Clark, a writer, art historian and critic who pieced together the history of Occidental culture, beginning with Charlemagne in

France, the Vikings in Norway and the Celtic Hebrides thru to the present day. Some may question the validity of its title, as the series ignores the great civilizations of Asia, India and the Americas — it would probably be better titled, "Western Civilization." But despite the program's obvious Eurocentrism, it is still an engrossing examination of our past which visits 117 sites, 18 major libraries and 118 museums. The 13 episodes are presented on seven tapes: two episodes per video with exception to Volume Seven. Each episode runs 50 min and each tape retails for $29.99. The entire boxed set may be purchased for $149.99. ★★★

Claire of the Moon

(1992, 106 min, US, Nicole Conn) While not the breakthrough lesbian film which many had hoped, *Claire of the Moon* is an earnest, if amateurish drama of simmering female sexual desire and equally strong denial. At an oceanside women writers' retreat in Oregon, Dr. Noel Benedict (Karen Trumbo), a brooding psychologist and lesbian author of "serious" books (reminding one of a constipated Carol Burnett), finds herself rooming with her opposite — Claire (Trisha Wood), a willowy yet cynical straight blonde woman who is determinedly messy and fun-loving. Their budding relationship becomes a tense and inadvertently amusing cat-and-mouse game of "I want you...I don't want you" as they alternately try to overcome their insecurities, accept their true feelings and pounce on each other. A refreshingly intimate lesbian romance that works as a love story despite being a talky and didactic soap full of typical lesbian stereotypes and featuring a wooden script, stilted acting, and an overload of lingering glances. ★★ $29.99

Claire's Knee

(1970, 106 min, France, Eric Rohmer) The fifth in director Rohmer's series of "Moral Tales," *Claire's Knee* is a sophisticated comedy of lust, unfulfilled desire and fidelity. The film tells the story of a young diplomat, recently engaged, who harbors a peculiar obsession for the teenage sister of his fiancée. A literate satire on sexual temptations with fine cinematography by Nestor Alemendros. (French with English subtitles) ★★★ $19.99

Clara's Heart

(1988, 108 min, US, Robert Mulligan) A heartwarming performance by Whoopi Goldberg dominates this uneven drama about a Jamaican maid whose loving influence on a young boy (Neil Patrick Harris) helps him through family difficulties. Michael Ontkean and Kathleen Quinlan are the youth's parents — grief-stricken over the death of their infant — who inadvertently ignore their other child. ★★ $9.99

Clash by Night

(1952, 105 min, US, Fritz Lang) Barbara Stanwyck gives a dynamic performance in this steamy psychodrama as the penned-up wife of a boring fishing boat captain (Paul Douglas) whose yearning for excitement leads her to her husband's best friend (Robert Ryan). A youthful Marilyn Monroe and Keith Andes give good support as a young couple. ★★★ $19.99

Clash of the Titans

(1981, 118 min, GB, Desmond Davis) Special effects by Ray Harryhausen (his final film before retirement) highlight this appealing if listless Greek mythology adventure set during ancient times. Starring Harry Hamlin, Judi Bowker, Laurence Olivier and Maggie Smith. ★★ $14.99

Class

(1983, 98 min, US, Lewis John Carlino) Jacqueline Bisset finds herself unknowingly involved with her son's college roommate. Rob Lowe is her offspring, Andrew McCarthy is her youthful lover. Bisset brings more class to this uninspired teen comedy than it deserves. ★½

Class Act

(1992, 98 min, US, Randall Miller) Blend the kinetic filming style of TV's "Parker Lewis," with the hip hop hijinks of Kid 'n Play's previous hit, *House Party*; throw in a little of the antic, slap-and-ouch comedy of the Three Stooges and a 1990s black version of Hope and Crosby, and you get some idea of what is in store in this agreeably inane teen comedy. *The Prince and the Pauper* goes inner city when teen genius Kid (Christopher Reid) finds himself in a foul-up that has him changing places with one of his school's fun-loving bums, Play (Christopher Martin). Although all of the goings-on are predictable, the film's infectious desire to entertain and amuse pays off, creating a harmless, anti-drug comedy that is pure fun. ★★★ $19.99

Class Action

(1991, 110 min, US, Michael Apted) Gene Hackman's dominant performance highlights this routine though intriguing courtroom drama – though he's not on screen nearly enough. Hackman plays a dedicated attorney who on behalf of an injured motorist takes a powerful corporation to court – with his daughter Mary Elizabeth Mastrantonio as the opposing council. Part mystery and part courtroom intrigue, the film has moments of interest, but some of the twists are rather contrived. ★★ $9.99

Class of 1984

(1982, 93 min, US, Mark L. Lester) The new teacher (Perry King) gets tormented by his students – and by Timothy Van Patten in particular – at an inner city high school. Also with Roddy McDowall and a young Michael J. Fox. Without the pretentions of a serious-minded examination of teacher-student relations, this half-baked, violent actioner is strictly for thrills – though it produces only a few. ★★

Class of 1999

(1989, 99 min, US, Mark L. Lester) In the wake of *The Terminator* comes this not-too-shabby ripoff (but ripoff nonetheless) about a high school from hell where gang-bangers meet their match in a group of malfunctioning renegade robot teachers (Pam Grier, Patrick Kilpatrick, John P. Ryan). Malcolm McDowell co-stars with Stacy Keach (who adds yet another leering psycho to his resume). ★★½ $14.99

The Class of Miss MacMichael

(1978, 93 min, GB, Silvio Narizzano) Glenda Jackson stars as a fiesty trade schoolteacher who struggles to gain the respect of her unruly students. Oliver Reed plays the school's menacing principal. The combination of comedy and melodrama is ill-served here. ★½ $9.99

Class of Nuke 'Em High

(1986, 84 min, US, Richard W. Haines & Samuel Weil) From the cinematic genii who gave us *The Toxic Avenger* comes their greatest masterpiece yet. High school students exposed to toxic waste become hideous mutants. Oh, the horror of it all. Is there no one who can save them? ★½ $12.99

Clean and Sober

(1988, 121 min, US, Glenn Gordon Caron) Michael Keaton, in a departure from his usual eccentric comic portrayals, gives a first-rate performance as a drug-addicted businessman who hides out in a drug re-hab; this forces him to come to terms with his addiction. While lacking the strong narrative of *The Lost Weekend* or *The Days of Wine and Roses*, the film nevertheless is a forceful drama told in a truthful, no-holds-barred manner. Excellent support from Morgan Freeman as a dedicated counselor and Kathy Baker as a weary addict. ★★★ $19.99

Clean, Shaven

(1995, 109 min, US, Lodge Kerrigan) Kerrigan's first film is a vivid, gut-wrenching study of paranoid schizophrenia, told from the point of view of the disturbed individual. Peter Greene stars as a recently released mental patient who begins an obsessive quest to find his young daughter, now living with an adopted mother. When his tortured journey takes a murderous turn, a manhunt begins and he is pursued by an equally obsessive detective. The film's soundtrack is particularly innovative, layering various elements such as radio broadcasts, overheard conversations and random noises within and around the dialogue itself. This cacophony, approximating what the mentally disturbed hear every day, is the single most powerful element contributing to the film's success. The director sets out to dramatize the experiences of the paranoid schizophrenic, and as the viewer is assailed by these sights and sounds, we come somewhat closer to understanding the character's plight. Very experimental in nature, and definitely not for the squeamish, *Clean, Shaven* is a highly original vision which succeeds as both social commentary and as a radically new method of exposition. ★★★ $19.99

Clean Slate

(1994, 107 min, US, Mick Jackson) This amusing, gimmick-ridden piffle stars Dana Carvey as a mild-mannered private eye whose plans to testify against a crime boss are thwarted when a rare form of amnesia makes him forget everything that happened the day before. Not very memorable, and that's the point. Valeria Golina is the Mary Astor-like client who hires him, and James Earl Jones also stars as a wheelchair-bound district attorney. ★★½ $9.99

Clear and Present Danger

(1994, 142 min, US, Phillip Noyce) Harrison Ford reprises his role from *Patriot Games* in this third Jack Ryan tale. An efficient and exciting thriller, *Danger* is based on Tom Clancy's novel which involves Ryan with South American drug dealers and political cover-ups. The story begins as Ryan takes over as acting deputy director of the CIA. He soon finds himself in political hot water and immediate danger when he uncovers evidence of White House duplicity with a drug cartel. Though the film is slightly overlong, it never fails to entertain, and there's a slam-bang ambush scene which is breathtaking. As usual, Ford is a commanding presence and his heroic Everyman character is well served here. Willem Dafoe also appears as a soldier of fortune, and Anne Archer (however briefly) and James Earl Jones also return. More thrilling than *Games* and on par with *Hunt for Red October*, *Danger* is a helluva ride. (Available letterboxed and pan & scan) ★★★½ $14.99

Clearcut

(1992, 98 min, Canada, Richard Bucaski) Graham Greene stars in this Native American *Deliverance* which serves as an impassioned cry against environmental atrocities committed in the Canadian wilderness by big timber and paper companies. Greene plays Arthur, an irate Native who, upon learning of yet another court decision against his tribe, takes matters into his own hands and abducts the foreman of the local paper mill and the lawyer representing his tribe and takes them to the forest for a harrowing lesson in humility. Greene gives a sturdy performance in this compelling drama. ★★½ $89.99

Cleo from 5 to 7 (Cleo de cinq à sept)

(1961, 90 min, France, Agnès Varda) An intelligent and absorbing film which examines a woman at the crossroads of life. A successful Parisian songstress, fearing the worst, is forced to reevaluate her life while waiting two hours for a medical report on her health. (French with English subtitles) ★★★½

Cleopatra

(1963, 243 min, US, Joseph L. Mankiewicz) Notorious epic about the queen of the Nile. Whether it's more noted for the Elizabeth Taylor-Richard Burton angle (they met and fell in love) or the colossal sum spent on it or the dreary notices it received, the film, though spectacular looking, is a tough four-hour viewing. However, it does feature two award-calibre performances by Rex Harrison and Roddy McDowall. ★★ $29.99

Cleopatra Jones

(1973, 89 min, US, Jack Starrett) There's lots of action in this violent adventure with Tamara Dobson as a lovely but lethal martial arts-trained government agent out to bust drug kingpins – including the hilariously preposterous Shelley Winters. ★★½ $14.99

Cleopatra Jones and the Casino of Gold

(1975, 94 min, US, Chuck Bail) Don't let an incoherent plot and ludicrous acting keep you away from this fun if less than stellar follow-up to *Cleopatra Jones*. The leggy Tamara Dobson returns as the brave and sexy drug agent out to wipe out a notorious Hong Kong drug ring. Stella Stevens camps it up as the villainous "Dragon Lady." ★★ $14.99

Clerks

(1994, 89 min, US, Kevin Smith) The two-store location in *Clerks*, a ferociously entertaining gem, doesn't even count as a mall — it's just a parking lot anchored by a third-rate video store and a Wawa-wannabe convenience store. To work in either establishment is more serving time than being employed. The convenience store clerk tries to maintain a sense of direction in the face of futility; the video store guy has abandoned hope long ago — when he opens the store at all it's to show contempt for his customers. Waiting in limbo, without even the comforting illusion of Godot, these Generation Xers structure their pointless day with corpse abuse, analyses of working-class exploitation, unrequited love and sponging friends. This original, highly inventive low-budget surprise stirs its disparate elements into a '90s examination of meaning and purpose. It all culminates with the delivery of spontaneous satori in the face of existential despair. And it's damn funny, too. ★★★½ $19.99

The Client

(1994, 124 min, US, Joel Schumacher) This adaptation of John Grisham's novel falls short of its expectations. Susan Sarandon stars as a struggling Memphis attorney who sees a golden opportunity walk in her door in the person of a young boy — a witness to the suicide of a mob lawyer — who hires her to help keep the Feds off his back. Of course, the bad guys show up, and the little guy finds himself on the run from both relentless G-man Tommy Lee Jones and villainous underworld kingpin Anthony LaPaglia. While at times entertaining, the film suffers from too many incredulities and a slack plot full of deadly breaks in the action. Sarandon and Jones put in fine performances as always and Mary-Louise Parker puts in a nice turn as the boy's white-trash mom. ★★½ $19.99

Cliffhanger

(1993, 118 min, US, Renny Harlin) Sylvester Stallone teams with *Die Hard 2* director Harlin for this unbelievably hair-raising, excessively violent actioner which, when flexing its special effects and cinematographic muscles, is nothing short of remarkable. However, these first-rate action scenes are offset by one-dimensional characters, clichéd plot developments and flat dialogue (Sly co-wrote the screenplay). Fortunately, *Cliffhanger* is much more action than talk. Stallone plays an expert mountain climber haunted by the edge-of-your-seat opening tragedy. Reluctantly, he returns to the same locale when skyjackers crash land in the mountains. Stallone and buddy Michael Rooker are then forced to help the sadistic John Lithgow retrieve stolen cash. Thrills, lots of blood, gruesome deaths, amazing climbing

footage and a cave-load of bats await them. Janine Turner ("Northern Exposure") also stars. ★★½ $14.99

The Clinic

(1984, 93 min, Australia, David Stevens) A comedy about social disease? It may sound strange, possibly in bad taste and potentially off-putting, but *The Clinic* is a surprisingly fresh and funny frolic about one day in the life of a Sydney V.D. clinic. Chock full of bawdy doctor/patient vignettes, the film is never derisive and maintains a gentle understanding for the afflicted denizens of this madcap milieu. One critic called it "an Aussie 'St. Elsewhere.'" ★★★

Cloak and Dagger

(1946, 106 min, US, Fritz Lang) Lang directed this competent spy thriller, which is more cloak than dagger. Gary Cooper stars as an American scientist who is sent to Germany during WWII to uncover military secrets. Lili Palmer is the femme fatale with whom he becomes involved. ★★½ $19.99

Cloak and Dagger

(1984, 101 min, US, Richard Franklin) Enjoyable and even suspenseful children's thriller with Henry Thomas (*E.T.*) as a young boy who becomes involved with spies when he obtains secret microfilm. Dabney Coleman plays dual roles as his father and his imaginary James Bond-ish playmate. ★★½ $19.99

The Clock

(1945, 90 min, US, Vincente Minnelli) A lovely romantic drama featuring one of Judy Garland's best dramatic performances. Judy plays an office worker who meets soldier Robert Walker while he's on a two-day pass; the two fall in love while spending the day together. ★★★½ $19.99

Clockers

(1995, 129 min, US, Spike Lee) Lee's adaptation of Richard Price's best-selling novel marks his first collaboration with that other famous ethnic New York filmmaker, Martin Scorsese (who produced). In an astonishingly good debut performance, Mekhi Phifer plays Strike, a smart youth with a love for trains who has gotten involved with a local crime lord, Rodney (Delroy Lindo). Strike is a "clocker," a dealer who can be found working around the clock from his perch on a park bench. The film opens with a terrific sequence which introduces the inner workings of the dealers (much like Scorsese's *Casino*). When a murder occurs, a sympathetic homicide detective (Harvey Keitel) on the case refuses to believe the self-defense story given by Strike's brother, who has confessed to the crime. The officer probes deeper into Strike's world, pressuring the young man to come clean and give up Rodney. Price and Lee weave a complex tale of loyalty, betrayal and honor, and despite a confusing ending, its multi-dimensional characters and relationships draw the viewer into a meticulously constructed world. Powerful without being maudlin, *Clockers* may not be particularly distinguished, but it is entertaining, engrossing and enlightening. ★★★ $19.99

The Clockmaker

(1973, 105 min, France, Bertrand Tavernier) Based on a novel by Georges Simenon, this fascinating and thought-provoking drama stars Philippe Noiret as a clockmaker in Lyon whose life is drastically changed after he learns that his son was involved in leftist terrorist acts. With the arrest of his son, the man's placid and ordered life must be reviewed as he tries to understand his role in the world. One of the finest French films of the 1970s. (French with English subtitles) ★★★★

Clockwise

(1986, 98 min, GB, Christopher Morahan) Monty Python's John Cleese is in rare comic form in this delightful and uproarious comedy as a fastidious headmaster whose perfunctory life is turned upside-down when he boards the wrong train for an important conference. ★★★½ $14.99

A Clockwork Orange

(1971, 135 min, GB, Stanley Kubrick) Little Alex and his grazhny droogs prowl the streets in search of sldky devotchkas. Kubrick's brilliant adaptation of the Anthony Burgess novel assualts the screen with snakes, Ludwig von, the old in-out and oodles more. Don't be oddy-knocky, take this tape home and villy the meaning of it, all my brothers. ★★★★ $19.99

Close Encounters of the Third Kind

(1977, 152 min, US, Steven Spielberg) Spielberg's classic sci-fi film. Richard Dreyfuss and Melinda Dillon are just two of the many Earthlings to see an alien craft — and are compelled to travel to Devil's Tower in Wyoming. The special effects, including the mother ship and the aliens, are second to none, and John Williams' lush, magical score is extraordinary. (This is the "special edition," which includes scenes not in the original 1977 release.) ★★★★ $14.99

Close to Eden

(1992, 106 min, Russia, Nikita Mikhalkov) This exquisitely rendered fable examines the effects of modernization on a family living on the Mongolian steppes just inside the Chinese border. After giving shelter to a stranded Russian truck driver, the family begins to question their own traditional lifestyles, leading the father to make a hilarious yet sobering

A Clockwork Orange

journey to the nearest big city in search of such modern amenities as a television and condoms. Russian director Mikhalkov (*Dark Eyes, Burnt by the Sun*) masterfully depicts their simple yet noble lives as contrasted with the polluted degradation of the industrialized city and keeps the pace lively despite the film's essentially static nature. At times mirthful and humorous, at other times serious and ponderous, the film charms the viewer with several marvelous flights of fantasy; one of which finds the husband coming face to face with Gunga Din. (Russian with English subtitles) ★★★★ $89.99

Alicia Silverstone (foreground) and Justin Walker in *Clueless*

Closely Watched Trains

(1966, 89 min, Czechoslovakia, Jiri Menzel) This Oscar-winning Best Foreign Film is a charming, bittersweet tragicomedy about a young, naive train dispatcher and his attempts to find love during the Nazi occupation. (Czechoslovakian with English subtitles) ★★★½ $19.99

Closet Land

(1991, 95 min, US, Radha Bharadwaj) In a nameless country and an unspecified year, a woman, the writer of children's books, is taken to a secluded room with no apparent exit or entrance. There she is interrogated by a seemingly benign officer. But when his requests for a confession to political subversion are denied, he becomes increasingly violent, inflicting mental and physical torture to achieve his goal. Madeleine Stowe and Alan Rickman give tremendous performances in this political allegory, a powerful and fascinating study of the individual struggle to control one's own thoughts, and an acknowledgement of the resiliency of the human spirit. ★★★ $92.99

The Clouded Yellow

(1951, 85 min, GB, Ralph Thomas) Though its title is obtuse, there's nothing incomprehensible about this exciting psychological thriller and whodunit. Trevor Howard plays a British secret agent who is forced into retirement. He accepts a job in the country looking forward to peace and relaxation. There he meets emotionally scarred Jean Simmons, who becomes the prime suspect in the murder of a hired hand. Together, Howard and Simmons flee the countryside in a determined effort to prove her innocence. The film takes its time setting up characterization, but once the chase begins, *The Clouded Yellow* (named after an elusive butterfly) shifts gears and becomes an unpredictable Hitchcock-like chase story which stays suspenseful until the final credits. ★★★½ $39.99

Clouds over Europe

(1939, 78 min, GB, Tim Whelan) Laurence Olivier and especially Ralph Richardson are both in terrific form in this taut, little-known espionage thriller which — à la *The Thin Man* — combines unusually witty comedy with a darn good mystery. Set in England at the start of WWII, the film stars Richardson as a government agent who is investigating the disappearance of top secret British aircraft. Olivier is one of the pilots who helps crack both the case and the skulls of the Nazis behind the scurrilous plot. Also with Valerie Hobson as Richardson's reporter sibling. (aka: *Q Planes*) ★★★½ $19.99

The Clowns

(1970, 90 min, Italy, Federico Fellini) This "documentary" within a film is a three-ring circus of spectacle, slapstick and sensation. Fellini (acting in the film as head of the camera crew) lovingly pays homage to the circus clowns of his childhood. (Italian with English subtitles) ★★★ $39.99

The Club

(1980, 93 min, Australia, Bruce Beresford) This unheralded Beresford find is not considered one of his best, but proves to be an entertaining if pedestrian sports drama. Jack Thompson is terrific as the inspirational coach of a soccer club who must change his team's losing ways and rally them to a championship. The film's not brain surgery but at least it's better than *The Fish That Saved Pittsburgh*. ★★½

Club des Femmes

(1936, 90 min, France, Jacques Deval) Danielle Darrieux stars as a nightclub entertainer who lives with several other women in a hotel in Paris where men are banned. The women's lives and fates unravel in this entertaining, playfully energetic farce. (French with English subtitles) ★★★

Club Extinction

(1990, 112 min, France/West Germany/Italy, Claude Chabrol) A stunning futuristic tale about a German society plagued by a series of violent, unexplained suicides. Originally titled *Dr. M.* (perhaps in homage to Fritz Lang's entropic character), the film stars Alan Bates as the megalomaniacal Dr. Marsfeldt, head of an all-powerful media organization and self-professed "travel agent" for whom death is the ultimate vacation. Jennifer Beals is oddly (but effectively) cast as Marsfeldt's unwitting ally and the useless Andrew McCarthy has a brief cameo as an assassin. Fans of the cerebral science fiction of the '70s will find this a welcome treat. ★★★ $89.99

Club Paradise

(1986, 96 min, US, Harold Ramis) A good cast isn't enough to totally save this waterlogged comedy about a disabled firefighter (Robin Williams) who becomes partners with a reggae nightclub owner (Jimmy Cliff) in a broken-down Caribbean resort. Peter O'Toole, Rick Moranis, Twiggy, Adolph Caesar and Joanna Cassidy also star. ★★ $9.99

Clue — The Movie

(1985, 96 min, US, Jonathan Lynn) A good cast is wasted in this limp, gimmicky mystery-comedy based on the popular board game. Eileen Brennan, Tim Curry, Madeline Kahn, Christopher Lloyd, Michael McKean and Lesley Ann Warren are on hand to find out if it was Mrs. Peacock in the library with the candlestick. Or was it Col. Mustard in the hall with the rope? Who cares? ★ $14.99

Clueless

(1995, 97 min, US, Amy Heckerling) What writer-director Heckerling did for the 1980s with *Fast Times at Ridgemont High* she does for the '90s in this hilariously witty send-up of high school life and adolescence (California upper-middle class specifically). The superficial but naively intelligent Cher (Alicia Silverstone), a carefree 15-year-old beauty with not much on her mind but clothes, social standing and boys, comes to a life decision to use her good looks and popularity for good causes. Aided by her two vacuous friends Dionne (she and Cher are both "named after a great singer of the past who now has an infomercial") and new student Tai, Cher sets out on a glorious quest to play matchmaker and good samaritan to anyone within arm's reach — but will she herself find true love? Heckerling's delicious screenplay, an updating of Jane Austen's "Emma," is one mirthful exposition after another, playfully lampooning the teenage milieu — there's a gallery of funny one-liners and comic vignettes. Bringing more depth and humor to Cher than would ever be expected, Silverstone proves herself an impeccable comedienne giving a cheerful, uproarious performance. ★★★½ $14.99

Coal Miner's Daughter

(1980, 125 min, US, Michael Apted) Sissy Spacek won an Oscar for her stirring portrait of country singer Loretta Lynn in this accomplished musical biography. The film follows Lynn's rise from a poor Kentucky mining town to country music superstar. Tommy Lee Jones gives a fine performance as Lynn's husband, and Beverly D'Angelo is sensational as Patsy Cline. ★★★½ $14.99

Cobb

(1994, 128 min, US, Ron Shelton) Ty Cobb was one of the greats on the field, but off it he was despised by the players and public alike. *Cobb*, Shelton's demanding and intriguing adaptation of Al Stump's myth-shaking novel, makes it easy to see why. Tommy Lee Jones gives a big, brash performance as the baseball great, now in his 70s. He's just hired second-string reporter Stump (Robert Wuhl) to write his biography. But as Stump gathers biographical information, he soon comes to realize that the legend of Ty Cobb is greatly contradicted by the actions of the man — a violent bigot. With Jones raging like a venom-spewing dragon, Shelton takes the chance of alienating most viewers. But it only underscores his story about the demystification of our heroes, and the price it extracts. Shelton could have even gone further at showing Cobb's ugly side, but here less is more. Playing William Holden to Jones' Gloria Swanson, Wuhl's one-dimensional portrayal is the major weakness of the film. ★★★ $19.99

Cobra

(1986, 87 min, US, Sylvester Stallone) Sylvester Stallone does his *Dirty Harry* bit with far less successful results as a Los Angeles detective hunting a serial killer. Dramatically sloppy and very gory. ★ $9.99

The Coca-Cola Kid

(1985, 94 min, Australia/US, Dusan Makavejev) Makavejev directed this strangely enjoyable, captialist/sexual comedy which stars Eric Roberts as an overly motivated American corporate whiz kid in search of new markets. Landing in Australia, he encounters difficulty with several stubbornly eccentric Aussies. Makavejev weaves his plot with characteristic absurdity and sensuality. Co-starring Greta Scacchi. ★★★ $14.99

Cocaine Cowboys

(1979, 87 min, US, Ulli Lommel) A strange story of a rock 'n' roll band who smuggle cocaine to help pay their expenses. They fall into trouble with their underworld financiers when a shipment of coke is lost in the ocean. Starring Jack Palance, and produced by Andy Warhol. ★

El Cochecito

(1960, 90 min, Spain, Marco Ferreri) This tragi-comedy is something of a perverse one-joke film — old dad, perfectly fit, nonetheless demands from his son a motorized wheelchair in order to socialize properly with his crippled

friends. This film wears thin after a while, but it does contain moments of truly bizarre black comedy while making points about the elderly and their loneliness. (Spanish with English subtitles) ★★

Cock & Bull Story

(1992, 80 min, US, Billy Hayes) "Midnight Express" author Hayes directed this potent two-man drama which was performed by the San Quentin Drama Workshop and video-taped before a live audience. The story is set in a small English town in a gym locker room where Jacko (Mark Sheppard), a boxer with hopes of making it big in London, trains for an upcoming event. His best mate, the fast-talking Travis (Trevor Goddard), hangs around and they engage in a series of tension-filled, sexually charged admissions and revelations about their personal feelings. Amidst the taunts and the macho posturing by the working-class youths comes the reality that the two can only express themselves through violence, despite their deep feelings to the contrary. Flat sound quality due to the live recording mars this otherwise gripping story. ★★★

Cockfighter

(1974, 83 min, US, Monte Hellman) Warren Oates stars as a trainer of fighting cocks whose illegal profession threatens his relationship with girlfriend Patricia Pearcy. A fascinating, offbeat drama directed by Hellman (*Two-Lane Blacktop*). ★★★

Cocktail

(1988, 100 min, US, Roger Donaldson) A completely witless, slick and formulaic piece of celluloid junk food. Tom Cruise stars as a young go-getter who arrives in the Big Apple, ready to cut himself a slice of the Wall Street action. To his dismay, he ends up working in a trendy Uptown bar where — under the tutelage of master bartender and part-time philosopher Bryan Brown — he's seduced by the life of quick money and easy women. ★½ $9.99

The Cocoanuts

(1929, 96 min, US, Joseph Santley) The Marx Brothers' first cinematic exercise in mayhem has the feel of the Vaudeville stage where they cut their teeth. The setting is a Florida hotel rapidly losing money under Groucho's management. All the elements of inspired madness are here, not the least of which is rapid-fire double-talk. ★★★ $14.99

Cocoon

(1985, 117 min, US, Ron Howard) Endearing, sentimental sci-fi fantasy about a group of Florida senior citizens who discover a fountain of youth — courtesy of the planet-hopping aliens next door. Exceptional cast of veteran performers includes Jessica Tandy, Hume Cronyn, Wilford Brimley, Jack Gilford, Maureen Stapleton, Gwen Verdon, Brian Dennehy, and an Oscar-winning turn by breakdancer extraordinaire Don Ameche. ★★★ $9.99

Cocoon: The Return

(1988, 116 min, US, Daniel Petrie) All the stars of the highly successful *Cocoon* return in this frequently charming though ordinary sequel which brings Don Ameche, Wilford

Brimley, Maureen Stapleton, Jessica Tandy, Hume Cronyn and Gwen Verdon back to Earth for a four-day visit. The plot borrows greatly from the original and the story is too syrupy and heavy-handed, but the cast helps to capture a little of the magic of the first film. ★★ $9.99

Un Coeur en Hiver

(1992, 100 min, France, Claude Sautet) Sautet's emotionally cool and complex film is a startling look at love, passion and miscommunication. Andre Dussollier plays a man who leaves his wife for a young, beautiful concert violinist, played by Emmanuelle Beart. After meeting her lover's business partner (Daniel Auteuil), she soon falls in love with him. Set in the world of contemporary classical music, *Un Coeur en Hiver* is a fascinating film and rewarding experience. Auteuil's performance as the cold and emotionally void object of affection is an underrated gem. (French with English subtitles) ★★★½ $9.99

Cold Comfort Farm

Coffy

(1973, 91 min, US, Jack Hill) Duck for cover! Hipswinging Pam Grier, the queen of blaxploitation, is packing and out for violent revenge! Spurred by her little sister's drug overdose, nurse Coffy becomes a one-woman execution squad as she seeks out the people responsible. Sexy, smart and always willing to bare her considerable assets in the line of duty, our sweet heroine poses as a prostitute as she battles crooked politicians, L.A. cops on the take (the more things change...), Italian drug pushers and Super Fly-attired pimps. She blows them all away in this violent, action-packed thriller. ★★½ $9.99

Cold Blood

(1978, 90 min, West Germany, Ralf Gregan & Gunter Vaesse) It is truly amazing how many mediocre Rutger Hauer films (*Fatal Error*, *Dandelions*, *Mysteries*, *Cold Blood*) are turning up from the dusty film vaults of Holland and Germany. But as every Rutger fan knows, as long as our handsome star is in it, and he sheds his clothes at least once, it's worth watching. This "dishonor among thieves" drama features a hot-blooded, miniskirt clad young woman who falls for the charming but coldly opportunistic Rutger and ends up in a nightmarish adventure. The film keeps one's attention, but the ending is ridiculous. (Dubbed) ★★ $9.99

Cold Comfort Farm

(1995, 99 min, GB, John Schlesinger) What begins as a seemingly familiar "Masterpiece Theatre"/Merchant Ivory-style upper-class English drama soon turns into a raucously funny satire that must be considered as one of director Schlesinger's best efforts. In the 1930s, pretty but naive Flora Poste (Kate Beckinsale) finds herself an orphan (and penniless), so she decides to claim her "rights" by moving from her posh London home to the estate of her rural relatives, the Starkadders of Sussex. And that is where the drawing room familiarity ends; for the doom-laden Starkadders, saddled by an ancient curse, are one sorry lot. They live in medieval squalor, talk in olde English and are far from accomodating to their high-falooting cousin. But Flora, who sees a "project" with them, rolls up her sleeves and, with a smile on her pretty face, pulls the family into the 20th century. Adapted from Stella Gibbons' 1932 parody, this delightful film also stars Ian McKellen as the curmudgeon father, Stephen Fry as a bungling writer hopelessly smitten with Flora, and Joanna Lumley as her comically supercilious aunt. ★★★★ $14.99

A Cold Coming

(1992, 70 min, US, David Gadberry) Earnest intention from playwright Howard Casner and director-star Gadberry cannot breathe life into this stagebound gay drama. Lovers for more than three years, Dave and John find themselves stranded one day at a train station during a blizzard. It is there that they begin to confront the reality that, despite emotional ties, their relationship is crumbling. Through flashbacks of their happier courtship days, the couple discusses, kvetches and argues on what has gone wrong while attempting a reconciliation. A low-budget production that is marred by being short on dramatic punch. Note: The sound clarity and volume fluctuate during the second half of the film. ★★ $59.99

Cold Feet

(1984, 96 min, US, Bruce van Dusen) Griffin Dunne and Marissa Chibas, both involved in non-gratifying relationships, take a chance on each other in a final stab at romance. Blanche Baker has some good scenes as Dunne's ex-wife in this otherwise static comedy. ★★ $59.99

Cold Feet

(1989, 94 min, US, Robert Dornhelm) Screenwriter and novelist Tom McGuane's engrossing comedy, set in Montana, stars Keith Carradine as the sanest in a trio of modern-day desperados whose partners include his over-sexed wife-to-be Sally Kirkland and Tom Waits as a charming but dangerous killer bent on revenge after being jilted out of the money from their last heist. The couple's attempts to settle down in

anonymity with their loot prove to be as elusive as the law, and their own lust and greed finally undermine their demented idea of the American Dream. This outrageous comedy is engaging and fun, although the writing seems forced at times with zany characters trying a bit too hard to be "weird." ★★★ $89.99

Cold Fever

(1995, 85 min, Iceland, Fridrik Thor Fridriksson) A young Japanese executive, Atsuhi Hirata (Masatoshi Nagase), forgoes a sunny golfing holiday in Hawaii in order to conduct a traditional memorial ceremony in honor of his dead parents. To complete this ritual, he must travel to the harsh, wintry wilderness of Iceland, where he meets an oddball assortment of eccentric characters as unpredictable and disarming as the untamed landscape itself. As Hirata travels through the frozen wasteland, his journey of making peace with the dead becomes a personal quest for inner solace, made all the more powerful and mesmerizing by the film's spellbinding cinematography. Thoroughly absorbing, *Cold Fever* shifts from quirky comedy to contemplative, existential drama and coalesces into a meditative, heady comment on spirituality and an individual's place in the world. Nagase starred in *Mystery Train*, but the most familiar faces are Lili Taylor and Fisher Stevens, who show up as obnoxious American tourists. (In English and Japanese and Icelandic with English subtitles) ★★★½ $94.99

Cold Heaven

(1992, 105 min, US, Nicolas Roeg) Anyone who thinks the age of chivalry is dead should take a look at the career of director Roeg who, after 21 years of living on the cutting edge of cinema, now seems content to simply make movies to keep his wife (actress Theresa Russell) employed. Case in point: this unabashedly moralistic drama that veers wildly between being a supernatural thriller and a Hallmark greeting card. Russell essays the role of an unfaithful wife who experiences extreme Catholic guilt when her husband (Mark Harmon) is killed before she can make amends. Also with Talia Shire and Will Patton. ★ $14.99

Cold Sassy Tree

(1989, 100 min, US, Joan Tewkesbury) Faye Dunaway and Richard Widmark give affecting performances in this wonderful May-December romance about Northerner Dunaway and widower Widmark's affair shocking his turn-of-the-century Southern town. ★★★ $14.99

Cold Turkey

(1971, 99 min, US, Norman Lear) A '60s-ish comedy about a small town and their efforts to stop smoking for a month to win $25 million in prize money. A pleasant romp, with Dick Van Dyke as the priest spearheading the campaign, and a good supporting cast including Bob Newhart, Tom Poston, Vincent Gardenia, Jean Stapleton and Edward Everett Horton. ★★★ $19.99

Colegas

(1980, 117 min, Spain, Eloy de la Iglesia) A fine drama about the friendship between

three teenagers in present-day Madrid. Jose and Antonio have been friends for most of their lives, but their relationship is severely tested after it is discovered that Antonio's sister, Rosario, is pregnant by Jose. Their efforts to get an abortion in Catholic Spain lead them to Morocco and the dangerous drug trade. (Spanish with English subtitles) ★★★ $89.99

The Collection

(1978, 64 min, GB, Michael Apted) Laurence Olivier, Alan Bates, Malcolm McDowell and Helen Mirren deliver outstanding performances in this gripping adaptation of Harold Pinter's critically acclaimed 1960 play. Harry (Olivier) and Bill (McDowell) are an embittered gay couple who come under attack from the menacing Bates when he accuses the younger Bill of sleeping with his wife (Mirren). Veiled threats and jealousy give way to deception, disappointment and betrayal as all four characters become trapped in a series of recriminations. Olivier called the play one of the best of the British stage. ★★★½

La Collectionneuse

(1966, 88 min, France, Eric Rohmer) Rohmer's *La Collectionneuse* is an interesting investigation of gender politics as well as modern notions of art, beauty and truth. Subtitled as a "fable," the fourth in a series of six, the film offers an unusual parable for those unschooled in the complex games of sexual pairing. *La Collectionneuse* is a "moral" film to the extent that its characters are concerned with their own psychological motivations. Rohmer's attention to thought process is evident both in his story and its structure. The story revolves around Adrian, a self-important would-be gallery owner, his painter friend Daniel and a Lolita-esque nymphette (Haydeé Politoff). Adrian attempts to protect his solitude after he finds himself sharing a villa with the others on the Riviera. Though he first resists her, Adrian later becomes obsessed with the young girl's charms. The story unfolds through Adrian's voice-over with a minimal and beautiful use of visual explication. Though the narrative is at times overbearing and didactic, the film maintains an even pace, thorough characterization and a solid story. (French with English subtitles) ★★★ $19.99

The Collector

(1965, 119 min, US, William Wyler) Searing psychological thriller with Terence Stamp kidnapping Samantha Eggar and keeping her prisoner in his basement. Superior performances from the two leads. ★★★½ $59.99

College

(1927, 65 min, US, James W. Horne) Buster Keaton stars as a scholar who looks down on athletics but is forced to participate in order to win the attention of his girl. Compared to other Keaton comedies, this is minor, but it is elevated by some memorable gags. ★★★ $29.99

College Swing

(1938, 86 min, US, Raoul Walsh) Bob Hope's second film, in which he receives fourth billing behind co-stars George Burns, Gracie Allen and Martha Raye, is an intermittently amusing hodge-podge of music, laughs, swing, academia and romance. It's palatable when the four leads and Edward Everett Horton are on screen. But some of the musical numbers, an icky romance subplot, and a few comic sequences are rough going. However, it's one of the few films from the 1930s to actually show living and breathing teenagers. They're the real *Swing Kids*. ★★ $14.99

Colonel Redl

(1984, 144 min, Hungary/West Germany, István Szabó) Klaus Maria Brandauer (*Mephisto*) gives a bravura performance as a man driven by a lust for power to rise from the son of a poor railway worker to become head of military intelligence and commander of the 8th Army in Prague. A sweeping historical epic of intrigue, love and treason set in Austria during the turbulent years leading up to World War I. Winner — Jury Prize, Cannes Film Festival, 1985. (German with English subtitles) ★★★

Color Me Blood Red

(1965, 74 min, US, Hershell Gordon Lewis) The third of Lewis' gore films stars Don Joseph as a struggling artist who finds that blood supplies the perfect color for his newest painting. Upon realizing that he has only so much... With the usual bad acting and homemade (but always disturbing) gore F/X. ★ $29.99

The Color of Money

(1986, 119 min, US, Martin Scorsese) Paul Newman won an Oscar for re-creating his acclaimed role as *The Hustler*, "Fast Eddie" Felsen, ex-pool hustler turned liquor retailer, who vicariously relives the glory days of his youth through a hotshot pool player (Tom Cruise). With Scorsese's inventive direction and Robbie Robertson's smoky score, this is a rare film experience. ★★★★ $9.99

Color of Night

(1994, 120 min, US, Richard Rush) Sigmund Freud meets a limp *Die Hard* in this mildly diverting but far from mysterious murder mystery starring Bruce Willis as a troubled psychologist who gets caught up in a series of murders. After one of his patients throws herself from his New York penthouse, Willis moves to L.A. where he becomes involved in murder, car chases, a group therapy session from hell, and a mystery woman. Willis tries to play off his "tough guy" image (his character is a gun-fearing Clark Kent-type), but it doesn't last long. This video release is the "director's cut" and runs 15 minutes longer. Included are the controversial frontal nude scenes of Willis. Will the prospect of capturing a glimpse of Willis' willy cause thousands of TLA customers to abandon good taste and rent this film? We certainly hope so — but be prepared to be disappointed. ★★ $14.99

The Color of Pomegranates

(1969, 80 min, USSR/Armenia, Sergei Paradjanov) Shelved after being termed "hermetic and obscure" by Soviet authorities, this poetic masterpiece was the last film director Paradjanov made before his five-year imprisonment in 1974 on trumped up charges of "incitement to suicide, speculation in foreign currency, spreading venereal disease, homosexuality and speculation in art objects." *The Color of Pomegranates* focuses on the powerful works and spiritual odyssey of 17th-century Armenian poet Sayat Nova. Filled with oblique, symbolic imagery, this exotic mosaic of a film is divided into eight sections, each depicting — from childhood to death — a period of the poet's life. A tribute not only to Nova but to the spirituality of the Armenian people, Paradjanov's film is for specialized tastes and those devotees who have a knowlegde of or interest in the poet and Armenia. (Armenian with English subtitles) ★★★½ $29.99

The Color Purple

(1985, 152 min, US, Steven Spielberg) Spielberg's acclaimed though controversial screen version of Alice Walker's Pulitzer Prize-winning novel. Whoopi Goldberg made a triumphant film debut as a black woman who tries to overcome the hardships of her arranged marriage to ill-tempered Danny Glover to find her own identity. Oprah Winfrey and Margaret Avery are both terrific in support as, respectively, the live-in maid to an oppressive white family, and Glover's mistress, a cabaret singer who contributes greatly to Goldberg's flourishing. (Available letterboxed and pan & scan) ★★★½ $19.99

Colors

(1988, 120 min, US, Dennis Hopper) A clamorous vision of gang warfare in Los Angeles directed by Hopper, with his patented flair for the unusual and bizarre. Robert Duvall and Sean Penn are fine in their roles as L.A. cops, but what really gives the film its edge is the presence of actual gang members whom Hopper cast to play the Bloods and the Crips — the city's largest rival gangs. Without totally departing from action movie conventions, *Colors* brims with flavor and detail and features a tremendous soundtrack. ★★★ $9.99

Coma

(1978, 113 min, US, Michael Crichton) Solid medical thriller adapted and directed by former med student Crichton. Genevieve Bujold is a Boston doctor whose investigations into a series of inexplicable hospital deaths leads her to a horrifying conspiracy. Michael Douglas is her disbelieving boyfriend, and Richard Widmark is well-cast as a hospital administrator. ★★★ $14.99

Combination Platter

(1993, 85 min, US/China, Tony Chan) Director Chan elicits finely drawn characterizations with minimal exposition in this low-budget independent feature. Centering around the efforts of a young, newly arrived Hong Kong emigré to get his green card, the deceptively simple story line allows a good ensemble cast to reveal the distinct personalities of a group of restaurant employees dealing with interpersonal conflicts, annoying customers, Department of Immigration agents and familial expectations. A small film, but knowing and direct in its execution. (In English and Chinese with English subtitles) ★★★ $89.99

Come and Get It

(1936, 99 min, US, Howard Hawks, William Wyler) An aggressive entrepreneur abandons the Northwest timber country for the boss' daughter. Many years later, through a quirky trick of fate, he's deluded into believing that he can revoke that decision of youth. Robust performances throughout, especially Frances Farmer in a dual role, Edward Arnold, Joel McCrea and Walter Brennan, who won an Oscar for Best Supporting Actor. ★★★ $19.99

Come and See

(1985, 142 min, USSR, Elem Klimov) The theatrical availability in 1987 of this remarkably powerful Russian film by the long-ostracized director Elem Klimov was one of the first tangible results of *glasnost* in the Soviet Union. Told with a barrage of some of the most harrowing and electrifying imagery in modern cinema, *Come and See* is an account of the brutal invasion suffered by the Russians at the hands of Hitler. Episodes shift back and forth between the ultra-realistic and a dreamlike surrealism which borders on hallucinogenic. As seen through the eyes of a young boy, the Nazi atrocities against his village, including its ultimate destruction, burn the screen with fierce images which will linger in our consciousness for a long time to come. A powerful cinematic achievement. (Russian with English subtitles) ★★★★ $59.99

Come Back, Little Sheba

(1952, 99 min, US, Daniel Mann) Though she'll probably always be remembered as TV's "Hazel," Shirley Booth's finest hour came when she set the stage and screen afire with her unforgettable Oscar-winning performance as the down-trodden wife of an alcoholic (Burt Lancaster). In this brilliant screen version of William Inge's play, Booth and Lancaster rent their home to young Terry Moore, setting the stage for jealousy and recriminations. ★★★★ $19.99

Come Back to the 5 & Dime, Jimmy Dean, Jimmy Dean

(1982, 110 min, US, Robert Altman) Sandy Dennis, Cher, Karen Black and Kathy Bates are the participants in the emotional warfare of a James Dean Fan Club reunion in a dust-bowl Texas town. Sandy's psyche, Cher's chest, Karen's contours and Kathy's sobriety are all in question as every skeleton tumbles from the closet in Altman's bitchy, Southern cat fight. ★★★

Come See the Paradise

(1990, 138 min, US, Alan Parker) Parker follows up *Mississippi Burning* by setting his sights once again on racial intolerance in this story of the internment of Japanese-Americans in camps during WWII. Parker gets credit for tackling a subject heretofore untouched by any American film, though one wishes the story had more dramatic structure. The first half of the film follows the love affair between a projectionist (Dennis Quaid) and his Asian boss' daughter (Tamlyn Tomita). Married for only a short time, they are separated after the bombing of Pearl Harbor. Quaid is drafted, and

Tomita and her entire family are uprooted and sent to the camps. The remainder of the film centers on the heartbreaking conditions they face, only to be remedied by the end of the war. ★★★ $19.99

The Comedy of Terrors

(1963, 84 min, US, Jacques Tourneur) This outstanding horror/comedy has all the hallmarks and crew members of a Roger Corman production, but was instead directed by Val Lewton's disciple Tourneur. Vincent Price and Peter Lorre star as two bumbling undertakers who supplement their business by murdering elderly potential clientel. Boris Karloff also stars as Price's father-in-law, and Basil Rathbone plays a vengeful landlord who accidentally becomes an on-again, off-again customer. With a hilarious and extremely literate script by Richard Matheson, superb art direction, beautiful cinematography (by Floyd Crosby) and an impressive score, The Comedy of Terrors stands alongside Corman's best Price/Poe films. It's a devious send-up of the best Shakespearean tragedies which succeeds as both black comedy and tongue-in-cheek horror camp. ★★★½ $14.99

Comes a Horseman

(1978, 118 min, US, Alan J. Pakula) In Montana after the second world war, ranch owner Jason Robards wants Jane Fonda's spread because he knows something she doesn't – there's oil under her land. The only thing stopping him: tough cowboy James Caan. Featuring a great supporting performance by Richard Farnsworth as Fonda's dedicated ranch hand. ★★★ $14.99

Comfort and Joy

(1984, 90 min, GB, Bill Forsyth) Forsyth called this whimsical odyssey a mixture of "Alice in Wonderland" and Sullivan's Travels. When his kleptomaniac, live-in lover abandons him, Alan (a cheerfully bland Glasgow radio personality) falls into a frightful funk and, aimlessly searching for salvation, stumbles into the midst of a gangland battle between rival factions of an ice cream cartel. ★★★ $69.99

The Comfort of Strangers

(1991, 102 min, US, Paul Schrader) Director Schrader (Patty Hearst) once again delves into the dark side of human nature with this visually exquisite production of Harold Pinter's screenplay about a young English couple (Rupert Everett, Natasha Richardson) who retreat to Venice to re-evaluate their relationship, and find themselves pawns in the twisted games of an Italian nobleman and his invalid wife (Christopher Walken, Helen Mirren). Marred only slightly by a seemingly unmotivated shock ending, this quirky entertainment. ★★★ $89.99

Comic Book Confidential

(1990, 85 min, US, Ron Mann) For devotees of animation, comic books and the creative forces behind them, this fascinating and delightful documentary is required viewing. The film combines historical footage, montages of comic art and a series of amusing interviews with many of the leading independent anima-

tors of the last 20 years, including William M. Gaines (of Mad Magazine fame), Stan Lee, Robert Crumb, Linda Barry, Art Spiegelman and many others. From the very first comic, "Funnies on Parade," to the very latest, "Raw," the film provides an entertaining and informational peek behind the animated doors of comics and their creators. ★★★ $29.99

Coming Home

(1978, 127 min, US, Hal Ashby) The stunning, Oscar-winning performances of Jon Voight and Jane Fonda dominate this moving Vietnam war drama about disabled Voight beginning an affair with married Fonda, whose husband Bruce Dern is overseas. A poignant love story and gripping anti-war film which unfortunately over-dramatizes some of its key scenes. ★★★ $14.99

Coming Out under Fire

(1994, 71 min, US, Arthur Dong) Adding yet another significant chapter in transposing oral lesbian/gay history onto film/video, this entertaining and eye-opening documentary centers on nine lesbians and gay men and their experiences as "undesirables" in the armed forces during World War II. Based on Allen Berube's book "Coming Out under Fire: The History of Gay Men and Women in World War II," the film provides both a historical overview of the American government's shifting attitudes towards gays in the military as well as allowing the interviewees to describe vivid personal experiences of the discriminatory practices of their own government. The film comes alive when the often eloquent vets recount both their good times (camaraderie with other gays/lesbians, wartime romances) and bad (arrests and discharges) living as closeted homosexuals in an organization that viewed them as either unfit for service, morally suspect or potentially hazardous to morale. At least 9,000 gay men and women were dishonorably discharged during WWII. ★★★ $29.99

Coming to America

(1988, 116 min, US, John Landis) Only sporadically funny, this Eddie Murphy comedy is surprisingly good-natured, a change of pace for the comic. Murphy stars as an African prince engaged to a native woman who decides to leave his home and head to New York in search of true love. Arsenio Hall also stars as his "man Friday" who accompanies the prince on his quest. What ensues is a rather formulaic fish-out-of-water tale with most of its jokes telegraphed hours before they arrive. ★★½ $14.99

Coming Up Roses

(1986, 93 min, GB, Stephen Bayly) This Welsh-language comedy is a mildly amusing updating of The Smallest Show on Earth. Against the grim landscape of Thatcher's England, three employees of a dilapidated movie theatre struggle to save the old house. (Welsh with English subtitles) ★★½ $29.99

Command Decision

(1949, 113 min, US, Sam Wood) Clark Gable stars as an Air Force general wrestling with his conscience about sending young men off to a certain death in order to achieve a strategic

victory. Walter Pidgeon plays Gable's superior officer, and Van Johnson is a raw recruit. A gripping and thoughtful war adventure based on the '40s stage hit. ★★★ $19.99

Commando

(1985, 90 min, US, Mark L. Lester) This fast-paced and often amusing adventure thriller is one of Arnold Schwarzenegger's best action films from the early part of his career. Arnold plays a retired Army colonel who sets out to rescue his young daughter, kidnapped by an exiled Latin American dictator. ★★ $9.99

Commercial Mania

(1950s-60s, 60 min, US) In this TeeVee Time Capsule, Rhino Video argues for our side in the debate "Resolved: Communism is dead because Wonderbread builds strong bodies twelve ways." Reddy Kilowat touts the adventure of electricity from the atom, Lucy and Desi push cancer sticks, and a former ex-president shills for soap in his most challenging role. $19.99

The Commies Are Coming!
The Commies Are Coming!

(1950s, US) This is a tape every American must see, and if you don't rent this tape, it will be known by those whose job it is to prevent the onslaught of commie decay from within. Jack Webb hosts two cautionary tales that could happen here. What would it be like if your typical family woke up one day only to find that the Reds had taken over? What would you do? The second is a searing exposé torn from the headlines of tomorrow about a Red training camp that looks like Anytown, USA, where commie spys are trained to live just like you and me. Ever wonder about that guy next door, the one who has lots of strange male visitors at all hours of the day and night and puts out lots of empty wine bottles on trash day? You are America's first line of defense! $39.99

Commissar

(1967, 105 min, USSR, Alexander Askoldov) Banned for 21 years by Soviet authorities, this remarkable human drama shocked the censors with its bold themes of anti-Semitism and women's rights. Set in 1920 during the austere Russian Civil War, the story follows the austere Claudia, whose military career as a Red Army Commander is jeopardized when she becomes pregnant by a comrade. Needing to hide this unwanted pregnancy from officials, she moves in with a poor Jewish family in the countryside until the child is born. Initially hostile to the family's religion and peasant ways, she soon finds herself softening and appreciating the cultural differences they have as well as the common bonds they all share. After the child is born, she faces the difficult choice of staying or rejoining the army. (Russian with English subtitles) ★★★½ $59.99

Commissioner of the Sewers

(1986, 60 min, US, Klaus Maeck) From the publication of his novel "Junkie" in 1963 through the present with the Hollywood-backed film version of his "Naked Lunch," William S. Burroughs has remained a controversial and fascinating figure. This documentary doesn't uncover anything new for seasoned Burroughs-philes, but for the uninitiated, it will prove to be enlightening as Burroughs, with his deadpan wit and outlandish theories, pontificates on everything from his beliefs on death after life, art and artists, to the meaning of his cut-up style of writing. He reads excerpts from his book "The Western Lands" and concludes with a reading of his now famous, and bitterly sarcastic, "Thanksgiving Prayer." ★★½ $29.99

The Commitments
(1991, 116 min, Ireland, Alan Parker) Parker's exuberant homage to the Dublin music scene has at its heart a highly talented cast of non-actors recruited for their musical skills. The story follows Jimmy, a determined young hustler who can't rest until he realizes his dreams of putting together a soul group. What the film lacks in plot is more than amply made up for in raw energy and outstanding musical numbers, all of which were actually performed by the cast. It may be hard to believe, but some of the versions of soul standards ("Try a Little Tenderness" and "Mustang Sally" to name just a few) compare very favorably with the originals. ★★★½ $19.99

Committed
(1984, 77 min, US, Sheila McLaughlin & Lynne Tillman) Committed tells the striking story of film star/leftist iconoclast Frances Farmer (Come and Get It, The Toast of New York). While dealing with the same subject as the 1982 Hollywood feature Frances, with Jessica Lange, this independent production avoids some of the theatrics in this feminist interpretation of her life. In 1935, Farmer was an overnight Hollywood sensation; within ten years she was in a state mental hospital. From stardom to a locked ward to a lobotomy, the film reconstructs a compelling and many-layered look at the life and repression of this culturally defiant woman. ★★★ $59.99

Common Threads: Stories from the Quilt
(1989, 79 min, US, Robert Epstein & Jeffrey Friedman) An Academy Award-winning documentary from the director of the acclaimed The Times of Harvey Milk. Epstein and co-director Friedman talk with surviving relatives and friends of five people who died of AIDS and were memorialized by the AIDS Quilt. Narrated by Dustin Hoffman, the film presents an emotionally charged look into their lives, as told by those left behind through recollection, photographs and film. Of course, there is great poignancy to these stories. But the storytellers also infuse a spirit of being to the departed which obviously helps keep the memory of those loved-ones alive. Not a eulogistic memorial, but rather personal and heartfelt reminiscences. ★★★½ $19.99

Common-Law Cabin
(1967, 83 min, US, Russ Meyer) Alaina Capri (42-24-36) as "Sheila" — a roman candle too hot to hold — goes through men like a box of matches! Babette Bardot (42-24-36) as "Babette," an uncommon common-law wife, is caught up in the lovelust of a man for his daughter! Adele Rein (42-24-36) is "Coral," an

innocent girl, lost in the body of a woman coveted by three men...one her father! $79.99

Communion
(1989, 109 min, US, Philippe Mora) Based on Whitley Strieber's best-seller, which detailed his experiences with alien beings, this serious-minded science-fiction thriller is far more interesting for the allegations presented by the author than for any noteworthy achievements from either the director or the cast. Christopher Walken, usually adept at playing eccentric characters, gives a truly strange performance as Strieber. The only cast member to really come out of this muddle totally unscathed is Frances Sternhagen, who plays a psychiatrist all-too-familiar with close encounters of the third kind. ★★

The Company of Wolves
(1985, 95 min, GB, Neil Jordan) An offbeat Freudian adaptation of "Little Red Riding Hood" which intriguingly explores some of the adult subtexts of the classic story. Angela Lansbury and David Warner star in this atmospheric mixture of dreams and fantasy. While the film teeters on the edge of the downright bizarre, it remains a frighteningly mysterious and slightly sexy thriller. Also with Stephen Rea. ★★★ $19.99

Company: Original Cast Album
(1970, 53 min, US, D.A. Pennebaker) Behind-the-scenes look at the recording sessions of Stephen Sondheim's award-winning Broadway musical "Company." The original Broadway cast, including Elaine Stritch, Barbara Barrie and Charles Kimbrough (TV's "Murphy Brown"), and Dean Jones, who replaced lead Larry Kert after three weeks, shine and grind it out in this truly revealing documentary of the creative process at work. To anyone who cherishes the cast recording, and especially Stritch's classic rendering of "The Ladies Who Lunch," this is a must. ★★★ $14.99

Les Comperes
(1983, 92 min, France, Francis Vèber) This very funny farce features the odd-couple Gérard Depardieu and Pierre Richard as the two former lovers of a woman who is desperately looking for her runaway son and who enlists each of them to help find him by telling them both that he is the child's father. Depardieu, as an ox-like journalist, and Richard, as a bumbling depressive, prove to be a winning combo. An inferior American remake, Pure Luck, stars Martin Short and Danny Glover. (French with English subtitles) ★★★½

The Competition
(1984, 129 min, US, Joel Olianski) Concert pianists Amy Irving and Richard Dreyfuss compete against one another for the same prize — only to find romance blossoming between them. It's predictable melodramatics, but the two stars are sincere and the concert footage nicely balances the film. With Lee Remick and Sam Wanamaker. ★★½ $9.99

The Compleat Beatles
(1984, 120 min, GB, Patrick Montgomery) A thorough documentary of the Fab Four, especially strong in its tracing of the group's origins from 1956 Liverpool to their British breakthrough in 1962. George Martin, Billy Preston, Marianne Faithful, Tony Sheridan and Billy J. Kramer are among those who offer up their views and there is, of course, a glut of excellent concert footage. Narrated by Malcolm McDowell. ★★★ $14.99

Le Complot
(1973, 120 min, France, René Granville) Based on recent French history, this taut espionage thriller is not in the same class as Z or Day of the Jackal (based on the same historical episode), but is still gripping entertainment. In 1960, Charles DeGaulle, frustrated by its bloody insurrection, granted Algeria independence, much to the shock of millions of Frenchmen who viewed Algeria as an integral part of French domain. The political unrest spawned by DeGualle's actions resulted in an underground terrorist movement, organized by French-Algerians, fanatical right-wing patriots and disillusioned officers formerly stationed in the North African colony. The labyrinthine webs of alliances, surveillance, deceit and betrayal are revealed as the film follows police and government agencies seeking to destroy the terrorist organization before the Republican order is threatened. Jean Rochefort plays the insurrectionists' leader and Michel Bouquet is the police captain determined to destroy his organization. (French with English subtitles) ★★★

Compromising Positions
(1985, 98 min, US, Frank Perry) This offbeat comic mystery is, for the most part, an entertaining sleeper with the terrific Susan Sarandon as a Long Island housewife who sets out to find just who killed dentist Joe Mantegna. As her investigation ensues, she discovers the womanizing doctor could have been done in by any one of his female patients. Though the film's resolution is not up to par, it's certainly fun getting there. Among the supporting cast, Judith Ivey is terrific as Sarandon's acerbic friend. Raul Julia, Edward Herrmann and Mary Beth Hurt also star. ★★★ $14.99

Compulsion
(1959, 105 min, US, Richard Fleischer) An outstanding, thought-provoking and ultimately suspenseful account of the Leopold-Loeb murder case, Compulsion is an enthralling, three-part, fictionalized telling of the notorious murder trial. Not as experimental as Rope or sexually suggestive as Swoon — two other stories based on the case — the film stars Dean Stockwell and Bradley Dillman as Judd and Artie, two rich geniuses who, seemingly friendless, are involved in a "dangerously close" relationship ('50s code for gay). The first third of the film examines their friendship, with Judd a willing accomplice to Artie's psychological domination. In an attempt to prove a theory of superiority, they kidnap a local boy and murder him. The murder investigation fills the middle third of the film, and the inevitable murder trial follows. Orson Welles appears as their agnostic defense attorney, which is based on Clarence Darrow. Welles, in a magnificent portrayal, delivers some of the most moving

Nicolas Cage in *Con Air*

courtroom speeches outside of *Inherit the Wind*. The triumphant film deeply probes the psyches of the two men in an attempt to understand but not to excuse their actions. ★★★★ $19.99

Con Air

(1997, 115 min, US, Simon West) Producer Jerry Bruckheimer calls on Nicolas Cage to deliver more of the same high-octane excitement of their previous smash, *The Rock*. And more of the same is what you get with *Con Air*, a high-voltage, hyperventilating ride which copies much of *The Rock*'s action framework without necessarily improving upon it. Gritting much teeth, a buffed-up Cage plays a former Army ranger unjustly sentenced to prison. Upon his parole and flight home, his plane is commandeered by a group of ruthless criminals en route to maximum security. Under the leadership of psycho John Malkovich, they plan their getaway unaware that Cage is trying to sabotage their every move. Though *Con Air*'s premise is quite engaging and offers many slam-bang action sequences, the film somewhat suffers from the lack of truly inventive action set pieces – many scenes are edited in a slapdash manner, and some of the film's better stunts we've seen elsewhere. But *Con Air* also has a hip sense of humor, can be a lot of fun, and maintains a good degree of tension throughout. John Cusack nicely plays a U.S. Marshal, and Steve Buscemi nearly steals the show as a Hannibal Lecter-like killer. ★★½ $102.99

Conan the Barbarian

(1981, 129 min, US, John Milius) Robert E. Howard's pulp fantasy hero is given full fleshy form by Arnold Schwarzenegger in the role he was born to play. The story, very faithful to the tone of the original novels, takes us from Conan's barbarian boyhood and his enslavement and training as a pit fighter through sundry minor adventures and escapades, bringing it full circle as he confronts the murderer of his parents and destroyer of his village, the evil sorcerer Thulsa Doom (James Earl Jones). While *Conan* could not be called a particularly cerebral movie, it is without a doubt a rousing adventure and is plenty of chest-thumping, sword-hacking fun for those who appreciate its blend of blood, fantasy, male-bonding and revenge. The testosterone-laden script, by co-writers Milius and Oliver

Stone, wisely gives most of the lines to everyone *but* Arnold, and moves briskly along, alternating fairly evenly between swords and sorcery, the two primary elements of Howard's fiction. Add to this an adventurous musical score and Ron Cobb's outstanding "period fantasy" production design and *Conan* is sure to please. ★★★ $14.99

Conan the Destroyer

(1984, 103 min, US, Richard Fleischer) The emphasis is on comedy, rather than revenge, in this disappointing sequel to the engaging fantasy film debut of Arnold Schwarzenegger. This time around, Conan and cohorts (including a laughable Wilt Chamberlain) must rescue a princess from the clutches of an evil wizard and retrieve a valuable magical item for the princess' kingdom. This story, however, is needlessly complicated, lacking the simplicity and economy of the original film's script, which was its saving grace. *Destroyer*, however, is not without its pleasures: Grace Jones is well-cast as a warrior who becomes a fierce and loyal follower of Conan, and Mako returns from the original as a sometimes powerful, sometimes buffoonish magician. Arnold is given too many lines to say this time around, but manages an admirable performance when he sticks to swinging a sword and flexing his pecs. The final battle between Conan and the evil god is also exciting and in the adventurous spirit of Robert E. Howard's original stories, but is unfortunately not really worth the wait. ★½ $14.99

The Conductor

(1979, 110 min, Poland, Andrzej Wajda) Dubbed with a jarringly inappropriate Polish voice, John Gielgud nevertheless is quite commanding as an elderly Polish émigré and internationally renowned maestro who returns to his homeland after a fifty-year absence. There, he rouses the provincial Gdansk orchestra with a stirring version of Beethoven's "Fifth Symphony." Gielgud, in one of his few starring roles, is believable as the baton-twirling conductor although the film never comes together. (Polish with English subtitles) ★★ $79.99

Coneheads

(1993, 87 min, US, Steve Barron) Surprisingly sophisticated humor, winning performances and neat special effects redeem what might have been just another bastard child sprung from the loins of "Saturday Night Live." Dan Aykroyd and Jane Curtin reprise their roles as Beldar and Primaat Conehead, who become trapped in a world they never made when their ship crash lands in suburbia USA. What initially reads as a one-joke premise (and one of the more tedious of the SNL sketches) is adroitly expanded into ideal entertainment for those who like their comedy off-the-wall and on-the-floor. ★★★ $14.99

Confession of a Serial Killer

(1992, 80 min, US, Mark Blair) This disturbing fact-based account of self-confessed real-life mass murderer Henry Lee Lucas is vividly

and graphically told in flashback after his capture by Texas Rangers. This is a film so lurid and perverse that even avid fans of the genre may want to take a shower after watching. ★ $89.99

Confessions of a Blue Movie Star

(1972, 95 min, West Germany, Karl Martine) Deceptively titled by the video company, this "soft X-rated" pseudo-documentary provides a probing look into the German porn industry. Inadvertently funny, the film is ostensibly a behind-the-scenes look into the making of one particular porno movie: a freely adapted version of "Lysistrata," self-proclaimed as "...cinematic art on the flesh and death of the soul...featuring coitus scenes." With screenwriting credits belonging to none other than Roman Polanski, the film's determinedly serious stance produces many funny episodes, especially when the porn director, an Erich von Stroheim for the raincoat crowd, attempts to make art out of the slamming of naked bodies. (Dubbed with English narration) ★★½ $19.99

Confidentially Yours

(1984, 111 min, France, François Truffaut) Truffaut's final film is a joyously spirited blend of screwball antics and film noir intrigue. The zesty Fanny Ardant is an intrepid Girl Friday determined to clear her boss of a murder charge. This supremely stylish romantic comedy sparkles with the director's joie de vivre. (French with English subtitles) ★★★½ $29.99

Conflict

(1945, 86 min, US, Curtis Bernhardt) An interesting misfire for Humphrey Bogart. Bogie plays a wife-killer who becomes involved in a psychological cat-and-mouse game with psychiatrist Sydney Greenstreet, who devises a scheme to get the murderer to admit his guilt. Alexis Smith is especially good as the younger sister of Bogart's deceased wife. ★★ $19.99

The Conformist

(1969, 115 min, Italy, Bernardo Bertolucci) This fascinating exploration of the emotional roots of Fascism in pre-war Italy ranks as one of the best Italian films of the 1970s. Jean-Louis Trintignant stars as Marcello, a repressed homosexual traumatized by a childhood incident in which he shot the family chauffeur after a seduction attempt. Now as an adult, Marcello longs for conformity and appears to find it when he joins the Italian Fascist Secret Service and tries to hide his homosexuality by marrying a vapid, petite bourgeois woman he barely tolerates. Sent to assassinate his former professor who is now a leading dissident, he meets and is "attracted" to a lesbian and anti-fascist (the alluring Dominique Sanda), who eventually develops into the moral adversary to Marcello's perverted beliefs. Sanda, who performs an exhilarating tango with Stefania Sandrelli, is a strong counterweight to Trintignant's Marcello. (Italian with English subtitles) ★★★★

Congo

(1995, 109 min, US, Frank Marshall) An expedition into the Congo to return a talking ape (don't ask!) to her native habitat turns deadly

C

when the troop stumbles across a legendary diamond mine guarded by a race of killer gorillas. One might expect that such a premise by the author of *Jurassic Park* and handled by the director of *Arachnophobia* would have some degree of style, intelligence and suspense. But here it's three strikes and you're out. Marshall's uninspired direction and a hodge-podge screenplay adaptation by John Patrick Shanley (how'd he get this job?) strips away all but the barest of sci-fi nuance. The result is a frivolous Disney-style adventure which plays like *Swiss Family Robinson*. Ultimately, *Congo* is possibly Crichton's least successful book-to-screen transfer. An adequate ensemble includes Dylan Walsh, Tim Curry and Laura Linney; only Ernie Hudson's tongue-in-cheek portrayal of a "great white hunter" provides enjoyment. (Available letterboxed and pan & scan) ★★ $14.99

A Connecticut Yankee in King Arthur's Court

(1931, 95 min, US, David Butler) Mark Twain's novel gets the Hollywood treatment once over in this version starring Will Rogers. Rogers was a force to be reckoned with back in the 1930s, with his "I only know what I read in the papers" attitude softening the sting of his satire that would have gotten him branded a "fellow traveler" in the dark ages of the '50s. This version starts in a haunted house with radio repairman Rogers getting blasted back to the 6th century and ends with Model Ts riding to the rescue of King and country. Unlike the Bing Crosby version, Rogers never sings. Also with Maureen O'Sullivan and Myrna Loy. ★★★ $19.99

A Connecticut Yankee in King Arthur's Court

(1949, 107 min, US, Tay Garnett) Musicalized, pleasant third screen version of the Mark Twain tale, with Bing Crosby as a 20th-century blacksmith who is transported back in time to the court of King Arthur. With Rhonda Fleming and William Bendix. ★★½ $14.99

A Connecticut Yankee

The Conqueror Worm

(1968, 88 min, GB, Michael Reeves) Vincent Price stars as Matthew Hopkins in this fascinating historical drama originally known as *Witchfinder General*. Set in 17th-century England during the struggle between Cromwell and the Crown, it is about the zealous efforts of Hopkins and his associates to seek out and persecute "witches," as well as anyone else who incurs their wrath. When Hopkins executes the priest of a small town for being a warlock, he and his partner find themselves the target of the priest's niece's fiancé, a young heroic soldier who leaves his post in Cromwell's army to hunt down and kill the pair. The movie is immensely engrossing and captures the English period detail remarkably well for a low-budget production. Price is at his absolute best, immersing himself in what is possibly his most menacing and sadistic role. The only complaint with the film is that it has been released on video with its original orchestral score replaced by a totally inappropriate and repetitive synthesizer track. ★★★½ $9.99

Conquest

(1937, 112 min, US, Clarence Brown) Good romantic costumer with Greta Garbo as Napoleon's Polish mistress, Marie Walewska. Charles Boyer effectively plays the French conqueror. ★★★ $19.99

Conquest of the Planet of the Apes

(1972, 87 min, US, J. Lee Thompson) Fourth in the *Apes* series. Back on present-day Earth, domesticated apes, who have been made slave-like servants, begin to rebel against the humans. The appeal of the series had begun to run its course, but this still manages to entertain in spite of itself. Starring Roddy McDowall and Ricardo Montalban. ★★½ $19.99

Consenting Adult

(1985, 100 min, US, Gilbert Cates) A compelling, well-made TV movie based on the Laura Hobson ("Gentlemen's Agreement") best-seller, and updated by a decade to include such topics as AIDS and anti-gay crime. Marlo Thomas has one of her best roles as the mother of a college athlete who must come to terms with her son's homosexuality when she discovers he is gay. Martin Sheen ably plays Thomas' fearful husband and Barry Tubbs gives a fine performance as their son. ★★★

Consenting Adults

(1993, 99 min, US, Alan J. Pakula) Kevin Kline, whose talent extends to choosing good roles, is ill-served by this, yet another in the glut of "steamy erotic thrillers," this one from the director of *Presumed Innocent*. A night of passion erupts into murder and betrayal when a married man (Kline) finds his neighbor's wife (Rebecca Miller) too tempting to resist. Mary Elizabeth Mastrantonio is the betrayed wife, and a creepy Kevin Spacey is the cuckold husband — or is he? What could have been an A-1 thriller is defeated by ridiculous plot contrivances and oh-so-predictable twists and turns. Also with E.G. Marshall and Forest Whitaker. ★½ $9.99

Consolation Marriage

(1931, 82 min, US, Paul Sloane) Irene Dunne and Pat O'Brien offer appealing performances in this standard romantic drama about jilted lovers who meet and marry, only to question their love when their former partners return. ★★½ $19.99

Consuming Passions

(1988, 98 min, GB, Giles Foster) A floundering family-owned chocolate factory finds the recipe for success when three employees take an accidental dip in the mixing vats. If this sounds like an absurd premise, it is, but still there are occasional flashes of hilarity. Vanessa Redgrave and Jonathan Pryce lend their talents. Based on a short play by Terry Jones and Michael Palin. ★★½

Contempt

(1963, 103 min, France/Italy, Jean-Luc Godard) A piercing, alienating film about film. Godard tackles communication problems and the difficulties of creating a motion picture — the compromises, frustration, idiocy and sacrifice. Brigitte Bardot is the contemptuous wife of a writer (Michel Piccoli) who sells out. (Available dubbed and in French with English subtitles) ★★★½

Continental Divide

(1981, 103 min, US, Michael Apted) John Belushi shows his acting range in this likable little romantic comedy about a hard-nosed, cynical urbanite who travels to the Rockies to interview a reclusive, self-reliant ornithologist (Blair Brown). Written by Lawrence Kasdan. ★★½ $9.99

The Conversation

(1974, 113 min, US, Francis Ford Coppola) This harrowing and brilliant film on the ethical and moral dilemmas of wiretapping and its consequences on personal liberties is Coppola's best film outside of the *Godfather* series. Gene Hackman gives a bravura performance as a surveillance specialist who comes to question the propriety of his profession, only to become a victim himself. Hackman tearing his apartment to shreds is one of the most devastating sequences ever put to film. Supporting cast includes Robert Duvall, Allen Garfield, Frederic Forrest and a young Harrison Ford. ★★★★ $14.99

Conversation Piece

(1974, 122 min, Italy, Luchino Visconti) Burt Lancaster is memorable as a retired intellectual whose life of solitude amid his books, paintings and art is abruptly invaded by the arrival of a garish 'modern' family who move in upstairs. His old-world comforts are shattered as he is both drawn to and forced to participate in their tawdry and hedonistic lifestyle. The invading family (which brings a breath of fresh air, life and love into the professor's life) includes the enchanting countess (Silvana Mangano), her daughter (Claudia Marsani) and the Countess' student revolutionary boy-toy (Helmut Berger). (Filmed in English) ★★★

The Conviction

(1993, 92 min, Italy, Marco Bellocchio) Attempting to capture some of the money-generating controversy of his sexually explicit *Devil in the Flesh*, Bellocchio's *The Conviction* tackles the murky but volatile subject of sexual harassment. A man and a woman get locked in a castle/museum after closing. The man, Lorenzo, and the woman, Sandra, play out a cat and mouse dance of domination and submission that eventually leads to a furious sexual conclusion. When the passions are spent, Lorenzo produces a key, prompting Sandra to feel used and abused. She initiates legal action claiming she was raped. What follows is a debate on sexuality and the problems between the sexes. For anyone interested in the subject, the film should be riveting; but it's a trial for those who wince at lines like "You'll try to destroy me, as a child does at birth." (Italian with English subtitles) ★★½ $19.99

Bardot abed in *Contempt*

Coogan's Bluff

(1968, 100 min, US, Don Siegel) Siegel directs with his usual manic pace as Arizona sheriff Clint Eastwood becomes a fish out of water when he comes to the Big Apple to capture an escaped hood convicted of murder. With Lee J. Cobb, Susan Clark and Tisha Sterling as "the hippie." ★★★ $14.99

The Cook, the Thief, His Wife & Her Lover

(1990, 126 min, GB/Denmark/France, Peter Greenaway) One of the most controversial films in years, the title of this Jacobean revenge-tragedy, set in an upscale French restaurant, says it all. The restaurant is visited nightly by the sadistic Thief (played ferociously by Michael Gambon). His battered Wife (Helen Mirren) in a heartbreaking performance) seeks solace in her secret Lover whom she meets one evening while dining. The sympathetic Cook rounds out the cast. A surreal theatre piece combining moments of tender tragedy and stomach-turning physical and mental cruelty, the film suggests that revenge is not always sweet: it sometimes has a few bones. (Unrated version) (Available letterboxed and pan & scan) ★★★½ $14.99

Cookie

(1989, 93 min, US, Susan Seidelman) Seidelman gets a couple of spirited performances in this cute tale by Nora Ephron. Smart-ass teenager Emily Lloyd finally hooks up with the father she never knew when she becomes his chauffeur after he is released from jail. Peter Falk is the mobster dad, Dianne Wiest is his mistress, and Brenda Vaccaro, Jerry Lewis and Ricki Lake also star. ★★½ $14.99

Cool Hand Luke

(1967, 126 min, US, Stuart Rosenberg) Paul Newman is splendid as the chain gang convict who's always in trouble with the boss and subsequently becomes hero to all of his fellow prisoners. The film is highlighted by the now famous egg eating scene. An excellent supporting cast is headed up by George Kennedy, Anthony Zerbe, Harry Dean Stanton, Dennis Hopper and Strother Martin ("What we got here is a failure to communicate"). ★★★★ $14.99

Cool Runnings

(1993, 98 min, US, Jon Turtletaub) A surprise hit at the box office, this Disney interpretation of the true-life story of the Jamaican bobsled team is a slightly trivial but amusing and uplifting saga. Relying on the tried-and-true formula of the underdog competing against all odds, the story follows Derice, a determined young Jamaican sprinter whose bid for the Jamaican track team is tragically dashed. Intent on becoming an Olympian at any cost, he turns to the unlikely sport of bobsledding, assembling a rag-tag crew to man his chariot and turning to ex-Olympian John Candy for coaching. Briskly paced and well stocked with both funny and touching moments, the film deserves honorable mention for giving American moviegoers something far-too-little seen: four black male leads who are non-threatening. ★★★ $14.99

Cool World

(1992, 101 min, US, Ralph Bakshi) Gabriel Byrne stars as an ex-con and cartoonist who discovers that his cartoon creations have a life of their own in a parallel universe known as Cool World. Director Bakshi follows the Roger Rabbit lead and combines live-action actors with his visually wild animation. On a technical level, the film is fascinating; Bakshi's trademark dark and leering imagery is as hip as ever. But unlike his previous efforts, this film is curiously unsatisfying. Byrne and co-star Brad Pitt are competent in their roles, but Kim Basinger is sadly out-gunned by her cartoon alter ego. The story is muddled and the action is unfocused; and, even to aficionados of adult animation, there's nothing here to recommend. ★ $14.99

Cooley High

(1975, 107 min, US, Michael Schultz) Affectionate reminiscence about a group of black high school students in mid-1960s Chicago. With Glynn Turman and Lawrence Hilton-Jacobs. The basis for the TV series "What's Happening." ★★★ $9.99

Cop

(1987, 110 min, US, James B. Harris) Routine suspense thriller is given a boost by James Woods' over-the-top portrayal of a cop whose domestic strife interferes with his pursuit of a serial killer. Based on the novel "Blood on the Moon" by James Ellroy. Also starring Leslie Ann Warren and Charles Durning. ★★

Cop and a Half

(1993, 93 min, US, Henry Winkler) This unbearably wooden action comedy has more troubles than its star Burt Reynolds had in divorce court. Devon (Norman D. Golden II) is a precocious eight-year-old who idolizes policemen. When he becomes the sole witness to a mob hit, he strikes a deal with the local police: If they make him a cop, he'll tell them everything he knows. Reynolds plays the hard-nosed, rule-busting detective who is given the task of taking young Devon on patrol — and wouldn't you know it, Burt hates kids. The film offers only one half-decent punchline when Devon pulls over his school principal for speeding and informs him, "I'm your worst nightmare: an eight-year-old with a badge." Eddie Murphy eat your heart out. ★ $9.99

Copacabana

(1947, 92 min, US, Alfred E. Green) Carmen Miranda can't get a gig, until manager and erstwhile boyfriend Groucho Marx lands two jobs for her. At the same club. As two different people. It becomes a bit of a strain, what with one being Brazilian and the other French. There's lots of flashy musical production numbers, and the usual wise-cracking encounters with officious officials. ★★½ $19.99

Cops and Robbers

(1973, 93 min, US, Aram Avakian) Two fine performances from Joe Bologna and Cliff Gorman as two cops who decide to pull off one perfect heist and then retire highlight this caper film that manages to be both funny and suspenseful. From the novel by Donald Westlake. ★★★ $14.99

Cops and Robbersons

(1994, 95 min, US, Michael Ritchie) After a disastrous attempt at late night TV, Chevy Chase returns to the big screen as a suburban dad (and would-be detective) who sees his big break in the form of a crotchety ol' police captain (Jack Palance) who moves in with the family to stakeout the murderous counterfeiter (Robert Davi) next door. There are some amusing gags, and Palance's patented sneering and growling make this somewhat worthwhile, but the next time Chase sees a cop, he should report his career as missing. Also with quintessential movie mom Dianne Wiest. ★★ $14.99

Copycat

(1995, 123 min, US, Jon Amiel) Despite its derivative shocks and improbabilities, *Copycat* manages to serve a few chills which should give less-than-demanding thriller fans a cheap scare or two. Sigourney Weaver is a renowned author and criminologist who is nearly killed by a psycho (Harry Connick, Jr.). When a copycat serial killer begins terrorizing the city, cops Holly Hunter and Dermot Mulroney convince the agoraphobic and homebound expert to help track him. The film is full of twists (some predictable, some not) and actually makes an attempt to present some deep psychological profiles of its characters – this is by far the more interesting aspect of the film. But a few of the sequences needed to set up the next scare lack either credibility or depth. Weaver and Hunter play well off each other; both actresses give convincing portrayals of strength and vulnerability. ★★½ $19.99

Coquette

(1929, 75 min, US, Sam Taylor) Mary Pickford was the second recipient of a Best Actress Oscar, and with her win came the Academy's first controversy. Many at the time complained that voters ignored artistic merit in favor of a popularity contest, and Pickford's histrionic portrayal of a flirtatious Southern belle only confirms those critics' charges. Pickford does get to break down on the stand, and grieve over her lover's dead body, but this tale of the Old South creaks at the seams, and doesn't offer any well-defined characters. Johnny Mack Brown, a rugged favorite of the early talkies, plays the ne'er-do-well in love with Pickford. Beware of poor sound quality in certain scenes. ★★ $19.99

Le Corbeau (The Raven)

(1943, 90 min, France, Henri-Georges Clouzot) From the director of *Diabolique* and *Wages of Fear* comes this pessimistic thriller about a small-town physician who becomes the victim of a poison letter campaign that sets his entire town into a frenzy of paranoia. This uncompromising depiction of the French middle class caused quite a storm when it was released because it was made with the assistance of the Germans and was viewed by many as an anti-French propaganda film. (French with English subtitles) ★★½

The Corn Is Green

(1945, 114 min, US, Irving Rapper) Bette Davis shines in one of her most heartfelt performances as Miss Moffat, a lonely schoolteacher in a small Welsh mining town who dedicates herself to a gifted student (John Dall), with the hope that the youth will leave his oppressive environment and one day enter Oxford. A superior, sentimental adaptation of Emlyn Williams' play. Davis would reprise the role in the ill-fated musical "Miss Moffat," which closed in Philadelphia. Remade by George Cukor in 1979 with Katharine Hepburn in the Bette Davis role. ★★★ $19.99

Cornered

(1945, 102 min, US, Edward Dmytryk) In 1944, musical star Dick Powell changed his image forever with the classic *Murder My Sweet*. Proving it no fluke, Powell reaffirmed his tough-guy persona with this taut thriller set post-WWII. Powell plays a war veteran whose wife died at the hands of Nazi collaborators. He winds up in Buenos Aires after circling the globe in search of a group of escaped fascists – his wife's killer among them. ★★★ $19.99

Corrina, Corrina

(1994, 115 min, US, Jessie Nelson) In an impressive debut as both writer and director, Nelson has fashioned a charming, sweet and intelligent romantic comedy-drama and semi-autobiography. Set in the 1950s, the film stars Ray Liotta as a single father coping with both the recent death of his wife and raising his traumatized seven-year-old daughter (marvelously played by Tina Majorino). Whoopi Goldberg co-stars as their new housekeeper Corrina, who takes the young girl under her wing, and who eventually becomes involved in an interracial romance with Liotta. Both Liotta and Goldberg offer sensitive, understated performances; and the film is thankfully devoid of any hokiness and sentimentality which characterize most heartwarming stories. *Corrina* also only marginally examines the racial issue to instead focus on the relationship of the film's wonderful three leading characters. ★★★ $14.99

Corrupt

(1983, 99 min, Italy, Roberto Faenza) An auspicious film debut by the notorious Johnny Lydon (aka Rotten). A sleazy heir to wealth, Lydon insinuates himself into a sadomasochistic relationship with a N.Y.C. police inspector (Harvey Keitel), stripping his personality to the bone. Relentlessly demented and frequently bristling with hostile humor, this is a kinky, punkist policer. Also known as *Cop-Killer* and *Order of Death*. ★★★

The Cosmic Eye

(1985, 76 min, US, Faith Hubley) A charming feature from one of our great animators, Hubley, with the voices of Maureen Stapleton, Dizzy Gillespie and Linda Atkinson. Expanding on the work she did with her late husband John, Hubley creates a free-form visual poem about the rights and responsibilities of human-kind. Its positive message never gets old, and it seems so simple, too. ★★★ $19.99

Cosmic Slop

(1994, 90 min, US, Reginald Hudlin, Warrington Hudlin & Kevin Rodney Sullivan) The creators of the *House Party* series and *Boomerang* succeed on all levels with this hip, Afro-centric "Twilight Zone"-inspired trilogy hosted by master funkateer George Clinton. Provocative, funny and always socially aware, this trio of tales tackles many of today's important issues such as domestic violence, gun control, religion and racism in a light-handed and sometimes humorous fashion. Despite its casual attitude, this clever and off-beat film manages to provide enough entertainment to satisfy those in search of something a little different. ★★★ $19.99

The Cotton Club

(1984, 127 min, US, Francis Coppola) Coppola's musical gangster film is a visual tour de force betrayed by a lack of dramatic substance. The supporting cast, including Bob Hoskins, Lonette McKee and Gregory Hines, totally overshadows leads Richard Gere and Diane Lane. ★★½

Cotton Comes to Harlem

(1970, 97 min, US, Ossie Davis) Made just prior to the explosion of blaxploitation films in the '70s, this fine adaptation of the Chester Himes novel (whose novels were also the source for *A Rage in Harlem*) stars Godfrey Cambridge and Raymond St. Jacques as policemen Coffin Ed Johnson and Gravedigger Jones. Actor-turned-director Davis does a fine job in telling their story as they try to expose a radical back-to-Africa preacher who they believe "ain't nothing but a cheat." A splendid blend of action and comedy, the film is also a spirited re-creation of 1950s Harlem. ★★★ $14.99

The Couch Trip

(1988, 97 min, US, Michael Ritchie) Dan Aykroyd brings his considerable charms to this standard comedy about a mental patient who escapes by impersonating a radio talk show psychologist in Beverly Hills. With Walter Matthau, Charles Grodin and Donna Dixon. ★★½ $9.99

Count Dracula

(1970, 98 min, Italy/Spain/West Germany, Jesse Franco) Christopher Lee dons tooth and cape in this slowly paced but faithful updating of Bram Stoker's "Dracula." A lawyer and his fiancée encounter the prince of darkness in Transylvania. Also with Herbert Lom and Klaus Kinski. ★★½ $14.99

The Count of Old Town

(1935, 75 min, Sweden, Edvin Aldolphson & Sigurd Wallen) Ingrid Bergman made her film debut in this buoyant comedy as a maid in a cheap hotel who falls in love with a roguish thief. (Swedish with English subtitles) ★★★ $19.99

Country

(1984, 109 min, US, Richard Pearce) Jessica Lange and Sam Shepard star as farmers who fight to save their land when the government threatens foreclosure and who struggle to save their family from the ravages of crisis. A well-made and topical film. Lange's performance is remarkable. ★★★ $79.99

The Country Girl

(1954, 104 min, US, George Seaton) Three stand-out lead performances by Grace Kelly, Bing Crosby and William Holden distinguish this absorbing Clifford Odets adaptation with Kelly in her Oscar-winning role as the wife of alcoholic actor Crosby. Holden is the dedicated director trying to help him in his comeback, becoming romantically involved with Grace in the process. ★★★½ $14.99

Country Life

(1995, 114 min, Australia, Michael Blakemore) On the heels of Louis Malle's

Vanya on 42nd Street comes another, delectable interpretation of Chekhov's "Uncle Vanya." Concentrating more on the comedy of culture clash and romantic escapades than the drama of emotional chasms and interpersonal relationships, this sometimes giddy concoction is set on a sheep ranch in post-WWII Australia. A sweetly romantic Sam Neill stars as Dr. Askey, an idealistic boozer who falls in love with Deborah (Greta Scacchi), the young wife of the estate's owner (director Blakemore is a smashing performance) who has returned after a long absence. Unrequited love, social upheaval and regret are themes still present, though this comedy of manners treads softly. Jack Hargreaves nicely plays Uncle Jack, and Kerry Fox is Sally, Jack's niece who secretly loves Askey. Not every scene of this liberal translation reaches its potential, but as an immensely appealing ensemble proves, *Country Life* has its merits. ★★★½ $19.99

Countryman
(1982, 100 min, Jamaica/GB, Dickie Jobson) Although ladened with a poor script, unprofessional acting and muddled politics, this lively story of the power of the Rastafarian is still good entertainment. A peaceful Rastafarian fisherman, Countryman Hiram Keller, rescues two Americans from a plane crash. But instead of simple thanks, he is thrown into a caldron of political intrigue which forces him to flee into the lush Jamaican jungle. It is there that he attains supernatural powers and is able to battle the elements and foe alike. The film is highlighted with a sampler-style reggae soundtrack featuring the music of Bob Marley, Toots and the Maytals, Scratch Perry, Aswad and Steel Pulse. ★★½ $59.99

Coup de Grâce
(1976, 96 min, West Germany, Volker Schlöndorff) Understated, yet subtly disquieting, this drama by Schlöndorff explores destructive human behavior – both in personal relationships as well as politics. Set in 1919 in a forlorn country estate somewhere in a Baltic republic, the story traces the lives of a middle-aged woman (Margarethe von Trotta), her brother and a German lodger who find themselves slowly impoverished by the civil war and anxious over the advancement of Red troops on their land. The woman, desperate for affection, falls obsessively in love with a Soviet soldier, a man who does not return her love and is soon driven away by her erratic and at times virulent behavior. A serious portrait of bitterly restrained people caught in the whirlwind of change. (German with English subtitles) ★★★ $59.99

Coup de Tete (Hothead)
(1978, 100 min, France, Jean-Jacques Annaud) This engaging comedy follows the exploits of a crazed soccer player whose antics on and off the field cause him to lose his position, get fired and end up in jail. He gets out, however, and soon extracts his "revenge." A bristling comedy with Patrick Dewaere in one of his best roles. (Dubbed) ★★★

Coup de Torchon (Clean Slate)
(1981, 128 min, France, Bertrand Tavernier) A diabolical black comedy which spits in the face of morality. Philippe Noiret is the ineffectual law enforcer in an African village who one day abandons his policy of non-confrontation and embarks on a systematic shooting spree. Based on the novel "Pop. 1280" by Jim Thompson. Also with Isabelle Huppert and Stéphane Audran. (French with English subtitles) ★★★½

Coupe de Ville
(1990, 99 min, US, Joe Roth) A sentimental though engaging road movie – and a heart-on-the-sleeve tribute to Dad. Daniel Stern, Patrick Dempsey and Ayre Gross star as three estranged brothers who are reunited on a cross-country trip to deliver a birthday present, a 1954 Coupe de Ville, to their mom. Of course, en route, the boys not only discover a little something about each other, but about themselves as well. Though the film tries to be insightful, it borders on manipulative and, at times, heavy-handed sentimentality. However, thanks to an abundance of funny lines and attractive performances, this is mostly an enjoyable ride. ★★½ $14.99

Courage Mountain
(1990, 96 min, US, Christopher Leitch) A beautifully photographed family film, this new version of the famed "Heidi" story won't make anyone forget the beloved 1937 Shirley Temple classic, but it is nevertheless an earnest, well-paced and sincerely acted adventure which should more than entertain pre-adolescent viewers. Young Juliette Caton ably plays the little heroine who, on the eve of WWI, moves from her Swiss Alps home to a fancy boarding school across the border in Italy. Once there, however, Heidi and a group of friends are separated from their headmistress and are taken to a local orphanage and used for slave labor. Charlie Sheen co-stars as a Swiss soldier and Leslie Caron nicely plays the devoted headmistress. ★★★ $14.99

Courage under Fire
(1996, 115 min, US, Edward Zwick) Addressing themes previously unrepresented in serious filmmaking from Hollywood – the Gulf War and women in the military – the intelligent and perceptive *Courage under Fire* is more than up to the challenge of either. In a solid characterization, Denzel Washington plays an Army commander who is investigating the case of a posthumous Medal of Honor going to a female pilot (Meg Ryan) killed in action. What should be a simple process soon becomes complicated when witnesses begin to contradict each other's stories – and it's uncertain if she died a hero or a coward. As Washington, troubled by his own Gulf War experiences, digs deeper to uncover the truth (which places him in conflict with military brass), Ryan's story is told in riveting, *Rashomon*-like flashbacks. Highlighting a marvelous ensemble, Lou Diamond Phillips exceptional as a soldier who knows more than he's saying; and Ryan discards her "bubbly" personality to deliver a thoroughly convincing and forceful portrayal of true grit. Director Zwick (*Glory*) surely knows that war is hell, and that truth and bravery aren't always casualties of war. ★★★½ $14.99

Courage under Fire

The Court Jester
(1956, 101 min, US, Norman Panama & Melvin Frank) Danny Kaye has one of his best roles in this beloved comedy classic which rates as one of the funniest comedies of all time. To help restore the throne to its rightful heir, Kaye goes undercover, posing as a court jester; and in the process, of course, turns the palace upside-down. Basil Rathbone and young Glynis Johns and Angela Lansbury also star. And don't forget: "The pellet with the poison's in the vessel with the pestle." Or is that "the flagon with the dragon?" ★★★★ $14.99

The Courtesans of Bombay
(1974, 74 min, India, Ismail Merchant) An intriguing and entertaining story which follows the inhabitants of Pavanpul, the courtesan quarters, who by day carry on their daily domestic lives and by night, thrill and delight with exuberant singing, dancing and sex. Filmed in a pseudo-documentary style, the film is more of interest for its sociological stance rather than entertainment value. Merchant's directorial debut. ★★½ $19.99

Cousin Bobby
(1992, 69 min, US, Jonathan Demme) Proving himself to be a director of many talents, Demme followed his Academy Award-winning *The Silence of the Lambs* with this provocative and sincere documentary about his long-lost cousin, Bobby Castle, a politically radical Episcopal priest who militantly crusades for the poor African-American and Hispanic parishoners of his Harlem church. Demme goes about filming his story as if it were a home movie, documenting his own rediscovery of a distant relation with hand-held camera work and microphone booms exposed. Demme splits the film between this familial reunion and Castle's history as a civil rights leader, concentrating especially on his close friendship in the '60s with Black Panther Party member Isaiah Rowley, who was killed by the Jersey City police. Additionally, the film takes aim at the unspoken war being waged on poor minority communities today, making a huge pothole at a busy Harlem intersection a metaphor for the

Marie-France Pisier in *Cousin, Cousine*

people's struggle. Eloquent and outspoken, Castle, along with cousin Jonathan, makes a powerful and compelling case for economic equality and social justice. ★★★½

Cousin, Cousine

(1975, 95 min, France, Jean-Charles Tacchella) An engaging look at love among the members of a large French family. Trouble brews when two cousins by marriage discover they have more in common than their in-laws. A sexy, romantic comedy. An international hit which spawned an American remake (the inferior *Cousins*). (French with English subtitles) ★★★½ $19.99

Cousins

(1989, 110 min, US, Joel Schumacher) An amiable if unremarkable rehash of *Cousin, Cousine* highlighted by a handful of sincere and appealing performances, including Ted Danson and Isabella Rossellini, as two cousins who fall in love; Sean Young and William S. Petersen as their respective spouses who fall in lust; and especially Lloyd Bridges and Norma Aleandro, who both give the film a dash of vitality — which keeps it afloat — as a pair of high-spirited sexagenarian lovers. ★★½ $14.99

Cover Girl

(1944, 107 min, US, Charles Vidor) This delightful Kern-Gershwin musical has Gene Kelly's brilliant dancing, Phil Silvers' burlesque routines, Eve Arden's wisecracks and Rita Hayworth's beauty, all packaged in lush Technicolor by the sure hand of director Vidor. ★★★½ $19.99

Cover Me

(1995, 94 min, US, Michael Schroeder) Playboy Films' first video release is this tepid, seen-it-before murder mystery set amidst the sex industry of L.A. in which a serial killer stalks models who have appeared on the cover of a local skin magazine. The twist is that the killer is a transvestite with ambiguous sexual orientation (see *Silence of the Lambs* for a similarly developed character). Demi/Dimitri's (Stephen Nichols) MO is to don women's clothing, go to a strip club, pick up a prostitute/dancer and take her home presumably for a night of paid lesbian sex. But girl-girl lovemaking soon turns to boy-girl killing and it takes a sultry policewoman (Courtney Taylor) to go undercover to capture the sicko. ★ $91.99

Cover-Up

(1988, 76 min, US, Barbara Trent) After releasing the right-wing documentary *Oliver North*, distributor MPI Video then produced this left-leaning probe into the shady dealings of the Iran-Contra Affair. The story alleges that the 1980 Reagan-Bush campaign bargained with the Iranians to delay the hostages' release to insure a victory over President Carter. ★★★ $14.99

The Covered Wagon

(1923, 60 min, US, James Cruze) Beautifully photographed epic of the Old West, introducing some of the elements of the genre that others would later exploit more fully. One of the biggest box-office smashes of the 1920s. ★★★ $14.99

Le Crabe Tambour

(1977, 120 min, France, Pierre Schoendoerffer) Haunting and provocative, Schoendoerffer's unconventional war drama lays bare the primitive sentiments of men in battle. Based on the actual exploits of a legendary French officer, nicknamed Le Crabe Tambour (The Drummer Crab), the film furrows through the complexities of honor and military chivalry. Jacques Perrin portrays the title character with a fascinating elusiveness — projecting the oblique demeanor of a perennial soldier. Accentuating the rich performances is Raoul Coutard's boldy adventurous cinematography, with its many spellbinding evocations of the elements. (French with English subtitles) ★★★½ $59.99

Crackers

(1983, 91 min, US, Louis Malle) Malle's American remake of the Italian classic *Big Deal on Madonna Street* is long on charm, but falls short when it comes to delivering either story or laughs. The film centers around a group of losers who keep off the mean streets of San Francisco by hanging out at a local pawn shop. When they concoct a scheme to crack the safe in the shop, the comedy is supposed to gear up, but somehow, the film never really gets on track. Starring Donald Sutherland, Jack Warden, Sean Penn and Wallace Shawn. ★★ $59.99

The Craft

(1996, 100 min, US, Andrew Fleming) *Heathers* meets *Carrie* in this psychologically mature tale of teen angst and retribution about a circle of student misfits whose prankish use of witchcraft against their tormentors gets out of hand when one of them (Fairuza Balk) loses control of her own personal demons and becomes a bitch of a witch. Director Fleming takes what might have been more "Gen-X" dribble and invests it with surprisingly keen insight and malicious wit, making this junior effort light years ahead of his first two films, *Bad Dreams* and *Threesome*. ★★★ $19.99

Craig's Wife

(1936, 75 min, US, Dorothy Arzner) Rosalind Russell is outstanding as the selfish, materialistic wife whose obsessive social climbing ruins her marriage. Remade in 1950 as *Harriet Craig* with Joan Crawford. ★★★ $19.99

The Cranes Are Flying

(1957, 94 min, USSR, Mikhail Kalatozov) Made during the "thaw" of the Cold War that resulted in greater liberty for filmmakers, this lyrical and poignant love story is set during WWII and follows the sad tale of two young lovers who are separated by the war. Tragedies soon befall the girl after her sweetheart volunteers to fight, leaving her in the hands of his brutish cousin. With sweeping and lush camera work, moving performances and an unusual absence of political propaganda, this highly

Rita Hayworth in a pose from *Cover Girl*

acclaimed and award-winning film (Best Director, Best Picture and Best Actress Awards at Cannes) is a tender, realistic portrayal of a love that triumphs in the face of adversity. (Russian with English subtitles) ★★★½ $59.99

Crash

(1997, 100 min, Canada, David Cronenberg) Banned in London, shunned by New Line distribution honcho Ted Turner, and cheered and hissed at 1996's Cannes Film Festival (where it won a special award for "audacity"), Cronenberg's controversial adaptation of J.G. Ballard's novel rumbles on the fumes of its outlaw reputation. Like *Naked Lunch* and *Videodrome*, this eerie effort finds a netherworld where technology, obsession and sex meet; then it sets them against each other in the horrific battlefield of the mind. James Spader plays a Toronto film producer whose unquenchable sexual desires take a new turn after he's involved in a car accident that kills the husband of passenger Holly Hunter. Despite the tragedy and subsequent injuries, Hunter and Spader begin a carnal relationship that eventually leads to an unusual medical researcher (Elias Koteas), who gets his kicks staging the car accidents of the deceased and famous (James Dean, Jayne Mansfield). It seems that there's a growing cult of the auto-erotic fetishists, and Spader eventually brings wife Debra Unger into the fray. Story line and character development take a backseat to mood and the psychological surveying going on here. Cronenberg films the numerous, fairly explicit sex scenes – hetero, homo, self, group – with a sense of detachment. Heated yet chilly at the same time, they turn unsettling when played against the frenzy of the adrenalin-charged car crash sequences. With *Crash*, Cronenberg goes boldly where few directors have ever gone before. If you follow him, make sure your seatbelts are on tight. ★★★ $99.99

Crash Dive

(1943, 105 min, US, Archie Mayo) In the last film before his own WWII tour of duty, Tyrone Power stars as a naval officer who is assigned to commander Dana Andrews' sub. In between daring attacks on the Germans, he falls in love with Andrews' fiancée Anne Baxter. The story nicely mixes romance, comedy and wartime heroics, the special effects are commendable, and the film's rich color is an asset. ★★★ $19.99

The Crazies

(1973, 103 min, US, George Romero) An early thriller from director Romero about a bungled Army experiment contaminating a small town's water supply, turning its citizens into crazed killers. ★★

Crazy from the Heart

(1991, 94 min, US, Thomas Schlamme) Christine Lahti and Ruben Blades star in this compelling drama about a high-school teacher who falls for a Hispanic janitor, causing an uproar in their small town. Both Lahti and Blades give convincing performances in this examination of self-confidence and individuality. ★★★ $89.99

Crazy in Love

(1992, 93 min, US, Martha Coolidge) Director Coolidge has crafted a lyrical and mature examination of the bonds of family and the complications which arise out of compulsive passions. A fine ensemble cast is headed by Holly Hunter and features Gena Rowlands, Bill Pullman and Julian Sands. Hunter fears her husband (Pullman) is losing interest in their marriage when she meets an enchanting photographer, Sands. Frances McDormand lends support in a strong, if small, role as Hunter's sister. Filmed to good effect in and around Seattle, the film sports earnest dialogue and characterizations along with moments of touching intimacy. ★★½ $89.99

Crazy Mama

(1975, 82 min, US, Jonathan Demme) Director Demme's talents are very much in evidence in this early exploitation film made for Roger Corman. Three generations of women (Ann Sothern, Cloris Leachman, Linda Purl) go on a riotous crime spree from California to Arkansas. An action/comedy/drama similar to Demme's later *Married to the Mob*. ★★½

Crazy Moon

(1987, 98 min, Canada, Allan Eastman) "Sitting through *Crazy Moon* gives me an idea of what it is like to be in Purgatory." So said *Philadelphia Inquirer* film critic Desmond Ryan. A great quote, but a judgment a tad too harsh for this innocuous variation on the *Harold and Maude* theme (society misfits in love). Kiefer Sutherland stars as an '80s teenager caught up in '40s nostalgia who falls in love with a deaf girl. Cinema from the Great White North does not send Hollywood packing, but it's entertaining nonetheless. ★★½

Crazy People

(1990, 90 min, US, Tony Bill) Dudley Moore stars as an advertising executive whose policy of "truth in advertising" lands him in the loony bin. There he becomes mixed up with a group of fellow patients, teaching them advertising and self-worth, and they teach him one of life's many lessons. This is simply *The Dream Team* on Madison Avenue. When it is lampooning TV and print advertising, it is hilariously wicked. But unfortunately, the rest of it is awkward and maudlin. ★★ $14.99

The Crazy Ray/Entr'acte

(1923/1924, 36/14 min, France, René Clair) *The Crazy Ray*, Dadaist Clair's first film, is a fanciful and amusing story of a mad scientist who invents a ray gun and puts the entire city of Paris in suspended animation. *Entr'acte*, conceived as a filmic intermission to be shown during the Dada ballet "Relache," has endured well beyond the original intention to become one of the important surrealist films of the

Crash

period. Plotless, the film, in frantic movements designed to offend its original audience, includes a chase through Paris with a runaway hearse. (Silent with musical accompaniment) ★★★ $39.99

The Creation of Adam

(1993, 93 min, Russia, Yuri Pavlov) Heralded by its director as the first gay-themed film from Russia, this mystical drama will disappoint many by its oblique handling of the gay angle. Set in the industrialized port of St. Petersburg, the story follows handsome designer Andrei (Alexander Strizhenov) who is stuck in an unfulfilling relationship with his equally unhappy wife. After saving an effeminate teen from a group of queer-bashers, he is quickly accused – by both the thugs and his wife – of being homosexual. His life is transformed when he meets Philip, a mysterious, self-assured young man. Their ensuing relationship, handled in a weird, dreamlike manner, is one of both seduction and brotherlike guidance. (Russian with English subtitles) ★★½ $39.99

Creation of the Humanoids

(1962, 75 min, US, Wesley E. Barry) Andy Warhol's favorite film features Forrest J. Ackerman (creator of "Famous Monsters of Filmland") and makeup by Jack Pierce, who created all the great monsters like Frankenstein and The Wolfman. After the next big one, humanoids are created to replace all the dead Third World people who used to do our menial work. ★

Creator

(1985, 108 min, US, Ivan Passer) Middling sci-fi comedy with Peter O'Toole as a Nobel Prize-winning biologist who attempts to clone his long-deceased wife, with the help of a young med student (Vincent Spano). ★★ $69.99

The Creature from the Black Lagoon

(1954, 79 min, US, Jack Arnold) What '50s monster movie could be any good without Richard Carlson, Richard Denning or Whit Bissell? Well, this film's got all three! Plus the neatest monster this side of the sushi bar. Directed by Arnold (*The Incredible Shrinking Man*), this film exhibits a surprising lyricism in its underwater sequences, especially the aquatic *pas de deux* with the heroine. Features the classic line, "David, you still don't look like an ekistiologist." Originally shown in 3-D. ★★★ $14.99

The Creeper

(1948, 64 min, US, Jean Yarbrough) A surprisingly stylish low-budget horror film about a mad doctor whose nostrum turns men into killer cats. Onslow Stevens stars. ★★½

Creepers

(1984, 82 min, Italy, Dario Argento) A deranged killer stalks a young girl through the grounds of her boarding school, but little does he know this girl can communicate telepathically with all species of insects. Now, she and her allegiant minions have a bone to pick. ★★½ $14.99

The Creeping Flesh

(1970, 89 min, GB, Freddie Francis) A lesser Hammer Studios production perhaps, but any horror film with Peter Cushing and Christopher Lee is bound to provoke a few chills. The plot features (you guessed it) a mad scientist who is obsessed with harnessing the "essence of evil." It's an old-fashioned affair, filled with monsters, evil spirits and numerous subplots. ★★★ $49.99

Creepshow

(1982, 120 min, US, George Romero) Five horror stories written by Stephen King offer a few chills, especially the final one about paranoid high-rise dweller E.G. Marshall and his newly arrived guests — hundreds of cockroaches. Also with Hal Holbrook, Adrienne Barbeau, Ted Danson, Leslie Nielsen and Ed Harris. ★★★ $14.99

Creepshow 2

(1987, 89 min, US, Michael Gornick) Three more Stephen King stories, here adapted by George Romero. Doesn't deliver the same number of chills as the original, but undemanding horror fans shouldn't mind. With George Kennedy, Tom Savini and Dorothy Lamour(!). ★★ $14.99

Creole Giselle

(1988, 88 min, US/Denmark, Thomas Grimm) Making only minor changes in the story (changed to 1841 Louisiana), music and traditional choreography, the Dance Theatre of Harlem's acclaimed interpretation of the classic "Giselle" features Virginia Johnson in the lead role and Eddie J. Shellman as Albert. ★★★ $29.99

Cria!

(1985, 110 min, Spain, Carlos Saura) This beautifully acted, haunting film stars Ana Torrent as a nine-year-old heroine with an uncanny talent for observing scenes not meant for her eyes, specifically the death of her father. An evocative film about the darker side of childhood, superstition, knowledge and the inevitable loss of innocence. Costarring Geraldine Chaplin. (Spanish with English subtitles) ★★★½

Cries and Whispers

(1972, 106 min, Sweden, Ingmar Bergman) Ingmar Bergman delves into the tumultuous world of familial hates, longings and frustrations in this superbly acted classic starring Liv Ullmann and Ingrid Thulin. (Swedish with English subtitles) ★★★★ $39.99

Crime and Punishment

(1935, 110 min, France, Pierre Chenal) Dostoyevsky's complex, brooding novel is brilliantly brought to the screen in this haunting and menacing adaptation. Harry Bauer stars as Raskolnikov, a tormented student who murders a money lender and her daughter and soon finds himself stalked by the cunning magistrate Porfiry. Light years ahead of Joseph von Sternberg's Hollywood version released that same year, director Chenal stages most of the action in a claustrophobic and atmospheric studio set — the result being an almost airless and unrelentingly intense drama. (French with English subtitles) ★★★★

Crime and Punishment

(1935, 88 min, US, Josef von Sternberg) Not as intense as the French adaptation of Dostoyevsky's existential novel, von Sternberg's version is at least more palatable entertainment. Peter Lorre gives a stellar performance as the brooding intellectual, Raskolnikov, who murders a greedy pawnbroker, deeming her "unfit to live." The omission of the accidental killing of the pawnbroker's retarded daughter lessens the guilt Raskolnikov battles in the novel. The story is lightened just a bit by this and Lorre's character appears a little more amiable because of it. Filled with intellectual banter on crime, guilt, faith and the "superman vs. the herd" theory, this film version stands fine on its own, but pales compared to the novel. ★★½ $19.99

Crime and Punishment

(1970, 200 min, USSR, Lev Kulidzhanov) This Russian version of the Fyodor Dostoevsky literary classic about a student who murders a pawnbroker and her daughter is an authentic and brilliant translation of the much-filmed novel. The impoverished Raskolnikov, racked by guilt for his crimes, is eventually hunted down by the Police Inspector Porfiry and confesses to the crime. Much longer than the U.S., English and French versions, the film probes the intense mental anguish of Raskolnikov and provides a haunting image of the man's tortured soul. (Russian with English subtitles) ★★★½ $29.99

Crime of the Century

(1996, 110 min, US, Mark Rydell) In the 1930s, the Lindbergh baby kidnapping/murder case and its subsequent trial was an unprecedented media event. An entire nation poured over every world, clue and witness' account — the country would not see anything like it until O.J. tried on that bloody glove. When the trial was over, a German emigrant named Hauptmann was found guilty and executed. But through the years, many historians have speculated that Hauptmann may have been innocent, a victim of an inferior defense, a zealous police investigation and a prejudiced court system. The methodically paced but riveting Crime of the Century, a made-for-HBO drama, takes this view and succinctly presents the facts as they could have been. It not only makes for great viewing, but a damn good argument for a miscarriage of justice, as well.

Stephen Rea is perfectly subdued as Hauptmann, whose only crime may have been a poor choice of a business partner. Isabella Rossellini is also splendid as Hauptmann's wife, who steadfastly supported her husband. ★★★½ $92.99

Crime Story

(1993, 90 min, Hong Kong, Kirk Wong) A real-life incident serves as the inspiration for a rare dramatic turn by comedy kung fu star Jackie Chan. Jackie is an ace Hong Kong cop called in to work on a tough kidnapping case. Little does he know that his own partner (Kent Cheng) is involved in the scam. Featuring almost no comedy and none of Jackie's trademark funny faces, Crime Story is as serious as a heart attack. Jackie's frustration at the escalating human cost of the case burns stronger and stronger, reaching a fever pitch at the climax when he confronts his partner in a burning tenement building. Cheng, consumed with guilt over his association with the kidnappers, decides to commit suicide by staying in the burning building, leaving Jackie to rescue both the kidnap victims and his own partner. Very few Hong Kong action films reach the emotional intensity of this and several earlier scenes in the film. Highly recommended for traditional action fans and those looking for another side of Jackie's star persona. Unfortunately, the film has been released in an atrociously dubbed version by Miramax/Dimension Films, which severely detracts from its serious tone. (Dubbed into English) ★★★½ $102.99

Crime Zone

(1988, 93 min, US, Louis Llosa) A low-budget, futuristic Bonnie and Clyde, Crime Zone tells the tale of two young "sub-grades," Bone (Peter Nelson) and Helen (Sherilyn Fenn). They are hired by a mysterious man named Jason (David Carradine) to steal an important government computer disk and soon find themselves the targets of an all-out police dragnet. Roger Corman produced this imaginative, entertaining if somewhat cheesy sci-fi thriller. ★★½ $79.99

Crimes and Misdemeanors

(1989, 97 min, US, Woody Allen) Allen's fascinating blend of humor and gripping melodrama follows the intersecting stories of two men: a successful opthalmologist (Martin Landau), who arranges the murder of his mistress; and an out-of-work filmmaker (Woody Allen) who falls in love with his producer (Mia Farrow). It is Allen's remarkable irony that one man's deep-rooted religious principles are betrayed at an insignificant cost, and integrity is ill-rewarded. The excellent cast features Anjelica Huston as Landau's mistress, and Alan Alda, who has some of Allen's best gags in years. ★★★★ $14.99

The Crimes of M. Lange

(1935, 85 min, France, Jean Renoir) A delightfully droll black comedy, scripted by Jacques Prévert and Renoir, that mixes fantasy and politics in its story of a worker uprising. When the crooked and lecherous boss of a publishing house suddenly disappears, the exploited workers of the company unite to form a co-operative and succeed in making the company a huge success. When the boss returns to take over, he finds the workers, led by M. Lange, a timid writer of pulp westerns, united in opposition. (French with English subtitles) ★★★★ $59.99

Crimes of Passion

(1984, 112 min, US, Ken Russell) This sizzling tale of a sexually repressed street preacher and a mysterious prostitute carries as resounding a wallop as could only come from the inimitable talents of Ken Russell. Anthony Perkins stars as the deranged reverend who's hell-bent on saving the soul of China Blue (Kathleen Turner) – a well-respected fashion designer by day who becomes a slinky streetwalker at night. Overflowing with camp humor and bizarre twists, the film is a visual treat in which seductive waves of saturated neon splash across the screen. Definitely one of Russell's more unique (a term which may be redundant when describing his work) and unforgettable ventures. (Unrated version) ★★★ $14.99

Crimes of the Heart

(1986, 105 min, US, Bruce Beresford) In the 1940s, this offbeat comedy would have been classified as a "woman's picture"; today, it is called a "star vehicle." Sissy Spacek, Diane Keaton and Jessica Lange breathe life into Beth Henley's Pulitzer Prize-winning play about three Southern sisters reunited in time of crisis, and of their estrangement and reconciliation. A sweet-natured film which garnered Oscar nominations for Spacek, co-star Tess Harper and its screenplay adaptation. ★★★ $14.99

Crimetime

(1996, 95 min, GB, George Sluizer) Tabloid TV gets the *Network* treatment in this stylish looking thriller which very nearly sinks in its own smartness. With Marianne Faithfull singing two songs in a well-choreographed club scene opening, the film gets off to a good start. Pete Postlethwaite plays a serial killer who picks up his first victim. A rather gruesome murder, it catches the attention of a TV magazine show (run by Karen Black doing her worst Faye Dunaway imitation) which re-stages sensationalistic crimes. Stephen Baldwin is the actor who gets his 15 minutes playing the murderer. Alternating between black comedy and suspense, *Crimetime* becomes more bizarre as the murders continue and Baldwin and Postlethwaite form an actor/mentor bond. There may be a message there somewhere, but it gets lost in all the blood and melodrama. Baldwin hasn't mastered the rage scene yet, but looks comfortable in his many nude scenes. Postlethwaite appears to be having fun hamming it up. ★★ $96.99

Crimewave

(1986, 83 min, US, Sam Raimi) Long before *Darkman* or *Miller's Crossing*, Sam Raimi and the Coen Brothers – Joel and Ethan – joined forces to make this alternately amusing black farce about a couple of bungling rat exterminators who set their sights on two-legged mammals instead. Louise Lasser, Paul L. Smith and Bruce Campbell star. ★★½

Criminal Law

(1989, 117 min, US, Martin Campbell) Gary Oldman and Kevin Bacon dance a psychotic *pas de deux* in this muddled thriller about a rich-kid serial killer (Bacon) who, having been caught, tried, and found not guilty, taunts his defense attorney (Oldman) with the knowledge that he's really guilty and plans to kill again. Britisher Oldman does a knock-out American accent, but it's not enough to overcome the shaky story line and plotting. Also stars Karen Young, Tess Harper and Joe Don Baker. ★★½ $14.99

The Criminal Life of Archibaldo de la Cruz

(1955, 91 min, Mexico, Luis Buñuel) Director Buñuel ended his self-exile in Mexico with this slyly humorous black comedy of one man's dark, sexual and murderous obsessions. After a traumatic experience in which a boy enjoys a secret sexual thrill on the accidental death of the family maid, he grows up one sick little pup. Years later he is now an aristocratic gentleman, and Archibaldo's secret thoughts harbor a guilt-fueled fantasy of sexual kinkiness, crime and murder against women; but, in true Buñuelian fashion, his criminal desires are thwarted at every turn. With surrealistic touches and macabre fetishism, Buñuel pokes wicked fun at the bourgeoisie, Catholicism and the Latino male. (Spanish with English subtitles) ★★★★ $29.99

The Crimson Pirate

(1952, 104 min, US, Robert Siodmak) Burt Lancaster is in top form, both as actor and athlete, in this supremely entertaining swashbuckler with Lancaster and fellow acrobat Nick Cravat fighting the bad guys in the Mediterranean. ★★★ $14.99

Crimson Tide

(1995, 113 min, US, Tony Scott) If *The Hunt for Red October* brought an end to the Cold War at a theatre near you, then another submarine thriller, *Crimson Tide*, certainly tries to rekindle the sleepy politics of paranoia. And it does so in an exceedingly efficient manner. Denzel Washington stars as the newly appointed second-in-command of the nuclear submarine *USS Alabama*. He and the crew serve under the watchful eye of hard-nosed captain Gene Hackman (giving one of his patented blustery performances). Things heat up, however, when a renegade Russian general takes control of a Soviet sub and threatens nuclear war. In no time, Washington and Hackman are at odds with each other over possible retaliation, and *Red October* gives way to *The Caine Mutiny*. Fairly authentic and exciting throughout, *Crimson Tide* is less jingoistic and more credible than director Scott's other military saga *Top Gun*, though Michael Schiffer's soldierly screenplay did get some help from the likes of Quentin Tarantino and Robert Towne. ★★★ $14.99

Critical Condition

(1987, 100 min, US, Peter Faiman) Harmless though silly Richard Pryor comedy with Pryor as a developer who feigns insanity to stay out of jail. But when he escapes from the mental

ward, he is mistaken for a doctor and proceeds to turn the hospital topsy-turvy. ★★ $14.99

Critters

(1986, 86 min, US, Stephen Herek) Offbeat comic horror film about some hairy tumbleweed-like monsters who arrive from another planet and terrorize a small Kansas town. An enjoyable, silly romp with both laughs and chills going for it. ★★½ $14.99

Critters 2

(1988, 87 min, US, Mick Garris) More toothy, glandular fur-balls terrorize the populace. Though in the same style of the original, it's not nearly as fun. ★½ $14.99

"Crocodile" Dundee

(1986, 95 min, Australia, Peter Faiman) A surprise and huge box-office hit upon its release, *"Crocodile" Dundee* is a tepid comedy about an Australian Everyman (played by Paul Hogan, which would be like saying Sylvester Stallone is an American Everyman!) who finds adventure in the wilds of New York City. Dundee is an Aussie crocodile poacher and local legend who becomes the subject of an article by American reporter Linda Kozlowski. She invites him back to the States, and together they become involved in urban intrigue and romance. Admittedly Hogan has a genial charm to him (if you can ignore his homophobia), but the film casts him in too many clichéd antics, and most of the comedy just isn't funny. ★★ $14.99

"Crocodile" Dundee II

(1988, 111 min, US\Australia, John Cornell) For the record, Mick "Crocodile" Dundee (Paul Hogan) must save his girlfriend (Linda Kozlowski) from ruthless drug dealers. For the record, this is a witless, though very profitable sequel. For those who liked the original, there's probably nothing we can say to dissuade you from watching this (and there's a lot of you). For those who didn't, avoid this at all costs. ★ $14.99

Cronica del Alba

(1982, 82 min, Spain, Antonio J. Betancor) Like Truffaut's Antoine Donel series, *Cronica del Alba* is the second film on the life story of a young boy growing into manhood. Jose Garces, or "Pepe," last seen as a youngster in love in *Valentina*, is now 15 years old and in his first year at the university. The setting is Zaragoza in 1919, on the eve of the anarchist rebellion, and our hero is caught between his continued love for the now ravishing Valentina, his bourgeois origins and his developing revolutionary ideals. Adapted from the novel by Ramon J. Sender, winner of Spain's National Literature Award in 1936. (Spanish with English subtitles) ★★★

Cronos

(1993, 92 min, Mexico, Guillermo Del Toro) This delicious and chilling little oddity from Mexico tells the tale of an aging antique dealer who happens upon an ancient device, built by an alchemist bent on achieving immortality, which transforms its user into a vampire. Upon accidentally discovering the scarab-shaped machine's purpose, the old man becomes addicted to its power and is soon on the road to ruin. Into the picture comes a wealthy American industrialist who is dying of cancer and will stop at nothing to get his hands on the box. As the old man, unable to break free of the contraption's spell, struggles to keep it to himself, his eight-year-old granddaughter becomes his only ally. Though at times gruesome and grisly, the film has a fair share of good humor and at its core is a touching tale about the relationship between the old man and his grandchild. (Spanish with English subtitles) ★★★ $14.99

Crooklyn

(1994, 114 min, US, Spike Lee) Occasionally funny and at times abrasive, this semiautobiographical film directed by Spike and co-written by Lee and his siblings focuses on the Carmichael family as they experience a summer in their crowded but comfortable Brooklyn neighborhood. Centering on the relationship between the Carmichael's matriarch (Alfre Woodard) and her young daughter (skillfully played by Zelda Harris), this patchwork quilt pieced together with vintage "Soul Train" footage, Afro Sheen commercials and a few wonderful moments may be entertaining for some but a little on the long side for those with short attention spans. Note: One painfully long sequence is shot in Cinemascope, so do not attempt to adjust your sets. ★★★ $19.99

The Cross and the Star

(1990, 53 min, US, John J. Michalczyk) The role of Christianity (especially Catholicism) in the Holocaust, a subject long shrouded in mystery and conflicting opinions, is the contentious subject explored in this informative documentary directed by Michalczyk, a former Jesuit. Interviewed are Jews and Christians alike — from scholars, clergy and Holocaust survivors but sadly not with now-dead government and religious leaders of the time. A thought-provoking historical and political exploration in anti-Semitism and religious animosity. ★★★ $59.99

Cross Creek

(1983, 122 min, US, Martin Ritt) Based on the memoirs of Marjorie Rawlings ("The Yearling"), this compelling drama stars Mary Steenburgen as the authoress, who ventures into Florida's backwoods and composes the novel which life there inspired. Sterling support from Rip Torn and Alfre Woodard. ★★★ $14.99

Cross My Heart

(1987, 100 min, US, Armyan Bernstein) Martin Short and Annette O'Toole are well-cast as two romantics on a first date — where everything goes wrong. An insightful though slow-moving comedy not without a considerable charm. ★★½ $14.99

Cross My Heart

(1990, 105 min, France, Jacques Fansten) French films don't come any sweeter than this charming, offbeat story about a group of classmates united in protecting a fellow student after his mother suddenly dies. Reminiscent of *My Life as a Dog* and *Small Change*, *Cross My Heart* offers its own delightful pleasures. When his young mother inexplicably dies one evening, 12-year-old Martin, fearful that he will be sent to an orphanage, tries to cover up her death. His resourceful classmates soon discover the situation, swear secrecy and begin an elaborate plan to keep Martin away from the authorities by tutoring him, supplying food and money, forging letters to an increasingly suspicious principal and even burying mom in an old grandfather's clock! Their unity in keeping the secret from untrustworthy adults and their unswerving loyalty to their dependent friend is quite atypical in an era when gunshots replace bells in many schoolyards. A heartwarming and winsome tale of growing up. (French with English subtitles) ★★★ $19.99

Cross of Iron

(1977, 120 min, GB/West Germany, Sam Peckinpah) Notable for being the great action director Sam Peckinpah's first war film, this nonetheless represents the director's decline and is only intermittently interesting. It tells the story of a group of German soldiers on the Russian front in 1943 — a compelling idea which isn't given its full due. There is, however, a brilliantly staged battle scene near the end of the film which may, or may not, make it worth sitting through. Stars James Coburn, Maximilian Schell and James Mason. ★★

Crossfire

(1947, 85 min, US, Edward Dmytryk) One of the first Hollywood films to deal with racial bigotry, this low-budget but engrossing thriller shot entirely at night stars Robert Ryan, Robert Mitchum, Robert Young and Gloria Graham. In a New York City hotel, a Jewish man is murdered and three G.I.s just back from the war are suspected. Interestingly, the original victim in the Richard Brooks novel, "The Brick Foxhole," on which the film is based, was a homosexual. Ryan (in an Oscar-nominated role) is especially good as a bigoted soldier. ★★★★ $19.99

Crossing Delancey

(1988, 97 min, US, Joan Micklin Silver) A charming tale of a "modern" woman searching for love and identity in an all-too-often inhumane "modern" world. Amy Irving is radiant as a young urbanite who has fled her ethnic roots to become a member of the "in" Greenwich Village literary scene. When her aging Lower East Side Jewish grandmother, Bubbie, hires a matchmaker to find her a hubbie — a local pickle maker (wonderfully portrayed by Peter Riegert) — her flight becomes all the more urgent. But despite all of her efforts to deny him, he possesses an undeniably sincere charm which plunges her into a true crisis of identity. Reizl Bozyk is a delight as the overbearing but lovable Bubbie. ★★★ $14.99

The Crossing Guard

(1995, 114 min, US, Sean Penn) Writer-director Penn has crafted an actors' vehicle in this somber treatment of guilt and redemption. The story opens on the day John Booth (David Morse) is released from prison after serving his sentence for the drunk driving death of a young girl, whose father Freddy Gale (Jack Nicholson) has vowed revenge. Both Morse and Nicholson deliver powerful yet nuanced performances as each struggles with his own personal hell. Anjelica Huston is equally compelling as Mary, the child's mother, who has attempted to move beyond her own numbing loss and reconnect with life. As the characters confront and rebuff each other, a more complete version of their lives emerges, especially regarding Freddy, whose guilt is as great as his grief. A solid supporting cast and exquisite cinematography propel a sometimes lumbering story line to its resolution, unexpected in its emotional release. A worthy follow-up to Penn's directorial debut *The Indian Runner*. ★★★ $19.99

Crossing the Borders: The Journey of Carlos Fuentes

(1989, 60 min, Canada, John Saffa) Author of the classic novel of the Mexican Revolution, "The Death of Artemio Cruz" and the best-selling "Old Gringo," Carlos Fuentes, one of Latin America's most outspoken novelists, is the subject in this provocative filmed interview. Fuentes freely discusses his views on art, sex and politics as well as offering an entertaining travelogue of Aztec ruins and the unique attractions of Mexico City. ★★½ $19.99

Winona Ryder and Daniel Day-Lewis in *The Crucible*

Crossing the Bridge

(1992, 103 min, US, Mike Binder) Detroit, 1975, is the setting for this rambling, finally-coming-of-age drama about three high school buddies drifting nowhere three years after graduation. Told through the eyes of Mort (an aspiring Jewish writer who sleeps until noon and hangs out with his dopey ex-jock friends), the story concerns the growing up that occurs when the gang considers smuggling drugs from Canada. Writer-director Binder's film comes off as a dramatically enhanced autobiography depicting what might have been his "good old days," but the screenplay at its worst gives way to clichés about tough, young adulthood. The cast, Josh Charles as Mort, Stephen Baldwin and Jason Gedrick as his friends, is competent but it's not nearly enough to lift the film above the excessive weight of its mood and the diverting classic rock soundtrack. ★★ $9.99

Crossover Dreams

(1985, 85 min, US, Leon Ichaso) Although American made, the Latin setting in New York's Spanish Harlem gives a feel of America as a foreign land. Salsa superstar Ruben Blades delivers a mesmerizing acting and singing performance in this gritty, bittersweet comedy about a musician who vainly strives to "cross over" to the pop music mainstream. This is a compelling tale about betraying one's roots and friends for the sake of success, and marks an impressive screen introduction for Blades. ★★★

Crossroads

(1986, 100 min, US, Walter Hill) Ralph Macchio is a musical prodigy who, with the help of a legendary bluesman, hits the road for fame and fortune. He also battles the Devil for his immortal soul. Ry Cooder wrote the score; good as it may be, it doesn't help. ★½ $19.99

The Crow

(1994, 105 min, US, Alex Proyas) *The Crow* was expected to be Brandon Lee's breakout film. Instead, he was killed on the set. He was 28. Ironically, his father, Bruce Lee, also died at an early age when his film career was expected to explode. The film itself is almost overshadowed by these events, but stands on its own as an entertaining actioner with a driving love story. In a darkly luminous, decaying inner city, Lee and his fiancée are brutally murdered for standing up to a slimy urban developer. Lee emerges from his grave after a year's regeneration, seeking vengeance to gain his final peace. Driven by an overpowering moral imperative, he hunts down the perpetrators of the crime against him. Lee exhibits an engaging screen presence in this well-paced, starkly shot neo-noir. His future work would have been eagerly anticipated. ★★★½ $14.99

The Crow: City of Angels

(1996, 86 min, US, Tim Pope) Using the same mythology created in the original but building a completely separate story from it, a new team of filmmakers has brought us a darker vision of the undead avenger. French actor Vincent Perez stars as Ash, a single father who is killed, along with his son, for accidentally witnessing a murder one night. Out of this senseless tragedy, the vengeance of the Crow rises. Ash is informed of his dark purpose by Sarah (Mia Kirshner), the only character to appear in both films, and soon sets his sights on Judah, a drug lord and sadist, and his crew of messengers and murderers (including Iggy Pop in a fantastic performance). Looking like a music video spawned in Clive Barker's nightmares, this sequel is filled with ritualistic tattoos, piercings, and enough religious imagery and symbolism to elevate it above its pulp-action roots. Lacking the sense of fun (and tragedy) Brandon Lee brought to the first production, *City of Angels* is nevertheless a fine effort when considered on its own dark merits. ★★★ $19.99

The Crowd

(1928, 104 min, US, King Vidor) This classic silent drama tells the tale of a newlywed couple's hard times in New York City. Eleanor Boardman and James Murray give refreshingly subtle performances as the young lovers who learn that it is their love for each other that prevents them from being swallowed up in the big city's faceless crowd. ★★★★ $29.99

The Crucible

(1996, 123 min, US, Nicholas Hytner) Arthur Miller's 1953 play about the Salem witch-hunts was a thinly veiled allegory on McCarthyism, and the critical reception to it was lukewarm at best: perhaps critics feared that by supporting the play with the hearings still going on, they too would be suspect. In time, McCarthyism died along with him, the Red Menace faded and the play was recognized as a masterwork of the American theatre. Adapted for the screen by Miller himself, this ominous, viscerally powerful film version is faithful to the text and yet, even though much of the action unfolds in claustrophobic interiors, the film maintains a larger-than-life feel. The story centers on the hysteria which results when lovestruck teen Abigail Williams (Winona Ryder) falsely accuses neighbors of witchcraft – which ultimately leads to John Proctor (Daniel Day-Lewis) and his wife Elizabeth (the terrific Joan Allen). The cast is sheer perfection. Ryder is unforgettable as the vengeful Abigail; she can make a venomous character seem so vulnerable and compelling. Though Communism is now dead, there needn't be a topical political or social relevance to appreciate this remarkable film; it exists as a chilling reminder of the pervasive paranoia during the Cold War, and provides an acidly ironic contrast to contemporary trials in which, rather than the innocent being persecuted, the guilty are set free. ★★★★ $102.99

The Cruel Sea

(1953, 121 min, GB, Charles Frend) Recalling the 1940s classic British war films in both its pacing and structure, the sometimes riveting *The Cruel Sea* follows the wartime experiences of the crew of a British warship patrolling the Atlantic during WWII. Jack Hawkins stars as the ship's captain who witnesses the sacrifice and dehumanizing effect of combat as he and his men battle a literally unseen enemy underneath the ocean, the German U-boats. From the young faces of the dead to a mesmerizing sequence of a ship sinking, the film delves into the often harsh daily lives of men at war, on the sea and, to a lesser extent, on land. The

Crumb

film features stunning cinematography to tell its potent story, and its location shooting and actual war footage only accentuates the realism the film successfully conveys. Donald Sinden makes a stalwart Number One, and a young and handsome Denholm Elliott also stars as one of the ship's officers. ★★★½

Cruel Story of Youth

(1960, 97 min, Japan, Nagisa Oshima) Dazzling, audacious and strangely contemporary over 30 years after its initial release, Oshima's (*In the Realm of the Senses*) second feature is a searing depiction of youthful alienation. Centered around the doomed affair of two teenaged lovers, the film shows a perversely Americanized post-WWII Japan and a disillusioned generation of reckless thrill-seekers. Behind his Ray Bans and his cat-that-ate-the-bird grin, the lead character charts a course toward a tragic end and drags his sexually exploited girlfriend down with him. (Japanese with English subtitles) ★★★★ $29.99

Cruising

(1980, 106 min, US, William Friedkin) Al Pacino goes undercover in the Village's gay community and director Friedkin lets loose a homophobic assault. Pacino plays a police officer assigned to investigate a series of murders committed against gay men. So he dons leather cap and jacket and hits the clubs. This thriller has been aptly described as a "gay horror story," for Friedkin's vision of the gay world is both horrific and inaccurate. ★ $14.99

Crumb

(1995, 119 min, US, Terry Zwigoff) R. Crumb certainly never wore any flowers in his hair that Summer of Love when he invented Underground Comics. Indeed, in each succeeding issue of *Zap* he spewed forth page after foolscap page of Hogarthian bile documenting the delusional nature of our Aquarian innocence. Director Zwigoff has captured the complexity of this man in his straightforward documentary, allowing the helplessly voluble Crumb to tell us more than he ever meant to — just like he does in his comics. Oddly for such a misanthrope, Crumb is as hard on himself as he is on us. His childhood is the fodder for any number of "Sally Jesse Raphael"'s. Indeed, she would probably give him the entire week during sweeps. Only his art has allowed him to come to terms with his "eccentricities," an outlet not available to his two brothers; one of whom finally killed himself after many attempts. The two family members who make the strongest impression by their absence are Crumb's sisters, who wisely declined to participate. ★★★½ $19.99

Crush

(1992, 97 min, New Zealand, Alison MacLean) This unnerving psychological thriller is infused with a brooding sense of doom. Set against the bubbling geysers of rural New Zealand, the story examines themes of passion, betrayal, desire, jealousy, seduction and revenge. Two women, Lane (Marcia Gay Harden) and Christina (Donough Rees), are involved in a car accident, leaving Christina severely injured and Lane (whose carelessness was the cause of the accident) unscathed. Lane inexplicably abandons her comatose friend, eventually befriending a novelist, Colin, and his 15-year-old boyish daughter, Angela. Angela, in turn, befriends the slowly recovering Christina, thereby precipitating an emotional showdown between the characters. A twisted, stylish, tension-filled feature film debut for MacLean, which works best when delving into the three women's constantly shifting relationships and subtle sexual games. ★★★ $19.99

The Crush

(1993, 89 min, US, Alan Shapiro) When a handsome young journalist (Cary Elwes) rents the guest house of an affluent couple, he becomes the object of their precocious teenage daughter's (Alicia Silverstone) dangerously obsessive affections. With a sexy 14-year-old seductress as the protagonist, a victim who is so clueless that one is tempted to yell "just get out of the house already stupid," and a wonderfully inane plot twist involving a used condom, *The Crush* has a sort of shamelessness about its own cheesiness. Silverstone bats her eyes, flirts and connives like a pint-sized Sharon Stone, and Jennifer Rubin adds a nice touch of earthiness as Elwes' of-age love interest. Elwes himself is tall, blond, handsome and a little too wooden, relying on his aforementioned attributes and a self-effacing smile to carry him through. ★★½ $9.99

Crusoe

(1989, 95 min, US, Caleb Deschanel) "Just sit right back and you'll hear a tale, the tale of a fateful trip..." This is indeed a fateful trip into the darkened heart of the colonial imperialist. A trip on which director Deschanel perilously sets out to explore the moral ineptitude of a 19th-century slave trader. Not that this isn't a noble purpose, but what results here is an overburdened and laboring rendition of the Robinson Crusoe story. The film is not entirely without merit, however: the cinematography offers a splendid view of the Seychelles and Aidan Quinn is compelling as a Crusoe who is forced to reevaluate his assumptions about life, power and greed. ★★

Cry Freedom

(1987, 157 min, GB, Richard Attenborough) Attenborough's superbly rendered film about the life and death of South African activist Stephen Biko is a compelling vision of the violence and strife which tears at the heart of the black townships. The story is told through the eyes of Biko's white journalist friend, Donald Woods (excellently portrayed by Kevin Kline). As Biko, Denzel Washington delivers one of his finest and most moving performances. The film was criticized for concentrating more on the plight of Woods and his family than on black South Africa, but in fact, the film stands as a stirring portrait of how injustice for some leads to injustice for all. ★★★½ $19.99

A Cry in the Dark

(1988, 121 min, Australia, Fred Schepisi) With an astonishing characterization, here portraying a mother on trial for the murder of her child, Meryl Streep once again gives proof that she is the finest actress of her generation. Set in Australia, and based on an actual incident which polemically divided that country, the film stars Streep as Lindy Chamberlain, a housewife and mother who is wrongfully arrested when her baby is killed by a dingo. The film recounts the tragedy and its aftermath, and not only explores the unbelievable strain on the Chamberlain household during the trial, but also the power of public opinion and a cynical press. A serious and intelligent film directed with a subtle hand. Sam Neill is excellent as Streep's husband. ★★★½ $14.99

A Cry in the Wild

(1990, 82 min, US, Mark Griffiths) A familiar but compelling family adventure about a young boy who survives a plane crash and now must fight for survival alone in a remote Canadian wilderness. Jared Rushton (*Big*), Ned Beatty and Pamela Sue Martin star. ★★½ $14.99

Cry of the Banshee

(1970, 92 min, GB, Gordon Hessler) This bad period horror film has virtually no redeeming value save the performance of

Vincent Price, who is clearly working well below his talent here. Price stars as a village magistrate who sadistically persecutes those he suspects of witchcraft and runs a strict household filled with incest, rape and treachery. His sons assist him in his nefarious work and give their horrible father a run for his money in the scum department. When Price exterminates a group of heathens who turn out to be Satan-worshippers, he has a curse placed upon his household by the leader of the group. The film then turns into a sort of slasher/monster movie, with various members of his household being dispatched in various gory ways. Though lots of the production design of the film is fairly good, it hardly contributes to the ludicrous and offensive script, which includes lots of nudity and gore to appeal to a mass market crowd. A very low point in Price's career. ★ $9.99

Cry, the Beloved Country

(1951, 111 min, GB, Zoltan Korda) One of the first films to confront the injustices of Apartheid in South Africa, this Korda classic, based on the Alan Paton novel, tells the tale of a black rural priest (Canada Lee) who travels to Johannesburg to find his son. Once there, he is confronted by the brutal realities of urban crime and the dehumanizing conditions of the segregationist townships. Sidney Poitier co-stars as an urban cleric who helps Lee in his search. ★★★½ $69.99

Cry, the Beloved Country

(1996, 109 min, US/South Africa, Darrell James Roodt) A second screen version of Alan Paton's novel of racial inequality in 1940s South Africa, *Cry, the Beloved Country* is compassionate storytelling which though lacking a thoroughly fluid narrative is enriched by two terrific actors in their prime. James Earl Jones plays Rev. Stephen Kumalo, a rural priest who embarks on an odyssey of discovery when he travels to Johannesburg in search of his lost son and sister. Through a little detective work, he soon learns his son is on trial for killing a white man in a robbery attempt. Richard

The Crying Game

C

Harris plays James Jarvis, the victim's father, a supremacist and neighbor of Rev. Kumalo. As the story constructs each grieving father's journey, it eventually leads to their paths crossing, enacted in an extremely poignant scene. A reverent, almost solemn adaptation, the film's strengths lie not only in Jones and Harris' remarkable performances, but from a dramatically involving story which examines from the heart and the mind the plight of both fathers and their eventual reconciliation with their sons. ★★★ $19.99

Cry-Baby

(1990, 85 min, US, John Waters) Waters' musical spoof of 1950s teen flicks is set (where else?) in Baltimore and stars Johnny Depp as "Cry-Baby" Walker, a tough-as-nails, pretty-boy delinquent and leader of the ultra-cool Drapes who falls in love with Allison, a squeaky clean rich girl who has that itch to go "bad." But for those of us who were teased by the uproarious *Hairspray* and have been waiting for his definitive "suburban mall period" classic, sadly, this is not the one. Although it falls a little flat, it is still enjoyable, especially for its many Waters touches. Cameos include Willem Dafoe, Troy Donahue, David Nelson and porn queen Tracie Lords; and Kim McGuire as the hideously unforgettable Hatchet-Face. ★★★ $14.99

The Crying Game

(1992, 112 min, GB, Neil Jordan) In a brilliant marketing coup, the folks at Miramax Films released this film strongly advising people not to give away its "secret." Word of this "secret" quickly swept the nation and everybody was dying to see what would have otherwise been another *Defence of the Realm* or *Hidden Agenda*. Thankfully, director Jordan's tautly realized political thriller is worthy of all the praise and press it generated. Stephen Rea received an Oscar nomination for his role as an IRA terrorist with a troubled conscience who promises a captured British soldier (Forest Whitaker) that he'll look after his girlfriend. Sometime later, Rea has opted out of the terror game and is trying to lead a quiet life of obscurity in London, where he decides to look her up. Newcomer Jaye Davidson's portrayal of the slender and exotic hairdresser is a knockout and also garnered an Oscar nomination. Trouble comes in spades when one of Rea's old Republican comrades, Miranda Richardson (who, as an actress, redefines the word versatile), shows up to test his loyalties. An exciting and highly entertaining story sprinkled with drama, comedy and plenty of intrigue. ★★★★ $9.99

Cthulhu Mansion

(1991, 92 min, US, J.P. Simon) Cheesy story about a gang of fugitives who invade the home of a carnival magician (Frank Finlay) and unwittingly unleash an evil force lying dormant in the basement. ★ $9.99

Cuba

(1979, 126 min, US, Richard Lester) Director Lester (*The Three Musketeers*, *Help!*) imbues a high style to this political thriller about a doomed love affair between Sean Connery and Brooke Adams as the Batista government collapses around them. ★★★ $14.99

Cujo

(1983, 91 min, US, Lewis Teague) Only Stephen King could write a book about a mother and son trapped in a broken-down car and being terrorized by a rabid St. Bernard and get away with it. If you think this premise sounds silly, think again because not only is King's book gripping, but this ably-made film adaptation is at times terrifying and filled with tension which builds to an excellent climax. Dee Wallace stars as the stalwart mom. ★★★ $9.99

Cup Final

(1991, 107 min, Israel, Brian Riklis) This quiet and slightly comic examination of the futile hatred between Israelis and Palestinians is one of the more refreshing films to come from Israel in recent years. The story follows Cohen, a young nebbishy Jewish soldier whose planned trip to Spain for the World Cup soccer finals is dashed when he is captured by a PLO band during the 1982 invasion of Lebanon. Forced to join them on their trek to Beirut, where they hope to find safe haven, he slowly overcomes his resentment towards his captors and even finds room to bond with them when he discovers that he and their charismatic commander, Ziad, are both rooting for the Italian team in the Cup Final. Filled with irony and gentle humor, the film exploits the situation to expose the prejudices of both sides while offering a glimmer of hope that their conflict is not intractable. (Hebrew and Arabic with English subtitles) ★★★ $59.99

Curdled

(1996, 94 min, US, Reb Braddock) In an enticing but bizarre performance, Angela Jones (the sultry cabdriver in *Pulp Fiction*) stars as Gabriela, a young woman fascinated by the sight and smell of human blood. In order to satisfy this craving for gore, she takes a job with a cleaning service specializing in post-forensic jobs. Their latest moneymaker is cleaning up after the "Blueblood Killer," a serial killer preying on wealthy socialites. After she finds a clue to his identity lurking beneath a pool of coagulated blood, she becomes the target of the murderer. Brilliant in its conception but flawed in execution, *Curdled* nevertheless remains satisfying entertainment for those who can stomach its subject matter. One could complain, however, that the filmmakers did not take the premise far enough; instead of being an obsessive misfit with a taste for the macabre, Gabriela eventually becomes a garden-variety Nancy Drew, piecing together bits before the police do. The ending, however, is terrifically macabre — make sure you stay tuned after the credits. ★★½ $99.99

The Cure

(1995, 95 min, US, Peter Horton) Two of Hollywood's biggest box-office kids of the '90s team up in this heartwarming story of a boy with AIDS and his friendship with a precocious neighbor. Brad Renfro (*The Client*) and Joseph Mazzello (*Jurassic Park*) are the kids of single mothers who happen to be as different as water and wine. Diana Scarwid, in a role which has her paralleling the bitchy, jilted mother she hated in *Mommie Dearest*, and Annabella Sciorra are the flatly drawn mothers. Mazzello has that likable quality and wins

over not only the friendship of the punky Renfro, but also the viewer's heart. On a quest to find a cure, the story ends up as almost a pre-teen version of *Midnight Cowboy* complete with bus rides and sickness, stealing and shivering. Though *The Cure* sounds of TV movie-of-the-week quality, the writing and acting has a sensitivity not usually associated with the small screen. ★★★ $19.99

Curly Sue

(1991, 102 min, US, John Hughes) Hughes butchers the memory of *Paper Moon* with this maudlin rehash about a father and daughter con artist team on the grift. Drifter James Belushi and young Alisan Porter hit Chicago and immediately put the sting on yuppie lawyer Kelly Lynch. After hitting Belushi twice with her car, she invites them to stay at her luxury penthouse. Once together, of course, she falls victim to their charm, and vice versa. Hughes' screenplay is ludicrous and manipulative (even for him), and his attempts to mix the bittersweet with slapstick are ill-served. Hughes has gone to the same well once too often. ★ $9.99

The Curse

(1987, 92 min, US, David Keith) An alien meteorite lands on a Tennessee farm, setting off a battle between the young boy who lives there and the surrounding neighbors, who have now been driven crazy from the meteor's effects. An interesting sci-fi tale directed by the actor Keith, and based on H.P. Lovecraft's "The Color Out of Space," which was previously filmed as *Die, Monster, Die*. ★★ $14.99

The Curse of Frankenstein

(1957, 93 min, GB, Terence Fisher) When their programmer *The Quatermass Experiment* became a "monster" hit, Hammer Studios wanted to know why. Was it the sci-fi? Or the monster? Marketing research came back with charts to prove that it was the latter, so Fisher was assigned to direct a new version of Mary Shelley's classic — this time with all the blood and guts that Eastman color and an X certificate would allow. The results made Peter Cushing and Christopher Lee stars and Hammer Studios the Universal of the Thames. This doctor is no madman, just intellect personified; and in this series of films it is he, not the monster, that is the unifying thread. ★★★½ $14.99

The Curse of Her Flesh

(1968, 75 min, US, Michael and Roberta Findlay) Take a little New York avant-garde theatre, blend in some psychedelic '60s sexual revolutionism and some purely gratuitous "T&A" action and the result is this entertainingly weird low-budgeter that, at times, seems to be a straight man's wet dream of lesbian S&M. So for those who never got over the closing of the old Troc and for those who appreciate lines like, "I was once told by a girlfriend that my big toe was better than any man's," this video was made for you. Oh, and the plot? Something about a nightclub owner on a killing spree. ★★ $19.99

The Curse of the Cat People

(1944, 73 min, US, Robert Wise & Gunther von Fritsche) This moody sequel to the classic

Cat People is an effective psychological thriller about a young girl who is befriended by the spirit of her father's deceased first wife. Simone Simon returns from the original as the ghostly visitor; and Kent Smith and Jane Randolph repeat their roles. ★★★ $19.99

Curse of the Demon

(1957, 81 min, GB, Jacques Tourneur) From the director of the original *Cat People* comes this low-budget, terrifying tale about a psychologist who investigates the death of a colleague, who may have been the victim of an ancient curse. Dana Andrews is the sleuthing shrink. A wonderfully atmospheric film which is marred only by its wooden-looking monster, included at the insistence of its American distributors. ★★★½ $14.99

Curse of the Queerwolf

(1987, 90 min, US, Mark Pirro) One of the funnier low-budget horror/sexploitation flicks to come around in some time, this wacky variation on the werewolf legend is, at times, a genuinely hilarious spoof that is marred only by an insidious streak of homophobia. The story follows Larry, a typical straight-as-an-arrow guy who, much to his horror, is bitten on the ass by a pretty "girl," turning him into a queerwolf — male by day and tarty, heavily rouged "lady" by full moon. The target of the film's antic humor is primarily gay men (watch out ACT-UP and Queer Nation members) and innocent little dogs. But while offensive to some, it is more harmless camp than incendiary hatred. ★★ $14.99

The Curse of the Starving Class

(1994, 102 min, US, J. Michael McClay) Ostensibly a quirky, comedy-tinged family melodrama about a clan of failing Nevada farmers, this adaptation of Sam Shepard's stage play stands instead, sadly, as proof that Shepard's work does not translate well to the screen. Indeed, Bruce Beresford's screenplay feels mushy, contrived and disjointed in its examination of a po' white trash family. James Woods is the alchoholic, good-for-nothing dad, who has been exiled from home by his more sober, but no-less-dysfunctional wife, Kathy Bates. Both seem to derive sick pleasure from not only tormenting each other, but their cowboy son, Henry Thomas and precocious daughter, Kristin Fiorella, as well. At issue is the family farm, which both parents are plotting to sell behind each other's backs. He's looking for quick cash from local honky tonk owner Louis Gossett, Jr. and she dreams of trips to Paris with her "lawyer," Randy Quaid, the shyster who sent Woods into the gutter to begin with. With the talent involved, one could reasonably expect much more than this anemic, aimless fluff. ★★ $14.99

The Custodian

(1993, 110 min, Australia, John Dingwall) This stinging indictment of police corruption stars Anthony LaPaglia as an honest cop who implicates himself in an internal affairs investigation as part of a scheme to bring down his crooked partner (Hugo Weaving). Top-notch performances and nail-biting suspense make this a most pleasant surprise. ★★★½ $92.99

Cutter's Way

(1981, 105 min, US, Ivan Passer) Passer's taut and complex thriller has a trio of social misfits stalking a possible murderer for their own muddled purposes. John Heard lends poignancy to the role of a crippled Vietnam War vet and Jeff Bridges is his drifting Ivy League buddy. ★★★ $19.99

Cutthroat Island

(1995, 118 min, US, Renny Harlin) Director Harlin's attempt to make his wife Geena Davis into a blockbuster action heroine is fun for awhile, but this pirate adventure is without a brain in its well-costumed head. A return to the swashbuckling sagas and serials of the 1930s, *Cutthroat Island* is the familiar story of buried treasure, coded maps, uneasy alliances, treacherous kin, barroom brawls and narrow escapes and capped by a big sea battle at the end. The real draw of the movie is not its script (frankly, each time an actor opens his or her mouth the viewer is likely to wince), but its spectacle. And the film succeeds in its several setpiece action scenes, including a bar fight, the climactic ship-to-ship battle and a carriage chase through a crowded market. Unfortunately, the few merits the film does have will probably be lost on the small screen. Davis and Matthew Modine do most of their own stunts, which the director — in Jackie Chan-style — makes obvious with a zooming camera. *Cutthroat Island* is proof, however entertaining it may be, that they don't make 'em like they used to. They should probably stop trying. (Available letterboxed and pan & scan) ★★ $14.99

Cyber Ninja

(1991, 80 min, Japan, Keita Amemiya) Non-stop cartoon-like action and outrageous special effects are sure to keep you on your toes in this highly original and bizarre *Star Wars* inspired sci-fi/martial arts epic. With the story taking place amid the chaos of a destructive war, a warrior princess is kidnapped by the underlings of a dark overlord. Intended to be the main course in a blood sacrifice which will unleash evil upon the land, the princess' only hope is a rebel band of soldiers and the mysterious Cyber Ninja to rescue her before it's too late. In spite of the familiar plot, this film manages to save itself by spicing things up with the use of some truly hallucinatory visuals and unexpected twists. ★★★ $19.99

Cyborg

(1989, 86 min, US, Albert Pyun) Silly and violent sci-fi actioner with Jean-Claude Van Damme fighting vicious gangs in the post-apocalyptic future. ★ $9.99

Cyborg 2

(1993, 99 min, US, Michael Schroder) Once again a cyborg (Angelina Joelie) chooses a hero (Elias Koteas) to be her protector as she tries to escape her creators. Koteas is no Van Damme, and this time it's the cyborg who's the fighting machine and routinely helps the hero out of hot spots. Jack Palance periodically appears on video monitors as guidance for the desperate duo and even has his own action sequence, though he doesn't perform any one-armed push-ups. While this movie is by no means the kick-and-punch fest its predecessor was, it does feature some good effects. ★★ $94.99

Cyrano de Bergerac

(1950, 113 min, US, Michael Gordon) Jose Ferrer won an Oscar for his stirring portrayal of one of literature's favorite heroes: the swashbuckling poet with the protruding proboscis — Cyrano de Bergerac. Though the film is technically uneven, it is more than made up for by Ferrer's classically flamboyant performance. Steve Martin (*Roxanne*), Gérard Depardieu and Derek Jacobi all appear in other versions of the Edmond Rostand classic (all of which are on video); and each actor is singularly brilliant. ★★★ $19.99

Cyrano de Bergerac

(1984, 176 min, GB, Terry Hands) The Royal Shakespeare Company's elaborate and stunning 1984 Broadway production of Edmond Rostand's classic. Derek Jacobi is mesmerizingly brilliant in the title role (he won a Tony Award), and an exceptional supporting cast includes Sinead Cusack and Pete Postlethwaite. ★★★★ $29.99

Cyrano de Bergerac

(1990, 135 min, France, Jean-Paul Rappeneau) Rappeneau's outstanding realization of Edmond Rostand's classic play is an overwhelming cinematic achievement, made only more so by the monolithic screen presence of Gérard Depardieu in the title role. For his part, Depardieu delivers the performance of a lifetime as he sinks his teeth into the romantic heart of Cyrano with panache and punctuates every action with a flourish. Everything else in the film falls into place around him: the lavish set pieces, the swashbuckling action, the beautiful rhyming verse and the brilliant cinematography. A most exciting and emotionally rewarding film experience. (French with English subtitles) ★★★★ $19.99

D3: The Mighty Ducks

(1996, 104 min, US, Robert Lieberman) Adolescents who enjoyed the first two *Ducks* films will probably like this third, lesser entry — notwithstanding the addition of some elements of the *Revenge of the Nerds* formula. This time out the quacking heroes are enrolled as a new Junior Varsity team on a full scholarship at Eaton Hall, a snobby prep school where they are (surprise!) the school underdogs and disdained by the status quo, particularly the Varsity team. The team's captain, Charlie, gets to fight with a new coach as Estevez has such a small role that it barely justifies his star billing. And Charlie, once again, comes to love and respect (surprise!) the new coach and the team comes from behind to (surprise!) beat the bullies and save their scholarship. The end (or is it?)... ★★ $22.99

D.A.R.Y.L.

(1985, 99 min, US, Simon Wincer) An engaging if low-keyed children's fantasy about a young boy, half-android, who runs away from his government lab and is befriended by a childless couple. Barret Oliver nicely plays the youth, and Mary Beth Hurt and Michael McKean are the couple who take him in. ★★½ $9.99

D.O.A.

(1950, 83 min, US, Rudolph Mate) Edmond O'Brien walks into a police station and reports a murder: his own. Thus begins Mate's tense, enthralling mystery about a man (O'Brien) who only has three days to find out who gave him a slow-acting lethal poison. Filmed on location in Los Angeles and San Francisco, this classic film noir will have you on the edge of your seat right up to the end. ★★★½ $19.99

D.O.A.

(1988, 96 min, US, Rocky Morton & Annabel Jankel) Co-directors Morton and Jankel's music video background is much in evidence in this slick style-over-substance remake of the 1950 film noir classic about a man (Dennis Quaid) who spends his final hours of life looking for the person who slipped him a slow-acting poison. Though much maligned as a remake, the film is an enjoyable thriller in its own right. Also with Meg Ryan, Charlotte Rampling and Daniel Stern. ★★★ $9.99

Da

(1988, 102 min, US, Matt Clark) Barnard Hughes reprises his award-winning stage role in this endearing adaptation about a man (Martin Sheen) who returns to his native Ireland for his estranged father's funeral; coming to terms with his deceased parent when the man materializes after the funeral. A rewarding, funny examination of familial responsibilities and misgivings. ★★★ $79.99

Dad

(1989, 117 min, US, Gary David Goldberg) As with the similarly themed *Da*, a son attempts to reconcile himself with his father, though in this instance his dad is not deceased but dying. Though not as successful as Matt Clark's comedy, Jack Lemmon's terrific performance compensates for the film's occasional dramatic lapses. Ted Danson and Olympia Dukakis also star. ★★½ $19.99

Daddy and the Muscle Academy

(1992, 60 min, Finland, Ilppo Pohjola) This involving documentary on the life and art of Tom of Finland has enjoyed acclaim both in lesbian and gay film festivals as well as from mainstream critics through its several theatrical engagements in the United States. The film explores the evolution of Tom's art from his crude but sexy drawing of German soldiers during Finland's Nazi occupation to his work as one of the most popular illustrators of gay erotic images; reaching a point in his craft that he has become an icon in the realm of gay male erotica. Tom himself is interviewed, shortly before his death in 1991 at the age of 71. He reminisces about his unusual childhood obsessions, the influences on his work and his interest in erotic-romantic images that are filled with uniforms, leather and chains, and muscle-bound, well-endowed men. Hundreds of his drawings are shown in this almost adulatory film on this celebrated artist. ★★★ $49.99

Daddy Long Legs

(1955, 126 min, US, Jean Negulesco) An enchanting musical romance with playboy Fred Astaire anonymously sponsoring orphan Leslie Caron's education, the two eventually falling in love. Score includes "Something's Got to Give." ★★★ $19.99

Daddy Nostalgia

(1990, 105 min, France/GB, Bertrand Tavernier) In this tender and wise story of the complex relationship between an aging, sick father, his wife and their daughter, Dirk Bogarde — in what may be his valedictorian performance — is simply brilliant as the fastidious and at times insufferable father. Jane Birkin plays his gangly screenwriter daughter who travels to her parents' sun-splashed Côte d'Azur villa when her father takes ill. Completing the trio is Bogarde's wife (Odette Laurie), a French woman who has become distant after enduring years with her grouchy, emotionally diffident husband. Director Tavernier insightfully delves into the characters' lives, thoughts and feelings as they attempt to understand each other and express their love. *Daddy Nostalgia* is emotionally devastating, yet never maudlin. ★★★★ $29.99

Daddy's Dyin'...Who's Got the Will?

(1990, 97 min, US, Jack Fisk) A wacky Texas family reunites at Daddy's deathbed, where secrets, accusations and grudges spew forth as its members wait to see exactly what they're gonna git. Amiable shenanigans with Beau Bridges, Beverly D'Angelo, Tess Harper, Judge Reinhold, Amy Wright and Keith Carradine. ★★½ $14.99

Daisy Miller

(1974, 93 min, US, Peter Bogdanovich) Visually striking adaptation of Henry James' novel with Cybill Shepherd as the 19th-century heroine Daisy, a young American woman who shocks European high society with her liberated sexual attitudes. Though Shepherd's flirtatious performance fails to fully capture the spirit and complexity of James' character, she is surrounded by a first-rate supporting cast, including Cloris Leachman as Daisy's mother, and especially Eileen Brennan as a snobbish socialite. ★★★ $14.99

Damage

(1993, 112 min, GB, Louis Malle) *Damage* is an arousing film, not just for the voyeuristic thrill of the much ballyhooed sex scenes between Jeremy Irons and Juliette Binoche, but for the peek into the sumptuous London flats, elegant country estates and luxurious antiqued European hotels which serve as the film's backdrop. Irons plays an English cabinet minister who finds himself drawn to his son's exquisite and emotionally bruised new lover (Binoche). Miranda Richardson earned an Oscar nomination for her role as Iron's restrained but ultimately tortured wife, and Rupert Graves rounds out the cast as the betrayed son and lover. Not much in terms of plot, but high on atmosphere and tension (both carnal and familial), *Damage* is at times an almost savage look into the sexual psyche. ★★★ $19.99

Fred Astaire and Leslie Caron in *Daddy Long Legs*

Dames

(1934, 90 min, US, Ray Enright) One of the best of the 1930s musicals, this backstage tuner features some great standards ("I Only Have Eyes for You," and the title tune among them) and those terrific Busby Berkeley dance routines. Forget the plot – it's another "let's put on a show" – it's the singing and dancing and comedy that's the main attraction here, and it's a hoot. The cast includes Dick Powell, Ruby Keeler, Zasu Pitts, and the great Joan Blondell. ★★★ $19.99

Damn the Defiant!

(1962, 101 min, GB, Lewis Gilbert) Alec Guinness is stellar as a British naval captain who must fend off a challenge for power by his first mate (Dirk Bogarde), a fierce and merciless officer who is reviled by the crew. Set during the Napoleonic wars, the movie was filmed with an acute sense of historical detail. ★★★ $14.99

Damn Yankees

(1958, 110 min, US, George Abbott) "Whatever Lola wants, Lola gets," and what Lola gets is this sparkling screen adaptation of the Tony Award-winning Broadway musical. Tab Hunter is Joe Hardy, the youthful reincarnate of a middle-aged die-hard Washington Senators fan who makes a pact with the Devil so he can help beat those damn New York Yankees. Re-creating their award-winning stage roles are the miraculous Gwen Verdon as Lola, who helps the Devil tame Joe, and Ray Walston, who gives an irrepressible comic performance as the Devil. With splashy choreography by Bob Fosse (who also appears in one dance sequence), a good-natured and memorable score and appealing characters, *Damn Yankees* is a definite winner. ★★★ $19.99

The Damned

(1969, 155 min, Italy/West Germany, Luchino Visconti) A frantic international cast depicts Visconti's panorama of pre-war German decadence and Nazi narcissism. Visconti captures all the horrors of the era, culminating with the infamous slaughter of the "Night of the Long Knives." Helmut Berger is exceptional with his elaborate impersonation of Marlene Dietrich. Also starring Dirk Bogarde, Ingrid Thulin and Charlotte Rampling. (Filmed in English) ★★★½ $59.99

A Damsel in Distress

(1937, 101 min, US, George Stevens) Fred Astaire's best musical of the 1930s made without Ginger Rogers. Though Joan Fontaine lacks Ginger's musical skill and screen charm, co-stars George Burns and especially Gracie Allen make one forget about the leading lady with their delightful supporting turns. Fred plays a famous dancer performing in London who falls for Lady Joan. The film contains one of the most remarkable musical production numbers ever conceived, "The Funhouse" sequence, and other Gershwin numbers include "A Foggy Day" and "Nice Work If You Can Get It." ★★★½ $19.99

Dance, Girl, Dance

(1940, 90 min, US, Dorothy Arzner) In possibly her most explicitly feminist film, director Arzner pairs Maureen O'Hara, as an idealistic young woman who dreams of becoming a ballerina, with Lucille Ball, the tough-as-leather show girl who doesn't take any shit from her leering, drunken audience. Ball convinces O'Hara to become partners in a burlesque troupe in this entertaining "the vamp and the virgin" comedy-drama. As "Bubbles," Ball is in great form. ★★★ $19.99

Dance Me Outside

(1994, 91 min, Canada, Bruce McDonald) Energized and completely unaffected performances from a talented young cast imbue a finely crafted coming-of-age story with gritty realism. Set in the present day on a Canadian Indian reservation, a young woman's murder is the focal point of many intertwining stories of relationship, family, friendship, racial prejudice and the search for identity and purpose. Ryan Black and Adam Beach play two young men trying to get into an auto mechanics school in Toronto. They need to write an essay as part of the entrance exam, but have nothing to say until the brutal murder of one of their friends provides the material – not only for the essay, but for their own personal quests for definition and adulthood. This independent gem details the course of many lives with humor, insight and compassion, without maudlin sentimentality or gilded heroics. This is a world of real people with real-life problems, who carve out solutions as they're needed. *Dance Me Outside* is surprisingly powerful and unexpectedly involving. ★★★½ $14.99

Dance of Hope

(1990, 75 min, US, Deborah Shaffer) The brutal excesses of power of the Argentine military government and the heart-rending plight of *los desaparacidos* have been well documented. But the equally repressive actions of the Pinochet regime in neighboring Chile is only now being uncovered. This film by Academy Award-winning director Shaffer probes the sad story of the relatives of the thousands of people who "disappeared" in the past ten years and their efforts to get the government to provide answers. The title of the film refers to the *cueca*, Chile's national dance of passion and courtship: the mothers, wives and relatives of the missing citizens perform this dance alone to emphasize the loss of their partner. The film features Sting performing his hit song, "They Dance Alone," with Peter Gabriel in an Amnesty International concert. (Spanish with English subtitles) ★★★ $59.99

Dance with a Stranger

(1985, 101 min, GB, Mike Newell) This critically acclaimed tale of passion and mystery follows the path of the romantic self-destruction of Ruth Ellis, the last woman to be executed in Great Britain. This gripping examination of a murderous romance stars Miranda Richardson (in a sensational film debut) as a dance hall girl who murders her abusive lover. As the selfish murdered boyfriend, Rupert Everett gives a convincing and sensual performance of an emotionally shallow upper-class beauty whose slumming leads to his demise. Ian Holm is outstanding in support as another of Ellis' men. ★★★½

Dancers

(1987, 98 min, US, Herbert Ross) From the director and star of *The Turning Point* comes this inferior tale of an egocentric ballet star (Mikhail Baryshnikov) who tends to seduce every young woman with whom he dances. When he turns his eye towards a young ballerina, he gets an unexpected lesson in love. ★ $14.99

Dances with Wolves

(1990, 183 min, US, Kevin Costner) Costner's directorial debut is this emotionally charged Academy Award-winning tribute to the Sioux Indians of the Dakota plains. Costner himself stars as Lt. John Dunbar of the Union Army, a man whose life is changed forever when he befriends the Lakota. At the close of the Civil War, Costner applies for service in the Western frontier. When he finally arrives at his outpost, finding it deserted, he settles in and begins to explore the territory. It is here that he makes contact with the Lakota. Beautifully photographed and filled with amazing stunts, *Dances with Wolves* presents a majestically sweeping vision of the grandeur of the great American West. The acting throughout is wonderful with Costner giving great depth to the humanistic Lt. Dunbar. Graham Greene is superb as Kicking Bird, Mary McDonnell is Stands with a Fist and Rodney A. Grant is Wind in His Hair. A wonderful cinematic achievement in which Costner brings back the epic western. (Costner's original four-hour version is also available for $29.99) (English and Lokata with English subtitles) ★★★★ $14.99

Dancing in the Dark

(1986, 98 min, Canada, Leon Marr) Martha Henry gives a mesmerizing performance as a woman whose life is defined by the minutiae of her 20-year marriage. When her protective shell of illusion cracks, she forfeits her tenu-

George Burns and Gracie Allen join Fred Astaire in
A Damsel in Distress

ous grasp on reality for a moment of catharsis. Well-crafted and somber, with able support from Neil Munro and thoughtful direction by Marr. ★★★ $14.99

Dancing Lady

(1933, 94 min, US, Robert Z. Leonard) An appealing M-G-M musical about chorus girl Joan Crawford making it to the top while involved with stage director Clark Gable and playboy Franchot Tone. Fred Astaire made his film debut, and Nelson Eddy and The Three Stooges also star. ★★½ $19.99

Dandelions

(1974, 92 min, The Netherlands, Adrian Hoven) A very young Rutger Hauer stars in this cartoonish sex drama that is dubbed in a style reminiscent of *What's Up, Tiger Lily?*. Rutger appears as a boozing, womanizing, self-hating low-life — or as one of the women he torments in the film calls him, "a cesspool of depravity." The characters, when they are not naked or gyrating in sexual contortions, are clothed in outlandish `70s mod outfits. Did people really dress like that? Anyway, our hero, underneath it all, is really only looking for true love. Will he find it? ★★

Dangaio

(1988, 45 min, Japan, Toshihiro Hirano) With names like Ramba and Pi Thunder, this cross-cultural animated space story involves four Esper-Warriors (three teenage girls and a boy), who are brainwashed and then altered into "augmented humans" or androids by a cunning scientist. This samurai-influenced story follows their adventures through space as they fight a powerfully evil blond cyborg as well as other galactic despots, all the while seeking truth to their actual identities. The battles are mostly in space, but in one funny sequence, poor Tokyo again finds itself an impotent victim to a Godzilla-like thrashing as the space wars settle down onto the unfortunate city. ★★★ $34.99

Danger: Diabolik

(1968, 99 min, Italy, Mario Bava) In this campy, colorful, hilariously wild adaptation of a popular Italian comic book, director Bava, better known for his seminal horror films *Black Sunday* amd *Black Sabbath*, collaborates with producer Dino De Laurentiis to produce a fun romp which echoes and spoofs everything from James Bond to "The Man from U.N.C.L.E." to "big heist" films of the early 1960s. John Phillip Law plays Diabolik, a master criminal who surrounds himself with electronic gadgets, beautiful women and wealth. During the course of the film, he steals ten million dollars, a priceless emerald necklace and a twenty-ton ingot of gold — and he manages to elude both the police and the underworld syndicate which has put a price on his head. Too much fun to seriously criticize and too ludicrous to take too seriously, the movie succeeds at just the level it was meant to: as a live-action comic book which has the viewer constantly rooting for its ultimate super (anti) hero. (Filmed in English) ★★★ $9.99

Dangerous

(1935, 72 min, US, Alfred E. Green) Bette Davis won an Oscar for her performance in this glossy soaper, but it was more for the snub the year earlier when she was overlooked for *Of Human Bondage* (Bette herself admitted the Oscar *should* have gone to Katharine Hepburn for *Alice Adams*). However, Davis is quite good as an actress on the skids who captivates architect Franchot Tone. ★★½ $19.99

Dangerous Game

(1993, 107 min, US, Abel Ferrara) Ferrara continues his examination of moral ambiguity (*Bad Lieutenant*) with this verité *pas de trois* between a film director (Harvey Keitel) and his two leads (Madonna and James Russo). They're working on a nauseating little film in which Russo plays a husband who continually abuses his wife (Madonna) and subsequently both attempt to escape their life of drug abuse and debauchery. Using the device of a film within a film, Ferrara warps the distinction between illusion and reality as the three principals become ever more enmeshed in their on- and off-the-set shenanigans. Keitel, Russo and Madonna all perform well, and Ferrara shows a deft directorial hand, but that won't help most viewers overcome the film's repugnant core and unrelentingly nihilistic viewpoint. (Unrated version) ★½ $96.99

Dangerous Liaisons

(1988, 120 min, US, Stephen Frears) Sexual corruption, insidious power games, deceitful duplicity and seductively witty dialogue are some of the unusual ingredients in this sumptuously enticing film. Glenn Close stars as the Marquise de Merteuil, an elegantly detached woman who along with her former lover, the similarly cunning Valmont (John Malkovich), enters into a wager on whether he can seduce the innocent Michelle Pfeiffer. Their amoral sexual sport entangles them and all who enter their lives as it follows its inevitably destructive course. Close revels in the role of the acrimonious aristocrat, and Malkovich, although cast against type, still captures the dangerously seductive charms of a snake dressed in gentleman's clothing. A special cinematic treat that should entertain the entire spectrum of tastes — from the romantic to the Machiavellian. ★★★★ $14.99

Dangerous Liaisons 1960

(1960, 111 min, France, Roger Vadim) Roger Vadim's 1960 version of Choderlos De Laclos' decadent tale of the sexual games of the morally bankrupt is set within the chic and smoky jazz clubs of modern-day Paris. Jeanne Moreau and Gerard Philip are the wealthy couple in a marriage where adultery and deceit are allowed and even encouraged just as long as love is absent. Philip's Valmont is a debonair, mysterious manipulator whose conquests are recounted to, and equalled by, Moreau — his wickedly duplicitous wife Juliette. The film, possibly Vadim's best, pulsates with sexual energy and excitement with its cool mood enhanced by a sultry jazz score by Thelonious Monk with Art Blakey and the Jazz Messengers. "C'est la guerre." "Tres bien, la guerre!" (French with English subtitles) ★★★½ $79.99

Dangerous Minds

(1995, 94 min, US, John N. Smith) As gritty as a high school prom, *Dangerous Minds*, based on LouAnne Johnson's autobiography "My Posse Don't Do Homework," treads the well-worn hallways and classrooms of nearly every self-sacrificing teacher film from *The Corn Is Green* to *Blackboard Jungle* to *Stand and Deliver*. And while *Minds* is clichéd, predictable and sentimental, it offers Michelle Pfeiffer as Johnson a chance to deliver an affecting performance — it's a portrayal which helps immeasurably to gloss over the film's otherwise formulaic structure. Pfeiffer plays the spirited teacher who turns around the lives of her apathetic, "socially troubled" students (mostly black and Hispanic) while battling school administration and other outside forces. Johnson is written as so compassionate her character almost borders on liberal, do-gooder parody, but Pfeiffer manages to wring some honest emotions in spite of it all. The unruly students are mostly Screenplay 101 concoctions — their tongues may be sharp but what makes them tick is noticeably absent. ★★½ $14.99

Dangerous Moonlight

(1941, 83 min, GB, Brian Desmond Hurst) This wartime classic by director Hurst (*Playboy of the Western World*) tells the story of a Polish concert pianist (Anton Walbrook) who, against the strenuous objections of his wife, puts aside his music and flies for the RAF. Wonderfully directed and superbly acted, the film makes excellent use of its classical music score. ★★★½ $19.99

Dangerous Moves

(1983, 110 min, Switzerland, Richard Dembo) Set amid the tranquil lakeside of Geneva at the site of an international chess match, this Academy Award-winning film is imbued with a power, literacy and complexity that belies its sedate environment. The physical movements may be minimal but the tension between the two grand masters is visceral and exciting. Starring Michel Piccoli, Leslie Caron and Liv Ullmann. (Dubbed) ★★★

A Dangerous Woman

(1993, 99 min, US, Stephen Gyllenhaal) One of the screen's great chameleons, Debra Winger is riveting as an innocent, child-like woman living in a small Southern town. Though somewhat shielded by her sister's (Barbara Hershey) position of power and influence, her naive inability to tell socially expected lies throws her into conflict with others in her community. She is also ill-equipped to deal with the emotional upheaval she experiences at the hands of an itinerant laborer (Gabriel Byrne). Ironically, her turmoil mirrors that of her sister's conflicted relationship with a married man, offering acerbic commentary on our lack of control in affairs of the heart. Though the narrative gets somewhat muddled, the film is ably carried by a fine ensemble cast, which includes David Strathairn, Chloe Webb and Laurie Metcalf. ★★½ $19.99

Daniel

(1983, 129 min, US, Sidney Lumet) This gripping political drama based on the Julius and Ethel Rosenberg case divides its story between two eras: the 1950s, when the Rosenbergs were (unjustly?) sentenced to death; and the late 1960s, where their surviving children grapple with the memory of their parents.

Timothy Hutton plays the title character, whose search for the truth about his mom and dad ushers a wave of recollections about them. Mandy Patinkin and Lindsay Crouse play the Rosenbergs (here called the Isaacsons), Amanda Plummer is their troubled daughter, and Ed Asner plays their dedicated lawyer up against a bigoted system. Expertly acted, this rewarding film moves slowly, but never fails to move the viewer. ★★★ $59.99

Danny Boy

(1984, 92 min, Ireland, Neil Jordan) This bleak Irish drama is a taut portrait of a young saxophone player who witnesses the murder of his manager. Haunted by violent images of one of the assailants, he sets out to hunt him down and avenge the atrocity. A dark and moody character study whose style is too self-serving and which is only occasionally intriguing. Stephen Rea appears in his film debut (he and director Jordan would reunite on *The Crying Game*) as the young musician. ★★ $59.99

Dante's Inferno

(1969, 90 min, GB, Ken Russell) Russell's filmic fascination with artists tortured by personal weaknesses (*The Music Lovers, Mahler, Valentino*) is amply evident in this early, rarely seen film. Oliver Reed plays Dante Gabriel Rossetti — a morose, brilliant and drunken painter-poet who, as Russell sees it, was more interested in his flamboyant and excessive lifestyle than his artistic output. Rossetti drew into his circle some of the most prominent figures of the late 19th-century: William Morris and his wife Jane, the poet Swinburne, his poetess sister Christina Rossetti and the critic John Ruskin. Russell re-creates the period wonderfully in this engrossing tale of art, poetry, booze and sex. ★★★ $19.99

Dante's Peak

(1997, 100 min, US, Roger Donaldson) After the spectacular effects of the two F/X film releases (*ID4, Twister*) which came before it, *Dante's Peak* should have been a blast. After all, the technology is only supposed to get better. But with only adequate effects and a story so transparent and cluttered as to make *Twister's* screenplay resemble *Sling Blade*, this disaster adventure — the first and least of 1997's volcano movies — disappoints on all levels. Clearly needing lunch money, Pierce Brosnan plays a scientist who predicts a major volcanic eruption in the Pacific Northwest. No one believes him, except the spunky mayor (Linda Hamilton) of the town located next to the mountain he thinks is ready to blow. The film teases throughout until the eventual explosion, but only after a stockpile of clichéd characters and plot lines limp across the screen. There's one very good effect involving a river overtaking a bridge, but the rest look like *Earthquake* outtakes. ★ $102.99

Danton

(1982, 136 min, Poland/France, Andrzej Wajda) Wajda directs his camera toward the social upheaval and political treachery of the French Revolution, and by doing so, draws an obvious allegory to the political situation in his native Poland in the 1980s. Gérard Depardieu is the boisterous people's champion, Danton, who is betrayed by the coldly civilized Robespierre as they maneuver for leadership of the New Republic. (French with English subtitles) ★★★★

Danzón

(1991, 103 min, Mexico, Maria Novaro) The sudden disappearance of her longtime dancing partner compels Julia (the endearing Maria Rojo), a demure Mexico City telephone operator, to begin a search which escalates into a personal odyssey, transforming her staid, habitual life with a flourish of self-discovery. She begins her road trip guarded and aloof, but before long is getting invaluable fashion advice from a cabaret-performer transvestite and warm emotional support from her hotel's craggy concièrge as well as the resident ladies of the evening. She greets this cavalcade of intriguing characters and exotic circumstances with a newly informed independence and a revitalized sense of self. Dance music pulsates throughout the film; the cultural significance of the dancehall is especially evident in one scene in which Julia explains the nuances of *danzón* (a particular kind of dance) to an admiring young man. A grown-up fairy tale awash with light and vibrant color. (Spanish with English subtitles) ★★★ $19.99

Darby O'Gill and the Little People

(1959, 93 min, US, Robert Stevenson) Albert Sharpe is the Irish caretaker whose tendency to spin the blarney causes no one to believe him when he becomes the guest of the Leprechauns in their underground home. Great special effects create a timeless atmosphere of charm and fantasy. Featuring a young Sean Connery. ★★★ $14.99

The Dark Angel

(1987, 148 min, GB, Peter Hammond) Peter O'Toole is an indulgent study of heavy-lidded menace in this wonderfully Gothic tale of a trusting maiden, a tragic death, a large inheritance, a mysterious and nasty Frenchwoman and a deceptively helpful uncle. This is all based on J.S. LeFanu's "Uncle Silas," written in 1864, which is generally regarded as the first psychological thriller. Encroaching danger is presaged by the strange French governess' incessant probing of her innocent charge, Maude (Jane Lapotaire), regarding the existence of her father's will. Maude's father reveals to her the key to the chest in the library, but not enough family secrets to save her from horrific malice from those she's been told to trust. The cast revels in their deliciously exaggerated characterizations, and the production is a feast of fine detail, from the crumbling decadence of Bartram Haugh to the lace and buttons of the gowns. ★★★ $19.99

Dark City

(1990, 98 min, Zimbabwe/GB, Chris Curling) The struggle of black South Africans for justice and equality in their own land is the theme of

Danton

this impassioned political thriller filmed entirely in Zimbabwe with a cast made up primarily of the members of Johannesburg's Market Theatre. When a peaceful march to the mayor's house of a black township turns violent, the police begin a crackdown, arresting seven innocent people. As they are put on trial in a kangaroo court, the black leaders are faced with accepting the injustice or fighting back. Victor, a naive and peaceful young man, is the center of the story as he becomes intricately involved after his friend is killed in cold blood and his brother imprisoned. The film focuses not only on his struggles over whether to continue non-violent protest or to take up a more violent approach, but also examines the rifts within the black independence movement which often ferment violence within the community, pitting black against black and rarely involving the true antagonists: the white authorities. ★★★ $29.99

The Dark Corner

(1946, 99 min, US, Henry Hathaway) Lucille Ball and Clifton Webb star in this unfairly neglected film noir mystery which is both exciting and well-acted. Lucy plays a secretary who sets out to prove the innocence of her private detective boss (Mark Stevens), who's been framed for murder. Webb co-stars as the caustic, wealthy art dealer who's behind the frame-up. ★★★ $59.99

The Dark Crystal

(1983, 94 min, GB, Jim Henson & Frank Oz) Muppet masters Henson and Oz deliver their take on a Tolkien-esque world peopled with furry dwarf creatures and evil sorcerers with their unmistakable zaniness and a healthy dose of plain-old good storytelling. The story concerns Jen, a young male "Gelfling," who sets out on a harrowing and heroic journey to rid his magical realm of the evil rule of the "Skeksis," a bilious and physically repugnant race that resemble decaying vultures. While a little short on plot, the film's characterizations are top-notch and should delight adults as well as kids. ★★★ $12.99

Dark Eyes

(1987, 115 min, Italy, Nikita Mikhalkov) Marcello Mastroianni is nothing short of brilliant as Romano, an irresolute dreamer seduced by both love and money in this charming romantic fable by Russian émigré Mikhalkov (*Slave of Love, Oblomov*). The story begins on an ocean liner where the garrulous Romano recounts his tumultuous and tragic life story to a rapt elderly newlywed. His tale is one of lost ambitions, luxury and boredom changed forever after he meets and falls deliriously in love with a mysterious Russian beauty. A funny, enchanting and, most of all, entertaining film. (Italian with English subtitles) ★★★½

Dark Habits

(1983, 96 min, Spain, Pedro Almodóvar) While not Almodóvar's best work, *Dark Habits* nonetheless manages to carry the director's unparalleled sense of twisted, subversive and blacker-than-black humor. When Yolanda's boyfreind dies of an overdose of heroin, she decides it's better to run and hide than face the law. She winds up at the doorstep of the "Humble Redeemers," an order of heroin-addicted nuns who specialize in cases like hers — indeed they were all once cases like her! The cast includes some of the familiar Almodóvites: Julietta Serrano stars as the Mother Superior and Carmen Maura appears as the cloister's resident tiger keeper, Sister Sin. (Spanish with English subtitles) ★★½ $39.99

The Dark Half

(1993, 121 min, US, George Romero) Timothy Hutton stars in this well-mounted but uninvolving story from the undisputed master of recycled horror, Stephen King. Hutton is adequate in the role of a "serious" author who is forced by a blackmailer to publicly bury his cheesy pulp fiction-writing pseudonym, "George Stark." But, like most dead things in horror movies, Stark doesn't take extinction lying down; he springs to life and goes on a killing spree. Romero's sure-footed direction is light years away from the low-budget material that he has come to be associated with, and quality performances from Hutton, Amy Madigan and Michael Rooker raises this head-and-shoulders above the usual King juvenilia — it just isn't very scary. Also with Julie Harris. ★★½ $14.99

Dark Horse

(1992, 98 min, US) Ari Meyers plays a teenager whose father (Ed Begley, Jr.) relocates the family from Los Angeles to a small town following her mother's death. After falling in with a bad crowd, she winds up in court and is sentenced to community service on a horse ranch, owned by a vet (Mimi Rogers). There she meets and falls in love with Jet, the "dark horse." Tragedy befalls both Allie and the horse, leading to an inspiring climax, complete with swelling string music. An admirable cast (including Donovan Leitch and Samanatha Eggar) and gorgeous scenery almost compensate for a tepid, melodramatic story line. ★★½ $14.99

The Dark Mirror

(1946, 85 min, US, Robert Siodmak) Olivia deHavilland, in a dual role, gives an entertainingly over-the-top performance as identical twins: one a virtuous young lady, the other a psychotic, deranged murderer. This Freudian thriller, both tense and fast-paced, revolves around the police and a psychiatrist's baffled efforts to determine which of the two women is innocent and which is the killer. ★★★ $14.99

Dark Passage

(1947, 106 min, US, Delmer Daves) Humphrey Bogart stars in this stylish film noir as a falsely accused convict who escapes prison and changes his appearance (via plastic surgery) in order to smoke out the real culprit. Lauren Bacall is on hand as the socialite who believes in him. Also starring the inimitable Agnes Moorehead. Good use of subjective camerawork, in which the first half hour of the film is shown from the point of view of the escaped con — whose face we don't see until he becomes Bogart. ★★★ $19.99

Dark Romances, Pts. 1 & 2

(1990, 235 min, US, Mark Shepard/Patricia Miller/Samuel Oldham/Rod Matsui/et. al.) This entertaining and perverse seven-story anthology features scream queen Brinke Stevens and adult film starlet/Hustler magazine covergirl Elle Rio. It's a fast-paced sex-and gore-laden epic which delivers the goods and then some, with subjects ranging from failed DNA experiments, hen-pecked husbands, masturbating teenage boys, S&M domination, murder, deception and many other fun topics. ★★½ $59.99

Dark Victory

(1939, 106 min, US, Edmund Goulding) Bette Davis, in one of her greatest triumphs, stars in this classic soaper as a jet-setting socialite who discovers she has only a few months to live. As she slowly accepts her fate, she becomes more responsible, living her remaining months "beautifully and finely," as her doctor/lover (George Brent) suggests. The fine supporting cast includes Geraldine Fitzgerald, an oddly-cast Humphrey Bogart and Ronald Reagan as Davis' happily betrothed suitor. ★★★½ $19.99

The Dark Wind

(1993, 111 min, US, Errol Morris) Director Morris imbues *Dark Wind* with the same hypnotic realism which permeated his 1988 documentary, *The Thin Blue Line*. Lou Diamond Phillips is arguably the best he's ever been as Jim Chee, the Navajo cop who studies to be a medicine man. A corpse mutilated by a Navajo skinwalker is found on Hopi ground, involving the police in intertribal politics and the spectre of witchcraft. The FBI and major drug transactions rapidly surface in this tale of a long-festering lust for revenge and rampant greed. Neil Jiminez (*The Waterdance*) co-wrote the story based on one of Tony Hillerman's many books set in the Arizona territories. ★★★ $9.99

Darkman

(1990, 120 min, US, Sam Raimi) Spectacular stunts and excellent special effects highlight this superhero adventure story. Liam Neeson stars as a scientist whose unfortunate run-in with the mob leaves him horribly disfigured and transforms him into a shadowy crime fighter. Director Raimi (the *Evil Dead* trilogy) continues to impress with his inventiveness as he and his scriptwriters unleash a slew of clever plot twists and come up with at least a half-dozen new ways to dispose of the bad guys. Colin Friels

and Frances McDormand offer fine support as, respectively, an evil real estate tycoon and Neeson's lawyer girlfriend. ★★★ $14.99

Darling

(1965, 122 min, GB, John Schlesinger) This highly influential classic brilliantly captures many of the manners, morals, and mores of mod mid-`60s London. Julie Christie, who is nothing less than radiant, deservedly won an Oscar for her portrayal of a young London model who quickly climbs the social ladder by strategically jumping in and out of assorted beds. Dirk Bogarde also stars as one of her conquests, and Laurence Harvey is featured as one who escapes her enticing trap. Schlesinger received an Oscar nomination for his perceptive direction, and the film itself was a Best Picture nominee. ★★★★

Daughters of Darkness

(1971, 96 min, Belgium, Harry Kumel) One from the vaults! Delphine Seyrig stars as a Hungarian countess and present-day vampiress who, in order to continue her daily blood baths (a youth and beauty preservative), must continually prowl for nubile virgins. Her blood-gathering soirees take her to Belgium where she, along with her lesbian secretary, seductively stalks the hotel for a quick fix. Bela Lugosi she's not. Campy, funny and erotic, this Gothic tale explores the darker side of sexuality with shocking frankness. (Filmed in English) ★★★

Daughters of the Dust

(1991, 114 min, US, Julie Dash) Independent filmmaker Dash has fashioned a lyrical, visually stunning drama about an African Gullah family off the coast of Georgia, circa 1902. Centering on the family's struggles, the film shows how half the family wants to move to the mainland, while the other half worry that their traditional African culture will be forever lost. Critically acclaimed and an art-house hit, *Daughters of the Dust* is not only one of the most gorgeous and vital films of recent years, it signals the arrival of a major talent. Exquisite. ★★★½ $24.99

Dave

(1993, 110 min, US, Ivan Reitman) A crowd-pleaser in every sense of the word, *Dave* is a fabulously funny comedy worthy of bipartisan support. In a particularly appealing performance, Kevin Kline plays Dave, a likable, good-

Daughters of the Dust

David Holzman's Diary

hearted schmoe who's a dead-ringer for the President of the United States. Which is why, when the Commander-in-Chief suffers a stroke, he's chosen to impersonate him. Under the tutelage of the scheming Chief of Staff (a wonderfully nasty Frank Langella), Dave charms all, including his First Lady (Sigourney Weaver), as he sets forth his own political agenda. Writer Gary Ross revels in the fish-out-of-water scenario, and taps into a Capra-esque tone — minus the sentimentality — in celebration of the Average Joe. In support, Kevin Dunn and Ving Rhames are commendable as, respectively, Press Secretary and the President's personal bodyguard. There's also four score and seven cameo appearances — and to give one of them away is grounds for impeachment. ★★★½ $9.99

David

(1979, 106 min, West Germany, Peter Lilienthal) Winner of the Best Film at the Berlin Film Festival, *David* is a suspenseful, understated account of the devastating rise of fascism and its effect on one particular family. David, a Jewish teenager growing up in Berlin in the 1930s, is temporarily insulated from the Nazis' horrific policies by his naively optimistic middle-class family. Told on a human scale, the film follows David as he witnesses the destruction of his community and home; is separated from his parents; and experiences personal persecution by brutal authorities and neighbors. His will to survive is well-portrayed in this moving drama. (German with English subtitles) ★★★ $79.99

David and Lisa

(1962, 94 min, US, Frank Perry) Perry's acclaimed drama about the relationship between two mentally ill teenagers, played with great sensitivity by Keir Dullea and Janet Margolin, is a sympathetic, rewarding look at young love and institutionalization. Howard da Silva gives a wonderful performance as their sympathetic doctor. ★★★½ $69.99

David Copperfield

(1935, 130 min, US, George Cukor) Cukor's superbly crafted adaptation of Charles Dickens' classic novel (the author's favorite among his own work) was one of the box-office giants of the 1930s, and with good reason. Freddie Bartholemew, in perhaps his finest role, heads a stellar all-star cast as Dickens' young hero, experiencing the hardships and

sorrows of orphaned life in 19th-century England. W.C. Fields is the perfect incarnation of Micawber, David's ne'er-do-well mentor; Edna May Oliver is splendid as David's eccentric Aunt Betsy; and Lionel Barrymore, Maureen O'Sullivan, Roland Young and Basil Rathbone are just a few of the outstanding supporting players. One of the finest filmic interpretations of classic literature. ★★★★ $19.99

David Copperfield

(1970, 100 min, GB, Delbert Mann) A good cast is featured in this darker version of Dickens' classic, including Ralph Richardson, Michael Redgrave, Edith Evans, Richard Attenborough and Laurence Olivier. Though it's an intriguing production, the 1935 George Cukor film remains the definitive translation. ★★★ $12.99

David Hockney: Portrait of an Artist

(1985, 52 min, GB) David Hockney is the most popular British painter of his generation, but in recent years, his painting has taken a back seat to photography. We are invited into the London studio of the artist where we witness his applications of still photography innovations to moving pictures. The result, on camera, is Hockney's first experiment in making "fine art" out of cinematography. $39.99

David Holzman's Diary

(1967, 74 min, US, Jim McBride) Selected as one of the American cultural treasures in the Library of Congress' National Film Registry, this amazingly self-assured and uncomfortably perceptive first film by Jim McBride (*The Big Easy*) is an audacious, groundbreaking independent film. David, an obsessively neurotic aspiring filmmaker attempting to unravel the mysteries of life, decides to make a movie on his life — to record on film "truth at 24 frames a second" and thereby capture the essence of his everyday events and people. But instead of learning from the study, the young man's film diary becomes his undoing, alienating his friends and girlfriend, distorting any real meaning and finally turning him into an alienated, frustrated and voyeuristic basketcase. L.M. Kit Carson is perfect as the passionate fool and Louise Levine is equally good in the "Anna Karenina role" of being his alternately demure and sensuous girlfriend. Filmed in a wickedly *faux* cinema verité style, this clever satire captures both the feeling of the tumultuous '60s era and the folly of its self-seeking "artists." ★★★★ $19.99

David Lynch's Hotel Room

(1992, 100 min, US, David Lynch/James Signorelli) A documentary about the places director Lynch stays when he travels — now *that* would be interesting! Here, rather, is a collection of three odd tales set in the same hotel room in various eras. *Tricks* is a basic weird-for-the-sake-of-weird story involving Harry Dean Stanton, hooker Glenne Headly and an unexpected guest checking into room 603 in 1969. An ominous tone and mysterious mood permeate, but nothing really adds up. *Blackout*, the

third segment and set in 1936, finds Lynch mining the spirit, but not the style, of *Eraserhead* to produce an awkward conversation between a young Oklahoma couple (Alicia Witt and Crispin Glover). The second segment provides the only real spark in the program. Directed by Signorelli (the other two were directed by Lynch), *Getting Rid of Robert* is a campy black comedy concerning three young socialites (Deborah Unger, Chelsea Field, Mariska Hartigay) as they anticipate the arrival of soon-to-be ex-boyfriend Griffin Dunne. ★★ $89.99

Dawn of the Dead

(1979, 125 min, US, George Romero) In this second installment of the *Night of the Living Dead* trilogy, the zombies get their just desserts when a Philadelphia SWAT team gets trapped in their hang-out — a large suburban shopping mall. There's lots of sly humor, blood and guts, making this bizarrely entertaining horror film a classic of the genre. (The remastered director's cut shown in letterbox format.) ★★★½ $14.99

The Dawn Patrol

(1938, 103 min, US, Edmund Goulding) Errol Flynn had one of his best roles as a WWI flying ace assigned to keep the Germans behind enemy lines. Basil Rathbone is in good form as a tough officer who must send new recruits to almost certain death. David Niven also stars. ★★★ $19.99

The Dawning

(1991, 96 min, GB, Robert Knights) Anthony Hopkins stars with newcomer Rebecca Pidgeon in this affecting tale about a young woman coming-of-age in 1920s Ireland and a mysterious man who she thinks may be her long-lost father. Set just outside Dublin at the height of the Republican campaign for independence, the story centers around Nancy, who lives with her aunt and grandfather on a beautiful country estate. Surrounded by wealth, she has little knowledge of the political violence and turmoil engulfing her country until, on her 18th birthday, she enounters a rough-hewn rogue (Hopkins) in her secret hideaway by the beach. Reminiscent of many a Masterpiece Theatre production, the film sports some able performances and is thoroughly enjoyable viewing although ultimately it glosses over the political and emotional issues it purports to address. Also with Jean Simmons, Hugh Grant and Trevor Howard. ★★ $89.99

The Day After

(1983, 126 min, US, Nicholas Meyer) Powerful made-for-TV movie detailing life in a small Kansas town before and after a nuclear strike. Powerful images fill the screen with what Americans would have to look forward to in the case of the unthinkable. Jason Robards, JoBeth Williams, Steve Guttenberg, John Cullum, John Lithgow and Amy Madigan head a first-rate cast. Though not as subtle as the similarly themed *Testament*, it is, however, not as devastatingly graphic as the haunting British counterpart, *Threads*. ★★★ $14.99

The Day After Trinity

(1980, 89 min, US, Joe Else) The scientific research which ushered in the dawn of the nuclear era is examined in this penetrating documentary. The site is Los Alamos, New Mexico, where, in 1941, J. Robert Oppenheimer and a group of brilliant scientists worked on a government project to end the war — with the results being a weapon of such power and destructive capability that its use in 1945 irrevocably changed the world. With footage of actual explosions and interviews with the people involved in the research, the film explores the moral anguish experienced by the naive scientists whose peace-inspired work resulted in the creation of a new generation of terrifying weapons. ★★★ $39.99

A Day at the Races

(1937, 111 min, US, Sam Wood) Fair maiden Maureen O'Sullivan is about to lose her health spa unless she receives financial assistance from hypochondriac millionairess Margaret Dumont. And who best to woo the symptom-laden lady than the ever-amorous Dr. Hugo C. Hackenbush, played by — guess who? — Groucho Marx. Chico and Harpo masquerade as his medical assistants, and the day is saved by a horse. ★★★½ $19.99

Day for Night

(1973, 120 min, France, François Truffaut) A loving ode to the intricacies of filmmaking. Truffaut portrays the compassionate director of a beleaguered production. Jean-Pierre Léaud is a spoiled young actor and Jacqueline Bisset is the beautiful heroine of the film within a film. An exhilarating and affectionate satire that captured the Best Foreign Film Oscar. (English language version) ★★★★ $59.99

A Day in the Country

(1936, 40 min, France, Jean Renoir) A Parisian mother and daughter are seduced during an afternoon outing, but what exhilarates one proves to be a rude awakening for the other. Renoir's lyrical, impressionistic work is taken from a de Maupassant short story. (French with English subtitles) ★★★★

A Day in the Death of Joe Egg

(1972, 106 min, GB, Peter Medak) Alan Bates and Janet Suzman give intense performances as a couple whose marriage is coming undone by the stress of caring for their spasmodic daughter. A black comedy of the darkest imaginable shade. ★★★ $69.99

Day of the Dead

(1985, 102 min, US, George Romero) Romero's final entry in his "zombie" series, following *Night of the Living Dead* and *Dawn of the Dead*. A group of scientists and military personnel become trapped in an underground missile silo, and hordes of the living dead lie between them and freedom. This claustrophobic horror film lacks the suspense of the first film and the special effects wizardry of the second. ★½ $9.99

The Day of the Jackal

(1973, 141 min, GB, Fred Zinnemann) Zinnemann's taut political thriller chronicles the international manhunt for a professional assassin (Edward Fox) on assignment to kill Charles DeGaulle. Though history tells us of the assassin's failure, the film maintains a remarkable tension throughout, and builds to an incredibly suspenseful ending. ★★★½ $59.99

The Day of the Locust

(1975, 144 min, US, John Schlesinger) A powerful, beautifully filmed screen version of Nathaniel West's novel of aspirations and forgotten dreams in 1930s Hollywood. Karen Black gives one of her best performances as an opportunistic, aspiring actress involved with both young studio set director William Atherton and lonely, slightly slow-witted Donald Sutherland (in a mesmerizing portrayal). Burgess Meredith received a well-deserved Oscar nomination as Black's boozing, sickly ex-vaudevillian father. An unforgettable though demanding film experience; the Hollywood premiere at the finale remains one of the most chilling sequences ever put to film. ★★★½ $14.99

The Day of the Triffids

(1963, 94 min, GB, Steve Sekely) Lying in a London hospital bed with bandages around his eyes, Howard Keel is one of the few people on Earth to miss a spectacular meteor display in the skies. He wakes up the next morning to discover that most of the population has disappeared and the few remaining people have lost their sight. And to make matters worse, man-eating plants are slowly taking over the city. This is the fascinating premise of this low-budget but smart sci-fi thriller which puts as much accent on characterization and plot as it does on chills (of which there are plenty). The killer plants are kind of cheesy, but that only adds to the fun. ★★★ $9.99

A Day on the Grand Canal with the Emperor of China

(1990, 60 min, US, David Hockney, Philip Haas) One of the most accessible documentaries on art available, this unusual film is a vivid journey down a 72-foot long 17th-century Chinese scroll. Narrated by artist David Hockney as he unrolls the elaborately painted and richly detailed scroll, the life of Emperor Kangxi as well as the bustling life of his kingdom come alive. Hockney also spins an interesting discourse on Eastern and Western perspectives and their relationship to his own artistic vision. ★★★½ $39.99

The Day the Earth Stood Still

(1951, 92 min, US, Robert Wise) 1950s science fiction doesn't come any better than this classic tale of alien beings and Earth's redemption. Michael Rennie plays Klaatu, an emissary from outer space who arrives in the nation's capital to deliver a message of doom. Shot on sight and tiring of lip service from the political hacks (it *is* Washington, D.C.), he decides to mingle with the general population, and befriends widow Patricia Neal and her precocious son Billy Gray. Meanwhile, there's the matter of the eight-foot robot, Gort, standing guard of Klaatu's spaceship, and his mission of peace. Made at a time when most sci-fi stories featured killer aliens, Wise's poetic, cautionary film presented a benevolent spaceman, and it did so in a suspenseful manner with touches of wit and political awareness. Sam Jaffe's enlightened scientist is particularly appealing. Klaatu Barada Nikto. ★★★★ $14.99

The Day the Sun Turned Cold

(1994, 99 min, China/Hong Kong, Yim Ho) This coproduction between mainland China and Hong Kong filmmakers is a powerful and sad exploration of grief, regret and responsibility which is haunting in its stark emotions. Set in a tiny rural area in northern China, the story centers on a patriotic young factory worker who, seeking to be a good, loyal, law-abiding Communist, goes back to his childhood village to accuse his mother of secretly poisoning his father many years before. Through flashback, we learn of the stern habits of the father, a possible extramarital affair by the mother, and a kindly stranger who may have been a catalyst for the supposed murder. Partially a film noir mystery and partially a meditation on individual responsibility and the nature of human goodness, *The Day the Sun Turned Cold* is never heady or pretentious. It moves at a languid pace, allowing the time to savor all its emotions. While uninvolving on a visual level (minimal camera movement captures the whites and browns of the snowy landscape), the film is thoroughly engrossing through its well-developed characters and thought-provoking story. A very good sign for the prosperous future of the Chinese film industry. (Mandarin with English subtitles) ★★★★ $79.99

Daybreak

(1993, 91 min, US, Stephen Tolkin) Tolkin's adaptation of the off-Broadway play "Beirut" is set in the near future of New York City as an epidemic sweeps across the nation infecting hundreds of thousands of people. The government places the "positive" individuals into isolation camps. Moira Kelly plays a young woman whose eyes are opened to what really is happening when she meets a group of resistance fighters led by Cuba Gooding, Jr., who tend and care for the infected. While this made-for-cable film is an obvious AIDS metaphor, it never really etches itself into believability despite competent performances by the leads. ★★ $94.99

Daylight

(1996, 115 min, US, Rob Cohen) Dull and dreary from start to finish, this is less "*Die Hard* in a tunnel" and more "*The Poseidon Adventure* underground." Sylvester Stallone is a New York emergency services specialist who now works as a cabbie because of his expulsion from the force on political grounds. Lucky for us, he is on the scene when the Lincoln Tunnel collapses after a freak traffic accident, killing dozens of motorists and trapping a handful of motley commuters inside. Sly must enter the tunnel (the best sequence in the film, unfortunately at the very beginning) and lead the dazed survivors out. But after the spectacular tunnel collapse and Stallone's entry, the film goes steadily downhill. The victims are a mixed bag of stereotypical disaster movie characters and most of the film's surprises have been done before in better movies. After inevitably becoming laden down with clichés and inane situations, the most welcome daylight in the film is the one the viewer will see after the end credits begin to roll. ★½ $19.99

D

The Days of Being Dumb

(1992, 98 min, Hong Kong) This charmingly slap-dash comedy is a fun example of Hong Kong action/comedy features. Fred (Jacky Cheung Hok-Yau) and Keith (Tony Leung Chiu-Wai) are inseparable boyhood friends and inept gangster wannabes. Their attempts to join the Hong Kong underworld are hampered because every time they join, they accidentally cause the quick death of their crime boss. Try as they might, the two just can't stay in a gang and soon earn the reputation as jinxes. They decide to go independent, but their first scheme – pimping – turns into a disaster when their first prostitute from Singapore turns out to be a lovelorn lesbian. Not of "international" standards, the film is nonetheless great, mindless fun. ★★½ $59.99

Days of Heaven

(1978, 95 min, US, Terrence Malick) Malick's lyrical film of a triangular love affair is set in the Eden-like vistas of the golden wheat fields of Texas. Richard Gere stars as a Depression-era drifter who with his sister Linda Manz and girlfriend Brooke Adams finds employment on the farm of lonely landowner Sam Shepard. A beautiful, haunting version of the pastoral dream. ★★★★ $14.99

Days of Thunder

(1990, 107 min, US, Tony Scott) Tom Cruise, who acquired Paul Newman's fascination for race driving when they appeared together in *The Color of Money*, takes to the track in this heavily clichéd racing drama. Cruise plays a boy wonder behind the wheel and under the sheets. Robert Duvall and Nicole Kidman benefit from his areas of expertise. ★★ $14.99

Days of Wine and Roses

(1962, 117 min, US, Blake Edwards) Though he is mainly considered a comedic filmmaker, Edwards directed two impressive dramas in the early 1960s: *Experiment in Terror*, and this harrowing story about alcohol abuse. Jack Lemmon and Lee Remick give outstanding performances as a newly married couple whose lives are devastated by the rigors of their incessant drinking bouts. On par with Billy Wilder's *The Lost Weekend*. ★★★½ $19.99

The Daytrippers

(1997, 87 min, US, Greg Mottola) Writer and director Mottola's first feature-length film is a prime example of what independent filmmaking should be. Take a simple story about a highly dysfunctional family and shoot it on location for next to no money, hire a bunch of established, but lesser-known actors and put together a compelling little comedy drama. The action begins when Hope Davis discovers a cryptic post card – filled with allusions to forbidden love – that's fallen from husband Stanley Tucci's (*Big Night*) night stand. She takes the card to her mother and father (Anne Meara and Pat McNamara), and they in turn suggest they all go into the city and confront Tucci with it. Hope's younger sister Parker Posey and her boyfriend Liev Schreiber tag along and thus begins a smartly concocted and at times hilarious, picaresque ride from Long Island to Manhattan and environs. At times it seems that there won't be enough material to

pull it off, but whenever things seem about to fizzle, Mattola's ingeniously written script unveils another intricate exploration of family dynamics as it heads towards a couple of dramatic denouements. ★★★½ $99.99

Dazed and Confused

(1993, 113 min, US, Richard Linklater) *Dazed and Confused*, the second film by director Linklater, moves at a slacker's pace, ambling here, ambling there, all the while telling the eclectic and engaging tale of a group of teenagers celebrating the last day of school in 1976. The pacing befits the film's message, which basically says that the '70s suck and nothing happens." With a virtually nonexistent plot, the story follows a core cast of eight teenagers through their haze of alcohol, music, drugs (lots-o-pot), minor rebellions and bizarre school initiations. The young actors, most notably newcomer Wiley Wiggins, have understated styles that make their boredom seem genuine and their anticipation of the "coolness of the Eighties" seem slightly pathetic. If none of the characters in this film seem familiar to you, your teenage years were definitely spent pre-Woodstock. ★★★ $14.99

The Dead

(1987, 88 min, US, John Huston) Huston's last film is a remarkable tribute to the poetic mastery of James Joyce. Deftly capturing the essence of Joyce's prose, Huston has fashioned a film brimming with incredible detail and richly imbued with the Irish spirit. The story may be a disappointment to some, however; for no matter how one approaches it, the viewer is simply an uninvited guest to a Christmas dinner party at which nothing really happens. Huston saves any emotional wallop for the film's ending passage in which the narrative poetry finally draws the audience into a long-awaited catharsis; considering the film's rich atmosphere, it's a worthwhile wait. ★★★½ $14.99

Dead Again

(1991, 107 min, US, Kenneth Branagh) Following his triumphant interpretation of Shakespeare's *Henry V*, actor-director Branagh goes giddy in this wildly imaginative comedy-thriller. Branagh stars as Mike Church, a Los Angeles detective who comes to the aid of a mysterious amnesiac woman (his then off-screen wife Emma Thompson). She is haunted by memories from 40 years earlier in which a renowned composer (Branagh again) may have murdered his wife (Thompson again). Derek Jacobi co-stars as a psychic who tries to help them sort things out. Branagh uses this preternatural premise and runs it over-the-top, taking the audience on a wonderfully tongue-in-cheek roller-coaster ride replete with surprise twists and a Hitchcockian ending. Robin Williams and Hannah Schygulla also star. ★★★½ $14.99

Dead Ahead: The Exxon Valdez Disaster

(1992, 90 min, US/GB, Paul Seed) Meticulously researched, superbly acted and thoroughly engrossing, this HBO/BBC production is a fast-paced exposé on the chain of events set in motion when the Exxon tanker Valdez dumped millions of gallons of crude

oil into the pristine Alaskan waters of Prince Williams Sound. The accident itself, caused by drunken carelessness, was horrible enough; even more terrifying was the response to it. The film presents a parade of company executives and government and military officials more interested in spin-doctoring than solving the problem of dead wildlife and contaminated wetlands. Christopher Lloyd, John Heard, Michael Murphy and Rip Torn head a fine ensemble cast that brings to life and makes comprehensible a complex and multi-layered story which ranges from the boardrooms of the mighty to the homes of the families who have yet to recover from a disaster they were assured could never happen. ★★★½ $89.99

Dead Alive

(1991, 97 min, New Zealand, Peter Jackson) Before *Heavenly Creatures*, Jackson made this wild zombie-splatterthon that ranks without a doubt as the goriest film ever made, bar none! Originally filmed as *Brain Dead*, this coal-black comedy barrage of pus-spewing, entrail-eating wackiness follows the story of an overbearing mother, her charming but somewhat wimpy son, his spicy Latina lover, a kung fu-fighting priest and a very rabid Sumatran rat-monkey. This highly entertaining, limb-shredding homage to such directors as George Romero and Sam Raimi is a must-see for those who like heavy doses of slapstick mixed with their horror. ★★★½ $14.99

Dead Calm

(1989, 96 min, Australia, Phillip Noyce) Nail-biting suspense abounds in this high-seas thriller about a married couple who take to the Pacific in their yacht to find peace of mind after the death of their infant son. Their tranquility is shattered, however, when they take aboard the lone passenger of a sinking yacht, unaware that the man is a psychopath. Director Noyce effectively uses the tiny confines of the boat to develop a frenzied atmosphere of claustrophobia and terror. Sam Neill and Nicole Kidman give grounded performances as the victimized couple, and Billy Zane is a perfect embodiment of evil as the maniacal visitor. ★★★ $9.99

Dead Connection

(1993, 93 min, US, Nigel Dick) Michael Madsen (*Reservoir Dogs*) is a cop on a mission in this mean-spirited suspenser about a vicious psychopath (Gary Stretch) who uses his exceptional good looks to attract women; then, he beats them to death and rapes them (in that order). Interesting characterizations and twists help the story along, but the connection between music video impresario/director Dick and the necessary talent to pull this one off is a dead one, indeed. Also with Lisa Bonet. ★★ $94.99

Dead End

(1937, 93 min, US, William Wyler) Director Wyler elicits remarkable performances from his entire cast in this classic drama, based on Sidney Kingsley's Broadway hit, about life in a New York City tenement. The cast includes Humphrey Bogart, Sylvia Sidney, Joel McCrea, Claire Trevor and the Dead End Kids; and Lillian Hellman wrote the screenplay adaptation. ★★★½ $19.99

Dead Presidents

Dead Heat

(1988, 86 min, US, Mark Goldblatt) Treat Williams and Joe Piscopo are L.A. cops investigating a series of robberies only to discover the culprits are the living dead. The criminals may have been brought back to life, but this film is dead and buried. An embarrassment for the otherwise respectable Williams. ★ $14.99

Dead Man

(1996, 120 min, US, Jim Jarmusch) Director Jarmusch uses the elements of the traditional western to craft a grim and gritty tale of one man's odyssey through a harrowing, alien environment to his inevitable resolution. Johnny Depp is the perfect embodiment of a wanderer adrift in a world he never made, searching for meaning and direction in a hostile landscape fraught with danger, studded with pitfalls, and muddled by one miscommunication after another. *Dead Man* is part existential allegory, part fairy tale; and in it Depp is basically the knight errant who must overcome a series of trials on his path. But there's no Holy Grail, no Golden Fleece at the end of the journey; the reward is just getting through it. The film yet manages to convey the whimsy of *Celine and Julie Go Boating* and the airy enchantment of *The Magic Flute*, two films with which it has little else in common. In its starkness and simplicity, *Dead Man* returns to the crystalline laconicism of Jarmusch's *Stranger Than Paradise*; and though we may sense that this saga is essentially without hope, we are still wryly bemused and frequently amused. When one of the twin marshalls on Depp's trail calls his partner "Lee," you know that *his* name is "Marvin." ★★★ $19.99

Dead Man Walking

(1995, 125 min, US, Tim Robbins) Powerful performances from Sean Penn and Susan Sarandon and the deft directorial touch of sophomore helmer Robbins distinguish this gripping examination of capital punishment. Sarandon stars as Sister Helen Prejean (upon whose book the film is based), a Louisiana nun who, having devoted her life to ministering to the poor, finds her world turned upside-down by a plea for help from death row inmate Matthew Poncelet (Penn). Most of the film revolves around these two characters as Sister Helen tries to draw out some shred of humanity and redemption from the remorseless Poncelet. As an analysis of a hot political issue, *Dead Man Walking* manages, remarkably, to find the center by concentrating on the totality of the human tragedy in both the initial crime and the concept of execution — ultimately, there are no winners in this story. Sarandon and Penn play off each other brilliantly, both giving career performances (Sarandon won an Academy Award; Penn was nominated) in a film that depends heavily on the intimate and emotionally gut-wrenching scenes between the two of them. Good support comes from Robert Prosky as a world-weary attorney and Raymond J. Barry as a grieving father. A thought-provoking film that will spark many a debate rather than settle them. (Available letterboxed and pan & scan) ★★★★ $19.99

Dead Men Don't Wear Plaid

(1982, 89 min, US, Carl Reiner) A vastly entertaining and clever mystery spoof with Steve Martin as a private eye who mixes it up on screen with Humphrey Bogart, Bette Davis, Barbara Stanwyck, Burt Lancaster and Alan Ladd – thanks to old movie clips and ingenious editing. Rachel Ward is his client. ★★★ $9.99

Dead of Night

(1945, 102 min, GB, Basil Dearden/ Robert Hamer/Charles Crichton/Alberto Cavalcanti) An eerie and chilling horror masterpiece about five people gathered together to tell strange tales. Made in 1945, the film was the standard for all subsequent horror anthologies to follow. The highlight is the final tale with Michael Redgrave as a ventriloquist – it'll definitely leave you hearing all of those things that go bump in the night. ★★★★ $9.99

Dead of Winter

(1987, 100 min, US, Arthur Penn) Mary Steenburgen has a field day playing three roles in this tense chiller from the director of *Bonnie and Clyde*. Steenburgen as an out-of-work actress who must fight for her life when she accepts a part in a movie being produced by an eccentric recluse (Jan Rubes) at his remote country mansion. Roddy McDowall is splendid as a mild-mannered though psychotic henchman. ★★★ $14.99

Dead Poets Society

(1989, 128 min, US, Peter Weir) Director Weir's surprise hit is an often hilarious, sometimes deeply moving and somber treatise on the fires of youth and the creative spirit which they enkindle. Robin Williams gives a spirited performance as Jack Keating — an unconventional English teacher at a New England boarding school for boys who finds himself at odds with the school's administration. And while no one here will deny the brilliance of Williams' work, the movie really doesn't belong to him: it belongs to the young actors who play his students. Robert Sean Leonard and Ethan Hawke head the ensemble of talented teenagers who make this movie a true success; their performances, as a group, are nothing less than marvelous. ★★★ $9.99

The Dead Pool

(1988, 91 min, US, Buddy Van Horn) In his fifth appearance as detective Harry Callahan, Eastwood finds himself hunting down the perpetrator(s) of a hit list known as the "dead pool." Not as exciting as its predecessors, still the film has all of the action and gunplay one comes to expect from *Dirty Harry* movies. Liam Neeson co-stars as one of Hallahan's prime suspects. ★★½ $19.99

Dead Presidents

(1995, 119 min, US, Allen and Albert Hughes) The Hughes Brothers follow their scintillating debut *Menace II Society* with this less impressive though not uninteresting morality tale about a young black Vietnam vet trying to build a life after the war. Anyone who's seen the trailer knows the predictable outcome: that pressed by his inevitable failure to find decent work, his pursuit of money turns criminal. The film has all the elements required to be a fascinating study of this young man's struggle to reintegrate, and his fall from virtue to disgrace. But the film can't seem to decide what to be: Is it a touching ghetto melodrama; harrowing Vietnam War exposé; or shoot 'em up heist flick? Alternately, it tries to be each of these things (literally in that order), but the transitions are not smooth and many of the characters are one-dimensional stereotypes. Larenz Tate (also of *Menace*) proves himself to be more than a one-time wonder as he imbues his role with more complexity than seems to have been in the script. The Hughes' once again employ a hands-off approach to their characters' moral integrity, a stance that paid off in *Menace* but here backfires in the face of the lead's questionable final choices. ★★½ $14.99

Dead Reckoning

(1947, 100 min, US, John Cromwell) Departing slightly from his tough guy roles, Humphrey Bogart plays a noir hero who, when he investigates the disappearance of an Army buddy, becomes entangled in a web of intrigue well beyond his control. A cynical tale where the hunter becomes the hunted. Lizabeth Scott is luminously attractive as the duplicitous young lady who entraps Bogie. Although this thriller doesn't rank among Bogart's best or more well-known works, it's nevertheless a taut mystery which will keep you guessing right up to the end. ★★★ $19.99

Dead Ringer

(1964, 115 min, US, Paul Henreid) Bette Davis' follow-up to her smash hit *Whatever Happened to Baby Jane?* may be a silly psychological thriller, but thanks to Davis' histrionics, it's certainly a lot of fun. Bette chews the scenery as estranged twins: one good and one evil. When the latter kills the former, she changes places with her wealthy sister to live the good life. Will anyone suspect the imposter? Boyfriend Peter Lawford and police inspector Karl Malden have their doubts. ★★★ $14.99

D

Dead Ringers

(1988, 115 min, Canada, David Cronenberg) The good twin-bad twin genre gets an unusual and fascinating once-over in this intense, often gruesome and quite disturbing psychological horror film masterfully directed by Cronenberg. Based on an actual incident, the film stars Jeremy Irons as identical twin brothers whose drug dependency and romantic involvement with the same woman (Genevieve Bujold) triggers their emotional and professional decline and eventual self-destruction. Irons gives a truly magnificent performance as the two doctors, giving each brother a distinctive and subtle shading. Bujold is excellent as the actress caught between them. The faint of heart beware. ★★★½ $9.99

Dead Tired (Grosse Fatigue)

(1994, 85 min, France, Michel Blanc) Director and writer Blanc plays dual roles as himself and a mischievous double in this wicked little farce dotted with actors, directors and the occasional agent, all playing themselves. Blanc finds himself in a waking nightmare, accused of nefarious deeds by friends and acquaintances of long standing. He retreats to the countryside to regain his composure, but that only leads him deeper into the abyss. Spurred into action by his friend Carole Bouquet, they embark on an odyssey to discover the source of his inexplicable predicament. Blanc nicely portrays the utter bewilderment of an unsuspecting man plunged into a jarring, unfamiliar world without preparation or understanding. Bouquet infuses the film with the magical charm of the classic *Celine and Julie Go Boating*. A delightful romp with many sly observances on fame and the cult of celebrity. (French with English subtitles) ★★★ $19.99

The Dead Zone

(1983, 103 min, US, David Cronenberg) From "goremeister" Cronenberg comes this unusually tame yet excellent adaptation of the Stephen King novel about an average Joe (Christopher Walken) who wakes from a five-year coma with the ability to see the future of anyone he touches. Also with Martin Sheen, Brooke Adams, Herbert Lom, Colleen Dewhurst and Anthony Zerbe. ★★★ $14.99

Deadline at Dawn

(1946, 83 min, US, Harold Clurman) With a crackling screenplay by Clifford Odets and an ominous and steamy New York-at-night backdrop, this fast-paced murder mystery stars Susan Hayward as a streetwise but soft-hearted dance hall girl who gets involved with a naive sailor in their frantic search for the killer of a female blackmailer. She soon becomes enmeshed in a maze of suspects and seedy characters all offering good reasons for having knocked off the broad. ★★★ $19.99

Deadlock

(1991, 103 min, US, Lewis Teague) *The Defiant Ones* with a twist: Rutger Hauer and Mimi Rogers co-star in this slick, entertaining made-for-cable thriller about a pair of criminals, shackled together at their necks by an explosive collar, who must escape from an experimental maximum security prison to recover $25 million in stolen diamonds from Hauer's double-crossing partners in crime (Joan Chen, James Remar). ★★★ $19.99

The Deadly Companions

(1961, 90 min, US, Sam Peckinpah) Peckinpah's first film lacks the director's later accomplished visual style, but this is nevertheless an interesting western drama. Maureen O'Hara is a pioneer woman whose young son is accidentally killed; Brian Keith is the ex-Army officer responsible for the boy's death, who escorts the woman cross-country for the boy's burial. ★★★ $14.99

Deadly Currents

(1991, 114 min, Canada, Simcha Jacobovici) An involving documentary concerning the Israeli-Palestinian conflict, this surprisingly evenhanded examination gives equal time to both sides, as well as three people caught in the middle. Soldiers, policemen, children, political leaders and terrorists all have their say — and the film avoids both sentimentality and a politically correct viewpoint. The conflict is seen through the eyes of its protagonists, not the eyes of (Western) onlookers. This aspect alone makes the film invaluable, but *Deadly Currents* offers something more: an intimate look at everyday life in the West Bank, an existence marked by the commonality of violence and hatred. The myriad ways in which people here deal with the stress is presented — submersion into military life with Rambo-like zeal, performance art, theatre and dance, terrorism. No pat resolutions, here; no one offers a viable solution to the conflict, and few offer any hope. *Deadly Currents* is an extremely worthwhile, important film. (Hebrew and Arabic with English subtitles) ★★★½ $89.99

Deadly Friend

(1986, 99 min, US, Wes Craven) Teenage genius implants a chip into the brain of a dead friend, bringing her back to life — as a rampaging killer. Craven has certainly done better. ★ $14.99

The Deadly Mantis

(1957, 78 min, US, Nathan Juran) Released by an earthquake in the Arctic, a giant praying mantis hops to the East Coast, causing destruction in Washington, D.C. and New York City before being gassed to death in the Holland Tunnel. Fun 1950s schlock with good F/X, lots of stock footage and a reliable cast including Craig Stevens and William Hopper. ★★½ $14.99

Deadtime Stories

(1986, 83 min, US, Jeffrey S. Delman) Scott Valentine heads the cast of this average horror trilogy, whose stories of witches, werewolves and murderesses is highlighted by the final and funny "Goldilocks" story. ★★

Deal of the Century

(1983, 99 min, US, William Friedkin) Chevy Chase, Sigourney Weaver and Gregory Hines are featured in this embarrassing political comedy about weapons dealers involved with the Third World. ★ $14.99

Dear Boys

(1980, 90 min, The Netherlands, Paul de Lussanet) This Dutch oddity about an aging gay Don Juan and his entourage is a lusty and humorous story of sexual obsession. Wolf, a novelist plagued by writer's block and an aging sexual adventurer and self-proclaimed "servant of beauty," finds his creative juices flowing once again after he meets and becomes helplessly smitten by Muscrat, an attractive but indifferent young man. In his attempt at seduction, Wolf lures him (along with his ancient Sugar Daddy) to his country house, where he lives with his handsome "ex," Tiger. And there in his den, the persistent Wolf stalks his prey. When straightforward seduction fails, our horny hero resorts to telling imaginative homoerotic fantasies to Muscrat hoping to stimulate, arouse and dispel the diffidence of his new-found love. A funny and candid look at one gay man's frantic attempts at keeping his sexual mystique and grasping an unattainable love. (Dutch with English subtitles) ★★★ $69.99

Dear God

(1996, 112 min, US, Garry Marshall) Can a lovable con man redeem himself by playing Santa Claus to the have-nots and find true romance at the same time? If anyone has to really think about the answer, then they may be able to unearth a smidgen of enjoyment from this otherwise labored, unfunny comedy. Very nearly smirking his way to cynically cool, Greg Kinnear is nevertheless submerged in the same sap and nonsense he so adroitly lampooned on "Talk Soup." He plays a scam artist who is forced to take a job at the post office's dead letter department. There, he begins reading letters written to God — and inadvertently helps the beleaguered authors (the letter writers, not the script writers) in an escalating "do-good" campaign. Marshall's wooden direction only underscores the screenplay's lack of laughs, though Laurie Metcalfe is able to overcome some of the dreariness with a lively performance. In his first starring role, Kinnear is quite affable, but the screenplay gives him little to work with. John Henson: take notice! ★★ $14.99

Death and the Maiden

(1994, 103 min, GB, Roman Polanski) A grim, involving chamber piece based on Ariel Dorfman's stage play, *Death and the Maiden* stars Sigourney Weaver as a former brutalized political prisoner. Now living peacefully with her husband (Stuart Wilson), whom she had protected, Weaver's seemingly calm exterior is shattered one night when she hears the voice of an acquaintance of her husband — the man who had tortured her. Thus sets in motion a game of revenge as the man (a marvelously controlled Ben Kingsley), now being held hostage, firmly denies being him and Weaver will do anything to prove that he is. But who is right? As the film sets out to answer that question, director Polanski brings a minimum of suspense to a situation which should have its audience uncertain throughout. However, Weaver's forceful but one-note portrayal and Polanski's stage-bound direction don't completely undermine an otherwise compelling scenario. ★★½ $19.99

Death Becomes Her

(1992, 115 min, US, Robert Zemeckis) Vanity, thy name is woman — or, more specifically,

Meryl Streep and Goldie Hawn in this hilariously vicious black comedy. Streep gives a priceless performance, and Hawn and Bruce Willis are both sparkling, with Willis finally abandoning his annoying cinematic smirk for actual characterization – this is his most engaging comic performance to date. Youthful lovers Hawn and Willis are engaged; that's until Broadway star Streep gets in the way. Years later, Hawn plots her revenge: Streep's death. But there's a catch – Streep has found the secret to immortality. Black comedy doesn't often get sharper than this, and there are some staggering special effects to help underscore the film's delightful nastiness. Streep once again amazes as she revels in the role of a vain, aging actress; her satiric performance is at once subtle, cunning and totally brilliant. And wait until you see Goldie as a 400-pound eating machine – it alone is worth the rental fee. ★★★½ $9.99

Death in Brunswick

(1990, 106 min, Australia, John Ruane) Sam Neill is Cal, a 34-year-old unemployed cook under the thumb of his meddling mom and living in squalor with no clear ambitions. A job in a sleazy night club introduces him to a vibrant young woman and a set of circumstances which transform his muddle through life into a dead-long propulsion for survival. His odyssey involves inadvertent murder, a crazed bouncer, illicit drugs, corpse defilement, firebombing and signs from God. A darkly funny, low-budget surprise, with the gritty sense of realism often present in Australian films, this small film is a wryly amusing look at the curse of human fraility, the gift of unquestioning friendship and the redeeming power of true love. Neill is matched by the supporting cast in whimsical portrayals of marginal small-town characters who handle life's eccentricities with more heart than reason. ★★★ $96.89

Death in the Garden
(La Mort en ce Jardin)

(1956, 90 min, Mexico, Luis Buñuel) Eschewing his signature style in favor of a more conventional narrative, Buñuel's *Death in the Garden* may prove a disappointment to fans of the great surrealist director. Based on a novel by Jose Andre Lacour, the film tells the story of diamond miners in post-WWII South America. When military officials announce that all mining will be controlled by the government, the town erupts into riotous chaos. At first glance a story of a power struggle, the film's loose and shifting perspective leaves political matters unresolved. Instead, the film dissolves into a story of interpersonal relationships among a group of mostly unlikable characters – a motley group of refugees who eventually flee the militia on a riverboat for Brazil. In what could be a less compelling predecessor to *Aguirre, the Wrath of God*, the crew wanders through the jungle, their notions of identity and power stripped by the brutal conditions of travel. Ultimately the film's structure breaks down to reveal what is an existential polemic, rather than a social critique – and at best, an interesting historical document that testifies to the dangers of colonialism. (French and Spanish with English subtitles) ★★½ $59.99

Death in Venice

(1971, 130 min, Italy, Luchino Visconti) Visconti's adaptation of the Thomas Mann novella of an artist in search of purity and beauty but who ultimately becomes fatally obsessed with an exquisite teenaged boy is a melancholy experience. Set in turn-of-the-century Venice, this languidly paced, darkly atmospheric film stars Dirk Bogarde as Aschenbach, an older man enamored with a flirtatious but unattainable blind youth (Björn Andresen), and who is gradually weakened by the cholera epidemic sweeping the city. Visconti changed Aschenbach's profession from writer to composer, enabling him to fill a largely wordless film with the wondrous music of Gustav Mahler. (Filmed in English) ★★★ $59.99

Death of a Bureaucrat

(1966, 87 min, Cuba, Tomás Gutiérrez Alea) When it comes to uproarious comedies, one rarely identifies the films of the Communist bloc, in general, and Castro's Cuba, in particular, as a source. But this madcap comedy is nothing if not a joy from beginning to end. Paying homage to the surrealist humor of Luis Buñuel and the pratfall antics of Harold Lloyd and Buster Keaton, Alea's story concerns a young man whose recently widowed mother finds that she cannot receive her pension without his father's union card – which was buried with him! He finds himself in a classic Catch-22 as he tackles an endless array of red-tape in his bewildering efforts to first get his father exhumed and then to get him reburied. A very funny black comedy which pokes wildly subversive fun at the powers-that-be. From the director of *Strawberry and Chocolate*. (Spanish with English subtitles) ★★★½ $69.99

Death of a Prophet: The Last Days Of Malcolm X

(1991, 60 min, US, Woodie King, Jr.) Ossie Davis narrates this dramatic re-creation of the last 24 hours of controversial black activist Malcolm X. Morgan Freeman stars in this critically acclaimed piece, along with Yolanda King (daughter of Rev. Martin Luther King, Jr.). ★★★ $29.99

Death of a Salesman

(1985, 150 min, US, Volker Schlöndorff) Remarkably successful play-on-film version of Arthur Miller's classic drama, with Dustin Hoffman giving a stunning performance as Willy Loman, the aging Brooklyn salesman whose career and home life slowly unravel about him. A superior supporting cast includes John Malkovich and Stephen Lang as his sons, and Kate Reid as his loyal wife. ★★★★ $19.99

Death of a Soldier

(1985, 93 min, Australia, Philippe Mora) A well-mounted recounting of the true story of a U.S. Army private stationed in Australia during WWII who murders three local women, and of his subsequent trial and execution. Starring James Coburn, Reb Brown and Bill Hunter. ★★½ $79.99

Death on the Beach

(1988, 101 min, Mexico, Enrique Gomez) Repressed homosexuality, vicious murders

and lovely bronzed bodies dominate this silly melodramatic thriller set under the Acapulcan sun. The story revolves around a handsome but misunderstood teenager who returns home (a mansion overlooking the Pacific) to find his domineeringly buxom mother shacking up with a fiercely heterosexual lover. The boy, sexually and emotionally confused, becomes agitated when they begin to introduce a succession of young girls to him. Instead of saying, "No, thanks, Mom," the boy's pent-up and unspent passions erupt in a violent and unpredictable way. A film not for card-carrying members of ACT-UP, for the filmmaker equates homosexuality with deranged, psychopathic behavior. Take the politics out, however, and you have a generally silly but fun sexual thriller. (Spanish with English subtitles) ★★ $79.99

Death on the Nile

(1978, 135 min, GB, John Guillermin) Lavish Agatha Christie mystery highlighted by sumptuous locales and a solid cast. Peter Ustinov is a delightful Hercule Poirot, who investigates the shipboard murder of a spoiled heiress. Who done it: David Niven, Bette Davis, Maggie Smith, Angela Lansbury, Mia Farrow, George Kennedy, Simon MacCorkindale or Jack Warden? We'll never tell. Lansbury is a stand-out among these accomplished performers. ★★★ $14.99

Death Race 2000

(1975, 80 min, US, Paul Bartel) Frankenstein (played by David Carradine) is the survivor of a number of deadly crashes, outfitted with a number of artificial limbs and devices taking on his challenger Machine Gun Viterbo (Sylvester Stallone) in this funny, somewhat campy but exciting action-satire. ★★★ $14.99

Death Warrant

(1990, 90 min, Canada, Deran Sarafian) Jean-Claude Van Damme stars as a cop who goes undercover in a violent penitentiary, seeking out those responsible for a series of brutal prison murders. Violent and only sporadically interesting. Cynthia Gibb and Robert Guillaume co-star. ★★ $9.99

Death Wish

(1974, 93 min, US, Michael Winner) In the film which started the "vigilante" action genre, Charles Bronson stars as a New York businessman who seeks vengeance against society's criminal underworld for the death of his wife and the rape of his daughter. The film tries to balance gritty, violent action sequences with a supposedly thoughtful treatise on crime and punishment, but it's nothing more than an excuse for Bronson to blow away punks and street scum and having the audience cheer him while he's doing it. As a detective on Bronson's trail, Vincent Gardenia is actually quite good, giving more conviction to his part than it deserves. ★★½ $14.99

Deathtrap

(1982, 116 min, US, Sidney Lumet) Ira Levin's hit Broadway murder mystery is brought to the screen in only a satisfactory adaptation. Michael Caine plays a down-on-his-luck playwright who sees a chance at reclaim-

D

ing success when a former student (Christopher Reeve) shows up with a sure hit script. Caine plots to murder him and take the play as his own. But plot twists and red herings await them. Dyan Cannon also stars as Caine's wife. The two twist endings are neatly written, but the entire production suffers from a dreariness due, in most part, to Lumet's stagebound direction. ★★½ $19.99

Deathwatch

(1980, 128 min, France/West Germany, Bertrand Tavernier) This unusual, present-day science-fiction film features Romy Schneider as a terminally ill woman whose slow death is being witnessed by a mass audience through a tiny video camera implanted in the eyes of an undercover TV reporter (Harvey Keitel). A fascinating film which speculates on the abuses of the media as well as the rise of Big Brother. (Filmed in English) ★★★

The Decameron

(1970, 111 min, Italy, Pier Paolo Pasolini) Boccaccio's bawdy and earthy stories of sexual adventures during the 14th century receive the Pasolini treatment. Told in several episodes, the stories illustrate the different facets of uninhibited human sexuality. The film takes special pleasure in depicting the Church's sexually repressed clerics frolicking lecherously amongst their flocks. *The Decameron*, Pasolini's first film in his trilogy of medieval tales, is perhaps his funniest and is certainly one of the director's best films. (Italian with English subtitles) ★★★½ $79.99

Deceived

(1991, 103 min, US, Damian Harris) While this film was the best of 1991's "mystery spouse" thrillers, its psycho-in-search-of-the-American-Dream story line might seem, especially to fans of *The Stepfather*, very familiar. Goldie Hawn delivers a strong, understated performance as a woman who slowly comes to discover that her recently deceased husband (perennial yuppie bad-guy John Heard) may not have been all the good things that she thought he was. In fact, he may not even be dead. Crisp direction and stylish settings keep a predictable plot moving briskly. ★★½ $9.99

The Deceivers

(1988, 112 min, GB, Nicholas Meyer) Pierce Brosnan stars as a 19th-century British officer who goes undercover to investigate a series of ritual killings by a secret brotherhood known as the Thuggees (who the British fought in the classic *Gunga Din*). Posing as an Indian, the officer infiltrates the fiendish sect and finds himself mysteriously drawn into its power, endangering not only his mission, but his life as well. At times a bit muddled, the film nonetheless is an often exciting and interesting sojourn to a little-traveled time in history. ★★½ $14.99

December Flower

(1984, 65 min, GB, Judy Allen) This tender story about the flowering relationship between a middle-aged widow and her aging aunt is a beautiful tribute to the resilience of the elderly. Jean Simmons and Mona Washbourne (*Stevie*) star. ★★★ $14.99

Deception

(1946, 112 min, US, Irving Rapper) Bette Davis is in great form as a suffering pianist torn between Claude Rains and Paul Henreid. Rains matches La Davis every step of the way with a grand portrayal of her mentor. One of Davis' most entertaining soaps. ★★★ $19.99

Deception

(1992, 90 min, US, Graeme Clifford) What could elevate this by-the-book mystery about a harried housewife (Andie MacDowell) who crisscrosses the globe in search of answers after her flyboy husband dies surrounded by shady dealings? Why Liam Neeson, as a shyly charismatic "Feed the World" worker, of course. Not to be corny, but Neeson has a smile that's akin to Paul Newman's eyes; it almost doesn't matter what sort of muck is surrounding the body part in question. The muck in this instance is MacDowell, who gives, as usual, a one-note performance. ★★½ $14.99

The Decline of the American Empire

(1986, 101 min, Canada, Denys Arcand) Arcand's comically incisive film examines a group of male and female French Canadian academicians as they analyse the worlds of sex and human mortality. As their discussion unfolds, many in the group arrive at varying degrees of self-discovery. Arcand skillfully weaves his way through the many viewpoints and compassionately presents his characters as they turn to sexuality as a hedge against death. (French with English subtitles) ★★★ $79.99

The Decline of Western Civilization

(1980, 100 min, US, Penelope Spheeris) Spheeris' absorbing, close-up look at the hard core lifestyle on the wild and wooly West Coast features the serene sounds of X, Black Flag, Fear, Germs and Catholic Discipline. ★★★

The Decline of Western Civilization, Pt. 2: The Metal Years

(1988, 90 min, US, Penelope Spheeris) Director Spheeris' raucous follow-up to her acclaimed docu-musical on the Los Angeles punk rock scene probes the headbanging fans and fast-living stars of the heavy metal world. Plenty of music and amusing interviews with demi-gods Ozzy Ozbourne, Aerosmith, Gene Simmons, Alice Cooper and Chris Holmes of W.A.S.P. Fans of the music as well as those intrigued by the appeal of the distinctive sound should be greatly entertained. ★★½

Decoration Day

(1990, 99 min, US, Robert Markowitz) James Garner stars in this made-for-television drama about a retired Georgia judge who reluctantly searches for his estranged boyhood friend, a black WWII vet who refuses to accept a long overdue Congressional Medal of Honor. An intelligent screenplay, incisive direction and exceptional performances from Garner, Bill Cobbs, Judith Ivey, Ruby Dee and Lawrence Fishburne contribute to elevate this well above standard TV-movie fare. ★★★½ $14.99

The Deep

(1977, 123 min, US, Peter Yates) Nick Nolte and Jacqueline Bisset play lovers on a romantic vacation in Bermuda who stumble upon a

sunken wreck from WWII and get entangled with a Haitian drug dealer (Louis Gossett, Jr.) and an old treasure hunter (Robert Shaw). The cinematography captures the lushness of the surroundings, but a flat screenplay sinks to the bottom. ★★ $14.99

Deep Cover

(1980, 81 min, GB, Richard Loncraine) Dennis Potter wrote the screenplay for this mysterious made-for-TV drama which mixes cryptic dialogue, paranoia, sexual duplicity and a notorious 1930s British scandal. Donald Pleasence stars as a reclusive former Cambridge professor and author whose home is visited by an enigmatic stranger (Tom Conti), claiming to be writing his thesis on one of his books. As he ingratiates himself into the household, including tempting the author's wife and daughter, it becomes apparent that he has ulterior motives. Potter sets the pace of his scenario slowly as characters playfully banter back and forth, with the author playfully giving bits of information only when needed. The cinematography gives the film a storybook glow which belies the characters' malevolent intents. Denholm Elliott also stars as Pleasence's personal secretary, both sharing a dark secret which ultimately comes to light. (aka: *Blade on the Feather*) ★★★

Deep Cover

(1992, 107 min, US, Bill Duke) Fresh from his triumphant portrayal of an inner-city father protecting his son from the rigors of the drug trade in *Boyz N the Hood*, the chameleon-like Laurence Fishburne crosses the "mean streets" in this gritty urban thriller from the director of *A Rage in Harlem*. Fishburne is magnetic as a cop who finds himself being seduced by a life of crime when he is sent into "deep cover" as a drug dealer. With a story as streetwise as anything this side of Scorsese, the screenplay by maverick writer Michael Tolkin (*The Player*) adds an extra level of depth and decadence to the characterizations — particularly Jeff Goldblum's turn as an ultra-smarmy attorney who wants to market his own designer drug. Also with Clarence Williams III, Gregory Sierra and Charles Martin Smith. ★★★½ $9.99

Deep in My Heart

(1954, 132 min, US, Stanley Donen) Entertaining production numbers highlight this otherwise by-the-books musical biography of Hungarian composer Sigmund Romberg ("The Student Prince," "The Desert Song"), with Jose Ferrer as the songwriter. Cast includes Merle Oberon and Paul Henreid, with guest appearances by Gene Kelly and Cyd Charisse. ★★½ $19.99

Deep Red

(1975, 98 min, Italy, Dario Argento) David Hemmings stars in this chilling horror-mystery as a British musician in Rome who witnesses the "Hatchet Murder" of a psycho. He then becomes obsessed with solving the case, finding clues, corpses and some bizarre drawings along the way. Filled with tension and atmosphere. ★★★ $19.99

D

Deep Throat

(1970, 70 min, US, Jerry Gerard) Linda Lovelace, upon discovering an anatomical shortcoming, works hard to overcome her liability. Harry Reems co-stars in this Capraesque tale of self-improvement. A testament to the will of man.

DeepStar Six

(1988, 103 min, US, Sean S. Cunningham) A group of deep-sea explorers attempt to establish a secret naval base on the ocean floor, but they discover there's a terror in the ocean depths. Nothing could be as scary, though, as this film's screenplay, acting and directing. ★★ $14.99

The Deer Hunter

(1978, 183 min, US, Michael Cimino) This Oscar-winning Best Picture is an unusual Vietnam War film in that it shows its characters before, during and after their war experience. The Vietnam episode is only a third of the film, but it is so devastating that it stays with you until the film's end. Among its gifted cast, Robert De Niro, Meryl Streep, John Cazale and Oscar-winner Christopher Walken give tremendous performances. ★★★★ $29.99

Def by Temptation

(1990, 95 min, US, James Bond III) An all-black cast invigorates this original treatment about a virginal "man of God" (James Bond III) who must avenge his father's downfall by doing battle with a demon (Cynthia Bond, the director's sister) who preys on sexually dishonest souls. Director/star Bond makes the most of his low, low budget while serving up a horror treat that harks back to the "blaxploitation" era of *Blacula* and *Blackenstein*, but without the gratuitous exploitation of that genre. ★★★ $89.99

Defence of the Realm

(1987, 96 min, GB, David Drury) Engrossing political thriller about a journalist who uncovers an explosive sex scandal involving a Minister of Parliament and a KGB agent, which leads the reporter on the trail of a governmental cover-up of a nuclear mishap on an American military base. The cast includes Gabriel Byrne, Greta Scacchi, and Denholm Elliott in a smashing performance as Byrne's seasoned editor. ★★★

Defending Your Life

(1991, 112 min, US, Albert Brooks) One of the most innovative and freshest comedies of the '90s, this low-key, quirky and very funny fantasy follows businessman Albert Brooks' adventures in the hereafter. Killed in a car accident, Brooks goes on trial to determine his next plane of existence. During his stay at Judgment City — where you can eat as much as you like and never gain weight — he falls in love with Meryl Streep, who is certainly on a higher spiritual plateau. The film, written and directed by Brooks, finds most of its humor with our conceptions concerning death, love and commitment. A particular highlight is Streep eating pasta, and there's a cameo which alone is worth the price of the rental. ★★★½ $14.99

The Defiant Ones

(1958, 97 min, US, Stanley Kramer) Kramer had a thing for films about prejudice (*Guess Who's Coming to Dinner*, *Judgment at Nuremberg*), but this taut drama is probably the best of them all. Tony Curtis and Sidney Poitier play two escaped convicts cuffed to each other, fleeing the police in the South. Curtis and Poitier's performances are remarkably well-defined. ★★★★ $19.99

The Delicate Delinquent

(1957, 90 min, US, Don McGuire) Jerry Lewis plays a bumbling (what else?) janitor who hangs out with the crowd from the wrong side of the tracks but ends up becoming a police officer. His first movie without Dean. ★★★ $14.99

Delicatessen

(1991, 97 min, France, Jean-Pierre Jeunet & Marc Caro) Displaying a playfully inventive virtuosity with the camera, and offering as its theme the socially indigestible subject of cannibalism, *Delicatessen* is a hilariously witty and sweetly outrageous story of a fairy-tale romance set amidst the ruins of a post-apocalyptic world. Set in the near future, in a Europe destroyed by an unnamed war where the days are thrown into perpetual dusk and food is scarce, the story revolves around an enterprising butcher who stays in business by adding some human flesh and by-products to his eagerly bought meats and sausages. Life changes for the butcher and the odd-ball tenants in the ramshackle flats above his shop when Louison (Dominique Pinon), a sweet-natured, rubber-faced clown-on-the-lam comes looking for a job and a place to live. Before your can say, "*filet mignon au poivre*," Louison falls in love with Julie, the butcher's willowy, near-sighted daughter. As poor Louison has to stay one step ahead of the butcher's cleaver, lest he become a tasty meat loaf for the butcher's rapacious customers, the directors gleefully notch up the speed and unleash a flurry of chaos as the film races to an inspired comic-book conclusion. While not for all tastes, this furiously paced tale is a deliciously outrageous comedy which brims with mischievous visual lunacy. (French with English subtitles) ★★★★ $89.99

Delirious

(1983, 70 min, US) Eddie Murphy live in concert, recorded in Washington D.C. in 1983, at the beginning of his phenomenal film career. Brimming with the humor — adult-oriented, often side-splitting and usually offensive — which has become the comic's trademark. $14.99

Deliverance

(1972, 109 min, US, John Boorman) James Dickey's best-seller makes for a stirring adventure-drama about four business associates whose weekend in the wilds turns tragic. Jon Voight and Burt Reynolds are fine as two of the execs, and completing the quartet, Ned Beatty and Ronny Cox both make impressive film debuts. ★★★½ $14.99

The Deluge

(1974, 183 min, Poland, Jerzy Hoffman) Set in the mountainous ravines of the Carpathians and filled with burning villages, opulent castles and spurting blood, this 17th-century war epic chronicles the patriotic glory and bloody violence during the Polish-Swedish War. The story is told through the romantic eyes of Andrzej, a courageous adventurer who finds more than a little time for amorous interludes. Based on the novel by Nobel Prize-winning author Henryk Sienkiewicz, this Polish *Tom Jones* was nominated for the Academy Award for Best Foreign Language Film in 1974. (Polish with English subtitles) ★★★ $59.99

Delusion

(1990, 95 min, US, Carl Colpaert) On a trip to Reno through a preternaturally desolate expanse, an altruistically motivated embezzler gives a lift to the wrong young couple. The eerily depopulated, incandescent desert becomes a mute observer as the mob lackey with a bad stomach and his would-be chanteuse kidnap the executive and introduce

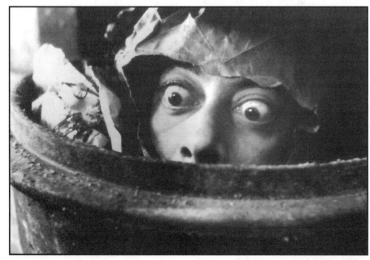

Delicatessen

a slight detour into his travel plans. An engaging cast (Jim Metzler, Jennifer Rubin and Kyle Secor), a clever script and attentive direction combine to create a nifty noir-ish mystery with an existential slant. ★★★ $89.99

Delusions of Grandeur

(1976, 85 min, France, Gerard Oury) A delightful, fast-paced comedy of royal intrigue in 17th-century Spain. Louis De Funes (*The Mad Adventures of Rabbi Jacob*) is an evil, all-powerful minister of the king who, when exiled by the queen, plots to get even. He is aided by his clever, good-natured servant, Blaze (Yves Montand). (French with English subtitles) ★★★

Dementia 13

(1963, 81 min, US, Francis Ford Coppola) Coppola made his feature film debut with this Roger Corman cheapie about an ax-murderer on the loose in an Irish castle. Often very gory, Coppola effectively uses black and white to enhance the horror of this Gothic thriller. Worth a look as both low-budget horror film and as first film for a major American director. Coppola once recollected: "Roger wanted sort of a copy of *Psycho*, with some kind of terrible knife scene thrown in. So I wrote the script to order." ★★★

Demetrius and the Gladiators

(1954, 101 min, US, Delmer Daves) An all-star cast (including Victor Mature, Susan Hayward, Anne Bancroft and Ernest Borgnine) is featured in this inferior sequel to 1953's *The Robe*, which centers on the search for the robe that Christ wore before he was crucified. ★★ $19.99

Demolition Man

(1993, 114 min, US, Marco Brambilla) In this surprisingly effective and comical action film, Sylvester Stallone plays a renegade cop whose battle with bad-guy Wesley Snipes leads to the deaths of innocent civilians. Both are frozen as punishment. Thirty-five years later, in a grotesquely funny fascist Utopian society, Snipes escapes, and an ill-equipped police department defrosts Sly to help them catch him. First-time director Brambilla has a good eye in creating an off-center future, and his action sequences are well-staged. As the over-the-top villain, Snipes clearly seems to be enjoying himself. ★★★ $9.99

Demon Barber of Fleet Street

(1936, 68 min, GB, George King) The cruelties of man are more wondrous than Peru in this true story of barber Sweeney Todd, who would kill bad-tipping customers and turn them into meat pies. (No singing in this film.) Todd Slaughter's most famous exercise in the Grand Guignol, rumored to feature asylum inmates in minor roles (mostly in front of the camera). ★★½ $9.99

Demon Knight

(1995, 93 min, US, Ernest Dickerson) The Crypt Keeper, that dapper and handsome host of the TV series "Tales from the Crypt," makes his way to the big screen in this tongue-in-cheek tale. The film, like the series, is alternately ghoulish, coolish and humorous, but it doesn't quite succeed in becoming the triple threat it so wants to be. Director Dickerson

clearly has a talent for creating a chilling atmosphere and maintaining a quick pace — only if the story line were as developed. It has to do with the Devil (Billy Zane) battling the mortal guardian (William Sadler) of a key containing the blood of Christ. Zane has a devilishly good time hunting his prey to a small New Mexico hotel and then tormenting all in his reach. Gory effects and macabre humor follow as he plays a demonic game of Ten Little Indians. ★★ $14.99

Demon Seed

(1977, 97 min, US, Donald Cammell) Julie Christie plays a housewife who's caught in the deadly plot of a powerful computer system (voice supplied by Robert Vaughn) as it attempts to secure immortality and take over the world. ★★½ $14.99

Demons

(1986, 89 min, Italy, Lamberto Brava) Stylish, eerie (if somewhat implausible) horror film co-written and produced by Italian horror master Argento about a movie preview audience watching a slasher film, while the horror on screen extends itself into the real world. ★★★

Demons in the Garden

(1982, 100 min, Spain, Manuel Gutiérrez Aragón) A child's magical memory of his father's hypocrisy and deceit is the subject of this engrossing tale about life after the end of the Spanish Civil War. A young boy grows up spoiled and manipulative as his mother, aunt and grandmother vie for influence over him. A trio of Spain's finest actresses etch memorable portraits that embody the divided nature of the Spanish character. Starring Angela Molina, Ana Belen and Eusebio Lazáro. (Spanish with English subtitles) ★★★ $79.99

Denis Leary: No Cure for Cancer

(1992, 63 min, US, Ted Demme) Exorcize your festering hostilities by proxy, courtesy of Denis Leary in this vehement, excruciatingly funny adaptation of his acclaimed off-Broadway show. Everybody's favorite bad boy spews his rants in a chain-smoking, beer-swilling, anti-PC frenzy, taking on heavy metal, suicide, red meat, drugs, NyQuil, dysfunctional families, health clubs, alcohol, and many other elements of contemporary American culture with hyperbole, venom and song. Amid the raucous and often guilty laughter are moments of surprising emotional effect in this hour-long, one-man barrage. Do you feel the urge to kill? Watch this instead. ★★★½ $12.99

Dennis Potter: The Last Interview

(1996, 70 min, GB) Betrayed by his body, sipping morphine from a flask, Dennis Potter, writer of such masterworks as "The Singing Detective," "Pennies from Heaven" and "Brimstone and Treacle," talks about his life, his art and his impending death in this often fascinating interview. The location for this gentle interrogation is appropriate: a TV studio empty save for two chairs, a small table, the interviewer and his clipboard, and Potter himself. Only minutes into the program, the playwright can no longer maintain his adopted role as Britian's bitterish curmudgeon — or perhaps, like so many of the characters who

Demolition Man

populate his plays, he just gives it more complexity and greater depth. ★★★ $29.99

Dennis the Menace

(1993, 94 min, US, Nick Castle) This updating of the "Dennis the Menace" saga definitely has its moments, like the one where Dennis (Mason Gamble) explains to Mrs. Wilson why his parents want to be left alone for their weekly Sunday morning "wrestling" sessions. Unfortunately, moments like these are few and far between and the story consequently sags around John Hughes' by now worn-out plot involving a burglar (Christopher Lloyd) who gets nailed by a precocious eight-year-old. Most of the performances are as bland as the film's suburban manicured setting, with the exception of Walter Matthau as the curmudgeonly Mr. Wilson and Joan Plowright as his understanding wife. ★★½ $19.99

The Dentist

(1996, 93 min, US, Brian Yuzna) Rather than being a *Dr. Giggles*-like slasher movie, this ambitious but failed project is more along the lines of a psychological thriller with teeth. Corbin Bernsen stars as a successful dentist with a beautiful wife, luxurious home and lucrative practice. This, however, is all an illusion; his wife is having an affair, he owes back taxes, and every insignificant blemish in his life becomes magnified to a stain of colossal proportions. While there is some effective satire, the film unfortunately concentrates too much on the collapse of the doctor's mind. Fans expecting a slasher pic will be sorely disappointed, and the writers (who also penned *Re-Animator*) are not up to the challenge of a subtle examination of professional psychosis. Dentistry was more chilling in *Marathon Man* and the abuse of the medical profession was more deeply examined in *Dead Ringers*. This movie is more like celluloid novocaine. ★★ $93.99

Le Départ

(1966, 90 min, Belgium, Jerzy Skolimowski) Mark (Jean-Pierre Léaud) is a 19-year-old with a mania for Porsches and car racing. His determination to enter a race (and find a Porsche in the process) is undermined when he meets and falls in love with Michele. A funny, visually eclectic story of one's dreams confronting reality. (French with English subtitles) ★★★

Deranged
(1974, 88 min, US, Bob Clark & Alan Ormsby) Based on the real-life activities of Wisconsin necrophile/murderer Ed Gein, *Deranged* stars Roberts Blossom as Ezra Cobb, "the butcher of Woodside," a mother-obsessed weirdo who digs up his mom, stuffs her and soon begins to kill other women to keep her company. Shocking, graphic, and at times semi-humorous, this unusual release is truly a "you've got to see it to believe it," but is recommended only to horror fans with a strong stomach. ★★ $39.99

Deranged
(1987, 85 min, US, Chuck Vincent) Ex-porn star Veronica Hart (now Jane Hamilton) plays a woman (sexually abused as a child) whose mental breakdown is further hastened by a ski-masked burglar breaking into her apartment. Pretty bad right down the line. Directed by porn "auteur" Vincent and co-starring porn regulars Jerry Butler and Jamie Gillis. ★ $14.99

Le Dernier Combat (The Last Battle)
(1983, 93 min, France, Luc Besson) Besson makes an impressive directorial debut with this offbeat, black-and-white sci-fi adventure set in a post-nuclear world where the few surviving men battle each other over territory and the last remaining women on Earth. Though Besson's film, which has no dialogue, follows the conventions of the post-apocalyptic genre, his visuals are striking and he creates a disturbing sense of atmosphere. ★★★

Dersu Uzala
(1975, 160 min, Japan/USSR, Akira Kurosawa) Kurosawa's Oscar-winning epic, a magnificent and sweeping production, explores the tremendous bond between an early 20th-century Russian explorer and his faithful guide Dersu. Kurosawa's immense visual artistry vividly captures nature's beauty and wrath. (Japanese with English subtitles) ★★★★ $39.99

Desert Bloom
(1986, 103 min, US, Eugene Corr) This underrated, extremely well-acted drama is set in 1950s Nevada at the dawn of the A-Bomb testing. Annabelle Gish offers a sincere performance as a young girl coming-of-age living with her mom (JoBeth Williams) and troubled stepdad (Jon Voight). Ellen Barkin is terrific as Gish's sympathetic, flamboyant aunt. ★★★½ $9.99

The Desert Fox
(1951, 88 min, US, Henry Hathaway) A tour de force performance by James Mason highlights this stand-out WWII war drama about Field Marshall Rommel and the Nazi general's defeat in the African campaign. ★★★½ $19.99

Desert Hearts
(1985, 93 min, US, Donna Deitch) Truly a landmark film in its positive and very realistic depiction of a love affair between two attractive and intelligent women, offering the viewer a human-scale, tender treatment of two women in love. A dude ranch in Reno, Nevada, in 1959 is the setting for the meeting of an uptight Columbia University professor awaiting her divorce and a free-spirited and openly gay sculptress who lives on the ranch. Helen Shaver and Patrice Charbonneau both give warm, expansive performances. ★★★½ $19.99

The Desert Rats
(1953, 88 min, US, Robert Wise) James Mason repeats his role from *The Desert Fox* as Field Marshal Rommel in this exciting WWII actioner. Set in North Africa, Rommel wages a battle of wits with a British commander (Richard Burton) in the Allied offensive at Tobruk. ★★★ $19.99

Designing Woman
(1957, 118 min, US, Vincente Minnelli) Gregory Peck and Lauren Bacall star in this pleasant romantic comedy reminiscent of *Woman of the Year*. Sportswriter Peck and fashion designer Bacall fall in love and marry while visiting California. Once back in their native New York, however, the honeymoon is over as the mismatched couple must contend with each other's crazy friends, jealous former partners and big city thugs. It's an engaging romp brightened by two star performances, but lacks the depth of the Spencer Tracy-Katharine Hepburn comedies it imitates. Mickey Shaughnessy has a few good scenes as a punchy boxer and the film features (probably) the first choreographed kickboxing scene — by a fey dancer, no less. ★★★ $19.99

Desire
(1989, 88 min, GB, Stuart Marshall) Utilizing incredible archival footage as well as interviews, this intense talk-fest documentary chronicles the birth, growth and eventual suppression of Germany's gay/lesbian movement, from 1910 thru Hitler's crackdown. Marshall takes an intellectual approach in his exploration of the emerging gay culture and birth of the "erotic idealism" inherent in the movement that flourished in the 1920s and '30s before ending when it was outlawed by the Nazis, resulting in the systematic oppression and eventual imprisonment of its members in concentration camps. Also explored is turn-of-the-century Germany's scientific "discovery" of homosexuality and how people reacted to this "breakthrough." Through interviews with expert sociologists, sexologists, historians and actual lesbian and gay survivors of the camps, the film offers a fascinating glimpse into a relatively unknown subject and proves to be a vital document in queer history. ★★★ $39.99

Desire
(1993, 108 min, Canada/France/W. Germany, Andrew Birkin) With its gorgeous multi-continental locales, attractive cast, and the beginnings of a passionate "lost love"-type story, *Desire* starts off with a romantic bang, but slowly peters out into just another repetitive romp in the proverbial sand. Greta Scacchi plays the daughter of European intellectuals who spend their holidays in the Scottish countryside. One summer Scacchi experiences a sexual awakening with farmer/fisherman Vincent D'Onofrio. Their subsequent brief encounters haunt Scacchi through her marriage, divorce and move to America. ★★ $89.99

Desire and Hell at Sunset Motel
(1992, 87 min, US, Alien Castle) A bickering young couple (Sherilyn Fenn, Whip Hubley) take a room in a moderately sleazy motel in sun-baked Southern California in 1958. Their contemptuous combat is punctuated with periods of blackout, flashbacks (flashforwards?), illicit and would-be lovers, a peeping-tom motel manager and a disappearing body in the pool. You won't know who's loyal to whom until the very end. David Hewlett, David Johansen and Paul Bartel also star in this intriguing look at the dark side of Ozzie and Harriet America. Director Castle also wrote the satisfyingly convoluted script. ★★½ $9.99

Desire under the Elms
(1958, 111 min, US, Delbert Mann) A curiously uneven but seductive adaptation of Eugene O'Neill's drama. Set in mid-19th-century New England, the film stars Anthony Perkins as the son of farmer Burl Ives. He begins an affair with his stepmother (the miscast but alluring Sophia Loren). ★★½ $19.99

Desiree
(1954, 110 min, US, Henry Koster) A rather muddled costume drama chronicling the love affair between young officer Napoleon and his mistress Desiree. More attention was paid to sets and costumes than historical accuracy, and the film suffers for it. Marlon Brando is an animated Napoleon, Jean Simmons is a lovely Desiree, and Merle Oberon is quite stunning as Josephine, but even these talents can't help salvage this production from mediocrity. ★★ $19.99

Desk Set
(1957, 103 min, US, Walter Lang) Spencer Tracy and Katharine Hepburn, in their eighth film together, are both splendid in this spirited version of the Broadway hit. Kate runs the research department of a TV network; Spencer is the efficiency expert whose computer is about to replace her and her staff. And though they're initially at odds, romance ensues. Joan Blondell is particularly snappy in support. ★★★½ $14.99

Desolation Angels
(1995, 90 min, US, Tim McCann) It seems nearly every independent film released these days falls into one of two camps — the touchy-feely twentysomething relationship movie, or the gritty, cynical "this-is-reality" cinema verité. *Desolation Angels*, detailing a working-class man's pursuit of vengeance for the alleged rape of his girlfriend, neatly falls into the latter category. With its constant handheld camerawork, real locations and unpleasant situations, the film aims for harsh realism, and succeeds much of the time. But the two male leads are thinly drawn and uninteresting, and the supporting characters are stock; so much so that the only role of note is the girlfriend, played by Jennifer Thomas, who gives the only performance of merit. Depressing if fairly accomplished, the film has to its credit many tense

moments and a strong ending. But like many of its ilk, it leaves one wondering if these meager rewards are worth the effort. ★★½ $94.99

Despair

(1978, 119 min, West Germany, Rainer Werner Fassbinder) The first of Fassbinder's two English-language films (the other being *Querelle*), this critically maligned psychological drama, based on Tom Stoppard's adaptation of a Vladimir Nabokov novel, is an interesting, even riveting but ultimately muddled puzzle. Dirk Bogarde stars as Russian émigré Hermann Hermann, a 1930s chocolate manufacturer who attempts to elude the Nazis by exchanging identities with a working-class double. The French title, *The Mistake*, might better describe Hermann's unbalanced schizoid state of mind when he concocts a plan of murdering his "double," collecting the insurance and then fleeing to Switzerland using the dead man's identity papers. (Filmed in English) ★★½

Desperado

(1995, 106 min, US, Robert Rodriguez) Sophmore director Rodriguez returns to the scene of the crime with this occasionally dazzling sequel to his refreshing low-budget debut, *El Mariachi*. Rodriguez has all the right elements in place to make *Desperado* a superlative action classic: sexy Antonio Banderas; a strikingly beautiful yet uncharacteristicly strong female lead in Salma Hayek; and a budget for enough pyrotechnics to blow up an entire city block. Sadly, however, *Desperado*, though flawlessly filmed and edited (by Rodriguez himself), fails to capture the good-humored slapstick zaniness of its predecessor and commits the sin of taking itself too seriously. The film certainly starts off with a bang: Following a wonderfully moody setup in which Steve Buscemi tells some tall tales to bartender Cheech Marin and the trigger-happy denizens of his sleezy Mexican bar, Banderas (taking up the role of the Mariachi from the first film) breezes into town seeking vengeance. The ensuing gun battles will stand up proudly against the best of John Woo for their outstanding choreography and bubblegum hilarity. But Rodriguez blows all his ammunition in the first 40 minutes and the remaining hour sees the action become increasingly sporadic and inane. Still, Banderas, with his unshorn locks and rough-hewn machismo, exudes pure charisma and is a savory pleasure to watch. (Available letterboxed and pan & scan) ★★½ $19.99

Desperate

(1947, 73 min, US, Anthony Mann) Refusing to take the rap for a fur heist he was conned into, honest ex-vet Steve Randell is forced to flee from both the police as well as the thug ringleader (the unsettlingly villainous Raymond Burr). His life on the lam is fraught with danger for him and his pregnant wife until he decides to fight back. A taut and engrossing low-budget drama with a film noir theme of an innocent man thrown into a sick world of evil. ★★★ $19.99

Desperate Characters

(1971, 88 min, US, Frank D. Gilroy) As seen through the eyes of the characters of this edgy drama, New York City seems to be a breeding ground of lives of quiet desperation. Addressing burgeoning themes whose topicality have not faded, Gilroy's adaptation of Paula Fox's novel is a moody character study which taps into the white fears of urban living in the early 1970s. The story follows the tedium that is the life of married couple Shirley MacLaine and Kenneth Mars as they eke out a daily existence. That the film is never tedious is as much a credit to director Gilroy's deft touch as it is to the two excellent performances by MacLaine and Mars. Giving one of her most accomplished portrayals, MacLaine has rarely been as powerfully understated. Mars — largely known for his comedic roles — is equally commanding in his dramatic debut. Gerald O'Loughlin and Sada Thompson offer great support. ★★★ $19.99

The Desperate Hours

(1955, 112 min, US, William Wyler) A suburban nightmare movie that pre-dates *Blue Velvet*. Humphrey Bogart is an ex-con who holds a perfect Eisenhower-era family (suit-and-tie dad, doting mom, attractive daughter and precocious young son) hostage in their own home. Fredric March is the strong-willed father, afraid for his family's safety, who wages a battle of wits and guts with Bogey. Far superior to the 1990 Michael Cimino-Mickey Rourke remake. ★★★½ $14.99

The Desperate Hours

(1990, 105 min, US, Michael Cimino) Director Cimino and actor Mickey Rourke team for this disappointing remake of the 1955 Humphrey Bogart thriller. Rourke stars as a psychotic who, with the help of his laywer, busts out of jail. They hide out in the house of a recently separated couple (Anthony Hopkins and Mimi Rogers). Lindsay Crouse is a tough-talking FBI agent hot on Rourke's tail. For his part, Cimino fails to deliver on what could have been a taut little thriller, choosing unwisely to "open" the film up; but he does manage to keep the suspense high and deliver some jarring moments. ★★ $14.99

Desperate Journey

(1942, 107 min, US, Raoul Walsh) A rather exciting war adventure which mixes suspense, comedy and patriotism. Errol Flynn plays an Australian commander who leads a group of Allied airmen (including wise-cracking Ronald Reagan) on a bombing mission in Germany. When they're shot down over enemy territory, he leads them on a perilous journey across Germany — in-between acts of sabotage and imprisonment — to England and freedom. Alan Hale provides the comic relief, and Raymond Massey is a relentless Nazi officer on their trail. ★★★ $19.99

Desperate Living

(1977, 90 min, US, John Waters) A motion picture malignancy which "spread like cancer in Waters' brain." Mink Stole stars as a dame on the lam with her 400-pound maid Grizelda. They find refuge in Mortville, a haven for perverts, murderers and worse, ruled over by porcine despot Queen Carlotta (Edith Massey). A high-volume, determinedly offensive camp comedy. ★★ $19.99

Desperate Remedies

(1993, 92 min, New Zealand, Stewart Main & Peter Wells) Campy to an outrageously shameless fault, this deliriously enjoyable and visually explosive costume romp is infused with more than its fair share of hyperventilating passions, luscious bosom-popping women and seductively thick-lipped men yearning for fulfillment. All this presented in blinding colors and with a convoluted plot that seems to have combined a dozen Harlequin romance novels. Set in Hope, a rugged 19th-century New Zealand pioneer seaport (strongly reminiscent of the setting of Fassbinder's *Querelle*), the story revolves around the efforts of Doretha (Jennifer Ward-Lealand), a strong-willed rich girl, and a sneering fop, Fraser (Cliff Curtis), to set up her pregnant opium-and-love-addicted sister Anna with the newly arrived but befuddled hunk Lawrence (Kevin Smith). The operatic plot soon falls to the background as the heaving breasts, lust-filled eyes and seething passions of all concerned envelop the viewer. A delightful romp that should have all howling with laughter. ★★★ $91.99

Desperately Seeking Susan

(1985, 104 min, US, Susan Seidelman) This hip comic adventure stars Rosanna Arquette as a bored New Jersey housewife thrust into the heart of Greenwich Village bohemianism by a konk on the head. Madonna made her feature film debut as Susan, the free spirit whose life Arquette follows through the personals in *The Village Voice*. Also with Aidan Quinn, Laurie Metcalf, Steven Wright, Ann Magnuson and John Turturro. ★★★ $9.99

Destination Toyko

(1943, 135 min, US, Delmer Daves) Cary Grant heads a good cast in this taut WWII submarine tale about the crew whose invasion of mainland Japan laid the groundwork for the aerial bombing of Tokyo (for that story, see *Thirty Seconds over Tokyo*). Though the characters are pure 1940s caricatures of fighting men, the sincerity of the actors portraying them and the solid action and suspense more than compensate. John Garfield and Alan Hale also star. ★★★½ $19.99

Destiny Turns on the Radio

(1995, 101 min, US, Jack Baran) Julian (Dylan McDermott) breaks out of jail after three years to find out from his partner in crime Thoreau (James LeGross) that the money from their bank job is gone and his girl (Nancy Travis) has taken up with another (James Belushi). Reality is heightened by confluences of chance and predestination; forays into the supernatural can be initiated by filling up the pool, and maintaining a healthy respect for animistic spirits and 20th-century rituals. And everyone agrees that Las Vegas is a town of limitless possibilities – a man can make his mark with a fair degree of patience and a pair of non-conducting rubber-soled boots. The cast, which also includes the likes of Richard Edson, Allen Garfield and Bobcat Goldthwaite, is uniformly engaging, and Baran provides some witty directorial touches to the tragically hip script. Some will not be amused, but if *Blood and Concrete* or *Delusion* were your cup of tea, try this. ★★½ $19.99

Destry Rides Again

(1939, 94 min, US, George Marshall) A gunslinger spoof — with a serious side — starring James Stewart as a non-violent sheriff who tames a Wild West town. There's plenty of action, lots of laughs and Marlene Dietrich, as a sexy saloon singer, even gets to sing a song or two. ★★★★ $14.99

Details of a Duel

(1989, 97 min, Argentina, Sergio Cabera) A teacher and a butcher leave home to go about their business of the day, including preparing for death. Contrary to their true nature, one must kill the other by mid-afternoon. Egged on by the clergy, the militia and the town's bureaucrats, the private conflict between the two men is soon escalated into a gladiatorial spectacle. Set in the Argentine Andes in the 1950s, this wry and subtle comedy mischievously exposes the machismo code of honor, a tradition that dictates a duel and possible death — all in the name of manly protocol. (Spanish with English subtitles) ★★★ $59.99

The Detective (Father Brown)

(1954, 91 min, GB, Robert Hamer) A sterling adaptation of the G.K. Chesterton novel. Alec Guinness is in masterful form in this lively comedy-thriller as the priest-turned-sleuth on the trail of stolen religious artifacts. Also with Peter Finch, Joan Greenwood and Cecil Parker. ★★★ $19.99

Detour

(1945, 68 min, US, Edgar G. Ulmer) Made for almost nothing in only five days by a small-time studio, this film noir classic probes the plight of an "innocent" man trapped in circumstances beyond his control. While hitchhiking across the U.S. to meet his girlfriend in Los Angeles, a man is accused of murder by a tough-talking tomato, who threatens to tell the police if he does not follow her every demand. Entrapped by this increasingly dangerous psychopath, the man must plot his escape. Infused with snappy dialogue, fog-shrouded city streets and a wonderfully evil femme fatale, this dark drama will prove to be a delight for all noir fans. ★★★½ $12.99

Devi

(1960, 96 min, India, Satyajit Ray) Ray's dreamily sensual film is about a Bengalese girl of astounding beauty who is declared to be a reincarnation of a goddess by her wealthy father-in-law. When he starts a cult of worship in her honor, she gradually becomes convinced of her own divinity. This ironic examination of India's decadent upper classes was banned from export until the intercession of Nehru. (Bengali with English subtitles) ★★★ $24.99

The Devil and Daniel Webster

(1941, 109 min, US, William Dieterle) Terrific screen version of Steven Vincent Benet's novel with Edward Arnold and Walter Huston giving terrific performances as Daniel Webster and Mr. Scratch (aka The Devil), respectively. The famous statesman defends a farmer who has sold his soul. The case is prosecuted by Scratch and the jurors are the cursed from Hell. (aka: *All That Money Can Buy*) ★★★½ $24.99

The Devil and Max Devlin

(1981, 95 min, US, Steven Hillard Stern) After getting pummeled by a bus, the deceased Max Devlin (Elliott Gould) strikes a deal with the Devil (Bill Cosby) to have his life restored if he can convince three people to sell their souls. An unexciting execution of a time-worn premise. ★★

The Devil and Miss Jones

(1941, 92 min, US, Sam Wood) Captivating Capra-esque comedy about a millionaire (Charles Coburn) who goes undercover at his own department store to find out what his disgruntled employees are complaining about. The strength of Norman Krasna's script and the charm of stars Jean Arthur, Robert Cummings and Coburn transcend the clichés and make for a most enjoyable romp. ★★★ $19.99

Devil in a Blue Dress

The Devil Bat

(1941, 69 min, US, Jean Yarbrough) Bela Lugosi charges up his giant bats with electricity and then sics them on people wearing his specially formulated cologne, only to be done in by a father of three wearing too much Old Spice. ★★½ $12.99

Devil Girl from Mars

(1954, 77 min, GB, David MacDonald) A Scottish inn and its inhabitants are terrorized by a beautiful but ruthless Martian (Patricia Laffan) in black leather. One of the first films with aliens seeking Earthlings for breeding stock. ★★ $14.99

Devil Hunter Yohko

(1990, 45 min, Japan, Tetsuro Aoki) This violent, sexy, supernatural animation story follows a pretty young woman named Yohko Mano who finds herself confronted with a series of perplexing questions: What do you do when your high school principal is a witch who wants you dead? What to do when one of your best friends has been turned into a zombie? And, what about your ninja grandmother? Find out the answers to these and many more questions in an amazingly fast-paced, entertaining package which will leave you wanting more. ★★★½ $29.99

Devil in a Blue Dress

(1995, 102 min, US, Carl Franklin) Denzel Washington, that master of subtle characterization, has created another persona rooted in a specific time and place with striking authenticity. Washington is Easy Rawlins (the character in Walter Mosley's books), a WWII vet whose recent unemployment coupled with mortgage payments induces him to agree to DeWitt Albright's (Tom Sizemore) request to locate Daphne Money (Jennifer Beals). She's an enigmatic beauty publicly tied to a local politico, and she's recently dropped out of sight. Rawlins finds that he's fallen down the rabbit hole. He's drawn into deeper mysteries, nothing is what it seems, people are murdered, and he's become a convenient target for unseen forces. He calls on an old acquaintance for support, Don Cheadle in a hyperkinetic turn as Mouse, who shoots first and rarely asks questions. Director Franklin has delivered a fitting follow-up to *One False Move*, meticulously re-creating late 1940s Los Angeles and bathing it in the golden glow of reminiscence. A smartly constructed film and satisfying noir entertainment. ★★★½ $19.99

Devil in the Flesh (Le Diable au Corps)

(1947, 110 min, France, Claude Autant-Lara) A beautifully acted and exquisitely filmed tale of the passionate and tragic involvement between a young student and a mature married woman set during World War I. While relatively calm by today's jaded standards, this shocking love story caused quite a controversy when it was first released. Remade by Marco Bellochio. (Dubbed) ★★★½ $34.99

Devil in the Flesh

(1987, 110 min, Italy/France, Marco Bellocchio) Bellocchio's notorious updating of the classic Maurice Radiquet novel tells the story of a sizzling love triangle between an imprisoned terrorist, his sultry girlfriend, and a teenage boy she lures right from the schoolyard. The themes of political intrigue, betrayal and madness take a back seat to the erotic couplings and explicit oral sex scenes between the sensuous young woman, Maruschke Detmers, and her enamored young victim, the handsome Federio Pitzalis. The film shocked the international film community and was tagged with an X rating in the U.S. This tape is the unedited version. (Italian with English subtitles) ★★★ $19.99

The Devil, Probably

(1977, 95 min, France, Robert Bresson) In a world dying from human pollution, young, angelic Charles (Antoine Monnier) finds no solace in radical politics, religion, sex, psychology or the arts. Unanchored, he vacilates between two women who love him: Edwige (Laetitia Carcano), who waits for him stoically, and Alberte (Tina Irissari), who leaves her lover Michel (Henri de Maublanc) to care for the increasingly alienated Charles. His death wish is a microcosm of the planet's unraveling, and the combined support and caring of his friends and lovers have no impact on his downward spiral. Young, attractive, intelligent and loved, why is Charles suicidal? But then, why are we killing ourselves as a species? Bresson's

Grace Kelly caught unaware in *Dial M for Murder*

polemic on the human penchant for self-destruction and inability to commit is kaleidoscopic, visionary; at once frenetic and stilted, energized and stolid, blistering and melancholy. Made in 1977, it defines problems without offering solutions — problems no closer to resolution today. A thought-provoking and disquieting examination of the human condition. (French with English subtitles) ★★★½ $89.99

The Devil's Disciple

(1959, 83 min, US, Guy Hamilton) Burt Lancaster, Kirk Douglas and Laurence Olivier (just the thought of these three acting together makes the head spin) bring splendor to the words of George Bernard Shaw in this glorious Revolutionary tale based on Shaw's play. Lancaster plays a small-town pastor, indifferent to the war around him, who gets a loud wake-up call to arms when he crosses paths with an American rebel (Douglas) and British General Burgoyne (Olivier). There's wit and vitality to Shaw's clever dialogue: no boring discourse here. The performances of the three actors befit their legendary stature; and an impressive supporting cast includes Harry Andrews, Janette Scott and George Rose, among others. ★★★½ $19.99

The Devil's Eye

(1960, 90 min, Sweden, Ingmar Bergman) One of Bergman's few comedies, this captivating adaptation of G. B. Shaw's "Don Juan in Hell" begins with the old Irish proverb, which says, "A maid's chastity is a sty in the eye of the Devil." We follow the determined efforts of Satan who, on a promise of reduced time in Hell, sends Don Juan to earth in order to rob the virginity of bride-to-be Bibi Andersson. Will the Devil's eye problem clear up, or will human goodness triumph? (Available dubbed and in Swedish with English subtitles) ★★★ $19.99

The Devil's Own

(1997, 110 min, US, Alan J. Pakula) The teaming of Harrison Ford and Brad Pitt — each

arguably their generations' best leading man — works surprisingly well to create an absorbing if somber drama which balances social and moral issues, good action sequences, and an affecting tale of a surrogate father and son. Showing few signs of its high-profile on-set difficulties, *The Devil's Own* casts Pitt as an IRA commander whose latest battle with the British (a well-executed scene) forces him into hiding in America. He is placed with unsuspecting New York cop Ford, and while playing the part of the gracious visitor he is actually preparing a return to Ireland with a boatload of missiles. Director Pakula is less interested in shoot 'em ups (though there are a few, non-gratuitous ones) and concentrates more on the father-son relationship between the two men. The strong performances by Ford and Pitt (who gives what may be his best portrayal to date) firmly establish their bond of friendship and the sting of its eventual betrayal. While producing sympathy for Pitt's character, the film never becomes a polemic. Its screenplay sometimes looks patchy (it was often written daily), but the overall finished product is sleek and engrossing. In support, Treat Williams makes for a cool, calculated villain. ★★★ $102.99

The Devil's Playground

(1976, 105 min, Australia, Fred Schepisi) This compelling drama, set in a boys' seminary, probes the torment of young students and their instructors as they grapple with sexual yearning and the harsh codes of religious discipline. The story concerns one particular boy's struggle to deal with both his divine calling and his pent-up sexual needs. A sometimes funny, always hard-hitting indictment of repression. ★★★

The Devil's Wanton

(1949, 78 min, Sweden, Ingmar Bergman) Bergman's sixth film is a sober interpretation of hell on earth, told from the point of view of a girl trying to find happiness with a man who was deserted by his wife after her lover had their

baby killed. This arty drama is filled with many of the master's signatures and cinematic techniques. (Swedish with English subtitles) ★★½

The Devil-Doll

(1936, 79 min, US, Tod Browning) Lionel Barrymore has a field day in this fun horror film as a scientist who shrinks humans to the size of dolls to get even with his enemies. Maureen O'Sullivan co-stars. ★★★ $19.99

The Devils

(1971, 109 min, GB, Ken Russell) Oliver Reed is the martyred cleric and Vanessa Redgrave is the sexually repressed nun in Russell's gruesome and graphic account of witchcraft hysteria in the 17th-century. Both Reed and Redgrave are superb in this frenzied adaptation of Aldous Huxley's book "The Devils of Loudon." Filmed with Russell's usual sobriety and reserve. ★★★½ $19.99

Diabolically Yours

(1967, 94 min, France, Julien Duvivier) Rivaling Brigitte Bardot for the title for the greatest number of forgettable, grade-B French films, dashing Alain Delon gives his all in this psycho thriller about a man's desperate search for his sanity. After a near-fatal car accident that left him in a coma for three weeks, Delon awakens to find that his memory is completely lost. Paranoia overwhelms him when he begins to suspect that the woman who claims to be his loving wife, the doctor who is supposed to be his best friend and the relatives who visit are merely staging an elaborate charade in some kind of secret conspiracy to drive him crazy. Senta Berger co-stars in this Hitchcockian suspense film from the director of *Pepe Le Moko*. (Dubbed) ★★½ $59.99

Diabolique
(Les Diaboliques; or The Fiends)

(1954, 107 min, France, Henri-Georges Clouzot) This white-knuckled thriller is set in a shabby boys' school and stars Simone Signoret as a battered mistress who plots a murder with her lover's wife (Vera Clouzot). In grisly fashion, they drug the husband, drown him in the tub and dump the corpse in a pool. But mysteriously, the body disappears and evidence of their crime begins to haunt them. The heart-stopping climax and twist ending will have you on the edge of your seat. (An inferior, updated American version was made in 1996 starring Sharon Stone and Isabelle Adjani) (French with English subtitles) ★★★★ $29.99

Dial M for Murder

(1954, 105 min, US, Alfred Hitchcock) Grace Kelly is the rich and beautiful wife of the diabolical Ray Milland. He hires a hit man to bump her off, but she kills the would-be assassin and faces the electric chair. In his inimitable fashion, Hitchcock forces the culprit husband to reveal his guilt. (Filmed in 3-D) ★★★ $19.99

Diamonds Are Forever

(1971, 119 min, GB, Guy Hamilton) Sean Connery returns for his next-to-last appearance as 007. His mission: to track down a diamond smuggler; which, of course, requires a whirlwind, world-wide adventure through

Amsterdam, Los Angeles and Las Vegas. Lots of fun. Also starring Jill St. John. ★★★ $14.99

Diary of a Chambermaid

(1946, 86 min, US, Jean Renoir) This bewitching but distinctively odd adaptation of the Octave Mirbeau novel was one of Renoir's last films made during his sojourn in Hollywood during the war. Co-produced and scripted by Burgess Meredith, this romantic comedy stars Paulette Goddard as the keyhole-peeping, gold-digging chambermaid whose arrival at a provincial mansion brings havoc to its decadent inhabitants. The film features Meredith as an eccentric, flower-eating neighbor and Judith Anderson as the matriarch of the household who rules with an iron fist. Though not as bitterly savage as the Luis Buñuel version, Renoir's film is still sharp in its satire of the upper classes. (Filmed in English) ★★½ $19.99

Diary of a Chambermaid

(1964, 79 min, France, Luis Buñuel) Jeanne Moreau stars as a reserved and well-cultured woman from Paris who begins to work for an upper-class family in the Provinces in 1939. The new maid soon discovers that the family is a thoroughly decadent group of characters as she finds herself enmeshed in the midst of a hotbed of hypocrisy and perversion. Their seemingly innocuous habits, like the grandfather's foot fetish, prove to be not-so-harmless when a young girl is found murdered and Moreau becomes obsessed with exposing the killer. Buñuel's sly comic touches are in evidence, but the film retains a biting edge as he equates the gentry's oppression with the rise of fascism. (French with English subtitles) ★★★½

Diary of a Country Priest

(1950, 120 min, France, Robert Bresson) Bresson's uniquely austere style of filmmaking is beautifully rendered in this somber work on the life and death of a young priest and his unsuccessful attempts to minister his first parish. (French with English subtitles) ★★★½ $59.99

Diary of a Hitman

(1991, 90 min, US, Roy London) Forest Whitaker, though miscast, makes a good showing as a hit man who studiously saves the earnings from his murderous profession for a down payment on his co-op apartment. Sherilyn Fenn co-stars as a drug-addicted cheerleader wannabe who stands in Whitaker's way for one last completed assignment. An intriguing premise executed with style, and it's fairly suspenseful. ★★★ $14.99

Diary of a Lost Girl

(1929, 100 min, Germany, G.W. Pabst) The alluring and enigmatic Louise Brooks stars in this parable of a woman's road to ruin. Brooks is a wronged innocent who is banished from respectability for having a baby out of wedlock. Forced to stay in a hellish house of correction, she escapes only to land in a brothel where she finds her ultimate redemption. (Silent with musical soundtrack) ★★★½ $29.99

Diary of a Mad Housewife

(1970, 94 min, US, Frank Perry) A perceptive study of housewife Carrie Snodgress' psychological deterioration at the hands of social

climbing, philandering husband Richard Benjamin and charmingly egocentric writer Frank Langella, with whom she has a brief, tempestuous affair. Superb performance by Snodgress and good support from Langella. ★★★ $69.99

Diary of a Mad Old Man

(1987, 90 min, France/Belgium, Ralph Michael) Filmed in English, this Ingmar Bergman-influenced drama is a tepid examination of an old man as he nears the end of his life. Marcel is a rich and self-absorbed businessman who forsakes the love of his devoted wife for a never-consummated sexual obsession with his son's attractive wife. The indignities of the aging process do not stop him from pursuing the young woman, even at the expense of his family and health. For a better look at sexual obsession, stick to Lolita and for an old man's reflection on his nearly completed life, watch Wild Strawberries. ★½ $29.99

The Diary of Anne Frank

(1959, 156 min, US, George Stevens) One of the most gripping and heartfelt stories to emerge from the Holocaust, this magnificent adaptation of the acclaimed play is based on the writings of Dutch teenager Anne Frank, whose diaries documenting years of hiding during WWII captured the hearts of millions around the world. Millie Perkins deftly plays Anne, who hid with her family in the attic of an Amsterdam warehouse to elude the Nazis. A superior supporting cast includes Joseph Schildkraut as her adoring father, Ed Wynn, in a rare and touching dramatic performance, and Oscar winner Shelley Winters. Diary is a testament to individual courage and a bitter history lesson we should never forget. ★★★★ $24.99

Diary of Forbidden Dreams

(1972, 94 min, Italy, Roman Polanski) Originally titled What?, this Polanski oddity is a ribald comedy about the sexual misadventures of an innocent but irresistible young woman. Her bizarre ordeal begins when she seeks shelter in an eccentric's mansion on the Italian Riviera. Her docile host turns lecherous tiger — but that only opens up a can of sexual worms as several other weird men descend for a bite. Funny and just a bit strange. Stars Marcello Mastroianni and Sydne Rome. (Dubbed) ★★½

Dick Tracy

(1990, 104 min, US, Warren Beatty) Beatty's colorful adaptation of the Chester Gould comic strip is a dazzling display of costumery and scenery. The performances in the film are, for the most part, splendid. Al Pacino's rendition of Tracy's arch-rival Big Boy Caprice is sensational. In the title role, Beatty delivers an appropriately heroic performance; Glenne Headly is charming as his girlfriend Tess Trueheart; Dustin Hoffman is hilarious as Tracy's informant, Mumbles; and Madonna gets to sing a couple of breathy show tunes penned by the inimitable Stephen Sondheim, and all of her other attributes are used to perfection. A highly entertaining romp — maybe now we can forget about Ishtar. ★★★ $9.99

Dick Tracy, Detective

(1945, 62 min, US, William Berke) Don't expect elaborate makeup effects or musical numbers from this installment in the original Dick Tracy series, and you won't be disappointed. The plot is a whole lot goofier and creepier than Warren Beatty's version, and the villains are just as perverse. Tracy's refreshingly pedestrian approach to crime-solving and his bizarre domestic situation add quirky appeal to this film. ★★★ $12.99

Dick Tracy Meets Gruesome

(1947, 65 min, US, John Rawlins) Boris Karloff stars as Gruesome, an ex-con with a diabolical plan to take over the city. The atmosphere is stark and Ralph Byrd is splendid as comic strip hero Tracy in this irresistible crime caper. ★★★ $9.99

Die Hard

(1988, 131 min, US, John McTiernan) First-rate action thriller starring Bruce Willis as a tough New York City policeman, on vacation and visiting his estranged wife (Bonnie Bedelia) in Los Angeles. His vacation is short-lived, however, as — armed only with his wits — he finds himself up against a group of terrorists who have taken control of a 40-story office building, among whose hostages include his wife. The action scenes are extremely well-directed and maximize suspense, and Willis' cynical cop is afforded some great one-liners as he battles the bad guys. (Letterboxed version available for $19.99) ★★★½ $14.99

Die Hard 2

(1990, 122 min, US, Renny Harlin) Bruce Willis is back in this fast-paced pyrotechnic sequel to his thrilling, claustrophobic high-rise original. This time, he's at Dulles Airport in Washington, D.C. waiting for his wife (Bonnie Bedelia) to land, when the place is taken over by a mercenary commando squad trying to hijack a Noriega-like dictator to safety. Not as tense, or as comprehensible, as the first film, but the large scale special effects and stunt work are amazing and the film packs a visceral jolt. (Letterboxed version available for $19.99) ★★★ $14.99

Die Hard with a Vengeance

(1995, 112 min, US, John McTiernan) Bruce Willis returns as New York City cop John McClane who — after finding adventure in Los Angeles and Washington D.C. — gets to play on his home turf in this action-packed if derivative third entry. McClane is called into a terrorist bombing case when the perp (Jeremy Irons), the brother of one of McClane's victims in the first film, seeks vengeance by playing cat-and-mouse all over the city with our hapless hero. Before you can say Lethal Weapon, McClane is partnered with a Harlem store owner (Samuel L. Jackson) who, after saving McClane's life, is now forced to help track down the bomber. As with the first two films, With a Vengeance features some extraordinary action sequences, each designed to top what came before it. On that level, the film is non-stop excitement; but even in light of the likable pairing of Willis and Jackson, the screenplay offers little of the strong narrative and character development offered in the first two films. (Available letterboxed and pan & scan) ★★½ $19.99

Die Watching

(1993, 92 min, US, Charles Davis) Christopher Atkins stars as a wannabe video director in this cliché-ridden erotic thriller. With the promise of work and fame, Atkins lures aspiring silicone-endowed actresses into his loft for auditions/screen tests and then kills them. Hard to believe...but wait, there's more: He soon meets his artist neighbor and falls in love, which, as you may have guessed by now, causes a conflict between the brewing love affair and his violent hobby. Die watching...we did...of extreme boredom. ★ $14.99

A Different Kind of Love

(1981, 60 min, GB, Brian Mills) After a slow start, this heart-wrenching BBC production about a man coming out to his mother picks up some emotional steam. Joyce Redman is appropriately overbearing as the domineering mother of Peter, a recently divorced father. She vainly attempts to set him up with available women, blind to the possibility that her 30-year-old son, now living with another man, might not be interested. Pinter-esque in dialogue, the film succeeds in capturing the inarticulate tensions between mother, son and lover. The gay men, who look indistinguishable, are not as finely detailed as the regal, ball-busting mum — which might be the point as the mother refuses to allow her son his own identity. Made for TV, the film is a quietly revealing drama of the stereotypical relationship between a gay man and his mother. ★★★

A Different Story

(1978, 108 min, US, Paul Aaron) A gay man (Perry King) and a lesbian (Meg Foster) marry to prevent his deportation, and then fall in love, have kids and go straight — each surrendering his/her sexual identity. The film uses the gay subtext simply as a gimmick, dwelling little on their original sexual orientation and more on their male-female love. Valerie Curtin is shrill and offensive as Foster's former lover; some of the other characters are merely stereotypes, as well. Offering no compassion towards the gay lifestyle, the film — sexual politics aside — just isn't that funny and presents its boring plot developments in a very sitcomish fashion. Addressing the sexual politics, the film is questionable in the notion that queers can be cured with a good heterosexual fuck. ★½

Diggstown

(1992, 98 min, US, Michael Ritchie) James Woods offers a sturdy performance in this familiar but likable Runyon-esque comedy about a grifter par excellence, his semi-retired partner (Louis Gossett, Jr.), and their screwball scheme to swindle an entire town. Though not as intricately plotted as *The Sting*, nor as stylish, the film offers good performances by the two leads, with sound support by Bruce Dern, and some nice action sequences. ★★½ $14.99

Dim Sum: A Little Bit of Heart

(1984, 89 min, US, Wayne Wang) Once again, director Wang reveals the communality of human experience through a sharply focused examination of a distinctive culture. The rela-

Diva

tionship between a Chinese-American mother and daughter is central to this warm observation of the familial bonds and cultural strengths of an Asian family in San Francisco. ★★★

Diner

(1982, 110 min, US, Barry Levinson) A scintillating slice-of-life served with a sprinkling of `50s nostalgia and a robust helping of male camaraderie. Levinson has created one of the most charming and humorous documentations of the often awkward transition from youth to adulthood. Impeccable ensemble acting from a cast including Steve Guttenberg, Daniel Stern, Mickey Rourke, Kevin Bacon and Ellen Barkin. ★★★★ $14.99

Dinner at Eight

(1933, 111 min, US, George Cukor) An all-star cast highlights this elegant Cukor classic based on George S. Kaufman and Edna Ferber's stage hit. Park Avenue shipping magnate Lionel Barrymore and his social-climbing wife Billie Burke throw a dinner party for a visiting British lord. On the guest list are fading screen idol John Barrymore (before his own decline); aging stage legend Marie Dressler; obnoxious financier Wallace Beery and his blowsy wife Jean Harlow; and family physician Edmund Lowe. How their lives and problems intertwine is the stuff that great moviemaking is made of. Dressler and Harlow steal the show. ★★★★ $19.99

Dinosaurs: I'm the Baby

(1991, 50 min, US) This double feature combines two episodes from the TV series which highlight the rambunctious baby of the dinosaur family. "Switched at Birth" is a comic take-off on the more tragic story of the same name in which Baby may or may not be Earl and Fran's baby. A Solomon-like solution ultimately settles the fate of both families involved, to almost everyone's satisfaction. In "Baby Calls," we learn that even dinosaurs have to potty train their little ones and are not immune to the same stubborn toddler reactions, with amusing one-liners and quite unusual results. It's easy to see why this video was a winner of a 1991 Parents' Choice Award. ★★★ $12.99

Diplomaniacs

(1933, 63 min, US, William A. Seiter) The comedy team of Bert Wheeler and Robert Woolsey star in one of their best comic outings, a totally crazy and hilarious romp (in every sense of the word) with W&W as barbers on an Indian reservation, being mistaken for diplomats and sent to Geneva to attend a peace conference. Silly and quite enjoyable fun. ★★★ $19.99

El Diputado (The Deputy)

(1979, 110 min, Spain, Eloy de la Iglesia) This highly praised and powerful thriller follows the political and sexual coming-out of a young married politician in post-Franco Spain. A congressman's repressed homosexual desires are awakened while serving a brief prison term for a political matter. After a first encounter, he furtively seeks out sexual partners until he falls in love with a 16-year-old street hustler. The film deals with the delicate balance between his life, his loving wife and his political goals. (Spanish with English subtitles) ★★★ $69.99

Directed by Andrei Tarkovsky

(1988, 105 min, USSR, Michel Leszczylowski) This "investigative" documentary into the life and works of the Soviet Union's greatest modern director was produced by the Swedish Film Institute and directed by Andrei Tarkovsky's longtime friend and editor Leszczylowski. Filmed in Sweden during the making of his final feature, *The Sacrifice*, and while he was gravely ill with cancer, the film attempts to capture, through interviews and footage from his films, the essence behind this brooding intellectual genius. ★★★ $59.99

Dirty Dancing

(1987, 97 min, US, Emile Ardolino) This sleeper hit of 1987 is a wonderfully nostalgic coming-of-age tale set in a Catskill Mountains resort in 1963. Patrick Swayze became a star thanks to his role as the handsome dance instructor who becomes involved with innocent teenager Jennifer Grey. Some good dancing and golden oldies highlight the film. ★★★ $14.99

Dirty Dishes

(1982, 99 min, France, Joyce Buñuel) After ten years of cooking, cleaning and taking care of her husband, a housewife's life has become so dulled by these domestic chores that even an affair with a younger man and other incidents can not seem to break her out of her crazed boredom. A deceptively comic *Diary of a Mad Housewife*. Directed by Luis Buñuel's daughter-in-law, Joyce Buñuel. (French with English subtitles) ★★★

The Dirty Dozen

(1967, 150 min, US, Robert Aldrich) Classic WWII adventure with Lee Marvin leading 12 condemned prisoners on a daring raid of a Nazi stronghold. Not a dull moment in its two-and-a-half hours, the first half of the film follows the rigorous training the men go through, and the second covers the crackerjack assault. Charles Bronson, John Cassavetes, Donald Sutherland and Telly Savalas are some of the dirty dozen, and Ernest Borgnine, Robert Ryan and George Kennedy are some of the military bigwigs. ★★★½ $19.99

Dirty Hands

(1976, 102 min, France, Claude Chabrol) Chabrol, France's master of the suppressed but always torrid urges and desires of the bourgeoisie, directed this familiar though atmospheric tale of treachery, murder and mystery. A woman and her lover plot to murder her husband — but with unexpected results. (Dubbed) ★★

Dirty Harry

(1971, 103 min, US, Don Siegel) The first of Clint Eastwood's *Dirty Harry* series is a classic action-thriller. In this flavorful and exciting police story, Harry Callahan chases after a psychopathic rooftop sniper. ★★★ $14.99

Dirty Pair: Affair on Nolandia

(1985, 57 min, Japan, Masahara Okuwaki) Laced with wild action and humor, this animated adventure begins on the planet Ukbar where the "Pair" start an investigation into some bizarre psychic occurrences. Along the way, they deal with attempted murder, sabotage, a series of "mindgames" and a pair of high-tech villains. ★★½ $24.99

Dirty Rotten Scoundrels

(1988, 110 min, US, Frank Oz) Michael Caine and Steve Martin make an unlikely but very funny and effective comic duo in this hilarious yarn about a couple of con men competing for control of a town on the French Riviera. Caine is superb as the established swindler who masquerades as a deposed prince. When rival Martin (who is in his element as the rude and crude American) lands on the scene, Caine is faced with a serious challenge to the control of his turf; where the two become enmeshed in a wacky series of attempts to outscheme each other. This remake of the 1962 film *Bedtime Stories*, starring Marlon Brando and David Niven, is expertly directed under the watchful eye of Oz. ★★★½ $9.99

Disclosure

(1994, 128 min, US, Barry Levinson) Michael Douglas, the self-appointed spokesman for the victimized white heterosexual male, is cast as such once again as a successful computer engineer and all-around good guy who is sexually harassed by his new boss and ex-flame Demi Moore. She in turn brings charges against him. Thus sets in motion a battle to prove his innocence. Forgetting the obvious complaint of a female aggressor in Hollywood's first film about sexual harassment, there are other points which make *Disclosure* an irritating piece of trash. Though slickly made by Levinson, and not without its entertaining moments, the film is a cheap sleight of hand which is no more about harassment than *Philadelphia* is about AIDS. Lacking the courage of its convictions, the film is ultimately about corporate intrigue, and even then misses the mark as a biting indictment. It's a misogynist, calculated foray into sexual politics whose only point is that women as much as men can abuse power. Roma Maffia provides the only shining moment as Douglas' attorney. ★★ $14.99

The Discreet Charm of the Bourgeoisie

(1972, 100 min, France, Luis Buñuel) A witty anarchistic social comedy about six upper-crust Parisians and their unsuccessful attempts to dine in a civilized manner. Buñuel's sardonic statement on the amoral world of the ruling class. (French with English subtitles) ★★★★

The Disorderly Orderly

(1964, 90 min, US, Frank Tashlin) Jerry Lewis is a young practicing med student who seems to have more of a flair for comedy than healing (unless you believe in the healing power of laughter). ★★★ $14.99

Disorganized Crime

(1989, 101 min, US, Jim Kouf) Disorganized comedy about a group of small-time criminals who attempt the ultimate heist, but who are faced with a few problems, such as the loss of their leader and no plan whatsoever. ★★ $9.99

Disraeli

(1929, 87 min, US, Alfred E. Green) George Arliss, such a distinguished actor of his day that in this film he is billed "Mr. George Arliss," won a much-deserved Best Actor Oscar for re-creating his legendary Broadway performance. This intelligent, if stagey adaptation centers on England's Jewish Prime Minister of the late 19th century and his efforts to secure the Suez Canal for Britain — which includes going head-to-head with Russian spies and anti-Semitism. Arliss' wife Florence is ideally cast as Disraeli's spouse, and a lovely Joan Bennett nicely plays a friend of the family for whom Disraeli plays matchmaker. Arliss had played the role once before in a 1921 silent. ★★★½ $19.99

Distant Thunder

(1973, 92 min, India, Satyajit Ray) Set in a remote village in Bengal during the outbreak of World War II, this harsh and vividly filmed story chronicles the lives of several families when the area is shaken by a famine and their world is disastrously uprooted. A riveting drama of great scope and power. (Hindi with English subtitles) ★★★½ $39.99

Distant Thunder

(1988, 114 min, US, Rick Rosenthal) An emotionally scarred Vietnam vet (John Lithgow) leaves his secluded life in Washington's rain forest to see the son (Ralph Macchio) he hasn't seen in fifteen years. Lithgow's sensitive performance can't offset the sentimental melodramatics and clichéd characterizations. ★★ $14.99

Distant Voices, Still Lives

(1988, 85 min, GB, Terence Davies) Davies' autobiographical and unblinking account of a family's oppressive lifestyle in pre- and postwar England. A timeworn photo album on film, the story traces the adolescence of Davies and his older sisters struggling to mature despite their abusive father's tyranny; and also the grown children's disenchantment, told through song at the local pub. *Distant Voices, Still Lives* is a passionate and rich film. ★★★½ $89.99

The Distinguished Gentleman

(1993, 112 min, US, Jonathan Lynn) More homogenized humor from the man who should have learned by now that politically correct comedy is not his forté, former four-letter-wordsmith Eddie Murphy. This time out he tackles the role of a grifter who scams his way into Congress in search of streets paved with gold, only to discover that he has a heart of gold himself. Awww, shucks. It's pretty funny, though, even without the profanity. Also stars Sheryl Lee Ralph, Joe Don Baker, Grant Shaud and Lane Smith. ★★½ $9.99

Le Distrait (The Daydreamer)

(1978, 101 min, France, Pierre Richard) Pierre Richard (*Tall Blond Man...*, *Les Comperes*) continues his bungling and frantically funny misadventures in this Gallic farce about an ad executive who just can't keep fantasy away from reality. Richard himself directed this funny escapade. (French with English subtitles) ★★★

Diva

(1981, 123 min, France, Jean-Jacques Beineix) Beineix's stunning film debut is a dashing, eclectic adventure that shimmers with style and humor. The unpredictable escapades begin when a young postal messenger secretly tapes the performance of a determinedly unrecorded operatic star. The chase begins when he flees from a skinhead punk, a pair of inescapable Taiwanese record pirates, and the police. A rapturous thriller that is an amalgam of pop culture paraphernalia, B-movie clichés and prodigious flair. (French with English subtitles) ★★★½ $29.99

Dive Bomber

(1941, 130 min, US, Michael Curtiz) Errol Flynn stars as a dashing young Navy flight doctor attempting to discover a way to prevent "pilot blackout" at the end of a power-dive. Fred MacMurray and Ralph Bellamy are a veteran pilot and chief flight doctor, respectively. Their interaction with Flynn is good, but this film follows conventions like there's no tomorrow. Spectacular aerial photography highlight an otherwise solid by-the-numbers film. ★★★ $19.99

D

Divine Madness

(1980, 95 min, US, Michael Ritchie) La Belle Bette, the Divine Miss Midler, in concert. No joke is too cheap, no gag too crass as evidenced by the raunchy stage performance of Bette and her Harlettes. And she sings, too. ★★★ $9.99

The Divine Nymph

(1979, 90 min, Italy, G.P. Griffi) This sexy romp features Laura Antonelli as a young and sensuous woman who becomes involved in a tragic love triangle with Marcello Mastroianni and Terence Stamp. A predictable story of decadence, obsession and deception. (Dubbed) ★★

Divorce — Italian Style

(1961, 104 min, Italy, Pietro Germi) Marcello Mastroianni is pure magic in this frantic satire on love and marriage — the first, and best, of the Italian sex comedies of the 1960s. Mastroianni plays an aging nobleman who, in order to marry his vivacious teenage cousin, must first get rid of his wife — a difficult task in a no-divorce country. His convoluted plan soon involves him acting as a jealous husband who, on finding his wife in bed with another man, kills her off in a fit of passion — the only problem is finding the "other man." A delightful comedy that was nominated for three Academy Awards and won for Best Original Screenplay. (Available dubbed and in Italian with English subtitles) ★★★★ $39.99

The Divorce of Lady X

(1938, 91 min, GB, Tim Whelan) This witty, sophisticated comedy examines the problems of a London barrister who allows a pretty young lady to spend an "innocent" night in his flat, only to later be named as a correspondent in a subsequent divorce action. This frothy comedy stars Laurence Olivier, Merle Oberon and Ralph Richardson. ★★★ $19.99

The Divorcee

(1930, 83 min, US, Robert Z. Leonard) Norma Shearer won an Oscar for her portrayal of a married woman who suffers through her husband's infidelity before deciding to give him a taste of his own medicine. ★★½ $19.99

Do the Right Thing

(1989, 120 min, US, Spike Lee) Lee's brilliant, controversial and thought-provoking *Do the Right Thing* bulldozed its way into the American consciousness — forcing people to take sides on many of Lee's radical assertions and making race relations the hot topic of the summer of '89. The story revolves around a single street in the Bed-Stuy section of Brooklyn during one of the hottest days of summer. Spike's attention is given to the citizens of the street from 'da Mayor (Ossie Davis is terrific as the suds-soaked elder who offers snatches of street wisdom) to Mookie (Lee is his rambunctious self as the un-enlightened delivery boy for Sal's Pizzeria). Danny Aiello also shines as Sal. Superbly acted and filmed, *Do the Right Thing* is not simply incendiary — it is downright great filmmaking. ★★★★ $19.99

Do You Remember Dolly Bell?

(1981, 105 min, Yugoslavia, Emir Kusturica) Made a a few years before his highly successful *When Father Was Away on Business*, director Kusturica's perceptive and amusing coming-of-age drama is set in 1960s Sarajevo. The story centers around the family life of Dino, an amiable 16-year-old who befriends a caustic but engaging young prostitute, nicknamed Dolly Bell. An engrossing film which delves into Yugoslavia's ever-shifting nature of non-aligned Communism and its effect on the family, especially the young. (Serbian with English subtitles) ★★★

Doc Hollywood

(1991, 105 min, US, Michael Caton-Jones) A hotshot big-city doctor is forced to offer his services to a small, backwoods town populated with a collection of offbeat and endearing characters. No, it's not "Northern Exposure." It's *Doc Hollywood*, a surprisingly charming comedy with Michael J. Fox as the doctor in question, a Washington D.C. surgeon waylaid in a Southern community on his trek west. And though the film does share similarities with the hit TV series, in no way is this a rip-off or re-hash. Fox gives an attractive performance as the Doc, possibly his best to date; he maintains his boyish qualities while discovering a maturity on-screen heretofore unseen. ★★★ $9.99

Docks of New York

(1928, 76 min, US, Josef von Sternberg) Lacking the mannered bombast of his later melodramas, von Sternberg's efficient, superb drama chronicles a stevedore's developing love for a woman he saved from suicide. The director's mastery of the language of silent film is most evident in his slow dissolves — either to compress time, or to accentuate the internal turmoil of a character. It was to be for the last time: sound required a less obtrusive vocabulary. ★★★★ $29.99

The Doctor

(1991, 125 min, US, Randa Haines) Yet another er in 1991's spate of moral redemption films (*Regarding Henry, The Fisher King, Doc Hollywood*), *The Doctor* features a solid performance by William Hurt, who again teams up with *Children of a Lesser God* director Haines. Hurt plays Jack McKee, a successful and respected heart surgeon who finds himself on the other side of the emergency room door when he is diagnosed with throat cancer. In coming to grips with both his illness and the indifference of his colleagues, he soon realizes his own shortcomings as a doctor and husband. Hurt's performance is incredibly nuanced; even at his most glib, McKee is a sympathetic and all-too-real character. Elizabeth Perkins also excels as a terminally ill woman. While not on par with Haine's Oscar-winning debut, *The Doctor* is an impressive follow-up nonetheless. ★★★ $9.99

The Doctor and the Devils

(1985, 93 min, GB, Freddie Francis) Another unusual production from Brooksfilms (Mel Brooks' production company), this Gothic tale is based on a 1940s screenplay by Dylan Thomas. It concerns two of the most famous villains in British history, Broom and Fallen, who provided corpses for the anatomical research of Dr. Thomas Rock. Timothy Dalton, Jonathan Pryce and Twiggy star in this grisly tale which evokes images of the old Hammer classics. ★★★ $79.99

Dr. Bethune

(1990, 115 min, Canada/China/France, Phillip Borsos) In a mesmerizing performance, Donald Sutherland brings subtle shading to the many facets of Dr. Norman Bethune, a complex man whose rude arrogance is tempered by his compassionate devotion to the cause of universal medical treatment. With a history as social and medical crusader, Bethune is summoned in 1938 to Yunan by Chairman Mao to be chief medical advisor to 100,000 troops. In flashbacks, the film concentrates on his efforts toward; and his prior achievements, as well. Beautifully photographed in Canada, Spain and China, this finely crafted, formally structured film is highlighted by performances from Helen Mirren, Helen Shaver, Guo Da and Anouk Aimee, among others. ★★★½ $19.99

Doctor Butcher M.D.

(1979, 81 min, Italy/US, Francesco Martino) An extremely gory cannibal adventure, with flesh-eating Indonesians attacking investigating Americans, while an insane doctor (M.D. — Medical Deviate) performs lobotomies on whoever he can get his hands on. ★★ $39.99

Dr. Caligari

(1991, 80 min, US, Stephen Sayadian) The director of the stylish porno-punk *Cafe Flesh* goes "legit" with this colorful takeoff on the classic German silent *The Cabinet of Dr. Caligari*. Now it is his granddaughter who is in charge of the asylum and her radical new form of therapy consists of gender bending until the patient snaps from severe mental fatigue. ★★ $14.99

Dr. Cyclops

(1945, 75 min, US, Ernest Schoedsack) Until the late 1950s, it was rare for color films to have many special effects. It was even rarer for a horror film to be made in color. Albert Dekker plays a mad doctor living in the jungle who shrinks anyone who visits him for no other reason than because he can. ★★★ $14.99

Doctor Detroit

(1983, 91 min, US, Michael Pressman) Dan Aykroyd plays a mild-mannered college professor who finds himself caught up in a power struggle with the Chicago mob when he takes care of five beautiful prostitutes. Some good laughs in this playful comedy. ★★½ $14.99

Doctor Dolittle

(1967, 144 min, US, Richard Fleischer) Rex Harrison talks to the animals and sails around the world in a giant snail. Children may enjoy this musical fable, though adults will find some of it difficult to take. A beguiling score includes "Talk to the Animals" (Oscar winner). ★★½ $14.99

Dr. Faustus

(1968, 93 min, GB, Richard Burton) Colorful rendering of the Faustus legend with first-time director Burton in the title role as a man who sells his soul to the Devil for personal gain.

While not the best telling of the tale, the film is notable for a cameo appearance by the director's wife, Elizabeth Taylor, in the role of "Helen of Troy." ★★ $19.99

Dr. Giggles

(1992, 96 min, US, Manny Coto) With a razor-thin scalpel in hand, a menacingly diabolical giggle and a penchant for involuntary organ transplants, Dr. Giggles is no ordinary Marcus Welby. Larry Drake draws more than just a few chuckles as the deranged son of a mad doctor who escapes from an asylum and sets out to exact vengeance on the town that killed his father. Soon, however, he finds higher moral purpose: To find a new heart for a vivacious young teenager with a defective valve — too bad the donors didn't get a chance to sign the consent form. While it fails to deliver the goods for hardcore splatter aficionados, this amusing horror spoof will have some viewers placing their hands over their eyes...when not holding on to vital organ parts. ★★ $19.99

Doctor in the House

(1954, 92 min, GB, Ralph Thomas) Dirk Bogarde stars in this hilarious farce about medical school students based on the story of Richard Gordon. This was the first of a series of sophisticated takeoffs on the *Carry On* films. ★★★

Dr. Jekyll and Mr. Hyde

(1920, 96 min, US, John S. Robertson) John Barrymore gives a virtuoso performance as Robert Louis Stevenson's tormented doctor in this silent classic. Filmed many times since, including the 1932 Fredric March version which has yet to be surpassed. ★★★ $29.99

Dr. Jekyll and Mr. Hyde

(1932, 82 min, US, Rouben Mamoulian) Robert Louis Stevenson's classic thriller of split personality and dementia has been done so many times and on so many different levels, that it, like "Frankenstein," has somehow lost not only its freshness, but also its ability to cause fear or to shock. This 1932 version is an exception. Fredric March, who won the Oscar for Best Actor, brings both tenderness and ferocity to the character that, despite the film's age, makes it hard to imagine anyone else in the role. Miriam Hopkins is unforgettable as the doomed prostitute who takes up with Mr. Hyde, and had there been a Supporting Actress category in 1932, she probably would have been an Oscar winner as well. Armenian-born director Mamoulian used his innovative camerawork and direction to create a truly tragic figure. One of the all-time greats in horror — a must-see. ★★★★ $19.99

Dr. Jekyll and Mr. Hyde

(1941, 114 min, US, Victor Fleming) Slick remake of the Robert Louis Stevenson story with Spencer Tracy as the mad doc, Ingrid Bergman as Hyde's ill-fated Cockney mistress and Lana Turner as Jekyll's bride-to-be. ★★★ $19.99

Dr. Jekyll and Sister Hyde

(1972, 94 min, GB, Roy Ward Baker) Friends of Freud should have a field day with this intriguing, but at times lifeless, variation of the Robert Louis Stevenson chiller starring Ralph Bates as the insanely curious doctor who manages to isolate his dark side only to find that it is actually feminine! As with most treatises on the nature of good and evil, evil is more fun as evidenced by Martine Beswick's villainous performance as Sister Hyde. ★★★ $9.99

Dr. Jekyll & Ms. Hyde

(1995, 95 min, US, David Price) When network television shows nothing but "Hee-Haw," when an ushers' strike closes down the cinema, when martial law closes the bookstores, and when video stores are stocked with only Sylvester Stallone flicks, then and only then should this ludicrous film be popped into the VCR. A tired variation of the Jekyll and Hyde tale, this insipid comedy features Tim Daly as a poor, eccentric scientist who, in his work making perfume fragrances, accidentally turns into a power-hungry woman (in the personage of Sean Young). Yes, sexual hijinks ensue as men fall under his/her murderous attractiveness. Harvey Fierstein ruins his already tattered acting career as a fey office worker. The best thing that can be said about this film is that it does not cause cancer (although not all of the studies are in). ★ $19.99

Dr. No

(1963, 111 min, GB, Terence Young) Sean Connery stars in the first and foremost James Bond adventure. There's sex, violence, exotic locales and the master-fiend Dr. No. This is agent 007 at his finest. Co-starring the luscious Ursula Andress. ★★★½ $14.99

Dr. Phibes Rises Again

(1972, 89 min, GB, Robert Fuest) A disfigured madman (Vincent Price) and his deceased wife go boating down the Underground River of the Dead in this sequel to *The Abominable Dr. Phibes*. Everybody's in it for the laughs: Terry-Thomas, Peter Cushing, Beryl Reed — even the set designer. ★★½ $9.99

Dr. Strangelove

(1964, 93 min, GB, Stanley Kubrick) Kubrick's unforgettable and hilarious black comedy is undeniably one of the greatest indictments of the Cold War ever to be seen in the cinema. From the legendary performances by Peter Sellers, Sterling Hayden, George C. Scott and Slim Pickens to Kubrick's brilliant use of the cinematic form, the film is an undaunted piece of mastery. The film's profound message about the dangers of aggression in the nuclear age is as timely now as it was when it was released — a superior cinematic achievement. (Available letterboxed or pan & scan) ★★★★ $19.99

Dr. Syn, Alias the Scarecrow

(1962, 129 min, US, James Neilson) Set in 1736 England, Patrick McGoohan plays the vicar Dr. Syn who, disguised as "The Scarecrow," defends the struggling farmers and villagers against the oppressive King George III, whose heavy taxes have led the commoners to revolt. ★★½

Dr. Terror's House of Horrors

(1965, 98 min, GB, Freddie Francis) Intriguing, episodic horror film from director Francis (*The Doctor and the Devils*). Five fellow travelers have their tarots read by a mysterious doctor as they ride on a train headed — where? Francis directs a strong cast including Peter Cushing, Christopher Lee and Donald Sutherland. ★★★ $14.99

Dr. Who — Pyramids of Mars

(1975, 91 min, GB, Paddy Russell) The Doctor (Tom Baker) and his companion Sarah (Elisabeth Sladen) face an invisible force field and robot mummies in their efforts to save the universe from Sutekh, an ancient, insane Egyptian with god-like powers (Horus' brother). A must see for Whovians and/or Egyptologists. ★★★ $19.99

Dr. Who and the Daleks

(1965, 84 min, GB, Gordon Fleming) The tremendous popularity, via PBS, of the "Dr. Who" TV series helped to resurrect this prehistoric version which stars Peter Cushing. As all good fans well know, the Daleks are a continuing nuisance to the Doctor and this film offers a chance to see them in one of their earliest forms. ★★½ $29.99

Doctor Zhivago

(1965, 180 min, GB, David Lean) Through his retelling of Boris Pasternak's novel of the Russian Revolution, Lean succeeds in creating both a mammoth spectacle and an impressive and absorbing account of one of the most fascinating and important periods in human history. An incredible ensemble is headed by the exceptional Julie Christie. Other luminaries include Omar Sharif, Geraldine Chaplin, Alec Guinness, Tom Courtenay, Rita Tushingham, Rod Steiger and Ralph Richardson — now that's a cast! (Available letterboxed and pan & scan) ★★★½ $24.99

Document of the Dead

(1979/1989, 76 min, US, Roy Frumkes) Directed by Frumkes (co-producer and writer of *Street Trash*) and narrated by Warhol favorite Susan Tyrrell, *Document of the Dead* is a documentary on director George Romero (dealing mainly with, and on the sets of *Dawn of the Dead*). A must for Romero (and Tom Savini) fans and for those interested in F/X and low-budget film production. ★★½ $19.99

Dodes'ka-den

(1970, 140 min, Japan, Akira Kurosawa) A stunning and masterful examination of the down-trodden lives and glorious dreams of a number of Tokyo slum dwellers. Kurosawa's first film in color is an eloquent and impassioned affirmation of life and the awesome power of hope. Oddly, the film was not very well received by the critics and was a big disappointment at the box office, causing Kurosawa to abandon filmmaking for several years. (Japanese with English subtitles) ★★★ $29.99

Dodge City

(1939, 101 min, US, Michael Curtiz) Errol Flynn trades in his sword and tights for a pistol and cowboy boots as the new sheriff in a trigger-happy town. Olivia deHavilland and Ann Sheridan also star. Flavorful western fun. ★★★ $19.99

D

Dodsworth

(1936, 101 min, US, William Wyler) Superb film version of Sinclair Lewis' novel about a retired industrialist and his wife who travel abroad; each coming to re-examine the purpose and value of their lives. Walter Huston, Ruth Chatterton and Mary Astor give outstanding performances, and David Niven, Paul Lukas and Oscar-nominee Maria Ouspenskaya also star. ★★★★ $19.99

Dog Day (Canicule)

(1983, 101 min, France, Yves Boisset) This gritty, macabre little gem is a pristine manifestation of the Gallic infatuation with American gangsters. Lee Marvin stars as Jimmy Cobb, a chiseled-faced personification of the amoral yet honorable hood, who is on the run after a botched stick-up job. He finds himself at the dubious mercy of a farming family, whose interrelationships and sense of loyalties make the word "criminal" inoperative. Like Godard's *Alphaville* and Melville's *Bob le Flambeur*, this is a parable of existential man told against the backdrop of the chimerical safety of small-caliber weapons and the illusive salvation of the big score. Also starring Miou-Miou and Jean Carmet. (Dubbed) ★★★½

Dog Day Afternoon

(1975, 130 min, US, Sidney Lumet) Before Al Pacino embarrassed himself *Cruising* the leather bars, he gave a first-rate performance as a gay thief whose attempt to rob a bank (to pay for his lover's sex change) brings the city of New York to a standstill. An often delightful comedy, director Lumet flavors his film with warm characters and deft humor. In supporting roles, Charles Durning as a police liaison and Oscar-nominee Chris Sarandon as Pacino's lover are standouts. Based on a true incident. ★★★½ $14.99

Dogfight

(1991, 92 min, US, Nancy Savoca) The heavily anticipated second effort from director Savoca is every bit as marvelous as her debut, *True Love*. River Phoenix stars as a young Marine who sets out with his buddies on a dogfight — a search for the ugliest girl in town to escort her to a dance. He charms Lili Taylor, a plump and awkward aspiring folk singer who soon discovers his cruel deception. To make amends, he convinces her to go on a "real" date and they wind up spending the night together — a night of revelation and intimacy which neither would soon forget. Phoenix, as always, is first-rate, but it is Taylor's superb portrayal which elevates the film. *Dogfight* is an honest slice-of-'60s life captured with sensitivity and awareness. ★★★½ $19.99

Dogs in Space

(1987, 109 min, Australia, Richard Lowenstein) This "drugged-up punks in love" picture explores the underground subculture of Australia's alienated youth, circa 1978. Michael Hutchence, lead singer of INXS, stars as the immovably passive leader of a commune of punks and hangers-on living in comfortable squalor in a ramshackle house in Melbourne. Infused with loud music, countless subplots and characters, the film, like its denizens, is incoherent and rambling. Yet, despite the problems, it is entertaining and amusing. Lovers of classical Australian cinema, beware! ★★½ $79.99

The Dogs of War

(1980, 101 min, GB, John Irvin) This film stretches the boundaries of political reason by idolizing a group of mercenaries who are hired to overthrow the dictator of a newly formed West African nation. This somber, but solid adaptation of Frederick Forsythe's novel stars Christopher Walken, Colin Blakely, Tom Berenger and JoBeth Williams. ★★★ $14.99

Doin' Time on Planet Earth

(1988, 83 min, US, Charles Matthau) A harmless, dopey comedy about teenage alienation — as in alien from outer space. Matt Adler is trapped in a dull, small Arizona town. Life seems aimless. Until he comes to the conclusion he's really from another planet. He meets up with Adam West and Candy Azzara, who convince him not only that he is right, but he's their leader who's destined to take them home. The film pokes fun at the extraterrestrial craze, and produces a few smiles. Directed by Matthau (Walter's son), who doesn't embarrass himself with his directorial debut. ★★½ $19.99

La Dolce Vita

(1961, 175 min, Italy, Federico Fellini) A staggering, trendsetting film that examines the hollow lives of Rome's decadent upper crust through the eyes of a cynical columnist. Marcello Mastroianni became an international star thanks to his swaggering portrayal of the lustful gossip columnist, and Fellini sharply observes the mores and morals of a generation. (Italian with English subtitles) ★★★★ $24.99

Dolemite

(1974, 88 min, US, D'Urville Martin) He's bad, the man is out-a-sight...he's Dolemite! Spewing hilarious invective-filled poetry that would make Eddie Murphy blush, Rudy Ray Moore single-handedly brings back those halycon days at the Goldman Theatre when pimps in fluorescent polyester jumpsuits, fur hats and gravity-defying afros ruled the cinematic land. Ignore the ludicrous acting and production values and just sit back and enjoy Dolemite as he faces crooked white cops, double-dealing thugs and scantily clad "hos" in this blaxploitation classic. Can you dig it? ★★★ $19.99

Doll Squad

(1973, 90 min, US, Ted V. Mikels) This fast-paced, cultish actioner features sultry Tura Satana (*Faster Pussycat Kill, Kill*) as a member of a Charlie's Angels-esque CIA assassin squad. Armed with flame-throwing lipstick tubes, bullet-bras and kung fu training, our heroines battle a group of saboteurs who want to take over the world by spreading a deadly virus. ★★★ $94.99

A Doll's House

(1973, 87 min, GB, Joseph Losey) Jane Fonda's controversial interpretation of Henrik Ibsen's 19th-century liberated woman is the centerpiece of Losey's cinematic adaptation of the classic play. Fonda plays Nora, who risks destruction in order to save her husband only to suddenly and dramatically have to assert her independence when she confronts their unabashed male arrogance. Trevor Howard and David Warner co-star. ★★★

Dollar

(1938, 78 min, Sweden, Gustaf Molander) An uncharacteristically light *Rules of the Game*-like comedy about three society couples who set out on a group skiing vacation. Starring Ingrid Bergman. (Swedish with English subtitles) ★★½ $19.99

The Dollmaker

(1984, 140 min, US, Daniel Petrie) Jane Fonda won an Emmy Award for her stirring performance in this first-rate TV drama as an impoverished farm woman who moves her family to Detroit when her husband lands a factory job. The film evokes a fine feel for 1940s America, and a stellar supporting cast includes Geraldine Page, Amanda Plummer and Levon Helm. ★★★½ $14.99

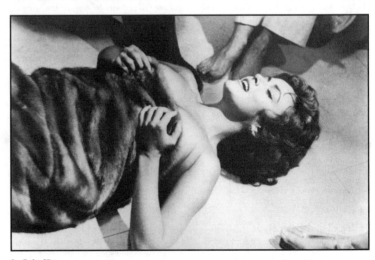

La Dolce Vita

Dollman vs. Demonic Toys

(1993, 64 min, US, Charles Band) *Dollman vs. Moronic Toys* might have been a better title for this shameless excuse of a film. This time the foul-mouthed toys are back and cranky heroine Tracy Scoggins enlists the aid of Dollman, a pint-sized cop from the planet Arthurus, and Dollchick (from another Full Moon Pictures disaster, *Bad Channels*) to help put them away for good. Padded with enough flashback footage to take up much of the 64 minute running time, this tepid thriller is paced so slow that only a funeral procession moving backwards could equal it. ★ $89.99

Dolly Dearest

(1992, 94 min, US, Maria Lease) Only above-par special effects distinguish this unimaginative horror pic best described as "*Child's Play* in drag." Sam Bottoms and Denise Crosby do time as the harried parents of a precocious little girl who, when forced to relocate to a small Mexican town, finds a best friend in a demonic doll. Even "Chucky" wouldn't take this doll out. ★★ $9.99

Dolores Claiborne

(1995, 125 min, US, Taylor Hackford) This heartfelt adaptation of Stephen King's best-seller is distinguished by yet another Oscar-caliber performance by Kathy Bates (who won for King's *Misery*) as a downtrodden New England housewife who must vindicate herself in the murder of her employer even as she unlocks the secrets that separate her from her neurotic, chain-smoking daughter (Jennifer Jason Leigh). Hackford deftly and seamlessly switches from present day to flashback, creating a richly woven tapestry of mystery and suspense laced with a sensitivity towards women (and motherhood) not usually associated with the author. As was demonstrated by *Stand by Me* and *The Shawshank Redemption*, it seems King's best screen adaptations are those which concentrate more on intimate relationships and less with horror. David Strathairn appears in the crucial role of Bates' deceased husband, and Christopher Plummer is icy cold as the sheriff suspicious of Bates. Danny Elfman wrote the wonderfully somber score. (Letterboxed version) ★★★½ $19.99

The Dolphin (O Boto)

(1987, 95 min, Brazil, Walter Lima, Jr.) This steamy fantasy is derived from a Brazilian myth about "O Boto," a lustful "were-dolphin" who, on the night of the full moon, becomes a handsome young man and lures unsuspecting women to the water where he bewitches and seduces them. Set in a small village on the northern coast of Brazil, the film tells the tale of Tereza, the daughter of a fisherman who falls under "O Boto"'s spell. When she gives birth to his son, the town becomes victim to a terrible curse in which the local waters become devoid of fish. Tinged with a smattering of black humor, this erotic drama is filmed in sensuous shades of midnight blue and is reminiscent in tone, though not on the same level, as the classic *Dona Flor and Her Two Husbands*. (Portuguese with English subtitles) ★★★ $19.99

Dominick and Eugene

(1988, 111 min, US, Robert M. Young) *Rain Man* has nothing on this similarly themed, criminally neglected drama. Set in Pittsburgh, the film details the complex relationship between twin brothers who have a dark secret buried in their past. Dominick (Tom Hulce) is a slow-witted man-child whose job as a trash collector subsidizes his brother's medical school tuition. Eugene (Ray Liotta) realizes his financial dependence on his brother — and Dominick's emotional dependence on him — is becoming burdensome, forcing him to consider some tough decisions about their future. Hulce gives a brilliantly textured performance and it probably should have been him, not Dustin Hoffman, to win that year's Oscar for a portrayal of a mentally disabled sibling. ★★★★ $19.99

Dominion Tank Police

(1988, 85 min, Japan, Koichi Mashimo) Act 1: "The Crime Corps" (45 min); Act 2: "The Crime War" (40 min). Startling animation is featured in this sci-fi tale set on a toxic cloud-covered Earth in 2010. The story concerns the attempts of the Tank Police to capture the notorious Buaku (a half-human, half-cyborg killer) and his ruthless partners (the bio-engineered cat sisters, Annapuma and Unipuma). $19.99 ea. ★★★

Don Giovanni

(1979, 185 min, France/Italy, Joseph Losey) Losey's brilliant screen adaptation of Mozart's operatic masterpiece features what amounts to an all-star cast of singers including Jose van Dam, Kiri Te Kanawa, Ruggero Raimondi and Teresa Berganza. Using a subtle blend of commedia dell'arte and morality play, Losey's interpretation of this Don Juan-based legend is a beautiful and bold marriage of opera and cinema. Sumptuously photographed on location in Venice, *Don Giovanni* is a visual treat. (Italian with English subtitles) ★★★★ $24.99

Don Juan

(1926, 111 min, US, Alan Crosland) The first sound feature (only music and sound effects, no dialogue thus no mention in the history books). John Barrymore is at his swashbuckling best, running when others would walk, jumping when others would sit down. If he weren't such a kinetic ball of energy, he would get lost in the sumptuous sets. ★★★½ $29.99

Don Juan deMarco

(1995, 90 min, US, Jeremy Leven) Johnny Depp gives yet another standout performance in this deliriously romantic fable about the power and magic of love. Depp stars as a possibly delusional young man who, insisting that he is the legendary lover Don Juan, decides to end his life because he cannot have the one woman he truly loves. Enter Marlon Brando as the retiring psychiatrist who tries to unlock the mystery of "the greatest lover that ever lived," all the while being seduced by the rhapsodic tales Depp spins during his therapy. First-time director Leven (a clinical psychologist and author) serves up possibly the most delicious mixture of erotic love and comedy since *Like Water for Chocolate*, and the film welcomes back to the big screen the ever-radiant Faye

Don Juan deMarco

Dunaway as Brando's loving but neglected wife. Even in light of Dunaway being underutilized and Brando being a sometimes cumbersome presence, *Don Juan* is a natural charmer — as only Depp could play him. ★★★ $14.99

Don Juan My Love

(1990, 96 min, Spain, Antonio Mercero) Beginning with an inventive variation on the presentation of the opening credits, this delightful fable is a thoroughly enjoyable and, at times, hilariously wicked comedy. The date is October 31, All Souls' Day eve, when the tormented ghost of the womanizing Don Juan rises from his grave and, as he has been doing for hundreds of years, begins a 24-hour attempt to end his term in purgatory by doing a good deed. The comedy of errors begins when he is mistaken for an obnoxious actor who is playing Don Juan in a theatrical production. Drug-smuggling actors, corpulent knife-wielding grandmothers, castanet-speaking production assistants and coke-filled angels all pop up in this wild romp which juxtaposes the romantic memory of old Spain with the harsh reality of a modern one. (Spanish with English subtitles) ★★★ $19.99

Don Quixote

(1973, 110 min, US, Rudolf Nureyev/Robert Helpmann) The film version of Marius Petipas' colorful ballet was co-directed by Nureyev (who also plays Basilio) and Robert Helpmann (who appears in the title role). Featuring the Australian Ballet, scored by Ludwig Minkus and lavishly filmed by cinematographer Geoffrey Unsworth. ★★★½ $39.99

Don Segundo Sombra

(1969, 110 min, Spain, Manuel Antin) Based on Ricardo Guiraldes' novel, the title character narrates the story of Fabio Caceres as he grows into adulthood. Don Segundo Sombra, an old "gaucho," is his mentor and model: he teaches the youth moral and human values through his behavior, his stories and his example. (Spanish with English subtitles) ★★½

Don's Party

(1976, 91 min, Australia, Bruce Beresford) A hilariously vulgar, 100-proof comedy which directs an unrelenting attack on Australian politics and suburbia. Don invites his friends over for an election night party but what begins as a quiet victory celebration soon succumbs to riotous boozing, arguments, partner-swapping, fights and marriages crumbling. Great fun! ★★★ $19.99

Don't Do It

(1994, 95 min, US, Eugene Hess) Essentially a series of vignettes, this uninspired look at twentysomething relationships advertises itself as "The Generation X Comedy," with a display box that says more about the musical score than the story line. For good reason. Ill-using its large group of up-and-coming actors, many of whom have previously given competent performances, the film tries to be a contemporary comedy of manners, complete with requisite AIDS reference; but it collapses in on itself with derivative tedium. The cast includes Alexis Arquette, Heather Graham, James LeGros, Sheryl Lee and Esai Morales. If you are a completist regarding any one of them, proceed with caution. Otherwise: Don't Watch It! ★ $92.99

Don't Drink the Water

(1969, 100 min, US, Howard Morris) Mildly entertaining version of Woody Allen's hit play with Jackie Gleason and Estelle Parsons as American tourists on an European vacation who are accused of spying and held captive in the Iron Curtain country of Vulgaria. ★★½

Don't Look Back

(1967, 96 min, US, D.A. Pennebaker) D.A. Pennebaker's intimate portrait of a young Bob Dylan follows the iconoclastic troubadour on his 1965 British tour as he encounters adoring fans, skeptical critics and bothersome comparisons to Donovan. ★★★½ $29.99

Don't Look Now

(1973, 110 min, GB, Nicolas Roeg) This stylish, visually beautiful mystery established Roeg as a leading auteur. In addition to creating one of the most famous sex scenes in the history of the cinema, Roeg brilliantly taps into one of the most primal fears of many adults — the death of a child. Based on a novel by Daphne du Maurier, the film stars Julie Christie and Donald Sutherland as bereaved parents who attempt to contact their child through a medium. Roeg's haunting imagery of winter in Venice is breathtaking. ★★★½ $49.99

Don't Play Us Cheap

(1972, 95 min, US, Melvin Van Peebles) In-between the vitriol of his blaxploitation films, director Van Peebles wrote and directed an endearing stage musical celebrating through song and dance the resilience of the African-American culture. Though slightly dated and unable to expand upon the staginess of the show, this filmic adaptation nicely captures the essence of the original piece and the spirit of a people. Featuring the original cast, the film is the playful and comic tale of two minions of the Devil whose perpetual assignment of breaking up parties leads them to crash a festive Saturday night get-together in Harlem. Esther Rolle (before she became famous on "Good Times") is the hostess, and she and her guests unknowingly and successfully counter each and every serve thrown at them. Van Peebles experiments with editing and over-laping, which he sometimes allows to go on too long. He also wrote the music: Some songs are energetic and tuneful, others are laborious. Tony Award nominee Avon Long is particularly memorable as a devil's disciple. ★★★ $79.99

Don't Tell Mom the Babysitter's Dead

(1991, 105 min, US, Stephen Herek) Left in the care of a tyrannical babysitter for the summer while their mother is away, Christina Applegate (TV's "Married...with Children") and siblings get a reprieve when nanny unexpectedly dies. With no money to live on, the kids take matters into their own hands and send sis into the working world. Though the premise smacks of a John Hughes knock-off, the film actually more resembles *The Secret of My Success*, as the story mostly concerns Applegate's business charade. There are a few laughs, but this amiable comedy is very one-note. Joanna Cassidy helps make it all bearable with a nice turn as Applegate's boss. ★★ $14.99

Doña Barbara

(1943, 138 min, Mexico, Emilio Fernandez) Adapted from Romulo Gallegos' passionate novel, this tense drama of power and love concerns a confrontation over land rights between a lawyer and the feared Doña Barbara, a wealthy landowner. The situation is further complicated when Doña Barbara, as well as her daughter, falls in love with the young man attempting to wrest control of their land. (Spanish with English subtitles) ★★★

Doña Flor and Her Two Husbands

(1976, 106 min, Brazil, Bruno Barreto) The humorous account of a young woman (Sonia Braga) whose first husband is beckoned from the grave when her second fails to satisfy her sexual needs. Barreto's hedonistic excursion simmers with the sights and sensuality of Brazil. (Available dubbed and in Portuguese with English subtitles) ★★★ $19.99

Doña Herlinda and Her Son

(1986, 90 min, Mexico, Jaime Humberto Hermosillo) A funny and subversively heart-warming love story about Doña Herlinda, a shrewd yet always placid mother who wishes for her son only that he live happily with Mom, his wife... and another man if need be. Her son, a sexually confused surgeon, is having a relationship with Ramon, a handsome music student. When Mom realizes that their relationship is romantic and deep, she helps things out by inviting her son's lover to stay with them, reasoning "Rodolpho has such a large bed!" A wickedly funny and uplifting Mexican comedy-of-manners which sympathetically portrays gay love. (Spanish with English subtitles) ★★★½ $79.99

Donkey Skin

(1970, 90 min, France, Jacques Demy) This enchanting and lyrical fairy tale is set in a small kingdom where the beloved queen is dying. Her final wish is that her husband, the king, only marry someone who is as beautiful as she. To the king's consternation, the only woman is his daughter! Filmed in sumptuous color, this adaptation of Charles Perrault's story is consistently entertaining. (French with English subtitles) ★★★ $29.99

Donnie Brasco

(1997, 115 min, US, Mike Newell) That British director Newell so concisely captures the nuance and flavor of 1970s gangland New York only serves to underscore the unexpected accomplishment of his crisp, extremely well-acted gangster drama. Based on the real-life experiences of undercover FBI agent Joe Pistone, *Donnie Brasco* casts Johnny Depp as the title character, the alias used by Pistone to infiltrate the mob. Befriending mid-level wiseguy Lefty Ruggiero (Pacino), Donnie secures a place for himself with Lefty as his mentor, all the while dispatching vital information. The strength of the film isn't in stylized bloodletting or technical wizardry, but the intrinsic relationship between Donnie and Lefty, and the human face placed on all its characters. The best of these is Pacino's Lefty, a middle-aged hit man who will never rise within the ranks — an anonymous foot soldier who sees in Donnie a chance to pass along his limited worldly wisdom. Michael Corleone he's not, and Pacino is superb in etching the fragile shadings of unfulfilled ambition. Depp is equally adept in relaying the inner conflict of a man slowly losing his emotional grip to a brutal underworld. Absorbing and vigorous, *Donnie Brasco* brings a fresh attitude to an often overplayed genre. ★★★½ $102.99

Donovan's Brain

(1953, 83 min, US, Felix Feist) Another scientist with a social problem. This one is Lew Ayres, and he's being controlled by the disembodied and quite living brain of an evil industrialist. Nancy (Reagan) Davis also stars. ★★★ $14.99

The Doom Generation

(1995, 85 min, US, Gregg Araki) Any fears that the bad boy of New Queer Cinema would sell out in this, his self-acknowledged "heterosexual film," can rest easy, for although Araki has a larger budget (and its accompanying

Donnie Brasco

need for a larger audience), this teens-on-the-run epic is dripping with homoerotic undertones, foul language, and violence that borders on the sadistic. On what was supposed to be a simple date, the tough-as-nails Amy (Rose McGowan), an angry Valley Girl with a checkered past, and Jordan (James Duval), a sweetly naive cutie, meet up with the dangerously sexy X (Johnathan Schaech). He soon gets them involved in a Quickie Mart robbery that turns deadly. And with bloody Twinkies in hand, the three escape into the neon night. Of course, just like those horny mall rats of suburbia, sex is always on the minds of our attractive protagonists, resulting in various couplings. Ultimately, *The Doom Generation* is a rollicking satire which unrepentantly revels in mocking all the values Middle America holds near and dear. So you better buckle up, for this viciously funny, tumultously nihilistic ride through a hellish California delivers undiluted, near hallucinogenic fun. ★★★½ $14.99

Doomed Megalopolis — Part 1, The Haunting of Tokyo

(1992, 50 min, Japan, Carl Macek & Rin Taro) This boldly original Japanimation is set in Tokyo in the early part of the 20th century, where an evil ghost-like Satanist, Kato, attempts to resurrect the body of a powerful spirit trapped in a ceremonial grave. If the spirit can be reborn, then Kato will become the most powerful "black angel" in Japan. ★★★ $19.99

The Doors

(1991, 141 min, US, Oliver Stone) A daring, provocative and hallucinogenic tribute, ostensibly a biography but much more, of the founding member of the 1960s rock group The Doors — Jim Morrison. Director Stone sees Morrison as a lost poet of his generation, which he probably was, and the film never condescends to either the era (which is difficult to recapture on film, but Stone has done so amazingly) or Morrison himself. Val Kilmer is an uncanny look-alike of the singer, but his portrayal goes far beyond simple impersonation; Kilmer embodies the passion and the firebrand of the pop star which was Jim Morrison. As the other members of The Doors, Kevin Dillon, Kyle MacLachlan and Frank Whaley all look the part, but their roles are merely foils for the fiery Morrison. The live performances are particularly impressive, featuring most of the group's classic material. ★★★½ $9.99

Double Dragon

(1994, 96 min, US, James Yukich) Hollywood launches another witless, empty attempt to cash in on the success of a video game by turning it into a live-action film. The results are just a cut above a Saturday morning cartoon. Set in post-apocalyptic Los Angeles where street gangs rule and even the cops are afraid to go out after dark, the film stars Robert Patrick (looking like a refugee from a Prince video) as the nefarious Koga Shuko who, along with his whip-wielding sidekick Lash and a steroid-enhanced mutant, attempt to wrest the second half of a mystical medallion from the two perky kickboxing orphans (Mark Dacascos and Scott Wolf) charged with protecting it. Anemic

Fred MacMurray and Barbara Stanwyck steam the screen in *Double Indemnity*

fighting sequences and only one decent special effect make this strictly for the pre-teen set. ★½ $19.99

Double Face

(1977, 84 min, Italy/West Germany/GB, Robert Hampton) Atrocious in so many ways — cheesy special effects, cartoonish acting, overly serious plot and the just-not-quite-right dubbing — this baffling and hyperventilating murder mystery is nevertheless strangely enjoyable. Klaus Kinski gives a wonderfully constipated, clenched-jaw, Nosferatu-like performance as the cuckold husband of a wealthy industrialist who dies in a suspicious car accident. Did she die innocently or was she killed or better yet, was her death faked with her now secretly living with her lesbian lover?! Not content to simply run the company and enjoy the money, our hero begins his own investigation into the byzantine circumstances and finds out more than he ever wanted to know. Great trash. (Dubbed) ★★ $49.99

Double Happiness

(1995, 87 min, Canada/China, Mina Shum) This delightfully offbeat drama-comedy is a promising feature film debut from writer-director Shum. Set in Vancouver, the story follows Jade Li (Sandra Oh), a spunky 22-year-old Chinese-Canadian woman who, when not working for her big break in acting, tries to find romance — two goals that upset her traditional-minded parents who just want her to find a "nice Chinese man and settle down." Interracial romance blooms when Jade falls for a cutely dorky white guy (Callum Rennie) while her parents (Stephen Chang and Alannah Ong) desperately try to set her up with a handsome, debonair and Chinese (but gay) lawyer (Johnny Mah). The complex family dynamics of an immigrant family clinging to the ways of the old world are wonderfully exposed in this spirited, thoughtful film. ★★★ $19.99

Double Impact

(1992, 107 min, US, Sheldon Lettich) The "Muscles from Brussels" is back in spades in this surprisingly effective kickfest. Jean-Claude Van Damme really cuts his acting teeth as twin brothers separated at birth who reunite years later to avenge the brutal murder of their parents. Though not a horror movie, it's scary to think that Van Damme actually does seem to be two different people. ★★ $14.99

Double Indemnity

(1944, 106 min, US, Billy Wilder) Considered to be the definitive film noir. The stunning Barbara Stanwyck plays an alluring vixen who cons unsuspecting insurance investigator Fred MacMurray into a murderous web of intrigue. A very sexy film, rich in subtlety. Director Wilder at his best. ★★★★ $14.99

A Double Life

(1947, 104 min, US, George Cukor) Ronald Colman won an Oscar for his triumphant performance as an acclaimed stage actor who can no longer separate his on- and offstage lives — and now he's playing "Othello." Shelley Winters is terrific in support as his fateful girlfriend. A superior suspense drama directed with great relish by Cukor. ★★★½ $14.99

The Double Life of Veronique

(1991, 97 min, Poland/France, Krzysztof Kieslowski) Irene Jacob is mesmerizing in the dual performance that won her the Best Actress Award at the 1991 Cannes Film Festival. This beautifully photographed, dream-like exploration of psychic bonds and parallel lives is flooded with sensual imagery and a haunting, evocative atmosphere. Jacob plays two women, born at the same time but a thousand miles apart, who are as inextricably bound as Siamese twins. Lush, golden lighting imparts an ethereal sense of myth and fairy tale as Veronique/Veronika searches for an understanding of her pervasive emotional reality. A revelatory inquiry into the transience

153

D

of human existence and the devastation of loss. (French and Polish with English subtitles) ★★★½ $79.99

Double Suicide

(1969, 105 min, Japan, Masahiro Shinoda) Set in 18th-century Japan and faithful to the Bunraku puppet theatre tradition for which it was originally written, this delicate, stylistic and erotic film tells the tragic tale of a middle-class merchant who, blinded by passion, loses his family and business in his relentless pursuit of an alluring prostitute. Based upon a work by Japan's greatest playwright, Monzaemon Chikamatsu (1653-1724), *Double Suicide* moves continually between the realistic and the formality of the Banruku Puppet Theatre which links it to the original play. (Japanese with English subtitles) ★★★

Double Team

(1997, 100 min, US, Tsui Hark) Lightning strikes a fourth time, as the extremely popular and talented Hong Kong action and fantasy director Tsui Hark succumbs to the brainless, dubious talents of star Jean-Claude Van Damme (Yuen Kwai, John Woo and Ringo Lam were the three previous casualties). This time around, Van Damme is a covert agent and assassin who is wounded while trying to off a particularly nasty terrorist (a musclebound Mickey Rourke). His identity is erased and he is sent to a top-secret island facility called the Colony, sort of a retirement home for government spooks. In the movie's only moderately well-written action set-piece, he escapes; thus begins the hunt for his nemesis, this time with the aid of a tattooed and hair-dyed weapons expert named Yaz (the similarly attired Dennis Rodman). Despite a surprisingly okay performance by Rodman, the movie goes nowhere. Only a furious kung fu fight between Van Damme and Chinese stuntman and movie villain Xiong Xin-Xin will quicken the pulse but, alas, it too falls prey to poor writing. Even Hark's trademark wild visuals are absent. ★½ $99.99

Double Wedding

(1937, 87 min, US, Richard Thorpe) Asking the probing question, "Why do Bohemians have to stay up all night?," this breezy screwball comedy pairs the incomparable duo William Powell and Myrna Loy. Powell plays an eccentric artist who crosses paths with rigid businesswoman Loy when she thinks Powell is in love with her younger sister (Florence Rice). A slew of zany characters are thrown into the stew as the two slowly fall in love. These include John Beal, a catatonic wonder, as Rice's real fiancé, and Jessie Ralph as a fiery old broad and friend to Powell. The ending is right out of a Marx Brothers film, and the crazy shenanigans which abound is ample cause for smiling. Based on the play "Great Love" by Ferenc Molnar ("The Guardsman"). ★★★ $19.99

Doubting Thomas

(1935, 78 min, US, David Butler) It's comedy of a high order when Will Rogers' wife Billie Burke gets the lead in a small-town amateur theatrical production. One of Rogers' best films is a truly funny adaptation of George Kelly's play, "The Torch Bearers." A good starter for those unfamiliar with the wonderful, homespun Rogers. ★★★ $19.99

Doug: Pattie, You're the Mayonnaise for Me

(1993, 40 min, US) *Doug* (a Nickelodean production) is one of the best cartoons of the '90s: witty, urbane, a bit gawky and very politically correct. In this trio of tales featuring his big love, Pattie Mayonnaise, he joins her rag-tag baseball team, asks her out for the first time and even eats (gasp) liver and onions on her behalf. If that's not love, what is? Also in the series: *Doug: How Did I Get Into This Mess?* $9.99

Le Doulos

(1962, 108 min, France, Jean-Pierre Melville) Melville's remarkable 1962 "nocturnal western" is adapted from a French detective novel and set in the French underworld. Jean-Paul Belmondo stars as a mysterious, cryptic informer caught up in the complex relationship between criminal and policeman. In this tightly written and subtly acted film, Melville has created a man's world rich with male rituals and solidly sensuous women, all involved in a Pirandellian plot that none of the characters fully understands. Stylishly and brilliantly photographed in black and white, and filled with Melville's passionate love of film noir and the language of film. (French with English subtitles) ★★★ $59.99

Down and Dirty

(1976, 115 min, Italy, Ettore Scola) Can you believe that Scola, the esteemed director of such high-brow hits as *Passion D'Amore* and *La Nuit de Varennes*, would also be responsible for this hilarious Italian "version" of *Pink Flamingos*!? Italy's urban poor, long ennobilized in neorealist films, are seen in an entirely different light in this demented and scathing black comedy. Nino Manfredi stars as the brutish patriarch of a morally depraved family whose interests include adultery, murder, revenge and incest. This thoroughly sick, no-holds-barred romp about Rome's low-life will have you crossing the street screaming the next time you are approached by a vagrant. (Italian with English subtitles) ★★★ $29.99

Down and Out in Beverly Hills

(1986, 97 min, US, Paul Mazursky) Mazursky's boisterously funny social comedy stars Nick Nolte as a street person who is taken in by a nouveau riche Beverly Hills family when he tries to drown himself in their swimming pool. Richard Dreyfuss and Bette Midler are in top form as the husband and wife whose lives are turned upside-down by their new boarder. Modern remake of the Jean Renoir 1932 classic *Boudu Saved from Drowning*. ★★★ $9.99

Down by Law

(1986, 107 min, US, Jim Jarmusch) Jarmusch continues on the theme of alienated outsiders in this razor-sharp and decidedly different "road picture." John Lurie and Tom Waits (wonderfully cast as a gravel-voice D.J./hipster) meet up in a Louisiana prison where they team with an irrepressible Italian tourist who leads them on a jailbreak through a stark eerie swamp and beyond. An offbeat comedy from one of the most original American filmmakers of today. ★★★ $14.99

Down Periscope

(1996, 92 min, US, David S. Ward) Another in the slew of 1996 casualties of TV stars who bombed in their big-screen starring debuts, "Frasier"'s Kelsey Grammer forgoes his very funny TV persona for a smug submarine commander on his first, disaster-prone mission. The usual assortment of misfits and slackers are on hand, with a slightly bemused Grammer enduring his crew's shenanigans; after all, damn it, they're a great bunch of guys. The story has to do with war games and a general (Bruce Dern) who has it out for Grammer. Director Ward does manage to inject some humor, though for the most part the laughs are infrequent and when they do occur they are of the knucklehead variety. As a radio engineer suffering numerous electrocutions and offering a few amusing impersonations, Toby Huss comes off the best out of the entire cast. ★★ $14.99

Downhill Racer

(1969, 102 min, US, Michael Ritchie) Robert Redford is the ski bum who gets a chance for

Leslie Nielsen is down for the count in *Dracula: Dead and Loving It*

an Olympic tryout. Gene Hackman is the compassionate coach. An involving drama heightened by superior ski sequences. ★★★ $14.99

Downtown

(1990, 96 min, US, Richard Benjamin) Though both Anthony Edwards and Forest Whitaker are extremely likable actors, there's little to recommend in this buddy-cop comedy set in urban Philadelphia (though locals may not recognize all the scenery). Edwards is the naive white cop partnered with streetwise black cop Whitaker, together tracking down a stolen-car ring. Stick to *Lethal Weapon*. ★★ $19.99

Dracula

(1931, 75 min, US, Tod Browning) Classic Hollywood horror film with Bela Lugosi as the quintessential Count Dracula, that pain-in-the-neck vampire who here is on the loose in foggy old London. Dwight Frye makes a memorable Renfield. ★★★½ $14.99

Dracula: The Spanish Version

(1931, 104 min, US, George Melford) One from the vaults! Filmed simultaneously with the original 1931 Bela Lugosi classic, this long-lost gem features the same sets and script translated into Spanish. Ripe with sensuality and atmosphere, many feel this version is more chilling than its English-language counterpart. With Carlos Villarias as the infamous Count. (Spanish with English subtitles) ★★★½ $14.99

Dracula

(1973, 100 min, US, Dan Curtis) Having made a fortune serializing the vampire legend with "Dark Shadows," producer-director Curtis returns to the original source with this made-for-TV adaptation of the Bram Stoker novel. Hollywood ham Jack Palance dusts off his formal attire for the title role of the count who...well, you know the story. Also with Simon Ward and Nigel Davenport. Teleplay by Richard Matheson. ★★½ $59.99

Dracula

(1979, 109 min, US, John Badham) This cinematic interpretation of the Broadway hit highlights the sexual subtext which is really at the heart of the vampire legends. Still, director Badham doesn't ignore the frights in this dark romance featuring Frank Langella as the sensual count locked in immortal combat with Dr. Van Helsing (Laurence Olivier). Features an excellent score by John Williams. ★★★ $14.99

Dracula: Dead and Loving It

(1995, 90 min, US, Mel Brooks) After a few comic misfires, Brooks is close to speed once more with this funny if sometimes obvious spoof on vampire films. It's no *Young Frankenstein*, but it is silly and over-the-top fun. An old hambone with this sort of comedy by now, Leslie Nielsen clearly is enjoying himself as the Count, neatly satirizing every vamp from Lugosi to Oldman. The story is basically the same: Dracula comes to England, and becomes a real pain in the neck until Professor Van Helsing (Brooks) gets on his trail. Brooks and his co-writers aren't on target with every joke, but many of the ones which do work are surprisingly fresh (such as Dracula dancing in front of a mirror or a hysterical scene of a staking). Brooks' supporting cast is altogether reli-

able, though Peter MacNicol steals the show with his joyfully demented turn as Renfield — luncheon in the garden will never be the same. ★★½ $19.99

Dracula Has Risen from the Grave

(1968, 92 min, GB, Freddie Francis) In this Hammer vampire horror tale, Christopher Lee emerges from a watery hibernation — looking more constipated than usual — to take sweet vengeance on a haughty monsignor (Rupert Davies) by claiming his beautiful niece. Hokey, campy fun. ★★½ $14.99

Dracula's Daughter

(1936, 70 min, US, Lambert Hillyer) With a decided taste for female blood, the screen's first vampire of the fairer sex, Gloria Holden, stars in this moody sequel to the Bela Lugosi classic. Holden stars as the titular vampire, whose attempts to escape her bloodthirsty inclinations (through the help of a sympathetic doctor) are dashed when she develops an affinity for a young woman whom she seduces and vampirizes. The first of what would be a long line of lesbian-themed vampire films. ★★★ $14.99

Dragnet

(1954, 89 min, US, Jack Webb) Jack Webb is Sergeant Joe Friday and Ben Alexander is Officer Frank Smith in this first film version of two Los Angeles detectives, here investigating a mob slaying. Webb teamed up with Harry Morgan in the original TV series. Made into a comedy in 1987 with Tom Hanks and Dan Aykroyd, it reappeared in 1991, again as a syndicated TV series. The others can't compare. ★★½ $14.99

Dragnet

(1987, 106 min, US, Tom Mankiewicz) "Just the facts..." Okay, this mediocre comic remake of the movie and famed TV series is a bust. Tom Hanks and Dan Aykroyd try their best to bring some lightheartedness into their roles, but they just aren't given any good material. Neither are Harry Morgan returning as Bill Gannon, or co-stars Christopher Plummer, Elizabeth Ashley and Dabney Coleman. ★½ $14.99

Dragon Chow

(1987, 75 min, West Germany, Jan Schütte) Schütte's evocative and moving study of the hopes and ambitions of a pair of immigrant Pakistanis in Hamburg, West Germany, is as unpretentious and pristine as its simple black-and-white photography. The story follows Shezad and Rashid, who live in a barren welfare hotel filled with Hamburg's *gastarbeiter* (guest workers). Shezad's dream is to break into the restaurant business. He gets his start when he lands a job at a local Chinese restaurant and joins forces with one of the waiters, Xiao. Together, they set out to open their own business, but find the West German environment less than hospitable. Schütte's story is simple and understated, but his treatment of this stranger-in-a-strange-land theme is flavorful and at times captivating. (German with English subtitles) ★★★½ $69.99

Dragon Fist

(1984, 95 min, Hong Kong, Lo Wei) Jackie Chan stars as kung fu artist Yuan, who seeks

vengeance for the death of his master. Traveling with the master's widow and her daughter, they journey to a distant village where they uncover the killer. To their surprise, however, he has mutilated himself out of guilt for his deed. Revenge, honor, soap-opera melodrama and great fight scenes galore make this an above average, entertaining treat for Jackie Chan fans. ★★★ $19.99

Dragon Seed

(1944, 149 min, US, Jack Conway & Harold S. Bucquet) Pearl S. Buck's novel of patriotism and heroism in war-torn China is the basis for this Katharine Hepburn vehicle. Kate plays a young Chinese peasant who becomes a guerrilla fighter when the Japanese army invades her small village. Also starring Walter Huston and Agnes Moorehead. Anglo-Americans portraying Asians may disarm some viewers, but this well-intentioned war drama did serve as allegory and morale booster for the American fight against Nazism at the time. ★★½ $19.99

Dragon: The Bruce Lee Story

(1993, 119 min, US, Rob Cohen) This rousing chop-socky story of Bruce Lee rises above its mediocre bio-pic roots thanks to the winning combination of its undeniably exciting subject, a breezy and witty screenplay, elaborately staged fight sequences, and the riveting presence of Jason Scott Lee in the lead role. The film follows B. Lee from his early days in Hong Kong to his life as an ambitious American immigrant, determined to overcome racial prejudices and personal demons on his way to success. Fame beckons when he is discovered by an appropriately sleazy Robert Wagner to co-star as Kato in the TV series "The Green Hornet." After its cancellation, and after losing the lead role in "Kung Fu" to *gweilo* David Carradine, he moves back to Hong Kong to begin a short career as a martial artist, suddenly dying at age 32. J.S. Lee's winning smile, chiseled body and effervescent personality carry the adulatory movie, adapted from the book by Lee's widow, Linda Lee Cadwell. While the film's love story is "nice," it is the fight sequences that are mesmeric — capturing the exaggerated look of kung fu fights, with their gravity-defying leaps, flailing legs and fists, hissing and crowing noises, and physical punishment that would pulverize any mere mortal. ★★★½ $14.99

Dragonheart

(1996, 108 min, US, Rob Cohen) This film will be remembered, at the very least, for featuring the first completely computer-generated main character, Draco the Dragon (voiced by Sean Connery). It is unfortunate, however, that this is the best thing about the movie. Dennis Quaid stars as an errant knight who lives to slay dragons, having been betrayed by one years earlier (in a too-obviously meaningful prologue). He meets his match in Draco, whom he discovers is the last of his kind. These two heroes soon learn they both share a dark secret: They are each partially responsible for the evil deeds and villainy of the country's tyrannical ruler (David Thewlis). Naturally, they join forces to destroy the evil king and restore goodness to the land. While the computer effects are stupendous and the

D

scenes between Draco and Quaid are the best of the film, the overall tone of the movie is far too juvenile for adults and too heavy, even dull at times, for kids. *Dragonheart* would have been a much better movie if it had known exactly what it wanted to be. (Available letterboxed and pan & scan) ★★½ $19.99

Dragonslayer

(1981, 108 min, US, Matthew Robbins) When his mentor suddenly shuffles off his mortal coil, a young sorcerer's apprentice finds himself thrust into battle with a massive serpent. This exciting tale will be sure to please fans of medieval myth and fantasy as well as lovers of good action-adventure. Ralph Richardson appears as the necromancer and Peter MacNichol stars as the brave young lad. The dragon sequences are terrific. ★★★ $14.99

The Draughtsman's Contract

(1982, 103 min, GB, Peter Greenaway) This bizarre tale of adultery, blackmail and murder is set amidst the genteel countryside of late 17th-century England. An early effort from director Greenaway (*The Cook, The Thief...*), this provocative and ribald puzzle of a film concerns an artist's rather unusual bargain to sketch the estate of a wealthy landowner: £8 per drawing and the use of the man's wife for sexual favors. ★★★ $19.99

Drawing the Line: Keith Haring

(1990, 30 min, US) When artist Keith Haring died in February 1990, of complications due to AIDS, he left behind an astounding artistic legacy. In his 31 years, Haring had gone from being an anonymous graffitist who drew chalk figures on New York City subway posters to being a popular and outspoken artist, with his work hailed as the successor to Andy Warhol and Roy Lichtenstein. Haring's hieroglyphic-like drawings, which have become an ubiquitous sight around New York, incorporated social issues such as the fight against Apartheid, crack and AIDS. This revealing profile contains interviews with gallery owners, fellow artists and actor Dennis Hopper as well as a close-up look into Keith Haring's passionate art. ★★★½ $19.99

Dream Lover

(1994, 103 min, US, Nicholas Kazan) James Spader plays a successsful architect who meets in the person of Mädchen Amick his dream woman. Low-keyed and set at a lethargic pace, the film (ever so) slowly has Spader soon wondering if his new wife and the mother of his child is not only having an affair but if she is really who she says she is. Part *Suspicion* and part *Body Heat* without the dramatic flair of either film, *Dream Lover* does become mildly interesting when the con becomes evident, and builds to a rather neat twist ending. ★★ $14.99

Dream Man

(1991, 75 min, US, David Edwards) Gay theatre at its most provocative, this premiere release in The Pride Playhouse Collection, featuring landmark gay-themed plays on video, is a savagely funny and intensely moving play written by James Carroll Pickett. Michael Kearns stars as an over-the-hill hustler, an acid-tongued purveyor of phone-sex fantasies, who

Dragonheart

confronts his customers' more perverse requests. ★★★ $24.99

A Dream of Passion

(1978, 106 min, Greece, Jules Dassin) This interesting film focuses on the parallel Medea-like lives of two women in modern day Athens. Ellen Burstyn delivers a powerful performance as an American woman jailed in Greece for murdering her three children in a fit of rage over her unfaithful husband. Melina Mercouri is an international actress who returns to Greece to play the role of Medea in a play. She soon becomes obsessed with Burstyn's plight and the two women's lives become inextricably connected through tragedy. (Filmed in English) ★★

The Dream Team

(1989, 113 min, US, Howard Zieff) Michael Keaton heads a solid cast in this literally crazy comedy about the misadventures of four mental patients on the loose in New York City. Christopher Lloyd, Stephen Furst and the scene-stealing Peter Boyle also star as Keaton's fellow psychiatric inmates who are left to fend for themselves on the mean streets when their doctor witnesses a murder and is left for dead. ★★★ $19.99

Dreamchild

(1985, 94 min, GB, Gavin Millar) This lavish fantasy/drama tells the story of the 80-year-old Alice Hargreaves who, as a child, had inspired Lewis Carroll to write his immortal "Alice in Wonderland." As Mrs. Hargreaves prepares to attend a symposium at Columbia University celebrating the 100th anniversary of Carroll's birth, she becomes haunted by fantastic images of the classic story, her youth, and her relationship with Mr. Carroll. Ian Holm is superb as the stuttering Carroll, and Coral Brown is unforgettable as the elder Alice. ★★★½ $14.99

Dreamers of the Day

(1990, 94 min, Canada, Patricia Spencer & Philip Wood) From the *Claire of the Moon* school of lesbian love and sexual coming out is this enjoyable if a bit amateurish drama. Set in Toronto, the story revolves around the friendship between openly lesbian Andra (Lorna Harding), an aspiring filmmaker, and Claire (Julie Lemieux), a married, profession-

ally successful film producer. The film follows their budding friendship which is undermined by Andra's attraction to the "straight" Claire, who is unable to deal with the sexually tinged relationship. Despite their repeated assertions of being "just friends," a romantic relationship ensues. A tender and believable love story, the film suffers a bit from a standard story line, often stilted acting, and a static camera. ★★ $39.99

Dreaming of Rita

(1994, 108 min, Sweden, Jon Lindstrom) From the less serious side of Swedish filmmaking, which most recently brought us the delightful *House of Angels*, comes this wacky, but sadly not entirely successful, road comedy. The action kicks off when the recently widowed Bob (Per Oscarson) flips his lid, and runs off in search of a Danish sweetheart of some thirty years earlier. This precipitates a chase in which his daughter, Rita (named after Bob's screen idol Miss Hayworth), tracks him down and together they journey on to Copenhagen all the while exploring their past à la *Wild Strawberries*. Rita, in turn, has left behind her still-nursing baby with husband Steff, who, with baby and teen daughter in tow, hits the road in search of familial mending. Along the way they all get the loopy advice of Eric XIV, a later-day computer-hacking roadside prophet who seems bent on getting Rita into bed. The film ultimately lands nowhere and its pat ending leads to no revelations; still *Dreaming of Rita*'s amiable atmosphere and curious characters make it amusing, if not wholly worthwhile, viewing. ★★½ $59.99

Dreams

(1955, 86 min, Sweden, Ingmar Bergman) This probing study into the psychology of desire follows the activities of a photography agency head and her top model who, while visiting another city for work, each have an affair. The setting is but a pretense for Bergman to explore women's dreams, torments and sexual obsessions; and how all of this affects their relationships with men. (Swedish with English subtitles) ★★★ $29.99

Dreamscape

(1984, 99 min, US, Joseph Ruben) Telepathic spies romp through the president's nightmares in this imaginative sci-fi thriller starring

Dennis Quaid, Max von Sydow, Christopher Plummer and Eddie Albert. ★★★

Dress Gray

(1986, 208 min, US, Glenn Jordan) This riveting murder mystery set in a military academy during the Vietnam War is based on the novel by Lucian K. Truscott IV and adapted by Gore Vidal. Alec Baldwin stars as a cadet who becomes embroiled in a cover-up over the mysterious death of another cadet who had been raped before his murder. Fearing a scandal involving homosexuality and murder, the embarrassed commandant (Hal Holbrook) and his staff cover up the death as a simple drowning. But as the truth slowly begins to unravel, Baldwin — the secret object of the dead, gay cadet's affections — becomes a suspect and handcuffed by the military's code of honor. Like a high stakes Hardy Boys mystery, Baldwin attempts to clear his name and uncover the real killer with the mystery unraveling in a genuinely tense and exciting fashion. *Dress Gray* is both a well-told story and a well-developed allegory for America's involvement in Vietnam. ★★★½ $24.99

Dressed to Kill

(1979, 105 min, US, Brian De Palma) De Palma's homage to Hitchcock stars Michael Caine as an inquisitive psychiatrist and Angie Dickinson as a woman whose promiscuity leads her to become the first victim of a schizophrenic transvestite murderer. De Palma succeeds in creating both atmosphere and suspense. ★★★ $19.99

The Dresser

(1983, 118 min, GB, Peter Yates) Albert Finney and Tom Courtenay are both outstanding as, respectively, a grandiloquent, aging actor and his devoted dresser. Finney is the head of a second-rate touring company besieged by financial and wartime woes; Courtenay is his gay confidant/secretary/valet who watches over him with the eye of a hawk and the perseverance of a den mother. A brilliant, moving and often funny peek behind the curtain of theatre life. ★★★½ $9.99

The Dressmaker

(1989, 92 min, GB, Jim O'Brien) Set in Liverpool in 1944, this intricate character study subtly probes the complexities of three women. When Rita, a timid, young waif, befriends a randy American soldier who is stationed in town, a bitter struggle for her soul ensues between her two aunts: the fun-loving Margo (beautifully played by Billie Whitelaw) and the disapproving, repressed spinster Nellie (icily portrayed by Joan Plowright), whose heart is as cold as her knitting needles. Based on the novel by Beryl Bainbridge, this extremely well-acted and absorbing family drama is taunt with sexual tensions and impending disaster. ★★★ $79.99

Drifting

(1983, 80 min, Israel, Amos Gutman) Gutman's acclaimed first feature is also the first gay film made in Israel. The story follows Robi, a 24-year-old would-be filmmaker who isolates himself completely in the gay world and grows increasingly troubled; not by the

political turmoil in his country, but by his increasingly aimless and frustrated life. His ennui causes him to reject his friends and lover and withdraw into self-destruction. A sensitive and moving drama. (Hebrew with English subtitles) ★★★ $69.99

Drifting Weeds (Floating Weeds)

(1959, 119 min, Japan, Yasujiro Ozu) A remake of his own silent film *A Story of Silent Weeds*, Ozu's lyrical drama is about rivalries among a traveling acting troupe. The film is marked by Ozu's spare directorial style and the beautiful photography by Daiei cameraman Miyagawa. (Japanese with English subtitles) ★★★½

The Driver

(1978, 131 min, US, Walter Hill) Some spectacular car chase sequences highlight this unusual action-adventure with Bruce Dern as a cop obsessed with catching jewel thief Ryan O'Neal. ★★★ $59.99

Driving Miss Daisy

(1989, 99 min, US, Bruce Beresford) Based on Alfred Uhry's play, this is an extremely well-acted and literate examination of the four-decade relationship between an elderly, Southern Jewish widow and her ever-patient black chauffeur. Oscar-winner Jessica Tandy and Morgan Freeman give magnificent performances as Daisy and Hoke, whose working relationship, beginning in 1948, slowly develops into one of friendship; reflecting the changing social mores around them. Oscar winner for Best Picture, though there were far more worthy films nominated that year. ★★★½ $19.99

Drop Dead Fred

(1991, 98 min, US, Ate De Jong) A poor man's *Beetlejuice*, this sporadically funny though silly and at times annoying comedy manages to entertain in spite of itself. Phoebe Cates returns home to her shrewish mother (Marsha Mason) after her husband dumps her. There she is revisited by her "imaginary" childhood friend, Drop Dead Fred. As played by Rik Mayall (of "The Young Ones"), Fred is a nose-picking, mischievous tornado of activity, eager to help straighten out the life of his former friend — whether sinking her best friend's houseboat or creating a ruckus at an exclusive restaurant (one of the best scenes in the movie). Mayall's over-the-top mugging will either cause chuckles or spasms, but there's no denying when he's on the screen, the film comes alive. ★★ $9.99

Drop Squad

(1994, 88 min, US, D. Clark Johnson) The DROP Squad — Deprogramming and Restoration of Pride — kidnaps co-opted blacks and re-educates them. But the Squad has hit a wall: their methods have lost effectiveness and they're at a crossroads. Eriq LaSalle (from TV's "E.R.") plays an advertising exec whose kidnapping is set up by his sister. Vondie Curtis-Hall, founder and leader of the Squad, is facing a crisis of confidence and seeking new direction. Ving Rhames and Vanessa Williams (no, not *that* one) are among the ensemble of strong supporting actors. With

this satire, director Johnson explores issues of personal responsibilities vs. community awareness. Many astute observations are delivered with a sure hand in this intriguing film executive produced by Spike Lee. ★★★ $19.99

Drop Zone

(1994, 101 min, US, John Badham) Exhilarating aerial photography punctuates this otherwise by-the-numbers rehash of *Die Hard* and *Point Break*. Wesley Snipes stars as a U.S. Marshall who goes undercover in the world of skydiving to locate a gang of gonzo parachutists (headed by *uber*villain Gary Busey) planning to "drop in" on the DEA, steal the names of every undercover agent working in the field, and sell them to the highest bidder. Obviously this is the kind of film where macho posturing replaces acting and stunt-work supplants action, but Snipes and Busey make the best of it. Michael Jeter provides comic support, and Yancy Butler and Grace Zabriskie also star. ★★½ $14.99

Drowning by Numbers

(1987, 118 min, GB, Peter Greenaway) For those repulsed by the scatalogical debauchery of *The Cook, The Thief...* or bewildered by the visually dazzling *Prospero's Books*, this earlier Greenaway effort will prove far more palatable. Wildly imaginative and entertaining, this offbeat comedy is a decidedly different twist on the battle between the sexes. The film follows the saga of three women (all named Cissie) who drown their husbands and then, attempting to cover-up their crimes, engage in a bizarre game of sexual innuendo with the local coroner, Madgett. This outrageous tryst becomes the centerpiece of Greenaway's operative metaphor; namely, the games people play. The film is literally filled with games, mostly played by Madgett and his pre-pubescent son. Additionally, the film itself is one long game of numerical hide-and-seek — video viewers beware, the small screen may make it difficult to participate. Joan Plowright, Juliet Stevenson, Joely Richardson and Bernard Hill deliver a terrific ensemble performance. ★★★½ $19.99

The Drowning Pool

(1976, 108 min, US, Stuart Rosenberg) This sequel to *Harper* finds Paul Newman deep in the heart of Dixie trying to help old lover Joanne Woodward out of a jam and only making matters worse. Melanie Griffith makes a delightful film debut as Woodward's precocious daughter. ★★½ $14.99

Drugstore Cowboy

(1989, 100 min, US, Gus Van Sant) Van Sant's gritty and provocative exposé of the down-and-out lives of four drug addicts living in the Pacific Northwest in the 1970s is one of the most highly original and profoundly honest films to come around in some time. Matt Dillon is perfectly cast as an icy-cool and unrepenting "drug fiend" who plays daddy to a rogue family of three fellow junkies — Kelly Lynch as his statuesque wife and James Le Gross and Heather Graham as his mindless junkie pals. Drawing its power from a surprisingly wry sense of humor and its wholly unapologetic tone, the film follows Dillon and

Duck Soup

crew as they wantonly romp from town to town and burgle the drugs they need from local apothecaries. It seems inconceivable that in the Reagan-Bush era of rampant anti-drug hysteria a film so brazenly non-judgmental on this issue could have been made, much less enjoy the tremendous acclaim which this film deservedly received. William S. Burroughs has a terrific cameo as a weathered drug addict. ★★★★ $14.99

Drums

(1938, 104 min, GB, Zoltan Korda) Korda's beautifully filmed colonial adventure features Roger Livesey as a patriotic British officer who forms an alliance with a young Indian prince (Sabu) to help him battle his scheming uncle (Raymond Massey). ★★★ $19.99

Drums along the Mohawk

(1939, 103 min, US, John Ford) Released the same year as his classic western *Stagecoach*, Ford heads East with this sumptuous historical drama mixed with humor and rousing adventure sequences. Henry Fonda and Claudette Colbert star as colonists during the Revolutionary War who must protect themselves from Indian uprisings in the backwoods of upstate New York. Cast includes Edna May Oliver (Oscar nominee) and John Carradine. Gorgeous cinematography in glorious Technicolor. ★★★ $19.99

Drunken Angel

(1948, 102 min, Japan, Akira Kurosawa) An older doctor attempts to cure and rehabilitate a tubercular young gangster (Toshiro Mifune) in this sinister and disturbing allegory on the human condition. This early Kurosawa work pays tribute to American film noir. (Japanese with English subtitles) ★★★

Drunks

(1997, 88 min, US, Peter Cohn) A small group of recovering alcoholics gather in the basement of a Times Square church for an intense AA meeting. One member (Richard Lewis) ducks out early to walk the streets of New York City — will he revert to his old ways? Well-intentioned but rather flat, *Drunks* barely qualifies as a movie; it's basically a succession of talking heads, each giving his or her story of addiction and misery. This is an adaptation of the play "Blackout," and its theatrical origins show;

director Cohn attempts to "open up" the play with shots of Lewis walking the gritty, cold streets but its staginess is still intact. The acting is uniformly good (including Faye Dunaway, Dianne Wiest and Harold Rollins), with individual moments of power, but the overall effect is artificial and unconvincing. It has the feel of an actor's workshop, and screams to be left on the stage. Extremely uncinematic, *Drunks* will be best appreciated by those who love acting for acting's sake. ★★ $97.99

A Dry White Season

(1989, 97 min, US, Euzhan Palcy) South African director Palcy (whose first film was the eloquent *Sugar Cane Alley*) powerfully confronts the violence and inhuman brutality of Apartheid. Donald Sutherland is excellent as Ben du Toit, a well-respected Afrikaner schoolteacher asked to use his influence to help find his gardener's missing son. Du Toit quickly finds himself entangled with the dreaded Special Branch — a rather noxious element of the South African security system. The movie draws its power as we witness du Toit, ostracized, humiliated and beaten, in his transformation from ignorant patriot to outraged citizen. Excellent support comes from Zakes Mokae, Jurgen Prochnow, Susan Sarandon and Marlon Brando. ★★★½ $19.99

DuBarry Was a Lady

(1943, 100 min, US, Roy Del Ruth) Those two crowned heads of comic tomfoolery, Red Skelton and Lucille Ball, take over the Bert Lahr and Ethel Merman roles of this entertaining adaptation of the Cole Porter musical. And though Red and Lucy are just fine, Hollywood once again outsmarted itself in the translation of a stage musical, here keeping only three of Porter's songs ("Friendship," "Do I Love You" and "Katie Went to Haiti"). Red's in love with nightclub entertainer Lucy. He sips a mickey and dreams he's Louis XV of France to Lucy's Madame DuBarry. Also with Gene Kelly and Zero Mostel. ★★★ $19.99

duBEAT-E-O

(1984, 84 min, US, Alan Sacks) Punky, irreverent and cocky, but marred by a nasty misogynist, violent and anti-gay streak, this low-budget musical-comedy is a wonderful illustration of the vastly different independent filmmaking worlds of L.A. and New York. Ray Sharkey plays a sleaze-ball filmmaker who, on the "forceful" insistence of his producer, must finish his rock opus on Joan Jett within 31 hours. With offscreen narration and commentary by the actual filmmaker and his friends, the film's hipper-than-thou approach will remind many of the much funnier and similarly themed *Tapeheads*. Featuring the music of Joan Jett, Social Distortion and The Lounge Lizards. ★★½ $59.99

Duck Soup

(1933, 70 min, US, Leo McCarey) The best Marx Brothers by most standards, this wacky tale follows the boys' exploits in the tiny coun-

try of Freedonia (Land of the Spree and Home of the Knave). Groucho is memorable as the celebrated Rufus T. Firefly, newly appointed president; Harpo and Chico are enemy spies, and Zeppo is a tenor. Margaret Dumont is her usual resilient self. ★★★★ $14.99

Duck Tales, the Movie: Treasure of the Lost Lamp

(1990, 74 min, US, Bob Hathcock) Full-length animated feature with Scrooge McDuck, Huey, Dewey and Louie and Webigail Vanderquack uncovering the legendary lost treasure of Collie baba. Family fun from the Disney crew. ★★½ $14.99

Duel

(1971, 90 min, US, Steven Spielberg) Spielberg's career-launching film is a first-rate made-for-TV thriller starring Dennis Weaver as a businessman being terrorized by an unseen truck driver who is apparently, and for no known reason, out to kill him. Inventive and highly suspenseful. ★★★ $14.99

Duel at Diablo

(1966, 103 min, US, Ralph Nelson) An exciting western with James Garner as an Indian scout, seeking revenge for the murder of his wife, who helps transport guns across Indian territory. Sidney Poitier is an ex-Army officer. Together, they hold off an Indian attack. ★★★ $19.99

Duel in the Sun

(1946, 130 min, US, King Vidor) Producer David O. Selznick's sexy epic western about the rivalry between two brothers (Gregory Peck and Joseph Cotten) for the love of a beautiful half-breed Indian girl, played with sultry authority by Jennifer Jones. One of the most popular films of the 1940s, the film, though very entertaining, sometimes seems to border on high camp. ★★★ $14.99

Duel to the Death

(1982, 100 min, Hong Kong, Ching Siu-Tung) Two outstanding swordsmen from rival schools, one Japanese and one Chinese, are forced to do battle in a traditional tournament which is held once every 100 years. But these are not ordinary swordsmen; they can fly through the air and summon supernatural powers to aid them in combat. Unexpectedly, the two become friends, combining their awesome abilities to defeat their enemy. This debut film from Hong Kong action director Ching, who also helmed the *Chinese Ghost Story* and *Swordsman* series, features all the trademark attractions of his later works: gravity-defying swordsmen, chaotic camerawork, themes of loyalty and duty, a bit of humor to lighten the drama and sumptuous visuals. Kimono-clad warriors stand atop rocky atolls, swooping down over the sea to attack their opponents; black ninjas sail through the forest on kites or burrow underground; and shaolin monks fight weaponless in a furious display of punches and kicks. A great introduction to Hong Kong action cinema, but also a forgotten gem sure to please even veteran fans. (Cantonese with English subtitles) ★★★½ $59.99

The Duellists

(1977, 100 min, GB, Ridley Scott) Scott's first feature film is an eccentric rendering of the Joseph Conrad story about an inexplicable feud between two officers of the Napoleonic army. Keith Carradine and Harvey Keitel personify the passion, honor and violence which are the heart of Conrad's story. An excellent supporting cast includes Albert Finney, Edward Fox and Tom Conti. A visually stunning film. ★★★½ $14.99

Duet for One

(1986, 107 min, GB, Andrei Konchalovsky) Julie Andrews, taking a break from musical comedy, gives a sensitive performance in this routine tragic tale of a world-renowned concert violinist whose career is brought to an abrupt end with the onset of multiple sclerosis. Alan Bates also stars as her unfaithful husband and Rupert von Sydow plays her psychiatrist and Rupert Everett is her embittered protégé. ★★½ $14.99

Duke of the Derby
(Le Gentleman D'Epsom)

(1962, 83 min, France, Jacques Juranville) Veteran French actor Jean Gabin breezes his way through this lightweight but entertaining comedy-drama as a charming old snob who lives in the sordid world of horse racing and gambling. Similar to the trend-setting *Bob le Flambeur*, the film follows him through the betting cirles and races as he charismatically scams his way through every crisis that confronts him. (French with English subtitles) ★★½

Dulces Navajas (Navajeros)

(1981, 100 min, Spain, Eloy de la Iglesia) Within the slums and bordellos of Madrid, an illiterate 16-year-old gang leader battles police, prison authorities and rival youth gangs for love and acceptance. A hard-hitting, sexually charged film based on a true story. Mexican actress Isela Vega is featured. (Spanish with English subtitles) ★★★

Dumb and Dumber

(1994, 106 min, US, Peter Farrelly) *Dumb and Dumber* certainly is. This may not be an original or even clever criticism, but then a film lacking originality or cleverness deserves neither. Jim Carrey and Jeff Daniels star in this sophomoric, scatological road comedy as Lloyd and Harry, two bumbling, dimwitted roommates who travel cross-country to locate Lloyd's dream woman (Lauren Holly). On the way, their stupid shenanigans involve them with blackmailers, murderers and high society. Anyone who has seen a Jerry Lewis or Bob Hope comedy has seen this all before. Ironically, for a Carrey vehicle it's Daniels as Harry who supplies most of the laughs, including a hilarious sequence set on the slopes of Aspen with Holly as a Margaret Dumont-like foil. Carrey, in turn, gives a hammy performance which captures none of the golden timing demonstrated in *The Mask*. ★½ $14.99

Dumbo

(1941, 64 min, US, Ben Sharpsteen) After the (initial) financial disappointment of *Fantasia*, Disney needed some cash, and fast, or his studio was going to be converted into a hospital.

This film was made quick and cheap, and that's what gives it its energy and charm. Clean and simple design, charming songs, and all the vitality of the classic shorts, *Dumbo* found Disney returning to form. ★★★★ $24.99

Dune

(1984, 137 min, US, David Lynch) Lynch brings Frank Herbert's sci-fi classic to the screen in this wildly uneven but thought-provoking adaptation. In the distant future, the most coveted substance is the drug-like spice known as Melange. Valued for its mind-expanding properties, the sole source of the spice is the desert planet Arrakis, or Dune. Thus, the superpowers clash over the control of Arrakis; for whoever owns the spice owns the universe. Although inconsistent, the set and costume design, as well as Lynch's directorial touches, make *Dune* a film that challenges the imagination. A box-office disappointment, the film seems to have found its niche on the small screen. (Available letterboxed and pan & scan) ★★½ $14.99

The Dunera Boys

(1985, 150 min, Australia, Sam Lewin) Bob Hoskins stars in this film about a group of Jewish refugees during WWII who are suspected of being Nazi informants in the British army. They are deported to a prison camp in Australia. Hoskins is absolutely brilliant as one of the refugees who is forced to prove his loyalty to England. Marred only by its length, this is an intelligently written and powerfully acted film. ★★★ $79.99

Dunston Checks In

(1995, 85 min, US, Ken Kwapis) Parents, beware: When Dunston checks in, your brain checks out. Dunston is an orangutan whose owner (Rupert Everett) passes for a British lord but who is in fact a thief with a primate assistant. The two of them check into a five-star hotel run by Jason Alexander. And then the shenanigans begin. Alexander's two sons befriend the monkey and try to save him from his life of crime (shades of *Monkey Trouble*) while their father contends with Faye Dunaway, the hotel owner's wife, who is anxious to obtain the new and elusive six-star status awarded to the best hotels. Of course, the chaos in the background leads to predictably disastrous consequences. Neither the strong cast nor the excellent production values can overcome the convoluted and drawn out story line. Paul Reubens' brief appearance is a waste but the orangutan and the youngest boy (Eric Lloyd) are endearing all the same. Kids should probably enjoy most of the film despite its many problems. ★★ $19.99

The Dunwich Horror

(1969, 90 min, US, Daniel Haller) Roger Corman produced this effective adaptation of the classic H.P. Lovecraft story. Dean Stockwell's interest in a rare book called "The Necronomicon" soon requires more than an attentive reading and begins to impinge on his relationship with girlfriend Sandra Dee. Ed Begley, in his last role, is the professor who puts a stop to all this evil. ★★½

Dust

(1985, 88 min, Belgium/France, Marion Hansel) Set on an isolated South African farm, this Venice Film Festival winner charts, with fearful precision, the mental disintegration of a lonely and sexually desperate young woman (Jane Birkin) who murders her tyrannical father (Trevor Howard). Based on J.M. Cotzee's novel, "In the Heart of the Country." ★★★

Dust Devil

(1992, 87 min, GB, Richard Stanley) From the writer-director of the visually interesting (but ultimately disappointing) *Hardware* comes this mystical tale of a demon (Robert Burke) who walks the South African veld looking for doomed souls to revitalize his life force. Once again, style tends to overpower director Stanley's story line, thereby lessening the chill factor of an otherwise gripping horror film. Chelsea Field and Zakes Mokae also star. Note: There is allegedly 15 minutes of gory footage missing from the video release of this film; there are no plans to release an extended version on tape. ★★ $89.99

Dusty

(1985, 89 min, Australia, John Richardson) A heartwarming tale of an aging Outback prospector, played by Bill Kerr (*Gallipoli*), who befriends a half-wild sheepdog named Dusty. A moving family adventure in the tradition of *Old Yeller*. ★★★ $39.99

Dutch

(1991, 105 min, US, Peter Faiman) John Hughes returns to one of his successful formulas (*Planes, Trains and Automobiles*) with considerably less successful results. Working-class stiff Ed O'Neill is engaged to upper-crust JoBeth Williams. It's Thanksgiving vacation, and Williams' preppy teenage son is stuck at school. So O'Neill is sent to escort the lad home. You won't need a crystal ball to predict plot developments, such as the two of them won't hit it off, or the cross-country trip becomes a comedy of errors, or the two become best buddies at film's end. In his first big screen starring role, O'Neill gives a likable performance, and, as the young boy, Ethan Randall is appropriately obnoxious — to the point of wanting to hit him with a snow shovel. ★★ $9.99

Dying Young

(1991, 105 min, US, Joel Schumacher) Director Schumacher and star Julia Roberts reunite after their successful *Flatliners*, though their experience with near-death here is catatonic. In a terribly written role (which shamelessly bears too many similarities to her *Pretty Woman*), Roberts is a working-class woman who takes a job as nurse to a terminally ill man (Campbell Scott). As the rich man intellectually enlightens her, she brings a much-needed spark of energy to an otherwise privileged, lonely person. Set in San Francisco and full of AIDS awareness messages in the background, the film is a tedious allegory for that disease and its wasting of young lives — if only the filmmakers had the guts to make the movie which this self-consciously tries to be. Scott is better than the film deserves, and his real-life mother, Colleen Dewhurst, appears in her final film. ★ $9.99

D

E.T. The Extra-Terrestrial

(1982, 115 min, US, Steven Spielberg) A classic sci-fi adventure, and one of the most popular pictures of all time. An alien lands in suburban California and is befriended by a ten-year-old boy (Henry Thomas), who helps the space traveler return home. It's magical, mystical, funny and extremely touching; and E.T. itself is a marvel of makeup and effects. Drew Barrymore is a delight as Thomas' younger sister. This is our generation's *The Wizard of Oz*. (Letterboxed version available for $19.99) ★★★★ $14.99

Each Dawn I Die

(1939, 92 min, US, William Keighley) James Cagney plays a reporter who is framed and sent to prison. George Raft is the tough con he tangles with. This routine Warner programmer features its stars in good form but is mired by a convoluted second half. ★★½ $19.99

The Eagle

(1925, 77 min, US, Clarence Brown) Full of romance, action and adventure, this silent costume adventure yarn was adapted from an Alexander Pushkin story. Rudolph Valentino plays a young Russian officer who rejects the advances of the evil Czarina (Louise Dresser). As a result, he is banished. But he returns as The Eagle, a Tartar Robin Hood out to take vengeance against the Czarina as well as win the hand of the woman (Vilma Banky) he loves. Great fun and Valentino cuts a fine swash. ★★★½

The Eagle Has Landed

(1977, 123 min, GB, John Sturges) Fast-moving, intricately plotted and solidly entertaining, this WWII action-adventure makes full use of an excellent cast, which includes Michael Caine, Donald Sutherland, Robert Duvall, Donald Pleasence, Treat Williams and Larry Hagman. Based on the novel by Jack Higgins about an attempt by the Germans to kidnap Winston Churchill. ★★★ $19.99

The Eagle Has Two Heads
(L'Aigle à Deux Têtes)

(1947, 99 min, France, Jean Cocteau) This extravagant and romantic melodrama was adapted from Cocteau's hugely successful play. Set in the 19th century, the film stars Jean Marais as a lederhosen-clad poet/anarchist (and double for the dead king) who sets out to assassinate the beautiful queen (Edwige Feuillére), but when the two lock eyes, it is love at first sight. In keeping with Cocteau's passion for linking love with death, the couple meets a tragic end. Probably the least successful of Cocteau's films. (French with English subtitles) ★★½ $29.99

An Early Frost

(1985, 100 min, US, John Erman) The first TV movie to deal with the subject of AIDS, *An Early Frost* is a thoughtful and undeniably powerful drama. Aidan Quinn stars as Michael, a successful gay lawyer who learns he has been infected with the HIV virus. He decides to tell his family, who do not even know he is gay. The effect of his announcement on him and his family is at the core of the heartfelt story. Quinn gives a sensitive though commanding performance, and Gena Rowlands, Ben Gazzara and especially Sylvia Sydney offer strong support as his parents and grandmother. John Glover is remarkable as a dying patient Michael befriends. An Emmy Award winner for Best Screenplay. ★★★½ $19.99

Early Summer (Bakushu)

(1951, 135 min, Japan, Yasujiro Ozu) The essence of Japanese family life is masterfully captured in this illuminating, passionate and, at times, humorous work that must be considered one of director Ozu's best post-war films. Noriko, an intelligent and independent woman of 28, is faced with an arranged marriage to an unloved and unloving man, but her sense of individualism conflicts with her feelings of obligation towards her family. She wants to please others but at the same time make her own way in life. A restrained, succinct observation on the inevitable tides of change on family traditions and bonds, and their effect on Japanese culture. (Japanese with English subtitles) ★★★★ $29.99

The Earrings of Madame de...

(1945, 105 min, France, Max Ophüls) This wonderfully captivating Ophüls film tells the ironic and ultimately tragic tale of a woman and a set of diamond earrings which are given to her by her husband, pawned by him when in debt, and then given again to her, but this time by her lover. A remarkable portrait of the vanity and frivolous nature of the upper classes in 19th-century Paris. (French with English subtitles) ★★★ $14.99

Earth

(1930, 90 min, USSR, Alexander Dovzhenko) One of the last silent movies and a masterpiece in Soviet cinema, *Earth* is a lyrically-told poem to man's love of nature, his endeavors to adapt it to his needs, and of man's death as part of the cycle of life. In Ukraine, a collective of poor peasants attempt to farm the vast lands of the Kulaks, the landed gentry, who in turn oppose them. Dovzhenko paints an indelible portrait of a people's struggle against superstition, rich landowners and nature itself in their fight to make their dreams reality. (Silent with orchestral accompaniment) ★★★★ $29.99

Earth Girls Are Easy

(1989, 102 min, US, Julien Temple) After dissecting 1950s London with a rock beat in the brilliant *Absolute Beginners*, director Temple takes a look at 1980s California, complete with valley girls, dudes and aliens — from outer space. Geena Davis awakens to find a spaceship in her swimming pool; a ship with shaggy Jeff Goldblum, Jim Carrey and Damon Wayans aboard. Doing her best for interplanetary relations, she takes the visitors under her wing, and in the process falls in love with Captain Jeff. The film never reaches the comic fever pitch it sets out to capture, though the cast manages to make the most of the uneven screenplay. ★★½ $14.99

Earth vs. the Flying Saucers

(1956, 83 min, US, Fred F. Sears) Splendid special effects by wizard Ray Harryhausen highlight this sci-fi favorite about aliens demanding Earth's surrender. ★★★ $9.99

Earthquake

(1974, 129 min, US, Mark Robson) Well, it *did* win an Oscar for some outstanding special effects, but aside from a dexterity at leveling miniature models of L.A., the film offers little else. Charlton Heston, George Kennedy, Genevieve Bujold, Richard Roundtree, Ava Gardner, Lorne Greene (as Gardner's father!) and evangelist Marjoe Gortner all star. ★★ $9.99

The East Is Red

(1992, 95 min, Hong Kong, Ching Siu-Tung) Move over Supergirl. Your days are numbered, Wonder Woman. Asia the Invincible, the first transsexual lesbian superhero, is now the reigning queen. This spectacular kung fu fantasy is 95 minutes of non-stop action featuring awesome special effects and enough

Dennis Hopper (l.) and Peter Fonda cruising in *Easy Rider*

flailing bodies and exhilarating fight sequences to keep any fan of the genre enthralled. With magical powers (including flying across the screen and flinging killer needles at her foes), Asia (Brigitte Lin Ching-Hsia) is a fiery villain/hero who goes on rampage, fighting neighboring armies, Spanish conquistadors and even a bevy of fake Asias, to regain the hand of Snow, the woman she loves. ★★★ $89.99

East of Eden
(1955, 115 min, US, Elia Kazan) James Dean gives an affecting and sincere performance as a rebel with a cause in this Kazan classic. Based on John Steinbeck's novel, this was Dean's starring debut as a misunderstood youth, yearning for his father's approval while searching for the truth about his mysteriously absent mother. Julie Harris and Raymond Massey give fine performances in support, and Jo Van Fleet was an Oscar winner for her portrayal of Dean's bitter mom. ★★★★ $19.99

East of the Sun, West of the Moon
(1991, 30 min, Sweden) Narrated by Max von Sydow, this Scandinavian fairy tale is brought to life through brilliantly illustrated cel animation. The story follows the mythic journey of a poor, beautiful maiden and a big white bear. Winner of several prestigious children's television awards. ★★★ $9.99

East Side, West Side
(1949, 108 min, US, Mervyn LeRoy) The foibles of New York's society darlings are under scrutiny in this capable though shallow melodrama based on the Marcia Davenport novel. Barbara Stanwyck and James Mason are a wealthy couple whose marriage is coming apart, especially with Ava Gardner and Van Heflin waiting for them in the wings. Good performances by all help gloss over the occasional dramatic potholes. ★★½ $19.99

Easter Parade
(1948, 104 min, US, Charles Walters) Tuneful Irving Berlin musical with Fred Astaire and Judy Garland as a song-and-dance team during the early 1900s. Songs include "Steppin' Out with My Baby," "A Couple of Swells" and the title tune; and Ann Miller and Peter Lawford co-star. ★★★½ $19.99

The Easy Life (Il Sorpasso)
(1963, 105 min, Italy, Dino Risi) Capturing the optimistic and carefree outlook in a rapidly modernizing Italy, this comedy-drama stars Vittorio Gassman as a pleasure-seeking middle-aged playboy who meets his opposite in a young Jean-Louis Trintignant, a meek, serious law student whom he takes under his wing. The fast-talking and equally fast-driving Gassman convinces the young man to accompany him on a trip to northern Italy and taste life's sweet offerings. A likable, offbeat film, well-played by the two charming leads. (Letterboxed version) (Italian with English subtitles) ★★★ $59.99

Easy Living
(1949, 77 min, US, Jacques Tourneur) Victor Mature plays an aging football star facing retirement. Lucille Ball plays the team secretary in love with him. Lizabeth Scott plays Mature's

possessive wife. A compelling and thoughtful drama accented by three smart performances. (Not to be confused with the similarly titled Jean Arthur classic comedy.) ★★★ $19.99

Easy Money
(1983, 95 min, US, James Signorelli) Rodney Dangerfield delivers some good laughs in this easy-going comedy about a slobbish baby photographer who stands to inherit millions — if he can give up drinking, smoking, gambling and over-eating. Co-starring Candy Azzara, Joe Pesci and Geraldine Fitzgerald. ★★★

Easy Rider
(1969, 94 min, US, Dennis Hopper) This low-budget phenom sent shock waves through Hollywood and the nation. Peter Fonda and Dennis Hopper are the hippie bikers whose trek across America blithely caught the mood of the times. Jack Nicholson is unforgettable as the alcoholic lawyer with an itch to drop out. ★★★½ $19.99

Easy Virtue
(1927, 79 min, GB, Alfred Hitchcock) Hitchcock meets Noël Coward. It's tempting to simply leave it at that. Based on a story by Coward, this early silent Hitchcock feature comes up a little short dramatically, but it does have flashes of the director's later style. The story has to do with the melodramatic sufferings an alcoholic's wife (Isabel Jeans) endures. ★★½ $12.99

Eat a Bowl of Tea
(1989, 102 min, US, Wayne Wang) Shortly after WWII, young Ben Loy is sent to Hong Kong by his father, Wah Gay, to find a bride. He returns with Mei Oi — a very modern and independent young woman with whom he has fallen deeply in love. Unfortunately, the choice is not one which sits so well with Wah Gay who finds his dearly held traditions threatened. What follows is a wry and irreverent, often offbeat and always endearing treatise on the struggle between old and new in the Chinese community. It is pulled together with the dizzyingly frantic pace of a 1930s screwball comedy. Once again, Wang has succeeded in making a purely Chinese-American movie which will appeal to all. (English and Chinese with English subtitles) ★★★ $19.99

Eat Drink Man Woman
(1994, 120 min, Taiwan, Ang Lee) On the heels on his well-received The Wedding Banquet, director Lee returns to his native Taiwan for this heartfelt and humorous examination of the romantic aspirations of an aging widower and his daughters. Featuring the most visually sumptuous cinematic food since Like Water for Chocolate and Babette's Feast, the film opens with a bang — the viewer being drawn into an ornate ritual of food prep as old Tao Chu (once the master chef of all Taipei) readies an "average" Sunday family dinner. His three daughters are a study in diversity: Jia-Jen, the eldest, is a devoutly Christian schoolteacher; Jia-Chien, the middle, is a rebellious spitfire and successful businesswoman; Jia-Ning, the youngest, seemingly infatuated with American "mall culture," works at Wendy's and is caught in the throes of puppy love. Lee's acute eye for

Eat Drink Man Woman

character uses this quartet to paint a stirring and highly humorous picture of emotional isolation against a backdrop of Taiwan's rapidly modernizing culture. (Mandarin with English subtitles) ★★★★ $19.99

Eat the Peach
(1986, 95 min, Ireland, Peter Ormrod) Two unemployed Irish fellows, inspired by a scene in Elvis Presley's bike movie, Roustabout, conspire to construct a "Wall of Death" upon which they will ride their cycles and defy gravity. Of course, their families and friends think they've gone mad, but Vinnie and Arthur persevere, resorting to smuggling and petty theft to realize their dream. An amiable comedy, filled with down home Irish charm. ★★½ $79.99

Eat the Rich
(1988, 92 min, GB, Peter Richardson) The outrageous British comedy troupe The Comic Strip (The Supergrass) serves some heaping portions of over-the-top comedy in this biting attack on England's class system. Having been fired from a very posh and unbearably snobby London restaurant, a transsexual waiter gangs up with a couple of fellow disenfranchised citizens and vows to start the revolution. They begin by taking over the restaurant and renaming it "Eat the Rich" — which, as it turns out, is exactly what the patrons unwittingly do. A marvelous example of Thatcher-era humor. ★★★ $19.99

Eaten Alive
(1976, 96 min, US, Tobe Hooper) From the director of The Texas Chainsaw Massacre comes this horror outing about a psychopathic hotel owner who has a bad habit of feeding his guests to his pet crocodile. Hooper's debut feature is bizarre though occasionally scary. ★★

Eating
(1990, 110 min, US, Henry Jaglom) Idiosyncratic director Jaglom (New Year's Day) takes us on a wonderfully entertaining afternoon outing to a fine suburban L.A. home where a group of women come together for a birthday party and where everyone's favorite topic of discussion is food, food, food. Filmed with an all-female cast, the comedy is much more consistent and funnier than Jaglom's previous outings as the wacky cast of Left Coast caricatures chatter, bemoan and marvel in their

collective guilt for and obsession of food and eating. The film is loosely structured, allowing the actresses to improvise, with the results being many hilariously memorable and perceptive lines. A note of caution – this film should either be seen on a full stomach or with a bunch of fattening munchies piled high on your lap. Go on a diet after the film! ★★★½ $94.99

Eating Raoul

(1982, 83 min, US, Paul Bartel) Paul and Mary Bland, a mild-mannered couple, devise a diabolical scheme to raise funds for their entrepreneurial dreams. Placing an ad in the local sex publication, they lure unsuspecting degenerates to their abode, club them with a frying pan and empty their wallets. Hunky Robert Beltran also stars as the not-as-clever-as-he-thinks-he-is hustler Raoul who may become their next victim. Bartel's cannibalistic comedy serves up a healthy portion of laughs in his most consistently outrageous comedy. ★★★½ $19.99

The Ebony Tower

(1987, 80 min, GB, Robert Knights) Laurence Olivier stars as an aging painter who, out of disdain for the art world, cloisters himself with two beautiful female art students in a remote French chateau. Their peaceful retreat is sent into chaos, however, by the arrival of a young artist (Roger Rees). This John Mortimer adaptation of the John Fowles novel also stars Greta Scacchi and Toyah Wilcox as Olivier's companions. ★★★

Echo Park

(1986, 92 min, US, Robert Dornhelm) An offbeat charmer about a would-be actress (Susan Dey) and her relationship with two boarders, a songwriting pizza delivery man (the very likable Tom Hulce) and a budding body-builder (Michael Bowen), both of whom share her rundown duplex in East Los Angeles. ★★★ $14.99

Echoes of Paradise

(1987, 92 min, Australia, Phillip Noyce) Wendy Hughes stars as a happily married mother of three whose idyllic suburban life is shattered after she discovers that her husband has been in a series of affairs for years. In an effort to escape the emotional turmoil at home, she travels with a friend to exotic Thailand where she meets a handsome Balinese dancer (John Lone). Her repressed desires and attitudes are slowly shed (as are her clothes) as she enters into a liberating relationship with the worldly and sweet-as-honey Lone. Similar in theme to *A Passage to India* and *The Sheltering Sky*, the film treads no new territory; and with seductive lines like, "You look tense. Let me give you a massage," the viewer should take the film more as a beautiful travelogue and less as anything insightful. ★★ $14.99

The Eclipse (L'Eclisse)

(1962, 123 min, Italy, Michelangelo Antonioni) The concluding film in Antonioni's existential trilogy, which includes *L'Avventura* and *La Notte*, continues with the theme of the barriers to human communication as part of an increasingly stark contemporary world. The film stars Monica Vitti as a young woman who, hours after leaving her old lover, meets a passionate young man (played by Alain Delon).

Johnny Depp as *Ed Wood*

Whether she'll really end her old affair or if the fledgling new one will even begin is at the heart of the conflict in this existential "art" film. The plot, however, takes a back seat to Antonioni's experimental film techniques and abstract style. (Letterbox format) (Italian with English subtitles) ★★★ $29.99

Ecstasy

(1933, 82 min, Czechoslovakia, Gutsav Machaty) A true curiosity! This slow-moving, predictable Czech film would have long been used for landfill had it not been for its scandalizing nude scenes of a pre-Hollywood Hedy Lamarr. Long unavailable, this uncut version has Lamarr in all her natural beauty as a young woman whose marriage to a fastidious older man sours on their wedding night. She soon leaves him and finds solace in the arms of a handsome young engineer. Filmed mostly as a silent film, with only about 20 words spoken, the acting is overly expressive by today's standards. (German with English subtitles) ★ $29.99

Ed Wood

(1994, 128 min, US, Tim Burton) Johnny Depp stars as the titular character in this ideally crafted biopic of the 1950s film director who single-handedly molded the grade-B aesthetic. Shot in black and white and imitating the cheesy production values of Wood's immortal cult classics (such as *Glen or Glenda*), the film is a perfect tribute to the man whose charming incompetence as a filmmaker was equally matched by an unrelenting enthusiasm for the medium. Depp's portrayal of Wood, a WWII vet with an insatiable appetite for angora and women's clothing, is right on the money, but it is Martin Landau's astonishing portrait of Bela Lugosi that steals the show. As the drug-addicted fallen star, Landau's performance transforms the film from simple biography to an inspirational tale of friendship and redemption. Fortunately, director Burton tempers the film's serious underbelly with generous doses of hilarity and wit, or to quote Depp as Wood, "Transvestites! Get me transvestites!" Also with Bill Murray, Sarah Jessica Parker, Patricia Arquette and Jeffrey Jones. ★★★★ $9.99

Ed Wood: Look Back in Angora

(1994, 50 min, US, Ted Newsom) A fitting companion piece to Tim Burton's *Ed Wood*, this engagingly frenetic examination of the blazingly eccentric director-writer-actor crosscuts clips from his one-of-a-kind movies with interviews from those who knew him. Interviewees include an ex-Marine who fought with him in the Pacific during WWII; movie industry types of the most marginal sort; and his long-suffering, ever-devoted wife. Director Newsom lets Wood's films speak for the tormented, would-be auteur, creating an affectionate and intimate biography of an obsessive whose ambitions greatly exceeded his talents. A stirring tribute to the man who created some of the worst movies ever made. ★★★½ $9.99

Eddie

(1996, 100 min, US, Steve Rash) The tolerance level of *Eddie*, a predictable if amiable sports comedy, begins and ends with one's appreciation (or lack thereof) of its star Whoopi Goldberg. Surely its premise of a die-hard New York Knicks fan becoming the slumping team's head coach bears no more originality or plausibility than similarly themed kids films like *Rookie of the Year* and *Little Big League*. And like those two films, the enjoyment factor is dictated by the suppression of one's common sense. Unfortunately, *Eddie* promises more than it delivers. Which is not to fault Whoopi. She's agreeable and often amusing, but her comic prowess alone cannot keep this comedy courtside. Even a seasoned comic needs more from a script than just the occasional cut-up line; just ask Jim Carrey. *Eddie* is strictly for Whoopi fans, who may graciously overlook the Formula 101 story; there are laughs to be had, just don't expect a winning season. ★★½ $19.99

Eddie and the Cruisers

(1983, 92 min, US, Martin Davidson) Tom Berenger, Ellen Barkin and Michael Paré star in this story of a popular 1960s rock band whose leader presumably died in an accident — but he may have faked his death and returned to his old neighborhood. Barkin is the TV reporter investigating the story; Paré is the legendary Eddie. Paré returned in the 1989 sequel, *Eddie and the Cruisers II*. ★★½ $14.99

Eddie Murphy — Raw

(1987, 90 min, US, Robert Townsend) This aptly titled movie is Eddie Murphy's first concert film. He's often very funny and has a great deal of energy, but he's as enamored with his anatomy as ever. If you like Murphy and enjoy his style of humor, this R-rated (well-justified) romp is the one for you. ★★ $14.99

Edge of Darkness

(1943, 120 min, US, Lewis Milestone) From the director of the classic anti-war film *All Quiet on the Western Front* comes that film's antithesis, a gripping WWII drama and passionate call-to-arms. Errol Flynn and Ann Sheridan head a splendid ensemble cast as leaders of the underground movement of their small Norwegian village, which the Nazis occupy. Featuring exceptional cinematography, this well-detailed film examines daily life under oppressive German rule and the birth of the town's Resistance movement. A dashing Flynn, a no-nonsense Sheridan, Walter Huston, Judith Anderson, and a heart-tugging performance by Ruth Gordon all contribute to make *Edge of Darkness* stand out among other war-era films. ★★★½ $19.99

Edge of Darkness

(1986, 307 min, GB, Martin Campbell) This stylishly produced BBC thriller is filled with espionage and intrigue and won six British "Emmy" Awards. Bob Peck stars as a London police detective whose life is brutally torn apart when his young daughter is found murdered. As he follows the trail of her killer(s), he uncovers a tangled web of conspiracy involving government agents, a maverick CIA operative, multinational corporations and a radical environmental group. Good, solid action entertainment starring Joanne Whaley and Joe Don Baker. ★★★ $29.99

Edge of Sanity

(1988, 90 min, GB, Gerald Kikoine) Turgid, uninvolving and ineptly directed, this Dr. Jekyll and Mr. Hyde horror spin-off features a bug-eyed Anthony Perkins as a doctor who accidentally concocts a mixture that turns him into a pasty-faced killer with a predilection for sleazy prostitutes. Set in Victorian London, this updated version of the Stevenson classic offers few thrills, tepid chills and not enough blood to keep the viewer from keeping a finger on fast-forward. A disappointment that is not enjoyable even on a camp level. ★ $9.99

Edison the Man

(1940, 107 min, US, Clarence Brown) Fine sequel to *Young Tom Edison* (which starred a youthful Mickey Rooney) with Spencer Tracy as the adult inventor. The film follows Edison's fascination with devices, and though some of the story is Hollywood-ized, it's a rewarding homage to the American genius. ★★★ $19.99

Edith and Marcel

(1983, 140 min, France, Claude Lelouch) The love affair between singer Edith Piaf and boxing champion Marcel Cerdan, who died in a plane crash in 1944, is romantically brought to the screen by Lelouch. The entrancing music of actual Piaf recordings and the casting of real-life son Marcel Cerdan, Jr. in the lead role adds pathos to this tragic love story. (French with English subtitles) ★★½

Educating Rita

(1983, 110 min, GB, Lewis Gilbert) Julie Walters is delightful as the Cockney dynamo who enrolls in a course at the Open University and comes under the tutelage of the cynical and boozy Michael Caine. Driven by her thirst for knowledge, Rita exchanges the chatter of the ladies' hair salon for discussions on Chekov and Blake, while at the same time breathing new life into her moribund teacher. A warm and witty comedy from Willy Russell's hit West End play. ★★★½ $9.99

Edvard Munch

(1974, 167 min, Norway, Peter Watkins) Though labeled by his contemporaries as a sick madman, Edvard Munch (1863-1944) is considered one of the most important and influential painters in the Expressionistic Movement. This abstract examination into the psyche of the artist traces Munch's professional and private lives through the combination of narrative and dialogue (some taken directly from his diary), reenactments, and documentary-like interviews. The collage design of the film produces an overlaying of image and sound, a hodge-podge of short scenes and repetition of events that its running time of 167 minutes may push some viewers to wonder if they could be the model for Munch's most famous work: The Scream. (Norweigan and German with English subtitles) ★★½ $29.99

Edward II

(1991, 91 min, GB, Derek Jarman) Director Jarman has reworked Christopher Marlowe's play into a homoerotic, sexually charged, radically relevant work for our times. Steven Waddington stars as the tragic King Edward, Andrew Teirnan as his beloved Gaveston, Nigel Terry as the villainous Mortimer and Tilda Swinton is the jealous and destructive Queen Isabella (for which she won the Best Actress Award at the Venice Film Festival). Graphically brutal, moving, surprisingly funny and always erotic, Jarman blends Marlowe's prose with contemporary jargon and costumes, replete with positive portrayals of queer sex, profanity and ACT-UP activists for a truly mesmerizing experience. One of the film's most surprising sequences occurs when Annie Lennox appears crooning Cole Porter's classic "Ev'ry Time We Say Goodbye," the piece she performed in the AIDS benefit "Red, Hot and Blue." Brilliant, daring and innovative, *Edward II* is contemporary filmmaking at its finest, and one of the best examples of modern queer cinema. A must see. ★★★★ $19.99

Edward Scissorhands

(1990, 98 min, US, Tim Burton) Having paid his dues to Hollywood several times over with

Batman, director Burton presents this small-scale gem about a boy with scissors for hands. Johnny Depp is admirable in the title role and Winona Ryder, Alan Arkin and the "quintessential movie-mom," Dianne Wiest, give ample support. The legendary Vincent Price has a cameo as the inventor. This heartbreaking and highly original parable on conformity casts Depp as a social misfit who's taken by Wiest to live in her "average suburban household" where he falls in love for the first time, becomes all the rage as a hairdresser to the neighborhood's wives, and learns the high cost for societal conventions. Burton has fashioned in this beautifully filmed and comic fantasy the ultimate tale of the outsider as misunderstood and victimized innocent. ★★★½ $14.99

Effi Briest

(1974, 140 min, West Germany, Rainer Werner Fassbinder) Hanna Schygulla is luminous as the title character in Fassbinder's accomplished adaptation of the 1895 novel by Theodore Fontane. Fassbinder once again explores the subject of societal restraints in this beautifully photographed and elegantly mounted production. When Effi's much-older husband finds evidence of a long-dead affair, a chain of events is inexorably initiated, and Effi is its primary victim. Schygulla's performace is subtle, delicately layered and compelling. One of the director's best works. (German with English subtitles) ★★★★ $79.99

The Efficiency Expert

(1992, 85 min, Australia, Mark Joffe) In the tradition of *Local Hero* comes this warm, low-key comedy from Australia. Set in 1960s Melbourne, the film is about a management specialist's (Anthony Hopkins) efforts to "update and modernize" a small, family run moccasin company. Instead of focusing on the ins-and-outs of the efficiency business, director Joffe's film is about decent working people trying to treat each other decently. In a richly textured but subtly moving performance, Hopkins plays a man in the midst of both a personal and a professional crisis of ethics. While the film may not break any new ground, it treads familiar territory gently and pleasantly. ★★★ $14.99

Egg

(1988, 58 min, Holland, Danniel Danniel) This engaging and delightful short film centers around a sweet but lonely 35-year-old baker whose quietly efficient life is put in turmoil after a personal ad he placed in an out-of-town newspaper produces a determined woman at his doorstep. Their tenuous attempts at a relationship soon involve the entire town's population. A humorous fable that takes a subdued approach and relies more on the actions of the characters rather than dialogue to tell its tale. A good double feature both in theme and style would be *Tampopo*. (Dutch with English subtitles) ★★★ $59.99

The Egg and I

(1947, 108 min, US, Chester Erskine) Big city socialite Claudette Colbert experiences culture shock at new hubby Fred MacMurray's chicken farm. Colbert sparkles; she and MacMurray highlight a strong supporting cast of seasoned character actors in this delightful, witty and fun excursion into the green acres of the American heartland. One of the smash hits of the 1940s, the film introduced Marjorie Main and Percy Kilbride as "Ma and Pa Kettle." ★★★ $14.99

The Egyptian

(1954, 140 min, US, Michael Curtiz) Hollywood doesn't make 'em like this anymore – and for most of us that's probably good news. An abandoned baby grows up to be the Pharaoh's physician. Based on a true story. Starring Victor Mature, Edmund Purdon, Jean Simmons and Peter Ustinov. ★ $19.99

The Eiger Sanction

(1975, 128 min, US, Clint Eastwood) Clint Eastwood is a college art professor and part-time government assassin in this somewhat "Bond-esque" movie of spies and espionage. Features some splendid mountain climbing scenes. Also with George Kennedy and Jack Cassidy as an offensively gay killer. ★★ $14.99

8½

(1963, 135 min, Italy, Federico Fellini) Fellini's masterful statement on his life and art stars Marcello Mastroianni as a filmmaker paralyzed by creative block and slipping deeper into a world of dream and fantasy. Claudia Cardinale portrays his sensuous apparition. (Available both dubbed and in Italian with English subtitles) ★★★★ $19.99

Eight Men Out

(1988, 119 min, US, John Sayles) A beautiful period piece rich in emotion about the infamous "Black Sox Scandal" of 1919. It was a time when baseball players were the heroes of the day, until the underpaid and underappreciated players of the Chicago White Sox threw the World Series and brought shame to our national pastime. Examining the events which led up to the darkest days in the history of American sports, Sayles has assembled a fine team of young, talented actors. Sayles should be commended as both writer and director for the depth and clarity he brings to the almost 20 characters whose individual stories seem to effortlessly intertwine to tell this fascinating and sorrowful tale. ★★★★ $9.99

8 Million Ways to Die

(1986, 115 min, US, Hal Ashby) Slick though unremarkable crime thriller with Jeff Bridges as an ex-Los Angeles sheriff who tries to crack a cocaine ring and help a prostitute (Rosanna Arquette) break free of her obsessive pimp. Andy Garcia is terrific as Arquette's menacing pimp. ★★★ $19.99

1860

(1934, 75 min, Italy, Alessandro Blasetti) The struggle for the unification of Italy, and especially the Sicilian peasant revolt against the Prince of Naples, provide the historical backdrop to this elegant war drama. Using non-professional actors, location shooting and natural lighting, the film brings an almost documentary feel to the story of one peasant's role during the battles and is considered a stylistic precursor to the Italian neorealist movement of the 1940s. (Italian with English subtitles) ★★★ $29.99

The Eighth Day

(1996, 114 min, France, Jaco van Dormael) Optimistic Belgian director van Dormael is given over to some wonderful flights of fancy, but his message about living life to the fullest is still cliché now matter how he dresses it up. *The Eighth Day* introduces George (Pascal Duquenne), a young man with Down's Syndrome who has a childlike sense of wonder, and Harry (Daniel Auteuil), an uptight salesman who fails to appreciate what he has. When these two characters meet in an accident one stormy night, they, of course, have a transforming effect on one another. Van Dormael can achieve great moments of sadness and magic in the film, much like his previous *Toto the Hero*, but there is too much filler between the scenes that truly captivate. However, the acting is superb. Duquenne is truly inspired as George, and he makes his naive character sympathetic without being saccharine. The range of emotions he displays is remarkable. Likewise, Auteuil deftly shows how Harry melts from his cold, unfeeling personality into a caring human being. The actors shared the Best Actor prize at Cannes. ★★½ $102.99

84 Charing Cross Road

(1987, 97 min, US/GB, David Jones) Anne Bancroft and Anthony Hopkins give spendid performances in this lovely film version of Hugh Whitemore's play (based on the memoirs of Helen Hanff) about the 20-year, transatlantic correspondence between a London bookseller (Hopkins) and one of his customers, a New York City woman (Bancroft). ★★★½ $19.99

Eijanaika

(1981, 151 min, Japan, Shohei Imamura) This chaotic portrait of Japanese society in the throes of a violent transition is masterfully directed by Imamura (*The Ballad of Narayama, Vengeance Is Mine, Black Rain*). Set in a bustling 19th-century Tokyo, the film depicts the loss of power by the Samurai Class at the hands of the new Imperial forces as well as outside business interests. Filmed against a backdrop of corruption, anarchy, bloodshed and eroticism, the story follows Genji, who returns to Tokyo after a five-year absence and finds that his wife has run off with a gangster. This mosaic portrait of Japanese culture run amok climaxes in a revolutionary frenzy and one of the most highly charged and dramatic spectacles in modern Japanese cinema. (Japanese with English subtitles) ★★★½ $79.99

El (This Strange Passion)

(1952, 82 min, Mexico, Luis Buñuel) This overheated story of passion, jealousy and violence is one of Buñuel's most entertaining films from his Mexican period. A biting anti-clerical satire full of bizarre touches and one that continues his theme of *amour fou*, which he first dealt with in *L'Age D'Or*. Francisco, a seemingly normal and devout aristocrat (but secret foot fetishist), becomes obsessed with a woman he sees in church. He pursues her and eventually marries the woman, but soon changes from a loving husband to a man crazed with murderous and unjustifiable jealousy. Buñuel's wry sense of humor is clearly intact in this memorable black comedy. Please note that there is a

Marcello Mastroianni in *8½*

slight problem with reading the white subtitles when there is a white background. (Spanish with English subtitles) ★★★ $59.99

El Cid

(1961, 184 min, US, Anthony Mann) Sprawling historical epic with Charlton Heston as the legendary Spanish hero who drove the Moors from his homeland. Sophia Loren also stars in this smart costume epic complete with impressive battle sequences, a better-than-average romance, and a story line none-too-difficult to follow. ★★★ $29.99

El Dorado

(1967, 126 min, US, Howard Hawks) Hawks' follow-up to his classic western *Rio Bravo*, *El Dorado* is an exciting western adventure with fine touches of comedy. The memorable cast includes John Wayne, Robert Mitchum and James Caan as the good guys; and Ed Asner and Christopher George as the bad guys. Aging gunfighter Wayne and sheriff Mitchum team up against a ruthless cattle baron. ★★★ $14.99

El Norte

(1983, 139 min, US, Gregory Nava & Anna Thompson) After their parents are murdered by a government death squad, a brother and sister flee their remote Guatemalan village and begin a hazardous trek to the "promised land" of America. A stunning, poetic tale of survival. ★★★½

El Super

(1979, 80 min, US, Leon Ichaso & Orlando Jiminez-Leal) Made in New York, this humorous, non-sentimental story of the trials of a homesick Cuban immigrant is both accomplished and heartwarming. Roberto, a Cuban exile for 10 years, works as a super in a New York apartment house and lives in its basement. Still not assimilated into this strange new land of snow, garbage and crime, he dreams of the palm trees, warmth and friendliness of his former land. This comical sad tale of a reluctant émigré is reminiscent of Franco

Brusati's very funny *Bread and Chocolate*. (Spanish with English subtitles) ★★★ $79.99

The Eleanor Roosevelt Story

(1965, 90 min, US, Richard Kaplan) When a Boswell, due to propriety, chooses to ignore the defining crisis in its subject's life, then any possibility of framing a coherent profile is relinquished. This by-the-numbers collage of newsreel footage and snapshots narrated with an almost comically stentorian voice-over by Eric Sevareid won an Academy Award as Best Documentary in 1965. Now "freshened up" for home video with a few pointless words from Hillary Rodham Clinton (who unfortunately shares none of the bon mots that surely must have passed between these two first ladies from their beyond-the-grave conversations), *The Eleanor Roosevelt Story* is hindered by an incessant tone of veneration, endemic of its era before television. We only learn what she did; never really *why*. What was it that caused this sheltered woman of privilege to suddenly betray her class and become a rare advocate for the poor and disenfranchised? And nothing is mentioned about her husband's infidelities nor her longtime relationship with Lerena Hickok. Maybe such things weren't discussed during the mid-'60s, but in ignoring the more controversial issues, their absence is only magnified. ★★ $29.99

The Electric Horseman

(1979, 120 min, US, Sydney Pollack) Robert Redford and Jane Fonda star in this unusual though entertaining drama about a cowboy (Redford) who steals a $12 million horse and escapes into the Nevada desert. There he is followed by TV reporter Fonda and romance ensues. ★★★ $9.99

The Elegant Criminal

(1991, 120 min, France, Francis Girod) Long dependent on Hollywood for its cinematic diet of lurid depictions of evil (Dr. Hannibal Lecter in *Silence of the Lambs*, Max Cady in Scorsese's *Cape Fear*, etc.), the French now have an evil genius to call their own. In this fascinating portrait, based on the true story of the notorious 19th-century murderer Pierre-Francois Lacenaire, director Girod (*The Infernal Trio, L'etat Sauvage*) has avoided the cheap, gory route and instead has fashioned an intimate, witty and complex look into the dark abyss of unrepentant evil. Daniel Auteil (*Jean De Florette, Manon of the Spring*) is riveting as Lacenaire — a failed playwright, refined gentleman, persuasive conversationalist, homosexual, as well as thief, con man and knife-wielding mass murderer — who despite (or because of) it all, received the respect of his jailers and became a national celebrity. (French with English subtitles) ★★★ $19.99

The Element of Crime

(1989, 104 min, Denmark, Lars Von Trier) This dark and brooding police thriller follows the story of an emotionally fragile cop who, after spending years in self-exile in Egypt, returns to a post-nuclear Europe — a continent plunged into inexplicable darkness, constant rain, and which is crumbling into chaos and senseless crime. Hired to track down the elusive killer responsible for a series of horrifying mutilations of young girls, the detective attempts to solve the killings by using the revolutionary theory of his former mentor: re-creating the exact events leading up to each murder. Filmed in mute black and white, the film's labyrinthine plot and bizarre imagery combine to make this a beguiling yet satisfying murder-mystery. (Filmed in English) ★★★ $79.99

Eléna and Her Men

(1956, 98 min, France, Jean Renoir) A blithely old-fashioned, highly stylized creation from director Renoir starring Ingrid Bergman as an impoverished 1880s Polish countess. Set on Bastille Day in Paris, Bergman becomes romantically involved with a debonaire count and a high-ranking soldier. This lush *fantaisie musicale* follows the countess' days as she must choose between the men and, of course, live happily ever after. This film, which Bergman specifically asked the director to make for her, was long thought lost. This is the full-length, restored version. (French with English subtitles) (aka: *Paris Does Strange Things*) ★★★ $59.99

Eleni

(1985, 117 min, US, Peter Yates) Based on Nicholas Gage's autobiographical best-seller, this uninvolving adaptation stars John Malkovich as a *New York Times* reporter who returns to his native Greece to investigate the death of his mother at the hands of Communist guerrillas 30 years earlier. Kate Nelligan is excellent as Gage's mother, whose story is told in flashback. ★★

The Elephant Man

(1980, 125 min, US, David Lynch) John Hurt, Anne Bancroft and Anthony Hopkins star in Lynch's eerie and hypnotic account of the life of John Merrick — a man so hideously deformed by disease that he was forced to make a living as a sideshow freak. Filmed in stark black and white, Lynch's camera acutely captures the darker corners of Victorian London and draws us into a world of shadows and despair. ★★★★

Elephant Walk

(1954, 103 min, US, William Dieterle) A new wife travels to her husband's exotic plantation, where a battle ensues with nature. No, it's not *The Naked Jungle*, which had those neat killer ants, but the inferior *Elephant Walk*, which can only boast rampaging elephants. Elizabeth Taylor joins husband Peter Finch on his Ceylon tea plantation. There, she falls for foreman Dana Andrews, and contends with epidemic, drought, her husband's wrath and the aforementioned pachyderms. ★★ $14.99

11 Harrowhouse

(1974, 95 min, GB, Aram Avakiam) Charles Grodin stars as a diamond salesman enlisted by a crazy millionaire (Trevor Howard) to steal one million dollars worth of diamonds. This unusual action spoof also stars Candice Bergen, James Mason and John Gielgud. ★★½ $59.99

Elmer Gantry

(1960, 146 min, US, Richard Brooks) Burt Lancaster won a Best Actor Oscar for his dynamic portrayal of a shady evangelist who charms himself into a religious troupe and the heart of Jean Simmons. Shirley Jones also won an Oscar for her sensational performance as Lancaster's former girlfriend-turned-prostitute. Based on Sinclair Lewis' best-seller. ★★★½ $19.99

Elmore Leonard's Criminal Records

(1991, 61 min, Canada, Mike Dibb) Elmore "Dutch" Leonard, king of the crime novel ("Cat Chaser," "City Primeval"), reveals the tricks of his trade as well as the meticulous research that goes into his works in this revealing documentary. A former writer of westerns and Hollywood screenplays (*52 Pick Up, Hombre, 3:10 to Yuma, Valdez Is Coming*) who turned to crime, Leonard talks about his writing and reminisces about the strange people and eerie places that have inspired his work. ★★★½ $19.99

The Elusive Corporal

(1962, 106 min, France, Jean Renoir) This intentionally lighthearted comedy about various attempts of three French soldiers to escape from a POW camp during World War II may bring to mind Renoir's anti-war classic *La Grande Illusion*. But the intent of the director was less on the examination of class and regional differences and more on the solidarity and friendship of his characters. Jean-Pierre Cassel is the charming and educated corporal who dedicates himself to breaking out of prison by any means possible. A wry, gentle comedy, featuring lively performances, and one of Renoir's most entertaining films. (French with English subtitles) ★★★½ $59.99

The Elusive Pimpernel

(1950, 107 min, GB, Michael Powell & Emeric Pressburger) Longtime collaborators Powell and Pressburger's excellent version of the daring exploits of Baroness Orczy's famous character is every bit as entertaining as the 1935 original, *The Scarlet Pimpernel*. David Niven is excellent as the heroic adventurer who rescues French aristocrats from the guillotine while doubling as an "indolent dandy of London." Originally filmed as a musical, all of the numbers were edited out, which is probably all the better. A fine supporting cast includes Margaret Leighton and Cyril Cusack. ★★★ $39.99

Elvira Madigan

(1967, 89 min, Sweden, Bo Widenberg) Considered one of the cinema's most beautiful films, this tale of star-crossed love follows a young officer who meets a beautiful circus dancer and takes off to create a fragile life in isolation which must surely destroy them both. This exquisitely photographed, superbly performed film explores the consequences of love in a lyrical, poignant manner. (Swedish with English subtitles) ★★★★ $24.99

Elvira — Mistress of the Dark

(1988, 96 min, US, James Signorelli) A feature film may seem like an unlikely vehicle for Elvira, the late night horror show hostess. It does not take long, however, for this disarming comedy to win you over. In the same vein as Pee-wee Herman, Cassandra Peterson's outrageous alter ego travels to Salem, Massachusetts, to collect an inheritance. Her confrontations with the straight-laced residents are funny and surreal. ★★½ $14.99

Gwyneth Paltrow as *Emma*

Emerald Cities

(1984, 90 min, US, Richard Schmidt) A film by California filmmaker Schmidt that, all in one film, juxtaposes the Santa Claus myth, nuclear war, punk rock, hypnotic self-analysis, psychedelic drugs and video manipulation. This visual cacophony is all presented with background music by Flipper and The Mutants. ★★★ $59.99

The Emerald Forest

(1985, 113 min, US, John Boorman) Director Boorman's son Charley plays the kidnapped child of an American engineer stationed deep within the Amazon. Boorman captures the beauty and mystery of these precious rain forests, while weaving subtle messages of the importance of cultural diversity and environmental respect into this taut action-packed adventure. Powers Booth plays the father who spends ten years searching for his son. ★★★½

Emma

(1996, 111 min, GB, Douglas McGrath) Another entry in the avalanche of Jane Austenmania that swept theatres in 1996 is this absolutely charming, albeit somewhat commerical, rendition of her 1815 novel about a meddlesome young woman whose attempts to sow the seeds of romance go hopelessly awry. A radiantly charming Gwyneth Paltrow brings an abundance of youthful exuberance to the title role while exceeding all expectations of her American pop film pedigree. There's an army of British talent surrounding Paltrow, of course, and all excel in supporting roles while lending that air of authenticity that only British actors can. And while her Emma is a peppy, somewhat modernized interpretation (for a more true Austen-esque turn see Kate Beckinsale in the recent A&E version), in the context of director McGrath's fanciful take on the tale, it's right on the money. In other words, though Austen purists might turn up their noses at this film's rather loose spin on the mores of Austen's era, there's simply no reason one shouldn't just get swept up in the sheer fun of it all — and if there's one thing this film has in abundance, it's fun. ★★★½ $19.99

Emma

(1996, 107 min, GB, Diarmuid Lawrence) Will this Jane Austen craze never end? Let's hope not. As long as productions continue to live up to the caliber of this sterling television adaptation, there's room for plenty more. Kate Beckinsale upstages Gwyneth Paltrow's recent take on the title character (though Paltrow brings her own sparkle) with a very mannered but nonetheless mischievous look at Austen's would-be Cupid. Having found true love for her one-time nanny, Emma Woodhouse declares herself a bonafide matchmaker and sets out to sew the seeds of amorous bliss for her best friend. Her plan goes terribly awry, however, and in the end, she's squarely confronted with her own shortcomings. It's a marvelously moral tale that is presented here with all the manners and propriety that Austen herself could have hoped for. Prim and proper, but with just the right mix of impetuous pride and feminine vulnerability, Beckinsale is the ideal choice for Emma and all who enjoy her here should be sure to take in her turn as Flora Poste (a 20th-century Emma) in the hilariously satirical *Cold Comfort Farm* and while you're at it pick up Paltrow's version of *Emma* and enjoy the overdose! ★★★★ $19.99

Emma's Shadow

(1988, 93 min, Denmark, Soeren Kragh-Jacobsen) The unlikely friendship between a willful, lonely 11-year-old girl with a slow-thinking, middle-aged sewer worker is the center of this small but affecting drama set in 1930s Copenhagen. Little rich girl Emma, frustrated by her parents' inattention, stages her own kidnapping and runs away from home, eventually hiding out at Malthe's ramshackle flat in the poor section of town. They form an unlikely alliance — with the clumsy but affectionate man passing the little girl off to his friends and neighbors as his niece. This 1988 Cannes Film Festival winner is a touching, gentle, lyrical movie about two lonely outcasts who find love and understanding. (Danish with English subtitles) ★★★ $19.99

Emmanuelle

(1974, 94 min, France, Just Jaeckin) Until Perrier hit these shores, director Jaeckin's classy come-on reigned as France's most popular export. Sylvia Kristel plays the inquisitive neophyte who sets out to satiate her carnal desires. A film classic which depicts virtually every variation on sexual activity as the heroine pursures the peaks of pleasure and desire. (Dubbed) ★★½

The Emperor Jones

(1933, 72 min, US, Dudley Murphy) The great African-American actor Paul Robeson stars in this film version of Eugene O'Neill's stage play. Robeson plays Brutus Jones, a strong-willed, egotistical railroad pullman who becomes king on a small island in the South Seas. Though the film is rather stagey, it is well worth a look for Robeson's incredibly commanding performance. ★★★ $19.99

Empire of Passion

(1978, 110 min, Japan, Nagisa Oshima) From the director of *Merry Christmas, Mr. Lawrence* and *In the Realm of the Senses* comes this erotic ghost story of unremitting passion and impending doom. A young married peasant woman has an affair with another man. Together, they kill her husband; but, twisting the *Ghost* theme on an ominous tilt, the angry husband comes back to haunt the two. Subtle, visually beautiful and a restrained work. (aka: *In the Realm of Passion*) (Japanese with English subtitles) ★★★ $79.99

Empire of the Air: The Men Who Made Radio

(1991, 120 min, US, Ken Burns) From the maker of the acclaimed "Civil War" series comes this made-for-PBS documentary which details the pioneering work of the inventors who created radio. Covering the years between 1906 and 1955, the film shows not only the developing technologies, including the creation of FM, but it also explores how this new and magical tool united the nation during the Depression and two World Wars as well as dramatically and irrevocably changed our notion of communications. ★★★ $19.99

Empire of the Sun

(1987, 152 min, US, Steven Spielberg) Spielberg's ambitious project is an enthralling, spectacularly filmed if not totally successful tale of a young, privileged British boy (Christian Bale) living in 1940s China who is separated from his parents when the Japanese invade. Sent to an internment camp, the youth quickly adapts to his environment; aided, in part, by sleazy American John Malkovich and frustrated Miranda Richardson. ★★★½ $19.99

Empire State

(1987, 104 min, GB, Ron Peck) Independent filmmaker Peck (*Nighthawks, Strip Jack Naked*) goes "mainstream" with this underworld crime thriller set amidst the 1980s boom of the rapidly gentrifying docklands of London's East End. Seemingly countless characters and subplots are weaved through this violent tale of drugs, scheming real estate speculation, greedy yuppies, bruising boxers, male prostitutes and elegant moles. The central story follows the attempt of a young turk and former male prostitute to try to take over a glitzy gay/straight nightclub. Martin Landau co-stars as a bisexual American businessman who likes rough trade and is willing to pay for it. The provocative though uneven film opens promisingly, but concludes in a mess of unanswered questions. ★★½ $79.99

The Empire Strikes Back

(1980, 124 min, US, Irvin Kershner) This second and best installment of George Lucas' *Star Wars* trilogy picks up the story as the Rebellion, fresh from its destruction of the Death Star, is consolidating its power and internal structure. An Imperial probe droid soon interrupts their work and puts them on the defensive against a newly reorganized and newly vengeful Empire, led by the evil Darth Vader. The Rebel leaders disperse, Luke heading off to a swamp planet to complete his Jedi training, in order to be prepared for the inevitable confrontation with Vader, and Han and Leia taking an extended detour with the droids through an asteroid belt and a city in the clouds. As the title says, however, Darth

E

Vader has been controlling events all along, and he has surprises in store for our heroes, particularly Luke. By far the darkest of the trilogy, *Empire* is the best because there exists, more than in the other two films, the real possibility of evil triumphant. This sustains a high level of tension throughout the film, up until its cliffhanger ending. *Empire* also has the best script of the three, without the western movie clichés of the first film and the commercial pandering of the third. *Empire* improves upon the original and leaves the viewer wanting more, more, more. ★★★★ $19.99

Employees' Entrance

(1933, 75 min, US, Roy Del Ruth) This Depression-era melodrama puts *Wall Street* to shame. Warren William stars as a department store manager who fires employees at the drop of a hat and is constantly fighting the managing directors, but he also keeps profits up. Loretta Young is a new employee who finds herself at odds with him when her fiancé becomes his assistant. Can she keep him from becoming as unscrupulous as the boss? Another in the series "Forbidden Hollywood," there's some racy dialogue and humorous moments. It's a thinly veiled debate about management's treatment of labor and its lack of morality. ★★★ $19.99

An Empty Bed

(1986, 60 min, US, Mark Gasper) This rarity among gay-themed films, focusing on the concerns of elderly gay men, features John Wylie as a gay man in his sixties. The story follows his reflections on his younger days, the choices he has made, and the prospect of an empty bed; for he lives alone, having been unable to commit himself to a relationship. He looks back, not with regret or bitterness, but with a feeling that things could have turned out differently. ★★★ $29.99

Empty Canvas

(1964, 118 min, Italy, Damiano Damiani) International casting of stars for film productions was quite the rage in Europe in the mid-Sixties. Which explains how Bette Davis, with a Southern accent and blond Dutchboy wig, ended up in this interesting but convoluted Italian production. Art student Horst Bucholz's love for a seductive model is frustrated by his domineering and blustery and immensely wealthy mother (Davis). A treat for Davis fans, but overall the story fails to excite. (Filmed in English) ★★

Empty Suitcases

(1980, 55 min, US, Bette Gordon) The politicalization and radicalization of an indecisive young woman is the thread that holds together this absorbing experimental short film by Gordon, director of *Variety*. Utilizing repetitive images, still photography and offscreen narration by a series of different women, the film explores the search for self-discovery and is as well a call-to-arms in the struggle against various forms of oppression. ★★★

Enamorada (In Love)

(1965, 81 min, Mexico, Emilio Fernandez) A classic of the Mexican cinema. Beatriz is the beautiful daughter of a very wealthy man. Jose,

a general committed to social and political change, is deeply in love with her. But the woman, blinded by a life's teaching that class is more important than love, has only contempt for this peasant-born young man. A fiery and passionate tale of love overcoming social pressures. (Spanish with English subtitles) ★★★½

Enchanted April

(1991, 104 min, US, Mike Newell) A heartwarming adaptation of Elizabeth von Arnim's 1922 romantic comedy about four English women who run off to an Italian seaside castle for emotional revitalization. The theme is a familiar one to English literature (uptight Brits flee their rainy island to the Italian sun where they finally let loose, a little) and its done full justice here. Josie Lawrence, Miranda Richardson, Joan Plowright and Polly Walker comprise the foursome which makes the getaway, with Lawrence acting as their divine yet humble inspiration. Alfred Molina, Jim Broadbent and Michael Kitchen give wonderful support as the various men in the women's lives. Filmed in the actual villa in Portofino, Italy, where von Armin penned her book, the film lovingly re-creates the ambience of the era while telling its charming tale of four women who start off as unlikely traveling companions and wind up best of friends. ★★★★ $19.99

The Enchanted Cottage

(1945, 92 min, US, John Cromwell) Isolated from society by physical deformities resulting from different sets of circumstances, a young man and woman learn to see themselves through each other's eyes. Touching performances from Dorothy McGuire and Robert Young elevate what could have been mawkish melodrama. Instead, this is a fantasy parable about the healing power of unconditional love. This film was used as an allegorical reference in Joseph Wambaugh's "The Secrets of Harry Bright." ★★★ $19.99

Encino Man

(1992, 88 min, US, Les Mayfield) In a move that might seem tantamount to box-office suicide, Hollywood has given us a movie starring quite possibly the most irritating creature ever put before the camera: MTV's Pauly Shore. The punchline is...for the most part, it works. Shore plays the world's oldest-looking high school student who becomes part of the in-crowd when his best friend (Sean Astin) unearths a prehistoric man in his backyard. Though a wee bit lethargic in the laughs department, a debuting Brendan Fraser steals the pic hands down with his money's-worth performance as the title character. ★★½ $9.99

Encore

(1952, 87 min, GB, Pat Jackson, Anthony Pelissier & Harold French) An intriguing tril-

Enchanted April

E

ogy based on three short stories by W. Somerset Maugham. In the first, a playboy battles with his brother over money; in the second, an irascible spinster makes life miserable for the unfortunate passengers on an ocean crossing; in the third, a circus high-diver gets the jitters. The cast includes Glynis Johns, Kay Walsh and Nigel Patrick. ★★★½

The End

(1978, 100 min, US, Burt Reynolds) Scandalously funny, this wicked black comedy features Burt Reynolds as a man who is told that he has only a few months to live and decides to commit suicide. Featuring hilarious appearances by Sally Field, Dom DeLuise (particularly deranged as Reynolds' schizophrenic best friend), Joanne Woodward, Carl Reiner, David Steinberg, Kristy McNichol and Robby Benson, who plays a naive priest turned on by Reynolds' "final" confession. The film takes a sharp satiric swipe at the hypocrisy of compassion as well as the sanctity of life. ★★★

The End of St. Petersberg

(1927, 69 min, USSR, Vsevolod Pudovkin) Made on the commemoration of the Tenth Anniversary of the 1917 Revolution, this ambitious drama follows the plight of a common laborer who is forced to leave his failing farm only to then suffer at the hands of capitalist factory owners and eventually witness the horrors of war. The film, in not a subtle fashion, details the pains and humiliation the people had to endure before experiencing the social upheavals and resulting freedoms of the Revolution. (Silent with orchestral accompaniment) ★★★ $29.99

Endangered Species

(1982, 92 min, US, Alan Rudolph) Low-keyed performances enhance this fact-based suspense thriller about a New York detective (Robert Urich) assigned to investigate a string of bizarre cattle mutilations out West. JoBeth Williams co-stars as the country sheriff also on the case. Slow-moving at times, but the patient viewer will be rewarded. Also stars Hoyt Axton. ★★★

Endgame

See: Beckett Directs

Endless Love

(1981, 115 min, US, Franco Zeffirelli) The film which will always be remembered as the butt of Bette Midler's classic Oscar-night joke: "That endless bore – *Endless Love*." It's about two teenagers (Brooke Shields, Martin Hewitt) with the hots for each other. ★ $14.99

Endless Night

(1971, 95 min, GB, Sidney Gilliat) Suspenseful Agatha Christie thriller about a rich American girl (Hayley Mills) who marries her chauffeur (Hywel Bennett). When they move into her mansion, their new life is anything but blissful when blackmail and murder enter the scene. ★★★ $9.99

Endurance

(1985, 90 min, Japan) For those of you who still mourn the cancellation of "The Gong Show," who find derisive pleasure in the misfortunes of others or are glued to the tube

watching the pitiful antics of game show contestants...this is the tape for you! Basically a condensed version of several episodes from one of Japan's favorite TV shows, "Endurance" is a game show of unbelievable sadism – out to prove that every man and woman has their price. The contestants are put through a series of stupid stunts designed to gauge their endurance level for pain, with tactics such as the agonies of the human rack, cannonballs to the backside and consumption of strange, semi-living food. The contestants are driven to ridiculous levels of humiliation all for the chance to be a finalist and win a few million yen. If you view the Japanese as a group of hard-working, serious people, you'll have to rethink that image after you see this wacky and determinedly stupid 90 minutes. ★★½

Enemies: A Love Story

(1989, 119 min, US, Paul Mazursky) Featuring a superb evocation of post-WWII New York, director Mazursky has created a career milestone with this darkly comic tale about a Jewish immigrant (Ron Silver), scarred from his wartime experiences, who suddenly finds himself with three wives. An extraordinary cast includes Anjelica Huston as his strong-willed first wife thought killed in the camps; Margaret Sophie Stein as his gentile, slave-like second; and the remarkable Lena Olin as a lusty socialist whose passion most ignites the stolid Silver. ★★★★ $9.99

The Enemy Below

(1957, 98 min, US, Dick Powell) Solid WWII yarn with Robert Mitchum as an American warship commander, and Curt Jurgens as a Nazi U-boat captain engaged in a battle of wits as the Yanks hunt down a German sub. As in the much-later *The Hunt for Red October*, the film explores the interpersonal relationships between the men of both crews, and also features Oscar-winning special effects. ★★★ $19.99

Enemy Mine

(1985, 108 min, US, Wolfgang Petersen) From the director of *Das Boot* comes this visually striking sci-fi adventure about two interplanetary enemies, a pilot from Earth and a warrior from the planet Drac, who become stranded together on a distant, deserted planet. Dennis Quaid and Lou Gossett, Jr. star in this space-age *Hell in the Pacific*. ★★★ $9.99

The Enemy Within

(1994, 86 min, US, Jonathan Darby) In this updated remake of *Seven Days in May*, the president (Sam Waterston) has seven days to sign a bill which increases the military budget by 30%. He does not intend to sign it. Forest Whitaker turns in a solid performance as the colonel who inadvertently uncovers a plot to overthrow the presidency – perpetrated by the U.S. military. Jason Robards exudes controlled mania as the general who orchestrates the mil-

L'Enfer

itary maneuvers to be executed in support of a manipulation of the Constitution. The strong cast includes Josef Sommers, George Dzundza and Dana Delany. A tautly paced and finely detailed HBO production – let's hope Newt doesn't watch it. ★★★ $19.99

Les Enfants Terribles

(1950, 107 min, France, Jean-Pierre Melville) A landmark of French cinema and a strong influence on the New Wave filmmakers, this collaboration with Jean Cocteau (who scripted the film and oversaw its production) is a haunting cinematic poem about the love and confused narcissism of a brother and sister, whose passion for each other is so intense that it flowers into perversity and eventual death. Please note that the only available videos of this classic, taken from a 16mm film, are in only fair condition. (French with English subtitles) ★★★ $29.99

L'Enfer

(1993, 100 min, France, Claude Chabrol) There's an unsettling discord between the open, sun-drenched country inn where *l'Enfer* is set, and the spiralling descent into madness which the film depicts. A husband (François Cluzet) becomes increasingly obsessional regarding his wife's (Emmanuelle Béart) supposed infidelities. While the film is sometimes ambivalent about her actual culpability, there is no doubt that Cluzet has crossed into a reality of his own making. Chabrol's masterly command of the medium allows the viewer to enter the mind of a man driven to hallucinatory extremes fueled by his paranoid distrust. The great director Henri-Georges Clouzot wrote the screenplay in 1963 with the intent of directing it. Although this rendition is different in tone from what we could have expected from that treatment, *L'Enfer* still retains Clouzot's dark edge. This is a spectacularly wrought mystery and a frightening examination of one man's self-induced hell. (French with English subtitles) ★★★★ $19.99

The Enforcer

(1951, 87 min, US, Bretaigne Windust) Tough Humphrey Bogart drama with Bogey as a hard-boiled district attorney out to break a crime ring. Zero Mostel and Everett Sloane co-star. (Not to be confused with the Clint Eastwood police drama.) ★★★ $19.99

The Enforcer

(1976, 96 min, US, James Fargo) Clint Eastwood encores as Dirty Harry in this third installment of the series. Tyne Daly co-stars as his partner as they comb San Francisco in search of a terrorist group. ★★★ $14.99

The English Patient

(1996, 162 min, GB, Anthony Minghella) From its opening frames, *The English Patient* evokes an exhilarating sense of time and place. Told with sweeping economy and the lyricism and tempo that only great art can author, this breathlessly romantic and impassioned epic is a rare reminder of the pleasures made available from consummate filmmaking. Intimate in scope but set within a sprawling framework, the story effortlessly narrates two time periods: pre-war Northern Africa and war-torn WWII Italy. In a superb, brooding portrayal both sensuous and aloof, Ralph Fiennes plays a severely burned amnesiac. Tended by a caring nurse (the wonderful, Oscar-winning Juliette Binoche) dealing with her own scars, his love affair with a married woman is told through flashback. Kristin Scott Thomas revels in the role of the beautiful sophisticate, giving a smart, alluring performance. Adapted from Michael Ondaatje's celebrated novel by director Minghella, *The English Patient* is keenly observed and replete with the kind of romanticism and intelligent dialogue audiences ache for. Minghella's visual style is extraordinary — his filmic instinct here suggests no less an artist than David Lean. Winner of 9 Academy Awards, including Best Picture and Best Director. ★★★★ $102.99

An Englishman Abroad

(1985, 63 min, GB, John Schlesinger) Alan Bates gives a riveting performance in this brilliantly staged drama made for British TV. Based on a true incident, the film casts Bates as Guy Burgess, the infamous British spy, traitor and gay outcast who defected to Russia in the 1940s. During a 1958 theatrical performance in Moscow featuring visiting actress Coral Browne (appearing as herself), a drunken Burgess promptly crashes backstage and sets up a friendship with the actress — desperate for Anglo companionship, cigarettes, drink and gossip from home. Browne, who is intrigued by this disheveled and eccentric outsider, comes to pity, despise and assist him after he invites her to his shabby flat — and comes to understand this almost broken man. A touching and humorous film with a witty, concise screenplay. ★★★★ $49.99

The Englishman Who Went Up a Hill, But Came Down a Mountain

(1995, 99 min, GB, Christopher Monger) Recalling the effervescence and whimsy of those wonderful Ealing comedies of the '50s and '60s, *The Englishman Who Went Up a Hill...* is a thoroughly engaging if understated romp which charms at the most unexpected moments. Set in 1917, the film stars Hugh Grant as an English mapmaker who travels to a small Welsh village to measure the town's mountain, which appears to be the only source of pride for the villagers. When they discover their mountain's height only qualifies as a hill, and will therefore be ineligible to be included on the map, the entire populace engages in a crazy scheme to make up the difference and to keep Grant in town to remeasure it. Director Monger sets an easygoing pace which befits the story's unconventional comedy and budding romance, and an excellent supporting cast — including Colm Meaney as a randy barkeeper, Ian Hart as a shell-shocked youth, Tara Fitzgerald as a beautiful decoy, and the very amusing Kenneth Griffiths as the local priest — displays an abundance of character and wit. ★★★ $19.99

Enjo

(1958, 98 min, Japan, Kon Ichikawa) Although *Enjo* takes place in a world that is alien to most of us, there are emotions explored that transcend all bounderies. Goichi Mizoguchi (Raizo Ichikawa) is a young monk who is lonely and misunderstood. After his father's death, Mizoguchi leaves his poor temple and arrives at the famous Shukaku temple. He is accepted at first by the head priest who is an old friend of his father's. But Mizoguchi soon proves to be inept at most everything he tries, with exception to his love for the temple. While political infighting and scandal dominate the rest of the monks' time, Mizoguchi only wants to care for Shukaku. A stutterer who soon withdraws into a silent world, Mizoguchi becomes ostracized. It is only years later in a defiant act that Mizoguchi can keep his beloved temple pure. Told almost entirely in tiered flashbacks and beautifully shot, *Enjo* is another masterpiece from Ichikawa (*The Burmese Harp*). Based on Yukio Mishima's novel. (Japanese with English subtitles) ★★★½ $79.99

Enormous Changes at the Last Minute

(1983, 115 min, US, Mirra Bank & Ellen Hovde) Based on the charming, humanistic tales of novelist Grace Paley, *Enormous Changes...* unites a crisp John Sayles-Susan Rice script and glorious performances by Ellen Barkin, Kevin Bacon, Maria Tucci and Lynn Milgran. This trilogy from Paley's second collection glistens with the dignity of contemporary urban women struggling against setbacks but determined to get their fair share from life. A funny, gracefully optimistic work. ★★★ $79.99

Enter the Dragon

(1973, 98 min, US, Robert Clouse) The first American/Hong Kong co-production is arguably the best martial arts film ever made. Starring Bruce Lee (in his last film), with Americans John Saxon, Jim Kelly and Bob Wall with an ensemble of international karate champions. ★★★½ $14.99

The Entertainer

(1960, 97 min, GB, Tony Richardson) Laurence Olivier gives an extraordinary performance in Richardson's depiction of a seedy vaudevillian on the skids who unwittingly destroys those around him. As the egotistical Archie Rice, Olivier captures the grotesque demeanor and futile yearnings of a defeated man. Based on John Osborne's play. ★★★½ $9.99

Entertaining Mr. Sloane

(1970, 94 min, GB, Douglas Hickox) Playwright Joe Orton's scathing black comedy about a young stud's entry into the lives of a middle-aged brother and sister. Beryl Reid is the sex-starved, man-hungry sister, Harry Andrews is her latently homosexual brother and Peter McEnery is the menacing hustler. This is a superbly acted and boldly presented rendition of one of Britain's most daring late-great playwrights. ★★★

Entre Nous

(1983, 110 min, France, Diane Kurys) Kurys' largely autobiographical work is a beautiful rendering of the strength and complexity of friendship. Isabelle Huppert portrays Lena, a reticent housewife resigned to the numbing security of her husband and family. Through a chance encounter, she meets Madeleine (Miou-Miou), a vibrantly bohemian sculptress whose

The English Patient

Entertaining Mr. Sloan

love and companionship open the door to Lena's self-discovery. The film radiates with the delicate nuances of a woman's sensibility and sensuality. (French with English subtitles) ★★★★ $19.99

Equinox

(1993, 107 min, US, Alan Rudolph) An elderly, indigent woman lies dying in a New York City street. She clutches a scrap of paper, closed with sealing wax, which catches the eye of a curious, would-be-writer morgue attendant, initiating a quest to uncover the truth behind a 30-year-old blind trust. Director Rudolph's relentless pacing is magnified by the constant, pounding ambient noise which underscores the desperation of characters tightly interwoven by proximity but with no emotional contact. As is usual with Rudolph films, there's an eclectic mix of talented players, here including Matthew Modine, Lara Flynn Boyle, Tyra Ferrell, Marisa Tomei, Kevin J. O'Connor, M. Emmet Walsh and Fred Ward. Modine is especially effective in a dual role, careening from frightened helplessness to cold-blooded tough guy to goofy dreamer. Every element of the production is on-target and highlighted by a mesmerizing soundtrack. The closing shot is a knock-out. ★★★½ $19.99

Equinox Flower

(1958, 118 min, Japan, Yasujiro Ozu) Ozu's deceptively serene style of filmmaking is showcased in this family drama about the post-war generation gap between a tradition-bound businessman and his more modern-minded daughter. Although sympathetic to the independence of his friends' children, Hirayama confronts rebellion in his own family after his daughter announces her engagement to a young man without seeking his approval. Shooting from about three feet from the ground with a rock-steady camera and featuring a bold use of color (his first film in color), Ozu provides a gentle drama of familial misunderstanding and reconciliation, a beautifully designed and moving work. (Japanese with English subtitles) ★★★ $69.99

Equus

(1977, 138 min, US, Sidney Lumet) Peter Shaffer's shattering play is faithfully brought to the screen with Richard Burton as the troubled psychiatrist who attempts to unlock the secret which triggered a disturbed stable boy (Peter Firth) to blind six horses. ★★★ $14.99

Eraser

(1996, 115 min, US, Charles Russell) Arnold Schwarzenegger's megabudget action movies are now so ingrained in the American consciousness that they have nearly attained a status not unlike Greek mythology: Everybody knows the stories and how they'll end. So the spectacle of getting from start to finish is what matters — just add explosions. This story-lite, gun-heavy vehicle is one of the worst offenders. Combining plot elements from a half-dozen earlier (and better) Schwarze-negger efforts with a dash of industrial/secret government espionage from *Mission: Impossible* (which is also much better), *Eraser* gives us Arnold as a U.S. Marshal charged with protecting star witness Vanessa Williams. He's usually good at witness protection and relocation, but this time our heroic "tree trunk" is up against one of his own guys. *Eraser* works on a (very) brainless level: it's relatively full of stunts and explosions, but even these are of the by-the-numbers variety. It's all been done before, and will only entertain diehard fans. ★★ $19.99

Eraserhead

(1977, 90 min, US, David Lynch) Lynch's fiendish cult classic adopts the logic of dreams and nightmares as layers of reality dissolve, sucking you into the eerie world of a warped mind. The befuddled "hero" Henry struggles against the powers of the shrinking mutant slab in this demented gem which promises that in heaven, everything is fine. Starring Jack Nance, and based, in part, on the director's brief stay in Philadelphia. ★★★½

Erendira

(1982, 103 min, Mexico/France/West Germany, Ruy Guerra) Director Guerra paints a surreal fresco of passion and revenge in this darkly humorous tale of a young girl forced into prostitution by her demented grandmother (Irene Papas). Based on a short story by Gabriel García Márquez. (Spanish with English subtitles) ★★★ $24.99

Erik the Viking

(1989, 100 min, GB, Terry Jones) Monty Python-ite Jones directed this funny, offbeat comic adventure which dares to ask the pertinent question, "Why rape, pillage and kill if you don't really feel like it?" Tim Robbins stars as the sensitive Norseman, Erik, who questions the rather violent way of life of a 12th-century Viking after he is affected by a woman he has accidentally killed. Also starring are Mickey Rooney as Erik's gnarled, slam-on-the-back father, John Cleese as the epitome of a calculating dark lord, and director Jones as the king of an island teeming with Julie Andrews wannabes. ★★½ $9.99

Ermo

(1995, 93 min, China, Zhou Xiaowen) Not the uproarious comedy the video box would imply, *Ermo* is actually a scathing social satire on the rapidly changing economic and political changes currently underway in Communist China. Set in that country's impoverished rural interior, the story focuses on Ermo, a pretty young woman who, despite a husband and children, becomes determined to "keep up with the Jones'" in her effort to own the biggest (and almost only) television in the village. In order to get the money for her dream appliance, Ermo becomes the epitome of a capitalist-crazed entrepreneur when she turns her simple homemade noodles into an ever-expanding enterprise — determined to leave no pot un-noodled in this quest. For the politicos, it can be seen as an indictment on the encroaching (and soulless) consumerism and for others less didactically inclined, simply a wry comedy-drama about ambition, family and the hidden joys of the simple ways of life. (Mandarin with English subtitles) ★★★ $99.99

The Ernest Green Story

(1991, 101 min, US) This stirring, superb production from the Disney family entertainment line tells the true story of the first black student to graduate from a white high school in the South. Battling intense hatred, the Arkansas government and even the Arkansas National Guard, nine brave teenagers chose to take a stand for equal education by leaving the safety of their black high school to enroll in a prestigious white Little Rock school. Ossie Davis, CCH Pounder and Morris Chestnut top an excellent cast of relative unknowns to produce a flawless reenactment of these almost forgotten heroes. ★★★★ $39.99

Ernestine: Peak Performances

(1969-1985, 15 min, US) With a running time of only 15 minutes, it is hard to figure out why this collection of clips of Lily Tomlin's hilarious character, Ernestine, was not added onto another tape. Short in running time, but long on laughs, Ernestine appears in all of her tacky obnoxiousness in skits from "Laugh-In," "Saturday Night Live" and an Emmy Awards ceremony. ★★★ $19.99

Ernesto

(1979, 95 min, Italy, Salvatore Samperi) This lush period drama revolves around the emotional and sexual coming-of-age of an impetuous Italian teenager who quickly discovers the power of youth, beauty and money. Set in the town of Trieste in 1911, the story follows Ernesto, the son of a wealthy merchant who, wielding his emerging sexuality with wanton abandon, becomes involved with a hunky stevedore, only to cruelly discard him. The lad immediately enters into an unlikely love triangle with a younger boy and his twin sister. Throughout his amorous romps, Ernesto — not a particularly likable youth — remains a figure of vacillating loyalties and reckless sexuality. The handsome Michele Placido is perfectly cast as the helplessly infatuated workman. (Italian with English subtitles) ★★★ $79.99

Erotic in Nature

(1985, 90 min, US, Cris Cassidy & Lee Rothermund) Soft-core porn for New Age Dykes. Tigress Productions serves up this story about two lovers, Kit Marseilles and Cris

Cassidy, as they explore each other's passions and bodies. ★★

Erotikus: History of the Gay Movie

(1975, 70 min, US, L. Brooks) The birth, maturation and eventual proliferation of gay erotic cinema is chronicled in this dated but interesting documentary narrated by superstar porno director Fred Halsted. The film explores the beginnings of gay erotica with physique magazines of the '50s and '60s and its evolution onto the big screen with the "innocent" bodybuilding films from the Apollo and Guild Studios. The film's historical approach to the evolution of gay filmmaking goes from the suggestive to the explicit when the film segues into a sexual montage of highlights from several hard-core films of the 1970s. Halsted's humorous recounting of this "art form" keeps it interesting but doesn't explore the explosion of male adult films in the '80s which has been brought about by the video revolution. ★★½ $19.99

Erotique

(1994, 120 min, US/Germany/Hong Kong, Lizzie Borden, Monika Treut, Ana Maria Magalhäes & Clara Law) A vastly uneven omnibus film that features four 30-minute shorts by women directors all of which share the theme of sexual fantasies as seen through feminist eyes/imagination. Borden's *Let's Talk about Sex* follows a feisty Latina woman who, while working as a phone-sex operator, becomes obsessed with one of her male customers. It is interesting more for what it attempts than for what it accomplishes. *Taboo Parlor*, by Treut, is a wonderfully decadent if controversial tale of female exploitation by a pair of lipstick lesbians. The two lovers decide to add spice to their already active sex life by picking up a posturing male and having their way with him. Though it's sensual and surprisingly funny, some may either miss or not appreciate its sardonic viewpoint (heterosexual men especially). *Final Call*, by Magalhäes, is a minor story of a woman getting it on with

Escape from L.A.

the man who rescued her from a sexual assault. The young lovers do have some steamy scenes. Probably the most accomplished of the four is Law's *Wonton Soup*, a witty, atmospheric story of two college lovers reunited in Hong Kong. The acting has warmth and depth, and the writing is clever. And it's damn steamy, too. ★★ $89.99

Escape from Alcatraz

(1980, 112 min, US, Don Siegel) A true story of the only three men ever to escape from Alcatraz. Clint Eastwood stars as Frank Morris, the bank robber who masterminds the escape. An exciting and accomplished thriller. ★★★½ $14.99

Escape from L.A.

(1996, 100 min, US, John Carpenter) Both a remake and a sequel to his 1981 cult classic *Escape from New York*, Carpenter's *Escape from L.A.* marks the return of the world's most unlikely one-eyed hero, Snake Plissken (Kurt Russell). This time, he must enter the island of Los Angeles, now serving as a spot of exile for those deemed undesirable to the fascist regime ruling what remains of the United States. There he has to retrieve both a lethal satellite control mechanism and the president's loony daughter, in that order. Standing in his way are a revolutionary leader within the fallen city, and a variety of ne'er-do-wells including a braindead surfer (Peter Fonda), Map to the Stars Eddie (Steve Buscemi), and a transsexual soldier named Hershey (Pam Grier). Unfortunately, the movie itself does not live up to this grand premise. Fans of the first film may be entertained as Carpenter and Russell cover much of the same ground in a slightly different way, but overall the lackluster computer effects, forced humor and sense of "we've seen all this before" work too much against it. ★★½ $14.99

Escape from New York

(1981, 106 min, US, John Carpenter) In 1997, New York City is a walled, barricaded maximum security prison. Air Force One, with the president aboard, is hijacked and crash lands inside the prison. Snake Plissken (Kurt Russell), one-time war hero and just sentenced to life, is volunteered as a one-man rescue team. *Escape from New York* effectively blends action-adventure and tongue-in-cheek comedy with consistently engaging performances from its cast. Imbued with trademark Carpenter directorial touches, not the least of which is the musical score, this director's cut includes the original trailer and a revealing interview with Carpenter; and the availability of letterboxing for the first time allows full appreciation of the director's ability to frame a shot. (The director's cut version) ★★★½ $19.99

Escape from the Planet of the Apes

(1971, 97 min, US, J. Lee Thompson) In the third entry of the *Apes* series, futuristic apes Roddy McDowall and Kim Hunter travel back in time to present-day Los Angeles. Though all the *Ape* sequels lack the energy and creative spark of the first film, this is nevertheless a lot of fun and the simian cast is clearly enjoying itself. Also with Ricardo Montalban and Sal Mineo. ★★★ $19.99

Escape Me Never

(1947, 103 min, US, Peter Godfrey) Ida Lupino sparkles as the waif with a heart o' gold in this musical melodrama set in northern Italy. She's a single mother crooning for her cappucino while her beau, charming composer Errol Flynn, smooth-operates on aristocrat Eleanor Parker. Even after making an honest woman out of Lupino, Flynn can't curb his lust for artistic freedom, or for Parker. Will he choose Fanella, the cool high-society girl, or Gemma, the one who truly understands the cad and his concertinas? Predictable yes, but Lupino is a delight. ★★½ $19.99

Escape to Witch Mountain

(1975, 97 min, US, John Hough) Two orphans with psychic powers search for their origins with the help of Eddie Albert, in one of Disney's better mystery/fantasies. With Donald Pleasence as a psychic investigator and Ray Milland as an evil tycoon. ★★★ $19.99

L'Etat Sauvage

(1978, 111 min, France, Francis Girod) An unusually hard-hitting French political thriller that deals with the ambiguous relationship and underlying racism between France and one of her former colonies — a developing central African country. Set in the early 1960s, the story revolves around a young French couple who find themselves adrift in the politically charged atmosphere of a recently established black state. The man (Jacques Dutronc) is an UNESCO official who finds that his wife (Marie-Christine Barrault) is having an illicit affair with the powerful Minister of Health. Filmed under the punishing sun of French Guinea, the film is an accomplished and taut drama of corruption, hatred and deceit. Michel Piccoli gives a memorable performance as a shrewd and deliberately impotent police chief. (French with English subtitles) ★★★

L'Été Meurtrier (One Deadly Summer)

(1983, 134 min, France, Jean Becker) This sizzling psychological drama captured four Césars in 1983, including the Best Actress Award for Isabelle Adjani. The story is set in a provincial village where a cartoonish tramp, played to the hilt by Adjani, struts into town throwing male libidos into a frenzy. Though dismissed as a whore by the townsfolk, little do they know that beneath the unpredictable exterior lurks a cunningly vengeful woman, determined to wipe away the remembrances of a haunting personal tragedy. (French with English subtitles) ★★★

The Eternal Return

(1943, 100 min, France, Jean Delannoy) Written by Jean Cocteau, this modern retelling of the Tristan and Isolde legend is a lavishly romantic and tender love story. Jean Marais is Patrice, the nephew of a wealthy widower, who arranges a marriage (albeit loveless) between Nathalie, a beautiful young woman he meets, and his uncle. With the help of a love potion, Patrice and Nathalie are irrevocably attracted to each other, threatening the family with their forbidden love. A poetic fable of tragic love reminiscent of Cocteau's classic, *Beauty and the*

171

Beast. (French with English subtitles) (aka: *Love Eternal)* ★★★ $29.99

Ethan Frome

(1993, 107 min, US, John Madden) Anyone who has read Edith Wharton's bleak tale of one man's catastrophic grasp at passion knows its movie adaptation is not destined to be "the feel good hit of the season." Liam Neeson is perfectly cast as the poor farmer whose desire for his wife's cousin (Patricia Arquette) ends in a tragic accident. Neeson's face transforms from twisted and bitter to smooth and handsome as this classic tale flashes between post- and pre-accident. Arquette is similarly well-suited, eschewing coquettishness for a more heart-pounding, lump-in-your-throat, clumsy sense of desire. As one would expect, the pace is slow and there is rarely any relief from the oppressiveness of the story, but the superb acting and intensity of its emotions more than compensate. ★★★ $19.99

Eubie!

(1979, 85 min, US, Julianne Boyd) Live version of the Broadway musical, a rousing tribute to the legendary composer Eubie Blake. Gregory and Maurice Hines repeat their acclaimed stage roles in a series of songs and dances, featuring Blake's best-loved works, including "I'm Just Wild About Harry," "In Honeysuckle Time" and "Shuffle Along," among many others. ★★★½

Eureka

(1983, 130 min, GB, Nicolas Roeg) Roeg's tale of a gold prospector (Gene Hackman) who strikes it rich in the Yukon and, years later, must fight gangsters and a son-in-law who might be a sorcerer is told in the director's familiar mythic style. His trademarks — breath-taking cinematography, jagged editing, and temporal jumps — are all present in this mystical story of greed and lust. ★★½ $14.99

Europa, Europa

(1991, 110 min, France/Germany, Agnieszka Holland) This sweeping statement on the resilience of the human spirit is one of the most powerful films to address the Holocaust in recent years. A brilliant mix of gut-wrenching drama and dark humor, *Europa, Europa* is based on the harrowing true story of Solomon Perel, a Jewish teenager who miraculously survived the war by passing himself off as Aryan; so well, in fact, that he unwittingly wound up in the Nazi Youth. Similar in theme to Jerzy Kozinski's novel, "The Painted Bird," the film features a young protagonist set adrift in a historical tide of events beyond his control, desperately clinging to his identity while at the same time having to forsake it. It's a moral dilemma which would push most to the breaking point. Polish filmmaker Holland adeptly seizes Solomon's story and punctuates the horror of his situation without overemphasizing the psychological strain such an ordeal might have had on its young hero. (German and Russian with English subtitles) ★★★★ $19.99

The Europeans

(1979, 92 min, US, James Ivory) Lee Remick stars in this lush adaptation of Henry James' novel about a 19th-century New England family whose lives are disrupted by the arrival of two European cousins — one a meddlesome, fortune-hunting countess. ★★★

Europa, Europa

Eve and the Handyman

(1960, 65 min, US, Russ Meyer) At times reminiscent of a Buster Keaton silent comedy, this early work by Meyer emphasizes sight gags and features a detective novel-style narrative by Eve Meyer as she tracks her man through his daily routine, noting his attempts to ignore a series of trademark Meyer women. Filmed on location in San Francisco, and featuring a thumping strip-tease soundtrack, *Eve and the Handyman* comments on sex and society in a lighter fashion than Meyer's later works. ★★½ $79.99

Eve of Destruction

(1991, 95 min, US, Duncan Gibbons) Renee Soutendijk, sexy star of *Spetters* and *The 4th Man*, is superbly preposterous as a spike-heeled, nuclear warhead-equipped humanoid on the loose in this otherwise disappointing sci-fi thriller. Eve VIII, an experimental cyborg invented by a sexually repressed doctor (also played by Soutendijk), is accidentally activated and becomes stuck in her "Battlefield mode" of programming. With single-minded determination, our supercharged heroine is every misogynist's worst nightmare as she plows her way cross country, destroying all in her path. A stiff Gregory Hines, acting as though this were Shakespearean drama, is ridiculous as the determined cop on her bloody trail. A great idea never realized. ★½ $14.99

Even Cowgirls Get the Blues

(1994, 100 min, US, Gus Van Sant) A disappointingly vapid and lifeless misfire, this attempt to capture the hippie-dippy effervescence of Tom Robbins' 1976 novel completely fails to come to cinematic life. Uma Thurman plays the pleasant if vacuous Sissy Hankshaw, a young beauty who is blessed/cursed with abnormally large thumbs and who lives the free life of the road. Encouraged by "The Countess" (an over-the-top faggy John Hurt) to visit his dude ranch, Sissy soon becomes embroiled in a cowgirl uprising headed by the "charismatic" Bonanza Jellybean (the catatonic Rain Phoenix). The two become romantically involved, and their affair is the best-handled aspect of the film. Though a failure on every level, and saddled by its attempts to be both post-modern camp and politically and sexually relevant, *Cowgirls* is nonetheless easy to watch and does sport moments of fun. ★★ $19.99

The Evening Star

(1996, 129 min, US, Robert Harling) Shirley MacLaine repeats her *Terms of Endearment* Oscar-winning role as Aurora Greenway in this strained if occasionally compelling sequel. *The Evening Star* takes place 13 years after the death of Aurora's daughter Emma (played in the original by Debra Winger). Aurora has raised her three grandchildren, but they are mostly problem kids who have little time or affection for their meddling grandmother. As the jagged, episodic story introduces its characters, Aurora tentatively initiates an affair with a younger man (Bill Paxton); her teenaged granddaughter (Juliette Lewis) is ready to run away to Los Angeles; and Emma's best friend Patsy (Miranda Richardson) is still around to raise Aurora's ire. *The Evening Star*, though often funny, doesn't have the original's rich material exploring the complex relationship between mother and daughter. And it's manipulative and sentimental. But it has a surprising emotional impact, probably due to the very able cast. MacLaine has lost none of Aurora's sting, and Marion Ross is delectable as the family housekeeper. Oh, Jack's back, too. ★★½ $102.99

An Evening with Quentin Crisp

(1980, 91 min, US, James Cady & Arthur Mele) Floridly disclaiming to be simply "a straight talk from a bent speaker," Quentin Crisp's performance piece/lecture filmed in front of an appreciative audience is full of the celebrity's Wildean witticisms and droll reflections on living as a gay man in the late 20th century. Patently outrageous and always entertaining, the British-born author ("The Naked Civil Servant" and "How to Watch Movies"), promising "a consultation with a psychiatrist who is madder than you are," holds court as he offers helpful hints, droll opinions and practical advice on such subjects as the avoidance of dreary housework, how to be yourself, how to dress and look smart, and how, generally, to live with style regardless of one's economic situation. Introduced by John Hurt, who memorably played him in the film version of his book, *The Naked Civil Servant*. ★★★

Evergreen

(1934, 91 min, GB, Victor Saville) Saville's musical comedy features a dazzling performance from Jessie Matthews as a young unemployed chorus girl who rises to fame by imitating her long-retired, but once-famous, mother. Fabulous set pieces make a wonderful backdrop for Matthews' splendid dancing. Punctuated by a lively Rodgers and Hart score. ★★★½ $39.99

The Everlasting Secret Family

(1987, 93 min, Australia, Michael Thornhill) With an outrageous premise – a highly organized secret society of pederasts stalk area schools for young male victims whom they then ravage and reprogram to their way of life – this is an enjoyably ludicrous drama that despite its sinister idea, still makes for strangely riveting, erotically charged entertainment. Mark Lee (*Gallipoli*) plays a gorgeous young boy who is spirited away by a wealthy middle-aged senator. He soon tolerates the sex and begins to enjoy the power and prestige he attains as the "boy-toy" of the politician. But as is wont for a finicky pederast, the senator soon drops him for younger flesh. Now fully indoctrinated into the society, and aging rapidly, Mark must go off himself in search of an innocent victim; and the boy he chooses is the senator's young son! Enjoyable camp once you ignore its incendiary harangues. ★★ $79.99

Every Day's a Holiday

(1937, 79 min, US, A. Edward Sutherland) The imitable Mae West tips her hat to the screwball genre with this amusing romp set at the turn of the century. Written by West, the story follows Mae as con artist/performer Peaches O'Day and her series of misadventures trying to elude the police, masquerade as a dark-haired French chanteuse, and organize a mayoral race. Mae manages to turn a catch-phrase or two ("Keep a diary, and someday it'll

keep you"), but most of the film's comedy is courtesy of lots of hair-brained hijinks. This may be the best supporting cast West has worked with, and it includes Walter Catlett, Charles Butterworth, and Charles Winninger as a society gent whose gallop is one in a million. Louis Armstrong appears in a cameo, and Mae proves herself quite handy with a pair of drumsticks. ★★★ $14.99

Every Girl Should Be Married

(1948, 84 min, US, Don Hartman) In a role reversal from most `30s and `40s comedies, shopgirl Betsy Drake sets her eyes on eligible bachelor Cary Grant, and *she* pursues *him*. Of course, Grant is happily unmarried with a preference to stay that way, and Drake has her hands full convincing him otherwise. Grant's charm makes this ordinary comedy more frothy than it really is. ★★½ $19.99

Every Man for Himself and God Against All

(1974, 110 min, West Germany, Werner Herzog) A young man, imprisoned in a cellar and locked away from society for most of his life, reemerges and must begin the arduous task of readjusting to an illogical and iniquitous world. Bruno S. gives an astounding performance as Kasper Hauser. The film is also known as *The Mystery of Kasper Hauser*. (German with English subtitles) ★★★½ $59.99

Every Which Way But Loose

(1978, 115 min, US, James Fargo) Amazingly, this boisterous, feeble backwoods comic adventure of a barroom brawler and his pet orangutan is Clint Eastwood's most successful film in terms of ticket sales to date. Go figure. Clint has certainly done better (and so has Clyde). Followed by a sequel, *Any Which Way You Can*. ★★ $14.99

Everybody Wins

(1990, 98 min, US, Karel Reisz) Nick Nolte is a small-town private investigator hired by local free-spirit Debra Winger to prove a friend innocent of murder. Ill-conceived from the start, the ludicrous screenplay is by Arthur Miller. Not even Nolte and Winger can salvage this disaster. ★ $89.99

Everybody's All-American

(1988, 127 min, US, Taylor Hackford) An involving drama about love and broken dreams with Dennis Quaid as a college football star and Jessica Lange as his beauty queen girlfriend who marry and search for the American Dream. ★★★ $14.99

Everybody's Fine

(1991, 115 min, Italy, Giuseppe Tornatore) Much less saccharine than his delightful arthouse hit *Cinema Paradiso*, director Tornatore's family drama is a bittersweet tale of illusion and disenchantment. Marcello Mastroianni stars as a simple old man who decides to visit his five "successful and happy" grown children who are dispersed throughout Italy. Unprepared for his surprise visits, his children try to bolster his mistaken belief that they lead problem-free lives, but their charades quickly fall apart forcing him to come to grips with reality and let go of his cherished and ideal-

ized images of their childhoods. (Italian with English subtitles) ★★★ $19.99

Everyone Says I Love You

(1996, 100 min, US, Woody Allen) Not everyone will be echoing the sentiments of the title of Allen's musical comedy valentine to New York, Paris and big city neurotics. Often entertaining and funny though insubstantial with lightweight character development, the film is a pastiche of bygone Hollywood musicals where characters just break into song. But whereas those musicals featured performers with good voices, here actors not known for their singing talents (and for good reason) use their own voices. A few are used to good effect (Goldie Hawn, Edward Norton), but most are not. It's a distracting gimmick, and an audience (especially with the high cost of movie tickets) has a right to expect professionalism in all aspects of the filmmaking process. Hawn is radiant as Allen's ex-wife, and the two engage in a wonderful dance sequence on the banks of the Seine. There's also a nifty song-and-dance number at Harry Winston's; however, even in light of several lively numbers, the effect as a whole is less satisfying. ★★½ $102.99

Everything You Always Wanted to Know About Sex...

(1972, 87 min, US, Woody Allen) Allen's hilarious assault on Dr. David Reuben's ridiculous best-seller is full of crude jokes, potentially obscene skits and Woody's unforgettable portrayal of the reluctant, existential sperm. Woody is aided and abetted by the likes of Burt Reynolds, Gene Wilder, Tony Randall, Lynn Redgrave and Lou Jacobi. ★★★ $14.99

Evil Cat

(1987, 90 min, Hong Kong, Dennis Yu) Incredible fantasy-based martial arts/horror flick where an ancient cat-like being enters our world from a subterranean home to unleash its destruction of our society. ★★★½ $59.99

The Evil Dead

(1983, 85 min, US, Sam Raimi) This low-budget horror film has more scares in it than all the *Friday the 13th*'s put together. Five friends head to the woods for a secluded, quiet weekend. However, things are anything but quiet when they awaken a demonic spirit. Director Raimi concentrates more on the suspense than the gore (though there's plenty of that, too), which immediately separates it from the usual, mindless horror film. Bruce Campbell stars, and returns in the sequel. ★★★

Evil Dead II

(1987, 85 min, US, Sam Raimi) In this spectacularly entertaining and frightening horror sequel, director Raimi accomplishes the near-impossible: he tops his terrific original. Bruce Campbell returns once again to battle the demonic spirits at that secluded cabin in the woods. There's a lot more humor here, and the special effects are sensational. Campbell gives an over-the-top performance which helps immensely in the enjoyment of this outrageously original chiller. Followed by *Army of Darkness*. (Letterboxed version) ★★★½ $14.99

The Evil of Frankenstein

(1964, 98 min, GB, Freddie Francis) Dr. Frankenstein discovers that his monster has been preserved in ice, but has fallen under the spell of a hypnotist and is rampaging once again. Peter Cushing plays Doctor Frank in this entertaining Hammer Films production. ★★ $14.99

Evil under the Sun

(1982, 112 min, GB, Guy Hamilton) Peter Ustinov returns as Hercule Poirot in this Agatha Christie mystery. Though not up to par with *Murder on the Orient Express* or *Death on the Nile*, this effective whodunit will nevertheless keep you guessing right up to the end. Poirot investigates the murder of a bitchy actress. Maggie Smith, Roddy McDowall, James Mason, Diana Rigg and Sylvia Miles are featured. ★★½ $14.99

Evita

(1996, 134 min, US, Alan Parker) Never having given a truly tantalizing performance on-screen despite having a superstar profile, Madonna finally hits the big time in the movies. She gives an extremely capable performance as Argentina's first lady Eva Peron in this big, splashy, well-crafted adaptation of Andrew Lloyd Webber's Tony Award-winning Broadway musical. Though Parker's direction sometimes teeters on overkill, he has staged some knockout musical sequences, the like of which audiences haven't seen in years. Closely following the stage show, the story follows the rise of Eva Duarte from poor beginnings to stardom as a (second-rate) actress to becoming her country's first lady and sometime spiritual voice. Webber acknowledges Eva's status as a controversial figure, but straddles the fence in political terms. Still, the music is his best, and Madonna and friends give it their all. Madonna gives a sensational rendering of "Don't Cry for Me Argentina," and though she doesn't fully explore the role's emotional range, she is most credible. The real surprise is Antonio Banderas, who is splendid in both voice and performance as the story's narrator and social conscience. ★★★½ $102.99

The Ex-Mrs. Bradford

(1936, 80 min, US, Stephen Roberts) William Powell goes sleuthing with ex-wife Jean Arthur. Is Powell ever not suave and debonair? Is Arthur ever not sparkling and charming? Apparently not. Stylish, witty fun, with a darned clever resolution to the murders at hand. Powell is in familiar Nick Charles territory here. ★★★ $19.99

Excalibur

(1981, 140 min, GB, John Boorman) This spellbinding saga is steeped in the rich lore of gallant knights and sinister sorcery. A lavish production, aswirl with sensuous colors and breathtaking imagery, *Excalibur* is a superlative rendition of the Arthurian legend with added mystical and sexual overtones. It is a brilliant illumination of why these tales have survived so vividly in our imaginations. ★★★★ $9.99

Executioners (The Heroic Trio 2)

(1993, 90 min, Hong Kong, Ching Siu-Tung & Johnny To) The female superhero trio is back, but this time in a sober, nihilistic post-apocalyptic world of the future where water is a precious commodity and power-mad politicians vie for the support of the beleaguered population. De-emphasizing the comedy almost to an extreme, this sequel is satisfying in its own way, but lacks the campy fun and vivaciousness of the first film. Our three original heroines return, but do not team up as the Trio proper until nearly the end. Anthony Wong returns as the semi-human killer, but now he is enslaved to Michelle Yeoh's Invisible Girl instead of the androgynous demon of the original film. Without as much action or comedy as its predecessor, *Executioners* relies instead on its bleak tone and future-noir art direction to retain interest; it is, however, more stylishly shot and edited that the first *Trio* film. (Cantonese with English subtitles) ★★½ $89.99

Executive Decision

(1996, 132 min, US, Stuart Baird) It would be easy to call *Executive Decision* another *Die Hard* or *Under Siege* clone, for it does bear many similarities: terrorists have taken control of a mode of transportation and it's up to our hero (Kurt Russell) to set things right. But this exciting actioner relies less on explosions and shoot-'em-ups (though it's not totally devoid of them) and more on suspense, paying greater attention to how they do it. Mideast terrorists have taken control of an American airliner, and in a daring mid-flight link-up, the good guys board the plane in their effort to thwart the bad guys' plans to possibly bomb Washington, D.C. and the Eastern seaboard. As a think-tank specialist out of his league, Russell carries much of the action by giving an understated characterization rather than playing it like, say, Steven Seagal, who appears briefly as a commando. Halle Berry makes a most convincing heroine. ★★★ $19.99

Executive Suite

(1954, 104 min, US, Robert Wise) When the president of a major furniture-manufacturing company suddenly dies, the members of the Board scramble to replace him quickly and quietly. Each man is driven by his own motives, be it avarice or altruism. An all-star cast, including William Holden, Barbara Stanwyck, Fredric March and June Allyson, are entangled in many subplots, which complement the big business focus. Adapted from Cameron Hawley's best-selling novel. ★★★ $19.99

The Exiles

(1990, 116 min, US, Richard Kaplan) While most documentaries on Nazi Germany deal with the Holocaust and/or the military aspect of the war, few deal with the plight of non-Jewish, free-thinking German citizens who also faced the threat of imprisonment in concentration camps for their beliefs. This documentary focuses not on the Nazi threat to bohemians or homosexuals (a subject touched on briefly in *Cabaret* and more in depth in the documentary *Enchanted*), but on the artists and intellectuals who fled Hitler and found freedom and sanctuary in the United States. One learns about the increasingly repressive political climate in 1930s Germany — a situation which soon became intolerable for many, with the most recognizable name being the director Billy Wilder. *The Exiles* is comprised of archival footage and interviews with the dissidents, many still alive and living in America, as they vividly recount their situation in Nazi Germany, the difficult decision to emigrate, and their new life in a foreign land. An interesting and illuminating film on an overlooked subject. ★★★ $59.99

Exit to Eden

(1994, 113 min, US, Garry Marshall) Based on the Anne Rice novel, with a new subplot thrown in for not-so-good measure, *Exit to Eden* is a tedious comedy which mixes mild S/M fantasy with a ridiculous story of jewel thieves. Paul Mercurio stars as a hunky photographer with specialized sexual tastes (read: S/M) who unknowingly takes photos of two thieves (Iman and Stuart Wilson) in the middle of a heist. Pursued by cops Dan Aykroyd and

Evita

Rosie O'Donnell, the bad guys follow Mercurio to a tropical island resort named Eden, a kinky sexual Disneyland run by dominatrix Dana Delany. Director Marshall tries to create a sophisticated, wacky romp when all the characters come together, but this contrived flop is enough to give sex a bad name. It's surprising that Rice didn't raise a stink equal to the one she made about another adaptation of one of her books. ★ $14.99

Exodus

(1960, 213 min, US, Otto Preminger) An epic version of Leon Uris' mammoth novel detailing the struggles of the new Israeli state. Paul Newman plays an Israeli resistance leader, involved with Army nurse Eva Marie Saint. The supporting cast includes Ralph Richardson, Sal Mineo, Lee J. Cobb and Peter Lawford. (Available letterboxed and pan & scan) ★★★ $24.99

The Exorcist

(1973, 121 min, US, William Friedkin) The film that brought the devil back into vogue and spurred a host of imitations. The lovely Linda Blair gives her all in a role that requires her to turn green and rotate her head 360 degrees. Don't say we didn't warn you. ★★★½ $14.99

Exorcist II: The Heretic

(1977, 110 min, US, John Boorman) It's a few years after the infamous possession, and Linda Blair's being visited by unwanted guests again. Richard Burton is the priest who tries to evict 'em in Boorman's over-the-top sequel featuring some really wild special effects, campy performances and lots of silly religious mumbojumbo. With Max von Sydow, Ellen Burstyn and Lee J. Cobb. ★½ $14.99

The Exorcist III

(1990, 110 min, US, William Peter Blatty) Author William Peter Blatty takes matters into his own (directorial) hands with this adaptation of his "Exorcist" sequel, "Legion." Police detective Lt. Kinderman returns (now in the persona of George C. Scott), and is on the trail of a serial killer. When evidence suggests that the killings are the handiwork of more than one person (including an executed murderer), he begins to suspect the presence of greater evil (could it be...oh, I don't know...Satan?). The plot, undone by its own complexity, does manage to work up a good chill. ★★½ $19.99

Exotica

(1995, 104 min, Canada, Atom Egoyan) Although beguilingly cryptic, this haunting psychological thriller is director Egoyan's (*The Adjuster, Family Viewing*) most accessible film to date. In Robert Altman-style, he weaves several characters and their stories together as he explores such ominous themes as voyeurism, grief, betrayal and the search for healing, forgiveness and salvation. There is Thomas, a gay pet shop owner involved in illegal importation of exotic bird eggs; Francis (Bruce Greenwood), a tax advisor who spends his sullen nights at a strip club called Exotica where he quietly obsesses over one particular dancer, Christina (Mia Kirshner). She, in turn, is involved in a relationship with Zoe, the club owner and object of jealous affection by the

Mia Kirshner in *Exotica*

violent D.J., Eric (Elias Koteas). Nothing is as it seems as Egoyan stingily offers bits of information to the byzantine connections that thread the characters together. An intelligent, even mesmerizing black comedy, *Exotica* will entrance those with the patience to consider the complexities of this demanding film. ★★★½ $19.99

Experience Preferred...But Not Essential

(1983, 80 min, GB, Peter Duffell) A delightful little comedy about a schoolgirl's summer experiences at a resort hotel on the Welsh coast. Annie (Elizabeth Edmonds) begins her life's education when she encounters the eccentric and slightly daft employees of the Hotel Grand. Included in the colorful crew are the Scottish cook who romances her out of her "Wellies" and a burly somnambulist prone to nocturnal wanderings in the nude. A warm, charming film with unexpectedly good performances. ★★★

Experiment in Terror

(1962, 123 min, US, Blake Edwards) Good performances highlight this exciting thriller about a psychopath who kidnaps a bank teller's sister, thus blackmailing the woman into stealing from her employer. Glenn Ford is the agent assigned to the case, and Stephanie Powers is the abducted sister. As the cashier, Lee Remick is first-rate, and Ross Martin — long before his celebrated "Wild Wild West" good-guy role on TV — is chilling as the killer. ★★★ $9.99

Explorers

(1985, 100 min, US, Joe Dante) This lighthearted and wacky sci-fi comedy follows the adventures of three young boys who build a make-shift spacecraft and head for the stars. River Phoenix (as the brainy nerd!), Ethan Hawke and Jason Presson are the kids, and

their confrontation with alien creatures is delightful. ★★★ $14.99

Exquisite Corpses

(1989, 95 min, US, Temistocles Lopez) A young man with a trombone and a stetson, fresh from the American heartland, gets off the bus in New York City. In no time at all, he's had his luggage stolen and found out that his fiancée is shacked up with another guy. In not very much more time, he's subjected to every con and con artist in the book (all those guys in ponytails); but he also gets a dose of urban myth and magic. Before long, our newly issued midnight cowboy is *the* hot new cabaret star. But the path of our hero's quest to become the new idol for the jaded masses is littered with dead bodies. Writer-producer-director Lopez has fashioned a witty, sly, sardonic little gem, peopled with characters only slightly exaggerated. The production is obviously low-budget, but Lopez makes maximum use of the Big Apple's rotting environment. ★★★

The Exterminating Angel

(1962, 95 min, Mexico, Luis Buñuel) Buñuel's scathing wit is amply displayed in one of his most complex works. The guests of a dinner party are simply unable to leave their host's home when they are ready to depart. Within this claustrophobic microcosm, Buñuel lampoons society's decadence and corruption. (Spanish with English subtitles) ★★★★ $24.99

Extramuros (Beyond the Walls)

(1985, 120 min, Spain, Miguel Picazo) Carmen Maura, long a favorite of Pedro Almodóvar, stars in this fascinating and strange story of lesbian love and lusty ambition behind a convent's walls. While the Plague ravages all around, a poverty-stricken convent becomes the center of attention after Sister Angela injures her hands and fakes the miracle of Stigmata. The nun, with her lover

Sister Ana (Maura), staves off the despotic Mother Superior to eventually become prioress herself, until the members of the Inquisition pay a not-so-friendly visit to the "saint." Throughout the bizarre ordeal, the two nuns' love for each other remains sensual, true and strong. An unusual melodrama that borders on the deliriously unreal — a curious mix of the combined excesses of Ken Russell's *The Devils* and the Watergate conspiracy. (Spanish with English subtitles) ★★★ $39.99

The Extraordinary Adventures of Mr. West in the Land of the Bolsheviks

(1924, 78 min, USSR, Lev Kuleshov) This sharply satiric comedy has all of the action and pratfalls of a Chaplin film in telling its story about the wildly misconceived notions Americans had (and still possess) of Soviet Russia. Mr. West, a naive and nervous American, travels to Russia to see firsthand this nation of raging Bolsheviks and deranged radicals. But with the "help" of some mischievous pranksters, his travels turn into a wild adventure peopled by an increasingly strange procession of weirdos. An inspired and still timely farce. (Silent with orchestral accompaniment) ★★★ $29.99

Extreme Justice

(1993, 105 min, US, Mark L. Lester) Interesting but highly uneven — and at times wooden — drama about the L.A.P.D.'s unique crime-fighting task force, the S.I.S. (Special Investigation Squad) and their highly unorthodox methods of taking hard-core criminals off the streets. The story that unfolds is all-the-more frightening considering the L.A.P.D.'s gung-ho presence in African-American and Latino communities. Originally made for cable and then released in theatres, the film features Lou Diamond Phillips, Scott Glenn and Yaphet Kotto. ★★ $14.99

Extreme Measures

(1996, 117 min, US, Michael Apted) A blurry look at the halls of medicine, *Extreme Measures* asks if the ends can justify the means when one prominent doctor (Gene Hackman in another skilled portrayal) takes both lives and short cuts to find a cure for the incurable. Hugh Grant, with his charm and perfectly just-out-of-place hair, is the unknowing physician caught in the conspiracy. This stunted wandering never reaches a vasteness of any thrill, with its frequent plot turns leaving viewers knowing where it will lead without a proper explanation of how it arrived there. Though Danny Elfman has composed a wonderful score, there's a complete lack of presence and believability in costar Sarah Jessica Parker, and the film's main antagonist (David Morse) separates good from

evil in a movie whose engaging qualities tend to be its own ambiguity. ★★ $99.99

Extreme Prejudice

(1987, 104 min, US, Walter Hill) Appealing actioner with boyhood friends Nick Nolte and Powers Booth finding themselves at odds when one grows up to be a drug king and the other a Texas Ranger. ★★½ $14.99

Extremities

(1986, 90 min, US, Robert M. Young) Farrah Fawcett, who appeared in William Mastrosimone's hit off-Broadway play, repeats her stage role as an attempted rape victim who overcomes her attacker and holds him hostage. Farrah's attempt to prove herself a serious actress, for the most part, is a success: she gives a compelling performance. Alfre Woodard and Diana Scarwid ably play Farrah's roommates caught in the moral dilemma, and James Russo makes an intense psycho. ★★½

Eye for an Eye

(1996, 105 min, US, John Schlesinger) Sally Field assumes the Charles Bronson role from the *Death Wish* series as a mother who seeks vengeance against the man who raped and murdered her daughter, and then walked free. About as dramatically defined as any of the Bronson sequels, *Eye for an Eye* features incredibly overdrawn characters who all wear their caricatures on their sleeves. Field is the devoted mother who — in the film's only truly good scene — hears her daughter's murder over her car phone. Kiefer Sutherland is the sleazy suspect cleared on a technicality (Why make him so obviously guilty when trying to build suspense as to who did it?). The film could have veered into an interesting examination of the mother's dilemma, but opts for the ridiculous scenario of a gun-toting Field stalking the low-rent district of L.A.'s downtown (rich people = good; poor people = bad). ★½ $14.99

Eye of the Needle

(1981, 112 min, US, Richard Marquand) Excellent WWII spy thriller starring Donald Sutherland (in one of his best roles) as the notorious Nazi assassin, "The Needle," who must keep his identity secret when he becomes stranded on an island inhabited by a war-wounded Brit and his lonely and frustrated wife (Kate Nelligan). Based on the best-selling novel by Ken Follett. Riveting from start to its pulse-pounding finish. ★★★½ $14.99

Eye of the Storm

(1991, 98 min, US, Yuri Zeltser) Adequate performances and a flashy build-up somehow can't quite sustain this stylish exercise in suspense that stars Lara Flynn Boyle ("Twin Peaks") as a downtrodden wife who takes a wrong turn when she and her abusive husband

(Dennis Hopper, renewing his "psycho" patent) pull into a lonely desert hotel run by a strange young man (Craig Sheffer) and his blind brother (Bradley Gregg). ★★ $14.99

Eyes of Laura Mars

(1978, 104 min, US, Irvin Kershner) Bondage chic goes commercial in Kershner's tale of a psychic fashion photographer (Faye Dunaway) and a troubled policeman (Tommy Lee Jones) searching for the identity of an ice pick murderer. Jon Peters' first major job as a producer after giving up giving blow drys to the stars. ★★½ $9.99

Eyes on the Prize, Vols. 1-6

(1989, 60 ea. min, US) This fascinating, award-winning PBS series documents the African-American civil rights movement from 1954 to 1965. Easily one of the best and most comprehensive works on the subject, the six episodes are: "Awakenings," "Fighting Back," "Ain't Scared of Your Jails," "No Easy Walk," "Is This America" and "Bridge to Freedom." 19.99 each ★★★★

The Eyes, the Mouth

(1982, 100 min, Italy/France, Marco Bellocchio) A compelling examination of a family ravaged by the suicide of a brother, and of the lengths that the brother's twin must go to to separate himself from the crippling ties of the past. Extraordinary performances by Lou Castel, Angela Molina and Emmanuelle Riva. (Italian with English subtitles) ★★★ $19.99

Eyes without a Face

(1959, 90 min, France, Georges Franju) Originally titled *The Horror Chamber of Dr. Faustus* for its U.S. release, this elegantly moody horror film concerns a deranged plastic surgeon who, after being responsible for a car accident that leaves his young daughter hideously disfigured, becomes determined to give her a new face — a face whose skin is grafted from the bodies of beautiful women his assistant kidnaps off the streets of Paris. A macabre and frightening story that creates its horror not through histrionics or blood but through an elegantly dark style, similar to the works of Jean Cocteau and the early German expressionists. (French with English subtitles) ★★★½ $29.99

Eyewitness

(1981, 102 min, US, Peter Yates) William Hurt and Sigourney Weaver star in this slickly produced murder mystery about a janitor (Hurt) who pretends to have knowledge of a murder being investigated by a hotshot reporter (Weaver), in order to become involved with the beautiful journalist. Also with James Woods, Christopher Plummer and Irene Worth. ★★★ $14.99

F/X

(1986, 106 min, US, Robert Mandel) Imaginative and taut thriller with Bryan Brown as a movie special effects expert who is hired by the Justice Department to fake the assassination of a mobster, only to be framed for the murder. The film features fine F/X, and makes good use of New York City locales. Brian Dennehy is particularly good as a cop on Brown's trail. ★★★ $9.99

F/X 2

(1991, 109 min, US, Richard Franklin) This more-than-capable sequel to the 1986 hit picks up five years later. F/X expert, and now toy manufacturer, Bryan Brown is convinced to help his girlfriend's ex-husband in a police sting. But when the latter is killed, Brown discovers a cover-up and enlists the help of pal Brian Dennehy to find out what happened. Though not entirely as successful as the original, the film nevertheless is an exciting mystery story peppered with some good special effects. Watch out for a real killer clown. Also with Rachel Ticotin, Joanna Gleason, Philip Bosco, Kevin J. O'Connor, and Jose DeGuzman returning as Velez. ★★½ $9.99

The Fable of the Beautiful Pigeon Fancier

(1988, 73 min, Brazil/Spain, Roy Guerra) From Gabriel Garcia Marquez comes this lyrical, dreamlike fable, filled with mystical forboding, dealing with the love of an older man for an alluringly mysterious woman. Don Orestes, a Dali-esque dandy of a man, lives off the wealth of his family in a poverty-stricken town in 19th-century Brazil. His highly structured life, dominated by his mother, is thrown into a whirlwind after he meets and falls in love with Fulvia (Claudia Ohana of *Erendira*), a beautiful dark-haired woman who tends pigeons and lives in seclusion on the edge of town with her husband and baby. The two are inexplicably drawn together, culminating in a fateful conclusion. Note: This film, made for Spanish television, was filmed in Brazil. The actors spoke Portuguese which was then dubbed into Spanish. (Spanish with English subtitles) ★★★ $19.99

The Fabulous Baker Boys

(1989, 113 min, US, Steve Kloves) This vibrant and sexy romantic comedy-drama stars the fabulous Bridges boys, Jeff and Beau, and the beautiful Michelle Pfeiffer. Don't let the title mislead you; this is an extremely well-written, acted and executed adult entertainment set against the sometimes tacky world of the lounge act. Pfeiffer, an actress of stunning beauty and incomparable talent, gives an intelligent, smoldering performance as Susie Diamond, the singer who enters the lives of two brothers whose piano act is dying a slow death. The film follows the love affair between cynical Jeff and sultry Michelle, almost effortlessly evoking the mood of those great 1940s screen romances. The smokey atmosphere is further enhanced by Dave Grusin's outstanding jazz score. ★★★½ $9.99

A Face in the Crowd

(1957, 126 min, US, Elia Kazan) The writer (Budd Schulberg) and director (Elia Kazan) of *On the Waterfront* were reunited for this compelling drama about a home-spun hillbilly entertainer whose TV success transforms him into a power-hungry demagogue. Andy Griffith is quite good in his film debut, and is given fine support by Patricia Neal, Walter Matthau and Lee Remick. ★★★½ $19.99

Face of Another

(1966, 124 min, Japan, Hiroshi Teshigahara) A scientist, his face horribly disfigured in an industrial accident, is fitted with a handsome mask; but instead of gaining renewed confidence and self-esteem, he retreats into self-pity and mistrust, eventually seducing his wife and then accusing her of adultery. Using surreal techniques, this psychological drama examines the dehumanization and isolation of man in present-day Japan. A chilling and fatalistic tale of alienation that was co-scripted by Teshigahara and Kobo Abe, whose previous collaboration was *Woman in the Dunes*. (Japanese with English subtitles) ★★★ $59.99

Faces

(1968, 129 min, US, John Cassavetes) Cassavetes was a master of truth-telling without compromise, whose unrepentant exposure of human hypocrisy was tempered by his astounding empathy for human suffering — even when self-inflicted. This is an unflinching examination of a middle-aged, middle-class couple in the throes of marital breakup, and the emotionally ravaging effects of their mid-life attempts to establish new relationships. The couple (Lynn Carlin, John Marley), their friends and acquaintances (Gena Rowlands is devastating as the other woman) are fully revealed as they confront the artificial confines of their societal roles. The film is brutal in its depiction of the underlying assumptions of the sexual mores of the time, which now seem almost Victorian yet uncomfortably familiar. An arresting drama that pulls no punches as it divulges one couple's painful confrontation with stifling confinement and lack of communication: a confrontation which acts as metaphor for the social structures of the era. ★★★½ $19.99

Faces of Women

(1987, 103 min, Ivory Coast, Désiré Ecaré) This debut effort by director Ecaré is an exuberant blend of raucous comedy, pulsating African music and dance, and steamy eroticism. Two stories, filmed ten years apart with two separate casts, are woven together with the chants and dances of an energetic female chorus. Both segments concern the place of African women in marriage, sex and society. The first and pivotal story offers an erotic, feminist slant on lust and cuckolding, with lovemaking so candid that the film was barred for many years from its native country. The

Julie Christie and Oskar Werner in *Fahrenheit 451*

second tale focuses on a middle-aged successful businesswoman confronting resistance from a stern patriarchal society that maintains that "women and money don't go together." Having created a bold, vibrant film, Ecaré emerges as a fresh African voice, using a new wave-influenced directorial style to examine the eternal battle of the sexes. (French with English subtitles) ★★★ $79.99

Face/Off

(1997, 135 min, US, John Woo) After two disappointing starts, director Woo has finally hit his stride in American cinema with this highly textured, complicated film which nearly equals the excellent work he did in Hong Kong. The inventive script sets up a situation that, although it is completely implausible, plays right into Woo's strength: an intimate conflict between two inextricably connected men of action. John Travolta is Sean Archer, an FBI agent committed to the capture of terrorist Castor Troy (Nicolas Cage), who murdered Archer's son in a botched assassination attempt. Troy is captured, but put into a coma, and Archer assumes his identity in order to learn the location of a secretly placed bomb. But Troy is not as sick as he looks and soon wakes up, assumes Archer's identity and takes over his old life. The two men eventually learn that their original perceptions of each other were not entirely accurate and find that they share a bond which is more complex than that of traditional hero and villain. The action sequences are brilliantly staged and the dramatic content of the film — Joan Allen brings a quiet strength to the role of Archer's wife — finally lives up to Woo's famous pyrotechnic sequences. ★★★½ $99.99

Fahrenheit 451

(1967, 111 min, France, François Truffaut) This intriguing adaptation of the famed Ray

Bradbury novel is a frightening vision of a not-too-distant future where books are outlawed and firemen incinerate "anti-social rubbish." Truffaut creates an eerie atmosphere of repression in this intelligent sci-fi tale. Starring Julie Christie and Oskar Werner. (Filmed in English) ★★★ $14.99

Fail-Safe

(1964, 111 min, US, Sidney Lumet) One of the most effective films yet made about the futility and horror of nuclear war, this taut and suspenseful adaptation of Burdick-Wheeler's best-seller is a nightmare "what-if" scenario: Through computer error, we have sent a plane to bomb Moscow — and the President must convince the Russians it was an accident and also decide how to rectify the situation. Henry Fonda is appropriately low-keyed as the Commander-in-Chief, and a young Larry Hagman ably plays the interpreter. This is the serious side of *Dr. Strangelove*, and every bit as gripping. Also with Walter Matthau and Dom DeLuise. ★★★½ $9.99

Fair Game

(1985, 90 min, Australia, Mario Andreacchio) Mindless revenge flick about an outback animal preservationist who finds herself in a sadistic game of one-upmanship with a psychotic poacher and his brain-dead cohorts. *Fair Game* isn't as exploitative as it sounds; however, one cannot help wondering if this is not yet another heroine trying to follow in the lucrative footsteps of *Alien*'s Sigourney Weaver. ★ $79.99

Fair Game

(1995, 90 min, US, Andrew Sipes) Acting more with the variety of T-shirts she wears than with her emotions, Cindy Crawford makes her acting debut as a divorce lawyer who is hunted by an Interpol-wanted, ex-KGB agent involved in pilfering millions from off-shore banks. This latest Eurotrash villain (Steven Berkoff) and his gang of thugs (looking like they didn't make final call for *Cliffhanger*) try to blow up Cindy because she is inadvertently delving too deep in their business. William Baldwin is the chummy cop-on-the-edge who rescues her, and the two run for their lives, pursued by the bad guys. Predictably, they argue and then fall in lust. The action sequences are boring, the acting is bad, the script and direction are nonexistent, and even the sight of a villain targeting Baldwin's ass-crack with a laser sight while he bangs away at Crawford in a moving boxcar cannot enliven this bloated mess. ★ $19.99

The Falcon and the Snowman

(1985, 131 min, US, John Schlesinger) Acclaimed espionage thriller based on the true-life story of Christopher Boyce and Dalton Lee, who sold national secrets to the Soviets. Timothy Hutton and Sean Penn are outstanding as Boyce and Lee. ★★★ $9.99

The Fall of the House of Usher

(1960, 85 min, US, Roger Corman) Corman graduated (for a time, anyway) from quickly produced horror and comedy exploitation pictures to seriously considered and scripted, heavily atmospheric, adult-themed horror films with this, his first of eight film adaptations of the works of Edgar Allan Poe. Vincent Price stars as the tragic Roderick, last in the doomed line of Ushers, who is stricken with a painful sensitivity and burdened with an all-encompassing sense of doom for his family, his home and his future. Philip Winthrop (Mark Damon) arrives at the House of Usher to sweep away his fiancée Madeline, Roderick's sister. Roderick, however, will not allow her to leave, and Damon becomes a hopeless bystander, able only to watch helplessly as the madness and destruction of the Usher legacy consumes Madeline, Roderick and the House itself. *House of Usher* is an unusually realized Gothic horror story; its expertly executed art direction, cinematography and musical score all contribute to its eloquence, and Richard Matheson's chilling screenplay was also a remarkable beginning in a line of Poe adaptations. ★★★ $14.99

Fall of the Romanov Dynasty

(1927, 90 min, USSR, Ether Shub) With innovative editing of remarkable archival footage, this is the first historical documentary produced in the Soviet Union. It's a stirring account of the events that led up to the overthrow of the Czarist regime and the subsequent rise of the people's republic. Director Shub skillfully utilizes newsreel footage as well as Czar Nicholas' home movies in bringing to life those fateful years between 1912 and 1917. (Silent with piano accompaniment) ★★★ $29.99

Fall Time

(1994, 88 min, US, Paul Warner) This kinky crime thriller uses Tarantino-style violence and a bevy of pretty boys to create an improbable tale dripping with homoerotic undertones. Leon (Stephen Baldwin) and Florence (Mickey Rourke) are two gun-toting crooks (and possible lovers) looking to hit a bank in a Southern town. Their scheme is foiled when three freshly scrubbed teens, out to fake their own robbery, get in the way. The boys — ringleader David (David Arquette), cute Joe (Jonah Blechman) and chiseled beauty Tim (Jason London) — are soon held hostage by the hoods. The film then takes a decidedly S&M bent as knives and guns are brandished (often times toward their captives' mouths — duh, symbolism?), pants are dropped and a bondage fantasy right out of a violent porn novel is acted out as Leon and Florence torment the youths while figuring out their next move. ★★★ $89.99

Fallen Angels, Vol. 1

(1993, 90 min, US, Tom Cruise/Alfonso Cuaron/Jonathan Kaplan) Three stories from Showtime's six-episode series of noirish treats. *The Frightening Frammis*, directed by Cruise, takes noir out of the back alleys and smoke-filled rooms and into the blazing sun of the desert in an intriguing tale of seduction and betrayal from a short story by Jim Thompson. Peter Gallagher plays a grifter who meets his match in the person of Isabella Rossellini. (★★★) *Murder, Obliquely*, directed by Cuaron, speaks of obsessive love and murderously bad behavior. Laura Dern's studies with noir master David Lynch are evident as she delivers a moody performance as a woman who falls

hard for a playboy who may have murdered his former girlfriend (Diane Lane). (★★★½) *Since I Don't Have You*, directed by Kaplan, is a spicy and semi-historical account of the underbelly of Hollywood in the '40s. Gary Busey plays a tough Guy Friday who works for both Howard Hughes (Tim Matheson) and gangster Mickey Cohen (James Woods). Trouble surfaces when both men hire him to find the same underage girl. (★★★) $14.99

Fallen Angels, Vol. 2

(1993, 90 min, US, Phil Joanou/Tom Hanks/Steven Soderbergh) Three stories from Showtime's six-episode series of noirish treats. *Dead-End for Delia*, directed by Joanou, is an effective mystery with Gary Oldman as a street cop who investigates the murder of his estranged wife (Gabrielle Anwar), leading him to her girlfriend (Meg Tilly). (★★★) *I'll Be Waiting*, directed by Hanks, is possibly the weakest of the grouping. Bruno Kirby plays a hotel detective who becomes involved with prison widow Marg Helgenberger and murder. (★★) *The Quiet Room*, directed by Soderbergh, is a taut psychological drama starring Joe Mantegna and Bonnie Bedelia as two crooked police officers whose shakedowns lead to tragedy. (★★★) $14.99

Fallen Champ: The Mike Tyson Story

(1993, 93 min, US, Barbara Kopple) Mike Tyson went from Brownsville, Brooklyn, welfare kid to Heavyweight Champion of the World to convicted rapist, all before his 25th birthday. Academy Award-winning producer-director Kopple (*Harlan County, U.S.A.*) traces the many influences in his life which led him from obscurity to adulation, and ultimately, to his incarceration. Powerful, lucid and unflinching, this documentary offers compelling commentary on Tyson as an individual as well as on being black in America. ★★★ $14.99

The Fallen Idol

(1948, 95 min, GB, Carol Reed) Ralph Richardson stars in this outstanding realization of Graham Greene's story about the friendship between an upper-class boy and a house servant who is suspected of murder. Reed skillfully probes the psychological depths of his characters while creating a fascinating examination of the schism between adults and children in their views of reality. ★★★★ $14.99

Falling Down

(1993, 112 min, US, Joel Schumacher) Director Schumacher and actor Michael Douglas take a walk on the wild side in this over-the-edge, misanthropic black comedy. Douglas plays a slightly psychotic, unemployed defense worker whose pent up hostilities against what he perceives as an increasingly foreign society explode in the sweltering heat and insufferable traffic jams of Los Angeles. At times wildly entertaining, at others shockingly violent and disturbing, the film follows Douglas as he abandons his car on the freeway and treks across L.A. towards the home of his estranged wife (Barbara Hershey). Along the way, he unleashes his fury on Latinos, Asians, neo-Nazis and other "bogeymen" standing between him and the American dream. Robert Duvall injects a voice of reason in the film as a

Yoshimitsu Morita's *The Family Game*

hen-pecked cop who must come to grips with his own sense of inadequacy before confronting Douglas. A reactionary though simple message of white fear in an increasingly non-white society. ★★★ $9.99

Falling from Grace

(1992, 100 min, US, John Mellencamp) Brooding heartland musician Mellencamp makes his acting/directing debut in this insightful and entertaining drama about... a brooding heartland musician. Bud Parks, Jr. (Mellencamp) is an ambivalent, restless superstar who tries to return home for his grandfather's 80th birthday. But when he decides to extend his visit and even considers staying permanently, family tensions and secrets surface, wreaking emotional havoc on all concerned. A fine supporting cast includes Mariel Hemingway, Kay Lenz, songwriter Larry Crane and, in a standout performance, Claude Akins. Mellencamp, for his part, puts in a solid turn bringing dimension to his character, setting an appropriate tone and keeping a lively pace. ★★½ $19.99

Falling in Love

(1984, 107 min, US, Ulu Grosbard) A curiously unaffecting film, given the high-power cast. Robert De Niro and Meryl Streep allow a chance encounter on a commuter train to blossom into an affair. They provide their usual professional performances, as do supporting players Harvey Keitel and Dianne Wiest, among others. There just isn't very much to work with. Interesting as evidence of a seldom-exposed aspect of the De Niro persona and a chance to see Streep do a toned-down, suburban Annie Hall. ★★½ $14.99

Fame

(1980, 134 min, US, Alan Parker) Parker follows a group of students at the New York High School of the Performing Arts from their auditions in dance, voice, drama and music through their graduation ceremony. Hot lunches, hard lessons and dancing in the street. Irene Cara sings the Oscar-winning title song. ★★★ $19.99

The Family

(1987, 130 min, Italy, Ettore Scola) Scola, director of the anarchic *Down and Dirty*, the allegorical *Le Bal* as well as the ambitiously political *La Nuit De Varennes*, chooses in this thoughtful drama a more relaxed and intimate style in chronicling the 80 years of one typical family's life, loves and losses. By confining the entire story within the walls of a grand Roman apartment, Scola's attention is not on the tumultuous events of the 20th century but rather on the more mundane but equally compelling story of a middle-class family headed by Vittorio Gassman. A touching and finely detailed soap opera which includes among the family members Fanny Ardant and Philippe Noiret. (Italian with English subtitles) ★★★ $19.99

Family Business

(1989, 115 min, US, Sidney Lumet) Endearing misfire written by Vincent Patrick (*The Pope of Greenwich Village*) about three generations of small-time crooks (Sean Connery, Dustin Hoffman and Matthew Broderick) who decide to pull one last heist together. Though Patrick's screenplay has the same "homespun" feel that made *Pope* such a joy, the three strong leads tend to overpower the material. Efficiently directed by Lumet. ★★ $11.99

The Family Game

(1983, 107 min, Japan, Yoshimitsu Morita) The contemporary Japanese middle class are mercilessly lampooned in this hilarious farce. The story, brimming with style and invention – from its extraordinary visual design to its incredulously quirky soundtrack – revolves around a family's decision to hire a tutor for their academically troubled son. The unorthodox and anarchistic instructor proceeds to wreak havoc in their previously tranquil lives. A wickedly satiric and endlessly surprising film. (Japanese with English subtitles) ★★★ $59.99

Family Life (Wednesday's Child)

(1971, 108 min, GB, Ken Loach) This fictional documentary by Loach details the deteriorating mental state of a severely disturbed 19-year-old girl and the influence her family has on

her. A harrowing portrait of mental illness and one that comes down hard against drug treatments and electro-shock therapy. ★★★ $59.99

Family Plot

(1976, 120 min, US, Alfred Hitchcock) The 53rd and final film in Alfred Hitchcock's illustrious career is a quirky blend of sinister humor and mystery. Barbara Harris, in a wonderfully kooky performance, is a phony (?) medium who, along with boyfriend Bruce Dern, stumbles onto the kidnapping pastime of diabolical William Devane and Karen Black. A supremely droll study of coincidence and the criminal urge. ★★★½ $14.99

A Family Thing

(1996, 110 min, US, Richard Pearce) James Earl Jones and Robert Duvall deliver subtle, finely drawn characterizations as half-brothers who are reunited after a separation of many decades, hundreds of miles, and the chasm of American racial relationships. Raised as white in a small Arkansas town, Duvall receives a posthumous letter from the woman whom he believed to be his mother informing him that in fact his birth mother was a black woman who worked for the family and who died at his birth. In unacknowledged, tightly controlled emotional upheaval and within shouting distance of old age, he embarks on an odyssey of self-discovery, traveling to Chicago to find his brother and his history. The script, wonderfully understated and studded with wry, poignant glimpses at human foibles, was cowritten by Billy Bob Thornton (*One False Move*, *Sling Blade*). The supporting cast is uniformly competent, including Michael Beach as Jones' disheartened son, and Irma P. Hall in a standout performance as Aunt T., the family's backbone and historian. *A Family Thing* is a small gem of surprising emotional impact, a story of ordinary people which encapsulates larger issues in a personal framework. ★★★½ $19.99

Family Viewing

(1987, 86 min, Canada, Atom Egoyan) Canadian independent filmmaking has been singularly brought back to life by the innovative and droll techniques of director Egoyan. Told with salacious humor and effective drama, this unusual black comedy is an award-winning observation of the goings-on of a denuclearized family. Dad is a middle-class sadomasochistic VCR repairman who, after driving his wife away with his obsession for kinky phone sex, lives in domestic bliss with his sexy bimbo. His son, Stan, is a pasty-faced teenage couch potato. The son finally escapes from his father and moves in with his girlfriend who, unbeknownst to him, works at the phone sex company and has a peculiar sexual relationship with his father. This story of contemporary familial corruption is an intelligent and promising start for a talented filmmaker. ★★★ $19.99

The Fan

(1981, 95 min, US, Edward Bianchi) Lauren Bacall plays a legendary stage and screen star who is stalked by a psychotic fan. A creepy and rather unlikable thriller based on Bob Randell's novel. Also with Maureen Stapleton, Michael Biehn and James Garner. ★½ $14.99

The Fan

(1996, 116 min, US, Tony Scott) As slick, cold and transparent as ice, *The Fan* is a twisted, by-the-books thriller which offers few thrills or any redeeming qualities. Robert De Niro is a Willy Loman-like salesman and obsessed San Francisco Giants fan about to lose his grip. Wesley Snipes is the Ken Griffey-like superstar who becomes De Niro's object of obsession. The suspense supposedly starts when they cross paths, but it's more like a lesson in Screenplay Coincidence 101. De Niro has played this part so often he can wring emotion from the most ill-defined role — which is exactly what he does. Ellen Barkin has little to do as a sports announcer, and Snipes plays his ballplayer as both friend and foe. The background baseball sequences, even with the addition of real players such as John Kruk, add little excitement and offer no rebuttle to the complaint that baseball in movies is boring. ★½ $19.99

Fancy Pants

(1950, 92 min, US, George Marshall) Bob Hope and Lucille Ball are in good form in this spirited remake of *Ruggles of Red Gap*. Bob is the cowardly valet who heads West with wild-and-woolly Lucy. She also sings the title song. ★★★ $14.99

Fandango

(1985, 91 min, US, Kevin Reynolds) Five college roommates, having just graduated, go on a last fling together across the Texas Badlands. An interesting youth drama with good performances from Judd Nelson, Kevin Costner and Sam Robards. ★★½ $14.99

Fanny

(1932, 120 min, France, Marc Allégret) In this second segment of the remarkable Pagnol Trilogy, Marius' father César (played by the unforgettable character actor Raimu) comforts Fanny after being deserted by his son. Pregnant, she accepts the hand of Panisse, a kindly but older friend of César. The film provides a rich portrait of complex

Fanny and Alexander

familial relationships. (French with English subtitles) ★★★½ $39.99

Fanny

(1961, 133 min, US, Joshua Logan) Acclaimed reworking of Marcel Pagnol's timeless story, based on the Broadway musical but *without* the songs (similar to 1963's *Irma La Douce*), with Leslie Caron as the young waif abandoned by a sailor. Enchanting performances by Caron, Maurice Chevalier and Charles Boyer help immeasurably. ★★★ $14.99

Fanny and Alexander

(1982, 197 min, Sweden, Ingmar Bergman) Bergman's joyous and engrossing portrait of a civilized Swedish family gracefully details the trauma and triumphs they encounter over the course of a year. Abandoning the dour tone of his earlier works, Bergman creates an enchanting tapestry of life's amplitude in this wise and witty Academy Award winner. (Available dubbed and in Swedish with English subtitles) ★★★★ $29.99

Fanny Hill

(1983, 80 min, GB, Gerry O'Hara) The extremely curvaceous Lisa Raines stars in this bawdy Playboy production rendition of the famous English folktale. The story follows the adventures of Fanny, a young country girl, orphaned in her adolescence, who moves to London where she falls into the good graces of Mrs. Cole (Shelley Winters), the cheerful proprietress of a house of pleasure. Special appearance by Oliver Reed. ★★ $79.99

Fantasia

(1940, 120 min, US, Joe Grant & Dick Huemer) This Walt Disney masterpiece is a consummate collection of seven animated shorts, each utilizing a classical score for their background, and all under the direction of Leopold Stokowski. The selections include "The Sorcerer's Apprentice," starring Mickey Mouse; the brilliantly animated "The Rites of Spring"; and the stirring finale, "A Night on Bald Mountain." ★★★★ $49.99

Fantastic Planet

(1973, 72 min, France, René Laloux) An unusual and provocative combination of science fiction and animation. Jammed with original ideas and visualizations, this French production is an imaginative allegorical tale about a futuristic planet where men are tolerated as tame, tiny pets. (In English) ★★★ $29.99

Fantastic Voyage

(1966, 100 min, US, Richard Fleischer) The special effects in this highly entertaining mid-'60s sci-fi classic may seem simple by today's standards, but at the time, they were nothing less than breathtaking. Stephen Boyd, Raquel Welch, Edmond O'Brien and Donald Pleasence star as members of a medical team which is miniaturized and then injected into the body of the president in order to perform some truly up-close surgery. ★★★½ $14.99

Far and Away

(1992, 140 min, US, Ron Howard) Husband and wife Tom Cruise and Nicole Kidman manage to ignite a few sparks in this handsomely produced romantic epic set in late 19th-century Ireland and America. Essentially a three-act story, the first part, set in Ireland, finds poor farmer Cruise and rich landowner's daughter Kidman meeting after he attempts to murder her father. The second act takes place in Boston, where the two have emigrated, finding only poverty and corruption. The final is set in the Old West, where all have surfaced to strike a claim. Though the film's Boston scenes are overly melodramatic, it is the first and last acts in which director Howard distinguishes himself. The lush Irish landscapes and the vast Western skies provide a thrilling backdrop for what becomes, ultimately, a surprisingly rousing entertainment. (Available letterboxed and pan & scan) ★★★ $19.99

Far Away, So Close

(1993, 140 min, Germany, Wim Wenders) Wenders continues his "Angels over Berlin" saga with this less-than-successful follow-up to the brilliant *Wings of Desire*. Where Bruno Ganz's Ariel in *Wings* was an angel whose selfish need to be human made him physically manifest, *Far Away*'s Cassiel (Otto Sander) comes down to earth because he wants to make things better. Instead, he falls victim to all of the human ailments he had hoped to remedy. Wenders takes a very grim view of the post-Cold War world, using Berlin as the perfect setting for a tale of impending social anarchy brought about by the collapse of old systems. Too often, however, Wenders allows his narrative to run wild and his flights of fancy can't keep things interesting. Cameos include Lou Reed, Peter Falk and Mikhail Gorbachev (for real!), and Willem Dafoe appears as a sleazy devil figure named Emit Flesti (*time itself* spelled backwards). (German with English subtitles) ★★ $94.99

The Far Country

(1955, 97 min, US, Anthony Mann) A sturdy western adventure with James Stewart in typically good form as a cowboy whose cattle drive to Alaska turns disastrous when he is swindled by outlaws. Good scenery and character interplay highlight this exciting tale. Also starring Walter Brennan and Ruth Roman. ★★★ $14.99

Far East

(1982, 90 min, Australia, John Duigan) Tepid drama about the owner of a sleazy tourist bar in Southeast Asia and his relationship with the wife of a crusading journalist. This mixture of political intrigue and romance has been done time and time again — with better results. Starring Helen Morse and Bryan Brown. ★ $9.99

Far from Home

(1989, 86 min, US, Meiert Avis) Drew Barrymore headlines this standard B-thriller about a budding teenaged nymphet who is stalked by an unknown killer while vacationing with her estranged father (Matt Frewer). Nothing special, but a few unexpected touches (including a well-handled lesbian couple) spice things up. Also starring Richard Masur, Susan Tyrrell and Jennifer Tilly. ★★ $14.99

Far from Home: The Adventures of Yellow Dog

(1995, 81 min, US, Phillip Borso) An adolescent boy is lost in the wilds and faces certain horrors as he attempts to find his way back home. Set at a lethargic pace and given to clichés of the genre, *Far from Home*'s main appeal is the "boy and his dog" story which punctuates the survival dramatics. Jesse Bradford, who was so engaging in *King of the Hill*, stars as the 14-year-old who becomes separated from his father's boat excursion during a storm. The film offers beautiful scenery (shot on location in British Columbia), but fails to maintain any excitement in the boy's rescue attempts. Bruce Davison and Mimi Rogers also star as the worried parents. ★★ $14.99

Far from Poland

(1984, 106 min, US, Jill Godmilow) Denied a visa to shoot a film in Poland, left-leaning independent filmmaker Godmilow (*Waiting for the Moon*) is forced to construct her documentary on the Solidarity movement from her studio in New York. This serious, non-fiction film delves into the perception and representation of "truth" as it charts the rise of the Solidarity movement in the shipyards of Damansk in early 1980 to its suppression by martial law in December 1981. From a number of various angles, Godmilow aims to present the reality of the situation without succumbing to easy, prejudicial conclusions. ★★★ $69.99

Far from the Madding Crowd

(1967, 169 min, GB, John Schlesinger) Julie Christie stars as a ravashing femme fatale who manages to make emotional mince meat out of three men's lives (Alan Bates, Peter Finch and Terence Stamp). Director Schlesinger's masterful touch combined with the brilliant cinematography of Nicolas Roeg make this an extraordinary viewing experience. ★★★½ $29.99

Far North

(1988, 92 min, US, Sam Shepard) Jessica Lange and Charles Durning lend a strong cast in this allegorical tale written by Shepard, here making his directorial debut. When the head of a Minnesota farming family is almost killed by one of his most obstinate horses, he wants his strong-willed daughter to destroy the dangerous animal, with unexpected consequences. ★★★ $19.99

A Far Off Place

(1993, 105 min, US, Mikael Salomon) Based on a pair of novels by Laurens van der Post, this passable Disney adaptation recounts the adventures of a pair of white teenagers and their Bushman friend who, in order to evade a gang of murderous poachers, flee into southern Africa's Kalihari Desert. Van der Post's story of orphaned children fleeing evil adults appears to be the perfect Disney fit; but despite this, or perhaps because of it, the film occasionally gets bogged down in formulaic predictability. Reese Witherspoon does a fine job as Nonnie Parker, an Africanized white girl, and Sarel Bok pulls a page right out of *The Gods Must Be Crazy* as the young bushman. Jack Thompson and Maximilian Schell lend some weight as adults on opposite sides of the law. ★★½ $14.99

Zhang Fengyi (l.) and Leslie Cheung in *Farewell My Concubine*

The Far Pavillions

(1983, 108 min, GB, Peter Duffell) Ben Cross and Amy Irving star in this epic love story about a British officer who falls in love with an Indian princess during the colonial era. The supporting cast includes Omar Sharif and Christopher Lee. ★★★

Farewell My Concubine

(1993, 154 min, China, Chen Kaige) Told on an epic scale, this big-budget spectacle recounts the tempestuous relationship between two Peking Opera stars as they live through five decades of turbulent Chinese history. In a repressive 1920s opera school, an androgynous young boy, Dieyi, begins a lifelong involvement with another student, Xiaolou. Years later, the two achieve national stardom, best known for their rendition of the tragic opera "Farewell My Concubine," in which the now-adult Dieyi (Leslie Cheung) plays the part of a woman. As their professional lives soar, their relationship becomes strained as the gay Dieyi falls in love with his affectionate but heterosexual co-star. Even after Xiaolou (Zhang Fengyi) marries a fiery former prostitute (superbly played by Gong Li), the two men's lives remain intractably intertwined. Exotic locations, sweeping photography, colorful costumes and an emotional story line make this a riveting experience. (Chinese with English subtitles) ★★★★ $19.99

Farewell, My Lovely

(1975, 97 min, GB, Dick Richards) Wonderfully evoking the time and mood of Raymond Chandler's 1940s Los Angeles, this film noir detective drama stars Robert Mitchum as an aging, down-on-his-heels Philip Marlowe who is pursuaded to take on a case involving a nightclub singer missing for six years. Charlotte Rampling is confusingly and destructively alluring as the femme fatale and Sylvia Miles is unforgettable as an alcoholic floozy who "sings" for a bottle. A complex, dark and entertaining film that more than

holds its own with the original, *Murder My Sweet* with Dick Powell. ★★★½

Farewell to the King

(1989, 117 min, US, John Milius) From the macho writer-director Milius (*The Wind and the Lion, Red Dawn*) comes this visually stunning, thematically stunted adventure epic of a WWII Army deserter (Nick Nolte) who faces a crisis of conscience when the island paradise he has ruled in peace is invaded by the British-Japanese conflict. Based on a novel by Pierre Schoendoerffer, the film co-stars Nigel Havers and James Fox. ★★ $14.99

Fargo

(1996, 90 min, US, Joel Coen) The peculiarly heightened reality that is a trademark of Coen Brothers' films is well-suited to this bizarre, true-life tale of a seemingly solid, middle-class man (William H. Macy) whose proximity to financial ruin precipitates a hair-brained scheme for quick monetary reward. His plan — to arrange his wife's kidnapping thereby splitting the ransom to be paid by his wealthy father-in-law — is conceived in gnawing greed and blind stupidity, and culminates in horrific tragedy imbued with macabre humor. All of the performances are remarkable, overtly broad yet cunningly subtle. Macy is an accomplished journeyman actor, and he renders an authentic and pathetic character. Steve Buscemi and Peter Stormare as the henchmen. But the absolute delight is Oscar-winning Frances McDormand as Margie the pregnant police chief, offhandedly battling morning sickness as she examines a triple-homicide crime scene. Minnesota's vast frozen expanses endow physicality to the desperate isolation which underlies this winter's tale. An unnerving study of human frailty and deception. ★★★★ $19.99

Farinelli

(1994, 110 min, Belgium, Gerard Corbiau) The tumultuous life of castrato singer Farinelli (nee Carlo Broschi), along with his co-dependent relationship with his brother, is bombasti-

F

cally explored in this absorbing if predictable period drama. Set in 18th-century France, the story revolves around the passionate, ambitious and handsome singer (played by Stefano Dionisi), whose beautiful voice — preserved through a traumatic castration as a boy — becomes his instrument for success. Riding the coattails of that success is his brother Ricardo (Enrico Lo Verso), a much less talented composer, and their intense love/hate relationship extends to their careers and romantic affairs. Jeroen Krabbé is very good as composer Handel who both admires, envies and admonishes the young singer. An elegant drama of unchecked ambition that sadly suffers from operatic excess, *Farinelli* could be called the *Lisztomania* for the opera set. (French and Italian with English subtitles) ★★½ $19.99

Fast Talking

(1986, 93 min, Australia, Ken Cameron) A sensitive comedy about the coming-of-age of a streetwise Australian youth who yearns to break out of the restricting confines of school and family life. A movie about hope, defiance and emotional honesty. ★★½ $19.99

Fast Times at Ridgemont High

(1982, 92 min, US, Amy Heckerling) "Hey dude, let's party." With these infamous four words, Sean Penn introduced the California Valley boy in this entertaining, wacky comedy whose moments of insight into the rigors of growing up elevate it far above the usual teenager-obsessed-with-sex flick. Some of the students who would go on to make a name for themselves include Jennifer Jason Leigh, Judge Reinhold, Phoebe Cates, Forest Whitaker, Eric Stoltz and Anthony Edwards. (Not a bad graduating class.) Heckerling's directorial debut. ★★★ $14.99

Faster, Pussycat, Kill! Kill!

(1966, 83 min, US, Russ Meyer) The best of Russ' black-and-white period. Tura Satana as Varla, the leader of a trio of wild go-go girls, is unforgettable; as is the dialogue, which defies description. A must-see! ★★★ $79.99

Fat City

(1973, 96 min, US, John Huston) After a period of intermittent critical and commercial success, Huston delivered this powerful portrayal of lonely outcasts on the fringes of the boxing world in California. Stacy Keach plays a down-and-out veteran of the ring and Jeff Bridges is a hungry newcomer. Susan Tyrrell is outstanding in support, giving a heartbreaking performance as a boisterous barfly. ★★★½ $19.99

Fat Man and Little Boy

(1989, 126 min, US, Roland Joffé) An absorbing drama about the birth of the atom bomb. Paul Newman, in an uncharacteristically unsympathetic and cold portrayal, stars as General Leslie Groves, the military leader who oversaw the project headed by the scientist J. Robert Oppenheimer. From this project would come the bombs which would be dropped on Hiroshima and Nagasaki. The film tries to create a mood of suspense in whether the scientists will succeed, but is far more interesting for the cat-and-mouse psychological games played between Groves and Oppenheimer in

their race to develop and ultimately use the bombs. ★★½ $14.99

Fatal Attraction

(1987, 119 min, US, Adrian Lyne) A box-office sensation, this psychological thriller is a not-too-subtle cautionary tale about adultery in the age of AIDS. Married exec Michael Douglas has a one-night stand with Glenn Close and lives to regret it. Anne Archer is the wife who is most hurt (literally) by the indiscretion. The film received a Best Picture nomination — a nod more to the socio-political impact of the story than a recognition of great filmmaking. (The Director's Cut is available for $29.99) ★★★ $14.99

Fatal Beauty

(1987, 104 min, US, Tom Holland) This attempt to cash in on the success of *Beverly Hills Cop* stars Whoopi Goldberg as an L.A. cop who's tracking down the source of a lethal batch of cocaine known as "Fatal Beauty." Very few thrills and an inferior story line is only partially offset by Goldberg's mugging. ★½ $9.99

Fatal Error

(1980, 90 min, The Netherlands, Wim Verstappen) As imaginative as its title, this limp cop caper is another of the seemingly endless stream of grade-B European action flicks Rutger Hauer made before he found fame (and better scripts) Stateside. This Dutch *Lethal Weapon* has a boyish Rutger as a bungling but charming detective who, with his partner, becomes embroiled in the mysterious suicide of a heroin dealer. Convinced that foul play was involved, the two try to uncover the killer by delving into the violent underbelly of Amsterdam's drug subculture. Inadvertently funny, the film proves that the Americans are best when it comes to crime thrillers, but nevertheless it's made all the more enjoyable by the irrepressible Hauer. (aka: *The Outsider*) (Dubbed) ★★

Fatal Instinct

(1993, 85 min, US, Carl Reiner) Unjustly maligned upon its release, *Fatal Instinct* is a sometimes very funny takeoff on film noir — and some of the targets include *Body Heat*, *Fatal Attraction*, *Basic Instinct* and *Double Indemnity*. Though no Leslie Nielsen, Armand Assante proves himself quite adept at parody, playing a cop/lawyer whose work for client Sean Young puts him on the road to danger. Kate Nelligan also stars as his wife, who's planning to knock off her husband and run off with her mechanic. As with most comedies of this sort, not all the gags work, but there's an abundance of laughs which do, thanks to a cast which clearly is having a lot of fun. Our favorite gag: Young's *Fatal Attraction* roller coaster ride. ★★★ $14.99

Fatal Vision

(1984, 192 min, US, David Greene) Critically acclaimed adaptation of the Joe McGinniss best-seller in which an ex-Green Beret is accused of murdering his pregnant wife and two young daughters, and his in-laws' relentless search for justice. Based on a true story. Good cast includes Karl Malden, Eva Marie Saint,

Father

Gary Cole, Barry Newman and Andy Griffith. ★★★ $29.99

Fate of Lee Khan

(1973, 105 min, Hong Kong, King Hu) Set during the Mongol-ruled Huan Dynasty, this exhilarating martial arts actioner is considered by many to be a classic of the genre. The story centers around Lee Khan, who finds himself in possession of a map needed by a band of Chinese patriots (mostly women) in their efforts at revolutionary uprising. Done with humor, operatic swordplay and choreographed fighting, *Khan* follows its hero's dilemma as he must decide to which side to pledge his allegiance. (Cantonese with English subtitles) ★★★½ $39.99

Father

(1966, 89 min, Hungary, István Szabó) A sensitive and involving look at a young man's maturation as he searches for the real conditions that caused his father's death in World War II. (Hungarian with English subtitles) ★★★

Father

(1991, 106 min, Australia, John Power) Set in modern-day Melbourne, this touching, emotional story concentrates on a middle-class family, including a young mother, her husband and their young daughters, who run a small hotel and restaurant, along with her aging father who built the place many years ago. An anonymous phone call urges the woman to watch a TV documentary one night, so as to learn the "real past" of her father. In a riveting moment, the woman is forced to delve into her father's questionable past: Was her father involved in a hideous and brutal war crime, and if so, then what has he been pretending to be all these years? Reminiscent of Costa-Gavras' much slicker *Music Box*, *Father* is smaller in scale, but packs more power, due in large part to Max von Sydow's tortured and pained portrayal of a man confronting himself, a confused daughter and a possibly heinous past. ★★★ $19.99

Father Goose

(1964, 116 min, US, Ralph Nelson) Cary Grant goes beach bum in this entertaining, sporadically funny comic adventure, the next-to-the-last film the actor would make. Set during WWII, the film casts Grant as a beachcomber living alone on a small South Seas island who is "drafted" by the Australian navy as a lookout. Complications, romance and some laughs arise when he rescues a French schoolmistress and six refugee children adrift at sea. Leslie Caron and Trevor Howard also star in this Oscar winner (Best Screenplay). ★★★ $19.99

Father of the Bride

(1950, 93 min, US, Vincente Minnelli) In this delightful family comedy, Spencer Tracy may have proved the inspiration for every sitcom father who has ever had to deal with a teenager. But few have done it better; it's hard to believe someone could be so funny just lifting an eyebrow. The story follows father Tracy and mother Joan Bennett readying for daughter Elizabeth Taylor's wedding. ★★★½ $14.99

Father of the Bride

(1991, 105 min, US, Charles Shyer) Steve Martin takes over the Spencer Tracy role from the 1950 classic comedy about a family preparing for their eldest daughter's wedding. Martin, who doesn't attempt to compete with Tracy, gives a very funny performance as the exasperated dad, but the film manages to be only mildly amusing even with Martin's presence. As with the original, Mom (played endearingly by Diane Keaton) and Dad become overwhelmed by all the arrangements – both financial and otherwise – for their daughter's wedding. From the in-laws to the caterers (Martin Short and B.D. Wong in offensively gay stereotypes), it's a never-ending calamity while the father of the bride handles with one-liners, pratfalls and humiliation. Putting aside expectations, this *Father* knows how to charm when it wants to, but it's only a stand-in for the original. ★★½ $14.99

Father of the Bride, Part II

(1995, 106 min, US, Charles Shyer) This painfully unfunny, sugar-coated "comedy" about the travails of a rich family will send hypoglycemics into shock and anyone else possessing an even mildly cynical nature to seek out a large barf bag. A follow-up to the 1991 hit and based on the screenplay of the 1951 film *Father's Little Dividend*, this flimsy excuse for a movie stars Steve Martin as George Banks, the grumpy and whiny husband of Nina (an often-in-soft-focus Dianne Keaton), the 1950s idea of the perfect wife. The premise is that both his wife and daughter become pregnant (and that's it folks – that's the plot – they each deliver a baby and then the movie ends!). Martin Short and B.D. Wong return from the '91 original reprising their offensive roles as swishy and shrill decorators. ★ $14.99

Father's Day

(1997, 98 min, US, Ivan Reitman) Admittedly, the thought of Robin Williams and Billy Crystal costarring in their first film together would seem almost heaven-sent. No other contemporary comics can equal their collective gift for delivery, ad-libbing, character and timing. Their annual "Comic Relief" appearances are convulsive. Expectations aside, however, their first joint venture is only occasionally funny, and director Reitman doesn't give his stars ample room in which to explore the

comic possibilities of the scenario. Based on the French comedy *Les Comperes*, the story begins when former lover Nastassja Kinski tells both Williams and Crystal that her missing son is his. They eventually unite to locate the teenager, and their incompatability sets the stage for a few laughs. On-screen together for most of the film's running time, the two stars – as would be expected – have a great rapport; they're the Lemmon and Matthau of the '90s. But the screenplay just isn't consistently funny. And what should have been non-stop hilarity is instead a cute comedy-of-errors with two incredibly gifted but underused leads. ★★½ $99.99

Father's Little Dividend

(1951, 82 min, US, Vincente Minnelli) Cheerful sequel to the hit comedy *Father of the Bride*. Spencer Tracy, Elizabeth Taylor, Joan Bennett and Billie Burke all repeat their roles as newlywed Taylor returns home – expecting. ★★★ $19.99

Fatherland

(1994, 100 min, US, Christopher Menaue) It's 1964. Hitler, having won WWII, dominates Europe (now known as Germania), but is still battling guerrillas in Russia. Needing an alliance with the United States, Germany opens its borders to American journalists for the first time since the war. The Reich readies for a celebration of the Fuhrer's 75th birthday, and there are rumors of a summit with U.S. President Joseph Kennedy, Sr. SS Major Rutger Hauer (the SS is now the peacetime police), through unusual elements in a murder investigation, and U.S. journalist Miranda Richardson, spurred by a stranger's communication, cross paths while tracking down a decades-old mystery. This HBO production is a well-executed thriller which makes good use of an intriguing premise and is uncomfortably effective in imagining life in a prosperous authoritarian state. ★★★½ $19.99

Fatso

(1980, 94 min, US, Anne Bancroft) First-time director Bancroft treads into husband Mel Brooks' territory with this occasionally amusing though disappointing comedy about an obese man's attempts to diet. Dom DeLuise makes the most of the material ("Get the honey!"), but even his larger-than-life comedic talents aren't enough to warrant a recommendation. ★★ $14.99

Faust

(1994, 97 min, Czech Republic, Jan Svankmajer) A warped, hypnotic retelling of the Faust legend. Anyone familiar with Czech animator Svankmajer knows he's not going to helm the next *Winnie the Pooh* episode. His films are adult, dark, obsessive and truly surreal. *Faust* is definitely no exception. Making use of marionettes, live action and stop-motion animation, Svankmajer arguably has made his most mature, haunting and affecting film to date – after a slow start, this becomes fascinating and enthralling. Svankmajer is able to take clay figures and clunky puppets and creak memorable images that are disturbing and hilarious, revolting and gorgeous. A real pleasure for fans of the bizarre. ★★★½ $79.99

The Favor

(1994, 97 min, US, Donald Petrie) When married Kathy (Harley Jane Kozak) can't get her old flame (Ken Wahl) out of her amorous fantasies, she convinces her semi-single friend Emily (Elizabeth McGovern) to act as her...well, as her proxy in love, thereby being able to enjoy an extramarital affair vicariously. Of course, a few problems arise, like the protests of Emily's young beau (Brad Pitt). A tepid comedy buoyed by McGovern's quirky charms, *The Favor* was shelved for a few years and its ultimate theatrical release was no doubt prompted by Pitt's new matinee idol status. ★★ $14.99

The Favor, the Watch and the Very Big Fish

(1991, 89 min, GB, Ben Lewin) Bob Hoskins photographs religious tableaus for the greater glory of the Mother Church. He's given the assignment to find a new Christ on the same day a friend asks a favor, in the execution of which he meets Natasha Richardson, an enchanting young woman with an incredible story about a watch. Michel Blanc and Jeff Goldblum join them in this fanciful and irreverent tale of the foibles of belief and the dangers of misplaced faith, with side commentary on the commercial manufacture of sublime images. Lewin directs his delightful script with wit and vigor, and the cast is engaging. As the two guys at the river bank note, "I just saw someone trying to walk on the water." "It happens. Go to sleep." ★★★ $9.99

Fawlty Towers

(90 min ea., GB) Basil Fawlty (John Cleese) is a pompous, overbearing, neurotic, repressed, condescending, snobbish martinet. He owns and runs Fawlty Towers, a hotel in the resort town of Torque ("...on the British Riviera"), serving a clientele which includes con artists, the hard of hearing, psychiatrists, spoon salesmen and Germans. His wife and staff work hard to protect the hotel's operation from the effects of Basil's misconceptions and prejudices. John Cleese, with his then-wife Connie Booth, wrote 12 perfect episodes chronicling the exploits of these intrepid hoteliers. Booth also plays Polly, the waitress/maid/desk clerk and occasional voice of reason. Prunella Scales as Basil's wife, Sybil, is a magnificent combination of iron-fisted expediency and air-headed self-indulgence. Andrew Sachs as the waiter, Manuel, combines guileless innocence with a wide-eyed wonder at the intricacies of the English language. This is hilarious in any language or accent, and it's unsurpassed for sheer pleasure. ★★★★ $14.99 each

Vol. 1: Basil wins big at the track and has "Communications Problems" trying to keep his good fortune from his wife; Thinking Basil has forgotten "The Anniversary," Sybil is a no-show at her surprise party; In "Basil the Rat," Manuel's pet rat is lost somewhere in the dining room just as the health inspector arrives.

Vol. 2: High society shows up at Fawlty Towers for "Gourmet Night," but the chef is plastered and it's up to Basil to make the meal; An American guest who can't get a "Waldorf Salad" makes life miserable for the entire staff; A guest dies during breakfast and Basil tries to keep anyone from finding out in "The Kipper and the Corpse."

Vol. 3: "The Builders" are fixing the hotel but they're so inept they make Basil look competent; Basil thinks "The Wedding Party" is behaving immorally and acts like a second-rate hotel detective; "The Psychiatrist" may have enough for a second novel after his stay at Fawlty Towers.

Vol. 4: Basil thinks a rude guest is one of the "Hotel Inspectors" and bends over backwards to please him; "The Germans" have arrived and the hotel is in chaos; Basil tries to bring "A Touch of Class" to the hotel when high society shows up.

Fear

(1954, 84 min, Italy, Roberto Rossellini) Rossellini's last and darkest film stars Ingrid Bergman and shows a marriage stumbling across lines of suspicion, mistrust and fear. Unfaithful wife Bergman is blackmailed by her lover's ex-girlfriend (and husband?). Her guilt drives her further into a series of lies leading to tragedy. (Filmed in English) ★★½

Fear

(1990, 98 min, US, Rockne O'Bannon) Ally Sheedy stars in this intriguing suspenser as a psychic police consultant who meets her match in a nefarious serial killer (is there any other kind?) who shares her mind-reading capabilities. This made-for-cable thriller should be appreciated by mystery fans for its taut scenes of mental cat-and-mouse. Also with Lauren Hutton, Michael O'Keefe and Stan Shaw. ★★★ $9.99

Fear

(1996, 95 min, US, James Foley) Director Foley, occasionally hot (*After Dark My Sweet, Glengarry Glen Ross*), occasionally not (*Reckless, Who's That Girl*), finds his career cooling behind the camera of the lastest ".....from Hell" film. When adorable adolescent Reese Witherspoon finds herself the object of obsession of bad-boy Mark Wahlberg, bad things ensue, especially bad things for — surprise — the family pet and the sensitive best friend. The screenplay appears to have been written with much help from a psychology textbook as there is no shortage of *quien es mas macho* posturing between boyfriend and Mr. Father Knows Best (William L. Petersen) and a "You're not my mother" conflict between daughter and stepmom. *Fear* is not so bad as much as it is a standard, predictable genre thriller. Sadly, though, of all the homicidal Wife/Mistress/Roommate/Nanny movies, the psycho boyfriend story is probably the one with the strongest connection to the real world and it deserves to have yielded a better film. ★½ $14.99

Fear City

(1984, 93 min, US, Abel Ferrara) From the director of *The King of New York* comes this grade-B thriller about New York City strippers getting sliced and diced by a self-righteous martial arts expert hell-bent on cleansing the city. The film features a surprisingly high-profile cast which includes Melanie Griffith, Tom Berenger, Billy Dee Williams, Rae Dawn

Chong, Jack Scalia and Maria Conchita Alonso in an uncredited role. ★★½

The Fear Inside

(1992, 100 min, US, Leon Ichaso) The ever-underrated Christine Lahti headlines this sterling nail-biter about a woman suffering from acute agoraphobia, making it impossible for her to leave the house — even when it is taken over by a psychotic couple on the run. Nostalgia fans will undoubtedly recognize this as an updating of the 1964 cult classic *Lady in a Cage*, which starred Olivia deHavilland as an invalid trapped in her home elevator. By changing the prison from a physical one to one of the mind, the terror and helplessness are made all the more real. Also featuring Dylan McDermott and a scene-stealing performance by Jennifer Rubin. ★★★ $9.99

Fear of a Black Hat

(1994, 86 min, US, Rusty Cundieff) First-time director Cundieff wears many hats, including writer and star, in this often hilarious, sophisticated *This Is Spinal Tap*-like parody about the making of a documentary of a "rags to riches" Public Enemy-like rap group called N.W.H. ("Niggaz with Hats"), whose members display an obscene fascination for "booty," guns and hats. The insipid head of the group, Ice Cold (Cundieff), and his daffy cohorts are seen in interviews and personal moments, all of them blistering funny. But the film's true genius lies in its scathing skewering of rap industry infighting, as well as the group's off-the-cuff, outlandish "PC" justifications for the sexism, misogyny, racism amd violence strewn throughout their music (as exampled in one of their songs, "Come and Pet the P.U.S.S.Y."). Mark Christopher Lawrence and Larry B. Scott are the other members of the group, Kasi Lemmons is the director of the documentary, and all are first-rate. ★★★½ $14.99

Fear Strikes Out

(1957, 100 min, US, Robert Mulligan) Unflinching examination of baseball player Jimmy Piersall, whose battle with mental illness is tensely brought to the screen by a standout portrayal from Anthony Perkins. Another strong performance from veteran Karl Malden as Piersall's father. ★★★ $14.99

Fearless

(1993, 122 min, US, Peter Weir) Weir returns to form with this unnerving character study, reminiscent of the director's more complex Australian works. In his second powerhouse performance of 1993, Jeff Bridges is remarkable as an airplane crash survivor who undergoes a dramatic change of personality. Having saved several lives on the plane, Bridges begins to assume a Christ-like persona as he moves further away from his loved ones and forms a bond with another survivor (Rosie Perez in an unexpectedly controlled and riveting performance), a mother whose two-year-old died in the crash. Perez and Bridges' scenes together possess a rare intensity, and both actors are the driving force of the film. Weir is successful in both examining the damaged psyches of his characters, and keeping a firm hand on an extremely well-directed crash sequence, told mostly through flashback. ★★★½ $14.99

The Fearless Vampire Killers

(1967, 107 min, GB, Roman Polanski) The restored version of this horror comedy adds over fifteen minutes of material to Polanski's loving tribute to the vampire films of Hammer Studios. Polanski himself plays one of the hunters out to rid the world of vampirism. Also starring Jack MacGowran and Sharon Tate. The full title is *The Fearless Vampire Killers or Pardon Me, But Your Teeth Are in My Neck.* ★★★ $14.99

Feast of July

(1995, 118 min, GB, Christopher Menaul) While this Ismail Merchant production would be but a minor addition to the oeuvre of his directing partner James Ivory, it is a fine first outing for British TV helmer Menaul. True to decorative detail and languid rhythms we associate with that era, *Feast of July* is a wistful pleasantry along the lines of *A Room with a View* and those other genteel romances, needing only Alastair Cooke's gently guiding introduction to make one feel certain it is a quiet Sunday evening and "Masterpiece Theatre" is on the telly. Embeth Davidtz embodies the broken and battered Bella Ford, a woman led astray in a town and a time not known to be forgiving. She is forced to bury her stillborn baby in the rough earth and seek sanctuary in the house of a lamplighter and his marriageable sons. Whether tragedy or happiness is to be found there is wherein hangs the tale, one that is engrossing during its telling but forgotten at its end. ★★½ $19.99

Fedora

(1978, 114 min, West Germany/US, Billy Wilder) This fascinating curiosity from Wilder, towards the end of his career, stars William Holden as an independent film producer who goes to Greece in search of Fedora, an actress from Hollywood's glamour years who now lives in a secluded villa. The film demonstrates a more romantic side of Wilder, but his potshots at contemporary Hollywood lack the bite of his more classic turns in the director's chair, most notably *Sunset Boulevard*. ★★★ $19.99

Feed

(1992, 76 min, US, Kevin Rafferty & James Ridgeway) A must-see for anyone who claims to be politically aware, *Feed* is a wittily edited montage of satellite footage filmed during the 1992 presidential campaign. Offering a glimpse of what goes on "prior" to some of the speeches and interviews of various presidential candidates, the film captures Jerry Brown being snippy and narcissistic, Bush flubbing and Clinton being slick. A highlight comes during an interview with Gennifer Flowers when Howard Stern employee Stuttering John asks if Clinton used a rubber and if she planned on sleeping with any other presidential candidates. A great film to watch with others, it's almost as comical as the 1992 presidential and vice-presidential debates. ★★★½ $29.99

Feeling Minnesota

(1996, 95 min, US, Steven Baigelman) As pseduo-hip and annoying as the worst Tarantino rip-off, *Feeling Minnesota* fails as thriller, Generation X road movie, and Tarantino-wannabe. The dull plot concerns a prodigal son named Jjaks (gosh, how cool!) who returns home for his loathsome brother's wedding to a bombshell (Cameron Diaz, who's forced to marry the lout as punishment for stealing from the local baddie), only to run off with sister-in-law. A corrupt cop (played terribly by Dan Aykroyd) and a friendly waitress (very well played by Courtney Love) also pop in and out of the film, which is basically a series of fistfights and shouting matches set to an alternative beat. With the exception of Love's waitress, all the characters are scum, and the "big twist" is as illogical and obvious as the surprise ending of a minor "Hart to Hart" episode. Vincent D'Onofrio's Method-y bully is irritating in the extreme, allowing Keanu Reeves' "subdude" performance to appear almost inspired. It's not, and neither is this tepid film. ★½ $101.89

Fellini Satyricon

(1969, 129 min, Italy, Federico Fellini) A wild and shocking phantamagoria set in a world of hermaphrodites, dwarves, prostitutes, nymphomaniacs and homosexual youths. Boldly bizarre in the unmistakable Fellini manner. (Italian with English subtitles) ★★★½ $19.99

Fellini's Roma

(1972, 128 min, Italy, Federico Fellini) Nostalgic and lavishly impressionistic, this "story of a city" is an engrossing tour of the Eternal City. Spanning from the '30s to the turbulent Rome of the '70s, Fellini offers a diverse view of his home through a mélange of deeply personal images of this vital, passionate land. ★★★ $19.99

Fellow Traveler

(1989, 97 min, GB, Philip Saville) *Fellow Traveler* is a totally engrossing psychological mystery about a blacklisted Hollywood writer living in England who learns of the suicide of his best friend. Ron Silver is splendid as the writer who, haunted by the memory of his friend (Hart Bochner), tries to piece together the reason and circumstance of his death — even at the risk of his own safety. Daniel J. Travanti is fine as Silver's former psychiatrist who may hold the key to the tragedy. An intriguing glimpse into the days of blacklisting

and anti-Communist hysteria, and of the pain endured by those blacklisted. ★★★

Female

(1933, 60 min, US, Michael Curtiz) This early directorial effort by Curtiz is a foreshadowing of his greatness to come (*Casablanca, Mildred Pierce*, etc.). Ruth Chatterton is Alison Drake, head of an automobile factory. She's never found a man who's an equal match, although she's had some fun along the way. George Brent (Chatterton's real-life husband) plays a new employee who's not afraid to say no to her. Of course, this is exactly what she needs. Looking for a man who wants her for herself and not her money, she struggles with her identity: can she be a hard-working woman and still be "feminine?" Never too melodramatic and surprisingly explicit, the film's subject matter is still relevant today. ★★★½ $19.99

Female Jungle

(1956, 73 min, US, Bruno Vesota) A booze-binging cop (Lawrence Tierney) may or may not have committed a murder during an alcoholic blackout, and only a footloose model (Jayne Mansfield) holds the key to the mystery. John Carradine appears as a venomous gossip columnist. ★★ $29.99

Female Misbehavior

(1983-92, 80 min, Germany/US, Monica Treut) Amusing and provocative, this series of four shorts explores the expanding boundaries of female sexuality by focusing on four unique and divergent women, all outcasts from conventional society as well as outlaws from mainstream feminism. *Bondage* (1983, 20 min) features an unidentified woman explaining the pleasures of bondage and tit torture and the "very warm, very safe, very secure" feeling that comes with it. *Annie* (1989, 10 min) stars ex-porn actress and performance artist (and self-declared "post-porn modernist") Annie Sprinkle, who offers an entertaining segment in which she transforms "average" women into sex stars and invites the audience to join her in examining and admiring her cervix with the aid of a flashlight and a speculum. *Dr. Paglia*

(1992, 23 min) features Dr. Camile Paglia, professor of Humanities at Philadelphia's University of the Arts, who came into contentious prominence with the publication of her best-selling book, "Sexual Personae," in 1990. The narcissistic, "anti-feminist" feminist and "academic rottweiler" discusses her theories as well as her disastrous sex life. *Max* (1992, 27 min) is perhaps the most fascinating of the segments. Interviewed is Native American Anita Valerio, who was formerly a stunningly beautiful lesbian but who now, thanks to surgery, is Max, a handsome heterosexual "almost" male. His discussion of the power of testosterone is highly amusing. ★★★ $29.99

Female Trouble

(1974, 95 min, US, John Waters) Follow the trials and tribulations of Dawn Davenport (Divine): from cha-cha heel obsessed teen to rape victim to murderess to electric chair victim. Waters' ode to misguided teen traumas and prison melodrama includes satirical blasts at middle-class values, performance art, and really bad makeup. ★★★ $59.99

La Femme Nikita

(1990, 117 min, France, Luc Besson) Action-packed and filled with mega-violence, Besson's wonderfully entertaining romantic thriller is one part *Clockwork Orange*, and two parts "Pygmalion." The seductively pouty and dazzlingly leggy Anne Parillaud debuts as Nikita, a modern-day Liza Doolittle with a vicious mean streak. Besson's story follows her somewhat Orwellian transformation from savagely criminal, punked-out heroin addict to well-groomed, statuesque and cold-blooded assassin for the French government. Soon, however, she begins to experience stirrings of humanity, which elevates *La Femme Nikita* above its action-adventure status. True to his "Boutique Cinema" roots, Besson bathes his visuals in neon-drenched colors and captures the action with a high-fashion, nouveau-chic panache. (American remake: *Point of No Return*) (French with English subtitles) ★★★½ $14.99

Femmes de Paris (Peek-a-Boo)

(1953, 83 min, France, Jean Loubignac) A delightful backstage comedy set in a burlesque hall and featuring the "Bluebell Girls" who provide the beauty (and some daring nudity!) and Louis de Funes who delivers the comedy. Adapted from the play "Ah, Les Belles Bacchantes." (French with English subtitles) ★★★

Ferngully — The Last Rainforest

(1992, 72 min, US, Bill Kroyer) Superb animation, an excellent cast and a very timely message more than compensate for the relatively weak tale of fairies and humans engaged in a power struggle over the valuable rainforest. The fairies and their friends (most notably Robin Williams as Batty Bat) are happily living in a magical rainforest until the humans, while thoughtlessly cutting down trees, unleash the mysterious, evil monster Hexxus (nastily vocalized by Tim Curry). The humans and fairies must then band together to fight him, learning to respect each other along the way. While over-simplistic, the themes serve to promote ecological awareness at an early age. ★★★ $14.99

Anne Parillaud in *La Femme Nikita*

F

Ferris Bueller's Day Off

(1986, 103 min, US, John Hughes) Often hilarious Hughes teen comedy with Matthew Broderick in great form as a high school student whose charm and ingenuity are able to get him into — and out of — any situation of his choosing. The story follows Bueller and his friends playing hooky and visiting downtown Chicago. ★★★½ $14.99

A Few Good Men

(1992, 138 min, US, Rob Reiner) Tom Cruise's high-octane performance as a cocky but lovable underdog (a role he's played before) helps energize an already compelling courtroom drama and murder mystery. Cruise plays a Navy lawyer who is chosen to defend two Marines accused of killing a fellow soldier. The question is: Were the two young cadets acting on their own, or were they under orders from a superior officer? As Cruise and fellow lawyers Demi Moore (who is actually fully clothed here) and Kevin Pollak feverishly investigate the killing, they are thwarted by military red tape and uncooperative soldiers at every turn. In a small but pivotal role, Jack Nicholson is the essence of the quintessential military mindset and gives a spellbinding performance as an over-zealous commander. Also with Kiefer Sutherland and Kevin Bacon. (Available letterboxed and pan & scan) ★★★½ $14.99

ffolkes

(1980, 99 min, GB, Andrew V. McLaglen) A surprisingly entertaining high-seas actioner with Anthony Perkins chewing the scenery as the leader of a group of terrorists who have taken over a supply ship. Roger Moore, in a playful mood, is the disheveled hero out to stop them. ★★★ $59.99

Fiddler on the Roof

(1971, 181 min, US, Norman Jewison) Magnificent screen version of the smash Broadway musical based on the stories of Sholem Aleichem. Chaim Topol plays Tevye the milkman (and he almost makes one forget about Zero Mostel), a poor Jewish husband and father of five who grapples with changing religious and social mores in Czarist Russia. The musical sequences are outstanding, and the classic score includes "If I Were a Rich Man" and "Sunrise, Sunset." (Available letterboxed and pan & scan) ★★★★ $24.99

The Field

(1990, 110 min, Ireland, Jim Sheridan) Richard Harris' excellent performance dominates this emotionally satisfying, leisurely paced and beautifully filmed story of obsession and murder. Harris plays (appropriately named) Bull McCabe, a poor farmer working the fields of the gorgeous Irish countryside whose determination and inflexibility towards acquiring a piece of land — one he had been cultivating for decades — leads to tragedy. An able supporting cast includes John Hurt as the town lackey, Sean Bean as Bull's less-than-bright son, Brenda Fricker as Bull's wife and Tom Berenger as "the American." ★★★½ $9.99

Field of Dreams

(1989, 106 min, US, Phil Alden Robinson) "If you build it, he will come." This is what novice farmer Kevin Costner hears in his cornfield one day, accompanied by a vision for him to build a baseball field. Acting on faith alone, he builds it, and "he" does come; he being the ghost of the great "Shoeless" Joe Jackson. This warm and humorous fantasy is a profoundly moving and magical fable about faith, redemption and our national pastime. Costner, the closest embodiment of idealism we've seen on the screen since that of young James Stewart or Henry Fonda, excels as the farmer; as does James Earl Jones as a reclusive, iconoclastic 1960s author who journeys with Costner. This is our generation's *It's a Wonderful Life*. ★★★★ $9.99

Field of Honor

(1988, 87 min, France, Jean-Pierre Denis) Set in 1870 France, this subtle but moving drama concerns a naive farm boy who, as was common at the time, is paid by a rich merchant to take the place of his son in the army. But he is soon disillusioned once he witnesses the horrors of war. (French with English subtitles) ★★★ $19.99

Fiend without a Face

(1958, 74 min, GB, Arthur Crabtree) Lifting a lesson from the Krell, a scientist using simple everyday objects manages to materialize his thoughts. Unfortunately, he's thinking about brains that crawl around on their spinal cords and suck the mental matter out of the heads of the local villagers who are revolted and revolt. The special effects are surprisingly good, and the film is both very effective and frightening. ★★★ $19.99

Fierce Creatures

(1997, 98 min, GB/US, Robert Young & Fred Schepisi) The cast of 1988's wacky Monty Python-esque comedy classic *A Fish Called Wanda* reunites for this not-really-a-sequel. The plot concerns a rich Australian tycoon (Kevin Kline) who overtakes a British company that controls, among other things, a zoo. Kline also plays the tycoon's oversexed, ne'er-do-well son, and he and the sexy Jamie Lee Curtis supervise the promotional overhaul of the zoo, set in motion by the rigid and seemingly animal-hating new director (John Cleese). In an effort to boost profits and give patrons the carnage they *really* want, only fierce animals are to be kept on hand. This sets up all sorts of comic situations in which the animal caretakers try to B.S. their way into convincing Cleese that various cute little critters are actually rabid, carnivorous vermin. The film has a few clever bits but, ultimately, it's not nearly as funny as *Wanda*, simply because the pitch-black humor and cheerful malevolence of the first film was substituted for cute, family-friendly hijinks. Very uneven, but the cast really shines, and it's obvious that they had a lot of fun working together again. ★★½ $102.99

The Fifth Element

(1997, 127 min, US, Luc Besson) Besson's Gallic sensibilities serve him well once again (as they did before in *The Professional*) in this sci-fi near-epic starring Bruce Willis as a cab driver who saves the world. Corbin Dallas, a decorated ex-soldier, is called upon to do his duty again when a gigantic, intelligent ball of indestructible black flame is discovered to be advancing toward the Earth. Luckily, Corbin has the assistance of the Fifth Element, the Supreme Being of the Universe, who also happens to be a very cute and very deadly, orange-haired young alien lady (Milla Jovovich). Standing in their way is a weapons magnate (Gary Oldman) with big buck teeth and an accent to rival Foghorn Leghorn's. Sound strange? It certainly is, but the special effects and overall visual design of the film are stunning, creating one of the best and most completely conceived future worlds seen on-screen since *Blade Runner*. And the mostly French crew bring a mindset to the film which would be absent if it had been a wholly American production. Unfortunately, the story itself does not live up to its look and feel. Alternately goofy and flashy, and sometimes too serious for its own good, it succeeds as fantastic popcorn entertainment, but falls short of being a speculative science fiction classic. ★★★ $99.99

The Fifth Monkey

(1990, 93 min, GB/Brazil, Eric Rochat) A lushly photographed though slow-moving version of Jacques Zibi's novel, "Le Cinquieme Singe." Ben Kingsley, in another of his patented eccentric characterizations, plays a peasant animal trader whose discovery of four chimpanzees in the Brazilian wilderness seems to be the answer to his matrimonial money problems. En route through the jungles to sell the animals, however, Kingsley comes up against mercenaries and corrupt officials; and in the process, of course — thanks to his simian compadres — learns the value of true friendship. ★★ $89.99

55 Days at Peking

(1963, 154 min, US, Nicholas Ray) Sprawling, exciting epic with Charlton Heston, Ava Gardner and David Niven as a group of Europeans involved in the Chinese Boxer Rebellion of 1900. ★★★ $29.99

52 Pick-Up

(1986, 114 min, US, John Frankenheimer) Elmore Leonard's best-selling novel makes for an exciting screen thriller. Roy Scheider plays a successful businessman who takes on a group of blackmailing pornographers. Solid support from John Glover as the villainous ringleader. ★★★ $9.99

Fight for Us

(1989, 92 min, The Philippines, Lino Brocka) Filmed clandestinely, director Brocka's stirring drama explores the political chaos and repression in The Philippines after a bloody revolution brings down a dictator only to install an equally corrupt "democracy." Jimmy Cordero is a former priest and dissident freed from jail after Marcos' downfall. He finds his efforts to resume a normal life interrupted when he is forced to confront a group of vigilantes who commit mass murders all under the name of democracy and anti-Communism. His efforts to bring these men to justice and to expose their connection to the government embroils him in a bloody fight that threatens an entire village as well as his wife, friends and children. ★★★ $79.99

The Films of James Broughton: Erotic Celebrations

The physical meets the philosophical in this collection of shorts directed by Broughton. *The*

Fierce Creatures

Bed (1968, 20 min) is a delightfully lyrical homage to the bed and the various roles it plays in our lives. Broughton's inspiration for the film came when "I couldn't get out of my mind how all the great events in my life take place in bed." In *Erogeny* (1976, 6 min), sensual touch is compared to the exploration of landscapes. *Herme's Bird* (1979, 11 min) glorifies the male phallus; and *Song of the Goodbody* (1977, 10 min) is a sly attack on sexual taboos. $29.99

The Films of James Broughton: Rituals of Play

Three early avant-garde works by director Broughton. *Mother's Day* (1948, 22 min) is an ironic nostalgic collection of pranks, fetishes amd rituals of a childhood dominated by a narcissistic mother obsessed with mirrors, big hats and proper behavior. *Four in the Afternoon* (1951, 15 min) tells of four people's search for love, based on Broughton's own poetry. Dylan Thomas described the film as "lovely and delicious; true cinematic poetry." The final short is *Loony Tom, the Happy Lover* (1951, 15 min), an homage to Mack Sennett. This slapstick comedy and Cannes Festival winner is about a woman-seducing tramp played by mime artist Kermit Sheets and is what Broughton calls "an impudent testimony to the liberating spirit of Pan." $29.99

The Films of James Broughton: The Pleasure Garden

Made in Great Britain (1953, 38 min) and winner of a special prize for poetic fantasy at Canner in 1954, this comic fairy tale, produced by Lindsay Anderson, was filmed at the ruined gardens of London's Crystal Palace. $29.99

The Films of James Broughton: Autobiographical Mysteries

The world according to Broughton is told in *Testament* (1974, 20 min), a complex collage of personal imagery, songs and dreams. *Devotions* (1983, 22 min), co-directed with Joel Singer, is a personal vision of a world of brotherly love. *Scattered Remains* (1983, 22 min) is a filmed performance piece of Singer "doing" Broughton. $29.99

The Films of James Broughton: Parables of Wonder

In this series of short films, Broughton deals with metaphysical themes, especially Zen Buddhism and Lao-Tzu. Total running time is 56 minutes and it includes *The Golden Positions* (1970, 32 min), a lovely, erotic and humorous blending of anatomical tableaus and pantomine; *The Gardener of Eden*; and *The Water Circle*. $29.99

The Films of James Broughton: Dreamwood

Dreamwood (1972, 45 min) is a spiritual odyssey into the landscape of a dream. Its poet hero, setting forth to rescue the bride of his soul, embarks on a voyage to a strange island where in a magical forest, he faces the most improbable experience of his life. $29.99

Final Analysis

(1992, 124 min, US, Phil Joanou) First teamed in *No Mercy*, where they caused very few sparks, Richard Gere and Kim Basinger are together again in this routine but flashy thriller. An unusually low-key Gere plays a successful San Francisco psychiatrist who, faster than you can say "Prince of Tides," becomes involved with a relative of one of his patients. The patient: Uma Thurman, who weekly shows up with new and interesting stories. The relative: Basinger, a beauty who could use a few hours on the couch herself. As Gere becomes spellbound by Basinger, he finds himself caught in a deadly game of cat and mouse between Basinger and her gangster husband Eric Roberts. Director Joanou pays homage to *Vertigo* in a crucial scene, and, in an ironic development, there's a peculiar plot device which figured heavily in Basinger's *Blind Date*. ★★½ $9.99

The Final Countdown

(1980, 104 min, US, Don Taylor) Intriguing and imaginative sci-fi outing with Kirk Douglas as the commander of an aircraft carrier who is suddenly transported — with his ship and crew — back to the Pacific just days before the Pearl Harbor attack. Also with Martin Sheen, Katharine Ross and James Farentino. ★★★

Finders Keepers, Lovers Weepers

(1968, 72 min, US, Russ Meyer) Inspired by Don Siegel's gangster movies, *Finders Keepers, Lovers Weepers* is about a robbery attempt in a go-go dance bar that gets out of hand. There's a memorable sequence of a couple making love out with a demolition derby. Starring the bosom brigade of Ann Chapman, Lavelle Roby and Jan Sinclair. ★★ $79.99

A Fine Madness

(1966, 104 min, US, Irvin Kershner) Elliot Baker did a fine adaptation of his own satiric novel, retaining much of its bite and a lot of its slapstick. Taking a break from his role as 007, Sean Connery plays an egocentric poet at odds with the world, including wife Joanne Woodward. ★★★ $14.99

A Fine Mess

(1986, 100 min, US, Blake Edwards) Ted Danson and Howie Mandel are two get-rich-quick schemers chased throughout Los Angeles by two petty, inept thieves. Unfortunately, there is nothing worth recommending in this stupid and unfunny comedy. ★ $19.99

Fingers

(1978, 91 min, US, James Toback) Gritty Scorsese-esque character study of an aspiring concert pianist (Harvey Keitel) who moonlights as a debt collector for his aging mafioso father. Though favorably reviewed upon its initial release, the film failed to receive audience support, and over the years has attained a certain cult status. Also with Jim Brown and Tisa Farrow. ★★★ $29.99

Finian's Rainbow

(1968, 145 min, US, Francis Ford Coppola) Coppola's glossy but rather stilted song-and-dance is based on the Burton Lane-E.Y. Harburg Broadway musical. Fred Astaire, bringing a touch of dignity and immeasurable charm, the scene-stealing Tommy Steele, and Petula Clark as Astaire's spirited daughter, star in this story of racism, lephrechuans and a stolen crock of gold. ★★½ $19.99

Finnegan Begin Again

(1984, 112 min, US, Joan Micklin Silver) Mary Tyler Moore and especially Robert Preston offer strong performances in this delightful made-for-cable movie about the relationship between a sixtysomething newspaper man and a 40-ish schoolteacher. Also starring Sam Waterston and Sylvia Sydney. ★★★ $29.99

Fiorile

(1992, 118 min, Italy, Paolo & Vittorio Taviani) A wonderful tale spanning three hundred years in a family's history of unrequited love. A poor farmer's daughter, Fiorile Benedetti, falls in love with a soldier of Napoleon's troops sent to insure safe passage of a chest of gold. While they tryst, her brother finds the gold on the back of a stray mule. Rather than return the gold, the brother keeps it, prompting the French to kill the soldier;

which, in turn, leaves Fiorile listless and pregnant. She places a curse on the person who caused her lover to be killed. This sets off the continuation of the theme through every other generation of Benedettis. Sibling rivalry, greed, power and the rest of the expected fare are featured in this beautifully photographed, sweeping costume drama. (Italian with English subtitles) (aka: *Wildflower*) ★★★ $19.99

Fire and Ice

(1983, 83 min, US, Ralph Bakshi) This sword & sorcery film is many cuts above its usual live-action brethren thanks to a fine script from ace comic scripters Roy Thomas and Gerry Conway, striking graphic designs by Frank Frazetta and powerful animation by Ralph Bakshi. ★★★ $24.99

Fire Down Below

(1957, 116 min, US, Robert Parrish) Solid performances from Jack Lemmon and Robert Mitchum and the particularly hypnotic presence of Rita Hayworth barely compensate for the wooden direction from Parrish in what should have been a rollicking scorcher of a movie. Refugee Hayworth has no papers. Seafaring buddies Lemmon and Mitchum are paid to smuggle her from one Carribean island to another. During the voyage, both fall for her. Hard. ★★½ $19.99

Fire in the Sky

(1993, 111 min, US, Robert Lieberman) In a small Southwestern town, five loggers report the disappearance of their co-worker. But what has the police and community up in arms is their story — that he was abducted by a UFO. Based on an actual sighting, *Fire in the Sky* is a surprisingly engrossing and credible recounting of the young man's story and the dilemma faced by his friends. The film's success is due in large part to its focus on the community and its reactions to the alleged event. Well-crafted and nicely acted by a strong cast which includes James Garner, D.B. Sweeney, Robert Patrick, Craig Sheffer, Henry Thomas and Peter Berg, this underrated and unexpectedly engaging film is worth checking out by skeptics and believers alike. The scenes aboard the spacecraft are particularly effective. ★★★ $19.99

The Fire Within (Le Feu Follet)

(1963, 104 min, France, Louis Malle) Stylish photography — perfectly capturing the "Swinging Paris" so familiar in the New Wave films of Godard, Truffaut and Rivette — is contrasted with an austere, melancholy account of a young man's final 48 hours in this, one of Malle's best works. Alain (Maurice Ronet), a handsome man of about thirty, is a recovering alcoholic about to release himself from a clinic. Disinterested in his former lifestyle as a bon vivant, and infused with an existential angst, he seeks out his friends in a dispirited attempt in finding some reason to live. A serious, somber drama of emptiness, regret and lost love. (French with English subtitles) ★★★½ $69.99

Firefox

(1982, 124 min, US, Clint Eastwood) Eastwood's lukewarm espionage thriller concerns a retired U.S. pilot who sneaks behind Russian lines to steal their latest MiG. The film

Richard Gere and Sean Connery in *First Knight*

is peppered with occasional sparks of high-flying action and, despite its plodding pace, provides some entertaining moments. ★★ $9.99

The Fireman's Ball

(1967, 73 min, Czechoslovakia, Milos Forman) Forman aims his satiric wit at Slavic bureaucracy in this, one of his earliest films. The setting is a ball honoring an aged fire chief, but he is quickly forgotten and it gives way to a torrent of disasters, including one of the funniest and most wonderfully demoralizing beauty contests ever conceived. (Dubbed) ★★★ $39.99

Fires on the Plain

(1959, 105 min, Japan, Kon Ichikawa) This hard-hitting anti-war outcry revolves around the retreat of a group of Japanese soldiers in the Philippines during WWII. Hiding in the hills, the soldiers must resort to cannibalism in order to survive. A harrowing, depressing and graphic account of the horrors of war. (Japanese with English subtitles) ★★★ $29.99

Fires Within

(1991, 90 min, US, Gillian Armstrong) Jimmy Smits and Greta Scacchi score high marks based on sex-appeal quotient in this slow-moving though compelling romantic love triangle set against the backdrop of political imprisonment and social injustice. Having just been released from eight years of prison in Castro's Cuba, Smits joins his family in Miami only to find that his wife (Scacchi) has become involved with a local (Vincent D'Onofrio) and his young daughter cannot remember him. In his struggle to assimilate and win back his family's love, Smits finds he must choose between his new life and the old comrades of his homeland. ★★½ $14.99

Firestarter

(1984, 115 min, US, Mark Lester) George C. Scott and Drew Barrymore strike sparks in this Stephen King horror story about a little girl who can induce a conflagration through mere thought. ★★½ $14.99

The Firm

(1993, 153 min, US, Sydney Pollack) In this exciting adaptation of John Grisham's best-selling novel of corporate intrigue, Tom Cruise plays a Harvard law graduate who accepts a golden opportunity job with an upscale Memphis firm. However, Cruise soon learns all is not as it appears when the Orwellian company not only has a firm grasp on his and wife Jeanne Tripplehorn's lives, but may have even murdered employees. As this relentless thriller unfolds, Cruise finds himself caught between government agents and hired killers who are on his trail. *The Firm* is a constant source of pulse-pounding suspense, and benefits greatly from an outstanding ensemble cast. Gene Hackman heads this group as a seasoned lawyer who takes Cruise under his wing. Also memorable are the shimmering Holly Hunter as a helpful and wily secretary and Wilford Brimley as a lethal security chief. Director Pollack keeps the action at a brisk pace which belies the two-and-a-half-hour running time. ★★★½ $9.99

First Blood

(1982, 97 min, US, Ted Kotcheff) The film which introduced Rambo. Sylvester Stallone plays an ex-Green Beret who is falsely arrested by small town authorities (led by Brian Dennehy); he exacts his revenge in particularly violent ways. Though it's not saying much, this mindless, violent actioner is the "best" of the trilogy. ★★ $14.99

The First Deadly Sin

(1980, 112 min, US, Brian G. Hutton) Frank Sinatra stars as a New York City police detective trying to uncover a serial killer while at the same time trying to cope with his wife's impending death. Faye Dunaway plays his bed-ridden spouse. Too sluggish to be an interesting action film and too convoluted to be of interest as a thriller. ★★ $14.99

First Family

(1980, 104 min, US, Buck Henry) Henry wrote and directed this aimless political satire

188

about a time in our not-too-distant future (perhaps even in your lifetime) when we have an ineffectual president (Bob Newhart), with a dipsomaniac first lady (Madeline Kahn) and a promiscuous daughter (Gilda Radner), and his funny adventures with that ever wacky Third World. With Harvey Korman, Julie Harris and Rip Torn. ★★ $14.99

First Kid

(1996, 101 min, US, David Mickey) A mildly amusing family comedy, *First Kid* is sort of a *Guarding Tess* for the prepubescent set. Sinbad plays a Secret Service agent who wants to guard the president. But he's assigned to the Commander-in-Chief's bratty, trouble-making adolescent son instead. The film manages to produce a few laughs at the expense of Sinbad and his efforts to hide his charge's mischievous nature. But a lot of time is also spent on the youth's self-pitying which would bore even its target audience. Sinbad and young Brock Pierce actually have a pleasant rapport; and of the many sentimental scenes, Sinbad's mentoring in boxing, dancing and dating works to better advantage. ★★ $19.99

First Knight

(1995, 132 min, US, Jerry Zucker) With *First Knight*, one actually gets two movies in one sitting. The first is the familiar though nicely played story of King Arthur (played with gusto by Sean Connery) and his reign at Camelot, fighting evil knights for the sake of queen and country. The second concentrates on the love story between Lancelot and Guinevere – and it's a preposterous one at that. Richard Gere stars as Lancelot, who travels across the land without a care until it's love-at-first-fight when he spots and rescues Guinevere (Julia Ormand) from the bad guys. Resembling Indiana Jones rather than a noble knight, Gere's Lancelot is a swaggering *Yankee in King Arthur's Court* who acts more like Fred Astaire pursuing Ginger Rogers than a man burnt by the embers of love. Set against an impressive evocative backdrop, *First Knight* features good battle scenes, a hammy villain in the form of Ben Cross, and a sincere Connery, but it's still not quite enough to offset Gere's miscasting and a ludicrous screenplay. ★★½ $19.99

First Love

(1970, 90 min, GB, Maximilian Schell) Based on a story by Russian novelist Ivan Turgenev, this lyrical and original drama was directed by and stars Schell. Photographed by Sven Nykvist, the film features a very attractive love interest in Dominique Sanda and John Moulder-Brown. Set in a Russian dacha during the calm before World War I, the story involves a teenager's (Moulder-Brown) first love with the lovely yet bedeviling daughter of an impoverished and eccentric old woman who moves in next door. Our lovesick young man's attempts to capture her interest are thrown into confusion when he discovers that she is his father's mistress! The excitement, pain and mystery of young love are captured in this Barry Levinson-produced film. ★★★ $49.99

First Men in the Moon

(1964, 103 min, GB, Nathan Juran) Master stop-motion animator Ray Harryhausen adapts H.G. Wells' speculative novel to his own needs adding lots of grasshopper-like moon-men, giant slug-cows and huge underground factories. Lionel Jeffries gives an amusing performance as the bumbling scientist, as does Edward Judd as his unwilling compatriot; and Martha Hyer is the requisite stowaway love interest. ★★★ $14.99

First Name: Carmen

(1983, 87 min, France/Switzerland, Jean-Luc Godard) This deconstructionist version of Merimee's classic tale finds Godard, loopy and pithy as ever, transforming the gypsy femme fatale into a filmmaker-cum-bank robbing revolutionary whose politics aren't nearly as well developed as are her libidinal urges. Joseph is the befuddled bank guard who is captivated by her sexual charms in the midst of a botched heist. Offering his asides and snide observations is her uncle, a washed-up fraud of a film director named Jean-Luc Godard, played with understated conviction by Godard himself! (French with English subtitles) ★★★ $29.99

The First Power

(1990, 99 min, US, Robert Resnikoff) Lackluster horror film offers little in chills or originality as L.A. cop Lou Diamond Phillips is up against the spirit of a recently executed murderer. ★ $19.99

The First Wives Club

(1996, 102 min, US, Hugh Wilson) If Hell hath no fury like a woman scorned, then the three divas of comedy hath more than their fair share of fun in *The First Wives Club*, a funny, spirited romp which postulates that revenge is not only sweet but profitable. With not an ego in sight, Bette Midler, Goldie Hawn and Diane Keaton play former college roommates who are reunited after 25 years when a friend commits suicide. Sharing in common insensitive, philandering ex-husbands, they form a bond (and later a company) to get even with their not-so-better halves. Based on Olivia Goldsmith's best-seller, the buoyant screenplay mixes physical comedy with sharp one-liners – some of them accentuating the feminist context, and the remainder firing bullets into the body-bag residue of male-female relationships (especially of those over age 40). But the real story here is the impeccable timing and teaming of Midler, Hawn and Keaton; singularly and together they ignite the film with sparkling energy and wit. Even with a few lapses in tempo, *The First Wives Club* is a club all should want to join. ★★★ $14.99

A Fish Called Wanda

(1988, 108 min, GB, Charles Crichton) What happens when two scheming American jewel thieves join forces with a pair of double-crossing British thugs? All hell breaks loose, that's what. This slapdash,

high-speed comedy is certainly one of the funniest film of the 1980s. John Cleese is wonderful as an uptight barrister who inadvertently gets tangled in the mess. Michael Palin has some very funny scenes as the bumbling, stuttering sidekick, and Jamie Lee Curtis simply enchants as the manipulative American bombshell. But the laurels go to Oscar winner Kevin Kline, who as Curtis' psychotic boyfriend ("Don't call me stupid"), climbs all over the screen in one of the finest comic performances in years. A fabulously entertaining caper comedy featuring a wickedly funny running gag about some very unlucky dogs. ★★★½ $14.99

The Fisher King

(1991, 138 min, US, Terry Gilliam) Gilliam's magical fable for modern times is an original and delightful masterwork complete with love, desperation and redemption. A hypnotic and exceptionally funny parable, the film stars Jeff Bridges as a hotshot D.J. whose world collapses when he feels responsible for a restaurant shooting. A few years later, he finds possible salvation in the form of street person Robin Williams, a former professor whose wife was killed in the slayings. In a quest worthy of the Holy Grail, Bridges sets out to make amends for two of the lives touched by the tragedy. Williams gives one of his best performances: his manic, machine-gun comic delivery is much in evidence, of course, but never has the actor demonstrated such vulnerability and tenderness. Bridges, in a very subdued role, is equally impressive and Oscar-winner Mercedes Ruehl is smashing as his lusty girlfriend. Special mention also goes to Amanda Plummer and Michael Jeter for their fine supporting turns. ★★★★ $14.99

Fist of the Northstar

(1990, 100 min, Japan, Toyoo Ashida) After a nuclear war, the few survivors huddle in the ruins of the cities where they are preyed upon by outlaw bikers, insane mutants and would-be dictators. Ken, our hero, is the top student of the deadliest school of martial arts. He has been chosen by the school's master to re-establish the peace. See fists fly, bones splinter, blood spurt and much more in this extremely violent though thrilling animated epic. (Dubbed) ★★★½ $19.99

A Fistful of Dollars

(1964, 96 min, Italy, Sergio Leone) The first of Leone's "spaghetti westerns" is an exciting

Diane Keaton, Goldie Hawn and Bette Midler in *The First Wives Club*

and entertaining working of Kurosawa's *Yojimbo*. Clint Eastwood became a star thanks to his role as the "Man with No Name," a mysterious stranger who gets involved in a feud between two rival families. ★★★ $14.99

A Fistful of Dynamite

(1971, 138 min, Italy, Sergio Leone) James Coburn stars in this high-voltage war adventure as an Irish terrorist who hooks up with peasant Rod Steiger during the Mexican Revolution. (aka: *Duck You Sucker*.) ★★★ $14.99

Fit to Kill

(1993, 94 min, US, Andy Sidaris) Former ABC sports director Sidaris returns with yet another film where the action isn't the only thing that's packed. *Playboy* alumnae Dona Speir and Roberta Vasquez reprise their roles as "double D-cup" federal agents who are on the trail of an old nemesis who possesses a valuable diamond called The Alexa Stone. Our two heroines spend a great deal of time removing their blouses while ducking both bullets and treacherous double agents in this mindlessly entertaining jiggle fest. ★★ $89.99

Fitzcarraldo

(1982, 158 min, West Germany, Werner Herzog) Herzog chronicles the bizarre history of a strong-willed visionary whose dream is to construct an opera house in the heart of the Peruvian jungle. A beguiling tale laced with the director's usual dose of mysticism and madness and featuring yet another appropriately lunatic performance by Herzog favorite Klaus Kinski in the title role. (German with English subtitles) ★★★★ $69.99

Five Card Stud

(1968, 103 min, US, Henry Hathaway) Dean Martin and Robert Mitchum star in this tame western adventure with Martin as a gunslinger (and part-time gambler) investigating the murders of the members of a lynch gang. ★★ $14.99

Five Corners

(1988, 98 min, US, Tony Bill) With plot developments as capricious as life itself, this story of five teenagers living in the Bronx in 1964 is writer John Patrick Shanley's follow-up to *Moonstruck*. John Turturro gives a stand-out performance as a psychotic ex-con whose infatuation with Jodie Foster leads to an evening of tragedy. Also starring Tim Robbins and Elizabeth Berridge. ★★★ $14.99

Five Days One Summer

(1983, 108 min, US, Fred Zinnemann) Sean Connery plays a middle-aged doctor vacationing in a remote Swiss village in the early 1930s. There he is accompanied by a young woman (Betsy Brantley), who is posing as his wife. However, as their relationship is explored, their dark secrets soon surface. This soap opera is set at a lethargic pace, and even Connery can't make you feel for the characters' plight. ★★ $14.99

Five Easy Pieces

(1970, 98 min, US, Bob Rafelson) This fascinating character study follows an aimless drifter who abandons the accoutrements of middle-class existence (and a promising musi-

cal career) for a life on the road spent amongst the squalor of cheap bars and shabby motels. Jack Nicholson gives a virtuoso, career-making performance, and Karen Black and especially Lois Smith as Nicholson's sister are outstanding in support. ★★★★ $14.99

Five Fingers

(1952, 108 min, US, Joseph L. Mankiewicz) The allegedly true story of how the Nazis came upon the plans for the Allied's Normandy invasion makes for a riveting and witty spy story which forgoes cloak and dagger in favor of an intelligent character study. James Mason is excellent as the suave valet to a high-ranking British diplomat who finances his planned retirement by selling secrets to the Germans. Michael Rennie is the agent on his trail. A complex tale of espionage which explores class differences as well, *Five Fingers* has not one but two great twists at its exciting finale. ★★★★ $19.99

Five Fingers of Death

(1973, 100 min, Hong Kong, Cheng Chang Ho) The film that opened the floodgates of the martial arts/kung fu flicks which became popular in the 1970s comes complete with gravity defying fight scenes, the usual vengeance plot and the inept dubbing that will make you wonder if the voices were borrowed from a 1960s Hercules film. Great fun, and one of the best of the genre. ★★★

Five Graves to Cairo

(1943, 96 min, US, Billy Wilder) With a wit and style usually not associated with WWII dramas, director Wilder has crafted a suspenseful espionage tale that is at once taut and relaxed. Franchot Tone stars as a British corporal who is stranded in the North African desert. Stumbling upon a hotel run by Akim Tamiroff and Anne Baxter, he is forced to impersonate a German agent when Field Marshal Rommel arrives in his push towards Cairo. Erich von Stroheim ably plays Rommel as a blustery, egocentric militarist; and this would be the first time during the war that a real-life Nazi appeared as a leading character in a Hollywood film. Tone is quite affable as an ordinary man thrust into danger — he would have been quite at home in *The 39 Steps* or *The Lady Vanishes*. In fact, Wilder's splendid blend of action, humor and intrigue is very Hitchcockian — though Wilder's celebrated cynicism was firmly taking root, and his singular gift for dialogue distinguishes the film. ★★★½ $14.99

The Five Heartbeats

(1991, 122 min, US, Robert Townsend) Townsend's flavorful but uneven musical drama is about the rise and fall of a black singing group in the 1960s. Townsend, who wrote the screenplay with Keenan Ivory Wayans, plays the group's leader and songwriter, who takes The Five Heartbeats from obscurity to stardom. There are many fine moments, especially the musical sequences which have an indestructible energy; but some of the film's dramatic scenes are heavy-handed and border on music industry cliché. From the group, Michael Wright and Tico Wells are in exceptional voice. ★★½ $19.99

Five Million Years to Earth

(1968, 98 min, GB, Roy Ward Baker) The third of the "Quatermass" films from Hammer Studios and screenwriter Nigel Kneale is arguably the best one, and certainly the most imaginative, successfully bringing together the odd combination of common sci-fi elements and more heady philosophical issues (such as a physical basis for good and evil). Andrew Keir is rocket scientist Quatermass, called to the site of a strange discovery: an eons-old spacecraft buried beneath a London subway station. Its inhabitants and some curious ape-like fossils found nearby hint at a startling truth: that humanity is descended from a race of beings genetically altered by ancient Martians. And some of us still bear the deep psychological scars of our Martian background! A freak accident unleashes the stored-up energy of the ship, giving more susceptible Londoners strange psychic abilities which they turn on their less-fortunate neighbors. Chaos ensues and Quatermass and company barely save the day, in one of the most downbeat and mind-numbingly powerful climaxes of any sci-fi film of the 1960s. (a.k.a.: *Quatermass and the Pit*) ★★★½ $14.99

The 5,000 Fingers of Dr. T.

(1953, 88 min, US, Roy Rowland) Dr. Seuss wrote this imaginative and unusual children's entertainment about a young boy (Peter Lind Hayes) who fantasizes that his piano teacher (Hans Conreid) is really the diabolical Dr. T., who kidnaps and imprisons youths, forcing them to participate in daily piano rehearsals. Clever set designs, wild choreography and an abundance of youthful escapades make this curiosity all the more intriguing. ★★★ $14.99

The Flamingo Kid

(1984, 98 min, US, Garry Marshall) Matt Dillon is well-cast in this endearing teen comedy about a Brooklyn high school grad who takes a summer job at an exclusive Long Island club. The film abandons the usual sex-obsessed hijinks of most teen comedies, opting instead for a surprisingly sweet reminiscence of the times. An excellent supporting cast includes Hector Elizondo as Dillon's dad, Jessica Walter as a snobbish patron, and, in a dynamic performance, Richard Crenna as an unscrupulous car salesman whose influence on the naive Dillon proves to be an eye-opener. ★★★ $14.99

Flamingo Road

(1949, 94 min, US, Michael Curtiz) Joan Crawford gives one of her better performances in this highly entertaining melodrama which skewers small town Americana and the political process. Crawford plays a carnival dancer who becomes stranded in Smalltown, USA. There, she falls in love with the town deputy (Zachary Scott), but the sheriff and town boss (the ever-evil Sydney Greenstreet) have other ideas. When the latter frames Joan and sends her to prison, it's get-even time when Joan is released. Crawford suffers gallantly, and is ever-ready with the next witty barb. ★★★ $19.99

Flash Gordon

(1980, 110 min, US, Mike Hodges) Though this updated sci-fi adventure failed to set a spark at the box office, it's a guaranteed fun ride as football hero Flash Gordon (Sam J. Jones) and reporter Dale Arden (Melody Anderson) travel to the planet Mongo with Dr. Zarkov (Topol) to stop the destruction of Earth at the hands of evil emperor Ming (the Merciless, that is), played with great relish by Max von Sydow. Features splendid sets and costumes, good special effects and a wonderful comic touch to the action. Score by Queen. Also with Timothy Dalton, Mariangelo Melato, Ornella Muti and Brian Blessed. ★★★ $9.99

Flash Gordon Conquers the Universe

(1940, 87 min, US, Ray Taylor, Ford Beebe) Now experience the first six chapters in this classic matinee serial as Buster Crabbe fights off the nefarious Ming the Merciless who plans to spread *The Purple Death from Outer Space* (the film's alternate title). ★★½ $29.99

A Flash of Green

(1985, 122 min, US, Victor Nunez) In this compassionate tale of corruption and greed, an investigative journalist (Ed Harris) becomes involved in a local real estate dispute between a corrupt politician and a homeowner. Also with Blair Brown, Richard Jordan and John Glover. ★★★ $59.99

Flashback

(1990, 108 min, US, Franco Amurri) Dennis Hopper makes the most of his role as a '60s fugitive captured by the FBI in this slight comedy. It's Hopper's show all the way, actually, playing an Abbie Hoffman-like radical who is being transported by uptight agent Kiefer Sutherland. It's sort of a poor man's *Midnight Run* with a political flavor as Hopper continually outwits his guardian till each discovers a respect for the other. ★★½ $14.99

Flashdance

(1983, 96 min, US, Adrian Lyne) Gnash your teeth if you will, but there's no denying this film's impact on Hollywood and pop culture (not to mention the welding industry). You certainly didn't find torn sweatshirts at Bloomie's before. In spite of its stilted plot, *Flashdance* is a viscerally entertaining musical with imaginative dance routines and a pulsating score. C'mon now, "What a feeling..." Starring Jennifer Beals and Michael Nouri. ★★ $9.99

Flatliners

(1990, 105 min, US, Joel Schumacher) This psychological thriller, about a group of medical students who embark on a series of otherworldly experiments, brims with a dark sense of dread and classic horror. Kiefer Sutherland is ideally cast as Nelson, a slightly demented intern who dreams up the idea of killing himself so that his fellow classmates can bring him back to life — thereby experiencing death. Kevin Bacon, Julia Roberts and William Baldwin deliver strong performances as his accomplices. One by one, they go under for longer and longer periods, but as they return from death, these modern-day Frankensteins find that they don't always come back alone. Filled with psychological underpinnings, *Flatliners* is as much about healing childhood wounds as it is a horror film. The excellent production design consists of dimly lit halls

which overflow with murky details of gargoyle-like statuary evoking universal images of Gothic terror. The equally creepy cinematography explores dark alleyways and roams narrow passages where unknown dangers lurk. ★★★½ $9.99

The Flavor of Corn

(1991, 93 min, Italy, Gianni da Campo) Similar in theme to the more explicit Dutch film *For a Lost Soldier*, this tender drama of friendship and enveloping love between a teacher and a 12-year-old boy is hampered by amateurish acting and an overly serious tone. University student Lorenzo (Lorenzo Lena) travels to a rural region of northern Italy for his first teaching assignment. He discovers that one of his pupils, Duilio (Marco Mestriner), is in "puppy love" with him. They become friends, and after Lorenzo breaks up with his girlfriend, he considers a sexual attraction to the youth. A surprisingly tasteful, restrained and bittersweet tale of first love and the internal conflict of accepting one's sexual feelings. (Italian with English subtitles) ★★½ $69.99

Fled

(1996, 98 min, US, Kevin Hooks) A low-rent knock-off of *The Defiant Ones*, *Fled* pits a black and white man against each other, both of whom are escaped convicts and handcuffed together. But wait — this isn't an old boring examination of moral conflict or a complex story of two men grappling with prejudice and inner pain. This is an action movie. Set in the high-tech '90s. Where computer software replaces human interest. Giving much too credibility to a role lacking in it, Laurence Fishburne is saddled with dopey Stephen Baldwin, together fleeing police and mysterious underworld figures on their trail. They bicker, they argue, they fight, they fall down a lot — they do everything but walk into the sunset together. For a couple of guys constantly on the move, they sure don't have a lot to do. ★★ $102.99

Flesh

(1969, 105 min, US, Paul Morrissey) A true artifact of the `60s sexual revolution as well as a great example of the quirky New York independent filmmaking that came out of the Warhol film factory. The film is an homage to the personality and body (with the emphasis on body) of Joe Dallesandro. The plot is simply a day-in-the-life of gay hustler Joe who utters immortal lines such as, "How am I going to make any money without clean underwear!" The story is told in vignettes and features old Warholian favorites Candy Darling and Jackie Curtis. There are priceless drug-induced dialogues throughout including the great philosophical thought, "The more you learn the more depressed you get." ★★★

Flesh & Blood

(1985, 126 min, The Netherlands, Paul Verhoeven) Given a big budget for the first time, Verhoeven weaves a colorful, erotic and gritty story of a rag-tag group of mercenary soldiers during Europe's feudal wars. This rowdy adventure tale lives up to its title and fascinates us with battles at castle gates, treacherous kings and princesses in distress. Rutger Hauer and

Jennifer Jason Leigh are standouts. Don't miss this one. (Filmed in English) ★★★½ $9.99

Flesh and Bone

(1993, 124 min, US, Steve Kloves) From its intense opening sequence to its haunting end, *Flesh and Bone* manages to be stylish and suspenseful without being flashy or shocking. Dennis Quaid is mesmerizing as a lonely Texas vending-machine supplier whose dark past suddenly sneaks up on him. The top-notch cast includes Meg Ryan, James Caan, and newcomer Gwyneth Paltrow (Blythe Danner's daughter) in a delightfully droll and dangerous performance. As in his first film, *The Fabulous Baker Boys*, writer-director Kloves frames his eye just below the surface of the ordinary to reveal secret things we wish we hadn't seen. ★★★ $19.99

Flesh and the Devil

(1926, 95 min, US, Clarence Brown) Greta Garbo gives a seductive performance in her first American film as a beautiful schemer who comes between life-long friends John Gilbert and Lars Hanson. Garbo and Gilbert are an inspired romantic duo. ★★½ $29.99

Flesh Gordon

(1974, 70 min, US, Howard Ziehm & Michael Benveniste) Flesh and his companions Prince Precious and Dr. Jerkoff explore the inner and outer regions of space. Late-nite cult fun which parodies the story's sci-fi origins, and includes lots of sex and cheesy sets and F/X. ★★ $29.99

Flesh Gordon Meets the Cosmic Cheerleaders

(1992, 103 min, US, Howard Ziehm) Battling galactic impotence, his latest nemesis, super sex-hero Flesh Gordon returns, along with his girlfriend Dale Ardor and Dr. Flexi Jerkoff, for a laugh-packed series of adventures that include a journey through a belt of farting ass-teroids, encounters with the infamous Queen Fridged, the well-endowed Robonda Hooters, slimy turd people and a galaxy of other sex weirdos. ★★½ $14.99

Fletch

(1985, 98 min, US, Michael Ritchie) This may be Chevy Chase's funniest screen comedy. Chevy plays an investigative reporter who, while undercover, is offered $50,000 by a millionaire (Tim Matheson) to murder him. Plenty of sharp dialogue and Chase is very funny. ★★★ $9.99

Fletch Lives

(1989, 95 min, US, Michael Ritchie) In this surprisingly funny sequel, Chevy Chase returns as the glib, wise-cracking reporter Fletch who here travels to the heart of Dixie when he inherits an old Southern mansion. There, he quickly becomes involved with the Klan, toxic waste, a TV evangelist, and murder. Chase can deliver a put-down with the best of them, and his impersonations of an array of characters are quite amusing. ★★★ $14.99

A Flight of Rainbirds

(1981, 94 min, The Netherlands, Ate De Jong) From the director of *Drop Dead Fred* and *Highway to Hell* comes this serio-comedy about love, sex and religion. Reportedly one of the highest grossing films in Dutch history, *A Flight of Rainbirds* stars Jeroen Krabbé in dual roles. In one, he is a timid and repressed scientist who one night dreams that he must lose his virginity in seven days or die. His more debonair alter ego is hence forced to come to the rescue. (Dutch with English subtitles) ★★½ $29.99

Flight of the Dragons

(1992, 98 min, US) Rankin and Bass animated this story of four wizard brothers in the time of King Arthur who band together to preserve the disappearing world of magic. Although they are aided by dragons, knights, and even a man from the 20th century, they are thwarted by one of the evil brothers who sees this as an opportunity to take all of the magic for his own malevolent purposes. While the voices of Harry Morgan, James Earl Jones and John Ritter add solidity, the animation's poor quality pulls the production down. ★★½ $14.99

The Flight of the Eagle

(1982, 139 min, Sweden, Jan Troell) This Swedish epic by Troell (*The Emigrants*) chronicles the brave but foolhardy trek of several men who attempt a balloon mission to the North Pole in 1897. Max von Sydow heads the group who are stranded in the frozen North and are confronted with eerie silence and the very real possibility that they will not survive. A gripping existential drama. (Swedish with English subtitles) ★★★

Flight of the Innocent

(1993, 105 min, Italy, Carlo Carlei) When a loving 10-year-old boy witnesses the murder of his entire gangster family by a rival crime syndicate, the stage is set for this edge-of-your-seat, run-for-your-life thriller that marks the auspicious debut of director Carlei. While inarguably the best foreign actioner to come out of Europe since *La Femme Nikita*, the film also merits strong praise as an art film for its masterful juxtaposition of gorgeous dreamlike imagery with scenes of horrendous violence reminiscent of Peckinpah at his peak. Young Manuci Colao gives a striking performance as the boy evading both the mob and the police. (Italian with English subtitles) ★★★★ $92.99

Flight of the Intruder

(1991, 115 min, US, John Milius) Vietnam War adventure film with Danny Glover as a Navy commander saddled with hotshot pilots Brad Johnson and Willem Dafoe, who disobey orders and fight the enemy in the way they think they should be fought. Plays like a right-wing fantasy, and a boring one, at that. ★ $14.99

Flight of the Navigator

(1986, 90 min, US, Randal Kleiser) Enjoyable science-fiction tale about a 12-year-old boy who is kidnapped by an alien spacecraft and accidentally returned – unchanged – eight years later. Joey Cramer plays the youth, and Veronica Cartwright and Cliff de Young are his parents. Paul Reubens supplies the voice of the spacecraft's computer. ★★½ $14.99

The Flight of the Phoenix

(1965, 147 min, US, Robert Aldrich) First-rate adventure film about a group of plane crash survivors stranded in the Sahara Desert. James

Stewart heads a good cast which includes Richard Attenborough, Peter Finch, Hardy Kruger, Ernest Borgnine and Oscar-nominee Ian Bannen. ★★★½ $19.99

The Flintstones

(1994, 92 min, US, Brian Levant) With as much about it to like as to dislike, *The Flintstones* is an appropriately cartoonish live-action version of the adored 1960s animated TV series. Featuring some neat special effects, playful performances and a less-than-beguiling script, the film is aided nicely by the near-perfect casting of John Goodman and Elizabeth Perkins as Fred and Wilma, and Rick Moranis and Rosie O'Donnell as Barney and Betty. The sluggish story has to do with Fred being promoted and used as a patsy by his devious supervisor. Sad to say, some of the TV episodes had more humor. But the film does have that wonderful cast, Elizabeth Taylor as Fred's mother-in-law, and a sincere desire to entertain. ★★½ $14.99

Flipper

(1963, 90 min, US, James Clark) Irresistible to children, this charming family film became the basis of the popular TV series. A fast bond develops between young Luke and Flipper after the boy saves the dolphin's life. ★★½ $14.99

Flipper

(1996, 96 min, US, Alan Shapiro) Originally a feature film in 1963, then a popular TV series, the story of a boy and his dolphin is back in this updated, benign family adventure which takes the innocence of the earlier versions and contrasts it with the greedy and immoral 1990s. No longer a tale of a father and his sons, this time a young divorce orphan spends a summer with his bohemian uncle on a remote Caribbean island. It is here he befriends Flipper, who has lost his mate due to an evil fisherman. Of course, Flipper helps in exposing him, and makes new friends in the process. The underwater sequences of *Flipper* are rather impressive, and the locales are beautiful. Children should be entertained, and the film has a pro-ecology message which surely should be of comfort to parents. There is a shark attack which may frighten the very wee ones. ★★½ $19.99

Flirt

(1995, 85 min, US, Hal Hartley) Hartley tells a short story of a love affair at the brink of commitment. He tells it three times, in three cities with three casts, using much of the same dialogue each time. In each retelling, there's a gun and a defining moment, changing one protagonist's life unalterably. And yet, it's a commonplace occurrence, whether in New York or Berlin or Tokyo. The repetition, across cultural boundaries, across issues of sexual orientation and class identity, serves to emphasize the story's universality. Before an extended separation, one partner asks another if they have a future as a couple. Before that person can answer, each must ask someone else the same question. Daffy and romantic, *Flirt* is about love's pain and exaltation, its nature as solid as a rock and as ephemeral as happiness; it's also about flirting and flirting's role in human relations. Look for a brief discourse on the subject in one interlude featuring three German construction workers who succinctly analyze the film's premise and success in exposition. Godardian in nature, *Flirt* is an energetic delight, filled with wry observance and urbane compassion. ★★★ $98.99

Flirtation Walk

(1934, 98 min, US, Frank Borzage) With more in common with *This Is the Army* than *42nd Street*, this cornball, Oscar-nominated musical is a singing Armed Forces advertisement for a peacetime America. Dick Powell plays a flip Army private who falls for the general's daughter, the non-dancing Ruby Keeler. But Cupid is momentarily against them, and he ships himself off to West Point to forget about her. When Daddy takes command of the school, however, they are reunited and, naturally, put on a show. Powell's repartee and most of the comedy are passable, but when buddy Pat O'Brien starts crying amid an extended military parade, it's all too much. ★★½ $19.99

Flirting

(1990, 100 min, Australia, John Duigan) Director Duigan's follow-up to *The Year My Voice Broke* is one of those purely delightful cinematic surprises. Rather than the puerile teen comedy the previews made it out to be, *Flirting*

The Flower of My Secret

is an insightful, intelligent and superbly crafted tale of coming-of-age. Set in early 1960s Australia, the story follows Danny Embling, a pimply-faced youth with leftist leanings and a commanding intellect who is suffering through his time at a posh, all-boys boarding school. Scandal ensues when he becomes involved with Thandiwe Adjewa, a Ugandan student (whose father is fleeing the regime of Idi Amin) from the sister school across the lake. Nicole Kidman offers a solid pre-"stardom" performance in support as a bitchy student who tries, at first, to sabotage their relationship. Filled with humor, mirth and unwavering humanism, *Flirting* is a small gem of a movie which should not be missed. ★★★★ $12.99

Flirting with Disaster

(1996, 92 min, US, David O. Russell) Ben Stiller and Patricia Arquette star in this relentlessly funny film about a young couple who set out on a cross-country drive in search of a name for their new baby. The trouble begins when Stiller (an adoptee) becomes obsessed with finding his birth parents before bestowing his newborn son with an appelation. In steps Téa Leoni, a long-legged, ravishing and slightly batty psychology student who's sent by the adoption agency to help him in his search. Along the way several uproarious blunders and mistaken identities are made and Stiller and Leoni do a little of their own "flirting with disaster." Into the mix are thrown a pair of federal agents, one of whom happens to be Arquette's former boyfriend, and the sexual hijinks really begin to heat up. Hilarious supporting work comes from Mary Tyler Moore and George Segal as Stiller's adoptive parents and Alan Alda and Lily Tomlin as his real ones. As written and directed by Russell (*Spanking the Monkey*), the film is a rollicking, quixotic journey that unleashes a barrage of side-splitting gags and awkward situations, culminating in a mind-bending denouement that will warm the cockles of any ex-hippie's heart. ★★★★ $19.99

A Florida Enchantment

(1914, 63 min, US, Sidney Drew) Considered one of the earliest films to feature ambiguous sexual attraction, this cross-dressing comedy, based on an 1896 Broadway play, is set at an elegant Florida resort. A young woman (Edith Storey), frustrated at her fiancé's philandering, ingests magic seeds from the African Tree of Sexual Change which quickly transforms women into men and vice versa. While she remains feminine looking (though she does sprout a cute mustache), she immediately assumes the behavior of a man: swaggering belligerently, smoking furiously and making repeated advances on other women. The seeds ultimately fall into the hands of her former finacé, who becomes an effeminate female in a male body. An ahead-of-its-time comedy which humorously explores men and women's sexual roles. ★★★ $39.99

Floundering

(1994, 97 min, US, Peter McCarthy) McCarthy, who produced *Repo Man* and *Sid & Nancy*, makes his directorial debut with this upteenth "Generation X" comedy which plays like "This Is Your Life." Set in the seedy surroundings of Venice Beach, California, the

films stars James LeGros as John Boyz, a twentysomething slacker who aimlessly wanders the streets of Venice. As friends pretentiously philosophize the meaning of their existence, the possibility of a plot rears its ugly head — John's failing attempts to find work. The film has some very funny moments, especially the cameos by John Cusack and Steve Buscemi. Even Ethan Hawke's appearance as John's strung out brother is surprisingly touching. But the generic screenplay is hit-or-miss, turning the film into a series of vignettes rather than a full-length feature. ★★ $14.99

Flower Drum Song

(1961, 133 min, US, Henry Koster) Though not one of Rodgers and Hammerstein's best musicals, this pleasant adaptation of their Broadway show manages to capture some lightheartedness and whimsical spirits. Nancy Kwan and James Shigetta star in a tale about the conflict of old and new traditions in San Francisco's Chinatown district. The score's best songs include "I Enjoy Being a Girl" and "A Hundred Million Miracles." ★★½ $19.99

The Flower of My Secret

(1995, 105 min, Spain, Pedro Almodóvar) Almodóvar continues his fascination with women on the verge in this uncharacteristically serious, even somber tale of lost love. The gorgeous and wealthy Leo (Marisa Paredes), a disenchanted writer of trash romance novels, is in the midst of the painful dissolution of her marriage. To make matters worse, her best friend is having an affair with Leo's husband; her housekeeper is a former renowned flamenco dancer (thinking of a comeback) whose son has been stealing from her; and her mother and sister — played with true familial tragicomedy by Chus Lampreave and Rossy De Palma — are perennially at each other's throats. Needing a change in her life, Leo becomes a literary critic, but under a pseudonym. Her first assignment: do a negative review of her most recent novel. While short on a coherent plot, the characters are engaging, as Almodóvar takes a more mature approach to love and the lack of it. (Spanish with English subtitles) ★★½ $19.99

Flowers in the Attic

(1987, 95 min, US, Jeffrye Bloom) Four children are brought by their mother to stay at their grandmother's and are locked in the attic, presumably not to be let out again. The best-selling novel is given a flat screen translation, and the drab performances of Victoria Tennant and Louise Fletcher (who can be tremendous in these types of roles) dampen an already preposterous film. ★ $14.99

Fluke

(1995, 96 min, US, Carlo Carlei) Italian helmer Carlei takes a radical turn from his Mafia drama *Flight of the Innocent* with this slightly surreal family film. The story follows Matthew Modine (or his voice anyway), who in the first scene dies in a fiery car crash and, in a bizarre twist on *Ghost* and *The Incredible Journey*, is reincarnated — as a puppy. After befriending a bag lady (who names him Fluke), he finds a mentor in a big old mutt named Rumpo. Life goes on for Fluke, but he is continually haunted by thoughts of his former wife (Nancy Travis) and

son (Max Pomeranc) and by some foreboding evil that seems linked to his former business partner (Eric Stoltz). At times supremely silly (especially in the middle half when the two dogs "talk" to each other telepathically), the film straddles the line, with varying degrees of success, between kid's fantasy comedy and adult melodrama. Still, it's all such feel-good fun, you can't help but like it. Samuel L. Jackson gives a goofy and garrulous turn as the voice of the streetwise Rumpo. $19.99

The Fly

(1958, 94 min, US, Kurt Neumann) Perhaps the ultimate sci-fi shocker of its day, Al (David) Hedison stars as a scientist whose matter transference experiments go horribly awry when he accidentally integrates his own gene patterns with those of a common housefly. Also starring Vincent Price and Herbert Marshall, and contains the famous spider scene ("Help me, help me"). Screenplay by "Shogun" author James Clavell. ★★★ $14.99

The Fly

(1986, 96 min, US, David Cronenberg) Cronenberg's remake of the 1958 Vincent Price semi-classic is a terrifying thriller highlighted by both Jeff Goldblum's virtuoso performance as the scientist experiencing a metamorphosis and incredible makeup effects. An intense and gory horror film, and not for everyone. Also starring Geena Davis. Followed by an inferior sequel. ★★★½ $19.99

The Fly II

(1989, 105 min, US, Chris Walas) Fans of slash-trash should appreciate this slickly made though moronic sequel to David Cronenberg's now-classic *The Fly*, which, like the original, is dripping with globs of gooey gore. Little did we know that the dream sequence in the original film was real: there really is a son of fly. Within weeks, Baby Brundle-fly grows into the fully developed Eric Stoltz, displaying amazing strength and intelligence. But there's a fly in the ointment here: he's being controlled and exploited by an evil scientist. ★ $19.99

Fly Away Home

(1996, 105 min, US, Carroll Ballard) After her mother is killed in an auto accident (a potentially disturbing scene handled with great subtlety), a 13-year-old Australian girl (Anna Paquin) is sent to Canada to live with her estranged father (Jeff Daniels), an eccentric inventor. What follows would usually be an excruciating visit to sentimental overkill, but in the hands of director Ballard and a very appealing cast, the semi-factual *Fly Away Home* is an uplifting and endearing family drama which celebrates life and its' wayward souls. The story has to do with Paquin raising a family of orphaned geese, who think the youngster their mother. When they are threatened with possible captivity or worse, father and daughter devise an improbable plan to allow the domesticated geese to migrate over a thousand miles away. Probably the most skilled and enjoyable non-Disney family film since *Babe*, *Fly Away Home* is enhanced by extraordinary cinematography and a lovely score. Paquin is adorable, and the geese are kinda cute, too. A genuinely satisfying work which could, once again, give family films a good name. ★★★½ $22.99

193

The Flying Deuces

(1939, 67 min, US, Edward Sutherland) Funny Laurel and Hardy feature with Stan and Ollie joining the French Foreign Legion to forget Ollie's ill-fated romance. ★★★ $9.99

Flying Down to Rio

(1933, 89 min, US, Thornton Freeland) The film that first paired Fred Astaire and Ginger Rogers. Delores Del Rio and Gene Raymond are the stars in this lively tuner about a dance band in Rio. Fred and Ginger's dancing is tops, and there's a knockout of a finale with chorines dancing on the wings of a moving plane. ★★★ $19.99

Flying Saucers over Hollywood: The Plan 9 Companion

(1992, 111 min, US, Mark Patrick Carducci) Legendary cult movie writer-director Edward D. Wood, Jr. is profiled with amazingly meticulous detail in this entertaining and intriguing peek into the life of the cross-dressing creator of many B-film classics, including his incredible and charmingly inept *Plan 9 from Outer Space*. Packed with rare footage, interviews and background info on his rag-tag group of Hollywood friends and misfits (including Bela Lugosi, TV horror hostess Vampira and gentle giant Tor Johnson), this film proves to be a definite must see for "Psychotronic" movie buffs, as well as those who crave something different. ★★★ $29.99

The Fog

(1980, 90 min, US, John Carpenter) Carpenter's follow-up to *Halloween* reunites him with that film's star, Jamie Lee Curtis, in this effective horror tale about a New England coastal town terrorized by a mysterious killer fog. Also with Adrienne Barbeau, Hal Holbrook and Janet Leigh. ★★★

Follow Me Quietly

(1949, 59 min, US, Richard Fleischer) The eternal confrontation between good and evil is re-enacted in this well-made crime melodrama. In the dark heart of a big city, a psychopathic serial killer, called "The Judge," stalks his innocent prey, leaving only a trail of corpses in his wake. The police are stymied until one detective uses an unorthodox method of constructing a dummy of the suspect, culled from evidence and witnesses, to trap the maniacal killer. ★★★ $19.99

Follow the Fleet

(1936, 110 min, US, Mark Sandrich) Sheer musical enchantment as sailors Fred Astaire and Randolph Scott court sisters Ginger Rogers and Harriet Hilliard (aka Harriet Nelson). Irving Berlin songs include "Let Yourself Go" and "Let's Face the Music and Dance." ★★★½ $19.99

Fool for Love

(1986, 105 min, US, Robert Altman) Sam Shepard's raw, elemental tragicomedy has been skillfully transferred from the stage to the screen by the ever-inventive Altman. This tale of obsessive love, set in a neon-drenched motel at the edge of the Mojave Desert, stars Shepard, the gorgeous and hot-tempered Kim Basinger and Harry Dean Stanton. ★★★ $14.99

The Fool Killer

(1965, 100 min, US, Servando Gonzalles) Shortly after the American Civil War, an abused child (Edward Albert) runs away from home and befriends an amnesiac war veteran (Anthony Perkins) — who may or may not be a mythical killer. A moody, provocative mystery drama. ★★★ $19.99

Foolish Wives

(1922, 95 min, US, Erich von Stroheim) Set in a Monte Carlo we have never known, von Stroheim's third film is chock full of adultery, seduction, blackmail, lechery and suicide, all seasoned with a heavy hand of symbolism. Would be high camp if it weren't for the perceptive characterizations with real psychological depth. Starring the director himself, Maud George and Mae Busch. ★★★ $29.99

Fools of Fortune

(1990, 104 min, Ireland, Pat O'Connor) Set against the backdrop of the bloody battle for Irish independence, this engrossing film tells the tale of a family ruined by war and reunited by courage and faith. Mary Elizabeth Mastrantonio stars as a young English woman whose love for her Irish cousin (Iain Glen of *Mountains of the Moon*) draws her into the midst of the fray. Julie Christie co-stars as her aunt, a British woman fighting for the Republican cause. ★★★ $89.99

Fools Rush In

(1997, 109 min, US, Andy Tennant) Another in the ever-growing line of theatrical films featuring the stars of TV's "Friends" (anybody remember *Ed?*), this romantic comedy stars Chandler (Matthew Perry, that is) as a New Yorker working in a nightclub in Las Vegas who has a one-night stand with Salma Hayek, an earthy, aspiring photographer. Before the bacon and eggs are made in the morning, she takes off, only to reappear a few months later, pregnant. They marry (at the sort of Vegas where Elvis is sighted daily), and problems immediately kick in: culture clashes, coastal clashes, religious clashes. There's no way this relationship should work. And, until the screenwriters settle for a syrupy, storybook finale, it doesn't. There are so many differences between the characters, you wonder where the romance comes into the romantic comedy. Hayek steals the show as the hot tamale; Perry plays it befuddled throughout. Though caricatures, Jill Clayburgh as Perry's mother and Tomas Milian as Hayek's father have the film's funniest moments. As an old song once asked, "Why do fools fall in love?" After watching this, your answer may be: "Who cares?" ★★ $99.99

Footlight Parade

(1933, 104 min, US, Lloyd Bacon) James Cagney is in *42nd Street* territory as a stage director putting on a Broadway show. Joan Blondell is the faithful secretary, and she's a delight. Great musical numbers (by Busby Berkeley) include "Honeymoon Hotel," "By a Waterfall" and Cagney in "Shanghai Lil." Also with Ruby Keeler and Dick Powell, and Guy Kibbee as an angel (that's theatrical parlance for a show's financial backer). ★★★½ $19.99

Footloose

(1984, 107 min, US, Herbert Ross) Clichéd musical drama about a city boy (Kevin Bacon) who moves to Iowa and comes up against the town's powerful minister (John Lithgow), who was instrumental in banning school dances. Also with Lori Singer and Dianne Wiest. ★★ $9.99

For a Few Dollars More

(1964, 130 min, Italy, Sergio Leone) Clint Eastwood stars as "The Man with No Name," who forms an uneasy alliance with Lee Van Cleef in a search for the bandit "Indio." The good guys and bad guys, so easy to identify in the Hollywood western thanks to the wardrobe department, become as ambiguous as the landscape yet as omnipresent as Ennio Morricone's haunting score. ★★★ $14.99

For a Lost Soldier

(1993, 92 min, The Netherlands, Roeland Kerbosch) The potentially explosive subject of man-boy love is delicately handled in this touchingly romantic drama of a boy's coming-of-age during WWII. Jeroen (Maarten Smit), a handsome 13-year-old, is sent by his mother to the countryside. It is there that his adolescent sexual yearnings for those of his own sex begin to take hold. Initially interested in his girl-crazy best friend, Jeroen finds true love with the older Walt (Andrew Kelley), a Canadian soldier stationed in the area. A gay version of *Summer of '42*, this wonderful love story is never sexually graphic, but the achingly romantic lovemaking scene between Jeroen and Walt is certain to shock, especially with its cavalier, naturalistic view of their tender love. (Dutch with English subtitles) ★★★½ $19.99

For Keeps

(1988, 98 min, US, John G. Avildsen) Straight-A student Molly Ringwald lets her high school crush on fellow student Randall Batkinoff lead her to the altar and the maternity ward as she learns that life can be a good deal harder than college prep algebra. With Kenneth Mars. ★ $14.99

For Love of Ivy

(1968, 102 min, US, Daniel Mann) When their maid Ivy announces she's leaving, Carroll O'Connor's children (Beau Bridges and Lauri Peters) try to fix her up with small-time gambler Sidney Poitier in this charming comedy-drama. ★★★ $14.99

For Love or Money

(1993, 96 min, US, Barry Sonnenfeld) The sad thing about cinematographers-turned-directors is that they tend to litter their resumes with features that look great and have nothing to say, while ignoring their lower-profile works. Such is the case with Sonnenfeld, whose two *Addams Family* features turned into Gothic gold mines, while this stylish, old-fashioned romantic comedy was undeservedly vanquished to video oblivion. Michael J. Fox resurfaces as a concierge extraordinaire whose dream of owning his own hotel is jeopardized when he falls for his principal investor's mistress (Gabrielle Anwar). Sure, it's been done before, but this fun frolic should warm many a heart. ★★★ $14.99

For Me and My Gal

(1942, 104 min, US, Busby Berkeley) Gene Kelly made his film debut opposite Judy Garland in this enjoyable backstage musical. They play a vaudeville couple during WWI hoping to make it big...which, of course, they do. Songs include "After You've Gone" and the title tune. ★★★ $19.99

For Our Children: The Concert

(1992, 85 min, US) This worthwhile benefit project from Disney will contribute all profits from this September 26, 1992 concert and subsequent video and album sales to the Pediatric AIDS Foundation. The star-studded cast includes Paula Abdul doing a very Michael Jackson-like rendition of "Zip-A-Dee-Do-Dah," Celine Dion and Maurice Davis belting out "Beauty and the Beast," Melissa Etheridge doing a very charming version of "The Green Grass Grew All Around," and Salt N' Pepa providing a very spicy version of "This Old Man." While Michael Bolton and Woody Harrelson were a bit slow, there were several spectacular show-stoppers that deserve special mention. Bobby McFerrin does a wonderul version of "Wizard of Oz" that was really the highlight of the show. Two other outstanding acts are relative unknowns: Mat Plendl does things with a hula hoop you never thought were possible and Craig & Company sing a hair-raising tribute to a "Haircut." ★★★ $19.99

For the Boys

(1991, 148 min, US, Mark Rydell) Though she has long been associated with the music of the 1940s ("Boogie Woogie Bugle Boy," etc.), this is Bette Midler's first on-screen foray into that decade. Unfortunately, it's not the perfect match one might have hoped for. Midler is paired with the miscast James Caan in this tale about the turbulent partnership of a song and dance duo – from their meeting during WWII to the present. When set in the '40s, the film has vitality and purpose, but it is overly ambitious and none-too-successful in tackling the Hollywood blacklist, and the Korean and Vietnam wars. As the bawdy Dixie Leonard, Midler is in excellent voice and her acting far outshines the rest of the cast, thereby propelling this otherwise mediocre film. A good soundtrack is amongst the film's few other outstanding attractions. ★★½ $9.99

For the Moment

(1993, 120 min, Canada, Aaron Kim Johnston) This softly romantic film is set in Maitoba in 1942, and explores the relationship between a young woman (Christianne Hirt), whose husband of one week has been overseas for two years, and an equally young fighter pilot-in-training (Russell Crowe). Their mutual attraction is conflicted by her loyalty to her absent husband and the tenuous nature of their current circumstances. There's not much new ground here, but the film does possess an authentic feel for the era. Several strong performances (Crowe and Hirt are especially appealing) counteract some hackneyed stereotypes and clichéd vignettes, and the film effectively conveys the war's effect on everyday life in this small farming community. A gentle and affectionate reminiscence of a time of great sacrifice and personal loss. ★★½ $89.99

For Whom the Bell Tolls

(1943, 186 min, US, Sam Wood) A critical and commerical hit upon its initial release, *For Whom the Bell Tolls* is a beautifully photographed adaptation of Ernest Hemingway's novel which hasn't held up quite as well as other films from its era. Shot in a stylized and fragmented fashion, the film stars Gary Cooper as an American fighting with the Spanish partisans in 1937 during their Civil War. Assigned to blow up a strategic bridge, he's teamed with peasant guerrillas, led by Akim Tamiroff and his stalwart wife Katina Paxinou (in a dynamic Oscar-winning performance), and including refugee Ingrid Bergman. As Cooper and Bergman fall in love, their future is threatened by the severity of their mission. Bergman looks impossibly beautiful, complemented more by the gorgeous Technicolor. While the power of Hemingway's story is evident throughout, and the two stars make appealing romantic leads, the film nonetheless is curiously distant. ★★★ $19.99

For Your Eyes Only

(1981, 128 min, GB, John Glen) The 12th James Bond thriller marked a deliberate return to a trimmed down plot and a minimum of histrionic gadgetry. While subsequent productions have been prone to such diversions, this effort is much closer to the stylistic intentions of the series' creator Ian Fleming. The film still features many of the Bond trademarks — spectacular chase scenes, mind-boggling stunts and a bevy of beautiful women. With Roger Moore. ★★★ $14.99

Forbidden Choices

(1994, 109 min, US, Jennifer Warren) Based on Carolyn Chute's novel "The Beans of Egypt, Maine," which was the title when released in theatres, this drama of love and poverty can be aptly described as second-rate Dickens for 20th-century America. Martha Plimpton stars as Earlene, an alienated, waifish young woman whose fascination with her white-trash neighbors, the Bean family, forms the core of the story. Rutger Hauer is Reuben, the unlikely Bean patriarch, Kelly Lynch is Roberta, Reuben's fertile common-law wife, and Patrick McGaw is Beal, the handsome rogue who initially inspires Earlene's romantic fantasies and who eventually becomes her husband. While the performances are uniformly fine, director Warren seems to wallow in the misfortune of the characters' lives to such an extent that you'll hear yourself saying "now what" with each passing plot development. ★★ $92.99

Forbidden Games

(1952, 87 min, France, René Clément) Clément directed this poignant anti-war outcry which follows two French children who become playmates during the German occupation in 1940 and soon begin to imitate the cruelty of the adult world that surrounds them. An unforgettable film experience. (French with English subtitles) ★★★★ $29.99

Forbidden Love — The Unashamed Stories of Lesbian Lives

(1992, 85 min, Canada, Aerlyn Weissman & Lynne Fernie) If at all possible, see this very funny and insightful documentary with an audience of queers because its perceptive approach to a serious and under-documented subject (Canadian lesbian history) will certainly ignite the crowd. The filmmakers weave archival footage, amusing interviews with older lesbians, and a reenactment of one particularly lurid tale of love in fleshing out what life was like for lesbians in the repressed Canada of the 1950s and '60s. Interspersed throughout are shots of hilariously cheesy covers from lesbian potboilers from days gone by. An unforgettable and compelling film with many memorable lines, including "I think that post-menstrual women should run the world!" ★★★ $69.99

Forbidden Planet

(1956, 98 min, US, Fred McLeod Wilcox) Leslie Nielson heads a group of space travelers who land on the planet Altair Four and encounter a "mad" scientist (Walter Pidgeon), his alluring daughter (Anne Francis), Robbie the Robot and the power of Id. An unusually intelligent sci-fi yarn with nifty F/X, good scenic design, and a plot borrowed from Shakespeare's "The Tempest." (Available letterboxed and pan & scan) ★★★½ $14.99

Forbidden Zone

(1984, 75 min, US, Richard Elfman) Horny midgets, transvestite schoolteachers, a half-chicken/half-boy, savage nymphomaniacs, obese maidens in bikinis and a dancing frog all inhabit the Forbidden Zone! Little Frenchy should never have opened that door. This ferocious farce defies description and promises to render you speechless. Original music by Danny Elfman and the Mystic Knights of the Oingo Boingo. Features Susan Tyrrell and the inimitable Herve Villachaize. ★★½

Force of Evil

(1948, 78 min, US, Abraham Polonsky) Blacklisted director Polonsky's last film for over twenty years casts John Garfield as a corrupt lawyer working for the mob in this powerful film noir classic. ★★★½ $14.99

Force 10 from Navarone

(1978, 118 min, GB, Guy Hamilton) Inferior sequel to *The Guns of Navarone* finds the likes of Robert Shaw, Harrison Ford and Carl Weathers teaming with other members of Allied forces to blow up a bridge crucial to the Nazi war effort. ★★ $9.99

Forced March

(1989, 104 min, US, Rick King) Chris Sarandon plays an actor who finds the walls dissolving between himself and the character he is playing, Hungarian poet Mikilos Radnoli who was killed in a Nazi concentration camp. The film evokes a certain power but the ambitious story line cannot fully explore the various subjects it presents. ★★½ $9.99

Foreign Body

(1986, 108 min, GB, Ronald Neame) Victor Banerjee (*A Passage to India*) plays an Indian immigrant in London who, upon the prodding of a friend, finds himself posing as a chiropractor. Banerjee displays a cunning knack for comedy as he is overcome by the advances of his wealthy female patients. A tribute to the early British sex comedies of the 1950s. ★★½

Foreign Correspondent

(1940, 119 min, US, Alfred Hitchcock) Joel McCrea is an American newspaperman stationed in London who becomes involved with a Nazi spy ring and is plunged into a series of terrifying adventures. This enthralling suspenser features a host of Hitchcock's most imaginative scenes, including the windmills that turn backward, an assassination attempt in Westminster Cathedral and a spectacular plane wreck at sea. Splendid performances by McCrea, Laraine Day, George Sanders and Herbert Marshall. ★★★★ $19.99

A Foreign Field

(1993, 90 min, GB, Charles Sturridge) An enchanting international cast distinguishes this impeccably produced made-for-TV BBC drama which, though subdued and deliberately paced, is charming nonetheless. Infused with amiable moments of comedy, the film follows the connecting stories of several people visiting the shores of Normandy 50 years after D-Day. The ensemble includes Leo McKern as a former British infantryman, Alec Guinness as a mentally disabled veteran, Lauren Bacall as a different kind of war widow, John Randolph as an American ex-G.I., Geraldine Chaplin and Edward Herrmann and his daughter and son-in-law, and Jeanne Moreau as a former flame of both McKern and Randolph's. ★★★ $91.99

Foreign Student

(1994, 96 min, US/GB, Eva Sereny) Based on the novel by Philippe Labro, this low-key adaptation examines an interracial romance in the 1950s. Marco Hofschneider plays a Parisian exchange student who spends a semester at a Southern college. There he meets a beautiful black woman (Robin Givens), a teacher who works as a maid at the home of one of his professors. Blind to the segregation and racism of the times, he pursues her, and the two fall in love. The bittersweet story has the youth exploring Southern culture as well, though any interesting dramatics is countered by rather listless pacing. Hofschneider, who spoke several languages as the young hero in *Europa, Europa*, effectively handles two more here. ★★ $14.99

Forest of Little Bear

(1979, 124 min, Japan, Toshio Goto) In the early spring of 1928, Ginzo returns to his village to discover that his only son was killed in action during a Siberian expedition. With the household now suffering from severe financial difficulties, Ginzo decides to go after the reward being offered for the head of "one-eared Itazu," a man-eating bear that has been terrorizing the snow-covered village. Determined in his righteousness of the task, the man becomes hunter only to discover the complexity of the relationship between man and beast and the universal sanctity of life. A deeply affecting drama offset by lush cinematography and beautiful locations. (Japanese with English subtitles) ★★★ $59.99

Forever and a Day

(1943, 105 min, US, Various Directors) This impressive episodic drama chronicles the lives of several generations of a family and their London home. Spanning the century-and-a-

half from 1804 to the German Blitz, the film was produced as a post-war fundraiser for British reconstruction and features just about every Hollywood actor with English roots, including Ray Milland, Merle Oberon, Charles Laughton, Robert Cummings and Nigel Young. Directors include René Clair, Frank Lloyd and Cedric Hardwicke. ★★★½ $19.99

Forever Female

(1953, 93 min, US, Irving Rapper) An engaging cast including Ginger Rogers, William Holden and Paul Douglas adds sparkle to this pleasant backstage comedy, written by Julius and Philip Epstein (*Casablanca, The Man Who Came to Dinner*). Rogers plays a middle-aged Broadway actress still playing the ingenue. She meets writer Holden, whose new play's characters include a 19-year-old daughter and a 50-year-old mother. Guess which one Rogers wants to play. As Rogers' ex-husband, Douglas gives the film's best performance; he can sling a one-liner with the best of them. ★★★ $9.99

Forever Lulu

(1987, 85 min, US, Amos Kollek) Alec Baldwin made his theatrical film debut in this tale about a New York City novelist (Hanna Schygulla) who begins investigating the goings-on of a gangster's moll (Debbie Harry). A forgettable, sloppy ripoff of *Desperately Seeking Susan* with no originality of its own. ★ $79.99

Forever Mary

(1990, 100 min, Italy, Marco Risi) A tougher look into modern urban Italian life than one usually sees. This hard-hitting prison drama, set in a Palermo juvenile detention center, takes an unflinching look at the "rehabilitation" of a group of teenagers. Essentially a spaghetti *To Sir with Love*, the story follows Marco (Michele Placido), a taciturn yet dedicated teacher who volunteers to spend some time trying to educate a clamorous group of teenagers. Their initial scorn soon turns to respect and much to the director's credit, the story avoids sentimental pitfalls and retains its hard edge. The title refers to Mario, a transvestite prostitute who falls in (puppy) love with the teacher. (Italian with English subtitles) ★★★ $79.99

Forever Young

(1983, 85 min, GB, David Drury) This David Putnam (*Chariots of Fire, Local Hero*) production is an intimate and compelling story about the relationship between a 12-year-old boy and a young priest who attempts to shield him from a painful secret. ★★★

Forever Young

(1992, 115 min, US, Steve Miner) Following in the footsteps of the charming independent feature *Late for Dinner* comes this likable comedy-drama of cryogenics and lost love. Mel Gibson plays a nice guy test pilot in 1939 who, after his fiancée becomes comatose, agrees to be a human guinea pig for scientist/pal George Wendt's experiment — to be frozen alive for a year. Fifty years later, Gibson is awakened by young Elijah Wood. As Gibson acclimates to life in the '90s, he tries to track down his long-lost friend and is romantically pursued by Wood's single mom, Jamie Lee Curtis. Alternately funny and shamelessly sentimental, *Forever*

Tom Hanks as *Forrest Gump*

Young is the kind of popular mainstream entertainment which can unapologetically make one laugh and cry. It's a good time without having to feel too guilty for enjoying such manipulative Hollywood fare. ★★★ $14.99

Forget Mozart

(1985, 93 min, Germany, Slavo Luter) Armin Mueller-Stahl stars in this intellectual music lover's answer to *Amadeus* which pays far more attention to historical fact than Hollywood passions. The character of Salieri is again prominent in this story, but blame for Mozart's death is attributed to disease, a failed marriage, alcoholism and the government's inattentiveness. Mueller-Stahl is perfect as the state's investigator into Mozart's untimely demise. Focusing on the historical and political backdrop to Mozart's life, the film explores Mozart's connections with the Freemasons and their influence in this era of revolutionary change in Europe. (German with English subtitles) ★★★ $29.99

Forget Paris

(1995, 101 min, US, Billy Crystal) Crystal wears several hats as producer/director /writer/star of this amiable romantic comedy which offers quite a few laughs in Crystal's inimitable comedic style but is also very familiar. The on-again, off-again love affair of Crystal and Debra Winger is told in flashbacks as friends' dinner conversation. When his deceased father's coffin is lost in Paris, NBA ref Crystal meets airline manager Winger; they fall in love, marry and return to the States. But conflicting schedules and misunderstandings sabotage their happiness, and what follows is a series of breakups and reconciliations. More serious in tone than his other romances, Crystal's film does offer many laughs, but it takes longer to get to them and what's in-between verges on the mundane. The acting is extremely competent, with Winger a delight. ★★½ $19.99

Forgotten Tune for a Flute

(1987, 131 min, USSR, Eldar Ryazanov) The Soviet Union is a society in rapid change and this breezy comedy about a bureaucrat who rediscovers a lost and suppressed part of his life is a wonderful and hopeful symbol of what direction the country is heading to. Lenny is a high-ranking government employee "happily" married to the daughter of another functionary who, after a mild heart attack, begins an affair with a sensible nurse. She, in turn, encourages him to broaden his life and take up another passion long forgotten: playing the flute. A delightful, post-*glasnost* social satire. (Russian with English subtitles) ★★★ $19.99

Forrest Gump

(1994, 142 min, US, Robert Zemeckis) With the nugget of folk wisdom "Life is like a box of chocolates," Tom Hanks launches into the epic telling of the life of Forrest Gump, a small-town simpleton who finds himself at the center of just about every significant cultural event in the latter half of the 20th century. He meets Presidents, goes to Vietnam and, among other things, starts the jogging craze of the '80s. It's a fine premise, and it leads to a host of entertaining moments. But it's all so shallow one wonders if it isn't merely the ideal contrivance to lure baby boomers to the box office — which it did in droves. Hanks' Gump is more than just an "enlightened idiot" of the Chauncy Gardner variety; he's a pure-of-heart all-American boy who never questions authority and prospers as a result. And therein lies its fundamental message which seems to offer absolution to boomers in a sweeping apology for the bad old days of the 1960s. In support, Gary Sinise stands out as Gump's sergeant, Mykelti Williamson is great as Gump's African-American mirror image, Robin Wright is Gump's longtime love, and Sally Field is his mom. Forget the Gump-isms and their residue, for though you may hate some of the contents you may appreciate the packaging. (Available letterboxed and pan & scan) ★★½ $14.99

Forsaking All Others

(1934, 84 min, US, W.S. Van Dyke) Always an intoxicating duo, Joan Crawford and Clark Gable reteam for this satisfying romantic melodrama. Crawford finds her marriage to Gable on the dull side (Gable dull?), so she looks for excitement in the arms of dashing Robert Montgomery. Will she leave her husband or realize they were meant for each other all along? The stars outperform their material. ★★½ $19.99

Fort Apache

(1948, 125 min, US, John Ford) The first of director Ford's cavalry trilogy (followed by *She Wore a Yellow Ribbon* and *Rio Grande*) stars Henry Fonda as a strict military commander at odds with both his men and neighboring Indians. John Wayne is the more compassionate officer caught between loyalty to the soldiers in his command and duty to the martinet under whom he serves. ★★★ $19.99

Fort Apache, the Bronx

(1981, 125 min, US, Daniel Petrie) Paul Newman is the cop facing a conflict of conscience when he witnesses two policemen throw a Hispanic man off a tenement roof. Ed Asner is the precinct captain trying to hold on to his outpost in the center of the crime-torn South Bronx (where the film was shot with

much protest from the community who didn't care for the portrayal of their neighborhood). Pam Grier steals the film with her performance as a drug-crazed prostitute. Ken Wahl is Newman's young partner. ★★★ $9.99

Fortress

(1993, 92 min, US, Stuart Gordon) The director of the cult horror hit *Re-Animator* shows us his vision of the future: an authoritarian world where, due to overpopulation, couples are limited to one child — offenders are duly sentenced to lengthy stays in corporate-managed, computer-controlled prisons. Christopher Lambert and Loryn Locklin play a husband and wife who find themselves imprisoned. She must fend off the obsessive advances of the bioengineered warden (a creepy Kurtwood Smith), while he has to contend with the wrath of some violent fellow inmates. Lambert soon assembles a group of prisoners to help him rescue his wife and escape the fortress. Gordon showers the set with blood, and introduces such grisly futuristic innovations as a neutron cannon (called "the splatter gun" by the inmates) and Intestinators (explosive security devices installed into each inmate's abdomen). While not for the squeamish, *Fortress* is nevertheless an enjoyable sci-fi/action hybrid. Lambert is perfectly adequate, too, as the hero, and Gordon regular Jeffrey Combs has an amusing supporting role as a techno-whiz cellmate. ★★½ $9.99

Fortunata y Jacinta

(1969, 108 min, Spain/Italy, Angelino Fons) Based on the 1877 novel, "Historia de Dos Casadas," by Benito Perez Galdos, this elegant but shrill melodrama recounts the tragic story of two very dissimilar women who vie for the love of the same man. Juan, a young Rock Hudson look-alike, leads a privileged life, with his future assured by the planned marriage to his beautiful cousin Yacinta. That ordered existence, however, takes a cruel turn after he meets and becomes obsessed with the earthy, sexually charged peasant woman Fortunata. Their entangled loves and passions lead inevitably to heartbreak and loss. The attempt by the filmmaker to tell the entire novel in the span of two hours gives the film a frantic, Cliffnotes feel, but irregardless, this ageless story of insuppressible passion is still engaging. (Spanish with English subtitles) ★★½

Fortune and Men's Eyes

(1971, 102 min, Canada/US, Harvey Hart) John Hubert's play about homosexual brutality in prison comes to the screen in this taut, claustrophobic and sensationalistic drama. The story follows young first-timer Smitty (Wendell Burton) who finds himself the prized sexual catch to a thuggish Rocky (Zooey Hall). Sexual humiliation, domination and abuse fill the halls of the seemingly guardless prison as the inmates enact a frenzied dance for power and gratification. Michael Greer (the swishy queen in *The Gay Deceivers*) is alternately hilarious and terrorizing as Queeny, the affectionate, limp-wristed fairy cell mate to Rocky and Smitty who, when threatened, turns into a dangerously violent psychopath. ★★★ $19.99

The Fortune Cookie

(1966, 125 min, US, Billy Wilder) Walter Matthau won an Oscar for his performance as a shyster lawyer out to parlay Jack Lemmon's minor injury into some really big bucks. A funny, biting comedy from the pens of Billy Wilder and partner I.A.L. Diamond. ★★★ $19.99

Fortunes of War

(1987, 180 min, GB, James Cellan Jones) This BBC production stars that consummate husband-and-wife team of Kenneth Branagh and Emma Thompson as a British couple swept up in the struggle against Fascism in 1939 Romania. Based on the autobiographical accounts of Olivia Manning, the story follows the pair as they reluctantly and increasingly become involved with the British Secret Service. With Branagh and Thompson in the leads, the acting is, as would be expected, top-notch and this epic production whisks the viewer through such exotic locales as Bucharest, Athens and Cairo. ★★★ $29.99

Forty Carats

(1973, 110 min, US, Milton Katselas) Lackluster version of the Broadway hit with Liv Ullmann as a 40-ish New Yorker who begins an affair with 20-ish Edward Albert while on holiday in Greece. Though Ullmann is miscast, and Albert is rather emotionless, there's good support from Gene Kelly and Binni Barnes. ★★ $59.99

48 Hrs.

(1983, 97 min, US, Walter Hill) Eddie Murphy's dazzling big-screen debut elevates this cop and convict caper above the usual urban action-drama. Murphy and the comically gruff Nick Nolte join forces to track a pair of homicidal heavies in Hill's jagged-edged comedy-thriller. ★★★½ $14.99

The 49th Parallel

(1941, 107 min, GB, Michael Powell) A stirring WWII suspense drama which was one of the first of the great 1940s British films detailing both the physical and moral fight against the Nazis. When a German U-boat is sunk off the coast of Canada, its five survivors embark on a murderous, ruthless trail from one community to another in their quest to cross into the United States. This political allegory follows the stalwart fight of civilians and servicemen alike to keep the German soldiers from accomplishing their mission. Cast includes Laurence Olivier, Leslie Howard, Raymond Massey, Glynis Johns and Anton Walbrook. (aka: *The Invaders*) ★★★★ $19.99

42nd Street

(1933, 89 min, US, Lloyd Bacon) Classic backstage musical with Warner Baxter as the driven director and Ruby Keeler as the chorine who subs for the injured leading lady and "comes back a star." It's a little creaky by today's standards, but who cares — it's got those terrific Busby Berkeley dance numbers and a fine Warren-Dubin score. ★★★★ $19.99

The 47 Ronin, Parts 1 & 2

(1942, 111/113 min, Japan, Kenji Mizoguchi) Taking his inspiration from one of the most admired tales of Japanese folklore, Mizoguchi adapts for the screen the true story of the 47 masterless samurai who, in 1703, all mysteriously killed themselves by committing *seppuku*. The two-part film begins with the Lord Asano who, in anger, draws his sword and strikes an arrogant but superior lord. With this act of insolence, he must kill himself which leaves his loyal samurai without a leader. The ronin vow to avenge their young lord's death. And with this background our story takes off. Successfully created to inspire wartime patriotism for the war-weary public, the film reinforces traditional Japanese values, as well as reminding the people of their heroism and warrior spirit. (Japanese with English subtitles) (Each volume sells singularly for $29.99) ★★★ $49.99

Foul Play

(1978, 116 min, US, Colin Higgins) Goldie Hawn stars in this funny mystery comedy as a San Francisco librarian who becomes involved with detective Chevy Chase and a plot to assassinate the Pope. Also with Dudley Moore and Burgess Meredith. ★★★ $14.99

The Fountainhead

(1949, 114 min, US, King Vidor) This highly stylized film version of the Ayn Rand novel stars Gary Cooper as an architect, modeled after Frank Lloyd Wright, whose ideas are ahead of their time. A rugged individualist, Cooper takes on a group of federal housing bureaucrats in a struggle over the perversion of his designs. Patricia Neal co-stars as Cooper's romantic interest. ★★★ $19.99

The 400 Blows

Four Adventures of Reinette and Mirabelle

(1986, 95 min, France, Eric Rohmer) Sophisticated humor and two disarmingly charming leads highlight this low-budget account of the up-and-down relationship between two young students. Reinette, a rigorously principled, naive country girl who is studying ethnology at the Sorbonne, meets Mirabelle, a pragmatic, worldly Parisian art student, and they decide to become flatmates.

Together, they have four adventures involving several characters from the streets of Paris. As always, this Rohmer tale is a talk-fest (but entertainingly so) as the two unknown teenage actresses give beguilingly naturalistic performances. An intelligent drama filled with wisdom, idealism and beauty. (French with English subtitles) ★★★½ $29.99

Four Days in July

(1984, 99 min, GB, Mike Leigh) This quirky comedy-drama is set in Northern Ireland during the middle of July, when the Protestants celebrate their national pride. Director Leigh deftly interweaves the lives of two couples, one Protestant and the other Catholic, and both expecting their first child. In his typical cinema verité manner, Leigh gently exposes the nuances of these disparate elements of Ulster society employing only simple living room conversation and other trivial daily chores — it is a quietly evocative exposé on a territory torn by strife. Look for Stephen Rea in a bit role as Dixie, the window washer. ★★★½ $29.99

Four Eyes and Six-Guns

(1992, 92 min, US, Piers Haggard) This entertaining family fare features an engaging performance from Judge Reinhold as Ernest Allbright, a naive, idealistic New York City optometrist who follows his dream to Wyatt Earp's Tombstone, Arizona. Before he gets there, his examination equipment is trashed while he's brutalized in a train robbery; after he arrives, he's bilked out of his life savings and winds up broke in a tumble-down shack. Of course, goodness and righteousness eventually triumph over adversity and deceit — aided in large part by Allbright's uncanny and unorthodox expertise with a six-gun. Trusty Fred Ward delivers a workmanlike portrayal of Marshall Earp. A delightful evocation of old-time western serials, with detailed costuming and set design, and not a cuss word within earshot. Suitable for all ages. ★★½ $9.99

The Four Feathers

(1939, 115 min, GB, Zoltan Korda) A.E.W. Mason's story about a young aristocrat who resigns his military commission on the eve of an expedition to the Sudan. He is subsequently branded a coward by friends and lover alike. To prove his worthiness he joins the group and helps battle the Sudanese uprising. A great epic of British imperialism. With Ralph Richardson and John Clements. ★★★½ $14.99

Four Horsemen of the Apocalypse

(1961, 153 min, US, Vincente Minnelli) Remake of the Rudolph Valentino silent box-office hit, with much less success, about brothers fighting on opposite sides of the war; here updated to WWII. Stars Glenn Ford, Ingrid Thulin, Charles Boyer, Lee J. Cobb and Paul Henried. ★★ $19.99

The 400 Blows

(1959, 99 min, France, François Truffaut) Arguably the finest in a long line of cinematic coming-of-age efforts, *The 400 Blows* marked the emergence of a brilliant young directorial talent. Truffaut's largely autobiographical feature film debut commenced the wonderful saga of Antoine Doinel (Jean-Pierre Léaud), the

Four Weddings and a Funeral

director's alter ego. Oppressed by the demands of parents and teachers, the young Antoine ventures out on his own only to discover the unsettling bleakness of personal freedom. (French with English subtitles) ★★★★ $29.99

The Four Musketeers

(1974, 106 min, GB, Richard Lester) Lester's impressive follow-up to *The Three Musketeers*, his romping vision of the Dumas classic, was filmed simultaneously with the original. While darker in tone than the first film, and less emphatic in its physical comedy, it is still filled with incisive period wit and lots of rollicking adventure. ★★★

Four Rooms

(1996, 98 min, US, Allison Anders, Alex Rockwell, Robert Rodriguez & Quentin Tarantino) Anthology films are sometimes very good, but are almost always uneven. In this case, it is much worse than that — the whole is much less than the sum of its parts. While two of the four segments are moderately good, the other two are so abysmally bad that they very nearly make the entire project a failure. The film takes place on New Year's Eve and tells four different bizarre stories, happening in four different rooms of a hotel serviced by one very overworked bellboy (Tim Roth in an ingratiatingly mugging performance). Anders' segment concerns a coven of witches who gather to perform a ritual and is boring from start to finish, seeming to have been written mainly as an excuse to use some mildly frank sexual language. Rockwell's bit is equally bad: It stars Jennifer Beals as the victim of a twisted bondage and power game and is actually painful to watch. The film livens up substantially in Rodriguez's segment, about two children in a room by themselves, nominally supervised by Roth. And Tarantino's segment tops off the weird mix with a macabre tale of a bet made in flesh. ★½ $19.99

The Four Seasons

(1981, 107 min, US, Alan Alda) A genuinely funny comedy on romance and relationships, director Alda has yet to equal this story about a group of friends who spend their vacations together. As the couples,

Alda and Carol Burnett, Jack Weston and Rita Moreno, and Len Cariou and Sandy Dennis and then Bess Armstrong, all offer delightful performances. A witty, even perceptive script by Alda. ★★★ $19.99

Four Weddings and a Funeral

(1994, 116 min, GB, Mike Newell) Proving that he is almost as effortlessly charming as a namesake called Cary, Hugh Grant gives a career-making performance in this enchanting romantic comedy playing a likable Britisher whose biggest flaw seems to be his fear of commitment. Fulfilling its titular promise, the film follows Grant and a wonderful group of friends as they wind their way from one ceremony to another imparting blithe observations on love, relationships and fear of both. Featuring a marvelously written screenplay, the film only loses control at its finale with an abrupt, simplistic ending which belies the intelligence which came before it. Andie McDowell is the film's only other flaw, giving a lifeless performance as the woman of Grant's dreams. However, Simon Callow and John Hannah, as devoted lovers, and Rowan Atkinson, immensely funny as a tongue-tied priest, are exceptional in support. ★★★½ $14.99

1492: Conquest of Paradise

(1992, 150 min, GB/France/US, Ridley Scott) The better of 1992's two dramatizations (the other being *Christopher Columbus: The Discovery*) about Christopher Columbus being discovered by Native Americans when he got lost trying to find a quicker trade route to Asia. Gérard Depardieu gives a fine performance as the explorer who betrays and is eventually betrayed, ultimately ending his years in obscurity and poverty. Director Scott's eye for the striking visual serves him well in enlivening this revisionist epic which unfortunately suffers from delusions of profundity. Also with Sigourney Weaver and Armand Assante. (Available letterboxed and pan & scan) ★★ $29.99

The 4th Man

(1983, 110 min, The Netherlands, Paul Verhoeven) A wonderful hallucinatory thriller that bristles with dark, forboding humor and sexual paranoia. The story concerns a brooding novelist (Jeroen Krabbé) entwined in the web of a mysterious beautician and her handsomely sculpted lover. Starring the hauntingly beautiful Renée Soutendijk. (Available dubbed and in Dutch with English subtitles) ★★★½ $19.99

The Fourth Protocol

(1987, 100 min, GB, John MacKenzie) A superior political thriller with Michael Caine as a government agent who stumbles upon a plot by a renegade Soviet general to destroy an American airbase in England. Based on Frederick Forsyth's novel, the film, as with the author's *The Day of the Jackal*, builds an unrelenting tension until its shattering conclusion. Pierce Brosnan is the KGB agent assigned to the deadly task, and Joanna Cassidy is radiant as his contact. ★★★½ $9.99

The Fourth War

(1990, 91 min, US, John Frankenheimer) Roy Scheider and Jürgen Prochnow battle it out as the last of the Cold War militarists in this competent though unexciting thriller. Scheider plays an American colonel and Prochnow is a Russian commander, both willing to start WWIII for the sake of psyching out the other. ★★½ $14.99

Fox and His Friends

(1975, 123 min, West Germany, Rainer Werner Fassbinder) Fassbinder's first specifically male gay-themed film is a richly textured and powerful drama of the relationship between two gay men of vastly different social backgrounds. A lower-class carnival entertainer, Fox (played by Fassbinder), finds himself suddenly flush after winning 500,000DM in a lottery. He soon becomes involved in an ill-fated romance with gold-digging Eugen, a rich, manipulative young man. The eternal class struggle and the continued exploitation of the poor and working class is tragically played out as the unwitting Fox is swindled out of his money and self-respect by his bourgeois lover and his family. (German with English subtitles) ★★★★ $29.99

1492: Conquest of Paradise

The Fox and the Hound

(1981, 83 min, US) While the music of this potential classic is not up to Disney's current standards, this tale of friendship between the hunter and the hunted is timeless and timely. Tod is an orphaned fox cub who befriends Copper, a hound puppy who will eventually be trained to hunt foxes. Although they become best friends, their relationship is threatened by Copper's owner, who is determined to kill Tod. The thrilling climax proves that friendship is indeed more powerful than hate or revenge, and reminds kids that differences need not be dividers. The animation is first-rate and the voices of Kurt Russell, Mickey Rooney, Sandy Duncan and Corey Feldman provide star quality. ★★★ $39.99

Foxes

(1980, 106 min, US, Adrian Lyne) Jodie Foster stars as one of four girls who share an apartment in the Los Angeles suburbs in this sociological study which poignantly examines the restless lives of today's youths, although it presents more questions than answers. With Sally Kellerman, Randy Quaid and Scott Baio. ★★½ $14.99

Foxfire

(1996, 102 min, US, Annette Haywood-Carter) A disappointing adaptation of Joyce Carol Oates' novel about a girl gang, *Foxfire* waters down important issues such as sexual harassment, drug addiction and female teenage angst as it depicts the actions of five rebellious high school girls coming to terms with their identities. Suspended from school for attacking a teacher, these disparate teens embark on a series of crimes that escalate in their severity. Like *Girls Town*, *Foxfire* takes the perspective of young women on the verge of adulthood, but much of the drama is heavy-handed and unpleasant. Often forgoing logic for the sake of dramatic effect, the film is as irresponsible as its heroines. Director Haywood-Carter succeeds in generating a palpable sexual tension between two of the girls, but is unable to coax a single decent performance from the cast. And though there's nifty camerawork and a fine alternative soundtrack, this is a case of style masking substance. What could have been a fiery display of female solidarity quickly becomes a frustrating one. ★★ $97.69

Foxy Brown

(1974, 94 min, US, Jack Hill) Mob queenpin Miss Katherine finds her harem reduced to mince meat when Pam Grier goes after those responsible for her brutal rape and the death of her brother. Grier is certainly a sight, but this early blaxploitation actioner is very violent and muddled. ★★ $9.99

Frameup

(1993, 91 min, US, Jon Jost) It's no big secret that the works of Jost are an acquired taste: his minimalistic, free-form films test the patience of most viewers and are probably of interest only to experimental filmmakers and fans thereof. *Frameup*, a monotonous, pretentiously artsy examination of a *Badlands*-like couple, holds true to the director's reputation. Husband and wife Howard Swain and Nancy Carlin star as the ill-fated couple, who meet in Idaho and head West for relaxation, sex and murder. Comprised of a series of narrations framed by a motionless camera, the film is all talk and very little action. Carlin gives a grating performance; Swain nearly captures the essence of a bad guy. He also has a tattoo on his penis spelling "Wow" — if there was truth in advertising it would have said "This Sucks." ★ $24.99

Framing Lesbian Fashion

(1992, 58 min, US, Karen Everett) Beginning with a montage of various outfits and "uniforms" worn by lesbians over the last four decades, this entertaining documentary traces the herstory of how apparel has helped shape and define the lesbian mystique — its attitudes, politics, sociology and personal role-playing. By tracing the fashion trends of lesbians, the films touches on such themes as the traditional butch and femme look, lesbian clones of the '70s and the Birkenstock-and-flannel radfems to today's world of greater freedom and individuality where fashion definition has been blurred and where lipstick lesbians and dykes with long hair, makeup and dresses are as much a part of the lesbian culture as women into body piercing, leather and even corporate drag. Intercutting archival photos with clips from movies (Katharine Hepburn and Marlene Dietrich in drag) and interviews, director Everett leads a fascinating journalistic tour of the evolving lesbian community, its culture and its shifting self-identity. ★★★ $24.99

Frances

(1982, 140 min, US, Graeme Clifford) Jessica Lange gives a powerful performance as Frances Farmer, the radiant Hollywood starlet of the `30s whose nonconformity launched a tragic succession of injustices. This chilling bio-pic delineates the demise of Farmer's promising film career and discloses the terrifying conditions of her imposed institutionalization. ★★★ $14.99

Francesco

(1989, 105 min, Italy, Liliana Cavani) A pre-puffy faced, before-his-boxing-career-skids-days Mickey Rourke is featured in this religious drama giving an emotionally raw and stirring performance as Francesco, the egotistical son of a wealthy merchant. After reading one of the first non-Latin translations of the Bible, Francesco takes the gospels literally. He gives up everything to live and suffer with the poor, gains "peace," starts the Franciscan order and becomes a saint. Rourke is joined on his quest for enlightenment by Helena Bonham Carter, who with her gaunt face, saucer eyes and translucent skin, makes the perfect ascetic. An elegantly told biblical epic that proves captivating even for non-believers. ★★★ $89.99

Francis

(1950, 91 min, US, Arthur Lubin) The first in the popular 1950s comedy series (seven films in all) about the comic hijinks of Francis, the talking mule. Before dazzling audiences with his fancy footwork in *Singin' in the Rain*, Donald O'Connor had one of his first big hits as a G.I. who is befriended by the chatty and wise-cracking animal. The entire series is dated but mindless fun, and this first entry is the best of them. Also released on video: *Francis Goes to the Races, Francis Joins the WACS* and *Francis in the Navy*. Incidentally, director Lubin went on to produce the similarly themed TV series "Mr. Ed." ★★½ $14.99

François Truffaut: Stolen Portraits

(1993, 93 min, France, Serge Toubiana & Michel Pascal) When director Eric Rohmer comes across his name on one of the hundreds of folders in the late Truffaut's study, he is nonplussed, irritated and a little bit frightened ("What's this?" he exclaims. "I don't keep a file on Truffaut in *my* office!"). Seemingly everyone who ever met was clipped, codified and arranged alphabetically in case the prolific director needed — somehow, to some degree — something of them in one of his cinematic tapestries. Well-chosen clips from the more famous of his works act as a kind of Greek chorus to the ex-wives, boyhood friends, actors and directors (Gérard Depardieu, Claude Chabrol and Bertrand Tavernier among them) who tell many tales — some flattering, some not so. Obviously 90 minutes is not enough time to develop a full portrait of Truffaut, whose many contradictions — as a man and as an artist —

invigorated so many of his movies. ★★★ $19.99

Frankenhooker

(1990, 85 min, US, Frank Henenlotter) From the director of *Basket Case* and its sequels comes this tale of a girl who is dismembered by a lawn mower at her own birthday party and the efforts of her boyfriend to get her back together. While keeping her head on ice in the family freezer, he goes shopping for parts on 42nd Street to see what he can pick up. Great sick fun. The unrated version. ★★½ $89.99

Frankenstein

(1931, 72 min, US, James Whale) The grand-daddy of all horror films. This classic stars Boris Karloff as the man-made monster, Colin Clive as the scientist who creates him ("It's alive!"), and Mae Clark as the requisite damsel in distress. A masterpiece of suspense, atmosphere and design. This is the restored version. ★★★★ $14.99

Frankenstein

(1993, 100 min, US/GB, David Wickes) The good Dr. Frankenstein (Patrick Bergin) is chased by his evil creation to the Arctic, where he is stranded on an immobile ship. There, he recounts his tragic tale to the captain one night as the monster (an unrecognizable Randy Quaid) waits for the dawn to attack. Because this film was made for television, its minimal use of blood and gore leaves the viewer free to look past the surface tension and delve into the motivations of the characters' actions. The doctor, in this version of Mary Shelley's renowned novel, is not bent on playing God for his own benefit, but rather sees mankind as the beneficiary of his study of science. ★★★ $92.98

Frankenstein Meets the Wolf Man

(1942, 73 min, US, Roy William Neill) It's Bela Lugosi meets Lon Chaney, Jr. in this fifth entry in the *Frankenstein* series, and sequel to *The Wolf Man*. This eerie, well-made story has Chaney searching to end his curse, only to do battle with the monster. As with the majority of the Universal horror films of the '30s and '40s, it's chilling to the bone. ★★★ $14.99

Frankenweenie

(27 min, US, Tim Burton) Director Burton gives his special treatment to a young boy's undying devotion to his dog. Shelley Duvall and Daniel Stern are Barret Oliver's (*The NeverEnding Story*) parents in this dark, brooding examination of heartfelt loyalty in the face of rabid persecution. You'll see early glimmerings of *Edward Scissorhands* and *Batman*, evidence of Burton's already-strong signature. A very polished effort and O.K. for kids despite its somber tone. ★★★½ $12.99

Frankie and Johnny

(1991, 118 min, US, Garry Marshall) Al Pacino and Michele Pfeiffer turn in a pair of charming performances in this pleasing romantic comedy about an ex-con (Pacino) who takes a job as a short order cook in a greasy-spoon diner and falls for the waitress (Pfeiffer). Excellent support comes from Hector Elizondo as the diner's owner, Kate Nelligan as an oversexed waitress, and Nathan

Lane as Pfeiffer's gay best friend. Marshall's directing is overly sentimental and TV-ish, as with his previous outing, *Pretty Woman*, but Terrence McNally's adaptation of his own stage play, "Frankie and Johnny in the Claire De Lune," is strong enough to make this a thoroughly enjoyable outing. ★★★ $9.99

Frankie Starlight

(1995, 101 min, Ireland/GB, Michael Lindsay-Hogg) This bittersweet Irish yarn tells the tale of a slightly psychic young French girl (Anne Parillaud) and her Irish-born dwarf son. The film opens with an adult Frank Bois (Corban Walker), her diminutive descendent, hawking a manuscript that depcits her life to a literary agent. We are then transported back to occupied Normandy, weeks before D-Day where Parillaud makes the disastrous error of predicting the invasion a day early. Stricken with grief, she stows away on an American troop ship only to be dropped off in Ireland, pregnant. She finds a benefactor in a kindly customs officer (Gabriel Byrne) who helps her through hard times and becomes a surrogate father to Frankie, and plants in the young boy a love of stargazing. Later, G.I. Matt Dillon shows up and woos them both with his Yankee charm. Not a lot transpires in *Frankie Starlight*, but its likable characters and generally mirthful outlook make it a completely enjoyable lark. Parillaud and Byrne both give beautifully understated performances and as the young Frank, Alan Pentony is quite alluring. ★★★ $96.89

Frantic

(1958, 94 min, France, Louis Malle) Malle's first film is an elegant thriller about what can happen to the perfect crime. Jeanne Moreau's lover is trapped in an elevator after murdering her husband. Subsequently, they become incriminated in a series of crimes they neither committed nor can deny, when their getaway car is stolen by a delinquent Parisian couple and is used for a rampage. A stylish film noir with a great Miles Davis score. (French with English subtitles) ★★★

Frantic

(1988, 120 min, US, Roman Polanski) Harrison Ford gives a controlled but compelling performance as an American whose wife (Betty Buckley) disappears the first day of their French vacation. He discovers the sleazy underbelly of Paris at night as he unrelentingly searches for his missing wife. ★★★ $9.99

Franz

(1972, 88 min, France, Jacques Brel) The past tangles with the present in this dark drama about the residents of a French boarding house. The residence, previously all-male, is thrown upside down when two women move in and begin to affect the men's lifestyles. (French with English subtitles) ★★½ $19.99

Frauds

(1993, 94 min, GB, Stephan Elliott) Guilt, fate and the "Peter Pan Syndrome" collide in this dark British comedy that gives new meaning to the term "death by misadventure." Singer Phil Collins earns his acting wings as a game-playing insurance investigator who makes out like a bandit blackmailing a young couple (Hugo

A boy and his whale: Free Willy

Weaver and Josephine Byrnes) who are guilty of insurance fraud – until the two find the prankster's own Achilles' heel. Good set design, winning performances and coal-black humor easily elevate this film above the level of standard "B-movie" fare. ★★★ $49.99

Freaked

(1993, 85 min, US, Tom Stern & Alex Winter) Winter (the *other* guy from *Bill & Ted's Excellent Adventure*) co-directed and co-wrote this highly original, laugh-laden comedy. He plays a self-absorbed TV star who, upon being named spokesperson for the nefarious E.E.S. Corporation (Everything Except Shoes), is sent to the tropical paradise Santa Flan to curb rumors about the side effects of the company's toxic product. It is there he and a group of innocents are turned into sideshow freaks by a demented scientist/carnival owner (Randy Quaid). Amazingly creative in its use of special effects and casting (Brooke Shields, Bobcat Goldthwait, Mr. T), this unusual film stands alone as a true laugh-a-thon. ★★★½ $96.99

Freaks

(1931, 64 min, US, Tod Browning) Browning's shocking story of circus freaks who wreak vengeance against their cruel exploiters. Sometimes gruesome, yet a sympathetic look at society's outcasts driven by abuse to an act of terror. ★★★ $19.99

Freaky Friday

(1977, 95 min, US, Gary Nelson) Long before the body-switching craze of the late 1980s, Barbara Harris and Jodie Foster played mother and daughter who switched identities for predictable comic results. This Disney comedy is charmingly done and benefits greatly from sparkling performances from the two ladies. ★★★ $9.99

Freddy's Dead: Nightmare on Elm Street 6

(1991, 96 min, US, Rachel Talalay) Freddy Krueger (Robert Englund) camps it up again in this inane, effects-heavy sequel. Lisa Zane plays a child psychologist who leads a group of troubled teens into their dream worlds to get to the bottom of their recurring nightmares – all star-

ring Freddy! Yaphet Kotto co-stars, with cameos by Roseanne, Tom Arnold, Alice Cooper and Johnny Depp. ★ $14.99

A Free Soul

(1931, 91 min, US, Clarence Brown) Lionel Barrymore won an Oscar for his solid portrayal of a lawyer defending mobster Clark Gable on a murder charge. Norma Shearer plays the attorney's daughter, who falls in love with Gable. Also with Leslie Howard and James Gleason, the film is impeccably acted, and helped launch Gable on the road to stardom. ★★★ $19.99

Free Willy

(1993, 111 min, US, Simon Wincer) Director Wincer pulls every cheap emotional trick out of his bag in this tale of a boy and his whale and, surprisingly, he succeeds in his efforts. Kind of an *E.T.* of the sea, the film follows a runaway (Jason James Richter) from the foster care system who, after vandalizing a local marine park, is taken under the wing of the park's employees and befriended by their charge, an unhappy whale named Willy. But when the park's greedy owner sees profits in killing the whale and collecting the insurance, our young hero is pressed into action to save his friend. Yes, it reeks of tear-jerking formulaity, but the film is nevertheless a winner amongst its target audience – kids. Lori Petty co-stars as Willy's trainer and Michael Madsen plays against type as the kid's foster father. ★★½ $19.99

Free Willy 2: The Adventure Home

(1995, 96 min, US, Dwight Little) Jesse (Jason James Richter) and his whale pal Willy are reunited for more adventure in this amiable sequel which ambitiously tackles ecological, Native American and coming-of-age themes. While on a family camping trip, complete with a newfound brother (Francis Capra), Jesse makes contact with Willy who has been reunited with his family. When an oil tanker runs aground and spills its contents, Willy and his family's lives are threatened by the spill. The first half of the film takes its time setting up the plot, and the human story of Jesse and his new brother and their mother's death is maudlin. However, the scenes with Jesse and Willy have an excitement to them, especially the film's finale which pits Jesse against greedy industrialists and a deadly oil fire. Jesse also finds first love, but with his hormones in high gear, that's to be expected. Most of the original cast returns. ★★½ $19.99

Freedom Is Paradise

(1989, 75 min, Russia, Sergei Bodrov) The innocent young boy in search "of freedom" or "of his father" has been a consistent theme in Russian filmmaking. Films like *Lessons at the End of Spring; Kindergarten; Freeze, Die, Come to Life* and *Come and See* all use the boy as a symbol of a new, true Russia lost in a harsh post-Communist world. This harrowing yet lyrical drama centers on 13-year-old Sasha who, after his mother dies, takes a journey through the barren worlds of Alma Ata in middle Asia to the outskirts of Leningrad, all in a determined quest to find his long-imprisoned father.

Filmed on location and at actual Soviet prisons, the story follows the boy as he is put in a reform school for orphans, escapes (only to be betrayed and then beaten by authorities) and, finally, through the intervention and help of strangers, arrives at a Gulag-like prison. A serious and gripping tale of persistence and perseverance. (Russian with English subtitles) ★★★½ $69.99

Freefall

(1993, 96 min, US, John Irvin) B-movie bad-boys Jeff Fahey and Eric Roberts co-star in this engaging espionage thriller about a photographer (Pamela Gidley) who becomes an unwitting pawn in a game of international cat & mouse when she launches into an affair with a rakish CIA operative (Roberts) who has taken a professional interest in her publishing mogul fiancé (Fahey). Despite the *Cliffhanger*-esque packaging, this fresh spy tale from the director of *The Dogs of War* is a non-stop joyride that keeps the pulse pounding right up to the very end. ★★★ $94.99

Freejack

(1991, 110 min, US, Geoff Murphy) An insipidly entertaining sci-fi thriller from the producer/co-writer of *Alien* and *Total Recall*. With special effects which far outshine the acting, the story features a catatonic Emilio Estevez as a cocky race car driver who is taken from the 20th century into the future by the lunar-faced Mick Jagger, who sports a smirk throughout the film as if to say "And I get paid thousands for this!" Jagger is the hired hand of an evil industrialist who wants to prolong his life by transferring the life juices of our young hero into his dying body. Anthony Hopkins lends some class to the production in a small role. ★½ $9.99

Freeze, Die, Come to Life

(1990, 105 min, Russia, Vitaly Kanevski) A brutal and uncompromising look at Soviet life under the Stalin regime as seen through the eyes of a young boy. The Party faithful are rallying villagers for a May Day celebration amid the abysmal poverty and unceasingly overcast skies in a remote Siberian outpost. The young protagonist, a pint-sized rebel and unwilling scapegoat, struggles gamely against hypocrisy, toadyism and bureaucratic myopia while maintaining his high spirits and fierce sense of individuality. Filmed with a raw, documentary-like feel, the film is sometimes bitter, often funny and insightful, and has moments of touching tenderness. It's also reminiscent of the equally superlative *Come and See*. ★★★½ $19.99

French Can-Can

(1955, 102 min, France, Jean Renoir) Set during La Belle Epoque in Paris' lively Montemartre, Renoir's gloriously vibrant tribute to the music hall shimmers with the brilliant colors of the director's palate. *French Can-Can* weaves a tale of jilted lovers, ambitious artists and scheming "angels." Jean Gabin, the Gallic Bogart, portrays an amorous impresario with a dream to revive the can-can in a renovated nightclub, which will become the legendary Moulin Rouge. Surrounding him is a circus of dance, love and music, and the people swept up in the exhilarating rhythms of

F

the theatre. (French with English subtitles) ★★★★ $59.99

The French Connection

(1971, 104 min, US, William Friedkin) Gene Hackman's tour de force performance as real-life New York City detective Popeye Doyle dominates this slam-bang police adventure about Doyle hunting down an international narcotics ring. Roy Scheider also stars as Hackman's partner. Winner of five Academy Awards, including Best Picture. ★★★½ $14.99

The French Connection II

(1975, 119 min, US, John Frankenheimer) Gene Hackman returns in this exciting sequel to the original Oscar winner. Popeye Doyle continues his search for an international drug ring, headed by Fernando Rey (who also returns from the first film). ★★★ $19.99

The French Detective

(1975, 100 min, France, Pierre Granier-Deferre) An entertaining police story which pits a determined middle-aged cop (Lino Ventura) and his cynical young partner (Patrick Dewaere) against a ruthless and elusive politician. (French with English subtitles) ★★★

French Kiss

(1995, 111 min, US, Lawrence Kasdan) Meg Ryan plays an American émigré who's engaged to Canadian doctor Timothy Hutton. He flies to Paris for a business trip. Since she's afraid to fly, she stays home. Bad move. He meets a beautiful French woman and breaks the engagement. This sends her abroad to win back her man. On the flight, she meets French jewel thief Kevin Kline, who uses her to help smuggle his latest booty. In an effort to keep track of her and the jewels, he pretends to help her win Hutton back. Of course after numerous escapades throughout Paris and the French countryside, the two soon fall in love. *French Kiss* is a lot more funny and endearing than the formulaic plot suggests, thanks to the frothy pace set by director Kasdan and the pleasant performances by its two stars. And if both actors are in familiar territory, it only works to the advantage of the film that both Ryan and Kline wrangle fresh interpretations of parts they evidently know so well. ★★★ $14.99

French Lesson

(1986, 90 min, GB, Brian Gilbert) Jane Snowden stars in this amusing little comedy of manners about a young English woman who sojourns to France where she receives a schooling in affairs of the heart. ★★½ $14.99

The French Lieutenant's Woman

(1981, 124 min, GB, Karel Reisz) This passionate tale of a mysterious woman's obsession shines with the excellent acting of Meryl Streep and Jeremy Irons, and the intriguingly complex screenplay by Harold Pinter. ★★★ $9.99

French Twist

(1995, 100 min, France, Josiane Balasko) This whimsical French farce with a lesbian twist nicely blends all the outrageousness of its genre with some finely drawn subtleties to create a highly amusing divertimento that is peppered throughout with touching moments. Victoria Abril is Loli, the dutiful (and evident-

ly happily housebound) Spanish wife of a boorish French real estate broker (Alain Chabat) who prides himself on his profusion of extra-marital affairs. Marijo (Josiane Balasko), a bohemian, cigar-smoking dyke from Paris, lands on their doorstep in the South of France with a broken-down VW minivan and, after a bit of small talk, makes a pass at Loli. Starved for the attentions of her philandering husband, Loli responds warmly to these advances, much to his outrage. But when *his* indiscretions come to light the whole situation really blows up and Loli retaliates in a most unusual way. Filled with the standard burlesque guffaws, *French Twist* is most impressive for its even-handed treatment of its characters. Balasko is quite fetching as a boyishly macho lesbian, Abril's range of emotion is sensational and her radiance is enough to capture the heart of any sexual persuasion. Even Chabat is given a fair shake as he struggles to reconcile his sexual urges with his emotional desires. (French with English subtitles) ★★★ $99.99

The French Way

(1952, 72 min, France, Michel Deville) This wartime musical comedy is generally pedestrian fare, but the presense of Josephine Baker helps make it of interest. Ms. Baker, who sings five songs in the film, plays cupid to two young lovers who cannot marry because of their feuding parents. (French with English subtitles) ★★

French Woman

(1979, 97 min, France, Just Jaeckin) A shocking sex scandal rocks the French government in this tale of blackmail and murder. Franciose Fabian stars as the real-life madam whose clientele included some of the world's most influential leaders. Also starring Klaus Kinski. From the director of *Emmanuelle* and *The Story of "O"*. (aka: *Madame Claude*) (Dubbed) ★★

Frenzy

(1972, 116 min, GB, Alfred Hitchcock) Brilliant latter-day Hitchcock. A suave London strangler ingeniously incriminates an innocent man in a wave of murders. A bold and crafty reassertion of Hitch's mastery of the suspense genre. Stars Jon Finch and Vivien Merchant. ★★★★ $14.99

Fresh

(1994, 115 min, US, Boaz Yakin) Starkly realized and ingeniously crafted, this urban coming-of-age drama follows an inner-city youth as he struggles to ride out life in the mean streets of Harlem and outwit the neighborhood gangstas. Sean Nelson delivers a disturbing portrayal as Fresh, a tensomething chess wizard (and a hardened drug runner) who is teetering on the edge of a life of crime. His dispassionate, calculating approach to life offers the viewer a sobering look at a vanquished generation, and his Machiavellian maneuvers and innovative survival skills make this much more than just another blighted urban/teen melodrama. Excellent support comes from Giancarlo Esposito as Fresh's Latino drug dealer employer/mentor and Samuel L. Jackson puts in another fine performance as his unemployed father, a fallen chess master to whom the boy regularly turns for advice. ★★★½ $19.99

Fresh Horses

(1988, 105 min, US, David Anspaugh) After she turned on *The Pick-Up Artist* and he scored *Less Than Zero*, it was uncertain if Molly Ringwald and Andrew McCarthy could sink any lower in their careers. And we were worried; of course they could. Essentially a wrong-side-of-the-tracks romantic drama, this totally contrived and suprisingly moribund film, about rich college student McCarthy falling for poor but sexy Ringwald, isn't even for fans of the two stars. ★ $89.99

The Freshman

(1990, 102 min, US, Andrew Bergman) This delightfully droll comedy stars Matthew Broderick as a film student who takes a job as a messenger to a presumed Mafia don (Marlon Brando). Brando, with no apologies, patterns his role after another Mafia don he made famous in a cinema classic back in the '70s — and he's terrifically funny. Look for a show-stopping cameo by Bert Parks. ★★★½ $9.99

Frida

(1984, 108 min, Mexico, Paul Leduc) The life of painter, revolutionary and woman-of-the-world Frida Kahlo is brilliantly brought to the screen in this insightful and poetic biography. Told from her deathbed in surreal flashbacks reminiscent of her own canvases, the film recalls Frida's stormy relationship with muralist Diego Rivera, her dealings with Leon Trotsky, her involvement with the cultural renaissance in Mexico in the 1930s, as well as captures the spirit and determination of one of the dominant painters of the 20th century. (Spanish with English subtitles) ★★★ $79.99

Friday

(1995, 96 min, US, F. Gary Gray) Starring rapper Ice Cube and comedian Chris Tucker, this well-written (by Cube and DJ Pooh) hip-hop comedy chronicles a day-in-the-life of a pair of homeboys in South Central Los Angeles who try to raise enough money to pay a debt to a pot dealer. Spiced with acid-tongued dialogue and a fine supporting cast that includes Johnny Witherspoon, Tiny Lister and a cameo by the legendary La Wanda Paige, *Friday* is a most amusing, energetic romp. ★★★ $19.99

Friday the 13th

(1980, 96 min, US, Sean S. Cunningham) Director Cunningham started the slasher genre with this gory though unexciting thriller about an unknown killer stalking camp counselors at Camp Crystal Lake. Jason would come back for seven more helpings. ★★ $9.99

Fried Green Tomatoes

(1991, 130 min, US, Jon Avnet) Based on Fannie Flagg's novel, this heartwarming, touching (don't let these words scare you) and funny film revolves around two separate stories: one present day and one set in the 1930s. Ignored housewife Kathy Bates meets charmer Jessica Tandy at a retirement home. It is there Tandy tells her the story of Idgy and Ruth, two friends from her youth in a small, nearby Alabama town. It is the latter story which is at the core of this tender, remarkable film. And as these two women, the incredible Mary Stuart Masterson and the wonderful Mary-

F

Louise Parker deliver multilayered performances worthy of their storyteller's adulation. The focus of Idgy and Ruth's story is their enduring friendship and love for each other (a greater love is hinted at but never revealed). And through these stories Bates is inspired to instill in herself newfound self-esteem. A lovely piece of filmmaking with indelible performances by a gifted cast. ★★★½ $14.99

Fried Shoes Cooked Diamonds

(1978, 55 min, US, Constanzo Allione) The reunion of the Beat poets at Naropa Institute in Boulder, Colorado. With Allen Ginsberg, William Burroughs, Timothy Leary, Meredith Monk, Miguel Pinero, Gregory Corso, Diane Di Prima, Peter Orlovsky, Amiri Baraka, Anne Waldman, Miguel Algarin and Chogyan Trungpa Rinpoche. $29.99

Friend of the Family

(1995, 98 min, US, Edward Holzman) *Mary Poppins* meets Pasolini's *Teorema* in this watchable soft-core melodrama. The setting is a rich but dysfunctional L.A. household where Dad (C.T. Miller) is a workaholic lawyer with little time for his sex-starved wife Linda (Annelyn Griffin Drew), his sex-kitten daughter Montana (Lissa Boyle) and his sex-starved son Josh (Will Potter). All are miserable until the arrival of Elke (Shauna O'Brien), a raven-haired beauty (and *Penthouse* centerfold) who, with nonchalant sultriness, seduces mom, personally instructs dad on the pleasures of sex, teaches the nymphette daughter not to be a slut and leads the nerdy son into the arms of a woman his own age – very '90s PC! Cheesy, fleshy fun! ★★½ $89.99

Friendly Persuasion

(1956, 138 min, US, William Wyler) Wyler's absorbing and sensitive adaptation of Jessamyn West's novel is about a Quaker family trying to maintain their religious beliefs during the days of the Civil War. An exceptional cast is headed by Gary Cooper, Dorothy McGuire and Anthony Perkins. ★★★½ $29.99

Friends Forever

(1986, 95 min, Denmark, Stefan Christian Henszelman) A teenage boy's sexual and emotional development is the theme in this pleasant Danish drama by Henszelman. Shy Kristian is a gangly and innocent 16-year-old who becomes friends with two very different boys – Henrik, a slightly effeminate and determinedly non-conformist student, and Patrick, a blond thug. When Patrick tells him that he is gay and introduces him to his older lover, Kristian is thrown into emotional turmoil. Similar to Denmark's other adolescent gay drama *You Are Not Alone*, this simple yet unpredictable story presents a positive outlook on a young man's sexual coming out and its effect on his friends. (Danish with English subtitles) ★★★ $69.99

Fright Night

(1985, 105 min, US, Tom Holland) First-time writer-director Holland takes the Gothic out of vampire lore and plops it right down in the middle of the American suburbs. The results are wonderful. In a toothsome twist on the "Boy Who Cried Wolf" story, Holland's script finds a young teen desperately trying to convince peo-

ple that his new neighbor is not the handsome ladykiller he seems to be – except the part about "ladykiller," of course. He finally enlists the reluctant help of a washed-up TV horror show host (Roddy McDowall). Chris Sarandon is exquisite as the vampire and William Ragsdale lends an over-the-top urgency to the young ghoul-chaser. ★★★ $14.99

Fright Night Pt 2

(1988, 101 min, US, Tommy Lee Wallace) The sister of the vampire killed in the original is out for blood against those who killed him – including TV horror film host Peter Vincent (Roddy McDowall); until she finally sees the light about what's at stake with her degenerate lifestyle. ★★ $14.99

The Frighteners

(1996, 110 min, US, Peter Jackson) Peter Jackson proves once again that he is one of the most original filmmakers working today with his latest amalgam of genres, this time a horror/suspense/private eye/love story/serial killer/comedy! Michael J. Fox stars as Frank Bannister, a con man ghost-hunter whose unique power to see the dearly departed stems from a terrible accident he had several years before, which killed his new wife and left him a shell of a man. Frank stumbles into the middle of a series of murders being committed by a ghastly apparition only he can see. Able to determine who will be next on this soultaker's list, he decides to use his gift to stop the malevolent spirit when a beautiful young widow (Trini Alvarado) shows up with a number on her head. Exhilarating from start to finish, *The Frighteners* features the most computer-generated special effects in any film to date and is a brilliant fusion of comedy and horror, alternately hilarious and downright shocking. Not for all tastes, but highly recommended for fans of Jackson and for those looking for something definitely different. ★★★½ $19.99

The Fringe Dwellers

(1986, 101 min, Australia, Bruce Beresford) This exotic film concerns Australia's Aborigines, whose story is similar to that of the American Indian, and the sad and frustrating fact that their tribal roots are disintegrating as they become displaced in their own land. The story follows Trilby, an Aborigine who seeks to leave her community to live out her dreams of romance and high living in the big city. ★★★ $79.99

The Frisco Kid

(1979, 122 min, US, Robert Aldrich) Aldrich captures the warmth and poignancy that could have so easily been lost in this tale of the Old West set in the 1850s. Bank robber Harrison Ford becomes the reluctant guide for rabbi Gene Wilder on his way to join his congregation in California. A nice mixture of comedy and sentimental dramatics. ★★★ $14.99

Frisk

(1995, 83 min, US, Todd Verow) Verow makes a memorable if controversial feature film debut with this adaptation of Dennis Cooper's 1991 novel of homosexuality, sadism and murder. Dennis (Michel Gunther) is a young gay man who experiences problems with his sexual persona – he harbors an increasingly obses-

sive and sadistic approach to gay sex. His fantasies soon become reality when he meets Henry (Craig Chester), a drugged-out masochist with no self-esteem. What begins as playfully violent sexual antics culminates in a murder. Dennis eventually takes up with a demented couple who share his homicidal bent. Graphic in its gay sex scenes, the film escalates to an almost unwatchable intensity as the violence becomes all too real – or is it simply imagined? Technically proficient and intelligently made, *Frisk*'s ominous content prompts the question of what is being said about gay men. In a jarring New Queer Cinema style, the film's exploration into the dark recesses of gay male desire results in a confusing conclusion: Is it a legitimate take on the complexity of sexuality, or a depiction of gays as sadists and killers? No easy answers here. ★★★ $59.99

Fritz the Cat

(1972, 78 min, US, Ralph Bakshi) R. Crumb's raunchy feline comes to life in this full-length X-rated cartoon crammed with good humor and bad taste. Whips up more obscenity and violence than Disney dared dream of. ★★★

From Beyond

(1986, 85 min, US, Stuart Gordon) Gordon's effective follow-up to his acclaimed *Re-Animator*. Once again borrowing from the works of H.P. Lovecraft, Gordon fills his film with outstanding and quite eerie special effects for his story about a doctor, investigating the death of a scientist, who becomes obsessed with the dead man's experiments with the "beyond." Jeffrey Combs also encores from *Re-Animator*. ★★★ $9.99

From Beyond the Grave

(1973, 97 min, GB, Kevin Connor) Another Amicus horror anthology, this time built around an antique shop run by an eerie proprietor played, once again with dignity and wit, by Peter Cushing. Four customers each try to rip off Cushing in some way, and – as is always the case in these kinds of films – get their just desserts in various macabre and supernatural ways. Donald Pleasence stars in one episode as a beggar and match salesman who helps fulfill an unhappy husband's secret wish, until the husband realizes that his fate is at the mercy of someone else's wishes. Another segment casts David Warner as a depraved collector who forms an unnatural bond with a spirit residing in an antique mirror. The best story, however, involves an old doorway that opens a portal into a sinister world which threatens to suck in and destroy a young married couple. A final coda involves Cushing's revenge on an attempted burglar and murderer. Lots of ghoulish fun and great entertainment on a dark night. ★★½ $14.99

From Dusk Till Dawn

(1996, 107 min, US, Robert Rodriguez) The beleaguered horror genre receives a welcome shot – this time in the neck – from Hollywood's two wunderkind *du jour*, screenwriter Quentin Tarantino and director Rodriguez. Easily the most entertaining horror/action/comedy since *Evil Dead 2*, *From Dusk Till Dawn* harkens back to pre-*Dogs* days for Tarantino, who wrote the script while still a video clerk. He and George Clooney star as Richie and Seth Gecko, two homicidal brothers and criminals-on-the-lam who take a lapsed Baptist minister (Harvey Keitel) and his family hostage on their run to the Mexican border. Once across, the only thing that stands between them and freedom is one night in a rough-and-tumble biker/trucker bar called the Titty Twister. Unbeknowst to them, the bar is home to a horde of shape-shifting vampires (including gorgeous vampiress Salma Hayek). Screenwriter Tarantino effortlessly combines the best elements of two genres — the film begins as an escaped convicts-road movie and turns on a dime into the realm of zombie and vampire flick. Gory and very adult themed, *From Dusk Till Dawn* is entertaining on all levels, and will leave its audience alternately gasping, screaming and laughing. ★★★½ $19.99

From Here to Eternity

(1953, 118 min, US, Fred Zinnemann) A brilliant cast brings to the screen James Jones' novel of pre-WWII life in an outstanding adaptation in which everything clicks — from the multi-layered screenplay to director Zinnemann's focused eye to a gallery of indelible performances. Set in Pearl Harbor just before the Japanese attack, the film follows the lives of a group of soldiers stationed in Hawaii. Burt Lancaster excels as the impassioned sergeant involved with commander's wife Deborah Kerr. In what is the performance of his career, Montgomery Clift plays a trumpet-playing G.I. whose soul-searching is at odds with military sensibility. Frank Sinatra and Donna Reed both won Oscars in support as, respectively, a private and a dance-hall hostess. Lancaster and Kerr appear in one of the most famous lovemaking scenes of all time: sand, saltwater and seaweed never looked so good. ★★★★ $19.99

From Mao to Mozart

(1980, 84 min, US, Murray Lerner) This Academy Award-winning documentary follows Isaac Stern on his 1979 tour of Communist China. Whether on stage performing, or encouraging budding violinists to feel their playing, Stern is always an electrifying presence. ★★★½ $59.99

From Russia with Love

(1964, 118 min, GB, Terence Young) Super spy James Bond (Sean Connery) must retrieve a top secret decoder machine and return it to England. The second, and many say the best, of the Bond adventures has Lotte Lenya as a sinister spy determined to terminate Agent 007. Plenty of suspense and hair-raising encounters. ★★★½ $14.99

From the Earth to the Moon

(1958, 100 min, US, Byron Haskin) Joseph Cotten and George Sanders play rival munitions manufacturers teaming up to reach the moon in this unusually faithful adaptation (except for the stowaway love interest) of the Jules Verne story. Director Haskin (*War of the Worlds*) captures a good sense of place and era that imbues the film with charm, if not scientific accuracy. ★★½ $19.99

From the Hip

(1987, 111 min, US, Bob Clark) From the director of *Porky's* comes this courtroom comedy that turns rather suspenseful at the end. Judd Nelson is the brash upstart lawyer whose courtroom theatrics would embarrass even F. Lee Bailey, as he is faced with defending a repellent murder suspect (John Hurt at his most flamboyant). ★★½

From the Life of Marionettes

(1980, 104 min, West Germany, Ingmar Bergman) This harrowing and provocative film was made in West Germany during Bergman's celebrated self-exile from Sweden for tax-evasion charges. His troubled mental state could be a clue to his harrowing story of a successful but dangerously psychotic businessman who is obsessed with killing his unfaithful wife. This obsession leads him into the sleazy world of sex clubs where he brutally murders a prostitute. An unsettling film, not for everyone, but insightful for Bergman-philes. (German with English subtitles) ★★½ $29.99

The Front

(1976, 94 min, US, Martin Ritt) This dramatization doesn't stray from the real-life situation that too many American artists found themselves in during the Truman and Eisenhower years — a reality that seems to be re-emerging in other forms today (Jesse Helms, take a bow). In this drama with comedic overtones, director Ritt captures an era permeated with fear, necessitating Woody Allen to front for desperate writers blacklisted for having Communist associations. The film is all the more powerful knowing that director Ritt, co-stars Zero Mostel (in a terrific supporting turn), Herschel Bernardi, Joshua Shelley, Lloyd Gough and writer Walter Bernstein were all victims of the Hollywood witchhunt. ★★★½ $9.99

The Front Page

(1931, 103 min, US, Lewis Milestone) This early talkie starts talking and doesn't stop. Adolphe Menjou plays the ruthless newspaper editor who will do anything to beat the rival papers covering the execution of a convicted murderer. Pat O'Brien is his reporter who will abandon his fiancée and his ethics to get that interview by helping the convict escape. This

Burt Lancaster and Deborah Kerr's quintessential embrace in *From Here to Eternity*

first filming of the Hecht/MacArthur comedy — later gender-switched into *His Girl Friday* and again remade by Billy Wilder — is fast and funny and as cynical as a *National Enquirer* headline. ★★★½ $19.99

Frozen Assets

(1992, 96 min, US, George Miller) This thematic mishmash manages somehow to combine plot lines about a bordello-like sperm bank, a stud-of-the-year contest and frustrated unemployed prostitutes into what appears to be a family comedy. Corbin Bernsen is a low-level executive sent to a small town to improve the finances of the community sperm bank as his last chance to make vice president. Shelley Long is the uptight biochemical engineer in charge of the "bank," who gets to make those long-winded, cloying speeches that have come to be her trademark. Of course, they hate each other immediately and are in love by the end of the movie. The only real "asset" is Larry Miller, who gives a hilariously understated performance as a seemingly dim-witted local lunatic who befriends Bernsen and saves the day. ★ $94.99

Fruits of Passion

(1981, 100 min, France/Japan, Shuji Terayama) The story of "O" continues in the Orient in this stunningly photographed sequel to Pauline Réage's novel of sexual domination. Sir Stephen (Klaus Kinski) takes "O" to a Chinese bordello and forces her to submit to moral degradation in order to prove her spiritual love to him. A kinky voyage for the sexually adventurous. (In English) ★★

The Fugitive

(1947, 104 min, US, John Ford) Affecting political allegory set in an anti-clerical, totalitarian Mexican state about a priest (Henry Fonda) on the run from zealous government officials. Director Ford's classic tale, told with foreboding and awash with shadows, is a subdued but nevertheless arresting portrait of a corrupt state versus the indomitable faith of its people. Filmed on location in Mexico. ★★★½ $19.99

The Fugitive

(1993, 127 min, US, Andrew Davis) Though not the first, nor last, film in the recent trend of TV-to-big screen adaptations, *The Fugitive* is certainly the final word. Harrison Ford takes over the part once immortalized by David Janssen in the classic 1960s TV show: Dr. Richard Kimble, a successful surgeon falsely convicted of murdering his wife. En route to prison, Kimble escapes, setting into motion a massive manhunt led by the relentless Det. Gerard (marvelously played by Oscar winner Tommy Lee Jones). As Kimble searches for the infamous one-armed man who actually committed the murder, Gerard combs the countryside in an epic quest. Rather than simply rehash the original series, director Davis and his writers have updated and re-energized a quintessential TV drama with remarkable success. A breathtaking adventure and a fascinating detective story told at breakneck speed, *The Fugitive* also features some of the best chase sequences in recent memory. (Available letterboxed and pan & scan) ★★★★ $19.99

The Fugitive Kind
(1959, 135 min, US, Sidney Lumet) Disappointing though gritty version of Tennessee Williams' play, "Orpheus Descending." Marlon Brando stars as a Mississippi drifter who becomes involved with two women (Anna Magnani and Joanne Woodward) while staying at a small Southern town. ★★ $19.99

Fugitive Samurai
(1984, 92 min, Japan, Minoru Matsushima & Akinori Matsuo) A samurai is betrayed by those close to the Shogun. He is falsely accused of treason and is set to die an unhonorable death. But he escapes and, with his young son in a baby cart, begins a violent quest of righteous revenge as he seeks to destroy those who would disgrace his family name. (Dubbed) ★★ $59.99

Full Contact
(1992, 90 min, Hong Kong, Ringo Lam) Chow Yun-Fat stars in this brutal Hong Kong action film from director Lam, who also directed Chow's *City on Fire* (the finale of which is the inspiration for *Reservoir Dogs*). Chow plays a buzz-cut, tattooed biker and petty thief who teams up with Judge (Simon Yam), a creepy associate of his cousin (Anthony Wong), for a big heist. They pull off the heist, but Judge double-crosses Chow and kills his young friend and partner, leaving Chow for dead in an unfortunate bystander's burning home. Chow slowly recovers, building his strength and wrath for another confrontation with Judge and his traitorous cousin. A radical departure for American audiences used to John Woo's highly stylized, melodramatic and tragic blood operas. Lam's work is more Western and story-driven. His eruptions of violence are also filmed in a less balletic way, particularly in this film, where the final showdown between Chow and Judge involves point-of-view shots of the bullets speeding across the room into furniture and human skulls. Not for everyone, but certainly a dramatic action film of high caliber and one of Chow and Lam's best works, together or separately. ★★★ $14.99

Full Eclipse
(1993, 97 min, US, Anthony Hickox) Horror film auteur Hickox (*Hellraiser III: Hell on Earth, Warlock: The Armageddon*) strengthens his hold on the genre with this made-for-cable shocker about a do-good cop (Mario Van Peebles) whose initiation into a super-elite police squad includes injecting a serum which turns the squad into a pack of werewolves. Atmospheric cinematography, outrageous special effects and kinky animalistic sex make this one not to miss. Also starring Patsy Kensit, Bruce Payne and Anthony Denison. ★★★ $14.99

Full Metal Jacket
(1987, 120 min, US, Stanley Kubrick) Kubrick's brilliantly realized Vietnam War drama, told with such grace and subtlety it practically discredits all similarly themed films which precede it. Kubrick divides his film into two equally devastating parts: a brutal boot camp training sequence and a horrific war piece set amidst the rubble of the 1968 Tet Offensive. Matthew Modine and Adam Baldwin star, supported by two incredible performances by Vincent D'Onofrio (who à la Robert De Niro gained 60 pounds for the part) as a dim-witted recruit, and Lee Ermey as a merciless drill sergeant. ★★★★ $19.99

Full Moon in Blue Water
(1988, 95 min, US, Peter Masterson) Playwright Bill Bozzone wrote this muddled screenplay about a widower (Gene Hackman) haunted by the past and the effect it has on his relationship with his girlfriend (Teri Garr), his father-in-law (Burgess Meredith) and his failing business on the coast of Texas. ★★ $9.99

Full Moon in Paris
(1984, 102 min, France, Eric Rohmer) Sharp dialogue and the beguiling presence of Pascale Ogier help make this Rohmer philosophical romance a gem. A headstrong self-absorbed woman, bored of her live-in lover, finds a second flat and begins another affair. (French with English subtitles) ★★★½ $24.99

The Fuller Brush Girl
(1950, 85 min, US, Lloyd Bacon) Lucille Ball and Eddie Albert star in this hilarious follow-up the *The Fuller Brush Man*. Ball and Albert play a pair of young lovers trying to scrape together enough money to buy their dream house — for $500 dollars down! Albert gets a promotion at the steamship company where they both work, but after Ball blows up the switchboard, she's fired. Desperate for money, she jumps into door-to-door cosmetics sales with disastrous results. The plot is slight and some of the hijinx are a little too over-the-top, but Ball's talent for outrageous slapstick carries the day, making this an all-around good time. Red Skelton has a cameo, reprising his role as the Fuller Brush Man. ★★★ $19.99

The Fuller Brush Man
(1948, 93 min, US, S. Sylvan Simon) Red Skelton gets a lot of mileage from this wacky, slapstick comedy with the gifted comedian uncovering a murder while going door-to-door. ★★★ $14.99

Fun Down There
(1989, 89 min, US, Roger Stigliano) Notwithstanding Vincent Canby's effusively upbeat review, this independently produced drama is notable only for its gay coming-of-age theme and should be of interest solely to an audience that accepts the film's earnest intentions and ignores its less-than-professional acting, plot and production values. A gangling young man, feeling frustrated and alone in his upstate New York town, moves to New York City determined to explore his gay tendencies, bottled inside for so long. Although not really attractive and possessing the personality of a piece of driftwood, the neophyte lover finds sexual success and excess in the Village. ★★ $39.99

Fun with Dick and Jane
(1977, 95 min, US, Ted Kotcheff) Jane Fonda and George Segal bring a lot of life to the 1970s social comedy as a married couple who turn to robbery to maintain their way of life after hubby Segal gets fired. ★★★ $9.99

The Funeral
(1984, 124 min, Japan, Juzo Itami) Made before his wonderfully quirky and popular hit *Tampopo*, this story is about the complex, confusing and often bizarre happenings during the preparation of a traditional Buddhist funeral by an affluent bourgeois couple (Tsutomu Yamazaki and Nobuko Miyamoto, the stars of both *Tampopo* and *A Taxing Woman*). This black comedy details both the sorrow as well as the callousness of the old man's family as they stumble about trying to mourn him, bury him, and then get back to their own lives. *The Funeral* is at once comic, sad and moving. (Japanese with English subtitles) ★★★½

The Funeral
(1996, 99 min, US, Abel Ferrara) Director Ferrara and screenwriter Nicholas St. John continue their exploration of morality and personal responsibility, but with a much greater degree of success than their previous collaboration, the awful *The Addiction*. This time around, the gangster genre is the target, and the pair fashion a tale of organized crime in the 1930s, where the families of two surviving brothers (Christopher Walken and Chris Penn) come together at the untimely funeral of a third. Unfortunately, St. John and Ferrara have a lot more to tell their audience than a basic tale of family loyalty and revenge. While *The Funeral* is interesting and its ensemble achieves an almost Coppola-level of success in the period gangster film genre, the film is overburdened with moralizing philosophy, much of it steeped in Catholicism, which turns characters into mere mouthpieces for divergent ideologies. And the heavy-handed ending undermines the successful drama and tragedy the fine cast worked so hard to establish. Ferrara is a good filmmaker, but he needs to concentrate more on the story and less on his philosophical agenda. ★★½ $89.99

Funeral in Berlin
(1966, 102 min, GB, Guy Hamilton) Michael Caine is the British operative who must arrange the defection of a top-level Russian military officer in Berlin. The second of the "Harry Palmer" spy thrillers, filmed on loca-

F

Funny Bones

tion in Berlin, has a few exciting scenes but isn't as effective as *The Ipcress File*. Based on the novel by Len Deighton. ★★½ $14.99

The Funhouse

(1981, 96 min, US, Tobe Hooper) A group of teenagers decide to spend a night in a carnival funhouse and are stalked by a ghoulish creature. Not very spooky, the film relies on the occasional shock for its chills. ★★ $14.99

Funny Bones

(1995, 128 min, GB, Peter Chelsom) Tommy Fawkes (Oliver Platt) is a failing comic who lives in the shadow of his near-legendary father George (Jerry Lewis). When Tommy's act bombs in Las Vegas, he immediately disappears, only to turn up in a small coastal town in England where he grew up. But what does this have to do with the opening sequence of a half-witted comedian (Lee Evans) who's left adrift at sea? Well, to tell any more would be to give away some of the zaniest jokes, sight gags and plot developments since Mel Brooks was in his prime. An alternately hilarious and dark comedy which seems to revel in both typical British drollness and over-the-edge Pythonish pranks, *Funny Bones* is a boldly original if lunatic peek into the artistic process which at the same time tries to answer that age-old question: What is funny? As the talented nut case, Evans gives an uproarious performance combining superlative physical schtick with a sympathetic portrait of a fragile mind. Leslie Caron and Oliver Reed (in a strange cameo) also star, and Lewis is quite effective. ★★★★ $19.99

Funny Dirty Little War

(1983, 80 min, Argentina, Hector Olivera) This anarchic and ruthless black comedy dissects the political absurdities and petty bureaucracy of a small Argentine village during the post-Peron years in the late 1950s. A full-scale civil war erupts in an otherwise peaceful, though disordered town when a local administrator becomes involved in a fanatical conflict with his governmental associates. As each political faction doggedly pursues victory, the corruption and dehumanization of war takes its toll when all involved increasingly become efficient in the practices of torture

and murder. A blistering anti-war satire which is both witty and tragic. (Spanish with English subtitles) ★★★½ $29.99

Funny Face

(1957, 103 min, US, Stanley Donen) All Paris becomes fixated when photographer Fred Astaire pulls out all the stops to capture the heart of his new model, the radiant Audrey Hepburn. This charming musical, from the director of *Singin' in the Rain*, features a fine score by George Gershwin, including "How Long Has This Been Going On?" and "S'Wonderful." ★★★½ $14.99

Funny Farm

(1988, 101 min, US, George Roy Hill) More dumb hijinks with Chevy Chase, here as a city-bred writer whose move to the country isn't exactly what he thought it would be. Some of the jokes are very funny, but many fall flat. ★★ $14.99

Funny Girl

(1968, 155 min, US, William Wyler) Barbra Streisand's Oscar-winning film debut, repeating her acclaimed stage role, as the legendary performer Fanny Brice. Though the film is somewhat melodramatic for a musical biography, Streisand's singing and clowning make it all worthwhile. Good period design, and Barbra sings "My Man," "People" and "Don't Rain on My Parade." Also with Omar Sharif, Kaye Medford, Walter Pidgeon (as Ziegfeld) and Anne Francis. ★★★ $19.99

Funny Lady

(1975, 137 min, US, Herbert Ross) This okay sequel to Barbra Streisand's smash musical *Funny Girl* finds Barbra in excellent voice reprising her role as legendary performer Fanny Brice. With Nicky in prison, Fanny takes up with Billy Rose, who would become her second husband. James Caan plays Billy, Omar Sharif has a small role encoring as Nicky, and Ben Vereen is a standout performing "Goodtime Charley." ★★½ $14.99

Funny People

(1978, 88 min, South Africa, Jamie Uys) "Candid Camera" — South African style! Uys,

director of the two *The Gods Must Be Crazy* films, keeps the laughs rolling in this funny, though a little long, series of Allen Funt-inspired vignettes of pulling stunts on unsuspecting people with a hidden camera recording their reactions. All of the standard gags are here, but what makes this comedy different is the South African setting which, far from the expected racially repressive environment, one sees a land more akin to a suburban Australian mall, where both blacks and whites, quite friendly and familiar to each other, are involved in the stunts, suggesting (like his other movies) a land of racial equality. Propaganda or not, the film, for those not over-exposed to this type of humor, is infectious and a little mean-spirited fun. ★★★

A Funny Thing Happened on the Way to the Forum

(1966, 99 min, US, Richard Lester) A rip-roaring, bawdy and hilarious adaptation of the hit Broadway musical. Zero Mostel (with the exception of "Fiddler on the Roof") had his best role on-stage, and here on-screen, as a conniving Roman slave who sets out to obtain his freedom. Sexual innuendo, slapstick and feverish chases are the order of the day as Mostel uses every trick in the book in his glorious quest. Jack Gilford also repeats his stage role as a fellow slave, and Michael Crawford is their young, love-struck master. Also with the zany Phil Silvers and Buster Keaton. Score by Stephen Sondheim. ★★★½ $19.99

Fury

(1936, 94 min, US, Fritz Lang) Lang's masterful exposé of mob violence with Spencer Tracy in a powerful portrayal of an innocent man unjustly accused of murder. Sylvia Sidney is splendid as Tracy's fiancée. ★★★½ $19.99

The Fury

(1978, 118 min, US, Brian De Palma) Set in the paranoid post-Watergate `70s, *The Fury* tells the story of two young psychics, Andrew Stevens and Amy Irving, who are being manipulated by a covert government agency attempting to harness their awesome powers. Stevens' father, Kirk Douglas, comes to their aid, battling the evil John Cassavetes. Director De Palma's film, as with most of his work, is highly stylized and often very violent. Rick Baker's makeup wizardry is outstanding. ★★★ $9.99

Fury Is a Woman

(1962, 95 min, Yugoslavia, Andrzej Wajda) Also known as *Siberian Lady Macbeth*, this lusty, bombastic melodrama is great pre-"Dynasty" fun. Set in turn-of-the-century Russia, the story focuses on Katarina, a beautiful but bored wife of an often out-of-town merchant whose life takes a decidedly tumultuous and erotic turn after she meets a boisterous wanderer. In a very short time, she dispatches her tyrannical father-in-law (with rat poison), takes her compliant peasant as a live-in lover and plots to kill her soon-to-return husband — it's all in a week's fun in this passion-fueled tale of murder, sex, madness and violence. (Serbo-Croatian with English subtitles) ★★★ $59.99

Gabriel over the White House

(1933, 78 min, US, Gregory La Cava) Imagine that George Bush, shortly after being elected, was in a high-speed car accident and wound up in a deep coma. And, that when he came out of it, he began a program to wipe out poverty, erase organized crime and eliminate war. If you can picture this, you'll have some idea of what this unabashed Depression-era propaganda piece is all about. Walter Huston stars as the president, elected by fraud and entrenched in a corrupt party system until his conversion at the hands of God. Thereafter he sets out to dissolve Congress and institute a kind of bleeding-heart liberalist dictatorship where all of the evils of the world can be eradicated. For those of us who respect the balance of power created by a trilateral government, it's a pretty frightening picture. Still, the film offers some fascinating glimpses at the social agenda in the early days of Roosevelt as well as makes some ominous predictions about the horrors of future world wars. ★★½ $19.99

Gabriela

(1983, 102 min, Brazil, Bruno Barreto) Brazilian beauty Sonia Braga swaggers through this dreamy sex comedy as the hard-to-hold wife of a Turkish bar owner (Marcello Mastroianni) who sets an entire two-bit town on its ear. Barreto smoothly directs Jorge Amado's tale of primitive passion and derailed amour. (Portuguese with English subtitles) ★★★ $79.99

Gal Young 'Un

(1979, 105 min, US, Victor Nunez) Based on a story by Marjorie Kinnan Rawlings ("The Yearling," "Cross Creek"), and set in Florida during Prohibition, this passionate film follows a lonely widow (Dana Preu) who erupts into violence when she realizes that she has been victimized by a fast-talking con man (David Peck). ★★★

Gall Force — Eternal Story

(1986, 86 min, Japan, Katsuhito Akiyama) Somewhere in space, an ancient war rages between the all-female Solonoid race and the bio-mechanical Paranoid civilization. Evocative of an all-female *Magnificent Seven*, and with overtones of *Star Wars* and *Alien*, this well-crafted animated action-adventure will please fans of the genre. (Dubbed) ★★★ $39.99

Gall Force 2 — Destruction

(1987/1993, 50 min, Japan, Katsuhito Akiyama) The battle rages on between the monstrous Paranoids and the female Solonoids in this action-packed sequel to *Gall Force - Eternal Story*. This time, ace pilot Lufy, survivor of the ill-fated Starleaf, rejoins the Solonoid army just as it learns that the two waring planets have been destroyed. With neither planet safe, our hero soon discovers that the next world targeted for destruction has been selected for a wild experiment that could end the fighting forever. ★★ $39.99

Gallipoli

(1981, 110 min, Australia, Peter Weir) A visually striking and emotionally jarring war drama focusing on the camaraderie of two young Australians who naively enlist in the army only to meet the savage realities of World War I. Mel Gibson and Mark Lee star as a pair of budding athletes who encounter the butchery of trench warfare up close on a stretch of godforsaken Turkish coastline known as Gallipoli. Weir holds no punches in delivering a stinging indictment of military leadership and war in general. ★★★★ $14.99

The Gambling Samurai

(1960, 93 min, Japan, Senkichi Taniguchi) Toshiro Mifune stars as Chuji, a gambling swordsman who breaks into a government warehouse, steals the rice, and then distributes the precious food to the starving farmers who inhabit his village. By this brave act, he becomes known as Japan's Robin Hood, and he sets out across the countryside avenging the cruel rape and murder of his sister by a vindictive local magistrate. (Japanese with English subtitles) ★★½

The Game Is Over

(1966, 96 min, France, Roger Vadim) Jane Fonda's first dramatic role features her as a neglected wife who falls passionately in love with her stepson (Peter McEnery). Her husband, Michel Piccoli, learns of the affair and viciously plots revenge. Swinging '60s Paris comes alive in this electrifying story of decadence directed by Fonda's then-husband. (Filmed in English) ★★★

Game of Seduction

(1985, 95 min, France, Roger Vadim) A steamy frolic amid the boudoirs and satin bedsheets of the always decadent French bourgeoisie. Sylvia Kristel stars as a sultry and beautiful woman who is happily married. Her fidelity to her husband is severely tested when a cold-blooded killer and equally cunning noblewoman place a bet that he can seduce her. Also starring Nathalie Delon and Jon Finch. (Filmed in English) ★★½

Gandhi

(1982, 200 min, GB, Richard Attenborough) Ben Kingsley brilliantly portrays Mahatma Gandhi, the spiritual and political leader of India who, driven by his dream of an independent India and guided by principles of non-violence, struggled a lifetime to rid his country of British imperialism. A fascinating and moving portrait of a man whose commitment to non-violence has served as a shining example to people all over the world. Winner of 8 Academy Awards. ★★★★ $29.99

Gang in Blue

(1996, 99 min, US, Melvin Van Peebles & Mario Van Peebles) The Van Peebles — father Melvin and son Mario — team up as codirectors and costars for this made-for-cable drama. A racist band of big-city cops has been harassing — and murdering — minorities for years. One black cop (Mario) has had enough. He tries to enlist the aid of his ex-lover (Cynda Williams, who was so strong in *One False Move* but who hardly registers here), now an FBI agent, but she's disinterested. Then he's assigned a new partner — a redneck ex-Marine. This fact-based cop drama is by the numbers at times, rather heavy-handed at others, but it has some kick to it and is certainly never dull. It falls in the trap, however, of presenting racists as one-dimensional characters; a little more development would have given the film more of an edge. ★★½ $99.99

Gang of Souls

(1988, 60 min, US, Maria Beatty) This tribute to the Beat Generation is comprised of various interviews with members of the first generation of the '50s movement (William Burroughs, Allen Ginsberg, Gregory Corso) as well as its leading adherents a generation later (Marianne Faithfull, Lydia Lunch, Richard Hell). With quotes like "'Howl' overcame censorship trials to become one of the most widely read works of this century," the documentary is prone to hyperbole and self-boasting, but nonetheless presents a vivid hour exploring the recollections and observations of today's performers and poets who together give us a teasing glimpse into creativity in the key of Beat. ★★½ $49.99

Gallipoli

The Gangster

(1947, 84 min, US, Gordon Wiles) A cynical gangster (Barry Sullivan) is confronted with a vicious out-of-towner who tries to muscle in on his territory. A tough, intriguing character study with Sullivan giving a commanding portrayal of a nefarious hood. With John Ireland, Henry Morgan and Leif Erickson. ★★★ $14.99

Garbo Talks

(1984, 104 min, US, Sidney Lumet) Anne Bancroft's spirited performance dominates this bittersweet comedy about a son (Ron Silver) who goes through heaven and hell to make his dying mother's last wish come true: to meet Greta Garbo. An episodic tale which features charming touches, though the film does move at a slow pace. ★★½ $19.99

The Garden

(1990, 88 min, GB, Derek Jarman) As director Jarman fitfully sleeps in his garden, his cryptic dreams — culled from his subconscious and his fevered imagination — are played out in their fullest, queerest glory. The lyrical images of male love, tenderness and art are interspersed with visions of natural beauty but collide against a background of homophobia, persecution and death. An allegory for AIDS, and his friends who have died from it, the film's main narrative thrust depicts two young male lovers as they, in the manner of Jesus Christ, are taunted, arrested, tortured and then crucified for their beliefs. A stunningly filmed work of art, full of poetic images and fueled by an intense longing for understanding, peace and brotherhood. Supported by a haunting score by Simon Fisher Turner, the film also features Tilda Swinton. ★★★ $19.99

The Garden of Earthly Delights

(1970, 95 min, Spain, Carlos Saura) Saura drastically changes pace and theme with this bizarre black comedy on Spanish society. This cynical tale is about a rich and ruthless old man who loses his memory and suffers from paralysis after an auto accident. His monstrously greedy relatives, desperate to find out the location of his fortune, stage disturbing scenes from his boyhood in their efforts to shock him into remembering. All the while, the old man silently plots his revenge. (Spanish with English subtitles) ★★★ $29.99

The Garden of the Finzi-Continis

(1970, 95 min, Italy, Vittorio De Sica) Set in fascist Italy, De Sica's Oscar-winning Best Foreign Film depicts an aristocratic Jewish family's confrontation with sweeping anti-Semitism. Based on the semiautobiography by Giorgio Bassani, this exquisitely photographed film explores the horrors of pre-war and war-torn Italy, and the complacency taken by the Finzi-Continis family who lock themselves in the comfort of their mansion's garden away from the realities outside their walls. Starring Dominique Sanda and Helmut Berger. Remastered. (Italian with English subtitles) ★★★½ $89.99

Gardens of Stone

(1987, 112 min, US, Francis Coppola) Coppola's passionate though heavy-handed Vietnam War film is a showcase for some four-star acting. James Caan and James Earl Jones deliver powerful performances as cynical Arlington Honor Guard officers who refer to themselves as "toy soldiers" — powerless to do anything about the onslaught of body bags except give them elegant funerals. D.B. Sweeney is the young officer itching to go to Vietnam: a gung-ho youngster who may not be ready for the experience. Anjelica Huston also stars in an ill-conceived role as Caan's romantic interest. ★★½ $19.99

Garlic Is as Good as Ten Mothers

(1980, 51 min, US, Les Blank) Did you know that Eleanor Roosevelt used to eat three cloves of chocolate-covered garlic every day? This and other tidbits are exposed by Blank as he explores the historical, culinary and horticultural aspects of garlic in this documentary that will linger with you a long time. ★★★ $59.99

Gas Food Lodging

(1992, 102 min, US, Allison Anders) In her debut film, director Anders tears a page out of Wim Wenders' *Paris, Texas* (on which she was an assistant director) with this heartfelt and emotionally penetrating tale of familial discord and redemption set against the backdrop of the American Southwest desert. Young Shade (winsomely portrayed by Fairuza Balk) lives with her single mother (Brooke Adams) and her teenage sister (Ione Skye). She spends her afternoons alternately haunting the town's deserted cinema (watching her favorite Mexican screen heroine in a series of cheesy romances), hanging out with her androgynous friend, Darius, and dreaming of her long-lost father. Both her sister and mother are similarly consumed with finding a man to fulfill their lives — a fact which has drawn the fire of some feminists, but which could indicate an innate contention that their romantic compulsions are actually a yearning for the absent father. Sprinkled throughout with a wry sense of humor, the film sports some enjoyably whimsical moments, especially when Shade bridges the town's racial barrier and befriends a young Mexican boy and his deaf mother. A truly enjoyable, exquisitely rendered drama. ★★★½ $19.99

Gaslight

(1944, 114 min, US, George Cukor) Charles Boyer is an effectively sinister counterpoint to Ingrid Bergman's fragile, luminous innocence in Cukor's classic treatment of manipulation and betrayed love. Boyer has a hidden purpose when he woos and weds orphan Bergman; to protect his secret, he begins a systematic attempt to drive her insane. Strong support from Joseph Cotten and a very tarty Angela Lansbury (in her film debut). ★★★½ $19.99

The Gate

(1987, 92 min, US, Tibor Takacs) *The Gate*, which delivers a few effective frights, follows a pair of young teens who accidentally unleash a horde of demons upon their neighborhood by playing the Satanic messages of a heavy metal record. The embarrassing plot is really just an excuse to showcase the film's spectacular low-budget effects, which include a very scary walking corpse and a towering King Demon which succumbs to an expertly wielded model rocket. Told from the point of view of the two

Derek Jarman's *The Garden*

friends, it uniquely abandons the familiar horror devices of finding solace or protection in one's parents, such isolation making it all the more frightening. Entertaining and quite scary at times, particularly for younger audiences for whom it is aimed. ★★

Gate of Hell

(1953, 89 min, Japan, Teinosuke Kinugasa) A handsomely photographed historical drama set during the 12th-century Japanese rebellion about a samurai warrior who invades a small town, falls in love with and is rejected by a married woman. Academy Award for Best Foreign Film. (Japanese with English subtitles) ★★★½ $29.99

Gates of Heaven

(1978, 82 min, US, Errol Morris) An appealingly funny documentary about pet owners and the trauma they face when their pet cemetary is sold and their animals' remains are transfered to another plot. A truly original meditation on the American soul. ★★★½ $19.99

A Gathering of Men

(1989, 90 min,) An interview between journalist Bill Moyers and poet Robert Bly. Combined with footage of a Men's Workshop led by Bly and storyteller Michael Meade, the program exposes the stifling influence which modern industrial life has had on the male spirit. Originally aired on PBS, this landmark video, along with Bly's best-selling book "Iron John," helped catapult the small but growing "Men's Movement" to national prominence. ★★★ $29.99

A Gathering of Old Men

(1987, 91 min, US, Volker Schlöndorff) Written by the Pulitzer Prize-winning Philadelphian Charles Fuller (*A Soldier's Story*), this is a powerful drama of racial tensions in the New South. Set amidst the sugar cane fields of a searingly hot Louisiana, the film stars Holly Hunter as a liberal plantation owner who galvanizes a group of long down-trodden black farmers and fishermen to militantly defend a fellow black man who claims that he killed a white man in self-defense. Impressive acting from the ensemble of elderly African-American men and a deft touch from German director Schlöndorff highlight this absorbing story of unity and courage. Louis Gossett, Jr. and Richard Widmark co-star as, respectively, a farmer and a complacently abusive Southern marshal. (aka: *Murder on the Bayou*) ★★★½ $14.99

The Gauntlet

(1977, 109 min, US, Clint Eastwood) Clint Eastwood is cop Ben Shockley who thinks he is escorting an ordinary witness (Sondra Locke) back to Phoenix for a trial. But he soon finds there are plenty who want to stop her from testifying against an organized crime family. A flavorful, exciting action tale nicely handled by director and star Eastwood. ★★★ $19.99

The Gay Deceivers

(1969, 99 min, US, Bruce Kessler) What has time done to this low-budget '60s comedy about two "perfectly normal" guys who try to evade the draft by posing as homosexual lovers? Is it offensively homophobic drivel or simply a frequently hilarious, naively camp curiosity? Filmed in a contemporary sitcom style, the film's funniest scenes come when our hapless heroes, under investigation by a suspicious Army recruiter, must move in to a gay bungalow complex, populated by the most outrageous gay stereotypes this side of Fairyland. Michael Greer adds both a campy humor and surprising gay dignity as he steals the show as Malcolm, the boys' gay landlord. If you mind swishy, lisping, prancing, mincing "fags" and the jokes that come with them, avoid this at all costs. For others, this anachronistic sex comedy will provide some laughs and an appreciation of how much things have changed in 25 years. ★★ $14.99

The Gay Divorcee

(1934, 107 min, US, Mark Sandrich) In their second film together (their first as legitimate leads), Fred Astaire and Ginger Rogers demonstrate such chemistry in both dancing and non-musical scenes that it only makes sense that they'd be paired another eight times. Fred plays a noted dancer who meets and pursues Ginger all over London. But she's unhappily married and hires Fred's best friend, lawyer Edward Everett Horton, to set up an infidelity scam to initiate a divorce. That's all the plot that's needed to provide several exquisite dance numbers and very lively comedy. Among the routines, Fred and Ginger perform "The Continental" and "Night and Day."

Vittorio De Sica in *General Della Rovere*

It's amazing what they can do with a couch, chair or table. The hilariously effete Horton and scatterbrained Alice Brady offer wonderful support, with Horton actually getting to perform a song ("Let's Knock Knees") and Brady given such amusing lines as "Divorces make me so sentimental." ★★★½ $19.99

Gay Purr-ee

(1962, 85 min, US, Abe Levitow) Judy Garland is in exceptionally good voice as Musette, the fairest feline in all of France. This animated tale follows her flight from country abode to the big city in search of fame and fortune. Her jilted suitor (Robert Goulet) and small friend (Red Buttons) prowl after her in hot pursuit and arrive just in time to save her from the clutches of the villain Meowrice (Paul Frees). ★★½ $14.99

The Gene Krupa Story

(1959, 101 min, US, Don Weis) Sal Mineo gives a good performance as the famous jazz drumman in this uneven musical biography examining Krupa's professional career and his personal life, including an almost career-ending drug addiction. Along with Susan Kohner, teen heartthrob James Darren, "Batgirl" Yvonne Craig and musicians Red Nichols and Buddy Lester. ★★ $19.99

The General

(1927, 74 min, US, Buster Keaton) Keaton plays a Confederate engineer with two great loves: a sweet Southern belle, and his train. When both are kidnapped by Yankee spies, Buster sets out on an uproarious quest to rescue them. Keaton uses his impeccable timing and acrobatic expertise to create many of silent comedy's definitive routines. The stunts here, often involving cannons and moving trains, demonstrate what a fearless performer Keaton was. ★★★★ $29.99

General Della Rovere

(1959, 129 min, Italy, Roberto Rossellini) Brilliantly acted by Vittorio De Sica, this tragic story revolves around an opportunistic con man who is persuaded by the Germans to impersonate a dead Resistance leader. Their plan backfires, however, when the man begins to assume the characteristics of the general. De Sica's transformation from scoundrel to hero and martyr is riveting. (Italian with English subtitles) ★★★★ $29.99

The General Died at Dawn

(1936, 97 min, US, Lewis Milestone) Top-notch romantic adventure with Gary Cooper as a mercenary in the Far East who becomes involved with spy Madeleine Carroll and fights treacherous warlord Akim Tamiroff. Script by Clifford Odets. ★★★½ $14.99

A Generation

(1954, 85 min, Poland, Andrzej Wajda) The first of Wajda's "War Trilogy" (which includes *Ashes and Diamonds* and *Kanal*), this is a compelling, exceptionally told story of the underground youth movement afoot in Nazi-occupied Poland. A young man and hires by a pretty face, helps the Resistance by aiding escapees from the Warsaw Ghetto. The naiveté of the youthful freedom fighters is shown in their understanding of war as a game. Their view is

soon changed with the realities of death as their innocent lives are corrupted and forever scarred. Wajda creates a mood of urgent and threatening angst. A young Roman Polanski is featured as one of the many youthful members of the Resistance. ★★★★ $24.99

The Genesis Children

(1972, 84 min, US/Italy, Anthony Aikmen) Tough call on this one: Is *The Genesis Children* a celebration of the beauty and innocence of youth and a bold expression of naturism or is this crudely made independent feature merely a thinly veiled excuse to leer at the naked bodies of the many boys shown in the film? With poor production values, chintzy tourist footage and terrible acting from the leads, this semi-home movie follows the frolicking antics of a group of mostly naked boys aged 10 to 15. What keeps the movie from being soft-core kiddie porn is the absence of any overt or implied sexuality. ★½ $69.99

A Gentle Woman
(Une Femme Douce)

(1969, 89 min, France, Robert Bresson) Bresson's first color film opens as an achingly beautiful 17-year-old Dominique Sanda leaps from her window to her death in the Paris streets below. Her husband recounts their brief courtship and marriage in a curious monotone with no emotional affect. This self-deluded, self-important man sees her (she's never given a name) only as a "sweet girl," not as an evolving personality; as an object to be alternately vilified and adored. She is a young and impoverished orphan, leaving relatives whom she describes as sinister. He is a methodical man without spontaneity or joy, who becomes obsessive when she fails to be totally compliant. The subtle though involving film maintains a sterile atmosphere, employing no score; the only music is fragmented, ultized as ambient sound as she changes her records from pop to classical when she enters the room. The viewer is witness to two lives which intersect with no real connection, and the man is left with his version of the truth. (French with English subtitles) ★★★ $29.99

Gentleman Jim

(1942, 104 min, US, Raoul Walsh) Errol Flynn is in good form as turn-of-the-century boxer Jim Corbett. Interesting look at the early days of boxing. Also with Alexis Smith, Jack Carson, Alan Hale and William Frawley. ★★★ $19.99

Gentleman's Agreement

(1947, 118 min, US, Elia Kazan) Gregory Peck stars as Skyler Green, a journalist who goes undercover as a Jew in order to collect information on anti-Semitism in this multi-Academy Award-winning film (including Best Picture). The premise has a tendency towards preachiness but sadly many of the issues concerning prejudice brought up in this 1947 film are still raging through today's headlines. From the cynical vantage point of the 1990s, Skyler can appear overly earnest as he discovers anti-Semitism at almost every turn. Easing some of the heavier moments in the film, however, is Celeste Holm, who won a Best Supporting Actress Oscar for her delightful portrayal of Ann, a wisecracking, life-of-the-party fashion editor who befriends Skyler. Also starring John Garfield and a very young Dean Stockwell as Peck's confused son. A powerful, earnest treatise on prejudice. ★★★½ $19.99

Gentlemen Prefer Blondes

(1953, 91 min, US, Howard Hawks) Marilyn Monroe is the gold-digging Lorelei Lee, who's just a little girl from Little Rock. She and best pal Jane Russell head to Paris in search of well-heeled husbands. Though Hawks' direction is sometimes static, and he may not fully understand the intricacies of the Hollywood musical, he nevertheless has created a bright and brassy musical comedy. Featuring unbeatable humor and the classic "Diamonds Are a Girl's Best Friend" production number, *Gentlemen*'s wonderful story line and snappy dialogue shine through. Marilyn gives one of her most endearing performances. And Russell, who has the funniest line about a hat, is at her best. ★★★ $14.99

Genuine Risk

(1989, 86 min, US, Kurt Voss) A by-the-books erotic thriller involving a fatal love triangle. The lusty girlfriend (Michelle Johnson) of an underworld kingpin (Terence Stamp) seduces his brooding bodyguard, igniting jealousy, rage and murder. Peter Berg also stars. ★★½ $89.99

George Stevens: A Filmmaker's Journey

(1984, 100 min, US, George Stevens, Jr.) A thoroughly engaging and heartfelt documentary written and directed by Stevens, Jr. about the life and career of his father, the noted film director. The program includes scenes from such Stevens classics as *Gunga Din, Woman of the Year, A Place in the Sun* and *Giant*. Stevens' approach to filmmaking is explored, and the film also includes rare color footage taken by the director during WWII. ★★★ $14.99

George Washington Slept Here

(1942, 91 min, US, William Keighley) Before Cary Grant as Mr. Blandings built his dream house, or Oliver and Lisa said "goodbye city life" in "Green Acres," Jack Benny and Ann Sheridan tore apart the countryside in this amusing comedic romp. Antique-buff Sheridan surprises city-loving husband Benny by buying a colonial home in the country. It's dilapidated, but it's okay: for George Washington once slept there. They soon find, however, that the place hasn't been touched since then as they prepare to refurbish it. Benny delivers his one-liners with zeal; and if there is a clinker among them, don't worry — there's a better one just a few lines away. Based on the Kaufman and Hart play. ★★★ $19.99

Georgia

(1987, 90 min, Australia, Ben Lewin) Judy Davis is an intelligent, witty, eccentric and captivating actress. And she brings all of these attributes to this slightly mystifying story of Nina Baily, an Australian tax lawyer who discovers that her biological mother was not the woman who raised her, but instead was Georgia, an erratic high society photographer who died amid tabloid rumors: "Accident or murder?" Though at times the facts are a bit hard to keep straight through the characters' thick Australian accents, the compelling story

Jane Russell (l.) and Marilyn Monroe in *Gentlemen Prefer Blondes*

and rich characterizations make *Georgia* an extremely satisfying mystery. ★★★ $19.99

Georgia

(1995, 117 min, US, Ulu Grosbard) Sibling rivalry achieves new heights in this courageous but ultimately disappointing musical drama which examines the fragile relationship between two sisters. Giving a no-holds-barred performance which is as gutsy as it is excessive, Jennifer Jason Leigh plays Sadie, an untalented rock singer struggling to make a name for herself in the grunge clubs of Seattle. Her sister, Georgia (Mare Winningham), however, has made a name for herself, a success which Sadie both resents and desperately strives for. *Georgia* is at its best when exploring their unstable relationship — Georgia is somewhat intolerant but protective, Sadie constantly seeking independence and approval. But the film also seems to revel in Sadie's professional and personal inadequacies, often exposing raw emotions in a dramatically involving series of events but without benefit of much subtlety; and her failed concerts become as painful for the viewer as they must be for Sadie's audience. However, Sadie's final indignity is that a film about her is named after Georgia. ★★½ $19.99

Georgy Girl

(1966, 100 min, GB, Silvio Narizzano) Lynn Redgrave delivers a delightful performance in this uncommon British comedy about a frumpy young woman who's satisfied to live life vicariously through her swinging London roommate (Charlotte Rampling). A delightful adult comedy-drama of modern-day morals. James Mason stars as a wealthy man who desires the ugly-duckling Georgy as his mistress. ★★★½ $19.99

Germany Year Zero

(1947, 75 min, Italy/West Germany, Roberto Rossellini) This grim vision of destruction and chaos forms one of Rossellini's war trilogy which includes *Open City* and *Paisan*. The setting for this neorealist classic is the ruined city of Berlin after the war where survivors struggle to live peacefully in an environment where their self-respect, even their humanity, is destroyed. The dispassionate camera follows 12-year-old Edmund (Edmund Moeschke), a boy whose family lives in a cramped war-damaged flat with four other families. As Edmond scavenges the city for coal, money and food, he meets Mr. Enning, a creepy middle-aged man and former Nazi schoolteacher. The old man soon involves the boy in the black market and ultimately eggs the youth to a heinous crime, an act which destroys the boy's innocence and proves the pervading power of lingering Fascism. (German with English subtitles) ★★★½

Germinal

(1993, 160 min, France/Italy/Belgium, Claude Berri) Based on Emile Zola's gripping novel about coal miners in the 19th century, *Germinal* provides director Berri with yet another exquisite literary adaptation. Miou-Miou and Gérard Depardieu are wonderfully type-cast as the working-class hero and his wife who struggle through the tense conditions that lead to a workers revolt. With sweeping camerawork and a pervading sense of doom, the film expertly captures the feeling of claustrophobia as to recall the power and anxiety of *Das Boot*. Berri is a true master of detail and period work, and nowhere is it more evident than this epic saga. (French with English subtitles) ★★★½ $19.99

Geronimo: An American Legend

(1993, 115 min, US, Walter Hill) Jason Patric's talents have, thus far, been under-utilized by Hollywood: he possesses an intensity and intelligence that marks each of his performances. He stars with Wes Studi in this haunting examination of Geronimo, the Apache who was the last Native American leader to elude the government's attempt to confine the Indian nations to reservations. Shot amid the dusty Utah vistas, Patric — complete with gentle Southern drawl — plays the cavalry officer who is sent to bring in Geronimo (Studi) upon his surrender. Though short on the taut dramatics typical of effective westerns, *Geronimo* is filled with forceful performances by Patric, Studi, Robert Duvall and Gene Hackman. The last scenes in the film paint a vivid portrait of some of the most shameful injustices in the history of the West. ★★★ $14.99

Gervaise

(1956, 110 min, France, René Clément) Based on the Emile Zola novel "L'Assommoir," this superbly acted drama of a laundrywoman's bleak life in 19th-century Paris achieves moments of brilliant realism and spellbinding dramatics but is overshadowed by the depressing lives of its characters. Nominated for Best Foreign-Language Film, *Gervaise* stars Maria Schell in a heartbreaking performance as a crippled woman who starts life anew with her two children after her philandering husband leaves her. Happiness is short-lived, however, as her second husband turns to drink and ruins both their lives. This is a devastating tale of betrayal, revenge and star-crossed love. Remade in 1993 as *Germinal*. (French with English subtitles) ★★★ $29.99

Get Crazy

(1983, 98 min, US, Allan Arkush) The *crazy* in the title is not misleading as a rock promoter for a Fillmore East-like theatre gets more than he bargained for when he stages a New Year's Eve concert. Starring Malcolm McDowell, Ed Begley, Jr., Lou Reed, Fabian and Daniel Stern, plus a few "in" cameos by famous music personalities. ★★★

Get on the Bus

(1996, 121 min, US, Spike Lee) A group of 20 or so African-American men hop on a commercial bus in Los Angeles and head to the Million Man March in Washington, D.C. Along the way, friendships are forged, fights break out, and the very purpose of this cross-country trek is discussed. Director Lee gathers together a collection of "types" (ex-gang banger, wise elder, buppie, gay couple, deadbeat dad) in an enclosed space for a period of time, and like a fascinating sociological experiment, observes the results. Lee avoids heavy moralizing for the most part, concentrating instead on delicious debates on a broad range of topics concerning black males: racism, misogyny, homophobia, upward mobility, self-respect, and even the O.J. verdict. This is a well-acted (especially by Andre Braugher, Ossie Davis and Charles S. Dutton), involving, fast-paced effort marred only by a dramatically unsatisfying, clunky ending. Until that point, *Get on the Bus* is worthwhile and intelligent entertainment. ★★★ $19.99

Get Out Your Handkerchiefs

(1978, 109 min, France, Bertrand Blier) A farcical comedy on unconventional love and sex. Gérard Depardieu is a husband aiming to please, Carole Laurie is his enigmatic wife and Patrick Dewaere is a lover brought in to lift her out of her depression. An insightful look into the sexual roles of the modern relationship; both witty and perceptive. (Available dubbed and in French with English subtitles) ★★★½ $59.99

Get Rita

(1972, 90 min, Italy, Giorgio Capitini) In the mood for a scoop of Italian gelato? Try the cinematic equivalent in this light, endearingly terrible comedy. Sophia Loren is Poopsie, a Milanese prostitute who finds herself "bought" by Charlie (Marcello Mastroianni), an abusive, big-time gangster. Poopsie proves to be a lot tougher than her nemesis as she seeks to undermine the low-life kingpin. Sounds serious? Don't be fooled — everyone overacts in this wacky comedy whose highlight is Loren's imitation of a dancing and singing Rita Hayworth. (Dubbed) ★½

Get Shorty

(1995, 105 min, US, Barry Sonnenfeld) Fresh from his success in *Pulp Fiction*, a triumphant John Travolta finds himself on the wrong side of the law once more in this thoroughly entertaining, hip and refreshing gangster comedy which takes aim at Hollywood and its players. Giving a scintillating performance which further demonstrates his range, Travolta plays Chili Palmer, a low-level but self-assured Miami mobster whose debt collection assignment takes him to Hollywood. An acknowledged film buff, Chili is soon pitching a movie deal to sleazy producer Harry Zimm (a hilarious Gene Hackman) rather than collecting his debt. In an ever-spiraling comedic vortex of industry machinations, Chili becomes involved with Zimm's leading lady (Rene Russo), a pretentious star (Danny DeVito) intrigued by Chili's facial expressions, a rival gangster (Delroy Lindo) also wanting a piece of Zimm, and a Miami gangland boss (Dennis Farina in a marvelously antic performance) out for revenge.

Based on the novel by Elmore Leonard, *Get Shorty* is smart, cynical and fabulously funny; its satire goes for the jugular in the most unexpected and gratifying ways. ★★★★ $19.99

Get to Know Your Rabbit

(1972, 91 min, US, Brian De Palma) Quirky, smirky, mischievous and very '70s, this oddball comedy (actually filmed in 1970) was made during De Palma's inventive independent period, when he made such films as *Hi Mom!*, *Greetings* and *Sisters*. Tommy Smothers plays a '70s version of a yuppie who chucks the pressures of executive life and "drops out" to become a tap-dancing magician. Orson Welles (who was an amateur magician) is his strange teacher, a bug-eyed John Astin (Gomez from TV's "The Addams Family") is his former boss and Allen Garfield is a swinger with a brassiere fetish. The film is filled with wacky humor that does not always hit the mark, but overall it's a fine example of the kind of exuberant comedy popular at the time. ★★★ $19.99

The Getaway

(1972, 122 min, US, Sam Peckinpah) Ali MacGraw and Steve McQueen capture on-screen the sparks they were striking offscreen in this violent tale of an ex-con hired by the mob to pull off a simple bank job. Even though the heist goes awry, the mob still wants their money — and they're holding his wife until they get it. This time out, director Peckinpah's penchant for balletic violence is subservient to the story and suspenseful action sequences. ★★★ $9.99

The Getaway

(1994, 114 min, US, Roger Donaldson) From the director of *No Way Out* comes this glamorous, highly entertaining remake of the grungy Sam Peckinpah actioner starring real-life husband and wife Alec Baldwin and Kim Basinger in the roles originally played by real-life couple Steve McQueen and Ali MacGraw. Both are evenly matched as a bickering, larcenous couple on the run from a botched heist and the accomplices that set them up (including Michael Madsen as a red-headed psycho). Also with James Woods and David Morse, and special mention goes to Jennifer Tilly in the comic role originally played by Sally Struthers. (Includes footage not shown in theatrical version.) ★★★ $19.99

Gervaise

Getting Away with Murder

(1996, 92 min, US, Harvey Miller) What was probably intended as an acerbic commentary on contemporary morals, *Getting Away with Murder* is merely plodding and muddled. Mild-mannered history professor Dan Aykroyd suspects next-door neighbor Jack Lemmon to be a Nazi war criminal. His interest is misread as support by Lemmon and daughter Lily Tomlin, leading to Aykroyd's further involvement in ensuing events. However, instead of a wry, twisting morality tale, this unfocused and weak effort telegraphs its punches way too early and without a power delivery. Director-writer Miller gets away with murder with a wretched waste of a fine cast and a potentially exciting story concept. ★ $14.99

Getting Even with Dad

(1994, 108 min, US, Howard Deutch) A promising premise, that of a precocious 12-year-old son blackmailing his criminal dad to go straight, hasn't been exploited at all and both lifeless direction and an awful script make this a tedious bore. Ted Danson plays an ex-con who masterminds a robbery which seems to be foolproof — only he didn't allow for a visitation from his estranged son (Macaulay Culkin). The kid gets wise to Dad's plans, and forces him to spend time with him, hoping he'll forget his life of crime. Danson seems lost, and Culkin is still a brat, though Saul Rubinek as Danson's partner and Glenne Headly as a cop rise above the material. ★½ $14.99

Getting It Right

(1989, 105 min, GB, Randal Kleiser) This English comedy about a man's sexual and emotional awakening is a surprisingly touching and consistently funny coming-of-age film. Gavin Lamb (the perfectly cast Jesse Birdsall) is a slightly awkward but handsome 31-year-old London hairdresser who lives at home and dreams of one day losing his virginity. In a whirlwind two weeks his structured life is shattered when he is thrown into the arms, and beds, of three very different women. Lynn Redgrave is smashing as the "older woman" who introduces our young hero to the pleasures of the flesh. ★★★ $9.99

The Getting of Wisdom

(1977, 100 min, Australia, Bruce Beresford) A spirited girl encounters unhappiness at a snobbish Melbourne girls' academy in Beresford's pleasant if unimaginative coming-of-age drama. Set before the turn of the century, the story follows intelligent but impetuous Laura (Susannah Fowle), who leaves her rural home for higher education in the big city. There, she overcomes the school's petty regulations, schoolgirl rivalries and the authority's herd mentality. Barry Humphries, the alter ego to Dame Edna Everage, appears as the school's principal in a wasted performance. ★★½ $19.99

Gettysburg

(1993, 248 min, US, Ronald F. Maxwell) An epic re-creation of the Battle of Gettysburg, this four-hour drama may not belie its running time, but it certainly captures the flavor of its time, and brilliantly stages in painstaking detail the endless battles which marked the Civil War. Earnest performances from an ensemble cast including Martin Sheen, Tom Berenger, Stephen Lang, Sam Elliott and Kevin Conway distinguish the production, though Jeff Daniels and Richard Jordan excel in their characterizations of ethical men caught in the confines of bloody combat. Though *Gettysburg's* dramatic scenes aren't on par with its battle sequences, the film features outstanding production values, and also some truly awful makeup. ★★★ $24.99

Ghost

(1990, 127 min, US, Jerry Zucker) A metaphysical romance/thriller/comedy, *Ghost* is a guaranteed crowd-pleaser filled with supernatural intrigue and lots of laughs. Patrick Swayze and Demi Moore star as Sam and Molly, a yuppie couple whose picture-perfect romance is broken up when Sam is suddenly dispatched to the other side. As he becomes stuck between dimensions, Sam's spirit roams the streets of Manhattan in search of answers. Whoopi Goldberg's Oscar-winning performance as Oda Mae Brown, a storefront spiritual advisor who becomes Swayze's reluctant link to the world of the living, is hilarious. Director Zucker moves the action along at a lively pace and makes the most of Goldberg's enormous comedic talents. Aside from a simplistic version of life in the hereafter, the film has few flaws and will leave even the most skeptical viewer smiling. ★★★ $14.99

The Ghost and Mrs. Muir

(1947, 104 min, US, Joseph L. Mankiewicz) Gene Tierney, Rex Harrison and George Sanders star in this charming fantasy about a widow (Tierney) who is romanced by a crusty if ethereal sea captain (Harrison), the once and present occupant of her New England cottage. A felicitous mixture of make-believe with an acute observation of human foibles, and requiring very little suspension of disbelief. Scripted by Philip Dunne, with music by Bernard Herrmann. ★★★ $19.99

The Ghost and the Darkness

(1996, 110 min, US, Stephen Hopkins) Though he doesn't appear on screen until a half-hour into the film, Michael Douglas' big-game hunter adds just the right kick to an otherwise familiar, occasionally exciting jungle adventure. Set in late-1890s East Africa, and amazingly based on a true story, *The Ghost and the Darkness* follows the attempts to build a railroad by a British firm whose crew has come under attack by two particularly ferocious lions (who in real life killed over a hundred men). Val Kilmer is the engineer sent to oversee construction and the elimination of the animals. The title refers to the nicknames the local workers have given to the two lions, somewhat spiritual but appropriate monikers as they prove terribly elusive. Kilmer is a little too white-man-knows-it-all, but he gives an earnest interpretation; Douglas at least has some fun with a slant on the great-white-hunter adventurer. The scenery is spectacular, and the cinematography captures the beauty of the land and the terror of the beasts. Once again, nature rules. ★★½ $14.99

The Ghost Breakers

(1940, 85 min, US, George Marshall) Though short on plot, there's plenty of laughs to this uproarious Bob Hope ghost comedy. After their great success in *The Cat and the Canary* the year before, Hope and the lovely Paulette Goddard reteamed for more high-spirited shenanigans. Radio journalist Bob helps Paulette — who's just inherited a haunted castle in Cuba — battle the bad guys and some prankish poltergeists. And Hope's got a one-liner for every occasion ("The girls call me Pilgrim, because every time I dance with one I make a little progress"): Some are merely funny; others are just hilarious. Willie Best makes the most of the unflattering role of the "scared Negro" (Best does get a few zingers of his own), and Goddard is captivating. Remade as *Scared Stiff* — almost shot for shot — with Martin and Lewis. ★★★½ $14.99

Ghost Dad

(1990, 84 min, US, Sidney Poitier) Bill Cosby plays a widowed father who dies and comes back to life, given a couple of days to straighten out his affairs for the sake of his children. Though Cosby hams it up, there's little that works in this tired ghost comedy. ★★ $12.99

The Ghost Goes West

(1936, 82 min, GB, René Clair) Delightful ghost comedy about a 200-year-old spirit who, refusing to leave the Scottish castle he haunts, travels to America when it is sold and shipped abroad. Written by Robert E. Sherwood, with Robert Donat as charming as ever in dual roles as the poltergeist and his descendant. ★★★½ $19.99

Ghost in the Machine

(1994, 90 min, US, Rachel Talalay) *The Lawnmower Man* meets *Shocker* meets *The Horror Show* ad infinitum ad nauseam (emphasis on "nauseam") as a serial killer on the brink of death is uploaded into a municipal mainframe enabling him to kill anyone who's paid their electric bill. State-of-the-art effects and a couple of creatively grisly deaths can't help shock this one back to life. Starring Karen Allen and Chris Mulkey. ★½ $96.89

Ghost in the Noonday Sun

(1973, 93 min, GB, Peter Medak) It is rumored that Peter Sellers and director Medak had a falling out which led to the demise of this blundering pirate comedy. Sellers stars as a rogue pirate who leads his men in search of hidden treasure, but finds that the booty is protected by a less than friendly ghost. Peter Boyle and Anthony Franciosa also star. ★

Ghost in the Shell

(1995, 80 min, Japan, Mamoru Oshii) Based on the cyberpunk manga by Masamune Shirow, *Ghost in the Shell* is a cerebral animated sci-fi tale that mixes philosophy with high-octane action. In a future dominated by technology, where human and machine mix without incident, the definition of humanity is questioned. A female cyborg, Major Motoko Kusanagi, is investigating a series of computer-hacking crimes with her special police unit, when it is revealed that their opponent is a new cybernetic life form. Known as the

Puppet Master, it is a sentient being created in a web of computer information, and it wishes to be free of its human creators. Director Oshii, who also helmed the spectacular *Patlabor 1 & 2*, brings his distinct style of visual storytelling to this feature through a mix of computer and traditional cel animation. The results are breathtaking, creating an animated vision on par with other classic Japanese anime like *Akira* and *The WIngs of Honnemaise*. (Japanese with English subtitles) (Dubbed version is available for $19.99) ★★★½ $29.99

Ghost Story

(1981, 85 min, US, John Irvin) The old guard of Hollywood showed up to make this horror film as generic as its title. Fred Astaire (in his last film), Melvyn Douglas, Douglas Fairbanks, Jr. and John Houseman teeter through this film about a shared secret from 50 years ago that is back for revenge. ★½ $19.99

Ghostbusters

(1984, 107 min, US, Ivan Reitman) One of the highest-grossing comedies of all time. Bill Murray, Dan Aykroyd and Harold Ramis play bumbling "paranormal investigators" who save the world, or at least New York City, from demonic apparitions. The special effects are state-of-the-art, and both high-brow and low-brow humor abounds. Fine comic performances from supporting cast Sigourney Weaver and Rick Moranis. ★★★ $14.99

Ghostbusters II

(1989, 102 min, US, Ivan Reitman) This formulaic sequel has, as in the original, an evil spirit from the past haunting the present – this time in the form of a truly ugly medieval monarch who is trapped in a less than flattering Renaissance painting. In conjunction with his imminent release the city of New York is being inundated by the now familiar ooze called "slime." All of the characters have returned from the first film – kudos go to Sigourney Weaver for being the only one in the bunch to have actually developed her character from the original. ★★½ $14.99

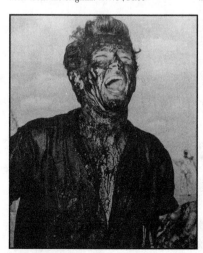

James Dean celebrates in *Giant*

Ghosts of Mississippi

(1996, 123 min, US, Rob Reiner) In 1963, civil rights activist Medgar Evers was assassinated in front of his Mississippi home. The murderer went free after two hung juries couldn't come to a verdict. Thirty years later, Evers' widow pushed for a new trial, eventually bringing her husband's killer to justice. This sad chapter of America's past is the focus of Reiner's commendable if unremarkable film, a detective and courtroom drama which doesn't quite have the passion of its convictions. Alec Baldwin plays the Assistant District Attorney in charge of the case, and Whoopi Goldberg is Myrlie Evers. Like so many Hollywood films about racial prejudice against African-Americans, the story is seen through the eyes of a white person – here Baldwin. But whereas a film like *Mississippi Burning* has energy and focus, *Ghosts of Mississippi* has professionalism but little heart. Baldwin is adequate in fleshing out his character, but Goldberg is so subdued as Mrs. Evers, and has so little to work with from the script, there's no room for any shading. James Woods is very good as the killer. ★★½ $102.99

Ghostwriter

(1993, 105 min, US) From Children's Television Workshop comes this high quality, entertaining and educational series. This first entry introduces us to the Ghostwriters team of young teens who solve mysteries with the help of the enigmatic title figure, a ghost who communicates by writing messages visible only to the team members. The video encourages reading and writing skills and has a very necessary coolness factor to appeal to a preteen audience. ★★★ $14.99

Giant

(1956, 198 min, US, George Stevens) Over 40 years after his tragic death, James Dean remains a mythic icon of youthful rebelliousness and alienation. This sprawling saga of Texas oil aristocracy provided Dean his final and most challenging role as the arrogant ranch hand, Jett Rink. A Best Director Oscar went to Stevens while Rock Hudson earned a nomination for his finest screen work and Liz Taylor won acclaim as Hudson's compassionate wife. *Giant* is an epic-sized drama of greed, jealousy and loyalty, but its stars seem to outshine the penetrating screenplay and thoughtful direction. ★★★½ $29.99

The Giant Gila Monster

(1959, 74 min, US, Ray Kellogg) Giant Gila monsters with funny glued-on fins attack kids in New Mexico as they listen to rock 'n' roll in their hot rods. Youth wins out. ★★ $9.99

Giant Robo – Episodes 1-4

(1992-1995, 45 each min, Japan, Yasuhiro Imagawa) Set on a retro-futuristic Earth, the *Giant Robo* series blends high-quality cartoon-style animation with action-adventure, science fiction, superheroics, giant robots, high drama, social commentary, and just about any other genre you can imagine. The plot line for the first four episodes of the series deals with the con-

flict between the Experts of Justice, the super-hero good guys, and Big Fire, a terrorist organization with its own evil, superpowered beings. Giant Robo, a titanic robot, and his young master, Daisaku, are members of the Experts. They find themselves embroiled in a conflict of global proportions, as the two groups struggle for control of the world's energy supply. *Giant Robo* is a truly unique anime series. It has amazing animation, a gripping story, and is incredibly fun to watch. The only problem is waiting for the next episode. Note: *Giant Robo* is based on the same *manga* that also produced the live-action *Johnny Sokko & His Giant Robot*. (Dubbed) ★★★½ $19.99

Gidget

(1959, 95 min, US, Paul Wendkos) First of the popular series with Sandra Dee as the innocent young beach groupie in love with surfer James Darren. Also with Cliff Robertson, who plays a beach bum, himself smitten by our little heroine. It's kinda sappy in a kinda cute way, but remember that it's *not* a documentary! ★★½ $9.99

The Gift

(1982, 195 min, France, Michel Lang) A harried bank worker meets and falls in love with a beautiful and alluring mystery woman (Clio Goldsmith), only to discover that his co-workers "bought" her for him as a retirement gift. Though the premise is promising, this sex farce barely ignites any sparks. (Dubbed) ★★

The Gig

(1985, 92 min, US, Frank Gilroy) Wayne Rogers heads a cast of wonderful actors in this engaging comedy-drama about a group of friends who get together to play jazz. All's well until they get their first professional gig. Also with Cleavon Little. ★★★ $19.99

Gigi

(1958, 116 min, US, Vincente Minnelli) Enchanting Oscar-winning musical about a French girl (Leslie Caron), being groomed to be a courtesan, and her romance with a handsome playboy (Louis Jordan). Maurice Chevalier also stars and is most memorable as young Gigi's guardian. Winner of nine Academy Awards, including Best Picture. Terrific Lerner & Lowe score includes "Thank Heaven for Little Girls" and "I Remember It Well." (Available letter-boxed and pan & scan) ★★★★ $14.99

Gilda

(1946, 110 min, US, Charles Vidor) A steamy, hard-boiled classic with the ravishing Rita Hayworth driving husband George MacReady and ex-lover Glenn Ford into frenzies of lust. Boldly adventurous in its day, *Gilda* holds up as a sizzling cauldron of perverse eroticism and social aberration. Featured is Rita's grinding performance of "Put the Blame on Mame," in which she loosens libidos with the removal of a single glove. ★★★½ $19.99

The Gin Game

(1982, 82 min, US) Jessica Tandy and Hume Cronyn repeat their award-winning performances in this lovely comedy-drama, a live version of their early 1980s stage hit. Written by D.L. Coburn, the play casts Tandy and Cronyn as elderly residents at a rest home whose developing relationship is put to the test during a series of lively, almost cutthroat gin games. Though the play does occasionally lapse into heavy dramatics, it is nonetheless poignant, insightful and vastly amusing. Its two legendary performers are remarkably fine. ★★★ $39.99

Ginger and Fred

(1986, 126 min, Italy, Federico Fellini) Fellini's best since *Amarcord* is a refreshingly whimsical story of two aging hoofers who are reunited after 30 years to appear on a TV variety show that is a cross between "This Is Your Life" and "The Gong Show." Both Giulietta Masina and Marcello Mastroianni are entrancing as the two out-of-their-element dancers. (Italian with English subtitles) ★★★ $19.99

The Girl

(1968, 86 min, Hungary, Márta Mészáros) Mészáros, one of Hungary's first internationally recognized directors, scored her first success with this absorbing drama of a young woman who leaves a state orphanage to search for her parents. The film manages to be touching without resorting to histrionics, and there's a bittersweet mood which Mészáros maintains throughout. (Hungarian with English subtitles) ★★★ $69.99

The Girl

(1987, 104 min, Sweden, Arne Mattsson) Cheesy soft-core erotic thriller starring Franco Nero as a successful, married lawyer who falls under the alluring spell of an unusually lascivious 14-year-old girl. His Lolita-esque affair soon becomes his undoing, however, when his passion leads to cross-European intrigue and murder. Christopher Lee, obviously in need of lunch money, makes an appearance in this unintentionally funny international mess. (Filmed in English) ★

The Girl Can't Help It

(1956, 99 min, US, Frank Tashlin) Jayne Mansfield stars as the quintessential "dumb blonde" in this classic cult musical. Tom Ewell plays a talent agent hired by Mansfield's gangster boyfriend (Edmond O'Brien) to make her a famous singing star. Jayne's attributes are more visual than vocal, but included in the film are some wonderful vintage performances by Fats Domino, Gene Vincent and The Platters. ★★★ $59.99

Girl Crazy

(1943, 100 min, US, Norman Taurog) A terrific George and Ira Gershwin score highlight this enjoyable Judy Garland-Mickey Rooney musical with Mickey as a rich kid who's sent to an all-male school to forget about girls, only to fall for Judy on arrival. Songs include "I Got Rhythm" and "But Not for Me." Choreography by Busby Berkeley; June Allyson and Nancy Walker co-star. ★★★½ $19.99

Girl from Hunan

(1986, 99 min, China, Xie Fei & U Lan) Spectacular landscapes of Chinese villages, mountains and rice fields provide the lush backdrop to this powerful drama of a young woman struggling to overcome sexist repression in rural China at the turn of the century. Sent to a nearby village in a pre-arranged marriage, 14-year-old Xiao Xiao finds herself

engaged to a little boy of two. Pampered by her future father-in-law, yet independent-minded, the girl cares for her toddling husband-to-be, but as her teenage years progress, she begins to think of him more in brotherly ways and directs her budding sexual curiosities toward older men, setting up a confrontation with clan elders who strictly enforce laws against adultery. Featuring elaborately staged tribal ceremonies for marriage and death in a male-dominated society, the film's theme, much repeated in Chinese and Japanese cinema, that "women were born to suffer," is nevertheless quite powerful. (Mandarin with English subtitles) ★★★½ $79.99

The Girl in a Swing

(1989, 112 min, GB/US, Gorgon Hessler) A repressed middle-aged businessman marries a mysterious German secretary (Meg Tilly) after a whirlwind romance and gets more than he bargained for. Unfortunately, the viewer gets less than he/she hoped for in this tepid "sexy" drama, based on the 1979 novel by Richard Adams ("Watership Down"). The film is filled with many tedious tearful outbursts (by both Tilly and, in all likelihood, the viewer) as well as some strange hallucinatory episodes. What is the terrible secret she is hiding? When it is revealed, it's disappointing. ★ $89.99

The Girl in the Picture

(1985, 90 min, GB, Cary Parker) John Gordon Sinclair, the gangly star of *Gregory's Girl*, stars in this lighthearted comedy about the frailties of modern love. Sinclair plays a young photo shop clerk who is involved in a tumultuous on-again, off-again relationship with a young college student. ★★ $79.99

Girl 6

(1996, 107 min, US, Spike Lee) Myriad cameo appearances by the terminally hip (Madonna, Quentin Tarantino, etc.) and the engaging presence of Theresa Randle can't save this disjointed morality tale. Randle plays a young woman who, to pay the rent until she gets her break in show business, accepts a phone sex job. Now a number on a switchboard — Girl 6

— not a name, she sinks into the milieu, losing sight of goals as they devolve into fantasies. Clips of Dorothy Dandridge and '70s blaxploitation flicks are interspersed throughout *Girl 6*, and the closing scene is a tip of the hat to Fellini's *8½*. Is this a parable equating acting and moviemaking with prostitution? Probably. But even such touches as the visual pun of Naomi Campbell in a T-shirt bearing the legend "Models Suck" can't salvage this unfocused amalgam of vignettes punctuated by an insistent, intrusive score by Prince. If you're in the mood for a Spike Lee joint, rewatch *Malcolm X*. ★★ $19.99

Girl Talk

(1987, 85 min, US, Kate Davis) Pinky is a spunky 13-year-old who is continually threatened with lock-up for not going to school. Sometimes she chooses to sleep in the streets rather than go home. Mars has found a surrogate family among fellow employees at a strip joint. They're actually more supportive than her own family. Martha is a single 19-year-old with an infant son. She's struggling with the effects of a sexually abusive father and an institutionalized mother. Director Davis examines the lives of these three young women, the products of sexual and psychological abuse; and looks at the failure of the existing systems created to address these problems. Though the film suffers slightly from an occasional lack of focus, it is often searing in the pain it reveals. The director offers no solutions or panaceas, but simply exposes the realities of the daily lives of these women, inviting understanding and compassion. ★★★ $79.99

The Girl with the Hatbox

(1927, 67 min, USSR, Boris Barnet) With heavily politicalized diatribes being the norm in early Soviet filmmaking, it is an even greater pleasure to view this cheery "American style" comedy. Anna Stern, who later starred in films at Goldwyn, plays a poor, naive factory girl who is given a seemingly worthless lottery ticket in lieu of pay by her unscrupulous boss, only to discover that she is a winner. The money, she soon discovers, elicits not only pleasure

Lili Taylor (l.) Anna Grace (c.) and Bruklin Harris in *Girls Town*

but the greed of those around her and devious lovers as well. (Silent with orchestral accompaniment) ★★★ $29.99

Girlfriends

(1978, 86 min, US, Claudia Weill) A flawless performance from Melanie Mayron as a photographer who makes it "on her own" after her best friend and roommate gets married makes this independent drama well-worth watching. Susan (Mayron) finds success as an artist while Ann (Anita Skinner) struggles to balance being a wife and mother with a writing career. Weill's film touchingly and accurately explores the two women's friendship and their singular ambitions without sentimentality or heavy-handedness. ★★★ $19.99

Girlfriends

(1993, 80 min, US, Mark Bosko & Wayne Harold) This kinky tale of a pair of likable lesbian serial killers is an inventive, low-budget combination of *Henry: Portrait of a Serial Killer* and *Pink Flamingos*. Pearl (Lori Scarlet) and her butch lover Wanda (Nina Angeloff) make a modest living picking up a variety of men, blowing their heads off and making off with their wallets. In the midst of the casual carnage, Pearl decides she wants to have a baby – pity the poor father-to-be. *Girlfriends*, not to be confused with the Claudia Weill film, is an ironic thriller loaded with shockingly graphic splatter effects, sly humor and a surprise ending. Lesbian empowerment has never been so unnerving – for the males in the audience! ★★★ $59.99

Girls Just Want to Have Fun

(1985, 90 min, US, Alan Metter) Enjoyable, better-than-average teen comedy with Sarah Jessica Parker giving a charming performance as a teenage girl determined to enter the big video dance contest despite protestations from family and church. ★★★ $14.99

Girls on Top

(1985, 50 min, GB, Paul Jackson) Two episodes from the popular British Central Independent Television sitcom featuring Tracey Ullman. Similar in concept to "The Young Ones," this time with girls, the story follows the comedic escapades of four disparate roomates – a disco airhead, a militant feminist, a lackluster dolt and a loudmouthed American – who endure each other's quirks and share adventures while handling their daffy landlady. The broadly sketched characterizations are essayed by Ullman, Dawn French, Jennifer Saunders, Ruby Wax and Joan Greenwood. ★★★ $19.99

Girls Town

(1996, 90 min, US, Jim McKay) Winner of the Filmmakers Trophy and a Special Jury Prize at Sundance, *Girls Town* rests mostly on the terrific chemistry of its ensemble cast. Touching upon issues important to young women, such as date rape, spousal abuse, teen pregnancy and abortion, the story provides an intimate look at a tight-knit band of female high school seniors anxiously awaiting their last day of educational captivity. The film initially looks as if it might become painfully aimless and meandering; but when an unexpected tragedy befalls the group, *Girls Town* comes sharply into focus and the

young women set out to vent their rage at the men who have screwed up their nascent lives. Set somewhere in the quasi-urban environs of Queens, the film's heroines are an unlikely mix of race and social backgrounds that have coalesced around a pride in their citified toughness and an inane rebelliousness. The performances are top-notch, with Lili Taylor being the obvious headliner, and Anna Grace leading the way as the emotional trailblazer for the posse. There's a nice hip-hop soundtrack, and the film avoids the maudlin, Afterschool Special mentality. ★★★½ $98.99

Giselle

(1977, 95 min, US, David Blair) Dance great Mikhail Baryshnikov and the greatest "Giselle" of all time, Natalia Markova, give us classical ballet at its finest in this Lincoln Center performance directed by Blair, the former principal of the Royal Ballet. ★★★½ $29.99

Giselle

(USSR) Filmed at the world famous Bolshoi Theatre in Moscow, the classic love story, "Giselle" is performed by the Bolshoi Company. With Natalja Bessmerthnova in the title role and Michail Lavrosky as Count Albrecht. ★★★ $39.99

Gladiator

(1992, 98 min, US, Rowdy Herrington) From the director of *Road House* comes this surprisingly sensitive blood-and-guts'er focusing on the friendship between two inner-city youths (Cuba Gooding, Jr. and James Marshall) and their entanglement with a crooked underground fight promoter (Brian Dennehy at his most demonic). It's silly and predictable, but fans of the genre should enjoy it. Also with Ossie Davis, Robert Loggia and John Heard. ★★ $19.99

The Glass Bottom Boat

(1966, 100 min, US, Frank Tashlin) Though the times they were a changin', Doris Day, in one of her last films, steered straight ahead with this familiar and silly slapstick comedy. Doris plays a widow whose work relationship with scientist Rod Taylor leads to romance and spies. A good supporting cast includes Paul Lynde, John McGiver, Edward Andrews, Dom DeLuise and Arthur Godfrey. Fun for those wishing to wax a nostalgic good time. ★★½ $19.99

The Glass Key

(1942, 85 min, US, Stuart Heisler) Tough-as-nails remake of the 1935 film, adapted from a Dashiell Hammett story, about a politician (Brian Donlevy) who is implicated in a murder; Alan Ladd is his "henchman" who tries to clear his name. Also with Veronica Lake and William Bendix. ★★★½ $14.99

The Glass Menagerie

(1987, 134 min, US, Paul Newman) The sterling performances of Joanne Woodward, John Malkovich, Karen Allen and James Naughton elevate this handsome production based on Tennessee Williams' classic play. Allen brings a heart-wrenching vulnerability to Laura, the lonely and lame daughter of faded Southern belle Woodward. Malkovich is well-cast as Woodward's troubled son Tom, and Naughton rounds out the cast as the Gentleman Caller. ★★★ $19.99

The Glass Key

The Glass Shield

(1995, 101 min, US, Charles Burnett) *The Glass Shield* begins with comic book strips of police officers on the job, but these one-dimensional figures unfortunately carry over to the live action. In this well-intentioned though heavy-handed examination of racism in police ranks, Michael Boatman and Lori Petty are newly placed officers (both there as tokens) who band together to expose corruption and widespread racism in their department. The story occasionally moves, but the rogue cops are drawn with such broad strokes they have about as much depth as a villain on a "Kojak" episode. These cardboard characters act with single-minded determination, and the authors evidently think that having one of them dying of cancer gives all of them characterization. There's a better story to be told here – just because a premise has merit doesn't necessarily make it good storytelling. ★★ $99.99

Gleaming the Cube

(1989, 105 min, US, Graeme Clifford) This skateboard thriller is of interest because of its lead performer, Christian Slater. With a hip delivery, reminiscent of Jack Nicholson, Slater brings a coolness to his role of the eternally rebellious youth who investigates the murder of his half-brother, a Vietnamese honor student. An interesting look at sibling rivalry and cultural clashes, with particularly impressive skateboarding scenes. ★★½ $9.99

Glen and Randa

(1971, 94 min, US, Jim McBride) A low-budget, post-apocalyptic tale, this early feature by McBride (*The Big Easy*) follows the travels of a primitive "Adam and Eve" couple scrounging for survival and looking for the fabled city of Metropolis. Clearly made in the heyday of the hippie movement, this minimalist parable is slowly paced but nevertheless intriguing in director McBride's quirky visual style. (Originally rated "X" in its theatrical release – solely for a prolonged nude scene.) ★★★ $59.99

Glen or Glenda?

(1953, 67 min, US, Edward D. Wood, Jr.) "Beevare the beeg green dragin!" Thus we are warned by narrator Bela Lugosi who introduces us to the hopelessly confused Glen, possessed with an uncontrollable urge to don female garb. Wood's (a John Waters favorite) unredeemable schlock-umentary is one of the most ill-conceived and funniest works of all time. "Vat are little boys made ov? Is it puppy dog tails? Big fat snails? Or maybe *brassieres! garters!...*" ★ $14.99

Glengarry Glen Ross

(1992, 100 min, US, James Foley) David Mamet's riveting adaptation of his own Pulitzer Prize-winning play is marvelously brought to the screen by Foley (*After Dark, My Sweet*). Al Pacino, Jack Lemmon, Ed Harris, Alan Arkin and Kevin Spacey star as a group of seedy real estate men who scratch out a living selling Florida vacation tracts to retirees, and Alec Baldwin puts in a short but brilliant turn as a callous head honcho who gives this rag-tag sales force a merciless tongue-lashing. With the proverbial "axe" hanging over their heads, they find themselves in a dog-eat-dog fight for their jobs. Mamet's screenplay, which bristles with his usual razor-sharp dialogue, tells a compelling and timely story of greed, avarice and the rich getting richer. While the entire cast is brilliant, special kudos go to both Lemmon and Pacino for their gutsy handling of Mamet's barrage of profanities. ★★★★ $14.99

The Glenn Miller Story

(1954, 113 min, US, Anthony Mann) James Stewart had one of his more popular roles in this affectionate tribute to the great swing time bandleader Glenn Miller. The film follows Miller's rise to become one of the major influences in popular music in the 1930s and '40s. June Allyson plays Mrs. Miller, and the score includes such standards as "Chattanooga Choo-Choo" and "Pennsylvania 6-5000." ★★★ $19.99

The Glimmer Man

(1996, 92 min, US, John Gray) The latest Steven Seagal slugfest is not quite his worst movie (that honor still belongs to *On Deadly Ground*), but this tired retread of dozens of other action/thriller buddy movies features none of the qualities which have served him in the past. Instead of an interesting twist or plot, we get Seagal as a mysterious homicide detective who is skilled in martial arts and practices Chinese medicine, and Keenan Ivory Wayans as his beleaguered partner and stand-in for the audience. They happen upon the trail of a mysterious cover-up involving a serial killer, the CIA and Seagal's shadowy past. The outcome, however, is boring and unimaginative and not worth the buildup. And instead of anticipated martial arts sequences from Seagal, the viewer is subjected to run-of-the-mill car chases, escapes, explosions and shootouts, none of which are done with any style or originality. Wayans is completely out of place and even Seagal's dubious talents are ultimately wasted. ★½ $102.99

Glitter Goddess of Sunset Strip

(1993, 115 min, US, Dick Campbell) An innovative, autobiographical psychodrama about the life and times of ex-glam rock groupie and sexual maverick Llana Lloyd. Born in 1952 into the strange, domineering world of a man-loathing lesbian mother and a schizophrenic father, Lloyd turned her psyche-tested, tormented existence into a positive learning experience and made it her claim to fame. With the story being told through a series of John Waters-influenced dramatic "reenactments" and talk-show footage (some featuring an Afro-endowed Oprah Winfrey), we get a unique fly-on-the-wall perspective into a complex world of gender role-playing and ahead-of-its-time sexual politics, with Lloyd and real-life daughter Alana playing the mother/daughter roles. ★★★ $69.99

Go Fish

Gloria

(1980, 121 min, US, John Cassavetes) Cassavetes' whirlwind thriller features a remarkable performance from Gena Rowlands as an ex-gangster's moll who begrudgingly takes charge of her neighbors' kid after they are brutally massacred by the mob. As she and the kid flee would-be assassins, Cassavetes' camera masterfully captures the gritty underbelly of New York City. ★★★ $69.99

Glory

(1989, 122 min, US, Edward Zwick) This powerful Civil War drama is the startlingly good, impressive and long-overdue story about a little-known chapter in American history: the first black combat unit. Matthew Broderick heads a first-rate cast as the white commander of the 54th Massachusetts Regiment, an all-black fighting unit comprised of enlisted men who were initially denied the basic rights of other soldiers; they were then forced to prove themselves in order to be treated equally. Morgan Freeman offers solid support as the company's wise sergeant and Oscar winner Denzel Washington is outstanding as a former slave. Based on the letters of Colonel Robert Gould Shaw, whom Broderick portrays. (Available letterboxed and pan & scan) ★★★★ $14.99

Glory! Glory!

(1988, 152 min, US, Lindsay Anderson) Anderson's potent satire of televangelism stars Richard Thomas as Bobby Joe Stuckey, an electronic preacher whose ministry is in disarray. His contributions are dwindling and cash flow is low. Things are so bad, in fact, that he hires a sexy rock 'n' roll singer (Ellen Greene) to help boost profits, and that's when the word of the Lord really starts to get turned upside-down. ★★★ $59.99

The Gnome-Mobile

(1967, 90 min, US, Robert Stevenson) Bright Disney fluff by the director of *Mary Poppins*. Walter Brennan, Matthew Garber and Karen Dotrice are out to protect forest gnomes from the grasp of a greedy circus owner. ★★★

Go Fish

(1994, 85 min, US, Rose Troche) An unlikely candidate to join the ranks of epochal lesbian-themed films, this delightful yet knowing independent romantic comedy by first-time Chicago filmmakers Troche (co-writer/director) and Guinevere Turner (co-writer) is more than simply the *Desert Hearts* for the '90s. Made on an extremely low budget, filmed in black and white, and featuring primarily non-professionals in major roles, *Go Fish*'s grittiness helps in making its characters more honest and accessible. Seriously cute and boyishly hip Max (Turner), after a drought of ten months, is looking for love. She possibly finds it in the person of Ely (V.S. Brodie), a semi-dorky, slightly older woman. How the two women meet, court and maybe even get together is wonderfully handled in a light, effervescent fashion that combines to paint a finely detailed and on-target depiction of young lesbian life. What the film lacks in professional pizzazz and slickness is more than made up by its vividly drawn characters and witty screenplay. ★★★½ $19.99

Go Tell the Spartans

(1978, 114 min, US, Ted Post) Burt Lancaster gives a well-modulated performance as an "advisory group commander" trying to keep his doubts to himself and his men alive as they traipse through the jungles of Vietnam on another pointless mission. One of the first films to look at our involvement in that war. ★★★½ $14.99

Go West

(1940, 81 min, US, Edward Buzzell) Groucho, Chico and Harpo take Horace Greely's advice and head west to make their fortune, and find themselves in the middle of a land swindle involving property wanted by the railroad. Even if not quite up to the standard of their earlier films, there are lots of funny bits, especially the spectacular closing train scene. ★★½ $19.99

Go West, Young Man

(1936, 80 min, US, Henry Hathaway) Though this backwoods Mae West comedy is not on par with her best known comedies, Mae's quips, a young Randolph Scott and a jab or two at Hollywood and stardom make *Go West, Young Man* worthy of interest. West, who wrote the screenplay adaptation, plays a famous movie actress on tour promoting her newest film. En route to Harrisburg, she and press agent Warren William become stranded in a small town where her arrival quickly turns everything topsy-turvy. Scott is the hunkish ('30s style) garage mechanic who makes Mae's weekend in the country all the more enjoyable. Those expecting a western romp will be disappointed, as the punny title refers to La West and not to geographic location. ★★½ $14.99

The Go-Masters

(1982, 134 min, China, Duan Ji-Shun & Junja Sata) The first Chinese-Japanese film co-production, *The Go-Masters* is a sprawling political/historical epic spanning the turbulent years of the 1920s thru the 1950s, and a poignant exploration of love, loyalty and destiny — pitting pride against national power. The story focuses on the relationship of two families, one Japanese and the other Chinese. The son of the Chinese family is an aspiring master of Go, a chess-like strategy game, who moves to Japan under the tutelage of a Japanese Go champion. When war erupts, he is thrown into a political maelstrom, forced to choose between his allegiance to his birthplace and to his adopted land. (Chinese and Japanese with English subtitles) ★★★½ $59.99

The Goalie's Anxiety at the Penalty Kick

(1971, 101 min, West Germany, Wim Wenders) After being suspended for missing a penalty kick, a goalie wanders around Vienna aimlessly. He picks up a cinema cashier and, for no apparent reason, kills her. While waiting for the inevitable arrest, he searches his soul, but finds only alienation and ennui. Although slow-going, this early Wenders film is a must for his fans. The filmmaker explores the existential territory of Camus' "The Stranger" and Sartre's "Nausea." (German with English subtitles) ★★★

God Is My Witness (Khuda Gawah)

(1994, 193 min, India, Mukul S. Anand) This dazzling action/adventure/romance/musical/melodrama is a heady, thrilling experience for modern Westerners, but Indian audiences have been flocking to this type of hybrid for years. *God Is My Witness* is a terrific introduction to this over-the-top style, sort of "Sergio Leone meets Stanley Donen in Bombay." The epic story involves Badshah Khan (played by Indian superstar Amitabh Bachchan), a cocky, noble Pathan chieftan who flips for the beautiful woman warrior Benazir (Sridevi), who won't marry him until he brings her the head of her father's murderer. Nearly all Indian films have a musical number every 20 minutes or so — no matter the genre. *God Is My Witness* is full of song-and-dance numbers, but wisely — and beautifully — uses them to further the story and flesh out characterizations. This attitude culminates in the operatic climax, a deliriously romantic, kitchen-sink crescendo rife with explosions, gunfire, reconciliations, swordplay, revenge and declarations of adulation. For those who mourn the loss of golden-age Hollywood; it didn't die, it just moved to India. (Letterboxed version) (Hindi with English subtitles) ★★★★ $99.99

God Told Me To

(1977, 91 min, US, Larry Cohen) New York City is besieged by a series of unrelated sniper attacks, committed by seemingly ordinary citizens who said they were ordered by God to kill. Tony LoBianco is the police detective whose investigation leads him to otherworldly powers. An imaginative if bizarre thriller which manages quite a few eerie moments. (aka: *Demon*) ★★½

The Godfather

(1972, 175 min, US, Francis Ford Coppola) In Coppola's brilliant crime saga, the director transformed the lowly gangster drama into an American epic capable of rivaling the western. From the wedding of Connie Corleone, to the end of her brother Michael's marriage, *The Godfather* is richly imbued with the texture of life, the allure of power and the basic corruptness of capitalism. Add to this the sheer visceral pleasure of watching top actors giving superlative performances and you've got one of the masterpieces of American cinema. Marlon Brando salvaged his career as the ruthless Don Corleone, and Al Pacino became a star playing his son Michael. Robert Duvall, James Caan, Sterling Hayden, John Cazale and Diane Keaton make up just a small part of what is truly an all-star cast. (Remastered in THX and available letterboxed and pan & scan) ★★★★ $24.99

Marlon Brando in The Godfather

The Godfather, Part II

(1974, 200 min, US, Francis Ford Coppola) Following the success of the original, Coppola felt free to delve more deeply and lyrically into the inherent roots of corruption, power and greed. By cross-cutting his two major stories — the rise of Vito Corleone and the fall of Michael — Coppola creates a dialectical narrative which elevates the movie above its low genre birthright. Also, this was the first film to contradict the much abused notion that sequels must be "parts" of a larger story. The stunning cast includes Al Pacino, Robert De Niro, Michael Gazzo, Robert Duvall, Lee Strasberg and Talia Shire. (Remastered in THX and available letterboxed and pan & scan) ★★★★ $24.99

The Godfather III

(1990, 161 min, US, Francis Ford Coppola) The third and final entry in Coppola's *Godfather* trilogy is a worthy, if flawed, finale — though it certainly isn't in the same league as the two classics which came before it. Al Pacino, in a forceful performance, returns as the reluctant Mafia boss, Michael Corleone, who is lulled back into gangland activities after

trying to go "legit." Also returning are Diane Keaton and Talia Shire as Michael's ex-wife and sister. If the picture has one major flaw, it is the casting of Coppola's daughter Sofia in the pivotal role of Michael's beloved daughter, Mary. The actress doesn't have the depth required, and in some scenes other actors can be noticed "holding back." It is Sofia's weakness which diminishes somewhat the power of the film's ending. Andy Garcia, however, as Michael's illegitimate nephew, is exceptional as a low-level criminal with loftier ambitions. (Remastered in THX and available letterboxed and pan & scan) ★★★ $24.99

The Gods Must Be Crazy

(1980, 89 min, South Africa, Jamie Uys) All this fuss over a Coke bottle? After viewing it, one can see why this small-budget gem became such a huge international hit. On a peaceful day in Botswana's Kalahari desert, a Coca-Cola bottle falls to earth and disrupts the life of a simple tribe of Bushmen. Their efforts to return the bottle from whence it came unleashe a tide of savage satire and slapstick comedy from which virtually no one escapes. ★★★½ $19.99

The Gods Must Be Crazy II

(1990, 97 min, South Africa, Jamie Uys) It's a shame that this hilarious sequel failed to achieve the box-office success of its predecessor; for *Crazy II* contains the same elements as the original including a propensity for sure-fire slapstick comedy. Bushman Xixo — played by N!xau, retaining the charm and genial sincerity which made the original such a success — returns, here having a series of misadventures searching for his two missing children. Meanwhile, a temperamental New York anthropologist is stranded in the desert with a local naturalist, and she's having a doozy of a time with the wildlife. Director Uys again displays a talent for precise choreographed visual comedy. ★★★ $19.99

Gods of the Plague

(1969, 92 min, West Germany, Rainer Werner Fassbinder) Deep in the backstreets of a sunless Munich, a den of sleazy gangsters and their molls stealthily plot their big heist only for it to end in betrayal and failure. Fassbinder has created a stunning and knowing tribute to film noir and the American gangster genre, combining swift camerawork with a suspenseful story line. Starring Hanna Schygulla, Harry Baer and Margarethe von Trotta. (German with English subtitles) ★★★½ $19.99

The Godson

(1967, 86 min, France, Jean-Pierre Melville) Drained of bright colors and told in a crisp, tight style, this definitive hard-boiled gangster film features Alain Delon as an emotionless and solitary hired killer whose airtight alibi for one of his jobs is slowly unraveled by authorities after he makes the mistake of falling in love. A classic tale of a man whose existence is as rigid, romantic and outdated as that of the Japanese samurai. (Dubbed) ★★★

Godunov: The World to Dance In

(1983, 90 min, Peter Rosen) This compelling docudrama is a portrait of Alexander

Godunov, from his fatherless childhood to his defection and subsequent superstardom in the West. Featuring dazzling performances, including a duet with Cynthia Gregory. ★★★ $19.99

Godzilla, King of Monsters

(1956, 80 min, Japan, Inoshiro Honda, Terry Morse) This original A-bomb allegory, and the first and best Godzilla film to date, features surprisingly effective special effects for its time, and a dark and somber tone absent from its many sequels. Godzilla, not one of the good guys in this original incarnation, rises from the sea belching radioactive breath. The inadvertent by-product of a nuclear accident, he wreaks total destruction at every turn, including the entire city of Tokyo. Edited for U.S. consumption, this version features spliced-in sequences with Raymond Burr as a reporter (named Steve Martin!) covering the events. The original Japanese release (which had a brief theatrical stint here in the early '80s) is unfortunately not yet available on video. ★★½ $9.99

Godzilla vs. Biollante

(1989, 105 min, Japan, Kazuki Ohmori) Disappointing entry in the Godzilla series pits the monster hero against a giant plant creature constructed from his own radioactive blood cells. The film falls short of the loony campiness of other Godzilla films, but worst of all, Godzy barely ever roars. ★★ $19.99

Godzilla vs. the Sea Monster

(1966, 88 min, Japan, Jun Fukuda) Godzilla's on our side now (but he's still as clumsy as ever), fighting a giant shrimp that's really just a prawn in a plot to take over the world. ★★ $9.99

Godzilla vs. the Smog Monster

(1972, 87 min, Japan, Yoshimitsu Banno) Our evil ways catch up with us when the smog monster comes to dine on our dumps and draining ditches. After becoming intoxicated on factory fumes, he gets belligerent and starts biting the hands that feed him — smashing up the place and ignoring our polite entreaties to stop. So Godzilla bounces the bore out. ★★ $19.99

Goin' South

(1978, 109 min, US, Jack Nicholson) Nicholson is a horse thief who is saved from the noose by a little-known law, giving him the opportunity to marry a widow (Mary Steenburgen) and take up the habits of a good prairie husband. However, he soon finds his past returning to haunt him. Christopher Lloyd, John Belushi and Veronica Cartwright also star. This is Nicholson's second directorial effort, the first being the little-known Drive, He Said. ★★★ $14.99

Goin' to Town

(1935, 71 min, US, Alexander Hall) Here's a sight to behold: A sequined Mae West dressed all in white riding a horse across the fruited plains. And darn if she doesn't look natural doing it. Mae plays a saloon singer who agrees to marry an oil tycoon/cattle rustler. When he gets killed on their wedding day, she inherits everything, and soon falls for a British earl who snubs her crude Western ways. So, the widow West heads to Buenos Aires for a crash course in society manners, horseracing and love. West's screenplay is peppered with her patented

one-liners, and she spices up the mix with a little murder and a few romantic twists. An enjoyable concoction with West in her element as a rustic flirt trying to make good. ★★★ $14.99

Going in Style

(1979, 96 min, US, Martin Brest) George Burns gives a rich performance as a senior citizen who talks his buddies Art Carney and Lee Strasberg into helping him rob a bank because they feel bored and forgotten. While the humorous sequences are sitcom funny, it's the tragic subtext about growing old in America which gives this small comic gem an unexpected resonance. ★★★½ $14.99

Going My Way

(1944, 130 min, US, Leo McCarey) Bing Crosby gives his most winning performance (it even won him an Oscar) as Father O'Malley, whose progressive ideas don't go down well with the street punks or the old parish priest. Bing sings "Swing on a Star," and there are plenty of familiar faces, including Oscar winner Barry Fitzgerald, Gene Lockhart and William Frawley. ★★★ $14.99

Going Places

(1974, 117 min, France, Bertrand Blier) Blier's energetic account of two loutish drifters who steal, molest and terrorize until they encounter a beautiful ex-convict who undermines their entire lifestyle. A weirder French film you will never see. Starring Patrick Dewaere, Gérard Depardieu, Miou-Miou and Jeanne Moreau. (Available dubbed and in French with English subtitles) ★★★ $59.99

Gold Diggers of 1933

(1933, 96 min, US, Mervyn LeRoy) Classic Berkeley backstage musical. Here it's Joan Blondell, Ruby Keeler, Dick Powell, Aline MacMahon, Guy Kibbee and Ginger Rogers putting on a Broadway show. Songs include "We're in the Money" (in pig Latin!) and "Forgotten Man." Berkeley's production numbers are sensational. ★★★½ $19.99

Gold Diggers of 1935

(1935, 95 min, US, Busby Berkeley) That "let's put on a show" gang is back, here in the forms of Dick Powell, Adophe Menjou, Gloria Stuart, Alice Brady and Glenda Farrell. Berkeley's production numbers are first-rate, and included is the remarkable "Lullabye of Broadway" (one of the great musical sequences of all time). ★★★ $29.99

The Gold of Naples

(1954, 107 min, Italy, Vittorio De Sica) Departing from his neorealist tradition, De Sica constructs four vignettes ranging from the comic to the tragic in this poignant, perceptive slice of Napleanic life. A 20-year-old Sophia Loren stars as a philandering wife who loses her wedding ring during a rendezvous with a lover and convinces her baker husband that she lost it in a pizza. Toto stars in another episode as a meek husband whose house is occupied by an arrogant racketeer. De Sica himself is featured in a third story of an avid gambler who is outsmarted in cards by an eight-year-old and the final segment has Silvana Mangano as a prostitute who enters into a strange marriage with a mentally unbal-

anced young man. (Italian with English subtitles) ★★★ $59.99

The Gold Rush

(1925, 100 min, US, Charlie Chaplin) This is quintessential Chaplin. This immortal comedy features some of the Little Tramp's most memorable routines including the dance of the dinner rolls and the shoe-eating sequence. Charlie plays a lone prospector, adrift in the frenzy of the Klondike gold rush. ★★★★

The Golden Boat

(1993, 90 min, France/US, Râúl Ruiz) Ruiz, the Paris-based Chilean expatriate, has developed a strong European cult following with his many uniquely told tales of passionate living. Blending surrealism with avant-garde deconstructionism and dreamlike images, Ruiz's films almost defy logical description. The barebones outline of this, his first English-language film, follows a young philosophy student and part-time rock critic for The Village Voice, Israel, who encounters an older homeless man, Austin, in a back alley on the Lower East Side. Before Israel can respond, Austin stabs himself and, while bleeding profusely, leads Israel on a bizarre journey through the streets of New York, all in a quest to find his true love, a Mexican soap opera star. Along the way, philosophy is discussed even while Austin compulsively kills several people — all of whom seem to come back to life in future scenes. Beguilingly obscure yet strangely wonderful, this black comedy features many interesting cameos including Annie Sprinkle, Barbet Schroeder and Jim Jarmusch. ★★★ $59.99

Golden Boy

(1939, 99 min, US, Rouben Mamoulian) Clifford Odets' searing story of a youth (William Holden in his breakthrough role) torn between his love of music and his boxing career. Also with Barbara Stanwyck and Lee J. Cobb. ★★★ $9.99

The Golden Child

(1986, 93 min, US, Michael Ritchie) A movie that doesn't attempt to go beyond a finger-paint-user's idea of humor; but if you like Eddie Murphy, you may find it amusing. Jokes involve "boogers" and Pepsi cans, while Eddie looks for the "Golden Child," the kidnapped savior of the world. ★ $14.99

The Golden Coach

(1952, 105 min, Italy, Jean Renoir) Renoir peppered this luxuriant fable set in 19th-century South America, which follows the three transient loves of a tempestuous actress (forcefully played by Anna Magnani), with an uncharacteristic tone of biting irony. Renoir joyfully expresses his love for the theater and theater life as he follows the "comedia dell'arte" through their lives and loves. As with Elena and Her Men and The River, this film is a fine example of "late Renoir." (Filmed in English) ★★★½ $59.99

Golden Demon

(1953, 91 min, Japan, Koji Shina) A spectacular look at the destructive effect of wealth in today's society. A poor young man falls in love with a middle-class woman but is rejected. Determined not to be hurt again, the man com-

Gone with the Wind

mits his life to the ruthless pursuit of wealth. After escaping a loveless marriage, the woman seeks out her old love but finds a changed person. A sensitive yet hard-hitting love story. (Japanese with English subtitles) ★★★

The Golden Voyage of Sinbad

(1974, 105 min, GB, Gordon Hessler) A delightful rehashing of the adventures of Sinbad the sailor, which features some of Ray Harryhausen's finest "dynamation" effects including a ship's figurehead that comes to life and, even more impressive, a six-armed statue that does battle with Sinbad. A wonderfully entertaining throwback to the days of Saturday afternoon matinees. ★★★ $14.99

Golden Years

(1991, 232 min, US) Stephen King tells the story of Harlan Williams, an elderly janitor who is accidentally exposed to a strange green dust in an explosion at a government defense lab. Shortly thereafter, he begins going through a series of mysterious changes which slowly turn him younger. Following this, of course, the big bad Feds show up and will stop at nothing to capture his newfound lab rat. Keith Szarabajka plays the first aged, then youthful hall sweeper. Frances Sternhagen is solid in support as his wife. Phillip Lenkowsky puts in a hilarious turn as a janitor-turned-lab assistant. Originally seven hours on TV, the continuity suffers somewhat in this heavily edited edition. ★★★ $24.99

Goldeneye

(1995, 127 min, GB, Martin Campbell) Pierce Brosnan has some pretty big shoes to fill with this, the 18th film to showcase the exploits of a certain "Bond, James Bond" — and those shoes fit like a glove. This time, it's personal as Bond goes after an "00" double agent (Sean Bean) who plans to topple the world economy using a pirated weapons satellite (codename: Goldeneye). There are, of course, the usual death-defying stunts, beautiful women and arch humor — series veteran Desmond Llewllyn as Q, the harried weapons master, is particularly funny. But Brosnan makes the film his own, creating a Bond who is more mature

and introspective than his predecessors. His 007 is more interested in fighting than loving, much to the dismay of villainous vixen Famke Janssen, and the film's violence is a bit more relentless as compared to the previous adventures. Noted British stage actress Judi Dench is M, the new head of M16. (Available letter-boxed and pan & scan) ★★★ $19.99

Goldfinger

(1964, 111 min, GB, Guy Hamilton) Her majesty's finest, Agent 007, combats the wicked genius with the Midas touch and his evil Asian henchman with the deadly derby. The third in the Bond series, complete with scads of gadgetry, loads of lovelies and Sean Connery in top form. One of the very best of the series. ★★★½ $14.99

The Goldwyn Follies

(1938, 120 min, US, George Marshall) George Gershwin's last film score highlights this okay musical about a Hollywood producer who searches for a "typical" moviegoer to judge his work. With Adolphe Menjou, Andrea Leeds and the Ritz Brothers. ★★ $19.99

The Golem

(1920, 75 min, Germany, Paul Wegener & Carl Boese) A classic tale of a rabbi who conjures up a cannibalistic monster of Jewish legend in order to avert an oppressive policy against Jews in Hapsburg. But once brought to life, the Golem breaks free from his master's spell and rampages through the town, causing havoc that appears to be beyond anyone's ability to stop. (Silent) ★★★½ $39.99

Gone with the Wind

(1939, 222 min, US, Victor Fleming) This is the big one! Based on Margaret Mitchell's epic Civil War novel, Vivien Leigh stars as Scarlett O'Hara, a beautiful, spoiled and determined Southern belle who meets her match in Rhett Butler (Clark Gable), a dashing and rebellious charmer. Also starring Olivia deHavilland and Leslie Howard. Academy Awards for Best Picture, Actress (Leigh), and eight others. *GWTW* has myriad characters, wonderful production values, and is the definitive example of old, big-studio moviemaking. Little wonder this movie has been woven into the fabric of our culture. ★★★★ $89.99

Gonza the Spearman

(1986, 126 min, Japan, Masahiro Shinoda) Filmed with stunning visuals, Shinoda's (*Double Suicide*) period piece is a vivid and engrossing account of what life was like during the samurai era. Gonza, a handsome but overly ambitious samurai, breaks off his engagement with a woman in order to better his position by marrying the clan leader's daughter. The brother of Gonza's former fiancée, a fellow lanceman, vows revenge for the insult to his sister and family. A classic tale of love, honor and tragedy that won the Silver Bear Award at the Berlin Film Festival. (Japanese with English subtitles) ★★★ $79.99

The Good Earth

(1937, 138 min, US, Sidney Franklin) Pearl S. Buck's novel of peasant farmers in China has been brilliantly brought to the screen to create one of the 1930s greatest films. In two mag-

nificent performances, Paul Muni and Oscar winner Luise Rainer portray Wang and O-Lan, respectively, who at the story's beginning are first introduced to each other on their wedding day. In a gripping series of events, they endure famine, revolution, the death of a child, betrayal, life as refugees and, in a classic sequence, a swarm of locusts. The mixing of Asian and Anglo cast members surprisingly detracts nothing from the film's power and credibility. This is due, in no small amount, to Muni and Rainer's portrayals. Franklin's direction is self-assured and his epic stagings of a mass exodus, political riot and the locust swarm are superbly juxtaposed by deeply effecting scenes of interpersonal relationships and familial conflict which would resonate in any language or culture. ★★★★ $19.99

Good Evening, Mr. Wallenberg

(1990, 115 min, Sweden, Kjell Grede) An ambitious, compelling drama, *Good Evening, Mr. Wallenberg* is based on the true-life experiences of Raoul Wallenberg (Stellan Skarsgord), a Swedish diplomat who attempted to save tens of thousands of Jews in Nazi-occupied Budapest near the end of WWII. Encountering Nazi bureaucrats, Hungarian collaborators and civilian hostility, Wallenberg's difficult path is detailed, and the story in unflinching honesty depicts the brutal, anti-Semitic realities of the time. Though the film may lack the epic feel and fluid narrative of the similarly themed *Schindler's List*, a wrenching power exists all the same. (Swedish, German and Hungarian with English subtitles) ★★★ $19.99

The Good Father

(1987, 90 min, GB, Mike Newell) Anthony Hopkins gives a multi-layered performance as a recently separated father exorcising his own demons through an acquaintance's custody battle. An intelligent, adult, considered exploration of male-female relationships and the dissolution of marriage. Fine support by Jim Broadbent and Simon Callow and nicely directed by Newell. ★★★

The Good Fight

(1982, 98 min, US, Noel Buckner, Mary Doe & Sam Sills) A stirring portrait of the men and women who made up the Lincoln Brigade, a group of 3,200 Americans who fought for the Spanish Republic against Franco and his fascist supporters in Spain's civil war. Told through newsreel footage, a Hollywood film and interviews with Brigade veterans, this absorbing documentary fills in the gaps of our social history and celebrates the passion and idealism of these real-life heroes. ★★★½ $69.99

A Good Man in Africa

(1994, 93 min, GB, Bruce Beresford) After such films as *White Mischief* and *The Kitchen Toto*, two of the better stories exploring British imperialism in Africa, it would take a film of great skill and freshness to expound on the theme. Unfortunately, *A Good Man in Africa* is not that film. Not entirely, anyway. The affable Colin Friels stars as a British diplomatic attache whose disastrous attempts to keep order backfire at every turn. A good support-

G

ng cast includes Louis Gossett, Jr. as a presidential nominee needing a rather dishonest favor from Friels; Joanne Whalley-Kilmer as Gossett's wife; John Lithgow as an uproariously pompous dignitary; and Sean Connery as a dedicated doctor and the titular good man. *A Good Man* is low-key and often flat, but it also contains many small charms at the most unexpected moments. ★★½ $94.99

Good Morning Babylon

(1987, 115 min, Italy, Paolo & Vittorio Taviani) The Taviani brothers' first film in English is a modern fable which chronicles the ambitions, dreams and loves of two brothers. Gifted artisans, the brothers leave their native Italy, emigrate to America and eventually work on the making of the sets for D.W. Griffith's *Intolerance*. Vincent Spano and Joaqui De Almeida are the siblings (and alter egos of the directors) in this funny yet poetic homage to the magic of the cinema. (Filmed in English) ★★★ $79.99

Good Morning, Vietnam

(1987, 120 min, US, Barry Levinson) Robin Williams sparkles as Adrian Cronauer, a real-life radio D.J. who found himself plunked down against his will in Saigon, 1965. What Levinson's film lacks by way of plot is more than made up for by Williams' sensational talents – his on-air scenes are pure comic genius. Forest Whitaker and Bruno Kirby co-star. ★★★ $9.99

The Good Mother

(1988, 103 min, US, Leonard Nimoy) Diane Keaton's remarkable performance elevates this involving melodrama about a divorced mother who begins an affair with a free-spirited artist; her ex-husband retaliates with child abuse charges. Liam Neeson, Jason Robards and James Naughton also star. ★★★ $9.99

Good Neighbor Sam

(1964, 130 min, US, David Swift) Jack Lemmon proves his mastery of physical comedy when he agrees to help the woman next door claim her inheritance by posing as her husband – much to his wife's annoyance. With Edward G. Robinson and Dorothy Provine. ★★½ $9.99

Good Night Michelangelo

(1989, 91 min, Canada, Carlo Liconti) A charming and offbeat film, this gentle comedy follows the lives of a family of immigrants in 1957 Toronto. Narrated by six-year-old Michelangelo, the film details the struggles, loves and misadventures of this boisterous family as they try to assimilate into the new English-speaking world. The family includes a grumpy grandfather, a hot-blooded widowed mother who rules with an iron fist, and an amorous Italian boarder, mischievously played by Giancarlo Giannini. Told with humor and a knowing nod to the family's difficulties, this Italian *Parenthood* is a pleasant portrait of a family in transition. (English language) ★★★

Good Sam

(1948, 128 min, US, Leo McCarey) A good samaritan (Gary Cooper) has the knack for getting into trouble with each good deed he performs. A minor comedy from the other-

wise sterling career of writer-director McCarey. Also stars Ann Sheridan. ★★ $19.99

The Good Son

(1993, 87 min, US, Joseph Ruben) Director Ruben follows his muddled box-office hit *Sleeping with the Enemy* with this equally contrived thriller, which still should manage to give a few chills to those who enjoyed his previous work. Playing against his *Home Alone* image, Macaulay Culkin reinterprets "The Bad Seed" for the '90s; he's a cherub-faced demon who delights in killing dogs, instigating a 12-car pileup and threatening the life and limb of his loved ones. Elijah Wood plays the young cousin who comes to live with Culkin and his family, and who soon discovers the truth about the little psycho. It is Wood's performance which gives the film its interest. A startling ten-minute ending sequence is evidently the film's only excuse for being made. ★★ $9.99

The Good, the Bad and the Ugly

(1967, 161 min, Italy/Spain, Sergio Leone) The final installment of the trilogy about "The Man with No Name" finds Clint Eastwood reluctantly teaming up with low-life Eli Wallach in order to beat bad guy Lee Van Cleef to a buried fortune in Confederate gold. The film rambles along like the shaggy dog tale that it is, always visually interesting, often very funny, with *the* classic film score by Ennio Morricone. ★★★½ $29.99

The Good Wife

(1987, 97 min, Australia, Ken Cameron) Rachel Ward, Bryan Brown and Sam Neill star in this pre-WWII drama set in a small Australian town. The story concerns the secretive love affair between an unhappily married woman and a handsome and attentive stranger. ★★½

Goodbye, Columbus

(1969, 105 min, US, Larry Peerce) It's Richard Benjamin (in his film debut) saying so long to university life when he falls for Jewish American Princess Ali MacGraw in this, the best adaptation of any of Phillip Roth's books. ★★★ $14.99

The Goodbye Girl

(1977, 110 min, US, Herbert Ross) Snappy Neil Simon comedy with Marsha Mason as a divorced mother who is forced to share her apartment with an egocentric actor (Richard Dreyfuss in his Oscar-winning role). Quinn Cummings deftly plays Mason's sharp-tongued young daughter. ★★★ $14.99

Goodbye, Mr. Chips

(1939, 115 min, US, Sam Wood) Extraordinary adaptation of James Hilton's novel about the life of a dedicated, shy schoolmaster. Robert Donat gives a remarkable Oscar-winning performance as Chips, and Greer Garson is exceptional in her film debut as his young wife. One of the greatest achievements of the incredible film year of 1939. ★★★★ $19.99

Goodbye, Mr. Chips

(1969, 151 min, US, Herbert Ross) Peter O'Toole's likable performance highlights this uninspired musical remake of the 1939 classic Robert Donat-Greer Garson drama, based on

the James Hilton novel. Also with Petula Clark, Michael Redgrave and Sian Phillips. ★★ $19.99

Goodbye, New York

(1985, 90 min, Israel, Amos Kollek) The comic talents of Julie Hagerty are fully realized in this charming Israeli comedy about a ditsy New Yorker who leaves her unfaithful husband, quits her job and flees to Paris. Fate intervenes, however, as she oversleeps at the Paris stopover and ends up, without luggage or money, in the totally foreign land of Israel. She is soon befriended by a good-natured but lascivious cab driver who guides her through comic misadventures and her second education in the Holy Land. (Filmed in English) ★★★

The Goodbye People

(1986, 104 min, US, Herb Gardner) Bittersweet tale of a 70-year-old retiree (Martin Balsam) who decides to re-open his Coney Island beachfront hot dog stand; aided by his estranged daughter (Pamela Reed) and an eccentric artist (Judd Hirsch). Based on director Gardner's play. ★★ $14.99

Goodbye Pork Pie

(1981, 105 min, New Zealand, Geoff Murphy) A wild adventure comedy about two young men and their thousand-mile excursion in a stolen car. As the police follow in hot pursuit, the two become newsmedia heroes as a result of their reckless escapades. ★★★ $69.99

GoodFellas

(1990, 146 min, US, Martin Scorsese) Ray Liotta delivers a gritty and charismatic performance as a young mob functionary in this based-on-fact, superbly crafted and high-energy look at the rise and fall of a mob insider. The film brilliantly illustrates the seduction of Liotta's early initiations, the headiness of his status as "goodfella" and the hellishness of his inevitable fall from grace. As Liotta's cold-blooded comrades, Robert De Niro and especially Oscar-winner Joe Pesci are mesmerizing; and Lorraine Bracco sparkles as Liotta's tough-as-nails wife. Scorsese has created a modern masterpiece, as well as one of the finest gangster movies of all time. ★★★★ $19.99

A Goofy Movie

(1995, 76 min, US, Kevin Lima) Goofy makes his big screen debut, but unfortunately his first starring vehicle is this mediocre entry which really misses its audience. While aimed at the under-ten set, the story line is about the preteen trials and tribulations of Goofy's son, Max. The youth's first date is ruined by his well-meaning father who decides at that moment they need a "bonding" cross-country trek together. The rest of the film focuses on Max's rebellion towards his father's parental overtures. Though the animation, story and musical numbers are only average, wee ones may enjoy the film, though it certainly lacks the appeal of other Disney titles. ★★ $22.99

The Goonies

(1985, 111 min, US, Richard Donner) This fun-filled if loud children's adventure follows the comic exploits of a group of adolescents who go searching for buried treasure to save their parents' homes. Youthful cast includes Sean Astin, Josh Brolin, Corey Feldman,

Martha Plimpton, Kelli Green, and Anne Ramsey as the head of the ruthless gang on their trail. ★★½ $19.99

Gore-Gore Girls

(1972, 70 min, US, Hershell Gordon Lewis) Lewis goes all out to gross out in his final and goriest film. Henny Youngman (!) is the owner of a nightclub whose dancers are butchered in various gruesome fashions. Graphic (and relatively lengthy) mutilation sequences made this one of the first films ever to receive an X rating for violence. ★

The Gorgeous Hussy

(1936, 102 min, US, Clarence Brown) Other than its catchy title, the best that can be said for this opulent costumer is that it features superior production values. Joan Crawford stars as Peggy Eaton, the infamous "Belle of Washington" during President Andrew Jackson's administration. The film traces her rise in political circles, and the scandal she caused, though it's not as interesting as it sounds. ★½ $19.99

Gorgo

(1961, 78 min, GB, Eugene Lourie) When Toho Studios made a knock-off of director Lourie's *The Beast from 20 Thousand Fathoms* called *Godzilla*, he decided to return the favor by making this man-in-a-rubber-monster-suit film, to much better results. When a traveling circus captures a giant prehistoric beast off the Scottish Sea and exhibits it in London, it becomes an instant smash – until mom comes looking for Jr. ★★½ $14.99

The Gorgon

(1961, 83 min, GB, Terence Fisher) This Hammer film has all the talent in their stable: Peter Cushing, Christopher Lee and Barbara Shelley under the steady hand of director Fisher. Cushing's ward has a problem: this beauty's a Medusa, first breaking men's hearts, then turning them into stone – literally. ★★½ $9.99

Gorillas in the Mist

(1988, 129 min, US, Michael Apted) Sigourney Weaver's outstanding performance is the heart and soul of this well-produced biography on anthropologist Dian Fossey. The story covers the nearly 20 years Fossey dedicated to the

mountain gorillas of central Africa, from her arrival on the continent as a census taker to her unprecedented work with the animals to her tragic murder. Bryan Brown also stars as a *National Geographic* cinematographer (and Fossey's lover) whose films on the naturalist's accomplishments helped bring about her international renown. Efficient, commanding direction from Apted. ★★★ $19.99

Gorky Park

(1983, 126 min, US, Michael Apted) Three corpses are found in Moscow's Gorky Park with their faces removed to make identification nearly impossible. But the key word here to Russian policeman William Hurt is "nearly." And he sets out to solve the murders with Sherlockian reasoning. Lee Marvin is chillingly effective as a shady American businessman. A taut and clever thriller from the pen of Martin Cruz Smith, with gritty yet stylish direction from Apted. ★★★½

Gospel

(1983, 92 min, US, David Leivick & Fred A. Ritzenberg) A rousing, non-stop musical assault on your senses and soul. Fully capturing the excitement generated by gospel music, this exhilarating concert performance film features The Mighty Clouds of Joy, James Cleveland, Walter Hawkins, The Clark Sisters and more. ★★★ $39.99

The Gospel According to Al Green

(1984, 90 min, US, Robert Mugge) Philadelphia filmmaker Mugge directed this exultant, fascinating portrait of pop superstar-turned Pentacostal preacher extraordinaire Al Green. Throughout his career, Green has incorporated both a spirituality and a sensuality that moves audiences to ecstatic heights of joy and release. Mugge captures Green both in concert and on the pulpit, hypnotizing his audience with the intensity and majesty of his performance. His dedication and desire to help his audience find happiness on this planet give this spine-tingling documentary an electric, revelatory energy rarely captured on film. ★★★½ $24.99

The Gospel According to St. Matthew

(1964, 135 min, Italy, Pier Paolo Pasolini) Dedicated to the memory of Pope John XXIII, Pasolini's remarkable film is a modern interpretation of the last days of Christ. Using non-professionals and filmed in a realistic, pseudo-documentary fashion in the arid regions of Calabria in southern Italy, the film depicts Jesus Christ as a man of the people and a revolutionary, fighting the social injustices of the time. Yet despite his faithful use of the scriptures, the film is imbued with a Marxist ideology, a situation which produced confused acclaim from Church leaders. (Available dubbed and in Italian with English subtitles) ★★★★ $29.99

Gospel According to Vic

(1986, 95 min, Scotland, Charles Gormley) Tom Conti and Helen Mirren star in this irreverent Scottish comedy. Conti brings his prototypical comic flair to the role of Father Cobb, a chaplain who is two miracles short of suc-

cessfully pleading Sainthood for a certain Blessed Edith. ★★★ $79.99

The Gospel at Colonus

(1986, 90 min, US, Lee Breuer) Based on the stage musical, this is an exhilarating gospel version of Sophocles' "Oedipus at Colonus," following the journey of Oedipus and his children to Colonus where the elder has come to die. The energetic cast includes Morgan Freeman, Clarence Fountain and the Five Blind Boys of Alabama, Robert Earl Jones and Carl Lumbly. Music by Bob Telson. ★★★

Gotcha!

(1985, 97 min, US, Jeff Kanew) The very likable Anthony Edwards plays a college kid on European vacation who becomes involved in political intrigue. Linda Fiorentino is very much a part of that intrigue. The film never really connects, but the Edwards-Farentino teaming and some amusing espionage bits compensate. ★★½ $14.99

Gothic

(1987, 90 min, GB, Ken Russell) Russell takes another step beyond the edge with this unusual, dreamlike psychological thriller. Set in the 1800s at Lord Byron's villa, the film depicts one hellish night spent by Byron and his guests, who included P.B. Shelley, his lover Mary, and author Dr. Polidori. The film suggests this fateful evening inspired Polidori to write "The Vampyre" and Mary (who would later marry her paramour) to pen "Frankenstein." Gabriel Byrne, Julian Sands and Natasha Richardson star. ★★★ $14.99

Grace of My Heart

(1996, 115 min, US, Allison Anders) Illena Douglas turns in a captivating performance as a woman searching for professional achievement and personal fulfillment in the fiercely competitive music industry. Opening in 1958 and spanning a decade and a half, the film sweeps across the shifting tides of contemporary popular culture while exploring the life of Edna Buxton (Douglas): naive, overprotected child of privilege with an unexpected reserve of strength. Director Anders successfully captures the look and feel of the varying eras and locales, as well as conveying the nature of the creative process as Edna's songs increasingly reflect her experiences and observations. Edna, dubbed with the stage name Denise Waverly, battles against the not-so-subtle ways women are relegated to secondary status when partnered with men, as well as the societal conventions which restrict artistic self-expression. Spot the subtext in the Bridget Fonda sequence, as she sings lyrics which encode material too inflammatory for the mores of the times. The cast is uniformly strong in their portrayals, and the film is densely packed and leisurely paced, losing focus only briefly during the California segment. *Grace of My Heart* pays equal respect to Edna and the music. ★★★ $94.99

Grace Quigley

(1985, 87 min, US, Anthony Harvey) Katharine Hepburn witnesses a murder committed by Nick Nolte. Appreciating the professional touch, she hires him – to kill her. In the course of making the financial arrangements,

Grace of My Heart

a lucrative enterprise evolves; you might call it a growth industry. A quirky reflection on the perils of old age that fluctuates between farce and pathos, the film could have been better. Strong performances by Hepburn and Nolte seem ill-served by director Harvey. Another edit of the film exists, but not on video. In all this, one question is left unanswered: How can Hepburn still look that good? ★★ $14.99

The Graduate

(1967, 105 min, US, Mike Nichols) Nichols' landmark comedy made stars of Dustin Hoffman and Simon & Garfunkel, and cleared the path for the cinematic concerns of the younger generation. Effortlessly poignant and humorous, the film follows recent grad Benjamin (Hoffman) as he contemplates the future (plastics?) and becomes romantically involved with the sultry Mrs. Robinson (Anne Bancroft in a smashing portrayal) and then her daughter (Katharine Ross). A perceptive and double-edged examination of mores and morals in 1960s America. ★★★★

Graffiti Bridge

(1990, 91 min, US, Prince) Prince wrote, directed and stars in this awful sequel to his 1984 hit *Purple Rain*, detailing the further musical adventures of "The Kid." Look for Morris Day and The Time, along with Mavis Staples, George Clinton and Ingrid Chavez. ★ $14.99

Grain of Sand

(1983, 90 min, France, Promme Meffre) Delphine Seyrig finds herself sinking into a morass of self-doubt when she loses her job after 14 years. Her only hope: locate an old lover from her past now living on the island of Corsica. Meffre makes a striking directorial debut, deftly handling the subtle psychology of a woman unsettled just as she comes to the precipice of encroaching old age. (French with English subtitles) ★★★ $59.99

Grand Canyon

(1991, 135 min, US, Lawrence Kasdan) Writer-director Kasdan turns his discerning eye to the fears and frustrations facing the American society in the '90s. An epic assignment, to be sure, but Kasdan and co-writer and wife Meg have fashioned an insightful and powerful examination of our times. Heading a dream cast, Kevin Kline plays a successful L.A. lawyer whose wrong turn driving home leads to an altercation with a street gang. He is rescued by truck driver Danny Glover. The two men befriend each other, ultimately opening a wide panorama of issues and concerns facing not only them but Kline's wife Mary McDonnell, his best friend, filmmaker Steve Martin, his secretary Mary-Louise Parker, Glover's new girlfriend Alfre Woodard, and his sister and nephew. The film tackles disparate themes such as racism, child abandonment, crime, violence, family mores, just to name a few, and all are handled with sensitivity and thoughtfulness. A beautiful achievement from Kasdan and his excellent ensemble cast. ★★★½ $19.99

Le Grand Chemin

(1987, 104 min, France, Jean-Loup Hubert) Poignant and tender without being maudlin,

this delightful coming-of-age drama tells the story of a sensitive nine-year-old Parisian boy's experiences in the countryside after his mother leaves him with friends for the summer. The couple, a prissy but insolent woman and a rough and tumble drunkard, dote on the boy but incessantly argue as they are constantly reminded of their own child who tragically died a few years before. Rounding out the boy's education and introduction into the grown-up world is a rambunctious and wise-beyond-words tomboy. Remade as *Paradise*. (French with English subtitles) ★★★½ $29.99

Grand Hotel

(1932, 113 min, US, Edmund Goulding) Greta Garbo heads an all-star cast as the melancholic ballerina who "vants to be alone." John Barrymore is the debonair jewel thief who romances her. Also featured in this Academy Award-winning picture are Joan Crawford, Lionel Barrymore and Wallace Beery. ★★★★ $19.99

Grand Illusion

(1937, 111 min, France, Jean Renoir) Renoir's humanistic masterpiece examines the chivalry and codes of honor among French POWs during WWI and their elegant German commandant (Erich von Stroheim), divided by nationality but united by class. A monumental indictment of the savagery of war. (French with English subtitles) ★★★★ $29.99

Grand Prix

(1966, 171 min, US, John Frankenheimer) Oscar-winning Special Effects and Editing highlight this otherwise plodding racing drama about the lives and rivalries of four drivers competing for the World Championship. Cast includes James Garner, Eva Marie Saint, Yves Montand, Toshiro Mifune and Jessica Walter. (Available letterboxed and pan & scan) ★★½ $24.99

Grand Tour: Disaster in Time

(1992, 99 min, US, David Twohy) Science-fiction buffs have reason to cheer in this edge-of-your-seat thriller penned (and directed) by Twohy, one of the legion of screenwriters credited on *Alien3*. Jeff Daniels stars as "the boy who cried aliens" when his quaint New England town is visited by time-traveling "disaster groupies" who get their kicks playing spectator to mankind's greatest tragedies. Nail-biting suspense makes this more than just another tedious morality play in the "Star Trek" mold. ★★★ $14.99

La Grande Bouffe

(1973, 125 min, France/Italy, Marco Ferreri) Director Ferreri, who can be as unrelenting and as vicious as Jonathan Swift, performs an autopsy on a dying class. Marcello Mastroianni, Ugo Tognazzi, Michel Piccoli and Philippe Noiret play four bored businessmen all named after their actors' counterparts. Victims of a terminal case of ennui brought on by the limitations inherent in bourgeois sensibilities, these gourmets become gourmands and decide to end it all by eating themselves to death. Ferreri vividly exposes the desperation among aging males as they attempt to retain their privileged positions — if not in the real world, than in one of their own creation. Though

the director evidences an attention to the scatological detail and an insistence at amplifying events to absurd proportions, these traditional elements of satire only heighten the film's comic possibilities. The big questions are asked, but only little ones are answered — unsatisfying perhaps, but then it's expected in these superficial times. (French with English subtitles) ★★★½ $79.99

La Grande Bourgeoise (The Murri Affair)

(1977, 115 min, Italy, Mauro Bolognini) The repressed lust and violent emotions of the Italian upper classes in turn-of-the-century Rome make this stylish drama of love, murder and betrayal a fascinating drama. Catherine Deneuve marries older man Fernando Rey but her disturbed brother Giancarlo Giannini can't accept them and plots his murder. A lush, wonderfully photographed and costumed period piece. (Available dubbed and in Italian with English subtitles) ★★★

La Grande Guerra

(1959, 118 min, Italy, Mario Monicelli) A pardoned criminal (Vittorio Gassman) becomes an unlikely soldier and together with his friend and fellow conscript, the cowardly Alberto Sordi, they find themselves becoming reluctant heroes in this diverting comedy set during World War I. (Italian with English subtitles) ★★½ $59.99

Grandview, U.S.A.

(1984, 97 min, US, Randal Kleiser) Patrick Swayze, Jamie Lee Curtis, C. Thomas Howell and Jennifer Jason Leigh supply the star power for this series of intertwining tales set in a small Midwestern town, with most of the action centering around the family-run auto derby. ★★ $19.99

The Grapes Of Wrath

(1940, 129 min, US, John Ford) A monumental achievement in American film history, this superb adaptation of John Steinbeck's novel received compassionate and visionary guidance from director Ford, and remarkable contributions from the entire cast. Set during the Depression, the unforgettable story follows the hardships of a poor Oklahoma family, the Joads, who migrate from their dust-bowl farm to California and the promise of a better future. The outstanding cast includes Henry Fonda, in the performance of his career, as the Joads' idealistic son, Tom; Jane Darwell as the stalwart matriarch; John Carradine, Charlie Grapewin and John Qualen. Oscars went to Ford and Darwell. ★★★★ $19.99

The Grass Harp

(1996, 107 min, US, Charles Matthau) An affecting adaptation of Truman Capote's touching novel of life in the South a couple generations ago, *The Grass Harp* is as tranquil as a calm summers' eve, which doesn't always accentuate the story's plucky characters or whimsical situations. Partly autobiographical, Capote's warm tale centers on Collin, an orphaned youth who is sent to live with his two maiden aunts. Sissy Spacek plays Verena, the younger but controlling sister, and Piper Laurie is Dolly, a cheerful, childlike recluse. Much of the episodic story concentrates on

G

The Great Dictator

Collin and Dolly's deep friendship, and the impact an argument between Dolly and Verena not only has on them but on the whole town. One of the strengths of *The Grass Harp* is the fine ensemble cast director Charles Matthau has assembled, including his father Walter in a wonderful turn as Dolly's suitor. Only Edward Furlong is unable to fully flesh out his character as the teenaged Collin, and his central character somewhat diminishes the effect. But Laurie and Spacek are terrific, and the film's gentle motion befits Capote's wistful recollections. ★★★ $99.99

The Grass Is Greener
(1961, 105 min, US, Stanley Donen) Stagey but mostly entertaining drawing room comedy with Cary Grant as an English earl whose jealousy sparks a calamitous weekend affair when wife Deborah Kerr is given the royal treatment by visiting American millionaire Robert Mitchum. Jean Simmons also stars as Mitchum's wife who has her own designs on Grant. Music and lyrics by Noël Coward. ★★½ $19.99

Grease
(1978, 110 min, US, Randal Kleiser) John Travolta and Olivia Newton-John created a small sensation in the late 1970s with this lively version of the long-running Broadway musical. Set in the late 1950s, the film brought Travolta fame as a high school "greaser" who tries to hide his romance with "uncool" new girl Newton-John. Spirited dance numbers and a pleasant score are the main attraction here. Stockard Channing steals the show as the leader of the girl greasers, and it's always nice to see the likes of Eve Arden, Sid Caesar, Joan Blondell and Alice Ghostley. ★★½ $14.99

Grease 2
(1982, 114 min, US, Patricia Birch) Birch, who choreographed the appealing dance sequences in the original *Grease*, directed this very unappealing sequel. Maxwell Caulfield and a young Michelle Pfeiffer are the high school kids in love. Featuring Lorna Luft, Eve Arden and Sid Caesar. ★ $14.99

Greaser's Palace
(1972, 91 min, US, Robert Downey) Downey's irreverent version of the Christ Story set in the Wild West. Our Savior's descent comes in the form of Zoot Suit, a gentle song-and-dance man who arrives by parachute to work miracles and bring peace and harmony to the world. ★★½ $29.99

Great Balls of Fire
(1989, 108 min, US, Jim McBride) A high-energy, slick bio on rock 'n' roll legend Jerry Lee Lewis. Dennis Quaid, in a gutsy though rather one-dimensional performance, plays the rock pioneer, whose life is traced from his meteoric rise on the music scene to his controversial marriage to his teenage cousin to the infamous British tour which nearly ruined his career. Though the film is short on dramatic development, and its characters behave as music biz/Southern stereotypes, it is at its best (and agreeably entertaining) in the superior and razzle-dazzle musical numbers featuring some of Lewis' greatest hits. Winona Ryder deftly plays Lewis' child bride. ★★★ $9.99

The Great Chase
(1963, 77 min, US) Was it really the editors of *Reader's Digest* Condensed Books who took their snips to the Silents, leaving just the good parts of Buster Keaton's *The General*, Douglas Fairbanks' *Mark of Zorro*, D.W. Griffith's *Way Down East*, among others? No annoying intertitles, no unpleasant subplots; just laffs, thrills and excitement in this fun introduction to cinema's formative years. ★★★ $19.99

A Great Day in Harlem
(1994, 60 min, US) It was a beautiful day, that June morning in 1958, when fledgling photographer Art Kane and the film director Robert Benton, then editor of *Esquire*, assembled some of the greatest jazz legends for a group photograph. This marked the first time that many of the greatest drummers, trumpet, piano and sax players were at the same place at the same time where none of them were playing. Milt Hinton and his wife Mona took 8mm home movies of the event and other people took candid photos, never before seen of the gathering. Kane sets the organizational scene while Sonny Rollins, Dizzy Gillespie and Hinton nostalgically recall their view on the event. Included are scenes of these jazz greats performing. Egos can get in the way with performers, but at least the artists discuss the other performers with mutual respect and include an interesting glimpse into the after-hours "party" that took place on the front stoop of 125th St. that summer day. ★★★ $19.99

The Great Dictator
(1940, 128 min, US, Charles Chaplin) Chaplin's first talkie stands as one of his greatest achievements. In this touching and often hilarious political spoof on the Third Reich, Chaplin plays dual roles: a poor Jew from the ghetto and Hynkel, the Hitler-inspired leader. Jack Oakie is hilarious as Italian dictator "Napolini." ★★★★

The Great Escape
(1963, 168 min, US, John Sturges) Blockbuster adventure, based on a true story, about a group of Allied POWs who plan a daring escape from a German camp during WWII. A terrific all-star cast includes Steve McQueen, James Garner, Richard Attenborough, James Coburn, Charles Bronson, Donald Pleasence and David McCallum. (Available letterboxed and pan & scan) ★★★½ $24.99

Great Expectations
(1946, 118 min, GB, David Lean) One of the finest literary adaptations ever put to film, this stunning version of the Charles Dickens classic about a young orphan and his mysterious benefactor stars John Mills, Valerie Hobson, Bernard Miles, Alec Guinness, Jean Simmons and Martita Hunt. Masterful direction by Lean. ★★★★ $14.99

Great Expectations: The Untold Story
(1987, 287 min, Australia, Tim Burstall) At first glance, the viewer might wonder why make another version of this classic Dickens tale? After all, there are already several superb takes on it, not the least of which is the David Lean masterpiece. But a closer look reveals that this Australian spin concerns itself not with the story of young master Pip but, taking a page from Tom Stoppard's "Rosencrantz and Guildenstern Are Dead," centers on Magwitch, the escaped convict who becomes his benefactor. The result is a surprisingly interesting and well-produced drama which in some ways goes farther than the original in pointing out the injustices and inhumanity of Britain's legal and class system of the time. ★★★ $29.99

Great Expectations
(1989, 310 min, US, Kevin Conner) Walt Disney's classy made-for-TV version of Charles Dickens' timeless masterpiece about Pip, the penniless orphan who inherits a fortune from an undisclosed source. Stars include Jean Simmons, John Rhys-Davies, Ray McAnally and a special appearance by Anthony Hopkins as Magwitch. ★★★ $49.99

The Great Gatsby
(1974, 144 min, US, Jack Clayton) Francis Ford Coppola adapted F. Scott Fitzgerald's classic for the screen with Robert Redford as the titular character, a self-made man accepted into Long Island society back in the jazz age. The film captures neither the sensuality nor excitement of the novel, though it's a faithful adaptation. Redford and Mia Farrow as Daisy are well-matched if curiously subdued. With Bruce Dern, Karen Black and Sam Waterston. ★★½ $14.99

The Great Imposter

(1960, 112 min, US, Robert Mulligan) Tony Curtis stars in this true story of Ferdinand Waldo Demara, Jr., who in the 1950s successfully impersonated a monk, a college professor, a prison warden, a naval surgeon and a schoolteacher all before being caught and arrested. Curtis is in good form, though the episodic story only occasionally delivers. ★★½ $14.99

The Great Lie

(1941, 107 min, US, Edmund Goulding) Competent soaper with Bette Davis marrying George Brent, who used to be involved with Mary Astor. He disappears in a plane crash, Mary is pregnant, and Bette then raises the child as her own. Though Bette is her usual indomitable self, the acting honors go to Academy Award winner Astor. ★★½ $19.99

The Great Madcap (El Gran Calavera)

(1949, 90 min, Mexico, Luis Buñuel) One of the most commercial films of his career, Buñuel's engaging and gentle social comedy takes a playful look at the insensitive and irresponsible bourgeoisie, a constant theme he explores in a much more surrealist and biting fashion in *The Discreet Charm of the Bourgeoisie*. Fernando Soler plays a wealthy industrialist who, after a period of drunken carousing and free-spending ways, suffers a heart attack. On recovery, he realizes that his ingratiating and fast-living wife, son and even servants, long accustomed to milking him of money and favors, need a good lesson on the value of money and the need to work. The plot has been done before, but the story remains fresh and lively with Buñuel's satiric touch. (Spanish with English subtitles) ★★★ $79.99

The Great Man Votes

(1939, 72 min, US, Garson Kanin) Through an ironic bit of casting, John Barrymore, whose career was virtually ruined because of his drinking, had his greatest late-career role as an alcoholic given one last chance at redemption. In this wonderful mix of comedy and pathos, Barrymore plays a former professor whose wife's death leads to his drinking and decline. As he fights for custody of his two children, the now-night watchman gets a second chance: His is the deciding vote in the town's mayoral race, making him a very popular constituent. ★★★½ $19.99

The Great McGinty

(1940, 81 min, US, Preston Sturges) In a flea-bitten Mexican cantina, a man who lost it all in a moment of dishonesty hears the story of a man who lost it all the first time he tried to go straight. Brian Donlevy is terrific as McGinty, who goes from hobo to governor to bartender-on-the-lam. Great support from Akim Tamiroff, William Demarest, Muriel Angelus and Louis Jean Heydt. Sturges won an Oscar for the screenplay of this, his first directorial effort. ★★★½ $14.99

The Great Moment

(1944, 83 min, US, Preston Sturges) Joel McCrea plays Dr. W.T.G. Morton, a 19th-century dentist who discovered anaesthesia, but was not credited with such during his lifetime.

Sturges' intriguing biography is an interesting failure, marred mostly by disorienting flashbacks and out-of-place slapstick. ★★ $14.99

The Great Mouse Detective

(1986, 74 min, US, John Musker) Boasting impeccable animation by Disney, this delightful detective story follows the exploits of a spirited murine sleuth. Kids of all ages and adults will enjoy this gentle parody of Arthur Conan Doyle's Sherlock Holmes. Featuring the appropriately villainous voice of Vincent Price. It may not be one of Disney's best, but it will certainly entertain. ★★★

The Great Muppet Caper

(1981, 95 min, GB, Jim Henson) The standard Muppet buffoonery makes for loads of fun as they try to solve a jewel robbery. Miss Piggy steals the show with her musical numbers (so reminiscent of Marilyn in *Gentlemen Prefer Blondes*), but the star-studded list of cameos is still impressive: Charles Grodin, Diana Rigg, John Cleese, Robert Morley, Peter Ustinov and Jack Warden. ★★★ $14.99

The Great Outdoors

(1988, 90 min, US, Howard Deutch) Very minor John Hughes scripted comedy with John Candy planning to spend a relaxing family vacation in the woods, not counting on cumbersome Dan Aykroyd. ★½ $9.99

The Great Race

(1965, 150 min, US, Blake Edwards) Epic-sized comedy from director Edwards about an intercontinental race and of the wacky participants. Though some of the jokes don't make the grade, there are plenty that do. Jack Lemmon and Peter Falk are the bad guys (boo, hiss) up against good guys Tony Curtis and Natalie Wood. ★★★ $19.99

The Great Rock n' Roll Swindle

(1980, 103 min, GB, Julien Temple) Our only question is why the powers that be changed the title of this film from the original *Who Killed Bambi?* The original ad campaign pictured a mutilated fawn and let's face it, what better way could one summarize the insane destructiveness of the legendary Sex Pistols? This fascinating documentary features the lunacy of Johnny Rotten, Sid Vicious, Malcolm McLaren and the rest of the gang. Temple would go on to direct *Absolute Beginners*. Trash and burn was never like this before. ★★★

The Great Santini

(1979, 116 min, US, Lewis John Carlino) An immensely absorbing family drama starring Robert Duvall as a no-nonsense military man whose toughest battle is waged with his troubled son. Outstanding performances by Duvall, Blythe Danner and Michael O'Keefe. ★★★½ $9.99

The Great Train Robbery

(1979, 111 min, US, Michael Crichton) An outlandishly entertaining, knock-your-socks-off caper film from writer-director Crichton, based on an actual incident from the mid-1800s. Sean Connery is well-cast as the mastermind behind a daring train robbery who enlists the help of Donald Sutherland and Leslie-Anne Down in the pursuit of a large

gold shipment. Just try to sit still during the shaving scene! ★★★½ $14.99

The Great Unpleasantness

(1993, 80 min, US, Dorne Pentes) From North Carolina's independent filmmaker Pentes comes this quirky and enjoyable tale of two young, unconventional couples. Not the slick style of Jarmuschian cinema one has come to expect of New York independent cinema, this tale takes a leisurely approach in telling its slight story, spending more time fleshing out its four main characters. Errol and Isabel are two pseudo-punks sharing a rickety house with an often feuding gay couple from South Carolina. When the building is threatened with demolition (from Errol's dad of all people), they are forced to defend their lifestyle and their right to live undisturbed. Although the acting is only fair and the dialogue borders at times on hackneyed, the film's unusual setting and its likably goofy characters make for painless viewing. ★★½ $79.99

The Great Waldo Pepper

(1975, 109 min, US, George Roy Hill) Entertaining comic adventure starring Robert Redford as a daredevil pilot in the Roaring '20s. He's ably assisted by Susan Sarandon and Margot Kidder. Good aerial photography. ★★★ $14.99

A Great Wall

(1986, 100 min, China/US, Peter Wang) The first Chinese/United States co-production is a good natured comedy about the cultural clashes confronting a Chinese-American family when they make their first trip back to the family's hometown in mainland China. (English and Chinese with English subtitles) ★★½ $19.99

The Great White Hope

(1970, 101 min, US, Martin Ritt) James Earl Jones repeats his award-winning stage role in this commanding adaptation. Jones gives a truly magnificent performance as turn-of-the-century boxer Jack Johnson (called Jefferson here), facing as many challenges outside the ring as inside it. Jane Alexander also repeats her stage role in a brilliant portrayal of Johnson's white mistress. ★★★ $39.99

The Great White Hype

(1996, 87 min, US, Reginald Hudlin) A playful if unruly racial and sports farce which at times goes over the edge of tastefulness and at others doesn't go far enough. Playing what could be Don King, Samuel L. Jackson stars as a shameless boxing promoter who engineers a championship bout to save his sagging empire — have a white opponent face his black champion (Damon Wayans), thereby creating a racial climate to the fight. He picks a has-been boxer-turned-rock singer (Peter Berg), and proceeds to try to get the out-of-shape contender into a reasonable facsimile of a fighter. Parts of *Great White Hype* are very funny, especially when lampooning the boxing industry and skewering race relations. But often the film, which was written by Ron Shelton (*Bull Durham, White Men Can't Jump*), is undisciplined and characterizations tend to be too broad. Still, it offers many a laugh, and

Jackson and his fellow cast members are highly spirited. ★★½ $19.99

The Great Ziegfeld

(1936, 176 min, US, Robert Z. Leonard) Lavish musical biography of legendary showman Florenz Ziegfeld. William Powell is a perfect incarnation of Ziegfeld, and Luise Rainer justifiably won an Oscar as his first wife Anne Held. Myrna Loy has a good supporting role as second wife Billie Burke (though she can't duplicate Burke's marvelous vocal quiver). It undeservedly won a Best Picture Oscar (over *Modern Times* and *Mr. Deeds Goes to Town*), but is nevertheless grand entertainment. ★★★½ $29.99

The Greatest Show on Earth

(1952, 153 min, US, Cecil B. DeMille) The title says it all and it's not just fairway hyperbole when Cecil gives the DeMille treatment to the circus. All thrills and spectacle, with about as much of a plot as one would find in any bigtop performance. A huge cast including Jimmy Stewart (as a clown), Charlton Heston, Betty Hutton and Dorothy Lamour keep all three rings busy in this Oscar winner for Best Picture (though it really didn't deserve it over such classics as *High Noon* or *The Quiet Man*). ★★★ $29.99

The Greatest Story Ever Told

(1965, 141 min, US, George Stevens) An all-star cast highlights this glossy though tired biblical epic about the life of Jesus. John Wayne is the Roman centurian overseeing Christ's crucifixion (hope we didn't give away the ending). Max von Sydow plays Jesus; and Charlton Heston, Carroll Baker, Angela Lansbury, Sidney Poitier, Shelley Winters, Ed Wynn and Telly Savalas also star. (Available letterboxed and pan & scan) ★★ $24.99

Greed

(1924, 133 min, US, Erich von Stroheim) Probably the most complete version of this psychological epic we will ever get to see, von Stroheim's masterpiece achieves a depth of characterization through an almost obsessive use of objective correlatives. A love triangle with a gold filling, the film starts high in the mountains and ends on a burning desert. Originally over nine hours long, cut by the studio to just over two, Brownlow & Gill have restored only minutes – but important minutes – including the prologue in the mine (where much of the symbolism is set up). Features another fabulous score by Carl Davis. (Silent) ★★★★ $29.99

Greedy

(1994, 109 min, US, Jonathan Lynn) From the writers of *Parenthood* comes more dysfunctional family humor – and though the results aren't equal to that film, this is nevertheless an appealing, though predictable comedy sporting a wicked bent. Michael J. Fox plays an estranged nephew who returns to the estate of his rich, dying uncle (the crotchety Kirk Douglas) at the insistence of his greedy cousins. The film is at its most entertaining when these vulturous family members (including the devilishly funny Phil Hartman) are at each other's throats in venomous one-upsmanship. Both Fox and Douglas give the tale a

pleasant edge; though this could have been a little more substantial. ★★½ $14.99

The Greek Tycoon

(1978, 112 min, US, J. Lee Thompson) Jacqueline Bisset plays the young widow of an assassinated American president who ends up marrying the richest man in the world (played by a crusty Anthony Quinn). This little-camouflaged story of the Kennedy-Onassis affair offers little of interest save some exotic locations. ★ $14.99

The Green Berets

(1968, 141 min, US, John Wayne & Ray Kellogg) John Wayne appeared in a few turkeys in his long career, but none more than this Vietnam War drama. Made at the infancy of the anti-war movement, this cliché-filled story is amazing in its stupidity, and even failed as a patronage to the titular fighting force. (And yes, that *is* the sun setting in the East!) ★ $19.99

Green Card

(1990, 108 min, US, Peter Weir) The American debut of French superstar Gérard Depardieu is this abortive tale of illegal immigration which co-stars Andie MacDowell. Depardieu, while not in peak form (possibly due to language barriers), carries the film for MacDowell who, though so wonderful in *sex, lies and videotape*, here, unfortunately, falls flat. A definite step backwards for Weir. ★★ $9.99

Green for Danger

(1946, 93 min, GB, Sidney Gilliat) Alastair Sim camps it up as an eccentric Scotland Yard inspector investigating a series of murders in a WWII hospital unit somewhere in the English countryside. Great fun for aficionados of the classic "drawing room/country house" murder mysteries made famous by Agatha Christie. Also starring a young Trevor Howard as one of the suspects. ★★★½ $39.99

Green Grow the Rushes

(1951, 79 min, GB, Derek Twist) Set in postwar rural England, *Green Grow the Rushes* is a film of charming mannerisms which takes its own good time setting up its peculiar story; but once that story is in motion it's unpredictably funny. In his last pre-Hollywood film, a youthfully handsome Richard Burton plays a fisherman involved in the local smuggling of alcohol. Once the scene stumbles roving reporter Honor Blackman, determined to find a story...anywhere. Also on hand for this gentle send-up of bureaucracy are various local authorities and government officials – some in on the scam, others trying to uncover it. Procedure gives way to lunacy as a routine pick-up literally lands itself in the middle of the town for all to see. As a crafty sea captain who handles any situation with a wry retort and deadpan diplomacy, Roger Livesey steals the show. ★★★ $39.99

Green Hornet, the TV Series

(1960s, 90 min, US, William Beaudine) Three episodes of the popular 1960s cult favorite featuring martial arts legend Bruce Lee and, as a bonus, Mr. Lee's original screen test for the show with behind-the-scenes making-of footage from the film *Enter the Dragon*. ★★½ $24.99

The Green Man

(1991, 150 min, GB, Elijah Moshinsky) Adapted from a Kingsley Amis novel, this elegantly sexy thriller/ghost story stars Albert Finney as a charming but overweight, sex-obsessed, middle-aged boozer. Along with his hard-working and all-too-understanding wife, he operates a cottage hotel outside of London that is famous for its reported ghostly visitations. Having used this ghost lore as an entertaining promotional lure, Finney, in a drunken haze, one day hallucinates that he actually sees a real ghost. After talking with the spectre, and doing some biddings for him, our inebriated hero discovers the apparition's evil intentions. A thoroughly entertaining, sophisticated and ghoulish delight. ★★★½ $24.99

The Green Pastures

(1936, 92 min, US, William Keighley & Marc Connelly) First he created a Broadway hit from the writings of Roark Bradford, then Connelly took them to Hollywood in this imaginative fable on how heaven *ought* to be. Rex Ingram stands out in the all-star black cast that includes Eddie Anderson and Oscar Polk. Today, one less generous might see the performances as your typical "Negro" stereotype – if the film made any attempt at realism. But *Green Pastures* has the benevolence of a child dreaming in Sunday school on a warm summer's day. The play's text is actually rather subversive: The Lord God Jehovah finally gets to move from the Old Testament to the New when he learns the meaning of mercy from his most disappointing creation, Man. The film features wall-to-wall spirituals, scored by Erich Wolfgang Korngold and performed by The Hal Johnson Choir. ★★★ $19.99

The Green Room

(1978, 95 min, France, François Truffaut) Truffaut stars as a journalist obsessed with his mortality and the deaths of his WWI comrades. An eerie, atmospheric departure for the director. Based on the writings of Henry James. (French with English subtitles) ★★½ $19.99

The Green Slime

(1968, 89 min, US/Japan, Kinji Fukasaku) An oozing, bubbling, slithering green slime, terrorizing an outer space station, threatens to invade Earth and wipe out civilization. With Robert Horton, Richard Jaeckel and Luciana Paluzzi. Oh, the horror! ★ $19.99

The Green Wall

(1969, 110 min, Peru, Armando Robles Godoy) This acclaimed and much honored drama is a stirring autobiographical tale of an urban family who, in a back-to-nature move, leave the pressures of Lima to hack out a new life in the challenging environment of the Peruvian jungle – the green wall. The film records their successes and obstacles, both natural and man-made, as they become determined to survive in this idyllic but cruel, rich but unyielding world. A film of spellbinding power and beauty. (Spanish with English subtitles) ★★★ $79.99

Greetings

(1968, 88 min, US, Brian De Palma) The talents of De Palma are wonderfully previewed

G

225

in this early directorial effort. Clearly showing his film school background, De Palma structures this witty satire on the '60s counterculture in a series of vignettes. A very young Robert De Niro stars as one of three friends living in New York City. The story follows their resourceful attempts to keep one of them from being drafted. Consistently funny and inventive, the film was co-written by De Palma and Charles Hirsch, and was soon followed by *Hi, Mom!* ★★★ $79.99

Gregory's Girl
(1982, 99 min, GB, Bill Forsyth) Teetering on the brink of adulthood, a gangly Scottish schoolboy discovers the pleasures and perils of infatuation as he falls for a leggy lass on the soccer team. Forsyth's spirited comedy deftly conveys the invigorating effects of young love. ★★★ $14.99

Gremlins
(1984, 106 min, US, Joe Dante) Offbeat humor and garish horror successfully blend together in this box-office hit. Young Zach Galligan gets a pet mogwai (*mog-why*) from his dad. The cute, cuddly animal (after the three rules have been ignored) spawns terrifying gremlins which proceed to destroy the town. Lots of in-jokes and neat special effects; and more importantly, the film demonstrates the many uses for a blender. ★★★ $14.99

Gremlins 2: The New Batch
(1990, 106 min, US, Joe Dante) The original *Gremlins* was a well-made thriller filled with a scathing, dark sense of humor, but much of its horror was too intense for smaller children. In *Gremlins 2*, Dante may have found what he was looking for when he made the first film. This hilarious romp is filled with hysterical self-reference and reaches such heights of absurdity that even little ones know it's all in good fun. This time around, the little nasties are set loose on a New York office tower, The Clamp Centre (aptly modeled, owner and all, after the Trump Plaza). Phoebe Cates and Zach Galligan reprise their roles from the first movie and Christopher Lee puts in a delightfully droll cameo appearance as a crazed genetic researcher. ★★★½ $14.99

Grendel, Grendel, Grendel
(1980, 90 min, Australia, Alexander Stitt) A charming animated fable about Grendel, a sympathetic and philosophic monster — 12 feet tall, green and spotted — who may bite human heads off but is immensely lovable. The film is adapted from John Gardner's popular novel which retells the story of Beowulf from the monster's point of view. Peter Ustinov is the voice of Grendel. The film is imaginative enough to fascinate children yet sophisticated enough to entertain their parents. ★★★

The Grey Fox
(1982, 92 min, Canada, Philip Borsos) Very successful western/character study of convicted stagecoach robber Bill Miner (Richard Farnsworth) who emerges from prison after 30 years to find that the world has left him behind. With robbery his only acknowledged trade, and horses and stagecoaches having

been supplanted by steam engines and trains, what's a guy to do? Though the pacing may be a little slow for some tastes, Farnsworth's portrayal of "the gentleman bandit" is in itself worth the price of rental. Director Borsos ably mixes the inherent humor of the situation (imagine, an 80-year-old train robber) with the pathos of the character to create a film that is touching without being maudlin, and a must-see for film lovers who wax nostalgic about the way movies used to be. ★★★½

Grey Gardens
(1976, 95 min, US, David & Albert Maysles) The lives of Edith Bouvier Beale and her adult daughter Edie are the subject of this moving documentary by the Maysles brothers. Secluded in their decaying Long Island mansion, these two eccentric women allow the morbid spectacle of their private melodrama to simply play itself out in front of the camera. Some have charged the directors with exploitation, although by revealing their subjects so unsparingly they go beyond voyeurism and challenge us to feel true compassion for these lonely human beings. ★★★ $59.99

Greystoke: The Legend of Tarzan
(1984, 129 min, GB, Hugh Hudson) Director Hudson followed his Academy Award-winning *Chariots of Fire* with this liberally adapted retelling of the Edgar Rice Burroughs Tarzan tale. Ralph Richardson is captivating in his swan song performance and Christopher Lambert became an international sex symbol through his portrayal of the Lord of the Jungle. A visual treat and the first Tarzan film to try to bring a sophistication to the tale. ★★★ $14.99

Gridlock'd
(1997, 90 min, US, Vondie Curtis-Hall) A frustration comedy about two junkies who run into bureaucratic roadblocks while trying to get clean, *Gridlock'd* is an engrossing but not quite heady trip. Mesmerizing performances by Tim Roth (slumming it up again in another of his patented transformations) and Thandie Newton (as a sultry overdoser) prevent this potentially downbeat film from becoming a trite antidrug message movie. Yet it is the heartbreaking presence of the late rapper Tupac Shakur that really makes this gritty, dark urban tale valuable. The film's weakest element is the subplot about buddies Spoon (Shakur) and Stretch (Roth) being chased by D-Reper (director Curtis-Hall), a gangster they wronged. But at least this story line puts the rest of *Gridlock'd*'s terrific accomplishments in bold relief. Watching these losers try to gain some self-respect and pull themselves together is amusing in its sheer exasperation. Politicized to a degree, the film makes its points within an interesting and entirely constructive framework. ★★★ $102.99

Il Grido (The Outcry)
(1957, 115 min, Italy, Michelangelo Antonioni) A compelling, slow moving, if not totally successful film about a man and his daughter who wander about aimlessly when their lives are placed in upheaval after the sudden departure of his fiancée. One of director Antonioni's earlier works is a moody look at psychological breakdowns and the lack of per-

sonal communication. (Italian with English subtitles) ★★½ $59.99

Grief
(1993, 92 min, US, Richard Glatzer) With the same quirky, endearing qualities which distinguished producer Yoram Mandel's first film *Parting Glances*, writer-director Glatzer has taken his personal experiences as a writer for TV's "Divorce Court" and fashioned an engaging and funny comedy-drama about friendship, love, bereavement and trash TV. Set during an eventful workweek, the film follows the misadventures of Mark (Craig Chester), a writer for a daytime TV show, as he comes to grips with his co-workers, office politics, an office crush, homophobia and the loss of his lover. Jackie Beat (in a "Divine" bit of casting) plays the show's overbearing but maternal producer. Alexis Arquette also stars as a bisexual employee involved in a secret office romance. Highlighting the film are campy renditions of the TV soap opera, which includes everything from lesbian circus performers to schizophrenic divas. ★★★ $89.99

Grievous Bodily Harm
(1988, 96 min, Australia, Mark Joffe) Don't let the artwork on the video box fool you: this gritty, nicely acted and sexy thriller is very much *not* the grade-C exploitation film which the cover suggests. Colin Friels plays a seedy Sydney newspaper reporter covering the murder of a porn star. Bruno Lawrence is the policeman investigating the case. And John Waters (not the American director), in a first-rate performance, is the killer whose search for his presumedly dead wife leads the three men on an intersecting road to danger. ★★★ $19.99

The Grifters
(1990, 110 min, GB, Stephen Frears) Director Frears' foray into the degenerate world of novelist Jim Thompson is a compelling look at life on the fringe. The story centers around a three-way power struggle between Roy, a small-time grifter, and the two women in his life: his mother and his girlfriend. John Cusack sinks his teeth into the role of Roy with intense complexity. Anjelica Huston dazzles as Roy's mother, Lily, a ruthless swindler who works the odds at the track for the mob. Annette Bening is Myra, Cusack's part-time-prostitute girlfriend, who tries to lure him into the big-stakes world of the "long con." Though theirs is a world filled with mistrust and betrayal, Frears' vision of their lives is tempered with occasional moral twists and underlying humanity. Superbly acted and directed, *The Grifters* is peppered with moments of shocking brutality as it careens toward its tragic conclusion. ★★★★ $9.99

The Grim Reaper (La Commare Secca)
(1962, 89 min, Italy, Bernardo Bertolucci) This rarely seen work, based on a five-page outline by Pier Paolo Pasolini, was 22-year-old Bertolucci's first film as a director. Set in Rome's seedy underworld, the story involves the investigation of the police into the brutal murder of a prostitute. As they go through the list of possible suspects, the police find a beguiling maze of alibis as well as widely different recountings of the events leading up to the

woman's last day. An interesting debut and one that the director admits was made by "...someone who had never shot one foot of 35mm before but who had seen lots and lots of films." (Italian with English subtitles) ★★★ $79.99

Gross Anatomy

(1989, 107 min, US, Thom Eberhardt) *The Paper Chase* goes to medical school in this uneven but appealing comedy-drama. Matthew Modine is in fine form as the initially cocky doctor-in-training who eventually comes to learn about more than just medicine. Christine Lahti does as well as possible in the cliché-ridden John Houseman role of tormentor/supporter. ★★½ $9.99

Grosse Pointe Blank

(1997, 106 min, US, George Armitage) In his most dramatic and grittiest role to date, John Cusack played an unrepentant con artist in *The Grifters*. Now, in his best film since that Stephen Frears classic, Cusack plays another outlaw, as an angst-ridden assassin – happily this dark comedy is played strictly for laughs. And it is funny. Wearing a few hats, including cowriter and coproducer, Cusack plays Martin Blank, a successful hit man who returns to his high school's tenth reunion. There he is reunited with Debi (the very engaging Minnie Driver), his former sweetheart who he stood up on prom night (never to be heard from again). Having federal agents and a rival hit man (Dan Aykroyd) on his trail is nothing compared to the task at hand in making amends with Debi. And then there's the school dance! Like his *Miami Blues*, director Armitage brings his own, wonderful offbeat humor and rhythm to the film, and *Grosse Pointe Blank* revels in these moments of fancy. Cusack has become the master of understatement, and he gives a ripe, humorous performance. Joan Cusack has some funny scenes as a wily secretary, and Alan Arkin is hilariously crusty as Martin's reluctant psychiatrist. ★★★½ $99.99

Ground Zero

(1987, 109 min, Australia, Michael Pattison) Receiving limited theatrical exposure here in the States, this suspenseful political thriller was a critical and commercial hit in its native Australia. Colin Friels (*Malcolm, High Tide*) stars as a cinematographer who unwittingly becomes involved in political intrigue when he searches for the truth about the death of his father – a noted WWII cameraman killed under mysterious circumstances – and in the process uncovers a British secret service cover-up from decades before. A thoroughly satisfying mystery with ample portions of social commentary and suspense. ★★★ $14.99

Groundhog Day

(1993, 103 min, US, Harold Ramis) On the heels of his whimsical turn in *What About Bob?*, Bill Murray tops himself with this extremely funny and surprisingly sweet romantic comedy, with the glib comedian giving one of his most likable and funniest performances. It's Groundhog Day, and cynical TV weatherman Murray has been sent to Punxsutawney, Pa., to cover the festivities for his Pittsburgh station. But there's one small problem: he seems to be reliving the day over and over and over again. Writer-director Ramis and co-writer Danny

Rubin have milked this inventive premise for all it's worth, and they've given some hilarious and irresistible moments to Murray and his merry band of cohorts. Andie MacDowell co-stars as his producer, and she's a good foil for the ever-increasing insanity that surrounds her. ★★★ $14.99

The Group

(1966, 150 min, US, Sidney Lumet) Candice Bergen, Joan Hackett and Hal Holbrook made their film debuts in Lumet's adaptation of Mary McCarthy's novel. Following the intertwining lives of eight graduates of an exclusive women's college, the story examines each character's development as they enter adult life. In much the same way as George Cukor's *The Women*, the film is revelatory in exposing its underlying assumptions regarding women's nature and women's place. It also may be the first film since Cukor's classic to have such a high number of female protagonists as its focal point. While it may sometimes play like a soap opera, it's an interesting document of its time. ★★★ $19.99

Grown Ups

(1980, 95 min, GB, Mike Leigh) Featuring intricate characterizations and plenty of incisive humor, Leigh's comedy-drama, though slowly paced (as are most of Leigh's earlier films), is a meticulous and startling examination of Thatcher's England. The story focuses on a young lower-middle-class couple who have just moved into their first home and are besieged by the wife's batty sister. Not helping matters is the fact that their next-door neighbor is their former high school teacher. Not a lot happens as far as plot is concerned, but Leigh's camera and sly wit make this of interest. ★★★ $29.99

Grumpier Old Men

(1995, 100 min, US, Howard Deutch) Jack Lemmon and Walter Matthau are at it again in this sophomoric though often funny sequel to *Grumpy Old Men* which should definitely tickle the funny bone of those who found enjoyment in the first film. With the two characters now friends and father-in-laws to be, the film introduces a new character to the small Minnesota town to feel their wrath: the impossibly beautiful Sophia Loren. She has taken over the local bait shop and is preparing to turn it into an Italian restaurant. Thus begins a war of wills as dedicated fishermen Lemmon and Matthau turn to every dirty trick in the book to sabotage her opening; that is until Loren turns to her feminine wiles and turns Matthau into putty. As with the first film, many of the jokes are of the sexual and flatulent variety, though in the hands of this very able cast you can't help but laugh out loud. Time may have aged the appearances of the cast, but certainly not their comic timing; and how wonderful to see romantic characters above the age of 50. ★★½ $19.99

Grumpy Old Men

(1993, 105 min, US, Donald Petrie) Jack Lemmon and Walter Matthau reunite for the

Grosse Pointe Blank

first time in 12 years and it's a pleasure to report they've lost none of the chemistry which has made them one of the screen's great comedy teams. And if the script isn't exactly on par with most of their previous works, their bouyant performances make this a lively comedy. They play neighbors who have been feuding since childhood. Into their lives breezes eccentric artist Ann-Margret (looking lovely but none-too-bohemian) and the race is on to capture her affection. Though many of the film's lines are on the Bart Simpson scale ("Eat my shorts," etc.), the entire cast (including Ossie Davis, Daryl Hannah, Burgess Meredith and Kevin Pollak) manages to sustain a playful cheerfulness despite what the title may suggest. ★★½ $14.99

The Guardian

(1990, 93 min, US, William Friedkin) Jenny Seagrove is the nanny from hell, offering newborns to an evil oak in this, Friedkin's first horror tale since *The Exorcist*. The story is ridiculous, the chills are non-existent, and Friedkin's pacing is lethargic. Also with Dwier Brown, who fared much better playing Kevin Costner's father in *Field of Dreams*. ★ $19.99

Guarding Tess

(1994, 98 min, US, Hugh Wilson) Masquerading as a gentle comedy about the tumultuous relationship between a former First Lady and one of her Secret Service agents, *Guarding Tess* quickly deteriorates into an implausible, yawn-provoking thriller without the thrills. Shirley MacLaine is right at home with her role as the widow of a former President – part Nancy Reagan, part bulldog (is that redundant?). She gets particular joy in playfully tormenting agent Nicolas Cage, a serious young man who can't wait for his time to be up. As they bicker and eventually come to understand each other, it becomes clear that someone is out to kill her. Short on laughs and slowly paced, *Tess* is a one-term comedy. ★★ $14.99

The Guardsman

(1931, 83 min, US, Sidney Franklin) Stage legends Alfred Lunt and Lynn Fontanne make a rare screen appearance in this thoroughly entertaining version of Ferenc Molnar's classic comedy. Reprising their acclaimed stage roles, the Lunts play a husband and wife acting team. Certain she is unfaithful to him, Lunt impersonates a dashing soldier and woos his own wife. And to his horror, she acquiesces. Though stage and screen require different acting styles, the very theatrical Lunts adapt to film with great skill. They are wonderful farceurs — what a shame they didn't return to Hollywood. Roland Young is splendid in support as a critic who watches this comedy of errors. Remade as *The Chocolate Soldier* and *Lily in Love*. ★★★★ $19.99

Guerilla Brigade

(1939, 90 min, USSR, Igor Savchanko) Ukrainian filmmaker Savchanko, who was a colleague of both Eisenstein and Dovzhenko, sets this inspirational war drama in his native Ukraine during the Civil War. It poetically depicts the struggles and triumph of the Ukrainian and Russian people as they join together in a struggle for liberty. (Russian with English subtitles) ★★★ $69.99

Guess Who's Coming to Dinner

(1967, 108 min, US, Stanley Kramer) Katharine Hepburn and Spencer Tracy appeared together for the last time in this acclaimed social comedy whose theme of interracial marriage may seem tame by today's standards but in 1967 created quite a stir. Sidney Poitier is wed to Tracy and Hepburn's daughter Katherine Houghton, causing varying reactions from both their families. Hepburn won an Oscar for Best Actress, and this was Tracy's final film. Houghton, incidentally, is Hepburn's real-life niece. ★★★ $14.99

Guido Manuli: Animator

(60 min, Guido Manuli) The equal to Bruno Bozzetto, and his collaborator on *Allegro Non Troppo*, Guido Manuli now has his own collection of his most important short works. From "The Erection" to "S.O.S.," Manuli tackles adult concerns with a wit and charm that bite but don't draw blood. ★★★ $39.99

Guilty as Sin

(1993, 107 min, US, Sidney Lumet) From the director of *Q&A* comes this uneven but trashily entertaining nail-biter starring Rebecca DeMornay and, in a wonderfully hammy performance, movie mannequin doll Don Johnson. DeMornay is well-cast as a career-and-ego-driven defense attorney who bites off more than she can chew when she takes on the case of a sleek lothario (Johnson) accused of killing his wife. To say more would be to give too much away as this murder mystery snakes along with more twists than DeMornay's pistol-driven swagger. Though steamy when it wants to be, *Guilty as Sin* is a little too slick and a little too obvious. ★★ $9.99

Guilty by Suspicion

(1991, 105 min, US, Irwin Winkler) The Hollywood blacklist of the 1950s, though mostly ignored over the years until the 1970s — which produced *The Way We Were* and *The Front* — is the subject of this compassionate drama. Robert De Niro is compelling as a successful film director whose personal and professional lives fall apart when he refuses to cooperate with the House Committee on Un-American Activities. Writer-director Winkler's film is full of remarkable detail, presenting its unsettling, effective story with finesse and subtlety. Annette Bening is very good as De Niro's

wife, and George Wendt, Martin Scorsese and Sam Wanamaker (a real-life victim of the witchhunts) also star. ★★★ $14.99

Gulliver's Travels

(1939, 74 min, US, Max & Dave Fleischer) The Fleischer Studios, home of the brilliant animated shorts of Popeye and Betty Boop, knew that they would have to follow Disney's lead and make feature-length cartoons if they wanted to stay in business. This "adaptation" of Swift's satire retains only the narrative and none of the bite with the introduction of new characters (like "Gabby") and new songs ("All's Well"). The commercial indifference to this film initiated a series of events that culminated in the Fleischers' losing their studio and Disney losing his only serious rival. ★★½ $14.99

Gulliver's Travels

(1996, 175 min, GB, Charles Sturridge) Like Lewis Carroll's "Alice" books, Jonathan Swift's 1726 classic defies translation into other media. Today we would say that the story lacks an "arc," that the targets for his vitriol are now lost to the ages, and his pessimistic outlook is too unsettling in an era when we must all feel each other's pain. Perhaps it should not be surprising that this biting attack against a bulging bourgeoisie has been carved down to a harmless little fairy tale. Who, then, would have imagined a made-for-TV production would be the most faithful and entertaining adaptation yet? And whoever OK'd Ted Danson for the role of the good ship's doctor is either a man of vision or a fool for Q ratings. But Danson does give a very good performance in a very difficult role, wisely choosing not to attempt an English accent. The all-star cast includes such stunt casting as Mary Steenburgen as his wife (she, too, is excellent and *does* do an English accent) and a veteran group of performers. Of course, the *real* stars are the special effects, here supplied by Jim Henson's always reliable people. While some of Swift's rapier raillery gets dulled down a bit, this bygone burlesque still manages to deliver a potent message. ★★★½ $24.99

Gumshoe

(1972, 88 min, GB, Stephen Frears) A capricious comedy about a small-time vaudevillian who's seen too many Bogart films and decides to try some sleuthing of his own. Albert Finney and Billie Whitelaw star in this intriguing little crime story. ★★★ $69.99

Gun Crazy

(1949, 87 min, US, Joseph H. Lewis) After a lifetime being obsessed with guns, a young man (John Dall) meets the love of his life in the form of a sexy, gun-toting carnival performer. The tough-talking dame (Peggy Cummins), a dangerous femme fatale in the most literal sense, craves the good things in life and coaxes the man into a violent series of armed robberies and eventually murder. An entertaining cult favorite, seemingly years ahead of its time, that is stylishly filmed and offers an unflinching peek, in the *Bonnie and Clyde* tradition, at ill-fated fugitives on the lam. ★★★½ $19.99

Gun Crazy

(1992, 97 min, US, Tamra Davis) Like a magnum in a velvet glove, Drew Barrymore blows away this touching love-and-bullets drama which proves that sometimes a cigar really is more than just a cigar, but a gun is just a gun. Barrymore slips comfortably into the role of a trailer park girl with a heart of lead who discovers the joys of gun play when she murders her touchy-feely stepfather (Joe Dallesandro) and falls in love with the world's only male virgin, James LeGros. This made-for-cable remake owes less to the original 1949 classic of the same title than it does to Terence Malick's *Badlands* or Arthur Penn's immortal *Bonnie and Clyde*, but it is destined to stand in its own right as an exceptional entry into the "love-on-the-run" genre. Also starring Ione Skye, Billy Drago and Michael Ironside. ★★★½ $89.99

The Gun in Betty Lou's Handbag

(1992, 89 min, US, Allan Moyle) Disney's take on female empowerment and self-worth won't please very many hard-core feminists, but anyone looking for a lightweight action comedy should take notice. Penelope Ann Miller stars as the title character, a small-town underdog who makes a desperate bid for attention by confessing to a crime she didn't commit. Then things get really out of hand when crime boss William Forsythe comes looking for her. Also stars Eric Thal and perennial favorites Alfre Woodard and Cathy Moriarty. ★★ $19.99

Gunbuster

(1990, 55 min, Japan, Hideaki Anno) This futuristic animated space adventure follows the story of Norika, a young girl who wants to follow in her hero father's footsteps and become a Mecha pilot. Sort of a Nipponized version of Luke Skywalker, Norika must learn to overcome her fears and insecurities, as well as the jealousies of her fellow trainees, in order to master the skills needed to join the elite group of fighter pilots who will defend the Earth Space force against alien invasion. An intelligent and involving story which should entertain all fans. For parents, please note that there is an innocent sequence featuring nudity in a shower. The inventive designs are by Haruhiko Mikimoto, creator of *Macross*. (Japanese with English subtitles) ★★★ $34.99

Gunfight at the O.K. Corral

(1957, 122 min, US, John Sturges) Expert telling of the infamous gunfight between Doc Holliday-Wyatt Earp and the Clanton gang. Burt Lancaster and Kirk Douglas star. Also with Rhonda Fleming, Jo Van Fleet, Earl Holliman and DeForest Kelley. A good companion piece covering the same story is John Ford's classic *My Darling Clementine*. ★★★½ $14.99

The Gunfighter

(1950, 84 min, US, Henry King) A splendid western tale with Gregory Peck in fine form as a former gunfighter unable to rid himself of his past. The look and feel of the film is remarkably authentic, and Peck is ably supported by Helen Westcott, Karl Malden, Millard Mitchell and Ellen Corby. ★★★½ $14.99

Gung Ho

(1986, 111 min, US, Ron Howard) Pleasant comedy examining the cultural clash between Japanese and American workers. Michael Keaton is certainly in his element as a Pennsylvania auto employee who convinces a Japanese interest to reopen his town's closed plant. Made a few years before the numerous headline-making Japanese takeovers. Gedde Watanabe steals the show as a harried Japanese exec. ★★½ $14.99

Gunga Din

(1939, 117 min, US, George Stevens) Three rowdy, hard-fisted British soldiers enjoy adventures in 19th-century India battling the Thugees and dropping wisecracks all the way. Cary Grant, Victor McLaglen and Douglas Fairbanks, Jr. are wonderful foils for each other in this rousing adventure film: the one which all others are judged by. Also with Joan Fontaine as Fairbank's fiancée and the splendid Sam Jaffe as the most famous water carrier in literature. Based on Rudyard Kipling's poem. ★★★★ $19.99

Gunmen

(1993, 97 min, US, Deran Sarafian) A slightly above average adventure which excels in borrowing story lines from many other action films. A renegade DEA agent (Mario Van Peebles) searching for $400 million belonging to a South American drug lord (Patrick Stewart) enlists the help of down-and-out Christopher Lambert, taking the pair on a wild chase with chain-smoking, wise-cracking Denis Leary as their hunter. In spite of the fast pacing and over-the-top performances by Stewart and cast mates Sally Kirkland and Kadeem Hardison, the film is curiously aloof considering its theme and genre. ★★½ $19.99

The Gunrunner

(1984, 92 min, Canada, Nardo Castillo) A then-unknown Kevin Costner stars as an idealist, circa 1926, who tries to finance guns for the Chinese Nationalist Revolution by selling bootleg liquor in Montreal. A very minor gangster saga which is of interest solely because of Costner's early-career appearance. ★ $14.99

The Guns of Navarone

(1961, 157 min, US, J. Lee Thompson) The special effects won an Oscar, and everything else about this fast-moving, involving and action-packed WWII adventure is up to the same standard. Gregory Peck, David Niven and Anthony Quinn head a strong international cast as the Allies go after a strategic Nazi placement of big guns. Based on the novel by Alistair MacLean. (Available letterboxed and pan & scan) ★★★½ $19.99

A Guy Named Joe

(1943, 120 min, US, Victor Fleming) Spielberg liked this film so much he remade it in 1989 as *Always* and used a film clip in 1982's *Poltergeist*. And it's hard to blame him. After being killed in action during WWII, pilot Spencer Tracy is sent back to Earth to look after young Van Johnson, who has become involved with Tracy's ex-girl Irene Dunne.

Okay, so the idea may sound silly, but who's to say it's not true. Pure romantic fluff, this 1940s morale booster may be sticky around the edges, but it certainly has heart. ★★½ $19.99

Guys and Dolls

(1955, 150 min, US, Joseph L. Mankiewicz) The Broadway musical based on Damon Runyon's colorful characters and featuring the music of Frank Loesser comes to the screen in this lavish and entertaining film. The story centers on gambler and rogue Sky Masterson's (Marlon Brando) budding affair with an innocent Salvation Army volunteer (Jean Simmons). A razor-thin Frank Sinatra also stars as a fellow gambler who has to find a site for their crap game. Vivian Blaine is unforgettable as Sinatra's squeaky-voiced girlfriend who stops the show with her rendition of "Adelaide's Lament." Brando in a singing role, the mesmerizing Runyon dialogue and great music combine to create an unusual, fun musical. (Available letterboxed and pan & scan) ★★★ $19.99

The Guyver

(1991, 92 min, US, Screaming Mad George & Steve Wang) When a college student finds himself the unwitting owner of an alien device that turns him into a super soldier, he becomes the only obstacle standing between world domination and an evil band of shape-shifting mutants. This hyper-kinetic monster fest is based on the Japanese animation series of the same name. ★★½ $14.99

The Guyver, Episodes 1 & 2

(1989, 60 min, Japan, Koichi Ishiguro) This over-the-top cyberpunk animated adventure follows the exploits of a high school student named Sho who accidentally finds a mysterious bio-mechanical alien-designed armour called the Guyver that interfaces with human subjects when activated, transforming them into powerful combatants. When three Guyver units are stolen from the Chronos Corporation, our reluctant hero Sho becomes the Guyver and battles corporate evil, biomorphic creatures and more. Great action and story clearly makes this one of the best of the anime releases. ★★★½ $14.99

Guyver 2: Dark Hero

(1994, 127 min, US, Steve Wang) Wisely abandoning the juvenile humor of its predecessor, *Dark Hero* returns to its origins in the popular Japanese animated and comic book series. Sort of a combination remake/sequel, the film is about a young man who has become fused with a biomechanical alien weapon called the Guyver unit. When he activates this unit, an armored skin envelops him, making him impervious to almost any attack. In his new role as a superhero, he must ward off the attacks of the evil Zoanoids, sent by the sinister Chronos Corporation, which wants the Guyver unit for its own weapons development division. *Dark Hero* also brings into the mix the discovery of an alien spaceship which may be the source of the bizarre bioweapon. Wang, who co-directed the original film, gives its sequel a much darker tone (hence the title) and develops its characters more fully, exploring the dual bless-

Bette Midler in *Gypsy*

ing/curse having such powers would bring. Though the film is on the long side, it features good special effects and includes some fantastic battle scenes between the Guyver and various monsters. ★★½ $19.99

Gypsy

(1962, 149 min, US, Mervyn LeRoy) Based on the Broadway landmark — itself based on the memoirs of stripper Gypsy Rose Lee — this stagey but entertaining musical stars Rosalind Russell in the famed Ethel Merman role. Russell plays Rose, the driving force behind and mother of two child stars of the 1920s, one of whom becomes burlesque's reigning queen. Natalie Wood is the young Gypsy. Classic Stephen Sondheim-Jules Styne score includes "Everything's Coming Up Roses" and "Let Me Entertain You." ★★★ $19.99

Gypsy

(1993, 140 min, US, Emile Ardolino) Bette Midler stars in this faithful and exhilarating made-for-TV adaptation of the Broadway classic. Taking over one of the most demanding and rewarding roles in musical theatre, that of the hard-driven stage mother Rose, Midler delivers a tour de force performance. It is to her credit that with the ghosts of Ethel Merman, Rosalind Russell, Angela Lansbury and Tyne Daly circling overhead (all had previously played Rose), she is able to give a fresh interpretation of a time-honored role which more than one actress had stamped her name upon. Though this small-screen version may somewhat lack the energy and excitement of a live performance, there's little doubt that the story of Mama Rose and her daughter, actress/stripper Gypsy Rose Lee, is one of the greatest of all American musicals. ★★★½ $14.99

The Gypsy

(1975, 90 min, France, Jose Giovanni) The eternally sexy Alain Delon plays a gypsy Robin Hood, a dashing thief who would steal anything for his beleaguered people. His criminal exploits and his valiant attempts to stay one step ahead of the police help make this an exciting and entertaining adventure film. (Dubbed) ★★★

H

Hackers

(1995, 105 min, US, Iain Softley) Much like director Softley's terrific *Backbeat*, his cyber thriller *Hackers* has a stimulating visual style to it, but it is there all comparisons end. About as plausible as *Johnny Mnemonic* and as exciting as *The Net*, the film stars the sullen Jonny Lee Miller as a gifted high school hacker (and former child prodigy/criminal) who moves to New York and quickly falls in with fellow and trendy computer nerds. When one of their own accidentally hacks some private and incriminating files, a corporate bad guy (Fisher Stevens) and his goons set out to retrieve the disc and frame the kids. This, of course, inspires them to band together, prove their innocence and expose the culprits. In spite of the film's sometimes dazzling visuals and an impressive knowledge of cyberspace, *Hackers* allows its clichéd teen characters' misfit hijinks to substitute for character development — and ultimately these kids are more hackneyed than hackers. ★★ $96.89

Hail, Hero!

(1969, 97 min, US, David Miller) Michael Douglas makes his film debut in this tense though plodding drama about an anti-war protester who enlists during the Vietnam War. With Arthur Kennedy and Teresa Wright, and featuring music by Gordon Lightfoot. ★★ $59.99

Hail Mary

(1985, 90 min, France, Jean-Luc Godard) This controversial film, which caused quite an uproar when it premiered at TLA in the winter of 1986, is truly not as blasphemous or shocking as it has been made out to be. Rather, *Je Vous Salue, Marie* is a reverent modern retelling of the Incarnation and Virgin Birth of Christ. The setting is 1980s France where Mary works at her father's gas station. Her selection to be the Mother of Christ, and how she deals with this, provides the central theme to this religious work. (French with English subtitles) ★★★

Hail the Conquering Hero

(1944, 101 min, US, Preston Sturges) Sturges' miraculous satire stars Eddie Bracken as the conquering hero of the title, a medically discharged Marine whose small hometown thinks him a war hero. Sturges lets loose a comic assault on politics, mother love and popular opinion as Bracken's Woodrow Truesmith gallantly tries to set the record straight, but is sabotaged at every turn. Bracken (as in Sturges' *Miracle of Morgan's Creek*) is priceless, and William Demarest shines as a "real" war hero trying to make Bracken look the part in his mother and sweetheart's eyes. ★★★★ $14.99

Hair

(1979, 121 min, US, Milos Forman) Forman's exuberant adaptation of the '60s landmark play shines with a wealth of cinematic finesse, heightened by Twyla Tharp's visceral choreography and the inspired performances of Treat Williams, Beverly D'Angelo and John Savage. They said it was unfilmable, and Forman proved them wrong. ★★★★ $14.99

Hairspray

(1988, 94 min, US, John Waters) Waters, the Prince of Puke and sleazemaster extraordinaire, put aside his odious ways to make this glorious sendup of the "teen scene" movies of the late '50s and early '60s. Set in Baltimore (where else?), the story follows Tracy Turnblad (Ricki Lake), a heavyset teen whose main ambition in life is to be on a local TV dance program. But she is soon faced with a moral dilemma when the producers ban her black friends from attending. Waters proves up to the task of exploring the racial issue, but wisely keeps the lid on all-out polemic and heavy-handedness by sticking with his strength — namely outrageous comedy. Masterful casting finds the likes of Pia Zadora, Rik Ocasek, Sonny Bono, Debbie Harry and of course, in his final role, the incomparable Divine. ★★★ $14.99

Half a Loaf of Kung Fu

(1985, 96 min, Hong Kong, Chen Chi-Hwa) The incomparable Jackie Chan stars as a buf-

foonish drifter looking for work, wisdom and the ultimate kung fu master in Imperial China. From the opening credits, you'll know that this self-parodying kung fu epic approaches its subject with tongue planted firmly in cheek. ★★★ $39.99

Half Moon Street

(1986, 90 min, GB, Bob Swaim) Muddled adaptation of Paul Theroux's novel "Dr. Slaughter," with Sigourney Weaver in the role of a financially depressed American PhD in London who tries to make ends meet by becoming an "escort" for politically influential clientele — in this case, the ubiquitous Michael Caine as a high-powered British diplomat. Anyone who's ever fantasized about the statuesque Ms. Weaver will find this a guilty pleasure at best, as nudity seems to have been written into her contract. ★

Half of Heaven

(1987, 127 min, Spain, Gutierrez Aragon) This charming story of a young woman's growth, loves and successes reads like a modern-day fairy tale with characters including two mean and ugly sisters and a grandmother imbued with special powers. Set in 1960s Franco Spain, our story follows Rosa (Angela Molina), an ambitious and self-reliant young widow who, with her daughter, leaves her family and the peasant lifestyle to find opportunities in the city. A wonderful story of one woman determined to make it on her own. While lulling you with the film's light and entertaining style, the director throws in biting commentary on Franco Spain, imbued with a fine Buñuelian sense of humor. (Spanish with English subtitles) ★★★

Halfmoon

(1995, 90 min, Germany, Frieder Schlaich & Irene von Alberti) Paul Bowles provides the short stories, offscreen narration and on-screen comments to this three-story film that, while atmospheric in look and dreamy in execution, fails to truly excite. It works best as an anthropological glimpse into a simpler, quite exotic world. "Merkala Beach" is a tale involving two young men and friends who fall in love with the same woman, a situation which leads to their violent separation. "Call at Corazón" is the second short and taken from an early work by Bowles. A husband and wife, their relationship already on shaky ground, take a cruise to the middle of nowhere. "Allal" ends the trilogy and tells a mystical story of a dusty village, a basketful of snakes and a young boy who is fascinated by them. (In English and Arabic with English subtitles) ★★ $59.99

Hallelujah!

(1929, 90 min, US, King Vidor) Though not the first film to feature an all-black cast, this simple morality tale is probably the best of its genre and generation, an era which saw African-American performers only fit for portraying maids and scared manservants. One must look beyond the patronizing and stereotypes, for at work here is quite an accessible story of an honest man caught in the clutches of evil and of his redemption. Heading a very dedicated cast, Daniel L. Haynes plays a trusting cotton-pickin' farmer who is led down the

Hail the Conquering Hero

path of temptation by vixen Nina Mae McKinney. When tragedy strikes, Haynes turns to God, only to be once again led astray. Director Vidor has crafted a gripping work, and there are spellbinding scenes which equal or surpass any film of the day, including one of a crowd being worked into a religious frenzy. There are several accomplished musical numbers as well. ★★★½ $19.99

Halloween

(1978, 90 min, US, John Carpenter) Carpenter's celebrated horror film is credited with starting the "slasher" genre, which has given way to Freddy, Jason and the likes. There's more than just blood and guts here, though, in this suspenseful tale of little Michael Meyers returning to his small home town to pick off Jamie Lee Curtis and friends. Donald Pleasence is the alarmed doctor trying to warn anyone who will listen. Followed by five sequels, none of which capture the style or chills of the original. ★★★

Hamlet

(1948, 153 min, GB, Laurence Olivier) Olivier directed and stars in this superlative adaptation of Shakespeare's tragedy. Olivier embodies the melancholy Hamlet, as much a victim of his lack of decisiveness as of his circumstances. The supporting players match him in their assumptions of their roles; among them Eileen Herlie, Basil Sydney, Feliz Aylmer, Jean Simmons, Stanley Holloway and Peter Cushing. Oscar for Best Picture; Olivier won as Best Actor. ★★★★ $19.99

Hamlet

(1969, 114 min, GB, Tony Richardson) With Mel Gibson's impassioned version still fresh in one's mind and Olivier's Hamlet considered the definitive portrayal of the tormented Danish prince, Nicol Williamson's little seen, imaginative interpretation is available for comparison purposes. Filmed at the Round House, London's equivalent of off-Broadway, the film is done in period dress but has a contemporary feel to it accented by dark, claustrophobic staging with little movement of the actors and a concentration on the intense faces of the leads, which include Anthony Hopkins and Marianne Faithful as Ophelia. Williamson's performance of a confused Hamlet, full of neurotic twitches and personal uncertainties, is riveting. ★★½ $19.99

Hamlet

(1990, 135 min, GB, Franco Zeffirelli) Taking an extreme career risk, Mel Gibson – Mad Max himself – takes on Shakespeare's most challenging role – that of the mad Prince Hamlet. Well, there's nothing mad or risky in the casting. In a sumptuous retelling of the classic tragedy, Gibson gives a fiery, credible and even inspired interpretation of the Melancholy Dane. And he is given remarkable support. Glenn Close is superlative as Hamlet's mother, Gertrude, who unknowingly marries her husband's murderer. Alan Bates makes an arresting Claudius, Helena Bonham-Carter is a fragile Ophelia and Ian Holm is a most amusing Polonius. Director Zeffirelli brings great energy to the work, and his stag-

ings are carefully conceived and executed. ★★★½ $14.99

Hamlet

(1996, 242 min, GB, Kenneth Branagh) Attempting to film the entire four-hour verse of Shakespeare's masterpiece, the first time the entire play has been adapted for the screen, director-star Branagh has created one of the most thrilling and accessible adaptations of Hamlet to date. Fairly extravagant in detail but significally intimate in emotion, Branagh's version is a star-studded spectacle which fills in the gaps from other translations with a style and tempo all its own. And in addition to his articulate direction, Branagh as actor is revelatory as the mad Prince of Denmark – no other contemporary artist on either side of the camera can communicate Shakespeare as he. His performance never waivers in intensity or focus, and he is able to extract lighter moments heretofore unrealized. The supporting cast for the most part is examplary. Derek Jacobi absolutely scintillates as the calculating Claudius, Julie Christie is a regal Gertrude, and Richard Briers' exhilaratingly new interpretation of Polonius is more politician than fool. The stunt casting of American actors is hit (Charlton Heston's actor, Billy Crystal's gravedigger) and miss (Jack Lemmon's guard). ★★★★ $102.99

Hammett

(1983, 97 min, US, Wim Wenders) After interminable delays in production, editing and distribution, Wenders' first American feature is a surprisingly intriguing, hard-boiled yarn stemming from the fictional exploits of pulp novelist extraordinaire Dashiell Hammett (Frederic Forrest). As with the best gumshoe tales, the plot is a foggy series of double-crossings and blackmail schemes. The film boasts an impressive gallery of supporting players and stylish, shadowy sets. ★★★

The Hand

(1981, 104 min, US, Oliver Stone) When cartoonist Michael Caine's hand is severed in a car accident, it follows him around and kills his enemies – or does it? Stone keeps his trademark stylistic flourishes well concealed in this early directorial outing. ★ $9.99

The Hand That Rocks the Cradle

(1992, 110 min, US, Curtis Hanson) A parents' nightmare makes for an enjoyably trashy if somewhat contrived thriller. Having sent chills up and down spines with The Bedroom Window and created a sense of dread in Bad Influence, director Hanson resorts to all the tricks to give a potent scare or two. Annabella Sciorra and Matt McCoy are almost the perfect new-age couple. They're madly in love, have a perfect home, perfect children...gee, the perfect life. Into their home comes what they think to be the perfect nanny, Rebecca DeMornay. But she blames Sciorra for her husband's death and now has a score to settle. DeMornay is actually quite good as a demented Mary Poppins, and her effective performance is at the heart of Cradle's success. ★★½ $9.99

A Handful of Dust

(1988, 118 min, GB, Charles Sturridge) A delight for all fans of "Masterpiece Theatre", "Brideshead Revisited," A Room with a View, the books of Evelyn Waugh and of films which opulently depict the trials, tribulations and eventual decay of England's landed gentry in the early part of this century. James Wilby stars as a naively contented land owner who unwittingly loses both his loves and his serenity when he allows his restless wife a "weekend" flat in London. The fun loving woman (Kristin Scott Thomas) soon falls for a penniless charmer in her frantic search for freedom and passion. Not as witty as Waugh's "Black Mischief" or "Decline and Fall," the story is nonetheless classy entertainment highlighted by some amusing cameos by Judi Dench, Anjelica Huston and Alec Guinness. ★★★ $19.99

Handgun

(1994, 90 min, US, Whitney Ransick) First-time director Ransick follows the well-trod footsteps of gangster chronicler Martin Scorsese with this gritty urban slice-of-life about a career criminal whose big score proves to be his last. Seymour Cassel stars as the lone survivor of an ill-fated heist who, wounded in the ensuing gun battle, tells each of his two sons, Treat Williams and Paul Schulze, different clues as to the whereabouts of the stolen loot, thereby forming an uneasy and treacherous alliance between the two. Ransick mixes jarring violence with well-drawn characters to create a tale that is both entertaining and insightful. Williams' charismatic performance is not to be missed. ★★★ $9.99

The Handmaid's Tale

(1990, 109 min, US, Volker Schlöndorff) Imagine a world so closely conformed to Phyllis Schlafly's dictates that even she couldn't get out of the house. In the near future, excessive environmental pollution has sterilized a majority of the population. The ruling reactionary theocracy therefore sends fertile females to the households of the ruling elite, where they are expected to copulate and procreate for the greater glory of God and state. Schlöndorff directs Harold Pinter's adaptation of Margaret Atwood's novel, fully utilizing the consumate talents of a gifted cast, which includes Natasha Richardson, Robert Duvall, Elizabeth McGovern and Aidan Quinn. ★★★ $14.99

Hang 'em High

(1968, 114 min, US, Ted Post) When his lynching doesn't take, Clint Eastwood wants satisfaction from the guys who did such a lousy job. This American take on Leone's spaghetti westerns lacks that director's stylish flourishes, but this still manages to entertain. With Ben Johnson, Dennis Hopper and Alan Hale, Jr. ★★½ $14.99

Hangin' with the Homeboys

(1991, 89 min, US, Joseph Vasquez) Vasquez's film won the Grand Prize at the Sundance Film Festival and was one of the more interesting entries in the Black Renaissance of the early '90s. The story follows four homeboys whose search for a good time on a Friday night takes them from the South Bronx to Manhattan. It's a simple premise, but Vasquez

H

uses it to good effect in chronicling the world view of disaffected black and Hispanic youths. Produced on a shoestring budget, the film suffers slightly from an unfocused script and some inconsistent performances (with the exception of John Leguizamo — who offers some of the more poignant moments), but it still manages to entertain in spite of its shortcomings. ★★★ $14.99

The Hanging Tree

(1959, 108 min, US, Delmer Daves) In one of his final roles, Gary Cooper brings a quiet strength to this involving western which casts the legendary star as a mysterious stranger who takes residence at an 1870s Montana gold mining town. Cooper plays a doctor with an uncertain past. Among those who cross his path are blinded immigrant Maria Schell, seedy prospector Karl Malden, and in their film debuts, George C. Scott as a malicious preacher, and stage actor Ben Piazza as a potential lynch-mob victim whom Cooper saves. ★★★

Hanna K.

(1983, 108 min, France, Constantin Costa-Gavras) Jill Clayburgh stars as a lawyer torn between her conflicting involvement with an Israeli lover (the District Attorney of Jerusalem) and an enigmatic Palestinian whom she defends against him in court. Caught up in the political strife, her perceptions of herself, her relationships and Israel, her adopted land, are profoundly altered. The film presents many questions which, though well-meaning, are clumsily handled. (Filmed in English) ★★ $59.99

Hannah and Her Sisters

(1986, 107 min, US, Woody Allen) Brilliantly scripted and directed, *Hannah and Her Sisters* stands as one of Allen's greatest accomplishments. Featuring Mia Farrow, an ascendant Barbara Hershey and the Oscar-winning Dianne Wiest as three sisters — whose lives are inextricably entwined amongst a host of friends, relatives, and lovers — *Hannah* is a skillful and subtle exploration of human interdependencies. This illuminating work features superb support acting by Allen, Lloyd Nolan, Maureen O'Sullivan, Max von Sydow and Oscar winner Michael Caine. ★★★★ $9.99

The Happiest Days of Your Life

Hanover Street

(1979, 109 min, US, Peter Hyams) American soldier Harrison Ford finds love in war-torn Britain with a married woman (Lesley-Anne Down) in this uninspired romantic drama set during WWII. ★★ $9.99

Hans Christian Andersen

(1952, 120 min, US, Charles Vidor) Danny Kaye lends considerable charm to this wondrous children's tale about storyteller Hans Christian Andersen. Frank Loesser's score includes "Inch Worm" and "Ugly Duckling." ★★★ $19.99

Hanussen

(1989, 140 min, Hungary/West Germany, István Szabó) Following *Mephisto* and *Colonel Redl*, this third collaboration between Szabó and actor Klaus Maria Brandauer stars Brandauer as an Austrian soldier in WWI who acquires an unsettlingly accurate ability to foretell the future. Settling in Berlin, he becomes a successful magician and clairvoyant. His comfortable life becomes entangled when he foresees fascism's rise and the persecution of the Jews, and must decide on keeping quiet or exposing them. Nominated for an Academy Award for Best Foreign Film, the film offers little dramatic punch but is beautifully photographed and has Brandauer giving a riveting performance as an ordinary man caught between powerful forces. (German with English subtitles) ★★★ $19.99

The Happiest Days of Your Life

(1950, 81 min, GB, Frank Launder) A charming example of post-war British comedy, this small but delightfully droll and often hilarious tale stars those two British national treasures: Alastair Sim and Margaret Rutherford. It's a new school year at the Nutbourne Academy for Boys, and when 100 girls arrive to share accomodations, it's anything but business as usual. Sim smartly plays the befuddled Nutbourne schoolmaster, and Rutherford is wonderful as his girls' school counterpart. The film's first half is full of entendres and puns (some may be lost on American audiences); the second half hits a frenzied, screwball pitch as students and faculty in both camps attempt to simultaneously conceal Nutbourne's co-ed status from rival school personnel and visiting parents. ★★★ $39.99

Happily Ever After

(1986, 92 min, Brazil, Bruno Barreto) This electrifying drama borrows elements from such films as *After Hours* and *Montenegro* to create a slightly surreal and sexually charged atmosphere, where the unexpected can always happen and people fall prey to their own desires. Barreto fashions a humorous, suspenseful tale of a woman's unlikely experience with a man she first meets in a dream. Regina Duarte delivers a powerfully controlled performance. Barreto's taut direction prevents the film from degenerating into just another skin flick. Menacing landscapes and Buñuelian adventures with a steady undercurrent of sexual excitement. (Portuguese with English subtitles) ★★★½ $69.99

Happily Ever After

(1990, 74 min, US, John Howley) Would you believe this is a star-studded animated sequel to "Snow White" that replaces the dwarfs with dwarfellas (Tracey Ullman, Sally Kellerman and Carol Channing, among others) and features Snow White saving the Prince? A Snow White for feminists! Irene Cara as Snow White, Ed Asner as Scowl the Owl, Phyllis Diller as Mother Nature and Malcolm McDowell as the Wicked Queen's brother round out the excellent cast. Its few weak moments (who thought Phyllis Diller should sing?) are overcome by the quality of the animation and the untraditional plot. ★★ $14.99

Happiness

(1934, 69 min, USSR, Alexander Medvedkin) Subtitled "A Tale About a Hapless Mercenary Loser, His Wife, His Well-Fed Neighbor, a Priest, a Nun, and Other Old Relics," this free-wheeling slapstick farce stops at nothing in presenting its own skewed version of reality. Infused with elements of vaudeville, burlesque and even surrealism, the comedy, based on folklore, revolves around a farmer who finds a purse filled with money. Believing that he has found everlasting happiness, the farmer finds instead bizarre disaster every which way he turns. Banned in Russia for over 40 years, this satire on man's and society's greed features everything from polka-dotted horses to nuns in see-through tunics. (Silent with orchestral accompaniment) ★★★ $29.99

Happy Birthday, Gemini

(1980, 107 min, US, Richard Benner) Ridiculous stereotypes, terrible acting and a tired script make this film version of Albert Innaurato's 1970s Broadway comedy "Gemini" a messy failure. Set in the row houses of Italian South Philadelphia, the story revolves around a closet case, Francis (Alan Rosenberg) who, while in the midst of a sexual identity crisis, must contend with his wacky neighbors, overbearing father and the unexpected arrival of two of his WASPish Harvard friends. Problems arise when schoolmate Judith (Sarah Molcomb) wants to resume their tentative college affair, but Francis is actually attracted to her blond brother Randy (David Marshall Grant). His tormented indecision finally comes to a head as he begins to accept his homosexuality. Included in the constantly screaming and bickering menagerie of grotesques are Rita Moreno and Madeline Kahn. From the director of *Outrageous*. ★ $14.99

Happy Gilmore

(1996, 92 min, US, Dennis Dugan) After the abysmal *Billy Madison*, Adam Sandler grows up ever so slightly in this equally moronic golf comedy which produces but a few (insipid) laughs. Happy Gilmore (Sandler) is a hockey nut/player with no talent for the game; in fact, he has no talent for any sport except golf, which he discovers accidentally. When his grandmother is in danger of losing her house, he sets out to win a few bucks in golf tournaments. A puerile smart aleck and perpetual loser, Happy's disregard for convention and his surprising ability make him a hero as he turns the golfing world topsy-turvy. Though *Happy Gilmore* is only marginally better than *Madison*, the jokes are still aimed at pre-pubescents, and in his few film appearances Sandler has only honed the skill of being annoying. ★½ $14.99

Happy New Year (La Bonne Annee)

(1973, 112 min, France, Claude Lelouch) Veering away from his usual saccharine tendencies, Lelouch's bright romantic caper features a gangster (Lino Ventura) who, although just paroled, plans a big robbery but instead of riches, finds instead his true love. (French with English subtitles) ★★★ $79.99

Harakiri

(1962, 134 min, Japan, Masaki Kobayashi) Set in 17th-century Japan after a long series of civil wars, *Harakiri* centers on the life of the Samurai in peacetime. Having no lord to serve and no war to fight, the Samurai can either live in poverty or commit harakiri, the suicide ritual. A young Samurai appears at the door of a rich lord's castle asking permission to perform the ritual, hoping instead the lord will offer him money to get rid of him. When the lord calls the soldier's bluff, the youth's father-in-law petitions the lord to take his son-in-law's place, but not before telling the tale of how the boy warrior came to be a Samurai. Kobayashi brilliantly weaves the many stories together as he effortlessly slips back and forth through time, aided greatly by the gorgeous black-and-white cinematography of Yoshio Miyajima. *Harakiri* is a classic waiting to find its cult. (Japanese with English subtitles) ★★★★ $39.99

Hard Boiled

(1992, 127 min, China, John Woo) After an exhilarating teaming in *The Killer*, the Chinese Scorsese and De Niro, John Woo and Chow Yun-Fat, triumph again with this spectacular amphetamin-overdriven thriller. Yun-Fat plays a renegade cop named Tequila, whose mission is to halt the operation of an ultra-violent gun smuggling ring. From the incredible opening shootout, which packs more punch than ten *Lethal Weapon*s, to the everything-but-the-kitchen-sink ending, this action epic succeeds on many levels thanks to the multi-layered characterizations and story, focused and creative direction, and pulse-pounding action sequences that thrust this pulp melodrama into near-operatic grandeur. (Cantonese with English subtitles) ★★★★ $19.99

Hard Choices

(1968, 90 min, US, Rick King) A teenager (Gary McCleery) enters the criminal justice system through an innocent involvement with a robbery, and becomes involved with the social worker (Margaret Klenck) assigned to his case. An interesting look at the process of enforcement and corrections in this country, and highlighted by an intriguing portrayal by John Sayles of a jaded, flippant drug smuggler. Based on a true story. Also starring Spalding Gray. ★★½ $19.99

Jean-Claude Van Damme in *Hard Target*

A Hard Day's Night

(1964, 85 min, GB, Richard Lester) Though 12 songs and filler would have made a hit, The Beatles and director Lester instead fashioned this inventive musical comedy classic filled with the frenzied emotion of early Beatlemania. Lester's early style shines through in this playful day-in-the-life look at the emerging rock stars. ★★★★ $19.99

Hard Target

(1993, 92 min, US, John Woo) The Balanchine of Bullets, Hong Kong action-meister Woo, has his first stateside effort and the result is a mostly successful, if somewhat uneven, reworking of *The Most Dangerous Game*. Jean-Claude Van Damme is up against bad-guy Lance Henriksen (steadily becoming a career villain), who sets up hunts for wealthy thrill seekers. The game: down-and-out combat veterans. Van Damme plays a hapless merchant marine who just wants to get out of New Orleans, but instead gets pulled into the intrigue when enlisted by a young woman whose father has disappeared. The film's first half is choppy, fraught with staccato dialogue and sporadic action. But once the chase is on, the action rises to a non-stop pitch. Woo finds his stride and delivers the goods with a flourish. ★★★ $14.99

Hard Times

(1975, 97 min, US, Walter Hill) Hill's directorial debut is also one of his best films. Charles Bronson takes on all comers in bare-knuckle fights. James Coburn plays his manager, and Jill Ireland also stars. Lots of action. ★★★ $9.99

The Hard Way

(1991, 115 min, US, John Badham) Though really nothing more than a formula buddy-cop comedy, the teaming of Michael J. Fox and James Woods proves to be a saving grace. Fox plays a spoiled Hollywood actor who is partnered with hard-boiled New York detective Woods when the former requests training for his next film assignment. Constantly at odds, Fox and Woods milk the situation dry; eliciting laughs even when the script doesn't warrant them. An amiable, harmless romp. ★★½ $9.99

Hardcore

(1979, 108 min, US, Paul Schrader) It's every father's nightmare when George C. Scott, playing a Calvinist from the Midwest (as is director Schrader), finds his runaway daughter making porno movies in the big city. Schrader captures the sleazy, degrading lifestyle often associated with these sorts of enterprises, but doesn't have the courage of his convictions when it comes to the ending. ★★½ $9.99

Hardcore

(1984-1991, 90 min, US, Richard Kern) Performance art, New York independent film-making and hard-core sex and violence collide in this shocking, determinedly self-indulgent and patently offensive series of shorts. Wallowing in punk-induced nihilism and featuring punk queen Lydia Lunch (as well as her poetry), the films, with background punk music by the Butthole Surfers and Sonic Youth, set out to offend all viewers with cheesy depictions of suicide, necrophilia, deviant sexual acts and really sloppy East Village apartments. ★★ $29.99

Hardcore #2 — The Films of R. Kern

(1983-91, 90 min, US, Richard Kern) With pulsating rock music, raunchy images of sex and violence, a brutal penchant for depicting sadomasochism and a "fuck you" punk sensibility, director Kern has determinedly stayed clear of mainstream filmmaking. This volume features eight of his shorts, all of which share a common theme of characters on the edge who don't give a damn. Included are: *Goodbye 42nd Street*, a leisurely photographic stroll through the hellhole that was once 42nd Street; and the infamous *Fingered*, a tale of sexual obsession that makes *Last Tango in Paris* seem like simple kindergarten fun. Rock star and professional slut Lydia Lunch stars in the film as she out-Madonnas Madonna with her sexual exhibitionism that sets out to shock, titillate and disturb. ★★★ $29.99

The Harder They Come

(1973, 98 min, Jamaica, Perry Penzelle) The age-old story of a country boy seeking riches in the big city, of urban corruption and coming to a bad end – reggae style! Jimmy Cliff is striking as the marijuana-running punk who kills a cop in a drug bust and becomes a folk hero. Features a hypnotic reggae soundtrack. ★★★ $19.99

Hardware

(1990, 94 min, GB, Richard Stanley) Style-over-substance defeats this *Alien/Terminator* derivative about a post-apocalyptic metal-worker (Stacey Travis) whose latest sculpture turns lethal when the scrap robot head given to her by her boyfriend (Dylan McDermott) reactivates and reassembles itself. Sounds great, but never manages to overcome the director's obvious music video background. ★ $9.99

Harem

(1987, 107 min, France/US, Arthur Joffe) This curiosity never received full theatrical distribution in the United States. The story has Ben Kingsley as an OPEC oil minister who becomes enraptured by Nastassja Kinski while on a business trip to America. Kingsley must have the beauty and right before he leaves, he ruthlessly kidnaps her and then places her among his 30-member harem. Passions explode when past meets present in this bizarre romantic comedy. (Filmed in English) ★ $79.99

Harlan County, U.S.A.

(1977, 103 min, US, Barbara Kopple) This Academy Award-winning documentary compellingly involves the viewer in the plight of Kentucky coal miners up against the Eastover Mining Company. The strikers are presented forthrightly, without condescension or glamorization, and with dignity. Surprisingly effective and immediate, the film retains its relevance regarding the conditions affecting American workers today. Highly recommended. ★★★★ $29.99

Harlem Nights

(1989, 115 min, US, Eddie Murphy) Murphy wrote, directed and stars in this gangster comedy set in late-1930s Harlem. Richard Pryor and his "adopted" son Murphy are up against a crooked cop and a white mob kingpin who want a piece of their lucrative nightspot. Superlative sets and costumes can't mask an unfunny screenplay, in which most of the humor is one character cursing at another. Director Murphy's film lacks the energy needed to sustain the farcical romp to wants to be; however, writer Murphy is to be applauded for giving Pryor the plum part of the film – and the veteran comic makes the most of it. With Redd Foxx, Della Reese, Arsenio Hall and the amusing Stan Shaw as a punch-drunk boxer. ★★ $14.99

Harley Davidson and the Marlboro Man

(1991, 98 min, US, Simon Wincer) Q: What do you get when you team Don Johnson and Mickey Rourke? A: A cinematic tour de force...NOT! Director Wincer (*Quigley Down Under*) makes a valiant effort, but this tale of two outlaw misfits who join forces to save a neighborhood bar from greedy developers is lost in a whirlwind of lackluster performances, overblown action sequences and an undernourished script. Hard-core Rourke fans might enjoy this oddity – others beware. ★½ $14.99

Harmagedon

(1983, 132 min, Japan, Taro Rin) Princess Luna of Transylvania is en route to the U.S. when a mysterious asteroid collides with her plane. Luna is then hurled into a pure psychic state where she learns the truth about her own mental powers and the evil doings of King Phantom, who has already destroyed Tokyo and plans to destroy the world. Drawn together by ESP, Luna and a rag-tag group comprised of a cyborg soldier, a young Japanese baseball player and a black kid named Sonny, team up to overcome the evil King Phantom. ★★★½ $39.99

Harold and Maude

(1971, 90 min, US, Hal Ashby) He's 20 and obsessed with death; she's 80 and full of joie de vivre. Together they combat the doldrums of life. Ruth Gordon shines as the vivacious Maude and Bud Cort is playfully grim as the morbid young Harold. Black comedy at its darkest, this wonderful love story features the music of Cat Stevens and features a hilarious supporting role by Vivian Pickles as Harold's daffy mother. One of the most popular films ever to play TLA Cinema. ★★★★ $14.99

Harper

(1966, 121 min, US, Jack Smight) Paul Newman stars as Louis Harper, a cynical Los Angeles detective hired for a missing persons case. A perfect '60s thriller, complete with scenery, California atmosphere and Newman's charisma. Lauren Bacall co-stars as the bedridden widow who hires Harper and she make the most of her femme fatale charm. Robert Wagner is also very entertaining as a pseudo-rich playboy. Janet Leigh plays Newman's estranged wife. Sharp direction from Smith and a witty script by William Goldman make for a most entertaining thriller. ★★★½ $14.99

Harriet the Spy

(1996, 96 min, US, Bronwen Hughes) Harriet is a precocious 11-year-old girl whose independent outlook has made her a bit of an outcast. Her beloved nanny instills in Harriet individualism and an appreciation for life. Which explains Harriet's penchant for writing in her notebook everything she sees. It's her observations and thoughts which lead to trouble in the sweet and enjoyable *Harriet the Spy*, a spirited adaptation of the Louise Fitzhugh children's book. Michelle Trachtenberg makes a very appealing Harriet; she neither down-plays Harriet's peculiarities nor does she immerse herself in them. Rosie O'Donnell is wonderful as Harriet's nanny, who imparts on the young girl sage advice while serving as loyal best friend. A nicely paced frolic of youthful custom and a particularly encouraging portrait of one young girl who discovers the importance of just being her. ★★★ $19.99

Harry and the Hendersons

(1987, 110 min, US, William Dear) This amusing little comedy about a suburban Seattle family who find themselves host to Bigfoot is filled with warmhearted humor. John Lithgow puts in yet another solid (and yet unsung) performance as Dad. Rick Baker's makeup for the giant Harry won him an Academy Award. ★★½ $14.99

Harry and Tonto

(1974, 115 min, US, Paul Mazursky) A Best Actor Academy Award went to Art Carney for his portrayal of an old man who, after eviction from his apartment building (about to be torn down around his ears), sets out on a cross-country odyssey with his cat. Touching, warm, humorous and sometimes very sad. In addition to *The Late Show*, perhaps the fullest use of Mr. Carney's mature talents. A lovely supporting cast includes Ellen Burstyn, Larry Hagman, Geraldine Fitzgerald and Melanie Mayron. ★★★½ $14.99

Harvest

(1937, 129 min, France, Marcel Pagnol) Orane Demazis and Fernandel, the stars of *Angele*, are reunited in this Pagnolian human drama about a peasant family and their struggle for existence. An itinerant hunter, wishing to have a family, coaxes a down-on-her-luck cabaret singer to leave her abusive companion and set up house with him in a deserted, decaying mountain village. The unlikely lovers struggle, against all odds, to till the land and keep the village alive. Innocently told by today's standards, this film was originally banned by French censors on moral grounds. (French with English subtitles) ★★★★ $59.99

The Harvest

(1992, 97 min, US, David Marconi) Miguel Ferrer stars as a screenwriter who travels to a Mexican resort town to get away from it all and rewrite his newest screenplay. Once there, he becomes involved in a convoluted series of events which lead to illegal organ transplants, murder and cover-ups. A finely crafted neo-noir thriller, *The Harvest* is an intricate puzzle that's fun to watch unfold. ★★★ $14.99

Harvey

(1950, 104 min, US, Henry Koster) James Stewart gives one of his best performances as the tipsolated Elwood P. Dowd, whose best friend, Harvey, just happens to be a six-foot rabbit (he's actually a pooka, but why quibble). Based on Mary Chase's Pulitzer Prize-winning Broadway play, the film is a faithful and delightful adaptation, capturing all the warmth, humor and craziness which made the play one of the great sensations of the late 1940s. As Elwood's exasperated sister, Josephine Hull had the role of her career and won an Oscar for it. ★★★½ $14.99

The Harvey Girls

(1946, 101 min, US, George Sidney) Judy Garland sings "Atchison, Topeka and the Santa Fe" as she and other well-bred young ladies head West to be waitresses at the new Fred Harvey railroad station restaurants. Though the story is pure hokum, Judy and a talented cast – including Ray Bolger and Angela Lansbury – plus enjoyable musical numbers make this a pleasant ride. ★★★ $19.99

The Hasty Heart

(1949, 104 min, GB, Vincent Sherman) Based on John Patrick's sentimental stage play, this affecting tearjerker is as sappy as it is captivating. Richard Todd gives an immense performance as a proud Scottish soldier staying at a Burmese hospital during WWII. Arrogant and cantankerous, he makes enemies of all around him until it is learned he only has a few weeks to live. Patricia Neal is quite good as the nurse looking after him, and even the presence of Ronald Reagan as an American G.I. doesn't compromise the integrity or enjoyment level of this polished, bittersweet tale. ★★★½ $19.99

Hatchet for a Honeymoon

(1967, 93 min, Italy, Mario Bava) Strong on visual imagery and short on plot, Italian horror master Bava tells the tale of a cross-dressing psycho killer/fashion mogul who murders brides while haunted by the ghost of his own wife. ★★½ $39.99

Hate (La Haine)

(1995, 94 min, France, Mathieu Kassovitz) Three marginalized French youths – one black, one Arab, one Jew, and all unlikely friends – spend a night on the mean streets of Paris in this stunning black-and-white feature by actor/director Kassovitz. The day after a massive street riot during which a well-liked gang member was put into a coma by a police beating, the three friends set out on their normal daily activities. But there's a twist: a policeman lost his pistol during the melee and one of the three now has it. In a society where privately owned firearms are a rarity, the other two are shocked and fascinated by the new toy. Vowing revenge if the coma-stricken youth dies, the now gun-toting punk struts his stuff and makes promises about killing himself a cop. The countdown begins. Violence lurks around every corner in *Hate*, and only after expectations have subsided does it show its ugly head. Low-budget though shot and edited remarkably well, the film is alternately harrowing and sad, and paints a very bleak picture of the future of urban society via its treatment of its youth. (French with English subtitles) (Letterboxed) ★★★★ $19.99

Haunted

(1995, 107 min, GB, Lewis Gilbert) The patient viewer will be rewarded by this slow-moving yet haunting ghost story about an arrogant turn-of-the-century college professor (Aidan Quinn) who, having been haunted as a child by the accidental death of his younger sister, has dedicated his life to proving there's no such things as ghosts. But when he takes up the challenge of exorcising a country estate, he uncovers a supernatural scandal so horrifying even Casper would run screaming. Having such classic fare as *Alfie* and *Educating Rita* to his credit, director Gilbert is in uncharted territory with this poltergeist patchwork, but he compensates the unlikely pace and familiar scare techniques with a good screenplay (based on the novel by James Herbert), winning performances and that great shock ending. ★★½ $9.99

Haunted Honeymoon

(1986, 83 min, US, Gene Wilder) A sometimes amusing mystery spoof with Gene Wilder and Gilda Radner as two 1930s radio stars who visit Wilder's aunt (Dom DeLuise in drag) at the family estate, becoming targets for murder. Though the pairing of Wilder and Radner is irresistible, they really aren't given any good material. ★★ $14.99

The Haunting

Haunted Summer

(1988, 106 min, US, Ivan Passer) Languid (read: boring), beautifully filmed (read: the countryside is more interesting that the characters), evocative period piece (read: pretentious costume drama drivel) and shocking (read: a failed attempt at titillation), this drama retreads the often-traveled grounds of the fateful summer that Percy Shelley, his lover and future wife Mary Goodwin, her half-sister Claire Claimont and the roguish poet Lord Byron spent together on the shores of Lake Geneva in 1816. Shelley is portrayed by a flower-sniffing, sonnet-espousing Eric Stoltz, the abused Claire is played by Laura Dern, Lord Byron is played by Philip Anglim, who is seen alternately as seductive and obnoxious, a mixture that entices Mary (Alice Krige) and ensnares the homosexual Dr. Polidori (Alex Winter). For a much better film on the same subject, Ken Russell's dreamlike psychological thriller *Gothic* is a must. ★ $9.99

The Haunting

(1963, 112 min, US, Robert Wise) Wise's classic ghost story about a team of researchers investigating a haunted house. Julie Harris and Claire Bloom are both splendid as psychic investigators, and Wise can get more scares from a door than Jason or Freddy can scrape together with an assortment of knives and axes. Based on Shirley Jackson's "The Haunting of Hill House," this is a frightening, genuinely creepy and well-made chiller. ★★★★ $19.99

The Haunting of Julia

(1976, 96 min, GB/Canada, Richard Loncraine) Moody and seductive supernatural thriller with Mia Farrow as a mother haunted by the death of her young daughter, whose spirit has now returned from the dead. ★★½

The Haunting of Morella

(1991, 82 min, US, Jim Wynorski) Roger Corman strikes again, and strikes out, in this dismal Poe adaptation that's a far cry from his 1960s efforts. David McCallum is the dopey, dedicated hubby of a condemned sorceress who returns to possess their virginal daughter.

This campy mix of buxom starlets and T&A in lieu of talent was helmed by Corman house director Wynorski (*Not of This Earth*). ★ $89.99

Havana

(1990, 145 min, US, Sydney Pollack) The sixth collaboration between actor Robert Redford and director Pollack features intelligent acting and competent direction, but is plagued by an insufferably poor script. The story follows the exploits of Redford as a big-stakes American gambler who's hanging around Havana on the eve of the Communist takeover. All he's interested in is a good poker game, but when he becomes smitten with the wife of a wealthy revolutionary (Lena Olin), he is inextricably sucked into the political fray. The film borrows heavily from classics like *Casablanca*, right down to the Scandinavian-born leading lady, but falls mighty short of that film's greatness. ★★ $19.99

Hawaii

(1966, 171 min, US, George Roy Hill) Epic film version of James Michener's novel set in the 1800s about settlers in our 50th state and how they shaped the territory. Max von Sydow is appropriately dour as a missionary, Julie Andrews is his personable wife, and Richard Harris is the sea captain in love with Andrews. Also with Gene Hackman, Carroll O'Connor and John Cullum. (Available letterboxed and pan & scan) ★★★ $24.99

The Hawk

(1993, 84 min, GB, David Hayman) Helen Mirren stars as an uptight suburban housewife in this clichéd, muddled thriller. When a serial killer begins to terrorize the normally peaceful English countryside with a series of brutal murders, she soon begins to suspect her traveling salesman husband (George Castigan), due to the many similarities between her own life and the killer's victims. The tired script, which occasionally succeeds by creating suspenseful moments, fails just as often by giving obvious clues and plot twists. Though the film rescues itself by allowing Mirren to deliver a strong performance, it is unfortunate that this is not enough to make what could have been an excellent film. ★★½ $19.99

Hawks

(1988, 100 min, GB, Robert Ellis Miller) Quirky comedy-drama with Timothy Dalton and Anthony Edwards as two terminally ill cancer patients who escape from their hospital ward in search of adventure. Dalton and Edwards bring great pathos to their roles; and though the last third of the film veers on a rather strange course, this can be rewarding, if offbeat, entertainment. ★★½ $92.99

The Hawks and the Sparrows

(1965, 88 min, Italy, Pier Paolo Pasolini) This post-neorealist parable is an unconventional story featuring Italy's beloved stone-faced clown Toto as an Everyman who, with his empty-headed son, travels the road of life accompanied by a talking crow, who waxes philosophically and amusingly on the passing scene. Pasolini presents a tragic fable which shows two delightful innocents caught between the Church and Marxism. (Italian with English subtitles) ★★★ $29.99

Hayfever

(1990, 105 min, US, Cristen Lee Rothermund) This lesbian comedy tells the tale of two women who must collect their inheritance from a great aunt at a roundup. On the way, there is plenty of adventure, sexual and otherwise, including a run-in with a mysterious villain who would foil their plans. Full of different types of women, music, dancing and sex. ★★½ $54.99

He and She

(1994, 90 min, Hong Kong, Cheng Dan Shui) Gay costume designer Tai (Tony Leung Kar-Fei) finds his sexuality blurred after he enters into a marriage of convenience with a pregnant friend. Happily homosexual, Tai soon begins to feel troublingly attracted to his new roommate Yee (Cherie Chung Chu-Hung). When the married biological father challenges the validity of the marriage and fights for child custody in court, Tai is forced to acknowledge his gayness and admit the marriage was unconsummated. Despite having the marriage annulled by the court, Tai realizes that he does indeed feel heterosexual yearnings for Yee and gathers that he doesn't love women in general, just Yee. Although leaning on the soap operaish side, this drama is quite interesting in its realistic depiction and social acceptance of a gay man – although his eventual "conversion" will leave many unconvinced. ★★½ $89.99

He Said, She Said

(1991, 115 min, US, Ken Kwapis & Marisa Silver) Lightweight comedy which is actually two films in one. The story centers on the relationship of journalists Kevin Bacon and Elizabeth Perkins – told through the eyes of each of them. Kwapis directed the "male" point-of-view, and Silver directed the "female" counterpart. ★★ $14.99

He Walked by Night

(1948, 80 min, US, Alfred L. Werker) This seminal noir policer showcases the use of forensic science as the LAPD tracks a vicious and highly intelligent cop killer. Starkly shot

and tautly written, the film follows the police investigation as it pieces together minute scraps of evidence, following leads with state-of-the-art technology of the time. This focus on the technical aspect of criminal investigation was unique in films by 1949, and apparently made a big impression on the actor portraying the crime lab scientist – Jack Webb. The film's introductory voice-over opens with a description of Los Angeles and tells us that what we are about to see is a true story – only the names have been changed...and taken from the files of the detective division. Sound familiar? It's the prototype for Webb's TV series, "Dragnet"; a term, incidentally, pointedly used several times in the film. ★★★ $29.99

Head

(1968, 86 min, US, Bob Rafelson) "Hey, hey, it's the Monkees!" The prefabricated four cavort with an all-star cast including Victor Mature (that hunk of yore), Annette Funicello, Frank Zappa and Jack Nicholson (who also co-scripted) in this psychedelic explosion of drug-induced humor. ★★★ $19.99

Head Against the Wall
(La Tete Contre les Murs)

(1958, France, Georges Franju) Franju, along with Jean-Pierre Melville, made consistently intriguing films in the `40s and `50s that anticipated the French New Wave. Franju, co-founder of the Cinematique Francaise in 1938, was known mostly for his documentaries and shorts; this was his first feature. Taking the theme of repression and rebellion, the story – possibly influenced by James Dean's alienated youth films – follows a young man's (Jean-Pierre Mocky, who also wrote the script) escape from an insane asylum in his efforts to locate his girlfriend (Anouk Aimée) and avoid his father's desperate attempts to recommit him. Co-starring Charles Aznavour. (French with English subtitles) ★★★

Head of the Family

(1970, 105 min, Italy, Nanni Loy) Set in post-war Rome, this sensitive drama concerns a woman (Leslie Caron) whose marriage of ten years has become loveless. She must face the prospect of life alone, dealing with both its pleasures and anxieties. Also starring Nino Manfredi and Ugo Tognazzi. (Dubbed) ★★½ $89.99

Head over Heels (A Coeur Joie!)

(1967, 89 min, France, Serge Bourguignon) Brigitte Bardot is a happily married woman who, through several years of marriage, has never cheated on her husband. Her fidelity is severely tested when, in London on a business trip, Bardot finds herself pursued by a handsome young man and must decide on staying faithful or having a "short" love affair. This drama, made for the French domestic market, is still an entertaining and knowledgeable look into the labyrinthine world of love. (French with English subtitles) ★★★

Hear My Song

(1991, 115 min, Ireland, Peter Chelsom) Made in the tradition of the Ealing Studio comedies with a splash of Local Hero thrown in, Hear My Song is a delightful frolic about a

sprightly young Irishman trying to make a go of it as a nightclub operator in Liverpool. After making a series of disastrous bookings, he is forced to try and save his venue by luring the famed Irish tenor Josef Locke (Ned Beatty) back from Ireland where he's been avoiding British tax collectors. Adrian Dunbar (who co-wrote the screenplay with first-time director Chelsom) delivers a winning performance as the music promoter Mickey O'Neill. Beatty is marvelous as Locke, putting in one of his best performances. ★★★½ $19.99

Hear No Evil

(1993, 97 min, US, Robert Greenwald) Marlee Matlin stars in this insipid thriller as a deaf aerobics instructor who inadvertently becomes involved in a murderous robbery scheme. It seems one of her clients, investigative reporter John C. McGinley, picks up a scoop about a stolen coin worth a million dollars. And the police department of Portland, Oregon, has a rotten apple in the form of sergeant Martin Sheen, who's involved in the heist. Sheen and his cronies then terrorize everyone in sight, and Matlin becomes the object of the bad guy's ire. McGinley's pal D.B. Sweeney shows up to play knight to her damsel in distress – like she needs one, she runs marathons for Christ's sake! Just once, we'd like to see a strong woman take care of herself; of course, that wouldn't leave any room for the sappy love interest. Making matters worse, director Greenwald can't decide whether he's making a thriller or a music video as he inserts several numbers which completely break the tension. ★½ $9.99

Hearing Voices

(1990, 89 min, US, Sharon Greytak) Numbed into quiet boredom by the shallow, manipulative world of fashion modeling, and physically scarred after reconstructive surgery, Erika floats aimlessly through her successful but empty life. She is saved emotionally after meeting Lee (sort of a Pauly Shore on Prozac), the gay lover of her doctor. Their relationship (sexual?), infused with tender caresses and revealing intimacies, is an unusual love, which while not altogether fulfilling, and ultimately doomed, does help in their respective healing processes. This story, of a "romance" between a gay man and a straight woman, provides a great premise; but the film, hampered by languid pacing and stilted acting, becomes a ponderous exercise in Bergman-esque "message cinema," reducing it to an earnest but lifeless viewing experience. ★★ $79.99

Heart and Souls

(1993, 103 min, US, Ron Underwood) While its scale may be more fitting for the small screen rather than the large one, this Robert Downey, Jr. comedy is really quite a charmer. Kyra Sedgwick, Tom Sizemore, Alfre Woodard and Charles Grodin are lost souls. They unexplainedly find themselves watching over a youngster, who grows up to be a harried businessman Downey. As they try to put his life right, they also are given a chance to tie up the loose ends of their own lives, which each failed to do before their deaths. As he demonstrated in Chaplin, Downey has a real knack for physical comedy; which comes in handy since the spirits – recalling Steve Martin's All *of Me* – possess Downey's body for much of the film. ★★★ $14.99

Heart Beat

(1980, 109 min, US, John Byrum) Fictionalized though rewarding account of the friendship of Beat poet Jack Kerouac and Carolyn & Neal Cassady. John Heard is the author, and Sissy Spacek and Nick Nolte are the Cassadys. Ray Sharkey is a standout in support as a Ginsberg-like writer. ★★½ $19.99

Heart Condition

(1990, 98 min, US, James D. Parriott) Instantly forgettable yet strangely enjoyable while it lasts, this phantasmal comedy about a racist cop who is befriended by a congenial black ghost is the perfect example of the "concept" idea of screenwriting. Bob Hoskins, at his gruffest and most lovable, is a down-at-the-heels cop who suffers a heart attack. Denzel Washington is the recently deceased man who spectrally returns to earth after his heart is transplanted into Hoskins' body. The two form an unlikely team as they attempt to track down Washington's drug-lord killers. ★★½ $14.99

Heart Like a Wheel

(1983, 113 min, US, Jonathan Kaplan) This triumphant, true-life saga chronicles the uphill struggle of stock car driver Shirley Muldowney (Bonnie Bedelia) to gain acceptance in the male-dominated world of motorsport racing. A thrilling tale of determination and perseverance. Bedelia gives an outstanding performance; Beau Bridges is exceptional as racer Connie Kalitte. ★★★½ $9.99

Heart of Dixie

(1989, 95 min, US, Martin Davidson) Another in the long line of well-meaning social dramas about racial discrimination in our country's past. A worthy subject to be sure, but the film lacks a perspective and a strong narrative needed to make it of interest. Ally Sheedy gives a sincere performance as a white college student given a jolting political lesson in racial injustice. ★★½ $19.99

Heart of Dragon

(1985, 85 min, Hong Kong, Samo Hung) In one of his earliest dramatic roles, Jackie Chan is cast as a police officer who is constantly taking care of his mentally retarded brother (director Hung), and running into myriad troubles while doing so. This HK version of *Rain Man* begins slowly, but builds to a grueling twenty-minute action climax set in a construction site which finds Jackie fighting at his fiercest to rescue his kidnapped brother. But fight scenes are not what this movie is about; it is more about Jackie's recognition of his love and responsibility for his unfortunate sibling. The two actors (who were schoolmates together) have several tender and dramatic moments together and Samo proves that he can be sentimental without becoming maudlin, both as a director and as an actor. Jackie as well handles the dramatic scenes with skill and shows an uncharacteristic face of rage and frustration during the climactic fight. *Heart* is not the kind of Hong Kong movie American fans are used to, but it will not disappoint the patient.

(Cantonese with English subtitles) ★★★ $19.99

Heart of Tibet

(1991, 60 min, US, David Cherniak) Introduced by none other than Jimmy Carter, this inspirational portrait of the 14th Dalai Lama follows the religious leader, spiritual teacher and Nobel Prize laureate on his almost surreal visit to Los Angeles. Revered by his followers as a "Living Buddha," the Dalai Lama, in exile from his Chinese-occupied Tibet for almost 30 years, has continued his quest for freedom for his country, but in a non-violent fashion. A bit reverential, exposing its biased slant, the film offers a brief history of the political turmoil affecting Tibet, the Dalai Lama's activities since his escape to India as well as offering an intimate look at the man himself – a powerful leader who has retained his simplicity and spirituality, and has a refreshing self-deprecating humor and joy for life. ★★½ $29.99

Heartaches

(1981, 93 min, Canada, Donald Shebib) This winsome romantic comedy and female buddy movie stars Annie Potts as a woman who after finding herself pregnant, and not by her racing-car enthusiast boyfriend David Carradine, abandons him and goes on the road. It doesn't take her long to meet up with a zany, streetwise woman (Margot Kidder) who takes her under her wing, and together they set up house in Toronto. Kidder gives an enjoyably manic performance in the plum role of the man-crazed peroxide blonde who takes the frumpy Potts on an unwilling series of adventures. ★★★

Heartbreak House

(1985, 122 min, US, Anthony Page) This surprisingly affecting and amusingly intelligent Showtime production of the George Bernard Shaw play stars Rex Harrison, Rosemary Harris and Amy Irving. Irving and her fiancé accept an invitation to a family weekend in the country from Harris, her fanciful and attractive friend. Undercurrents of conflict arise between fathers and daughters, husbands and wives, men and women, industrialist and activist as Shaw unleashes his razor-sharp wit in this insightful and often comedic exploration of human relationships. Harrison is especially engaging as the land-bound sea captain who is seeking the seventh degree of concentration. Based on the successful 1985 Broadway revival. ★★★ $14.99

The Heartbreak Kid

(1972, 106 min, US, Elaine May) One of the best American comedies to come out of the 1970s, this Neil Simon scripted film from a Bruce Jay Friedman story features Charles Grodin as Lenny, a nice if self-absorbed Jewish *schlemiel* who, realizing on his honeymoon that he has made a fatal mistake in marrying his sunburned, cake-guzzling wife (hilariously and pathetically played by Jeannie Berlin), makes the decision to dump her for the WASPish ice-queen goddess in the body of Cybill Shepherd. His frantic efforts to bow out of his marriage and his ensuing relentless pursuit of his unattainable dream woman is mercilessly lampooned by director May. ★★★½ $9.99

Heartbreak Ridge

(1986, 130 min, US, Clint Eastwood) Vigorous war adventure, with an accent on humor during its well-paced boot camp sequence, stars director Eastwood as a rough-talking, old-school Marine sergeant in charge of a platoon of new recruits. ★★½ $9.99

Heartburn

(1986, 108 min, US, Mike Nichols) Jack Nicholson and Meryl Streep deliver earnest performances in this faithful film version of Nora Ephron's autobiographical best-seller about a writer (Streep) who discovers that her husband (Nicholson) is having an affair both during and after her pregnancy. A grueling commentary on deception and its consequences. ★★½ $14.99

Heartland

(1979, 96 min, US, Richard Pearce) Magnificent independent production set in the early 1900s about a widow (Conchata Ferrell) who heads to Wyoming to become housekeeper for a cantankerous rancher (Rip Torn). A beautifully filmed story of pioneer life with sterling performances by Ferrell (whose film roles have been too few), Torn and Lilia Skala as a stalwart neighbor. ★★★½

Hearts and Minds

(1974, 110 min, US, Peter Davis) This Oscar-winning documentary examines the American psyche in the wake of the Vietnam War. A series of heartrending interviews of veterans (and others who were sucked up into the war's madness) is intercut with some of the most horrifying footage of the war to create a brutally emotional viewing experience. ★★★★ $19.99

Hearts of Darkness: A Filmmaker's Apocalypse

(1991, 96 min, US, Fax Bahr, George Hickenlooper & Eleanor Coppola) This mesmerizing documentary on the making of Francis Ford Coppola's *Apocalypse Now* was culled from over 60 hours of footage shot by Coppola's wife, Eleanor, while on location in the Philippine jungle. The film follows Coppola and crew as they wend their way up river and almost enter the eerie world of Joseph Conrad's "Heart of Darkness" themselves. Documented

Hearts of Darkness: Marlon Brando on the set of *Apocalypse Now*

are all of the troubles which beset the film: Martin Sheen's near-fatal heart attack in the middle of shooting; sets being destroyed by tropical monsoons; and the delays caused when the Filipino Air Force helicopters being used as props would leave to engage in real combat with that country's Communist rebels. Coppola's quip to reporters at Cannes sums up the film best, "We had access to too much money, too much equipment and we slowly went insane." ★★★½ $14.99

Hearts of the West

(1975, 103 min, US, Howard Zieff) Underrated western spoof with Jeff Bridges as a farmboy who heads to Hollywood and becomes a star of Grade-B cowboy movies. The terrific cast includes Andy Griffith, Blythe Danner and the hilarious Alan Arkin as an eccentric director. ★★★ $19.99

Heat

(1995, 172 min, US, Michael Mann) Continuing themes he introduced in 1981's *Thief*, writer-director Mann has created a self-described "Los Angeles crime saga" which features, among other pleasures, the first on-screen meeting between thespian heavyweights Robert De Niro and Al Pacino. De Niro plays a cool, icily competent thief whose credo "Have no attachments, nothing you can't walk away from" has served him well. Into his life come two new developments, one in the form of a pretty young bookseller (Amy Brenneman), the other in the weathered face of an equally cool L.A. homicide detective (Pacino) obsessed with his capture. Most of the film is a buildup to the inevitable showdown between the two men, neither of whom is willing to back down or give up. Mann's script brings the tired cliché of "honor among thieves" to a new level as it contrasts both men. Unfortunately, the overlong film is bogged down by far too many unnecessary subplots. Also hindering the success of the film is Pacino's out-of-control performance. Despite the flaws, however, Mann's exceptional visual style shines with slickly staged chases, rob-

Heat

beries and confrontations, making this a satisfying and moving crime drama. (Letterboxed version available for $24.99) ★★★ $19.99

Heat and Dust

(1983, 130 min, GB, James Ivory) Ivory's lush and romantic tale of two British women's parallel absorption into the mystical and carnal realm of the Far East. Julie Christie is the independent, contemporary woman tracing her roots and Greta Scacchi makes a dazzling debut as her scandalous great aunt. ★★★ $59.99

Heat and Sunlight

(1987, 98 min, US, Rob Nilsson) The final 16 hours of a relationship between an aging, leather-clad photographer (Nilsson) and a beautiful young dancer is explored in this slow-moving, improvisational melodrama. Bringing new meaning to the phrase "vanity production," director Nilsson plays the brooding, jealous, obsessive man who is slow in realizing that his girlfriend is just not interested. ★½ $79.99

Heat of Desire (Plein sud)

(1985, 91 min, France, Luc Beraud) This unexpectedly unpredictable tale of obsessive love follows university professor Patrick Dewaere as he meets sensuous siren Clio Goldsmith and immediately throws off the life he had lived to that point. His involvement with her grows to include her shady family (Guy Marchand and Jeanne Moreau) and an improbable scam that they are preparing. (French with English subtitles) ★★★ $19.99

The Heat of the Day

(1991, 120 min, GB, Christopher Morahan) Made for "Masterpiece Theatre," this romantic spy thriller, set against the backdrop of the London Blitz, stars Patricia Hodge as a middle-aged woman who is drawn into the espionage biz against her will. When a very mysterious and elusive Michael Gambon (*The Cook, The Thief...*) shows up at her door and insinuates that her lover (Michael York) is a Nazi spy, Hodge finds herself in a sticky ethical dilemma. Then, Gambon complicates things with his amorous advances. The three veteran actors breathe life into an otherwise moribund Harold Pinter screenplay. ★★½ $19.99

Heathers

(1989, 102 min, US, Michael Lehmann) Comedy comes no blacker than in this bitingly sharp satire on teenage suicide and murder. First-time director Lehmann and writer Daniel Waters have fashioned a refreshing antidote to all of those disgustingly sweet Brat Pack flicks that presume to tell Middle America what the white youth of today are thinking. The story revolves around three bitchy, self-obsessed beauties all named Heather who prance about their high school terrorizing the geeks and cock-teasing the jocks. Their newest member Veronica (Winona Ryder) takes part in the pranks, but feels somehow empty until she meets J.D. (Christian Slater), a decidedly different teen whose cool looks and demented sense of a good time propels her into a whirlwind week of murder, terrorism and funerals. When Veronica writes in her diary, "Suddenly my teenage angst bullshit has a body count," you know that this is no ordinary coming-of-age movie. ★★★★ $14.99

Heatwave

(1983, 99 min, Australia, Phillip Noyce) Set amidst a blistering city heatwave, this complex thriller about the abuses of corporate power escalates to a stirring, nerve-shattering climax. Judy Davis is especially good as a community organizer who opposes the uncontrolled and insensitive policies of an expansionist development company. ★★★

Heaven

(1987, 80 min, US, Diane Keaton) A light-hearted look at what lies ahead after this lifetime, from first-time director Keaton. Includes a mix of interviews and film footage addressing the subject of Heaven. ★★½ $9.99

Heaven and Earth

(1993, 135 min, US, Oliver Stone) The third film in director Stone's Vietnam trilogy (*Platoon* and *Born on the Fourth of July*), based on the true-life perils of a Vietnamese peasant, Le Ly Hayslip (Hiep Thi Le). Unique because this intensely melodramatic story looks at the war through the eyes of a woman, viewers will find themselves physically and emotionally drained as the film examines in minute detail the main character's trials which include torture, rape, prostitution and a failed marriage to an American G.I. (Tommy Lee Jones). Lushly photographed and laced with fine performances by Le, Jones and Joan Chen, this fiercely impassioned film shows another side of the Vietnam conflict with insight and understanding. ★★★ $19.99

Heaven Can Wait

(1943, 112 min, US, Ernst Lubitsch) Superbly entertaining comic fantasy from Lubitsch with Don Ameche as the recently departed, retelling the story of his youthful romantic intrigues to the Devil himself. Also starring the beautiful Gene Tierney, Charles Coburn and Marjorie Main. (Not associated with the similarly titled Warren Beatty comedy.) ★★★½ $19.99

Heaven Can Wait

(1978, 101 min, US, Warren Beatty & Buck Henry) Beatty is in fine form as both director and star in this exceptional remake of the 1941 classic *Here Comes Mr. Jordan*. Beatty plays a pro football player who dies before his time, and with the help of angel James Mason, finds a new body to inhabit. Great supporting cast, including Julie Christie, Jack Warden and especially Dyan Cannon and Charles Grodin as murderous and quite excitable paramours. ★★★½ $14.99

Heaven Help Us

(1985, 104 min, US, Michael Dinner) An above average and quite entertaining coming-of-age comedy set in mid-1960s Brooklyn. The story follows the exploits of a group of Catholic high school boys, and features an appealing cast including Andrew McCarthy,

Mary Stuart Masterson, Donald Sutherland, John Heard, Kevin Dillon, Wallace Shawn and Patrick Dempsey. ★★★

Heaven on Earth

(1986, 100 min, Canada, Allan Kroeker) This compelling and sensitive drama is based on a little known historical episode. Between the years 1867 and 1914, during the social upheaval of the Industrial Revolution, England found itself with many unwanted, abandoned and orphaned children. In an effort to alleviate the problem, these "home children," as they became known, were sent to Canada to begin new lives. This is the story of five of these children; innocents who, faced with a demanding and often times cruel existence, soon realized that their dreams of heaven on Earth were not to be realized in their new adopted land. ★★★ $79.99

Heaven's a Drag

(1994, 96 min, GB, Peter Mackenzie Litten) Marketed as Britain's first gay mainstream movie, this romantic comedy about commitment, AIDS, death, mourning and recovery, though well-intentioned, disappoints on many levels. The London-set comedy is labored, the acting is shrill, and the story line shockingly familiar, seemingly lifted in chunks from such better films as *Ghost, Blithe Spirit* and *Truly, Madly, Deeply*. Stereotypical drag queen Mark (Ian Williams) dies from AIDS but his hunky lover Simon (Thomas Arlie) seems unable to mourn his loss and proceeds to return to his life of good times, discos and anonymous sex. That is, until a "vengeful" Mark returns from the grave to offer his former lover advice — from keeping his apartment clean to expressing his true feelings. The usual "only I can see him" ghost shenanigans ensue. ★½ $29.99

Heaven's Gate

(1980, 220 min, US, Michael Cimino) Whadda you care how much this notorious $50 million bomb cost? It costs the same to rent as any of Corman's two-day wonders. Cimino (*The Deer Hunter*) lavishes his attention on the evolution of the community of Heaven's Gate — from its rough and tumble mining town origins to that of a full-blown city, as civilization begins to tame the wild frontier. Starring Kris Kristofferson, Jeff Bridges, Isabelle Huppert, Joseph Cotten, Christopher Walken and Wyoming. (Available letterboxed and pan & scan) ★★ $24.99

Heaven's Prisoners

(1996, 126 min, US, Phil Joanou) A troubled, recovering-alcoholic ex-cop (Alec Baldwin) and his wife (Kelly Lynch) enter a hazy world of drug trafficking, cover-up and disloyalty when a small plane crashes into the Bayou not far from their boat. The only survivor is a very young Salvadorian refugee, whom the couple take into their home. The arrival of a DEA agent leads Baldwin to old childhood friend Eric Roberts, now a drug dealer, and his perpetually intoxicated wife Teri Hatcher. Also involved is Mary Stuart Masterson, who struggles valiantly with her miscasted role as a stripper. As the story progresses, layers of deceit are peeled away. Baldwin's attempts to secure the orphaned girl's safety lead him too close to

Heavy Metal

the activities of a drug-smuggling ring, placing those closest to him in imminent danger. Though overly long, the film adroitly defines a mood of despondency and captures the feel of the Louisiana Bayou. And though not entirely successful in its execution, the film remains an adult and thoughtful examination of what we choose to value in life, what drives us, and what we sacrifice for our beliefs. ★★½ $14.99

Heavenly Creatures

(1994, 99 min, Australia, Peter Jackson) *Heavenly Creatures* is the provocative, imaginative true-life story of how the intense and passionate relationship of 1950s teenagers Pauline Parker and Juliet Hulme led to the grisly murder of Pauline's mother. The film realistically and fantastically portrays the friendship of the teens with newcomers Melanie Lynskey and Kate Winslet giving outstanding and believable performances as Pauline and Juliet, respectively. The parents of both teens worry about their daughters' "unnatural" relationship and things go terribly wrong when they are eventually separated. Only one solution remains for the two friends. Director Jackson, best known for the cult horror film *Dead Alive*, endows the film with such vision and substance (in addition to some amazing special effects) that the viewer is easily and quickly drawn into the lives of the lead characters. It's the most thrilling story of matricide since *Psycho*. Of interest: After serving time, Juliet became a best-selling murder mystery author using the name Anne Perry. ★★★★ $19.99

Heavens Above

(1963, 105 min, GB, John & Roy Boulting) Peter Sellers displays his usual comic genius as an idealistic and naive young vicar who is accidentally assigned to a small country parish. When, upon arriving, he is met with a less-than-Christian zeal by the townsfolk, he cheerfully sets out to breed a healthier atmosphere — much to the chagrin of the local power structure. This scathing satire pointedly accuses the Anglican church of acquiescing to the estab-

lishment. The film's only drawback is its somewhat heavy-handed Christian message. ★★★½

Heavy

(1996, 105 min, US, James Mangold) Like a more modest "*Marty* for the '90s," *Heavy* is a nicely observed, small slice-of-lifer, set mostly in an out-of-the-way greasy spoon in upstate New York, about the unrequited love between an overweight cook and a beautiful new waitress. Pruitt Taylor Vince is excellent as Victor, the terribly shy but good-hearted mama's boy who dreams of both becoming a gourmet chef and having a relationship with the very appealing Callie (Liv Tyler). Director Mangold captures many telling details that ring true — the silly, insecure gestures and childish fantasies we have when we're pining after someone seemingly unattainable. Many things in *Heavy* feel truthful — the dreary, small town atmosphere, for example, is spot on, but stops short of becoming oppressive. Though not as rich in character as one would want, Mangold makes a strong debut with this moody tale, and gets terrific support from Deborah Harry, Joe Grifasi and especially Shelley Winters as Victor's mother. ★★★ $98.39

Heavy Metal

(1981, 93 min, Canada, Gerald Potterton) After 15 years, the long-overdue *Heavy Metal* is finally on video with a new short segment and a remastered soundtrack. An animated anthology film, *Heavy Metal* is a series of fantasy and sci-fi tales which have the common theme of breasts, broadswords, badass aliens and bodacious rock 'n' roll. Source of countless adolescent erotic fantasies, the film's animation is primitive compared to contemporary works, but its nostalgic charm and historical value are hard to deny. The segments range from the terrific ("B17" and Richard Corben's "Den") and funny ("So Beautiful, So Dangerous" and Berni Wrightson's "Captain Sternn") to the overlong ("Taarna") and trite ("Harry Canyon"). The best rely on animation and music to tell the story, rather than dialogue. Heavily rotoscoped (where animated cels are drawn over existing live-action footage), the film has a singular

Hedd Wynn

look, though is reminiscent of the works of Ralph Bakshi. Boasting a soundtrack of the best of the late '70s and early '80s rock music, *Heavy Metal* is a sexy, gory, violent, fun-filled ride whose qualities will not diminish on repeated viewing. ★★★ $24.99

Heavy Petting

(1989, 85 min, US, Obie Benz) Amusing and entertaining satire on our country's repression of and obsession with sex; chronicling those "innocent" days (when "good girls didn't") with clips from '50s "B" movies and with funny, insightful and occasionally stupid anecdotes from the likes of David Byrne, Sandra Bernhard, Ann Magnuson, Josh Mostel, Laurie Anderson and Spalding Gray. ★★★ $14.99

Heavy Traffic

(1973, 76 min, US, Ralph Bakshi) Animator Bakshi's most ambitious project of his early career, this boldly original and revolutionary work combines live-action and animation to tell the story of a New York youth who escapes the confines of his surroundings by drawing the people around him – creating a devastating portrait of the underside of city life. Rated X. ★★★

Hedd Wyn

(1995, 123 min, Wales, Paul Turner) From a country where poets are revered as much as sports figures are in America comes this handsome and affecting film based on a true story. Told in a series of flashbacks remembered by a soldier wounded in battle in WWI, *Hedd Wyn* recounts the story of Ellis, a young farmer living with his large family in an impoverished Welsh village whose talent for prose has made him somewhat of a local celebrity. As he pursues the local lasses with religious fervor, Ellis – whose pen name is Hedd Wyn – tries to accomplish a poet's highest honor – winning a chair for poetry. While most of the story concentrates on Ellis' romantic and literary agendas, the film also reflects upon the Welsh tradition and speaks to the misfortunes of war (for both soldier and family left behind) in a series of carefully detailed battle scenes. Hedd Wyn's poetry frames the story which manages to also comment on the author's life. Huw Garmon, a good-looking and efficient actor, brings to Ellis a good-natured charm. (Welsh with English subtitles) ★★★ $89.99

Hedda

(1975, 100 min, GB, Trevor Nunn) Glenda Jackson dominates this powerful film version of Henrik Ibsen's classic play "Hedda Gabler." Taken directly from the Royal Shakespeare Company's stage rendition, Jackson's Hedda is a Nordic femme fatale – a neurotic, iron-willed controller who is nevertheless alluring to the local men. Also stars Timothy West and Jennie Linden. ★★★

Heidi

(1937, 88 min, US, Allan Dawn) Little Shirley Temple shines as the young Swiss girl taken away from her loving grandfather. ★★½ $19.99

The Heidi Chronicles

(1995, 94 min, US, Paul Bogart) Based on a play by Wendy Wasserstein (who also wrote this made-for-cable adaptation), this bittersweet drama chronicles the maturation of art historian Heidi Holland (Jamie Lee Curtis), a tirelessly average woman naively caught up in the politics and fads of American life. The story begins with her high school prom in the early 1960s and then fastforwards her through the hippie and anti-war periods, the feminist decade of the '70s, and the '80s "Me Generation." Through the years, she sets forth on a voyage of self-discovery, though to her regret she doesn't always find the most satisfactory romances. Curtis gives a pleasing performance as the sometimes hapless Heidi, and if she and other characters fit nicely into easily recognized categories, it's their journey together which is most appealing of all. Tom Hulce gives a solid performance in support as Heidi's gay friend Peter, who approaches his complex character with good humor and a level-headedness. ★★★ $14.99

Heidi Fleiss: Hollywood Madam

(1995, 106 min, US, Nick Broomfield) This weirdly funny, satirical documentary – a perhaps unintentional parody of the exploitative TV newsmagazines whose clips it uses – is the perfect vehicle for this tale of Hollywood's swarmy excesses. The film concentrates on convicted panderer Heidi Fleiss' relationships with Ivan Nagy, her lover, nemesis and alleged pimp; and Madam Alex, Hollywood's grand madam for 20 years and Heidi's one-time employer and mentor. Each of the three refutes allegations from the other two, yet they all seem inextricably linked. L.A.P.D. is represented by Daryl Gates, whose brother is openly acknowledged as using such professional services. Gates details his fervor to prosecute pimps rather than johns. Yet the department has a history of protecting pimps and madams if they're good informants, a role which Fleiss apparently refused to play. Contradictory stories rebound until every utterance seems a self-serving lie. Wickedly enjoyable yet ultimately unsettling, it demonstrates wretched excess permeates every aspect of this latest entry into the annals of Babylon. You'll feel the need to bathe after viewing. ★★★ $19.99

Helen Keller: In Her Own Story

(1955, 50 min, US, Nancy Hamilton) Helen Keller has stood as *the* prime example of a person conquering seemingly insurmountable odds. Blind, deaf and mute from infancy, Ms. Keller went on to overcome her disabilities (with the help of her incredible teacher and confidant Anne Sullivan) and become a champion of the handicapped and a symbol of good will for the world. This documentary, shot in 1953, explores Ms. Keller's private world, beyond the press coverage and behind the scenes. Following her throughout her home and watching her live her usually unseen "normal" life, we see how she lived and worked. Featuring never before seen footage, including the only known clip of Anne Sullivan speaking with Helen, this informative, if somewhat dated film, sheds some more light on one of the most important and amazing women of this century. ★★★ $29.99

Hell Comes to Frogtown

(1988, 86 min, US, R.J. Kizer) Enjoyable low-budget sci-fi adventure starring "Rowdy" Roddy Piper as a post-apocalyptic mercenary (and one of the few remaining fertile men) who must rescue a group of similarly potent women. ★★½ $9.99

Hell in the Pacific

(1968, 103 min, US, John Boorman) Director Boorman takes a microcosm of WWII and extrapolates a parable on the insanity of war. An American and a Japanese soldier find themselves washed up on a deserted island in the Pacific. Their mutual dependence necessitates the suppression of their hostilities. Both Lee Marvin and Toshiro Mifune are superb, managing to be both ethnic representatives and universal Everymen. Boorman directs with a sure hand. ★★★½ $14.99

Hell Is for Heroes

(1962, 90 min, US, Don Siegel) A fine cast of young actors is featured in this taut WWII drama about a small American company caught behind enemy lines. Starring Steve McQueen, Bobby Darin, Harry Guardino, James Coburn, Nick Adams and Bob Newhart. ★★★ $14.99

Hell Up in Harlem

(1973, 96 min, US, Larry Cohen) Fred Williamson sets out, in his own annihilating way, to make the ghetto safe from detestable murderers and druggies in this entertainingly violent sequel to *Black Caesar*. One of the best scenes features black maids force-feeding soul food to Mafia children. ★★ $9.99

Hell's Angels on Wheels

(1967, 95 min, US, Richard Rush) Four bikers tangle with rival roadies and local thugs. A young Jack Nicholson plays a brooding gas station attendant named Poet who discovers the joys of a hog. Trashy biker pic still manages to entertain in a guilty pleasure sort of way. ★★

Hellbound: Hellraiser II

(1988, 97 min, GB, Tony Randel) With this extremely gruesome sequel, British author Clive Barker continues to redefine the modern horror genre. Picking up where the original

H

left off, Kirsty wakes up in a mental hospital. Intent on saving her father's damned soul, she enlists the help of a fellow patient, and together they descend into the bowels of Hell. Very graphic and violent – not suggested for the faint-hearted. ★★★ $14.99

Hello, Dolly!

(1969, 146 min, US, Gene Kelly) Barbra Streisand shines in this elaborate and entertaining screen version of the hit Broadway musical comedy. Streisand plays turn-of-the-century matchmaker Dolly Levi, who sets her own sights on grocery store owner Horace Vandergelder (the agreeably gruff Walter Matthau). There are wonderful dance numbers, and a whimsical score by Jerry Herman. Though some of the production is rather overblown, it detracts nothing from the film's enjoyment. Also with Michael Crawford and Tommy Tune. Based on Thornton Wilder's comedy, "The Matchmaker." ★★★½ $19.99

Hellraiser

(1987, 93 min, GB, Clive Barker) Barker's riveting directorial debut is unquestionably one of the most serious and intelligent horror films in recent memory. Told from the perspective of Kirsty, our teenage heroine, this phantasmagorical tale of gruesome family secrets finds its beginnings with her Uncle Frank, a sinister sensualist who cracks the code of a mysterious Chinese puzzle box and thereby opens the door to another dimension. Through this threshold come the dreaded Cenobites (led by the menacing Pinhead), a punked-out crew of otherworldly sadists with a penchant for ripped flesh and steaming entrails. Followed by two equally intense and gory sequels. ★★★½ $14.99

Hellraiser: Bloodline

(1996, 90 min, US, Alan Smithee) Makeup effects artist Kevin Yagher originally conceived and directed this fourth installment in the *Hellraiser* series as a three-part anthology film, showing the various problems that people throughout the ages have gotten into when they irresponsibly play with a Lament Configuration (the infamous puzzle box of the inventor Lemarchand). Studio executives, however, decided to re-edit the film into a linear narrative with flashbacks. Primarily set in the future, the film is now about the current

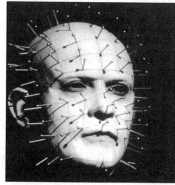

Pinhead in *Hellraiser*

Lemarchand's attempt to destroy Pinhead forever. While undoubtedly better in its original form, the studio version has its moments of interest and terror–it is still fascinating to see *Hellraiser* stories set in 19th century France and in a space station in the future. Mildly atmospheric and definitely better than the third installment of the series (*Hellraiser 3: Hell on Earth*), *Bloodline* is worth a die-hard horror fan's passing glance, but no more. ★★ $19.99

Help!

(1965, 90 min, GB, Richard Lester) It's hard to top a masterpiece. Lester and The Beatles united again in this attempt to recapture the mad-cap brilliance of *A Hard Day's Night*, and while the effort is a decidedly good one, it falls short of its predecessor. Still, any fan of The Beatles or Lester's slap-dash comic style will revel in this rockin' romp. ★★★½ $19.99

Helter Skelter

(1976, 119 min, US, Tom Gries) Based on the best-selling novel by prosecuting attorney Vincent Bugliosi, this exceptional made-for-TV movie is a truly disturbing docu-drama about Charles Manson and his family of disciples. Steve Railsback's intense portrayal of Charlie is stunning. ★★★½

Henessey

(1957, 103 min, GB, Don Sharp) Rod Steiger stars in this high-paced political thriller as an Irish demolitions expert who sets out to avenge his daughter's death by bombing the Parliament on opening day – when the Royal Family attends. The action gets hot when both the IRA and the British Secret Service try to stop him. ★★★ $19.99

Henry IV

(1985, 94 min, Italy, Marco Bellocchio) Driven mad by unrequited love, a man (Marcello Mastroianni) spends 20 years believing himself to be a medieval emperor. A finely crafted tale of passion and illusion from Nobel Prize winner Luigi Pirandello. (Italian with English subtitles) ★★★ $24.99

Henry V

(1946, 137 min, GB, Laurence Olivier) A stirring version of Shakespeare's historical drama. Olivier directed as well as stars as the heroic king who fights for his kingdom in France. Filmed in Technicolor, Olivier introduces the viewer to his play on film by opening with an impressive aerial shot of a re-creation of London's 17th-century Globe Theatre. ★★★★ $19.99

Henry V

(1989, 137 min, GB, Kenneth Branagh) Branagh's astonishing directorial debut remakes Shakespeare's classic which Laurence Olivier had all but stamped his name upon. Everything about this film works. Branagh delivers a bravura performance as the young King Henry which is nothing short of inspirational. His supporting cast is as good as they come and includes Ian Holm as Luelen, Paul Scofield as the King of France and Derek Jacobi as the Chorus. Branagh's direction is crisp and clean, his command of the dialogue is perfect and he masterfully works

Kenneth Branagh as *Henry V*

Shakespeare's subtle sense of humor into the movie. ★★★★

Henry & June

(1990, 140 min, US, Philip Kaufman) The first film to earn the MPAA's NC-17 rating, director Kaufman's steamy adaptation of Anais Nin's novel about the passionate love triangle between herself, writer Henry Miller and his wife June is a glorious sexual and literary odyssey through the streets of 1930s Paris. Exquisitely photographed, *Henry & June* sumptuously evokes a frenzied carnival atmosphere and makes for an extraordinary sensual cinematic experience. Newcomer Maria de Medeiros is dazzling as the doe-eyed Anais, a prolific diarist who vigorously committed herself to the pursuit of complete sexual abandon. As Miller, Fred Ward is excellent, exuding a sleazy sexuality and the tenderness of a love-struck poet. Uma Thurman gives a lusty portrayal of the voluptuous bombshell June. ★★★½ $19.99

Henry: Portrait of a Serial Killer

(1986, 105 min, US, John McNaughton) Initially dismissed by its producers as not having enough blood and action to please the *Friday the 13th* horror crowd, this harrowing portrait of a psychotic killer was not successful until the art audience discovered it. Henry, recently released from prison for killing his mother, moves in with his old buddy Otis and his sister, Becky. Henry soon resumes his random killings, eventually initiating a more-than-willing Otis in his frenzied rampages. The real horror in the film is not the actual killings, but rather in the sympathetic and non-judgmental approach the film takes as it follows Henry on his cooly detached and senseless pursuit of death. ★★★ $19.99

Her Summer Vacation

(1972, 90 min, Brazil/France, Victor di Mello) Passions erupt, clothes shed and sexual taboos are thrown on the bedroom floor after Giselle, a young Maria Schneider look-alike, spends the summer learning all about sex at her father's Brazilian ranch. Our Latin American nymphette, imbued with an insatiable and "anything goes" sexual appetite, soon develops torrid relationships with her lovely stepmother, the ranch's handyman, her bisexual cousin and even an all-too-willing former baby-sitter. All kinds of sexual proclivities are gleefully displayed in this soft "X" sexual smorgasbord including bisexuality, lesbianism, incest, voyeurism, rape, and pedophilia, with a hint of bestiality thrown in as well. Art? Hell no! But it is enjoyable fun for those who associate "art" films with yearning naked bodies set against exotic locales. (Dubbed) ★★ $29.99

Hercules
(1959, 107 min, Italy, Pietro Francisci) Muscleman Steve Reeves stars in this sleek adventure film as the Greek hero Hercules. The film which started the "gladiator" genre which was so popular in the early '60s. ★★½

Hercules in New York
(1970, 91 min, US, Arthur Allan Seidelman) Arnold Schwarzenegger's film debut finds him pitted against Arnold Stang in a grade-Z *Clash of the Titans*-like production. The picture cuts between New York and Mt. Olympus (actually a mound of rock in Central Park) as Arnie disobeys Zeus' order not to hang out with mortals. The spectacular production values in this one might have even cost as much as $100. All of the acting is bottom-of-the-barrel and Arnie's accent was so thick at the time that all of his lines are badly dubbed. Yes, it's trash, but hey, you must admit, this is the ultimate Saturday night party tape as well as a prime candidate for "Mystery Science Theatre 3000." ★ $19.99

Herdsmen of the Sun
(1988, 52 min, France, Werner Herzog) Narrated in English by director Herzog, this fascinating, anthropologic documentary focuses on the Woodabes, a Saharan nomadic tribe. The highlight of the film is the strange mating ceremony staged by the young male members, all with exotically handsome, mesmeric features, who don fancy dress and elaborate make-up for an unusual beauty pageant that is judged by the women of the tribe. ★★★ $59.99

Here Comes Mr. Jordan
(1941, 93 min, US, Alexander Hall) Classic supernatural comedy with Robert Montgomery in a splendid performance as a boxer who dies before his time; forced to look for another body to inhabit with the help of heavenly Mr. Jordan (Claude Rains). Special mention goes to James Gleason as Montgomery's exasperated coach. Remade in 1978 as *Heaven Can Wait*. ★★★½ $19.99

Hero
(1992, 112 min, US, Stephen Frears) There's a lot to like, and a lot to digest, in Frears' satire on heroism and the media. In the tradition of such classic comedies as *Nothing Sacred* and *Hail the Conquering Hero*, *Hero* is about a case of mistaken identity magnified to the Nth degree. And although it's not in the same class as those two comic gems, this nevertheless possesses a certain style and wit. Dustin Hoffman returns to Ratso Rizzo territory with a glorious sly performance as a petty crook who, in spite of himself, rescues a planeload of passengers after an aircraft crashes right in front of him. One of those he saves is TV reporter Geena Davis, who turns the city topsy-turvy looking for the "hero" who vanished into the night. When a substantial award is offered for him to come forward, onto the scene comes grifter and too-good-to-be-true

Andy Garcia. Not getting his due, Hoffman tries to convince anyone who will listen that he really is the hero, but no one will believe him. ★★★ $14.99

The Heroic Trio
(1993, 87 min, Hong Kong, Ching Siu-Tung & Johnny To) Only the wild world of Hong Kong action cinema could have produced this dizzying comic book-style movie about three female superheroes and their battle against an androgynous demon which is trying to breed a new, evil Emperor of China. Anita Mui (*Rumble in the Bronx*) is the mask-wearing Wonder Woman, who runs across electrical power lines and throws razor-sharp darts into her foes. The astonishing Michelle Yeoh (*Supercop*) is the kung fu mistress Invisible Girl, who is at first allied with the demon, but who soon learns she has a mysterious past connection with Wonder Woman. Maggie Cheung (also of *Supercop*) plays Thief Catcher, a motorcycle-riding, shotgun-toting, leather-clad tough chick who only does good when the pay is right. An outrageous, colorful and campy romp, *Heroic Trio* is cinema for the sheer fun of it, with flying heroes/heroines and villains, gravity-defying fight scenes, and an ending shamelessly ripped off from *The Terminator* — which is curiously improved upon in its inimitable Hong Kong style. (Cantonese with English subtitles) ★★★ $89.99

Hester Street
(1975, 90 min, US, Joan Micklin Silver) The first feature by Silver (*Crossing Delancy, Between the Lines*) weaves a rich tapestry of ghetto life in New York City's Bowery at the turn of the century. Carol Kane was given a well-deserved Academy Award nomination for her performance as Gilt, a Jewish émigré trying to assimilate as quietly as possible into her new country while still being supportive of her husband as he experiences a cultural identity crisis. ★★★ $29.99

Hexed
(1993, 91 min, US, Alan Spencer) Ayre Gross stars as a nerdish hotel clerk who fancies himself a trendy big-wig. Telling fellow workers of his famous (albeit ficticious) associations with celebs, he's put to the test when one of them shows up at the hotel. She's a model with secrets of her own — one of them being that she's a murderess. Too bad she didn't take aim at the script. Director-writer Spencer tries to create a frantic farce in the mistaken identity, door-slamming tradition; what he gives life to, however, Dr. Frankenstein wouldn't lay claim to. ★ $19.99

Hey Babu Riba
(1986, 109 min, Yugoslavia, Jovan Acin) Set in 1950s Yugoslavia, this charming and funny film recounts the days of innocence of four close friends and rowing partners who all fall in love with the same girl, their beautiful blonde coxswain. The young girl, flattered by all of the attention, likes them all and wishes to remain friends but rejects their advances only to unwisely fall in love with an ambitious mem-

The Hidden Fortress

ber of the Communist Party. A decidedly different coming-of-age film: one that explores the tender pain of first love and the bonds of loyal friendship, yet set against the political turmoil of a recently formed Communist government. (Serbo-Croatian with English subtitles) ★★★½ $19.99

Hi, Mom!
(1970, 87 min, US, Brian De Palma) Anarchy reigns in De Palma's frenzied sequel to *Greetings*. Robert De Niro stars as a returning Vietnam vet who takes on the roles of urban guerrilla, porno filmmaker and insurance salesman. Add to the fray a spoof of 1970s "encounter theatre" called "Be Black Baby," in which a group of black militants terrorize their white audience, and you've got a loopy and totally frantic vision of New York at the height of the counterculture generation. ★★★

The Hidden
(1987, 98 min, US, Jack Sholder) Alien Kyle MacLachlan gives L.A. cop Michael Nouri a hand in capturing an incredibly violence-prone extraterrestrial hiding out in the bodies of various citizens. Stylish, clever and full of action. ★★★ $14.99

The Hidden 2
(1994, 91 min, US, Seth Pinsker) Fans of the 1987 cult fave about an alien parasite whose presence causes radically violent behavior in its host have little to cheer in this unworthy sequel that features none of the original cast (though there is considerable footage from the first film) — and none of the originality. This time around, Raphael Sbarge stars as an alien cop sent to Earth as backup to stop the original alien from reproducing and turning the world into a party planet (darn!). He gets some help from "Nicole Kidman-wannabe" Kate Hodge. Though it's as bad as it sounds, it may be worth a look for fans of the horror genre. ★★ $14.99

Hidden Agenda
(1990, 106 min, GB, Ken Loach) Based on an amalgamation of actual scandals, this fictionalized account of official corruption in Northern Ireland is a superb addition to the already substantial library of British films which explore the machinations of the "secret" government. The tightly woven thread of intrigue begins when an American civil rights activist (Brad Dourif) is assassinated in Belfast. Frances McDormand and Brian Cox are both

excellent as, respectively, Dourif's girlfriend and an incorruptible Scotland Yard detective who together uncover the biggest political scandal since Watergate and Iran/Contra. ★★★½ $14.99

The Hidden Fortress

(1958, 126 min, Japan, Akira Kurosawa) One of Kurosawa's most entertaining works, *The Hidden Fortress* concerns a shrewd general (Toshiro Mifune) attempting to smuggle a petulant princess and her treasure trove of gold through enemy territory. Augmented by a bungling pair of peasants, the divergent group encounters enough hair-raising obstacles to sap the power of a light saber. Much in evidence is Kurosawa's sense of humor, largely embodied by Mifune's warrior who flails, cajoles and berates his ragtag crew. The inspiration for *Star Wars*. (Japanese with English subtitles) ★★★½ $39.99

Hidden Pleasures (Los Placeres Ocultos)

(1977, 95 min, Spain, Eloy de la Iglesia) Soon after his death, Franco's vice-like grip on cultural freedoms relaxed and artists like de la Iglesia were soon able to explore previously forbidden themes. De la Iglesia, the director of *El Diputado* and *Colegas*, produced this, Spain's first openly gay film: an impassioned drama about a closeted bank director who prowls the street of Madrid in search of male teenage prostitutes. His life is changed after he meets and falls in love with a straight young man. The controlled, placid surface of their relationship is shattered by contradictory and sometimes violent interplay concerning differences of class, intellect and convention. (Spanish with English subtitles) ★★★ $69.99

Hide and Seek

(1980, 90 min, Israel, Dan Wolman) A study of adolescents in the throes of self-discovery, this film explores the sensitive issue of forbidden love. Set in the late 1940s, the crucial years before the birth of the state of Israel, the film deals with the youthful quests and adjurations of a generation which would become the backbone of the new nation. (Hebrew with English subtitles) ★★★

Hero

Hide in Plain Sight

(1980, 98 min, US, James Caan) Caan made an impressive directorial debut with this based-on-fact story about a divorced man (Caan) who loses his children when his ex-wife's husband is relocated after testifying against the mob. ★★★ $19.99

Hideaway

(1995, 112 min, US, Brett Leonard) Jeff Goldblum stars in this uneventful thriller about a man who returns from the brink of death with the ability to see through the eyes of a serial killer (Jeremy Sisto). Good thing, too, because the killer's next victim is: (ta-da!) Goldblum's daughter (Alicia Silverstone). Dean R. Koontz's best-selling novel is reduced to pop/psychobabble drivel centering around Goldblum's need to make amends for the accidental death of his youngest daughter by risking everything to save his eldest. Director Leonard, who helmed *The Lawnmower Man*, gratuitously uses state-of-the-art F/X, but it's a clear attempt to disguise that there's nothing much going on here. Christine Lahti is wasted as Goldblum's wife. ★½ $19.99

Hiding Out

(1987, 98 min, US, Bob Giraldi) Jon Cryer's likable performance is the sole reason to see this amiable though lifeless comedy about a stockbroker who masquerades as a high school senior to hide from the mob. Also starring Keith Coogan as his cousin. ★★ $19.99

The Hiding Place

(1975, 145 min, US, James F. Collier) A moving true story about a Dutch family sent to a German concentration camp for hiding Jews during WWII. Produced by Billy Graham's Evangelistic Association, the film, though overtly religious, is not in any way "preachy" — and presents an unrelenting view of camp life. Good performances by Julie Harris, Eileen Heckart and Arthur O'Connell. ★★★ $19.99

High and Low

(1962, 142 min, Japan, Akira Kurosawa) This carefully paced thriller by Kurosawa stars Toshiro Mifune as a business executive who is forced to pay ransom to kidnappers who mistakenly stole his chauffeur's son. Adapted from the Ed McBain novel "King's Ransom," Kurosawa vividly captures the extent to which Mifune, an innocent bystander, has to accept responsibility for the actions of the repellent kidnappers. (Japanese with English subtitles) ★★★½

High Anxiety

(1977, 94 min, US, Mel Brooks) Perceptive Hitchcock spoof from director Brooks about a psychiatrist (Brooks) who becomes the new chief of an asylum with murderously funny results. Harvey Korman and Cloris Leachman are wonderful as kinky co-conspirators, and Madeline Kahn delectably brings to life the "icy blonde" persona of a 1930s namesake, Madeleine Carroll. Great fun for playing "spot the plot" with Hitchcock scholars. ★★★ $9.99

High Fidelity

(1989, 85 min, US, Allan Miller) *High Fidelity*, the latest collaboration from the team that

produced *From Mao to Mozart: Isaac Stern in China*, is a wonderfully humorous and spirited account of the working of the Guarneri String Quartet, the oldest string quartet in the U.S. which still maintains its original membership. Filled with the music of Haydn, Schubert and Beethoven, this documentary follows the quartet through rehearsals and recording sessions as well as performances in Prague, Venice, Baden-Baden and across the United States. ★★★½ $39.99

High Heels

(1972, 100 min, France, Claude Chabrol) A great cast can't save this minor Chabrol comedy mystery. Playboy doctor Jean-Paul Belmondo courts and weds Mia Farrow, only to then meet and fall in love with her sister, Laura Antonelli. Belmondo then goes about the task of eliminating Miss Antonelli's many suitors. (Dubbed) ★½

High Heels

(1991, 115 min, Spain, Pedro Almodóvar) On the heels (no pun intended) of his notorious *Tie Me Up! Tie Me Down!*, Almodóvar moves into new territory by looking a bit more closely at the human motives and desires he usually savages. The story revolves around a volatile estranged mother-daughter relationship; upon reuniting, they come to realize that they have been sharing the same man. Quicker than you can say *Women on the Verge*, the film fires headfirst into a series of alternately hilarious and tragic situations. The luminous Victoria Abril (*Tie Me Up! Tie Me Down!*) plays the successful but emotionally bankrupt daughter Becky. Marisa Paredes gives a virtuoso Joan Crawford-style performance as Becky's domineering, cold but ultimately caring mother. Almodóvar's trademark visuals blend with tragic and comedic melodrama to wonderful effect; he continues to be one of the most original and inventive directors working today. (Spanish with English subtitles) ★★★ $89.99

High Hopes

(1989, 110 min, GB, Mike Leigh) This bitingly sarcastic and yet poignant survival guide to Thatcher's England is often funny and always thought provoking. The story revolves around Cyril and Shirley, two lovers attempting to stay true to their leftist ideals and lifestyle despite the rising tide of heartless capitalism. The cast of memorable characters includes Cyril's embittered mother, teetering on senility; his hysterical sister, bent on obliterating her working-class roots with the plastic comforts of suburbia; and two willfully funny upper-class twits who blindly romp amidst the decay of Thatcher's New Society. ★★★½ $29.99

High Noon

(1952, 84 min, US, Fred Zinnemann) Gary Cooper won a second Oscar for his stirring performance in this western classic as a retiring small-town marshall who is abandoned by the townspeople when a murderer he sent away to prison returns to seek vengeance. The gunfight finale is arguably the best showdown in film. Also starring Grace Kelly and Thomas Mitchell. ★★★★ $19.99

High Plains Drifter

(1973, 105 min, US, Clint Eastwood) A solid western tale from Eastwood about the title character (Eastwood) protecting a small town from a group of prison parolees out for vengeance. With Verna Bloom and Marianna Hill. ★★★ $14.99

High Road to China

(1983, 120 min, US, Brian G. Hutton) Having been the first choice, and unavailable, for *Raiders of the Lost Ark*, Tom Selleck finally starred in a big-screen, tongue-in-cheek adventure – unfortunately for him, it was this pleasant but minor film. Selleck plays a daredevil flyer hired by Bess Armstrong to find her missing father. ★★ $19.99

High School Confidential

(1958, 85 min, US, Jack Arnold) The legendary cult classic featuring "the smart aleck leader of the hot rod set," "the girl who has too much too soon," and "the glamorous teacher devoted to thwarting delinquency." Cast features Russ Tamblyn, Mamie Van Doren, Jan Sterling, John Drew Barrymore, Jackie Coogan and Jerry Lee Lewis. They don't make 'em like this anymore! ★★ $14.99

High School High

(1996, 90 min, US, Hart Bochner) In this *Airplane*-like parody of *Dangerous Minds* and *Stand and Deliver*, Jon Lovitz plays the idealistic son of the snobbish headmaster of a posh private school who takes a teaching job at Marion Berry High, the worst school in the city. The first third of the film is actually funny, alternating between sharp satire and so-dumb-it's-funny humor in true Z-A-Z fashion. Unfortunately, the writers run out of ideas far too quickly, and *High School High* ends up becoming a slightly comic variation of what it started out satirizing – a cheesy, feel-good, inspirational teen drama. Too bad, too; with a little more creativity and chutzpah, this could've been a nice surprise. As it is, it's barely a passable time-filler. ★★ $102.99

High Season

(1987, 92 min, GB, Clare Peploe) First-time director Peploe co-wrote (along with son Mark) this tepid mish-mash about the effects of tourism on a small Greek island. The beautiful Jacqueline Bisset competes with the scenery in her role as a photographer whose life is complicated by obnoxious tourists, inept spies and her self-important ex-husband (James Fox in a suitably hedonistic role). No doubt Britain's idea of "mindless entertainment." Also with Irene Papas and (look closely) Kenneth Branagh. ★★ $14.99

High Sierra

(1941, 100 min, US, Raoul Walsh) Humphrey Bogart is at his best in this stirring tale of a tired, aging killer on the lam from the police. The theme is an old one, but it is masterfully rejuvenated by Bogart's unforgettable performance. Also contributing to the overall excellence of the film are stand-out performances by Joan Leslie, as Bogey's goody-goody heartthrob, and Ida Lupino, as the not-so-goody moll who pines for his love. ★★★½ $19.99

High Society

(1956, 107 min, US, Charles Walters) Amiable musical remake of *The Philadelphia Story* with songs by Cole Porter. Grace Kelly, Bing Crosby and Frank Sinatra take over the Katharine Hepburn, Cary Grant and James Stewart roles. ★★★ $14.99

High Spirits

(1988, 97 min, US, Neil Jordan) Peter O'Toole, Daryl Hannah and Steve Guttenberg manage to wring a few laughs from this tepid ghost comedy with Guttenberg as an American tourist visiting an Irish castle who meets and falls in love with ghost Hannah. Also with Beverly D'Angelo and Liam Neeson. ★½

High Tide

(1987, 104 min, Australia, Gillian Armstrong) Judy Davis reteams with director Armstrong in this well-crafted, emotionally powerful story of a woman (Davis), stranded in a small coastal town, who befriends an adolescent girl. Armstrong's fine, sensitive direction elevates this absorbing drama well above the clichéd, maudlin soap opera it very well could have been. Davis, Claudia Karvan as the young girl, and especially Jan Adele as the girl's grandmother, all offer outstanding performances. ★★★½ $14.99

Higher Learning

(1995, 127 min, US, John Singleton) In *Boyz n the Hood*, director Singleton shaded his story with a subtlety which belied its incendiary theme. But in an effort to punctuate his thought-provoking *Higher Learning*, about campus strife in the '90s, he has given way to stereotypes and heavy-handedness. In remarkable detail, the story shows the fractious campus life awaiting a group of college freshman. As the students come to adhere to their own agendas – racial, sexual, political – the cookie-cutter story lays the way to a tragic but inevitable climax. Among a splendid cast are Omar Epps, very good as a black athlete on scholarship; Michael Rapaport, who makes the most of a one-dimensional fascist; and Kristy Swanson, who is sympathetic as a white bread "do-gooder" exploring her sexuality. Best of all, however, is Laurence Fishburne as a dedicated professor. *Higher Learning* may recall the best of the 1960s campus revolutionary flicks, but in doing so it is also doomed to repeat many of their mistakes. ★★½ $19.99

Highlander

(1986, 116 min, GB, Russell Mulcahy) Christopher Lambert stars as a Scottish member of a bizarre group of immortal warriors who do battle with each other down through the ages. The story skips around from 12th-century Scotland to modern-day Manhattan to 18th-century Boston (and so on) and, as a result, the film sometimes becomes narratively incoherent. But despite this shortcoming, the action is fantastic. Sean Connery is his usual marvelous self as Lambert's mentor and Clancy Brown is excellent as his menacing adversary. (Letterboxed director's cut retails for $19.99) ★★½ $14.99

High Plains Drifter

Highlander 2: The Quickening

(1990, 90 min, US, Russell Mulcahy) Good special effects (as well as some chintzy ones) help add to the cheesy fun of this inferior remake of the 1985 swashbuckling adventure. Sean Connery and Christopher Lambert dust off their broadswords as they do battle with alien assassins (led by the ever-leering Michael Ironside) out to destroy the Earth's fragile ecosystem. Also with Virginia Madsen and John C. McGinley. (Letterboxed director's cut retails for $19.99) ★★ $14.99

Highlander: The Final Dimension

(1994, 100 min, GB, Andy Morahan) Director Morahan should have applied the Highlander credo, "There can be only one," to the making of sequels and not served up this totally inept and unsatisfying conclusion to the cultish series about a race of immortals whose destiny is fulfilled only by decapitating each other and absorbing their power. Christopher Lambert reprises his role as the centuries-old swordsman who must now face his greatest challenge (next to career resuscitation) in the form of a recently unearthed immortal (Mario Van Peebles in an undisciplined performance). Offscreen beheadings, major plot holes and a totally gratuitous subplot about an old flame reincarnated as an antiquities expert (the fetching Deborah Unger) make this rehash about as ridiculous as it sounds. ★ $14.99

The Highest Honor

(1984, 99 min, Australia, Peter Maxwell) Compelling World War II drama which recounts the true story of the unique friendship between two enemies: a POW and his Japanese jailer, both torn by their sense of duty and sense of humanity. This action/drama is interesting but not as riveting as the similarly themed *Merry Christmas, Mr. Lawrence*. ★★½ $14.99

Highway 61

(1992, 99 min, Canada, Bruce McDonald) A Canadian independent feature, this road comedy contains much of the hip and anarchic humor which distinguishes Jim Jarmusch and Hal Hartley's works. Though not entirely successful in its send-ups and Lynch-like Americana admonishments, there's an abundance of offbeat and wildly satiric jabs at the denizens both on and off the road. Don McKellar, displaying a charmingly subdued persona, is a staid Canadian small-town barber taken on the ride of his life by "escapee from a heavy metal crew" roadie Valerie Buhagiar. En route to New Orleans transporting the dead body she claims to be her brother, and pursued by a man who identifies himself as Satan, the two disparate travelers wind their way down an erratic highway as loopy and disjointed as the eccentrics they meet. ★★★ $94.99

Highway of Heartache

(1994, 86 min, Canada, Gregory Wild) Excessively wacky, with cartoonish acting and set design, this defiantly offensive no-budget country musical aspires to be an intoxicating mixture of John Waters and Patsy Cline, but after a promising start (highlighted by the witty and catchy musical numbers) it soon falls flat. The story follows the tumultuous life of Wynona-Sue Turnpike (Barbara Chamberlain), an eternally optimistic if trigger-happy woman and aspiring superstar whose road to fameis littered with dead bodies. In between it all, there are plastic penises, musical numbers, big Baltimore-style hair and a weird Greek chorus in the form of two lip-synching drag queens who bitchily follow our heroine. Trying mightily to be an outrageous spoof, *Highway of Heartache* is saddled with a weak script, and though brainless fun, it ends up being a third-rate imitation of the master fo the genre, John Waters, and his *Female Trouble*. ★★ $79.99

Highway to Hell

(1992, 100 min, US, Ate De Jong) Chad Lowe (yes, Rob's little brother) and Kristy Swanson (*Buffy the Vampire Slayer*) star as a young couple on their way to Las Vegas for a secret wedding. Unknowingly, the pair find a passageway to Hell, and meet the Devil himself (played by Patrick Bergin). Filled with car chases, battles with zombie bikers, cannibal freaks and someone named Hell Cop, this fast-paced horror/adventure/comedy provides mindless fun and fright for all. ★★½ $19.99

Hill Number One

(1951, 57 min, US, Arthur Pierson) James Dean makes his first dramatic screen appearance (or at least so the box says) in this pietistic TV Easter sermon produced by St. Paul Films and sponsored by the Family Rosary Crusade. A group of soldiers shelling a hill in Korea (among them is Roddy McDowall) is getting fed up with the inhumanity of war when the company pastor shows up and gives them a homily on the victory won by Jesus on Easter Sunday at "Hill Number One." The story of the Resurrection is then acted out with all the dramatic flair of a high school Christmas pageant with Dean as John the Apostle, Ruth Hussey as the Virgin Mary and Michael Ansara as the converted centurion, Decius. In the end, the action returns to Korea, where the good chaplain reminds his men that Christ's victory over death gives them the green light to continue their shelling. Heady stuff by itself, but it's topped off with an advertisement in which we are all exhorted to pray the rosary. ★ $14.99

Hill 24 Doesn't Answer

(1959, 106 min, Israel, Thorton Dickinson) Hill 24 is one of the foothills dominating the approach to Jerusalem. Set in 1949, on the eve of the U.N. cease-fire imposed during the Israeli war of independence, this fiercely realistic drama follows the actions of four young Zionists who volunteer to defend the strategic hill in order to maintain access to the besieged city. A historically important film that successfully captures the tensions in the birth of a nation. (English dialogue) ★★★ $79.99

Hillbillies in a Haunted House

(1967, 88 min, US, Jean Yarbrough) Two country singers and their manager spend the night in a seemingly abandoned mansion. Little do they know that a gang of foreign spies is hiding out in the basement, poised to steal a secret formula for rocket propellant. Warning: Lots of songs! ★ $19.99

The Hills Have Eyes

(1977, 89 min, US, Wes Craven) Tense and gory horror film from director Craven (the original *A Nightmare on Elm Street*). A vacationing family makes a very wrong turn in the desert — and find themselves up against a group of psychotic cannibals (are there any other kind?). ★★★ $9.99

The Hills Have Eyes, Pt. 2

(1984, 86 min, US, Wes Craven) Sequel to Craven's cult horror film. This time out, it's some teenagers in trouble, as they travel through the desert. Lacks the suspense and style of the original. ★★ $14.99

Himatsuri

(1985, 115 min, Japan, Mitsuo Yangimachi) One of the Japanese New Wave's best efforts so far, *Himatsuri* brilliantly explores the complex mental landscape of modern Japan, torn between advanced technology and the superstitions and mystical undercurrents that pervade the Japanese subconscious. Set in a fishing village, it follows the spiritual transformation of a rough-hewn but affable lumberjack (the suberb Kinya Kitaoji) who moves from defiling the land to communication with the gods that inhabit it. (Japanese with English subtitles) ★★★½ $59.99

The Hindenberg

(1975, 125 min, US, Robert Wise) George C. Scott and Anne Bancroft head a good cast in this inflated disaster film, which speculates that the infamous Hindenburg crash of 1937 was actually sabotage. Outstanding special effects and actual footage interspersed heighten the tension at the end — and what a knockout ending it is. Also with William Atherton, Roy Thinnes, Gig Young, Burgess Meredith and Charles Durning. ★★ $14.99

The Hired Hand

(1971, 95 min, US, Peter Fonda) Fonda's follow-up to *Easy Rider* is this elegiac and subversive western which bombed at the box office. Fonda stars as a mysterious wanderer who returns to his wife (Verna Bloom) after a seven-year absence. Panned by critics, this lyrically filmed mood piece on loneliness, loyalty and the nature of love was lost in the flood of "trip-

py" films in the early '70s, but still, it compares favorably to other "modern westerns" championed by Peckinpah. ★★★ $14.99

Hiroshima

(1995, 165 min, Canada/Japan, Roger Spottiswoode & Koreyoshi Kurahara) Made-for-cable, this illuminating and extremely accomplished film is an even-handed depiction of the events leading to the dropping of the atomic bomb on Hiroshima and Nagasaki during WWII. Told in a quasi-documentary style, *Hiroshima* incorporates actual newsreel footage which has been masterfully tinted and juxtaposes it with an astonishingly authentic re-creation of the times and events — shot in subdued hues — to produce a jarring, fascinating narrative. Certain scenes are indistinguishable between real and re-enacted. Beginning with the death of FDR, the story is seen from Truman's perspective as the new Commander-in-Chief, and through the eyes of Japan's Prime Minister Suzuki as the Japanese high council debates their future war efforts. The film balances its time between the behind-the-scenes strategies of the two governments, the dilemma facing the scientists and pilots involved with the bomb, and moving interviews with those who were actually there. A large international cast excels, though Kenneth Welsh as Truman and Tatsuo Matsumura as Suzuki ground the film with their inspired portrayals. (English and Japanese with English subtitles) ★★★½ $19.99

Hiroshima Maiden

(1988, 58 min, US, Joan Darling) A young Japanese woman from Hiroshima comes to America in 1955 and stays with a family while she undergoes treatment for radiation burns. Everyone welcomes her except the oldest son, who is persuaded by his friends that she is a spy. This touching though slowly paced drama is inspired by the stories of the real-life "Hiroshima Maidens." With Tamlyn Tomita, Susan Blakely and Richard Masur. ★★½ $29.99

Hiroshima Mon Amour

(1959, 91 min, France, Alain Resnais) Obsessive pasts haunt the affair of a French woman and a Japanese architect in 1950s Hiroshima. The woman's memories of her scandalous involvement with a German soldier and the piercing recollections of nuclear horror both unite and repel the two lovers. Resnais' brilliant first film was scripted by Marguerite Duras. (French with English subtitles) ★★★★ $14.99

His Girl Friday

(1940, 92 min, US, Howard Hawks) Rosalind Russell and Cary Grant star in Hawks' fast-talking, wise-cracking, sex-change version of *The Front Page*. Russell is the ace reporter set to wed the less than dynamic Ralph Bellamy. Grant is her editor and ex-husband determined to thwart the match. A classic screwball comedy filmed at a machine-gun pace, the film's jokes are hilarious, the situations outlandish, and Grant and Russell are in terrific form. ★★★★ $19.99

H

History Is Made at Night

(1937, 98 min, US, Frank Borzage) Intriguing blend of romance, comedy and melodrama with Jean Arthur and Charles Boyer in fine form in the story of Arthur divorcing husband Colin Clive and falling in love with headwaiter Boyer. ★★½ $14.99

A History of Racist Animation

(90 min, US) See Popeye and Superman battle the Japanese; Bugs Bunny teasing a black hunter; the Chinese portrayed as idiot laundrymen and other racial stereotypes in this amazing collection of propaganda cartoons from the golden age of animation. $34.99

A History of the Blue Movie

(Alex De Renzy) Film and sex have long provided amusement for people of all sorts. This "educational" endeavor unites the two, providing a historical rundown of cinematic erotica. Director De Renzy covers the evolution of pornography from burlesque to fraternity house favorites to hard-core stag gems to other vintage essays into explicitness. Also included are excerpts from some classic scorchers, "Smart Aleck" (starring Candy Barr) and "The Nun's Story." ★★

History of the World Pt. I

(1981, 92 min, US, Mel Brooks) An alternately funny and fuzzy, sometimes vulgar history lesson from the not-so-professorial mind of Mel Brooks. Vignettes tell the progress of man from primitive cave dwellers to the Roman Empire to the French Revolution. In typical Brooks fashion, the film features outrageous comic situations, unbelievably silly jokes and an all-star cast. Among its stars are Gregory Hines, Dom DeLuise, Madeline Kahn, Harvey Korman, Cloris Leachman, Sid Caesar, Bea Arthur and Orson Welles as the narrator. ★★ $9.99

Hit!

(1973, 135 min, US, Sidney J. Furie) Embittered over the drug-related death of his daughter, U.S. agent Nick Allen (Billy Dee Williams) teams up with an underwater warfare expert (Richard Pryor) to seek vengence against a group of drug smugglers in Marseilles. Overly detailed and lengthy at times, but more-than-exciting action and witty dialogue help to keep this one moving. ★★½ $14.99

The Hit

(1985, 98 min, GB, Stephen Frears) Willie Parker (Terence Stamp) dropped a dime on his mobster cohorts. For his confession, the British magistrate granted him clemency and a new identity in a bucolic Spanish villa. Now, ten years later, he's being hunted down by a hired killer and appears doomed to pay for his finger-pointing. However, things go peculiarly astray when this condemned man's tranquil acceptance of his death sentence throws his edgy executioner (John Hurt) for a loop. In spite of its ominous subject matter and jagged action, The Hit harbors a sly undertow of dark humor which distinguishes it from simpler underworld thrillers. Also with Tim Roth and Laura del Sol. ★★★

The Hitch-Hiker

(1953, 71 min, US, Ida Lupino) Little-known but critically acclaimed film noir, co-written and directed by Lupino, about an ex-con who hitches rides, then robs and kills his captives. A tense psychological thriller. With Edmond O'Brien and Frank Lovejoy. ★★★ $24.99

The Hitcher

(1986, 97 min, US, Robert Harmon) Rutger Hauer is evil personified in this taut thriller about a young man who is terrorized by a maniacal hitchhiker. C. Thomas Howell, in what may easily be his best role to date, is the innocent driver whose trek across Nevada turns into a deadly game of cat and mouse. Filled with unrelenting suspense and seething with homoerotic imagery, this film, not for the faint of heart, will electrify fans of the genre. ★★★

Hitler's Children

(1943, 83 min, US, Edward Dmytryk) Though the title suggests They Saved Hitler's Brain rather than Watch on the Rhine, this compelling 1940s anti-Nazi propaganda drama is very much in the latter film's league in its cautionary tale of Nazi oppression. Sort of a "Romeo and Juliet" set in the Fatherland, the story follows the friendship and romance of a Nazi youth (Tim Holt) and an American girl (Bonita Granville) living in Germany. A big hit in its day, the title refers to the dictator's army of children undergoing fascist brainwashing. ★★★ $29.99

Hobson's Choice

(1954, 107 min, GB, David Lean) Charles Laughton offers a priceless performance in this delicious working-class comedy about a tyrannical bootmaker who struggles to maintain his dominion over his three daughters. Brenda de Banzie plays a strong-willed daughter who defies his authority by marrying the man of her choice. ★★★½ $29.99

Hocus Pocus

(1993, 96 min, US, Kenny Ortega) Released through Disney's children's distribution arm rather than its more adult-oriented subsidiaries, this very lightweight but amiable fantasy half-heartedly recaptures the frivolity of the Fred MacMurray comedies of the 1960s. Bette Midler, Kathy Najimy and Sarah Jessica Parker star as 17th-century witches who return to modern-day Salem and run "amok, amok, amok." With more hokum than hocus, the witches set out to steal the souls of the town's children. Their only opposition are three spunky kids. Most of the laughs are mild, and the film gives the impression of being more risque than it is – it's harmless fare. Though she's not given much to do, Midler generates some energy, and sings "I Put a Spell on You," the film's only real highlight. ★★½ $14.99

Hoffa

(1992, 100 min, US, Danny DeVito) This sprawling biography of the tough-as-nails labor leader benefits from a gutsy performance by Jack Nicholson in the title role, but it would have been better if it were more Hoffa and less Danny DeVito. There are few scenes here where the co-star/director's presence is not apparent, and that's the big problem: after nearly two-and-a-half hours, we know more

about DeVito's ficticious sidekick, Bobby Ciaro, than we do of James Hoffa – and that's no fault of Nicholson. The film traces Hoffa's rise to power, from his determined attempts to enlist truckers to the union to his prominence as the no-nonsense Teamsters president. With no thanks to David Mamet's script, DeVito – whose visual style apes Coppola – glosses over Hoffa's personal life in favor of mano-a-mano confrontations and feverish speeches that eventually grow repetitious. ★★ $9.99

The Holcroft Covenant

(1985, 112 min, GB, John Frankenheimer) Master suspense director Frankenheimer is not too successful in bringing Robert Ludlum's first novel to the screen. Michael Caine is led on a globe-trotting series of adventures as he searches for a fortune left behind by his dead father (a comrade-in-arms to Hitler). ★½ $14.99

Hold Me, Thrill Me, Kiss Me

(1993, 110 min, US, Joel Hershman) If one can pay homage to Pedro Almodóvar, Russ Meyer and Woody Allen in the same film, first-time director Hershman has done it with this quirky comedy. Quite a task, but Hershman has the prodigious and underexposed talents of Adrianne Shelley (Trust) to help him out. Set in a seedy trailer park, the plot is just the old "boy meets stripper, stripper handcuffs boy to bed, boy begins to fall for stripper's animal-loving little sis" story, with a little murder and mayhem thrown in for good measure. Also starring Diane Ladd and Sam Young. ★★★ $92.99

Hold That Ghost

(1941, 80 min, US, Arthur Lubin) In one of their best films, Abbott and Costello meet their comedic equal in Joan Davis when they spend the night in a house haunted not only by ghosts but by mobsters. A wonderful romp, and Davis is a particular delight. ★★★ $14.99

A Hole in the Head

(1959, 120 min, US, Frank Capra) Frank Sinatra sings "High Hopes" in this Capra sentimental favorite. Frank plays a down-on-his-heels motel owner raising a young son (Eddie Hodges) and trying to make ends meet. Edward G. Robinson, Eleanor Parker, Carolyn Jones and Thelma Ritter also star. ★★★ $19.99

The Holes (Les Gaspards)

(1981, 92 min, France/US, Pierre Tchernia) An all-star cast (Philippe Noiret, Michel Serrault, Gérard Depardieu) and a peculiarly un-French premise makes this fantasy/comedy a real find for Francophiles. The plot is as follows: Living in the labyrinthine maze of ancient tunnels and caves deep under the streets of Paris is a society of people who want to escape the world above. Their tranquility is disturbed, however, after an ambitious Minister of Public Works begins to dig up the city for his many pet construction projects, one being that the Seine would be paved over for conversion into a downtown highway! The mole people, led by an aristocratic Noiret, take matters into their own hands by kidnapping tourists, bicyclists and even policemen in a frantic effort to keep progress at bay. Laced

Holiday

with many funny moments and featuring a young, mop-headed Depardieu, this strange film is imaginatively executed and wackily entertaining. (Dubbed) ★★★ $79.99

Holiday

(1938, 94 min, US, George Cukor) The second and more popular version of Philip Barry's Broadway hit, this delightful comedy stars Katharine Hepburn and Cary Grant, in their third of four films together, as non-conformists up against an ever-restrictive world. Grant, at his most charming, plays a free spirit engaged to socialite Doris Nolan, soon discovering he has more in common with her sister Kate. Lew Ayres stands out as the alcoholic black sheep of the family, and Edward Everett Horton, repeating his role from the original 1930 film, is marvelous as Grant's mentor and friend. ★★★★ $19.99

Holiday Affair

(1949, 87 min, US, Don Hartman) A beautiful and young Janet Leigh plays a war widow who must decide between Robert Mitchum and Wendell Corey. A pleasant comedy-drama enhanced by two delightful performances by Leigh and Mitchum. ★★½ $14.99

Holiday Hotel

(1978, 109 min, France, Michel Lang) The French preoccupation with both love and summer vacation is wittily explored in this sexy, cheerful comedy. Guy Marchand (*Cousin, Cousine; Entre Nous*) is a frazzled father whose 16-year-old daughter is set loose at a small summer resort during August holiday. Lots of French skin and a giddy good time. (French with English subtitles) ★★½

Holiday Inn

(1942, 101 min, US, Mark Sandrich) Bing Crosby and Fred Astaire are the top-liners (can't get any bigger than that) at Bing's holiday resort (only open during holidays, naturally). As the romantic interest, Marjorie Reynolds is splendid; as is the Irving Berlin score (which includes "White Christmas"). Delightful. ★★★½ $14.99

Hollywood Erotic Film Festival

(1980s, 95 min, US) Erotic filmmaking, as opposed to the pornographic variety, is an all-too-rare style of approach to the eternal mysteries of sex and our lemming-like attraction to its fatal desire. This feature-length compilation of 12 short films is the perfect way to cap off a romantic evening with that special someone. Included in the program are "Strip Tease," a lustful animated piece by Bruno Bozzetto; "Erection," a riotous spoof on phallic power; and "Reproduction Cycles," which details the mating rituals of the little-known Martian microbe. $44.99

Hollywood Shuffle

(1987, 82 min, US, Robert Townsend) A series of side-splitting vignettes tell the tale of a struggling black actor's search for a serious role in Hollywood. Stand-up comic and first-time director Townsend redefined the term "shoestring budget" when he "maxed out" his credit cards in order to pay the final production costs for this spoof. His strategy paid off and the resulting lampoon on racial inequity in tinseltown went on to reap huge and well-deserved rewards at the box office. ★★★

The Holy Innocents

(1984, 108 min, Spain, Marto Camus) In Franco's Spain, 1962, the modern world has yet to arrive at many rural communities where the feudal system of landowning gentry and peasant laborers continue. This is the setting for Camus' powerful and rousing drama of oppression and revenge. Paco and Regula, husband and wife, are gatekeepers to an aristocratic family. Their struggles — raising a family, eking out a subsistence and maintaining some self-respect — provide the soul for this touching film. (Spanish with English subtitles) ★★★

Hombre

(1967, 111 min, US, Martin Ritt) Paul Newman has a sardonic cool about him as a white man living among the Indians who journeys with a group of travelers on a stagecoach line's final voyage. Set in the last days of the Old West, director Ritt's riveting parable (based on an Elmore Leonard story) probes racial intolerance against Indians and the price of humanism as Newman and co-riders Fredric March, Diane Cilento and Martin Balsam are up against bad guy Richard Boone, highwaymen and the elements. A thoroughly satisfying western, featuring a terrific performance from Cilento as a gutsy widow. ★★★½ $14.99

Home Alone

(1990, 103 min, US, Chris Columbus) John Hughes wrote the script for this box-office smash about an eight-year-old boy left behind when his family leaves for their European Christmas vacation. Little Macaulay Culkin plays Kevin, whose idyllic stay home alone is interrupted by two inept burglars. Much of the film centers on Kevin's ingenious defense ploys, and the hilariously sadistic acts of sabotage he institutes against the thieves. Joe Pesci and Daniel Stern are the unfortunate criminals. Catherine O'Hara and John Heard play his distraught parents, and John Candy has an amusing cameo as a polka king. However, it's youngster Culkin who captivates with a refreshing variation on the precocious youth; and his enormous contribution to this romp should not be overlooked. ★★★ $19.99

Home Alone 2: Lost in New York

(1992, 113 min, US, Chris Columbus) The lucrative adventures of young Kevin McAllister (Macaulay Culkin) continue in this by-the-numbers but amusing sequel. The action has been transplanted from the suburbs to the more exciting mean streets of Manhattan. Predictably, Kevin becomes separated from his family again, meets up with the recently escaped Wet Bandits (Joe Pesci and Daniel Stern) and sets out to creatively foil their plot to rob a toy store. Writer-producer John Hughes sticks to his winning formula like tar to a rooftop, though this time Kevin is less an innocent child and more a preachy know-it-all. Still, there's little denying Culkin's charm, the broad physical comedy of Pesci and Stern (and their stunt doubles) and the colorful, if underused, support of Tim Curry, Rob Schneider and Dana Ivey. However, this is much more violent than the first film. ★★½ $19.99

The Home and the World

(1984, 130 min, India, Satyajit Ray) Set in 1908 British-ruled India, this is a shattering yet measured study of emancipation, commitment and love. The story concerns a liberal man's desire to free his wife of purdah and allow her to mingle with his male friends. His plan backfires, however, when she becomes fascinated by an intelligent revolutionary politician. Ray intricately explores the shifting tides of emotion between the three in this exquisite drama. (Bengali with English subtitles) ★★★

Home for the Holidays

(1995, 105 min, US, Jodie Foster) Foster's directorial follow-up to *Little Man Tate* continues her examination of familial conflicts and off-the-fringe characters in this sometimes funny family comedy which proves "it's all relative." The slightly neurotic but sane Holly Hunter returns home for Thanksgiving holiday. To anyone who has suffered through family get-togethers, her anxiety is all the more empathetic as she is greeted by a varied assortment of relatives. Anne Bancroft and Charles Durning are her interfering though caring parents, Geraldine Chaplin is the flaky aunt, and in the film's most spirited portrayal, Robert Downey, Jr. is her jocular gay brother. Dylan McDermott is Downey's handsome dinner guest whose identity is meant to be a surprise. While all the characters have their peculiarities, Foster and writer W.D. Richter ultimately exploit their endearing characteristics as well. The film is at its best up to and during the eventful dinner scene — which provides some genuinely hilarious moments — but like a holiday meal, it leaves little room for expansion afterwards. The closing montage nicely brings the film together. ★★½ $19.99

A Home of Our Own

(1993, 104 min, US, Tony Bill) Kathy Bates' sturdy performance as a widowed mother of six elevates this sentimental drama, literally a poor woman's *Alice Doesn't Live Here Anymore*. Set in the early 1960s, the story follows Bates and her children as they leave their Los Angeles home

H

and head east for greener pastures. En route, they settle in Idaho, where they scrape out a living in a small rural town and try to come together as a family all the while trying to make the titular dream come true. As Shayne, the eldest son of the "Lacey tribe," Edward Furlong is impressive. ★★½ $19.99

Home of the Brave

(1949, 86 min, US, Mark Robson) Powerful WWII drama based on Arthur Laurents' play about a black soldier (James Edwards) experiencing prejudices from fellow G.I.s while fighting in the South Pacific. Produced by Stanley Kramer. ★★★½ $19.99

Homeboy

(1988, 118 min, US, Michael Seresin) After his daring performance in *Barfly*, Mickey Rourke goes even further over the edge with a highly unusual portrayal of an illiterate, monosyllabic boxer competing one last time for the title. Christopher Walken plays his unsavory manager. A downbeat but curiously appealing boxing drama which unfortunately gives in to many clichés of the genre. ★★½

Homecoming

(1948, 113 min, US, Mervyn LeRoy) In postwar roles, Clark Gable and Lana Turner both demonstrate a dramatic maturity together in comparison to their two earlier teamings. In this compelling if familiar wartime story, Gable stars as a society doctor who enlists and is sent overseas, where he eventually falls for headstrong nurse Turner. Anne Baxter is Gable's wife back home: she also serving who only stands and waits. Gable's character's name is Ulysses, which suggests the film's inspiration in the story of a soldier who returns home a changed man. Baxter's scenes are perfunctory, as Gable and Turner's romance and working relationship during the war are the film's main attraction. ★★½ $19.99

The Homecoming

(1973, 111 min, GB, Peter Hall) Hall's production of Harold Pinter's now-classic play is perhaps one of the finest stage-to-screen adaptations to come out of the American Film Theatre series. This riveting family saga about a young academic who returns to his parents' London home with his newlywed wife in tow is peppered with Pinter's wry humor as well as his incisive views on domestic strife. Outstanding performances abound from a cast which includes Cyril Cusack, Ian Holm, Michael Jayston and Vivien Merchant. ★★★★

Homer and Eddie

(1989, 100 min, US, Andrei Konchalovsky) James Belushi is Homer, a sheltered, child-like man. Whoopi Goldberg is Eddie, an already-crazed woman who just found out she has a month to live. Together, this unlikely pair take to the road and learn about themselves and each other. With Karen Black and Anne Ramsey. ★★ $9.99

Homeward Bound: The Incredible Journey

(1993, 90 min, US, DuWayne Dunham) If you wondered why the folks at Disney felt compelled to remake their classic 1963 adventure

film *The Incredible Journey*, your question will be answered 15 minutes into it. The perfectly cast voices of Michael J. Fox as the young pup Chance, Sally Field as the hilariously disdainful cat Sassy, and Don Ameche as the wise and faithful old dog Shadow, combined with the amazingly facile animal actors, create a winsome and charming experience. The three pets are left on a neighbor's ranch while their family is temporarily away. As time passes, they become convinced that the family is in trouble and decide to make their own way back to their old house, thus beginning their "incredible journey." This is indeed one of those rare family movies that will please everyone. ★★★ $19.99

Homeward Bound II: Lost in San Francisco

(1996, 89 min, US) With most of the original cast intact, this sequel lacks the spontaneous charm of the original. Part of the problem is that the transposition from the country to the city adds urban characters that are both contrived and formulaic. While the animals perform amazing tricks, they too often seem to be out of step with their expressions of emotions. On this family vacation, the three animals escape from their cages on the airport runway, fearing that they are going to a "bad place." They must then battle their way through the animalistic streets of San Francisco, making friends and saving a child and a kitten from a raging fire along the way. Not one of the better talking animal films available. ★★ $22.99

Homicide

(1991, 100 min, US, David Mamet) Award-winning playwright Mamet's third outing as director is a gritty crime drama about a Jewish homicide detective struggling with his ethnic identity. Mamet regular Joe Mantegna stars as Bobby Gold, a hard-nosed inner-city cop who is hot on the trail of a dangerous fugitive, and a probable promotion. But, when a Jewish shopkeeper is murdered, he gets lassoed into working the case by the deceased's family. Disavowing his heritage, he tries to get off the case and, at first, derides the family's hysteria over the possibly anti-Semitic nature of the crime. Mamet's characteristic terse dialogue punctuates this deftly made modern-day morality play. Mantegna's raw portrayal contributes greatly to the film's dark, moody atmosphere. ★★★★ $19.99

L'Homme Blesse

(1984, 105 min, France, Patrice Chereau) Adrift in the French underworld of hustlers and pick-ups, the innocent Henri (Jean-Hughes Anglade) experiences a brutal awakening to his gay sexuality. He witnesses a trick being beaten in the train station toilet, surrenders to the culprit's fierce embrace and finds himself hopelessly lost in ardor for this mysterious thug. Suddenly drawn to rough trade, Henri undergoes a number of hardships before finding liberation in a shocking final act of conquest. A disturbing yet powerful examination of sexual obsession and one man's personal sexual odyssey. (French with English subtitles) ★★★ $79.99

John Wayne in *Hondo*

Hondo

(1953, 84 min, US, John Farrow) Though not on the level of John Wayne's work with director John Ford, *Hondo* is an exciting and well-made western which features a sterling film debut by Geraldine Page. Wayne plays a half-Indian scout who befriends Page and her young son, who have been left alone on their ranch located dangerously close to an Apache camp. Wayne gives an overly mannered performance, but is countered by Oscar nominee Page, who gives a solid portrayal of a stalwart homesteader. ★★★ $19.99

Honey

(1978, 89 min, Italy/Spain, Gianfranco Angelucci) A sensual, erotic drama about a young woman novelist who takes her manuscript to a publisher's home and is asked to read passages from it. What unfolds is her steamy story of first sexual encounters and discovered pleasures. Starring Clio Goldsmith and Fernando Rey. (Dubbed) ★★

Honey, I Blew Up the Kid

(1992, 89 min, US, Randal Kleiser) Rick Moranis and Marcia Strassman reprise their roles in this mildly entertaining rehash of *Honey, I Shrunk the Kids*. This time, of course, scientist Moranis blunders in the opposite direction and winds up with a 100-foot tall, two-year-old behemoth, who threatens downtown Las Vegas (temper tantrums pose a real threat now!). While the original provided entertainment for all ages, this one will be infinitely more appealing to the little ones than adults. Another disappointment is the lack of a Roger Rabbit short which preceded the original. An instance in which bigger isn't necessarily better. ★★½ $9.99

Honey, I Shrunk the Kids

(1989, 93 min, US, Joe Johnston) Rick Moranis stars as a scientist dad whose attic project goes berserk one fine afternoon and miniaturizes not only his kids, but the neighbors' as well. As bad turns to worse, the little ones find themselves stranded across the backyard, and their only hope lies in trekking across the yard – which, for them, is now the size of Kansas and bears a striking resemblence to Oz. This is a pure fluff and fun comedy-fantasy which takes its simple premise and goes a long way. ★★★ $9.99

Honey We Shrunk Ourselves

(1997, 75 min, US, Dean Cundey) Moranis is the only remaining cast member in this third, and hopefully, final entry in the series. While mildly entertaining, the mediocre special effects and sappy plot dampen adult enjoyment. This episode pairs Moranis' family with his brother, sister-in-law, niece and nephew. The two wives are about to embark on a weekend getaway but discover their husbands have been accidentally shrunk – a fate they themselves suffer. Meanwhile the kids, thinking they have the house to themselves, proceed to party under the secret watch of their minute parents. Parents and children come to miss and respect each other in the inevitable warmhearted ending. Kids may find things to like, especially the scene in which the parents take a wild ride on a hot wheel track. ★★ $22.99

Honeymoon in Vegas

(1992, 92 min, US, Andrew Bergman) Can a film which features 34 Flying Elvises be all bad? Writer-director Bergman (The Freshman) has taken to task this age-old question, and in his capable hands, Honeymoon in Vegas, featuring those same 34 Flying Elvises, is a most pleasurable comedy. Nicolas Cage and Sarah Jessica Parker are madly in love, and have traveled to Las Vegas to wed. But big-time gambler James Caan sees Parker, who's a dead ringer for his late wife, and promptly tricks Cage into an arrangement to spend the weekend with her. From there it's an all-out free-for-all, as Cage, now certain he has lost his love, travels through hell and high water to get her back. Cage is at his most manic, handling each successive zany setback with frenzied comic abandon. Caan fares much better than he did in For the Boys, and Parker, as she was in L.A. Story, is a lovely and fiery comedienne. The 34 Flying Elvises, by the way, all perform admirably. ★★★ $19.99

The Honeymoon Killers

(1970, 108 min, US, Leonard Kastle) A crazed swindler and his 250-lb. lover prey on a host of lonely, gullible women for financial gain in this sinister and subversive cult classic. Starring Shirley Stoler and Tony LoBianco. ★★★

The Honeymoon Machine

(1961, 87 min, US, Richard Thorpe) Steve McQueen, in one of his first starring roles, plays an American sailor stationed in Venice who joins forces with scientist Jim Hutton in an elaborate scheme to use a Navy computer to win at the roulette table. In-between finetuning the system and collecting their winnings, both men find time for romance. It's slightly disorienting to see McQueen in such a farcical role, but he manages to wring a few laughs; as do supporting players Dean Jagger, the underrated Paula Prentiss, and the scene-stealing Jack Weston. ★★½ $19.99

Honky Tonk

(1941, 105 min, US, Jack Conway) The first of Clark Gable and Lana Turner's four films together is an appealing western drama. Gable is a con artist on the run who meets up with beauty Turner en route to a small Nevada town. There, Gable takes up residence, courting Turner for romance and the locals for business. Turner makes the most of her first starring role, and the dialogue is snappy and full of double-entendres. Frank Morgan and Claire Trevor offer good performances in support as, respectively, Turner's drunkard father and a dance-hall girl. ★★½ $19.99

Honkytonk Man

(1982, 122 min, US, Clint Eastwood) One of Eastwood's very few misfires. Clint plays a terminally ill, Depression-era country singer who packs up and heads on the road, hoping to make it to the Grand Old Opry. Clint's son Kyle plays his nephew who accompanies him on the trip. Featuring Marty Robbins and Verna Bloom. ★★ $14.99

The Honor of Dongfang Xu

(1988, 92 min, China, Xhang Huanxun) Kung Fu fans should enjoy the wonderfully operatic martial arts melees in this otherwise ordinary movie. Set in the early 1900s, when China was under the imperialistic domination of eight Western nations, the story revolves around Dongfang Xu, a gentle family man, whose combined martial arts agility and Zen-master's concentration lead him to be chosen to fight an "evil" Russian boxer. (Dubbed) ★★ $59.99

Hook

(1991, 144 min, US, Steven Spielberg) Who better to update the Peter Pan fairy tale than Hollywood's fantasy maven Spielberg? Who better indeed. Spielberg has fashioned a fun-loving romp through Never-Never-Land which will delight kids and have enough depth to captivate adults. Hook finds Peter Pan all grown up and in the form of Peter Banning (Robin Williams), a 40-year-old workaholic corporate raider-type who has no time for his kids let alone being one. When his old nemesis, Captain Hook (Dustin Hoffman), rears his ugly head and kidnaps Peter's tykes, he is forced to confront a past he doesn't even remember. The performances are splendid throughout: Williams revels in his boyish way; Hoffman camps it up as the decadent and snobbish Hook; Bob Hoskins nearly steals the show as Hook's comical henchman Smee; Julia Roberts brings a spark to Tinkerbell; and Maggie Smith is wonderful as the aging Wendy. ★★★ $14.99

Hoop Dreams

(1994, 171 min, US, Steve James, Frederick Marx & Peter Gilbert) This compelling look at the aspirations of two talented African-American high school basketball stars, Arthur Agee and William Gates, is both highly entertaining and deeply dis-

turbing. The film introduces the two as they are recruited to play for an exclusive suburban Catholic Academy, St. Joseph's (alma mater to NBA luminary Isaiah Thomas). Their paths eventually diverge as Arthur loses his scholarship and returns to public school while William is groomed to be the team's next "Isaiah." Assembled from over 250 hours of footage shot over five years, the film impressively pinpoints each young man's basketball highlights and lowlights, creating an urgent sense of athletic drama throughout. But the film's real triumph is in its depiction of their respective families and struggles; and in acknowledging the bitter irony that so many young men place their hopes in basketball, and reaching the NBA, as a ticket out of the ghetto, when really it's just another level of exploitation and marketing. Both William and Arthur are likable personalities and their basketball skills provide many an "ooh" and "ahh" for lovers of great hoops, but one is left ultimately wondering whether March Madness will ever seem the same again. ★★★★ $19.99

Hoosiers

(1986, 114 min, US, David Anspaugh) Gene Hackman gives a dynamic performance as the new coach to an Indiana high school basketball team, determined to get them to the championships. An exciting and involving drama, with great support from Barbara Hershey and Oscar nominee Dennis Hopper as a boozy fan. Even for those who avoid sports dramas, this is a must. Excellent score by Jerry Goldsmith. ★★★½ $9.99

Hope and Glory

(1987, 113 min, GB, John Boorman) Boorman's sweet, finely crafted and quite humorous recollection of his childhood days in England during WWII at the time of the German Blitz. Young Sebastian Rice-Edwards is Billy, the director's alter ego, through whose eyes we see a unique view of war-torn Britain. Sarah Miles is splendid as Billy's mother, who struggles to keep her family together in the wake of neighborhood bombings, extramarital affairs and indifferent adolescents. Perfectly

Hope and Glory

cast and boasting outstanding production values, this reminiscence, like Woody Allen's similarly themed *Radio Days*, is a brilliant evocation of early 1940s life. ★★★★

Hopscotch

(1980, 104 min, US, Ronald Neame) Walter Matthau and Glenda Jackson are reteamed (they first appeared together in *House Calls*) in this entertaining spy comedy with Matthau as a weary CIA agent who decides to publish his memoirs – and tell all. Ned Beatty is his boss who's not too keen on the idea. ★★★

The Horn Blows at Midnight

(1945, 78 min, US, Raoul Walsh) Though he often joked about this film being the turkey of the 1940s (and his career), Jack Benny's ascent into the heavens is actually quite funny. Benny plays an angel who is dispatched to Earth to destroy it with one blow from Gabriel's horn. Though *To Be or Not To Be* is unquestionably Benny's one film classic, *Horn* is a pure lark with the comedian in wonderful form. ★★★ $19.99

Horror of Dracula

(1958, 82 min, GB, Terence Fisher) The first of the British Hammer Films to feature Christopher Lee as Count Dracula and Peter Cushing as the tireless Dr. Van Helsing. In this outing, the Prince of Darkness ventures from Transylvania to London in search of new blood. A well-played and atmospheric horror tale that ably compares to the 1931 Bela Lugosi classic. ★★★½ $14.99

The Horror Show

(1989, 95 min, US, James Isaac) A serial killer who dies in the electric chair vows to take revenge on the cop who put him away. Now, as an unstoppable force, the killer returns to terrorize the cop and his family. With Lance Henriksen and Dedee Pfeiffer. ★½ $14.99

The Horse

(1983, 116 min, Turkey, Ali Ozgenturk) The incredible hardships endured by a father and son as they struggle against abject poverty is the plot of this compelling film. Reminiscent of *The Bicycle Thief*, the film, set in modern Turkey, details the father's attempts to earn enough money to send his son to school. A sensitive yet complex exposé of the grim realities of life, this film so upset the government that director Ozgenturk was sent to prison for several years. ★★★ $59.99

Horse Feathers

(1932, 68 min, US, Norman Z. McLeod) The password is "swordfish" as the Marx Brothers turn academia upside-down with Groucho as the head of Huxley College, preparing the school for the big game. Harpo and Chico are part-time students as well as spies. Thelma Todd is the "big girl on campus." With the exception of *Duck Soup*, this madcap romp is the funniest of all the Marx Brothers' movies. ★★★½ $14.99

Horse of Pride

(1980, 118 min, France, Claude Chabrol) Chabrol, France's best-known chronicler of the foibles of the bourgeoisie, turns his cinematic eye towards a drastically different type of people: the proud but poor peasants of

Brittany. Set in the early 1900s and adapted from the French best-selling novel by Pierre Jakez Helias, this earthy drama follows the rituals of birth, death, marriage and harvest in a Breton village during four seasons. Chabrol captures their values and mythology in a lifestyle that has been steadily dying. (Breton with English subtitles) ★★★½ $59.99

The Horse Soldiers

(1959, 119 min, US, John Ford) Brooding Civil War drama with John Wayne and William Holden as ideologically opposed Union soldiers who are on a sabotage mission deep within Confederate territory. Not one of Ford's best, but nevertheless intriguing. ★★½ $14.99

Horse Thief

(1986, 88 min, China, Tian Zhuangzhuang) Set in an isolated and impoverished village in Tibet, *Horse Thief* is a stirring yet simply told work of art. Nordo, a young and able man, is forced to steal in order to support his growing family. He is caught and, with family in tow, driven out of the village into nomadic life. In the harsh conditions of the countryside, his attempts to eke out an existence fail and he returns to repent. But he soon finds himself again attracted to theft. Full of mysterious religious rituals and haunted by images of death, this film eschews simple Communist doctrine and is more concerned with the ancient ways of dealing with the hardships and cruelties of life. (Mandarin with English subtitles) ★★★½ $59.99

The Horse's Mouth

(1958, 93 min, GB, Ronald Neame) Alec Guinness' flawless portrayal of Gulley Jimson, a crotchety and eccentric old artist whose love of painting leads him to incessant mischief, is unquestionably one of his finest comic performances. Kay Walsh is also brilliant as his reluctant cohabitant in this hilarious tribute to nonconformity and art. Guinness himself wrote the screenplay from a Joyce Cary novel. (Available letterboxed and pan & scan) ★★★½ $24.99

The Horseman on the Roof (Le Hussard sur le Toit)

(1996, 117 min, France, Jean-Paul Rappeneau) France's great cholera epidemic of 1832 would hardly suggest the backdrop to a gripping story of courage, loyalty and love, but with its exquisite cinematography, compelling performances and stirringly old-fashioned story line, *The Horseman on the Roof* is exactly that. Oliver Martinez stars as Angelo, handsome Colonel of the Hussards, revolutionary and Italian expatriate, who begins a Candide-like adventure in his attempt to return home to Italy. He is accompanied on his journey by Pauline de Théris (Juliette Binoche), a beautiful countess with her own agenda for fleeing the region. As small towns in Provence become ravaged by the enveloping epidemic (and in some cases gripped with hysteria), and quarantine has closed all borders, the two refugees encounter fear, death, intrigue, and their own hearts. Director Rappeneau (*Cyrano de Bergerac*) has crafted an ambitious epic both ravishing and penetrating which rarely falters in its intensity, and the

The Horse's Mouth

film is remarkably lucid in its many narrative transitions. Binoche offers a radiant performance, and Martinez is especially good as the dedicated soldier. (French with English subtitles) ★★★½ $99.99

The Hospital

(1971, 103 min, US, Arthur Hiller) Biting satire by Paddy Chayefsky with George C. Scott as a disillusioned doctor working at a New York City hospital who finds more ills in both administrative policy and his fellow physicians than he does in his patients. Diana Rigg and Barnard Hughes co-star. Chayefsky won an Oscar for his scathing screenplay. ★★★½ $19.99

Hot Pepper

(1973, 54 min, US, Les Blank) The music of Clifton Chenier, set against the backdrop of rural and urban Louisiana. Clifton, a French accordianist, mixes rock and blues with Zydeco, a combination of Cajun French with African undertones. $49.99

Hot Shots

(1991, 85 min, US, Jim Abrahams) From one of the directors of *Airplane!* and (sole director of) *Big Business* comes this often hilarious parody of military and pilot films, *Top Gun* in particular. The jokes are delivered at a machinegun pace and most of them succeed. Charlie Sheen, satirizing his *Navy SEALS* role, is the Tom Cruise-ish, hotshot pilot competing against arrogant Cary Elwes. Lloyd Bridges shows up as an admiral who is obviously related to Bridges' *Airplane!* air traffic controller. In fact, and quite obviously, all are in *Airplane!* territory, here. And though the film doesn't reach the comic heights of that classic, *Hot Shots* is nevertheless a high-flying romp. ★★★ $9.99

Hot Spell

(1958, 86 min, US, Daniel Mann) Exceptional performances by Shirley Booth, Anthony Quinn and Shirley MacLaine highlight this compelling drama. Booth plays a middle-aged housewife who must contend with her husband's extramarital affairs and her children's romantic problems. ★★★

The Hot Spot

(1990, 120 min, US, Dennis Hopper) Based on a Charles Williams pulp novel, this atmospheric and offbeat thriller tells a tale of robbery, murder, blackmail and "good-lookin'-but-dangerous dames" set in the dusty locales of a small Texas town. In the leading roles, Don Johnson as a low-life drifter and Virginia Madsen as a femme fatale fail to impress. The film is elevated, however, by a host of wonderful supporting actors and a bluesy score by John Lee Hooker and Miles Davis. ★★½ $14.99

Hot to Trot

(1988, 83 min, US, Michael Dinner) Bobcat Goldthwait (who is a great stand-up comedian but who has yet to find a suitable film role) dons the Donald O'Connor role from the *Francis* movies of the 1950s in this talking horse comedy. John Candy gives voice to his equine co-star. ★ $19.99

Hotel Colonial

(1987, 103 min, US, Dinzia T.H. Torrini) John Savage is called to Bogota, Colombia, to identify the body of his brother, who has supposedly committed suicide. But after trudging through the Amazonian jungle, Savage finds that his brother is actually living in a world of drugs and depravity. Robert Duvall and Rachel Ward also star. A dismal drama of betrayal and corruption. ★

The Hotel New Hampshire

(1984, 110 min, US, Tony Richardson) A felicitous actors' exercise which follows closely the John Irving novel. The serendipitous script examines the exploits of a highly unusual American family, both at home and abroad, and ranges in mood from the almost slapstick to the nearly tragic. While the direction tends to harbor self-indulgence, each actor's portrayal is inventive and endearing. With Rob Lowe, Jodie Foster, Beau Bridges and Nastassja Kinski. ★★★ $14.99

Hotel Reserve

(1944, 79 min, GB, Peter Glenville) James Mason stars in this gripping drama about an Austrian refugee at a seaside resort in the south of France during WWII who helps the local police hunt down a Nazi spy. ★★★ $19.99

Hotel Terminus

(1988, 267 min, US, Marcel Ophüls) Winner of both the Cannes International Critics Prize in 1988 as well as the Academy Award for Best Documentary, this groundbreaking film is a meticulous investigation into the life of Klaus Barbie, the "Butcher of Lyons," whose Nazi war crimes include the ordering of the deaths of

The Hours and Times

over 4,000 people as well as 44 children of Izieu. The film spans 70 years and traces the 40-year manhunt for the ruthless war criminal. An extraordinary film which is part detective story and part a study of the complex web of international political deceit. *Hotel Terminus* can be considered the final chapter in Ophüls' trilogy on World War II which includes *The Sorrow and the Pity* and *Memory of Justice*. ★★★★ $29.99

The Hound of the Baskervilles

(1939, 80 min, US, Sidney Lanfield) The sun never rises on the English moor; ominous foreboding permeates even broad daylight. Stark, brooding black-and-white cinematography establishes the ambience for Mr. Sherlock Holmes' unraveling of the centuries-old curse of the Baskerville family. This first pairing of Basil Rathbone and Nigel Bruce as Sherlock Holmes and Dr. Watson clicked so powerfully that it was followed by another 13 Sherlock Holmes films. Although it is said that Rathbone came to hate Mr. Holmes, he never faltered in his portrayal of Arthur Conan Doyle's detective. ★★★½ $14.99

The Hound of the Baskervilles

(1959, 88 min, GB, Terence Fisher) The horror masters at Hammer Studios chose Arthur Conan Doyle's most macabre mystery in what they had hoped would begin a new series for them. Peter Cushing, though a little too aged for the role of Sherlock Holmes, does a credible job, keeping the great detective cold as ice and sharp as a tack. Christopher Lee for once plays a good guy, in the role of Lord Baskerville. In the role of Dr. Watson, director Fisher utilized the talents of Andre Morell, who had recently played the title character in BBC-TV's "Quatermass and the Pit." The moor set would end up seeing double duty, being used later in the year in Fisher's remake of *The Mummy*. ★★★ $19.99

The Hound of the Baskervilles

(1977, 84 min, GB, Paul Morrissey) Basil Rathbone can rest easy as Morrissey's tepid spoof of Arthur Conan Doyle's classic novel falls laughlessly flat. Co-writers and stars Dudley Moore and Peter Cook should share the blame, as well, as their antics are deadly unfunny. Even a good supporting cast (Kenneth Williams, Denholm Elliott, Spike Milligan, Terry-Thomas and Prunella Scales) can't save this dud. Moore strikes a happy medium, the dog runs away with the picture, and careers must be salvaged. ★

Hour of the Star

(1986, 96 min, Brazil, Suzanna Amaral) On December 30, 1986, film critic Andrew Sarris announced that an unknown Brazilian feature, *Hour of the Star*, had already made his "Best of 1987" film list. The film then opened to universal critical acclaim. This deeply touching work harkens back to the grand neorealist style of *La Strada* and *The Bicycle Thief*, creating an unlikely heroine out of Macabea, an uneducated, obtuse girl from Brazil's northeastern provinces. Despite her impoverished surroundings, she carries herself with dignity and a surprising degree of wit. First-time director Amaral made the film when 52 years old, after raising nine children, then attending

N.Y.U. (Portuguese with English subtitles) ★★★½ $79.99

Hour of the Wolf

(1967, 89 min, Sweden, Ingmar Bergman) One of Bergman's most powerful works, *Hour of the Wolf* is a nightmarish drama of mental illness and creative intensity. A successful painter (Max von Sydow) and his loving wife (Liv Ullmann) spend the summer on a barren island where, spurred by insomnia and haunted by demons both real and imagined, the man's sanity slowly unravels while his distraught wife helplessly watches. A haunting psychological horror film which mixes surrealistic touches with old-fashioned Gothic terror to create a brilliant and unforgettable vision of madness. Also starring Ingrid Thulin and Erland Josephson. (Swedish with English subtitles) ★★★★ $19.99

The Hours and Times

(1991, 60 min, US, Christopher Münch) Taking the historic, seemingly unimportant fact that Beatles' manager, and early guiding force, Brian Epstein took John Lennon on a four-day vacation to Barcelona, Spain, just months before the meteoric rise of the Fab Four, director Münch has fashioned a fictional "what-might-have-happened" queer drama. Epstein – Jewish, upper-class and gay – and Lennon – a Liverpudlian working-class musician with unlimited but raw promise – seem an unlikely pair although their mentor/student relationship is rather intense. Their vastly different lifestyles attract and distance the two and is especially evident in Epstein's sexual attraction for the appreciative but hopelessly straight Lennon. This sexual tension provides the dramatic centerpiece in this understated and low-budget picture which works both as an engrossing exploration of the shifting nature and intensity of friendship and a touching example of unrequited love. Ian Hart, who portrays Lennon, would play him again in *Backbeat*. ★★★½ $19.99

House

(1986, 93 min, US, Steve Miner) Tongue-in-cheek horror film about a horror novelist (William Katt) who moves into the house of his deceased aunt to write about his Vietnam War experiences, and becomes terrorized by deadly, gruesome monsters. The film mixes decent horror effects with comedy, and the result is enjoyably silly. Also with George Wendt, Richard Moll and Kay Lenz. Followed by the inferior *House 2: The Second Story*. ★★½ $14.99

House Arrest

(1996, 108 min, US, Harry Winer) Jamie Lee Curtis and Kevin Pollak star as parents who, on their wedding anniversary, announce to their two children their intent to separate. Their seventh grade son Grover (Kyle Howard) decides to take radical steps and locks them in the basement in an attempt to force them to resolve their problems. The class bully, the class beauty and Grover's best friend all find out about the lock-up and force their parents to join the prisoners, creating a house of juvenile delinquents upstairs and disgruntled adults downstairs. The outcome is never in doubt as Grover constructs a makeshift family and conducts group therapy for the adults via video camera. Though the film has a certain charm and the cast is quite engaging, *House Arrest* is too long, the ending is too pat, and there's not an abundance of funny scenes to overcome the story's banalities. ★★ $99.99

House of Angels

(1993, 119 min, Sweden/GB, Colin Nutley) Some would say the term "Swedish comedy" is an oxymoron, but thanks to British director Nutley, this delightful Nordic romp should sway all naysayers. A pixie-like Helena Bergstrom stars as a young cabaret artist who returns to her mother's village to collect her inheritance, one of the town's prized estates. This, along with her leather-clad, motorcycle-straddling gay companion, Zac, turns the normally quiet little town into a beehive of gossip and curious disbelief. Sporting a wonderfully eccentric cast ranging from yokels to drag queens, the film is one of those marvelous contrivances which, though minor in scope, provides plenty of heartwarming good cheer. ★★★½ $19.99

House of Cards

(1993, 108 min, US, Michael Lessac) Utterly engrossing, *House of Cards* is a moving look into the mind of an exceptional child. While living in Mexico, seven-year-old Sally becomes influenced by the legends told to her by a native guide after her father dies in an accident at an archeological dig. Back in the States, Sally withdraws from her family, stops speaking and begins to exhibit spectacular feats of the mind and body leading doctors to diagnose her as autistic. Sally's mother (Kathleen Turner) refuses to accept the diagnosis and begins to devise a cure. Besides being a tense and well-acted drama of love and mysticism, *House of Cards* asks tough questions about what's "normal" and the process involved in "curing" a child with a brilliant mind. Also starring Tommy Lee Jones. ★★★½ $19.99

House of Dark Shadows

(1970, 96 min, US, Dan Curtis) Theatrical version of the popular 1960s daytime horror soap opera, "Dark Shadows." Jonathan Frid returns as Barnabas Collins, the 18th-century New England aristocrat-turned-vampire, here looking to end his curse. Some good chills, and recommended for fans of the TV show. ★★★ $19.99

House of Games

(1987, 102 min, US, David Mamet) Playright Mamet's directorial film debut is this superbly crafted story about an uptight psychiatrist (Lindsay Crouse) who goes thrill-seeking with a sophisticated con artist (Joe Mantegna). Filled with red herrings and unexpected twists, Mamet's ingenious screenplay imparts a keen sense of psychology doused with a hilarious and wry sense of humor. The acting is outstanding; Crouse is eerily emotionless as the famous shrink and Mantegna is both charming and alluring as the smooth-operating grifter. ★★★½ $19.99

The House of the Spirits

(1994, 132 min, US/Sweden, Bille August) Savagely received by the American film critics but embraced by the European press, this near-epic adaptation of Isabel Allende's acclaimed novel of thwarted love and class distinction fails to fully capture the essence of the original text. But for all its shortcomings, the film possesses a sense of poetry and conviction which counter the heavy dramatics. Set against the backdrop of political upheaval in an unnamed South American country (read: Chile), the story follows the lives of the multi-generational Trueba family: including an oppressive landowner father (Jeremy Irons); his innocent, clairvoyant wife (Meryl Streep); their young daughter (Winona Ryder), who is having an affair with a revolutionary (Antonio Banderas); and the family's repressed aunt (the remarkable Glenn Close), who has been banished by her unforgiving brother. Awash in mysticism amd romantic symbolism, the film will both intrigue and infuriate with its crystalline emotions and excesses. ★★★ $9.99

House of Wax

(1953, 88 min, US, Andre de Toth) A smash hit in its day, and originally shown in 3-D, this Vincent Price chiller has long been a horror favorite. Price plays a sculptor who resorts to real subjects to carve after a fire mishap leaves him disfigured. With Charles Bronson and Carolyn Jones in very early film roles. ★★★ $14.99

The House on Carroll Street

(1988, 100 min, US, Peter Yates) Intriguing thriller set during the McCarthy era as subversive "red" Kelly McGillis mixes it up with FBI agent Jeff Daniels when she unwittingly uncovers an underground Nazi organization. ★★½ $14.99

House on Chelouche Street

(1973, 120 min, Israel, Moshe Mizrahi) This family drama is set in Tel Aviv during the turbulent period of British rule just before the partition of Palestine. The film successfully captures the excitement and anxiety in a rapidly evolving country. (Hebrew with English subtitles) ★★★ $39.99

House on Haunted Hill

(1958, 75 min, US, William Castle) Semi-classic haunted house story with Vincent Price as an eccentric millionaire who offers a group of strangers $10,000 each to spend a night in his haunted mansion. Good, old-fashioned, eerie fun. ★★★ $14.99

The House on 92nd Street

(1945, 88 min, US, Henry Hathaway) Based on a real-life spy case during WWII, this exciting, low-keyed thriller is told in a taut semi-documentary style. Lloyd Nolan stars as an FBI chief who is put in charge of the case of Nazi and Fifth Columnist infiltration after it is discovered the Germans are obtaining secrets about the atom bomb. William Eythe is the American double agent setting up the Nazis, and Signe Hasso and Leo G. Carroll are two of the German agents. Beginning with a shot of J. Edgar Hoover busy at work, the film at times seems to be none-too-subtle propaganda for the government agency, but the story soon takes charge to deliver a well-detailed and crisp espionage adventure. Location footage helps in the film's general feeling of authenticity. ★★★½ $19.99

House Party

(1989, 96 min, US, Reginald Hudlin) A refreshingly hip and surprisingly innocent comedy about a day in the life of a group of black suburban teenagers who simply want to throw a party without getting hassled. The story revolves around Kid (Christopher Reid, from the rap duo Kid N' Play), who must sneak out of his house and avoid a gang of thugs. Although the plot is thin, this spirited and delightful musical/dance/comedy is even more impressive in that it shows black teens having fun without resorting to the stereotypes of them being druggies, criminals or impoverished. Robin Harris is hilarious as Kid's overprotective, Dolemite-loving father. ★★★ $14.99

House Party 2

(1991, 94 min, US, Doug McHenry & George Jackson) Fans of the original *House Party* might be disappointed by this politically correct, message-laden sequel to the 1990 hit starring rap stars Kid N' Play (Christopher Reid and Christopher Martin). Hip-hop hijinks ensue when Play connives to throw "the mother of all pajama parties" on the college campus where Kid is about to be expelled. Also with Tisha Campbell, Iman, Queen Latifah and Georg Stanford Brown. ★★ $14.99

House Party 3

(1994, 93 min, US, Eric Meza) Real-life rappers Kid N' Play return, here as L.A. record producers, in this truly tedious sequel. After receiving advance money from the record executive "Showboat" (Michael Colyar), the mixed-up duo decides to squander their newfound fortune on Kid's bachelor party. Wallowing in a sea of sexist and racial stereotypical humor, this foul-mouthed feature is saved on occasion by the energetic performances of chart-toppers TLC and pint-sized rappers Immature. ★½ $14.99

Houseboat

(1958, 110 min, US, Melville Shavelson) Charming romantic comedy starring Cary Grant as an overwhelmed widower who hires Sophia Loren as a maid (though she's really a socialite) to take care of his three children and their houseboat. The kind of enjoyable '50s romantic fluff which Grant seemed to have a patent on. Harry Guardino is a scene-stealer as the handyman. ★★★ $14.99

Houseguest

(1995, 108 min, US, Randall Miller) As is the case with Jim Carrey or Pauly Shore vehicles, the degree of enjoyment of their films lies in the appreciation and tolerance of the star. The same holds true with *Houseguest*, a genial comedy starring stand-up comic and sometime TV star Sinbad. The premise is an odd one: In order to get away from the thugs looking for him, our hero assumes the identity of another; here, the boyhood friend of Phil Hartman. As he is whisked away to the safe confines of suburbia, Sinbad ultimately enriches the lives of these strangers while they do the same for him. While the concept and even the execution is stale, both actors manage to wring what-

H

ever comic life is present. *Houseguest* may not be totally unwanted, but it comes dangerously close to overstaying its welcome. ★★ $19.99

Household Saints

(1993, 124 min, US, Nancy Savoca) In her previous feature-length outings (*True Love, Dogfight*), director Savoca evidenced an uncanny ability to capture the feel of the films' eras and environments. In *Household Saints*, she adds an element of the surreal which creates the mythic dimension with which we remember our childhoods and the stories our parents and grandparents told us. Vincent D'Onofrio and Tracey Ullman are winsome as the husband and wife (he wins her in a pinochle game) whose daughter (Lili Taylor) becomes the neighborhood saint in 1950s Brooklyn. The film is delightful, funny and entertaining. ★★★½ $94.99

Householder

(1962, 101 min, India, James Ivory) The first collaboration between director Ivory, producer Ismail Merchant and writer Ruth Prawer Jhabvala (who would go on to create, among others, *A Room with a View, Maurice* and *The Remains of the Day*) is this delightful and warmhearted but uneven comedy. Shashi Kapoor plays a young teacher who, pushed by his meddlesome mother, enters into an arranged marriage with a woman equally naive and inexperienced. Troubles begin for the couple as they find themselves unprepared for the difficulties of marriage and its financial responsibilities. While not one of the trio's best works, the film provides an interesting background for their future films. ★★½ $79.99

The Housekeeper

(1986, 106 min, Canada, Ousami Rawi) Rita Tushingham is excellent in the lead role as a dyslexic cleaning lady who goes on a murderously psychotic jag. Chilling suspense is accented by occasional forays into black humor in this sometimes confusing thriller. ★★½ $19.99

Housekeeping

(1987, 116 min, US, Bill Forsyth) Forsyth's first American film (shot in the Pacific Northwest) is a brilliantly quirky comedy about familial ties and individuality. Christine Lahti gives a sensational performance as vagabond Aunt Sylvie, who comes to stay to look after her recently orphaned nieces (nicely played by newcomers Sara Walker and Andrea Burchill). The film touchingly examines the close-knit relationship of the two sisters, and the influence Aunt Sylvie has on the two girls: one socially conscious and embarrassed by her aunt, and the other a soulmate. A film of rare sensitivity and character, with a haunting finale. ★★★★ $79.99

Housesitter

(1992, 102 min, US, Frank Oz) Steve Martin and Goldie Hawn star in this funny screwball romp about a woman who, through a web of lies and deceits, squirms her way into the life of an unsuspecting architect with side-splitting results. It's a plot which is vaguely reminiscent of classics like *Bringing Up Baby* and *Ball of Fire*. Of course, Hawn, admirable a job though she does, can never be compared to the great Kate, and Martin is certainly no Cary Grant;

but still, the film's outrageous humor and situations give these two modern-day comics plenty of good material to make for a thoroughly enjoyable laugh fest. ★★★ $9.99

How I Got into College

(1989, 89 min, US, Savage Steve Holland) Holland's occasionally funny but predictable and surprisingly lifeless comedy scores about a C-. Told in typical Savage Steve style, wacky characters and situations abound in this not-so-savage farce about the college entrance experience. Some of the jokes fall with a thud — but there are enough truly funny scenes to give this comedy a passing grade. Holland clearly remembers all the anxieties and hopes of the young adult years, but it's about time he grew up a little. ★★½ $89.99

How to Make an American Quilt

How I Won the War

(1967, 109 min, GB, Richard Lester) John Lennon stars in this funny and surreal portrait of one man's less than Rambo-like military career. This often hilarious presentation of the lives of a rag-tag group of WWII soldiers taps into the somewhat naive but joyously nihilistic anti-militarism of the time. The material is certainly "dated," but the heart of the piece is in the right place. ★★★ $59.99

How Tasty Was My Little Frenchman

(1973, 80 min, Brazil, Nelson Pereira dos Santos) As the French and Portuguese swarm the Brazilian coastline in the mid-1500s, the indigenous Indian tribes align themselves with their would-be conquerers according to their own local conflicts (the friend of my enemy is my enemy). One hapless Frenchman is left to drown by a Portuguese contingent. However, he wades to shore to be found by an Indian tribe friendly to the French. Unfortunately, they mistake him for a Portuguese, and they are cannibals. Much like colonialism itself, the victim is expected to participate in the ritual of exploitation — he has a speaking part in the cooking ceremony. He is given a wife to help him learn his lines, and is well-fed during his period of instruction. He is avidly attentive to

his education in tribal ways, hoping to endear himself to his captors. This delightful farce overcomes its low budget and sometimes haphazard construction with droll insight and a wicked sense of humor, courtesy of director dos Santos, a leading proponent of Brazil's Cinema Novo. (French and Tupi with English subtitles) ★★★ $79.99

How the West Was Won

(1962, 162 min, US, John Ford, Henry Hathaway & George Marshall) It took three directors to bring this overblown, epic western to the screen. One of the ultimate "all-star cast" extravaganzas released during the 1960s, this mammoth production was originally shown in 3-strip Cinerama, which is lost on the small screen. The story traces the lives of three generations of a pioneer family. Some outstanding action scenes (the river raft and train sequences in particular). Cast includes Henry Fonda, John Wayne, James Stewart, Gregory Peck, Richard Widmark, Debbie Reynolds, George Peppard, Robert Preston and Agnes Moorehead, just to name a few. (Available letterboxed and pan & scan) ★★★ $24.99

How to Beat the High Cost of Living

(1980, 105 min, US, Robert Scheerer) Jessica Lange, Jane Curtin and Susan Saint James are a trio of housewives who embark on a comedic caper to nab some cash from their local shopping mall. With Richard Benjamin, Fred Willard and Dabney Coleman. Though a good premise, even a agreeable cast can't make sense of this muddled farce. ★½

How to Get Ahead in Advertising

(1989, 95 min, GB, Bruce Robinson) A brilliant piece of rowdy leftist propoganda with shades of Monty Python, Kafka and Sigmund Freud. When ace London adman Dennis Bagley (Richard E. Grant) is unable to concoct that perfect pitch for a pimple remedy, his subconscious kicks in and produces a rapidly growing pimple on his neck. Yet this is no ordinary zit! This one talks and spews a wicked venom, both at Bagley and the viewer. As the pesky pimple grows larger, its rantings on behalf of unbridled materialism become uglier and its urge to take over our hero's body becomes stronger. Where will it end? The ever shining Rachel Ward plays Bagley's wife and is the perfect foil to the boisterous boil's grotesque humor. No adventurous viewer should dare miss this fiendish British satire. ★★★½ $14.99

How to Irritate People

(1973, 65 min, GB, Ian Fordyce) Out of the Flying Circus era of the Monty Python gang comes this humorous set of sketches narrated by John Cleese and featuring Pythonites Graham Chapman and Michael Palin as well as Connie Booth from "Fawlty Towers." The skits, all on the theme of how to irritate people right up to their boiling point, go on too long and vary greatly in the laughs department; but for Cleese and Python fanatics, this made-for-British TV show will prove to be a welcome howl. ★★ $14.99

How to Make an American Quilt

(1995, 109 min, US, Jocelyn Moorhouse) By no means a great film, *How to Make an*

American Quilt is probably the most successful of 1995's many female ensemble pieces (*Waiting to Exhale, Moonlight and Valentino, Now and Then*, etc.). While all of these films feature good performances and an engaging rapport between the costars, Moorhouse's drama has a definition of character and poignancy which elevates it. Winona Ryder is a college student who spends her summer vacation with her grandmother (the always tangy Anne Bancroft). As the young woman looks to set her romantic and academic lives in order, she becomes enmeshed in Bancroft's quilting circle, a group of mostly older women who all share a past of secrets, pain and camaraderie. With so many stories weaving through the narrative, one may be shortchanged (Alfre Woodard's for instance) and another not as dramatically exciting (Ryder's reunion with her mother Kate Capshaw), but each member of the film's terrific cast heartens the tale with a refreshing, robust liveliness. ★★★ $19.99

How to Marry a Millionaire

(1953, 95 min, US, Jean Negulesco) Hollywood's first Cinemascope comedy is a witty and stylish souffle starring Marilyn Monroe, Betty Grable and Lauren Bacall as three Manhattan gold diggers out to trap (and marry) unsuspecting millionaire bachelors. David Wayne, William Powell and Cameron Mitchell are the catches. ★★★ $14.99

How to Murder Your Wife

(1965, 118 min, US, Richard Quine) Typically funny 1960s sex farce with Jack Lemmon as a happily unmarried cartoonist who awakens one morning to find himself wed to the lovely Virna Lisi. He quickly devises numerous plans to get rid of her. ★★★ $19.99

How to Succeed in Business without Really Trying

(1967, 121 min, US, David Swift) Delightful screen version of the Tony Award and Pulitzer Prize-winning Broadway musical with Robert Morse re-creating his acclaimed stage role.

Morse stars as a mail room clerk who works his way up the corporate ladder in record time, thanks to the help of a little book and a lot of chutzpah. A terrific farce on big business, with great support from Rudy Vallee ("Ground hog!") and Michelle Lee. Frank Loesser's classic score includes "Brotherhood of Man" and "I Believe in You." Choreographed by Bob Fosse on stage, only one dance number remains. ★★★ $19.99

How U Like Me Now

(1992, 109 min, US, Darryl Roberts) First-time director Roberts proves to be a talent to be reckoned with with this charming low-budget urban comedy which recounts the professional and romantic struggles of twentysomething friends living in Chicago's South Side. Comprised of an ensemble cast that features Darnell Williams ("All My Children") and Salli Richardson (*Posse*), the film tackles many issues, including interracial romance, buppies, back-to-Africa politics, and others, without being heavy-handed or alienating like some films of this genre. ★★★ $89.99

Howard the Duck

(1986, 111 min, US, Willard Huyck) One of the infamous duds of the 1980s, this comic fantasy isn't the worst movie ever made; however, it is an overproduced mess. Based on the comic book, it's all about an alien duck who travels to Cleveland and is befriended by rock star Lea Thompson. In the immortal words of Groucho: "Why a duck?" ★ $9.99

Howards End

(1992, 140 min, GB, James Ivory) The third time certainly is a charm. Production partners James Ivory and Ismail Merchant (*A Room with a View, Maurice*) have outdone even themselves with this sumptuous re-creation of a third E.M. Forster novel, a tale of class struggle in the dying days of the Edwardian era. The story centers around the tragic confluence of three families from London's various social strata. Vanessa Redgrave and Anthony Hopkins personify the upper crust as the Wilcoxes. The Schlegel sisters (Emma Thompson and Helena Bonham Carter) represent the liberal middle class. And Leonard Bast (Sam West), an educated Cockney trying to make his way into the world of business, and his wife (Nicola Duffett) embody the lower depths. Filmed with all of the pomp and circumstance one has come to expect of Merchant Ivory productions, and acted with loving attention to both the mannerisms and prose of the era, *Howards End* is a truly marvelous and engaging period piece. Thompson won a well-deserved Oscar for her portrayal of the elder Schlegel, and is equally matched by Hopkins. ★★★★ $19.99

The Howling

(1981, 91 min, US, Joe Dante) From the director who loved horror films as a kid (and then never grew up), this werewolf tale is resplendent with in-jokes, character actors and good, scary special effects. Like Dante's other work (*Gremlins 1 & 2, Explorers*), *The Howling* takes off at full gallop and doesn't stop, reflecting his years cutting trailers for Roger Corman. Features Dee Wallace and Patrick Macnee. Co-written by John Sayles. ★★★

Howling II

(1985, 90 min, US, Philippe Mora) Sequel to Dante's *The Howling* lacks the original's style and hipness. After the death of the TV reporter in the original, her brother, a colleague and an occult expert head to Transylvania to kill the queen of the werewolves. Followed by four additional sequels, most of which have been relegated to direct-to-video. (aka: *Your Sister Is a Werewolf*) ★½ $14.99

The Hucksters

(1947, 120 min, US, Jack Conway) A glossy, satirical look at the business of advertising. Clark Gable is an idealistic go-getter who finds he must virtually sell his soul in order to succeed. The great cast is rounded out by Ava Gardner, Sydney Greenstreet, Adolphe Menjou, Edward Arnold and Deborah Kerr (in her first American film role). ★★★ $19.99

Hud

(1963, 112 min, US, Martin Ritt) Paul Newman gives a riveting performance as the disreputable son of Texas cattle rancher Melvyn Douglas in this outstanding modern-day western. Brilliantly photographed by James Wong Howe, the film centers on Newman's volatile relationships with his estranged father (who is faced with financial ruin), impressionable nephew Brandon de Wilde and world-weary housekeeper Patricia Neal. Oscars deservedly went to Neal as Best Actress and Douglas as Supporting Actor; in fact, the entire ensemble is superb. A film of such grit you can almost taste the dust. Based on a novel by Larry McMurtry ("The Last Picture Show," "Lonesome Dove"). ★★★★ $14.99

Hudson Hawk

(1991, 95 min, US, Michael Lehmann) A major disappointment from the director of *Heathers*. Bruce Willis stars in this half-hearted comic adventure as a cat burglar who is coerced into committing a series of robberies. Andie MacDowell is the Vatican spy he tangles

How to Marry a Millionaire

A Hungarian Fairy Tale

with, Danny Aiello is his partner, and James Coburn is the CIA renegade trying to stop him. In all fairness, the actors try to maintain a degree of wackiness and lightheartedness, but there's too much mugging and winking; the viewer is numbed by a cast going to extremes to show the good time they're (supposed to be) having. Even the always-fun Sandra Bernhard appears lost. ★½ $9.99

The Hudsucker Proxy

(1994, 111 min, US, Joel Coen) With their usual cinematic aplomb, the Coen Brothers open the floodgates and unleash a torrent of invigorating witticisms and dizzying visuals in this spectacular, over-the-top tribute to the 1940s screwball comedy. Tim Robbins stars as a beamish Midwestern rube who hits the streets of New York, circa 1947, looking to grab the lower rungs of any corporate ladder. He lands in the Orwellian mailroom of the Hudsucker Corporation, a megalithic industrial powerhouse headed up by a heartless and power-hungry Paul Newman. True to the genre, Robbins soon finds himself on a meteoric rise to power upon which he must learn life's hard lessons. Jennifer Jason Leigh, as a hard-nosed reporter, rat-a-tat-tats her lines at machine gun pace while paying splendid homage to Katharine Hepburn, Rosalind Russell and Barbara Stanwyck. A highly entertaining film, from its dramatic industrial Gothic scenery – seemingly straight out of Fritz Lang's *Metropolis* – to its Capra-esque finale. ★★★½ $9.99

Hugh Hefner: Once Upon a Time

(1992, 91 min, US, Robert Heath) Fascinating, entertaining account of the genesis and growth of entrepreneureal genius Hugh Hefner's $8,000 idea. While the film takes a keyhole look at the founder of the *Playboy* empire, seeing him as a pioneer in the sexual revolution, it also manages to show how the magazine argued for civil and gay/lesbian rights, an end to censorship, abortion rights, the decriminalization of drugs and other important political and social issues. A well-crafted, never-boring look at the American icon. ★★★ $19.99

Hullabaloo Over Georgie and Bonnie's Pictures

(1978, 82 min, India, James Ivory) This film is a lighthearted romp through royal India – a world of princesses, palaces, tourists, precious art objects and the people who wheel and deal with them. What's all the hullabaloo about? Georgie owns a priceless collection of ancient paintings which he loves, but his sister wants more practical objects and wants him to sell. Frantic art dealers are soon in hot pursuit as the royal couple are deluged with people who want to buy. A great double twist ending concludes this exotic film. ★★★ $19.99

The Human Comedy

(1943, 117 min, US, Clarence Brown) Exceptional adaptation of William Saroyan's best-seller about the trials and tribulations of small-town life during WWII. This slice-of-life drama stars Mickey Rooney in possibly his best dramatic performance as a sensitive teenager coming of age, and the terrific Frank Morgan, Fay Bainter and James Craig also star. ★★★½ $24.99

The Human Condition, Part 1

(1959, 200 min, Japan, Masaki Kobayashi) *The Human Condition* is an epic chronicle of one man's struggle to retain his humanity as he descends into the hypnotic, distorted reality of war. As Part 1 (*No Greater Love*) opens, production at a mining camp in occupied Manchuria is at a standstill. With a Japan desperate for raw resources for its war machine, Kaji, a pacifist who believes that effective management requires winning the hearts and minds of the workers, is given authority. (Japanese with English subtitles) ★★★ $59.99

The Human Condition, Part 2

(1960, 180 min, Japan, Masaki Kobayashi) Part 2 (*Road to Eternity*) begins with Kaji being tortured by the military police for having treated the Chinese humanely. Allowed one memorable night with his wife, Kaji is then ordered to the front. His records brand him "red" and his superiors mistreat him zealously. (Japanese with English subtitles) ★★★ $59.99

The Human Condition, Part 3

(1961, 190 min, Japan, Masaki Kobayashi) Part 3 (*A Soldier's Prayer*) commences as Kaji awakens to chaos and where the surviving Japanese soldiers savagely retreat from an equally brutal Soviet Army. Kaji's own moral standards are challenged when he is forced to kill to survive. The film's final section, set in a Russian POW camp, has our hero understanding that the socialist ideas that he has championed offer no shield to man's basest tendencies. (Japanese with English subtitles) ★★★ $59.99

The Human Tornado

(1975, 90 min, US) Rudy Ray Moore returns in this unintentionally hilarious sequel to *Dolemite*. The production values are still K-Mart quality and the cast seems to be dropouts from the Lee Majors School of Acting, but Rudy's foul-mouthed and virulent rap poetry and his imaginatively fluorescent fashion sense will hold all entranced. ★ $19.99

Humoresque

(1946, 125 min, US, Jean Negulesco) This superior soap opera stars Joan Crawford as a wealthy society woman becoming romantically involved with a young, talented musician (John Garfield). Crawford and Garfield (who each offer an accomplished performance) are engaging together, and the melodramatic story line is consistently entertaining. ★★★ $19.99

The Hunchback of Notre Dame

(1923, 137 min, US, Wallace Worsley) Lon Chaney enthralled a generation of filmgoers in this impressive silent film of the Victor Hugo classic about the deformed bell-ringer Quasimodo, and his love for a beautiful Gypsy girl. Chaney's characterization and makeup effects are outstanding. Remade several times, including the 1939 Charles Laughton version (still the best), and in 1957 with Anthony Quinn. ★★★½ $24.99

The Hunchback of Notre Dame

(1939, 117 min, US, William Dieterle) Outstanding version of the Victor Hugo classic with Charles Laughton in one of his best performances as the deformed bell-ringer Quasimodo. Maureen O'Hara is a lovely Esmerelda. The best of many screen versions. ★★★★ $19.99

The Hunchback of Notre Dame

(1996, 95 min, US, Gary Trousdale) After the high drama and pointed social lessons of the admirable *Pocahontas*, the animators at Disney have taken on an even darker text with this beautifully crafted feature film based on Victor Hugo's classic novel. Changing little of the story but reframing it to reflect Disney's traditional syle of storytelling, *Hunchback* is a brightly colored, tune-filled adaptation which manages to find quite a few laughs in a story not known for having them. Quasimodo (wonderfully voiced by Tom Hulce) is still ugly and deformed, but here he's not quite so grotesque as to frighten little ones, and he's given three gargoyle friends to pal around with, so he's not quite as pathetic and lonely. The music by Alan Menken and Stephen Schwartz is capable but not particularly memorable as other Menken scores. Esmerelda is a fiery heroine, and Demi Moore gives her good voice. Disney should be commended for tackling and succeeding in bringing a non-typical project to the screen. ★★★½ $29.99

A Hungarian Fairy Tale

(1986, 95 min, Hungary, Gyula Gazdag) Less fairy tale and more political fable, this magical film is a startling video find. Carried away on a cloud of romance after a performance of Mozart's "Magic Flute," a beautiful young woman with a Mona Lisa smile makes love with a handsome stranger. Their union produces a child, who is lovingly raised by the woman until she suddenly dies. The young boy, Andris, lost in the impersonal world of Budapest, begins an odyssey throughout Hungary searching for his father. Told with subtle humor and imbued with poetic beauty, this story of outsiders fleeing the confines of a conformist society is a remarkable achievement. Filmed in vivid black and white, this dreamlike and imaginative story will stay with

H

the viewer long after it is over. (Hungarian with English subtitles) ★★★★ $89.99

Hunger

(1966, 115 min, Denmark, Henning Carlsen) Per Oscarsson won the Best Actor Award at the Cannes Film Festival for his portrayal of a penniless and starving artist in 1890s Norway. This grim yet absorbing drama follows the young man who, despite being physically emaciated from lack of eating and prone to talking to his shoes, as well as to hallucinations, retains hope for his survival and optimism for his success as a writer as he tackles his hunger, waning self-respect and an overwhelming loneliness. The film does not have much of a plot, yet Oscarsson's performance keeps the viewer riveted. Based on the first novel by Nobel Laureate Knut Hamsun. (Danish with English subtitles) ★★★ $79.99

The Hunger

(1983, 99 min, GB, Tony Scott) Catherine Deneuve stars as Miriam, an icy, elegant vampiress, hundreds of years old, who goes on the prowl for a new mate after her 200-year lover (David Bowie) quickly ages. Her affections find their way to Sara (Susan Sarandon), a doctor who has written on the subject of accelerated aging. Dripping with cinematic style and chic sexual intrigue, *The Hunger* is both a chilling vampire tale and a sensuous drama of lesbian attraction and desire. The two romp, fall into each other's arms and make love — and, of course, share blood. The two stars create unprecedented sensual sizzle. ★★★½ $14.99

Hungry Hearts

(1989, 30 min, US, Nan Kinney & Debi Sundahl) Produced by Fatale Video, the leaders of lesbian erotica, this short tale is set at an ocean resort where two real-life strippers, Pepper and Reva, engage in sensual and passionate lovemaking. Made by women for women, this bawdy tale of sex includes a striptease, a much-used dildo, a harness and a most unusual bath. Lingerie lovers will love this one. $39.99

The Hunt

(1965, 93 min, Spain, Carlos Saura) Under a relentless sun which scorches the parched fields of central Spain, three apparently successful middle-aged men, all veterans of the Spanish Civil War, and a young man set off for a day of rabbit hunting. Fueled by the heat and long simmering tensions, the hunt escalates from petty fighting and bickering into eventual bloodshed as the men's jealousies, obsessions and hatreds rise to the surface. Saura's searing psychological thriller, spare in style, probes man's cruel nature so successfully that its tale should shock the viewer. (Spanish with English subtitles) ★★★½ $19.99

The Hunt for Red October

(1990, 135 min, US, John McTiernan) Director McTiernan's thrilling adaptation of Tom Clancy's best-seller is a well-paced and gripping Cold War drama filled with intrigue and exciting action. Sean Connery excels as a Soviet submarine skipper who steals a state-of-the-art sub from the Russian fleet and goes

AWOL. The question now facing the CIA is this: does he want to defect or is he going to single-handedly plunge the world into nuclear war? Costar Alec Baldwin is commanding as the CIA bookworm who is convinced of the defection theory. (Available letterboxed and pan & scan) ★★★½ $14.99

The Hunted

(1995, 111 min, US, J.F. Lawton) From the author of *Under Siege* comes this hokey actioner with lapses of excitement. Christopher Lambert stars as an American businessman in Japan who is on the run after witnessing the murder of a beautiful geisha (Joan Chen) by a villainous ninja assassin (John Lone). Violent almost to the point of slapstick, Lawton's film is yet another feeble attempt to cash in on the current "Asian cinemania" and as such features decent swordplay and a fast-paced (but ridiculous) script. ★★ $19.99

The Hurricane

(1937, 102 min, US, John Ford) Ford's classic adventure yarn has Dorothy Lamour (complete with sarong) and Jon Hall as tropical island lovers whose romance is interrupted by a devastating storm and island governor Raymond Massey. The film is noted for a spectacular climactic hurricane sequence. ★★★½ $19.99

The Hurried Man

(1977, 91 min, France, Edouard Molinaro) From the director of *La Cage aux Folles* comes this mildly interesting saga of a man driven to live his life in the fast lane. Alain Delon plays a 40-year-old playboy whose carefree lifestyle is threatened when a financial deal becomes more than he bargained for when part of the package includes marriage to a millionaire's daughter (Mireille Darc). Delon is delightful as a lifelong bachelor forced into responsibility. (Dubbed) ★★ $59.99

Husbands and Lovers

(1991, 94 min, Italy, Mauro Bolognini) If *Penthouse*'s Bob Guccione had been given a chance to direct *Who's Afraid of Virginia Woolf*, the result might have been something like this Italian-produced, English-language drama that will most likely be remembered for the unashamed full-frontal nudity of its well-known co-stars. Julian Sands bares all as the desperately lovelorn husband of an unfaithful wife (Joanna Pacula). Beautifully shot and mildly titillating, the film fails in its attempt at mixing erotica with character study, and relies too heavily on sexual content to mask the skimpy resolution. ★★ $89.99

Husbands and Wives

(1992, 110 min, US, Woody Allen) In an uncanny example of life imitating art, Allen's last collaboration with Mia Farrow is an often humorous, sometimes relentless examination of disintegrating marriages and fickle attractions between older men and younger women. Made in an almost documentary, cinema verité style (complete with hand-held camera work), the film is a kind of eavesdropping on the lives of two couples: Mia & Woody and Sydney Pollack & Judy Davis. In the opening scene, Davis and Pollack announce to Farrow

and Allen that they've decided to separate and from there, the film, in typical Allen fashion, meanders through all of the intellectual and emotional ramifications of marriage, fidelity and lust. Occasionally using talking head interviews with the characters, Allen probes their thoughts on all of these matrimonial ups-and-downs. Liam Neeson and Juliette Lewis costar as would-be marriage busters. ★★★½ $19.99

Hush...Hush, Sweet Charlotte

(1965, 133 min, US, Robert Aldrich) Motivated by the success of *Whatever Happened to Baby Jane?*, *Hush...* is yet another Grand Guignol thriller which was so common in the 1960s. Originally titled *Whatever Happened to Aunt Charlotte?*, Bette Davis, again in *Baby Jane* territory, stars as a very wealthy victimized hermit, haunted by the memories of a dead lover. The top-notch cast includes Olivia deHavilland, Joseph Cotten and Agnes Moorehead, who received an Oscar nomination for her unrecognizable slovenly housekeeper. ★★★ $19.99

Hustle

(1975, 120 min, US, Robert Aldrich) Burt Reynolds plays an old-fashioned L.A. cop who spends his days investigating suicides, porn rings and the mob, and spends his nights in the arms of a sexy Parisian call girl (Catherine Deneuve). Reynolds is personable, but he's just going through the motions in this below-average police thriller. With Ben Johnson, Paul Winfield, Eileen Brennan, Eddie Albert and Ernest Borgnine. ★½ $14.99

The Hustler

(1961, 135 min, US, Robert Rossen) Paul Newman has never been better than this! His classic portrayal of a disenchanted pool hustler who challenges the champ Minnesota Fats (Jackie Gleason) is set against the vivid backdrop of the seedy New York pool hall scene. Also starring Piper Laurie, in an unforgettable performance as Newman's crippled girlfriend; and George C. Scott, giving a brilliant characterization as a gruff promoter. A masterpiece of mood, character study and technique, with sharp direction by Rossen. ★★★★

Hypothesis of the Stolen Painting

(1978, 78 min, France, Râul Ruiz) Made for French TV (obviously light years ahead of its American counterpart), this intriguing and meditatively intellectual mystery-thriller was directed by the highly original and beguiling avant-garde director Ruiz, a Paris-based, Chilean expatriate. The "detective" story begins with a guide showing an unseen interviewer a series of paintings by Second Empire artist Frederic Tonnerre, in an effort to solve the mystery of a seventh painting. The paintings — actually *tableaux vivants*, live stagings of the works with the people in suspended animation — are only one of the many adventurous techniques used by Ruiz in his playful unraveling of his strange whodunit. A Ruiz short, *Dog's Dialogue*, precedes the feature. (French with English subtitles) ★★★ $59.99

I, a Woman

(1966, 92 min, Denmark/Sweden, Mac Ahlberg) Unlike the more famous but equally successful *I Am Curious Yellow* that hit American shores in 1968, this groundbreaking, sexually explicit drama of a woman's yearning sexuality has survived the sexual revolution quite well. Beautiful blonde Siv (Essy Persson) is an innocent country girl from a deeply religious family who drops her staid (no sex before marriage) boyfriend and the restrictiveness of provincial life to move to the big city and take care of her raging libido. Siv is a refreshing character – a beguilingly attractive temptress, she rejects conventional relationships and their obligations in a pursuit of simple pleasures and freedom. (Swedish with English subtitles) ★★★ $24.99

I Am a Camera

(1955, 98 min, GB, Henry Cornelius) John van Druten's theatrical interpretation of Christopher Isherwood's "Berlin Diaries" is brought to the screen with intelligence and wit. This marvelously acted piece features Julie Harris as Sally Bowles (a character later made truly famous by Liza Minnelli in Bob Fosse's *Cabaret*) as well as Laurence Harvey, Shelley Winters and Patrick McGoohan. ★★★ $24.99

I Am a Dancer

(1973, 93 min, GB, Pierre Jourdan & Bryan Forbes) An absorbing documentary portrait of one of this century's greatest dancers, Rudolf Nureyev. Once a favorite Sunday matinee at TLA Cinema, the film follows Nureyev through his training to his arrival on the international scene. Dance lovers won't want to miss the incredible performance footage including dances with Cynthia Gregory and Margot Fontaine. ★★★ $9.99

I Am a Fugitive from a Chain Gang

(1932, 93 min, US, Mervyn LeRoy) The best and most powerful of Warner Brothers' 1930s "social dramas." Paul Muni gives a tour de force performance as a WWI veteran unjustly imprisoned and sent to a Southern chain gang. Escaping the brutality of the system, Muni finds himself on the run, and never looking over his shoulder. A daring exposé of criminal injustice, the film was based on the autobiography of Thomas E. Burns. Glenda Farrell is impressive in a small part as Muni's fiancée. ★★★★ $19.99

I Am Cuba

(1964, 141 min, USSR/Cuba, Mikhail Kalatozov) *I Am Cuba* is a kaleidoscopic exposé of Batista's Cuba, a land of stark, diametric opposites, of great wealth and abject poverty, whose inequalities are flamboyantly juxtaposed by a perpetually moving camera as it reveals the conflicting lifestyles of the monied elite and the barely subsisting underclass. The stark black-and-white cinematography and an unabashed affection for the land are reminiscent of Sergei Eisenstein's *Que Viva Mexico!* The film's political agenda is unapologetic, and within the structure of four short stories of hardship and abuse, it presents the crushing exploitation of Cuba's people and

resources, revealing the underlying causes of Castro's revolution. The film counters timeless images with modern-day devices. There is an astounding 3½-minute shot that starts at street level, ascends several stories, travels through a workshop and out the window to follow a crowd moving through the streets below. Invigorating, inticing and sometimes brutal, the film shows equal affection to the teeming slums, the entertainment palaces and the fertile countryside. It's lyrical, joyous yet harsh and unwavering. (Spanish and Russian with English subtitles) ★★★★ $89.99

I Am Curious Blue

(1968, 103 min, Sweden, Vilgot Sjoman) With footage shot at the same time as *I Am Curious Yellow*, this tepid sequel continues the story of a sociologist's sexual study, though it looks as if *Yellow* features the more "interesting" takes. (Dubbed) ★★ $59.99

I Am Curious Yellow

(1967, 120 min, Sweden, Vilgot Sjoman) Adult film fans seeking titillations from this infamous breakthrough film should reconsider renting this Swedish curiosity. *I Am Curious Yellow* spends less time on sex and more in exploring the times and lifestyles of Swedish youth, specifically an adventurous young lady. (Dubbed) ★★½ $59.99

I Am My Own Woman

(1992, 90 min, Germany, Rosa von Praunheim) This wonderfully inspiring film of one person's determined efforts to be exactly what he wants to be is director von Praunheim's best work to date. A documentary with re-created dramatic scenes intercut throughout, the film tells the courageous story of Charlotte von Mahsldorf, born Lother Berfelde, a transvestite who realizes his dream of living life as a woman. The story follows the events of her life, from her teenage years during WWII to operating an East Berlin museum. Despite the repression of the Communists, attacks by skinheads and public

scorn, Miss Charlotte retains an amazingly sunny outlook as she freely goes about her life as a woman. Two actors play Charlotte as the young Lother/Charlotte, and Charlotte plays herself in the later years. An unforgettable portrait of a unique individual who bravely lived his life as she saw fit. (German with English subtitles) ★★★½ $79.99

I Can't Sleep

(1995, 110 min, France, Claire Denis) While films with positive gay and lesbian characters have multiplied in the '90s, so have depictions of queers as less than desirable members of society. With its depiction of a serial killing gay transvestite, *I Can't Sleep* joins the troubling latter group. However, it's difficult to say if this provocative, nihilistic French drama is homophobic because it is based on a true story of two gay "granny" killers. The story is set in the "New France" – not the familiar one of intellectual bourgeoisie contemplating infidelity or the meaning of life, but a France filled with poor immigrants and almost paralyzed by social ills. The story principally follows two brothers from Martinique: Theo (Alex Descas), a hard-working family man, and Camille (Richard Courcet), his strikingly beautiful gay drag queen brother. But Camille harbors a secret other than his sexuality: He and his white French lover (Line Renaud) have been terrorizing Paris with a series of brutal murders, all on older women. The story is based on Thierry Paulin, who killed more than 20 women between 1984-1987. He died from AIDS before coming to trial, and his lover is serving a 20-year sentence. (French with English subtitles) ★★½ $89.99

I Come in Peace

(1990, 92 min, US, Craig R. Baxley) Dolph Lundgren and Brina Benben star in this mildly entertaining but empty-headed science-fiction action movie as two police officers who must investigate a series of murders they soon discover are being committed by a drug-dealer from outer space. Once they discover the exact

Paul Muni (l.) in *I Am a Fugitive from a Chain Gang*

257

nature of what the alien is doing and encounter an alien cop tracking the druglord villain, they set out with some extraterrestrial weaponry to kick alien butt. Lundgren is about as good as he ever gets in this by-the-numbers movie, with Benben on hand to provide luke-warm comic relief. The plot is a mixture of the stories of several other, better sci-fi movies, and the special effects, though good, do not elevate the film above its low-rent feel. Baxley fared much better in 1994 with the highly original *Deep Red*. ★½ $9.99

I Confess

(1953, 95 min, US, Alfred Hitchcock) Montgomery Clift is a troubled priest held prisoner to the sacred vows of the confessional. By refusing to divulge the claims of a murderer, Clift becomes accused of the killer's crimes. Steeped with symbolism and laced with a telling commentary on the fine edge between guilt and purity. ★★★ $19.99

I Could Go on Singing

(1963, 99 min, GB, Ronald Neame) Judy Garland's last movie reveals the legendary singer in commanding voice as a famed entertainer who travels to England to retrieve her son, who is living with his father (Dirk Bogarde). The movie is pure melodrama, but Garland's vocal performances are pure magic. ★★½ $19.99

I Dismember Mama

(1972, 86 min, US, Paul Leder) Great titles do not great movies make. An escapee from a mental institution falls in love with an 11-year-old and seeks to "purify" his world. ★

I Don't Buy Kisses Anymore

(1992, 112 min, US, Robert Marcarelli) Though its title is quite clever, *I Don't Buy Kisses Anymore* is essentially an updated and rather sluggish *Marty*, without an abundance of that film's insight and wit. Jason Alexander stars as a lonely and overweight thirty-year-old shoe salesman who falls for an attractive psychology student (Nia Peeples). Though not attracted to him, she befriends him and feigns romantic interest for personal gain (for her thesis). Most of the characters are Jewish and Italian caricatures — they're not offensive, just lacking in dimension. Lou Jacobi saves the day with a crackling turn as a colorful family patriarch. *Kisses* (which refers to the chocolate) isn't all bad; it's just like the candy: you wish more was there under the wrappings. Filmed on location in Philadelphia. ★★ $89.99

I Don't Give a Damn

(1983, 94 min, Israel, Shmuel Imberman) This somber drama deals with the life of Rafi, a young soldier who is paralyzed in a terrorist explosion. Rafi finds that his vibrant, carefree lifestyle is drastically cut short, but he refuses to accept his future life confined to a wheelchair. First in a military hospital and later in his parents' home, his personality changes as he becomes disillusioned, bitter and self-pitying. He rejects his loving girlfriend who wants to look after him, berates his family and generally becomes a moody depressant who cannot live among the healthy. His despair gradually changes after he becomes interested in

photography, accepts his fate and reconciles with his loved ones. (Hebrew with English subtitles) ★★½

I Don't Want to Talk About It

(1994, 102 min, Argentina, Maria Luisa Bemberg) This amusing little fantasy stars Marcello Mastroianni as an Argentine gentleman who falls in love with a midget. Actually, the story revolves more around the relationship between the wee lady, Alejandra Podesta, and her mother, Luisina Brando, who tries desperately not to let her daughter know she's "different" — hence the film's title which refers to mama's response whenever anybody mentions her daughter's size. Lusciously filmed with a tinge of magical realism, the film enjoys fine performances and nice characterizations and is, for the most part, mildly enjoyable in spite of a weakened dramatic structure — it's cinematic cotton candy. The film features a hauntingly lyrical score by Nicola Piovani. (Spanish with English subtitles) ★★★ $19.99

I Hate Blondes

(1981, 89 min, Italy, Giorgio Capitani) An unexpectedly funny comedy about a ghost-writer of best-selling detective novels whose work inspires a series of real-life heists. A pretty blonde jewel thief becomes entangled in this web of comic mishaps. (Dubbed) ★★★

I Heard the Owl Call My Name

(1973, 79 min, US, Daryl Duke) A young Anglican priest (Tom Courtenay) is sent by his bishop (Dean Jagger) to live among the Indians of the Northwest, where he gains a new appreciation of human existence. Courtenay delivers a passionate performance in this moving made-for-TV drama. ★★★

I Killed Rasputin

(1967, 85 min, US, Robert Hossein) Cult favorite chronicling the life of legendary mystic Rasputin. In 1909 Russia, the mysterious Rasputin wins the favor of Empress Alexandra by saving the life of her son. But wary palace guards distrust the shadowy figure, and secretly plot his demise. With Gert Frobe, Peter McEnery and Geraldine Chaplin. ★ $59.99

I Know Where I'm Going

(1945, 92 min, GB, Michael Powell & Emeric Pressburger) The radiant Wendy Hiller plays a wealthy young woman who travels to the Scottish Hebrides to marry an older man, only to have her attentions diverted by a dashing young suitor. Splendid use of the Scottish countryside by directors Powell and Pressburger makes this a lyrically visual treat. ★★★★ $39.99

I Like It Like That

(1994, 105 min, US, Darnell Martin) Director Martin not only became the first black woman to gain the backing of a major studio with this explosively funny, poignant and precise look at life in the Bronx, she also made a flourishing entrance as a freshman director. Lauren Velez stars as Lisette, a twentysomething Latina with three kids and a jailed husband, Chino (Jon Seda), who thinks her penis is his passport to a woman's heart. Getting her first taste of freedom during his incarceration, and being more than a little put off by his macho posturing

I Like It Like That

upon his return, she kicks him out and is forced to fend for herself. Determined to make it, she lies her way into a job at a record company run by Griffin Dunne. It's a winning rags-to-a-decent-living story that is as hard-edged as it is likable. Martin shows a strong directorial hand and moves things along at a refreshing pace. Punctuated by pulsing hip-hop, salsa music and colorful camerawork, *I Like It Like That* is a dazzling debut. Also with Rita Moreno. ★★★½ $19.99

I Like You...I Like You Very Much

(1994, 58 min, Japan, Oki Hirojuki) Another "Pink Film" from Japanese New Queer Cinema, this very erotic low-budget drama is reminiscent of early Godard and others of awkward, pretentious soft-core porn. A young man is picked up at the train station by another. They have sex but commitment beyond the physical act is hampered when one of them pines for a third man he sees at the same station. Shaky, handheld camerawork adds to a certain raw realism but also induces a bit of queasiness. A bit less mournfulness and a bit more story could have saved this drama. (Japanese with English subtitles) ★★ $39.99

I Love Lucy, Vols. 1-12

(1951-1956, 51 min, US) America's favorite redhead, Lucille Ball, reigned supreme on the TV screen almost for the entire decade of the 1950s. Playing Lucy Ricardo, Ball shined as arguably the most beloved television character of all time. She was a mixture of innocence, kookiness and playfulness, and she was always resourceful in her misguided attempts to get in on the act despite her obvious lack of talent. Her then real-life husband, Desi Arnaz, played her husband Ricky, a Cuban bandleader who was constantly putting up with her crazy schemes. Co-starring William Frawley and Vivian Vance as Fred and Ethel Mertz, their constant friends and neighbors, "I Love Lucy" is a consummate production whose fresh, hilarious shows, week after week, year after year, excelled due to extremely developed scripts, the wackiest situations, and a cast — and a star — which was second to none. $14.99 ea.

Vol. 1: Lucy performs her classic "Vitameatavegamin" routine as "Lucy Does a TV Commerical" (1952); Lucy learns to stomp the grape in "Lucy's Italian Movie" (1956).

Vol. 2: This classic episode, "Job Switching" (1952), has Lucy and Ethel working in a chocolate candy factory; Lucy gets a bad case of sunburn just before the big "Fashion Show" (1955).

Vol. 3: In these two classic shows set in Hollywood, Lucy gets to meet William Holden in "L.A. at Last" (1955) and Harpo Marx (doing a terrific mirror pantomine scene) in "Lucy and Harpo Marx" (1955).

Vol. 4: In two pregnancy-themed shows, Lucy tells Ricky the good news in "Lucy Is Enciente" (1952) and Little Ricky is born in "Lucy Goes to the Hospital" (1953).

Vol. 5: Lucy spots Bob Hope at a baseball game and dons disguises to meet him in "Lucy and Bob Hope" (1956); Lucy disguises herself as Superman in "Lucy and Superman" (1957).

Vol. 6: Lucy and Ricky bet they can survive without modern appliances in "Pioneer Women" (1952); Lucy, Ricky, Ethel and Fred go on "The Camping Trip" (1953).

Vol. 7: It's the Ricardos against the Mertzes in "Never Do Business with Friends" (1953) and "The Courtroom" (1952).

Vol. 8: Lucy and Ricky are handcuffed just before he's set to appear on a big TV show in "The Handcuffs" (1952); Lucy masquerades as a ballet dancer to appear in Ricky's show in "The Ballet" (1952).

Vol. 9: Lucy gets a fake beard stuck to her face in "The Moustache" (1952); Lucy gets a trophy stuck on her head in "Lucy and the Loving Cup" (1957).

Vol. 10: Lucy bets she can not tell a fib for 24 hours in "Lucy Tells the Truth" (1953); Ricky thinks Lucy is "The Kleptomaniac" (1952) when he finds a closet full of items.

Vol. 11: In "Bonus Bucks" (1954), Lucy and Ethel fight over a lottery ticket; Lucy thinks "The Fur Coat" (1951) Ricky needs for his club act is an anniversary gift.

Vol. 12: When "Lucy Cries Wolf" (1954) once too often, no one will believe it when she's really kidnapped; In "Lucy Is Envious" (1954), Lucy dresses up as a woman from Mars and invades the Empire State Building (1954).

I Love Trouble

(1994, 120 min, US, Charles Shyer) Nancy Myers and Charles Shyer, the husband and wife writer-producer-director team, try to pull off the romantic comedy-action thriller thing (à la *Charade*). As rival reporters who reluctantly team up to crack a big story, Nick Nolte has never been so "leading man" and Julia Roberts returns to *Pretty Woman* mode as a doe-eyed woman with a great smile. One of Summer of '94's surprise bombs, this uneven mix of comedy and violence sporting a contrivance-riddled plot is entertaining in spite of itself. ★★½ $19.99

I Love You

(1982, 104 min, Brazil, Arnaldo Jabor) This colorful though pretentious erotic comedy features the stunning Sonia Braga as a housewife-cum-hooker drawn into a brief but intense encounter with a bankrupt bra manufacturer. Sparks fly as this whirlwind romance renews the vitality in both their lives. (Portuguese with English subtitles) ★★

I Love You Again

(1940, 99 min, US, W.S. Van Dyke II) William Powell and Myrna Loy are at it again and the results are joyously screwball. Powell plays a con man who discovers he's been a victim of amnesia for nine years and living under the identity of a fuddy-duddy pottery employee. Learning his alter ego has access to great wealth, he concocts a scam with newly acquired partner Frank McHugh. However, when he meets his wife Loy, who's about to divorce him, he plans to rekindle their marriage while setting up the good citizens of his small town. The Powell-Loy magic is ever present, but the lion's share of the laughs belong to Powell as he himself falls victim to a series of sight gags and humiliations. Loy is her usual classy persona. ★★★ $19.99

I Love You, Alice B. Toklas

(1968, 93 min, US, Hy Averback) Peter Sellers is at his loony best in this dated but hilarious comedy about a middle-aged L.A. lawyer who drops out and turns on. Leaving his bride-to-be at the altar not once, but twice, Sellers loses himself in a haze of drug-dosed cookies and a subsequent whirlwind tour of the hippie subculture. Paul Mazursky co-wrote the script. ★★★½ $14.99

I Love You Rosa

(1972, 84 min, Israel, Moshe Mizrahi) This feminist drama and tender love story is set in 1888 Jerusalem where a childless 20-year-old widow (Michal Bat-Adam) discovers that according to Deuteronomic Law she must marry her husband's brother — with the problem being that he is only 11 years old and determined to fulfill his duties. Rosa, forced to work in a bathhouse and sew for a living, must decide if she should follow the law and wait until the boy is eighteen or break with tradition and find another husband. Sentimental and charming, the story takes an insightful look at religious traditions, love, family and individual freedoms in this Oscar-nominated Best Foreign-Language Film. (Dubbed) ★★★ $39.99

I Love You to Death

(1990, 96 min, US, Lawrence Kasdan) Based on a true story, this sometimes funny, hit-or-miss black comedy is about a wife who discovers her husband is cheating on her and attempts to murder him — repeatedly. Kevin Kline gives a gloriously funny performance as the philandering husband. As the wronged wife, Tracey Ullman is given very little to do, and the talented comedienne is wasted. As her mother, Joan Plowright lets her hair down, and is obviously having some fun. Also with Keanu Reeves, River Phoenix and William Hurt. ★★★ $14.99

I, Madman

(1989, 95 min, US, Tibor Takacs) Director Takacs shows a flair for combining stop-motion monsters and live-action horror in this deliberately paced, moody mix of film noir and fright flick. Jenny Wright stars as a bookseller who unleashes a demon from the pages of a possessed book. Stylish camerawork and a clever script make this film an unusual but effective entry in the all-too-familiar horror lineup. ★★★ $89.99

I Married a Monster from Outer Space

(1958, 78 min, US, Gene Fowler, Jr.) When the major studios saw the grosses that AIP was getting from hot titles like *I Was a Teenage Werewolf* et. al., they decided to play that game too. The surprise is that this is quite a good little film. Atmospheric, effective special effects, a neat-looking bunch of papier-mâché aliens, and a word to young brides everywhere about the dangers of intergalactic miscegenation. ★★½ $49.99

I Married a Shadow

(1982, 110 min, France, Robin Davis) Nathalie Baye (*Return of Martin Guerre*) gives a strong performance as a mysterious woman with a false identity and a threatening past in this romantic suspense thriller. Pregnant, she leaves her abusive husband and travels to the South of France. Her train derails enroute, killing another pregnant woman. The in-laws of the dead woman, whom they have never met, take Baye home, thinking she is their daughter-in-law. Her new life is wonderful until she is threatened by the husband of her past. A compelling, seductive reworking of the 1949 Barbara Stanwyck soaper *No Man of Her Own*. (Dubbed) ★★★

I Married a Witch

(1942, 77 min, US, René Clair) Entertaining ghost comedy with Veronica Lake as a 17th-century Salem witch who comes back to haunt the descendant (Fredric March) of the man who had her burned at the stake. Based on a story by Thorne Smith ("Topper"). ★★★ $14.99

I Never Promised You a Rose Garden

(1977, 96 min, US, Anthony Page) Kathleen Quinlan's astonishing performance as a schizophrenic teenager undergoing treatment highlights this absorbing adaptation of Hannah Green's novel. Bibi Andersson ably plays her caring psychiatrist. ★★★

I Never Sang for My Father

(1970, 93 min, US, Gilbert Cates) A sterling version of Robert Anderson's play, with Gene Hackman in a fine performance as the estranged son of Melvyn Douglas who attempts reconciliation when his father becomes sick and unable to care for himself. Douglas, who in his later years became a brilliant character actor, is superb. Good support from Dorothy Stickney and Estelle Parsons. ★★★ $69.99

I Only Want You to Love Me

(1992, 96 min, Germany, Hans Günther Pflaum) Serious, analytical and as dry as the Sahara, this documentary on the life and work of Rainer Werner Fassbinder provides interesting information on the prolific and fast-living director; although in a stifling style that limits the film to die-hard fans. Essentially a talking heads documentary, the interviewees include fellow German directors Volker Schlöndorff, RWF regulars Ingrid Caven, Hanna Schygulla (looking uncharacteristically puffy and Morticia-like), Harry Bear, Kurt Raab (interviewed shortly before his death from AIDS), his mother Lilo Eder and several other friends and colleagues. There are also,

I Was a Male War Bride

in a helter-skelter fashion, excerpts from many of his movies. A bit tedious, the film sidesteps RWF's homosexuality as well as his drug and drinking problem. There is a fascinating film to be made on the enfant terrible of German cinema, but this isn't it. (German with English subtitles) ★★ $39.99

I Pagliacci
(1982, 70 min, Italy, Franco Zeffirelli) Placido Domingo stars in this exciting Leoncavallo opera. Georges Pretre conducts the orchestra and chorus of La Scala, and Teresa Stratas and Juan Pons co-star. (Italian with English subtitles) $24.99

I.Q.
(1994, 96 min, US, Fred Schepisi) From director Schepisi, who helmed one of the most beguiling romantic comedies of the 1980s, *Roxanne*, comes an almost equally enchanting confection. Walter Matthau, in a most amusing impersonation, plays Albert Einstein, the world renowned scientist now residing in Princeton, New Jersey. In a scenario recalling the whimsy and appeal of the great 1940s screwball comedies, Einstein plays matchmaker to his brainy but impassioned niece, nicely played by Meg Ryan. Though she's engaged to an egghead researcher (Stephen Fry), Uncle Albert coaches a good-natured garage mechanic (Tim Robbins) who has fallen under her spell. And much like the seven professors in *Ball of Fire*, Einstein and his four brainy pals take delight both scientifically and personally in their romantic experiment to bring the two together. Robbins continues to prove himself a cinematic natural resource giving a spirited, magnetic performance. ★★★½ $14.99

I Remember Mama
(1948, 134 min, US, George Stevens) Irene Dunne gives a captivating performance in this touching drama about an immigrant family living in San Francisco. Thanks to Dunne's sparkling performance and Stevens' delicate direction, the film is sweet and heartfelt without needless sentimentality, and has to it the

same flavor as Kazan's *A Tree Grows in Brooklyn*. ★★★½ $19.99

I Sent a Letter to My Love
(1981, 96 min, France, Moshe Mizrahi) A perceptive and unusual comedy-drama starring Simone Signoret as a formidable woman who has devoted her life to the care of her crippled brother. Being a bit lonely, she advertises in a personal column. Receiving a reply from a suitor whom she knows to be her brother, she continues the newspaper romance for her brother's sake. Mizrahi also directed Signoret in *Madame Rosa*. (Dubbed) ★★★

I Shot Andy Warhol
(1996, 106 min, US, Mary Harron) From its opening, which portrays the aftermath of the action of its title, *I Shot Andy Warhol* is a frantically paced and at times gripping chronicle of Valerie Solanas, Warhol's would-be assassin. Solanas (smartly played by Lili Taylor) was a semi-delusional lesbian feminist activist who slummed around Greenwich Village in the early '60s turning tricks to survive while peddling copies of her "S.C.U.M. (Society for Cutting Up Men) Manifesto." Essentially, Solanas comes off as a born loser, but one with an irrepressible and often brilliant intellect. In the film (though probably not in real life), she hangs around with transvestite Candy Darling (Stephen Dorff in an amazingly transformative role), who ultimately introduces her to Warhol and his milieu. For the most part, the film hits its mark, despite an overly long party scene at The Factory. Quite entertaining – in its own depressing way – it presents a most fascinating portrait of a woman who exemplified the phrase "a legend in her own mind." With a gritty streetwise demeanor, Taylor delivers rapid-fire speech at a relentless pace, and she's nothing short of first-rate. As Warhol, Jared Harris is an exquisite understatement of ethereal chic. ★★★½ $94.99

I Spit on Your Grave
(1989, 100 min, US, Meir Zarchi) A young woman takes a writing sabbatical to the country where she is brutally raped and beaten and

left for dead. But she survives and exacts bloody revenge. This low-budget exploiter manages to create quite a few suspenseful moments in between scenes of gratuitous violence. ★★

I, the Worst of All
(1990, 100 min, Argentina/France, Maria Luisa Bemberg) From the director of *Camila* and *Miss Mary* comes this unconventional story of 17th-century Mexican poet and nun Sor Juana inez de la Cruz. Confined to a prison-like cloister during the Spanish Inquisition, Sister Juana's passionate, philosophical poems become the "rage" amongst both the rich and poor, causing problems for the virtually sealed-off convent and prompting an intimate relationship (though mostly through bars) with a beautiful vicereine (Domenique Sanda). The film is elegant and intelligent, though the two women's relationship which is hinted at never goes beyond lingering glances. Based on the novel by Octavio Paz. (Spanish with English subtitles) ★★★ $29.99

I Wake Up Screaming
(1941, 82 min, US, Bruce Humberstone) Unusually stylish, this entertaining and moody thriller stars Betty Grable who, after her sister is murdered, teams up with the prime suspect (Victor Mature) to find the real killer. There are plenty of twists to keep the whodunit experts one body behind. The film features a fine performance by Laird Cregar as a sinister detective relentlessly out for his own form of demented justice. ★★★ $19.99

I Walked with a Zombie
(1943, 69 min, US, Jacques Tourneur) Don't let the title fool you – this is a first-rate thriller about a nurse (Frances Dee) who travels to the West Indies to care for a plantation owner's wife. She soon learns the woman is under the spell of a local voodoo priest. Lots of chills and remarkable camerawork and lighting. ★★★ $19.99

I Wanna Be Your Man
(1994, 97 min, Hong Kong, Chung Chi Shing) A Hong Kong drama that features a sensitive handling of a lesbian policewoman. Unlike the American film *Internal Affairs*, a policer that featured, as a side issue, Laurie Metcalf as a lesbian cop, *I Wanna Be Your Man* is much more interested in the lesbian theme rather than the crime action. Police Inspector Susan Wong (Christy Chung) is a beautiful, slightly butch lesbian cop who lives with her petulantly femme girlfriend Ron. The secret of her sexual orientation becomes accidentally known to Luk, an affably mediocre cop who, instead of telling his fellow officers that their boss is a dyke (an action that would ruin her), quickly becomes her friend and confidant. But Ron and Luk soon fall in love, a situation Susan is forced to accept. Better-than-average TV fare made interesting because of its setting and theme. ★★★ $89.99

I Wanna Hold Your Hand
(1978, 104 min, US, Robert Zemeckis) It's 1964 and The Beatles hit New York. The city is thrown into a panic as The Fab Four are to appear on "The Ed Sullivan Show," and every-

body scrambles for tickets. With this inspired premise, director Zemeckis lets go with a comic assault about a group of Jersey students who try to crash the show. A fine ensemble of young actors include Nancy Allen, Bobby DiCiccio, Marc McClure and Wendy Jo Sperber. ★★★ $9.99

I Want to Live

(1958, 122 min, US, Anthony Mann) Susan Hayward won an Oscar for her commanding performance in this true story of prostitute Barbara Graham, who, framed and convicted of murder, was sentenced to death. ★★★ $19.99

I Was a Male War Bride

(1949, 105 min, US, Howard Hawks) Though not on par with the best of either director Hawks or actor Cary Grant, an abundance of genuine laughs and skillful tomfoolery by its two stars make *I Was a Male War Bride* an appealing wartime comedy. Grant plays a French military attache who is teamed with no-nonsense American WAC Ann Sheridan. While on assignment, the bickering couple fall in love and marry. But complications and Army red tape arise when he tries to accompany his bride to the States — which includes a little trans-vestism on the part of Grant. ★★★ $19.99

I Was a Teenage Werewolf

(1957, 70 min, US, Gene Fowler) A youthful Michael Landon plays a juvenile delinquent who's got one on James Dean — he's a were-wolf (thanks to mad doc Whit Bissell). This low-budget horror flick is a campy pleasure in spite of the awkward acting and less-than-suc-cessful scares. ★★ $29.99

I Was a Zombie for the FBI

(1986, 105 min, US, Marius Penczner) Aliens plan to steal the formula for the world's most popular cola in order to turn Earth's population into subservient zombies. It's up to two crack FBI agents and a beautiful reporter to save the day. (Did they want a Pepsi or a Coke?) ★

I'll Cry Tomorrow

(1955, 117 min, US, Daniel Mann) Exemplary biography on entertainer Lillian Roth (based on her novel) about the singer's fight with alcoholism. Susan Hayward gives a magnifi-cent performance as Roth, and Jo Van Fleet is fine in support as her mother. ★★★½ $19.99

I'll Do Anything

(1994, 116 min, US, James L. Brooks) After brilliantly dissecting TV journalism in *Broadcast News*, writer-director Brooks turns his eye on the movie industry with less-than-satisfying results. Nick Nolte stars as a talented but unemployed actor who unexpectedly gains custody of his bratty six-year-old daughter. While trying to pursue both a coveted film role and a pretty, budding producer (Joely Richardson), he must also get to know his estranged child. When Brooks zeroes in on the movie-making process, the film is funny and diverting; however, the scenes concerning the reunion of father and daughter are maudlin at best. Originally intended as a musical, the film was edited after disappointing previews — iron-ic after Brooks nearly lampoons the process in his story. ★★½ $19.99

I'll Love You Forever...Tonight

(1992, 76 min, US, Edgar Michael Bravo) Made for under $100,000 by Bravo as his the-sis film for UCLA, this somber and searing drama, set in queer twentysomething L.A., revolves around the lives, loves and sexual rela-tions of a group of friends and acquaintances. Serious with occasional flashes of humor, the film delves into the loneliness, self-deception and self-loathing of its several gay male char-acters with an unflinching realism. Described as "Pinter-on-Fire Island" and "a queer *Big Chill*," this thought-provoking tale, filmed in shadowy black & white and which captures the tensions of today's post-AIDS male youth, is alternately compassionate and gritty but always perceptive. A TLA Video exclusive. ★★★ $29.99

I'm All Right, Jack

(1960, 104 min, GB, John & Roy Boulting) No word less than side-splitting will suffice in describing this scathing satire on labor relations in England. The inimitable Peter Sellers stars as a young man caught between the two sides of a bitter labor dispute. The essence of worker-man-agement relations, as practiced in England, are captured with the utmost clarity in this unre-lenting farce. Co-stars include Ian Carmichael, Terry-Thomas, Richard Attenborough and Margaret Rutherford. ★★★½ $19.99

I'm Almost Not Crazy

(1989, 56 min, US, Michael Ventura) A won-derful look at the life and professional career of maverick filmmaker John Cassavetes. Includes interviews with Cassavetes, his wife Gena Rowlands, Peter Falk and scenes from his films. ★★★ $29.99

I'm Dancing as Fast as I Can

(1982, 107 min, US, Jack Hofsiss) Based on Barbara Gordon's memoir, Jill Clayburgh stars as the TV documentary filmmaker who tries to put an end to her valium dependency — with great difficulty. Clayburgh is very good as Gordon, and gets splendid support from Nicol Williamson, Joe Pesci, Dianne Wiest and Geraldine Page. ★★½ $69.99

I'm Gonna Git You Sucka

(1988, 87 min, US, Keenan Ivory Wayans) Before he found success with his TV comedy series "In Living Color," Wayans made this good-natured spoof on the blaxploitation flicks of the 1970s. With a fine supporting cast of veterans, such as Isaac Hayes, Jim Brown and Bernie Casey, the film is about a young, idealistic soldier (Wayans) on leave. He returns home to find that his brother OG'd (died of an overdose of gold chains) and the mob wants to turn his sister to prostitution for some debts left behind by the departed Bro. Our hero, vowing to bring the bad guys to justice, assem-bles a motley band of "bad" dudes, and with the music of *Shaft* in the background, they bat-tle and kick some butt. ★★★ $14.99

I'm No Angel

(1933, 88 min, US, Wesley Ruggles) "It's not the men in your life, it's the life in your men." This is just one of the classic quips made by the one and only Mae West in this sparkling, bawdy pre-Code comedy. The 1930s sex goddess is at

her best as a carnival performer who finds it as much a breeze taming the men as she does the lions. Becoming the toast of the town upon her arrival in New York, she crosses paths with businessman Cary Grant, to whom she promis-es "When I'm good, I'm very good. But when I'm bad, I'm even better." Looking ravishing, West's every other line seems to be a dandy sexual entendre; even when she's not being suggestive, she's suggestive. Sixty years have not dampened the snap and sizzle of her retorts. She has the talk, and she has the walk. Also fea-turing the famous "grape" line, this is one of two West films which single-handedly saved Paramount Studios from near-bankruptcy in 1933. ★★★½ $14.99

I'm Not Rappaport

(1996, 135 min, US, Herb Gardner) Herb Gardner adapted and directed his Tony Award-winning play about the tender and comic rela-tionship between two disparate New York senior citizens. The stage show was more fluid, but this engaging character piece is buoyed by two endearing performances given by Walter Matthau and Ossie Davis. Nat (Matthau) is a rascally 80-year-old Jewish leftist who meets half-blind building custodian Midge (Davis), a black man his same age, dur-ing visits to Central Park. Though Midge real-ly wants nothing to do with them, Nat slowly ingratiates himself into Midge's life. The charm of the story is Gardner's wonderful characterizations of Nat and Midge, who when not feuding, telling jokes or fighting off pimps and gang members are impersonating mafia dons or becoming involved in the lives of some of the park's habitués. Through telling moments, Gardner imparts thoughtful obser-vances towards the realities of aging in urban America, while Matthau and Davis mine a rich comic text, producing laughs and poignant moments, alike. ★★★ $102.99

I'm the One You're Looking For

(1988, 85 min, Spain, Jaime Chavarri) A con-troversial film that explores the complicated range of feelings generated between a woman (Patricia Adrian) and the man who rapes her. The story begins when a beautiful but unhappy model is raped after she stops on a deserted road to help a handsome motorist. The traumatized young woman, fueled by either repulsion and revenge on her attacker or a strange physical attraction to him, becomes obsessed with the young man. With the aid of a ditsy middle-aged housewife and a sexually confused erotic dancer, she begins to hunt for him through the seedy and at times bizarre underworld of Barcelona. Saying things like, "I'll get raped a thousand times in order to find him," the young woman's motivations are complex and the viewer's response is certain to be wide-ranged in this absorbing psychological sus-pense thriller. Almodóvar regular Chus Lampreave is a scream as the outlandish woman who comes to our heroine's aid. (Spanish with English subtitles) ★★★ $79.99

I've Heard the Mermaids Singing

(1987, 81 min, Canada, Patricia Rozema) Sheila McCarthy, star of this enchanting com-edy, is nothing short of a revelation. The film

The Icicle Thief

itself is cute and whimsical but it is McCarthy, as Polly, the day-dreaming romantic Gal Friday, who steals the show as well as our hearts. An avid photographer who dwells in her own fantasy world, Polly secures a job as a temp in the office of an art collector. Her innocence and joie de vivre proves to be a bracing tonic in a world dulled by pretension and greed. A film and a performance that should lift your spirits. ★★★

Ice Palace

(1960, 143 min, US, Vincent Sherman) Richard Burton stars in this sprawling adaptation of Edna Ferber's novel about Alaska's drive toward statehood. Set at the end of WWII, the film casts Burton as a soldier who returns home to Seattle only to find his job has been given away. After roughing up his ex-boss, he heads for Alaska, where he teams up with Robert Ryan and Carolyn Jones in a fish canning enterprise and an ill-fated love triangle. ★★½ $19.99

The Ice Pirates

(1984, 93 min, US, Stewart Raffill) It is 10,000 years into the future, and an evil empire has gained control of the water supply for the entire universe. It is up to a band of rag-tag pirates, led by Robert Urich, to hijack the shipments of frozen ice blocks through space and thwart the evildoers. Mindless, familiar though occasionally kinda fun. With Anjelica Huston, Mary Crosby, John Matuszak and Ron Perlman. ★★ $14.99

Ice Station Zebra

(1968, 148 min, US, John Sturges) Potent Cold War thriller with Rock Hudson as a sub commander whose secret mission to the North Pole sets the stage for a showdown with the Russians. With Patrick McGoohan, Ernest Borgnine and Jim Brown. Based on an Alistair McLean novel. ★★½ $19.99

Iceman

(1984, 99 min, US, Fred Schepisi) Director Schepisi makes credible and arresting this story of a prehistoric man found frozen in the Arctic and discovered to be still alive by a scientific team. Timothy Hutton is one of the researchers who enters into an almost empathic relationship with the Neanderthal, who is remarkably portrayed by John Lone. Unusual and surprising. ★★★ $14.99

The Icicle Thief

(1989, 90 min, Italy, Maurizio Nichetti) Infectiously funny, this inventive and fast-paced satire on commercial television defies easy plot description. A bungling director (Nichetti himself) is interviewed at a TV station before the screening of his newest film, a black-and-white neorealist drama. The picture, a tender, affectionate tribute to *The Bicycle Thief*, tells the story of the many struggles of an unemployed man (Nichetti again), his beautiful wife and their son, an unbelievably hard-working boy of six. But the family finds that financial hardships are nothing in comparison to the confusion and disruption caused when a scantily clad, English-speaking platinum blonde in full color "falls" out of her bathing suit commercial and into their neorealist lives. Aghast that his touching tale has taken on a bizarre twist, the director is forced to break into his film in a vain attempt to make matters right. With tender humanism and a deft comic touch, Nichetti is a breath of fresh air. (Italian with English subtitles) ★★★½ $19.99

Idi Amin Dada

(1974, 90 min, France, Barbet Schroeder) The repellingly charismatic Idi Amin, brutal dictator of Uganda in the 1970s, secured an almost Hitlerian legacy as a blood-thirsty, power-hungry despot who pillaged the country's treasury and attempted to eliminate all opposition. It was even said that after his overthrow, human remains (presumably for midnight snacks) were found in his refrigerator. From this unlikely subject comes Schroeder's fascinating, funny and shocking documentary that was made with the full cooperation of Idi Amin (although who, after completion, threatened the director with death if certain cuts were not made). We witness a jovial, even likable bully who mugs for the camera, rebuts all of the murderous charges against him and attempts to charm his way into the viewers' hearts and minds. But beneath his friendly posturing, the reality of evil personified seeps through. ★★★ $59.99

The Idiot

(1951, 166 min, Japan, Akira Kurosawa) Made immediately after his international success *Rashomon*, Kurosawa faithfully transposed his favorite literary work to the screen with this engrossing adaptation of Fyodor Dostoevsky's complex tale of madness and jealousy. Changing the time and setting to a snow-battered, post-war Japan, the story follows a kept woman who is wanted for marriage by three different men, including the holy fool Prince Kameda and his raucous friend (Toshiro Mifune). The video transfer is especially good, highlighting Kurosawa's imaginatively lit black-and-white photography. (Japanese with English subtitles) ★★★½ $79.99

The Idolmaker

(1980, 119 min, US, Taylor Hackford) Ray Sharkey mesmerizes in this much-overlooked gem about a '50s rock impresario who stops at nothing to insure the success of his teen heart-throb protégés. Also with Peter Gallagher and Tovah Feldshuh. ★★★ $14.99

If...

(1969, 111 min, GB, Lindsay Anderson) Inspired by Jean Vigo's classic *Zero for Conduct*, this extraordinary allegorical film is set in a repressive public boarding school. Malcolm McDowell, who made his film debut in this explosive, furiously funny attack on the British establishment, stars as one of three unruly seniors whose refusal to conform ultimately leads to a full-scale student rebellion. Anderson's surreal and manic style seems the perfect cinematic exclamation point to the end of a turbulent decade. The alternating use of color and black-and-white cinematography is not an artistic statement, but more the fact that Anderson, who shot the film out of sequence, ran low on money and was forced to shoot in black and white. ★★★★ $49.99

If It's Tuesday, It Must Be Belgium

(1969, 99 min, US, Mel Stuart) Though its humor may be somewhat dated, this congenial comedy about a group of American tourists on the European vacation from hell manages to produce a few hearty laughs. Suzanne Pleshette, Mildred Natwick, Murray Hamilton, Peggy Cass, Norman Fell and Michael Constantine are just some of the beleaguered travelers visiting nine countries in 18 days. And it's the kind of trip — and comedy — where everything that can go wrong will. The film may not always keep time with the slap-dash pace it sets for itself, but as a time capsule of swinging '60s mod it's almost invaluable. Donovan sings the dreadful title tune, and appears in a cameo; Hamilton comes off the best from this large cast; and there's an irresistible running gag about the ultimate hotel towel thief. ★★½ $19.99

If Looks Could Kill

(1991, 105 min, US, William Dear) TV heartthrob Richard Grieco ("21 Jump Street") makes the jump to the big screen in this unexpectedly amiable spoof about a high school student studying in Europe who is mistaken for a James Bond-type superspy. Can he save the world in time for finals? Also with Linda Hunt in a delightfully campy turn as a whip-wielding villainess. ★★½ $14.99

If Lucy Fell

(1996, 93 min, US, Eric Schaeffer) An instantly forgettable but relatively painless "love-in-the-'90s" comedy. Sarah Jessica Parker (as a therapist — ha!) and Eric Schaeffer (co-director of *My Life's in Turnaround*) star as romantically challenged roomies who've made a pact to throw themselves off the Brooklyn Bridge within one month (Parker's character's 30th birthday) if they haven't found mate material. Wonder what'll happen, eh? Starts off dumb and pseudo hip (cameos by Hal Hartley regulars Bill Sage and Robert Burke, and Sirajul and Mujibar from "Letterman" only further this feeling), then becomes mildly involving in the middle third, then blows it by making the hugely predictable wrap-up really protracted. The usually annoying Parker is actually half-decent here, but Schaeffer isn't — you don't want him dead real, *real* bad; and Ben Stiller has some laughs as modern artist Bwick. The kind of film in which two weeks later you'll wonder out loud, "Did I see this?" ★★ $19.99

If She Says Yes, I Don't Say No

(1983, 95 min, France, Claude Vital & Marcel Julian) This is certainly a strange title but don't be put off. From the people who gave us the ménage à trois comes this ménage à quatre, a very funny sex comedy about a fiercely independent young woman and the attempts of the three men in her life to please her. Only the French could get away with this one! (French with English subtitles) ★★★

Ikiru

(1952, 143 min, Japan, Akira Kurosawa) Kurosawa's most affecting film, *Ikiru (To Live)* salvages great hope from intractable despair. Takashi Shimura is both pathetic and radiant as a minor bureaucrat who, about to die of cancer, realizes that he never really meant anything to anyone. The film deals with his attempts to make his existence meaningful. (Japanese with English subtitles) ★★★★ $39.99

Illegally Yours

(1988, 102 min, US, Peter Bogdanovich) Bogdanovich made a bold but futile attempt at a comeback with this whimsical but empty-headed romp about a juror (Rob Lowe donning the Ryan O'Neal-*What's Up Doc* persona) who sets out to clear the name of a former high school crush (Colleen Camp). ★★ $14.99

Illusions Travel by Streetcar

(1953, 90 min, Mexico, Luis Buñuel) A small, pleasant and surprisingly gentle comedy that revolves aroung two laid-off transit workers in Mexico City who, on learning that it is headed

for the scrap heap, commandeer an aging trolley and take it on one final, wild drunken ride. With class-conscious humor, Buñuel pokes gentle fun at the various passengers who board the train and become part of the wildly antic adventures through the city. (Spanish with English subtitles) ★★★ $59.99

Ilsa: Harem-Keeper of the Oil Shieks

(1983, 91 min, US, Don Edmonds) Ilsa, that wicked she-wolf of the S.S., is back! This time, she is the evil taskmaster heading up a harem for a greedy oil lord. With Dyanne Thorne and Mike Thayer. ★

Ilsa: She-Wolf of the S.S.

(1974, 92 min, US, Don Edmonds) Perverse kinky fare about Nazi Commandant Ilsa using prisoners in experiments to test her outlandish theories. Although sure to offend many, this is a bonanza for those who like to wallow in bad taste. Dyanne Thorne is uncanny in her embodiment of the lustful villainess. ★

Ikiru

The Image

(1990, 110 min, US, Peter Werner) A successful anchor/reporter for a "60 Minutes"-type news show — played by an engaging Albert Finney — and a wonderful strong cast strive for hidden truths and higher ratings. Finding that these goals don't often coincide, *The Image* explores TV's role in creating a public's view-

points and the pitfalls of making oneself a marketable product. A bit of stale New Age music and a somewhat preachy climax are the only drawbacks to this thought-provoking and enjoyably charming HBO production. ★★★ $89.99

Images

(1986, 54 min, US, Janet Liss) *Images* is a dramatic love story about a happy lesbian couple whose relationship is tested by "the other woman." This first-rate film portrays positive characters and combines a tender love story with gentle eroticism. ★★½ $44.99

Imaginary Crimes

(1994, 106 min, US, Anthony Drazan) Harvey Keitel delivers an involving and nuanced portrayal of a dreamer and con man whose flights of fancy are borne in silent disappointment by his wife and two daughters. Fairuza Balk is remarkably powerful as the eldest daughter who assumes the role of family caretaker when her mother (Kelly Lynch) dies; the story is told through her eyes. Reminiscent of *This Boy's Life*, *Imaginary Crimes* carefully evokes the same time period of the late '50s and early '60s. Seymour Cassel appears as one of Keitel's business partners, and Vincent D'Onofrio is Balk's teacher and mentor. Director Drazan has crafted a thoughtful and intimate study of the infinite human capacities for self-delusion and quiet strength. An unexpected surprise, and recommended. ★★★½ $19.99

Imagine: John Lennon

(1988, 103 min, US, Andrew Solt) This stirring documentary on the life of John Lennon is a well-balanced and detailed look at one of the greatest musical icons of our time. Drawing on exhaustive archives of footage, director Solt has pieced together an entertaining and, at times, extremely moving chronicle of Lennon's life and work — beginning with his traumatic childhood and inevitably culminating with his tragic death. Brimming with great music and Lennon's charismatic and candid screen presence, the film is more than a mere tribute to this incredible fallen artist. ★★★½ $24.99

Imitation of Life

(1959, 124 min, US, Douglas Sirk) Arguably the best of the '50s soap-operas, this second screen version of Fanny Hurst's novel stars Lana Turner and Juanita Moore as, respectively, an ambitious actress and her self-sacrificing black maid, who each find difficulty in raising their teenage daughters. Sandra Dee and Susan Kohner become the troublesome offspring. Moore and Kohner are standouts. A four-hanky tearjerker with the most famous funeral in the movies. ★★★½ $14.99

Immediate Family

(1989, 95 min, US, Jonathan Kaplan) Glenn Close and James Woods are a childless couple who are looking to adopt a baby. Mary Stuart Masterson and Kevin Dillon are having one, though they are unmarried and unprepared for parenthood. When these four expectant parents get together, the result is a charmingly sweet, innocuous comedy-drama about familial ties and the adoption process. The story, about a privileged couple trying to get to know the parents of their future child, alternates between insightful drama and gentle humor, and director Kaplan handles both with extreme affection. Masterson walks away with the acting honors, giving a sympathetic and intuitive performance as the young mother-to-be. ★★★ $9.99

El Immigrante Latino

(1972, 89 min, Colombia, Gustavo Nieto Roa) "El Gordo" Lopez, a classical musician from Bogota, decides that the musical opportunities are greater in the United States. So, with his life savings of $1,000, our innocent hero travels to New York on a visitor's visa. His naive hopes to find instant fame and fortune are deflated as he encounters a series of very funny disasters; what we call the "New York Experience." But hope and his good nature prevail as Gordo seeks to find a place in his new world. (Spanish with English subtitles) ★★½

The Immoral Mr. Teas

(1959, 63 min, US, Russ Meyer) The original "nudie-cutie" film which spawned nearly 150 imitations within a year of its release. Starring Russ' army buddy Bill Teas, and a bevy of bosomy beauties. ★★ $79.99

Immoral Tales

(1969, 90 min, France, Walerian Borowczyk) The allure, mystique and sensuality of the human flesh is explored in this provocative film. Divided up in four bawdy stories which are set between 1498 and 1970, this racy item observes the timelessness of love born and destroyed. Stars Paloma Picasso. (Dubbed) ★★½

The Immortal Bachelor

(1979, 94 min, Italy, Marcello Fondato) This lusty and altogether enjoyable sex farce stars Giancarlo Giannini as a hot-blooded Italian lover who just can't seem to get enough of the eternal allures of women, one of them the beautiful Monica Vitti. Also starring Claudia Cardinale. ★★★

Immortal Beloved

(1994, 121 min, GB, Bernard Rose) Gary Oldman stars as Ludwig van Beethoven in this somewhat trivial examination of the tempestuous composer's life and loves. Beginning with Beethoven's death, the story follows the travails of Beethoven's confidant (Jeroen Krabbé) who sets out to find the mysterious "Immortal Beloved" named as the composer's beneficiary. His search leads him across war-torn Europe to three prime candidates: Valeria Golino, the daughter of a mid-level nobleman; Isabella Rossellini, portraying a very sympathetic Hungarian Countess; and Johanna Ter Steege, the low-born upholsterer who was not only Ludwig's one-time playmate, but also the sister-in-law with whom he battled over the custody of his nephew. While all of the actors perform adequately, nothing of real consequence happens. And as the film is structured as a series of flashbacks, there is no foundation of dramatic tension. While the soundtrack is most pleasing, one can't help but wish that Ken Russell had been at the helm to take this film over the top and into the realm of the absurd, because that is where it wants to go. ★★½ $19.99

The Importance of Being Earnest

(1952, 95 min, GB, Anthony Asquith) Michael Redgrave, Dorothy Tutin, Edith Evans, Margaret Rutherford and Joan Greenwood star in this impeccable rendition of Oscar Wilde's classic farce. Wilde's play is certainly one of the hallmarks of British theatre and it represents the height of his genius. He joyously pokes and jabs at the hypocrisy of British society while using the most widely accepted conventions of the stage to present his most radical ideas and social criticisms. Sterling performances from the entire cast make this one of the most outstanding comedies to grace any screen, large or small. ★★★★ $19.99

Imposters

(1979, 110 min, US/West Germany, Mark Rappaport) Independent New York filmmaker Rappaport has fashioned, with the help of Charles Ludlam (the founder of New York's Ridiculous Theatre Company), an absurdist, convoluted and extremely strange "comedy" about two twin brothers (who are not twins) whose interests include magic, love triangles, assassinations and stolen Egyptian treasures. Produced on a miniscule budget and told episodically in a labyrinthine plot, this very "'70s" picture might seem rudderless and even senseless to many, but can also be quite entertaining and original. ★★½ $39.99

Impromptu

(1991, 95 min, GB, James Lapine) This enchanting and romantic period comedy examines the courtship between composer and pianist Frederic Chopin and novelist George Sand. Sand, a liberated woman long before her time, was easily one of the more feisty and bohemian writers of the late 19th century and she set about seducing the reclusive, sickly and fervently chaste Chopin with characteristic wit and charm. Judy Davis is splendid as the vivacious Sand and Hugh Grant delivers a wonderfully low-key performance as Chopin. The circle of artists and free-spirited souls with whom Sand mingled is played by an excellent supporting cast with Mandy Patinkin as her ex-lover, Alfred de Musset; Bernadette Peters as the scheming Marie d'Agoult; Julian Sands as composer Franz Liszt; Ralph Brown as the painter Eugen Delacroix; and Emma Thompson and Anton Rodgers as the Duke and Duchess of Antan. ★★★½

Improper Conduct (Mauvaise Conduite)

(1984, 110 min, France, Nestor Almendros & Orlando Jiminez-Leal) This provocative documentary investigates the oppression and abuse faced by Cuba's gay and intellectual populace under the hyper-machismic reign of Castro. Twenty-eight Cuban exiles — homosexuals, poets, artists and former government officials — are interviewed, each detailing their conflicts with a system that suppresses civil rights and considers homosexuality a crime. (English and Spanish with English subtitles) ★★★½ $19.99

Impulse

(1984, 91 min, US, Graham Baker) Interesting but inconclusive tale of two young lovers (Tim Matheson and Meg Tilly) who seek answers to the mysteriously erratic behavior of the residents of a small community, who suddenly engage in inexplicable actions for no apparent reason. Hume Cronyn also stars. ★★ $14.99

Impulse

(1990, 109 min, US, Sondra Locke) Director Locke's second feature is a tough, gritty portrait of a hard-edged undercover vice cop (Theresa Russell) who becomes both the number one suspect and next potential victim in a murder case. Jeff Fahey and George Dzundza co-star. ★★★ $19.99

Impure Thoughts

(1985, 87 min, US, Michael Simpson) Capturing a period from the filmmaker's experience, Simpson's Impure Thoughts is a thoughtful, funny film that both humorously satirizes and seriously reconsiders Catholic parochial education in the `60s and `70s. Flashbacks (confession, nuns with clickers and rulers, illicit lust, cheat sheets, "leaving room for the Holy Ghost" between dance partners) are beautifully integrated by Simpson into his higher purpose of contemplating such issues as life and death, sin, redemption, conscience and the hereafter. Starring Brad Dourif and the voice of Judith Anderson. ★★★

In a Glass Cage

(1986, 98 min, Spain, Agustin Villaronga) Although definitely not for the squeamish, this sexually bizarre and violent thriller is a real find for those aficionados of no-holds-barred horror. Set a few years after WWII, the story concerns a former Nazi doctor and child molester who, because of an accident, is confined to an iron lung. The tormentor becomes the tormented after a mysterious young man, employed to be the paralyzed man's nurse, is instead bent on revenge. Mixing the style of Diva with the graphic sadomasochism of Pasolini's Salo, the film treads on ideas rarely ventured in commercial films. An uncompromising psychosexual drama that is both erotic, painful and terrifying. (Spanish with English subtitles) ★★★ $79.99

In a Lonely Place

(1950, 91 min, US, Nicholas Ray) Humphrey Bogart gives a chilling and complex performance in this terrific and brooding film noir thriller. Bogey plays a mentally unstable Hollywood screenwriter, given to uncontrollable rage, who must clear his own name when he is suspected of murdering a hat-check girl. Gloria Grahame is perfectly cast as a starlet who begins an affair with Bogart, she being his only alibi. The film greatly benefits from Ray's expert, moody direction, and Bogart's strong, atypical portrayal. ★★★½ $69.99

In a Year of 13 Moons

(1979, 119 min, West Germany, Rainer Werner Fassbinder) A passionate and pessimistic account of the final period in the doomed life of a transsexual named Elvira (ex-Erwin), who underwent a sex change operation on impulse to please a rich eccentric who no longer loves him/her. Now alone, Elvira seeks help from friends and her former wife, only to be repulsed and/or betrayed. 13 Moons is one of Fassbinder's most chilling and captivating efforts. As with his other films, RFW challenges and disorients the viewer with his sporadic sentimentality and harsh detachment. Volker Spengler excels as Elvira, an innocent sexual casualty in a desperate, and ultimately futile, search of aid. (German with English subtitles) ★★★½ $29.99

In Celebration

(1974, 131 min, GB, Lindsay Anderson) Anderson's contribution to the American Film Theatre series is this rendition of David Story's loosely autobiographical play about three grown-up sons who return to their coal-mining home town to celebrate their parents' 40th anniversary. Alan Bates heads the original Royal Court Theatre cast. ★★★

In Cold Blood

(1967, 134 min, US, Richard Brooks) A truly remarkable screen adaptation of Truman Capote's novel. Straightforward presentation in moody black and white avoids sensationalizing the already potent story of random slaughter by two aimless, rootless lost boys (Robert Blake and Scott Wilson). Director Brooks, aided by a masterful script, conveys complex information and muted emotional states with assured skill and humane empathy. Unsettling, discomforting, rewarding. ★★★★

In Country

(1989, 120 min, US, Norman Jewison) Bruce Willis stars as a Vietnam vet whose emotional scars have yet to heal. Emily Lloyd gives a sparkling performance as his spirited niece who harbors her own grief due to the death of her father in combat. Though Willis is top-billed, his is really more of a supporting character, as the film belongs to Lloyd, in both character time and performance. The film, at times, is haunting, but too many scenes seem short-changed dramatically; writer Frank Pierson doesn't fully explore some of the profound themes he has addressed. The film's ending, however, taking place at the Vietnam memorial in Washington, D.C., is one of the most startlingly moving film sequences in memory. ★★½ $14.99

In Custody

(1994, 123 min, GB, Ismail Merchant) Producer Merchant returns to behind the camera for the first time since *The Courtesans of Bombay*, his 1982 feature directorial debut, with this pleasant comedy-of-manners set in a small town in northern India. A poor, under-appreciated schoolteacher is assigned to interview Nur (played by the wonderful Shashi Kapoor), a renowned Urdu poet. The teacher is greeted by a great artist near the end of his life – obese, sickly, cantankerous and confined primarily to his home. The film revolves around a series of aborted interviews (family, friends, food and sex always seem to interrupt). One suspects that this simple story is actually a pretext for Merchant to offer lively discussions on the fading Urdu culture and language, and to have his actors read from the writings of the great Urdu poet Faiz Ahmad Faiz. ★★★ $29.99

In Heaven There Is No Beer?

(1984, 51 min, US, Les Blank) A romp through the Polka subculture in America. Visit a Polkabration in Connecticut, attend an International Polka Association Convention, and witness a Polka Mass in Milwaukee. $59.99

In Love and War

(1987, 96 min, US, Paul Aaron) Fact-based drama with James Woods as a Navy pilot held prisoner for eight years during the Vietnam War and Jane Alexander as his loving wife who organizes other POW wives at home in order to get some straight answers from the government. Woods and Alexander offer compelling performances, though the absorbing story isn't quite as powerful as it could have been. With Haing S. Ngor. ★★½ $89.99

In Love and War

(1996, 115 min, US, Richard Attenborough) Ernest Hemingway's real-life WWI exploits were the inspiration for his classic novel "A Farewell to Arms." Rather than opting to remake a third film version of the classic story, director Attenborough instead adapts the book "Hemingway in Love and War." In fictionalizing certain aspects of his youth, Hemingway knew real-life facts does not a compelling story make, and he's proven right with this languid romantic drama. Chris O'Donnell plays the teenaged Hemingway, who lies about his age to join the Red Cross. Stationed in Italy and wounded on the front, he falls in love with his nurse Agnes von Kurowsky (Sandra Bullock). It's a bittersweet May-June romance which later would leave the author emotionally scarred. Usually personable on-screen, Bullock gives a flat portrayal, leaving one and all to wonder just why Hemingway would be haunted by this affair for the rest of his life. At least O'Donnell captures the enthusiasm of the writer, though not his drive. Attenborough's pacing is sluggish throughout, and for a film about a passionate affair, there's little passion. ★½ $102.99

In Memoriam

(1977, 89 min, Spain, Enrique Brasso) Geraldine Chaplin stars in this somber melodrama about commitment, obsessive love and jealousy. Essentially a three-person play, the film tells the story of a tangled love triangle between Luis, a celebrated novelist; Juan, a struggling writer; and Paulina, the woman they both love. Luis, who is incapable of expressing his deep love of Paulina, finds that he has lost her to the passionate and possessive love of Juan. Chaplin is beguiling as the woman torn between the two men – emotional and personality opposites. A Spanish soap opera that avoids the typical excesses of the genre and delves more into the psychological nuances of the characters. (Spanish with English subtitles) ★★½

In Name Only

(1939, 94 min, US, John Cromwell) Tearjerker starring Cary Grant as a wealthy businessman who is trapped in a loveless marriage to social climber Kay Francis. When Grant falls in love with Carole Lombard and asks for a divorce, scheming wife Francis refuses the request and sets on a ruthless course to foil their affair. A familiar romantic soaper highlighted by Grant

and Lombard's affectionate scenes together. ★★★ $19.99

In Old Chicago

(1938, 96 min, US, Henry King) With the great success of M-G-M's *San Francisco* in 1936, 20th Century-Fox released their own disaster spectacle and the result is a pleasing if fictionalized version of the great Chicago fire of 1871. Tyrone Power and Don Ameche play the O'Leary brothers – one a scalawag and the other the mayor. They're the sons of Mrs. O'Leary, who owned that famous cow. Alice Brady won an Oscar for her stalwart but sentimental portrayal of Ma, and Alice Faye also stars. The film features outstanding special effects – the finale depicting the raging firestorm and chaos which followed is impressive indeed. ★★★ $19.99

In the Army Now

In the Army Now

(1994, 91 min, US, Daniel Petrie, Jr.) Following in the military bootsteps of such comic luminaries as Bob Hope, Goldie Hawn, Abbott & Costello and Bill Murray, twentysomething clown Pauly Shore joins the service, disproving the slogan "Be all you can be." Toning down his annoying Valley-speak a tad, Shore plays a moronic lad who with his best friend joins the Army for the financial assistance available after his tour of duty. Once in uniform, of course, he mouths off, makes enemies, tears the place apart and saves the day. This is strictly standard issue, whose few jokes have already been done by those mentioned above. Shore and cohorts Lori Petty, David Alan Grier and Alan Dick try to enliven the film, but are sabotaged by a screenplay missing in action. ★★ $14.99

In the Belly of the Dragon

(1989, 100 min, Canada, Yves Simoneau) This plucky little surprise from our northern neighbors is evidence that life is absurd, corporations are out to get you and people are funny all over the world. A young man, in an effort to afford a new pair of cowboy boots, trades the everyday nightmare of his dead-end job distributing circulars door-to-door for the high-tech nightmare of being an experimental subject for biochemical brain research. He begins an odyssey wherein he learns the transient regard for human life, the power of a well-thrown dart and the absolute value of some really good friends. (Dubbed) ★★★ $29.99

In the Cold of the Night

(1990, 112 min, US, Nico Mastorakis) Glossy, high-tech suspenser about a man (Jeff Lester) whose nightly dreams of killing a beautiful stranger (Adrienne Sachs) begin to come true when she shows up on his doorstep. Also with Marc Singer, David Soul, John Beck and Tippi Hedren in a wonderfully silly cameo. ★★½ $89.99

In the Good Old Summertime

(1949, 102 min, US, Robert Z. Leonard) Charming musical remake of Ernst Lubitsch's *The Shop Around the Corner*. Judy Garland and Van Johnson are the bickering co-workers who unknowingly fall in love via the personals. Though the same story is the basis for the Broadway musical "She Loves Me," this musical and the show have different scores. ★★★ $19.99

In the Heat of the Night

(1967, 109 min, US, Norman Jewison) A Best Picture Oscar went to this exceptional mystery story about a black Philadelphia cop and his experiences with racial bigotry while helping the Sparta, Mississippi, police force solve a murder. Sidney Poitier is Virgil Tibbs, a savvy police detective whose assistance to the small town and captain Rod Steiger is ill-rewarded and unappreciated. Both actors are excellent, and Steiger won an Oscar for Best Actor as the racist policeman trying to do right. ★★★★ $14.99

In the Land of the War Canoes

(1914, 47 min, US/Canada, Edward S. Curtis) Photographer Edward S. Curtis, best known for his still photographs of Native Americans, spent three years with the Kwakiutl Indians of Vancouver Island in order to capture on film their lifestyle, ceremonial dances and religious rituals. This fascinating documentary is a meticulous re-creation of a tribal society before the invasion of the white man destroyed their culture. ★★★ $39.99

In the Line of Fire

(1993, 123 min, US, Wolfgang Petersen) Petersen follows his riveting and underrated *Shattered* with this superior suspense thriller which affords Clint Eastwood a second opportunity to deliver a career performance. Clint plays a seasoned Secret Service agent who was present at JFK's Dallas murder. He finds himself entangled in another presidential assassination scenario as a routine investigation puts him and partner Dylan McDermott on the trail of a potential killer, played with great menace by John Malkovich. Much of the film's enjoyment lies in the cat-and-mouse relationship Malkovich's would-be assassin nurtures between the agent and himself. Rarely has a screen duo's adversarial battle been as enthralling. For once, Eastwood leaves behind his laconic character, and Jeff Maguire's intelligent screenplay makes it a pleasure to hear the actor form complete sentences. (Letterboxed version available for $19.99) ★★★★ $14.99

In the Mood

(1987, 99 min, US, Phil Alden Robinson) Amiable comedy based on the real-life experiences of 15-year-old Sonny Wisecarver, who in the 1940s made headlines around the country by having affairs with two older women, one of whom he married. Patrick Dempsey is a delight as Carver, who was also known as "The Woo Woo Kid." ★★½ $14.99

In the Mouth of Madness

(1995, 95 min, US, John Carpenter) Carpenter's eagerly anticipated return to the horror genre is this startlingly original H.P. Lovecraft-based tale about a skeptical insurance investigator (Sam Neill) who sets out to prove that the disappearance of best-selling author Sutter Cane (Jürgen Prochnow) is a publicity stunt. As he digs deeper, he finds out that what Cane has been selling as fiction is actually fact-based memory transmitted by "the dark ones" — and that Cane's final novel will unleash Hell on Earth. What begins as a mature, well-visualized opus into madness and surrealism eventually clashes with the filmmaker's schlocky sense of atmosphere and "boo"-style horror gimmicks, creating a mixed-bag of chills and chuckles. But the film's reflexive ending (not to give anything away) rounds it out nicely, and should leave any viewer just the least bit paranoid. Charlton Heston and Julie Carmen also star. ★★ $19.99

In the Name of the Father

(1993, 127 min, Ireland, Jim Sheridan) Daniel Day-Lewis and Irish producer-writer-director Sheridan (*My Left Foot*) reteam and once again deliver the goods in a profound manner with this impassioned scream for justice which dramatizes the real-life plight of Gerry Conlon and his companions, a group of innocents known as the Guilford Four who spent 15 years in a British prison for an IRA bombing. Day-Lewis easily could have won his second Oscar for his fiery portrayal of the emotional Conlon, a petty thief and troublemaker from Belfast who, by sheer coincidence, was caught in the British government's legal net — which also picked up several members of his family and his friends including his father and aunt. And while Day-Lewis' performance sparkles, it is Pete Postlethwaite, in a riveting performance as his steadfastly principled father Giuseppe, who truly carries the film's moral message. Emma Thompson co-stars as a dedicated lawyer who finally uncovers the truth and helps free them. ★★★★ $19.99

In the Name of the Pope King

(1977, 105 min, Italy, Luigi Magni) Nino Manfredi, known more for his comedy roles, takes a successful stab at serious acting in this compelling story of intrigue, political conflict and murder. Set in 1867 during a turbulent period of peasant revolt and leftist bombings, the film stars Manfredi as Monsignor Colombo, a magistrate for the conservative papal state. He finds himself immersed in political turmoil when he discovers that his son might be involved in terrorist activity against the state. An interesting companion film to this fascinating political and personal drama is Bertrand Tavernier's similarly themed *The Clockmaker*. (Italian with English subtitles) ★★★ $59.99

In the Navy

(1941, 85 min, US, Arthur Lubin) Abbott and Costello are sailors who become involved with the escapades of crooner Dick Powell, who's joined the Navy to escape his adoring fans. Lou falls for Patty of The Andrews Sisters, and there's a photographer (Claire Dodd) masquerading as a sailor who's out to snap a shot of Powell in uniform. This A&C comedy isn't as consistently funny as some of their other romps, especially when the story concentrates on Powell. However, the boys do offer some funny bits (a shell game, proving 7 X 13 = 28), and Lou has a few amusing solo bits as well. Powell and The Andrews Sisters supply the songs, which are mostly forgettable. ★★½ $14.99

In the Realm of the Senses

(1976, 115 min, Japan, Nagisa Oshima) Oshima's most debated work in a career marked by controversy, *In the Realm of the Senses* is an unrelenting journey into the world of passion and eroticism. Oblivious to social restraints and public sentiment, a geisha and her lover engage in a torrid sexual spree, losing themselves in the fervor of their lovemaking and their quest for ultimate ecstasy. The ideology of male dominance and female submission

In the Name of the Father

Incident at Oglala

is thoroughly undermined as the obsessed lovers create a closed existence of incessant lovemaking and sadomasochistic experiments. This is an eerily beautiful examination of the intensity of physical desire. (Japanese with English subtitles) ★★★½ $19.99

In the Shadow of the Stars

(1992, 93 min, US, Irving Sarat & Allie Light) The 1992 Academy Award winner for Best Feature-Length Documentary, this witty and compassionate film goes behind the scenes of the San Francisco Opera Company and observes the lives and dreams of its aspiring young singers. A rare and unpretentious peek into the unreal world of opera. ★★★ $19.99

In the Shadows of Kilimanjaro

(1986, 94 min, US, Raju Patel) Timothy Bottoms and John Rhys-Davies are just two of the workers in the African desert who are attacked by 90,000 hungry baboons. Lunch! It's as silly as it sounds. ★ $19.99

In the Soup

(1993, 96 min, US, Alexandre Rockwell) Steve Buscemi, who created memorable characters in *Parting Glances, Barton Fink* and *Reservoir Dogs*, is finally given a chance to star in his own film with this enjoyably rag-tag independent comedy. Buscemi plays a down-on-his-luck aspiring (but possibly no-talent) filmmaker. His world is turned upside down after an eccentric "businessman" takes him under his dark wing and offers to finance his Tarkovsky/Godard-inspired opus. Strikingly similar to *Mistress*, the film is entertainingly wacky and features great performances by Buscemi as the befuddled loser sucked into a bizarre, criminal world, Seymour Cassel as his "savior," and Jennifer Beals as Buscemi's Puerto Rican *object d'amour*. While not as hilarious as it thinks it is, the film is still a lot of fun. Look for some funny cameo appearances by the director Jim Jarmusch and Carol Kane. (Available in both black-and-white and color versions) ★★★ $19.99

In the Spirit

(1990, 94 min, US, Sandra Seacat) A health nut (Marlo Thomas) and a socialite (Elaine May) stumble across the "datebook" of a deceased hooker, and comedic complications ensue. Soon, everyone is after the book. A likable cast rises above the forced material. With Peter Falk, Olympia Dukakis, Melanie Griffith and Jeannie Berlin. ★★½ $89.99

In the White City

(1983, 108 min, Switzerland/Portugal, Alain Tanner) Bruno Ganz stars in Tanner's haunting mood piece about a Swiss boat engineer who jumps ship in Lisbon and begins a personal quest of self-discovery. Roaming the streets and frequenting the watering holes, he dives head first into the foreignness and unfamiliarity of his new surroundings. Tanner turns this existential odyssey into a fascinating examination of solitude, freedom and self-estrangement as he unravels the psyche of a man's unstructured search for something real. (German and Portuguese with English subtitles) ★★★ $79.99

In This Our Life

(1942, 97 min, US, John Huston) Bette Davis lets loose as a neurotic hussy whose tantrums and plottings ruin the lives of sister Olivia deHavilland, husband George Brent and, finally, herself. Davis gives a commanding performance in this familiar melodrama, though the film suffers somewhat due to director Huston's unfamiliarity with the genre. ★★½ $19.99

The In-Laws

(1979, 103 min, US, Arthur Hiller) Alan Arkin and Peter Falk make an engaging comedy team in this spright comedy about a dentist who becomes involved in the wacky goings-on of his daughter's future father-in-law — a CIA agent. ★★★ $14.99

The Incident

(1967, 107 min, US, Larry Peerce) A gritty, well-done low-budget thriller set almost exclusively in a New York City subway car. A disparate group of passengers are terrorized by punks Martin Sheen and Tony Musante. Some of the riders include Beau Bridges (first-rate as an injured soldier), Jack Gilford, Thelma Ritter, Brock Peters, Ruby Dee and Ed McMahon. ★★★ $59.99

Incident at Map Grid 36-80

(1983, 80 min, USSR, Mikhail Tumanishvili) An interesting premise, sort of a Russian *Hunt for Red October*, and a rare look at Soviet military might help make this a compelling war thriller. While out on routine sea maneuvers, a Soviet squadron receives a distress call from an American submarine which is carrying a secret nuclear arsenal. The Soviets respond to the call but are warned not to approach. Complicating the already tense situation is a malfunctioning computer that sounds the alarm to launch the American sub's cruise missiles. The opposing admirals must decide on the fate of the submarine in a tense stalemate that could possibly trigger WWIII. (Russian with English subtitles) ★★★ $59.99

Incident at Oglala

(1992, 89 min, US, Michael Apted) This important and long-overdue documentary is about the events that occurred in 1975 on the Sioux Indian reservation in South Dakota. Shamefully, the film failed at the box office, yet its story of the U.S. government's (under the auspices of the Bureau of Indian Affairs) secret war against the American Indian Movement is one which needs to gain more public attention. The film asserts that the attack on two FBI agents which led to the stand-off was an act of self-defense and that those who were punished for it (Leonard Peltier remains the only person jailed in the incident) were innocent. The film also asserts that through a band of violent government cronies known as the "Goon Squads," an atmosphere of brutality and terror was maintained on the reservation, an atmosphere which ultimately led to the fateful confrontation. Robert Redford, who produced the film, also narrates. Apted also directed the fictionalized counterpart, *Thunderheart*, which puts a Hollywood spin on the whole affair. ★★★½ $19.99

An Inconvenient Woman

(1991, 200 min, US, Larry Elikann) One of those fun, luminary-infested TV movies, this darkly comic thriller is set among the elite of L.A. society. An attempt to make murder look like suicide is inadvertently disturbed by way of an ingenuous mistress. Jason Robards, Jill Eikenberry and Rebecca DeMornay head a large, big-name cast through this convoluted tale of murder, betrayal and deception. Based on the book by Dominick Dunne. ★★ $89.99

Incredible Manitoba Animation

(50 min, Canada) From Canada's "funniest, friendliest and flattest" province comes this series which features: *Get a Job*, a wonderful, doo-wop comedy on the pitfalls of unemployment for a down-on-his-paws Bob Dog; *The Cat Came Back*, a hilarious Oscar-nominated short about a house-destroying kitty; *The Big Snit*, another Oscar-nominated film that follows a squabbling, scrabble-playing couple in the shadow of a nuclear holocaust; and several others. ★★★ $29.99

The Incredible Mr. Limpet

(1964, 102 min, US, Arthur Lubin) Cute live-action and animated comedy starring Don Knotts, who falls off a Coney Island pier and becomes a fish — helping the U.S. Navy battle Nazi submarines. Also with Jack Weston and Carole Cook. ★★½ $19.99

The Incredible Sarah

(1976, 106 min, GB, Richard Fleischer) An outstanding performance by Glenda Jackson breathes life into this otherwise mediocre biopic on the life of the legendary French stage actress Sarah Bernhardt. ★★½

The Incredible Shrinking Man

(1957, 81 min, US, Jack Arnold) This existential sci-fi classic written by Richard Matheson has the courage of its convictions in its strange metaphysical climax as an ordinary Joe finds that he is growing smaller every day. Brilliant

Will Smith saves the world in *Independence Day*

special effects don't overshadow Grant Williams' performance. ★★★½ $14.99

The Incredibly Strange Creatures Who Stopped Living and Became Mixed-Up Zombies

(1963, 82 min, US, Ray Dennis Steckler) A great title highlights this camp gem full of bad acting, a stupid plot, neat zombies and atmospheric camera work thanks to Joe Micelli, Laszlo Kovacs and Vilmos Zsigmond. (aka: *The Teenage Psycho Meets Bloody Mary*) ★

The Incredibly True Adventure of Two Girls in Love

(1995, 95 min, US, Maria Maggenti) This thoroughly enjoyable lesbian first love story is a startling film debut by independent filmmaker Maggenti. Randy (Laurel Holloman) is a white high school tomboy living with her lesbian aunt. Evie (Nicole Parker) is a beautiful and pampered black deb from the right side of the tracks. They meet and love blossoms despite their differences. But trouble brews for the two as both of their families undertake to break the lovers apart. A long-awaited "wholesome lesbian comedy and romance" which ignores queer politics and prejudice and concentrates on the two young women's intense attraction for each other. Not as big city grunge as *Go Fish* nor as jaded as *Bar Girls*, *Two Girls* is a terrifically sweet low-budget romantic comedy that could be described as a "queer John Hughes comedy" — when he was in his prime, of course. ★★★ $19.99

The Incubus

(1982, 90 min, US, John Hough) A peaceful New England community is besieged by a series of demonic murders. John Cassavetes stars as an investigator who follows the demon's path to a frightened young man whose nightmares may hold the key to the mystery. Boring, confusing and not very exciting. ★

An Indecent Obsession

(1985, 106 min, Australia, Lex Marinos) Adapted from Colleen McCullough's (*The Thorn Birds*) best-selling novel, this hospital drama is set immediately after Japan's surren-
der in World War II. But for the war-ravaged psychiatric patients of Ward X, the end of the war makes little difference. Their troubled minds and battered spirits, held in check by the beautiful nurse Langtry (Wendy Hughes), are soon tested by the appearance of a mysterious man who is admitted into their wing. Vicious currents of lust, homophobia, jealousy, desire and violent death soon undermine them all. A hyperventilating soap opera that squanders its juicy material with a leaden hand; the film ultimately fizzles. ★★

Indecent Proposal

(1993, 118 min, US, Adrian Lyne) Director Lyne has never been accused of being a subtle director. But nothing he's done before hints at the heavy-handedness of this silly romantic drama. To be fair, Lyne establishes his film with some flair. Demi Moore and Woody Harrelson are a young married couple experiencing financial troubles. They head to Las Vegas and promptly lose everything. Then, Demi attracts the attention of zillionaire Robert Redford who offers a million dollars to spend the night with her. Aside from the incredulous offer is the disturbing subtheme of "women as chattel." The film really hits bottom, though, after the deed is done. The last hour is dedicated to an unlikable couple whining about everything and Redford acting like a lovesick teenager. As *Honeymoon in Vegas* demonstrated, it's a workable comic ploy, but as envisioned by Lyne and screenwriter Amy Hoden Jones (who made quite a few changes from the novel), it doesn't work in dramatic terms. A conceit of such calculation resembles a mathematical equation rather than a movie. ★★ $14.99

Independence Day

(1983, 110 min, US, Robert Mandel) A handful of strong performances dominate this telling drama about the day-to-day lives of a small Southwestern town. Kathleen Quinlan heads the cast as a young woman, involved with mechanic David Keith, who longs to escape the confines of her constrictive lifestyle. Dianne Wiest is superb in support as a battered wife. Also with Frances Sternhagen, Cliff De Young and Richard Farnsworth. ★★★ $19.99

Independence Day

(1996, 145 min, US, Roland Emmerich) Recalling the UFO paranoia/hysteria of those 1950s sci-fi films – the classic and cheesy, alike – in which dastardly aliens set out to destroy our benign planet, *Independence Day* is the ultimate Us vs. Them sci-fi encounter. Though the film sometimes crosses over the line of credibility, *ID4* boasts great special effects, a coherent story line, more laughs than anyone would have a right to expect, and a top-notch cast obviously enjoying themselves. Combining many plots and characters who all come together by story's end, the film's fun starts when several giant spaceships hover over Earth's major cities. As the president, the military and scientists engage in speculation, it soon becomes clear these aliens are no *E.T.*s. Among the ensemble, Bill Pullman is a wimpy president who discovers his resolve, Will Smith is a resourceful fighter pilot, Jeff Goldblum is a crafty mathematician, and Judd Hirsch and Randy Quaid nearly steal the show as two indomitable papas. Yes, *Star Wars* is slicker, and *Close Encounters* more visionary, but there's no denying *Independence Day* is a blast. (Letterboxed version available for $24.99) ★★★½ $22.99

The Indian in the Cupboard

(1995, 96 min, US, Frank Oz) Oz (*What About Bob?*) directs his first family-oriented feature with just the right amount of fantasy and magic added to a story of childhood friendship and trust. Based on Lynne Reid Banks' book, this charming adaptation stars Hal Scardino as Omri, the youngest of three children in a New York City household with lots of toys and two other boys. Omri's brother presents him with a cabinet in which Omri places an American Indian figure. The cupboard shakes awaking Omri and when he opens it he is surprised to find the Indian (played by Litefoot) alive. Omri is the personification of wonder and innocence as he learns through his friend to be brave and independent in the rough and troubled world at home and on the streets of New York. David Keith shines as a cowboy brought to life by Omri's new friend. His exuberance brings life and action when the film tends to momentarily drag. ★★★ $22.99

The Indian Runner

(1991, 127 min, US, Sean Penn) Maverick actor Sean Penn takes his talents behind the camera with this stunningly realized character study centering on the stormy relationship between a highway patrolman (Davis Morse) and his "loose cannon" of a brother (Viggo Mortensen). Though short on story, this loving tribute to the filmmaking of the '70s will reward the patient viewer with its detailed attention to time and place, and remarkable performances by Sandy Dennis and Charles Bronson. Also with Dennis Hopper, Valeria Golino and Patricia Arquette. ★★★ $14.99

Indian Summer

(1993, 98 min, US, Mike Binder) To anyone who never went to overnight camp, this congenial film will make you wish you had. *Indian Summer* is a *Big Chill*-like comedy which reunites seven old friends who attended Camp Tamakwa during its "golden age" in the early '70s. Invited back to their old stomping grounds by camp owner Alan Arkin, the friends get to work out some of their demons and share old secrets. Especially engaging are Diane Lane as Bethy, a woman whose husband (and camp sweetheart) died in a car crash the year before, and Bill Paxton, who as the rebel of the bunch got kicked out of camp one summer for mysterious reasons. With warmth and humor, *Indian Summer* brings back the sights, sounds, smells (oh, those smells), first kisses and first heartbreaks of summer camp. Also starring Elizabeth Perkins and Kevin Pollack. Based on director Binder's own experiences. ★★★ $9.99

Indiana Jones and the Last Crusade

(1989, 127 min, US, Steven Spielberg) Indiana Jones and director Spielberg are back in glorious form after the near-fiasco of *Temple of Doom*. Harrison Ford is as dashing as ever as Indy, who is off in search of the Holy Grail, and his missing father. Sean Connery is an absolute delight as Indy's dad. Playing against type from his Bond and macho roles, Connery's senior Dr. Jones is a timid scholarly type not really prepared for his son's more dangerous escapades. The humor and the pace is fast and furious and Indy's old enemies — the Nazis — are back to do battle once again. Every bit as enjoyable as the original *Raiders*. ★★★½ $14.99

Indiana Jones and the Temple of Doom

(1984, 118 min, US, Steven Spielberg) Spielberg attempts to outdo his success with *Raiders of the Lost Ark*. The perils are greater but the plot is weaker. The film is actually a prequel to *Raiders*, following Indy and sidekick Kate Capshaw in their adventures in the Far East. However disappointing, the opening sequence is worth the price of the rental: Capshaw singing a Mandarin version of "Anything Goes" — leading to a highly exciting and comical nightclub brawl. Perhaps Spielberg has a career in musicals. ★★½ $14.99

Indiscreet

(1958, 100 min, US, Stanley Donen) For couples wanting romance, this is the ticket. Ingrid Bergman plays a ravishing European actress who is courted by an equally ravishing Cary Grant. The fare is at times slow and perhaps even overly romantic, but the film is filled with an engaging sense of wry wit and humor — not to mention a seething sexual tension between its two stars. Bergman and Grant, as the urbane lovers, could not have been better cast. ★★★ $19.99

Indiscretion of an American Housewife

(1954, 63 min, Italy, Vittorio De Sica) The unusual teaming of American producer David O. Selznick and neorealist Italian director De Sica does not really work. The action centers in Rome's main railroad station and features Jennifer Jones as an adulterous wife who meets her lover Montgomery Clift for a final fling. It is no *Brief Encounter* but an interesting try. (aka: *Terminal Station*) (Filmed in English) ★★ $59.99

Indochine

(1992, 155 min, France, Regis Wargnier) An Academy Award winner for Best Foreign-Language Film, *Indochine* is a beautifully photographed and evocative love story set during the French colonization of Indochina. In a rapturous performance, the stunning Catherine Deneuve stars as the dowager of a successful rubber plantation. Though a strict foreman, she has an especially loving relationship with her adopted, Indochinese daughter (well played by Linh Dan Pham). Against the backdrop of social upheaval, their worlds collide when they both fall in love with the same man, a handsome French soldier (Vincent Perez). A poetic epic which balances romance and politics with equal finesse. (French with English subtitles) ★★★★ $19.99

The Infamous Daughter of Fanny Hill

(1987, 73 min, US, Arthur P. Stootsberry) In the decadent high society of 18th-century London, Kissy Hill takes up where her famous mother left off. But a jealous wife wants to put an end to Kissy's husband-stealing bedroom antics...permanently. Stacy Walker stars. ★ $29.99

Infernal Trio

(1974, 100 min, France, Francis Girod) While quite shocking and even scandalous in its initial release, time has not been kind to this macabre black comedy about a trio of amoral, larcenous lovers. Michel Piccoli plays a distinguished lawyer who entices two German sisters, Romy Schneider and Mascha Gomska, into marrying a series of rich older men. When the husbands die of natural causes or are "encouraged" to leave this life, the three share in the proceeds of the wealth and insurance money. Unevenly paced, the film fluctuates between serious drama, sexy romp and pitch-black comedy. This social satire, which sets out to intentionally shock its unsuspecting audience, delivers an enthusiastically shameless descent into the pleasures and profits of evil. (French with English subtitles) ★★½

Inferno

(1978, 107 min, Italy, Dario Argento) This sequel to the macabre maestro's *Suspiria* is an almost incomprehensible collection of bizarre images and fantastically realized setpiece murders. The lack of a linear narrative, however, does not detract from its overall ambiance of weirdness and terror. A young American poet discovers a book which she believes identifies her ancient New York apartment building as the residence of the Mater Tenebrarum, the mother of shadows, one of three witches who generate all the misery in the world. The first mother, Mater Suspiriorum, lives in Freiburg and was the subject of Argento's *Suspiria*. Radically different from any American horror or suspense film, *Inferno* is full of stylistic touches which overcome its narrative difficulties. One scene in particular, where the poet must descend into what appears to be a puddle on her basement floor, but turns out to be an entire series of underwater chambers, is audacious and magnificent. *Suspiria* and *Inferno* are the only two films Argento has made with purely supernatural plots, a fact which gives him the freedom to completely abandon all logic and submerge himself in the stylish, horrifying impulses which make him unique among horror film directors. ★★½ $59.99

The Infiltrator

(1995, 102 min, US, John MacKenzie) A powerful HBO film, *The Infiltrator* is based on the book "In Hitler's Shadow," the true-life story of Israeli journalist Yaron Svoray, who while on assignment in Germany went undercover to expose a neo-Nazi group. Oliver Platt plays Svoray, a writer living in America who is sent to report on the recent racially motivated attacks by skinheads in Germany. But as Svoray digs deeper, he discovers to his horror a well-organized, underground fascist political organization with growing public support. The film — in eye-opening detail — shows the extent of racial hatred permeating in modern Germany, directed at immigrant Turks, Jews, blacks and anyone else "non-white." Through the decades we've seen films featuring re-creations of 1940s Germany with Nazis spouting their hate, but it's doubly unsettling to see these same dispicable sentiments addressed in modern times — it can happen here. Platt is perfunctory, though Arliss Howard is splendid as Svoray's accomplice. ★★★ $14.99

The Informer

(1935, 91 min, US, John Ford) An eerie, dreamlike quality pervades director Ford's film of a dull-witted man who informs on his Irish Republican Army comrade in 1922 Dublin. Victor McLaglen won the Best Actor Oscar for his haunting portrayal of the pathetic misfit; Ford won for Best Director, Dudley Nichols for Best Screenplay and Max Steiner for Best Score. An evocative examination of the human condition. ★★★★ $19.99

Inherit the Wind

(1960, 127 min, US, Stanley Kramer) Spencer Tracy and Fredric March, possibly America's two greatest film actors, both give tour de force performances in this outstanding adaptation of the Lawrence-Lee stage play, based on the infamous Scopes Monkey Trial of 1925. Though the names are changed, Tracy is Clarence Darrow and March is William Jennings Bryan, each on opposite sides of the court when a teacher (Dick York) is arrested and tried for teaching the theories of Darwin.

Indochine

One of the finest, most literate screenplays to grace an American film, the enthralling court sequences are all the more topical today as the battle of separation between Church and State continues. Also with Gene Kelly, Florence Eldridge and Harry Morgan. ★★★★ $19.99

The Inheritance

(1977, 105 min, Italy, Mauro Bolognini) This well-acted drama, a bit trashy for European standards, features a sexy Dominique Sanda as a cooly calculating woman who marries into a wealthy family and begins a steamy affair with her dying father-in-law (Anthony Quinn). A titillating and erotic video find. Sanda won the Best Actress Award at the Cannes Film Festival for her role as the money-hungry vixen. (Dubbed) ★★½

The Inheritors (Die Erben)

(1982, 89 min, Austria, Walter Bannert) This critically acclaimed film exposed the terrifying resurgence of neo-fascist groups who prey on today's youth. Featured at the 1984 Cannes Film Festival and winner of the Jury Award for Best Cinematography at the World Film Festival in Montreal, this compelling look at a cancerous growth of hatred provides images that one can not easily forget. (Dubbed) ★★★ $19.99

The Inkwell

(1994, 112 min, US, Matty Rich) From the director of Straight Out of Brooklyn comes this gentle black version of Summer of '42. Larenz Tate plays Drew, a naive 16-year-old with a killer smile from the wrongish side of the tracks who comes of age during the summer of '76 while he is visiting his highbrow relatives at a ritzy (and primarily black) beach in Martha's Vineyard. On the arty side of an "After School Special," The Inkwell is not a particularly original film, but Tate gives such a fresh, guileless performance that one can forgive some of its more artificial moments. The bell-bottoms and mega-Afros are a must for all '70s enthusiasts. ★★½ $14.99

The Inner Circle

(1991, 139 min, US, Andrei Konchalovsky) A fascinating and moody examination of life under Stalin in 1930s Moscow. Based on a true story, the film stars Tom Hulce as a newlywed and loyal party member, who is whisked from his home on his wedding day to the great halls of the Kremlin. It is there he begins service to Stalin as his personal projectionist. Politically naive, it is during this regime that Hulce slowly becomes aware of the corruption and paranoia running rampant within the walls of Russia's party headquarters. The first American film to actually lens at the Kremlin, The Inner Circle — which refers to Stalin's elite group of companions — uses its Russian locations to better effect than did The Russia House. However, like that film, its locale sometimes seems to dwarf the narrative. Hulce delivers a solid portrayal of the innocent Ivan, and Lolita Davidovich scores well as his wife. ★★★ $19.99

Innerspace

(1987, 120 min, US, Joe Dante) All hell breaks loose when a miniaturized Dennis Quaid is accidentally injected into the body of highly

manic Martin Short. Hunted down by a pair of evil industrialists (hilariously portrayed by Kevin McCarthy and Fiona Lewis), the two hit the road where they develop a working relationship: with Quaid giving the orders and Short, the hypochondriac hero, responding with outrageous pratfalls. The film won an Academy Award for Special Effects. Meg Ryan also stars. ★★★ $9.99

Innocence Unprotected

(1968, 78 min, Yugoslavia, Dusan Makavejev) This inventive and, at times, hilarious film-within-a-film reunites and interviews the cast of Yugoslavia's first talky: a tacky, ridiculously naive melodrama. While the stars dreamily reminisce, we watch excerpts from the 1942 film, a story about a seemingly brainless woman saddled with a wicked stepmother and a lecherous older suitor who falls in love with a muscleman/daredevil. Makavejev mischievously intermixes footage of the horror of the war with the interviews and the film as he shows the illusion of fame and power. (Serbo-Croatian with English subtitles) ★★★ $59.99

The Innocent

(1976, 115 min, Italy, Luchino Visconti) Visconti's final masterpiece is set in turn-of-the-century Italy and features a fine cast, sumptuous photography and stunning sets and costumes. Giancarlo Giannini is a chauvinistic aristocrat who ignores his beautiful and loving wife (Laura Antonelli) in order to pursue his adulterous affair with his mistress (Jennifer O'Neill). Revenge is sweet, however, as the lonely and frustrated wife takes on a lover and turns the tables on her insensitive husband. (Italian with English subtitles) ★★★★

The Innocent

(1995, 119 min, GB, John Schlesinger) In one of director Schlesinger's lesser outings, the historic tearing down of the Berlin Wall sets in motion a bittersweet recollection of Cold War romance and intrigue. Campbell Scott plays a British telephone specialist who begins working for the Americans in their attempt to tap into Russian phone lines (by tunneling into East Berlin). Anthony Hopkins is the brash Yank commander overseeing the project who must contend with possible conspiracy when Scott falls for a local German woman (Isabella Rossellini) who may or may not be a spy. The espionage aspect of the film is quite compelling, as Scott is thrown into a volatile situation where events are out of his control. But as a romance the film sags, with Rossellini constantly defending her feelings to Scott while at the same time leading him on. And though the film features good period design, Schlesinger's sluggish pace helps detract from the scenario. American actor Scott is good as the young Brit, though Hopkins is sometimes unintelligible using a poor American accent. ★★ $19.99

Innocent Blood

(1992, 114 min, US, John Landis) Landis returns to American Werewolf in London territory with this anemic comic horror film which could be dubbed A French Vampire in Pittsburgh. Anne Parillaud, fresh from La Femme Nikita, plays a bloodsucker with a social conscience:

she only attacks criminals for her blood lust. But when she crosses paths with mob kingpin Robert Loggia and undercover cop Anthony LaPaglia, things go awry. As the mobster-turned-vampire, Loggia brings such needed vitality to an otherwise weary film that for a while, it seems he may turn it around. A high order even for someone of Loggia's talents. Much of the blame goes to Michael Wolk's thin screenplay; and to the ill-pairing of leads Parillaud and LaPaglia — Lily and Herman Munster generated more sparks. There's lots of blood and killings, though. ★★ $14.99

Innocent Lies

(1995, 88 min, GB, Patrick DeWolfe) Gabrielle Anwar and Stephen Dorff co-star in this absorbing and extremely well-made British-French period piece about a London detective (Adrian Dunbar) who is dispatched to a French fishing village, circa WWII, to investigate the mysterious death of his predecessor. He soon becomes entangled in the Freudian affairs of a brother and sister who love each other entirely too much. Boasting a magnificent evocation of the times, the film also features a stand-out performance by Joanna Lumley (of "Absolutely Fabulous") as the bitch goddess mother of the incestuous pair. DeWolfe's parable on the price of love is an ambitious and welcome offshoot from the erotic thriller genre, weaving its threads of anti-Semitism and incest into an Agatha Christie-like mystery. ★★★ $14.99

An Innocent Man

(1989, 113 min, US, Peter Yates) Tom Selleck stars in this ordinary, contrived innocent-man-behind-bars prison drama. Selleck is a successful aerospace engineer and loving husband who is framed by two cardboard-cutout dishonest undercover cops. Once incarcerated, he learns, with the kindly help of "lifer" F. Murray Abraham, that prison can be hell. This sort of thing has been done for decades, and done a helluva lot better. ★ $9.99

Innocent Victim

(1988, 89 min, GB, Giles Foster) Helen Shaver stars in this dull thriller about a best-selling author whose grief over the loss of her three-year-old son is complicated when her mentally unbalanced mother (Lauren Bacall) kidnaps a small boy to replace him. Based on a novel by Ruth Rendell. Also with Colin Firth and Paul McGann. (aka: Tree of Hands) ★ $79.99

Insect Woman

(1963, 123 min, Japan, Shohei Imamura) The sexual manipulation, subjugation and exploitation of women is the hard-hitting theme in this multi-award winning film that chronicles 45 years in the harsh life of a woman. Beginning as a child, where she is abused by her stepfather, through her illegitimate pregnancy and finally to her life in a sordid brothel, the film, like the director's Black Rain, displays little sentimentality in fleshing out this gripping but somber tale. (Japanese with English subtitles) ★★★ $79.99

Inserts

(1976, 117 min, US, John Byrum) Richard Dreyfuss is a fading silent screen star in 1930s Hollywood who turns to making blue movies to supplement his income. Bob Hoskins, Jessica Harper, Veronica Cartwright and Steven Davies are his cast of assorted oddball cronies. Despite its intriguing premise, a lackluster screenplay makes little of the scenario. ★★

Inside

(1996, 94 min, GB/US, Arthur Penn) A claustrophobic prison drama about human rights abuses in South Africa, *Inside* is an intense and at times agonizing viewing experience. The film deals with the lies and transgressions perpetrated by Col. Kruger (Nigel Hawthorne), an interrogator who brutalizes Marty (Eric Stoltz), a university professor he suspects of conspiracy, terrorism, treason and sabotage. Held in a sparse cell, Marty communicates with and observes the prison's other inmates through a peephole while he is tormented physically and mentally. *Inside* also depicts the investigation by one of these prisoners (Louis Gossett, Jr.) of Kruger's unjust treatment of Marty ten years after his incarceration. Made for Showtime, Penn's film is extremely effective and well-made, though it tends to suffer from occasional staginess. The three leads all contribute superlative performances, and the script, by Bima Stagg, is commendable for raising issues of truth and freedom in an appropriate and contemporary framework. ★★★ $89.99

Inside Hitchcock

(1984, 60 min, US, Richard Schickel) An excellent documentary on The Master of Suspense, Alfred Hitchcock, written and directed by Schickel. With scenes from such classics as *Psycho*, *North by Northwest* and *Notorious* intercut with Hitch himself explaining his cinematic theories, this fascinating profile is an insightful glimpse into the mind of one of the greatest filmmakers of all time. ★★★½ $39.99

Inside Monkey Zetterland

(1993, 98 min, US, Jefery Levy) With a cast that seems to come straight from the pages of *Details*, *Inside Monkey Zetterland* seems to care more about who is actually in the film rather than telling a story. Starring Patricia Arquette, Sofia Coppola, Sandra Bernhard, Ricki Lake and Rupert Everett, the film revolves around an ex-child star (played by writer-producer Steven Antin) whose lesbian sister has left her pregnant lover and moved into his house owned by their soap opera star mother. When radical terrorists come onto the scene, things start getting a little convoluted. Not without merit, *Zetterland* has that ever-popular "quirky charm" and features some good performances, especially by Arquette. ★★ $92.99

Inside the Third Reich

(1982, 240 min, US, Marvin J. Chomsky) Superior made-for-TV teledrama based on the autobiography of Hitler's confidant Albert Speer. Rutger Hauer stars as the brilliant architect who works his way through the ranks of 1930s Germany to become Hitler's right-hand man. Derek Jacobi is sensational as the maniacal dictator, and the international all-star cast includes John Gielgud, Blythe Danner, Trevor Howard, Viveca Lindfors, Ian Holm and Renee Soutendijk. ★★★½ $39.99

Insignificance

(1985, 110 min, GB, Nicolas Roeg) The always adventurous Roeg's apocalyptic farce is a surreal and sexually charged black comedy which records the hot summer night in 1954 that Marilyn Monroe and Albert Einstein spent together. Theresa Russell and Michael Emil are the blonde and the brain, Gary Busey and Tony Curtis costar as Joe DiMaggio and Sen. Joe McCarthy, respectively. ★★★

The Inspector General

(1949, 102 min, US, Henry Koster) Danny Kaye lets loose as an inept elixir salesman who is mistaken for the feared Inspector General by a small country village — whose citizens will do anything to please him. Plenty of laughs and Kaye gets to do a patter song or two. ★★★ $19.99

Inspiration

(1931, 74 min, US, Clarence Brown) Greta Garbo's third talkie is a minor romantic drama about love and sacrifice. Garbo's in her element as a Parisian artists' model whose past seems to get in the way with her new relationship with student Robert Montgomery. Though not one of her best, even a routine Garbo effort is worth a look. ★★ $19.99

Interiors

(1978, 93 min, US, Woody Allen) Allen's homage to Ingmar Bergman meticulously details the misunderstandings and growing collapse of an upper-middle-class family. Geraldine Page and E.G. Marshall are the repressive parents; Diane Keaton, Mary Beth Hurt and Kristin Griffith are the rival siblings; and Maureen Stapleton is the "ridiculous" woman who breathes new life into their anguished lives. ★★★½ $14.99

Intermezzo

(1937, 91 min, Sweden, Gustaf Molander) Ingrid Bergman is ravishing as an aspiring pianist whose career is interrupted when she falls tragically in love with a world-famous pianist. Despite the fact that he is already married, the two run off together in their interlude of love. Holding up remarkably well over the years, this entertaining love story was seen by producer David O. Selznick who immediately brought the young Bergman to Hollywood and remade this feature in 1939 in the film which launched her international career. (Swedish with English subtitles) ★★★ $19.99

Intermezzo

(1939, 70 min, US, Gregory Ratoff) Ingrid Bergman repeats the role from the 1936 Swedish romantic drama of the same name, which brought her international acclaim. Bergman plays a musical prodigy involved with her mentor, Leslie Howard. A beautifully crafted love story. ★★★ $19.99

Internal Affairs

(1990, 115 min, US, Mike Figgis) Brutally realistic violence, potent acting and intense psychological gameplaying combine to make this tough cop thriller a thoroughly engaging psychological thriller. Richard Gere sinks his teeth into the role of a decorated but menacingly corrupt cop who locks horns with Andy

Garcia, an internal affairs officer assigned to investigate wrongdoing on the L.A. police force. Garcia, a tightass "good cop" is teamed up with a lesbian partner (Laurie Metcalf) as they attempt to untangle a trail of payoffs, extortion and murder, all leading to the increasingly deranged and dangerous Gere. ★★★ $14.99

International House

(1933, 72 min, US, Edward Sutherland) W.C. Fields, Rudy Vallee, George Burns, Gracie Allen, Cab Calloway and his Orchestra and Bela Lugosi star in this sometimes hilarious and peculiar episodic comedy that has a Chinese scientist inventing TV, sending a wild assortment of interested buyers to the Orient (including Fields and Burns). ★★★ $14.99

Interrogation

(1982, 118 min, Poland, Richard Bugajski) Banned for almost eight years by the Polish Communist government, this scathing study of one woman's harassment and torture at the hands of her own government was finally released in 1990 with the star of the film, Krystyna Jarda, winning the Best Actress Award at Cannes. After a one-night stand with a military officer, a cabaret singer is imprisoned by the secret police, without ever being informed of her alleged crime. For the next five years, she is forced to become a survivor and not a victim in her efforts to maintain her dignity and sanity in the face of an oppressive Stalinist power. (Polish with English subtitles) ★★★½ $79.99

Intersection

(1994, 98 min, US, Mark Rydell) Yet another senseless American rehash of a French film, this time Claude Sautet's *Les Choses de la Vie* (*The Things of Life*). Richard Gere plays a whiny architect involved in a car accident. As he looks back at his life, the story concentrates on his relationships with his wife (Sharon Stone) and journalist mistress (Lolita Davidovich). Though Gere has in recent years acquired a newfound maturity and confidence on-screen, his presence alone does not warrant a remake. Stone gives the film's best performance as his beautiful but cold wife. ★★½ $19.99

Interview with the Vampire

(1994, 122 min, US, Neil Jordan) Rich in atmosphere and bristling with sexual tension and suspense, this highly stylized adaptation of Anne Rice's classic vampire story was the subject of much second guessing before its release. The biggest controversy was the casting of Tom Cruise as Lestat, the dapper vampire whose character would require the subtlety and depth of a Daniel Day-Lewis. Happily, Cruise acquits himself nicely and is handsomely complimented by the tormented Brad Pitt as Louis. Told in flashback, the story recounts the life of grieving widower and 18th-century plantation owner Louis who bids adieu to his beloved blue sky of morning for the dark shadows of night when Lestat makes him one of his own. As Louis desperately clings to the last vestiges of his humanity, he engages in a battle of conscience and will with his mentor Lestat. Though bloody and violent, the film relies on the psychological makeup of

Interview with the Vampire

its characters for its power, and detail to time and place is exemplary. Kirsten Dunst is remarkable as a youthful vampiress, and Christian Slater, Antonio Banderas and Stephen Rea also star. ★★★½ $19.99

Intervista

(1992, 108 min, Italy, Federico Fellini) Whereas *Amarcord* explores the director's childhood, *8½* his midlife creative crisis and *Fellini's Roma* the city he loves, *Intervista* is the master's nostalgic look at his youthful days at the famed Cinecitta — the film studio where he made all his films. Touchingly evocative and bubbling with magical stories from his past as well as capturing the director at work today, the film is Fellini's valentine to the movies and the filmmaking process. Opening with his return to Cinecitta to begin work on his film version of Franz Kafka's "Amerika," a Japanese TV crew doggedly interviews him, prompting the director to recall his life-changing first visit to Cinecitta. That visit, presented as a film-within-a-film, features a wide-eyed Fellini who, on assignment to interview a beautiful star, stumbles across a fantastic film city bustling with excitement, chaos and magic. Adding to this heady mixture is a touching scene near the end when Marcello Mastroianni and Anita Ekberg visit the set, and at one point watch some sensual and romantic moments from *La Dolce Vita*. A joyous celebration — all done in the director's ebullient and seductive style. (Italian with English subtitles) ★★★½ $29.99

An Intimate Story

(1983, 95 min, Israel, Nadar Levithan) Set in the close confines of a Kibbutz, this engrossing drama focuses on the problems of a childless couple who have been married for 10 years. Their shattered dreams, as well as the lack of privacy in the "extended family" atmosphere of the Kibbutz, force them to reevaluate their relationship. Charming but low-key. (Hebrew with English subtitles) ★★★ $79.99

Into the Night

(1985, 115 min, US, John Landis) Landis' off-center and very engaging comic thriller stars Jeff Goldblum as a likable Average Joe who gets tangled with beautiful Michelle Pfeiffer and Iranian terrorists. Good supporting cast includes David Bowie, Richard Farnsworth, Dan Aykroyd and cameos by 12 noted film directors. ★★★ $9.99

Into the West

(1993, 97 min, Ireland, Mike Newell) This harshly realistic and heartwrenching film begins in the urban squalor of Dublin. The story tells the tale of two boys who rescue a mystical white horse from an evil businessman and embark on a journey "into the west" of underdeveloped Ireland. In an almost magical escape, they elude the police across the countryside and come to terms with the death of their mother. Gabriel Byrne gives a moving performance as the boys' father, a misplaced "traveler," who does his own grieving as he searches for his sons. Although the breathtaking ending leaves some loose ends, each character is spiritually and emotionally matured by their experience. Written by Jim Sheridan. ★★★½ $9.99

Into the Woods

(1987, 153 min, US, James Lapine) Stephen Sondheim's astute and witty lyrics complement his melodious tunes in this effervescent musical which blends several children's fairy tales to produce one intertwining musical fable. Filmed from a live stage performance, the production features the original Broadway cast bringing to life the stories and characters from "Cinderella," "Jack and the Beanstalk," "Rapunzel" and "Little Red Riding Hood." Joanna Gleason (who deservedly won a Tony Award for her vibrant performance) and Chip Zien are a baker and his wife who set out to reverse the spell cast on them by the witch next door (the splendid Bernadette Peters), thereby meeting other fairy tale characters. Sondheim and author-director Lapine expand on the moralistic and mortality themes inherent in fairy tales creating a sumptuous union of comedy, dancing, music and myth. Deceptively innocent for children but complex and intuitive for adults. ★★★½ $24.99

Intolerance

(1916, 123 min, US, D.W. Griffith) Griffith's lavish spectacle is a landmark achievement in silent filmmaking. Following the popular success of *Birth of a Nation*, but stung by charges of racism, Griffith's theme in this classic is man's inhumanity to man. This intolerance and bigotry is illustrated in four interlocking tales from history: transpiring in ancient Babylon, biblical Judea, medieval France and modern America. Innovative film techniques, including the brilliant intercutting of the four stories, create an exciting climax. Starring Lillian Gish, Mae Marsh and Constance Talmadge. ★★★★ $29.99

The Intruder

(1975, 98 min, France, Serge Leroy) En route from Rome to Paris, a man and his young stepson are terrorized — for no apparent reason — by an unknown killer who is relentless in his pursuit and lethal to anyone coming between himself and his targets. This Hitchcockian suspense thriller stars Jean-Louis Trintignant, Mireille Darc and Bernard Fresson. (French with English subtitles) ★★★

Intruder in the Dust

(1949, 87 min, US, Clarence Brown) Released in the same year as *Lost Boundaries* and *Pinky*, two equally acclaimed social dramas examining racial prejudice, this is an exemplary, patient adaptation of William Faulkner's novel. The story is seen through the eyes of a white protagonist — as are films decades later — here a young boy (Claude Jarman, Jr.) from the South. There's a chilling, business-as-usual tone to the film's opening as the citizens of a small town gather to ceremoniously witness the lynching of accused murderer Juano Hernandez. Only four outcasts, including Jarman, come to his defense as the film balances non-preachy social observations with a crackerjack detective story. Hernandez brings unflinching dignity to the role of the alleged killer. An important cornerstone in the development of American cinema's social conscience. ★★★★ $19.99

Invaders from Mars

(1953, 78 min, US, William Cameron Menzies) Slick sci-fi tale about a young boy who witnesses an alien craft land and tries to convince those around him it really exists — those not already possessed by the other-worldly visitors, that is. Lots of fun, and a heck of a sight better than the 1986 remake. ★★★ $19.99

Invaders from Mars

(1986, 102 min, US, Tobe Hooper) Inferior remake of the 1953 classic sci-fi film about a young boy who tries to convince those around him that a Martian attack is under way. Real-life mom and son Karen Black and Hunter Carson play mom and son, and Louise Fletcher continues her patented villainous/strange character as a dastardly teacher. ★½

Invasion of the Body Snatchers

(1956, 80 min, US, Don Siegel) Classic '50s sci-fi chiller about pod people taking over the bodies of a small California community. Director Siegel's low budget belies the film's extraordinary composition and unrelenting tension. Top-notch cast includes Kevin McCarthy, Dana Wynter and Carolyn Jones. Remade in 1979. ★★★★ $19.99

Invasion of the Body Snatchers

(1979, 114 min, US, Philip Kaufman) One of the few instances in which a sequel does justice to the original. In this updated and refurbished remake, director Kaufman creates an unusually effective sense of dread to chillingly tell the story of pod people taking over the bodies of the citizens of San Francisco. Great cast includes Donald Sutherland, Brooke Adams, Jeff Goldblum and the marvelous Veronica Cartwright. Just try to forget that haunting (and unsettling) ending. ★★★½ $14.99

Invasion of the Bee Girls

(1974, 85 min, US, Denis Sanders) When the men of a small community are dying off due to excessive sexual activity, their wives are brought in for medical experimentation. In the lab, the women are irradiated, covered with bees and cocooned, where they emerge transformed into "Bee Girls." Written by Nicholas Meyer. ★★½

Invasion of the Scream Queens

(1992, 97 min, US, Donald Farmer) A funny and informative peek into the world of B-movie jiggle queens (past, present and future), complete with interviews and clips from the many horror/exploitation films they have appeared in. One segment of particular interest may be the Mary Woronov interview where she discusses her pre-Hollywood days with Andy Warhol and later work with Joe Dante and Paul Bartel. ★★★ $89.99

Investigation

(1983, 116 min, France, Etienne Perier) This action-packed murder mystery stars Victor Lanoux (*Cousin, Cousine*) as a rich, brooding man whose wife refuses his request to divorce him so that he may marry his pregnant mistress. The bloody murder that ensues is powerfully explored, with tantalizing and surprising results. (French with English subtitles) ★★★

Invisible Adversaries

(1977, 112 min, Austria, Valie Export) This low-budget feminist/art/science-fiction film can only be recommended to the cinematically adventurous or those with masochistic tendencies. Filled with a weird techno soundtrack, an aimlessly roaming camera and unattractive people having explicit sex, this feminist *Invasion of the Body Snatchers* has the "unique" premise of an alien power descending on the world. Anna, a Viennese photographer, unearths an insidious plot by "otherworldly powers" to infiltrate the minds of people and destroy them by raising their human aggression level. Much better done in *Liquid Sky*. (German with English subtitles) ★★ $59.99

The Invisible Man

(1933, 71 min, US, James Whale) Claude Rains made his debut in Whale's bewitching comic horror tale based on the H.G. Wells novel. Playfully funny and featuring dandy special effects, the film casts Rains as a scientist who has discovered the secret to invisibility — at the cost of his own sanity. As the local snoop, Una O'Connor proves she can scream with the best of them. ★★★ $14.99

Invitation au Voyage

(1982, 95 min, France, Peter Del Monte) An incestuous obsession between an introverted young ruffian and his punk rock star sister is rudely interrupted by her tragic death. With hypnotic images of her throbbing in his head, the teenager hits the road for points unknown. A striking rock score punctuates this visually arresting portrait of a young man's descent into dementia. (French with English subtitles) ★★★ $19.99

Invitation to a Wedding

(1983, 89 min, GB, Joseph Brooks) An American college student flies to England to attend a wedding and, during the dress rehearsal, is accidentally married to the bride by a bumbling country vicar (Ralph Richardson). The ensuing farce unfolds at a break-neck pace. John Gielgud makes a hilarious appearance as an Englishman-turned-Southern evangelist. ★★★

The Ipcress File

(1965, 108 min, GB, Sidney J. Furie) Michael Caine is impressive in his debut as Harry Palmer, an unemotional, Cockney crook-turned-secret agent. Considered the best of Len Deighton's Harry Palmer series, the film features a tense, complex plot revolving around a group of kidnapped scientists. This high-paced spy thriller is fascinating from start to finish. ★★★½ $14.99

Iphigenia

(1977, 129 min, Greece, Michael Cacoyannis) Based on Euripides' tragedy, "Iphigenia in the Bay of Aulis," this epic story concerns the fate of man and the demands of the gods. Agamemnon's army, set to sail to war, is immobile because of the lack of winds. In his attempts to appease the gods, he accidentally slays a sacred deer. For this offense, Agamemnon is told to sacrifice his young daughter, Iphigenia. This story of political intrigue unfolds behind the backdrop of Greece's ancient ruins. (Greek with English subtitles) ★★★

Irezumi

(1983, 88 min, Japan, Yokhi Takabayashi) The Japanese art of tattooing is the focal point of this intriguing and erotic contemplation of freedom, commitment and passion. Complying with her lover's demand, a young woman submits to a long and painful procedure in which an intricate tattoo is etched across her entire back. The master illustrator's somewhat unusual technique is to have the woman engage in sexual intercourse with her teenage assistant during the tattooing in order to arouse and prepare the skin. (Japanese with English subtitles) ★★½

The Irishman

(1978, 90 min, Australia, Donald Crombie) A sweeping tale of a family's futile battle against progress, this gripping frontier drama is set in 1920s North Queensland and features a young Bryan Brown in a small role. The story concerns Paddy Doolan, a proud Irish rancher, whose refusal to accept change and use motorized machinery pits one of his sons against the other. ★★★

Irma la Douce

(1963, 142 min, US, Billy Wilder) A lively though very broad farce from director Wilder. Jack Lemmon stars as a Parisian policeman who falls for streetwalker Shirley MacLaine. Determined to keep her "straight," Lemmon runs a comically ragged course as he doubles as both suitor and, by impersonating British royalty (shades of *The Lady Eve*), her only customer. And then there's the tale of the real British lord, but that's another story. Based on the Broadway musical — *sans* music. ★★★ $19.99

Iron and Silk

(1991, 91 min, US, Shirley Sun) Obvious sincerity and knowledge of the subject is not enough to lift this earnest drama about a young man's experience in China above an Afterschool Special. Based on Mark Salzman's autobiographical book, the film follows Salzman, a handsome American infused with a passion for all things Chinese, who goes to pre-Tiananmen Square China to study. His experiences in the country — learning to master martial arts, falling in love, attempting to win over the shy people, teaching eager Chinese English — is interesting; but without dramatic conflict, the film seems more a beautifully made travelogue than an insightful drama depicting the differences between East and West. ★★ $19.99

The Iron Crown

(1941, 100 min, Italy, Alessandro Blasetti) Attempting to create sort of an Italian saga similar to Fritz Lang's *Die Nibelungen*, Blasetti decided "more is better" by borrowing not only from Lang but Ariosto and the Grimm Brothers in this lavish pseudo-historical fantasy. Set in ancient times, this adventure spectacle includes a beautiful princess, a young hero raised by lions and a magical crown that rights injustice. (Italian with English subtitles) ★★½ $59.99

Iron Eagle

(1986, 117 min, US, Sidney J. Furie) Jason Gedrick, with the help of Louis Gossett, Jr., flies the unfriendly skies of the Middle East to rescue his father being held captive. This tepid *Top Gun* clone lacks that film's technical know-how (and makes it seem good in comparison). ★½ $14.99

Iron Maze

(1991, 102 min, US, Hiroaki Yoshida) A young man in a dying factory town (Jeff Fahey) discovers that his old flame (Bridget Fonda) is now married to the scion of the Japanese entrepreneur who just bought a decaying industrial complex. The son cannot understand community opposition to turning the

The Ipcress File

site into an amusement park. Co-produced by Oliver Stone, this well-acted and intelligently scripted film examines complex issues from multiple perspectives without stereotyping or condescension. Timely and pertinent, with a *Rashomon*-like style of exposition. ★★★ $89.99

The Iron Triangle

(1988, 94 min, US, Eric Weston) A U.S. Army captain (Beau Bridges) leads his men into a bloody battle to capture a Viet Cong stronghold along the Ho Chi Minh trail. A well-meaning if lethargic story which tries to reexamine the conflict of the Vietnam War. Haing S. Ngor co-stars. ★★

Iron Will

(1994, 104 min, US, Charles Haid) After their success with *White Fang*, Disney is back in the tundra with this equally appealing adventure film. Though heavy on the clichés, the likable story focuses on a teenaged Kansas farm boy, Will (Mackenzie Astin), who enters the big dog-sled race of 1917 in place of his deceased father. Competing and holding his own against seasoned adults, the youth quickly becomes a media sensation in his gritty attempt for victory. *Iron Will* has a nice period look to it, and director Haid keeps the action moving at a brisk pace. In the lead role, Astin is commendable, and Kevin Spacey and David Ogden Stiers appear in support. ★★★ $14.99

Ironweed

(1987, 144 min, US, Hector Babenco) A demanding, rather depressing but expertly acted and brilliant evocation of William Kennedy's Pulitzer Prize-winning novel. Set amongst the squalor of the poor and alcoholic street bums living in late-1930s Albany, the film features two mesmerizing performances by Jack Nicholson and Meryl Streep as two part-time lovers living on the skids; each concealing a secret from their past. Though it is certainly downbeat, the tour de force portrayals from Jack and Meryl make it a fascinating experience. (Watching Streep sing "She's My Gal" is alternately painful and exhilarating, and is one of the great movie moments of the 1980s.) ★★★ $14.99

Is It Easy to Be Young?

(1986, 85 min, USSR, Yuri Rodniek) Punks in black leather, anesthetized drug addicts and restless youths alienated by an unresponsive government might not seem so out of the ordinary for Americans, but the subject becomes much more interesting when the dissatisfied teens are Russians. With the Soviet Union facing dissolution, this boisterous documentary lends some insight into the thoughts and feelings of the Soviet youth seeking a different way. (Russian with English subtitles) ★★★ $59.99

Is Paris Burning?

(1966, 173 min, US/France, René Clément) An all-star cast highlights this epic WWII film about the liberation of Paris from the Germans, and the Nazis' attempt to level the city. The cast includes Jean-Paul Belmondo, Kirk Douglas, Simone Signoret, Charles Boyer, Leslie Caron, Orson Welles and Yves Montand, among many others. Hitler had commanded that the city be destroyed before the Germans left, and the title refers to his

constant inquiries as to that order's success. ★★½ $29.99

Is There Sex After Death?

(1971, 97 min, US, Jeanne & Alan Abel) Sometimes very funny and consistently raunchy sex parody on adult movies with Buck Henry, Holly Woodlawn and Marshall Efron. ★★★ $29.99

Isadora

(1968, 153 min, GB, Karel Reisz) Vanessa Redgrave's bravura performance highlights this gripping biography of dance innovator and free spirit Isadora Duncan. James Fox and Jason Robards offer excellent support, but it's Redgrave's show all the way. ★★★ $19.99

Ishtar

(1987, 107 min, US, Elaine May) This mega-bomb was doomed before it even hit the theatres due to production leaks and trade talk. With a reported cost of over $50 million, it didn't meet anyone's expectations. However, if you can erase all preconceptions, you may find it funny; particularly the intentionally horrendous Dustin Hoffman-Warren Beatty duets. A film you either love or hate. ★★ $14.99

The Island (Hodaka No Shima)

(1962, 96 min, Japan, Kaneto Shindo) An unusual work of art, made without dialogue. The story is told only through visuals, sounds and music. Beautifully photographed on a remote and barren island off Japan, the story follows a peasant family's daily struggle for survival. Their precarious existence is continually threatened by nature but the family never ceases its work. An engrossing, visually breathtaking tale told in documentary-like fashion. ★★★½

The Island

(1980, 114 min, US, Michael Ritchie) Laughable adventure film about modern-day pirates terrorizing the Caribbean. Michael Caine is a journalist investigating area disappearances who is captured by the seagoing bandits. Based on the novel by Peter Benchley ("Jaws"). ★ $19.99

The Island of Dr. Moreau

(1977, 104 min, US, Don Taylor) H.G. Wells' acclaimed novel comes to the screen in this mildly entertaining adaptation as Burt Lancaster plays a demented doctor who has created half-human animals. Michael York is the young man who discovers the humanoids. The film which asks the question, "Are we not men?" ("We are Devo.") For a more definitive version, see the 1933 *Island of Lost Souls* with Charles Laughton. ★★½

The Island of Dr. Moreau

(1996, 96 min, US, John Frankenheimer) Good and terrible from start to finish, this third version of H.G. Wells' story began with a troubled production history and wound up an incomprehensible mish-mash which stands as a testament to the vanity of the Hollywood actor and the stupidity of the Hollywood producer. The story is the same as before: David Thewlis is discovered drifting in the ocean and winds up on Moreau's island, where a brilliant, but disgraced scientist conducts experiments

into the animal nature of man and vice versa, attempting to create a perfect hybrid. Val Kilmer camps it up as Moreau's assistant and eventual successor. Frankenheimer and crew have created a mess: Kilmer overacts with abandon, Marlon Brando throws in a variety of astonishingly stupid bits of business, props, and costumes, Thewlis looks lost. The presence of the manimals and human oddities (some real, some makeup) only serves to drive the viewer deeper into the territory of the surreal. By the end, Kilmer is imitating Brando, Thewlis is throwing his hands up in exasperation and the viewer has wasted an hour and a half. This creation of the mad Dr. Frankenheimer is viewable for camp value only. ★½ $14.99

Islands

(1986, 57 min, US, Maysles Brothers) Remember Christo, that "wacko artist" who seemed possesed at the notion of "wrapping" a bunch of islands in Florida with pink plastic? Directed by the Maysles Brothers, this film follows Christo and his equally determined manager/wife as they try to overcome difficulties, skeptical governments and agencies, and other obstacles on their march toward their vision. Also included is footage shot as Christo and company seek permission from various governments to "wrap" the Pont-Neuf in France and the Reichstag in Germany. A fascinating, entertaining and moving document of the triumphs of the human will and spirit. ★★★ $59.99

Islands in the Stream

(1977, 110 min, US, Franklin J. Schaffner) George C. Scott is most effective as a father reunited with his sons after a self-imposed exile in the Bahamas at the outbreak of World War II. Based on the novel by Ernest Hemingway. With David Hemmings and Claire Bloom. ★★½ $14.99

Isle of the Dead

(1945, 72 min, US, Mark Robson) Boris Karloff gives a passionate portrayal of a Greek army commander who is trapped, along with several others, on an island hit by plague. This atmospheric chiller bears more than a slight resemblence to Jacques Tourneur's *I Walked with a Zombie* in content and technique, for director Robson worked on that and other Val Lewton classics as editor. ★★★ $19.99

It

(1990, 193 min, US, Tommy Lee Wallace) Frightmaster Stephen King continues to provide cinematic sustenance for a horror-starved market with this small-screen "Monster Piece Theatre" production about a group of childhood friends who reunite as adults to face their own "big chill" — an evil presence that lurks beneath their hometown and manifests as their innermost fear, a demonic killer clown (played by Tim Curry). Curry gives a *con brio* performance, far superior to the usual made-for-TV readings, but horror elements bear the burden of commercial sponsorship and are less than eye-clenching. Still, die-hard scarebears won't be disappointed and the uninitiated will find this one a good place to start. The cast includes John Ritter, Harry Anderson, Richard Thomas, Annette O'Toole, Dennis Christopher and Tim Reid. ★★½ $24.99

It Could Happen to You

It Came from Hollywood

(1982, 80 min, US, Andrew Solt & Malcolm Leo) A humerous look at the bad sci-fi movies that emerged in the 1950s. Hosted by Dan Aykroyd, John Candy, Cheech and Chong and Gilda Radner. ★★½ $59.99

It Conquered the World

(1956, 71 min, US, Roger Corman) Drive-in classic with a creepy monster that releases bloodsucking bats, whose bites reduce people to zombies. This picture is often equated with films from this time period in which the story line mimicks the "Red Scare" which was sweeping 1950s America. ★★

It Could Happen to You

(1994, 101 min, US, Andrew Bergman) For all those who bemoan "they don't make them like they used to" comes this gentle romantic comedy. Nicolas Cage stars as a super honest New York City cop who gives half of his winning lottery ticket to a perpetually down-on-her-luck waitress (Bridget Fonda) as a tip. A charming modern fairy tale without much depth and a Gump-like belief in the triumph of goodness, *It Could Happen to You* relies heavily on the charisma of its two stars, and both deliver affable, slightly kooky performances. Rosie Perez, on the other hand, goes completely overboard in a screechingly annoying turn as Cage's money-grubbing wife. ★★★ $19.99

It Happened in the Park

(1956, 87 min, Italy/France, Gianni Franciolini) Told in a series of vignettes, this simple but affecting drama takes the premise of filming a day in the life of Villa Borghese, the beautiful landscaped park in Rome. The stories revolve mostly around *amore*: budding romances, illicit affairs and bickering lovers. Also included is a touching drama of a teacher revealing to a pupil that he is going blind; and the best episode is the finale, about two warring prostitutes who, on the run from the police, find themselves competing in a Miss Cinema pageant. Please note that the sound is only fair and the subtitles sometimes fall below the screen; but this is the only version currently available. (French with English subtitles) ★★★

It Happened One Night

(1934, 105 min, US, Frank Capra) Predicted as a box-office bomb, this hugely entertaining comedy was the smash hit of 1934, not only winning Oscars for almost everyone involved (Best Actor – Clark Gable, Best Actress – Claudette Colbert, Best Director – Frank Capra), but also managing to snag the Best Picture Oscar as well; it ushered in a whole new style of Hollywood comedy. This romantic comedy concerns the adventures of a runaway heiress (Colbert) and a newspaperman (Gable) who discovers her identity and helps her by "marrying" her. Full of rapid-fire one-liners and ingenious gags, this enduring classic is every bit as delightful as its reputation suggests. ★★★★ $19.99

It Happens Every Spring

(1949, 128 min, US, Lloyd Bacon) Ray Milland plays a scientist who discovers a serum which repels wood. To determine its effectiveness, he tries out as a big-league pitcher – and becomes the major's new ace. Paul Douglas is terrific as his team's weathered, hen-pecked manager. A lighthearted, funny romp which is one of the semi-classics of the era's many baseball films. ★★★ $19.99

It Lives Again

(1978, 91 min, US, Larry Cohen) Dreadful sequel to *It's Alive* finds another young couple experiencing the mutant baby syndrome. But this time, the mother gives birth to triplets. Frederic Forrest, Kathleen Lloyd, John Marley and John Ryan star. ★ $14.99

It Should Happen to You

(1954, 87 min, US, George Cukor) Charming fluff about a New York City woman, Gladys Glover (Judy Holliday), who rents a Columbus Circle billboard – just to put her name on it. She then becomes a media sensation. In his film debut, Jack Lemmon plays a filmmaker involved with the wacky Gladys. Holliday, of course, is nothing short of delightful. ★★★ $14.99

It Started in Naples

(1960, 100 min, US, Melville Shavelson) Clark Gable stars as a stuffy Philadelphia attorney who arrives in Italy to bring home his orphaned nephew. But cultures clash when he runs up against the boy's fiery Italian aunt (Sophia Loren). A sunny Mediterranean romp. ★★★ $14.99

It Started with a Kiss

(1959, 104 min, US, George Marshall) Debbie Reynolds is the kooky, man-hunting chorine. Glenn Ford is the Army sergeant who, after much ado, steals her heart. After one day, they marry, and he is soon transferred to Spain. There they discover the downside of love at first sight, as they try to get to know each other. To make matters worse, she is pursued by handsome matador Gustavo Rojo; he is pursued by countess Eva Gabor; and colonel Fred Clark is constantly on their case. A fluffy romantic comedy, not without a few chuckles, which tries to be both sexy and innocent. It settles for sappy. For a really good '50s sex farce, check out *Ask Any Girl*. ★★½ $19.99

It Takes Two

(1995, 101 min, US, Andy Tennant) It's contrived, it's cutesy, and, egaad, it's the Olsen twins...and yet, it's surprisingly charming. A rare romantic family comedy, *It Takes Two* has appealing elements for both the kids and the adults. In this update of *The Prince and the Pauper*, Mary-Kate and Ashley are the identical kids who have grown up under completely different circumstances. One has been raised wealthy and cultured, the daughter of the widowed Steve Guttenberg. The other is an orphan befriended by the unmarried Kirstie Alley. Once the twins meet each other, and faster than you can say *The Parent Trap*, they try to bring Kirstie and Steve together. The plan is complicated by the fact that Guttenberg is about to get married to a very unpleasant socialite, so they must act fast. The plot thins out a bit at this point, but the characters are likable enough to amuse. ★★½ $19.99

It! The Terror from Beyond Space

(1958, 69 min, US, Edward L. Cahn) Space explorers land on Mars and pick up a monstrous hitchhiker on their return to Earth, which is bent on their destruction. The inspiration for *Alien*. ★★ $19.99

It's a Gift

(1934, 73 min, US, Norman Z. McLeod) One of W.C. Fields funniest films, here Bill plays a grocery clerk who goes to California, discovering a funny and wild, wild West. ★★★

It's a Mad, Mad, Mad, Mad World

(1963, 154 min, US, Stanley Kramer) One of the top box-office hits of the 1960s, this overlong Cinemascope extravaganza was director Kramer's attempt to revive the silent slapstick comedies of years gone by. For the most part, it works. Spencer Tracy, in one of his last screen appearances, heads an all-star cast looking for an elusive "W" marking the spot of a buried fortune. The cast, really just second-bananas to a series of hilarious stunts and car chases, includes Mickey Rooney, Jonathan Winters, Sid Caesar, Milton Berle, Phil Silvers, Buddy Hackett and, in a hilarious performance as the mother-in-law from hell, Ethel Merman. Still good for some genuine laughs, the film is representative of the overblown all-star epics which marked the mid-'60s. (Letterboxed) ★★★½ $24.99

It's a Wonderful Life

(1946, 130 min, US, Frank Capra) Capra's immortal classic with James Stewart as the father who wished he'd never been born – and who gets his wish. Capra as director and Stewart as actor were at the peak of their talents. Donna Reed, Thomas Mitchell, Lionel Barrymore and Henry Travers, as moviedom's most endearing angel, also star. ★★★★ $14.99

It's Alive

(1974, 91 min, US, Larry Cohen) Cult fave about an expectant couple and the birth of their new baby – a hideous mutant killer. John Ryan, Sharon Farrell and Michael Ansara star. ★★½ $14.99

It's Alive III: Island of the Alive

(12987, 95 min, US, Larry Cohen) The *It's Alive* babies are back! This time, more distraught parents have watched the government banish their mutant children to a remote island. Years later, these teenage mutants want to come back to the society that created them. Michael Moriarty, Karen Black, Neal Israel and MacDonald Carey star. ★★ $14.99

It's Always Fair Weather

(1955, 102 min, US, Gene Kelly & Stanley Donen) *Singin' in the Rain* directors Kelly and Donen and writers Betty Comden and Adolph Green reunited for this cheerful, entertaining musical about three former Army buddies who meet 10 years after the end of WWII. There are great dance sequences, a good score, and Kelly, Dan Daily, Cyd Charisse, Michael Kidd and Dolores Gray are all fine. It's amazing what Kelly can do with a garbage can lid. ★★★½ $19.99

It's in the Bag

(1945, 87 min, US, Richard Wallace) Popular 1940s radio star Fred Allen is featured in this funny and crazy romp about flea trainer Allen inheriting a small fortune – only the money is hidden in one of five chairs scattered throughout the city. Jack Benny makes a hilarious extended cameo (the entire scene is priceless), and Don Ameche and Rudy Vallee also appear as themselves (as down-on-their-luck cabaret singers!). Similar in plot to Mel Brooks' *The 12 Chairs*. ★★★ $19.99

It's My Party

(1996, 91 min, US, Randal Kleiser) Based on the true story of his lover of eight years, director Kleiser has made an emotionally candid, very personal AIDS and suicide drama which is short of dramatic structure but overpowering in the honest emotions it establishes. Giving a remarkably subtle and heartfelt performance, Eric Roberts stars as Nick, an architect and gay man with AIDS who decides to kill himself upon learning he has PMI, a debilitating disease which kills in a matter of days. But beforehand, he decides to throw a farewell bash – attended by family and friends, and his ex-lover Brandon (Gregory Harrison) who has crashed the party. The story focuses on Nick's various relationships (some are superficially explored, others are rather tender) and a possible reconciliation with Brandon all the while joking with gallows humor of the inevitable. With a large supporting cast, many are slighted in terms of definition, but the ensemble is sincere in a story which obviously touches all. Though not as polished as the high-profile AIDS drama *Philadelphia*, *It's My Party* is more aware, and can be sentimental without being maudlin. ★★★ $19.99

It's Pat

(1994, 77 min, US, Adam Bernstein) Julia Sweeney stars in this annoying, one-joke comedy, based on her "Saturday Night Live" sketch, as Pat, an androgynous, bothersome loser who keeps one and all guessing as to his/her gender. Whereas this comic concept inspired a few funny five-minute bits, as a feature-length movie it is interminable. The story has to do with Pat finding love (in the form of an equally androgynous David Foley from "The Kids in the Hall") and endlessly searching for the right career. Though the film contains a number of laughs, it is saved from total abomination by Charles Rocket, who is actually quite good as Pat's neighbor who slowly goes insane trying to determine Pat's sex. ★½ $9.99

The Italian Straw Hat

(1927, 101 min, France, René Clair) Clair's madcap comedy based on the Labiche-Michel farce about a groom, minutes before his marriage, who goes on a frantic search for the identical hat his horse has just eaten. The sometimes hilarious escapades are superbly exploited by Clair. (Silent with musical accompaniment) ★★★½ $19.99

Italianamerican/The Big Shave

(1974/78, 54 min, US, Martin Scorsese) Two short films from Scorsese. *Italianamerican* features the director's irrepressible mother and father, Catherine and Charles, in an intimate conversation at their Little Italy home in New York. A funny look at one family's ancestry, life and accomplishments. In *The Big Shave*, a young man nicks himself shaving and suddenly, an ordinary morning is transformed into a frightening religious experience. Scorsese's black humor is much in evidence, even at an early age, and encapsulates his obsessions with religion, suffering and blood. ★★★ $24.99

Ivan & Abraham

(1993, 105 min, France, Yolande Zauberman) The poignant and enduring friendship of two adolescent boys – one Jewish and one Christian – makes for a haunting, lyrical coming-of-age tale set against the turbulent backdrop of rising anti-Semitism in 1930s Poland. Beautifully shot in stark black and white, *Ivan & Abraham* is set in a *shtetl*, or small Jewish community. Ivan (Roma Alexandrovitch) is a Catholic youth apprenticing at the home of Abraham (Sacha Iakovlev), and the two are inseparable friends. When Abraham's strict grandfather forbids his grandson to see Ivan, the two run away together. Pursuing them are Aaron, an escaped political prisoner ready to leave the country, and Rachel, Abraham's older sister who is in love with Aaron (though she is promised in marriage to another). With a poetic and focused eye, the film juxtaposes the story of the boys' life on the road; the disturbing, escalating tensions in the village; and the passage of customs for an uncertain future. The performances of the two boys are remarkably assured. (Yiddish, Polish, Russian and Gypsy dialect with English subtitles) ★★★½ $89.99

Ivan the Terrible, Part I

(1943, 94 min, USSR, Sergei Eisenstein) Eisenstein's epic biography of Ivan Grozny IV, proclaimed Russia's first Czar in the middle of the 16th century. The film, the first of two parts, traces the emperor's coronation, his defeat and his eventual reinstatement. The film features an original score by Sergei Prokofiev. (Russian with English subtitles) ★★★½ $29.99

Ivan the Terrible, Part II

(1946, 90 min, USSR, Sergei Eisenstein) Eisenstein's follow-up to his 1943 classic chronicles Ivan's reign in the late 16th century and his revenge on those who had denounced him. (Russian with English subtitles) ★★★½ $29.99

Ivanhoe

(1952, 106 min, US, Richard Thorpe) A young and absolutely ravishing Elizabeth Taylor stars in this rendition of Walter Scott's epic tale of Saxon honor and Norman villainy in middle-age England. Robert Taylor stars as Ivanhoe, a young knight torn between the honorable Rowena and the Jewess Rebecca, while at the same time trying to bring the good King Richard back to England. Joan Fontaine and George Sanders co-star in this beautifully filmed historical drama. ★★★ $19.99

Ivanhoe

(1982, 142 min, GB, Douglas Camfield) Lavish version of Walter Scott's classic story of knighthood, love, Richard the Lionhearted and 12th-century England. Starring James Mason, Anthony Andrews, Sam Neill and Olivia Hussey. Earlier version made in 1952 with Elizabeth Taylor and Robert Taylor. ★★★ $19.99

J'Accuse

(1937, 125 min, France, Abel Gance) A lost masterpiece from the director of *Napoleon*, this, Gance's sound remake of his 1919 film of the same title, is a virulent antiwar film that was originally banned by the French government as being potentially treasonous. An epic of love and the catastrophic effects of war on one man's spirits, this powerful and disturbing cry against man's inhumanity to his fellow man features a particularly chilling sequence where a man calls upon millions of dead soldiers to rise from their graves and march on Paris. (French with English subtitles) ★★★½ $19.99

J'ai Été au Bal

(1990, 114 min, US, Les Blank) Independent documentary filmmaker Blank, who has produced several films about Cajun and Zydeco music culture (*Hot Pepper* and *Dry Wood*), has joined forces with ethnic music producer Chris Strachwits to deliver his most coherent and comprehensive effort to date. From the sounds of the 1920s and Joe Falcon to the rock 'n' roll beat of Wayne Toups (the Cajun Bruce Springsteen) to the flamboyance of the "King of Zydeco" Clifton Chenier, *J'ai Été au Bal* captures the raw spirit of rural Louisiana through a fascinating blend of archival and current footage. A deeply felt understanding of why and how this infective music has come to be the wonderful gumbo that it is. (French with English subtitles) ★★★ $49.99

Jabberwocky

Jabberwocky

(1977, 100 min, GB, Terry Gilliam) "T'was brillig and the slithy toves..." Gilliam uses the resources of his friends in the Monty Python gang to bring Lewis Carroll's classic poem to the screen with great aplomb. Michael Palin stars in this tale of a medieval kingdom's search for a brave young lad to slay a nasty, scaly beast. Featuring the same bloody absurdities of life as in *Holy Grail*. ★★★ $19.99

Jack

(1996, 113 min, US, Francis Ford Coppola) Jack is a young boy whose body isn't really his own. This didn't happen by wishing, or even the result of an ancient artifact. Nothing bewitching here. He's suffering from a disease which makes his body grow four times its normal rate. Which is only one of the missteps with *Jack*, a sullen fable short on magic and

humor, two essential ingredients of the genre. Robin Williams plays the title character, a ten-year-old whose body is that of a 40-year-old. Sheltered by his doting mom, Jack eventually makes his way to school and the outside world, where hurt, friends and experience await him. As directed by Coppola, *Jack* is too encompassing in what it tries to accomplish — it's operatic where it should be frolicsome and only occasionally does the story capture the whimsical cadence of childhood. However, Williams makes a spirited child, and the bittersweet observations of the film very nearly tug at a heartstring or two. ★★ $19.99

Jack Be Nimble

(1993, 93 min, New Zealand, Garth Maxwell) Creepy "everything-but-the-kitchen-sink" thriller about a young girl (Sarah Smuts-Kennedy) who uses her latent psychic powers to find the brother she lost through adoption (played as an adult by Alexis Arquette). Of course, this happens just as he murders his abusive adoptive parents and is stalked by his four psycho stepsisters. Eerie photography and a totally twisted story line make this an excellent horror film for the art-house set and a welcome import from the land down under. Also with Bruno Lawrence. ★★★ $14.99

Jack Kerouac's Road

(1987, 55 min, Canada, Hermenegilde Chaisson) Through photographs, archival footage, interviews and skillful reconstruction of events, this documentary-cum-docudrama delves into the often treaded subject of Jack Kerouac, the gifted but troubled Beat writer and author of "On the Road," "The Dharma Bums" and "Satori." (French with English subtitles) ★★★ $49.99

Jack the Bear

(1993, 98 min, US, Marshall Herskowitz) This is a film with a sneaky left hook. Just when you think you're awash in a mushy "Wonder Years"-for-the-big-screen rip-off, *Jack the Bear* surprises you with some down-to-earth honesty about growing up (and old) with big doses of rage and guilt. Danny DeVito stars as a widowed dad in the early '70s who makes his living as the host of a local TV station's late movie show and who must contend with a possible psycho neighbor. Though it does have a definite sugary "how many times have I seen this before" side, the heart-tugging performances of DeVito's two sons (Robert Steinmiller and Miko Hughes) make this a definite seven on the tearjerker scale. ★★½ $19.99

Jack the Giant Killer

(1962, 92 min, US, Nathan Juran) After completing Ray Harryhausen's *The Seventh Voyage of Sinbad*, a lot of the same people went to work on this film, which explains why it has the feel of a knockoff. Still, the special effects (by Jim Danforth) are good; featuring a giant, another giant (this one with two heads), a flying dragon, witches, ghouls and a sea monster — in short, the usual Saturday night South Street crowd. ★★ $14.99

Jack's Back

(1988, 97 min, US, Rowdy Herrington) James Spader gives a solid portrayal of a troubled

young man investigating the murder of his twin brother in this very effective update (set in Los Angeles) of the Jack the Ripper tale. A vastly underrated mystery with lots of chills to it. ★★★ $14.99

Jackie Chan's First Strike

(1996, 88 min, Hong Kong, Stanley Tong) Originally released in Hong Kong as *Police Story 4*, (*Supercop* was the third of the series), *First Strike* once again casts Jackie Chan as a Hong Kong police officer who must this time travel the globe in order to stop some arms dealers who are in league with the Russian mafia. More a tribute to James Bond films than a traditional Jackie Chan vehicle, the film visits several exotic locales and showcases several large stunt sequences (a chase on skis and snowmobiles, an underwater fight in a shark tank and a rollicking chase through Chinatown streets on stilts). Only one "traditional" kung fu fight is included in the film, but it is a doozy as Jackie beats up a group of bad guys with a ten-foot aluminum stepladder! Jackie's age, however, is beginning to show and he seems to be increasingly "Americanizing" his movies with less kung fu and more Hollywood-type stunts. Nevertheless, he is the best in the world at what he does and *First Strike* is another totally entertaining piece of escapist cinema. (Partially dubbed in English) ★★★ $102.99

Jackie Mason on Broadway

(1988, 60 min, US) Jackie Mason stars in this hilarious video presentation of his Tony Award-winning one-man show. Filmed during a Broadway performance, this one-hour comedy routine features Mason's perceptive and unique view of the world, from the differences between Jews and gentiles to politics to Hollywood. Mason, who staged a comeback of sorts with this highly successful show, assaults his audience with a constant barrage of one-liners and anecdotes. Nothing is sacred in the world according to Mason. ★★★½ $14.99

Jacknife

(1989, 102 min, US, David Jones) An extremely compelling drama about two Vietnam vets coming to terms with their tour of duty and the death of an old friend. Robert De Niro visits his old Army buddy Ed Harris, together exorcising their demons; De Niro then becomes involved with Harris' sister Kathy Bates. The three stars give excellent performances, which makes this oft-told tale seem all the more fresh. ★★★ $19.99

Jacko and Lise

(1982, 92 min, France, Walter Bal) Jacko and Freddie are inseparable friends whose lives are free of responsibility. Their friendship and their outlook on life change, however, when Jacko falls in love with a young woman and decides to better himself. A story of a young man's growth from a carefree youth into adulthood. (French with English subtitles) ★★½

Jacob's Ladder

(1990, 113 min, US, Adrian Lyne) From the writer of *Ghost*, Bruce Joel Rubin, and the director of *Fatal Attraction*, Lyne, comes this harrowing, roller-coaster ride about a Vietnam vet terrorized by his own demons. Tim Robbins plays Jacob Singer, who tries to reconcile his past, both as a soldier and as a father devastated by family tragedy. In doing so, he is haunted by freakish hallucinations that threaten both his sanity and his life. A dark, psychological thriller, Lyne's camera gives terror a gruesome yet sylish look. ★★★ $14.99

Jacquot

(1991, 118 min, France, Agnès Varda) Varda's loving tribute to her partner, Jacques Demy (*The Umbrellas of Cherbourg*), is a mixture of flashbacks, personal narratives and scenes from his films, which together create a vivid picture of his early interest in film. Varda presents a detailed exposé on Demy's (nicknamed "Jacquot") experience during the war and especially his early film projects as a youth. The performances are remarkably genuine, especially the three actors who portray Demy. *Jacquot* marks the only collaboration between the two directors, ending with Demy's death in 1990. The film's final scene owes tribute to François Truffaut's *The 400 Blows*. (French with English subtitles) ★★★½ $19.99

Jade

(1995, 95 min, US, William Friedkin) *Basic Instinct* meets *Jagged Edge* in this worthless and uninspired outing from the author of both better films, Joe Eszterhas. Linda Fiorentino plays the wife of a high-powered defense attorney (Chazz Palminteri) who becomes the prime suspect when a wealthy politico is murdered during an act of kinky sex with an unknown femme fatale known only as "Jade." David Caruso plays the cop/ex-lover determined to get to the bottom of it all. Friedkin's thriller is a well-mounted but raucous mess, with action sequences that far outshine the ridiculous screenplay. Palminteri, who was such a breath of fresh air in *Bullets over Broadway*, is overbearing and redundant, and Caruso and Fiorentino are merely placeholders in this tedious exercise. ★½ $14.99

Jagged Edge

(1985, 108 min, US, Richard Marquand) An embittered Glenn Close defends a charismatic San Francisco newspaper publisher, played

with sleek charm by Jeff Bridges, in this well-crafted murder mystery/courtroom drama. Peter Coyote almost steals the show as the skeptical D.A. who steadfastly refuses to believe Bridges' protestations of innocence of his wife's murder. Close gives a fine, believable performance in both the courtroom encounters and in her romantic involvement with Bridges. Robert Loggia received an Oscar nomination for his salty-tongued investigator. ★★★ $9.99

Jail Bait

(1954, 70 min, US, Edward D. Wood, Jr.) Unlike its title's suggestion, this is not a tale of oversexed, underage teens. Instead, it's a melodrama about small-time crooks in constant runins with the law. This notoriously bad film noir piece was shot in four days. From the director of *Plan 9 from Outer Space*. With Steve Reeves (pre-*Hercules*) and Lyle Talbot. ★½ $9.99

Jailbirds' Vacation

(1965, 125 min, France, Robert Enrico) Lino Ventura stars in this middling drama about the desperate lengths a man will go to keep his business afloat. Hector Valentin's financial struggles with his family's sawmill company is greatly helped after he hires two strangers to help operate the factory. On the suggestion of the two, the owner begins to hire several parolees from the local prison only to discover a dark motive behind the scheme. (French with English subtitles) ★★

Jailhouse Rock

(1957, 96 min, US, Richard Thorpe) Arguably Elvis Presley's best musical has the King as a former convict who tries to make it as a rock 'n' roll star – think he succeeds? The musical number "Jailhouse Rock" is a classic. ★★★ $14.99

Jamaica Inn

(1939, 90 min, GB, Alfred Hitchcock) This tense, suspenseful melodrama by Hitchcock, starring Charles Laughton and Maureen O'Hara, is based on the best-selling novel by Daphne Du Maurier. The story is set in the 18th century and is about a country squire

(Laughton) who is secretly the head of a band of pirates who wreck ships and ransom them. This was Hitchcock's last film in England before he began his "Hollywood period." ★★★ $24.99

James and the Giant Peach

(1996, 80 min, US, Henry Selick) Roald Dahl's charming children's story makes for an equally charming animated tale, though not quite as inventive or groundbreaking as director Selick's debut feature *The Nightmare Before Christmas*. When young James loses his parents, he is forced to live with his two oppressive aunts (Joanna Lumley and Miriam Margolyes camping it up). That is until a giant peach miraculously appears in their garden, offering James flight across the ocean. Using the same stop-motion animation as in *Nightmare*, Selick and his staff are able to incorporate live-action material, as well, to good effect. Hindered only by an unmemorable score (as contrasted to *Nightmare*'s excellent musical numbers), *James and the Giant Peach* is an affectionate fantasy which is capable of winning the hearts of children and parents alike. ★★★ $22.99

The James Dean Story

(1957, 80 min, US, Robert Altman & George W. George) Documentary on `50s screen legend James Dean, including interviews with friends, associates and family. A rather one-dimensional portrait, *The James Dean Story* captures neither the mystery nor the power of the actor. For a more complete portrait of Dean, check out *James Dean: The Last American Teenager*. ★★ $12.99

James Joyce's Women

(1986, 91 min, GB, Michael Pearce) Through a series of haunting, often erotically charged vignettes, the remarkable Fionnula Flanagan offers a true tour de force as she portrays six fascinating women – three from Joyce's writings and three from his life. The film intelligently and successfully captures the spirit of James Joyce and is a one-of-a-kind theatrical experience. ★★★ $69.99

Jamon Jamon

(1992, 96 min, Spain, Bigas Luna) Dripping with Freudian tension, director Luna's loony erotic comedy rips a page of Pedro Almodóvar's book as it delves into the abyss of *l'amour fou*. Set on a lonesome strip of highway in a dusty and deserted Spain, the story begins with a passionate teen tryst between the lower-class Silvia (Penelope Cruz) and Jose Luis (Jordi Molla), the son of an underwear tycoon. Insisting that he marry within his class, Jose Luis' overbearing mother (a marvelously camp Stephania Sandrelli) hires the strapping Raul (Javier Bardem) to lure Silvia away from her son. But her plan backfires when she herself falls prey to Raul's smoldering masculine wiles. Luna's script plays out like an absurdist Greek tragedy, overflowing with sexual jealousies, and some paternal ambiguities for good measure. At times as perplexing as it is hilarious, the film features a nude midnight bullfighting scene which is not to be missed. (Spanish with English subtitles) ★★★ $19.99

Jamon Jamon

Jan Svankmajer, Alchemist of the Surreal

Jan Svankmajer, Alchemist of the Surreal

(1964-1982, 60 min, Czechoslovakia, Jan Svankmajer) From the lyrical mysticism of his first film, "The Last Trick," to the joyously tactile experience of "Dimensions of Dialogue," Svankmajer exploits every technique of animation to its fullest, creating worlds beholden only to their own internal logic. ★★★ $24.99

Jane Austen in Manhattan

(1980, 108 min, GB, James Ivory) Two rival New York theatre companies vie for the rights to produce a recently unearthed manuscript by Jane Austen. One wants to produce the piece as a period operetta, the other wants to make it an avant-garde performance piece. It's an interesting premise; however, the film is not one of the best to come out of the Merchant Ivory mill. ★★

Jane Campion Shorts

(1983-86, 49 min, Australia, Jane Campion) Campion, director of *The Piano* and *An Angel at My Table*, made an unprecedented debut at the 1986 Cannes Film Festival with these three short films, all made while she was still a film student. They are all distinguished by her mischievous sense of comic irony. *Passionless Moments* (13 min) is a series of vignettes which humorously examine the seemingly unimportant private moments of everyday living. *A Girl's Own Story* (27 min) tells of a girl's childhood in the 1960s. *Peel* (9 min) tells of a mother and her young son and daughter who take a drive in the country only to be met by disaster. ★★★½ $29.99

Jane Eyre

(1944, 96 min, US, Robert Stevenson) This almost film noirish adaptation of Charlotte Brontë's novel about an unloved orphan girl who grows up to become a governess in a mysterious manor is a shadowy Gothic affair. Joan Fontaine and Orson Welles give such brooding performances, they seem like two Elizabethan actors gone mad. Also, be on the lookout for a very young Elizabeth Taylor. ★★★ $19.99

Jane Eyre

(1983, 239 min, GB, Julian Amyes) Dread not the thought of being tied down for four hours of tedious BBC drama, for this retelling of the Charlotte Brontë classic is a motivating and powerful drama. This rapturous tale of two lovers frustrated by social mores and misty pasts stars Timothy Dalton and Zelah Clarke, who are nothing less than superb as the star-crossed lovers, and their performances infuse the story with unrivaled immediacy and emotion. ★★★½ $24.99

The January Man

(1989, 97 min, US, Pat O'Connor) John Patrick Shanley (*Moonstruck*) wrote this mystery-comedy about a serial killer terrorizing New York. Kevin Kline is police chief Danny Aiello's brother who helps his sibling solve the case. Susan Sarandon, Mary Elizabeth Mastrantonio, Harvey Keitel, Rod Steiger and Alan Rickman also star; and though it's a great cast, the story is so muddled, they are mostly wasted. ★★ $9.99

Jason and the Argonauts

(1963, 104 min, GB, Don Chaffey) Spectacular special effects by Ray Harryhausen and a beautiful Bernard Herrmann score are the highlights of this otherwise predictable action-adventure fable about Jason's hazardous and monster-filled search for the Golden Fleece. The forgettable stars are Todd Armstrong and Nancy Kovack. The real stars are Harryhausen's sword-fighting skeletons, multi-headed Hydra, and malevolent Harpies. ★★½ $14.99

Jason's Lyric

(1994, 119 min, US, Doug McHenry) Allen Payne and Jada Pinkett star as the titular couple in yet another tense/tragic urban melodrama, with one exception being that this is actually entertaining. Smart, hard-working Jason (Payne) and his thuggish malt liquor-swilling sibling Josh (skillfully played by rapper Bokeem Woodbine) are bonded by the memory of their slain father (Forest Whitaker). But they are also separated by the opposite paths they choose for themselves. When Jason meets Lyric (Pinkett), she inspires him to leave their town and start a peaceful life together; psychobro stands between them, dangerous and out of control. Powerful dialogue, fine performances, an intelligent script and eyeglass fogging lovemaking scenes more than compensate for the occasional cliché. ★★★ $19.99

Jaws

(1975, 120 min, US, Steven Spielberg) One of the great box-office hits of all time is also one of the best horror films in the last few decades. Spielberg's classic shark story, based on Peter Benchley's novel, kept millions out of the water during the summer of '75. Roy Scheider, Richard Dreyfuss and the great Robert Shaw go shark hunting off the New England coast and find Melvillian adventure. A classic combination of suspense, effects, editing, cinematography, score and bristling characterizations. (Available letterboxed and pan & scan) ★★★★ $19.99

Jaws 2

(1978, 117 min, US, Jeannot Szwarc) Flimsy sequel has a couple of scares to it, but there is absolutely no comparison to the original. Roy Scheider and Lorraine Gary return (and are much classier than this film deserves) as another great white shark terrorizes Amity Island. On the menu: *teenager du jour*. ★★ $19.99

The Jazz Singer

(1980, 115 min, US, Richard Fleischer) Second remake of Al Jolson's "first talkie" about a cantor's son (Neil Diamond) who goes against his father's wishes and becomes a rock star. Pretty bad stuff; even Laurence Olivier is embarrassing. ★ $14.99

Jazzman

(1983, 80 min, USSR, Karen Shakhnazarov) With a deft touch and gentle satiric outlook, this pleasant comedy, set in the 1920s, focuses on a musical conservatory student who wants to study jazz. Reacting to the official stance that jazz is a "monstrous product of bourgeois society," our young hero quits school to start his own jazz band. Teaming up with two colorful street musicians and a saxophonist, the young musicians struggle to gain acceptance for this "anti-revolutionary" music form. Filled with Dixieland, ragtime and swing sounds, the film joyfully preaches the universality of music. (Russian with English subtitles) ★★★ $59.99

je tu il elle

(1976, 95 min, Belgium/France, Chantal Akerman) This first feature film by Belgium-born director Akerman is a charming yet demanding, innovative psychodrama that places her in the same avant-garde company as Alain Robbes-Grillet and Marguerite Duras. The film, whose title means "I...you...he...she," opens with director/heroine Akerman lying alone and naked in bed eating from a bag of sugar. From this follows a deceptively simple story told in three segments, each containing an element of the traditional depiction of women. Initially, she is writing a sad letter to an (ex?)lover; another is a brief sexual encounter with a truck driver; and, finally, a sexual relationship with another woman. While eschewing traditional narrative, Akerman thinks out such ideas as loss and separation, solitary introspection and voyeurism with startling clarity. (French with English subtitles) ★★★ $29.99

Jean de Florette

(1986, 122 min, France, Claude Berri) Adapted from two of Marcel Pagnol's novels (author of the popular trilogy "Marius," "Fanny" and "César"), this powerful and absorbing tale of greed, betrayal, idealism and love was an art-house hit across the country. Yves Montand gives an unsettling performance as "Papet," an evil old peasant intent on swindling some valuable land from his neighbor. After accidentally killing the original owner of the property, he must now deal with Jean (Gérard Depardieu), a city-bred hunchback who optimistically brings his family to the farm and dreams of a new life. Followed by *Manon of the Spring*. (French with English subtitles) ★★★★ $19.99

Jefferson in Paris

(1995, 140 min, GB, James Ivory) Director Ivory and longtime writing partner Ruth Prawer Jhabvala, responsible for the brilliant *The Remains of the Day* among many others, have fashioned a film which, while a superior evocation of late-1700s Paris, examines in a dispassionate, casual manner the five-year service of Thomas Jefferson as American ambassador to France. Ivory's works have usually demonstrated extraordinary characterizations, but here the film concentrates on Jefferson's libido while ignoring the essence of a great man living in a troubled time. As Jefferson, Nick Nolte is more lumberjack than patrician; he makes a clever lover but a dubious patriot. Greta Scacchi and Thandee Newton are his love interests, and Simon Callow and Gwyneth Paltrow offer good support. ★★½ $19.99

Jeffrey

(1995, 92 min, US, Christopher Ashley) Paul Rudnick has adapted his own off-Broadway hit with this witty if slightly flawed comedy. Jeffrey (the chipper Steven Weber), a gay aspiring actor, has come to a momentous decision: In the age of AIDS, he's going to become celibate. Then he meets the devastatingly handsome Steve (Michael T. Weiss). As these two men tentatively begin a relationship, Jeffrey learns of Steve's HIV-positive status, which only complicates his fear of commitment. The success of Rudnick's play (and to a large degree the film) lies, partially, in creating a comedy centered around the subject of AIDS, and endowing it with an acerbic, even sardonic sense of humor. And when *Jeffrey* is funny (which it is most of the time), it is very, very funny. But in the filmization, certain dramatic scenes only magnify their less-than developed emotions. Patrick Stewart gloriously camps it up as Jeffrey's rich, designer friend Sterling, bringing unexpected depth to his role. Bryan Batt reprises his stage role as Sterling's PWA lover, and cameos include Sigourney Weaver, Kathy Najimy, Olympia Dukakis and a scene-stealing Nathan Lane. ★★★ $19.99

Jeffrey Dahmer — The Secret Life

(1993, 95 min, US, David R. Bowen) Gross, obscene and revolting, this low-budget bio-pic on serial killer Jeffrey Dahmer is a horribly sick film experience that sympathetically portrays the killer; it is saved only by the possibility that it might actually be an inadvertently black, black comedy. Screenwriter Carl Crew stars as Dahmer, a misunderstood man who, mistreated by his unloving parents and ignored by an insensitive government, takes his childhood fascination with cutting up dead animals, combines it with his kinky homosexual desires and proceeds to kill, mutilate and dismember at least 17 young men. Incredibly, Dahmer is the narrator, recounting his "troubles" and explaining his actions. The acting is terrible and the plodding story line only adds to the difficulty of watching Dahmer prowl gay bars, picking up men with the promise of photographing them for money, drug them and then kill them. ★ $39.99

Jennifer 8

(1992, 127 min, US, Bruce Robinson) Two good performers get wasted in this muddled thriller. Andy Garcia is a burnt-out L.A. cop who takes a job in a small town only to fall onto the trail of a serial killer. Uma Thurman is a blind schoolteacher who Garcia thinks is going to be the killer's next victim. To give away any of the leaps of logic, or amazing coincidences on which this film relies to unravel its plot, would destroy the little bits of mystery it does manage

to create. Suffice to say that you would have to be a lot more than blind not to see this movie killer coming from a mile away. ★★ $14.99

Jeremiah Johnson

(1972, 116 min, US, Sydney Pollack) Robert Redford is Johnson, the legendary mountain man and trapper who made war on the Blackfoot Indians after they murdered everything he loved. While taking some liberties with the original story (Johnson actually ate the livers of the Blackfeet he killed), the film is nevertheless an inspired and entertaining tale of a man who cannot abide modern society's rules and restrictions. Abandoning life in the city for the natural wonder of the mountains, young Johnson heads for the hills and nearly dies because of his own incompetence. After a short series of lessons from a veteran mountain man, Johnson gets the knack of life in the wild and sets out on a series of adventures until the aforementioned tragedy interrupts his idyllic life. The film is beautiful testament to the possibility of man's oneness with the natural world and an ode to the indomitable, individual spirit. It is also an uncharacteristic western in a genre which had, at the time it was released, grown tired and repetitive. ★★★ $14.99

The Jerk

(1979, 94 min, US, Carl Reiner) Steve Martin had his first starring role and his first big screen success in this very funny and incredibly silly rags-to-riches-to-rags-back-to-riches comedy. Steve plays a hapless schmoe who finds and loses (and finds again?) happiness and Bernadette Peters. ★★½ $9.99

Jerker

(1991, 90 min, US, Hugh Harrison) Robert Chesley's controversial homoerotic play about two men who, through a series of sexually charged telephone calls, begin to become friends and learn something about themselves is alternately intriguing, sexy and emotionally hard-hitting. The story begins when a young man is woken up by a stranger who wants telephone sex. He obliges, and through a series of these calls, their talks shift slowly from mere sexual games and into monologues and conversations about personal ambitions and frustrations. The alternate title is "Helping Hand – A Pornographic Elegy in Twenty Telephone Calls, Many of Them Dirty." This video features, at the conclusion, an in-depth interview with Chesley on the writing and production of his play. ★★★ $24.99

The Jerky Boys

(1995, 82 min, US, James Melkonian) Having achieved mixed commercial success in the conversion of TV sitcoms, cartoons and comic books to the silver screen, Hollywood once again sets its sights on the recording industry (after the great popularity of Cheech & Chong) and the result is this featherweight comedy featuring the debut of The Jerky Boys. Johnny Brennan and Kamal Ahmed play a pair of ne'er-do-well phone pranksters who bluff and insult their way into Mafia high society, incurring the wrath of a New York crime boss (Alan Arkin). What may have been funny on their two platinum-selling comedy albums suffers greatly from a skeletal screenplay and a paucity of

Jerry Maguire

comic inspiration. Even cameos by Tom Jones and William Hickey can't help. ★½ $19.99

Jerry Maguire

(1996, 138 min, US, Cameron Crowe) Can a heartless sports agent find redemption, true love and riches at the box office? When the agent is Jerry Maguire and played with considerable magnetism by Tom Cruise, evidently the answer was never in doubt. An appealing romantic comedy with a thing or two to say about the cutthroat industry that is modern-day sports, *Jerry Maguire* firmly reinforces Cruise's bankability and stature as one of America's foremost leading men. Though given to excessive shouting every now and then, Cruise has rarely been better as Jerry Maguire, a sports agent whose night of conscience (and wordy "mission statement" decrying his firm's greediness) casts him into the unknown waters of solo artist. With an admiring accountant (a charming Renee Zellweger) in tow, Maguire takes his one client (Oscar winner Cuba Gooding, Jr.) and attempts to go one-on-one with the big boys. Writer-director Crowe, whose *Say Anything* is a knowing romance, has created likable characters who all get to say and do things within a very romantic framework. His is a smart, lively, funny work. As Maguire's exuberant client, Gooding is sensational, bringing humor and spontaneity to what could have been a nondescript role. ★★★ $21.99

Jesse James

(1939, 105 min, US, Henry King) Exciting western focusing on the unlawful exploits of outlaws Jesse and Frank James. Tyrone Power and Henry Fonda play the brothers, and Randolph Scott and Brian Donlevy also star. Fonda would repeat the role a year later in *The Return of Frank James*. ★★★ $19.99

Jesus Christ Superstar

(1973, 103 min, US, Norman Jewison) Vibrant screen version of the Andrew Lloyd Webber-Tim Rice rock opera (which appeared on Broadway) about the last days of Jesus Christ. Jewison brings a contemporary flavor to the biblical story, which features Ted Neeley, Carl Anderson and Yvonne Elliman. ★★★ $19.99

Jesus of Montreal

(1990, 119 min, Canada, Denys Arcand) From the director of the wickedly sarcastic *Decline and Fall of the American Empire* comes this serious, intelligent and satiric update of the persecution and crucifixion of Jesus Christ. Set in present-day Montreal, a priest hires a young actor to revamp and modernize his parish's annual Passion Play. Daniel (Lothaire Bluteau), a serenely intense young man, takes his task quite seriously. With him in the lead as Christ, he and a ragtag collection of his friends present a radical and, in the Church's eyes, scandalous production which soon becomes a hit with the public. Although the story parallels the Bible's account closely, the film never sinks to mere rehashing, and offers interesting and, at times, humorous thoughts on spiritualism in the modern world, the function of art, the perils of fame and the struggle to retain one's personal integrity. (French with English subtitles) ★★★½ $19.99

Jetsons: The Movie

(1990, 81 min, US, William Hanna & Joseph Barbera) Disappointing feature-length version of the popular animated TV series. "Meet George Jetson. Jane, his wife. Their boy Elroy. Daughter Judy." Kids should enjoy it, though adults will probably be bored. ★½ $12.99

The Jewel of the Nile

(1985, 104 min, US, Lewis Teague) Entertaining sequel to *Romancing the Stone* picks up six months later after Michael Douglas and Kathleen Turner have sailed into the sunset. Douglas once again comes to Turner's rescue after she is held captive by an Arab ruler. Lots of laughs and action and Danny DeVito, as well. ★★½ $14.99

Jezebel

(1938, 103 min, US, William Wyler) Though many believe Bette Davis won her first Oscar (for *Dangerous*) as a consolation prize, there's no doubt whatsoever that she deserved her second one for *Jezebel*. Davis is brilliant as a Southern belle whose flirtations and fickleness drive away boyfriend Henry Fonda; she is then forced to come to terms with her own faults when he returns with a new wife. The ballroom sequence is especially noteworthy. Fay Bainter also won an Oscar as Davis' aunt. ★★★½ $19.99

Jesus Christ Superstar

JFK

(1991, 189 min, US, Oliver Stone) No stranger to controversy, Stone serves up a volatile mix of politics and conspiracy. Technically brilliant and impressively acted, Stone's triumphant speculative drama is based on New Orleans District Attorney Jim Garrison's experience in bringing charges — the only ones ever leveled against any individual — for the murder of John F. Kennedy. Fiercely debated, the film suggests that Lee Harvey Oswald was merely a patsy for other criminally responsible organizations, including government agencies. Whether or not you believe Stone's version of that fateful day's events, there's no denying *JFK* is a labor of love for the director, and he has crafted a fascinating and often spellbinding dissertation. Kevin Costner is well-cast as the impassioned D.A., giving what may be his finest dramatic performance to date. Among a first-rate supporting cast, Tommy Lee Jones, Kevin Bacon, Gary Oldman and particularly Donald Sutherland are impressive. ★★★★ $24.99

The Jigsaw Man

(1984, 91 min, GB, Terence Young) The delicious chemistry and edge-of-your seat excitement which arose out of the pairing of Laurence Olivier and Michael Caine in *Sleuth* is unfortunately not evident in this effort which co-stars Susan George and Robert Powell. Caine plays an ex-British Secret Service agent who defects to Russia, submits to extensive plastic surgery, and comes back to England for one final mission. Predictable and, sadly, not very exciting. ★★ $14.99

The Jim Bailey Experience

(1990, 54 min, US, Compiled by Stephen Campbell & Rick Flynn) Culled primarily from old TV clips (including an appearance on "The Lucy Show"), this fluffy promotional documentary focuses on actor-illusionist Jim Bailey, arguably the most well-known of the female impersonators/impressionists today. Included are segments from his acts, whose subjects include Barbra Streisand, Phyllis Diller, Peggy Lee, Judy Garland and, in an effort to stay current, Madonna. ★★½ $39.99

Jimmy Hollywood

(1994, 110 min, US, Barry Levinson) You can't judge a video by its cover or even its theatrical run, since director Levinson reedited this film for home video viewing. The result is an interesting though not very engaging comedy-drama about an actor-wannabe (Joe Pesci) who becomes a vigilante after his girlfriend is mugged on the mean streets of Hollywood. On the heels of films such as *The Chase* and *Serial Mom*, the film tries to examine the power of celebrity criminals, as Pesci's Jimmy Hollywood is partially inspired by the media coverage of his deeds. The surprise of the film is Christian Slater's quirky, low-key performance as Pesci's friend (and henchman) who has lost (and continues to lose) various parts of his memory. ★★½ $19.99

Jingle All the Way

(1996, 85 min, US, Brian Levant) If it's holiday cheer you're looking for, you'll have to look elsewhere, for *Jingle All the Way* gets down and dirty. Some of the time, that is — for it's

also rather sappy. But when it's funny, it's cynically so; producing the kind of nasty laughs and sight gags usually associated with executive producer Chris Columbus (director of the *Home Alone* movies). Its high-concept premise works for awhile: Arnold Schwarzenegger is a workaholic father who forgets to buy his son's Christmas present, a popular action figure. He sets out on Christmas Eve for the impossible task of finding one. This scenario, and a rivalry with fellow dad Sinbad on a similar mission, sets in motion some very funny comedy, where everyone takes a pratfall or suffers some physical humiliation. But the film soon runs out of steam — and ideas — and turns into a feel-good free-for-all. With jokes about postal workers, mail bombs, pedophilia, consumerism and crooked Santas, it couldn't have possibly kept pace and entertained the masses. ★★

Jinxed

(1983, 103 min, US, Don Siegel) This muddled black comedy about blackmail, blackjack and murder stars Bette Midler, in her pre-Touchstone days, as a Las Vegas singer and Ken Wahl as a gambler who hooks up with her. Rip Torn also stars as a dealer, he the "jinxed" of the title. This film is known more for the conflicts on the set than for what is presented on the screen. ★★ $9.99

Jo Jo Dancer, Your Life Is Calling

(1986, 97 min, US, Richard Pryor) Pryor wrote, directed and stars in this autobiographical story of the rise and fall of a talented black comedian, whose drug habit nearly kills him. Though Pryor commendably opens up some deep wounds, and the comic's early years are well captured, much of the film suffers from a lack of energy and soul. ★★ $9.99

Joan of Arc

(1948, 100 min, US, Victor Fleming) Ingrid Bergman gives a passionate performance as the peasant girl who led the French armies to victory. Based on the Maxwell Anderson play. Also starring Jose Ferrer (an Oscar nominee). ★★½ $19.99

Joan of Paris

(1942, 91 min, US, Robert Stevenson) Extraordinary "B" WWII drama with Michelle Morgan as a young Parisian woman who sacrifices herself so that a group of British pilots can escape the Gestapo in Occupied France. With Paul Henreid and Alan Ladd. ★★★½ $19.99

Jock Peterson

(1974, 97 min, Australia, Tim Burstall) Jack Thompson stars as an electrician who quits his job and enrolls in college. His education is not limited to books, however, as he soon becomes embroiled in an affair with his English professor's wife (Wendy Hughes). An amiable tale with unpredictable appeal, bolstered by Hughes' winning performance. ★★½

Joe

(1970, 90 min, US, John G. Avildsen) Hard-hitting though dated generation gap drama with Peter Boyle giving a sensational performance as a bigoted New York construction worker (hard hat) whose prejudice leads to tragedy. Susan Sarandon made her debut as his daughter, who becomes involved with a group of "hippies." ★★★ $14.99

Joe Versus the Volcano

(1990, 99 min, US, John Patrick Shanley) Tom Hanks plays Joe, a grim factory worker who learns he is terminally ill. When a tycoon learns of his condition, Joe is given a chance to live like a king for six weeks in exchange for his services as a human sacrifice to a live volcano. (It sounds crazy, but plotwise it actually makes sense.). En route, he takes up with the tycoon's two daughters (both played exceedingly well by Meg Ryan), and finds true love, adventure and a complete luggage set. The first half of the film is occasionally inspired, but the last half is as lost as its hero, adrift at sea with no direction in mind. ★★½ $9.99

Joe's Apartment

(1996, 90 min, US, John Payson) With the exception of *Shinbone Alley*, movies starring singing and dancing cockroaches are rare birds indeed. Unfortunately, *Joe's Apartment* — which had the chance to be the *Citizen Kane* of its genre — takes its unusual and potentially camp classic premise and squanders it. Based on an MTV-produced short film, *Joe's Apartment* casts Jerry O'Connell as Joe, a country bumpkin newly arrived in the big city. It turns out his New York apartment is overrun by roaches. Only these aren't ordinary bugs — these sing, dance, crack jokes, give romantic advice and party on. Obviously, the film's best moments feature the computer-animated roaches doing their thing — and a lot of it is both sick and funny. But they only occupy a third of the film. It's the human element which drags the film to a halt. The filmmakers sharpened their focus on the *Cuca Blattodea* and forgot to flesh out the *Homo Sapiens*. Maybe next time they should feature live roaches and animate everyone else. ★★ $14.99

Joe's Bed-Stuy Barbershop

(1982, 60 min, US, Spike Lee) Spike Lee was still a student at NYU when he made this satirical, slice-of-life tale of bookmaking, murder and trying to make it big; all set at a corner barbershop in the Bed-Stuy section of Brooklyn. ★★★

Joe's Apartment

Joey Breaker

(1993, 92 min, US, Stephen Starr) Because of its show business setting, comparisons to *The Player* are inevitable. But while Robert Altman's film is about how those possessing power can get away with murder, *Joey Breaker* is about how there is more to life than the art of the deal. Joey is a fast-talking New York talent agent whose pace is slowed down after he meets a Jamaican waitress played by Cedella Marley (Bob's daughter). All of the film's characters feel as though they were picked up off a SoHo street corner: a hip-hop comedian, a man infected with AIDS, interracial couples, gay lovers; and the film treats them as the everyday people they are. Richard Edson (*Do the Right Thing*) is charismatic and compelling as Breaker, and with his flattened out nose and crooked smile, he proves that you don't have to have movie-star perfect looks to play a romantic lead effectively. *Joey Breaker* is an exuberant and invigorating comedy which dances happily to a reggae beat. ★★★½ $92.99

John & Yoko — The Bed-In

(1970, 72 min, GB, John Lennon & Yoko Ono) Refused an entry visa to the United States in 1969 due to their anti-Vietnam War stance, John Lennon and Yoko Ono decided to travel to Montreal's Queen Elizabeth Hotel and, on the doorstep of America and within easy earshot of the powerful U.S. media, they began, as they had earlier in Amsterdam, a much-publicized bed-in. Extolling a plea for world peace and presented in a way "expending the least energy to maximum effect," the couple, in their pajamas, entertained the press, conducted interviews and engaged in political discussions with such divergent celebrities as Al Capp, Tommy Smothers and Timothy Leary. The film culminates with a rousing bedroom recording of "Give Peace a Chance." What made the admittedly commercial stunt successful was the self-proclaimed, "perverted pop star" Lennon's irreverent, witty and humanistic approach to a serious plea. ★★½ $24.99

Johnny Be Good

(1988, 84 min, US, Bud Smith) Robert Downey, Jr., once again, is the saving grace in an otherwise awful comedy, this one about high school jock Anthony Michael Hall being wooed by various colleges. ★ $19.99

Johnny Belinda

(1948, 103 min, US, Jean Negulesco) Jane Wyman won an Oscar for her sensitive performance as a deaf-mute woman who is taught to communicate by a compassionate doctor (Lew Ayres). Also with Charles Bickford and Agnes Moorehead. ★★★½ $19.99

Johnny Eager

(1941, 107 min, US, Mervyn Taylor) Though Robert Taylor and a young Lana Turner are its stars, it's the Oscar-winning performance of Van Heflin which elevates this standard but glossy underworld melodrama. Taylor plays a heel of a petty crime boss who becomes involved with D.A.'s daughter Turner. It's a contrivance of the plot that we're expected to believe Turner as a sociology student (and a well-dolled

one at that) who blindly and knowingly ignores Taylor's life of crime all for a pretty face. Taking advantage of the only well-crafted role in the film, Heflin revels as Taylor's alcoholic, scholarly, self-pitying friend. It's a tender yet wrenching performance. ★★ $19.99

Johnny Got His Gun

(1971, 111 min, US, Dalton Trumbo) Dalton Trumbo did a disservice to his classic anti-war novel with this sometimes moving but ultimately sluggish adaptation. Timothy Bottoms is the severely disabled soldier. ★★½

Johnny Guitar

(1954, 110 min, US, Nicholas Ray) A true original from Ray, this is the story of a cowboy who carries a guitar instead of a pistol and believes that "...when you boil it all down, all a man needs is a good smoke and a cup of coffee." Joan Crawford plays a saloon keeper who enlists Johnny's aid, and Mercedes McCambridge is incomparable as the local crusader who simply cannot rest until she sees them all hang. Insightful and intoxicating, the film has been cited as a source of inspiration by such contemporaries as Wim Wenders and Jim Jarmusch. ★★★½ $14.99

Johnny Handsome

(1989, 95 min, US, Walter Hill) Mickey Rourke stars in this stylish, gritty thriller as a petty thief — whose facial disfiguration has given him the unkindly nickname of "Johnny Handsome" — who is double-crossed by fellow gang members during a robbery. In prison, he undergoes cosmetic surgery, and with a new face and a release from jail, sets out to get revenge. Among the film's supporting cast, Ellen Barkin and Lance Henriksen as Rourke's vicious ex-mates, Morgan Freeman as a cop not fooled by a pretty face and Forest Whitaker as the doctor who performs the surgery, are all first-rate. ★★★ $14.99

Johnny Mnemonic

(1995, 98 min, US, Robert Longo) It's a meeting of '90s chic and aesthetic: visual artist Robert Longo and cyberpunk William Gibson team on the film adaptation of the latter's tech-nothriller short story. But somewhere, somehow, some computer-generated wires got mighty crossed. Keanu Reeves stars as the title character, a high-tech courier working in a bleak future blatantly reminiscent of *Blade Runner*'s Los Angeles. With a computer-friendly head full of chips and wires, Johnny accepts one final assignment to transport some delicate information. But the ruthless Yakuza are on his trail, and they're after both the data and his head. Beyond the intriguing premise, *Johnny Mnemonic* offers little. It's set at a lethargic pace, the action scenes are boring, the actors look distracted, and the story rambles from one pointless predicament to another. As a hired killer, Dolph Lundgren overshadows the rest of the cast — and that about says it all. ★ $19.99

Johnny 100 Pesos

(1993, 95 min, Spain, Gustavo Graef-Marino) A mildly diverting suspense thriller which is based on a true incident. Teenager Johnny Garcia (Armando Araiza) takes part in his first armed robbery with four ex-cons. The plan goes sour, and the five are forced to take hostages. The police are called in, they surround the place, and a media circus unfolds. The film starts off well, with some quirky details and amusing satire. But it soon becomes predicatable and rather unexciting. Johnny is uninteresting, and his character rarely goes beyond the "young thug" stage. With little more insight than a newspaper headline, *Johnny 100 Pesos* appears to have stayed close to the actual events, which does not work in its favor. (Spanish with English subtitles) ★★ $89.99

Johnny Stecchino

Johnny Stecchino

(1991, 105 min, Italy, Roberto Begnini) This amiable farce about a bumbling schoolbus driver who is mistaken for a Mafia leader enjoyed at one time the distinction of being the highest-grossing film in Italian history. Director, co-writer and star Begnini (best known for his work in *Down by Law* and *Night on Earth*) is the centerpiece of the hilarious tale in which the hopelessly inept Dante (Begnini) is lured to Palermo by the wife of notorious mobster Johnny Stecchino (Begnini again) to be used as his double. Of course, Dante is completely unaware of the deception, which leads him into a hilarious series of misadventures with rival gang members and the police. As an actor, Begnini's comic schtick is almost flawless, while as a director his timing is occasionally suspect. Still, the humor builds throughout reaching a fever pitch by film's end and leaving those in need of good comedy well sated. (Italian with English subtitles) ★★★ $19.99

Johnny Suede

(1991, 95 min, US, Tom DiCillo) A preternaturally coifed Brad Pitt stars in this meandering oddity about a down-and-out, would-be rocker set in Manhattan's lower depths. First-time director DiCillo's tale of post-punk nihilism finds its roots in Susan Seidelman's 1982 *Smithereens* as it follows the insufferably image-conscious Johnny Suede (pre-stardom Brad Pitt) in his vain attempts at relationship, putting together a Rockabilly band and pulling off an armed robbery. These proceedings are precipitated when a pair of suede shoes falls from the sky and into his life thereby providing him the "magical" keys to some unknown subcultural kingdom until he winds up in a relationship with the down-to-earth Yvonne, who challenges all of his vain instincts. Pitt's

narcoleptic portrayal of the title character provides most of the amusement in an otherwise static affair as he bums his way around Manhattan's lonely dock district "a legend in his own mind, who could have been a contender." Also with Tina Louise and rocker Nick Cave. ★★½ $89.99

johns

(1997, 97 min, US, Scott Silver) Lukas Haas and David Arquette star as two Santa Monica Boulevard street hustlers in this lyrical, sobering tale of self-respect and friendship amidst L.A.'s seedy underworld of male prostitution. Reminiscent of both *Midnight Cowboy* and *My Own Private Idaho*, johns is set on Christmas Eve where 20-year-old John (Arquette) has anxiously anticipated spending the holiday (and his birthday) in a posh hotel. His dream is quashed, however, when his lucky sneakers and the money in them are stolen. Determined to raise the cash, he solicits the help of his pal Donner (Haas), a fellow hustler who is quietly in love with John. Harsh realism merges with dreamy romanticism and quirky humor in this compelling tragi-drama that features standout performances from the two leads. Haas is affecting as the delicate, doe-eyed gay teen, and Arquette is equally good as the nominally straight John. Elliott Gould is terrific in a cameo as a lustful former client. ★★★ $102.99

A Joke of Destiny

(1984, 105 min, Italy, Lina Wertmüller) Wertmüller's underrated political satire follows the almost surreal situation of an Italian official's attempts to release a cabinet minister who becomes trapped in his new computerized car. Some really funny moments highlight this subversive little gem. (Italian with English subtitles) ★★★

The Jolson Story

(1946, 128 min, US, Alfred E. Green) Classic '40s musical of legendary singer Al Jolson, with Larry Parks giving a star-making performance as the showman. Songs (dubbed by Jolson himself) include "Swanee," "April Showers" and "Mammy." One of the biggest hits of the decade. Followed by *Jolson Sings Again*. ★★★ $19.99

Jonah Who Will Be 25 in the Year 2000

(1976, 110 min, Switzerland, Alain Tanner) Before *The Return of the Secaucus Seven*, *The Big Chill* or even "thirtysomething," there was Tanner's fascinating political comedy which follows a disparate group of post-May '68 "Coke/Marxists" who, each in their own individualistic fashion, must come to grips with a changing political and social scene brought on by the more conservative period of the '70s. The characters, among them a quiet, subversive schoolteacher, a supermarket cashier with a soft spot for pensioners and a wildly opinionated farm hand, all must begin making a living but all the while trying to retain their political commitments in an increasingly repressive environment. The ensemble actors, which include Miou-Miou, Jean-Luc Bideau and Myriam Boyer, are uniformly excellent, and the dialogue is quick, fascinating and challenging. A remarkably relevant film for any

political climate. (French with English subtitles) ★★★★ $29.99

Joseph Andrews

(1976, 104 min, GB, Tony Richardson) Even if this comedy had been great, which it isn't, director Richardson would have been hard pressed to match the achievements of his earlier excursion into the novels of Henry Fielding (*Tom Jones*). Here, Peter Firth plays a lowly functionary who rejects the advances of the voluptuous Lady Booby (Ann-Margret) in favor of a lowly peasant girl. ★★ $49.99

Joseph Conrad's The Secret Agent

(1996, 94 min, GB, Christopher Hampton) By both its title and opening proclaimer suggesting that 1880s London was a haven for foreign spies, *Joseph Conrad's The Secret Agent* immediately brings to mind images of high-tension espionage and back-alley intrigue. But this intellectual discourse on politics and morality (or the lack of) never really satisfies with its slow pacing and confusing narrative. Bob Hoskins plays a London shopkeeper and part-time spy for the Russians. When he is ordered to bomb Greenwich Park, it ends in tragedy; this leads to a series of escalating, out-of-control events. Director Hampton creates an effectively enigmatic London, where things aren't always as they appear and uncertainty grips all the players. But art direction alone can't substitute for story, and the sometimes affecting familial drama at the core of a more somber spy tale has difficulty resonating. Philip Glass has written an extraordinary score, and an uncredited Robin Williams gives the film's best performance as the only true anarchist of the bunch. Conrad's story was the basis for Alfred Hitchcock's far superior 1936 thriller *Sabotage*. ★★ $99.99

Josepha

(1982, 103 min, France, Christopher Frank) Set amid the turbulence of the theatre, director and author Frank's intimate psychological drama stars Claude Brasseur and Miou-Miou as a thespian couple whose marital roles are ones they can't quite master. Following Brasseur's affair with another woman, their union begins a slow and painful disintegration as they are forced to enact a bitter resolution. A glistening portrait of personal triumph, sacrifice and determination that manages both humor and poignancy. (Dubbed) ★★★

The Josephine Baker Story

(1991, 120 min, US, Brian Gibson) Lynn Whitfield excels in her award-winning performance as the legendary Josephine Baker. The story focuses on the singer's rise to stardom in Paris, her ongoing struggles with racism in America, and two affairs: one with an Italian count, played by Ruben Blades, and the other with orchestra leader Jo Bouillon (David Dukes). Also with Louis Gossett, Jr. and Craig T. Nelson as Walter Winchell. ★★★ $14.99

Jour de Fête

(1949, 70 min, France, Jacques Tati) Tati, France's answer to Chaplin, stars in his first directorial effort. The story concerns the bungling adventures of a small town mailman who, after hearing about the efficiency of the

The Joy Luck Club

American Postal Service, decides that it is time to do the same. His manic new delivery system, set out to modernize, brings about the opposite result. Great fun in this vintage Tati. (French with English subtitles) ★★★½ $29.99

Le Jour se Lève

(1939, 85 min, France, Marcel Carné) From the makers of *Children of Paradise* comes this model of French poetic realism. Jean Gabin is a criminal trapped in an attic. With the police closing in, he flashes back on the events that drove him to commit murder. A thoughtful, intelligent film. (French with English subtitles) ★★★½

The Journey of August King

(1995, 91 min, US, John Duigan) August King (Jason Patric) is a widowed farmer living in North Carolina's Appalachian Mountains in the early 19th century. Grieving over the death of his wife, King lives a lonely, mundane existence devoid of human contact or emotion. As this compelling, leisurely paced film recounts a three-day journey home, August regains his humanity in a humane though illegal act of moral rightness. Thandee Newton, who played a similar role in *Jefferson in Paris*, is Annalees, a runaway slave escaping the brutality of her father/master (Larry Drake). Knowing that death possibly awaits her, King hides Annalees in his wagon as half the county searches for her (with a price on her head). As the journey becomes more perilous, the indifferent King becomes more adamant about aiding the young woman in her attempt to head north and to freedom. Patric gives a beautifully understated performance which takes time to grow on the viewer; and as his character blooms, so does this quietly powerful film. Newton is first-rate in bringing to Annalees unfailing determination and a wrenching vulnerability. ★★★ $19.99

Journey of Hope

(1990, 110 min, Switzerland, Xavier Koller) Winner of the 1990 Academy Award for Best Foreign-Language Film, *Journey of Hope* is an exquisitely photographed, heartbreakingly tragic yet surprisingly uninvolving tale about a Kurdish family residing in a small mountain village in southeastern Turkey. Unable to provide his family with a decent life, the father decides to uproot the entire clan and journey to Switzerland to join a relative and live in "paradise." Seemingly gleaned from today's headlines, the film bogs down in endless scenes involving harrowing escapes from border patrols and snowbound mountain crossings. While certainly well-meaning, the Academy must have been influenced by the timing of the Gulf War to have chosen this piece over such vastly superior works as Michael Verhoeven's *The Nasty Girl* and Zhang Yimou's *Ju Dou*. (In Kurdish, Turkish, German and Italian with English subtitles) ★★½ $19.99

The Journey of Natty Gann

(1985, 101 min, US, Jeremy Paul Kagan) Fine (if underrated) family film about the adventures of a teenaged girl who travels cross-country during the Depression in search of her father. Good cast includes Meredith Salenger, John Cusack, Lainie Kazan, Barry Miller and Scatman Crothers. ★★★ $9.99

Journey to the Center of the Earth

(1959, 132 min, US, Henry Levin) Entertaining (and old-fashioned) fantasy based on the Jules Verne novel. James Mason leads a group of scientists to the Earth's core, where they discover a prehistoric world. ★★★ $14.99

Joy House (Les Felins)

(1964, 98 min, France, René Clément) A macabre suspense story about the strange happenings in a Riviera villa operated by two American cousins (Jane Fonda and Lola Albright). The women's offer of refuge to the on-the-run Alain Delon seals his fate and slowly turns this "safe house" into an oppressive prison. An interesting, but minor, Clément work. (English language version) ★★

The Joy Luck Club

(1993, 135 min, US, Wayne Wang) Director Wang's absorbing adaptation of the Amy Tan novel is a decidedly emotional affair. Faithfully following Tan's novel, with only a few omissions and changes, the film tells the separate tales of four Chinese-American women and their American-born daughters. The mothers' sagas are the foundation of the film as they relate the misogynist nature of traditional Chinese society and the harrowing journeys which ultimately led them to America. By comparison, the daughters' yuppie, thirtysomething problems may seem meager, but the real aim of both Tan's book and Wang's movie is to examine mothers and daughters with hugely disparate upbringings as they discover common ground. The result is deeply moving and highly effective. All of the performances from the ensemble crew are good, especially Ming-Na Wen as the Tan alter ego. ★★★½ $9.99

Joy of Living

(1938, 90 min, US, Tay Garnett) Captivating screwball musical comedy with the ever-delightful Irene Dunne as a famous singer being romanced by playboy Douglas Fairbanks, Jr. Also starring are Lucille Ball, Alice Brady and Guy Kibbee. (Though it's released on the "Lucy Signature" Collection, Lucy really has a supporting role.) ★★★ $19.99

The Joyless Street

(1925, 96 min, Germany, G.W. Pabst) Famous as the film that brought Greta Garbo to international fame, this grimly realistic depiction of the contrasting social conditions in postwar, hyper-inflationary Vienna is also noted for its innovative use of editing and camera work. Pabst films with an unflinching eye to this story about the hunger, destitution and misery of a deteriorating middle class while also showing the moral excesses of the rich. A striking landmark in social realism. Restored with material found in film vaults in Europe, this edition is closer to the original than any version available in the U.S. until now. (Silent) ★★★½ $29.99

Ju Dou

(1990, 93 min, China, Zhang Yimou) Filmed in striking primary colors, this folktale and political allegory is an erotic tale of tangled passions between two lovers and the bitter consequences of their forbidden love. Set in a small village in 1920s China, a rich and tyrannical middle-aged man operates a cloth dye works. He has just recently married his third wife, Ju Dou, a young beauty who, like the others before her, is brutalized and degraded by her impotent husband. She soon falls in love with her husband's hardworking but simple nephew. Their illicit affair and illegitimate child soon has the town ablaze with gossip; especially after an accident leaves her husband paralyzed, allowing the couple to take over the factory, silence her incensed husband and brazenly display their affair. But fate is not kind to the obsessed lovers in this dramatic tale of oppression, desire and vengeance. (Chinese with English subtitles) ★★★½ $19.99

Juarez

(1939, 132 min, US, William Dieterle) Engrossing, well-produced biography (Hollywood style) of Mexican revolutionary leader Juarez, smartly played by Paul Muni. With Bette Davis, Brian Aherne, John Garfield, and a smashing turn by Claude Rains as Napoleon III. ★★★ $19.99

Jubilee

(1984, 103 min, GB, Derek Jarman) Jarman's wildly inventive, highly personal punk fantasy of a post-apocalyptic future of a dying England takes off where *A Clockwork Orange* ended. The Queen is dead, Buckingham Palace is a recording studio and the police have it off with each other when they're not breaking the heads of young men. In a nod to *Civilization*, Queen Elizabeth I is transported by her astrologer to the close of the 20th century to witness the disintegration of order and the explosion of destruction and chaos. The cast of wasted, punked-out characters include a passively receptive and sexually mesmeric Adam Ant, Little Nell (of *Rocky Horror Picture Show*), and a strong-willed Toyah Wilcox. A punk rock version of "Rule Britannia" is a musical highlight, with additional music by Adam and the Ants, Siouxie and the Banshees, and Brian Eno. A fascinating culture shock look at a pre-Thatcherized England. ★★★ $24.99

Jude

(1996, 123 min, GB, Michael Winterbottom) A warning to those looking for happy tales of love among Britain's upper classes in the 19th century, à la Jane Austen: This somber and austere adaptation of Thomas Hardy's "Jude the Obscure" is nothing less than Austen's antidote. Hardy, the son of a stonemason, provides a harrowing vision of an England on the verge of industrial revolution and still mired in an unjust class system. Clearly somewhat autobiographical, the story follows Jude (superbly played by Christopher Eccleston), an eternally optimistic and socially daring young stonemason who breaks class taboo by pursuing a university education. He further pushes the bounds of societal tolerance when he takes up with his atheist schoolteacher cousin (Kate Winslet), despite his being married. The film's first third is a jumble of vignettes as it appears the filmmakers tried to hurry through a mountain of plot points, and character development suffers as a result. The film's last half provides a much more intricate peek at its protagonists and the social mores of the day. And there are some truly horrifying plot twists near the end not for the faint of heart. This tragic romantic drama is both a thought-provoking history lesson and gloomy period piece. ★★½ $99.99

Judex

(1963, 100 min, France, Georges Franju) A faithful remake of an early French serial which follows the mysterious adventures of the black-cloaked hero/avenger, Judex (The Judge), as he rights wrongs, battles an evil banker and brings the guilty to justice. (French with English subtitles) ★★½

The Judge and the Assassin

(1976, 125 min, France, Bertrand Tavernier) This provocative psychological drama, set in 1890s France, follows the lives of two dissimilar men: Judge Rousseau, a respected magistrate from the ruling elite; and a demented ex-army sergeant who roams the country-side indiscriminately raping and killing young women and children. Their lives cross when the crazed killer is arrested and the judge embarks on a frenzied pursuit to prove that the man is sane and guilty. Philippe Noiret is perfect as the

hell-bent moralizer whose actions, all in the name of justice, are equally repellant as that of the sick killer. Isabelle Huppert makes one of her earliest appearances as the poor mistress of the judge who slowly begins to see through his "virtuous" actions. (French with English subtitles) ★★★½ $79.99

Judge Dredd

(1995, 91 min, US, Danny Cannon) Based on the popular British comic book series, *Judge Dredd* is a visually stunning though empty-headed visceral ride into a bleak future. Sylvester Stallone finds himself in similar territory as his entertaining *Demolition Man* as a good guy who's framed and must battle a wicked villain in a futuristic society. Whereas *Man* is lots of fun thanks to Wesley Snipes' scene-stealing and a good amount of comedy, this trek is a muddled array of action scenes, posturing (by Stallone), lethargic pacing and humorless bits. But the film does exhibit superior production design, and the effects are quite startling as rocket-powered skijets roam a *Blade Runner*-influenced city sky. Stallone is nothing more than a parody of himself. Max von Sydow is on hand to try to lend a bit of dignity, Armand Assante hams it up as the heavy, and Rob Schneider's comic relief — while funny at first — becomes tiresome. (Available letterboxed and pan & scan) ★★½ $14.99

Judgment

(1990, 89 min, US, Tom Topor) The sexual abuse of minors by priests is the delicate issue handled quite effectively in this serious and focused HBO drama. Keith Carradine and Blyth Danner star as devout Catholics whose faith in both the law and the Church are shattered when their son reveals that he has been sexually abused by a priest (David Strathairn). Along with other parents in the parish, they begin a persistent but painful campaign to remove him and have him prosecuted as a sex offender. The challenges they face include a reluctant legal system and a secretive Church hierarchy bent on denial and self-preservation. An all-too-true and sad story which is given expert handling here, with all of the personalities treated fairly — even the perpetrator is seen as a victim. ★★★ $89.99

Judgment at Nuremberg

(1961, 178 min, US, Stanley Kramer) Hailed by critics and nominated for a car-load of Oscars, Kramer's massive epic on the atrocities committed by the Nazi Third Reich of WWII holds up surprisingly well. A chronicle of the famous Nuremberg trials of war crimes by Nazi officers, the film boasts some terrific performances, namely Maximilian Schell in an Oscar-winning performance as the German defense attorney. Though unneccesarily overlong (some subplots involving extraneous characters, while certainly historically vital, bog down the film at times), the actual "trials," featuring Spencer Tracy as the American judge presiding over the hearings, are mesmerizing. Also featured are Burt Lancaster, Richard Widmark, Marlene Dietrich, Judy Garland and Montgomery Clift. (Available letterboxed and pan & scan) ★★★★ $24.99

Judgment in Berlin

(1988, 92 min, US, Leo Penn) An East German couple hijacks an airliner with a toy gun to defect to the West in this pre-*glasnost* thriller. Martin Sheen stars as the American judge called in to preside over the court case. The compelling scenario is sometimes short-changed dramatically, but Sheen offers a strong performance, and Sean Penn is terrific in a cameo as a witness. ★★½ $19.99

Judgment Night

(1993, 110 min, US, Stephen Hopkins) Emilio Estevez and Cuba Gooding, Jr. star in this luke-warm action thriller. Four clean-cut suburbanites decide to venture into the city for an evening of beer drinking, swearing and a boxing match. Quicker than you can say *Grand Canyon*, they find themselves lost in the bad part of town. While trying to find their way home, the boys wreck their vehicle and become involuntary witnesses to a drug hit, spending the rest of the evening being hunted by a wise-cracking psychotic killer (Denis Leary). Cliché-ridden dreck with a script so horrible it repeats on you like a bad meal. ★½ $12.99

Juice

(1992, 95 min, US, Ernest R. Dickerson) The directorial debut of Spike Lee's longtime cinematographer, Ernest R. Dickerson, is a moving drama about power, respect and loyalty on the streets of Harlem. The story, which follows the lives of four friends, each with a different set of priorities, is somewhat like a rehashed *Cooley High* for about the first 40 minutes. But it then changes abruptly and becomes an intense examination of the struggle for survival in a decaying urban structure created by an unsympathetic and unaware society. ★★★ $14.99

Jules and Jim

(1962, 110 min, France, François Truffaut) One of the most beautifully lyrical works in the history of the French cinema, Truffaut's classic saga of an ill-fated ménage à trois captures the sweet melancholia of love's ebb and flow. Jeanne Moreau gives a performance of stunning grace and power as the tempestuous Catherine, the volatile apex of the love triangle. Oskar Werner and Henri Serre star as the two close friends who succumb to Catherine's charms. (French with English subtitles) ★★★★ $29.99

Julia

(1977, 118 min, UA, Fred Zinnemann) From director Zinnemann, a name long associated with the highest-quality filmmaking (*From Here to Eternity, High Noon, A Man for All Seasons*), comes this sterling adaptation of author Lillian Hellman's memoir, "Pentimento." Vanessa Redgrave plays the title role of the WWII Resistance fighter whose friendship involves Hellman (magnificently played by Jane Fonda) in danger and intrigue. Also starring Jason Robards as Dashiell Hammett, Maximilian Schell, Hal Holbrook and (if you look quick) Meryl Streep in her debut. Oscars went to Robards, Redgrave and screenwriter Alvin Sargent. ★★★★ $19.99

Julia and Julia

(1988, 98 min, US, Peter Del Monte) Set in Italy, this moody, interesting but not quite successful tale is about a woman seemingly losing her grip on reality. Kathleen Turner is the heroine who is apparently living out two different existences: one in a happy marriage with Gabriel Byrne and the other involved in a dangerous love affair with a jealous boyfriend, played by Sting. ★★½ $19.99

Julia Has Two Lovers

(1991, 87 min, US, Bashar Shbib) Daphna Kastner co-wrote and stars in this offbeat, erotically charged comedy about a woman on the verge of a convenient marriage to her dull, old-fashioned fiancé (David Charles), who is given food for thought via a day-long phone conversation with an amorous wrong number (David Duchovny). ★★ $14.99

Juliet of the Spirits

(1965, 142 min, Italy, Federico Fellini) A lavishly colorful baroque fantasy with Giulietta Masina as a middle-aged woman haunted by hallucinations from her past and subconscious. In an effort to prevent her world from crumbling, she confronts these spectres and then is freed from the fantasies that have imprisoned her throughout life. A richly symbolic work, plunging into the depths of the human psyche. (Italian with English subtitles) ★★★½ $29.99

Julius Caesar

(1953, 120 min, US, Joseph L. Mankiewicz) Classic translation of the Shakespeare play, with an astonishing cast including Marlon Brando as Marc Antony, James Mason as Brutus, John Gielgud, Louis Calhern, Edmond O'Brien, Greer Garson and Deborah Kerr. ★★★½ $19.99

Julius Caesar

(1970, 117 min, US, Stuart Burge) After parting the Red Sea and proving himself rather adept at chariot racing, Charlton Heston tackles the classics with surprisingly satisfactory results. Good performances highlight this version of Shakespeare's classic, also with Jason Robards, John Gielgud, Diana Rigg, Richard Johnson, Richard Chamberlain and Robert Vaughn. (Though the 1953 version is still the definitive production.) ★★★ $19.99

Jumanji

(1995, 104 min, US, Joe Johnston) Featuring computer graphics special effects of rampaging animals terrorizing its cast, which includes two precocious children, *Jumanji* is a *Jurassic Park*-inspired fantasy which is heavy on the F/X, midway on the ingenuity, and light on the execution. A magical board game, *Jumanji* takes its young players and places them in the center of a jungle adventure, which usually manifests itself in the playing area of its participants. When an adolescent boy disappears into the game, he returns 25 years later (as Robin Williams) when two orphaned children begin play. Immediately, the three of them are thrust into danger when jungle animals materialize and begin to destroy their hometown; they set out to return the animals back to the game. When not relying too heavily on its many F/X creations, the film has a spirited playfulness and a rather engaging cast. However, *Jumanji* falters when it allows the

effects to take center stage at the expense of its human players. Certain scenes may frighten very young ones, but it should entertain most children. ★★½ $22.99

Jumpin' at the Boneyard

(1992, 107 min, US, Jeff Stanzler) Another in the early '90s string of lower-budget urban dramas, this film stands out as one of the best efforts. Two brothers (outstandingly played by Tim Roth and Alexis Arquette) come together after several years apart. One is a drug addict, the other a divorcé. The older one (Roth) tries to get his brother off of drugs by taking him back to their old neighborhood, the Bronx. Not only has the neighborhood changed, but so have they. They relive old memories and try to deal with their own demons. It's a gritty, no-nonsense portrayal, highlighted by realistic dialogue and intense acting. Danitra Vance and Samuel L. Jackson are among the excellent actors in the supporting cast. ★★★½ $94.99

Jumpin' Jack Flash

(1986, 100 min, US, Penny Marshall) Marshall's directorial debut is an alternately amusing spy comedy with Whoopi Goldberg as a computer operator who comes to the aid of a British agent held prisoner behind the Iron Curtain. Though Marshall was much more successful with her next film, *Big*, this is nevertheless an enjoyable piece of fluff thanks mostly to Goldberg's comic antics. ★★½ $14.99

June Bride

(1948, 97 min, US, Bretaigne Windust) Bette Davis gets to show off her comedic skills in this lively battle-of-the-sexes romantic comedy. Davis plays a magazine editor who is accompanied by ex-lover and writer Robert Montgomery to cover a wedding at an Indiana small town. Montgomery, always at home with a glib remark, and Davis make for a most enjoyable team. ★★★ $19.99

June Night

(1938, 90 min, Sweden, Per Lindberg) Ingrid Bergman plays a promiscuous small town girl who moves to Stockholm and changes her name after being involved in a shooting. Finding success in her displaced home, she is soon haunted by shadows of the past when the shooting victim and a reporter each threaten to expose her and ruin her newfound happiness. This routine romancer is highlighted by a lovely performance by Bergman. (Swedish with English subtitles) ★★½ $19.99

Jung on Film

(1990, 77 min, US, John W. Meaney) An interview with pioneering analytical psychologist Carl Jung, conducted in August 1957. Jung discusses his work, his life and his collaboration with Sigmund Freud. (For two other works on Jung, see *A Matter of Heart* and *The Wisdom of the Dream*.) $29.99

The Jungle Book

(1942, 105 min, US, Alexander Korda) Beautifully filmed, live-action version of Rudyard Kipling's classic about Mowgli, the jungle boy, who is raised by a pack of wolves after the death of his parents. Sabu plays young Mowgli. ★★★ $14.99

The Jungle Book

(1967, 78 min, US, Wolfgang Reitherman) Charming Disney animated feature, based on Kipling's tales, about Mowgli, a young human boy, and his adventures with jungle animals. Wonderful score includes "Bare Necessities" and "I Wanna Be Like You." Voices include Phil Harris and Sebastian Cabot. ★★★ $26.99

The Jungle Book

Starring Jason Scott Lee
See: Rudyard Kipling's The Jungle Book

Jungle Fever

(1991, 132 min, US, Spike Lee) Much like his *Do the Right Thing*, Lee's explosive *Jungle Fever* is a stirring and thought-provoking drama about race relations in modern society. Wesley Snipes stars as an aspiring African-American architect who begins an affair with Annabella Sciorra, his Italian-American secretary. The film explores not only the doomed-from-the-start relationship, but also the reactions (almost totally negative) of those affected by the affair. For Lee, the contentious theme of a mixed-race relationship proves simply to be a springboard for his goal of exploring such divergent topics as tensions within African-American families, drug abuse, the tempestuous relationships between men and women, and the widening social schism between the blacks who attain middle-class "respectability" and the ones left behind. Samuel L. Jackson is riveting in support as Snipes' addict brother. ★★★½ $19.99

Junior

(1994, 110 min, US, Ivan Reitman) Having not learned a lesson with the infamously bad *Rabbit Test*, Hollywood delivers yet another tepid comedy about a man who becomes pregnant. But this time it's not just any man, it's Arnold Schwarzenegger. What a concept: *The Terminator* with child. Arnold plays a scientist who impregnates himself with an embryo. With the help of co-hort Danny DeVito, he carries to term. And along the way, he falls for fellow researcher Emma Thompson (who seems above all this nonsense). *Junior* isn't without its share of laughs, most of them at the expense of Arnold's newly found motherhood (morning sickness, maternal sensibilities and even a surprisingly pro-choice sentiment). But it's all so labored (sorry); and the unimaginative screenplay does little to humorously exploit the situation. ★★ $19.99

Junior Bonner

(1972, 103 min, US, Sam Peckinpah) Peckinpah directed this vibrant western comedy-drama with Steve McQueen as an ex-rodeo star who returns home to enter a local rodeo contest. McQueen has rarely been better, and Robert Preston and Ida Lupino are superb as his estranged parents. ★★★ $14.99

Jupiter's Thigh

(1981, 96 min, France, Philippe De Broca) Director De Broca (*King of Hearts*) mixes adventure, romance and comedy in this pleasant sequel to *Dear Inspector*. Philippe Noiret and Annie Girardot star as honeymooners who stumble upon a rare statue whose missing thigh triggers a humorous chain of wild events. (French with English subtitles) ★★½

Jupiter's Wife

(1994, 78 min, US, Michael Negropont) Filmmaker Negropont spent two years exploring the mystery of Maggie, a schizophrenic homeless woman he finds living in Central Park with her huge family of stray dogs. Fascinated by the intricate mythology that Maggie has built up around herself, Negropont does an outstanding job as both cultural anthropologist and psychological detective as he carefully cajoles ever-more-detailed information from her – the result is a riveting piece of real-life drama that was a winner of a Sundance Special Jury Prize. Maggie claims to be the daughter of actor Robert Ryan and the wife of the god Jupiter. Surprisingly articulate and outgoing, Maggie has established an unexpectedly viable life on the streets, and her natural ingenuity is supplemented by the support of a cadre of Upper East Side friends. The film thus touches on some of the deeper issues of how society deals with those of limited capacity: Are her friends merely enablers whose association keeps Maggie trapped in her life or do they provide her only lifeline to the world outside her fantasies? Maggie herself is an amazing character and the film's examination of her is at once revelatory and life-affirming and unalterably sad. ★★★½ $24.99

Jurassic Park

(1993, 126 min, US, Steven Spielberg) A spectacular, state-of-the-art fantasy film based on the Michael Crichton best-seller, *Jurassic Park* is a dizzying display of special effects, the likes of which the movies have never seen. Sam Neill and Laura Dern are paleontologists who agree to preview a newly constructed outdoor theme park built by millionaire Richard Attenborough. With mathematician Jeff Goldblum along for the ride, all are dazzled by the genetic engineering Attenborough has achieved: dinosaurs have been re-created and are roaming about on his tropical island paradise. However, the thrills begin when the carnivorous dinosaurs escape their confines and pit man against beast. With this scenario, Spielberg has crafted one heart-pounding episode after another, and his film is a high-flying blend of high-tech F/X and non-stop excitement. Followed by a 1997 sequel *The Lost World*. (Available letterboxed and pan & scan) ★★★½ $9.99

Jury Duty

(1995, 86 min, US, John Fortenberry) Not that his prior films would ever challenge *Some Like It Hot* or *Airplane!* in comic stature, but Pauly Shore's first three films look like comic masterpieces compared to *Jury Duty*, a horrendous and unbelievably unfunny comedy. Shore stars as a ne'er-do-well who is called for jury duty. Homeless and jobless and assigned to a high-profile case, Shore prolongs the court proceedings to take advantage of the room and board. Along the way, he also courts fellow juror Tia Carrere. With a story line and joke cannister equally deficient, *Jury Duty* is guilty of atrocious writing, bad acting, lifeless direction and a despicable "sense of humor." ★ $14.99

Just a Gigolo

(1980, 105 min, West Germany, David Hemmings) Amid the glittery milieu of decadent post World War I Germany, David Bowie is a debonair "escort" to a host of society women. Kim Novak wants his body, David Hemmings wants his body and his soul while Marlene Dietrich (in her final film appearance) observes the goings-on while belting out the title tune. ★★½ $59.99

Just Another Girl on the I.R.T.

(1993, 92 min, US, Leslie Harris) Harris makes her film debut with this low-budget independent drama that, while very rough around the edges, vibrates with energy, tension and humor. Harris has given a strong cinematic voice to a segment of the population long ignored – the black female teenager. And what a voice. Chantel (Ariyan Johnson in a dazzling debut) is one of the smartest kids at her Brooklyn high school but she is loud, obnoxious, self-centered and not nearly as mature as she thinks. When the ambitious, promising Chantel finds herself faced with an unwanted pregnancy, a common situation too rarely depicted in film, Harris portrays a story as poignant, scary, frustrating and moving as real life. ★★★ $14.99

Just Another Pretty Face

(1958, 110 min, France, Marc Allégret) Made right before the cinematic explosion of the French New Wave, this action/melodrama can be seen as typical entertainment fare for France in the 1950s. The film stars Henri Vidal as a police detective bent on solving a smuggling ring. The situation becomes more difficult when he falls in love with a beautiful member of the smuggling gang. Watch for brief appearances by the very young Jean-Paul Belmondo and Alain Delon. (French with English subtitles) ★★½

Just Between Friends

(1986, 120 min, US, Allan Burns) Attractive performances by Mary Tyler Moore, Ted Danson and especially Christine Lahti elevate this ordinary romantic comedy-drama about a suburban housewife (Moore) who begins a friendship with the woman having an affair with her husband. ★★½ $14.99

Just Cause

(1995, 102 min, US, Arne Glimcher) Part social drama and part thriller (without much thrills), *Just Cause* stars Sean Connery as a Harvard Law professor who attempts to prove the innocence of a young black man (Blair Underwood) convicted of murder and sentenced to die. When Connery travels to Underwood's small Florida town to investigate, he comes in conflict with the town's redneck black sheriff (Laurence Fishburne) who helped put the youth away. Similar to *Malice* insofar that the film starts in one direction and switches gears halfway through, *Just Cause*'s change is not for the better: What begins as an involving story of injustice gives way to a ridiculous revenge fantasy. Executive producer Connery attacks his role with an integrity lacking in the rest of the production, Fishburne is appropriately adversarial, and Ed Harris has a small but forceful cameo as a serial killer. ★★ $14.99

Just Like a Woman

(1994, 90 min, GB, Christopher Monger) Adrian Pasdar stars in this gentle, cross-dressing comedy about an American banker living in London whose penchant for lingerie gets him in trouble with his wife, who thinks he's seeing another woman. She kicks him out, and he winds up lodging with an older woman (Julie Walters) who's just ended a 22-year marriage. After they strike up a relationship, he divulges his secret to her and rather than react with revulsion she helps him fulfill his fantasies. The film follows Pasdar, whose heterosexuality is never called into question, on a trip to a transvestite club and depicts his humiliating arrest by the police. While basically a straight love story, the film nonetheless is an entertaining examination of gender roles in relationships. Based on Monica Jay's book "Geraldine." ★★★ $14.99

Just Like Weather

(1986, 98 min, Hong Kong, Allen Fong) A fascinating independent feature about a couple who, in an effort to save their crumbling marriage, decide to travel to New York for a second honeymoon. What makes the film different is that in the midst of this drama, the director interviews the two about themselves and their worries about their relationship. A thinly veiled allegory about Hong Kong's impending return to the control of Communist China. (Cantonese with English subtitles) ★★★ $39.99

Just Tell Me What You Want

(1980, 114 min, US, Sidney Lumet) A witty comedy with Alan King as an overbearing tycoon who tries to win back the mistress (Ali MacGraw) who walked out on him. King has never been funnier, and Myrna Loy has some great moments as his secretary. ★★★ $14.99

Just the Two of Us

(1970, 82 min, US, Barbara Peters) Quite possibly the most unheralded lesbian-themed film ever made in the United States, *Just the Two of Us* tenderly tells the love story between two married women. The film features low production values and sub-par acting, but it rises above these flaws with an engaging pro-lesbian script (much like the '90s sensation *Go Fish*). Pretty and sensible Denise (Alicia Courtney) and the sweetly ditsy blonde Adria (Elizabeth Plumb) are lonely housewives living in suburban L.A. who become close friends. While lunching at a restaurant, they notice two women at another table kissing. Both women are transfixed, and a romance between them ensues. However, what is a fling to one becomes much more to the other. A thoughtful examination of passion and identity, *Just the Two of Us*, with its non-traditional ending, should bring a collective smile on the faces of any lesbian audience. ★★★

Justine

(1969, 115 min, GB, George Cukor) Interesting character study of a lusty woman (Anouk Aimée) who seduces men while helping arm Palestinian Jews poised to revolt against British rule. Michael York, Dirk Bogarde and Robert Forster co-star. ★★½ $59.99

K

K-2

(1992, 111 min, GB, Franc Roddam) Michael Biehn and Matt Craven star in this surprisingly engrossing action/drama about a pair of buddies from Seattle who join an expedition to climb one of the Himalayas' most daunting peaks – K2. Based on the award-winning Broadway play by Peter Meyers, the film, shot in breathtaking locations in Pakistan, is filled with exceptionally photographed action sequences which dramatically illustrate the exhilaration and dangers of hard-core mountain-climbing. ★★★ $14.99

K-9

(1989, 102 min, US, Rod Daniel) Inept mandog buddy comedy (in the same vein as *Turner and Hooch*), with James Belushi as a cop saddled with a mean-tempered German shepherd. You know you're in trouble when one of the film's "best" laughs comes from two dogs doing it. ★½ $14.99

Kaddish

(1984, 92 min, US, Steve Brand) A superb, multileveled documentary which details the effects of the Holocaust on a Hungarian survivor and his American-born son. By focusing on the son, Vossi, *Kaddish* enables us to observe a heretofore little examined legacy of the Holocaust: the process by which children come to terms with the parents from whom they've inherited an unimaginable nightmare. It explores how children who were told bedtime stories about concentration camps learn to view a world in which they truly feel that "it can happen here." Filled with unexpected humor, tenderness and a sense of the strength between a father and son, *Kaddish* is a moving portrait of a young man coming to terms with an overwhelming personal and historical tragedy. ★★★½ $39.99

Kafka

(1992, 88 min, US, Steven Soderbergh) The sophomore jinx has claimed yet another victim in Soderbergh's (*sex, lies and videotape*) ambitiously adventurous second feature. Jeremy Irons stars as Kafka, a mild-mannered insurance clerk by day and aspiring writer by night, who becomes involved in a complex web of murder and bureaucracy gone wild, as well as diabolical plans for human reconditioning. While his friends and acquaintances are regularly killed off, Kafka assumes a "Woody Allen-doing-James Bond" persona in his quest to get to the bottom of all the evil. Initially intriguing, but ultimately frustrating, the story has little to do with the writings and life of Franz Kafka ("The Castle," "Metamorphosis") and instead becomes a somewhat pedestrian murder mystery. Theresa Russell is miscast as the femme fatale (just hearing her Valley Girl twang is painful). While the film doesn't succeed in attaining its lofty pretentions, its startling, mostly black-and-white cinematography, realistic locales in the brooding city of Prague and several playful surrealistic episodes help keep the story moving (but to where?). ★★½ $94.99

Kagemusha: The Shadow Warrior

(1980, 160 min, Japan, Akira Kurosawa) Kurosawa's sweeping historical drama weaves elaborate battle sequences with tranquil interior scenes, marvelously displaying the director's artistry. A film of great scope, power and detail. (Japanese with English subtitles) ★★★½ $19.99

Kalifornia

(1993, 110 min, US, Dominic Sena) Brad Pitt and Juliette Lewis headline this unnerving and at times nauseating thriller for the art-house set. David Duchovny costars and narrates as a free-lance writer with a fascination for serial killers. Bereft of ideas for his book, he and his photographer girlfriend (Michelle Forbes) plan a road trip from Georgia to L.A. visiting the sites of famous murders along the way. Short on cash, they solicit a rideshare and wind up with Pitt and Lewis, the poorest white trash to hit the screen since *Pink Flamingos*. Put these two couples in a '60s Lincoln convertible and you've got the recipe for a nightmarish ride across the Southern heartland. Lewis fits snugly (perhaps a bit too) in her role as the innocent, uneducated airhead who worships her abusive boyfriend; Pitt in the meantime redefines the term psychopath with his portrayal of a filthy, beer-guzzling, grizzle-faced parolee (for what we never learn). Director Sena creates a cinematic pastiche, straddling the line between hip atmospheric character study and pure quease-inducing ter-

ror. (Letterboxed version sells for $19.99) ★★★ $14.99

Kameradschaft (Comradship)

(1930, 89 min, Germany, G.W. Pabst) Although WWI had been over for more than a decade, and Hitler had not yet risen to power, the hostility and tensions between the French and the Germans in 1930 were strained. The melting of this mistrust is the subject of *Kameradschaft*. Tragedy strikes a mining community near the French-German border when a cave-in traps over 400 French miners. Through the efforts of the townspeople and especially the neighboring Germans, disaster is averted and communication is opened. (German with English subtitles) ★★★½

Kamikaze '89

(1982, 106 min, West Germany, Wolf Gremm) This very strange and tense fantasy thriller is based on Per Wahloo's best-selling novel "Murder on the 31st Floor" and features Rainer Werner Fassbinder's final screen appearance. He plays a detective who has four days to solve a mystery before a bomb explodes. (German with English subtitles) ★★½

Kamikaze Hearts

(1986, 80 min, US, Juliet Bashore) Reality and fiction are intriguingly merged in this fascinating film-within-a-film-within-a-film about two women working in the porno business. Sharon (Mitch) Mitchell is an unusually sexy woman who travels to San Francisco to star in a porn film. Mitch is also the subject of a documentary (*Truth or Fiction*), and the film crew observes her professional and private life. Tigr Mennett is Mitch's lover, who accompanies Mitch to the City of Hills, where a strain between the two women begins to surface. A complex, sexually explicit love story that is also a revealing exposé of the adult film industry. ★★★ $59.99

Kanal

(1957, 90 min, Poland, Andrzej Wajda) Wajda's intense World War II drama is the second of his trilogy which includes *A Generation* and *Ashes and Diamonds*. The story follows the heroic but grim actions of a group of Polish soldiers and patriots who attempt to escape Nazi-occupied Warsaw through the underground sewer system. (Polish with English subtitles) ★★★½ $24.99

Kangaroo

(1986, 105 min, Australia, Tim Burstall) Based on D.H. Lawrence's semiautobiographical novel, Colin Friels and Judy Davis star as an idealistic English writer and his wife who move to Australia in the early 1920s in the hopes of finding a more tolerant world in which to rebuild their lives. However, when the leader of a secret fascist group puts pressure on them to join their ranks, they discover the harmony they thought they had found has given way to the same social and political friction they thought they had left behind. Despite its incendiary theme, the film lacks any emotional spark. ★★ $79.99

Kansas

(1988, 108 min, US, David Stevens) From the director of *A Town Like Alice* comes this unen-

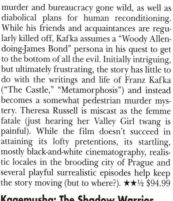

Jeremy Irons in *Kafka*

gaging drama about a mild-mannered drifter (Andrew McCarthy) who is tricked into committing a bank robbery by a "friendly" sociopath (Matt Dillon). ★

Kansas City

(1996, 110 min, US, Robert Altman) A small-time hood crosses a gangster (an effective Harry Belafonte) in Depression-era Kansas City. The hood's wife (Jennifer Jason Leigh) wants her husband back after the mob boss' men nab him, so she kidnaps a wealthy, opium-addicted "socialite" (Miranda Richardson) to ensure his release. *Kansas City* may not be anywhere near *Nashville* on the map, but it's certainly no *O.C. and Stiggs* either. The film has the director's visual eye for character detail, as well as his pointed examinations of life's realities and ironies. These observations create a depressing, hopeless tone that makes this tough going, despite energetic performances (with a typically mannered, bizarre turn by Leigh) and a compelling, more traditional narrative. A jazz background offers a splendid score, and there's a terrific tenor sax duel. The film is packed from beginning to end with some great period tunes. ★★½ $99.99

Kaos

(1984, 188 min, Italy, Paolo & Vittorio Taviani) Set against the stunning backdrop of a sun-bleached, nearly barren Italian landscape, the Taviani brothers' adaptation of five stories by Luigi Pirandello together form a fascinating dramatic quilt. All of the stories, ranging from comedy to tragedy, focus on peasant life in turn-of-the-century Sicily and are stunningly photographed. Never succumbing to maudlin sentimentality, the folk tales are richly told with an embracing celebration of life. (Italian with English subtitles) ★★★★ $29.99

The Karate Kid

(1984, 126 min, US, John G. Avildsen) A fatherless teenager living in Los Angeles, bullied by the local gang, learns karate from the family handyman. Ralph Macchio and Noriyuki "Pat" Morita are both very likable in this first outing of the popular trilogy. ★★★ $14.99

The Karate Kid, Part II

(1986, 113 min, US, John G. Avildsen) Sequel to the 1984 sleeper with Ralph Macchio and Noriyuki "Pat" Morita reprising their roles as student and mentor. In Okinawa, Ralph goes up against a local hood. The first one had charm, this one has counter-charm (but it's not as bad as *III*). ★★ $14.99

The Karate Kid, Part III

(1989, 111 min, US, John G. Avildsen) Ralph Macchio returns a third time (isn't he a little too old to play a teenager?) to do battle; enough already. ★ $14.99

Kasaramu Ce (This Land Is Ours)

(1991, 84 min, Nigeria, Saddik Balewa) A political tale of greed and power. Sani, a young farmer, is moved to act when his grandfather is killed by a money-hungry businessman who, finding precious stones throughout a village, tries to buy up all of the property. This film breaks one of the most important elements of a thriller when the mystery of the conspirators

is revealed in the first 15 minutes. The lack of female characters provides a glimpse into the powerlessness of women in this Muslim community. The acting is quite natural and the editing keeps the story moving well, despite its predictability. (English and Hausa with English subtitles) ★★ $29.99

Katherine

(1975, 98 min, US, Jeremy Paul Kagan) Sissy Spacek stars as an overprivileged girl who, rejecting her affluent birthright, transforms from innocent to activist to revolutionary during the turbulent 1960s and early 1970s. A compelling drama of conscience and commitment, highlighted by Spacek's compassionate performance. Henry Winkler, Julie Kavner, Jane Wyatt and Art Carney also star. ★★★

The Keep

(1983, 96 min, US, Michael Mann) From the director of *Manhunter* comes this stylish-looking but empty-headed horror film set during WWII about Nazi soldiers holing up at an ancient site — where a demonic creature has lain dormant. ★½ $79.99

Keeper of the City

(1992, 96 min, US, Bobby Roth) Louis Gossett, Jr. stars as a tough-nosed police detective. Peter Coyote plays a crime reporter. Anthony LaPaglia co-stars as the son of a deceased Mafia kingpin who can no longer live in the shadow of his father's crooked past and begins murdering the leaders of Mafia families. When the lives of these three men intersect, it makes for an interesting, if familiar, police thriller. LaPaglia's performance, though credible, is slightly reminiscent of Robert De Niro's *Taxi Driver* character Travis Bickle. Gossett performs admirably. ★★½ $9.99

Keeper of the Flame

(1942, 100 min, US, George Cukor) Solid performances by Spencer Tracy and Katharine Hepburn distinguish this intriguing drama about reporter Tracy investigating the life of a deceased politician, only to uncover a dark secret about the man. Kate is the widow. ★★★ $19.99

Keetje Tippel (Kathi's Passion)

(1975, 104 min, The Netherlands, Paul Verhoeven) This early Dutch effort by Verhoeven is a passionate and sensual story of lost innocence. Set in 1880 Amsterdam, the film stars Rutger Hauer and centers on the life and struggles of a free-spirited young woman (Monique van de Ven) who is forced into prostitution by her destitute family. A worthy resurrection of early 20th-century social fiction which exhibits wit, detail and conscience. (Available dubbed and in Dutch with English subtitles) ★★★

Kelly's Heroes

(1970, 145 min, US, Brian G. Hutton) Though not in the same league as *The Dirty Dozen*, this WWII adventure is nevertheless an entertaining romp with Clint Eastwood, Telly Savalas and other Army buddies planning a gold heist behind enemy lines. With Donald Sutherland, Carroll O'Connor and Don Rickles. ★★½ $14.99

Kenneth Anger: The Magic Lantern Cycle, Vols. 1-4

(1947-80, 40 min each, US, Kenneth Anger) Kenneth Anger has been in the forefront of American independent filmmaking since he started making experimental shorts in his late teens in the 1940s. While few of these films have recieved any theatrical exhibition, Anger's own curated retrospective referred to as *The Magic Lantern Cycle* is available on video in four volumes. These films have been controversial, confiscated by the police for being "obscene," and have had no less a fan than Jean Cocteau, with whom Anger briefly apprenticed in the early 1950s. In addition to his filmmaking, Anger is also known as the (infamous) author of the "Hollywood Babylon" books which skewer the filmmaking capital with its sordid and gossipy anecdotes and myths.

Vol. 1: Fireworks (1947) is a homoerotic masterpiece, made when Anger was just 17 years old. Titled so for the seminal image of a sailor's erection that ejaculates like a roman candle. The short chronicles Anger's descent into the night as he scours the waterfront looking for rough trade. *Rabbit's Moon* (1950) is Anger's tribute to Méliès. It's set in an iridescent forest where the sad clown prince Peirrot despondently dances in the cadence of a silent film, bathing in the cool blue lunar light. *Eaux d'Artifice* (1950) is set in a magical garden of fountains and fauna. It's a visual fugue complemented by Vivaldi's music, and is probably Anger's most beautifully constructed film.

Vol. 2: Inauguration of the Pleasure Dome was first shot in 1954 and recut over a period of 12 years, to the form which exists today. It's based on one of Aleister Crowley's bacchanals, and features writer Anais Nin in the role of Astarte. Anger's first overtly religious piece, it incorporates unused footage from the short *Puce Moments*.

Vol. 3: Scorpio Rising (1963) is perhaps his best-known and arguably the quintessential underground short of the 1960s. A homoerotic ritual to that "masculine fascination with the Thing that Goes," *Rising* found its Greek chorus in Top 40 radio, using the music of everyone from Bobby Vinton to The Rondells (illegally, however, prompting countless lawsuits). Against its pop score, some rough trade gently polishes his hot rod car. The film was denounced by both the L.A.P.D. and the American Nazi Party! *Puce Moments* (1948) is an early short about an aging actress dressing to go out. *Kustom Kar Kommandoes* (1965) continues Anger's camp sensibilities. It's only a fragment of what was meant to be "an oneiric vision of contemporary American (and specifically California) teenage experience."

Vol. 4: Invocation of My Demon Brother (1967) is the second part of Anger's Aleister Crowley trilogy (though much of the footage had been stolen by the film's star and Manson follower Bobby Beausoleil). As the Magus dances, Lucifer, the Bringer of Light, arrives reconciling opposites. Mick Jagger supplied the lackluster synthesizer music. *Lucifer Rising* (1969) is the final chapter of his black trilogy. The long-dead Egyptian gods Isis and Osiris are summoned at sacred grounds around the

K

289

world until they appear in their pink flying saucers over the ancient pyramids of the Valley of Kings. It's one of Anger's most iridescent images put to film. $29.99

The Kentuckian

(1955, 104 min, US, Burt Lancaster) In his only directorial effort, Lancaster wears dual coonskin hats in this dramatically awkward but scenic adventure. Set in Kentucky during the 1820s, the film has Lancaster as a backwoodsman who, with his young son, sets out for Texas and the rugged but rewarding life. On the way, he becomes sidetracked by indentured servant Dianne Foster, schoolteacher Diana Lynn, villainous merchant Walter Matthau (in his debut), and two feuding Klansmen on his trail. Director Lancaster is none-too-subtle in the "simple-life-is-better" motif, and his actor counterpart doesn't fare much better giving a stiff characterization. ★★ $19.99

Kerouac

(1984, 100 min, US, Steve Allen & William S. Burroughs) This fascinating and revealing glimpse into the life of Beat novelist Jack Kerouac ("On the Road," "Dharma Bums") effectively merges a docudrama format (featuring Kerouac look-alike Jack Coulter) with actual footage of Kerouac as well as Allen Ginsberg, William Burroughs, Carolyn Cassady and others. ★★★

The Key

(1983, 116 min, Italy, Tinto Brass) Soft-core porn for viewers of intellectual pretensions, this Brass (*Caligula, Salon Kitty*) production features loads of nudity as well as the vigorous caressing of bare cheeks, sexy women in black lace and enough kinky sex to give justification to its "X" rating. Set in Venice in 1940, the film stars British actor Frank Finlay as a sexually obsessed aristocrat who chronicles his many exploits and voyeuristic excursions in a diary that is read ravenously by his equally active wife. Accompanied by a lively score by Ennio Morricone, this teasingly erotic tour through the boudoirs of the sexually adventurous is nothing if not tantalizing and just a little bit "dirty." (English and Italian with English subtitles) ★★

Key Largo

(1948, 101 min, US, John Huston) Humphrey Bogart and Lauren Bacall star in this exciting screen version of Maxwell Anderson's hit play. Edward G. Robinson costars as the ruthless gangster who takes refuge in an isolated hotel during a storm and terrorizes the patrons and staff. Claire Trevor won an Oscar as Robinson's pathetic, alcoholic moll. ★★★½ $19.99

The Keys of the Kingdom

(1944, 137 min, US, John M. Stahl) One of Gregory Peck's earliest efforts casts him as a priest doing missionary work in 19th-century China in this moving adaptation of A.J. Cronin's novel. Slightly overlong, but compelling nonetheless. With Thomas Mitchell, Vincent Price, Edmund Gwenn and Roddy McDowall. ★★★ $19.99

Khartoum

(1966, 136 min, GB, Basil Dearden) Charlton Heston and Laurence Olivier square off in this retelling of the 1883 siege at Khartoum, in the British Sudan. Punctuated with magnificently choreographed battle scenes, this epic adventure finds Olivier in peak form as the fanatical Arab leader who incites his people to rise up against the British presence. Heston delivers one of his best performances as the English general who opposes him. ★★★ $19.99

Kicking and Screaming

(1995, 96 min, US, Noah Baumbach) Set in that post-Bachelors' Degree, pre-gainful employment, Twilight Zone time of life, *Kicking and Screaming* follows several newly minted college grads as they haphazardly grapple with deteriorating personal relationships, exacerbating family expectations and a nonexistent job market (with clerking in a video store once again serving as a metaphor). No new material here, but director Baumbach crafts an engaging, unpretentious treatment of familiar themes. A sometimes intelligent, sharply observed script and witty performances combine to deliver a fresh entertainment, similar to *The Brothers McMullen* in its unexpected charm. The cast works well as an ensemble, and Harvard and its environs are the perfect backdrop to evoke the womb-like ambience of university life. The characters are recognizable without being clichéd, and their various responses to academia, separation and anxiety illicit pangs of nostalgia — even in those viewers a decade or two removed from the experience. ★★★ $94.99

The Kid

(1921, 90 min, US, Charlie Chaplin) Chaplin's first true feature-length film tells the saga of an abandoned infant who's adopted by Charlie and, ultimately, becomes his streetwise sidekick. Chaplin expertly mixes slapstick and sentimental melodrama to create a timeless comic experience. Chaplin had defined his Little Tramp role with his priceless performance, and little Jackie Coogan could bring you to laughter or tears with just a look. ★★★½

A Kid for Two Farthings

(1955, 96 min, GB, Carol Reed) Reed's heartwarming fable about the hopes and aspirations of an impoverished lad is filled with insights about the human condition. In a play on "Jack and the Beanstalk," the young boy is sent to market where he buys a goat with an odd deformity — a single horn is growing out of its head. Convinced that the kid is a magical, wish-granting unicorn, the boy's head fills with fantasies about ending his family's poverty. ★★★½ $39.99

The Kid from Brooklyn

(1946, 113 min, US, Norman Z. McLeod) Danny Kaye is a comic dynamo as a timid milkman who unwittingly becomes a prize fighter. There are plenty of laughs, and Kaye (as usual) is a delight. Virginia Mayo also stars. Remake of the Harold Lloyd 1936 comedy, *The Milky Way*. ★★★ $19.99

The Kid from Brooklyn

A Kid in King Arthur's Court

(1995, 89 min, US, Michael Gottlieb) Mark Twain's classic time travel tale is dusted off for a third time (Will Rogers and Bing Crosby also found medieval adventure) to produce a particularly unimaginative and silly retelling. Thomas Ian Nicholas (he brought some life to *Rookie of the Year* but the young actor can only mug here) is Calvin, a 20th-century little league player who finds himself hurled back into the 6th century and the court of Camelot. There he finds romance, adventure, intrigue and manages to boost his own sagging self-confidence through a series of lifeless episodes and smirky comedy. Though the idea of the update is intriguing, Disney once again condescends to its adolescent audience, even toying with the Camelot legend. Joss Ackland plays an unappropriately dim-witted king, no doubt made senseless after reading the script. ★★ $14.99

Kidnapped

(1960, 97 min, US, Robert Stevenson) Disney, after its great success ten years earlier with Robert Louis Stevenson's *Treasure Island*, returns to another Stevenson source with exciting results. Peter Finch and James MacArthur star together as Alan Breck and David Balfour, respectively the 18th-century adventurer and the young kidnap victim, who join forces to battle pirates and the Redcoats. Not *the* definitive Stevenson adaptation, but entertaining nonetheless. Peter O'Toole's film debut. ★★★ $19.99

Kids

(1995, 90 min, US, Larry Clark) This unrelenting cinema verité look at a group of Manhattan teenagers seems destined to shock even the most hardened sensibilities. The assault begins even before the film's opening shot as we hear the distinct and magnified sounds of two teens ferociously sucking face. The ensuing scene, in which the film's anti-hero, Telly, talks his way into "fuckin'" a virgin, basically sets the tone for the whole film. As we follow him, his buddy Casper, and a bunch of other delinquents through 18 hours of unbridled hedonism, Telly boasts about previous virginal conquests and plots his next — when he's not suckin' on a 40, smoking a blunt, kicking the shit out of some poor guy or harassing fags. Unlike other films about youth at risk (*Christiane F., Pixote*), *Kids* offers no moral imperatives and makes no apologies.

Director Clark (who made a name for himself photographing his fellow heroin addicts) employs astounding camerawork and a well-thought out narrative structure to present a disturbingly real picture of these wayward youths. The result is socially compelling though bordering on nauseating to watch and may leave one contemplating a vasectomy or tubal ligation. ★★ $14.99

The Kids Are Alright

(1979, 108 min, US, Jeff Stein) This frantically paced rockumentary paean to The Who will delight both their hard-core fans and those with a strong appreciation of good rock. Culled from interviews, concert footage and appearances on numerous TV variety shows (most notably "The Smothers Brothers"), the film offers a vivacious look at the group and their notorious hijinks, especially those of drummer Keith Moon, who proves to be beyond control. ★★★ $19.99

Kids in the Hall: Brain Candy

(1996, 90 min, Canada, Kelly Makin) Canada's five-man comic arsenal The Kids in the Hall, who found great success on TV with their hilarious sketches, make their big-screen debut with this witty, on-target satire of American society in the '90s (with Prozac a particular target). The basic setup involves an unscrupulous pharmaceutical company which releases an untested "happiness" drug to an unsuspecting public and all the wackiness that ensues. In true Kids fashion, pain and anger are turned into laughter as the Kids skewer America's mindset towards the elderly, drugs, the handicapped, grunge bands, MTV — and there's a terrific, uproarious "coming out" song-and-dance number. The cast is great, with everyone playing multiple roles as they did in the show — some favorite characters from TV even return. Though it may not always reach the hilarity level or deliver the many belly laughs the TV show managed to produce, *Brain Candy* is a consistently funny and inventive romp that is leagues above most contemporary comedies. ★★★ $14.99

Kika

(1993, 90 min, Spain, Pedro Almodóvar) Almodóvar's latest is a big-budget comedy-drama filled with outlandish costuming, neon-bright colors and wild characters, all filmed at the director's trademark, frenetic pace. Alternating between farce and an examination of urban crises, the film stars Verónica Forqué as Kika, a sweet, sexy makeup artist who is forced to confront urban rape, multiple murders and intrusion of her privacy by the media's prying eyes. When Kiki is raped, it is caught on camera by a neighbor. The tape falls into the clutches of Andrea (Victoria Abril), the hostess of Madrid's "Cops"-like TV show called "Today's Worst." And Andrea — who can be found clothed in black rubber with a robotic camera helmet on her head and arc lights covering her breasts — wants to air the tape on national TV! This story of voyeurism and media manipulation also stars statuesque transsexual Bibi Andersen and Rossy DiPalma, who is fine as Kika's lesbian maid. (Available dubbed and in Spanish with English subtitles) ★★★ $14.99

Kill Me Again

(1989, 94 min, US, John Dahl) This nifty little thriller is a small, engaging film noir/mystery which bypassed theatrical play. Val Kilmer plays a private investigator who is hired by femme fatale Joanne Whalley to fake her murder — she's being pursued by a boyfriend she's double-crossed. The murder is so convincing that the police now suspect the P.I., and the woman is nowhere to be found. Though one or two of the twists may be predictable to the mystery buff, there's more than enough intrigue and suspense for the rest of us. The love scenes between the future Mr. and Mrs. Kilmer are rather tame, however. ★★★ $19.99

The Killer

(1983, 110 min, Hong Kong, John Woo) Fasten your seat belt and get ready to blast off into nonstop action and rip-roaring entertainment in this relentlessly paced and extremely funny tongue-in-cheek exercise in slapstick violence which might be called *The Keystone Cops with Uzis*. The story follows a veteran assassin (Chow Yun-Fat) who, in the course of performing one last job before retiring, inadvertently blinds a young cabaret singer. Overwrought with guilt, he decides to devote his life to helping her, but the cops and the mob just won't let this killer-with-a-heart-of-gold go straight. Eventually, he teams up with a maverick cop and they embark on an adventure in which bullets fly like popcorn and the hilarity goes to extremes. Director Woo, one the the most exciting directors to come out of the burgeoning Hong Kong film market, has fashioned a film lover's dream — a perfect blend of art, action and comedy which Martin Scorsese called "one of the best of a new genre of film." Highly recommended. (Available in Cantonese with English subtitles or dubbed) (Available letterboxed or pan & scan) ★★★★ $19.99

Killer — A Journal of Murder

(1996, 90 min, US, Tim Metcalfe) Awkwardly narrated, *Killer: A Journal of Murder* is "based" on a true story about a trusting new prison guard (Robert Sean Leonard) at Leavenworth and his misplaced friendship with a sociopathic prisoner (James Woods). Produced by Oliver Stone, the movie raises many questions about our penal system — both past and present — without the pretension of trying to answer them. Yet when needed the most, the writing perches on the fence about whether treating these criminals kindly is the act of a fool or a saint. In killing a killer (and all the implications therein), the violent acts are embellished for shock value in an increasing attempt to evoke emotion; these acts eventually give way to the sensationalism the film at one point condemns. Featuring familiar faces throughout, both in tale and performer, *Killer* surpasses expectations but avoids its own potential. ★★ $95.49

The Killer Inside Me

(1975, 99 min, US, Burt Kennedy) While not as searing as the Jim Thompson novel on which it is based, *The Killer Inside Me* is still a gripping psychological thriller. Stacy Keach stars as the seemingly rock-steady keeper of the law in a small California town whose long-simmering anger caused by a traumatic childhood incident finally explodes. Keach is at his best as the deranged yet sympathetic murderer, and Susan Tyrell is equally sharp as the white-trash prostitute who triggers his violence. ★★½ $99.99

The Killer Shrews

(1959, 71 min, US, Ray Kellogg) Ken Curtis (Festus of TV's "Gunsmoke") produced and stars in this tale of shrews the size of dogs — mainly because they *were* dogs, dressed in Pat Nixon's old cloth coat and wearing plastic fangs. Every bit as good as director Kellogg's other feature, *The Giant Gila Monster*, but lacking the sure hand he exhibited in his John Wayne opus *The Green Berets*, where the sun sets in the East (but that's another story for another time). ★ $9.99

Killer's Kiss

(1955, 67 min, US, Stanley Kubrick) This early Kubrick curiosity stars Frank Silvera as a farm-bred boxer at the end of a short-lived fighting career. He falls fast and hard for a dance-hall girl. Her job is a self-imposed penance for past "sins," and her sleazy boss' obsessive interest in her results in murder. Kubrick's second feature includes a short but noteworthy nightmare

The Killer

K

The Killers

sequence; not only did he direct, but he co-produced, edited, photographed and wrote the story as well. ★★★ $19.99

The Killers

(1964, 95 min, US, Don Siegel) Lee Marvin and Clu Gulager fulfill the terms of their contract by gunning down John Cassavetes. But Marvin needs to know why the doomed man didn't try to run. The killers begin a search for the man who ordered the hit, and uncover several dirty little secrets along the way. Based on a short story by Ernest Hemingway. Also with Angie Dickinson and Ronald Reagan as a bad guy (before his years in Washington). ★★★ $14.99

The Killing

(1956, 83 min, US, Stanley Kubrick) Kubrick's first feature film is a taut thriller about an attempted heist at a race track. Filmed in exquisitely noir-ish black-and-white tones, the film stars Sterling Hayden as the stone-faced ringleader who pulls together a gang of noncriminals to conspire on the multimillion dollar job. Though not as exuberant as his later works, Kubrick's touches nonetheless permeate this highly stylized tale of human aspiration undone by avarice and deceit. An excellent group of stock supporting actors deliver a conglomeration of superbly melodramatic and emotionally cool performances. ★★★½ $19.99

Killing Cars

(1986, 104 min, West Germany, Michael Verhoeven) Director Verhoeven, who has come into American prominence with *The Nasty Girl*, has shown great progress since this mildly interesting action/intrigue film. Jürgen Prochnow (*Das Boot*) plays Ralph, an amazingly unlikable hot-rod car designer whose work on a top secret "super car" becomes the target for industrial sabotage and other types of intrigue too numerous to recount. As the plot thickens, our hyperventilating hero (who is a surprisingly inept driver) is forced to confront

a roving band of punks, double-crossing lovers and insidious coworkers in his efforts to get his car made. It's all smoke and no fire in this "thinking man's" thriller – after seeing this film, it is easy to understand why American filmmakers reign supreme around the world in the action genre. An interesting note for viewers: for some inexplicable reason, two voices are used for Prochnow – one is his natural German-accented voice, the other a studio-produced American voice. (English language version) ★½ $14.99

The Killing Fields

(1984, 141 min, GB, Roland Joffé) This highly emotional and often terrifying examination of Cambodia in the aftermath of the American evacuation stars Sam Waterston as Sidney Schanberg, a Western journalist who stayed behind to witness the takeover of the brutally repressive Khmer Rouge. Haing S. Ngor (a native of Cambodia who in real life was tortured by the Pol Pot regime) received a much-deserved Oscar for his moving portrayal of Schanberg's translator, Dith Pran. Athol Fugard, John Malkovich and Spalding Gray also star in this nightmarish vision of one of history's darkest moments. ★★★★ $19.99

The Killing Heat

(1984, 104 min, Australia, Michael Raeburn) An intense, provocative version of Doris Lessing's novel "The Grass Is Singing." Karen Black stars as a city girl who marries a farmer, only to find herself unprepared for the rigors of country life. Through her affair with a black farm hand and her husband's violent reaction, director Raeburn is pointedly commenting on the realities of African Colonialism. ★★★

The Killing of a Chinese Bookie

(1976, 109 min, US, John Cassavetes) Sure to be the most feared entry at a Gamblers Anonymous Film Festival, *The Killing of a Chinese Bookie* stars Ben Gazzara as Cosmo, the

owner/MC of a sleazy nightclub-cum-strip joint whose bad luck at a Mafia-operated poker game throws him into a violent web of extortion, double dealings and contract killings. A tough-talking but oddly moral man with a flashy lifestyle and a penchant for pretty ladies, Cosmo finds that his T&A showplace is a church compared to the treachery of organized crime. Director Cassavetes' hand-held camera and seemingly improvised dialogue create a repressively realistic atmosphere where one cannot escape. A riveting, sweat-producing drama that was dismissed on its initial run (and will certainly have its detractors today) but now must rank as one of Cassavetes' best films. ★★★ $19.99

The Killing of Angel Street

(1981, 101 min, Australia, Donald Crombie) Based on actual events, this is the compelling story of corruption and the people who fought against it. A young activist battles to save her neighborhood from developers and becomes embroiled in a web of intrigue. Starring John Hargreaves and Liz Alexander. ★★½

The Killing of Sister George

(1968, 138 min, GB, Robert Aldrich) One of the great and infamous lesbian "breakthrough" films of the 1960s, this story of an aging lesbian who loses her job and her young lover is a shrill, even grotesque exposé on lesbian lifestyles. Beryl Reid is magnetic in her portrayal of George, the loud and aggressive, cigar-chomping dyke whose girl-chasing ways (she even accosts a cab full of nuns!) and domineering personality drive away all who care for her. The triangle of lesbian stereotypes include: butch George; the predatory, sophisticated middle-aged lesbian (Coral Brown); and Childie, the kittenish but neurotic femme (Susannah York). An entertainingly dated tale of love and loneliness that treads a strange line between comedy and sensationalist, perverted drama. Some scenes were shot in the London lesbian bar Getaway Club. ★★

Killing Zoe

(1994, 96 min, US, Roger Avary) Eric Stoltz stars in this Luc Besson-influenced splatter film about an American safecracker (Stoltz) who travels to Paris to help his childhood friend (Jean-Hugues Anglade) knock off a bank. Stoltz soon finds himself trapped in a nightmare that makes Griffin Dunne's wild taxi ride in *After Hours* feel like a sunny stroll through a garden. Anglade and his comrades, a self-proclaimed band of political freedom fighters, force the wary Stoltz into a wild night of drinking, smoking hash and shooting heroin. Julie Delpy plays a call girl whom Stoltz hires his first night in town and who later, it turns out, is a secretary at the targeted bank. All style and no substance, the film has a few entertaining moments, but is ultimately unfulfilling and pointless. ★½ $14.99

Kim

(1950, 113 min, US, Victor Saville) Stirring adaptation of Rudyard Kipling's adventure story about a young English boy who becomes involved with a British secret agent in 19th-century India. Dean Stockwell plays the young title character, and Errol Flynn's then-faltering career was saved by his winning portrait of the daring soldier-spy. ★★★ $19.99

Kind Hearts and Coronets

(1949, 104 min, GB, Robert Hamer) Alec Guinness created a sensation with his portrayal of all eight members of an aristocratic family who are eliminated one by one by a wayward relative who's bent on claiming the family's royal title. A delicious Ealing Studio comedy with a droll and macabre world view. Featuring a zesty costar performance by Dennis Price as the ambitious social climber. ★★★★ $9.99

A Kind of Loving

(1962, 112 min, GB, John Schlesinger) Schlesinger's first feature film is a sensitive drama about a young couple who marry because of pregnancy. While the film was unfortunately lost in the shuffle, having been released after its sensational "kitchen sink" counterparts *Room at the Top* and *Saturday Night, Sunday Morning*, it is a nonetheless witty, frank and poignant study of a lust gone awry. Featuring sterling performances by Alan Bates and June Ritchie as the young couple. ★★★½

Kindergarten

(1987, 143 min, USSR, Yevgeny Yevtushenko) Poet and neophyte filmmaker Yevtushenko has taken an overused theme – the destructiveness of war as seen through the eyes of a child – and has fashioned from it a completely original and exciting autobiographical work. The setting is 1941 during the evacuation of Moscow. A mother sends her ten-year-old son to the safety of relatives in a Siberian village. En route, however, the youth's train is bombed, and the boy's journey becomes a vivid and harrowing odyssey through a war-charred landscape. The poet emerges from the filmmaker in this sentimental, bombastic and emotional film. (Russian with English subtitles) ★★★½ $59.99

Kindergarten Cop

(1990, 111 min, US, Ivan Reitman) Arnold Schwarzenegger mixes comedy and action as a tough Los Angeles cop who is forced to go undercover as a kindergarten teacher in hopes of capturing the criminal father of one of the

kids. Schwarzenegger goes through the usual comic humilities playing baby-sitter to a group of precocious five-year-olds. The comedy doesn't always work, and the action is less than exciting, but in spite of it all the film maintains a certain level of enjoyment, though none of it is credible. Arnold is Arnold, which is probably enough to please his fans. Pamela Reed, however, as his partner, is the film's biggest asset giving a spirited performance who can make the unbelievable convincing. Penelope Ann Miller also stars as a fellow teacher and the ex-wife of the man they're searching for. ★★½ $14.99

The Kindred

(1987, 92 min, US, Jeffrey Obrow & Stephen Carpenter) Rod Steiger, Kim Hunter and Amanda Pays give some class to this mostly entertaining, derivative horror film about a scientific experiment which spawns a half-human sea creature. ★★ $14.99

The King and I

(1956, 134 min, US, Walter Lang) "Shall We Dance?" That question will be difficult not to ask after viewing this sumptuous film version of Rodgers and Hammerstein's stage classic. Yul Brynner gives an unforgettable and timeless performance as the King of Siam in this story of a proper British schoolteacher who, tutoring the court's children, falls in love with the monarch. Deborah Kerr is radiant as the governess, and the great score includes "Getting to Know You" and "Hello Young Lovers." Brynner won a Best Actor Oscar. ★★★½ $19.99

King David

(1985, 114 min, US, Bruce Beresford) Richard Gere plays the young David, from the famous fight with Goliath to his time as King. Beresford approaches this with a seriousness which separates it from those lavish 1950s biblical epics; though the first half, featuring Edward Woodward as King Saul, is much more successful than the latter half. ★★½ $14.99

King for a Day

(1980, 88 min, Israel, Asi Dayan) Although Israeli film production is not high in the international filmmaking standards, their films are made for domestic use and are usually fun, light, family entertainment. In *King for a Day*, the story revolves around the return of an older man's daughter to Jerusalem. The problem is that she thinks that he is a rich man so, with the help of his friends, he plays a game of wealth. (Hebrew with English subtitles) ★★½

A King in New York

(1957, 105 min, GB, Charles Chaplin) Often misunderstood, Chaplin's last starring film is a bittersweet political satire about a deposed European monarch who visits America amidst the McCarthy anti-Communist hysteria. Not at all "anti-American" as its detractors at the time claimed, this somewhat uneven but

remarkable stab at social madness is filled with hilarious moments and has much to say about our nuclear and technological insanity. Chaplin's son Michael is featured as a young political malcontent. ★★★

King Kong

(1933, 100 min, US, Merian C. Cooper & Ernest B. Schoedsack) He is billed as "the eighth wonder of the world" and, in the sixty years since the movie's release, animator Willis O'Brien's awesome creature has all but lived up to that title. There are ample reasons why this parable about the notorious giant ape let loose in New York City has had such an enduring notoriety. As enormous and unwieldy as the whole project is, the simple fable around which the story is built continues to be resonant. As an adventure-fantasy, *King Kong* has yet to be outdone. ★★★★ $19.99

King Kong

(1976, 134 min, US, John Guillermin) Perhaps the most hyped film of the 1970s, especially for its supposedly spectacular mechanical effects. Despite winning an honorary Oscar, the effects are anything but special. Whatever possessed filmmaker Dino De Laurentiis, the king of the bloated epic, to remake the 1933 classic is beyond human (or simian) comprehension. The only redeeming factor of this remake is the launching of Jessica Lange's career and the end of De Laurentiis'. "When my monkey die, everybody gonna cry." ★ $14.99

King Lear

(1971, 137 min, GB, Peter Brook) Stark black-and-white cinematography and a somber Danish landscape underscore director Brook's heavy treatment of the Shakespearian tragedy. Paul Scofield as the King heads an exceptional ensemble, including Irene Worth, Jack MacGowran, Cyril Cusack and Patrick Magee. ★★★½ $19.99

King Lear

(1984, 158 min, GB, Michael Elloit) Who better to play Lear than Laurence Olivier in his later life? This Emmy Award-winning Granada Video production might be one of the finest versions of Shakespeare's play available. The outstanding cast includes John Hurt, Diana Rigg, Dorothy Tutin and Leo McKern. ★★★★ $29.99

King Lear

(1987, 90 min, US/Switzerland, Jean-Luc Godard) Even for hard-core Godardians, this incomprehensible version of Shakespeare's classic might prove to be tough going, the end result sadly suggesting that perhaps we already have seen all of the exciting filmic innovations from France's most innovative director. The oddball cast of Molly Ringwald, Woody Allen, Peter Sellers, Burgess Meredith and Norman Mailer meander through the various scenes with Godard himself starring as a crazed professor with a penchant for strange headgear. ★½ $24.99

The King of Comedy

(1983, 139 min, US, Martin Scorsese) Robert De Niro is Rupert Pupkin, an aspiring but psychotic comedian, who schemes his way onto network TV and instant celebrity. Scorsese

Alec Guinness in Kind Hearts and Coronets

K

293

The King of Marvin Gardens

directs a finely tuned cast, including Jerry Lewis as a cynical dean of the airwaves and Sandra Bernhard as Pupkin's rubber-faced accomplice. ★★★ $19.99

King of Hearts

(1967, 102 min, France, Philippe de Broca) A perennial favorite at TLA, De Broca's classic comedy is a moving celebration of the triumph of innocence. Alan Bates stars as a Scottish soldier dispatched to a small French village where the only remaining inhabitants are the inmates of the local asylum. (English and French with English subtitles) ★★★½

King of Kings

(1961, 168 min, US, Nicholas Ray) Ray, an accomplished veteran of noir and mysteries, turned his talents to the story of Christ in this beautifully filmed religious epic. Jeffrey Hunter plays Jesus, and is supported by Siobhan McKenna, Robert Ryan and Rip Torn. A better spectacle and far more successful in its storytelling than 1965's similarly themed *The Greatest Story Ever Told*. (Available letterboxed and pan & scan) ★★★½ $24.99

The King of Marvin Gardens

(1972, 104 min, US, Bob Rafelson) An enthralling drama fueled by a poignant story of the American Dream lost and the dynamic acting of Jack Nicholson, Bruce Dern and especially Ellen Burstyn. Nicholson is David Stabler, a quiet, almost mousy late night Philly D.J. who is pulled out of his staid life when his volatile, always-in-trouble brother (Dern) calls from an Atlantic City jail. Traveling to an off-season, geriatric-filled pre-casino A.C., David is sucked into his brother's grandiose scheme of easy money, willing women and ownership of a small Hawaiian island. Nicholson ably plays off his boisterous image as the shy loser given one last chance. Dern is maniacal as the naive dreamer/crook and Burstyn, in perhaps her most affecting role, plays a wacked-out, aging beauty queen fearful that she's run out of chances and who slowly realizes that her

Prince Charming is only a double-dealing toad. Another star of the film is Atlantic City itself, a seedy, forlorn dead end at the edge of a cold, empty ocean. One of the most underrated and accomplished films of the 1970s. ★★★★ $19.99

King of New York

(1990, 106 min, US, Abel Ferrara) Christopher Walken stars in this savage exposé of a ruthless drug kingpin who fancies himself a modern day Robin Hood. Upon his release from prison, Walken begins a campaign, using a veil of moral superiority, to eliminate all of the "bad" elements from the drug trade. Ferrara's film, intensely gratuitous in its violence, has an undeniable power in its examination of corruption and betrayal. The supporting cast, all of whom would go on to some degree of success, includes David Caruso, Laurence Fishburne, Giancarlo Esposito and Wesley Snipes. ★★★ $14.99

King of the Gypsies

(1978, 112 min, US, Frank Pierson) Eric Roberts takes over leadership of his Gypsy tribe when his grandfather dies; which doesn't sit too well with Roberts' father Judd Hirsch. Susan Sarandon is Hirsch's wife who defies her husband and gives her support to her son. Also starring Sterling Hayden, Annette O'Toole and Shelley Winters. ★★½ $14.99

King of the Hill

(1993, 115 min, US, Steven Soderbergh) Set in Depression-era St. Louis, *King of the Hill* is based on the memoirs of A.E. Hotchener and tells the tale of a boy who is essentially abandoned by well-meaning but desperate parents. While not ignoring the realities of the period, director Soderbergh (*sex, lies, and videotape*) manages to pick out the story's joyous moments without ever getting sickeningly sentimental. Much credit has to go to 13-year-old Jesse Bradford who stars as Aaron, a boy who begins to lose everything but always keeps his sense of fairness, fun and dignity. Bradford's soulful eyes reveal his thoughts with a subtlety

that's remarkable for an actor of any age. With an impeccable eye, Soderbergh has taken a small story and given it quiet, resonant power. ★★★½ $19.99

King, Queen, Knave

(1972, 92 min, GB, Jerzy Skolimowski) Undeservedly maligned by critics, this surreal adaptation of Victor Nabokov's novel is filled with stinging black humor. The story concerns an impish young lad who falls in love with his aunt (Gina Lollobrigida); and together they plot to murder her husband (David Niven). ★★★

King Ralph

(1991, 97 min, US, David S. Ward) John Goodman has his first starring role in this lightweight but engaging comedy. Goodman plays a Las Vegas lounge singer (who does a mean Little Richard) who, after an accident wipes out the entire royal family, becomes the King of England. Most of the comedy centers on the big guy's "fish out of water" comedy of errors. Peter O'Toole also stars as the royal secretary who acts as baby-sitter and cultural guide to King Ralph. ★★½ $9.99

King Rat

(1965, 133 min, US, Bryan Forbes) A gritty, first-rate drama, based on James Clavell's novel. Set at a POW camp in Malaysia during WWII, the story focuses on the rigors of captivity facing Allied prisoners, and the high cost they pay for their dignity and survival. George Segal stars as a mercenary American G.I. financially benefitting from the hunger and sickness around him; and James Fox is terrific as his principled, British right-hand man (the film hints at more but never follows up on it). Good cast includes Tom Courtenay as an officious security officer, and John Mills and Denholm Elliott (who was a real-life POW) as ranking officers. ★★★½ $19.99

King Solomon's Mines

(1937, 80 min, GB, Robert Stevenson) This exciting adventure story tells of the search for a legendary diamond mine deep in the heart of Africa. The robust and legendary Paul Robeson fills the screen with star quality as a mysterious African chieftan. Based on a novel by H. Rider Haggard. ★★★ $39.99

King's Row

(1942, 127 min, US, Sam Wood) Ronald Reagan's best performance (excluding his portrayal of the "I can't remember" president) is featured in this gripping and well-made drama. Set in a small Midwestern town, the story follows the friendship of Ann Sheridan, Robert Cummings and Reagan from childhood to young adulthood — as Cummings studies medicine overseas, Sheridan and Reagan stay behind, with tragedy in store for Reagan. Sheridan and Betty Field (as a reclusive childhood friend) excel. ★★★½ $19.99

The King's Whore

(1992, 111 min, US/Italy/West Germany, Axel Corti) "Masterpiece Theatre" meets Danielle Steele in this lavishly produced variation on the "Dangerous Liaisons" theme. Timothy Dalton stars as a 19th-century Italian king who stops at nothing in the pursuit of his chancellor's wife (Valeria Golina). The film is surprisingly well-made and entertaining to the end, and definitely qualifies as a "guilty pleasure." ★★½ $19.99

The Kingdom

(1994, 279 min, Denmark, Lars von Trier) You may have your "E.R.," America, but look away: *The Kingdom*, a joyfully creepy and surrealistic Danish medical thriller/satire, is full of jaded New Age practices, a crying for mother Casper, a nationalistic neurologist longing for his homeland through binoculars, a spiritualist has-been finally in touch to a clue of an afterlife, and more information about voodoo than one would expect in a waiting room. Udo Kier stars as the new staff member to a Copenhagen hospital, where patients and doctors, alike, engage in totally unexpected behavior. Though comparisons have been made to "E.R." and David Lynch's "Twin Peaks," and they may even exist, *The Kingdom* is a singular effort. Director von Trier has his own agenda – he even makes a carnival barker pitch between episodes accentuating the ever-continuing battle between good and evil. At four-and-a-half hours, the film is hardly dull or repetitive, and if expectations are put on hold, von Trier's stylistic smorgasbord can be as compelling and visually hypnotic as his earlier work *Zentropa*. (Danish with English subtitles) ★★★½ $24.99

Kingfish – A Story of Huey P. Long

(1995, 96 min, US, Thomas Schlamme) Huey Long, the Kingfish, emerged from the morass of Louisiana politics in the 1930s to become a national figure crusading for a redistribution of wealth and power. He formed a third party called Share Our Wealth, proselytizing exactly that, moving from Governor to the U.S. Senate with his eyes on the White House. He was larger than life, bombastic and rambunctious, and capable of making friends and enemies, and John Goodman is an on-target choice to portray this flawed giant. Unfortunately, the characterizations in *Kingfish* are sketched too broadly, almost buffoonishly, and the film suffers a heavy-handedness present in many Turner productions. While the visual production values exhibit attention to detail and an effective use of location, the script is weak and an intrusive musical score is particularly annoying. Stick with

King of the Hill

All the King's Men, which was based on the life of Long. ★★ $14.99

Kingpin

(1996, 113 min, US, Peter Farrelly & Bobby Farrelly) A one-handed bowling wiz takes a moronic Amish farmer and tries to turn him into the next champion. What sounds like a pitch from *The Player* actually turns out to be an unexpectedly funny, dark-edged entry from the "dumb" school of comedy filmmaking. Woody Harrelson plays a potential champion bowler whose brush with rival Bill Murray ends up with his bowling hand being cut off. Years later and now an alcoholic grifter, Harrelson stumbles upon Randy Quaid, a talented Amish bowler who hides his ability from his family. With just the sparest of double talk, Harrelson and Quaid are on the road to Reno to enter the national championship. Much of *Kingpin* is in the stupid vein, and does it wallow in it. But it's also very cynical, and much as you may, you can't help but laugh. *Kingpin*'s also of note for three prominent stars having desperately bad hair days. ★★★ $14.99

Kings Go Forth

(1958, 109 min, US, Delmer Daves) An intriguing war story that explores racial bigotry. Frank Sinatra and Tony Curtis are American G.I.s fighting in France during WWII who both fall in love with Natalie Wood. When they discover she is half black, their prejudices come to the fore, forcing them to face and examine their bigotry. All three stars give fine performances in this penetrating melodrama. ★★★ $19.99

Kings of the Road

(1976, 176 min, West Germany, Wim Wenders) This early Wenders masterpiece is a somber tale of a projector repairman and a friend who slowly thread through the barren landscape of the border regions of West and East Germany visiting shattered movie theatres, listening to rock 'n' roll and encountering strangers with strange stories. The "New" Germany that Wenders paints is one of a vast and underpopulated hinterland which proves to be both empty and imprisoning. (German with English subtitles) ★★★½ $29.99

Kipperbang

(1982, 80 min, GB, Michael Apted) This lightweight comedy details the romantic fantasies of a group of young teens and their teachers in 1948 Britain. *Kipperbang* evokes the mood of a Bill Forsyth film, but lacks resonance and sense of direction. ★★½ $59.99

Kipps

(1941, 82 min, GB, Carol Reed) Michael Redgrave puts in a solid performance as Mr. Kipps, a shopkeeper who, upon inheriting a fortune, attempts to enter into high society. Sidney Gilliat's screenplay is faithfully adapted from the H.G. Wells novel. (Later made into the Broadway musical "Half a Sixpence.") ★★★½

Kiss Me Deadly

(1955, 105 min, US, Robert Aldrich) With the despairing plea "Remember me" from a soon-to-be-dead dame echoing in his head, private eye Mike Hammer (Ralph Meeker) becomes

involved in a convoluted case of torture, murder and a stolen, white-hot Pandora's box. Hammer, a sometimes sadistic and violent man, attempts to find the killers of a frantic, near-naked woman (Cloris Leachman) whom he picks up in his car one night. A great, fast-moving plot, loads of unforgettable characters and creative photography contribute in making this Mickey Spillane detective story (and Cold War allegory) a classic of late film noir. ★★★½ $19.99

Kiss Me Kate

(1953, 119 min, US, George Sidney) One of Cole Porter's best scores highlights this vibrant adaptation of the Broadway musical about a divorced theatrical couple who are reunited for a performance of Shakespeare's "The Taming of the Shrew." Howard Keel and Kathryn Grayson are wonderful as the estranged husband and wife; and the dance sequences featuring Ann Miller, Bob Fosse, Tommy Rall and Bobby Van are terrific. ★★★½ $19.99

Kiss Me Stupid

(1964, 126 min, US, Billy Wilder) A rollicking sex farce unfairly maligned on its initial release, this wicked comedy offers many a nasty swipe at sexual politics. Dean Martin plays a successful, womanizing singer ending a tour. En route through a small Nevada town, Martin is "shanghaied" by struggling composer Ray Walston, who will do anything to have Dino hear his music – including hiring prostitute Kim Novak to masquerade as his wife, hoping Dean will take a fancy to her. ★★★ $19.99

Kiss of Death

(1947, 98 min, US, Henry Hathaway) Victor Mature, in his best role, is Nick Bianco, a hard-luck crook who turns state's evidence only to find himself stalked by a vengeful hoodlum. Richard Widmark, in his screen debut, steals the show as a sadistic, psycho hood with a demonic giggle and a propensity for throwing old ladies in wheelchairs down flights of stairs. ★★★½ $14.99

Kiss of Death

(1971, 80 min, GB, Mike Leigh) A minor film from the early career of director Leigh, *Kiss of Death* is essentially the dead-end story about the dead-end life of Trevor, a pathetic and slightly sociopathic Manchester youth. Trevor hangs out with his best friend, makes a half-hearted, and mean-spirited, stab at dating and keeps up his work as a mortuary assistant. As slice-of-life and character study, the film exhibits Leigh's innate talents, but its story goes nowhere and lacks any shred of motivating interest. ★★ $29.99

Kiss of Death

(1995, 101 min, US, Barbet Schroeder) An accomplished, intense and satisfying crime thriller, director Schroeder's gritty updating of the 1947 film noir classic is a high-octane ride through New York City's underworld. David Caruso makes a credible, satisfying leading man debut as a Queens ex-con trying to stay legit but who's pulled back into crime out of a misguided sense of loyalty. Much like Victor Mature's imprisoned jewel thief in the original, Caruso's Jimmy Kilmartin wants nothing to do with the assistant D.A.; that is until his family is directly affected by his partners-in-crime. Turning on them in an ingenious manner, he infiltrates a gang led by low-level mob figure Junior Brown (Nicolas Cage), while at the same time coping with a cop with a grudge (Samuel L. Jackson). Cage is a marvel as Junior, giving an extraordinary portrayal of a sadistic sociopath who's as complex as he is lethal. Schroeder's taut direction, a lean, multilayered screenplay and first-rate performances all combine to thrust this into the genre's upper echelon. ★★★½ $96.89

Kiss of the Spider Woman

(1985, 120 min, Brazil, Hector Babenco) Babenco's spellbinding meditation on political idealism and self-delusion stars William Hurt (who won a Best Actor Oscar) and Raul Julia, who portray two dramatically opposite inmates thrown together in a dungeon-like cell somewhere in South America. Julia, a cold political realist and activist, is forced to endure the fantasies of Hurt, a hopelessly romantic and politically naive homosexual. An exotic Sonia Braga plays both Julia's one-time lover and Hurt's imagined heroine. (Filmed in English) ★★★½ $14.99

Kiss Tomorrow Goodbye

(1950, 102 min, US, Gordon Douglas) A cold-blooded mobster (James Cagney) escapes from prison and embarks on a crime spree with his love-struck gun moll. But when he murders her brother and dumps her for a classy debutante, Cagney learns the hard way that hell hath no fury like a gun moll scorned. ★★★ $19.99

Kissed

(1997, 75 min, Canada, Lynne Stopkewich) You would think that a movie about a necrophiliac woman working as an embalmer would be fairly controversial, shocking or at least push some uncomfortable buttons within the viewer. This may be true with a poorly executed, low-budget horror film like *Nekromantik*, but it is unfortunately not the case with this glossier production based on a short story from a book of women's erotica. Molly Parker stars as a curious young woman who happens to be sexually attracted to youthful, fresh male corpses. While in embalming school, she meets a med student (Peter Outerbridge) who becomes attracted to her obsession and eventually begins to share her

Raul Julia (l.) and William Hurt in *Kiss of the Spider Woman*

compulsion for cadavers. He, however, wants to cross the line that only she has been able to find and his measures turn drastic when she cannot help him realize his fantasy. Fairly tame and placid, the film attempts to explore its subject obliquely, without showing too much in the way of sex and gore. Too bad, because this restraint works against the movie, since the ability of the first-time filmmakers is not up to the challenge of conveying an uncomfortable point without graphically showing it. ★★½ $99.99

The Kitchen Toto

(1988, 96 min, GB, Harry Hook) Offering an uncompromising child's eye view of 1950s Kenya, when that state was still very much a colony of Great Britain, *The Kitchen Toto* is a mesmerizing and at times harrowing examination of a land imprisoned by the boundaries of cultural and racial alienation. The title refers to a kitchen helper, in this case Mwangi (Edwin Mahinda), a young Kenyan of the Kikuyu tribe who leaves his widowed mother to work in the house of the British chief of police. Scorned by both colonialist and tribesmen, Mwangi tries peacefully to find his way through a turbulent world where violence is the norm. ★★★½ $19.99

Kitty and the Bagman

(1982, 95 min, Australia, Donald Crombie) The glory days of the Warner Brothers back lot are revived in this colorful Aussie Roaring Twenties comedy, full of flappers, gamblers and an earnest interest in the dishonestly earned dollar. Set in Sydney, it follows a beautiful innocent young bride, Kitty O'Rourke, who turns to the oldest profession in order to spring her small-time hood husband from jail. ★★½

Kitty Foyle

(1940, 105 min, US, Sam Wood) Ginger Rogers won an Oscar (beating Katharine Hepburn in *The Philadelphia Story*) for her strong portrait of a career woman torn between two men of different social backgrounds. Dalton Trumbo adapted the screenplay from Christopher Morley's novel. ★★★ $19.99

The Klansman

(1974, 112 min, US, Terence Young) With a cast including Richard Burton and Lee Marvin, a script cowritten by Samuel Fuller and a topic as important as race relations in the deep South, one would expect something from this film. Don't. It's almost impossible to convey the disappointment of this embarrassingly trashy and exploitative little oddity. Fuller was set to direct, but took an early walk. ★ $14.99

Klondike Annie

(1936, 77 min, US, Raoul Walsh) Mae West adapted her own stage play and stars in this unusual comedy-drama and morality tale. West plays an entertainer who murders her possessive lover and escapes on a steamer bound for Alaska. On board, she meets

Kitty Foyle

love-struck captain Victor McLaglen and missionary Helen Jerome Eddy. With the police hot on her trail, and Eddy dying at sea, West changes identities with the dead woman and, on arrival in Alaska, is forced to continue the charade. The tone is more somber compared to West's other movies, and though Mae still manages to knock off a few "West-ern" zingers, its do-good, sentimental attitude doesn't altogether mix with West's brazen character. ★★ $14.99

Klute

(1971, 114 min, US, Alan J. Pakula) Jane Fonda won an Academy Award for her mesmerizing portrayal of a high-priced New York call girl in this psychological thriller. Donald Sutherland stars in the title role of an out-of-town cop on the trail of a missing husband who may have been a client of Fonda's. An outstanding use of sound and editing, along with the sexual frankness of the script, make this one of the landmark films of the '70s. Also starring Roy Scheider and Charles Cioffi. ★★★★ $14.99

Knife in the Head

(1978, 108 min, West Germany, Reinhard Huff) Bruno Ganz (*Wings of Desire*) stars in this well-paced mystery as Hoffman, a scientist who is shot in the head at a local radical hang-out while searching for his estranged wife. The injury leaves him partially paralyzed and causes him to lose much of his memory. As Hoffman tries to uncover the truth about the shooting, he is caught between the radicals and police who each want to exploit him for their own purposes. Brilliant acting and a great script make this a top-notch thriller. (German with English subtitles) ★★★ $29.99

Knife in the Water

(1962, 95 min, Poland, Roman Polanski) Polanski's extraordinary study of three characters interacting on a small boat and how an innocent yachting weekend is transformed into a journey of mistrust and adultery. Polanski's first film, a fascinating study of sexual obsession, is riveting in its narrative, and creates a tension-filled atmosphere throughout. (Polish with English subtitles) ★★★★ $29.99

Knight Moves

(1992, 90 min, US, Carl Schenkel) This psycho-thriller is an effective, bone-chilling mystery about a serial killer who gives clues to an international chess master about where and when his next victim will die because he wants to play against the best. Christopher Lambert is very convincing as the champion and Tom Skerritt, in a sturdy performance, is the local police chief who both suspects and helps him. The standard thriller ending doesn't detract from the film; in fact, it's very intense despite its predictability. If you can figure out who the killer is before he's revealed, you're a bit of a chess master yourself. ★★★ $9.99

Knight without Armour

(1937, 107 min, GB, Jacques Feyder) This cross-cultural oddity was produced by British movie mogul Alexander Korda, directed by Frenchman Feyder, takes place in Russia, and stars Marlene Dietrich and Robert Donat. The story concerns an aristocratic Russian woman who is rescued from the Bolshevik Revolution by a British undercover agent. Based on a novel by James Hilton, the film is imbued with sumptuous production values, charismatic acting and lots of romance and atmosphere. ★★★ $19.99

Knightriders

(1981, 145 min, US, George Romero) This nonhorror feature from the director of the *Living Dead* trilogy is a deeply personal, idealistic but perhaps naive moral tale about the difficulties of remaining true to one's personal beliefs. It follows King Billy (Ed Harris) and his troop of knights, who travel around the country putting on motorcycle-jousting competitions and medieval fairs for middle American spectators. The members of the group follow Billy and live this lifestyle because they want a respite from the pressures and temptations of the modern world. Ironically, their growing popularity brings these same pressures to bear upon their group, fragmenting it in the process. The entire film can be seen as a metaphor for Romero's career as an independent filmmaker and succeeds on many levels: as a rousing action-adventure picture, as an allegory, and as an exploration of the possibility of maintaining one's idealism. Harris is terrific in an early, pre-star performance, and a huge cast of supporting players lend authenticity. ★★★ $19.99

Knights

(1993, 89 min, US, Albert Pyun) It's cyborg vs. man in yet another predictable sci-fi actioner. With the usual ravaged wasteland serving as a backdrop, cyborg leader Kris Kristofferson has discovered that enemy robo (Lance Henriksen) has discovered a new source of fuel: human blood. Hero Kris teams up with a vengeance-seeking human (Kathy Long) in a disjointed frenzy of kickboxing chaos, saving the day, but not the amount of brian cells lost while watching this. ★ $14.99

Kojiro

(1967, 152 min, Japan, Hiroshi Inagaki) Kojiro is a young man with an attitude. Taken into a home as a foundling, he chafes under the rough authority of the family's son, Hyosuké, with whom he has been raised as a brother. He gains Hyosuké's mortal enmity when he runs off with his sister, Toné. Hyosuké pursues his sister and our hero, even though Toma, Toné's fiancé and Kojiro's best

friend, refuses to do so, wanting only Toné's happiness. With Hyosuké in hot pursuit, Kojiro vows to Toné to become famous and secure their position in society. To do this, he challenges a martial arts school, and wins by flying in the face of tradition. When the instructor commits suicide in disgrace, the students take off after Kojiro. A late-night indulgence of flying fists, flashing swords, bruised egos and flailing passions, where the characters are either tributes to order and decorum or totally at the mercy of their emotions. Warning: inferior subtitles. But don't worry; you'll get the idea without getting all the text. (Japanese with English subtitles) ★★½ $49.99

Koko: A Talking Gorilla

(1978, 81 min, France, Barbet Schroeder) This fascinating documentary has director Schroeder and cinematographer Nestor Almendros traveling to laboratories at Stanford University to take a close look at Koko, a female gorilla that has been taught to talk through sign language. The film also probes the controversial techniques used by the scientists and captures the excitement of this rare breakthrough in communication. (English and French with English subtitles) ★★★ $59.99

Koko the Clown Cartoons

(1927-29, 70 min, US, Max & Dave Fleischer) Max and Dave Fleischer, animation's great innovators and creators of Betty Boop and Popeye, were instrumental in transforming animation from simple drawings and stories and elevating it to a pop culture art form. While the Disney studios were releasing wholesome cartoons, the Fleischer brothers combined animation with live-action, contemporary music, social issues and even surrealism to bring their cartoons to life. This series of ten silent, black-and-white cartoons all feature their early creation, and future favorite, Koko the Clown. ★★★ $19.99

Kolya

(1996, 111 min, Czechoslovakia, Jan Sverak) This Academy Award winner for Best Foreign Language Film is a sweetly rendered fable about a washed-up, middle-aged classical cellist and compulsive womanizer who's struggling to make ends meet in 1988 Prague. Having been booted off the state Philharmonia for having too many close relatives who've "immigrated" to the West, Frantisek Louka (Zdenek Sverak) ekes out a living by playing funerals and touching up gravestones. Out of desperation, he agrees to a fake marriage to a Russian émigré for a substantial sum of money. Louka finds himself up a tree, however, when she splits town leaving him with her 5-year-old boy, Kolya (Andrej Chalimon), and a suspicious police inspector who seems determined to lock him up. *Kolya*, of course, is a simple story and though it doesn't cover any new ground, its charm lies in Louka's gradual warming to fatherhood (or grandfatherhood as it were) as set against Prague's gradual warming to the Velvet Revolution. Ultimately, the film avoids the maudlin trap and delivers a tender and subtly profound look at the latter days of Communism and Soviet occupation in the Czech Republic. (Czech with English subtitles) ★★★½ $102.99

Korczak

(1990, 118 min, Poland, Andrzej Wajda) Wajda returns to his roots with this haunting story of Janusz Korczak, a well-known Jewish doctor and poet who ran an orphanage for 200 children in the Warsaw ghetto. Realizing that his wards would surely be sent to the camps, he vowed to stay with them until the end, despite repeated efforts by members of Poland's intelligentsia to convince him to run to freedom. Stylistically the film resembles Wajda's 1950s classics *Ashes and Diamonds* and *Kanal*, including shadowy black-and-white camera work by Robby Müller and the

K

Kolya

The Krays

scratchy sound quality. The screenplay by Agnieska Holland (director of *Europa, Europa*) is heavy-handed at times, but is nonetheless powerful in conveying the overwhelming love which Korzcak gave to his children. Actor Wojtec Pszoniak instills in Korczak an almost messianic quality, portraying him as a gentle but at times angry defender of righteousness and human dignity. (Polish with English subtitles) ★★★★ $79.99

Kostas

(1986, 88 min, Australia, Paul Cox) A Greek immigrant taxi driver and a wealthy socialite fall in love. When pressure from friends and family threaten their relationship, they must decide whether to live by the rules or by their hearts. Wendy Hughes' passionate performance highlights this otherwise standard star-crossed romantic drama. ★★½ $69.99

Koyaanisqatsi

(1983, 90 min, US, Godfrey Reggio) A remarkable and riveting cinematic poem that astonishes the viewer with its aural and visual splendor. This nonconventional, non-narrative feature is a mesmerizing compilation of images; a study of awesome natural and man-made landscapes observed and presented in an invigorating fashion through the use of speeded-up, time-lapse and slow-motion photography. Few films have offered such a rich integration of sounds, ideas and images. Composer Philip Glass has provided a hypnotic score which serves as an amplification of the visuals' power. ★★★½

Kramer vs. Kramer

(1979, 104 min, US, Robert Benton) Hollywood takes a movie-of-the-week "topical" subject — Mom takes off to find herself and Dad is left with the kid — and with solid performances from Dustin Hoffman, Meryl Streep and Jane Alexander, an unexpectedly fine performance from a very young Justin Henry, beautiful cinematography and competent scripting and direction from Benton, transforms it into a compassionate study of urban life and family ties, not to mention a media sensation. Oscars for Best Picture, Best Direction, Best Actor, Best Supporting Actress and Best Screenplay. ★★★★ $14.99

Krapp's Last Tape

See: Beckett Directs

The Krays

(1990, 119 min, GB, Peter Medak) A highly original and haunting account of the true-life rise to power of two of England's most notorious thugs — the Kray twins. Under the loving care of their tough-as-nails mum (played with a down-to-earth forcefulness by Billie Whitelaw), the brothers ride a wave of unthinkable violence and terror, becoming the most feared men in the ganglands of 1960s London. Filmed with an eerie and atmospheric sense of the surreal, director Medak's vision of the Krays' sadistic reign offers a fascinating psychological profile of these ruthless killers. Despite their differing sexual orientations, they are ultimately bound to each other and to their mother. Gary and Martin Kemp both deliver excellent low-key performances as the twins. ★★★½ $14.99

Krush Groove

(1988, 97 min, US, Michael Schultz) Although saddled with a formula plot, this infectious hip-hop and rap musical still has a fresh, exciting feel mostly as a result of the spirited music of Sheila E., the Fat Boys and Kurtis Blow. The story centers around some ambitious but naive renegades who want to set up their own record label dedicated to the sounds of the inner city, but who soon find themselves immersed in the loansharking and drug underworld. The Fat Boys are very funny in their Three Stooges-like comedy relief. ★★½ $14.99

Kuffs

(1992, 102 min, US, Bruce A. Evans) After a bit of an acting stretch in *Robin Hood* and *Mobsters*, Christian Slater returns to his most recognizable screen persona, that of the glib, wise-cracking rebel. Slater plays the brother of a San Francisco Police Patrol captain who inherits the security agency business after his sibling is murdered. Partnered with suspended cop Tony Goldwyn (*Ghost*), Slater takes on the killer and the slimy businessman he works for. The film is reminiscent of *Beverly Hills Cop*, especially in pacing, editing and musical score. And like Eddie Murphy's hit, mixes action, suspense and lots of comedy; though not as successfully. ★★ $9.99

Kung Fu Rascals

(1991, 110 min, US, Steve Wang) A kingdom is threatened by total destruction as an evil tyrant gathers his troops for a crushing attack, and the only ones who can stop him are three guys named Chen Chow Mein, Reepo, and Lao Zee. An incredible array of special F/X by director Wang (F/X director of *Predator*, *Batman Returns*), action that rivals such films as *The Seventh Voyage of Sinbad*, slapstick humor and martial arts hijinks galore make this action-adventure a real find. ★★★ $29.99

Kurt Vonnegut's Monkey House

(1992, 100 min, US) Four involving, humorous and thought-provoking episodes of Kurt Vonnegut's series are compiled for video release. "All the King's Men" is the first and best of these stories. It's a powerful exercise in acting and storytelling which creates an entirely new aesthetic for a good game of chess. ★★★ $79.99

Kwaidan

(1964, 164 min, Japan, Masaki Kobayashi) This legendary Japanese film is a superb anthology of four terrifying tales of the supernatural. Filmed with exquisite visual sensitivity, this distinctive work of art is filled with dreamlike settings, elaborately stylized action and haunting sound effects. (Japanese with English subtitles) (Letterboxed version) ★★★½ $29.99

L.627

(1992, 145 min, France, Bertrand Tavernier) A gritty, semidocumentary-like look at the day-to-day lives of undercover narcotic agents in a Paris most tourists will never see, *L.627* is a disturbing, overlong and possibly racist examination which despite its flaws still manages to be compelling. Capably directed by veteran filmmaker Tavernier (*Round Midnight, A Sunday in the Country*), the film centers on a rogue cop named Lulu (Didier Bezace), who has been transferred to an overworked precinct. Unlike American films of this sort, there are no shootouts, car chases or gratuitous violence. The story's power is accumulative in the relationship of the officers and Lulu's personal and professional life. However, it is difficult to determine if the film panders to racial stereotypes as all of the dealers tracked by Lulu and his associates are either black or Arab – which is defended by Tavernier as what he saw when accompanying real police officers on assignment. (French with English subtitles) ★★★ $79.99

L.A. Story

(1991, 95 min, US, Mick Jackson) Steve Martin, after a less-than-spectacular outing in *My Blue Heaven*, wrote the screenplay for and stars in this fabulously witty satire on life in Los Angeles' fast lane. Martin plays a wacked-out TV weatherman who loses his job, and begins affairs with two dissimilar women: Valley girl Sarah Jessica Parker (in a wonderfully comic turn) and British reporter Victoria Tennant. Martin's screenplay is full of on-target jabs, lively slapstick and metaphysical revelations (our favorite: the two very different lines at an Automatic Teller Machine). Martin's best work since *Roxanne*, and a pure delight. ★★★½ $9.99

Labyrinth

(1986, 101 min, US, Jim Henson) George Lucas has combined his talents with the magical puppet artistry of Jim Henson to create this imaginative fantasy. A young girl (Jennifer Connelly), searching for her kidnapped brother, is forced to weave her way through a treacherous maze where she encounters the deliciously maniacal elfin-like David Bowie. This *Wizard of Oz*-like odyssey features adorable puppetry, catchy tunes, and a rather complex story line which only slightly detracts from its whimsical tone. ★★★

Labyrinth of Passion

(1982, 100 min, Spain, Pedro Almodóvar) Almodóvar's second feature film is a dazzling display of a great future talent in its rawest form. The story centers around both Riza Niro, the son of a deposed Middle Eastern tyrant who likes to hang around with Madrid's sleazier denizens, and Sexi, an aspiring rock singer and unabashed nymphomaniac. The two fall for each other and decide to run away, but first they must deal with their respective rock groups, a group of terrorists who are bent on kidnapping Riza, and a whole host of other outrageous plot twists. Bristling with loony humor, the film lacks the visual punch and flawless timing of his later works, but still it is a frantic, if somewhat uneven, portrait of Almodóvar's explosive potential. (Spanish with English subtitles) ★★½ $79.99

The Lacemaker

(1977, 108 min, France, Claude Goretta) A very young Isabelle Huppert stars as an inexperienced shopgirl who meets a bourgeois student on the deserted beaches of an off-season Normandy resort. They return to Paris where their romance strains under the weight of class and intellectual differences. Huppert, who rocketed to international stardom thanks to her portrayal, is breathtakingly beautiful and gives a tender portrait of love. Lovingly filmed by Goretta. (French with English subtitles) (Letterboxed version) ★★★½ $29.99

Ladies of the Chorus

(1949, 61 min, US, Phil Karlson) Though Marilyn Monroe gets star billing on the video box, she really has a secondary role in this, her second film. MM is a burlesque dancer who's looking for a ticket out; and if a wealthy bachelor can help, so be it. Adele Jergens plays her mother who has been there before and tries to help her daughter not make the same mistakes. Marilyn sings some songs, and looks great, but it's a minor vehicle nonetheless. ★★ $19.99

Ladies on the Rocks

(1983, 100 min, Denmark) Two women – Misha, stuck with a good-for-nothing boyfriend, and Laura, married with kids – decide to chuck the domestic scene and join forces, become a cabaret comedy team and take their act on the road. This Danish "*Thelma and Louise*-meets-*Punchline*" follows the aspiring comediennes as they fine-tune their revue in the small clubs which dot rural Denmark. The two women, who also cowrote the script, center their strange but amusing schtick on stereotypically pre-feminist obsessions: their far-from-perfect bodies, men, love and more about men. An unusual comedydrama about two self-determined women. (Danish with English subtitles) ★★½ $29.99

Lady and the Tramp

(1955, 75 min, US, Hamilton Luske) Beloved Disney classic rates as one of the studio's top animated features. Who can forget the spaghetti scene, which is more romantic than most modern "love stories." ★★★★

Lady by Choice

(1934, 77 min, US, David Burton) In a role quite similar to her brilliant success a year earlier in *Lady for a Day*, May Robson encores as a cantankerous, scraggy old lady who gets the onceover. Carole Lombard is a fan dancer looking to cool her image. So her press agent gets the idea to "adopt a mother," and guess who gets chosen. This is a bright, appealing comedy, and Lombard and Robson work extremely well together. ★★★ $19.99

Lady Chatterley's Lover

(1955, 102 min, France, Marc Allégret) Danielle Darrieux stars as the repressed Lady Chatterley who enjoys a sexual awakening and personal freedom when she meets a handsome, muscular workman in this fine French version of D.H. Lawrence's classic novel. Although when viewed today the film is quite tasteful, it caused a storm in the U.S. in the 1950s and was banned by the New York State Board of Censors. (French with English subtitles) ★★½

The Lady Eve

(1941, 93 min, US, Preston Sturges) Sturges, the most prolific and arguably the greatest comic filmmaker of the 1940s, wrote and directed this hilarious screwball comedy, one of the director's finest achievements. Barbara Stanwyck, in a great comic performance, is a cardsharp who sets out to hook gullible millionaire Henry Fonda. They fall in love, but when he gets wise she gets dumped, and Stanwyck devises a scheme to get him back – by impersonating royalty. The first-rate supporting cast includes Charles Coburn, William Demarest and the very funny Eugene Pallette as Fonda's exasperated father. ★★★★ $14.99

Lady for a Day

(1933, 96 min, US, Frank Capra) Capra's enchanting comedy based on Damon Runyon's story "Madame La Gimp," about a group of Broadway denizens who come together to help an old apple seller. Character actress May Robson has her greatest screen role as "Annie," and she makes the most of it. Capra's deft touch helps immeasurably in the film's enjoyment. Capra remade the story in 1961 as *A Pocketful of Miracles*. ★★★½ $79.99

The Lady Eve

The Lady From Shanghai

(1948, 87 min, US, Orson Welles) Rita Hayworth is the scorching femme fatale with a heavenly body and a devilish mind in this fascinating murder mystery. Welles himself plays her prime victim who, with a skull as thick as his Irish brogue, steps right into her trap. ★★★ $19.99

Lady in a Cage

(1964, 93 min, US, Walter Grauman) James Caan's first starring role. He plays the sadistic leader of a vicious gang of thieves who trap Olivia deHavilland in her own home. This fast-paced, lurid melodrama really delivers in the finale. With Jeff Corey, Scatman Crothers and Ann Sothern. ★★½ $49.99

Lady in Cement

(1968, 93 min, US, Gordon Douglas) Frank Sinatra is back in this sequel to *Tony Rome* as the titular detective, investigating the death of a nude woman who went swimming wearing only cement overshoes. Sinatra could play this role in his sleep – which he looks like he's doing throughout. Few thrills punctuate this standard mystery. With Raquel Welch, Dan Blocker and Joe E. Lewis. ★★ $59.99

The Lady in the Lake

(1946, 104 min, US, Robert Montgomery) Montgomery stars as private dick Phillip Marlowe searching for a missing wife and discovering a different woman's corpse floating in a mountain lake. Montgomery, who also directed, uses first person camera angles from Marlowe's point of view. Complete with Raymond Chandler's standards of gritty dialogue between troublesome cops and L.A. lowlifes. With Audrey Trotter, Lloyd Nolan and Jayne Meadows. ★★★ $19.99

Lady in White

(1988, 112 min, US, Frank LaLoggia) A real find. Young Lukas Haas gets locked in school overnight and uncovers – with the help of a young girl's spirit – the mystery of the legendary "Lady in White"; not to mention the identity of the girl's murderer. An extremely accomplished ghost story, with a great visual

Lady in a Cage

style. Though some may guess who the killer is before the denouement, it detracts nothing from the suspense and total enjoyment of this first-rate sleeper. Also with Alex Rocco, Len Cariou and Katherine Helmond. ★★★½ $9.99

Lady Jane

(1985, 117 min, GB, Trevor Nunn) Overlooked in its initial release, this elegant and absorbing romance is about the real-life adolescent aristocrat Lady Jane, who ascended to the British throne for a brief and tragic nine days. Starring Helena Bonham Carter and Cary Elwes. A bittersweet historical drama. ★★★ $79.99

Lady of Burlesque

(1943, 91 min, US, William Wellman) Barbara Stanwyck brings plenty of pizzazz to this sassy and enjoyable comic mystery based on Gypsy Rose Lee's "The G-String Murders." Stanwyck plays a burlesque dancer who sets out to solve who's killing her fellow strippers. ★★★ $9.99

Lady on the Bus

(1978, 102 min, Brazil, Neville D'Almeida) Sonia Braga, Brazil's voluptuous first lady of soft-core sex films, stars in this spicy romp. Sonia plays a frigid young married woman who can't seem to make it with her new husband. Seeking a cure, our heroine seeks the sexual help of her husband's male friends and even strangers in her determined efforts to loosen up. Why not? A charming and entertaining diversion. (Dubbed) ★★½

Lady Sings the Blues

(1972, 144 min, US, Sidney J. Furie) Diana Ross makes a sensational film debut as the legendary blues singer Billie Holiday. The film has all the dramatic trappings of a standard Hollywood biography; Ross, however, is in great voice. Billy Dee Williams and Richard Pryor (a stand out as Ross' piano player) also star. ★★★ $29.99

The Lady Vanishes

(1938, 97 min, GB, Alfred Hitchcock) The quintessential train murder mystery starring Michael Redgrave and Margaret Lockwood as a pair of travelers who undertake a search for a missing passenger – a diminutive old woman who holds secrects of international espionage. Upon vanishing, only a name on a window and a haunting melody serve as proof of her existence. ★★★★ $24.99

The Lady with the Dog

(1960, 89 min, USSR, Josef Heifitz) Thought to be one of the few films to capture the essence of Anton Chekov, this much admired romantic yet bittersweet love story is set in turn-of-the-century Russia. While vacationing at a resort in Yalta, a married, middle-aged banker meets a beautiful but sad young woman who, having left her husband behind in the city, has come on holiday accompanied only by her little dog. Attracted to one another, they begin an affair and eventually fall in love. Resolving to continue their affair after the holiday, they meet for years clandestinely in Moscow, but knowing full well that their love and relationship is doomed. (Russian with English subtitles) ★★★ $29.99

Ladybird, Ladybird

(1994, 102 min, GB, Ken Loach) Director Loach once again turns a quasi-documentary lens on the British underclass in this disarming, well-wrought drama based on a true story. Crissy Rock is unerringly authentic as a young mother who loses several children to state care – a woman whose pick of men mirrors her abusive childhood and whose love of her children is outstripped by bad choices, circumstances and a social welfare system which loses the human element in a sea of categorization. A cycle of childbirth, beatings and stays in women's refuges is broken by a chance encounter with a Paraguayan political refugee (portrayed with quiet passion by Vladimir Vega), a victim of an even more repressive state. Rock is shattering in a performance notable for a lack of melodrama or saccharine sentiment, straightforwardly depicting a life often lived out of bags and suitcases. The film recalls *American Heart* in exploring the strengths and frailties of family bonds, but offers more hope in its resolution. ★★★½ $14.99

Ladybugs

(1992, 89 min, US, Sidney J. Furie) There is only one Rodney Dangerfield and that is all you get when you see any one of his movies, tired old routines rehashed for the umpteenth time. The amazing thing is that it usually works, over and over again – although to a much lesser dergree here. Mr. No Respect finds himself as the coach of a girls' soccer team in this distant cousin of *The Bad News Bears*, where all the stereotypes and clichés are firmly in place. This often silly though surprisingly entertaining and moralizing film showcases a kinder, gentler Rodney (the film is rated PG-13), but parents should be warned that there are some naughty words, risque innuendos and a dream sequence that borderlines on tastelessness. ★★ $14.99

Ladyhawke

(1985, 121 min, US, Richard Donner) An entertaining medieval fantasy which combines adventure, romance and magic to produce an exciting story. Rutger Hauer stars as a knight deeply in love with a beautiful maiden (Michelle Pfeiffer), but the two are cursed by an evil bishop with a terrible spell. The lovers are eternally separated – for in the day, the young woman is turned into a hawk and in the night, when she is transformed back into human form, he is changed into a wolf. It takes a young pickpocket (a delightfully funny Matthew Broderick) to assist them in breaking the curse. ★★★ $14.99

The Ladykillers

(1955, 90 min, GB, Alexander MacKendrick) Another mordant comedy classic from the Ealing Studios with Alec Guinness leading a group of maladroit thieves whose plans are undone by a sweetly obtuse little old lady (superbly portayed by Katie Johnson). The other members of this bumbling gang of hoods are played by an impressive and well-seasoned cast: Peter Sellers, Herbert Lom, Cecil Parker and Danny Green. ★★★★ $9.99

L

The Lair of the White Worm

(1988, 94 min, GB, Ken Russell) Russell's intoxicating adaptation of Bram Stoker's final work is a tongue-in-cheek romp into the world of Gothic horror. Amanda Donohoe offers up a truly kinky performance as a mysterious snake lady who slithers her way into modern England in search of virgins to feed to her giant worm god. Hugh Grant, Sammi Davis and Peter Capaldi make up the group of locals determined to stamp out this ancient evil. Russell's flair isn't lost as this slimy tale of rampant vampirism oozes with an abundance of camp humor, serpentine symbolism, and just about every daft snake joke in the book — oh, and let's not forget those requisite Russellian hallucinations. ★★★½ $9.99

Lake Consequence

(1992, 90 min, US, Rafael Eiseman) "Hey honey, did you catch any fish?" is undoubtedly the most memorable line in *Lake Consequence*, though you'll have to watch the film to figure out why. But this is not a movie that's counting on its witty repartee to capture the viewer's interest; it's a plain and simple *9½ Weeks*/Zalman King/soft-core erotica portrayal of a woman's plunge into sexual abandon. The cast includes some blindingly attractive performers: Billy Zane is the strong silent landscaper/requisite drifter, Joan Severance is the requisite repressed housewife, and May Karasun is the requisite bisexual exhibitionist, who form a brief but fiery ménage-à-trois. ★★ $9.99

Lakki — The Boy Who Grew Wings

(1992, 104 min, Norway, Svend Wam) Wam's film about a troubled youth's struggle towards spiritual ascent is about as obvious as the mysterious wings that grow on young Lakki's back. Yes, the film actually depicts scenes of sprouting feathers and dreams of flight as Lakki tries to come to grips with his parents' separation, his father's new fiancée, his mother's flagrant sexual behavior, and perhaps his own sexual orientation. The symbolism is so heavy-handed that it almost becomes insulting, but the cinematography itself merits the film a look. Winner of Best Picture at the 1992 Giffoni Film Festival. (Norwegian with English subtitles) ★★ $59.99

Lancelot of the Lake

(1974, 80 min, France, Robert Bresson) Hailed in its day as a magnificent cinematic achievement, this austere examination of the end of chivalry and the dissolution of King Arthur's Court is more a cinematic relic from a bygone cinematic era. Stark and somber in atmosphere, the film follows Lancelot as he returns empty-handed from his quest for the Holy Grail filled with foreboding that his failure is linked to his illicit love for Queen Guinevere. Bresson's approach is stylistically minimal to the extreme as the film features barren dialogue and severely restrained performances which, though seemingly wooden, disguise a bristling subtext. Bresson also seems fascinated with the sound of men clanking around in metal suits as they wander aimlessly throughout the film. It's of a style that was all the rage in the art-houses of the era, but the success of its translation to the small

Amanda Donohoe in *Lair of the White Worm*

screen of the '90s is less than certain. (French with English subtitles) ★★½ $79.99

Land and Freedom

(1995, 109 min, GB, Ken Loach) Loach offers a powerful and heartrending look at the Spanish Civil War as seen through the eyes of an earnest young Liverpudlian. The film opens with the fatal heart attack of an elderly man in present-day England. As his bereaved granddaughter sifts through his belongings, the story focuses on his involvement as a youth in the volunteer brigades in Spain. Young David (portrayed with engaging sincerity by Ian Hart) begins his journey as an ardent unionist and card carrying member of the Communist Party. Upon his arrival in Spain, he is swept up into the POUM movement, a rather freely organized and highly egalitarian sector of the Resistance, and graduates to a front-line "militia" where he and his group make occasional incursions into Francoista territory and liberate villages. The film's real focus is on the betrayal of POUM and other grass-roots groups by Stalinist-led international forces — Loach holds no punches in branding Stalin and The Party as mercenary traitors to the workers' cause. Ever the left-wing agitator, Loach once again has created a brilliant blend of personal history and political treatise that is riveting and intellectually fascinating. ★★★★ $14.99

The Land Before Time

(1988, 66 min, US, Don Bluth) This rather short but charming animated feature should entertain younger children with its story of a baby dinosaur, Littlefoot, who becomes separated from his parents. Like the director's previous animated film, *An American Tail*, the story centers on the little lost hero's search for home. The animation, though less than superlative, is fine for the film's simplistic story and the plotline should be easy for young ones to follow. ★★★ $19.99

The Land Before Time II: The Great Valley Adventure

(1994, 74 min, US) This straight-to-video sequel is a wonderful addition to the world of animated children's films. We are reunited with Little Foot and his friends in a valley that

is almost completely cut off from predatory dinosaurs. Into this peaceful playground roam two egg-hunting dinosaurs who are chased by the young group into the "mysterious beyond." They bring back the wrong egg and find themselves the proud "parents" of a tiny T-Rex, teaching them a lesson about responsibility along the way. Their various adventures are thrilling and educational. ★★★ $19.99

Land Before Time III

(1995, 71 min, US) Children who enjoyed the first two *Land Before Time* films should appreciate this third entry as well. The five young heroes have returned in another adventure that combines fun, songs and valuable lessons. In this episode, meteors have fallen to Earth and cut off the water supply to the Great Valley. Upset by the ensuing squabbling among the various adult dinosaur tribe members, the kids go exploring for other water sources to ease the tension. Three bullying teen dinosaurs try to stop them, only to find themselves in need of help from their young targets as predators invade the valley. Unity in the face of adversity and peaceful solutions to problems underline a strong plot that will engage the kids while they learn. ★★★ $19.99

Land Before Time IV — Journey Through the Mists

(1996, 74 min, US) Littlefoot is back with all his friends in this fourth installment of the popular animated dinosaur series. This time his beloved grandfather has fallen ill and desperately needs a remedy than can only be found outside of their protected valley. Littlefoot and the gang make the perilous journey and, of course, save the day. If your kids liked the others in this series, they will surely like this episode. ★★★ $19.99

The Land of Faraway

(1988, 95 min, Norway/Sweden, Vladimir Grammatikov) A young boy in Stockholm is whisked away by a friendly spirit to meet the father he has never known — the King of the Land of Faraway. Soon, the boy is embroiled in a desperate bid to save the children of Faraway from an evil knight who has kidnapped them. Timothy Bottoms, Susannah York, Christopher Lee and Christian Bale star. ★★½ $9.99

Land of Look Behind

(1982, 88 min, Jamaica/US, Alan Greenberg) The lush sensuality of Jamaica, the Rastafarian faith and the mystical fervor of reggae are the subjects of this impressionistic documentary/fantasy. Director Greenberg journeys into the hearts and minds of the island people and chronicles their cultural and religious beliefs. This magical meditation on Jamaican life evolved from a planned documentary on Bob Marley's funeral, and includes the music of Marley, performances by Gregory Isaacs and Lui Lepki and dub poet Mutaburuka. ★★★ $19.99

The Langoliers

(1995, 150 min, US, Tom Holland) There's an unusually effective eeriness to the opening of *The Langoliers*, a made-for-TV adaptation of Stephen King's novel. A select group of passengers on a red-eye from Los Angeles to Boston awaken mid-flight to discover their fellow passengers and the crew have literally disappeared into thin air (leaving behind glasses, false teeth, wigs, etc.). As they try to solve the puzzle of their intriguing "Twilight Zone"-like dilemma, the story unfortunately veers into the realm of *Forbidden Planet* and *Nightmare on Elm Street* — and without the style of either — as one person's fragile mental state puts all in danger. What follows is a silly, lethargic story of parallel universes and cartoon monsters from the subconscious out to eat everything in sight. None of the cast really helps, and Bronson Pinchot is saddled with a terribly conceived character which only underscores the story's weaknesses. ★★ $19.99

Larger Than Life

(1996, 93 min, US, Howard Franklin) Bill Murray inherits an elephant from the father he never knew, then must decide whether to sell her to Linda Fiorentino's sexy but unscrupulous animal talent agent or allow sensible zoologist Janeane Garofalo to take her to Sri Lanka to be in her natural habitat. Have no idea what'll happen? Then you must see *Larger Than Life*. Otherwise, there isn't much to recommend, although the film — save for some goopy sentimentality — is painless enough. The elephant has its requisite cutesy/funny moments, and even a slumming Murray is still entertaining, though Garofalo is once again under- (and mis-) used, and the middle third really drags. Kids may enjoy it, and adults have the added "bonus" of witnessing a car-wreck of a performance by Matthew McConaughey as a freakish, paranoid redneck. But still, you can't help wonder: What were the makers (and especially Murray) thinking? ★★ $19.99

Larks on a String

(1968, 96 min, Czechoslavakia, Jiri Menzel) From the director of *Closely Watched Trains* comes this surprisingly timely, playfully subversive allegory on the crumbling of the Communist State. Made in 1968 immediately after the Soviet invasion of Hungary, the film was promptly banned and not made available until 23 years later. Set in an almost surreal scrap heap, the story follows the work, thoughts and loves of a group of prisoners — professors, musicians, union organizers and Jews — who are caught in the crackdown,

believed to pose a "threat to the state." The guards and government officials are disorganized, demoralized and corrupt, and seem to be simply waiting for the people's revolution to begin. Although thoroughly political, the satire retains a light, almost joyful stance, taking particular delight in the love interest between two prisoners — a simple boy and a pretty young woman. (Czechoslovakian with English subtitles) ★★★½ $19.99

Las Vegas Hillbillys

(1966, 90 min, US, Arthur C. Pierce) Jayne Mansfield and Mamie Van Doren need plenty of support in this story about a busted Las Vegas bar invigorated when it is inherited by a hayseed who starts booking it with country acts. Musical performances by Bill Anderson, Sonny James and Del Reeves. ★

Laserman

(1990, 92 min, US, Peter Wang) Intelligent, eccentric multicultural comedy-thriller about a Chinese-American scientist who accidentally kills his lab assistant in an experiment, resulting in the loss of his job. His "grifting" brother-in-law convinces him to sell his new laser device to some "business associates" — actually hit men for a terrorist organization. All the while, police inspector Lu (director Wang) is on their trail as the hero reluctantly enters the black market of high-tech weapons, mistaken identities, telepathic orgasms and more! ★★★ $19.99

Lassie

(1994, 95 min, US, Daniel Petrie) This heartwarming, old-fashioned family film is a real gem. This time, the family finds Lassie on the side of the road after its sheep-rearing owner is killed in a truck accident. This is handy since the new owners eventually decide to raise sheep themselves. While certainly more intelligent than most people, Lassie is so darn noble that she (he?) is likable anyway. The supporting cast (Thomas Guiry, Helen Slater, Jon Tenney and Richard Farnsworth) are excellent and Frederic Forrest is a wonderfully villainous sheep herder. ★★★ $14.99

Lassiter

(1984, 100 min, US, Roger Young) Tom Selleck tries his hand at *Bond*age in this slick if derivative spy thriller about a notorious 1930s cat burglar pressed into service by the British government to steal a cache of diamonds from the Nazis. The usual thrills and chills abound, with Jane Seymour and Lauren Hutton providing more than an eyeful of stylish spectacle. Also with Bob Hoskins. ★★½

Last Action Hero

(1993, 130 min, US, John McTiernan) Arnold Schwarzenegger finally bombed with this disappointing action-parody, sort of a *Purple Rose of Cairo* meets *Lethal Weapon*. A 12-year-old kid is magically transported by a magical movie ticket into the celluloid world of his favorite film hero, Jack Slater. The trouble really starts, however, when they both emerge in the real world on this side of the screen. The film is an endless barrage of gags referring to the insipidness of many Hollywood actioners: hundreds of smashing cars; tons of insufficient backup officers; plastic-looking blonde-haired,

blue-eyed babes; Arnold Schwarzenegger; African-American police captains; and any other readily available clich, of cop-action flicks. Suffering from lackluster direction, *Last Action Hero* is a good joke with a really awful punchline. Joan Plowright and Ian McKellen stand-out in cameos. ★★ $9.99

The Last American Hero

(1973, 100 min, US, Lamont Johnson) Jeff Bridges gives a commanding performance as stock car champion Junior Jackson in this vibrant racing drama based on a series of articles by Tom Wolfe. The story follows backwoods moonshiner Jackson from his running whiskey to his determined bid for the championship on the independent circuit. Bridges brings to mind a young Paul Newman with an icy cool portrayal of swaggering confidence. Also with Valerie Perrine, Gary Busey and Geraldine Fitzgerald as Jackson's feisty mother. On par with another splendid racing feature, *Heart Like a Wheel*. ★★★½ $59.99

The Last Boy Scout

(1991, 105 min, US, Tony Scott) Here's another live action cartoon from the *Lethal Weapon/Die Hard* factory. Bruce Willis is a Secret Service agent turned private investigator who teams up with Damon Wayans, a burned-out former football star. Together they take on a gang of well-dressed bad guys conspiring to...do you really need to know? This mishmash of implausibility and macho posturing could be totally dismissed if only *Lethal Weapon* screenwriter Shane Black hadn't created such dimensional bad characters and director Scott's slam-bang action sequences had been less than dazzling. Easily offended law enforcement officers, African-Americans, athletes, homosexuals, pacifists, women and others may need to take this one with a grain or two of salt. ★★ $14.99

The Last Butterfly

(1993, 106 min, Czechoslavakia/GB, Karel Kachyna) In a sincere and moving performance, Tom Courtenay plays a renowned Parisian mime artist who is coerced by the Nazis to perform at Terezin, Czechoslavakia, or "city of the Jews" — a propaganda community established by the Germans. A virtual prisoner himself, the apolitical performer soon discovers the truth about the town (it's a midway point for the camps). Unable to communicate with the visiting Red Cross, he tries to alert them the best way he knows how: through his art. These final scenes, a harrowing, updated adaptation of "Hansel and Gretel," are mesmerizing and give the film its emotional power. (In English) ★★★ $19.99

Last Call at Maud's

(1993, 75 min, US, Paris Poirier) The 1989 closing of Maud's Study, a lesbian bar and institution in San Francisco since 1966, propelled filmmaker Poirier to explore the 23-year life of the bar and its patrons as well as offer a fascinating minihistory of recent (post-WWII) lesbian life and the role that lesbian bars played in it. Many longtime patrons of Maud's are interviewed, providing vivid case histories as they nostalgically recall their first experiences in a lesbian bar. Their recollections offer a lively and informative account of lesbian life from the 1940s to the present, with stories of the many raids and police harassment of "queer" bars which surprisingly lasted until the early '70s, even in San Francisco. An engaging and informative documentary which celebrates lesbian life and provides an essential chapter in the social and political history of lesbians. ★★★ $39.99

The Last Days of Chez Nous
(1992, 96 min, Australia, Gillian Armstrong) Armstrong's charming character study of a dysfunctional Sydney family stars Lisa Harrow as Beth, an underpaid novelist and the unofficial matron of Chez Nous, a household comprised of her, her French husband J.P. (Bruno Ganz) and her teenage daughter from a previous marriage, Anna (Miranda Otto). Into the soup comes her carefree sister and a gawky young male boarder. What follows is a fundamentally plotless, but nevertheless engaging and entertaining examination of the ways that people fail to communicate in spite of their desire for human contact — hmmm, could be a Wim Wenders film. *Last Days* is a sincere and well-drawn portrait of family life. ★★★ $19.99

The Last Detail
(1973, 105 min, US, Hal Ashby) Jack Nicholson received his third Academy Award nomination for his portrayal of "Bad Ass" Buddusky, one of two "lifer" sailors who are given the detail of escorting a young recruit convicted of stealing to Portsmouth Naval Prison. Ashby's direction and Michael Chapman's cinematography give this film a gritty look that complements its cynical, uncompromising atmosphere. One of Nicholson's most fully realized characterizations. ★★★½ $9.99

The Last Dragon
(1985, 108 min, US, Michael Schultz) Martial arts meets Motown in this silly though enjoyable tale of a black kung fu student who explores the streets of New York. Berry Gordy served as executive producer. With Taimak, Julius J. Carry III and Vanity. ★★ $79.99

Last Embrace
(1979, 102 min, US, Jonathan Demme) Engaging thriller à la Hitchcock about a CIA

Last Exit to Brooklyn

agent (Roy Scheider) who, believing himself to be a target for assassination after his wife is murdered, finds himself entrapped in the mystery of his own identity. To say more would give the show away. Also starring Janet Margolin, John Glover and Christopher Walken. The climax is a shocker. ★★★ $14.99

The Last Emperor
(1987, 164 min, US/Italy, Bernardo Bertolucci) Winner of nine Academy Awards, this sweeping historical epic chronicles the turbulent life and times of China's last emperor, Pu Yi. John Lone is mesmerizing as the weak-willed monarch, a man ascended to the Dragon Throne at the age of three, only to abdicate at six and then coerced to spend his early life within the opulent walls of China's Forbidden City. His story — from "Lord of 10,000 years" to playboy, prisoner, political puppet and finally common gardener — is told by Bertolucci in the grandest of cinematic traditions. An enthralling and extravagant story of one rather simple man engulfed by the events of his times. (Filmed in English) ★★★★

Last Exit to Brooklyn
(1990, 103 min, West Germany, Uli Edel) This German production of Hubert Selby, Jr.'s 1957 underground classic is a hard-hitting, no-holds-barred look at life in hell along the docks of Brooklyn in the early '50s. This isn't just Ozzie and Harriet in reverse; it's an all-out indictment of the American experience as seen through the eyes of Brooklyn's lower depths. It's not pretty — it is, however, a gripping and undeniably overwhelming drama. Stephen Lang is excellent as a bewildered union leader who is painfully forced to come to grips with his repressed homosexuality. Jennifer Jason Leigh is dazzling as the teenage hooker Tralala who enforces her womanhood at the end of the film in one of the most disturbing scenes ever filmed. (Filmed in English) ★★★½ $89.99

The Last Five Days
(1982, 112 min, West Germany, Percy Adlon) Belying his trademark playful touch, Adlon (*Sugarbaby*, *Bagdad Cafe*) goes for much weightier subject matter in telling the shattering true story of a young girl and her brother who are executed by the Nazis for distributing anti-fascist propaganda. Lena Stoltze (*The Nasty Girl*) plays Sophie Scholl, the woman compelled to almost suicidal political action against the Nazis in 1943 in this restrained, precise film of crushing emotional impact. (German with English subtitles) ★★★ $79.99

Last House on the Left
(1972, 91 min, US, Wes Craven) Two young women are abducted and brutalized by some buffoonish escaped convicts in this economic but severely dated horror outing which launched the careers of both Craven and Sean S. Cunningham (*Friday the 13th*). Whether or not this appeals to you depends on your tolerance for corny humor and amateurish acting. ★

The Last Hurrah
(1958, 121 min, US, John Ford) Spencer Tracy gives an outstanding performance in this excellent version of Edwin O'Connor's novel

about the last days of a political boss. Great supporting cast includes Basil Rathbone, Pat O'Brien, James Gleason, Donald Crisp and Ed Brophy. ★★★★ $19.99

Last Hurrah for Chivalry
(1978, 108 min, Hong Kong, John Woo) Just before he reinvented the gangster movie with his phenomenally successful *A Better Tomorrow*, writer-director Woo bid farewell to the "heroic swordplay" movies with which he began his career with this fun, well-written story of two killers-for-hire who foreshadow the honorable criminals of his modern blood operas. Damian Lau and Wei Pai are master swordsmen who have no allegiances and adhere strictly to the code of their personal art. When they both decide to help out a wealthy local who is seeking revenge against an evil kung fu master, they discover that few hold honor, duty and friendship in the same high esteem. Featuring some exciting, traditional swordfights (no modern wire work here) interspersed with its themes of male bonding and righteous sacrifice, *Last Hurrah* is Woo's point of transition from being a contract director of comedies and kung fu movies to the pioneer of action cinema he is today. ★★★ $59.99

The Last Klezmer
(1994, 84 min, US/Poland, Yale Strom) Leopold Kozlowski, a teacher of music and klezmer musician, returns home for the first time in fifty years to his home town in Poland. This intimate portrait and homecoming documentary is poignant in its sincerity and insightful in director Strom's focus on Kozlowski's passion of teaching the art of klezmer to opera and piano students. It reminds one of teaching jazz to a classically trained musician. Kozlowski's inevitable return is shot in a style reminiscent of a war film, catching all of his reactions as he sees what has become of his home and meets some of his friends from his youth. Most of the powerful moments come with his reunions with friends and drunken nostalgic talks. Absence of klezmer music — which has been called "Jewish jazz" — is apparent in the stark landscape of post-WWII and post-Communist Poland, and it is this vacancy which serves to underscore the messages of both Kozlowski and the filmmaker. (In English and Polish, Yiddish & Russian with English subtitles) ★★★ $79.99

The Last Laugh
(1924, 73 min, Germany, F.W. Murnau) One of the classics from Germany's "Golden Era," *The Last Laugh* features the great Emil Jannings as a proud doorman of a luxury hotel who is demoted to washroom attendant. Once envied and respected by his neighbors, the baffled old man sees his world and status crumble; but in a surprising ending, he still gets the last laugh. German actress Lotte Eisner once said of the film, "This is a German tragedy that can only be understood in a country where uniform is king, not to say god." (Silent) ★★★★ $24.99

Last Man Standing
(1996, 100 min, US, Walter Hill) Combining the gangster and western genres and using a ghost town during the rough-and-tumble

1930s as its setting, *Last Man Standing* is a particularly stylish reworking of *Yojimbo* whose narrative isn't quite as accomplished as its visuals. As the perennial Man-with-No-Name, Bruce Willis is a mysterious drifter who arrives in a near-deserted Texas town and immediately gets caught between two feuding mob factions. Seeing a quick buck, he plays both sides from the middle; that is, until they get wise and he eventually sets out to clean up the town. Visually, *Last Man Standing* may be director Hill's best looking film. The golden-hued cinematography nicely captures the dusty landscape, and the gunfight sequences are well staged. But the drama nestled in-between the fights and shootouts are slowly paced, and having the story told several times in other, better films, there's not much new here. ★★½ $19.99

The Last Metro

(1980, 135 min, France, François Truffaut) Truffaut's poignant account of Parisian theatre under the Nazi thumb stars Catherine Deneuve and Gérard Depardieu as members of an acting troupe struggling through the Occupation. Heinz Bennett plays Deneuve's husband and stage director, forced underground because of his Jewish heritage. (French with English subtitles) ★★★ $29.99

The Last Movie

(1971, 110 min, US, Dennis Hopper) After his phenomenal success with *Easy Rider*, the powers-that-be in Hollywood believed that they had found the voice of the young, restless America in Hopper. Universal Pictures bankrolled the neophyte director's next project and gave him carte blanche to produce his next "blockbuster." The result, however, was an "artsy," possibly drug-induced and complicated (some said incomprehensible) mess. The film, starring Sam Fuller, Peter Fonda, Michelle Phillips and Dean Stockwell, revolves around the happenings of an American movie crew filming a western in a small Peruvian village. ★★

The Last of England

(1988, 87 min, GB, Derek Jarman) Uncompromising in its vision, *The Last of England* is a beautifully photographed fragmented poem structured within a series of cross-cutting vignettes. Filled with homoerotic images, the film deals with the destruction of our physical and emotional world by the ravages of Thatcherism and the callousness of Man. Accompanied by Nigel Terry's baleful narration, the visuals include shots of Jarman, male prostitutes and scenes of urban squalor and decay, as well as references to the Queen and the Falklands. It's a baffling but interesting work, reminiscent of Jean Cocteau. ★★★ $24.99

The Last of His Tribe

(1992, 90 min, US, Harry Hook) This made-for-HBO drama stars Graham Greene (*Dances with Wolves*) as Ishi, the last known survivor of the Yahi people. His tribe having been wiped out in the slaughter of California's natives (a decimation which brought the total Indian population of the state from 300,000 in 1800 to 20,000 in 1900), Ishi is discovered by the "civilized" world in 1911. Jon Voight plays the

eager anthropologist who ventures to save the Yahi ways and traditions for posterity. David Ogden Stiers and Anne Archer also co-star. ★★½ $19.99

The Last of Mrs. Cheyney

(1937, 98 min, US, Richard Boleslawski) Joan Crawford had one of her biggest hits of the 1930s with this fairly entertaining remake of the 1929 Norma Shearer success. Crawford is in her element as an American jewel thief working her way through the cream of British high society. What she finds besides stolen gems is love. Also starring William Powell and Robert Montgomery. ★★½ $19.99

The Last of Phillip Banter

(1986, 100 min, US/Spain, Herve Hachuel) This limp thriller about a man's mental breakup lacks both tension and complexity. Set in Madrid amidst the American community working there, the story centers on Phillip Banter, a world-weary drunk whose marriage to the boss' daughter is deteriorating. Is this handsome but obnoxious self-pitying bore really losing his marbles or is there a conspiracy out there determined to undermine his mental stability? By the time the viewer discovers the truth, it is too late — you'll be sound asleep. A wooden Tony Curtis, who seems surprised to be in this film, co-stars. ★ $79.99

The Last of Sheila

(1973, 120 min, US, Herbert Ross) Entertainingly puzzling to the very end, this star-studded murder-mystery features James Coburn as a game-obsessed film producer who invites six of his Hollywood jet-set "friends" on a cruise in the Mediterranean where a mean-spirited game, begun by him and designed to expose a dark secret of each member, backfires. Twists and turns abound in this plexus story written by real-life puzzle freaks Anthony Perkins and Stephen Sondheim. The "innocent" guests include James Mason, Dyan Cannon, Joan Hackett, Richard Benjamin and Raquel Welch. ★★★ $14.99

The Last of the Finest

(1990, 97 min, US, John MacKenzie) Though its title may be a little too self-congratulatory, this is a surprisingly effective and taut police adventure. Brian Dennehy stars as the leader of a special unit of the L.A. Police Department who accidentally stumbles upon a drug operation which may be linked to high-ranking government officials. Taken off the case when they get too close, Dennehy and his partners continue the unwanted investigation after one of their own is killed. This is the first Oliver North-inspired action-adventure which clearly does not see patriotism as an excuse for unlawfulness. ★★★ $14.99

Last of the Mohicans

(1992, 112 min, US, Michael Mann) In transfering James Fenimore Cooper's novel of Colonial America to the screen, director Mann (*Manhunter*) wouldn't immediately spring to mind: a tale set in 1757 during the French and Indian Wars doesn't exactly fit Mann's cinematic M.O. Which is what makes this efficient, terribly exciting adaptation all the more rewarding. Daniel Day-Lewis is cast as Indian

scout Hawkeye, and he so immerses himself in the part it's easy to forget he's not really an American. It's Day-Lewis' determined portrayal, well-staged action sequences, astonishing camerawork and a splendid re-creation of pre-Revolutionary times which make *Mohicans* the lump-in-your-throat adventure that it is. And it's bloody romantic, too. Madeleine Stowe plays a British major's daughter, whom Hawkeye escorts through the wilderness and eventually falls in love with. Especially good in support is Jodhi May as Stowe's younger and ultimately brave sister. (Letterboxed version sells for $19.99) ★★★½ $14.99

Last of the Red Hot Lovers

(1972, 98 min, US, Gene Saks) Minor screen adaptation of Neil Simon's play with Alan Arkin as a restaurant owner desperately trying for an extramarital affair. Sally Kellerman, Paula Prentiss and Renee Taylor are the women in his life. ★★ $14.99

The Last Party

(1993, 96 min, US, Mark Benjamin & Marc Levin) Purported to be a study of the political ideas of the "twentysomething" generation, this masturbatory documentary follows Robert Downey, Jr. to the 1992 political conventions, where he interviews a mishmash of government figures. Besides these unrevealing segments, the film consists of Downey speaking "candidly" about his own upbringing, or shots of the star stripping down to his "tighty-whities" in public as a demonstration against "boredom." Downey may be a wholly watchable personality under most circumstances, but this is such a mess, one can only hope it's some weird practical joke. ★½ $89.99

The Last Picture Show

(1971, 118 min, US, Peter Bogdanovich) Bogdanovich's brilliant adaptation of Larry McMurtry's novel is regarded as one of the definitive coming-of-age sagas: not only in its depiction of the "end of innocence" for its characters, but for an entire way of life. Set in a one-horse town in 1950s Texas, the film stars Joseph Bottoms and Jeff Bridges as heatstruck teens sweltering in the dustbowl of their own lives. Cybill Shepherd, Ellen Burstyn and Oscar winners Cloris Leachman and Ben Johnson round out the cast. Bogdanovich's eye for the period and place paints a picture of a ghost town more chilling than any horror movie. (Followed by an inferior sequel, *Texasville*) ★★★★ $19.99

The Last Remake of Beau Geste

(1977, 85 min, US, Marty Feldman) Feldman directed, wrote and stars in this uneven though sometimes funny spoof on Foreign Legion movies — *Beau Geste* in particular. Michael York plays Marty's twin brother (and Arnold and Danny thought they had an original idea) who accompanies his sibling to the legendary French outpost in Morocco. Ann-Margret, James Earl Jones and Peter Ustinov also star. ★★ $14.99

The Last Seduction

(1994, 110 min, US, John Dahl) Linda Fiorentino is in nightmarishly good form as Bridget Gregory, the ultimate femme fatale and the bane of every heterosexual man who crosses her path. When her New York med-school husband (Bill Pullman) comes home with the proceeds of a major drug deal, she scampers with the loot and heads upstate. And oh, you boys upstate better beware! Filled with delightful twists and turns, *The Last Seduction* follows Bridget as she sets up shop in the sleepy little burg of Beston where she gets Mike (Peter Berg) in her talons. Mike is a perfect rube for Bridget. He's so bent on getting out of small town life, and so in love with her as his way out, that he falls squarely into every trap she sets, and they are numerous. Fiorentino is incredibly sharp as Bridget. She's the arch woman, viewing men occasionally as sex toys, but always as completely subordinate to her will. Ultimately, what makes this film so seductive is Bridget's completely unapologetic nature: she's the woman who's been wronged by men and is going to take everything she can to make up for it. And what makes it all so much fun is that we're rooting for *her*. ★★★★ $19.99

The Last Starfighter

(1984, 100 min, US, Nick Castle) Amiable sci-fi adventure with Lance Guest as a small-town youth who yearns for excitement — and finds it when he is recruited by a space promoter (Robert Preston) to help in the fight against an evil conquerer. Preston is tops in a slight variation of his *Music Man* con man. ★★½ $9.99

Last Summer

(1969, 97 min, US, Frank Perry) Poignant coming-of-age drama about three restless teenagers (Barbara Hershey, Bruce Davison and Richard Thomas) and their summer of discovery at a private beach. Oscar-nominee Cathy Burns is a stand-out in support. Stunning photography by Gerald Hirschfield. ★★★ $59.99

The Last Supper

(1976, 110 min, Cuba, Tomás Gutiérrez Alea) Reminiscent of Buñuel's delightfully vicious *Viridiana*, this sardonic political allegory is about a pious slaveholder at the turn of the century who, feeling the pangs of guilt, tries to cleanse his soul in front of God by staging a re-enactment of the Last Supper. Asking his slaves to forget their shackles for a night, the plantation owner "enlists" twelve of them to play the apostles. Told with caustic wit and blasphemous irony, this dazzling tour de force features a powerful black cast and a not-so-subtle preaching of imminent political revolt. Winner of the Grand Prize — Chicago International Film Festival. (Spanish with English subtitles) ★★★½ $69.99

The Last Supper

(1995, 94 min, US, Stacy Title) An unexpected murder over Sunday dinner leads a group of five grad students to a unique course of political action. They alter their weekly ritual of inviting a sixth person for dinner and conversation by choosing as their guest someone they believe the world would be better off without. What begins by happenstance and an abstract discussion (If you met Hitler in 1909...) soon escalates out of their control. As the freshly dug mounds of earth in their back yard steadily increase in number, the members of the group go through disconcerting changes of their own, each finding that final

The Last Supper

solutions have fearsome effects on the perpetrators as well as the victims. A subplot involving a missing child is ironic counterpoint to their ongoing analysis of their PC, let's-make-the-world-a-better-place housekeeping. While the film raises some intriguing questions, its potency is undercut by uneven performances and inconsistent plot developments. Still, it might be just the thing the next time you have the gang over for Sunday dinner. Starring Bill Paxton, Jason Alexander and Courtney B. Vance. ★★½ $97.69

Last Tango in Paris

(1973, 129 min, Italy, Bernardo Bertolucci) An aging expatriate (Marlon Brando) becomes involved in a doomed sexual liaison with a young French woman (Maria Scheider). A landmark film which lays bare the primal nature of man. Brando equals his greatest performances as a seeker of truth, seething with sexual anger and drunk with self-loathing and contempt. (Filmed in English and French) ★★★★ $19.99

The Last Temptation of Christ

(1988, 164 min, US, Martin Scorsese) Scorsese's adaptation of the Nikos Kazantzkais novel is a controversial telling of the Christ story, but for many a believer and non-believer alike this epic exploration of the man behind the myth has proven to be a true article of faith. Willem Dafoe delivers a stylistically brilliant portrayal of a Jesus who, uncertain whether the voices he hears are from God or Satan, is locked in an agonizing battle with his own destiny. Supporting cast includes Harvey Keitel as a lower East-Side Judas, Barbara Hershey as Mary Magdalene, Harry Dean Stanton as Paul, Andre Gregory as John the Baptist and David Bowie as Pontius Pilate. Scorsese has succeeded in crafting a truly elegant and thought-provoking treatise on spirituality and existence — clearly a labor of love. ★★★★ $19.99

The Last Time I Saw Paris

(1954, 116 min, US, Richard Brooks) Romance blossoms between a young Army writer (Van Johnson) and a fun-loving socialite

(Elizabeth Taylor) in post-war Paris. This uneven drama is enhanced by slick production values and Taylor's charm and beauty. Donna Reed and Walter Pidgeon co-star. Based on the novel "Babylon Revisited" by F. Scott Fitzgerald. ★★ $19.99

The Last Tycoon

(1976, 125 min, US, Elia Kazan) Robert De Niro stars in this screen version of F. Scott Fitzgerald's unfinished novel. An accomplished film for its acting alone, it still seems unfinished, although Harold Pinter's script does the best it can. Worth seeing if only for De Niro's performance. Jack Nicholson has a memorable small part as a script writer trying to start a union. ★★½ $14.99

The Last Waltz

(1978, 117 min, US, Martin Scorsese) Scorsese's dazzling documentation of The Band's momentous farewell performance on Thanksgiving Day, 1976. Concluding over a decade and a half of playing together, the group is joined on stage by a wealth of guest artists: Bob Dylan, Eric Clapton, Neil Young, Van Morrison and many others. Songs include "The Weight," "Up on Cripple Creek" and "The Night They Drove Old Dixie Down." The first film to fully utilize the Dolby stereo surround process. ★★★½ $14.99

The Last Wave

(1978, 106 min, Australia, Peter Weir) Richard Chamberlain plays a Sydney lawyer who, while defending a group of Aborigines accused of murder, becomes entangled in the labyrinthine world of ancient tribal magic, rituals and spiritualism. Atmospheric and moody, Weir's cerebral exercise in psychological horror is sometimes too ambitious but nevertheless has an ingenuity which heralded the director as a major player in the Australian film community. ★★★ $19.99

The Last Winter

(1984, 92 min, Israel, Riki Shelach) A patriotic Israeli living in America returns to his homeland to fight in the Yom-Kippur War of 1973. After he is reported missing in action, his distraught American wife flies to Tel Aviv in search of answers. Her friendship with another MIA wife helps alleviate the pain and frustration of her wait. A serious, thoughtful and absorbing drama. (Filmed in English) ★★★

Last Year at Marienbad

(1961, 93 min, France, Alain Resnais) At the spa in Marienbad a man (X) confronts a woman (A) with the conviction that they had an affair the previous year. Resnais transcends the limits of spatial and temporal storytelling rules. A classic of innovative cinema. Scripted by Alain Robbes-Grillet. (French with English subtitles) ★★★½ $29.99

Latcho Drom

(1993, 103 min, France, Tony Gatlif) This pulsating musical and visual odyssey should be required viewing for all whose ears tingle when they encounter similarities in musical and social mores across cultures. An ode to the gypsy life, the film initially chronicles Europe's modern vagabonds who began their journey westward 1,000 years ago as a nomadic tribe from the north of India. It then launches into a series of MTV-inspired segments of ethnic music and dance — with stops in Egypt, Turkey, Romania, Hungary, Slovakia and Spain. As a kind of cultural travelogue mapping the source of musical inspiration from Asia to Europe — and linking those continents — the film is fascinating; the first three (Asian) segments are riveting. But as the film's focus ventures westward, its outlook becomes as bleak as its subjects', ultimately disintegrating into shameless and maudlin political propaganda bemoaning the plight of Europe's migratory underclass. Though probably valid, the film's polemic eventually loses its persuasiveness due to a lack of subtlety. Still, a fascinating trip for lovers of music, rhythm and dance. ★★½ $89.99

Late Chrysanthemums

(1954, 101 min, Japan, Mikio Naruse) This moving portrait of three retired geishas and their struggle to earn a living and retain respect long after the bloom of youth has gone is a detailed and poignant tragicomedy. Adapted from three Fumiko Hayashi stories, director Naruse masterfully depicts the subtle nuances of the women's emotionally intertwined relationships. Despite their meager living conditions and declining years, they determinedly fight for their dignity. (Japanese with English subtitles) ★★★½ $19.99

Late for Dinner

(1991, 92 min, US, W.D. Richter) Director Richter followed up The Adventures of Buckaroo Banzai (seven years later) with this subtly moving tale that mixes science fiction, romance and comedy to produce one of 1991's great films that nobody saw. Brian Wimmer and Peter Berg play best buddies who wind up "frozen" by a scientist as they run from the law in 1962. When the pair are thawed out nearly thirty years later, they have to contend with a society that has left them behind. More significantly, they have to rediscover and reconcile with the people they love. We've all seen this Rip Van Winkle, Back to the Future stuff before,

Late Chrysanthemums

but rarely has it been done with such care, depth, sensitivity and soul. ★★★½ $14.99

The Late Show

(1977, 94 min, US, Robert Benton) Two superior performances by Art Carney and Lily Tomlin highlight this winning mystery comedy written and directed by Benton (Kramer vs. Kramer, Places in the Heart). Carney plays an aging private eye who is thrown together with slightly daffy Tomlin as he investigates the death of his partner. Thoroughly enjoyable and a terrific homage to those great detective mysteries of the 1940s. ★★★½ $14.99

Late Spring

(1949, 108 min, Japan, Yasujiro Ozu) Director Ozu brings great subtlety and elegance to this beautifully crafted film about a young woman with an unhealthy attachment to her aging, widowed father. Fearful that she will become an old maid on his account, the old man pretends that he himself is going to wed and tricks her into marriage. Unfortunately, the grandeur of Ozu's exquisite but slow-paced style does not translate well to video — much of the beauty of Ozu's films come from his discerning eye for black-and-white imagery. Still, his finely drawn characters and meticulous study of familial relations make this unequalled viewing for lovers of great drama. ★★★★ $69.99

Late Summer Blues

(1987, 101 min, Israel, Renen Schorr) Set in 1970 during the War of Attrition at the Suez Canal, this moving drama chronicles the bittersweet dilemma facing a group of seven teenage students who, just finishing their final exams and high school, face impending induction into the Israeli armed forces. Sobered by the gruesome realities of war, the film focuses on the enthusiastic innocence and idealism of these youths as they are thrust into adulthood. (Hebrew with English subtitles) ★★★ $29.99

Laugh for Joy

(1954, 106 min, Italy, Mario Monicelli) Anna Magnani, in one of the best performances of her career, stars in this moving and bitter drama as a movie extra in Rome's Cinecittà Studio who becomes entangled in a messy rela-

tionship with two men: an American executive (Ben Gazzara) and a crafty con man. From the director of Big Deal on Madonna Street. (Italian with English subtitles) ★★★ $59.99

Laughing Sinners

(1931, 72 min, US, Harry Beaumont) Top-billed Joan Crawford and Clark Gable appear for the first time together in this predictable pre-Hays melodrama, based on the romantic Broadway play "Torch Song," which goes a long way to describe the romantic suffering Crawford endures. Joan plays a nightclub singer who is madly in love with traveling salesman Neil Hamilton. However, when he dumps her, she tries to commit suicide, but is saved by Salvation Army preacher Gable. Just when it seems Joan has found happiness, back into her life comes Hamilton...and temptation. This morality tale is a little rough around the edges, but is nonetheless appealing for its antiquated posture. ★★½ $19.99

Laughing Target

(1991, 52 min, Japan, Tohru Matsuzono) This bizarre animated action/adventure/supernatural/romance begins with the prearranged marriage of six-year-old cousins Yuzuru and Azusa. After ten years, Yuzuru is now dating Satomi and they seem like a normal couple; until Azusa returns and expects Yuzuru to fulfill his childhood vow, forming the strangest of love triangles. Now a weird presence is making itself felt, along with a series of strange accidents, and Azusa is the key. With its H.P. Lovecraft overtones and soap opera-like story, this is quite an entertaining change from the usual giant robot/space war-type stories that are so common in the Japanese animation genre. ★★★½ $19.99

Laura

(1944, 85 min, US, Otto Preminger) With the question of "Who killed Laura?" (and not Palmer), Preminger sets the stage for a complex, riveting and one-of-a-kind murder mystery. Dana Andrews plays a police detective investigating the murder of successful businesswoman Laura Hunt (the beautiful Gene Tierney). Through a series of flashbacks, cynical columnist Waldo Lydecker (Clifton Webb) recalls Laura's life up to the murder. Among

L

the suspects are Webb, fiancé Vincent Price and socialite Judith Anderson. Featuring extraordinary photography, a haunting score, unexpected twists, remarkable performances and a scalpel-sharp wit, *Laura* is not to be missed. Webb gives a quintessential performance as the acerbic Lydecker ("I write with a goose quill dipped in venom"), and Tierney is simply exquisite. ★★★★ $19.99

The Lavender Hill Mob

(1951, 82 min, GB, Charles Crichton) Yet another of the Ealing Studio greats, this mischievous comedy features a stand-up performance by Alec Guinness as a mild-mannered bank employee who dreams up what he thinks is a foolproof plan to steal one million British pounds in gold from the Bank of England. Winner of a Best Screenplay Oscar, this zany comedy climaxes with a madcap chase and features Audrey Hepburn in a bit part. ★★★★ $9.99

Law Breakers
(Les Assassins de L'Ordre)

(1971, 107 min, France, Marcel Carné) An engrossing and sobering exploration into police corruption in the French judicial system. A burglary suspect is brought in for questioning, but hours later, is found dead in his cell, his body badly battered. All the officials in the prison deny any misconduct and the case seems unsolvable until the judge (Jacques Brel) assigned to the case takes a special interest in bringing the guilty to justice, even at the expense of his friends and his personal safety. (French with English subtitles) ★★★

Law of Desire

(1987, 100 min, Spain, Pedro Almodóvar) Almodóvar's foray into sexual obsession is a wonderfully overheated sexual melodrama which basks in its farcical intentions. The story revolves around Pablo, a popular gay filmmaker, and his sister Tina (Carmen Maura), who used to be his brother until he changed his sex in order to please his lover – their father! Antonio Banderas also stars as a darkly handsome but demented fan who attempts to win the director's heart by any means possible. Their loves, passions and wild adventures are splashed on the screen with the uninhibited eroticism, camp and outlandish wit that one would expect from the Spanish equivalent to Warhol. (Spanish with English subtitles) ★★★½ $79.99

Lawman

(1971, 95 min, US, Michael Winner) In the same mold as *Unforgiven*, this solid though at times slowly paced western abandons the usual fight of good vs. evil for the ambiguous shades of a grey moral study. Burt Lancaster heads a first-rate cast as a marshal who travels to a neighboring town to bring in seven cowpokes on a charge of murder. As Lancaster tracks the mostly law-abiding men, he battles with vigilante citizens, and comes to question his inflexible allegiance to the letter of the law – much like Javert in "Les Miserables." Robert Ryan plays the impotent town sheriff who reluctantly aids Lancaster, Lee J. Cobb is a ranch boss, and Robert Duvall is one of the men who vainly goes up against Burt. ★★★½ $19.99

The Lawnmower Man

(1992, 132 min, US, Brett Leonard) Originally released in theatres under the banner *Stephen King's Lawnmower Man*, this virtual reality, sci-fi thriller was in fact only based in small part of one of the horror maven's stories. King went to court and got his name removed from the title and it's easy to see why. Though the film features some outstanding computer-generated special effects, the story is incredibly thin. Pierce Brosnan stars as a scientist who uses his dim-witted gardener (Jeff Fahey) as a guinea pig in a virtual reality-based experiment aimed at expanding mental capacity. As with all mad scientists' schemes, things go hopelessly awry and Brosnan is sent scrambling to undo the damage. This release is the director's cut containing 34 extra minutes, making it more coherent than its theatrical release. ★½ $14.99

Lawnmower Man 2: Jobe's War

(1995, 93 min, US, Farhad Mann) Having little connection with the equally bad *The Lawnmower Man*, this awful sequel begins as Jobe (Matt Frewer) survives the cataclysmic destruction of the virtual reality labs where he has been given superhuman intelligence and powers. Gone is his lordship over the electronic netscape. This time, Jobe seems to be an honest, caring human being who becomes dependent upon electronic technology because of physical handicaps. Also mysteriously gone is Pierce Brosnan's character – he's been replaced by Ben (Patrick Bergen), the creator of a new kind of microchip which (of course) will revolutionize computer technology. Ben teams up with a group of lovable street urchins in order to stop the company which now has control of the superchip and which is using Jobe to complete Ben's work. A complete waste of time, without even the interesting computer graphics which supported the silly first film, *Lawnmower Man 2* is an embarrassment for all involved. ★ $99.99

Lawrence of Arabia

(1962, 222 min, GB, David Lean) Peter O'Toole is possessed as T.E. Lawrence in this biography of a man who almost single-handedly helped the Arabs to escape their Turkish bondage in a brilliant saga of courage, sun and sand. The breathtaking Cinemascope photography is sadly lost on the small screen, but Lean's brilliant direction and the peerless performances of Omar Sharif, Alec Guinness, Anthony Quinn and Claude Rains will quickly put this out of mind. ★★★★ $29.99

Laws of Gravity

(1992, 100 min, US, Nick Gomez) Director Gomez makes a startling debut with this high-voltage independent film that bears more than a passing resemblance to *Mean Streets* as it tracks the ups and downs of a group of small-time Brooklyn hoods whose livelihood gets in the way of the big score. Peter Greene stars as an aging "reservoir pup" whose day-to-day dealings in "the hood" collide with keeping his hot-headed, gun-running buddy (Adam Trese) out of hot water. Gomez's deft mixture of sure-footed performances from a cast of unknowns, a blisteringly improvisational script and frenetic camerawork that defies all laws of gravi-

ty suggest the arrival of a new streetwise master. ★★★½ $9.99

The League of Gentlemen

(1960, 115 min, GB, Basil Dearden) Jack Hawkins, Nigel Patrick and Richard Attenborough star in this exciting and briskly paced escapade about a group of ex-army officers who use their military talents to rob a bank. Imbued with a light sense of humor, the film is peppered with classic British witticisms. ★★★½ $39.99

A League of Their Own

(1992, 127 min, US, Penny Marshall) A marvelously entertaining baseball comedy, *A League of Their Own* is inspired by the real-life antics of the all-girls baseball league founded in 1943, when most of the major league's players were away at war. Geena Davis and Lori Petty star as country-girl sisters who are discovered by ever-acerbic scout Jon Lovitz. Whisked off to Chicago, they join Madonna and Rosie O'Donnell on the Rockford Peaches. There they're under the watchful bloodshot eyes of the team's over-the-hill, boozing manager Tom Hanks, who gives one of his richest characterizations (his lecture about "crying in baseball" is one of the funniest moments of his career). The entire cast, in fact, is excellent. As the sisters whose sibling rivalry would make Joan Fontaine and Olivia deHavilland blush, Davis and Petty offer splendid performances. And it doesn't hurt that they look good in uniform and can handle a ball and glove. As she demonstrated in *Big*, director Marshall has a wonderful sense of comic timing, and she has crafted a sweet and funny valentine of a film. (Available letterboxed and pan & scan) ★★★½ $14.99

Lean on Me

(1989, 104 min, US, John G. Avildsen) Director Avildsen (*Karate Kid*) takes his "go for it" attitude and puts it in the classroom with mostly unsatisfactory results. Morgan Freeman gives a powerhouse performance as real-life principal Joe Clark, who took control of a Paterson, New Jersey, high school overrun by drugs, violence and apathy. You want to root for him but when he starts bullying those around him, and violates city and fire ordinances – and lies about doing so – he is clearly not the kind of hero who warrants such an idealized tribute. The film is at its best when it is not lionizing Clark as crusader, but rather showing his earnest commitment to his students. ★★ $9.99

Leap of Faith

(1992, 110 min, US, Richard Pearce) Despite the immeasurable comedic talents of Steve Martin and a perfect premise for skewering evangelical preachers, this dramatic comedy falls short of its mark. When their bus breaks down, Martin (doing his best Jim Bakker) and company set up shop in a depressed farming community. The town's crops are being devastated by drought and, quicker than you can say *The Rainmaker*, its inhabitants are primed for Martin's promises of divine intervention. Despite this ideal setup, Martin never really clicks, primarily because it's so hard to believe someone so smarmy could convince anyone he's on God's side. The romance between Debra Winger (Martin's fellow filmflam artist) and the town's sheriff Liam Neeson provides some charming moments, but the most interesting thing about *Leap of Faith* is its behind-the-scenes look at how preachers make those miracles. ★★½ $14.99

The Leather Boys

(1963, 105 min, GB, Sidney J. Furie) Rita Tushingham (*A Taste of Honey*) stars as a woman trapped in an incompatible marriage to a motorcycle-loving mechanic in this compelling and uncompromising study of compulsive behavior. Focusing on their opposing viewpoints and sleazy environment, the film chronicles the ever-widening rift which leads to infidelity and unhappiness. Co-stars Dudley Sutton. ★★★

Leather Jackets

(1992, 90 min, US, Lee Drysdale) Even the buoyant presence of Bridget Fonda cannot keep this inane thriller from drowning under the weight of its attitude-heavy, cliché-ridden plot. Writer-director Drysdale aims low and misses with a shopworn tale of two former friends, one of whom (D.B. Sweeney) is a reformed petty thief. The other (Cary Elwes), however, still enjoys a life of crime until he finds himself on the run from a gang whose leader he has just killed. Fonda does what she can in the thankless role of the girl in the middle, Sweeney just broods a lot and Elwes hams it up, caricaturing every overblown, doomed movie rebel without a cause. Drysdale manages a couple of capable action sequences early on, but the pace slows and interest wanes considerably by the time he attempts to add some dimension to the characters and meaning to the story. ★½ $89.99

Leaving Las Vegas

(1995, 112 min, US, Mike Figgis) In bringing John O'Brien's decidedly downbeat novel about a man bent on suicide through alcohol to the screen, director Figgis and his two co-stars Nicolas Cage and Elizabeth Shue took a huge cinematic risk that pays off in spades. This sultry and sometimes subversively funny examination of a self-declared loser (Cage) and the proverbial "hooker with a heart of gold" (Shue) who befriends him is on the one hand as depressing a film as has been made and on the other remarkably refreshing and engrossing for its undaunted emotional honesty. Cage plays Ben, a self-destructive minor Hollywood player who, upon getting fired for alcoholism, hops in his "Beemer" and heads for a final showdown with the bottle in Vegas. Once there, he takes up with Sera (Shue), a buff streetwalker who takes him in – on the condition that she never try to convert him. Both principals are at the top of their form: Cage won a highly deserved Oscar for his unflinching portrayal, and Shue took advantage to shatter her *Adventures in Babysitting* image with a nuanced, rock solid performance. With its morbid outlook on life, *Leaving Las Vegas* is certainly not for all tastes, but for those who are undeterred by a journey into the heart of inebriation, it is clearly among the best films of 1995. (Available letterboxed and pan & scan) ★★★★ $14.99

Leaving Normal

(1992, 110 min, US, Edward Zwick) The first of the *Thelma and Louise* "clones," *Leaving Normal* is a quirky, affectionate if uneven road movie about two uncertain women coming to terms with themselves. Featuring two sumptuous performances by Christine Lahti and Meg Tilly, the film follows the misadventures taken by Darly (Lahti), a quick-witted cocktail waitress and Marianne (Tilly), a waifish divorcee, who cross paths and decide to set out together on the road to Alaska. In contrast to *T & L*, most of the characters they encounter are comic foils, someone for the two lead characters to react to rather than gain any personal or interpersonal insight. Nevertheless, *Leaving Normal* is a journey with more than its share of appealing diversions; one of whom, Patrika Darbo, is splendid as a waitress named 66. ★★½ $19.99

La Lectrice (The Reader)

(1988, 98 min, France, Michel Deville) Miou-Miou is enchanting in this labyrinthine tale of a woman who reads to her husband the story of a woman who reads to those who can't read for themselves. Her motley clients include a boy in a wheelchair, the neglected daughter of a businesswoman, a bedridden war widow, and an impotent businessman – each seeking more than just a fairy tale. While not nearly as confusing as it sounds, director Deville's choices of the texts of Tolstoy, Beaudelaire, de Maupassant and Carroll tend to render this a trying (albeit welcome) challenge for even the most literate filmgoer. However, the mixture of humor and pathos, and the general zaniness of the characters and situations, make it as much fun as curling up with a good book. (French with English subtitles) ★★★ $19.99

The Left Hand of God

(1955, 87 min, US, Edward Dmytryk) Humphrey Bogart stars as a downed WWII pilot who enters a Catholic mission posing as a priest to escape a vengeful Chinese warlord (Lee J. Cobb). Gene Tierney costars as a beautiful missionary whose heart sees through his disguise. Also with E.G. Marshall and Agnes Moorehead. ★★½ $19.99

The Left-Handed Gun

(1958, 102 min, US, Arthur Penn) Penn's directorial debut is a stylistic, provocative if not totally successful adaptation of Gore Vidal's story about Billy the Kid. The depiction of Billy by the intensely handsome Paul Newman is that of a pensive, misunderstood but hot-headed loner – a tormented youth in the fashion of James Dean and Hamlet. After his boss is murdered, Billy and his two best friends, Tom (James Best) and Charlie (James Congdon), become obsessed with gunning down the man's killer. Penn's emphasis is more on psychological development rather than the traditional western good guys vs. bad guys, bringing an originality rarely seen to the time-honored genre. ★★½ $14.99

The Legacy

(1979, 100 min, US, Richard Marquand) Six strangers are invited to a remote English mansion when they suddenly begin dying off. A supernatural presence is in the air and is using the process of elimination to select an heir. This *Omen*-inspired horror tale lacks suspense or a plot but tries to make up for it with gore and nonsense. With Katherine Ross and Sam Elliott. ★★ $19.99

Legal Eagles

(1986, 116 min, US, Ivan Reitman) Earnest performances from Robert Redford and Debra Winger save this genial though disappointing comedy. Redford and Winger play, respectively, a successful district attorney and an eccentric lawyer who team to defend a SoHo performance artist (Daryl Hannah) accused of murder. It's not really all that bad, but with that cast, it doesn't meet expectations. ★★½ $14.99

Legend

(1985, 89 min, GB, Ridley Scott) Sexual undercurrents abound in this lavishly mounted and incredibly handsome fantasy about the Devil's attempts to gain control over a young girl. The film has its moments as a modern rendition of Grimm's Fairy Tales. It is symptomatic, however, of Scott's post-*Alien* inability to provide a forceful, powerful narrative in addition to his typical wealth of visual detail. Starring Tom Cruise, Mia Sara and Tim Curry. ★★½ $14.99

The Legend of Dolemite!

(1994, 75 min, US, Foster Corder) The Godfather of Rap, the black Lenny Bruce and the inspiration for comedians Richard Pryor and Eddie Murphy, recording artist, satirist/comedian and film star Rudy Ray Moore is surprisingly unknown outside his rabid group of fans. With a tongue filthier than Richard Nixon on a bad day, Rudy Ray (aka Dolemite) has parlayed his macho urban braggadocio to a hilarious art form. This low-budget video, while technically below average, does feature interviews with Rudy Ray, scenes from his nightclub act (not to be missed is a disgustingly funny joke about Bill and Hillary Clinton), interviews with admirers (Ice-T, Eazy-E) and clips from his now-classic 1970s blaxploitation films. For fans a must; for neophytes, a coarse but entertaining eye-opener. ★★½ $19.99

Legend of 8 Samurai

(1984, 130 min, Japan, Kinji Fukasaku) This action-adventure film features Japanese folklore and fantasy to tell the story of Princess Shizu, who is the only survivor of an attack by the phantoms of another clan. She is rescued by two masterless samurai and they flee, but the curse laid upon her family stays. She is told that it will take eight samurai to do battle with the phantoms to lift the curse. (Dubbed) ★★½

The Legend of Hell House

(1973, 95 min, GB, John Hough) Four psychics agree to spend a week at a haunted mansion to discover why their colleagues, conducting experiments at the house years earlier, were murdered. One of the best of its genre, this is quite suspenseful and the scares are many. Starring Roddy McDowall, Clive Revill and Pamela Franklin. ★★★ $19.99

The Legend of the Suram Fortress

(1985, 87 min, USSR, Sergei Paradjanov) Based on ancient Georgian legend and dedicated to all Georgian warriors killed in defense of the Motherland, this unique, but for most viewers inscrutable, tale has minimal dialogue and dazzling visuals. When a newly built Georgian fortress mysteriously collapses, the townspeople are at a loss and vulnerable to attack. An aging soothsayer claims that the only way to keep the walls standing is to have the son of the lover who jilted her buried alive inside the walls. (Georgian with English subtitles) ★★★ $59.99

Legends

(1992, 54 min, US, Ilana Bar-Din) Beginning as a straightforward documentary on the enormously popular Vegas show Legends — a "glitzy" show of professional impersonators performing dead megastars like Marilyn Monroe, Elvis Presley and Judy Garland — this film at one point takes a delightfully funny, revealingly perceptive and almost painfully sarcastic turn when it goes behind the stage and interviews its "stars" and producer. Allowing the impersonators and the megalomaniacal producer to hang themselves with their own thoughts of self-importance and capturing the mean-spirited backbiting among them, the film becomes a uniquely unreal glimpse of tacky Americana at its most bizarre — a real life Spinal Tap! ★★★ $19.99

Legends of the Fall

(1994, 133 min, US, Edward Zwick) Like those fondly remembered soapers of the 1940s, whose stars could help gloss over any screenplay contrivance, Legends of the Fall is a gloriously old-fashioned melodrama which, while occasionally overdone in its dramatic construction, never fails to entertain. It's a near-epic tale where everything and everyone looks great. Beginning just before the start of WWI, the film stars Brad Pitt as one of three sons of a stalwart Montana rancher (Anthony Hopkins). When their youngest brother (Henry Thomas) returns home with a beautiful fiancée (Julia Ormond), siblings Pitt and Aidan Quinn nuture romantic feelings for her. Thus sets in motion an encompassing story of love, betrayal, war and familial ties. Director Zwick (Glory) allows his actors full range of emotions, and however good the ensemble is, all are upstaged by the sprawling locales and the film's gorgeous cinematography. (Available letterboxed and pan & scan) ★★★½ $14.99

The Lemon Sisters

(1990, 93 min, US, Joyce Chopra) A pleasant, low-key comedy with an accent on characterizations more than story, with Diane Keaton, Carol Kane and Kathryn Grody as three childhood pals who are members of a singing group known as the Lemon Sisters; they're looking to make their mark in the nightclubs of Atlantic City. The performances are fine, though Kane steals the film with her delightful portrayal of the wacky and hopelessly mediocre singer (her solo performance is a highlight). Supporting cast includes Elliott Gould, Aidan Quinn and Ruben Blades. ★★½ $9.99

Leningrad Cowboys Go America

(1990, 80 min, Finland, Aki Kaurismäki) Infused with his trademark droll sense of humor and peopled by an arresting cast of weirdos sporting gravity-defying hair and razor-sharp shoes, this Finnish comedy is a successful, albeit one-note, cultural satire. Beginning in the frozen tundra of Finland, a group of aspiring but not very good rock musicians decide to tour America seeking fame and fortune. An inopportune death, gigs in seedy Louisiana bars, and dumbfounded or bored-to-tears audiences prove to be little deterrence to these beer-guzzling aliens bent on becoming an overnight American success. Told with little dialogue and in neat vignettes, this misfits-on-the-road movie will prove to be a grinning delight for adventurous videophiles. ★★★ $19.99

Lenny

(1974, 112 min, US, Bob Fosse) Adapted from Julian Barry's play, Lenny is a powerful and often touching portrait of the troubled and controversial comedian Lenny Bruce. Filmed in a richly textured black and white, Lenny features superb performances by Dustin Hoffman as the comic and Valerie Perrine as his wife, stripper Honey Harlowe. ★★★½ $19.99

Lenny Bruce — Without Tears

(1972, 75 min, US, Fred Baker) Lenny Bruce was as much a performance artist as comic — and his performances would continue even after he left the stage. Director Baker has fashioned the best documentary yet on this seminal artist, interspersing rare interviews with extended excerpts from his "concerts" and TV appearances, one of which is a very bizarre pilot for his own variety show! With comments from Paul Krasner, Mort Sahl, Kenneth Tynan, Nat Hentoff and, of course, Steve "I've just written another song" Allen. ★★★ $19.99

Lenny Bruce Performance Film

(1973, US) A complete nightclub performance from the hipster satirist whose risque topics and language brought about police raids and a New York City obscenity trial. Bruce at his peak. $19.99

Lensman

(1984, 107 min, Japan) Based on the classic sci-fi novels of E.E. "Doc" Smith (1890-1965), this action-packed animation marvel utilizes state-of-the-art technology to render its story of 25th-century intergalactic wars. Since Star Wars was influenced by Smith's work, the story will be familiar to fans, but the innovative, 3-D effects should enthrall every viewer. ★★★ $29.99

Leo Tolstoy

(1984, 103 min, USSR, Sergei Garasimov) The turbulent personal life and prodigious professional career of Leo Tolstoy (nee Count Lev Nikolayevich), one of the greatest writers of the 19th century and author of "War and Peace," is explored in this remarkable documentary. The film delves into his pampered childhood and his stormy marriage, as well as the forces that fueled the novelist's creative drive. (Russian with English subtitles) ★★★ $59.99

Léolo

(1992, 115 min, Canada, Jean-Claude Lauzon) Director Lauzon's follow-up to Night Zoo is a wonderful and rather bizarre coming-of-age tale, telling the story of an imaginative 12-year-old boy who believes he is the offspring of a Sicilian tomato (yes, the fruit). A clever mixture of reality and imagination, the film follows the exploits of young Léolo and his dysfunctional family: his parents who are obsessed with bowel movements; a dim-witted weight lifting brother; a sister calmed only by her secret bug collection; and a demented grandfather. The imagery is haunting, beautiful, disgusting and often hysterical, and the film is enhanced by beautiful cinematography and a soundtrack featuring Tom Waits and The Rolling Stones. (French with English subtitles) ★★★½ $19.99

Léon Morin, Priest

(1961, 118 min, France, Jean-Pierre Melville) Emmanuelle Riva stars as a lonely young widow with anticlerical, atheist and Communist views who meets and befriends a handsome young priest (Jean-Paul Belmondo). Their lively exchange of ideas on religion and life soon results — almost against her will — in an "invasion by God" into her soul, and the process of conversion into Catholicism begins. Set during the German and Italian Occupation and the beginning days of the Liberation, this austere, intense lesson of independence, love and faith is reminiscent of Robert Bresson's works and is a great departure from the hard-boiled gangster films usually associated with director Melville. While Belmondo's role as the almost saintly priest is glazed over, it is Riva's Barny — a determinedly independent, opinionated woman — that is quite memorable in this moving religious, political and allegorical drama. (French with English subtitles) ★★★ $59.99

Leon the Pig Farmer

(1993, 98 min, GB, Vadim Jean & Gary Sinyor) A witty take on the Jewish mother syndrome, but this time from the British. Leon is an unsuccessful real estate dealer who is neither married nor rich, much to the chagrin of his successful parents. Fired from his job for botching a large deal, Leon takes a job with his mother's kosher catering service. While on a delivery to a local fertility clinic, he happens to find out that he was conceived by artificial insemination. What's a nice Jewish boy to do when he discovers that his father is in reality a pig farmer from a small English hamlet? Why, get to know his newly discovered parent, of course. The film features plenty of laughs, and Mark Frankel is wonderful as Leon. Good support comes from Connie Booth, Janet Suzman and Maryam D'Abo. ★★★ $19.99

The Leopard Man

(1943, 66 min, US, Jacques Tourneur) Val Lewton's follow-up to his highly successful Cat People is another first-rate, low-budget chiller, also directed by Tourneur. Set in a small New Mexico town, the search is on for an escaped leopard, which may be responsible for a series of gruesome killings. ★★★

Les Miserables ('95)

The Leopard Son

(1996, 87 min, GB, Hugo van Lawick) This pseudo-documentary (á la *The Bear*) tracks the coming of age of a young leopard cub in the wilds of the Serengeti under the watchful and concerned eye of a wildlife cinematographer. Narrated by John Gielgud, this personal and comprehensive story follows the cub from birth to independence as he learns the way of the plains. While the graphic depiction of death and dining by the local predators may be a bit much for the small ones, the scenes between mother and son are charming and universal. A standout among nature films. ★★★ $89.99

Leprechaun

(1990, 91 min, US, Mark Jones) A playfully sadistic munchkin wreaks havoc when his personal possessions are threatened. No, it's not the latest entry in the *Home Alone* series, but the "magically delicious" tale of a leprechaun (Warwick Davis) from Ireland who goes on a (dare we say it?) "cereal" killing spree to reclaim his stolen bag of gold. Having sat on the shelf for three years before its gratuitous theatrical release, the strictly rudimentary "insert fiend here" screenplay bears the distinction of being quite possibly the only horror movie to be set in rural North Dakota. Oooh, scary... With Jennifer Aniston. ★★ $14.99

Les Girls

(1957, 114 min, US, George Cukor) Three showgirls take their former dancing partner to court; but during testimony, can't agree as to what really happened. A joyously entertaining musical with Gene Kelly in good form as the hoofer, and Mitzi Gaynor, Kay Kendall and Tiana Elg as his ex-mates. ★★★ $19.99

Les Miserables

(1935, 108 min, US, Richard Boleslawski) Excellent adaptation of Victor Hugo's classic novel with Fredric March and Charles Laughton giving great performances as, respectively, petty thief Valjean and relentless police inspector Javert. Remade several times, including as a Broadway musical. ★★★½ $59.99

Les Misérables: Stage by Stage

(1989, 60 min,) A behind-the-scenes look at the various world-wide productions of the acclaimed musical "Les Misérables." Features many scenes (not whole production numbers, however) from the show, many of which are in foreign tongues. A fascinating documentary, especially for those who have seen (and loved) the Tony Award-winning musical. ★★★ $19.99

Les Misérables

(1995, 174 min, France, Claude Lelouch) Victor Hugo's classic treatise on social injustice gets a radical updating by director Lelouch. Venturing well beyond mere adaptation into the realm of liberal interpretation, Lelouch's daring, invigorating and spellbinding three-hour epic opens at a New Year's ball on the eve of the 20th century where a trusted chauffeur, Henri Fortin (Jean-Paul Belmondo), helps his Count make a run from justice. Fate, of course, intervenes and it is Fortin who serves prison time, leaving his wife and son to fend for themselves. Jumping many years forward to the Nazi Occupation, the story revolves around Fortin, Jr. (again Belmondo). Having retired from a career as a prize fighter, he makes his living as a mover and winds up helping a Jewish family make a run for the Swiss border. Fortin, an illiterate, has become fascinated with the parallels between himself and Hugo's hero Jean Valjean, and so he has his Jewish riders read the novel out loud for him. Lelouch then enacts these readings (with Belmondo playing Valjean) and draws the obvious analogies between Hugo's characters and those of Vichy France. Belmondo revels in his multiple roles, and his rich performance combined with Lelouch's ingenious screenplay makes for one of the best offerings from France in many a year. (French with English subtitles) ★★★★ $29.99

Les Misérables — In Concert

(1995, 160 min, GB, Ken Caswell) To celebrate the 10th anniversary of his award-winning stage musical "Les Misérables," producer Cameron Mackintosh assembled an extraordinary cast (including original members from the London and New York stages) for a special performance of the show at the Royal Albert Hall. Featuring most of the musical's three-hour plus score and including film excerpts from the original staging, this enthralling live concert is about as close as one can get to experiencing the thrill of sitting in a theatre watching a live performance without actually having paid $65 for a front row seat. Colm Wilkinson, who created the role of petty thief Jean Valjean, is in great voice leading a remarkable group of performers, who include Tony Award winner Michael Maguire and "Miss Saigon"'s Lea Salonga. As this concert reminds us, "Les Misérables" is the greatest musical production of the last two decades, and the assembled "dream cast" certainly lives up to the billing. ★★★★ $24.99

Lesbionage

(1988, 90 min, US, Joyce Compton) This low-budget lesbian thriller centers around two bickering, interracial lovers whose relationship and private detective partnership are revitalized when they are employed by a blackmailed lesbian congresswoman. The cast of suspects in this humorous and sexy sleuther includes her three jealous lovers, and the case soon involves the KGB, a kidnapping and government corruption. ★★½ $59.99

Less Than Zero

(1987, 96 min, US, Marek Kanievska) Never has a title more aptly fit its film. A creative void by all concerned has made this limp attempt to be the *Easy Rider* of the rich, alienated teens of the '80s nothing more than a sad curiosity piece. Purging the ennui, drug taking and bisexuality of the novel for cheap moralistic posturing, the film is almost an antithesis of the Bret Easton Ellis best-seller. Robert Downey, Jr. is the only cast member with an active pulse while Andrew McCarthy and Jami Gertz listlessly cruise the highways of L.A. as zombies in search of motivation, direction and characterization. ★ $19.99

A Lesson in Love

(1954, 95 min, Sweden, Ingmar Bergman) This Bergman romantic comedy, lightweight but nonetheless satisfying, details the marital tensions and break up of a middle-aged gynecologist who, although happily married for 15 years, has a short affair with a patient. His wife finds out and abruptly leaves him to live with her former lover, his best friend. (Swedish with English subtitles) ★★★

Lessons at the End of Spring

(1989, 75 min, Russia, Oleg Kavan) The triumph of the human spirit over repression and injustice is the theme of this emotionally powerful drama set in a Khrushchev-era Soviet Union. A 13-year-old boy is mistakenly thrown into an adult prison where begins a harrowing odyssey in which inhuman treatment of the prisoners is the norm. Despite this, our young hero retains, throughout, his naive sense of justice as well as his defiant survival instincts. Similar to the Russian films *My Name Is Ivan* and *Kindergarten*, the film is not only great storytelling, but is startling in its unflinching criticism of the Soviet state. (Russian with English subtitles) ★★★½ $59.99

L

Let Him Have It

(1991, 115 min, GB, Peter Medak) This chilling and engrossing drama is based on an actual incident which led Great Britain to reevaluate, and eventually abolish, its death penalty. Set in the '50s, amidst the ruins of a bombed-out London still recovering from the war, the story follows the demise of a quiet, learning-disabled and epileptic young man who naively falls in with a group of Hollywood gangster-influenced, would-be thugs. When a bungled robbery attempt leads to the cold-blooded killing of a policeman, he finds himself not only implicated in the murder, but also subject to the wrath of a vengeful society seeking blood. ★★★½ $14.99

Let It Be

(1970, 80 min, GB, Michael Lindsay-Hogg) A fascinating look at the final days of the world's most famous rock group, punctuated by The Beatles' great songs and the legendary "rooftop" concert sequence. It is a wistful film, full of portentous glances, asides and remarks. It captures the group at the moment before the end, and is important viewing for all music fans. ★★★

Let It Ride

(1989, 91 min, US, Joe Pytka) When you read the box ("He drinks. He smokes. He curses.") for this zany comedy, don't let the inane ad copy dissuade you from an appealing, thoroughly enjoyable lark. Richard Dreyfuss is a winner as a race track gambler whose wish for a "great day" comes true when he becomes privy to a hot tip. Teri Garr has some nice moments as his long-suffering wife, Jennifer Tilly is her usual delightful self as a gambler's gal and Robbie Coltrane is a scene-stealer as a track cashier. ★★★ $14.99

Let's Dance

(1950, 112 min, US, Norman Z. McLeod) Fred Astaire is the song-and-dance man who helps ex-partner Betty Hutton battle her deceased husband's grandmother for custody of her young son. Some good dance sequences get lost in the sentimental story. ★★ $14.99

Let's Do It Again

(1975, 112 min, US, Sidney Poitier) Sidney Poitier and Bill Cosby are back together again in this very funny sequel to *Uptown Saturday Night*. This time around, Poitier and Cosby scheme to turn nebbish Jimmie Walker into a champion boxer – through hypnosis – in order to save their lodge. High spirited and lots of fun. ★★★ $14.99

Let's Get Lost

(1987, 119 min, US, Bruce Weber) The life and music of jazz great Chet Baker is the subject of this poignant, fascinating documentary by noted photographer Weber. In fact, Weber's roots show to tremendous effect as this examination of a tortured artist's genius and self-destruction looks every bit as handsome as its subject in his early years. Weber splendidly intercuts rare recording sessions, interviews with family and friends, and even includes clips from Baker's short-lived movie career in the 1950s. The scenes of Baker's later years are heartbreakingly sad as the ravages of

drug addiction had clearly taken its toll on this legendary trumpeter. ★★★½

Let's Make Love

(1960, 118 min, US, George Cukor) A well-intentioned misfire, this sporadically amusing musical stars Yves Montand as a millionaire who learns he is to be parodied in an off-Broadway show. He becomes intent on closing the show until he sees leading lady Marilyn Monroe, and, well, you know the rest. This could have been a lot more palatable had anyone other than Montand starred as the millionaire. ★★

Lethal Weapon

(1987, 110 min, US, Richard Donner) After several sincere and well-intentioned flops (*The River*, *Mrs. Soffel*), Mel Gibson returns to his Mad Max days and unleashes his charismatically explosive action persona in this rousing and violent cop vs. druggies movie. He plays an emotionally off-balanced undercover cop with Danny Glover co-starring as his stable, family man partner; and together, they become embroiled in a series of tense and exciting situations. There are two not-to-be-forgotten scenes for fans: the shot of Mel's cute hairy buns and his hilarious, psychotic imitation of the Three Stooges' Curly. (Available letterboxed and pan & scan) ★★★½ $19.99

Lethal Weapon 2

(1989, 113 min, US, Richard Donner) Mel Gibson and Danny Glover are back, and as the old movie ads used to say, they're bigger and better than ever. As in the original, Gibson and Glover have redefined the genre with a spontaneous, fresh repartee which is as entertaining as it is humorous. Plot really takes a back seat to the fast, frantic (sometimes violent) action scenes and the delectable rapport between the two stars. But for the record, Roger and Martin find themselves up against a ruthless South African diplomat, who happens to be a part-time drug dealer. Joe Pesci does the impossible by stealing the show as a loquacious, ingratiating accountant being protected by Mel and Danny. (Available letterboxed and pan & scan) ★★★½ $19.99

Lethal Weapon 3

(1992, 118 min, US, Richard Donner) Mel Gibson and Danny Glover are back as detectives Martin Riggs and Roger Murtaugh in this average third installment in the *Lethal Weapon* series. Just days away from his retirement, Rog (Glover) once again gets unwittingly sucked into harm's way by his loose cannon partner (Gibson). Together they find themselves uncovering a scheme to steal high-powered weaponry from police storage, with the prime suspect being a corrupt ex-cop. Along the way they are investigated by a sexy Internal Affairs officer (Rene Russo) who conveniently winds up with the hots for Riggs (you didn't really think they would let Mel go without a love interest, did you?). Joe Pesci reprises his role as low-life Leo Getz and delivers some of the film's best one-liners. Despite a screenplay which resists all logic, director Donner's flair for humor and chase scenes, along with Gibson and Glover's charisma and on-screen chemistry, makes for a mindless though enter-

taining ride. (Available letterboxed and pan & scan) ★★½ $19.99

The Letter

(1940, 95 min, US, William Wyler) Bette Davis and director Wyler's second film together (after their success with *Jezebel*) is a knock-out adaptation (and second screen version) of W. Somerset Maugham's novel about a tycoon's wife who murders her lover and claims self-defense; only to be a victim of blackmail when "the letter" proves otherwise. Also starring Herbert Marshall as Davis' husband and James Stephenson as her lover (Marshall played the Stephenson role in the 1929 version). ★★★½ $19.99

Letter from an Unknown Woman

(1948, 90 min, US, Max Ophüls) Lush romantic drama with Joan Fontaine suffering from cinema's worst case of unrequited love as she is obsessed with musician Louis Jordan. A film of visual splendor; and one that, thanks to director Ophüls' sturdy direction, avoids the clichés usually found in melodramas. ★★★ $14.99

Letter to Brezhnev

(1985, 94 min, GB, Chris Bernard) A bawdy, low-budget comedy about two Liverpool girls, looking for sex and romance, who chance upon two Soviet sailors in a local disco. It offers a vibrant, gritty portrait of young people in the harsh industrial wasteland of northern England as they look for love and dream of escape from their dreary daily lives. The film is graced by fine performances from Peter Firth, Alfred Molina, Alexander Prigg and Margi Clarke. ★★★

A Letter to Three Wives

(1949, 103 min, US, Joseph L. Mankiewicz) A year before he would write and direct the classic *All About Eve*, Mankiewicz won two Oscars for both writing and directing this scintillating and extremely witty comedy-drama which dissects and devours, among other things, marriage, education, consumerism and social strata. Three suburban matrons learn that one of their husbands has run off with another woman. Told in three flashbacks, the story focuses on each couple's shaky marital history while giving clues as to whom the dastardly Addie (who is never seen) betrayed. Though an extremely well-acted ensemble piece, it's Ann Sothern who runs away with the picture as the socially ambitious wife of happy-to-be-just-a-teacher Kirk Douglas. The exotic Linda Darnell and wholesome Jeanne Crain are the other wives, and Paul Douglas (in a terrific film debut) and Jeffrey Lynn are their respective husbands. ★★★★ $19.99

Letters from My Windmill

(1954, 100 min, France, Marcel Pagnol) Pagnol's splendid trilogy of short tales. "Three Low Masses": The Devil takes over the body of a dunce and torments a priest. "The Elixer of Father Gaushet": Brother Gauchier inherits some home-made brew and begins to sell the wine for charitable purposes. "The Secret of Master Cornielle": A sentimental story of an ancient miller who for 18 years has been pretending to compete with a modern steam mill. (French with English subtitles) ★★★

L

Lianna

Letters from the Park

(1988, 85 min, Cuba, Tomás Gutiérrez Alea) Adapted from a Gabriel Garcia Marquez short story, this elegant tale of innocence, romance and forbidden love is set in turn-of-the-century Cuba. The story revolves around two shy young lovers, Juan and Maria. Though attracted to one another, each finds it impossible to articulate their feelings. Unaware of the other's actions, they each enlist an older man to compose beautifully poetic love letters to the other, letters that eventually bring the two together. Problems arise after the poet, swept away with their romance and his own repressed feelings, falls in love with the young woman but is forced to keep his feelings silent. This Spanish "Cyrano de Bergerac" — without the nose — is a wonderfully enchanting, dreamy and seemingly universal story. (Spanish with English subtitles) ★★★ $19.99

Leviathan

(1989, 98 min, US, George Pan Cosmatos) The director's in over his head and the actors out of their depth trying to pump life into this tale about a monster terrorizing an undersea community. With Peter Weller, Richard Crenna, Amanda Pays and Daniel Stern. ★ $14.99

Li'l Abner

(1959, 113 min, US, Melvin Frank) Colorful screen version of the hit Broadway musical, based on Al Capp's comic strip, about the eccentric citizens of Dogpatch, USA. The story follows Li'l Abner, a muscle-bound loafer, and his romantic near-misses with beautiful girlfriend Daisy Mae. The story and lyrics are as witty and sardonic as Capp's strip often was. Songs include "Bring 'em Back" and the politically astute "The Country's in the Very Best of Hands." With Peter Palmer, Leslie Parrish and the always splendid Stubby Kaye. ★★★ $14.99

Lianna

(1982, 110 min, US, John Sayles) Director-writer Sayles' exceptional and humorous exploration of the coming out of the "good wife" offers a compassionate view of lesbianism, self-determination and unrest. Lianna (Linda Griffiths) confronts her husband's infidelity, falls in love with her graduate instructor and sets out on her own. Sayles directs with a sensitive hand, and his perceptive screenplay contains many vulnerable and tender moments examining one woman's budding lesbian self-realization. ★★★

Liar, Liar

(1997, 100 min, US, Tom Shadyac) In *The Nutty Professor*, director Shadyac found a kindler, gentler Eddie Murphy with rousing comedic results. In *Liar, Liar*, an often hilarious but frequently mawkish comedy, Shadyac attempts to unearth the same qualities in Jim Carrey — and though they are there, Carrey proves the nastier the nicer. Carrey plays a divorced father and unscrupulous lawyer; unfortunately for his adoring five-year-old son, not in that order. Making a birthday wish, young Justin Cooper wishes his father could go one day without telling a lie. This starts a terrific premise which is realized most of the time. Watching Carrey blurt out the truth at the most inopportune times, or writhe in scores of facial and vocal contortions, brings a new appreciation for his comic skills (under control as much as Jim Carrey can be, this is the best work he's done since *The Mask*). And his boardroom rant is classic. However, most of the scenes with his son and ex-wife are maudlin; you expect Carrey to skewer this kind of sap, not embrace it. But truth being stranger than fiction, Carrey can ultimately make a believer out of anyone. ★★★ $22.99

Liar's Moon

(1983, 106 min, US, David Fisher) A teen from the wrong side of the tracks (Matt Dillon) falls for the richest girl in town (Cindy Fisher), much against the wishes of both families, who carry a dark secret that could ruin the lovers' chance at happiness. Dillon's passionate performance elevates this otherwise familiar, star-crossed lovers romantic drama. With Yvonne DeCarlo, Susan Tyrrell, Hoyt Axton and Broderick Crawford. ★★½

Libeled Lady

(1936, 98 min, US, Jack Conway) Classic screwball comedy featuring an impeccable cast. Spencer Tracy is a scheming newspaper editor looking for a story; he hires William Powell (a hilarious performance and what a great fisherman!) to implicate heiress Myrna Loy in a romantic scandal. Jean Harlow rounds out the powerhouse cast as Tracy's long-suffering fiancée. ★★★½ $19.99

The Liberation of L.B. Jones

(1969, 101 min, US, William Wyler) A race-conscious town in Tennessee is divided over the scandalous divorce of a black lawyer and his adulterous wife, who has been having an affair with a white cop. Wyler deftly demonstrates the sexual and racial passions boiling over in the tiny town, but the screenplay can't overcome its melodramatic roots. Lee J. Cobb, Roscoe Lee Browne, Lola Falana, Barbara Hershey and Yaphet Kotto star. ★★½ $59.99

Licence to Kill

(1989, 133 min, GB, John Glen) Timothy Dalton makes his second appearance as agent 007, and while he may not make anyone forget the one and only Sean Connery, he proves once and for all that Moore is less. In this terrifically exciting and well-produced adventure, set mostly in Miami and Central America, Bond loses his "licence to kill" when he sets out to avenge the murder of his friend's wife. There are, to be sure, hair-raising action

scenes and the trademark Bond humor, plus two beautiful co-stars in Talisa Soto and Carey Lowell — the latter demonstrating that Bond women have finally grown up and can definitely hold their own with the big guys. Robert Davi makes a most memorable villain as a ruthless druglord. ★★★ $14.99

Lie Down with Dogs

(1995, 86 min, US, Wally White) With the enticing promise of being a refreshing comic alternative to typical AIDS dramas and New Queer Cinema artiness that many gay-themed films offer, this surprisingly amateurish production disappoints on many levels. Though this low-budget comedy does have its share of laughs, it's saddled with poor acting and a plot line you couldn't hang your Calvin Kleins on. A relentlessly grinning Tommie (writer-director White) decides to chuck his job in sweaty New York for three months of pleasure in gay mecca Provincetown. He tries to find a job as a houseboy ("In Provincetown, you don't apply, you audition!"), and quickly dives into a series of sexual escapades. The film's most interesting character is that of Tom, a handsome, Brazilian mooch (played by Randy Becker) — possibly because Becker is the only one that can act. Marketed exclusively towards gay men, *Lie Down with Dogs* could offer a mindless good time for that audience, but artistic expectations should be put on hold. ★★ $19.99

Liebelei

(1932, 83 min, Germany, Max Ophüls) Suppressed by the Nazis for years and subsequently rarely seen, *Liebelei* finds Ophüls' visual style yet to exhibit the long, languid tracking shots of his later works such as *La Ronde* or *The Earrings of Madame de...*, though it shares with them a common theme. This, his first big success, is another of his meditation on the nature of love — here a love blocked not so much by class strata, but by class custom. In late 19th-century Vienna, where a man's word or a withheld hand meant something, a philandering lieutenant vows to mend his ways when he falls for a woman of a more modest station. Unfortunately, he soon becomes the victim of his past — a past that no longer holds meaning now, save for some vague requirement of "honor." Though *Liebelei* is not remarkable in either story or storytelling, Ophüls' unsteady but promising directorial hand allows this somber love story to be of historical interest. (German with English subtitles) ★★½ $39.99

Liebestraum

(1991, 105 min, US, Mike Figgis) Don't be put off by its puzzling title (taken from Franz Liszt's love song), for this Figgis production is an absorbing, noir-influenced thriller which skillfully merges two violent, obsessive love triangles, 40 years apart. Kevin Anderson is an architectural journalist who, while on a visit to his home town to see his dying mother (Kim Novak in a wonderful supporting role), meets an old friend, Paul (Bill Pullman). Paul is a real estate developer in the process of tearing down a main street department store which has been shuttered for 40 years after the gruesome double murder of its owner and his mistress. The writer's interest in the building and its mysterious past causes him to become romantically involved with Paul's wife, who is photographing the building's destruction. The result is a torrid tale of lust and jealousy. This is the director's cut, seven minutes longer than the theatrical version. ★★★ $14.99

The Life and Death of Colonel Blimp

(1943, 115 min, GB, Michael Powell & Emeric Pressburger) A memorable British wartime classic which follows the long and eventful life of a prosperous, old-fashioned officer of the British Army. At 115 minutes, the video version of this tale, which winds its way through several wars and four different women (all played by Deborah Kerr!), is regrettably a full 48 minutes shorter than the theatrical cut. ★★★★ $19.99

Life and Nothing But

(1990, 135 min, France, Bertrand Tavernier) Tavernier's film is a somber, meditative yet romantic exploration of war, loneliness and love. Philippe Noiret stars as a cynical army officer assigned to catalogue the dead, injured and missing French soldiers at the end of WWI. The story revolves around two women, one an elegant lady and the other a young waitress, who both travel to the rain-drenched and battle-scarred fields of the front and solicit the aid of Noiret in finding their missing husbands. A thoughtful film on the emotional healing process. (French with English subtitles) ★★★½ $19.99

The Life and Times of Allen Ginsberg

(1993, 83 min, US, Jerry Aronson) Enlightening and highly entertaining, this intimate portrait of visionary Beat poet and self-proclaimed "faggot and individualist" Allen Ginsberg seeks to venture beyond his fame and controversy to explore the man who has dedicated his work and life "to ease the pain of living." Through photos and interviews with relatives, friends and Ginsberg himself, the film begins with his influential childhood and follows him to his Greenwich Village days and initial success as a poet (and his friendship with Beat poets Jack Kerouac and William Burroughs). The film also touches

upon his anti-Vietnam War activities, and the mellower years which followed. While the historical accounts are fascinating, it is Ginsberg's readings of his poetry which stir and move. ★★★ $29.99

The Life and Times of Judge Roy Bean

(1972, 120 min, US, John Huston) Paul Newman plays the legendary outlaw in this not-quite-a-western. It's an interesting, unusually self-aware but slightly uneven film, with a star-studded cast — Victoria Principal, Jacqueline Bisset, Anthony Perkins, Tab Hunter, Ned Beatty, Roddy McDowall, John Huston, Stacy Keach as "Bad Bob," and Ava Gardner as Lily Langtry. ★★½ $14.99

Life Classes

(1987, 117 min, Canada, William D. MacGillivray) This simple yet poignant film tells the inspiring story of a woman's burgeoning self-discovery and personal fulfillment. After learning that she is pregnant, 30-year-old Mary (Jacinta Cormier), deadened by the narrow-mindedness and boredom of her Nova Scotia village, decides to leave her family and mindless job and move to Halifax. It is there, with a baby in tow, that she finds a job as a nude model in an art school and begins to explore her own unrealized artistic talents. A quiet celebration of each individual's potential for beauty and expression. ★★½ $99.99

A Life in the Theatre

(1993, 78 min, US, Gregory Mosher) Jack Lemmon and Matthew Broderick offer fine performances in this very capable made-for-cable adaptation of David Mamet's play. The comedic piece is more of an excuse for Mamet to offer a portrait of actors fretting their hour upon the stage rather than a conventional story. Here, more so than in most of Mamet's film works, it is clearly the rhythm of his dialogue that is the real star. Though plot and characterization are very subtle here, both stars appear proficient and quite comfortable with Mamet-speak (even allowing themselves to be upstaged by it), which only further elevates the production. ★★★ $92.99

Life Is a Long Quiet River

(1987, 89 min, France, Etienne Chatiliez) The Quesnoys are a well-bred, bourgeois Catholic family living in France. Everything is wonderful and polite in their lives until one fateful day when they discover that, in the delivery room twelve years prior, their doctor had switched their son with the daughter of the Groseille family, a sordid group of low-income slobs from The Other Side of Town. What ensues is an entertaining farce as the Groseilles attempt to get every penny they can out of the "accident" and the Quesnoys struggle to keep their family values intact. A comic and often caustic commentary on social classes and the family unit. (French with English subtitles) ★★★½ $79.99

Life Is Beautiful

(1981, 102 min, Italy, Grigorig Ciukhrai) The title of this tense and electrifying drama is purely ironic. Set during the politically unstable situation in pre-revolutionary Lisbon, the story concerns itself with the false arrest of a man. He is beaten, imprisoned and kept away from his wife and family. His political neutrality and personal sanity are severely tested by his abusive jailers. (Dubbed) ★★★

Life Is Sweet

(1991, 102 min, GB, Mike Leigh) British director Leigh follows his wickedly satirical *High Hopes* with this mirthful and touching slice of middle-class life set in the English Midlands. Taking on the notion of family dysfunctionality, the film follows the daily trials of a middle-aged couple (Allison Steadman and Jim Broadbent) and their twentysomething twin daughters — one an aspiring plumber (Claire Skinner), the other an aspiring radical feminist (Jane Horrocks). The common obsession in the film is food. Dad's a chef in a hotel kitchen, family friend Aubrey (Timothy Spall) is gonzo over the gourmet restaurant he's opening and Horrocks is an anorexic/bulimic. Leigh masterfully takes this soap opera situation and creates a wry, witty comedy filled with social commentary and a surprising amount of tender moments. The acting throughout is wonderful, but Horrocks deserves special attention for her portrayal of the family's scapegoat. ★★★½ $14.99

The Life of Emile Zola

(1937, 116 min, US, William Dieterle) In one of the best of the 1930s Hollywood biographies, Paul Muni gives a remarkably controlled performance as the famed French author. Gale Sondergaard is well-cast as his wife, and Joseph Schildkraut won a supporting Oscar as the wrongly accused Captain Dreyfus, for whom Zola intervened. Oscar winner for Best Picture. ★★★★ $19.99

A Life of Her Own

(1950, 108 min, US, George Cukor) Cukor stays true to his reputation as a woman's director by coaxing an assured, textured performance from Lana Turner. It's too bad Isobel Lennart's (*Funny Girl*) screenplay wasn't as inspired. Lana plays a Midwestern girl who moves to New York to start a career in modeling. In no time, she's on all the magazine covers. She also becomes involved with married tycoon Ray Milland, with whom there can be

Life Is Sweet

no happy ending. The film's beginning sizzles as it peeks behind the scenes of the Big Apple's modeling circles, but it quickly changes gears and fizzles into another routine melodrama focusing almost entirely on Turner's affair as the other woman. Ann Dvorak nearly steals the show as an aging model who briefly takes Turner under her wing — she leaves the story all too quickly. ★★½ $19.99

The Life of Leonardo Da Vinci

(1972, 270 min, Italy, Renato Castellani) Poorly dubbed and strangely constructed, this nonetheless compelling film biography of Leonardo Da Vinci, one of the great geniuses of the Renaissance, is a curious and exhaustive made-for-TV production that "historically" dramatizes the life of the renowned painter, scientist, astronomer and engineer. The film begins with Da Vinci's birth in 1475 and proceeds to his death in 1564. The film concentrates on his prodigious artistic output in painting and architecture and his many inventions. Hokey at times, and speculative other times (the film ignores Da Vinci's homosexuality), *The Life of Leonardo Da Vinci* should be of great appeal for anyone interested in the life and artistic output of this fascinating man. ★★★ $59.99

Life of Oharu

(1952, 137 min, Japan, Kenji Mizoguchi) One of the most enduring masterpieces of world cinema, this is an exquisitely rendered portrait of a woman who is tragically victimized by the brutal strictures of 17th-century feudal Japanese society. The director shows remarkable insight into the psychology of his female protagonist and fills the screen with hauntingly beautiful camera work. (Japanese with English subtitles) ★★★★ $29.99

Life of Sin

(1990, 112 min, US, Efrin Lopez Neris) The short, stationary shots in the opening sequence of *Life of Sin* establish a moody, almost dreamlike quality which permeates the rest of the film. Miriam Colón is engrossing as the peasant woman who gains fame and fortune during an unhappy and unfulfilled life. In a role which could easily have engendered histrionics, her understated and measured portrayal is all the more powerful. Raul Julia is

strong in support as Colón's lifelong friend, whose loyalty is unquestioning until a tragic, unnecessary confrontation. Jose Ferrer is a pleasure in the small role of the Catholic bishop who will accept Colón's donation to the Church, but not with his own hand; and will remain unforgiving of her sins after her death. An interesting study of hypocrisy and societal double standards, though somewhat marred by an unclear resolution. ★★½ $89.99

Life Stinks

(1991, 95 min, US, Mel Brooks) Brooks hits rock bottom with this comedy — a sad, humorless and offensive parody of homelessness and big business. Brooks plays a multimillionaire who bets he can live penniless and homeless on the streets of Los Angeles for one month. Once there, director-writer Brooks lets loose an incredible array of comic vulgarities, none of which are the least bit amusing or original. Two or three funny scenes cannot justify this film, which does nothing more than belittle and mock a serious issue. *Sullivan's Travels* it's not. If he really wanted to help, Brooks should have donated the cost of the film to charity. ★ $9.99

Life with Mikey

(1993, 91 min, US, James Lapine) Michael J. Fox stars as an ex-child actor who opens his own kiddie talent agency. The biggest belly laughs in this lazy comedy come when Fox holds open auditions to find the next Macaulay Culkin and ends up with tiny tots spouting *The Odd Couple*, baton twirlers and Ethel Merman's bastard daughter. Unfortunately, the movie gets mired down in its own plot about a street-smart kid (Christina Vidal) who, by the sheer force of her uninhibited charm, nabs a major cookie commercial and saves the agency from impending doom. However, Vidal has all the personality of a wet graham cracker and when mixed with Fox's affable but lackluster performance the picture turns into pure mush. Nathan Lane is good in support as Fox's business partner. ★★ $9.99

Lifeboat

(1944, 96 min, US, Alfred Hitchcock) After an ocean liner is torpedoed by a German sub, a handful of disparate survivors are left adrift in a cramped lifeboat. When a final castaway appears, one of the Nazi crew members and the only individual aboard with any navigational skill, the group is caught in an equally cramped moral dilemma. A cinematically daring work which, though confined to a single setting, is never claustrophobic, and is suspenseful and intriguing throughout. John Steinbeck wrote the screenplay. Acting awards went to Tallulah Bankhead for her only truly satisfying screen appearance. ★★★★ $14.99

Lifeforce

(1985, 100 min, US, Tobe Hooper) Some elaborate special effects can't hide the silliness of the plot and ineffec-

Tallulah Bankhead in *Lifeboat*

tiveness of Hooper's direction. Space vampires are terrorizing London. An intriguing premise gone sour. ★ $14.99

Lifetime Commitment

(1987, 30 min, US, Kiki Zeldes) Despite its static, almost amateur direction, this moving story of Karen Thompson's struggles for legal acceptability and access to her hospitalized lover proves to be a compelling tale. Sharon Kowalski was critically injured in an auto accident in 1983 resulting in her needing constant medical attention. Despite the fact that Karen and Sharon were living together for four years, exchanged rings and made a lifetime commitment to each other, Sharon's parents, denying that their daughter was a lesbian and backed by the courts, denied Karen many rights traditionally accorded a family member. Karen recounts her frustration with trying to care for her lover and charts her personal growth from a closeted woman, afraid of going to a lesbian bar, to becoming national advocate for lesbian and gay partnership rights. Since the film was made, Karen won her case in a December 1991 Minnesota court ruling which stated that a "family of affinity...ought to be accorded respect." ★★★ $39.99

The Lift

(1985, 95 min, The Netherlands, Dick Maas) A Dutch thriller about an elevator in a high-tech office building with a murderous mind of its own. The highlight of this film was probably the ad which said: "Take the stairs! Take the stairs! For God's sake, take the stairs!" Great premise that holds up for a while, but when it comes to horror and splatter films, nothing beats the Americans. (Dubbed) ★★

Light of Day

(1987, 107 min, US, Paul Schrader) Michael J. Fox and Joan Jett play a brother and sister who perform together in a local Cleveland rock band, trying to make it big time. Gena Rowlands is their dying mother, at odds with her carefree daughter. Full of clichés in both its family drama and trying-to-get-ahead show business story. ★★ $14.99

Life of Emile Zola (previous page)

Light Sleeper

(1992, 103 min, US, Paul Schrader) Despite the heavy-handedness of Schrader's direction and its unsatisfying sugarcoated ending, *Light Sleeper* is an engrossing and intriguing drama. Essentially the story of the midlife crisis of alienated 40-year-old drug runner John LeTour (Willem Dafoe), the story is punched up by an entertainingly frantic, amphetamine-driven performance by Susan Sarandon as the brains and balls behind a high-class New York drug ring. LeTour is a loyal and decent but slumberous man (sort of a thinking man's Travis Bickle) who, after years of delivering the goods to the yuppies, posers and rich lowlifes, begins to question it all. Under Schrader's direction, the denizens of this seedy world of drug pushers, users and abusers become a metaphor for the world at large. A serious, arty, flawed (the music soundtrack by Michael Been is terrible) yet entertaining drama. ★★★ $14.99

Light Years

(1987, 80 min, US, Renee Laloux) "In a thousand years, Gandahar was destroyed. A thousand years ago, Gandahar will be saved." With this intriguing mathematical paradox, acclaimed director Laloux (*Fantastic Planet*) and master science fiction writer Isaac Asimov combine their formidable talents to produce a captivating and truly original animated sci-fi adventure. This rewarding odyssey of sight and sound is brought to the screen with a boundless imagination which tips its hat to some of the great animated classics before it, from *Yellow Submarine* to *Lord of the Rings*. Featuring the voices of Glenn Close, Christopher Plummer and others. ★★★ $14.99

The Lighthorsemen

(1988, 115 min, Australia, Simon Wincer) The thrilling true story of the Australian Light Brigade's military exploits during World War I, and especially their assault on thousands of German and Turkish troops in Beersheba, is the focus of this sweeping saga. Wincer impressively directs the elaborately staged battle sequences, although some of the widescreen spectacle will be lost on video. While the characters are all too simply drawn and its heavy-handed clichés of "war is hell" get tiring, fans of military adventure films will overlook this and become absorbed in the sweeping action of this epic. ★★½ $14.99

Lightning Jack

(1994, 101 min, US, Simon Wincer) Wincer takes the helm to direct his fellow Aussie Paul Hogan in this insipid comedy set in the Old West. Hogan plays Lightning Jack Kane, an aging outlaw who teams up with a deaf and mute Cuba Gooding, Jr. to knock off a few banks. Gooding tries to liven things up with his physical schtick, and he might have succeeded if only his material was elevated anywhere above insulting (to African-Americans, the physically challenged, Native Americans, etc.). For his part, Hogan makes us yearn for the less-nauseating "Crocodile" Dundee, and Beverly D'Angelo makes the most embarrassing appearance of her career as the virtuous whore who pines for him. This is Muzak filmmaking — the film's cheesy humor and fluffy plot line leave one with that kind of hollow feeling otherwise found only in elevators and supermarkets. ★ $14.99

Lightning over Water

(1980/81, 91 min, US, Wim Wenders & Nicholas Ray) While not a documentary, this unusual film chronicles the last days of famed director Ray who was dying of cancer. While visiting Ray in his SoHo loft, Wenders listens to a story Ray would like to film. They decide to film that story, as it is being lived. The result is a film about friendship as well as a rather unfocused look at a man attempting to finish his life and work with the help of those around him. ★★★

The Lightship

(1985, 89 min, US, Jerzy Skolimowski) What might have been a standard good vs. evil allegory is elevated to a B-grade suspense thriller starring the chameleonic Robert Duvall as an effeminate bank robber who, along with two sadistic partners, escapes from the law by hijacking a lightship piloted by a pacifist captain (Klaus Maria Brandauer). Duvall's excessively flamboyant performance makes this worthwhile viewing. ★★½ $79.99

Like Father, Like Son

(1987, 98 min, US, Ron Daniel) One of the least successful of the "body switching" comedies, with harried surgeon Dudley Moore and teenage son Kirk Cameron switching bodies thanks to an ancient potion. ★★ $9.99

Like Water for Chocolate

(1992, 113 min, Mexico, Alfonso Arau) An immensely satisfying cinematic experience in every regard, this runaway art-house hit is at the same time whimsical, romantic, comic, tragic, sensuous and, above all, pure in spirit. In the grandest Latin American tradition of magical realism, the film tells the tale of Tita, a young woman who is condemned to a lonely and passionless life by her family's cruel tradition that the youngest daughter must care for her mother until she dies. Denied her one true love, Pedro (who Mama arranges to marry Tita's older sister), and forced into servitude, she responds by pouring her emotions into the recipes she is forced to cook for the family, resulting in witches' brews that have a profound effect on all who partake. Filled with marvelously entertaining flights of fancy, the film takes one wild turn after another while revolving around the magnificent feasts that Tita prepares. It's mouth-watering good fun, sprinkled with intrigue and a heavy dash of passion. (Available dubbed and in Spanish with English subtitles) ★★★★ $19.99

Lili

(1953, 87 min, US, Charles Walters) An absolute delight! Leslie Caron gives an enchanting performance as a 16-year-old French orphan who joins a traveling carnival. There she falls in love with the magician (Jean-Pierre Aumont), and is given a valuable lesson in life and love from a crippled puppeteer (Mel Ferrer), who uses his small creatures to cheer the sorrowful Lili. Oscar-winning score includes the wonderful "Hi-Lili, Hi-Lo." Perfect for children of all ages. ★★★★ $19.99

Lilies of the Field

(1963, 95 min, US, Ralph Nelson) Sidney Poitier won an Oscar for Best Actor with his portrayal of a carpenter who reluctantly becomes involved in helping a group of German nuns. Poitier meets the nuns by chance after his car breaks down in front of their decaying convent. The sisters take this as a sign from God that he is the one who will save their home and build them a new chapel. Poitier's performance is full of charm and Lilia Skala is wonderful as the mother superior. A good, lighthearted film that is as inspiring as it is entertaining. ★★★½ $19.99

Lily for President

(1992, 50 min, US, Tom Trbovich) While out promoting her upcoming movie, *The Seven Ages of Woman*, Lily Tomlin finds herself caught up in a political whirlwind which eventually sweeps her into the White House! All of her stock characters, along with James Coco, Pee-wee Herman and a host of other celebrities, help her in her pursuit of the highest office. Imagine if you will: Lily as Pres, Ernestine as the White House switchboard operator, Judith Beasley as Lily's Consumer Advisor, Trudy the Bag Lady as the Chief of Stuff and, most importantly, five-year-old Edith Ann as the Secretary of the Future. It's enough to give Jesse Helms nightmares! While not on par with her best work, and unfortunately shot directly on video, this briskly-paced political satire is still a lot of fun and will provide plenty of amusement for any Tomlin fan. ★★★ $19.99

Lily in Love

(1985, 104 min, GB, Karoly Makk) Maggie Smith and Christopher Plummer offer engaging performances in this minor though enjoyable update of Molnar's comedy "The Guardsman." Plummer plays an aging classical actor who disguises himself as a younger man to get the lead in a film written by his wife (Smith). When he lands the role, his wife

Pedro and Tita in *Like Water for Chocolate*

315

becomes attracted to the "young man," unaware of his true identity. ★★½

Lily: Sold Out

(1981, 50 min, US, Bill Davis) Possibly the weakest of Lily Tomlin's performance videos despite the presence of several of her trademark characters and the cameo appearances of Paul Anka, Dolly Parton, Liberace and Joan Rivers. With the lure of gobs of money, Lily agrees to do the "Strip" and venture into the tacky world of Vegas. She soon finds out, however, that her subtle "message-laden" character comedy is no match for the glitzy pizazz of Vegas superstar-lounge lizard Tommy Velour (Lily doing an on-target spoof of Wayne Newton) and his gaudy, megacharged ilk. But Lily decides to sell out and the result is a show that would make any polyester-wearing grandmother from Indiana flush with excitement. However, this parody of an already existing parody proves to be tiresome and makes one yearn for Lily to return to her "highbrow" comedy schtick. ★★½ $19.99

Lily Tomlin: Appearing Nitely

(1979, 70 min, US, Wendy Apple) Lily Tomlin's made-for-HBO special is a live recording of her one-woman show, "Appearing Nitely." Alternately hilarious and poignant, Lily goes on an almost stream-of-consciousness tear as she mines remembrances from her childhood and youth to create a series of memorable characters and situations. She loses herself in the skits, becoming the shopping bag lady, the bratty adolescent and the geeky suburban girl ready to experiment in the whacked-out '60s. After the performance, the camera ventures backstage for a peek into her dressing room which is filled with famous well-wishers. And keep watching, for at the end there is a wonderful segment of Tomlin accepting an award at the Tony Awards and reliving her life-long dream: not of stardom, but of becoming a waitress! ★★★½ $19.99

Limelight

(1952, 145 min, US, Charles Chaplin) In this, his last American film, Chaplin returned to the London music halls of his childhood. This bittersweet tale tells the story of an aging performer who triumphs over his own foibles (declining popularity and his own mortality) and "passes the torch," so to speak, by curing a young, aspiring ballet dancer of her paralysis

Little Caesar

and thus launching her career (and ending his). The film is certainly overlong and, at times, sluggishly paced; but even this Chaplin "failure" is still a moving tribute to those with whom Chaplin has always sympathized: the underprivileged. A dark and nostalgic piece from one of the screen's all-time greats. ★★★

The Linguini Incident

(1992, 100 min, US, Richard Shepard) Monty (David Bowie), the new British bartender at the latest New York theme park restaurant (a palace of trend), needs to marry to get a green card. Or so it seems. Rosanna Arquette, Eszter Balint, Buck Henry, Andre Gregory, Viveca Lindfors and Marlee Matlin are some of the characters in this giddy, convoluted and very entertaining foray into the world of Manhattan's super-rich, super-chic and wannabes. Escape artistry, Mrs. Houdini's wedding ring and some very serious wagers are a few of the backdrops to tell the tale of deception, survival and monetary gain in a place where robbery becomes performance art if you're wearing the right bra. A nifty score underlines the fun; and everybody looks good, too. ★★★

The Lion in Winter

(1968, 135 min, GB, Anthony Harvey) Katharine Hepburn and Peter O'Toole are both at their fiery best as Eleanor of Aquitaine and King Henry II of England. With undaunted ferocity, the two engage in a bitter battle over who will be the successor to the throne while their children surreptitiously battle each other for the position. Unparalleled performances in the supporting roles are turned in by Anthony Hopkins, Nigel Terry, John Castle, Timothy Dalton and Jane Merrow making this an overall acting gem. Based on James Goldman's Broadway play. (Available letter-boxed or full-screen) ★★★★

A Lion Is in the Streets

(1953, 88 min, US, Raoul Walsh) James Cagney's brisk performance brings unexpected life to this interesting but otherwise average political potboiler. Cagney plays a drifter from the Deep South who becomes a favorite son and runs for Governor. As he gains power and influence, he becomes more corrupt and ruthless, which sets the stage for a final showdown. ★★ $19.99

The Lion King

(1994, 84 min, US, Roger Allers & Rob Minkoff) Highly overrated and the subject of much undeserving ballyhoo, this feather in Disney's animated cap, despite its many flaws, found millions rushing to rent in record numbers. The story revolves around young Simba, the crown Prince of Pride Rock, where all of the beasts live in peace and harmony under the benevolent dictatorship of his father, Mufasa (the voice of James Earl Jones). When the King's evil brother Scar (Jeremy Irons) conspires to murder his royal sibling, Mufasa's son Simba, thinking

himself responsible for the inevitable tragedy, goes into self-imposed exile, only to return when the kingdom is on the verge of ecological ruin. Its weak plot aside, what really leaves *The Lion King* lacking in the light of its immediate predecessors *The Little Mermaid*, *Beauty and the Beast* and *Aladdin* is its score. Elton John and Tim Rice sprinkle the proceedings with sappy pop musical numbers that are completely lacking the razzmatazz and good-natured fun of their forebears Alan Menken and Howard Ashman. ★★½ $49.99

Lionheart

(1991, 115 min, US, Sheldon Lettich) Jean-Claude Van Damme plays a member of the French Foreign Legion who travels to America when he learns his brother is dying. En route in New York City, he becomes involved in the financially lucrative but deadly sport of street-fighting, where he is champion and in great demand. Typical Van Damme actioner: lots of fights and little sense. ★★ $14.99

Lip Gloss

(1993, 70 min, Canada, Lois Siegel) Montreal's surprisingly bustling world of drag shows, transvestites, female impersonators and drag queens takes center stage in this low-budget documentary. Interviewed are the stars (many older and heavyweight), including Armand Monroe, Guilda, Bobette, and Derek of the comedy drag ballet troupe Les Ballets Trockadero de Monte Carlo. As a document of a fringe gay lifestyle, the film is interesting, if somewhat downbeat. However, the interviews "drag" on a bit (in the bad sense of the word) and the film depicts a disturbing misogynistic streak among many of the interviewees. This "*Montreal Is Burning*" took almost eight years to complete and captures the spirit of the city's gay and transgender population. ★★½ $39.99

Lipstick

(1976, 89 min, US, Lamont Johnson) Inferior revenge film and ridiculous social drama with Margaux Hemingway taking on rapist Chris Sarandon. Mariel Hemingway is her little sister; Anne Bancroft plays an attorney. ★ $59.99

Lipstick on Your Collar

(1993, 360 min, GB, Renny Rye) As with Dennis Potter's *The Singing Detective* and *Pennies from Heaven*, *Lipstick on Your Collar* is a multilayered, intricately structured exploration of the human psyche. Director Rye utilizes every aspect of the medium and every nuance of interpersonal relationships to relate the intertwined stories of several proper Englishmen at work in a military intelligence office at the height of Cold War paranoia. The men spend their 9 to 5 days translating, deciphering, analyzing and decoding information about Russian troop movements from sources disparate and arcane in bureaucratic isolation. Their personal lives are spent in a threadbare England still recovering from WWII. These private and professional worlds collide when the newest member of the intelligence group, a naive private, finds himself living in the same building as his corporal — and his corporal's beautiful, ill-treated wife. Dull, utter normalcy is bizarrely juxtaposed with outbursts of pop tunes, sublimely choreographed under satu-

L

Lipstick on Your Collar

rated lighting: the subconscious made manifest. The cast is uniformly excellent, each one delivering a performance which bridges the impossible chasm between characterization and caricature. Potter has delivered another adventurous examination of the human condition. ★★★★ $59.99

Liquid Sky

(1983, 112 min, US, Slava Tsukerman) Flying saucers, fatal orgasms, rampant androgyny and relentless nihilism make *Liquid Sky* one of the most original and hallucinatory films in memory. Co-author Anne Carlisle stars in dual roles as Jimmy, a snarling junkie, and Margaret, his female nemesis, a languid model with an unusual kiss of death. Perched atop Margaret's penthouse terrace are mite-sized aliens who crave the sensation of a heroin rush, which, it seems, is duplicated organically during human orgasm. A stunning cultural collage that offers an alien's-eye view of Manhattan's lurid clubs, majestic skyline and jaded populace. ★★★

The List of Adrian Messenger

(1963, 98 min, US, John Huston) George C. Scott heads an all-star cast in this potent Agatha Christie-like murder mystery about a maniac (and master of disguise) who is killing off potential heirs to a family fortune. Scott plays the detective on the case. With Kirk Douglas, Burt Lancaster, Tony Curtis, Robert Mitchum and Frank Sinatra. ★★★ $19.99

Lisztomania

(1975, 104 min, GB, Ken Russell) Franz Liszt, classical composer, gets the full treatment from Russell in this outlandish visual and sexual assault on historical accuracy and biographical detail. The presumption is that Liszt was a precursor to the rock superstars of today and in unabashed Russell fashion, he turns this into a garish, psychosexual extravaganza. Roger Daltrey brings a certain Adonis-like quality to his role as Liszt, but a guest appearance by Ringo Starr as the Pope is heresy in anybody's book. ★★ $14.99

Little Big League

(1994, 119 min, US, Andrew Scheinman) *Little Big League* is equal parts *Rookie of the Year* and *The Kid from Left Field*, and despite its lack of originality it still manages to produce a cer-

tain charm all its own. The story has to do with an 11-year-old baseball fanatic inheriting the Minnesota Twins when his beloved grandfather dies. The youth quickly appoints himself manager, and for the rest of the film he must prove his worth and inspire his players towards the inevitable championship showdown. Though the kid is a boorish walking baseball encyclopedia, you can't help rooting for him; and he's surrounded by some entertaining and zany players, most of whom seem to be *Major League* rejects. ★★★ $14.99

Little Big Man

(1970, 150 min, US, Arthur Penn) Dustin Hoffman stars as the 121-year-old Jack Crabbe, who recounts his experiences with General Custer, Wild Bill Hickok, Indians and medicine show con men. An epic comedy, with touches of drama and a perfect cast that includes Faye Dunaway, Chief Dan George, Richard Mulligan and Martin Balsam. ★★★½ $9.99

Little Buddha

(1994, 123 min, US, Bernardo Bertolucci) Beautifully photographed and emotionally uplifting, Bertolucci's surprisingly accessible story of spiritual enlightenment has the grand sweep of his *The Last Emperor* but on a smaller scale. Interweaving the modern-day story of a young boy who may or may not be the reincarnation of the Dalai Lama, and the ravishing telling of the origins and tenets of Buddhism and specifically the coming-of-age of the prophet Siddhartha, the film is insightful throughout and amazingly balances both worlds with equal artistry. As the parents of the young child (played with authority by Alex Wiesendanger), Bridget Fonda and Chris Isaak bring compassion to their roles, and Ying Ruocheng is charming as the monk who discovers the possible identity of the boy. But the real treat is Keanu Reeves as the young Indian prince Siddhartha — and while traces of his California dude are present, he nevertheless is believable...and he looks great in mascara, too. ★★★½ $19.99

Little Caesar

(1930, 80 min, US, Mervyn LeRoy) Edward G. Robinson gives a live-wire performance as Caesar Enrico Bandella, one of moviedom's most infamous and ruthless criminals. Robinson has been caricatured as this persona so often that it takes a while to realize how subtle his performance really is. Rico is as classless, cold-blooded and blindly ambitious as the real gangsters we read about; and the film, the first of the 1930s crime movies, traces his bloody rise and bloody fall. The place to start for anyone studying mob films. ★★★★ $19.99

Little Dorrit — Pts. I & II

(1988, 177 & 183 min, GB, Christine Edzard) A magnificent two-part adaptation of Charles Dickens' classic novel, released in two separate volumes (it is recommended that they be viewed in their correct order). The film, set in

early 19th-century London, tells the story of the Dorrit family: from their internment in debtor's prison to their eventual rescue and financial security, and of their relationship with the rich Clennam family, in particular the family's idealistic son, Arthur. Part One, *Nobody's Fault*, is told through the eyes of Arthur, and Part Two, *Little Dorrit's Story*, is seen through the eyes of young Amy, the title character. The film abounds with remarkable performances, but standing out are Derek Jacobi as Arthur, Oscar-nominee Alec Guinness as William Dorrit, Miriam Margolyes as Arthur's former lover and Sarah Pickering as Little Dorrit. ★★★½ $24.99

The Little Drummer Girl

(1984, 130 min, US, George Roy Hill) A stirring if overlong political thriller, based on John LeCarre's novel, exploring the volatile situation in the Middle East, the complexities of personal allegiance and one woman's emotional dismantling as the result of her involvement with sparring terrorist forces. Diane Keaton gives a remarkable performance as an actress who is "hired" to pose as an agent, thrusting her into political intrigue. ★★★ $14.99

The Little Foxes

(1941, 116 min, US, William Wyler) Terrific screen version of Lillian Hellman's Broadway smash. Bette Davis is at her bitchy best as Regina, the matriarch of a bickering Southern clan facing financial ruin. Patricia Collinge gives a heartbreaking performance as the kind-hearted aunt, and Teresa Wright and Herbert Marshall also offer top support. ★★★½ $19.99

Little Fugitive

(1953, 75 min, US, Ray Ashley, Morris Engel & Ruth Orkin) One of the first American independent films, *Little Fugitive* is a wonderful mix of cinema verité, funny observations of youth, and touching reflections of familial relationships. Shot on location on the streets of New York City, which gives it a hauntingly nostalgic, almost ethereal look, *Little Fugitive* follows two adventurous days of Joey (Richie Andrusco), a seven-year-old Brooklyn youth and constantly harassed little brother. When his older brother Lennie (Rickie Brewster) and friends make Joey believe he's killed Lennie, Joey runs away to Coney Island where he's left to fend for himself. Capturing the frenzy and delight of New York's amusement institution or the minutiae of urban life are only minor accomplishments compared to the presence of young Andrusco. He's a marvel; the youngster is so at ease in front of the camera the film appears more documentary than fictional. Little Joey's escapades are certain to enthrall, to the point that the significant contributions of *Little Fugitive* to the birth of American independent filmmaking are easily overlooked. ★★★½ $79.99

Little Giants

(1994, 106 min, US, Duwayne Dunham) This may not have done well at the box office, but children who liked *Mighty Ducks* or *Bad News Bears* should like this football version of the same story. Rick Moranis and Ed O'Neill play highly competitive brothers — one can't play sports and the other is a little league football

L

coach. While Moranis may have no athletic ability, his daughter (nicknamed Icebox) is a natural but is rejected for uncle O'Neill's team solely because she's a girl. Eventually a team of other outcasts is born, with Moranis as its coach. While the ending is predictable, there are some good laughs along the way, and everyone will cheer as Icebox creams the competition. ★★½ $19.99

Little Man Tate

(1991, 99 min, US, Jodie Foster) Foster's impressive directorial debut is a quirky, entertaining comedy/melodrama about a seven-year-old genius who gets caught in a tug-of-war between his working-class mom (Foster) and a determined educator (Dianne Weist). The story centers around young Fred Tate's lack of social skills (a trait invariably attached to child prodigies), and his leaving his mother to study at an academy for gifted children living under Weist's supervision. Both Foster and Weist give strong performances and newcomer Adam Hann-Byrd is affecting as Fred. Harry Connick, Jr. has a nice cameo appearance as a college student who befriends the precocious brainiac. ★★★ $14.99

The Little Mermaid

(1989, 82 min, US, John Musker & Ron Clements) From the masters at Disney studios comes the company's best film since *Mary Poppins*, and the finest full-length animated feature since *Cinderella*. Howard Ashman and Alan Menken have written a joyously tuneful score to tell the tale of a young mermaid who falls in love with a handsome human prince, much to the chagrin of her father. The film features outstanding animation, a witty, thoroughly enjoyable story, the delightful Oscar-winning song "Under the Sea," and a bewitching cast of characters. *The Little Mermaid* will come to be cherished for years as *Snow White*, *Bambi* and *Pinocchio* have been before it: it is certainly as accomplished. ★★★★

Little Monsters

(1989, 103 min, US, Richard Alan Greenberg) The movie that proves there really are monsters under our beds! Fred Savage meets Maurice (Howie Mandel), the zany monster that lives under *his* bed, and wacky misadventures ensue. Not as cute as the premise suggests, the cast tries hard to overcome a pedestrian screenplay. Daniel Stern, Margaret Whitton and Frank Whaley also star. ★★ $14.99

Little Murders

(1971, 110 min, US, Alan Arkin) Arkin directed this blackest of black comedies about urban decay, both physical and moral. Elliott Gould is the catatonic photographer; Vincent Gardenia, his paranoid father-in-law; Donald Sutherland, the hippie priest; and Arkin, the schizophrenic detective in a frighteningly funny vision of a not-so-distant present. ★★★ $59.99

Little Nemo: Adventures in Slumberland

(1990, 86 min, Japan, Misami Hata & William T. Hurtz) This mildly entertaining tale of Little Nemo (a young boy whose best friend is a squirrel) and his adventures into Slumberland is most notable for its excellent

A Little Princess

animation. Nemo's dreams take him to a magic land where he befriends the king and his daughter and is given the key to the kingdom with the warning not to use it on a forbidden door. Of course, he unlocks the door and unleashes the king's evil nemesis who imprisons all of Nemo's friends. Nemo learns a valuable lesson and grows up along the way as he saves Slumberland. Melissa Manchester sings the theme song and Mickey Rooney and Rene Auberjonois supply two of the voices of the main characters. Richard M. and Robert S. Sherman (*Mary Poppins*) wrote the musical score. ★★½ $14.99

A Little Night Music

(1978, 124 min, US, Harold Prince) A rather mediocre adaptation of the brilliant Tony Award-winning musical written by Stephen Sondheim (which was based on Ingmar Bergman's *Smiles of a Summer's Night*). Elizabeth Taylor is miscast as Desiree, the actress who re-enters the life of newly married Len Cariou (repeating his stage role). Diana Rigg steals the show as the wife of soldier Lawrence Guittard, who is having an affair with Taylor. The film captures none of the magic which made the Bergman film and the stage play great hits. Though "A Weekend in the Country" is performed quite admirably. ★½

Little Nikita

(1988, 98 min, US, Richard Benjamin) Mommie's a Commie (and Daddy, too) in this contrived thriller with young River Phoenix unaware of his parents' political sympathies; all of them under investigation by FBI agent Sidney Poitier. Both Phoenix and Poitier deliver strong performances but the muddled screenplay takes its time setting up the barebones action. ★★ $14.99

Little Odessa

(1995, 98 min, US, James Gray) This brooding, pungent exploration of familial loyalties and personal isolation is Gray's astonishing directorial debut. Tim Roth is arresting as Joshua, hit man for the Russian mafia, whose profession has estranged him from his Russian Jewish family; particularly his father (Maximilian Schell), who is watching his wife (Vanessa Redgrave) die of a brain tumor. Like his brother, the younger son Reuben (Edward

Furlong) is caught between ancestral custom and assimilation into American culture; and Joshua, who kills without thought or hesitation, is in some ways an icon of that assimilation. Disconnection and self-doubt imbue all attempts at communication with futility, immersed in an indefinable Slavic melancholy. Thoughtful and deliberate direction guides uniformly remarkable performances through this haunting examination of the painful human longing to make contact. Deftly orchestrated clashes of violence lead to an anguished denouement at once inevitable and equivocal. ★★★★ $96.89

The Little Prince

(1974, 88 min, GB, Stanley Donen) Antoine de Saint-Exupery's magical book had all the trappings of a great film and you'd think that by putting Donen (*Singin' in the Rain*) in the director's chair, assembling the quirky cast of Richard Kiley, Gene Wilder and Bob Fosse, and adding a musical score by Lerner and Loewe that you'd have a winner. But the film is a disappointment. The story of a neurotic aviator who counsels a young boy from outer space about such Earthly matters as love and life is presented coyly and lacks affection. ★★ $14.99

A Little Princess

(1995, 100 min, US, Alfonso Cuaron) Based on the novel by Frances Hodgson Burnett, which was filmed once before in 1939 as *The Little Princess* with Shirley Temple, *A Little Princess* is an excellent adaptation embracing the themes of loneliness and courage. A young girl, Sara, is moved from her home in India to the same private girls' school in New York City attended by her deceased mother when her doting father joins the military ranks of WWI. Her fairy-tale existence is abruptly ended when he is pronounced killed in action and all of his assets are seized by the British government, leaving Sara penniless. The headmistress, played with delicious disdain by Eleanor Bron (so memorable in such '60s classics as *Help* and *Bedazzled*), forces her to become a serving girl. Sara learns to keep her faith in miracles and inspires the other girls along the way until the wonderful tear-laden ending. ★★★½ $19.99

L

The Little Rascals

(1994, 83 min, US, Penelope Spheeris) Coaxing charming performances from an almost all-child cast, Spheeris has made a most entertaining and updated big-screen version of the *Our Gang* comedies. With no real plot to speak of, the story centers on the antics of the "He Man Womun Haters Club," and the fateful day when one of their own (Alfalfa) falls in love...with a girl. A pint-sized "battle of the sexes" comedy, *Little Rascals*'s amusing screenplay gives the children ample opportunity to mug, flirt, sing, dance, race go-carts, blow bubbles and act like little big people — all of which they do with an endearing quality. Adults Mel Brooks, Whoopi Goldberg and Daryl Hannah make cameo appearances, but it's the kids who take center stage. ★★★ $14.99

A Little Romance

(1979, 108 min, US, George Roy Hill) Charming coming-of-age tale about the budding romance between an American girl (Diane Lane) living in Paris and a young French boy (Thelonious Bernard). The two of them run away to Venice together, under the eye of kindly con man Laurence Olivier. ★★★ $14.99

Little Shop of Horrors

(1960, 70 min, US, Roger Corman) This cult comedy, shot in a mind-boggling two-and-a-half days, is a delightful grab bag of goofy gags and kooky characters. Mel Welles is the skid row florist, Jack Nicholson is the masochistic dentist's patient and Audrey, Jr. is the bizarre begonia with a diet of human blood. Remade in 1986 as a musical. ★★★ $19.99

Little Shop of Horrors

(1986, 88 min, US, Frank Oz) "He's a mean, green mother from outer space and he's bad!" Science fiction, comedy and musical doo-wop blend wonderfully in this screen version of the hit off-Broadway musical based on Roger Corman's 1960 exploitation flick. Audrey II, the alien Venus Flytrap with an appetite for human blood, befriends a nerdish Rick Moranis in its fiendish plot to take over. The many show-stopping scenes include a maniacal Steve Martin as a sadistic dentist who meets his match in Bill Murray's hilariously masochistic patient. ★★★½ $9.99

The Little Theatre of Jean Renoir

(1968, 100 min, France, Jean Renoir) Renoir's final film, in a career that spanned over 50 years and 36 features, is a lovely gem told in three episodes with each story recalling Renoir's favorite themes and styles and introduced by the filmmaker himself. The first episode, "The Last Christmas Dinner," follows a tramp looking for a Christmas dinner. The second, "The Electric Floor Polisher," is an amusing tale of a woman in love with a home appliance and her two husbands who object. The concluding segment, "The Virtue of Tolerance," is about an elderly man who must accept the affairs of his wife. Jeanne Moreau makes a memorable appearance as a solemnly untalented music hall performer. (French with English subtitles) ★★★½ $59.99

Little Vera

(1987, 109 min, USSR, Vasily Pichul) Hailed as a breakthrough film, *Little Vera* is one of the first Soviet movies to show nudity as well as expose the internal problems confronting the working class in the USSR. Natalya Negoda is wonderful as Vera, a pouty, sultry and restless teenager who falls in love with an older student. Problems erupt after he moves in with Vera, her nervous mother and alcoholic father. This is a fascinating work, showing a Russia not bent on the destruction of the capitalist world, but one embroiled in ethnic strife, where rebellious, Western-influenced teens seek a new life and where the family unit is threatened by the freedoms and sexual promiscuity of the free world. (Russian with English subtitles) ★★★ $29.99

Little Women

(1933, 115 min, US, George Cukor) A thoughtful, and very faithful adaptation of Louisa May Alcott's classic book, with a wonderful performance by Katharine Hepburn as Jo, one of four sisters growing up in pre-Civil War New England. Joan Bennett, Paul Lukas, Frances Dee and Spring Byington also star. An impeccable production, with superb direction from Cukor. ★★★★ $19.99

Little Women

(1994, 115 min, US, Gillian Armstrong) Winona Ryder stars in this winsome adaptation of the Louisa May Alcott classic that, though bearing little resemblance, compares favorably to George Cukor's classic 1933 screen version starring Katharine Hepburn. Indeed, under the keen direction of Armstrong, and with various liberties taken in Robert Swicord's excellent screenplay, the film becomes more autobiographical in nature than Alcott's book ever was. The result is masterful as the film not only tells the familiar tale of Little Jo, her three sisters and their Marmee, it becomes an examination of the roots of "liberalism" as experienced by Alcott, who grew up imbued in the Transcendentalist movement of Walden Pond. For her part, Ryder makes a wonderful Jo, though period acting still seems a stretch for her, and Susan Sarandon is a powerful presence as Marmee, a feminist mom way before her time. Kirsten Dunst is mesmerizing as the young Amy, but Samantha Mathis can't parlay her take on the same character years later. Putting in a powerful performance as the sickly Beth is Claire Danes. ★★★★ $19.99

Live and Let Die

(1973, 121 min, GB, Guy Hamilton) Roger Moore's first outing as 007 takes us on an excursion to the Caribbean where he unearths a heroin ring masterminded by Yaphet Kotto. The tropical climate allows for ample unveiling of female décolletage, principally Jane Seymour, and the usual bevy of would-be starlets. Perhaps not the best of the Bond series, but certainly worth a look for anyone interested in a good action-adventure flick. (Available letterboxed and pan & scan) ★★½ $14.99

Live Wire

(1992, 87 min, US, Christian Duguay) Pierce Brosnan is the renegade cop, Ron Silver the slimy U.S. senator and Ben Cross the obsessed terrorist in this formulaic but mindlessly entertaining action-thriller. The explosive *du jour* is a colorless, tasteless liquid, convenient for single servings or punch bowls, which leaves no trace in the scattered remains of its victims. Washington D.C. is the natural setting for this slick and cynical commentary on the abuse of position and privilege, and the disastrous consequences of unbridled greed. ★★ $14.99

Lives of a Bengal Lancer

(1935, 109 min, US, Henry Hathaway) A rousing adventure film comparable with the similarly themed *Gunga Din* and *Beau Geste*. Gary Cooper stars as a Canadian serving in the British army in the parched desert of colonial India. Excitement and danger await him and fellow officer Franchot Tone as they serve under a cold-hearted commander, attempt to reconcile their leader and his naive son, and battle the crafty enemy. Good action sequences are offset by well-etched characterizations, unexpected comedy and a fair amount of suspense, all of which are under the tight direction of Hathaway. ★★★½ $14.99

Livin' Large

(1991, 96 min, US, Michael Schultz) What begins as a surprisingly amusing satire on racial relationships and television journalism quickly deteriorates into a questionable and misogynist sitcom. Terence (T.C.) Carson brings a lot of life to his role of a young black man who gets a chance to fulfill his dream when he is groomed to be the next superstar reporter for an Atlanta TV station. He soon finds that his success comes with a price, however, which includes ignoring his own cultural identity. The first half of the film is complete with good humor and truthful revelations about the TV industry. But the film's creators sabotage their efforts with their less-than-congenial depiction of the only two white women in the cast, whose "crime" is wanting to succeed in a "white man's world." From the film's distorted viewpoint, it doesn't matter if you're black or white, as long as you're male. ★★ $14.99

The Living Daylights

(1987, 130 min, GB, John Glen) Timothy Dalton takes over the reigns as super British agent 007. James Bond is up against a KGB defector who's really a double agent, and an American arms dealer. Dalton is a fabulous choice for Bond, bringing a sophistication to the part Roger Moore never dreamed of — more in line with Sean Connery's interpretation. Lots of great action and stunts, coupled with Dalton's dashing presence, make this one of the best of the Bonds. ★★★ $14.99

The Living End

(1992, 84 min, US, Gregg Araki) With its opening close-up shot of a bumper sticker that reads "Choose Death," one can rest assured that this self-described "irresponsible" black comedy about two HIV-positive men who set out on a lawless road adventure will not hesitate to cajole, provoke and otherwise incite strong reactions from the audience. Produced on a miniscule budget, the film presents an in-your-face reaction to society's disregard for the plight of HIV-positive people. Jon is a whiny, urban gay – a film writer and critic – who happens into a relationship with fellow "positive" Luke, a free-spirited and rageful drifter who precipitates their angst-driven journey into anarchy. It's best to ignore the film's thinly written script, awkward scenes and less-than-professional acting and concentrate instead on its irresistable "Yeah, I'm HIV-positive and I blame society!" message; for despite its faults, it's a totally entertaining effort. ★★★ $29.99

Living in Oblivion
(1995, 91 min, US, Tom DiCillo) A delightful and ingenious comedy that chronicles a disastrous three-day period on the set of an independent film production. Steve Buscemi is perfectly cast as Nick, the high-strung director who desperatley tries to tie down all the loose ends and nail down a few scenes with his eager, but at times maladroit, cast and crew. His accomplices are a hilarious Dermot Mulroney as the hulking cinematographer, Wolf; Danielle Von Zerneck as the bossy assistant director, Wanda; and Catherine Keener as the leading lady, Nicole, who can't remember the simplest of lines. The capper, however, is James LeGros, who blows onto the set as one-time indie hack, newfound Hollywood darling, Chad Palomino – an inspired caricature of Brad Pitt (who starred in DiCillo's first film, *Johnny Suede*). DiCillo's inventive script is filled with fantastical – almost Pirendellian – surprise twists, bristling humor and plenty of good-natured skewering of the film industry. ★★★½ $96.89

Living on Toyko Time
(1987, 83 min, US, Steve Okazaki) Offbeat and charming romantic comedy about a Japanese girl who marries – to stay stateside – a Japanese-American rock musician, who has little interest in anything but rock 'n' roll and a vegetative lifestyle. ★★★

Living Proof: HIV and the Pursuit of Happiness
(1993, 70 min, US, Kermit Cole) Refusing to pessimistically portray people with AIDS simply as victims of a deadly disease, this documentary focuses on some of the many HIV-positive men, women and children who are living life to the fullest. Buoyantly upbeat, *Living Proof* centers around one man, George DeSipio, who, after being diagnosed with AIDS in 1990, teamed with photographer Carolyn Jones to work on a photo essay that would offer positive role models for PWAs and celebrate the lives of those infected. In all, over 40 people from all walks of life talk about how the knowledge of being HIV-positive is far from being a death sentence. ★★★ $59.99

Loaded
(1996, 105 min, New Zealand, Anna Campion) Jane Campion's little sister Anna makes an inauspicious directorial debut with this dreary psychological thriller, an uneventful discourse whose one-dimensional characters substitute pretense with pretension. With its film-within-a-film backdrop, the story centers on a group of friends who weekend at a country mansion to make a horror movie. As the dynamics and romantic couplings of the group change, a death underscores the partic-

ipants' anxieties and uncertain allegiances. *Day for Night* it's not. Unfortunately for director Campion, she's working from her own flat screenplay. It's one of those stories in which the viewer impatiently waits for *something* to happen. It doesn't. But Campion does demonstrate some imaginative camerawork, and a tripping scene is about the only sequence of interest. ★½ $19.99

Loaded Weapon 1
(1993, 82 min, US, Gene Quintano) Looks like a case of an older brother trying to keep up with a younger sibling. After Charlie Sheen's spoofing of Tom Cruise in *Hot Shots*, Emilio Estevez takes on the lighter side of Mel Gibson in this amiable spoof. Samuel L. Jackson joins him as the other half of the *Lethal Weapon* team. The film is perhaps a little too self-aware and does not have the rapid fire-delivery of some of the more successful films in this genre, like *The Naked Gun* series. However, even though it doesn't go far enough, the film does provide some serious chuckles at the expense of the Gibson/Glover team. Tim Curry has some amusing scenes as, initially, a killer girl scout, and William Shatner hams it up as a bad guy. (aka: *National Lampoon's Loaded Weapon 1*) ★★½ $9.99

Local Hero
(1983, 111 min, GB, Bill Forsyth) Forsyth's enchanting comedy stars Peter Reigert as a reluctant Texas oil company executive who is sent overseas to purchase an idyllic Scottish village. Almost to his chagrin, the townsfolk, one of the strangest assortment of oddballs ever to hit the screen, seem all too eager to sell. All but one, that is. Burt Lancaster makes a commanding appearance as the company's owner who gets helicoptered in to take over the negotiations. This clever concoction, with its pastoral settings and a ubiquitous air of affable humor, offers a gentle treatise on the continuing march of progress and what we stand to lose by it. ★★★★ $9.99

Lock Up
(1989, 106 min, US, John Flynn) Even Sylvester Stallone has rarely sunk this low. Stallone plays a convict who is transferred to a new prison, run by mean warden Donald Sutherland – who's got a grudge to settle with Sly. ★ $14.99

The Lodger
(1926, 75 min, GB, Alfred Hitchcock) Hitchcock's mastery of narrative and atmosphere is stylishly evident in this silent thriller about a mysterious rooming house tenant who is suspected of being Jack the Ripper. Although not his first film, *The Lodger* ostensibly begins the Hitchcock oeuvre, for it was his first commercial success, first thriller, first cameo appearance and the first use of his favorite "innocent man falsely accused" plot line. ★★★ $12.99

Logan's Run
(1976, 120 min, US, Michael Anderson) Michael York plays Logan, a man with a problem: He's a 29-year-old bounty hunter who collects the people who didn't submit to state mandated euthanasia when they hit the age of 30 – and tomorrow is *his* birthday. Large futur-

istic sets, great special effects and Peter Ustinov highlight this episodic, intriguing vision of the near future. Also starring Jenny Agutter. ★★★ $19.99

Lola
(1960, 91 min, France, Jacques Demy) With its breezy tone, distinctive editing and innovative cinematography (thanks to Raoul Coutard), this New Wave-influenced fairy tale proved to be an audacious debut for Demy, a director who, with the exception of *The Umbrellas of Cherbourg*, never achieved his potential. Owing much to *On the Town* and the works of Max Ophuls (to whom it is dedicated), this fanciful love story stars Anouk Aimée as a free-spirited nightclub singer who is faced with the enviable dilemma of choosing between a trio of lovers. Framed within a series of coincidences and chance encounters and offering the notion that love is transient, the story never bogs down in "realities" and takes the wonderfully innocent approach that love conquers all. (French with English subtitles) ★★★½ $59.99

Lola
(1969, 98 min, GB/Italy, Richard Donner) Charles Bronson stars as a 40-something American porno writer who has a tempestuous affair with a liberated 16-year-old girl. This early effort of director Donner also stars Susan George as the irrepressible young Lola. Not as provocative as it would like to be, though Bronson and George offer appealing performances. ★★ $9.99

Lola Montes
(1955, 110 min, France, Max Ophüls) In a 19th-century circus in Vienna, the famous Lola Montes, fleeing scandal, is reduced to living out the highlights of her exotic life for the pleasure of the masses and at the urging of a forceful ringmaster. Ophüls' first film is a scintillating tale of excess and regret, and is beautifully photographed. (French with English subtitles) ★★★½

Lolita
(1962, 152 min, GB, Stanley Kubrick) Kubrick's screen adaptation of Vladimir Nabokov's provocative novel, though not a complete success, effectively captures the author's sense of black humor and features outlandish performances by Peter Sellers and Shelley Winters. James Mason is a college professor who marries a lonely widow only for the opportunity it offers to seduce the sexually precocious Sue Lyons. This peculiar tale of murder and lust is an example of earlier Kubrick efforts where powerful and eccentric characters ruled the screen. ★★★ $19.99

London Kills Me
(1992, 107 min, GB, Hanif Kureishi) Where screenwriter Kureishi's *My Beautiful Laundrette* dealt with working-class aspirations, sexuality and morality in a racist, Thatcherized London, director Kureishi's *London Kills Me* goes a few rungs down the economic ladder in a humorous exploration of life on the fringe underbelly of a post-punk, beyond-hope society. The story follows Clint, a pale, emaciated, sexually abused-as-a-child 20-year-old who,

L

Lone Star

despite being mired in a seemingly hopeless world of drugs, homelessness, petty thievery and prostitution, retains a cheery, optimistic approach to his prospects of survival and success. Hope springs eternal after an exasperated owner of an upscale Portabello Road restaurant promises the bedraggled Clint a job if he comes in the following week with a new pair of shoes. Clint's odyssey, following this promise of respectability, becomes his repeated and increasingly frantic attempts to acquire this elusive pair of shoes. A fascinating yet flawed comedy-drama that despite a tagged-on happy ending that borders on the bizarre is fun nonetheless and vividly captures this part of London. ★★★½ $89.99

Lone Star

(1996, 135 min, US, John Sayles) As the American independent cinema's guiding light, director Sayles has continually surprised us with his versatility, writing, producing, directing and costarring in a legion of intelligent, complex and personal films over the last two decades. He's moved easily from genre to genre, putting a human face on such subjects as racism, labor and inner-city politics. *Lone Star*, possibly his best film to date, is a brilliant distillation of the director's themes and feelings over the years – a gripping mystery-thriller with so many simmering emotions under its surface that it's in constant threat of either self-destructing or losing its way. Thankfully, it does neither. Chris Cooper, a Sayles regular, plays Sam Deeds, a low-keyed sheriff in a small Texas town investigating some skeletal remains and a lawman's rusty badge found in the desert. The son of Buddy Deeds, a much-revered sheriff, Sam believes his father (played in flashbacks by Matthew McConaughey) may have had something to do with the findings. He soon discovers that the more digging he does, the more skeletons he finds. Moving fluidly from the past to the present, *Lone Star* is a compelling, quietly powerful work that stays with you long after its stunning but daringly conceived secret is revealed. This is stirring stuff from a filmmaker who would have it no other way. ★★★★ $19.99

Lone Wolf and Child Series

Based on a popular Japanese comic book or *manga* by Kazuo Koike and Goseki Kojima, this incredible series tells the ongoing tale of Itto Ogami (Tomisaburo Wakayama), the Shogun's official executioner, who is disgraced by a rival family's plot and forced to walk "the road to Hell" with his young son after the murder of his wife and ostracism of his entire clan. Ogami becomes an assassin for hire, wheeling young Daigoro (Akihiro Tomikawa) around in a wooden cart, which is accessorized with a multitude of weapons (and which has given the films the alternate title of the "Baby Cart" series) and selling his formidable swordplay skills. Always on the lookout for enemy ninja, the films tell the stories of Ogami's encounters with various characters in feudal Japanese life and his usually heroic adventures, all the while teaching Daigoro the meaning of courage and sacrifice. The films were first introduced to American audiences in the re-edit *Shogun Assassin*, which emphasized some of the campiness and cult value of the story. The Japanese originals, however, are deadly serious. They tell a tale of honor surviving through disgrace and redemption made possible only through wholesale slaughter. Each individual film is a masterpiece of the samurai genre, and together they form a collection which ranks as one of the best film series in world cinema.

Sword of Vengeance

(1972, 83 min, Japan, Kenji Misumi) The first film tells the origin story of the Lone Wolf and of his expulsion from his home at the hands of the duplicitous Yagyu clan. After his wife is murdered, Ogami, one of the Shogun's most loyal servants, is falsely accused of conspiring against his Lord and is ordered to commit *harakiri*. Refusing to comply with the royal decree, he becomes a "demon on the road to Hell," with no future and no hope for escape from his chosen fate. Along for the ride is his infant son Daigoro, whom, in one of the best scenes of the film, Ogami gives the choice between joining his mother in death (by choosing a ball placed before him) or joining his father in his bloody journey (by choosing a sword). Its beautiful widescreen photography is filled with dazzling visuals and breathtaking colors, but are rather staid compared to the wild carnage which is to come. (Japanese with English subtitles) ★★★★ $29.99

Baby Cart at the River Styx

(1972, 81 min, Japan, Kenji Misumi) This time around, Ogami faces two of the most colorful villains of the entire series. The first is a clan of female ninja, sent to kill Ogami after they prove their mettle by systematically dismembering one of the Yagyu clan's best assassins. The second villains, however, are even better: the three "Gods of Death" whom John Carpenter paid homage to in his *Big Trouble in Little China*. Assigned to protect an official whom Ogami has been hired to kill, each wields his own hand-to-hand weapon with fearsome skill and is a master killer in his own right; together they are unbeatable, until they meet Lone Wolf and Child. Again featuring the trademark geysers of blood which distinguishes the series, *Lone Wolf 2* is fantastic, featuring even more action than its predecessor,

and delving deeper into the complex character of Ogami. Possibly the best, and certainly the most fun entry in the series. (Japanese with English subtitles) ★★★★ $29.99

Baby Cart to Hades

(1972, 89 min, Japan, Kenji Misumi) The third film in the blood-filled samurai series finds Ogami paralleled with a disgraced ronin warrior who has become a thug-for-hire in order to make a living. Both are shown as men trying to act within their codes of honor, having been made outcasts by society at large. After he gets involved in a dispute between two rival clans, the climax of the film finds Itto fighting a veritable army of soldiers, some armed with early firearms. But the Lone Wolf's accessorized baby cart holds a few more surprises for the unsuspecting foe! And after the carnage subsides, Ogami must face off against the ronin who has shadowed him throughout the film, in a mortal test of honor. One of the more philosophically complex episodes of the series. Originally released in the U.S. in a dubbed version called both *Lightning Swords of Death* and *Lupine Wolf*. (Japanese with English subtitles) ★★★★ $29.99

Baby Cart in Peril

(1973, 81 min, Japan, Buichi Saito) Second only to the "Gods of Death" from the second film in the series, this entry's main villain is both beautiful and deadly: the tattooed female assassin Oyuki. Hired to kill her early in the film, Ogami later learns that, far from being a bloodthirsty killer, Oyuki is a desperate woman who has been severely wronged — raped and betrayed by her teacher — and began life as an assassin only because she was forced to. Sympathizing with her, Ogami must nevertheless carry out his assignment: his code of *bushido* requires it. But before he does so, he allows Oyuki revenge against those who had previously despoiled her. The film also features a confrontation between Ogami and Gunbei Yagyu, son of the Lone Wolf's bitterest enemy, who was previously thought to be dead, but has actually been part of a grand deception on the part of the entire Yagyu clan. (Japanese with English subtitles) ★★★★ $29.99

Baby Cart in the Land of Demons

(1973, 89 min, Japan, Kenji Misumi) A series of messengers, each with a part of the final orders to hire Ogami, confront the Lone Wolf as he makes his way across the landscape. Killing each of them, he pieces his mission together and, along with the viewer, slowly learns the entire story: an insane local leader has substituted his young daughter, raised as a boy, as the clan's legitimate heir. Ogami has been hired to kill the clan leaders and prevent such an unconventional transfer of power from occurring. A side-story highlight of the film is a scene in which Daigoro is publicly tortured for not revealing the identity of a pickpocket who forced him into giving her aid. His stoic courage under the magistrate's interrogation is extremely moving, and signals his transition to adulthood. Ogami's reaction is also highly dramatic, and contrary to what many Western viewers would expect. One of the more complex episodes of the series. (Japanese with English subtitles) ★★★★ $29.99

L

White Heaven in Hell

(1974, 85 min, Japan, Yoshiyuki Kuroda) This final episode, unfortunately, does not feature any major confrontation between Ogami and his archenemy Retsudo Yagyu, but that does not prevent it from being as entertaining as the five preceding it. Yagyu has sent two of his remaining children to kill Ogami, one of whom is a bastard child who spurns any connection to his father, instead preferring to kill Ogami for his own glorification. With the assistance of three supernatural warriors, he dogs Ogami's heels, killing any innocent people Lone Wolf and Child come in contact with, thus assuring his complete isolation from the rest of humanity. Ogami retreats to the frozen wastelands, where a gigantic battle between him and what remains of the Yagyu clan is staged. An exciting fight on skis (with the baby cart on a sled!) follows, where the white of the snow is stained by the series' ever-present crimson blood. A fine end to a fantastic series. (Japanese with English subtitles) ★★★★ $29.99

The Loneliness of the Long Distance Runner

(1962, 103 min, GB, Tony Richardson) Alan Silitoe's classic short story about a rebellious reform-school boy whose athletic prowess earns him a shot at the Olympics is lovingly brought to life by director Richardson. Tom Courtenay excels as the young runner and Michael Redgrave is superb as the school warden who takes him under his wing. A classic example of the British "kitchen sink" drama of the early '60s. ★★★½ $19.99

Lonely Are the Brave

(1962, 107 min, US, David Miller) A riveting modern-day western with cowboy and escaped prisoner Kirk Douglas on the lam, pursued by a relentless sheriff's department. With Walter Matthau, Gena Rowlands, Carroll O'Connor and George Kennedy. ★★★ $14.99

The Lonely Guy

(1984, 90 min, US, Arthur Hiller) When Steve Martin is dumped by his girlfriend, he takes up with similarly fated Charles Grodin, who introduces him to the wonderful world of bachelorhood. Based on the book by Bruce Jay Friedman, and adapted by Neil Simon, this offbeat, low-keyed comedy offers some comic insights into romance but is a little too introverted for its own good. ★★½ $9.99

The Lonely Lady

(1983, 92 min, US, Peter Sasdy) Tacky, tasteless and completely satisfying in a campy way, this Hollywood exposé, adapted from the Harold Robbins novel, was made to showcase the talent and body of the spunky Pia Zadora. The story begins with young Pia, a talented high school virgin (now that's great acting), who after being raped by a garden hose wielded by a Hollywood brat, quickly learns that being good is not all that it's cracked up to be. On recovery, she is determined to become a successful writer in the sleazy world of show business. Sleeping her way to the top, our chipmunk-faced Pia achieves the success she sought, only to find emptiness and remorse, proving that it is indeed a lonely road up the ladder of fame and fortune. Champagne bottles are popped, lesbianism is hinted, breasts are bared and phallic images abound in this Zadora-ized "star" vehicle. ★ $59.99

The Lonely Man

(1957, 87 min, US, Henry Levin) Jack Palance grimaces and clenches his jaw through most of this lean western as a retired gunfighter trying to make peace. Emulating Henry King's outstanding The Gunfighter, though with only partially satisfying results, the story centers on Palance. Going blind and hunted by various gangs, he wants to forget his "triggering" days and reconcile with his estranged son Anthony Perkins, but the Law of the West and his son's hatred won't allow either. It's almost funny to hear Perkins spout a Norman Bates-like devotion to his mother, and Palance lassoing and hog-tying Perkins has got to be seen to be believed. ★★½ $14.99

The Lonely Passion of Judith Hearne

(1987, 116 min, GB, Jack Clayton) Brian Moore's 1955 novel is brought to the screen with a pair of outstanding performances. Maggie Smith stars as the title character, a crestfallen middle-aged woman who suffers because of her undying and somewhat misplaced faith in the church and whose life is stalled in rundown boarding houses. Bob Hoskins is superb as her self-effacing suitor. ★★★ $79.99

Lonelyhearts

(1958, 101 min, US, Vincent J. Donehue) Good performances highlight this occasionally moving Nathaniel West story with Montgomery Clift taking over the "Miss Lonelyhearts" newspaper column, becoming involved with the lives of his readers. With Robert Ryan, Myrna Loy and Maureen Stapleton (Oscar nominee). ★★½ $19.99

Lonesome Dove

(1989, 180 min, US, Simon Wincer) Parts one and two of the highly-rated TV miniseries, hailed by critics and audiences alike, and based on the Pulitzer Prize-winning novel by Larry McMurtry. Two former Texas rangers leave their small town to take on an epic 2,500-mile cattle drive north to Montana. Episodes include "Leaving" and "On the Trail." Besides winning seven Emmys, this miniseries proved to be a cinematic shot-in-the-arm for the western genre. Standout cast includes Robert Duvall, Tommy Lee Jones, Danny Glover, Diane Lane, Robert Urich, Frederic Forrest, Rick Schroeder, D.B. Sweeney and Anjelica Huston. ★★★½ $39.99

Long Ago Tomorrow

(1971, 111 min, GB, Bryan Forbes) Filmgoers used to Malcolm McDowell's screen persona as a virile, sometimes violent, young man, will be surprised by this subdued melodrama in which he plays a paraplegic involved in a love affair with another disabled person. Surprisingly engaging with powerful performances from both McDowell and Nanette Newman. ★★★ $59.99

Long Awaited Pleasure

(1989, 90 min, US, Giovanna Manana) Lois Weaver and Peggy Shaw, co-founders of the inventive lesbian comedy/musical troupe Split Breaches, are the saving graces in this low-budget production that follows two women who meet and fall in love. Rory, a gangly thirtyish New York dentist, moves to a small Southern city after breaking up with her longtime lover. It is there that she meets Sue, a willowy blonde undertaker anxious for a partner. The simple story deals primarily with their initial, tentative talks and dates, which lead up to the dramatic moment of their first kiss and the beginning stages of a love affair. A fine, honest depiction of the awkward moments and exhilarating highs of a nascent lesbian relationship. ★★½ $39.99

The Long Day Closes

(1992, 83 min, GB, Terence Davies) Somber, melancholy and haunting, this restrained drama of a young boy's maturation is a very effective mood piece recalling director Davies' childhood. Filmed in a leisurely, almost floating style and obviously autobiographical, the story concerns Bud (Leigh McCormack), a preadolescent boy living with his close-knit family in 1950s Liverpool. A thoughtful but shy boy with few friends, Bud immerses himself in escapist Hollywood musicals and develops an especially close relationship with his mother. There's surprisingly little dialogue, and not much happens in the way of dramatic excitement or tension. Yet this poetic style of filmmaking is both entrancing and pensive. ★★★½ $19.99

Long Day's Journey into Night

(1962, 170 min, US, Sidney Lumet) A staggering adaptation of Eugene O'Neill's classic autobiographical play detailing his explosive homelife in early 1900s New England. In a tour de force performance, Katharine Hepburn stars as O'Neill's drug-addicted mother whose grasp on reality slowly dissipates to the helpless horror of those around her. Ralph Richardson masterfully portrays the patriarch of the family — an aging, alcoholic actor who'd rather reminisce on a glorious past than face the truths of the present. As their sons, Dean Stockwell plays the youngest brother stricken by TB, and Jason Robards is a powerful presence as the troubled author witnessing his family's decay. ★★★★ $19.99

Long Day's Journey into Night

(1987, 169 min, US, Jonathan Miller) Jack Lemmon re-creates his acclaimed performance from the Broadway revival in this expert production of Eugene O'Neill's classic drama. Bethel Leslie also stars as Lemmon's drug-addicted wife, and Peter Gallagher and Kevin Spacey are both fine as their sons. ★★★

Long Gone

(1987, 110 min, US, Martin Davidson) From the director of Apartment Zero comes this wonderful made-for-cable production, an offshoot of Bull Durham, about the manager of a minor league team whipping his players into shape for a run at the championship. William L. Petersen deftly plays the manager, and Virginia Madsen is the beauty queen with an eye for marriage. A delightful surprise. ★★★ $14.99

L

The Long Good Friday

(1980, 105 min, GB, John MacKenzie) A powerful English mobster suddenly finds himself and his empire victims of a bloody battle decree and desperately seeks its source. This taut gangster saga stars Bob Hoskins as the besieged underworld head, Helen Mirren as his sturdy mistress and Eddie Constantine as an influential American investor. ★★★½ $14.99

The Long Goodbye

(1973, 112 min, US, Robert Altman) Elliott Gould gives one of his best performances as a burned-out Philip Marlowe out to find out if and why he was framed by a good friend (Jim Bouton) for a woman's murder. Altman takes the tired, used-up detective film genre and fills it with quirky, nasty characters and bizarre humor. Look for *On Golden Pond* director Mark Rydell as an incredibly sadistic, dry-witted gangster who can injure his loved ones just to show what he can do to people he hates. ★★★½ $19.99

The Long Hot Summer

(1958, 117 min, US, Martin Ritt) Ritt directed this engaging film, a successful translation of William Faulkner's story. Paul Newman became a star thanks to his stand-out performance as Ben Quick, a wandering farmhand who becomes involved with the Varner family, headed by a domineering father (Orson Welles). From first encounter, Ben takes a shine to the elegant but aloof Varner daughter (Joanne Woodward), which suits Daddy just fine, since he's hankerin' for plenty of Varner heirs. Whether under the scorching sun or the shade of the front porch, the all-star cast deliver fiery performances, especially Newman as the lusty opportunist. ★★★½ $14.99

The Long Kiss Goodnight

(1996, 120 min, US, Renny Harlin) After the mishap of *Cutthroat Island*, husband and wife Geena Davis and Harlin are back in good form with this consistently entertaining and always unpredictable (if farfetched) mystery/suspenser. Giving as much attention to thrills as to offbeat characterizations, director Harlin has crafted a rollercoaster ride of intrigue. Davis stars as a mild-mannered housewife who suffers from amnesia. When she is involved in a car accident, bits of memory begin to surface – like how to accurately throw a knife and an alter ego named Charlie. When a private investigator (Samuel L. Jackson) she had previously hired stumbles across a clue to her identity, the two set out to uncover the truth...with some very nasty secret agents on their trail. Davis and Jackson have a wonderful rapport, which aids greatly in the film's overall enjoyment. There's lots of chases and explosions and predicaments which we really know no one could get (in or) out of. We may not always believe what Harlin asks us to, but what fun we have trying. ★★★ $19.99

The Long, Long Trailer

(1954, 103 min, US, Vincente Minnelli) Released at the height of their TV popularity, Lucille Ball and Desi Arnaz star in this comic romp about a newly married couple's adventures on the road in the titular vehicle. Lots of fun. ★★★ $14.99

The Long Riders

(1980, 100 min, US, Walter Hill) Sometimes stunt casting works, as in this film which features Stacy and James Keach as the outlaws The James Brothers; David, Keith and Robert Carradine as The Younger Brothers; Randy and Dennis Quaid as the brothers Miller; and Christopher and Nicholas Guest as the Fords. Director Hill captures the melancholy in the passing of the Old West, while not ignoring the shoot-outs and chases as The James Gang face the penalty for one withdrawal too many. ★★★ $14.99

The Long Voyage Home

(1940, 104 min, US, John Ford) Director Ford's slightly stagey but brilliantly cinematic rendering of four Eugene O'Neill one-acts depicts life on a merchant ship, following the day-to-day affairs of a group of seamen whose loneliness and frustrations give way to suspicion and the off-shore frivolities which bring about tragedy. John Wayne, in a very uncharacteristic portrayal, plays a naive Swede; and Thomas Mitchell is unforgettable as a seasoned old salt. Outstanding black-and-white cinematography by Gregg Toland (*Citizen Kane*). ★★★½ $14.99

The Longest Day

(1962, 169 min, US, Andrew Marton, Bernhard Wicki & Ken Annakin) Classic WWII epic which accounts the Allied invasion of Normandy. One might think that at nearly three hours in length this could be a tedious affair, but the action here is carried at a brisk pace and with great attention to detail. The all-star cast delivers a plethora of strong performances from the likes of John Wayne, Henry Fonda, Sal Mineo, Richard Burton, Robert Ryan, Mel Ferrer, Red Buttons and the list goes on. One of the best WWII dramas ever made. ★★★★ $24.99

The Longest Yard

(1974, 123 min, US, Robert Aldrich) Former pro Burt Reynolds gets incarcerated and heads the prison football team to victory. Some good laughs and lots of action in this forceful comedy. ★★★ $14.99

Longtime Companion

(1990, 96 min, US, Norman René) One of the first American films to address the AIDS crisis, *Longtime Companion* is an exceptional look into the lives of a group of gay friends, and how the disease affects them, both collectively and singularly. Director René and writer Craig Lucas succeed in creating full-dimensioned characters and the film is rich in sharp observations and keen wit. There is a terrific ensemble cast, but Bruce Davison must be given a special mention for his superlative portrayal of the lover who slowly watches his longtime companion succumb. ★★★½ $14.99

Look Back in Anger

(1958, 99 min, GB, Tony Richardson) John Osborne's play made theatre history in England as a rebellious attack against the rigidity of the English establishment. Bristling with heated dialogue, the play represents the first signs of post-war dissatisfaction with the social immobility of life in a dying Empire. Brilliantly performed by Richard Burton, Claire Bloom, Mary Ure and Donald Pleasence, this trend-setting "angry young man" drama is a must for lovers of great writing and excellent acting. ★★★½

Look Back in Anger

(1980, 101 min, GB, Lindsay Anderson) Malcolm McDowell once again teams up with Anderson in this compelling remake of John Osborne's explosive "angry young man" play. McDowell offers a passionate performance as Jimmy Porter, and Anderson deftly directs the action. ★★★

Look Back in Anger

(1990, 114 min, GB, David Jones) Kenneth Branagh stars in this version of John Osborne's powerful "kitchen sink" drama based on Judi Dench's West End revival. Branagh re-creates the role made famous by Richard Burton as Jimmy Porter, a young man whose poor position in life results in a simmering rage that is directed towards both his wife (nicely played by Emma Thompson) and to the indifferent world that surrounds him. Branagh's excellent performance is the core of the piece offering a blistering portrayal of frustration and passion. ★★★ $19.99

Look Who's Talking

(1989, 90 min, US, Amy Heckerling) The surprise hit of 1989, this mostly amusing comedy is consistently charming due partially to two great gimmicks: a talking baby whose thoughts are heard on screen, and the ever-glib Bruce Willis as the vocal incarnation of the little tyke, Mikey. Kirstie Alley is Mikey's mom, a single accountant having an affair with married business associate George Segal. While waiting for him to leave his wife, she ignores the attentions of a helpful and obviously made-for-each-other taxi driver. John Travolta delivers a wonderful comic performance as the cabbie; here he reminds you why he was the #1 box office attraction of the late 1970s. ★★½ $14.99

Look Who's Talking Too

(1990, 81 min, US, Amy Heckerling) Talking baby Mikey now has a talking sister. Inferior sequel to the surprise comedy hit finds now-married John Travolta and Kirstie Alley with a new daughter (voiced by Roseanne), while facing matrimonial problems. Travolta has a good scene dancing in a playroom, but otherwise the film is without charm or wit. Bruce Willis encores as the voice of Mikey, and Damon Wayans is the voice of a neighborhood friend. ★½ $14.99

Looker

(1981, 94 min, US, Michael Crichton) From the creator of *Coma* and *Westworld* comes this sci-fi satire about beautiful models who are murdered and then reconstituted by a computer hoping to produce the perfect spokesperson. (No, this is *not* the Vanna White story.) With Susan Dey as the model out for vengeance, Albert Finney as the plastic surgeon going out of business and James Coburn as the C.E.O. ★★½ $14.99

Looking for Langston

(1989, 45 min, GB, Isaac Julien) This pensive yet celebratory meditation on black poet

L

Langston Hughes is an original work of cinematic art. Stylish and sexy, the film incorporates the lyrical poetry of Essex Hemphill and Bruce Nugent with archival footage of the Harlem Renaissance of the 1920s. Re-enacted Cotton Club scenes, romantic shots of two intertwined lovers, Robert Mapplethorpe's photographs of beautiful black men and the pounding disco beat of "Can You Feel It" are also used in telling the story of black consciousness in a culturally evolving America. ★★★½ $39.99

Looking for Mr. Goodbar

(1977, 136 min, US, Richard Brooks) Diane Keaton's terrific performance isn't enough to sustain this horrid adaptation of Judith Rossner's best-seller about a repressed schoolteacher who turns to nightly bar-hopping for sexual and personal fulfillment. Also with Richard Gere, Tuesday Weld and Richard Kiley. ★ $14.99

Looking for Richard

(1996, 118 min, US, Al Pacino) It's long been a presumption that Yanks can't do Shakespeare. And for the most part American actors have carried that on their shoulders and scarred psyches with the foreboding of Hamlet's ghost. The debunking and playful spoofing of this theatrical myth is only one of the delicious treats in store in *Looking for Richard*, a scintillating peek behind the theatrical curtain and into the soul of Shakespeare's evil prince. Making an assured directorial debut, Pacino leads his crew (and audience) on an odyssey to discover the inner workings of "Richard III," both the play and the man. Intercutting actual scenes performed by the likes of Alec Baldwin (especially good as Clarence), Winona Ryder, Kevin Spacey and Penelope Allen (terrific as the Queen), with Pacino a forceful Richard, the actor talks to everyone from an American Average Joe to some of England's acting royalty to come to an understanding of the Bard. Comical and always fascinating, *Looking for Richard* — much to its success — actually makes Shakespeare accessible, and for those (of us) not able to fully comprehend the play, it nicely fills in any and all gaps. In fact, everyone in Pacino's cast is so good, it makes one yearn for a filmed feature-length rendering. (That's a hint, Al.) ★★★★ $102.99

Loose Cannons

(1990, 94 min, US, Bob Clark) Gene Hackman makes so many movies a year, the odds are that occasionally a clinker is going to get through. This is one of them. Mis-matched cops (now *there's* an original idea) Hackman and Dan Aykroyd are up against modern-day Nazis in Washington D.C. ★ $14.99

Loose Connections

(1983, 90 min, GB, Richard Eyre) A delightful little road comedy about a dedicated feminist who decides to drive across Europe to attend a women's conference in Munich. She winds up with Harry, a less-than-savory traveling companion whose outright chauvinism tests her nerve all the way down the Autobahn. ★★★ $29.99

Loot

(1972, 101 min, GB, Silvio Narizzano) Joe Orton's frantically paced, door slamming farce/black comedy — by far one of the most original and uproarious plays ever to grace the British stage — is presented here with all the outrageousness it deserves. The story concerns a pair of misguided youths who, having knocked over a bank, hide the swag in mom's coffin. All hell breaks loose as the distraught duo tries to retrieve their booty. Inspired performances abound from a crackerjack cast: Lee Remick, Roy Holder, Hywell Bennett and Milo O'Shea. ★★★

Lord Jim

(1965, 154 min, GB, Richard Brooks) Peter O'Toole is Jim, a romantic young English seaman whose life is irrevocably altered when he violates his personal code of honor by a single act of cowardice. In subsequent attempts to erase his guilt, he finds himself in the middle of a massive Indonesian labor dispute and incipient rebellion. O'Toole gives an outstanding performance under the direction of Brooks, who scripted from the Joseph Conrad novel. Featuring James Mason, Curt Jurgens, Eli Wallach and Jack Hawkins. ★★★ $19.99

Lord of Illusions

(1995, 108 min, US, Clive Barker) Very disappointing third feature from director Barker, who made the outstanding *Hellraiser* and the also-disappointing *Nightbreed*. Scott Bakula stars as Harry D'Amour, a private investigator who becomes embroiled in a bizarre series of murders involving an illusionist whose high-profile act turns out to be inspired by real magic. Harry follows the trail through its twists and turns until he learns the truth: the illusionist Swann was the disciple and eventual murderer of an evil magician named Nix, whose resurrection is being engineered by a murderous cult. Adapted from his superb short story "The Last Illusion," Barker's film shows obvious signs of tampering: Harry's dark and occult side, mentioned at the beginning of the film, is abandoned in favor of making him a more traditional film noir hero; his relationship with Swann's wife seems to be curtailed; and an entire end sequence has been edited into an incomprehensible mess. The basic story itself, though, is promising and original and, given the talent involved, should have turned out better. Still radically different from most horror films, it was perhaps too far ahead of its time to please the studio powers-that-be. ★½ $19.99

Lord of the Dance

(1996, 93 min, Ireland, Michael Flatley) Michael Flatley's follow-up to *Riverdance* is more of the same, only glitzier, with higher production values, snazzier costumes, and a smattering of drama to work with this time. But once again, the dancing's the thing, and it's the same terrific, rousing dancing played to a Dublin crowd prone to jubilant outbursts worthy of rabid ringside fans. The only drawback to this production is the too frequent cutting and dissolving of shots — we barely have time to register an individual image when another takes its place — just let the dancers do their thing. With that said, however, *Lord of the*

Dance is quite entertaining, an impressive collection of musical numbers. And while one may have the urge to titter at the sight of raging egomaniac Flatley, bare-chested and oiled down at the climax, there's no denying the man can dance. ★★★ $24.99

Lord of the Flies

(1963, 91 min, GB, Peter Brook) A haunting and powerful adaptation of William Golding's novel brought to the screen by the incomparably daring British stage director Brook. Unlike his masterful *Marat/Sade*, which exploded on the screen with theatrical brilliance, here the "theatre" tends to slightly overshadow the strength of the story. However, this allegory of English schoolboys who slowly revert to brutal savagery when stranded on an island is still a fascinating and disturbing film in its own right. ★★★

Lord of the Flies

(1990, 90 min, GB, Harry Hook) Deep greens and beautiful forests dominate the frames of this remake, complete with yowling children and war paint. Director Hook displays his true forte, cinematography, paying more attention to picture than content. Detailing the regression of shipwrecked boys from an ordered existence into primitive, warring factions, this slightly updated version of William Golding's allegorical novel makes it to the screen with little change, except that the boys run around with glow-sticks instead of torches. ★★½ $19.99

Lord of the Rings

(1978, 133 min, US, Ralph Bakshi) Bakshi's ambitious adaptation of J.R.R. Tolkien's classic fantasy trilogy covers only one-half of the series. Filmed in rotoscope (live-action enhanced with animation — a technique better utilized in his later work *American Pop*), *Lord of the Rings* tells of the War of the Rings within the mystical land, Middle Earth. Despite any shortcomings for the book's enthusiasts, it's a joy to see Tolkien's creations, such as Frodo and Gollum, on film. ★★★

The Lords of Discipline

(1983, 102 min, US, Franc Roddam) A cast of up-and-coming young stars (Michael Biehn, Rick Rossovich, Judge Reinhold, Bill Paxton) populate this sensationalistic thriller about a senior (David Keith) at a 1964 South Carolina military academy charged with protecting the school's first black student (Mark Breland) from a mysterious hazing organization known as "The Ten." Based on Pat Conroy's semiautobiographical novel. Also with Matt Frewer, Barbara Babcock and Jason Connery. ★★½ $14.99

Lorenzo's Oil

(1992, 135 min, US, George Miller) Susan Sarandon and Nick Nolte star in director Miller's (*The Witches of Eastwick*, the *Mad Max* films) stirring adaptation of the real-life story of Michaela and Agusto Odone whose son Lorenzo was stricken by an incurable, and fatal, disease known as ALD. Rising above its mushy "disease-of-the-week" roots, *Lorenzo's Oil* is more riveting scientific detective story than melodrama as it follows the Odones in their relentless search for a scintilla of hope while battling a complacent medical establishment. Both Sarandon and Nolte put in superb

L

performances (with Nolte doing an Italian accent!) as the beleaguered parents whose love for their son drives them to feverishly search for their own cure. ★★★½ $19.99

Lorna

(1964, 78 min, US, Russ Meyer) The first film in which Russ added violence to spice up the sex. Lorna Maitland is a sexually frustrated housewife who becomes involved with an escaped convict. The first of Russ' black and whites. ★★ $79.99

Losing Isaiah

(1995, 108 min, US, Stephen Gyllenhaal) With its made-for-TV premise of a child custody battle, the compelling *Losing Isaiah* tugs at the heart while prodding the mind. Halle Berry, in an exceptionally fine performance, plays a crack-addicted mother who throws her newborn baby in the trash (later thinking him dead). Jessica Lange, in a passionate portrayal, plays a hospital social worker who adopts the child. Four years later, however, after Berry has gone through rehab, she discovers the baby is alive, and takes Lange to court to obtain custody. In addressing the contentious social issues of interracial adoption, the film smartly and effectively acknowledges that no easy or even correct answers are readily available. Samuel L. Jackson is very credible as Berry's lawyer, Cuba Gooding, Jr. appears as her boyfriend, and David Strathairn nicely plays Lange's supportive husband. ★★★ $14.99

Lost and Found

(1979, 112 min, US, Melvin Frank) Attempting to capitalize on their success in *A Touch of Class*, Glenda Jackson and George Segal pair up once again for this mordant comedy on married life. While not quite as funny or lively as the first go-round, Jackson and Segal do have a certain screen chemistry which makes this worthwhile viewing. ★★½

Lost Boundaries

(1949, 105 min, US, Alfred L. Werker) A postwar social drama made at a time when American cinema was rediscovering (however briefly before McCarthyism) its political voice, *Lost Boundaries* is the affecting, if slightly slow-moving, story of racial intolerance in rural America. In his debut, Mel Ferrer plays a dedicated light-skinned black doctor who, with his wife, "passes" for white in order to accept the lucrative position of town physician in an all-white New Hampshire town. Based on a true story, the film recounts the couple's dilemma as they must deny their cultural heritage but are afforded the opportunity to give their children a privileged upbringing. The film is directed at an even pace throughout, but there are times one would wish for the action to move a bit more briskly. However, the message is uncompromising and important. Oddly enough, the son's reaction to the news and his trip to Harlem illustrate the best and worst aspects of the storytelling. ★★★ $19.99

The Lost Boys

(1987, 98 min, US, Joel Schumacher) Hip vampire tale about a family moving to a small California coastal town, and discovering the city is populated with teenage vampires. Jason Patric and Corey Haim are the brothers bat-

Losing Isaiah

tling bloodsuckers Kiefer Sutherland and friends. Dianne Wiest is the boys' mom, and Bernard Hughes is the coolest grandfather this side of Grandpa Munster. (Even if it did bring together "the Coreys" [Haim and Feldman], it's still good fun.) ★★★ $9.99

Lost Highway

(1997, 134 min, US, David Lynch) Making the excesses and narrative of *Blue Velvet* seem the model of restraint by comparison, Lynch's *Lost Highway* is eerie, scary, enigmatic, weird and provocative. Sometimes the film is all of these at once, when it's in high gear; and sometimes it just tries too hard to evoke just one of those moods, stalling in its tracks. Graced by beautiful cinematography by Peter Deming, *Lost Highway* is the bizarre, often incomprehensible but nevertheless hypnotic story of a murder, a jazz musician and his wife, a youth in over his head, and the ability to phone someone while standing right next to them without being on the phone. Story coherency is of little consequence in *Lost Highway*; Lynch and cowriter Barry Gifford go out of their way to give bits of traditional narrative structure and then rub your face in it the very next minute. Sometimes the film is weird Lynchisms for weird's sake; then he constructs a gem of a scene to remind you exactly what he's capable of doing. The cast includes Bill Pullman, Patricia Arquette (in a dual role), Balthazar Getty, Robert Loggia, and, in an effectively creepy portrayal, Robert Blake. ★★½ $102.99

The Lost Honor of Katharina Blum

(1975, 95 min, West Germany, Volker Schlöndorff & Margarethe von Trotta) A political thriller which examines the havoc wrought by West Germany's yellow journalism. A woman is victimized and traumatized by the relentless press coverage of an evening she spent with a suspected terrorist. Directed by the husband-wife team of Schlöndorff (*The Tin Drum*) and von Trotta. (German with English subtitles) ★★★

Lost Horizon

(1937, 132 min, US, Frank Capra) The restoration of Capra's exotic fantasy about the fabled kingdom of Shangri-La is in itself an epic of sorts: a 13-year search of worldwide archives to locate some 20 minutes of lost footage, cut following the film's original 1937 release. Capra, then at the peak of his fame

and very much the Spielberg of his day, had a staggering budget of $4 million (equivalent to over $80 million today) to re-create James Hilton's utopian novel about a noted British diplomat (Ronald Colman) who is abducted so that he can succeed a dying High Lama (Sam Jaffe) at a remote Himalayan paradise. Great supporting cast includes Jane Wyatt and Edward Everett Horton. ★★★★ $19.99

Lost in a Harem

(1944, 89 min, US, Charles Riesner) It's hijinks aplenty as Abbott and Costello run amok in the Middle East with some occasionally funny results. Bud and Lou are magicians stranded in the desert who become involved with sultan Douglas Dumbrille and harem beauty Marilyn Maxwell. Mideast relations have never been the same. Also with the Jimmy Dorsey Orchestra. ★★½ $14.99

Lost in America

(1985, 91 min, US, Albert Brooks) Brooks hilariously stars as an upwardly mobile young ad executive who loses a big promotion and decides to turn his back on yuppiedom to discover the "real" America (in a $40,000 Winnebago). Julie Hagerty is his accepting wife in this sharply detailed comedy on the American Dream/Nightmare. ★★★½ $14.99

Lost in Yonkers

(1993, 112 min, US, Martha Coolidge) Neil Simon's Pulitzer Prize-winning and Tony Award-winning play loses some of its luster in this appealing if uneven adaptation. Award winners Mercedes Ruehl and Irene Worth repeat their stage roles in this nostalgic tale about two adolescent brothers who go to live with their stern grandmother (Worth) and endearing, slow-witted aunt (Ruehl). As a childhood remembrance, the film is funny and sweet, with Brad Stoll and Mike Damus as very likable youths. Halfway through, however, the film runs out of energy, and even a canister of Simon one-liners is not sufficient to give it a full recharge. As the fearsome matriarch, Worth gives a gallant characterization, but she's such a one-note holy terror, the film plays like *Throw Grandmomma from the Train* whenever she's on screen. Ruehl gives an earnest performance as Aunt Bella, whose child-like innocence endows her with pathos and charm. ★★½ $19.99

The Lost Language of Cranes

(1992, 90 min, GB, Nigel Finch) Changing locales from a Jewish Upper West Side Manhattan family to a WASPy suburban London one surprisingly does not tarnish David Leavitt's critically acclaimed novel. For this BBC feature film production successfully retains the book's powerfully emotional central story of a troubled family's crisis with homosexuality. Phillip, a young, handsome gay man, falls in love and begins to feel the need to tell his parents about his true sexual self. The twist is that the young man's father, Owen, a successful middle-aged professor, is also gay/bisexual but keeps his yearning closeted from his wife and family — finding release in weekend cottaging in dark movie theatres and anonymous bars. The parallel stories of these two men and the emotionally distraught wife and mother caught in-between results in an undeniably painful melodrama that is exceptionally sensitive to the issues of homosexuality, coming out and familial miscommunication. The director John Schlesinger and Rene Auberjonois are featured in small but humorously touching roles as the unconventional "parents" of Phillip's lover. ★★★★ $19.99

The Lost Moment

(1947, 88 min, US, Martin Gabel) An involving drama based on Henry James' "The Aspern Papers," with Robert Cummings as an American publisher in Venice looking for a deceased writer's lost love letters, finding the woman he sent them to (Agnes Moorehead) and becoming involved with her niece (Susan Hayward). ★★★ $14.99

The Lost Patrol

(1934, 74 min, US, John Ford) Ford's rousing adventure film about a small British army unit, lost in the Mesopotamian desert, which comes under attack by Arab forces. Victor McLaglen stars as the unit's commander, and Boris Karloff has a field day as a religious fanatic. ★★★½ $19.99

The Lost Weekend

(1945, 101 min, US, Billy Wilder) Wilder's uncompromising and devastating social drama on alcoholism startled audiences in its day with its brutally honest depiction of life on the bottle. Ray Milland won a much-deserved Oscar for his intense performance as a writer whose two-day alcoholic binge becomes a descent into hell. Supporting cast includes Jane Wyman, Howard Da Silva in a stand-out performance as a disapproving bartender, and Frank Faylen (probably best known as Dobie Gillis' dad on TV) as a psychiatric ward attendant. Winner of 4 Academy Awards including Best Picture and Best Director. ★★★★ $14.99

The Lost World: Jurassic Park

(1997, 134 min, US, Steven Spielberg) In Spielberg's frenzied, hard-edged sequel to *Jurassic Park*, claws are definitely sharper, teeth have more of a bite, and the horror is more horrific. Those man-made dinosaurs have returned to wreak havoc and scare the humans out of their wits — both on and off the screen. Displaying even more impressive effects than in the first film, but lacking a developed story line and having a Swiss cheese-like plot, The

Lost World finds Dr. Ian Malcolm (Jeff Goldblum) returning to take on those deadly prehistoric beasts. It seems there was another island populated by the dinosaurs, and there are those who would capture them and bring them to the U.S. (didn't they see *King Kong*?). Julianne Moore is Sarah, Malcolm's scientist girlfriend who is studying the dinosaurs and in imminent danger. That's all the plot that's needed to produce great scares (including a classic, hold-your-breath scene in a camper) and greater visuals (wait till you see the knock-'em dead finale and nod to *Godzilla*). Goldblum gets to say some funny one-liners, but that's the screenplay's biggest asset. Though if it's thrills and chills you're looking for, this is the place to be. ★★★ $22.99

Louisiana

(1984, 206 min, US, Philippe de Broca) In 1836, a young woman (Margot Kidder) returns to Louisiana after 11 years in Paris, expecting great wealth from her father's estate. She finds that the bank has foreclosed, the land and slaves have been sold and all that's left are a house badly in need of repair and one spectacular necklace. Her response to her circumstances is played out against the realities of a slave economy and a brutally enforced caste system. It's possible that director de Broca wanted this film to comment on the slave trade as *King of Hearts* commented on WWI; unfortunately, it misses the mark. The simplicity and broadly drawn characters, which charmed in *Hearts*, are an embarrassment here, and at times almost trivialize the profound subject matter. The cast, however, including Ian Charleson and Len Cariou, is uniformly fine; and the period is handsomely re-created. An earnest attempt to examine the range of opinions and emotions which govern human relationships. ★★ $29.99

Louisiana Purchase

(1941, 98 min, US, Irving Cummings) Politics takes it on the chin in this mildly entertaining Bob Hope comedy. Bob plays an elected official who takes the rap for illegal goings-on by his associates. A senator is sent to investigate, and Hope and pals will try anything to save their skins. Hope is in his element as a wise-cracking dupe, but it's Victor Moore's marvelous stint as the visiting senator which saves this comedy from the mundane. Hope's filibuster is a particular highlight. ★★½ $14.99

Louisiana Story

(1948, 77 min, US, Robert J. Flaherty) Produced by Standard Oil on a "no-strings-attached" policy, Flaherty's final film focuses on the story of a young Cajun boy who watches his Bayou sanctuary being invaded when an oil rig begins drilling in the swamp. Filming in an almost poetic style, Flaherty captures the mysterious appeal of the pristine paradise and offers a stirring tribute to the Bayou people. This beautiful and heartfelt semidocumentary was shot by Richard Leacock with a Pulitzer award-winning score by Virgil Thompson. ★★★½ $29.99

LouLou

(1980, 110 min, France, Maurice Pialat) An engrossing look at a wife who spurns the comforts of bourgeois security for the pleasures of

a bohemian lifestyle with a dangerously charming, drunken and chain-smoking womanizer. Gérard Depardieu, perfecting the loutish drifter character he played so well in *Going Places*, is LouLou and Isabelle Huppert is Nelly, the bright but bored wife of the sappy Guy Marchant, whose demure behavior unravels in the face of the unabashed sexual excesses offered by LouLou. Riding a sexual and emotional rollercoaster, the incongruous pair slowly discover real love and affection. A rambling road movie that captures life on the edge, yet all the while, never leaving the streets of Paris. (French with English subtitles) ★★★ $79.99

Love

(1971, 92 min, Hungary, Karoly Makk) Legendary Hungarian actress Lili Darvas, in her final film, is mesmerizing in this funny, touching and politically astute Academy Award nominee. After her husband is imprisoned on political charges, his wife keeps his memory alive and his sick elderly mother happy by telling the woman that her son had emigrated to America. The daughter-in-law continues the illusion by faking letters from her husband about America, as well as his fabulous success there as a movie director, and sending them to the old woman, who is kept alive by the excitement and happiness of her son. The film is about both personal and political falsehoods as well as a family's love and compassion. (Hungarian with English subtitles) ★★★★ $59.99

Love Affair

(1994, 108 min, US, Glenn Gordon Caron) Third time's almost a charm. Robert Towne wrote the screenplay for this easy-going romantic drama, based on the 1939 classic *Love Affair*, which itself was remade in 1957 as *An Affair to Remember*. Though moderately updated, the plot is basically the same with Warren Beatty and Annette Bening, both engaged to other partners, meeting and ultimately enjoying a shipboard romance. The two stars' relaxed and natural delivery give the film a pleasant edge, though they are a sometime victim to a glib screenplay which clearly tries too hard to be hip. As Beatty's beloved aunt, Katharine Hepburn makes a memorable appearance, looking frail but resolute; and there's a movie first as Kate utters the "f" word. Nice support from Garry Shandling, Brenda Vaccaro and Chloe Webb. ★★½ $19.99

Love Affair: Or...The Missing Switchboard Operator

(1967, 70 min, Yugoslavia, Dusan Makavejev) A bizarre and unpredictable curiousity from Yugoslavia's greatest filmmaker. The story, both an unusual love story and a political parable, follows the budding relationship of a vivacious young woman and her rat-exterminating boyfriend. All is well until she allows herself to be seduced by a man of higher means. A daring work. (Serbo-Croatian with English subtitles) ★★★

Love Among the Ruins

(1975, 100 min, US, George Cukor) An exceptional TV movie starring film legends Katharine Hepburn and Laurence Olivier at their regal best as former lovers reunited years later when barrister Olivier defends aging actress Hepburn in court. A delightful and totally grand romantic comedy, directed with panache by Cukor. ★★★½ $14.99

Love and a .45

(1994, 90 min, US, C.M. Talkington) Aiming for sardonic, hip commentary on today's modern world and life on the edge, *Love and a .45* never quite escapes its derivative origins and unoriginal execution. Some interesting people pop up — *Re-Animator*'s Jeffrey Combs, *Eraserhead* Jack Nance, Peter Fonda — but the viewer is never moved from mild interest to involvement. This ain't no *True Romance*, but if you're into the genre, you might want to check out the random assortment of marginal characters who flit in and out of the precarious lives of this would-be Bonnie and Clyde team. ★★ $14.99

Love and Anarchy

(1973, 100 min, Italy, Lina Wertmüller) An enormously powerful political drama about Italian Fascism during the 1930s, brilliantly written and directed by Wertmüller. Giancarlo Giannini stars as a Venetian peasant who takes up residence in a brothel as he awaits his opportunity to assassinate Mussolini. Music by Nino Rota. (Italian with English subtitles) ★★★½ $29.99

Love and Death

(1975, 82 min, US, Woody Allen) Tolstoy, Dostoevsky, Bergman (Ingmar) and the history books take a beating in Allen's hilarious comedic assault on 1800s Russia. Also starring Diane Keaton. ★★★½ $14.99

Love and Faith

(1978, 154 min, Japan, Kei Kumai) This moving Japanese period drama stars Toshiro Mifune and Takashi Shimura. The rise of Christianity in 16th-century Japan is used as a backdrop for a tragic romance involving the beautiful stepdaughter of Japan's leading tea master, whose love for a young Christian lord precipitates a conflict with vile warlord Mifune. (Japanese with English subtitles) ★★★

Love and Human Remains

(1993, 100 min, Canada, Denys Arcand) Adapted from Brad Fraser's play "Unidentified Human Remains and the True Nature of Love," this somber drama might also be titled "Sex and Human Alienation." The story takes place in a nameless Canadian city populated by attractive, sexually active but world-weary young people of all sorts of sexual orientations. There is the gay David (Thomas Gibson), a former actor now contented waiter who roams the clubs of the city participating in but not really enjoying anonymous sex. His roommate is Candy (Ruth Marshall), a pretty and intelligent young woman in love with the indifferent David (they once had a fling) and who soon gets involved with both a straight man and an especially intense lesbian schoolteacher (Joanne Vannicola). Ladies' man Bernie (Cameron Bancroft) is the troubled yuppie and Kane (Matthew Ferguson) is a sexually confused teenager fixated on the older David. Amidst it all a serial killer is on the prowl. Weaving its tale of souls emotionally adrift, Arcand's first English-language film effectively goes from one character to another charting their collective ennui and their valiant attempts to use sex as a facilitator toward intimacy, fulfillment and happiness. ★★★ $19.99

Love and Other Catastrophes

(1996, 90 min, Australia, Emma-Kate Croghan) Funky and hip from the very start, this amusing little Australian screwball comedy follows one mixed-up day in the life of a group of grad students in Melbourne. At the center are Alice (Alice Garner), a sprightly young woman who is four years late with her dissertation on "Doris Day as Feminist Warrior," and her lesbian roommate Mia (Frances O'Conner), who finds herself caught in the bureaucratic nightmare of trying to change her department. The film zips around through their respective days while introducing a slew of supporting oddballs, especially in regards to their search for a new, third roommate. Of course, each has trouble on the love front with Mia on the outs with her girlfriend Dannie

(Radha Mitchell), and Alice nursing a school-girl crush on campus hunk (and part-time gigolo!) Ari (Matthew Dyktysnki). Director and cowriter Croghan demonstrates a marvelous sense of character while delivering occasionally cracking dialogue, and Garner and O'Conner both make thoroughly engaging protagonists. The film is refreshing, too, for its depiction of a campus environment that is seemingly neither gay nor straight, but decidedly and very integratedly both. ★★★ $99.99

Love at First Bite

(1979, 96 min, US, Stan Dragoti) Very enjoyable take-off on the Dracula legend with George Hamilton as the Count searching New York City for new victims — finding Susan Saint James. Lots of laughs in this parody which isn't afraid to use every bat joke in the book. ★★★ $9.99

Love at Large

(1990, 97 min, US, Alan Rudolph) For the first 60 minutes, this stylish homage to '40s film noir is nearly perfect: Tom Berenger is a wonderfully befuddled and rumpled detective; there is a labyrinthine and duplicitous plot; and enough femme fatales to enrapture a slew of Sam Spades. Regrettably, however, this Rudolph-scripted mystery cannot sustain its initial high level and slowly unravels near the end. Gravel-voiced P.I. Harry Dobbs (Berenger) is hired to tail a possibly two-timing husband, but follows the wrong person — a man who leads the private eye into an increasingly sordid mess of murder, bigamy and deception. Elizabeth Perkins and Anne Archer also star. ★★½ $89.99

Love Crazy

(1941, 99 min, US, Jack Conway) Nick and Nora Charles' better halves, William Powell and Myrna Loy, appear in their tenth film together (they would make three more). A lively and zany screwball comedy, the story follows the merry exploits of Powell and Loy on their fourth anniversary. When she gets jealous over hubby's former girlfriend moving in upstairs, Loy files for divorce. Concocting a loony plan to get her back, Powell feigns insanity...and he's so convincing she has him committed. But we've already given away too much. Powell and Loy are, of course, terrific. Powell suffers almost every indignity (the elevator scene is a hoot) with his customary élan. ★★★ $19.99

Love Crimes

(1992, 85 min, US, Lizzie Borden) Sean Young stars as an unorthodox District Attorney trying to build a case against a mysterious man who is impersonating a well-known photographer and is taking advantage of a number of unsuspecting and vulnerable women. Patrick Bergin plays yet another deranged and sadistic villain — not much of a stretch from Julia Roberts' abusive husband in *Sleeping with the Enemy*. Look for a solid portrayal of the assistant D.A. from Arnetia Walker. Overall, independent feminist filmmaker Borden's (*Working Girls*) attempt to enter the mainstream, while slightly perplexing and uneven, is an interesting and watchable thriller. Unrated version. ★★ $14.99

Love Crazy

Love Field

(1992, 104 min, US, Jonathan Kaplan) Michelle Pfeiffer's Oscar-nominated performance more than redeems the few plot holes in this otherwise endearing drama. Pfeiffer plays Lurene, a Dallas housewife who, upon the assassination of JFK, buses to Washington for his funeral. Enroute, she inadvertently involves a fellow passenger, a black man (Dennis Haysbert), with the police. Traveling with his young daughter, the father and child hit the back roads to elude the authorities, accompanied by the naive, good-intentioned Lurene. What follows is a charming road movie with touches of whimsy, romance and history lessons on racial attitudes, 1960s-style. Haysbert and young Stephanie McFadden, as his daughter, give especially pleasing performances. But this is Pfeiffer's film. As the giddy Lurene, she never patronizes the part. Her strength is her honest emotion, and the film is more lovely for it. ★★★ $14.99

Love Film

(1970, 130 min, Hungary, István Szabó) Although unknown by most American audiences, this poignant human drama, political allegory and romantic love story is considered a pivotal film in Hungary's post-war cinema. Twenty-seven-year-old Jancsi boards a train in Budapest on a journey to be reunited with his childhood sweetheart, Kata, who fled after the 1956 uprising. The trip also proves to be a journey into his pain-filled past — of innocent childhood moments, romantic rendezvous, as well as haunting images of WWII airraids, Communist youth rallies and the suffering caused by the Russian suppression of the Budapest Spring. (Hungarian with English subtitles) ★★★½ $39.99

Love from a Stranger

(1947, 81 min, US, Richard Whorf) Newly married Sylvia Sidney marries wholesome John Hodiak, only to begin to suspect he may be a killer — and she may be his next victim. Based on an Agatha Christie story, which bears a resemblance to Alfred Hitchcock's *Suspicion*. It's a familiar story line with a degree of suspense. An earlier version was made in Great Britain in 1937 with Ann Harding and Basil Rathbone. ★★½ $14.99

Love Happy

(1949, 91 min, US, David Miller) Some swell kids want to put on a show, but the money's run out. But wait — the spectacular Romanov diamonds are in the can of sardines that the cat is dining on... Chico and Harpo track down the gems as Groucho tracks down the sullen but fabulously wealthy Ilona Massey, who's also after the loot. Vera-Ellen and Raymond Burr dance up a storm (yes, Raymond Burr), and Marilyn Monroe has a walk-on that makes up in intensity what it lacks in length. Ben Hecht was one of the scriptwriters for this occasionally funny Marx Brothers romp. ★★½ $19.99

Love Hurts

(1989, 110 min, US, Bud Yorkin) Another lost Vestron Picture title, *Love Hurts* is a beguiling if familiar comedy-drama about a family coming together for a weekend wedding. Jeff Daniels heads a fine cast as a newly divorced insurance agent who returns home for his sister's nuptials. Complicating the visit are his ex-wife (Cynthia Sikes) and children, who have just moved in. The story focuses on Daniels' various relationships with his family, including his estranged young daughter, drunken father and wary ex-wife. As in his excellent family drama *Twice in a Lifetime*, director Yorkin handles familial trauma, rich characters and warm humor all with equal command. John Mahoney and Cloris Leachman are extremely appealing as Daniels' colorful parents, and the wondrous Judith Ivey has a small but effective bit as a family friend. ★★★ $14.99

Love in a Fallen City

(1984, 97 min, Hong Kong, Ann Hui) This compelling romantic wartime drama centers on the troubled love affair between a young divorcée and a rich, Westernized playboy right at the time of Hong Kong's fall to the Japanese in 1941. (Cantonese with English subtitles) ★★½ $39.99

A Love in Germany

(1984, 110 min, West Germany, Andrzej Wajda) Amid the sweeping crush of the Nazi terror, a German shopkeeper (Hanna Schygulla) falls in love with a Polish POW and suffers the grave consequences of the illicit affair. Director Wajda conveys the poignance of personal tragedy overshadowed by the grand obscenity of war. (German with English subtitles) ★★★½ $19.99

Love in the Afternoon

(1957, 130 min, US, Billy Wilder) Audrey Hepburn is captivating as a young Parisian artist whose curiosity and romanticism leads to romance in Wilder's enchanting and sardonic comedy. Maurice Chevalier is a private eye who is hired to tail American playboy Gary Cooper, who is having an affair with a married woman. Starry-eyed Audrey hears that the cuckold husband may resort to firearms, and sets out to warn the Casanova. Romance ensues as the innocent Audrey gets philandering Gary to change his ways. Wilder casts a sarcastic eye towards romance and relationships while ultimately creating a sweetly caring one between Hepburn and Cooper — who have a wonderful chemistry together. Here, Chevalier reminds one why he was one of France's biggest stars, and who could forget the wonderful train sequence? ★★★½ $14.99

Love in the City

(1953, 90 min, Italy, Various) This six-episode film is based on a very interesting idea: the director of each segment is "sent off" to capture, cinema verité style, an aspect of love and romance in the Eternal City. This hidden camera technique has each director act as a secret reporter out to explore typical Italian life. The Michelangelo Antonioni and Federico Fellini segments provide a fascinating hint to their future filmmaking careers. Other directors include Cesare Zavattini, Dino Risi, Alberto Lattuada and Francesco Maselli. Stars Ugo Tognazzi and Maresa Gallo. (English narration) ★★★

Love Is a Many Splendored Thing

(1955, 102 min, US, Henry King) Based on the autobiographical best-seller by Han Suyin, this slick but hokey romantic drama is, at best, a partially splendored thing. Set in Hong Kong before the start of the Korean War, the film stars Jennifer Jones as an Eurasian doctor involved in an affair with married American correspondent William Holden. Their love flourishes in the face of obstacles such as interracial prejudice and Holden's wife's refusal to divorce. Jones and Holden both offer tender, captivating performances, but the film is slow moving, and John Patrick's dialogue, in trying to capture the mysticism and beauty of Chinese culture, borders on the clichéd; though a line such as "Let us have tea and talk of absurdities" is hard to resist. A Best Picture nominee. ★★½ $19.99

Love Me or Leave Me

(1955, 122 min, US, Charles Vidor) James Cagney and Doris Day (in her best film role) both give terrific performances in this musical biography of 1920s torch singer Ruth Etting. Cagney plays her gangster boyfriend. Score includes "Ten Cents a Dance" and "Shaking the Blues Away." ★★½ $19.99

Love Me Tender

(1956, 89 min, US, Robert D. Webb) Elvis Presley's film debut is an acceptable Civil War drama about a Southern family taking different sides in the conflict. Also with Debra Pagent and Richard Egan. Elvis sings the title tune and "Let Me," among others. ★★½ $14.99

Love Meetings

(1964, 90 min, Italy, Pier Paolo Pasolini) *Love Meetings* is a gritty, cinema verité-style investigation of sex in Italy. The film includes appearances by author Alberto Moravia and noted psychologist Cesare Musatti. Pasolini appears as the interviewer and asks a wide range of individuals to share their tales of love — including their thoughts on prostitution, homosexuality, marital and nonmarital liaisons. (Italian with English subtitles) ★★★ $29.99

Love on the Run

(1979, 93 min, France, François Truffaut) Jean-Pierre Léaud makes his final appearance as Antoine Doinel in Truffaut's complex, bittersweet concluding installment of the Doinel saga. Through a marvelous sequence of flashbacks from earlier films, Truffaut documents Doinel's rocky road to adulthood. Truffaut's untimely death makes this cinematic "summing up" seem particularly appropriate. (French with English subtitles) ★★★ $29.99

Love Potion #9

(1992, 90 min, US, Dale Launer) This lightweight fluff written and directed by the creator of *My Cousin Vinny* and *Ruthless People* is a far cry from the classic screwball comedies it wants most desperately to be — but then any movie that takes its inspiration from a '60s pop tune can't hope for much. Hormonal hijinks ensue when a pair of nerdy scientists (Tate Donovan and Sandra Bullock) accidentally discover a love potion. While utterly predictable from start to finish, the film is redeemed somewhat by director Launer's hip take on the subject matter. Watch for another nifty cameo by the timeless Anne Bancroft. ★★ $9.99

L

Love Songs

(1986, 107 min, France, Elie Chouraqui) Catherine Deneuve and Christopher Lambert are enticingly matched as the ill-fated lovers in this entertaining and perceptive drama set in the rock music world of Paris. Deneuve is a successful talent agent, married to an American writer for 12 years and mother of two children, who reluctantly succumbs to a persistent and alluringly charming client, rock singer Lambert. The film's appeal could rest solely on the sexually charged love affair, but director Chouraqui also focuses on the people affected by the relationship. ★★★

Love Story

(1970, 99 min, US, Arthur Hiller) This box-office sensation is either classic romantic drama or ridiculous foolishness – depending on your tastes. Ryan O'Neal is the guy from the right side of the tracks, in love with Ali McGraw, who's from the wrong side of town and has a fatal disease. No matter what you think of this, it's better than the sequel *Oliver's Story.* ★★½ $14.99

Love, Strange Love

(1982, 120 min, Brazil, Walter Khouri) This controversial film, about a young boy's sexual awakening in a brothel, caused quite a storm several years back when it played the film festival circuit. Possibly because of its subject matter, it never was released theatrically in the U.S., but is now on video in a complete unedited version. The story follows the development and growth of a young boy who is sent to live at his aunt's brothel. The enticing girls prove too much for the curious boy as he adjusts to this strange world. (Dubbed) ★★½

Love Streams

(1986, 122 min, US, John Cassavetes) Two offbeat siblings, both desperate for some kind of happiness in their lonely existences, address their erratic ways in this examination of contemporary lifestyles. Cassavetes also appears as the hedonistic brother; Gena Rowlands is the overly loving sister. Both Cassavetes and Rowlands are compelling in this insightful glimpse into two slightly neurotic romantic psyches. ★★★

Love! Valour! Compassion!

(1997, 120 min, US, Joe Mantello) Terrence McNally's Tony Award-winning play, trimmed from its three-hour running time, makes for an affecting, low-keyed tragicomedy which offers alternately insightful, heartrending and funny moments, but this film adaptation just misses in capturing the play's passion and greatness. A group of gay friends from New York spend their summer holiday weekends in the country at the beautiful lakeside estate of lovers Gregory and Bobby. They include longtime companions Arthur and Perry, the witty show queen Buzz (who has AIDS), and John, an overbearing composer who is accompanied by his handsome young lover Ramon. With a discerning eye and ear, McNally explores the bonds and boundaries of friendships and romantic relationships which is perceptive drama no matter what sexual orientation the characters may be. But *Love! Valour! Compassion!* is also stirringly gay, as well, and it

unceremoniously celebrates queer humor and custom. The ensemble is terrific. All but Jason Alexander (as Buzz) starred in the Broadway production, and he effortlessly fits in giving a tender, funny portrait. John Glover is exceptional as John, and, in a dual role, his twin brother James, a sweet-natured, flamboyant PWA. Randy Becker is an attractive and often nude Ramon. ★★★ $99.99

Love with the Proper Stranger

(1963, 100 min, US, Robert Mulligan) Natalie Wood and Steve McQueen's impassioned performances dominate this hearty romantic comedy-drama about the love affair between shopgirl Wood and musician McQueen. Edie Adams and Tom Bosley also star. ★★★ $19.99

Love without Pity

(1990, 95 min, France, Eric Rachont) A delightfully witty drama of romantic love in the land of existentialism. Hippo – young, handsome, and with a seductive Belmondo-cool attitude – leads a carefree bohemian life; living with friends, bumming money and casually picking up women, only to drop them when his interest flags. A sexist pig certainly, but a charming one. But his "love 'em and leave 'em" attitude towards women comes back to haunt him when he meets a professional woman who does not immediately succumb to his charms. Intrigued by this evasive victim, he goes all out, only to find himself smitten with love, jealousy and obsession, all traits that mean nothing to the young lady. (French with English subtitles) ★★★ $19.99

The Loved One

(1965, 116 min, US, Tony Richardson) Evelyn Waugh's audacious satire on the Southern California way of life (and death) was adapted for the screen by Terry Southern and Christopher Isherwood ("I Am a Camera"). This classic black comedy, which was billed as "the film with something to offend everyone," follows the sometimes surreal journey of a young man as he makes his way through studio intrigue, romance and a mystical funeral parlor. Robert Morse is the Candide-like nephew who travels to L.A. to visit his uncle; John Gielgud is his dearly departed relative; Rod Steiger is the Oedipal Mr. Joyboy; Liberace is a fastidious casket salesman; and Tab Hunter, Roddy McDowall and Jonathan Winters round out the talented cast. A refreshing slap in the face to both normality and eccentricity. ★★★½

The Lover

(1992, 119 min, France, Jean-Jacques Annaud) No stranger to exotic locations, director Annaud (*The Bear, Black and White in Color*) must have felt right at home with this screen adaptation of Marguerite Duras' novel. Set in Vietnam in 1929, this story about a French schoolgirl is a sensual feast for the eyes and ears. The girl, struggling to gain independence from her difficult family life and trying to understand her own sexual awakening, begins a torrid and illicit affair with a wealthy Chinese man. Although they don't really approve of the affair, her family tries to manipulate the situation for their own benefit. Annaud skillfully captures the tension-filled colonial setting that

serves as a backdrop for these displaced persons, and the film is aided by gorgeous cinematography. Jeanne Moreau provides insightful narration as the girl, now a woman living in France, remembering her life in another country. (Filmed in English) ★★★½ $14.99

Loverboy

(1989, 98 min, US, Joan Micklin Silver) After her tremendous success with *Crossing Delancey*, Silver's irresponsible and unfunny sex farce rates as a major disappointment. Patrick Dempsey plays a teenager who becomes the romantic idol of a group of older women – jumping in and out of bed with each of them. Cast includes Kate Jackson, Kirstie Alley and Robert Ginty. ★★ $14.99

Lovers (Amantes)

(1991, 105 min, Spain, Vincente Aranda) In a story that makes the films of Pedro Almodóvar seem innocuously tame, this sexually charged, hyperventilating melodrama is a lurid tale of a love triangle gone dangerously awry. Fresh from a stint in the military, the broodingly handsome Paco finds his well-planned life with his prim and virginal fiancée shattered when his sultry, widowed landlady seduces him. Luisa, the luscious "older woman" (Victoria Abril of *High Heels; Tie Me Up, Tie Me Down*), proves to be a seasoned sexual dynamo and a tough opponent for Trini, Paco's inexperienced girlfriend. But faced with losing him, she decides that, "if you can't beat 'em, join 'em" and begins her own assault to capture the heart and loins of our young hero. Paco, unable to decide between the two hellcats, soon finds the choice made for him. What self-respecting foreign film lover would miss a film seething with a plethora of out-of-control Latino passions, sexual deception, bloody revenge and a fist-clenching scene with a strategically stuffed handkerchief? (Spanish with English subtitles) ★★★½ $14.99

The Lovers

(1958, 89 min, France, Louis Malle) Boasting a casual view of adultery, this early Malle melodrama became famous mostly for censorship problems and court cases on its initial United States release. Jeanne Moreau stars as a restless woman, bored by the privileges of her Pernod-and-caviar provincial life and trapped in a loveless marriage. Weekly sojourns into the elegant world of Parisian society produce some diversion as well as a polo-playing lover, but her unhappiness remains until one day she meets an unpretentious young student who offers her sexual fulfillment and temporary relief from her emptiness. Moreau, with her sad, sultry beauty, was made an international star by the film, which also won the Special Jury Prize at Venice. Letterboxed format. (French with English subtitles) ★★★ $24.99

Lovers and Liars

(1981, 93 min, Italy, Mario Monice) A disappointing black comedy about the ill-fated and calamity-prone romance of American tourist Goldie Hawn and married businessman Giancarlo Giannini. The two make an interesting couple as they wind their way through a series of comic disasters and arguments on the way to true love, but neither have much to work with. (Dubbed) ★★ $14.99

Loves of a Blonde

(1965, 88 min, Czechoslovakia, Milos Forman) Years before his international success with such films as *Amadeus, Cuckoo's Nest* and *Ragtime*, Forman directed a series of quirky, funny films from his Eastern European homeland. This film depicts life in a small factory town near Prague with a curious social injustice: the women outnumber the men ten to one. A visit by a group of army reservists allows Anduka, the blonde in question, to enjoy a welcomed but bittersweet respite. (Czechoslovakian with English subtitles) ★★★½ $39.99

The Loves of Carmen

(1948, 99 min, US, Charles Vidor) Bizet's famous opera about a soldier who becomes obsessed with a comely Gypsy woman is so flamboyant and loaded with such sensuous music that one must wonder why anyone would want to turn it into a nonmusical drama. This rendition of the tragic tale will leave one wondering. On the up side, however, Rita Hayworth's dazzling beauty is enough to make this easy viewing. ★★½ $19.99

A Low Down Dirty Shame

(1994, 110 min, US, Keenan Ivory Wayans) Those expecting an action-packed tribute to the blaxploitation films of the '70s will surely be disappointed by this mind-numbing disaster. Director-writer-actor Wayans plays a former cop-turned-private investigator who is hired by ex-partner Charles Dutton to take on a nefarious drug lord. Jada Pinkett plays his eager assistant. With a cast such as this, one would expect at least a competent production, instead of the insipid, offensive dreck which Wayans has created. Those who are brave enough to sit through this are sure to feel that it's a low down dirty shame a film this bad was made in the first place. ★½ $14.99

The Low Life

(1996, 98 min, US, George Hickenlooper) Director and cowriter Hickenlooper graduates from a filmmaking documentary (*Hearts of Darkness*) and a Civil War horror story (the underrated *Ghost Brigade*) to the twentysomething genre. Partially based on the director's own experiences after graduating from Yale, *The Low Life* follows a recent grad and aspiring writer (Rory Cochran) through demeaning temp jobs and a frustrating relationship with a manic-depressive Southern belle beauty (Kyra Sedgwick doing her best in a basically unplayable role). And this being a GenX movie, there are obligatory bar scenes, with Cochran and cohorts discussing pop culture, philosophy and life's injustices. Cochran is good in an extremely low-key role, and he's ably supported by James LeGros, Christian Meoli and especially Sean Astin, who's great as Cochran's annoying but ultimately sympathetic roommate. *The Low Life* has many flaws, but it's moving and insightful and doesn't condescend. ★★★ $19.99

The Lower Depths

(1957, 125 min, Japan, Akira Kurosawa) Kurosawa's compelling adaptation of Maxim Gorky's classic play. The story concerns a group of peasants living in absolute squalor. Crammed in on top of each other, the tenants are locked in a constant battle of wits: some clinging desperately to their broken dreams while others viciously shoot them down. This truly touching tale features an exceptional ensemble cast headed by the incomparable Toshiro Mifune. (Japanese with English subtitles) ★★★ $59.99

Loyalties

(1986, 98 min, Canada, Anne Wheeler) An interesting, if not predictable, psycho-feminist drama that probes the evolving friendship between two women of wildly different backgrounds. An upper-class British family, fleeing from a secret trauma, moves to a small town in Alberta. The wife, Lily (Susan Wooldridge), hires a hell-raising Indian woman (Rosanne Ladoceur) as their housekeeper. Despite a stormy beginning, the two overcome barriers of race and class to forge a strong friendship. ★★½ $9.99

Lucas

(1986, 100 min, US, David Seltzer) One of the pleasant surprises of 1986, this charming teen comedy follows the romantic misadventures of a love-struck 14-year-old (played with wide-eyed innocence by Corey Haim) who falls for the new girl in town, a newly acquainted friend who has set her sights on the football team captain (Charlie Sheen). Haim, before he had his 15 minutes of fame as one of the two Coreys, is wonderful; and Winona Ryder shows that, even before she hit it big, she had star quality. ★★★ $14.99

Lulu in Berlin

(1985, 50 min, US, Richard Leacock & Susan Woll) Louise Brooks' life and film work, which took her from Hollywood to pre-Hitler Germany and 1930s France, was exciting and controversial. Her remarkable career is recounted in this absorbing documentary that features the only filmed interview with Ms. Brooks as well as clips from several of her films. The filmmakers, renowned documentarians, capture the radiance of this articulate, seductive and beguiling woman. ★★★½ $59.99

Lumiere

(1976, 95 min, France, Jeanne Moreau) Moreau's warm and endearing directorial debut chronicles the lives, loves, careers and friendships of four women of different ages all living in Paris. Starring François Simon, Bruno Ganz and Moreau, the film's affectionate yet insightful look at these people produces a wonderful human drama. (French with English subtitles) ★★★

Lumiere and Company

(1995, 88 min,) A fascinating collection of 40 short films by 40 filmmakers from around the world. All the films are 52 seconds in length, and shot with the original camera built by the Lumiere Brothers at the turn of the century. It's a terrific challenge, and exciting to see how the various directors use the very brief running time and primitive technology to their advantage. The results range from the dull and uninspired, to the brilliant and beautiful. The best efforts seem to come from expected sources — John Boorman, Claude Lelouch, and especially Zhany Yimou and David Lynch. Some of the lesser-known directors contribute strong pieces as well. Interspersed throughout are the filmmakers' equally varied responses to questions such as "Why do you film?" and "Is film mortal?" An absolute must for serious film buffs. ★★★½ $59.99

Luna Park

(1993, 108 min, Russia, Pavel Lounguine) Employing the same herky-jerky, low-budget look of his earlier *Taxi Blues*, director Lounguine has created a gritty, nightmarish and all-too-real treatise on Russia's seemingly inevitable slide into total social chaos. The story follows Andrei, a neo-Nazi thug who hangs with a loosely organized band in a Moscow amusement park. Upon learning that he is half Jewish, he begins a desperate search for his Semitic father, finally landing upon Naoum, an aging intellectual, songwriter and esthete. As Andrei struggles with his emotions (should he murder Naoum or embrace him as his father?), Lounguine evokes a terrifying image of Russia on the edge where class differences, deep-rooted anti-Semitism, xenophobia, and a complete lack of state control are giving rise to unspeakable violence. (Russian with English subtitles) ★★★ $29.99

Lupo

(1970, 100 min, Israel, Menahem Golan) Fifty-year-old Lupo, widower and neighborhood character, stands up to city hall when his dilapidated but beloved community is threatened with demolition. A zesty, unpredictable comedy. (Filmed in English) ★★★ $59.99

Lust for Life

(1956, 122 min, US, Vincente Minnelli) Kirk Douglas gives possibly his best performance as painter Vincent Van Gogh in this riveting drama about the artist's tortured life. Anthony Quinn won an Oscar as Van Gogh's compadre, Paul Gauguin. Minnelli's film avoids the clichés of the artist at work, and succinctly presents the tale with subtlety and a narrative coherency. ★★★½ $19.99

Lust in the Dust

(1985, 85 min, US, Paul Bartel) Gold lies somewhere in the squalid town of Chile Verde and the person who can line up the asses of Divine and Lainie Kazan will be able to follow the map tattooed thereon (half a map per cheek) to the treasure's whereabouts. A wildly funny spoof of westerns also starring Tab Hunter. ★★★ $14.99

Luzia

(1987, 112 min, Brazil, Fabio Barreto) Substituting for Sonia Braga in the saucy, sensuous and beguiling role, Claudia Ohana (one of Brazil's biggest stars) more than fills her place in this exciting Brazilian western. Ohana is a rodeo cowgirl caught in a clash between squatters and the powerful ranch owners. (Portuguese with English subtitles) ★★½ $19.99

L

M

(1931, 99 min, Germany, Fritz Lang) Lang's harrowing psychological drama has Peter Lorre, in his screen debut, as a child murderer being hunted by the police as well as the Berlin underworld. Based on an actual incident which haunted a Dusseldorf community in 1929. Lorre, in contrast to the eye-popping, campy performances he would give later in his career, is nothing short of spellbinding. ★★★★ $19.99

M*A*S*H

(1970, 116 min, US, Robert Altman) One of the most devastating black comedies and potent antiwar films ever to hit the screen, Altman's blisteringly funny, anarchic romp rocketed him to stardom and set the tone for a generation of irreverent filmmakers. Set during the Korean War, the film stars Elliott Gould (back when he had screen presence) and Donald Sutherland as two hotshot, unconventional doctors assigned to a Mobile Army Surgical Hospital. In between the blood and death of war and surgery, they let loose in binges marked by drinking, sex, disobedience and other flagrant actions of nonmilitary behavior. Sally Kellerman has never been better as "Hot Lips" Houlihan, Robert Duvall is the inept Frank Burns, and Tom Skerritt, Gary Burghoff, Bud Cort, Fred Williamson and Rene Auberjonois all lend able support. The film was made into a successful TV series which only partially retained the film's hard edge and biting cynicism. ★★★★ $9.99

M. Butterfly

(1993, 100 min, US, David Cronenberg) The much-anticipated screen version of David Henry Hwang's hit play is something of a letdown. Inspired by a true story, the tragic tale is about a man's self-delusional love for and betrayal by an alluring Chinese woman who is actually a man. A deer-in-the-headlights-like

Jeremy Irons stars as Rene Gallimard, a nebbish accountant at the French Embassy who falls in love with an opera singer, Song Liling (John Lone). As the two begin an affair, Gallimard rises in rank at the embassy, unknowingly disseminating government secrets. The action unfolds slowly and the film's emotional level never seems to rise above the simmering point of grand tragedy; though the relationship between Irons and Lone is romantic, tender and touching. Lone, in heavy makeup and beautifully dressed, plays a convincingly demure woman. ★★½ $14.99

M.D. Geist

(1986, 45 min, Japan, Hayheo Ikeda) On a distant planet, powers clash and wars rage. When the bio-engineered M.D. Geist shows up in this animated sci-fi adventure, things really get going, especially when he takes on a gang of vicious motorcycle villains. High-tech visuals and bone-crunching violence highlight this Japanese animated tale. ★★½ $19.99

Mac

(1993, 120 min, US, John Turturro) Actor Turturro makes an extremely impressive directorial debut with this drama about three Italian-American brothers who start their own construction company. Set in mid-1950s Queens, the film tells of the enterprising brothers' struggle against rival developers, procedural setbacks and most often each other. Turturro (who also coscripted the film) plays the eldest — the trio's inspiration and ultimately their leader. Michael Badalucco and Carl Capotorto put in superb work as his younger brothers. Turturro's real-life wife, Katherine Borowitz, stars as his on-screen wife, and Ellen Barkin appears as a whacked-out hep-cat gal. Meticulously crafted and carefully photographed, the film's tight-knit ensemble of actors provide outstanding, rich and multilayered characterizations. As a director, Turturro shows a strong, clear vision as he keeps the pace lively and tells his story with precision. Winner of the Camera D'Or at Cannes. ★★★★ $19.99

Macao

(1952, 81 min, US, Joseph von Sternberg) In the notorious Far East, a mysterious American adventurer helps a detective hunt down an elusive gangster. A seedy atmosphere and a fair amount of tension heightens this noirish tale. Robert Mitchum, Ava Gardner and William Bendix star. ★★★ $19.99

Macario

(1960, 91 min, Mexico, Roberto Gavaldon) A poetic fairy tale, the story follows Macario, an impoverished woodcutter who, with his young wife and four children, struggles to eke out an existence in rural Mexico. Plagued by a sense of failure, our hero vows not to eat again until he can have a turkey all for himself. On the Day of the Dead, his wife steals a bird, cooks it and gives it to him as he goes into the forest to work, where he is confronted by the Devil, God and

Death, all asking him to share his prized meal. He eventually chooses Death, and in return receives magical powers to heal the sick and dying. His life changes as he accumulates wealth and possessions, all the while attracting the attention of the Church's local inquisition. Based on a story by B. Traven (author of "The Treasure of the Sierra Madre"). ★★★ $79.99

Macaroni

(1985, 104 min, Italy, Ettore Scola) Jack Lemmon plays a weary business executive who returns to Naples for the first time since WWII. There he is reunited with a wartime acquaintance (Marcello Mastroianni), who has been sending his own sister forged letters from the serviceman since the war ended. The two stars overcome an intriguing story which is only half-heartedly explored. (Filmed in English) ★★½ $79.99

MacArthur

(1977, 130 min, US, Joseph Sargent) In an attempt to reproduce the sweep and historical significance of 1970's *Patton*, the filmmakers set their sights on another controversial military leader of World War II: General Douglas MacArthur. Even with an actor of Gregory Peck's caliber in the title role, the film is only mildly interesting. The story covers in episodic, sometimes melodramatic fashion, the career of the general from WWII thru Korea. Peck gives a compelling performance, but lacks the necessary panache befitting the larger-than-life commander. Ed Flanders is quite good, however, as President Truman. ★★½ $19.99

MacArthur's Children

(1985, 115 min, Japan, Masahiro Shinoda) The effects of America's victory over Japan and subsequent occupation and cultural domination of this proud nation are the themes of Shinoda's poignant and funny film. Set in a small fishing village immediately after World War II, the film explores the relationship and attitudes of the townspeople to their foreign "rulers." The film is not a biting indictment against Americans, but rather a loving remembrance of these strange people who came and changed Japan forever. (Japanese with English subtitles) ★★★

Macbeth

(1948, 112 min, US, Orson Welles) A presentiment of evil overshadows every frame of Welles' *Macbeth*. A most faithful adaptation, both to Shakespeare's writing and to the historical era depicted. Welles makes optimum use of lighting and set design, and he is as much Macbeth as he was Kane. Jeanette Nolan epitomizes the woman whose desire for power can be exercised only through her husband. Able support from Dan O'Herlihy, Edgar Barrier and Roddy McDowall. ★★★½ $19.99

Macbeth

(1971, 140 min, GB, Roman Polanski) Who knows what evil lurked in the heart of the Bard when he penned this murderous tale of treachery and violence? In any case, Polanski's grim and gory conception of Shakespeare's bloody drama is not only one of his greatest film achievements, but is one of the truest rendi-

Peter Lorre in *M*

M

tions of this sordid tale. Gripping and highly atmospheric, the film was greeted by an uproar fueled by its extreme (but not unwarranted) violence, a speech by Lady Macbeth in the nude, and problems in Polanski's personal life. ★★★½ $19.99

Macho Dancer

(1988, 136 min, The Philippines, Lino Brocka) The eternal tale of the naive country boy who is seduced and corrupted by the evils of the big city is played out in this fascinating and erotic drama. Paul, a somnambulistic teenage beauty, is drawn to Manila after his American lover and supporter of his family returns to the U.S. Young Paul is enamored by the city's notorious gay bars and nightclubs and is seduced into a world of prostitution, sexually explicit dancing and "brown slavery." The film offers a voyeuristic glimpse into the tacky yet lascivious gay underground where sexual acts are performed on stage and then bought and sold off stage. (Tagalog with English subtitles) ★★★ $69.99

The Mack

(1973, 110 min, US, Michael Campus) One of the most popular of the '70s blaxploitation flicks, this gritty, misogynous actioner is the story of Goldie, a likable but sleazy ex-convict who aspires and attains his lofty goal of being a superpimp – "the meanest 'mack' in town." With an envious stable of fine 'hos, plenty of muscle and a cutthroat business attitude, our hero soon discovers that pimping's profitable but, "what gains a man to win the world and lose his own soul." Heavy, man. ★★ $9.99

Mack the Knife

(1989, 122 min, GB, Menahem Golan) Raul Julia stars in this misbegotten version of "The Threepenny Opera," about the numerous, unsuccessful attempts of London's street people to keep England's most notorious criminal behind bars. With Richard Harris, Julie Walters and Roger Daltrey. ★½ $89.99

The Mackintosh Man

(1973, 105 min, GB, John Huston) Paul Newman and James Mason are on opposite sides of the fence in this derivative though enjoyable spy thriller about a freelance agent (Newman) who must ferret out a Communist traitor high in the ranks of the British government. Also starring Dominique Sanda, Harry Andrews and Ian Bannen. ★★½ $14.99

Macross Two, Episodes 1 & 2

(1990, 55 min, Japan, Kenichi Yatagai) Action-packed animated sci-fi/adventure that tells the tale of a news reporter who is after a story involving a Valkyrie ace named Silvie Gena and the quickly changing events in his life as an invading alien force enters the solar system. The reporter Hibiki and an exotic alien woman, Ishtar, then join forces not only to learn about each other's cultures, but also to learn the secrets of Macross. ★★½ $19.99

Mad Dog and Glory

(1993, 96 min, US, John McNaughton) Robert De Niro stars as an extremely mild-mannered police photographer who, after he saves the life of mobster/stand-up comic Bill Murray, is given – as a little "thank you" – the service of

Mad Max Beyond Thunderdome

Uma Thurman for one week. This amiable comedy-drama finds its niche as a character study, focusing on how the harsh world can bring very different people together. De Niro and Thurman are both endearing and funny, in a clumsy sort of way, and Murray puts an oddly menacing (if not fully believable) air. Despite its charms, however, *Mad Dog and Glory* is yet another example of the "women as chattel" theme explored in films afar afield as *Indecent Proposal* and *Honeymoon in Vegas*. David Caruso, before his one-year-wonder stint on TV's "N.Y.P.D. Blue," is especially good as De Niro's police buddy. ★★★ $19.99

Mad Dog Morgan

(1978, 93 min, Australia, Philippe Mora) Dennis Hopper, a few years before he was accepted back in the Hollywood fraternity with *Blue Velvet*, traveled Down Under to make a few bucks in this explosively violent "western" saga. Playing the role with maniacal intensity, Hopper's Morgan is a man who, after killing a police chief, becomes an outlaw on the run and famous throughout the land for his daring and improbable escapes from the noose. An unusual but exciting actioner with Hopper in good form. ★★★

Mad Dogs and Englishmen

(1971, 119 min, GB, Pierre Adidge) Joe Cocker's (as mad an Englishman as ever there was) 1970 American tour with Leon Russell is put to film with excellence and flair. With both of the musicians at the pinnacles of their careers, the film shows Cocker belting out his classic renditions of "Feeling Alright," "With a Little Help from My Friends," and a legendary version of "The Letter." Russell is a master band leader, piano player and a Very Mysterious Presence. Great band, great vibes in one of the best "rockumentaries" ever made. ★★★

Mad Love

(1995, 99 min, US, Antonia Bird) Drew Barrymore and Chris O'Donnell star in what could have been, and should have been, a fun-loving teen rebel romp across the American

West, but is instead a tedious, soppy melodrama that makes a half-hearted attempt to address mental illness. O'Donnell plays the grade-A high school senior who helps his single dad keep the family together. Barrymore is the new kid in town, a raging rebel who spells trouble from the start. It's not hard to guess that O'Donnell falls for her and forsakes his comfy chemistry exam-laden life for the dangerous female newcomer. In and of itself, this is a well-worn and time-honored film contrivance. Add to it, however, an oh-too-trendy Seattle backdrop and a relentless grunge soundtrack that spits up a new song every 40 seconds and you get the feeling that the producers threw this together with tired formulas and Scotch tape. It just gets to be too much. ★ $14.99

Mad Max

(1979, 93 min, Australia, George Miller) The original adventures of Max, the Road Warrior, valiant law enforcer combatting the deranged highway marauders of a not-too-distant future. Mel Gibson stars in this nerve-bending classic of automotive madness. (Dubbed from Australian English into "American") ★★★

Mad Max Beyond Thunderdome

(1985, 106 min, Australia, George Miller & George Ogilvie) The last and least of the *Mad Max* trilogy, this movie still delivers some exciting action sequences, or at least half of it does. Directed in two parts by two different directors, the lines of division and talent show very clearly. While the first half of the film, directed by series veteran Miller, is along the lines of the previous two, with an angry Max (Mel Gibson) trying to survive in an authoritarian community called Bartertown, it later drags to a crawl when Max goes off into the desert and encounters a band of post-apocalyptic children awaiting the appearance of a savior, who turns out to look a lot like Max. The second half of the film is not terribly bad, but completely out of place with what preceeds it. The latter half's action sequences also pale in comparison to the flying duels Max must fight with a violent giant called Master Blaster in Bartertown's Thunderdome. The fun of the first half of the movie is also fueled by the presence of Tina Turner in her wildly overblown performance as Auntie Entity. Not a bad film altogether, but a sputtering end to what had been a high-octane series. ★★½ $14.99

The Mad Miss Manton

(1938, 80 min, US, Leigh Jason) Barbara Stanwyck and Henry Fonda appeared together for the first time (they were reunited in *You Belong to Me* and Preston Sturges' marvelous *The Lady Eve*) in this madcap mystery-screwball comedy. Stanwyck plays a zany socialite who, along with a group of friends, investigates a murder. Lots of fun. ★★★

Mad Monster Party

(1967, 94 min, US, Jules Bass) This off-the-wall oddity defies categorization: it's a tongue-in-cheek musical monster movie done in stop-motion animation. Dr. Frankenstien (appropriately vocalized by Boris Karloff) has decided to retire and invites all the monsters under his leadership to a convention where he will announce an heir to his evil throne. The cast, such as it is, includes the Mummy, Dracula, the Frankenstein monster and his mate (hilariously rendered by Phyllis Diller), the Werewolf and others. The plot is paper thin, but the one-liners and take-offs are witty and amusing. ★★★

Madame Bovary

(1934, 117 min, France, Jean Renoir) While not considered one of Renoir's best works, this faithful retelling of the Gustave Flaubert novel is still interesting for fans of both artists. In 1840, a young woman, eager to escape her dreary provincial life, marries a dull country doctor. As her situation becomes more desperate, however, she begins a series of affairs with other men; actions that cause her to become a tragic victim of her own romantic illusions and aspirations. Several reasons have been given for this film's failure: some point to the fact that Renoir was forced to cut over one hour from his final version, and others look to the inappropriate casting (too old for the part and excessively dramatic) of Valentine Tessier in the title role. (French with English subtitles) ★★½ $59.99

Madame Bovary

(1949, 115 min, US, Vincente Minnelli) Lavish screen version of Flaubert's celebrated novel about a 19th-century French housewife whose lust for social and financial power brings on her own doom. Jennifer Jones makes an alluring heroine, and James Mason, Van Heflin and Louis Jourdan also star. ★★★ $19.99

Madame Bovary

(1991, 130 min, France, Claude Chabrol) Isabelle Huppert stars in Chabrol's lushly photographed yet starkly realized adaptation of Gustave Flaubert's classic. Huppert delivers a restrained performance as Emma Bovary, a 19th-century woman whose lust for self-fulfillment sets her against a hypocritically pietistic society amd ultimately leads her to adultery. Her character is filled with contradictions, sometimes cold, calculating and intensely materialistic; other times convivial, passionate and vulnerable. Filmed in the countryside surrounding Rouen, the film convincingly cap-

tures the mood of Flaubert's France. (French with English subtitles) ★★½ $9.99

Madame Butterfly

(1996, 129 min, France, Frédéric Mitterrand) A sumptuous, wrenching filmization of Puccini's heartbreaking opera. Philadelphia's own Richard Troxell is quite good as that slime, Lt. Pinkerton, a horny jerk who buys a gorgeous fifteen-year-old geisha's hand in marriage, only to abandon her. Mitterand's camera direction is a bit uninspired in the early scenes, allowing only the beautiful exteriors and editing to tell us this ain't no stage version. In fact, the first act of the film is, while certainly engaging, a bit stagey; but the film is more assured and stylish as it progresses, becoming a rich, cinematic jewel of a film. The music is, of course, terrific, and Ying Huang is wonderful in the title role. She has a stunning voice, but she's not of the plant-my-feet-and-belt-it-out school of opera performance. She gives a full-blown, dramatic portrayal, and if you find yourself scrambling for a tissue by film's end, she's to blame. (Italian with English subtitles) ★★★½ $24.99

Madame Rosa

(1977, 105 min, France, Moshe Mizrahi) The touching story of a loving relationship between an aging Holocaust victim and former prostitute (Simone Signoret) and a young Arab boy she tends. Academy Award-winning Best Foreign Film, 1978. Also stars Constantin Costa-Gavras. (Dubbed) ★★★½ $24.99

Madame Satan

(1930, 116 min, US, Cecil B. DeMille) Not entirely successful in some of its parts, *Madame Satan* is a fascinating excursion into '30s cinema. Rather than displaying director DeMille's characteristically heavy touches, the film is reminiscent of Ernst Lubitsch, Noël Coward, Busby Berkeley and Alfred Hitchcock. Now that's a combination. Kay Johnson plays a wife who learns of husband's Reginald Denny's unfaithfulness. Feigning ignorance, she forces her husband's mistress Lillian Roth and his sidekick Roland Young (in a terrific performance) into a series of comedic escapades. But after Denny leaves her, Johnson is masquerading as the mysterious Madame Satan to get him back. After viewing a spectacular musical production number taking place en route and aboard a high-flying zeppelin, one would think they've seen it all. But DeMille has another wild card up his sleeve for an unbelievable finale. A pre-Code production, the film's themes of sexuality and adultery would have assured it could not have been made as is after 1934. ★★★½ $19.99

Madame Sin

(1971, 90 min, US, David Greene) Bette Davis has the title role in this made-for-TV espionage flick à la James Bond. Robert Wagner plays a former CIA agent deluded into assisting the evil Madame Sin in the theft of a Polaris submarine. Production design and sets nearly rival those of the Bond films and, for a change, good doesn't triumph over evil. Also with Denholm Elliott as Madame Sin's evil henchman. ★★½ $9.99

Madame Sousatzka

(1988, 122 min, GB, John Schlesinger) Shirley MacLaine gives a spirited performance as an eccentric and demanding piano teacher who dedicates herself to her new student – a gifted 15-year-old Indian boy. A lovely, lyrical film directed by Schlesinger with great sensitivity. Also with Peggy Ashcroft, Twiggy and Navin Chowdhry as the youth. ★★★ $19.99

Madame X

(1966, 100 min, US, David Lowell Rich) Sixth screen version of the weepy chestnut, this time around with Lana Turner as the woman with a past who sacrifices all for the sake of her son. Keir Dullea plays her offspring, a lawyer who unknowingly defends his mother. ★★ $14.99

Mädchen in Uniform

(1931, 89 min, Germany, Leontine Sagan) This landmark film dealing with a lesbian relationship between a sensitive student and her teacher still retains both its timeliness and power in dealing with this controversial subject. Written by Christa Winsloe, this legendary film is a sympathetically handled account of one girl's rebellion against suffocating discipline and sexual repression in a Prussian boarding school. (German with English subtitles) ★★★½ $24.99

Made for Each Other

(1939, 85 min, US, John Cromwell) Sentimental, heartwarming melodrama with James Stewart and Carole Lombard as newlyweds battling illness, poverty and a meddling mother-in-law (Lucille Watson). ★★½ $19.99

Made in America

(1993, 110 min, US, Richard Benjaman) Thanks to a couple of winning performances from Ted Danson and Whoopi Goldberg, what might easily have been just another insipid comedy from the Hollywood mill is instead a fun-loving, briskly paced and often hilarious romp. When Goldberg's daughter, Zora (Nia Long), discovers that she is the result of artificial insemination, she investigates only to discover that not only is her father white, but worse, he's Hal Jackson, the obnoxious, egotistical car dealer whose insane TV advertisements plague the local airwaves. She quickly goes to confront him with the fact and the hilarity begins. Of course, Danson and Goldberg slowly warm to each other and...well, you can guess the rest – life really did imitate art (for awhile, anyway). Will Smith savors his role as Zora's gawky but pure-hearted best friend. ★★★ $9.99

Made in Heaven

(1987, 103 min, US, Alan Rudolph) Sweetly romantic fantasy about a young man (Timothy Hutton) who dies, goes to Heaven, and falls in love with a new spirit (Kelly McGillis), who is about to be sent to Earth. Unbalanced but interesting handling of the subject of predestination from the director of *Choose Me* and *Trouble in Mind*. Watch for uncredited performances from Debra Winger and Ellen Barkin. ★★½ $9.99

M

Mademoiselle Striptease (or Please! Mr. Balzac)

(1957, 99 min, France, Marc Allégret) This amusing Brigitte Bardot romp has our buxom beauty as the daughter of a French official who seems to get into all kinds of trouble. First, she enters an amateur striptease contest and then becomes involved in the theft of a rare book from the Balzac museum. The film will not strain your mental capacity, but it's an enjoyable vehicle for BB fans. (French with English subtitles) ★★½

Madhouse

(1990, 90 min, US, Tom Ropelewski) A paltry black comedy about a married couple whose lives are turned upside-down by visiting relatives, neighbors, etc. There are about 15 minutes in the middle of this film which are truly funny, but the rest of the film is as uninviting as Kirstie Alley and John Larroquette's pain-in-the-ass houseguests. If these two successful TV stars continue to appear in trash like this, they'll never get off the small screen. ★½ $9.99

The Madness of King George

(1994, 105 min, GB, Nicholas Hytner) In one of the most entertaining, witty and literate history lessons one will ever encounter, author Alan Bennett's adaptation of his stage hit "The Madness of George III" is a sumptuously filmed and costumed historical epic which royally details the madness of a king, backstage power struggles, and the frivolity of ceremony. Giving a performance of great substance, emotional depth and humor, Nigel Hawthorne excels as George III, the British monarch who has just lost the American colonies and who is about to lose his mind. As the king succumbs to increasingly bizarre behavior under the watchful eye of his doctor (Ian Holm), a bemused court looks on, ambitious princes plot, and the faithful Queen Charlotte (the wonderful Helen Mirren) performs 18th-century damage control. In an impressive debut, director Hytner has a sharp eye for pageant and is meticulous in forging the relationships of his characters while simultaneously exposing Bennett's sardonic edge. On a side note, is it really true they changed the play's title for the American market because they thought filmgoers would think this a sequel? ★★★★ $19.99

Madonna: The Girly Show

(1993, 120 min, US) Filmed on location in Sydney, Australia, seductress/songstress Madonna bumps and grinds her way through a well-chosen selection of her hits, past and present. Highlights include the expected costume changes; a strip-bar opening number complete with topless dancer; a bacchanalian celebration of sexuality climaxing with Ms. Cicconne collapsing into a heap of writhing/undulating bodies; a '70s disco get-down session featuring an entrance atop a mirror ball; and a unique version of the song "Like a Virgin" that evokes images of a Marlene Dietrich cabaret performance. The bottom line: This video is hot! ★★★ $29.99

Madonna: Truth or Dare

(1991, 118 min, US, Alek Keshishian) Though not technically a documentary, this fascinating behind-the-scenes look at pop icon Madonna's worldwide "Blonde Ambition" tour seeks to reveal the singer in on- and offstage actions and interactions. And though she is the executive producer, therefore with much at stake, Madonna is to be credited with "opening up" and revealing much about herself in front of the camera — calculated as that may be. That same camera also captures some fabulous live performances, with Madonna singing some of her greatest hits. Also on hand are Madonna's dancers, relatives and friends; not to mention a gallery of famous names, from then-beau Warren Beatty to Sandra Bernhard to Kevin Costner, to whom Madonna "disses." Even those who aren't fans will come away with an appreciation of the talented and savvy entertainer. ★★★½ $14.99

The Madwoman of Chaillot

(1969, 132 min, US, Bryan Forbes) Katharine Hepburn heads an all-star cast in this hokey adaptation of the Jean Giradoux play. Kate is an eccentric "countess" no longer able to cope with the world's loss of innocence. With her streetpeople cohorts, she concocts a plan to get even with the corporate world. You really want to like it, but the film's good intentions get in its way — but oh, what a cast! Charles Boyer, Edith Evans, Paul Henreid, Yul Brynner, Richard Chamberlain and Danny Kaye are just a few of the featured luminaries. The basis for the Broadway musical "Dear World." ★★ $19.99

The Magic Christian

(1970, 95 min, GB, Joseph McGrath) The hilarious escapades of Peter Sellers as the world's wealthiest man, and Ringo Starr as his handpicked messiah, as they embark on a zany scheme to expose society's corruptibility. Cameo appearances by Raquel Welch, Yul Brynner, Roman Polanski and Christopher Lee round out an eccentric, all-star cast. This scathing indictment of avarice and the lust for power is dated in style, but not in substance. ★★★ $14.99

The Magic Flute

(1974, 134 min, Sweden, Ingmar Bergman) Bergman's sensuous adaptation of Mozart's magical operatic tale about a star-crossed couple and an impish man in search of a mate. Exquisitely performed and filmed. (German with Swedish and English subtitles) ★★★★ $29.99

Magic in the Water

(1995, 101 min, US, Rick Stevenson) An underwater E.T., this girl-meets-lake monster tale replaces Reeses with Oreos, substitutes the divorced mom with a divorced dad, and saves a lot of special effects money by hardly ever showing the creature. All that aside, this is a gentle family film about two kids and their dad, who while on vacation in northern Canada, encounter a mysterious underwater serpent who helps heal some family wounds and who exposes illegal toxic dumping at the same time. Mark Harmon heads a competent cast which includes a lovely performance by Sarah Wayne as the young girl. ★★ $19.99

The Magic Sword

(1962, 80 min, US, Bert I. Gordon) Loosely based on the story of St. George and the dragon, this romantic fairy tale unfolds when a young knight (Gary Lockwood) vows to rescue a damsel in distress. Armed with a magic sword, he begins a dangerous journey through an enchanted forest where seven deadly curses await him. The film also stars Basil Rathbone, Ed Wood, Jr., and TV horror movie hostess Vampira in a small role. ★★ $14.99

Magic Town

(1947, 103 min, US, William Wellman) Director Wellman invades Frank Capra's territory in this story of a pollster who finds a small, quiet town the perfect barometer for national polls. That is, until the town's notoriety changes everyone's outlook. With Capra's favorite actor, James Stewart, and Jane Wyman. ★★★ $19.99

Magical Mystery Tour

(1967, 60 min, GB, The Beatles) Sometimes called a rock Un Chien Andalou, The Fab Four's charmingly surreal musical chronicles their escapades on a psychedelic bus trip. Songs include "The Fool on the Hill," "I Am the Walrus" and the title tune. $19.99

The Magician

(1959, 102 min, Sweden, Ingmar Bergman) Set in 19th-century Sweden, this richly Gothic and visually exciting "thinking man's horror film" follows the supernatural exploits of a magician (Max von Sydow) and his troupe who are detained in a small village when his magical powers are disbelieved. The clash between truth and illusion, reality versus the supernatural and the dramatic contrasting the comic all contribute to make The Magician a landmark in film history. (Swedish with English subtitles) ★★★½ $29.99

The Magick Lantern Cycle

See: Kenneth Anger

The Magnificent Ambersons

(1942, 88 min, US, Orson Welles) Welles' follow-up to Citizen Kane is a shattering adaptation of Booth Tarkington's novel about the self-destruction of a turn-of-the-century aristocratic family. Joseph Cotten, Tim Holt, Anne Baxter and Agnes Moorehead, in a mesmerizing performance as Holt's maiden aunt, star in this butchered masterpiece (the studio edited 20 minutes from Welles' final cut). ★★★★ $19.99

Magnificent Obsession

(1954, 108 min, US, Douglas Sirk) One of the best of the '50s soap operas, and the first Ross Hunter-Douglas Sirk collaboration. Rock Hudson, in the role which made him a star, gives a strong portrayal of a careless playboy whose wastrel ways lead to an auto accident that blinds Jane Wyman. Dedicating his life to a "magnificent obsession," Hudson becomes a surgeon determined to restore Wyman's sight. Barbara Rush and especially Agnes Moorehead as Wyman's nurse are tops in support. Remake of the 1935 Irene Dunne-Robert Taylor tearjerker. ★★★ $14.99

The Magnificent Seven

(1960, 128 min, US, John Sturges) This American remake of Akira Kurosawa's *The Seven Samurai* stars Yul Brynner, Steve McQueen, James Coburn, Robert Vaughn, Charles Bronson, Horst Bucholtz and Brad Dexter as the title characters (there's a good trivia question!). There's action aplenty as seven American gunslingers come to the aid of a small Mexican village being terrorized by bandits (led by Eli Wallach). Crisp direction by Sturges and a memorable score by Elmer Bernstein. ★★★½ $14.99

The Magnificent Ambersons

Le Magnifique

(1974, 86 min, France, Philippe de Broca) Jean-Paul Belmondo plays a double role as both a hapless hack novelist and his macho fictional alter ego in this action-filled spoof of the super-spy genre. Jacqueline Bisset is his glamourous assistant with whom he falls in love. It's not art, and it isn't even *That Man from Rio*, but it is a fun adventure comedy. (Dubbed) ★★½

Magnum Force

(1973, 124 min, US, Ted Post) Clint Eastwood returns in this second Dirty Harry film, trying to uncover a conspiracy within the San Francisco police department involving a group of vigilante officers who execute notorious criminal suspects. Hal Holbrook costars as Harry's superior, who disagrees with Harry's unorthodox methods, which he equates with those of the vigilantes. While nothing could match the power and intensity of Don Siegel's original *Dirty Harry*, this sequel nevertheless

works as an entertaining, average action film. Eastwood is his usual laconic self, and a group of young police sharpshooters are admirably portrayed by a very young Tim Matheson, Robert Urich and David Soul. The film's most interesting point is its distinction between the work of the vigilantes and the violent work of Harry himself — a fine line indeed — and seems to be an attempt to explain the subtleties of the first film to its critics. Unfortunately, this film lacks the persuasive power it needs; the only people convinced of its merits and its message will be those who saw and enjoyed its predecessor. ★★½ $14.99

The Mahabharata

(1989, 318 min, GB, Peter Brook) Brook's epic undertaking of the Mahabharata, the Hindu story of the origins of the world, a massive tome which is over 15 times longer than the Bible. The result is nothing less than what we've come to expect from Brook: a brilliantly acted and thoughtfully directed epic with an ensemble cast from over 19 different countries and every continent. The running time of close to six hours — short considering the subject — has been broken down into three separate stories for the video release: "The Game of Dice" (97 min), "Exile in the Forest" (111 min) and "The War" (110 min). ★★★½ $99.99

Mahler

(1974, 115 min, GB, Ken Russell) Russell kept his normal excesses to a minimum in this sumptuously filmed and costumed biography of the famed Swedish composer Gustav Mahler. The film is a dazzling evocation of the loves, moods and music of the artist. Through flashbacks and beautiful dream imagery, it focuses on the tormented life and turbulent relationship he endured with his wife. Such Russellisms as a dream sequence with a Nazi Pope (a Nazi Pope?) do sneak through. On the whole, however, this is Russell in a mellow mood. ★★★

Mahogany

(1975, 109 min, US, Berry Gordy) An inferior, even ridiculous drama set in the fashion world with Diana Ross making it big as a model. Billy Dee Williams is her boyfriend, a community activist who disapproves of her profession. Looking like a fey Bernard Goetz, Anthony Perkins plays the photographer who discovers her and then goes all bitchy and neurotic when she rebukes his romantic overtures. Perkins presumedly plays a bisexual, as gossipy associates infer and from the suggestion of an awfully staged fight scene — which looks like a bad imitation of the wrestling match in *Women in Love* — between Perkins and Williams in which the latter inserts a phallic-shaped gun in the mouth of his almost willing adversary. Pure trash and not even fun on a camp level. ★ $14.99

Maid to Order

(1987, 92 min, US, Amy Jones) Agreeable Cinderella comedy with Ally Sheedy as a pampered rich girl whose father wishes she had never been born — and with the help of fairy godmother Beverly D'Angelo, it comes true. Kinda cute if you don't think about it too much. ★★½ $9.99

The Main Event

(1979, 109 min, US, Howard Zieff) Barbra Streisand and Ryan O'Neal reunited (after *What's Up Doc?*) for this tired comedy about a bankrupt perfume manufacturer who inherits the contract of a retired boxer. Not very funny, implausible with none of the chemistry between the two stars in their earlier outing, this is tough going even for die-hard Streisand fans. ★½ $14.99

Maitresse

(1976, 112 min, France, Barbet Schroeder) The kinky underground world of sado-masochism is revealed in this enjoyably shocking drama that will remind many of the sexual outlandishness of *Last Tango in Paris*. Gérard Depardieu stars as a burglar who breaks into the flat of Bulle Ogier, a professional sadist who, as a leather-clad, whip-snapping dominatrix, rules over her compliant stable of wealthy clients. A wickedly tantalizing fable about the darker side of love. An interesting item about the film is that the featured customers (all masked) are real Parisian masochists who paid to be in the film. (French with English subtitles) ★★★ $59.99

Major Barbara

(1941, 131 min, GB, Gabriel Pascal) George Bernard Shaw collaborated with director Pascal on this superb rendition of his poignant social comedy. Wendy Hiller is excellent as the daughter of a wealthy munitions manufacturer who, disillusioned with her father's world, joins the Salvation Army. A brilliant cast is rounded out by Rex Harrison, Robert Newton, Robert Morley and, in her film debut, Deborah Kerr. Filled with Shaw's unswerving and razor-sharp commentary. ★★★★ $39.99

Major League

(1989, 107 min, US, David S. Ward) Contrived though amiable baseball comedy with a few well-placed laughs about the new owner of the Cleveland Indians (Margaret Whitton) purposely making her team lose so she can move the team to Florida. Tom Berenger, Charlie Sheen, Corbin Bernsen and Wesley Snipes are just a few of the reasons they're so bad. ★★½ $9.99

Major League 2

(1994, 100 min, US, David S. Ward) Those who enjoyed the original baseball comedy should find many a laugh with this retread sequel. All the characters are back, but as the film opens, most have gone through changes. Charlie Sheen's "Wild Thing" has gone yuppie, Tom Berenger's seasoned catcher is now a coach, and Corbin Bernsen owns the team. The rest of the club is in misfit territory, too. And like in the first film, they have to band together to win. There's enough humor to satisfy the undemanding baseball fan, though Bob Uecker as a radio announcer and Randy Quaid as an initially gung-ho fan steal the share of laughs. ★★½ $9.99

Major Payne

(1995, 97 min, US, Nick Castle) About as funny as a night in war-torn Bosnia, *Major Payne* is a pointless remake of the so-so 1955 Charlton Heston military comedy *The Private War of Major Benson*, with an incredibly insipid

Denzel Washington as *Malcolm X*

Damon Wayans in the title role. Payne is a seemingly slow-witted career soldier who is booted out of the Army and sent to command a group of junior ROTC cadets. With a scenario that makes *Renaissance Man* seem like *M*A*S*H* by comparison, the story follows his mean-spirited efforts to help them win a military competition. Though there's enough blame to go around, most of the film's faults lie with Wayans's capacities as actor and co-author. The latter has given the former absolutely nothing to work with, and as such his performance is tedious and irritating. The script? At one point, Payne attempts to literally break the fingers of a five-year-old. Such wit. ★ $14.99

A Majority of One

(1962, 149 min, US, Mervyn LeRoy) An intimate stage piece, this schmaltzy but nevertheless beguiling comedy-drama only slightly misses its mark in the screen adaptation. Rosalind Russell – taking over the Tony Award-winning role played by Molly Goldberg herself, Gertrude Berg – plays Mrs. Jacoby, a Jewish widow from Brooklyn who accompanies her daughter and diplomat son-in-law to Japan, where she is romanced by a high-ranking Japanese businessman (played by Alec Guinness). It's distracting having Anglo thespian Guinness (as good as he may be) playing an Asian, but the film's observations on love, culture clashes and bigotry compensate. In support, Mae Questel and Marc Marno repeat their stage roles, with Marno very appealing as Eddie, a hipster servant. ★★½ $19.99

Make Mine Mink

(1960, 101 min, GB, Robert Asher) Terry-Thomas stars in this often hilarious farce about a retired army officer who becomes the leader of a philanthropic band of fur thieves. ★★★½

Make Room for Tomorrow

(1981, 106 min, France, Peter Kassovitz) The generation gap is explored in this comedy-drama about four generations of a family who gather to celebrate the birthday of their great grandfather. At the reunion, the eccentricities

of each seem just a little more outrageous than the last. (French with English subtitles) ★★★

Making Love

(1982, 113 min, US, Arthur Hiller) Sort of a breakthrough for American films, this slick but superficial romantic drama features Michael Ontkean as a successful doctor who leaves his wife (Kate Jackson) for a handsome writer (Harry Hamlin). One of the first Hollywood films to feature well-adjusted gay characters in nonsupporting roles, and to show two men kissing. With all its "good intentions," the story is at times soap opera-ish, but involving nonetheless. Good performances from its three lead players. ★★½ $69.99

Making Mr. Right

(1987, 95 min, US, Susan Seidelman) The ingredients for this film sure seemed right: John Malkovich and offbeat comic Ann Magnuson starring in Susan Seidelman's follow-up to *Desperately Seeking Susan*; what could go wrong? Well, just about everything, but the real tragedy here is the script. Magnuson plays a P.R. expert who is hired to help develop a human image for Chemtech Corporation's new android (Malkovich), but ends up clashing with the android's creator (also Malkovich) when she falls in love with the machine. ★ $14.99

The Making of Miss Saigon

(1991, 75 min, GB) "Miss Saigon," the London stage spectacular produced by Cameron Mitchell ("Les Misérables"), opened April 1991 on Broadway with advance ticket sales of over $30 million. What in this show could create such theatrical hysteria and unprecedented anticipation? This documentary attempts to explain its appeal and phenomenal success. By taking the camera behind the footlights and with interviews, rehearsal scenes and actual footage from the show, it helps reveal the creative powers and mechanical ingenuity that combine to create a spellbinding musical extravaganza. ★★★ $29.99

The Makioka Sisters

(1983, 110 min, Japan, Kon Ichikawa) Director Ichikawa breathtakingly adapted Junichiro Tanizaki's best-selling novel about the lives and loves of four sisters in 1930s Osaka. Brilliantly photographed, the film explores the sisters' efforts to sustain and come to terms with the passing of their proud customs, which have slowly slipped away – victims to encroaching Westernization in the ever-changing days of pre-war Japan. The story follows the two married sisters' valiant attempts to find a suitable husband for the third sister while the youngest one, rebelliously promiscuous, discovers and embraces the new freedoms available. (Japanese with English subtitles) ★★★★ $59.99

Malcolm

(1986, 86 min, Australia, Nadia Tass) This refreshingly funny Aussie import follows the madcap antics of part-time inventor Malcolm (played with elfish charm by Colin Friels), a naive young man who, after teaming up with a bank robber and his moll, uses his technical wizardry to pull off a series of hilarious heists. ★★★ $79.99

Malcolm X

(1992, 201 min, US, Spike Lee) Director Lee's most ambitious work to date, *Malcolm X* is an intense and highly accomplished biography of the slain religious and community leader. Featuring a tour de force performance by Denzel Washington as Malcolm, the film traces his life from his zoot suited-youth in the 1940s; to his imprisonment, where he was first introduced to the Muslim faith; to his rise as a disciple of Elijah Muhammad, the Supreme Minister of the Nation of Islam; to his life-changing pilgramage to Mecca; to his tragic assassination. Lee's film succinctly examines these stages of Malcolm's life, creating a fluid transition from each period to the next. As a storyteller, Lee has never been more focused, capturing Malcolm's conviction and the unrest of the era while viewing Malcolm's evolutionary process with unexpected objectivity. *Malcolm X* is not as incendiary as would be expected nor is it as controversial. Lee's big, complex and powerful film befits the life and legend of such a complicated and fervent man. ★★★★ $24.99

Male of the Century

(1979, 101 min, France, Claude Berri) Berri, the Renaissance man of "French Cinema Souffle," directed, wrote and stars in this pleasant comedy. It is the story of a befuddled chauvinist whose liberated wife is kidnapped by bank robbers. Taken from an idea by Milos Forman. (French with English subtitles) ★★½

Malice

(1993, 107 min, US, Harold Becker) Alec Baldwin plays a brilliant surgeon newly arrived to a small New England town. He rents a room from married couple Nicole Kidman and college professor Bill Pullman. In a nasty series of events, Baldwin unnecessarily operates on Kidman, initiating a multimillion dollar lawsuit. But this is only half of it. And what begins as a slow-paced melodrama quickly blossoms into a cagey psychological thriller complete with figure-eight plot twists and baffling detective work. Though the denouement may not surprise hard-core fans of mysteries in the *Body Heat* mold, the film takes wicked delight in its crafty composition. Baldwin and Kidman are admirable, but it's Pullman who ties the film together with his sleuthing academic. ★★★ $19.99

Malicious

(1973, 97 min, Italy, Salvatore Samperi) Laura Antonelli stars in this spicy though abrasive sex comedy as a housekeeper hired by a widower to look after him and his three sons. But she soon becomes the object of desire for all the men in the house, including the youngest, a 14-year-old coming of age, and the father, with his own plans for courtship and marriage. (Dubbed) ★★½ $49.99

Mallrats

(1995, 96 min, US, Kevin Smith) Director Smith's follow-up to his witty *Clerks* is a disappointing but not entirely unentertaining entry into the disaffected youth genre. The action is moved from Hell's shopping strip to Hell's suburban shopping mall, from black and white to color reminiscent of colorization. The film opens as the two central characters, Brodie and T.S. (Jeremy London and Jason Lee), are dumped by their respective girlfriends Rene and Brandi (Shannon Doherty and Claire Forlani). Our protagonists would get on with their lives if they had any. That not being the case, they speed to their local mall, where fate, chance and an odd assortment of henchmen...er, characters (many in exile from *Clerks*) provide our antiheroes with the means of retribution and reconciliation. The film opens flatly and often feels forced, though it does deliver a few authentic moments at the most unexpected times. ★★ $19.99

Malou

(1983, 94 min, West Germany, Jeanine Meerapfel) Hannah lives with her husband in West Germany. Her life and marriage are affected, however, by her obsession with her dead mother, Malou, whose frantic life included a marriage to a Jew during Hitler's reign and her efforts to save him. Told through flashbacks, the film explores the relationship between the two women's lives and how Hannah deals with her present condition. The slow pacing and obvious dramatics rarely live up to its promising premise. (German with English subtitles) ★★

The Maltese Falcon

(1941, 100 min, US, John Huston) Huston made his impressive directorial debut with this classic mystery and third screen version of Dashiell Hammett's novel. Humphrey Bogart stars as Sam Spade, tough-guy private eye whose investigation into the death of his partner leads him to tangle with femme fatale Brigid O'Shaughnessy (the ravishing Mary Astor) and underworld art collector Kasper Gutman (Sydney Greenstreet in his Oscar-nominated film debut). Huston's film is awash in shadowy black and white which only heightens the tension brought about by the mysterious goings-on in the search for the elusive black bird, a jewel-encrusted statuette which

leaves a trail of corpses in its wake. One of the first films of the budding noir genre, and one of the best. ★★★★ $19.99

Mama, There's a Man in Your Bed

(1989, 111 min, France, Coline Serreau) Released theatrically under its less wieldy French title, *Romuald et Juliette*, this engaging social comedy, directed by Serreau (*Three Men and a Cradle*), is the story of a very unlikely love between a CEO from the "white" side of the tracks and a poor black cleaning lady with five kids (all from different husbands). Cuckolded by his wife and ousted from his executive position in a yogurt company, our privileged young man finds comfort, sympathy and a comrade-in-arms with the charming black woman. Their alliance soon blossoms into romantic love in this sweet, surprisingly entertaining farce that features several spirited performances and a fine blues soundtrack. (French with English subtitles) ★★★ $89.99

Mama Turns 100

(1978, 100 min, Spain, Carlos Saura) Wildly imaginative, this sly black comedy is set in a cavernous house in rural Spain where a family prepares to celebrate the 100th birthday of their elderly matriarch. But this familial celebration is not as innocent as one might expect: the wacky children are bent on making this birthday her last, but the eccentric and shrewd Mama has her own devious plans. Geraldine Chaplin stars in this circuitous tale of greed, power and money. (Spanish with English subtitles) ★★★ $59.99

The Mambo Kings

(1992, 104 min, US, Arne Glimcher) Set to the pulsating rhythms of a Latin beat, *The Mambo Kings* opens like gangbusters and rarely lets go. Based on the Pulitzer Prize-winning novel "The Mambo Kings Play Songs of Love," by Oscar Hijuelos, this stirring film adaptation has the look and feel of a 1950s musical, which only enhances its style. Armand Assante and heartthrob Antonio Banderas are musician brothers from Cuba who flee their homeland and venture to the uncertainty of New York City's nightclubs and ballrooms. Most of the film centers on the brothers' attempts to get ahead, which culminates into a lucky break: an appearance on "I Love Lucy" (Desi Arnaz, Jr. appears as his father). If the film falters at all, it's during the last half hour, which echoes tragic melodramatic moments from musicals past. But it's easily overlooked. There's an outstanding film score, featuring some terrific mambo numbers, and a haunting ballad, "Beautiful Maria of My Soul." ★★★½ $9.99

Mambo Mouth

(1992, 60 min, US, Thomas Schlamme) With razor-sharp satire and hilariously inspired portrayals of the diverse personas of the American Latino, John Leguizamo proves that he is a talent to be reckoned with in this hugely entertaining video adapted from his off-Broadway show. A skilled critic, Leguizamo creates six different aspects of the Latino — from the sexual bravura of a misogynist macho male, to a goofy 14-year-old homeboy's first sexual experience with a prostitute, as well as an acid-tongued, hip-swiveling prosti-

tute. A wonderfully revealing commentary on the self-image and perceptions of the Latino in America. ★★★ $19.99

Mame

(1974, 131 min, US, Gene Saks) The Broadway musical "Mame" is one of the most endearing of all stage shows — which benefitted greatly from Angela Lansbury's immortal performance. Unfortunately, there's little magic to this flat screen verison, with Lucille Ball miscast as Auntie Mame. Robert Preston makes a good Beau, and Bea Arthur and Jane Connell repeat their roles as, respectively, Vera and Agnes Gooch. Another instance in which Hollywood outsmarted itself by replacing the star of a stage hit. ★★½ $14.99

Mamma Roma

(1962, 110 min, Italy, Pier Paolo Pasolini) Anna Magnani is a heartrending revelation in this intensely moving neorealist urban drama. Magnani plays a poor but tenacious individualist who, despite her sad eyes and an arduous life, never loses her vitality, her hearty laugh nor the passionate love she has for her son. A former prostitute, she longs for a middle-class existence for her long estranged teenaged son, but when a former pimp threatens to expose her past, she is forced back on the streets. A disquieting tale set amidst the gloom of a crime- and poverty-plagued modern high-rised Rome. In his second feature, Pasolini adheres to the serious filmmaking style evident in his debut *Accatone!* — characterized by a tough, uncompromising narrative and a simplistic though well-crafted visual acumen — rather than the elaborate and stylistic flourishes of his later works. (Italian with English subtitles) ★★★½ $79.99

A Man, a Woman and a Killer

(1975, 95 min, US, Rick Schmidt & Wayne Wang) This collaboration with northern California filmmaker Schmidt and Wang is a beguiling, Godard-influenced meditation of a film about the making of the film. Essentially a two-character story, the film explores the relationship, both within the story as well as the rehearsals, between a paranoid man, his girlfriend and his imagined assassin. The pacing is slow and the "cut and paste" narrative style will agitate some, but overall the film is an interesting primer for Wang's future films. ★★ $59.99

A Man and a Woman

(1966, 102 min, France, Claude Lelouch) This Oscar-winning film is a joy to watch and a must for all people in love. Anouk Aimée and Jean-Louis Trintignant are wonderful as a widow and widower who meet at a boarding school for their children. A simple and heartwarming contemporary love story. (Dubbed) ★★★½ $19.99

A Man and a Woman: 20 Years Later

(1986, 120 min, France, Claude Lelouch) Anouk Aimee and Jean-Louis Trintignant reprise their wonderful characters from Lelouch's classic love story, *A Man and a Woman*. But the 20 years have both dimmed their attractiveness as well as the ability and even sanity of the director. The two ex-lovers are reunited in an attempt to make a film

M

Man Bites Dog

about their long-gone love affair. Throw in an escaped mental patient, a murder and a desert scene and you end up with a true mess. (French with English subtitles) ★½ $19.99

Man Bites Dog

(1992, 96 min, The Netherlands, Remy Belvaux) Morbidly funny is probably the best way to describe this amoral mockumentary about a poetry-reciting serial killer with a heart of gold whose sadistic exploits are recorded by a film crew. While finding themselves both repulsed and fascinated, the filmmakers in this "cinema veritasteless" spoof are drawn into the likable maniac's perverse pastime. Some viewers may be put off by the film's excruciatingly slow pace, but it seems a necessary device for the filmmakers to capture the rhythm of this maniac's life. A brutal, vulgar, repellent open sore of a film that pushes its NC-17 rating to the furthest. ★★★ $19.99

A Man Called Peter

(1955, 119 min, US, Henry Koster) A remarkable performance by Richard Todd highlights this sensitive biography of Peter Marshall, a Scottish minister who became chaplain to the U.S. Senate. ★★★ $19.99

A Man Escaped

(1956, 102 min, France, Robert Bresson) A riveting drama set almost entirely within a prison cell, *A Man Escaped* stars François Leterrier as a Resistance fighter who is captured and imprisoned by the Nazis and is sentenced to be executed. As he charts his plans for escape, a young boy is placed in his cell, and the man must decide whether to trust the youth or kill him as a possible spy. Rather than resorting to artificial film devices to create tension (music, editing), the film successfully relies entirely on the central character and his studied actions. Based on a true story. (French with English subtitles) ★★★½ $29.99

Man Facing Southeast

(1987, 108 min, Argentina, Elisio Subiela) A fascinating sci-fi drama exploring the role of psychiatry in the modern world and the struggle of the individual vs. society. At a Buenos Aires mental institution, a man mysteriously appears, claiming he is from another planet. Though not officially a patient, he is regarded

as just another delirious paranoid by his psychiatrist and the staff. It is only after a series of intellectual verbal sparrings between patient and doctor, and an otherworldly spiritual calm he casts on the other inmates, that the doctor begins to suspect that his story could very well be true. A compassionate, grown-up fairy tale. (Spanish with English subtitles) ★★★

A Man for All Seasons

(1966, 120 min, GB, Fred Zinnemann) This splendid film version of Robert Bolt's play about the conflict between Sir Thomas More and King Henry VIII is one of the outstanding films of the decade. Paul Scofield gives a mesmerizing, Oscar-winning performance as More, and is brilliantly supported by the likes of Robert Shaw as Henry, Orson Welles as Cardinal Wolsey and Wendy Hiller as More's devoted wife. The film was awarded six Oscars and is a must for all those interested in rich, historical dramas. ★★★★ $19.99

A Man for All Seasons

(1988, 150 min, US, Charlton Heston) Sturdy remake of the classic 1966 film, with Charlton Heston in a fine performance as Britain's ill-fated Chancellor of England, Thomas More. Also with Vanessa Redgrave, Richard Johnson and John Gielgud. ★★★ $79.99

The Man from Nowhere (L'Homme de Nulle Part)

(1937, 98 min, France, Pierre Chenal) This unjustly forgotten black comedy deftly combines elements of Pagnol's rural tales like "The Fanny Trilogy" with Carné's satirical bent in *Bizarre, Bizarre*. When a quiet young man, married to an unforgiving wife and henpecked by his shrewish mother, is mistaken for being dead, he decides to remain in that state and start life anew in Rome. Unfortunately with his new identity comes new problems. Adapted from Luigi Pirandello's only novel and filmed entirely in Italy. (French with English subtitles) ★★★ $59.99

The Man from Snowy River

(1982, 115 min, Australia, George Miller) Based on a beloved Australian poem, Miller's splendid adventure film spins the tale of a young mountain horseman who faces the challenge of snaring a valuable runaway colt. Tom Burlinson and Kirk Douglas (in a dual role) star in this inspirational paean to the majesty of the Australian landscape and the ruggedness of its inhabitants. ★★★ $14.99

A Man in Love

(1987, 108 min, France, Diane Kurys) Kurys' long anticipated follow-up to her critically acclaimed *Entre Nous* is a mildly disappointing but interesting love story set within the filming of a movie in Italy. This film-within-a-film stars Peter Coyote as a married American actor who

falls in love with Greta Scacchi, his on-screen lover. Kurys creates a romantic and sensual world where the fantasies of film overtake reality. Jamie Lee Curtis co-stars as Coyote's abandoned wife. (Filmed in English) ★★½

The Man in the Gray Flannel Suit

(1956, 153 min, US, Nunnally Johnson) Extremely competent film version of Sloan Wilson's novel examining Madison Avenue mores, as seen through the eyes of go-getter Gregory Peck. A fine cast includes Jennifer Jones, Fredric March, Marisa Pavan and Lee J. Cobb. ★★★ $39.99

The Man in the Iron Mask

(1939, 119 min, US, James Whale) Alexander Dumas' swashbuckling tale of sibling rivalry between France's King Louis XIV and his twin brother, raised by the Three Musketeers, makes for high-spirited adventure. Whale directs with a sure hand, making the production both exciting and smart. ★★★ $14.99

The Man in the Moon

(1991, 99 min, US, Robert Mulligan) From director Mulligan comes a sweet-natured, gentle family drama set in the rural South. With the same locale, tone and youthful themes explored in his classic *To Kill a Mockingbird*, Mulligan's thoroughly satisfying coming-of-age tale centers on two sisters growing up in the 1950s. As the two siblings who fall in love with the same boy-next-door, Reese Witherspoon and Emily Warfield give glowing portrayals of teenage uncertainty and familial anxiety. Sam Waterston gives a passionately intense performance as their father. Though *Man in the Moon* is not in a league with *Mockingbird*, it does suggest Mulligan has artistically returned to peak form. ★★★ $14.99

The Man in the Silk Hat

(1983, 96 min, France, Maud Linder) Max Linder, France's most popular comedian of the silent era, is lovingly remembered in this funny and insightful documentary made by his 50-year-old daughter, Maud. Through numerous excerpts from his two-reelers and features, we rediscover Linder's comic genius and enjoy his infectious humor. From his slapstick antics and pratfalls to his work behind the camera, we learn of a man of whom Charles Chaplin once said, "He was my professor." (Narrated in English) ★★★ $24.99

The Man in the White Suit

(1952, 84 min, GB, Alexander MacKendrick) Another one of Alec Guinness' peerless '50s comedies. Here he stars as an unassuming lab assistant who invents a miracle fabric that can be woven into indestructible cloth. The potential catastrophe that this poses for clothing manufacturers pits Guinness against the industry in a Chaplinesque battle which serves as a witty and incisive chastisement against the greed of capitalism. ★★★★ $9.99

The Man Inside

(1990, 93 min, US, Bobby Roth) Intriguing political thriller with Jürgen Prochnow as a German reporter who goes undercover at a right-wing tabloid to expose its unethical operating practices. Peter Coyote costars as an embittered veteran at the rag who takes

Prochnow under his wing. Also with Nathalie Baye and Philip Anglim. ★★★ $19.99

Man Is Not a Bird

(1965, 80 min, Yugoslavia, Dusan Makavejev) The *enfant terrible* of Eastern European cinema, this, Makavejev's first feature, is a delirious satire on the state of Communism as well as a humorous celebration of guiltless eroticism (a theme which runs throughout all his works). An engineer gets a job in a bleak industrial town and there, meets and falls in love with his landlord's daughter. The young woman, a carefree and impetuous individual, proves to be the undoing of the man. An amusing highpoint in all of the wild proceedings is the crosscutting of Beethoven's "Ode to Joy" being performed in a factory with our heroes frantically making love. (Serbian with English subtitles) ★★★½ $69.99

A Man Like Eva

(1983, 89 min, West Germany, Radu Gabrea) Eva Mattes turns in a startling opposite-gender performance as a thinly disguised R.W. Fassbinder-like film director who loves, dominates and even terrorizes his cast and crew. This absorbing drama charts the inevitable self-destruction of an artist who longed for love but could not receive it. (German with English subtitles) ★★½ $79.99

Man of a Thousand Faces

(1957, 122 min, US, Joseph Pevney) James Cagney scores another triumph in a biographical role, this time as silent screen star Lon Chaney. The film divides its time between Chaney's personal life and his career: effectively re-creating some of Chaney's best-known roles; and, somewhat melodramatically, detailing his two marriages. Dorothy Malone plays his first, troubled wife; and Jane Greer is his beloved second wife. Like Cagney's *Yankee Doodle Dandy*, this film is an affectionate tribute to its subject. ★★★ $14.99

Man of Aran

(1934, 77 min, US, Robert J. Flaherty) Flaherty's lifelong cinematic interest in documenting the resilient efforts of man in his battle against a hostile enviornment continues in this brilliant chronicle set in the barren wind- and surf-swept islands of Aran — situated off the western coast of Ireland. Two years in the making, the film dramatically captures the constant struggle of the independently minded people who must conquer the rough forces of nature to insure their simple survival. ★★★★ $29.99

Man of Flowers

(1984, 110 min, Australia, Paul Cox) An unusual Australian black comedy. Norman Kaye stars as a sexually repressed lover of art and flowers who, each Wednesday, pays a beautiful artist's model to perform an impassioned striptease to the strains of classical music. His lonely life, caused by childhood sexual traumas, is enlivened and upset as he reluctantly becomes involved with her tumultuous personal life. Weirdly funny, with a hypnotic, ever-present classical score. ★★★

Man of La Mancha

(1972, 130 min, US, Arthur Hiller) Another in a long line of dreadful screen adaptations of classic Broadway musicals. In the same league as *Mame*, *A Chorus Line* and *A Little Night Music*, this is probably the worst offender, as a brilliant theatre piece has been reduced to a deadened bore. Peter O'Toole, who was so good in the musical *Goodbye, Mr. Chips*, is embarrassingly bad as Don Quixote; though not half as embarrassing as Sophia Loren as Dulcinea. Only James Coco as Sancho captures the spirit of the stage production. Where, oh where, was Richard Kiley? ★ $19.99

Man of Marble

(1977, 160 min, Poland, Andrzej Wajda) Made just before the emergence of the Solidarity movement, Wajda's look at the fate of the worker in Communist Poland was slightly ahead of its time. Employing a documentary-like style, Wajda follows a young filmmaker as she unearths the history of Radziwiloowicz, a bricklayer who, in the Stalinist 1950s, was exalted to the lionized stature of worker-hero only to be later crushed as an enemy of the state. Well-directed and well-acted, the film is a fascinating look into the machinations of the Polish bureaucracy, but it unfortunately suffers as a result of its weighty running time. ★★★½ $29.99

A Man of No Importance

(1994, 98 min, GB, Suri Krishnamma) Albert Finney shines in this slender but engrossing drama as Alfie Byrne, a seemingly happy-go-lucky bus conductor who undergoes a late midlife crisis and reawakening. Set in Dublin in the early 1960s, the story follows bachelor and deeply closeted gay man Alfie, who quietly lives with his sister (Brenda Fricker), keeps his passengers amused with poetry readings, and harbors a crush for Bobby (Rufus Sewell), a handsome coworker. Alfie's life takes a turn when he organizes a community theatre presentation of Oscar Wilde's "Salome," which ultimately inspires him to confront his true sexual desires. A character study of limited insight which celebrates life and individuality, *A Man of No Importance* manages to succeed in spite of its dramatic shortcomings by the sheer force of Finney's acting prowess. Tara Fitzgerald also stars as a passenger Alfie persuades to star in his production and with whom he falls unrealistically in puppy love. ★★½ $19.99

Man of the House

(1995, 98 min, US, James Orr) Attempting a film comeback, Chevy Chase abandons his smart-aleck screen persona and instead goes the Disney route appearing as yet another adult upstaged and outsmarted by a precocious adolescent. Where's *Fletch* when you really need him? TV's "Home Improvement" co-star and teen idol *du jour* Jonathan Taylor Thomas plays 12-year-old son to Farrah Fawcett's divorced mom. Their years of togetherness is intruded upon when U.S. Attorney Chase moves in with hopes of marrying Fawcett. But Thomas has other plans, which includes keeping the adults in separate beds and forcing Chevy to join a father-son Indian scout troop to further humiliate him. With

only a few laughs scattered about, the film isn't helped by Thomas' whining or flat direction by Orr. ★★ $14.99

Man of the Year

(1995, 90 min, US, Dirk Shafer) A *Spinal Tap* for the homo set! Witty, dramatic and slyly humorous, this faux documentary follows the unrobing success and sexual coming out of Dirk Shafer, *Playgirl's* 1992 Man of the Year. Cleverly structed by Shafer, the film turns the tables on his real-life achievements by restaging them in documentary fashion. Ruggedly handsome with piercing blue eyes, blond hair and delicately rippling muscles, Dirk ascended the ranks of "straight" nude modeling to become one of *Playgirl's* favorite pin-ups. The tale unfolds as Dirk comes out and the film proceeds to recount the event leading up to the "hoax." Adding to the "reality" of the film is actual footage from numerous TV talk shows and interviews with his parents (both played by actors). The slapdash comedy works more often than not, though the film drags a bit near the end and is quite prudish, but nonetheless *Man of the Year* works as an example for any gay or lesbian person coming to public grips with their sexuality. ★★★ $59.99

The Man on the Eiffel Tower

(1949, 85 min, US, Burgess Meredith) A highly suspenseful psychological thriller about a police inspector (Charles Laughton) playing mental cat-and-mouse games with a suspected murderer (Franchot Tone). Filmed in Paris. ★★★½ $19.99

Man Trouble

(1992, 90 min, US, Bob Rafelson) Check your expectations at the door for this romantic comedy that heralds the reunion of superstar Jack Nicholson and the man who directed him in *Five Easy Pieces* and *The Postman Always Rings Twice*. Nicholson stars as a dog trainer who becomes involved with a prima donna (Ellen Barkin) caught up in underworld affairs. Though critically lambasted upon its theatrical release, the film is not so much bad as it is disappointing; it simply cannot sustain the burden of being a "minor" movie with

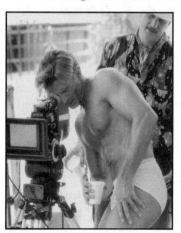

Man of the Year

M

major talent. Also with Beverly D'Angelo, Harry Dean Stanton, Michael McKean and Veronica Cartwright. ★★ $19.99

The Man Who Came to Dinner

(1941, 112 min, US, William Keighley) Monty Woolley re-creates his acclaimed stage role in this gloriously funny adaptation of the Kaufman and Hart stage hit. Woolley is at his acerbic best as a famed critic who visits the small-town home of Billie Burke and family and is forced to stay after an accident makes him immobile. The epitome of the unwanted house guest, he proceeds to run everyone's life and sends the household into hysteria. Bette Davis took a supporting role as Woolley's secretary, and Ann Sheridan, Jimmy Durante and Mary Wickes also star. But this is Woolley's show all the way, and it is one of the funniest performances of the 1940s. ★★★½ $19.99

The Man Who Captured Eichmann

(1996, 96 min, US, William A. Graham) The true story of the Israeli Mossad agent who led the operation to capture the mastermind behind the system used to transport millions of Jews to the Nazi death camps makes for a thrilling and thought-provoking made-for-cable movie. Adolf Eichmann (Robert Duvall in a terrific performance) is living in anonymity in Argentina with his family. After a concentration camp survivor reports meeting someone who may be Eichmann at a cafe, a commando squad is sent to Buenos Aires to kidnap him and bring him back to Israel to stand trial. Equally divided between action and dialogue, the first half of the film concerns the mechanics of grabbing the Nazi while the second half examines the team's wait for an opportunity to leave the country. This wait gives the lead commando (Arliss Howard) the chance to examine his own personal motivation for taking the mission while at the same time interrogating Eichmann and trying to understand how a human being could do what he did. Far from being the monster everyone believes, he discovers that Eichmann is really only a petty bureaucrat ultimately concerned with meeting his quotas. A fascinating look at the banality of evil. ★★★½ $102.99

The Man Who Could Work Miracles

(1937, 86 min, US, Lothar Mendes) Enchanting adaptaion of H.G. Wells' story about an "ordinary little fellow" endowed with the power to work miracles. Roland Young (best known as Topper) is engaging as the mild-mannered miracle man. ★★★ $19.99

The Man Who Fell to Earth

(1976, 140 min, GB, Nicolas Roeg) David Bowie stars as the frail and mysterious visitor from another planet who unknowingly threatens American industry with his powers. A tremendously original sci-fi drama presented with the surreal and mind-boggling sensitivities of Nicolas Roeg. Also stars Candy Clark, Buck Henry and Rip Torn. ★★★ $19.99

The Man Who Knew Too Much

(1934, 75 min, GB, Alfred Hitchcock) Based on a Bulldog Drummond story, this fast-paced thriller stars a villainous Peter Lorre (in his first English-speaking role) as a kidnapper who snares an innocent couple's child in order to insure their silence about a planned assassination attempt. Film historians have long argued the comparative merits of this version versus its 1956 remake; see for yourself the different approaches Hitchcock took at varied points in his career. ★★★ $12.99

The Man Who Knew Too Much

(1956, 120 min, US, Alfred Hitchcock) While vacationing in French Morocco, James Stewart and wife Doris Day become embroiled in a case of international intrigue, and with the kidnapping of their youngest son, are thrust into the very heart of a dangerously murderous scheme. An invigorating and suspenseful remake of Hitchcock's own 1934 thriller. Stewart and Day offer typically endearing performances which add to the flavor of this slick bag of tricks. ★★★½ $14.99

The Man Who Loved Women

(1978, 119 min, France, François Truffaut) This bittersweet comedy, the inspiration for the American remake (remember, the one with Burt Reynolds?) is most aptly served by Truffaut. Gallic enchantment as the female of the species plagues Charles Denner, the continually tempted skirt-chaser who seeks to transcribe his romantic legacy. (French with English subtitles) ★★★ $19.99

The Man Who Shot Liberty Valance

(1962, 122 min, US, John Ford) A classic study of the character of man and the nature of convenient truths. James Stewart is catapulted into political prominence when he's credited with ridding a frontier town of a murderous villain. Stewart and John Wayne represent different codes of honor; Lee Marvin is the common evil, to be dealt with as conscience dictates; and Vera Miles is the woman sought as helpmate and prize. Strong support by an exceptional cast, including Edmond O'Brien, Andy Devine, Woody Strode, Strother Martin, Lee Van Cleef and Jeanette Nolan. Excellent direction by Ford. ★★★★ $14.99

The Man Who Would Be King

(1975, 127 min, US, John Huston) Rudyard Kipling's exhilarating yarn of the daring exploits of two English soldiers in colonial India. Sean Connery and Michael Caine star as the ambitious explorers who attempt to infiltrate an ancient land and establish themselves as deities. Exotic locales, hair-raising adventures and deft direction make this one of Huston's finest. (Available letterboxed and pan & scan) ★★★½ $19.99

Man with a Cross

(1943, 88 min, Italy, Roberto Rossellini) Made under Fascist control and later rejected by Rossellini, this drama deals with the Italian expeditionary forces on the Russian Front during the summer of 1942. The story focuses on a saintly chaplain who tends to both the spiritual and physical needs of the Italian soldiers, as well as to the peasants during a Russian artillery bombing. (Italian with English subtitles) ★★½ $59.99

Man with a Movie Camera

(1928, 90 min, USSR, Dziga Vertov) A seminal and still controversial film which attempts to create a cinematic reality by "simply" depicting a day in the life of Moscow. But director Vertov, fascinated by the possibilities of the medium, utilizes editing, fast/slow motion, split screen and superimposition to distort the very reality he seeks to represent. An exciting, surreal compendium which explores the relation between cinema, actuality and history. ★★★½ $74.99

The Man with Bogart's Face

(1980, 111 min, US, Robert Day) Bogie look-alike Robert Sacchi stars as a fledgling private eye whose business increases dramatically due to his unique chiseled features. Soon, he finds himself deluged with requests to locate a pair of priceless blue sapphires in a Maltese Falcon-esque caper. A pleasant if inconsequential mystery comedy which playfully acknowledges its noir roots. The cast includes Franco Nero, Michelle Phillips, Olivia Hussey, Sybil Danning and Herbert Lom. ★★½ $59.99

The Man with One Red Shoe

(1985, 100 min, US, Stan Dragoti) One of the least successful of the many American adaptations of French comedies — in this instance, The Tall Blond Man with One Black Shoe. Tom Hanks plays a violinist mistaken for a secret agent. Also with Lori Singer, Jim Belushi and Carrie Fisher. ★½ $9.99

The Man with the Golden Arm

(1955, 119 min, US, Otto Preminger) Frank Sinatra received an Oscar nomination for his powerful performance as a drug addict trying to go straight. Preminger's stirring drama pulls no punches. Eleanor Parker is terrific as Sinatra's handicapped wife. ★★★ $19.99

The Man with the Golden Gun

(1974, 125 min, GB, Guy Hamilton) Roger Moore's second outing as 007 finds him a little more comfortable in the role that he soon got too comfortable with. A distant cousin of Bond creator Ian Fleming, Christopher Lee, plays the titular character, a paid assassin named Scaramanga, abetted in no small way by his major domo Nick Nack (Herve Villechaize). ★★½ $14.99

The Man with Two Brains

(1983, 90 min, US, Carl Reiner) Steve Martin and Reiner struck comic gold a third time in this improbable but hilarious spoof with Martin as a scientist who falls in love with a brain in a jar, and begins the search for the perfect body to harbor it. Kathleen Turner also stars as Martin's faithless wife, and Sissy Spacek gives voice to the brain. ★★★ $9.99

The Man without a Face

(1993, 125 min, US, Mel Gibson) In an unusual choice to make his directorial debut, Gibson stars in this involving, surprisingly downbeat adaptation of Isabelle Holland's novel. Gibson plays a disfigured loner whose life and appearance are a mystery to his New England neighbors. When young Nick Stahl learns of Gibson's possible past as a teacher, he lobbies him for private tutoring. Against his better judgment, Gibson agrees, and a frienship soon develops between the two. Gibson serves as a commendable mentor and friend until news of previous child molestation charges begin to surface. Gibson gives an earnest performance as the compassionate tutor, but the film, though competently produced, is sometimes as evasive as its titular character. ★★½ $14.99

Man's Best Friend

(1993, 87 min, US, John Lafia) One of the best "killer animal" movies since *Jaws*, this extremely well-mounted sci-fi shocker stars Ally Sheedy as an ambitious TV reporter who goes after an exclusive on a suspected animal rights violator (Lance Henricksen) and winds up in the possession of his prize experiment: a genetically altered superdog with a psychotic streak and a short fuse. Special mention goes to newcomer Max the Canine Terminator, whose performance makes Lassie look like a dog and renders Barney's acting efforts positively prehistoric! ★★★ $14.99

Man's Favorite Sport

(1963, 121 min, US, Howard Hawks) Rock Hudson stars in this entertaining, amusing comedy as a renowned fishing expert who really can't stand the sport or the great outdoors. When he agrees to make an appearance at a fishing tournament, public relations director Paula Prentiss has her hands full making Rock an outdoorsman. An amusing spoof on sports and manhood with many well-placed jabs. ★★★ $14.99

The Manchurian Candidate

(1962, 126 min, US, John Frankenheimer) Richard Condon's best-seller about a brainwashed Korean War vet out to do our country dirt is superbly brought to the screen by Frankenheimer, who would explore similar territory two years later with *Seven Days in May*. Laurence Harvey, Janet Leigh, Frank Sinatra and Henry Silva star, with Angela Lansbury as the ruthless wife of a McCarthy-esque politician, giving a most chilling and mesmerizing performance of deception and betrayal. ★★★★ $19.99

Mandela

(1987, 135 min, US, Philip Saville) Gripping, first-rate made-for-cable production about the life of South African leader Nelson Mandela. Danny Glover brilliantly portrays the jailed activist, whose lifelong battle against Apartheid served as a rallying cry around the world. Alfre Woodard is remarkable as Nelson's wife, Winnie. ★★★

Mandingo

(1975, 127 min, US, Richard Fleischer) A steamy love story set on a slave breeding plantation. It's just like *Gone with the Wind*, only all the characters are in heat. Starring James Mason, Ken Norton, and Susan George as the nymphomaniac "white girl." Trashy, awful and a definite guilty pleasure. ★ $14.99

Mandroid

(1992, 81 min, US, Jack Ersgard) Clichéd but entertaining sci-fi adventure romp, featuring two scientists who develop the Mandroid, a high-tech robot controlled by a virtual reality headset. One of the pair, Drago, is evil and he steals the robot when a lab explosion disfigures him. Saved by a slightly better than usual script and brisk pacing, this film could be a lot of fun for starting sci-fi fans. ★★ $89.99

The Mangler

(1995, 95 min, US, Tobe Hooper) Robert Englund stars in this atmospheric misfire (based on yet another Stephen King short story) about a sweatshop bedsheet folding machine that develops a taste for human flesh when an accidental combination of circumstances awakens the demon residing within. It's as silly as it sounds. Englund's campy performance as the Scrooge-like caretaker of The Mangler, and director Hooper's Grand Guignol treatment of the subject matter, along with some really grotesque death sequences, almost compensate for the skimpy screenplay and poor performances. ★★ $19.99

The Mango Tree

(1982, 92 min, Australia, Kevin Dobson) Starring Geraldine Fitzgerald, this is the story of a young man's coming-of-age as he, his family, and his friends experience the tumultuous changes of the early 1900s in a small Australian town. Sweetly done but not out of the ordinary. ★★½ $69.99

Manhattan

(1979, 93 min, US, Woody Allen) Allen is at his most insightful with this valentine of a film which pays tribute to his favorite city, romance, Gershwin, neuroses and bungled love affairs. Arguably his best film (some would say *Annie Hall*), *Manhattan* follows the jagged course of love taken by a group of New York sophisticates. Shot in a romanticized black and white, the film is both deliriously comic and assuredly dramatic while exploring romantic indiscretions, misjudgments and betrayals. Allen plays a TV writer who is involved with high schooler Mariel Hemingway. His married best friend Michael Murphy is involved with pseudo-intellectual magazine editor Diane Keaton. As these romantics crisscross and grapple with the frailties of relationships, Allen succinctly addresses the nature of romance and its tenacious grip on us all. Meryl Streep also stars as Allen's lesbian ex-wife. ★★★★ $14.99

Manhattan Melodrama

(1934, 93 min, US, W.S. Van Dyke) Though best known as the movie John Dillinger saw before being gunned down, this crime saga is actually quite good (it won an Oscar for Best Screenplay). Clark Gable and William Powell are childhood pals who find themselves on opposite sides of the law. And they're both in love with Myrna Loy. Yeah, it's a familiar theme, but this was one of the first films to use it. One of Gable's better '30s outings, and the first pairing of Powell and Loy. ★★★ $19.99

Manhattan Murder Mystery

(1993, 108 min, US, Woody Allen) In his first post-Mia production, Allen reteams with his old partner Diane Keaton to bring about this engaging and genuinely funny whodunit in the tradition of *The Thin Man*. Allen and Keaton play a calcified middle-aged couple who befriend the seemingly blissful older couple down the hall. But when the wife suddenly drops dead of a heart attack, Keaton suspects her husband of murder and takes it on herself to uncover the truth, setting off a hilarious and, at times, tense mystery. Alan Alda costars as a friend who plays along with Keaton's theory while Allen thinks she's just deranged. Throughout, Allen serves up his usual repertoire of quips and one-liners and they consistently amuse. Keaton seems right at home, picking up her Annie Hall persona without missing a beat. *Manhattan* is an enjoyable affair that does Nick and Nora Charles proud, albeit without the 15 martinis per scene. ★★★½ $19.99

The Manhattan Project

(1986, 117 min, US, Marshall Brickman) Quirky sci-fi comedy about a teenager (Christopher Collet) who builds an atomic bomb in hopes of exposing a secret nuclear plant in his neighborhood. John Lithgow plays a scientist who befriends the youngster. ★★½ $14.99

Manhunter

(1986, 119 min, US, Michael Mann) Stylish, gritty police thriller based on Thomas Harris'

Diane Keaton (l.) and Woody Allen in *Manhattan*

M

"Red Dragon." William L. Petersen stars as an unorthodox ex-FBI agent – he is able to think exactly like a criminal and thereby deduce his next move – who comes out of retirement to track down a serial killer. The character of Dr. Hannibal Lecter, played by Brian Cox, would surface a few years later as the psychopath in *The Silence of the Lambs*, played by Anthony Hopkins. ★★★ $14.99

Maniac

(1962, 86 min, GB, Michael Carreras) Hammer Studio head Carreras takes a turn as director in this stylish knock-off of *Psycho*, about an American (Kerwin Matthews) in Paris who runs into problems with his girlfriend's family. Fairly suspenseful and rather coherent considering its derivative roots. ★★★ $49.99

Maniac

(1981, 87 min, US, William Lustig) A terrifying and extremely gross film with Joe Spinell as a schizophrenic who takes to the streets at night to kill at random. The horror of the killings is intensified by Spinell's sympathetic portrayal of the killer. Recommended for gore fans only. ★ $14.99

Maniac Cop

(1988, 92 min, US, William Lustig) New York is being terrorized by a series of mutilation murders, and the public breaks out in a panic when the killer is discovered to be a police officer. Bloody and violent, this horror tale is slightly elevated by its intriguing premise and few scares. With Tom Atkins, Bruce Campbell, Richard Roundtree, William Smith and Sheree North. Written and produced by cult fave Larry Cohen. ★★ $14.99

Mannequin

(1938, 95 min, US, Frank Borzage) An extremely competent performance by Joan Crawford is the main attraction of this otherwise ordinary romantic drama. Joan is a working girl from a Hester Street tenement in New York who marries ne'er-do-well Alan Curtis to escape her poverty. At her wedding party, she meets wealthy shipping magnate Spencer Tracy, who immediately falls for her. Though she loves her husband, she's torn between both men – that is until Curtis gets a nasty idea to frame Tracy. In support, Leo Gorcy has some good scenes as Crawford's younger brother; so that's how a 1930s teenager behaved. ★★ $19.99

Mannequin

(1987, 89 min, US, Michael Gottlieb) Set at Wanamaker's in Philadelphia, this lifeless comedy stars Andrew McCarthy as a store employee who discovers that a mannequin (Kim Cattrall) has come to life – but only he can see her. That's about the calibre of the jokes, if you don't include Meshach Taylor's caricature of a lisping, limp-wristed flamboyantly gay window dresser. Followed by an equally inane sequel. ★ $9.99

Manny & Lo

(1996, 90 min, US, Lisa Krueger) A mesmerizing fairy tale of two sisters on the run which is brought to life by three enthralling performances. Living in different foster homes, Lo (Aleska Palladino) rescues her sister Manny

(Scarlett Johansson) from the household who had her sleeping in the garage. They take to the road in their deceased mom's car, shoplifting what they need. Manny takes family photographs from the houses they break into, and Lo is in denial about her pregnancy. Finally accepting that birth is imminent, they kidnap a clerk (Mary Kay Place) from a children's store to aid them in the delivery. Place's understated construction of the repressed, tightly wound Elaine is all the more powerful for its subtle control, as Elaine's relationship with the captors evolves into the mutually sustained bond of outcasts. Director Krueger has constructed a wryly observant film illuminated by insightful moments in which a person's life is delineated in a few words or a chance gesture. That chimeric element of magic in childhood metamorphizes into wish fulfillment and paranoia for children forced into adult roles with no example of adult behavior. A remarkable film with unexpected warmth and humor, and a loving respect for its three protagonists. ★★★½ $19.99

Noam Chomsky in *Manufacturing Consent*

Manon of the Spring

(1986, 112 min, France, Claude Berri) Set 10 years after the conclusion of *Jean de Florette*, this sequel unfolds with César (Yves Montand) and his nephew Ugolin now tilling the soil they stole from Jean de Florette. Manon, Jean's daughter, has grown into a beautiful, untamed woman who roams the countryside tending goats. The drama concerns Manon's efforts to reclaim the land and renounce the men who were responsible for her father's demise. The conclusion to this epic of revenge and treachery is riveting drama and is a superlative finale to two exquisite stories. (French with English subtitles) ★★★★ $19.99

Mansfield Park

(1986, 261 min, GB, David Giles) Jane Austen's classic novel is brought to the small screen in this excellent BBC adaptation. Set in 18th-century England, the story follows Fanny Price, a destitute young woman, who struggles to be accepted by her wealthy cousin's family. ★★★½ $29.99

The Manster

(1959, 91 min, Japan, Kenneth B. Crane & George P. Breakstone) It took two directors to make this movie about an American reporter in Japan who is given an injection by mad Dr. Suzuki. When an eyeball appears on his shoulder, he looks the other way. But things soon come to a head when an entire face forms and starts growing in his ear! So they decide to split up and go their separate ways. ★ $9.99

Mantis in Lace

(1968, 88 min, US, William Rotsler) This classic psycho-killer-LSD-nudie flick stars Susan Stewart as Lila, a topless dancer who takes too much acid. This seductive black widow lures unsuspecting studs to her candlelit love shack for sex and a little chemical excitement, only to have her prey find out that death is the payoff. Filmed by Laszlo Kovacs, who did *Easy Rider* the following year. ★★½ $24.99

Manufacturing Consent: Noam Chomsky and the Media

(1993, 166 min, Canada, Mark Achbar & Peter Wintonick) Noam Chomsky, probably one of the greatest thinkers of the late 20th century, is examined, discussed, explored and even ridiculed in this engrossing, well-paced and humorous documentary. The film chronicles Chomsky's rise to fame as well as his fall from grace as a controversial author and professor of linguistics, and examines the inequities in American television journalism and the problems with the medium of television itself. In interviews, Chomsky covers everything from World War II to sports to basic communication theories. This film stands as a wonderful testament to a truly thought-provoking and incredibly astute political and philosophical thinker. ★★★★ $39.99

The Manxman

(1929, 90 min, GB, Alfred Hitchcock) Hitchcock's last silent film is an appealing romantic melodrama about a rich lawyer and an indigent fisherman in love with the same woman. ★★★ $49.99

Map of the Human Heart

(1993, 109 min, Canada/Australia, Vincent Ward) Director Ward has crafted a dense web of dusky, beautiful images in this story of a love affair that spans 30 years and three continents. Arvik, a half-Inuit boy suffering from tuberculosis, is whisked away from the Arctic by a visiting mapmaker who takes him to a Catholic orphanage in Canada. There, Arvik befriends a young girl of mixed Native American and French Canadian heritage, who shares his feelings of displacement being caught between two worlds. Many years later as adults (played by Jason Scott Lee and Anne Parillaud), they meet again in WWII London, where both are engaged in the fight against Germany. Arvik is a fighter pilot whose last mission – the bombing of Dresden – goes awry in a powerful, disturbing scene. The film's expansiveness of time and place unfortunately results in a distancing of the characters, yet Ward succeeds in provoking thought on the people, places and events that shape one's life. ★★★ $14.99

Marat/Sade

(1967, 118 min, GB, Peter Brook) Peter Weiss' play (the full title of which is "The Persecution and Assassination of Jean-Paul Marat as Performed by the Inmates of the Asylum of Charenton Under the Direction of the Marquie de Sade") is brought to the screen with lurid intensity by the Royal Shakespeare Company. The play is, as its title says, the story of the manipulation of the inmates by the Marquis in order to destroy his most hated political enemy: Marat. Glenda Jackson is stunning in her film debut as Charlotte Corday (the unwitting tool of Patrick Magee's truly maniacal de Sade). This dark and disturbing film is a powerful allegory of the cruelty and abuse inherent in the wielding of political power. ★★★½ $29.99

Marathon Man

(1976, 125 min, US, John Schlesinger) Nail-biting thriller with Dustin Hoffman as a Columbia University student who unwittingly becomes involved with the CIA, Nazi war criminals and the beautiful Marthe Keller. Laurence Olivier is chilling as one of the screen's most vicious villains, and Roy Scheider also stars as Hoffman's secret agent brother. Does for dentists what *Psycho* did for showers. Based on the William Goldman novel. ★★★½ $14.99

March of the Wooden Soldiers

(1934, 73 min, US, Gus Meins) Laurel and Hardy's classic musical comedy is based on the Victor Herbert operetta "Babes in Toyland." Stan and Ollie are Santa's hapless helpers, who help save Toyland with their giant wooden soldiers. ★★★ $19.99

Maria Chapdelaine

(1984, 108 min, Canada, Gilles Carle) A family's hardships and determined pioneering spirit against the stark, brutal wilderness of North Canada is the theme of this lyrical drama based on the novel that has become a literary cornerstone of French-Canadian culture. Set against the breathtaking backdrop of the unspoiled beauty of Quebec's upper Gatineau region, the lovely Maria is the object of affection of two young men, one of whom offers escape from the difficult life in the snow-covered north. (French with English subtitles) ★★★

El Mariachi

(1992, 81 min, US, Robert Rodriguez) While the story of the funding for this $7,000 film is almost legendary, it cannot prepare one for the exciting, inventive and entertaining fun that first-time director Rodriguez creates. Displaying dazzling visual virtuosity and a playful, almost mocking approach, *El Mariachi* tells the tale of a congenial mariachi singer who, with his beloved guitar in hand, arrives in a dusty, nameless Mexican town seeking a place to sing. But, before he can even quench his thirst and strum his first note, he is mistaken for a gun-toting, vengence-seeking criminal and is thrown into the midst of an unbelievably bloody battle between warring gangs. Acrobatic gunfights and flailing bodies are never far away, as he slugs it out (and more than holds his own) with the bad guys. A thrilling western that belies its low budget in

delivering an exhilarating and often hilarious film. (Available dubbed and in Spanish with English subtitles) ★★★½ $14.99

Marianela

(1972, 108 min, Spain, Angelino Fons) Based on the novel by Benito-Perez Galdos, this touching story, set in late-19th-century Spain, tells of a young disfigured woman whose only solace is to serve as guide to a young, handsome blind man. However, when his eyesight is restored, her fragile world is shattered. (Spanish with English subtitles) ★★½

Marie

(1985, 112 min, US, Roger Donaldson) Sissy Spacek gives a fine performance in this true story of Marie Ragghianti, a divorced mother who becomes the chairman of the Tennessee State Board of Pardons and Paroles, and whose exposure of political corruption led to the ousting of a governor. Also starring Jeff Daniels and Morgan Freeman, and Ragghianti's real-life lawyer, Fred Thompson, appears as himself. ★★★ $79.99

Marie Antoinette

(1938, 149 min, US, W.S. Van Dyke II) Grand M-G-M costumer about the life of the doomed 18th-century French queen. Norma Shearer plays the title role, and Tyrone Power, John Barrymore, Gladys George and Robert Morley (outstanding as Louis XVI) co-star. ★★★ $19.99

Marius

(1931, 123 min, France, Alexander Korda) This first film of the legendary Pagnol Trilogy introduces Marseilles cafe owner César and his son Marius. Marius loves Fanny but leaves her for a life at sea. Shortly afterwards, Fanny finds herself pregnant. The joy and hardship of the simple people of Provence are splendidly captured. This is followed by *Fanny* and *César*. ★★★★ $39.99

Mark of the Devil

(1970, 90 min, West Germany/GB, Michael Armstrong) During the 18th century, a corrupt, impotent witch hunter has his way with women in more grotesque ways than can be imagined. This once *cause célèbre* is really much ado about nothing, as it offers gross instead of scares. Herbert Lom, Reggie Nalder and Udo Kier star. ★ $14.99

Mark of the Vampire

(1935, 61 min, US, Tod Browning) An eerie horror tale by *Dracula* director Browning about vampire expert Lionel Barrymore and police detective Lionel Atwill investigating a series of attacks in a small rural village. Also starring Bela Lugosi. ★★★ $19.99

The Mark of Zorro

(1920, 90 min, US, Fred Niblo) Douglas Fairbanks in another of his patented swashbuckling roles. Lots of great sword fights, lots of great sets and lots of people running around a lot. ★★★ $19.99

Marked for Death

(1990, 93 min, US, Dwight H. Little) It's voodoo and violence as Steven Seagal plays a tough DEA agent who finds he and his family

are targets of a vicious drug lord. Needless to say, martial arts action ensues. The little bit of action can't compensate for the ridiculous story or Seagal's awful acting. ★ $9.99

Marked Woman

(1937, 97 min, US, Lloyd Bacon) Loosely based on the trial of New York crime boss "Lucky" Luciano, this taut gangster drama stars Bette Davis as a clip joint hostess who is persuaded by D.A. Humphrey Bogart to testify against the racketeer boss responsible for her sister's disappearance. Davis is terrific in this crisp tale which is as enthralling as it is cynical. ★★★ $19.99

Marlene

(1986, 91 min, West Germany, Maximilian Schell) Marlene Dietrich, screen legend and public recluse, is the subject of this fascinating, amusing and insightful portrait. Miss Dietrich agreed to make the film with the unusual stipulation that director Schell not film her. So with only microphone in hand, the resourceful Schell interviews, confronts, compliments and does battle with this tough yet vulnerable lady. An unconventional portrait of one of Hollywood's greatest stars. (Filmed mostly in English) ★★★½

Marlowe

(1969, 95 min, US, Paul Bogart) A director named Bogart (no relation) brings famed detective Philip Marlowe to the 1960s in this neat little thriller starring James Garner in the title role. The plot has something to do with Marlowe investigating the disappearance of a young man. With Rita Moreno, Jackie Coogan, Carroll O'Connor and Bruce Lee, who makes kindling out of Marlowe's office. ★★★ $19.99

Marnie

(1964, 129 min, US, Alfred Hitchcock) Initially misunderstood, *Marnie* has been reevaluated as a continued exploration of the themes explicated in *Vertigo*: sexual inhibition and anxiety, the complex network of communication between men and women, and the tyranny of the past over the present. Tippi Hedren essays the man-hating heroine and Sean Connery is her prey and predator. ★★★ $14.99

Marooned

(1969, 134 min, US, John Sturges) Low-key sci-fi adventure with Gregory Peck as a panicky aerospace chief trying to get three stranded astronauts back to Earth. With Richard Crenna, James Franciscus, Gene Hackman and Lee Grant. Oscar for Best Special Effects. ★★½ $9.99

Marquez: Tales Beyond Solitude

(1989, 59 min, Canada, Holly Aylett) Dazzling storyteller, master of "magical realism" and Nobel Prize laureate Garbriel Garcia Marquez is the subject of this fascinating documentary. Featuring a rare interview with Marquez, the film focuses on the author's novels, including "One Hundred Years of Solitude," "Love in the Time of Cholera" and "The Autumn of the Patriarch" as well as his film adaptations, many of which are available on video. An impressive portrait of one of the greatest writers of Latin American literature. ★★★ $19.99

M

M

Marquis

(1990, 80 min, France, Henru Xhonneux) Sort of an X-rated Ren & Stimpy-visit-the-French Revolution, and arguably one of the strangest films of the last few years, this bizarre tale tells of the Marquis de Sade's imprisonment in the Bastille during the upheaval of 1789 — with the twist being that all of the cast play out their roles in grotesque animal costumes. Devilishly witty and shockingly vulgar, this bestial satire's cast includes, in a leading role, Colin, de Sade's frisky and dialectically opinionated penis; the Marquis himself (a horny but pensive hound-faced intellectual); a lusty prison guard in love with the Marquis who is intent on being buggered by him; and a whip-wielding, horse-faced dominatrix who flails at the flanks of the decadent rulers. Despite being bogged down by the intricate 18th-century French politics, any film that delights in wallowing in excessive perversity and politics (is there a connection here?) will certainly shock some, and entertain, amuse and titillate others. From the producers of the equally inventive *Delicatessen*. (French with English subtitles) ★★★½ $29.99

The Marriage of Maria Braun

(1978, 110 min, West Germany, Rainer Werner Fassbinder) Fassbinder's superb mixture of historical epic, offbeat comedy and social commentary stars Hanna Schygulla as the enterprising heroine who rises from the ashes of post-war Germany to become a captain of industry. (German with English subtitles) ★★★★ $29.99

Married to It!

(1993, 112 min, US, Arthur Hiller) If *Married to It!* were a person, it would never get asked to the prom. It's whiny, pretentious and tries way too hard to be popular. With "something for everyone," the story revolves around three couples: rich and materialistic Ron Silver and Cybill Shepherd; socially conscious, old hippies Beau Bridges and Stockard Channing; and newlyweds Robert Sean Leonard and Mary Stuart Masterson. Like a Woody Allen film with all of the complaining but none of the insights, *Married to It!* is redeemed only by the buoyant presence of Masterson, who brings energy, charm and definite offbeat prom-queen potential to all of her roles. ★★ $14.99

Married to the Mob

(1988, 105 min, US, Jonathan Demme) Michelle Pfeiffer reveals her considerable comic talents in this vibrant and colorful comedy, directed by Demme and awash with trendy pop music, cool ethnic types and hip American iconography. Pfeiffer stars as a "mob" widow who sets out to leave "the family" behind her. But her late husband's boss has other ideas about it, and goes to great lengths to let her know it. Into her life comes FBI agent Matthew Modine, who thinks she has yet to sever the umbilical, and sees a chance to nab the nefarious don — by romancing the frustrated widow. Dean Stockwell gives a hilariously sleazy performance as the don and Mercedes Ruehl is terrific as Stockwell's manically jealous wife. ★★★ $9.99

A Married Woman
(Une Femme Mariée)

(1964, 94 min, France, Jean-Luc Godard) *A Married Woman* is a fine example of Godard's wild experimentation with narrative, sound usage, editing, and literary allusions. Subtitled, "Fragments of a Film Shot in 1964," the film begins with a concern for woman's role in society but he is really much more interested in ideas of memory, the present and intelligence. (French with English subtitles) ★★★½

Marry Me! Marry Me!

(1968, 96 min, France, Claude Berri) A charming romantic comedy produced, directed, written by and starring Berri. It's an offbeat story about European Jewish families, and follows Claude, a Jewish encyclopedia salesman in Paris, as he inconveniently falls in love with a pregnant Belgian girl. Berri unfolds the story with gentle, perceptive humor. (Dubbed) ★★★

The Marrying Man

(1991, 115 min, US, Jerry Rees) Plagued by controversy, this Neil Simon-scripted comedy misses the mark as an affectionate tribute to the screwball comedies of the '30s and '40s. Groom-to-be Alec Baldwin is caught philandering with Kim Basinger by her gangster beau. Forced to marry her, Baldwin's engagement to heiress Elisabeth Shue is cancelled and he's left distraught...until he's re-engaged to Shue and meets Basinger again. Baldwin is competent, but Basinger appears to be imitating Michelle Pfeiffer in *The Fabulous Baker Boys*, especially in her musical numbers. Paul Reiser scores well as what could be the Neil Simon character. ★★ $9.99

Mars Attacks!

(1996, 103 min, US, Tim Burton) Combining some gleefully twisted black humor with plenty of homages and references to schlocky (and not-so-schlocky) alien invasion and sci-fi flicks of the 1950s and '60s, director Burton's magnum opus (and first widescreen film) is the perfect companion piece to his eloquent, intimate masterwork *Ed Wood*. A parody of the kind of movie Ed Wood only wishes he could have afforded to make, *Mars Attacks!* is the story of some funny-looking but terribly ill-tempered aliens who declare war on the Earth. Why? Because it's there! An all-star cast plays various hapless Earthlings, most of whom deserve their fate. But a small group of heroes (led by Jim Brown, Lukas Haas and Tom Jones) are able to withstand the alien assault and devise a weapon powerful enough to halt their malicious advance. Great special effects, deliberately designed to evoke memories of afternoon sci-fi matinees (the saucers look terrific), an outstanding score by Danny Elfman and campy, wild-eyed performances by everyone involved all add up to a fantastic "A" budget "B" movie. Hipper and more entertaining than its '96 counterpart *ID4*, and ten times funnier — stock up on your Slim Whitman records! ★★★½ $19.99

La Marseillaise

(1937, 130 min, France, Jean Renoir) This grand epic chronicles the events of the French

The Marriage of Maria Braun

Revolution of 1789. This is a stirring account of the events which led to the uprising, and Renoir has filmed it in a episodic, tense fashion. (French with English subtitles) ★★★ $59.99

Martha & Ethel

(1995, 80 min, US, Jyll Johnstone) A highly personalized labor of love, this endearing documentary offers two radically different portraits of the filmmakers' childhood nannies. Director Johnstone and producer Ettinger examine each of their families' interactions with their paid child rearers and uncover a fascinating study of family dynamics as well as an entertaining exposé on the lives of the wealthy. Martha (of the Johnstone family), a cranky 87-year-old German immigrant, is a stern disciplinarian who was feared by the children. Interwoven with her story is Ethel's (the Ettingers' nanny), an extraordinarily resilient and graceful 92-year-old daughter of South Carolina sharecroppers who bemusedly informs the camera that she is "b-l-a-c-k." Ethel is a stark contrast to Martha: She treats her charges with kindness and is beloved by the Ettinger children as if she were their own mother. Though the stories of these two remarkable women have little in common, their differing styles and the clearly divergent attitudes of their employers make this captivating viewing. *Martha and Ethel* is a film of pure honesty, and is propelled by the personal charm of its two subjects. ★★★½ $96.89

The Martian Chronicles, Vols. 1-3

(1979, 97 min, US, Michael Anderson) Rock Hudson stars in this lively and popular television miniseries of Ray Bradbury's sci-fi tome. Three volumes tell the story of expeditions to Mars and the fate which awaits them. Darren McGavin, Bernadette Peters, Christopher Connelly, Roddy McDowall, Bernie Casey and Nicholas Hammond also star.

Vol. 1: The Expeditions: It's 1999 and Earth faces extinction. Three separate expeditions are launched towards Mars in the hopes of colonization and learning some of the mysteries that shroud the red planet.

Vol. 2: The Settlers: The year is now 2006. Human settlers have landed on Mars, and it appears germs transported from Earth have destroyed the Martian civilization. But colonel Hudson believes they still exist in an unknown form. Meanwhile, Earth is destroyed as a result of nuclear war.

Vol. 3: The Martians: As the final chapter opens, Earth has been destroyed and the few colonists on Mars are the only hope of survival for mankind. ★★★ $14.99

Martin

(1978, 95 min, US, George Romero) A witty and sardonic updating of the Dracula legend about a young man with a troublesome fondness for blood. What distinguishes Romero's work is an ability to maintain an atmosphere of terror and suspense while simultaneously indulging in a most kinky sense of humor. ★★★

Marty

(1955, 91 min, US, Delbert Mann) Oscar-winning Best Picture about a shy butcher who finds true love, and a glimpse into the lives of two ordinary, lonely people who meet by chance in a dance hall. Ernest Borgnine won an Oscar for his poignant portrayal of the title character, a hapless Everyman, and is given solid support by Betsy Blair and Joe Mantell. Screenplay by Paddy Chayefsky (Best Screenplay Award). ★★★★ $14.99

Marvin and Tige

(1982, 104 min, US, Eric Weston) John Cassavetes stars as an alcoholic ad exec who meets an embittered, streetwise 11-year-old contemplating suicide because of his mother's recent death. Cassavetes takes an interest in the child, and tries to reunite him with his estranged father (Billy Dee Williams). A film which wears its heart on its sleeve in its well-meaning examination of racial intolerance. ★★½

Marvin's Room

(1996, 105 min, US, Jerry Zaks) Diane Keaton and Meryl Streep are sisters estranged for 20 years, brought together by Keaton's onset of leukemia after a lifetime as family caretaker. The younger Lee (Streep) jumped ship when the responsibilities for ailing, elderly relatives became a numbing reality of respirators and myriad pill bottles; the older Bessie (Keaton) was included in the medical rituals, initiating a life defined by the illnesses of others. As the sisters mutually contrast each other — Bessie is compliant and selfless; Lee is defiant and con-

trary — so do Lee's sons choose opposing coping mechanisms. Young Charlie (Hal Scardino) attempts to conform and adapt. But the teenaged Hank (Leonardo DiCaprio) matches his mother's confrontational stance, in active defiance to her emotional flareups. From the first awkward reacquaintance of the two sisters, united by blood yet strangers to each other, the uncanny symbiosis of familial interrelationships ameliorates the harsh edges of conflict, imparting a blessed balance to both sisters and both brothers. This actors' vehicle suffers somewhat from stage director Zaks' unfamiliarity with the medium and a curiously toned-down script. But the strength and honesty of the ensemble portrayals rise above these failings with unexpected humor and warmth of emotion without artifice. ★★★ $102.99

Mary My Dearest (Maria de Mi Corazón)

(1983, 100 min, Mexico, Jaime Humberto Hermosillo) This Mexican soap opera, adapted from a story by Gabriel Garcia Marquez, is a moderately interesting black comedy of ill-fated love, produced independently by one of Mexico's most popular directors. After a mysterious eight-year absence, Maria, a beautiful young magician, returns to the home of small-time crook Hector. The couple fall in love for a second time, but are soon separated when Maria, in a bizarre mix-up, is placed in an insane asylum and can't get out. (Spanish with English subtitles) ★★½ $59.99

Mary Poppins

(1964, 140 min, US, Robert Stevenson) "In every job that must be done, there is an element of fun." And there could be no greater fun than Walt Disney's classic live-action and animated musical. Julie Andrews won an Oscar for her delightful performance as everyone's favorite magical nanny, Mary Poppins, who arrives at the Banks household to oversee two young children. Wonderful support by Dick Van Dyke (as long as you overlook his accent), David Tomlinson, Glynis Johns and Ed Wynn. Quick — can you say supercalifragilisticexpialidocious backwards? ★★★★ $22.99

Mary Reilly

(1996, 118 min, GB, Stephen Frears) Director Frears' disjointed adaptation of the tale of Dr. Jekyll and Mr. Hyde (John Malkovich) uses the intriguing premise of following the action from the point of view of the good doctor's maidservant, Mary Reilly (Julia Roberts). This might have been (should have been) an excellent launch pad for a new examination of the intricacies of good and evil. Though the script has some elements that lead in that direction, it ultimately shies away from any substantive exploration of amorality. One of the film's few virtues is Mary's somewhat involuntary yet compulsive attraction to the evil in Mr. Hyde, made clear by flashbacks to childhood abuses suffered at the hands of her drunken and incestuous father (Michael Gambon). But the film bogs down in the tête-à-tête between Reilly and Hyde and becomes a claustrophobic and uninteresting spine-tingler along the lines of another British Gothic film, *The Turn of the Screw*. Also primary to the film's laconic pace is Malkovich's stoic performance; though a fine actor, his heavy, theatrical style varies little from film to film, character to character, ergo, Jekyll to Hyde. This makes him an inelegant choice to play dual characters, especially so when they are supposed to be diametrical opposites. Roberts, usually the one to pick on critically, gives an able performance, mildly believable Irish accent and all. ★★ $101.89

Mary Shelley's Frankenstein

(1994, 123 min, GB, Kenneth Branagh) Branagh, Britain's wunderkind *du jour*, sets his sights away from Shakespeare and onto less fanciful fare with this egocentric and grisly adaptation of the time-honored tale which takes the notion "the sins of the father..." to a truly horrific level. Returning to the original source and the central theme that man was not meant to play God, Branagh delivers an emotionally complex portrayal of Dr. Frankenstein as a man who creates life and then turns his back on it, thus setting the stage for a Gothic tragedy of Shakespearean proportions. There are, of course, Branagh's trademark histrionics — dizzying, non-stop

Mars Attacks!

camerwork, a booming and somewhat distracting score, and some shameless overacting by the director-star — but heartfelt performances by Robert De Niro as the monster and Helena Bonham Carter as "the Bride" help put this one over the top. ★★★ $14.99

Masala

(1993, 100 min, Canada, Srinivas Krishna) Temple Universtiy graduate Krishna's ingenious feature debut is this wildly entertaining brew which examines the difficulties of assimilation for Indian immigrants in North America. Krishna himself stars as a thuggish young hunk who dabbles in drugs and petty crime. When his entire family is killed in a plane crash, he moves to Toronto to live with his ruthlessly greedy uncle (Saeed Jaffrey). He strikes up a relationship with the daughter of a financially strapped postman (Jaffrey in a multiple role), whose mother has candid conversations with her favorite deity Krishna (Jaffrey again) through her VCR. The film wonderfully resembles its namesake presenting a tasty mélange of spicy subplots, twists and characters including some bizarre yet amusing musical numbers mounted in the tradition of classic Indian religious dramas. Colorful and wild, the film presents a wholly original take on the struggles of Indian immigrants to retain their cultural identity. ★★★½ $19.99

Mascara

(1987, 99 min, Belgium, Patrick Conrad) Michael Sarrazin stars as a sexually repressed police inspector on the brink of insanity in this stylishly shot thriller. Charlotte Rampling co-stars as his sister and the object of his incestuous desires. Filled with themes of lust, love, transvestism and transexuality, the film features some scenes in a kinky after hours club which are worthy of one of Ken Russell's fevered dream sequences. ★★★ $19.99

Masculin-Feminin

(1966, 103 min, France, Jean-Luc Godard) Starting from a Du Maupassant short story, Godard fashions a remarkable portrait of French youth in the `60s — "the children of

Srinivas Krishna in *Masala*

Marx and Coca Cola." A blending of experimental fiction with documentary segments aims to drive the "political truth" home to the workers. Jean-Pierre Léaud is an aimless revolutionary who wants answers but sees nothing in the political turmoil that surrounds him. Godard's "fifteen precise facts" on the problems of the younger generation. (French with English subtitles) ★★★½ $29.99

Mask

(1985, 120 min, US, Peter Bogdanovich) Cher gives a stirring performance as the mother of Rocky Dennis, a teenager afflicted with a disfiguring congenital condition. Director Bogdanovich effectively paints a sympathetic portrait of the young man's life, and Eric Stoltz gives a commendable performance as Dennis. ★★★ $14.99

The Mask

(1994, 102 min, US, Charles Russell) Rubber-faced Jim Carrey, who in one year has gone from TV chump to box-office champ, gets totally bent out of shape (with the help of F/X meister Greg Cannom) in this eagerly anticipated and totally enjoyable follow-up to his debut *Ace Ventura*. The one-dimensional story, which is really an excuse to get from one special effect to another, is the standard "under-dog has his day" scenario, with Carrey as a beleaguered nebbish who finds an ancient mask that turns him into a green-faced, zoot-suited, whacked-out super-hormonal super-hero. But under the direction of Russell, what amazing effects they are. Carrey's world becomes a Tex Avery-style cartoon replete with side-splitting computer-generated F/X and technicolored, show-stopping musical numbers. As such, *The Mask* defies you not to be entertained, and it's almost impossible not to be. Featured in support are goddess-in-waiting Cameron Diaz and Peter Riegert. ★★★ $14.99

The Mask of Fu Manchu

(1932, 72 min, US, Charles Babin) Considered to be the best movie adapted from the Fu Manchu novels, this very fun adventure yarn stars Boris Karloff as the evil mastermind intent on world domination and Lewis Stone as the hero dedicated to stopping him. The film moves along at a good pace and is highlighted by a stupendous pyrotechnic show, reminiscent of that in *Frankenstein* a year earlier, as Fu tries to determine the authenticity of a powerful sword brought to him. Archaic racial stereotypes notwithstanding, Karloff's performance is the real treat here — he obviously relishes playing such a juicy role of mad genius and diabolical villain rolled into one. It is also historically interesting watching him in a central speaking role for M-G-M when at Universal he was almost typecast into mute villains (in *The Mummy* and the two later *Frankenstein* sequels he made). Dated and old-fashioned, but enjoyable nonetheless. Also with Myrna Loy. ★★½ $19.99

Masque of the Red Death

(1989, 83 min, US, Larry Brand) A deadly plague spreading across the land prompts a medieval prince to lock himself and his aristocratic friends inside a castle. But no one is safe from an evil masked man on a horse, who brings despair and death in his wake. Roger

Corman produced this updating of his 1964 semiclassic adaptation of Edgar Allan Poe's chilling tale, but the results are not as satisfying. Patrick Macnee, Tracy Reiner and Adrian Paul star. ★★ $14.99

Masque of the Red Death

(1991, 83 min, US, Alan Birkinshaw) In this minor, updated version of Edgar Allan Poe's short story, Herbert Lom plays a dying patriarch who throws one last grand ball — if he's gotta go he's determined to take his friends along with him. Brenda Vaccaro, as a foul-mouthed matron, and Frank Stallone, one of her men in arms, are just two of the guests who would rather not accompany him. ★★ $89.99

Mass Appeal

(1984, 99 min, US, Glenn Jordan) Jack Lemmon gives a commanding performance in this appealing adaptation of the Broadway comedy-drama about the clash of wills between a well-to-do priest (Lemmon) and an outspoken seminarian (Zeljko Ivanek). The film touches upon clashes between the old Church and the younger ideology — some of it is superficial and some of it is surprisingly thorough. ★★½ $19.99

Massacre at Central High

(1976, 87 min, US, Renee Daalder) Cult favorite with Andrew Stevens as the new kid in school who begins a one-man campaign of terror against a brutal student gang. Also stars Robert Carradine in one of his first roles. ★★½

Master Harold and the Boys

(1985, 105 min, GB/US, Michael Lindsay-Hogg) This powerful film written by South Africa's eminent playwright, Athol Fugard, concerns a South African white youth whose "special friendship" with two black men is adversely affected by the return of his father to the family-owned tea room. The youth's uncovered, heretofore unrecognized racism helps us understand the difficulty in escaping the values that surround us as we grow to personhood. ★★★½ $19.99

Master Killer

(1979, 115 min, Hong Kong, Liu Chia Liang) This high-flying kung fu actioner tells the tale of a young man (Liu Chia Hui) who, having managed to escape the evil Manchus, takes refuge in a Shaolin temple where he learns the deadly martial arts and becomes a fighting monk. Finally, he leaves the temple intent on exacting revenge against the Manchus. Aside from its run-of-the-mill story, the film features some well-choreographed fighting sequences. The final death match between Liu and kung fu master Lo Lieh features eye-popping acrobatics and heart-stopping swordplay. In fact, this fight alone makes up for the bad dubbing. (Dubbed) ★★★ $39.99

Master of the World

(1961, 104 min, US, Roger Corman) One of Corman's most entertaining and effective films. Vincent Price plays Robur the Conquerer in this Jules Verne story about a peace activist out to destroy the armies of the world from his flying ship. Charles Bronson co-stars. ★★ $14.99

The Mask

Mastergate

(1992, 90 min, US, Michael Engler) With the subheading "A Play on Words," writer Larry Gelbart's hilarious political farce is just that, a wondrous whirlwind of words, doublespeak and raillery. Taking aim at network news, Washington, the military and Hollywood, *Mastergate* asks the seemingly familiar question, "What did the President know — and did he have any idea that he knew it?" The story centers on a Congressional hearing into illegal arms delivered to Central American rebels funded through a movie's $1.3 billion budget. Though the satire is obvious, it is Gelbart's scintillating dialogue — which easily could have been penned by Stoppard or Chayefsky — which propels the film, creating an uproarious verbal confrontation of half-truths and evasions. Among a terrific cast all in on the joke, Richard Kiley and David Ogden Stiers play Congressional leaders, James Coburn could be Oliver North, Tim Reid is a newscaster, Ed Begley, Jr. and Bruno Kirby are low-level scapegoats, and Dennis Weaver might be George Bush. Though enjoyable on any level, this is a must for politicos. ★★★½ $19.99

Masters of the Universe

(1987, 106 min, US, Gary Goddard) Dolph Lundgren flexes his muscles as a space-age warrior whose battle with evil lord Frank Langella brings him to Earth. Pretty inept in all departments. ★½ $9.99

Mata Hari

(1931, 100 min, US, George Fitzmaurice) Garbo never looked lovelier than as the famed WWI spy whose exotic looks seduced every male she met. Ramon Navarro and Lionel Barrymore are just two who fall victim to this woman's wiles. Navarro utters the famous line, "What's the matter, Mata?" ★★★ $19.99

Matador

(1988, 102 min, Spain, Pedro Almodóvar) This wickedly satiric romp is a decidedly twisted and thoroughly amusing wallow in the world of sexual desires. A series of bizarre sexual murders are baffling the police in Madrid until young Angel — the son of an ultra-right-wing, religiously obsessive mother — turns himself in to the police. The problem is that he is innocent and has been experiencing the killings clairvoyantly. His femme-fatale attorney is aware of his innocence, as is his bullfighting instructor: for they are each responsible for the grisly murders. Director Almodóvar rips away the facade of human behavior and reveals a hilarious, sometimes frightening, subterranean view of a world ruled by passion and death. (Spanish with English subtitles) ★★★½ $79.99

The Match Factory Girl

(1989, 70 min, Finland, Aki Kaurismaki) A bleak little saga about a mousy factory worker whose dreary life includes living at home with her mother and stepfather while desperately seeking male companionship despite her bland looks and nondescript personality. Kaurismaki's film is every bit as personality-less as its main character. What is so perplexing is that the film contains not one scintilla of emotion, not even a blip — granted, life in Helsinki may be unbearably innocuous at times, especially for the underprivileged proletariat, but it is hard to fathom life on the level Kaurismaki presents it. Even so, the film lacks the director's subtle sense of humor and incisive commentary usually found in his other works; it only displays an effective use of minimalism. (Finnish with English subtitles) ★★ $79.99

The Matchmaker

(1958, 101 min, US, Joseph Anthony) Enjoyable screen version of Thornton Wilder's play, with Shirley Booth giving a wonderful performance as turn-of-the-century matchmaker Dolly Levi. As Horace Vandergelder, one of her clients and romantic interest, Paul Ford is in good form. Also with Anthony Perkins and Shirley MacLaine as youthful lovers, and Robert Morse as Perkins' sidekick. The basis for the musical "Hello, Dolly." ★★★ $19.99

La Maternelle

(1933, 83 min, France, Jean Benoit-Levy & Maria Epstein) A society girl down on her luck becomes a maid in "la maternelle," a kindergarten which provides a temporary refuge for the poor children of a Parisian slum. The compassionate young woman befriends and mothers the children, many of them victims of abuse, and takes into her home a lonely waif abandoned by her "working girl" mother. An affectionate and heartwarming, yet grimly realistic drama. (French with English subtitles) ★★★ $29.99

Matewan

(1987, 132 min, US, John Sayles) The dramatic retelling of a 1920s coal strike in West Virginia has been sensitively written and directed by Sayles and beautifully photographed by Haskell Wexler. This compelling story of solidarity and martyrdom amidst the grime and dust of the coal town features fine performances by James Earl Jones, Mary McDonnell and Chris Cooper. ★★★½ $14.99

Matilda

(1996, 90 min, US, Danny DeVito) Matilda is a little girl with serious problems: Her parents never wanted her in the first place and treat her with great disdain. After refusing to let her go to school (someone has to stay home and accept the boxes of illegal car parts!), they finally send her to a school where the principal loves to torment the students. Luckily, Matilda has discovered she has telekinetic powers that allow her to exact a very satisfying revenge on the adults who mistreated her — and this is done without becoming malicious or mean, which is part of the film's success. Mara Wilson, who was precious in *Mrs. Doubtfire*, is simply terrific as Matilda, acting with both a maturity and innocence that is utterly endearing. Director DeVito and Rhea Perlman hilariously play her parents, and the story is told with wit and style. ★★★½ $22.99

Matinee

(1993, 107 min, US, Joe Dante) Dante shows just where he cut his teeth as a youthful movie fan with this playful homage to '60s schlock films. Set during the Cuban Missile Crisis, the story revolves around a teenager (Simon Fenton), an avid creature feature fan, who becomes assistant to John Goodman's big-hearted film director — part Alfred Hitchcock, part William Castle. Goodman has come to the youth's small Florida town to screen his newest, grade-Z creation, *Mant* (Half Man, Half Ant, All Terror!). Dante and writer Charlie Haas clearly are enjoying their sometimes hilarious send-ups of the dreadful matinee horror films of decades yore, and their film-within-a-film has some delectable scenes. Cathy Moriarty has a good time as the film's scream queen, and Dante's supporting cast includes Dick Miller, Kevin McCarthy, Jesse White and William Schallert. ★★★ $9.99

The Mating Game

(1959, 96 min, US, George Marshall) Anyone wishing for an old-fashioned comic confection should appreciate this homespun romantic comedy. All others, however, beware: insulin shock ahead. Debbie Reynolds is the red-blooded, eldest daughter of farmer/trader Paul Douglas' Maryland brood. When IRS agent Tony Randall comes to investigate Douglas' 20-year nonpayment of taxes, her parents do their darndest to match Reynolds and their educated visitor. There's no shortage of good spirits, thanks to a dedicated cast (Randall is especially good); but it's all so damn cute this was probably corn when released in 1959. ★★½ $19.99

A Matter of Heart

(1983, 107 min, US, Mark Whitney) Carl Gustav Jung discovered powers of healing and

Matewan

guidance in his studies of the dream world, contributing to a philosophy of Western thinking which radically transformed the nature of modern psychology. His remarkable genius is captured with exquisite tenderness in this fascinating film which helps reveal the relationship between his thought and his life. ★★★½ $79.99

Maurice

(1987, 140 min, GB, James Ivory) With the same reverence and regal authority he brought to *A Room with a View*, director Ivory has created a personal triumph with this exquisite adaptation of E. M. Forster's semiautobiography. Set in pre-WWI England, the film examines the social and sexual repression of the era in this story of the emotional conflict facing a college student coming to terms with his homosexuality. James Wilby is perfectly cast in the title role, Hugh Grant gives a precise performance as his platonic lover who transforms from free spirit to social prig, and Rupert Graves is splendid as the handsome gardener who awakens Maurice's dormant feelings. ★★★★ $14.99

Mauvaise Graine

(1933, 77 min, France, Billy Wilder & Alexander Esway) When his rich, indulgent daddy takes the roadster away, spoiled, amoral Henry (Pierre Mingand) gets himself mixed up with a fast woman (Danielle Darrieux) and a ring of car thieves. Shot on location in and around a Paris of the early Thirties, *Mauvaise Graine* captures a city at the height of its beauty and a career about to burst into bloom. Like many, screenwriter and director Billy Wilder had to leave a Germany about to go insane. The director who would find greatness in America a few years later managed to raise enough money with co-director Esway to shoot a low-budget action film starring then-unknown Darrieux (*La Ronde*). Exhibiting many of the narrative touches that would become Wilder's trademarks (and can be traced back to his unsuspecting mentor Ernst Lubitsch), the film is fast-paced and action-packed, recklessly driven along by a jazzy score from Franz Waxman (like Wilder himself, to be bound for Hollywood). (French with English subtitles) ★★★ $39.99

Maverick

(1994, 120 min, US, Richard Donner) In their initial meeting, Jodie Foster — as an alluring con artist — sums up her impression of dashing gambler Bret Maverick, played by Mel Gibson: "Irritating and likable." This also ably describes this pleasant if inconsistent big screen version of the popular 1960s TV series. Gibson takes over the James Garner role, and he gives an amiable account of the rascal/cardsharp who only wants to play in the big poker tournament but who gets sidetracked at every turn. Foster is uncharacteristically breezy as Maverick's equally roguish partner. Both are eclipsed, however, by Garner, who appears as a crusty lawman. The actor's effortless charm is a reminder of what distinguished the TV show, and what the film is more in need of. *Maverick* may not totally capture the effervescence of its prototype, but it does contain many enjoyable moments of nonsensical whimsy. (Available letterboxed and pan & scan) ★★★ $19.99

The Maverick Queen

(1956, 92 min, US, Joseph Kane) Faithful screen version of a Zane Grey novel with Barbara Stanwyck as a lady bandit who falls in love with the Pinkerton detective (Barry Sullivan) sent to track her down. ★★½ $14.99

Max Dugan Returns

(1983, 98 min, US, Herbert Ross) Amiable, even charming Neil Simon comedy with Jason Robards, as Marsha Mason's long-lost father, who reenters his daughter's life. Matthew Broderick debuts as Mason's teenage son, and Donald Sutherland also stars; Kiefer Sutherland has a small role. ★★★ $59.99

Max Headroom

(1985, GB, Rocky Morton & Annabel Jankel) Inventive, glitzy cult favorite about a television reporter who accidentally becomes the world's first computer-generated TV host — Max Headroom. Flashy special effects add to this haunting, cynical vision of the powerful role television plays in our future. Matt Frewer stars. ★★★★

Max Mon Amour

(1986, 97 min, France/US, Nagisa Oshima) The attention-grabbing premise of this film — that a sophisticated Parisian woman falls in love with a chimpanzee — should generate some interest in this unusual satire by Japanese director Oshima. Margaret (Charlotte Rampling) and English diplomat Peter (Anthony Higgens) are an unhappy couple opulently living in Paris. Their marriage is strained when the husband discovers that his wife is having an affair not with another man, but with a chimpanzee. Trying to be liberal and understanding, he asks his wife to bring hairy Max home, creating a bizarre nuclear family. Even with its premise, the film disappoints; for after Max is introduced, there is nothing more to shock, and every time the story approaches a surreal level, it steps back, embracing conventionality. (In English and French with English subtitles) ★★ $89.99

Maxie

(1985, 98 min, US, Paul Aaron) The considerable talents of Glenn Close and Mandy Patinkin are not enough to save this mediocre ghost comedy. Close and Patinkin play a married couple whose lives are interrupted when the spirit of a flapper — murdered in the 1920s — inhabits the body of the former. It's nice to see Close let down her hair, but the flimsy screenplay just doesn't give her enough to do. The last film of the great Ruth Gordon. ★½ $9.99

Maximum Overdrive

(1986, 97 min, US, Stephen King) Author King stepped behind the camera for the first time to direct his story of rampaging trucks — and this is so bad it may be some time before he steps there again. Emilio Estevez, Pat Hingle and Laura Harrington are some of the people trapped in a cafe terrorized by those murderous 18-wheelers. ★ $14.99

Maximum Risk

(1996, 101 min, US, Ringo Lam) The Jean-Claude Van Damme curse continues for former Hong Kong directors as ace action auteur

Lam (*City on Fire, Full Contact*) is brought low by the Muscles from Brussels. After kickboxing the careers of Corey Yuen Kwai (*No Retreat, No Surrender*) and John Woo (*Hard Target*), Van Damme stars in this lame, brainless chase picture about a former French soldier who discovers he had a twin brother involved in some shady dealings with the Russian mob. Another surprise awaits Jean-Claude when he meets his bro's girlfriend (Natasha Henstridge), who turns out to be very resourceful at avoiding professional killers. The two of them must unravel the convoluted plot before the audience does, or at least before it gets bored enough to turn them off. Not even stylishly shot, it displays none of the talent or promise which probably got its director the job in the first place and is a complete disappointment. ★ $14.99

May Fools

(1990, 108 min, France, Louis Malle) A mildly entertaining comedy of manners about the family squabbles of a petit bourgeois clan. Set against the backdrop of the 1968 student uprising in Paris (an event which toppled the government of Charles DeGaulle), the film follows the Vieusacs as they converge on their ancestral country mansion to pick through the possessions of a recently deceased matriarch. Michel Piccoli stars as Milou, the hopelessly romantic father of the remaining kin, and the only family member who opposes the sale of the house and surrounding vineyard. Malle shows the family bickering as a microcosm of the era's social turmoil with Milou's idealism and joie de vivre representing the country's heart and soul. The results are mixed, but Piccoli's performance is pure gold. The always lovely Miou-Miou also stars as Milou's ultra-materialistic daughter. ★★ $19.99

Maya Deren: Divine Horsemen — Living Gods of Haiti

(1950s, 52 min, US, Maya Deren) Maya Deren's documentary journey to Haiti, examining the practice of voodoo.

Maya Deren, Her Experimental Films

(1943-1957, US, Maya Deren) Unfairly neglected and largely forgotten today, Maya Deren was one of the first to rigorously analyze the nature of film, in both her films and her writings. While many of the stylistic devices that she developed were quickly appropriated by others, her nascent feminist concerns were not, leaving her the lone voice of woman in a rampantly sexist medium. Includes: *Meshes in the Afternoon, At Land, Ritual in Transfigured Time* and *The Very Eye of Night*.

Maybe...Maybe Not (Der bewegte Mann)

(1994, 93 min, Germany, Sönke Wortmann) This slick sex comedy follows the antics of the blond, womanizing Axel (Til Schweiger). After being caught in the act one too many times, the handsome young man is thrown out of his girlfriend's flat. With no one to turn to, the desperate Axel is forced to accept the kindness of strangers — although in this case, the strangers are a group of starry-eyed gay men. Axel moves in with one of them, Norbert (Joachim Krol), a fastidious, shy gay man. The story then follows their developing friendship, Axel's increasing involvement with the gay world, and his ex-girlfriend Doro's efforts to get her man back. The goings-on soon escalate into a laughably frantic farce as Axel tries to assure Doro that he is straight...despite being caught naked in bed with Norbert. The gay caricatures — and that they are — are meant for fun as the humor lampoons both the gay and straight worlds. A huge popular success in Germany, the comedy's based on a comic book (by cartoonist Ralf König) and plans are reportedly in the works for an American remake. (German with English subtitles) ★★½ $96.89

Mayerling

(1935, 91 min, France, Anatole Litvak) The passion and agony of two doomed lovers is explored in this sumptuous true story which stars Charles Boyer as the Crown Prince Rudolph of Austria who falls under the trance of the stunningly beautiful Danielle Darrieux. A shimmering romance that sadly, yet inevitably, leads to tragedy. (French with English subtitles) ★★★ $14.99

McBain

(1991, 104 min, US, James Glikenhaus) All action, no frills...that's the strength of this lean, compact action drama. Christopher Walken goes the avenging-vet route as he and his 'Nam buddies team with a beautiful revolutionary (the typecast Maria Conchita Alonso) to overthrow an evil Central American dictator. Although it's no *Dogs of War*, it does feature nice directorial touches and a strong supporting cast (Steve James, Michael Ironside and D.B. Sweeney). ★★½ $9.99

McCabe and Mrs. Miller

(1971, 121 min, US, Robert Altman) One of Altman's best, *McCabe and Mrs. Miller* is a wonderfully poignant drama which explores ambition, greed, love and alienation, all within a decidedly quirky western setting. Warren Beatty is the cocky McCabe, a naively optimistic gambler who builds a town and hires Julie Christie to set up a high-class brothel. Featured is a haunting Leonard Cohen soundtrack. ★★★½ $14.99

The McGuffin

(1985, 95 min, GB, Colin Bucksey) This tribute to Hitchcock's *Rear Window* derives its title from the phrase coined by the late mystery master. The story concerns a film critic whose nagging curiosity leads him to become embroiled in a murder plot being perpetrated by his neighbors. The film lacks a cohesiveness and delivers few thrills. ★★

McVicar

(1980, 111 min, GB, Tom Clegg) The Who Films presents this portrayal of John McVicar (Roger Daltrey), whose real-life escape from the high-security wing of a British prison led to his being dubbed "Public Enemy No.1" by the British press. This tough and tense prison drama won the critics' raves, but failed to find a crossover audience in the U.S. Excellent support from Adam Faith and soundtrack by Jeff Wayne and The Who. ★★★

Me and Him

(1989, 94 min, US, Doris Dorrie) An up-and-coming architect (Griffin Dunne) finds his life turned upside-down when he wakes up one morning and finds his penis starts talking to him. An ironically tame film despite its controversial nature. Cast includes Craig T. Nelson and the voice of Mark Linn-Baker. From the director of *Men*. ★★ $79.99

The Mean Season

(1985, 106 min, US, Phillip Borsos) Intriguing mystery thriller with Kurt Russell as a Miami newspaper reporter who becomes involved with a serial killer when the latter offers him an "exclusive" story. This puts both the reporter and his girlfriend (Mariel Hemingway) in danger. ★★½ $14.99

Mean Streets

(1973, 110 min, US, Martin Scorsese) Scorsese's early masterpiece, set in New York's Little Italy, features a tremendous cast headed by Harvey Keitel and Robert De Niro. Keitel, an aspiring mobster, finds his Catholic background, his love for a young woman and his attachment to an irresponsible friend hindering his fledgling Mafia career. Well integrated into the story is a superlative `60s soundtrack. Scorsese's gritty portrayal of gangland life and his superlative photographic and editing techniques have made this bristling drama often imitated but rarely equalled. ★★★★ $19.99

Meatballs

(1979, 94 min, Canada, Ivan Reitman) Bill Murray's first hit comedy. Alternately funny and ridiculous, the film follows the comic exploits of counselor Murray at summer camp. (Followed by two inferior sequels.) ★★½ $9.99

The Meatrack

(1969, 90 min, US, Michael Thomas) This pre-porn find is an intriguing drama about the sordid life of a young bisexual man "forced" into male prostitution. First seen hitchhiking to San Francisco and immediately being picked up by a salivating older man, the curly-haired, tight-jeaned J.C. (David Calder) proves to be an interesting case study of alienation and sexual denial/confusion. Much like Joe Buck in *Midnight Cowboy* and Joe Dallesandro in *Flesh*, J.T. embarks on a fees-paying sexual odyssey, hooking up with a variety of clients, all of whom are seen in less than flattering light. J.T.'s only glimmer of happiness is offered when he falls in love with innocent Jane (Donna Troy); but like all such urban tales of life on the fringe, his happiness is only fleeting. A little heavy-handed in the moralistic "woe is me the homosexual" angle, this time capsule is nonetheless watchable and, at times, eye-opening. ★★½ $29.99

The Mechanic

(1972, 100 min, US, Michael Winner) This average Charles Bronson suspense/action film casts the stone-faced actor as an aging hit man who reluctantly takes on an apprentice (Jan-Michael Vincent) in order to pass on his bloody craft. Winner, who also directed Bronson in the notorious but successful *Death Wish*, is a competent director who knows how to tell a story — even one which is not particu-

larly full of meaning — and the basic framework of this film is simple yet engaging. Bronson's confident muttering and quiet strength make his cookie-cutter character more interesting than it ought to be, which keeps the viewer's attention riveted to his performance and diverts it from Vincent's hyperactive hit man wannabe. Winner is also able to sustain a sufficient level of tension throughout the film's slow points, ending the movie with a literal bang and a surprise which will satisfy even the most charitable viewer's thirst for revenge. ★★½ $14.99

Medea

(1959, 107 min, US, Jose Quintero) Despite a below-average video transfer, this black-and-white television adaptation of Euripides' classical Greek tragedy about a wronged woman's fury and revenge is nonetheless fascinating. In a role that she played on Broadway, Judith Anderson is Medea, a woman who, fueled by a passionate love for Jason in her youth, stole the Golden Fleece for him, betrayed her country and killed her brother. But now, years later, Jason has abandoned Medea and plans to marry the young daughter of Creon, King of Corinth. Creon, fearful of the magical powers of Medea, banishes her along with her two young sons fathered by Jason. It is here that the story begins, as the age-ravaged Medea, now bitter and scornful, plots strategies for survival as well as to exact a terrible revenge on her enemies. The frenzied, theatrical acting in this filmed stage production is dated and the direction is awkward at times, but Dame Anderson creates a memorable image of a mercurial woman filled with unbridled rage and passion. Produced by David Susskind with Bob Rafelson as the script editor. A statuesque Colleen Dewhurst is featured in support. ★★★ $29.99

Medea

(1971, 100 min, Italy, Pier Paolo Pasolini) With *Medea*, Pasolini presents a troubling vision of Euripides' classic tragedy. Soprano Maria Callas, in her only non-musical role, gives an intense and fascinating interpretation of the woman who murders her children and poisons her husband. (Italian with English subtitles) ★★½ $39.99

Medicine Man

(1992, 104 min, US, John McTiernan) Director McTiernan (*The Hunt for Red October*, *Die Hard*) sets out to save the Venezuelan rain forest, but after this mess, he'll be lucky to salvage his career. Sean Connery, looking great in ponytail, plays an eccentric botanist who retreats into the jungle and discovers the cure for cancer. Enter Lorraine Bracco, Brooklyn scientist, who's been sent to find him. There, they exchange barbs, lose the cancer cure, befriend the natives, battle greedy land developers destroying the forests and fall in love. Sad to say, even Connery's ever-commanding presence isn't enough to make this worthwhile. And Bracco is sorely miscast. This otherwise talented actress' screeching and *kvetching* will have one wishing she'd fall off the nearest hilltop. Though the story has a good premise, *Medicine Man* is one doc whose license should be revoked. ★★ $9.99

Mediterraneo

(1991, 92 min, Italy, Gabriele Salvatores) Catering unashamedly to the saccharin-loving moviegoer, this winner of the Academy Award for Best Foreign-Language Film takes Hollywood's penchant for "feel good" movies, throws in some exotic locales and produces an entertaining but mindlessly unrealistic comedy-drama. Early in WWII, a bungling platoon of Italian military misfits become stranded on a beautiful Greek island. Cut off from the war, this motley assortment of Italian stereotypes find themselves not in battle, but in an idyllic land, filled with eager-to-please, life-loving Greeks (mostly young beautiful women). Greek-Italian relations have never been closer than in this "cultural fantasy." (Italian with English subtitles) ★★½ $19.99

Medium Cool

(1969, 110 min, US, Haskell Wexler) Acclaimed cinematographer Wexler directed this fascinating political drama set against the turbulent backdrop of the 1968 Chicago Democratic Convention. A TV news cameraman (Robert Forster) finds that the dispassion by which he covers his news stories is beginning to be the way he deals with his personal life. A unique blend of fictionalized narrative juxtaposed with the real world. ★★★★ $14.99

Medusa: Dare to Be Truthful

(1992, 51 min, US, John Fortenberry) Julie Brown, spooftress extraordinaire, first made herself known to the world via her "Just Say Julie" show on MTV, and later in the camp-farce musical Earth Girls Are Easy. And now, her masterpiece. Yes, too strong a word; but her send-up of pop icon Madonna's documentary Truth or Dare is dead-on and brilliant. From the oh-so pretentious black-and-white photography, to the letter-perfect costumes and production, right down to the "I'm queen bitch of the world" tantrums and diatribes Ms. M. is famous for, Brown has it down. Highlights include a hilarious (and unbelievably rude) take on Madonna's infamous visit to her mother's gravesite — including a sidesplitting sight gag (watch for the shovel) — and a take-off on "Vogue" entitled, smartly enough, "Vague,"

Mediterraneo

that is a jaw-dropper. Familiarity with *Truth or Dare* is a requirement, so get comfy, watch them back to back, and go into pop culture overdrive. ★★★½ $14.99

Meet John Doe

(1941, 123 min, US, Frank Capra) Capra's social drama stars Barbara Stanwyck as a newspaper reporter who turns hayseed drifter Gary Cooper into a national hero. Edward Arnold offers his usual strong support as a corrupt politician benefitting from Stanwyck's mock grassroots campaign. Capra offers his usual "common man vs. the corporate mindset" in a most capable setting, and the two stars certainly help. ★★★ $19.99

Meet Me in St. Louis

(1944, 114 min, US, Vincente Minnelli) Judy Garland had one of her biggest hits with this charmingly old-fashioned, sentimental musical — a loving reminiscence of turn-of-the-century family life. Mary Astor and Leon Ames are Judy's parents, and little Margaret O'Brien as her sister demonstrates rare and extraordinary emotion for a five-year-old. Judy sings "The Trolley Song" and "Have Yourself a Merry Little Christmas." ★★★★ $19.99

Meet the Feebles

(1992, 92 min, New Zealand, Peter Jackson) If you've ever wondered what becomes of Muppets when they go bad, then this determinedly disgusting (but unfunny) comedy reveals all. Marketed as "one of the sickest movies ever made," this drug, sex and bodily fluid-immersed backstage tale includes such characters as lovelorn Heidi Hippo (a big-titted serial-killing Miss Piggy); a drug-addicted, knife-throwing frog; a promiscuous bunny who contracts AIDS; a fey gay fox who belts out a musical number called "Sodomy"; and many other animal grotesques. A film to offend just about everyone which wallows in its own distastefulness. ★ $89.99

Meeting Venus

(1991, 124 min, US/GB, István Szabó) Hungarian director Szabó, highly acclaimed for his German trilogy of human nature (*Colonel Redl*, the Academy Award-winning *Mephisto* and *Hanussen*), changes his tune with this romantic drama about the efforts of a world-renowned conductor (Niels Arestrup) to mount a multinational production of Wagner's "Tannhauser" while maintaining an amorous affair with his temperamental diva (Glenn Close). While there are a few great moments of tenderness and passion between the leads, Close's character is otherwise wooden and the dubbing of her operatic performances (actually performed by Kiri Te Kanawa) is painfully obvious. ★★½ $19.99

Meetings with Remarkable Men

(1979, 107 min, GB, Peter Brook) The astounding tale of G.I. Gurdjieff, a man driven by a quest for knowledge and the answers to the meaning of existence. Beautifully photographed on location in the mountains of Afghanistan, Brook's illuminating vision stars Terence Stamp and Dragan Maksimovic. ★★★ $69.99

Meet John Doe

Mein Kampf

(1961, 117 min, Sweden, Tore Sjoberg) The rise and fall of Hitler and Nazi Germany is graphically detailed in this powerful documentary. Unusually restrained, the film relies less on sermonizing and allows the images, culled from newsreels and from the extensive footage shot by the Nazis, to speak for themselves. An effective historical foray into the nature of evil, *Mein Kampf* is an invaluable primer for those interested in World War II. ★★★ $39.99

Melvin and Howard

(1980, 95 min, US, Jonathan Demme) A "slice of life" film that looks so spontaneous it borders on voyeurism. A sweet-natured study of Melvin Dummar, who claimed to have given a ride to Howard Hughes one night; later he's mentioned as one of Hughes' heirs for his effort. Paul Le Mat gives a sturdy performance as Melvin, and Mary Steenburgen won an Oscar as his mostly estranged wife. Jason Robards is Howard Hughes. ★★★★ $14.99

Memoirs of an Invisible Man

(1992, 95 min, US, John Carpenter) You'd think Hollywood would have learned by now. There hasn't been a really good "invisible man" movie since the original Claude Rains thriller in 1933 (*Topper* and *Harvey* don't count). Chevy Chase stars as a San Francisco businessman who falls asleep during a business meeting and thanks to a neighboring nuclear fusion accident, wakes up invisible. And to make matters worse, he's got CIA heavy Sam Neill after him. Some good special effects and visual humor help hide a transparent plot, though director Carpenter seems more interested in playing politics than creating a definitive "invisible" comedy. ★½ $9.99

Memories of a Marriage

(1989, 90 min, Denmark, Kaspar Rostrup) Nominated for an Academy Award for Best Foreign Film, this romantic drama is a love story which depicts the joys, sorrows and conflicts of a love affair which lasted a lifetime. Sort of a mix between Bergman's *Scenes of a Marriage* and Merchant Ivory's *Mr. and Mrs. Bridge*, the film's star Ghita Norby won

Denmark's Best Actress Award for her performance. The film itself won the "Film of the Year" award in Germany. (Danish with English subtitles) ★★★ $19.99

Memories of Me

(1988, 105 min, US, Henry Winkler) Alan King's flamboyant performance highlights this pleasant comedy-drama about a heart surgeon (Billy Crystal) who tries to mend the severed relationship with his father (King). Also with JoBeth Williams. ★★★ $9.99

Memories of Underdevelopment

(1968, 97 min, Cuba, Tomás Gutiérrez Alea) The first film from post-revolutionary Cuba to be released in the United States, this wise and fascinating tale of a man finding himself a stranger in his own land was produced by the Cuban Film Institute, but does not contain the doctrinal politicking one would expect from a film sponsored by a young Communist country. The story, set in 1961, revolves around a young man from a bourgeois Europeanized family who, instead of fleeing to Miami with the rest of his family, decides to stay and come to terms with the revolution. Wanting to adapt to the new society, the man, however, finds himself incapable of shedding his bad capitalistic habits and turning over a new socialist leaf. (Spanish with English subtitles) ★★★½ $69.99

Men

(1985, 99 min, West Germany, Doris Dorrie) A shrewdly comic satire about an advertising man who loses his wife to a surly young bohemian. In order to discover where he went wrong, he moves in with his wife's new beau (unbeknownst to her) and thus sets the stage for this scintillating behavioral comedy. The lively script is loaded with outrageous comic asides and intelligent wit. (German with English subtitles) ★★★½ $79.99

The Men

(1950, 85 min, US, Fred Zinnemann) Marlon Brando's screen presence is immediately evident in this, his debut film performance. He's a WWII vet battling the consequences of a wartime injury. Solid acting all around; Jack Webb and Richard Erdman as fellow patients and Everett Sloane as the head doctor offer key support. ★★★½ $19.99

Men Don't Leave

(1990, 113 min, US, Paul Brickman) After her husband's accidental death, suburban mother Jessica Lange is forced to sell her home and, with her two sons (Chris O'Donnell and Tom Mason), she moves to Baltimore for a better-paying job. All three endure their own adjustment to the unfamiliar urban environment, via a parade of teenaged video pirates, elementary school rip-off artists, bitchy gourmet shop owners, one very strange nurse (a quirky characterization by Joan Cusack) and a "professional musician" (Arliss Howard). Brickman's direction seems a bit diffuse early on, but tightens up as the story progresses to a satisfying, believable conclusion. Life does go on, with or without a fairy-tale white knight. ★★★ $19.99

Men in Black

(1997, 95 min, US, Barry Sonnenfeld) In *Independence Day*, which was *the* movie of

Summer '96, Will Smith gallantly saves Earth from hordes of invading aliens. Nothing he did in *ID4*, however, could have prepared Smith for the sheer fun and exhilaration awaiting him, Tommy Lee Jones and especially the viewer in director Sonnenfeld's uproariously entertaining *Men in Black*, which is *the* movie of Summer '97. Smith and Jones play government agents whose task is to monitor illegal aliens — as in the extraterrestrial kind. Playing roles they both do well, Smith is the new, cocky recruit and Jones is the stoic, seasoned vet. When a nasty alien assassin (a giant bug who literally takes the form of Vincent D'Onofrio) arrives to murder one of the many aliens living incognito in New York, our men in black hunt him down like the pesky cockroach he is. Sonnenfeld crams more humor, excitement and terrific effects into the film's efficiently brisk 95-minute running time than the vast majority of box office smashes can manage at any length. *MIB* is funny, hip and a technical wonder. It also nicely explains how and why certain celebrities in our culture achieved their success. That's the *real* scary part. ★★★½ $22.99

Men of Respect

(1991, 113 min, US, William Reilly) Reilly's directorial debut is this stunning take on Shakespeare's "Macbeth," a frenzied gangland tragedy about the bloody rise and fall of a self-destructive and ambitious young man. The film is uneven at times, but has a visceral intensity that should be savored. John Turturro is possessed in the lead role and his real-life wife, Katherine Borowitz, is alluringly deadly as the Lady Macbeth character. Also starring Peter Boyle and Rod Steiger. ★★½ $11.99

The Men Who Tread on the Tiger's Tail

(1945, 60 min, Japan, Akira Kurosawa) Based on a traditional Kabuki theatre piece, this early Kurosawa fable in set in late 12th-century feudal Japan. Having led the Genji Army to victory in battle, Yoshitsune returns home only to incur the wrath of his jealous Shogun brother. With a price on his head, Yoshitsune and his faithful bodyguard/monk Benkei engage a group of warriors to help Yoshitune regain his lordly stature. Thus begins Kurosawa's short (one-hour) though engaging film which follows Yoshitsune's trek across the stylized Japanese countryside to return to his city, now under guard. Dressed as monks, the six warriors (and their comic porter) peacefully march to an almost assuredly violent confrontation. But there are no battles here. Kurosawa revels in the power of the spoken word, eschewing action for the dynamics of personal conflict, and his usage of editing and sound substitutes for swordplay. Simplistic in its storytelling, *Men* produces a tension and lyricism through cunning and myth. Denjiro Okochi is superb as the mentor-like Benkei. (Japanese with English subtitles) ★★★ $39.99

The Men's Club

(1986, 100 min, US, Peter Medak) A group of middle-aged men gath-

er for an evening to discuss their lives, and end up at a whorehouse. Mediocre version of Leonard Michael's novel. A cast including Roy Scheider, Treat Williams, Frank Langella and Harvey Keitel can't help matters. ★

Menace II Society

(1993, 90 min, US, Allen & Albert Hughes) Going several steps beyond its more tame cousin, *Boyz N the Hood*, *Menace II Society* is a gripping and unapologetic view of life on the mean streets of L.A.'s Compton. The film centers on Caine, an archetypal, disenfranchised '90s urban youth who follows the street's kill-or-be-killed code with an eerily dispassionate degree of stoicism — it all seems to be beyond his scope of caring, or as his homey O-Dog puts it, "I'm America's nightmare: young, black and I don't give a fuck." Featuring superb ensemble acting and a seamless visual acumen, the film may indeed prove frightening to some as it gives witness to the brutality which shapes young lives without so much as a hint of judgment: There are no heroes or villains in this story, just average people living average lives. A scary thought, perhaps, but it is what gives the film its brilliance. ★★★★ $14.99

Ménage

(1986, 84 min, France, Bertrand Blier) Family values are turned inside-out in this outrageously wacky sexual farce that takes demonic delight in its vulgarity, misogyny and demented sexual mores. Life changes abruptly for the feuding, poverty striken couple Antoine (Michel Blanc) and his wife Monique (Miou-Miou) after they meet the bombastic and dangerously exciting Bob (Gérard Depardieu), who showers them with money and promises of the good life — made possible by inviting them to his nightly burglary raids of rich homes. But the rewards of the bourgeois life has its price, especially after the burly Bob falls passionately in love with...no, not the sexy Monique, but the bald, mousy and frantically tight-lipped Antoine! Watching Depardieu wax poetic and become all girlish in front of the bewildered Antoine is a hilariously priceless moment in French cinema. (French with English subtitles) ★★★½ $29.99

Mephisto

(1981, 135 min, West Germany, István Szabó) A riveting portrait of the artist as opportunist. Klaus Maria Brandauer turns in a breathtaking

Men in Black

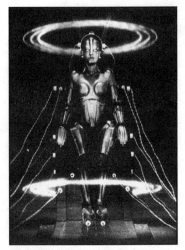

Metropolis

performance as an actor whose burning ambition leads him to compromise his artistry, relationships and well-being. Director Szabó captures the grand spectacle and subtle nuances of a man obsessed. (Dubbed) ★★★½ $14.99

The Mephisto Waltz

(1971, 108 min, US, Paul Wendkos) Very effective satanic chiller with Alan Alda as a journalist who experiences changes after interviewing dying musician Curt Jurgens. Jacqueline Bisset plays Alda's wife. ★★★ $59.99

The Merchant of Four Seasons

(1972, 88 min, West Germany, Rainer Werner Fassbinder) Fassbinder's first widely recognized film concerns the life struggle of Hans: a born loser who is rejected by his bourgeois family, spurned by his "one true love," married to an unfaithful wife, cheated by his friends and reduced to peddling fruit to sustain a meager existence. A superb mixture of black humor, melodrama and satire with an unforgettable and haunting ending. (German with English subtitles) ★★★★ $29.99

Mere Jeevan Saathi (My Life Partner)

(1965, 126 min, India, Ravee Nagaich) Although India produces hundreds of films each year, the very few that ever reach our shores are almost exclusively limited to the works of Satyajit Ray. And while the vast majority of these releases are produced solely for domestic viewing, there are many that can be enjoyed by an international audience. *Mere Jeevan Saathi*, an exuberant romance/comedy/musical which details a businessman's sudden rise and fall, is a good example of modern Indian filmmaking. (Hindi with English subtitles) ★★★

Meridian

(1990, 91 min, US, Charles Band) Sexy Sherilyn Fenn stars as an artist who returns to her family's ancestral estate in Italy, where she finds and falls in love with a gentle yet hideous

creature. Soon, she learns that the castle is under the spell of an ancient curse that only she can dispel. ★★½ $19.99

Mermaids

(1990, 115 min, US, Richard Benjamin) A pair of winning performances from Cher and Winona Ryder punctuate this pleasantly quirky coming-of-age comedy-drama about a thoroughly unconventional single mother and her abundantly confused and zealously pious teenage daughter. Along with baby sister Kate (Christina Ricci), they uproot and move to a small New England town, circa 1963, where neighbors duly observe that they are not the typical nuclear family. Bob Hoskins lends his considerable talents as a local shoe merchant who falls for Cher and wants to help her discover familial bliss. Ryder's saturnine portrayal of adolescence is quickly becoming a thing of legend and her ability to deliver sullen, dead-pan one-liners transforms *Mermaids* from potentially gooey family melodrama to often hilarious, sometimes heartwarming comedy. ★★★ $14.99

Merrill's Mauraders

(1962, 98 min, US, Samuel Fuller) Director Fuller delivers another solid WWII actioner set in the Pacific Theatre. Jeff Chandler leads a war-weary battalion in the Burmese jungle on an arduous trek through hostile terrain populated by deadly, well-concealed Japanese troops. Based on the actual exploits of Brigadier General Frank D. Merrill. ★★★ $14.99

Merry Christmas Mr. Lawrence

(1983, 122 min, GB/Japan, Nagisa Oshima) Oshima's mesmerizing drama studies the conflicting cultures of East and West, which surface within the confines of a WWII POW camp. David Bowie is a captured New Zealander whose stiff-lipped bravery and rebellious nature perplex his Japanese guards and intrigue the compound's commanding officer, who is gravely smitten by Bowie's allure. (Filmed in English) ★★★ $19.99

The Merry Widow

(1934, 99 min, US, Ernst Lubitsch) The great Lubitsch had the right "touch" with this delightfully sophisticated, tongue-in-cheek adaptation of the Franz Lehar operetta. Maurice Chevalier is at his best as the dashing nobleman who tries to woo a rich widow from Paris to her homeland where the bankrupt country is in desperate need of her funds. Jeanette MacDonald plays the title role. ★★★½ $19.99

Meteor

(1979, 105 min, US, Ronald Neame) The worst special effects you've ever seen highlight this strangely intriguing disaster film, one of the last in the line of buildings, ships, killer quakes and other forces of nature. Sean Connery brings unexpected humor to this mishmash as a scientist who has six days to prevent a giant meteor from destroying most of Earth. Brian Keith, as Connery's Soviet counterpart, also rises above the script and direction to give a funny performance. Natalie Wood, Karl Malden and Henry Fonda also star. ★★

Meteor Man

(1993, 100 min, US, Robert Townsend) Absolute silliness from actor/director Townsend (*Hollywood Shuffle*), who stars as a young urban idealist who believes in a better life for his ghetto community. Opportunity comes knocking one day when he is hit by a meteor and given the supernatural powers needed to rid his neighborhood of drug dealers. Hokey beyond reckoning, the film is not without its endearing moments and occasionally Townsend's comic genius shines through — a particularly hilarious moment finds Townsend and his nemesis doing battle on the streets using runway modeling moves. ★★ $14.99

Metro

(1997, 117 min, US, Thomas Carter) At the heart of this Eddie Murphy action/comedy is a terrific car chase down the precarious streets of San Francisco, involving two cops, a killer, a runaway cable car and a trolley full of screaming bystanders. Logic and crashed cars are tossed through the air like matchbox toys, but this sequence is a hyperkinetic, giddily over-the-top piece of Hollywood stunt craftsmanship — and excess. A lesson from the school of bigger and louder is better. But as *Metro* zooms along, it feels more like the film was written "around" this spectacular chase scene. Murphy plays a police hostage negotiator who runs afoul of a vicious killer after a botched robbery. Michael Rapaport is his new trainee, who merely turns up whenever Murphy needs an extra pair of eyes or a sharpshooter or a lipreader (don't ask). By now, it's safe to assume that most Hollywood police thrillers are identical with little variation on the film-by-numbers plots, and *Metro* is one of these. Murphy is in fine comic form, but after his brilliant comeback in *The Nutty Professor*, this is a step backwards. He should be growing as an actor, not chasing his own tail in rote action movies like this. ★★ $102.99

Metropolis

(1926, 120 min, Germany, Fritz Lang) Lang's spectacularly stunning vision of a world ruled by machines and controlled by Big Brother is one of the most important works to come out of the German Expressionist Film Movement in the 1920s. Its continued popular appeal lies in the fact that so many of Lang's images of

Mi Vida Loca

future society still capture our imagination. Print quality is good, and is accompanied by a classical misic soundtrack. ★★★★ $29.99

Metropolis
(Giorgio Moroder Version)

(1926, 129 min, Germany, Fritz Lang) Giorgio Moroder's restored and tinted edition of Lang's futuristic classic is a beauty to watch. His trick is in replacing the usual classical soundtrack for this silent film with modern rock songs, which will either have people turning up their volume or frantically running to throw their speakers out the window! The print itself is in mint condition.

Metropolitan

(1990, 108 min, US, Whit Stillman) A cast of unknowns breathes life into first-time writer-director Stillman's Oscar nominated screenplay about a preppie "divorce orphan," from the less-than-fashionable Upper West Side, who falls in with the right crowd for a season of meaningless social events. He mocks their empty lifestyle with a refreshing no-holds-barred honesty, which, while not comedic in content, transforms *Metropolitan* into hilarious social satire. ★★★½ $19.99

Mexican Bus Ride
(Ascent to Heaven)

(1951, 73 min, Mexico, Luis Buñuel) The misadventures of an innocent young man who is sent to the mountains to fetch the family lawyer to his dying mother is delightfully brought to the screen by the always mischievous, irreverent and surrealistic Buñuel. (Dubbed) ★★★

Mi Vida Loca   (My Crazy Life)

(1994, 92 min, US, Allison Anders) Writer-director Anders' follow-up to her hit art-house film *Gas Food Lodging* is an insightful look into the lives of young Latino gangsters living in Echo Park, Los Angeles. The film is divided into three main segments that intertwine to tell the story of a gangland community from the perspective of the main characters. Differing from the usual gang picture in that it is told from a primarily female vantage point, *Mi Vida Loca* centers around two best friends, Sad Girl and Mousey, and the man they both love, Ernesto. The well-written script emotionally portrays the struggle of gangland females to raise children in a world where most fathers are dead or in jail by adulthood. This film does not rely on a big-budget or graphic violence to tell its powerful story; instead it is done with well-written dialogue, an interesting story and excellent acting. ★★★★ $19.99

Miami Blues

(1990, 97 min, US, George Armitage) Alec Baldwin, sporting a crew cut and oftentimes a topless torso, stars in this offbeat, funny and wildly enjoyable comedy-thriller as a recently paroled killer and pathological liar who poses as a cop to save crime victims before he himself rips them off. He soon meets a gullible young prostitute, Jennifer Jason Leigh, and together they play house, with Leigh cooking and cleaning and Baldwin leaving in the morning for his day of crime. Fred Ward also stars as the slovenly cop, who, after losing his gun

Alan Rickman (l.), Liam Neeson (c.) and Aidan Quinn in *Michael Collins*

and false teeth to Baldwin, is determined to bring him to justice. All have fun with their roles, but Leigh is almost too good for the film, bringing heartbreaking depth in an unusually moving performance. ★★★½ $9.99

Miami Rhapsody

(1995, 95 min, US, David Frankel) Yes, it's truly ironic that Mia Farrow appears in this fluffy romantic comedy which is about as close to a Woody Allen film as one can get without having Allen's name on the credits. But that's not to suggest that *Miami Rhapsody* bears a resemblance either artistic or comical to the Woodman: This is most definitely "Woody Lite." Trying to act more sophisticated than she really is, Sarah Jessica Parker plays a twentysomething writer whose impending marriage opens her eyes to the failings of the relationships of those around her. These include her mother Farrow, who is actually quite good as a middle-aged housewife having an affair with nurse Antonio Banderas; father Paul Mazursky; and brother Kevin Pollak, who has a pregnant wife and a roving eye. There are some amusing moments and one-liners to this *Rhapsody*, but the characters' and story's lack of development makes it half-a-beat off. ★★½ $19.99

Michael

(1996, 105 min, US, Nora Ephron) As if his otherworldly role in *Phenomenon* wasn't enough, John Travolta now takes on the part of an angel — a wisecracking, crotch-scratching, barhopping one at that — in this sloppy romantic comedy. William Hurt, Andie MacDowell and Robert Pastorelli are reporters for a supermarket tabloid who respond to Iowa housewife Jean Stapleton's letter about her angel houseguest Michael (Travolta). Low and behold, he's the real thing. As they set out to return to their Chicago offices with Michael in tow, all are affected in one way or another by their heavenly traveling companion. Travolta once again proves that he's such an engaging presence on-screen that he can rise above such dribble, and he alone is the saving grace of this inexplicable box office hit. Hurt and MacDowell have a budding romance that is

both unbelievable and shabbily conceived, and the plot point isn't helped by MacDowell's one-note performance. ★★ $102.99

Michael Caine — Acting in Film

Renowned actor Michael Caine, veteran of countless film roles, is a surprisingly perceptive and engrossing teacher in this short film in which he offers tips and fundamental techniques for effective acting in front of the camera. Before a class of six students, a live audience and the video viewer, Caine intructs them on the subtleties of film acting — from close-up reaction shots to line reading and even demonstrating the importance of eye movement to a scene. Fascinating for both acting students as well as the general movie-going public. ★★★½ $39.99

Michael Collins

(1996, 127 min, Ireland, Neil Jordan) In a role befitting his larger-than-life screen presence, Liam Neeson gives his best performance since *Schindler's List* playing another real-life character who overcomes odds to carve a niche for himself in history. Superbly directed by Jordan (who also wrote the intelligent screenplay), *Michael Collins* is the passionate, remarkably detailed story of the Irish revolutionary who sought to seek Ireland's independence from British rule. Though comparisons could be made to 1995's Oscar winner *Braveheart*, this more contemporary tale utilizes both speech and action to convey the commitment of its battle-scarred hero. With the complex political issues of the formation of the Irish Republican Army at its core, the film traces the rise of Collins as a party official whose legend and determination led to brief peace and an Ireland which still exists today. Neeson is surrounded by an expert supporting cast, including Aidan Quinn as his right-hand man, Alan Rickman as the leader of the Army, Stephen Rea as a police detective, and, in a surprisingly effective portrayal, Julia Roberts as Collins' girlfriend. An impressive achievement on all levels, *Michael Collins* is stirring as both history and cinema. ★★★★ $19.99

The Midas Touch

(1989, 100 min, Hungary, Geza Beremenyi) Winner of the 1990 European Film Award for Best Director, this involving political drama unfolds in Budapest in the early 1950s. Monori is a quick-thinking merchant with a penchant for making a quick profit – from the sale of anything from apples to lentils. His schemes and techniques are severly tested with the approaching turmoil of 1956. (Hungarian with English subtitles) ★★★ $79.99

Midnight

(1939, 94 min, US, Mitchell Leisen) "Every Cinderella has her midnight" says imposter Claudette Colbert, and in trying to escape hers a breezy, sophisticated romp is born. Cleverly written by Billy Wilder and Charles Brackett, this effervescent romantic comedy stars Colbert as a penniless showgirl newly arrived to Paris. She befriends cabbie Don Ameche, who soon falls for her. But true love must wait when Colbert is hired by baron John Barrymore (in a spirited comeback performance) to impersonate a countess – it seems his wife Mary Astor is involved in a romantic indiscretion with playboy Francis Lederer, and it's up to Colbert to come between them. Director Leisen sets a brisk pace, though the film's theme of mistaken identity and the screenplay's sexual innuendo is pure Wilder. Colbert, as usual, is a delight. ★★★★ $14.99

A Midnight Clear

(1992, 107 min, US, Keith Gordon) Gordon's second directorial feature, after The Chocolate War, is a vigorous and very polished antiwar drama, and a much more assured piece of filmmaking than his debut. Set during the last months of WWII, the story traces the emotional toll taken on a group of weary, young G.I.s at the front line who come in contact with a group of German soldiers. The equally tired enemy soon makes clear their desire for surrender. As each side cautiously builds to a ceasefire, both armies enjoy a respite from the hell around them. But for how long? Gordon handles his young cast very well, who include Ethan Hawke, Kevin Dillon, Frank Whaley, Arye Gross and Peter Berg. Gary Sinise has a pivotal role as an older and much-beloved platoon member. ★★★½ $19.99

Midnight Cowboy

(1969, 113 min, US, John Schlesinger) No longer the shocking tale it was when first released, this classic slice of pop culture has evolved into a somewhat nostalgic reminder of the `60s mindset, capturing the naiveté and upheaval of a society enduring growing pains. Jon Voight and Dustin Hoffman create a pair of legendary screen losers: Joe Buck, the aspiring stud-for-hire; and Ratso Rizzo, his rodent-like mentor. ★★★★ $14.99

Midnight Crossing

(1988, 104 min, US, Roger Holzberg) Tedious thriller with Faye Dunaway and Daniel J. Travanti as a husband and wife who are searching for buried loot he had stashed away years before. ★ $89.99

Midnight Dancers

(1994, 100 min, The Philippines, Mel Chionglo) This eye-opening but over-the-top mess of melodramatic excess explores the tumultuous life and unconventional loves of "macho dancers" – male prostitutes who work as dancers and hustlers in Manila's gay bars. A more chaste and unrefined take on these young men than Lino Brocka's luridly watchable Macho Dancers, the tale begins when young country-bred Sonny (Lawrence David) rejoins his family in Manila. He learns that his two brothers both earn a living dancing and prostituting themselves. They oddly approach this sleazy lifestyle as simply a way to make easy money, an attitude shared by their parents. Sonny becomes intrigued by the scene and begins to work there, ultimately beginning an affair with a sultry transvestite. Prostitution and homosexuality are approached so casually, that the filmmaker can't use them as dramatic devices; and that's the problem, for the simple story lacks dramatic tension or focus. However, despite the awkward, over-ambitious handling of the many social themes it explores, the drama proves to be impassioned, sexy and involving. (Filipino with English subtitles) ★★½ $29.99

Midnight Express

(1978, 121 min, US, Alan Parker) Based on the autobiography of Billy Hayes, this intense film explores the hellish years Hayes spent in a Turkish prison for drug smuggling. Brad Davis gives a remarkably complex performance as Hayes, and a good cast includes John Hurt and Randy Quaid. Violent, raw and powerful, Midnight Express works on both an emotional level as Hayes witnesses, experiences and fights back against the brutality of the prison staff, and as an exposé on corruption and examination of camaraderie. The film does contain one false note, however, as in real life Hayes was lovers with a fellow prisoner, but here he is politely brushed aside. Oscar-winning screenplay by Oliver Stone. ★★★½ $12.99

Midnight Run

(1988, 122 min, US, Martin Briest) Robert De Niro stars as a modern-day bounty hunter who is hired to escort mob accountant Charles Grodin from New York to Los Angeles to stand trial. What begins as a simple plane ride turns into a no-holds-barred cross-country free-for-all involving the FBI, the Mafia, hit men and rival bounty hunters. Highlighted by well-staged shootouts and chase scenes, and quite humorous and delightfully venomous sparring between the two stars. ★★★ $14.99

A Midsummer Night's Dream

(1935, 117 min, US, Max Reinhardt) Captivating version of Shakespeare's classic, with an all-star cast including James Cagney (as Bottom), Mickey Rooney (who steals the show as Puck), Olivia deHavilland, Dick Powell and Joe E. Brown. ★★★ $19.99

A Midsummer Night's Dream

(1968, 124 min, GB, Peter Hall) Shakespeare goes Mod! The Royal Shakespeare Company's frolicking rendition of the Bard's masterful farce is indeed a daring departure from the norm, but is in every way true to the author's intent. A must for fans of theatre. A splendid cast includes Diana Rigg, David Warner, Ian Richardson, Judi Dench and Ian Holm as the mischievous Puck. ★★★ $24.99

A Midsummer Night's Sex Comedy

(1982, 88 min, US, Woody Allen) Allen ponders the foibles of sex, love and courtship in this whimsical period piece. Six couples engage in a romantic roundelay during an idyllic country outing. Starring Mia Farrow, Tony Roberts, Mary Steenburgen and Jose Ferrer. ★★★ $14.99

A Midwinter's Tale

(1995, 98 min, GB, Kenneth Branagh) Lovers of theatre will rejoice in this uproarious and frenetic look at the inner-workings of a haphazardly slapped together theatre troupe and their attempt to mount a production of "Hamlet" – on Christmas Eve! Made by Branagh no doubt as a study for his subsequent film adaptation of the play, A Midwinter's Tale opens with a perky rendition of Noël Coward singing his "Why Must the Show Go On?" which immediately sets an irreverent tone. The madness begins when out-of-work actor-director Joe Harper (Michael Maloney, who played Laertes in Branagh's Hamlet) begs his agent (Joan Collins) for some money to stage "Hamlet." He quickly assembles a cast of theatre rejects that includes Richard Briers (who played Polonius in Hamlet) as Claudius; Julia Sawalha (Saffron of "Absolutely Fabulous") as Ophelia; Nicholas Farrell (Horatio in Hamlet) as Laertes; John Sessions as a drag queen Gertrude; and, in perhaps the most hilarious turn, Celia Imrie as a designer so ethereal, her concept doesn't occur to her until opening night. With just two weeks to rehearse, the question becomes "how can the show possibly go on?" Branagh's cast does a crackling job exploring the tenuous relations of so many super-egos, and the film becomes increasingly riveting as their collective cool breaks down. ★★★½ $99.99

Mighty Aphrodite

(1995, 95 min, US, Woody Allen) Perhaps reacting to the seriousness of his personal life, Allen's comedy of a married couple who adopt, and of the middle-aged father's obsession with the young birth mother, is not as complex in character and narrative as Allen's former films, but is nevertheless consistently funny and thoroughly entertaining. Allen plays a sports writer married to an ambitious art gallery employee (Helena Bonham Carter). They decide to adopt, and as the exceptional child grows, Allen becomes determined to locate the real mother. All his preconceptions about familial lineage and genes are smashed when he meets a ditsy prostitute/porn actress (marvelously played by Oscar winner Mira Sorvino), and then becomes involved in her life. As in his Play It Again, Sam, Allen's subconscious comes to life, here in the form of F. Murray Abraham as a member of a Greek chorus who'd be more at home on Broadway than the Acropolis. In fact, many of Allen's signature themes – neurosis, infidelity and upperclass New York anxieties – are on display. They may not cut as deep, but they run wild just the same. ★★★ $14.99

M

The Mighty Ducks

(1992, 104 min, US, Stephen Herek) This amiable Disney farce stars Emilio Estevez as Gordon Bombay, a high-powered schmuck of a lawyer whose dubious philosophy of life is suitably summed up by his personalized license plate – JUSTWIN. His winning streak comes to an end, however, when he is arrested for D.W.I. and sentenced to community service as the coach of a public league hockey team in Minneapolis' poorest neighborhood. Of course, this is the perfect setup for the type-A, egomaniacal Gordon to come to terms with his fall from grace as a child hockey star and learn the traditional virtue that "winning isn't everything." Purely formulaic, *The Mighty Ducks* goes out of its way to be predictable schmaltz and nonetheless, if one suspends one's normal critical faculties for an hour-and-a-half, the film is enjoyable and contains all of the right elements to thoroughly entertain the kids – which it did in droves in its theatrical run. Joss Ackland appears as a hockey shop owner and Gordon's childhood mentor. (Followed by two sequels) ★★½ $9.99

Mighty Joe Young

(1949, 94 min, US, Ernest B. Schoedsack) Schoedsack and Robert Armstrong, the director and star of *King Kong* and *Son of Kong*, are back together; yet again sharing the spotlight with an ape. This cult favorite, which features good special effects, is about a young girl and her pet gorilla. Lots of fun. ★★★ $19.99

Mighty Morphin Power Rangers: The Movie

(1995, 95 min, US, Bryan Spicer) So it's short on character development. So the plot is so thin it's almost transparent. Its target audience will certainly love this movie. In honor of the transition to the large screen, this adaptation of the popular TV series features a new villain, Ivan Ooze (Paul Freeman), who has been freed from six thousand years of captivity forced upon him by Teen Rangers of yore. (The plot avoids the history lesson on who exactly inhabited North America 4,000 B.C.) The Rangers get new zords and really cool outfits in the process of saving the day, helped by a scantily clad sorceress. The climax reveals the new, improved fighting giant, the Ninja Falcon Mehazord, which, of course, means a new set of film-related merchandise just in time for the holidays. The female Rangers on the TV series are as strong and able as their male counterparts, but curiously here they scream for help and need to be rescued, belying their usual equal status. ★★ $22.99

The Mighty Quinn

(1989, 98 min, US, Carl Shenkel) Here's a film which, while it's not going to win any awards, will provide the viewer with a mildly entertaining evening of mystery and fun. Denzel Washington stars as Xavier Quinn, a police chief on a small Carribean island. Determined to clear the name of his childhood friend – now a somewhat notorious local criminal (Robert Townsend) – Quinn tenaciously probes the murder of a white businessman on the island. In a somewhat predictable twist, he runs into a lot of opposition from some of the island's more prestigious constituents. ★★½ $9.99

The Mikado

(1990, 131 min, GB, John Michael Phillips) For his highly acclaimed rendition of the Gilbert and Sullivan opera, British stage producer Jonathan Miller moved the play's action from Japan to England in the 1920s and '30s. Filmed before a live audience at the London Coliseum, this sensational production features Monty Python's Eric Idle as Ko-Ko. ★★★½ $39.99

Mikey and Nicky

(1976, 105 min, US, Elaine May) This acclaimed drama written and directed by May (which was re-released ten years after its initial run to critical praise) stars John Cassavetes and Peter Falk as two small-time hoods who try to avoid a mob hit man (Ned Beatty). Quirky and very appealing. ★★★ $29.99

Mildred Pierce

(1945, 111 min, US, Michael Curtiz) An Oscar-winning performance by Joan Crawford highlights this high-gloss soaper about a long-suffering mom who competes with her ungrateful little minx of a daughter for the affections of the same man. Ann Blyth is wonderfully rotten as daughter Vida, and the always reliable Eve Arden is a scene-stealer as Joan's best friend. ★★★½ $19.99

Milk Money

(1994, 110 min, US, Richard Benjamin) Part *Pretty Woman* and part adolescent coming-of-age fantasy, *Milk Money* is an innocuous comedy about prostitution, suburbia, Grace Kelly and parenthood. Michael Patrick Carter plays a 12-year-old boy who with two friends goes searching for a prostitute in the big city. There he meets good-hearted Melanie Griffith who, through a series of circumstances, comes to stay at his place in the burbs, prompting the youth to try to set her up with his widowed father (Ed Harris). The film is a little too grown up for kids and too childish for adults, and there's its problem: *Milk Money* isn't sure what it wants to be. But thanks to some appealing performances (especially Harris' goofy, lighthearted absent-minded dad), there are smiles in the offing. ★★½ $14.99

The Milky Way

(1936, 89 min, US, Leo McCarey) Harold Lloyd's best talkie has the silent clown as a mild-mannered milkman who becomes an unlikely boxing sensation when he accidentally knocks out the champ. Remade in 1946 as *The Kid from Brooklyn* with Danny Kaye. ★★★ $24.99

The Milky Way

(1969, 102 min, France, Luis Buñuel) The religious pilgrimage of two tramps traveling from France to Spain is the pretense of a plot in this savagely funny and continually imaginative heretical assault on organized religion. The folly of man's continual adherence to the insanities of Church dogma are portrayed through the tramps' surrealistic encounters with the Virgin Mary and Jesus Christ, as well as the Marquis de Sade. (French with English subtitles) ★★★★ $24.99

Mille Bolle Blu

(1993, 83 min, Italy, Leone Pompucci) Like a palimpsest used once too often, this breezy little comedy is mared by a faded familiarity that comes from having seen this all before. It is 1961. All Rome awaits the projected solar eclipse. The summer's warmth forces open the windows and doors on an archtypical street in the heart of the city. Imagine, if you will, Alfred Hitchcock's *Rear Window* with lots of yelling and gesticulation; no one has any secrets for long, and everyone has a colorful story. Someone dies. Someone marries. Characters are drawn with Fellini-esque broad strokes: endearing, entertaining, and as flat and as fleeting as the color comics section on Sunday. (Italian with English subtitles) ★★½ $89.99

Millennium

(1989, 95 min, US, Michael Anderson) An intriguing concept for a science-fiction adventure – about a group of aliens who rescue passengers of airplanes right before they crash – is given an uneven treatment in this occasionally entertaining thriller. Cheryl Ladd stars as a benign extraterrestrial from an underpopulated, dying planet whose scientists keep track of crashes, whisking away the doomed passengers to help repopulate their own world. Kris Kristofferson also stars as an airline inspector who becomes involved with time-hopping stewardess Ladd. ★★½ $14.99

Miller's Crossing

(1990, 115 min, US, Joel Coen) This thoroughly engrossing and brilliantly produced gangland sendup overflows with sardonic wit, bristling dialogue and operatic violence. Gabriel Byrne heads an excellent cast as Tom, a mob insider whose endless scheming provides the plot with an abundance of unexpected twists, double-crosses and red herrings. The story follows a fight for control of City Hall between Tom's boss, Leo (confidently portrayed by Albert Finney), and an arch-rival. In the midst of the fray is Bernie Bernbaum, a weasely small-time hood who's trying to muscle in on both men's numbers racket. As Bernie, John Turturro delivers a tantalizingly over-the-top performance. In her cinematic debut, Marcia Gay Harden is superb as the hard-as-nails Verna, who is both Bernie's sister and Leo's girlfriend. ★★★★ $14.99

Millhouse: A White Comedy

(1971, 92 min, US, Emile De Antonio) Richard Milhous Nixon gets the De Antonio treatment in this biting "documentary" satire that exposes, through creative use of newsreel footage and interviews, the abominations of our 37th president. Made before the Watergate scandal, we view a calculating, opportunistic and amoral Nixon who, on occasion, has advocated the death penalty for drug dealers and a nuclear assault on Southeast Asia. A funny but sobering view of an American megalomaniac. ★★★ $39.99

Le Million

(1931, 85 min, France, René Clair) A finely tuned musical comedy which follows the wild adventures of a penniless and creditor-hounded painter who wins a million francs in a lottery but loses the winning ticket in a pair of pants he had pawned. His hurried attempts to retrieve the ticket, while keeping just one step ahead of his creditors, make this a delightful film. (French with English subtitles) ★★★½

Min and Bill

(1930, 66 min, US, George Hill) Marie Dressler won an Oscar for her heartbreaking performance as a feisty waterfront hotel proprietress who fights to keep the abandoned girl, whom she has raised as her own, from being taken away. In one of the big hits of the 1930s, Dressler and co-star Wallace Beery make a great team. ★★★ $19.99

Mina Tannenbaum

(1994, 128 min, France, Martine Dugowson) A rich, layered film, *Mina Tannenbaum* charts the winding path of a relationship between two women. Mina, a rebellious painter (Romane Bohringer), meets Ethel (Elsa Zylberstein) in dance class at age seven. Alongside their relational development, the film conquers such issues as ethnic identity, mental illness and the power of familial history. In addition, the two women must resolve their struggles with art and feminism in face of a dominant and conformist culture. Though thematically the film bites off more than it can chew, each of these issues is handled with subtlety and sensitivity. Director Dugowson, who also wrote the screenplay, treats her subject matter with imagination and humor, often taking interesting filmic risks. (French with English subtitles) ★★★ $89.99

Minbo (Or the Gentle Art of Japanese Extortion)

(1994, 123 min, Japan, Juzo Itami) When a high-class hotel comes under siege from a gang of mobsters known in Japan as the Yakuza, it takes the savvy of a strong-willed woman to face them down. Beginning as a whimsical comedy that slowly turns into an intense exposé on the wiliness of the criminal world, this biting satire makes for spirited and entertaining fun. The Hotel Europa and its employees become the object of elaborate extortion plots from cartoonish thugs, despite the efforts of the meek accountant-turned-security head. But instead of guns and the police, help arrives in the form of Mahiru Inoue, a small, well-dressed young woman and attorney-at-law who goes to battle with nothing more than her devilish grin, disarming wit and tons of *chutzpa*. While some of the film's reliance on the Japanese honor code and their fear of losing face might distance some viewers, this daring film should intrigue most. Director Itami (*Tampopo, A Taxing Woman*) was attacked and injured by outraged Yakuzas during its making yet he finished the film and it became one of Japan's highest-grossing films. (Japanese with English subtitles) ★★★ $79.99

The Mind's Eye

(1990, 40 min,) Engaging, visually stunning collection of computer animated shorts, spanning in content from the dawn of creation into the distant future. ★★★ $14.99

Mindwalk

(1991, 110 min, US, Bernt Capra) Written by theoretical physicist Fritjof Capra ("The Tao of Physics") and directed by his brother Bernt, this intriguing environmental talk-fest is certainly no masterpiece of drama, but for lovers of "Nova" and other PBS science programs, as well as environmentalists and New Age adherents, this will undoubtedly prove to be both fascinating and entertaining. Sam Waterston is a liberal politician who, having just lost a bid for the White House, travels to France to visit his old '60s buddy, poet John Heard. As they walk aroung the medieval Iles de St. Michel, they happen upon Liv Ullmann, a semi-retired Norwegian quantum physicist. This chance meeting gives way to what can best be described as *My Dinner with Andre* meets *A Brief History of Time* as Ullmann lectures the two men on the history of physics and how Cartesian and Newtonian mechanical thinking has led us to our current environmental crisis. ★★½ $19.99

The Miniver Story

(1950, 104 min, US, H.C. Potter) Released eight years after the classic *Mrs. Miniver*, this decidedly inferior sequel features that film's two stars, Greer Garson and Walter Pidgeon. Beginning on VE-Day, the film follows the postwar life of Mrs. Miniver as she welcomes back her husband and family separated during the war. The story introduces a possible extramarital affair for Mrs. M. in the beginning, but quickly forgets it after her husband arrives. Mr. M., unlike other post-war film characters, has no difficulty adjusting to civilian life — it's as if he's been on an extended fishing trip rather than fighting abroad. Whereas the original explored war-time issues with intelligence, this post-war saga is artificial and meandering. That's James Fox as the young son. ★★ $19.99

Miracle at Moreaux

(1985, 58 min, US, Paul Shapiro) Loretta Swit stars as a nun in WWII France. Based on a true incident, the story follows Swit and her students as they risk their lives to enable three Jewish children to escape from the Nazis — a process which forces them to overcome their own prejudices and fears. The gripping drama and endearing characters make the film both highly entertaining and educational. ★★★ $14.99

Miracle Down Under

(1987, 106 min, Australia, George Miller) Directed by Miller (*The Man from Snowy River*, not *Mad Max*, etc.), this compelling Australian drama follows the adventures and personal conflicts of a group of settlers exploring the uncharted southeastern Australian territory in the late 1800s. Dee Wallace Stone and John Waters (no, not *that* John Waters) star. ★★★ $29.99

Miracle in Milan

(1951, 96 min, Italy, Vittorio De Sica) Merging his trademark style of Neorealism with an enchanting urban fable, De Sica succeeds in creating a politically charged yet endearing poetic tale. The story begins when a poor old lady finds a baby abandoned in a cabbage field. The orphan, Toto, grows up a smiling, accepting and generous young man, despite the abject poverty that surrounds him in war-ravaged Milan. Toto, with the help of the city's homeless, constructs a squatter city, only to see it threatened by greedy developers. Hope is not lost, however, for with the aid of a magical dove given to him by his departed stepmother, he tries to save their beloved home town. A humorous story of survival told without bitterness, from one of Italy's greatest filmmakers. (Italian with English subtitles) ★★★½ $29.99

Miracle in Rome

(1989, 76 min, Colombia, Lisandro Duque Naranjo) This wonderfully tender and heart-rending story of faith, hope and love is set in a small town in Colombia. A man's seven-year-old daughter, Evelia, dies suddenly in his arms. She is buried, but 12 years later the man, Margarito, is forced to exhume the body when the area is slated for development. To his amazement, her body is just as he left it, with Evelia seemingly only asleep. The town soon claims a miracle and declares her a saint; but the area's bishop, wanting to avoid red tape, would rather have her quickly reburied and forgotten. Resisting the pressure, Margarito goes off to Rome, with the girl's body in tow, to plead his case for beatification to the Pope; only to be greeted by indifference and a labyrinthine religious bureaucracy. But his faith and love for his child keep him resolute as he soon realizes that a miracle of a different order is needed. Adapted from a story by Gabriel Garcia Marquez. (Spanish with English subtitles) ★★★ $19.99

Miracle Mile

(1989, 102 min, US, Steve DeJarnatt) An off-the-wall, strangely upbeat (not to mention off-beat) and thoroughly entertaining nuclear annihilation yarn about a pair of young lovers caught in the madness of the final few hours before the dawn of the Mad Max Millenium. DeJarnatt's madcap vision of impending doom takes off when Anthony Edwards picks up a ringing pay phone only to hear what seems to be the frantic voice of an Air Force silo operator who is desperately trying to reach his father and warn him that the unthinkable has been made real. The ensuing whirlwind of mayhem is brimming with acerbic wit and hilarious black comedy, and offers a refreshing perspective on what things may be like as we sink back into the primordial ooze. ★★★½ $14.99

The Miracle of Morgan's Creek

(1944, 99 min, US, Preston Sturges) Writer-director Sturges had a field day with this brilliantly funny farce starring Betty Hutton and Eddie Bracken. Hutton gets impregnated by a G.I. leaving for overseas, and the unwed mother-to-be can't remember who the soldier was. It was a miracle that Sturges got this past the censors. ★★★★ $14.99

Miracle on 34th Street

(1947, 97 min, US, George Seaton) Classic Christmas story about a Macy's Santa Claus who insists he's the real Kris Kringle — sending New York City into a frenzy. Edmund Gwenn deservedly won an Oscar for his delightful and definitive portrayal of Santa, and young Natalie Wood is charming as a disbelieving youngster who is befriended by St. Nick. ★★★½ $14.99

The Miracle of Morgan's Creek

Miracle on 34th Street

(1994, 114 min, US, Les Mayfield) With exception to Richard Attenborough's lively interpretation of Santa Claus, and a charming performance by Mara Wilson as the youngster who under his guidance learns to believe, there's little else to recommend about this updated remake of George Seaton's 1947 holiday classic. New York's 34th Street is still the setting for this tale of a department store Santa who insists he's the genuine article, but now the competing stores are fictional, which sets the tone for a story devoid of real emotion. Elizabeth Perkins plays the Maureen O'Hara role, a repressed store manager, and Dylan McDermott is the rich, handsome, seemingly perfect neighbor in love with her. Both their roles are lifeless '90s creations. Writer John Hughes alternates between sappiness and caricature, neither of which characterized the original sentimental fantasy. ★★ $14.99

The Miracle Worker

(1962, 107 min, US, Arthur Penn) Brilliant screen version of William Gibson's acclaimed play which heartbreakingly details Helen Keller's fight to speak. Anne Bancroft gives a stunning performance as Annie Sullivan, the half-blind teacher whose guidance enables the young Helen to communicate. Patty Duke as Helen matches Bancroft all the way, and both actresses deservedly won Oscars. ★★★★ $19.99

Mirage

(1965, 109 min, US, Edward Dmytryk) Intriguing Hitchcockian thriller with Gregory Peck as an amnesia victim who becomes entangled in a murder mystery while trying to regain his memory. Also with Diane Baker, Walter Matthau and Kevin McCarthy. ★★★

The Mirror (Zerkalo)

(1974, 106 min, USSR, Andrei Tarkovsky) Fusing personal memories of his childhood as a wartime exile with fragments of his adult life and reflecting on his mother's experience with political terror, Tarkovsky has fashioned a haunting dreamlike puzzler that might best be described as an autobiographical poem. The director reflects on three generations of his family, as well as the painful experience of his parents' marital breakup, in making this deeply moving, powerful and challenging film. An intense and very personal film. (Russian with English subtitles) ★★★½ $59.99

The Mirror Crack'd

(1980, 105 min, GB, Guy Hamilton) Before she went sleuthing in "Murder She Wrote," Angela Lansbury appeared as Agatha Christie's crack sleuth Miss Marple in this enjoyable, if slight, mystery. Elizabeth Taylor and Kim Novak are well-cast as rival and catty movie queens, and Rock Hudson, Tony Curtis and Geraldine Chaplin round out the cast as Miss Marple becomes involved with show people when Taylor is almost murdered. ★★ $14.99

The Mirror Has Two Faces

(1996, 126 min, US, Barbra Streisand) In order for an ugly duckling story to work, before the duckling symbolically turns into a swan, the duckling should be, well, undesireable. It is this basic premise of the folklore principle which director Streisand has forgotten in this sometimes giddy, sometimes overbearing romantic comedy. Streisand plays a supposedly unattractive college professor — fact is that she's not ugly. Jeff Bridges, in an extremely likable performance, is a fellow professor looking for an asexual relationship. So he searches for a plain Jane to not feel sexually aroused. He finds Babs, and, of course, she falls in love with him; she fixes herself up; he falls in love with her; mix-ups and hijinks ensue. There are quite a few appealing comedic moments to the film, and Streisand is a congenial professor and mate. But the whole setup of the movie doesn't work, which magnifies not only Streisand's ego (her refusal to look really "bad") but the often fluffy, routine comedy as well. ★★½ $19.99

Mirror Images II

(1993, 92 min, US, Gregory Hippolyte) In this sex-filled thriller, two identical sisters lock heads with each other. Carrie is a sexually uptight woman traumatized by a childhood murder, while Terri is her evil, thought-to-be-dead bisexual twin sister (both played by Shannon Whirry). Terri, when not working as a prostitute, enjoys seducing Carrie's boyfriends, employees and eventually her husband; taking devilish delight in the rouse. Then sibling rivalry turns deadly. Hippolyte, the director of such lesbian-tinged exploitation flicks as *The Other Woman* and *Sexual Intent*, is the unquestioned king of lesbian titilation of soft-core erotica, and he delivers once again with a nonjudmental, sensitive and sensual seduction scene. ★★ $92.99

The Misadventures of Mr. Wilt

(1990, 84 min, GB, Michael Tuchner) Although not nearly as funny as the wildly absurd Tom Sharpe novel, "Wilt," from which it is based, this frantic comedy still has its moments. Henry Wilt spends his days teaching English Lit in a second-rate community college and his nights fantasizing about elaborate ways to kill his fad-obsessed wife. When she disappears, he learns the police suspect *him* of doing her in and disposing of her body in a cement-covered pit. Sinking him further in the mess are Wilt's doings on the night of the disappearance which include a much-witnessed sexual tryst with a full-sized anatomically correct doll. Griff Rhys Jones is perfect as the hapless Wilt in this rollicking black comedy and Mel Smith is unusually good as the bungling detective assigned to the strange case. ★★★ $89.99

Misery

(1990, 107 min, US, Rob Reiner) Director Reiner returns to Stephen King territory (after the wonderful *Stand by Me*) leading Kathy Bates to a well-earned Best Actress Oscar for her creepy portrayal of a schizophrenic fan who first rescues, then imprisons her favorite author (James Caan) when he kills off her favorite romance novel character. Reiner once again demonstrates that horror need not be all blood and guts. Also with Lauren Bacall, Richard Farnsworth and Frances Sternhagen. ★★★ $14.99

The Misfits

(1961, 124 min, US, John Huston) A stark, poignant film with Clark Gable, Montgomery Clift and Eli Wallach as modern-day cowboys, and Marilyn Monroe as a delicate divorcée entangled in their games of camaraderie and machismo. Scripted largely for Monroe by husband Arthur Miller, *The Misfits* marked her and Gable's final screen roles. ★★★ $19.99

Mishima: A Life in Four Chapters

(1985, 121 min, US/Japan, Paul Schrader) Yukio Mishima, Japan's most celebrated novelist, stunned his country in 1970 when, after a bizarre attempt at a political overthrow, he committed *seppuku* (ritual suicide). With this puzzling event at its center, Schrader has created a daring film that tries to understand the man through his writings. With the final day of Mishima's life as the background, the film is

Rita Hayworth knocks 'em dead in *Miss Sadie Thompson*

intercut with three stylized episodes from his novels. A fascinating look at an obsessed artist. (Japanese with English subtitles) ★★★ $79.99

Miss Firecracker

(1989, 102 min, US, Thomas Schlamme) Welcome to Yazoo City, Mississippi. What more likely setting for playwright Beth Henley (*Crimes of the Heart*) to serve up this thoroughly charming piece of American pie filled with a cast of characteristically odder-than-odd characters. A crackerjack ensemble of actors is headed by Holly Hunter as a slightly eccentric "girl with a past," whose one dream in life is to win the annual Miss Firecracker Beauty Pageant. Sparks fly when her rapacious cousins Mary Steenburgen and Tim Robbins descend on her fragile ego with a ferocity that only family members can muster. Alfre Woodard adds comic zip as Hunter's daffy seamstress with a penchant for hearing voices through her eyeballs. ★★★ $9.99

Miss Julie

(1985, 90 min, Sweden, Alf Sloberg) This dazzling adaptation of Strindberg's riveting play concerns one woman's social and sexual domination. Miss Julie, a noblewoman, allows her butler to seduce her after her engagement is broken. Her actions then lead to a haunting and unremitting exploration of how the woman's disgrace begins to destroy her. Outstanding performances and magnificent cinematography enhance the intensity of this story. (Swedish with English subtitles) ★★★

Miss Rose White

(1991, 95 min, US, Joseph Sargent) This Emmy Award winner is a brilliant and sensitive tale of a young Jewish immigrant who must come to terms with her ethnicity when her sister, a Holocaust survivor, comes to join her and her father in America just after the second World War. Kyra Sedgwick is marvelous as the title character and Maximilian Schell boasts a strong supporting performance as her father, as does the always wonderful Amanda Plummer as her sister. D.B.

Sweeney and Maureen Stapleton round out a strong supporting cast. Based on the off-Broadway play "A Shayna Maidel" by Barbara Lebow. ★★★½ $14.99

Miss Sadie Thompson

(1953, 93 min, US, Curtis Bernhardt) Although Rita Hayworth's Sadie Thompson won't make anyone forget *Gilda*, she nevertheless gives a sparkling performance in this musical remake of W. Somerset Maugham's story "Rain" (the 1932 version starred Joan Crawford). Rita plays a "good time" entertainer who, while stranded on a tropical island during WWII, becomes involved with a brawny G.I. (Aldo Ray) and a hypocritical minister (Jose Ferrer) whose obsession with Sadie's salvation cloaks other desires. (Timely, isn't it?) ★★★ $19.99

Missing

(1982, 122 min, US, Constantin Costa-Gavras) Costa-Gavras' award-winning thriller probes the mysterious disappearance of a young American writer during the bloody political upheaval in Chile. Sissy Spacek and Jack Lemmon star as the wife and father whose persistent search uncovers some frightening facts on U.S. involvement in South America. ★★★½ $19.99

The Mission

(1986, 125 min, GB, Roland Joffé) A Best Picture nomination went to this acclaimed, based-on-fact historical drama, set in 18th-century South America. Jeremy Irons stars as a Jesuit priest who leads a tribe of native Indians in a revolt against mercenary colonialists. Robert De Niro also stars as a soldier whose social conscience leads him to become involved on behalf of Irons and his cause — an act which draws him into an insurmountable challenge and inevitable tragedy. Gorgeous Oscar-winning cinematography. ★★★½ $14.99

Mission: Impossible

(1996, 111 min, US, Brian De Palma) The popular, award-winning 1960s TV drama

"Mission: Impossible" gets a '90s facelift with this exciting, extremely well executed though somewhat dense thriller. Serving as producer and star, Tom Cruise plays Ethan Hunt, a member of the elite undercover team. Jon Voight plays Jim Phelps, the team's leader and a carryover character from the TV series. On a mission Mr. Phelps decides to accept, most of the members are killed, with Hunt the only likely survivor. It soon becomes apparent that they were set up, and Hunt — who is now the number one suspect — goes underground to discover the identity of the mole. With exception of some unnecessary collegiate bantering which looks like outtakes from *Top Gun*, this big-screen update is serious about its own mission: to deliver fast-moving and intricate entertainment. Maybe it's a little too intricate for its own good, but the twists are unpredictable, the action plentiful; and among several terrific sequences, there's a hold-your-breath ending. The Cold War may be dead, but good political espionage is not. (Available letterboxed and pan & scan) ★★★ $21.99

The Missionary

(1982, 93 min, GB, Richard Loncraine) Monty Pythonite Michael Palin stars in this eccentric comedy-drama as a naive English missionary just returned from Africa and assigned to rehabilitate the fallen women of Edwardian London. Maggie Smith costars as his lascivious benefactor in this refined satire. ★★★½ $19.99

Mississippi Blues

(1983, 96 min, France/US, Bertrand Tavernier & Robert Parrish) French director Tavernier and Georgia-born independent filmmaker Parrish combine their talents in approaching the people and music of the Mississippi Delta. This charming, affable film explores the ever-shifting landscape, the lives of the people in the river towns, their customs and most wonderfully, their musical traditions of Delta Blues and gospel. ★★★ $19.99

Mississippi Burning

(1988, 125 min, US, Alan Parker) This gut-wrenching masterwork is one of the most powerful American film to date to explore racial prejudice. Based on the actual 1964 murders of three civil rights workers, the film presents a fictionalized account of the investigation. Gene Hackman and Willem Dafoe star as two FBI agents assigned to the case. At odds with each other from the start, together the two men confront a hostile white community either unwilling or unable to cooperate, and an oppressed black community impregnated with fear of reprisal at the hands of the ruthless white bigots controlling the town. Dafoe is very good as the conventional FBI man, but it is Hackman's virtuoso performance which forms the core of the film. ★★★★ $9.99

Mississippi Masala

(1992, 118 min, US, Mira Nair) Director Nair (*Salaam Bombay!*) sets her sights on the subtleties of insidious racism in this affecting modern-day "Romeo and Juliet" set in the deep South. The story follows the forbidden love that blossoms between a young Indian woman (Sarita Choudhury), whose family fled

Idi Amin's Uganda, and an African-American carpet cleaner (Denzel Washington). Nair expertly exposes the unspoken and unacknowledged racism that permeates the Indian community. Washington and newcomer Choudhury give heartfelt performances and Nair puts her stunning looks to good use. Roshan Seth (*Gandhi, Sammy & Rosie Get Laid*) delivers yet another superb supporting performance as Choudhury's lawyer father who yearns to return to Uganda. ★★★ $14.99

Mississippi Mermaid

(1969, 123 min, France, François Truffaut) This intriguing but tame romantic thriller was one of the director's few certifiable flops, despite the superstar casting of Jean-Paul Belmondo and Catherine Deneuve. The story concerns a tobacco plant owner (Belmondo) on an African island who gets more than he bargained for after the arrival of his mysterious mail-order bride (Deneuve). The Hitchcock-inspired plot is elaborately presented, but the film lacks needed tension and fails to reach its intended suspense. (French with English subtitles) ★★ $19.99

The Missouri Breaks

(1976, 126 min, US, Arthur Penn) Marlon Brando plays a sadistic gunslinger hired to kill horse thief Jack Nicholson and his gang (Randy Quaid, Harry Dean Stanton). Set in the late 1880s in Montana hill country, where Brando and Nicholson play a deadly game of cat-and-mouse, this bizarre western was a financial disappointment upon release. It has, over the years, taken on cult status thanks to its two stars. ★★ $19.99

Mr. and Mrs. Bridge

(1990, 105 min, US, James Ivory) A leisurely, fine character study highlighted by two bravura performances from Paul Newman and especially Joanne Woodward as an upper-middle-class Kansas City husband and wife. Based on two Evan S. Connell novels, "Mr. Bridge" and "Mrs. Bridge," the film, set in the years between the two World Wars, examines with razor-sharp intensity and formidible wit the couple's everyday, and even mundane, existence. A series of continuing and perfectly constructed stories, the film's most memorable scenes include Newman's "battle" with a tornado and Woodward's astonishing reaction at her son's Boy Scout meeting. ★★★½ $9.99

Mr. and Mrs. Smith

(1941, 95 min, US, Alfred Hitchcock) A rarely seen Hitchcock anomaly, this madcap comedy stars Carole Lombard and Robert Montgomery as a husband and wife who discover their marriage isn't legal. ★★★ $19.99

Mr. Arkadin

(1955, 94 min, GB, Orson Welles) Welles takes a factual mysterious occurrence and weaves a mesmerizing, convoluted tale of intrigue, deception and false identity. Welles plays Gregory Arkadin, a man of immense wealth and power, who commissions a petty gangster to compile a dossier on the origins of...Gregory Arkadin. Pay attention: the action moves very swiftly. ★★★ $24.99

Mr. Baseball

(1992, 108 min, US, Fred Schepisi) A lackluster confection about a bad-boy baseballer (Tom "What Happened to My Career?" Selleck) whose losing streak and outfield antics get him traded to Japan. There he becomes involved in the obligatory misunderstandings, misadventures, romance and culture clashes. Schepisi's sure-footed direction is the saving grace of this mediocre addition to the "stranger in a strange land" body of filmmaking. Also starring is Ken Takakura, Japan's answer to...well...Tom Selleck. ★★ $9.99

Mr. Blandings Builds His Dream House

(1948, 94 min, US, H.C. Potter) Cary Grant and Myrna Loy star in this delightful screwball comedy. Grant is Mr. Blandings, a city-bred man who yearns for the "good life" — to be a country boy with a big, old country house in the idyllic Connecticut countryside. But Mr. Blandings soon discovers that the "good life" isn't quite what he expected... and the fun begins. Forget the remake with Tom Hanks and Shelley Long, *The Money Pit*; this is the real thing. ★★★ $19.99

Mr. Deeds Goes to Town

(1936, 115 min, US, Frank Capra) One of director Capra's great achievements, this delightfully entertaining and "pixilated" social comedy stars Gary Cooper as Longfellow Deeds, a small-town boy who becomes heir to a fortune; when he decides to give it away to the needy, he goes on trial for insanity. Jean Arthur, in the first of her three Capra films, shines as a newspaper reporter who gets the first scoop on Mr. Deeds. One of Cooper's best and most charming performances. ★★★★ $19.99

Mr. Destiny

(1990, 105 min, US, James Orr) This modern-day *It's a Wonderful Life* stars James Belushi as Larry Burrows, a 35-year-old Average Joe who's down on his luck. Along comes Mr. Destiny (Michael Caine) in the guise of a bartender with an attentive ear. He slips Larry a magic potion which allows him to see how his life would have turned out if he'd managed to hit the ball in that fateful little league game 20 years earlier — in reality he had struck out, of course. Despite its total predictability, the film still holds a certain charm and is mildly entertaining. Belushi delivers a very likable performance and, as usual, Caine carries the film with his commanding screen presence. ★★ $9.99

Mr. Frost

(1989, 92 min, GB, Philip Setbon) Jeff Goldblum plays an icy killer who hasn't spoken in two years. Alan Bates is the cop out to find his true identity and Kathy Baker is the psychiatrist caught in the middle. In trying to create uncertainty in Mr. Frost's identity, the film only manages to occasionally intrigue with its slow pace and strange occurrences. ★★ $89.99

Mr. Hobbs Takes a Vacation

(1962, 116 min, US, Henry Koster) James Stewart brings considerable charm to this genial comedy about Stewart and wife Maureen O'Hara taking the kids on vacation, where nothing turns out the way they expect. ★★½ $19.99

Mr. Holland's Opus

(1995, 142 min, US, Stephen Herek) Though movies featuring dedicated teachers are most assuredly a dime a dozen, and most of them, including *Mr. Holland's Opus*, frequently languish in sentimentality, it's Richard Dreyfuss' solid portrayal which distinguishes this alternately clichéd and absorbing drama. The story follows 30 years in the career of Mr. Holland (Dreyfuss), a budding composer who accepts a seemingly temporary position as a high school music teacher. Flashing through several time periods, the film examines both the extraordinary effect Mr. Holland has on his many students, and his sometimes rocky home life, which includes a child being born deaf and a possible extramarital affair. Dreyfuss ages in the part quite effectively, bringing maturity to Mr. Holland's later years as compared to the younger character's impulsive dreamer; and his serenade to his son, singing John Lennon's "Beautiful Boy," could bring tears to a stone. Glenne Headly as Mr. Holland's wife is slyly understated. This *Opus* may shamelessly tug at the heart strings, but does so with warmth and efficiency. ★★½ $14.99

Mr. Hulot's Holiday

(1953, 86 min, France, Jacques Tati) Tati, one of the greatest mime and visual artists since Chaplin and Keaton, stars as Mr. Hulot, that charming and totally naive fool who creates disorder wherever he wanders. A French seaside resort is the setting for the Hulot pratfalls in this captivating comedy classic. ★★★★ $29.99

Mister Johnson

(1991, 100 min, GB, Bruce Beresford) A well-intentioned but disappointing adaptation of Joyce Cary's novel about colonial Africa. Set in

Mission: Impossible

the African bush in the 1920s, the film tells the story of Mr. Johnson, a mischievous black clerk who, in his zealousness to be accepted as an Englishman, manipulates, lies and steals. Despite some strong performances, especially from Pierce Brosnan as Mr. Johnson's boss, Beresford's vision seems blurred and it's unclear whether he is making a film about a man who turns his back on his people, the diabolical nature of British colonialism, or the incumbent tragedy in the forced modernization of tribal cultures. Whatever his intent, the result is a bleak and almost misanthropic muddle. ★★ $89.99

Mr. Jones

(1993, 114 min, US, Mike Figgis) In a highly flamboyant role, Richard Gere gives an appropriately over-the-top performance as a charming manic-depressive; but even the star's energetic bravado can't elevate this standard romantic drama. Following a suicide attempt, Gere is hospitalized and placed under the care of psychiatrist Lena Olin. As she attempts to treat his neurosis, the two become romantically involved. The implications of a doctor-patient relationship is glossed over in favor of two wayward lovers at odds with the world — which only negates the power of a potentially involving drama. Olin is never quite able to define her poorly conceived role, and is constantly overshadowed by her indomitable co-star. ★★½ $14.99

Mr. Klein

(1977, 122 min, France, Joseph Losey) A disturbing mystery-drama about a self-centered, amoral man (Alain Delon) in Nazi-occupied Paris. He takes advantage of the sweeping anti-Semitism until his world is suddenly shattered when he is mistaken for another — a Jewish Klein. A powerful indictment well-acted and thoughtfully directed. (Dubbed) ★★★

Mr. Lucky

(1943, 99 min, US, H.C. Potter) Cary Grant stars in this romantic comedy-drama as the owner of a gambling ship who sets out to sting Laraine Day, but ends up falling in love with her and trying to go straight instead. Not one of Grant's better efforts, but mildly entertaining. ★★½ $19.99

Mr. Majestyk

(1974, 104 min, US, Richard Fleischer) Surprisingly flavorful Charles Bronson actioner about an ex-con trying to run a straight business, but is pushed too far by local corrupt law enforcers and a sinister Mafia hit man. With Linda Cristal and Lee Purcell. Elmore Leonard penned the script. ★★½ $14.99

Mr. Mom

(1983, 92 min, US, Stan Dragoti) Written by John Hughes, this amiable comedy stars Michael Keaton as a brand new househusband who must contend with housework and wife Teri Garr working 9 to 5. Yes, it's been done before, though Keaton's comic finesse makes most of this familiar territory seem fresh. ★★½

Mr. North

(1988, 92 min, US, Danny Huston) John Huston's son Danny took over the reigns of this quirky comedy when his legendary father died just before the start of production. Anthony Edwards plays the ingratiating title character, who warms himself to the flaky citizens of Newport's upper class. Also with Robert Mitchum, Lauren Bacall, Anjelica Huston, Mary Stuart Masterson and Harry Dean Stanton. A real charmer. Based on Thornton Wilder's "Theophilus North." ★★★

Mr. Reliable

(1996, 110 min, Australia, Nadia Tass) Based on a true story, *Mr. Reliable* is an undistinguished Australian comedy which could have been a sleeper but turns out to be more of a snore. Colin Friels stars as Wally, an ex-con who unexpectedly stages a hostage crisis during a nasty heatwave in the summer of 1968. Director Tass (*Malcolm*) strives for whimsy by making the police buffoons and the various neighbors "lovable" eccentrics. But these characters — like Wally himself and his "hostage" Beryl (Jaqueline McKenzie) — are a one-dimensional bunch. There's nothing particularly funny about this overblown siege. *Mr. Reliable* only becomes diverting during the final third, when the temperature rises, tempers flare and actions are taken. A usually dependable actor, Friels seems lost in the title role, though McKenzie is quite engaging as Beryl. ★½ $99.99

Mister Roberts

(1955, 120 min, US, John Ford & Mervyn Le Roy) Classic film version of Thomas Heggen and Joshua Logan's Broadway smash about life aboard a military cargo ship during WWII. Henry Fonda, in one of his best roles, plays the title character, a dedicated naval officer who yearns for combat service. James Cagney is terrific as the small-minded ship's captain who's more concerned with his treasured palm tree than with the anxieties of his men. Jack Lemmon won an Oscar for his memorable comic turn as Ensign Pulver, the ship's laundry and morale officer. William Powell also stars as the worldly medical officer. ★★★★ $14.99

Mr. Saturday Night

(1992, 114 min, US, Billy Crystal) Crystal makes his directorial debut with this disappointing comedy of a Catskills comedian who flirts with stardom. Reminiscent of Neil Simon's *The Sunshine Boys*, the story follows the tumultuous personal life and career of fictional stand-up comic Buddy Young, Jr. (whose catch-phrase "Don't get me started" is as catchy as it is annoying). As played by Crystal, Young is a self-destructive one-man arsenal of one-liners who can no more handle personal relationships than he can the success he spends a lifetime trying to achieve. Though there are plenty of funny lines, most of *Mr. Saturday Night* is an overly ambitious and shallow examination of Young's offstage life. And the scenes with Crystal as an old timer (complete with bad aging makeup) are maudlin. Buddy's brother and manager, with whom he is constantly at odds, Oscar nominee David Paymer is particularly noteworthy. ★★ $19.99

Mr. Skeffington

(1944, 146 min, US, Vincent Sherman) A sensational Bette Davis performance is the heart of this grand soap opera with Davis in rare form as a youthful beauty who marries Claude Rains for money and position circa mid-1910s. The film, spanning several decades, follows Davis as she ages and discovers the true meaning of love and loyalty. Rains is terrific as her devoted spouse. ★★★ $19.99

Mr. Smith Goes to Washington

(1939, 129 min, US, Frank Capra) Fresh from their success the year before in *You Can't Take It with You*, director Capra and star James Stewart reteamed to create, arguably, their finest achievement. Stewart gives a superb performance as an idealistic, newly appointed U.S. Senator and political dupe to Claude Rains (terrific as a corrupt senator) and Edward Arnold (a powerful characterization as boss Taylor). Once there, he uncovers — with more than a little help from secretary Jean Arthur — political wrongdoings, and sets out to expose them. Though Capra is known to be somewhat excessive in patriotic zeal and sentimentality, here they work to his advantage as his characters act according to their moral dictates. This Capra masterpiece features one of the finest ensemble casts ever assembled, and in addition to those above, Thomas Mitchell, Harry Carey, Jr. and Beulah Bondi also star. ★★★★ $19.99

Mr. Stitch

(1995, 90 min, US, Roger Avary) Originally meant to be a TV movie, this direct-to-video release is an ambitious, intelligent sci-fi thriller which adapts the Frankenstein myth to a near-future setting and adds an interesting wrinkle to it. The second feature of writer-director Avary (co-writer of *Pulp Fiction* and director of *Killing Zoe*), the film stars Rutger Hauer as a scientist who creates a composite human being from the parts of corpses. His creation (Wil Wheaton), who names himself Lazarus, is superior to a normal human in both intellect and strength, but is wracked by nightmares. Under the supervision of a psychiatrist (Nia Peeples), Lazarus becomes obsessed with determining the cause of his nightmares and discovering what lies beyond the doors of his white-walled cell. Alternately fascinating and innovative, *Mr. Stitch* does succumb late in its story to a clichéd showdown between science and the military, and loses its sense of awe when the reason of Lazarus' creation is discovered. But the cast works well together, the design is breathtaking, and Avary truly makes the viewer care about Lazarus' plight. ★★★ $92.99

Mr. Wonderful

(1993, 98 min, US, Anthony Minghella) After his charming first film *Truly, Madly, Deeply*, director Minghella's second feature rates as a disappointment. A pleasant though insubstantial comedy, the film casts Matt Dillon as a working-class divorcé whose alimony payments stand between him and a happy new life. Evoking the spirits of films afar afield as *The Awful Truth* and *Send Me No Flowers*, Dillon begins an exhaustive search for his ex's (Annabella Sciorra) perfect match. William Hurt, Mary Louise Parker and Vincent D'Onofrio also star. Director Minghella's next film would be the Oscar-winning *The English Patient*. ★★½ $19.99

Mr. Wrong

(1996, 92 min, US, Nick Castle) Making her big screen starring debut, Ellen DeGeneres manages to utilize the waifish charm she demonstrates on her TV sitcom, but unfortunately her smiles, grimaces and rolling eyes can't sustain a lackluster screenplay. Ellen plays a successful TV producer (for a tacky San Diego morning talk show) who meets whom she thinks is Mr. Right (Bill Pullman). But as he shows his true and obnoxious colors, she is unsuccessful in getting rid of him or getting him to understand the meaning of "it's over." Had this been a drama, it probably would have starred Michael Douglas and Demi Moore; as a comedy, it's only marginally more tolerable. There are few laughs to be had, and the story meanders from mediocre to bad; though the two stars do occasionally generate a degree of compatibility. For DeGeneres, however, this first film is definitely made of the *Wrong* stuff. ★★ $19.99

Mr. Wrong

Mistress

(1992, 109 min, US, Barry Primus) Where Robert Altman's *The Player* relentlessly lampooned the world of Hollywood's movers and shakers, Primus' low-budget, independent *Mistress* pokes lighthearted fun at the making of low-budget, independent films. Robert Wuhl stars as a washed-up writer-director who one day receives a call from retired studio hack Martin Landau, who has unearthed one of Wuhl's old scripts. Together, they take the script and run the gauntlet of potential money brokers (Robert De Niro, Danny Aiello and Eli Wallach), each of whom, of course, has a mistress they want in the film. Directed with care and wit by first-timer Primus, the film astutely delves into the challenges facing would-be filmmakers who want to maintain the artistic integrity of their scripts. All of this is done with a good dose of humor and an earnest sense of moral vision. The terrific ensemble also includes Laurie Metcalf as Wuhl's ex-wife, and Jace Alexander, who is hilarious as Wuhl's motor-mouthed, hotshot assistant. ★★★½ $9.99

The Mistress

(1953, 106 min, Japan, Shiro Toyoda) This deeply affecting film is not only a beautiful cinematic work, but also an exceptional study of female psychology. A woman believes that she is married to a prosperous man, but discovers that he is already married and that she is no more than his mistress. Set in a period when Japan was moving toward industrialization, *The Mistress* explores the conflict between the demands of society and individual freedom. (Japanese with English subtitles) ★★★

Mixed Blood

(1985, 97 min, US, Paul Morrissey) A jet-black comedy from director Morrissey (*Andy Warhol's Frankenstein*, *Andy Warhol's Dracula*) set in New York's notorious Alphabet City about a gang of drug-running youths, under the guidance of a Fagan-like protector and her hunkish son, who set out to control the neighborhood drug trade. Stars Marilia Pera (*Pixote*), Richard Ulacia and Linda Kerridge. ★★★

Mixed Nuts

(1994, 97 min, US, Nora Ephron) From the director of *Sleepless in Seattle* comes what must be a contender for the worst film of 1994. Steve Martin headlines this so-called comedy about the wacky (and grim) happenings that befall a band of miserable misfits at a suicide prevention center on Christmas Eve. But wait, it gets funnier: There's an unwed, screw-loose mother-to-be (Juliette Lewis), her homicidal/suicidal boyfriend (Anthony LaPaglia), a beleaguered widow (Madeline Kahn), a mysterious serial killer, and a pathetic transvestite who sets his sights on Martin. Considering the cast (which also includes Rob Reiner, Adam Sandler and Garry Shandling), one can't but wonder what blackmail-worthy dirt Ephron may have had on everyone involved to get this "nightmare before Christmas" made. Boring and unsightly, these *Mixed Nuts* should have stayed in the can. ★ $19.99

Mo' Better Blues

(1990, 135 min, US, Spike Lee) Despite the engaging presence of Denzel Washington and a catchy jazz score by Bill Lee and Branford Marsalis, Lee's story of jazz musicians — and follow-up to his incisive and controversial *Do the Right Thing* — must be considered a disappointment. Saddled with an uninvolving script, Spike fails to capture the creative spark and passion of the jazz world and its habitués. Washington plays Bleek Gilliam, a moderately successful trumpet player and singer who, to the detriment of the plot, is a really "nice guy" whose only flaw seems to be his inability to settle down with just one girlfriend. Don't be completely turned off by this criticism, however, for even Lee's failures are more interesting and enjoyable than most of the stuff that comes out of Hollywood. The one truly inexcusable aspect of the movie is Lee's heinously anti-Semitic depiction of the exploitive Jewish club owners. Their hateful portrayal is an embarrassment to the talents of one of our most promising film artists. ★★ $19.99

Mo' Money

(1992, 91 min, US, Peter MacDonald) With the success of many "Saturday Night Live" spin-offs, it would follow that giving big-screen treatment to the lovably dysfunctional characters created by "In Loving Color's" Damon Wayans would produce a natural hit. Unfortunately, the forced insertion of the comic crazies into a cut-and-paste action plot proves to be more "ho-hum" than "ha-ha." Wayans stars (along with brother Marlon) as a con man whose first legitimate job lands him smack in the middle of a major credit card scam. As with most middle-of-the-road productions of this kind, this action-comedy is neither funny enough, nor exciting enough to garner anything more than the occasional bemused chuckle. ★★ $14.99

Mobsters

(1991, 104 min, US, Michael Karbelnikoff) A stylishly made but flat underworld crime saga riddled with uneven characterizations and lots of bullets. The story follows the beginnings of the youthful partners-in-crime "Lucky" Luciano (Christian Slater), Meyer Lansky (Patrick Dempsey) and "Bugsy" Siegel (Richard Grieco). Ostensibly about the birth of a national organized crime syndicate, the film is content to be merely a glossy, bloody shoot 'em up. Even with an admirable re-creation of 1920s New York, *Mobsters* is recommended only for those who can't get enough of gangster stories. ★★ $14.99

Moby Dick

(1956, 116 min, US, John Huston) It is generally agreed that Gregory Peck was miscast in the role of Captain Ahab, but his performance detracts nothing from Huston's masterful interpretation of Herman Melville's classic novel. Extraordinary action scenes abound in this immortal sea epic. Also starring Richard Basehart and featuring a cameo appearance by Orson Welles. ★★★½ $19.99

Modern Problems

(1981, 91 min, US, Ken Shapiro) Chevy Chase lets loose as an air traffic controller who acquires telekinetic powers after exposure to nuclear waste. Some funny bits thanks to Chase's mugging, but very silly. ★★ $9.99

Modern Romance

(1980, 100 min, US, Albert Brooks) An insightful and playfully funny therapeutic comedy session written and directed by Brooks. Brooks plays a highly neurotic film editor looking for romance, but obsessively drawn to Kathryn Harrold. As with most Brooks films, his deadpan though manic observations are not for everyone; but he has such a unique view of the world, it's hard to resist his charms. Also with Bruno Kirby and the director James L. Brooks, for whom A. Brooks worked in the classic *Broadcast News*. ★★★ $9.99

Modern Times

(1936, 89 min, US, Charles Chaplin) When the backers of Rene Clair's *À Nos la Liberté* prepared to sue Chaplin over the similarities they found in *Modern Times*, Clair wouldn't hear of it, as he was honored by the homage — though over the years Chaplin did find himself in hot water over the film's supposed Commie leanings. At any rate, this extraordinary silent comedy (Chaplin's last silent) is a wildly funny and touching social satire. Victimized by the machine age, Chaplin goes berserk and inadvertently leads a factory riot. The radiant Paulette Goddard plays the orphan waif with whom he falls in love. ★★★★

The Moderns

(1988, 128 min, US, Alan Rudolph) An exquisite-looking period drama set against the backdrop of the Paris art scene of the 1920s. Keith Carradine, Linda Fiorentino and John Lone are American expatriates who become involved in romantic intrigue as well as an art forgery scam. Genevieve Bujold steals the film as an art dealer, and Kevin J. O'Connor makes a splendid Hemingway. ★★★

Mogambo

(1953, 115 min, US, John Ford) Solid remake of 1932's *Red Dust*, with Clark Gable repeating his role from that film as a hunter in the wilds of Africa who's involved with both earthy Ava Gardner and society girl Grace Kelly. Gardner is especially good as the brassy showgirl. ★★★ $19.99

The Mole People

(1956, 78 min, US, Virgil Vogel) 1950s B-film thespian John Agar and Hugh Beaumont (Beaver's dad) star as explorers who climb down a hole in Asia and find a lost underground civilization of albino Sumerians, who have the half-human Mole People as their slaves. But their minions revolt and save our brave captive heroes from the surface. ★½ $14.99

Moliere

(1984, 112 min, GB, Bill Alexander) The Royal Shakespeare Company's version of Dusty Hughes' working of Mikhail Bulgakov's comedy-drama about the tumultuous life of the great French playwright Moliere. Antony Sher is splendid as the famed comic dramatist. ★★★ $39.99

Moll Flanders

(1996, 123 min, US, Pen Densham) Daniel Defoe's classic novel has been dumbed-down so that every man, woman, child or frog in the audience can understand it. Badly paced, this updating (last filmed in 1965) awkwardly stumbles around the story of an orphaned young woman doing her best to survive in 18th-century London. Potentially potent material is pureed into an insipid source for cheers of "You go, girl" from the Oprah crowd. Director Densham complained that summer audiences passed over his costume drama in favor of loud, special effects-laden action films. The sad truth is, a popcorn-muncher like *Mission: Impossible* has more to say about an innocent trying to survive in a corrupt, cynical world than this "important" film. Not a total disaster, there are some affecting moments, and Morgan Freeman and Robin Wright give their best to undeserving material. ★½ $19.99

The Molly Maguires

(1970, 123 min, US, Martin Ritt) Sean Connery and Richard Harris give earnest performances in this gritty drama of clashing coal miners in Pennsylvania during the 1870s. Solid direction by Ritt (*Sounder*). ★★★ $14.99

Modern Times

Mom and Dad Save the World

(1992, 88 min, US, Greg Beeman) Some nice special effects can't help this mildy amusing sci-fi adventure/spoof. Teri Garr and Jeffrey Jones (playing a beleaguered husband similar to his role in *Beetlejuice*) are celebrating 20 years of marriage with a weekend getaway when the evil Jon Lovitz, petty dictator of a far-away planet, kidnaps them with the intent to marry Garr. (He happened to fall in love with her while scoping out the planet for global domination.) As it turns out, his planet is inhabited by imbeciles (the screenwriters must hail from there, too), so Mom and Dad's job is markedly easier than it might have been. Jones and Garr are appealing, but Lovitz's performance is all over the place. ★★ $14.99

Moments — The Making of Claire of the Moon

(1992, 70 min, US) Fans of the independent lesbian feature *Claire of the Moon* and those simply interested in the filmmaking process will enjoy this behind-the-scenes documentary. Essentially a video scrapbook, it takes the viewer into the initial casting sessions through the frantic, on-location shooting and concludes with the film's enthusiastically received theatrical premiere. Outtakes from the film, five years in the making, and interviews with the beleaguered but determined director Nicole Conn are also included. Some cynics might see this film as simply a vanity production (for the film was made by the same company as *Claire of the Moon*), but it becomes, on its own merit, an interesting peek into how an independent film is made. ★★½ $39.99

Mommie Dearest

(1981, 129 min, US, Frank Perry) The campy, spirited version of Christine Crawford's novel detailing her abused childhood as the adopted daughter of actress Joan Crawford. Faye Dunaway pulls out all the stops in a no-holds-barred portrayal of the movie queen. (Ironically, Crawford herself remarked that if her life story were ever filmed, she wanted Dunaway to play her.) The

film which immortalized the line, "No wire hangers!" ★★★ $14.99

Mon Oncle

(1958, 116 min, France, Jacques Tati) Tati's bumbling M. Hulot confronts modern architecture in this hilarious pratfall comedy. Without relying on dialogue, Tati has created a true classic in visual farce. (Various languages) ★★★★ $29.99

Mon Oncle Antoine

(1971, 104 min, Canada, Claude Jutra) The Canadian film industry has had its ups and downs over the years, but this lyrical masterpiece is one of its crowning jewels. Filmed entirely on location in the backwoods of northern Quebec, this deeply moving coming-of-age story bears a resemblance to *My Life as a Dog* even though it pre-dates that film by almost 15 years. Using local inhabitants as extras, director Jutra employs the bleakness of life in a depressed mining town to capture the universality of the experiences of a 15-year-old boy who is struggling with issues of life, love and desire. (French with English subtitles) ★★★½ $39.99

Mon Oncle D'Amerique

(1980, 123 min, France, Alain Resnais) A brilliant and witty contemporary comedy on the human condition. The title refers to the proverbial French uncle who, fortune made, will return with his riches to solve every problem. A comedy about the drama of life that weaves its way through a metaphysical maze in its attempt to understand the motivations, ambitions and frustrations of man. (French with English subtitles) ★★★★ $29.99

Mona Lisa

(1986, 104 min, GB, Neil Jordan) Bob Hoskins won international acclaim for his searing performance as a dim-witted Cockney thug who falls hopelessly in love with a beautiful prostitute (Cathy Tyson). Initially hired as her chauffeur, a warm relationship develops between the two, and the ex-con moonlights as detective to track down her missing girlfriend. Michael Caine also stars as a slimy crime boss. A film bristling with sardonic humor and unnerving suspense. ★★★½ $14.99

Mondo New York

(1988, 83 min, US, Harvey Keith) Lock up the children, throw away your inhibitions and most of all, hide your pet mice before you descend into the rotten core of the Big Apple in this bustling tour of New York's entertainment underbelly. Amusing, nauseating yet always fascinating, first-time director Keith takes us on a voyeuristic journey to the clubs and back-alley downtown venues to observe performance artists and other assorted nocturnal denizens perform their bizarre, twisted and scandalous acts to appreciative audiences. The extraordinaire Dean and the Weenies will have you rushing to the rewind control to listen again to their infamous post-punk anthem, "Fuck You!" Let the weak of stomach be warned – this ain't Kansas, Dorothy! ★★★ $14.99

Mondo Topless

(1966, 60 min, US, Russ Meyer) A documentary on the topless craze of the Sixties. Meyer's trademark deep-voiced narration is truly hilarious. With a cast of cantilevered cuties including big-busted Babette Bardot, capaciously domed Darla Paris and the "buxotic" Darlene Grey. ★★ $79.99

Mondo Trasho

(1969, 95 min, US, John Waters) This celluloid atrocity by America's Father of Filth, Waters, is visual assault and battery, laying waste an already crumbling civilization. Explore a world oozing with sex, violence and overwhelming seaminess. It's just another day in the life of a 300-pound transvestite. Divine, in skin-tight, gold lamé Capri pants, runs over Mary Vivian Pearce in a 1959 Cadillac and commits other acts of mayhem. There's also sightings of the Virgin Mary, drug-addicted doctors, nasty 1950s rock tunes, nods to *The Wizard of Oz* and *Freaks*, and dismemberment of feet and hands that would make *Boxing Helena* gasp. ★★

Money for Nothing

(1993, 90 min, US, Ramon Menendez) Based on the amazingly true story of Joey Coyle (played by John Cusack), a Philadelphia Average Joe who stumbles upon mountains of cash, *Money for Nothing* totally ignores the fact that in real life, Joey had a history of drug and psychological problems – an explanation needed as to why Joey totally goes off kilter when money becomes no object. Even without the subtext, however, this comedy-drama still fails – its attempts to extricate humor from Joey's moral dilemma come off pathetic rather than farcical. Michael Madsen shines in this otherwise pointless film. ★½ $19.99

The Money Pit

(1986, 91 min, US, Richard Benjamin) A modern reworking of the Cary Grant comedy *Mr. Blandings Builds His Dream House.* Tom Hanks and Shelley Long buy a suburban New York home real cheap, and after moving in and starting remodeling, discover why the low cost. Very few of the gags work here; most of

this is predictable, unfunny and terribly overproduced. Stick to the original. ★½ $14.99

Money Train

(1995, 110 min, US, Joseph Ruben) *Money Train* is an actioner/heist movie which doesn't deliver on either aspect. With a contrived screenplay which rarely makes sense, mugging from its two stars, and a misrepresented plot development, about the only thing this has going for it is its impressive location shooting and the occasional chemistry of Misters Wesley Snipes and Woody Harrelson. They play transit cops (and foster brothers) who work for the New York City transit system. Rebellious and always in trouble (though Woody is the perpetual screwup), they consistently come under the wrath of their mean-spirited boss (Robert Blake), in between their undercover assignments (which are actually the most interesting segments of the film). Trouble brews when they talk of robbing the "money train" (the payroll car), and the plans for such are set in motion. The two actors demonstrate none of the comic zing from *White Men Can't Jump*, though due in large part to the silly dialogue they are forced to scream at one another. And expectations should be put on hold for a slam-bang heist adventure, for here the film is nothing but a tease. ★★ $19.99

Monika

(1952, 82 min, Sweden, Ingmar Bergman) A sultry, irresponsible teenager (Harriet Andersson) from a working-class district in Stockholm spends an idyllic summer with a shy and poetic boy on the tranquil islands off the Swedish coast. Basking in the sun and living for the moment, the two lovers explore their emotions and sensuality until the cold winds of autumn sweep away their innocent dreams and force them back to the city where Monika, saddled with an unwanted pregnancy, is forced to marry and settle down. This early Bergman effort is a tender yet unsentimental look at a love affair extinguished all too suddenly. (Swedish with English subtitles) ★★★ $29.99

Monkey Business

(1931, 77 min, US, Norman Z. McLeod) Those wild and zany Marx Brothers start out as stowaways on an ocean liner and end up rescuing a kidnapped damsel in a run-down barn, all the while spewing out some of their best lines of anarchistic, iconoclastic chatter. The first of their movies written directly for the screen is a sheer delight, with gun-toting tough guys, disgruntled molls, befuddled shipboard officers and a bevy of beauties who live to be chased by the ever-lecherous Harpo. Zeppo exudes warmth and charm as a man in love; Groucho and Chico exhibit a physical agility matched only by the running of their mouths. A fine madness. ★★★½ $14.99

Monkey Business

(1952, 97 min, US, Howard Hawks) Cary Grant is the archetypal absent-minded professor searching for the drug of eternal youth. Both he and wife Ginger Rogers give the elixir a test spin, along with their new roadster; youth is fleeting, and mercifully so. Marilyn Monroe is the secretary of every corporate executive's dream – like the boss says, anybody can type. Director Hawks has great fun with this happy exercise in regression. ★★★ $19.99

Monkey Grip

(1982, 101 min, Australia, Ken Cameron) *Monkey Grip* is the story of Nora (Noni Hazlehurst), an independent, strong-willed woman trying to raise a daughter alone amidst the underground world of musicians, actors and writers. The film follows unconventional Nora as she becomes involved with a brooding, sexually volcanic man (Colin Friels) whose fascination with her becomes dangerously obsessive. Good performances by Hazlehurst and Friels help gloss over the story's melodramatics. ★★½

Monkey Trouble

(1994, 93 min, US, Franco Amurri) *Monkey Trouble* is a nice family film: The parents can enjoy Harvey Keitel's inspired performance as

The Marx Brothers are a barrel of laughs in *Monkey Business*

363

a drunken Gypsy thief, and the kids can both enjoy and learn from the young heroine and everyone will love the monkey. Dodger, a kleptomaniac simian, runs away from Keitel and a life of crime and straight into the arms of Thora Birch, a young girl who longs for a pet. She soon discovers the primate's propensity for pickpocketing and retrains him. Keitel is determined to get Dodger back and get even, with hilarious and satisfying results. Mimi Rogers and Christopher McDonald also star. ★★★ $14.99

Monsieur Beaucaire

(1946, 93 min, US, George Marshall) Booth Tarkington's novel of court intrigue gets the Bob Hope treatment, and the result is a consistently funny romp. Set in 18th-century Europe, the story has Bob playing a barber who is forced to impersonate royalty, much against his will. And, of course, the charade puts him in constant danger. At this point in his career, Hope could do this sort of comedy in his sleep. But to his credit, he gives an engaging comic performance, and he gets to recite some dandy one-liners. ★★★ $14.99

Monsieur Hire

(1990, 81 min, France, Patrice Leconte) Michel Blanc delivers an exquisitely understated performance as the voyeuristic anti-hero in this haunting thriller. Suspected of murdering a young woman, Blanc's favorite pastime is to spy on his attractive neighbor, Alice (Sandrine Bonnaire). She soon becomes aware of his fixation and, much to his horror, tries to befriend him. Alice's boyfriend, Emile (Luc Thuillier), seems to have no objection to her flirtations, for reasons which become obvious only at the film's clever conclusion. Director Leconte exhibits a fine sense of detail and imbues the film with a compellingly eerie atmosphere. Based on a 1933 novel by George Simenon, which was first adapted for the screen in Julien Duvivier's 1946 Panique. (French with English subtitles) ★★★ $19.99

Monsieur Verdoux

(1947, 128 min, US, Charles Chaplin) From an idea suggested by Orson Welles, Chaplin fashioned Hollywood's first black comedy about a wife murderer who feels amateurish compared to what the governments of the world were doing. Chaplin took a long time to make talkies; but when he did, he made certain that they talked! Fortunately the long passages of philosophical digressions, while obvious, are interesting and make a nice binder 'twixt the comedy set pieces. Martha Raye holds her own against the acknowledged master of physical comedy as he tries many ways to murder her. ★★★½

Monsieur Vincent

(1947, 112 min, France, Leon Carre) This excellent biography of St. Vincent de Paul, who gave up his worldly possessions and devoted his life to the poor, preaching charity and understanding, won an Oscar for Best Foreign Film of 1948. Set in 17th-century France, the film successfully avoids the sententious piety which permeates most religious bios, weaving instead with quiet fervor and ineffable grace a story of a saintly hero with the courage of his

convictions. Pierre Fresnay portrays the title role with a masterful performance. (French with English subtitles) ★★★½ $29.99

Monster from Green Hell

(1957, 71 min, US, Kenneth Crane) Jim Davis stars in this cheapie B-movie about a government rocket that crashes in the Congo, spawning mutant insects. To keep production costs down, director Crane actually lifted some scenes straight from his past films. ★ $14.99

Monster in a Box

(1992, 96 min, US, Nick Broomfield) Renowned storyteller/actor Spalding Gray returns to the screen to perform yet another of his insightful and hilarious monologues (the uninitiated should most definitely see Swimming to Cambodia). Sitting in front of a live audience, Gray engagingly prattles on about the difficulties he encountered over the past several years while trotting around the globe in a desperate attempt to escape his "monster in a box," a monolithic 1,800-page autobiographical manuscript which has, lurking in its pages, the death of his mother. In his typical fashion, Gray intricately weaves his tales of joy and woe, along the way evoking in his audience a myriad of emotional responses ranging from outright hilarity to somber reflection. Veteran documentarist Broomfield directs the film with enough vigor to compensate for its essentially static nature, making it thoroughly enchanting viewing. ★★★ $19.99

Monster in a Box

Monster in the Closet

(1986, 87 min, US, Bob Dahlin) "Destroy All Closets!" No, this isn't the rallying cry of ACT-UP, but the battle hymn for the gallant cast of characters belonging to this low-keyed, low-budget horror parody. Spoofing *Superman*, *King Kong* and *The Exorcist*, among many others, *Monster in the Closet* is probably the first film to feature a monster with a decidedly alternative sexual preference. A Clark Kent-type reporter investigates a series of killings in a small town, aided by a teacher and her young

son. There are few laughs, though many in-jokes; and for a Troma release, the film is surprisingly inoffensive. ★★ $14.99

Monte Walsh

(1970, 100 min, US, William A. Fraker) Aging cowboys Lee Marvin and Jack Palance watch the West they knew being bought up by Eastern conglomerates and trivialized in traveling Wild West shows. As the open ranges get fenced in, some give up and settle down, some become outlaws and some just hang on. Perceptive characterizations and stunning location photography combine to deliver a bittersweet ode to a dying way of life. Also starring Jeanne Moreau. ★★★ $14.99

Montenegro

(1981, 98 min, Sweden, Dusan Makavejev) This marvelously anarchic and subversive black comedy stars Susan Anspach as a sexually frustrated housewife who is lured away from her beautiful home and family and tumbles into the Zanzibar, a Yugoslavian bar filled with a carnival world of misfits and twisted characters. Filmed in Sweden by a Yugoslavian director in the English language. ★★★ $19.99

Monterey Pop

(1969, 88 min, US, D.A. Pennebaker) The first and the best of the great rock festivals features the dynamic performances of Jimi Hendrix, The Who, Jefferson Airplane, Janis Joplin, Otis Redding and The Animals. ★★★

A Month by the Lake

(1995, 92 min, GB, John Irvin) As a genre, tales of hapless Brits seeking solar solace in the Italian countryside have provided the film canon with some esteemed gems — A Room with a View and Enchanted April to name but a few. This tiresome comedy will not be among them. Vanessa Redgrave plays Miss Bentley, a single, middle-aged woman who, during the spring of 1937, travels to the Lake Como resort of her youth. There she meets the distinctly unlikable and rather pompous Major Wilshaw (James Fox) and inexplicably chases after him with the chutzpah of a schoolgirl. Uma Thurman comes on the scene as the American nanny of a boisterous Italian family and she immediately bedazzles Wilshaw. The film's inept script and awkward direction attempt to make broad comedy out of the generational rivalry between Redgrave and Thurman, but the result is mostly silly, irksome and — especially for an actress of Redgrave's stature — embarrassing. ★½ $19.99

A Month in the Country

(1988, 96 min, GB, Pat O'Connor) A beautifully filmed, sensitive adaptation of J.L. Carr's novel about two WWI veterans who, emotionally ravaged by their wartime experiences, come to terms with their past during an idyllic summer in the English countryside. Colin Firth and Kenneth Branagh both offer outstanding performances as the men; Natasha Richardson also stars as the daughter of the local vicar who falls in love with Firth. ★★★½ $19.99

Monty Python and the Holy Grail

(1974, 90 min, GB, Terry Gilliam & Terry Jones) The Python troupe takes on King Arthur in this insane farce set amongst the castles, lochs and moors of Scotland. Like the early works of Woody Allen, this is a scattershot affair with gags flying at every turn; miraculously, most hit their mark. The result is a hilarious and inspired excursion into knighthood, medieval pagentry, religious sentiment and transvestism. (Available letterboxed and pan & scan) ★★★½ $19.99

Monty Python Live at the Hollywood Bowl

(1982, 78 min, GB, Terry Hughes) Britain's premiere loonies invade Los Angeles with this madcap series of sketches and routines. All of their favorite concerns, including God, death, and life in heaven, are hilariously explored. The film also features footage with Carol Cleveland and Neil Innes. A must for Python fans. ★★★ $14.99

Monty Python's Flying Circus, Vols. 1-22

(1969-74, 60 each min, GB, Ian MacNaughton) Over a five-year period, beginning in 1969, five British comedians and one American animator who called themselves "Monty Python's Flying Circus" appeared on the BBC in a series of TV comedy shows which featured hilarious, zany and absurdist sketches. They would eventually revolutionize TV and movie comedy for a generation to come. Graham Chapman, John Cleese, Terry Gilliam, Eric Idle, Terry Jones and Michael Palin were the culprits. Sporting goofy humor and silly sight gags, the show was a throwback to the comedy of The Goon Squad, a British comic staple of the 1950s. This collection features the best (and worst) of the sketches performed, many of which have become part of our vocabulary and collective comedic experience. ★★★★ $19.99 each

Monty Python's Life of Brian

(1979, 93 min, GB, Terry Jones) The Gospel According to Monty Python! This side-splitting spoof lampoons 2,000 years of religious thought and mankind's hysterical hankering for a good Messiah. Perhaps Python's best feature. Just remember — always look on the bright side of life. ★★★½ $14.99

Monty Python's The Meaning of Life

(1983, 101 min, GB, Terry Jones) This effort from the Python troupe is a wild collection of vignettes on the humorous aspects of existence — from conception through demise. Included are the educational song and dance production, "Every Sperm Is Sacred," and an unforgettable restaurant retching sketch. ★★★ $14.99

Moon 44

(1989, 102 min, West Germany/US, Roland Emmerich) Michael Paré headlines this outer space actioner about yet another corporate conspiracy in a future where profit is the bottom line and the workers are expendable. Light years better than anyone would expect it to be, with serious performances and a wholehearted attempt at special effects. Not just another money-making Star Wars clone. Also features, in a glorified cameo appearance, Malcolm McDowell. ★★½ $14.99

The Moon in the Gutter

(1983, 126 min, France, Jean-Jacques Beineix) After the incredible promise of Diva, Beineix's eerie follow-up was greeted with puzzled shrugs by the most sympathetic critics. Its reputation aside, however, this sordid tale of obsession is bristling with technical wizardry and sinuous noirism. A fascinating failure. Stars Nastassja Kinski and Gérard Depardieu. (French with English subtitles) ★★

Moon over Miami

(1941, 91 min, US, Walter Lang) Enjoyable Betty Grable musical about two sisters (Grable, Carole Landis) who go millionaire hunting in Miami. They find Don Ameche, Robert Cummings and Jack Haley. Charlotte Greenwood is a particular delight as Grable's cohort who joins Betty and her sister on their quest. ★★½ $19.99

Moon over Parador

(1988, 105 min, US, Paul Mazursky) Energetic though silly comedy from Mazursky set in the small (fictional) Latin American country of Parador whose hated dictator dies, and is replaced by a look-alike — an American actor. Richard Dreyfuss has a field day as the politically naive actor who gets a quick lesson in politics and love when he impersonates the country's ruler. Sonia Braga and Raul Julia also star. ★★½ $19.99

Moonlight and Valentino

(1995, 105 min, US, David Anspaugh) A familiar story of a woman coming to terms with the death of her husband and of her relationship with her supportive friends and family, Moonlight and Valentino is a congenial female buddy movie which is more heart than soul, more emotion than intellect. Elizabeth Perkins plays a woman whose husband is killed in a morning jog. As her sister (Gwyneth Paltrow), best friend (Whoopi Goldberg) and stepmother (Kathleen Turner) gather — sometimes collectively and sometimes singularly — to give her comfort, she has a degree of difficulty in trying to get on with her life. The story takes place over a two-year period, and the characters enter and exit in a sitcomish manner. The widow Perkins rarely shows emotion — to either her husband's untimely death or her caring though sometimes interfering mates — which immediately distances her character from the viewer. But as written by Ellen Simon (Neil's daughter), the film also exhibits a genuine bond between the women, and they're given some good dialogue to recite. Jon Bon Jovi makes an impressive debut as Perkins' hunky house painter. ★★½ $19.99

Moonlighting

(1982, 97 min, GB, Jerzy Skolimowski) Working illegally in London, a group of Polish

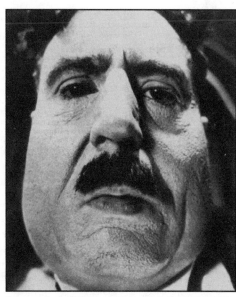

"Better get a bucket!" Mr. Creosote in Monty Python's the Meaning of Life

laborers are brutally cut off from home and family when martial law is declared in their country. Skolimowski's moving and imaginative parable of the Polish struggle stars Jeremy Irons as the only member of the group who can speak English. ★★★½ $49.99

Moonraker

(1979, 126 min, GB, Lewis Gilbert) In this, the 11th outing of agent 007, Roger Moore is on the trail of a wealthy industrialist (Michael Lonsdale) who plans to poison the human race from the safety of his own private space station. Jaws (Richard Kiel) returns, and Lois Chiles is Dr. Holly Goodhead. Gimmicky but still fun. ★★★ $14.99

Moonrise

(1948, 90 min, US, Frank Borzage) This grim psychological melodrama is a brooding tale of a young man who, after years of being taunted about things from his and his father's past, accidentally kills a banker's son. Dane Clark, Lloyd Bridges and Ethel Barrymore star in this rural drama of violence, insanity and revenge. ★★★ $19.99

Moonstruck

(1987, 102 min, US, Norman Jewison) Cher won an Oscar for her performance as a young Italian-American widow in this loopy tale about the power of love over reason. Nicolas Cage delivers an inspired over-the-top performance as her misfit brother-in-law-to-be to whom she is inexplicably attracted. Jewison's direction of John Patrick Shanley's Oscar-winning screenplay "hits your eye like a big pizza pie!" Olympia Dukakis also won an Oscar in support as Cher's no-nonsense mother. Other excellent supporting work comes from Vincent Gardenia, Danny Aiello, Julie Bovasso and John Mahoney. ★★★½ $14.99

More

(1969, 110 min, Luxembourg, Barbet Schroeder) The energy, excitement, innocence and eventual demise of the hippie/youth movement of the '60s is wonderfully captured in Schroeder's first film. The story is a tender tale of a West German student who travels across Europe – from the cafes of Paris to the sun-drenched beaches of Ibiza – searching for love and adventure. Schroeder provides a definitive image of this improbable era where peace, revolt, sex, drugs and rock 'n' roll reign supreme. The soundtrack features great music by Pink Floyd. (English and French, German, and Spanish with English subtitles) ★★★½ $59.99

The More the Merrier

(1943, 104 min, US, George Stevens) A sparkling comedy from director Stevens. In overcrowded, wartime Washington D.C., Jean Arthur shares her small, one-bedroom apartment with Joel McCrea and Charles Coburn; the latter playing matchmaker. Coburn deservedly won a Best Supporting Oscar as the lovable Mr. Dingle; Arthur (though a nominee) probably should have won Best Actress for her captivating portrayal. Stevens also won an Oscar as Best Director. ★★★★ $19.99

Morgan!

(1966, 92 min, GB, Karel Reisz) One of the finest and funniest black comedies ever to hail from the shores of Great Britain, *Morgan!* stars David Warner as an artist teetering on the precipice of total insanity. After his wife (Vanessa Redgrave) divorces him, he sets out on a series of lunatic escapades in an effort to reconcile himself to his new status. Filled with truth and pathos, this is a very funny look at the process of "breaking up." ★★★★

Morgan Stewart's Coming Home

(1987, 96 min, US, Alan Smithee) Maybe he should have stayed where he was... he might have had better luck. The usually reliable Jon Cryer gives it the old college try playing a student who returns home to aid his father's election bid – turning the campaign upside down. Director Paul Aaron took his name off the film, replacing it with "Alan Smithee," the industry moniker for such occasions. ★½

Morituri

(1965, 128 min, US, Bernhard Wicki) One of Marlon Brando's more fascinating failures from the 1960s (a decade in which the star took many chances in his film roles – most of which foundered). Brando plays an anti-Nazi German demolitions expert who is "recruited" by the British to help them seize a German freighter which is booby-trapped to explode upon capture. Yul Brynner also stars as the ship's captain. (*aka: The Saboteur* and *The Saboteur, Code Name Morituri*) ★★ $19.99

The Morning After

(1986, 103 min, US, Sidney Lumet) Jane Fonda's bravura performance as an alcoholic actress on the skids highlights this predictable though gritty mystery thriller. Fonda awakes one morning to discover a corpse beside her – and she can't remember anything about the night before. Jeff Bridges helps her find out the truth. ★★½ $14.99

Morning Glory

(1933, 73 min, US, Lowell Sherman) Katharine Hepburn won her first Oscar for her glorious performance as a starstruck actress determined to succeed on the New York stage. In a role similar to the one she would play in *Stage Door* a few years later, Hepburn shines in this compelling theatrical drama as Eva Lovelace, a small-town girl with stars in her eyes, and enough determination and talent to make sure her dreams come true. ★★★ $19.99

Morocco

(1930, 92 min, US, Josef Von Sternberg) The impossibly seductive Marlene Dietrich made her American film debut as a cabaret singer in Morocco, torn between Foreign Legionnaire Gary Cooper and wealthy Adolphe Menjou. Romantic and very interesting. ★★★½ $14.99

Moron Movies

(1985, 75 min, US, Len Cella) A hilariously stupid collection of vignettes by Lansdowne-based Cella. The shorts include *The Advantage of Having Warts, How to Know If You're Ugly, How to Clean the Toilet without Gagging* and, of course, the answer to the eternal question, *Why Animals Should Wear Underwear.* $19.99

Morons from Outer Space

(1985, 87 min, GB, Mike Hodges) They came, they saw, they did a little shopping. The title says it all: four not-quite-right-in-the-head humanoids from the planet Blob crash Earth, where these pinheads are treated as media heroes and eventually become successful rock stars. The trousers of the well-known British reserve are ceremoniously dropped in this daffy sci-fi comedy. ★★½ $14.99

Mortal Kombat

(1995, 101 min, US, Paul Anderson) The most successful video game-to-film transfer yet (though that's not saying much), this movie is a fun ride through strange worlds and raucous martial arts competitions which wisely abandons any aspirations to plot or character development; everything in this movie is at the service of its action scenes. These scenes, therefore, are well-staged and exciting, pitting three human heroes against a variety of evil humans, monsters and sorcerers. Sonya Blade, Liu Kang and Johnny Cage must travel to Outworld to compete in the biggest martial arts competition of them all: Mortal Kombat. Each has his or her own reasons for traveling to the tournament, but Lord Rayden (Christopher Lambert) knows the truth: the game will decide the future of our world. Aficionados of the video game series will appreciate the film's many in-jokes, but a knowledge of the game is not necessary to enjoy the movie's many thrills. Spectacular computer effects highlight its fight scenes, and the set design, also computer-aided, is very impressive. *Mortal Kombat* is brainless fun for all ages, which is all it tries to be. ★★½ $19.99

Mortal Thoughts

(1991, 102 min, US, Alan Rudolph) A stylish, gripping psychological thriller dripping in atmosphere and tension. Set in Bayonne, New Jersey, the film stars Demi Moore and Glenne Headley as lifelong friends and business partners; the latter is married to abusive Bruce Willis (thankfully underplaying his role). In an accident, he dies and the two cover up his death. But was it an accident? And who really did it? Harvey Keitel is the police detective grilling Moore for the answers – reliving the story through flashbacks right up to the unexpected ending. Though Moore's screen work here is most accomplished, Headley steals the show with a hypnotic performance as the suspected murderess. ★★★ $14.99

Moscow Does Not Believe in Tears

(1980, 152 min, USSR, Vladimir Menshov) This surprise Oscar winner of 1981 is a light and charming look into contemporary Soviet life. The story concerns three young provincial girls' move to Moscow and their search for work, love and marriage. The first half could very well be a *How to Marry a Millionaire* – Soviet style! (Russian with English subtitles) ★★★ $59.99

Moscow on the Hudson

(1984, 115 min, US, Paul Mazursky) Robin Williams gives an endearingly sweet performance as a Russian musician who defects to America in the middle of Bloomingdale's. Writer-director Mazursky fills this benign satire with interesting eccentrics and amusing anecdotes as the befuddled defector suffers some severe culture shock. A totally winning social comedy with good support from Maria Conchita Alonso and Cleavant Derricks. ★★★½ $14.99

The Mosquito Coast

(1986, 119 min, US, Peter Weir) Harrison Ford is well cast as Pennsylvania inventor Allie Fox, whose disgust with the direction of American culture prompts him to upheave his family to a primitive island off the Central American coast to begin a utopian society. But for Fox, there is no escaping civilization. Once they reach their paradise, the society left behind begins to rear its ugly head, sending the determined father deeper into a paranoiac state and eventual madness. River Phoenix gives a strong performance as the teenage son who must protect his family when their paradise turns to hell. An ambitious treatise on man's psyche and his desire to get back to nature. ★★★ $9.99

Mother

(1926, 90 min, USSR, V.I. Pudoukin) Set during the unsuccessful workers' rebellion of 1905, Pudoukin's engrossing story is about one family's hardships under the cruel czarist regime. A technically impressive allegory for Russia's conversion to Communism. (Silent with musical soundtrack) ★★★

Mother

(1952, 98 min, Japan, Mikio Naruse) A compelling portrait of a working-class woman's struggle to resurrect her family from post-war ruins. Told through the eyes of her daughter, the mother possesses a tenacious will and resilient spirit as she, a woman alone, sacrifices and tirelessly works for the welfare of her family. An incisive allegory for a nation that had to rise from the ashes of WWII. (Japanese with English subtitles) ★★★

Mother

(1996, 104 min, US, Albert Brooks) Albert Brooks sets out to prove that even though she may not wear Army boots, there's still plenty to fear from that dear old materfamilias, especially when you're a middle-aged dime store novelist who's recently divorced and caught in the throes of depression. Brooks is in his element as a quintessential schnook and author of cheap sci-fi thrillers (that nobody reads) who decides that the only way to get his life back in gear is to move back in with his mother. So, he hops in the car and cruises from L.A. to Sausolito and begs ma to let him have his old room back. Debbie Reynolds (in her first screen appearance in 25 years) is superb as his put-upon mom who just can't understand what all his fussing is about anyway. "Let the past stay the past," she tells him. Brooks' script does a fine job skewering mother-son stereotypes, delivering several big laughs at the expense of just about everybody from cheap pop psychologists to mom herself, including a hilarious bit where she tries to serve him two-year-old ice cream. Brooks has done this character before, but Reynolds gives a strikingly nuanced portrayal of a woman who is much deeper that her surface gloss suggests. With this wonderful lark, Brooks proves *Mother* knows best. ★★★½ $102.99

Mother Kusters Goes to Heaven

(1976, 108 min, West Germany, Rainer Werner Fassbinder) Brigitte Mira is outstanding as Mother Kusters, an older woman whose sedate, ordinary life is thrown into turmoil when her husband goes mad at work, killing the paymaster, and then committing suicide. As she struggles to understand what happened to her husband, the emotional poverty of her life is revealed in her casual comments regarding her husband's lack of communication, her daughter's ability to turn the media attention to career advantage and her son's inability to counter his wife's desire to distance herself from the embarrassment. As the media vultures descend, the facts of her prosaic life are twisted and sensationalized to sell papers. Mother Kusters' outrage over the desecration of her husband's memory makes her a willing target for third-rate politicos promising the means of retribution. Mira's entirely believable performance and Fassbinder's unerring cynical eye deliver a powerful treatise on the human propensity toward exploitation. (German with English subtitles) ★★★½ $79.99

Mother Night

(1996, 113 min, US, Keith Gordon) A wonderfully wry and unexpectedly romantic adaptation of Kurt Vonnegut's 1974 novel, *Mother Night* marks another successful behind-the-camera turn for actor-turned-director Gordon (*A Midnight Clear*). Using flashback to recall the life of an American double agent living in Nazi Germany, the story begins with Howard Campbell (Nick Nolte) serving time in an Israeli prison. An outspoken Nazi sympathizer and playwright, Campbell was in fact a spy for the Allies who would use his weekly anti-

Semitic and anti-American radio hour to convey encoded secret information. Traveling back and forth in time (much like Vonnegut's *Slaughterhouse-Five*), the film focuses on Campbell's post-war life as a desolate, lonely widower in New York whose name perversely comes before the public once more. All during the story, Vonnegut takes a moral dilemma and devours it, spitting out chunks of ambiguity and the bizarre with devilish delight. Sheryl Lee is luminous as Campbell's German wife, and John Goodman is the mysterious American agent who enlists Campbell's help. ★★★½ $102.99

Mother's Boys

(1994, 95 min, US, Yves Simoneau) Jamie Lee Curtis toplines this Freudian suspenser about a well-bred sociopath who, having abandoned her husband (Peter Gallagher) and children years earlier, tries to reclaim them using her eldest son as leverage. Curtis is suitably creepy as a woman who will stop at nothing — even sexual intimidation — to win back her family. However, the film ultimately deteriorates into standard shock fare. Joanne Whalley-Kilmer and Vanessa Redgrave also star. ★★½ $19.99

Mothra

(1962, 100 min, Japan, Inoshiro Honda) The director of the first *Godzilla* movie created this cute fairy tale about two twin six-inch princesses kidnapped from their throne on Infant Island and exhibited on Tokyo television singing their siren song — a song that calls their giant moth to come and save them, at the city's expense. Featuring Japanese recording stars "Peanuts" as the princesses. ★★ $12.99

Motor Psycho

(1965, 65 min, US, Russ Meyer) Three bikers, led by a crazed Vietnam vet, go on an unstoppable orgy of rape and murder, until a vengeful husband gets on their trail and forces a showdown. Made between *Mudhoney* and *Faster, Pussycat, Kill! Kill!* and featuring the alluring Haji, *Motor Psycho* is Meyer's entry into the biker genre and presages *Faster, Pussycat's* theme of rampaging maniacs in the desert terrorizing hapless strangers. ★★ $79.99

Mouchette

(1966, 90 min, France, Robert Bresson) The last 24 hours in the life of a 14-year-old peasant girl is starkly presented without pity and without offering a single glimmer of hope. This moving story of humiliation and defeat traces the experiences of Mouchette, a bewildered youngster who is victimized at home by her drunken father, alienated at school, isolated from a hostile world and who is finally driven to suicide. A simply told, overwhelming story whose strong narrative and technical virtuosity transcends the unrelentingly grim dramatics. (French with English subtitles) ★★★½ $59.99

Moulin Rouge

(1952, 123 min, US, John Huston) A fascinating film biography, rich in color and detail, about the life of 19th-century French painter Henri de Toulouse-Lautrec. Jose Ferrer gives a stunning portrayal of the troubled artist, whose growth impediment was impetus to his flagrant lifestyle and art. ★★★½ $19.99

The Mountain

(1956, 105 min, US, Edward Dmytryk) Spencer Tracy and Robert Wagner star as two brothers at odds while climbing a treacherous peak to reach an aircraft that crashed. Claire Trevor also stars. Tracy's sincere performance highlights this familiar tale of familial conflict. ★★½ $14.99

Mountains of the Moon

(1990, 135 min, US, Bob Rafelson) Inspired by the journals of 19th-century explorers Richard Burton and Jack Speke, this is a stirring account of the torturous and famous expedition taken by the two adventurers to discover the source of the Nile. With the majestic sweep usually associated with the works of David Lean, director Rafelson meticulously re-creates the worlds of privileged Britain and small-tribe Africa, and has fashioned an exhilarating adventure film of the highest order. Patrick Bergin and Iain Glen give outstanding performances as Burton and Speke, respectively, whose sometimes perilous and always enlightening journey began in 1854, and ended many years and thousands of miles later in betrayal and death. ★★★★ $14.99

The Mouse That Roared

(1959, 83 min, GB, Jack Arnold) This hilarious satire on the idiocies of foreign policy involves the miniscule Grand Duchy of Fenwick which declares war on the United States with the intention of losing in order to receive foreign aid. This is a film which could have only been made in the pre-Vietnam era, when America was still basking in its Marshall Plan glow. Featuring Peter Sellers in three amusing roles, and a pre-opening sequence which ranks as a classic. ★★★½ $19.99

Movie in Your Face

(1990, 85 min, US) HBO stand-up comic fave Tommy Sledge is featured as a narrator and voice-over actor in this romp inspired by the classic *What's Up Tiger Lily?* Once again, new dialogue has been dubbed in to replace the original language in what appears to already be a comedy; but nonetheless the end result is very funny and will appeal to comedy fans everywhere. ★★★ $39.99

Moving

(1988, 89 min, US, Alan Metter) New Jerseyites Richard Pryor and family pack up and move to Idaho when Dad lands a great job. Most of this is of the predictable sort, but Pryor's manic reactions and character make it tolerable. ★★ $19.99

Moving the Mountain

(1995, 83 min, US/China, Michael Apted) Director Apted, who effortlessly focuses his talents on successful documentaries (*Incident at Oglala*) and popular theatrical films (*Nell*), continues his insightful exploration of the human condition with this powerful documentary. Chronicling several people in leadership positions during the Tiananmen Square protests, the film recounts their involvement and gives a history of the events which led to the killing of thousands and the reawakening of an undercurrent of change within China.

M

The empassioned Li Lu, one of the student leaders, is profiled with reenactments of his life from childhood and actual news footage of the events surrounding the protests. *Moving the Mountain* is a sobering view of these now-exiled students, and the film is enhanced by stylish editing, engaging principals, and inspirational stories. ★★★½ $92.99

Mozart — A Childhood Chronicle

(1976, 224 min, West Germany, Klaus Kirscher) A German new wave exploration of an artist in the style of Hans-Jurgen Syberberg's *Parsifal*, this original documentary uses as its entire script the letters written by Wolfgang Amadeus Mozart, his father, mother and oldest sister. Combining readings of the personal letters, authentic costumes and locations and Mozart's finest music, this complex, moving film traces the development of the young composer from the age of seven to his death at thirty-five. (German with English subtitles) ★★★ $79.99

The Mozart Brothers

(1986, 98 min, Sweden, Suzanne Osten) An often hilarious view of the artistic process choosing to draw upon the Marx Brothers' *A Night at the Opera* for inspiration. The story concerns a radically innovative production of Mozart's "Don Giovanni" as done by a Stockholm opera company. We are given a profound look at the trials of Walter, the fanatically avant-garde theatre director, whose attempts to win the hearts of the intransigent singers often result in some of the film's funniest moments. In a somewhat Bergman-esque touch, the ghost of Mozart offers Walter encouragement and advice through nocturnal visitations. For fans of opera, theatre and music alike, this is a wonderful flight of fancy which will surely not disappoint. (Swedish with English subtitles) ★★★ $24.99

Mr.

See: Mister

Mrs. Brown, You've Got a Lovely Daughter

(1968, 110 min, GB, Saul Swimmer) This lightweight vehicle for '60s pop group Herman and the Hermits co-stars Mona Washbourne and Stanley Holloway. The band of course sings the title song along with their other hit, "There's a Kind of Hush All Over the World." This jump on the Beatles' *A Hard Day's Night* bandwagon is only intermittently entertaining. ★★

Mrs. Doubtfire

(1993, 105 min, US, Chris Columbus) Heavy on the laughter as well as the sentiment, *Mrs. Doubtfire* is an appealing comedy in spite of its sprinkling of Afterschool Special schmaltz. Featuring a very funny performance by Robin Williams, this genuinely entertaining, high-concept comedy casts Williams as a recently divorced actor. Losing a custody battle over his three children, Williams takes advantage of ex-wife Sally Field's search for a housekeeper — and impersonates a sixty-ish British nanny. It takes a half-hour for the beguiling Mrs. Doubtfire to make her appearance, but when she does, Williams and the film become nearly inspired. Often recalling *Tootsie*, *Mrs.*

Doubtfire isn't on that film's level, but it does firmly stand on its own two orthopedic pumps. ★★★ $14.99

Mrs. Miniver

(1942, 134 min, US, William Wyler) A beautifully filmed, exceptionally acted drama of a British family facing the rigors of WWII. Greer Garson won a Best Actress Oscar as the title character, a formidable wife and mother who does her best to keep her family together in the wake of separation and tragedy. Walter Pidgeon is fine as Mr. Miniver, and Teresa Wright is lovely as their daughter-in-law. Winner of seven Oscars, including Film and Director. ★★★½ $19.99

Mrs. Parker & the Vicious Circle

(1994, 123 min, US, Alan Rudolph) Jennifer Jason Leigh gives a tour de force performance as Algonquin wit and writer Dorothy Parker. In this extremely humorous though slightly downbeat examination of a troubled soul, director Rudolph has brilliantly reconstructed 1920s New York — a time when a select group of Manhattan's literary set convened to sling the next bon mot. In a series of flashbacks, the story follows Parker's rise as an author, her relationships with humorist Robert Benchley (Campbell Scott) and playwright Charles MacArthur (Matthew Broderick), and the formation of the legendary Algonquin Round Table. Leigh's portrayal of the lonely and acerbic Parker is very much the pulse of the film. She inhabits Parker as if possessed, conveying an eerie worldliness and heartbreaking vulnerability. Though physically miscast, Scott is excellent in capturing Benchley's goofy mannerisms and subtle comedy — his "Treasurer's Report" is perfection. ★★★½ $19.99

Mrs. Parkington

(1944, 124 min, US, Tay Garnett) A dedicated cast led by Greer Garson and Walter Pidgeon enlivens this compelling soap opera. Spanning the course of 60 years in the life of the title character, the film features Garson as a wealthy New York family matriarch who is faced with a familial crisis. Remembering the past for guidance, Mrs. Parkington recalls her life and marriage to her "scoundrel" industrialist husband, played by Pidgeon. Although the dramatics is routine, it is the earnest performances from the entire cast which elevate it. Oscar nominee Garson is noble and lovely, but one could question her character's devotion to such a cold-hearted businessman. Agnes Moorehead, who also received a nomination, gives a splendid characterization as Pidgeon's wise ex-mistress. ★★½ $19.99

Mrs. Soffel

(1985, 110 min, US, Gillian Armstrong) Diane Keaton is the sheltered wife of a stern prison warden who surrenders to the powerful attraction of a death-row convict (Mel Gibson); both become the object of a massive hunt when she helps him escape and they run away together. The attractive pairing of Keaton and Gibson and a good evocation of the period aren't sufficient enough to mask a dreary story and a passionless directorial style. (Available letterboxed and pan & scan) ★★ $14.99

Ms. Don Juan

(1973, 87 min, France, Roger Vadim) Vadim, mediocre filmmaker but successful promotor of such sex sirens as Jane Fonda, Brigitte Bardot and Catherine Deneuve, directed this half-baked tale of murder and passion. BB stars as an evil seductress with an insatiable sexual appetite and hypnotic charms who devours and destroys everyone in sight. A sexual switch of the Don Juan story. (Dubbed) ★★

Ms. 45

(1981, 84 min, US, Abel Ferrara) A Freudian, feminist revenge fantasy. Zoe Tamerlis is riveting as a victimized deaf-mute who adopts the Charles Bronson method of street sanitation and wages a war against the male scum population. ★★★

Much Ado About Nothing

(1993, 110 min, GB, Kenneth Branagh) Returning to the familiar soil of Shakespeare (*Henry V*), actor-director Branagh springs forth with a delightfully giddy and frantic romp set in the sun-drenched fields of Tuscany. Shakespeare's bawdy comic tale of love torn assunder casts Branagh and then-real-life wife Emma Thompson as the sharp-witted, acerbic would-be lovers Benedick and Beatrice, whose course of true love is not a tranquil one. Branagh and Thompson, radiant together, elevate the Bard's prose to resplendent levels of ecstasy. Featuring a splendid ensemble cast, including Denzel Washington, Robert Sean Leonard, Keanu Reeves and Michael Keaton (in a funny comic turn as Constable Dogberry), the film is peppered with brilliant comic timing and seasoned with moments of overwhelming romanticism. *Much Ado* is truly a to do: a joyous celebration of unbridled passions. ★★★★ $14.99

Mudhoney

(1965, 92 min, US, Russ Meyer) A black-and-white profile of rural Missouri lowlife in the '30s, which rails against American morality and religious hypocrisy. Stars Lorna Maitland, Rena Horten ("the embodiment of the body") and the buxom Lee Ballard. ★½ $79.99

El Muerto

(1979, 105 min, Argentina, Hector Olivera) Taken from the short story by Jorge Luis Borges, this South American western is set in the late 19th century when revolution and civil war overwhelmed the land. After killing a man in a street fight, Benjamin Otalora flees Buenos Aires for the interior of Uruguay where he is soon taken under the wing of a ruthless gun smuggler and becomes part of his well-organized gang who provides arms to both sides of the conflict. Handsome, calculating and blinded by ambition, our hero belligerently jockeys for power, even to the point of becoming the lover of his boss' wife. The older man, growing sick, must decide whether to turn over power to the brash young man or fight him in order to retain it. (Spanish with English subtitles) ★★★

Mulholland Falls

(1996, 107 min, US, Lee Tamahori) In 1950s Los Angeles, a renegade group of cops known as the "Hat Squad" implemented their own individual brand of justice against criminals with an unlawful but patriotic zeal. Had they ever seen this muddled though frequently exciting exposé of vigilantism and cover-up suggested by their real-life exploits, the filmmakers may have been next to be "escorted" out of town. Nick Nolte heads the cast as the leader of a group of elite cops who — upon the investigation of a murdered woman — become entangled in a complex mystery which ultimately leads to military conspiracy. Shot in a golden, nostalgic soft-focus, this excellent evocation of post-war L.A. is unfortunately a bargain basement *Chinatown*, which only belies its novel premise. Fellow cops Michael Madsen and Chris Penn have literally nothing to do, and soon disappear; of the large cast, only Chazz Palminteri as the fourth member of the squad brings life to his character. New Zealand director Tamahori (*Once Were Warriors*) has a great feel for time and place but isn't able to jump start a contrived script. ★★½ $99.99

Multiple Maniacs

(1971, 94 min, US, John Waters) The film Waters claimed "flushed religion out of my system" is so irredeemable that even describing it offends public standards of morality. But we'll try. A traveling carnival called "Lady Divine's Cavalcade of Perversions" lands in Baltimore and disrupts the lives of the creeps living there. We're treated to a junkie shooting up on a church altar, bearded transvestites, the semi-classic scene of Divine being raped by a 15-foot lobster, Mink Stole's rosary beads, cannibalism, Kate Smith's rendition of "God Bless America" and, perhaps most disturbing of all, shots of downtown Baltimore. ★★½

Multiplicity

(1996, 110 min, US, Harold Ramis) Michael Keaton gets cloned and essentially plays with himself in this amiable though lackluster comedy whose cute premise is never fully realized. Harking back to *Mr. Mom* and *Beetlejuice* with his characterizations, Keaton plays a harried construction foreman who doesn't have enough hours in the day for his professional or private lives. After a chance meeting with a scientist, Keaton is cloned, enabling the original to spend more quality time with the wife (Andie MacDowell) and kids while the "xerox copy" shows up at work. In time, there are four Keatons running around on the screen, engaging in predictable shenanigans. The special effects are terrific, and Keaton creates distinct personalities for his four "Dougs." But the screenplay doesn't come close to the film's F/X wizardry, and the laugh quotient is surprisingly low. MacDowell has little to do, and the supporting cast is wasted. ★★ $19.99

The Mummy

(1932, 72 min, US, Karl Freund) Noted cinematographer Freund (*Metropolis*, *Dracula*) made his directorial debut in Boris Karloff's second greatest horror role. Buried alive for trying to restore life to his great love, it is he who is accidentally revived by an overeager archaeologist. Moody and foreboding, this tragic tale of love lost over the centuries moves ceaselessly forward towards its inevitable destiny. ★★★½ $14.99

The Mummy

(1959, 86 min, GB, Terence Fisher) Journeyman director Fisher brings his usual panache to the remake of the Karloff classic based on an early draft for that film. Christopher Lee is the resurrected avenger out for archaeologist Peter Cushing's blood in this, one of Hammer Films' most stylish efforts. ★★★ $14.99

The Mummy's Hand

(1940, 67 min, US, Christy Cabanne) Before passing the role to Lon Chaney, Tom Tyler starred as Kharis, the mummy, in this first of a series. The action takes place at an archaeological dig where explorers find the sacred tomb of an Egyptian princess still guarded by Kharis. Excellent set design and good acting combine to make this a classic from the golden age of horror films. Trivia buffs take note: look for ten minutes of footage from Karloff's *The Mummy* (1932), used here as flashback. ★★★ $14.99

The Muppet Movie

(1979, 94 min, US, James Frawley) The first of the Muppet films, this sweet, entertaining children's film follows the trail of Kermit the Frog on his way to stardom. Miss Piggy, Fozzie, Gonzo and the rest of the gang tag along. Cameos by Steve Martin, Carol Kane, Orson Welles and many more. There's a charming musical score by Paul Williams. ★★★ $14.99

Muppet Treasure Island

(1996, 99 min, US, Brian Henson) The always-welcome Muppets return in an energetic retelling of the Stevenson classic. Gonzo and Rizzo the Rat take center stage joined by Muppet faves Kermit, Miss Piggy and Fozzie (playing a lunatic whose best friend lives in his index finger); Tim Curry, Kevin Bishop and Billy Connelly lend human support. While not as wildly inventive or consistently funny as their latest TV incarnation, "Muppets Tonite!" (which is coming soon to video), *Treasure Island* is a wholly entertaining lark, thanks to both the kooky antics in which the characters engage, and the fact that the creators play the story straight (as they did in the even better *Muppet Christmas Carol*). Not without its slow moments, the film nevertheless has wondrous bits, such as the musical numbers "Cabin Fever" (a Carmen Miranda-inspired free-for-all performed by pirates and Muppets in drag), and "Love Led Us Here," a heartfelt ballad sung by Kermit and Miss Piggy while hanging upside-down over a cliff. ★★★ $22.99

The Muppets Christmas Carol

(1992, 85 min, US, Brian Henson) Jim Henson may be gone, but his legacy continues through his son Brian in this latest adaptation of the Dickens classic. Michael Caine (looking very well, thank you) stars as Ebenezer Scrooge, and Kermit and Miss Piggy star as Bob and Emily Crachit. This could easily become a perennial family favorite with the familiar characters intact, but toned down just slightly for the younger set. Narration by Gonzo as Dickens himself helps introduce the plot lines and add some background. It's funny, touching and, of course, a technical marvel, seamlessly blending Muppet characters with the humans. ★★★½ $14.99

The Muppets Take Manhattan

(1984, 94 min, US, Frank Oz) The title is more than lived up to as Kermit, Miss Piggy and the rest of the gang head to New York to put on a Broadway musical. Lots of fun. Guest stars include Art Carney, James Coco, Joan Rivers and many more. ★★★ $14.99

Murder

(1930, 92 min, GB, Alfred Hitchcock) A fast-paced and inventive whodunit about a juror in an actress' murder trial who becomes convinced of the woman's innocence and sets out for some amateur sleuthing. The bizarre truth is ultimately revealed with an extraordinary twist. ★★★ $12.99

Murder at 1600

(1997, 107 min, US, Dwight H. Little) On the heels of the more involving *Absolute Power*,

Robin Williams lets loose as *Mrs. Doubtfire*

M

Murder at 1600 is a by-the-books but competently made thriller which also suggests that there's more shenanigans going on in the White House than seances and shredding parties. Unlike Clint Eastwood's thriller in which, like "Columbo," we know the identity of the killer, *Murder at 1600* plays more like a "Murder She Wrote" episode as a body is found but we're not sure who did it. Wesley Snipes plays a D.C. homicide detective investigating the murder who is up against constant interference from Secret Service chief Daniel Benzali and staff, including agent Diane Lane who eventually becomes Snipes' ally. There are a couple of unpredictable twists and a few red herrings, but director Little seems more concerned with chases and the rudiments of the action film than laying the foundation for a good mystery. Ronny Cox plays a president who also didn't serve in the military, and Alan Alda is the oily National Security chief. ★★½ $102.99

Murder by Death

(1976, 94 min, US, Robert Moore) Neil Simon wrote the screenplay for this delightfully zany spoof on movie detectives; with an all-star cast doing a number on Nick and Nora Charles (David Niven and Maggie Smith), Miss Marple (Elsa Lanchester), Charlie Chan (Peter Sellers), Hercule Poirot (James Coco) and Sam Spade (Peter Falk). Plenty of laughs and lots of fun. ★★★ $19.99

Murder by Decree

(1979, 121 min, Canada/GB, Bob Clark) A superior, dark-edged Sherlock Holmes mystery with Christopher Plummer as the famous sleuth, and James Mason as Dr. Watson. An investigation into the murders of Jack the Ripper suggest involvement by a member of the Royal family. Also with Candy Clark, Genevieve Bujold, Donald Sutherland and John Gielgud. Plummer makes a most convincing Holmes, and Mason is a wondrous Watson. ★★★½

Murder by Natural Causes

(1979, 96 min, US, Richard Day) Exceptional made-for-TV thriller about a well-known psychic (Hal Holbrook) and the unfaithful wife (Katharine Ross) who is literally trying to scare him to death. Written by Richard Levinson and William Link (*That Certain Summer, My Sweet Charlie*, etc.). ★★★

Murder in the First

(1994, 122 min, US, Marc Rocco) Kevin Bacon shines in this somber and tragic slice of history about Henri Young who, in 1937, after a botched escape attempt lands him three years naked and freezing in the bowels of Alcatraz, murders in plain sight the stool pigeon who turned him in. Christian Slater is the fledgling public defender who turns a simple open-and-shut case into an indictment against the prison system and Alcatraz itself. Director Rocco (*Where the Day Takes You*) enhances what would normally be deemed "made-for-TV" fare with gripping scenes of prison brutality. This violence is characterized by yet another showy performance from Gary Oldman as the sadistic associate warden. Kyra Sedgwick (the real-life Mrs. Bacon) has an interesting cameo as a hooker paid by Slater to give Bacon his first taste of sex. ★★★ $14.99

Murder, My Sweet

(1944, 95 min, US, Edward Dmytryk) One of the classics of film noir, this adaptation of Raymond Chandler's "Farewell, My Lovely" is a raw but exhilarating murder mystery where hard-boiled, wise-cracking detective Phillip Marlowe (Dick Powell) becomes immersed in a duplicitous world of evil where everyone is a suspect and no one should be trusted. After taking on the case of finding ex-con Moose Malloy's missing girlfriend Velma, Marlowe soon is over his head in a sordid and ever more confusing maze of kidnappers, liars and ruthless killers. Superb dialogue and a great story highlight this stylish, trend-setting mystery. ★★★½ $19.99

Murder on the Orient Express

(1974, 127 min, GB, Sidney Lumet) Agatha Christie's popular novel makes for a sumptuous ride on the Orient Express in this big-budget, large-scaled, all-star murder mystery. Albert Finney, obviously enjoying himself, stars as Hercule Poirot, that famed Belgian detective who finds himself investigating the murder of an American industrialist (Richard Widmark) while a passenger on the famed luxury train. With more than enough suspects to go around, Poirot systematically interrogates and eliminates until the final and very surprising conclusion. The suspects? Ingrid Bergman as a dyslexic governess, Lauren Bacall as a famed actress, Sean Connery as a former soldier, Anthony Perkins as a personal secretary, John Gielgud as a manservant, Michael York and Jacqueline Bisset as lovers, Vanessa Redgrave, Martin Balsam, Wendy Hiller, Rachel Roberts...a truly impressive cast. Lumet's pace is even throughout, which doesn't give rise to too many overly exciting scenes, but he keeps the whodunit aspect absolutely entrancing. ★★★½ $29.99

Murder, She Said

(1962, 87 min, GB, George Pollock) While dozing on a train, Miss Jane Marple awakens to witness a murder on a passing train. The police don't believe her. We, however, know better. Margaret Rutherford made her debut as Agatha Christie's famous sleuth. Arthur Kennedy co-stars. ★★★ $19.99

Murderers Are Among Us

(1946, 85 min, Germany, Wolfgang Stoudte) Filmed in the rubble of Berlin at the end of WWII, *Murderers Are Among Us* is both a casebook example of the neorealist style and an unsettling historical document. A young woman recently released from a concentration camp returns to her apartment to find it occupied by a surgeon traumatized and embittered by his war experiences. Her stalwart resolve to begin life anew is in diametric opposition to his disillusionment: He who once saved lives no longer believes mankind worth saving. He encounters his former superior officer, a butcher of a man thriving in the devastation and at no loss for new opportunities for exploitation. The surgeon sees this encounter as a chance for retribution, and finds redemption instead. Especially revealing are the references to the atrocities, the camps and mass executions, which amazingly some question the reality of even now, 50 years later. It seems there was no doubt of their existence in 1946, when this film was made. A startling and revelatory piece of filmmaking, and a testament to the human ability to salvage hope from utter desolation. (German with English subtitles) ★★★ $39.99

Muriel

(1963, 111 min, France/Italy, Alain Resnais) Resnais continues his exploration of the theme of the relationship between present and past in this serious film about the concrete realities of everyday life. Helen, a 40-year-old antique dealer, disillusioned with her situation, attempts to relive her past be renewing a relationship with a lover of 20 years before. (French with English subtitles) ★★★ $59.99

Muriel's Wedding

(1995, 105 min, Australia, P.J. Hogan) Toni Collette gives a magical performance as the overweight, unemployed Muriel who desperately wants to fit in with the popular girls from high school. Her obsession with the clique prompts her to finance a vacation with her father's money to visit a popular resort just to be with them. When the theft is discovered, she leaves her family home in Porpoise Spit, Australia, for the big city life of Sydney. There she reacquaints herself with high school buddy Rhonda (brilliantly played by Rachel Griffiths), who is a social butterfly to Muriel's demure homebody. After repeated attempts at relationships, she marries a South African swimmer — who needs his citizenship to compete in the Olympics — to realize her lifelong dream of marriage. The sometimes despairing events in Muriel's life are played out against extremely funny and often cynical comedy, humor which seems to take the sting out of her forlorn life. And as with other "ugly duckling" tales, the release of the swan inside allows for both humor and pathos. Bill Hunter is his usual evil self as Muriel's father and the supporting characters of the other siblings and Muriel's mother are excellent. ★★★½ $19.99

Murmur of the Heart

(1971, 118 min, France, Louis Malle) Although tame by today's standards, Malle's infectious comedy about a boy's sexual coming-of-age and his relationship with his carelessly sensual mother caused quite a sensation when first released in 1971, creating much controversy due to the film's matter-of-fact attitude about incest. Set in France in 1954, the story follows the day-to-day lives of a bourgeois family and especially Laurent, a precocious 14-year-old boy whose interests lie mainly in the jazz music of Charlie Parker and attempting to lose his virginity. His success in love takes an unexpected turn when he, accompanied by his free-spirited mother, is sent to a spa to recover from rheumatic fever. A tender and funny film which affectionately satirizes familial relationships. (French with English subtitles) ★★★½ $19.99

Murphy's Romance

(1985, 107 min, US, Martin Ritt) James Garner received an Oscar nomination for his delightful performance in this simple and charming romantic comedy. Garner plays a

The Music Man

small-town pharmacist who romances a recently divorced mother (Sally Field), much to the dismay of her ne'er-do-well ex-husband (Brian Kerwin). Corey Haim appears as Field's young son. ★★★ $9.99

Murphy's War

(1971, 106 min, GB, Peter Yates) When a British merchant ship is sunk by German torpedoes off the coast of Venezuela at the end of WWII, Peter O'Toole finds himself in the unenviable position of being the sole survivor. For the remainder of the film, he dedicates himself to hunting down and destroying the U-boat responsible for the tragedy. Superbly staged action sequences and O'Toole's formidable presence make this a highly entertaining adventure film. Also starring Philippe Noiret. ★★★ $14.99

Music Box

(1989, 128 min, US, Costa-Gavras) Director Costa-Gavras delivers another taut political thriller based on co-producer Joe Esterhas' finely drawn script. Lawyer Jessica Lange takes on her Hungarian-émigré father's case when he is accused of Nazi collaboration and heinous atrocities during WWII. Her firm belief that her father is innocent, however, gradually erodes as the evidence against him accumulates. A suspenseful, thoughtful exploration of the conflict between familial devotion and the strength of ethical belief. Fine ensemble acting is highlighted by the performances of Oscar-nominee Lange, Armin Mueller-Stahl as her father, and Frederic Forrest as the prosecuting attorney. ★★★ $14.99

The Music Lovers

(1971, 122 min, GB, Ken Russell) This extravagant account of the life of Tchiakovsky is classic Russell — wonderfully overacted and filled with wildly overstated imagery. Richard Chamberlain stars as the tortured, repressed homosexual composer; Christopher Gable is his clinging blond boyfriend; and Glenda Jackson, in a ferocious performance, plays his mad, nymphomaniac wife. Set in turn-of-the-

century Russia, the film is impressively costumed and feverishly presented — with the hilarious, phallic and symbolism-laden "1812 Overture" dream sequence a particular highlight. ★★★ $19.99

The Music Man

(1962, 151 min, US, Morton Da Costa) This outstanding adaptation of Meredith Willson's Broadway smash is one of the great American musicals. Robert Preston reprised his triumphant stage role to give the performance of his career as turn-of-the-century con man Prof. Harold Hill, who comes to River City, Iowa, to form a boys' band. Classic score includes "Trouble," "76 Trombones" and "Till There Was You." Shirley Jones is in good voice as Marion the Librarian, and Buddy Hackett, Paul Ford, Hermione Gingold and a very young Ron Howard offer good support. ★★★★ $19.99

The Music of Chance

(1993, 98 min, US, Philip Haas) With the intricacies of a good symphony and the eerie mystery of the best campfire stories, *The Music of Chance*, based on the Paul Auster novel, is a complex and superbly acted tale of happenstance. James Spader, taking a break from his usual well-groomed yuppie roles, plays a polyester-clad cardshark who is plucked from the mouth of despair by a drifter of another sort, Mandy Patinkin. The two embark on a road trip to a card game where Spader has set up two rich marks, Joel Grey and Charles Durning. When Spader and Patinkin arrive at the remote mansion of the eccentric billionaires, their lives are set on a dangerous and ludicrous path. Spader occasionally goes a little over-the-top in his weasel-like performance, but Patinkin, as a man of morals set adrift in a world of skewed honor, has a depth of character that anchors the ephemeral story. ★★★½ $19.99

The Music Teacher

(1989, 100 min, Belgium, Gerard Corbiau) This opulent yet winsome drama is set in turn-of-the-century France where a world renowned opera singer suddenly announces his departure from the stage and retires to his estate in the countryside. It is there that he establishes a private school and selects two aspiring singers to be his pupils. The aspiring singers, a shy young woman and a poor but proud thief, are tutored by the older man, all in an effort to be ready for a singing competition hosted by the maestro's long-time enemy. Infused with humor, pathos and an innocently blossoming love story, this charming story features musical excerpts from Mahler, Verdi, Mozart, Schubert and Puccini. (French with English subtitles) ★★★ $19.99

Musica Proibita (Forbidden Music)

(1943, 93 min, Italy, Carlo Camogalliani) This interesting find was a typical example of the filmmaking style in Italy before the arrival of Neorealism in the late 1940s. The melodrama is set in the world of Italian opera and tells the haunting story of the love affair between a young conductor and the woman he loves. But their relationship is forbidden by the girl's grandmother when she learns of the identity of the man's father. An explosive tale of

romance, murder, revenge and passion. (Italian with English subtitles) ★★½

Mussolini and I

(1985, 130 min, Italy/US, Alberto Negrin) Susan Sarandon, Anthony Hopkins and Bob Hoskins head an international cast in this made-for-cable treatment of the conflicts between Mussolini (Hoskins) and his son-in-law Count Galeazzo Ciano, Minister of Foreign Affairs (Hopkins). Sarandon plays Benito's daughter in this sumptuously photographed and enjoyably overblown escapist entertainment. Cut down from its TV running time of 192 minutes, the film was originally titled *Mussolini: The Decline and Fall*. ★★½ $19.99

Mute Witness

(1995, 92 min, US, Anthony Waller) A mute American F/X artist working on a low-budget slasher film in Russia witnesses her coworkers seemingly making an after-hours snuff film and is accidentally locked in the studio with them. She is then stalked through the hallways in a brilliantly conceived, tension-laden extended chase sequence which is unrelenting in its suspense and unrivaled in its execution. First-time director Waller, in an obvious though unacknowledged homage, infuses the film with the nail-biting suspense and horrific violence of De Palma and Argento to create a highly stylized and visceral thriller. The film's second half, however, becomes needlessly convoluted as an attempt to add humor puts it starkly at odds with the constant terror which comes before it. Slightly off target, *Mute Witness* is witty and inventive nevertheless. ★★★ $19.99

Mutiny on the Bounty

(1935, 132 min, US, Frank Lloyd) The first, and best, of the three *Bounty* pictures about the tyrannical Captain Bligh, his 18th-century voyage to Tahiti, and the events leading up the the notorious mutiny, led by First Officer Mister Christian. Charles Laughton gives a tour de force performance as the severe Bligh, and Clark Gable is well-cast as Christian. Oscar for Best Picture. Remade in 1962 (with Marlon Brando and Trevor Howard) and 1984 (with Mel Gibson and Anthony Hopkins). ★★★★ $14.99

Mutiny on the Bounty

(1962, 179 min, US, Lewis Milestone) This grandiose, self-important, often ludicrous movie manages to be thoroughly entertaining almost in spite of itself. Lush tropical locations help as does Marlon Brando's campy, bemused performance. Trevor Howard plays the sadistic Captain Bligh with tremendous relish. The two stars reportedly disliked each other, leading to on-set confrontations that rivaled those aboard the Bounty. ★★½ $29.99

My American Cousin

(1985, 95 min, Canada, Sandy Wilson) The time and setting for this enjoyable story is 1959 in the quiet outback of western Canada, where rock `n' roll, hot rods and James Dean-influenced teens are still American phenomena. It's home, however, for Sandy, a precocious 12-year-old whose life takes a heated turn when Butch, her hip, handsome teenage cousin from

America, visits. A humorous coming-of-age drama that explores first love as well as the dreams and frustrations of two very different people. ★★★ $9.99

My Beautiful Laundrette

(1986, 94 min, GB, Stephen Frears) An unpredictable and charming social comedy which follows the unlikely success story of a young English-born Pakistani (and budding capitalist) and his punk lover (Daniel Day-Lewis). Together they brave the ugly spectre of racism and transform a dingy East Side laundrette into a glitzy and profitable laundry emporium. ★★★★

My Best Friend's Girl

(1984, 110 min, France, Bertrand Blier) Isabelle Huppert gives an erotically charged performance in Blier's whimsical look at male-bonding set around the ski resorts of Switzerland. Coluche co-stars with sexy ski-shop proprietor Thierry L'hermitte (*My New Partner*) as the fast friends who share an enthusiasm for femme fatale Huppert. (French with English subtitles) ★★½

My Blue Heaven

(1990, 95 min, US, Herbert Ross) Ross' funny though uneven look at the witness protection program run amok may be considered the demented "what-if" sequel to *GoodFellas*. Steve Martin is an ex-gangster with a new identity relocated to suburbia and Rick Moranis is a G-Man who has to keep an eye on him. Good idea. Good cast. Even scriptwriter in Nora Ephron, who wrote *When Harry Met Sally*. So what happened? We think director Ross should leave the dopey high-concept comedies to Ivan Reitman and John Hughes. ★★ $9.99

My Bodyguard

(1980, 96 min, US, Tony Bill) A youngster (Chris Makepeace) hires the biggest kid in his class (Adam Baldwin) as his bodyguard to protect him from a gang of bullies. Martin Mull plays the little guy's dad, Ruth Gordon his grandmom, and Matt Dillon is one of the toughs. ★★½ $14.99

My Brilliant Career

(1979, 101 min, Australia, Gillian Armstrong) A radiant Judy Davis stars in this period drama about a young woman in Australian outback at the turn of the century who is torn between marrying a local landowner (Sam Neil) and pursuing her career as a writer. Lovingly photographed and directed by director Armstrong, the film is a marvelously understated look at a Victorian woman's struggle with the constraints of her social position. ★★★½

My Cousin Vinny

(1992, 119 min, US, Jonathan Lynn) Joe Pesci plays a fish-out-of-water in this good-natured comedy about a smallfry Brooklyn lawyer who travels to a backwoods Southern town to save his cousin (perpetual teenager Ralph Macchio) from a murder rap. Marisa Tomei's Oscar-winning, over-the-top performance as Pesci's gum-popping girlfriend easily outshines the rest of the goings-on in this small movie that acquits itself nicely. Fred Gwynne has some fun as the incredulous judge. ★★★ $14.99

My Darling Clementine

(1946, 97 min, US, John Ford) The often-told tale of Wyatt Earp, the Clanton Gang and the infamous fight at the O.K. Corral. This western is blessed with the sure hand of director Ford, who imbues his story with such a visual splendor and poetic grace it ranks among his finest works. Henry Fonda is the famed marshall who, with Doc Holliday (Victor Mature), cleans up the town of Tombstone. Also starring Linda Darnell and Walter Brennan. ★★★★ $14.99

My Dinner with Andre

(1981, 110 min, US, Louis Malle) Malle serves up a delectable duet by the quest-crazed Andre Gregory (former artistic director of TLA) and the pragmatic Wallace Shawn. A supremely intelligent film which asks the question, "Is there any more reality on the top of Mount Everest than there is in the cigar shop next door?" ★★★½

My Fair Lady

(1964, 170 min, US, George Cukor) Although much will be lost in watching this enchanting musical extravaganza on the little screen, *My Fair Lady* still dazzles the viewer with spectacular sets and costumes, an inspired Lerner & Loewe score and wonderful performances by Rex Harrison and Audrey Hepburn. Winner of eight Academy Awards, this musical version of George Bernard Shaw's "Pygmalion" tells the now familiar tale of Professor Henry Higgins, an arrogant linguist, who takes Cockney flower waif Eliza Doolittle under his wing on a bet that he can transform her into a lady. ★★★★ $19.99

My Family (Mi Familia)

(1995, 125 min, US, Gregory Nava) A sometimes engrossing but ultimately shallow and unfocused three-generational family saga, this failed attempt at a Mexican-American *Godfather* was unsurprisingly produced by Francis Coppola and pays homage to his epic. Following a Mexican-American immigrant's life from his arrival in Los Angeles until the time his last grandchild leaves his household, the film tries to show the strength of its characters through heartbreaking tragedy, inflicting upon them one horrible event after another. While still entertaining and populated with quirky and interesting characters — Edward James Olmos and Jimmy Smits are fine as two brothers with different destinies — the weepy and maudlin story is at its best when it balances the heavy drama with a lighter tone supplied by Olmos as its narrator/writer. An adequate film whose ambitions exceed its capabilities, *My Family* vividly captures several decades in a period East Los Angeles, the dust of which contrasts sharply with the art deco shine of a white West L.A. ★★½ $19.99

My Father Is Coming

(1991, 82 min, US, Monika Treut) In this comical story of sexual confusion and self-discovery, Treut (*The Virgin Machine, Seduction: The Cruel Woman*) proves to be one of the more exciting of the New York-based independent filmmakers. Vicky, an aspiring actress and struggling waitress, finds her life in turmoil when she becomes involved with both a mysterious man and a female coworker at the time her German father comes over for a visit. Having given the impression that she is a successful actress and happily married, Vicky vainly tries to impress her sour and demanding father, even resorting to getting a Latino-loving gay friend to be her "husband." But papa doesn't get a chance to complain, for he is immediately swept up in a whirlwind of romance, TV commercial appearances and kinky sex in an odyssey that eventually leads to the bed of a lovely sex guru, Annie Sprinkle. The many characters in this charming comedy cover the spectrum of sexuality — from gay and straight to female-to-male transsexuals, with the results being an exuberant slice of life, New York style. (In English and German with English subtitles) ★★★ $29.99

My Father's Glory

(1991, 110 min, France, Yves Robert) The cherished childhood memories of author Marcel Pagnol are tenderly told in this enchanting and romantic tale set in turn-of-the-century Marseilles and Provence. The story follows Marcel, an 11-year-old boy who, along with his loving mother, schoolteacher father and other relatives, spends an idyllic summer in the rugged but beautiful terrain of southern France. It is there, amidst the tranquil hills, that the boy begins to learn about nature, friendship and life. A deceptively simple film, with great insights into familial relationships set in an era long ago lost to progress. The story continues in *My Mother's Castle*. (French with English subtitles) ★★★½ $19.99

My Favorite Blonde

(1942, 78 min, US, Sidney Lanfield) In his old radio show, Bob Hope made so many compliments about Madeleine Carroll it was almost a running gag. How appropriate, then, he co-

Wallace Shawn and Andre Gregory in *My Dinner with Andre*

stars with her in this very funny spy comedy which pays homage to Carroll's classic thriller *The 39 Steps*. Hope stars as a second-rate entertainer (his partner, a penguin, has far more talent) who becomes involved with British agent Carroll, who must transport secret bombing information cross-country. And, of course, the enemy is in hot pursuit. Hope and Carroll make such wonderful foils for each other one could be tempted to second-guess Paramount's casting of Dorothy Lamour in the *Road* movies. Clever one-liners, non-stop adventure and a breezy pace all contribute to make this arguably Hope's best comedy outside of the *Road* series. ★★★½ $14.99

My Favorite Brunette

(1947, 87 min, US, Elliott Nugent) A funny Bob Hope romp with Bob as a baby photographer who really wants to be a private eye; and through mistaken identity, gets his chance. Costars (surprise!) Dorothy Lamour. Peter Lorre and Lon Chaney, Jr also star. In-joke cameos include Alan Ladd and Der Bingle. ★★★ $14.99

My Favorite Wife

(1940, 88 min, US, Garson Kanin) Cary Grant and Irene Dunne star in this fabulously funny comedy, their second of three films together. Dunne returns home after seven years lost at sea to discover husband Grant has just remarried. Randolph Scott is the handsome hunk who was marooned with Dunne, much to Grant's chagrin. A joy from beginning to end. Remade in 1963 as *Move Over Darling*. ★★★½ $14.99

My Favorite Year

(1982, 92 min, US, Richard Benjamin) A delightful comedic reflection on the early years of television. Peter O'Toole runs wild as a swashbuckling celluloid hero (patterned after Errol Flynn) brought to his knees by the prospect of a live TV appearance. Sparkling support by Joseph Bologna as an ersatz Sid Caesar and Mark Linn-Baker as O'Toole's impressionable escort. O'Toole has probably never been funnier, and the screenplay offers hilarious observations on stardom and the grind of behind-the-scenes TV. ★★★★ $14.99

My Fellow Americans

(1996, 101 min, US, Peter Segal) Call it what you may: *Grumpy Old Presidents*, *The American Grumps* or *In the Line of Fire of Grumpy Old Men*; but *My Fellow Americans*, a predictable, puerile comedy about two feuding, ex-presidents on the run, manages to produce a few laughs in spite of itself. Jack Lemmon and James Garner, two of the most agreeable comic actors of their generation, rely mainly on their invaluable comedic instincts to almost pull this off. They play former commander-in-chiefs (and opponents) who, having individually discovered a cover-up by the current president (Dan Aykroyd), flee together when they are almost assassinated by the Secret Service. Most of the film consists of them bickering as they try to elude the hit men, and each handles the one-liners and put-downs with charm and ease. If only the screenplay were worthy of their talents. Though the story line does sneak

My Favorite Year

in a few partisan viewpoints of gay rights and immigration, this is basically for those who found enjoyment in the *Grumpy Old Men* series. ★★½ $19.99

My First Wife

(1984, 89 min, Australia, Paul Cox) John Hargreaves and Wendy Hughes give powerful, anguished performances in Cox's award-winning drama about the disintegration of a ten-year marriage. Told from "the man's point of view," this portrait of the disemboweling of their union is gutsy and emotionally involving. ★★★

My Forbidden Past

(1951, 72 min, US, Robert Stevenson) Ava Gardner seeks to marry a promising young doctor, but family members disrupt her nuptial plans. When Ava later attempts to rekindle the affair, she finds her lover has since married. Robert Mitchum and Melvyn Douglas are the men in her life. An uninvolving soaper which barely rises above its melodramatic story line. ★★ $19.99

My Girl

(1991, 102 min, US, Howard Zieff) Alternating between comedy and drama, *My Girl* is an ever-so-cute, very sentimental "kids" movie" (from its marketing advertising) which may prove to be too intense in certain scenes for particularly young viewers. Of course, the scene in question is the much-talked about death of the Macaulay Culkin character; which, though handled awkwardly in dramatic terms, is sensitively portrayed. Little Anna Chlumsky stars as an 11-year-old girl living with her father Dan Aykroyd, a funeral director. The story follows her summer vacation, where she befriends Culkin, reluctantly witnesses her father fall in love with Jamie Lee Curtis, and other assorted summer-related activities. There are a few laughs to be had (the grandmother seems to get the best scenes), though this is more dramatic than the ads suggest. ★★½ $14.99

My Girl 2

(1994, 99 min, US, Howard Zieff) What might have been an affecting tale of a young girl's quest to discover the history of her deceased mother is instead overwhelmed by heavy-handed sentimentality and a mawkish sensibility which makes the frequently saccharine original seem like something from Abel Ferrara by comparison. Dan Aykroyd and Jamie Lee Curtis sleepwalk through their reprised roles as "My Girl" Vada's (Anna Chlumsky) parents. For her part, Chlumsky shows evidence — as she did in the first film — that she could deliver an arresting performance if she had something to work with. The film's only redeeming quality is that it avoids attacking those who don't fit into the Quayle Family Values it so heartily celebrates. ★½ $14.99

My Heroes Have Always Been Cowboys

(1991, 106 min, US, Stuart Rosenberg) Scott Glenn plays an aging rodeo circuit bullrider who returns to his small Texas home town for the first time in 20 years after an accident leaves him injured. There, he picks up the pieces he left behind, taking care of his invalid father, rebuilding the family's deserted ranch and renewing a romance with an old flame. Glenn is particularly good in this involving though choppy tale of familial conflict and loyalty. With Kate Capshaw, Ben Johnson, Tess Harper and Gary Busey. ★★½ $9.99

My Left Foot

(1989, 103 min, Ireland, Jim Sheridan) It came as no surprise when Daniel Day-Lewis walked away with an Oscar for Best Actor for his portrayal of the severely handicapped Irish painter/author Christy Brown. Born with cerebral palsy, Brown never gained the use of his limbs except for his left foot, with which he brushed canvases so stunning they earned him recognition as an acclaimed artist. With acute sensitivity, Day-Lewis depicts Brown as an intense, brooding, complicated and restless soul with a zest for life far beyond that of most

River Phoenix (l.) and Keanu Reeves in *My Own Private Idaho*

people. Fine support comes from Brenda Fricker, who also won a much-deserved Oscar for her gutsy performance as Christy's resilient mother. A stunning portrait both passionate and intelligent. ★★★★ $14.99

My Life

(1993, 112 min, US, Bruce Joel Rubin) With the screenplays for both *Ghost* and *Jacob's Ladder* to his credit, Rubin, making his directorial debut, is in familiar waters with this emotional and surprisingly persuasive drama about life and death. Michael Keaton stars as a successful L.A. executive dying of cancer. About to become a first-time parent, he decides to leave a video autobiography for his child, whom he will probably not live to meet. As he and his wife (Nicole Kidman) anticipate the birth of their new baby, each must come to terms with Keaton's impending demise. Although a little too steeped in ancient mysticism for its own good, Rubin's text is moving and probably has more to say about the dying process than the high-profile *Philadelphia*. Keaton's performance is uncommonly good. ★★★ $14.99

My Life and Times with Antonin Artaud

(1993, 98 min, France, Gérard Mordillat) Based on the diaries of Parisian poet Jacques Prevel, this fictionalized account follows a young Prevel (Marc Barbé) as he develops a tentative relationship with Antonin Artaud (Sami Frey). Undoubtedly one of the more twisted and perverse geniuses among the pantheon of theatre innovators, Artaud and his treatises on "Theatre of Cruelty" and "Theatre and the Plague" have influenced modern performing arts more than, perhaps, most would like to think. Prevel himself is a piece of work, a down-and-out philanderer who spends most of his time in a flophouse with his emotionally strung-out girlfriend and occasionally spending time with his inexplicably devoted wife. When he hears of Artaud's release from an insane asylum, he finagles an introduction in hopes of developing fame by association. Filmed in black and white, the film does a fine job of evoking a sumptuous post-war imagery and has a stylish, Euro-chic appeal. But it is a sadly inappropriate memorial to Artaud to present his final days so harmlessly — no suffering in the fires of his own internal hell here. Instead, the film understands Artaud as a dying legend through the eyes of a new, more upbeat generation — it's just too safe. (French with English subtitles) ★★½ $19.99

My Life as a Dog

(1985, 101 min, Sweden, Lasse Hallström) A captivating and heartwarming look at the trials and tribulations of a 12-year-old boy who, in the wake of his mother's death, is shipped off to live with his uncle in a rural Swedish village in the 1950s. Touching drama is sprinkled with poignant comedy as the boy battles his feelings of self-abasement and despair. A truly winning insight into the joys and sorrows of childhood which features outstanding performances from its two child stars. (Available dubbed and in Swedish with English subtitles) ★★★★ $19.99

My Life's in Turnaround

(1994, 84 min, US, Eric Schaeffer & Donald Lardner Ward) This ultra no-budget impromptu, along with the more highly acclaimed *Clerks*, should serve as inspiration to all those budding filmmakers out there who are struggling for both money and ideas. The beauty of *My Life...* is that its two actor/writer/producer/directors, Schaeffer and Ward, really had no idea what to make a film about, so they made a film about exactly that — two burnt-out denizens of lower Manhattan's grunge art scene searching to make a film deal. It's a contrivance that on face value is not the least bit clever, but in this duo's hands it somehow becomes ingenious. Think of it, these guys make an asset out of their dearth of creative inspiration! What makes it all work is their infectious personalities and the hilarious and incessant banter between them — what develops is actually a thoughtful look at their friendship. Along the way they try to woo John Sayles, Casey

Siemaszko, Martha Plimpton and Phoebe Cates into their project. ★★★ $89.99

My Little Chickadee

(1940, 83 min, US, Eddie Cline) W.C. Fields was an alcoholic; Mae West practiced abstinence. The two did not get along. Fields wrote his scenes; she hers. Count the number of times they're in the same shot together. Perhaps it was this animosity that goaded them to do some of their best work in this tale of a woman of easy virtue entering into a marriage of convenience with a con man. It is in this film that Fields says that the only thing worse than being in Philadelphia is being hanged. ★★★ $14.99

My Little Girl

(1986, 118 min, US, Connie Kaiserman) Mary Stuart Masterson once again proves that she's one of the best young actresses around today with her touching performance in this absorbing drama of an overprivileged miss who tries to make a difference by working with disadvantaged young girls. Geraldine Page costars as her supportive grandmother. With James Earl Jones, Anne Meara and Peter Gallagher. Portions filmed in the Main Line area of Philadelphia. ★★★

My Man Godfrey

(1936, 96 min, US, Gregory La Cava) Classic screwball comedy with Carole Lombard giving a priceless performance as a daffy heiress who meets a hobo on a scavenger hunt, and hires him as the family butler, unaware that he is actually a successful businessman. William Powell is dapper as ever as the title character, and there's great comic support from Eugene Pallette, Alice Brady and the hilarious Mischa Auer, who earned an Oscar nomination for, among other things, imitating a monkey. ★★★★

My Michael

(1975, 95 min, Israel, Dan Wolman) Two intelligent young adults find each other and marry in a divided Jerusalem in the late 1950s. Michael, a responsible and hard-working scientist, is comfortable in the arrangement, in contrast to Hanna, who finds herself unfulfilled by the petit-bourgeois life she is leading. Loneliness and fantasy take over in this gentle, yet controversial rendering of the Amos Oz novel. (Hebrew with English subtitles) ★★★ $79.99

My Mother's Castle

(1991, 98 min, France, Yves Robert) The childhood remembrances of young Marcel continue in this captivating story which begins where *My Father's Glory* ends. Marcel's family returns to the city after their magical summer in Provence, only to decide later to make their country cottage a weekend and holiday retreat. It is there, in the barren, parched hills, that Marcel discovers the joy and pain of first love as well as a deep affection for and understanding of his loving parents. Possibly a bit too saccharine for hardened existential French videophiles, this unpretentious, heartwarming drama should prove to be a treasured delight for others. (French with English subtitles) ★★★ $19.99

My Name Is Bill W.

(1989, 118 min, US, Daniel Petrie) James Woods gives one of his trademark on-target performances as Bill Wilson, cofounder of Alcoholics Anonymous. An intensely driven businessman and alcoholic, Wilson is literally kept alive by his wife (JoBeth Williams) until he finds treatment which handles his condition as a disease, not a lack of will. By chance he meets Dr. Robert Smith (James Garner), fellow drunk; together they formulate what will develop into the 12-step program. This TV production has a fine eye for period detail and enjoys good performances from the entire cast. But it is, as usual, Woods who captures your attention, delivering a multifaceted and engrossing portrayal. ★★★ $19.99

My Name Is Ivan

(1962, 84 min, USSR, Andrei Tarkovsky) The first film by this visionary Russian director is a poetic, sad story of a young boy caught up in World War II. Following the death of his mother during the early days of the war, 12-year-old Ivan's childhood is quickly ended when he joins the ranks of youths working as intelligence scouts for the army. The film is made in a style which moves from terrifying realism to lyrical impressionism. A haunting film experience. (Russian with English subtitles) ★★★½ $19.99

My Neighbor Totoro

(1994, 87 min, Japan) This superbly animated tale is both an enchanting story and a terrific look at Japanese life in the country. Two young girls move out of the city with their father while their mother recuperates from a long illness in a distant hospital. In their new home they meet two large, furry and lovable totoros, creatures visible only to the children. When the youngest girl mistakenly starts to fear that her mother is going to die, she runs away to find the hospital and is rescued by the totoros. The film won an award of excellence from the Film Advisory Board. (Dubbed) ★★★½ $14.99

My New Gun

(1992, 99 min, US, Stacy Cochran) Diane Lane stars in this quirky comedy as a yuppie, suburban housewife who doesn't know how to react when her husband (Stephen Collins) gives her a .38 revolver for protection — so she gives it to her wacky new neighbor (James LeGros). LeGros, with *Drugstore Cowboy* and *Gun Crazy* behind him, inches ever closer to being awarded a patent for his emotionless, zoned-out drifter character, who in this case purports to need a gun to protect his mother. Brimming with suspicion, and a possible infatuation, Lane starts to snoop around his house in search of clues about his real motives. Is he a drug dealer? A Mafia hit man? What she finds only confuses her more. First-time director Cochran keeps the action moving at a snappy pace and gives the film just the right amount of skewed humor to make it most refreshing viewing. ★★★ $94.99

My New Partner

(1985, 104 min, France, Claude Zidi) A delightful French farce about the antics of a charmingly amoral cop. Philippe Noiret stars as the veteran "flic" who must teach the ways of the world to his new partner, a scrupulously innocent rookie. Noiret and Thierry L'hermitte offer engaging performances. (French with English subtitles) ★★★

My Night at Maud's

(1970, 105 min, France, Eric Rohmer) Scintillating conversation on life, love and morality forms the bedroom talk in Rohmer's witty and fascinating comedy of manners. Jean-Louis Trintignant plays the staunch Catholic who finds his principles tested when he is invited by the charming but free-spirited Maud (Françoise Fabian) to spend the night in her nonexistent spare room. The focus is not how they get together, but rather, how they manage not to. The third of Rohmer's Six Moral Tales and one of the director's most

captivating works. (French with English subtitles) ★★★½ $19.99

My Other Husband

(1985, 110 min, France, Georges Lautner) This story, about a frantic woman who has a husband and child in Paris and a lover and two children in the country, has the potential of being just another *comédie soufflé*. But happily, coupled with a funny script, some great supporting characters and the exhilarating presence of Miou-Miou in the starring role, the film rises above the situation comedy and becomes not only a successfully zany farce but also a sensitive feminist look at one woman's life. (French with English subtitles) ★★★ $59.99

My Own Private Idaho

(1991, 105 min, US, Gus Van Sant) "I always know where I am by the way the road looks..." —River Phoenix as Mike Waters. With his third film, Van Sant has proven himself one of the most daring, innovative and accomplished directors of the day. Phoenix's portrayal of Mike, a solitary, narcoleptic street hustler searching for his long-lost mother is brilliant. Van Sant deftly weaves in a subplot based on Shakespeare's "Henry IV, Pt II," even borrowing a smattering of the Bard's dialogue. Keanu Reeves gives strong support as Mike's Prince Hal-like friend and William Richert is superb as the Falstaff-derived Bob Pigeon. Dreamily photographed, with mood ranging from hilarious to tragic to highly erotic, *Idaho* is a modern classic. ★★★★ $19.99

My Science Project

(1985, 95 min, US, Jonathan Betuel) A high school senior working on a class project creates a device which can alter time and space. It's not really as fun as it sounds. With John Stockwell, Fisher Stevens and Dennis Hopper. ★½

My Sister Eileen

(1955, 108 min, US, Richard Quine) In 1942, Rosalind Russell starred in *My Sister Eileen*, a film comedy based on Ruth McKinney's stage hit. Eleven years later, Russell reprised her role in the Broadway musical adaptation, retitled "Wonderful Town," written by Comden and Green and scored by Leonard Bernstein. However, a new musical score was written when the story returned to the screen in this musical form in 1955. Though the music is not on par with "Wonderful Town," it's nevertheless snappy and engaging. Betty Garrett and Janet Leigh play sisters from Ohio who move to Greenwich Village, hoping to find fame and fortune. They find Jack Lemmon and Bob Fosse. Fosse choreographed the film, and his fledgling trademark movements are in evidence. The best musical sequence is a terrific Kelly/O'Connor-type number featuring Fosse and that fabulous dancer Tommy Rall. ★★★ $19.99

My Summer Story

(1994, 85 min, US, Bob Clark) Jean Shepherd's childhood reminiscences are continued the summer following the delightful *A Christmas Story*. Unfortunately, the results aren't nearly as lively or inspired. This time around, family members (here portrayed by Charles Grodin, Mary Steenburgen, and two more Culkins: Kieran and Christian) each have a personal

My Night at Maud's

M

quest. The eldest son wants to find the perfect killer top. Mom wants to collect a complete set of movie theatre giveaway china. And Dad sets out to vanquish an obscenely extended family of miscreant neighbors. As with the first *Story*, Clark directs and Shepherd provides the narration. But this effort lacks the consumate charm and whimsy of *Christmas*; the characters are too broadly drawn, and lack the warmth and accessibility which make the first film a perennial favorite. Still, there are some enjoyable moments and the film qualifies as safe family fare. ★★ $14.99

My 20th Century

(1989, 104 min, Hungary, Ildiko Enyedi) Crisscrossing confusion and strange coincidence propel this lighthearted fairy tale about twin sisters, separated at birth, who are reunited years later. Set against the tumultuous chaos of turn-of-the-century Hungary, as well as many other exotic locales throughout Europe, the story has the twins meeting once again on the Orient Express — one, a wealthy courtesan; the other, an anarchist carrying explosives. While unknown to one another, each woman is having an affair with the same man. (Hungarian with English subtitles) ★★★ $19.99

Myra Breckinridge

(1970, 94 min, US, Michael Sarne) An outrageous X-rated version of Gore Vidal's "scandalously" satiric transsexual novel that has taken on mythic proportions for being such a bomb. Red Reed and Raquel Welch are the male and female embodiment of the same person — before and after the operation. John Huston, Mae West, Farrah Fawcett and Tom Selleck are just some of the casting oddities. Combine them with a talentless director, and a screenplay imbued with a slap-dash Sixties mentality, and the result had critics running to their thesauruses looking for stronger words than "atrocious." Yes, it's bad. But in a campy, smirky, hipper-than-fag sort of way. Why, either the lesbian scene between Welch and Fawcett or the tasteless sequence in which Welch rapes a strapping stud of a cowboy (Roger Herren) is worth the price of rental. It really has to be seen to be believed. (★★★★ Camp Value) ★

Mysteries

(1978, 93 min, The Netherlands) Rutger Hauer stars in this rather stiff but absorbing film version of Nobel Prize-winning Knut Hamsun's novel. On the Isle of Man late in the 19th century, a mysterious, lonely, and possibly insane young stranger (Hauer) arrives in a small coastal community and begins to upset the townspeople's well-ordered lives. Sylvia Kristel and Rita Tushingham play the unattainable women he falls in love with. A bit muddled in execution and Rutger's dubbing is poor, but the film successfully creates an eerie, somber world where love and understanding prove to be tantalizingly elusive. (Dubbed) ★★

Mysterious Island

(1961, 101 min, GB, Cy Endfield) Ray Harryhausen created some of his best work in this adaptation of the Jules Verne novel about Confederate prisoners whose escape attempt leaves them stranded on an island infested with giant animals. Bernard Herrmann's score is outstanding. Lots of fun. ★★★ $14.99

Mystery Date

(1991, 98 min, US, Jonathan Wacks) Ethan Hawke stars in this high-energy action/comedy which resembles Martin Scorsese's *After Hours*. When a young man on his dream date finds himself mistaken for his older brother, sparks fly and his world is turned upside down. The film is filled with implausibilities so common to the teen comedy, but the laughs make it well worth a look. ★★½ $14.99

The Mystery of Alexina

(1985, 84 min, France, René Feret) This literate, beautifully photographed film, based on a mid-19th-century memoir, tells the tale of a convent-bred teacher at a girls' elementary school. She falls in love with another girl, but soon discovers that she herself is a man. This fascinating love story poses intriguing questions of identity and character in a romantic, stylish setting. Screenplay by Jean Gruault (*Jules and Jim*, *The Wild Child*). (French with English subtitles) ★★★

The Mystery of Picasso

(1956, 77 min, France, Henri-Georges Clouzot) Declared a national treasure by the French government, this fascinating documentary features Pablo Picasso at work, creating over 15 works before the camera's eyes. The paintings were destroyed after the filming so this is the only opportunity to view them. An absorbing look at one of the greatest artists of the 20th century as well as a study of an artist's vision and its physical results. Picasso's mind and artistic motivations are wonderfully and forever on view. (French with English subtitles) ★★★★

The Mystery of Rampo

(1995, 100 min, Japan, Kazuyoshi Okuyama) A challenging contemporary Japanese film which explores the connections between fiction and reality, *The Mystery of Rampo* tells the story of a well-known but misunderstood writer, Rampo. In a beautiful animated segment, we see one of his stories come to life: An invalid father accidentally locks himself in a lacquer cabinet while playing hide-and-seek with his children, and when his wife discovers him, she allows him to suffocate. Although the story is never published, Rampo learns that a real-life situation has mirrored his story. Rampo becomes obsessed with the wife, eventually incorporating her (as his previous character) into another story. Real life and fantasy merge as Rampo assumes the identity of his

most popular character, a seemingly invincible police inspector, who investigates the widow and soon falls in love with her. Fascinating, thought-provoking, and even an absorbing mystery, *Rampo* is a feast for the senses. It also warns us that as our fantasies gain greater importance in our lives, we may sacrifice our grip on reality and our ability to determine our futures. (Japanese with English subtitles) ★★★½ $19.99

Mystery Science Theatre 3000

(1996, 73 min, US, Jim Mallon) An "average Joe" (Michael J. Nelson) and his two robot pals, Crow and Tom Servo, are forced by a mad scientist to watch the worst films ever made (in this case, the 1954 sci-fi flick *This Island Earth* — which really isn't *that* bad). Of course, instead of writhing in pain, the trio has a high time comically ridiculing the film. This big-screen version of the cult TV series is basically your average episode, only *shortened* by 20 minutes. To make matters worse, there seems to be even more time spent on the breaks — short comic sketches that break up the movie-within-the-movie-watching — which were never that funny anyway, even when series creator Joel (the "good Darrin" of MST3K) was host of the show. (Interesting that these guys can rip others' work to shreds brilliantly, and yet can't create an even mildly amusing two-minute sketch on their own.) Still, there are some belly laughs to be had, along with a lot of chuckles and giggles (as well as a few groans); those who love the TV series should like the movie. ★★½ $14.99

Mystery Train

(1989, 113 min, US, Jim Jarmusch) Jarmusch continues to explore the theme of strangers in even stranger lands. This time out he uses Memphis, Tennessee, as the backdrop for three interwoven stories which collide in a run-down hotel in the sleazy part of town. The episodes follow a young and very hip Japanese couple who have come to pray at the temple of rock 'n' roll; three Memphis low-lifes on a drunken, brawling and murderous night of debauchery; and a young Italian woman, stranded by the death of her husband and waiting to accompany his coffin back to Italy. Jarmusch delights in the odd-ball quirkiness of his characters. ★★★ $19.99

Mystic Pizza

(1988, 102 min, US, Donald Petrie) This fresh and winning romantic comedy-drama follows the ups and downs of three young waitresses trying to come to terms with their impending adulthood. Along the way, they fall in love, play some pool, and even pass out at their own weddings — all the while serving the best damn pizza in the state of Connecticut. A young, talented cast includes Julia Roberts, Annabeth Gish, Lili Taylor, Vincent D'Onofrio, William R. Moses and Adam Storke, and the veteran and always delightful Conchata Ferrell also stars. ★★★ $14.99

Nadine

(1987, 83 min, US, Robert Benton) Sweet-natured comic thriller set in 1954 Texas starring Jeff Bridges and Kim Basinger as a separated husband and wife who unwittingly become involved with a local gangster when Basinger witnesses a murder and mistakenly takes possession of secret documents. Rip Torn is a most spirited villain. ★★★

Nadja

(1995, 92 min, US, Michael Almereyda) This bloodless, art-house vampire film aspires to be innovative in both its narrative and its cinematography, but is not completely successful in either respect. Nadja (the cadaverous Elina Lowensohn), a Romanian vampire transplanted to New York City lives a life of coffeehouse ennui and predatory hunting. She begins a lesbian relationship with a similarly disaffected twentysomething burnout married to a likable but dimwitted amateur boxer, who just happens to be the nephew of the vampire-hunter who slew Nadja's father! As if this weren't needlessly convoluted enough, Nadja has a twin brother, who is in the loving care of a nurse who is the boxer's sister! The film's tone veers wildly from angst-ridden to campy humor, particularly when the vampire hunter (embarrassingly played by Peter Fonda) is on-screen. It also attempts to create a sort of "vampire-vision" through the use of a Fisher Price PixelCam, which fragments the picture — it resembles looking through a rain-soaked windshield. Though the production design is very good, and the narrative occasionally maintains an even dramatic tone to create an interesting though unoriginal variation on the vampire myth, Nadja ultimately is too pretentious for its own good. ★★ $14.99

Naked

(1993, 126 min, GB, Mike Leigh) Though Leigh's films could never be accused of being upbeat, nothing he has done before can prepare one for this brilliant, terrifying and undeniably real vision of the welfare state. Leigh takes us on a picaresque journey following Johnny (David Thewlis in a stunning performance), our 27-year-old protagonist (or is that antagonist?), an embittered, overly loquacious ne'er-do-well who spews forth a relentlessly nihilistic tirade against man, God and society. After sexually assaulting a woman in Manchester, he flees to London and insinuates himself on his former girlfriend, Louise, and immediately beds her roommate, Sophie. Quickly tiring of their company, he hits the streets for a midnight sojourn, on which he waxes eloquent with every stranger about his apocalyptic philosophies. Leigh does a brilliant job of framing Johnny's rage against a backdrop of urban decay, and completes the picture with a truly vicious characterization of the ruling elite in the form of Louise's sexually sadistic landlord, Jeremy. ★★★★ $19.99

The Naked and the Dead

(1958, 131 min, US, Raoul Walsh) A tough and gritty film version of Norman Mailer's novel about a group of WWII soldiers stationed in the Pacific; though its familiar, disparate characters have surfaced in just about every "platoon" film. With Aldo Ray, Cliff Robertson, Raymond Massey and Joey Bishop. ★★½

Naked City

(1948, 96 min, US, Jules Dassin) In a trend-setting, "just the facts, ma'am," semidocumentary style seen in countless films and TV shows since, this gripping crime thriller follows a police investigation's probe into the brutal murder of a beautiful young model. Barry Fitzgerald plays the folksy, pipe-smoking Lieutenant Muldoon who, along with his strikingly handsome assistant (Don Taylor), combs the classy veneer of Upper West Side society in an attempt to crack open the case. Noteworthy and quite fascinating is the film's entirely on location shooting in old New York, a rarity at a time when Hollywood stuck with studio sets. The finale, a chase through the Lower East Side, culminating atop the Williamsburg Bridge, is action filmmaking at its best. ★★★ $29.99

The Naked Civil Servant

(1980, 80 min, GB, Jack Gold) Based on the autobiography of Quentin Crisp, this is a witty examination of the process of growing up gay in the repressive England of the 1930s and '40s. John Hurt's portrayal of Crisp is nothing less than superb as he fights back against society's intolerance, ostracism and violence with pointed, razor-sharp humor. ★★★½ $19.99

The Naked Country

(1985, 90 min, Australia, Tim Burstall) Forget the box art picturing a scantily clad woman baking in the Australian sun, for rather than cheesy erotica this is nothing more than a run-of-the-mill action/melodrama set in the Australian Outback. The story centers around a white rancher who has come into conflict with the local tribe of Aborigines over grazing rights. Into the picture comes the local constabulary in the form of a drunken bush policeman who is more likely to side with the natives than the whites. And then there's the rancher's neglected wife who, for one night, can't control her desires for the copper. It all culminates in a showdown between rancher and natives which unsuccessfully aspires to the magical imagery of The Last Wave. ★★ $14.99

The Naked Edge

(1961, 97 min, GB, Michael Anderson) Gary Cooper's last film is a disappointing psychological thriller borrowing much from Alfred Hitchcock's Suspicion. Deborah Kerr costars as Cooper's wife, who slowly begins to suspect her husband is a murderer. It seems Cooper's testimony about his employer's murder sent a coworker to prison; and now it looks like the wrong man may have been incarcerated. Though the film contains a few stylish touches, its pace is, for the most part, sluggish and the twists are unexciting. ★★ $19.99

The Naked Gun

(1988, 85 min, US, David Zucker) From the makers of Airplane!, Airplane 2 and the cult TV show "Police Squad," comes this zany, irreverent and anarchistic comedy. Stonefaced Leslie Nielsen is Lieutenant Drebin — a hilarious mixture of the bungling innocence of Mr. Magoo

Naked Gun 33⅓

and Maxwell Smart with the ruthlessness and often sadistic crimefighting tactics of a Philly cop (no letters please!). Here we find Lt. Drebin investigating a plot to assassinate the Queen of England while she is on a visit to America. The story line, however, serves simply as a backdrop for the wild cavalcades of silly, sick and stupid jokes that we have come to expect from the Zucker/Abrahams/Zucker team. ★★★ $9.99

Naked Gun 2½: The Smell of Fear

(1991, 85 min, US, David Zucker) From the brother of the director of Ghost...no, make that from the partner of the director of Airplane!...no, that ain't right, either. From the director of...oh, hell, you know who he is! Leslie Nielsen returns as that lethal weapon Lt. Frank Drebin in this consistently funny sequel. Lt. Drebin is on the case in Washington, D.C. and he's up against greedy industrialists determined to sabotage our nation's antipollution measures. Though the film is not as hilarious as the original Naked Gun or Airplane! — both films seem to produce a never-ending stream of guffaws — 2½ is nevertheless a constant pleasure. And its White House opening scene is priceless. Who needs the Democrats for Bush-bashing when Drebin is around? ★★★ $14.99

Naked Gun 33⅓: The Final Insult

(1994, 83 min, US, Peter Segal) Leslie Nielsen and company are back for another side-splitting round of slapstick hijinks and stupid puns in this third Naked Gun film co-written by David Zucker and Pat Proft and helmed by first-time director Segal. Frank Drebin, now enjoying the bliss of retirement as his wife (Priscilla Presley) goes to work, is persuaded by old pals George Kennedy and O.J. Simpson to help them on a case. This leads him to prison where he befriends a terrorist and he eventually helps save that American institution: the Academy Awards. As would be expected, the laughs are fast and furious, and Nielsen's comic timing and mugging is priceless. With everything from sperm banks to Hollywood neatly spoofed, all involved prove this is one series which has yet to run out of breath. ★★★ $14.99

Naked in New York

(1994, 91 min, US, Dan Algrant) The story of a young writer's rites of passage, *Naked in New York* is appealing only in a dilapidated, disorganized sort of way. Eric Stoltz stars as a bohemian Jewish New York playwright who meets a WASPy photographer (Mary-Louise Parker) while in college and proceeds to set up housekeeping. Billed as a romantic comedy, *Naked* lacks the focus to be much of anything but a series of amusingly eclectic scenes tied together by Stoltz's artsy, philosophical angst. However, Kathleen Turner steals the movie with her exuberant portrait of a boozy, pot-smoking seductress/actress. Check out Woody Allen's *Bullets over Broadway* for the same movie with more substance and comic flair. ★★½ $19.99

The Naked Jungle

(1954, 95 min, US, Byron Haskin) This is the one with the ants! Plantation owner Charlton Heston tries to make a go of it in South America; he loses to the elements and Eleanor Parker. Though silly at times, it's a lot of fun and even manages to offer some high moments of jungle adventure. ★★½ $19.99

The Naked Kiss

(1965, 90 min, US, Samuel Fuller) From its electrifying opening sequence — in which an enraged bald-headed prostitute (Constance Towers) beats a man senseless with a telephone — through its exposé of corruption and vice in "Small Town, USA," this torrid melodrama never lets up. Towers is Kelly, a hip-swinging, eye-flirting floozy who "escapes" to a bucolic backwater town to begin life anew as a nurse to handicapped children. But an unforgiving and hypocritical society hounds her and just won't let a bad girl go good. Fuller fans won't be able to supress a smile throughout this deliciously enjoyable cult potboiler. ★★★½ $29.99

Naked Lunch

(1991, 115 min, US, David Cronenberg) William Burroughs' 1950s free-form classic, with its non-linear narration and shocking imagery, had long been thought "unfilmable." Director Cronenberg has done the impossible, for this hallucinatory horror/sci-fi/comedy/drama is a witty and imaginative interpretation. Peter Weller stars as Burroughs' monosyllabic alter ego, Bill Lee, a bug exterminator who, along with his sharp-tongued wife (the amazing Judy Davis), gets hooked on his own bug powder. Lee, swimming in a narcotics-induced paranoia, sees his Remington typewriter come alive in the form of a slimy, bug-shaped creature who informs him that he is really an underground agent on a mission to fight a worldwide "Interzone" conspiracy. This leads him to "travel" to Morocco, where he meets other agents Ian Holm, Julian Sands and, in an additional role, Davis. An audacious and demanding foray into the psyche of a drug-addicted artist that will prove for some to be disgusting and incomprehensible — a response that would have delighted Burroughs. ★★★★ $94.99

The Naked Prey

(1966, 94 min, US, Cornel Wilde) Rather exciting action film with Cornel Wilde as an African safari guide who becomes human prey to a group of tribal hunters. ★★★ $19.99

The Naked Spur

(1952, 93 min, US, Anthony Mann) Flavorful, exciting western with James Stewart as a bounty hunter obsessed with tracking down outlaw Robert Ryan and his companion Janet Leigh. ★★★ $19.99

The Naked Sun

(1985, 90 min, Brazil/Italy, Tonio Cervi) The colorful and sensual excitement of Rio's Carnival is the setting for this sexy love story about a young man who flees both Italy and his creditors, winding up in Rio where he becomes involved in a torrid love affair with a beautiful, mysterious woman. (Dubbed) ★★½

Naked Tango

(1991, 90 min, US, Leonard Schrader) Set in 1924, this surreal thriller — reminiscent of *Apartment Zero*, which is also set in Buenos Aires — stars the ravishing Mathilda May as a scheming woman who unwittingly becomes involved with two feuding brothers (Esai Morales and the sensually brutal Vincent D'Onofrio), both of whom are stylishly murderous criminals. Boasting lush camerawork, stunning production design and the erotic world of the Tango, this sexually charged though slow-moving thriller is a treat. Co-produced by Oscar-winning costume designer Milena Canonero, the film is dedicated to "Kiss of the Spider Woman" author Mañuel Puig, whose work the film has been obviously influenced by. ★★★ $99.99

Naked Youth

(1959, 80 min, US, John F. Schreyer) Three teens bust out of their juvenile detention center and head south of the border, where they encounter "dangerous drugs, thugs, gun molls, dope dolls and bad guys." Mamie Van Doren hosts. ★ $9.99

The Name of the Rose

(1986, 128 min, Italy/West Germany/France, Jean-Jacques Annaud) Sean Connery stars in this visually rich medieval murder mystery set in a remote monastary. A monk falls from a high tower: was it suicide or murder? As other brothers are found dead, visiting monk Connery investigates the series of bizarre deaths. Full of tongue-in-cheek allusions to Sherlock Holmes (Connery's sleuthing monk is named William of Baskerville), this film may be a disappointment to those who have read the novel; but the film perfectly captures the atmosphere of the era and maintains a sufficient amount of suspense. Also with F. Murray Abraham and Christian Slater as Connery's youthful apprentice. (Filmed in English) ★★★

Nana

(1980, 92 min, Italy, Don Walman) Emile Zola's classic erotic novel about a Parisian streetwalker who, by seducing the rich and powerful, becomes the toast of Parisian society, is successfully brought to the screen. The sensuous Katya Berger plays the lusty and ambitious woman with Jean-Pierre Aumont also starring as her most ardent and long-suffering lover. (Dubbed) ★★½

Nanami: First Love

(1968, 104 min, Japan, Susumu Hani) This unusual, erotic drama is a spellbinding tale of passionate desire and psychological turbulence. A troubled young man becomes obsessed with Nanami, a sensuous nude model and prostitute. The man suffers, however, from impotence and from a series of complex, puzzle-like flashbacks, which help explain his

Peter Weller plays William Burroughs' literary alter ego in *Naked Lunch*

Abel Gance's *Napoleon*

psychosexual problems. (Japanese with English subtitles) ★★★ $24.99

Nanook of the North

(1922, 69 min, US, Robert J. Flaherty) The first and possibly the finest of Flaherty's social documentaries, this simply constructed but trailblazing film was named as one of the 25 outstanding films worthy of historical preservation by the U.S. Congress in 1990. Set in the frozen vastness of Alaska, the story follows Eskimo Nanook's heartrending daily struggle for survival as he and his family battle nature for only the barest essentials of life. An absorbing classic that has been restored to its original condition and graced with a new musical score by The Tashis Ensemble. A sad note to this film is that Nanook died of hunger shortly after the film was released. ★★★★ $29.99

Napoleon

(1927, 235 min, France, Abel Gance) Gance's overwhelming historical saga charts the French leader's youth, rise to power and triumphant Italian campaign. Meticulously reconstructed over the years, this silent classic remains a monument of technical innovation and virtuosity. ★★★★ $29.99

Narda or the Summer

(1968, 90 min, Mexico, Juan Guerra) Notwithstanding its terrible title, this harmless sex comedy, set in a Mexico eerily devoid of any real Mexicans, tells the tale of two naive young men, with Southern California good looks, who decide to share a woman. So off they go in their sports car to sunny Acapulco where they meet up with the mysterious Narda, a blonde beauty who proves to be too much for the would-be swingers. A '60s oddity which, while amusing and even intriguing, is probably mostly of interest to anyone studying intermediate Spanish! (Spanish with English subtitles) ★★ $24.99

Narrow Margin

(1990, 97 min, US, Peter Hyams) This remake of the 1952 thriller of the same name bears all of the action and suspense associated with some of director Hyams' earlier films (*Outland*), but lacks the substance. Gene Hackman stars as an FBI agent assigned to escort the reluctant eyewitness of a mob killing (Anne Archer) from Canada to Los Angeles in safety. With hit men hot on their trail, the two board a train and — the rest you can guess. The film carries a fair number of thrills and the interplay between the characters is enjoyable enough, but there's nothing new here. ★★½ $14.99

The Narrow Margin

(1952, 70 min, US, Richard Fleischer) Well-acted, well-paced thriller about a detective (Charles McGraw) assigned to protect a mobster's widow traveling by train from a gang of hoods who want her dead. Marie Windsor costars as the targeted woman under McGraw's wing. (Remade in 1990 with Gene Hackman and Anne Archer.) ★★★ $19.99

Nashville

(1975, 159 min, US, Robert Altman) Altman's masterful, multilayered mosaic of 1970s Americana. A wonderful ensemble of 24 characters interact at a Tennessee political rally resulting in comedic and often poignant vignettes. One of the greatest achievements of the decade, the film's stellar cast includes Lily Tomlin, Ronee Blakely, Henry Gibson, Keith Carradine, Barbara Harris, Barbara Baxley and Allen Garfield. Carradine won an Oscar for his song, "I'm Easy." ★★★★ $29.99

The Nasty Girl

(1990, 95 min, Germany, Michael Verhoeven) Teasing the viewer into thinking that this is a simple, modern-day Bavarian fairy tale, Verhoeven's hugely enjoyable satire soon becomes much more. Dealing with fascism, terrorism and people's secretive, guilty pasts, the film amazingly never becomes didatic or boring. The story begins with sweet-faced Sonja, the daughter of a nice middle-class couple, entering an essay contest proposing as her theme "My Town in the Third Reich." The seemingly tranquil community's guilty memory is jolted and, faced with an exposition of their fascist-collaborative past, begin efforts, including threats of violence and a firebombing, to stop the determined young lady's goal of uncovering the truth. An invigorating mixture of comedy, investigative journalism, history lesson and moral heroism; all done in a lilting and audacious style of filmmaking. One of the most entertaining films to come out of Germany in years. (German with English subtitles) ★★★½ $89.99

Nasty Habits

(1976, 91 min, GB, Michael Lindsay-Hogg) This odd comic allegory transposes Nixon and his Watergate cronies to a Philadelphia convent and was produced and distributed by Brut Productions (yes, the perfume company). It stars a fine comic cast with Glenda Jackson as Nixon, Sandy Dennis as John Dean, Anne Meara as Gerald Ford, and Geraldine Page as Robert Haldeman. It's an offbeat affair with

some good laughs, but not enough for a feature film. ★★

National Lampoon's Animal House

(1978, 109 min, US, John Landis) John Belushi made the most of his film debut, giving a truly funny performance, in this raucous, sophomoric comedy about an anarchic college fraternity's comic exploits. Cast of then-youthful performers include Tim Matheson, Tom Hulce, Peter Riegert, Karen Allen and Kevin Bacon. ★★★ $14.99

National Lampoon's Christmas Vacation

(1989, 97 min, US, Jeremiah S. Chechik) This third entry of the *National Lampoon Vacation* series, continuing the saga of the hapless Griswold family, finds Clark, Ellen and family home for the holidays. The laughs are surprisingly plentiful as they prepare for a family gathering where, of course, nothing goes right. Returning as patriarch Clark is Chevy Chase, a master of pratfall and schtick, and the comedian has some good sightgags here. ★★★ $14.99

National Velvet

(1944, 125 min, US, Clarence Brown) Lovely family drama with Elizabeth Taylor and Mickey Rooney training their horses for the Grand National Steeplechase competition. Terrific entertainment. ★★★★ $14.99

Native Son

(1986, 112 min, US, Jerold Freedman) This second film version of Richard Wright's best-seller is a capable production made by "American Playhouse." The story is about a poor black youth living in 1930s Chicago who accidentally kills a rich white girl and is sentenced to death. Victor Love plays Bigger Thomas, the embittered youth, and Matt Dillon, Elizabeth McGovern, Geraldine Page and Oprah Winfrey are also featured. Filmed in 1951 with author Wright as Thomas. ★★★ $14.99

The Natural

(1984, 134 min, US, Barry Levinson) Astonishing cinematography highlights this affecting fantasy drama with Robert Redford as a mystical 1930s ballplayer; his career is cut short in his youth and he returns to the game later in life. Grand support from Wilford Brimley, Richard Farnsworth, Glenn Close, Robert Duvall and Kim Basinger. ★★½ $14.99

Natural Born Killers

(1994, 119 min, US, Oliver Stone) Stone's hallucinatory roller-coaster ride follows a pair of unrepentant serial killers (Woody Harrelson and Juliette Lewis) on a cross-country spree of wanton carnage and mind-bending schizoid dementia. Ultimately joining them is Robert Downey, Jr. as the Kiwi-accented host of a sensationalist TV tabloid show who is determined to get their story at any cost. Quentin Tarantino's inventive script has the two homicidal lovebirds consummating their relationship with the murder of her abusive father (Rodney Dangerfield) in a bizarre and hilarious skit that parodies TV sitcoms. But Stone has trouble finding the humor in the rest of Tarantino's tale and the result is yet another exercise in bashing the audience over the head — this time about our culture's love affair with violence and the media's mercenary job of feeding that appetite. In light of Tarantino's more entertaining *Pulp Fiction*, one wonders what might have been the result had someone else with more humor directed *Killers*. (Available letterboxed and pan & scan in a special director's version) ★★½ $29.99

The Natural History of Parking Lots

(1990, 92 min, US, Everett Lewis) The title is probably the most intriguing aspect of this independent black-and-white film. Dripping "L.A. cool" attitude, the drama revolves around the relationship of two troubled brothers — the boyish Chris (Charlie Bean) and the elder, hunky Lance (b. Wyatt). The two live together in an opulent home without their divorced parents and occupy their time languidly laying about in their jockeys, teasing each other in a troubling, pseudo-homosexual incestuous fashion — but nothing comes of this fleshy posturing (if it did, then there might have been a plot). With terrible post dubbing, an early Jarmusch scenario rip-off and an affected artsy approach, the film is trying but not altogether worthless, especially for aspiring filmmakers and Bruce Weber fans. ★★ $29.99

Naughty Marietta

(1935, 106 min, US, W.S. Van Dyke) Jeanette MacDonald-Nelson Eddy musical (their first together) with the two falling in love in the American wilderness. Score includes "Tramp, Tramp, Tramp" and "Ah, Sweet Mystery of Life." MacDonald and Eddy make an appealing romantic and singing duo, though the story is overly sentimental. (And she's not *that* naughty!) ★★½ $19.99

The Naughty Nineties

(1945, 76 min, US, Jean Yarbrough) The classic skit "Who's on First" highlights this otherwise average Abbott and Costello romp, with the boys trying their luck as Mississippi gamblers. ★★ $14.99

The Navigator/The Boat/The Love Nest

(1921-24, 102 min, US, Buster Keaton, Eddie Cline, Donald Crisp) A collection of three Buster Keaton comedies. *The Navigator* (1924, 60 min) is a masterful comedy directed by Keaton and Donald Crisp. Featuring exceptional comic visuals, great running gags and inventive plot twists, the film casts Keaton as a rich slacker who finds himself stranded on an ocean liner with the woman (Kathryn McGuire) who has jilted him. Adrift at sea, the two are beset by problems ranging from making morning breakfast to finding suitable sleeping accomodations. One remarkable scene finds Keaton underwater fighting with swordfish and an octopus, and, as usual, Keaton's stunts are without peer. This is classic comedy. (★★★★) *The Boat* (1921, 23 min) continues the volume's nautical theme, with Keaton and family losing home, car and dignity to live on their homemade houseboat (the *Damfino*). Clever slapstick and funny vignettes combine to make this a delight. (★★★1/2) *The Love Nest* (1923, 20 min) is a cute high seas comedy with Keaton being rescued by a tyran-

nical captain and turning his ship upside-down with uninhibited buffoonery. (★★★) $29.99

The Navigator

(1989, 92 min, New Zealand, Vincent Ward) A thinking person's fantasy is a rare breed, indeed; which makes this totally original and captivating time-travel odyssey all the more praiseworthy. Set in the 14th century besieged by the Black Plague, a small village free of the disease fears that it too will succumb. Its only hope lies in a young boy with psychic powers who, accompanied by his older brother and four villagers, makes a perilous trek across his land to fulfill a vision — only to find himself in modern-day New Zealand. This accomplished production belies its low budget, featuring splendid photography and an impressive first-rate cast and technical know-how. ★★★½ $59.99

Navy SEALS

(1990, 113 min, US, Lewis Teague) A Navy SEAL team (SEa, Air, Land) on a mission to free U.S. hostages in the Middle East discovers a terrorist's arsenal of missiles. Mindless, even confusing, action adventure with cardboard caricatures in uniforms performing derring-do in combat. Charlie Sheen, Michael Biehn, Joanne Whalley-Kilmer, Bill Paxton and Rick Rossovich star. (Letterboxed version sells for $19.99) ★½ $9.99

Nazarin

(1958, 91 min, Mexico, Luis Buñuel) Religious hypocrisy is the theme in this, one of Buñuel's most powerful, realistic and yet often overlooked films. An eccentric young priest, imbued with the teachings of Christ, sets out to live a life of purity outside the confines of the church. Yet his journey through the land is met with hostility, indifference and confusion by those he encounters. For (in the Buñuelian world) the idealistic precepts of love and simplicity are no match in a world dominated by physical needs and limitations. A grim religious satire and winner of the Best Film Award as Cannes. (Spanish with English subtitles) ★★★★ $69.99

Néa — The Young Emmanuelle

(1976, 103 min, France/West Germany, Nelly Kaplan) At 16, Sybille (Ann Zacharias) becomes a best-selling author of erotic literature; though she's a virgin, she uses her fantasies and observes others for material. Soon, Sybille grows tired of being inexperienced and a voyeur. She convinces her publisher (Sami Frey) that they should sleep together in order to give her more material for her next book. Their relationship sours, however, when she falls in love with him and he starts to take credit for the book's success. In between their encounters, she encourages her bisexual mother to leave her father for her female lover. A sensual, intriguing coming-of-age story which balances its erotic story line with the more conventional trappings of romance and sexual politics. (French with English subtitles) ★★★ $59.99

Near Dark

(1987, 95 min, US, Kathryn Bigelow) This stylish, gritty vampire tale is one of the better horror films of the 1980s. Young Adrian

Pasdar falls for Jenny Wright, who's part of a traveling group of nightstalkers — including Lance Henriksen, Bill Paxton and Jenette Goldstein (who all worked together in *Aliens*). When he gets bitten, he joins them on their reign of terror throughout the West. Though the film takes some liberties with the vampire legend, it's one of the most intense shockers of the genre. ★★★½ $9.99

Necessary Roughness

(1991, 108 min, US, Stan Dragoti) It's *Back to School* meets *Semi-Tough* as a misfit college football team attempts to win a game. Scott Bakula (TV's "Quantum Leap") is a 37-year-old farmer and former high school football star who enrolls at a Texas university to become their quarterback. Under the guidance of new, straight-arrow coach Hector Elizondo and assistant Robert Loggia, the team learns to band together for what, of course, will be the big game at the finale. The film shares much with the baseball farce *Major League*, though it is far more congenial. ★★½ $14.99

Necronomicon: The Book of the Dead

(1996, 90 min, US, Christophe Gans, Shusuke Kaneko, Brian Yuzna) This triptych of episodes based on stories by the great horror/fantasy writer H.P. Lovecraft can be classified along with most other attempts to bring his highly imaginative works to the big screen, as a nice try. Producer and codirector Yuzna (*Bride of Re-Animator*, *Society*) directs the last and probably the best episode, based on "The Whisperer in Darkness." The first episode (by French director Gans), "The Drowned", is trite and marred by poorly-executed special makeup effects. The middle episode, "The Cold" (based on "Cool Air"), directed by Kaneko (*Gamera 1995*) is admirable, but its modern ending works at cross-purposes with its Lovecraftian beginning. Yuzna also directed the amusing wraparound segment, starring Jeffrey Combs (*Re-Animator*) as HPL himself. Fans of Lovecraftian lore will either be overjoyed or outraged, and more casual viewers will probably be mildly entertained. ★★ $94.99

Ned Kelly

(1970, 100 min, GB, Tony Richardson) Set in 19th-century Australia, this ambitious Outback western features the screen acting debut of Mick Jagger. He plays Ned Kelly, Australia's most notorious outlaw, who with his band of fellow Irishmen does battle against the repressive British authorities. Jagger, much better used as the decadent rock star in Nicolas Roeg's *Performance*, is out of place in this film. A bit too scrawny for the role, he does not possess the needed screen presence and his painful attempt at an Irish brogue doesn't help either. Lightning does not strike twice for director Richardson in his attempt to mold the rude rocker in the fashion of "lovable rogue" as he did with Albert Finney in *Tom Jones*. Featuring music by Waylon Jennings. ★★½ $14.99

Needful Things

(1993, 120 min, US, Fraser C. Heston) Stephen King's "tale *du jour*" is stylishly served up by first-time director Heston (the son of Charlton). Heston's quasi-operatic production boasts a knock'em-dead performance by veteran actor

Max von Sydow as Leland Gaunt, a satanic salesman whose curio shop, Needful Things, springs up out of nowhere causing all hell to break loose in the small New England town of Castle Rock. Kudos also to Amanda Plummer as a downtrodden spinster who becomes enmeshed in the soul-stealing machinations of the demonic Mr. Gaunt. ★★½ $14.99

Negatives

(1968, 90 min, GB, Peter Medak) Medak's (*The Ruling Class*) first directorial effort is a macabre and erotic tale about a young couple with a somewhat more than kinky sexual bent. They encounter a glamorous photographer with an equally warped sense of bedroom play and enter an even stranger world of sexual fantasy. This stylish and unusual film stars Glenda Jackson, Peter McEnery and the heart-stopping Diane Cilento. ★★★

Neighbors

(1981, 91 min, US, John G. Avildsen) John Belushi's last film finds him the straight man as Dan Aykroyd, for once, gets a chance to cut loose as the maniac who moves in next door and make life a living hell. This reverse casting is indicative of the chances this film was willing to take, especially in the decision to maintain the novel's dark and unrelenting tone. While it provides comedic moments of dark-edged humor, the overall effect is one of a tired, over ambitious project. ★★ $9.99

Nekromantik

(1991, 75 min, Germany, Jörg Buttgereit) This unrelenting gore fest is a disgusting exercise in shock cinema. A mild-mannered corpse-retriever for an ambulance company, whose hobbies include collecting body parts and organs from crash victims, at-home autopsies and viewing tapes of bunny rabbit slaughter, slowly becomes unglued after his girlfriend leaves him. Not as much fun as the sequel, *Nekromantik 2*. (German with English subtitles) ★ $29.99

Nekromantik 2

(1991, 100 min, Germany, Jörg Buttgereit) Not for the faint-of-heart (nor for unsuspecting German film fans), this repugnant, puerile yet perversely enjoyable film is a low-budget descent into the porno/necrographic world where death and decay meet sexual obsession. A young woman exhumes her recently deceased boyfriend, cleans him up and, voila!, has a more than compliant sexual partner. The film has plenty of disgusting sexual acts, as well as gory mutilations to satisfy any splatter fan and, as a bonus, there's a brilliant spoof on European art films. What sick mind makes these films? And what sick mind watches them? It's a film that would make Herschel Gordon Lewis proud. (German with English subtitles) ★★ $29.99

Nell

(1994, 113 min, US, Michael Apted) Jodie Foster's remarkably nuanced performance highlights this otherwise dispassionate, ordinary tale of a "wild child" discovered in the backwoods of North Carolina. Liam Neeson costars as a caring physician who has his hands full when Foster is found living wild and speaking a language no one understands.

Successfully arguing against having her institutionalized, Neeson moves in nearby and dedicates himself to deciphering her broken English and introducing her to civilization. Though the dramatics lead to tender moments between the two characters, the film is strangely devoid of emotion, and both a town populated by stereotypes and a subplot about psychologist Natasha Richardson's romantic involvement with Neeson detract from the rhythm of the story. However, the mystery of Foster's condition and the actress' unearthly inhabitation of the title character make *Nell* at the very least a compelling watch. ★★½ $14.99

Nelly and Monsieur Arnaud

(1995, 103 min, France, Claude Sautet) A talky though quietly powerful examination of unspoken desire, *Nelly and Monsieur Arnaud* concerns the relationship between a despondent young woman and a wealthy older man. Yet despite any prurient overtones, the film mines this nonsexual romance for its high emotional content. Nelly (Emmanuelle Béart, star of director Sautet's *Un Couer en Hiver*) is a young Parisian who owes six months back rent and is trapped in a loveless marriage. A friend introduces her to Monsieur Arnaud (Michel Serrault), a judge who needs help writing his memoirs. Smitten by the beautiful woman, he offers her money and a word processing job with "no strings attached." Meeting on a daily basis, a power struggle masquerading as a flirtation develops. As these characters move closer to realizing their destinies, their jealousies come into bold relief. Ultimately, Nelly and Monsieur Arnaud engage in a pas de deux with ironic consequences. The performances by both leads are quite moving, full of gentle, realistic nuances. Sautet has crafted an intelligent French chamber drama that aches with the resonance of heartbreak. (Letterboxed version) (French with English subtitles) ★★★½ $99.99

Nemesis

(1992, 92 min, US, Albert Pyun) In the not-too-distant future, Japan and the U.S. have merged politically and economically and, through the use of cybernetic parts, humans can repair or replace damaged body parts. Enlisted to battle corrupt government officials and the more-than-human citizens that want to take over the world, Olivier Gruner stars as a semiretired cyber-cop who saves the day in this slick, sci-fi treat, which features some above-average action sequences and a fine supporting cast which includes Tim Thomerson, Deborah Shelton and perennial bad guy Brion James. ★★½ $14.99

The Neon Bible

(1995, 92 min, GB, Terence Davies) While director Davies' pensive, even heart-wrenching mood pieces (*Distant Voices, Still Lives* and *The Long Day Closes*) seem perfectly placed in the urban landscape of post-war Liverpool, that same style when transposed to a diametrically opposed locale – in this case rural American South – results in a much less satisfactory experience. Based on a story by John Kennedy O'Toole, the film is one which is of obvious attraction to Davies: A coming-of-age tale of a sensitive teenage boy brought up in a household dominated by loving women. Set in 1940s

Georgia, the story centers on David, who is brought up in a stifling Christian Fundamentalist household headed by his father (Denis Leary in an effective dramatic role). His only real communication comes when his big city aunt (Gena Rowlands) – a former showgirl – comes for an extended visit. Not much happens as the strangely friendless, sad-eyed David floats from one incident to another developing a longing for something different. Davies films in his trademark haunting style, but the meandering story ultimately produces a less-than-successful film. ★★ $89.99

The Nest

(1980, 109 min, Spain, Jaime de Arminan) A passionate and haunting film that depicts the complex relationship between a lonely 60-year-old widower and a captivating and intelligent 12-year-old girl. A moody, sensitive portrait about the meaning of friendship and love as he follows this relationship to its inevitable, tragic conclusion. (Spanish with English subtitles) ★★★

The Nest

(1987, 89 min, US, Terence H. Winkless) A genetic experiment goes awry and turns ordinary cockroaches into bloodthirsty carnivores. The creepy bugs will definitely make one's skin crawl, and the film, while giving in to horror genre clichés, uses its multilegged stars to good effect. Get out the industrial-strength Raid! ★★ $14.99

The Net

(1995, 118 min, US, Irwin Winkler) The considerable charm of its leading lady Sandra Bullock is barely enough to keep this muddled computer-age thriller afloat. *The Net* consists of lots of computer talk, computer gadgets and hackers lovingly doting on their computers, but what it doesn't feature is a well-developed screenplay, and the film lacks memorable suspense or a credible story line. Bullock plays a lonely computer whiz who becomes involved in a high-tech conspiracy when she gets hold of a disc able to enter any system (shades of *Sneakers*). After the bad guys erase her identity in a particularly eerie sequence, she spends the rest of the film trying to elude them while seeking help from anyone that will listen (shades of *The Pelican Brief*). The chase scenes are rather flat, though the computer-babble will engage those who spend a lot of time at the keyboard. ★★ $19.99

Network

(1976, 121 min, US, Sidney Lumet) A boisterous, brilliantly savage satire on television, America's fickle viewing habits and the corporate mentality. Paddy Chayevsky's scathing script is given extraordinary life by a remarkable cast to tell the story of the rise of a fourth network. Peter Finch won an Oscar as the weary newsman who loses his sanity and becomes a guru; Faye Dunaway also won an Oscar as the ruthless news department head whose aphrodisiac is high ratings. William Holden gives a tremendous performance as the ex-department chief, who impotently witnesses the craziness around him. Also with Robert Duvall, Ned Beatty and Beatrice Straight, who won a Supporting Oscar as

Holden's neglected wife. An original and breathtaking masterwork. ★★★★ $14.99

Nevada Smith

(1966, 135 min, US, Henry Hathaway) Exciting western with Steve McQueen in the title role — based on a character from Harold Robbins' "The Carpetbaggers" — as a cowboy who tracks down the gang who murdered his parents. ★★★ $14.99

Never Cry Wolf

(1983, 105 min, US, Carroll Ballard) Farley Mowat's stirring novel about his trek through the Canadian tundra to study the Arctic wolf is brought beautifully to the screen in this Disney production. The film capitalizes on the book's romantic vision of the frozen wilderness through breathtaking landscapes and a sense of daring high adventure. Charles Martin Smith stars as the Mowat character. ★★★½ $14.99

Never Give a Sucker an Even Break

(1941, 71 min, US, Edward Cline) W.C. Fields' last starring film, with a script reportedly written on the back of an envelope, is a sometimes hilarious collection of gags, with Fields playing himself; aided by Margaret Dumont and Franklin Pangborn. ★★★½

Never on Sunday

(1959, 97 min, Greece, Jules Dassin) This Greek *Pygmalion* was a huge international hit when first released and was considered quite daring in its day. Melina Mercouri is unforgettable as an exuberant and carefree prostitute who meets up with an American tourist (Jules Dassin) who falls in love with her and attempts to educate her to the finer things in life. Mercouri won the Best Actress Award at Cannes and the film won an Academy Award for Best Song. A thoroughly entertaining romp with wonderful location shooting in Piraeus and the Greek countryside. (Filmed in English) ★★★½ $19.99

Never Say Never Again

(1983, 137 min, GB, Irvin Kershner) Sean Connery will never say never to Bond, James Bond... He's back after 12 years and dives into this remake of *Thunderball*. If you missed this exciting spy adventure, see it; Connery is as suave and debonair as ever, proving Moore isn't necessarily more. Also with Barbara Carrera, Klaus Maria Brandauer, Max von Sydow and Kim Basinger. (Available letterboxed and pan & scan) ★★★ $19.99

Never Talk to Strangers

(1995, 86 min, US, Peter Hall) Rebecca De Mornay plays a psychiatrist who specializes in multiple personality disorder. While treating a serial killer (Harry Dean Stanton), she meets and begins an affair with a mysterious and sexy surveillance specialist (Antonio Banderas). And while her upstairs neighbor (Dennis Miller) pines away for her, and her estranged father (Len Cariou) tries to rekindle their relationship, she becomes the target for a series of deadly threats from an anonymous source. This "erotic thriller" is both predictable and tame, offering few chills and only one steamy encounter of note. De Mornay acts as if she were on tranquilizers, and Banderas, who seems to be doing a variation of the same

unpredictable character he played in two equally bad 1995 films, *Assassins* and *Four Rooms*, is in danger of wearing out his American welcome. To anyone who really thinks about it, the identity of the stalker is obvious. ★★ $19.99

The Neverending Story

(1984, 92 min, GB, Wolfgang Petersen) Petersen's first English-language film is a near-classic fairy tale about a young boy who becomes so immersed in the book he's reading that he is magically drawn into the story and must help save the tale's world from destruction. Wonderful children's fare, perhaps a bit scary for the wee-est of tykes, but filled with good special effects and an earnest young hero. Only a slight clumsiness and not-too-subtle allegorical message keep this from the highest pantheon of children's film. ★★★½ $14.99

The Neverending Story II: The Next Chapter

(1990, 90 min, US, George Miller) Sequel to the 1984 family favorite about a young boy transported to a magical land within the pages of his book. Now, the boy must return to the fantasy world to save his old friends from an evil sorceress, and finds the courage that he lacks in real life. Not as entrancing as the original, but still entertaining. Includes the original five-minute Warner Brothers cartoon "Box Office Bunny." ★★½ $19.99

The New Age

(1994, 110 min, US, Michael Tolkin) Judy Davis and Peter Weller are well-suited in their roles as a pair of wanton yuppies whose comfortable material world comes crashing down around them. Their marriage is too hip for words, they live in a multi-zillion dollar house in the hills, and hobnob with the rich and famous. But it all falls apart and they are forced to search for some deeper meaning to their lives, leading them to new sex partners and a succession of New Age gurus (Patrick

Bauchau and Rachel Rosenthal provide excellent portraits) who can only pose more questions than answers. Writer-director Tolkin (who penned *The Player*) evokes the same eerie atmosphere of his earlier work, *The Rapture*, as he unfolds this tale of spiritual emptiness in a world of decadence and consumption. Adam West puts in a fine turn as Weller's playboy father, and Samuel L. Jackson proves his range as the motivational manager of a telephone salesforce. ★★★ $19.99

The New Centurions

(1972, 103 min, US, Richard Fleischer) Stinging depiction of cop life: George C. Scott is a veteran officer who dreads retiring; Stacy Keach is a young cop whose work comes before everything, including his wife. Based on the novel by Joseph Wambaugh. With Jane Alexander and Rosalind Cash. ★★★ $14.99

New Fists of Fury

(1984, 120 min, Hong Kong, Lo Wei) Jackie Chan plays a former pickpocket during WWII who is forced to fight for his life when his fiancée's school is destroyed and its master savagely murdered. With her help, he learns a new and deadly fighting art and together they exact vengeance for the death of her master. A brutal ballet of martial arts mayhem. (Dubbed) ★★★ $9.99

New Jack City

(1991, 101 min, US, Mario Van Peebles) Pulsating with the music, life and ever-present violence of a drug-infested inner city, this tough gangster thriller, ostensibly a black *Scarface*, should keep even the most taciturn viewer riveted to his seat. The city is New York, where a vicious crack dealer (villainously played by Wesley Snipes) is driving his way to the top of the drug underworld. It takes two renegade cops (Ice T and Judd Nelson) to try to bring him and his sordid empire down. Van Peebles' first film is a tough, exciting and impressive work that successfully straddles the fine line of glorifying the drug culture while

Next Stop, Greenwich Village

also presenting a stringent anti-drug message. ★★★ $9.99

New Jersey Drive

(1995, 86 min, US, Nick Gomez) Based on a true story of police corruption in Newark, New Jersey, this Spike Lee-produced tale centers around a young "boy in the hood" (Sharron Corley) who finds himself thrust into the middle of a turf war between his car thief friends and the law when one of them steals a policeman's private car. Gomez's violent, flashy and somewhat predictable second effort falls short of his gritty and well-characterized debut film *Laws of Gravity*, and *New Jersey Drive*'s reliance on stock characters, flashy MTV-style camerawork and overbearing rap music soundtrack only weakens the "urban action" genre instead of enhancing it. ★★ $19.99

A New Leaf

(1971, 102 min, US, Elaine May) May wrote, directed and stars in this comedy about a rich but clumsy woman (May) who is courted by a bankrupt playboy (Walter Matthau), who's only after her money. Both stars are in good form, and the film offers many a well-placed laugh. ★★★ $14.99

A New Life

(1988, 104 min, US, Alan Alda) Alan Alda goes through middle-aged angst as he and wife Ann-Margret divorce and find new loves. Alda retreads familiar territory here, but he and a good cast wring some life out of the unremarkable material. With Hal Linden, John Shea and Veronica Hamel. ★★½ $14.99

New Wave (Nouvelle Vague)

(1990, 89 min, France, Jean-Luc Godard) The eternal war between the sexes and the classes is given the Godard treatment in this dense, meandering and ultimately enigmatic drama/thriller. Beginning with the quote, "Women are in love, men are in solitude, mutually they steal love and solitude from each other," the story begins when a befuddled Alain Delon is almost run over by the wealthy daughter of an industrialist. She picks him up and takes him home, but is it love or does she have something else in mind for him? Never simply content to tell a singular story, Godard infuses the film's soundtrack with layers of overlapping dialogue, poetry and music while the camera roams, circles and pans during each scene. While the earnest film enthusiast might see "art" and meaning in all of this complexity from the enfant terrible of the French New Wave, others, including casual viewers and the more cynical cinéaste, will conclude that the master has run out of new ideas; with his most recent films, including this, "full of sound and fury, signifying nothing." (French with English subtitles) ★★ $79.99

New Year's Day

(1990, US, Henry Jaglom) While the films of Jaglom (the poor man's David Mamet) are not everyone's idea of entertainment and fun, there is an unwavering flock (however small) of devotees who actually enjoy his personal style of angst-ridden filmmaking. Jaglom appears as a recently divorced Los Angelino who flees to New York on New Year's day. His new apart-

ment, however, is still occupied by the old tenants, three young women who invite him to stay while they pack and throw a farewell party. At the party, peopled by a diverse assortment of oddball New Yorkers, our lecherous and unsympathetic hero views the proceedings with a detached air as he dispenses advice and tries to pick up women. He also begins to listen and learn some things about himself. While the caliber of the acting varies, Gwen Milles is especially affecting as the fragile Anne. Awkward at times, repetitive and something of a vanity production, the film nevertheless holds one's attention. ★★★ $79.99

New York, New York

(1977, 137 min, US, Martin Scorsese) Liza Minnelli and Robert De Niro meet at a WWII victory party; the innocent pop singer and volatile jazz musician wed. As she reaches stardom, his fortunes decline, further straining an already combative marriage. The potent performances are ably underscored by a superb evocation of the era, though the story line is at times predictable and given to backstage clichés. Another dark look at human relations from director Scorsese. (Available letterboxed and pan & scan) ★★½ $24.99

New York Stories

(1989, 123 min, US, Martin Scorsese/Francis Coppola/Woody Allen) Three-part film by New York directors Scorsese, Coppola and Allen. Scorsese's *Life Lessons* stars Nick Nolte as a moody and talented painter tormented by the end of his relationship with his apprentice/lover Rosanna Arquette. The second segment, Coppola`s *Life without Zoe*, is a cold story of a bratty child's indulgent birthday party. The final film, Allen's *Oedipus Wrecks*, is the lifesaver of the three, and one of Allen's funniest works. Allen stars as a successful lawyer who is haunted, nagged and criticized by his ever-present mother, wonderfully portrayed by Mae Questel (the original voice of Betty Boop). Not wholly successful, but still an interesting venture. ★★½ $9.99

News from Home

(1976, 85 min, Belgium/France, Chantal Akerman) Avant-gardist Akerman has produced in this static, repetitive exercise her own unique filmic symphony to New York City. Attempting to explore the differences between European myths of the city against its gritty reality, cinematographer Babette Mangolte captures the strangely stark beauty of an alienated, lifeless world while offscreen Akerman occasionally reads, in a monotone voice, letters from a Belgian mother to her daughter living in New York. A difficult, abstract work of art. (French with English subtitles) ★★½ $24.99

Newsfront

(1978, 110 min, Australia, Phillip Noyce) This much celebrated and award-winning film vividly re-creates the glory days of newsreels and the men who captured the turbulent war years of the 1940s. Director Noyce intercuts a fictional story with actual news events to create this spirited true-life adventure. The fine cast includes Bill Hunter, Wendy Hughes, Gerard Kennedy, Angela Punch and Bryan Brown. ★★★

Newsies

(1992, 121 min, US, Kenny Ortega) This Disney musical about a group of newsboys who strike against a corrupt newspaper mogul boasts a wonderful cast of young talent, but unfortunately the story drags between musical numbers leaving the viewer mostly dispassionate. Even the always magnetic screen presences of Robert Duvall and Ann-Margret can't liven up this one. The cast includes Christian Bale, Bill Pullman and Michael Lerner. ★½ $9.99

Next Door

(1994, 95 min, US, Tony Bill) From the director of such minor gems as *My Bodyguard* and *Five Corners* comes this made-for-cable, mean-spirited retread of the 1981 turkey *Neighbors*. The story centers on a violently escalating feud between a nerdy college professor (James Woods) and his sociopathic "white trash" next-door neighbor (Randy Quaid). This dark comedy, also starring Kate Capshaw, is short on laughs and totally unnecessary. ★½ $93.99

The Next Karate Kid

(1994, 104 min, US, Christopher Cain) Originality and reality are sorely missing in this blatant rip-off of all the other *Karate Kid* movies. Yes, they did replace Ralph Macchio with Hilary Swank, but many of the lines are lifted directly out of the first film. The excesses are beyond belief. The school security chief runs a paramilitary gang of kids whom he eggs on to horrible extremes of power and brutality. Of course, he and Noriyuki "Pat" Morita have it out in the end and you can guess who wins. Even the parts of the film which could have been funny, like a group of monks zen bowling, are pushed so far that they are ridiculous. This gender-switching *Karate Kid* should be the last of the series. ★ $96.89

Next of Kin

(1984, 72 min, Canada, Atom Egoyan) Egoyan's fascination with family relations and the effects of electronic media on one's life are explored in this sly, off-the-wall comedy-drama. Peter, in most respects a normal young man, finds his relationship with his tyrannical WASP family to be unbearable. After a session of video therapy, he sees a video about a troubled Armenian family that had lost a baby to adoption 20 years before. Deciding that a new family is in order, he acts out the role of their long-lost son. Inspired lunacy reigns in this brilliant and original directorial debut that explores not only family tensions but ideas of displacement, cultural stereotypes and role playing. ★★★½ $79.99

Next Stop, Greenwich Village

(1976, 109 min, US, Paul Mazursky) Mazursky's excellent semiautobiographical account of his early adulthood in 1950s Greenwich Village is one of the first American films in which a writer-director looks back at his youth. Lenny Baker gives a rich characterization as an aspiring actor who leaves his Brooklyn home for the unknown wilds of the Village. There, he befriends an eccentric group while waiting for his big break. Mazursky sees the era as a magical time, and his affection shows. The director's evocation of an almost mythical period is first-rate; it's as if Marty McFly grabbed a camera and took the DeLorean for another ride. Ellen Greene co-stars as Baker's girlfriend, and Christopher Walken, Dori Brenner, Antonio Fargas, Lois Smith, Lou Jacobi and (look quick) Jeff Goldblum are strong in support; but the acting honors go to Shelley Winters for her hilarious turn as Baker's quintessential overprotective mom (wait till you see her tap dance!). Though not as well known as some of his other films, *Next Stop, Greenwich Village* is possibly Mazursky's best. ★★★★ $59.99

Next Summer

(1986, 100 min, France, Nadine Trintignant) An all-star cast of Fanny Ardant, Philippe Noiret, Jean-Louis Trintignant and Claudia Cardinale sadly cannot save this pretentious drivel which claims to give a penetrating humanistic insight into familial relationships. In a rambling country house, the extended family of patriarch Noiret live, love, argue and reconcile (and all within 100 minutes!). French fluff at its most nauseating. (French with English subtitles) ★★ $69.99

The Next Voice You Hear

(1950, 83 min, US, William Wellman) An odd drama about the voice of God being heard on the radio and the effect it has on the residents of a small town. The execution is not quite up to the premise, yet the film is strangely moving if one releases all cynical thoughts. With James Whitmore and Nancy (Reagan) Davis. ★★½ $19.99

Next Year If All Goes Well

(1983, 97 min, France, Jean-Loup Hubert) Isabelle Adjani and Thierry L'hermitte star in this whimsical romantic comedy as a modern couple involved in an ambivalent affair. While Adjani, a pragmatic career woman, longs for a comfortable domestic life, L'hermitte, a boyish cartoonist, quakes at the mere mention of parenthood and retreats to the safer realm of his outer space comic strip. A megahit in France, *Next Year...* is an often riotous glimpse at marriage and infidelity. (Dubbed) ★★★ $69.99

Niagara

(1953, 89 min, US, Henry Hathaway) The turning point in Marilyn Monroe's career, this taut suspenser gave Marilyn her first big break towards stardom, and hinted at the legendary persona which would soon emerge. While vacationing at Niagara Falls, a faithless wife (MM) plots to murder her husband (Joseph Cotten) and run off with her lover; but when the distraught husband gets wise, he has other ideas. The importance of this film in MM's career usually overshadows the fact that this is quite an accomplished thriller. ★★★ $14.99

Die Nibelungen

(1924, 195 min, Germany, Fritz Lang) **Part 1: Siegfried (100 min); Part 2: Kriemhilde's Revenge (95 min)** This masterpiece of the silent cinema was one of the most elaborate German productions of its time. Director Lang offers a pictorial feast with magical forests, huge castles and wondrous creatures of the woods. While each part of *Die Nibelungen* is complete unto itself, together they take on a resonance that only enriches the viewing expe-

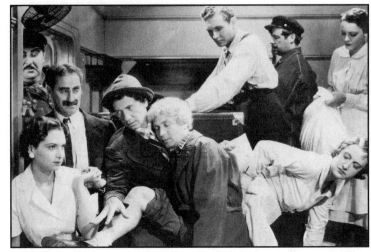

A Night at the Opera

rience. Set at the dawn of time, this mythical drama follows Siegfried, a handsome young warrior, who is given magical powers by a race of gnomes called The Nibelungen as a reward for slaying a dragon. ★★★★

Nicholas and Alexandra

(1971, 183 min, GB, Franklin J. Schaffner) This lavish chronicle of the Russian Revolution is rich with scenery, costumery, and even some good acting, though at a three-hour running time it's a little on the long side. The film stars Michael Jayston and Janet Suzman (who earned an Academy Award nomination) and offers a sprawling and often interesting look at the Russian monarchy during the 14 years leading to the revolution which proved its undoing. Tom Baker appears as Rasputin and cameos are put in by Laurence Olivier, Michael Redgrave and Jack Hawkins. ★★★ $29.99

Nicholas Nickleby

(1947, 95 min, GB, Alberto Cavalcanti) In the mid-1980s, when the Royal Shakespeare Company produced an 8½-hour stage version of Charles Dickens' classic story, interest in this earlier (and considerably shorter) film version was rekindled. Starring Derek Bond and Cedric Hardwicke, the story is of a young man's struggle to protect himself and his family from a scheming and miserly uncle. It's a story full of resonance and emotional power and the film stands as a faithful rendition. ★★★ $14.99

Nick of Time

(1995, 89 min, US, John Badham) Filmed in the gimmicky fashion of real time, *Nick of Time* is a not-so-plausible but nevertheless intriguing political thriller which manages to offer a few thrills along the way. Johnny Depp plays a father whose daughter (Courtenay Chase) is abducted upon arriving by train to Los Angeles. Christopher Walken and Roma Moffia are the kidnappers, assassins who have been hired to kill the incumbent governor of California (Marsha Mason) who's running for

reelection. As they hold his daughter captive, Depp is coerced to pull the trigger with a maniacal Walken following his every move. The film sets up an interesting dilemma for the loving father, which it only occasionally explores. However, Walken's mugging and the filler between action scenes are compensated by some genuine suspense and a how-will-he-do-it scenario. In a departure for him, Depp captures the anxiety of a father caught in a nightmare, though he seems to be better served by his outsider roles. Charles S. Dutton appears as a wily shoeshine man who helps Depp. ★★½ $14.99

Night after Night

(1932, 73 min, US, Archie Mayo) Mae West appears in her film debut, and though she's only on screen for about 15 minutes, it's easy to see why she became a hit. A young, Valentino-looking George Raft gets star billing in this light underworld comedy-drama as a speakeasy owner who has his hands full with rival gangs and old girlfriends. Though he's just "a mug trying to be a gentleman," Raft falls for society girl Constance Cummings, much to the disdain of former g.f. Wynne Gibson. West plays yet another former girlfriend, and when she steps on screen, an otherwise pedestrian film suddenly comes alive with energy and humor. West, who had yet to fully hone her campy, staccato delivery and "Diamond Lil" persona, says her archtypical line "Goodness had nothing to do with it, dearie." In the believe-it-or-not department, Raft has a seminude scene. ★★½ $14.99

Night and Day

(1946, 128 min, US, Michael Curtiz) As Hollywood fiction, this is pretty entertaining stuff; but as the true biography of legendary songwriter Cole Porter, it's laughably inaccurate. And though no one ever complained about seeing Cary Grant in a film, he's not exactly the perfect choice to play the composer. With Alexis Smith as Mrs. Porter (his wife, not mom), and Monty Woolley plays himself as Cole's best friend. Mary Martin has a small scene singing "My Heart Belongs to Daddy." Of course, a film made in 1946 would never have even hinted at Porter's well-known homosexuality. ★★½ $19.99

Night and Fog

(1956, 50 min, France, Alain Resnais) Resnais' disturbing documentary examines the horrors of the German concentration camps. The images will haunt the viewer, but will also help preserve the memory of "...the cry that never ends." (English language narration) ★★★★

Night and the City

(1950, 101 min, US, Jules Dassin) Richard Widmark is unnerving as a small-time hustler scouring the rubble of a decimated London barely recovered from the ravages of WWII. He facilitates small cons, setting up traveling businessmen for the benefit of his objectionable bar-owning boss. He thinks he sees a way out, a way to challenge the city-wide controller of the wrestling game and buy a ticket out of squalor. With blind frenzy, he steals from the woman who loves him (Gene Tierney), connives the woman who would provide him with a lucrative set-up and betrays the employer who supports him. He comes very close to pulling it all off before the threads unravel and he faces unprotected the accumulated rage of those whom he has used. Widmark scurries like a rat over London's bombed-out remains with an enthralling, hyperkinetic desperation used to great effect by director Dassin. ★★★½ $89.99

Night and the City

(1992, 104 min, US, Irwin Winkler) Winkler's visceral, punchy direction propels outstanding performances from Robert De Niro, Jessica Lange, Cliff Gorman, Jack Warden and Alan King through Richard Price's frenetic screenplay. This slick and clever update of the 1950 Richard Widmark classic, which captures the feel of contemporary urban noir, provides De Niro with the vehicle for one of his finest performances; he's Harry Fabian, the quintessential street-smart, fast-talking hustler – the *Mean Streets* wise guy all grown up. After a lifetime of taking the money and running, he decides to go for the big score in the fight game. In going up against the major players, he enters an unfamiliar world with rules he barely understands and unwittingly disrupts an uneasy truce in a decades-old familial conflict. He's in over his head, and takes down with him the one person who trusts him. As the married woman who becomes involved with Fabian, Lange is luminous, portraying just the right balance of big-city knowing and innocent naiveté. ★★★½ $19.99

A Night at the Opera

(1935, 92 min, US, Sam Wood) Groucho Marx, as Otis B. Driftwood, con artist extraordinaire and Margaret Dumont's financial advisor, hooks up with an opera company on its way from Italy to America via luxury liner. Complete with young lovers, scurrilous cads, pompous fools, stowaways Chico and Harpo, and the often imitated but never duplicated stateroom scene. ★★★½ $19.99

Night Crossing

(1981, 106 min, GB, Delbert Mann) Fairly entertaining true story about two families who plan an escape from East Berlin by hot-air balloon. Starring Beau Bridges, John Hurt, Jane Alexander and Glynnis O'Connor. ★★

Night Falls on Manhattan

(1997, 114 min, US, Sidney Lumet) After *A Stranger Among Us* and *Guilty as Sin*, it appeared director Lumet may have had lost his once-commanding abilities. But in returning to the city and theme in which he has previously excelled, Lumet has crafted an intoxicating police procedural and courtroom drama. A worthy follow-up to his terrific crooked cop tales *Serpico* and *Prince of the City*, the deceptively complex *Night Falls on Manhattan* sees New York City assistant D.A. Andy Garcia is given his first case – prosecuting the drug lord responsible for the shooting of his policeman father (Ian Holm). The court case is the only thing that's cut-and-dry in the story, for Lumet has more in mind than just a routine trial. His screenplay (based on Robert Daley's "Tainted Evidence") explores the subtleties of racial stereotype, the duplicity of familial and professional loyalties, and the accepted boundaries of duty and corruption. Holm excels as Garcia's father, a decent man whose own son is uncertain of his level of culpability; and Ron Leibman makes a most spirited district attorney who's wiser than he acts. The only false note of *Night Falls on Manhattan* is Lena Olin's rather contrived romance with Garcia. ★★★½ $99.99

Night Full of Rain

(1978, 104 min, Italy, Lina Wertmüller) In this Italian-language battle-of-the-sexes drama, Giancarlo Giannini stars as an Italian Communist journalist trapped in a rocky marriage to Candice Bergen, an American photographer and feminist. Director Wertmüller attempts to wring life out of the clash between an old-world chauvinist intent on keeping his wife in check and a liberated woman equally determined to continue her career. Set in Italy and San Francisco, the film has moments of visual spectacle, insight and humor, but the confused plot undermines it all. The full title is *The End of the World in Our Usual Bed in a Night Full of Rain*. (Italian with English subtitles) ★★½ $19.99

Night Games

(1980, 100 min, France, Roger Vadim) A turgid little drama about a Beverly Hills housewife who, after her husband leaves her, experiences a fantasy sexual relationship with a "presence" that visits her nightly. Cindy Pickett stars as the sexually disoriented woman, and Joanna Cassidy and Barry Primus also star. (Filmed in English) ★½

A Night in Casablanca

(1946, 85 min, US, Archie Mayo) Groucho, Chico and Harpo battle Nazis and uncover stolen loot in the exotic if seedy Hotel Casablanca. There's a young couple in love, a femme fatale, a dastardly villain, some bungling idiots and the usual suspects. Not on par with the Marx Brothers' earlier works, but entertaining just the same. ★★½

A Night in the Life of Jimmy Reardon

(1988, 90 min, US, William Richert) Young River Phoenix explores his sexuality with various women as he decides between college and his girlfriend. An irresponsible sexual coming-of-age comedy which alternates between near-kiddie porn and adult romantic comedy. With Ann Magnuson, Meredith Salenger and Ione Skye. ★★ $19.99

Night Is My Future

(1947, 87 min, Sweden, Ingmar Bergman) An upper-class pianist is blinded in an accident on a firing range and is cared for by his maid, with whom he falls in love. This little-known Bergman film is done with craftsmanship and taste, and contains a powerful dream/nightmare sequence. (Swedish with English subtitles) ★★½

'Night, Mother

(1986, 97 min, US, Tom Moore) Sissy Spacek and Anne Bancroft offer good performances as mother and daughter in this adaptation of Marsha Norman's Pulitzer Prize-winning play. Spacek plays a troubled woman intent on committing suicide; Bancroft plays her mother who desperately tries to talk her out of it. The film can't overcome its depressing theme, but the two actresses make the drama involving. ★★½ $79.99

Night Moves

(1975, 95 min, US, Arthur Penn) Gene Hackman excels in this gripping psycho-thriller from the pen of Alan Sharp. Hackman plays an emotionally on-the-edge private detective who is hired to track down a wayward daughter (Melanie Griffith) in Florida. Penn provides able direction in this pessimistic film which captures the sanguine mood of post-Watergate America. ★★★ $19.99

Night of Dark Shadows

(1971, 97 min, US, Dan Curtis) Even though Jonathan Frid and Joan Bennett are gone, this sequel to *House of Dark Shadows* hasn't lost its bite when Kate Jackson tries to understand just why Laura Parker was hanged as a witch. ★★½ $14.99

Night of the Comet

(1984, 95 min, US, Thom Eberhardt) Entertaining, clever "B" sci-fi comedy about two Valley Girls who seem to be the last survivors of a killer comet. After an exhausting shopping spree at the local mall, however, they soon realize they are not alone: zombies! Starring Catherine Mary Stewart and Kelli Maroney. ★★½

Night of the Day of the Dawn of...

(1992, 98 min, US, Lowell Mason) Full Title: *Night of the Day of the Dawn of the Son of the Bride of the Return of the Revenge of the Terror of the Attack of the Evil Mutant Hellbound Flesh Eating Subhumanoid Living Dead Part 2*. George Romero's *Night of the Living Dead* is turned upside down in this brain-cauterizing attempt at spoof. Inspired by Woody Allen's *What's Up Tiger Lily?*, director Mason has taken the original *N.O.T.L.D.*, excised the soundtrack and redubbed it as an alleged comedy. The result is over 90 minutes of non-stop insults and juvenile laughs. The film is produced by Jyvass Productions. How appropriate. ★½ $89.99

Night of the Demons 2

(1994, 96 min, US, Brian Trenchard-Smith) Good special effects and a wicked sense of humor permeate this predictable but effective frightfest about the usual group of bad-egg Catholic college brats who decide to throw a Halloween party in the town's most notorious haunted house. Needless to say, all hell breaks loose in the form of a seductive demoness out to steal her virginal sister's soul. Possibly the only horror film in history to feature a "nunja" (that's ninja nun) as its hero — and it works! ★★½ $9.99

The Night of the Following Day

(1969, 93 min, US, Hubert Cornfield) A dated but intriguing drama about four professional criminals and their "foolproof" kidnapping scheme that goes horribly wrong when fate and human nature conspire against them. As the leader of the group, Marlon Brando (obviously in the middle of a bad hair day) drinks heavily from the method acting well, and is outshined by Richard Boone, who gives a splendid performance as a sadistic psychopath. Rita Moreno and Jess Hahn round out the nefarious group. Pamela Franklin also stars as their helpless victim. ★★½ $89.99

The Night of the Generals

(1966, 148 min, GB, Anatole Litvak) Peter O'Toole and Omar Sharif star in this WWII thriller about a Nazi intelligence officer hot on the trail of a psychotic general suspected of murdering prostitutes. Over-the-top performance by O'Toole makes a laughable script interesting. The supporting cast includes Tom Courtenay, Donald Pleasence and Philippe Noiret. ★★ $9.99

The Night of the Hunter

(1955, 93 min, US, Charles Laughton) This enigmatic suspense thriller is the distinguished actor Charles Laughton's sole directorial effort; and he succeeds magnificently. A dreamlike, disturbing fable in which two children are pursued by a madman, The Night of the Hunter is full of haunting images. The psychotic preacher with L-O-V-E and H-A-T-E tattooed on his knuckles is chillingly portrayed by Robert Mitchum and the black-and-white cinematography is incredibly lyrical. ★★★★ $19.99

Night of the Iguana

(1964, 118 min, US, John Huston) In this expertly acted film version of Tennessee Williams' steamy Broadway play, Richard Burton, Ava Gardner and Deborah Kerr give stellar performances as participants in a love triangle in a small Mexican resort town. Burton plays a defrocked priest-turned-bus tour guide who becomes involved with young nymphette Sue Lyon, sexually repressed Kerr and fiery hotel proprietor Gardner (who is stunning in possibly her best screen portrayal). Grayson Hall (TV's "Dark Shadows") received an Oscar nomination for her stirring portrait of Lyon's lesbian guardian who engages Burton in a psychological battle for her soul. ★★★ $19.99

Night of the Living Dead

(1968, 96 min, US, George A. Romero) The foremost fright film ever. On a ghoulish summer night in Pittsburgh, decomposing corpses return to life to devour the living. Graphically gruesome and morosely funny, this gem established director Romero as a master of the genre. ★★★★ $9.99

Night of the Living Dead

(1990, 95 min, US, Tom Savini) Makeup master Savini directs this color remake of George Romero's black-and-white horror classic. It's virtually shot-for-shot. The only difference is that Barbara, the catatonic female lead from the original, is now in the Sigourney Weaver-Linda Hamilton school of film heroines. Ironically, the film loses some of its tension in color; but nevertheless delivers the goods. ★★½ $14.99

Night of the Shooting Stars

(1982, 106 min, Italy, Paolo & Vittorio Taviani) A fascinating probe into the collective consciousness of post-war Italy. Filtered through the memory of a woman whose childhood was spent during the period, it is the tale of the war's closing days in a small Italian town. Poetic, enthralling and magnificently crafted. (Italian with English subtitles) ★★★½

Night on Earth

(1991, 125 min, US, Jim Jarmusch) Director Jarmusch explores the subculture of the taxi cab with this enchanting series of five offbeat vignettes set respectively in Los Angeles, New York, Paris, Rome and Helsinki; each centering around a cabbie and their fare(s). The film features an international all-star cast of Gena Rowlands and Winona Ryder (L.A.); Armin Mueller-Stahl, Giancarlo Esposito and Rosie Perez (N.Y.); Béatrice Dalle and Isaach de Bankolé (Paris); Roberto Benigni and Paolo Bonacelli (Rome); and Matti Pellonpää, Kari Väänänen and Sakari Kousmanen (with names like that, where else but Helsinki?). While each of the stories is entertaining, the standouts are Mueller-Stahl and Esposito's hilarious cultural collision in the New York episode and Benigni's outrageous portrayal of a loopy Italian who speeds around Rome in the middle of the night while wearing dark sunglasses and entertaining himself with an endless series of one-liners. (Filmed in English, French, Italian and Finnish with English subtitles) (Available letterboxed and pan & scan) ★★★½ $14.99

The Night Porter

(1974, 115 min, Italy, Liliana Cavani) Few films equal the unrelenting intensity of Cavani's disturbing drama. Years after surviving sexual imprisonment under a Nazi stormtrooper, a woman inadvertently encounters her former torturer/lover working as a night porter at a Viennese hotel. Despite their reversed positions of power, they ultimately reenact their sadomasochistic roles in a gruesomely lecherous dance of death. (Filmed in English) ★★

Night Shift

(1982, 106 min, US, Ron Howard) Howard's directorial debut produced this funny comedy about a fast-talking city morgue assistant (Michael Keaton in his debut) who turns his

Armin Mueller-Stahl in *Night on Earth*

workplace into a bordello. Also starring Henry Winkler and Shelley Long. ★★★ $9.99

The Night Stalker

(1971, 73 min, US, John Llewellyn Moxey) An immensely enjoyable made-for-TV vampire tale (the pilot for the short-lived TV series) with Darren McGavin as a hard-boiled investigative reporter who unearths a story about a modern-day bloodsucker terrorizing Las Vegas. The film successfully combines the style of a 1940s noir mystery with comedy and horror; and McGavin is tops as the cynical journalist. ★★★ $9.99

The Night They Raided Minsky's

(1968, 99 min, US, William Friedkin) A fine comic romp heralding the infamous days of Burlesque, with Jason Robards as a vaudeville comic who becomes involved with Pennsylvania Dutch girl Britt Ekland. The film captures the flavor of the bawdy comics and comely strippers, and provides a fascinating glimpse of life both on- and offstage during this bygone era. Norman Wisdom is especially good as a stage comic, and Bert Lahr also stars, though he died mid-production and a double was used in certain scenes. ★★★½ $19.99

Night Tide

(1963, 84 min, US, Curtis Harrington) Inspired by Val Lewton's Cat People and starring a baby-faced Dennis Hopper, this surreal fantasy tells the story of a young sailor (Hopper) who falls in love with a strange woman posing as a mermaid in a seafront carnival. She believes herself to be a descendant of the "sea people" who must kill during the full moon. This moody chiller features a fine supporting cast that includes Luana Anders (Dementia 13) and Roger Corman regular Bruno Ve Sota, fine black-and-white cinematography and a special cameo by Ed Wood, Jr.'s rubber octopus from Bride of the Monster, who's seen wrestling with Hopper during a nightmare sequence. ★★★ $19.99

A Night to Remember

(1958, 123 min, GB, Roy Baker) A first-rate drama about the infamous night the luxury liner Titanic hit an iceberg and sank in the freezing waters of the Atlantic, killing over

1,500 passengers and crew. Kenneth More, exceptional as the ship's captain, heads a highly competent cast including Honor Blackman, David McCallum and George Rose. A riveting, meticulous production told in semidocumentary style, which only adds to the overall authority of the film. ★★★★ $14.99

Night Train to Munich

(1940, 95 min, GB, Carol Reed) Long unavailable on home video, Reed's thrilling reworking of Hitchcock's *The Lady Vanishes* is a pleasure to watch. A spy/chase thriller of the highest order, it tells the story of a pair of undercover agents (Rex Harrison and Paul Henried) who are both after a prominent industrialist and his daughter (Margaret Lockwood). Bouncing back and forth from Germany to England and in-between, the plot is full of captures, escapes and recaptures. Most movies are content with one or two nail-biting sequences: this is full of them. Even the somewhat dated comic relief of a pair of English comics (Basil Radford and Naunton Wayne) is welcome; their tension-filled one-liners perfectly reflect the audience's anxiety. From the titular train ride to the climax on a mountaintop cablecar, the film is suspenseful from start to finish. The beginning of the film also deftly interweaves stock footage of German armies advancing across the European continent to reinforce the feeling of desperate isolation it tries to give its heroes. ★★★★ $24.99

Night Train to Venice

(1993, 98 min, Italy/Germany, Carlo U. Quinterio) Beware the film extricated from the vaults when its leading man becomes a star! That's the warning label that should be slapped on each and every box of this excruciating psychothriller starring heartthrob *du jour* Hugh Grant. Trying to pass itself off as stylish through a mishmash (nay, a cacophony!) of images, *Night Train...* assaults the viewer for 98 minutes with an endless parade of meaningless drivel about a group of skinheads terrorizing the Orient Express on its way to Venice. Ultimately, through unabashed and silly symbolism, the film makes the assertion that Nazis are associated with the "devil" and those fighting them are bound to God! Malcolm McDowell tries to keep a straight face portraying a thinly veiled Mephistopheles. Save this for the film class on how *not* to make a movie. ★ $9.99

The Night Walker

(1964, 86 min, US, William Castle) Barbara Stanwyck (in her last theatrical feature) and real-life ex-hubby Robert Taylor star in this tense psychological thriller. Stanwyck portrays a wealthy widow who has strange recurring dreams about her lost husband. The $1.99 special effects during the dream sequences and *Psycho* author Robert Bloch's mind-numbing screenplay help to do for Barbara what *Trog* did for Joan Crawford, which easily could explain her quick leap to TV and "The Big Valley." The film does have its moments, though. ★★½ $14.99

The Night We Never Met

(1993, 99 min, US, Warren Leight) Fans of sweet romantic comedies should enjoy this delightful surprise from writer-director Leight. The comings and goings of three strangers who time-share a New York apartment without meeting sets the stage for a very entertaining comedy of convenient coincidence – i.e. light on convincing plot, heavy on funny lines and scenes. Matthew Broderick delivers a droll yet engaging performance as a heartbroken would-be gourmet chef. Annabella Sciorra, as a semi-happily married dental hygienist, and Kevin Anderson, as a loutish, immature stockbroker, shine as Broderick's mystery roommates. The three contrasting lifestyles provide spark as does the supporting cast which includes Justine Bateman and Jeanne Tripplehorn who, as Broderick's performance artist "ex," nearly steals the show. ★★★ $9.99

Night Zoo

(1987, 117 min, Canada, Jean-Claude Lauzon) A schizophrenic film if there ever was one – is it a darkly violent crime thriller or a heartwarming human drama of the rapprochement of a man with his father? The film focuses on both themes and suffers for it. After being released from prison, Marcel, an angry punk of questionable sexuality, tries to readjust to life on the outside but his efforts are thwarted by two sleazy gay cops. While Marcel is getting into hot water with thugs and lowlifes, he also tries to reach out to old dad; you know, the one with the whizzing ticker. Set in a dark and dangerous Montreal, the film's action sequences are exciting, but generally the film bogs down when it deals with the sappy familial angle. (French with English subtitles) ★★½

Nightbreaker

(1989, 100 min, US, Peter Markle) Martin Sheen and son Emilio Estevez star in this gripping thriller about lethal government testing. Sheen and Estevez play the same character – in the 1950s and the 1980s – a doctor who was involved in atomic experiments in the Nevada desert using – and endangering – American military personnel. Also with Lea Thompson and Melinda Dillon. ★★★ $9.99

Nightbreed

(1990, 93 min, GB, Clive Barker) Barker's second feature, based on his novella "Cabal," is as ambitious as his first feature *Hellraiser* but falls short in its execution. Hidden away in a deserted cemetery is a mythical civilization of ghoulish outcasts: both friend and foe, they are a formidable presence. A young man, Boone (Craig Sheffer), has horrific visions of these creatures and in an act of poor judgment seeks treatment from a creepy psychiatrist (played by David Cronenberg), who frames Boone for a series of killings he himself is committing. Boone is killed and then reincarnated as one of the Nightbreed, a race of underground monsters who are readying themselves for battle against their human oppressors. Though Barker's inten-

tions are good, and the story is a nice metaphor for any marginalized group (and probably a reconstruction of Barker's growing up a fantasy-loving, artistically minded gay youth in straightlaced Britain), the film is sluggish and meandering, and the director fails to create any palpable suspense. However, the design and execution of the creatures are excellent. ★★

The Nightcomers

(1972, 96 min, US, Michael Winner) Tired thriller which attempts to hint at why the children of Henry James' "The Turn of the Screw" became the way they did. Marlon Brando is a sadistic and sexually abusive gardener who serves as perverse mentor; Stephanie Beacham is the governess involved in a kinky relationship with Brando. The sexual aspect of the film predates the similarly themed Brando film *Last Tango in Paris*, but lacks that classic's detailed character development or cinematic stylization. ★★

Nighthawks

(1981, 99 min, US, Bruce Malmuth) The suspense is riveting in this little-seen police thriller starring Sylvester Stallone and Billy Dee Williams as a pair of New York cops on the trail of a ruthless international terrorist. Rutger Hauer shines as the terrorist Wulfgar, in a role which prefigures his sadistic killer in *The Hitcher* five years later. Also starring Persis Khambatta and Lindsay Wagner. Even Stallone's presence can't ruin this gem of a film. ★★★ $14.99

The Nightmare Before Christmas

(1993, 74 min, US, Henry Selick) This enchanting animated musical bears the trademark of its producer Tim Burton, for it's a daring and imaginative entertainment. Made in cooperation with and released by Disney studios, *Nightmare* features the best in stop-motion animation to tell the tale of Jack Skellington and his fellow inhabitants of Halloweentown who band together to bring their own special ghoulish flavor to Christmas. Kidnapping Santa Claus, Jack takes over the reins of Santa's sleigh and delivers a holiday to remember. Determinedly dark and decidedly funny, *Nightmare* boasts a devilishly playful score by Danny Elfman, and the voices of Elfman, Catherine O'Hara, Chris Sarandon

The Nightmare Before Christmas

and Paul Reubens bring to life these wonderfully macabre characters. ★★★½ $14.99

A Nightmare on Elm Street

(1984, 91 min, US, Wes Craven) When the psychosexual desires of young girls come out in their dreams, the result is a blood-crazed apparition with razor sharp, phallic-like talons. This is surely one of the most frightening films of the 1980s, due primarily to its inventive premise of this villain literally escaping from the victims' minds, rather than from the local insane asylum. ★★★ $9.99

A Nightmare on Elm Street, Pt. 2

(1985, 87 min, US, Jack Sholder) The second entry in the *Elm Street* saga is the weakest of the series. It's five years later, and Freddy is back trying to possess a teenage boy in order to continue his murderous ways. ★½ $9.99

A Nightmare on Elm Street 3: Dream Warriors

(1987, 96 min, US, Chuck Russell) One of the most popular of the *Nightmare* series, this imaginative and sometimes wickedly funny sequel has Freddy back tormenting more hapless teens, here being cared for by Heather Langenkamp from the original. Robert Englund, of course, returns as Mr. Krueger, and Dick Cavett and Zsa Zsa Gabor appear in cameos. ★★★ $9.99

A Nightmare on Elm Street 4: The Dream Master

(1988, 92 min, US, Renny Harlin) You can't keep a good mass-murderer-from-beyond-the-grave down. Freddy returns once again to wreak havoc on poor, unsuspecting teenagers. Very stylish, with a few good scares. Director Harlin would go on to direct the explosive *Die Hard 2*. ★★½ $9.99

A Nightmare on Elm Street 5: The Dream Child

(1989, 89 min, US, Stephen Hopkins) Freddy Krueger goes surreal. Freddy teams up with an unborn child to continue his murderous ways. Good visuals but not much more. ★★ $9.99

Nights of Cabiria

(1957, 110 min, Italy, Federico Fellini) This Academy Award-winning film is a grim but very moving drama from Fellini's early career. The film lacks the flash and fantasy of the director's later films but has a power and intensity that is sadly lacking in his final works. This is a poignant tale of a naive prostitute who searches for love and fulfillment in every man she meets. The waifish streetwalker is wonderfully portrayed by Giulietta Masina. The story would form the basis for the musical *Sweet Charity*. (Italian with English subtitles) ★★★★

Nijinsky

(1980, 125 min, GB, Herbert Ross) Ross, who scored a major triumph with *The Turning Point*, once again turns to the world of ballet with this expertly acted, rather melodramatic but intriguing biography about the legendary dancer Nijinsky (George de la Pena) and his professional and private relationship with his mentor/lover Sergei Diaghilev (impressively

played by Alan Bates). Supporting cast includes Leslie Brown, Colin Blakely, Jeremy Irons, Janet Suzman, and Alan Badel in an outstanding performance as a wealthy patron of the arts. ★★½ $14.99

9½ Weeks

(1986, 113 min, US, Adrian Lyne) Mickey Rourke and Kim Basinger star as two SoHo yuppies who meet by chance and quickly find themselves entangled in a highly erotic sadomasochistic relationship. Rourke is well-cast as the domineering, slightly sinister commodities broker who draws Basinger, a sexy art dealer, into a series of kinky, sex-for-sex's-sake adventures. Whether in a back alley or a clock tower, the heat from these attractive actors is enough to make the screen sweat, though not enough to produce a totally comprehensible film. ★★½ $19.99

Nine Months

(1995, 102 min, US, Chris Columbus) This occasionally funny but always obvious comedy stars the now-inevitable Hugh Grant as a reluctant father-to-be who loses the woman he loves (Julianne Moore) before realizing that, damn it, there's nothing better than "family values." Director Columbus' cloying tribute to masculinity follows on the heels of earlier box office successes *Mrs. Doubtfire* and *Home Alone*, but claims none of the pacing, style or humor of either film. Sadly, brilliant actress Moore (*Vanya on 42nd Street, Safe*) is relegated to playing second fiddle and the film fails to showcase her talents. Comic relief comes from Jeff Goldblum, Tom Arnold, Joan Cusack, and the always overstated Robin Williams. ★★ $14.99

976-Evil

(1988, 89 min, US, Robert Englund) Robert Englund (alias Freddy Krueger) directed this effective horror outing about an outcast teenager (Stephen Geoffreys) who acquires demonic powers thanks to a 976 phone number. ★★½ $14.99

9 to 5

(1980, 110 min, US, Colin Higgins) Jane Fonda, Lily Tomlin and Dolly Parton proved to be a formidable team in this amusing and topical hit comedy. Three secretaries get even with their sexist, insensitive boss (Dabney Coleman); and raise office efficiency and productivity to new highs in his absence. Tomlin's cartoon fantasy sequence is a hilarious highlight. ★★½ $9.99

1918

(1985, 89 min, US, Ken Harrison) Two-time Academy Award-winning screenwriter Horton Foote (*To Kill a Mockingbird, Tender Mercies*) adapted his own play about the frustrations and loss of innocence of a small Texas town during the final months of WWI. Extremely well-acted, this somber story is a little too leisurely paced, which sometimes distracts from the heartfelt dramatics. Starring Matthew Broderick, William Converse-

Nitrate Kisses

Roberts and Hallie Foote. (A sequel followed, *Valentine's Day*.) ★★½

1984

(1984, 115 min, GB, Michael Bradford) After watching this excruciating, but unequalled, version of George Orwell's classic novel, one may well be expected to seek counseling. Gripping performances by John Hurt, Richard Burton (in his last screen appearance) and Suzanna Hamilton along with impressive production design and grainy, muted cinematography, power this overwhelming and gloomy depiction of Orwell's futuristic nightmare world. A harrowing film experience. ★★★ $14.99

1941

(1979, 118 min, US, Steven Spielberg) Although labeled as Spielberg's first "flop," this epic WWII comedy is definitely not the dud it was proclaimed to be. Over-produced as it may be (it's the *It's a Mad, Mad, Mad, Mad World* of the '70s), there are some very funny sequences in this story of wartime hysteria in Los Angeles. The film is highlighted by great special effects, and an all-star cast including John Belushi, Dan Aykroyd, Treat Williams, Tim Matheson and Nancy Allen. ★★½ $14.99

1900

(1977, 234 min, Italy, Bernardo Bertolucci) Bertolucci examines the intertwined lives of Robert De Niro and Gérard Depardieu, both born on the same day at the turn of the century; one to a landowner, one to a peasant household. This grand, sweeping yet personal epic follows them through the rise of Fascism in Italy, and beyond. Studded with exceptional performances, among them: Dominique Sanda, Donald Sutherland, Burt Lancaster and Sterling Hayden. (English-language version) ★★★½

1990: The Bronx Warriors

(1983, 84 min, Italy, Enzo G. Castellari) So this is what they thought 1990 would look like back in 1983. It's after the bomb and local thugs take on corporate evil-doers. With Vic Morrow, Christopher Connelly and Fred Williamson. ★ $19.99

1969

(1988, 93 min, US, Ernest Thompson) A good cast featuring Kiefer Sutherland, Robert Downey, Jr., Winona Ryder and Bruce Dern is mostly the reason to see this sincere though dramatically impotent teen drama set against the backdrop of the '60s anti-war protests. ★★

90° South

(1933, 72 min, GB, Herbert G. Ponting) A spellbinding chronicle of Captain Robert Scott's heroic but ultimately tragic race for the South Pole – not only did Norwegian explorer Amundsen reach the goal first, but Scott and his entire expedition died on the trip. Originally released in 1913, photographer Herbert G. Ponting remade the film in 1933, adding narration taken from the journal found next to Captain Scott's frozen body. ★★★ $39.99

99 Women

(1969, 90 min, Spain/West Germany/GB/Italy, Jess Franco) The women-in-prison genre gets the European "art" treatment in this lurid drama set in a bizarre, fortress-like castle on a Mediterranean island. Sexy, scantily clad women are hauled to prison and are greeted by a hellish superintendent (Mercedes McCambridge). Inside, they are abused and succumb to injustices until the inevitable breakout. The usual ingredients of the genre are present: beautiful women, cat fights, lots of skin and sex, and a veritable hotbed of lesbian encounters. Ridiculous, though enjoyable trash. ★

92 in the Shade

(1976, 91 min, US, Thomas McGuane) McGuane (*Cold Feet*) adapted and directed this flavorful version of his acclaimed novel. Peter Fonda plays a fishing boat captain who finds romance and rivalry in the Florida Keys. Margot Kidder, Burgess Meredith, Warren Oates and Harry Dean Stanton round out this well-cast drama. ★★★ $59.99

Los Niños Abandonados

(1974, 65 min, Colombia/US, Danny Lyon) This unbelievably depressing documentary is a slice-of-life story of the brutal living conditions of the young orphans of Bogata, Columbia, who, abandoned by the State and ignored by the people, are forced to eke out their existence on the streets. The filmmaker follows several of the boys through their daily activi-

Anthony Hopkins and Joan Allen are Richard M. and Pat in *Nixon*

ties: begging for money and food, playing amid the rubble of the slums and swimming in a nearby stream. An unrelenting and harrowing portrait that offers little hope for either the children or society. For unlike other films of similar theme (*Pixote, Streetwise* and *Los Olvidados*), this film fails in achieving an empathy with and compassion for the children as well as explaining the social reasons responsible for this sad situation. (Spanish with English subtitles and English narration) ★★½

Ninotchka

(1939, 110 min, US, Ernst Lubitsch) The ads read "Garbo laughs," and so she does in Lubitsch's witty and captivating comedy. As a rigid Russian agent, Comrade Greta risks honor and career when she falls for Paris and playboy Melvyn Douglas. Impeccable direction from Lubitsch, and scintillating dialogue co-written by Billy Wilder. ★★★★ $19.99

The Ninth Configuration

(1979, 115 min, US, William Peter Blatty) Before he retreated back to familiar territory with *The Exorcist III*, author Blatty made an impressive directorial debut with this creepy, surrealistic adaptation of his novel "Twinkle, Twinkle, Killer Kane." Stacy Keach plays a psychiatrist treating a group of military outcasts at an isolated mental hospital. A sometimes funny and very disturbing psychothriller. ★★★ $14.99

Nitrate Kisses

(1992, 63 min, US, Barbara Hammer) Thematically returning to her seminal short film on lesbian sexuality, *Dyketactics*, Hammer's first feature film challenges the viewer with her thoughts on the loss of queer history as well as an unapologetic foray into both lesbian and gay sensuality and sexuality. The story begins with a short biography of writer Willa Cather, a presumed lesbian who destroyed all her personal records before her death. With this willful destruction of historical information, Hammer explores the life and sex of several older lesbians and makes a plea for gays and lesbians to record and rediscover their own history. And all this set against some amazingly queer blues songs. *Kisses* is a demanding yet lyrical documentary and filmgoing experience. ★★★ $39.99

Nixon

(1995, 190 min, US, Oliver Stone) If moviemaking is this century's conveyance of contemporary folklore, *Nixon* mythologizes a historical figure deeply imbedded over decades in the American consciousness. And few personalities elicit such polar extremes of reaction as President Richard Milhous Nixon, a deeply conflicted man with true world vision yet bogged down in consuming, petty hatreds and beset by driving personal demons. He was a man who left his imprint, for better *and* worse, on the 20th century's political landscape. Anthony Hopkins approaches the formidable task of portraying a public figure whose every vocal inflection is known by millions with a consummate actor's creation of a multilayered, contradictory and often baffling personality, a man as inherently discordant as the reactions he provokes. Stone's technical

filmmaking expertise exploits the innermost soul of an individual against the backdrop of a nation's psyche; if you hold his political interpretation as indulgence, you must allow an auteur's sure hand at his medium. In support, Joan Allen stands out as Pat Nixon, the one person who saw it all yet was least seen by the public eye. ★★★½ $19.99

No Escape

(1994, 118 min, US, Martin Campbell) A slumming Ray Liotta stars in this futuristic action-thriller, sort of *Escape from New York* meets *Lord of the Flies*. After killing his superior officer, ex-soldier Liotta is sent to a secret island prison where he's caught between two warring factions. He reluctantly joins forces with Lance Henrikson and the more "civilized" prisoners in their fight against Stuart Wilson (playing a flamboyantly evil leader) and his band of cutthroats. Gory and not without a few thrills, *No Escape* is a by-the-book adventure story which should satisfy any action fan searching for a brainless two hours. ★★½ $14.99

No Fear, No Die

(1992, 97 min, France, Claire Denis) Denis' follow-up to the popular *Chocolat* is a gritty, ugly and surprisingly slow-moving tale of the underground world of cockfighting. Dah and Jocelyn are two trainers who work for a sleazy club owner and his wife. What ensues is a tangled web of deceit and greed between the four characters. Unfortunately, the film spends too much time depicting disturbingly graphic scenes of cockfighting and not enough time developing the relationships between the characters and the metaphorical values of the cockfights. An excellent cast (including Isaach de Bankolé and Solveig Dommartin) and great cinematography cannot overcome the underdeveloped script. End titles claim that no animals were injured or killed, but you be the judge. (French with English subtitles) ★★ $29.99

No Highway in the Sky

(1951, 98 min, GB, Henry Koster) Giving the kind of performance that has endeared him to movie audiences for decades, James Stewart is in top form as an absent-minded scientist whose investigation into the structural weaknesses of a new airplane turns him into a one-man crusader. As an expatriate American living in England, Stewart's airplane researcher tries to convince his superiors that a crash is imminent. As he sets off to prove his theory, he finds himself on one of the doomed aircraft. The film nicely balances benign comic episodes with a story both suspenseful and gripping. Marlene Dietrich costars in a part not unlike herself, that of a cynical, famous movie actress – she's made-to-order and nearly defines the word glamorous. Glynis Johns is also very appealing as a stewardess who falls in love with Stewart. ★★★ $19.99

No, I Have No Regrets

(1973, 75 min, GB, Michael Houldey) The indomitable spirit and mesmeric talents of the legendary French singer and songwriter Edith Piaf are showcased in this captivating musical biography. From her beginning singing on the back streets of Pigalle through her rise to international stardom, Piaf's life was anything but

Z

ordinary. The film features many performances as well as exploring the diminutive Piaf's tumultuous private life which entranced the people of France for over 20 years. Interviewed are several of her friends (Eddie Constantine) as well as a former husband (Yves Montand) who all recount anecdotes on the beloved pop songstress who tragically died at age 43 in 1965. Narrated in English and produced for the BBC, the film should delight fans and win over more than a few converts. Please note that the video is taken from a 16mm print, with the result being below average quality. ★★★½

No Man of Her Own
(1950, 98 min, US, Mitchell Leisen) Barbara Stanwyck's gripping performance distinguishes this seductive, moody noir melodrama. Surviving a train crash and on the lam, Stanwyck assumes the identity of a woman who, about to meet her deceased husband's family for the first time, is killed in the accident. Taken in by the family, Stanwyck's newfound happiness is short-lived, however, as a blackmailing ex-boyfriend enters the picture. Though the plot and execution of the drama is pure soap opera, Stanwyck's gutsy portrayal makes it all the more involving. (Remade as the French film I Married a Shadow) ★★★

No Man's Land
(1987, 107 min, US, Peter Werner) An undercover rookie cop (D.B. Sweeney) investigates a charming high-class car thief (Charlie Sheen) and finds himself being seduced by the deadly, fast-paced world of money, power and corruption. ★★ $14.99

No Mercy
(1986, 105 min, US, Richard Pearce) Routine police thriller benefitting from the teaming of Richard Gere and Kim Basinger. Gere plays an undercover cop who investigates the murder of his partner, leading him to the sultry, mysterious Basinger. ★★ $9.99

No Regrets for Our Youth
(1946, 111 min, Japan, Akira Kurosawa) This, the master's first major work, an epic drama of feminist self-discovery, is set in 1930s Japan — a time of growing nationalism and right-wing militarism. Yukie, a vivacious young woman, falls in love with her father's most outspoken left-wing law student. She gives up a life of ease to move to Tokyo and support his dangerous antiwar activities, only to see him executed for espionage. Her own life undergoes an amazing transformation after his death as she retreats to the countryside of her ancestors to begin a new life, alone. (Japanese with English subtitles) ★★★½

No Skin off My Ass
(1990, 85 min, Canada, Bruce La Bruce) The onslaught of New Queer Cinema (Swoon, Poison, The Living End among them) continues with this wry, low-budget and sexually explicit comedy about a punkish hairdresser who, in an homage to Robert Altman's That Cold Day in the Park, becomes obsessed with a tough-looking but shy skinhead. Filmed in grainy black and white and blown up from Super-8, the story opens when the coiffeur (who also

narrates) invites the seemingly lost, baby-faced skinhead home. Sort of a fag version of the beautiful and near-catatonic Joe Dallesandro in Trash, the skinhead passively and diffidently accepts his offers of a bubblebath and a place to live. Rounding out the cast of characters is the skinhead's lesbian sister who gets cheap thrills by undressing her brother in front of her friends. While the gay sex is hardcore at times, it is also romantic. The film was the victim of censorship in both England and its native Canada (the film was seized by the Morality Squad of Toronto and charged with three violations: bondage, nudity, and the sucking of toes!). ★★★½ $39.99

No Surrender
(1986, 100 min, GB, Peter Smith) This no-holds-barred satire examines (and skewers) the political and religious passions that are rife in today's England. Three busloads of senior citizens descend on a seedy Liverpool nightclub for their New Year's Eve celebration. They add to the already volatile mix of Irish Protestant loyalists, Irish Catholics, punks and an inept magician (Elvis Costello) to make the laconic manager's evening a nightmare. The film hilariously dives into the fray and observes the pitiful state of human relations. ★★★½

Paul Newman is Nobody's Fool

No Time for Sergeants
(1958, 119 min, US, Mervyn LeRoy) Andy Griffith, repeating the acclaimed stage role which brought him prominence, gives a wonderful performance as bumpkin Will Stockdale, the Georgia farmboy who takes the U.S. Air Force (after Will gets finished that's U.S. Air Farce) by surprise. Full of down-home, folksy humor, the story revolves around the series of misadventures which befall Will and his co-horts, including Nick Adams and Murray Hamilton. Don Knotts, who would team with Griffith a few years later on TV, repeats his stage role with a funny turn as camp psychiatrist. ★★★ $14.99

No Way Out
(1987, 116 min, US, Roger Donaldson) Complex political thriller starring Kevin Costner as a naval officer who is assigned to the Pentagon. There he becomes involved with his boss' mistress, leading to murder and political cover-up. Gene Hackman, Sean Young and Bill Paxton also star. Remake of the 1948 film noir classic The Big Clock. (Letterboxed version sells for $19.99) ★★½ $14.99

No Way to Treat a Lady
(1968, 108 min, US, Jack Smight) Rod Steiger gives a bravura performance in this extremely well-done thriller as a psychopath who uses various impersonations to make contact with his victims. George Segal is the cop on the case, and Lee Remick is caught between them. ★★★½ $14.99

Noa at Seventeen
(1982, 86 min, Israel, Isaac Yeshurun) It is 1951, and Noa, a 17-year-old girl, struggles for autonomy as the ideological debate over the future of kibbutz socialism tears her family apart. Should she finish high school or follow her youth movement friends to kibbutz? Will Israel's labor movement follow Moscow blindly or turn its attention to the West? This sophisticated allegory penetrates the very essence of the bond which fused the personal and political in the early years of the state. (Hebrew with English subtitles) ★★ $79.99

Nobody's Daughter
(1976, 90 min, Hungary, Laszlo Ranody) Csore is an eight-year-old orphaned girl who is adopted by a poor farming family. However, her chance for happiness is thwarted as the family is only interested in their government allocation. Running away from their cruelty to search for her real mother, Csore finds herself, once again, back at the orphanage. When she is adopted by a rich family, she is treated even worse. It is young Csore's struggle to overcome the odds against her which makes for a poignant, heartbreaking tale of courage and resilience. (Hungarian with English subtitles) ★★★ $59.99

Nobody's Fool
(1994, 101 min, US, Robert Benton) Paul Newman's superlative performance distinguishes this excellent and at times humorous character study of an aging rambler who tries to piece together the loose ends of his life. In one of his most accomplished screen portrayals, Newman plays Sully, a sixty-ish handyman with a bum leg who lives in a small New York town. Divorced and estranged from his family, this lothario who refuses to acknowledge the passing of time has been seemingly content with both odd jobs thrown his way and his own meager existence. But when he is reunited with his son and forced to reexamine his life, Sully's soul-searching leads to magnificent, introspective dramatics. An exceptional supporting cast includes Bruce Willis as Newman's shifty boss; Melanie Griffith as Willis' wife; Jessica Tandy as Newman's landlady; and Gene Saks as a one-legged lawyer. Based on Richard Russo's novel and skillfully adapted by director Benton, Nobody's Fool is a grand, intimate day-in-the-life which pays trib-

The classic crop-dusting scene in
North by Northwest

ute to the ordinary in a most extraordinary way. ★★★★ $14.99

Noir et Blanc

(1986, 80 min, France, Claire Devers) This understated yet bizarre drama, adapted from Tennessee Williams' "Desire and the Black Masseur," deals with an increasingly intense sadomasochistic relationship between two men. Infused with oblique "meaning" and sexual ambiguity, and strangely compelling, the black-and-white tale begins when a mousy but not unattractive white accountant begins working at a health club. Seemingly heterosexual (he has a girlfriend), the shy man begins taking advantage of the gym's perks, especially the free massages given by a silent, muscular black masseur. Their sessions begin to take on violent elements, resulting in damaged skin and broken bones; but the two participants, unable to break away from the intoxicating relationship, continue their fatal dance of violence. A dark story of a curious, passionate relationship with an ending designed to shock. ★★½ $79.99

Noises Off!

(1992, 101 min, US, Peter Bogdanovich) If ever video could provide a deserving film a second chance, this is it. Bogdanovich must have been sure that this screen adaptation of Michael Frayn's hilarious, Tony Award-winning farce was going to fire up his directorial comeback. And by all rights it should have, but for some reason audiences stayed away from this superbly directed, well-acted and screamingly funny romp. Michael Caine heads an all-star ensemble of actors, including Carol Burnett, John Ritter, Christopher Reeve, Denholm Elliott, Marilu Henner, Nicolette Sheridan, Julie Hagerty and Mark Linn-Baker. Together, they form the cast and crew (with Caine as director) of an incestuous touring company of an English drawing room farce. Following Frayn's script nearly to the letter, the action proceeds through three acts in which we see the play first at rehearsal, then a side-splitting view of a performance from backstage and finally a full performance in which all of the company's foibles and sexual trysts result in complete utter confusion. ★★★½ $9.99

Nomads

(1986, 95 min, US, John McTiernan) From the director of *Die Hard* comes this imaginative but flat chiller with Pierce Brosnan as the inevitable victim of ghoulish phantoms; Leslie-Anne Down is the psychiatrist who tries to help him, only to experience first-hand his ordeal. ★★

Nomigi Pass

(1979, 154 min, Japan, Satsuo Yamamoto) The abuses and brutal conditions of Japan's silk mills of the early 1900s are brought to realistic life in this memorable drama. The story follows a group of young girls who are hired to work in the mills and the hardships, loves and tragedies they must endure. (Japanese with English subtitles) ★★★

None But the Brave

(1965, 106 min, US, Frank Sinatra) Ol' Blue Eyes directs and stars in this tale of two enemy platoons, one American and one Japanese, who find themselves stranded on a remote island in the Pacific at the height of World War II. Lots of war film clichés, though Sinatra gives an especially appealing performance. Clint Walker, Tommy Sands and Tony Bill costar. ★★ $14.99

None But the Lonely Heart

(1944, 113 min, US, Clifford Odets) It is ironic that Cary Grant, a peerless comedian whose impeccable comic timing would create upteen comedy classics, received his only two Oscar nominations for dramas. One of these is Clifford Odets' moody melodrama set in the 1930s about a Cockney drifter who returns home to look after his dying mother. Ethel Barrymore won an Oscar as Grant's mum. ★★★ $14.99

Norma Rae

(1979, 113 min, US, Martin Ritt) Sally Field won an Oscar (and newfound respect) for her triumphant portrayal of a Southern mother and textile worker who defies the abusive management of her company and organizes a union. Ron Liebman plays the New York labor organizer who introduces Field to the idea, and Beau Bridges is her husband who feels the neglect and ostracism of his wife's activism. Based on a true story. ★★★½ $9.99

Normal Life

(1996, 108 min, US, John MacNaughton) MacNaughton (*Henry: Portrait of a Serial Killer*) directed this fact-based crime drama about a white-trash couple who turn to crime to solve their financial and marital woes. Luke Perry's surprisingly persuasive performance and Ashley Judd's dead-on, energetic portrayal go a long way toward making these unappealing characters sympathetic. The screenplay is less successful, offering spotty characterizations and obvious satire. It's the powerful acting and strong direction that make this of interest. Though not as effectively disturbing as *Henry*, *Normal Life* does display the director's deft touch with uncomfortable scenes of rage and violence. By turns witty, stupid, sexy, annoy-

ing, thrilling and flat, this mixed bag is, in the end, a well-made TV movie-of-the-week with hot sex and strong violence. ★★½ $96.89

The Norman Conquests I, II, & III

(1980, 108/93/100 min, GB) British playwright Alan Ayckbourn's brilliant comic trilogy goes beyond the standards of your average drawing room farce by presenting the same story from three different rooms in a country manor. Tom Conti establishes himself as a comic genius with his performance as the lustful Norman, who foppishly charms and cajoles his way into the hearts of his wife's two sisters. The trilogy comes on three tapes which are to be rented separately. ★★★★

Norman, Is That You?

(1976, 92 min, US, George Schlatter) This gay sex farce tries to have it both ways — making fun of faggots while espousing a what-will-be-will-be sexual philosophy — and the result is a surprisingly inoffensive and politically incorrect comedy. The story revolves around Norman (Michael Warren), a handsome black man who lives with Garson (Dennis Dugan), his cute, swishy white lover in West Hollywood. Trouble brews when Norman's father, and eventually his mother (Redd Foxx, Pearl Bailey), land at the doorstep of their presumedly straight son. The film's dialogue is at time funny despite some lame jokes, stupid stereotypes and a regular lexicon of innocuous gay name-calling. Wayland Flowers and his sassy puppet Madam add to the campy humor. ★★½ $19.99

Norman Loves Rose

(1982, 98 min, Australia, Henri Safran) Carol Kane is very good as the wildly attractive sister-in-law of a 14-year-old boy who develops a tremendous crush on her. A little fooling around was nice, but problems arise when Kane becomes pregnant — and the father is not her husband! ★★½ $69.99

North

(1994, 87 min, US, Rob Reiner) *North*, the story of a child who "divorces" his parents and searches for new ones, is too close in theme to *Irreconcilable Differences* to be original. And its execution is part sentimental and part *Naked Gun*, and the two don't mix. Evidently it was doomed from the start. Elijah Wood plays North, whose search takes him around the world. On the way, he meets the likes of Dan Aykroyd, Jon Lovitz and Bruce Willis. Much like Dorothy in *The Wizard of Oz*, he soon realizes he was better off at home but has difficulty getting there. Though the reason for North leaving France is hilarious, the film is a misfire no matter where on Earth it's set. ★½ $19.99

North by Northwest

(1959, 136 min, US, Alfred Hitchcock) Hitchcock returns to his favorite theme of an innocent man falsely accused in this terrifically exciting, funny and suspenseful thriller. Cary Grant is the epitome of cool sophistication as a Madison Avenue ad executive mistaken for a spy. James Mason is a perfect villain and Eva Marie Saint is the perennial icy blonde beauty. Classic Hitchcock touches include the crop-dusting scene and the Mt. Rushmore finale. ★★★★ $19.99

North Dallas Forty

(1979, 119 min, US, Ted Kotcheff) An entertaining, perceptive football comedy following the careers (on and off the field) of NFL players Nick Nolte and Mac Davis. Great cast includes Charles Durning, John Matuszak, Bo Svenson and Dabney Coleman; and Davis makes an impressive screen debut. ★★★ $14.99

The North Star

(1943, 106 min, US, Lewis Milestone) Involving WWII drama about the efforts of a small Eastern Russian village who fight off the invading Nazis. Written by Lillian Hellman. Stars Dana Andrews, Anne Baxter, Walter Huston and Erich von Stroheim. ★★★ $39.99

North to Alaska

(1960, 122 min, US, Henry Hathaway) Sprawling comic western with John Wayne, Stewart Granger, Fabian, Capucine and Ernie Kovacs prospecting for gold in our northernmost state. Kovacs is particularly good as a con man out to fleece partners Wayne and Granger. ★★★ $14.99

Northern Exposure

(1991/92, 46 min, US, Peter O'Fallon/Rob Thompson) What can one say about a TV series which makes consistent reference to the likes of Jung, Nietzsche, Kafka and other literary and philosophical giants? Refreshing and thought-provoking are adjectives which come to mind. While the series was not without its ups and downs, many episodes stand out for their inventiveness and sheer amusement value. Set in a small town in Alaska, the show revolves around a group of quirky characters, most notably Dr. Joel Fleischman (Rob Morrow), a young doctor from New York City who is indebted to the state for his medical education. $14.99 each

Aurora Borealis: A cleverly written episode which revolves around Chris (John Corbett), the town's existential redneck D.J., who is obsessed with a massive sculpture he is trying to complete when into his life comes a young, black tax accountant from Portland. The two immediately discover a bizarre psychic connection between them which culminates in a hilarious shared dream sequence. This episode also introduces Adam (Adam Arkin), a legendary Bigfoot-like being who turns out to be quite human (and a great cook). ★★★★

Cicely: We learn of the roots of the town, founded at the turn of the century by a lesbian couple (Jo Anderson and Yvonne Suhor – a truly radical notion for a highly rated TV show). All of the regular actors portray their alter egos from their arrival in a lawless backwater to the transformation of it into a flourishing center of the arts and intellectual activity. This episode is one of the show's finest hours. ★★★★

Seoul Mates: The show focuses primarily on die-hard patriot, former astronaut Maurice Minnefield (Barry Corbin) and his reaction when a young Korean man shows up claiming to be his son. Corbin portrays one of the more realistically complex characters in an ensem-

ble of well-conceived roles, and the range of emotion he demonstrates in this situation resonates. ★★★½

Thanksgiving: The distinctly Anglo holiday comes to Cicely, Alaska – a remote town populated largely by Native Americans with their own good-natured but serious take on what Thanksgiving represents. The town newcomer, hard-core New Yorker Joel Fleischman (Rob Morrow), experiences the holiday from another perspective – as an unwilling participant in a ritual which involves throwing tomatoes. In a series noted for being intelligent, amusing and offbeat, this particular episode stands out. ★★★★

Northern Pursuit

(1943, 94 min, US, Raoul Walsh) Errol Flynn does his part as a Canadian Mountie who hunts a crashed Nazi pilot through the wilderness. Exciting in places, but nothing out of the ordinary. ★★½ $19.99

Nosferatu

(1922, 63 min, Germany, F.W. Murnau) Murnau's "symphony of horror" was the first, and most macabre, of the film versions of the legendary vampire, Count Dracula. Max Schreck's loathsome count, with his bald head, rodent face, long pointed ears, skeleton-like frame and talons will chill the most callous viewer. (Silent with musical soundtrack) ★★★½ $29.99

Nostradamus

(1994, 118 min, US, Roger Christian) Born into a Europe ravaged by plague and the persecution of the Inquisition, physician Michel de Nostradame garnered a reputation as a mystic and seer, acquiring fervent enemies and attracting powerful friends from the monarchy and from secret societies of learning. The rabid suppression of knowledge by the establishment religion necessitated that information be passed in secrecy, under sworn oaths of silence. This workmanlike exposition of Nostradamus' life and times is enhanced by beautiful cinematography and exquisitely detailed period costume. A fine ensemble includes Rutger Hauer, Amanda Plummer and F. Murray Abraham; and as Nostradamus, Tcheky Karyo has no trouble carrying the film with arrestingly modulated intensity. Though the film opens slowly, it's worth a bit of patience; the viewer is amply rewarded. ★★★ $19.99

Not Angels But Angels

(1994, 80 min, Czech Republic/France, Wiktor Grodecki) The world of male prostitutes in the recently democratized Czech Republic is the lurid subject of this absorbing, nonjudgmental talking-heads documentary

The incomparable Max Schreck in *Nosferatu*

(that throws in shots of hard-core pornography as well). With either rap or somber classical music playing in the background, the director interviews more than ten boys, ranging in age from 14 to 19 years old, who work the train station, discos and streets of Prague. They answer questions about their family background (most come from broken homes), how they got their start selling themselves, what they do to a john and for how much, whether they consider themselves gay or not (50/50), their fear of AIDS, and what their aspirations are. The boys' responses offer a fascinating glimpse into a seldom seen world – although one gets the uncomfortable feeling that both the viewer and the filmmaker are involved as well in the exploitation of these vulnerable young men. ★★★ $39.99

Not as a Stranger

(1955, 136 min, US, Stanley Kramer) After a distinguished career as a producer, Stanley Kramer made his directorial debut with this sometimes compelling version of the Morton Thompson novel. The story traces the career and private life of dedicated but impersonal medical student Robert Mitchum who, about to be kicked out of medical school for lack of tuition, marries nurse Olivia deHavilland to finance his education. Frank Sinatra costars as Mitchum's med school roommate. and Charles Bickford is especially good as a country doctor with whom Mitchum partners. The film is at its best when concentrating on Mitchum's professional life, featuring some gripping doctor-patient scenes. It is standard soap opera, however, when not in the office or hospital. ★★½ $19.99

Not for Publication

(1984, 87 min, US, Paul Bartel) Cult favorite Bartel takes on the tabloids in this offbeat tale of muckraking journalism and political scandal. Nancy Allen is a moonlighting reporter who discovers her boss, the incumbent mayor of New York, at an orgy she is assigned to cover. David Naughton, Laurence Luckenbill and Alice Ghostley also star. ★★½ $69.99

Not of This Earth

(1988, 80 min, US, Jim Wynorski) This remake of one of Roger Corman's great trashy movies is now slightly trashier as teen porn performer Traci Lords keeps her pants on (but not her top) in her legit debut. Rent the original. ★ $14.99

Not without My Daughter

(1991, 117 min, US, Brian Gilbert) Sally Field stars as an American mother, married to an Iranian husband, who becomes trapped in Iran when they visit his family for a two-week vacation. Two years later, after being forced to endure the oppressive Islamic life, she tries to escape with her daughter back to America. Based on a true story, the film nevertheless indulges cultural stereotypes, though Field gives an impassioned performance which heightens the story's intrigue. ★★ $9.99

Notebook on Cities and Clothes

(1990, 80 min, France, Wim Wenders) Ostensibly a documentary about Japanese fashion designer Yohji Yamamoto, this Wenders film is really a reflection on art and the creative process. Filmed in and around Paris, the filmmaker and designer engage the viewer in contemplation about the nature of visual communication and the creation of images. The opening sequence establishes the nature of the inquiry with narration which ponders the believability of photographs and other images in the digital age. ★★★ $59.99

Notes for an African Orestes

(1970, 75 min, Italy, Pier Paolo Pasolini) This fascinating look at the artistic process of one of the world's most daring and creative filmmakers is, simply put, a cinematic notebook. We follow Pasolini as he treks around East Africa scouring remote villages and crowded marketplaces for raw footage and discusses all of the possibilities for what he hoped would be a production of "The Orestia." Aeschylus' myth is truly one of the materpieces of ancient Greek theatre and Pasolini's idea was to set the story in a rapidly modernizing Africa as a grand allegory for the painful and awkward period of development which swept through the Third World in the 1960s. For fans of Pasolini, this will prove to be a mesmerizing and poetic view of underdevelopment and the quest for modernization which plagues the Third World today. (Dubbed) ★★★½ $29.99

Nothing in Common

(1986, 130 min, US, Garry Marshall) Bittersweet comedy-drama with Tom Hanks as an advertising exec caught in the middle of his parents' separation. Jackie Gleason gives a terrific performance as Hanks' gruff father, and Eva Marie Saint nicely plays his mom. ★★★

Nothing Sacred

(1937, 75 min, US, William Wellman) The delightful Carole Lombard, a small town girl, thinks she's dying of a rare disease and is turned into the "Sweetheart of New York" by scheming reporter Fredric March. This riotous and cynical battle-of-the-sexes classic was written by Ben Hecht. Presented in three-strip Technicolor for the first time on video, and digitally remastered from archive prints. ★★★½ $24.99

Notorious

(1946, 101 min, US, Alfred Hitchcock) Romance and intrigue are the ingredients in this Hitchcock thriller set in post-war Brazil. American secret agent Ingrid Bergman marries an elderly spy (Claude Rains) to gain information on Nazi activity. Cary Grant is her contact in Rio and her partner in a seething love affair. Grant and Bergman are ravishing, but it is Rains who steals the show. ★★★½ $9.99

The Notorious Daughter of Fanny Hill

(1966, 74 min, US) In this audaciously adult grade-Z "no budget" nudie film, super-sexy Stacey Walker stars as Kissy Hill, the teenage offspring of Fanny. Tutored in the art of love-making and other bedroom games, she goes on to play hanky-panky with the best of them (the Duchess of Roxbury and the Marquis de Sade included). ★★

La Notte

(1961, 120 min, West Germany/Italy, Michelangelo Antonioni) Antonioni's exploration of noncommunication, boredom and inpenetrable loneliness features Jeanne Moreau and Marcello Mastroianni as a troubled married couple who have stopped understanding each other and themselves. Set in one night in Milan, this unforgettable mood piece is classic Antonioni. (Italian with English subtitles) ★★★

Nous N'Irons Plus au Bois

(1982, 88 min, France, George Dumoulin) During the Spring of 1944 in a Nazi-occupied forest in northern France, a Resistance group of several Frenchmen hold out. Their unity and purpose are put to the test when they come upon several German deserters. The group is divided on whether they are indeed deserters, and if they are, what should they do with them? (French with English subtitles) ★★★

Now and Then

(1995, 96 min, US, Lesli Linka Glatter) Essentially a derivative, inferior female *Stand by Me*, *Now and Then* features four inseparable friends who obsess over a dead body, with all of this set against an (obtrusive) oldies soundtrack. Demi Moore, Melanie Griffith, Rosie O'Donnell and Rita Wilson get together for the birth of the latter's baby; this is the cue for the flashback to the childhood summer which cemented their friendship. Like Rob Reiner's sweet-natured coming-of-age film, not a lot happens to the four protagonists. The basic plot is the girls' determined efforts to get to the mystery of a deceased boy, whose spirit they think they've brought back to life. And their journey of discovery includes themselves, as well. But whereas *Stand by Me* was punctuated by subtle direction and a marvelous screenplay, *Now and Then* only offers the infrequent but admittedly amusing observation of adolescence. The four young actresses (especially Christina Ricci and Gaby Hoffmann) are personable and endearing; their adult counterparts have very little to do. ★★ $19.99

Now Voyager

(1942, 117 min, US, Irving Rapper) Bette Davis received a Best Actress nomination for her portrayal of a lonely spinster who, with the help of a caring analyst, changes from an ugly duckling to a high-flying swan. Claude Rains and Paul Henreid also star as the doctor and love interest, respectively. Bette's stunning transformation, memorable dialogue and a lush Max Steiner score highlight this classic tearjerker. ★★★½ $19.99

Nowhere to Run

(1992, 95 min, US, Robert Harmon) Jean-Claude Van Damme attempts to do something different in this film: act. Trying to show off his sensitive side as an escaped convict, he befriends a family being coerced by evil land developers into selling their land. Van Damme's acting is low-key to say the least. Rosanna Arquette plays the lonely widowed mother and Kieran Culkin (Macaulay's younger brother) is actually quite good as her son. The film starts off well enough, but suffers from extreme predictability and dull action sequences. It's a disappointing action film even for fans of the "Muscles from Brussels." ★½ $14.99

Nude on the Moon

(1961, 78 min, US, Doris Wishman) B-grade nudist camp flick about a pair of rocket scientists who fly to the moon and discover it populated with half-naked "moon dolls," sporting pipe cleaner antennae growing out of their bouffant hairdos. ★ $19.99

Nueba Yol

(1996, 104 min, Dominican Republic, Angel Muñiz) Never certain why, a recent widower feels compelled to leave behind the comforts of his friends and home in the Dominican Republic to make a success of himself in New York City. Needless to say, a workable definition of "success" is not to be learned on *those* mean streets. Warm and funny, *Nueba Yol* is also honest and real, recalling the best cinema can be: full of life in all its joyfulness and sorrow. Like Renoir or Ozu, director Muñiz lets the camera quietly eavesdrop on people too genuine to be giving performances, a rarity these days when too much of world cinema looks to emulate the latest from a Hollywood grown out of touch. (Spanish with English subtitles) ★★★½ $19.99

La Nuit de Varennes

(1982, 133 min, Italy/France, Ettore Scola) Scola's brilliant historical drama is set in 1791 on the night of Louis XVI and Marie Antoinette's flight from Paris. First-hand witnesses to the revolution against the ancient regime include the ribald Restif (Jean-Louis Barrault), the aging Casanova (Marcello Mastroianni), Thomas Paine (Harvey Keitel), and a lady-in-waiting (Hanna Schugulla). (French with English subtitles) ★★★½

Number Seventeen

(1932, 83 min, GB, Alfred Hitchcock) This strange and entertaining comedy-thriller about jewel thieves is first set in a spooky abandoned house and concludes with an exciting cross-country chase involving a hijacked train, a bus, a ferry and lots of water. ★★★ $9.99

The Nun (La Religieuse)

(1965, 140 min, France, Jacques Rivette) From Rivette, director of the cult classic *Celine and Julie Go Boating* (which is *not* on video), comes this intensely somber drama about a young woman who suffers physical and psychological anguish at the hands of her family, a religious order and society. Set in 18th-century France, the film stars the beautiful Anna Karina as Suzanne, who, unable to marry because of the lack of a dowry, is sent unwillingly to a convent. Lacking a calling for the religious life, Suzanne stubbornly refuses to take her vows which results in her being beaten and semi-starved. After being transferred to another convent where its Mother Superior attempts to entrap her in a lesbian relationship, she escapes; but she soon finds that her new freedom leads only to more suffering. Banned by the French government for its "anticlerical" stance, this unsentimental film is uncompromising in presenting a world bereft of compassion and understanding. (French with English subtitles) ★★★ $59.99

The Nun's Story

(1959, 149 min, US, Fred Zinnemann) Excellent adaptation of the Kathryn Hulme novel following the life of a young novice from the convent to service in the Belgian Congo. Audrey Hepburn is simply magnificent as the dedicated nun, who endures great hardships working with doctor Peter Finch (in an admirable performance) in the jungle. A fine supporting cast includes Edith Evans, Peggy Ashcroft, Dean Jagger, Mildred Dunnock,

The Nun

Patricia Collinge, Beatrice Straight and Colleen Dewhurst. ★★★★ $19.99

Nuns on the Run

(1990, 90 min, GB, Jonathan Lynn) Ex-Python Eric Idle and veteran BBC-TV comic Robbie Coltrane are great together as entry-level gangsters who find themselves wanted by both the police and the mob. After they are set up and marked for murder by "Mr. Big," they turn the tables and run off with the mob's ill-gotten booty; and in the process cross a rival gang, as well. Where do the boys choose to hide out? In the nearest convent, naturally. Donning habit and attitude, they masquerade as two novices, and proceed to turn the well-ordered order upside-down. Lighthearted, mindless fun. ★★½ $19.99

The Nutcracker: The Motion Picture

(1984, US, Carroll Ballard) The magical music and joyful dance of Tchaikovsky's legendary holiday ballet "The Nutcracker Suite" is brought to the screen in this production designed by Maurice Sendak and performed by the Pacific Northwest Ballet. $9.99

The Nutcracker

(1993, 96 min, US, Emile Ardolino) Box-office champ Macaulay Culkin suffered his first financial bomb in his role as the Nutcracker Prince in this screen version of ballet's Christmas favorite. Staged at SUNY Purchase by Peter Martins, the film is unimaginative, even dull; its biggest problem being its straightforward shooting which stagnates the action and does not utilize the possibilities of opening up the play. ★★ $19.99

Nuts

(1987, 116 min, US, Martin Ritt) Based on Tom Topor's stage hit, this highly successful courtroom drama features one of Barbra Streisand's most accomplished dramatic performances. Streisand plays a high-priced prostitute on trial for murdering a john; however, while she insists it was self-defense, her family petitions to have her certified mentally incompetent. Richard Dreyfuss is terrific as the lawyer who defends Streisand's right to a trial. With Maureen Stapleton, Eli Wallach, James Whitmore and Karl Malden. ★★★ $14.99

Nuts in May

(1976, 84 min, GB, Mike Leigh) Alison Steadman stars with Roger Sloman as a young couple on holiday in East Anglia. A pair of highly compulsive, vegetarian neatniks, they check into a campground for some communing with nature, but immediately come into conflict with their neighbors. The film

A transformed Eddie Murphy in *The Nutty Professor*

lazily meanders with them as their well-planned holiday slowly unravels. ★★ $29.99

The Nutty Professor

(1963, 107 min, US, M. Gerald Lewis) Fifty million Frenchmen can't be wrong. This is *the* Jerry Lewis film for those who don't like Jerry Lewis (let's see hands). Mild-mannered professor Lewis becomes lounge lizard Buddy Love thanks to a potion he quaffs accidentally. Lots of brilliant sight gags and a good use of color give proof that this is a director in control of his medium. (Remade in 1996 starring Eddie Murphy) ★★★ $14.99

The Nutty Professor

(1996, 95 min, US, Tom Shadyac) This hilarious remake of the 1963 Jerry Lewis semiclassic is a twofold success: Eddie Murphy has finally delivered on the promise he demonstrated in *48 HRS.* and *Trading Places*, and — a rarity — a remake is worthy of (and possibly better than) the original. Murphy plays Sherman Klump, a brilliant, 400-pound chemistry professor. Clumsy, lonely though very likable, Sherman is supervising a DNA experiment to curb obesity which he tries on himself after meeting lovely associate Jada Pinkett. Sherman's Mr. Hyde turns out to be Buddy Love, a slim, attractive, testosterone-driven alter ego who is so over the top Murphy almost seems to be doing a self-parody of his own image. *The Nutty Professor* is consistently funny complete with humorous sight gags, snappy dialogue and good special effects: it's rollicking good fun. Murphy is splendid, playing seven parts including four family members at a convulsive dinner; but it's his creation of Sherman which sustains the comedy. The actor is never condescending nor does he go after the easy, cheap joke. Even behind the extraordinary makeup, Murphy's comic luminance shines through. ★★★ $19.99

O Lucky Man!

(1973, 173 min, GB, Lindsay Anderson) Anderson's mammoth and brilliant allegory stars Malcolm McDowell as a latter-day Candide, buoyed by optimism in a sea of sham and corruption. A young coffee salesman pushes his way to the top only to fall and rise and fall yet again. A tremendous score is provided by Alan Price and sparkling support by Arthur Lowe, Ralph Richardson and Rachel Roberts. ★★★★ $24.99

O.C. and Stiggs

(1987, 95 min, US, Robert Altman) Altman has long been known for a frantic style of filmmaking in which his camera seems to eavesdrop on the frenzied proceedings of inexplicably insane characters. In the cases of M*A*S*H and Nashville, this style readily lent itself to creating scathing satires filled with social and political content. Now Altman attempts the teen comedy. The spirit of revolution runs deep in this one, folks, but Altman's flourish can't save this meaningless yarn about a couple of kids whose passion in life is to humiliate a wealthy insurance tycoon and his family while skipping to the beat of King Sunny Ade. ★★

The Object of Beauty

(1991, 101 min, US/GB, Michael Lindsay-Hogg) John Malkovich and Andie MacDowell are an American couple living at an expensive London hotel. Their financial crunch leads them to an insurance swindle – only before they are able to institute the hoax, someone beats them to it. A very low-key comedy with few laughs, and two rather annoying people as the principal characters. ★★½ $9.99

Objective, Burma!

(1945, 142 min, US, Raoul Walsh) Errol Flynn leads a familiar ragtag unit of soldiers into the Burmese jungle to destroy a Japanese stronghold. The film scored well with wartime American audiences as a rather suspenseful first-rate morale booster. But across the sea, our British allies were less-than-enthusiastic as the film ignores the contributions of the Allied forces, including the long-suffering British 14th Army, which had spearheaded the Burmese campaign. Still, a well-made, if jingoistic, war story. ★★★ $19.99

Oblomov

(1979, 140 min, USSR, Nikita Mikhalkov) This delightful social satire and sensitive character study of a likable but lazy aristocrat was adapted from the 1859 Russian novel by Ivan Goncharov. Oblomov, a good-natured and indolent landowner in Czarist Russia who has never worked a day in his life, decides that he has no reason for getting out of bed and finds himself in a melancholy stupor and paralyzed with lethargy. While a procession of friends fail to change his slothful ways, it is his passionate love for a woman named Olga that energizes him and gives the man a new lease on life. (Russian with English subtitles) ★★★ $59.99

Observations under the Volcano

(1983, 82 min, US, Christopher Blackwood) An engrossing behind-the-scenes look at the making of John Huston's 1984 film Under the Volcano, shot in Mexico. Includes interviews with stars Albert Finney and Jacqueline Bisset, members of the crew and, of course, larger-than-life director John Huston.

Obsession

(1976, 104 min, US, Brian De Palma) De Palma's elegant thriller is one of the most underrated films of the 1970s, largely because it is always unjustly relegated to the category of "Hitchcock rip-off." Cliff Robertson stars as a man who feels responsible for the death of his wife in a kidnapping tragedy and seeks to resurrect her in the form of another woman (Genevieve Bujold, in a dual role). Sound familiar? Don't be misled. True, the film owes a great deal to Hitchcock's Vertigo, but its strength lies in its ability to work independently as a mystery on its own merits. Also with John Lithgow. Magnificent score by Bernard Herrmann. ★★★½ $9.99

Occurrence at Owl Creek Bridge

(1962, 29 min, France, Roberto Enrico) Winner of both an Academy Award and the Grand Prix, this is an expert adaptation of the Ambrose Bierce short story about a Civil War soldier's short-lived escape from the hangman's noose. Brilliantly using every cinematic technique available to manipulate time and space, this is an oft-used example in film schools of how to do a literary adaptation. (In English) ★★★★

Ocean's 11

(1960, 127 min, US, Lewis Milestone) The "Rat Pack" is in full bloom in this enjoyable caper comedy. Frank Sinatra, Dean Martin, Sammy Davis, Jr., Peter Lawford and Joey Bishop come up with a foolproof plan to rob five Las Vegas casinos – at the same time! Also with Angie Dickinson and Cesar Romero. ★★★ $14.99

October
(Ten Days That Shook the World)

(1928, 99 min, USSR, Sergei Eisenstein) Commissioned to celebrate the tenth anniversary of the revolution, this stirring portrait of an entire nation set on the edge of change is taken from American John Reed's writings. Director Eisenstein had endless resources to make the film and with the virtual absence of any footage of the real events of 1917, this powerful epic is elevated into the realm of historical importance. (Silent with musical soundtrack) ★★★★ $29.99

Octopussy

(1983, 130 min, GB, John Glen) The 13th Broccoli Bond production found itself up against itself as Sean Connery returned to the role in the competing project Never Say Never Again. Roger Moore is confronted with several villains including the title character, played by Maud Adams, who may or may not be working for any one side at any moment. This isn't one of the better films in the series; though the stunts are adequate, and the customary

tongue-in-cheek humor is considerably low-brow. ★★½ $14.99

The Odd Couple

(1968, 106 min, US, Gene Saks) The laughs are plentiful in this first-class adaptation of Neil Simon's Broadway hit. Jack Lemmon and Walter Matthau are in great form as Felix and Oscar, the two most unlikely and mismatched roommates in New York City. ★★★½ $14.99

Odd Man Out

(1947, 113 min, GB, Carol Reed) Under cover after escaping from prison, James Mason plans a payroll heist to finance IRA operations. During its execution, he kills a man. In the process of escaping the scene of the crime, he briefly enters the lives of many people, eliciting a gamut of reactions and exposing a wide range of human idiosyncrasies. A perceptive examination of values and morality, incisively directed by Reed and with excellent performances by Mason, Kathleen Ryan, Robert Newton and Dan O'Herlihy. ★★★★

Odd Obsession

(1959, 110 min, Japan, Kon Ichikawa) Director Ichikawa's disturbing drama about the strained marital relations between an ex-beauty queen and her elderly husband who keeps himself going sexually with injections, jealousy and by taking photos of his nude, sleeping wife. The couple's twisted story has a surprise ending. (aka: The Key) (Japanese with English subtitles) ★★★

The Odessa File

(1974, 128 min, GB, Ronald Neame) Frederick Forsyth's best-seller comes to the big screen with Jon Voight as a German journalist who is on the track of Nazis in the early 1960s. Voight gives a solid performance which single-handedly elevates an otherwise muddled mystery. With Maximilian Schell and Derek Jacobi. Music by Andrew Lloyd Weber. ★★½

Oedipus Rex

(1967, 110 min, Italy, Pier Paolo Pasolini) Filmed in and around an awesome, 15th-century adobe city in the Moroccan desert, Pasolini's version of the Oedipus legend retain's the basic elements of Sophocles' classic tragedy. A young man, abandoned at birth by his parents, is foretold of his doomed fate by an oracle; nontheless, he unknowingly murders his father and marries his mother. This tragic story of a man's intractable road to his destiny shimmers with lavish costumes, bloody sword fights, sun-drenched locales and the expressive performances of Franco Citti and Silvana Mangano. (Italian with English subtitles) ★★★ $59.99

Of Human Bondage

(1934, 83 min, US, John Cromwell) This low-key treatment of the W. Somerset Maugham novel is enlivened by the striking presence of a truly luminous and effectively trashy Bette Davis. Leslie Howard is his usual earnest self as a failed artist turned medical student who becomes obsessed with Davis' aloof, uncaring waitress. A scandal ensued when Davis was overlooked as a Best Actress nominee – causing a massive write-in campaign and, some say, a consolation Oscar for Bette the following year. ★★★ $19.99

Of Human Bondage

(1964, 100 min, US, Ken Hughes) W. Somerset Maugham's celebrated novel of a doctor (Laurence Harvey) whose passion for a crude waitress (Kim Novak) leads to tragedy is given inferior treatment in this third screen adaptation. Stick to the 1934 Bette Davis version (unless you're really a fan of one of the two stars). ★★ $24.99

Of Mice and Men

(1992, 110 min, US, Gary Sinise) Coproducer, costar and director Sinise's retelling of John Steinbeck's classic novel is an absorbing, brilliantly acted film. Sinise stars as the world-weary drifter George, opposite John Malkovich's thoroughly convincing portrayal of the helpless man-child Lenny. Horton Foote's literary screenplay beautifully translates the novel to film. Heightened by marvelous supporting performances from Ray Walston, Joe Morton, Casey Siemaszko, Sherilyn Fenn and John Terry, *Of Mice and Men* ranks with *A Midnight Clear* as another excellent overlooked film of 1992. ★★★½ $19.99

Off Beat

(1986, 92 min, US, Michael Dinner) Judge Reinhold, who played the young officer in *Beverly Hills Cop*, is back in uniform — but with little success — as a New York library clerk who masquerades as a police officer to win the affection of policewoman Meg Tilly. ★★ $9.99

Off Limits

(1988, 102 min, US, Christopher Crowe) Senseless actioner with Willem Dafoe and Gregory Hines as two military policemen looking for a murderer in 1968 Saigon. ★ $14.99

An Officer and a Gentleman

(1982, 126 min, US, Taylor Hackford) Three outstanding performances by Richard Gere, Debra Winger and Lou Gossett, Jr. highlight this compelling romantic drama about a naval officer who begins an affair with a girl from the wrong side of the tracks. Gossett won an Oscar for his tough-as-nails performance as Gere's drill instructor. ★★★ $14.99

The Official Story

(1985, 112 min, Argentina, Luis Puenzo) 1985's Academy Award winner is a politically explosive and emotionally draining drama set in the tumultuous period after the Falkland's debacle. Norma Aleandro is mesmerizing as a comfortably middle-class woman who is determined to find out the truth about "los desaparecidos," the many people who disappeared during the military dictatorship. (Spanish with English subtitles) ★★★★ $19.99

Oh Dad, Poor Dad, Mama's Hung You in the Closet and I'm Feeling So Sad

(1966, 86 min, US, Richard Quine) Zany black comedy about a "typical" American family: a domineering mother, several Venus flytraps, piranhas, a weirdo baby-faced son, a lecherous baby sitter, and a father who happens to be a stuffed corpse hanging in

the closet. With Rosalind Russell, Robert Morse, Barbara Harris, Hugh Griffith and Jonathan Winters as "Dad." ★★½ $49.99

Oh, God!

(1977, 98 min, US, Carl Reiner) Pleasant family comedy with George Burns as The Almighty visiting Earth and summoning supermarket manager John Denver to spread His word. (Followed by two sequels) ★★½ $9.99

Oh! My Three Guys

(1994, 96 min, Hong Kong, Chiu Sung Kee) While Hollywood at best keeps gay/lesbian characters on the periphery, the burgeoning cinema of Hong Kong has been much more willing to include them into a film's story line — albeit with varying degrees of success and empathy. This touching comedy/melodrama goes one step further than the standard HK film by singularly focusing on the lives and loves of three young gay men who live together as roommates. Their stories involve spurned male lovers, AIDS, suicide, drag queens and a woman determined to change one of them. A shrill but entertaining and sensitive melodrama. ★★½ $89.99

Oklahoma!

(1955, 145 min, US, Fred Zinnemann) Sprawling though unremarkable film version of the landmark Rodgers and Hammerstein Broadway musical. Gordon MacRae and Shirley Jones are the youthful lovers; their romance interrupted by hired hand Rod Steiger. A great score complements the immortal Agnes de Mille dance sequences. Good supporting cast includes the always-fine Charlotte Greenwood, Gloria Graham as Ado Annie, and Eddie Albert. ★★★ $19.99

Okoge

(1992, 120 min, Japan, Takehiro Murata) Japan's teeming if still underground gay life is explored and celebrated in this pleasant story of the relationship between two gay lovers and the effervescent woman who befriends them. The story revolves around Goh, a young, self-employed man, and Tochi, an older married corporate worker. Their inability to find a suitable location for their lovemaking is solved by Sayoko, a naive young woman who inexplicably finds herself drawn to gay men. She offers her small apartment as a convenient love-pad. Funny but deceptively lighthearted, the film addresses the serious theme of homophobia which is pervading Japan. A note on the title: *Okama* is Japanese for a rice pot and a slang insult against gays; *Okoge* is the rice that sticks to the bottom of a pot and is Japanese for "fag hag." (Japanese with English subtitles) ★★★ $79.99

Old Boyfriends

(1977, 103 min, US, Joan Tewkesbury) Talia Shire stars in this bittersweet story of a woman who seeks out her past lovers in an attempt to learn more about herself. A mixed bag of romance and identity which is ambitious but

The Old Dark House

not always successful. Richard Jordan, Keith Carradine and John Belushi are her former flames. John Houseman and Buck Henry also appear. ★★

The Old Dark House

(1932, 72 min, US, James Whale) *It was a dark and stormy night...* Five weary travelers are stranded in the ancestral home of the Femm family. Horace Femm (Ernest Thesiger) is an athiest so frightened of God that he trembles at every thunderbolt. His sister Rebecca (Eva Moore) taunts him and their unwanted company with sermons against the sins of the flesh. Morgan, their mute and malevolent butler (Boris Karloff), is either their protector or prisoner, depending on his intake of gin. Whale has fashioned a sardonic comic essay on rot and decay, as intricate and delicate as a fugue. The film cunningly balances cheap thrills against metaphysical chills; Whale looks into the abyss, forces a laugh, and hides his anguish behind a witty bon mot. Among the superb ensemble, Charles Laughton, in his American film debut, gives a well-modulated performance as a loutish lord; Raymond Massey is the clueless sophisticate; and Melvyn Douglas is the war vet who already knows too much about death. ★★★½ $24.99

Old Enough

(1984, 91 min, US, Marisa Silver) Sarah Boyd and Rainbow Harvest star in this coming-of-age drama about two New York City girls, one from Park Avenue and the other from Brooklyn, who befriend each other. A meandering look at adolescence which can't overcome — despite accurate moments of insight — its stereotypes. ★★

Old Gringo

(1989, 119 min, US, Luis Puenzo) Jane Fonda, Gregory Peck and Jimmy Smits star in this period romance set against the backdrop of Pancho Villa's Mexican uprising in 1913. Fonda plays a spinster who travels south of the border, where she becomes involved with revolutionary Smits and writer Ambrose Bierce (played with perfection by Peck). Though the story lacks a coherent structure, it has an undeniable emotional power; and the chemistry between the three leads is palatable. Peck's soliloquy on love is a reminder of the power and excitement of great acting. ★★½ $9.99

The Old Gun

(1980, 141 min, France, Robert Enrico) Winner of three César Awards, this riveting drama stars Philippe Noiret and Romy Schneider. The story is set in World War II France where a Frenchman's huge estate is taken over by the Germans. The brutality of the Nazis result in his wife and child being murdered. Noiret's quiet life is forever destroyed which results in his methodical vengence against the killers. (Dubbed) ★★★

Old Ironsides

(1926, 111 min, US, James Cruze) Wallace Beery is as hammy as ever in this silent tale about Merchant Marines battling pirates in the early 1800s. Great action and great fun — even Boris Karloff in a small role. ★★★ $29.99

The Old Maid

(1939, 95 min, US, Edmund Goulding) Bette Davis plays to the hilt the role of an unwed mother who, after her boyfriend is killed in the Civil War, gives up her child to be raised by her cousin (Miriam Hopkins). It's an acting tour de force as Davis and Hopkins battle it out with each other over daughter Jane Bryan. ★★★ $19.99

Old Yeller

(1957, 83 min, US, Robert Stevenson) Life on a Texas farm, circa 1859, highlights this popular Disney tale of a boy and his dog, based on Fred Gipson's well-liked novel. With Tommy Kirk, Fess Parker and Dorothy McGuire. ★★★ $19.99

The Oldest Profession

(1967, 97 min, France/West Germany/Italy, Various) Six chronological stories, all directed and starring different artists, humorously probe the history of prostitution from prehistoric times to the present and beyond. The final segment, "Anticipation," by Jean-Luc Godard, is an especially good short film that speculates on aliens from outer space and their Parisian sex habits. (Dubbed) ★★½

Oleanna

(1994, 101 min, US, David Mamet) Granted, a play by Mamet about sexual harassment is kind of like letting the fox guard the chickens, but that's not what makes this examination of campus politics a failure. The problem is more dramatic in nature. Mamet's patented dialogue, brash and stacatto to the extreme, is usually what makes his plays so dynamic, but in this two-actor setting, it falls flat, ultimately rendering his characters unbelievable. The first act finds John (William H. Macy), an arrogant, self-serving college professor who is up for tenure, locking horns with Carol (Deborah Eisenstadt), a student who wants to know why she has failed his class. His career is put in peril in act two when she submits a scathing letter to the tenure review board full of accusations of impropriety. Mamet has conjured up the perfect white male "victim" — it turns

out, of course, that Carol is under the influence of a campus feminist group. But thankfully, John's character does not escape unscathed as he is shown to be truly a lout. Still, not since August Strindberg's "Miss Julie" has the stage or screen seen a woman more determined to ruin a man, just for the sake of doing it. ★½ $19.99

Oliver!

(1968, 153 min, GB, Carol Reed) This elaborate musical rendition of the Charles Dickens tale about a young boy swept into a gang of thieves is as close to flawless as a movie can get. Its frolicking score, splendid re-creation of 1830s London and an unforgettable performance by Ron Moody as the scurrilous Fagan helped win it five Oscars, including Best Picture and Best Director. A trifle long, the film nonetheless holds the attention of even young viewers throughout. ★★★★ $19.99

Oliver & Company

(1988, 72 min, US, George Scribner) While *Oliver & Company* will probably not acquire the classic status of so many Disney animated films, it is a strong and enjoyable entry into the family film arena. Loosely based on Dickens' "Oliver Twist," this version features Oliver as a tabby kitten lost in New York City. He is befriended by a gang of dogs engaged in working scams on behalf of Einstein, their bumbling human owner who is indebted to a villainous loan shark. Along the way, Oliver is adopted by a rich girl and plot twists ensue as Einstein tries to get the money to pay off his debt. Enlivened by the music of Billy Joel (who voices Dodger), the film benefits from a good ensemble, though Bette Midler steals the show as the snooty French poodle Georgette. ★★★ $29.99

Oliver Twist

(1948, 116 min, GB, David Lean) This brilliant adaptation of Charles Dickens' classic novel stands as the finest cinematic treatment

of all the screen versions to tell Dickens' story of a young orphan's adventures in 18th-century London. Alec Guinness gives a captivating performance as Fagin; and the remarkable cast includes Robert Newton, Francis L. Sullivan, Kay Walsh and a young Anthony Newley as the Artful Dodger. ★★★★ $19.99

Olivier, Olivier

(1991, 109 min, France, Agnieszka Holland) Olivier, a precocious nine-year-old coddled by his doting mother, one day mysteriously disappears without a trace. His family is torn apart by the loss, but are reunited six years later when a 15-year-old homosexual prostitute claims to be their long-lost son. The family, especially the mother, desperately wants to believe that this savvy teen is indeed the innocent of years past. As in the similarly themed *Return of Martin Guerre*, doubts soon emerge as to the true identity of the youth. This engrossing drama creates suspense as to why he disappeared, and tenderly unfolds a tale of a boy learning about love and trust. (French with English subtitles) ★★★ $19.99

Los Olvidados (The Young and the Damned)

(1950, 88 min, Mexico, Luis Buñuel) Buñuel's social protest film is set in a Mexico populated by juvenile delinquents, beggers, cripples and other physically and/or socially deformed characters. The story centers around a particular boy as he learns the skills of survival within an oppressive society. (Spanish with English subtitles) ★★★★

Olympia, Pts. 1 & 2

(1936, 220 min, Germany, Leni Riefenstahl) This magnificent account of the Berlin Olympic Games of 1936 transcends a typical documentary of a sporting event. Through imaginative use of editing and camera movement, as well as spectacular photography, Riefenstahl's film achieves its goal of being a Nazi propaganda film but more importantly, it

Los Olvidados

is a graceful, nonpolitical look at the majestic beauty of the athletes. (German with English subtitles) ★★★★

The Omen

(1976, 111 min, US, Richard Donner) Gregory Peck and Lee Remick star in this blockbuster thriller that set the trend in horror films for years to come. Peck and Remick play the newly appointed American ambassador to England and his wife, who unwittingly become the parents of the Antichrist, Damien. Billie Whitelaw also stars as the satanic nanny who stops at nothing to protect her charge. Definitely not for the squeamish. ★★★ $9.99

On a Clear Day You Can See Forever

(1970, 129 min, US, Vincente Minnelli) Based on the Broadway musical, this splashy if occasionally muddled adaptation stars Barbra Streisand as a woman who learns of a past life when under hypnosis. Yves Montand is her psychiatrist, who falls in love with her — only the woman she was, not the woman she is. Streisand gives a good performance in the "dual" role, though Montand is woefully miscast. Also with Bob Newhart, Larry Blyden and Jack Nicholson as Barbra's guitar-playing brother. Score by Alan Jay Lerner and Burton Lane. ★★½ $14.99

On Borrowed Time

(1939, 99 min, US, Harold S. Bucquet) This sentimental variation of *Death Takes a Holiday* is pure '30s corn, but underneath the folksy interplay there's a thoroughly intriguing fantasy at work. Death (played by Cedric Hardwicke) has just taken a married couple. And now he's set his sights on the rest of the family. This includes patriarch Lionel Barrymore, sweet-as-sugar grandmother Buelah Bondi, and an annoyingly precocious child (Bobs Watson). But Grandpa Barrymore has a trick or two in store for the Grim Reaper when he comes to call. ★★★ $19.99

On Common Ground

(1992, 70 min, US, Hugh Harrison) Using the format of a low-budget soap opera, this charming, funny yet politically savvy film chronicles the changing nature and maturity of a divergent group of denizens of the gay bar The Purple Parrot. We follow them from the pre-Stonewall time of naiveté and repression through the sex-filled disco days of the '70s and ending in the '80s where AIDS casts a shadow on them all. The acting sometimes falls short of being professional and the video production values are bare bones, but they prove to be of little importance as the earnestness of the cast and director shines through as they tackle a violent police crackdown, premature death, racism within the community, gay/lesbian rage and eventual political activism. The film is followed by a short documentary entitled *On Common Ground – The Real Story*. The 30-minute film is a series of interviews with older lesbian and gay activists who reminisce about "the life," the underground bar scene and police harassment in the 1940s through the '60s. ★★★ $14.99

On Dangerous Ground

(1951, 82 min, US, Nicholas Ray) Ray's second collaboration with producer John Houseman is this brilliant exposé of a tough, inner-city policeman (Robert Ryan) who falls prey to the violence of the urban jungle. So much so, that he is sent for a cooling off period to upstate New York where the real intrigue begins when he falls in with a blind woman (Ida Lupino) and her mentally retarded brother (Summer Williams). Bernard Hermann's score was reportedly his favorite. ★★★½ $19.99

On Deadly Ground

(1994, 100 min, US, Steven Seagal) In this pretentious and ridiculous eco-thriller, Steven Seagal's P.C. action hero asks several questions, such as "What is the essence of a man?" and "How much wealth is enough?" He should have been inquiring how to make a movie. In his directorial debut, Seagal plays a born-again environmentalist who takes on his former boss, an evil oil magnate (Michael Caine). But the best director Seagal and his writers can muster are one-dimensional heroes, cardboard villains, and a predictable story line. And actor Seagal couldn't be more wooden if he were a totem pole. Obviously, Seagal wasn't taking notes during the shoot of the exciting and highly entertaining *Under Siege*. ★ $14.99

On Golden Pond

(1981, 109 min, US, Mark Rydell) Both Katharine Hepburn and Henry Fonda received Oscars for their affecting, expansive performances in this thoughtful, sentimental comedy-drama. Fonda stars as Norman Thayer, an 80-year-old retired teacher preoccupied with death, whose birthday celebration only triggers his fear of old age and dying. Hepburn is Ethel, Norman's devoted wife, who dutifully contends with her husband's cantankerous moods and encompassing anxiety. Jane Fonda, in her only film appearance with her father, plays the couple's alienated daughter vying for her father's affection. ★★★ $14.99

On Her Majesty's Secret Service

(1969, 140 min, GB, Peter Hunt) Despite the fact that George Lazenby was an unimpressive, and very temporary, James Bond, incredible action and location photography make this one of the finest and most exciting entries in the series. The usual mayhem is given an unusual twist as Bond marries a Spanish contessa (Diana Rigg). (Available letterboxed and full-screen) ★★★ $14.99

On Moonlight Bay

(1951, 95 min, US, Roy Del Ruth) Comparisons to *Meet Me in St. Louis* are inevitable as this bright, wholesome musical has the same folksy (okay, corny if you must) charm as that Judy Garland classic. It also has Leon Ames as a father whose decision to move has disrupted his loving family. Doris Day plays a tomboy who acquires feminine ways when she meets new neighbor Gordon MacRea. Their course of true love is a rocky one, but it is tuneful; though Doris doesn't sing much since the accent is on comedy. Billy Gray does a nice turn on the mischievous youth, Rosemary de Camp is the mother, and Mary Wickes, as a wise-cracking maid, is a wel-

come addition to any household. It's sappy, but it's fun. ★★★ $19.99

On the Beach

(1959, 133 min, US, Stanley Kramer) One of the first films to seriously address the issues of a nuclear apocalypse, this first-rate adaptation of Nevile Shute's novel tells the tale of an American submarine crew who find themselves in Australia awaiting the fallout with the rest of the inhabitants. Gregory Peck, Ava Gardner, Fred Astaire (in his first dramatic role) and Tony Perkins star. ★★★½ $19.99

On the Town

(1949, 98 min, US, Gene Kelly & Stanley Donen) A grand, energetic and immensely enjoyable adaptation of the popular Broadway musical. With a score by Leonard Bernstein and a book by Betty Comden & Adolphe Greene, directors Kelly and Donen have opened up, with location shooting, this exuberant group of three sailors on a 24-hour pass, and of their romantic adventures in New York City. Kelly, Frank Sinatra and Jules Munchin are the men in uniform; and Vera-Ellen, Betty Garrett and Ann Miller are the women with whom they meet and fall in love. Includes "New York, New York" and "Come Up to My Place." ★★★★ $19.99

On the Waterfront

(1954, 108 min, US, Elia Kazan) Marlon Brando became a legitimate contender with this textbook study of Method acting. After he sings to the law about dockside corruption, the union mob comes down hard on him. Lee J. Cobb is the waterfront godfather, Karl Malden is the street-smart priest, Rod Steiger is Brando's spineless brother and Eva Marie Saint is the troubled girlfriend. A rare combination of a superlative ensemble, exact direction, topical story line and a brilliantly structured screenplay played out in a singular vision. ★★★★ $19.99

On Top of the Whale

(1982, 93 min, The Netherlands, Râùl Ruiz) Ruiz, a Chilean expatriate based in France, has produced over fifty films since 1968. This, his first available on video, is a demanding, complex and imaginatively photographed film, both unusually invigorating and a challenging entertainment. The bare bones plot outline is as follows: a Dutch anthropologist and his girlfriend meet up with Narcisso, an eccentric millionaire who claims to have the last survivors of a lost Indian tribe in his summer home in Patagonia. The three, along with the woman's daughter, travel to this bleak country house and there the anthropologist attempts to understand the Indians' bizarre language, a language consisting of one word, spoken with different inflections. With all of the characters arbitrarily switching from English, French, Spanish, German, Dutch and the cryptic Indian dialect, Ruiz has made an amusing exercise on the mysteries of language and communication. ★★★ $59.99

On Valentine's Day

(1986, 105 min, US, Ken Harrison) Writer Horton Foote's satisfactory prequel to *1918*. Set in a small texas town one year earlier, the film traces the emotional struggle and reconciliation of young Elizabeth (Hallie Foote), disowned by her family for marrying against their wishes. Matthew Broderick has a cameo, reprising his role as Elizabeth's brother. ★★½ $14.99

Once a Thief

(1991, 90 min, Hong Kong, John Woo) Fans of Woo won't want to miss this over-the-top comedy about a trio of Chinese art thieves. The action follows Chow Yun Fat (Woo's baby-faced lead man), Leslie Cheung (*Farewell My Concubine*) and Cherie Chung as sophisticated larcenists of European art treasures. Through flashbacks, we learn that the three were orphans together, raised under the watchful eye of two surrogate father figures: one a ruthless crime lord and the other a caring cop who constantly pushes them to go straight. The film's first hour, filmed on location in Paris, is at times insufferably uneven — one senses that Woo and his crew weren't well-suited to the demands of location shooting so far from their familiar Hong Kong. But the action explodes about halfway through when Chow and Cheung botch a job and wind up in a dizzyingly exciting chase scene, ultimately leading them back to Hong Kong where Woo turns to his patented knack for turning gut-wrenchingly violent action sequences into side-splitting laugh fests. (Cantonese with English subtitles) ★★★½ $39.99

Once Around

(1991, 115 min, US, Lasse Hallström) From the director of *My Life as a Dog* comes this endearing and offbeat romantic comedy, with Richard Dreyfuss and Holly Hunter reteaming after *Always* as mismatched lovers who marry and settle down. Danny Aiello and Gena Rowlands play Hunter's exasperated parents, at odds with their decidedly different, and same-age, son-in-law. Good performances help compensate occasional lapses in the script. ★★½ $9.99

Once Bitten

(1985, 93 min, US, Howard Storm) Atrocious comedy with vampire Lauren Hutton on the lookout for a virgin in present-day Los Angeles — having trouble finding one. Also with Jim Carrey and Cleavon Little. ★ $9.99

Once Upon a Forest

(1993, 71 min, US, Charles Grosvenor) Near Dapplewood Forest, a gas truck overturns and a young badger is overcome by the fumes leaking out. Her family is killed, the other animals have mysteriously disappeared and her three young friends, a mole, a hedgehog and a mouse, embark upon an adventure to find the herbs that will save her life. The animation is superb, the story line is engaging and the characters are very likable in this Disney-like tale. It shows the effects of humans on the forest and the pain of losing your family without being preachy or heavy-handed. ★★★ $14.99

Once Upon a Honeymoon

(1942, 116 min, US, Leo McCarey) Ex-burlesque queen Ginger Rogers marries Nazi spy Walter Slezak — only she's not aware of his true identity. However, reporter Cary Grant is, and he pursues them on their honeymoon to

Charles Bronson (in background) meets his welcoming committee in *Once Upon a Time in the West*

expose the German agent and rescue Rogers from possible assassination. A curious mix of adventure, drama and comedy from director McCarey. ★★½ $19.99

Once Upon a Time in America

(1984, 227 min, US, Sergio Leone) Leone's epic is a fascinating analysis of unyielding ambition, moral decay and the predatory nature of the past. Through an opium-induced haze, Robert De Niro traces the events of a lifetime led on the wrong side of the law. ★★★½ $29.99

Once Upon a Time in the West

(1969, 165 min, Italy, Sergio Leone) Expanding upon the plot line of *Johnny Guitar*, Leone and story collaborators Dario Argento and Bernardo Bertolucci produce a polemic that is stunning in its grandeur, funny in its cynical sense of humor — using the horse opera as a metaphor for all that is wrong with the American capitalist system. Henry Fonda had one of his greatest roles as one of the most cold-blooded killers in westerns ("I never trust a man who wears a belt with suspenders"). Charles Bronson is in fine form as "The Man with the Harmonica" out for revenge. Another brilliant score by Ennio Morricone. ★★★★ $29.99

Once Upon a Time...When We Were Colored

(1996, 112 min, US, Tim Reid) First-time director Reid has crafted an affectionate and richly textured portrait of life in a black community in 1940s Mississippi. At a time when the dominate white society provided no legal or moral recourse for prejudice and brutality, African-Americans bonded to nurture and protect themselves in an environment which institutionalized restrictions dictated by hate and fear. The psychological ramifications of this poisonous atmosphere are poignantly evoked by some trenchant performances from the able ensemble of actors. Seen through the eyes of a boy on the cusp of manhood, the film

is remarkable in its ability to convey the internal reality of its protagonists, to enable the viewer to see these people as they see themselves and the world around them. This warmly told story of strength and solidarity captures the special intonations of a particular time and place, with compassionate understanding of the people who inhabited it. ★★★½ $14.99

Once Were Warriors

(1995, 102 min, New Zealand, Lee Tamahori) At once searingly brutal and lyrically poetic, *Once Were Warriors* is an unflinching examination of one exceptionally strong woman's struggle to keep her family whole while battling a husband mired in drink and violence. In an unforgiving urban wasteland — where abandoned children live in rusted-out, abandoned cars, the state puts children into institutions, and women expect the brutality they invariably receive — the young still attempt to forge identities with purpose and dignity, despite all restrictions of class, race and economics. The performances are so vital and authentic that the film seems more documentary than drama; especially noteworthy are Rena Owen and Temuera Morrison as the parents, and the remarkable Mamaengaroa Kerr-Bell as 13-year-old Grace, the family's soul with love and in tragedy. Director Tamahori has crafted a potent and volatile exploration of one family's survival in an environment devoid of hope or expectation — as alien as Maori tattooing and as familiar as the exhaust fumes outside your window. ★★★★ $19.99

One Crazy Summer

(1986, 94 min, US, Savage Steve Holland) Though not as successful as his hilarious *Better Off Dead*, this crazy comedy is nonetheless an entertaining if uneven spoof with John Cusack as a teenager spending summer vacation in Nantucket — surrounded by a gang of wackos. Also starring Demi Moore, Bobcat Goldthwait and Curtis Armstrong. ★★½ $19.99

One Day in the Life of Ivan Denisovich

(1971, 100 min, GB, Caspar Wrede) An earnest, literate adaptation of Alexander Solzhenitsyn's epic novel about life in a Siberian labor camp during the early 1950s. Though a difficult book to translate to film, director Wrede has crafted a mesmerizing look at the hardships of a prisoner serving the last years of a ten-year sentence. In the title role, Tom Courtenay is nothing short of brilliant. Beautiful cinematography by Sven Nykvist. ★★★½ $19.99

One False Move

(1992, 105 min, US, Carl Franklin) This film's opening 10 minutes are so violently disturbing that it's enough to make one stop viewing it. However, stick with this one for *One False Move* is an intense, original thriller. The story follows a gang of three ruthless Los Angeles drug dealers who, having raided their rivals, make off with a bag full of cash and blow, and hit the road for Arkansas in search of a place to lie low. Waiting at the other end are Dale "Hurricane" Dixon (Bill Paxton), the country "bumpkin" local sheriff in Star City, Ark., and a couple of L.A. cops who have reason to believe the bad guys are headed their way. While the tension mounts, the filmmakers use the situation to deftly probe the underbelly of American life, from racial tensions to the inherent conflict between rural and urban values. The film features excellent performances from its entire cast, but Paxton's bravura portrayal is a standout. ★★★½ $19.99

One Fine Day

(1996, 100 min, US, Michael Hoffman) Though they exude great charm and have a wonderful chemistry between them, Michelle Pfeiffer and George Clooney just aren't able to give an added boost to this convoluted romantic comedy which is short on both romance and comedy. But if *One Fine Day* doesn't completely work, it's not because everyone in the cast doesn't try; and no one tries more than its two personable stars. They play divorced parents who come together when their children miss the class trip. Each having a professional crisis looming, they take turns babysitting both kids. Of course, they're antagonistic in the beginning, but soon they succumb to each other's magnetism. This losing battle-of-the-sexes does on occasion please, but it's due more to Clooney and Pfeiffer's rapport than any screenplay manipulation. They'd probably be better matched the next time Catwoman and Batman meet. And to show that they're both great parents, they never lose their temper with two of the brattiest kids. Parents may experience some empathy; non-parents may quickly scribble a donation to the nearest Planned Parenthood. ★★ $102.99

One Flew Over the Cuckoo's Nest

(1975, 133 min, US, Milos Forman) Jack Nicholson gives a triumphant performance as the dangerously sane Randall P. McMurphy, the feisty ringleader of an asylum's inmates. Forman adapts Ken Kesey's eloquent novel with boundless zeal and multi-award-winning results. Louise Fletcher won an Oscar (as did Nicholson) for her unforgettably adversarial head nurse whose unwavering strictness leads to defiance and tragedy. ★★★★ $14.99

One from the Heart

(1982, 100 min, US, Francis Ford Coppola) Coppola's celebrated bomb (costing some $25 million) stars Frederic Forrest and Teri Garr as lovers who split after five years. They find new lovers, only to realize they were really meant for each other. Nothing more than a stylized, full-length music video which lacks any dramatic structure. Co-stars Raul Julia and Nastassja Kinski. Music by Tom Waits. ★★

One Good Cop

(1991, 100 min, US, Heywood Gould) Michael Keaton gives a competent performance in a relatively lackluster treatment of the good-cop-loses-partner-and-has-a-crisis-of-faith formula. The occasional sparks generated by the cast can't quite compensate for the flat, predictable script and mundane direction. ★★ $9.99

101 Dalmatians

(1961, 80 min, US, Wolfgang Reitherman, H.S. Luske & Clyde Geronimi) An enchanting Disney classic, this animated tale follows the adventures of a faithful dalmatian, Pongo, and his mate as they attempt to stop one of Disney's best villains, Cruella DeVil, from kidnapping a truckload of pups and turning them into fur coats. The animation is splendid, and the comical story is one of Disney's best. (An inferior live-action version was made in 1996 starring Glenn Close) ★★★½

101 Dalmatians

(1996, 103 min, US, Stephen Herek) The names are the same and so essentially is the story. But wait! The lively animated characters, mean, colorful villainess and cuddly spotted canines have been replaced by real people. So who can fault the suits at Disney for taking this golden marketing opportunity by the tail and racing with it. The story's the same: Dalmatians Pongo and Perdy play matchmaker for their respective owners. After the humans are hitched, the dogs give birth to 15 precocious kids, which attract the attention of Cruella DeVil (Glenn Close). She has plans to manufacture dalmatian coats, and intends to add Pongo and Perdy's brood to the other 84 pooches she's stolen. There are some charming moments here, particularly in the film's first hour. And Close's dazzling grand-old-dame turn as flamboyantly dressed "uber-bitch" Cruella would make RuPaul and Dennis Rodman jealous. But Disney handed the writing and producing bone for this baby to John Hughes. Blame him for failing to give the speechless pups easily identifiable personalities, and for some insipid slapstick humor that eventually turns this puppy into *Dog Home Alone*. ★★ $26.99

One Magic Christmas

(1985, 100 min, US, Phillip Borsos) This poignant family fantasy draws much of its inspiration from both *It's a Wonderful Life* and *A Christmas Carol*. Mary Steenburgen stars as a housewife whose lost Christmas spirit is found with the help of an unlikely guardian angel, played by Harry Dean Stanton. ★★★ $19.99

One Nation Under God

(1993, 84 min, US, Teodoro Maniaci & Francine Rzeznick) Providing another invaluable piece of queer history, this low-budget documentary investigates the organizations and people who try to "cure" gays and lesbians. The film offers screen time to both sides of the debate including interviews with the directors of "recovery programs," professionals opposed to their work, ex-gays who claim they are now straight, and the former ex-gays who claim that it is all a farce. The film's most eloquent and perceptive speakers are Michael and Gary, founding members of Exodus and now former ex-gays who voice the strongest condemnation of these organizations that expose radical "curative" treatment. Though the film is pro-gay, it would have been enough just to allow these religious zealots a forum to debunk their own notions. ★★★ $29.99

One False Move

One Night of Love

(1934, 80 min, US, Victor Schertzinger) A captivating musical with Grace Moore in a wonderful performance as an American opera singer who studies and falls in love with Italian maestro Tullio Carminati. ★★★ $19.99

One Sings, the Other Doesn't

(1977, 90 min, France, Agnès Varda) Varda's feminist triumph follows the friendship and developing self-fulfillment of two young women in Paris from 1962 to 1976. Pauline is a free-spirited singer while Susanne becomes an organizer in a family planning clinic and both succeed through the love and support of each other. This warm and thoughtful film blends fact, fiction and feeling to sing its song in praise of women. (French with English subtitles) ★★★

One Touch of Venus

(1948, 81 min, US, William A. Seiter) Long before *Mannequin* came this charming musical comedy with Ava Gardner as a department store statue that magically comes to life and is romanced by window dresser Robert Walker. ★★★ $19.99

One Trick Pony

(1980, 98 min, US, Robert M. Young) Paul Simon stars in this bittersweet, unfulfilled story of an aging rock star trying to salvage his marriage and his flagging career. Simon also wrote the script. Blair Brown, Rip Torn, Joan Hackett and Lou Reed also star. ★★ $14.99

One, Two, Three

(1961, 110 min, US, Billy Wilder) A hilarious, lightning-paced (this may be the fastest comedy since Howard Hawks' *His Girl Friday*) political farce from director Wilder, made during the heyday of the Cold War. James Cagney — who would not make another film for 20 years — is in top form as the harried Coca-Cola executive stationed in West Berlin who must contend with card-carrying Commies, ex-Nazis and Southern belles when the boss' daughter secretly marries a young Communist. All this and Pepsi-Cola, too. ★★★★ $19.99

One Wild Moment

(1977, 88 min, France, Claude Berri) An engaging French farce that follows the adventures of a recently divorced 44-year-old man who goes on vacation in the hope of having an affair with some beautiful young girl. His fantasy comes true, but he then realizes that the young beauty that seduced him is the daughter of his best friend. The inspiration for the American comedy *Blame It on Rio*. (French with English subtitles) ★★½

One Woman or Two

(1986, 97 min, France, Daniel Vigne) A curious international cast of Gérard Depardieu, Sigourney Weaver and Dr. Ruth Westheimer team up in this silly, occasionally funny remake of the classic *Bringing Up Baby*. Depardieu plays a foggy paleontologist who finds what he thinks to be the fossilized remains of the first Frenchwoman. Weaver is the opportunistic ad exec who wants to market the discovery in a perfume advertising campaign. And if this wasn't enough, Dr. Ruth plays an American philanthropist... well, maybe she should stick to just giving out sexual advice. (French with English subtitles) ★★

One-Eyed Jacks

(1961, 141 min, US, Marlon Brando) Brando's only directorial effort pits him as an outlaw against sheriff Karl Malden in a psychological tug-of-war. Slim Pickens, Pina Pellicer, Katy Jurado, Ben Johnson and Elisha Cook, Jr. also star in this unusual, intriguing western morality tale. ★★★ $19.99

One-Eyed Swordsman

(1963, 95 min, Japan, Seiichiro Uchikawa) This action/fantasy film is set during Japan's age of the Shoguns and features the heroic efforts of a mysterious one-eyed, one-armed samurai who fights to defend the underdog while on his search for a magic sword. (Japanese with English subtitles) ★★½

Onibaba

(1965, 103 min, Japan, Kaneto Shindo) This exotic and macabre story is set in medieval Japan, a land ravaged by continual upheavals and bloody battles between powerful warlords and where suffering peasants in the pillaged villages grow more and more desperate in the struggle to survive. An elderly woman and her son's wife eke out their existence by searching for wounded soldiers, killing them — if necessary — and stripping them of their armour which they exchange for food. When a friend returns from the war with news of her son's death, the old lady becomes suspicious, both of the returning soldier and of her daughter-in-law — neither of whom seem in the least upset by his untimely demise. When the two begin a passionate affair, the old lady calls upon the demons and spirits to help her punish her daughter-in-law. *Onibaba* is a disturbing tale of deceit and survival, suspensefully told by director Shindo (*The Island*). (Japanese with English subtitles) ★★★½ $29.99

The Onion Field

(1979, 122 min, US, Harold Becker) Powerful film version of Joseph Wambaugh's fact-based novel about the killing of a policeman and his partner's eventual breakdown. James Woods' electrifying performance as the psychopathic hood brought him international acclaim. With John Savage, Franklyn Seales and Ted Danson. ★★★ $14.99

Only Angels Have Wings

(1939, 121 min, US, Howard Hawks) Top-flight adventure with pilot Cary Grant running a small airline in the South American jungle, resisting the considerable charms of the ever-charming Jean Arthur. Good support from Thomas Mitchell, a young Rita Hayworth and silent screen star Richard Barthelmess. Solid direction from Hawks. ★★★½ $19.99

Only One Night

(1939, 90 min, Sweden, Gustaf Molander) This intense melodrama stars Ingrid Bergman as a repressed young woman, who, in order to

Onibaba

please her father, becomes involved with a rich, philandering older man. (Swedish with English subtitles) ★★½ $19.99

Only the Lonely

(1991, 102 min, US, Chris Columbus) John Candy gives possibly his best performance in this low-keyed comedy-drama written and directed by Columbus and produced by John Hughes. Candy, effectively underplaying his part, stars as a thirtysomething, single Chicago cop, still living at home with his mother, who falls in love with Ally Sheedy: only problem is he just can't break away from mom. In her first screen appearance in 20 years, Maureen O'Hara returns as Candy's feisty mother. Much credit goes to O'Hara for her solid portrayal of the basically unlikable, prejudiced and outspoken Rose; the actress never attempts to belittle or dilute the character, and creates a three-dimensional, totally complex woman. Also with Anthony Quinn, James Belushi and Milo O'Shea. ★★½ $9.99

Only Two Can Play

(1962, 106 min, GB, Sidney Gilliat) This highly entertaining sex comedy is a wonderful example of early '60s British cinema. Peter Sellers stars as a Welsh librarian who has soured on married life and spends his days dreaming of naughty affairs with other women. When he gets his wish in the form of a vivacious socialite, Mai Zetterling, he finds it might be more than he can handle. Both Sellers and Zetterling deliver wonderful performances. An excellent supporting cast includes Virginia Maskell and Richard Attenborough. ★★★ $69.99

Only When I Laugh

(1981, 120 min, US, Glenn Jordan) Neil Simon's screenplay, based on his play "The Gingerbread Lady," rates as one of his best and most underrated. Marsha Mason excels in this serio-comic gem as an alcoholic actress, just released from a sanitarium, who tries to stay off the bottle. Kristy McNichol is her teenage daughter; and James Coco and Joan Hackett both give outstanding performances in support as, respectively, a struggling gay actor and a mentally unstable socialite. ★★★½ $19.99

Only You

(1994, 108 min, US, Norman Jewison) From the director of *Moonstruck* comes this totally infectious story of a young woman (Marisa

Tilda Swinton is *Orlando*

Tomei) who, ten days before her wedding, takes off for Italy to find the man who she thinks is her ultimate destiny (when she was 11 a Ouija board predicted her future mate). Once abroad, she engages in a series of misadventures searching for Mr. Right, while roguish American Robert Downey, Jr. pursues her under false pretenses. Though Tomei can occasionally step on the line between endearing and cloying, Downey has a sparkling charm, ease and elegance that harkens back to the movie stars of yore. Cynics may wonder if Tomei would really have such an extensive ready-to-travel wardrobe in her meager closet; others will just bask in the film's witty dialogue and warm Italian sunshine. ★★★ $19.99

Open City

(1946, 105 min, Italy, Roberto Rossellini) Rossellini's classic, which marked the beginning of Italian Neorealism, is about the underground movement operating in Rome during the Nazi occupation. The brilliant performance by Anna Magnani brought her international acclaim. Coscripted by Federico Fellini. (Italian with English subtitles) ★★★★ $24.99

Open Doors

(1990, 109 min, Italy, Gianni Amelio) Exactingly paced, this psychological drama on the nature of justice is a thoughtful film which is quite similar in theme to Bertrand Tavernier's *The Judge and the Assassin*. Set in 1937, the film begins with a man going to a government office and calmly killing his former boss, his seemingly supportive successor, and later, raping and killing his wife. He is arrested, says little, shows no regret and simply awaits his punishment. One of the judges assigned to the case, an older, wealthy patrician, becomes intrigued by the man and, risking his reputation and against the wishes of the defendant, tries to find out what caused the man to resort to such violence. The title refers to the Fascist promise that with their harsh penal code, people would be able to

sleep with their doors open. (Italian with English subtitles) ★★★ $19.99

Opening Night

(1977, 144 min, US, John Cassavetes) Complex, emotional, disquieting and at times exasperating, *Opening Night* is a none-too-subtle but riveting drama of the midlife crisis of an aging actress (Gena Rowlands) as she works in a play about a woman quite like herself. As the star, Rowlands is a talented but high-strung alcoholic who teeters on the verge of a nervous breakdown while costar and ex John Cassavetes, harried director Ben Gazzara and sympathetic but tough playwright Joan Blondell helplessly watch. The theatre world and its inevitable tantrums and backstage theatrics provide an ideal location for Cassavetes' exploration of a husband and family-less woman facing middle age in a profession that idolizes youth and discards the "old." The acting is superb, from Rowlands' intense emoting to Gazzara's subtle nuances and taut facial expressions. Possibly a bit too long, but for fans, a treat. ★★★ $19.99

Opera do Malandro

(1986, 105 min, Brazil, Ruy Guerra) This Brazilian reworking of "Three Penny Opera" is set in the slums of Rio in 1942 and is a highly stylized, tango-influenced homage to the splashy M-G-M musicals of the '50s. Our hero is Max Oversees, a charming scoundrel whose heart is divided between his longtime ex-prostitute lover and a young, convent-trained beauty who is also the daughter of the local crime boss. Guerra (*Erendira*) directed this exuberant and highly enjoyable musical; the highlights of which include a flamenco-style duel (read: cat fight) between the two leading ladies and an imaginative musical number amidst the urinals in a nightclub's men's room. (Portuguese with English subtitles) ★★★ $79.99

Operation Dumbo Drop

(1995, 108 min, US, Simon Wincer) After the soul-searching demonstrated in such films as

Platoon and *Casualties of War*, which attempt to examine our involvement in Vietnam, Disney offers this cardboard paste-up of a film which plays like "*The Absent-Minded Professor Goes to War*." And though it's based on a true story, a screenplay stuck in neutral and eye-rolling shenanigans keep this from attaining much comic mileage. The story centers on a group of Green Berets stationed in Vietnam who are assigned to transport an elephant from the jungle to a friendly village, which needs the animal for a traditional ceremony. Of course, things go awry, tempers flair, and eventually they succeed. Yes, the sight of an elephant being parachuted from an airplane is a rather funny sight. But the film relies too heavily on obvious elephant jokes, and rarely gives its human actors anything equally amusing to say or do. Danny Glover, Ray Liotta and Denis Leary play off each other as best they can. ★★ $14.99

Operation Petticoat

(1959, 120 min, US, Blake Edwards) In *Some Like It Hot*, besides donning a wig, Tony Curtis gave a rather skillful Cary Grant imitation. It is therefore fitting that he would that same year costar with the master comedian. This sometimes hilarious comedy, which was one of the box-office smashes of the 1950s, stars Grant as the captain of a crippled WWII submarine who has his hands full not only making his ship seaworthy but also looking after five nurses rescued at sea. Directed with flair by Edwards. ★★★½ $19.99

Opportunity Knocks

(1990, 105 min, US, Donald Petrie) Opportunity wasn't knocking too loud for comedian Dana Carvey's starring debut. Carvey's mastery of mimicry and sketch comedy isn't well-served in this story of a con man who ingratiates himself into the family of a wealthy industrialist. Also with Robert Loggia and Todd Graff. ★★ $14.99

The Opposite Sex

(1956, 117 min, US, David Miller) Musical updating of *The Women* (with men in this version). Cast features June Allyson, Joan Collins, Ann Sheridan, Ann Miller, Joan Blondell, Jim Backus and Agnes Moorehead. The film, which lacks the supreme artistry of the original, does possess a charm all its own, and the performers all appear to be in their element. ★★★ $19.99

Oranges Are Not the Only Fruit

(1989, 165 min, GB, Beeban Kidron) Adapted for BBC-TV by Jeanette Winterson from her novel of the same name, director Kidron's (*To Wong Foo...*) three-part production chronicles the coming-of-age of a young British lesbian, Jess (Geraldine McEwan). In her turbulent struggles with her domineering evangelist mother (Charlotte Coleman), Jess grows up to be a fiercely independent young woman. This poignant story features a marvelous ensemble cast and charming performances from its two leads. ★★★½ $29.99

Ordeal by Innocence

(1984, 87 min, GB, Desmond Davis) The outstanding cast of Donald Sutherland, Faye Dunaway, Christopher Plummer and Sarah

Miles barely manage to salvage this marginal Agatha Christie mystery from the video junk heap. Sutherland stars as an American who sleuths his way about a 1950s English hamlet. See it for the cast, but don't expect much more. ★★ $79.99

Ordet

(1954, 126 min, Denmark, Carl Dreyer) A gripping, award-winning drama about two families, separated by religious beliefs, who must come to terms with their children's love for each other. (Danish with English subtitles) ★★★½

Ordinary People

(1980, 123 min, US, Robert Redford) A collection of great performances are featured in this gripping, Oscar-winning Best Picture exploring a family's disintegration in the wake of their eldest son's death. Timothy Hutton won an Oscar for his sensitive portrayal of a teenager coming to terms with his brother's passing. Mary Tyler Moore and Donald Sutherland have never been better as the parents; and Judd Hirsch is outstanding as Hutton's caring psychiatrist. Redford's directorial debut is remarkably assured. ★★★★ $14.99

The Organization

(1971, 107 min, US, Don Medford) Sidney Poitier appears for a third time as Virgil Tibbs, the quick-witted police detective he first introduced in *In the Heat of the Night*. Set in San Francisco, the story centers on Tibbs' investigation of a group of kidnappers-vigilantes, who have concocted an elaborate plan to bring down drug-peddling underworld figures. There's a really good ten-minute opening robbery sequence, and the film, though it does lag in certain scenes, is peppered by exciting chases and a few twists. Of course, Poitier's heroic presence helps immeasurably. A supporting cast of actors who went on to varying degrees of success include Raul Julia, Demond Wilson, Daniel J. Travanti and Ron O'Neal. ★★★ $14.99

Organized Crime and Triad Bureau

(1993, 91 min, Hong Kong, Kirk Wong) A combination of a John Woo-style "heroic

Orphans of the Storm

bloodshed" film and an American police procedurial, this semi-sequel to Jackie Chan's *Crime Story* follows an unconventional cop (Danny Lee, co-star of Woo's *The Killer*) who relentlessly pursues an underworld gang leader (Anthony Wong) and his moll (Cecilia Yip). After several battles, escapes and legal loopholes, Lee corners Wong on a small island. A massive search ensues, in which the criminal becomes as much of a victim as the people he's blackmailed and killed. An interesting variation of the crime thriller, *Bureau* presents a basically unsympathetic cop and a more sympathetic bad guy — one cannot help but feel sorry for him as he crawls through the grimy landscape. Not as viscerally thrilling as Ringo Lam's crime movies (*City on Fire, Full Contract*) nor as artistic as Woo's bullet ballets, *Bureau* is still a highly original and entertaining by-the-numbers story of cops and criminals. (Cantonese with English subtitles) ★★★½ $89.99

Orguss, Episodes 1 & 2

(1983, 80 min, Japan, Noboia Ishiguro) Highly entertaining *Star Wars*-influenced animated space opera that takes place in the year 2062, when Earth's two superpowers are battling over something called the Orbital Elevator, a structure which could shift the balance of the planet's political and economic climate. Dimensional space/time distortion, space gypsies and more are featured in this complex story. ★★★ $19.99

Orgy of the Dead

(1966, 90 min, US, Edward D. Wood, Jr.) Just when you thought it was safe to be dead comes this campy mess of zombie girls and tortured teens in bondage. Starring Criswell and Ghoulita, and filmed in "Astravision" and "Sexicolor." From the creator of *Plan 9 from Outer Space*, which says it all. ★ $9.99

Oriane

(1984, 88 min, Venezuela/France, Fina Torres) First-time director Torres' beautiful and hauntingly romantic film studies the relationship between a young woman and her deceased aunt through a series of mesmerizing flashbacks and surrealistic fantasy. The story follows Marie, who must venture through the jungle and other wilderness to arrive at the remote hacienda which she has just inherited from her aunt, Oriane. As she rummages through all of the relics and artifacts in the house, memories are stirred within her and slowly, a mysterious family secret comes to the fore. (Spanish with English subtitles) ★★★ $79.99

The Original Fabulous Adventures of Baron Munchausen

(1961, 110 min, Germany, Karel Zeman) This gorgeous film looks like a cross between a Georges Melies fantasy and a Gustav Doré engraving, as live actors perform in an animated world full of cross-hatchings. When men finally land on the moon, who should they come across but that teller of tall tales, The Baron, having tea with Jules Verne. Every bit as fanciful as the Terry Gilliam version, but a lot less morbid. ★★★

Original Gangstas

(1996, 98 min, US, Larry Cohen) A very nasty gang, the Rebels, is taking over the dying town of Gary, Indiana. The police and city hall are powerless and apathetic, and the citizens are too scared to stop them. It's up to the founders of the Rebels — now in their fifties — to put an end to this nonsense! Yeah, you'll be cheerin' on Fred Williamson and the gang as they whip some ragamuffin butt in this very entertaining throwback to the '70s blaxploitation films. Reuniting a whole slew of African-American performers who starred in those films, Cohen (himself the director of *Black Caesar*) uses them to full advantage, allowing everyone to strut their tuff-ass moment. Jim Brown is quite good, Williamson is a load of fun (his entrance is a howl), and the supporting cast is energetic. Subtle it's not — this is a B-movie through and through. But it's fast-paced fun, and while they may be past their prime, these original gangstas put most of the newer crop of action stars to shame. ★★★ $96.89

Orlando

(1993, 93 min, GB/Russia/France/Italy, Sally Porter) Adapted from Virginia Woolf's 1928 modernist novel, this wholly original, stunningly filmed comedy of sexual mores, attitudes and gender switching stars the luminous Tilda Swinton in the title role. The tale begins in 1600, when the bewitchingly androgynous Orlando captures the eye of the aging Queen Elizabeth I (regally played to the hilt by Quentin Crisp), who promises the nobleman the deed to his family's estate on the condition that he retain his beauty and does not age. As the centuries roll by, the immortal Orlando strolls through the elaborate pageant of English history. During this quest for love and self-discovery, Orlando changes sexes while still retaining his/her personality, independence, kind heart and droll sense of humor. Spectacularly staged and costumed, and featuring a hypnotic soundtrack (including Jimmy Somerville), this witty, enchanting film is infused with wry jokes and emotional truths and is a thrilling odyssey that should not be missed. ★★★★ $19.99

Orphans

(1965, 105 min, USSR, Nikolai Gubenko) Winner of the Special Jury Prize, Cannes Film Festival, this tender and revealing film is set in a boys' boarding school and follows the growth, education and budding sexuality of a young boy. (Russian with English subtitles) ★★★

Orphans

(1987, 115 min, US, Alan J. Pakula) This extremely well-acted drama, starring Albert Finney, Matthew Modine and Kevin Anderson, tells the story of two orphaned brothers, on the edge of society, who live in a broken-down house in Newark and survive through petty thievery. Their lives are dramatically transformed when their plan to rob a drunk goes haywire. That drunk, a wealthy gangster, superbly played by Finney, is intrigued by the two youths and turns the tables a bit by developing a close father-son relationship with the boys. Based on Lyle Kessler's successful stage play. A unique, rewarding film experience. ★★★ $19.99

Orpheus

Orphans of the Storm

(1921, 126 min, US, D.W. Griffith) This powerful melodrama about two girls caught up in the French Revolution stars real-life sisters Dorothy and Lillian Gish, playing two sisters in Paris in search of a cure for one's blindness. A classic from the silent era, from the director of *Birth of a Nation*. ★★★★ $19.99

Orpheus

(1949, 95 min, France, Jean Cocteau) Cocteau's allegorical update of the Orpheus myth is a mesmerizing blend of the natural and the fantastic, poetry and science fiction. Jean Marais stars as the successful poet who becomes enamored with the Princess Death — who travels between this world and the next via chauffeur-driven Rolls Royce. The director's major achievement in cinema. (French with English subtitles) ★★★★ $29.99

Orpheus Descending

(1990, 117 min, GB, Peter Hall) Hall's searing screen adaptation of Tennessee Williams' drama about a forbidden love in a sleepy Southern town. Vanessa Redgrave stars as Lady Torrence, a very unhappily married woman whose repressed sexual passions erupt when she encounters a mysterious, young drifter (Kevin Anderson). As the two revel in their tryst, her tyrannical, bedridden husband plots his revenge. ★★★ $79.99

Osaka Elegy

(1936, 71 min, Japan, Kenji Mizoguchi) One of the earliest surviving films from Mizoguchi's early film career, this drama is a subtle examination of Japanese cultural mores and a indictment of the country's mistreatment of women. Told in realistic fashion, the story follows the travails of Ayako, a good-hearted young woman who, in order to repay the debt of her drunken father and support her school-age brother, reluctantly becomes involved with her boss, a henpecked and unsavory lout. She eventually sinks into prostitution and is both exploited and condemned by society. The film also marks the initial collaboration between Mizoguchi and Yeshitaka Yoda, an enduring relationship that lasted for 20 pictures. (Japanese with English subtitles) ★★★½ $39.99

Ossessione

(1942, 135 min, Italy, Luchino Visconti) For this, his first feature film, Visconti adapted James M. Cain's powerful tale of ill-fated love, "The Postman Always Rings Twice," and transplanted it to wartime rural Italy. Gino, a virile young drifter, meets and falls in love with Giovanna, a beautiful yet desperately unhappy woman who is trapped in a loveless marriage with an older man. The two begin a doomed affair, conceived in passion and lust, but ending in greed, murder and recrimination. This remarkable neorealist debut was banned by Mussolini during the war, and because it was an unauthorized version of the Cain novel, it was not permitted into the United States until 1975. (Italian with English subtitles) ★★★½ $29.99

The Osterman Weekend

(1983, 102 min, US, Sam Peckinpah) Peckinpah's final film is a sometimes intriguing but rather confusing thriller about a TV reporter (Rutger Hauer) who is used by CIA agent John Hurt to spy on three of his friends — suspected Soviet agents. Also with Burt Lancaster, Craig T. Nelson, Dennis Hopper, Chris Sarandon and Meg Foster. ★★½ $14.99

Otello

(1986, 123 min, Italy, Franco Zeffirelli) The dark treacheries and intense passions of Shakespeare's classic is vividly brought to the operatic screen by Zeffirelli. Set in an unreal Mediterranean locale, this soaring and lavish production stars Placido Domingo as the tragic, crazed king. (Sung in Italian with English subtitles) ★★★½ $24.99

Othello

(1952, 107 min, US, Orson Welles) Welles' masterful interpretation of Shakespeare's tale of murder, jealousy, betrayal and racism was thought to have been lost forever. Thanks to the determination of his daughter Beatrice Welles-Smith, however, the film's negatives were unearthed in a New Jersey vault, restored and seen by audiences in 1992 for the first time since 1955. Extremely stylish in production and exquisitely filmed in highly contrasted black-and-white cinematography, the film has the feel of an Eisenstein epic, an effect which is enhanced by the poor sound quality — apparently, when found, the negatives were in excellent condition, but the soundtrack was not. Welles himself stars as the Moor of Venice who ill-advisedly allows his evil sidekick, Iago (Michael MacLiammor), to convince him that his newlywed wife, Desdemona (Suzanne Cloutier), is having an affair with Casio (Robert Coote). Tragic in every detail, Welles portrays the deceived lover with bravado. Winner of the Palme D'Or at the 1952 Cannes Film Festival. ★★★½ $89.99

Othello

(1995, 124 min, GB, Oliver Parker) First-time director Parker's brooding, sexy adaptation of one of Shakespeare's most enduring works bears the distinction of being the first theatrical film version to use an African-American actor (Laurence Fishburne) in the role of the Moorish general. The story, of course, centers on Othello's manipulation by the power-hungry lieutenant Iago (Kenneth Branagh), who makes Othello believe his new bride (Irene Jacob) is guilty of infidelity and, ultimately, drives him to madness. Though *Othello* was unduly criticized for being a Cliff's Notes version of the play (relying on approximately half the original text) and for its explicit interracial scenes, the film is nevertheless an enthralling reworking which gives power to Shakespeare's written word and the emotions they harness. Fishburne's acting prowess has never been in question, but his mastery of Shakespeare's poetry coupled with the range of emotions spanned by the character is a further testimony to his ability. Branagh (who obviously slid from the womb quoting the Bard) is mesmerizing as the evil Iago, and Jacob makes for a tragically beautiful Desdemona. The story centuries later resonates and has lost none of its universality. ★★★½ $19.99

The Other

(1972, 100 min, US, Robert Mulligan) A sleepy New England town in 1935 is the setting for this first-rate psychological thriller about two twin boys, one of whom is a murderer. Based on Thomas Tryon's best-seller. With Uta Hagen and Diana Muldaur. ★★★ $59.99

Other People's Money

(1991, 115 min, US, Norman Jewison) Danny DeVito delights as Larry "The Liquidator" Garfield, a heartless, greed-driven corporate raider who is the centerpiece of this amusing adaptation of Jerry Sterner's off-Broadway hit. The latest subject of Larry's insatiable takeover fancies is the New England Wire & Cable Company, a small "mom & pop" factory run by a paternal Gregory Peck. Jewison's direction uses the showdown between small-time family capitalist and Wall Street power-broker to deliver a predictably Capra-esque message, but the film does have one surprisingly candid moment when DeVito delivers an impassioned speech to the stockholders of the little company. ★★½ $9.99

The Other Side of Midnight

(1977, 165 min, US, Charles Jarrott) Trashy melodrama based on Sidney Sheldon's novel. Set before, during and after WWII, the story centers on a steamy love affair between an American pilot and a married French actress, and the deadly revenge exacted on them by her husband. Starring Marie-France Pisier, John Beck and Susan Sarandon. ★½ $59.99

Our Daily Bread

(1934, 73 min, US, King Vidor) When no Hollywood studio would make this paean to communal living, Vidor risked his own money and made it himself. While as a socialist tract it's embarrassingly simplistic, to audiences suffering under the full wallop of the Depression it must have been as uplifting as a Berkeley musical number. An unemployed laborer and his wife are given a second chance when a rich uncle lets them squat on a bankrupt farm. They soon turn it into a cooperative, recruiting other victims of the crash. Vidor, the director of such silent classics as *The Crowd*, brings all his dramatist skills to the meager plot, setting off his striking visuals with a dynamic montage style right out of Eisenstein. ★★★½

Our Miss Fred

(1975, 96 min, GB, Bob Kellett) A guilty, campy pleasure if there ever was one, starring female impersonator Danny LaRue as a soldier who, during WWII, is caught in drag just when the Germans invade France. The admittedly ridiculous story follows his inventive attempts to get through Nazi-infested lands (under the *nom de guerre* of Frederika) without the Germans catching on to his identity – sort of a slapstick/drag version of *Europa, Europa*! Determinedly heterosexual, although there are plenty of double-entendres to the contrary, our wonderfully fashion-accessorized heroine, who "has every little thing a woman should have and more," traipses through the countryside dazzling the enemy (and even a few horny Frenchmen) with her fabulously outrageous frocks, wigs and sharp-tongued wit. ★★★ $99.99

Our Sons

(1991, 100 min, US, John Erman) From the director of *An Early Frost* comes this intelligent and moving made-for-TV AIDS drama. Julie Andrews and Ann-Margret star as the respective mothers of gay lovers Hugh Grant and Zeljko Ivanek. Andrews is a wealthy businesswoman who remained close to her son after he came out, while A-M, a barmaid from Arkansas, refuses to accept or even acknowledge her son's sexuality and rejects him. When Ivanek becomes sick with AIDS, Andrews is persuaded by her son to meet his lover's mother and try to get the two to reunite. A serious, straightforward story which, while suffering a bit from a talking heads-style of filmmaking, remains compelling and compassionate. ★★★ $19.99

Our Vines Have Tender Grapes

(1945, 105 min, US, Roy Rowland) This earnest, folksy drama does not hold up quite as well as other similarly themed films – *Our Town* or *The Human Comedy* for instance – which bestow blessings upon the virtues of American small-town life. In a bit of flagrant nontypecasting which happily works, Edward G. Robinson plays a kindly Norwegian farmer

Laurence Fishburne (l.) and Kenneth Branagh in *Othello*

living with wife Agnes Moorehead and daughter Margaret O'Brien. Though not much really happens, the story follows one year in the lives of the family, mostly centering on seven-year-old O'Brien (whose cheerfulness would put Pollyanna to shame). Adapted by soon-to-be blacklisted writer Dalton Trumbo, who paints Americana with broad, sentimental strokes. ★★½ $19.99

Out Cold

(1989, 92 min, US, Malcolm Mowbray) This delightfully sick comedy stars Teri Garr as a slightly demented housewife who, after finding out that husband Ernie is cheating on her, locks him in his butcher shop's freezer. Her frenzied attempts to get rid of her frozen hubbie entangles John Lithgow, the nerdish partner of Ernie as well as a bungling private eye, Randy Quaid. ★★★ $89.99

Out of Africa

(1985, 160 min, US, Sydney Pollack) Gorgeous cinematography by David Watkin, a tremendous performance by Meryl Streep, a moving score by John Barry, and subtle direction by Pollack make this film worthy of its several Academy Awards. Based on the life and works of Isak Dinesen, it's the story of a Danish woman, Karen Blixen (Streep), who moves to Nairobi with her aristocratic husband. There, she falls in love with Africa and with a handsome British explorer (Robert Redford minus the accent). A beautiful film. ★★★★ $19.99

Out of Bounds

(1986, 93 min, US, Richard Tuggle) Inept thriller with Anthony Michael Hall as an Iowa farmboy who unwittingly becomes involved with drug pushers on his first visit to Los Angeles. ★ $79.99

Out of Order

(1985, 90 min, The Netherlands, Carl Schenkel) When two films about killer elevators (the other being *The Lift*) are released from the same country in the same year, it

would be prudent to avoid entering tall buildings while visiting that land. Anyway, this intense thriller is miles ahead in terror than *The Lift* and features Renee Soutendijk. The story is set in a deserted office building where four people discover, to their horror, that the lift is...*out of order*! Excitement for us, but a nightmarish hell for the trapped occupants! (Dubbed) ★★★

Out of the Blue

(1947, 86 min, US, Leigh Jason) Enjoyable screwball comedy with George Brent as a henpecked husband who has some explaining to do when wacky Ann Dvorak is found unconscious in his apartment. ★★½ $19.99

Out of the Blue

(1980, 93 min, US, Dennis Hopper) Before Dennis Hopper burst back onto the Hollywood scene, he made this gritty and extraordinary low-budget feature about a nihilistic, punked-out teenager. With an alcoholic truck driver (Hopper) for a dad and a junkie mom (Sharon Farrell), the young Linda Manz gets all of her life experience in seedy roadhouses and various watering holes. Excellent performances make this a harrowing experience of the emptiness of life on the edge. ★★★½ $9.99

Out of the Past

(1947, 96 min, US, Jacques Tourneur) Robert Mitchum is memorable as a retired private eye, living as a gas station owner, who is lured back to his old job by gangster Kirk Douglas (wonderfully greasy) to find his dame who ran off with his heart as well as his money. Our fated hero's sleuthing leads him to Mexico where he not only finds his prey (Jane Greer, cunningly seductive as the femme fatale), but falls in love with her as well. A riveting drama of double dealings, *amour mort* and pervasive corruption. A '40s film noir classic. (Remade in 1984 as *Against All Odds*.) ★★★½ $19.99

Out on a Limb

(1992, 82 min, US, Francis Vèber) Matthew Broderick stars in this awful screwball comedy from the director of *Three Fugitives*. Broderick is miscast as a hotshot Manhattan stockbroker who pays a visit to his hometown en route to complete a multimillion dollar deal and runs afoul of the murderous activities of his stepfather. Director Veber's interesting use of narration and flashback adds nothing to the mundane plot. Also with Jeffrey Jones. ★ $9.99

The Out-of-Towners

(1970, 97 min, US, Arthur Hiller) The laughs are plentiful (and very close to home) in this Neil Simon romp with Jack Lemmon and Sandy Dennis as the title couple, an Ohio exec and his wife visiting New York City, where they encounter one disaster after another. ★★★ $14.99

Outbreak

(1995, 127 min, US, Wolfgang Petersen) Dustin Hoffman stars in this fact-based and very exciting topical thriller as a cantankerous Army doctor who, along with his ex-wife (Rene Russo), a newly appointed bigwig at the CDC, races against time (and a top-level military conspiracy) to stop the spread of a highly infectious mutant virus that kills within 24 hours of contact. While short on characterization and guilty of eventually deteriorating into a standard "good guys vs. bad guys" actioner, the film as directed by Petersen displays the director's knack for mixing tension, claustrophobia and doom (as demonstrated in *Das Boot* and *In the Line of Fire*). As such, it's quite successful in its gruesome depiction of the ultimate end-of-the-world scenario; and in an era of AIDS and Ebola, all-too believable. Among a fine supporting cast, Donald Sutherland costars as military evil incarnate, Morgan Freeman is his unwitting co-conspirator, and Kevin Spacey appears as Hoffman's spirited coworker. ★★★ $14.99

Outcasts

(1986, 102 min, Taiwan, Yu Kan Ping) After being caught having sex with another student, young Ah Ching is both expelled from school and beaten out of his home by his father. Befriended by a middle-aged photographer as well as by other young gays, Ah rebuilds his life with the help of his new surrogate family and begins to explore his own sexuality. The first film from Taiwan with a gay theme, *Outcasts* is, at times, unintentionally funny in its heavy-handed melodramatic excesses, but is nonetheless a powerful and sensual look at youth finding a place in an uncaring and insensitive world. (Mandarin with English subtitles) ★★★ $49.99

The Outer Limits

(1963-1965, 52 min, US) Unfairly overshadowed by "The Twilight Zone," this series at its best — which was most of the time — created a dark moody vision of the universe only somewhat leavened with hope. In truth, the series reflected more the vision of supervising producer Joseph Stefano, who had scripted *Psycho* for Alfred Hitchcock a few years earlier, than that of series creator Leslie Stevens, star of "Peter Gunn." With rich film noir photography, stylized sets, dark political intrigue and brilliant scripts, "The Outer Limits" required too much thought for what was supposed to be just an hour of monster, which probably doomed it to only a two-year run. But the series now stands as one of the most original and effective sci-fi/fantasy shows ever put on the air. $12.99 each

Outland

(1981, 109 min, US, Peter Hyams) Sean Connery gives one of his best performances in this taut sci-fi thriller as a lone cop determined to smash a drug ring on Io, the ninth moon of Jupiter. Peter Boyle is the slimy, corrupt executive who wants to buy his badge. Director Hyams presents an isolated world where law is practically extinct and capitalism reigns supreme. This underrated jewel was affectionately dubbed "*High Noon*" in Space" by critics upon its theatrical release. ★★★ $9.99

The Outlaw

(1943, 117 min, US, Howard Hawks) Jane Russell made a notorious film debut (though the film was shot in 1941) in this legendary (and at the time scandalous) western adventure about Billy the Kid and his girlfriend. Though most of the attention over the years

Cuba Gooding, Jr. (l.) and Dustin Hoffman search for a cure in *Outbreak*

has been focused on Russell's ample bosom, not to be overlooked is Walter Huston's showy turn as Billy. ★★★ $19.99

The Outlaw and His Wife

(1917, 73 min, Sweden, Victor Sjostrom) Sjostrom directed and stars in this superbly acted and visually stunning drama which gave Sweden its breakthrough after WWI. The setting is Iceland in the 19th century where a farmer and his wife are being hunted by the police for a petty crime. Fleeing to the mountains and fjord hills to escape detection, they soon succumb to the brutal forces of nature. Color tinted, this video version features a full orchestral score and was beautifully restored in 1986 by the Swedish Film Institute. ★★★½ $29.99

The Outlaw Josey Wales

(1976, 135 min, US, Clint Eastwood) Exciting post-Civil War adventure about a Confederate renegade (Clint Eastwood) on a trail of vengeance against the Union soldiers who murdered his wife and son. ★★★½ $19.99

Outrage

(1994, 108 min, Spain, Carlos Saura) Don't believe the hype — this is not some sex-drenched, exotic shoot-'em-up which could be misinterpreted, but a thoughtful, moderately paced examination of a young woman's reaction to a brutal violation. Francesca Neri is compelling as a circus sharpshooter, the victim of three young thugs whose advances she rejects. Antonio Banderas delivers an effective, subdued performance as a reporter captivated by the vivacious woman. In physical and emotional shock from the severity of the attack on her, she turns instinctively to a familiar weapon, near at hand, to execute her act of vengeance. Certainly not a great film, but compassionate in its depiction of one woman's response to an act of carnage that shatters her life. (Spanish with English subtitles) ★★½ $14.99

Outrageous

(1977, 100 min, Canada, Richard Benner) A wildly funny and affecting Canadian film about a female impersonator and his touching friendship with a schizophrenic girl. Craig Russell's impressions of Streisand, Garland, Midler, West and others are flawless, and Hollis McLaren is captivating as the young woman. ★★★½

Outrageous Fortune

(1987, 92 min, US, Arthur Hiller) One of the most hilarious films of the 1980s, *Outrageous Fortune* finds its success in the ingenious pairing of pretty, prim and proper bitch Shelley Long with flamboyant, aggressive floozy Bette Midler (and, as with Olivier's *Hamlet*, a role the Divine Miss M was born to play). The fireworks given off by these two are priceless. The truly outrageous plot finds the female odd couple searching for a "missing" boyfriend; they become involved with the CIA, Russian agents, biochemical warfare, and George Carlin. ★★★½ $9.99

The Outside Chance of Maximilian Glick

(1989, 95 min, Canada, Allan A. Goldstein) This low-budget Canadian film set in 1960 is a charming coming-of-age comedy which plays as sort of a "Jewish Wonder Years." Making an impressive film debut, Noam Zylberman stars as a 13-year-old boy who is readying for his bar mitzvah. The film follows the days before, when Max experiences first love with a pretty gentile girl; befriends the new, unorthodox, Orthodox rabbi; and for the first time rebels against his family. Jan Rubes co-stars, and Saul Rubinek is a total delight as the new rabbi whose candor and sense of humor turns an entire town on its ear. ★★★

The Outside Man

(1973, 104 min, US, Jacques Deray) It's killer vs. killer in this dated actioner about a sad-eyed assassin (Jean-Louis Trintignant) who finds himself at the wrong end of a gun when his latest employer (Angie Dickinson) embraces the philosophy that "dead men tell no tales." Roy Scheider gives another surefire performance as the hit man whose credo is "there's no honor among thieves," and Ann-Margret is on target as the helpful floosie whose philosophy is "leave it to cleavage." ★★½ $14.99

The Outsiders

(1983, 91 min, US, Francis Ford Coppola) S.E. Hinton's best-selling teen novel about kids from the wrong side of the tracks in the early 1960s is transformed into a stylish and visually rich film by director Coppola. The cast is interesting to watch — it includes several well-knowns before they hit it big: C. Thomas Howell, Matt Dillon, Ralph Maccio, Patrick Swayze, Rob Lowe, Diane Lane, Emilio Estevez and Tom Cruise, among others. ★★½ $9.99

Over the Brooklyn Bridge

(1983, 108 min, US, Menachem Golan) A Brooklyn luncheonette owner (Elliott Gould) needs to borrow money to open a posh Manhattan eatery. His uncle (Sid Caesar) is willing to loan him the cash — if he drops his current Christian girl (Margaux Hemingway) and settles down with a nice Jewish girl (Carol Kane). Unmemorable and not all that funny, either. With Shelley Winters and Burt Young. ★½

Over the Edge

(1979, 95 min, US, Jonathan Kaplan) Aimless violence is the result of the frustration and alienation of suburban youths in director Kaplan's dynamic youth-in-revolt film. The hard-rock soundtrack with Cheap Trick, The Ramones and Jimi Hendrix heightens the ten-

sion in this powerful sleeper. With Matt Dillon and Michael Kramer. ★★★ $14.99

Overboard

(1987, 112 min, US, Garry Marshall) Pleasant Goldie Hawn comedy with Goldie as an obnoxious society woman who gets amnesia and is convinced by workman Kurt Russell that she is his wife and the mother of his three wild children. One of Goldie's better comedies with a fair share of laughs. ★★★ $9.99

The Overcoat (Shinel)

(1959, 73 min, USSR, Aleksei Batalov) This faithful adaptation of Nikolai Gogol's tragi-comic story follows a beleaguered clerk, whose dreams of a glorious new coat are not only realized, but change his destiny. The setting is 19th-century czarist St. Petersberg in this simple yet moving story. (Russian with English subtitles) ★★★½ $59.99

Overindulgence

(1987, 95 min, GB, Ross Devenish) This retelling of the scandalous murder trial of a wealthy British expatriate in 1941 colonial East Africa has its moments, but it can't compare to *White Mischief*, which is based on the same incident. ★★

The Owl and the Pussycat

(1970, 95 min, US, Herbert Ross) Barbra Streisand and George Segal are terrific together in this raucous and very funny screen version of Bill Manoff's Broadway play. Streisand, in sensational form, plays a hooker who is kicked out of her apartment after complaints made by neighboring writer Segal; so she moves in with him. ★★★½ $9.99

The Ox

(1992, 91 min, Sweden, Sven Nykvist) Ingmar Bergman's longtime cinematographer Nykvist made his directorial debut with this grim parable about the day-to-day struggles for life in 1860s famine-stricken Sweden. The film's opening scene introduces Helge (Stellan Skarsgard), a destitute tenant farmer who, in a fit of desperation over his family's poverty, brutally bludgeons one of his landlord's two remaining oxen, quickly butchering the animal and hiding the evidence. Of course, Helge and his wife Elfrida (Ewa Froling, looking remarkably like a young Liv Ullmann) go on to suffer the guilt that their devious act, coupled with the austere piety of Nordic Christianity, must inevitably bring to bear. Based on a true incident, the film is yet another example of the life-is-so-grim-above-the-Arctic-Circle school of Swedish filmmaking which here is mildly unengaging. Max von Sydow brings a small breath of life to the film as the town's humanistic vicar. (Swedish with English subtitles) ★★ $19.99

The Ox-Bow Incident

(1943, 75 min, US, William Wellman) A classic western morality play. Henry Fonda and Henry (Harry) Morgan ride into town just in time to experience the formation of a lynch mob. The scene in which they question the "rustlers" who are one wrong answer from a hangman's noose is suitably tense. With Anthony Quinn and Dana Andrews as the accused. ★★★★ $19.99

Oxford Blues

(1984, 97 min, US, Robert Boris) Updated, sloppy version of the 1938 hit *A Yank at Oxford*, with Rob Lowe, in the Robert Taylor role, as an American rower enrolled at Oxford and in love with Amanda Pays. ★½

Pacific Heights

(1990, 102 min, US, John Schlesinger) A "yupwardly mobile" couple (Matthew Modine and Melanie Griffith) pool their resources to purchase and renovate a large Victorian home (complete with two rental units) in an upscale San Francisco neighborhood. Enter Michael Keaton as sociopath Carter Hayes, a tenant from hell who seems to know that a lodger can do just about anything to his landlords and not be evicted – including nonpayment of rent and destruction of property and cockroach breeding. An infuriating blend of "who says life is fair anyway" legal procedures and sweaty-palm psychological warfare, and the film really doesn't work on either level. ★★ $9.99

The Package

(1989, 108 min, US, Andrew Davis) This taut political thriller stars the ideally cast Gene Hackman as an Army Security specialist stationed in Germany who is assigned to escort a wayward soldier (Tommy Lee Jones) back to the United States for a court-martial. This apparantly routine mission comes unglued when his "package" gives him the slip. As Hackman sets out on the trail of his charge, he is framed and becomes the subject of a murder investigation forcing the on-the-lam officer to hunt down Jones himself. Joanna Cassidy is tops as Hackman's estranged wife who winds up joining him in his adventure. ★★★ $9.99

Padre Nuestro

(1986, 90 min, Spain, Francisco Rabal) Fernando Rey stars as a powerful Vatican Cardinal who, upon learning he has only one year to live, returns to the village of his youth in order to settle the errors of his mischievous childhood. Thus is set in motion a series of richly comic confrontations with the people of his past: his sexually repressed brother, his domineering mother, the peasant woman who 30 years earlier bore his illegitimate child, and his prostitute daughter, "La Cardenala," portrayed with unabashed sensual zeal by Victoria Abril (*Tie Me Up! Tie Me Down!*). Director Rabal, in the tradition of Luis Buñuel, has painted a colorful portrait of Spanish society which, through a mixture of comedy and drama, exposes the country's struggles with the demands of the church, the flesh and the aristocracy. (Spanish with English subtitles) ★★★ $79.99

Padre Padrone

(1977, 114 min, Italy, Vittorio & Paolo Taviani) The moving struggles of an illiterate shepherd who overcomes hardships to become a successful scholar are wonderfully recounted in this Taviani brothers classic. Autobiographical in nature, the story revolves around the relationship of a young man who has a yearning for knowledge and the brutalizations inflicted on him by his tyrannical father who fears both education and civilization. (Italian with English subtitles) ★★★½ $59.99

The Pagemaster

(1994, 85 min, US, Joe Johnston & Maurice Hunt) An able cast, respectable animation and an extremely enjoyable story line all work together to create a pleasant children's tale which mixes live-action and animation. Macaulay Culkin stars as an overly timid boy who, after getting caught in a rainstorm, takes shelter in a library. There, thanks to a knock on the head, he is transformed into a cartoon character thereupon meeting The Pagemaster (Christopher Lloyd). His mission: to find his way out of the library and through the plots of several well-known novels with the help of some engaging, talking books. His experiences along the way help him face his fears, and learn the value of reading. Whoopi Goldberg, Patrick Stewart and Leonard Nimoy skillfully lend their voices. ★★★ $14.99

I Pagliacci

(1982, 70 min, Italy, Franco Zeffirelli) Placido Domingo stars in this exciting version of the Leoncavallo opera. Georges Pretre conducts the orchestra and chorus of La Scala, and Teresa Stratas and Juan Pons co-star. (Italian with English subtitles) ★★★ $24.99

A Pain in the A—

(1974, 90 min, France/Italy, Edouard Molinaro) Jacques Brel and Lino Ventura star in this hilarious story of a hired killer who crosses paths with a suicidal shirt salesman. An odd friendship ensues as the contract killer attempts to protect the hapless salesman from his attempts at self-destruction. Music by Jacques Brel. Remade by Billy Wilder as *Buddy Buddy*. (French with English subtitles) ★★★ $29.99

Paint It Black

(1989, 101 min, US, Tim Hunter) A hunky sculptor (Rick Rossovich) is "discovered" by a sexy gallery owner (Sally Kirkland) who has more on her mind than art. However, obsession soon escalates into a web of intrigue and murder. A rather effective thriller buoyed by a good performance by Kirkland and a nicely written screenplay. Martin Landau, Julie Carmen and Doug Savant co-star. From the director of *River's Edge*. ★★★ $89.99

The Paint Job

(1992, 90 min, US, Michael Taav) Will Patton stars as Wesley, a lonely man who falls in love with his neighbor's wife (Bebe Neuwirth). The problem is she's married to his boss and best friend Willy (Robert Pastorelli). The dark past of one of these central characters mixes with primal urges, leading to deadly consequences boiling to a violent climax. A slightly above average psychological thriller which offers a couple of jolts and an unexpected plot twist. ★★½ $89.99

Paint Your Wagon

(1969, 166 min, US, Joshua Logan) Lee Marvin and Clint Eastwood (two unlikely musical stars but certainly at home with the western) play a pair of California gold prospectors in the Old West, both involved with Jean Seberg and looking for a fortune. Harve Presnell gets the plaudits for his singing (including the standard "They Call the Wind Maria") in this sturdy adaptation of the Broadway musical. ★★★ $29.99

Painters Painting

(1972, 116 min, US, Emile De Antonio) A fascinating survey of modern art which probes the creative spirits of such contemporary masters as de Kooning, Johns, Rauchenberg, Motherwell, Pollack, Warhol and many more. An entertaining and informative introduction – more of an homage than a critique – to the world of modern art. ★★★ $29.99

Paisan

(1946, 90 min, Italy, Roberto Rossellini) Written by Rossellini and Federico Fellini, this gritty, neorealist classic is set up in six vignettes, all dealing with the relationship between the Americans and Italians during the liberation of Italy in WWII. Rossellini used

Preston Sturges (c.) leads his cast of *The Palm Beach Story*

mostly nonprofessional actors for the roles and he presents the stories in a style reminiscent of a wartime documentary. (Italian with English subtitles) ★★★★ $29.99

The Pajama Game

(1957, 101 min, US, George Abbott & Stanley Donen) Snappy choreography from Bob Fosse is only one of the highlights of this effervescent musical starring Doris Day, whose love-hate relationship with John Raitt is mirrored by labor unrest between the workers and managers of a pajama factory. Songs include Carol Haney's knockout "Steam Heat," and the standards "Hernando's Hideaway" and "Hey, There." One of the better stage-to-screen adaptations of a Broadway musical. ★★★½

Pal Joey

(1957, 109 min, US, George Sidney) Lively film version of the Rodgers and Hart musical with Frank Sinatra as a cabaret entertainer involved with socialite Rita Hayworth and dancer Kim Novak. Songs include "The Lady is a Tramp" and "Bewitched, Bothered and Bewildered." ★★★ $19.99

Pale Rider

(1985, 116 min, US, Clint Eastwood) Eastwood wears two hats as director and actor in this first-rate western adventure, Eastwood's homage to *Shane*. Clint stars as the mysterious stranger who comes to the aid of a gold prospecting community being harassed by an unscrupulous land baron. Michael Moriarty and Carrie Snodgress also star in this gorgeously photographed film. ★★★ $19.99

The Paleface

(1948, 91 min, US, Norman Z. McLeod) The one-and-only Bob Hope plays a cowardly dentist out West who becomes involved with sharpshooter Jane Russell. Loaded with very funny gags. An even funnier sequel followed in 1952, *Son of Paleface*. ★★★ $14.99

The Pallbearer

(1996, 97 min, US, Matt Reeves) Only intermittently funny with a suspect comic intuition, *The Pallbearer* will do little to repair the image of the Generation X'er as a slacker and a whiner. This plays more like a dramatic (and lurid) study of alienation than a quirky comedy of errors. "Friends" star David Schwimmer makes a big-screen starring debut portraying a character not much different from his small-screen persona. In what could have been a "Friends" plot line (it did made a good "Murphy Brown" episode), Schwimmer is invited to be a pallbearer — and then give the eulogy — for a former classmate he can't remember. He soon becomes romantically involved with the deceased man's grieving mother (Barbara Hershey) while at the same time trying to initiate a relationship with Gwyneth Paltrow. Of course, events get out of control. Besides the absence of much humor, the screenplay's handling of Hershey as the "older woman" is despicably insensitive; and though sometimes personable, Schwimmer's act soon grows tiresome. ★★ $19.99

The Palm Beach Story

(1942, 90 min, US, Preston Sturges) Claudette Colbert decides that her beloved inventor hus-band Joel McCrea would be better off without a wife to support; she skips down to Palm Beach to divorce him and find a millionaire husband who can finance his inventions. On the train... But before we get to the train, keep your eyes open during the opening credits, where more happens than during the entirety of some contemporary films. Of course, so much else happens that you may forget the beginning until the end, when everything is resolved. Or is it? Mary Astor, Rudy Vallee, William Demarest and Franklin Pangborn contribute to this madness, written and directed by — who else? — Preston Sturges. ★★★★ $14.99

Palookaville

(1996, 92 min, US, Alan Taylor) Three losers try to better their financial situations by staging an armored car robbery in this adequate low-budget, independent comedy. William Forsythe, Vincent Gallo and Adam Trese are three friends, all down on their luck and all without the resources (both financial and intellectual) to better their situations. A botched jewelry store heist and an abortive attempt to start a private cab company are only the latest in a string of failures for the trio, whose love lives are as miserable as their monetary ones. After saving the life of an armored car driver who suffers a heart attack on the road, they later get the idea to rob the same company in what passes for a master criminal plan among the three of them. Almost annoyingly quirky, the film still has its merits. A hesitant romance between Forsythe's character, a shlump whose main companions are his two stinky dogs, and an equally down-on-her-luck clothing store clerk is the sweetest and most satisfying part of the film. Also noteworthy is Gallo's subplot, about his unhappy home life and his frequent escapes to the arms of his cute but underage neighbor. ★★½ $89.99

The Panama Deception

(1992, 91 min, US, Barbara Trent) This well-crafted, meticulously researched and tightly structured documentary is a clear and lucid presentation of a complex analysis of the U.S. invasion of Panama and the press coverage which was made available to the American people. On December 19, 1989, 20,000 U.S. troops launched a midnight attack. The official story of that incursion, voiced through interviews with Gen. Maxwell Thurmond, Commander of the Southern Command, and Guillermo Ford, President of Panama, among others, is juxtaposed with testimony from eyewitness Panamanian citizens, various analysts such as Ramsey Clark, and the camera's evidence. U.S. media had no coverage of the thousands of civilians killed, the almost 20,000 people left homeless, indications of the use of experimental weaponry, or the continued use of overwhelming deadly force after stated objectives were achieved. This is an important and fascinating exposé, and required viewing for anyone interested in an independent press and a responsible military. ★★★★ $79.99

Pandora's Box

(1928, 110 min, Germany, G.W. Pabst) This expressionistic classic from Pabst features a luminous Louise Brooks, with her haunting beauty, sexual mystique and trademark helmet

Louise Brooks in *Pandora's Box*

of black bobbed hair, as the sexually insatiable Lulu, a prostitute who ensnares a series of men (and one woman) with her fectching beauty and beguiling indifference. Lulu's cavalier approach to love results in a self-destructive path — but not before she unwittingly destroys all who come close to her. (Silent) ★★★★ $24.99

Panic in the Streets

(1950, 93 min, US, Elia Kazan) When a corpse in New Orleans is found to be carrying the plague, a desperate search begins to track down its source. Richard Widmark is terrific as a health official supervising the hunt, and Jack Palance is memorable as an edgy psychopath who unwittingly holds the key to the mystery. A superb film noir thriller, directed in crisp, crackling fashion by Kazan. ★★★★ $39.99

Panic in Year Zero

(1962, 95 min, US, Ray Milland) Milland is both director and star of this low-budget but surprisingly effective and entertaining post-Apocalypse chiller. Milland, wife Jean Hagen and family take a vacation in the mountains. While there, a nuclear bomb strikes their city home nearby, and as they attempt to return to civilization, they stumble upon a newly ravaged society with terribly impolite manners. Milland is stiff upper-lipped as the heroic father, and his direction is equally rigid. But the film's premise, setting, cast of characters and cheesy cinematography and score all combine to make this a real panic. ★★★ $14.99

Panique (Panic)

(1946, 82 min, France, Julien Duvivier) From the novel by Georges Simenon, France's master of suspense, this clever study of mob psychology is set in the slums of Paris during the aftermath of WWII. Two lovers frame a stranger for a murder, but is the plan as perfect as they think? (French with English subtitles) ★★★½

409

Panther

(1995, 124 min, US, Mario Van Peebles) Denounced by real-life Panther Bobby Seale for its shameless inaccuracies, this clichéd melodrama not only manages to rewrite history, it also reduces a revolutionary group's actions to the level of a common street gang. Even the group's positive activities are handled as an afterthought. In spite of the terrific performances by Marcus Chong as Huey Newton and Courtenay B. Vance as Bobby Seale, *Panther* only occasionally hits its mark as it unevenly presents its social and political thoughts. ★★ $19.99

The Paper

(1994, 112 min, US, Ron Howard) A solid ensemble cast including Michael Keaton, Glenn Close, Robert Duvall, Marisa Tomei and Randy Quaid help bring to life this otherwise ordinary but involving newspaper comedy-drama. In this a-day-in-the-life-of-a-journalist, Keaton stars as the city editor of a New York daily tabloid who is caught in a dilemma when his managing editor (the wonderfully steely Close) wants to publish a story proclaiming two black youths guilty of murder when there's a chance they might be innocent. It becomes a battle of business vs. ethics when the two literally fight it out. Duvall nicely plays the paper's editor, Tomei is Keaton's pregnant wife, and Quaid has some funny scenes as a paranoid photographer who may not be that paranoid after all. ★★½ $14.99

The Paper Chase

(1973, 111 min, US, James Bridges) Exceptional study of academia with Timothy Bottoms as a Harvard Law student and John Houseman (in his brilliant Oscar-winning performance) as his professor and adversary. Also with Lindsay Wagner (as Bottoms' girlfriend and Houseman's daughter), Edward Herrmann and James Naughton. ★★★½ $19.99

Paper Moon

(1973, 103 min, US, Peter Bogdanovich) Bogdanovich's triumphant follow-up to *The Last Picture Show* and *What's Up Doc*, his other two classics, is, unfortunately, his last great work. One of the most charming comedies of the 1970s, Ryan O'Neal (one of the few times he's been likable) and Oscar winner Tatum O'Neal star as Depression-era Bible-selling grifters working their way through the Midwest. Excellent support from Madeline Kahn, P.J. Johnson and John Hillerman. ★★★★ $14.99

A Paper Wedding

(1991, 90 min, Canada, Michel Brault) A Canuck *Green Card*, this predictable but nevertheless charming drama features a deceptively impassive performance by Genevieve Bujold. Bujold is an unmarried university professor who, in order to help her immigration lawyer-sister, agrees to a marriage of convenience with a Chilean dissident who hopes to avoid deportation. The paper wedding becomes complicated, however, after immigration officials begin an investigation, forcing the unlikely couple to live together. Is love just around the bend? (French with English subtitles) ★★★ $79.99

Harry Dean Stanton in *Paris, Texas*

Paperhouse

(1989, 92 min, GB, Bernard Rose) First-time director Rose has fashioned an engrossing, surreal and frightening psychological horror film about an 11-year-old girl whose vivid imagination propels her from the safety of her bedroom to an eerie world conjured up by her own subconscious fears. Confined to bed because of recurring fainting spells, Anna spends her time drawing and becomes especially interested in finishing her sketch of a lonely house. But when she is asleep, she is transported to this house to find a paralyzed young boy and an unseen yet palpable evil. Vivid images, ominous landscapes and an ending to rattle even the most impassive viewer. ★★★

Papillon

(1973, 150 min, US, Franklin J. Schaffner) Steve McQueen gives what may be his best performance as the Devil's Island convict who is determined to escape, no matter what the cost. Easily one of the best "escape" films ever made. Dustin Hoffman gives magnificent support as a wise and easily contented prisoner. An intense and beautiful film. ★★★★ $14.99

Parade

(1973, 88 min, France, Jacques Tati) Newly rediscovered and restored, Tati's final film (made a year before he went bankrupt) was shot on video and was originally made for Swedish television. While not ranking with his best work, the film features many gloriously funny visual gags as Tati takes us through the many acts of a circus troupe who perform for an appreciative audience of two small children. This celebration of innocence and simple entertainment has clowns, magicians, acrobats and mimes who all take center stage for a time. A witty and humorously entertaining film with minimal dialogue and maximum enjoyment. ★★★ $29.99

The Paradine Case

(1948, 116 min, US, Alfred Hitchcock) Attorney Gregory Peck risks his marriage and profession when he falls in love with the enigmatic Mrs. Paradine, on trial for murdering her rich, blind husband. This talky but fascinating did-she-or-didn't-she also stars Ethel Barrymore, with Charles Laughton as the delightfully lascivious judge. ★★★ $14.99

Paradise

(1991, 115 min, US, Mary Agnes Donoghue) A surprisingly effective remake of the French hit *Le Grand Chemin*. Don Johnson and Melanie Griffith play a troubled rural couple who take care of a friend's young son for the summer. The shy, sheltered youth (well played by Elijah Wood) befriends a young tomboy (Thora Birch), who helps the boy emerge from his shell. And, in turn, the youth helps the couple come to terms with the death of their baby. A low-key, rather sweet coming-of-age tale. ★★★ $9.99

Paradise Alley

(1978, 109 min, US, Sylvester Stallone) Stallone wrote, directed and stars in this gritty though contrived story of three brothers from Hell's Kitchen who enter the world of wrestling to escape their New York City ghetto environment. ★★ $9.99

Paradise Lost: The Child Murders at Robin Hood Hills

(1996, 150 min, US, Joel Berlinger & Bruce Sinofsky) Picking up where they left off with *My Brother's Keeper*, directors Berlinger & Sinofsky once again travel to small-town America to cover a sensational murder trial. In this case, the locale is West Memphis, Arkansas (basically a broken down trailer park suburb of Graceland on the other side of the mighty Mississippi), and the trial is that of three teens who are accused of the brutal satanic ritual murder of three 8-year-old boys. The chief defendant is Damien Wayne Echols, a black-clad 18-year-old outcast, who the D.A. prosecutes along with Jason Baldwin, 16, based on the confession of their alleged accomplice Jessie Lloyd Misskelly. Originally shot for HBO and shown at film festivals around the country, the film's excessive running time will seem all-too-brief as Berlinger and Sinofsky do a brilliant job of presenting the myriad points of view and stringing them together into a riveting narrative. At one point, they even get stuck in a documentarian's nightmare when one of their interviewees presents them with evidence potentially damaging to the prosecution's case. The film's undisputed star, however, is Damien. Both villain and hero, he projects an intellect that clearly sets him apart from his home town, and his eerie cool on the witness stand makes for gripping viewing and is sure to leave the viewer wondering – did he or didn't he? ★★★★ $59.99

Paradise Road

(1997, 113 min, GB/US, Bruce Beresford) There's a telling moment in *Paradise Road* which transcends traditional POW films. British prisoner Glenn Close is taken into the jungle by the guard who has beaten her. Instead of another attack, this heretofore monster reveals an unexpected humanity which takes her by surprise – she still hates this man, but through the universality of music, there is the slightest glimmer of hope. And it is through music that the prisoners of *Paradise Road* retain their faith and the will to survive. Based on actual incidents which occured in a Japanese POW camp during WWII, this is the affecting, hard-hitting story of a group of female Allied prisoners who for nearly three years suffered at the hands of the often brutal Japanese. Under the leadership of Close, the women form a "vocal orchestra" to show the enemy "they still have life to them." Though it sometimes approaches sappy and clichéd waters, it is quite touching and affirming. Director Beresford pulls no punches in the depiction of the cruelty; similarly themed films from the 1940s and '50s, such as the very good *Three Came Home*, could have never shown such things. Close's stirring performance is the film's center of gravity, and Pauline Collins as a missionary excels in support. ★★★ $99.99

The Parallax View

(1974, 102 min, US, Alan J. Pakula) Complicated and fascinating political thriller with Warren Beatty as a newspaper reporter investigating the assassination of a senator. As he digs further into the story, his own life and the lives of witnesses and those around him become increasingly in danger. ★★★½ $14.99

Pardon Mon Affaire

(1977, 105 min, France, Yves Robert) Miserably remade by Gene Wilder as *The Woman in Red*, this lovely, wry French boudoir comedy follows four buddies who undergo a series of complicated comic adventures through the streets and bedrooms of Paris. Jean Rochefort stars in a wonderful comic performance as the ringleader and chief erotic provocateur. (Dubbed) ★★★

Pardon Mon Affaire, Too

(1977, 110 min, France, Yves Robert) A film that pokes fun at marriage, fidelity, love and friendship, is a zestful continuation of the extramarital affairs of Jean Rochefort and his middle-aged friends. Their appetites for inflated fantasies and faded dreams are insightfully explored in this gently satiric farce. (Dubbed) ★★½

Pardon My Trunk
(Buongiorno, Elefante!)

(1952, 85 min, Italy, Gianni Franciolini) Vittorio De Sica turns in a fine performance in this wild though uneven satire of a Italian schoolteacher who receives an unwanted gift of an elephant from a wealthy prince. His efforts to rid himself of the bulky present set off a series of comic vignettes. (Dubbed) ★★½

The Parent Trap

(1961, 127 min, US, David Swift) Cute though sentimental Disney comedy with Hayley Mills doubling as long-lost twin sisters who meet at summer camp and devise a plan to reunite their divorced parents Brian Keith and Maureen O'Hara. ★★½ $19.99

Parenthood

(1989, 124 min, US, Ron Howard) An all-star cast shines in Howard's charming and very funny family comedy. Howard and cowriters Lowell Ganz and Babaloo Mandel examine American middle-class family life as seen through the not-so-ordinary eyes of the multi-generational Buckman clan. Steve Martin stars as Gil, a worrisome father who is ever-aware of personal shortcomings with his own father and is determined not to repeat the same with his troubled son. Jason Robards, Mary Steenburgen and the wonderful Dianne Wiest also star. ★★★ $14.99

Parents

(1989, 90 min, US, Bob Balaban) First-time director Balaban serves up a wild postmodern feast that may leave you with a bad taste in your mouth but a grin on your face. Young Bryan Madorsky discovers his Ozzie and Harriet parents have a terrible secret and it's hardly appetizing. Starring Randy Quaid, Mary Beth Hurt and the scene-stealing Sandy Dennis. Not for everyone, but if you prefer your filmmaking adventurous, give it a nibble. ★★★ $14.99

Paris Belongs to Us

(1959, 138 min, France, Jacques Rivette) New Wave director Rivette's (*Celine and Julie Go Boating, The Nun*) first feature is this low-budget drama starring Jean-Claude Brialy and features cameos by fellow filmmakers Jean-Luc Godard, Claude Chabrol (who was also the cameraman) and Jacques Demy. The story is set in a near-deserted Paris one summer where a group of enthusiastic young amateurs get together in an effort to present a production of Shakespeare's "Pericles." But the death of the composer, suicide of the producer and mounting political and sexual tensions between the actors undermine their efforts. A spare and moody tale of optimism and doom. (French with English subtitles) ★★★ $29.99

Paris Blues

(1961, 98 min, US, Martin Ritt) Jazz and romance in the City of Lights, as musicians Paul Newman and Sidney Poitier court Joanne Woodward and Diahann Carroll. The film makes good use of a fine Duke Ellington score. Entertaining and well done. ★★★ $19.99

Paris Express

(1953, 80 min, GB, Harold French) Claude Rains stars as a low-level clerk who embezzles from his business in hopes of going on extended holiday, but instead finds himself lured by a femme fatale into a web of robbery, murder and intrigue. Rains' good performance and a moody atmosphere compensate for the sometimes muddled narrative. ★★½

Paris, France

(1993, 111 min, Canada, Gérard Ciccoritti) Deliriously paced and entertainingly saturated with numerous and inventively diverse sexual couplings, this tale of mid-life crisis, regret, longing and sexual repression is anything but your standard melodrama. Set in Toronto, the story involves the three owners of a small publishing company: a married couple, Lucy and Michael, and their business partner, William. The stability of their lives is thrown into an emotional maelstrom with the arrival of Sloan, a former boxer turned writer. As Sloan becomes involved with both the sexually starved Lucy and the openly gay William, his sexual needs lead to confusion: Is he a gay top man or a straight bottom boy (with Lucy administering the half-nelsons and whip-snappings)? Beyond the steamy sex scenes is the uninhibited notion of exploring all of one's many sexual needs. ★★★ $14.99

Paris Is Burning

(1990, 78 min, US, Jennie Livingston) Welcome to the world of the Ball, where everyone is Cinderella. The balls in question are the voguing and drag-balls of Harlem, the subject of director Livingston's award-winning and sensationally entertaining documentary. Voguing, an underground dance invented by black and Latino queers, burst upon the pop scene when Madonna "took" voguing for herself and popularized it. But it's the originators of the form who are the film's subject. Voguers, or "ball walkers," affiliate themselves with "Houses," the equivalent of nonviolent gay street gangs, and compete for trophies at the late-nite balls. For some, these balls are the only escape they have from their otherwise poverty-stricken lives. Livingston uses sensitivity and compassion in documenting her stars. From legendary drag queen Dorian Corey, to multi-grand prize winner Pepper Labeija, to hot-voguer Willi Ninja, all are fierce, friendly and for real. Snubbed at the Oscars, *Paris* is one of the liveliest and most touching movies of 1990; Madonna's production company financed it out of limbo and into video release. ★★★½ $19.99

Paris, Texas

(1984, 150 min, US, Wim Wenders) Wenders' understated exploration of human loneliness and vulnerability features Harry Dean Stanton as a near-catatonic wanderer who is somewhat snapped out of his stupor by his brother (Dean Stockwell). Upon reuniting with his young son, he and the boy set off in search of their long-lost wife and mother, Nastassja Kinski. Sam Shepard's screenplay and Robby Müller's camera keenly map out the desert of the human soul as set against the bleak Texas landscape; Ry Cooder's haunting slide guitar finishes off the effect. ★★★ $19.99

Passione d'Amore

Paris Trout

(1991, 100 min, US, Stephen Gyllenhaal) A stunning made-for-cable adaptation of Pete Dexter's award-winning novel. Dennis Hopper is outstanding as the title character, a racist 1940s Southern storekeeper who kills a young black girl, the sister of a man Trout cheated in a car sale, and who now stands trial for murder. Barbara Hershey is terrific as Hopper's abused wife, whose moral outrage to her husband's actions sends her into the arms of lawyer Ed Harris (in a wonderful characterization). ★★★★ $19.99

Paris When It Sizzles

(1964, 110 min, US, Richard Quine) Despite an engaging premise and a first-rate cast, this forced comedy offers little in laughs or enjoyment. Screenwriter William Holden and secretary Audrey Hepburn romp around Paris in a series of fantasies acting out his new script. ★½ $29.99

Parsifal

(1982, 255 min, West Germany, Hans-Jürgen Syberberg) Syberberg, director of *Our Hitler*, has created a spectacular and provocative film experience with this version of Richard Wagner's splendid opera. The eternal drama of the search for the Holy Grail is imaginatively enacted within the crevices and crannies of a mammoth replica of Wagner's death mask, with the character of Parsifal portrayed by both a man (Michael Kutter) and a woman (Karen Krick). The film, while a note-complete performance of the opera, is anything but conventional and is a must for all opera fans and adventurous film enthusiasts. ★★★½ $44.99

Parting Glances

(1986, 90 min, US, Bill Sherwood) A wonderfully rich and seductively appealing independent production which definitely rates as one of the best of all gay-themed films. The action takes place in a 24-hour period and centers around Michael (Richard Ganoung) and Robert (John Bolger), a gay New York couple who are about to temporarily separate as Robert is transferred overseas. Their attempts to keep the relationship strong and to understand each other is the core of this simple but wise comedy-drama. The supporting cast of mainly gay friends who throw a farewell party for Robert are all finely drawn, but it's Steve Buscemi who steals the film with a bravado performance as Nick, a rock singer and Michael's ex-lover who's dying of AIDS. Produced on a low budget, the film's strengths lie in its simple and honest moments — a loving embrace or a telling confession. A joyful, knowing gay love story. ★★★★ $29.99

Partisans of Vilna

(1986, 130 min, France, Josh Waletzky) This stirring documentary examines the Jewish resistance during WWII. Interspersing interviews with former freedom fighters from around the world with rare archival footage from the war years, the film spellbindingly introduces us to the Jewish youths who organized an underground resistance in the Vilna ghetto and fought as partisans against the Nazis. A powerful, heartrending tribute to courage in the face of unrelenting adversity.

(French, English, Hebrew and Yiddish with English subtitles) ★★★½

Partner

(1968, 112 min, Italy, Bernardo Bertolucci) Madness, romanticism, theatre and politics are the theme in *Partner*, a surprisingly noncommercial film director Bertolucci now repudiates. Greatly influenced by the 1968 student rebellions which swept Europe as well as the political cinema of Jean-Luc Godard and the theatrical devices developed by Julian Beck's Living Theatre, the film is a free adaptation of Dostoevsky's "The Double." Pierre Clementi stars as a repressed art teacher who is possessed and ultimately driven mad by his alter ego, a political revolutionary. A beautiful but off-setting film that is a must for fans of Bertolucci and followers of political cinema. (Italian with English subtitles) ★★★½ $39.99

The Party

(1968, 99 min, US, Blake Edwards) Peter Sellers gives one of his funniest performances as a clumsy Indian actor invited to a private Hollywood party. Edwards directs with the same comic assurance that he exercised in the *Pink Panther* series: inventive sight gags and crazy comedy abound. ★★★½ $14.99

Pascali's Island

(1988, 104 min, GB, James Dearden) Ben Kingsley gives an admirable performance in this rather slowly paced drama set on a small Greek island during the last days of the fading Ottoman Empire. Kingsley plays a local eccentric and Turkish spy who unwittingly becomes involved with a suave British archeologist (Charles Dance) and his plot to steal a precious artifact from the isle. Also caught up in the intrigue is an Austrian expatriate (Helen Mirren in a captivating performance), a lonely artist who falls in love with the handsome adventurer with tragic results. In addition to Kingsley and Mirren's first-rate portrayals, the film is highlighted by sumptuous cinematography and beautiful locales. ★★ $14.99

A Passage to India

(1984, 163 min, GB, David Lean) Master filmmaker Lean proves himself capable of pulling yet another beautifully crafted "big" picture out of his hat with this meticulous adaptation of the E. M. Forster novel about the clash between British and Indian cultures and classes in the colonial India of the 1920s. A superlative cast (Judy Davis, Victor Banerjee, Peggy Ashcroft, James Fox and Alec Guinness) plays against the brilliance of Lean's craft, with which he imbues each and every backdrop with flavor and nuance. Very satisfying. ★★★★ $19.99

Passage to Marseille

(1944, 109 min, US, Michael Curtiz) Curtiz, the director of *Casablanca*, reteamed with that film's star, Humphrey Bogart, and many of its supporting cast (including Claude Rains, Sydney Greenstreet and Peter Lorre) in hopes of repeating that classic's critical and commercial success. Although they didn't succeed on either level, *Passage to Marseille* is nonetheless an acceptable WWII adventure about escaped Devil's Island convicts who join the Free French in the fight against the Nazis. Confusing flashbacks-within-flashbacks keep this film from being the first-rate production Curtiz and company had hoped. ★★½ $19.99

La Passante

(1982, 106 min, France, Jacques Rouffio) Romy Schneider is wonderful in a dual role in this, her final film. It is the story of two lovers who are mysteriously compelled for political actions to become involved in the assassination of a South American ambassador who may have been a former Nazi leader. (French with English subtitles) ★★½

The Passenger

(1975, 123 min, Italy, Michelangelo Antonioni) Jack Nicholson stars in this hypnotic thriller as a discontented reporter who changes his identity for a dead man. A brilliant portrayal of alienation's pangs and the barren landscape of one man's soul. ★★★½

P

Passenger 57

(1992, 84 min, US, Kevin Hooks) A *Die Hard* clone, Hooks' cartoonish action film has the friendly skies substituting for the skyscraper as the backdrop for the act of terrorism. Wesley Snipes stars as an ex-secret service agent-turned-airline security consultant who battles a group of deadly international skyjackers. While the script is laughably illogical at points, Snipes shows what a good actor can do with a bland script, as opposed to a good action film with a bland actor (i.e. Steven Seagal in *Under Siege*). ★★ $9.99

Passion Fish

(1992, 136 min, US, John Sayles) Sayles' upbeat comic melodrama explores the rigors of adjusting to life as a paraplegic. Mary McDonnell stars as May-Alice, a famous soap opera star who, after being crippled by a New York taxi, returns to her home town on the Louisiana bayou to wallow in self-pity, drown herself in booze and heap abuse on a succession of unsuspecting house nurses. She finally meets her match, however, when the agency sends her the equally uncompromising and obstinate Chantelle (Alfre Woodard). Sayles wrings every ounce of humanity and wry humor from the clash of these two emotional tyrants as they slowly warm to each other. Marvelously photographed on location, the film sports a trio of splendid performances from McDonnell (who was nominated for an Oscar), from Woodard (who should have been) and David Strathairn as a local Cajun handyman who takes an obvious shine to McDonnell. ★★★½ $19.99

Passion for Life

(1948, 89 min, France, Jean-Paul Chanois) A sincere young teacher (Bernard Blier), impassioned with progressive ideas, comes to a provincial village where he meets opposition from the stodgy parents. Predating *Dead Poets Society* and *Stand and Deliver* by many decades, this sincere though sentimental tale follows the teacher as he must not only prove his worth but his methods as well after he promises that every one of the students in his class will pass a national test. (French with English subtitles) ★★½ $59.99

The Passion of Anna

(1969, 100 min, Sweden, Ingmar Bergman) Bergman continues with the recurring theme of a couple (or couples) isolated from society yet under attack from either, or both, outside forces as well as within their own selves. In this deeply textured psychological drama, Max von Sydow moves to a sparsely populated island where he meets a widowed young woman (the remarkable Liv Ullmann) and an architect (Erland Josephson) and his wife (Bibi Andersson). Complex emotional and spiritual fears are brought to the surface as the four develop revealing relationships that lay bare their despair and protective self-deceptions. (Swedish with English subtitles) ★★★★ $19.99

The Passion of Joan of Arc

(1928, 77 min, France, Carl Dreyer) Based on the actual transcripts of the historical trial and using innovative close-ups that have made film history, Dreyer's extraordinary film of the Inquisition, trial and death of Joan of Arc remains as fresh and powerful today as it was over 60 years ago. (Silent with musical accompaniment) ★★★★ $29.99

The Passionate Thief

(1962, 100 min, Italy, Mario Monicello) The director of *Big Deal on Madonna Street* brings his comedic talents to this entertaining story of larceny and love. Italian favorite Toto is a small-time bit player who repeatedly thwarts the efforts of a pickpocket (Ben Gazzara) to earn his living one New Year's Eve night. Anna Magnani co-stars in this minor, but worthwhile comedy of errors. (Italian with English subtitles) ★★½ $19.99

Passione d'Amore

(1982, 117 min, Italy, Ettore Scola) A handsome and witty tale about the ironies and intricacies of love and beauty. In 19th-century Italy, a dashing young cavalry officer engages in an adulterous affair with a voluptuous woman only to become involved with his commanding officer's homely, cantankerous cousin. This sardonic, dark comedy received a special jury prize at the Cannes Film Festival. The basis for the Stephen Sondheim musical "Passion." (Dubbed) ★★★½ $24.99

Passport to Pimlico

(1948, 85 min, GB, Henry Cornelius) This wonderful little British comedy has an anarchic "little man battling the establishment" attitude. A fish store proprietor unearths an ancient treaty that establishes Pimlico as a part of Burgundy, instead of London, thus releasing store owners from both the post-war rationing and British licensing laws. A wonderful parody of the postwar state of Europe starring Stanley Holloway, Basil Radford, and the great Maragret Rutherford. ★★★½ $14.99

Past Midnight

(1992, 100 min, US, Jan Eliasberg) This made-for-cable mystery is about a social worker (Natasha Richardson) who falls for her latest case, a paroled wife killer (Rutger Hauer) whom she believes was wrongly accused — or was he? A few interesting turns and a trio of seasoned performances (rounded out by Clancy Brown) can't overcome a plot line more basic than *Basic Instinct*, but it's not bad for a B-grade attempt. ★★½ $14.99

Pastime

(1991, 95 min, US, Robin B. Armstrong) Tucked in between the theatrical releases of *Field of Dreams* and *A League of Their Own*, this small-scaled, bittersweet drama is not in the same league as those two gems, but is nevertheless an appealing, carefully rendered character study. In a splendid performance, William Russ makes the most of his first starring role with a gorgeous turn as a veteran minor league ballplayer at the end of his career. Having had a brief stint in the majors, and after twenty years in the minors, Russ is now the butt of his teammates' jokes, not fully aware of his own shortcomings and still hoping to make it back to "the Bigs." When he befriends a young, talented pitcher, both men strike a friendship to help each other face their uncertain futures. ★★½ $14.99

Pat and Mike

(1952, 95 min, US, George Cukor) This enjoyable sports comedy doesn't rate with the best of the Katharine Hepburn-Spencer Tracy films, but it is nevertheless a pleasant tale with Kate as a sports pro and Spencer as her manager. ★★★ $19.99

Pat Garrett and Billy the Kid

(1973, 122 min, US, Sam Peckinpah) Outlaw-turned-lawman Pat Garrett (James Coburn) stalks Billy the Kid (Kris Kristofferson) across the New Mexican desert in this vivid Peckinpah western. Cast features Jason Robards, Slim Pickens, Rita Coolidge and Bob Dylan (in his acting debut). This is the restored version. ★★½ $19.99

A Patch of Blue

(1965, 105 min, US, Guy Green) A moving, sensitive drama of a blind white woman (Elizabeth Hartman) falling in love with a black man (Sidney Poitier). Fine acting accen-

Spencer Tracy and Katharine Hepburn in *Pat and Mike*

tuates this story; Shelley Winters won an Oscar as Hartman's overbearing mother. (Available letterboxed and pan & scan) ★★★ $19.99

Pather Panchali

(1955, 115 min, India, Satyajit Ray) This first film of Ray's widely acclaimed Apu Trilogy tells of Apu's childhood as a member of a poverty-stricken family in a Bengali village. The film is grippingly realistic and, although the locales are exotic, the human situation it portrays is shattering. (Bengali with English subtitles) ★★★★ $19.99

Pathfinder

(1988, 88 min, Norway, Nils Gaup) Set in the bitter cold and snow-covered tundra of northern Finland, this exciting, violent and emotional adventure story, taken from a 1,000-year-old legend, concerns an unusually dramatic coming-of-age of a teenage boy whose family is massacred by a rampaging band of thieves. Young Aigin flees to another village but finds that the killers are on his trail. He must decide whether to flee with the others, stand and fight a hopeless battle or join forces with the village's elderly but still powerful "pathfinder." Infused with the cultural mysticism and superstitions of the nomadic Lapp people, this Academy Award-nominated tale tells of the eternal battle of man against his own forces of evil. (Lapp with English subtitles) ★★★½ $19.99

Paths of Glory

(1957, 86 min, GB, Stanley Kubrick) Kubrick's first true masterpiece combines superb direction with outstanding performances and remains one of the most shattering studies of the insanity of war to date. Kirk Douglas, George Macready, Adolphe Menjou and Ralph Meeker star in this WWI story about a French general who orders his men on a futile mission. When they return in failure, he picks three soldiers to be tried and executed for cowardice. This scathing attack on the hypocrisies of war is, so far as we know, still banned in France. ★★★★ $19.99

Patriot Games

(1992, 118 min, US, Philip Noyce) A very capable sequel to the hit thriller *The Hunt for Red October*, with Harrison Ford taking over the role of CIA agent Jack Ryan first introduced by Alec Baldwin. While on a lecture

Pather Panchali

tour in London, Ryan thwarts an attempted Royal Family assassination, killing one of the terrorists in the process. This makes him and his family a target of the dead man's brother. Punctuated by a series of well-mounted and exciting action scenes, the film is marred only by a hastily tacked-on ending which belies what came before it. Whereas Baldwin's Jack Ryan was a protagonist driven by rational thought, Ford's Ryan is a reluctant but nevertheless visceral hero to be reckoned with. *Fatal Attraction*'s Anne Archer costars as Ford's wife, and she suffers similarly. (Available letterboxed and pan & scan) ★★★ $14.99

Pattes Blanches

(1949, 92 min, France, Jean Grémillon) Set against lovingly rendered Breton landscapes, this perverse melodrama of obsessive rivalry is a twisted mesh of sexual jealousies, intrigues, violence and revenge. Director Grémillon, best known for his documentaries and for presiding over the Cinémathèque, fills his film with strange scenes and a wonderful trick ending. The film follows the sordid story of two sons who fight for the love of a pretty but vicious innkeeper's mistress. The title refers to the white spats worn by a reclusive aristocrat who is ridiculed and loathed by the villagers. (French with English subtitles) ★★½ $59.99

Patti Rocks

(1988, 105 min, US, David Burton Morris) An original and quite controversial dissection of the attitudes and misconceptions of what some men feel about women. Billy (Chris Mulkey), a 30-year-old married dock worker, convinces his old friend Eddie (John Jennings) to accompany him on a long ride to Billy's pregnant girlfriend's house, to help him break off their relationship. The first half of the film is the car ride, as the two men exchange their conflicting views on women and life in vivid, locker-room talk. The second-half takes place at Patti's apartment, where the men discover an independent and compassionate woman who has her own ideas on her future with Billy and the baby. ★★★

Patton

(1970, 170 min, US, Franklin J. Schaffner) George C. Scott won (and refused) an Oscar for his powerhouse performance of the controversial WWII commander, General George Patton, in this superior wartime biography. The film, which won seven Oscars including Best Picture, follows Patton's campaign in Europe and Northern Africa. ★★★★ $19.99

Patty Hearst

(1988, 108 min, US, Paul Schrader) Natasha Richardson plays the title role in this dark, gritty version of Patty Hearst's story about the young heiress being kidnapped and brainwashed by the Symbionese Liberation Army; then being forced to participate in a series of bank robberies. With William Forsythe and Dana Delaney. ★★½

Paul Bowles in Morocco

(1970, 57 min, GB, Gary Conklin) "If life is a question of being...then the best thing for him was to sit back and be, and whatever happened, he still was." Paul Bowles, acclaimed writer ("The Sheltering Sky," "Let It Come Down") and composer, is spotlighted in this intriguing documentary. Having left the United States in the 1940s to travel around the world, Mr. Bowles eventually settled in Morocco and it is there, in Tangier, that the filmmaker finds this urbane and fascinating man. Reading passages from his novels, recounting exotic stories from his past, visiting his favorite haunts and philosophizing about the Moroccan people and their lifestyle, Bowles rambles, but what captivating rambling it is. Interestingly, the film at times is less about the writer and more about the strange appeal of this mysterious Arab culture and land. ★★★ $29.99

Paul Cadmus: Enfant Terribles at 80

(1984, 64 min, US, David Sutherland) In his Connecticut studio as he draws a nude, Paul Cadmus reminisces about his background, his artistic inspirations and the techniques of his work in a career which saw his brash, satirical and sexually provocative paintings create scandal and controversy as far back as the 1930s.

Pathfinder

This award-winning documentary lets Cadmus do all the talking as the erudite artist takes us through his stormy career and explains his paintings and drawings as well as the people who inspired him. ★★★ $39.99

Paul Robeson

(1978, 118 min, US, Lloyd Richards) James Earl Jones, accompanied only by Burt Wallace on piano, holds the stage for nearly two hours as Paul Robeson, recounting a remarkable life in a mesmerizing performance. Jones adeptly shifts mood and tone from episode to episode as Robeson responds to indignity and prejudice with good humor and a well-justified anger tempered by a towering intellect. Written by Phillip Hayes Dean, the story's first act covers Robeson's undergraduate days at Rutgers to his rise as a star in the London production of "Showboat." In Act Two, his brilliant theatrical career dissolves as the rise of Fascism alters the face of Europe. He returns home only to face racism and the House Un-American Activities Committee. This complex, courageous man of integrity is given full voice with Jones' vital, stirring portrayal; and this play on film is satisfying both dramatically and as history. ★★★½ $59.99

Paul Strand — Under the Dark Cloth

(1989, 81 min, Canada, John Walker) Pioneer filmmaker, cameraman and trendsetting still photographer Paul Strand (1890-1976) is the fascinating subject of this involving documentary. Influenced by modernist painters such as Matisse and Picasso, the young Strand revolutionized photography in the 1920s by moving from simple landscape photography to creating works that were abstract interpretations of movement. Through interviews with friends and co-workers such as Georgia O'Keefe, Fred Zinnemann and Leo Hurwitz, as well as viewing and dissecting many of his most celebrated works, we begin to understand the driving creative force that has produced a startling and complex portfolio of images. Sergei Eisentein once said, "Paul Strand is one of the greatest photographers in the world." ★★★ $29.99

Pauline at the Beach

(1983, 94 min, France, Eric Rohmer) This effervescent sex farce follows the amorous escapades of a precocious young girl, her stunningly beautiful cousin, an adventurous rogue and a beleaguered beachcomber. A witty meditation on the folly of love and the quest for romance. (French with English subtitles) ★★★ $24.99

The Pawnbroker

(1965, 116 min, US, Sidney Lumet) Gripping drama of a New York pawnbroker haunted by the memory of his imprisonment at a Nazi camp during WWII. Rod Steiger gives a virtuoso performance as the embittered prison camp survivor. Remarkably realized by director Lumet. ★★★★ $14.99

Payday

(1972, 98 min, US, Daryl Duke) Rip Torn plays an aging country music star who, tied to the seedy world of life on the road, seeks out the few people in his life who aren't trying to squeeze him for something. A terrific perfor-

mance by Torn dominates this insightful, arresting drama. ★★★

PCU

(1994, 85 min, US, Hart Bochner) A lot funnier than it has a right to be, this *Animal House* rip-off for the '90s follows to the letter the rules of the campus comedy (especially pitting uptight students and administration against fun-loving misfits), which makes *PCU* just another teenage comedy clone. However, that's only half the story. For as a satire on political correctness, this is a surprisingly funny, predictably sophomoric romp which takes pot shots at all of the sacred cows of the 1990s. It could even bring a smile or two to PCers (with a sense of humor). ★★½ $96.89

The Pebble and the Penguin

(1995, 74 min, US, Don Bluth) In this entry from Don Bluth (*All Dogs Go to Heaven*) and company, there seems to be a determination to generate a Broadway-like production in both style and content. And while Barry Manilow's music is actually quite good, it often seems like fill-in for a fairly thin plot. Shy boy penguin Hubie (voiced by Martin Short) meets girl penguin Marina (Annie Golden), and they fall in love. But evil penguin Drake (Tim Curry) stands in their way, and he vanquishes Hubie who struggles for the rest of the film to return to his love — with the help of new pal penguin Rocco (James Belushi). The cast provide good voices, and the animation is first-rate, but a little more intrigue would have been welcome. ★★½ $14.99

The Pedestrian

(1974, 97 min, West Germany, Maximilian Schell) An excellent drama examining the guilt of Nazi crimes against humanity and their effects on German society 45 years later. A wealthy industrialist is involved in a car accident in which his son is killed. The ensuing publicity brings out a story that he might have participated in the slaughter of a Greek village during the war. The circumstantial evidence

linking him to the crimes and the country's reaction to the news combine to indict the man. But is he guilty? (Dubbed) ★★★½

Pee-wee's Big Adventure

(1985, 90 min, US, Tim Burton) There are things about him you wouldn't understand, there are things you couldn't understand, things you shouldn't understand. He's Pee-wee Herman, loner and rebel. Paul Reubens' triumphant characterization is the ultimate child of the Eighties. Follow Pee-wee as he desperately searches for his most prized possession: his recently stolen bicycle. Anti-intelligence was never so brilliant. ★★★½ $9.99

Peeping Tom

(1960, 109 min, GB, Michael Powell) Powell's long-suppressed masterpiece is a lucid, slyly witty thriller about a deranged cameraman's obsession with photographing beautiful women as he murders them. So hostilely received at the time of its release, this film virtually ended this great director's career. (Letterboxed version) ★★★½ $29.99

Peggy Sue Got Married

(1986, 104 min, US, Francis Coppola) A separated 43-year-old mother (Kathleen Turner) travels back in time to her senior year in high school — where she attempts to set the future right. Nicolas Cage is her once and future husband. A sweet-natured blend of fantasy, comedy and drama, which, for the most part, works beautifully. Turner is most engaging. ★★★

Peking Opera Blues

(1986, 104 min, Hong Kong, Tsui Hark) One of the best of the recent crop of Hong Kong imports, this entertaining satirical adventure film features stunning set design, gold-digging dames, plots and counterplots, assassinations, singers and soldiers, all coming together in furiously paced, breathlessly choreographed action sequences. Set in 1913, the frenetic comedy features three young women who become enmeshed in dangerous intrigue

Pee-wee's Big Adventure

P

involving efforts to topple a general. Director Tsui has been quoted as saying that the film is a satire on "Chinese ignorance of Democracy," but it doesn't stop the fun in this tongue-in-cheek farce. (Cantonese with English subtitles) ★★★½ $59.99

The Pelican Brief

(1993, 125 min, US, Alan J. Pakula) *The Pelican Brief*, which could be dubbed *Murder Most Fowl*, stars Julia Roberts as a law student who uncovers the diabolical plot behind the assassination of two Supreme Court justices. Jokingly – but accurately – called a Nancy Drew for the '90s, this slick but lackadaisical film version of John Grisham's best-seller lacks the excitement and tension which made his other '93 movie adaptation, *The Firm*, so enjoyable. Denzel Washington costars as a journalist who helps Roberts stay alive after her savvy detective work puts her life in peril. This is the sort of paranoia-conspiracy thriller in which once a character befriends the hero(ine), you know they're gonna end up dead in the next reel. ★★½ $14.99

Pelle the Conqueror

(1988, 160 min, Denmark, Bille August) Winner of the Academy Award for Best Foreign Picture, this epic drama about human resilience stars the hypnotic Max von Sydow as a poor, but never downtrodden widower who emigrates with his young son from the economically depressed Sweden to Denmark at the turn of the century. His illusory quest for the good life leads only to a straw bed in the cold barn of a brutally insensitive farmer. The story centers around the close relationship between the father and son as they attempt to eke out a happy life amid crushing oppression. ★★★ $19.99

Pennies from Heaven

(1981, 107 min, US, Herbert Ross) Steve Martin, trying to escape his "wild and crazy guy" persona, had long wanted to do this transplanted version of Dennis Potter's tale of a Depression-era sheet music salesman whose dreary life is in stark contrast to the cheerful songs he sells. With the original recordings of the songs of the era acting as a Greek chorus, Potter's world remains every bit as bleak here as in his other works ("The Singing Detective," "Dreamchild"). Beautifully photographed by Gordon Willis, on stylized sets designed by Ken Adams. And Christopher Walken's dance sequence is a show-stopper. ★★★½ $19.99

Penny Serenade

(1941, 95 min, US, George Stevens) Cary Grant and Irene Dunne give compelling performances in this first-rate tearjerker with Grant and Dunne as a couple whose attempts to adopt after the death of their baby brings about tragedy. A three-hankier. Fine support from Beulah Bondi as a sympathetic adoption official and Edgar Buchanan as the couple's best friend. ★★★ $19.99

The People That Time Forgot

(1977, 90 min, US, Kevin Connor) Patrick Wayne, Doug McClure and Sarah Douglas battle prehistoric monsters and savage tribespeople while searching for a lost adventurer. This

sequel to *The Land That Time Forgot* is forgettable though silly fun. Based on a story by Edgar Rice Burroughs. ★★

The People vs. Larry Flynt

(1996, 127 min, US, Milos Forman) The most controversial film of its year, *The People vs. Larry Flynt* is also one of its best. It's a film full of surprises – from the caliber of its acting to the persuasiveness of its message to the agility and energy of its storytelling. As unlikely a hero to the Constitution as any in modern America, Larry Flynt started as publisher of *Hustler* magazine, initiated as a "racier" alternative to *Playboy*. Tasteless and exploitative, the magazine brought him notoriety and many brushes with the law. As the film succinctly recalls, one of these brushes landed him in front of the Supreme Court in a historic case. Faced with the difficult task of relating the story of a man whose moral life is probably undeserving of one, director Forman and writers Scott Alexander and Larry Karaszewski (*Ed Wood*) never lionize Flynt (like the film's detractors have complained). It's balanced writing and Flynt is no more than a sleazy publisher who happened to make a significant social contribution. But the beauty of the film is that the story is always appealing. As Flynt, Woody Harrelson has never been more effective; and Courtney Love is absolutely riveting as his wife. Forman has crafted a cunning biography, timely political fable, and, most surprisingly, a crushing story of romantic loss. ★★★★ $102.99

The People vs. Paul Crump

(1968, 60 min, US, William Friedkin) Originally made for TV, this powerful criminal investigative documentary was made by a young Friedkin (*The Boys in the Band*, *The Exorcist*) decades before Errol Morris' similarly themed *The Thin Blue Line*. The film investigates the crime and prosecution of Paul Crump, a black man convicted of murder and sentenced to die in the electric chair. Reenacting the crime and murder in dramatic fashion, in which $20,000 was stolen, several employees beaten and a security guard killed,

action returns to Crump in jail, where even his jailers acknowledge that he is a rehabilitated man. The film is less concerned about his involvement in the murder and more on the man himself, the function of prison and a possible conspiracy by officials to continue to seek his death. ★★★ $39.99

Pépé le Moko

(1936, 86 min, France, Julien Duvivier) Set in the Algerian Casbah, this sumptuously photographed, *tres* complex, fascinating story follows a hardened gangster's (Jean Gabin) successful ploy to elude the police. The melodramatic story observes his attraction to a beautiful femme fatale (Mirielle Balin) who eventually causes his undoing. (French with English subtitles) ★★★½ $14.99

Pepi, Luci, Bom y Otras

(1980, 86 min, Spain, Pedro Almodóvar) Spanish bad-boy director Almodóvar's 1980 feature debut, a mock-pornographic farce, is rude, funny and *very* nasty. The inimitable Carmen Maura (who would work many times with Almodóvar) plays the heiress Pepi, who seeks revenge on the cop who deflowered her by becoming involved with his masochistic wife Luci and her lesbian rock-star friend Bom. Replete with drugs, erection-measuring parties, beatings and body fluids, this low-budget, raw and crude camp piece lacks the frenetic pace and lush panoramic color scheme of his later works; but as a curio, it is a must for Almodóvar fans. (Spanish with English subtitles) ★★ $79.99

Peppermint Soda

(1977, 94 min, France, Diane Kurys) An arthouse favorite for years, this engaging comedy about growing up is set in Paris in the early 1960s. The story follows the lives of two spirited sisters, 12-year-old Anne and 15-year-old Frederique. Writer-director Kurys (*Entre Nous*) manages to examine those often explored topics of teendom (first loves, strict parents, fascist teachers and "becoming a woman") with a freshness and honesty that is an absolute delight. Especially good is Eléonore Klarwein,

The People vs. Larry Flynt

Peppermint Soda

who as Anne has a kind of sulky, impertinent charm and a devastatingly impish smile. Kurys followed this autobiographical film with *Cocktail Molotov*. (French with English subtitles) ★★★½ $29.99

The Perez Family

(1995, 112 min, US, Mira Nair) This sensual and hypnotic comedy of errors and culture clash is set during the 1980 Mariel boat-lift (during which thousands of Cuban political prisoners were released and placed in American holding centers to await citizenship). Marisa Tomei stars as Dorita Perez, a sultry Cuban floozy who tries to scam her way out of the American internment camp by claiming to be the wife of Juan Raul Perez (Alfred Molina), a once dapper, now bedraggled wreck who wants nothing more than to be reunited with his wife of 20 years, Carmela (Anjelica Huston), who doesn't even know he's been released. Nair's follow-up to her debut film, *Mississippi Masala*, is an intoxicating blend of humor, irony and romance enhanced by gorgeous cinematography but marred only by her distracting but effective use of non-Hispanic actors in the lead roles. Also starring Chazz Palminteri and Trini Alvarado. ★★★ $19.99

Perfect

(1985, 120 min, US, James Bridges) John Travolta plays a *Rolling Stone* reporter who is writing an exposé on Los Angeles health clubs and becomes infatuated with a club owner (Jamie Lee Curtis). A real stinker. ★ $9.99

A Perfect World

(1993, 137 min, US, Clint Eastwood) Eastwood's *A Perfect World*, which surprisingly garnered so-so box-office results, is an unusual and worthy follow-up to the director's Oscar-winning *Unforgiven*. In an electric and atypically malevolent performance, Kevin Costner plays an escaped prisoner who kidnaps an eight-year-old boy and holds him hostage as he tries to outrun the police. Eastwood and Laura Dern play a Texas lawman and criminologist, respectively, tracking them across the state. The film has a dark edge to it, and Eastwood's deliberate pacing only accentuates the tension produced by both the examination of the symbiotic relationship which develops between captive and convict

and an unnerving fifteen-minute attempted murder sequence. ★★★½ $9.99

Perfectly Normal

(1991, 106 min, Canada, Yves Simoneau) British laughmeister Robbie Coltrane (*Nuns on the Run, The Pope Must Die*) stars in this quirky sleeper about an opera-loving brewery worker (Michael Riley) who is conned by Coltrane into using his inheritance to open a restaurant staffed by aria-singing waiters. Imaginative visuals by Alain Dotsie. ★★★

Performance

(1970, 106 min, GB, Nicolas Roeg & Donald Cammell) James Fox is a gangster on the run drawn into the richly decadent, hallucinatory and erotic life of a retired rock idol — portrayed by Mick Jagger with androgynous glee. Using this alien world for refuge, he finds himself surrounded by an atmosphere of sex and violence which puts even his hardened senses on edge. A fascinating, yet repellent, visual experience. ★★★ $19.99

Perfumed Nightmare

(1978, 91 min, The Philippines, Kidlat Tahinik) Tahinik's treatise on the abuse of power and technology in the Third World for so-called "progress" was a winner of the International Critics Award at the Berlin Film Festival. This semiautobiographical fable follows a young Filipino through his awakening to, and reaction against, American cultural colonialism. Filmed in a quasi-documentary style, the film is a sometimes humorous, often compelling look at the insanity of unchecked industrial expansion. (English and Tagalog with English subtitles) ★★★ $39.99

Peril

(1985, 100 min, France, Michael Deville) A provocative, erotic thriller about a wealthy industrialist family who hires a musician to give lessons to their precocious daughter. The plot thickens as the wife of the industrialist seduces the young man and uses him as a pawn in a deadly, mysterious game of lust. An enigmatic tale of sexual duplicity. (French with English subtitles) ★★★ $19.99

Period of Adjustment

(1962, 111 min, US, George Roy Hill) Hill made his directorial debut with this lively film version of Tennessee Williams' successful stage comedy. In one of her first starring roles, Jane Fonda plays the newlywed wife of war veteran Jim Hutton. However, en route to Miami, their honeymoon trip is anything but sweet. Constantly at odds with each other, they stop at the home of Hutton's war buddy Tony Franciosa, himself experiencing marital difficulties with wife Lois Nettleton. What follows is a comic and tender exploration of love, marriage, male bravado and sexual compatibility. The four principals perform exceedingly well, with Nettleton a standout. ★★★ $19.99

Permanent Record

(1988, 92 min, US, Marisa Silver) Keanu Reeves delivers a compelling performance in this moving, sensitive drama as a tormented youth who can't figure out why his best friend

killed himself. Capable cast includes Alan Boyce, Barry Corbin, Michelle Meyrink and Kathy Baker. ★★★ $89.99

Permanent Vacation

(1980, 87 min, US, Jim Jarmusch) The aimlessness and ennui of the "post-punk generation" is the theme of Jarmusch's first feature film. Drawing from the now-familiar world of the Lower East Side, the film follows the dreamlike odyssey of a 16-year-old (Chris Parker of The Blank Generation) as he looks for meaning in his surroundings and his relationships with his girlfriend, acquaintances and parents. Utilizing the logic of a walking dream, Jarmusch has created a gritty, oppressive yet fascinating world. The film is dedicated to Nicholas Ray and features a jazzy score by John Lurie. ★★★

Permission to Kill

(1975, 96 min, GB, Cyril Frankel) International intrigue abounds in this complex spy thriller. Dirk Bogarde stars as the world-weary head of a spy consortium who must prevent a political expatriate (Bekim Fehmiu) from returning to his fascist homeland where certain death awaits. Also with Ava Gardner, Timothy Dalton and Frederic Forrest. ★★★

Persona

(1966, 83 min, Sweden, Ingmar Bergman) Bergman probes the depths of human psychology in this absorbing study of spiritual anguish. Liv Ullmann plays an actress who suffers a nervous breakdown and falls mute. A young nurse (Bibi Andersson) is employed to help, but instead, a deep emotional attachment is formed between the two as Andersson tries to bring her out of her silence and back into the world. This fascinating, complex film is erotically charged and remarkably intuitive, and beautifully shot in black and white. Ullmann gives a stunning, haunting performance without uttering one word. (Swedish with English subtitles) ★★★★ $19.99

Personal Best

(1982, 124 min, US, Robert Towne) Two women become friends and lovers during tryouts for the Olympics. Mariel Hemingway plays the fast but feckless Chris who gets a chance to make the team through her involvement with Tori (Patrice Donnelly). They become romantically involved, even though Chris denies the true nature of their romance, which only exasperates Tori. Their jealous, bitter coach (Scott Glenn) adds to their relationship's problems by eventually pitting them against each other personally and professionally. The film runs a bit too long and the cinematography is unimpressive with too many lingering group shower scenes and crotch close-ups, though the interpersonal relationship between the two women is sensitively handled. ★★★ $14.99

Personal Services

(1987, 105 min, GB, Terry Jones) Julie Walters, whose debut in *Educating Rita* captured the hearts of those who saw it, gives another delightful performance in this irreverent, hilarious satire on British mores. Walters plays a waitress who opens a successful

Pete Kelly's Blues

London brothel, whose customers are some of England's highest-ranking officials. Based on the real-life exploits of madam Cynthia Payne. (*Wish You Were Here* follows the adventures of a younger Cynthia Payne.) ★★★ $29.99

Persuasion

(1995, 103 min, GB, Roger Mitchell) Lost amidst the hype and fanfare surrounding Emma Thompson's adaptation of Jane Austen's *Sense and Sensibility* (or perhaps seen because of it), this superlative though admittedly modest BBC production of the author's lesser-known novel is in many regards equal to, and in some ways superior to, its more pedigreed cousin. Enchanced by an unfaltering cast that delivers a host of performances with the uttermost sincerity and charm, the story revolves around the failing fortunes of the Elliot family and specifically of their as yet unmarried daughter Anne (Amanda Root). Shortly after the family has given up its manor, Anne (who is periously close to middle age) is reunited with her one former true love, Frederick Wentworth (Ciaran Hinds). Some years prior, she had broken her engagement, but clearly she is still in love. Romance follows, and oh, does it make for a swooning good time. Root and Hinds are not your typical screen beauties, and that is precisely what makes them so appealing – their radiance comes from within and it infects the entire film. Furthering the film's charm is its gritty, mud-strewn look at life in the English countryside circa 1810. This is a film in which skirt hems and coattails are downright soiled by the end of a stroll in the woods – how truly refreshing. ★★★★ $19.99

The Pest

(1997, 90 min, US, Paul Miller) Through his one-man off-Broadway shows, comedy specials and supporting turns in comedies such as *To Wong Foo...*, John Leguizamo has proven himself to be a resourceful, disciplined comedian. However, in *The Pest*, his first starring role, all restraints have been removed, and Leguizamo

is so over the top he often makes Jim Carrey appear subtle by comparison. As with Carrey, Leguizamo shows he has the talent, all he needs is the right material – which he doesn't get here. In this updated, '90s comic version of *The Most Dangerous Game*, Leguizamo plays a small-time con artist who agrees to be hunted by big-game hunter Jeffrey Jones for $50,000. This premise is all Leguizamo needs to offer a hyperventilating series of impersonations, jokes and pratfalls which rarely offer a punch line and are so tiring that even when they're funny there's no time to catch your breath. Leguizamo is a comic whirlwind, a human Tasmanian Devil, but ultimately *The Pest* is about as substantial as hot air. ★½ $99.99

Pet Sematary

(1989, 102 min, US, Mary Lambert) One of Stephen King's scariest books makes for one of his least successful screen adaptations. When his young son is accidentally killed, a grieving father uses a magical graveyard to bring him back to life, though he's not the same fun kid he used to be. ★★ $14.99

Pet Sematary II

(1993, 102 min, US, Mary Lambert) When is a music video not a music video? When it's this, the derivative sequel to the successful Stephen King adaptation by former rock music video director Lambert (who also directed the original). Edward Furlong (*Terminator 2*) stars as a troubled teen who must cope with the accidental death of his mother, a bullying sheriff (Clancey Brown) and the dark secrets of an ancient Indian burial ground with the power to restore life – almost. Though better written (and acted) than the first, director Lambert seems unable to resist flaunting her heavy metal roots, investing any moments of genuine horror that might exist with a slick, rock-n-roll flair. Here's hoping this fright franchise has found its final resting place. Also with Anthony Edwards. ★½ $14.99

Pet Shop

(1994, 88 min, US, Hope Perello) What do you get when you cross an alien fur ball with your average Earth-type household pet? The answer: The changelings featured in this nice addition to the family film genre from the makers of *Dragonworld*. Under the witness protection program, a Bronx family has just moved to a small town in Arizona where their teenage daughter struggles to fit in. Meanwhile, aliens have taken over the local pet shop and have given away pets who change into their alien form once the kids get them home. An intergalactic couple plot to kidnap the kids and the fun begins. ★★½ $14.99

Pete Kelly's Blues

(1955, 95 min, US, Jack Webb) Webb and Lee Marvin play Roaring '20s jazz musicians trying to keep ahead of the mob. This beautiful looking film is as stiff as Webb's demeanor; however, it is still worth a look for both a rare and wonderful dramatic performance by Peggy Lee as a doomed lounge singer, and two numbers by Ella Fitzgerald. Also starring Janet Leigh and Martin Milner. ★★½ $14.99

Pete 'n' Tillie

(1973, 100 min, US, Martin Ritt) Low-key though very engaging comedy-drama about the courtship and marriage of unlikely partners Walter Matthau and Carol Burnett. Geraldine Page is terrific in support as Burnett's bitchy friend (she received an Oscar nomination), and Rene Auberjonois is fine as her gay confidant. ★★½ $14.99

Pete's Dragon

(1977, 128 min, US, Don Chaffey) Charming live-action and animated Disney musical about an orphaned boy and his friendship with Elliott, the magic dragon. Starring Helen Reddy, Jim Dale and Mickey Rooney. ★★★ $24.99

Peter Pan

(1953, 78 min, US, Walt Disney) Even by today's standards of super-techno-FX and computer-generated wizardry, Disney's classic *Peter Pan* maintains its stature as an acme in animation technique. And the story is equally dazzling. The airborne hero takes Wendy and her brothers to Never-never Land, an island beyond space and frozen in time; where a determined, ticking crocodile stalks the nefarious Captain Hook, who in turn stalks the boy who will never grow up. How joyful to return to a time and place where – if we believe, and think happy thoughts – we can fly, we can fly, we can fly. ★★★½

Peter Pan

(1955, 100 min, US, Vincent J. Donohue) Mary Martin's timeless performance highlights this 1955 Emmy Award-winning television broadcast of the Broadway musical. Martin sparkles as the young boy determined never to grow up, and Cyril Ritchard is on-hand as the troublesome Captain Hook. Favorite songs inlcude "I Won't Grow Up," "Never Never Land" and, of course, "I'm Flying." ★★★½

P

Peter's Friends

(1992, 102 min, GB, Kenneth Branagh) Attempting to be a British *Big Chill* meets *The Rules of the Game* by way of "Writing Comedy for the Movies 101" outline, the story is set in a large English manor where six old university friends meet for a ten-year reunion. This cast of "wacky" stock characters includes director-star Branagh as a talented writer who sells himself off for money in Hollywood; his vulgar, loud-mouthed wife Rita Rudner (the film's cowriter); Stephen Fry as the lumbering host harboring a "secret"; and Emma Thompson (who outshines them all) as a gawky, eccentric woman trying desperately to change. Infused with admittedly funny, even witty one-liners, the film suffers from an all-too-familiar sitcom feel. The film's final "revelation" that the bisexual Peter is infected with HIV is a cheap, exploitative device aimed at triggering sappy, liberal sympathies. It's a heavy price for the viewer to pay for the preceeding moments of humor. ★½ $14.99

Le Petit Amour

(1987, 80 min, France, Agnès Varda) Varda's sad tale of a 40-year-old divorcée who takes comfort in the innocent arms of her daughter's best friend, even though he is only fifteen. Aware that the relationship is doomed from the beginning ("I know you won't be around when you start shaving," she tells him), she finds herself unable to resist the charms of what should have been an uncomplicated fling. (French with English subtitles) ★★½ $79.99

Petit Con

(1984, 90 min, France, Gérard Lauzier) Whereas most teenage comedies worship their young protagonists, *Petit Con* offers welcome relief with its pungent ironic humor that sends up both its adolescent hero and the values he blithely adheres to. Bernard Brieux gives a painfully acute performance as Michel, an 18-year-old cauldron of horniness, oversensitivity and naive politics who tries to find his niche

Lon Chaney in *Phantom of the Opera*

amongst the charlatans, hoods and weirdos of Paris. A Feifferesque observation of post-Sixties culture. (French with English subtitles) ★★★

La Petite Bande

(1984, 91 min, France, Michel Deville) This delightfully cheery romp follows the fantastic adventures of a group of English school children who play mass hooky and sneak off to France. Their travels take them through towns and countryside. All the while, they are an elusive target for the police who are intent on sending them home. (No dialogue - music and sound effects) ★★★ $59.99

La Petite Sirene (The Little Mermaid)

(1980, 104 min, France, Roger Andrieux) They're at it again! While sexual encounters between adults and teenagers are morally forbidden fruit in the states, for French filmmakers, it's almost a way of life. And this tantalizing Nabokovian drama, infused with engaging humor, is no exception. Philippe Leotard (*La Balance*) stars as a middle-aged auto mechanic who becomes the befuddled object of desire to a rich, spoiled 14-year-old obsessed with a fairy tale, "The Little Mermaid." (French with English subtitles) ★★½ $19.99

The Petrified Forest

(1936, 83 min, US, Archie Mayo) Bette Davis shines as an Arizona cafe waitress who meets up with English drifter and poet Leslie Howard. There at the cafe, they and a small party are held hostage by escaped felon Humphrey Bogart. A sterling adaptation of Robert Sherwood's hit play. ★★★½ $19.99

Peyton Place

(1957, 157 min, US, Mark Robson) This box-office smash (which served as the basis for the popular TV series) is a well-made screen version of the Grace Metalious novel. A quintessential soap opera, the story follows the lives of the citizens of a small New England town. Good cast includes Lana Turner, Hope Lange, Lloyd Nolan, Arthur Kennedy and Russ Tamblyn. ★★★ $14.99

Phantasm

(1979, 87 min, US, Don Coscarelli) Watch out for that flying silver ball! Two brothers decide to investigate the strange goings-on at a mausoleum and become the prey of a demonic figure. Gory, inventive and very unusual. ★★★

Phantasm II

(1988, 90 min, US, Don Coscarelli) Sequel to the cult horror hit has the "Tall Man" returning, traveling around the country stealing dead bodies for his demonic purposes. The survivors from the original are out to stop him. Though as gory as the original, it's not quite as effective. ★★ $14.99

The Phantom

(1996, 96 min, US, Simon Wincer) Underrated and overlooked in a crowded Summer of '96, *The Phantom* is an endearingly cheesy, old-fashioned and enjoyable throwback to the cliffhanger serials of the 1930s and '40s. Billy Zane is the dashing hero in purple tights, who is up against a

millionaire – Treat Williams is a hoot as the mustache-twirling villain – determined to own three magic skulls which would give him ultimate power. Director Wincer, his production team and the entire cast capture the flavor of the comic book, succeeding where the similarly themed *The Shadow* failed. In fact, if the film were in black and white, it would seem lifted from an ongoing serial, with nary a trace of '90s sensibility (save the slight camp approach). This is what makes *The Phantom* so appealing. It may not be as hip or brooding or cyncial as recent adventure films, but its wholesome, derring-do spirit promises a fun time. ★★★ $14.99

The Phantom of Liberty

(1974, 104 min, France, Luis Buñuel) Well into his 70s, Buñuel continued to cinematically pinch our noses with his playful surreal satires on the middle class, democracy and love. "I am fed up with symmetry." So says a character early on in this montage of episodes, dreams and nightmares – each of which makes fun of man's idealistic notions of freedom. Filmed in an almost stream-of-consciousness style, this subversive little comedy is a delight. (French with English subtitles) ★★★½

Phantom of the Opera

(1925, 90 min, US, Rupert Julian) One of the greatest of all silent films, this chillingly atmospheric adaptation of the classic horror tale stars Lon Chaney in a tour de force performance as the masked composer haunting a Parisian opera house. ★★★½ $24.99

The Phantom of the Opera

(1943, 93 min, US, Arthur Lubin) Good remake of the classic silent film. Claude Rains gives a fine performance as the masked phantom living in the sewers beneath the Paris Opera House. Suzanna Foster and Nelson Eddy also star as the young lovers. ★★★ $14.99

Phantom of the Opera

(1990, 90 min, US, Dwight H. Little) Slice-n-dice remake of the horror classic about the cursed opera house dweller and his lady love. Robert Englund (aka Freddy Krueger) barely changes his makeup. Has *no* relation to the Broadway version. ★½ $14.99

The Phantom of the Paradise

(1974, 92 min, US, Brian De Palma) The first Faust-influenced horror, rock-musical comedy. A thwarted songwriter sells his soul to the Devil (an astute casting of Paul Williams) for rock 'n' roll success and Jessica Harper. A witty satire on at least a dozen different films and genres. De Palma directs many memorable scenes and performers including Beef, a hilarious rock superstar parody played by Gerritt Graham. ★★★ $14.99

Phar Lap

(1983, 108 min, Australia, Simon Wincer) An inspirational and entertaining account of the rise and fall of one of history's most phenomenal race horses, Phar Lap, who became a Depression-era hero to the Australian people. Ron Liebman stars as the Jewish-American owner who does battle with the high-brow, anti-Semitic Aussie racing elite. ★★★ $14.99

P

Phase IV

(1974, 86 min, US, Saul Bass) Famed title designer Bass (he did a lot of work with Preminger and Hitchcock) directed this cerebral sci-fi tale about a colony of ants that learn the power of their numbers as they fight man for supremacy of the planet. ★★½ $39.99

Phedre

(1968, 92 min, France, Pierre Jourdan) Jean Racine's Greek tragedy was first staged in Paris in 1677. This film version was theatrically filmed and powerfully presents the sad story of the consuming passion of Phedre, who falls in love with her stepson Hippolyte. Torn with remorse, she is compelled to confess her love to her husband. Starring 68-year-old Marie Bell. ★★★

Phenomenon

(1996, 117 min, US, Jon Turtletaub) After playing a couple of tough guys in *Pulp Fiction* and *Get Shorty*, John Travolta softens his image and goes the *Charly* route with mixed results. Travolta is George, an auto mechanic with not much going for him but who's very likable. When he sees what appears to be an extraterrestrial light in the sky, he is infused with a super intelligence and powers of telepathy. In between predicting earthquakes and saving lives, George also pursues Lace (Kyra Sedgwick), a mother of two who's always meeting the wrong man and who's determined not to meet any more. As a fantasy, *Phenomenon* beguiles. It's as personable as George himself – yes, he could be smarter but you kinda like what you see. And a good cast of supporting characters punctuates the film's playful spiritedness. But the romance between George and Lace drags, despite an engaging chemistry between Travolta and Sedgwick. And the ending is a cheat, a cop-out. *Phenomenon* tries to be magical but ultimately settles for common. ★★½ $19.99

Philadelphia

(1993, 120 min, US, Jonathan Demme) Tom Hanks won a Best Actor Oscar for his performance as a high-powered gay lawyer at a prestigious Philadelphia law firm who is stricken with AIDS. When his employers catch wind of this, they sabotage his work and fire him on false pretense. He retaliates with a lawsuit, soliciting a homophobic ambulance chaser (Denzel Washington) to represent him. The first Hollywood film about AIDS, *Philadelphia* delivers a strong emotional punch despite suffering from some procedural flaws, including underdeveloped relationships between characters – nowhere is this more felt than between Hanks and his lover Antonio Banderas. Additionally, the film's courtroom scenes are lacking in the expected drama, primarily because there is almost no doubt as to the outcome. Nothing can detract, however, from the film's hopeful and compassionate core, and the result is a very moving experience. ★★★ $14.99

The Philadelphia Experiment

(1984, 102 min, US, Stewart Raffill) Intriguing sci-fi thriller about two WWII sailors who are catapulted into the 1980s. Nancy Allen brings a nice no-nonsense sensibility to the modern girl who befriends time travelers Michael Paré and Bobby Di Cicco. ★★½ $14.99

The Philadelphia Experiment 2

(1993, 98 min, US, Stephen Cornwell) Brad Johnson (*Always*) stars in this inventive if static science-fiction thriller. Johnson assumes the role of an ex-naval pilot (originally played by Michael Paré) whose present-day existence becomes a nightmare when a military madman (Gerrit Graham) orchestrates a time shift that sends a Stealth Bomber back to WWII Germany enabling the Nazis to win the war. Watch for the David Lynch-inspired sequence with Graham trying to choose musical accompaniment for his Nazi propaganda film. ★★ $14.99

The Philadelphia Story

(1940, 112 min, US, George Cukor) Cukor's dedication to character, Philip Barry's delicious dialogue, and three of the most enchanting lead performances ever to grace the screen all combine to create the wittiest and most sophisticated comedy of the 1940s. Katharine Hepburn repeats her stage role as the Philadelphia socialite faced with a dilemma on her wedding day: who to marry. James Stewart won an Oscar for his delightful performance as a reporter covering Hepburn's wedding; and Cary Grant is the essence of charm as Kate's ex-husband. ★★★★ $14.99

Phobia

(1980, 91 min, US, John Huston) The phobia-ridden patients of a psychiatrist are being murdered one by one. The problem is – everyone appears guilty. Paul Michael Glaser stars. It's hard to believe this mess was directed by the great John Huston. ★ $79.99

The Phoenix

(1978, 137 min, Japan, Kon Ichikawa) Set thousands of years ago, this mystical and exciting film tells the story of the quest by an aging queen for the blood of the elusive phoenix, which she believes will give her eternal life. A fantasy-adventure combining live action and animation by world-famous cartoonist Osamu Tezuka. (Japanese with English subtitles) ★★★ $89.99

Phone Call from a Stranger

(1952, 96 min, US, Jean Negulesco) A survivor of a plane crash (Gary Merrill) visits the families of various victims, and receives understanding from a kindly, invalid widow, played by Bette Davis. Shelley Winters, Keenan Wynn and Michael Rennie also star. ★★★ $19.99

Physical Evidence

(1989, 99 min, US, Michael Crichton) Burt Reynolds plays a suspended, washed-up cop, awash in booze and self-pity, who is the prime suspect in the murder of an old criminal adversary. Prospects look grim when the defender's office assigns the neophyte "little rich girl" Theresa Russell as his lawyer. Did he kill during a drunken fury or was he set up? You may know the answer long before the final resolution, but the film's deft action and Reynolds' always-present self-deprecating humor helps gloss over the film's inconsistencies with plot to produce a mindless escapist entertainment. ★★½ $14.99

Piaf

(1981, 115 min, US, Howard Davies) Jane LaPortaire won a Tony Award for her touching portrayal of the legendary French songstress Edith Piaf. Ballads are woven closely together to re-create the bittersweet life of the woman who so captivated the world with her voice and life. Written by Pam Gems. ★★★

The Piano

(1993, 121 min, New Zealand, Jane Campion) Set in 19th-century New Zealand, this sumptuously photographed and atmospheric tale of repressed passions stars Oscar winner Holly

The Philadelphia Story

Hunter as Ada, a mute Scottish woman who is forced into an arranged marriage. She and her illegitimate daughter, Flora (the Puck-like Anna Paquin, who also won an Oscar), arrive at their new home with their worldly possessions – including Ada's prized piano. However, Ada's pious new husband, Stewart (Sam Neill), refuses to carry the instrument through the bush, and abandons it on the beach. He then sells the piano to an illiterate settler (Harvey Keitel), who in turn agrees to sell it back to Ada in exchange for lessons. His true intentions, however, involve Ada in a bizarre but passionate affair. Campion masterfully uses the power struggles between all of the characters to explore the various themes of colonialism and the plight of women while sketching a mesmerizing and emotionally involving story. ★★★★ $9.99

The Piano Lesson

(1995, 99 min, US, Lloyd Richards) August Wilson's Pulitzer Prize-winning Broadway drama is given an excellent realization in this made-for-TV adaptation. Re-creating his acclaimed stage role, Charles S. Dutton stars as Boy Willie, a 1930s black sharecropper with dreams of buying the land his family had once worked as slaves. He travels to Pittsburgh to convince his sister Berniece (Alfre Woodard) to sell the family's prized piano to pay for the farm. Thus sets in motion a passionate, heartfelt series of soul-searching and familial confrontations and reminiscences as Berniece refuses to part with the piano – a legacy of their servile past. As befits a great storyteller, Wilson's dialogue conjures another time and place, evoking through hearty though poetic anecdotes and conversations the history of a family. As Boy Willie, Dutton gives an outstanding performance, creating one of the theatre's most memorable, larger-than-life characters. Woodard, on the other hand, superbly underplays Berniece, the family's backbone still attempting to come to terms with the past. ★★★★ $14.99

The Pick-Up Artist

(1987, 81 min, US, James Toback) A good cast valiantly tries to bring some life to this otherwise lifeless drama. Robert Downey, Jr. is the title character, setting his sights on Molly Ringwald. With Dennis Hopper, Danny Aiello, Harvey Keitel and Mildred Dunnock. ★★ $19.99

The Pickle

(1993, 103 min, US, Paul Mazursky) Since Mazursky has dabbled with autobiographical material in the past, and had a big flop with *Scenes from a Mall*, the obvious question is whether this comedy about a desperately out of work auteur springs from some personal experience. Danny Aiello effectively assumes the role of Harry Stone, the hedonistic yet weary director who reluctantly checks his integrity and accepts a job at the helm of a movie about a giant pickle from outer space. This low-key comedy centers on Stone's return to his hometown of New York City and the tension-filled hours before the world premiere of his film. Though *The Pickle* is a curious mix of genuine drama and broad sitcom humor that never quite gels, it is entertaining and more

The Piano

than holds its own amidst the crowded giant vegetable genre. ★★½ $19.99

Pickpocket

(1959, 75 min, France, Robert Bresson) This austere meditation on the life of a petty thief is classic Bresson. Loosely based on Dostoevsky's "Crime and Punishment," this somber, static and emotionally distanced existential drama follows a man who, against the goodly advice of many, leads a life of crime. Our defiant protagonist's lifestyle leads him to prison where, removed from the world, he finds freedom and salvation. Set on the very real streets of Paris, this fascinating story finely details the planning and execution of crime and will remind some viewers of the work of Jean Genet as well as Camus' "The Stranger." (French with English subtitles) ★★★½

Pickup on South Street

(1953, 81 min, US, Samuel Fuller) Richard Widmark stars in this classic film noir spy thriller as a small-time pickpocket whose latest sting unwittingly involves him in political espionage. Director Fuller expertly extorts maximum tension from its novel premise; and Thelma Ritter gives a sensational performance as the pathetic, streetwise fence. ★★★½ $19.99

Picnic

(1955, 115 min, US, Joshua Logan) Riveting film version of William Inge's play about the sexual frustrations and longings in a small Kansas town. William Holden is the beefy drifter who sets hearts aflutter; Cliff Robertson is his old college friend; Kim Novak is Robertson's girlfriend who prefers Holden; and Rosalind Russell gives an electrifying performance as a spinster schoolteacher. Russell would have probably won a Supporting Actress statue but she refused to be in that category. ★★★★

Picnic at Hanging Rock

(1977, 115 min, Australia, Peter Weir) This dreamlike puzzle revolves around the disappearance of three schoolgirls and their teacher on an afternoon outing. Imbued with a swooning atmosphere of sexual mystery and ominous desire. ★★★½

Picnic on the Grass

(1959, 95 min, France, Jean Renoir) Set near the ancestral home of his painter father, Auguste, and filmed in an impressionistic style, Renoir has made a "filmed poem" to the mystery and power of nature. The story centers on a hardened biologist and candidate for President of the United States of Europe whose dedication to genetic engineering and the power of science is broken by the love of a peasant girl. (French with English subtitles) ★★★ $59.99

Picture Bride

(1995, 101 min, US, Kayo Hatta) Director Hatta has fashioned a subtle, deliberately paced and seductively involving portrait of one young woman's long, protracted journey across land, oceans and the terrain of the heart. Youki Kudoh is luminous as Riyo, one of the more than 26,000 Asian women who in the early 1900s traveled to Hawaii to marry men farming the cane fields. The couples were known to each other only by photos and letters, and both Riyo and her new husband Matsuji (played with earthiness and practicality by Akira Takayama) had concealed secrets from each other in their postal communications. Tamlyn Tomita (*The Joy Luck Club*) is memorable as a cane field worker whose great strength and determination are fully required to bear her load in life; and Toshiro Mifune has a cameo as the head of a traveling cinema. Meticulously produced, lushly photographed and presented with love and heart, the film presents even the most terrible hardships in an amber glow of reminiscence, leaving the viewer with a sense of the warmth of fond memory. ★★★½ $19.99

Picture Windows

(1995, 95 min, US, Norman Jewison/Peter Bogdanovich/Jonathan Kaplan) This selection from the ongoing Showtime production of short films features three entries from this uniformly well-executed series. *Soir Bleu*, directed by Jewison: A traveling central European circus creates a hallucinogenic world of saturated colors, fantastic costumes and death-defying feats, lending an air of

Jeanne Crain and Ethel Waters in *Pinky*

hyperrealism to this tale of love and betrayal inspired by "Il Pagliacci." This is the brutal backdrop to the love of a sad clown for a fading trapeze artist trapped in an abusive marriage. *Song of Songs*, directed by Bogdanovich: George Segal is a fussy, judgmental baker experiencing midlife crisis in this witty morality tale. His outrage at the opening of an intimate apparel shop across the street changes to awe when he meets the shop's spectacularly endowed owner (Sally Kirkland). His undoing, however, is provided by his long-suffering wife (Brooke Adams). *Language of the Heart*, directed by Kaplan: A whimsical, soul-satisfying tale of romance with a talented ballerina, an accomplished violinist who plies his trade in the street, and a lecherous old maestro who, as it turns out, has a heart of gold. An artfully re-created 1920s setting enchances this happy story. ★★★ $90.49

Pictures from a Revolution — A Memoir of the Nicaraguan Conflict

(1991, 93 min, US, Susan Meidelas, Richard P. Rogers & Alfred Guzzetti) As a photojournalist for *The New York Times*, Susan Meidelas covered the Sandinista Revolution in 1981. In this film, she returns to Nicaragua ten years later in search of the guerrillas, socialists and bystanders from her original photographs. As she retraces her steps and interviews survivors and their families, her journey becomes something of an odyssey into the human heart of a war-ravaged nation. It is an unusual political documentary which sketches out a minihistory of the Sandinista Revolution — from its idealistic founding, the United States' support of the Contras, and its eventual loss in elections. ★★★ $29.99

Pie in the Sky

(1996, 94 min, US, Bryan Gordon) *Threesome* star Josh Charles plays a young man with two obsessions: his childhood love, Amy (Anne Heche), and traffic. Conceived while his parents were stuck in a traffic jam, he feels it's his life's work, and dreams of meeting his idol, traffic reporter Alan Davenport (John Goodman). Meanwhile, he and Amy have an on-again, off-again romance. A mildly enjoyable romantic comedy, *Pie in the Sky* is slightly

disappointing considering director Gordon's previous film, the Oscar-winning short *Ray's Male Heterosexual Dance Hall*. This isn't as whimsical or romantic as it wants to be, nor as edgy or energetic as it should be, but the traffic-obsession angle lends it a nice, quirky feel, and it remains highly watchable throughout. The two leads are just this side of bland, but Goodman, Peter Riegert and especially Christine Lahti add sparkle. ★★½ $93.69

A Piece of the Action

(1977, 135 min, US, Sidney Poitier) Con men Sidney Poitier and Bill Cosby do their best to help a group of ghetto children. Overlong film mixes the crazy criminal antics of Cosby and Poitier with the social drama of life in the ghetto. For the most part, it doesn't work. Also with James Earl Jones and Denise Nicholas. ★★ $14.99

Pierrot le Fou

(1965, 90 min, France, Jean-Luc Godard) Godard's ebullience for life and his fascination with the possibilities of film are wonderfully displayed in this frantic and stylized tale of love, intrigue and betrayal. Jean-Paul Belmondo and Anna Karina star as two young lovers who involve themselves in a murder and begin an idyllic flight from justice. Filming without a script, Godard embellishes his story of doomed romantic love with splashy colors, exotic settings in the south of France, his trademark use of jump-cuts, classical music and literary references. (French with English subtitles) ★★★½ $59.99

Pillow Talk

(1959, 105 min, US, Michael Gordon) A box-office sensation in 1959, this delightful sex farce teamed Rock Hudson and Doris Day in the first and best of their "battle of the sexes." Though they can't stand each other in person, Rock and Doris unknowingly fall in love on their party line. Great support from Tony Randall and the always reliable Thelma Ritter. ★★★½ $14.99

Ping Pong

(1987, 95 min, GB, Po Chih Liong) From the mysterious nocturnal streets of London's Chinatown comes this exotic, noirish comedy-

thriller about a young Anglo-Chinese law student who is whisked into the tantalizingly complex task of executing a traditional Chinese will. Simple at first, but because of an intricate web of conditions and bequests, it falls to a vivacious young woman to piece together some unresolved mysteries. A richly textured and often comical portrait of a transplanted society caught between tradition and transition, flavored with a striking visual flair and moments of magic and fantasy. ★★★

Pink Cadillac

(1989, 122 min, US, Clint Eastwood) This change-of-pace comedy is a misfire for director Eastwood. He plays a bail-bond bounty hunter who becomes unlikely partners with the wife of one of his prey (Bernadette Peters). Peters is a cute and perky foil for the stoic Clint, but the part does little to display her fine comic talents. Not as abysmal as some critics have complained, there are some entertaining moments in the film — especially when Eastwood is afforded the chance to masquerade as various characters. But those hoping for a "make-my-day" Clint or rock'em-sock'em action would do better to look elsewhere. ★★ $14.99

Pink Flamingos

(1972, 95 min, US, John Waters) The sleazo-porn-trash extravaganza that made the fabulous Divine a household word and Waters an object of fear, awe and nausea all over the world. In one of the most disgusting and perversely funny films ever made, zaftig matriarch Babs Johnson (Divine) and her family of egg-adoring Mom (Edith Massey) and chicken-loving son (Danny Mils) battle the repugnant Connie and Raymond Marble (Mink Stole and David Lochary) for the title of "filthiest person alive." Restored version with additional footage. ★★½ $19.99

Pink Floyd: The Wall

(1982, 99 min, GB, Alan Parker) Pink Floyd's mammoth rock 'n' roll allegory is vividly brought to the screen by Alan Parker in this visually impressive and sonically explosive epic. Bob Geldof (Mr. Live Aid) is the embodiment of a frazzled rock idol as the down and out Pink. ★★★ $14.99

Pink Narcissus

(1971, 78 min, US, Anonymous) A longtime favorite of gay audiences in Europe, this legendary erotic creation was rediscovered in the U.S. in 1972. Made by Anonymous, the film was reportedly shot over a seven-year period and is reminiscent of the 1960s New York Underground and Kenneth Anger. Straddling the line between underground art and gay porn, the film is a classic of gay male erotica. The hero, teenage beauty Bobby Kendall, drifts into slumber and his dreams, fueled by a lively imagination and sexual fantasy, take on a surreal and amatory air. Poetic, tender yet sexually potent, we are taken through his erotic reveries: from scenes of Bobby becoming a toreador, a Roman slave, and eventually involved in Arabian Nights debauchery. ★★★ $39.99

The Pink Panther

(1964, 113 min, GB, Blake Edwards) This delightful comedy caper introduced Peter

P

Sellers' now-famous characterization of the bumbling Inspector Clouseau. While not the best of the Pink Panther series (that honor goes to *A Shot in the Dark*), this is still a zesty and sophisticated farce with many of the "trademarks" of Sellers' unsurpassed comic ability. Costars David Niven, Herbert Lom, Robert Wagner and Claudia Cardinale. ★★★½ $14.99

The Pink Panther Strikes Again

(1976, 103 min, GB, Blake Edwards) This hilarious fourth installment in the *Pink Panther* series is one of the best of the bunch. The Inspector's former boss, chief Dreyfuss (Herbert Lom), has gone off the deep end and will stop at nothing, including holding the entire world hostage with a giant death ray, to see Clouseau dead. Sellers, as always, is hysterical, especially in the Munich Octoberfest scene. ★★★½ $14.99

Pink Ulysses

(1989, 98 min, The Netherlands, Eric deKuyper) Using Ulysses' return from 20 years of exile in Troy as its nucleus, this sex-drenched oddity from the director of *Naughty Boys* and *Casta Diva* goes where no Steve Reeves vehicle dared to venture. The film features the obligatory loin-clothed beefcakes, and stirring the kinetic mix is a cheap esthetic which permeates this visual mélange. A sure bet for late-nite cult status. ★★½ $39.99

Pinky

(1949, 102 min, US, Elia Kazan) Jeanne Crain stars as a Southern black woman who passes for white when she leaves her home to live in the big city, finds work as a nurse and becomes romantically involved with a white doctor. After her mother (Ethel Waters) takes ill, she returns home to care for her and is confronted with racism and her own personal identity crisis centering around the acceptance of her own blackness. Tightly directed by Kazan and featuring standout performances by Oscar nominees Crain, Waters and Ethel Barrymore, this melodramatic masterpiece is a must-see for those seeking drama that hits hard and doesn't let up until the last Kleenex is used. An ideal double feature would be *Imitation of Life*. ★★★★ $19.99

Pinocchio

(1940, 88 min, US, Ben Sharpsteen, Hamilton Luske) Disney's second animated feature is filled with fantastical imagery and a wild carnival-like atmosphere as Geppetto's little wooden boy goes on an almost picaresque journey toward a more fleshy existence. While the film is guaranteed to inspire delight (let us not forget Jiminy Cricket), the story's invective morality along with Disney's at times horrific representation of killer whales and an underwater purgatory for little boys who lie may prove a tad frightening for many a tot. Still, as with all vintage Disney, this is a must-see. ★★★★ $59.99

Pinocchio and the Emperor of the Night

(1987, 91 min, US, Hal Sutherland) Pinocchio embarks on a magical trip when a mysterious carnival comes to town. A disappointing version with only adequate animation and a curious aimlessness to the story's telling. Featuring the voices of Edward Asner, James Earl Jones, Rickie Lee Jones and Don Knotts. ★★ $14.99

Pippin

(1981, 120 min, US, David Sheehan) First-rate production of Bob Fosse's Tony Award-winning musical. One of Fosse's greatest stage triumphs, "Pippin" is a jubilant, colorful and tuneful look at Pippin, son of King Charlamagne, and his search for fulfillment and love. Ben Vereen re-creates his award-winning role as the Narrator, and is joined by William Katt as Pippin, Eric Berry (also repeating his stage role) as the King, Chita Rivera as the Queen, and Martha Raye as Pippin's vivacious grandmother. Fosse's dance numbers are outstanding, and Stephen Schwartz's score is earthy, witty and vibrant. ★★★½

Pirahna

(1978, 92 min, US, Joe Dante) Director Dante and writer John Sayles teamed for the first time (they encored with *The Howling*) for this engaging horror spoof. You'll regret it if you pass up this biting tale of mutant, man-eating fish making julienne fries of beach-loving teens. Promises lots of laughs and chills, and contains the immortal line, "Excuse me sir, the fish are eating the guests." ★★★

Piranha II: The Spawning

(1981, 88 min, US, James Cameron) This sequel to *Piranha* takes its stylistic cues from *Wolfen*, mixes in a bunch of Roger Corman camp and resembles *Jaws* in substance. Put it all together and you have an amazingly silly but enjoyable horror movie... and yes, it was directed by *that* James Cameron (*The Terminator*, *Terminator 2: Judgment Day*). He shows nothing of the greatness which would follow. ★★

The Pirate

(1948, 102 min, US, Vincente Minnelli) Gene Kelly's thrilling dance numbers highlight this charming musical about traveling acrobat Kelly being mistaken for a notorious pirate by love-struck Judy Garland. Cole Porter's score includes "Be a Clown" and the Nicholas Brothers are sensational in support. ★★★ $19.99

Pirates

(1986, 124 min, France/US, Roman Polanski) A fun if convoluted pirate comedy with Walter Matthau in good form as a ruthless scalawag in search of a famed treasure. Also with Charlotte Lewis and Cris Campion. ★★½ $14.99

The Pirates of Penzance

(1983, 112 min, US, Wilford Leach) All of the exuberance and rollicking sense of fun of the 1980s hit Broadway revival of Gilbert and Sullivan's operetta has been joyously captured on screen in this vastly underrated musical. Kevin Kline repeats his Tony Award-winning role as the Pirate King, with Rex Smith as the "slave to duty" pirate apprentice, Angela Lansbury as his guardian, the wonderful George Rose as "the very model of a modern major general," and Linda Rondstadt as Rose's beautiful daughter who falls in love with Smith. Kline is in terrific form, both as singer and physical comedian; and the colorful sets are a major asset. ★★★½ $19.99

The Pit and the Pendulum

(1991, 97 min, US, Stuart Gordon) From the director of the cult classic *Re-Animator* comes this stylishly sadistic remake of the Edgar Allan Poe horror classic. Lance Henriksen stars as Torquemada, the mad monk of the Spanish Inquisition, who goes to extreme lengths to suppress his awakening sexual desires for a beautiful peasant girl. Director Gordon sacrifices atmosphere for hard-core shocks with surprisingly effective results. ★★½ $89.99

The Pitfall

(1948, 86 min, US, Andre de Toth) The Great American Dream gone sour is the theme of this intriguing moral tale. The bored husband of Jane Wyatt, Dick Powell forgets his idyllic suburban family to enjoy a brief fling with a sexy siren (Lizabeth Scott) — an action that soon brings violence, deceit, tragedy and sudden death. Raymond Burr is memorable as the hulking private eye. ★★★ $19.99

Pixote

(1981, 127 min, Brazil, Hector Babenco) A brilliant, disturbing film about a band of youths who escape a brutal detention center to resume their desperate lives of petty crime in the slums of São Paulo and blaze a trail of violence. Our hero Pixote (Fernando Ramos da Silva), a gun-toting 10-year-old outcast, and his youthful friends get involved in a drug smuggling scheme and soon befriend an aging alcoholic prostitute (the riveting Marilia Pera), who offers them a brief respite of tenderness as a mother figure and a lover. Pixote, a desperate boy in a winless situation, struggles against the hardships of an environment deprived of hope and ruled by casual brutality. From the director of *Kiss of the Spider Woman* and from a novel by Jose Louzeiro. Da Silva was murdered by police when he was 19-years-old for suspected drug and gang activity. (Portuguese with English subtitles) ★★★★ $89.99

Pixote

A Place in the Sun

(1951, 122 min, US, George Stevens) An ambitious effort, and one of the few movies of its day to address the subject of class conflict in America. Montgomery Clift gives a great performance as a young man content to climb the social ladder by ordinary means. That is, until he meets rich society girl Elizabeth Taylor. Although occasionally heavy and slow-moving, and the impending tragedy is perhaps all too inevitable, this is still poignant material, and Clift and Taylor express genuine tenderness and passion. Shelley Winters is memorable as the girlfriend who Clift wishes would vanish. Based on Theodore Dreiser's "An American Tragedy." ★★★½ $14.99

A Place of Weeping

(1986, 88 min, South Africa, Darrell James Roodt) A powerful human drama of one woman's personal fight for freedom and her battles against the hatred and resentment of a people, as well as the oppressive hand of the Apartheid system. A heroic story of her bravery and emotional traumas against undignified abuse. ★★★

Places in the Heart

(1984, 113 min, US, Robert Benton) Outstanding autobiographical drama from director Benton with Sally Field in her (second) Oscar-winning role as a stalwart widow, raising her young son in Depression-era Texas, who partners with a black transient (the terrific Danny Glover) to raise cotton. A superb supporting cast includes John Malkovich as a blind boarder, Ed Harris, Lindsay Crouse and Amy Madigan. ★★★½ $19.99

The Plague

(1991, 105 min, GB/France/Argentina, Luis Puenzo) Albert Camus' haunting novel of the anarchy, suffering and isolation that befalls a city when the plague resurfaces is brought to the screen in this serious, well-intentioned effort. The film focuses more on personal traumas and human nobility than Camus' greater existential thought. An all-star cast includes William Hurt as a dedicated doctor, Robert Duvall as a life-loving old codger, Raul Julia plays an enterprising opportunist, and, adding a little sex and a love interest in the otherwise bleak tale is Sandrine Bonnaire, who plays a vain reporter stranded in the quarantined city. The film tries hard not to be too grim, concentrating instead on the human interests of the people whose courage and selflessness shine during the tragedy. A worthy attempt to translate such a distressing story to the screen. ★★★ $14.99

Le Plaisir

(1951, 96 min, France, Max Ophüls) These three stories from Guy De Maupassant all deal with man's eternal search for pleasure. The first story contrasts pleasure and old age, the second pleasure and purity, and the third pleasure and marriage. Ophüls' stylish, brilliant film, set in 1890s France, playfully speculates on man's alternating natures and conventions. (French with English subtitles) ★★★½ $14.99

Plan 9 from Outer Space

(1959, 79 min, US, Edward Wood, Jr.) As TV psychic Criswell admits, "There comes a time in every man's life when he just can't believe his eyes." Rent this and your time has come. Based on sworn testimony, this opus, often considered the worst movie ever made, tells about some silly suited space alien's latest attempt at taking over the world after failing the eight previous tries (makes you wonder why we even bother to keep watching the skies). Bela Lugosi died shortly after shooting commenced, so a chiropractor half his age and twice his size acted as his stand-in, disguising himself by holding a cape over his face the whole time. We could go on... ★ $9.99

Planes, Trains and Automobiles

(1987, 93 min, US, John Hughes) Teenmeister Hughes wrote and directed this funny tale of uptight businessman Steve Martin trying to get home to Chicago for Thanksgiving, only to face disaster at every attempt. John Candy is endearing as a bumbling chatterbox who becomes Martin's unwanted traveling companion. ★★★ $14.99

Planet of the Apes

(1967, 112 min, US, Franklin J. Schaffner) Classic sci-fi adventure with Charlton Heston as a modern-day astronaut hurled centuries into the future to a planet where apes rule and man is hunted for sport. Roddy McDowall, Kim Hunter and Maurice Evans, all under some incredible makeup effects, appear as adversarial and not-so-adversarial simians. Followed by four sequels. ★★★½ $19.99

Planet of the Vampires

(1965, 86 min, Italy, Mario Bava) The crew of an interplanetary spacecraft crash land on a mysterious planet and must defend themselves from a race of formless creatures determined to take over their bodies. Mindless schlock that only occasionally delivers the horror goods. ★★ $14.99

The Planets

(1983, 50 min, GB, Ken Russell) Spectacular MTV for the classical set. August Eugene Ormandy and the Philadelphia Orchestra provide the musical accompaniment and "mad" director Russell supplies the wonderfully bombastic visuals as they team up to present Gustav Holst's "The Planets." Russell's vivid interpretation juxtaposes mankind's curiously violent and dangerous nature against its sensual, lyrical, adventurous and playful spirit. At times shocking as well as beautiful, this made-for-British-TV film is both captivating and enthralling. ★★★ $14.99

Platinum Blonde

(1931, 86 min, US, Frank Capra) One of Frank Capra's biggest commercial and critical successes pre-*It Happened One Night*, this bright comedy may be stagey but never fails to entertain. Jean Harlow stars as an heiress who decides to do Pygmalion one better by marrying her subject — down-to-earth newspaper reporter Robert Williams. She vows to make him a gentleman, but finds her work cut out for her. Loretta Young is Williams' fellow reporter, who is secretly in love with him.

Though Harlow's delightful performance would make her a full-fledged star (her nickname "platinum blonde" would stick till her untimely death), it is Williams who is the main attraction. With his Will Rogers-like plainness, Williams has a natural screen presence; tragically, he died a year later at the age of 35. ★★★ $19.99

Platoon

(1986, 120 min, US, Oliver Stone) Stone's numbing Vietnam War drama is one of the finest war films ever made, and is the best film made about the experiences of American infantrymen in that war. Charlie Sheen plays a young recruit torn between sergeants Willem Dafoe and Tom Berenger. Stone won an Oscar for this masterful achievement, and he would win another one for his equally brilliant companion piece, *Born on the Fourth of July*. ★★★★ $9.99

Play It Again, Sam

(1982, 84 min, US, Herbert Ross) Woody Allen is a hapless girl chaser who depends on the ghost of his hero, Humphrey Bogart, to guide him in matters of the heart. And he needs all the help he can get! Also starring Diane Keaton, Susan Anspach and Tony Roberts. Scripted by Allen. ★★★½ $14.99

Play Misty for Me

(1971, 102 min, US, Clint Eastwood) Clint Eastwood's directorial debut is an accomplished thriller about a California D.J. (Eastwood) and his number one fan (Jessica Walter), who loves the song "Misty" and whose fatal attraction for the radio jock puts him and those around him in danger. Lots of chills; Walter is terrific as the obsessed fan. ★★★ $14.99

Playboy of the Western World

(1962, 100 min, Ireland, Brian Desmond Hurst) This is a beautiful and lyrical film version of J.M. Synge's classic Irish play about a boyish young man who captivates a small village with his tale of how he did in his dad. Synge's soaring poetry is faithfully translated

The Playboys

Jean Harlow (c.) captures the attention of all in *Platinum Blonde*

to the screen and the film is inestimably aided by a transcendent performance by Siobhan McKenna – one of the great Irish actresses of her day. ★★★½

The Playboys

(1992, 110 min, Ireland, Gillies MacKennon) This sweet comic fable stars the ever-luminous Robin Wright as the strong-willed Tara, a young woman who defies her small Irish town by having a baby out of wedlock. Determined not to let a man influence her life, Tara nevertheless finds herself drawn to one of the vaudevillians in an Irish acting group. The man (strongly played by handsome Aidan Quinn) vies for Tara's attention along with the local heavy-drinking constable (Albert Finney, in yet another powerful turn), whose obsession with Tara leads to a series of tragic circumstances. Written by Shane Connaughton (*My Left Foot*), the film suffers from some truly sappy dialogue and the main plot point can be seen a mile away. But it does offer sumptuous settings (circa 1957) and a truly awe-inspiring performance from Finney. ★★★ $14.99

The Player

(1992, 123 min, US, Robert Altman) *The Player* is a trenchant black comedy about a young film studio executive named Griffin Mill (played with unnerving restraint by Tim Robbins) who finds his fax-filled, mineral water-drinking, Range Rover-driving life coming apart after he receives death threats from a screenwriter he has shunned. As he dives deeper into paranoia, we learn more and more about an industry that thrives on schmoozing, back-stabbing and green-lighting multimillion dollar projects that are pitched in 25 words or less. With Robbins, one of today's finest natural actors, in the lead, and a brilliant, pointedly satiric script by Michael Tolkin, who adapted his own cult novel, *The Player* marks the return to power of its iconoclast director Altman. There's also the miraculous supporting cast that includes Whoopi Goldberg, country star Lyle Lovett, Fred Ward and Greta

Scacchi as a beautiful and heady painter from Iceland (?) with the impossible name of June Gudmunsdottir. And then there are the cameos – scores of them – from the likes of Cher, Lily Tomlin, Jack Lemmon and others too numerous, and too revealing, to name. A sublime movie-going experience, *The Player* is filled with cinematic jazz riffs that transcend all expectations. ★★★★ $14.99

Playing Away

(1986, 102 min, GB, Horace Ove) Lightweight though amiable "culture-shock" comedy about a country village's attempts to prove its liberalness by challenging a rough-and-tumble Jamaican cricket team from Brixton in honor of their "Third World Week." ★★½

Playing for Time

(1980, 150 min, GB, Daniel Mann) Vanessa Redgrave and Jane Alexander star in this brutally honest account of the real-life story of Fania Fanelon (Redgrave), a survivor of the Auschwitz death camp. Both actresses and playwright Arthur Miller (who scripted this American production) won Emmy Awards for their contributions to this unusually powerful telemovie. ★★★★

Playtime

(1967, 108 min, France, Jacques Tati) Hilarious chaos befalls an antiseptically modern Paris when Mr. Hulot comes to town. Sight and sound gags abound as Tati deftly observes Modern Man bungling in his glass and steel cage. ★★★★ $39.99

Plaza Suite

(1971, 115 min, US, Arthur Hiller) Walter Matthau plays the roles of three different men in this engaging Neil Simon comedy, based on his stage play. Matthau plays a businessman, a Hollywood producer and the father of a would-be bride, and is ably supported by Barbara Harris, Lee Grant and Maureen Stapleton. ★★★ $14.99

Plenty

(1985, 119 min, US, Fred Schepisi) Schepisi brings an elegant directorial style to David Hare's acidic drama about England after WWII. As Susan Traherne, a complex woman whose psychological breakdown mirrors Britain's own post-war decay, star Meryl Streep is riveting. Also featuring Sting, Sam Neill, John Gielgud and Tracy Ullman. ★★★ $14.99

The Plot Against Harry

(1969/1990, 80 min, US, Michael Roemer) Made by NYU film professor Roemer, this witty and amazingly insightful social comedy was originally shot in 1969 under the title *Nothing But a Man*, but money problems kept it in the can until 1990 when Roemer reedited the film. The result is a joyous, cooly observed and, at times, hilarious story about the tales of woe that befall Harry Plotnick, a modern-day Job and small-time Jewish gangster. Released from prison, he finds his protection racket being taken over by the Italian mob and discovers a daughter he never knew he had. Martin Priest is wonderfully droll as the always nonplussed Harry. Roemer's direction, sort of pre-Jarmusch Jarmusch, is astute; especially his uncanny eye for capturing '60s kitsch as well as the impending changes brought on New York by drugs and violence. Unfortunately, Roemer retreated back to the world of academia and has yet to make another feature. ★★★½ $29.99

The Ploughman's Lunch

(1983, 100 min, GB, Richard Eyre) This cutting inquiry into the devious opportunism of a BBC journalist scans the subconscious mood of Britain behind the false huzzahs of the Thatcher brigade. Jonathan Pryce is the cold-hearted protagonist who will stop at no romantic treachery or professional hypocrisy in his claw up the social ladder. Tim Curry co-stars. ★★★

The Plumber

(1980, 76 min, Australia, Peter Weir) A sinister comedy-drama that presents the case of an unexpected and unknown visitor, a manipulative plumber, who invades the home of a medical researcher and his wife and instigates emotional turmoil. A darkly funny thriller. ★★★

Pocahontas

(1995, 80 min, US, Mike Gabriel & Eric Goldberg) The animators at Disney, after the huge popular success with the politically sensitive if artistically commonplace *The Lion King*, have made a film even more serious in tone and social awareness but more satisfying in its story and execution. Disney's first animated feature based on real-life characters recalls the tale of the young, feisty Indian princess Pocahontas who falls in love with British explorer John Smith. This mythic "Romeo and Juliet" romance is set in the New World's colony of Virginia, where a greedy English governor has arrived intent on wiping out the Algonquin nation in his search for treasure. Less comedic than other Disney films (though a raccoon sidekick does supply many a chuckle), *Pocahontas* through story and song relays powerful messages of prejudice, avarice, spirituality and environmental concerns which makes this one of the company's most thoughtful productions.

P

Point of No Return

While the animation is lovely to look at, the score is less than spectacular with exception to two marvelous numbers, "Round the River Bend" and an almost stunning parable of hatred, "Savages." ★★★½ $39.99

Pocket Money

(1972, 102 min, US, Stuart Rosenberg) Two marginal, modern-day cowpokes go for the big score with a larcenous cattle deal in this sardonic, existential western. Paul Newman and Lee Marvin are particularly delicious in this Terence Malick-scripted fable about the quest for salvation (read: "big money"). Fine cinematography by Lazlo Kovacs. Also starring Strother Martin. ★★★ $14.99

Pocketful of Miracles

(1961, 136 min, US, Frank Capra) Entertaining remake of director Capra's own 1934 hit *Lady for a Day*. Bette Davis chews much scenery as Apple Annie, the poor, old apple seller who masquerades as a rich matron – with a little help from her friends – for the sake of her daughter (Ann-Margret in her film debut). Glenn Ford and Hope Lange also star, and Oscar-nominee Peter Falk is a scene-stealer. ★★★ $14.99

Poetic Justice

(1993, 108 min, US, John Singleton) Singleton follows his sizzling debut, *Boyz N the Hood*, with this disappointing drama starring Janet Jackson as a hairdresser and part-time poet who is wooed by tough guy Tupac Shakur. Though hampered by an anemic plot, Singleton gets some nice work out of both Jackson and Shakur (whose easy-going demeanor belies his real-life character). Sadly, though, Jackson fails to breathe adequate life into her screen persona's poetry, written in real life by Maya Angelou. ★★ $14.99

Poetry in Motion

(1985, 90 min, US, Ron Mann) William Burroughs, John Cage, Allen Ginsberg, Tom Waits, Charles Bukowski and Amiri Baraka are just some of the 25 artists featured in this compilation documentary/performance film in which these celebrated poets recite their own works. Includes Ginsberg offering a rousing rock poetry session, Cage passionately reading and discussing Henry David Thoreau, and Burroughs reading from his writings in his trademark deadpan animated style. ★★★ $39.99

The Point

(1985, 74 min, US, Fred Wolf) Animated fable set in the land of "Point," a place where everyone and everything has a point. A young boy, the first and only round-headed child ever born there, is subsequently banished to the Pointless Forest, where he meets new and exciting creatures. Narrated by Ringo Starr, with songs by Harry Nilsson. ★★★ $14.99

Point Blank

(1967, 92 min, US, John Boorman) Director Boorman creates a stylish new form of film noir using wide screen and color in this cynical thriller. Lee Marvin is at his meanest as a man shot and left for dead by his unfaithful wife and her mobster lover. Now he's back and out for revenge against the businessmen and mobsters who did him wrong. Also features Angie Dickinson, Keenan Wynn and Carroll O'Connor. ★★★½ $19.99

Point Break

(1991, 122 min, US, Kathryn Bigelow) A slam-bang, action-packed and incredibly silly adventure film from director Bigelow (*Near Dark*). Keanu Reeves plays a novice FBI agent who goes undercover on the Southern California beaches to infiltrate a group of surfers suspected of being The Ex-Presidents – a highly successful gang of bank robbers whose masks feature the likenesses of President Bush's four predecessors. Patrick Swayze is the philosophy-quoting, mystical gang leader whose series of macho stunts of one-upmanship with Reeves creates several astonishing action scenes – including a hold-your-breath, how-did-they-do-that sky jumping scene, a prolonged but impressive surfing sequence and a lengthy chase scene amid the back alleys of Los Angeles. ★★½ $9.99

Point of No Return

(1993, 109 min, US, John Badham) For those who saw Luc Besson's dazzling *La Femme Nikita*, it is difficult to recommend this faithful remake. Though the film copies the original nearly shot-for-shot, it lacks its predecessor's visual panache and chilling neo-pop style. Still, the film fared well at the box office, and standing on its own, it is not an unworthy effort. Bridget Fonda is fine in the lead role of a societal throwaway who is saved from the executioner by a shadowy government official who wants to make a super assassin out of her. Still, she's no match for the pouty and vulnerable Anne Parillaud, who originated the role. So still we wonder, why watch a watered-down remake when you can see the original, subtitles and all? It's yet another case of Hollywood not being able to leave well enough alone. ★★½ $14.99

The Pointsman

(1987, 95 min, The Netherlands, Jos Stelling) In the dead of winter, a beautiful, fashionably attired French woman accidentally gets off a train in the remote Scottish Highlands where she encounters a strange recluse who lives and works at the desolate train station. In this "artsy," quirky and complex story, the two, neither speaking the other's language, begin a strange relationship – one which initially makes her a "prisoner," but later develops into friendship and eventually ill-fated passion. This unconventional tale is a visually stunning mood piece which, for those with the patience, proves to be an absorbing and thoughtful treatise on the vagrancies of love and communication. ★★★

Poison

(1991, 85 min, US, Todd Haynes) Winner of the Grand Jury Prize at the Sundance Film Festival, this amazingly self-assured first feature by director Haynes proved to be quite a controversial work upon its release. Interweaving three seemingly unconnected stories, each with its own individual filmmaking style, this low-budget independent effort will mesmerize many, perplex others and disgust more than a few. *Hero*, the first tale, told in a semidocumentary form, recounts a young boy's killing of his abusive father and his miraculous flight away. *Horror*, filmed in a '50s sci-fi horror flick manner, follows the tragedy that strikes a scientist after he successfully isolates the human sex drive in liquid form. The final tale, adapted from the writings of Jean Genet, is *Homo*, an intensely sensual and lyrical story of obsessive, unrequited love set in a prison. *Poison* is a wholly original, provocative, unsettling and intelligent film that is a must-see for adventurous videophiles. ★★★½ $19.99

Poison Ivy

(1992, 89 min, US, Katt Shea Ruben) Writer-director Ruben's entry into the "from hell" genre stars Drew Barrymore as the mysterious, seductive, possibly naughty Ivy, who insinuates herself into the dysfunctional family of an awkward and angry classmate, Sylvie, played convincingly by Sara Gilbert. A familiar battle for identity ensues as the two outcasts venture to see if a slut and an intellectual can maintain a friendship. Ivy soon manipulates her way into Sylvie's wealthy family and sets her sights on seducing dad (Tom Skerritt), whose wife (Cheryl Ladd) is dying of emphysema. Though Ruben's film gets bogged down in narrative schizophrenia deciding whether it's an erotic or psychological thriller, it certainly tries to please everyone with several steamy (though somewhat motiveless) sex scenes and a few chills in the third act that almost comes together enough to be effectively thrilling. *Poison Ivy* may be melodramatic, predictable and based on many unfortunate stereotypes, but it sure makes for amusing trash. ★★ $14.99

Police

(1984, 113 min, France, Maurice Pialat) On the surface, Pialat's (*À Nos Amours*) tensely exciting "policier" is about a brutal Paris cop's (Gérard Depardieu) efforts to break up a North African drug ring. But Pialat, who combines ferocious rawness with pristine formality, goes further than anyone before him in establishing the policeman's physical, moral and emotional intimacy with the criminals he interrogates and brutalizes. Depardieu is at the top of his form as the course, crude cop. A film of stunningly vivid temperment that is less a typical, action-packed thriller and more a psychological probe done with exacting realism. (French with English subtitles) ★★★½ $29.99

Police Academy

(1984, 97 min, US, Hugh Wilson) An insipidly funny slapstick comedy which amazingly spawned five sequels, though once was (more than) enough. Steve Guttenberg, Bubba Smith and Kim Cattrall are three of the zany misfit police cadets let loose on an unsuspecting public. This combination of low-brow hijinks and sophomoric schtick does contain many a laugh, but this imitative romp is years behind other "dumb" comedies such as *Airplane!* ★★½ $14.99

Police Story
(Jackie Chan's Police Force)

(1985, 100 min, Hong Kong, Jackie Chan) Asia's biggest box-office attraction for years, the boyishly charming Jackie Chan combines the physical dexterity of Bruce Lee with the comedic talents of Tom Hanks. Chan is a decidedly exciting talent; for those unfamiliar with his work, *Police Force* is certain to amaze, delight and entertain. The plot has Jackie as a policeman on the trail of drug smugglers, but story matters little for it is the action-comedy sequences, with Jackie doing all of his own death-defying stunts, that capture one's attention. From dangling on a runaway bus with only an umbrella handle to his balletic dance on speed boats, Jackie Chan's stunts should excite even the most jaded action fan. Interestingly, *Police Force* was a hit at the 1988 New York Film Festival. (Dubbed) ★★★½ $14.99

Pollyanna

(1960, 134 min, US, David Swift) Cute children's tale about a beguiling young girl (Hayley Mills) who captures the hearts of an entire New England town with her warm and sunny disposition. With Jane Wyman and Agnes Moorehead. ★★★ $19.99

Poltergeist

(1982, 114 min, US, Tobe Hooper) A classic horror story from director Hooper, this film owes much to its writer and producer, Steven Spielberg. When spirits from the "other side" kidnap their young daughter (the adorable Heather O'Rourke), an ordinary suburban family goes through Heaven and Hell to get her back. JoBeth Williams and Craig T. Nelson offer the right blend of playfulness and seriousness as the hapless parents, and Beatrice Straight and Zelda Rubinstein are the best ghostbusters yet. This is the finest ghost story since *The Haunting*, and the special effects are terrific. ★★★★ $19.99

Poltergeist 2: The Other Side

(1986, 90 min, US, Brian Gibson) This average sequel once again finds the Freling family battling for the safety of little Carol Ann (Heather O'Rourke). JoBeth Williams and Craig T. Nelson return, but even they aren't enough to help. There are, however, some nifty special effects, and Julian Beck is absolutely eerie as a ghostly visitor. ★★ $14.99

Poltergeist 3

(1988, 97 min, US, Gary Sherman) Abysmal third and final entry of the *Poltergeist* films has Carol Ann (Heather O'Rourke) visiting relatives in Chicago, once again bothered by evil spirits. There is no suspense and poor effects, and Tom Skerritt and Nancy Allen are lost with the material. Sadly, this was O'Rourke's last film. ★ $14.99

Polyester

(1981, 86 min, US, John Waters) In this odorized ode to suburban decay, Divine is a campy delight as Baltimore housewife Francine Fishpaw, who experiences her own private hell when hubby-with-a-bad-toupee has an affair, her daughter turns out to be a slut, and her revered son is cited as the notorious foot-stomper. Then, Golden Boy Tab Tomorrow (Tab Hunter) comes into her life. Waters tones down the crudeness to win new fans and succeeds — although number two on the scratch-and-sniff card is a doozy. ★★★ $19.99

Pool Hustlers

(1984, 101 min, Italy, Maurizio Ponzi) The smoke-filled rooms of pool halls provide the unlikely backdrop to this charming comedy-drama. Francesco, a poor man's Pierre Richard, is a mop-headed amateur billiards wizard who gets himself hustled out of thousands of dollars by an unscrupulous champion. His efforts to pay off the debt, first by stealing and second by competing in a high-stakes billiards contest, is the basic plot. But it is our bungling hero's endearing personality and his sweet romance with a sexy saxophone player that gives the film its appeal. (Italian with English subtitles) ★★★ $24.99

Poor White Trash

(1962, 84 min, US, Harold Daniels) Cajun camp starring Peter Graves as a self-righteous city slicker, and Tim Carey (the sharpshooter in Kubrick's *The Killing*) as a bayou bully. So controversial upon its release that armed guards were posted at the drive-ins to keep out minors! ★

Popcorn

(1990, 93 min, US, Mark Herrier) Clever twist to the "crazed killer" genre, where a horror film festival is the setting for a killer stalking members of the audience who believe his escapades are all just a part of the show. Cast features Jill Schoelen, Tom Villard, Dee Wallace Stone, Ray Walston and Tony Roberts. ★★½ $89.99

The Pope Must Die(t)

(1991, 89 min, GB, Peter Richardson) British comic Robbie Coltrane stars in this rollicking poke at the Catholic Church, the Vatican and the men who occupy its hallowed halls. Coltrane plays a this-close-to-being-defrocked priest who, through a misspelling made by a near-deaf dictation clerk, is accidentally catapulted into the Papacy. What follows is a sometimes hilarious commentary on the role of the Church in late-20th-century life as this new Pope promulgates his liberal philosophies on birth control, abortion and the use of Vatican money. Beverly D'Angelo and Paul Bartel also star. ★★★ $19.99

The Pope of Greenwich Village

(1984, 120 min, US, Stuart Rosenberg) A tough, gritty crime drama with Mickey Rourke and Eric Roberts as two small-time hoods trying to make a name for themselves in New York Mafioso territory. Rourke and Roberts are very good, as is Geraldine Page in a sensational supporting role as a crooked cop's slovenly mother. ★★★ $19.99

Popeye

(1980, 114 min, US, Robert Altman) Though this musical based on the famous comic strip and cartoon is not without its momentary enjoyments, the story of Popeye the Sailor, his "goil" friend Olive Oyl and lifelong nemesis Bluto is mostly an ill-conceived, overblown extravaganza. Robin Williams gets "A" for effort for his daring performance as Popeye, and Shelley Duvall is a perfect Olive, but Harry Nilsson's forgettable score and Altman's clumsy direction offer little to recommend. ★★ $14.99

Porcile (Pigsty)

(1968, 99 min, Italy/France, Pier Paolo Pasolini) Two contrasting stories are interwoven in a single narrative in Pasolini's biting satire on society's darker nature and the entrenched powers that be who are compelled to squash it. One tale, set in a barren, mountainous land in medieval times, features Pierre Clementi as a wandering soldier who descends into cannibalism, eventually recruiting a cult of followers who feed to the fiery volcano Mt. Etna the heads of their victims. The contrasting story, set in modern times, stars Jean-Pierre Leaud as the bourgeois son of a former Nazi, now a wealthy industrialist, who is politically and sexually confused — so confused as to prefer the sexual companionship of his neighboring peasants' pigs to his attractive (and frustrated) fiancée Anne Wiazemsky. While not as explicitly outrageous as *Salo: 120 Days of Sodom*, nor as whimsical as *The Decameron*, this brutal allegory of savage "innocents" and their threat to organized soci-

Police

Portrait of a Woman, Nude

ety is intense and involving. (Italian with English subtitles) ★★★ $29.99

Porky's

(1981, 94 min, US/Canada, Bob Clark) Sophomoric sex comedy manages a few laughs but is mostly lamebrained. Set in 1954 Florida, the story tells of a group of high school teenagers who play practical jokes and try to get laid. ★★ $9.99

The Pornographers

(1966, 128 min, Japan, Shohei Imamura) Imamura's wonderful black comedy focuses on a group of diligent 8mm porno filmmakers, struggling with the high risks and low production values inherent to Japan's booming underground sex trade. Imbued with Imamura's mordant philosophical sensibility, and populated with his stock company of misfits, the film is a hilarious and scathing look at modern Japanese society. (Japanese with English subtitles) ★★★½ $79.99

Port of Call

(1948, 100 min, Sweden, Ingmar Bergman) A minor Bergman drama of morality, love and self-awareness which is significant as one of the director's first attempts at Neorealism. The story traces – in an almost documentary fashion – the relationship between a bitter, resigned "experienced" woman and the sailor who falls in love with her. (Swedish with English subtitles) ★★

Portnoy's Complaint

(1972, 101 min, US, Ernest Lehman) Richard Benjamin is a discontented Jewish boy whose doting parents (Lee Grant and Jack Somack) refuse to let him grow up. Karen Black, Jill Clayburgh and Jeannie Berlin costar. This cinematic atrocity is based on Philip Roth's bestseller. ★ $14.99

The Portrait of a Lady

(1996, 144 min, GB/US, Jane Campion) Director Campion's adaptation of Henry James' 19th-century novel opens with a black screen accompanied by voiceovers of modern young women talking about love and sex; this is immediately followed by a montage of chic

black-and-white images of these young women. Right away, we know that Campion has more in mind than a straightforward read on James' tale of the willful young American Isabel Archer, a woman who sets out to rise above the conventions of her day only to suffer at the hands of her own naïveté. While Campion keeps true to the period, presenting an exquisitely detailed picture of late-19th-century Europe, she takes a few detours along the way in the form of a couple of fantastically realized sexual fantasy sequences. Nicole Kidman's portrait of Archer is at once compelling and enigmatic; having rejected two suitable suitors on the grounds of wanting to explore life, she sets out on a transcontinental trek only to embrace the advances of slithering malcontent Gilbert Osmand (John Malkovich). For his part, Malkovich's performance is tired; he's proving himself an actor of very limited range. Barbara Hershey delivers one of the film's more compelling turns as Madame Serena Merle, a dangerously alluring friend of Osmand's, and Martin Donovan is excellent as Isabel's consumptive cousin Ralph Touchett. (Available letterboxed and pan & scan) ★★★ $99.99

Portrait of a Woman, Nude (Nudo di Donna)

(1983, 112 min, Italy, Nino Manfredi) Manfredi directed and stars in this erotically charged comedy of sexual illusions and delusions. Set against an incomparable Venice, the film casts Manfredi as a husband who suspects that his wife is the model for a life-size portrait in a photographer's palazzo. His torments, as he struggles for the truth, are a marvel of sexual paranoia and comic energy. (Italian with English subtitles) ★★★

Portrait of Jason

(1967, 100 min, US, Shirley Clarke) This striking documentary is a look into the life, loves and philosophy of an articulate black gay street hustler. Clark simply places a camera in front of Jason Holiday (née Aaron Payne), prods him with a few offscreen questions and lets him take over. Drinking throughout the film, Jason, a natural and animated storyteller, brings us into his world – a gritty, troublesome place where fantasy blends seamlessly into reality. His tragic-comedic story is peppered with witty comments and observations, but the minimalist approach taken by Clarke might prove to be troublesome to those who are not taken in by the antics of the roguish Jason. ★★★ $39.99

Portrait of Jennie

(1948, 86 min, US, William Dieterle) A beautifully filmed romantic fantasy with the lovely Jennifer Jones inspiring struggling artist Joseph Cotten; the latter believing she may be the spirit of a deceased woman. ★★★ $39.99

Portrait of Teresa

(1979, 115 min, Cuba, Pastor Vega) Perhaps one of the most controversial films to emerge from post-revolutionary Cuba, this cinema verité drama centers around the life of Teresa, a housewife and mother who works in a textile

factory by day and attends political and cultural meetings in the evenings. With compassion and authenticity, the film probes the problems of her household, as her husband becomes increasingly frustrated and resentful towards his nontraditional wife – a beleaguered yet determined woman resolved to make a life of her own. A revealing look into sexism and women's struggles in the face of ingrained traditions of machismo in a country that boldly proclaims their liberation. (Spanish with English subtitles) ★★★ $69.99

Portrait of the Artist as a Young Man

(1977, 93 min, GB, Joseph Strick) This beautifully filmed though slow-moving adaptation of James Joyce's autobiographical novel stars Bosco Hogan as Stephen Dedalus, a young man who is forced to question and confront his Irish Catholic upbringing before he sets out on life's journey. Age-old issues such as sexual guilt, familial repression and Church oppression are met with rebellion by the young man. John Gielgud provides a highlight (and should wake up the nappers) with his spirited hellfire speech from the pulpit. ★★½ $29.99

The Poseidon Adventure

(1972, 117 min, US, Ronald Neame) One of the more enjoyable entries of the 1970s disaster films. Gene Hackman plays a priest who joins Ernest Borgnine, Stella Stevens, Red Buttons, Carol Lynley and Shelley Winters ("Manny, Manny") on an upside-down tour of their luxury liner when a tidal wave capsizes the ship. Great sets. ★★½ $19.99

Positive

(1990, 80 min, US, Rosa von Praunheim & Phil Zwickler) *Positive* follows *Silence = Death* as the second part of von Praunheim's trilogy about AIDS and activism (the third, *Asses on Fire*, was never released). This film powerfully documents New York City's gay community's response to the AIDS crisis as they are forced to organize themselves after the government's failure to stem the epidemic. Activists interviewed include playwright Larry Kramer, People with AIDS Coalition co-founder Michael Callen, New York filmmaker and journalist Phil Zwickler, as well as representitives from ACT-UP, Queer Nation and the Gay Men's Health Crisis. ★★★½ $29.99

Positive I.D.

(1987, 95 min, US, Andy Anderson) On a shoestring budget, director Anderson has fashioned a complex and fascinating thriller about a Texas woman whose rape leads her to live a second life – with a new identity and all. The film's look is clearly low-budget, but the story, twists and directorial style are first-rate. ★★★ $79.99

Posse

(1975, 94 min, US, Kirk Douglas) Douglas produced, directed and stars in this amiable tale of a U.S. cavalry marshall out to nab a vicious criminal – not for justice's sake, but so he can get elected to the Senate. Bruce Dern, Bo Hopkins and James Stacy co-star. ★★★ $9.99

Posse

(1993, 113 min, US, Mario Van Peebles) On the heels of Kevin Costner and Clint

Eastwood's Oscar-winning, revisionist westerns comes director Van Peebles' distinctive, anachronistic updating of the genre. And though this "MTV" rap-style telling lacks the verisimilitude and attention to detail of either Costner or Eastwood's epic sagas, *Posse* is certainly a lot of fun. Van Peebles stars as a "mysterious drifter" who leads a down 'n' dirty posse of Army deserters in escaping from a renegade colonel (Billy Zane) and engaging in a leprechaunic quest for stolen gold. And while the film historically acknowledges the presence of black cowboys on the American frontier in much the same way *Glory* did for the Civil War, it is most effective when viewed as Hollywood escapist fare. Also with Stephen Baldwin, Tone Loc, Big Daddy Kane and Blair Underwood. ★★★ $14.99

Possessed

(1931, 77 min, US, Clarence Brown) Joan Crawford, in one of her patented tough-gal roles, plays an ambitious factory worker who dreams of a better life. Clark Gable is an influential New York lawyer with an aversion to marriage who can give her the life she wants. Lots of snappy dialogue. ★★★ $19.99

Postcards from America

(1994, 93 min, GB, Steve McLean) Based on the life and works of the late artist and AIDS activist David Wojnarowicz who died in 1992, this stylized drama (not a biopic) brilliantly portrays the life of this tortured gay soul on a desperate, life-long search for love and the supportive family he never had. The episodic story intercuts three periods in David's life: his abused childhood (as played by Olmo Tighe); his 1970s late teens years as a Times Square hustler and petty thief (Michael Tighe); and his emotionally adrift life as an adult (James Lyons) who substitutes furtive, anonymous sex for love and whose rage and alienation eventually takes to the road. A dreamy, meditative,

Lana Turner and John Garfield in *The Postman Always Rings Twice*

melancholy and gripping experience whose story and fragmented structure is reminiscent of Cyril Collard's *Savage Nights* and Todd Haynes' *Poison*. McLean collaborated with Wojnarowicz before his death and based the film on two of his autobiographical writings, "Close to the Knives" and "Memories That Smell Like Gasoline." ★★★½ $59.99

Postcards from the Edge

(1990, 101 min, US, Mike Nichols) Actress Carrie Fisher's first attempt at screenwriting is this breezy comedy based on her true-life battle with alchohol and drug abuse. Meryl Streep and Shirley MacLaine are fabulously funny as the struggling Hollywood daughter and her aging celebrity mom. Fisher's screenplay deftly confronts the serious side of substance abuse while not straying from her comedic intent. ★★★ $9.99

The Postman (Il Postino)

(1993, 108 min, Italy, Michael Radford) British director Radford (*1984, White Mischief*) went international to create this sublime divertimento about a simple-minded Italian postman and his budding relationship with the exiled Chilean poet and socialist Pablo Neruda. The film stars French acting giant Philippe Noiret as Neruda, who seeks political refuge on a tiny Mediterranean island. Mario (Massimo Troisi) is the unemployed fisherman's son who takes a job with the postal service, the sole purpose of which is to deliver Neruda's mail. Ultimately, Mario approaches "Don Pablo" seeking advice about his unrequited love for the local barmaid, Beatrice (Maria Grazia Cicinotta). Carefully avoiding becoming Mario's Cyrano, Neruda gently mentors him in the ways of both love and "metaphors," also nurturing his budding Communist leanings along the way. Noiret logs another unflappable performance that is beautifully complemented by Troisi's shy and awkward Mario. Troisi's performance is made all the more remarkable by the fact that he was losing his battle to cancer and died the day after principal shooting ended — it is a touching and unforgettable swan song. (Italian with English subtitles) ★★★½ $99.99

The Postman Always Rings Twice

(1946, 113 min, US, Tay Garnett) Both John Garfield and Lana Turner had rough-and-tumble lives off-camera: Garfield spent his childhood in various Bronx gangs and Turner landed in Hollywood as a 16-year-old orphan. Perhaps it was the reflection of their real-life dramas that smolders in their definitive portrayals of the ultimate drifter and the unhappily married woman whose passions lead to betrayal and murder. James M. Cain's book inspired four films, but not even Jack Nicholson and Jessica Lange, in the most recent remake, were able to give it the gritty

intensity captured in this classic film noir. ★★★½ $19.99

The Postman Always Rings Twice

(1981, 123 min, US, Bob Rafelson) A loner on the skids (Jack Nicholson) and a suacy waitresss (Jessica Lange) become a sexually ravenous pair driven to murder in Rafelson's sexy if uneven adaptation of the James M. Cain novel. Both performers give impassioned portrayals of lust-blinded lovers with fogged-up moral compasses. ★★½ $14.99

Powaqqatsi

(1988, 99 min, US, Godfrey Reggio) Following the phenomenal success of their art-house hit *Koyaanisqatsi*, director Reggio and cinematographers Leonidas Zourdoumis and Graham Berry reconvened to create this whirlwind vision of life in the Third World. Employing the same time-lapse photography techniques and yet another dazzling score from composer Philip Glass, the filmmakers delve into the myriad issues affecting developing countries as the forces of international capitalism forever change the quality and pace of life for the people. ★★★

Powder

(1995, 111 min, US, Victor Salva) Recalling the social outcast theme of *Edward Scissorhands*, but without that film's satiric dark edge, *Powder* is the sometimes affecting, very sentimental and often bizarre fantasy of a strange teenager suffering from a case of extreme albinism. Orphaned and alone, Jeremy (Sean Patrick Flanery), nicknamed "Powder," is taken to a state home under the guidance of its kindly director (Mary Steenburgen). There, he is soon forced to confront the cruelty of mankind, and discovers he possesses special powers. *Powder* contains certain scenes of heartrending drama which give it an emotional center absent in some other outcast-themed films (such as *Nell*), and the supporting cast ranges from compelling (Lance Henriksen as a small-town sheriff) to stock (Jeff Goldblum as one of Jeremy's teachers). But overshadowing the film is the disclosure of director Salva's conviction of child molestation and prison sentence. It brings a different perspective to the subtly homoerotic film which, though maybe unfair to Salva as an artist, only magnifies Powder's alienation and ostracism. ★★½ $14.99

Power

(1986, 111 min, US, Sidney Lumet) Richard Gere stars as a hotshot political consultant in this muddled exposé of politics and the media. Julie Christie plays his ex-wife, Gene Hackman is his former partner, and Denzel Washington and Kate Capshaw also star. ★★½ $14.99

The Power of One

(1992, 111 min, US, John G. Avildsen) Critically destroyed and a commercial bomb, this high-profile dud does have one thing going for it: Morgan Freeman. Set during the early days of Apartheid, the film follows PK, a young boy of English descent who is sent to an Afrikaner boarding school. Witnessing racial injustice, this "Great White Hope" takes it upon himself to battle oppression and right the wrongs of the world via native music and boxing! (Why not?) Directed by Avildsen with about as much subtlety as his *Karate Kid* movies, this pretentious, dull and slightly racist stinker (even more glaring because of the film's subject matter) is watchable only for the cinematography, shot on location. The aforementioned Freeman, as PK's loving mentor, makes quite an impression despite the truly wretched "well-meaning" dialogue he's forced to spout. A high-profile cast, including Armin Mueller-Stahl, John Gielgud and pretty-boy newcomer Stephen Dorff as PK, do nothing to bring this mess to life. ★½ $19.99

Powwow Highway

(1988, 91 min, US, Jonathan Wacks) A delightful, heartfelt and poignant examination of the problems facing Native Americans today. A lumbering Cheyenne buys a battered Buick from the local junkyard and, with a buddy (a radical Indian Rights activist) in tow, sets out on a modern-day "vision quest." As the two wayfarers stray farther and farther from the safety of their reservation, the film exposes not only the distrust and racial hatred they encounter, but also the deep rifts in their own community. ★★★ $89.99

Practice Makes Perfect (Le Cavaleur)

(1980, 105 min, France, Philippe De Broca) Jean Rochefort's comic talents are put to fine use in this wry, graceful comedy about a philandering concert pianist. The journey to his inevitable comeuppance is filled with lustful encounters with present and former wives, agents, mistresses, and daughters of former girlfriends. (French with English subtitles) ★★★

Prancer

(1989, 103 min, US, John Hancock) A nice holiday film for the kiddies with a hopeful message and some sweet spirit. It's the story of a young girl who finds a wounded reindeer in the woods and, believing it's Prancer, nurses it back to health so she can return it to Santa. Cute, old-fashioned and a welcome change of pace from all that drivel the kids watch on Saturday mornings. ★★½ $14.99

A Prayer for the Dying

(1987, 107 min, GB, Mike Hodges) Mickey Rourke delivers a subdued performance as a guilt-ridden IRA assassin in Hodges' adaptation of Jack Higgins' novel. With their usual skill, Bob Hoskins, as a feisty priest, and Alan Bates, as a cold-blooded racketeer, lend strong support. Though not as thrilling as its source, the film offers insight into the power of forgiveness and man's atonement for his sins. ★★½

The Preacher's Wife

(1996, 124 min, US, Penny Marshall) In this update of the 1947 classic *The Bishop's Wife*, Denzel Washington takes over the Cary Grant role as an angel who is sent to aid a minister having a crisis of faith. Great casting: Denzel is possibly the Cary Grant of his generation — charismatic, debonair and effortlessly romantic. And here he is all these and more. But unfortunately Washington's presence alone

isn't enough to make *The Preacher's Wife* a wholehearted success. Endearing, rather uneven and very sentimental, the film casts Whitney Houston as the title character. After a few starring roles, she still is stiff on camera, with exception to a couple musical numbers. And therein lies one of the film's problems. Maybe the biggest liability is changing the magical aspect of the film. Denzel is an angel who isn't afforded many opportunities to strut his stuff: that was one of the many pleasures of the original. But the film does boast a fine supporting cast (Courtney B. Vance and Jenifer Lewis are wonderful), and the inherent charm of the original story is still evident. ★★½ $19.99

Predator

(1987, 107 min, US, John McTiernan) Gory science-fiction thriller with Arnold Schwarzenegger as the leader of an elite government fighting unit whose mission to rescue political prisoners from the jungles of South America turns deadly when they are stalked by a lethal, unseen enemy. ★★★ $14.99

Predator 2

(1990, 108 min, US, Stephen Hopkins) An extraterrestial lands in L.A. in the future and is confronted by a jungle far different than that of the original *Predator*. Danny Glover stars as a police officer who, forced to take time out from his busy drug war schedule, finds himself pitted against something slightly more destructive than a Jamaican with an Uzi. Though the story is very thin, the film is saved by great action sequences and a good cast (including Ruben Blades, Maria Conchita Alonso and Gary Busey). ★★½ $9.99

Prehysteria

(1993, 86 min, US) This hokey and mediocre family film is best viewed by kids who love dinosaurs. A museum-owning scavenger in a safari suit goes looking for treasure in a South American jungle, where he finds and steals some sacred dinosaur eggs that are accidentally hatched by the family dog. The father and his two children fight to keep the miniature dinosaurs from being exploited by the museum owner. While the special effects are acceptable, the minute, whimpering and supposedly adorable dinosaurs are annoying at times. ★★ $14.99

Prelude to a Kiss

(1992, 110 min, US, Norman René) Based on the Tony Award-nominated play, this opened-up film version loses very little of the passion and charm of the original stage production. In this captivating romantic fantasy, Alec Baldwin (reprising his Broadway role) and Meg Ryan star as a couple who meet, fall in love and marry. However, on their wedding day, the souls of Ryan and an uninvited guest, a seventy-year-old man (played with high spirits by Sydney Walker), are transposed. As this AIDS allegory continues, Baldwin suddenly finds his mate, once young and healthy, now sickly and old virtually overnight. But how to get them to switch? Adapting his own play for the screen, Craig Lucas imbues this tale with great good humor, and gives thoughtful testament to the responsibility, resilience and consummate

power of love. From the writing-directing team who made *Longtime Companion*. ★★★ $9.99

Premonition

(1978, 83 min, US, Alan Rudolph) Director Rudolph makes his debut with this largely unknown "glorified" student film about a musician whose nightmares of his own death cause him to question his hedonistic life and his sanity. Though Rudolph, an acknowledged protégé of Robert Altman, has become known as one of our more liberal directors, this somehow winds up being a "Say No to Drugs" treatise rather than the paranoid thriller the box promises. All in all, a must-see for film buffs and Rudolph fans alike. ★★½

The President's Analyst

(1967, 104 min, US, Theodore J. Flicker) Supremely entertaining political romp with James Coburn as the title character deciding he no longer wants the position; eluding various American and world-wide government agents who either want to kill him or want to know the chief executive's inner-most secrets. Godfrey Cambridge and Severn Dardern are particularly funny in support as a CIA agent and his Russian counterpart. ★★★½ $14.99

The Presidio

(1988, 97 min, US, Peter Hyams) San Francisco cop Mark Harmon squares off against military base commander Sean Connery over the policeman's murder investigation and Connery's daughter Meg Ryan, with whom Harmon is romantically involved. Few sparks, though Connery is, as usual, commanding. ★★½ $14.99

Pressure Point

(1962, 88 min, US, Hubert Cornfield) After their great success with *The Defiant Ones*, producer Stanley Kramer and Sidney Poitier reteamed for this stimulating and hard-hitting psychological drama. Set during WWII, Poitier plays a prison psychiatrist who treats American Nazi Bobby Darin, jailed for sedition. As Poitier tries to get to the root of Darin's chronic sleeping disorder, the black doctor must contend with his white patient's continual racial and ethnic assaults. Poitier gives a good performance, though much of his role is simply to react to Darin's childhood traumas and fascist ravings. Darin, though his films numbered few, had his best part in this movie. It's a subtle, chilling performance. Darin would be back conversing with a shrink a year later in *Captain Newman, M.D.* ★★★ $19.99

Presumed Innocent

(1990, 127 min, US, Alan J. Pakula) Harrison Ford stars in this taut thriller about a veteran prosecutor whose life is abruptly shattered when he is accused of brutally raping and murdering a colleague (Greta Scacchi). Against an avalanche of damning evidence, Ford proclaims his innocence only to discover that the judicial process, in which he so steadfastly believed, is rife with corruption and political intrigue. Ford's portrayal, filled with anxiety and pathos, will keep the viewer guessing from beginning to end as to his guilt. Bonnie Bedelia is terrific as his wife, and Raul Julia gives a stellar performance as Ford's suave defense attorney. ★★★½ $9.99

Pretty Baby

(1978, 109 min, US, Louis Malle) Malle's controversial film is a sensitively handled story of a 12-year-old girl (Brooke Shields) born and raised in Storyville, New Orleans' old whorehouse district. Keith Carradine, in one of his most effective performances, plays the photographer who becomes obsessed with her. Malle's impressive evocation of WWI Louisiana is complemented by a remarkably textured examination of sexual proclivity. Susan Sarandon is especially good as Shields' floozy mother. ★★★½ $14.99

Pretty Boy

(1993, 86 min, The Netherlands, Carsten Sonder) This dark, kinky and violent tale of one youth's tough coming-of-age takes place amidst the lurid world of teenage male prostitution. Nick (Christian Tafdrup) is a handsome and innocent 13-year-old runaway who quickly falls in with the wrong crowd when he arrives in Amsterdam. Befriended by a hardened, violence-prone gang of teen hustlers, Nick is soon immersed in a world where middle-aged pederasts prowl the train stations and parks for boys, and where sex is performed only for money and love rarely comes into play. (Danish with English subtitles) ★★½ $69.99

Pretty in Pink

(1986, 96 min, US, Howard Deutch) Molly Ringwald — John Hughes' Liv Ullmann? — stars in this witty comedy-drama scripted by Hughes as a girl from the "other side of the tracks" who braces the taunts of her snobby classmates and lets herself be wooed by class dreamboat Andrew McCarthy. Jon Cryer is a standout as Ringwald's wacky cohort, and Harry Dean Stanton, James Spader and Annie Potts also star. ★★★ $9.99

Pretty Woman

(1990, 117 min, US, Garry Marshall) This Cinderella story about a Los Angeles hooker-with-a-heart-of-gold who becomes involved with a repressed New York tycoon borrows much from better films before it. But few of them featured as charming a performance as that of Julia Roberts. Though it's an oft-used cliché: It's a star-making portrayal. As the businessman, Richard Gere reacts nicely and looks quite handsome with his greying hair, but his role is simply a foil for the enchanting Ms. Roberts. ★★½ $9.99

Prick Up Your Ears

(1987, 108 min, GB, Stephen Frears) This chilling and graphic portrayal of the life and death of British playwright Joe Orton is a masterful tribute to a man who fearlessly attacked English morals and custom. Cut down in his prime, Orton's legacy is well remembered here through scathingly witty dialogue and stand-out performances by Gary Oldman (as Orton) and Alfred Molina (as Kenneth Halliwell — Orton's tormented lover who brutally murdered him in 1967). A brilliantly candid look at the gay scene in London during the late '50s and early '60s. ★★★★

Pride and Prejudice

(1940, 118 min, US, Robert Z. Leonard) Exquisite comedy of manners based on Jane Austen's classic novel about five sisters' search for husbands. Laurence Olivier and Greer Garson are splendid as young lovers, and the film features a fine evocation of 19th-century England. Also starring Edna May Oliver, Edmund Gwenn, Mary Boland and Maureen O'Sullivan. ★★★½ $19.99

Pride and Prejudice

(1995, 300 min, GB, Simon Langton) While most will content themselves with a look at *Sense and Sensibility* or *Persuasion*, this absolutely charming BBC adaptation of Jane Austen's classic should not be missed. Jennifer Ehle is completely enchanting as Elizabeth Bennet who, with her three sisters, suffers a mixed social standing because their father married low. As always with Austen, the central paradox is how hazily off these undesireables while at the same time skewering the very class snobbery that makes their chance at marriage so precarious. Ehle's Elizabeth is a spunky and cavalier protagonist whose forthrightness leads her to an inevitably strained courtship with Mr. Darcy (Colin Firth), who is both the richest and preeminent snob of the county. Their contentious flirtings make for the most engaging and satisfying meetings of the minds. In support, Alison Steadman is uproariously grating as the Bennet girls' embarrassingly lower-class mom. An enjoyable and engrossing romantic drama that may occasionally show its low-born roots but is really as flawless as its upper-crust, recent cousins. ★★★★ $99.99

The Pride and the Passion

(1957, 132 min, US, Stanley Kramer) Not even the talents of Cary Grant, Frank Sinatra and Sophia Loren can elevate this laughable war epic. Set in Spain after Napoleon's conquest of that country, the story follows the efforts of a group of Spanish peasants, led by Sinatra, to transport a cannon, certain to defeat any enemy, to a French occupied town. Grant is a British officer who helps them. Loren is there to look lovely, which she does; and to create a romantic triangle. And on those dusty roads, she never gets dirty, either. The film offers some impressive battle sequences, but little else. ★½ $19.99

The Pride of St. Louis

(1952, 93 min, US, Harmon Jones) The professional and personal life of St. Louis pitching great Dizzy Dean is given the Hollywood treatment in this very likable baseball biography. Dan Dailey had one of his best roles as the famous pitcher, who created a stir whether on the field or in the radio booth. ★★½ $19.99

The Pride of the Yankees

(1942, 127 min, US, Sam Wood) The best of all the baseball biographies, and — until *Field of Dreams* came along — the best of all sports-themed films. Gary Cooper gives a terrific performance as New York Yankees legend Lou Gehrig, whose remarkable career was ended by sickness. Teresa Wright is splendid as Mrs. Gehrig, and there's good support from Babe Ruth (as himself), Walter Brennan and Dan Duryea. ★★★★ $19.99

Priest

(1995, 97 min, GB, Antonia Bird) Not quite as incendiary as its theme would suggest, nor as blasphemous as religious conservative protestors called it, *Priest* is the moving, provocative and quite powerful story of one clergyman's struggle for sexual identity and religious idealism. Linus Roache gives a stirring performance as Father Greg, a newly transferred priest assigned to a parish in a working-class neighborhood of Liverpool. As he comes in conflict with the liberal Father Matthew (Tom Wilkinson in a terrific portrayal), who is having an affair with the housekeeper (Cathy Tyson), Father Greg tries to come to terms with his emerging gay sexuality. This was the crux of the film's controversy, and though writer Jimmy McGovern and director Bird present a realistic and no-holds-barred examination of his coming out, the heart of the film is the touching story of a sexually abused teen who confides in Father Greg, thus engaging him in a crisis of conscience of whether to break his vow. In her debut, Bird has fashioned a remarkably compelling debate on religious dogma, one intended to provoke thought as it stirs one's emotions. ★★★★ $19.99

Priest of Love

(1981, 125 min, GB, Christopher Miles) An elegantly photographed biography of D.H. Lawrence's final days. Detailed are the author's self-exile to New Mexico, his sojourn to Italy to write "Lady Chatterley's Lover," and the tempestuous relationship with his Frieda (Janet Suzman). Ian McKellen gives a stirring portrait of the author. Co-starring John Gielgud, Ava Gardner and Sarah Miles. ★★★ $79.99

Primal Fear

(1996, 130 min, US, Gregory Hoblit) Richard Gere gives a high-voltage portrayal of a cocky, glory-seeking defense attorney who bites off more than he can chew when he finagles his way into the case of a backwoods, "butter-wouldn't-melt-in-his-mouth" alter boy (Edward Norton) accused of murdering a beloved archbishop. Having cut his teeth on TV's "L.A. Law," director Hoblit's complex whodunit combines compelling courtroom drama with a stellar supporting cast (Laura Linney and Frances McDormand are both excellent as the ex-girlfriend/prosecuting attorney and criminal psychologist, respectively), but this is clearly a showcase for newcomer Norton whose character navigates the film's ever-increasing maze of plot twists to its shocking conclusion. ★★★ $14.99

Prime Cut

(1972, 86 min, US, Michael Ritchie) Lee Marvin and Gene Hackman make the most of this gritty, tongue-in-cheek gangland drama about a Kansas City mobster in deep trouble when an enforcer from Chicago is sent to collect a debt. Sissy Spacek makes her film debut. ★★★ $59.99

The Princess Bride

The Prime of Miss Jean Brodie

(1969, 116 min, GB, Ronald Neame) Maggie Smith won a much-deserved Best Actress Oscar (edging out Jane Fonda's staggering portrayal in *They Shoot Horses, Don't They*) for her magnificent performance as an eccentric schoolteacher in 1930s Edinburgh. Based on Muriel Spark's novel, the story centers on the schoolmistress' life in and out of the classroom, where she exerts an enormous influence on her young, impressionable girls. A sincere and absorbing character study also starring Celia Johnson, Pamela Franklin and Jane Carr. ★★★½ $19.99

Prime Suspect

(1992, 230 min, GB, John Strickland) A deserved Emmy Award winner for Best Miniseries, "Prime Suspect" is a tremendous, gripping tale which combines mystery and the politics of gender. Helen Mirren gives an outstanding performance as Detective Chief Inspector Jane Tennison, a policewoman who is able to confront rampant sexism in the police department when she is given the opportunity to head the search for a serial killer terrorizing London. She must also continually prove herself to both her male superiors and the men under her command. An intelligent, suspenseful and extremely well-acted film, followed by two equally successful sequels. ★★★★ $29.99

Prime Suspect 2

(1993, 230 min, GB, John Strickland) Helen Mirren returns as Detective Chief Inspector Jane Tennison. Though she has gained the respect of the men under her command, her superiors continue to keep her under a magnifying glass. A new investigation has Tennison investigating the discovery of a dead body in the black community. As tensions mount from the outcry of racism, the police bring a black detective onto the case against her wishes — he happens to be her ex-lover. A startling, complex examination of race and racism intertwined with a gripping murder mystery. ★★★★ $29.99

Prime Suspect 3

(1994, 205 min, GB, David Drury) Helen Mirren returns as Jane Tennison, who has now been promoted to Detetive Chief Inspector and transferred from the criminal division to the vice squad at a Charing Cross police station. There, she is confronted with the mysterious death/murder of a 15-year-old homeless rent boy who perished in a fire. Fighting sexual discrimination, interference in her own department and her own personal crisis, D.C.I. Tennison continues the investigation; one that hints at police and political complicity. David Thewlis also stars as the main suspect, a villainous opportunist who haunts the city's train stations recruiting wayward boys into a life of petty crime and prostitution. A riveting, groundbreaking and compulsively watchable drama that, although it doesn't paint a positive picture of gay lifestyles, doesn't succumb to homophobia or exploitation — a rare achievement for such a contentious subject. In fact, with its unflinching themes of pedophilia, teenage prostituion, gay policemen and child pornography, it's a surprise this TV crime drama was ever produced. ★★★★ $39.99

The Primrose Path

(1940, 93 min, US, Gregory La Cava) Ginger Rogers stars in this involving comedy-drama as a girl from the "wrong side of the tracks" and a family of prostitutes, who falls in love with straight-arrow proprietor Joel McCrea. Marjorie Rambeau is splendid as Rogers' mother. From the director of *Stage Door* and *My Man Godfrey*. ★★★ $19.99

The Prince and the Pauper

(1937, 120 min, US, William Keighley) The classic Mark Twain novel is given royal treatment in this story about a young prince and a look-alike peasant boy trading places. With Billy and Bobby Mauch as the youths, and Errol Flynn, Claude Rains and Alan Hale. ★★★ $19.99

The Prince and the Pauper

(1978, 113 min, US, Richard Fleischer) Mark Lester plays the dual roles in this uninspiring version of the Mark Twain story. With Charlton Heston, Oliver Reed, Raquel Welch and Rex Harrison. (aka: *Crossed Swords*) ★★ $19.99

The Prince and the Showgirl

(1957, 117 min, GB, Laurence Olivier) By all reports, there was no love lost between Laurence Olivier and Marilyn Monroe on the set of this light romantic comedy. There was nothing lost on the screen, however. As a pair, they work magnificently together with Monroe playing an American chorus girl who is courted by Olivier's Balkan prince at the coronation of King George V in London. Terrence Rattigan provides a vivacious script based on his hit play "The Sleeping Prince." ★★★ $14.99

Prince of Darkness

(1987, 110 min, US, John Carpenter) Priest Donald Pleasence is up against Satan in the form of an icky goo; he, a college professor and his students are out to stop the demon's return to earth. Director Carpenter has certainly done better. ★½ $14.99

The Prince of Pennsylvania

(1988, 93 min, US, Ron Nyswaner) An offbeat dude (Keanu Reeves) wants to avoid following in his blue-collar father's footsteps, so he kidnaps his pop and holds him for ransom. The problem? No one wants him back. Fred Ward, Bonnie Bedelia and Amy Madigan co-star. Director Nyswaner also wrote the cult hit *Smithereens*. ★★½ $14.99

Prince of the City

(1981, 167 min, US, Sidney Lumet) Director Lumet returns to *Serpico* territory in this riveting, epic police drama which is based on a true story. Treat Williams gives a truly remarkable performance as a New York City narcotics officer who risks his job, friendships and safety when he reports widespread department corruption. Jerry Orbach is terrific in support as Williams' friend and fellow cop. ★★★½ $24.99

The Prince of Tides

(1991, 132 min, US, Barbra Streisand) Streisand's acclaimed second directorial effort (the wonderful *Yentl* was her first), *The Prince of Tides* is a lush, exceptional-looking film version of Pat Conroy's novel. It was also 1991's biggest Oscar controversy when the film garnered seven nominations but not one for helmer Streisand. In the performance of his career, Nick Nolte is outstanding as a married, Southern high school coach who travels to New York when his sister is admitted to a psychiatric hospital. There he meets her doctor (Streisand), and the two begin a brief affair. Though Streisand's character was less conspicuous in the book, here the doctor has a greater presence — which is one of the few disservices to this otherwise laudatory adaptation. A touching romance and a rather harrowing childhood memory piece, *The Prince of Tides* will certainly satisfy the romantics in most of us; though those more cynical will probably be less impressed. Kate Nelligan excels in support as Nolte's mother. ★★★½ $14.99

The Princess and the Pirate

(1944, 94 min, US, David Butler) One of Bob Hope's funniest films *sans* Bing, this hilarious pirate spoof stars Bob as a traveling entertainer who becomes mixed up with a runaway princess (Virginia Mayo) and a band of cut-throat pirates. The laughs seem to come about every 15 seconds, and a highlight has Bob dressing up as an old hag, being romantically pursued by Walter Brennan! And that's not to mention the typical Hope barrage of puns, double-entendres and silly one-liners. (First Mate: "We should head South, Captain. We have friends there." Hope: "Oh, Democrats.") ★★★½ $19.99

The Princess Bride

(1987, 98 min, US, Rob Reiner) Reiner faithfully adapts William Goldman's tale of love and swashbuckling adventure with style, wit and just the right amount of "mushy stuff." Cary Elwes stars as a stable boy; Robin Wright is the beauty in love with him. As with most fairy tales, the course of true love does not run smooth until story's end. Mandy Patinkin steals the show as swordsman Inigo Montaya, out to avenge his father's death. ★★★½

Princess Caraboo

(1994, 96 min, GB, Michael Austin) Phoebe Cates stars in this picturesque but uneven swipe at aristocratic hypocrisy that might best be described as *Anastasia*-lite. Cates plays an enigmatic beauty found wandering the English countryside and, speaking no English, is taken in by a social-climbing couple (Wendy Hughes and Jim Broadbent) who assume her to be foreign royalty. Stephen Rea costars as an inquisitive journalist enchanted by her innocence but intent on solving the mystery of her identity. This based-on-fact story also stars Kevin Kline and John Lithgow. ★★ $19.99

Princess Tam Tam

(1935, 80 min, France, Edmond Greville) It's a musical Parisian Pygmalion! A French novelist travels to North Africa seeking inspiration but instead finds himself becoming steadily more infatuated and entranced by a native girl (Josephine Baker). She accompanies him back to Paris where, to everyone's amazement, she is the toast of the town. (French with English subtitles) ★★★ $29.99

Josephine Baker in *Princess Tam Tam*

Princess Yang Kwei Fei

(1955, 91 min, Japan, Kenji Mizoguchi) An eighth-century Chinese Cinderella story, *Princess Yang Kwei Fei* tells the tale of an unspoiled stepsister who is unwittingly used by an ambitious gentleman who wants to get in with the emperor. Soon the emperor himself becomes enchanted by this beautiful and talented woman and makes her his wife. Featuring beautiful sets and stunning visuals, this historical love story's slow pace may lose some viewers; but for lovers of Mizoguchi's meticulous style, the leisurely pace proves to be a virtue. (Japanese with English subtitles) ★★★ $29.99

The Principal

(1987, 109 min, US, Christopher Cain) New inner-city high school principal James Belushi goes head to head with the bad dudes in his school. Belushi and his co-star Louis Gossett, Jr. play well off each other in this effort to make a difference, but the script is full of high school-thug clichés and an inconsistent mix of comedy and drama. ★★ $14.99

Prison

(1988, 102 min, US, Renny Harlin) There's quite a few chills in this nifty, stylish horror film from director Harlin (*Die Hard 2*). The spirit of a prisoner wrongfully executed two decades before comes back to get even with his former guard (Lane Smith) — who's now the warden. Also starring Viggo Mortensen and Chelsea Field. ★★½

Prison Stories: Women on the Inside

(1990, 94 min, US, Donna Deitch/Joan Micklin Silver/Penelope Spheeris) Three gritty, nonexploitative, slice-of-life stories of women behind bars. Rae Dawn Chong and Annabella Sciorra are partners in crime whose friendship is now put to the test while in jail; Rachel Ticotin, an inmate herself, tries to keep her young son from sharing a similar fate; and Lolita Davidovich, who murdered her abusive husband, is now facing parole and is terrified at the prospect of freedom. Grace Zabriskie and Talisa Soto also star. ★★★ $92.99

Prisoner of Honor

(1991, 88 min, US, Ken Russell) Russell is unusually restrained in this made-for-HBO retelling of "The Dreyfus Affair," a scandalous incident of anti-Semitism in 19th-century France. Richard Dreyfuss stars as an officer who refuses to allow his army to betray its honor by framing an innocent Jewish officer for treason. A good companion piece to *The Life of Emile Zola*. ★★★ $89.99

The Prisoner of Second Avenue

(1975, 105 min, US, Melvin Frank) One of the best of the Neil Simon stage-to-screen adaptations, this gloriously funny and, at times, bittersweet comedy benefits greatly from two superlative performances from Jack Lemmon and Anne Bancroft. Lemmon plays a recently unemployed exec who suffers a breakdown, which prompts wife Bancroft back into the work place. All the while, they contend with noisy neighbors, robberies, attempted muggings, a 14th-floor walk-up, picky cab drivers, trash, and the sweltering summer heat; every-

thing, in fact, which makes living in New York a singular experience. A treat from beginning to end. ★★★½ $14.99

Prisoner of the Mountains

(1996, 99 min, Russia, Sergei Bodrov) This gritty adaptation of Tolstoy's 150-year-old tale "Prisoner of the Caucasus" is a stirring anti-war drama that offers Western audiences an unprecedented and incredibly lucid look into the little-seen world of the Caucasus Mountain region. The story follows two Russian soldiers (Oleg Menshikov and Sergei Bodrov, Jr.) who are captured by a local Muslim patriarch (Jemal Sikharulidze). Chained together in Sikharulidze's barn, the two are a study in opposites: Menshikov is a hard-nosed veteran who views the villagers as enemies and Bodrov is a gawky new recruit who innocently (and perhaps foolishly) believes in his captors' humanity. It is Bodrov who strikes up a touching relationship with Sikharulidze's young daughter (the captivating Susanna Mekhralieva). Hoping to cut a deal to get his son out of a Russian prison, Sikharulidze steadfastly resists the relentless pressure from his townspeople to execute his charges. Bleak beyond imagination and yet unparalleled in grandeur, the mountain backdrop for this tale will give one an instant appreciation for the fierce reputation of its people who, for centuries, have given expansionist-minded Russians more than they bargained for. Director Bodrov, Sr. never misses a beat in delivering his heart-rending message on the insanity of war. (Russian with English subtitles) ★★★½ $99.99

The Prisoner of Zenda

(1937, 101 min, US, John Cromwell) This third of many screen versions of Anthony Hope's celebrated novel is by far the best of the bunch. Ronald Colman had one of his most popular roles as both the King of Ruritania and his look-alike cousin, who impersonates H.R.M. when the ruler is kidnapped. Madeleine Carroll, Mary Astor, Douglas Fairbanks, Jr and David Niven all offer strong support in this exciting adventure film. ★★★½ $19.99

The Prisoner of Zenda

(1952, 101 min, US, Richard Thorpe) Not as exciting as the 1937 Ronald Colman version, this extravagant though lifeless remake stars Stewart Granger and Deborah Kerr in the story of a commoner who doubles for the King. ★★½ $19.99

The Prisoner of Zenda

(1979, 108 min, US, Richard Quine) Even Peter Sellers' comic mastery can't save this farcical remake of Anthony Hope's swashbuckling novel about a king's double who is forced to step into the royal shoes when his highness is kidnapped. Not a high point in Sellers' career. ★ $14.99

Prisoners of Inertia

(1989, 92 min, US, J. Noyes Scher) What starts out as a simple Sunday brunch date deteriorates into an *After Hours*-style nightmare for a young Manhattan couple (Amanda

P

Plummer, Christopher Rich) in this mildly amusing independent film. ★★½ $79.99

Private Benjamin

(1980, 110 min, US, Howard Zieff) Goldie Hawn's effervescent performance highlights this hit comedy about a pampered "Jewish American Princess" who enlists in the Army — only to find it wasn't what she expected. Eileen Brennan gives a solid comic turn as Hawn's ever-suffering captain. ★★★ $9.99

A Private Function

(1985, 93 min, GB, Malcolm Mowbray) Class snobbery, petty vice and social climbing are given a sharp satiric examination in this grand British black comedy. Set in post-war England, the film stars Michael Palin and Maggie Smith as a couple who kidnap a pig earmarked for the nuptials of Princess Elizabeth and Prince Phillip. ★★★½ $19.99

Private Life

(1982, 102 min, USSR, Yuli Raizman) Reminiscent of Arthur Miller's "Death of a Salesman," this sensitive drama of an older man forced to reevaluate his life values after being unexpectedly dismissed from his lifelong job, was made by 80-year-old Soviet director Raizman. Sergei, a taciturn manager of a large factory, finds himself baffled by his enforced retirement and at a loss regarding what to do with his "endless string of Sundays." Quickly, he realizes that he has been insensitive to the importance in his life of his wife, relatives and friends. Symbolic of Russia at the time, the man begins a personal awakening to both the joys of life and of human relations. Nominated for the 1983 Foreign Film Oscar. (Russian with English subtitles) ★★★ $59.99

The Private Life of Henry VIII

(1933, 97 min, GB, Alexander Korda) This sweeping historical chronicle of the 16th-century British monarch features a robust performance by Charles Laughton as the ever-hitchable king. The film had a major impact on the image of British cinema around the world as it featured then-unexpected tongue-in-cheek humor which set it apart from the usual dour historical drama. Co-stars Elsa Lanchester. ★★★★ $19.99

The Private Life of Sherlock Holmes

(1970, 125 min, US, Billy Wilder) Thoroughly engaging film about, well, the title says it all. When a famous Russian ballerina wants Holmes to be the father of her child, he cleverly sidesteps her invitation by suggesting that he and Dr. Watson are more than just roommates. A convenient lie or the truth? You decide. To complicate matters, there's the mystery of the Belgian amnesiac, her missing husband and the Loch Ness monster. Served up as only Wilder can. ★★★ $19.99

Private Lives

(1931, 84 min, US, Sidney Franklin) One of Noël Coward's most delightful stage comedies is given sparkling treatment in this very funny screen adaptation. Norma Shearer and Robert Montgomery are a divorced couple who meet each other on their respective second-marriage honeymoons. In a flash, they leave their spouses and run off to rekindle their relation-

ship — and their bickering. The film is ripe with those scintillating Coward witticisms, and if Shearer and Montgomery aren't the perfect choices to recite them (the Lunts made *The Guardsman* that same year), they nevertheless handle this sophisticated hilarity with great charm. ★★★★ $19.99

The Private Lives of Elizabeth and Essex

(1939, 106 min, US, Michael Curtiz) A must-see for fans of Bette Davis, this screen version of Maxwell Anderson's play may be short on historical accuracy, but it remains an excellent period costume drama. Davis is superb as Queen Elizabeth I whose love for the dashing Earl of Essex (Errol Flynn) is put to rest by political neccessity. The film also stars Olivia deHavilland and Vincent Price. ★★★

A Private Matter

(1992, 100 min, US, Joan Micklin Silver) Director Silver tackles the true story of an abortion case that gained national attention in 1964. Sissy Spacek delivers a strong, measured portrayal of the mother who, while pregnant with her fifth child, weighs the option of abortion when the effects of Thalidomide on fetuses begins to be disclosed. As she and her husband (Aidan Quinn, in another competent performance) are catapulted into the national spotlight, their personal lives become political fodder. Both parents lose their jobs, and the family struggles against the strains of media scrutiny and interest group pressure. A powerful examination of an issue that has lost none of its potency in the intervening 30-plus years. Another noteworthy HBO production. ★★★½ $89.99

Private Parts

(1997, 111 min, US, Betty Thomas) Controversial radio and TV shock jock Howard Stern acquits himself rather nicely in this film "bio" of his rise to fame, based on his bestseller. After several directors took a stab at it, *Private Parts* finally landed in the capable hands of Betty Thomas, who — with this film, *The Brady Bunch Movie* and *The Late Shift* — has carved a wonderful niche for herself as a director of pop culture comedies. Thomas keeps the pace brisk, wrangles quite a few laughs and gets a winning performance from Stern, who's just as good at his patented "offensive" schtick as he is as a romantic lead (!) in the film's surprisingly affecting love story. Not all of *Private Parts* clicks, but it's nevertheless a funny, entertaining comedy which can be enjoyed even by those who aren't fans of his radio show. And the story of Stern's stalwart refusal to compromise and his insistence on pushing the envelope is — in a rather anarchic way — inspiring. A pleasant surprise. ★★★ $99.99

Privates on Parade

(1984, 95 min, GB, Michael Blakemore) Alternately hilarious and heartwarming, this romp covers the comic adventures of a theatri-

Howard Stern in *Private Parts*

cal troupe of British soldiers tap-dancing their way through WWII. Monty Pythonite John Cleese stars as the commander of this motley crew and Denis Quilley is ferociously funny as the director whose productions would make a USO show look like Shakespeare-in-the-Park. Don't miss the uproarious closing credits sequence. ★★★ $19.99

Prix de Beaute

(1931, 93 min, France, Augusto Genina) Louise Brooks' final starring vehicle, and her only film made in France, has her as a bored young office worker who, against the wishes of her boyfriend, seeks fame and fortune by becoming an entrant in the Miss Europa beauty contest. A standard melodrama that is highlighted by another luminous performance by the enigmatic international star. The film, co-scripted by director Genina and René Clair, features the voice of Edith Piaf who sings for Ms. Brooks. (French with English subtitles) ★★ $59.99

The Prize

(1963, 135 min, US, Mark Robson) An entertaining Cold-War spy thriller, *The Prize* is the sort of fun, mindless romp typical of the halycon days of the mid-1960s. Paul Newman plays a Nobel Prize-winning author who becomes entangled in international intrigue when he attends the Nobel ceremonies in Stockholm. He suspects that kindly nuclear physicist Edward G. Robinson has been kidnapped and replaced with an imposter. Anyone who's seen *Foreign Correspondent* knows it's the truth. Elke Sommer, Diane Baker and everybody's favorite spy Leo G. Carroll also star. This is the one where Newman attends a nudist meeting. ★★★ $19.99

Prizzi's Honor

(1985, 129 min, US, John Huston) Jack Nicholson stars as Charlie Pantana, a lonely and confused hit man who falls hopelessly in love with mysterious and alluring femme fatale Kathleen Turner. Anjelica Huston won the Oscar for Best Supporting Actress as Nicholson's once-betrothed. Director Huston infuses this wry black comedy with his characteristic joie de vivre. ★★★★ $14.99

Problem Child

(1990, 81 min, US, Dennis Dugan) Bastard precursor to *Home Alone*, about an adopted

P

seven-year-old who tortures his new parents after they whisk him away to the suburbs from an orphanage thrilled to see him gone. John Ritter is the oh-so-happy dad who believes his psycho-loving son is just in need of affection. The movie's tone is surprisingly mean-spirited; however, there are a number of slapstick laughs. ★★ $14.99

Problem Child 2

(1991, 91 min, US, Brian Levant) That tiny terror of the suburbs is back in this equally tasteless sequel. John Ritter and little Michael Oliver return as the hapless father and "devil" child, who have now relocated to another town. It doesn't take long for the imp to return to his prankish ways, especially when another orphaned child enters the scene — and *she's* hellbent for mischief, too. However, "double your pleasure" does not apply here. ★½ $19.99

The Producers

(1968, 88 min, US, Mel Brooks) Brooks' hysterical farce is certainly one of the funniest films of all time. Zero Mostel gloriously chews the scenery, the furniture and whatever else is in sight as a Broadway producer aching for a hit. He schemes with meek accountant Gene Wilder to produce a flop and make a fortune. They happen upon "Springtime for Hitler" and its crazed Nazi author (Kenneth Mars). The rest, as they say, is history. ★★★★

The Professional

(1994, 109 min, US/France, Luc Besson) Besson retools his art-house hit *La Femme Nikita* for an American audience, expanding the role of "Victor the Cleaner" into that of a cuddly, lovable hit man who becomes the reluctant guardian and mentor of a precocious 12-year-old (Natalie Portman) when her family is executed by a psychotic, drug-dealing cop (Gary Oldman in a role so over-the-top that Nicolas Cage probably fired his agent for not getting him the part). The twist comes when, hellbent for revenge, she asks him to teach her to kill. What might have been *La Femme Lolita* is instead this two-headed hybrid whose Euro-American sensibilities muddle the impact of the story. Besson's impression of police action is decidedly European, while his shying away from the evolution of the young girl into junior assassin (which reeks of the American inability to accept justifiable violence especially from children) leaves a feeling of irreconciliation. (Available letterboxed and pan & scan) ★★½ $19.99

The Professionals

(1966, 117 min, US, Richard Brooks) A rollicking adventure tale expertly directed by Brooks. Burt Lancaster heads the cast as a soldier who is hired to rescue the kidnapped wife of millionaire rancher Ralph Bellamy. Lee Marvin, Robert Ryan and Woody Strode are Lancaster's cohorts, and Jack Palance is the villain holding Claudia Cardinale captive. ★★★½

Profumo di Donna
(Scent of a Woman)

(1975, 103 min, Italy, Dino Risi) Vittorio Gassman was winner of the Best Actor Award at Cannes for his portrayal of a blind, one-armed ex-army captain who resourcefully uses his other senses to savor the beguiling attractions of the other sex. With a young army cadet acting as his eyes, our pleasure-seeking hero travels to Naples in search of love. An Italian farce with undercurrents of drama as well as a decidedly chauvinist attitude to women and relationships. Remade in 1992 with Al Pacino and Chris O'Donnell. (Italian with English subtitles) ★★★

Project A (Part 1)

(1983, 83 min, Hong Kong, Jackie Chan) Jackie Chan, the charismatic and physically adroit superstar of Asian cinema, has starred in and directed countless films in Hong Kong including the critically acclaimed *Jackie Chan's Police Force*. In this period comedy, Jackie plays an honest marine cadet in turn-of-the-century Hong Kong who battles dastardly drug smugglers. Sit back and be amazed by his sensationalistic, death-defying stunts which border on the unreal. (Cantonese with English subtitles) ★★★½ $39.99

Project A (Part 2)

(1987, 101 min, Hong Kong, Jackie Chan) For those who can't get enough of Jackie Chan's operatic, single-stunt comes this new set of adventures of Dragon Ma, the only noncorrupt cop in turn-of-the-century Hong Kong. (Cantonese with English subtitles) ★★★ $39.99

Prom Night

(1980, 91 min, Canada, Paul Lynch) A group of teenagers readying for the high school prom are stalked by a mysterious killer in this run-of-the-mill slasher pick. With Jamie Lee Curtis, who continues her reign as scream queen of the '80s. Also with Leslie Nielsen, who plays it relatively straight here. ★★ $9.99

Prom Night II: Hello Mary Lou

(1987, 97 min, US, Bruce Pittman) It's "Peggy Sue on Elm Street" as a long-dead prom queen returns from the dead to reclaim her title. ★★

The Promise

(1995, 115 min, Germany/France, Margarethe von Trotta) Von Trotta's misguided love story is nothing more than a melodramatic tale of love between cement slabs that made up the Berlin Wall. Accompanying his girlfriend Sophie and several friends, teenager Konrad is torn apart when he trips and misses his chance for escape into West Germany. Left behind, Konrad years later becomes a scientist who is kept under the thumb of the government, while Sophie becomes a tour guide of historic buildings. Through the years and several chance meetings, their love is tested, stretched, rekindled and finally quashed under the weight of the opposing countries. The good vs. evil parallel is very heavy-handed, with the Westerners being portrayed as completely caring and glamorous, and the Eastern extremely over-played. Though their romance occasionally moves, the soap opera pacing, contrived plot developments and wooden acting make this all the more disappointing from the usually reliable director of *Rosa Luxemburg*. (German with English subtitles) ★★ $91.99

Promises! Promises!

(1963, 90 min, US, King Donovan) Jayne Mansfield plays a happy housewife who takes an ocean cruise with her overworked husband, hoping to get pregnant. Notable for Mansfield's bathtub nude scene, which caused a stir during the film's original release. ★

The Promoter

(1952, 89 min, GB, Ronald Neame) Alec Guinness stars in this engaging comdey about a young man who climbs out of his lowly social rank and rises to the pinnacle of power in his small town. (British title: *The Card*) ★★★ $39.99

Proof

(1991, 91 min, Australia, Jocelyn Moorhouse) This spellbinding little oddity from Australia was one of the year's most pleasant surprises. It tells the twisted tale of Martin, a neurotic, blind photographer — no, that's not a typo — who's convinced that everyone lies to him about his surroundings. He snaps off photos as physical evidence that he hopes will one day expose this alleged deceit. When he befriends a young man named Andy, he finds a companion to whom he entrusts the job of describing photographs. But his housekeeper Celia, an obsessive woman who is secretly in love with him (which she shows in the bizarre behavior of moving his furniture around in order to keep him dependent on her), does everything in her power to sabotage their friendship. Director Moorhouse gets great performances from her ensemble in this fascinating, taut and well-made psychological examination of trust, perceived childhood wounds and sexual obsession which questions our emotional attachment to our perceptions of reality. A great companion piece to Antonioni's classic *Blow-Up*. ★★★★ $19.99

Prophecy

(1979, 95 min, US, John Frankenheimer) An ecological horror film with more emphasis on the eco than logical. Nuclear pollutants are turning our fresh-water friends into oversized and very upset monsters. ★★ $19.99

The Prophecy

(1995, 95 min, US, Gregory Widen) This very original horror film about a second war in Heaven stars Christopher Walken as the archangel Gabriel, who has come to Earth to steal the soul of a dying warrior in order to enlist his aid in a war Gabriel and other renegade angels are waging against God and his loyal servants. Eric Stoltz plays a lesser angel who has come to stop Gabriel and to protect the human beings Gabriel will destroy in his crusade. As Gabriel, Walken exudes menace and spews contempt at the "talking monkeys" he must deal with on his quest. But the film's low-budget origins prevent its grand premise from being realized and a lackluster and confusing ending makes the viewer regret having accepted it in the first place. Though the film will be especially enjoyable to anyone familiar with the particular mythos the film is exploring — such as Gabriel's trumpet and how people acquired the cleft under their noses. Viggo Mortensen also turns up at the end in an interesting twist to the film, as the "original Angel" who intervenes in the war with an agenda of his own. *The Prophecy* is a good idea which unfortunately fails in its execution. ★★ $19.99

Prospero's Books

(1991, 129 min, GB/The Netherlands, Peter Greenaway) Greenaway's kaleidoscopic, hallucinatory spin on Shakespeare's "The Tempest" is sure to leave the viewer with a visceral reaction — some will delight in his orgiastic vision, while others may be nauseated and others still will simply be left dumbfounded. Whatever the reaction, there is no denying the sheer audacity of Greenaway's achievement as he splatters the screen with an endless procession of naked bodies and a level of bacchanalian spectacle never before seen in cinema. Sir John Gielgud, in what may well be his swan song, not only stars as Prospero but also gives voice to every other character in the film. While the film sketchily follows the narrative, Greenaway pays more attention to the thematic content of the Bard's work and plays it up as an allegory for the conquering of the magical New World (read: the Americas) by the intellectual rationality of the West. For adventurous viewers of cinema, this is a must, but be warned that a knowledge of "The Tempest" is extremely helpful in one's comprehension of the film. ★★★½ $19.99

Protocol

(1984, 96 min, US, Herbert Ross) Goldie Hawn's endearing charm elevates this average comedy about a Washington waitress who saves the life of a diplomat and becomes involved in international diplomacy and intrigue. ★★½ $9.99

Prototype X29A

(1992, 98 min, US, Phillip Roth) Another excursion into quasi-mystic cyberpunk sensibilities (à la *Robocop*, et al), this technoparable on human duality is set in L.A. 2057 A.D., where totally cybernetic Prototypes are programmed to destroy Omegas, cybernetically altered humans. The requisite elements are all here: stark Cathedral lighting in debris-riddled, ravaged interiors; painfully bright, ozone-depleted, barren wasteland exteriors, *Road Warrior* costumes, casual violence and electronic takes on Gregorian chants. You've seen it all before, and yet, the young cast gives it their best shot and the story offers wry commentary on the human tendency towards self-destruction through technology. ★★ $89.99

Providence

(1977, 104 min, France, Alain Resnais) John Gielgud creates a vivid character in the person of Clive Langham, a noted elderly author, in this fascinating story on creativity and imagination by French director Resnais. In what many consider to be his finest screen role, Gielgud plays the often drunk, foul-mouthed old man, who despite suffering from a fatal disease, spends a night hallucinating about members of his family while trying to plot out his next novel. Fact, fantasy and his unconscious thoughts and feelings as well as his growing senility are incorporated into the fabric of his tale. Filmed in English, this literate and involving film costars Dirk Bogarde, Ellen Burstyn and David Warner. ★★★

Amanda Plummer and Tim Roth in *Pulp Fiction*

Provincial Actors

(1980, 104 min, Poland, Agnieszka Holland) In her debut feature, director Holland (who would go on to helm *Europa, Europa* and *The Secret Garden*) takes the trials and tribulations of a rural theatre troupe and politicizes in a meandering fashion their attempt to produce a play. Christopher, the leading actor of the troupe, is a dedicated artist — to the extent he ignores his impatient wife Anna, herself a former actress but now relegated to children's puppet shows. In the course of rehearsals and performances, Christopher experiences marital problems and a near-mental breakdown as he idealistically strives for perfection in his craft and contemplates a move to the big city and possible stardom. Holland demonstrates little of the dramatic structure or a fluent style evident in her later works, but the film does offer an interesting glimpse into the mind and the relationship of the artist. (Polish with English subtitles) ★★ $79.99

Psych-Out

(1968, 95 min, US, Richard Rush) A deaf runaway (Susan Strasberg) searches the streets looking for her brother amidst the psychedelic world of the 1960s. Cast includes Jack Nicholson, Bruce Dern, Dean Stockwell and the Strawberry Alarm Clock. ★★½

Psycho

(1960, 109 min, US, Alfred Hitchcock) What more can be said about this classic shocker that has forever altered the sanctity of the shower (not to mention tainted the reputations of taxidermists and loving sons)? Anthony Perkins made his mark with the jagged-edged portrait of mild-mannered hotel proprietor Norman Bates. A masterpiece of both suspense and narrative form, *Psycho* is Hitchcock at his best. ★★★★ $14.99

Psycho II

(1983, 113 min, US, Richard Franklin) Anthony Perkins returns as Norman Bates. It's 20 years later, and Norman has been released from the asylum, trying to keep his hands (not to mention the shower) clean. With Vera Miles

(returning from the original classic), Meg Tilly and Robert Loggia. ★★½ $14.99

Psycho III

(1986, 96 min, US, Anthony Perkins) The Bates Motel is open for business once more. Anthony Perkins returns as Norman, who here becomes attracted to Diana Scarwid, his new assistant manager, who bears a striking resemblence to the ill-fated Marion Crane. Some scenes are played strictly for laughs. ★★ $14.99

Puberty Blues

(1981, 86 min, Australia, Bruce Beresford) Beresford's comic, risqué look at the coming-of-age of two teenage girls around the surfing beaches outside Sydney. It offers an insightful look at adolescent rites of passage, told from the female point of view. ★★½ $59.99

Public Access

(1992, 86 min, US, Bryan Singer) An intriguing but ultimately unfulfilled thriller, *Public Access* is the promising first feature film by director Singer and writer Christopher McQuarrie, the team behind 1995's brilliant *The Usual Suspects*. The slickly handsome Ron Marquette is Whiley Pritcher, an enigmatic stranger who comes to the sleepy middle American town of Brewster with a mission: to expose its dark underbelly and tear apart the town from within. He buys time on the local public access channel, hosting a show ironically called "Our Town," and asks the question, "What's wrong with Brewster?" Soon a bevy of semi-lunatic callers tell on their neighbors, venting their anger at Whiley and threatening to uncover a scandal lurking beneath Brewster's surface. Though Singer and McQuarrie fail to find a satisfying resolution to the questions they pose, the ending — which doesn't mesh with the creepy buildup which precedes it — is nevertheless thought-provoking and unique. The film combines parts of *Talk Radio* and *Blue Velvet* to show the depravity and selfishness which hide behind the friendly small-town smile. ★★½ $92.99

Public Enemy

(1931, 83 min, US, William Wellman) Classic 1930s gangster film with James Cagney giving a star-making performance as a slum kid who rises to the top of the underworld. First-rate cast includes Jean Harlow, Joan Blondell and, of course, Mae Clarke, who was the recipient of that famous grapefruit. ★★★½ $19.99

The Public Eye

(1992, 99 min, US, Howard Franklin) Fireball Joe Pesci reveals a seldom-seen sensitivity in this atmospheric biography based on the life of '40s tabloid photographer Leon Bernstein. Pesci is "The Great Bernzini," a papparazzi prototype whose photojournalistic aspirations get him embroiled with the cops, the mob and a sultry femme fatale (Barbara Hershey). While the "beauty and the beast" angle wears thin at times, writer-director Franklin leads Pesci through an otherwise picture-perfect tableau of a life that was at once touching and wondrous; and Peter Suschitzky's dead-on mixture of black-and-white photography with color cinematography perfectly captures the gritty milieu of the 1940s New York underworld. (Not to be confused with the 1972 Mia Farrow romantic comedy of the same name.) ★★½ $19.99

Pulp Fiction

(1994, 153 min, US, Quentin Tarantino) Tarantino's audacious, art-house actioner is perhaps the only American film so story-intensive that it deserves the title "the *Gone with the Wind* of action movies." John Travolta and Samuel L. Jackson never been better than as a pair of gregarious hit men whose day-to-day activities take them through an interlocking series of darkly comic and horrific scenarios ranging from an accidental drug overdose to a graphic (and unexpected) rape sequence. As with his debut film *Reservoir Dogs*, Tarantino introduces a rogue's gallery of well-drawn characters into a labyrinthine story line, playing with perspective, time and place to create perhaps the most original American film since *Citizen Kane*. Overlong without ever being boring, this gritty walk on the wild side features an astounding ensemble including Uma Thurman, Bruce Willis (his best screen portrayal), Harvey Keitel, Tim Roth, Amanda Plummer, Ving Rhames, and Christopher Walken in a scene-stealing cameo. (Includes additional footage not shown theatrically) (Available letterboxed and pan & scan) ★★★★ $14.99

Pump Up the Volume

(1990, 100 min, US, Allan Moyle) Christian Slater, fresh from his success in *Heathers*, dons the troubled youth persona once again, and though this subversive teen comedy-drama has none of that near-classic's devilish wit, it's dead on target in capturing teenage disillusionment in the land of "white bread." Slater plays a shy high school student (and new kid in town) who lets go and "talks hard" as Harry Hard-on, an irreverent pirate D.J. His voice in tune to both the misfits and the hip of his school, Harry soon becomes an unwilling guru to his classmates, and a "threat" to school and local authorities. *Pump Up the Volume* is brimming with great dialogue and an excellent musical score, and like *Heathers*, casts an iconoclastic glance towards today's teens. ★★★ $9.99

Pumping Iron

(1977, 85 min, US, George Butler & Robert Fiore) A sometimes mesmerizing glimpse into the little-dissected world of bodybuilding, this part-adulatory, part-voyeuristic documentary centers on the Mr. Olympia contest and on its two main competitors – Arnold Schwarzenegger and Lou Ferrigno. There's lots of scenes of bulging biceps and sweaty faces as the directors interview the men in and out of the gym, and cinematically eavesdrop on conversations and workouts. ★★★ $14.99

Pumping Iron II – The Women

(1985, 107 min, US, George Butler) Several years after *Pumping Iron*, Butler returned to the gyms in this engaging look at female bodybuilding. As the camera ogles the bronzed women pumping up, champions Rachel McLish, Bev Francis and a dozen others discuss their commitment to the sport and demonstrate their physical prowess. ★★★ $19.99

Pumpkinhead

(1988, 87 min, US, Stan Winston) This Gothic-like horror film is a cut above the typical teen slasher film. Directed by Winston (the F/X wizard behind *Alien*), *Pumpkinhead* provides creepy fun which relies more on suspense than gore (although the film does have its share). A group of city kids go "wilding" in the country and accidentally kill one of the young locals. The dead child's father (Lance Henriksen) wants revenge and summons a mythical demon, which comes to life and inhabits the surrounding mountains. ★★½ $14.99

Punchline

(1988, 128 min, US, David Seltzer) This intriguing and often hilarious comedy-drama stars Tom Hanks (in an unusual departure from his other film roles) as a self-centered medical student drop-out determined to make it in the world of stand-up comedy. Sally Field nicely plays a New Jersey housewife (patterned on Roseanne?) who yearns to make people laugh. The film entertainingly explores both the milieu of the comic and the touching story of the friendship and ill-fated romance between Hanks and Field. John Goodman plays Field's supportive husband, a role he'd play for nine years with you-know-who on TV. ★★★ $9.99

The Punisher

(1990, 92 min, US/Australia, Mark Goldblatt) Dolph Lundgren stars as a policeman who turns vigilante after the murder of his family, becoming yet another comic book hero. The film is a good example of the B-movie actioner, filled with bone-crunching violence, explosions, kidnappings and ninjas. Louis Gossett, Jr. costars as Lundgren's ex-partner, and Kim Niori is featured as the ice-princess leader of the Japanese mob. ★★ $9.99

The Punk Rock Movie

(1978, 90 min, GB, Don Letts) Sid Vicious, Johnny Rotten, The Clash, The Slits, Generation X (with, Billy Idol), Siouxie & The Banshees, Wayne Country and many other "trash and burn" attractions all explode on the screen with raucous and explosive vitality in this crude Super 8mm blow-up. ★★

The Puppet Masters

(1994, 95 min, US, Stuart Orme) Sci-fi visionary Robert A. Heinlein's gripping cold war parable about alien possession is updated and streamlined into this tense if derivative chiller with more than a passing resemblance to *Invasion of the Body Snatchers*. This time out the alien is a parasite that attaches itself to the spinal cord of its victim and drills into the brain, rendering the host unable to exercise free will. Though we've seen it all before, the film benefits from a fast-paced script, good special effects and a commanding performance by Donald Sutherland as the resident know-it-all science expert called in to stem the tide of alien domination. Also with Eric Thal, Julie Warner and Yaphet Kotto. ★★★ $9.99

The Puppetoon Movie

(1986, 80 min, US, George Pal) Do you remember when you first saw *Pinocchio* or *Fantasia*? When an animated feature was a magical escape in a darkened movie palace? When timeless stories, breathtaking music and dazzling craftsmanship filled the big screen in Technicolor hues? *The Puppetoon Movie* is a collection of the works of legendary fantasy filmmaker George Pal (*War of the Worlds, The Time Machine*). Pal's unique form of animation employed an army of individually carved wooden figures – usually over 9,000 puppets for an average short! Take a trip back to the days when artists meticulously crafted every frame of film and created a world that was truly magical in its scope. ★★★ $12.99

A Pure Formality

(1994, 108 min, France/Italy, Giuseppe Tornatore) An arresting opening sequence of murder and flight begins an intricately constructed battle of intellect and will between two formidable opponents. As the prime suspect, a rain-soaked and disheveled Gérard Depardieu emits a raw intensity reminiscent of his performance in *Going Places*. As Police Inspector Bogart, Roman Polanski seems to carry the burden of his personal experiences with police procedures. The conflict between these evenly matched protagonists, which starts in an isolated, threadbare provincial police station, maintains a frenetic pace of visceral animosity in this sly game of cat and mouse. Tornatore keeps a tight ship, deftly utilizing all the materials at his disposal – not the least of which is Ennio Morricone's score. The film's resolution is satisfying in its ambiguity, a wry treatise on the many-layered nature of reality. (French with English subtitles) ★★★½ $96.89

Pure Luck

(1991, 96 min, US, Nadia Tass) Yet another attempt by Hollywood to capitalize on the success of lesser-known foreign films, this limp remake of the hilarious French comedy *La Chevre* falls decidedly flat. When the accident-prone daughter of a wealthy industrialist disappears at a Mexican resort, the company's psychologist (Harry Shearer) suggests that the only person capable of finding her is the equally maladroit and bumbling Martin Short. Danny Glover is the company detective who

Putney Swope

reluctantly accepts him as a partner in the search. The pairing doesn't seem like a bad one, but this comic duo simply can't match the sidesplitting slapstick achieved by Gérard Depardieu and Pierre Richard in the original. Though Short being stung by a bee is very funny. ★★ $9.99

Purlie Victorious

(1963, 105 min, US, Nicholas Webster) Leisurely film version of Ossie Davis' Broadway satire about a free-wheeling preacher (Davis) who goes up against an oppressive, bigoted landowner (Sorrell Booke). Also starring Ruby Dee, Godfrey Cambridge and Alan Alda. The basis for the award-winning musical "Purlie." (aka: *Gone Are the Days*) ★★★

The Purple Heart

(1944, 99 min, US, Lewis Milestone) This WWII drama doubles as a fascinating piece of war-time propaganda and an interesting examination of individual heroism. Dana Andrews, Farley Granger and Richard Conte are just three of a group of U.S. pilots captured and held prisoner by the Japanese Army. ★★★ $14.99

Purple Noon (Plein Soleil)

(1960, 118 min, France, René Clément) This stylish, gorgeously photographed and sexy thriller, made nearly four decades ago, is far from being dated and is possibly more impressive when viewed today. Set amidst the opulent, sun-drenched locales of the Mediterranean, the film's serpentine plot involves the tangled affairs of three young "beautiful people." Alain Delon is the stunningly handsome Tom, a friend and hanger-on to Phillip (Maurice Ronet), a brattily rich American playboy cruising the warm blue waters in his sailboat with his long-suffering girlfriend (Marie Laforet) and Tom. But this surface beauty and tranquility only masks a deadly scheme of revenge and murder as Tom concocts a plot to take over his friend's life and love. Hitchcockian in detail and twists, *Purple Noon*, adapted from Patricia Highsmith's "The Talented Mr. Ripley," is certain to enthrall devotees of murder/mysteries as well as interest fans of a style of European filmmaking now sadly gone. (French and Italian with English subtitles) ★★★½ $102.99

Purple Rain

(1984, 111 min, US, Albert Magnoli) Prince makes an prodigous film debut as The Kid, a young band leader with an alcoholic father, an uptight attitude and problems with women. Filled with outrageous production numbers and pulsating music by Prince and the Revolution as well as Morris Day and the Time. The film's treatment of women is suspect, but the question arises, is it unmitigated misogyny or a comment on the ravages of spousal abuse? You decide. ★★½ $9.99

The Purple Rose of Cairo

(1985, 82 min, US, Woody Allen) Mia Farrow stars as a waifish Depression-era waitress who is swept off her feet by Jeff Daniels, the star of her favorite movie. The catch, of course, is that he literally walks off the movie screen to get to her! A delicious concept, done full justice by Allen. "I'm in love with a wonderful man — he's fictional, but you can't have everything." ★★★★ $14.99

The Purple Taxi

(1977, 107 min, France/Italy/Ireland, Yves Boisset) An unusual French drama with an international cast featuring Fred Astaire, Charlotte Rampling, Peter Ustinov and Philippe Noiret, as a group of expatriates who live in Ireland and are involved in a complicated ménage of relationships. (Filmed in English) ★★

The Pursuit of D.B. Cooper

(1981, 100 min, US, Roger Spottiswoode) A fictionalized account of a real-life event, this appealing caper comedy stars Robert Duvall and Treat Williams in a story which tries to speculate what "really" happened to infamous hijacker D.B. Cooper in 1971. Williams is the thief, and Duvall is the policeman hot on his trail. ★★½ $9.99

Pushing Hands

(1992, 100 min, US, Ang Lee) *Pushing Hands* is a Tai Chi exercise of ebb and flow, accomodation and imposition, a physical manifestation of the quest for balance. In director Lee's first film, the balance of the Chu household is disrupted when Alex (Bo Z. Wang) brings his father (Sihung Lung), a Tai chi master in China, to New York to live with him, his Caucasian wife and their child. Circumstances force father and daughter-in-law (Deb Snyder) into unrelentingly close contact, exacerbating generational and cultural differences. The ongoing conflict eventually erupts, resulting in the disruption and dissolution of the precarious familial bonds. Master Chu embarks on a solo journey into this strange new world, and his quest is delicately considered with compassion and sharp observance by the director. A small gem of a film whose resolution offers warmth without naiveté. (In English and Mandarin with English subtitles) ★★★ $92.99

Putney Swope

(1969, 88 min, US, Robert Downey) While the liberal wing of Hollywood was making a big show out of taking Sidney Poitier home to dinner, Downey was preaching true equality when he argued that given half the chance blacks could be every bit as corrupt as whites. Having spent the better part of a decade directing TV commercials, Downey set his fable in the milieu he knew well — Madison Avenue advertising. When token black Swope is accidentally elected the agency's new president, change is in the air. First up, a corporate make over, starting with the name. Now called "Truth & Soul," the company vows not to accept any politically incorrect clients — until the cash flow gets tight. Downey mixes faux commercials with a wild narrative style that influenced mainstream movies for years to come. ★★★ $19.99

Pygmalion

(1938, 96 min, GB, Anthony Asquith & Leslie Howard) George Bernard Shaw helped write the screenplay for this first real expert film translation of one of his plays. Wendy Hiller is captivating as Eliza Doolittle, the guttersnipe flower seller who is transformed into a proper socialite by the efforts of Professor Henry Higgins (Leslie Howard). Unfortunately lost in the shuffle since the international success of the musical "My Fair Lady" on which it is based, this earlier, more modest, version is exemplary of "classic" British cinema. ★★★★ $24.99

A Pyromaniac's Love Story

(1995, 96 min, US, Joshua Brand) From the creator of TV's "Northern Exposure" comes this cloying comedy of errors about a poor schlub (John Leguizamo) who takes the blame for setting a fire he didn't commit in exchange for the $20,000 he needs to run away with his beloved (Sadie Frost) who'll now have nothing to do with him. Enter the real culprit (William Baldwin) who set the fire as a tribute to his beloved (Erika Eleniak) and now wants proper credit! Part O'Henry and part Wilde, without the flair of either, Brand's quirky and miscast mishmash relies on the kinetic energy of rising star Leguizamo to sustain it, and though he and most of the cast are cheerful, the screenplay doesn't make it worth the effort. ★★ $94.99

Q

(1982, 93 min, US, Larry Cohen) From the fertile mind of Cohen (*It's Alive*) comes this very exciting half monster movie/half cop story about an ancient winged creature that's alive and well and living atop the Chrysler Building. Michael Moriarty is great as a two-bit loser who discovers the nest and then blackmails the city for millions to divulge the location. David Carradine, Richard Roundtree and Candy Clark also star. ★★★ $9.99

Q & A

(1990, 132 min, US, Sidney Lumet) Director Lumet scrutinizes the mean streets of New York City in this powerful but insensitive urban drama. In a forceful and maniacal performance, Nick Nolte stars as a racist, homophobic cop whose murder of a suspect is being investigated by young assistant D.A. Timothy Hutton, who uncovers a web of political corruption. Lumet, whose *Serpico* and *Prince of the City* have explored similar themes, pulls no punches either in his depiction of racism or political dirty dealings. Armand Assante is commanding as a gangster being investigated by Hutton. As unflinching as the drama is in its examination of bigotry, *Q & A* is shockingly callous in its depiction of gays. ★★½ $9.99

Quackser Fortune Has a Cousin in the Bronx

(1970, 90 min, Ireland, Waris Hussein) Gene Wilder delivers an exceptionally subdued performance as a man who follows horses around the streets of Dublin and sells their manure for gardening. A charming and offbeat comic love story which also stars Margot Kidder as an American coed who becomes the center of Wilder's amorous attentions. ★★★

Quadrophenia

(1979, 115 min, GB, Franc Roddam) It's Mods versus Rockers in The Who's gripping portrait of teenage anguish and anger played out in '60s Britain amid pill-popping, gang warfare and rock 'n' roll. This vibrantly-paced film is filled with great music and features the momentous film debut of Sting as an ace face. ★★★½ $14.99

Quality Street

(1937, 84 min, US, George Stevens) Fanciful screen version of James Barrie's whimsical play of mistaken identity and romantic trickery. Katharine Hepburn stars as a beautiful society girl whose fiancé goes off to the Napoleonic Wars. When he returns 10 years later, he doesn't recognize his former girlfriend, whose beauty has somewhat faded. So she masquerades as her own high-spirited niece to win him back. Franchot Tone and Fay Bainter also star. ★★★ $19.99

Quartet

(1948, 120 min, GB, Ken Annakin) First-rate episodic drama featuring four W. Somerset Maugham short stories, which are introduced by the author himself. The stories are: *The Facts of Life*, *The Alien Corn*, *The Kite* and *The Colonel's Lady*. The cast includes Dirk Bogarde, Mai Zetterling, Basil Radfors, Ian Fleming and Honor Blackman. ★★★½

Quartet

(1981, 101 min, GB/France, James Ivory) Ivory's adaptation of Jean Rhys' novel stars Isabelle Adjani as a young woman who, upon being stranded in Paris, falls prey to a beguiling British couple played by Alan Bates and Maggie Smith. Excellent performances and Ivory's steady hand at the helm make this tale of hedonism and treachery a spine-tingling treat. ★★★ $19.99

Que Viva Mexico!

(1930/1984, 90 min, USSR, Sergei Eisenstein) This famous aborted project has endured a long, rocky history. In 1930, Eisenstein traveled to Mexico in an effort to make a film on that country. The project was suspended after a dispute with his producer, the writer Upton Sinclair. With filming only partially completed, Eisenstein left for the Soviet Union expecting the rushes to be sent to him for completion; but they never arrived and the project languished for over 40 years until Grigory Alexandrov, his former editor, obtained the rushes (from MoMA, of all places) and constructed a version Eisenstein might have done. The result is a glorious and compelling vision of a mystical Mexico. Told in five segments, Eisenstein explores different aspects of Indian life as well as their plight after the Spanish conquest and Catholic indoctrination. Strikingly photographed, this poetic and vivid film explores both the beauty and the underlying tragedy of this fascinating country. (Russian with English subtitles) ★★★ $59.99

The Queen

(1968, 80 min, US, Frank Simon) This outlandish behind-the-scenes look at the drag Miss All American Beauty Pageant of 1967 has only improved with age, offering the viewer a fascinating and humorous peek into the world of drag, its memorable participants and a glimpse at one aspect of pre-Stonewall gay life. Staged in New York, the film captures the frantic days of preparation for the elaborately staged finals as the 40 regional contestants arrive, meet the exacting Edith Head-like coordinator, rehearse their stage entrance and dance numbers, and exchange makeup, fashion and beauty secrets. The pageant itself is a glamorous, sensational affair which gives center stage to these beauties, especially Philadelphia's Harlow. After the crowning of the new queen, many of the attitude-throwing,

Quadrophenia

jealous losers bare their sharp claws and venomous tongues, bitching about the winner and her oh-so-tacky dress. Meow! A camp delight and finger-snapping fun. ★★★ $29.99

Queen Bee

(1955, 95 min, US, Ranald MacDougall) Joan Crawford is at her fire-breathing best in this soaper about the machinations of the manipulative matriarch of a dysfunctional Southern family who destroys the lives of those around her (in between costume changes). More fashion show than film, *Queen Bee* sparkles with the cattiest dialogue this side of *All About Eve* and should find a home on the shelf of every Crawford devotee. Barry Sullivan, as her long-suffering husband, John Ireland and Fay Wray (who in Joan hadn't met such a monster since *King Kong*) also star. ★★★ $19.99

Queen Christina

(1933, 97 min, US, Rouben Mamoulian) In one of her most intoxicating performances, Greta Garbo radiates sensuality and regal authority as the lonely but compassionate 17th-century Swedish monarch — who renounced her throne rather than be forced to wed and produce an heir. Exquisitely photographed, the film also features John Gilbert as her intended, who can't understand her reluctance and constant wearing of men's trousers. Mamoulian's classic works as both historical epic and examination of individual expression, and Garbo posed sphinx-like at the bow of a ship is unforgettable. ★★★★ $19.99

Queen Kelly

(1929, 96 min, US, Erich von Stroheim) Let's dish some dirt! Even though von Stroheim was supposed to be nothing more than her bimbo director, he still managed to make this Gloria Swanson vehicle into something of his own before the plug was pulled. A handsome prince falls for a cute little convent girl, only to lose her when she is shipped off to an East African brothel run by her aunt. It's Cinderella with a few kinks; but the film is never really com-

Greta Garbo as *Queen Christina*

pleted after Swanson had a snit about a scene where a syphilitic cripple drools tobacco juice on her in bed. Needless to say, it's the kind of fun only von Stroheim could create. Some scenes cropped up in Billy Wilder's *Sunset Boulevard* twenty years later. ★★★½ $39.99

Queen Margot

(1994, 140 min, France, Patrice Chereau) This lavishly produced French epic, based on a novel by Alexandre Dumas, examines the bloody history of the struggle between France's Catholics and Protestants in the late 16th century. Opening with the marriage of the Catholic Margot (the unbelievably radiant Isabelle Adjani) to the Protestant Henri of Navarre (Daniel Auteuil), the film details the events leading up to and following the St. Bartholomew's Day massacre in Paris, when the Catholic guard slaughtered over 6,000 Huguenots. Brimming with more palace intrigue than the best of Shakespeare, the story's central villainess is the Queen Mother, Catherine de Medici (Virna Lisi), who is constantly hatching plots to dispatch poor Henri and keep her three sons, King Charles (Jean-Hugues Anglade), massacre mastermind Anjou (Pascal Gregory) and Alencon (Julien Rassam) in power. Amidst all the rabble is Margot who is insanely in love with the son of a slain Huguenot leader, La Môle (the smoldering Vincent Perez) and thus grudgingly sides with her husband, Henri. Marvelously acted and filled with graphic images of brutal violence, the film is a superb costume drama and will delight lovers of history. (French with English subtitles) ★★★½ $19.99

Queen of Hearts

(1989, 112 min, GB, Jon Amiel) Wonderfully wacky tale from the director of *The Singing Detective* (not yet available on video) about an Italian couple who elope to London to escape an arranged marriage, only to be tracked down by the vengeful would-be groom. Director Amiel ably mixes whimsical ideas with dead-on characterizations. ★★★½

The Queen of Spades

(1948, 95 min, GB, Thorold Dickinson) Anton Walbrook stars as a young Russian officer who is consumed by an obsession to learn the secret of winning at cards from a diabolical old countess (a bravura performance by Edith Evans). Based on a story by Alexander Pushkin, the film is infused with an eerie atmosphere of the macabre. ★★★ $39.99

Queens Logic

(1991, 116 min, US, Steve Rash) A remarkable ensemble cast breathes life into this *Big Chill*-like, thought-provoking examination of growing up and growing apart. A group of friends return to the old neighborhood for a wedding which may or may not happen. As events accelerate toward a fateful bachelor party, the childhood friends discover how the world has changed, and how they've remained the same. The cast includes Joe Mantegna, Kevin Bacon, John Malkovich, Linda Fiorentino, Ken Olin, Chloe Webb and Jamie Lee Curtis. ★★½ $9.99

Querelle

(1982, 106 min, West Germany, Rainer Werner Fassbinder) Some say that Fassbinder was past the point of dissipation as he worked on Jean Genet's homoerotic story of lust and murder. There is no denying that the final result lacks the cohesion of the director's greatest works. But its ominously dark and determinedly artificial sets, the pervasive homosexual iconography and the stylized acting all gel to create a brooding, melancholy mood quite fitting with the classic novel. Brad Davis is Querelle, a ruggedly handsome, narcissistic and sexually confused sailor who exploits and even kills the ones who lust after him. Peter Nero is perfect as the commander who secretly worships him while Jeanne Moreau is completely miscast as Querelle's part-time lover and brothel madam. (English language version) ★★½ $19.99

The Quest

(1996, 95 min, US, Jean-Claude Van Damme) Jean-Claude Van Damme proves that he can be as bad a director as he is an actor in this, his debut behind the camera. He stars in this period tale as the leader of a group of kiddie thieves who becomes entangled with a debonair pirate (in the form of Roger Moore). He's then sold into slavery and then becomes a martial arts master. He later meets Moore again, and they are soon both after a priceless golden dragon which can only be won by being the sole survivor of an invitation-only fighting contest. If you've played Mortal Kombat or another similar video game, you know the story already. All that hooey only serves to bring the slow-moving story to the final competition, which is actually staged rather well. ★★ $14.99

Quest for Fire

(1982, 97 min, France/Canada, Jean-Jacques Annaud) An enthralling supposition on the evolution of mankind, skillfully and imaginatively crafted by Annaud. Novelist Anthony Burgess ("A Clockwork Orange") and Desmond Morris collaborated to create the original language and body movement of prehistoric man in this unique mesh of fantasy and pop-archaeology. ★★★½ $69.99

A Question of Love

(1978, 104 min, US, Jerry Thorpe) Based on a true story about a nurse in Ohio who moved in with her female lover with her two sons in tow. When the older child wants to go back to his father, a tempestuous and hard-fought court battle ensues. Great performances are delivered by both Gena Rowlands and Jane Alexander. ★★★

A Question of Silence

(1983, 92 min, The Netherlands, Marleen Gorris) This production is surely one of the most controversial and provocative films released in some time. Ostensibly a feminist thriller, the film chronicles the seemingly unmotivated murder of a male shopkeeper by three middle-aged women who had never met before and did not know their victim. A woman psychologist tries to piece together the puzzle of why they killed the man. Was it senseless murder or a political act — the rage

Ralph Fiennes in Quiz Show

of women against a male dominated society? (Dutch with English subtitles) ★★★ $29.99

Quick

(1993, 99 min, US, Rick King) Teri Polo stars as a hit woman nicknamed "Quick" in this very entertaining "boobs and bullets" adventure. She's hired to take out an embezzling Mafia accountant (Martin Donovan) who's stolen $3 million from crime boss Robert Davi. In a series of bizarre events, Quick is not only seduced by the lure of money, she also falls prey to the charms of her intended target, sending her corrupt policeman/boyfriend (Jeff Fahey) into a jealous frenzy. Leaving a cross-country trail of carnage, the pair soon find themselves pursued by the remaining cast in this strange but recommended surprise. ★★ $92.99

The Quick and the Dead

(1995, 103 min, US, Sam Raimi) From the director of the *Evil Dead* trilogy comes this underrated homage to the Sergio Leone spaghetti westerns of yore. A deglamorized Sharon Stone (who coproduced) stars as a vengeful gunslinger who rides into the dustball town of Redemption (no symbolism there) looking for the man responsible for her father's murder. She winds up smack-dab in the middle of the annual "Fastest Gun in the West" contest. Gene Hackman, in a nod to his role in *Unforgiven*, gives an over-the-top performance as the sadistic town overlord who, until now, has won the contest hands down. Needless to say, he's the man she's looking for. Though it's mostly predictable fun, what distinguishes the film is director Raimi's patented inventive technical prowess: using camera angles and impossible POV shots, he deftly meshes gruesome violence with side-splitting humor. It's a visual and darkly comic feast. Also with Leonardo DiCaprio as Hackman's son, Russell Crowe, Lance Henriksen and Gary Sinise. ★★★ $19.99

Quick Change

(1990, 88 min, US, Howard Franklin) Likable caper comedy with Bill Murray, Geena Davis and Randy Quaid pulling off a perfect bank robbery — but their troubles begin when they try to make it out of New York City. Jason Robards is the cop assigned to the case, and veteran stage actor Philip Bosco has some good moments as a fastidious bus driver. ★★½ $9.99

Quicksilver

(1986, 106 min, US, Tom Donnelly) Routine youth pic with Kevin Bacon as a burned-out stockbroker who takes a job with a bicycle messenger service, unwittingly becoming involved with drug dealers. ★½ $79.99

The Quiet Earth

(1985, 110 min, New Zealand, Geoff Murphy) Bruno Lawrence stars in this thought-provoking sci-fi tale as a scientist who awakens one morning to find himself the last person on earth. An imaginative film with an ending as haunting as that of *2001*, *The Quiet Earth* has much to say about man's race towards self-destruction. ★★★

The Quiet Man

(1952, 129 min, US, John Ford) You will be amazed by John Wayne's nuanced performance as *The Quiet Man*, the Irishman returning home to Inisfree after years in Pittsburgh steel mills. The entire cast is a delight, and the camera caresses the Irish countryside. Ford won a Best Director Oscar for this one. Also starring Maureen O'Hara, Barry Fitzgerald, Victor McLaglen, Ward Bond and Jack MacGowran. ★★★★ $19.99

Quigley Down Under

(1990, 120 min, US, Simon Wincer) Tom Selleck stars in this appealing western as an American cowboy who travels to mid-19th century Australia to work for ruthless ranch owner Alan Rickman. When Selleck refuses to be a paid assassin, he's left for dead in the Outback and extracts vengence against his former boss. (Available letterboxed and pan & scan) ★★★ $14.99

The Quiller Memorandum

(1966, 105 min, GB, Michael Anderson) Harold Pinter provided an entertaining though not particularly suspenseful screenplay for this espionage thriller about an American operative rooting out neo-Nazis in modern-day Berlin. The first-rate cast includes Alec Guinness, George Segal, Max Von Sydow and Senta Berger. ★★½ $59.99

Quilombo

(1984, 120 min, Brazil, Carlos Diegues) Diegues' (*Bye Bye, Brazil*) historical saga is a stirring fusion of folklore, political impact and dynamic storytelling. Based on historical fact, the setting is 17th-century Brazil where groups of runaway black slaves escaped into the jungle where they formed self-governing communities. Set on the border line between history and legend, between mountains and the sky, *Quilombo* is a powerful vision of paradise — sensual and alive, with exotic scenery and spectacular blood-and-thunder bat-

tles, all touched with a bit of the mystical and surreal. (Portuguese with English subtitles) ★★★ $29.99

Quintet

(1979, 110 min, US, Robert Altman) Atmospheric but confusing fantasy about the survivors of a new ice age who pass the time playing Quintet, a game where all the losers end up dead and there is only one winner. Paul Newman stars with Vittorio Gassman and Fernando Rey. ★★ $19.99

Quiz Show

(1994, 130 min, US, Robert Redford) It's 1958, and "Twenty-One" is the most popular game show on TV. Herb Stempel (John Turturro) is its long-running champion; that is until he is forced to "take a dive," making handsome challenger Charles Van Doren (Ralph Fiennes) its newest winner. Initially unaware of any wrongdoing, Van Doren slowly learns of the show's fix but succumbs to the easy winnings. This forces Stempel to go public and brings Congressional investigator Richard Goodwin (Rob Morrow) onto the scene. In adapting the real-life story of the quiz show scandal to the screen (based on Goodwin's autobiography), director Redford has fashioned an immaculate, evocative drama of self-delusion, investigation and conspiracy and superbly juxtaposes it with a stinging allegory of America's loss of innocence. As Van Doren, Fiennes is extraordinary in capturing the moral dilemma of an honest man caught in the claws of bribery and adulation, and is evenly matched by Turturro's gutsy portrayal of the vindictive but ultimately wronged Stempel. As Van Doren's Pulitzer Prize-winning father, Paul Scofield is devastatingly brilliant. ★★★★ $14.99

Quo Vadis

(1951, 171 min, US, Mervyn LeRoy) Epic M-G-M production about the love affair between a Roman soldier (Robert Taylor) and a Christian woman (Deborah Kerr). Peter Ustinov gives a great performance as Roman emporer Nero. Everything about this box-office smash is done on a grand scale, from its art direction and costumes to its story and screenplay which manages to rise above religious film clichés. ★★★½ $24.99

Quilombo

R

Rabbit Test

(1978, 86 min, US, Joan Rivers) Occasionally tasteless, episodic comedy with Billy Crystal as the world's first pregnant man. Joan Rivers, who also cowrote the screenplay, extracts one or two amusing scenarios from this premise, but most of it is abysmal. ★½

Rabid

(1972, 90 min, Canada, David Cronenberg) Porn queen Marilyn Chambers stars as a young woman who undergoes experimental skin-graft surgery after a motorcycle accident. One month later, she emerges from a coma with an insatiable appetite for blood which she obtains though the use of a spiked organ growing out of very sexual-looking orifice in her armpit. Her victims then become rabid vampires themselves, attacking all who come near them until they, too, go into a coma and die. Cronenberg's themes of "venereal horror" and medical experimentation are evident here, albeit in somewhat embryonic form, as is his fascination with the superficial and vain concerns of the modern industrial world. Chambers is surprisingly good in her Typhoid Mary-like role, and the irony in the very sexual scenes when she feeds on her victims is certainly the reason Cronenberg cast her in this non-pornographic role. Less cerebral and more reliant on standard shocks for its success, *Rabid* is nevertheless a highly original exploration of the familiar vampire and living dead genres. ★★½

The Rachel Papers

(1989, 92 min, GB, Damian Harris) Charles Highway (Dexter Fletcher) can have any girl he chooses, guided by his customized computer program, "Conquests and Techniques," an assortment of enticing props including appropriate clothing and home decor, and sensitive poetic quotations. But when he meets Rachel Noyce (Ione Skye), all his irresistible schemes fail; Charles must reveal his true self to win her. *The Rachel Papers* is candid, funny and touching, a charming story of young lust and love with a remarkably grown-up sensibility. Featuring Jonathan Pryce and James Spader. ★★★

Rachel, Rachel

(1968, 101 min, US, Paul Newman) An intensely somber but affecting drama of a woman who, after years of self-imposed fear, decides to experience life. Joanne Woodward, in a poignant and carefully realized performance, plays Rachel, a 35-year-old schoolteacher and walking tinderbox of repressed emotions and sexual frustration. Newman's directorial debut is a film of great subtlety and beauty. Estelle Parsons gives a tender portrait of a closeted lesbian in love with Rachel. ★★★★ $19.99

Racing with the Moon

(1984, 108 min, US, Richard Benjamin) Benjamin's bittersweet tale of youthful yearnings and indecision boasts strong performances by Sean Penn and Nicolas Cage as a pair of buddies biding their freedom on the eve of military duty. Elizabeth McGovern is beguiling as a young woman involved with Penn. Ripe with the gentle air of innocence and a warmhearted sense of humor. ★★★ $14.99

The Racket

(1951, 88 min, US, John Cromwell) The professional and personal battle between two former friends now on opposing sides of the law is the story in this hard-hitting crime drama. Robert Mitchum is a tough-as-nails precinct captain determined to keep his turf clean from the likes of Robert Ryan, his old chum who stops at nothing in his quest for expansion of his crime kingdom. Lizabeth Scott co-stars as the love interest, and some scenes were directed by Nicholas Ray. ★★★ $19.99

Radio Days

(1986, 85 min, US, Woody Allen) Allen's loosely structured but powerfully envisioned series of fables and vignettes takes us back to the halcyon days of radio. Through a series of hilarious, and often magical, reminiscences about his childhood, Allen eavesdrops on the lives of actors, singers, talk show hosts, and even the cigarette girl who made good. As usual, Allen deftly utilizes what has become his stock company of actors — Mia Farrow, Diane Keaton, Jeff Daniels, Tony Roberts, and the luminescent Dianne Wiest. ★★★★ $14.99

Radio Flyer

(1992, 114 min, US, Richard Donner) *Radio Flyer* has the look of an affectionate childhood memory piece — but these reminiscences are sweetened with bitter recollections belying its innocent tone. Elijah Wood and Joseph Mazzello (both child actors give admirable performances) play two brothers whose divorced mom (Lorraine Bracco) remarries. Unbeknownst to her, the kids' new stepdad turns out to be a child abuser, and the boys devise a plan to escape his brutality: to take flight by making their red radio flyer wagon airworthy. *Radio Flyer* has many moments of genuine interest, especially when recalling the fantasies and peculiarities of youth. But the underlying child abuse theme is clearly out of place in this otherwise Spielberg-esque fantasy. Parents should be prepared to answer a few questions from preadolescent viewers. Tom Hanks has a cameo and serves as narrator. ★★½ $9.99

Radio Inside

(1994, 102 min, US, Jeffrey Bell) Though the story line is virtually nonexistent (a love triangle involving two radically different brothers), *Radio Inside* has a nonchalant quirkiness that ultimately makes it watchable. Take for instance the way the one brother (William McNamara), an un-career oriented, guilt-ridden artist, off-handedly calls up Jesus (yes, that Jesus) on a pay phone to get advice when he falls for the girlfriend (Elisabeth Shue) of his yuppie sibling (Dylan Walsh). An engaging and idiosyncratic look at relationships, both romantic and familial. ★★½ $19.99

Radioland Murders

(1994, 112 min, US, Mel Smith) As modern filmmakers have expanded upon the film genres of noir, westerns and horror films, the screwball comedy remains elusive. Such is the case, once again, with *Radioland Murders*, an unstable though frenzied comedy set against the backdrop of radio during the late 1930s. Mary Stuart Masterson plays a secretary/manager of a new radio network. As they prepare for their opening night, she must contend with an estranged husband ("Dream On"'s Brian Benben) seeking reconciliation, inept cast members and technicians, and a series of murders. The film tries to achieve the madness and quick pace of a Marx Brothers movie — there's plenty of slamming doors, pratfalls and one-liners. But the actors have little to work with, and the film doesn't capture the excitement and popularity that was live radio. ★★ $19.99

Raga: Ravi Shankar

(1991, 95 min, US, Howard Worten) Ravi Shankar, teacher, philosopher and musician, has become the most recognized purveyor of classical Indian music in the world. He first

Harrison Ford makes the switch in *Raiders of the Lost Ark*

gained prominence in this country as the "musical guru" to ex-Beatle George Harrison in the early '70s, and has gone on to work with other musicians, most notably Peter Gabriel, with whom Shankar collaborated on the thrilling score for Martin Scorsese's *The Last Temptation of Christ*. *Raga*, a spiritual piece reflecting the hopes of the Indian people, follows Shankar as he returns to his native country to reunite with Baba, his musical guru. A glorious pilgrimage to a culture that is still foreign to most of this country, the film follows Shankar as he tries to pass on his teachings, even receiving a Doctorate of Arts from UCLA. A mystical and thought-provoking film. ★★★½ $19.99

Rage

(1972, 100 min, US, George C. Scott) George C. Scott, in a respectable first-time directing effort, stars as a Wyoming rancher who, with his son, is victim of a fatal dose of experimental nerve gas discharged in an accident. The nearby military installation initiates an immediate cover-up, inciting the dying man to acts of enraged vengeance. Also with Richard Basehart, Barnard Hughes and Martin Sheen. ★★½ $14.99

Rage and Honor

(1992, 93 min, US, Terence H. Winkless) Female empowerment is taken to the extreme in this otherwise standard karate action flick. Mighty-mite Cynthia Rothrock stars as a martial arts instructor who teams up with a renegade Aussie cop (Richard Norton) to bring down a villainous villainess (Terri Treas) and a lesbian kickboxing posse (led by the scene-stealing Alex Datcher), all under the employ of a nasty druglord (Brian Thompson) who just happens to be her brother! Chauvinists and rednecks need not apply. ★★ $19.99

A Rage in Harlem

(1991, 115 min, US, Bill Duke) A fine cast brings unexpected life to this boisterous and funny crime comedy set in 1950s Harlem. Forest Whitaker is well cast as a naive, religious virgin who becomes involved with luscious swindler Robin Givens after she arrives in New York with a shipment of gold from a Southern robbery. Her appearance sets off a wild series of events as seemingly everyone in the Big Apple is after the booty. In a surprising comic turn, Givens gives a wonderfully controlled and vampish performance as the foxy femme fatale. But this is very much an ensemble piece, and the likes of Gregory Hines, Danny Glover and Zakes Mokae all contribute greatly. A colorful version of a Chester Hines story, and every bit as successful as the author's *Cotton Comes to Harlem*. ★★★ $9.99

The Raggedy Rawney

(1987, 95 min, GB, Bob Hoskins) Actor Hoskins throws his hat into the directorial ring with this offbeat tale of a wartime deserter (Dexter Fletcher) who disguises himself as a woman to escape his vindictive superior. Hoskins also stars as the head of a Gypsy camp who mistakenly thinks Fletcher is a witch – a "rawney." Not completely successful, but a welcome change for the adventurous viewer. ★★★

Raging Bull

(1980, 128 min, US, Martin Scorsese) Robert De Niro is nothing short of astonishing as boxing champion Jake La Motta, who struck it rich in the ring then squandered his fortune and alienated his family and friends. Scorsese's most brooding work (and that's saying something), shot in vibrant tones of black and white, is a masterpiece of technical brilliance, excrutiatingly observant dialogue and almost mythical boxing sequences. Stand-out support by Joe Pesci and Cathy Moriarty. ★★★★ $14.99

Ragtime

(1981, 155 min, US, Milos Forman) Forman, a director who can take the most difficult source material (*One Flew Over the Cuckoo's Nest*, *Hair*) and create masterworks, has done it again with this remarkable screen version of E.L. Doctorow's complex novel. Set in New York City during the turbulent early 1900s, the story follows black musician Harold E. Rollins, Jr. (in an outstanding performance) and his quest for justice after being the victim of a racial attack. After a 20-year absence in films, James Cagney returned to the screen to play the Police Commissioner. A superb ensemble cast includes Elizabeth McGovern, Mary Steenburgen, Maureen Stapleton, Mandy Patinkin and the chilling Kenneth McMillan. ★★★½ $29.99

Raiders of the Lost Ark

(1981, 115 min, US, Steven Spielberg) From South American jungles to the mountains of Nepal to the North African desert, our hero, archeology prof and world-class adventurer Harrison Ford, deciphers mystical symbols in search of the Ark of the Covenant, battling scurrilous Nazis with intrepid helpmate, hard-drinking Karen Allen. Strong story line, solid performances and state-of-the-art moviemaking potently combine in a fast-paced, most enjoyable and intelligent action-adventure film. Written by Lawrence Kasdan from a story by George Lucas and Philip Kaufman. Followed by two sequels: *Indiana Jones and the Temple of Doom* and *Indiana Jones and the Last Crusade*. ★★★★ $14.99

Railroaded

(1947, 71 min, US, Anthony Mann) In the dark, crime-ridden jungle of an inner city where mobsters rule, a lone police detective begins a search for a killer on the lam from police, who, in a desperate fight for survival, involves an innocent youth. John Ireland stars as a ruthless gangster in this taut, suspenseful, low-budget crime melodrama. ★★★

The Railway Children

(1970, 104 min, GB, Lionel Jeffries) Distinguished character actor Jeffries directed this engaging film version of the Edwardian children's classic about three young kids who are determined to clear their father's name. A

Raining Stones

vivid and heartwarming look at turn-of-the-century British life filmed in the beautiful countryside of Yorkshire and filled with youthful determination. ★★★

Rain Man

(1988, 140 min, US, Barry Levinson) Dustin Hoffman gives a remarkable performance as an "idiot savant" who is virtually kidnapped by his younger brother (Tom Cruise) and taken on a cross-country trip. From beginning to end, the film is an emotionally overpowering experience told in a surprisingly stylish and entertaining fashion. Hoffman won all sorts of kudos for his portrayal, but not to be overlooked is the terrific contribution by young Cruise, who more than holds his own with the most honored actor of his generation. (Available letterboxed and pan & scan) ★★★½ $14.99

The Rain People

(1969, 102 min, US, Francis Ford Coppola) Made in 1969 when male "buddy" films were flourishing, this sensitive drama from Coppola tells the compassionate story of a pregnant woman who leaves her husband in search of self-fulfillment. Shirley Knight, in a beautifully restrained performance, is the young voyager who sets out on the road, befriending dim-witted James Caan along the way. An intimate work exploring one woman's social awakening and personal independence. ★★★ $19.99

The Rainbow

(1989, 104 min, GB, Ken Russell) An unusually restrained "classic" adaptation of D.H. Lawrence's novel. The setting is early 20th-century England and follows the sexual and spiritual liberation of young Ursula, the Jennie Linden character in *Women in Love*. Sammi Davis is great as the earnest and doe-eyed young woman whose sexuality and desires erupt, all the while yearning for true love, self-respect and independence in a society which frowns on all three. Amanda Donohoe is delightfully decadent as Ursula's gym instructor, seductress and mentor. The film also reunites Glenda Jackson and Christopher Gable (from *The Music Lovers*) as the parents of the restless, inquisitive Ursula. ★★½

Raining Stones

(1993, 90 min, GB, Ken Loach) Veteran filmmaker Loach, who has made a career flip-flopping between mainstream movie making and the radical fringes, has drummed up a veritable masterpiece of agitprop with this engaging tale of an out-of-work laborer who hatches a hundred lame-brained schemes to make ends meet. Through the comedic escapades of Bob (Bruce Jones), Loach sternly disabuses us all of the notion that the underclass are a bunch of boozing loafers uninterested in a hard day's work. A devout Catholic, Bob desperately needs money to buy his daughter a new outfit for her first communion. But rather than let Bob's conundrum stand merely as a condemnation of the Church, Loach passionately and with great force of conviction shows the Church also as his only shred of hope – it is the only thing that keeps Bob going. This conflict is at the heart of Loach's film and it is what gives it its beauty, helping it rise above simple dialectical materialism and touch on notions of spirit. It's the perfect companion piece to Mike Leigh's *Naked*, which, by contrast, rails against notions of things spiritual in the face of poverty. ★★★★ $19.99

The Rainmaker

(1956, 121 min, US, Joseph Anthony) Burt Lancaster and Katharine Hepburn offer terrific performances in this fine adaptation of the N. Richard Nash play. Set in 1913, the film casts Lancaster as con man who promises a small drought-ridden Kansas town he can deliver much-needed rain. Kate is the spinsterish farm girl who falls for the charming grifter. ★★★ $14.99

Raintree County

(1957, 175 min, US, Edward Dmytryk) Fanciful costume drama set during the Civil War with Elizabeth Taylor as a Southern belle and Montgomery Clift as her lover. M-G-M tried, but did not succeed in creating another *Gone with the Wind* – though there is much that is praiseworthy about this mammoth production. That includes the supporting cast of Eva Marie Saint, Rod Taylor, Lee Marvin and Agnes Moorehead. (Available letterboxed and pan & scan) ★★½ $24.99

Raise the Red Lantern

(1991, 125 min, China, Zhang Yimou) From the director of *Red Sorghum* and *Ju Dou* comes this lyrically haunting tale about a young educated woman who is sold into marriage against her will, becoming the newest of four concubines kept by a wealthy man. Immediately at odds with her three predecessors (who can scarcely conceal their jealousy of her) and bewildered by her strict and mysterious master, she reacts to her new situation with a mixture of rebellion and resignation. Director Zhang imbues the film with an extraordinary attention to detail, filming from the perspective of the fledgling concubine, giving the viewer a unique appreciation for the character's existential loneliness. Additionally, the film's understated dialogue and bewitching visual style amplify Zhang's compelling tale of the subjugation of women in feudal China. Chinese actress Gong Li is spellbinding as the young woman who finds herself trapped in the jaws of a regimented and unforgiving patriarchy. (Mandarin with English subtitles) ★★★★ $19.99

A Raisin in the Sun

(1961, 128 min, US, Daniel Petrie) Sidney Poitier stars as Walter Lee Yonger, a young African-American man struggling with his place in a white dominated society. Lena (Claudia McNeil), Walter's mother, receives a $10,000 insurance check and the family must decide how the money should be spent. Walter wants to invest with a friend in a liquor store, Lena wants to use the money to buy a house in a better neighborhood, while her daughter (Ruby Dee) wants to use the money to finish medical school. A powerful tale of a poor, proud black family living in a 1950s Chicago ghetto, facing the racist attitudes of America and the truth of the limited opportunities for blacks in this society. Based on the play by Lorraine Hansbury. ★★★★ $14.99

A Raisin in the Sun

(1989, 120 min, US, Bill Duke) Remake of the classic 1961 screen version of Lorraine Hansbury's play, and every bit as accomplished as that earlier adaptation. Danny Glover gives a tremendous performance as Walter Lee Younger; and as his recently widowed mother, Esther Rolle is wonderfully down to earth. Among the supporting cast, Kim Yancy gives a fine performance as Walter's sister. A remarkable work. ★★★½ $39.99

Raising Arizona

(1986, 94 min, US, Joel Coen) The Coen Brothers unleash a veritable grab bag of tricks and surprises as they unspool the hilarious tale of H.I. and Ed McDonough, would-be-parents who baby-nap a youngster from a recent batch of quintuplets in order to fulfill their parental urges. This truly offbeat, supremely comic film is loaded with crazy characters, wild chase scenes and inexhaustible energy. Nicolas Cage and Holly Hunter give antic yet touching performances as the barren but determined couple. ★★★★ $9.99

Raising Cain

(1992, 91 min, US, Brian De Palma) After the debacle of *Bonfire of the Vanities*, De Palma immediately returned to the genre he knows best – manipulative thrillers. John Lithgow stars in this hodge-podge of every other De Palma film (and some Hitchcock, of course) about a schizophrenic child psychologist who moonlights as a sociopathic baby-stealer. While nowhere near the caliber of filmmaking displayed in *Carrie* or *Dressed to Kill*, *Raising Cain* holds up fairly well when viewed as a black comedy rather than as the nail-biter it pretends to be. Also starring Lolita Davidovich and featuring a scene-stealing performance by Frances Sternhagen. ★★½ $19.99

Rambling Rose

(1991, 112 min, US, Martha Coolidge) Laura Dern earned a well-deserved Oscar nomination for her portrayal of Rose, a Depression-era orphan who is taken as a live-in maid by a respectable Southern family in 1930s Georgia. Her sexual energy bursting at the seams, Rose turns the family's traditional values upside-down and precipitates a dispute between Mom (Diane Ladd) and Dad (Robert Duvall) as to how best to deal with her. Ladd, Dern's real-life mom, was also an Oscar nominee for her splendid work as Rose's matronly advocate. As always, Duvall is solid as the sternly disciplinarian dad and Lukas Haas provides fine support as the family's sexually obsessed 13-year-old son. Charmingly humanistic in tone, the film is imbued with a wonderful sense of mirth and thereby avoids getting bogged down in the potentially melodramatic pitfalls of its subject matter. ★★★½ $14.99

Rambo: First Blood Pt 2

(1985, 93 min, US, George P. Cosmatos) Sylvester Stallone's sequel to *First Blood* is a ridiculous war film by any standards, but it did introduce an idiom (or is that idiot?) into our vocabulary and culture. For the record, Johnny Rambo returns to Vietnam to locate American POWs. ★½ $14.99

Rambo III

(1988, 101 min, US, Peter MacDonald) More inane and implausible action scenes from Sylvester Stallone as Superman Johnny Rambo. Rambo sets out to rescue captured Richard Crenna from behind enemy lines. ★ $14.99

Ran

Rampage

(1992, 97 min, US, William Friedkin) Michael Biehn stars as a liberal D.A. recovering from the accidental death of his young daughter in this tense courtroom drama about the capture and sentencing of a serial murderer (Alex McArthur). While the film shows the murders with luridly vivid detail, it does not handle them with the exploitative nature so many of these types of films tend to use. Instead, it deals more with the inner workings of our not always perfect judicial system. Laced with great visual jolts, fine performances and an unusual script, this film is one that will keep you gnawing at your fingernails. (Made in 1987 but not released until five years later.) ★★★ $14.99

Ramparts of Clay

(1971, 85 min, France/Algeria, Jean-Louis Bertucelli) Against the hauntingly beautiful setting of an isolated Tunisian village, this stunning, visually breathtaking fictional documentary portrays the struggles of a young woman to liberate herself from the subservient role her people's ancient customs demand. Her participation in a strike-like action against a local entrepreneur allows her a glimpse of life outside her rigidly structured village. (Berber with English subtitles) ★★★½

Ran

(1985, 160 min, Japan, Akira Kurosawa) 75-year-old Kurosawa has reached the culmination of his brilliant career with this majestic free-telling of Shakespeare's "King Lear." Set in the 16th century, the epic thunders with breathtaking scenery, boldly staged battle sequences and the tragic story of an old man's war with his sons. The love, death and treachery between both friends and adversaries is universal in theme and provides the human backdrop for this classic. (Japanese with English subtitles) ★★★★

Rancho Deluxe

(1974, 93 min, US, Frank Perry) Jeff Bridges and Sam Waterston star as two petty grifters; New West cowboys who decide to go after the big score. With intent to rustle some cattle, they team up with Harry Dean Stanton, hired hand to a couple of Easterners for whom the West is little more than a commodity. Sweeping Montana vistas offer mute witness to a delightful display of human foibles and crackling idiosyncracies as the crew sets about their business. Director Perry adeptly guides Tom McGuane's multilayered, sardonic and witty screenplay. Also starring Slim Pickens and Elizabeth Ashley. ★★★½ $19.99

Rancho Notorious

(1952, 89 min, US, Fritz Lang) Frontier love triangle develops between a breathy saloon songstress (Marlene Dietrich), a once-great gunslinger (Mel Ferrer) and a revenge-seeking cowpoke (Arthur Kennedy). An unusual and invigorating western which concentrates as much on character development as it does with the genre's other staples. ★★★½

Random Harvest

(1942, 124 min, US, Mervyn LeRoy) A grand, lush soap opera of the highest order with

Ronald Colman and Greer Garson in *Random Harvest*

Ronald Colman as a shell-shock and amnesiac WWI veteran who marries dance-hall girl Greer Garson. When he regains his memory, he returns to his old life but has no memory of his wife; who has now become his secretary in the hopes that he'll remember. Colman and Garson's compelling performances should capture the hearts of even the most cynical. ★★★½ $19.99

Ransom

(1996, 120 min, US, Ron Howard) The nightmare of a child's kidnapping has been turned into a slick, calculated thriller which intermittently conveys the pain and suspense of the situation. Mel Gibson plays a wealthy airline owner whose nine-year-old son is kidnapped. The story then focuses on the parents and FBI's attempts to deal with the criminals, and the conflict growing within the group of kidnappers. The screenplay (based on a 1956 Glenn Ford film) doesn't take much time setting things up as the kidnapping (a taut scene) occurs rather quickly in the film. From there there are lots of scenes of Gibson yelling, Rene Russo crying (the actress has been given very little else to do as the child's mother) and the FBI looking concerned. Unfortunately, the best plot point in the film, which happens halfway through, had already been given away in the film's trailers (probably a good marketing decision but a poor one from a viewer's point of view). A star vehicle all the way, Gibson makes the most of the anguished father; though the writers don't fully explore his own possibly criminal side. Director Howard uses New York locations to his advantage, and has a firm grasp of several tension-filled sequences. ★★½ $19.99

Raoni — The Fight for the Amazon

(1979, 82 min, France/Brazil, Jean-Pierre Dutilleux) The Amazon Indians' fight against the Brazilian government's genocidal land policies is the center of this engrossing film. With civilization rapidly encroaching into their isolated and simple lives, the many Indian tribes who populate the Amazonian rainforest are forced to either drastically change their lifestyle or fight. The filmmaker focuses his attention on one tribe, the Mekranotis, and is especially taken in by their charismatic and forceful chief, Raoni. With ethnographic footage of their village, we see the tribe's attempts to stop the decimation of the rainforest. An exhilarating adventure into a previously unseen world and a cautionary environmental tale. ★★★½ $29.99

Rapa Nui

(1994, 107 min, US, Kevin Reynolds) Jason Scott Lee stars in this well-intentioned but ultimately disappointing "ecological message movie" about the demise of the natives of Easter Island, site of the mysterious giant stone heads discovered by Captain Cooke in the 18th century. Call it a loinclothed "Romeo and Juliet" as Lee, a member of the "Long Ear" clan hotly pursues Sandrine Holt, a member of the subservient "Short Ears," much to the chagrin of Lee's childhood chum and now rival in love, Esai Morales (a "Short Ear" Tybalt?). The two clans clash as the Long Ears keep ordering the Short Ears to construct giant talismans in the hope that their ancestors will call them all home, a practice that ultimately leads to the deforestation of the entire island. Hokey in the extreme, the film does have its entertaining moments and, hey, with the entire cast parading around nearly stark naked, it can't be all bad. ★★½ $19.99

Rape of Love

(1977, 117 min, France, Yannick Bellon) A disturbing film with Nathalie Nell as a nurse who is ruthlessly raped by four drunkards. Tragically, she discovers this is only the beginning of her ordeal. A poignant account of insensitivity and injustice. (French with English subtitles) ★★½

Rapid Fire

(1992, 90 min, US, Dwight H. Little) Brandon Lee, son of legendary kick-meister Bruce Lee,

Rashomon

chops his way into the "B-movie" arena with this extremely mindless actioner that might just as easily been called *Vapid Fire*. Lee plays a peace-loving student who must fight for his life when he becomes a witness to some Mafia activity. Lee provides his own comic relief with a "valley girl" delivery guarenteed to leave the bad guys unsure whether to fight him or fuck him. ★★ $9.99

The Rapture

(1991, 100 min, US, Michael Tolkin) Unaccountably overlooked in its theatrical release, *The Rapture* is a startling philosophical drama that brings to light such weighty issues as religious zealousness, life after death and the search for faith. Mimi Rogers stars as a woman with a mind-numbing job as an L.A. telephone operator who seeks release from her existential emptiness in alcohol, drugs and anonymous group sex. Her life changes dramatically, however, after she discovers God through a religious awakening. Her newly inspired faith is put to the test in a series of Job-like trials culminating in a vision to go to the desert (with her young daughter in tow) and await the Second Coming. A thought-provoking film that offers many angles to the religious issues and an ending which forces viewers to decide for themselves. ★★★½ $14.99

The Rascals

(1981, 93 min, France, Bernard Revon) The French have been making films about the sexual awakening of young people years before the births of the American directors who are obsessed with the same theme. Rather than titillate the viewer with cheap sex jokes, the films usually focus more on the psychological and emotional problems of budding adulthood. This film, a thoroughly delightful comedy about the coming-of-age of an irrepressible boy in a Catholic school, deals with his first relationship with an older girl. (Dubbed or French with English subtitles) ★★★

Rashomon

(1951, 88 min, Japan, Akira Kurosawa) The film which opened the West to Japanese cinema, Kurosawa's brilliantly conceived Academy Award-winning classic delves into the mysteries of truth, reality and illusion, telling the story of a murder and rape through the conflicting testimony of all those involved: the "murdered" man, his ravished wife, the murderer, the arresting officer and a "neutral" bystander. The result is five completely different versions of the story. (Japanese with English subtitles) ★★★★ $29.99

Rasputin

(1978, 104 min, USSR, Elem Klimov) The demonic rise and bloody fall of Gregori Rasputin is explored in this fascinating and elaborate period piece. Although certainly not history, this Russian version of the Rasputin legend seems to be the definitive exposé of a man whose hypnotic spell over the royal family hastened their downfall. Set amidst the luxurious surroundings of the rich and powerful in Czarist Russia, the story follows Rasputin, a religious fanatic who not only craved power, but women and booze as well. Was he a prophet sent by God to be the only hope for the Russian aristocracy or was he simply a madman bent on self-destruction? Both sides of the man are explored in this mesmerizing melodrama. (Russian with English subtitles) ★★★½ $59.99

Rasputin and the Empress

(1933, 123 min, US, Richard Boleslawski) The legendary Barrymores — Ethel, John and Lionel — made only one film together: and the result is a static, well-acted and affecting historical drama of the Romanoffs. Set in Russia just before the Revolution, the film examines the calamitous reign as "the power behind the throne" of the notorious "priest" Rasputin, who contributed to the fall of the royal dynasty. Ethel plays Alexandra with a regal authority, and brother John is a chivalrous Colonel of the Guards. But it's Lionel's crafty portrayal of the opportunist spellbinder Rasputin which elevates the film. He's cunning and vile, and is exact in bringing to life a character who's "like a man-eating shark with a bible under his fin." ★★★ $19.99

Rate It X

(1985, 90 min, US, Lucy Winer & Paul De Koenigsberg) Fifteen years after the birth of the Women's Movement, independent filmmakers Winer and De Koenigsberg traveled across America to explore both subtle and graphic examples of sexism and chauvinism in our culture. *Rate It X* is a funny yet hair-raising documentary that, with both fringe characters and amiable "men-next-door," exposes the pervasive and endemic nature of sexist attitudes. But this is not a stern polemic; the male population, obviously being prodded by the filmmakers, can enjoy the witty, ironic exposure of their ridiculously outdated beliefs. Can't you? ★★★ $59.99

The Raven (Le Corbeau)

(1943, 92 min, France, Henri-Georges Clouzot) Clouzot, the director responsible for two of the most suspenseful films ever made, *Diabolique* and *Wages of Fear*, preceded those with this extremely dark and tense thriller about a small town in France beseiged by paranoia in the wake of a mysterious, poisonous letter campaign written by "The Raven" and addressed to the town's physician. The uncompromising depiction of the French middle class caused quite a storm when the film was released because it was made with the assistance of the Germans and was viewed by many as anti-French propaganda. (French with English subtitles) ★★★½ $39.99

The Raven

(1963, 86 min, US, Roger Corman) Set in 15th-century England, this satiric version of the Edgar Allan Poe work pits two magicians (Vincent Price, Peter Lorre) against a master sorcerer (Boris Karloff), who has absconded with Price's wife. Look for a young Jack Nicholson. ★★★

The Ravishing Idiot

(1965, 99 min, France, Edouard Molinaro) Anthony Perkins stars in this slapstick caper comedy as a bungling bank clerk who, with walking disaster area Brigitte Bardot, unwittingly becomes involved with a Soviet spy ring. Edouard Molinaro also directed the first two *La Cage aux Folles* films. ★★½

Raw Deal

(1948, 80 min, US, Anthony Mann) With tough-talking guys, hard-boiled dames, plenty of cross and double-cross, and a hero so gruff you almost expect to hear his street-smart moll call him a "lug," *Raw Deal* is a startling good noir thriller which doesn't pinch on action or characterization. It's so aware of itself, you'd think Quentin Tarantino had something to do with it. Dennis O'Keefe is a prisoner ready for the break. He took the rap for his creepy, sadistic boss Raymond Burr, who's helping in the escape. Only Burr doesn't want to see him succeed. And when O'Keefe gets wind, it's revenge time. To complicate matters, O'Keefe, accompanied by flame Claire Trevor, has taken his lawyer Marsha Hunt hostage, and he's soon torn between the two women. Sexual tensions simmer, jealousies erupt, and the line between right and wrong becomes blurred. Mann directs in a crisp, no-nonsense fashion, and the dialogue is priceless. ★★★½ $29.99

Raw Deal

(1986, 106 min, US, John Irvin) This violent and tongue-in-cheek thriller stars Arnold Schwarzenegger as a small-town sheriff (and former FBI agent) who single-handedly takes on the Chicago mob. ★★ $9.99

The Razor: Sword of Justice

(1972, 90 min, Japan, Kenji Misumi) An uncommon entry in the samurai genre, this unique film tells the story of Hanzo Itami (Katsu, star of the *Zatoichi* films), the only honest law official in Edo. He lets convicted criminals off the hook if they swear to become his assistants in his fight against crime and corruption and he subjects himself to police tor-

R

tures to test their effectiveness and to discipline his body and mind. He also has terrific swordplay skills, and is endowed with a huge "asset" which he brings to bear in especially difficult cases, particularly during interrogations. When Itami finds out that an exiled assassin has returned to town and is fooling around with a woman who is also linked to Itami's boss, he goes against orders and investigates. The plot he uncovers, however, is not nearly as exciting as the film's early buildup would suggest. Well-shot and featuring a couple of good swordplay scenes, the uneven tone and frequent penis humor work against the film's effectiveness, except as a campy cult flick. It is interesting, however, to see Katsu portray a character who is not blind. (Japanese with English subtitles) ★★½ $29.99

The Razor's Edge

(1946, 146 min, US, Edmund Goulding) Fine adaptation of W. Somerset Maugham's acclaimed novel with Tyrone Power going through heaven and hell in his search for spiritual truth. Anne Baxter won an Oscar for her heartbreaking alcoholic, and Clifton Webb should have won one as the cynical Elliott Templeton. (Mediocre remake in 1984 with Bill Murray) ★★★ $19.99

The Razor's Edge

(1984, 129 min, US, John Byrum) Bill Murray, in his dramatic debut, plays a disillusioned WWI vet who rejects his materialistic lifestyle and retreats to the Himalayas in search of truth. An inferior remake of the 1946 classic which doesn't work on any level. Theresa Russell, Catherine Hicks and Denholm Elliott star. ★ $14.99

Re-Animator

(1985, 86 min, US, Stuart Gordon) H.P. Lovecraft would turn over in his grave if: a) he took some of the re-animation serum developed by the mad scientist in this nifty film; or

b) he saw the liberties taken with his story. This film proves that director Gordon would beat George Romero hands down in a gross-out contest, as a decapitated body gives head both figuratively and literally. (Answer to the question: both.) This is the unrated version. ★★★½

Ready to Wear (Pret-a-Porter)

(1994, 132 min, US, Robert Altman) After his brilliant *The Player* and riveting *Short Cuts*, director Altman's take on the Paris fashion world rates as a disappointment in spite of being intermittently fascinating. Assembling (once again) an amazing all-star cast, Altman sets out to both satirize and demystify the carnival-like atmosphere of the *pret-a-porter* fashion shows, but sabotages himself by presenting too many players, the majority of which are dramatically shortchanged. However, some characters stand out, including Tim Robbins as an American sports writer, Julia Roberts as a rival reporter romantically involved with Robbins, Marcello Mastroianni and Sophia Loren as ex-flames, Linda Hunt as a magazine editor, Stephen Rea as a hot-shot photographer, and Kim Basinger, who nearly steals the film as a hilariously inept TV reporter. Lauren Bacall, Anouk Aimée, Rupert Everett, Tracey Ullman, and Forest Whitaker and Richard E. Grant as gay designers, are among the casualties. For Altman, Paris is no *Nashville*. ★★½ $14.99

Real Genius

(1985, 108 min, US, Martha Coolidge) Diverting teen comedy with Val Kilmer as a member of a group of super-intelligent teenagers who create a sophisticated laser system for a class project. However, when they discover that they have been working on a military secret, they devise an elaborate scheme to get revenge. ★★½ $14.99

The Real Glory

(1939, 95 min, US, Henry Hathaway) An exciting adventure film which bears more than

just a little resemblence to *Gunga Din*. Gary Cooper and David Niven are soldiers of fortune who assist the American Army in their battle against a guerrilla uprising in the Philippines just after the Spanish-American War. Director Hathaway excels at this type of filmmaking, and the action scenes are terrific. ★★★ $19.99

Real Life

(1979, 99 min, US, Albert Brooks) Director, writer and star Brooks attacks such suspect documentaries like PBS did to the Louds in "An American Family." Every bit as biting and as funny as *This is Spinal Tap*, Brooks plays a very egocentric documentary filmmaker who, after invading Charles Grodin's home, will stop at nothing to make this "reality" as interesting as possible. ★★★ $14.99

Reality Bites

(1994, 99 min, US, Ben Stiller) *Reality Bites* is a whimsical film that looks at some of life's more monumental choices, like who to love, what low-pay, low-reward job to take and which psychic hot line to call when you've really hit rock bottom. Winona Ryder is splendid as a recent college graduate whose life is thrown into a depressed frenzy when she has to find a new job and is confronted with one too many romantic decisions. Both Ethan Hawke and Ben Stiller (who also directed) make charming leading men as Ryder's bi-polar love interests, and stand-up comic Janeane Garofalo almost steals the show as her ironic, Gap-managing, '70s obsessed apartment mate. With cultural and "generational" references jammed into every corner, *Reality Bites* is an intriguing look at the way that some people under 30 deal with life, but it has an even more captivating and witty take on the way many people deal with love. ★★★½ $14.99

Rear Window

(1954, 112 min, US, Alfred Hitchcock) Hitchcock confronts the manifold by-products of voyeurism with this splendid study of a murder's detection. James Stewart is superlative as the intrusive observer who reflects our own sometimes dangerous desires. An uncommonly carnal Grace Kelly is his eager accomplice. ★★★★ $14.99

Rebecca

(1940, 115 min, US, Alfred Hitchcock) Hitchcock's first Hollywood movie is a Gothic masterpiece based on the book by Daphne Du Maurier. Joan Fontaine plays a passive and awkward paid companion ("friend of the bosom") for the snooty dowager Mrs. Van Hopper. While on vacation at Monte Carlo, she falls in love with the ominous and rich Maxim de Winter (Laurence Olivier) who whisks her off to his mansion. However, his mysterious attachment to his deceased first wife wreaks havoc upon their marriage. The most durable performance comes from Judith Anderson as the creepy Mrs. Danvers, the fanatically devoted housekeeper (paramour?) of the first Mrs. de Winter, whose eventual death/suicide echoes that of the "mad woman in the attic" in "Jane Eyre." A chilling script and superb acting and direction won *Rebecca* an Oscar for Best Picture. ★★★★ $9.99

R

Joan Fontaine (l.) is tormented by Judith Anderson in *Rebecca*

Rebel

(1985, 93 min, Australia, Michael Jenkins) Matt Dillon stars as a U.S. Marine stationed in Sydney and on the run from the military police. Complications arise when he falls in love with a nightclub singer. Bryan Brown is the stranger who offers a solution... for a price. Winner of 5 Australian Film Awards. ★★ $14.99

Rebel Rousers

(1967, 78 min, US, Martin B. Cohen) Bruce Dern is the philosophising leader of a pack of motley motorcyclists; he's the kind of guy who takes his hog everywhere – including into the cantina of the small Mexican town where he meets old high school buddy Cameron Mitchell. Mitchell is having paternity problems and looks about 20 years older than Dern. A biker flick typical of the era. Watch Jack Nicholson make lewd advances on a five-months-pregnant woman. Harry Dean Stanton also has a bit part. ★★ $9.99

Rebel without a Cause

(1955, 111 min, US, Nicholas Ray) A testament to adolescent angst with James Dean as the prototypical angry young man at odds with his parents, himself and the future. A brooding film that cemented the Dean legend. In her first adult role, Natalie Wood offers an incandescent performance as a soul mate; and Sal Mineo is especially touching as Plato, a friendless youth who has yet to come to terms with his latent sexuality, and who is secretly in love with Dean's charismatic character Jim. (Available letter-boxed and pan & scan) ★★★½ $19.99

Reckless

(1995, 100 min, US, Norman René) Mia Farrow is a howling delight in this wacky and inventive Christmas-themed fairy tale based on the play by Craig Lucas (*Longtime Companion*) and directed by her partner René. They've concocted a tale that careens from one weird character and plot device to another. Farrow plays Rachel, an idiotically sweet chatterbox housewife and mother who is forced out of her home on Christmas Eve when she discovers that her husband has put a contract out on her life. She is rescued by the superficially nice social worker Lucas (Scott Glenn) and his deaf paraplegic wife Pooty (Mary-Louise Parker). But for poor Rachel, her newfound happiness with the couple proves to be short-lived as poisoned champagne, dark secrets and a drunken Santa Claus test the limits of sanity. A droll, warped romp of self-discovery infused with purposefully cheesy special effects, oddball cameos and an intoxicating mix of comedy, fantasy and surreal nightmare. The film that comes closest to it is Lindsay Anderson's *O Lucky Man!*. ★★★ $14.99

Record of a Tenement Gentleman

(1947, 72 min, Japan, Yasujiro Ozu) A charming, melancholy portrait of life in Japan after the war, director Ozu's inspirational tale examines the alternately heartfelt and comic exploits of a young boy abandoned by his parents. Discovering the youth and feeling sorry for him, a tenement dweller brings him home only to find his flatmate will not allow him to keep the child in the apartment. After straws are drawn to see who takes care of the child among the neighbors, an older widow grudgingly ends up with him. She decides to take the child back to his parents, but his mother is dead and his father has left to find a job in an another area with no forwarding address. Against the odds, a close relationship soon develops between them nurtured by mutual understanding and respect. While it may seem cold compared to American standards of morality, the film holds true as a wonderful story of enriched lives and community living during a difficult time in history. (Japanese with English subtitles) ★★★★ $69.99

Red

(1994, 98 min, France, Krzysztof Kieslowski) The last of director Kieslowski's "color" trilogy (following *Blue* and *White*) is a sumptuous finale, and the most satisfying of the three films. A beautiful Irene Jacob stars as a model preparing a trip to reunite and reconcile with her traveling boyfriend. But events and emotions are skewed when she runs over a dog and seeks out the animal's owner. Who she eventually finds is Jean-Louis Trintignant, a burned-out, bitter ex-judge who spends his spare time spying on his neighbors. An unusual relationship develops between the two, culminating in an act of self-examination and moral responsibility. Bringing together both themes and characters from the first two films, Kieslowski weaves a compelling and haunting tale of communication, emotion and love gone awry, and it's all enhanced by a seductive, mysterious atmosphere. (French with English subtitles) ★★★½ $19.99

The Red and the Black

(1954, 140 min, France, Claude Autant-Lara) Stendhal's classic 1831 novel is adapted in this sumptuous period drama. Gérard Philipe is the ambitious Julian Sorel, whose plan for money and power have him deciding against the scarlet uniform of the soldier for the much more lucrative red robes of the clergy. In his headlong plunge to "greatness" our handsome hero quickly dispenses with the religious angle in order to seduce the rich women he tutors while ultimately falling in love with the beautiful Danielle Darrieux. (French with English subtitles) ★★★½

The Red and the White

(1968, 92 min, Hungary/USSR, Miklos Jansco) Hungary's premiere director Jansco sets this haunting antiwar drama in central Russia during the Civil War of 1918, in which the Red Army tangled with a counterrevolutionary threat from the Whites in the hills along the Volga River. The action centers around a monastery where a group of nurses do their best to conceal the identities of the wounded and administer equal care to all. Employing remarkable visuals, Jansco forges a compelling treatise on the absurdity of war and the humiliation of mechanical slaughter. (Hungarian with English subtitles) ★★★½ $79.99

The Red Balloon

(1956, 60 min, France, Albert Lamorisse) This highly acclaimed short film is a fantasy guaranteed to appeal to both adults and chil-

Red Dust

dren. It tells the story of Pascal, a lonely French boy who befriends a wondrous red balloon which follows him everywhere and fills his need for friendship. This beautiful film maintains a true sense of childish wonder and has much to say about the need for love. For the adults, one can view the film and interpret the Christ allegory that the balloon could represent. (No dialogue) ★★★★ $14.99

Red Beard

(1965, 185 min, Japan, Akira Kurosawa) Toshiro Mifune is the wise, pragmatic doctor who guides a young intern through the trials and frustrations of the profession. The humanistic education changes him from a conceited technician to a humble man who values each of his patients as a whole person. (Letterboxed version) (Japanese with English subtitles) ★★★½ $39.99

Red Dawn

(1984, 110 min, US, John Milius) Contrived (and often ridiculous) political action-adventure film about a group of teenage resistance fighters who do battle with the Communist invaders who have taken over their small town. Patrick Swayze, C. Thomas Howell, Charlie Sheen and Lea Thompson are some of the pint-sized Rambos. ★½ $19.99

Red Desert

(1965, 116 min, Italy, Michelangelo Antonioni) Antonioni's first color film is an intriguing study of the alienation of man. Against the backdrop of a sterilized, impersonal industrial landscape, a love affair is enacted out. Starring Richard Harris and Monica Vitti as the doomed lovers, the film deals with the impossibility of real communication between people entrapped in this modern, hostile environment and longs for a return to a more innocent era. (Italian with English subtitles) ★★★ $59.99

Red Dust

(1932, 83 min, US, Victor Fleming) Clark Gable stars as a rubber plantation worker in Indochina who romances good-time girl Jean

Harlow and a coworker's wife, Mary Astor. A pre-Code production simmering with sexuality and with its fair share of laughs for the usually rigid adventure genre. Gable and Harlow are particularly appealing together. Gable also appeared in the 1953 remake, *Mogambo*. ★★★½ $19.99

Red Firecracker, Green Firecracker

(1994, 111 min, China, He Ping) Director He's third feature is weakened by his inability to bring anything new to the overly familiar territory of the Chinese New Wave. Set against the country's transition into the 20th century, *Red Firecracker* is an epic lovers' triangle that, while being visually rewarding, is unfortunately emotionally hollow. Female child Chun Zhi (Ning Jing) is raised male in order to inherit the family fireworks business. Her reserved manner is only accentuated by the austerity of the man's garb she wears. But these years of repression melt with the arrival of Nie Bao (Wu Gang), an itinerant painter hired to help decorate the home for the New Year's holiday. Taking umbrage at this interloper is Man Dihong (Zhao Xiaorui), the house foreman who sees his long cherished dream of winning "the master's" hand turn quickly into a nightmare. As in other, better films (*To Live, The Blue Kite*), there are epic landscapes, but their use here as emotional correlatives is too obvious to be effective. (Mandarin with English subtitles) ★★½ $19.99

Red Heat

(1985, 104 min, US/West Germany, Robert Collector) Linda Blair and Sylvia Kristel team up in this pedestrian Cold War women-in-prison flick set in a nameless Communist country. Blair, an American innocent, is captured by Communists after inadvertently witnessing the abduction of a political dissident. She is sent to a hellhole women's prison which seems to be run by a lesbian prisoner (Kristel). Kristel camps it up as the red-haired, power-hungry vixen who reigns over a bevy of tattooed beauties with a mixture of cruelty and sexual control. The lifeless film contains the requisite hair-pulling-in-their-underwear fights and snippets of gratuitous nudity. Barely enjoyable on a camp level. ★½ $14.99

Red Heat

(1988, 106 min, US, Walter Hill) Arnold Schwarzenegger and James Belushi join forces in this tepid buddy cop action film, with Arnold as a rigid Russian officer teaming with free-wheeling Chicago cop Belushi to search for a Soviet drug dealer. (Available letterboxed and pan & scan) ★★ $14.99

Red King, White Knight

(1989, 106 min, GB, Geoff Murphy) Tom Skerritt stars as a seasoned CIA veteran who is sent into the Soviet Union to thwart a hardline general's planned assasination of Mikhail Gorbachev. He joins forces with his one-time nemesis, KGB agent Szaz (Max Von Sydow), and together they hunt down the conspirators. Helen Mirren also stars as a retired Russian operative and former lover to Skerritt. An exciting post-*glasnost* political thriller. ★★★ $19.99

Red Kiss (Rouge Baiser)

(1986, 100 min, France, Vera Belmont) Exploring the budding sexuality of teenagers, this sincere, charming and intelligent drama is punctuated by both its background setting (the turbulent political times in 1952 France) and its star, Charlotte Valandrey — a beguiling, dark-eyed beauty of fifteen. Committing as much time to championing the French Communist Party as she does carousing in a graveyard with friends, young Nadia's life begins to change when she meets a handsome apolitical fashion photographer. This young man's world of beautiful women and "cool" Gauloise-filled jazz clubs confuses and entices Nadia as her ardently idealistic beliefs clash with those of the real world. Marthe Keller is wonderful as Nadia's mother, a former Polish beauty with a mysterious past. (French with English subtitles) ★★★ $19.99

Red Lion

(1969, 115 min, Japan, Kihachi Okamoto) Toshiro Mifune gives a bravura performance as the scarlet-maned bumbler who returns to his village after a ten-year absence, only to discover that he is to be the one to liberate his villagers from their deceitful, oppressive government. The pace of the film changes from a humorous beginning to an action-packed violent ending, with much exciting swordplay. (Japanese with English subtitles) ★★★

Red Pomegranate

(1969, 75 min, USSR, Sergei Paradjanov) The powerful works of 17th-century Armenian poet Arutuin Sayadian are captured in this exotic mosaic of a film. Essentially a tribute to his life as well as to his dedication to the Armenian people, the film is divided into eight sections each depicting, from childhood to death, a period of the poet's life. Filled with oblique, symbolic imagery, this film is definitely only for specialized tastes and those devotees who have a knowledge of the poet and of Armenia. (Armenian with English subtitles) ★★★ $59.99

Red River

(1948, 133 min, US, Howard Hawks) Hawks' epic western rates as one of the finest of the genre. John Wayne, in an unsympathetic role, plays a rancher who heads a strenuous cattle drive along the Chisolm Trail. As the journey wears on, the other men, including his foster son Montgomery Clift, begin to question his ability as a leader, prompting a collision course between father and son. An astonishing accomplishment featuring gorgeous cinematography and brilliant direction by Hawks. (Remastered director's cut version.) ★★★★ $14.99

Red Rock West

(1993, 98 min, US, John Dahl) Nicolas Cage stars in this *Blood Simple*-esque thriller that offers more twists than a Philadelphia soft pretzel. The once-promising actor returns to form as an out-of-work wildcatter with a gimpy leg, a heart of gold and a pocketful of lint who sees dollar signs when a small-town bar owner (J.T. Walsh) mistakes him for the hit man he just hired to kill his wife (Lara Flynn Boyle). Then the real killer (perennial ham Dennis Hopper) shows up. Perhaps the only film ever to go from cable to video to a successful theatrical run, this sleeper is an expertly plotted game of cat-and-mouse and a well-studied tribute to the film noir era. ★★★½ $19.99

The Red Shoes

(1948, 133 min, GB, Michael Powell & Emeric Pressburger) This lavishly breathtaking realization of the classic fairy tale is a glorious ode to the wonders of dance and the pursuit of artistic and personal fullfillment. Featuring an exquisite performance by Moira Shearer as the doomed ballerina. Also starring Anton Walbrook. ★★★★ $14.99

Red Sonja

(1985, 89 min, US, Richard Fleischer) Arnold Schwarzenegger takes a back seat to Brigitte Nielsen in this sword and sorcery adventure with Nielsen as the fearless female warrior. Unmemorable action scenes and wooden acting only accentuate the laughable story line. ★ $19.99

Red Sorghum

(1988, 92 min, China, Zhang Yimou) The promise of a Chinese New Wave in filmmaking is much in evidence in this breathtaking epic of peasant life by first-time director Zhang. Visually stunning and filmed in Cinemascope (the power of which will be diminished on the small screen), the story revolves around the reminiscences of a young man for his grandparents — peasants who lived in a remote section of northwestern China during the 1920s and '30s. Nine (the beautiful and remarkable Gong Li) is a young beauty who, immediately prior to her arranged marriage with a leper, is saved by a heroic servant. They both fall in love and their ensuing relationship, through personal turmoils as well as Japan's invasion of their area, is dazzlingly dramatized. A visually stunning folk tale that celebrates the vitality and endurance of the peasant people. (Chinese with English subtitles) ★★★½ $79.99

The Red Squirrel (La Ardilla Roja)

(1993, 104 min, Spain, Julio Medem) In *The Red Squirrel*, love spirals inexorably down a vortex of forbidden love. Nancho Novo plays a rock star who takes advantage of a beautiful woman's amnesia — brought on by a motorcycle accident — to create another dream lover now that his song writing days are over. But is this dream lover (Emma Suarez) dreaming, too? Like some antipodal Hitchcock film — most obviously *Vertigo* — director Medem tightens the psychological threads until they are just about to break, then he begins to weave a tapestry that, while dark, is not bereft of life. Unfortunately, the white subtitles get lost during some of the lighter passages. (Spanish with English subtitles) ★★½ $89.99

The Red Tent

(1969, 121 min, Italy/USSR, Mikhail K. Kalatozov) An international all-star cast highlights this exciting adventure film detailing General Nobile's ill-fated 1928 Arctic expedition, where the survivors of a crashed dirigible struggle against nature and the odds while waiting to be rescued. Starring Sean Connery, Claudia Cardinale, Hardy Kruger and Peter Finch as Italian explorer Nobile. Similar in

R

theme to Jan Troell's memorable *Flight of the Eagle.* ★★★ $19.99

Red-Headed Woman

(1932, 81 min, US, Jack Conway) Jean Harlow is a sexy siren out to get the man she loves — her boss (Chester Morris). Look for an aspiring Charles Boyer in the small role of the chauffeur who befriends her. Vintage Harlow. ★★★ $19.99

Reds

(1981, 200 min, US, Warren Beatty) Beatty won a Best Director Oscar for this epic drama about the last years of John Reed, the American journalist who becomes involved in the Russian Revolution. Diane Keaton, in a finely controlled performance, is Louise Bryant, his wife. This long but interesting film serves as both lush romantic drama and political exposé. Jack Nicholson, as a heartbroken Eugene O'Neill, steals every scene he's in. Maureen Stapleton also won an Oscar as Best Supporting Actress. ★★★★ $29.99

Redwood Curtain

(1995, 99 min, US, John Korty) Playwright Lanford Wilson, who with *The 5th of July, The Hot l Baltimore* and *Talley's Folly* has demonstrated a remarkable ability to decipher and communicate the frailties of relationships and the need for human contact by characters on the fringe, delves into further exploration of identity and miscommunication in this extremely poignant made-for-TV adaptation of his play. Lea Salonga, who previously moved audiences in the stage musical "Miss Saigon," gives a touching portrayal of an adopted Vietnamese teen who, after the death of her troubled but adoring adoptive father (John Lithgow), sets out to find her biological parents. Director Korty's pacing is deliberate and absorptive, underscoring the fragile and uncertain search of the young girl. Jeff Daniels (who costarred in "5th of July") nicely handles the difficult role of a disturbed Vietnam vet who may hold the answer to the puzzle. A compassionate, rewarding piece of filmmaking. ★★★½ $14.99

Reefer Madness

(1936, 67 min, US, Louis Gasnier) The evils of marijuana exposed! Bill was a happy all-American high school student until that fatal puff of the deadly weed. The effects: wild parties, violence, sex and...insanity! Is it worth it? ★ $9.99

The Ref

(1994, 92 min, US, Ted Demme) Sporting a wit as nasty and as big as its star Denis Leary's devil-may-care grin, *The Ref* is a refreshingly funny and resourceful slant on *Desperate Hours*-type films. Leary stars as a hapless thief whose botched Christmas Eve burglary puts him on the run. He kidnaps bickering married couple Judy Davis and Kevin Spacey and hides out in their not-so-sweet home. However, nothing this streetwise criminal has seen in or out of prison can prepare him for the fireworks which erupt when the feuding husband and wife go at it. The characters may be in a near-constant state of screeching, but fortunately most of the wickedly delightful dialogue is

worth hearing. The performances from the three leads are as energetic as they are funny, and Glynis Johns is just right as the mother-in-law you love to hate. ★★★ $14.99

The Reflecting Skin

(1990, 98 min, Canada, Philip Ridley) This bizarre, independently produced horror movie owes more to Luis Buñuel than to Wes Craven. A young boy growing up in the Midwest must contend with a father who *may* be a child molester, a beautiful neighbor who *may* be a vampire, dead children, exploding frogs, a hidden human fetus and a mysterious black Cadillac. The film goes over the top at times (you can almost see the filmmakers snickering at their own outlandishness), but it is consistently interesting and offers more than a few good jolts. ★★½ $19.99

Reflections in a Golden Eye

(1967, 108 min, US, John Huston) Sexual repression abounds in this kinky version of Carson McCullers' novel. Marlon Brando is the latent homosexual Army officer and Elizabeth Taylor is his unsatisfied, contemptuous wife. Robert Forster is the hunky object of Brando's affection, and Zorro David is a fey houseboy. Not totally successful, the performances, however, make it slightly interesting. Unfortunately, the film suffers from being made at a time when there was a budding sexual freedom for all but gay characters; which made it impossible to fully explore Brando's character and sexual yearnings. The right director could make a helluva remake. ★★½ $19.99

Reform School Girls

(1986, 94 min, US, Tom DeSimone) Definitely one of the best and most outlandish films of the women-in-prison flicks. Innocent Jenny (Linda Carol) finds herself sent to Pridemore, a hellish reformatory/prison supervised by lecherous female gaurds and ruled over by Head Matron Edna (but she prefers to be called Eddie), a cartoonishly evil dyke bitch who takes malicious pleasure in tormenting the young girls. If that was not enough for our heroine, she also faces a dormitory filled with underwear-clad beauties headed by Charlie (Wendy O. Williams), a platinum blonde thug with a face only a near-sighted mother could love. The weight-lifting Charlie stays in good graces with authorities by being Eddie's bedmate. Oh yes, they're bad! There is plenty of nudity, riots, cat fights and break-outs to keep any fan entranced, and if that doesn't do it, the sight of Sybil Danning as the militaristic warden will. The title song says it all, "So Young, So Bad, So What." ★★ $9.99

Regarding Henry

(1991, 107 min, US, Mike Nichols) In one of the better "redemption" stories which haunted movie screens in the early 1990s (others include *The Doctor,*

The Super and the brilliant *Fisher King*), Harrison Ford stars as a very nasty corporate lawyer who is shot in a hold up, thereby drastically changing his life. Forced to undergo a lengthy healing and therapy process, Ford is changed "for the better" when he returns to his ignored wife (Annette Bening) and neglected adolescent daughter. Though clearly a "yuppie fantasy" for the '90s (no matter how ruthlessly or insensitively one acts, one can be redeemed in the end), there is much satisfaction in seeing Ford's transformation. And to his credit, Ford's beguiling performance (after the accident, of course) as the child-like family man makes the most of the manipulative screenplay. ★★★ $9.99

Reilly: Ace of Spies

(1984, 80 min, GB, Jim Goddard) From Thames Television comes this short but thrilling spy caper starring Aussie Sam Neill as Reilly, the poor man's James Bond — an international scoundrel and womanizing superspy. Leo McKern and Jeanne Crowley costar in this story of Eastern European intrigue, Russian oil and beautiful women. Watch it despite the fact that the director's next project was the disastrous Madonna-Sean Penn flop, *Shanghai Surprise*. (The entire four-part series is also available for $49.99 each or $149.99 for the set) ★★★ $14.99

The Reincarnation of Golden Lotus

(1989, 99 min, China, Clara Law) This tale of ill-fated love and the objectification of women is a kind of Chinese *Dead Again* without the whodunit subplot. Starting in Mainland China during the Cultural Revolution, the story follows a young Chinese woman who turns out to be the incarnation of the Golden Lotus, the wife of a wealthy landowner in feudal China. She is swept away to modern-day Hong Kong by a rich baker where she falls into the same traps of her previous life. Director Law skillfully shows the parallels between the mistreatment of women under Communism, in old Imperial China and in colonial Hong Kong. (Mandarin with English subtitles) ★★★ $79.99

The Reivers

(1969, 107 min, US, Mark Rydell) Totally charming screen version of William Faulkner's

The Reincarnation of Golden Lotus

R

story set in the early 1900s about an adventurous 12-year-old boy (Mitch Vogel) who travels from Mississippi to Tennessee with carefree Steve McQueen and pal Rupert Crosse by motorcar. ★★★ $14.99

Relentless

(1989, 92 min, US, William Lustig) Judd Nelson turns psycho in this surprisingly effective thriller written by one Jack T.D. Robinson, better known as Phil Alden Robinson (the director of *Field of Dreams*). Nelson sinks his teeth into the role of a Los Angeles serial killer who delights in showing up the baffled police. Robert Loggia is the seasoned detective assigned to the case, partners with the newly promoted Leo Rossi, himself anxious to do good. This should satisfy those looking for a couple of good chills. ★★½

The Relic

(1997, 110 min, US, Peter Hyams) Based on the terrific novel by Douglas Preston and Lincoln Child, this big-budget production boasts great special effects, an original and terrifying monster, and A (or A-) level talent. What it doesn't have in abundance is originality, but that's alright because its effective shocks and consistently high level of suspense and terror make up for any feeling of having seen it all before. Penelope Ann Miller is the brains and Tom Sizemore the brawn in a battle with a bizarre new life form accidentally brought back to the Chicago Museum of Natural History from the Amazon jungle. Kothoga, as the creature is known, stalks the dark and claustrophobic hallways of the dusty museum, making meals of guards and visitors alike. Leave it to the management to hold a gala reception one dark and stormy night while the creature is loose in the building. It's up to our heroes to stop the beast. Great fun, and it's a particular pleasure to see James Whitmore in a good supporting role as the wise, older scientist who figures out what's going on before anyone else does. Whitmore's real-life wife Audra Lindley has the line of the movie as a wise-cracking coroner. ★★★ $102.99

The Reluctant Debutante

(1958, 94 min, US, Vincente Minnelli) Rex Harrison and Kay Kendall bring a degree of respectability to this mildly amusing drawing-room comedy. A British couple ready their daughter (Sandra Dee), schooled in the States, for her society debut. A rather sappy and dated family film, rescued by the two stars' earnest performances, and by the always-reliable Angela Lansbury in support. ★★ $19.99

The Remains of the Day

(1993, 137 min, GB, James Ivory) The unequivocal masterpiece of producer Ismail Merchant and director Ivory. Spare in plot yet devastatingly powerful in its theme of repressed emotions and self-disillusionment, the deceptively simple story simmers with complex, unexpressed passions by its main characters. Adapted from Kazuo Ishiguro's novel, the story is set in a stately English manor with action being intercut from its 1930s heyday to its faded glory and near abandonment in the 1950s. In a magnificent performance, Anthony Hopkins stars as Stevens,

Anthony Hopkins (l.) and Emma Thompson in *The Remains of the Day*

the manor's longtime butler. With an unswerving and unquestioned devotion to his employer, Lord Darlington (James Fox), Stevens sacrifices any semblance of a personal life — including an unconsummated relationship with the estate's vivacious housekeeper, charmingly played by Emma Thompson. Devoid of heavy-handedness, the film is quite witty and entertaining, and is beautifully composed — its characters create almost unbearable tension and joy. ★★★★ $19.99

Rembrandt

(1936, 84 min, GB, Alexander Korda) Charles Laughton delivers an inspired and moving performance as the renowned Dutch painter. He portrays Rembrandt as a complex and multifaceted egotist whose deep religious faith drove him to ignore poverty and lack of sponsorship in pursuit of his art. Korda's direction imbues the screen with a plethora of stunning tableaux. ★★★½ $29.99

Rembrandt — 1669

(1977, 114 min, The Netherlands, Jos Stelling) Quite different in approach to Charles Laughton's lusty portrayal of the Dutch artist in the invigorating Alexander Korda biopic, this slow-moving drama painstakingly details the final year of the controversial and tumultuous life of the talented but troubled painter. Depicting Rembrandt as an egotistical, self-indulgent man prone to relying on his celebrity status, this film by Stelling (*The Pointsman*) authentically re-creates the period as well as captures Rembrandt's intense artistic drive. (Dutch with English subtitles) ★★ $79.99

Remo Williams

(1985, 121 min, US, Guy Hamilton) A New York policeman (Fred Ward) becomes a highly trained, top-secret government agent, with a little help from an elderly Korean master (played by Joel Grey). This entertaining adventure features well-staged action sequences, including a hold-your-breath fight atop the Statue of Liberty. ★★★

Renaissance Man

(1994, 129 min, US, Penny Marshall) After two smart successes with *Big* and *A League of Their Own*, Marshall fumbles the ball with this sappy service comedy starring Danny DeVito as a hapless, unemployed teacher who accepts an Army position to have his life changed for the better. DeVito takes charge of a group of military rejects, ultimately allowing his students to discover their own self-respect and at the same time putting his own life in order. There are some pleasurable moments to the film, but Marshall goes over the top with its sentimental message. The big surprise of the film is the effective performance given by Mark Wahlberg (aka Marky Mark) as a backwoods G.I. ★★½ $9.99

Les Rendez-Vous d'Anna

(1978, 122 min, Belgium/France, Chantal Akerman) Filmed in a minimalist style, this quietly moving drama of alienation features a young Belgian director, Anna, who travels by train through Europe publicizing her newest film. Along the way, she meets a stream of characters: friends, lovers, relatives and strangers. The pervading malaise enveloping Anna is brought out by Akerman's trademark style of static camera shots, understated images, monologues and silence. A grim portrait of one woman adrift as well as a vision of an insensate Europe. Starring Aurore Clement, Lea Massari, Helmut Griem and Jean-Pierre Cassel. (French with English subtitles) ★★½

Rendez-Vous

(1985, 83 min, France, André Téchiné) This stylish melodrama stars Juliette Binoche as a naive 18-year-old girl who moves from the provinces to Paris in order to seek independence and establish an acting career. She soon becomes entangled in two love affairs; one with an overly idealistic young man (Wadek Stanczak) and another with a self-destructive youth (Lambert Wilson). This chic, well-cast study of opposing forces in life and fate co-stars Jean-Louis Trintignant and was winner of the Best Director Award at Cannes. (French with English subtitles) ★★★ $79.99

R

Rendezvous in Paris

(1995, 100 min, France, Eric Rohmer) A trio of heartbreaking tales from director Rohmer – it should be a guaranteed pleasure for his legion of fans. Rohmer's protagonists are annoying and amusing in the way they say one thing – and then do another. This trait, combined with beautiful Parisian settings, unites the shorts in this fine collection. All of the films tackle themes of fidelity and trust, chance and coincidence, but none as well as the opening piece, *A 7 pm Rendezvous*. When a young woman learns that her boyfriend may be cheating on her, she arranges a meeting with a stranger in order to get at the truth. The second film, *The Benches of Paris*, depicts a romantic tug-of-war between a man who craves the affections of a woman who is merely using him to get back at her cheating husband. The last tale, *Mother and Child 1907*, tells of the improper seduction of an art student by a pick-up artist in the Picasso Museum. Driven by dialogue, each of these mini-films showcase attractive performers and, as always, Rohmer's graceful romantic touch. (French with English subtitles) ★★★ $102.99

Renegades

(1989, 106 min, US, Jack Sholder) Labored police thriller with Kiefer Sutherland as an undercover cop who teams with Lakota Indian Lou Diamond Phillips to track down killers who stole a sacred Indian artifact. Supposedly set in Philadelphia, but most of the scenes will be unrecognizable to natives. ★½ $12.99

Renoir Shorts

(1927, 52 min, France, Jean Renoir) Fans of Renoir should enjoy these two very early silent shorts which include *The Charleston* and *The Little Matchgirl*, an enchanting, impressionistic adaptation of Hans Christian Andersen's fairy tale. ★★★

Repentance

(1983, 151 min, USSR, Tengiz Abuladze) Thanks to *glasnost*, this nightmarish political allegory about the excesses of the Stalinist era was finally released. This savage, outrageous satire was a huge success in Russia and won the Special Jury Prize at Cannes. A mysterious old woman defies the law and repeatedly exhumes the body of a recently deceased local chieftain. In a series of flashbacks, we learn that the much loved Georgian mayor was actually a despotic ruler, a Stalinist bully – with the gestures of Mussolini and the mustache of Hitler – who was content only with power, no matter the cost. An important, thought-provoking film. (Russian with English subtitles) ★★★

Repo Man

(1983, 92 min, US, Alex Cox) Scorned, feared and ruthless...he's a breed apart...he's a repo man. This raunchy romp sideswipes white dopes on punk, life in the 'burbs, hot-blooded Puerto Ricans and alien-in-the-car flicks. 'Nuff said? Starring Harry Dean Stanton and Emilio Estevez. ★★★½ $9.99

Report to the Commissioner

(1975, 112 min, US, Milton Katselas) A high-tension police drama with Michael Moriarty as a rookie cop who accidentally kills an under-

Steve Buscemi and Harvey Keitel in a "John Woo-ish" standoff from *Reservoir Dogs*

cover policewoman, resulting in a departmental cover-up. Also with Yaphet Kotto, whose scene with Moriarty in an elevator is riveting. ★★★ $29.99

Repossessed

(1990, 95 min, US, Bob Logan) Linda Blair (and Satan) resurfaces in this funny comedy that borrows more from *Airplane!* and *The Naked Gun* than from *The Exorcist*. Leslie Nielsen stars as Father Mayii (pronounced "may I"), the retired priest who must once again do battle with Satan for the soul of a suburban housewife. More laughs than you can shake a cross at. ★★½ $14.99

Repulsion

(1965, 105 min, GB, Roman Polanski) An eerie, kaleidoscope profile of a troubled young girl, imprisoned by her sexual fears and splintered by her shattered psyche. When her sister leaves her alone for the weekend, she is thrust into a world of mental deterioration and hallucinatory nightmares. Polanski directs a profoundly moving performance by Catherine Deneuve as the demure manicurist plagued by frightening visions. ★★★★

Requiem for Dominic

(1990, 88 min, Germany/US, Robert Dornhelm) *Requiem for Dominic* is one of those "little" films that gets lost in the shuffle. Set amidst the December 1989 Romanian uprising which toppled Ceaucescu, this docudrama combines feature film sequences along with shocking and sometimes brutal documentary-style footage of the revolution with unrelenting realism. The story follows the true-life story of Dominic Paraschiv, a political activist wrongly accused of murdering 80 of his colleagues. A childhood friend (Paul Weiss) returns from exile to champion his cause. Director Dornheim (*Echo Park, Cold Feet*) delivers a potent and harrowing tale of political upheaval. (German with English subtitles) ★★★ $79.99

The Rescuers

(1977, 79 min, US, Wolfgang Reitherman, John Lounsberry & Art Stevens) The voices of Eva Gabor as Miss Bianca and Bob Newhart as Bernard in the title roles are appealing and humorously appropriate, as are the contributions of Geraldine Page, Joe Flynn and John McIntyre. A group of mice named the Rescue Aid Society find a bottle with an SOS from a little girl named Penny, who Miss Bianca and Bernard track down to a swamp in the bayou. They must save her from the evil Madame Medusa and her creepy crocodiles who plan to use Penny to retrieve a valuable diamond from a small cave. As usual, Disney's animation and musical score are excellent. ★★★

The Rescuers Down Under

(1990, 109 min, US, Hendel Butoy) This appealing sequel to Disney's *The Rescuers* finds mice Bernard and Miss Bianca traveling to Australia to rescue a young boy and a near-extinct eagle. ★★★

Reservoir Dogs

(1992, 99 min, US, Quentin Tarantino) With one of the most intense and original directing debuts in memory, Tarantino manages with great success to add a new tier to the gangster film genre. The film opens with the bloody aftermath of a failed jewelry heist during which the surviving thieves go to extreme lengths to root out the "rat" in their midst. Bolstered by an excellent ensemble cast led by Harvey Keitel, Tim Roth, Michael Madsen and Steve Buscemi, Tarantino effectively presents his story in an exciting and unique non-linear style. With gritty dialogue and a level of realistic violence which borders on pornographic, the film gives the viewer an unusual fly-on-the-wall perspective of a desperado lifestyle. (Available letterboxed and pan & scan) ★★★★ $14.99

The Respectful Prostitute

(1955, 75 min, France, Charles Brabant & Marcel Pagliero) The seething racial hatred of America's Deep South is the theme in this surprisingly hard-hitting melodrama adapted from a play by Jean-Paul Sartre. When a drunken white man, a senator's son, kills an innocent black bystander on a train, the police conspire to call it self-defense and begin a manhunt for the dead man's black friend. The only witness to the killing is a white woman who is embroiled in the controversy when the law resorts to bribes, blackmail and violence in an effort to get her to recant her testimony and save the killer. The woman, a tough, acid-tongued beauty from New York, is no friend of blacks, but feels compelled to stick to the truth, even when she herself is set up and implicated in a crime. Years ahead of its time, this fascinating story is a powerful and terribly disturbing look into the soulless void of man. (Dubbed) ★★★ $19.99

Restoration

(1995, 118 min, GB, Michael Hoffman) An unexpected and lavish period drama spectacular in design and intimate in scope, *Restoration* is an impressively mounted production rich in character and tone. It's mid-1600s England, a time when that country embraced the passions of the intellect and the sensuous. Young doctor Robert Merivel (Robert Downey, Jr.) balances his energies between hedonistic pursuits and his profession. A chance meeting with Charles II (Sam Neill) elevates the buffoonish Merivel to court physician. But his life of pageant is short-lived as he is coerced into marrying the king's mistress (Polly Walker), and suffers his majesty's wrath when he falls in love with her. Thus sets Merivel on a compelling and at times fascinating odyssey through the course of English history (the London fire, the great plague) which restores his and a country's humanity. Though Downey's casting as the frolicking Brit was risky, the actor rises to the occasion and gives a splendid portrayal of an ordinary man whose resolve is tested during the most extraordinary times. Despite its change of gears from frothy to serious (or maybe because of it), *Restoration* engages as it provokes, and is consistent in its irradiative vision. ★★★½ $19.99

The Resurrected

(1991, 108 min, US, Dan O'Bannon) Screenwriter Dan O'Bannon (*Alien*) tries a rather successful hand at directing this ghastly H.P. Lovecraft tale of a scientist (Chris Sarandon) who goes too far in his attempts to revive the dead. While a little too slow in getting started, the film is revitalized by some gruesome special effects. ★★½ $14.99

Resurrection

(1980, 103 min, US, Daniel Petrie) Ellen Burstyn gives a powerful performance as a woman who survives a near-fatal car accident, endowing her with the powers of spiritual healing and making her a target of religious fanatics. A graceful, beautiful drama, one of the most underrated films of the 1980s. Also stars Sam Shepard and stage legend Eva Legallienne as Burstyn's wise grandmother. ★★★★ $59.99

Return from Witch Mountain

(1978, 95 min, US, John Hough) Good special effects highlight this amiable sequel to *Escape To Witch Mountain* as Bette Davis and Christopher Lee kidnap two psychic alien chil-

dren to use them in robbing a museum (how does one kidnap a psychic, anyhow?). ★★½

The Return of Frank James

(1940, 92 min, US, Fritz Lang) Henry Fonda reprises his role as Jesse James is this excellent sequel which was nicely directed by Lang. This time he's out to get the man who shot his brother in the back. Gene Tierney co-stars in her film debut. ★★★½ $14.99

The Return of Jafar

(1994, 66 min, US) Of course *The Return of Jafar*, the made-for-video sequel to *Aladdin*, isn't as good as the original – who would expect it to be? After all, the film took seven years to make compared to the sequel's two years. *Jafar*'s animation is less spectacular, the songs aren't as catchy and the inimitable Robin Williams is not on hand to astound as the voice of the genie. However, the animation is still pretty darn eye-popping, and Dan Castellaneta (from "The Simpsons"), who took over for Williams, does bring the genie to life with a schizophrenic energy. And while it is really the lackluster songs that keep *The Return of Jafar* from being first-rate, this tale of high adventure and loyalty is still a real charmer for adults and kids alike. ★★★ $22.99

The Return of Martin Guerre

(1983, 111 min, France, Daniel Vigne) Gérard Depardieu and Nathalie Baye star in this sensuous saga of truth, desire and devotion. After a long absence, Martin Guerre returns to the village of his youth, and to a warm reception from its townspeople. However, his life takes an unexpected turn when his identity comes into question and he is brought to trial. An unabashedly romantic, yet never trite, statement on the strength of love. (French with English subtitles) ★★★½ $29.99

Return of the Fly

(1959, 80 min, US, Edward L. Bernds) Vincent Price returns in this satisfactory sequel to the semi-classic horror film. Brett Halsey, grown-up son of David Hedison, attempts to continue

his father's experiments – and guess what happens to him, too. ★★ $14.99

Return of the Jedi

(1983, 133 min, US, Richard Marquand) The final film of George Lucas' *Star Wars* trilogy lives up to its expectations as a nail-biting battle for the galaxy, but does not surpass what the first two movies achieved. Featuring the best special effects of the three, it is also unfortunately the most commercial of the group (its fuzzy little Ewoks are tailor-made for toy store shelves). The film begins with our heroes attempting to repair the damage of the Empire's strike back, by rescuing Han from the abode of the gangster-slug Jabba the Hut and getting Luke a new hand and a completion to his Jedi training with Yoda. The story then shifts to the Rebellion's grand plan: to destroy the new Death Star, the Emperor and Darth Vader in one final assault. The series goes out with a literal bang and ties all the characters' stories together into a happy ball of family, love and freedom. A bit sappy, perhaps, but the audience of the original *Star Wars* grew up between the first and third movies, and was not the target audience of *Jedi*. The popularity and influence of the series shows most obviously in *Jedi*, and this also probably upset the original fans, who preferred to have their illusions of fantasy unbroken. Nevertheless, it is a remarkable end to a remarkable phenomenon. ★★★½ $19.99

Return of the Living Dead

(1985, 90 min, US, Dan O'Bannon) Funny and gory horror spoof of "living dead" zombie movies. The dead are ready to party when a secret military chemical brings them back to life. The film which introduced those immortal words: "Send more cops!" ★★½ $14.99

Return of the Living Dead, Part II

(1988, 89 min, US, Ken Wiederhorn) Inferior sequel to the comic zombie film with a totally new bunch of corpses rising from the dead. As if James Karen and Thom Mathews didn't have enough trouble in the first outing, they're back to party once more. ★½ $14.99

The Return of Martin Guerre

Return of the Living Dead 3

(1994, 97 min, US, Brian Yuzna) Gruesome visuals (and vittles) characterize this splatter-fest from the producer of the *Re-Animator* series about what happens when an Army brat uses an experimental nerve gas to resuscitate his thrill-seeking girlfriend (Mindy Clark) thereby turning her into a brain-sucking por-cupine-woman. Also starring Kent McCord and J. Trevor Edmonds. ★★½ $94.99

The Return of the Pink Panther

(1975, 113 min, GB, Blake Edwards) After a six-year hiatus, Peter Sellers returns to the screen as the hilariously inept Inspector Clouseau. Like many of the post-*Shot in the Dark* sequels, Edwards tends to concentrate too heavily on big, violent sight gags and Sellers' peerless knack for slapstick and prat-falls. Still, this is one of those films that will keep you laughing throughout. Co-stars Herbert Lom. ★★★ $14.99

The Return of the Secaucus 7

(1980, 100 min, US, John Sayles) What hap-pens when seven former activists get together for a reunion is the focus of Sayles' first direc-torial work. Ten years after being jailed for a night on trumped-up protesting charges, these friends reminisce about the causes, concerns and convictions of their youth. Emotions flow as the weekend turns into a series of bitter-sweet realizations regarding the group's goals and accomplishments. ★★★★

The Return of the Soldier

(1985, 101 min, GB, Alan Bridges) The pow-erhouse cast of Alan Bates, Glenda Jackson, Julie Christie and Ann-Margret (yes!) high-lights this riveting psychological drama adapt-ed from Rebecca West's first novel. During World War I, a soldier (Bates) experiences shell shock and amnesia and returns to his country estate without the memory of his past 20 years. His only recollections are of a bucolic child-hood and a youthful love affair. Christie is won-derful as the pampered wife who is only famil-iar to her husband "like any other guest in the same hotel." A subtle, handsomely mounted and involving production. ★★★½

Return of the Swamp Thing

(1989, 87 min, US, Jim Wynorski) Campy *Swamp Thing* sequel once again pits Louis Jourdan against the infamous plant man, this time with Heather Locklear along for the ride. ★ $14.99

Return of the Tall Blonde Man with One Black Shoe

(1974, 84 min, France, Yves Robert) Pierre Richard revives his role as the incredibly clutzy and bumbling musician who accidentally stum-bles into international intrique. A hilarious spoof of spy movies. (Dubbed) ★★★ $19.99

Return of the Vampire

(1943, 69 min, US, Lew Landers) Columbia Studios tried to sneak into Universal's demi-monde with this atmospheric tale of a caped vampire named Armand Tesla, stalking the ruins of war-torn London. No matter what name you give the character, when Bela Lugosi plays a vampire, it's Dracula. ★★ $9.99

Return to Oz

(1985, 110 min, US, Walter Murch) Dark and rather depressing sequel to the classic *The Wizard of Oz*, with Dorothy returning to Oz (after a bout in a sanitarium) but finding things changed for the worst. With Nicol Williamson, Jean Marsh, Piper Laurie and lit-tle Fairuza Balk as Dorothy. ★★

Return to Salem's Lot

(1987, 96 min, US, Larry Cohen) Entertaining theatrical sequel to Stephen King's acclaimed TV miniseries. Michael Moriarty plays an anthropologist who, with his young son, travels to the small Northeastern town, overrun by vampires. Also with Samuel Fuller, Ricky Addison Reed and Andrew Duggan. ★★★ $14.99

Return to Snowy River

(1988, 97 min, Australia, Geoff Burrowes) While not as good as the original *Man from Snowy River*, this drama of romance and ambi-tion set against a backdrop of a horse ranch proves to be diverting, highlighted by lush photography of galloping horses and a nicely drawn villain in Brian Dennehy. The story fol-lows the love affair between young ranchhand Jim (Tom Burlinson) and Jessica, the lovely daughter of the ranch. Once again, Jim must prove his worth in order to win the young woman's hand. ★★½ $9.99

Reuben, Reuben

(1983, 101 min, US, Robert Ellis Miller) A wonderfully witty character study with the superb Tom Conti as a recklessly amorous, casually and usually inebriated Scottish poet. Though his last verses were conjured long ago, he suffers no lack of charm as he takes a New England college town by storm. ★★★

Revenge

(1990, 124 min, US, Tony Scott) This tepid romantic thriller stars Kevin Costner as a for-mer pilot who travels to Mexico to visit mil-lionaire gangster Anthony Quinn. Once there, the hotshot flyboy promptly falls in love with his host's beautiful, bored wife (Madeleine Stowe). As passions ignite, Quinn quickly learns of the couple's affair, and he initiates a near-fatal beating of the two (Revenge #1); then there's the Revenge of the Revenge, and so on and so on. Director Scott is an accom-plished visual stylist, but plot and characteri-zation are not his forte. ★ $9.99

Revenge of the Nerds

(1984, 90 min, US, Jeff Kanew) One of the more engaging of the silly teen sex comedies, with Robert Carradine and Anthony Edwards leading fellow campus nerds to form their own fraternity. With Curtis Armstrong, Julie Montgomery and Ted McGinley. More hijinks continued in a tepid sequel *Revenge of the Nerds 2*. ★★½ $9.99

The Revenge of the Pink Panther

(1978, 99 min, GB, Blake Edwards) Director Edwards had clearly run out of ideas by the time of this last Peter Sellers go-round as Inspector Clouseau. The film is barely redeemed by the usual pratfalls and a fine per-formance from Dyan Cannon. Quite unfortu-

Revolution: A Red Comedy

nately, Sellers gives a sloppy and ill-timed per-formance as even his comic genius is not able to save Edwards' lackluster material. ★★ $14.99

Reversal of Fortune

(1990, 120 min, US, Barbet Schroeder) Jeremy Irons won an Oscar for his stunning portrayal of Claus von Bulow in this remark-able satire on greed and the upper-class, based on the novel by von Bulow's lawyer, Alan Dershowitz. Accused of trying to murder his wife, Sunny, von Bulow was tried, convicted and then eventually acquitted. The film details in fascinating fashion the events leading up to this; all told with a dark and sometimes hilari-ous sense of humor. Glenn Close, who spends most of the film in a coma, is splendid as Sunny; and Ron Silver is terrific as Dershowitz, whose passionate defense for the unlikable von Bulow led to his release. And though both Close and Silver were shamelessly overlooked at Oscar time, it is Irons' masterful and cynical portrait which distinguishes this classic come-dy of manners. ★★★★ $14.99

The Revolt of Job

(1983, 97 min, Hungary, Imre Gyongyossy) Autobiographical in nature, this touching, compassonate film follows the actions of an elderly Jewish couple who, having lost all seven of their children during Nazi occupation, become determined to retain and pass on their proud heritage. They do so by illegally adopting a gentile boy. Their love and under-standing for the boy helps him see the world not as an ugly place, but in which nature, religion and love are one. Nominated for Best Foreign Film. (Hungarian with English subti-tles) ★★★

Revolution

(1985, 125 min, US, Hugh Hudson) Almost legendary bomb with Al Pacino as an illiterate trapper who becomes involved in the Revolutionary War when his 14-year-old son joins in the fight against the British. Donald Sutherland, Nastassja Kinski and Joan

Plowright are also featured. Stick to *1776* if you want to know the true story. ★ $14.99

Revolution: A Red Comedy

(1990, 84 min, US, Jeff Kahn) This intriguing and amusingly dry independent political satire is set in the Lower East Side of New York where two hip Marxist wannabes (Ollie, a rhetoric spewing, bathtub loving "revolutionary"; and Suzy, his sexy accomplice) recruit an overly effusive fellow student in their goal of spreading the works of Karl Marx and worldwide revolt throughout a land that really couldn't care less. Trouble brews for our would-be subversives when they can't seem to decide where to begin their violent overthrow – should they bomb the World Trade Center, rob rich relatives or simply pinch some candy from the local deli? Working on a very low budget, the film is reminiscent of Jean-Luc Godard's political films (*Weekend*, *Tout Va Bien*), but the somber pontificating and naive idealism of the master is replaced here with a witty cynicism more apt for our times. ★★★ $69.99

Rhapsody in August

(1991, 98 min, Japan, Akira Kurosawa) Japanese grand master Kurosawa's eloquent examination of the nuclear holocaust in Nagasaki – as seen through the eyes of a survivor and her four grandchildren 44 years later – is a highly emotional and engrossing drama. Sprinkled throughout with touches of wry humor, the film follows the four youngsters who, deposited by their parents with Grandma for the summer, constantly needle her for more information about the war and the bomb, allowing us to discover the grisly details through their innocent eyes – an especially moving scene comes when the children take a tour of Nagasaki's monuments to the victims. Ultimately, it is the old lady who takes center stage, however, as she falls into despair over the loss of her husband in the blast as its anniversary draws near. Richard Gere makes a surprisingly effective appearance as an Amerasian relative from Hawaii who comes to visit (and yes, he performs in Japanese). This understated film is a beautifully crafted and heartfelt requiem. (Japanese with English subtitles) ★★★½ $19.99

Rhapsody in Blue

(1945, 139 min, US, Irving Rapper) As with 1946's *Night and Day*, this biography of musical genius George Gershwin is a fictionalized account of an American icon's life. Robert Alda plays Gershwin, and the film's main interest is the great composer's classic music. *Rhapsody* is more melodramatic and not quite as much fun as the Porter bio. ★★ $19.99

Rich and Famous

(1981, 117 min, US, George Cukor) Cukor's last film is a likable, updated remake of *Old Acquaintance*, with Jacqueline Bisset and Candice Bergen taking over the Bette Davis-Miriam Hopkins roles as college friends and rivals. Both novelists, Bisset is the "serious" and single writer who careens from one sexual encounter to another, while Bergen is the housewife who finds acclaim, but loses a husband, by writing low-brow fiction. Also with David Selby, Hart Bochner and Meg Tilly. ★★★

Rich and Strange

(1934, 92 min, GB, Alfred Hitchcock) Hitchcock's favorite film from his British period is a suprisingly funny yarn about a bored couple who inherit a large sum of money and embark on a journey around the world. Their "idyllic" vacation is enlivened by adulteries, swindles, a shipwreck and a tasty meal that turns out to be a fried cat. ★★★ $12.99

Rich Boy, Poor Boy

(1992, 94 min, The Philippines, Piedro de San Paulo) Sort of a Filipino-style *Maurice*, this romantic and erotic gay love story, banned in The Philippines, is also a melancholy drama of the class problems afflicting the Third World. Mark, a rich, Americanized young man returns from the States to visit his mother at her country estate where he meets and falls in love with Pilo, a hunky, sincere servant. Their love blossoms despite Mark's mother's attempts to push young women in his direction and her eventual discovery of the affair. But it is the political turmoil in the countryside that proves to be an even larger obstacle to the naive lovers. Plus: A short film, *A Boy Named Cocoy*, also directed by de San Paulo, precedes the feature. This entertaining and erotic tale, which plays as a sort of Filipino J.O. fantasy, follows Cocoy, a 20-year-old country boy who arrives in the Big City only to lose all of his clothing and money to thieves. He is saved from a life in the streets by a friendly young man named Tony. And when Cocoy discovers that he is gay, he repays him in the only way he knows how! (Tagalog with English subtitles) ★★★ $69.99

The Rich Man's Wife

(1996, 100 min, US, Amy Holden Jones) Derivative, unbelievable and about as thrilling as looking for Iowa license plates on the L.A. Freeway, *The Rich Man's Wife* tries to be a provocative noir; anyone who has seen *any* film noir – either good or bad – will be able to see right through the clichés and oh-so predictable ending. Halle Berry is having marital problems with her rich husband (Christopher McDonald); while vacationing in the mountains, she meets one of the relatives from *Deliverance*. He begins to stalk her, and then her husband – who ends up dead. But what's the real story? The problem with *The Rich Man's Wife* is that there isn't any. In fact, there isn't much of anything. Even respectable actors like Berry and McDonald seem lost. So will the viewer. If you really need noir thrills, rewatch *Body Heat* and *Mortal Thoughts* – two good films this borrows from. ★ $19.99

Richard Pryor — Live in Concert

(1979, 78 min, US, Jeff Margolis) This concert film, showing the comic at the very peak of his talent, succeeds where most other "live" performance documentaries fall short. Many comedians have flashes of brilliance, but only Richard Pryor's comic tour de force lasts the entire length of the film. Re-creating everything from his heart attack to his pet monkey's sex drive, Pryor's act is, of course, excruciatingly funny. At the same time, the intimacy with which he discusses painful real-life experiences makes this a cathartic experience. ★★★½ $19.99

Richard Pryor Live on Sunset Strip

(1982, 82 min, US, Joe Layton) Live concert film which features Richard Pryor's first recount of the accident which nearly took his life – which he jokingly refers to as "Pryor on Fire." Consistently hilarious. ★★★½

Richard III

(1955, 158 min, GB, Laurence Olivier) Olivier leads a dream cast as the physically grotesque and completely villainous Richard III, King of England. Sir Larry seems to revel in his part as the vile and fiendish hellhound who cavorts his way into conquest on the battlefield and in the boudoir. With a supporting cast of Claire Bloom, Ralph Richardson and John Gielgud, this serves as a reunion of the Royal Academy of Dramatic Arts. ★★★★ $24.99

Richard III

(1995, 106 min, GB, Richard Loncraine) Ian McKellen wrote the screenplay adaptation and stars in this virbrant, often thrilling updating of Shakespeare's classic tragedy of betrayal and ambition; streamlined and set in the 1930s, it all makes perfect sense. The story traces the rise of Richard (McKellen in a malevolent and hypnotic performance), the ruthless prince who plots, lies and kills his way to the throne. McKellen and director Loncraine have created a Nazi-like society which Richard commands, and Shakespeare's story and dialogue superbly underscore Richard's oppressive regime and fascist roots. This is a brave and original interpretation of a time-honored work, and one which succeeds on nearly every level. Among the splendid supporting cast, Maggie Smith is simply great as Richard's mother who can barely conceal the contempt she holds for her son, Nigel Hawthorne is fine as Richard's brother Clarence, who is quickly dispatched to the tower, and Adrian Dunbar is appropriately amoral as Richard's hired thug. The outstanding production design complements the rampant hysteria of Richard's new order, which has been brilliantly maneuvered by Richard and envisioned by McKellen. ★★★★ $19.99

Richard's Things

(1980, 104 min, GB, Anthony Harvey) This made-for-TV drama wallows in somber pretentiousness and is unusually stagnant for its subject matter. Liv Ullmann stars as a widow who is seduced by her late husband's girlfriend. The two get together initially out of curiosity, a desire for companionship and to share their feelings. But a deeper relationship develops, and the two women fall in love. A good premise, but sexual seduction never looked so dreary as Ullmann goes through the film as if in the frozen existential wasteland of Bergmania. ★½

Richie Rich

(1994, 95 min, US, Donald Petrie) Based on the popular comic book, *Richie Rich* is weak on plot and heavy on the gimmicks, but it's also surprisingly entertaining. Macaulay Culkin is unusually understated as the richest kid in the world, Richie Rich, who has everything he could want but friends. The story follows his attempts to befriend a group of neighborhood kids, and foil bad guy John Larroquette who

R

has stolen the family fortune. Among the film's smaller riches are Edward Herrmann and Christine Ebersole, both charming as Richie's philanthropic parents, and the elaborate set design which is great eye candy. ★★★ $19.99

Ricochet

(1991, 97 min, US, Russell Mulcahy) A stylized action film starring John Lithgow as a crazed serial killer who plots the downfall of a politically ambitious buppie cop (Denzel Washington) who sends him to prison. The film is packed with enough non-stop action to please any fan of the genre. Ice-T offers strong support as a hip-hop crack-dealing revolutionary. ★★½ $9.99

Riddance

(1973, 84 min, Hungary, Márta Mészáros) A factory worker pretends to be a student when she meets a handsome scholar at the university. However, after they fall in love, she confesses her working-class background. Though caring little about her class, he will only introduce her to his parents as a fellow student. As she comes closer to acceptance, she realizes that she cannot live under false pretenses and chooses independence over social position. (Hungarian with English subtitles) ★★½ $69.99

The Riddle of the Dead Sea Scrolls

(1990, 80 min, GB, Richard Cassidy) The Dead Sea Scrolls were hidden during the Maccabean Wars by the Essenes. Their discovery by a shepherd in 1947 provided the worldwide academic community an unparalleled opportunity to examine 2,000-year-old documents with this amount of writing intact and in such good condition. At first dated roughly 150 years before the birth of Christ, later examination questions that. This fascinating documentary explores the implications inherent in the discrepancy between the two schools of thought regarding the dating of the scrolls, while outlining the history of the find and the process of making the manuscripts available for study. If the writing actually refers to John the Baptist and Jesus, they reveal a contemporary history of the establishment of Christianity which differs from the present mythology. *Riddle* is a well-considered exploration of issues which have archeological, historical and religious implications. ★★★ $24.99

The Riddle of the Sands

(1979, 102 min, GB, Tony Maylan) A rousing thinking-man's adventure film set in the early part of the 1900s which follows the fantastic adventures of two young British yachtsmen who, while on a pleasure cruise on the North Sea, stumble upon a German plot to invade England. Our daring heroes do what is expected of them − stop the nefarious Germans! Starring Michael York and Jenny Agutter. ★★★ $19.99

Ride the High Country

(1962, 94 min, US, Sam Peckinpah) Peckinpah's first masterwork and one of the great, classic westerns. Randolph Scott and Joel McCrea (who must have at least 50 westerns between them) are two aging ex-lawmen who have helped tame the West that no longer has a place for them. McCrea is hired to transport

gold from a mining community; he hires Scott and a young cowboy to help, unaware the two men are conspiring to steal the shipment. The literate script, beautiful locations and touching performances by Scott, McCrea and a young Mariette Hartley make this melancholy western linger in one's memory. ★★★½ $19.99

Rider on the Rain

(1970, 119 min, France, René Clément) This surprisingly good, nail-biting thriller by Clément (*Forbidden Games, And Hope to Die*) stars Charles Bronson and Jill Ireland. Bronson is Harry Dobbs, a police inspector in a small French village who unwittingly becomes involved in a bizarre murder mystery involving a mysterious drifter, rape and revenge. In a genre that all too often sinks to insipid levels, this intelligent and taut Hitchcockian puzzler is a refreshing alternative. (English language verison) ★★★

Riders of the Storm

(1986, 92 min, GB, Maurice Philips) Offbeat comedy about a group of high-flying Vietnam vets who set out to sabotage the presidential campaign of a conservative female candidate. With Dennis Hopper and Michael J. Pollard at their most eccentric. ★★½

Riders to the Sea

(1987, 45 min, Ireland, Ronan O'Leary) Geraldine Page stars (in her final performance) in this powerful rendition of J.M. Synge's classic one-act play about three women waiting in quiet desperation for word of a son who has disappeared at sea. Also starring Amanda Plummer and Sachi Parker. ★★★

Ridicule

(1996, 102 min, France, Patrice Leconte) With a barrage of pomp and circumstance and a pocketful of wit, this extravagant and delightful period piece follows the travails of an overly eager and naively optimistic young viscount, Ponceludon (Charles Berling), who sets out for the court of Louis XVI to petition the king. Most of his land being swamp, the young idealist is intent on winning the king's approval (and funding) to build a series of canals and dikes to drain the land and restore health and prosperity to his serfs. Of course, upon his arrival at Versailles, he discovers that he is regarded as nothing more than a country bumpkin not worth the time of day and thus begins a several years' journey into the bowels of a corrupt and ruthless system. Under the tutelage of a kindly old doctor (Jean Rochefort), a veteran of the court, he discovers that the greatest currency in the palace is repartee and that to achieve any hope of audience with the king, one must be a master of the rejoinder. He excels, of course, but this only brings the notice of Fanny Ardant, an influential countess whose friendship is as much a hazard as it is a help. Director Leconte, whose previous efforts (*M. Hire* and *The Hairdresser's Husband*) were sparse and lonely character studies, proves more at home in the regalia of costume spectacle. (French with English subtitles) ★★★½ $99.99

Riff Raff

(1992, 94 min, GB, Ken Loach) This is guerrilla filmmaking at its finest. Loach's ultra-

Ridicule

realistic, documentary-style peek into the lives of lower-class British construction workers is a marvelously subversive skewering of England's collapsing welfare state. The action centers around a young Glaswegian drifter named Stevie who arrives at a London construction site and is taken in by the regulars of the crew. Shortly after the crew sets him up in a suitable squat, he meets up with a bright-eyed Dublin beauty and they strike up a remarkably tender relationship which slowly gives way under the strains of their subcultural differences. Peppered with moments of deep insight as well as hilarious comedy, the film's fly-on-the-wall perspective offers a remarkably personal and unapologetic view of the people buried beneath the ashes of the British Empire. Featuring thick dialects from all over the U.K., the film's gritty dialogue is subtitled for American audiences. ★★★★ $19.99

Rififi

(1955, 116 min, France, Jules Dassin) The archetypal heist flick, this delightful movie concerns itself with four sleazy Montmartre jewel thieves who plan and execute a daring robbery but soon find that their fellow partners are more dangerous than the police. Director Dassin, who moved to France after being blacklisted in the States during the McCarthy era, meticulously enacts the robbery in a daring and wonderfully tense 25-minute sequence filmed in total silence. (French with English subtitles) ★★★★

The Right Stuff

(1983, 193 min, US, Philip Kaufman) All involved with this mammoth, sensational adaptation of Tom Wolfe's best-seller about the early days of America's space program certainly have the right stuff, too. A fabulous cast including Sam Shepard as pioneer pilot Chuck Yeager, and Ed Harris, Scott Glenn, Dennis Quaid and Fred Ward as our first astronauts are all mesmerizing in their depiction of the men whose courage and skill began our exploration into space. The film, which is over three hours long, seems half that running time thanks to exceptional editing and photography, a well-defined screenplay, enthralling aerospace sequences, and director Kaufman's keen eye for pacing and detail. ★★★★ $29.99

THE DISCERNING FILM LOVER'S GUIDE

Rikisha-Man

(1958, 105 min, Japan, Hiroshi Inagaki) This Venice Film Festival Grand Prix winner is a classic story of unrequited love. Toshiro Mifune stars as a feisty rikisha cart-puller who helps a lost boy home, where he falls hopelessly in love with the boy's beautiful mother. The cultural differences between the two preclude any relationship in this sad and unforgettable story. (Japanese with English subtitles) ★★★

Rikki and Pete

(1988, 107 min, Australia, Nadia Tass) From the director and writer (David Parker) of *Malcolm* comes this gadget-laden follow-up about an off-the-wall inventor and his geologist sister who escape the local sheriff by fleeing to the Outback. Suffice it to say, chaos ensues in this humorous though lightweight "Les Miserables Down Under." ★★½

Rikyu

(1991, 116 min, Japan, Hiroshi Teshigahara) From the director of *Woman in the Dunes* comes this intelligent drama on the strained relationship between the art of politics and the politics of art. Set in the 16th century, a power-hungry peasant rises to leadership after a powerful warlord is killed. Ignorant of the traditions of higher Japanese culture, he appoints Hideyoshi, a wise and elderly tea master, to teach him the Zen approach to Ikebana (flower arranging) as well as the delicate and mysterious tea ceremony. However, social and spiritual instruction soon evolve into political advice, a turn of events unforeseen by the taciturn old teacher. (Japanese with English subtitles) ★★★ $79.99

Rio Bravo

(1959, 141 min, US, Howard Hawks) Hawks' classic western with John Wayne as a small town sheriff determined to keep a killer confined to his jail, despite a limited source of man-power in the town. Dean Martin, Angie Dickinson, Ricky Nelson and Walter Brennan try to help. Flavorful direction from Hawks. ★★★½ $19.99

Riot

(1969, 97 min, US, Buzz Kulik) Jim Brown reluctantly helps fellow jailbird Gene Hackman start a riot to cover their prison breakout in this stereotyped, extremely violent jailhouse romp. Wonderfully clichéd performances (Ben Carruther's drooling psychopathic Indian, Gerald O'Loughlin's pants-wetting sadistic guard/hostage and Michael Byron's mincing gay character), hard-boiled dialogue and the prison's (Arizona State Penitentiary) real warden, personnel and inmates as performers combine to make this film an exploitative, entertaining treat. ★★½ $14.99

Riot in Cell Block 11

(1954, 80 min, US, Don Siegel) A collection of cutthroats seize control of their cellblock in this hardboiled crime flick. A gritty, early entry from the director of *Dirty Harry*. ★★★ $19.99

Ripping Yarns

(1983, 90 min, GB) Michael Palin and Terry Jones of the Monty Python clan wrote and star in this BBC series that satirizes British storytelling and legends. Though more uneven than some Python projects, there are enough outrageous scenes to please those who can't get enough of their irreverent hijinks. $14.99 each

Vol. 1 – Ripping Yarns: "Tomkinson's Schooldays" in a stuffy, traditional English boarding school is complete with a bizarre headmaster and school bully; a British officer attempts to "Escape from Stalag Luft 112B"; "Golden Gordon" sets out to help his favorite football team who have lost six years in a row.

Vol. 2 – More Ripping Yarns: In "The Testing of Eric Olthwaite," Eric's parents run away from home because their son is so boring; "Whinfrey's Last Case" happens just as the Germans are about to attack to start WWI; Gothic horror is spoofed in "The Curse of the Claw."

Vol. 3 – Even More Ripping Yarns: "Roger of the Raj" is thrust into war in India; Agatha Christie is spoofed when there's a "Murder at Moorstones Manor"; and finally, the indescribable "Across the Andes by Frog."

The Rise of Catherine the Great

(1934, 92 min, GB, Paul Czinner) A lavish though slowly paced historical drama about the Russian Czarina whose life was needlessly spoiled by a stolid planned marriage. The film does not depict the legend of her ultimate demise, which is so grotesque that we can all be thankful that Penthouse Productions (creators of the infamous *Caligula*) failed to complete their proposed telling of the story. Starring Douglas Fairbanks, Jr. and Elisabeth Bergner. ★★★½ $19.99

The Rise to Power of Louis XIV

(1966, 100 min, France, Roberto Rossellini) Rossellini's first in his series of historical dramas tells the story of Louis XIV's rise to power as well as his decline. Includes a memorable scene where he forces his court to watch him devour a 14-course meal. Made in only 23 days for French television, this is one of Rossellini's most important and influential works. (French with English subtitles) ★★★½

Rising Sun

(1993, 126 min, US, Philip Kaufman) Michael Crichton's adaptation of his Japan-bashing, high-tech best-seller is a tedious tale of corporate espionage. Sean Connery and Wesley Snipes are an unlikely duo as a pair of L.A.P.D. liaison officers sent to investigate a murder at the boardroom of a major Japanese multinational. Of course, their search for the killer leads them right into the middle of the trade wars between Japan and the United States. All the while, the older and wiser Connery must explain to Snipes all of the tricks the Japanese are using to bury the U.S. economically. Ultimately, the film can't decide whether it wants to be a full-fledged action-thriller or an overly worded primer on Japanese business treachery. The film does pick up some steam towards the end, but by then we've already figured out whodunit. The supporting cast includes Steve Buscemi, Tia Carrere and Harvey Keitel. ★★ $14.99

Risky Business

(1983, 99 min, US, Paul Brickman) Tom Cruise created a small sensation in his first starring role as a college-bound teenager who turns his upper-class Chicago home into a bordello while his parents are out of town. There are plenty of laughs, and a good, youthful supporting cast including Rebecca DeMornay, Curtis Armstrong and Bronson Pinchot. ★★★ $14.99

Rita, Sue and Bob Too

(1986, 93 min, GB, Alan Clarke) This interesting sex comedy with a dark edge features Siobhan Finneran and Michelle Holmes as Rita and Sue, two lower-class teenagers who baby-sit for nouveau riche yuppie Bob (George Costigan). Bob initiates both girls sexually in very quick succession and everything moves along quite happily until Rita becomes pregnant, signaling a turn for the worse for all parties concerned. The film captures the gritty hopelessness of the industrial midlands of England quite well, and is marred only slightly by a trite ending. ★★★

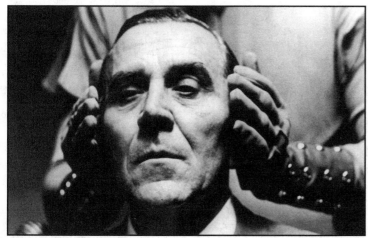

The Rite

457

R

The Rite

(1969, 75 min, Sweden, Igmar Bergman) Bergman's claustrophic treatise on censorship and the arts pits three members of a succesful cabaret act against a Kafka-esque magistrate (Eric Hell) who must determine whether a piece of their show is "obscene." The troupe is comprised of Ingrid Thulin (*The Silence, Cries and Whispers*), her husband Gunnar Bjornstrand (*Smiles of a Summer Night, The Seventh Seal*) and Anders Ek, with whom she is having a torrid affair. Their tryst is common knowledge to Bjronstrand, who feels emotionally dependedent on them both. As the judge individually interogates them, their stories unravel along with all of their interpersonal foibles and neuroses. The film culminates, naturally, with their performing the offending piece (a kind of sexually based pagan ritual) for the astonished judge. For lovers of Bergman and other serious cinephiles, this is probably must viewing. For most others, however, Bergman's opressive sense of ennui and cinematographer Sven Nyquist's briliant, but suffocating up-close camerawork may prove too much to bear, even considering the film's graciously short running time. ★★½ $39.99

Ritual of Death

(1985, 83 min, Brazil, Fauzi Mansur) When an acting company decides to stage an updated version of an Egyptian ritual involving human sacrifice, they accidentally unleash a dark, evil force. A satanic priestess then begins to use the troupe to recall the spirit of a cult leader who led his people to mass suicide. Soon the play becomes real and the cast members begin to disappear one by one in this Dario Argento-influenced thriller from Brazilian fright-master Mansur. ★★★ $24.99

The Ritz

(1976, 91 min, US, Richard Lester) Lester's riotous farce stars Jack Weston as a Cleveland garbage collector on the lam in a gay bathhouse. There he encounters Rita Moreno ("You thought I was a drag queen?"), Treat Williams ("You madicon hump!"), F. Murray Abraham, the Andrews Sisters and the ever-popular steam room. Not as hilarious or as refined as the Broadway production (written by Terrence McNally), but very entertaining nonetheless. ★★★ $19.99

The River

(1951, 99 min, India, Jean Renoir) In 1949 and 1950, Renoir traveled to Bengal to make his first color film, the story of a large British family living on the banks of the Ganges River. Though it has never attained the classic status of many of his earlier works, it remains one of Renoir's loveliest, drollest and most pleasing films. The film features outstanding cinematography by Jean's brother Claude. Also of special note is Renoir's assistant director for the production: Satyajit Ray. ★★★★ $29.99

The River

(1984, 124 min, US, Mark Rydell) Mel Gibson and Sissy Spacek play a farm couple struggling against nature and business interests to hold on to their home. Good production values (including lush cinematography by Vilmos Zsigmond) and earnest performances from the two leads can't make up for dramatic inconsistencies. The least of the trilogy of "farm films" released in 1984 (including *Places in the Heart* and *Country*). ★★ $9.99

River of No Return

(1954, 91 min, US, Otto Preminger) A big, sprawling western (shot in Cinemascope, which means some of the spectacular cinematography will be lost on the small screen) with Robert Mitchum as a farmer who is double-crossed by gambler Rory Calhoun and sets out, with his young son and saloon singer Marilyn Monroe, to even the score. There's explosive chemistry between Monroe and Mitchum which propels the film well beyond the usual western adventure. ★★★ $14.99

The River Rat

(1984, 93 min, US, Tom Rickman) *The River Rat* is a semi-involving, if not completely successful tale of a wrongly convicted man (Tommy Lee Jones) paroled from prison attempting to establish a relationship with the daughter (Martha Plimpton) he's never known. Jones and Plimpton give solid performances, but the film strays off into a subplot about a hidden fortune and an evil prison psychiatrist (Brian Dennehy) which is never as gripping as the genuine moments between father and daughter. ★★½ $14.99

A River Runs Through It

(1992, 123 min, US, Robert Redford) A meticulous and beautifully rendered adaptation of Norman MacLean's celebrated autobiographical novella, *A River Runs Through It*, with its romanticized view of aw-shucks country living and astonishing picturesque backdrops, leaves little doubt as to director Redford's interest in the story. The story follows the relationship between young MacLean, a straight-laced scholar played by Craig Sheffer and his wilder, younger brother, Paul (Brad Pitt in a terrific portrayal). Though opposites in temperament, the brothers share a passion for fly-fishing, taught by their stern preacher father (Tom Skerritt); it is their reverence for the sport which bonds them. As Norman travels to the East to attend college, Paul stays behind in Montana and lives the life of a boozing, cynical journalist. As the brothers are reunited, MacLean's text is movingly realized: "It is those we live with and love and should know who elude us." Though the entire cast is outstanding, it is Pitt whose star-making performance anchors the film. ★★★½ $14.99

The River Wild

(1994, 108 min, US, Curtis Hanson) Meryl Streep goes the Sigourney Weaver route and tackles the action adventure movie with rip-roaring results. Streep, husband David Strathairn and young son Joseph Mazzello go on a white water rafting vacation. Unbeknowst to any of them, neighboring rafter Kevin Bacon and his companions are actually escaped criminals on a getaway. And when the latter's guide "unexplainedly" vanishes, Streep and family are ultimately terrorized into helping with their escape. Though the plot is barely seaworthy, director Hanson (*The Hand That Rocks the Cradle*) keeps the film afloat with hair-raising action scenes, most of which have Streep doing her own stunts on obviously dangerous rapids. But it is Streep's performance which propels the film, making it easy to gloss over any inconsistencies. Bacon makes a most effective heavy. ★★★ $19.99

River's Edge

(1986, 99 min, US, Tim Hunter) A perfect counterpiece to Rob Reiner's *Stand by Me*, released the same year, *River's Edge* is the disturbing story of a group of burned-out '80s teens who find the body of a friend killed by a classmate, greeting the discovery with a lack of emotion or concern. A gripping story of youthful alienation and hopelessness. Keanu Reeves, Crispin Glover and Ione Skye star as the youths and Dennis Hopper costars as a half-crazed ex-biker and, interestingly, is the film's moral center. Based on an actual incident. ★★★

Riverdance

(1995, 71 min, Ireland, John McColgan) Choreographer/dancer extraordinaire Michael

The Road to Wellville

The Road Warrior

Flatley brings his unique blend of Irish folk dance and Gene Kelly showmanship to the stage in this extravaganza, taped in Dublin. With the impeccable timing, discipline and attention to detail worthy of the Marine Corps Silent Drill Team, Flatley's troupe is a visual delight, with enough tap shoes, toned legs and buff bodies clicking in precision to make Busby Berkeley jealous. Flatley, the star of the show (and boy, does he know it), is both a consummate show-off and dancer, and he's truly a joy to watch. The troupe's terrific dance numbers are broken up by short vocal performances by Irish sirens, a gospel choir, and the Harlem Tap Company. A must for dance or Irish music fans. (Flatley and his troupe returned in *Lord of the Dance*) ★★★½ $24.99

Road Games
(1982, 100 min, Australia, Richard Franklin) This early entry from the director of *Psycho II* deals with an Aussie psycho-killer and the trucker (Stacy Keach) who sets out to bring him in. A young Jamie Lee Curtis co-stars as a hitchhiker who finds herself in the middle of this "road game." Director Franklin, who at one time studied under Alfred Hitchcock, tries hard to deliver the same shocks and is not entirely unsuccessful. All in all, a decent thriller. ★★½

Road House
(1948, 95 min, US, Jean Negulesco) A torrid melodrama with Cornel Wilde and Richard Widmark as partners in a roadside bar who begin feuding when Widmark hires alluring singer Ida Lupino, only to have her fall in love with Wilde. From there, passions and jealousies erupt, leading to betrayal and murder. A solid drama rife with sexual tension, and featuring a slam-bang ending. Lupino is terrific as the raspy-voiced entertainer. ★★★½ $19.99

Road House
(1989, 114 min, US, Rowdy Harrington) Patrick Swayze plays a tough philosopher who takes a job as a bouncer at a rough 'n' tumble Midwest bar; he comes in conflict with crooked Ben Gazzara. About as dramatically

plausible as a philosophy major who doubles as a bouncer, and given to random violence which most assuredly would have upset its hero under any other circumstances. Also with Sam Elliott and Kelly Lynch. ★ $14.99

Road Scholar
(1993, 75 min, US, Roger Wesberg) A definite must-see for lovers of Romanian-born poet Andrei Codrescu's National Public Radio commentaries. Part documentary, part flight of fancy, the film is basically an extended series of observations by Codrescu on American culture as he motors in a huge Cadillac convertible across the country. First, he has to learn how to drive, an amusing episode in itself, and then he's off to the Big Apple to meet fellow poet Allen Ginsberg and to check out one of Brooklyn's famous Romanian eateries. On his journey across the continent, Codrescu finds an assortment of oddballs to interview including New Age "channelers," Las Vegas wedding vendors and the inhabitants of Biosphere Two, among others. Upon his arrival in San Francisco, the mood turns slightly more serious as he prepares to become a naturalized American — this allows commentary on the nature of American citizenship which actually verges on patriotic and is ultimately deeply moving — even for those of us who are hardened cynics (of whom Codrescu is certainly one). ★★★ $14.99

Road to Rio
(1947, 100 min, US, Norman Z. McLeod) One of the funnier Bob Hope-Bing Crosby-Dorothy Lamour "Road" pictures, with the boys as stowaways arriving in Rio, forming an "authentic" American jazz band, and helping Dorothy escape the influence of her evil aunt. Also with The Andrews Sisters and Gale Sondergaard. ★★★ $14.99

Road to Ruin
(1992, 90 min, US, Charlotte Brandstrom) Peter Weller shows his lighter side in this charming romantic comedy about a billionaire industrialist who feigns poverty when he begins to fear that the woman he has fallen in love with (Carey Lowell) is only after his money. ★★½ $14.99

Road to Utopia
(1945, 90 min, US, Hal Walker) A non-stop barrage of hilarity, *Utopia* probably rates as the best of the seven "Road" pictures. Bob Hope, Bing Crosby and Dorothy Lamour are off on the road to Alaska in search of gold and romance. What they find are outlaws, talking fish, scheming showgirls and lots of snow. The plot of Bob and Bing helping Dorothy retrieve her stolen gold mine from crooks plays a back seat to the crazy shenanigans, which produces a whirlwind combination of one-liners, impersonations, schtick and in-jokes. Robert Benchley supplies glib commentary throughout. One of our favorites: (Bob trying to act tough at a local bar) "Give me a lemonade...in a dirty glass." ★★★½ $14.99

The Road to Wellville
(1994, 120 min, US, Alan Parker) Part Bugs Bunny and part John Huston, Anthony Hopkins stars as Dr. John Harvey Kellogg, he of the cereal fame, who later in life ran the

spa/hospital Battle Creek Sanitorium. Kellogg's principles were based on the philosophy of "no meat and no sex," and that the key to good health lies in the constant cleansing of the bowels. With this premise, director Parker takes an outrageous journey down the halls of the sanitorium, where enemas both become a part of the daily routine and form the core of the humor of the film, whose cheap flatulation jokes become redundant. Among an engaging cast forced to make personal hygiene funny, Bridget Fonda plays a Kellogg devotee who drags husband Matthew Broderick to the spa, and John Cusack plays a budding tycoon who joins forces with Kellogg's idiot adopted son (Dana Carvey) to produce a new breakfast cereal. ★★ $19.99

The Road Warrior
(1982, 94 min, Australia, George Miller) He roams the barren plains of a post-apocalyptic wasteland, a tight-lipped, leather clad loner, living only for the ever-precious petrol. Mel Gibson writes the book on existential cool in Miller's violent vision of a fuel-less future. Suspenseful throughout, this boasts great action sequences and a stunning, futuristic look. ★★★½ $14.99

Roads to the South
(1978, 100 min, France, Joseph Losey) With cool directorial elegance and subtle perception, Losey creates a complex portrait of a man grappling with deep personal conflicts. Yves Montand stars as an exiled Spanish revolutionary who, after establishing himself as a successful screenwriter abroad, returns to his homeland to fight Fascism; but instead is forced to deal with a lifetime of personal deceptions, illusions and hypocrisies. Miou-Miou co-stars in this intense drama. (French with English subtitles) ★★★ $59.99

Roadside Prophets
(1992, 96 min, US, Abbe Wool) With the screenwriting credit of Alex Cox's quintessential punk movie *Sid and Nancy* attached to his resume, Wool's directorial debut is an all-the-more disappointing attempt at '90s hip. John Doe, of the L.A. band X, teams with Beastie Boy Adam Horovitz for this story of two reluctant heroes without a clear destination. Set against the motorcycle subculture and the lure of the open road, the film tries to blend the idealism of the '60s with the unanswered promises of the '90s. In their travels, the protagonists encounter assorted visionaries, freaks and philosophers, brought to life in unasked-for cameos by Arlo Guthrie, David Carradine, John Cusack (a disgusting but memorable moment) and, yes, Dr. Timothy Leary. With no memorable dramatics, *Roadside Prophets* at least features a great soundtrack, with The Pogues, Pray For Rain, Bug Lamp, Broken Homes and Excene Cervenka. ★½ $14.99

The Roaring Twenties
(1939, 106 min, US, Raoul Walsh) James Cagney stars as a WWI veteran who returns home to New York, becoming an underworld kingpin. Humphrey Bogart and Jeffrey Lynn are Cagney's war buddies who become his associates. One of the last of the great Warner Brothers gangster films. ★★★½ $19.99

Rob Roy

(1995, 139 min, GB, Michael Caton-Jones)
Liam Neeson dons the historical kilt of 18th-century Scottish hero Robert Roy MacGregor. And, though the film suggested by his life lacks a particular warmth and narrative strength, *Rob Roy*'s skirt fits Neeson like a glove. As the almost saint-like leader of the Clan MacGregor, Rob Roy must rescue hearth and home (in the form of Jessica Lange) from the nefarious clutches of the British, represented here by dishonest nobleman John Hurt and, in a scene-stealing turn as a dastardly dandy who slices through the Ten Commandments with a viciousness which belies his foppish demeanor, the exquisitely nasty Tim Roth. With such excellent films as *Scandal* and *This Boy's Life* to his credit, director Caton-Jones once again displays a flair for evocation and inducing richly textured performances from his cast, though the film's screenplay is in need of the necessary swashbuckle that generally makes these adventures so enduring. ★★½ $14.99

The Robe

(1953, 135 min, US, Henry Koster)
Extravagant, if over-produced, biblical epic with Richard Burton as a Roman guard overseeing Christ's Crucifixion who becomes haunted by his deed. Victor Mature is his Christian slave, and Jean Simmons and Michael Rennie also star. ★★½ $19.99

Robert et Robert

(1979, 105 min, France, Claude Lelouch)
Lelouch's humorous, affecting portrait of two lonely men: a middle-aged, hot-headed cab driver, and a bumbling rookie patrolman. Stood up at a dating service, they quickly develop a fast relationship. (French with English subtitles) ★★★

Roberta

(1935, 105 min, US, William A. Seiter)
Jerome Kern-Otto Harbach musical with Irene Dunne as a young heiress, Fred Astaire as a band leader, and Ginger Rogers masquerading as a countess. The story, to be honest, is fluffy even by '30s standards, but the sublime teaming of Astaire and Rogers elevates it – giving it a degree of unexpected charm. Songs include "Smoke Gets in Your Eyes" and "I Won't Dance." ★★★ $19.99

Robin and Marian

(1976, 112 min, GB, Richard Lester) A genuinely touching and affecting love story which offers a revisionist view of medieval history and our legendary friends from Sherwood Forest. Sean Connery and Audrey Hepburn are a magical pairing as the aging Robin Hood and Maid Marian in this telling of Robin's return to Sherwood after years of exile. The supporting cast is an incredible array of talent: Robert Shaw, Richard Harris, Nicol Williamson, Denholm Elliott and Ian Holm. ★★★ $19.99

Robin and the Seven Hoods

(1964, 103 min, US, Gordon Douglas) The Rat Pack is back (in their final outing) in this fairly entertaining comic romp about 1920s Chicago hoods Frank Sinatra, Dean Martin, Bing Crosby, Sammy Davis, Jr., Peter Falk and Edward G. Robinson. ★★½ $14.99

Robin Hood

(1973, 83 min, US, Wolfgang Reitherman)
Walt Disney's animated version of the Robin Hood legend, with the Bandit of Sherwood Forest as a cunning fox. Cute and well-done. ★★★ $24.99

Robin Hood

(1991, 104 min, US, John Irvin) Swashbuckling adventure with one of 1991's "Robin Hood" adaptations. In this version, Patrick Bergin plays the nobleman-turned-outlaw who robs from the rich and gives to the poor. Jürgen Prochnow, Jeroen Krabbe, Edward Fox and Uma Thurman star. ★★★ $19.99

Robin Hood: Men in Tights

(1993, 103 min, US, Mel Brooks) The once brilliant Brooks provides further proof that his comedic well ran dry long ago with this inane skewering of the legend of Sherwood Forest. Despite rolling out a barrel of half-decent one-liners and sight gags, the film clumsily plods from joke to joke, with very little of interest in between. Cary Elwes, doing his jolly best to add a spark as Robin of Loxley, constantly mugs for the camera and generally hams things up beyond all proportion. But Brooks' once impeccable sense of comic timing is nonexistent here, so much so that as the evil Prince John, even Richard Lewis' usually hilarious schtick falls curiously flat. ★½ $19.99

Robin Hood: Prince of Thieves

(1991, 145 min, US, Kevin Reynolds) The big question with this new version of *Robin Hood* is: Is it comparable to the 1938 Errol Flynn classic? The answer: No, it isn't. But it doesn't try to be. This big-hearted and very entertaining retelling of the Robin Hood legend has a whole new story to convey, and it does so winningly. Kevin Costner is the new Robin, and though he lacks the accent and sophistication we have all come to expect of the Bandit of Sherwood Forest, he nevertheless gives a believable portrait of the idealistic folk hero. The story pits Robin against the evil Sheriff of Nottingham, who attempts to seize control of the throne of England in King Richard's absence. The supporting cast includes Morgan Freeman, Mary Elizabeth Mastrantonio and Christian Slater; however, the honors go to Alan Rickman for his hysterical, over-the-top portrayal of the Sheriff – Rickman takes a role which Basil Rathbone had owned for nearly six decades and a creates an equally memorable, singular villain. (Available letterboxed and pan & scan) ★★★ $19.99

Robin Williams Live

(1986, 85 min, US) Robin Williams' tour de force comic performance recorded live at the Metropolitan Opera House. Williams' hilarious monologue includes barbs and insights into Reagan, drugs, fatherhood and Hollywood. ★★★½

Robocop

(1987, 103 min, US, Paul Verhoeven) When officer Murphy (Peter Weller) of the Detroit Police Department (its services now subcontracted out to a large, faceless corporation) is brutally executed in the line of duty, his brain and other body bits become the unwitting components for a new kind of law enforcement robot. Director Verhoeven marshalls an exciting array of stunning special effects, exciting action sequences and a razor sharp wit in delivering this scathingly funny, yet nightmarishly believable, parable of corporate capitalism run amok. (Letterboxed version available for $19.99) ★★★½ $9.99

Robocop 2

(1990, 118 min, US, Irvin Kershner) This follow-up to Verhoeven's brilliant original lacks the insightful political commentary and wit of the first film. On top of that, the film is excessively violent – to the point of mean-spiritedness. The special effects are excellent, particularly the animated face of the villainous Robocop 2, and the action moves at a spirited pace. ★★ $9.99

Robocop 3

(1993, 95 min, US, Fred Dekker) It's "half-man/half-machine" and all drivel in this rusty retread about the cyborg cop (exit Peter Weller, enter Robert Burke) whose humanity once again clashes with his state-inspired programming when he's caught in the crossfire between a militaristic police force, a renegade group of freedom fighters and a ninja! Burke's performance is (dare we say it?) mechanical at best, and the creaky screenplay (copenned by the director and comic book scribe Frank Miller) could have used a stiff injection of WD40 oil. Also with Nancy Allen, Rip Torn and CCH Pounder. ★½ $9.99

Robot Carnival

(1987, 90 min, Japan) *Robot Carnival* is an eye-opening collection of eight musical animation adventures by nine of Japan's top animation talents. Each was given creative freedom to produce a cartoon of about 10 minutes length with the only stipulation being that it would deal with robots. ★★★½ $19.99

Robot Monster

(1953, 63 min, US, Phil Tucker) Notoriously bad sci-fi horror film. This is the one where the monster has a diving helmet head and a gorilla-suit body. P.U. ★ $12.99

Rocco and His Brothers

(1960, 180 min, Italy, Luchino Visconti) Alain Delon and Claudia Cardinale star in this epic tale of five peasant brothers and their widowed mother who migrate from the impoverished south to northern Italy only to find their dreams of happiness shattered when they confront the mean streets of industrial Milan. This neorealist melodrama chronicles the family's struggle in their new world; a world where family values and loyalty are lost to the new morality and individualism of contemporary society. Told in four episodes, the story centers on Rocco (Delon), the gentle and withdrawn brother who tragically falls in love with Nadia (Annie Giradot), the girlfriend of his thuggish boxer brother. The escalating tensions between the two, fueled by the repressions and frustrations of an unfeeling land, build to a climax of rape and murder. A powerful operatic drama about opposing cultures, lust, greed

The Rocky Horror Picture Show

and the will to survive. (Italian with English subtitles) ★★★½

The Rock

(1996, 131 min, US, Michael Bay) Sean Connery helps agent Nicolas Cage break *in to* Alcatraz and in doing so helps create a cracking good, crackerjack action thriller — plot holes and all. When military man Ed Harris takes control of the defunct prison — holding hostages and threatening nuclear attacks on the city of San Francisco — FBI agent Cage enlists the help of longtime con Connery, who's the only man ever to have escaped from the notorious prison. With a small platoon in tow, they cavort through the catacombs and hallways of the prison, at odds with each other more than their prey. As would be expected with a high-profile studio film of this sort, there's plenty of explosions, deaths and mayhem. But *The Rock* is fortunately more than that. It has humor, suspense, and the good sense to give its three very personable stars the text and breathing room to do what they do best. And while *The Rock* may stretch the boundaries of plausibility with its sometimes contrived set pieces, it rocks and rolls to a rousing beat just the same. (Available letterboxed and pan & scan) ★★★ $19.99

Rock Baby, Rock It

(1957, 80 min, US, Murray Douglas Sporup) All the cool cats and slick chicks band together to save their local rock club from the mob. The ludicrous script is equalled by appalling performances and shoddy direction, though it certainly does qualify as top-of-the-list late-nite cult status. ★ $9.99

Rock Hudson's Home Movies

(1992, 63 min, US, Mark Rappaport) Often hilarious, highly original and utterly convincing, this revisionist interpretation of Rock Hudson's film career and life seeks to discover the "real" Hudson through his "reel" persona. Was this Hollywood hunk completely out of touch with his secreted sexuality, or did he throughout his career offer subtle — or not so subtle — hints at his homosexuality. Exploring this idea, Rappaport's insightful and unconventional biography cleverly dissects — through freeze-frame, slo-mo and replays —

Hudson's films, seeking clues and overtly gay signals. ★★★½ $39.99

Rock-a-Doodle

(1992, 75 min, US, Don Bluth) Don Bluth (*An American Tail, The Land Before Time*) continues to define his role as the "hip Disney" with this animated outing which combines live-action characters with cel animation. Edmund (a real-life boy) is sucked into his favorite book where the Grand Duke of Owls is plotting to extinguish the sun. The only person who can save the day is an Elvis-impersonating rooster who sings his way through his heroic deeds. ★★★ $14.99

Rocket Gilbraltar

(1988, 100 min, US, Daniel Petrie) Burt Lancaster's commanding presence distinguishes this moving tale about a family coming together to celebrate their dying patriarch's birthday. The film focuses on his special relationship with his young grandchildren who help him realize his last wish. A pre-*Home Alone* Macaulay Culkin makes a good impression as one of Lancaster's grandkids. The good cast also includes Suzy Amis, John Glover, Bill Pullman and Kevin Spacey. ★★★ $14.99

The Rocketeer

(1991, 108 min, US, Joe Johnston) Some great special effects highlight this lightweight though entertaining family adventure. Set in 1930s Hollywood, the story follows the beginnings of a comic book-like hero, The Rocketeer, who helps fight off the Nazis in Los Angeles (yes, they were there, too). Bill Campbell plays the likable title character, a down-and-out pilot whose discovery of a high-octane rocket pack turns him into a high-flying crime-fighter. Timothy Dalton seems to be having the most fun, playing a Hollywood superstar and Nazi spy, clearly patterned after Errol Flynn. Though the flying sequences are excellent, the script is no more than an ordinary good guys vs. bad guys scenario, offering little of the unpredictable derring-do which made the *Indiana Jones* films on-screen fireworks. What should have been a rollicking rollercoaster ride is merely a genial couple of turns on a carousel. Based on Dave Steven's '80s comic book. ★★½ $9.99

The Rocketship Reel

(1969-1988, 55 min, Canada) From International Rocketship Limited, the adventurous animation company in Vancouver, British Columbia, comes this outrageous compendium of Canadian short animated subjects. Highlights include the classic *Bambi Meets Godzilla* by Marv Newland; *Anijam*, an intriguing short by 22 different animators all doing a segment based on the last animator's final cell; and the offensively bloody *Lupo the Butcher*. ★★★ $29.99

Rocketship X-M

(1950, 77 min, US, Kurt Neuman) Even though Irving Block was only trying to capitalize on George Pal's publicity for *Destination Moon, Rocket Ship X-M*, while no match for *Moon*, holds up quite well as the Saturday matinee programmer it was intended to be. Lloyd Bridges and Hugh O'Brien are the astronauts

headed for the moon who accidentally overshoot it and end up on Mars, partying with the radiation mutants. ★★½ $19.99

The Rocking Horse Winner

(1950, 91 min, GB, Anthony Pelissier) Moody, though very successful adaptation of the D.H. Lawrence fable about a young boy who discovers that he can predict the winners of horse races by riding his rocking horse. Actor John Mills co-produced as well as co-stars, along with Valerie Hobson and John Howard Davies. ★★★½

Rocky

(1976, 119 min, US, John G. Avildsen) Sequels aside, let us not forget that this Oscar-winning, Capra-esque boxing drama is quite good, and introduced Sylvester Stallone to a wide audience, not to mention his popular creation: South Philly boxer Rocky Balboa. Rocky goes after the title against champion Apollo Creed (Carl Weathers); he's aided by trainer Burgess Meredith. Talia Shire is exquisite as Stallone's plain-Jane girlfriend. ★★★½ $9.99

Rocky II

(1979, 119 min, US, Sylvester Stallone) Sylvester Stallone returns as Rocky Balboa in this sequel to the Oscar-winning original. Rocky goes after yet another championship. Nothing new here, and not nearly as good as the first film. Talia Shire, Burgess Meredith and Carl Weathers return, and the film shows a new route to get from the Spectrum to a South Philadelphia hospital which should amuse locals. ★★ $9.99

Rocky III

(1982, 99 min, US, Sylvester Stallone) Sylvester Stallone's Rocky now takes on Mr. T in the third *Rocky* film. Here he's under the tutelage of former opponent Carl Weathers — whatever happened to old Burgess Meredith, you may ask (we won't tell). Also back are Talia Shire and Burt Young. ★★ $9.99

Rocky IV

(1985, 91 min, US, Sylvester Stallone) The fourth in the series, and probably the most ludicrous. Sylvester Stallone wraps himself in the flag as Rocky takes on a Russian superhuman competitor (played by Dolph Lundgren). ★ $9.99

Rocky V

(1990, 103 min, US, John G. Avildsen) Sylvester Stallone's fifth bout as boxer Rocky Balboa. Stallone stars with his own son Sage in this story pitting Rocky, now punch-drunk, penniless and back in his South Philly beginnings, against his former, youthful protégé, whom Rocky had been training. Talia Shire returns, yet again, as Mrs. Rocky. ★★ $9.99

The Rocky Horror Picture Show

(1975, 95 min, GB, Jim Sharman) "Come up to the lab, and see what's on the slab." In *the* cult-midnight show attraction, scientist, alien and bisexual transvestite Dr. Frank N. Furter is visited by average Americans Brad and Janet; the latter two giving themselves over to "absolute pleasure." A wacked-out, spoofy, goofy, hip and campy one-of-a-kind musical. Tim Curry is the Doc, with Susan Sarandon as

R

Janet, Barry Bostwick as Brad, Richard O'Brien as the hunchback valet Riff-Raff, Meatloaf (again!) as rock 'n' roller Eddie, Little Nell as Columbia, and Patricia Quinn as Magenta. Based on the British stage musical, with lyrics and music by O'Brien. "Let's do the Time Warp again!" (Followed by *Shock Treatment*) ★★★½ $19.99

Rodan

(1957, 70 min, Japan, Inoshiro Honda) This cousin to *Godzilla* is filled with the usual images of crumbling cities, people running and screaming, and out-of-synch dubbing. As such, it's a very entertaining post-war atomic paranoia fest featuring a giant pterodactyl who, after being hatched from an egg, dines on giant bugs in a mine, causing amazing amounts of destruction and more. ★★★ $9.99

Rodrigo D: No Future

(1990, 93 min, Colombia, Victor Gaviria) The first Colombian film to be selected for competition at the Cannes Film Festival is a shocking and timely portrayal of the youths who populate the rough and tumble slums of Medellin, Colombia — the murder capital of the world. (Spanish with English subtitles) ★★★ $79.99

Roe vs. Wade

(1989, 100 min, US, Gregory Hoblit) Two moving performances by Holly Hunter and Amy Madigan highlight this absorbing made-for-TV drama about the controversial Supreme Court battle concerning a woman's right to abortion, and the events which led to the historic decision. ★★★ $14.99

Roger & Me

(1989, 90 min, US, Michael Moore) Moore's hilarious "documentary" about the relationship between General Motors and the people of his hometown, Flint, Michigan, and the subsequent slow death of that town, is a highly personal statement of frustration in the face of the unyielding greed of America's megacorporations. The theme which ties the film together is Moore's relentless effort to get an interview with Roger Smith, the chairman of G.M. Along the way he settles for the townsfolk, assorted "native" celebrities like Bob Eubanks and other players in the plant closing game, many of whom provide mockeries of themselves or the situation in general. The film is rounded by Moore's narration, which he delivers in an unerring deadpan and adds all the more comic spice to the brew. ★★★★ $14.99

Rollerball

(1975, 123 min, US, Norman Jewison) Slick though violent and empty-headed sci-fi adventure, set in the 21st century, where man has eliminated crime, pollution and other social ills. Now, a violent form of entertainment is sought by the masses — a deadly physical contact sport called Rollerball. James Caan stars as a battle-scarred veteran, along with Maud Adams, Ralph Richardson and Moses Gunn. ★★ $14.99

Roman Holiday

(1953, 119 min, US, William Wyler) Captivating romantic comedy featuring Audrey Hepburn's magical Oscar-winning starring debut. Hepburn plays a princess

whose unofficial tour of Rome is aided by newsman Gregory Peck, who's after a hot story, but finds romance instead. Hepburn and Peck are simply wonderful together, and Eddie Albert ably supports them as Peck's quick-fingered photographer. ★★★★ $14.99

Roman Scandals

(1933, 92 min, US, Frank Tuttle) One of the unsung heroes of 1930s comedy, Eddie Cantor is a delight in this funny musical romp about Cantor finding himself back in Roman times. Busby Berkeley choreographed the dance sequences. ★★★ $19.99

The Roman Spring of Mrs. Stone

(1961, 104 min, US, Jose Quintero) Vivien Leigh is Karen Stone, a middle-aged widowed actress who retires and settles in Rome to live in peace and solitude. Through a vulgar procuress (Lotte Lenya, in a terrific performance), Mrs. Stone meets a swarthy young stud, Paolo (Warren Beatty). Before long, Mrs. Stone succumbs to the suave gigolo's chicanery, and she soon finds herself losing both her money and her self-respect. Beatty's accent may cause a chuckle or two, but the film, based on a Tennessee Williams novella, does come off, thanks to Leigh's tender portrayal. ★★★ $14.99

Romance

(1930, 76 min, US, Clarence Brown) Greta Garbo's second talkie is a stagey but compelling romantic melodrama with the diva as an opera star involved in an affair with young clergyman Gavin Gordon. Lewis Stone is particularly good as Gordon's best friend, who also becomes involved with Garbo. ★★½ $19.99

Romance of Book and Sword

(1987, 181 min, Hong Kong, Ann Hui) A gorgeous two-part historical epic, based on a popular novel by Jin Yun, that is set in 15th-century China and features the battles between Manchu Emperor Qianlong and a group of warriors dedicated to overthrowing his dynasty and replacing it with Chinese leaders. Filmed in exotic locales throughout China, this rousing action feature is also an interesting allegory to Hong Kong's present political situation. (Cantonese with English subtitles) ★★★ $39.99

Romance with a Double Bass

(1974, 40 min, GB, Robert Young) This hilarious mini-film stars John Cleese as a bass player scheduled to play in an orchestra at a Royal wedding. Arriving early, he takes a quick skinny-dip in the pool only to find that the Princess (Connie Booth) has done the same. From this improbable beginning, adventure and romance bloom. ★★★ $19.99

Romancing the Stone

(1984, 106 min, US, Robert Zemeckis) Frenetic comic adventure starring Kathleen Turner as a romance novelist whose fantasies come true when she travels to South America to rescue her kidnapped sister and meets a daring adventurer (Michael Douglas). Though Turner and Douglas play well off each other (inspiring a sequel and *The War of the Roses*), Turner's wonderfully comic turn is the core of this entertaining comedy. ★★★ $14.99

Romantic Comedy

(1983, 103 min, US, Arthur Hiller) Stilted adaptation of Bernard Slade's play about two playwriting partners who share successes, flops and repressed love. Dudley Moore and Mary Steenburgen do their best to carry it off, but in all, marginally romantic and not all that funny. ★★ $9.99

The Romantic Englishwoman

(1975, 115 min, GB, Joseph Losey) Michael Caine and Glenda Jackson star as a novelist and his wife who invite Helmut Berger into

Eddie Cantor (r.) in *Roman Scandals*

their home with the hopes that he will both share their bed and help Caine with his new novel. This elegant and underrated comedy-drama candidly explores many of our modern neuroses. Written by Tom Stoppard and Thomas Wiseman. ★★★½

Romeo and Juliet

(1954, 138 min, GB, Renato Castellani) This popular and beautifully filmed version of Shakespeare's tragic tale of star-crossed lovers unfortunately falls victim to miscasting in the lead roles. Laurence Harvey and Susan Shentall, like the 1936 pairing of Leslie Howard and Norma Shearer, are too old for their parts. Shakespeare's characters were teenagers, and were not effectively portrayed that way until the 1968 version. Nevertheless, Harvey and Shentall both give admirable performances. The film features sumptuous cinematography, and magically re-creates the atmosphere of Renaissance Verona. ★★★½ $19.99

Romeo and Juliet

(1968, 152 min, GB, Franco Zeffirelli) With an eye for romantic detail that is almost unsurpassed in the film industry, Franco Zeffirelli brings Shakespeare's immortal masterpiece to the screen with a flourish. Olivia Hussey and Leonard Whiting star as the ill-fated lovers and Milo O'Shea brings his mature wisdom to this visually ravishing production. Also starring Michael York as Tybalt. (Available letterboxed and pan & scan) ★★★★ $19.99

Romeo and Juliet

Starring Leonardo DiCaprio and Claire Danes
See: William Shakespeare's Romeo and Juliet

Romeo Is Bleeding

(1994, 110 min, US, Peter Medak) Romeo Is Bleeding has all the right elements: a nifty script about greed, corruption and sex; a grimy film noir feel that's tinged with a hallucinatory edge; a haunting jazz soundtrack; and a great cast that includes the always intriguing Gary Oldman as a crooked cop on the take from the mob, Annabella Sciorra as his good wife and Lena Olin as a devil-in-disguise cop killer. Unfortunately, the film lacks an overall cohesiveness as the disparate elements go on their merry way without ever really connecting to each other. Ultimately, Romeo leaves one entertained but unsatisfied. ★★★ $14.99

La Ronde

(1950, 97 min, France, Max Ophüls) Ophüls directed Anton Walbrook, Simone Signoret and Simone Simon among a stellar group of French actors in this witty, elaborate satire on sexual behavior. Ten sketches are presented, in which an interconnecting group of lovers change partners until their liaisons come full circle. This bemused view of affairs of the heart also features Danielle Darrieux and Jean-Louis Barrault. (French with English subtitles) ★★★½ $29.99

The Roof

(1956, 98 min, Italy, Vittorio De Sica) De Sica's realistic and gentle drama follows a poverty-striken young couple who must overcome red tape in trying to find a home and happiness in post-war Rome. (Italian with English subtitles) ★★★

The Rookie

(1990, 121 min, US, Clint Eastwood) A formulaic thriller directed by and starring Eastwood about a hardened veteran of the L.A.P.D. who is assigned a rookie partner. Following all of the guidelines for the good cop/bad cop buddy movie, The Rookie riddles the screen with bullets, car chases and blazing pyrotechnics. The film enjoys its share of wry, self-effacing humor and the pace is brisk. ★★½ $14.99

Room at the Top

(1959, 115 min, GB, Jack Clayton) This effervescent story about a low-born Brit's ruthless drive to reach the top of the ladder in a northern industrial town is powered by a gutsy performance by Laurence Harvey. Simone Signoret (who won an Oscar) co-stars as an unhappily married French woman who falls desperately in love with the determined young man. Considered a far-reaching, seminal work, the use of and attitude towards sex and language paved the way for the ultra-realistic "kitchen sink" school of British drama. ★★★★

Room Service

(1938, 78 min, US, William A. Seiter) Groucho Marx is a struggling producer with a potential hit show on his hands — all he needs is money. Which wouldn't hurt his hotel bill, either. Chico and Harpo add their usual dazzle, and Lucille Ball and Ann Miller are the love interests. The film is interesting in that, in addition to the trademark absurdist humor, there are definite indications of Groucho's acting potential, which was never fully utilized by Hollywood. Script by Morrie Ryskind. ★★★ $19.99

A Room with a View

(1985, 115 min, GB, James Ivory) Forster's classic novel of the sexual awakening of a young woman amidst the emotional repression of Victorian England is brilliantly captured in this comedy of manners. During a trip to Florence, the girl's simmering sensuality is exposed when she meets and falls in love with a free-spirited and handsome young man. The struggle between this love and the expectations of a "proper society" features outstanding performances by Helena Bonham Carter, Maggie Smith, Denholm Elliott, Daniel Day-Lewis and Julian Sands. ★★★★ $14.99

The Roommate

(1984, 96 min, US, Nell Cox) A collegiate "Odd Couple," as an ultraconservative (Lance Guest) is paired with a mantra-chanting yogist (Barry Miller) at Northwestern University in 1952. This funny, warm drama is based on a story by John Updike. ★★★ $69.99

Roommates

(1995, 109 min, US, Peter Yates) A sweet, old-fashioned though uneven examination of a grandfather and grandson's enduring relationship, Roommates gives Peter Falk one of the best film roles of his career. He plays Rocky, who at 75 years of age raises his young grandson Michael after the youth loses his parents. Their years together are spent happily until Michael, now an adult (played by D.B. Sweeney), is on his own. The two reunite when Rocky is evicted and moves in with his grandson. Much of the comedy stems from their

Felix and Oscar shenanigans, and from Rocky's jealousy of Michael's new relationship (the lovely Julianne Moore). But the film also wallows in its unpleasantness, and after a charming first half the story loses its good humor for a succession of tragedies which are clumsily handled. ★★½ $19.99

Rope

(1948, 80 min, US, Alfred Hitchcock) The Master of Suspense's audacious experimentation with real time and ten-minute takes gives this murder-thriller both a kinetic and claustrophobic atmosphere. Suggested by the Leopold-Loeb case, the story concerns two homosexuals (played by Farley Granger and John Dall) who murder an old schoolmate for the thrill of it, stuff his corpse in an old chest, and then proceed to hold a party around the makeshift casket with attendees including the victim's father and fiancée. The film's screenplay was written by Arthur Laurents (West Side Story, The Way We Were). (The Leopold-Loeb story has also been told in Compulsion and Swoon.) ★★★½ $14.99

Rorret

(1987, 105 min, Italy, Fulvio Wetzl) Inspired by the films of Alfred Hitchcock, this creepy thriller centers on a reclusive and voyeuristic owner of a cinema specializing in horror films who goes on a killing rampage whenever he gets "excited" by terror. The psychopathically deranged man's modus operandi is to meet women who share his horror interests and then kill them in theatrically filmic fashion. Although needlessly talky, the film has moments of tension and intrigue with the highlight being the film-within-a-film homages (re-creations) to famous horror sequences from Peeping Tom, Strangers on a Train, Psycho and Dial M for Murder. (Italian with English subtitles) ★★ $29.99

La Rosa Blanca

(1960, 100 min, Mexico, Roberto Gavaldon) Based on the controversial novel by B. Traven ("Treasure of the Sierra Madre," "Macario"), this compelling and impassioned film tells the story of the armed struggle that ensues between the land-thirsty Condor Oil Company and Don Jacinto, owner of the hacienda "La Rosa Blanca," an oil-rich land the company wants to expropriate. Contrasting the peasant's spiritualism and reverence for the land with the malfeasance and greed of the multinational, the film obviously takes sides but is very good drama nonetheless. (Spanish with English subtitles) ★★★

Rosa Luxemburg

(1986, 122 min, West Germany, Margarethe von Trotta) Von Trotta has created a mesmerizing epic on the personal and political life of Rosa Luxemburg, one of the most dynamic and passionate leaders of the socialist democracy in Germany. Barbara Sukowa gives a truly amazing performance as "Red Rosa," whose life is chronicled from her emergence in the Social Democratic Party to her loss of faith after WWI. Sukowa brings to life the role of the charismatic leader of the peace movement which inspired many in turn. A wonderfully produced portrait, the film has a starkness befitting a war picture which is juxtaposed with a realism rare to what are usually overblown period pieces. (German with English subtitles) ★★★★ $29.99

Rosalie Goes Shopping

(1990, 94 min, US, Percy Adlon) Director Adlon has teamed once again with hefty star Marianne Sagebrecht (*Sugarbaby*) to produce this pleasant but disappointingly thin satire on America's obsession with consumerism. Determined to provide everything "money" can buy for her children and loving husband (Brad Davis), Rosalie, our devoted and increasingly frenetic housewife, soon finds herself juggling 37 credit cards, several mortgage payments and writing out worthless checks. With the wolf soon baying at her comfortable suburban door, our intrepid consumer devises more and more ingenious ways, including computers and electronic mail, to stay a few steps ahead in her great pursuit of the American Dream. ★★

The Rosary Murders

(1987, 105 min, US, Fred Walton) Slow but interesting tale of a parish priest (Donald Sutherland) who hears the confession of a serial killer preying on priests and nuns, and finds himself torn between his sacred vows and the pursuit of justice. Charles Durning and Belinda Bauer co-star. ★★

The Rose

(1979, 134 min, US, Mark Rydell) Bette Midler made an impressive film debut as a hard-drinking, fast-living rock chanteuse – suggested by the life of Janis Joplin – struggling against the pressures of success. Alan Bates is her mean-spirited manager and Frederic Forrest is her on-again, off-again lover. The film's musical numbers contain a raw energy thanks to the conviction of the Divine Miss M, and her earthy performance avoids the usual industry clichés. ★★★ $9.99

The Rose Garden

(1989, 152 min, US/West Germany, Fons Rademakers) This gripping drama, which exposes the latent anti-Semitism in modern-day Germany, stars Liv Ullmann as a tenacious lawyer who is hired to defend a man (Maximilian Schell) accused of committing a seemingly unprovoked attack on an elderly businessman at the Berlin airport. As the drama unfolds, Ullmann uncovers the fact that the old man was a commandant of a Nazi concentration camp and presided over the death of many Jews and children. A serious, compassionate psychological drama that features fine performances by both Ullmann and Schell as well as an oddly cast Peter Fonda. From the director of the Oscar-winning film *The Assault*. (Filmed in English) ★★★ $89.99

The Rose Tattoo

(1955, 117 min, US, Daniel Mann) Anna Magnani gives an extraordinary performance in this riveting adaptation of Tennessee Williams' play as a widow, still obsessed with the memory of her late husband, who begins an affair with trucker Burt Lancaster. Magnani won the Oscar for her portrayal, and is

matched all the way by Lancaster. Marisa Pavan also stars. ★★★½ $19.99

Roseland

(1977, 103 min, US, James Ivory) Set in the famed New York dance hall, *Roseland* is a collection of three captivating short character vignettes studying the tattered lives of the people who gravitate to the club. Exceptional performances come from Christopher Walken, Joan Copeland, Lilia Skala and Helen Gallagher. ★★★

Rosemary's Baby

(1968, 136 min, US, Roman Polanski) Classic chiller from Polanski with newlyweds Mia Farrow and John Cassavetes unwittingly befriending devil worshippers Ruth Gordon and Sidney Blackmer in modern-day New York. Gordon won an Oscar for her performance, and the film contains many frightening moments. ★★★★ $14.99

Rosencrantz and Guildenstern Are Dead

(1991, 119 min, GB, Tom Stoppard) Adapting and directing his own play for the screen might have been too much for the talented Stoppard, but although the film is a bit stagebound, it still proves to be an exhilarating mental exercise with Stoppard toying with the English language in this witty, intellectual comedy. The story takes the ingenious ploy of changing the focus of "Hamlet" from the brooding Dane to two minor flunkies, Rosencrantz and Guildenstern. Tim Roth and Gary Oldman are scintillating as the lost and, at times, pathetic duo who are forced by circumstances to pontificate on their seemingly predetermined fate, the overall meaning of their existence as well as other existential points; all the while, playing their roles as the unwitting pawns of the king. Though he sometimes can be annoying in certain film roles, Richard Dreyfuss is a delight here as the Player King. All told – an audacious, verbally duelling metaphysical comedy. ★★★½ $19.99

Rosewood

(1997, 139 min, US, John Singleton) The story of a real-life tragedy is told with sledgehammer subtlety by director Singleton, who does history a disservice by sacrificing all ambiguity, character development and moral conflict for the sake of a shallow, easy political statement. Ving Rhames stars as an enigmatic WWI veteran who comes to Rosewood, Florida – a town built and populated almost entirely by black Americans – to buy some land and begin a peaceful life. Instead, a case of mistaken identity brings a mob of angry whites from a neighboring, poorer town to wreak a violent vengeance and retribution on Rosewood. Unfortunately, the film neglects historical drama in favor of crowd-pleasing sentiment and simplicity. Rosewood's citizens are angelic in their purity and goodness, and also completely unrealistic. Don Cheadle's talents are wasted as a musician and piano teacher who spends most of the film in hiding. Rhames does a decent job, but an interesting attempt to make into him a romantic leading man is quickly abandoned in favor of more shouting, crying and screaming. Singleton has taken a

fascinating, important and tragic story and made a terrible, albeit good-looking movie out of it. ★★ $102.99

Roswell — The U.F.O. Cover-Up

(1994, 91 min, US, Jeremy Kagan) In 1947, something crashed in the desert outside Roswell, New Mexico. The official government story called it a weather balloon. Kyle MacLachlan portrays one of the eyewitness military officers who maintained that the crash material was of an unknown substance displaying properties exhibited by no known metal...from *this* planet. An engaging speculative entertainment, *Roswell* opens at a 30-year commemoration of the event, utilizing flashbacks and adopting a quasi-documentary tone in this fictionalized account of an actual occurrence. This HBO production has the production values, attention to detail and quirkiness that have come to be expected of them. Martin Sheen, one of a strong ensemble cast, hovers on the fringes as the requisite Ominous Government Man. ★★½ $14.99

Rouge

(1988, 93 min, Hong Kong, Stanley Kwan) With stunning visuals and a great story, this supernatural love story alternates between the brothels and theatres of an opium-hazed 1930s Hong Kong and the sophisticated, bustling but vapid world of the present-day city. A courtesan, who died in a love-induced suicide, returns to earth years later seeking out her lover after he fails to join her in Heaven. A terrifically stylish movie. (Cantonese with English subtitles) ★★★½ $39.99

Round Midnight

(1986, 130 min, France/US, Bertrand Tavernier) Dexter Gordon gives a painfully touching performance as Dale Turner, a raspy-voiced saxophone player ravaged by drugs and booze, but who nonetheless retains his dignity and possesses the "elegant soul of a poet." Tavernier creates a moody and authentic world of American jazz exiles and the habitués of the smokey Parisian jazz clubs of the '50s. Wonderful music performed by Gordon, Herbie Hancock, Ron Carter, Tony Williams and John McLaughlin. ★★★½ $19.99

The Round Up

(1965, 89 min, Hungary, Miklos Jancso) A Hungarian film masterpiece that paints an unflinching portrait of fear, torture and oppression. Set in the mid-19th century after the establishment of the Austro-Hungarian empire, the camera acts as an unseen observer as several hundred Hungarian peasants, outlaws and herdsmen are rounded up, imprisoned and tortured by the Austrian authorities in an effort to uncover and crush the remaining rebel stronghold. The men are forced to confess and identify other freedom fighters before they themselves are eliminated. A harsh, disturbing chronicle of a demonic police state told with little dialogue and set in a timeless, bleak plain where routine terror reigns. (Letterbox format) (Hungarian with English subtitles) ★★★★ $59.99

Ruby in Paradise

Roustabout

(1964, 100 min, US, John Rich) Elvis Presley joins the carnival, run by none other than Barbara Stanwyck. Look quick for Raquel Welch as a college coed. Though not one of Elvis' best, it's kinda cute in that isn't-Elvis-the-living-end sort of way. Elvis sings "Hard Knocks," "It's a Wonderful World" and "Big Love, Big Heartache." ★★½ $14.99

Rover Dangerfield

(1991, 74 min, US, Jim George & Bob Seeley) Rodney Dangerfield's entry into the world of animation (he wrote the screenplay and co-wrote the songs with Harold Ramis) is surprisingly entertaining and well done. Some jokes will soar over the kids' heads, but they should enjoy the songs and story of the cynical city dog transported to the country, where he finds love and a family. ★★½ $14.99

Roxanne

(1987, 107 min, US, Fred Schepisi) Steve Martin's comic tour de force performance highlights this breathlessly funny updating of "Cyrano de Bergerac." Martin plays a small Northwestern town's fire chief whose elongated nose has kept him from romantic entanglements; that is, until he falls in love with beautiful astronomy student Daryl Hannah. Rick Rossovich is the handsome but vacuous hunk – himself terrified of romantic repartee – who speaks Martin's heartfelt words of love. Shelley Duvall offers wonderful support as Martin's confidant. Martin's "20 insults" is a classic. (Though Michael Douglas won the Oscar that year for *Wall Street*, Martin's performance was by far and away the year's best.) ★★★½ $9.99

Roy Lichtenstein — Portrait of an Artist

(1989, 55 min, US, Chris Hunt) This overview of Roy Lichtenstein's career in art spans his early influences from Picasso and Impressionism to his Pop Art career and experiments with comic book art. The interviews are somewhat insightful, but barely touch on his personal life and how it is reflected in his work. ★★ $39.99

Royal Wedding

(1951, 93 min, US, Stanley Donen) Light-hearted Fred Astaire musical with Fred and Jane Powell as a famous brother-and-sister act who travel to England to perform their show, coinciding with the marriage of Queen Elizabeth II. (Fred dances on the ceiling in this one.) ★★½ $19.99

Rubin and Ed

(1991, 90 min, US, Trent Harris) Ed (Howard Hesseman), a middle-aged, leisure-suited failure at life, must bring a new recruit to his highly charged motivational real estate seminar or face expulsion and the loss of promised riches, self-esteem and inner peace. His search leads him to Rubin (Crispin Glover), an oddly dressed malcontent under the thumb of an overbearing mom who agrees to go to the seminar if Ed will help him bury his dead cat. Hesseman and Glover bounce off each other with just the right amount of manic energy to make this delightfully quirky road-trip saga (a post-Reagan era exploration of the latest wrinkle in the American Dream) an audacious romp. ★★★ $89.99

Ruby

(1977, 84 min, US, Curtis Harrington) After her success in *Carrie*, Piper Laurie encored with another horror opus, though with considerably less results. The spirit of a murdered 1930s gangster returns to haunt the descendants of those responsible. A few thrills in this derivative chiller. ★★

Ruby

(1992, 100 min, US, John Mackenzie) Danny Aeillo stars as Jack Ruby, the Dallas nightclub owner who shot Lee Harvey Oswald, in this intriguing underworld look at the J.F.K. assassination. Following on the heels of Oliver Stone's *JFK*, *Ruby* details the events leading up to that fateful day in Dallas from Ruby's point of view, all the while portraying him as a small-time gangster who got in over his head. Sherilyn Fenn co-stars as a fictional floozy who wins over Ruby's heart. ★★½ $14.99

Ruby in Paradise

(1993, 115 min, US, Victor Nunez) Writer-director Nunez presents the simple story of Ruby, a young woman who flees a desolate life in rural Tennessee and settles on the Gulf Coast of Florida. Ashley Judd is a revelation as Ruby, who explores who she is while happily working in a tacky seaside gift shop. Her graceful performance is one of subtlety and nuance which, combined with Nunez' gentle direction, elevates what could have been a run-of-the-mill outing. Despite some minor screenplay contrivances, this is the kind of work that gives independent filmmaking its good name. ★★★½ $14.99

Rude

(1995, 90 min, Canada, Clement Virgo) This hard-hitting independent film delves beneath the surface of problem-plagued inner city life to explore the personal lives of those who are forced to live there. Filmed near the Toronto housing project where the Jamaican-born director grew up, Virgo's feature film debut tells three stories all set on an Easter Sunday

and all dealing with personal redemption and the struggle to survive and love in a tough world. The first is about an older black man and former drug dealer attempting to adjust to life after release from prison. The second looks at the loneliness of a young woman who, abandoned by her boyfriend, contemplates an abortion as she watches videos of her life in happier times. The third tale follows a handsome young boxer who must face the truth about himself and his own sexuality after participating in a gay-bashing. ★★★ $92.99

Rude Awakening

(1989, 100 min, US, Aaron Russo & David Greenwalt) Two hippies in hiding since the 1960s reemerge and find their old friends have become materialistic yuppies. A good premise isn't fully realized in this only occasionally funny comedy. With Eric Roberts, Cheech Marin, Julie Hagerty, Robert Carradine, Buck Henry, Louise Lasser and Cindy Williams. ★★ $14.99

Rude Boy

(1980, 120 min, GB, Jack Hazan & David Mingay) Pulsating with the trash-and-burn energy of late '70s London, this gritty punk-rock drama follows the saga of a rebelious young teen who's hired as a roadie for The Clash. Filmed in a documentary style, the film features live footage of some of the band's early concerts. Songs include "London's Burning," "White Riot," "The Prisoner" and "All the Young Freaks." ★★½

Rudy

(1993, 112 min, US, David Anspaugh) From the director of *Hoosiers* comes this likable *Knute Rockne* for the '90s. Nearly pouring on the sentiment as much as its 1940s counterpart, the film stars Sean Astin as Rudy, a mill worker who has dreamed his whole life of entering Notre Dame and playing for their football team. This based-on-fact story follows his attempts to realize both dreams, despite being short in stature and dyslexic. Though Astin's Rudy is almost to the point of annoying with his constant chatter of his beloved school, it's to the actor's credit he eventually wins you over by the end credits. Robert Prosky, Charles S. Dutton and Ned Beatty are very effective in supporting roles. ★★½ $9.99

Rudyard Kipling's The Jungle Book

(1994, 108 min, US, Stephen Sommers) A smashing live-action adaptation of Rudyard Kipling's classic tale, this Disney-produced adventure yarn is not only the most entertaining version of the story to date, but is also the best non-animated film released by Buena Vista in many a year. A loin-clothed and extremely fit Jason Scott Lee portrays Mowgli, the Indian boy who becomes lost in the jungle and is raised by animals. His carefree existence is shattered when he meets the humans he once knew as a child. These include Sam Neill as a colonel, John Cleese as a doctor, sinister soldier Cary Elwes and a lovely Lena Headey as Mowgli's grown-up childhood sweetheart. Director Sommers blissfully mixes Indian lore and Indiana Jones-type antics, all set against beautifully designed backgrounds of tropics, English pageantry and lost treasure. A high-flying adventure both smart and thrilling. ★★★½ $22.99

Ruggles of Red Gap

(1935, 92 min, US, Leo McCarey) Charles Laughton is priceless in this absolutely delightful comedy. He plays a proper English butler who heads to the American West to work for an unconventional family. Charlie Ruggles and Mary Boland offer terrific support as his new employers. Remade with Bob Hope and Lucille Ball as *Fancy Pants*. ★★★★ $14.99

Rugrats: Tales from the Crib

(1993, 40 min, US) Two very young friends, Tommy and Chuckie, brave a series of adventures together. Another excellent series from Nickelodeon, this episode finds the dynamic duo setting their sea monkeys free in the ocean; attempting exploratory surgery to see if Tommy's father is a robot; and getting trapped in a toy store, which turns out to be more of a nightmare than a dream come true. Also in this series: *Rugrats: A Baby's Gotta Do What a Baby's Gotta Do*. ★★★ $9.99

Rules of the Game

(1939, 110 min, France, Jean Renoir) Renoir's grand comedy of manners is a sublime study of social codes and crumbling morals. Within the confines of a lavish country estate, the intricate lives of the aristocracy and their servants undergo a dramatic unravelling. A marvel of ensemble acting and a perennial contender as one of the greatest films of all time. (French with English subtitles) ★★★★ $29.99

The Ruling Class

(1971, 139 min, GB, Peter Medak) Peter O'Toole gives a comically possessed performance as Jack, the 14th Earl of Guerney, who insists he's Jesus Christ. This irreverent and boisterous black comedy overflows with madness as people burst into song and assume whacked-out characters at the drop of a hat. Co-starring Alastair Sim as a befuddled bish-

op and Arthur Lowe as a bolshevik butler. ★★★½ $39.99

Rumble Fish

(1983, 94 min, US, Francis Coppola) Coppola's film adaptation of S.E. Hinton's novel was a financial and critical failure. Unlike his version of *The Outsiders*, this film lacks Coppola's usual glossiness. Mickey Rourke stars as "The Motorcycle Boy," who returns to his home town to try to stop his brother (Matt Dillon) from following in his legendary, wandering footsteps. This is a film which viewers will find either a pretentious bore or a rewarding film experience. (We found it the former.) Shot in black and white. ★½ $14.99

Rumble in the Bronx

(1994, 90 min, Hong Kong, Stanley Tong) International martial arts/comedy megastar Jackie Chan's third attempt to break into the U.S. film market proves to be the charm. A story-light, action-heavy, redubbed romp through Vancouver (doubling for New York), *Rumble in the Bronx* blows away Chan's two previous American-produced films (*The Big Brawl*, *The Protector*), but falls short of his best Hong Kong works. Chan plays Keung, who, while visiting his uncle in New York, runs afoul of a local multiethnic biker gang, who beat him up and trash his uncle's store. After making amends with the gang leader's girlfriend (Francoise Yip), both Chan and the gang must bury the hatchet in the face of a bigger threat: a group of homicidal mobsters searching for a bag of stolen diamonds. The bare-bones plot aspires only to be entertaining, and the film is just that; the martial arts and comedy scenes more than make up for any other deficiencies. As the amazing action scenes prove, Chan is the real thing; he's a charismatic superstar who can do his own stunts, perform successful physical comedy, and kick more butt than Seagal, Van Damme and Stallone combined. (Available letterboxed and pan & scan) ★★★ $19.99

A Rumor of War

(1980, 106 min, US, Richard T. Heffron) Brad Davis heads a terrific cast — which includes Keith Carradine, Michael O'Keefe and Brian Dennehy — in this outstanding made-for-TV Vietnam War drama. In a compelling and rich performance, Davis plays a newly arrived G.I. whose — like that of Tom Cruise in *Born on the Fourth of July* some nine years later — unblinking support of the war gives way to self-doubt and tragedy. ★★★½ $14.99

The Run of the Country

(1995, 116 min, Ireland, Peter Yates) This charming coming-of-age tale is set in the breathtaking Irish countryside, populated with believable characters and describing that tenuous time of life when children must separate from home before they can find a true connection with it. Matt Keeslar is authentic in his description of Danny, the bereaved young man whose recent loss of his mother is the traumatic catalyst to monumental changes in his life. Albert Finney is expectedly captivating as the domineering father whose own loss makes him even less receptive to his son's state of mind. Danny embarks on a road trip with an appropriately adventurous friend (Anthony Brophy), a trip of abandon and self-discovery which is enhanced by their meeting Annagh (Victoria Smurfit), whose beauty and joy of life are revelatory — she is Danny's first love. A touching story of loss and reconciliation with the wit to avoid the maudlin and the warmth to heal the heart. ★★★ $98.39

Runaway

(1984, 100 min, US, Michael Crichton) Futuristic thriller starring Tom Selleck as a bounty hunter tracking down defective, murderous robots. Crichton's story is a miss on practically all levels. Also starring Gene Simmons (of KISS), Kirstie Alley and Cynthia Rhodes. ★★ $9.99

Runaway Train

(1985, 107 min, US, Andrei Konchalovsky) High-voltage action film, based on a screenplay by Akira Kurosawa, with Jon Voight and Eric Roberts as two escaped prisoners who become trapped on a runaway train in the frozen wasteland of the Northwest. Terrific performances by Voight and Roberts (both received Oscar nominations — unusual for an action film), and Rebecca DeMornay and Kenneth McMillan also star. ★★★½ $14.99

The Runestone

(1991, 105 min, US, Williard Caroll) Why is it that the scientific geniuses in movies never recognize a potentially devastating circumstance as quickly as their less-intelligent observers do? Peter Riegert earns the dunce cap as an archaeologist whose discovery of an ancient runestone unleashes a blood-thirsty fur coat — er... wolfbeast — that only an animal rights activist could love. William Hickey, Joan Severance and Alexander Gudunov pay the rent with this one. ★ $14.99

The Runner Stumbles

(1979, 109 min, US, Stanley Kramer) In a small Washington mining town during the 1920s, a priest (Dick Van Dyke) is accused of

The Ruling Class

murdering a young nun. Considering the volatile subject matter, this is pretty tame stuff. Co-starring Kathleen Quinlan, Maureen Stapleton, Beau Bridges and Ray Bolger. ★★

The Running Man

(1987, 100 min, US, Paul Michael Glaser) Futuristic actioner with Arnold Schwarzenegger as a condemned prisoner whose one chance of hope lies in a torturous and deadly televised game where contestants are pitted against brutal opponents and impossible obstacles. Richard Dawson is well-cast as the game show host. ★★½ $14.99

Running Mates

(1992, 85 min, US, Michael Lindsay-Hogg) From the director of *Object of Beauty* comes this bittersweet comedy about love and loyalty in the whirlwind of a political campaign. The exceptionally photogenic Ed Harris stars as Hugh Hathaway, the Senator stud bucking for a Presidential nomination. Diane Keaton is Aggie Shaw, a charmingly kooky author who wins his heart (sound familiar?). However, the spin doctors aren't sure if Aggie is First Lady material, what with her outspoken demeanor and questionable past. Winning performances by both Harris and Keaton makes this love-conquers-all story a real delight. ★★★ $19.99

Running on Empty

(1988, 116 min, US, Sidney Lumet) Christine Lahti, Judd Hirsch and River Phoenix head an exceptional cast in this powerful and perceptive drama about a family's struggle to stay together. Lahti and Hirsch portray former '60s radicals wanted by the FBI who have been living underground for two decades. Borrowing the names of the deceased and able to move their family at a moment's notice, they must face the extra burden of separation when their eldest son, a gifted musician, applies for college – which would bring the boy into the open and guarantee his not seeing his parents again. A tour de force from all involved. ★★★★ $14.99

Running Scared

(1986, 106 min, US, Peter Hyams) Gregory Hines and Billy Crystal work well together in this effective police thriller as two streetwise undercover Chicago cops on the trail of a drug kingpin. The film is highlighted by funny dialogue and an exciting (if improbable) chase scene on the elevated line. ★★½ $14.99

Running Wild

(1928, 68 min, US, Eddie Cline) Even in this hilarious silent film, you can hear every word W.C. Fields is muttering under his breath. Once again sporting that sleazy little dab of a mustache that he seemed to favor in his silent films, Fields is a mere milquetoast of a man, emboldened by a chance encounter with a hypnotist. ★★★½ $29.99

Rush

(1991, 120 min, US, Lili Fini Zanuck) A dark, intense look at undercover cops in 1970s Texas, *Rush* has an unrelentingly grim outlook, which, though obstensibly about agents becoming lost in another world, comes off more as a 1980s "just-say-no" parable. In another long line of stand-out performances, Jennifer Jason Leigh stars as a novice police officer who is teamed with brooding Jason Patric to snare alleged drug kingpin Gregg Allman. As the two officers introduce themselves to the denizens of the underworld, they slowly become what they're hunting. It's a point, though well made, which would have been used to better dramatic effect if not for the blatant moralizing. Nevertheless, first-time director Zanuck (producer of *Driving Miss Daisy*) has created a sometimes devastating portrait of life on the edge. Allman doesn't say much but is an ominous presence, and young Max Perlich (so good in *Drugstore Cowboy*) is well cast as a dealer who's out of his league. ★★½ $9.99

The Russia House

(1990, 123 min, US, Fred Schepisi) An intriguing espionage thriller, based on John Le Carre's novel. Sean Connery plays a down-on-his-heels London publisher who is unwittingly thrust into political intrigue when a top secret Russian manuscript is sent to him. At the insistence of the British Secret Service, Connery travels to Moscow to uncover the story and its writer. Michelle Pfeiffer, complete with accent, ably plays the Russian liaison with whom the reluctant spy falls in love. As a spy story, *The Russia House* is at its best; but the romantic angle between Connery and Pfeiffer, though handsome, is not always believable. Great Russian locations enhance the atmosphere of this *glasnost* thriller. ★★½ $9.99

The Russians Are Coming, the Russians Are Coming!

(1966, 135 min, US, Norman Jewison) Hysteria breaks out in a small New England coastal town when a Russian submarine runs aground on their beach. Some hilarious moments from an inspired cast, including Oscar nominee Alan Arkin as a Russian sailor and Jonathan Winters as a gun-toting local. Also with Carl Reiner, Eva Marie Saint and Brian Keith. ★★★½ $19.99

Ruthless People

(1986, 93 min, US, Jim Abrahams, David Zucker & Jerry Zucker) Larceny, infidelity and murder among California's nouveau riche form the core of this hilarious comedy. Danny DeVito plays an unfaithful husband who plots to kill his overbearing wife, Bette Midler, who, fortunately for him, has been kidnapped by a not-so-ruthless couple whom DeVito swindled. Judge Reinhold and Helen Slater are the hapless couple. A hip, modern retelling of O'Henry's celebrated short story, "The Ransom of Red Chief." ★★★½ $9.99

The Rutles — All You Need Is Cash

(1978, 70 min, GB, Eric Idle & Gary Weis) Years before *This Is Spinal Tap*, Eric Idle of Monty Python fame concocted this "mockumentary" on the English rock group The Rutles. With Neil Innes (of the cult group The Bonzo Dog Band) providing the group's superb repertoire, this elaborate and playful satire of The Beatles is a must-see for Fab Four fans. With cameos by Mick Jagger and Paul Simon, along with original members of the Not Ready for Prime Time Players. ★★★ $14.99

Ryan's Daughter

(1970, 176 min, GB, David Lean) This unabashedly sentimental, wildly cinematic story was filmed in Northern Ireland and features Sarah Miles as a young girl who marries a simple, plodding schoolteacher (Robert Mitchum) only to have an affair with a British soldier (Christopher Jones). As directed by Lean, the film is brisk and stylish, but the simplicity of the story doesn't support the elephantine production values that Lean heaped upon it. M-G-M went out on a limb for $15 million on this extravaganza and was lucky it didn't bomb. (Available letterboxed and pan & scan) ★★★ $24.99

R

S.F.W.

(1995, 92 min, US, Jefery Levy) Stephen Dorff, in a Brad Pitt-ish turn, and Reese Witherspoon are the two surviving hostages of a 36-day incarceration at a Fun Stop convenience store, held captive by the terrorist group Split Image — a group savvy enough to bring video equipment but with no apparent message. *S.F.W.*, which stands for "So Fucking What," takes a swipe at every element of the machinery that turns a news story into a prime time event: the packaging of TV movies, instant analysis from "Nightline," psychobabble from shrinks, and groupies eager to bask in other people's 15 minutes of fame. While the film could be easily written off as a *Natural Born Killers* clone with B-movie execution, it does manage to juxtapose the horror of hostage taking with the banality of media hype. Uneven and awkward, but strangely satisfying. ★★½ $94.99

S.O.B.

(1981, 121 min, US, Blake Edwards) Edwards' brilliant, scathing indictment of Hollywood and the men and women behind and in front of the cameras. William Holden gives a sterling performance as a jaded director with a predilection for teenaged girls. Also starring Robert Preston as the wise-cracking doc, Julie Andrews as a superstar who bares all, and Robert Mulligan as Edwards' alter ego who discovers exactly what it takes to make a hit. One of the most underrated and misunderstood films of its decade. ★★★½ $9.99

Sabotage

(1936, 76 min, GB, Alfred Hitchcock) Freely adapted from Joseph Conrad's "Secret Agent," this elaborately detailed and disquieting film concerns a kindly movie theater manager who doubles as a dangerous foreign agent. The man's wife (Sylvia Sydney), after her younger brother is killed by a bomb, begins to develop suspicions and then has a little trouble carving the roast that evening. ★★★ $12.99

Sabrina ('54)

Saboteur

(1942, 108 min, US, Alfred Hitchcock) Robert Cummings is charged with the wartime sabotage of a munitions factory and forced into a hurried flight from misguided justice. Racing across the country, he pursues the true culprit, an elusive individual named Fry, and eventually confronts him atop the Statue of Liberty. One of Hitchcock's lesser-known works, this nonetheless is a tense, exciting spy story with many scenes which bear the Master's touch. ★★★½ $14.99

Sabrina

(1954, 113 min, US, Billy Wilder) Charming romantic comedy featuring the impeccable cast of Audrey Hepburn, Humphrey Bogart and William Holden. Holden is a rich playboy smitten with chauffeur's daughter Hepburn; but older brother Bogey steps in to separate the pair and falls in love with her himself. Based on Samuel Taylor's play "Sabrina Fair." Remade in 1995 with Harrison Ford and Julia Ormand. ★★★½ $14.99

Sabrina

(1995, 127 min, US, Sydney Pollack) One of the joys of Billy Wilder's 1954 romantic comedy *Sabrina* is the enchanting performance by Audrey Hepburn as the chauffeur's daughter who becomes involved with her father's employer. (Certainly William Holden and Humphrey Bogart don't hurt, either.) In taking over her role, no one expected Julia Ormand to be another Hepburn. But in Pollack's tranquil remake, sadly, the magic is just not there. However, all is not lost as Harrison Ford, not really known for his light romantic style, gives a choice, even charming portrayal of a likable cad. When the plain-looking Sabrina (Ormand) returns home from Paris looking beautiful, young tycoon David (Greg Kinnear) falls madly in love — which interferes with the business plans of older brother Linus (Ford). To break up the affair, the unemotional Linus courts Sabrina himself, which leads to unpredictable romance. Ormand is lovely, and in certain scenes demonstrates great allure, but she is unable to develop a lasting impression. Kinnear, in his debut, nicely captures David's carefree nature. Not without its own modest charms, *Sabrina* is an appealing though unnecessary remake. ★★½ $14.99

Sacco and Vanzetti

(1971, 120 min, France/Italy, Guiliano Montaldo) Told in pseudo-documentary style, this exposé of the famous 1920 trial of two Italian anarchists who were unjustly accused of crimes is a classic look at the American injustice system and the American penchant for mass political hysteria when it suits its leaders. A realistic and moving account with Joan Baez singing the title song. (Dubbed) ★★★

El Sacerdote (The Priest)

(1977, 100 min, Spain, Eloy de la Iglesia) Set during the repressive Franco regime (which acts as a symbol of the equally repressive Catholic Church), this involving drama follows the tortured life of a 36-year-old priest as he struggles with his vow of celibacy and his increasingly intense obsession with "sins of the flesh." Father Miguel (de la Iglesia regular Simon Andreu) is a conservative priest who blindly follows the restrictions of authority until he becomes troubled with his raging and unspent libido. Vowing to remain chaste, he begins to hallucinate about people having sex (including a priest with another man) which culminates in an act of near-pedophilia. Unable to find solace in either Christ or the arms of a married woman who loves him, the tormented man resorts to a horrible act in an attempt to solve his problems. Similar in tone and theme to 1994's *Priest*, this film stays more focused on the dilemma of a sincere man who must fight the conflicting forces of his religious calling and the calling of physical desire. (Spanish with English subtitles) ★★★ $79.99

The Sacrifice

(1986, 145 min, Sweden/USSR, Andrei Tarkovsky) Alexander's family is gathered to celebrate his 70th birthday. A quiet tension fills the air. When an uneasy silence is shattered by an emergency broadcast which reports an impending nuclear attack, they begin to fall apart. Alexander then learns of a way the disaster can be prevented... but is the world worth saving? In this, his final film, Tarkovsky forms a powerful vision of the future which will haunt the memory. Winner of the 1986 Cannes Film Festival Special Jury Prize. (Swedish with English subtitle) ★★★½

Sadie McKee

(1934, 90 min, US, Clarence Brown) Joan Crawford is in good form in this three-hanky weeper as a maid involved, at various times, with millionaire Edward Arnold, ne'er-do-well Gene Raymond and employer Franchot Tone. ★★★ $19.99

Sadie Thompson

(1928, 97 min, US, Raoul Walsh) W. Somerset Maugham's "Rain" gets a good workout as Gloria Swanson plays a whore in Pago Pago who takes up with reformer Lionel Barrymore. Director Walsh has fun on both sides of the camera playing the sailor who really loves her. Seldom seen, until the recent reconstruction of the lost last reel using surviving production stills and frame enlargements. ★★★½ $29.99

Safe

(1995, 121 min, US, Todd Haynes) Restrained but emotionally involving, this harrowing tale of a woman who physically suffers at the hands of "progress" is an accomplished drama that offers great promise for its director, Haynes (*Poison*). The deceptively simple story follows Carol White (the remarkable Julianne Moore), an out-of-touch, Stepford Wife-like Southern California housewife who, despite being buffeted by a wealth of material comforts and a loving husband, finds her body slowly ravaged by allergic reactions to everyday chemicals, fragrances and fumes. This transforms her seemingly protected upper-middle-class existence into a terror of everyday life. Her doctors can not find anything physically wrong with her, so Carol sets off to New Mexico for answers and a cure at a New Age-style spa/convalescence resort. With a bold yet austere visual style, Haynes chillingly explores suburban complacency and existential alienation and its ensuing

Julianne Moore (c.) is plagued by mysterious symptoms in *Safe*

lack of self-worth. Ultimately, *Safe* is anything but and is thought-provoking and quietly disturbing. ★★★½ $19.99

Safe Is Desire

(1993, 60 min, US, Debi Sundahl) Lesbian erotica gets no hotter, nor safer, than in this low-budget sizzler. Dianne and Allie are an interracial couple whose sexual attraction for each other gets a cold slap in the face when the two cannot agree on the need for safe sex. In an effort to win Dianne over to the joys and protections of safe sex, Allie takes her to a lesbian sex club. There a group of highly charged performers, The Safer Sex Sluts, demonstrate the pleasures inherent in dental dams, Saran Wrap, latex, role-playing and protected sex toys. Far from simple dyke porn, the film's graphic sex scenes are never (OK, rarely) gratuitous as it attempts to be both funny and informative in its depiction of lesbian romance coupled with sexual responsibility. ★★★ $39.99

Safe Passage

(1994, 97 min, US, Robert Allan Ackerman) Susan Sarandon received an Oscar nomination for her work in *The Client*; however, her valiant portrayal of a mother awaiting news of her Marine son is far more compelling. Sarandon plays mother to seven sons, one of whom is a soldier stationed in the Middle East. When word comes that his barracks has been bombed, the entire family comes together for the requisite tears and laughter, revelations and recriminations. Though there's nothing overtly original in either the film's plot line or execution, it's the conviction of the ensemble, headed by the radiant Sarandon, which gives *Safe Passage* its emotion. Sam Shepard co-stars as Sarandon's estranged husband, and Sean Astin, Robert Sean Leonard, Nick Stahl and Jason London are siblings. ★★★ $14.99

Saga of the Vagabonds

(1959, 115 min, Japan, Toshio Sugie) This samurai actioner stars Toshiro Mifune as a roving, down-on-his-heels ruffian who hesitantly becomes involved in the political infighting between two princes battling for control of their castle and territory. Sort of a Japanese western, the film features all the ingredients of a grade-B flick: a barroom (read: sakiroom) brawl, the cavalry to the rescue and a band of wild, thrill-seeking cowboys (samurai) who unite and fight the bad guys. Mifune humorously plays it to the hilt, blustering his way through the role of the "scoundrel with a heart." (Japanese with English subtitles) ★★½

Saigon: Year of the Cat

(1983, 106 min, GB, Stephen Frears) An American Embassy official (Frederic Forrest) in Saigon in 1974 begins a relationship with a British bank employee (Judi Dench), despite a feeling of foreboding regarding the progress of the war, and the frustration of his superiors' lack of reception to his views. This Thames Television production, scripted by David Hare, covers the final months before the fall of Saigon in 1975 — the year of the cat. ★★★ $14.99

The Sailor Who Fell from Grace with the Sea

(1976, 104 min, GB, Lewis John Carlino) This striking and erotic drama concerns itself with a group of young schoolboys who commit a ritual murder upon a visiting sailor. Sarah Miles plays a lonely widow who falls in love with the sailor (Kris Kristofferson) before his unfortunate demise. Filled with steamy love scenes (featured in *Playboy* at the time), this unusual and beautifully photographed film is based on a novella by Yukio Mishima. ★★★

The Saint

(1997, 110 min, US, Phillip Noyce) Simon Templar, aka The Saint, has been around for a long time. The hero of over 50 books, a film series in the 1940s, and a popular TV show starring Roger Moore in the 1960s, this guy has seen a lot of action. And while there's a bit of action, as well, in this update starring Val Kilmer as Templar, its formulaic and *Mission: Impossible*-convoluted story (without that film's

hyper-energy) keeps it from ever becoming a truly satisfying espionage adventure. A proficient thief with state-of-the-art gadgetry and an ability for impersonation, Templar is hired to locate and steal the cold-fusion formula of scientist Elisabeth Shue. Natch, he falls for her during the execution of his duties. Kilmer is quite good in his many disguises (though he's less creative with Templar), and Shue seems to be enjoying all the pretty sights of their location shoot in Russia and England. There's a couple of very competent action scenes, and a few laughs along the way, but *The Saint* never gets as flavorful and fun as its predecessors. ★★ $102.99

St. Elmo's Fire

(1985, 110 min, US, Joel Schumacher) Though it wants to be more, this drama of post-college grads struggling in Washington D.C. is nothing more than "The Little Chill." A who's-who cast of 1980s teen celebs is featured, including Emilio Estevez, Rob Lowe, Andrew McCarthy, Demi Moore, Judd Nelson, Ally Sheedy and Mare Winningham. ★★ $9.99

Saint Jack

(1979, 112 min, US, Peter Bogdanovich) An American businessman in Singapore (Ben Gazzara) aims to run the classiest whorehouse in town, but runs afoul of the Chinese mafia. Denholm Elliott and George Lazenby co-star in this well-played tale set against the seedier side of small-time operations. ★★★

St. Martin's Lane

(1938, 85 min, GB, Tim Whelan) Incorporating a Warner Brothers backstage musical with a British class melodrama, this touching and lively rags-to-riches tale is a bittersweet look at ambition and romance. The story follows the rise of a street gamine (Vivien Leigh) who is at first taken under the wing of a mediocre busker (street musician), marvelously played by Charles Laughton. Under his supervision, her natural talent blossoms. She eventually becomes the toast of the town, while in true *A Star Is Born* fashion, her former mentor flounders. Leigh, in a pre-*Gone with the Wind* role, creates a totally sympathetic character who does many unsympathetic things, and in an early role, Rex Harrison gives a nuanced performance as the sophisticated songwriter who spirits her away to fame, fortune, and his penthouse. ★★★ $24.99

The Saint of Fort Washington

(1993, 107 min, US, Tim Hunter) Danny Glover and Matt Dillon star in this poignant if familiar character study examining the friendship between two homeless men. Dillon plays a schizophrenic photographer newly homeless. At the prison-like shelter Fort Washington, he is befriended by Vietnam vet Glover, who takes him under his wing. With images of *Scarecrow* and *Midnight Cowboy* hovering overhead, the two confront an uncaring, suspicious and hostile society in their battle to survive on the streets. Both actors give strong performances, and the film succeeds in putting a face to the faceless army of the homeless; though its important message of "they're not criminals" is at times heavy-handed. ★★★ $19.99

Salaam Bombay!

(1988, 114 min, India/France, Mira Nair) A spectacular directorial debut for 31-year-old Nair, this shockingly graphic yet compassionate tale chronicles the wretched but ever resourceful life of 10-year-old Krishna, a boy thrown out from his house and forced to fend for himself. Initially scared and alienated, Krishna soon befriends the prostitutes, drug dealers and fellow street urchins of the red-light district and eventually becomes part of their milieu of exploitation, squalor and survival. Vividly drawn, using many non-professional actors and filming on the teeming streets of Bombay, this revelation avoids being preachy or heavy-handed in telling its realistic tale. (Hindi with English subtitles) ★★★

Salem's Lot: The Miniseries

(1979, 184 min, US, Tobe Hooper) Though still missing 16 minutes from the original miniseries telecast, this restored adaptation of the Stephen King novel easily qualifies as one of the scariest horror movies ever made for television. David Soul stars as a successful novelist who evidently never read Tom Wolfe's most famous admonition, "You can't go home again," and does just that. Unfortunately, his arrival coincides with that of a worldly antique dealer (James Mason in a superbly sinister performance) who has earmarked the inhabitants of Soul's small New England hometown as "fang fodder" – vampires. Also with Bonnie Bedelia, Lew Ayres, Lance Kerwin, and Reggie Nalder as the most hair-raising vampire this side of *Nosferatu*. Also available in the more violent 112-minute "European" version. ★★★½ $24.99

Salem's Lot: The Movie

(1979, 112 min, US, Tobe Hooper) First-rate made-for-TV adaptation of Stephen King's novel about a small New England town which is home to scores of vampires. David Soul is the hometown boy who returns after many years absence to uncover the dastardly doings. This chiller produces many a goose-bump, and features a good cast including James Mason, Bonnie Bedelia, Lance Kerwin, Lew Ayres, Ed Flanders and Reggie Nalder. (This is an edited version from the original 200-minute miniseries.) ★★★ $14.99

Sallah

(1963, 110 min, Israel, Ephraim Kishon) One of the best Israeli films ever made, *Sallah* was an Academy Award nominee for Best Foreign Film and won First Prize in the San Francisco International Film Festival. Chaim Topol (Tevya in *Fiddler on the Roof*) stars as the head of an immigrant family from North Africa who encounter nothing but frustration and disappointment during their period of transition in the Promised Land. (Hebrew with English subtitles) ★★★★ $79.99

Salmonberries

(1991, 94 min, Germany, Percy Adlon) Written and directed by Adlon (*Sugarbaby*), *Salmonberries* has much in common with his earlier effort *Bagdad Cafe* (surreal cinematic flights of fancy, a haunting soundtrack and lots of landscape). Set in the desolate, no-man's land of Alaska, this quirky drama examines the developing emotional bonds between two women of disparate backgrounds. Singer k.d. lang plays an orphaned Eskimo who hides her gender beneath baggy layers of clothing and who develops an attraction to Roswitha, the local librarian of the town of Kotzebue. Through much courting, Roswitha (Rosel Zech) resists her affections. Though not satisfying as a lesbian love story, the film is notable for the presence of lang and her beautiful soundtrack featuring the theme song, "Barefoot." ★★½ $29.99

Saló: 120 Days of Sodom

(1975, 117 min, Italy, Pier Paolo Pasolini) Pasolini's last film is an unbelievably bleak and depressing vision of the human condition which shocked audiences with its brutally graphic scenes of sexual degradation and oppresive violence. The director transposes the Marquis de Sade's novel about the debauching of the four pillars of 18th-century French society to World War II Italy (Saló was the site of Mussolini's brief puppet government in northern Italy). There, a group of four men, all fascist members of the power elite (a duke, a bishop, a banker and a judge), act out their lust for power and control. They kidnap sixteen teenage boys and girls and systematically and sadistically force them to engage in a variety of perverse and repugnant acts including coprophilia, necrophilia, torture, sexual debasement and, eventually, murder. The startled viewer is the voyeur in Pasolini's descent into the evils of the human spirit. Condemned by the Italian censors for its "aberrant and repugnant sexual perversion." ★★★½ $89.99

Salome

(1953, 103 min, US, William Dieterle) Rita Hayworth's lustrous beauty shines in this liberal retelling of the biblical story of Salome – daughter to Queen Herodia of Galilee – who offered herself to spare John the Baptist. Charles Laughton stars as King Herod who, for fear of a curse, cannot bring himself to silence the good Baptist despite the prodding of his wicked queen (Judith Anderson). Palace intrigue abounds as queen plots against king, king lusts after daughter-in-law and a Roman commander (Stewart Granger) must conceal his religious beliefs. While extremely well-acted and often entertaining, the film suffers from a heavy-handed treatment of its religious themes. ★★½ $19.99

Salome's Last Dance

(1988, 87 min, GB, Ken Russell) With his usual flair for decadence and depravity, Russell crafted this brilliant tribute to the literary genius of Oscar Wilde. The film follows Wilde to a male brothel where he is entertained by an "illegal" performance of his banned play, "Salome." The play itself represents Wilde's twisted vision of the fateful biblical encounter between Salome (daughter of King Herod) and John the Baptist. Here re-enacted full of pulsating sexual innuendo, Russell eagerly sinks his teeth into Wilde's poetry and renders the play, in its entirety, at a frenetic pace. Imogen Millais-Scott is devilishly alluring as the coquettish, cockneyed Salome, and Glenda Jackson is nothing short of perfect as the steely, evil Queen Herodias. ★★★

Salon Kitty

(1976, 110 min, West Germany, Tinto Brass) Made in the "grand" tradition of *Caligula, The Damned, Saló* and *The Night Porter*, this exploitative, sexually graphic shocker features a crazed Helmut Berger as a powerful SS officer who will do anything to get the dirt on his fellow Nazis and their wives. An erotic and, at times, disturbing probe into the sickness of man. (English language version) ★★½

Salsa: The Motion Picture

(1988, 97 min, US, Boaz Davidson) Horrendously – but at least laughably – bad, this misguided attempt to cash in during the "salsa craze" of the late 1980s features ex-Menudo star Bobby Rosa as a grease monkey with a twitch in his hips, an itch in his crotch and stars in his eyes. Rosa, with a chiseled body but a squeaky, Michael Jackson voice, can dance; but that alone can't save this insipid *Saturday Night Fever/Dirty Dancing* rip-off. ★ $14.99

Salt of the Earth

(1953, 94 min, US, Herbert Biberman) One of the classics of American independent film-making, this impassioned, pro-feminist drama chronicles the events in a bitter strike by Chicano zinc miners in New Mexico. When an injunction is issued against the workers, the wives of the strikers take to the picket line. Seemingly incomprehensible even in today's conservative climate, the film was boycotted by most cinemas on its release; with director Biberman, actor Will Geer, producer Paul Jarrico and screenwriter Michael Wilson all subsequently blacklisted for their part in its production. ★★★½ $29.99

Salut L'Artiste

(1973, 96 min, France, Yves Robert) Marcello Mastroianni's extraordinary talent to portray the "naive oaf" comes fully to life in this captivating and witty modern farce about a fumbling bit actor trying to live two lives at once. His mistress finally leaves him and so he sheepishly returns home to his wife only to discover that she is carrying someone else's child. Full of pratfalls and pitfalls, this engaging and sardonic comedy sparkles with effervescence. (French with English subtitles) ★★★

Salut Victor!

(1988, 83 min, Canada, Anne Claire Poirier) Made for TV, this French-Canadian gay love story, though a bit predictable, is a simply told and poignant tale about love in life's later years. Set in a retirement home, the film follows Philippe, a wealthy gentleman who begins to feel the pain and loneliness of losing his health and sense of freedom. He is reluctantly pulled out of his doldrums by his friendship with Victor, a talkative, exuberant man who recently lost his lover in a plane crash. These disparate men soon strike up an affecting, tender relationship as this delicate tearjerker adds new meaning to the term "old-fashioned," and breaks new ground through its portrait of older gay men. It ultimately charms one and all with its sentiment. (French with English subtitles) ★★★ $39.99

James Woods in *Salvador*

Salvador

(1986, 123 min, US, Oliver Stone) Released the same year as his classic *Platoon*, Stone wrote and directed this taut, hard-hitting political drama based on American photojournalist Richard Boyle's experiences in El Salvador in 1980. James Woods gives what may be his finest performance as Boyle, and James Belushi has certainly never been better as Boyle's sidekick just along for the ride. ★★★½

Samantha

(1992, 101 min, US, Stephen La Rocque) When Samantha is informed by her parents that they did not give birth to her, but actually found her on their doorstep 21 years earlier, she locks herself in her room by way of an elaborate booby trap involving a house plant, a dripping shower and her father's musket. Martha Plimpton plays Samantha, a young woman in search of her own identity in this comedy that tries slightly too hard to be off-beat. However, Plimpton gives an edgy, headstrong performance, and the charming, sexually tense relationship between Samantha and her cello-playing best friend Henry (Dermot Mulroney) nearly makes up for the sometimes ridiculous screenplay. ★½ $89.99

Sammy and Rosie Get Laid

(1987, 100 min, GB, Stephen Frears) Director Frears and writer Hanif Kureishi reunite after their triumphant *My Beautiful Laundrette* to fashion another brilliantly scathing portrait of present-day London. Sammy (Ayub Khan Din), the son of a right-wing Pakistani politician, is involved with a sexually liberated English woman (Frances Barber). When his father, fleeing political enemies, comes to live with them, their informal relationship begins to mirror the mounting social unrest in the streets outside their window. ★★★½ $14.99

Samson and Delilah

(1949, 128 min, US, Cecil B. DeMille) Hedy Lamarr is ready for her close-up as the seductive Delilah in this typically lush DeMille biblical drama. Victor Mature is quite good as strongman Samson who gets the "cut" from rejected lover Delilah. Angela Lansbury plays Delilah's sister, and George Sanders also stars as Saran. ★★★ $29.99

Samurai I

(1954, 92 min, Japan, Hiroshi Inagaki) Scintillating thrills and excitement are promised for fans of samurai and adventure films with this rousing trio called the "Samurai Trilogy," which is based upon the real-life adventures of legendary swordsman Miyamoto Musashi. The great Toshiro Mifune is the peasant who trains to become a master swordsman and protector of his people. This, the first part, introduces the aspiring samurai and examines his arduous training and indoctrination. (Japanese with English subtitles) ★★★ $19.99

Samurai II

(1955, 102 min, Japan, Hiroshi Inagaki) Part two of the "Samurai Trilogy" deals with the developing skills of samurai Toshiro Mifune and centers around a bloody duel with a particularly mean warrior. (Japanese with English subtitles) ★★★ $19.99

Samurai III

(1956, 102 min, Japan, Hiroshi Inagaki) In this, the concluding chapter of the "Samurai Trilogy," we follow our hero's romantic interlude as well as his defense of a village from a marauding horde. We also witness the inevitable showdown with his arch nemesis, Kojiro. Please note: Although the three films in the "Samurai Trilogy" follow a chronology, each film can be enjoyed and understood independently of each other. (Japanese with English subtitles) ★★★ $19.99

Samurai Reincarnation

(1981, 122 min, Japan, Kinji Fukasaku) In 1638, the Shimabara Revolt, which rose from the severely repressive measures taken against the Christians by the Shogunate government, ends after a series of bloody battles with 18,000 rioters exterminated. The leader of this uprising, Shiro, is beheaded and his face is put on public display. But after that night, in the midst of a violent thunderstorm, Shiro reincarnates. Casting aside the teachings of Jesus Christ, he now sets out to burn up the countryside with the fire of hatred and anger. (Japanese with English subtitles) ★★½ $39.99

Samurai Saga

(1959, 110 min, Japan, Hiroshi Inagaki) This love triangle between a very demanding princess and two warriors is set in war-torn Kyoto in 1599. Toshiro Mifune is one of the gallant swordsmen whose enormous nose is the only impediment to his capture of the elusive beauty. A classic story of romance and war. (Japanese with English subtitles) ★★★

San Francisco

(1936, 116 min, US, W.S. Van Dyke) One of the most popular films of the 1930s, this early disaster film stars Clark Gable as a saloon owner and Jeanette MacDonald as a singer who fall in love – all set right before the big earthquake of 1905. Spencer Tracy is excellent in support as Gable's best pal, and the special effects are quite good. ★★★ $19.99

Sand and Blood

(1987, 101 min, France, Jeanne Labrune) Coming on the heels of Pedro Almodóvar's exploration of sex and violence in the bullring

with *Matador* comes this much more thoughtful yet equally provocative, erotically charged drama. An upcoming matador from "the wrong side of the tracks" meets and befriends a wealthy doctor who is morally opposed to the violence of the bullfight. Their unlikely relationship affects both their lives and their families as together they confront their hidden secrets and fears. Be forewarned: the bullfighting and slaughterhouse scenes in the film contain bloody and graphic images of violence against animals. (French with English subtitles) ★★★ $79.99

The Sand Pebbles

(1966, 179 min, US, Robert Wise) This beautifully photographed, compelling drama features a splendid performance by Steve McQueen as a jaded sailor on an American gunboat on the Yangtze River in 1926. His increasing awareness of the volitile political situation contributes to his escalating confrontation with his superiors. A sprawling combination of action, romance and subtextual editorial comment. Also starring Richard Attenborough, Candice Bergen and Oscar nominee Mako. ★★★½ $29.99

Sandakan No. 8

(1974, 121 min, Japan, Kei Kumai) Winner of the Berlin Film Festival's Silver Bear Award, this heartrending drama follows a female journalist who befriends an impoverished old lady who recounts her anguished life as a prostitute in a brothel in Borneo in the early 1900s. (Japanese with English subtitles) ★★★½

Sanders of the River

(1935, 98 min, GB, Zoltan Korda) This outmoded adventure tale about the captain of a river patrol in colonial Africa is filled with caricature and offers little insight into the colonial mindset. Still, the film is made interesting by its early use of location shooting and the dominating screen presence of Paul Robeson. ★★½ $19.99

The Sandlot

(1993, 101 min, US, David Mickey Evans) It's the 1960s, and soon-to-be fifth grader Scotty Smalls is the new kid in town. An avid baseball fan, Scotty is befriended by a baseball-loving group of kids who all spend an idyllic summer playing our national pastime. Things go great for Scotty and his pals until Scotty's dad's prized baseball, autographed by Babe Ruth himself, lands in a junkyard guarded by the legendary "The Beast," a dog so ferocious his name alone sends shivers down the spine of children everywhere. This heartwarming family film is a wonderful coming-of-age tale which should entertain both child and adult. James Earl Jones, Denis Leary, Arliss Howard and Karen Allen appear in adult roles. ★★★ $14.99

Sanjuro

(1962, 96 min, Japan, Akira Kurosawa) Toshiro Mifune is at his scruffy, steely-eyed best as the leader of young revolutionaries. An action-packed adventure film, sequel to *Yojimbo*. (Japanese with English subtitles) ★★★ $29.99

Sans Soleil

(1983, 100 min, France, Chris Marker) Narrated in English by a woman reading from the lengthy memoirs of a friend's world-wide travels, this non-narrative, almost dreamy philosophical and sociological experimental film makes for an intense and demanding but rewarding film experience. The memoirs of the unnamed traveler expound on his travel impressions, mainly in Japan and in West Africa. As the narrator reads, the camera takes us to the amazingly contrasting locations, filled with weird and wondrous customs, sights and passions. The sense of contrasts, between the prosperous, industrialized Japan and the poor but teeming life in rural Africa, goes beyond simple ethnographic observation to become an intimate, almost mystical poem/portrait of mankind. ★★★ $29.99

Sanshiro Sugata

(1943, 80 min, Japan, Akira Kurosawa) Made under the watchful eye of censors, this first film by a 33-year-old Kurosawa helped establish him as a major director. Set in the late 19th century, the story revolves around Sanshiro Sugata, an eager student looking for a master to teach him the martial art of Ju-jitsu. He soon abandons this quest for the newer art of Judo, a form of fighting that requires the young man not just to learn the mere techniques of the art, but to attain a spiritual discipline as well. With explosive martial arts choreography, this understated philosophical film features the theme that runs throughout Kurosawa's work; that of a man who champions a principle despite an often hostile established order. (Japanese with English subtitles) ★★★ $19.99

Sansho the Baliff

(1954, 125 min, Japan, Kenji Mizoguchi) Set in the 11th century, this epic drama begins in a land ruled by a kindhearted provincial governor who is overthrown and exiled. His wife is reduced to prostitution while his children are kidnapped and sent into slavery. One of the children escapes and vows to establish a group of followers and return to his land in force. This sweeping drama, while played on a grand scale, retains the human quality in unfolding this sad yet beautiful tale. (Japanese with English subtitles) ★★★½ $39.99

Santa Claus — The Movie

(1985, 104 min, US, Jeannot Szwarc) Big-budget, clumsy but harmless children's story about one of Santa's elves falling prey to an evil toymaker, who may use "elfin" magic to control Christmas. David Huddleston is an appropriately larger-than-life Santa; however, Dudley Moore and John Lithgow appear very embarrassed by what's going on. ★★ $9.99

The Santa Clause

(1994, 95 min, US, John Pasquin) A satisfactory family comedy which is in need of a lot more laughs, The Santa Clause rarely demonstrates the caliber of humor suggested by its catchy title. TV's ratings king Tim Allen ("Home Improvement") plays a divorced dad who on Christmas Eve knocks Santa off the roof. Taking over Kris Kringle's holiday obligations, Allen learns in doing so he is now the new Santa — hence the Santa Clause. As his young son boasts of dad's new position, which prompts a visit to the psychiatrist, Allen

begins to take on the physical characteristics of Santa in preparation for next year's holiday season. While the story does occasionally live up to its enjoyable premise, and the North Pole set is real cool, the film never really ignites sparks in the laughs department, depending instead on F/X wizardry and the odd wink at the audience. ★★½ $14.99

Santa Sangre

(1990, 120 min, Italy/Mexico, Alejandro Jodorowsky) In the furiously imaginative tradition of his '70s cult classic El Topo comes this violent, bizarre and mystifying parable of a young man's ultimate Oedipal complex. Set in Mexico, the story begins in a circus where a young boy is witness to a brutal family incident: discovering her husband in bed with another, a woman throws acid on his privates only to have the man chop off her arms before he slits his own throat. Understandably affected, the neurotic boy spends his adolescence in an insane asylum, but soon escapes (or does he?) and is reunited with his armless mom. Together, they begin a killing rampage against any woman who comes close to him. Plot matters little here, for it is Jodorowsky's intense visuals, like a hallucinogenic Fellini spectacle, that assaults the viewer leaving one both exhausted and exalted by this nighmarish vision. Highly recommended for adventurous videophiles and fans of the surreal. (English language) ★★★ $19.99

The Saphead/The High Sign/One Week

(1920/21, 118 min, US, Herbert Blanche/Buster Keaton & Eddie Cline) A collection of three Buster Keaton comedies. The Saphead (1920, 78 min) was Keaton's first starring role. The film features Keaton as the title character, a Wall Street heir oblivious to life around him. The creaky plot has to do with Keaton's brother-in-law trying to steal the family fortune. Keaton shines in a lengthy, well-staged sequence about a run on the stock exchange. (★★1/2) One Week (1921, 19 min) was Keaton's first short as director and writer (with Eddie Cline), made directly after Saphead. It's a truly inventive, hilarious slapstick comedy about Keaton and his newlywed wife (Sybil Sealey) trying to build their pre-fab honeymoon home. Performing his own stunts, Keaton is a marvel. His stone face, comic timing, acrobatic skill and dexterity — marvelously on display here — make him the silent screen's greatest clown. (★★★★) The High Sign (1921, 21 min) is a humorous story of Keaton becoming involved with a gang of cutthroats. What makes this short memorable is an unbelievable finale in which Keaton takes on the gang with the help of a booby-trapped mansion. As he runs from room to room and floor to floor in seconds, notice there is no editing. Astonishing. (★★★) $29.99

Sarafina!

(1992, 99 min, US, Darrell James Roodt) Mbogeni Ngema's powerful musical play about the struggle for freedom amongst South Africa's black school children is brought to the screen with mixed results. The young Leleti Khumalo is superb in the title role of Sarafina, a teenage girl whose ambition is to play Nelson

Mandela in the school play, but instead finds herself caught up in a vicious conflagration of hatred towards the white oppressor. Whoopi Goldberg, however, in the role of a radical history teacher, fails to master the South African accent and therefore never achieves believability. The film also suffers from an almost schizophrenic vacillation between moments of profound emotional impact and almost trivial song-and-dance routines, as well as a propensity for studio dubbed sound which seems woefully out of place. Still, by its end the film imparts a potent message on the destructive nature of hatred. South African chanteuse Miriam Makeba makes a brief appearance as Sarafina's mother and John Kani plays the high school principal. ★★½ $9.99

Sartre Par Lui Meme

(1976, 190 min, France, Alexandre Astruc & Michel Contat) Jean-Paul Sartre, leading Existentialist and author of philosophical essays, plays and novels — many concerning the plight of man, alone in an alienating world — agreed to a filmed interview to speak of his work and his life. Filmed in his Montparnesse flat and featuring his longtime companion, Simone de Beauvior, this witty and insightful document ranges from such topics as the Occupation and May 1968, to Existentialism and the role of the intellectual. An engrossing three hours with one of the great minds of the 20th century. (French with English subtitles) ★★★

Satan Met a Lady

(1936, 75 min, US, William Dieterle) Second screen version of Dashiell Hammet's "The Maltese Falcon" — the first was filmed in 1931 — and not on par with John Huston's 1941 classic. Warren William plays the private eye, and Bette Davis is the mystery woman. ★★ $19.99

Satan's Brew

(1976, 112 min, West Germany, Rainer Werner Fassbinder) RFW's first comedy is a weird, vulgar and perverse story of the adventures of Walter Kranz (Kurt Raab), a "revolutionary" poet who imagines himself to be the 19th-century homosexual poet Stefan George. The film, shot in a black comedic slapstick style, boasts among its peculiar characters Kranz's butch wife (Ingrid Caven), a retarded brother, a wart-faced admirer and a troupe of prostitutes. (German with English subtitles) ★★½ $19.99

Satanic Attraction

(1990, 102 min, Brazil, Fauzi Mansur) Someone or something is murdering young women and using their blood for its own diabolical purposes. When the traces of satanic rituals are found near the crime scenes, police suspect they are dealing with a cult killer. Meanwhile, a radio mystery show begins to foreshadow the killings, making the cops believe there is a connection between the two. An effective horror outing from director Mansur. (Dubbed) ★★★ $24.99

Saturday Night and Sunday Morning

(1960, 89 min, GB, Karel Reisz) With a savage comic perspective and a totally realistic approach, this biting drama, one of the first and best of the British New Wave of the 1960s, is a classic of the "angry young man" genre. In a star-making role, a youthful and handsome Finney is mesmerizing as a Nottingham factory worker whose rebellious nature is neatly summarized by his opening narration, "What I want is a good time. The remainder is all propaganda." The story follows Finney as he lets off steam on the weekends through his drinking binges and two romantic affairs − one of them with a married woman (a magnificent Rachel Roberts). Though no Alfie, Finney doesn't tread lightly with his depiction of a likable cad; and he and director Reisz take such care in attention to time and place that the film nearly borders on eavesdropping. A remarkable, insightful canvas whose honesty and daring made possible films afar afield as *A Clockwork Orange, Absolute Beginners* and *Trainspotting.* ★★★★ $14.99

Saturday Night Fever

(1977, 118 min, US, John Badham) John Travolta created a cultural phenomenon as a Brooklyn youth who uses the disco dance floors to escape the tedium of his home and social life. Donna Pescow is exceptional as a local girl in love with Travolta. A tune-filled, trendsetting time capsule both compelling and hoary. Musical score by the Bee Gees. (Available in both PG- and R-rated versions.) ★★★ $14.99

Saturn 3

(1980, 88 min, GB, Stanley Donen) From the director of *Charade* comes this odd little sci-fi parable. Space-aged, hydroponic gardeners Kirk Douglas and Farrah Fawcett find their little astro-Eden no longer a lovely, verdant garden after that snake Harvey Keitel shows up with his psycho-robot Hector. ★★ $14.99

Savage Nights (Les Nuite Fauves)

(1992, 126 min, France, Cyril Collard) Possibly the most personal and controversial of all the films dealing with AIDS, *Savage Nights* is a startlingly knowing semiautobiographical melodrama by former rock star and writer Collard (who died from AIDS at the age of 36 in 1993 just four days before his film swept the César Awards). Collard stars as Jean,

a high-living bisexual photographer who discovers he is HIV-positive. He becomes involved with both love-sick 17-year-old Laura (Romane Bohringer) and S/M obsessed, neo-Nazi soccer player Sami (Carlos Lopez). The story revolves around these two tumultuous relationships as the outwardly calm Jean tries to forget about his illness through physical and sexual comforts. With its jagged, almost documentary feel, the film effectively and unapologetically delves into the life of a non-hero and his personal response to coping with AIDS. (French with English subtitles) ★★★ $14.99

The Savage Woman

(1991, 100 min, Canada, Léa Pool) After her suicide attempt in the raw, mountainous wilderness of France fails, Marianne, a young French-Canadian woman wanders the area, avoiding contact with people and slowly losing her civilized self. She is eventually befriended by Elyseé, a lonely engineer working nearby at a dam, who nurses her back to health. The unlikely couple, seemingly against their will, soon fall in love. But their deepening relationship is strained by Marianne's secret: she's wanted by the police for murder. Pool's deft directorial hand is best revealed in the touching, tentative relationship of the two lovers and the unraveling of the woman's mysterious past. A taut melodrama kept interesting right until the surprise ending. Winner of the Most Popular Film in the 1991 Montreal Film Festival. (French with English subtitles) ★★★ $39.99

Savages

(1982, 106 min, GB, James Ivory) By far the most offbeat result of the years of collaboration between Ivory and Ismail Merchant, this is the story of a group of clay covered savages who stumble across an abandoned mansion. Bit by bit, they assume the roles of the former, more civilized, inhabitants until finally they have constructed their own little microcosm of the landed gentry. This strange and hypnotic film evokes images of *King of Hearts* and *The Emerald Forest.* Starring Sam Waterston. ★★½

Save the Lifeguard

(1976, 90 min, Israel) This comedy of errors focuses on a married man who has a weakness

for bikini-clad young ladies and is put to the fidelity test by his suspicious father-in-law. The trap backfires as our hero resists the alluring charms of this feminine bait and stays true to his wife. (Hebrew with English subtitles) ★★½

Saving Grace

(1986, 112 min, US, Robert M. Young) With a tip of the hat to *Roman Holiday*, this muddled comedy stars Tom Conti as the Pope who, tiring of his rigid regime, unceremoniously leaves the Vatican to spend time with the common folk. Giancarlo Giannini, Erland Josephson and Edward James Olmos also star. ★★

Sawdust and Tinsel

(1953, 95 min, Sweden, Ingmar Bergman) Also known as *The Naked Light*, Bergman's powerful classic is set in the circus milieu and deals with the fluctuating love allegiances between a circus owner, his wife, his mistress and her other lover. For sheer spectacle, psychological accuracy and richness of composition, this dazzling film is unrivaled. (Swedish with English subtitles) ★★★½ $29.99

Say Anything

(1989, 100 min, US, Cameron Crowe) John Cusack stars in this intelligent, insightful and gloriously entertaining teen comedy as a high school grad who falls in love with the class valedictorian. Ione Skye is lovely as the class queen, and John Mahoney gives a stunning portrayal of her doting father. Credit writer and first-time director Crowe for making a "wrong side of the tracks" romance imbued with blithe observations on young adulthood and on the complexities of relationships − whether they be romantic or otherwise. ★★★½ $19.99

Sayonara

(1957, 147 min, US, Joshua Logan) Immensely popular upon its release, this romantic drama benefits from a commanding performance from Marlon Brando as an American pilot stationed in post-WWII Tokyo who falls in love with a Japanese woman (Miiko Taka). Red Buttons and Miyoshi Umecki both won Oscars for their moving portrayals of ill-fated lovers. ★★★½ $19.99

The Scalphunters

(1968, 102 min, US, Sydney Pollack) Rollicking comic western with Burt Lancaster as a fur trapper who teams with educated slave Ossie Davis when his furs are stolen. With Shelley Winters, Telly Savalas and Dabney Coleman. ★★★ $19.99

Scandal

(1989, 114 min, GB, Michael Caton-Jones) First-time director Caton-Jones' vivid enactment of the incredible sex scandal which brought a firmly entrenched, conservative British government to its knees in 1963. Joanne Whaley-Kilmer sparkles as Christine Keeler, a nightclub showgirl whose sexual dealings with the then-Minister of War, John Profumo (stoically portrayed by Ian McKellen), and a Soviet Naval Attache (Jeroen Krabbé) sparked what is still the biggest scandal in British political history. John Hurt is extraordinary as Stephen Ward, the socialite

Saturday Night and Sunday Morning

Scarecrow (U.S.S.R.)

and sexual provocateur whose manipulations brought about what came to be known as "The Profumo Affair." ★★★½ $14.99

Scandal Man

(1972, 86 min, France, Richard Balducci) The sordid world of yellow journalism is explored in this riveting, sometimes violent look at a photojournalist working in a Parisian version of the *New York Post*. The reporter, no stranger to sensationalistic coverage, finds himself in hot water when he creates a scandal by photographing a black man kissing a white American woman, who is the daughter of a leading Ku Klux Klan member. Conspiracy, murder and intrigue follow in this rarely seen crime drama. (French with English subtitles) ★★★

Scanner Cop

(1994, 94 min, Canada, Pierre David) While this rewarding third sequel to David Cronenberg's 1981 sci-fi classic *Scanners* borrows only the original concept, it nevertheless captures the flavor of the original more effectively than the second or third entries. Daniel Quinn stars as a rookie cop who must unleash his previously checked scanner powers when a mad scientist (Richard Lynch) targets the L.A.P.D. for extinction. Essentially a comic book on film, *Scanner Cop*'s special effects (by shockmeister John Carl Buechler) and over-the-top villainy make this a grisly return to form. ★★½ $9.99

Scanners

(1981, 102 min, Canada, David Cronenberg) Cronenberg first achieved wide notoriety with this tense horror film about amoral scientist Patrick McGoohan who keeps track of pharmaceutically created mutants who can read your mind or make your head explode. Warning: Not for the squeamish. ★★★

Scanners 2

(1991, 104 min, Canada, Christian Duguay) This well-intentioned sequel to David Cronenberg's 1981 gore-fest focuses more on optical effects than splatter shots in its tale of a reluctant scanner who becomes a pawn in the megalomaniacal schemes of a power-mad police official. With David Hewlett and Deborah Raffin. ★★ $9.99

Scanners III: The Takeover

(1991, 101 min, Canada, Christian Duguay) A scanner (Steve Parrish) must return from self-imposed exile when an experimental drug turns his sister (Liliana Komoroska) into a mind-bending megalomaniac. Very good special effects and Liliana Komoroska's over-the-top performance help compensate for the formulaic story. ★★½ $9.99

The Scar

(1948, 82 min, US, Steve Sekely) Paul Henreid is a fugitive who kills his look-alike psychiatrist and assumes his identity to see his plan backfire when the dead man's own crimes begin to surface and implicate him. Joan Bennett co-stars in this interesting low-budget thriller. (aka: *Hollow Triumph*) ★★★ $19.99

Scarecrow

(1973, 115 min, US, Jerry Schatzberg) Two towering performances by Gene Hackman and Al Pacino dominate this unusual but fascinating buddy film with Hackman and Pacino as drifters who team up together. Great supporting cast includes Eileen Brennan, Ann Wedgeworth and Dorothy Tristan. ★★★ $14.99

Scarecrow

(1983, 130 min, USSR, Roland Bykov) This extraordinary and haunting drama centers around the pretty Lena, a 12-year-old girl who, along with her eccentric grandfather, moves to a small city on the outskirts of Moscow. Although teased by her fellow sixth graders

and nicknamed "Scarecrow," Lena good-naturedly accepts it. But the pestering soon becomes mean and vicious after a school trip is cancelled and the blame is mistakenly directed at Lena. Reminiscent of *Lord of the Flies*, this powerful film is a chilling group portrait of the incredible tyranny and torment of which children are capable, as well as the strength of the individual against it. (Russian with English subtitles) ★★★½ $59.99

Scared Straight

(1978, 54 min, US, Arnold Shapiro) Peter Falk hosts this Academy Award-winning exposé about juveniles who are brought into a maximum security prison and taught by the "lifers" what prison existence is all about. Brutal in its honesty and sobering in its content. ★★★½

Scarface

(1932, 93 min, US, Howard Hawks) Hawks' classic crime drama is the definitive gangster film of the 1930s. Unrelenting in its delineation of a ruthless crime lord, Paul Muni excels as Tony Carmonte (loosely based on Al Capone), an ambitious hood who "climbs" his way to the top of the Chicago underworld in the 1920s. Expert direction by Hawks. Co-starring Ann Dvorak, George Raft and Boris Karloff. ★★★★ $19.99

Scarface

(1984, 170 min, US, Brian De Palma) Al Pacino is Tony Montana, a particularly vicious thug in the Cuban mafia, who, fueled by a perverse vision of the American Dream, rises to the top of the drug world. Director De Palma's controversial updating of the 1932 classic is excessive, bloody, lurid and lacking even a hint of subtlety. Yet it is also visually exciting, delivering salacious fun and complete enjoyment on a gut level. Also starring Michelle Pfeiffer in an early career role. ★★½ $19.99

The Scarlet Letter

(1972, 90 min, West Germany, Wim Wenders) Nathaniel Hawthorne's classic novel about a woman accused of adultery in 17th-century Salem, Massachusetts, receives the Wenders treatment. The film explores the "moral" Puritan virtues of the townspeople against the repressed passions which eventually erupt into chronic hysteria, violence and witchcraft. Strangely, this is Wenders' least favorite of his films, for it contained "The only lead character for whom I did not have any feelings." (German with English subtitles) ★★½

The Scarlet Letter

(1995, 135 min, US, Roland Joffé) Nathaniel Hawthorne's classic novel of romance, witchcraft and betrayal in colonial America is given a definite Cliffs Notes reworking in Joffé's muddled though handsome adaptation. In a rather one-dimensional portrayal, Demi Moore is Hester Prynne, the noble heroine who falls in love with the local pastor (Gary Oldman), bears a child out of wedlock, is forced to wear a scarlet "A" (for adultery), and must contend with her long-thought-dead husband (a hammy Robert Duvall) bent on revenge. Joffé's film, while looking authentic in design and costumes, has an irritating, disjointed feel to it, as if writer Douglas Day

S

Stewart may have skipped whole chapters and/or omitted instrumental, transitional paragraphs. Oldman looks like he'd rather be back in England, and Duvall looks embarrassed as Moore's husband who had lived with the Indians (the actor is laughable in his war dance). We won't even mention how they tampered with the ending. ★★ $14.99

The Scarlet Pimpernel

(1934, 95 min, GB, Harold Young) A stiff-lipped adventure classic with Leslie Howard, perfectly cast, as the elusive pimpernel who aids innocent victims of the French revolution while posing as a foppish member of British society. Co-stars Merle Oberon and Raymond Massey, produced by Alexander Korda. ★★★½ $19.99

Scarlet Street

(1945, 102 min, US, Fritz Lang) Originally judged to be immoral here in the United States, this Lang remake of Jean Renoir's *La Chienne* moves the action from Paris to Greenwich Village, as its story of obsession, manipulation and tortuous fate unfolds. Edward G. Robinson is a meek middle-aged cashier who becomes fatally attracted to the seductive charms of prostitute/actress Joan Bennett. Egged on by the deceptive but sexy vixen and her insidious boyfriend Dan Duryea, Robinson is driven to embezzlement and certain tragedy. Lang's darkest film is an expressionist moral tale and a fine example of psychological film noir. ★★★½ $19.99

Scene of the Crime

(1986, 90 min, France, André Téchiné) Catherine Deneuve delivers a wonderfully multilayered performance as a divorced woman living in the French countryside. Her frustrated dreams of love and fantasy become real when she meets up with a handsome young man, recently escaped from prison, who lures her into a passionate love affair and provides a way out of the deadening provincial life. A taut, well-structured suspense thriller. (French with English subtitles) ★★★ $24.99

Scent of a Woman

Scenes from a Mall

(1991, 87 min, US, Paul Mazursky) The casting of Woody Allen and Bette Midler as a married couple was inspired — on paper. And indeed, they work well together, but this lightweight farce, set against the glitz and glamour of the Beverly Mall, while providing the occasional laugh, is basically dull and flat. She's a high-powered psycholgist and he's a major promoter. They wend their way through the seemingly endless mall and go through a series of petty fights, major revelations and other assorted marital spats. Along the way, the film attempts to lampoon both their yuppie lifestyle, the obscenity of American consumerism and the shallowness of modern marriage. Director Mazursky tries to squeeze some life out of the bone-dry script, but if it weren't for the talents of Allen and Midler, this film would be only slightly less boring than going to the mall on a Saturday night. ★★ $9.99

Scenes from a Marriage

(1973, 168 min, Sweden, Ingmar Bergman) The long and prolific filmmaking career of Bergman is highlighted by many classics; this film, originally a five-hour Swedish television special, must certainly count as one of his best. The film examines the decay and disintegration of a marriage. An intimate and painful look at a couple's arguments, misunderstandings, and lovemaking, as well as their eventual divorce, ending with a new post-divorce friendship. Liv Ullmann and Joseph Erlandson excel as the wife and husband. A passionate and fascinating look at human relations. (Swedish with English subtitles) ★★★★ $39.99

Scenes from the Class Struggle in Beverly Hills

(1989, 95 min, US, Paul Bartel) Director Bartel stays true to his slap-dash style of comedy in this often hilarious, sometimes outlandish and always entertaining drawing-room farce. Jacqueline Bisset stars as a Beverly Hills widow who mourns the loss of her husband (Paul Mazursky) by plotting the sexual conquest of her Chicano male-servant...who has a bet with another servant on who can seduce the other's employer first...get the picture? The stage is set for a no-holds-barred explosion of comedy in which everyone is trying to get into bed with someone. The cast includes Ed Begley, Jr., Wallace Shawn, Bartel, and is rounded out by a terrific performance by Ray Sharkey as a bisexual butler. ★★★ $9.99

Scenes of the Surreal

(1988-90, 58 min, Czechoslovakia/GB, Jan Svankmajer & James Marsh) Three wildly inventive shorts by Czech animator Svankmajer and a BBC documentary on his life and work comprise this bizarrely enjoyable video. *Darkness, Light, Darkness* (1989, 7 min) deals with the wonders and terrors of the senses as a single clay hand begins to assemble the needed parts in making itself whole. Evolution surrealist style! *Virille Games* (1988, 14 min) finds Czech sportsmanship in soccer taking a bloody and deadly turn after the mischievous animator has one too many shots and beer. The techniques and hilarious violence will remind some of Monty Python. *Death of Stalinism in Bohemia* (1990, 10 min) has Stalin

and his Czech wannabe's and cohorts lampooned in this bitter political satire which questions the myth of change in a world of repression. In *Jan Svankmajer: The Animator of Prague* (1990, 27 min), Marsh interviews the erudite but mysterious animator who draws from childhood memories and the notion of magic to create his weird animated world. Featured are excerpts from many of his early shorts from the 1960s. ★★★ $59.99

Scent of a Woman

(1992, 137 min, US, Martin Brest) Al Pacino's tour de force, Oscar-winning performance is the heart and soul of this admittedly overlong and manipulative but nevertheless wickedly funny and touching comedy-drama based on the 1974 Italian comedy *Profumo di Donna*. Chris O'Donnell costars as a college student who is hired to watch cantankerous, blind vet Pacino for the weekend. What should be an uneventful stay at home gives way to a whirlwind tour of New York City as Pacino dupes his companion into accompanying him for a razzle-dazzle three-day getaway. The success of the film lies in Pacino's cynical, hard-bitten military man; and the actor, barking out orders and insults with the determination of a German shepherd on the attack, sinks his teeth into one of the juiciest roles of his career. As directed by Brest (*Midnight Run*), the film transpires at a crackling pace and no scene is allowed to wear out its welcome. ★★★½ $19.99

The Scent of Green Papaya

(1993, 104 min, Vietnam, Tran Anh Hung) Anh Hung's Oscar-nominated and Cannes Award-winning first film exquisitely portrays domestic life in Saigon through the eyes of a young Vietnamese country girl. Divided into two parts, the first and far more interesting segment shows the arrival of ten-year-old servant girl Mui. Despite the serene and beautiful surroundings, there is an internal strife amongst the family in which the innocent Mui becomes a part. Here the film accurately portrays the intimate moments of family life and the wonderment that Mui enjoys from nature and papaya trees in particular. The second part takes place ten years later. Mui has a new master with whom she has fallen in love; and the story concentrates on their romance. Though the film features beautiful cinematography throughout, the last half doesn't have the tension or joy of discovery which makes the first half so successful. Still, the film is a rare look into a culture and people, and its feelings of family and love are transcendent. (Vietnamese with English subtitles) ★★★ $19.99

Schindler

(1991, 80 min, GB, John Blair) Though Steven Spielberg's Oscar-winning *Schindler's List* had a documentary feel to it, this made-for-TV British film is a true documentary on the life of Oskar Schindler and the role he played in saving the lives of more than 1,000 Jews from Nazi concentration camps. The film includes German propaganda footage as well as what they recorded for their own meticulous record keeping, and interviews with survivors who knew both Schindler and Commandant Amon Goeth, including Schindler's widow and

S

Goeth's maid Helena (played by Embeth Davidtz in Spielberg's film). ★★★ $14.99

Schindler's List

(1993, 185 min, US, Steven Spielberg) In his boldest attempt to create a "cinematic masterpiece" and finally get noticed by a stubbornly disinterested Academy, Spielberg bypasses the heart and goes right for the jugular in this first ever big-budget Hollywood drama on the Holocaust. Undeniably driven by sincerity, Spielberg's Oscar-winning Best Picture is alternately impressive, maudlin, focused and well-acted. Filmed in black and white, the film deals with the Nazi extermination of Polish Jews and how one man, Oskar Schindler, transformed from a philandering opportunist (and Nazi profiteer) to a capitalist savior to 1,200 imprisoned Jews. With fluid camerawork, Spielberg re-creates life for Krakow's Jews during Nazi occupation – from resettlements in the ghetto to their internment in the camps. Schindler is ably portrayed by Liam Neeson, and Ben Kingsley as an accountant who aids Schindler and Ralph Fiennes as camp commander Amon Goeth are especially effective. Spielberg's scenes of Nazi atrocities are emotionally wrenching, but the film's pacing, the director's trademark sentimentality and an artificial ending keep Schindler's List from being the classic the director so fervently strived for. (Available letterboxed and pan & scan) ★★★ $29.99

School Daze

(1988, 114 min, US, Spike Lee) Lee's bold but ultimately unsatisfying social comedy-drama set at a black university centers on the friction between two cliques: the "wannabees" and the "jigaboos." Lee sets out to examine racial identity and self-discrimination in the black community; but his heavy-handed approach makes for little interest. The best scene is a musical fantasy number, which is alive with an energy unfortunately missing from the rest of the film. ★★½ $14.99

School Ties

(1992, 107 min, US, Robert Mandel) It is the 1950s and David Green, a lower middle-class kid from Scranton, is recruited by the exclusive St. Matthews School to help break their three-year losing streak in football. Handsome and an excellent athlete, David (Brendan Fraser) is quickly embraced by the school elite. But a situation presents itself: David is Jewish, a fact that he does not exactly go out of his way to reveal to his new anti-Semitic, joke-spewing friends. Originally released around the time of the L.A. riots, the film was promoted as a hard-nosed look at prejudice. But it is the underlying theme of what parts of ourselves we are willing to give up in order to fit in and "be a part of things" that gives this film its punch. While not original (it could be titled Scent of a Dead Poet), School Ties is a heartfelt and surprisingly entertaining story with just the right amount of nostalgia and sentimentality. ★★★ $19.99

Scorpio

(1972, 114 min, US, Michael Winner) French heartthrob Alain Delon is a CIA assassin who is contracted by the Agency to kill his one-time partner (Burt Lancaster) who they say is selling secrets to the Soviets. The acting in this film is, for the most part, wooden, with the exception of Paul Scofield's portrayal of a last-of-his-breed Russian super-spy living in Vienna. There are also many loose ends left hanging at the conclusion of the film, which could have been an intentional comment of how in the spy biz "all evidence is at best conjecture," but it's probably just poor screenwriting. There are, however, some nice location shots of Paris and Vienna, and a few neat non-weapons-related spy tricks to keep your mind off the hokiness of this thrill-less thriller. ★★ $14.99

The Scorpion Woman

(1989, 95 min, Austria, Susanne Zanke) The often scandalous yet strangely mesmeric theme of an older woman's relationship with a much younger man is explored once again in this interesting drama. Lisa, a 44-year-old magistrate living in Vienna, finds herself frustrated at her moribund relationship with her lover and soon takes up with a legal assistant twenty years her junior. This relationship soon affects her professional life after she is assigned a case in which an older woman, accused of assault on a young man, is found to have been romantically involved with the victim. (German with English subtitles) ★★½ $59.99

The Scout

(1994, 100 min, US, Michael Ritchie) Albert Brooks stars in this occasionally funny, improbable and mawkish baseball tale as a scout for the New York Yankees. Sent to Mexico, he discovers Brendan Fraser, who may possibly be one of the greatest players of the game. And before the film looks like another fish out of water comedy, Brooks brings him back to the States. That's when his and the film's problems begin. Fraser turns out to be mentally unstable, and Brooks and shrink Dianne Wiest attempt to get to the root of the problem. The film's beginning has a charm to it, thanks to Brooks' underplaying, and Fraser gives an appealing performance. But the last half is painfully bad, underscored by an incredulous ending. ★★ $96.89

Scream

(1996, 110 min, US, Wes Craven) Full of in-jokes and references to countless splatter movies from the 1980s, Wes Craven's best film since A Nightmare on Elm Street works as homage, spoof, and as one of the scariest mainstream horror films to be released in theaters in the last ten years. Beginning as a slasher movie (with a terrific scene during which top-billed Drew Barrymore exits the film), the movie soon becomes a murder mystery with enough red herrings to rival the work of Dario Argento. A masked killer is terrifying a town, killing teenagers and slowly working his (or her?) way to the traumatized daughter (Neve Campbell) of another local murder victim of a year ago. In order to escape the macabre mood of the town and have a little fun, the remaining teens gather at a big house in the woods to watch horror movies, drink and get laid. The killer, of course, is there and all hell breaks loose. Intelligent, witty and, at times, very scary, Scream is destined to become a postmodern horror movie classic which will

Ben Kingsley in Schindler's List

eventually be ranked along with Halloween and Dawn of the Dead. ★★★½ $102.99

Scream of Stone

(1990, 105 min, Canada/West Germany, Werner Herzog) In this, one of his most disciplined films, Herzog has again found his emotional correlative in nature: a monolith of a mountain in Argentina, a "scream of stone." Donald Sutherland has been hired to produce a live TV program as two of the world's greatest mountain climbers try to conquer unknown territory – both external and internal. Brad Dourif gives a rich performance as the one climber who has come to peace with The Mountain having tried to conquer it to win the affections of (the late) Mae West. ★★★

Screamers

(1996, 100 min, US, Christian Duguay) Peter Weller stars as a beleaguered colonel in this not uninteresting adaptation of a short story by Philip K. Dick (Blade Runner). Weller's laconic character commands a small group of soldiers stationed on the distant mining planet Sirius B, site of a battle in the latest futuristic corporate war. In the fight, biochemical entities known as "Screamers," small, multi-bladed machines, have mutated into larger, more human-looking warriors. The story focuses on Weller's attempts to cross the planet's wasteland to broker a truce. Not very original nor particularly good, Screamers does feature adequate production values for its low budget, and the limited special effects can be entertaining (such as in a sequence where a horde of Screamers stream from a doorway in a most innocuous form). ★★ $99.99

Scrooge

(1970, 118 min, GB, Ronald Neame) Though it won't replace Alastair Sim's 1951 A Christmas Carol as the definitive version of Dickens' novel, there's a lot to like in this musical adaptation. Albert Finney makes an appropriately cantankerous Ebenezer Scrooge, the miser and all-around-humbug who is visited by three spirits on Christmas Eve. With Alec

Guinness, Edith Evans and Kenneth More. A pleasant, if uninspired, score by Leslie Bricusse. ★★★ $14.99

Scrooged

(1988, 101 min, US, Richard Donner) A mildly entertaining updating of Dickens' "A Christmas Carol" with Bill Murray taking over the role of Scrooge, here as a heartless TV executive. It's not as funny as it could have been, but there are some good moments: especially Carol Kane as a whacked-out Ghost of Christmas Present and Bobcat Goldthwait as a 1980s Bob Cratchet. ★★½ $14.99

Scrubbers

(1982, 90 min, GB, Mai Zetterling) A comic and tragic tale about a tough crop of women inmates at a dingy British borstal. From the black lesbian lovers to the mute anorexic, the leather-jacketed tough girl and the baby-faced heroine, the performers are feisty and unforgettably human. ★★★

Scum

(1980, 98 min, GB, Alan Clarke) This harrowing British drama explores the physical, sexual and psychological violence in a borstal (prison) for youthful offenders. Phil Daniels and Ray Winstone, the mod and rocker stars of *Quadrophenia*, star in this powerful and disturbing tale. The film could have used a more palatable title for its commercial release. ★★★

The Sea Hawk

(1940, 127 min, US, Michael Curtiz) Classic sea adventure with Errol Flynn swashing-many-a-buck on the high seas as a pirate captain taking on the Spaniards in the name of England and Queen Elizabeth I. Claude Rains, Donald Crisp, Flora Robson and Alan Hale also star. Outstanding score by Erich Wolfgang Korngold. (This is the restored version.) ★★★½ $19.99

Sea of Grass

(1947, 131 min, US, Elia Kazan) Unusual western tale based on a Conrad Richter story about New Mexico grasslands and the fight to preserve them. Spencer Tracy, Katharine Hepburn, Melvyn Douglas and Robert Walker head a good cast, but much of the film is heavy going. ★★½ $19.99

Sea of Love

(1989, 112 min, US, Harold Becker) Al Pacino gives a solid performance as a veteran New York City detective assigned to catch a serial killer who makes contact through the personals. Placing an ad, Pacino goes undercover, setting up a rendezvous under the watchful eye of partner John Goodman. There he meets sexy prime suspect Ellen Barkin. The two begin a passionate affair; all the while clues point to her guilt. In addition to being an extraordinarily talented actress, Barkin is certainly one of the sexiest women in film today, and her steamy scenes with Pacino are electric. ★★★ $14.99

The Sea Wolf

(1941, 90 min, US, Michael Curtiz) Jack London's exciting tale of the sea and of the nefarious Captain Wolf Larsen makes for a riveting, atmospheric high-seas adventure. Adapted for the screen by Robert Rossen, the story plots the course of three civilians who find themselves on board the aptly-named, turn-of-the-century schooner "Ghost" helmed by the tyrannical Larsen. Edward G. Robinson, in a dynamic and complex portrayal, plays the hardened captain who finds it "Better to reign in Hell than serve in Heaven." As the newest members of this "hell ship," a lovely Ida Lupino and a handsome John Garfield are both fugitives from the law; and Alexander Knox is an idealistic writer forced to face the barbaric side of human nature. A rip-roaring action film which gives berth to both high adventure and intelligent characterizations. ★★★½ $19.99

The Sea Wolves

(1980, 120 min, GB/US, Andrew V. McLaglen) An engaging WWII adventure about a group of ex-British cavalry soldiers doing their part against the Nazis. Gregory Peck, Roger Moore, David Niven, Trevor Howard and Patrick Macnee go after a German radio transmitter with some suspenseful and funny results. ★★★ $14.99

Seance on a Wet Afternoon

(1964, 116 min, GB, Bryan Forbes) This enthralling psychological thriller breathes with an atmosphere of ever-building suspense that is unrelentingly sustained. A pair of superb performances are offered by Kim Stanley and Richard Attenborough as a medium and her husband who kidnap a child in order to publicize her clairvoyant skills. Written and directed by Forbes, it stands as one of the greatest and most unusual British films of the '60s. ★★★½

The Search

(1948, 104 min, US, Fred Zinnemann) A touching story, sensitive direction and a sobering theme all contribute to make this a classic post-war drama. Montgomery Clift gives a fine performance as an American soldier stationed in war-ravaged Germany who takes in a young Czech boy — a concentration camp survivor — when he finds the youth alone on the streets. Meanwhile, the boy's mother searches for her son from camp to camp. Filmed on location in Berlin amid the bombed out buildings, which only serves to enhance the poignant narrative. Little Ivan Jandl is a heartbreaker as the boy. ★★★★ $19.99

Search and Destroy

(1995, 90 min, US, David Salle) Griffin Dunne heads a cast of Hollywood's coolest in this self-consciously hip adaptation of the Broadway play about a Florida film producer, at odds with the IRS, who tries to orchestrate a movie deal based on the writings (and ravings) of an eccentric new-age guru (Dennis Hopper), the financing of a commodities/cocaine dealer (Christopher Walken) and the underworld contacts of a speed-freak yuppie (John Turturro). Possessed by moments of articulate insights, painter-turned-artist Salle's work is not altogether successful, relying too much on the gratuitously weird nature of the characters and situations to sustain it; rather than allowing his marvelous ensemble to breathe into it. Ileanna Douglas gives a heartfelt performance as Dunne's low self-esteem girlfriend, the film's producer Martin Scorsese appears in a cameo, and Rosanna Arquette and Ethan Hawke also star. ★★½ $19.99

The Search for Signs of Intelligent Life in the Universe

(1991, 120 min, US, Jane Wagner) This delightful and engaging Tony Award-winning two-hour, one-woman show can easily be considered Lily Tomlin's magnum opus. The show centers around Trudy the Bag Lady as she escorts a group of visiting aliens from outer space and attempts to enlighten them on human idiosyncracies. Using this premise, Lily jumps from one character to another amazingly giving life — without benefit of makeup or costume — to such Tomlin creations as Chrissie, making time at her aerobics workout; the punked-out Agnes Angst on a memorable visit to Grandma and Grandpa's; a male weightlifter; streetwalkers Tina and Brandi who entertain the press; and, as the centerpiece of all of this, Lynn, Marge and Edie (a middle-class white woman, a black radical and a drunken feminist), who make their way through the '70s and the early days of the women's movement. The best humor in the piece comes from Trudy, however, as she pontificates on her own unique brand of cosmology. Relying primarily on footage from the actual show, the film occasionally cuts to staged re-creations of the vignettes. ★★★½ $29.99

The Searchers

(1956, 119 min, US, John Ford) In a career rich with milestones, Ford achieved one of his greatest artistic triumphs with this beautifully filmed western. John Wayne had one of his most complex characters — possibly wanted by the law and consumed with racial hatred — as Ethan Edwards, who after his brother and sister-in-law are murdered by Indians, sets out to locate his kidnapped niece (played by a young Natalie Wood). Jeffery Hunter also stars as Wood's brother who accompanies Wayne on his relentless, years-long search. ★★★★ $19.99

Searching for Bobby Fisher

(1993, 110 min, US, Steven Zaillian) Every competitive endeavor, whether baseball, figure skating or chess, contains at its core artistry and purity. It's remarkable for a film to capture the passionate involvement of an activity's participants; even more so when the activity is as internal as that of chess. *Searching for Bobby Fisher* is profoundly successful in this. The story of a young boy's initiation into a glorious obsession with chess is intercut with an almost mythologized recounting of the career of Bobby Fisher. The film addresses the negative aspects of competition — the pressures, the ruthlessness — with a noticable absence of preaching and a good dose of sly wit. Joe Mantegna, Ben Kingsley, Laurence Fishburne and Joan Allen deliver impressive performances, and young Max Pomeranc is mesmerizing as Josh, the 10-year-old whose intuitive grasp of the game thrusts him into a world of rivalry, clashing egos and immense satisfactions. ★★★★ $14.99

S

Kate Maberly and Andrew Knott in Agnieszka Holland's *The Secret Garden (1993)*

Season of the Witch

(1976, 89 min, US, George A. Romero) The director of *Night of the Living Dead* takes on witchcraft with this boring tale of a young woman grappling to hang onto her sanity as she becomes enmeshed with members of a witches' coven. ★½

Sebastiane

(1976, 82 min, GB, Derek Jarman) Jarman's sensual, lushly photographed, highly erotic (and homoerotic) vision of the legend of St. Sebastian is filled with beautiful images of male bodies and graphic scenes of sex and torture. The lives of few saints are as shrouded in mystery as that of the celebrated martyr Sebastian, whose arrow-pierced body has become one of the most familiar images in Christian iconography. In this film, he is perceived as a Christian sympathizer who, sent into exile by the Emperor Diocletian, becomes involved in a sadomasochistic intrigue which ultimately results in his death. Music by Brian Eno. (Latin with English subtitles) ★★★ $79.99

Second Best

(1994, 105 min, GB, Chris Menges) A harrowing and at times bleak story of father-son relationships, *Second Best* stars William Hurt as an introverted Welsh postmaster who petitions to adopt a troubled ten-year-old. The story, which has as much to do with the adoption process as with interpersonal relationships, follows the rocky road on which Hurt must gain the trust and ultimately the affection of his young charge, who still envisions a reunion with his gaoled father. At the same time, Hurt must exorcise his own paternal demons as his father lies close to death. Hurt gives a controlled, sincere performance as a man clinging to life, and Chris Cleary Miles is startlingly good as the young boy. The two actors help smooth over some of the more choppy dramatics. ★★½ $19.99

Second Chance

(1953, 81 min, US, Rudolph Maté) Potent mystery thriller with Robert Mitchum as an ex-boxer who helps gangster's girlfriend Linda Darnell elude contract killer Jack Palance in Mexico. ★★½

Second Chorus

(1940, 83 min, US, H.C. Potter) Fred Astaire and Burgess Meredith are fellow musicians who set their sights on their lovely manager, Paulette Goddard. Not without its charms, but by no means one of Fred's better musicals. ★★½ $19.99

Seconds

(1966, 106 min, US, John Frankenheimer) Director Frankenheimer's long-unreleased classic thriller has finally made its way to home video, in a restored European cut. Rock Hudson stars, in what is arguably his best screen performance, as the "after" part of a bizarre transformational experiment. A middle-aged businessman, tired of his life, job and wife, goes to a mysterious organization which promises to remake him, to give him a second chance. After extensive surgery, he wakes up with a new face and identity, that of an artist. Settling into his new life, he eventually realizes that he will never find the happiness which he thought was waiting around the corner. So he returns to the organization for another try, with unfortunate results. This bizarre but simple story is itself transformed into a masterpiece of paranoia and horror by Frankenheimer's taut direction and James Wong Howe's dazzling, canted-angled, black-and-white cinematography. Faces are blown up to unreal proportions and even a simple cocktail party turns into a nightmare. Disturbing but brilliant, *Seconds* always remains plausible, its proposition desirable enough to make it seem very real. ★★★½ $79.99

Secret Admirer

(1986, 98 min, US, David Greenwall) An intriguing premise can't sustain this uneven sex comedy about a teenager (C. Thomas Howell) who wrongly assumes the identity of the sender of an anonymous love letter. When the letter falls into the hands of adults Cliff De Young, Dee Wallace Stone, Fred Ward and Leigh Taylor-Young, further complications arise. ★★

The Secret Agent

(1936, 86 min, GB, Alfred Hitchcock) Taken from an episode in "Ashenden," a W. Somerset Maugham novel, this gripping story follows agent John Gielgud, dispatched to Switzerland to terminate a spy whose identity he doesn't know. Director Hitchcock creates maximum suspense with his usual flair. Co-starring Madeleine Carroll, Peter Lorre and Robert Young. ★★★ $24.99

The Secret Agent

Starring Bob Hoskins
See: Joseph Conrad's The Secret Agent

Secret Ceremony

(1968, 109 min, US, Joseph Losey) This campy psychological thriller stars Elizabeth Taylor and Mia Farrow as strangers who create a fantasy world, living together as mother and daughter. Their relationship is threatened when Farrow's stepfather (Robert Mitchum) appears on the scene. Pamela Brown and Peggy Ashcroft co-star. ★★

The Secret Cinema/Naughty Nurse

(1966/1969, 29/8 min, US, Paul Bartel) The first film of cult director Bartel tells the tale of an actress unable to decipher if her life is real, or whether she is simply the filmed subject of a diabolical director. Also includes the Bartel short "Naughty Nurse." ★★½

Secret Fantasy

(1979, 88 min, Italy, Pasquale Festa Campanile) The beleaguered Nicolo (Lando Buzzanca) is a middle-aged cellist who becomes obsessed with the idea that his beautiful wife (Laura Antonelli) is running around with other men. At his wife's insistence, he visits a psychiatrist who advises our hero to relax and explore his own sexual fantasies. A steamy, erotic sexual fantasy for the adventurous. (Dubbed) ★★

The Secret File on J. Edgar Hoover

(1993, 60 min, US, William Cran) Originally broadcast on PBS, this hard-hitting exposé seeks to reveal the "depth of Hoover's personal corruption." The investigation hits on his gambling problems, the misappropriation of public funds for personal use, his unexplained laxity in battling the Mafia, and his hidden homosexuality. As FBI director for 48 years, Hoover enjoyed amazing popularity; after his death, however, reports have revealed his tyrannical control and abuse of power. The most lurid of the revelations concern his homosexuality and relationship with his assistant and constant companion, Clyde Tolson. Were the two simply lifelong, "monastic" bachelors and best friends, or were they "sex deviants" with Hoover being "terrorized by his urges?" Interviewing former FBI agents and eyewitnesses, the documentary lays claim that the two were not simply lovers but rather outlandish homosexuals who "held each other's hands"

S

and engaged in sex parties; and Hoover was being blackmailed by the Mafia with pictures of him giving head to Tolson! Whatever interest this documentary may hold is offset by its subtly anti-gay sentiments. ★★ $14.99

The Secret Garden

(1992, 100 min, US, Alan Grant) Based on the best-selling children's book of the same name, this Hallmark Hall of Fame production provides enchanting quality entertainment. Upon being orphaned, Young Mary is sent to an English estate to live with a family friend. Ill-treated by her new providers, she is sad and bitter until she discovers the estate's secret garden and all of its mysteries. Along with her newfound friends, the sickly Colin and the philosphical Dickon, she brings the garden back to life. This compelling story, along with the wonderfully talented young cast will charm the entire family. ★★★ $14.99

The Secret Garden

(1993, 101 min, US, Agnieszka Holland) Holland makes her English-language debut with this superlative adaptation of Frances Hodgson Burnett's 1909 children's classic. This must assuredly be considered the definitive screen translation of this oft-adapted tale. Ten-year-old Mary Lennox is sent to live in the gloomy estate of her uncle, Lord Craven. There she is chastened by the manor's obdurate housekeeper Mrs. Medlock (stonily portrayed by Maggie Smith) not to snoop, which, of course, she immediately does. Emotionally and visually rich in every detail, Holland's film probes the psychological aspects of the story as young Mary (flawlessly portrayed by Kate Maberly) uncovers the house's secrets and befriends both its sickly young master and a local farm boy with an affinity for animals. ★★★★ $19.99

Secret Honor

(1984, 90 min, US, Robert Altman) Philip Baker Hall gives a bravura performance in this lacerating Altman adaptation of an original screenplay about the political and personal demise of Richard Nixon. The action transpires in Nixon's private office, sometime after

his resignation. Embittered by his political fortunes, brimming with hatred and vengeance, he launches into a ferocious monologue about his obsessions and regrets. Throughout, we are given a sometimes touching, often repugnant, look at a frightfully complex man. Altman has once again proven his mastery of bringing ambitiously offbeat projects to the screen with astonishing results. ★★★½

The Secret Life of Walter Mitty

(1947, 110 min, US, Norman Z. McLeod) One of Danny Kaye's most popular films, this funny adaptation of James Thurber's comedy has Danny as the timid, day-dreaming hero whose constant fantasies get him involved in real-life adventures. Kaye's constant co-star Virginia Mayo is as lovely as ever, and Boris Karloff has an amusing supporting role as a psychiatrist. ★★★ $19.99

The Secret of My Success

(1987, 110 min, US, Herbert Ross) There are echoes of *How to Succeed in Business...* in this amiable though lowbrow comedy with Michael J. Fox coming to the big city and moving up the corporate ladder thanks to a little chicanery. Fox is the main attraction here. ★★½ $9.99

The Secret of N*I*M*H

(1982, 84 min, US, Don Bluth) Charming, low-keyed animated tale, based on Robert C. O'Brien's award-winning children's book, about a mother mouse who tries to save her home from being destroyed with the aid of her wacky animal friends. Featuring the voices of Dom DeLuise, John Carradine, Derek Jacobi and Peter Strauss. ★★★ $14.99

The Secret of Roan Inish

(1995, 103 min, US, John Sayles) Chameleonic director Sayles once again proves his range by venturing into virgin waters with this lyrical and enchanting Irish fairy tale. Based on the novel "Secret of Ron Mor Skerry" by Rosallie K. Fry, the story follows Fiona Coneelly, a young girl who is sent to live with her grandparents on Ireland's rugged and forbidding northwestern coast. Unperturbed by her change of scene, Fiona begins to pursue her

murky family history and long-lost baby brother. His mystery revolves around a remote island called Roan Inish, the ancestral stomping grounds of the Coneelly clan and home to Selkies, mystical half-seal and half-human sea creatures. With the help of cinematographer Haskell Wexler's haunting imagery, Sayles presents a flawless piece of storytelling that is as heartwarming as it is foreboding. Jeni Courtney gives a performance well beyond her years as Fiona, an intrepid adventuress into the realm of myth. As her grizzled grandpa and archetypally Irish grandma, Mick Lally and Eileen Colgan are both extraordinary — through them, Sayles pays brilliant homage to oral traditions. ★★★★ $19.99

Secret Places

(1985, 96 min, GB, Zelda Barron) Set in an English boarding school during WWII, this warm, often moving drama follows two schoolgirls from very different backgrounds who form an ill-fated friendship. A poignant and sensitive exposé of the chasms between social classes featuring a youthful dialogue on love, sex, philosophy and patriotism. ★★★ $79.99

The Secret Policeman's Other Ball

(1982, 92 min, GB, Julien Temple) Yet another benefit show for Amnesty International featuring the loonies of the Monty Python gang along with Peter Cook and other British wackos. An onslaught of hysterical skits is interspersed with the music of Pete Townshend of The Who. ★★★

The Secret Policeman's Private Parts

(1984, 77 min, GB, Julien Temple & Robert Graef Jr.) The zanies from the Monty Python gang are joined by Peter Cook, Connie Booth, Pete Townshend, Phil Collins, and Pope Bob Geldof in this Amnesty International Benefit Show. A variety of sketches, filmed live, are guaranteed to evoke a state of sublime silliness. ★★★

The Secret Rapture

(1994, 96 min, GB, Howard Davies) David Hare's masterful screen adaptation of his original play is this study of a young woman (Juliet Stevenson of *Truly, Madly, Deeply*) who must reevaluate her life when her father's death leaves her in the care of his manipulative, alcoholic widow (Joanne Whalley-Kilmer). The film is at once intimate and powerful and, flawed fourth act notwithstanding, is a welcome addition to the British film canon. In a remarkably textured performance that is sorrowful and triumphant, Stevenson joins the pantheon of previous Hare-oines that has included Meryl Streep (*Plenty*) and Vanessa Redgrave (*Wetherby*). Also with Penelope Wilton. ★★★½ $14.99

Secrets & Lies

(1996, 142 min, GB, Mike Leigh) Director Leigh, a consummate cinematic storyteller, can delineate a lifestyle by the length of a hemline and encapsulate a life history with a sentence fragment. He approaches his protagonists with heartfelt empathy delicately balanced with unflinching honesty. In this film, he brilliantly communicates two decades of one family's secrets and lies, brought to light by one

The Secret of Roan Inish

woman's search for her birth mother. Marianne Jean-Baptiste gives one of several superlative performances from the ensemble as Hortense, the daughter given up for adoption. Her quest to discover her biological mother injects Hortense into another family's intricate obfuscations and smoldering resentments. As her birth mother Cynthia, Brenda Blethyn perfectly embodies a woman at sea in the world, buffeted by circumstance, imbued with defeat and helplessness. Cynthia, who is white, is at first overwhelmed by the arrival of Hortense, who is black. But before long, the shock transforms to catharsis as Hortense, comfortably middle class, invites Cynthia to participate in a happier world, which Cynthia previously viewed only as an outsider. Timothy Spall delivers a deceptively understated performance as Cynthia's brother Maurice, the family's locus and diffuser of conflict. *Secrets & Lies* utilizes the grinding minutiae of daily living to underscore raw emotion and numbing regret, and yet acknowledges with joyous tribute the indomitable human spirit. ★★★★ $102.99

Secrets of Women

(1952, 108 min, Sweden, Ingmar Bergman) This early Bergman comedy is a thought-provoking and witty story of the indiscretions and foibles of man. Set in a summer home, three women confide in one another about their relationships with their husbands. Their extramarital affairs and the rapprochements with their men make for interesting conversation with amusing insights into the human condition. (Available dubbed and in Swedish with English subtitles) ★★★ $39.99

Seduced and Abandoned

(1964, 118 min, Italy, Pietro Germi) This witty yet bitter film studies the inequalities and injustices of the Sicilian moral code. A young woman is befriended and seduced by the fiancé of her sister. His denial of any responsibility and his abandonment destroys her. The film alternates between a bedroom farce and social realism and is a successful follow-up to the director's *Divorce, Italian Style*. (Italian with English subtitles) ★★★

The Seduction of Mimi

(1974, 89 min, Italy, Lina Wertmüller) A boisterous farce on machismo Italian-style with Giancarlo Giannini as the frustrated Mimi. Wertmüller's surgically sharp satire earned her a reputation on the international scene. (Italian with English subtitles) ★★★½ $29.99

Seduction: The Cruel Woman

(1985, 84 min, West Germany, Elfi Mikesch & Monica Treut) Treut and Mikesch's highly stylized and dreamlike exploration of sado-masochism stars Mechthild Grossmann as Wanda — a glamorous dominatrix and proprietor of the local "gallery" of bondage. As she moves from relationship to relationship, the film plumbs the depths of the dark side of sexual desire. Sheila McGlaughlin (*She Must Be Seeing Things*) also stars in this slick visual fantasy which is inspired as much by the photography of Helmut Newton as by Leopold Sacher-Masoch's 1869 work, "Venus in Furs." ★★★ $29.99

See No Evil, Hear No Evil

(1989, 103 min, US, Arthur Hiller) Richard Pryor and Gene Wilder team for a third time in this amiable and often funny comedy. The comics play two mismatched, prospective coworkers — the catch is that Pryor is blind and Wilder is deaf — who become suspects in a murder which they (sort of) witnessed. The film is mostly one long chase as the two try to elude the police while they try to track down the real killers. *See No Evil...* has questionable taste in a couple of its gags, but it is mostly an entertaining and humorous romp enlivened by two comic princes. ★★½ $14.99

See You in the Morning

(1989, 119 min, US, Alan J. Pakula) Jeff Bridges and Alice Krige star in this uneven romantic comedy-drama as a middle-aged couple struggling with issues of parenthood and past spouses. A slightly disappointing effort from Pakula. Also starring Farrah Fawcett, Linda Lavin, Drew Barrymore and Lucas Haas. ★★ $14.99

See You Monday

(1979, 100 min, Canada, Maurice Dugowson) With possibly the worst title song ever record-ed for a motion picture, this French-Canadian coproduction starts off on the wrong foot and never recovers. French actress Miou-Miou (in a definite career mistake) costars with '70s cute TV personality David Birney in this middle-of-the-road soap opera made in Montreal. Miou-Miou is a saccharine-sweet redhead who, along with her friend, realize that they are tired of getting involved with married men and become determined to change their ways. An oddity, and a poor one at that. ★

Seeding of a Ghost

(1989, 100 min, Hong Kong) This mind-bending, violent supernatural/horror film follows a taxi driver/adulterer who, through the use of witchcraft, takes vengeance for the brutal rape-murder of his also-cheating wife. Spiced with incredible F/X and a bizarre story line, and laced with some great martial arts street fights, this genre-blending tour de force may be one of the finest examples of Asian exploitation cinema. ★★★½ $59.99

Seems Like Old Times

(1980, 121 min, US, Jay Sandrich) Goldie Hawn and Chevy Chase reteamed after their successful *Foul Play* in this bright, funny Neil Simon comedy. Goldie plays a lawyer whose ex-husband (Chase) reenters the scene, much to the chagrin of new husband Charles Grodin. ★★★ $19.99

Seize the Day

(1986, 105 min, US, Fielder Cook) Compelling adaptation of Saul Bellow's novel starring Robin Williams in a fine dramatic performance as an unemployed 40-year-old divorcée who moves to New York City to begin life anew. There he is greeted by the brutality and corruption of the corporate world. ★★★ $29.99

Seizure

(1974, 93 min, Canada, Oliver Stone) A horror novelist (Jonathan Frid) invites several friends to his home for the weekend, where his sinister dreams come to life to torment his guests. This ordinary thriller marks Stone's first feature — he has done better since. Cast includes Troy Donahue, Mary Woronov, Herve Villechaize, Martine Beswicke and Christine Pickles. ★★

The Senator Was Indiscreet

(1947, 81 min, US, George S. Kaufman) In the great playwright George S. Kaufman's only directorial effort, William Powell is perfect as an incompetent, foolhardy senator who decides to run for President (that could never happen in *real* life); Powell's candidacy is sabotaged by a personal diary. An effervescent political satire. ★★★ $19.99

The Sender

(1982, 92 min, GB, Roger Christian) A suicidal mental patient (Zeljko Ivanek) turns his horrific nightmares into reality by choosing receivers for his demented thoughts. Some good chills in this unexpected thriller. Kathryn Harrold, Shirley Knight and Paul Freeman costar. ★★½ $19.99

Sense and Sensibility

(1986, 174 min, GB, Rodney Bennett) This excellent TV version of Jane Austen's first

The Seduction of Mimi

S

Sense and Sensibility ('95)

novel is a charming tale about two sisters — one well-mannered and restrained and the other outspoken and impetuous — who are looking for love and happiness amidst the rigid social mores of 18th-century England. Imbued with a lighthearted and amorous humor, the story follows their initial attempts at husband hunting and their ensuing disappointments. ★★★½ $29.99

Sense and Sensibility

(1995, 135 min, GB, Ang Lee) If Jane Austen had a Hollywood agent, she could be reaping in megabucks right now. Her popularity is at an all-time high (over the past 170 years, that is) and this luscious adaptation of one of her better known novels is sure to push it even higher. Emma Thompson produced and wrote the adaptation, and then hired the masterful Taiwanese director Lee (*The Wedding Banquet*) to helm — together they have made as seemly a rendering of Austen as one is likely to see. Thompson and Kate Winslet play the two Dashwood sisters who, legally unable to be the rightful heirs of their father's will, are forced out of their impressive estate (and "polite" society). Their dilemma, of course, is how to marry — after all, in early 19th-century society, women without dowries were hard to pawn off. Hence, the story revolves around their conundrum as they pin their hopes on a handful of suitors including the affable Hugh Grant, lovesick Alan Rickman and handsome Greg Wise. Though essentially a drama, Thompson's playful screenplay, in the hands of Lee, finds a great deal of good humor in Austen's story and makes the most of it. Awash with excellent performances, the film exhibits an economy of manners that would do Austen proud. (Available letterboxed and pan & scan) ★★★★ $19.99

A Sense of Freedom

(1978, 85 min, GB, John MacKenzie) Based on an autobiographical novel by Jimmy Boyle, an inveterate Glasgow gangster whose activities earned him a life sentence for homicide and whose violent disposition hardly abated once behind bars. Filmed for Scottish television, it features an intense, hard-edged performance by David Hagman as the pugilistic Boyle who revels in antagonizing prisoners and guards alike. ★★★

A Sense of Loss

(1978, 105 min, France, Marcel Ophüls) Ophüls, the director of *The Sorrow and the Pity*, made this searing but balanced documentary about the neverending conflict in Northern Ireland. The film reveals how this ageless tragedy creates a nightmarish society of hatred and violence. ★★★

Senso (Wanton Countess)

(1954, 120 min, Italy, Luchino Visconti) A lavish and tragic tale of love and war and one of the landmarks of post-war Italian cinema. The story concerns the careless actions of an aristocratic woman (Alida Valli) who sacrifices her marriage and security for a handsome but cowardly soldier (Farley Granger). This lavishly romantic story is set in Venice in 1866 on the eve of the great conflict between Venice and Austria. (Italian with English subtitles) ★★★½

Sensual Man

(1974, 90 min, Italy, Marco Vicario) The ubiquitous Giancarlo Giannini (the Gérard Depardieu of Italian films), stars as a lusty, irresponsible playboy whose life consists of a series of sexual episodes which include a relationship with the former mistress of Mussolini as well as a Communist member of Parliament. His fantasy-filled life ends when he falls in love and marries: his wife suffers from a psychological block which prevents her from consummating the marriage. Will he accept his purgatory on earth? (Dubbed) ★★

The Sentinel

(1977, 92 min, US, Michael Winner) A young model (Christina Raines) moves into a Brooklyn Heights brownstone, which happens to be the gateway to Hell. This hilariously hyperventilating mix of *The Exorcist* and *Rosemary's Baby* is enjoyably bizarre trash. Also with Chris Sarandon, Ava Gardner and Burgess Meredith. ★★ $14.99

A Separate Peace

(1972, 104 min, US, Larry Peerce) John Knowles' best-selling novel makes a not-altogether successful transition to film in this sunsplashed teenage drama of friendship, initiation and betrayal. Reminiscent of *Summer of '42* and the first part of *Brideshead Revisited*, the action, set at a prep school at the beginning of WWII, focuses on two roommates' developing friendship. Parker Stevenson is the freshly scrubbed narrator Gene who falls under the charismatic power of the athletic and domineering Finny (John Heyl). Their friendship is tested after a freak accident, possibly caused by Gene, injures Finny. His injury and the ensuing strain on their relationship forces the two to grow up and begin to face the harsh reality of the world outside the school's protective gates. While pretty to look at, the film tests the patience as it slows to an aimless crawl after the accident. ★★ $49.99

Separate Tables

(1958, 99 min, US, Delbert Mann) A superlative adaptation of two Terence Rattigan one-act plays, combined in one telling, about a group of vacationers at an English seaside resort. A miraculous ensemble includes Burt Lancaster and Rita Hayworth as a divorced

couple; David Niven (in his Oscar-winning role) as an ex-military hero who may or may not be a fraud; Deborah Kerr as a lonely spinster; and Oscar winner Wendy Hiller as Lancaster's long-suffering mistress. Also with Gladys Cooper, Rod Taylor and Cathleen Nesbitt. Though the entire cast is praiseworthy, it is Niven, Kerr and Hiller who walk away with the acting honors. ★★★★ $19.99

Separate Tables

(1983, 112 min, GB, John Schlesinger) Director Schlesinger's made-for-TV rendition of Terence Rattigan's pair of playlets is every bit as worthy as the 1958 film version with Burt Lancaster and Wendy Hiller. In "Table by the Window," Julie Christie plays an aging fashion model who travels to a seaside resort in the hopes of rekindling a relationship with her ex-husband (Alan Bates). In "Table Number Seven," Christie plays a woman who holds a secret love for an Army major (Bates) who is embroiled in a public scandal. Both Bates and Christie offer superb performances and excellent supporting work comes from Claire Bloom and Irene Worth. ★★★½ $59.99

September

(1987, 82 min, US, Woody Allen) Venturing into his *Interiors* ouvre, this yuckless, Chekhovian chamber piece concerns a group of six successful people who vent their frustrations, angst and regrets during a weekend retreat in Vermont. A fine but underutilized cast includes Denholm Elliott, Mia Farrow, Elaine Stritch, Sam Waterston, Jack Warden, Dianne Wiest and Allen himself. A seriously flawed work by Allen which is probably his least accomplished film. ★★ $14.99

September 30, 1955

(1977, 107 min, US, James Bridges) Richard Thomas heads a terrific youthful cast (which includes Lisa Blount, Tom Hulce, Dennis Quaid and Dennis Christopher) in this intriguing character study. The title refers to the day actor James Dean died, and the film traces the effect Dean's death has on an idolizing college student (Thomas) and his fellow classmates. The film alternates between the merry exploits of teenage hijinks and the drama of *East of Eden*-like soul searching. Leonard Rosenman's score from that film is used here to good effect, and writer-director Bridges has created compelling characters in this semiautobiography. In one of his few starring movie roles, Thomas is excellent and successfully captures the essence of teenage alienation. ★★★ $14.99

Sgt. Bilko

(1996, 94 min, US, Jonathan Lynn) If this sometimes funny version of the classic TV series doesn't sustain a consistent hilarity level, it does make up for it by an engaging cast who perform with unswerving energy. Taking over the role created by the immortal Phil Silvers, Steve Martin has big shoes to fill as Sgt. Bilko, military con man and bull artist extraordinaire. The story — what there is of it — has to do with Bilko and his gang facing the wrath of a visiting major, played to the hilt by Phil Hartman. Impersonations, pratfalls, silly sight gags and double speak are the order of the day as Bilko tries every trick in the book to rid himself of this major pain in the neck. Though the big-

S

The Servant

screen *Sgt. Bilko* lacks the lightning-fast pace of the show, and Martin can't duplicate Silver's inimitable breakneck delivery, there's still laughs to be found. One of the best of them has to do with the military's "Don't ask, don't tell" policy, an update which probably would have elicited a great double take from Silvers' usually collected sergeant. ★★½ $14.99

Sergeant Rutledge

(1960, 118 min, US, John Ford) Ford's tale of an African-American sergeant in the U.S. Cavalry standing trial for rape and murder. Ford's attempts to comment on racism are marred by the fact that the story is a muddled mix of the Old West and contemporary politics, and that the story really focuses on Jeffrey Hunter, the white lieutenant who defends Sergeant Rutledge. Woody Strode's quiet performance as the title character is engaging, but in the end is nothing more than a cliché. ★★½ $14.99

Sergeant York

(1941, 134 min, US, Howard Hawks) Gary Cooper won the first of his two Oscars for his stirring performance in this fact-based story of backwoodsman Alvin York, a pacifist drafted during World War I whose mental anguish and soul-searching leads him to reconcile his conflicting convictions, becoming a war hero on the battlefields of France. Expert direction by Hawks. ★★★★ $19.99

Serial Mom

(1994, 95 min, US, John Waters) Waters has created his most accessible film – a terrifically executed satire on suburbia, sex and violence, and our obsession with celebrity criminals. Kathleen Turner is delicious as a June Cleaverish housewife: She cooks, cleans, listens to Barry Manilow, and even recycles. And she's a serial killer, too. Not indiscriminately, however; this bloody mama only kills to protect family and hearth. As husband and kids begin to realize the truth and the police close in, Waters lets loose a series of comic salvos which

both tantalize and underscore his topical burlesque. You know you're in familiar Waters when Turner kills a victim with a leg of lamb while the score to *Annie* blares in the background. Longtime Waters co-hort Mink Stole is most memorable as a victimized neighbor. This twisted and defiantly hilarious comedy also serves as a cautionary tale to careless video renters: Rewind! ★★★½ $14.99

The Serpent's Egg

(1978, 120 min, West Germany/US, Ingmar Bergman) Bergman's troubled and frightening drama about survival in the dawn of Nazi Germany. Set in 1933 Berlin, the film is about a Jewish-American trapeze artist (David Carradine) and his sister-in-law (Liv Ullmann), threatened by a mad doctor who portends the Nazi catastrophe that is soon to befall Germany. (Filmed in English) ★★½

Serpico

(1973, 129 min, US, Sidney Lumet) Al Pacino gives a sterling performance in this based-on-fact story about a non-conformist New York City undercover cop who is ostracized by his fellow officers when he reports widespread police corruption. Director Lumet's first of his "corruption" films (followed by *Prince of the City*, *Q & A* and *Night Falls on Manhattan*) is a hard-hitting and exemplary look at one man's personal courage. Fine location shooting helps in the authenticity of the story. Based on Peter Maas' best-seller. ★★★½ $14.99

The Servant

(1963, 115 min, GB, Joseph Losey) Dirk Bogarde and Sarah Miles star in one of Losey's most tantalizing and complex films. Taken from Harold Pinter's first screenplay, it's a sardonic household study of the fickleness of the power and the daily moral hypocrisies of the British upper-class. ★★★½

Servants of Twilight

(1991, 96 min, US, Jeffrey Obrow) A mother and her young son are accosted by a wild-eyed,

disheveled woman in a parking garage who claims that the son is the child of Satan and must be destroyed. Frustrated by police inaction, the mother hires a private investigator to protect the boy from murderous attacks by crazed cult members. Strong acting and a well-scripted story line keep the action moving through various twists and turns as the viewer is deftly guided to a quite unexpected denouement. Grace Zabriskie and Carel Struycken (the giant from "Twin Peaks") are especially good as two of the lunatic cult members. Based on a best-seller by Dean R. Koontz. ★★½ $9.99

Set It Off

(1996, 120 min, US, F. Gary Gray) Four black women, close friends and sick and tired of being screwed by the system, decide to turn the tables by robbing some banks. An enjoyable caper film, *Set It Off* is never believable, but energetic and pulpy enough to satisfy. The social commentary is obvious, and the circumstances leading up to the ladies' fateful decision is as heavy-handed and generic as a stock gangster film from the '30s. In fact, the film resembles nothing so much as an updated Cagney flick with a race and gender change – complete with a "crime doesn't pay" message that feels pasted on. Once you can get past the "it's society's fault" exposition, however, *Set It Off* becomes a genuinely entertaining crime film which manages a few kinetic action scenes along the way. Queen Letifah steals the show as a kick-ass lesbian tough, and Jada Pinkett is quite affecting as a woman of conscience. ★★★ $102.99

The Set-Up

(1949, 72 min, US, Robert Wise) Robert Ryan is splendid as a washed-up boxer who, instead of throwing a big fight, rescues his pride but incures the wrath of mobsters. A stirring drama of rampant corruption and personal redemption. ★★★ $19.99

Seven

(1995, 125 min, US, David Fincher) *Seven* is a plummeting descent into the ink-black recesses of the human soul – and one human soul in particular so revolted by the casual and profane excesses of his fellow creatures that he devises a series of intricate and carefully produced executions/passion plays/performance pieces to express his revulsion. He re-creates each of the seven deadly sins in tableaux of rare irony and brutal torture. The police on his trail (Morgan Freeman, world-weary and bone tired and near retirement; and Brad Pitt, young and eager and newly transferred) are dogged and determined, but there is no moral redemption here. While the film at first seems textbook in its element – grizzled veteran, frisky new guy, crazed serial killer – the formula resolution is rejected for a darker vision. The film emanates rain-swept foreboding, and Freeman's performance is a study of nuance. A remarkable execution of extremely unsettling material. (Available letterboxed and pan & scan) ★★★½ $19.99

Seven Beauties

(1976, 115 min, Italy, Lina Wertmüller) Giancarlo Giannini is superb as Wertmüller's Everyman who lives through the horrors of

482

WWII and the concentration camps. Quite possibly her greatest achievement. (Dubbed) ★★★★

Seven Brides for Seven Brothers

(1954, 103 min, US, Stanley Donen) Donen (*Singin' in the Rain*) directed this classic M-G-M musical starring Howard Keel and Jane Powell. Keel plays the eldest of seven brothers who marries, prompting the other six to take wives – by kidnapping them. Superb dance sequences choreographed by Michael Kidd. Also starring Russ Tamblyn, Tommy Rall and Julie Newmar. ★★★★ $14.99

Seven Chances/Neighbors/ The Balloonatic

(1920-25, 96 min, US, Buster Keaton/Eddie Cline) A collection of three Buster Keaton comedies. *Seven Chances* (1925, 56 min) is a buoyant romp with Keaton as a sad sack who will inherit seven million dollars – but only if he weds by 7:00 PM that evening. Thus begins a wild scramble to find a willing wife. The film is highlighted by a hilarious prolonged chase sequence in which Keaton is pursued by hundreds of women through back alleys, city streets and across the countryside. (★★★1/2) *Neighbors* (1920, 18 min), written and directed by Keaton and Eddie Cline, is a delightful comedy with Keaton involved in a "Romeo and Juliet"-type romance with neighbor Virginia Fox. The two families, separated by a mutual back fence, try to put a stop to it. Keaton's ingenious ploys to woo and wed Fox are wonderful. The film's accent is on physical stunts, and all are remarkable. (★★★1/2) *The Balloonatic* (1923, 22 min) finds Keaton adrift in a hot air balloon, eventually crashing to earth and finding love and misadventures. (★★★) $29.99

Seven Days in May

(1964, 118 min, US, John Frankenheimer) This flawless political thriller is so frightening because it is so possible. Burt Lancaster is the Chairman of the Joint Chiefs of Staff planning a military coup if the President (Fredric March) goes ahead and signs that nuclear disarmament treaty with the Russians. A taut script from Rod Serling is accentuated by fine direction from Frankenheimer and terrific performances from Lancaster, March, Kirk Douglas and Edmond O'Brien. ★★★★ $19.99

Seven Deadly Sins

(1953, 127 min, Italy/France, Roberto Rossellini/Edouard Molinaro/Yves Allegret) A below-average video transfer, and white subtitles that fall below the screen many times, sadly mar this enjoyable moral comedy devoted to man's seven deadly sins – Avarice, Anger, Sloth, Lust, Envy, Gluttony and Pride. This omnibus is fashioned episodically, with each of the dangerously alluring vices made by a different director, including: Roberto Rossellini, Edouard Molinaro, Yves Allegret and Claude Autant-Lara. Surprisingly ribald, the film is hard going because of its low quality, but if you speak a little French or Italian (or both), or are not bothered by subtitle drop out, the film will prove to be a delightfully irreverent peek into man's baser nature. (French and Italian with English subtitles) ★★1/2 $29.99

The Seven Faces of Dr. Lao

(1964, 100 min, US, George Pal) Pal's fanciful fantasy with Tony Randall giving a tour de force performance as the proprietor of a traveling circus. Randall plays seven roles. Oscar-winner for Makeup Effects. ★★★

The Seven Percent Solution

(1976, 113 min, US, Herbert Ross) Sherlock Holmes' coke paranoia has gotten so bad that Dr. Watson (Robert Duvall) concocts a scheme, with the help of Prof. Moriarty (Laurence Olivier), to get Holmes (Nicol Williamson) to see Dr. Sigmund Freud (Alan Arkin) and take the cure. While in Vienna, he might as well solve a few mysteries while he's at it. Engrossing fun from the pen of Nicholas Meyer (*Time After Time*), directed with panache by Ross. ★★★1/2 $14.99

Seven Samurai

(1954, 200 min, Japan, Akira Kurosawa) A passionate, exhilarating epic that stands alone in the realm of adventure films. To defend a flock of villagers, a small band of mighty warriors combat a horde of invading bandits. Kurosawa studies the intricate code of honor among the fighting men and their uneasy alliance with the downtrodden farmers. The complete, uncut version. (Japanese with English subtitles) ★★★★ $34.99

Seven Thieves

(1960, 102 min, US, Henry Hathaway) A brilliant thief (Edward G. Robinson) gathers a crew of criminal cronies to help him pull off his final crowning heist: robbing the casino vault at Monte Carlo. Tension-filled with good characterizations. Also starring Rod Steiger, Joan Collins, Eli Wallach and Sebastian Cabot. ★★★ $39.99

The Seven Year Itch

(1955, 105 min, US, Billy Wilder) Wilder's witty and zany romp exposes the sexual fantasies of the middle-aged married man. Marilyn Monroe is the unintending temptress upstairs who becomes the object of Tom Ewell's Walter Mitty-ish, philandering escapades. ★★★1/2 $14.99

1776

(1972, 141 min, US, Peter H. Hunt) A sparkling version of the Tony Award-winning Broadway musical about the events leading up to the signing of the Declaration of Independence. Far from a detail-ridden history lesson, this rousing entertainment is a witty, clever and significant glance at the framing of a country. Most of the original stage stars repeat their roles, with William Daniels in his finest hour as the antagonistic lobbyist for independence, John Adams; he's smartly supported by the wonderful Howard da Silva as Ben Franklin, Ken Howard as Thomas Jefferson and John Cullum (TV's "Northern Exposure") as Edward Rutledge. ★★★1/2 $19.99

The Seventh Cross

(1944, 112 min, US, Fred Zinnemann) A superb melodrama with Spencer Tracy escaping from a Nazi concentration camp accompanied by six others. With Hume Cronyn, Agnes Moorehead and Jessica Tandy. ★★★1/2 $19.99

The Seventh Seal

(1956, 96 min, Sweden, Ingmar Bergman) Plague stalks 14th-century Sweden in this mystical classic, as a war-weary knight (Max von Sydow) encounters Death by the seaside and challenges him to a perilous chess match with his life in the balance. Unquestionably one of Bergman's greatest. (Swedish with English subtitles) ★★★★ $29.99

The Seventh Sign

(1988, 98 min, US, Carl Schultz) The premise of this occult thriller says the Bible foretells the destruction of the planet by seven warning signs. No matter how close you look in the Old or New Testaments, you won't find any warnings about bad horror films such as this. Demi Moore is the pregnant woman privy to the apocalyptic prophecies. ★ $11.99

The Seventh Victim

(1943, 71 min, US, Mark Robson) Exceptionally eerie occult thriller produces many a chill in this story of a woman (Kim Hunter) who unwittingly becomes involved with a satanic cult while searching for her missing sister in New York's Greenwich Village. One of Val Lewton's best films; the screenplay

The famous game of chess in *The Seventh Seal*

was written by the producer under the pseudonym "Carlos Keith." ★★★ $19.99

The 7th Voyage of Sinbad

(1958, 87 min, US, Nathan Juran) Though a little creaky around the edges, good special effects make this one of the more enjoyable of the Ray Harryhausen films. Hero Sinbad battles an evil magician to restore his girlfriend — who has been shrunk only inches tall — to her normal size. Bernard Herrmann did the score. ★★½ $14.99

Severed Ties

(1992, 95 min, US, Damon Santostefano) This direct-to-video Fangoria Film production tries to be part *Basket Case*, part *Street Trash*, part *Dead Alive*, but fails to be as witty, scary, or gory as any of them. A young scientist tries to perfect a formula for a plasma replacement which will allow spontaneous regeneration of any wounded limb or organ. His mother, however, is secretly manipulating him into selling the formula to an evil chemical company. He eventually escapes her clutches, losing his arm in the process, and falls in with a group of homeless people, led by Garrett Morris. His severed arm, naturally, provides the first experiment for his new medicine. The movie is passable entertainment, with a few interesting effects, but the performances by Elke Sommer as the evil mother and Oliver Reed as her cohort-in-scum are overdone and rambling. Morris is entertaining but underused, as is a promising subplot about the reptilian source of the young man's new arm. This device, which could have provided the filmmakers with a terrific, effects-laden finale, is cut off too soon. ★½ $14.99

Sex and Justice

(1993, 77 min, US, Julian Schlossman) One might assume that with Gloria Steinem narrating and offering commentary, this video of the edited highlights of the contentious 1991 Senate confirmation hearing of Judge Clarence Thomas and professor Anita Hill's allegations of sexual harassment would be far from unbiased. Happily, this is not the case as the video is impartial and in search of the truth. Cross-cutting the testimony of both Thomas and Hill before the all-white, all-male Senate committee, one's indignation falls less on the two and more on the high-handed theatrics, posturing and bullying of the "august" Senators. Fascinating stuff for people not already OD'ed on the subject. ★★★ $24.99

Sex Is...

(1992, 80 min, US, Marc Huestis & Lawrence Helman) Contemporary gay men's preoccupation with sex and its side and after effects (love, relationship, AIDS) is entertainingly explored in this verbally and visually graphic documentary. Essentially a film of talking heads with some additional footage (mostly hard-core sex scenes) added, the film records the thoughts and opinions of various gay men. At times funny and surprisingly insightful, the men (including co-director Huestis) recount their childhood sexual obsessions, fantasies, proclivities and dislikes while they all agree that sex is a principal aspect of their lives. Raunchy, blunt and unapologetic, *Sex Is...* is an

important testimony to gay men and their sexual lives before and during the age of AIDS. ★★★ $39.99

sex, lies, and videotape

(1989, 100 min, US, Steven Soderbergh) First-time writer and director Soderbergh's emotionally powerful and darkly comic examination of infidelity, honesty and the darker side of human sensuality suprised everyone when it walked away with the Grand Prize at the 1989 Cannes Film Festival. John (Peter Gallagher) and Ann Dellany (Andie MacDowell) are the perfect young American couple: he's a new partner in a successful law firm; she's a squeaky-clean and somewhat prudish housewife; and he's having a torrid affair with her sister (lustily played by the ravishing Laura San Giacomo). Into the fray comes John's old roommate Graham (who is portrayed with a quiet brilliance by James Spader), an austere and strangely pious wanderer who is returning home after years on the road. An eruption of hidden passions and untold secrets follow as the four move inevitably towards a final confrontation. The entire ensemble in this would-be love quadrangle is superb and Soderbergh's script and direction are bold, new and refreshing. ★★★★ $19.99

The Sex of the Stars
(Le Sexe Des Étoiles)

(1993, 100 min, Canada, Paule Baillargeon) This preachy Canadian melodrama details the difficult relationship between an adolescent girl and her estranged father, who returns to her life a transsexual woman. Twelve-year-old Camille is lost in the fantasy of her long-gone "perfect" father. He returns to Montreal after several years in New York City intent on rekindling, however awkwardly, their relationship. Camille accepts the obvious — that her father is now a woman called Marie-Pierre — but refuses to alter any of the traditional father-daughter dynamics that she so desperately wants. The film tries to be "feel good" in spirit, but it ultimately reinforces the notion that deviant homosexuality is a sad, violent and unfulfilling world whose characters must pay the price for living a grotesque lifestyle. (French with English subtitles) ★★ $59.99

Le Sex Shop

(1973, 92 min, France, Claude Berri) This congenial French satire wittily explores our modern preoccupation with sex, and our changing sexual mores. Claude, the owner of a sexual paraphernalia shop, decides to keep his own marriage in high gear by testing his merchandise "firsthand." Taking advice from his own manuals, he attempts to introduce his wife to swing clubs and a ménage à trois. (Dubbed) ★★½

Sextette

(1978, 91 min, US, Ken Hughes) Four on the floor is standard equipment with this classic beauty, as Mae West returns to the showroom after an absence of nearly 40 years, loaded with options and ready for action. Her turbocharged headers make it clear that this is one body built to go the distance in this camp classic about a vixen whose honeymoon keeps getting interrupted by her many ex-husbands. A

pre-James Bond Timothy Dalton faces his most dangerous challenge as Mae requires more servicing than a Buick Skylark. Ringo Starr, Tony Curtis, George Hamilton and Alice Cooper are just a few who take her out for a spin after a quick look under the hood. ★½ $19.99

Shack Out on 101

(1955, 80 min, US, Edward Dein) Hyperventilating Red paranoia at its most entertaining! Lee Marvin is Slob, a trouble-making hash-slinger (with a hidden agenda) in a remote greasy spoon operated by lug Keenan Wynn. Set almost entirely in the ramshackle beanery, the story features a great cast of oddball characters with the Marilyn Monroe-like Terry Moore as the saucy but determined blonde who uncovers a nefarious ring of traitors. ★★★ $19.99

Shadey

(1987, 90 min, GB, Philip Saville) Offbeat espionage spoof with Anthony Sher as a garage mechanic who agrees to use his special powers — the ability to read minds and project those images onto film — to finance his sex-change operation. Billie Whitelaw, Patrick MacNee and Katherine Helmond also star in this irreverent comedy. ★★½

The Shadow

(1994, 112 min, US, Russell Mulcahy) Based on the popular 1930s radio program, this lifeless cartoon "adventure" tale stars a grim Alec Baldwin as the avenging hero/bad guy Lamont Cranston, aka The Shadow. Borrowing the set design ideas of *Batman* without any of its excitement, the film is a series of awkward battle scenes and comic vignettes as The Shadow takes on a mystical madman (John Lone) bent on world domination. Penelope Ann Miller, Tim Curry and Ian McKellen also star, and none are able to overcome the ridiculous and soggy material. ★ $19.99

The Shadow Box

(1980, 100 min, US, Paul Newman) Joanne Woodward stars in this well-made and sensitive version of Michael Cristofer's Tony Award and Pulitzer Prize-winning play. The story follows the lives of three terminally ill patients as they and their families spend a day at an experimental retreat in the California mountains. Woodward gives a beautifully controlled performance, and Christopher Plummer is equally splendid as her gay ex-husband. Also with Valerie Harper, Sylvia Sydney, James Broderick and Melinda Dillon. Fine direction by Newman. ★★★

Shadow Catcher

(1974, 90 min, US, T.C. McLuhan) This engaging documentary details Edward Curtis in his life and work among the Native Americans of the Northwest during the early 1900s. Curtis' incredible passion for his craft and his commitment to his subject are described through journal entries, correspondence and, above all, his photographs. A special treat is Curtis' own film, shown in fragments, called *Life Among the Headhunters*, which is unique for both its artistic and historical content. ★★★ $29.99

Shadow Hunter

(1992, 98 min, US, J.S. Cardone) Scott Glenn is a burnt-out L.A. cop who is a perfect complement to the squalid urban decay he lives in. His marriage is breaking up and he's ready to quit the force when he's sent to Arizona to pick up a Native American wanted for murder. When Twobear (Benjamin Bratt in a chilling performance) escapes from his custody, Glenn enters into an odyssey in which his survival may well depend on the strength of his soul. A well-paced combination of psychological thriller and action/adventure, sprinkled with elements of Native American mysticism. Angela Alvarado and Robert Beltran highlight a good supporting cast, and the spectacular Arizona desert is beautifully captured. ★★½ $14.99

Shadow of a Doubt

(1943, 108 min, US, Alfred Hitchcock) Cited by Hitchcock as one of his personal favorites, this cat-and-mouse, spellbinding psychological thriller stars Joseph Cotten as an apparently ordinary fellow who visits his small-town kin. However, his diabolical past gradually becomes evident, and threatening, to his suspicious young niece (wonderfully played by a wide-eyed and innocent Teresa Wright). ★★★★ $14.99

Shadow of the Thin Man

See: The Thin Man Series

A Shadow You Soon Will Be (Una Sombra ya Pronto Seras)

(1994, 105 min, Argentina, Hector Olivera) Olivera explores the state of post-democratic Argentinian society through the means of allegory and metaphor. Based on a novel by Osvaldo Soriano, *A Shadow You Soon Will Be* follows the meanderings of an unemployed computer programmer (Miguel Angel Sola) through an eerily barren countryside. The director uses wide angle shots and a variety of editing styles to capture the disorientation of Argentina's social and political landscape. A true road movie in which every character is more bizarre than the last, the film looks like a hybrid child of Wenders and Fellini with a bit of surrealism thrown in for good measure. Our hero's travels lead him not towards any one particular tale (despite an intriguing run-in with a fortune teller), but rather towards an understanding of exactly how he has landed where he is. Not technically proficient, *Shadow* provides an ironic, amusing exploration of the "journey" for those philosophically inclined. (Spanish with English subtitles) ★★★ $89.99

Shadowlands

(1987, 73 min, GB, Norman Stone) A West End and Broadway hit, this moving love story stars Joss Ackland as writer C.S. Lewis, who finds that his ordered Don's life at Oxford is thrown into turmoil after he meets and falls in love with American poet Joy Gresham (Claire Bloom). Winner of two British Academy Awards. ★★★

Shadowlands

(1993, 130 min, GB, Richard Attenborough) Though Attenborough isn't exactly known for his light directorial touch (*A Bridge Too Far, Cry Freedom*), he brings unexpected poignancy and intelligence to this captivating romantic drama about the real-life love affair between author C.S. Lewis and writer Joy Gresham. Based on William Nicholson's hit stage play, the film stars Anthony Hopkins as Lewis, a proper British professor/lecturer whose ordered life takes a turn when American Gresham (Debra Winger) arrives on his doorsteps. As she insinuates herself into his life, they marry in order for Gresham to stay in the country — and ultimately and inevitably fall in love. Though it may sound like nothing more than a British *Green Card*, *Shadowlands*, which is also unexpectedly funny, is a beautifully told, exceptionally scripted story and features two remarkable performances by Hopkins and Oscar nominee Winger. ★★★★ $19.99

Shadows

(1960, 87 min, US, John Cassavetes) Cassavetes' directorial debut is a rough-hewn improvisation pulsating with hyperkenetic energy. The grainy black-and-white cinematography and Charlie Mingus score augment the quasi-documentary intimacy amd immediacy delivered by the competent cast. Lelia Goldini is a naive 20-year-old black woman living with her two brothers, one a ne'er-do-well (Ben Carruthers) and the other a struggling jazz musician (Hugh Herd) desperately trying to keep the family together. The complexities of racism are explored from their perspectives, as the brothers deal with the underside of the entertainment industry, and their light-skinned sister handles the emotional upheaval of a relationship with a Caucasian man who does not know she is an African-American. The low-budget production values (the film was originally shot in 16mm), which includes some non-sync sound and an effective use of ambient sound, are reminiscent of the British kitchen sink dramas of that time. Riveting and involving, and quintessential Cassavetes. ★★★ $19.99

Shadows and Fog

(1992, 86 min, US, Woody Allen) Lost amid the controversy surrounding the breakup of Woody Allen and Mia Farrow, this minor addition to Allen's filmography is nonetheless a very entertaining, well-made and often amusing ode to early German cinema. Based on Allen's stage play "Death," the story centers on Woody's hapless nebbish who becomes an object of a lynch mob's hunt for a serial killer. The action takes place in an archetypal pre-WWII European city on a foggy night and is shot in a stark black and white which is filled with visual references to the German Expressionist classics *M* and *Nosferatu*. An impressive supporting cast includes John Malkovich, Mia Farrow, John Cusack, Madonna (in a bit role), and Lily Tomlin, Jodie Foster and Kathy Bates, who steal the show in a hilarious scene as a trio of hookers who give Farrow a lesson in life. The superb soundtrack is composed of a delightful mélange of Kurt Weill cabaret tunes. ★★★ $92.99

Shadows of Forgotten Ancestors

(1964, 99 min, USSR, Sergei Paradjanov) The historical pageantry and epic legends of medieval times are enacted in this visually and musically vibrant love story. Set in 19th-century Ukraine, the drama centers around a young man who is trapped in a loveless marriage and haunted by his true but dead sweetheart. But make no mistake about its simple plot, for the film is a wonderful compendium of folk dances, religious zealousness and witchcraft. It is filmed in a psychedelic rampage and has more spectacular effects, spectacular camera movements, wild experiments with color and bizarre musical scenes than anyone would imagine in one film. (Ukrainian with English subtitles) ★★★★ $29.99

Shaft

(1971, 106 min, US, Gorden Parks) With Isaac Hayes' rhythmic score in the background, this sexy and violent (always a great combo in blaxploitation) crime story stars Richard Roundtree as John Shaft, a mean and resourceful private dick. Essentially a black *French Connection*, the story has Shaft hired by a ruthless drug lord (Moses Gunn) to find his daughter, who was kidnapped by the white Mafia. Slick, action-packed urban fun. ★★★ $14.99

Shaft's Big Score!

(1972, 105 min, US, Gordon Parks) The baddest mutha in town is back, in this well-paced action-packed sequel. While investigating the murder of a friend by an underworld crime figure, hero Shaft (Richard Roundtree) discovers that the money he was going to use to pay off his pal's gambling debt is missing. He then makes a deal with crime boss Stumpy (Moses Gunn) and makes the same deal with another boss, putting himself in the middle of an intense war. Stylish, never boring, well-acted Cadillac among blaxploitation films. ★★★ $14.99

Shakedown

(1988, 90 min, US, James Glickenhaus) Peter Weller and Sam Elliott are the mismatched partners in this routine actioner about a public defender (Weller) and a burned-out undercover cop (Elliott) who go after some corrupt policemen. Some good action scenes, but the plot makes little sense. ★★ $19.99

Shakes the Clown

(1991, 87 min, US, Bobcat Goldthwait) While never quite living up to *The Boston Globe*'s tantalizing tagline that this Bobcat Goldthwait-written and directed comedy is "The *Citizen Kane* of alcoholic clown movies," the film's story — that of a drunken, down-on-his-luck clown — drags a bit, but delivers many good laughs. Set in a semi-surrealistic town populated by all types of unemployed, has-been clowns, Goldthwait stars as a "good clown" whose love of booze eventually complicates him in a murder. The plot, however, comes secondary to the film's frantic, hit-or-miss style, with some highlights being the one-liners from a foul-mouthed black female clown, Julie Brown's hilarious turn as Goldthwait's lisping bowler-girlfriend and, in an unbilled cameo, Robin Williams' film-stealing role as a slightly fey yet militaristic mime instructor. Yes, the story itself is not very interesting nor well-constructed, some of the scenes and main characters are decidedly unfunny and much of the humor relies on cursing and bodily function jokes. But overall, a funny little oddity. ★★½ $89.99

S

Shakespeare Wallah

(1965, 120 min, India, James Ivory) The setting is India during the last days of the British Raj when the struggling nation was trying to free itself of colonial imperialism and cultural saturation by the British. Amidst all of this turmoil, an English Shakespearean acting troupe valiantly tours the countryside. The story concerns the budding love affair between the daughter of one of the actors and a young Indian. Their infatuation and innocence and persistence amidst the changes help make this a charming and delightful tale. ★★★ $19.99

Shall We Dance

(1937, 116 min, US, Mark Sandrich) Captivating Fred Astaire-Ginger Rogers musical with Fred and Ginger as a dance team pretending to be married; of course, they fall in love. Needless to say, there are great dance numbers, and the Gershwins' score includes "Let's Call the Whole Thing Off," "They All Laughed" and "They Can't Take That Away from Me." ★★★½ $19.99

Shallow Grave

(1994, 92 min, Scotland, Danny Boyle) This grisly Scottish black comedy tells an all-too familiar tale of greed-conquers-all, but an eccentric sense of style and some truly shocking twists make it a surprising and riveting thriller. The film follows three unlikable roommates: Alex (Ewan McGregor), David (Christopher Eccleston), and Juliet (Kerry Fox of *An Angel at My Table*). After verbally intimidating and humiliating possible lodgers to share their gigantic Edinburgh flat, they decide on a shady character (Keith Allen) whose irascible nature feeds their misanthropic appetites. Things unravel when he dies of a drug overdose and leaves them with a suitcase full of cash. They immediately go about hatching schemes to keep the money and dispose of the body (one of the film's more grotesque

scenes) and ultimately begin an inexorable descent into madness and greed. Of the three, David takes a true turn for the worse, holing himself up in the attic with the swag and threatening all comers with a hammer. Fledgling director Boyle shows great promise; his visual prowess and sprightly script keep the tension building right up to the excruciating climax. ★★★½ $19.99

Shame

(1968, 103 min, Sweden, Ingmar Bergman) The personal horrors of war are explored in this intense story of a couple caught up in a senselessly violent civil war. The setting is 1971, when a seemingly happy but quarrelsome couple (Max von Sydow and Liv Ullmann) have fled to a secluded farmhouse on a remote island to escape the unexplained war which is ravaging the mainland. Both orchestra musicians, von Sydow is a self-absorbed, emotionally fragile man and Ullmann his strong-willed wife. The war and its horrific violence soon spills into their world, trapping them and then brutally stripping them of their dignity as they desperately struggle for survival. Very powerful acting by von Sydow and Ullmann and a gripping, action-filled story make this powerful drama one of Bergman's best. (Swedish with English subtitles) ★★★★ $19.99

Shame

(1988, 90 min, Australia, Steve Jodrell) A taut, violent story of rape, murder and oppression. A woman, traveling alone on a motorcycle, encounters engine trouble and seeks help from the citizens of a small out-of-the-way town. Instead, she discovers a conspiracy of violence directed against many of the town's young women. Confronted with this terror, our heroine chooses to stay and fight. The ensuing sexual battle is told in the best Rambo-like style as this riveting film not only

delivers potent doses of action, but also explores the tumultuous relationship between the sexes. ★★★ $14.99

The Shameless Old Lady

(1966, 94 min, France, René Allio) Sylvie, a French character actress for almost 50 years, is finally the star in this touching and delightful film based on a Brecht short story. A 70-year-old widow, after devoting herself to her family during a drab, uneventful life, decides to change her ways and boisterously enjoy her remaining years. Shocking her children and neighbors, she buys a *Deux Chevaux*, joins a political group, befriends a prostitute and goes on holiday. (French with English subtitles) ★★★½

Shampoo

(1975, 112 min, US, Hal Ashby) Critically acclaimed social comedy about the romantic exploits of a bed-hopping Beverly Hills hairdresser (Warren Beatty). First-rate cast includes Julie Christie, Goldie Hawn, Jack Warden, Carrie Fisher and Oscar winner Lee Grant. ★★★ $9.99

Shane

(1953, 118 min, US, George Stevens) Director Stevens' classic western stars Alan Ladd as a mysterious gunfighter who comes to the aid of a homesteading family (Van Heflin and Jean Arthur), and is idolized by their young son (Brandon De Wilde). Jack Palance is a most memorable villian. ★★★★ $14.99

Shanghai Blues

(1984, 108 min, Hong Kong, Tsui Hark) Belying one's preconceived notions of Hong Kong's cinema, this gleefully anachronistic, gag-filled screwball comedy, set in 1937 and 1947 Shanghai, has a not-too-ordinary plot — boy meets girl, boy loses girl, boy and girl wind up as fueding neighbors without recognizing each other. A pretty cast and imaginatively wacky ideas fuel this enjoyable oddity. (Cantonese with English subtitles) ★★★ $39.99

Shanghai Surprise

(1986, 97 min, US, Jim Goddard) One of the candidates for Worst Film of the Decade, this laughable adventure film teamed then-husband and wife Sean Penn and Madonna in the story of a missionary in 1930s China who enlists the aid of a down-and-out adventurer to track a missing opium shipment. Just dreadful on every level. ★ $14.99

Shanghai Triad

(1995, 108 min, China, Zhang Yimou) Chinese master Zhang (*To Live, Raise the Red Lantern*) puts his artful spin on a 1930s crime period piece with mixed results. At times entrancing at others simply tediously trance-enducing, the film follows the first several days in the apprenticeship of young Tang Shuisheng, a 14-year-old "country bumpkin" (as he is repeatedly called). Thanks to his uncle Liu's influence, Shuisheng is to be the personal servant of Bijou (Gong Li), the extravagant moll of triad boss Mr. Tang. The film meanders through its first half, suffering from an absolutely sonambulistic editing pace and getting dragged down by a series of overly long singing numbers in which Bijou entertains at the Boss' nightclub. After an attack by rival

Shall We Dance: Will the real Ginger Rogers please step forward?

S

gang members sends Mr. Tang and his entourage to a small island to seek refuge, the film finally finds a narrative pace as it explores Bijou's process of personal transformation. Still, the film ultimately fails to provide the crystal clear social commentary that is so evident in all of Zhang's other films, which might have been OK had it served up the action-packed crime drama that it might have. (Mandarin with English subtitles) ★★½ $19.99

Sharky's Machine

(1981, 119 min, US, Burt Reynolds) A bit overlong but nevertheless a flavorful police thriller with police detective Burt Reynolds taking on sleazeball Vittorio Gassman. With Rachel Ward, Brian Keith and Charles Durning. ★★½ $9.99

Sharma and Beyond

(1984, 85 min, GB, Brian Gilbert) This installment of David Putnam's (*Chariots of Fire, The Killing Fields*) "First Love Series" is a winning and poignant exploration of the complex relationship that develops between a father, a daughter and her suitor. The young woman, recently wounded in love, is not at all sure whether this new young man, an aspiring sci-fi writer, is more interested in her, or in her father who is a famous author. ★★★

Shattered

(1991, 97 min, US, Wolfgang Petersen) A postmodern whodunit whose psychological complexities, which sometimes obscure the action, probably doomed this inventive, very exciting thriller at the box office. Tom Berenger is left an amnesiac after a near-fatal accident and there are twists aplenty as he tries to get some idea of who he used to be, who he is now and who he can trust to tell him the truth. Greta Scacchi is his loving wife (or is she?), Corbin Bernsen is his best friend (or his he?), and Bob Hoskins is the private detective trying to solve Berenger's intricate puzzle. A film rich in suspense and overflowing in atmosphere and style. ★★★½ $9.99

The Shawshank Redemption

(1994, 142 min, US, Frank Darabont) Put aside whatever preconceptions you may have about a two-and-a-half hour period prison story, for the Oscar nominated *The Shawshank Redemption* is not only emotionally moving but one of the best films of its year. Adapted from a Stephen King novella, this is the story of Andy Dufresne (Tim Robbins), a banker given life imprisonment for the murder of his wife. Sentenced to Shawshank Prison, Andy is brutalized regularly when not staying to himself. Life turns around for him when he befriends Red (Oscar nominee Morgan Freeman), a lifer with connections, and becomes financial broker for the crooked warden and his guards. As Andy serves his life sentence, he manages to sustain a hopefulness which affects the other prisoners as well. Director Darabont makes a very assured feature debut, the cinematography and other technical aspects are first-rate, and Robbins, Freeman and James Whitmore as a veteran con are remarkable. ★★★★ $14.99

She

(1935, 94 min, US, Irving Pichel & Lansing Holden) Deep within an Arctic glacier is the unknown land of Kor. With a hot temper and a colder heart, an ancient queen (Helen Gahagen) rules over this subterranean land while pining still for her long dead lover. She keeps at bay the ravages of the centuries by bathing in a fountain of flames. Finally her Romeo does return — reincarnated as Randolph Scott. Alas, love's embers quickly die when Scott has to go to Helen Mack for a little R&R. Produced by the same team that made *King Kong, She* is a marvelous mélange of matinee-movie dialogue, kitschy costumes and campy art deco sets. Gahagen is convincingly calculated as the ruthless monarch known only as *She Who Must Be Obeyed*. ★★★ $24.99

She

(1965, 106 min, GB, Robert Day) Great, campy, lost-world fun is to be had in this Hammer Films retelling of the old H. Rider Haggard story about a lost city, a doomed hero, slave sacrifices, an ancient cult and a beautiful, immortal queen. John Richardson stars as Leo, a post-WWI adventurer who has a vision of a beautiful queen (Ursula Andress) in her ancient land. Drawn inexplicably but inxorably to her, he enlists the aid of his wartime compatriots (including scholarly Peter Cushing, who's in fine form as always) and journeys across the desert in search of love. They eventually discover a lost city which at first seems a paradise, but becomes a prison when the despotic truth is revealed about the land's ageless ruler. As it turns out, Leo is the reincarnation of her lost love, who long ago betrayed her. Is he doomed to repeat the same mistake? Will he walk into the Eternal Flame to gain everlasting life. Would you want to live forever and spend a pleasure-seeking eternity with Ursula Andress? Where do I sign? ★★★ $19.99

She Done Him Wrong

(1933, 66 min, US, Lowell Sherman) A very young Cary Grant stars opposite Mae West, who co-authored this classic gay `90s spoof based on her stage hit "Diamond Lil." La West is at her buxom best as Lady Lou, diamond collector and man snatcher — which came first? Grant is the next-door missionary bent on saving her soul — or is he? Mae says it best — "Why don't you come up sometime and see me?" ★★★★ $14.99

She Must Be Seeing Things

(1988, 85 min, US, Sheila McLaughlin) Independent New York filmmaker McLaughlin's lesbian love story explores the complex sexual and emotional commitment of two women professionals. This interesting love story follows the rocky relationship of Agatha, a New York lawyer, and Jo, a filmmaker. While Jo is out of town, Agatha comes upon her diary and photos which suggest that she is developing an interest in men and may be unfaithful to her. Agatha's growing jealousy

John Richardson and Ursula Andress in *She* ('65)

and her frantic attempts to keep her wavering lover interested result in her donning men's clothing and spying on her unsuspecting partner. The drama is a bit stilted and not entirely successful, but there are moments of great insight and fine acting by Sheila Dabney and Lois Weaver. ★★½ $29.99

She Wore a Yellow Ribbon

(1949, 103 min, US, John Ford) The second (and more successful) film in director Ford's cavalry trilogy. John Wayne gives a commanding performance as an officer about to retire, experiencing emotional conflict in doing so. Also starring Joanne Dru, John Agar, Ben Johnson and Victor McLaglen. Oscar-winning cinematography. ★★★★ $19.99

She'll Be Wearing Pink Pyjamas

(1985, 90 min, GB, John Goldschmidt) Julie Walters is a delight in this amiable comic adventure about a group of professional women who volunteer to spend a week at a survival training camp. ★★½

She's Gotta Have It

(1986, 84 min, US, Spike Lee) Lee's inspired and raucous comedy about Nola Darling and her three boyfriends: Mars — "Please baby, please baby, baby, baby, please"; Jamie — "Wherever you want to go, I'll go, whatever you want to do, I'll do"; Greer — "Am I not beautiful darling?" This miraculous cinematic achievement was put together on a shoestring budget and shot over a period of 11 days in a two-square block area of Brooklyn, and yet it stands as one of the funniest and most poignant statements to date on a woman's sexual freedom and how it affects the men in her life. ★★★½ $14.99

She's Having a Baby

(1988, 106 min, US, John Hughes) Kevin Bacon and Elizabeth McGovern fall in love and marry, set up house and prepare for the blessed event; all the while contending with the rigors of married life. Hughes brings about as much character development to this stilted "adult" comedy-drama as he does to his lesser teen flicks. With Alec Baldwin and William Windom. ★★ $14.99

She's the One

(1996, 96 min, US, Edward Burns) In his sophomore outing, director Burns (*The Brothers McMullen*) offers another testosterone-centric examination of familial bonding and sibling rivalry in this sometimes contrived but always entertaining tale of two dissimilar brothers, one crusty dad, and the three women in their lives — four, if you count the never-seen mother. Francis (Mike McGlone) works on Wall Street and possesses a beautiful wife (Jennifer Aniston), a spectacular apartment and the morals of pond scum. Mickey (Edward Burns) drives a cab and lives in a ratty flat with a broken heart. Dad (the endearingly cantankerous John Mahoney) runs his waterfront dwelling as part boot camp and part locker room, and his one true love is his boat — fishing trips with his sons are fashioned as Iron Man rituals. This lively tale of miscommunication and erroneous assumptions is precipitated by Mickey's marriage to an intriguing stranger (Maxine Bahns) 24 hours after she flags his cab. He then crosses paths with his ex-fiancée (Cameron Diaz); setting in motion events which uncover a web of jealousies, secrets and lies revealed with Hal Hartley-esque juxtapositions and keen observations of human foibles. Lots of fun topped off with a sweet resolution. ★★★ $99.99

She-Devil

(1989, 99 min, US, Susan Seidelman) What's a slovenly, socially inept suburban housewife to do when her accountant husband starts a passionate affair with her favorite glamorous and achingly beautiful romance novelist? Take revenge...what else? When Roseanne dumps the kids and the dog on wandering hubby Ed Begley, Jr. and soft-focus sweetie Meryl Streep, she begins her metamorphosis from frump to take-charge woman (hear her roar). Streep reveals an unexplored panache for comedic understatement and Barr serves her role well. ★★½ $9.99

She-Devils on Wheels

(1968, 83 min, US, Hershell Gordon Lewis) Lewis' stab at the biker genre, about a violent female motorcycle gang with "guts as hard as the steel of their hogs!" The girls wage war with a rival (male) bike gang, pick their men from a "stud line" and have an all-around "real bad time!" ★ $19.99

The Sheep Has Five Legs

(1954, 95 min, France, Henri Verneuil) Fernandel, in a role that brought him international recognition, is both hilarious and believable in this comedy in which he plays six different roles. A town seeking publicity decides to reunite its oldest resident with his long-estranged quintuplet grandsons. Fernandel plays both the old man and all five sons — from a salty sea captain to an arrogant hair dresser. Bringing to mind (and equally as talented) the masters of multiple personalities,

Peter Sellers and Alec Guinness, the manic Fernandel is a marvel of comic deftness. (French with English subtitles) ★★★½ $39.99

The Sheltering Sky

(1990, 138 min, Italy/GB, Bernardo Bertolucci) Against the vast backdrop of the sweltering heat and punishing sky of Northern Africa, Bertolucci's intimate epic (adapted from Paul Bowles' classic novel) follows the lives of three American travelers during the early 1950s. A husband and wife (John Malkovich and Debra Winger) and their traveling companion (Campbell Scott) embark from Tangier in search of the "real" Morocco. Slow moving, with the sumptuous photography one would expect from the director of *The Last Emperor*, this sun-drenched existential journey did not please all on its initial release, but for those with the patience, this spectacular drama should enthrall. Malkovich is perfect as the arrogant and unfeeling husband who is overwhelmed by culture shock, and Winger's performance as a complacent woman who undergoes a radical transformation is mesmerizing. ★★★½ $19.99

Shenandoah

(1965, 105 min, US, Andrew V. McLaglen) An enormously satisfying Civil War drama blessed with one of James Stewart's most moving performances. Stewart plays a Virginia patriarch whose family is ripped apart by the conflict. With Doug McClure, Glenn Corbett, Patrick Wayne and Katharine Ross. The basis for the stirring Broadway musical of the same name (which starred John Cullum in the Stewart role). ★★★ $14.99

Sherlock, Jr./Our Hospitality

(1923/24, 119 min, US, Buster Keaton/John Blystone & Keaton) A collection of two Buster Keaton comedies. In *Sherlock, Jr.* (1924, 44 min), Keaton is less concerned with physical schtick and slapstick (though there is certainly enough to go around) and concentrates more on the possibilities of the medium of film. He plays a projectionist and amateur sleuth whose daydreaming puts him in the film he is projecting. There's a brilliant sequence in which Keaton is trapped on-screen as the film changes from one scene to another. And even better is the finale in which he rides driverless on the handlebars of a motorcycle through crowded streets and open countryside. (★★★★) *Our Hospitality* (1923, 75 min) is the winning story of Keaton returning to his Southern hometown and becoming involved in an on-going family feud. The story is more complex than most, there's an abundance of wonderful sight gags, and Keaton's stunts atop a waterfall are awe-inspiring. (★★★½) $29.99

Sherman's March

(1985, 155 min, US, Ross McElwee) What begins as a documentary chronicling the destruction and after-effects of General Sherman's march through the South during the Civil War soon turns into the director's own destructive Southern quest: a quest not of war but of love and romance. In this engaging non-fiction film, we follow McElwee, an energetic, self-indulgent optimist, and determined filmmaker, as he cuts a swath through the

affluent New South to find not the smoldering remains of the war but a formidable array of extravagant Southern belles. These women constantly distract, bewilder and ultimately conquer our intrepid hero during his disastrously hilarious search for romance, love and meaning. An entertaining and original film. ★★★½ $29.99

Shine

(1996, 105 min, Australia, Scott Hicks) Two parts biopic and one part fairy tale, this real-life drama about Australian pianist David Helfgott's triumph over a lifetime of mental illness and his subsequent return to the stage is as inspiring and emotionally satisfying as it is well-crafted and seamlessly put together. Told as flashback, the film's narrative walks through the three stages of Helfgott's life: A young prodigy (Alex Rafalowicz) who's driven by his stern Holocaust survivor father (Armin Mueller-Stahl) to play well beyond his years; a troubled but brilliant teen (Noah Taylor) who struggles to break free of his father's influence; and finally the broken adult (Geoffrey Rush) who has fallen into a mental collapse that includes endless rapid-fire mumbling. Rush scored a major coup (but by no means an undeserved one) when he snagged 1996 Oscar honors for Best Actor. While *Shine* necessarily walks the fine clichéd line of the typical victory-over-adversity tale, Taylor and Rush's dazzling portrayals, director Hicks' acute attention to detail and the rousing use of Rachmaninov's "Piano Concerto No. 3" make this one of the most gratifying cinematic experiences of the past several years. ★★★★ $102.99

The Shining

(1980, 142 min, GB, Stanley Kubrick) Jack Nicholson is at his absolute lunatic best as a once loving father who slips deeper and deeper into homicidal frenzy. His family is contracted to care for a snow-bound, and decidedly sinister, hotel and the descent into madness begins. For those who have read Stephen King's masterpiece of horror and suspense, Kubrick's treatment may be disappointing, but the film is worth a look for Nicholson's inspired ravings and for Garret Brown's stunning Steadicam photography. Also with Shelley Duvall. ★★★ $19.99

The Shining Hour

(1938, 80 min, US, Frank Borzage) A good cast is featured in this appealing romantic drama. Joan Crawford is at the center of a family crisis as a nightclub dancer who comes between two brothers when she becomes engaged to one of them. Melvyn Douglas and Robert Young are the feuding siblings, and Margaret Sullavan and Fay Bainter round out the talented cast. ★★★ $19.99

Shining Through

(1992, 127 min, US, David Seltzer) Those nasty Nazis are back and this time they're up against America's *Working Girl*, Melanie Griffith. Griffith encores the role of a secretary who wants more in life than just to take dictation. Here, she speaks German and can make a wicked strudel. Of course, these two qualifications are enough to send her off to Germany in the middle of World War II to obtain secret information. Just for good measure, she's in love with her boss, secret agent Michael Douglas. To be totally fair, there are some good moments to this slick but silly spy thriller. Especially when Liam Neeson, a standout as a Nazi official, is on screen. But don't look for a credible plot, because it's just not there. Griffith does make a good Sherlock Holmes in the film's decent beginning. ★★½ $9.99

Ship of Fools
(1965, 149 min, US, Stanley Kramer) Absorbing, well-made drama examining the lives of a group of shipboard passengers traveling from Mexico to Germany right before the start of WWII. Powerful performances by Simone Signoret, Oskar Werner, Vivien Leigh, Lee Marvin, Jose Ferrer, Elizabeth Ashley, Michael Dunn and George Segal. ★★★½ $19.99

Shipwrecked
(1990, 93 min, US, Nils Gaup) High-spirited adventure yarn about a young boy stranded on a tropical island, fighting for survival while trying to outwit a vicious gang of pirates. Gabriel Byrne and Stian Smestad star. From the director of *Pathfinder*. ★★★ $9.99

Shirley Valentine
(1989, 108 min, GB, Lewis Gilbert) Pauline Collins re-creates her award-winning West End and Broadway role as a London housewife who leaves her family in search of self-fulfillment. Collins gives an enchanting performance as Shirley, the vivacious homemaker whose outlook on life is as entertaining as the one-liners she joyously delivers to the camera. If the idea of a woman fleeing husband and hearth to gain her own independence is not exactly original, writer Willy Russell (*Educating Rita*) imbues both the story and its heroine with such a delightful sense of humor that it all seems as new and refreshing as Shirley's near-idyllic Greek island getaway. ★★★ $14.99

Shoah
(1985, 570 min, Israel, Claude Lanzmann) Lanzmann brings the unspeakable reality of the Holocaust down to human scale in this monumental epic that explores this deplorable page of human history through an examination of the particular physical details and specifics of mass genocide. In *Shoah*, Lanzmann rejects the notion that the Holocaust was a result of impersonal historical forces and grimly examines the harsher reality of it as being the actions of men against men. A landmark effort. (French, German and Polish with English subtitles) ★★★★ $299.99

Shock Corridor
(1963, 101 min, US, Samuel Fuller) In this wonderfully entertaining and over-the-top melodrama, Peter Brock stars as a Pulitzer Prize-hunting reporter who fakes madness in order to be admitted into an insane asylum and uncover the perpetrator of an unsolved murder. In the hospital, where the inmates represent a microcosm of a sick and violent society, his investigation bogs down as he himself slowly sinks into dementia. Constance Towers is terrific as his apprehensive stripper girlfriend. A gripping story told with frenzied fervor. ★★★½ $29.99

A Shock to the System
(1990, 87 min, US, Jan Egleson) Michael Caine shines as brilliantly as ever in this pitch black comedy. When his long overdue promotion is unexpectedly handed to a smarmy young hot shot, Caine is incensed. When he accidentally discovers the convenience and simplicity of murder, Caine is inspired. Director Egleson's tilted angles and offbeat camera movement serve the story well, depicting Caine's skewed view of a world in which he casually knocks off those who get in his way. A scathing indictment of the corporate sensibility, the film is fueled by an insightful, razor-sharp wit which in turn is contrasted with several moments of bone-chilling terror. Good supporting cast includes

Elizabeth McGovern, Peter Riegert and Swoosie Kurtz. ★★★½ $14.99

Shock Treatment
(1981, 90 min, US, Jim Sharman) This musical-comedy sequel to *The Rocky Horror Picture Show* finds Brad and Janet (now palyed by Cliff De Young and Jessica Harper) prisoners in demented Denton, home of happiness and TV game shows. Richard O'Brien leads the proceedings as a mentally suspect medic in this twisted satire on The American Way (greed, lust, media-manipulation and skimpy attire). ★★★ $14.99

Shocker
(1989, 110 min, US, Wes Craven) Director Craven only manages a few sparks in this grisly tale about a mass murderer who comes back from the grave to get even with the psychic teenager who helped fry him. Special effects are good, story is ridiculous and there's an amazing surrealistic chase scene which takes place inside a television set. Though Craven has certainly done better, *Shocker* has a lot more scares and a better look to it than the inferior, similarly themed *The Horror Show*. ★★ $19.99

The Shoes of the Fisherman
(1968, 152 min, US, Michael Anderson) Anthony Quinn heads an all-star cast in this labored epic as the first Russian-born Pope who tries to bring about world peace. Also starring Laurence Olivier, John Gielgud, David Jannsen, Leo McKern and Oskar Werner. (Available letterboxed and pan & scan) ★★ $24.99

Shoeshine
(1946, 92 min, Italy, Vittirio De Sica) This brutal but brilliantly conceived story about two boys surviving in the squalid conditions of post-war Italy is told in a tragic, neorealist style. Giuseppe and Pasquale are two shoeshine boys whose goal is to pool their savings and buy a horse. Their plans are interrupted, however, when they run afoul of the law and end up in a repressive reform school. Their friendship becomes strained and tragedy strikes as the desensitized adult world crushes their youthful innocence. (Italian with English subtitles) ★★★★ $29.99

Shogun Assassin
(1981, 86 min, Japan/US, Kenji Misumi & Robert Houston) An exciting installment of the Japanese "Sword of Vengeance" series about a samurai warrior who travels across the countryside pushing his young son in a heavily armed baby cart. Narrated by the child, the film is an absolutely stunning visual ballet of violence and bloodletting. (Dubbed) ★★★ $39.99

Shoot Loud, Louder... I Don't Understand!
(1966, 100 min, Italy, Eduardo De Filippo) Not to be confused with "great art," this Italian screwball comedy stars Marcello Mastroianni as an eccentric artist with an even stranger uncle, who together become involved in a series of zany escapades which result in seductions, fireworks and eventual betrayal and murder. Written and directed by Italy's best known playwright, De Filippo (*Marriage*

Shoeshine

Italian Style), this wild romp also stars the scantily-clad Raquel Welch and features the music of Nino Rota. (Dubbed) ★★½

Shoot the Moon

(1982, 123 min, US, Alan Parker) Parker's brutally honest film about the breakup of a Marin County family was a disappointment at the box office, which is a tragedy because it features impeccable performances by Albert Finney and Diane Keaton as the couple, and young Dana Hill as their daughter. Peter Weller and Karen Allen co-star. Not an "escapist" film by any means, its ending will send you reeling. ★★★½ $19.99

Shoot the Piano Player

(1962, 85 min, France, François Truffaut) Charles Aznavour is a timid pianist in a second-rate Parisian bistro who accidentally becomes entangled with the mob. Truffaut cavalierly mixes comedic element with a film noir tone in what is surely his quirkiest masterpiece. (French with English subtitles) ★★★★ $29.99

Shoot to Kill

(1988, 110 min, US, Roger Spottiswoode) Suspenseful thriller with Sidney Poitier on the trail of a ruthless killer, who is hiding out amid a mountain tour group. Tom Berenger is the mountain guide who teams with Poitier when it turns out his girlfriend Kirstie Alley is leading the group. ★★★ $9.99

The Shooting

(1967, 82 min, US, Monte Hellman) Jack Nicholson and Warren Oates are in uncomfortable alliance as the woman with no name (Millie Perkins) follows a trail and keeps her own counsel in this Old West tale of vengeance and morality. Gritty and atmospheric; you can feel the heat of the Southwestern desert. Nicholson also co-produced. ★★½

The Shooting Party

(1977, 105 min, Russia, Emil Loteaunu) *The Shooting Party* is a sumptuous realization of Anton Chekhov's early novella of the same name. This tale of passion, set amidst the absurd excesses of pre-Czarist Russian nobility, tells the story of a local magistrate who falls in love with a young woodsman's daughter (Galina Belyayeva). It's a gripping story of unrequited love, murder and the injustices of fate. (Not to be confused with the 1985 British drama.) (Russian with English subtitles) ★★★ $59.99

The Shooting Party

(1985, 108 min, GB, Alan Bridges) Set on a great English estate in the autumn of 1913, this entertaining and highly acclaimed film casts a slightly jaded eye towards both the landed gentry of an Edwardian England on the brink of World War I and the irrevocable changes that it produced. It marvelously identifies the petty ceremonies and traditions of a declining ruling class and is filled with the crisp conversation of a cast of well-defined, idiosyncratic individuals. Starring James Mason, John Gielgud, James Fox and Dorothy Tutin. ★★★½

Margaret Sullavan, Frank Morgan and James Stewart in *The Shop Around the Corner*

The Shootist

(1976, 99 min, US, Don Siegel) John Wayne's final film is an exemplary western tale set at the turn of the century with the Duke as a famed ex-gunfighter who learns he is dying of cancer. In this touching allegory for the death of the Old West, Wayne sets out to put his affairs in order, but is constantly haunted by his past. A first-rate cast includes Lauren Bacall, James Stewart, Ron Howard, Richard Boone, Hugh O'Brian and Harry Morgan. ★★★½ $14.99

The Shop Around the Corner

(1940, 97 min, US, Ernst Lubitsch) Very charming romantic comedy with James Stewart and Margaret Sullavan as feuding coworkers in a Budapest shop who unknowingly fall in love with each other when they begin corresponding after answering a lonely-hearts ad. Remade in 1949 as the musical *In the Good Old Summertime*. ★★★½ $19.99

The Shop on Main Street

(1966, 128 min, Czechoslovakia, Jan Kadar) This heartbreaking story follows the tragic relationship between an elderly Jewish woman and the Slovak man assigned by the Nazis to watch over her. This Academy Award-winning Best Foreign Film is not only a moving story but also an impassioned and heartrending plea for peace and understanding. (Czechoslovakian with English subtitles) ★★★★ $24.99

Shopping

(1993, 100 min, GB, Paul Anderson) Written and directed by music video auteur Anderson (the man behind 1995's *Mortal Kombat*), this hip, slick and colorful debut film takes an unsentimental look at the life of Billy (Jude Law), a young adrenaline junkie recently released from prison. Abandoned by both parents and society, he spends his time stealing cars and robbing shops with his friends, including Jo (Sadie Frost), an adoring young Irish girl who sees Billy's self-destructive nature but can do nothing to change it. At odds with the police (in the person of Jonathan Pryce) and a jealous chieftan (Sean Pertwee in a terrific and intense performance), Billy careens along his collision course with arrest and/or death with reckless abandon, living only for the high of the moment. Anderson brings a remarkable visual artistry to the film, imbuing it with equal parts MTV fast-cuts and Terry Gilliamesque urban British waste-scape. A modern techno-rock soundtrack blends seamlessly with the images to create a sobering vision of urban youth. ★★★ $92.98

Short Circuit

(1986, 98 min, US, John Badham) Pleasant sci-fi comedy about a state-of-the-art robot who escapes from the lab and teams up with a free-spirited artist (Ally Sheedy). Also starring Steve Guttenberg and Fisher Stevens. ★★½ $9.99

Short Circuit 2

(1988, 110 min, US, Kenneth Johnson) Number Five lives! This time, the robot searches for input about life in the big city, all the while ducking street hoods, greedy bankers and a gang of ruthless thieves. Not as appealing as the original. Fisher Stevens, Cynthia Gibb, Michael McKean and Jack Weston star. ★★ $14.99

Short Cuts

(1993, 189 min, US, Robert Altman) Based on nine short stories and a poem by Raymond Carver, *Short Cuts* immediately calls to mind one of Altman's masterpieces from the '70s, *Nashville*. But where *Nashville* is centered around a single event, *Short Cuts* examines the comings and goings of 22 characters connected simply by being part of the sprawl that is suburban Los Angeles, a microcosm of contemporary America. Altman explores the everyday lives of these characters with a cynical bite. He also has managed to put together one of the most impressive ensemble casts in American cinema (including Tim Robbins, Lily Tomlin, Jack Lemmon, Frances McDormand and Julianne Moore, just to name a few). A tremendous slice of life, *Short Cuts* is brilliant, audacious filmmaking. ★★★★ $19.99

Short Eyes

(1977, 104 min, US, Robert M. Young) Miguel Pinero's powerhouse play, scripted during his imprisonment in Sing Sing, is a gritty, nerverattling glimpse of life behind bars. When a white first-time offender (Bruce Davison) reveals his charge of child molesting, he becomes the target of a unified onslaught of abuse. ★★★ $19.99

Short Time

(1990, 100 min, US, Gregg Champion) Amiable comedy about how a mixed-up medical test has mistakenly convinced a police officer (Dabney Coleman) that he's dying. In order for his family to collect on his insurance policy, he's got to be killed in the line of duty. Now, he has become a "super cop," tracking down all sorts of vicious bad guys in an effort to get someone, anyone, to bump him off...quickly. Matt Frewer, Teri Garr, Barry Corbin and Joe Pantoliano also star. ★★½ $14.99

A Shot in the Dark

(1964, 101 min, GB, Blake Edwards) Edwards and Peter Sellers hit the mark with this hysterical "Pink Panther" masterpiece. Arguably the best of the series, the film is inundated with hilarious comedy, great stars, and an undaunted performance by Sellers. Inspector Clouseau ineptly sets out to prove that the ravishing Elke Sommer is innocent of murder despite all evidence to the contrary. When you come down with a bout of Pink Panther-itis, this is the one to rent! Costarring George Sanders and Herbert Lom. ★★★★ $14.99

The Shout

(1978, 87 min, GB, Jerzy Skolimowski) Alan Bates plays a mysterious intruder in an English couple's household. Susannah York co-stars as the woman who succumbs to his emotional and sexual domination in this chilling tale of overwhelming menace and aggression. John Hurt also stars as the high-strung husband in this adaptation of Robert Graves' ("I, Claudius") short story. ★★★

Shout at the Devil

(1976, 147 min, GB, Peter Hunt) Set in Mozambique at the outset of WWI, this overlong, but occasionally exciting, action film features the unlikely pairing of Lee Marvin and Roger Moore as an elephant poacher and an expatriate Englishman. Together, with Marvin's daughter (Barbara Perkins) in tow, they set out to sink a German battleship. ★★½

Show Boat

(1936, 113 min, US, James Whale) This second of three film versions of the Kern-Hammerstein perennial is the best of the bunch thanks to Whale's sensitive yet firm direction and a superb evocation of 1880s America. A first-rate cast includes Irene Dunne, Allan Jones, Charles Winninger, and, in unforgettable voice, Helen Morgan singing

"Bill" and Paul Robeson's staggering vocal of "Ol' Man River." ★★★½ $19.99

Show Boat

(1951, 107 min, US, George Sidney) Colorful version of the Kern-Hammerstein musical, though the 1936 version is by far the better of the two. With Kathryn Grayson, Ava Gardner, Howard Keel, Joe E. Brown and Agnes Moorehead. ★★★ $14.99

Show Business

(1944, 92 min, US, Edwin L. Marin) The inestimable comedic talents of the great Eddie Cantor and the hilarious Joan Davis are combined in this quite entertaining comedy with the two stars as vaudeville performers. ★★★

A Show of Force

(1990, 93 min, US, Bruno Barreto) An intriguing political thriller about a crusading TV journalist (Amy Irving) investigating one of Puerto Rico's biggest scandals: the brutal 1987 killing of two young men atop a mountainous broadcast tower. Were they terrorists, as the government claims, or were they student activists lured to their deaths by the FBI? Impressive cast includes Robert Duvall, Andy Garcia, Lou Diamond Phillips and Kevin Spacey. ★★½ $14.99

Show People

(1928, 81 min, US, King Vidor) Marion Davies stars in this wonderful silent comedy as a country girl who comes to Hollywood to be a "serious" actress, but finds unexpected success as a comedy star. ★★★ $29.99

Showdown in Little Tokyo

(1991, 79 min, US, Mark L. Lester) Heads roll and fingers fly as L.A. cop Dolph Lundgren teams up with Brandon Lee to stop evil, tattooed Japanese druglords from smuggling "ice" into the country, and to avenge the hideous murder of Dolph's parents. No ponderous moral messages in this one, just a lot of mindless action, despicable villains and a rocket-speed chase. ★★ $9.99

Showgirls

(1995, 131 min, US, Paul Verhoeven) Damned by critics, condemned by conservatives and ignored by the public, this relentlessly bad and wildly camp extravaganza is one of the most cheesily entertaining films to come out of Hollywood since *Myra Breckinridge* and *Beyond the Valley of the Dolls*. The rags-to-nipple clamps tale (and raunchy update of *All about Eve*) centers around the tough-talking white trash Nomi (Elizabeth Berkley), a brain-dead bleached blonde Barbie doll who is lured to the bright lights, fast living and tacky lifestyle of Las Vegas, home of high rollers and the $1.49 strawberry shortcake. Blessed with spunk, a curvaceous body and piston-gyrating hips, Nomi — beginning at a sleazy lap dance dive — steadily claws up the greased pole of success, going from trailer trash tramp to glittery star. Along this road kill of broken dreams, Nomi finds herself the object of interest from Crystal (Gina Gershon), the coke-sniffing, leering star/slut of the Vegas strip who happily wallows in her own hedonism. But Nomi sets her sights on Zack (Kyle MacLachlan in a look and hair-do that suggests

he's auditioning for the next Adolf Hitler bio), Crystal's boyfriend. Hearing lines like, "It must be weird not having anyone coming on you," Nomi knows she's made it to the top. (★★★★ Camp Rating) ★ $19.99

And what about some of the $40 million budget of *Showgirls?*

$12.00 — Acting Classes;
$150.00 — Various leather accessories;
$15,000 — Jewelry (check made out to K-Mart);
$50,000 — Research (paid in quarters);
$100,000 — Bikini wax kits;
$1,000,000 — Dr. Rabinowitz ("Implanter of the Stars");
$5,000,000 — Cheese;
$15,000,000 — Coke

Shy People

(1987, 119 min, US, Andrei Konchalovsky) Jill Clayburgh is a street-smart New York magazine writer working on an article about long-lost relatives who live deep within the Louisiana bayou. Barbara Hershey is the fierce marshland matriarch sheltering her brood from the outside world. Together, they clash big time. Martha Plimpton and Mare Winningham costar. ★★ $19.99

Siberiade

(1979, 206 min, Russia, Andrei Konchalovsky) The tumultuous events in Russia's 60-year history from 1900 to the 1960s provide the backdrop for this lavishly photographed and lyrically poetic saga of three generations of two families in a Siberian hamlet. Directed and cowritten by Koncholovsky (*A Slave of Love*), the film follows the day-to-day events of the poor Ustyuzhanin and the middle-class Solomin families, both virtually untouched by 19th-century progress. The Siberia pictured here isn't a vast frozen wasteland, but a vista of lush forests, cascading rivers and virgin land unpolluted by man's brutal touch. Feuds, affairs, murder and revenge transpire amid the social upheaval in this microcosm of a peasant Russia forced into the 20th century. Despite its length, *Siberiade* is a fast-moving and touching drama of the universal story of humanity caught in the turbulence of sweeping development. (Russian with English subtitles) ★★★★ $79.99

Showgirls

Gary Oldman does it his way in *Sid & Nancy*

Sibling Rivalry

(1990, 88 min, US, Carl Reiner) Kirstie Alley, who hasn't had much success with some of her film comedies, brings some life to this amusing black comedy as a doctor's wife whose sexual frustration leads her to an affair. However, things go from bad to worse when her lover dies in bed and she learns his true identity. Scott Bakula plays her hapless husband. ★★½ $19.99

The Sicilian

(1987, 146 min, US, Michael Cimino) A gangster takes on the mob by robbing the rich and distributing the wealth among the peasants in post-WWII Sicily. Needless to say, the Mafia is not happy. Christopher Lambert, Terence Stamp and John Turturro star in this misguided and lethargic crime saga. ★ $14.99

Sid and Nancy

(1986, 111 min, US, Alex Cox) Cox (*Repo Man*) takes the story of two self-destructive junkies, Sid Vicious of the Sex Pistols and Nancy Spungen, and sparks it up with savage energy and sardonic wit. It's no easy feat to romanticize, yet not idealize, these flamboyantly adolescent creatures. In spectacular performances, Gary Oldman and Chloe Webb bring a ferociousness to their roles that draws us to this doomed pair, if only to be repelled by their self-absorbed stupidity. ★★★½

Sideburns

(1990, 110 min, Russia, Yuri Mamin) Uncannily timely for a post-Communist Russia and a post-unification Germany, this exuberantly wacky yet cautionary political satire is a seriously funny film that, with its antic filmic style, will remind some of Dusan Makavejev's early works. Two geeks dressed in turn-of-the-century waistcoats, sporting bushy sideburns and brandishing canes, arrive in a backwater Russian city and begin winning adherents with their reactionary, Nazi-tinged political philosophy that idolizes poet Alexander Pushkin and seems to be against all change. The first target of their violent rampage for social conformity is the hippy-dippy "Children of Perestroika," but soon other reactionary groups spring up to vie for power and it takes the really bad guys

(the Communists) to restore "order" to the land. Director Mamin said of the film, "My goal is to make people laugh at reality before they die of horror." (Russian with English subtitles) ★★½ $59.99

Siesta

(1987, 105 min, US, Mary Lambert) Ellen Barkin stars as Claire, a professional daredevil who suddenly awakens to find herself lying on an airport runway covered in blood. Unable to recall her last three days and mystified by the origins of the blood, which is not her own, she begins an erotic and hallucinatory odyssey through a sun-bleached Spain where she encounters a menacingly horny cabbie, her now indifferent ex-lover and an eccentric group of intoxicated British "artists." This feature film debut by Lambert is a refreshingly complex, frenzied and enigmatic mystery-drama. Featuring Jodie Foster, Isabella Rossellini, Grace Jones and Julian Sands, with music by Miles Davis. ★★★ $14.99

The Sign of the Cross

(1932, 124 min, US, Cecil B. DeMille) DeMille's religious opus is a stylistically extravagant tale which mixes religious dogma with scenes of Roman excesses of sex and violence. In what could be the precursor to *The Robe* made 20 years later, the film centers on Roman big-wig Fredric March who falls in love with Christian do-gooder Elissa Landi. Then he spends the rest of the story trying to keep her from being lion bait. Far more interesting as characters are Charles Laughton, as an effeminate Nero, and Claudette Colbert, who gives a splendid performance as a cunning and sexy Poppaea (her nude bathing scene is a highlight). DeMille overplays the religious aspect but outdoes himself depicting the many torturous deaths in the arena (by elephant, alligator, gorilla) and with a sizzling lesbian seduction. ★★★ $14.99

Signal 7

(1983, 92 min, US, Rob Nilsson) From the director of *On the Edge* and *Heat and Sunlight* comes this rambling but sensitive portrayal of two middle-aged cab drivers who are going nowhere fast. Shot on videotape on a shoestring budget, this largely improvised drama can be uncomfortably revealing during its soul-baring scenes, reminding one of the early works of John Cassavetes, to whom the film is dedicated. ★★½ $79.99

La Signora di Tutti

(1934, 94 min, Italy, Max Ophüls) Ophüls' only Italian film, this sublime and powerful melodrama features Isa Miranda as Gaby Doriot, an aging film star who, at the top of her professional career but in the depths of despair in her private life, attempts suicide. Under anesthesia on the operating table, her sordid past, one of great excesses, ambitions and painful loves, is relived in her thoughts. (Italian with English subtitles) ★★★ $59.99

Signs of Life (Lebenszeichen)

(1968, 90 min, Germany, Werner Herzog) This early Herzog feature exhibits many of the director's signature touches, albeit sometimes haltingly utilized. During WWII, a wounded

German soldier is billeted to an occupied Greek island, removed from the conflict. He recuperates in the company of his Greek wife and two other German soldiers in a small, impoverished fishing village. At first seemingly idyllic, their lives bog down in tedium, heat and boredom. The young man unravels, his mental deterioriation leading him to the munitions dump in an attempt to shake his fist at God. The director's trademark static shots are not as effective in their conveyance of existential anguish as they would become in his later films; but the film is a valuable glimpse into the early development of a major filmmaker. (German with English subtitles) ★★½ $69.99

Signs of Life

(1989, 91 min, US, John David Coles) An extremely talented cast highlights this personal and touching drama about the final days of a boat-building business and how the closing affects those around it. Arthur Kennedy is remarkable as the patriarchal owner who refuses to accept the inevitable. Kevin J. O'Connor and Vincent D'Onofrio are both fine as the two young workers planning to leave their small town at the expense of a loved one. Also starring are Kate Reid as the business' loyal manager, Beau Bridges as a father faced with financial ruin, and the exceptional Michael Lewis as D'Onofrio's slow-witted younger brother. Though these types of films are usually described as "small," there is nothing miniature in the scope or achievement of this "little" gem. ★★★½ $14.99

The Silence

(1963, 95 min, Sweden, Ingmar Bergman) An intense story of two sisters, emotionally and physically united since childhood, who, while traveling together, begin the struggle of separation. The younger woman seeks freedom from her embittered sister by entering into a relationship with a stranger. Last of Bergman's trilogy on faith which includes *Through a Glass Darkly* and *Winter Light*. (Swedish with English subtitles) ★★★ $24.99

Silence = Death

(1990, 60 min, US, Rosa von Praunheim & Phil Zwickler) Avant-garde German filmmaker von Praunheim (*City of Lost Souls, A Virus Knows No Morals*) explores in this documentary the reactions and response of New York's artistic community to the ravages of AIDS. Activists interviewed include representatives from the many arts organizations that alert the public to the crisis through performance art, music, theatre and literature as well as artists David Wojnorowicz, Paul Smith and Rafael Gamba. Particularly entertaining segments include Keith Haring as he admits to nostalgic longing for the days of care-free sex and Allen Ginsberg's musing upon his shyer attitude about experimenting sexually. Even with the gentler voices, the film's undercurrent is an angry demand for action and recognition. ★★★ $29.99

The Silence of the Lambs

(1991, 118 min, US, Jonathan Demme) Demme's nerve-racking psychological chiller based on the novel by Thomas Harris stars Jodie Foster as Clarice Starling, a fledgling FBI agent who is assigned the daunting task of interviewing convicted psycho-killer, Dr. Hannibal Lecter (Anthony Hopkins) in the hopes that he can help her develop a profile of "Buffalo Bill" — a mass murderer who likes to skin his victims. Hopkins' portrayal of the maniacally twisted Lecter is sheer terrifying brilliance. Rarely has an actor exuded pure, malevolent evil with such seductive charm. For her part, Foster is equally stellar. Her Clarice is an intricate and subtly drawn character who finds herself in a dangerous *pas de deux* with Lecter. The scenes between the two of them are riveting. Demme's direction throughout is superb and this film firmly establishes him as one of the leading directors for the '90s. Also starring Scott Glenn. Winner of 5 Academy Awards including Best Picture, Director, Actress (Foster) and Actor (Hopkins). (Letterboxed version available for $19.99) ★★★★ $9.99

Silent Fall

(1994, 100 min, US, Bruce Beresford) Richard Dreyfuss stars as a noted psychiatrist who battles his own demons while helping a child come to terms with his. Ben Faulkner plays a ten-year-old autistic youth who is the sole witness to the murder of his parents and near-fatal stabbing of his sister (Liv Tyler). Dreyfuss is reluctantly called into the investigation to try to reach the boy, made more difficult by the child's silence, an interfering doctor (John Lithgow) and an impatient sheriff (J.T. Walsh). Beresford's subtle direction creates a suspenseful mood throughout, and though *Silent Fall* may by too clinical at times, it nonetheless is an engaging psychological mystery. Linda Hamilton also stars in the thankless role of Dreyfuss' wife. ★★★ $14.99

Silent Movie

(1976, 86 min, US, Mel Brooks) Although this Brooks spoof on Hollywood filmmaking is not on the comic level with his best works, it is nonetheless an enjoyable lark. Brooks plays a has-been producer who attempts a comeback by making a silent movie. All this, of course, is set within a silent film, more than living up to

its title. The cast includes Dom DeLuise, Marty Feldman, Bernadette Peters and Ron Carey; and includes cameos by Anne Bancroft, Paul Newman and Liza Minnelli, among others. ★★★ $9.99

The Silent Partner

(1978, 103 min, Canada, Daryl Duke) Christopher Plummer (whose enormous talents have rarely been utilized on screen) teams with Elliott Gould in this original and riveting suspense thriller. Gould plays a bank teller who figures out Plummer's plan to rob his bank, turning the tables on him. However, when the psychotic would-be robber figures out the double-cross, he sets out after Gould and the loot. With Susannah York and, in a small part, John Candy. ★★★

Silent Running

(1971, 89 min, US, Douglas Trumbull) Special effects master Trumbull (*2001*) directed this inventive though leisurely sci-fi/environmental tale with Bruce Dern tending a space garden when Earth has become barren, losing control when the powers that be decide to shut it down. Written by Michael Cimino, Steven Bochco (TV's "Hill Street Blues") and Deric Washburn. ★★★ $14.99

Silent Tongue

(1994, 98 min, US, Sam Shepard) The final theatrical release of River Phoenix, this involving though labored ghost story is slightly odd, but it achieves a poetic, mystical tone. Set in the Old West, the film casts Alan Bates as a slimy sideshow owner who traded his Indian daughter to pioneer Richard Harris for his son (Phoenix) to marry. However, after the woman dies in childbirth, Harris returns to negotiate for Bates' remaining daughter to comfort his near-mad, grieving son — whose refusal to bury his wife causes her spirit to return to seek vengeance. *Silent Tongue* is an unusual, slowly paced but nevertheless gripping treatise on 19th-century Western culture, and features showy but sound performances from the entire cast. Shepard's direction is thoughtful and carefully realized. ★★½ $14.99

The Silk Road

(1988, 99 min, Japan, Junya Sato) A "sukiyaki western" in the best sense of the term, this spectacular saga of love, heroism and war is set on the Silk Road (the ancient 5,000-mile trade route that stretches through the Asian desert). The story follows the adventures of a reluctant warrior, Zhao, a young man who rescues a captured princess (a young and beautiful one at that), but finds that his reward is only to be hunted down by a vengeful crown prince intent on killing both him and the princess. This exhilarating romantic adventure should not be confused with the similarly packaged, but somewhat less satisfying battle-filled epic, *Heaven and Earth*. (Japanese with English subtitles) ★★★½ $9.99

Silk Stockings

(1957, 117 min, US, Rouben Mamoulian) Charming musical remake of Ernst Lubitsch's *Ninotchka*, with Fred Astaire in the Melvyn Douglas role as a movie producer, and the lovely Cyd Charisse in the Garbo role as the Russian envoy. Score by Cole Porter. ★★★ $19.99

Silkwood

(1983, 128 min, US, Mike Nichols) In yet another remarkable performance, Meryl Streep stars as Karen Silkwood, the nuclear plant worker who died under mysterious circumstances after uncovering damaging information against the plant for which she worked. Kurt Russell as her boyfriend and Cher as her lesbian roommate both offer strong support in Nichols' tense, harrowing and compelling drama. ★★★½ $14.99

Silver Bullet

(1985, 95 min, US, Daniel Attias) Stylish version of Stephen King's story about a small town being terrorized by a werewolf, with Gary Busey and young Corey Haim determined to put a stop to it. ★★½ $14.99

Silver City

(1986, 110 min, Australia, Sophia Turkiewicz) At the end of the 1940s, thousands of war-weary refugees began landing on Australia's shores. This immigration onslaught was encouraged by the Australian government's vigorous campaign to increase the nation's population and expand its industrial capacity. The turbulent setting of the refugee settlement camps is where our story takes place. A Polish family's hardships and love interests are the focus of this touching film about displaced people trying to overcome a past which haunts them. ★★½

The Silver Stallion: King of the Wild Brumbies

(1993, 93 min, Australia) Herds of brumbies, or horses, run wild in the Australian Outback and are hunted by the local "cowboys." The Silver Stallion is the most sought after horse of all, coveted for his size, strength, and above all, his blond hair and golden mane. Caroline Goodall portrays an author who chronicles his story for both future publication and the enjoyment of her adolescent daughter as they work on their farm. The equestrian scenes are spectacular and the cinematography is superb. The high production quality and engaging

Meryl Streep (l.) and Cher share a tender moment in *Silkwood*

story line make this an excellent family film. ★★★ $14.99

Silver Streak

(1976, 113 min, US, Arthur Hiller) Gene Wilder and Richard Pryor team for the first time in this engaging and often hilarious comedy which tips its hat to Hitchcock and the mystery-aboard-a-train films. Passenger Wilder gets himself mixed up with Jill Clayburgh, FBI agents, murder, con artist Pryor and spies as he travels from Los Angeles to Chicago. Pryor is a standout, and the cast includes Patrick McGoohan, Ned Beatty, Ray Walston and Scatman Crothers. ★★★ $9.99

Silverado

(1985, 132 min, US, Lawrence Kasdan) Entertaining and very stylish western adventure with the "two Kevins" — Kline and Costner — and Danny Glover and Scott Glenn as four drifters who team up to battle a crooked town sheriff and the gang who controls him. Also with Brian Dennehy, Jeff Goldblum and Rosanna Arquette. ★★★ $14.99

Silverlake Life: The View from Here

(1992, 99 min, US, Tom Joslin & Peter Friedman) Arguably the most harrowing vision of death and dying ever recorded, this emotionally devastating video diary of two lovers living with and dying from AIDS is far from a morbid recording of one's own death. Rather, it's a celebration of life and of the enduring love the two men had for each other. Joslin, a film teacher, and his lover of 22 years, Mark Massi, decided to record their lives after the onslaught of AIDS-related illnesses. The camera follows them as they visit the doctor, buy medicine and herbal "cures" and other activities, but stays primarily in their apartment in the Silverlake section of Los Angeles. The two men attempt to continue leading productive lives despite the frustration of their physical incapacities. One's immediate feeling — after the sadness of their story — is an acknowledgement of their overriding commitment to each other, making this personal diary an astonishing love story. ★★★★ $19.99

Simon Bolivar

(1972, 120 min, Venezuela/Italy, Alessandro Blasetti) The adventurous and heroic life of Simon Bolivar, "el liberator" of South America, gets a boisterously operatic treatment in this Venezuelan/Italian coproduction. Maximilian Schell — normally very good — plays the role a bit too theatrically, shouting his lines and continuously flailing about his arms. Although this is not the definitive portrait of Bolivar, it is still an interesting story — that of one man, led by a vision of a unified continent, who struggles to unite a diverse and poverty-stricken people, forges an army and, against seemingly insurmountable odds, successfully battles colonialist Spain. Set in the early 1800s, the film needlessly splices the story with a subplot of his loves and his "all-too-human" side, but happily, this is brief. The film, originally in Cinemascope, is badly cropped in this video transfer. (Dubbed, although Schell's English is his own.) ★★½ $49.99

Simon of the Desert

(1965, 45 min, Mexico, Luis Buñuel) This comic and surreal attack on the Church is drawn from the life of Saint Simeon Stylites who, in order to lead the "correct Christian life," resided atop a pillar. Vain, self-important and sexually repressed, our hero soon finds that he is tempting prey for the cunning Devil. (Spanish with English subtitles) ★★★½ $29.99

Simone de Beauvoir

(1982, 105 min, France, Josee Dayan & Malka Robowska) Pioneer feminist, author ("The Second Sex", "Prime of Life"), philosopher, political activist and longtime companion of Jean-Paul Sartre, Simone de Beauvoir's life has been one of remarkable interests and insights. In this documentary, the filmmakers let Ms. Beauvoir speak freely, as she recounts her friendships (with the leading thinkers of her day), her political sympathies (including her thoughts on the 1968 student uprising), sexual fidelity, aging and death. Photos from Ms. Beauvoir's personal collection, archival footage and a fascinating conversation with Sartre are included in this candid portrait of a brilliant woman. (French with English subtitles) ★★★ $59.99

Simple Men

(1992, 105 min, US, Hal Hartley) Where other than in a Hartley film would you find such characters as a brawling, chain-smoking nun, a French-speaking, grunge-rocking gas-station attendant, and a beautiful Romanian epileptic? For the discriminating viewer, Hartley's films are unique and rewarding; but *Simple Men*, while worthy, lacks the cohesion of his previous, more successful efforts, *The Unbelievable Truth* and *Trust*. The story follows Bill, a petty criminal, and his kid brother Daniel on their search for their escaped-con dad, who may or may not have bombed the Pentagon 20 years earlier. Their quest leads them to the little town of Sagapawnac, Long Island, where each man, buoyed by Jim Beam and long-winded philosophical chit chat, realizes his destiny. Peppered with plenty of droll moments, the film suffers mainly from its somewhat meandering pace and a few too many incidental characters. ★★½ $19.99

A Simple Story

(1978, 110 min, France, Claude Sautet) Romy Schneider is an unalloyed pleasure in this subtle, incisive look at a woman's mid-life crisis. Though she's a successful designer with a teenage son and a sympathetic circle of friends, Schneider is plagued by doubts and fears about the path she has chosen, and can't figure out how to change things. Schneider won a French Academy Award for her gripping performance. (Dubbed) ★★★ $29.99

A Simple Twist of Fate

(1994, 106 min, US, Gillies MacKinnon) Mistakenly billed as a comedy, this drama inspired by "Silas Marner" follows one hard-luck and heartbreaking story after another for the first 30 minutes or so. To start with, Steve Martin finds out that the child his wife is expecting isn't his; then he moves to a small town where his fortune in gold coins is stolen; then a heroin addict dies in the snow outside

his house. Only after the woman's young daughter wanders into Martin's home and life does the film lighten up. He adopts her and things are fine for years, until her real father (Gabriel Byrne) decides to take her back, leading to an emotional ending. There is a lot of depth and tragicomedy in this worthwhile film, which also stars Catherine O'Hara and Stephen Baldwin. ★★½ $14.99

The Sin of Harold Diddlebock

(1947, 90 min, US, Preston Sturges) Sturges and Harold Lloyd share the dubious distinction of being two of America's most undervalued treasures. Writer-director Sturges is witty, hilarious, touching and intelligent; Lloyd's capable synthesis of subtle characterization and side-splitting slapstick is unmatched. The plot involves an ex-football star who, after 20 years in a dead-end job, uses his life savings to make a fortune at the track only to lose it at the circus. At the circus? Just watch it — you won't regret it. (aka: *Mad Wednesday*) ★★★

The Sin of Madelon Claudet

(1931, 73 min, US, Edgar Selwyn) Helen Hayes, the First Lady of the American Theatre, makes one of her rare screen appearances in this superb soap opera, and she won an Oscar for it. In the tradition of *Stella Dallas* and *Madame X*, Hayes, in a glorious performance, plays a mother who sacrifices all for the sake of her son. Sure it's been done before, even back then, but Hayes' portrayal and the sharp directorial style make it all the more refreshing. ★★★ $19.99

Sinbad and the Eye of the Tiger

(1977, 113 min, GB, Sam Wanamaker) The weakest of the whole Harryhausen/Sinbad series is saddled with a predictable plot, anemic characters, and (most surprisingly) less than spectacular special effects. For the record, the plot concerns Sinbad's quest to help a prince who's been transformed into a baboon by a sorceress' evil spell. ★½ $14.99

Since Stonewall

(1971-1991, 80 min, US) Independent gay and lesbian filmmakers are the focus in this entertaining ten-short compilation that deals, both seriously as well as humorously, with such topics as AIDS, female impersonation and coming out. Highlights include Gus Van Sant's *Discipline of DE* — (DE, or Do Easy, refers to an at-peace approach to life and inanimate objects inspired by William Burroughs); *Bust*, in which Holly Brown becomes a multiple-personalitied Bette Davis-type mother-in-law from hell; and *Queerdom*, an animated tale of a muscle man who wakes up one morning suddenly "feeling a little queer." Other shorts include *Final Solution* by Jerry Tartaglia, *Anton* by Robert Dunlap and *976*- by David Weissman. ★★★ $29.99

Since You Went Away

(1944, 172 min, US, John Cromwell) A tremendous cast brings life to this compelling and first-rate WWII soaper, a huge hit back in 1944. Sort of *Mrs. Miniver* with an American family, the story follows the struggles and daily lives of those on the homefront. Claudette Colbert shines as the mother and wife keeping a stiff upper lip while her husband is fighting overseas. Also with Jennifer Jones, Joseph Cotten, Shirley Temple, Monty Woolley, Hattie McDaniel and Agnes Moorehead. ★★★½ $39.99

Sincerely Charlotte

(1986, 92 min, France, Caroline Huppert) Isabelle Huppert camps it up as a beguiling nightclub singer who is on the lam for the suspected murder of her boyfriend. With the net closing, and in desperation, she reenters the life of her old boyfriend, now married. Smitten with the alluring Huppert, the man's attention is divided between his quiet domestic life and the carefree, dangerous but exciting world of his ex. Miss Huppert is wonderful as the femme fatale; part innocent, part liar and bitch — she's memorable! (French with English subtitles) ★★★

Un Singe en Hiver
(Monkey in Winter)

(1962, 105 min, France, Henri Verneuil) In theme and acting prowess, *Un Singe en Hiver* can be favorably compared to *The Color of Money*. Crusty old-timer Jean Gabin is wasting his days away in a small town. His life is reinvigorated when a young man (Jean-Paul Belmondo) moves into town, for Gabin sees in this wild drinker and dreamer fragments of his own vibrant youth. They join together for a few unforgettable adventures. (French with English subtitles) ★★½

Singin' in the Rain

(1952, 102 min, US, Gene Kelly & Stanley Donen) Movie musicals just don't come any better than this. A collection of superbly creative talents were at their peak with this spoof on 1920s Hollywood, with directors Kelly and Donen and writers Betty Comden and Adolphe Green combining forces after their success with *On the Town*. Kelly, who also choreographed, plays a popular silent screen star faced with the

advent of "talkies" and salvaging his new film. Debbie Reynolds is perfectly cast as the pert chorine romanced by the actor; Donald O'Connor is priceless as Kelly's childhood pal; and Jean Hagen's Lina Lamont is one of the great "dumb blondes" in movie history. It's hard to pinpoint just one highlight in a film rich in magical moments, but O'Connor's "Make 'Em Laugh" and Kelly's "Broadway Ballet" certainly stand out. ★★★★ $19.99

Singing the Blues in Red

(1987, 110 min, West Germany/GB, Ken Loach) Also known as *Fatherland*, this acerbic little gem is a flawed yet stimulating look at East-West relationships as seen through the unblinking eyes of a wary political émigré. Klaus, a celebrated political songwriter/singer from East Berlin, is kicked out of East Germany but is enthusiastically welcomed into the capitalist arms of the West. Always questioning and distrustful of those in power, Klaus soon finds his worst fears of the West confirmed and feels no compunction about biting the corrupt hands that feed him. In his first news conference in West Berlin, he condemns his "fascist" sponsors — his American record company and government officials. Documentarian Loach pulls no punches as he explores the disillusionment of the socialist dream as well as the myths and contradictions inherent in the "Free World." (English and German with English subtitles) ★★½

Single Room Furnished

(1968, 93 min, US, Matteo Ottaviano) Jayne Mansfield's last film features her as a tenement resident desperately looking for love after being deserted by the two men she cared for. With Dorothy Keller and Fabian Dean. ★ $19.99

Single White Female

(1992, 107 min, US, Barbet Schroeder) In his most commercial film to date, director Schroeder jumps on the Hollywood Formula

bandwagon, and thanks to his deft touch, what should have been a flimsy made-from-hell thriller is, for the most part, a potent psychological suspenser. Jennifer Jason Leigh is the aforementioned roomie, who answers Bridget Fonda's ad to share her New York apartment. A mousy woman with no discernable personality of her own, Leigh becomes infatuated with the hipness of Fonda's breezy demeanor. This "crush," however, soon gives way to jealousy when Fonda reenters the dating game. Though lacking the stylish trappings of a *Fatal Attraction*, or even that film's narrative strengths, it is Leigh and Fonda's strong performances which elevate this tale above the ordinary. ★★½ $14.99

Singles

(1992, 100 min, US, Cameron Crowe) This second feature from the director of *Say Anything* has been touted as "*The Big Chill* for the twentysomething generation" and features a post-Brat Pack ensemble cast (Bridget Fonda, Campbell Scott, Matt Dillon and Kyra Sedgwick) as a group of Seattle MTV spawn trying to cope with their disillusionment about life and, more importantly, dating. Crowe's humorous coverage of their adventures splashing around in the dating pool redeems what might have been yet another whiny, self-centered product of the "new enlightenment." Also with Bill Pullman. ★★★ $14.99

The Sinister Urge

(1962, 75 min, US, Edward D. Wood, Jr.) More schlock from the man who gave us *Glen or Glenda* and *Orgy of the Dead*. Here, a police officer investigates a series of porn star murders. Look out for the ruthless, evil, over-acting Mrs. Big (Jean Fontaine). Title could be used for a Wood bio on his ability to make awful films. ★

Sink the Bismark!

(1960, 97 min, GB, Lewis Gilbert) The British Navy launches an all-out effort to destroy the pride of Hitler's fleet. Excellent special effects help this well-made WWII action-drama. ★★★ $19.98

Sins of Rachel

(1972, 87 min, US, Richard Fontaine) Cheaply made, with acting well below professional standards, this clumsy murder mystery has some interest because it was one of only two feature films made by Richard Fontaine, one of the pioneers in gay male erotica in film. Bloated and aging rapidly, Rachel Waring is a faded nightclub "star" who is murdered just about the time her juicy memoirs are about to be published. Screenwriter Ann Noble campily plays the horny old bitch in sort of a Hermione Gingold imitation of an aging Bette Davis. The suspects include her cute son Jimmy (Bruce Campbell), a sexually confused young man who slept in his mother's bedroom, a stud who serviced the dead woman, her black publisher and others in the Peyton Place-like seaside town. ★½

Sirens

(1994, 94 min, Australia/GB, John Duigan) Filled with sun, sea, wine, sex and just the right amount of stimulating conversation,

Bridget Fonda (l.) and Matt Dillon in *Singles*

Sirens is like the perfect mini-vacation: not too taxing but very refreshing. Hugh Grant stars as an uptight preacher in the 1920s who must try to convince erotic painter Sam Neill to withdraw one of his "shocking" pictures from an exhibition. To achieve his task, Grant, accompanied by his wife Tara Fitzgerald, visits Neill and his lusty models (including supermodel Elle Macpherson), who do their best to get the couple to take the plunge into hedonism. Witty, nicely photographed and well acted, *Sirens* is eye candy for the Merchant Ivory set. ★★★ $14.99

Sirocco

(1951, 98 min, US, Curtis Bernhardt) Humphrey Bogart stars as a cynical, unscrupulous businessman and black marketeer without political convictions in French occupied Syria (sound familiar?). Lee J. Cobb is the French Lt. Colonel in charge of an investigation to discover who is supplying the Arab resistance with arms (you're only allowed one guess). Not one of Bogie's best, but he has a good world-weary presence. ★★ $9.99

Sister Act

(1992, 101 min, US, Emile Ardolino) Whoopi Goldberg is a comic delight in a film finally worthy of the comedienne's talents. Goldberg stars as a Reno lounge singer who, upon witnessing a gangland murder, is sent to hide out at a San Francisco convent, run by the inestimable Maggie Smith. Captivating the order one by one, Whoopi does anything but lay low when she takes control of the church's choir and turns them into an overnight sensation. As would be expected, a lot of the humor stems from the nuns engaging in very un-nun-like behavior. But most of the comedy is sharper than that suggests. And though the premise is strictly formulaic, it's one Hollywood formula which works. Among the great pleasures of the film is the sight of those nuns singing '60s pop tunes — "I Will Follow Him" takes on a whole new meaning. As an elderly nun, it's good to see Mary Wickes again, and Kathy Najimy steals every scene she's in as an unbelievably perky sister. This surprise box-office hit was originally written by Paul Rudnick for Bette Midler, but after she left the project, he took his name off the credits. ★★★½ $9.99

Sister Act 2: Back in the Habit

(1993, 112 min, US, Bill Duke) To say that *Sister Act 2* is formulaic would put one in danger of committing the unpardonable sin of understatement. That is not to say that the formula doesn't work. A little. Whoopi Goldberg is back as lounge singer Deloris Van Cartier; but this time, instead of having to save a bunch of nuns, she has to turn a rag-tag Catholic School music class into something resembling a choir. The charm of the first film was watching the nuns coming out of their shells; but how many times have we seen sassy, underachieving kids learn the meaning of self-respect because of a dedicated teacher. Nevertheless, the film does have its comedic moments, and the giggling Kathy Najimy and the impish Michael Jeter do add some holy spirit to this rather unimaginative sequel. ★★ $9.99

Sister, My Sister

(1994, 102 min, GB, Nancy Meckler) Inspired by the same story that prompted Jean Genet's "The Maids," this provocative and uneasy drama is set in 1930s France and stars Joely Richardson and Jodhi May as two repressed sisters who work as servants to an obsessively demanding madam (Julie Walters) who rules her house, and the life of her daughter, with a velvet-gloved iron fist. Held virtual prisoners in the claustrophobic house, the two young women soon become incestously involved with each other and their hot passions soon unravel their facade of orderliness. A highly sensual, intense, at times funny but ultimately unsettling tale. ★★★ $14.99

Sisters

(1973, 93 min, US, Brian De Palma) The beginning of director De Palma's sometimes overwhelming display of technical wizardry, this (dare we say it?) Hitchcockian tale follows the crisscrossing path of twin sisters (one good, one evil, both played by Margot Kidder) and a reporter (Jennifer Salt), who thinks she has witnessed a murder (shades of *Rear Window*). Scathing in its treatment of society as a breeding ground of thrill-seeking voyeurs, this appetizing but deadly serving of sibling rivalry is more than just another "evil twin" hors d'oeuvre. ★★★

Sitting Ducks

(1978, 90 min, US, Henry Jaglom) Michael Emil and Zack Norman are the zany and querulous odd couple in this delightfully wacky road comedy. After the whiny and fastidious Emil steals $750,000 from his employer, he and his co-hort Norman go on the road to Florida and from there Costa Rica. But along the way, these clashing nebbishes meet, befriend and take along for the ride a strange assortment of characters. Improvised dialogue and Jaglom's sympathetic eye and ear for misfits heighten an entertaining road movie. ★★★ $19.99

Six Degrees of Separation

(1993, 112 min, US, Fred Schepisi) Based on John Guare's acclaimed Broadway play, which itself was inspired by a strange but true story, this witty and involving exploration of self-deception is an exhilarating comedy. The charismatic Will Smith plays a gay con man who ingratiates himself into the households of several rich New Yorkers by claiming to be the son of Sidney Poitier. One of those scammed is art dealer Donald Sutherland and his wife Stockard Channing (brilliantly re-creating her award-winning stage role). As they recount their experiences in a series of anecdotal flashbacks, they play detective, ultimately learning the truth about their charming hoaxster. Guare, who wrote his own screenplay adaptation, has fashioned a modern masterwork dissecting the classes, race relations and, to a lesser degree, our desire as a society to appear in the film version of "Cats." ★★★★ $19.99

Sixteen Candles

(1984, 93 min, US, John Hughes) Charming, often funny and affecting coming-of-age tale with Molly Ringwald as a perplexed teen beseiged by creepy freshmen, spoiled siblings, confused parents and rampant hormones.

Slacker: A Madonna Pap smear anyone?

Cast includes Paul Dooley, Justin Henry, Blanche Baker and Anthony Michael Hall. ★★★ $14.99

Skateboard Kid

(1993, 83 min, US) A teenage skateboard fanatic moves from the city to a small country town with his dad (Timothy Busfield) and meets the mom (Bess Armstrong) and daughter match they've been looking for. Along the way, they battle father and son bad guys and, of course, win the day. Although the plot is predictable, the video will appeal to teens and especially skateboarders, as it does feature a lot of action shots set to the music of "The Trashkittens." ★★ $14.99

Sketch Artist

(1992, 89 min, US) Jeff Fahey (*The Lawnmower Man*) lays another brick in the road to B-movie stardom in this mundane mystery about a police sketch artist who involves himself in a murder investigation when the only suspect bears a startling resemblance to his wife (Sean Young). Also with Drew Barrymore, Charlotte Lewis and Tcheky Karyo. ★½ $9.99

Skin Deep

(1989, 101 min, US, Blake Edwards) Minor Edwards comedy with a few laughs, but mostly a disappointment for the writer-director. John Ritter is a writer who can't keep his mind off women. ★½ $9.99

Skin Game

(1971, 102 min, US, Paul Bogart) Extremely likable comedy set pre-Civil War with James Garner as a con man teaming with runaway slave Lou Gossett, Jr., the two posing as master and servant. ★★★ $14.99

The Skull

(1965, 83 min, GB, Freddie Francis) A collector of the occult who obtains the skull of the Marquis de Sade descends into a nightmare of murder and madness in this Amicus production starring the dynamic duo of Peter Cushing and Christopher Lee. Cushing plays the skeptical collector, who realizes too late the evil influence the skull is having on him. At first, the skull is the proud centerpiece of his collection, but as curiosity about its legend overtakes him, he unconsciously becomes part of a murderous nightly ritual. Suspected by the police, he is eventually consumed by the skull's evil. Lee plays a fellow collector whose help and warnings Cushing ignores until they can no longer do him any good. The film, set in the modern day, is properly atmospheric and tense but is hindered somewhat by lackluster special effects involving the skull. Director Francis has made better films for both Hammer and Amicus, but Cushing and Lee are stellar, as always, and manage to overcome the film's minor shortcomings enough to turn it into an entertaining horror story, complete with moral lesson. ★★★ $9.99

The Sky Above, the Mud Below

(1962, 92 min, France, Pierre-Dominique Gaisseau) This extraordinary documentary charts the enthralling yet dangerous expedition of a group of anthropologists through the jungles of Dutch New Guinea and into man's savage and violent past. Their endurance was tested daily as they encountered cannibals, headhunters and wild animals, as well as disease and death. Academy Award for Best Documentary Feature. (Narrated in English) ★★★★

The Sky's the Limit

(1943, 89 min, US, Edward H. Griffith) Fred Astaire musical with Fred as a war hero on leave in New York, falling in love with photographer Joan Leslie. Fred's dancing is the tops. ★★★ $14.99

Skyline

(1985, 84 min, Spain, Fernando Colomo) A witty, droll depiction of the adventures of a Spanish photographer who comes to Manhattan seeking fame and fortune. The problems he encounters, including an extremely competitive job market, the fast-track lifestyle, and the incomprehensible language of the natives, drive him into the company of the few Spanish friends he has in the city. The film is a fine comic study of one immigrant's problems in the land of opportunity. (English and Spanish with English subtitles) ★★★ $39.99

Skyscraper Souls

(1932, 99 min, US, Edgar Selwyn) Big business, middle class and working class are all struggling to strike it rich, or at least hold on to what they've got. Set in a skyscraper, the ultimate symbol of America in the '30s, the film follows the lives of several "souls" that live and work there. Warren William plays a sly and ruthless businessman, trying to gain total ownership of the building. A young Maureen O'Sullivan is the innocent secretary who is tempted by him. As events unfold, things come to a dramatic climax. Underneath the story, there is a darker, cynical side reflecting the mood of the times. Great art direction by M-G-M's Cedric Gibbons (who designed *Grand Hotel*) exquisitely captures the era of geometrics and chrome. ★★★ $19.99

Slacker

(1991, 97 min, US, Richard Linklater) First-time director Linklater takes us on a kaleidoscopic journey through the neo-beatnik scene of Austin, Texas. Using an interesting cinematic device, Linklater introduces the viewer to a series of random characters, following each one until some other interesting person pops up. The film literally weaves its way from one to the next without ever looking back. Starting with Linklater himself, as he steps off a bus, catches a taxi and begins babbling with the cabbie about the metaphysical implications of *The Wizard of Oz*, we meet a seamless string of vagabonds, pseudo-intellectuals, conspiracy theorists and even a woman hawking what she claims is a Madonna Pap smear. Filled with hilarious moments, the film is a fascinating document of a generation of would-be philosophers with nowhere to go and nothing to do. ★★★ $19.99

Slamdance

(1987, 100 min, US, Wayne Wang) Tom Hulce, Mary Elizabeth Mastrantonio, Virginia Madsen and Harry Dean Stanton star in this moody attempt at modern film noir. Hulce plays an artist who is suspected of murdering club-hopper Madsen. Director Wang offers a splash of style to the filmmaking, but can't save the muddled story. ★★½ $14.99

Slap Shot

(1977, 122 min, US, George Roy Hill) Racy comedy with Paul Newman as a hockey player on a losing minor league team. When they start playing rough, they find attendance booms, and they win as well. This is a very funny film, though the language is quite strong — those offended by such dialogue should take note. Also starring Michael Ontkean and Lindsay Crouse. ★★★ $14.99

Slate, Wyn & Me

(1987, 90 min, Australia, Don McLennan) Borrowing heavily on such American "mixed up, violent but attractive young people on the lam from the law" flicks as *Bonnie and Clyde*, *Thieves Like Us* and *Badlands*, this mindless Aussie road movie has moments of interest but is generally a below-average import. The story begins suspiciously with two bungling brothers who rob a bank, kill a cop and then kidnap a witness (the requisite sexy teenager). But the meandering drama, filled with a rock 'n' roll soundtrack and countless car chases, soon runs out of gas leaving the viewer in the dust. ★★

Slaughter of the Innocents

(1994, 104 min, US, James Glickenhaus) Former action hack director Glickenhaus (*McBain*) comes of age with this gripping FBI procedural that, in its no-holds-barred approach to the subject of a serial child rapist/killer, almost makes *Silence of the Lambs* look like "Little Bo Peep." Scott Glenn stars as a special agent thrust into the path of a maniac when his precocious, computer prodigy son (Jesse Cameron-Glickenhaus) makes a startling connection linking a recent killing to a 15-year-old series of grisly child slayings. Warning: Weak stomachs need not apply. ★★★½ $14.99

Slaughterhouse Five

(1972, 104 min, US, George Roy Hill) Kurt Vonnegut's hero Billy Pilgrim becomes unstuck in time — between his war experiences in Dresden, his life as an optometrist in `70s suburbia and as a member of a select zoo on the planet Tralfamadore. This very faithful adaptation is a visually stunning and emotionally satisfying trek in time which captures Vonnegut's irreverence, novelty and irony. Michael Sacks, Valerie Perrine and Ron Liebman star. ★★★½ $14.99

Slave Girls from Beyond Infinity

(1987, 73 min, US, Ken Dixon) When a buxom blonde bursts onto the screen in a tight close-up of her gifted abundance, one can almost see the director smirking in the background fully enjoying his cheesy yet entertaining homage to the fleshy grade-B flicks of Hollywood's past. Filled with a bevy of luscious actress-wannabees, the story is a sci-fi adventure where our curvaceous heroines must do battle with insidious aliens. In its best

S

Michael Sacks and Valerie Perrine on the planet Tralfamadore in *Slaughterhouse Five*

moments, this amusing spoof will remind one of a Russ Meyer film set in outer space, but the rest of the time it's pure, titillating exploitation. ★ $14.99

A Slave of Love

(1978, 94 min, USSR, Nikita Mikhalkov) A dazzling, imaginative tale set in 1919 concerning a White Russian film crew's trials and tribulations in completing a romantic melodrama amid the rising tide of the revolution. The stunning Elena Solovel, as the naive leading lady, is a revelation. (Russian with English subtitles) ★★★½ $59.99

Slaves of New York

(1989, 125 min, US, James Ivory) Disappointing screen version of Tama Janowitz's best-selling novel about the trendy New York art scene, with Bernadette Peters as a struggling hat designer involved with a self-centered artist. ★★ $89.99

Sleep with Me

(1994, 85 min, US, Rory Kelly) Fast becoming the crown prince of slacker-angst movies (*Naked in New York; Bodies, Rest and Motion*; etc.), Eric Stoltz headlines this loosely scripted tale of two best friends (Stoltz and Craig Sheffer) and the woman (Meg Tilly) they both love. With Tilly sputtering her lines in confused sentences and Stoltz sighing and smoking heavily while philosophizing irrationally, *Sleep with Me* takes on the rhythms, feel and humor of real life. Add to that an eclectic supporting cast and a beguilingly shy performance by Sheffer and this film almost begins to make up for its complete lack of control. Check out Quentin Tarantino as a party guest attempting to explain why *Top Gun* is homoerotic. ★★½ $14.99

Sleeper

(1973, 88 min, US, Woody Allen) Allen enters the hospital in 1973 for treatment of an ulcer and, because of "complications," reawakens after cryogenic sleep in the year 2173. Our hapless hero and latter-day Lazarus directs his wit to the future and his body to the orgasmitron. Consistently hilarious, and Allen and Diane Keaton make a perfect comedic team. ★★★½ $14.99

Sleepers

(1996, 152 min, US, Barry Levinson) Despite its talented high-profile cast, excellent evocation of 1960s New York and slick production values, *Sleepers*, a supposedly "true" story about torture, revenge and the loss of innocence, never overcomes the trappings of a gangster-themed dime novel. Levinson begins his story with command: it traces the boyhood friendship of four youths from Hell's Kitchen; they are eventually sent to reform school when a prank turns deadly. Their life there is a living hell as they are repeatedly physically and sexually assaulted. The story picks up years later when two of them kill one of their former attackers (Kevin Bacon) and are prosecuted by one of their old buddies (Brad Pitt), who plans to lose the case unbeknowst to them. The biggest controversy of *Sleepers* isn't its surprising homophobia but the fact that original author Lorenzo Carcaterra claimed this was a

biography — it later came to light that nothing in the story could be proved. As fact *Sleepers* is tragic history; as fiction it's an adolescent revenge fantasy. Also starring Robert De Niro and Dustin Hoffman. ★★½ $19.99

Sleeping Beauty

(1959, 75 min, US, Clyde Geronimi) Charming Disney animated feature based on the fairy tale classic about the princess who falls under the spell of the evil Maleficent. ★★★ $26.99

Sleeping Dogs

(1977, 107 min, New Zealand, Roger Donaldson) This political chase thriller is a suspenseful tale of paranoia, repression of freedom and one man's resistance. Sam Neill stars as Smith, a man who flees domestic trouble and finds solace on a quiet coastal island. His newfound peace is shattered when the right-wing government declares martial law and begins a crackdown on dissidents. Smith is jailed on trumped-up charges, escapes and begins a new life as a reluctant insurgent. ★★★

Sleeping with the Enemy

(1991, 99 min, US, Joseph Ruben) Julia Roberts brings a lot of energy to this ordinary thriller. She plays a mistreated wife, married to neurotic Patrick Bergin. Instead of divorce, she stages her own death, and moves to another town under a new identity. But her husband finds out the truth, and goes looking for her, stalking his spouse and planning his revenge. Short on thrills and credibility. ★★ $9.99

Sleepless in Seattle

(1993, 100 min, US, Nora Ephron) Ephron's second directorial feature basks in the romantic tradition of our cinematic past, and in doing so, she has created her quintessential comedy — warts and all — with just a little help from *An Affair to Remember*. Tom Hanks plays a Seattle widower who's still not over his wife's death. His young son (the likable Ross Malinger) calls a national radio talk show, forcing his dad to talk on the air. Meg Ryan, meanwhile, lives in Baltimore and though engaged, she realizes there's something missing in her life. When she hears Hanks, she thinks she's found it. The next 90 minutes is an appealing comedy in which these misplaced spirits try to connect. Thanks to Hanks and Ryan's enchanting performances, the film seems breezier and more substantial than it really is. Nevertheless, the performances and Ephron's light directorial touch are sufficient reward for anyone searching for a blissfully romantic morsel. (Available letterboxed and pan & scan) ★★★ $14.99

Sleepwalk

(1987, 90 min, US, Sara Driver) A lyrical and witty feature debut for director Driver, *Sleepwalk* has the logic and landscape of a dream, an open-ended fairy tale set in the margins of an imaginary New York. The theft of an ancient and sacred manuscript, one which a young woman is translating, leads to strange happenings — her fingers begin to bleed, the woman's roommate becomes bald, and a woman is killed just as the mysteries of the book are about to be solved. Ann Magnuson is memorably comic as the rapidly balding room-

mate. Driver has a sharp eye for color and light and imbues the film with a lively, humorous style. ★★★

The Slender Thread

(1966, 98 min, US, Sydney Pollack) Two sincere performances from Sidney Poitier and Anne Bancroft elevate this compelling drama. Poitier plays a college student who is a volunteer at a Seattle crisis center. What looks to be a slow night becomes a fight for survival when he gets a call from Bancroft — who's just taken an overdose of pills. As Poitier desperately tries to get Bancroft to reveal her location, the events leading to her suicide attempt are told in flashback. These scenes are rather routine, but the sequences involving Poitier's verbal rescue attempt are enthralling. Pollack's directorial debut. ★★½ $14.99

Sleuth

(1972, 138 min, GB, Joseph L. Mankiewicz) Laurence Olivier is an eccentric upper-class English cuckold who plans a confrontation with Michael Caine, the man who has not only stolen his wife's affections, but has the effrontery to be of the wrong class. Both Olivier and Caine give knockout performances in this royal battle of wit and wills. Screenplay by Anthony Shaffer from his play. Eclectic direction from Mankiewicz makes maximum use of a limited setting. ★★★½

A Slightly Pregnant Man

(1973, 92 min, France, Jacques Demy) A daffy, gender-bending comedy which features Marcello Mastroianni and Catherine Deneuve as a loving but childless couple whose lives are upturned when Marcello discovers that he is in the family way. There's exploitation of the notorious birth-to-be and the changing ways Catherine treats the pregnant and irritable Marcello are the ingredients for this enjoyable farce. (Dubbed) ★★½

Sling Blade

(1996, 135 min, US, Billy Bob Thornton) Writer-director Thornton crafts an unforgettable character in his portrayal of Carl Childers, a slightly retarded 37-year-old man newly released from a mental institution 25 years after murdering his mother and her lover. He reenters his small Arkansas home town with a repairman's job and a cot in a tool room and a new friend, young Frank Wheatley (played with amazing presence by Lucas Black). The details of Carl's history are revealed as he gets closer to Frank and his mom, Linda (Natalie Canerday), suggesting parallels and similarities, especially regarding Doyle (Dwight Yoakam), Linda's boyfriend and Frank's nemesis. Carl's simple, natural, instinctive bonding with the Wheatley family is in stark contrast to Doyle's manipulative, self-serving attempts at control, eventually placing Carl in the position of protector and avenging angel. In this unfolding drama of decent, unassuming people defending themselves in a hostile world, Carl becomes increasingly sane by becoming insane. John Ritter gives a strong turn as Vaughan, Linda's boss and caring gay friend, a man who is isolated from the community by his sexual preference as Carl is by his past deed. A superb, Oscar-winning screenplay, an effective minimalist musical score and a sure directorial hand describe this involving, heartfelt tale. A thought-provoking film essayed with wry wit and uncommon wisdom. ★★★★ $102.99

The Slingshot

(1994, 102 min, Sweden, Ake Sandgren) How many times must one be punched, hit, kicked and verbally abused before your resiliency of optimism is gone? You'll have to watch this abusive and not-so-happy coming-of-age film to find out. If you've seen *A Christmas Story*, *Leolo* and *My Life as a Dog*, you've caught all of the nuances of this film. Set in Sweden in the 1930s, the story centers on Roland, a precocious youngster who will do anything to get enough money for a bicycle, even sell slingshots made of contraband condoms. Great artistic design and good acting can't hide a lackluster film which can't deliver the final punch. (Swedish in English subtitles) ★★ $19.99

Sliver

(1993, 106 min, US, Phillip Noyce) No, the title doesn't refer to the amount of logic within the plot (though it easily could), but to a Manhattan luxury high-rise apartment building plagued by a series of unexplained deaths. Sharon Stone plays a recently divorced and sexually frustrated book editor (it could happen) who moves into the "horror high-rise" where romance and terror await in the form of William "Duh" Baldwin and Tom Berenger. As penned by Joe Eszterhas and stylishly directed by Noyce (*Patriot Games*), what might have been a trenchant study of voyeurism and social responsibility is reduced to a slick, trashy and befuddled whodunit whose dime-store resolution gets under the skin like a sliver of glass. Also with Martin Landau, Colleen Camp, CCH Pounder and Nina Foch. ★★½ $14.99

Slumber Party Massacre

(1982, 78 min, US, Amy Jones) Novelist Rita Mae Brown ("Rubyfruit Jungle") penned this horrific lampoon of mad-slasher films. If its tongue weren't firmly planted in cheek, it would probably get lopped off. ★★

Sluts and Goddesses Video Workshop

(1993, 52 min, US, Maria Beatty & Annie Sprinkle) Few will be prepared for this wildly entertaining, sexually frank and humorously tongue-in-cheek all-female video workshop which attempts to dispel and explore the myths of female sexuality. Former porno film star, now celebrated performance artist and nascent filmmaker, Annie Sprinkle is a delight as a demented sex education teacher/guru who takes us on an exploration into women's many pleasurable and exciting sexual personas. Sprinkle, along with her ten "transformation facilitators," offers helpful tips like, "When it comes to makeup, too much is never enough" to "You haven't lived fully until you've had your body painted." This enjoyable search for your "inner slut" also includes suggestions on how to have fun with body hair, body piercing, choosing a new name as well as essential sexercises — from group masturbation and female ejaculation demonstrations (featuring a five-minute orgasm!) to learning about your private parts ("Can you find your cervix?"). A

must for feminists and lesbians with a sense of humor (and yes, for you leering male voyeurs). ★★★ $39.99

Small Change

(1976, 104 min, France, François Truffaut) Truffaut's buoyant visual soufflé is a winning observation of youthful resiliency. Set in a tiny French town, *Small Change* follows a group of school children through their daily endeavors. (Dubbed) ★★★½ $19.99

Small Faces

(1996, 113 min, Scotland, Gillies MacKinnon) The incongruous glint of gunmetal in a heather-dappled, wooded lane belies the apparent tranquility of pastoral Glasgow, and serves as an emblem of the underlying tensions of gang affiliations which allow no neutrality and broker no dissent. Set in 1968, the story is told through the eyes of 13-year-old Lex (Iain Robertson), the youngest of three brothers, who is sucked into a vortex of conflicting allegiances. His brother Bobby (J.S. Duffy) is a member of one of the area gangs. Lex's other brother Alan (Joseph McFadden) is a promising art student of benign aspect and high expectations. Young Robertson brings intelligence and awareness to his character, who is thrown into a violent milieu just as that violence takes a quantum leap. Events unfold quickly and inexorably, leaving the adults to watch in stunned incomprehension and bitter helplessness, equally shocked by the acts of brutality and by the young ones' ease of adaptability to this new world. Director MacKinnon (*The Playboys*) adeptly utilizes a strong cast to explore one family's response to crisis and loss. A powerful and timeless film executed with youthful energy and compassionate understanding. ★★★½ $99.99

Small Wonders

(1996, 80 min, US, Allan Miller) One of the most disarming films about children since Truffaut's *Small Change*, Miller's modest but jubilant sleeper examines a divorced mother of two who teaches violin to Harlem elementary school kids. This straight-ahead, no frills, shot-on-video documentary may sound like a sappy, dull Afterschool Special, but *Small Wonders* is anything but. The film follows Roberta Guaspari-Tzavaras and her students from first meeting to their sold-out concert at Carnegie Hall (complete with guest violinists Isaac Stern and Itzhak Perlman). Guaspari-Tzavaras is inspirational, the kids are devoted, and become musicians. This is the real *Mr. Holland's Opus*, and offers a superb argument for the continued support of music and art in our public school systems. On a sidenote, and in the believe it or not department, horrormeister Wes Craven is developing a fiction version of the story. ★★★½ $102.99

The Smallest Show on Earth

(1957, 81 min, GB, Basil Dearden) This highly amusing little British comedy tells the tale of a young couple who inherit a run-down movie theatre. Bill Travers and Virginia McKenna are charming as the pair who are thrust against their will into the cinema business. Peter Sellers, as the drunken, near-sighted projectionist, and Margaret Rutherford, as the slow-moving octogenarian cashier, play two of the

ancient employees who come along with the theatre — both are magnificent as always. Filled with joie de vivre, the film imparts an alluring sense of nostalgia for anyone who considers themselves a dyed-in-the-wool cinema buff. ★★★ $14.99

Smash Palace

(1981, 100 min, New Zealand, Roger Donaldson) This highly acclaimed work by Donaldson is a compelling drama set in the cities and countryside of New Zealand. It is a powerful tale of a marriage jeopardized by a man's obsession with auto racing and a woman's overriding need for love and affection. ★★★½

Smash-Up

(1947, 103 min, US, Stuart Heisler) Susan Hayward shines in an Oscar-nominated role as a nightclub singer who turns to the bottle after giving up her career for marriage. Dramatically it's familiar territory but Hayward's performance more than compensates. (aka: *Smash-Up, the Story of a Woman*) ★★½ $12.99

Smile

(1975, 113 min, US, Michael Ritchie) Ritchie's best film is this hilariously biting satire of Americana. Bruce Dern stars as a small-town California car salesman who, with his perky and maniacally organized wife (Barbara Feldon), helps organize the Young Miss Beauty contest. The "behind the scenes" peek at the pretty contestants, their amazingly talentless talent and the lascivious judges are only a few of the highlights of this perceptive and witty film which features as two of the contestants, the very young Melanie Griffith and Annette O'Toole. ★★★½ $19.99

Smiles of a Summer Night

(1955, 108 min, Sweden, Ingmar Bergman) An exquisite carnal comedy about eight people who become four couples in turn-of-the-century Sweden. Bergman's witty treatise on changing partners under the midnight sun is filled with delightfully ironic humor. The basis for the Tony Award-winning musical "A Little Night Music," which was poorly adapted to film. (Swedish with English subtitles) ★★★★ $29.99

Smilla's Sense of Snow

(1997, 121 min, Denmark/Germany/Sweden, Bille August) This very disappointing adaptation of Peter Høeg's best-selling thriller stars Julia Ormond as the titular character, a half Dane, half Greenlander scientist whose obsession with the "accidental" death of a young boy leads her deeper into a web of murder and deception. For all the world, this could have been an interesting film, but somehow the characters, Ormond especially, seem to be wandering around in some kind of daze. With all deference to Ormond as an actress, it was perhaps an unachievable undertaking to convey to detailed inner workings of Smilla Jasperen's prickly personality, which was the most intriguing aspect of Høeg's novel. But, instead of a fascinating journey into the convoluted workings of her personality all we get is the icy exterior, a shortcoming that only makes her more perplexing. Gabriel Byrne,

Richard Harris, Vanessa Redgrave, Robert Loggia and Jim Broadbent all appear in support. August shows that he's more at home directing smaller, more personal movies although his locations and sense of mis-en-scène provide the film's best evocation of the book. ★★ $99.99

Smithereens

(1982, 93 min, US, Susan Seidelman) Wren is a legend in her own mind – a self-assured, narcissistic New Wave hanger-on with a yen for the big time. Seidelman (*Desperately Seeking Susan*) directed this gritty Greenwich Village odyssey. A distinctly modern version of the American Dream. ★★★ $29.99

Smoke

(1993, 90 min, US, Mark D'Auria) An initially intriguing but ultimately trying independent film, *Smoke* borrows heavily from Martin Scorsese's seminal drama *Mean Streets*. Michael, a puffy, almost handsome 30-ish man, is a bathroom attendant with a penchant for overweight older men. In a laborious and pretentious pacing style, the film examines Michael's kinky obsessions and sexual desires which clash with his Catholic guilt. The film is slow going and is of interest mainly to viewers searching for gay/lesbian-themed films. ★★ $39.99

Smoke

(1995, 113 min, US, Wayne Wang & Paul Auster) The divergent rhythms of New York come alive in the guise of this immensely satisfying slice-of-life comedy-drama centered around the habitués of a tobacco shop in the heart of Brooklyn. In a portrayal which perfectly captures the nuances and heartbeat of a likable Joe, Harvey Keitel plays an Italian chorus who becomes involved in the lives of some of his customers. As one of them, William Hurt exhibits the right amount of ennui and melancholy as a widowed WASPy author who befriends a black youth (nicely played by Harold Perrineau, Jr.) whose fabrications mask deep familial hurts. Forest Whitaker is splendid as the teen's long-lost father, an abrupt, pained man looking for a new start. As Keitel witnesses the dramas around him, he himself discovers a child he never knew when his former con artist girlfriend (the feisty Stockard

Channing) reenters his life. These stories effortlessly coalesce into a deeply affecting tale defined by rich characterizations and bouyant comedy – the least of which is the beautiful finale which explains Keitel's passion for photography. Followed by an anti-sequel, *Blue in the Face.* ★★★★ $19.99

Smooth Talk

(1985, 91 min, US, Joyce Chopra) Based on Joyce Carol Oates' short story "Where Are You Going, Where Have You Been," this compelling, gutsy coming-of-age drama explores a 15-year-old California girl's sexual awakening. Laura Dern is excellent as the budding teen, and Treat Williams exudes charm and malevolence as her seducer. ★★★

Snake and Crane Arts of Shaolin

(1978, 95 min, Hong Kong, Chen Chi Hwa) After nearly being killed a dozen times while trying to learn an ancient fighting technique developed by a group of Shaolin masters, student Hsu Yin Fung (Jackie Chan) is unjustly accused of killing the masters and destroying all records of their deadly art. When his girlfriend is murdered, he seeks the help of another master who finally teaches him the form which he in turn uses in his search for the true killer. Brisk kung fu chaos, enlivened by Chan's trademark stunt-laden style. ★★½ $19.99

The Snake Pit

(1948, 108 min, US, Anatole Litvak) An intelligent, fascinating drama about a young woman who experiences a nervous breakdown and is committed to a mental institution. It's a disturbing look into the life inside of a mental institution and even more chilling considering when the film was made. The film features some fantastic camerawork and a brilliant performance from Olivia deHavilland. ★★★★ $19.99

The Snapper

(1993, 95 min, Ireland, Stephen Frears) Written by Roddy Doyle (*The Commitments*), *The Snapper* is a wonderful character study full of laughs and tears. Tina Kellegher plays the strong-willed daughter of an Irish working-class family who becomes pregnant and refuses to reveal who is the father of the baby. Colm Meaney is outstanding as her good-hearted father and Ruth McCabe stands out as the loving mother who keeps her family together through it all. Marvelous acting and a humorous and insightful screenplay make this film a rare treat. Director Frears is in a playfully droll mood. (Followed in 1997 by *The Van*) ★★★★ $96.89

The Snapper

Sneakers

(1992, 105 min, US, Phil Alden Robinson) In his first film since the acclaimed *Field of Dreams*, director Robinson leaves the serenity of country life for the excitement of a big-city caper. A clever, humorous and complex computer-age thriller, the story centers on a group of professional thieves and computer hackers who are coerced by the U.S. government to steal a mysterious black box. Once it is in their possession, they learn the box is really the ultimate code breaker, able to decipher any computer program in the world. And now there are some very dangerous people out to retrieve it at any cost. Robert Redford and Sidney Poitier head a good ensemble cast which includes Dan Aykroyd, River Phoenix, Mary McDonnell, Ben Kingsley and David Strathairn. While not in the same class as *Topkapi* or *The Sting*, which it at times recalls, *Sneakers* is nevertheless exuberant, fun-filled and set at a rapid-fire pace. ★★★ $9.99

Sniper

(1993, 99 min, US, Luis Llosa) Just when you thought that there were no more action films around with a good surprise, along comes this hard-hitting character study set in the wilds of South America. Tom Berenger is back in the jungle, this time as a hard-as-nails, and possibly slightly crazy, government assassin. When his partner is killed during a hit, the higher-ups send in sharpshooter Billy Zane to keep him in line. Like 1988's *The Beast, Sniper* is more about what it is like to kill rather than being about how many people are killed and with what semi-automatic weapons. Berenger and Zane interact well, perhaps bonding just a little too quickly for the animosity their characters originally show each other. *Sniper* is an action film that actually ends up showing some humanity. ★★★ $19.99

Snow Country

(1957, 134 min, Japan, Shiro Toyoda) Based on the novel by Yasunari Kawabata, then Japan's only winner of the Nobel Prize for Literature, this passionate love story tells of the budding relationship between two people and the nagging cultural differences that pull them apart. Shimamura, an artist in Tokyo, escapes to the tranquil rural Honshu region in the northwestern part of the country for relaxation. There he meets and falls in love with Kumako, a charming young woman from the snow-covered village. The disparities in their upbringing as well as the antagonism of the

The Snake Pit

townsfolk kind of make this a Japanese "Romeo and Juliet." (Japanese with English subtitles) ★★★ $59.99

Snow White and the Seven Dwarfs

(1937, 83 min, US, Ben Sharpsteen) Arguably Disney's finest achievement (and his first feature-length animated film), *Snow White* is the perfect blend of animation, story and character utilizing charming songs and good humor. A huge smash at the box office in 1937, the film, of course, follows the adventures of Snow White, who does battle with an evil, jealous witch and who finds her prince, all the while living in the forest with seven adorable little men. Tamer than any cartoon made today, the film still captivates — it is one of the authentic masterpieces of American cinema. ★★★★ $39.99

So Fine

(1981, 91 min, US, Andrew Bergman) Ryan O'Neal plays a mild-mannered professor who accidentally creates a fashion sensation for his father, a clothing manufacturer: see-through pants. Jack Warden's spirited portrayal of O'Neal's father is the bright spot of this see-through comedy. ★★ $19.99

So I Married an Axe Murderer

(1993, 93 min, US, Thomas Schlamme) "Saturday Night Live" alumnus Mike Myers should be axed from the comedy register for this insultingly inept follow-up to the 1992 smash hit *Wayne's World*. Myers headlines as a so-bad-he's-good coffeehouse poet whose fear of marriage ends when he weds the quirky but beautiful owner (Nancy Travis) of the local butcher shop despite his mounting fears that she may be (drum roll, please) an axe murderer. Also with Brenda Fricker, Amanda Plummer and Anthony LaPaglia. Oh, how the mighty hath fallen (and they can't get up!). ★½ $19.99

So Proudly We Hail

(1943, 126 min, US, Mark Sandrich) One of the few WWII films to be seen through the eyes of women, this gallant, terse drama follows the sometimes heartbreaking role of nurses in combat. The sublime Claudette Colbert stars as an Army head nurse who, at the film's start, is catatonic and on her way home. The story then traces her path on the many battlefields of World War II, where romance, tragedy and camaraderie shape her life. Excellent in support are Paulette Goddard (who received an Oscar nomination) as Colbert's right-hand gal and Sonny Tufts as a soldier/Goddard's love interest who "never gets killed." Though high in 1940s and wartime sentiment, this is a no-nonsense, pleasurable melodrama. ★★★½ $14.99

Soapdish

(1991, 95 min, US, Michael Hoffman) A terrific comic cast makes the most of this sometimes very funny spoof of soap operas. Sally Field is the reigning Queen of the Soaps. Whoopi Goldberg is her writer and longtime friend. Kevin Kline is Field's ex-beau, who returns to the airwaves after a 20-year absence to be reunited with Sally — both on-screen and off. Robert Downey, Jr. is the inefficient producer, more worried about bedding second-string actress Cathy Moriarty than his show's quality. And Elizabeth Shue rounds out the cast as Field's niece who, unbeknownst to her aunt, has signed on with the show. The film's tempo is played as grand farce, and though not all of the humor works, it's a joyously loony romp. ★★★ $14.99

Society

(1989, 99 min, US, Brian Yuzna) This "Beverly Hills, 90210" from hell features a teenage boy who seems to have it all: nice family, nice car and a deadly debutante girlfriend with looks that kill — literally! After a few of his friends disappear, our reluctant hero soon discovers an underworld "society" complete with shape-shifting weirdos and a coming-out party where ritual sacrifice is the main attraction. Yuzna (*Re-Animator*) directed this horror-filled sweet sixteen with special effects by Screaming Mad George (*Poltergeist II*). ★★ $14.99

Sofie

(1993, 145 min, Sweden, Liv Ullmann) Taking on the mantle of her longtime director, Ingmar Bergman, actress Ullmann debuts behind the camera with this affecting, if somewhat overlong, saga about the life of an unassuming Jewish woman in turn-of-the-century Sweden. Early on, the film hinges on her choice between a fiery and passionate affair with a Christian painter or an arranged marriage to a dour Jewish man from the countryside. As she spends much of her time with her three spinster aunts, the film examines her struggle between virtue and spiritual freedom. Benefiting from a host of fine performances, most notably Karen-Lise Mynster in the lead role and Erland Josephson as her doting father, Ullmann's film often captures the whimsical nature of Bergman's *Fanny and Alexander*, but at 145 minutes, the film too often overstays its welcome. (Swedish with English subtitles) ★★½ $89.99

The Soft Skin

(1964, 118 min, France, François Truffaut) A mature, underrated work by Truffaut that explores the ill-fated fling with infidelity by a successful publisher and a pretty airline stewardess. Truffaut focuses on their day-to-day life in this precisely-told examination of a catastrophe-prone situation. (French with English subtitles) ★★★ $29.99

Solaris

(1972, 165 min, USSR, Andrei Tarkovsky) Hailed by its admirers as a visionary, philosophical work and by others (especially sci-fi fans) as a difficult, if not turgid, boring flick, this, Tarkovsky's best-known film, adapts the popular science-fiction theme of men lost in space to his own idiosyncratic style of filmmaking. Eschewing high-tech gimmickry and special effects, the story centers on a psychologist who is sent to investigate a series of unexplained deaths on a Russian space station that is orbiting the remote planet of Solaris. There he finds that the killers are not aliens but rather phantoms materialized from the cosmonauts' guilty past. Adapted by Tarkovksy from a Stanislaw Lem novel, the film is admittedly heavy going, weighted down by long static scenes, but it is also an imaginative, serious work about man's limits as well as his barely concealed fears and self-destructive nature. (Russian with English subtitles) ★★★½ $19.99

Soldat Duroc

(1975, 85 min, France, Michel Gerard) In September 1944, a few days after the liberation of Paris, a young French soldier secretly crosses the German lines in the middle of the night to rejoin his fiancée in Senlis, a small town still occupied by the German Army. His plans become unraveled, however, when he is captured by two soldiers, one American and the other French, who were sent by General Patton to help liberate the Nazi-held village. An absorbing and nicely told war drama. (French with English subtitles) ★★★

Veronica Lake (l.) and Claudette Colbert are nurses fighting during WWII in *So Proudly We Hail*

501

Soldier in the Rain

(1963, 88 min, US, Ralph Nelson) Blake Edwards adapted William Goldman's novel for this touching story about the friendship between a wheeling-dealing Army sergeant (Jackie Gleason) and his young sidekick (Steve McQueen). ★★★

Soldier of Orange

(1979, 165 min, The Netherlands, Paul Verhoeven) The title of this intelligent and engrossing adventure story refers to the House of Orange, The Netherlands' Royal Government which was put in exile after the Nazi invasion of their country. Verhoeven demonstrates his ability to both re-create an era pregnant with fear and danger as well as tell a hypnotic war story. Rutger Hauer and Jeroen Krabbé (*The 4th Man*) are aristocratic students who are caught up in the war effort and become dangerously involved in the Dutch resistance. (Dutch with English subtitles) ★★★½

A Soldier's Story

(1984, 102 min, US, Norman Jewison) Crackling with racial tension, Jewison's searing murder mystery probes the multifaceted dilemma of black advancement in a predominately white man's Army. Brilliantly acted with power and grace, Philadelphian Charles Fuller's Pulitzer Prize-winning play is a rare triumph of the stage to screen process. Adolph Caesar was Oscar nominated for his powerful portrayal of a much-disliked drill sergeant. Also starring Howard E. Rollins and Denzel Washington. ★★★★ $14.99

The Solid Gold Cadillac

(1956, 99 min, US, Richard Quine) In a role not unlike her wonderful turn in *It Should Happen to You*, that divine blithe spirit Judy Holliday is impeccably funny as a daffy blonde who takes on the corporate world. She stars as a minor shareholder in one of those giant, faceless New York corporations. When she learns of wrongdoing on the company's board, she sets out to straighten things up. Of course, bigwig Fred Clark and others have different ideas. Narrated by George Burns, the film is a continuing series of gentle swipes at big business framed by delightful comic vignettes with Judy at her best. Paul Douglas is in fine form as one of the board members who falls under Judy's luminous spell. ★★★½ $19.99

Solo

(1996, 106 min, US, Norberto Barba) With Hollywood's mega-action stars becoming as aged as some pungent French cheese, there exists a great opportunity for a young studling to emerge and take center stage. No, Mario, get off the pedestal; you're not the one. Despite an impressive set of pecs, Van Peebles just can't pull it off in this tediously flaccid sci-fi actioner. He plays an android with a heart (a novel idea...who approves these screenplays?) who discovers that his maker, the U.S. Army, is using him for something *really* bad. The pacing is deadly, the acting stultifying (Sofia Coppola would look good by comparison) and the story so hackneyed as to make *Daylight* seem like poetry. But there are video drones (present company excluded) who will rent the film,

turn off their minds, and gleefully waste 106 minutes — you have been warned. ★ $101.89

Some Came Running

(1958, 136 min, US, Vincente Minnelli) Frank Sinatra stars as an author who stirs things up in his sleepy hometown after several years away. Disillusioned, Sinatra steps off a bus with a good-natured floozy (Shirley MacLaine) in tow, and contrary to his family's wishes, manages to run into trouble at every turn. Dean Martin also stars as Sinatra's buddy, who accompanies the ex-G.I. on his self-destructive binges. Though the film has a few slow stretches, the first-rate performances and the stunning conclusion make it all worthwhile. ★★★ $19.99

Some Girls

(1988, 94 min, US, Michael Hoffman) This refreshingly offbeat youth comedy stars a hilariously deadpan Patrick Dempsey as a lovesick college student who visits his girlfriend (Jennifer Connelly) and her family during Christmas break. Dempsey expects a jolly good time, but gets more than he bargained for when he discovers that her family is more than a little eccentric. It's *You Can't Take It with You* meets *Risky Business*, and to director Hoffman and writer Rupert Walters' credit, the majority of the film's many gags score exceedingly well. ★★★ $19.99

Some Kind of Hero

(1982, 97 min, US, Michael Pressman) Based on James Kirkwood's novel, this disappointing adaptation stars Richard Pryor as a former Vietnam POW returning home after six years in captivity who finds trouble adjusting to civilian life. ★★ $14.99

Some Kind of Wonderful

(1987, 93 min, US, Howard Deutch) More teenage angst courtesy of John Hughes, with Eric Stoltz in love with Lea Thompson; Mary Stuart Masterson in love with Stoltz. Hughes' bucket from the well must be worn out by now. ★★ $14.99

Some Like It Hot

(1959, 122 min, US, Billy Wilder) Director Wilder's masterpiece rates as one of the funniest American comedies of all time, and it only gets better with age. Jack Lemmon and Tony Curtis, at their comic best, star as down-and-out musicians in 1920s Chicago who, upon witnessing the St. Valentine's Day Massacre, don wig and dress and join an all-female band to escape the murderous thugs looking for them. Marilyn Monroe is Sugar Kane, the band's beautiful blonde singer who the boys are enraptured by. Curtis romances MM (out of drag, of course) and Lemmon is courted by millionaire Joe E. Brown ("Well, nobody's perfect"). They just don't come any better than this. ★★★★ $14.99

Somebody Has to Shoot the Picture

(1990, 105 min, US, Frank Pierson) A death-row inmate hires a photographer to document his execution for a murder he says he did not commit. Roy Scheider is compelling as the photog who finds himself drawn into a maze of deception and cover-up in this intriguing examination of the duplicity and hidden agendas contaminating the U.S. judicial system. This

made-for-HBO production was scripted by photojournalist Doug Magee from his book "Slow Coming Dark." Also starring Bonnie Bedelia and Arliss Howard, who is riveting as the prisoner awaiting execution. ★★★½ $14.99

Somebody Up There Likes Me

(1956, 113 min, US, Robert Wise) Paul Newman's fine performance as boxer Rocky Graziano highlights this sturdy biography, tracing the fighter's life from youth to champion. With Pier Angeli, Sal Mineo, Robert Loggia and a young Steve McQueen. ★★★ $19.99

Someone to Love

(1987, 109 min, US, Henry Jaglom) The films of Jaglom are certainly a cinematically acquired taste. Dwelling on clearly autobiographical subjects, casting friends and lovers, as well as encouraging them to extemporize through the scenes, has given him the not-unfair moniker of being the poor man's Woody Allen. In *Someone to Love*, Jaglom hosts a party inviting all acquaintances who would find themselves alone on Valentine's Day. Desperately driven to understand why successful and attractive people find true love elusive, he "circulates" among the guests, probing their lives. Orson Welles, in his final screen appearance, hypnotizes the audience with his controversial views on the affairs of the heart. ★★★ $39.99

Someone to Watch Over Me

(1987, 113 min, US, Ridley Scott) The director of *Alien* and *Thelma and Louise* brings his hyperbolic visual sense to this tension-filled love story about a cop from Queens (Tom Berenger) who falls in love with the socialite-turned-mob informer (Mimi Rogers) he's been assigned to protect. Between the mobsters and his wife (the splendid Lorraine Bracco), his life is in constant jeopardy. ★★★ $14.99

Something for Everyone

(1970, 112 min, GB, Harold Prince) Broadway director Prince's directorial film debut is this witty black comedy that stars a seductive Michael York as a cunning, amoral opportunist who insinuates himself into the household of the flamboyant Countess von Ornstein of Bavaria (Angela Lansbury). Once inside, he proceeds to infiltrate the bedrooms of both her and her son. Lansbury camps it up wonderfully, acting as though she were a drag queen on stage at a New York fashion show, unveiling her fabulous frocks to an enraptured audience. Anthony Corlan plays Helmut, the countess' gay teenage son, whose dark and sullen good looks prove to be a nice contrast to York's fair complexion. Jane Carr plays Lansbury's corpulent daughter who has the last laugh. Sly fun and sophistication abound in this charming gem. ★★★½ $59.99

Something of Value

(1957, 113 min, US, Richard Brooks) Compelling screen version of Robert C. Ruark's best-selling novel about the Mau Mau uprising in Kenya and the effect it has on two friends, one black, one white. Starring Rock Hudson, Sidney Poitier and Wendy Hiller. ★★★ $24.99

Something to Talk About

(1995, 101 min, US, Lasse Hallström) Julia Roberts demonstrates a certain charm in her most adult role to date (she's a working mother and wife), but neither she nor a rather capable cast is able to gloss over a rather contrived and pedestrian screenplay. She plays a well-to-do wife who discovers her husband (Dennis Quaid) is having an affair. To figure things out, she retreats with her spunky adolescent daughter to the horse ranch run by her stoic father (Robert Duvall). The film concentrates on her state of indecision and her husband's attempts to win her back, and throws in a subplot of her good-natured mother (Gena Rowlands) discovering her father's past philandering for extra measure. Written by Callie Khouri (*Thelma and Louise*), the film is all-the-more disappointing as it tries to be a serious if comedic examination of adultery and reconciliation but can only address its concerns in superficial, episodic skits. Kyra Sedgwick steals the show with her dynamic, no-nonsense portrayal of Roberts' sister. ★★ $19.99

Something Wicked This Way Comes

(1983, 94 min, US, Jack Clayton) Ray Bradbury wrote the screenplay based on his own novel about a mysterious carnival's visit to a turn-of-the-century Midwestern town. Full of wonderfully magic moments, redolent with evil, this film captures the essence of a young boy's imagination — one who thinks the carnival's proprietor may have demonic origins. With Jason Robards, Pam Grier and Jonathan Pryce as "Mr. Dark." ★★★ $9.99

Something Wild

(1986, 113 min, US, Jonathan Demme) The screwball comedy is given a violent twist by director Demme. When businessman Jeff Daniels skips out on a lunch bill, he encounters sexy, wild Melanie Griffith, who proceeds to abduct him and take him on the ride of his life. Ray Liotta is a standout as Griffith's psychotic ex-husband. A totally original road movie which is something of a cross between *Bringing Up Baby* and *Blue Velvet*. ★★★½

Sometimes a Great Notion

(1971, 114 min, US, Paul Newman) A first-rate cast distinguishes the absorbing drama set in the Oregon woodlands about a logging family, headed by patriarch Henry Fonda, whose decision to ignore a local strike brings about tragedy. Paul Newman, Richard Jaeckel and Michael Sarrazin are Fonda's sons, and Lee Remick is Newman's wife. Jaeckel received a well-deserved Oscar nomination, due mostly to an amazing drowning scene. ★★★ $14.99

Sometimes Aunt Martha Does Dreadful Things

(1971, 95 min, US, Thomas Casey) Unintentional laughs abound in this little-known camp classic about a fugitive killer who both hides from the law and lives "in sin" with his young male lover by parading around in drag pretending to be the boy's aunt. As bad as it sounds, the film certainly gives in to gay stereotyping (and much more); but it's good for a laugh. ★

Sometimes They Come Back

(1991, 100 min, US, Tom McLoughlin) Whoever said "you can't go home again" never imparted this bit of wisdom to horror writer Stephen King, who once again returns to that tired — er, sleepy — New England town for this tale of a college professor/author (big stretch, eh?) who is haunted by ghosts from his past — literally. This made-for-TV movie boasts additional footage for the home video release. With Tim Matheson and Brooke Adams. ★★ $14.99

Somewhere I'll Find You

(1942, 117 min, US, Wesley Ruggles) After their box-office smash the year before in *Honky Tonk*, Clark Gable and Lana Turner reunited in this equally popular film, Gable's last before his four-year WWII tour of duty. Full of crackling dialogue, this handsome romantic adventure features the two stars in larger-than-life form in the story of correspondent Gable falling for reporter Turner, but who ignores his true feelings because his younger brother Robert Sterling is also in love with her. All three find themselves hurried from the safety of pre-Pearl Harbor America into the thick of war-torn Indochina. The abrasive ending befits the mindset of an America at war. ★★★ $19.99

Somewhere in Time

(1980, 103 min, US, Jeannot Szwarc) Old-fashioned romantic fantasy with Christopher Reeve as a contemporary playwright who falls in love with a turn-of-the-century actress (Jane Seymour) he sees in a portrait, and wills himself back in time. The film never quite delivers on its intriguing premise, though John Barry's beautiful score and the attractive scenery help. ★★½ $14.99

Sommersby

(1993, 117 min, US, Jon Amiel) This sweeping post-Civil War adaptation of *The Return of Martin Guerre* is a pleasant Hollywood rarity: an American remake of a European art-house hit which *doesn't* ruin all memory of the original. While the film is vastly different and more commercial than its predecessor, it is nonetheless a refreshing and enjoyable drama. Richard Gere plays Jack Sommersby, a wealthy Confederate landowner who returns to his little valley several years after the war. Long thought dead, he is greeted with a mixture of disbelief and cautious joy by both the townsfolk and his wife, marvelously portrayed by Jodie Foster. Ultimately, Gere's Sommersby is so gentle and loving that Foster can't believe he is really her husband, who had been an abusive alcoholic when he left for the war. Which raises the question: Is he who he claims to be? Director Amiel superbly recreates the antebellum South, but what makes it all worthwhile is the dazzling on-screen magnetism between Foster and Gere. ★★★½ $9.99

Son of Dracula

(1943, 78 min, US, Robert Siodmak) Lon Chaney, Jr., takes over for Bela Lugosi in this successful and very atmospheric sequel with Dracula now terrorizing the American South. $14.95

Son of Frankenstein

(1939, 99 min, US, Rowland V. Lee) Boris Karloff would appear as "The Monster" for the last time in this genuinely eerie chiller, the third in the *Frankenstein* series. Basil Rathbone is the chip off the old block who tries to make the monster "good" and clear the family name. Like father, like son, and things go awry. In an unexpected and effective performance, Bela Lugosi plays Ygor. ★★★ $14.99

Son of Godzilla

(1967, 86 min, Japan, Joh Fukuda) When Godzilla lays an egg in this movie, out pops another living butane lighter, this one called Minya. Godzilla and son decide to tear up the town in celebration of Jr.'s coming out party — even though Allstate doesn't cover acts of Godzilla. ★½ $9.99

Son of Kong

(1933, 70 min, US, Ernest B. Schoedsack) When *King Kong* became such a hit, RKO rushed this sequel out the same year — but it's still lots of fun. Carl Denham (Robert Armstrong), hounded by law suits for all the damages that big old ape did, flees New York for the solitude of Skull Island, only to run into Kong, Jr. Master animator Willis O'Brien continued his best work with lots of battles with giant animals of one era or another (some of it left over from the first film), with a heartrending ending accentuated by a fine Max Steiner score. ★★★ $19.99

Son of Paleface

(1952, 95 min, US, Frank Tashlin) This very funny sequel to the Bob Hope-Jane Russell hit comedy, *The Paleface*, tops the original. Bob plays a timid Harvard graduate who heads West to claim an inheritance and tangles with outlaws, Roy Rogers, Trigger and gorgeous showgirl Jane. ★★★ $14.99

Son of the Shark

(1995, 85 min, France, Agnes Merlet) Imagine if you will a kiddie version of *A Clockwork Orange*. Maybe a little *Natural Born Killers* thrown in and plenty of *The 400 Blows*, just to be considered an homage. Getting a clear picture yet? If you have one, you've got the story of Martin and Simon, two brothers abandoned by their mother, abused by their father and split up by the state because they are too dangerous together. The film is powerful, gritty and the children are full of anger and love for each other. The photography has a mist to it and is dark and depressing, as much of their life must be. These kids hold the whole town at bay while they watch movies at the local theatre, with one projecting the film while the other watches it eating popcorn. It must be tough to be a French parent these days. (French with English subtitles) ★★★ $19.99

Song of Love

(1947, 119 min, US, Clarence Brown) Katharine Hepburn stars in this glossy though dramatically uneven biography of Robert and Clara Schuman and their friendship with young composer Johannes Brahms (Robert Walker). With Paul Henreid as Schuman. $19.99

Song of the Loon

(1970, 90 min, US) Long considered a classic of independent gay filmmaking, *Song of the Loon* is an earnest tale of love and brotherhood among men as well as a naturalist's delight. Set in northern California in the 1870s, the story follows the odyssey of Ephraim McKeever, a young man in search of love and happiness. By using non-professional actors, not showing hard-core sex scenes and featuring such silly lines as "Dammit, you're beautiful," the film is at times awkward and dated, but it is also a welcome change from the normal X-rated fare that abounds. ★★ $24.99

Sonia Speaks — Going Farther Out of Our Minds

(1988, 100 min, US) In an exhilarating speech, videotaped at UC Santa Cruz, Sonia Johnson lectures on the theme of patriarchy and how women are enslaved and colonialized by 5,000 years of "violence and political terrorism" caused by the existing system. Rejecting the "practical" feminist approach of gaining power and eliciting change (i.e., working within the system), Sonia, as the vocal outsider, is compelled to seek a vision of women leaving the "senile patriarchial" society behind and beginning to live in a new world right now. Sonia's ideas are fascinating, insightful and do not become bogged in intellectual or metaphysical details. Women, watch it with some men in attendance and watch the fireworks! ★★½ $39.99

Sonny Boy

(1990, 96 min, US, Martin Carroll) This extremely weird film features a family that would feel right at home in John Waters' Mortville. A dark tale of family love gone berserk, *Sonny Boy* features Paul L. Smith as a 300-pound psychotic crook who with his wife, Pearl, raises an orphan boy to become an animal-like killing machine to advance their criminal enterprise. The role of the sweet, loving mother Pearl is played oddly enough by David Carradine, who plays the part entirely as a woman — wearing polka-dot dresses, makeup and jewelry and sensible hair, although she does like her occasional cigar. As they go about their murderous ways, all involved ignore the fact that Pearl is a transvestite, which only adds to the pleasure of this mean-spirited oddity. ★★½ $89.99

The Sons of Katie Elder

(1965, 122 min, US, Henry Hathaway) Solid western action with John Wayne, Dean Martin, Michael Anderson, Jr. and Earl Holliman as the title characters, out to avenge their mother's murder. ★★★ $14.99

Sons of the Desert

(1933, 69 min, US, William A. Seiter) Henpecked Laurel and Hardy want to go to the national convention of their lodge, the Sons of the Desert, but their wives won't let them. So like little boys are wont to do, they sneak off anyway, only to get caught when Stanley ends up in a newsreel. The title of this Laurel and Hardy masterpiece is also the name of their fan club — still in existence today! ★★★½

Sophie's Choice

(1982, 157 min, US, Alan J. Pakula) A tour de force Academy Award-winning performance by Meryl Streep distinguishes this powerful adaptation of William Styron's sweeping novel. Kevin Kline is Streep's volatile lover, who learns the horrid secret of Sophie's Auschwitz survival. Peter MacNicol is Stingo, a young author who falls in love with Sophie. The film is divided between Sophie's harrowing life at Auschwitz and her post-war years as a guilt-ridden survivor living in Brooklyn. Both time frames offer heartrending, compassionate drama, and in bringing Sophie to life in the two time periods, Streep delivers a portrayal of such nuance and emotion that it certainly ranks as one of the greatest performances ever given in the history of American cinema. ★★★½ $9.99

Sophisticated Ladies

(1982, 108 min, US) An unforgettable celebration of the genius of Duke Ellington, brought to vibrant life with incredible talents, award-winning costumes and all the lights of Broadway. Starring Phyllis Hyman and Hinton Battle (recent Tony Award winner for "Miss Saigon"). ★★★

Sorcerer

(1977, 122 min, US, William Friedkin) From the director of *The French Connection* comes this expensive remake of H.G. Clouzot's classic *Wages of Fear*. Just as spine-tingling but not nearly as involving as the original. Roy Scheider plays one of four desperate hoods now in hiding in a seedy Latin American town trying to buy their way out. Their only hope: help extinguish a raging oil fire by driving their trucks loaded with nitroglycerine on a suicide run over almost impassable roads. ★★½ $19.99

Sorceress

(1989, 98 min, France, Suzanne Schiffman) Though this is only her first film, Schiffman, longtime collaborator of François Truffaut, has made a decidedly self-assured and moving drama of religious beliefs, hypocrisy and persecution. Set in a peasant village during the 13th century, a young monk, sent by the Church to ferret out heretics, comes in conflict with a mysterious young woman who lives in the forest, who tends to the health of the villagers by making and administering herbal potions. This is a moving, complex drama that explores not only religious themes but also the role and persecution of women during the Middle Ages. (English language version) ★★★ $29.99

The Sorrow and the Pity

(1970, 260 min, France, Marcel Ophüls) A landmark film in cinema history, one of the most brilliant and shattering films ever made. Ophüls creates a sense of living history as he examines France's occupation by Germany during WWII, and France's complicity in the virulent racial and religious bigotry that defined the Third Reich. (Dubbed narration) ★★★★

Sorry, Wrong Number

(1948, 89 min, US, Anatole Litvak) Based on the acclaimed radio program (which starred Agnes Moorehead), this stylized thriller fea-

Sons of the Desert

tures Barbara Stanwyck in an electrifying performance as a bedridden wife who overhears a murder plot on her phone's party line — unaware that she is the intended victim. Burt Lancaster plays her husband. ★★★ $14.99

Sotto Sotto

(1984, 104 min, Italy, Lina Wertmüller) The prototypical machismo-obsessed Italian male must come to grips with the sexual freedoms and diversity of the late 20th century in this wild sexual comedy that is both illuminating and troubling in its depiction of two women in love with each other. Set in Naples, the story revolves around Ester and Adele, two friends who witness two women kissing. This initiates a revelation, and the two fall in (unconsummated) love. Then Ester's husband discovers his wife is in love with someone else, and sets out to discover who. ★★½ $19.99

Soul Man

(1986, 101 min, US, Steve Miner) Ineffectual social satire with C. Thomas Howell as a white student masquerading as an African-American in order to qualify for a scholarship to Harvard Law School. Rae Dawn Chong co-stars as Howell's girlfriend fooled by the charade. ★★

Soultaker

(1990, 94 min, US, Michael Rissi) Joe Estevez (yes, there's yet *another* one!) stars in this awful supernatural thriller about two lost souls attempting to reunite with their bedridden bodies while trying to elude the Angel of Death. ★ $14.99

The Sound of Music

(1965, 172 min, US, Robert Wise) This classic adaptation of Rodgers and Hammerstein's Broadway musical has long been a family favorite — and in terms of ticket sales, only *Gone with the Wind* has been seen by more people. Based on the true experiences of the Von Trapp family, the film stars Julie Andrews as Maria, an Austrian novice who becomes governess to seven children during the onset of WWII. A sentimental concoction of schmaltz and over-kill which still manages to work in spite of it all. Also with Christopher Plummer, Eleanor Parker and Angela Cartwright. The R&H score includes "Do Re Mi" and "Climb Every Mountain." Winner of four Academy Awards, including Best Picture. Remastered in THX. (The letterboxed version sells for $24.99) ★★★★ $19.99

S

Sounder

(1972, 105 min, US, Martin Ritt) Cicely Tyson and Paul Winfield both received much-deserved Oscar nominations for their superlative performances in this sensitive and beautifully crafted drama about a black sharecropping family's struggle in the early 1930s. As their young son, Kevin Hooks is outstanding. Also nominated for Best Picture. ★★★★ $14.99

South Central

(1991, 99 min, US, Steve Anderson) Set in 1981, this wildly violent and highly entertaining history of crack and L.A. street gangs is based on the real-life story of West Coast drug dealing gangsters, the Crips. The film's coke-addled hero, Bobby Johnson (Glenn Plummer), soon learns that killing rival pimps, freebasing, smoking angel dust and blowing out a deceitful woman's private parts with a .44 magnum isn't as cool as quietly reading Muslim literature and "rejecting the circle of hate that society inflicts on the black man." Covers much of the same ground nearly as effectively as *Boyz N the Hood*. ★★★ $14.99

South Pacific

(1958, 150 min, US, Joshua Logan) Rodgers and Hammerstein's landmark Broadway musical is given the royal treatment in this lush adaptation. Mitzi Gaynor (in the Mary Martin role) plays an American nurse who finds love while stationed in the South Seas during WWII. Rossano Brazzi, John Kerr, France Nuyen, Juanita Hall (singing the haunting "Bali H'ai") and Ray Walston also star. ★★★ $19.99

South Riding

(1938, 85 min, GB, Victor Saville) Trying to condense Winifred Holtby's sprawling tale of local political and social intrigue into a mere 85 minutes, *South Riding* moves along at a furious clip, setting up and then forgetting plot lines, suggesting others, painting in broad strokes this "typical" British community – leaving the details to be filled in by our own shared experiences. As an examination of the British class system, it is a little naive, but thanks to a quorum of fine performances, the film comes alive like some incipient episode of "Masterpiece Theatre." Ralph Richardson, land rich and cash poor, may soon lose the manor house, drained as he is by an institutionalized wife (Ann Todd) and a daughter (a spirited Glynis Johns) in dreadful need of public schooling. Mix in a consumptive commie (John Clements) who wants to erect public housing on the land, a disgraced school-teacher (Edna Best) in love above her station, and a corrupt businessman (Edmund Gwenn), well, surely then, you have an accurate depiction of any small town council. ★★★ $24.99

Southern Comfort

(1981, 106 min, US, Walter Hill) Competent action film (reminiscent of *Deliverance*) about a group of National Guardsmen who are forced to fight for their lives in the Louisiana swamps when gun-toting Cajuns come their way. With Keith Carradine, Powers Boothe, Fred Ward, Peter Coyote and Franklin Seales. ★★½

A Southern Yankee

(1948, 90 min, US, Edward Sedgwick) The ever-hilarious Red Skelton stars in this Civil War comedy about a buffoonish bellhop who is accidentally recruited to spy for the Union Army. Along the way, he falls for a Southern belle (Arlene Dahl), inadvertently foils the Rebels and immortalizes the line, "My, it's so nice to be among the magnolias again." Brian Donlevy also stars as Dahl's erstwhile suitor. ★★★ $19.99

Soviet Spy

(1961, 130 min, France, Yves Ciampi) This docudrama presents the case of Richard Sorge, a German journalist covering WWII in Japan. Official records show that Sorge was hanged as a Soviet spy in 1944. The film explores this mystery man's life, beginning with conflicting opinions by his associates on his alleged espionage activities and then moving up to a reenactment of the events that led to his capture. A very interesting exploration into the life and role of a possible Soviet spy. (French with English subtitles) ★★★

Soylent Green

(1973, 97 min, US, Richard Fleischer) This frighteningly prescient sci-fi tale about the dangers of the "greenhouse effect" was made long before the term became a popular buzzword. Charlton Heston plays a hardened New York cop who stumbles onto the secret of Soylent Green, a nutritional wafer used to feed the masses. Edward G. Robinson is excellent in his final role as Heston's aging roommate who can remember the halcyon days of Earth when it was still green. ★★½ $19.99

Space Jam

(1996, 87 min, US, Joe Pytka) Falling far short of its intended "Pro basketball meets *Roger Rabbit*" aspirations, Michael Jordan's debut does not bode well for his future success as a movie star, although fans of the sports legend will probably be satisfied and younger viewers will enjoy the loud, colorful basketball sequences. Jordan, whom the film treats as a near-deity, is forced to team up with a plethora of Looney Tunes characters in a game of intergalactic and multidimensional basketball when some evil (but very lovable) aliens try to kidnap Bugs Bunny and company. Unfortunately, the marketing of the movie seems to have taken precedence over its execution. The animation is good, but clumsily intercut with the live-action sequences and it's nothing we haven't seen before. The humor is forced and the film is padded out to feature length with some boring montage sequences. Several humorous scenes and a few funny digs at rival Disney are fun, however, and it is also a pleasure to see a host of seldom-used Looney Tunes characters lurking in the background of all the crowd sequences. It is a pity, however, that they couldn't have been given more to do. ★★ $22.99

Space Thing

(1968, 69 min, US, Cosmo Politan) A sci-fi buff dreams himself into a universe of intergalactic space-age sex and satellites, complete with an insatiable bisexual queen mother and her voluptuous female crew. The low-budget special F/X, set designs and acting, clearly

inspired by the Ed Wood, Jr. school of filmmaking, and spiced with healthy doses of humor, will send you into orbit. ★ $24.99

Spaceballs

(1987, 96 min, US, Mel Brooks) A misfire for Brooks, this lame and untimely parody of George Lucas' *Star Wars* series features the usual Brooks assault of visual and verbal puns, which more often than not fail to hit their desired target. Die-hard "Star-heads" may be amused, but *Hardware Wars* did it better and earlier. The best scene of the film is an on-target takeoff on *Alien* and the classic Warner Brothers cartoon "One Froggy Evening." (Available letterboxed and pan & scan) ★★ $14.99

Spacecamp

(1986, 108 min, US, Harry Winer) A group of teenagers attending a NASA summer camp are accidentally launched into space, where they're on their own to get back to Earth. Kate Capshaw and Lea Thompson star in this ordinary teen adventure. ★★ $14.99

Spaghetti House

(1982, 102 min, Italy/GB, Guilio Pardisi) Nino Manfredi, Italy's master of film comedy, abandons his usual persona to star in this drama of a bungled robbery attempt which results in a tense hostage situation. Manfredi stars as an outspoken Italian waiter in London who, along with four of his compatriots, is held hostage by three desperate black men. Although this film falls occasionally into depicting easy stereotypes, it also explores race relations, prejudices and the common oppression suffered by both immigrants and blacks in lily-white England. Costarring Rita Tushingham as Manfredi's stalwart wife. ★★½

Spanking the Monkey

(1994, 106 min, US, David O. Russell) Don't let the title fool you. Russell's film is an insightful and offbeat look at love, sexuality and incest. Jeremy Davies is convincing as a college freshman student, Ray, who must stay home on his summer vacation to take care of his bedridden mother instead of taking a prestigious internship. The relationship between the two becomes increasingly convoluted as the mother looks towards her son to fill the void left by a traveling husband, and Ray's sexual frustrations grow. *Monkey* boasts first-rate acting and a well-written script. And don't let the incest throw you — this is handled in such a subtle way the film went on to win the Audience Popularity Award at the 1994 Sundance Film Festival. ★★★ $19.99

Sparkle

(1976, 98 min, US, Sam O'Steen) The trials and tribulations of stardom, as experienced by three sisters (Lonette McKee, Irene Cara and Dwan Smith) during the 1950s rock era. Curtis Mayfield's rousing score highlights this sometimes clichéd story made all the more appealing by its musical numbers and sincere performances. Written by the director Joel Schumacher. ★★½ $14.99

Sparrows

(1926, 84 min, US, William Beaudine) A gaggle of orphans, a quicksand-infested swamp, a

Ingrid Bergman and Gregory Peck in *Spellbound*

Lindbergh-like kidnapping and 'gators. Fine fixin's for a melodrama. Mary Pickford, racing through her '30s, plays a waif half her age trying to get her brood out of the Bayou alive. One of the classics of the silent era, which the kids will love as much as the adults. ★★★½ $29.99

Spartacus

(1960, 184 min, US, Stanley Kubrick) This epic adventure is highlighted by remarkable action sequences and strongly developed characterizations, all set against the visual spectacle of Kubrick's discerning eye for locale and cinematic tone. The winner of four Academy Awards including Best Supporting Actor (Peter Ustinov) and Best Cinematography. Kirk Douglas stars in the title role as a rebel slave who leads the revolt against the Roman Republic. Also starring Laurence Olivier, Jean Simmons, John Gavin, Tony Curtis, Charles Laughton and a cast of (literally) thousands! Music by Alex North. (Available letterboxed and full-screen) ★★★★ $19.99

Speaking Parts

(1989, 93 min, Canada, Atom Egoyan) Similar in theme to *sex, lies, and videotape*, this perceptive look at the delicate balance between love and sex in the age of video features the entangled lives of three young people. Lance, a part-time actor and full-time bed-changer at a hotel, becomes the object of desire for both Clara, a scriptwriter intrigued by the physical similarities between Lance and her dead brother, and Lisa, a shy hotel maid who obsessively watches his minor appearances as an extra in films she rents on video. This quietly stylized drama is a dark glimpse into the way people act and how they show themselves to others. ★★★ $19.99

Special Bulletin

(1983, 105 min, US, Edward Zwick) Outstanding made-for-TV drama directed by Zwick (*Glory*) about a group of nuclear protestors who, holding a TV reporter and cameraman hostage, threaten to detonate nuclear bombs if warheads in Charleston, South

Carolina, are not disarmed. Like Orson Welles' "War of the Worlds," the film is presented as if it were a live news broadcast. Intelligently written, and expertly acted and directed. Ed Flanders ("St. Elsewhere"), Kathryn Walker, Roxanne Hart, David Clennon ("thirtysomething"), David Rasche and Rosalind Cash head the cast. ★★★½ $19.99

A Special Day

(1977, 110 min, Italy, Ettore Scola) The day Hitler arrives in Rome to meet with Mussolini is the time setting for this touching drama of an oppressed housewife (Sophia Loren) who meets and befriends a troubled homosexual (Marcello Mastroianni). Fine performances from the two as well as Scola's realistic treatment make this a memorable film. (Dubbed) ★★★

Special Effects

(1985, 90 min, US, Larry Cohen) Intriguing, top-notch Grade-B thriller with Eric Bogosian (*Talk Radio*) as a maniacal movie director who murders an actress, and then hires a look-alike and makes a movie about the killing. Also starring Zoe Tamerlis, who plays both actresses. ★★½

The Specialist

(1994, 115 min, US, Luis Llosa) Llosa, who also helmed *Sniper*, proves he is far better directing explosions than people with this hormone-driven soap opera that pleases the eye as it insults the intelligence. Sylvester Stallone plays an ex-CIA operative and explosives expert who is hired by hypersexy Sharon Stone to wipe out the men (a slumming Rod Steiger and "macho-prissy" Eric Roberts) responsible for her parents' death. But there's a hitch: The bad guys have hired Sly's vengeful ex-partner (the scene-stealing James Woods) as their security chief. The steamy shower scene between Stallone and Stone is, in itself, a sight to behold, but the incessant "cock-fighting" between Roberts and Stallone, Roberts and Woods, and ultimately Stallone and Woods,

leaves one guessing as to who wants to fight and who wants to fuck. ★★ $14.99

Species

(1995, 111 min, US, Roger Donaldson) Ben Kingsley and Michael Madsen topline this unintentionally funny horror film about a half-human, half-*Alien* creature whose attempts at perpetuating her own species by mating with a human male are hampered by a ragtag team of experts (including Forest Whitaker, Alfred Molina and Marg Helgenberger). Action-maven Donaldson's first foray into the field of horror is sabotaged by an incredibly clichéd script, hokey dialogue, and lackluster performances. In spite of its insipid, rip-off premise, *Species* does feature first-rate special effects, including H.R. Giger's *deja vu* alien design, and a fetching debut by Natasha Henstridge as the monstrous Sil. ★½ $19.99

Speechless

(1994, 98 min, US, Ron Underwood) Written before the high-profile relationship of politicos James Carvell and Mary Matalin, this frothy, lightweight battle-of-the-sexes comedy casts Michael Keaton and Geena Davis as rival candidate speechwriters who become romantically involved. Both suffering from insomnia, they meet cutesy late one night, though unaware of each other's political association. Of course, fireworks and misunderstandings fill the air when they learn the truth. It's difficult to fully appreciate a romantic comedy whose political observations are subtler and more compelling than the love story, but such is the case with *Speechless*. As the two love birds, Keaton and Davis rattle off some funny exchanges, but their chemistry appears lacking. ★★½ $9.99

Speed

(1994, 120 min, US, Jan De Bont) Keanu Reeves sheds his surfer-dude persona, with varying success, and enters the realm of action-hero-dom. Reeves stars as a rough-and-ready member of an elite L.A.P.D. SWAT team that specializes in disarming the handiwork of even the wiliest of terrorists — especially that zaniest movie star of them all, Dennis Hopper, who does himself proud as the film's mad bomber. In the film's terrifically staged and hyperventilating opening sequence, Reeves, with the help of his good buddy Jeff Daniels, foils Hopper's attempt to become a few million dollars richer. In response, Hopper brews up a brilliant scheme to extort money from the good citizens of L.A., while at the same time handing Reeves a fitting payback, by rigging a bus to blow sky-high if it slows down below 50 mph. Once Reeves boards the ill-fated vehicle and the winning Sandra Bullock, a courgeous passenger, takes the wheel, the race is on and the action never slows for a second. Despite several sequences that push the boundaries of believability, the film is an entertaining and often amusing diversion. So strap on your seat-belt and enjoy! (Bullock returned in a 1997 sequel, *Speed II: Cruise Control*) (Letterboxed version available for $19.99) ★★★ $14.99

Speed 2: Cruise Control

(1997, 100 min, US, Jan De Bont) By *not* appearing in a project, Keanu Reeves may have made the smartest decision of his career by saying "no" to reprising the role of Jack Traven from *Speed* for its sequel. Sandra Bullock, however, is not that lucky. She returns in this waterlogged, empty-headed encore, this time set on a cruise ship. She's got a new boyfriend (Jason Patric, who couldn't show less emotion if he were dead), also an L.A. cop, and once again she crosses paths with a mad bomber (the bug-eyed Willem Dafoe). Everything there was to like about the original is absent this second time around. Suspense? None. Excitement? Gone. Unpredictable thrills? Stick to the original. A clever villain? Watch *Die Hard* again. Even the personable Bullock is cheerless (she shouldn't have watched the dailies). There's a prolonged effects scene which is truly impressive that has two ships colliding. But it only lasts minutes, and getting there is like watching *Beyond the Poseidon Adventure*. Director De Bont had too much money, too much control, and too few ideas. ★ $99.99

Speed Racer: The Movie

(1967/1993, 80 min,) Turbo-charged pop nostalgia at its best, this feature includes two classic episodes, "The Car Hater" and "The Mammoth Car." Also featured in this highly entertaining package is a Colonel Bleep cartoon – a milestone in television created in 1956 that has the distinction of being the first TV cartoon produced in color. This well-paced feature is also tastefully peppered with vintage animated commercials and a music video that fetaures a "Techno" rendering of the Speed Racer theme song. So put on your P.F. Flyers and run, don't walk, to the video store. ★★★ $14.99

Spellbinder

(1988, 99 min, US, Janet Greek) Interesting if not quite successful suspenser about a lawyer (Timothy Daly) who comes to the aid of a damsel in distress (Kelly Preston), and learns she's on the run from a bloodthirsty coven of witches. With Rick Rossovich and Audra Lindley. ★★ $79.99

Spellbound

(1945, 111 min, US, Alfred Hitchcock) Gregory Peck stars as the victim of a troubling mental paralysis and Ingrid Bergman is the analyst determined to unlock the door to his mysterious past. An intriguing, trendsetting work with a dazzling dream sequence designed by Salvador Dali. ★★★½ $9.99

Spetters

(1981, 109 min, The Netherlands, Paul Verhoeven) Three Dutch youths find themselves at the crossroads of adulthood in this arresting drama. Seeking to escape their working-class destinies, they dream of fame and fortune racing motorcycles, but are sidetracked by the fateful intervention of a scheming hash-slinger (the sultry Renée Soutendijk). (Dubbed) ★★★ $19.99

Spices

(1986, 98 min, India, Ketan Mehta) Set in 1940s British-controlled India, this engaging melodrama deals with the beginnings of the nationalistic rumblings of the colony and specifically one community's reaction to the plight of an oppressed woman. Sanbai, a young, defiant beauty, spurns the advances of a sudebar, the military-backed tax collection force, and is forced to take refuge against his wrath. Initially fearful and reluctant to help, the men and women of the village must make a stand against the injustice and tyranny of a belligerent oppressor. (Hindi with English subtitles) ★★★ $29.99

The Spider's Stratagem

(1970, 97 min, Italy, Bernardo Bertolucci) This stylish and intelligent political thriller, taken from a Jorge Luis Borges short story, follows a young man's journey to the village of his youth. There he finds the statue of his father (a hero killed 30 years earlier by anti-fascists) has been defaced and the townsfolk mysteriously hostile. While attempting to discover the truth about his father, he soon finds himself entangled in an increasingly complex web of lies, mysteries and omens. Magnificently staged by director Bertolucci. (Italian with English subtitles) ★★★★ $29.99

Spiders

(1919, 137 min, Germany, Fritz Lang) Planned as the first installment of a four-part adventure serial, Lang produced only this one entry, a wildly exotic forerunner to the *Indiana Jones* trilogy. With tongue-in-cheek humor, our hero must battle the arch-criminal Lio-Shar and his unsavory gang, the Spiders, as they search for lost Inca treasure, diamonds shaped like the head of a Buddha, as well as devise a plan to dominate the world. Filled with scenes of lost civilizations, human sacrifice and pirates, this big-budget action silent is very interesting and one of the earliest surviving films of the great German filmmaker. (Silent with musical soundtrack) ★★★ $29.99

Spies

(1928, 88 min, Germany, Fritz Lang) Lang's fascination with futuristic technology, expressionistic design and sweeping adventure reaches a high point in this enthralling spy thriller featuring an evil criminal mastermind and agent #326, a suave super agent. (Silent) $29.99

Spies Like Us

(1985, 103 min, US, John Landis) Until *Nothing But Trouble* came along, this inferior spy comedy was at the bottom of the film pile for Chevy Chase and Dan Aykroyd. The guys play bumbling CIA agents who, let loose in the Middle East to serve as decoys, nearly start WWIII. ★½ $9.99

Spike of Bensonhurst

(1988, 100 min, US, Paul Morrissey) Written and directed by ex-Warholite Morrissey, this mob comedy stars Sasha Mitchell as Spike Fumo, an ambitiously arrogant yet charming two-bit boxer who, on sheer chutzpa, tries to climb his way to the top. Ernest Borgnine (in the best screen role he's had in decades) plays the befuddled neighborhood don who must contend with Spike after his WASPy daughter falls under his seductively dangerous charms. Geraldine Smith is unforgettable as Spike's lesbian mom and Sylvia Miles steals a few scenes as a coke-sniffing congresswoman. ★★★

The Spiral Staircase

(1975, 89 min, US, Peter Collinson) Okay remake of the 1946 Dorothy McGuire thriller with Jacqueline Bisset in the McGuire role as a mute woman terrorized by an unknown killer. Christopher Plummer, Sam Wanamaker, Mildred Dunnock and Elaine Stritch are possible suspects. ★★ $14.99

Spirit of '76

(1991, 82 min, US, Lucas Reiner) Time machine inventor David Cassidy (yes, that's right, David Cassidy!), along with two fellow scientists, sets sail back through time to the year 1776 to retrieve the Constitution of the United States — and other remnants of our past — with the hopes of saving Earth from a cold, grey future. By mistake, however, our travelers wind up in the year 1976 where they encounter a world of Pop Rocks, disco, Apache scarves, mood rings and (God forbid) Leif Garrett! Funny and entertaining, the film fea-

Keanu Reeves in *Speed*

tures a great supporting cast that has more familiar faces than a "Love Boat" episode and a foot-stomping soudtrack that'll make you want to do the Hustle! ★★ $89.99

The Spirit of St. Louis

(1957, 138 min, US, Billy Wilder) James Stewart's absorbing portrayal of aviator Charles Lindbergh highlights this interesting though overlong look at the flyer's early years and his historic, transatlantic flight. ★★½ $19.99

Spirit of the Beehive

(1973, 95 min, Spain, Victor Erice) An unforgettable and hypnotic drama by first-time director Erice, and one that features moving performances by two young girls, both non-professional actors. In a remote Castilian village, two children watching *Frankenstein* at a traveling film show become entranced by the image of the monster. The younger girl, a sensitive eight-year-old, believing that he is the spirit of the monster, discovers and befriends a fugitive soldier just before he is captured. A haunting and poetic mood piece. (Spanish with English subtitles) ★★★½ $29.99

Spirits of the Dead (Histoires Extraordinaires)

(1967, 117 min, France, Federico Fellini/Louis Malle/Roger Vadim) An anthology film nominally based on three short stories by Edgar Allan Poe, this mélange of '60s-style, Felliniesque grotesquerie and soft-core eroticism only lives up to its title in its final segment. Jane Fonda is the object of Vadim and his camera's obsession in the first story, "Metzengerstein," about a young countess who believes that her dead cousin has been reincarnated as a magnificent black horse. See Jane walk, see Jane ride, see Jane breathe...the only distinguishing feature of this otherwise boring segment is the casting of brother Peter Fonda as Jane's love. The second story, "William Wilson," by Malle, is much more interesting. It stars Alain Delon as a young libertine whose debaucheries are continually foiled by a mysterious doppelganger until he takes a decisive step which seals not only his double's fate, but his own as well. The third story is the best. "Toby Dammit," directed by Fellini, stars Terence Stamp as an alcoholic and egocentric English actor. His trip to Rome is haunted by the vision of an eerily beautiful young blonde girl playing with a bouncing ball. The film is indicative of the time it was made (costumes, hairstyles), and only Fellini's segment captures the true spirit of Poe. (French with English subtitles) (Letterboxed) ★★½ $59.99

Spitfire

(1934, 94 min, US, John Cromwell) Katharine Hepburn plays an uninhibited South Carolina mountain woman who evokes the wrath of the local townsfolk when she kidnaps a baby from its mother because she feels it's not being properly cared for. Unusual an occasionally compelling. Robert Young and Ralph Bellamy also star. ★★½

The Spitfire Grill

(1996, 111 min, US, Lee David Zlotoff) An audience favorite at 1996's Sundance Film Festival, writer-director Zlotoff's sentimental

film garnered more attention upon theatrical release for being funded by a Roman Catholic order than it did for its artistry. Nevertheless, this deliberately paced tale of an ex-con and her profound impact on the town of Gilead, Maine, is a heartwarming character study set in a gossipy but picturesque rural community. The multiple story lines of determined women trying to establish their place in the world may echo *Fried Green Tomatoes*, but *Spitfire Grill* distinguishes itself (much like *Tomatoes* did) with solid female bonding, homespun wisdom and beautiful scenery. Alison Elliott is a marvel as Percy, a stranger with a secret who acts as catalyst to unlock the mysteries of Gilead's most prominent residents. She is moving even in the hokiest of scenes. And though the film ties up its plots and characters in a most contrived conclusion, Zlotoff's subtlety makes for an absorbing little drama which may jerk a tear or two from those less cynical. ★★½ $99.99

Spitting Image

(1987, 60 min, GB) No American political satire is as witty, scathing, astute or plain darned funny as Britain's *Spitting Image*, the now-famous puppet show which uses grotesque caricatures of prominent public figures to lampoon their policies and pretensions. The programs are filled with fantastic images, rapid-fire dialogue and outrageous musical numbers. "Bumbledown," a review of Ronald Reagan's life and presidency, is painfully brilliant and possibly one of the most insightful analyses of his career. "The Sound of Maggie" is uproarious, even without a detailed knowledge of British politics. Each of the music video shorts hits its target squarely. Keep your eye on the screen — it moves fast. ★★★½ $24.99

Splash

(1984, 109 min, US, Ron Howard) Director Howard and stars Tom Hanks and Daryl Hannah hit it big with this charming comedy about a businessman (Hanks) who falls in love with a mermaid (Hannah). John Candy has some amusing scenes as Hank's co-hort. ★★★ $9.99

Splendor in the Grass

(1961, 124 min, US, Elia Kazan) Beginning with screendom's first French kiss, this lyrical and delicate examination of youthful love and the heartache and joy that accompanies it is somewhat sentimental, but after 30 years it's still a heartbreaking and timeless story. Natalie Wood, in her most accomplished performance, and Warren Beatty, in his screen debut, star as young lovers in 1920s Kansas who are hopelessly trapped by overbearing parents, social class lines and the boundaries of first love. Director Kazan handles his actors and story with great sensitivity, and William Inge won an Oscar for his insightful screenplay. Also making film debuts are Sandy Dennis and Phyllis Diller. ★★★½ $14.99

Split Decisions

(1988, 95 min, US, David Drury) Heavy-handed boxing drama about three generations of fighters, with a *Rocky* slant, as the youngest takes to the ring to avenge his brother's death. With Gene Hackman and Jeff Fahey. ★★ $14.99

The Spy Who Came in from the Cold

Split Image

(1982, 111 min, US, Ted Kotcheff) A well-acted drama with college student Michael O'Keefe joining Dennis Hopper's cult to be with Karen Allen. Dad Brian Dennehy hires deprogrammer James Woods to get him back. Good performances accentuate this compelling story. ★★★

Split: Portrait of a Drag Queen

(1992, 60 min, US, Andrew Weeks & Ellen Fisher Turk) The fascinating yet tragic "rags-to-riches-and-fabulous frocks" story of International Chrysis, a glamorous beauty who ran away from the poverty of his Brooklyn boyhood to become a charismatic drag artist, friend of Salvador Dali and underground celebrity, is recounted in this intriguing documentary. Through interviews with Chrysis, her fellow drag queen friends and archival and home movie footage, we learn of her inspiring rise to showgirl stardom only to succumb to cancer in 1990 at the age of 39, her death caused by the seepage of wax and silicone from her artificial breasts. Looking like a cross between Raquel Welch and Joan Collins, Chrysis' struggles and witty, fanciful tales are told in this tender and entertaining portrait of an unforgettable "chick with a dick." ★★★ $39.99

Split Second

(1992, 90 min, GB, Tony Maylam) London in the year 2008 is the setting for this *Lethal Weapon*-meets-*Alien* rip-off which, while woefully unoriginal, winds up being hugely entertaining and, at times, hilarious. A potbellied Rutger Hauer continually growls, grimaces, smokes and "lives on anxiety, caffeine and chocolate" in his pursuit of a serial killer. Neil Duncan, in a wonderfully witty performance, co-stars as Hauer's overeducated new partner and more than once the two actors appear to be on the verge of laughter and/or tongue kissing! Two questions: Why does the Dutch actor playing a British cop have an American accent and what is "Nights in White Satin" doing all over the soundtrack? ★★★ $9.99

Splitting Heirs

(1993, 86 min, US/GB, Robert Young) Eric Idle stars as a poor Cockney schlub who discovers one fateful day that he is the true heir to a vast dukedom and that the Pakistani family that raised him since infancy is not his real family (gasp!). Such is the level of humor in this execrable attempt at crossbreeding Monty Python with "The Corsican Brothers." Rick Moranis co-stars as the cretinous American yuppie who, having been switched at birth with the unfortunate heir, has usurped Idle's rightful title as "Duke of Something-or-Other" and is none too willing to return it. A more appropriate title would have been *Splitting Headaches*. Also starring Barbara Hershey and John Cleese. ★ $19.99

Spring Symphony

(1984, 102 min, West Germany, Peter Schamoni) The passionate life and musical genius of German composer Robert Schumann is featured in this interesting if familiar drama. While a student, Schumann becomes violently involved with his teacher's daughter, pianist Clare Wieck (Nastassja Kinski). Their affair threatens the teacher who becomes jealous and forces young Kinski to choose between family, love of her music and desire. (Filmed in English) ★★½

Springtime in the Rockies

(1942, 91 min, US, Irving Cummings) Betty Grable is at her best in this blithe musical comedy about a bickering theatrical couple at a mountain resort. With John Payne, Carmen Miranda (as delightful as ever), Charlotte Greenwood, Cesar Romero, Edward Everett Horton and Jackie Gleason. ★★★ $19.99

Der Sprinter

(1985, 90 min, West Germany, Christoph Böll) A witty social satire about a young closeted gay man who, in order to please his mother, decides to be "normal." Wieland Samolak portrays our confused hero, a pale, wide-eyed young man with expressionistic silent film star looks and a charming comedic touch. He chooses sports, specifically running, as his entrance into the straight world. His attempts at sports produce little until he meets and falls in love with a buxom butch female shot putter. Oh!, the price to pay for conformity! (German with English subtitles) ★★★

William Holden in *Stalag 17*

Sprout Wings and Fly

(1983, 30 min, US, Les Blank) A life-affirming profile of old-time Appalachian fiddler Tommy Jarrell. Filmed in the Blue Ridge Mountains of North Carolina. ★★★ $44.99

Spy Hard

(1996, 81 min, US, Rick Friedberg) This *really* stupid comedy, executive-produced by its star Leslie Nielsen, attempts to duplicate the hilarity level of the *Naked Gun* films, but misses most of the time. Nielsen plays Agent WD-40 (har har), assigned to stop his arch-nemesis (Andy Griffith) from blowing up the world. En route, the film lampoons almost every hit of the 1990s, from *Speed* to *Pulp Fiction* to *Cliffhanger*. There are a few laughs to be had, but even the best of these would only be middling fare in a *Naked Gun* comedy. It's a shame *Spy Hard* isn't funnier, because Nielsen tries so hard, you really want to like it. He's not afraid to try any joke in the book; unfortunately, the writers skipped many a chapter. The opening title sequence, directed and performed by "Weird" Al Yankovic, is by far the funniest bit, and proves he should have directed the rest of the film. ★★ $19.99

The Spy in Black

(1939, 82 min, GB, Michael Powell) Conrad Veidt plays a German naval officer and spy in this intriguing tale of espionage set amidst the moors of Scotland during WWI. Legendary director Powell adds his spice with a series of ingenious plot-twists and a keen eye for romance. ★★★

The Spy Who Came in from the Cold

(1965, 112 min, GB, Martin Ritt) This adaptation of John LeCarre's novel is every bit as cold as the Cold War intrigue it chronicles — and that's what makes it so good. Richard Burton is an embittered agent who's as much a sacrificial pawn as anything — and he knows it. Claire Bloom is the woman who can still see him through his alcoholic haze, only to be tragically betrayed. One of Burton's best performances. ★★★½ $19.99

The Spy Who Loved Me

(1977, 125 min, GB, Lewis Gilbert) One of the best of the Roger Moore Bond films, this scintillating spy thriller pairs 007 with a seductive Russian agent (Barbara Bach) to quash an arch-villain's plans for world destruction — does he ever do anything else? Richard Kiel is featured as the seven-foot henchman Jaws. (Available letterboxed and pan & scan) ★★★ $14.99

Square Dance

(1987, 112 min, US, Daniel Petrie) Well-acted drama about a young farm girl's coming of age when she runs away from home to live with her estranged mother in the city. Winona Ryder gives a superb performance as the young girl, as does Jane Alexander as her mom, and Jason Robards as her grandfather. Rob Lowe gives a surprisingly effective portrayal of a young retarded man. ★★★

The Squeeze

(1987, 102 min, US, Roger Young) Inferior comedy with Michael Keaton as a down-on-his-luck con man who joins forces with an

aspiring detective (Rae Dawn Chong) to investigate a murder which implicates Keaton's ex-wife. ★½ $14.99

Stage Door

(1937, 92 min, US, Gregory La Cava) Katharine Hepburn, Ginger Rogers, Andrea Leeds, Lucille Ball, Eve Arden and Ann Miller are some of the inhabitants of the Footlights Club, a boarding house for aspiring starlets. Fast, witty repartee and uniformly fine performances highlight this story of a wealthy newcomer (Hepburn) trying to break into show business and gain acceptance from her new companions. Adolphe Menjou is superb as a suave and lecherous producer. Based on the play by Edna Ferber and George S. Kaufman. ★★★★ $19.99

Stage Fright

(1950, 110 min, GB, Alfred Hitchcock) A clever, lighthearted thriller starring Marlene Dietrich as the mistress of the man accused of murdering her husband. But is he or she the true killer? Amid the backdrop of theatre life, innocence is pitted against duplicity, illustrating Hitchcock's fascination with both. ★★★ $19.99

Stage Struck

(1958, 95 min, US, Sidney Lumet) Mild remake of *Morning Glory*, suffering most from Susan Strasberg's less-than-inspired performance as a struggling actress determined to become a star. With Henry Fonda, Joan Greenwood and Christopher Plummer. ★★

Stagecoach

(1939, 97 min, US, John Ford) Director Ford, with one masterful stroke, took the western, heretofore a "B" programmer, and with sweeping panoramas, landmark use of camera and editing techniques, superlative action sequences and strong character development, elevated the genre to a singular American art form. John Wayne heads a consummate cast in this story of a group of disparate travelers heading west by stagecoach, besieged by Indian attacks and internal conflict. Also starring Claire Trevor, John Carradine, Andy Devine and Thomas Mitchell, who won an Oscar for his stirring portrayal of a drunken doctor. ★★★★ $14.99

Stakeout

(1987, 115 min, US, John Badham) Richard Dreyfuss and Emilio Estevez team up as a pair of cops assigned to keep an eye on a beautiful woman (Madeline Stowe) whose ex-boyfriend (Aidan Quinn) escaped from jail, leaving a trail of bodies behind him. Complications arise when Dreyfuss falls in love with their subject. Dreyfuss and Estevez have a wonderful chemistry which heightens the enjoyment of this accomplished comic thriller. Followed by a 1994 sequel, *Another Stakeout*. ★★★ $9.99

Stalag 17

(1953, 120 min, US, Billy Wilder) The quintessential POW film. William Holden deservedly won an Oscar for his knockout performance as a cynical prisoner of war suspected of leaking secrets to his German captors. Alternately funny and suspenseful, director Wilder keeps the action moving at a remarkable pace, and allows the viewer to feel the

S

confines of the barracks without a moment of claustrophobia. Top-notch supporting cast includes Don Taylor, Otto Preminger, Robert Strauss, Harvey Lembeck, Peter Graves and Sig Ruman. ★★★★ $14.99

Stalag Luft

(1994, 103 min, GB, Adrian Shergold) It's the surreal meets "Hogan's Heroes" as a group of British soldiers plot their escape from Stalag Luft. Stephen Fry stars as a pompous, ineffectual ranking officer at a German POW camp. With 23 escapes (and 23 recaptures) to his credit, he plans the impossible: to have all 327 prisoners escape. All goes well until the Germans inform them that not only do they know what they're planning, but that they want to go along, too! An extremely silly satire on prisoner-of-war films (*The Great Escape* in particular), *Stalag Luft* begins excruciatingly slow in setting up character and plot. The film picks up ever so slightly once the story's bizarre hook is set in motion, though only a few moments of whimsical comedy manage to come to life. Some of the jokes may be lost on an American audience. ★½ $34.99

Stalingrad

(1993, 150 min, Germany, Joseph Vilsmaier) This stunning German production follows a group of soldiers from Italy to the snowy steppes of Russia in their futile attempt to capture the city of Stalingrad in what was one of the bloodiest battles of WWII. Much like *Das Boot* or Sam Peckinpah's *Cross of Iron*, the film's narrative features some unlikely heroes (at least for an American audience): German soldiers. Vividly and authentically drawn, with a diversity of motivations and moralities, the script avoids making each character a cliché. While there are the requisite experienced veteran, green lieutenant, fresh-faced youth and craven coward, each of these stereotypes is fleshed out in various ways to keep the viewer constantly surprised. And the war sequences are appropriately nightmarish, giving a foxhole-eyed view of the street-to-street battles which claimed over two million German and Russian lives. The characters and dramatic situations are so well-drawn, though, that they remain in the mind long after the memory of the epic battle sequences have faded. (German with English subtitles) ★★★½ $89.99

Stalker

(1979, 160 min, Russia, Andrei Tarkovsky) A stark, hallucinatory work that formulates a tormented vision of post-apocalyptic existence. The film revolves around a mysterious, government-restricted "Zone" where a meteor shower has altered the rules of nature, creating an eerie wasteland of mirage and mindtraps. Rumor abounds that within the Zone is a "Room" which holds the "Truth" and can fulfill one's deepest desires, but it is only with the aid of a physically gifted guide, or "Stalker," that the dangerous, forbidden area can be reached. What this nightmarish sci-fi film lacks in pacing is made up in its startling, psychedelic imagery. (Russian with English subtitles) ★★★★ $19.99

The Stalking Moon

(1969, 109 min, US, Robert Mulligan) Gregory Peck plays an Army scout who

escorts Eva Marie Saint, captured years before by the Indians, and her young half-breed son home – with the boy's father in pursuit. The story's good premise is only occasionally realized, though the two stars work well together. ★★½ $14.99

The Stand

(1994, 360 min, US, Mick Garris) Based on the best-seller by Stephen King, this epic six-hour made-for-TV adaptation is typical King: fascinating, excessive, fantastical, impulsive and imaginative, with its fair share of slow moments. Set in modern times, the story begins as a virus (King wrote this years before the discovery of AIDS) wipes out 99% of the planet's population. While some survivors (mostly white) are spiritually drawn to a kindly, psychic old black woman (wonderfully played by Ruby Dee), others answer the calling of the devil incarnate. As all follow their chosen paths, the stage is set in true King fashion for the battle between good and evil. Among the large cast, Gary Sinise, Rob Lowe, Laura San Giacomo, Ossie Davis and Ray Walston are most memorable. ★★★ $39.99

Stand and Deliver

(1987, 105 min, US, Ramon Menendez) Edward James Olmos gives an outstanding performance as a strict public school math teacher who commits himself to his East L.A. students as they prepare for a difficult mathematics test. He is ultimately able to instill a pride and confidence in the previously unrecognized. Moving tribute to the tenacity of Jaime Escalante, the real-life teacher on whom the story is based. ★★★ $9.99

Stand by Me

(1986, 87 min, US, Rob Reiner) This sweet-natured reminiscence is set in the late 1950s and recounts the misadventures of four pubescent boys who set out in search of the body of a young boy killed in a train accident. Based on the Stephen King novella, "The Body." Wil Wheaton, River Phoenix, Corey Feldman and Jerry O'Connell are the young boys; Kiefer Sutherland co-stars as the town bully; and Richard Dreyfuss has a cameo as the narrator. Reiner's enchanting observation on the predilection of (specifically male) youth is winsome, articulate and refreshingly entertaining. ★★★½ $14.99

Stand-In

(1937, 91 min, US, Tay Garnett) Humphrey Bogart and Leslie Howard are reunited (*The Petrified Forest*) in this amusing show-biz comedy. Howard plays an efficiency expert who is dispatched to Hollywood to save a studio from financial ruin. Not knowing the business, he enlists the aid of former child star Joan Blondell and boozy producer Bogie. Bogart is surprisingly funny in his first comedic role, and Blondell is, as always, sassy and smart. ★★★

Stand-Off

(1989, 97 min, Hungary, Gyula Gazdag) Filmed in documentary-like fashion, this suspenseful thriller recounts the actions of an 18-year-old Hungarian youth who, along with his younger brother, enters a student dormitory near the Hungarian border and holds 16 girls

hostage. Their demands: a flight out of Budapest, $1,000,000 and eventual freedom in the West. The director István Szabó plays a key role as one of the negotiators in this intense drama. (Hungarian with English subtitles) ★★★ $79.99

Stanley & Iris

(1990, 103 min, US, Martin Ritt) The title protagonists have monotonous, dead-end factory jobs; Iris (Jane Fonda) on one of the production lines, Stanley (Robert De Niro) in the company kitchen. She's a widow raising two children and helping to support an unemployed sister and brother-in-law. He's trying to function in the world while hiding his illiteracy. The film develops a nice rhythm as the details of their separate lives start to intertwine and mesh, changing midway to an almost fairy-tale conclusion. As usual, Fonda and De Niro give exceptional performances. ★★★ $9.99

Stanley and Livingstone

(1939, 101 min, US, Henry King) Spencer Tracy gives a stirring performance as Stanley searching for missionary Livingstone (Cedric Hardwicke) lost in darkest Africa at the turn of the century. A vastly entertaining '30s biopic. ★★★ $39.99

The Star

(1952, 89 min, US, Stuart Heisler) A ninth Oscar nomination for Best Actress went to Bette Davis for her solid portrayal of a fading movie queen in this vitriolic Hollywood melodrama. Though Davis herself was at the time experiencing sort of a "comeback," there is no real parallel between the legendary actress and her character of Margaret Elliott, though certain similarities are open to interpretation. A young Natalie Wood plays Davis' adolescent daughter. ★★★ $19.99

The Star Chamber

(1983, 109 min, US, Peter Hyams) Michael Douglas is a judge frustrated at the number of lowlifes our judicial system lets free on mere technicalities. What will he do when he finds himself invited to join a clandestine organization of like-minded litigants? An intriguing premise is half-heartedly explored making this a thinking man's thriller without a lot of smarts to it. Hal Holbrook, Yaphet Kotto and Sharon Gless costar. ★★½ $9.99

Star 80

(1983, 102 min, US, Bob Fosse) Never one to avoid controversy, Fosse picks apart the trappings of the American Dream with this unsettling account of a fantasy gone haywire. Mariel Hemingway portrays Dorothy Stratten, the peaches-and-cream Canadian girl whose taste of stardom was all too brief. The film's greatest strength lies in the performance of Eric Roberts, whose calculating swagger and coiled intensity are frightfully ominous. ★★★½ $14.99

A Star Is Born

(1937, 111 min, US, William Wellman) The original of the story of Esther Blodgett, an aspiring actress who marries matinee idol Norman Maine: her career takes off, his career fizzles. Janet Gaynor had one of her best roles as Blodgett, bringing freshness and charm to

Star Trek VI: The Undiscovered Country

the role, and Fredric March is outstanding as the fading star Maine. Dorothy Parker and Alan Campbell were two of the writers. Remade in 1954 with Judy Garland and James Mason, and in 1976 with Barbra Streisand and Kris Kristofferson. Digitally remastered from an archives print. ★★★½ $24.99

A Star Is Born

(1954, 170 min, US, George Cukor) Director Cukor often referred to *A Star Is Born* as his "butchered masterpiece" because the studio cut nearly 30 minutes from the finished film just weeks after its successful opening in 1954. After years of painstaking research and compilation, the film is restored to its original release length. The immortal Judy Garland gives her finest performance, both vocally and dramatically, as Vicki Lester, the young songstress who rockets to stardom upon discovery by matinee idol James Mason. Mason is equally brilliant as Norman Maine, the fading star who falls in love with Judy. One of the many songs is the unforgettable "The Man That Got Away." ★★★★ $29.99

A Star Is Born

(1976, 140 min, US, Frank Pierson) Though this second remake of the classic romance was dubbed by those-less-kind as "A Bore Is Starred," it's not *quite* as bad as that suggests. Barbra Streisand takes over the Janet Gaynor/Judy Garland role as an aspiring singer whose romance with a faltering rock star leads to tragedy. Kris Kristofferson is the fading star. The least successful of the three screen versions. ★★½ $19.99

The Star Maker

(1995, 113 min, Italy, Giuseppe Tornatore) Director Tornatore returns to the theme of the magic of the cinema which was brilliantly examined in his *Cinema Paradiso* with this often wry fable. Sergio Castellitto stars as Morelli, a con man making his way through 1950s Sicily offering dreams of fame and fortune or, at the very least, escape to the poor villagers of the small towns he visits. For a nominal fee, he films any and all with the promise of sending these screen tests to the cinematic giants of Italian filmmaking. Of course, the tests go no further than the back of his dilapidated truck which trumpets his arrival in each town. Not an evil man per se, Morelli is nevertheless unmoved by the various, funny and sometimes touching stories he

is told, and it is too late when he realizes the special power he and the camera holds. Tornatore captures the flavor of the times with the same accuracy he demonstrated in *Paradiso*, and certain scenes featuring nudity are certainly sexy; however, as good as this morality tale is, it is by no means the sophisticated romp which the box art suggests. (Italian with English subtitles) ★★★ $19.99

Star Trek

In this TV series, on NBC from 1966 to 1969, Gene Roddenberry created the perfect vehicle to discuss his humanistic philosophy. Respect for the sanctity of all forms of life, the taking of pleasure in the diversities of cultures, the unquenchable thirst to understand and the human capacity for love are what gives this show its timelessness. William Shatner portrays the courageous Cpt. James T. Kirk, Leonard Nimoy is Mr. Spock, his Vulcan First Officer, DeForest Kelley is the compassionate Dr. McCoy, James Doohan plays the ship's crafty engineer Scotty, and George Takei, Nichelle Nichols, Walter Koenig, Majel Barrett and Grace Lee Whitney are the crew of the Enterprise. Long a cult favorite (spawning eight theatrical films and four TV spinoffs), all 79 episodes are available for rental and purchase. Each episode runs 52 minutes, and sells for $12.99 each (except for "The Cage" and the two-hour "The Menagerie" which sell for $14.99 each)

Star Trek — The Motion Picture

(1979, 143 min, US, Robert Wise) The first theatrical outing for the crew of the Starship Enterprise. Captain Kirk and friends are sent to stop a deadly energy field heading towards Earth. Not as exciting as its sequels, some good special effects help compensate for its extremely long running time. Still, if you're a "Star Trek" fan, you gotta love it. This is the extended edition, with 11 minutes added to the theatrical version. (Available letterboxed and pan & scan) ★★½ $14.99

Star Trek II: The Wrath of Khan

(1982, 113 min, US, Nicholas Meyer) The crew of the Starship Enterprise battle their old foe Khan (see "Star Trek" TV episode "Space Seed"), who is determined to get revenge against Captain Kirk for...(you have to see the TV show). *II* is a gloriously entertaining sci-fi adventure, containing splendid special effects. William Shatner, Leonard Nimoy, DeForest Kelley and the rest of the gang are all on hand; and Ricardo Montalban nicely plays Khan. (Available letterboxed and pan & scan) ★★★½ $14.99

Star Trek III: The Search for Spock

(1984, 105 min, US, Leonard Nimoy) With the possibility of Spock being regenerated on the fast-disintegrating planet Genesis, Admiral Kirk and company hijack their old ship and go out after their friend — no matter what he may have evolved into. Intriguing sci-fi notions and

a fast-paced story make this an enjoyable yarn. The usual cast plus John Larroquette, Dame Judith Anderson and Christopher Lloyd as Kruge, the Klingon. (Available letterboxed and pan & scan) ★★★ $14.99

Star Trek IV: The Voyage Home

(1986, 119 min, US, Leonard Nimoy) This fourth film in the *Star Trek* movie series is possibly the best of the bunch. The crew of the Starship Enterprise, on their way home for criminal prosecution, are diverted to 1980s San Francisco to prevent the destruction of Earth in the 23rd century — by saving the whales. Good special effects and terrific humor highlight this top science-fiction adventure. (Available letterboxed and pan & scan) ★★★½ $14.99

Star Trek V: The Final Frontier

(1989, 106 min, US, William Shatner) This fifth entry in the *Star Trek* series was savaged by the critics and overlooked by audiences because of the ludicrous plot line (the Enterprise must travel through the allegedly awesome Great Barrier in search of God — the great and powerful Oz was more ominous) and the corniness of Laurence Luckinbill as a Vulcan with a heart of gold. Put those things out of your head because the fact is, this film is still enjoyable. Humorous and often touching, *Star Trek V* works because it is another chance for us to see characters we've grown up with. Director Shatner may have some problems parlaying action scenes to the screen, but nobody knows the crew of the Enterprise better than he and for that, we can thank him. (Available letterboxed and pan & scan) ★★½ $14.99

Star Trek VI: The Undiscovered Country

(1991, 110 min, US, Nicholas Meyer) The aging crew of the Starship Enterprise is back for one last mission. Not wanting to end on a down note after the disappointment of *Star Trek V*, the producers brought them back for this superior adventure which stands up to the best of the series. Faced with a dwindling supply of oxygen on their home planet, the Klingons decide to make peace with the rest of the galaxy. Fittingly, Capt. Kirk is chosen as the emissary to negotiate this "new universal order." Unhappily for him and the rest of the crew, there are powerful forces at work on both sides which don't want to see an end to their warring ways. The entire cast has a blast with this clearcut allegory for our current international climate. (Available letterboxed and pan & scan) ★★★ $14.99

Star Trek: The Next Generation

Debuting 18 years after the cancellation of the popular TV series "Star Trek," this spinoff aired in syndication for seven years, often #1 in the ratings. Set 75 years later than the William Shatner episodes, *The Next Generation* stars Patrick Stewart as the bald-headed, principled though demanding Jean-Luc Picard, the Enterprise's stalwart captain who in character is light years away from Shatner's sentimental risk-taker James Kirk. The series boasts outstanding special effects, which by comparison make the original series' production values seem like a Roger Corman quickie. The show's

Patrick Stewart meets the Borg queen in Star Trek: First Contact

other emphasis is on intelligent, thoughtful scripts which explore the humanity of man (as did the original) while bringing more depth to the relationships of the crew members. The cast includes Jonathan Frakes as First Officer Riker; LeVar Burton as the ship's partially blind engineer Geordi LaForge; Denise Crosby as Security Chief Tasha Yar; Michael Dorn as Lt. Worf, a Klingon serving on the Enterprise; Brent Spiner as Data, an android desperately trying to be human; Gates McFadden as the dedicated Dr. Crusher; Wil Wheaton as her teenaged son; Marina Sirtis as the Betazoid empath Counselor Troi; and occasionally Whoopi Goldberg as the wise, centuries-old Guinan. Gene Roddenberry, who created the original series, served as executive producer. Each episode runs 48 minutes, and sells for $14.99 each. (The pilot episode runs 96 minutes and sells for $19.99)

Star Trek Generations

(1994, 118 min, US, David Carson) A new crew takes control of the Starship Enterprise's theatrical adventures, and as James T. Kirk passes the captain's chair to Jean-Luc Picard, *Generations* brings both men together in an enjoyably familiar sci-fi tale. Whereas the first six *Trek* films echoed the rhythms and themes of the 1960s TV series, *Generations* is very much a by-product of the popular syndicated show. The story begins with the mysterious death of Kirk, and then skips ahead three-quarters of a century where Picard and his able crew answer an SOS, rescuing, among others, loony scientist Malcolm McDowell, who spells trouble for all. As would be expected, the plot consists of lots of techno-babble, alternate universes and devious Klingons. The entire crew of "T.N.G." is on hand, though Data (Brent Spiner) gets the best share of both screen time and the laughs as he finally acquires long-elusive human emotions. Patrick Stewart is ever-commanding as Picard, William Shatner is at his best as Kirk, and there's a show-stopping crash scene worth seeing twice. (Available letterboxed and pan & scan) ★★★ $14.99

Star Trek: First Contact

(1996, 110 min, US, Jonathan Frakes) Captain Kirk is dead, and the *Star Trek* films are now on their own — but that's not such bad news based on *Star Trek: First Contact*, the first big-screen film in the series without any original cast member. In the hands of the "Next Generation" crew, the theatrical series is alive and well. Exciting, darker than expected and

still funny when you need it to be, *First Contact* reunites Captain Picard (Patrick Stewart) with the Borg, those ominous alien beings who a few years earlier had nearly "assimilated" the good captain on a fine two-part TV episode. To take the Borg on, the filmmakers take a cue from *Star Trek IV* and travel back in time to save Earth in the "present." The Borg are a terrific foil for Picard and company — dangerous, unpredictable and almost undefeatable — exactly what we have come to expect from good villains. The entire cast performs with accustomed efficiency, and even characters other than Data (Brent Spiner steals the show as usual) are allowed to earn a laugh. Technical credits are commendable, and there are a couple of cameos to bring on a smile. Director Frakes has done a yeoman's job. (Available letterboxed and pan & scan) ★★★ $14.99

Star Wars

(1977, 121 min, US, George Lucas) A little while ago and not too far away, a man nearly reinvented the American film industry. What can you say about a movie which is one of the biggest and most influential cultural phenomena of the late 20th century? This is no exaggeration, as dialogue, characters and situations from Lucas' trilogy have crept into the American psyche since this blockbuster first appeared on movie screens. Mark Hamill, Harrison Ford, Carrie Fisher, Alec Guinness and the voice of James Earl Jones are now icons, identified primarily (at least by anyone under the age of thirty) as their characters in *Star Wars*. One reason for this influence is the fact that Lucas himself was drawing on the myths and fables present in American film throughout its history, particularly in early serials and later Hollywood westerns. The story is nothing new, and was probably cribbed from various cowboy movies and Kurosawa's *The Hidden Fortress*: a group of motley adventurers must rescue a princess from the clutches of an evil tyrant, and then rally their forces to destroy his empire. What Lucas did was to combine this primal story line with dazzling (and cutting-edge at the time) special effects, sound, production design and an otherworldly galaxy of alien characters, thus making it appealing to everyone with a taste for adventure, fantasy, romance or fable. *Star Wars* shines, a rousing and wonderful entertainment for all ages, worthy of its status as groundbreaker and blockbuster. Followed by *The Empire Strikes Back* and *Return of the Jedi*. Remastered and re-released theatrically in 1997 with added footage (wait till you see Jabba!) and enhanced special effects. ★★★★ $19.99

Stardust Memories

(1980, 88 min, US, Woody Allen) Allen's autobiographical statement is a daring if rambling film which pits the artist against his audience. Allen plays a comedian/writer/director whose growing legion of fans crave more comedies while he is preoccupied with human suffering. Starring Charlotte Rampling, Marie-Christine Barrault and Jessica Harper. ★★½ $14.99

Stargate

(1994, 125 min, US, Roland Emmerich) From the director of *Universal Soldier* comes this entertaining if lightweight sci-fi thriller which plays like *Star Wars* meets *Indiana Jones*. Kurt Russell and the ever-engaging James Spader costar as a military burnout and nerdy Egyptologist, respectively, who are assigned to decipher the markings on an ancient discovery. When it turns out it's a galactic gateway, they travel to the other side where peace-loving desert tribes are enslaved by an evil, skin-shedding alien (Jaye Davidson, who here cannot muster more than a "strike a pose" method of acting). Though the story line is lackluster and the finale is more Stallone than sci-fi, the film is greatly benefited by an intriguing premise, impressive costumes and good special effects. A dress rehearsal for director Emmerich's next film, *Independence Day*. (Available letterboxed and pan & scan) ★★½ $14.99

Starlight Hotel

(1987, 94 min, New Zealand, Sam Pillsbury) Fine family fare about a 12-year-old waif who sets off across the New Zealand countryside in search of her father, and instead finds herself on the run with a fugitive from the law. Though lacking the panache of *The Journey of Natty Gann*, it nonetheless stands on its own as an interesting variation of the buddy-road movie. ★★★

Starman

(1984, 115 min, US, John Carpenter) Jeff Bridges' captivating performance highlights this good-natured and extremely satisfying Carpenter sci-fi adventure about an alien on the run from the authorities. Karen Allen plays a widow who is at first kidnapped by the extraterrestrial (who has taken on the form of her late husband), but who later helps and befriends him. ★★★½ $9.99

Stars and Bars

(1988, 94 min, US, Pat O'Connor) Wacky and offbeat comedy with Daniel Day-Lewis as a British art dealer who travels to the American South to purchase a prized painting and is introduced to one of the craziest families this side of the Vanderhoffs. With Harry Dean Stanton as the family patriarch, Martha Plimpton, Joan Cusack, Steven Wright, Laurie Metcalf, Glenne Headly and Spalding Gray. ★★ $19.99

The Stars Fell on Henrietta

(1995, 110 min, US, James Keach) Set in Depression-era Texas, this nostalgic if colorless character study gives Robert Duvall another chance to deliver a sterling portrayal of a gruff but lovable curmudgeon. He plays Mr. Cox, an aging wildcatter who happens upon the struggling farm of Mr. and Mrs. Day (Aidan Quinn and Frances Fisher), promptly claiming there's oil on their property. Mr. Cox sets about to raise the money (sometimes illegally) as Mr. Day falls under the spell cast by the self-proclaimed "oil man" and begins drilling, risking his farm in the process. Much like *The Rainmaker*, a stranger making promises puts the family at odds, though there's little doubt as to the outcome. With such an exploitable premise, the film is curiously tame, most scenes maintaining a listless pace, which inevitably works against its strong ensemble, good period design and lovely cinematography. ★★½ $9.99

The Stars Look Down

(1939, 110 min, GB, Carol Reed) Exquisite performances by Michael Redgrave and Margaret Lockwood highlight this searing film adaptation of A.J. Cronin's novel about a poor Welsh mining family's struggles and their son's resolution to run for public office. ★★★★ $14.99

Starstruck

(1982, 95 min, Australia, Gillian Armstrong) A zesty, new-wave musical brimming with infectious tunes, inspired choreography and enchanting performances. Jackie, a winsome waitress at the family pub in Sydney, has a hankering for stardom; and, with the help of her mite-sized manager/cousin, sets out to launch her singing career. Armstrong directed this ebullient Australian comedy with an abundance of flair and originality. ★★★½ $19.99

Start the Revolution without Me

(1970, 91 min, US, Bud Yorkin) Engaging spoof set during the French Revolution with Gene Wilder and Donald Sutherland chewing the scenery as two pairs of twins separated at birth; reunited years later resulting in cases of mistaken identity between the aristocracy and peasantry. ★★★ $14.99

State of Grace

(1990, 130 min, US, Phil Joanou) Gary Oldman and Sean Penn star in director Joanou's *Mean Streets*-like vision of the inner workings of Manhattan's Irish-American mob. Based on journalistic accounts of the "Westies," a real-life Hell's Kitchen band of thugs known for their brutal savagery, the film accurately depicts the erratic and unpredictable violence which rules the streets of New York. Oldman delivers a stellar performance as Jackie Flannery, a dangerously loose cannon in the gang. Sean Penn stars as a childhood friend who returns to the neighborhood after a long absence. Highly stylized, *State of Grace* centers on the attempted union of the "Westies" with the Italian mafia in the mid-'70s. Ed Harris is good in support as the leader of the Irish gang. ★★★ $9.99

State of Siege

(1973, 120 min, France, Constantin Costa-Gavras) This tense drama of the kidnapping of a U.S. "special advisor" provides the background for the uncovering of the United States' true role in the internal affairs of Latin America. (French with English subtitles) ★★★ $19.99

State of the Union

(1948, 122 min, US, Frank Capra) A well-scripted political comedy based on the Pulitzer Prize-winning play by Howard Lindsay and Russell Crouse. Spencer Tracy gives a commanding performance as an idealistic industrialist who is drafted as a presidential nominee. Katharine Hepburn is the estranged wife who returns to her husband for the sake of the campaign, where the candidate is torn between his ambition for office and the integrity of his wife's uncompromising and outspoken views.

Angela Lansbury is especially noteworthy as Tracy's rich sponsor. ★★★ $19.99

The State of Things

(1982, 110 min, West Germany/US, Wim Wenders) Wenders' *8½* is an imaginative and engrossing picture dealing with the condition of the European art film and its corrupting nemesis: Hollywood. The story concerns the crew and cast of a film who find themselves marooned in Portugal and their production money and film stock depleted. The crew, waiting for more money, must kill time. A compelling meditation on the inertia of the moviemaking process, creative impasses and the impossibility of telling stories anymore. (Filmed in English) ★★★

Static

(1985, 93 min, US, Mark Romanek) A young inventor (Keith Gordon) prepares to launch his earth-shattering new creation (a TV which gets pictures of Heaven) with the aid of his new-wave friend and his ex-Green Beret evangelist cousin. Gordon co-wrote the uneven though imaginative script. ★★

The Station

(1992, 92 min, Italy, Sergio Rubini) Charming, romantic and quintessentially European, *The Station* tells of an unlikely love between a nerdy railway station attendant and an elegant young woman. The fastidious young man, who lives on an elaborate timetable both in his work and in his life, finds his order coming to an end after the mysterious woman, seemingly on the run, enters the station in the middle of the night to wait for the morning train. Their relationship, first as a typical clerk to an indifferent customer, develops into more after trouble descends on the station and the man is forced to take drastic action to defend them. Deliberate in pacing, but rich in nuance and emotion, this quiet, gentle love story is a real delight. (Italian with English subtitles) ★★★½ $89.99

The Stationmaster's Wife (Bolwiessar)

(1977, 111 min, West Germany, Rainer Werner Fassbinder) Originally a two-part TV series running 200 minutes, this shorter version is Fassbinder's version of "Madame Bovary" in a Nazi Germany rotting from within. Kurt Raab is the sheepish, masochistic stationmaster who suspects his wife's infidelities. But not wanting to risk losing the small luxuries to which he has become accustomed, he chooses not to act upon his suspicions. Elisabeth Trissenaar gives a mesmerizing performance as a woman in love with her carnal desires and the power they give her. Fassbinder's visual style is rich, gorgeous, and suffocating, mirroring their bourgeois lifestyle. (German with English subtitles) ★★★ $29.99

Stavisky

(1974, 117 min, France, Alain Resnais) Starting off with the details from a real 1930s French political scandal, Resnais adroitly blends facts — from the real case with Leon Trotsky's arrival in exile — with fiction in presenting this absorbing drama about moral degeneracy and political corruption. Jean-Paul Belmondo plays Serge Alexandre (nee Sacha Stavisky), a suave, elegantly-attired con man who concocts a financial swindle that soon involves powerful government officials and high-ranking police. Resnais creates a visually breathtaking and chilling allegory of France's political situation on the eve of Fascist aggression. Costarring Charles Boyer. (French with English subtitles) ★★★½ $59.99

Stay Hungry

(1976, 103 min, US, Bob Rafelson) Jeff Bridges stars as a Southern pre-yuppie who buys a gym as part of a business deal, only to gain an appreciation for the people he exploits while learning something about himself as well. Also with Sally Field and Arnold

Starstruck

Schwarzenegger in his first major acting role. ★★½ $9.99

Stay Tuned

(1992, 89 min, US, Peter Hyams) The irony is delicious: former TV stars John Ritter and Pam Dawber finally make the transition to the big screen only to be sucked back into the "television from Hell" (and it really is) in this comical boob tube spoof. Ritter plays a video addict whose ritual TV watching is given a twist when Satan's helper (Jeffrey Jones) offers him 666 channels of the ultimate in interactive television – it's "You Bet Your Life" meets *The Running Man*. Though not as consistently savage as it might have been, *Stay Tuned* does offer some funny parodies – especially of "Three's Company" and an animated segment by Chuck Jones. ★★ $9.99

Stealing Beauty

(1996, 119 min, GB/Italy, Bernardo Bertolucci) Judging by the ad campaign, box art and trailer, one might expect this tale of sexual awakening in the sun-drenched hills of Tuscany to be no more than a panderous exercise in lechery on the part of aging director Bertolucci. And to whatever degree this is true (and it is, a little), *Stealing Beauty* is also a remarkably astute and touching examination of the young woman's innocent, oddly chaste, desire for sexual initiation. The story revolves around a 19-year-old American (Liv Tyler) staying with family friends at their homestead; a kind of remnant hippie artist commune nestled in the farmland outside of Siena. Clearly out of her element and surrounded by middle-aged adults, she turns to an ailing houseguest (Jeremy Irons) for solace and comfort. More style than substance, the film's lush settings and sensual photography give the impression that Bertolucci penned his script as an excuse to hang out filming at beautiful Tuscan villas for a summer. Nevertheless, the result is a very satisfying and refreshing look at romance amongst the privileged artist class. Delivering a marvelously natural performance, newcomer Tyler, who has no apparent fear of the camera, proves herself a worthy lead. ★★★ $99.99

Stealing Heaven

(1988, 108 min, GB, Clive Donner) Peter de Lint stars as Peter Abelard, a 12th-century French philosopher and churchman who broke taboo and secretly married one of his students, Heloise (Kim Thomson). Denholm Elliott co-stars as her wrathful father in this passionate tale of forbidden love. ★★★

Stealing Home

(1988, 98 min, US, Steven Kampmann) America's two favorite pastimes, baseball and sex, take it on the chin in this uneven though well-acted comedy-drama. Mark Harmon stars as a down-and-out ballplayer who, upon hearing of the death of a childhood friend, reminisces and reflects upon their relationship two decades earlier. Partially told in flashback, the film is equally divided between the present and past, and is far more successful in the scenes involving the latter. Jodie Foster gives a wonderful performance as Harmon's free-spirited mentor. ★★½ $19.99

Steamboat Bill, Jr.

(1927, 71 min, US, Charles Riesner) One of Buster Keaton's finest comedies casts him as a returning college graduate who must prove himself to his burly father, Steamboat Bill, Sr. The cyclone at the climax gives Keaton the chance to reconcile with his father and demonstrate the comic genius of one of the all-time great physical comedians. ★★★★ $29.99

Steaming

(1985, 95 min, GB, Joseph Losey) Losey's last film is an adaptation of the critically acclaimed play by Neal Dunn which features a stellar female cast of Vanessa Redgrave, Sarah Miles, Patti Love and Diana Dors (in her final role). Set on "ladies' day" at a London bathhouse, we find six women, of wildly divergent backgrounds, coming together to discuss their intimate secrets and commiserate about their place in the world. The production is perhaps a bit over-stagey, but it is carried by first-rate performances. ★★½

Steel Magnolias

(1989, 115 min, US, Herbert Ross) A fine ensemble cast including Sally Field, Shirley MacLaine, Olympia Dukakis, and Julia Roberts is featured in this heartrending, sentimental and funny comedy-drama. The story centers on the friendship of six women in a small Louisiana town who meet periodically at the local beauty shop. Field heads this terrific cast as mother of newlywed Roberts, whose marriage is much of the focus of the film. MacLaine is hilarious as the town curmudgeon; and Dukakis is splendid as the gossipy town matriarch. The first half of the film suffers from sloppy editing, and sometimes the characters seem interchangeable with other Southern-themed works, but the performances are so captivating the film's flaws can be overlooked. ★★½ $14.99

Steelyard Blues

(1973, 93 min, US, Alan Myerson) A group of misfits (including Jane Fonda, Donald Sutherland and Peter Boyle) band together to restore a vintage airplane, hoping to fly away to paradise. Amiable counterculture hijinks. Written by David S. Ward (*The Sting*). ★★½ $19.99

Stella

(1990, 109 min, US, John Erman) Even the great Bette Midler can strike out on occasion, as proved by this turgid remake of the perennial classic. Bette plays the sacrificing and (supposedly) slovenly mother of teenager Trini Alvarado; but she's more schizophrenic as one moment she's wise and creative and the next crude with no fashion sense. It just doesn't work in the 1990s. Stick with Barbara Stanwyck's 1937 version. John Goodman, Stephen Collins, Eileen Brennan and Marsha Mason co-star. ★½ $19.99

Stella Dallas

(1937, 111 min, US, King Vidor) Barbara Stanwyck gives a stellar performance in this classic tearjerker as a mother who sacrifices all for the sake of her daughter. Anne Shirley plays her daughter. Far superior to the 1990 remake with Bette Midler. ★★★½ $19.99

Step Lively

(1944, 88 min, US, Tim Whelan) Frank Sinatra and George Murphy star in this fast-paced musical version of the Marx Brothers' *Room Service*. Murphy plays the part of a Broadway producer who, despite no financial resources, schemes to put on a show. ★★★ $19.99

The Stepfather

(1987, 98 min, US, Joseph Ruben) This frightening thriller gets most of its chills because it could so easily be true. Terry O'Quinn is a meek little guy who wants a perfect family and home, and by damn, *he's going to have it* – no matter what the cost or who gets killed in the process. ★★★½

The Stepfather II

(1989, 86 min, US, Jeff Burr) Terry O'Quinn reprises the role of Daddy Dearest, now escaped from the loony bin, employed as a marriage counselor and looking for love (Meg Foster). An insipid rehash of the original. (Followed by an equally stupid third film in the series.) ★ $9.99

The Stepford Wives

(1975, 115 min, US, Bryan Forbes) Finally released on video more than twenty years after its initial theatrical run, this "domestic" horror film might be considered a misogynistic (or to use '70s-speak, "chauvinistic") fantasy seemingly out of date in the modern '90s. But its horrific themes take on an additional, unexpected resonance in the age of cloning and other innovations which were science fiction two decades ago. Katharine Ross stars as a young woman who moves to a seemingly perfect planned community with her hotshot lawyer husband. She soon finds, however, that her aspiration to become a professional photographer makes her stick out amongst the apron-clad hausfraus who smilingly serve their husbands' every need and whim. Digging a little deeper beneath the happy surface of Stepford, she and her equally-independent best friend (a wonderful Paula Prentiss) discover the horrifying secret of the Stepford Mens' Association and their man-made paradise. Perhaps a bit slow to begin with, the film delivers quite a few good shocks in its final reel. ★★★ $14.99

Stephen King's Thinner

(1996, 92 min, US, Tom Holland) A selfish lawyer accidentally but recklessly runs down the daughter of an ancient gypsy mystic and becomes the object of a sinister curse in this adaptation of a Stephen King story written under his "Richard Bachman" pseudonym. Extremely overweight and always unsuccessfully dieting, the lawyer (Robert John Burke) suddenly finds himself losing fat at an alarming rate. Pleased at first, he realizes the horror of his situation when he cannot stop or even slow down his wasting away. He must confront the old gypsy and, with the help of a mob contact (Joe Mantegna) he has defended in the past, persuade him to lift the curse. One could overanalyze this scenario, its moral implications and parallels to drug abuse or AIDS, but it's really just a basic horror film. Competently acted and produced, it's satisfying while it lasts but leaves no lasting impression. The fat-to-

S

Stonewall

thin makeup effects and Burke's performance are particularly well done. ★★½ $99.99

Steppenwolf

(1974, 105 min, US, Fred Haines) Max von Sydow, Dominique Sanda and Pierre Clementi star in this fascinating film about the psychological and philosophical pilgrimage of Herr Haller, a man torn between the bourgeois respectability he has achieved and his private anti-social impulses. Herman Hesse's novel is not an ideal novel for a film adaptation, though director Haines manages some impressive visual touches. ★★½ $59.99

The Sterile Cuckoo

(1969, 107 min, US, Alan J. Pakula) Liza Minnelli gives a heartrending performance as a lonely and eccentric college student searching for love and acceptance. She finds the former in the unlikely person of shy Wendell Burton. A perceptive and touching look at first love. ★★★½ $49.99

Stevie

(1978, 102 min, GB, Robert Enders) Glenda Jackson stars in this wonderful character study of British poetess Stevie Smith. Adapted from Hugh Whitemore's hit London play, the film co-stars Mona Washbourne and Alec McCowen, but it's Jackson's show as she celebrates love, family, and her own fascination with the English language. ★★★★

Sticky Fingers

(1988, 97 min, US, Catlin Adams) Two dizzy roommates "borrow" from the stash of cash they're holding for friend Loretta Devine, and go overboard. The film tries for the slap-dash energy of the crazy romps of yore, but it's mostly wasted in unfunny and contrived situations. Helen Slater and Melanie Mayron are the roommates. ★½

Still of the Night

(1982, 91 min, US, Robert Benton) Hitchcockian murder mystery about a psychiatrist (Roy Scheider) who tries to solve the murder of one of his patients, falling in love with the prime suspect (Meryl Streep) in the process. Streep chain-smokes and chews the scenery in this somewhat involved thriller

which, like most Hitchcock imitations, fails to measure up to the master. ★★½ $9.99

The Stilts (Los Zancos)

(1984, 95 min, Spain, Carlos Saura) Director Saura returns to the familiar surroundings of theatrical life and sexual obsession. An aging, recently widowed professor initiates an affair with his beautiful neighbor, who is married to the charismatic leader of a local theatre company. In an attempt to retain her affection, the professor writes a play for the troupe, which is performed on stilts. Against this backdrop, the trio play out an anguished and explosive scenario infused with unrestrained desires and emotional manipulation. (Spanish with English subtitles) ★★★ $24.99

The Sting

(1973, 129 min, US, George Roy Hill) Delightful Oscar-winning comedy set in 1930s Chicago with Paul Newman and Robert Redford as con artists out to "sting" gangster Robert Shaw. Marvelous supporting cast includes Eileen Brennan, Charles Durning, Ray Walston and Harold Gould. There's so many twists you won't know what's what or who's who. Winner of seven Oscars, including one for David S. Ward's first-rate screenplay. ★★★★ $19.99

Stir Crazy

(1980, 111 min, US, Sidney Poitier) The second and most popular of the Gene Wilder-Richard Pryor comedies, and it's very funny. The guys are two bungling thieves who are sent to prison; quite ill-prepared for life behind bars. With Georg Stanford Brown, JoBeth Williams and Craig T. Nelson. ★★★ $14.99

Stolen Kisses

(1968, 90 min, France, François Truffaut) The third episode in the Antoine Doinel series finds Jean-Pierre Léaud, our inept but lovable hero, doing what he must to stay on the furtive heels of love and romance. A poignant and comic tale at the foibles of romance. (Dubbed) ★★★½ $59.99

A Stolen Life

(1946, 107 min, US, Curtis Bernhardt) Bette Davis lets loose as a set of twins, one of whom

takes the other's place in marriage to the man they both loved when her sibling dies in a plane crash. Not Bette's best, but more than interesting thanks to La Davis' histrionics. ★★½ $19.99

The Stone Boy

(1984, 93 min, US, Christopher Cain) Robert Duvall and Glenn Close star as the confused parents of a young boy who kills his older brother in a hunting accident. Exceptionally portrayed by Jason Presson, the boy goes into shock and is unable to explain the circumstances leading up to the shooting, and sinks deep within a grim-faced exterior. Duvall delivers an understated performance as a Montana rancher caught in a situation beyond his understanding but compelled to muster the strength needed to heal his family and reconcile with his son. Excellent support by Wilford Brimley and Frederic Forrest contribute to make this atypical Hollywood film a beautiful and important achievement. ★★★ $59.99

Stones for Ibarra

(1988, 101 min, US, Jack Gold) An American couple (Glenn Close, Keith Carradine) escape the rat race of big city life and embark on a journey across rural Mexico in 1959. Their odyssey takes a 360 degree turn, however, when they learn one of them is suffering from a terminal disease. A thoughtful, tender drama elevated by touching performances from its leads. ★★½

Stonewall

(1996, 93 min, GB, Nigel Finch) Far from being a dry, fictionalized account of the people involved in the 1969 Stonewall Riots, this adaptation of Martin Duberman's book and the final film by director Finch (who died from AIDS during final editing) is instead a rollicking musical drama that successfully blends gay history and queer fabulousness to wonderful effect. This what-might-have-been-happening on the days before that fateful summer night's tale features Matty (Frederick Weller), a studly country boy who arrives in New York City and almost immediately becomes involved with a rambunctious group of black, white and Latino drag queens. He becomes romantically involved with one particular diva, La Miranda, a saucy and hopelessly romantic drag queen. As La Miranda and her friends suffer from police harassment and the mob-owned and operated bars, Matty begins to become politicized, and the two forces combined are not to be reckoned with! A passionate, spirited tale — torn from gay history — that is alternately funny, touching, upsetting and even a bit educational. ★★★ $94.99

Stop Making Sense

(1984, 99 min, US, Jonathan Demme) Visual wit and dynamic rhythms faithfully and inventively convey the near-religious fervor of a Talking Heads concert. Demme's rockumentary won laurels for being a new breed of performance film, one which showcases a band's unique personality rather than the director's pyrotechnics. Shunning clips of frothing crowds and backstage doodlings, Demme and figure-head David Byrne have constructed a film which builds to a rousing crescendo as additional performers join the stage with each successive song, augmenting what begins with a solo acoustic rendering of "Psycho Killer" by Byrne. Truly a scintillating celebration of rock `n' roll. ★★★★

Stop! or My Mom Will Shoot

(1992, 87 min, US, Roger Spottiswoode) It's the ultimate high-concept film: Sylvester Stallone and Estelle Getty star in this flat and predictable comedy about a Los Angeles police sergeant who (and here's the concept, folks) teams up with his sixtysomething mom. While visiting her son, she witnesses a murder and demands to be part of the investigation. Stallone, to his credit, is still trying to change his image, following *Oscar* with another comedy. But the only constant is that Stallone is stranded in yet another weak entry. Curiously, Stallone does give one of his better performances of the last few years. Hey Sly: You made some good movies in the '70s, but continue picking films like this, and it'll be *Stop! My Career Is Over.* ★½ $19.99

Stop the Church

(1990, 30 min, US, Robert Hilferty) Gaining notoriety after PBS rejected airing the program, this political film, with its sympathies clearly on the protesters' side, documents ACT-UP's discussions, planning and execution of a march and "die-in" at St. Patrick's Cathedral in 1989. With its stated goal of "offending" the church and its anti-gay New York diocese leader, Cardinal O'Conner, the action was organized to protest the Catholic Church's insensitive position on gay rights as well as AIDS awareness and treatment. With a shaky hand-held camera focused on the action, director Hilferty's best moments are at an ACT-UP meeting, where the morality and righteousness of a protest within the church building itself is heatedly discussed. Whether one approves of the ensuing protest (not to be confused with another demonstration in which protesters received and then spit out the Host), the film is a fascinating exposé of radical political thought and contentious action. ★★½ $39.99

Stop the World I Want to Get Off

(1966, 98 min, GB, Philip Saville) This lively film adaptation of Anthony Newley-Leslie Bricusse's smash London/Broadway musical is filmed directly from a staged performance, inexplicably minus its star Newley. Tony Tanner (who would go on to become a Broadway director) takes over the role of Littlechap, a British Everyman who, through song (and what classics they are), observes his life – including courtship, marriage and infidelity. This was one of the groundbreaking stage musicals of its era, and the film version nicely captures the play's originality and vitality. Songs include "What Kind of Fool Am I" and "Gonna Build a Mountain." ★★★ $19.99

Storm Boy

(1976, 90 min, Australia, Henri Safran) Set in the wind-swept wilderness area of South Australia, this children's story of discovery, friendship and growing up centers around a young boy who lives in isolation with his fisherman father. While exploring the dunes one

day, he meets and befriends an Aborigine teenager and a beautiful pelican and the three venture off and share many adventures. ★★½

The Storm Within (Les Parents Terribles)

(1948, 98 min, France, Jean Cocteau) This adaptation of Cocteau's play, considered by many to be his finest work, is a riveting psychological tragicomedy about the complicated tangle of sexuality, parental rivalry and jealousy within a troubled family. Cocteau creates a claustrophobic intimacy (only two sets, static camera, many close-ups, no exteriors) as this incestuously close family bares its soul. Yvonne deBray is wonderful as the domineering mother, Jean Marais plays the son, and Josette Day is the woman he (and his father) loves. (French with English subtitles) ★★★★ $29.99

Stormy Monday

(1988, 93 min, GB, Mike Figgis) Melanie Griffith and Sting (in one of his few good performances) star in this moody and atmospheric mystery-thriller set in the dreary city of Newcastle. Tommy Lee Jones plays an American businessman who is trying to take advantage of the town's depressed economy by snatching up real estate, including Sting's jazz club. ★★★ $14.99

Stormy Weather

(1943, 77 min, US, Andrew L. Stone) A dazzling, high-spirited tribute to the legendary Bill "Bojangles" Robinson. Featuring the music of Lena Horne, Cab Calloway and Fats Waller. Tunes include "Ain't Misbehavin'" and Lena's sultry version of the title number. ★★★ $19.99

The Story of a Three Day Pass

(1967, 87 min, France, Melvin van Peebles) Van Peebles' film about an African-American soldier's affair with a French woman while on leave in Paris in the 1960s is an entertaining love story. The two principals, Harry Baird and Nicole Berger act as conduits on a surreal journey exploring race relations in the military and how some American mores become irrational in other societies. While at times flawed, van Peebles' cut and camerawork stand out as he pays homage to Luis Buñuel and Jean Cocteau. ★★½ $19.99

The Story of Adele H.

(1975, 97 min, France, François Truffaut) Isabelle Adjani portrays the young heroine whose obsessive attachment to an uncaring scoundrel in the military drives her to the brink of madness...and beyond. An exceptionally told and acted drama based on the memoirs of the daughter of French literary giant Victor Hugo. (French with English subtitles) ★★★★ $19.99

The Story of Boys and Girls

(1991, 92 min, Italy, Pupi Avati) *The Story of Boys and Girls* is a sumptuously filmed parable about two disparate Italian families coming together for a nuptual banquet signifying the joining of the clans. Set for the most part on a small Italian farm, the film details the fabulous 20-course feast over which these two families (one of the intellectual city class, the other of rural peasant stock) meet for the

The Story of Qiu Ju

first time. Filled with some wonderfully mirthful moments, the film uses the festivities as the platform for some time-honored (especially in Italian filmmaking) commentary on class differences as well as the occasional amorous roll in the hay. (Italian with English subtitles) ★★★ $19.99

The Story of Louis Pasteur

(1936, 85 min, US, William Dieterle) Paul Muni won an Oscar for his detailed performance as French scientist Louis Pasteur. Hollywood storytelling and scientific heroics mesh perfectly in this first-rate biography. ★★★★ $19.99

The Story of "O"

(1975, 97 min, France, Just Jaeckin) Based on the classic novel by Pauline Reage, this controversial and, to many, shocking film introduces Corinne Clery as "O," a woman who must sexually surrender in total submission to her demanding lover. Followed by nine more "stories." (Dubbed) ★★

The Story of Qiu Ju

(1992, 100 min, China, Zhang Yimou) This collaboration between Zhang and actress Gong Li bears little resemblance to their previous period dramas such as *Raise the Red Lantern* and *Ju Dou*. Unlike those examinations of feudal China, *Qiu Ju* is an almost upbeat and decidedly proletarian look at one woman's crusade for justice. When her husband is severly beaten by the local party boss, Qiu Ju, a poor peasant woman, demands an apology. Upon his repeated refusals, she takes her case to ever-higher courts and encounters every stone wall the byzantine Chinese bureaucracy can put in her way. *Qiu Ju* is remarkable in its simplicity; Zhang has stripped his cinematic style to the bare minimum, eschewing the luxurious mise-en-scène and stunning photography of his other works. As a Chinese Mother Courage, Gong Li, in one of her best performances, offers a wry portrayal. (Chinese with English subtitles) ★★★½ $19.99

Story of Sin

(1975, 128 min, Poland, Walerian Borowczyk) From the director of *Immoral Tales* comes this elegant, full-bodied melodrama, set in turn-of-the-century Poland, tracing the life of a young girl, strictly raised, whose downfall is presaged when she opens her heart and soul to a married man. Misfortunes befall our innocent heroine as she becomes pregnant, is forced to get rid of the baby and slinks into degrading prostitution. Adopting the position that love has no place in an immoral, exploitative world, the harrowing drama takes an erotic, albeit sluggish, angle on *amour fou*. (Polish with English subtitles) ★★★

Story of the Late Chrysanthemum

(1939, 115 min, Japan, Kenji Mizoguchi) Bristling with passion and filmed with startling imagery, this poignant tale chronicles the life of a Kabuki actor in 1880s Tokyo. The young man, Kikunosuke, despondent after being ridiculed by other members of his father's famous troupe, returns home and begins an affair with a servant girl and, on his father's insistence, sets out on his own. The responsibility for both their survival and his eventual rise as a celebrated actor rests with his wife, Okoku, who sacrifices everything, even her health, for his success. This heartbreaker borders on over-sentimentality but is still a fascinating classic of doomed love. (Remastered print) (Japanese with English subtitles) ★★★½ $29.99

The Story of Vernon and Irene Castle

(1939, 93 min, US, H.C. Potter) The last of the Fred Astaire-Ginger Rogers 1930s musicals for RKO is an appealing bio of the early 20th-century dancing team. Fred and Ginger's dancing is up to par, but it certainly doesn't rate with their other 1930s classics. ★★½ $19.99

Story of Women

(1988, 110 min, France, Claude Chabrol) Isabelle Huppert delivers her most impressive performance since her debut in *The Lacemaker* in Chabrol's chilling and thought-provoking drama set in Vichy, France. Huppert plays a wife whose husband is away at the front. She is persuaded to perform an abortion on a dis-

traught neighbor. In a desperate attempt to support herself, she begins offering the service to others; but she is soon arrested by the fascist officials. The drama, based on a real-life criminal case, recounts the story without sentiment and flawlessly evokes the tense mood of an occupied people. But it is Huppert's spellbinding portrayal of an independent, vunerable and, at times, unsympathetic character which gives the film its lasting power. (French with English subtitles) ★★★½ $29.99

Storyville

(1992, 112 min, US, Mark Frost) Frost, who co-produced "Twin Peaks," debuts as a director with this tale of dirty politics, sex and murder set in a moody, steamy things-are-sort-of-different-around-these-parts atmosphere. James Spader plays an ambitious young man running for the Senate position recently vacated by the indictment, and later death, of his father. Jason Robards co-stars as Spader's more ambitious, self-serving and unscrupulous uncle, using his own private agenda as he guides the candidate's career. The campaign runs into trouble when Spader becomes involved in a murder investigation that threatens to expose more deep secrets than he could imagine. Instead of anticipating the quirks and whims of David Lynch, viewers should set their expectations to more mainstream fare and enjoy what winds up being an involving romantic courtroom mystery with a little gratuitous sex and violence thrown in. ★★½ $19.99

La Strada

(1954, 115 min, Italy, Federico Fellini) Fellini's tender and haunting tale of a brutish circus strongman (Anthony Quinn) and his sidekick (Giulietta Masina) whose loneliness and solitude bind them together in a tenuous relationship. A truly poetic classic and an Academy Award winner. (Italian with English subtitles) ★★★★ $29.99

Straight from the Heart

(1988, 92 min, Canada, Léa Pool) Returning from a harrowing trip to Nicaragua, where he

has witnessed and photographed the horrors of war, prize-winning photojournalist Pierre returns home to Montreal only to find that Sarah and David, his lovers in a ten-year ménage à trois, have both left him. This absorbing drama, unusual for its matter-of-fact approach to bisexuality, explores the man's devastated life — from his futile attempts to reunite the threesome, his pain and loneliness at being abandoned, his recovery through the love of a handsome deaf-mute and his wanderings through the city photographing urban decay. An intriguing, melancholy love story and quiet study of a man's emotional void, reminiscent in part of Alain Tanner's *In the White City*. (French with English subtitles) ★★★ $24.99

Straight Out of Brooklyn

(1991, 91 min, US, Matty Rich) Nineteen-year-old Rich wrote and directed this remarkable and highly personal exposé of life in the projects. The story follows Dennis, a teenager who thinks of nothing but getting out of the ghetto. Plagued by his savagely alcoholic father, and with nowhere to go, he ultimately concocts an outrageous and ill-advised scheme to rob a drug dealer. While lacking the power and sophistication of *Boyz n the Hood*, this gritty and hard-hitting film is nonetheless an important milestone in the development of African-American filmmaking in the 1990s. $14.99

Straight Talk

(1992, 91 min, US, Barnet Kellman) Dolly Parton stars in this mildly entertaining comedy about a good-hearted country girl who gets fired from her job as a dance instructor and decides that Chicago is the place she ought to be. Once she arrives in the Windy City, she manages to get herself a job as a telephone operator at a radio station. On her first day at the job, she searches for the bathroom and ends up in the control room where she's mistaken for the new on-air psychologist. Of course, she's a hit with the listeners, a profitable problem for the station manager (Griffin Dunne) and the subject of an investigation from cynical newspaper reporter James Woods, who is completely out-of-sync with the rest of the cast. Look for cameos from John Sayles and Spalding Gray. ★★ $9.99

Straight Time

(1977, 114 min, US, Ulu Grosbard) A recently released con (Dustin Hoffman) finds himself trapped between an indifferent criminal system and his own unconscious bent toward self-destruction. A provocative if ambitious drama helped by a strong supporting cast. With Theresa Russell, Gary Busey and Harry Dean Stanton. ★★½ $14.99

Straight to Hell

(1987, 86 min, US, Alex Cox) Director Cox (*Repo Man*) takes on the spaghetti western, as the bizarre citizens of a desert hamlet find themselves at the mercy of two rival gangs. Only partially successful, it's pretentious though occasionally very amusing. Cast includes Dennis Hopper, Grace Jones and Elvis Costello. ★★

Guilietta Masina (l.) and Anthony Quinn in Fellini's classic *La Strada*

Stranger Than Paradise

Strait-Jacket

(1964, 89 min, US, William Castle) "Have Ax Will Travel" as Joan Crawford plays an ax murderer recently released from prison. She moves to a community where it seems she's up to her old tricks. Crawford's Gothic horror follow-up to *Baby Jane* is alternately campy and occasionally effective – though its little success obviously is in the star's hammy playing. ★★½ $59.99

The Strange Affair of Uncle Harry

(1945, 80 min, US, Robert Siodmak) George Sanders is affecting as a shy man who must take drastic steps to get out of the domineering psychological grip of his two scheming sisters in this impressive Hitchcockian small-town thriller. Geraldine Fitzgerald co-stars in this gripping and intelligent drama of obsession, hypochondria and the recuperative powers of love. ★★★ $19.99

Strange Behavior

(1981, 98 min, New Zealand, Michael Laughlin) A small college town is rocked by a series of brutal murders, which appear to be strangely linked to a psychology class experiment with an auto-suggestive drug. Laughlin sustains an eerie mood throughout, but the film loses some steam in the final half. Louise Fletcher, Michael Murphy and Fionna Lewis star. ★★½ $19.99

Strange Days

(1995, 145 min, US, Kathryn Bigelow) *Strange Days* is full of visceral thrills from start to finish, efficiently realized by its director Bigelow, though in the end there's no mistaking the influence of co-writer James Cameron. Set in Los Angeles on the eve of the new millennium, this slam-bang, hallucinatory thriller stars Ralph Fiennes as Lenny, a former policeman who peddles virtual reality discs containing the experiences of others. However, when one of his clients is murdered, Lenny becomes involved in an out-of-control pursuit to find her murderer, track a serial killer, and expose a police cover-up of a racially motivated murder. Angela Bassett also stars as Mace, a body-

guard and friend who helps Lenny, and occasionally acts as moral compass. The two outstanding performances by Fiennes and Bassett help immeasurably in giving the film an intelligence and passion which clearly elevates this actioner much the same way Sigourney Weaver and cast propelled *Aliens*. Bigelow's direction, in fact, is reminiscent of that film, where one exciting scene is followed by another, and the suspense is unrelenting. There is, however, a brutal rape sequence which could offend many viewers. (Available letterboxed and pan & scan) ★★★½ $19.99

Strange Interlude

(1932, 111 min, US, Robert Z. Leonard) Eugene O'Neill's powerful Pulitzer Prize-winning play of deceit and unrequited love gets a poignant and sturdy film adaptation – surprising considering the film retains O'Neill's innovative theatrical device of characters speaking their innermost thoughts. Norma Shearer, not the greatest actress of her time, rises to the demands of her most challenging role. She plays a woman who is haunted by the death of her fiancé. Her grief allows her to marry not for love, and to betray her husband, ironically, out of love. Clark Gable gives the film's richest performance as Shearer's longtime friend and lover. The film, at half the running time of the play, still manages to capture the essence of O'Neill's complex work. ★★★½ $19.99

Strange Invaders

(1983, 94 min, US, Michael Laughlin) When a small town gets taken over by aliens that look just like you and me, how can anybody tell? And does it make any difference? Fifties icons Kenneth Tobey and June Lockhart show young turks Paul LeMat, Nancy Allen, Louise Fletcher and Wallace Shawn how one went about vanquishing spacemen back in the old days. A generally entertaining spoof. ★★★

The Strange Love of Martha Ivers

(1946, 117 min, US, Lewis Milestone) Though its title suggests a '40s "B" potboiler, this gritty

melodrama is anything but. Barbara Stanwyck gives a smashing performance as a wealthy, neurotic wife who is haunted by a murder in her past. Kirk Douglas makes a fine film debut as her spineless husband. Their lives come apart when old friend Van Heflin returns to town, digging up the paast. ★★★ $12.99

The Stranger

(1946, 95 min, US, Orson Welles) Well-crafted thriller with Edward G. Robinson, in an unusual role as a "good guy," as a government agent who is sent to a small college town in Connecticut to track down an escaped Nazi war criminal. Orson Welles, as the feared German, is the embodiment of evil; Loretta Young also stars as Welles' unsuspecting fiancée. ★★★½ $19.99

The Stranger

(1988, 93 min, US, Adolfo Aristarain) A woman (Bonnie Bedelia) stricken with amnesia slowly realizes she is the only witness to a series of brutal murders and must piece together the mystery before the killer can find her. An intriguing premise is well-played, though it's not as suspenseful as it could have been. Peter Riegert co-stars. ★★½ $79.99

The Stranger

(1991, 120 min, India, Satyajit Ray) Ray's swan song (completed just months before his death) is a wonderful and fitting tribute to the artist's legacy – using simple cinematic jestures to tell a simple tale while delivering ample emotional, spiritual and narrative clout. The film opens when Anila (Mamata Shankar) – a prototypical Indian middle-class housewife – receives a letter from her long-lost uncle (Utpal Dutt) announcing that he will be in Calcutta and wishes to visit. Filled with suspicion that he is not who he says, but an imposter attempting to freeload, she and her family become obsessed with verifying his true identity. Over time, however, her husband (Depankar De) slowly warms to him and her son (Bikram Bannerjee) becomes fully entranced by his charm. As played by Dutt, the uncle is as enchanting and worldly wise as he is enigmatic and impenetrable, all the while playing cat and mouse with the family's suspicions and filling their lives with mystery. He's a bit of a spiritual trickster, mildly mocking his hosts while gently guiding them towards some inner-awakening. (Bengali with English subtitles) ★★★★ $59.99

A Stranger Among Us

(1992, 109 min, US, Sidney Lumet) This Lumet dramatic thriller so resembles Peter Weir's *Witness* that it has been dubbed *Vitness*. Melanie Griffith stars as a street-hardened New York undercover cop (not exactly typecasting) who is sent into Brooklyn's Hasidic community to root out a jewel thief/killer. All too predictably, of course, all of her coarse, unladylike behavior is transformed by the gentle, loving touch of this quaint people, but not before she tries her best to lead the Rabbi's son to temptation (her name, incidentally, is Emily *Eden*!). While Griffith does her best to overcome her mousy voice and newcomer Eric Thal delivers a sparkling performance as the Rabbi's son Ariel, the film can't overcome its formulaic

S

shallowness and fails to rise above its gushy, adoring view of the Hasidim. ★★ $19.99

Stranger on the First Floor

(1940, 64 min, US, Boris Ingster) Thanks to the stunning art direction by Van Nest Polglase (whose next project would be *Citizen Kane*), this little sleeper is considered by many to be the first true film noir. Taxi driver Elisha Cook, Jr. is sentenced to the chair for a rather brutal murder on the testimony of press reporter John McGuire. Now the reporter is having some doubts... Peter Lorre as the titular character gives his best performance since *M*. ★★★ $19.99

Stranger Than Paradise

(1984, 90 min, US, Jim Jarmusch) From the scroungy anomie of New York's Lower East Side to the snowy desolation of Cleveland to the sunny listlessness of Florida, this poker-faced neo-comedy follows the stillborn adventures of three amiable misfits in search of a natural habitat. Director Jarmusch's cool shaggy-dog minimalism is absurdly funny and boldly original. ★★★★

Strangers in Good Company

(1991, 101 min, Canada, Cynthia Scott) This spirited, low-budget gem documents the travails of eight elderly women who become stranded in the wilderness when their tour bus breaks down. Using their resources, they find an abandoned house and begin foraging for food. Tremendously diverse in character and background (they have a lesbian, a Native American, an African-American and a retired nun), they each have a story to tell and the film allows them to do just that. Filmed entirely on location with an ensemble of non-actors who essentially play themselves, *Strangers in Good Company* is a wonderfully heartwarming homage to the spirit of these women, and to the wondrous application of one's continual self-discovery. ★★★½ $9.99

Strangers on a Train

(1951, 101 min, US, Alfred Hitchcock) Hitchcock's slick psycological thriller tackles blackmail, murder and latent homosexuality as Farley Granger meets Robert Walker on a train and soon becomes an unwilling partner in crime. A superior effort that features a knockout ending which is exemplary of the unrelenting tension the Master of Suspense could create. The basis for the spoof *Throw Mama from the Train*. (The British version with two additional minutes) ★★★★ $19.99

Strapless

(1989, 103 min, GB, David Hare) With lush settings and a dreamy score (including Nat King Cole's "When I Fall in Love"), writer-director Hare sets a romantic tone in this unconventional film. Blair Brown (Hare's wife) portrays an American physician living in Britain who discovers love and confusion in both her carefree sister (Bridget Fonda) and an enigmatic businessman (Bruno Ganz). Hare's direction is fluent, his dialogue graceful; Brown beautifully depicts a woman on the uneasy path to self-discovery. ★★★ $14.99

Straw Dogs

(1972, 113 min, GB, Sam Peckinpah) Dustin Hoffman is the meek mathematician who, when his wife and home are attacked, finds catharsis and renewed masculinity in a violent, bloody confrontation. Peckinpah at his best. ★★★½ $9.99

Strawberry and Chocolate

(1993, 110 min, Cuba, Tomás Gutiérrez Alea & Juan Carlos Tabio) This Oscar nominee is both a delightful comedy of friendship and love as well as a surprisingly critical political drama. Set in modern-day Havana, the story centers on the unlikely friendship between David (Jorge Perugoría), a shy, straight and lost soul who blindly believes in the righteousness of the Revolution, and Diego (Vladimir Cruz), a swishy but intelligent, witty and opinionated gay man. Diego, who initially lusts after the innocent college student, soon seduces him — not through sex, however, but by his free-thinking appreciation of art, the "enemy's drug" (Johnny Walker Red) and his effervescent personality. David learns to take his political blinders off and in the process opens himself up to the differences in people — both politically and sexually. Insightful, joyful and humorous, *Strawberry and Chocolate* is a celebration of individuality in the face of conformity. (Spanish with English subtitles) ★★★½ $19.99

Strawberry Blonde

(1941, 97 min, US, Raoul Walsh) James Cagney is terrific as a young dentist whose life becomes a chaotic, emotional maze when he falls for a ravishing gold-digger (Rita Hayworth) only to marry a more proper Olivia deHavilland. Director Walsh offers up a timely blend of laughter, nostalgia, action and romance. ★★★ $19.99

The Strawberry Statement

(1970, 109 min, US, Stuart Haggman) Dated but interesting version of James Kunen's novel of '60s campus protest. Bruce Davison stars as a college jock who becomes involved with Kim Darby and a campus strike. Featuring an outstanding soundtrack containing many '60s rock standards. ★★★ $69.99

Stray Dog

(1949, 122 min, Japan, Akira Kurosawa) This stylized, non-samurai work from Kurosawa is an intense police thriller set in a seamy, war-ravaged Tokyo. Toshiro Mifune plays a rookie detective who loses his gun to a pickpocket and, fearing the pistol will fall into the hands of a killer, begins a desperate search through the underworld in an attempt to find the pistol and the thief. An under-appreciated murder mystery from the master of Japanese cinema. (Japanese with English subtitles) ★★★

Streamers

(1983, 118 min, US, Robert Altman) Altman utilizes the intensity of the theatrical experience with the opportunities offered through film in this adaptation of David Rabe's award-winning play. *Streamers* is an ensemble piece, set in a claustrophobic Army barracks, featuring four ill-assorted young soldiers waiting for assignments to Vietnam. Hidden fears and prejudices generate sexual intolerance, racial distrust and a misunderstanding which leads to violence. David Alan Grier, Matthew Modine, Mitchell Lichtenstein and Michael Wright star. The entire cast won Golden Lion Awards for Best Acting at the Venice Film Festival. ★★★ $14.99

Street Fighter

(1994, 95 min, US, Steven E. deSouza) It's difficult to decide whether to hate this film more for perpetuating the awful trend of bringing video games to the big screen or for giving the late, great Raul Julia an unworthy final theatrical appearance. Come to think of it, there are plenty of other reasons to despise it. Jean-Claude Van Damme stars as the head of an elite military unit whose mission in life is to stop the nefarious General Bison (Julia), a dictator bent on global domination. With the help of martial arts experts who would look more at home broadcasting the weather on CNN, Van Damme plays a boring game of cat and mouse with his adversary until a prolonged and surprisingly unexciting fight finale. The terrible screenplay gives neither of its stars any material to work with — to such an extent that even an actor of Julia's capabilities is lost. ★ $19.99

Street Kid

(1990, 89 min, Germany, Peter Kern) With a lion's mane of pompadoured hair, skin-tight jeans, flashy cowboy boots and a cocky attitude, 14-year-old Axel prowls the mean streets of Dusseldorf selling his body to pederasts — all of whom are out to taste forbidden fruit. Similar to *Christiane F.* in depicting the gritty and harsh life of teenagers on the streets, the film's sardonic humor keeps it from being somber as it follows the bisexual Axel who, despite abusive parents (his own father rapes him at one point), possesses a fun-loving and tender attitude. Life takes an unexpected change for the boy after he meets an unhappily married man twice his age who falls in love with him. (German with English subtitles) ★★★ $69.99

Street Music

(1981, 88 min, US, Jenny Bowen) An ambitious street musician/singer (Elizabeth Daily) and her bus driver boyfriend (Larry Breeding) find themselves unlikely champions of the elderly when the run-down hotel in which they all live is about to be torn down. An intriguing mixture of social responsibility and musical aspiration that occasionally manages to rise above the clichés and its unusual scenario. ★★½ $69.99

Street of Shame

(1956, 88 min, Japan, Kenji Mizoguchi) Mizoguchi's final film is set in 1956 in a Tokyo brothel and explores the lives, dreams and hardships facing a group of prostitutes. This stirring portrait of the women delves not only into brothel life but follows them into the harsh streets of the city and into their homes. A penetrating study of love and sex and a powerful cinematic vision. (Japanese with English subtitles) ★★★½ $29.99

Street Smart

(1987, 95 min, US, Jerry Schatzberg) Morgan Freeman's blistering portrait of a ruthless pimp highlights this gritty urban drama about a newspaper reporter (Christopher Reeve in a change-of-pace role) who fabricates a story about the private life of a pimp – which turns out to be all too close to that of Freeman. Kathy Baker is exceptional as one of Freeman's working girls. ★★★

Street Trash

(1987, 90 min, US, Jim Muro) Entertaining and disgusting, *Street Trash* is not more than one step up from a student film, though it is very competently made and has good production values considering its setting. It explores two days in the life of various filthy, horrible, insane, violent, lecherous street people, the caricatured "trash" of the title. The minimal story is about both a toxic brand of cheap liquor which melts its imbibers from the inside out and the gang rape and accidental murder of a mob boss' young mistress by the inhabitants of a junkyard. The movie has a guilty pleasure feel about it, from its well-done and completely disgusting special makeup effects to its gallows humor (including Vietnam flashbacks) to its remarkably accurate depiction of life in the seediest part of town. *Street Trash* also features the only film occurrence we know about of a "keep-away" game played using a man's severed penis. Watch it if you dare. ★★ $79.99

The Street with No Name

(1948, 91 min, US, William Keighley) An exciting crime thriller with a chilling performance by Richard Widmark as an up-and-coming crime boss who targets an FBI agent for death when the feds get too close to his gang's operations. With Mark Stevens and Lloyd Nolan. ★★★ $19.99

A Streetcar Named Desire

(1951, 122 min, US, Elia Kazan) Marlon Brando is the brutish Stanley Kowalski, who psychologically strips his fragile sister-in-law Blanche (Vivien Leigh) until her breakdown is complete. Tennessee Williams' masterpiece is layered with sexual symbolism and haunting imagery, and features fine support from Karl Malden as a well-intentioned suitor and Kim Hunter as Stanley's beleaguered wife. Brando and Oscar winner Leigh's performances have over time become part of our cinematic heritage. This is the director's cut featuring mostly edited reaction shots which clearly give the story more of a sexual pitch. ★★★★ $19.99

The Streetfighter

(1975, 91 min, Japan, Seiji Ozawa) The success of Quentin Tarantino has had its share of fortunate side-effects, not the least of which is the rediscovery and greater availability of the films he himself enjoys. One of the more high profile of these is Sonny Chiba's *The Streetfighter*. While not quite deserving the reputation of a classic, this is nevertheless great entertainment, particularly for those who enjoy slightly cheesy 1970s martial arts films. Presented in its original, uncut version, the film is awash in brutal violence – limbs are broken, eyes gouged out, and genitalia pulled off, all by our hero Terry Tsurugi (Chiba). Terry is a killer-for-hire who helps rescue Junjo, an important gang member, from prison. After killing Junjo's associate during a double-cross attempt, Terry finds himself pursued by the criminals who hired him. Great martial arts fun is available in megadoses here, with Chiba killing nearly everyone in sight and basically grimacing his way through his role. Tsurugi's match with the master of a karate school is particularly well-done, and watch out for the infamous X-ray skull punch! Letterboxed version. (Dubbed in English) ★★★ $19.99

Streets of Fire

(1984, 93 min, US, Walter Hill) Kinda hip and fun rock 'n' roll fable with Michael Paré as a soldier of fortune who returns to his old neighborhood to rescue his ex-girlfriend from the clutches of a vicious motorcycle gang. Willem Dafoe, Diane Lane, Rick Moranis and Amy Madigan star. ★★★ $14.99

Streets of Gold

(1986, 95 min, US, Joe Roth) A sincere and passionate performance from Klaus Maria Brandauer elevates this ordinary boxing drama about a Russian fighter, now living in Brooklyn as a dishwasher, who trains two youths (Adrian Pasdar, Wesley Snipes) for the American team – in the hopes of competing against his former coach. ★★½ $9.99

Streetwise

(1985, 92 min, US, Martin Bell) An extraordinary documentary which chronicles the lives of nine young runaways, ages 13 to 19, who survive in the drug and tenderloin district of Seattle and support themselves by prostitution, pimping, panhandling and petty thievery. It's a bleak picture, but one that also captures sweet flirtatious moments and times of shared humor and experience as these kids try to create a niche for themselves. Oscar nominee for Best Documentary. ★★★★ $19.99

Strictly Ballroom

(1992, 94 min, Australia, Baz Luhrmann) Tapping into the Fred and Ginger in all of us, first-time director Luhrmann has crafted a glorious take on the elegant (but at times wacky) world of ballroom dancing. Newcomer Paul Mercurio stars as a bad-boy hoofer whose innovative technique flies in the face of the traditionalists, making him an outcast in a dance community where "ballroom" has been elevated to a religion. With a nod to *Dirty Dancing*, he takes up with an awkward dance student (Tara Morice) and the two set out to win the big dance competition. Of course, they fall in love while doing so. As by-the-books as it sounds, a laugh-out-loud, zany and enjoyable musical is born. The film's can't-keep-still soundtrack and rousing choreography may make ballroom dancing the new national craze. ★★★½ $14.99

Strictly Business

(1991, 83 min, US, Kevin Hooks) West Philly native Hooks has fashioned a warm and winning comedy about a dyed-in-the-wool "buppie" (Joseph C. Phillips) who enlists the aid of a mailroom clerk (Tommy Davidson of "In Living Color") to help him meet the girl of his dreams (Halle Berry). While yet another "message" movie from the black community for the black community, this one manages to mix a little sugar with the medicine, making its theme of unity and racial harmony an enjoyable pill to swallow. ★★½ $19.99

Strike

(1925, 82 min, USSR, Sergei Eisenstein) In a remarkable directorial debut, Eisenstein introduced radical innovations in editing, montage and camera work in presenting this impassioned film about the struggles of workers embroiled in a violent strike at a Moscow factory, set before the Revolution. He recounts the workers' hardships and exploitation as well as the devastating strike itself – the resulting hunger, the presence of predatory infiltrators and ultimately the bloody massacre by the militia. (Silent with orchestral accompaniment) ★★★★ $29.99

Striking Distance

(1993, 102 min, US, Rowdy Herrington) Bruce Willis is in good form in this interesting thriller about a by-the-books cop whose demotion to the Pittsburgh River patrol comes in handy when his ex-girlfriends start turning up as fishbait courtesy of a serial killer with an inside knowledge of police procedure. Also starring Sarah Jessica Parker. ★★½ $14.99

Stripes

(1981, 106 min, US, Ivan Reitman) Bill Murray and Harold Ramis team up with director Reitman in this mildly successful, pre-*Ghostbusters* comedy spoof on life in the Army. Murray and Ramis play a couple of losers who join under the assumption that life in the forces will be an easy overseas holiday. Along the way, they hoodwink their superiors and become inadvertent heroes. Goofy and sophomoric, Murray's charm and the spirited performances of the supporting cast, including John Candy, P.J. Soles, Warren Oates and

Striptease

Stuart Saves His Family

Judge Reinhold, provide this military farce with "a few good laughs." ★★½ $9.99

The Stripper

(1963, 95 min, US, Franklin J. Schaffner) Joanne Woodward's competent performance saves this William Inge melodrama about an aging stripper and her affair with a young man. Richard Beymer, Claire Trevor and Gypsy Rose Lee co-star. ★★½ $59.99

Striptease

(1996, 115 min, US, Andrew Bergman) It will come as no surprise that in *Striptease*, Demi Moore takes her clothes off; and it is of no cheer that Carl Hiaasen's cunning satirical novel has been stripped of its bite and wit to such an extent. When she loses custody of her child to her slimy husband, Moore takes a high-paying job at a Fort Lauderdale strip club to earn enough money to reopen the case. Becoming its star attraction, Moore becomes the unwilling object of lust from a local congressman (a spirited and funny Burt Reynolds) which leads to murder and run-ins with the mob. Director and adapter Bergman (*The Freshman*), who can be quite adept, is unable to capture the flavor of the book or convey the energy and tempo of good satirical comedy. And he's not helped by a sullen Moore, who attacks her part as if she were playing Lady Macbeth. Reynolds, on the other hand, appears to fully understand the nuances of farce, and he gives a most pleasurable performance; as does Ving Rhames as the club's heroic bouncer. ★½ $19.99

Stromboli

(1950, 81 min, Italy, Roberto Rossellini) This neorealist Rossellini drama stars Ingrid Bergman as a woman who escapes an internment camp only to marry an unresponsive fisherman and live on a barren, bleak island confronting poverty and a spiritual sort of prison. Although the film received excellent reviews, the Bergman/Rossellini extramarital affair during the time of the release doomed the picture commercially. (Filmed in English) ★★★

Stroszek

(1977, 108 min, West Germany, Werner Herzog) Three German misfits — a whore, a former mental patient and an eccentric old man — confront the American Dream in one of Herzog's funniest and most accessible films. Fleeing Berlin, the trio's wanderings lead them to the barren bleakness of Railroad Flats, Wisconsin. Setting up house in a mobile home bought on credit, they attempt to come to terms with the dubious splendors of American culture: TV, football, dancing chickens, and other oddball bits of Americana. A lyrical, perceptive and bittersweet comedy starring Bruno S. and Eva Mattes. (German with English subtitles) ★★★½ $29.99

Stuart Saves His Family

(1995, 97 min, US, Harold Ramis) What is hopefully the last of the "S.N.L." "skit-to-screen" vehicles stars Al Franken as the nebbishly New Age talk show host who's "good enough and smart enough...," until the cancellation of his cable-access show and the death of an aunt force him to come to terms with his own dysfunctional family. Alternately funny and even touching at times, Franken's screenplay pokes fun at the New Age and 12-step programs while also trying to reach a catharsis from their application, though he is more successful in his spoofing than the sometimes dreadful pathos. Franken clearly knows Stuart well, and Laura San Giacomo and Vincent D'Onofrio are good in support. ★★½ $14.99

The Stud

(1978, 95 min, GB, Quentin Masters) This semi-soft-core melodrama tells the story of a virile young nightclub manager whose obligations include servicing the boss' wife. Adapted from the novel by Jackie Collins, it stars her sister Joan. Very trashy, with an abundance of celebrity skin. ★

The Student Prince at Old Heidelberg

(1927, 105 min, US, Ernst Lubitsch) This silent film version doesn't really miss the music of Romberg's operetta, with its breezy charm that became known as the "Lubitsch Touch." Ramon Novarro is effervescent as the heir to the throne getting to cut loose for the first time now that he's away for college. Everything would have been fine if he hadn't fallen in love with bar-frau Norma Shearer at the fraternity beer bash. ★★★½ $29.99

The Stuff

(1985, 93 min, US, Larry Cohen) Playfully satiric horror film about a mysterious goo — the newest culinary fad — which turns those who eat it into zombies with an appetite. Starring Michael Moriarty, Andrea Marcovicci, Garrett Morris, Paul Sorvino and Danny Aiello. ★★ $9.99

The Stunt Man

(1980, 129 min, US, Richard Rush) Peter O'Toole is the maniacal film director who befriends then dominates a young man (Steve Railsback) on the run from the police. A fre-

netically paced, tautly edited story about paranoia and illusion versus reality. ★★★★ $19.99

The Substitute

(1996, 114 min, US, Robert Mandel) At one point in his illustrious career as shepherd of this country, Richard Nixon commissioned a study to determine if the American people would accept martial law. Had the answer been yes, this film might represent the prevailing model for public education. Tom Berenger's patented sensitive tough guy is this time an unemployed covert op. He assumes the cover of substitute teacher, replacing his on-again, off-again lover (Diane Venora) when her leg is broken by the school's reigning gang leader. Within a few days, this warrior-with-a-gentle-heart uncovers a nasty little secret on school grounds, which had amazingly gone undetected until his arrival. Enlisting the aid of his mercenary buddies, and providing the raison d'être for now-obligatory John Woo projectile shots, Berenger brings the war back home. Look for the scene in which Berenger is asked about his Vietnam War wounds. The class responds to his reply by displaying their own wounds, inflicted on the city streets by superior weaponry: fin de siècle Show and Tell. ★★ $14.99

Suburban Roulette

(1967, 70 min, US, Hershell Gordon Lewis) Although best known for his gore films, director Lewis also made a number of cheap exploitation flicks. In this one, Tom Wood stars as the father of the new family in suburbia, where the wives are swapping more than just recipes. Opening narration brings to mind fellow B-budget director Russ Meyer (similarities end there). ★ $12.99

Suburbia

(1984, 96 min, US, Penelope Spheeris) This archly funny anthem to punk nihilism captures the spirit of anomie rampant on the Mellow Coast. If only there were more social clubs, these kids wouldn't be going around ransacking neighborhood garages. ★★½

Subway

(1985, 103 min, France, Luc Besson) Tuxedoed punks, mondo body-builders, roller-skating purse snatchers and roving musicians stylishly adorn Besson's glimpse at Paris underground life. A brilliantly choreographed car chase romps and roars its way into the Paris Metro, where Christopher Lambert eludes his pursuers. Amidst the labyrinthine corridors and twisted passage ways of the cavernous underground, a wonderfully colorful world of outrageous misfits springs into bloom, highlighted by a luminously attired Isabelle Adjani. (Dubbed) ★★★½

Subway to the Stars

(1987, 103 min, Brazil, Carlos Diegues) Diegues, director of *Bye, Bye Brazil*, has fashioned this enchanting fable that is a modernization of the Orpheus legend. The story revolves around the young Vinicius, an innocent saxophonist who embarks on an odyssey through the seedy and sleazy underworld of Rio de Janeiro in search of his missing girlfriend. His journey brings him in contact with cops and bandits, slum dwellers and dreamers, prostitutes and poets. Although the settings are grim and his task seemingly endless, our young hero, as well as the demimondes of the slum, retains an optimistic and dreamy attitude. (Portuguese with English subtitles) ★★★

Success Is the Best Revenge

(1984, 90 min, GB, Jerzy Skolimowski) Director Skolimowski's follow-up to his widely successful *Moonlighting* continues to explore the plight of Polish immigrants in foreign lands. This time his view is slightly more autobiographical as he tells the tale of a Polish filmmaker (Michael York) living in exile in London. As he works feverishly to make a film about the growing unrest in his homeland, he becomes estranged from his rebellious teenage son. ★★★

Sudden Death

(1995, 110 min, US, Peter Hyams) What might simply be described as "*Die Hard* at a hockey game" is actually a highly enjoyable if predictable action thriller with Jean-Claude Van Damme as an ex-firefighter who, having been unable to rescue a little girl from a burning building in the film's opening, sees a chance for redemption when terrorists take his daughter — and the Vice-President — hostage at the Stanley Cup finals. Having worked well together on *Timecop*, director Hyams and Van Damme deliver another one-two punch with fast-paced action, elaborate stuntwork and massive explosions. Powers Boothe's performance as the *de rigeur* charismatic villain usually associated with this genre is a highlight, as is a fight sequence involving a manhating, kickboxing penguin. ★★★ $14.99

Sudden Impact

(1983, 117 min, US, Clint Eastwood) Eastwood's fourth go-round as San Francisco detective "Dirty" Harry Callahan puts him on the trail of a woman (Sondra Locke) who is getting revenge against the gang who raped her and her sister years before. The series is starting to show its age, but director Eastwood still manages to bring some life to the familiar tale. Go ahead, it'll make your day. ★★½ $9.99

Suddenly

(1954, 77 min, US, Lewis Allen) Frank Sinatra, in sort of a precursor to *The Manchurian Candidate*, plays the leader of a group of assassins in this suspenseful thriller. Little-seen for many years after the Kennedy assassination, the story concerns a group of gunmen who take over a house in a small town where the president is due. ★★★ $19.99

Suddenly, Last Summer

(1959, 114 min, US, Joseph L. Mankiewicz) A blistering Tennessee Williams drama (co-scripted by Gore Vidal) about psychiatrist Montgomery Clift investigating what caused Elizabeth Taylor to crack while on summer vacation with Katharine Hepburn's son Sebastian. Terrific performances by Taylor and Hepburn. ★★★ $19.99

Suffering Bastards

(1990, 90 min, US, Bernard McWilliams) Independent low-budget comedy about a pair of born-loser brothers (John C. McGinley, David Warshofsky) who rip off their low-life boss, Eric Bogosian, and use the money to buy back their dead mother's Atlantic City night club, revitalizing their lounge-singing careers. Unusual, uneven but not without an abundance of quirky charm. ★★★ $89.99

Sugar Cane Alley

(1984, 104 min, Martinique, Euzhan Palcy) This bittersweet Third World tale about French colonial exploitation during the 1930s focuses on Jose, a young boy who manages to escape shantytown poverty through intellectual pursuit and the aid of his indomitable grandmother. (French with English subtitles) ★★★ $29.99

Sugar Hill

(1994, 125 min, US, Leon Ichaso) With a marketing campaign that suggests it might be the next *New Jack City*, it is no wonder that *Sugar Hill* made no great strides upon its theatrical release. In point of fact, director Ichaso's sometimes grisly yet gripping character study owes more to the works of William Shakespeare than to its gangster roots. Wesley Snipes stars as a Harlem drug lord who, having seen both his parents destroyed by heroin, finally decides to get out, much to the dismay of his firebrand brother (Michael Wright in a typically drugged-out performance). While action fans may find this a little too talky, it is nonetheless extremely well-acted and a worthy addition to the gangster canon. ★★★ $96.89

Sugarbaby (Zuckerbaby)

(1985, 108 min, West Germany, Percy Adlon) This tender and endearing comedy stars Marianne Sägerbrecht as a sad, overweight mortuary attendant helplessly smitten with a slim blond subway conductor. The film radiates a fine erotic warmth as Marianne, taking leave of both her job and her senses, stalks and then captures her prey. An unusual and compassionate essay on the power of love and will. (German with English subtitles) ★★★ $39.99

The Sugarland Express

(1974, 109 min, US, Steven Spielberg) Based on a true story, Spielberg's theatrical debut is a vastly entertaining comedy-drama. In one of her best performances, Goldie Hawn plays a mother who helps her husband escape jail, and together they plan to kidnap their own baby, now a ward of the state. In the ensuing confusion, they take a state trooper hostage, and have the entire Texas police force on their trail as they attempt to retrieve their child. ★★★½ $14.99

Suite 16

(1994, 109 min, GB/The Netherlands, Dominique Deruddere) Psychological and sexual games run amock on the Côte D'Azur in this intriguingly sick English-language drama. Chris (Antoine Kamerling) is a handsome, self-assured German blond whose con is to seduce older women on the French Riviera and then rob them. After almost killing a robbery victim, he flees and finds temporary refuge in the opulent suite/apartment of Glover (Peter Postlethwaite), a rich but wheelchair-bound paraplegic. After a menacing first

Sugar Cane Alley

night, tables are turned as captor becomes captive when Glover offers the young man a lucrative offer to stay and have sex with women and allow him to watch. Chris (seen nude for most of the film) becomes comfortable with the arrangement, until the sexual antics with a bevy of slick prostitutes tire and Glover hires a thuggish, muscle-bound leather man to bring a new dimension to the sexual shenanigans. This kinky tale palpitates in homeroticism as its story of humiliation, greed, abuse and ultimately love unfolds. ★★★ $94.99

The Suitors

(1989, 106 min, US/GB, Ghasem Ebrahimian) This unpredictable and outrageous dark comedy tells the story of an Iranian woman, newly married and arrived in New York City. Mariyum arrives in the U.S. with her rich husband, Haji. But during a celebration, a friend's landlord mistakes a religious feast (in which a sheep is sacrificed) for a terrorist act, and a SWAT team accidentally shoots Haji, leaving the young émigré a widow. Alone in a strange land, and having tested some of the freedoms belonging to American women, Mariyum is courted by her late husband's four friends, who prove to be as relentless in their romantic attentions as they are in their desire for Mariyum to return to traditional Islamic values. ★★★ $59.99

Sullivan's Travels

(1941, 91 min, US, Preston Sturges) One of director Sturges' many great comedies of the 1940s, this brilliant probe into the psyche of a comedy filmmaker — decades before Woody Allen or Blake Edwards found success with the theme — is his most personal film and a classic road movie. Joel McCrea stars as a successful movie director who longs to direct a "serious" film — so he sets out on the road, dressed as a hobo, to see the "real world." He befriends Veronica Lake, an actress wannabe about to head back home, and learns a few valuable lessons on the resilience of man and the power of laughter. A masterful combination of razor-sharp satire and sentimentality. ★★★★ $14.99

The Sum of Us

(1994, 100 min, Australia, Kevin Dowling & Geoff Burton) From the 1991 off-Broadway play comes this endearing family comedy-drama about the unusual relationship between a father and son. Set in a working-class area of Sydney, the story centers on the widowed but fun-loving Harry (Jack Thompson) and his football-playing son Jeff (Russell Crowe). What makes their story so different is that dad not only knows that his twentysomething son is gay, but is quite enthusiastic and accepting of it – hoping that Jeff will eventually find Mr. Right. With great wit and charm, the two men's wacky home life is explored. And as Harry finds romance through a dating service, Jeff falls hard for a handsome gardener. Funny, tender though slightly maudlin towards the end, *The Sum of Us* makes many sexual stereotypes with its even portrayal of homosexuality. Best of all, however, are the terrific performances by Thompson and Crowe, who endow Harry and Jeff with humor, sympathy and sensibility. ★★★½ $19.99

Summer

(1986, 99 min, France, Eric Rohmer) Rohmer's illuminating and moving exploration of loneliness stands as one of his most accomplished works to date. An independent but melancholy Parisian secretary, recently separated from her boyfriend, seems unwilling, even incapable, of enjoying her two-week holiday. Her loneliness and frustrations are compounded by her shyness as well as a strong will that refuses to compromise. Rohmer paints a vivid portrait of this woman and her efforts to connect and enjoy life. (French with English subtitles) ★★★½

Summer and Smoke

(1961, 118 min, US, Peter Glenville) Geraldine Page repeats her acclaimed stage role in Tennessee Williams' searing drama, and she should have won an Oscar for it. In a tour de force performance, Page plays a sexually repressed minister's daughter who falls in love with dashing playboy Laurence Harvey. Set in a small Mississippi town in 1916, the story is a sensitive treatise on unrequited love and ignored passion. Also with Una Merkel, Pamela Tiffin, Earl Holliman and Rita Moreno. ★★★½ $19.99

Summer City

(1976, 83 min, Australia, Christopher Frazer) A very young Mel Gibson stars in this little known Australian sex comedy about the final free-for-all fling of four students who are on the prowl for girls, thrills and surf. Set in the early Sixties, this routine teen hijinks comedy is of interest for Gibson's film debut. ★★½ $9.99

The Summer House

(1993, 85 min, GB, Waris Hussein) This enchanting British comedy unites two of the grande dames of international cinema: Jeanne Moreau and Joan Plowright. Giving one of the most sparkling performances of her long career, Moreau plays the hard-drinking, high-spirited childhood friend of Julie Walters, who's preparing her daughter's marriage. When Moreau arrives for the wedding, she's shocked to discover that the intended groom is a boorish mama's boy. So entering into a mischievous co-conspiracy with the cantankerous mother of the groom, royally played by Plowright, she sets out to prevent the marriage from ever taking place. Though the film does-

n't sustain a high level of exuberance throughout, *The Summer House* compares favorably with recent British period romances, such as *Widows' Peak* and *Enchanted April*, which came before it; and Moreau's radiance even outshines the placid beauty of the local countryside. ★★★ $19.99

Summer Interlude

(1950, 94 min, Sweden, Ingmar Bergman) This early Bergman romantic drama, an affecting story told with the director's usual able hand but lacking in his visual expertise, is a bittersweet tale about a famed ballerina (Maj-Britt Nilson) who chances upon a deceased lover's diary, triggering memories of first love, happier days and tragic circumstance. (aka: *Illicit Interlude*) (Swedish with English subtitles) ★★★ $29.99

Summer Lovers

(1982, 98 min, US, Randal Kleiser) This exotic eye-pleaser, from the director of *The Blue Lagoon*, focuses on how three young people (Peter Gallagher, Daryl Hannah and Valerie Quennessen) spend their summer vacation. Not a lot of substance, but any movie about a ménage à trois in the Greek islands can't be all bad. ★★½ $9.99

Summer Night

(1987, 94 min, Italy, Lina Wertmüller) Director Wertmüller returns to the familiar terrain of sexual and political conflict in this enjoyably erotic comedy, reminiscent in many ways to her 1975 hit *Swept Away*. That film's star Mariangela Melato plays a bitchy millionairess who has the tables turned on a notorious terrorist responsible for a series of kidnappings. She kidnaps him and holds him captive on her isolated Mediterranean isle, where the two become locked in a lusty battle of the sexes – Wertmüller style. The handsome Michele Placido (*Ernesto, Big Business*) plays the befuddled kidnapper. ★★★ $19.99

Summer of '42

(1971, 102 min, US, Robert Mulligan) A captivating coming-of-age tale which concentrates more on character and emotion than sentimentality. Set in 1942, the film stars Gary Grimes as a teenager vacationing in New England who falls in love with beautiful and married Jennifer O'Neill, whose husband is overseas. What follows are blithe observations on first love and the teen years which should have anyone who's been through it smiling in recognition. ★★★ $14.99

The Summer of Miss Forbes

(1988, 87 min, Mexico, Jaime Humberto Hermosillo) A luminous Hanna Schygulla stars as a sexually repressed governess in this erotic, beautifully photographed but ultimately silly melodrama scripted by Gabriel Garcia Marquez. In a lush sea resort, a frenzied couple goes on a six-week cruise and hires Miss Forbes (Schygulla), a stern Prussian schoolteacher, to instill manners and discipline into their two chubby, calculating sons. Matronly dressed and militarily tough by day, Miss Forbes harbors another personality – for at night, she becomes a tequila-guzzling, cake-stuffing floozy, whose simmering sexual urges boil over. And while she is plotting the sexual

conquest of the boys' beautiful diving instructor, they concoct a plan to rid themselves of her forever. While enjoyable, the film never completely works, with Ms. Schygulla miscast as the barely-concealed basket case. (Spanish with English subtitles) ★★½ $19.99

Summer School

(1987, 98 min, US, Carl Reiner) Director Reiner manages to produce a few laughs in this otherwise ordinary comedy with Mark Harmon as a summer school teacher who'd rather be elsewhere. With Kirstie Alley and Robin Thomas. ★★ $14.99

Summer Stock

(1950, 109 min, US, Charles Walters) Judy Garland sings "Get Happy" in this entertaining musical about a theatrical troupe, including dancer Gene Kelly, who plan to turn her farm's barn into a theatre. Good supporting cast includes Eddie Bracken, Marjorie Main and Phil Silvers. ★★★ $19.99

A Summer to Remember

(1960, 78 min, USSR, G. Danelia & I. Talankin) Based on a young child's view and acceptance of the atmosphere that surrounds him, this film focuses on a six-year-old boy's relationship with his mother and stepfather. The stepfather is brilliantly played by Sergey Bondarchuk (director of *War and Peace*). (Russian with English subtitles) ★★★

Summer Vacation 1999

(1988, 90 min, Japan, Shusuke Kaneko) A provocative and lushly photographed tale of budding sexuality and the loss of innocence that owes more to French cinema than that of Japanese filmmaking. Four teenage boys (all intriguingly played by young girls) are left behind in their boarding school during the summer. Their idyllic world is forever changed after another youth, who bears an uncanny resemblance to a dead friend, joins them. By using women to play the leads, the film takes on an interestingly androgynous angle while at the same time hauntingly exploring the fragile period in time when youth is suspended between innocence and experience, uncomplicated friendships and the initial pangs of romantic love and sexual awareness. (Japanese with English subtitles) ★★★ $69.99

Summer Stock

S

Summer Wishes, Winter Dreams

(1973, 95 min, US, Gilbert Cates) A trio of outstanding performances by Joanne Woodward, Martin Balsam and Sylvia Sidney is the heart of this compelling drama about a housewife facing a midlife crisis. Both Woodward and Sidney received well-deserved Oscar nominations. ★★★ $14.99

Summertime

(1955, 99 min, US, David Lean) Big-budget Lean production starring Katharine Hepburn as a high-strung, lonely American spinster from Akron, Ohio, looking for romance in extremely photogenic Venice. Fortunately, Rossano Brazzi is nearby. ★★★½ $24.99

Sun Valley Serenade

(1941, 86 min, US, Bruce Humberstone) Sonja Henie and John Payne star in this lively musical about a Norwegian war refugee given shelter at the Idaho resort; but the main attraction is Glenn Miller and His Orchestra, and Milton Berle as their manager. Also with the marvelous Nicholas Brothers. Songs include "Chattanooga Choo-Choo" and "It Happened in Sun Valley." ★★★ $19.99

Sunchaser

(1996, 122 min, US, Michael Cimino) Director Cimino's career is still on hold with this weak entry in the "soulless-yuppie-finds-himself" sub-genre starring Woody Harrelson as a wealthy oncologist who's carjacked by Jon Seda, a terminally ill juvenile delinquent. They embark on a spiritual journey to a sacred mountain to cure Seda's cancer. Along the way, the disparate men find a shared humanity and learn "to get along." It's as hokey as it sounds. Cimino's post-Deer Hunter films have all shared a lack of focus, but none more so than Sunchaser. The concept is sentimental and unrealistic and the execution artificial and preachy. It strives to be P.C. with its Native-American subplot and the "he's-okay-after-all" juvey from the hood. Insulting and poorly shot, it makes one yearn for the bad-for-you thrills of a "good" exploitation film. ★½ $99.99

Sunday, Bloody Sunday

(1971, 110 min, GB, John Schlesinger) Glenda Jackson and Peter Finch are sparkling in this landmark work. A cause célèbre in the early 1970s, this moving drama centers around the troubled participants in a bisexual triangle. The kiss between Peter Finch and Murray Head aroused an audible gasp from the audience of the day. Marvelously directed by Schlesinger. ★★★★ $19.99

A Sunday in the Country

(1984, 94 min, France, Bertrand Tavernier) An illuminating, visually ravishing tale which centers around an elderly painter and the weekend visit paid to him by his children. Many primal issues of life are delicately handled in this subtle, masterfully crafted drama. (French with English subtitles) ★★★★ $19.99

Sunday in the Park with George

(1984, 140 min, US, James Lapine) Stephen Sondheim's Pulitzer Prize-winning Broadway musical, filmed directly from the stage, about the life of 19th-century French artist Georges Seurat, and his painting of the masterpiece "Sunday Afternoon on the Island of La Grand Jette." The original Broadway cast is featured in this superb production, including Mandy Patinkin, Bernadette Peters, Charles Kimbrough (now appearing on TV's "Murphy Brown") and Dana Ivey. ★★★★

Sunday Too Far Away

(1975, 95 min, Australia, Ken Hannam) A simple yet solid drama about the dangerous rivalries between the members of a group of macho sheep shearers. Jack Thompson is especially good as one of the group's hardened leaders. ★★★

Sunday's Children

(1994, 94 min, Sweden, Daniel Bergman) Daniel Bergman, the son of Ingmar Bergman, makes his directorial debut with this heartfelt, magical memory piece. An autobiography written by the elder Bergman, the story centers on the life of the eight-year-old Ingmar, here called Pu (played by the sullen Henrik Linnors), and the relationship with his distant but loving father (Thommy Berggren). As the story flashes from the past to the present, Pu must come to terms with his dying father while being haunted by images and recollections from his childhood. Though Daniel may lack his father's assured control of the medium, and Ingmar's script is fragmented, Sunday's Children is a beautifully crafted, eloquent and bittersweet stroll with one's ghosts and demons. (Swedish with English subtitles) ★★★ $59.99

Sundays and Cybele

(1962, 110 min, France, Serge Bourguignon) An intelligent and touching story of the developing relationship between an amnesiac man and a young orphan girl whom he befriends by telling her that he is her father. (French with English subtitles) ★★★★ $29.99

The Sundowners

(1960, 133 min, US, Fred Zinnemann) Exceptional adaptation of Jon Cleary's bestseller about a 1920s Australian sheepherding family. Robert Mitchum and Deborah Kerr give excellent performances, and the film features stunning cinematography. Also starring Peter Ustinov and Glynis Johns. ★★★★ $14.99

Sunrise at Campobello

(1960, 144 min, US, Vincent J. Donehue) Ralph Bellamy's tour de force performance accentuates this compelling look at the early life of President Franklin D. Roosevelt. The story focuses on Roosevelt's infancy in politics and his devastating battle against polio. Greer Garson is equally as impressive as Eleanor Roosevelt. Though Roosevelt's years as president aren't covered, there's more than enough potent drama here. ★★★ $19.99

Sunset

(1988, 107 min, US, Blake Edwards) This Edwards mystery comedy set in 1920s Hollywood is short on laughs but does contain considerable charm thanks entirely to James Garner's delectable turn as Wyatt Earp. The famous lawman helps investigate a bordello murder and crosses paths with Tom Mix (played by Bruce Willis) and a nefarious silent screen star obviously based on Charlie Chaplin. Also with Malcolm McDowell, Mariel Hemingway and Kathleen Quinlan. ★★½ $9.99

Sunset Boulevard

(1950, 110 min, US, Billy Wilder) Arguably the most vitriolic and macabre statement yet on the movie-making capital. Wilder uncovers the fractured dreams, withered ambitions and gruesome neuroses of Tinseltown's denizens. William Holden is the two-bit hack writer nursing a case of self-disgust and Gloria Swanson, in an astonishing performance, is the aging film queen secluded with her bitterness in a Gothic mansion. ★★★★ $14.99

Sunset Park

(1996, 100 min, US, Steve Gomer) Here's the pitch: A middle-class white schoolteacher picks up an extra gig coaching her inner city's high school basketball team (read: black male teenagers). Initially unaccepted in a hostile environment, she eventually makes contact with her alienated charges, learning from them as she instructs them, and leads them to the city championship game. "Seen it," you say? Well, yes, you have, and while any reservations there may be are probably well-founded, it somehow avoids being as bad as could be expected. Rhea Perlman's name is above the title in this vanity production (coproduced by husband Danny DeVito), and she delivers just enough earthy believability to an otherwise soft-focused effort. Sunset Park is also aided in no small measure by the supporting cast, especially Fredro Starr as the student who most clearly sees the team as a possible ticket up and out. Add some well-shot game sequences, and the result is an unexpectedly energetic if lightweight entertainment. ★★½ $19.99

The Sunshine Boys

(1975, 111 min, US, Herbert Ross) After an absence from the big screen of over 30 years, George Burns returned to join up with Walter Matthau as the famous vaudevillians, The Sunshine Boys, who broke up decades before. Now a big producer would like to have them do one of their classic routines on a television special. Burns received an Oscar for his performance in this engaging adaptation of Neil Simon's hit Broadway play. ★★★ $14.99

The Super

(1991, 90 min, US, Rod Daniel) By the sheer force of his personality, Joe Pesci saves this lightweight, formulaic comedy from the video junkpile. In his first starring role, Pesci plays a bigoted, unscrupulous New York ghetto landlord who is forced by the courts to live in one of his own ramshackle buildings. Of course, the misunderstood realtor comes to respect his tenants, each of whom discovers newfound compassion for him. Another '90s redemption story, and one not without a few laughs. However, the characters are pure stereotypes, and the film's ending would have made Frank Capra squirm. ★★ $9.99

Super 8½

(1994, 106 min, Canada, Bruce La Bruce) A mild disappointment after his audacious debut with No Skin Off My Ass, La Bruce's (BLaB) much anticipated second film is a surprisingly hard-core (much graphic sex), film-within-a-film autobiographical drama that, while containing fascinating scenes, is a structural mess. BLaB himself stars as a washed-up porn star/filmmaker, living off his hustler boyfriend. His life is changed when a lesbian underground filmmaker (Liza LaMonica) begins making an experimental movie on his life. La Bruce, who's reminiscent of a more romantic but sexually aggressive Gregg Araki, gets to show off his sexual prowess to good effect, but these scenes bog down the movement of a potentially interesting tale. Also with "Kids in the Hall" star Scott Thompson (as Buddy Cole) and fellow independent filmmaker R. Kern. ★★½ $39.99

Super Mario Brothers

(1993, 104 min, US, Rocky Morton) The super Mario Brothers are just two average plumbers from Brooklyn who find themselves defending the Earth against a bunch of humanoid dinosaur descendants from another dimension. The story is as flimsy as you would expect a movie based on a video game to be, but the dialogue has a nice, quirky style. And thanks to some competent acting by Bob Hoskins and John Leguizamo as the super plumbers, and an over-the-top Dennis Hopper as the slimy lizard king, this live-action comic book is an oddly entertaining if ridiculous action-comedy. ★★ $9.99

Supercop

(1996, 93 min, Hong Kong, Stanley Tong) Chan's masterful *Police Story 3* has been redubbed, reedited and renamed to serve as his follow-up to the hit *Rumble in the Bronx* (actually a newer film than *Supercop*) — and it's also a better movie, more accurately depicting the combination of action and humor which made Chan an international star. Jackie is a Hong Kong police officer sent undercover into Mainland China to spring a mobster from a prison camp and follow him back to Hong Kong, where Jackie can dismantle the crime organization from the inside. Things go well until his girlfriend (Maggie Cheung) is kidnapped and Jackie must blow his cover to save the day. Luckily, helping him out this time is a

tough-as-nails Mainland police officer (the sensational Michelle Khan). Nearly matching Jackie's kung-fu skills and equaling his charm and comic ability, Khan gives the film an added boost of adrenaline and even does her own stunts, too (including a breathtaking motorcycle jump onto a moving freight train). The climax of Jackie hanging from a ladder suspended beneath an airborne helicopter as it flies over Kuala Lumpur should satisfy even the most jaded American action movie fan. And if it doesn't, check your pulse. ★★★½ $99.99

Superfly

(1972, 98 min, US, Gordon Parks, Jr.) Picketed by blacks for its glorification of the drug underworld, *Superfly* was nonetheless a huge popular success and spurred several sequels. New York City is an urban wasteland which provides the gritty backdrop to this tawdry tale of one tough-talking, coke-sniffing pusher (O'Neal) who plots for one final mega-deal before retiring. With a hypnotic Curtis Mayfield score in the background, the film vividly captures the drug dealing world and, unlike most films of this type, takes no moral high ground — depicting a drug-ravaged city with the shakes waiting for its next score. ★★ $9.99

Superfly T.N.T.

(1973, 87 min, US, Ron O'Neal) O'Neal returns as the super-slick, super-bad hustler Priest in this charmingly inept sequel to the far superior *Superfly*. This time, Priest, retired and trying to clear his head in Rome, is enlisted into service by a freedom fighter from Africa to assist in a gun-running mission. This action fun-fest of color also features a good supporting cast that includes a brillo-pad, Afro-endowed Robert Guillaume (TV's "Benson") and Roscoe Lee Brown, a confused screenplay by Alex Haley ("Roots") and a slammin' soundtrack composed and performed by obscure 1970s funk supergroup Osibisa. ★★ $19.99

Supergirl

(1984, 114 min, GB, Jeannot Szwarc) This juvenile fantasy about Superman's comic book

cousin is barely saved from complete mediocrity by Faye Dunaway's ultra-campy portrayal of the arch villainess. Helen Slater is cute but shallow as the superhero, and the film really never gets off the ground. ★★

The Supergrass

(1987, 105 min, GB, Peter Richardson) Outrageous comedy about a young man who pretends to be a drug smuggler to impress his girlfriend, becoming involved with real smugglers and the police — who believe him to be a drug kingpin. The cast includes Adrian Edmondson, Nigel Planer and Alexi Sayle, all regulars on the hit BBC comedy series "The Young Ones"; and Jennifer Saunders of "Absolutely Fabulous." ★★½

Superman: The Movie

(1978, 143 min, US, Richard Donner) In a style reminiscent of a Spielberg or a Lucas, director Donner retells the Superman myth in a grand, often gaudy epic. Spectacular special effects, garish set design, an all-star cast and the obligatory John Williams score highlight this box-office smash. The film follows Superman from his origins on Planet Krypton to his adolescence in Smallville to his heroics in Metropolis. The cast includes Christopher Reeve, Marlon Brando, Margot Kidder and Gene Hackman. ★★★ $19.99

Superman II

(1981, 127 min, US, Richard Lester) Christopher Reeve returns as the Man of Steel in this rollicking sequel. Three fugitives from Krypton travel to Earth, and give Superman a great big headache. Gene Hackman returns as Lex Luthor, and he's as funny as he was in the original adventure. Also with Margot Kidder, Ned Beatty, Jackie Cooper and Valerie Perrine (all returning from *Superman* as well). ★★★ $19.99

Superman III

(1983, 123 min, US, Richard Lester) Christopher Reeve is back once more as the man from Krypton in this comedic Superman

S

Gloria Swanson is ready for her close-up in *Sunset Boulevard*

outing with Richard Pryor fronting for villain Robert Vaughn, out to defeat Clark Kent's alter ego. Some of this is funny, but mostly it's just laughable. (Where's Hackman when you need him?) ★★ $19.99

Superman IV: The Quest for Peace

(1987, 90 min, US, Sidney J. Furie) Superman decides to rid the world of its nuclear weapons; but his good deed backfires as Lex Luthor appropriates the warheads for an elaborate arms deal. Christopher Reeve and Gene Hackman star in this middling adventure with a timely message. ★★ $19.99

Supervixens

(1975, 106 min, US, Russ Meyer) The story of a young man who, wrongfully accused of having killed a woman, is running from the policeman (Charles Napier). Scenes such as the placing of a stick of dynamite between a bound Supervixen's spread legs marks Meyer's return to his tried and true mixture of sex and violence. ★★ $79.99

Support Your Local Gunfighter

(1971, 92 min, US, Burt Kennedy) After their success with the funny *Support Your Local Sheriff*, director Kennedy and James Garner team again for this amiable follow-up. On the lam, con man Garner chooses the small Western mining town of Purgatory to hide out. Upon his arrival, however, the locals think he is a notorious gunslinger, involving him in a war between two mining factions. Suzanne Pleshette is the cowgirl who falls for him. There's a lot of good humor, and familiar character actors like Joan Blondell, Harry Morgan, Dub Taylor and Jack Elam (very amusing as Garner's sidekick) aid in the film's overall enjoyment. ★★½ $19.99

Support Your Local Sheriff

(1969, 93 min, US, Burt Kennedy) Wonderful western spoof with James Garner a delight as a town's sheriff up against a lawless breed when gold is found in them thar hills. With Joan Hackett, Walter Brennan, Harry Morgan, Bruce Dern and Jack Elam. ★★★ $19.99

Sure Fire

(1993, 86 min, US, Jon Jost) Trouble is brewing in a small Southwestern town and mounting tensions erupt with tragic results in this Jost film. Unfortunately, the real trouble might have been on the other side of the camera, because it feels like the filmmakers could not strike a balance between art film and thriller. Although Jost may have had some comment on the human condition in mind here, and he certainly has a way with imagery, a slower, more monotonous 86-minute film would be hard to find. ★ $89.99

The Sure Thing

(1985, 94 min, US, Rob Reiner) Reiner's impressive follow-up to *This Is Spinal Tap* is an intelligent and fresh look at adolescent romance. It offers a distinct alternative to most youth-oriented comedies by presenting teenagers that are hip, witty and even sensitive. Sort of a modern reworking of *It Happened One Night*. John Cusack is terrific in one of his first starring roles. ★★★½

Surf Nazis Must Die

(1987, 88 min, US, Peter George) The Beaches Have Become Battlefields...The Waves Are a War Zone! Is there anyone to help us? Set after a devastating earthquake, the coastline becomes a battleground for control as rival gangs fight for the sand and the water. And a mother fights to avenge her son's death at the hands of these punk patrols...and for as long as she is alive — *Surf Nazis Must Die*. ★

Surrender

(1987, 95 min, US, Jerry Belson) Flat romantic comedy with Sally Field trying to choose between a caring but seemingly impoverished writer (Michael Caine) and a wealthy yuppie attorney (Steve Guttenberg). With Peter Boyle, Julie Kavner, Jackie Cooper, Louise Lasser and Iman. ★★ $9.99

Surviving Desire

(1992, 100 min, US, Hal Hartley) In this half-hour film made for PBS' American Playhouse, director Hartley tackles the themes of obsession, mismatched love and the varying degrees of self-worth which he explored in his feature films *The Unbelievable Truth, Trust* and *Simple Men*. The film stars Martin Donovan (a Hartley regular) as a moody young professor who falls for, pursues and learns a lesson from an attractive student. Newcomer Mary Ward is appealing, talented and seems to relish her part as the brash, brainy and fiercely independent young woman. Early in his career, Hartley concentrated on making short films, but found that there was no viable market for them. This program, however, contains two pieces from the pre-feature film days. The films display Hartley's stylish flair and talent for snappy wordplay, but it becomes clear that the feature-length format may be better suited to his studies of relationships and their place in, or out of, the world around them. ★★½ $19.99

Surviving Picasso

(1996, 123 min, GB, James Ivory) Genius, lover, sexist, bully, egotist, artist: these and other identifying traits of legendary painter Pablo Picasso are perfectly brought to life by Anthony Hopkins, who gives another in a long line of fabulously complex performances. But Hopkins' riveting portrayal is not quite enough to overcome director Ivory's static account of the final years of the artist's life and his love affairs. Suggested by the novel "Picasso: Creator and Destroyer" (its subtitle aptly describes one of the film's many point of views), *Surviving Picasso* is narrated by Picasso's longtime lover Francoise Gilot (nicely played by Natascha McElhone), mother to two of his children. (Interestingly, her biography of the same time period was not used.) The film almost ignores Picasso the artist in favor of his relationships with Gilot and others. That Picasso is possibly defined by his treatment of his mistresses and wife doesn't necessarily make for an articulate, clearer vision. But as was probably true in real life, Hopkins makes sure that Picasso is always center stage and cognizant of his place in the world. ★★½ $99.99

Surviving the Game

(1994, 94 min, US, Ernest Dickerson) Ice-T stars as a bum...er, residentially challenged person...who is recruited by an urban missionary (Charles S. Dutton) to lead a hunting party through the Northwest wilderness, only to find that he is (surprise!) the prey. Former Spike Lee cinematographer Dickerson adds nothing new to this shopworn premise — introduced in 1932 as *The Most Dangerous Game* — that has been tried by everyone from Robert Wise to John Woo and even on "Gilligan's Island." What the film lacks in story is more than compensated for in violence and hammy performances from Rutger Hauer, Gary Busey, F. Murray Abraham and John C. McGinley. ★★ $14.99

Susan and God

(1940, 117 min, US, George Cukor) Anita Loos (*The Women, Gentlemen Prefer Blondes*) adapted Rachel Crothers' stage hit, a curious blend of sophisticated comedy and family

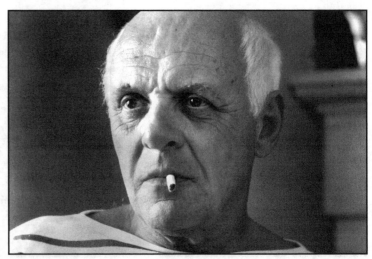

Surviving Picasso

drama. Joan Crawford stars as a flighty socialite who finds religion; she begins preaching love and God and interferes with her society friends' lives. Fredric March is Crawford's alcoholic and estranged husband who does not benefit from his wife's new spiritual awakening. Crawford gives an atypical daffy performance, here resembling a young Auntie Mame. ★★½ $19.99

Susan Lenox: Her Fall and Rise

(1931, 77 min, US, Robert Z. Leonard) The only pairing of screen legends Greta Garbo and Clark Gable is this blustery melodrama with Garbo as a poor farm girl forced to marry a brutish neighbor. She runs away, straight into the arms of a tall, handsome engineer (Gable). However, fate seems destined to keep the lovers apart. ★★½ $19.99

Susan Slept Here

(1954, 98 min, US, Frank Tashlin) A young troublemaker (Debbie Reynolds) finds herself the unlikely guest of a man-about-town writer (Dick Powell) and proceeds to complicate his bachelor existence. Anne Francis plays Powell's society beauty sweetheart. Kinda cute. ★★½

Susana

(1951, 82 min, Mexico, Luis Buñuel) A mischievous Buñuel focuses this subversive melodrama on a born-bad sexpot who escapes from prison and finds refuge in a hacienda with a kindly family. From the moment she enters the house, the wanton vamp does nothing but wreak havoc, sending just about every man within 20 miles to the brink of sexual frenzy. In a truly kinky ending, our heroine's bedeviling force is brought under control by the lady of the ranch with the aid of a studded riding crop. Brimming with sly humor and trademark touches, *Susana* is delicious fun for all Buñuel lovers. (Spanish with English subtitles) ★★★ $24.99

Suspect

(1987, 122 min, US, Peter Yates) This taut courtroom thriller stars Cher as a public defender who takes on the difficult case of a deaf derelict (Liam Neeson) who has been charged with murder. When a juror (Dennis Quaid) approaches her with helpful evidence, she finds herself not only facing an ethical dilemma, but is also drawn into a whirlwind of Hitchcockian intrigue. The film features solid performances from the entire cast including Philip Bosco and John Mahoney in support. ★★★ $14.99

Suspicion

(1941, 99 min, US, Alfred Hitchcock) Joan Fontaine won a belated Oscar as a shy girl who enters a hasty marriage with the charming but sinister (?) Cary Grant, and begins to believe that he could be a murderer — with her as his next victim. Of interest: the studio changed the ending to fit Grant's image, fearing the public would not accept the writer's original conclusion. Crisp direction from Hitchcock. ★★★ $19.99

Suspiria

(1976, 97 min, Italy, Dario Argento) Argento's classic horror film features mayhem galore at a swank private school in Europe complete with stormy nights, psychopaths and a frenzied soundtrack. Argento's plot is barely skin deep, but his highly stylized camerawork and editing, and the edge-of-your-seat suspense will leave one gasping. Look for a particularly effective homage to the French surreal masterpiece *Un Chien Andalou*. ★★★

Suture

(1994, 96 min, US, Scott McGehee & David Siegel) Unscrupulous patricidal Victor Towers (Michael Harris) sets up his long-lost, almost identical half-brother Clay Arlington (Dennis Haysbert), attempting to murder him and have it look as though he himself has been killed. But Clay survives, disfigured and amnesiac, and is accepted as Victor, who is now under suspicion for their father's murder. Clay's efforts to reinvent his persona are presented with kaleidoscopic images, memories layering and enveloping Clay in the course of his reconstruction. Adding a special dimension to this exploration of identity and self-knowing is that Clay is played by Haysbert, who is black, and Victor by Harris, who is white. Shot in stark black and white, and employing a pared-down but effective soundtrack, *Suture* is an interesting premise with an intriguing execution. Also with Mel Harris (who plays Dr. Renee Descartes) and Sab Shimono. ★★★ $14.99

Swamp Thing

(1982, 91 min, US, Wes Craven) Tongue-incheek monster movie with a scientist transformed into a half-man/half-vegetable when one of his experiments goes awry. Louis Jourdan camps it up as a fellow scientist, and Adrienne Barbeau is the woman Swamp Thing loves. ★★½

The Swan

(1956, 109 min, US, Charles Vidor) This beguiling comedy of manners begins as a European matriarch seeks to reverse her family's declining fortunes by marrying off her only daughter (Grace Kelly) to the country's crown prince (Alec Guinness). Louis Jourdan plays the young woman's tutor, who is disappointed to see that she is actually smitten with the prince. Agnes Moorehead, Leo G. Carroll and Estelle Winwood co-star. ★★★ $19.99

Swan Lake

(1980, 128 min, GB, John Michael Phillips) Natalia Markova (as Odette) and Anthony Dowell (as Prince Siegfried) bring their superb talents to Tchaikovsky's love story. Additional choreography by Rudolf Nureyev and Frederick Ashton and sets by surrealist Leslie Hurry. ★★★ $29.99

Swann in Love

(1984, 115 min, France, Volker Schlöndorff) Schlöndorff beautifully renders the emotional intricacies and period flavor of Marcel Proust's illustrious "Swann's Way." Jeremy Irons is the dashing, cultivated Charles Swann who loses his heart and esteem in a passionate tryst with a pouting courtesan (Ornella Muti). A sparkling ensemble of supporting players includes Alain Delon, Fanny Ardant and Marie-Christine Barrault. (Filmed in English) ★★★

Sweeney Todd

The Swap

(1979, 90 min, US, John Shade & John C. Broderick) An ambitious young filmmaker learns the power and perils of his medium when his homemade pornos of powerful friends are used for political blackmail. With Robert De Niro, Jennifer Warren, Lisa Blount and Sybil Danning. Originally filmed in 1969, reedited and rereleased in 1979. ★★½ $14.99

The Swashbuckler

(1979, 101 min, France, Jean-Paul Rappeneau) It is a shame that so many of Jean-Paul Belmondo's films never make it over to these shores because generally you can count on them being action-packed and full of adventure. However, the film distribution system being what it is, few of his recent efforts have received showings in the U.S. *The Swashbuckler* is an early '70s comedy/adventure that features the charismatic rogue as a man-on-the-run who gets involved in fighting in the American War for Independence. (French with English subtitles) ★★★

Swedenhielms

(1935, 88 min, Sweden, Gustaf Molander) Ingrid Bergman plays a young woman engaged to the son of a renowned aristocrat in line to win the Nobel Prize. When it becomes apparent, however, that the father will not be awarded the prestigious prize, the family is thrown into an emotional and financial crisis, affecting each family member, and the young Bergman, in disparate ways. (Swedish with English subtitles) ★★½ $19.99

Sweeney Todd

(1984, 140 min, US) Live performance of Stephen Sondheim's Tony Award-winning musical. Magnificently re-created for video, Angela Lansbury (also a Tony Award winner) and George Hearn repeat their stage roles as, respectively, the evil Mrs. Lovett and the demonic barber Sweeney, who together conspired to murder his customers and serve them up in her meat pies. An unusual topic for a musical, to be sure, but the genius of Sondheim's music and lyrics and Harold Prince's original staging combine to create a musical masterpiece. Lansbury and Hearn (who stepped into the role after Len Cariou)

S

give two of the greatest performances to be seen in the theatre in recent memory. An unforgettable theatre piece, and not to be missed. ★★★★ $39.99

Sweet Bird of Youth

(1962, 120 min, US, Richard Brooks) An expert adaptation of Tennesse Williams' critically acclaimed play. Geraldine Page excels as a former movie queen whose career has given way to achohol and compromise. Searching for seclusion, she arrives in a small Southern town accompanied by ne'er-do-well hometown boy Paul Newman. Ed Begley won an Oscar for his powerful portrayal of the town's corrupt boss who has it in for Newman. ★★★½ $19.99

Sweet Charity

(1969, 133 min, US, Bob Fosse) Fosse's first film as director is based on his hit Broadway musical, itself based on Fellini's *Nights of Cabiria*. Shirley MacLaine is at her best as dance hall hostess Charity Hope Valentine, the quintessential hooker with a heart of gold. Forever having her heart broken by Mr. Wrong, Charity finds solace in her never-ending optimism and joie de vivre while confronting a series of romantic adventures. Fosse's storytelling is highly stylized, with special emphasis on editing, and features memorable musical numbers. ★★★½ $14.99

Sweet Country

(1987, 150 min, US, Michael Cacoyannis) Some good actors can't save this unfortunate political thriller about an American couple who move to Chile after the Allende assassination, becoming involved in a Marxist underground movement. The cast includes Jane Alexander, John Cullum, Carole Laurie, Franco Nero and Irene Papas. ★½

Sweet Dreams

(1985, 115 min, US, Karel Reisz) Jessica Lange stars as country superstar Patsy Cline in this moving portrait of Cline's vibrant life, her climb to stardom and her untimely death. Ed Harris stars as Cline's husband Charley Dick, and Ann Wedgeworth gives a stirring performance as her mother. Lange received an Oscar nomination for her affecting performance. ★★★

Sweet Hearts Dance

(1988, 101 min, US, Robert Greenwald) A good cast adds some sparkle to this routine romantic comedy as husband and wife Don Johnson and Susan Sarandon decide to split; while friend Jeff Daniels begins an affair with Elizabeth Perkins. ★★½ $19.99

Sweet Liberty

(1986, 107 min, US, Alan Alda) The films of Alda are either hit (*The Four Seasons*) or miss (*A New Life*), but this pleasant comedy sits comfortably towards the former. Alda is a college professor whose book on American history is being made into a movie — and a wild assortment of film types descend upon his peaceful and unprepared town. Good cast includes Michael Caine, Bob Hoskins, Michelle Pfeiffer and Lillian Gish. ★★★ $19.99

Paula Kelly (l.), Shirley MacLaine (c.) and Chita Rivera in *Sweet Charity*

Sweet Lorraine

(1987, 91 min, US, Steve Gomer) Charming, bittersweet comedy-drama about the last days of an 80-year-old Catskills Mountain hotel. Maureen Stapleton gives a winning performance as the hotel's matriarchal owner. ★★★ $79.99

Sweet Movie

(1974, 105 min, Canada/France/West Germany, Dusan Makavejev) One woman's sexual initiation and her descent into the liberating pleasures of the flesh is just one of the stories in this bizarre and sensual celebration of political and sexual anarchism. Makavejev, a sort of Serbo-socialist John Waters, fuses several stories in trying to answer the question, "Is there life after birth?" The main story revolves around a virginal Miss World who, after fending off the lustful advances of her new husband, the richest man in the world and his black muscle-building bodyguard, finally finds her libido liberation on the top of the Eiffel Tower with a singing mariachi star. The film concludes with a delightfully disquieting, gluttonous, orgasmic and scatological feast. A wildly outrageous and original film that probably could not have been made in today's conservative climate. (In English, French, Dutch, German and Serbo-Croatian with English subtitles) ★★★

Sweet Nothing

(1996, 90 min, US, Gary Winick) A depressing but well-intentioned look into the life and mind of a Bronx crackhead, *Sweet Nothing* is based on diaries found in a New York apartment. The first (and weaker) half of this low-budget film depicts how Angelo (Michael Imperioli) gets caught in the vicious cycle of drug addiction. When he finally decides to kick the habit, the film — like its protagonist — begins to recover. Suddenly, the clichés disappear and Angelo's downward spiral starts earning the viewer's sympathy. As directed by Winick, *Sweet Nothing* does get occasionally preachy (particularly when Angelo reads from his diary in voice-over), but the film's message

is still important. Imperioli gives a full-bodied performance as Angelo, inhabiting the edginess of a man who can not resist the highs and lows drugs provide. He is ably supported by Mira Sorvino as his long-suffering wife, and Paul Calderon as his flashy business partner. Offering an unromanticized view of addiction and recovery, *Sweet Nothing* sometimes misfires, but at least maintains the courage of its convictions. ★★½ $99.99

Sweet Smell of Success

(1957, 96 min, US, Alexander MacKendrick) Burt Lancaster is J.J. Hunsecker, N.Y.C.'s most popular gossip columnist. Tony Curtis is the weaselly press agent who will do anything to keep his favor. Screenwriters Clifford Odets and Ernest Lehman worked overtime on the dialogue as each character spits words like knives in an attempt to get the "one up" on the next guy. Everyone gets their just desserts in this cynical masterwork. ★★★★ $19.99

Sweet Sweetback's Baadasssss Song

(1971, 97 min, US, Melvin Van Peebles) Van Peebles wrote, directed and stars in this trend-setting work — which initiated the "blaxploitation" film cycle of the 1970s — about an African-American on the run from "the Man." Violent and told with a discernable rage, the film is in some ways rather dated, with its long montages of Sweetback running and running (complete with split-screen, super-impositions and freeze frame), wall-to-wall, loud '70s jazz, and some stereotypes of its own (mostly women and gays). But the film has lost little of its power in depicting the brutal effects of racism, and even the film's dated score and technical aspects add to *Sweetback's* nightmarish quality. A historically important film that is well-worth seeing, and one that has far more bite than most contemporary films. ★★★ $19.99

Sweet William

(1980, 92 min, GB, Claude Whatham) Practically unseen in the U.S., this charming and sexy comedy features Sam Waterston as a promiscuous young playwright who becomes involved with a woman who refuses to accept his compulsive philandering. Waterston is beguiling and raffish, and is ably assisted by the strong performances of Jenny Agutter and Anna Massey. ★★★

Sweetie

(1990, 97 min, Australia, Jane Campion) First-time director Campion's spellbinding drama follows the story of Kay (Karen Colsten), a highly superstitious and emotionally repressed cafeteria worker whose once-blissful but slowly disintegrating relationship with a handsome co-worker is further rattled when her unpredictable sister Sweetie shows up on her doorstep. Mentally unstable and possibly schizophrenic, the ill-tempered Sweetie destroys Kay's routine; and when their parents show up, it's a virtual free-for-all. As Sweetie, Genevieve Lemon gives a devastating performance. ★★★★ $9.99

Swept Away

(1975, 116 min, Italy, Lina Wertmüller) A swarthy sailor and his beautiful, wealthy employer are cast adrift on the hot sands of a Mediterranean island. The sweeping blue waves and the blazing August sun thrust them together in a steamy, passionate affair. The battle of the sexes and class struggles are played out in this handsomely photographed drama. Starring Mariangela Melato and Giancarlo Giannini. (Remastered) (Italian with English subtitles) ★★★★ $29.99

The Swimmer

(1968, 94 min, US, Frank Perry) Burt Lancaster is splendid in this unusual but rewarding film about a businessman (Lancaster) whose disgust for his middle-class life prompts him to, one afternoon, swim his way home from one pool to another, reflecting upon his life. ★★★

Swimming to Cambodia

(1987, 85 min, US, Jonathan Demme) A unique fusion of stage and film, Spalding Gray's theatrical monologue about his experiences in Cambodia while filming a small role in *The Killing Fields*, makes for captivating and enlightening entertainment. Director Demme, who had already directed the quintessential live concert film *Stop Making Sense*, unleashes an attentive camera on Gray, who, in brilliantly comic and cerebral morsels of insight, hypnotically weaves a tale of life, the war, and the search for the perfect moment. ★★★★ $14.99

Swimming with Sharks

(1995, 93 min, US, George Huang) "The fastest way to get to the top is to work with someone already there." This is the advice taken to heart by ambitious but naive writer Guy (Frank Whaley) when he accepts the job as assistant to Buddy Ackerman (Kevin Spacey), the abusive V.P. of Production of Keystone Pictures. But daily dosages of insults take their toll as Guy takes Buddy hostage. And through a series of flashbacks, *Swimming with Sharks* tells the story of what drove Guy to this act and to possibly commit murder. Writer-director Huang's black comedy is of the darkest shade, a numbing satire whose venom penetrates to the bone. Though similar to though not quite as successful as *The Player*,

this viciously funny film forgoes playful swipes and even subtlety in its view of Hollywood and instead flaunts an industry where "punching below the belt is rewarded," which *Sharks* mercilessly does itself. Though Whaley's performance (and character) is rather one-dimensional, Spacey gives a dazzling portrayal of the acid-tongued, demanding exec; it's at once vile, funny, brutal and remarkably controlled. "Shut up, listen, and learn." ★★★ $14.99

Swing Kids

(1993, 112 min, US, Thomas Carter) A truly disappointing, even awful story of individualism, Nazism and swing music. Robert Sean Leonard plays a German teenager who is part of a youthful clique that includes Frank Whaley and Christian Bale. They spend their nights dancing to American swing and days avoiding the Hitler Youth. But these 1930s hipsters soon discover the Nazis are formidable foes as one by one they either join the movement or perish. There were so many situations available to screenwriter Jonathan Marc Feldman that it's doubly disheartening he gave his characters no moral dance steps to go along with their jitterbug, or any emotional depth as they try to sidestep the Nazis. The musical sequences (of which there are too few), however, do manage to capture the era's fascination for the dance craze, and feature some good standards. Barbara Hershey and an unbilled Kenneth Branagh also star. ★½ $9.99

Swing Shift

(1984, 100 min, US, Jonathan Demme) When America's men left to fight WWII, her women took their places on the job, altering the structure of the family and women's self-expectations. Goldie Hawn, Kurt Russell, Ed Harris and an exceptional Christine Lahti star in director Demme's examination of this little-explored aspect of that pivotal time. The film's uneveness is perhaps due to reported disagreements between Demme and Hawn as to her character's personality; it is nonetheless well-worth watching. ★★★ $9.99

Swing Time

(1936, 103 min, US, George Stevens) One of the best of the Astaire and Rogers musicals, with Fred and Ginger as a dance team in a romantic predicament — he's engaged to the girl back home. Extraordinary dance numbers, and the fine score includes "The Way You Look Tonight" and "Pick Yourself Up." ★★★★ $19.99

Swingers

(1996, 96 min, US, Doug Liman) In *Swingers*, men call women "babies," wear retro clothing, emulate Frank Sinatra and his Rat Pack crew, and worship at the altar of Tarantino, Travolta and Scorsese. Mixing retro 'tude with contemporary guy predicaments, Liman's debut is a surprisingly winning look at the romantic and social entanglements of a group of hepcat Los Angeles lounge lizards. The focus is on Mike (Jon Favreau, who also scripted), a New Yorker who has come to L.A. to try to make it as a comic. He joins ultra-slick Trent (Vince Vaughn) and some other pals for after-hour prowls of area clubs. Eventually, Mike realizes that meaningless one-nighters aren't for him:

He's longing for a real relationship. But can he find it with a martini in one hand and a bassa nova record in the other? *Swingers* celebrates and satirizes the macho tactics of club life at the same time. With dialogue that jives and characters that cook, you often feel like you're watching a documentary about the cool, cool world it depicts. This is one happy-and-a-half hour worth checking out. ★★★½ $102.99

Swiss Family Robinson

(1960, 126 min, US, Ken Annakin) Disney's exciting version of the classic adventure story about a family shipwrecked on a deserted island. With John Mills, Dorothy McGuire and James MacArthur. ★★★ $19.99

Switch

(1991, 103 min, US, Blake Edwards) Edwards wrote and directed this occasionally amusing though ordinary body-switching comedy. Ellen Barkin single-handedly saves the picture from mediocrity with a vibrant portrayal of a sexist philanderer who is murdered and comes back as a beautiful blonde. Perry King is what she used to look like; Jimmy Smits is his partner who is now attracted to his associate. In view of Edwards' brilliant sex farce *Victor/Victoria*, *Switch* is all the more disappointing. ★★ $14.99

Switchblade Sisters

(1975, 91 min, US, Jack Hill) Worth its weight in gold as a cultural artifact of an unfortunate time in American cinematic history, *Switchblade Sisters*, the second release in Quentin Tarantino's "Rolling Thunder" line of eclectic films, will undoubtedly entertain those audience members who are already in love with its dubious endowments: babes, bikers and blades. And no amount of argument from any one will convince them that the movie really is trash. The story is simple: teenage gang debutantes fight enemies within and without in a series of brawls, rape sequences and prison scenes (complete with lesbian guards). A new chickie, however, has come on the scene to challenge the authority of the ruthless gangleader. Are her switchblade skills up to par? Will her clothes come off in the climactic fight scene? Unfortunately, the movie is too bad to sit through to find out, serving mainly as proof that Tarantino's taste in films sometimes dips a bit too deeply into camp and crap. ★ $102.99

Switching Channels

(1988, 105 min, US, Ted Kotcheff) A bargain-basement remake of the classic *His Girl Friday*, with Burt Reynolds and Kathleen Turner in the Cary Grant and Rosalind Russell roles. The characters have been changed from newspaper to TV reporters. ★½ $14.99

Swoon

(1992, 95 min, US, Tom Kalin) The scandalous 1924 murder trial of Nathan Leopold and Richard Loeb for the inexplicable murder of a young boy is given a slightly tilted, definitely New Queer Cinema treatment in this intriguing independent feature that will certainly fascinate some and probably frustrate and upset others. Filmed in grainy black and white, homosexual lovers Leopold and Loeb, both intelligent college students from wealthy

Sylvia and the Phantom

Jewish families, get their visceral and sexual kicks in petty crimes. Their intense but perverted love culminates in a bungled scheme to kidnap a boy, resulting in the youth's cold-blooded killing. The two are eventually tracked down by the police, arrested, tried and sentenced to life in prison. But director Kalin's real interest lies less in the horrendous act of the unlikely criminals and more with the lovers' secretive, intense and self-destructive relationship. A controversial, compelling story, guaranteed to stir debate even within the gay community. Other films adapted from the notorious murder are Alfred Hitchcock's *Rope* and Richard Fleischer's *Compulsion*. ★★★ $19.99

The Sword and the Rose

(1953, 91 min, GB, Ken Annakin) Flavorful Disney adventure starring Richard Todd and Glynis Johns. Mary Tudor, unhappily betrothed to King Louis XII of France, falls for the dashing Palace Captain of the Guard. This incurs the wrath of the evil Duke of Buckingham, who stops at nothing to destroy the romance. ★★★ $19.99

The Sword and the Sorcerer

(1982, 100 min, US, Albert Pyun) A ruthless king summons a long-dormant sorcerer to aid him in his evil-doings, but a young prince (Lee Horsley) aims to stop him. Unexciting combination of adventure and sorcery. With Kathleen Beller, Simon MacCorkindale, George Maharis and Richard Moll. ★★

The Sword in the Stone

(1963, 79 min, US, Wolfgang Reitherman) Amiable Disney animated feature based on the Arthurian legend about young Arthur's search for the famed sword and his adventures with Merlin. Highlighted by bouncy songs and a great wizard duel between Merlin and Mad Madam Mim. ★★½ $24.99

Sword of Doom

(1967, 120 min, Japan, Kihachi Okamoto) Tatsuya Nakadai (*Kagemusha*, *Ran*) stars as an amoral, disaffected young samurai who shifts between moods of brooding nihilism and outbursts of extreme and random violence. After accidentally killing an opponent in a tourna-

ment duel, he leaves his village in disgrace and wanders the countryside in a seemingly pointless search to find an opponent worthy of his deadly swordplay skills. He is pursued by the vengeance-seeking brother of the man he killed, who has since become the student of a master swordsman (Toshiro Mifune). The vengeful samurai trains to master the art of the sword-thrust, the only attack which may defeat Nakadai's unconventional style. Beautifully filmed in stark widescreen black and white, the film is a dark exploration of the violent and base natures of humanity and features an astonishing fight sequence featuring Mifune defending himself against a botched assassination attempt on a bridge at night in the snow which will leave the viewer breathless. (Japanese with English subtitles) ★★★½ $29.99

Sword of Fury I

(1973, 90 min, Japan, Tai Kato) This dazzling film follows the exciting life of Japan's most famous swordsman of the 17th century, Musashi Miyamoto. It features almost unbelievable displays of swordsmanship and easily made Miyamoto one of Japan's most famous samurai. (Japanese with English subtitles) ★★★½

Sword of Fury II

(1973, 77 min, Japan, Tai Kato) This sequel follows samurai Musashi in his preparation for the battle against the notorious Kojiro to be Japan's premiere swordsman. Stars Hideki Takahashi and Jiro Tamiya. (Japanese with English subtitles) ★★★

Sword of the Valiant

(1984, 102 min, GB, Stephen Weeks) Sean Connery's brief but commanding presence is about the only reason to see this sword-and-sorcery adventure. Miles O'Keefe plays a knight (Sir Gawain) who goes up against the infamous Green Knight. ★★

Swords of Death

(1971, 76 min, Japan, Tomo Uchida) The short opening montage of this period piece is an introduction to sword master Musashi, the originator of the two-sword style of fighting. The main story unfolds as Musashi petitions instruction in a particular fighting technique

with the chain and sickle, a technique which will reveal to him the basic principles of two-sword fighting. What he doesn't know is that he's asked to be taught by the husband of the woman whose brother he killed at the battle of Sekigahara. The husband is a opportunistic mercenary who feeds off the conflicts of others. While Musashi believes himself to be enjoying the man's hospitality, the brigand has in fact sent for his band of marauders as back-up in his intention to exact vengeance. The ensuing melee gives new meaning to the idea of on-the-job training. A cautionary note: The video transfer is not of the highest quality, and the subtitles are not always easy to read. (Japanese with English subtitles) ★★½ $39.99

Sybil

(1976, 198 min, US, Daniel Petrie) Sally Field gives a virtuoso performance in this haunting and technically superior made-for-TV movie about a young woman's multiple personality disorder. Field left behind the ghost of "The Flying Nun" forever when she tackled this demanding and career-making role. Joanne Woodward is splendid as the psychiatrist trying to help the schizophrenic Sybil. ★★★★

Sylvia

(1986, 99 min, New Zealand, Michael Firth) A teacher's unorthodox yet highly successful methods meet strong opposition from local authorities. Eleanor David stars as the revolutionary educator Sylvia Ashton-Warner in this moving fact-based drama. ★★★ $79.99

Sylvia and the Phantom

(1950, 97 min, France, Claude Autant-Lara) Jacques Tati stars in this enchanting supernatural comedy. The story is set in a haunted castle where Tati and his 16-year-old daughter live. Trouble brews when his daughter falls in love with the ghost of her grandmother's long-deceased lover. Not your typical French film. (French with English subtitles) ★★★ $24.99

Sylvia Scarlett

(1936, 94 min, US, George Cukor) A rakish thief and his daughter (Edmund Gwenn and Katharine Hepburn) are on the run from the law, so Kate becomes a "he," and the pair hooks up with con artist Cary Grant. All the while, Kate maintains her secret identity, until she falls in love and must make a fateful decision. This is one of Cukor's fascinating misfires, which was crucified when released. Over the years, it has taken on cult status for its unusual premise and stylish tone. ★★½ $19.99

Sympathy for the Devil (One Plus One)

(1969-70, 110 min, France, Jean-Luc Godard) This fascinating "song of revolution" intercuts The Rolling Stones rehearsing "Sympathy for the Devil" while the always controversial Godard wanders among them with occasional interruptions, car crashes, political diatribes as well as a visit to a porn store as he attempts to expose a society in collapse. A whirling attack on and an examination of politics, society and cinema. (English and French with English subtitles) ★★★ $29.99

T-Men

(1948, 92 min, US, Anthony Mann) Return with us now to those thrilling days of yesteryear, when all government agents were square-jawed, clean-living, right-thinking white men fighting the evil nemesis of non-Anglo minorities washing upon our shores like scum in a bathtub. This pseudo-quasi-documentary opens with a technique brought to full flower by Ed Wood, Jr.: A voice-over introduces a professional representative of a really important organization – in this case, the U.S. Treasury (T-Men...get it?) – who in turn introduces a representative composite case. In this case it's the Shanghai Paper Case. Two stalwart protectors of our nation's security go undercover, infiltrating the loosely knit organization of ne'er-do-well counterfeiters who use high-quality paper almost identical with U.S. currency. Earnest orchestrations alternate with ingratiatingly banal incidental music to accompany images shot in extreme noir and with a penchant for highly reflective surfaces. A nostalgic reminder of a time when most people actually trusted the government. ★★½ $24.99

Tabu

(1931, 82 min, US/Tahiti, F.W. Murnau) Filmed entirely on the seemingly idyllic island of Tahiti, and made through the unusual collaboration between directors Murnau and Robert Flaherty, *Tabu* is an early, rarely seen masterpiece. Set amidst the glistening sun and fine sand beaches of the island, the film tells the tragic tale of two young lovers, forced to separate after a tribal edict calls the girl "tabu" to all the men of the village. The video transfer is taken from a strikingly beautiful print that was restored at the UCLA film archives. ★★★★ $39.99

Taffin

(1988, 96 min, GB, Francis Megahy) Pierce Brosnan stars as a reclusive heavy in a small Irish coastal town who makes his living collecting bills. He's better at shaking people down than serving legal papers so it's no wonder that he's not well-liked by the townsfolk. But when big business attempts to build a chemical plant in their backyard, the natives come begging for him to put up a fight. It's a fairly simple and oft-repeated premise, but the inventive ways in which Brosnan and the locals beat up on the corporate big boys offer some amusing moments and satisfy some sense of social justice. ★★ $14.99

Take Me Out to the Ball Game

(1949, 93 min, US, Busby Berkeley) Though it doesn't really rank with the best of the Kelly-Sinatra musicals, there's a lot to like in this flavorful romp with Gene and Frank as ball players greeting the new owner of their club: the aquatic Esther Williams. ★★★ $19.99

Take the Money and Run

(1969, 85 min, US, Woody Allen) Allen's first film as writer and director uses a documentary-like format, which he would use again in his later *Zelig*. This hilarious odyssey follows the misadventures of Virgil Starkwell, a bumbling thief who can't even write a holdup note without messing up (Gub? What's a gub?). A non-stop verbal assault featuring some of Allen's funniest sight gags. ★★★½ $14.99

Take 2

(1972, 100 min, Israel, Baruch Dienar) This breezy sex comedy follows the amorous adventures of Assi, an Israeli cinematographer whose interests lie not only in the commercials and documentaries he shoots but in the lovely actresses and models he comes in contact with. Although he is rough, arrogant and cynical, this proves to be no hindrance for the enterprising young ladies. His idyllic and lascivious affairs take an abrupt turn after he is forced to hire an assistant – a young American woman who not only disapproves of his lifestyle but of his professional work as well. Two total opposites who find themselves with nothing in common but...love. ★★½ $79.99

Taking Care of Business

(1990, 108 min, US, Arthur Hiller) Escaped con James Belushi assumes the identity of rich businessman Charles Grodin when the former finds the latter's appointment book/wallet, or filofax, and carries off the charade while enjoying the sweet life. There are a few laughs to be found in this genial comedy, though it's mostly predictable stuff. ★★ $9.99

The Taking of Pelham One Two Three

(1974, 104 min, US, Joseph Sargent) It's a mystery why this incredibly suspenseful thriller wasn't a box-office hit when released in the theatres. Robert Shaw heads a four-man gang who hijack a New York City subway car at rush hour and demand one million dollars in ransom – to be delivered in one hour. Walter Matthau is the transit inspector on the case, Martin Balsam is one of the gang members, and Shaw is at his malevolent best as the leader. Filmed on location, *One Two Three* is superb entertainment. ★★★½ $14.99

A Tale of Springtime

(1990, 107 min, France, Eric Rohmer) With the completion of his "Six Comedies and Proverbs," Rohmer's new series "Tales of the Four Seasons" begins auspiciously with this engaging, sophisticated drama starring his usual coterie of attractive, young intellectual Parisians. Jenny, a philosophy graduate, resolutely independent and set in her ways, is befriended by Natasha, a chatty young piano student. Jealous of her divorced father's girlfriend (the same age as she), Natasha manipulates, in a none-too-subtle maneuvering, to make her father and Jenny a couple, resulting in a rather awkward weekend of shifting allegiances for the foursome at the father's country house. A deceptively simple and entertaining story, brought to thought-provoking complexity through Rohmer's elegant style and his perceptive approach to human relations. (French with English subtitles) ★★★★ $19.99

A Tale of Two Cities

(1935, 121 min, US, Jack Conway) The best of the many screen versions of the Charles Dickens classic set during the French Revolution, which was "...the best of times, the worst of times." Ronald Colman is in fine form as the lawyer who does "...a far, far better thing than I have ever done before." ★★★½ $19.99

A Tale of Two Cities

(1958, 117 min, GB, Ralph Thomas) One of seven film versions of Charles Dickens' immortal classic about the French Revolution, this faithful adaptation falls just short of the 1935 version. A terrific cast, featuring Dirk Bogarde, Dorothy Tutin, Cecil Parker, Donald Pleasence and Christopher Lee, makes this a still worthwhile endeavor. ★★★ $19.99

A Tale of Winter

(1994, 114 min, France, Eric Rohmer) Told in his trademark spare style, Rohmer's deceptively simple story of the search for love varies from his usual talky, philosophical dramas by featuring a protagonist who lives through emotions, not by intellectual reason. Felicie (Charlotte Very) spends an idyllic summer in a passionate romance with Charles (Van Den Driessche). Through an accidental mix-up, however, they are separated and never see each other again. Five years pass with Felicie, now with a daughter (Charles' unbeknowst to him), still yearning for him – a passion kept alive by her feeling that they will be reunited. Felicie becomes emotionally and romantically lost – her true love is gone and her current lovers are unsatisfying. The film is held together by the wonderful creation that is Felicie, a vacillating but determined romantic whose ambition lies not in understanding the complexities of desire or emptiness but to simply be happy. An endearing *Sleepless in Seattle* for the Francophile set. (French with English subtitles) ★★★ $89.99

Talent for the Game

(1991, 91 min, US, Robert M. Young) Edward James Olmos brings much sincerity to the role of a veteran major league scout who happens upon a gifted, Midwestern pitcher. The focus of the story follows the young ball player's introduction into the majors and his exploitation at the hands of the team's new owner. The film is one long, predictable cliché, but Olmos and costar Lorraine Bracco, as Olmos' longtime girlfriend, are likable characters and director Young (*Dominick and Eugene*) fills his film with beguiling, personal moments. ★★½ $14.99

Tales from the Crypt

(1972, 92 min, GB, Freddie Francis) A chilling anthology of five frightening tales of deceit, mayhem, and treachery as experienced by five people lost in a catacomb. Joan Collins, Patrick Magee, Ian Hendry and Richard Greene are among the five wayward souls who are shown their futures by a mysterious and evil monk (Ralph Richardson). ★★★

Tales from the Darkside: The Movie

(1990, 95 min, US, John Harrison) Sporting a versatile cast that includes Deborah Harry, Christian Slater, and Rae Dawn Chong and stories by George Romero and Stephen King, among others, *Tales from the Darkside: The Movie* leaves behind the familiar, bloody turf covered by the likes of Freddy Krueger and Jason and instead calls upon evil housewives, gargoyles, mummies and a black cat to keep its audience on the edge of its seat. It's all good fun, but occasionally stumbles when it swings from a serious mood to tongue-in-cheek horror and back again. ★★★ $14.99

Tales from the Gimli Hospital

(1989, 72 min, Canada, Guy Maddin) Maddin's ferociously funny Gothic creation is set during the turn of the century in the small Icelandic village of Gimli during a smallpox epidemic. Filmed in an eerie black and white and featuring minimal dialogue, the film tells the story of two hospitalized patients, Einar and Gunnar, who battle each other over everything from telling the perfect story to winning the attentions of their Louise Brooks-lookalike nurses. Wildly impressionistic and surreal, the film will elicit the same kind of astonished chuckles and gasps as another cult classic, *Eraserhead*. ★★★ $79.99

Tales from the Hood

(1995, 97 min, US, Rusty Cundieff) With the same irreverence and stylish flourishes he brought to *Fear of a Black Hat*, director Cundieff has fashioned possibly the first horror anthology film with a social conscience. Not having to rely on monsters for his horrific tales, Cundieff uses the realities of life in the '90s – drug abuse, domestic violence, gang warfare, black-on-black crime, dishonest cops and racism – to create four ironic tales from the supernatural. A devilishly bug-eyed Clarence Williams III is the storyteller, whose audience of three drug-dealing youths listen impatiently to his scary yarns. These include a rollicking tale of a murdered civic leader who enacts revenge; a well-intentioned but heavy-handed story of an abusive "monster"; and the film's two best segments of a David Duke-like politician and an unrepentent gang member. Mixing chills with ills, Cundieff's *Hood* is fun for all; and it's great to see Williams and Rosalind Cash back on the big screen. ★★★ $19.99

The Tales of Hoffman

(1951, 112 min, GB, Michael Powell & Emeric Pressburger) This Powell and Pressburger follow-up to *The Red Shoes* has been given special treatment in its transfer to video, highlighting its lurid Technicolor. During intermission at the Nuremberg Opera House, a group of students gather in the *bierkeller* to drink, smoke and listen to the acclaimed poet Hoffman spin tales of love, loss, mystery and evil. Located somewhere between the poetic surrealism of Jean Cocteau and the highly stylized works of Peter Greenaway, this film version of Offenbach's operatic fantasy will appeal to music lovers and the casual viewer alike. Moira Shearer stars as a robotic ballerina and tenor Robert Rounseville plays the young Hoffman. The music is performed by the Royal Philharmonic Orchestra, conducted by Sir Thomas Beecham. (Filmed in English) ★★★ $39.99

Tales of Ordinary Madness

(1983, 107 min, Italy, Marco Ferreri) Italian director Ferreri provokes every reaction but boredom, and with a scenerio launched from the sordid musings of cult poet Charles Bukowski, he has perhaps found the vehicle best suited for his iconoclastic style. A grizzled Ben Gazzara is the derelict author stumbling through adventures in a sickeningly sun-drenched L.A. The tauntingly beautiful Ornella Muti adds a new dimension to screen masochism. (Filmed in English) ★★★ $69.99

Tales of Terror

(1963, 90 min, US, Roger Corman) In this portmanteau movie, Corman fashions four of Edgar Allan Poe's short stories into three episodes, each featuring Vincent Price. Vincent's daughter gets a strange mother's day surprise; Basil Rathbone is an evil mesmerist whose sultry looks turn Vincent to putty; and, in a comedic segment, Peter Lorre quells a wine taster before his time. ★★★ $14.99

Tales of the City, Vols. 1-3

(1993, 120 min each, US/GB, Alastair Reid) Taken from Armistead Maupin's endearing and popular novel, this boldly original and faithful adaptation follows the interconnected lives of a group of San Francisco eccentrics (both gay and straight) during the halcyon 1970s. This six-part miniseries centers around exotic Earth Mother Anna Madrigal (Olympia Dukakis), landlady of 28 Barbary Lane. Her colorful extended family of tenants includes innocent Mary Ann (Laura Linney), a recent arrival from Cincinnati; bisexual/fag hag Mona (Chloe Webb); and Michael (Marcus D'Amico), a hopeless romantic eternally searching for Mr. Right. The lives of these people and others come together in an amazingly complex series of eye-opening episodes which involve marital infidelity, ribald sexuality, recreational drug use and scenes of the emerging gay lifestyle. *Tales...* is funny, provocative and totally unpredictable. Cameos include Edie Adams, Lance Loud, Paul Bartel, Rod Steiger, Karen Black, Mary Kay Place and Ian McKellen.★★★★ Each vol.: $19.99 Set: $59.99

The Talk of the Town

(1942, 118 min, US, George Stevens) When discussing the movie career of Cary Grant, other films will undoubtedly spring to mind before *Talk of the Town*, but this little-known Stevens comedy is unquestionably one of the actor's best efforts. Grant stars as an escaped convict (framed, naturally) who hides out in the house of an old friend, the captivating Jean Arthur. But she has just rented it to Supreme Court nominee Ronald Colman. While Grant poses as the gardener, Arthur and an unsuspecting Colman attempt to prove Cary's innocence. Of course, both men fall in love with her, and Arthur herself is torn between them. Sparkling romantic comedy and potent social commentary as well. ★★★★ $19.99

Talk Radio

(1989, 119 min, US, Oliver Stone) After *Platoon* and *Wall Street*, Stone explores yet another kind of jungle in this hard-hitting, explosive look at the world of talk radio, public opinion and social intolerance. Loosely based on slain talk show host Alan Berg (a Denver radio personality killed by a neo-Nazi group), the film stars Eric Bogosian, in a dazzling performance as Barry Champlain, a popular late-nite radio host whose verbal sparrings with his audience, not to mention his unapologetic views spoken in rapid-fire delivery, keep his listeners coming back for more. Through a series of flashbacks chronicling his success on the air, the film examines Champlain's complex psychological makeup and his volatile relationships, both in the present and the past, with those closest to him. ★★★½ $19.99

Talkin' Dirty After Dark

(1991, 86 min, US, Topper Carew) Martin Lawrence stars in Carew's film about the lives of struggling black comics in Los Angeles. Lawrence does some excellent stand-up, but for the most part, the material is substandard. One might get the impression that the only things black comics make fun of is sex, what white folks do, sex, what brothers do, and...more sex. ★★ $14.99

The Tall Blond Man with One Black Shoe

(1972, 90 min, France, Yves Robert) A bungling young violinist unwittingly becomes involved with a bunch of would-be James Bonds and sets off a madcap chase of agents and

Tales from the Hood

assassins in this hilarious French farce. Starring Pierre Richard and Bernard Blier. (Dubbed and in French with English subtitles) ★★★

The Tall Guy

(1990, 92 min, GB, Mel Smith) Essentially a one-joke affair, the film follows Dexter King (Jeff Goldblum), an expatriate American stage actor living in London. Because of his above-average height, he is constantly cast in humiliating "fool" roles. Demonstrating a flair for physical comedy, Goldblum is at his best in the movie's real showstopper – a musical version of "The Elephant Man," one of the most tasteless and undeniably funny sequences ever put to film. Featuring Rowan Atkinson and Emma Thompson. ★★½ $19.99

Tall Tale: The Unbelievable Adventures of Pecos Bill

(1995, 96 min, US, Jeremiah Chechik) Not to be confused with Shelley's Duvall's Tall Tales productions, this Disney adventure starring Patrick Swayze as Pecos Bill is a heartwarming coming-of-age story featuring old-time western mythic heroes. When his family's farm and the nearby town are threatened by a ruthless railroad baron (played with magnificent maliciousness by Scott Glenn), a young boy (Nick Stahl) turns to Pecos Bill, Paul Bunyon and John Henry for help. Along the way, he learns the power of his own faith and commitment in the face of adversity. Largely ignored upon its theatrical release, *Tall Tale* is a terrific family film that is both fun and stimulating. Aimed primarily at boys, parents looking for similar encouragement for their girls might look to *A Little Princess*. ★★★ $14.99

Tamango

(1958, 98 min, France, John Berry) This standard seafaring yarn is rescued from certain obscurity by its theme of African slave-trading, black revolt and a "steamy" interracial love story. Curt Jurgens plays a ruthless sea captain of a Dutch slave ship in the 1820s who falls in love with a beautiful black slave (Dorothy Dandridge). Revolt simmers when one strong-willed and resourceful slave, and former warrior (Alex Cressan), attempts to break his chains and lead a rebellion. Despite poor English dubbing of some minor characters and Dandridge's strange, Hollywood diva-ish acting style, the film holds great interest with its depiction of a proud but enslaved village, with their collective will not yet broken by the brutality of forced servitude. The black warriors who lead the rebellion are depicted as especially strong and heroic. ★★½ $29.99

The Tamarind Seed

(1974, 123 min, GB, Blake Edwards) Edwards makes an infrequent foray into the world of drama with this espionage/romance starring Julie Andrews and Omar Sharif. The material isn't strong, but the locations (London, Paris and Barbados) are wonderful and the two stars have some fine moments as the Cold War Romeo and Juliet. ★★ $9.99

The Taming of the Shrew

(1967, 126 min, US/Italy, Franco Zeffirelli) Sumptuous screen version of Shakespeare's classic comedy with rich characterizations from Elizabeth Taylor and Richard Burton as the feuding couple; she an unmarried "wildcat" and he the only man in Padua willing to court her. The story, of course, is the basis for the Cole Porter musical "Kiss Me Kate." ★★★½ $19.99

Tampopo

(1987, 114 min, Japan, Juzo Itami) One of the most inspired and zaniest comedies to be released in years, this Japanese satire on food and sex is a delectable send-up of American westerns. A widow, who operates a noodle restaurant in Tokyo, is befriended by a transient truck driver. Together, in the search for the perfect noodle, they recruit a rag-tag team of social misfits to aid them in their quest. This appetizing comedy of epic proportions presents a world where the power of sex is second only to the power of – you've guessed it – the noodle! (Japanese with English subtitles) ★★★★

Tango and Cash

(1989, 105 min, US, Andrei Konchalovsky) Sylvester Stallone and Kurt Russell star in this slick formulaic police thriller about two super cops framed by a megalomaniac drug dealer. Skipping the standard love interest (or are the two stars the love interest?), the film includes enough car crashes to keep Detroit in the black for another five years. The money combination of a mangy and volatile Russell (à la Mel Gibson in *Lethal Weapon*) with a well-dressed, bespectacled Stallone allows both actors to play with their screen images and made the latter likable for the first time since *Rocky*. ★★½ $9.99

Tank Girl

(1995, 104 min, US, Rachel Talalay) This semi-likable mishmash is sure to elicit squeals of joy from a few while giving migraines to many as it pounds its way through 104 minutes of non sequitured one-liners and plotless shenanigans. Lori Petty springs to life as the title character, a buzz-cut grunge girl with a slightly phallic passion for tanks. Along for the ride is Naomi Watts as her sidekick Jet Girl. Together they join forces with the Rippers (a mutant band of half-human, half-kangaroo renegades) and battle the powerful Water and Power overlords (led by Malcolm McDowell) in the year 2033. Though as visually bombastic as the worst of MTV and as narratively challenged as a "Monkees" episode, the big-screen version of the popular comic book *might* prove fun for the less-discriminating viewer looking for a mindless yuk to accompany their inebriated state. ★★ $19.99

Tanner '88, Vols. 1-3

(1988, 120 ea. min, US, Robert Altman) In 1988, director Altman created a fictional Democratic presidential candidate and used the actual primary process as location shooting. Michael Murphy as Jack Tanner hits the campaign trail, shaking hands with Bob Dole, Gary Hart and Pat Robertson, who may or may not know it's only a movie. Tanner's flashes of brilliance in a quagmire of mediocrity (sometimes his own) are packaged for media consumption by his campaign staff. It's a cynical, intelligent and sardonic look at the photo ops, pollsters, spin doctors, petty sabotage, backbiting and pure chance that comprise the modern American political system. Written by Garry Trudeau, with Sidney Blumenthal as a political consultant, the film stars Pamela Reed, Kevin J. O'Connor, Veronica Cartwright and Cleavon Little, all making an exceptional ensemble cast. Vol. 1 includes "The Dark Horse," "For Real" and "Night of the Twinkies"; Vol. 2 includes "Moonwalker and Bookbag," "Bagels with Bruce," "Child's Play" and "The Great Escape"; Vol. 3 includes "The Girlfriend Factor," "Something Borrowed, Something Blue," "The Boiler Room" and "Reality Check." ★★★½ $79.99

Tap

(1989, 110 min, US, Nick Castle) A frenzied celebration of dance set against an urban backdrop, as a disillusioned tap dancer (Gregory Hines) is torn between his craft and a lucrative living as a thief. With Joe Morton and Sammy Davis, Jr. ★★★ $14.99

Tapeheads

(1988, 97 min, US, Bill Fishman) An exhilaratingly original and innovative spoof which will not disappoint. The film's story follows the unusual road to fame taken by two misfits: the deliciously sleazy John Cusack and the constantly bewildered Tim Robbins. They join forces and set up an independent video production company. Stymied by their failure to make rock videos, they subside on the fringe, making living (and not so living) with as well as taping funerals until their big break comes. The film is crammed with crazy comedy and peppered with unforgettable lines. There's some wild musical numbers and both Cusack and Robbins are wonderful farceurs – and if that's not enough, Junior Walker and Sam Moore appear as "The Swanky Modes." ★★★½

Taps

(1981, 124 min, US, Harold Becker) Military cadets seize control of their military academy when outside forces threaten to shut it down. Some of this is by-the-books, and slow going, but its young cast is enthusiastic. Timothy Hutton, George C. Scott, Sean Penn and Tom Cruise star. ★★ $9.99

Tarantula

(1955, 80 min, US, Jack Arnold) Leo G. Carroll ("The Man from U.N.C.L.E.") stars as a scientist whose secret growth formula works a little too well, resulting in a mutated spider which chews up the countryside and anything else that gets in its way. One of the best of the many 1950s giant/mutant schlock films, *Tarantula* features a credible story, spectacular F/X, and a cameo by a young Clint Eastwood as a squadron leader. Highly entertaining. ("I knew Leo G. Carroll was over a barrel when *Tarantula* took to the hills.") ★★★ $9.99

Target

(1985, 117 min, US, Arthur Penn) Director Penn and actor Gene Hackman are reunited for a third time in this satisfactory espionage thriller. Hackman plays a former CIA agent who, with son Matt Dillon, sets out to rescue his wife, kidnapped by enemy agents out for revenge. ★★½ $9.99

Targets

(1968, 90 min, US, Peter Bogdanovich) This contemporary horror film gave Boris Karloff his last great role as an aging horror film star who decides to retire because events in the real world have rendered his talents superfluous. As if to underscore the point, a soldier just back from Vietnam begins a rampage of killing which leads him to a drive-in, where the old star is making a public appearance. ★★★ $14.99

Tartuffe

(1984, 140 min, France, Gérard Depardieu) Depardieu makes his directorial debut with this version of Moliere's classic stage play about religious and sexual hypocrisy. Starring Depardieu himself in the lead role, the film also stars his wife Elizabeth as well as French stage actor François Perier. The story revolves around a rich merchant who, with his wife, comes under the manipulative spell of a cunning charismatic religious zealot. He is threatened with exposure after the husband discovers that the rascal had made love to his young, attractive wife. Similar to *Cyrano de Bergerac* in its use of poetic dialogue, this satire exposing man's greed and delusions is a skillfully faithful adaptation. (French with English subtitles) ★★★

Tarzan, the Ape Man

(1932, 99 min, US, W.S. Van Dyke) The first of the Johnny Weissmuller Tarzan pictures, with the Olympic swimmer as the definitive Ape Man, and Maureen O'Sullivan as a lovely Jane. Very entertaining adventure film. ★★★ $19.99

A Taste of Honey

(1962, 100 min, GB, Tony Richardson) This lovely, heartbreaking film is a "minor" masterpiece. Rita Tushingham stars in this earthy tale about a group of social rejects in Britain's bleak, industrial North. A poetic saga, which is aided by top-notch performances, and transcends lower-class cliché. ★★★½ $14.99

Taste the Blood of Dracula

(1970, 95 min, GB, Peter Sasdy) The fourth in the Hammer vampire stories. Dracula seeks vengeance against three Victorian thrill-seekers whose cowardice causes the death of a magician trying to resurrect the Prince of Darkness. More campy, hokey fun with Christopher Lee as the evil bloodsucker. ★★½ $14.99

Tatie Danielle

(1990, 100 min, France, Entienne Chatiliez) The supposed dignity and mellifluousness of one's "golden years" is the target of this sharply satirical black comedy. Seemingly innocent and helpless, our sinister heroine Tatie Danielle is, in actuality, a bitter, calculating and unrepentantly mean old lady who receives sick pleasure out of hurting and manipulating all who try to help her. Tatie meets her match one day when an equally manipulative young nurse (who is on to her tactics) arrives on the scene. The film, to its detriment, ignores the motives for Auntie's meanness, and instead takes devious delight in simply chronicling her often hilariously terroristic antics. (French with English subtitles) ★★½ $19.99

Taxi Blues

(1990, 110 min, Russia/France, Pavel Lounguine) This superbly rendered street-level saga about a unique friendship between a rough-hewn Moscow cab driver and an alcoholic saxophone player is a brutal but moving testament to the arduous process of change in the former Soviet Union. Filmed in the early-morning emptiness of Moscow's mean streets, the film uses these two characters to symbolize the faces of the new Russian psyche (the black marketeer and the newly freed intellectual). It is a sometimes humorous, often upsetting and uniformly bleak look at the hardships facing the common people as they struggle to move out of decades of stagnation. Director Lounguine won a well-deserved Best Director prize at Cannes for this very worthy effort. (Russian with English subtitles) ★★★★ $29.99

Taxi Driver

(1976, 113 min, US, Martin Scorsese) Robert De Niro is Travis Bickle, a lonely cab driver obsessed with the squalor and decay of New York City. He sets out on a one-man mission to clean the streets of its underworld of pimps, junkies and hookers. Scorsese directs this sordid and haunting film featuring Jodie Foster in the tragic and memorable role of a teenage prostitute. De Niro's quintessential performance, Scorsese's sardonic view of American urban life, and a mesmerizing and unsettling use of non-exploitative violence propels this masterwork to the forefront of American cinema. ★★★★ $14.99

Taxi Zum Klo

(1981, 107 min, West Germany, Frank Ripploh) Filmmaker and star Ripploh's witty social comedy offers an illuminating portrait of one man's gay lifestyle, his conflicting image in a straight-laced profession and his relationship with a monogamous lover, who disapproves of Frank's hedonistic promiscuity. Funny, charming and unflinchingly honest. (German with English subtitles) ★★★ $79.99

A Taxing Woman

(1988, 127 min, Japan, Juzo Itami) The Japanese post-Kurosawa New Wave continues in this sexy and whimsical comedy from the director of *Tampopo* and *The Funeral*. The story follows Ryoko (Nobuko Miyamoto), a diligent and resourceful female tax inspector who tackles the ever-ingenious tax evading efforts of the citizens. Her greatest challenge is presented by Gondo, a suave operator of "love hotels" whom she suspects is underreporting massive amounts of money. Her impassioned efforts to catch him in the act and his equally feverish schemes to evade detection bring this unlikely pair together in this highly charged comedy. (Japanese with English subtitles) ★★★½ $19.99

A Taxing Woman's Return

(1988, 127 min, Japan, Juzo Itami) This irreverent and free-wheeling comedy about the ingenious efforts of the Japanese to evade taxes and the tenacious tax collectors who are equally determined to ferret out every hidden taxable yen is a welcome follow-up to the hugely successful *A Taxing Woman*. Nobuko Miyamoto is again the charming tax inspector who this time investigates a corrupt funda-

Robert De Niro in *Taxi Driver*

mentalist religious order which might be a front for a real estate racket. While not as fresh as the original, this scathing satire from the director of *Tampopo* is, nevertheless, still a joy to watch. (Japanese with English subtitles) ★★★ $29.99

Tchaikovsky

(1970, 153 min, Russia/US, Igor Tlaankin) Though nominated for a Best Foreign-Language Oscar, this is a disappointing, standard bio of the famed composer Pyotr Ilyich Tchaikovsky. The film suffers from a below-average musical soundtrack (a sin for a film about and infused with classical music) and the lushly elegant Cinemascope visuals are all but lost in the non-letterbox video transfer. The story examines Tchaikovsky's life (from his tortured childhood to his struggles with loneliness and despair to his eventual renown) with an ice-cold austerity which gives little insight into the studious, intense and taciturn composer. Tchaikovsky's homosexuality has been completely ignored, omitting a vital element explaining his rocky romances and disastrous marriage. Produced by composer Dimitri Tiomkin, who also arranged and conducted the music, the film begs for the excesses of Ken Russell's *The Music Lovers*. (Russian with English subtitles) ★½ $59.99

Tchao Pantin

(1985, 94 min, France, Claude Berri) Berri a director noted for his light comedies (*Le Sex Shop*, *Male of the Century*), leaves behind his safe stories to probe the back alleys, sleazy bars and tenements of drug dealers and various other denizens of the Parisian underbelly. A darkly somber and intensely moving thriller about the relationship between an alienated old man, retired from everything around him, and a lonely punk youth. An exciting tale of survival in a heartless world. Winner of 5 Césars. (French with English subtitles) ★★★

Tea and Sympathy

(1956, 123 min, US, Vincente Minnelli) Adapted (and watered down) by Robert Anderson from his own Broadway play, this tale of a sensitive teen at a New England boarding school who is accused of being a homosexual is both involving and curiously tame. John Kerr plays the youth, who is suspected by his classmates of being a "sister boy." Deborah Kerr is the understanding wife of the headmaster who befriends the confused teen and who eventually exorcises any latent homosexual desires. ★★★ $19.99

Teacher's Pet

(1958, 120 min, US, George Stevens) Entertaining romantic farce with Clark Gable as a newspaperman and Doris Day as a teacher. Both come together when he takes her writing course. ★★★ $14.99

Teachers

(1984, 106 min, US, Arthur Hiller) A good cast is mostly wasted in this story of the everyday ups and downs of an urban high school. Starring Nick Nolte, JoBeth Williams, Judd Hirsch, Ralph Macchio, Morgan Freeman, Richard Mulligan and Laura Dern. ★★ $9.99

The Teahouse of the August Moon

(1956, 124 min, US, Daniel Mann) A mild-mannered Army captain (Glenn Ford) is left in charge of an occupied village in 1946 Okinawa, and wacky results ensue. Marlon Brando plays a wily Asian interpreter. ★★★ $19.99

Teaserama

(1955, 75 min, US, Irving Klaw) Fabulous '50s pin-up queen Betty Page and busty glamazon Tempest Storm are featured in this truly amazing burlesque presentation. Performances by pin-up faves Honey Baer, Trudy Wayne, Chris LaChris and Cherry Knight, campy comic routines by famed vaudeville player Joe E. Ross ("Sgt. Bilko," "Car 54, Where Are You?"), and a great dance/striptease by female impersonator Vicky Lynn combine to make this film a "Burly-Q" classic. ★★★ $24.99

Teen Wolf

(1985, 90 min, US, Rod Daniel) Though *Back to the Future* was released several months before it, this harmless teen comedy was Michael J. Fox's film debut. Fox plays a teenager who discovers he's really a werewolf. To its credit, there are a few laughs. Followed by an awful 1987 sequel, *Teen Wolf Too*, starring Jason Bateman. ★★½ $9.99

Teenage Confidential

(60 min,) Mamie Van Doren hosts this look at the juvenile deliquent films of the 1950s and 1960s, including clips from *Naked Youth*, *Teenage Devil Dolls*, *I Was a Teenage Psycho*, and more. Groovy! $9.99

Teenage Mutant Ninja Turtles

(1990, 93 min, US, Steve Barron) Long popular on video in cartoon form, these live-action Teenage Mutant Ninja Turtles proved to be just as popular on the big screen in this hokey but crowd-pleasing (if you're under 15) adventure-comedy. Here the TMNT find themselves up against a group of teenagers under the evil influence of a Japanese gangster. Cowabunga, dude. Though a bit sluggish throughout, there's still enough action to appeal to the younger set, and Jim Henson's full-size costumes are terrific. (Followed by two sequels.) ★★ $22.99

Telefon

(1977, 100 min, US, Don Siegel) Exciting espionage thriller with Charles Bronson playing a Russian agent sent to the U.S. to preserve detente by stopping a psychotic defector (Donald Pleasence) from activating scores of hypnotized saboteurs. A terrific cast includes Lee Remick, Tyne Daly and Patrick Magee. ★★★ $19.99

Tell Me a Riddle

(1980, 94 min, US, Lee Grant) A married couple, together for 47 years and lately grown apart, try to bring love back to their lives at the news of the wife's impending death. Excellent performances by Melvyn Douglas and Lila Kedrova as the husband and wife. ★★★

Tell Them Willie Boy Is Here

(1969, 96 min, US, Abraham Polonsky) Robert Blake stars as Willie Boy, an American Indian who becomes the object of a massive hunting party and a political scapegoat during the early 1900s. Set in the arid deserts of Southern California, the film begins with a drunken pool room fight involving Willie Boy and a white patron. From there, events start to snowball as Willie Boy kills the father of his girlfriend (a tanned Katharine Ross), and the two go on the run with a disinterested sheriff (Robert Redford) and a blood-thirsty posse on their trail. Director Polonsky – whose first feature this was since being blackballed during the McCarthy witch-hunts – sets an ominous tone as he effectively tells a tale of injustice and hysteria and juxtaposes it with an exciting chase story. ★★★ $14.99

The Temp

(1993, 99 min, US, Tom Holland) Timothy Hutton, an upwardly mobile marketing executive with a penchant for paranoia, is blown away by the skills of his new temporary secretary, played by Lara Flynn Boyle. She files, she types, she makes copies like nobody's business, and, unfortunately, she also may be bumping off most of Hutton's competition in the dog-eat-dog world of cookie manufacturing. The main problem with *The Temp* is that Boyle is so blatantly obvious in her manipulations of Hutton that the film loses a lot of its tension early on. Otherwise, there is nothing particularly wrong with this fairly standard thriller, and as a plus there is Faye Dunaway as Hutton's no-holds-barred boss. ★★ $19.99

The Tempest

(1982, 140 min, US, Paul Mazursky) Mazursky's contemporary treatment of Shakespeare's drama has John Cassavetes attempting to resolve his midlife crisis by abandoning his successful Manhattan existence to search for truth and beauty in the Greek isles. Beautiful location shooting and engaging performances compensate for weaknesses in the script. Also with Gena Rowlands, Susan Sarandon, Raul Julia and Molly Ringwald. ★★½ $9.99

Temptation of a Monk

(1994, 118 min, Hong Kong, Clara Law) While stylishly filmed, this tale of a betrayed general who must seek refuge in a temple is slow-moving and confusing. Joan Chen stars as

the siren princess who tempts a general of a royal family's army as he tries to atone for his errors in being accused a traitor. Lavish costumes, open landscapes and period music abound. The actors leave a good impression on a poorly written script. Though director Law (*Reincarnation of Golden Lotus*) has exhibited a fine edge with her prior works, she is unable to overcome a taxing story line and laborious characters in this well-intentioned but misguided effort. (Mandarin with English subtitles) ★★ $19.99

10

(1979, 121 min, US, Blake Edwards) Edwards wrote and directed this hit comedy about a famed composer (Dudley Moore) who becomes obsessed by a woman (Bo Derek) he rates a perfect "10." Moore is good at playing Edwards' slapstick, and Julie Andrews and Brian Dennehy offer good support. Robert Webber's self-pitying gay composer is a bit much, though. ★★★ $9.99

The Ten Commandments

(1923, 146 min, US, Cecil B. DeMille) Unfortunately DeMille never heeded the eleventh commandment which is: Thou shalt not make epic movies out of the Bible pandering to people's prurient interests. The first portion of this sprawling mess violates that edict, then goes on to tell a contemporary tale of two brothers – one good, one evil – and how the Word saves their souls. Great camp fun with two-strip Technicolor sequences. ★★★ $19.99

The Ten Commandments

(1956, 220 min, US, Cecil B. DeMille) Mammoth epic from DeMille, based on his silent classic. Charlton Heston dons beard and robe to portray Moses, leading the Jews out of Egypt. A spectacular production, though some scenes may cause a few smirks. An all-star cast includes Yul Brynner, Anne Baxter, Edward G. Robinson and Yvonne de Carlo. Even with today's state-of-the-art special effects, the parting of the Red Sea is still impressive. ★★★½ $29.99

Ten Days Wonder

(1971, 101 min, France, Claude Chabrol) Although not well received in its initial release in 1971, this oddity has been called by some a "fascinating theological thriller" and seen by others as a pretentiously arty mess. Whatever, the film is a distinctly original work that fans of Chabrol and of the avant-garde should enjoy. Adapted from an Ellery Queen story, the film stars Anthony Perkins as a mentally and emotionally disturbed young man who falls in love with his father's (Orson Welles) child bride. A bewildering mystery of madness, adultery and blackmail. (Filmed in English) ★★½

Ten from Your Show of Shows

(1973, 92 min, US, Max Liebman) For those of you who remember the classic TV comedy show of the 1950s, "Your Show of Shows," no more additional information is needed other than that this is a collection of their most hilarious routines. For those not familiar, these examples of the very best of TV sketch comedy, performed live each week, are not to be missed. Starring the madcap team of Sid Caesar, Imogene Coca and Carl Reiner, and with many skits written by Mel Brooks, the film concludes with a painfully funny parody of "This Is Your Life." ★★★★

Ten Little Indians

(1974, 98 min, GB, Peter Collinson) Second remake of the Agatha Christie mystery "And Then There Were None," this time set in a remote desert inn, where ten strangers are gathered and then murdered one by one. Lackluster pacing adds nothing new to this oft-told tale. Cast features Oliver Reed, Elke Sommer, Richard Attenborough and Gert Frobe. ★★

10 Rillington Place

(1971, 111 min, GB, Richard Fleischer) This gripping psychological thriller is another true-life murder case brought to the screen by director Fleischer (Compulsion, The Boston Strangler). The story centers on notorious mass-murderer John Christie (Richard Attenborough) and his unwitting pawn Timothy Evans (John Hurt). Sometimes too clinical to be completely successful as a thriller, the film manages to remain interesting nonetheless. ★★★ $19.99

10 Violent Women

(1979, 97 min, US, Ted V. Mikels) Bored with their jobs, ten female coal miners attempt to increase their income through a jewelry heist and by dealing cocaine. Director Mikels (Corpse Grinders, Girl in Gold Boots) has a cameo as a fence who suffers death by spiked heel. As campy and outrageous as it sounds. ★

The Tenant

(1976, 125 min, France/US, Roman Polanski) Polanski himself stars in this dark and eerie film noir about a social misfit who moves into a Parisian apartment and begins a bizarre descent into madness. Filled with paranoia and forboding, the film takes on its own twisted logic as it makes its way towards a truly outrageous denouement. ★★★ $49.99

Tender Mercies

(1982, 89 min, US, Bruce Beresford) Robert Duvall delivers a powerful, Oscar-winning performance as a country singer on the skids who is rescued from despair and the bottle by the quiet strength and sensitivity of a young widow. Australian Beresford (Breaker Morant) makes his American directorial debut with this humanistic drama. ★★★★ $14.99

The Tender Trap

(1955, 111 min, US, Charles Walters) Frank Sinatra stars in this engaging comedy about an insufferably unattached bachelor who falls for sweet young-and-innocent Broadway hopeful Debbie Reynolds and gets more than he bargained for. One of the better "sophisticated" comedies to come out of the '50s, this adaptation of the Max Schulman/Robert Paul Smith play features a bunch of winning musical numbers (especially the Cahn-Van Heusen title tune). Celeste Holm and David Wayne are excellent in support and Carolyn Jones is great in a small role. ★★★½ $19.99

Tendres Cousines

(1980, 90 min, France, David Hamilton) A funny, tender coming-of-age film which follows the sexual antics of a 14-year-old boy and his beautiful cousin. Master erotic photographer Hamilton (Bilitis) presents this romp of unrequited love amidst the haylofts of rural France. (Dubbed) ★★½

The Tenth Man

(1988, 100 min, GB, Jack Gold) Written by Graham Greene in 1944 while under contract with M-G-M, the manuscript for this riveting thriller, about a man's cowardly act, his punishment and eventual redemption, languished in the studio archives until it was rediscovered in 1983. The setting is Occupied France, 1941. Wealthy lawyer Jean-Louis Chavel (Anthony Hopkins) is imprisoned in a Nazi roundup. When a German officer is killed, the Nazis retaliate by killing one in ten prisoners, with the prisoners themselves choosing the victims. Chavel's revealing moment occurs after they draw lots and he loses. Fearful of death, he trades places with another man, offering his substantial fortune and property to his family. Years later, a penniless Chavel returns to his former chateau, now home to the dead man's lovely but forlorn sister and her ailing mother. Assuming a new identity, he becomes their gardener and friend – knowing full well their hatred of Chavel, the man who "killed" their son and brother. His secret shame remains hidden until one day a stranger arrives claiming that he is Chavel. ★★★★ $19.99

The Tenth Victim

(1965, 92 min, Italy, Elio Petre) A macabre yet compelling sci-fi tale set in the 21st century where killing has been ritualized in a sport where men and women pursue each other in a deadly game. Marcello Mastroianni and Ursula Andress star in this nightmarish thriller that blends just the right amount of satire in its exploration of the uneasy relationship between the individual and society. Miss Andress' bullet-firing brassiere is worth the price of the rental alone! (Dubbed) ★★★

Teorema

(1968, 98 min, Italy, Pier Paolo Pasolini) Pasolini's fusion of Marxism, sex and religion stars a very young and attractive Terence Stamp as a divine stranger who enters the household of a bourgeois family and profoundly affects their lives when he seduces the mother, father, son, daughter and maid. A surreal and sensual allegory with the Pasolini postulation that the ruling class can be undermined and destroyed by the one thing that it cannot control — sex. Winner of the Grand Prix at Venice, 1968. (Italian with English subtitles) ★★★ $19.99

Tequila Sunrise

(1988, 116 min, US, Robert Towne) Towne, who wrote the brilliant Chinatown, is the director and writer of this uneven but gorgeous-looking romantic thriller which tries to and occasionally succeeds in capturing the mood of the Roman Polanski classic. Mel Gibson stars as a former drug dealer trying to go straight, but is about to be busted by his high school chum Kurt Russell. The two men become embroiled in a game of cat-and-mouse as both fall in love with a beautiful restaurant owner, Michelle Pfeiffer. The three stars give earnest performances, but are unable to hide some of the contrivances of the script. ★★ $14.99

Terence Davies Trilogy

(1974-83, 101 min, GB, Terence Davies) Three short films, Madonna and Child, Children and Death and Transfiguration, were made by director Davies over a ten-year period (including time spent as a student at the National Film School) and were all inspired from his own life. The films examine the harsh life — from boyhood to the grave — of Robert Tucker, a gay Liverpudlian. While lacking in traditional narrative, this bleak yet stirring and powerful portrait follows one man's continual battle against the demons that drove him into loneliness and despair. Beginning in his bullied and tortured youth, Robert struggles with his conflicting homosexual desire

Terence Davies Trilogy

and the tight restraints and ensuing guilt of his Catholicism. Through a complex use of flash-forwards and flashbacks, he eventually comes out of the closet and sheds his childhood religion, but continues to be a haunted, mother-dominated adult — still tormented by his guilt-ridden sexuality and its emotional confusion. A richly evocative and ultimately unforgettable work. ★★★ $39.99

Teresa Venerdi

(1941, 90 min, Italy, Vittorio De Sica) A delectable comedy directed by and starring De Sica as a young physician working in an orphanage who finds himself innocently involved with three women. The magnificent Anna Magnani co-stars as a doctor's assistant who sets out to win the doctor herself. Filled with action, intrigue and jealousy, this legendary Italian comedy is sometimes known by the title, *Doctor Beware*. (Italian with English subtitles) ★★★

Terminal Bliss

(1992, 91 min, US, Jordan Allan) Before shooting to fame as a moody California rich kid on TV's "Beverly Hills 90210," teen heartthrob Luke Perry played a moody California rich kid in this pointless tale of adolescent decadence. While the sex and drugs sequences during the first 15 minutes offer generous helpings of delicious B-movie juvenile delinquency, the aimless, episodic structure of the film eventually grows tiresome. And as Southern California brats indulge in hard drugs, cheap sex and teenage angst, the film reaches its inevitably ludicrous anticlimax. Who needs plot, depth and style when you can hear lines like, "Mom, I'm going out to kill myself now. I'll be home late." (Made in 1987) ★ $19.99

The Terminal Man

(1974, 107 min, US, Mike Hodges) Interesting if flawed thriller based on Michael Crichton's novel with George Segal as a scientist who becomes controlled by a computer. Also starring Joan Hackett and Jill Clayburgh. ★★ $14.99

Terminal Velocity

(1994, 102 min, US, Deran Sarafian) This high-flying actioner starring Charlie Sheen as a devil-may-care sky diver and Nastassja Kinski as a Russian agent who lures him into helping her beat the bad guys is filled with implausibilities, bad dialogue, wretched acting and is still somehow great fun. Well, maybe not *great* fun, but even though Sheen (sporting a ridiculous D.A. hairdo) and Kinski demonstrate why their respective careers are in stasis, there are plenty of fist fights, gunplay, explosions (there's even a tribute to *Die Harder*) and general chaos to light up the night of any starving action fan. ★★½ $14.99

The Terminator

(1984, 108 min, US, James Cameron) Director Cameron and actor Arnold Schwarzenegger both burst on the action scene with this explosively entertaining and taut sci-fi thriller. Arnold plays a cyborg sent from the future to present-day Los Angeles to terminate the mother (Linda Hamilton) of a revolutionary. Michael Biehn is the soldier also from the

future sent to eliminate Arnold. (Letterboxed version available for $19.99) ★★★½ $14.99

Terminator 2: Judgment Day

(1991, 135 min, US, James Cameron) He's Back! Director Cameron and box-office superstar Arnold Schwarzenegger team up once again for this long-awaited follow-up. The 100 million dollar price tag on this impressive sci-fi extravaganza made a lot of jaws drop, but that's nothing compared to what the rip-roaring, non-stop action and eye-popping special effects do. The year is 1997. The evil cyborgs have sent the new, improved T-1000 terminator unit back through time on a mission to eliminate the future leader of the human resistance — a typical Southern California adolescent named John Conner (nicely played by Edward Furlong). But into the fray comes a second killing machine (guess who), reprogrammed by the humans and sent back to protect the lad. Together, they liberate his mom, Sarah (a very buff Linda Hamilton), who's been institutionalized for her babblings about robots from the future and impending apocalypse, and the relentless chase begins. Joe Morton adds excellent support as a computer scientist who *might* inadvertently develop a doomsday machine. (Letterboxed version available for $19.99) ★★★½ $14.99

Terms of Endearment

(1983, 132 min, US, James L. Brooks) A sensitive, funny and deeply touching examination of the tumultuous relationship between a mother and daughter. *Terms* virtually monopolized the Oscar ceremony, taking Best Picture and Best Director honors as well as (finally) acknowledging Shirley MacLaine for her crackling conception of a rigid matriarch. Debra Winger is sensational as her spunky daughter and Jack Nicholson rises to the occasion as the ex-astronaut next door with the wrong stuff. Followed in 1996 by an inferior sequel, *The Evening Star*. ★★★½ $9.99

Terra em Transe

(1966, 105 min, Brazil, Glauber Rocha) *Terra em Transe*, about the disillusionment and death of a young poet and journalist who is persuaded to become involved in the politics of his country, is a landmark of political cinema and a vivid example of Brazil's Cinema Novo movement. A powerful and quite personal film which was denounced by the Right as incendiary propaganda, hailed by the Left as an impassioned exposé, and banned by the government for some time. Winner of the International Film Critics Award at Cannes. (Portuguese with English subtitles) ★★★½ $59.99

La Terra Trema

(1948, 160 min, Italy, Luchino Visconti) Initially setting off to make a Communist Party-financed short documentary on the conditions of the peasants in poverty-stricken Sicily, Visconti soon abandoned this to work on an epic focusing on the harsh conditions of southern Italy's fishermen, factory workers and miners. He finished only this segment, "Episodes del Mare" — and the result is a neorealist masterpiece. Filmed on location with nonprofessional actors, the story tells of the conditions and struggles of an exploited

fisherman's family and the unsuccessful revolt by them and others against insurmountable odds. With startlingly beautiful images, a simple narrative and his focus on social reality, this, only Visconti's second feature, is considered one of his best works. (Italian with English subtitles) ★★★★ $69.99

The Terror

(1963, 81 min, US, Roger Corman) Effective Corman cheapie starring Boris Karloff and Jack Nicholson about an injured soldier from Napoleon's army recovering at an eerie castle with strange goings-on. ★★½ $9.99

The Terror Within

(1988, 89 min, US, Thierry Notz) A chemically-induced plague has ravaged the Earth and its remaining survivors are trapped in a laboratory 500 feet below the Mojave Desert. When a pregnant woman is found, the group soon learns that the baby she is carrying is an embryonic mutant. Just a little bit spooky, though its good premise isn't thoroughly realized. ★★½ $14.99

The Terrornauts

(1967, 75 min, GB, Montgomery Tully) Mysterious alien forces kidnap an entire building containing research scientists and transport them to another planet. There, a robot takes the Earthlings to yet another planet, where little green men show them the fate of Earth. Fun, low-budget British sci-fi based on the novel "The Wailing Asteroid." ★★½ $14.99

Tess

(1979, 180 min, GB/France, Roman Polanski) Polanski's Academy Award-winning interpretation of Thomas Hardy's novel features breathtaking cinematography and a strong, eloquent performance by Nastassja Kinski as a peasant girl who ruins and is ruined by two men. Polanski precisely and memorably portrays the moral rigidity of Victorian England and brilliantly moves this story to its inexorable climax. (Filmed in English) ★★★½ $29.99

Testament

(1983, 89 min, US, Lynne Littman) The devastation of a nuclear attack is powerfully conveyed via personal relationships rather than elaborate special effects in Littman's staggering drama. Jane Alexander gives a virtuoso performance as a housewife who helplessly watches the demise of family and friends. An extremely intense film which resists strident advocacy, opting for sensitivity and restraint in its warning of a nuclear nightmare. Also starring William Devane, Lukas Haas, Mako and Kevin Costner in a small role. ★★★½ $14.99

The Testament of Dr. Mabuse

(1933, 120 min, Germany, Fritz Lang) Banned in Germany soon after its release, Lang's brilliant thriller is a trenchant allegory on the rise of Nazism, as well as the thinking of its crazed leader. In this follow-up to Lang's 1922 silent classic *Dr. Mabuse: Der Spieler (The Gambler)*, Rudolph Klein-Rogge returns as the now lunatic underworld crime lord imprisoned in an insane asylum, spending his final days writing diabolical plans to create "an abyss of terror" in Germany. From his cell, these plans are carried out, much to the consternation of the police, even after his death. (German with English subtitles) ★★★½ $24.99

The Testament of Orpheus

(1959, 83 min, France, Jean Cocteau) "I shall present a striptease in which I shed my body to expose my soul." With this statement, Cocteau opens his final film, a farewell celebration to art. Cocteau himself takes the lead in this private diary which exposes the relationship between the artist, his work and his dreams. The arresting piece features appearances by such friends as Jean Marais, Yul Brynner, Pablo Picasso and Charles Aznavour. (French with English subtitles) ★★★½ $29.99

Tetsuo: The Iron Man

(1989, 67 min, Japan, Shinya Tsukamoto) Shockingly perverse techno-erotic splatterthon about a Japanese businessman who begins to metamorphose into a misshapen "Iron Man" after running over a "metal fetishist" in a hit-and-run accident. The next day, the offender discovers metal shards growing out of his face and his phallus turns into a two-foot homicidal corkscrew. The remainder of this surrealistic, cyberpunk epic concerns a battle between two "Iron Men" in what could be best described as *Eraserhead* meets *In the Realm of the Senses.* Also included is the 25-minute short film *Drum Struck* (**), directed by Greg Nickson and featuring actor Anthony Bevilacqua as a rock-n-roll drummer in search of the perfect beat in this strange David Lynch-influenced piece. ★★★★ $79.99

Tevye

(1939, 96 min, US, Maurice Schwartz) Taken from the famous Sholom Aleichem story from which *Fiddler on the Roof* is based, this moving human drama set in Czarist Russia (yet filmed on Long Island) will remind viewers less of the famous musical play and more of the works of such directors as Pagnol, Renoir and Bresson. Director and Yiddish stage actor Schwartz stars as Tevye, a deeply religious man thrown into a conflict between the rules of his religion and his love for his family after he discovers that his daughter Khave has fallen in love with a Gentile and plans to marry him. (Yiddish with English subtitles) ★★★ $79.99

Tex

(1982, 103 min, US, Tim Hunter) A young Matt Dillon gives a subdued and sensitive performance as a teenager on the verge of adulthood. Abandoned by their father, he and his brother struggle with responsibility and indecision. Based on S.E. Hinton's novel (Francis Coppola would find limited success with two other Hinton novels, *The Outsiders* and *Rumble Fish*). Hunter (*River's Edge*) directs with clarity. ★★★

Texas

(1941, 94 min, US, George Marshall) Solid western with William Holden and Glenn Ford as two drifters in search of love and fortune in the wilds of Texas. They find Claire Trevor. ★★★ $9.99

Texas Chainsaw Massacre

(1974, 81 min, US, Tobe Hooper) Hooper directed this horrific tale about the gruesome slaughter of a group of innocent youngsters by a family of maniacs, headed by "Leatherface." This much-imitated gorefest has yet to be equaled for its sheer terror and shocking but surprisingly non-bloody depictions of violence. You have been warned. ★★★ $19.99

Texas Chainsaw Massacre Part 2

(1986, 95 min, US, Tobe Hooper) Slick sequel to the Hooper cult hit stars Dennis Hopper as a retired Texas Ranger out to avenge the murder of his family, who were killed in the original film. A pretty awful follow-up with nary an authentic chill in sight. ★ $9.99

Texasville

(1990, 125 min, US, Peter Bogdanovich) Sad to report that as good as *The Last Picture Show* is, its sequel, *Texasville*, is as bad. In a small, dusty town in 1970s Texas, frumpy and double-chinned Jeff Bridges is in the throes of midlife crisis: he's disillusioned and broke, married to an unresponsive, verbally abusive Annie Potts and attracted to the returning Cybill ("look but don't touch") Shepherd. Strangely, the plot is lifeless, uninvolving and tepid, especially in light of the film's intended goal of being a torrid Southern sexual comedy. All of the stars from the original film return, including Cloris Leachman, Timothy Bottoms, Eileen Brennan and Randy Quaid. ★½ $19.99

Thank You and Goodnight

(1991, 77 min, US, Jan Oxenberg) "What is this thing called death? And what is eternity anyway?" Independent filmmaker Oxenberg breaks through the commercial film barrier with this humorous, irreverent, inventive and touching comedy-drama documenting her grandmother's death. Never maudlin nor morbid, Oxenberg tackles not only the life and personality of her 70-ish grandmother, a self-proclaimed kosher ham, but contemplates the mystery of death and the regret and sorrow of the living. The director intermixes interviews with her grandmother, a strong-willed, cranky Jewish New Yorker, along with her friends and family and interspersese these with imaginative use of life-size cut-outs of herself and others in dramatic remembrances from her childhood. An emotionally powerful yet humorously contemplative family autobiography that clutches at the heart and soul. ★★★★ $19.99

Thank Your Lucky Stars

(1943, 130 min, US, David Butler) Warner Brothers' entry into the all-star musical which the studio released during WWII to help the war effort. Eddie Cantor plays dual roles as himself and a show business hopeful, and there's plenty of 1940s stars: Bette Davis sings "They're Either Too Young or Too Old," Errol Flynn sings "That's What You Jolly Well Get" and Ida Lupino and Olivia deHavilland jitterbug! Humphrey Bogart, John Garfield and Ann Sheridan also appear. ★★★ $29.99

That Championship Season

(1982, 110 min, US, Jason Miller) A well-acted but static adaptation of the Pulitzer Prize-winning Broadway drama about the reunion of a championship high school basketball team. Robert Mitchum is their coach, and the team consists of Bruce Dern, Paul Sorvino (re-creat- ing his acclaimed stage role), Stacy Keach and Martin Sheen. ★★½ $79.99

That Cold Day in the Park

(1969, 113 min, US, Robert Altman) Sandy Dennis stars as a 32-year-old virgin who is attracted to a handsome young mute (Michael Burns) she meets in the park. However, when she takes him home to care for him, a sly psychological game begins between the sexually repressed woman and the prankish drifter. An occasionally unfocused though unsettling drama. ★★½ $14.99

That Darn Cat

(1965, 116 min, US, Robert Stevenson) Cute Disney comedy about a cat who helps solve a kidnapping mystery. With Dean Jones, Hayley Mills and Dorothy Provine. ★★½ $19.99

That Darn Cat

(1997, 100 min, US, Robert Spiers) This remake of Disney's popular 1965 family comedy retains very little of the appeal of the original. Even the presence of the usually adorable Christina Ricci can't bring to life the story of a cute feline which helps solve a kidnapping. Doug E. Doug appears as an FBI agent, and Dean Jones, who was in the original, costars. Slow, rarely funny, and ultimately a pointless retread. ★½ $26.99

That Hamilton Woman

(1941, 125 min, US, Alexander Korda) Good performances highlight this story of the ill-fated romance between Lord Admiral Nelson and Lady Emma Hamilton. The best of the three films made by then-husband and wife Laurence Olivier and Vivien Leigh. (The same story was retold in 1973 in *The Nelson Affair*, which is not available on video.) ★★★ $19.99

That Naughty Girl (Mam'zelle Pigale)

(1958, 77 min, France, Michel J. Boisrond) Brigitte Bardot, in a role that plays against her bombshell image, stars as an innocent but klutzy schoolgirl who finds herself the unwitting pawn in a cat-and-mouse chase between the police, a ring of counterfeiters and her ex-con father. Scantily clad in either a tight-fitting tennis outfit, a flimsy bikini, a bath towel or even, for a time, a Roman tunic, young Brigitte is both disarmingly likable and sexy in this minor but amusing film which features more than its fair share of tacky musical numbers. (Dubbed) ★★

That Obscure Object of Desire

(1977, 103 min, France, Luis Buñuel) Buñuel's surreal comedy of the sexes stars Fernando Rey as an aging aristocrat who falls obsessively in love with a beguiling but unapproachable woman, played by two different actresses: the detached Carole Bouquet and the voluptuous Angela Molina. Buñuel's final film takes us mischievously through the enigma of human passion. (French with English subtitles) ★★★½ $29.99

That Old Feeling

(1997, 107 min, US, Carl Reiner) They say love is better the second time around, but it would take quite a torrid affair to equal the sheer enjoyment experienced in watching *That Old Feeling*, an old-fashioned, delightfully funny battle-of-the-sexes comedy. Divorced for 15 loathing years, Bette Midler and Dennis Farina reunite for their daughter's wedding, hopefully with their claws retracted for the day. However, neither could have anticipated the reunion in store when old resentments give way to uncontrollable lust and they run away together. With his most entertaining film since *All of Me*, director Reiner wisely lets his wonderful cast cut loose. Midler is a master of the one-liner, and she's in top form. Finally given a lead role, Farina (who was robbed of an Oscar nomination for *Get Shorty*) rises to the occasion and is a marvelous comic presence. Lending solid support, Danny Nucci is a handsome tabloid photographer, and David Rasche is priceless as a babbling New Age therapist. Though some of the story loses its balance when it concentrates too much on the daughter, Midler and Farina make any old feeling seem new again. ★★★ $99.99

That Sinking Feeling

(1979, 82 min, Scotland, Bill Forsyth) This first feature by gifted Scottish director Forsyth only came to America after the successes of *Local Hero* and *Gregory's Girl*. In his characteristic way, Forsyth imbues this tale with amiable but lunatic teenagers and a host of daft adults. The story involves a gang of Glasgow youths who concoct a scheme to rob a warehouse full of stainless steel sinks. John Gordon Sinclair (*Gregory's Girl*) stars. ★★★

That Thing You Do!

(1996, 110 min, US, Tom Hanks) It should come as no surprise that the first film Tom Hanks has written and directed is a witty, nice, beguilingly old-fashioned movie-movie. After all, double Oscar winner Hanks is a witty, nice, old-fashioned movie star, perhaps the Jimmy Stewart of his generation. What may come as a surprise is that Hanks has also managed to make his first film so well-crafted and toe-tappingly charming. *That Thing You Do!* chronicles the rise, quick star status and even quicker slide of a pop band in 1964. Hailing from Erie, PA, and called The Wonders, the group consists of a jazz aficionado drummer (Tom Everett Scott), a self-absorbed songwriter (Johnathan Schaech), a goofy guitarist (Steve Zahn), and an anxious bass player (Ethan Embrey). Also along for the ride is Faye (Liv Tyler), Jimmy's perky girlfriend and the group's biggest fan. With Neco-wafer colored cinematography and lovingly rendered period detail, the film moves at a rapid clip tracking the group's roots in smalltown America and their ascension to the top. With *That Thing You Do!*, Hanks seems to know that sometimes it's hip to be square, and he's proud of it. ★★★½ $14.99

That Touch of Mink

(1962, 99 min, US, Delbert Mann) Doris Day made two "sex" comedies in 1962: this one costarring Cary Grant; and *Lover Come Back*, with Rock Hudson. Though *That Touch of Mink* is not nearly as funny or successful as *Lover Come Back*, it is nevertheless a pleasant enough nostalgia course for an era when women (nice girls, anyway) did everything possible to keep their virginity, and men did

That Obscure Object of Desire

everything they could to dissuade them. Tame stuff compared to today, but it did manage to curl a few lips "way back" in '62. ★★½ $19.99

That Uncertain Feeling

(1941, 84 min, US, Ernst Lubitsch) Sophisticated if lightweight romp from the great Lubitsch about a married couple's dilemma when the wife gets the hiccups. Merle Oberon and Melvyn Douglas give appealing performances as the husband and wife, and Burgess Meredith steals the show as their pianist neighbor. ★★½ $19.99

That Was Then, This Is Now

(1985, 103 min, US, Christopher Cain) Emilio Estevez stars in and adapted this routine version of S.E. Hinton's novel about a troubled teen's coming-of-age. Also starring Craig Sheffer, Kim Delaney and Morgan Freeman. (Hinton's other novels which have been filmed are "The Outsiders," "Tex" and "Rumble Fish.") ★★ $79.99

That'll Be the Day

(1974, 90 min, GB, Claude Whatham) An underrated and compelling drama of a British working-class youth (David Essex), and would-be rock and roller, as he moves through adolescence to adulthood. Set in the 1950s, this down-to-earth story of musical aspiration also stars Ringo Starr and includes a small performance by Keith Moon. The sequel, *Stardust*, follows the boy further into his love and music and its attendant trappings. ★★★ $14.99

That's Adequate

(1987, 80 min, US, Harry Hurwitz) This episodic low-budget movie parody actually contains several hilarious, if totally silly, skits. The cast includes Tony Randall, James Coco, Robert Townsend, Bruce Willis, Robert Downey, Jr., Jerry Stiller and Anne Meara. This is sort of a poor man's *Amazon Women on the Moon* and *The Groove Tube*, though it is just as funny. And the parodies of the Three Stooges, Adolph Hitler as a youth and an animated chil-

dren's show would be at home in a Python or Brooks film. Not for sophisticated tastes. ★★

That's Dancing

(1985, 105 min, US, Jack Haley, Jr.) Hodgepodge compilation of some of the movies' best dance sequences. Includes scenes from *West Side Story*, *42nd Street* and *Sweet Charity*, among many others. ★★½ $19.99

That's Entertainment

(1974, 132 min, US, Jack Haley, Jr.) Compilation of some of M-G-M's best musical moments. Includes clips from *The Wizard of Oz*, *Gigi* and *Singin' in the Rain*, among many others. Hosts include Fred Astaire, Gene Kelly, James Stewart and Elizabeth Taylor. The musical sequences that were chosen and the wealth of wonderful stars who appear combine to make this a delightfully nostalgic musical experience. ★★★½ $14.99

That's Entertainment, Part 2

(1976, 126 min, US, Gene Kelly) Kelly and Fred Astaire host this fond remembrance and sequel, looking back at more of the best M-G-M had to offer. Includes comedic and dramatic scenes, as well as musical clips. ★★★ $14.99

That's Life

(1986, 102 min, US, Blake Edwards) Edwards wrote and directed this absorbing drama starring Jack Lemmon in a remarkable performance as a successful architect facing emotional crisis as his 60th birthday nears. Julie Andrews gives a solid portrayal as his wife. ★★★ $14.99

Theatre of Blood

(1973, 105 min, GB, Douglas Hickox) Though its joke wears thin, this is nevertheless an entertaining horror film about a demented Shakespearean actor (Vincent Price) who takes a bloody revenge against the eight theatre critics who gave him "thumbs down." (Watch out Roger and Gene.) Cast includes Diana Rigg, Robert Morley and Jack Hawkins. ★★★ $14.99

Susan Sarandon (l.) and Geena Davis in *Thelma and Louise*

Thelma and Louise

(1991, 120 min, US, Ridley Scott) A wildly entertaining and remarkably accomplished road movie which features uncharacteristically sensitive and intuitive direction from Scott. Susan Sarandon and Geena Davis are the title characters, two friends who leave their male counterparts and head for a leisurely weekend getaway. En route, however, their trek turns deadly and they find themselves on the run from the police. Stylish and witty, Callie Khouri's Oscar-winning screenplay follows their series of escalating criminal adventures as the two women break away from the confines of a male-dominated society, searching for their own identity and independence. Sarandon and Davis are both outstanding, each creating enormously appealing, substantial and distinct characters. Representing a microcosm of male society, Harvey Keitel, Michael Madsen and Brad Pitt are the disparate men in Thelma and Louise's lives. (Available letterboxed and pan & scan) ★★★★ $14.99

Them!

(1954, 94 min, US, Gordon Douglas) A horror favorite for years, this is the one with the giant ants. Humongous insects are spotted in the desert, and they're working their way to Los Angeles. James Whitmore, Edmund Gwenn, Joan Weldon and James Arness are the crack team tracking them down. Lots of good old-fashioned chills. ★★★½ $9.99

Theme

(1979, 108 min, Russia, Gleb Panfilov) An early test case under *glasnost*, *Theme* was completed in 1979 only to be held out of release by Russian censors until 1988. Its crime: being too emotional. In retrospect, the most fascinating thing about this otherwise very standard drama is that anyone would ever find it worthy of suppression. The film's action centers around Kim Yesenin, a 54-year-old poet who is thoroughly under the wing of the Soviet bureaucracy. While seeking relaxation in the country, he is confronted by an alluring young woman who accuses him of selling out his artistic integrity to the state. Naturally, he finds himself smitten by both her and her uncompromising views and sets out to reform himself. While not particularly successful in its condemnation of Soviet artistic bureaucracy, the film is more interesting as a study of one man's struggle for artistic integrity. (Russian with English subtitles) ★★★½ $59.99

Theodora Goes Wild

(1936, 94 min, US, Richard Boleslawski) Though for some reason it's not one of the better known screwball comedies of the 1930s, *Theodora Goes Wild* is nevertheless a delightful and at times hilarious escapade with Irene Dunne (in an Oscar nominated performance) at her best. She plays a religious-bred New England woman who unbeknowst to her family and small town is actually the popular writer (under a pseudonym, of course) of a series of racy women's novels. Melvyn Douglas, exuding great charm in a role which is probably the precursor to his playboy in *Ninotchka*, plays the ne'er-do-well who thinks Dunne to be as provocative as the women in her novels, and who helps let her secret out when he comes a-courtin'. The laughs are plentiful, and the film even manages a friendly swipe or two at puritanism. This was Dunne's first real chance to play comedy, and she proved herself to be a peerless comedienne. ★★★½ $19.99

There Goes My Baby

(1994, 95 min, US, Floyd Mutrux) It's the early 1960s: The Vietnam War is still called a police action, the hippies are just gathering in San Francisco, Watts is on fire and the class of '65 is spending their last night together. Dermot Mulroney, Rick Schroder (who gives a surprisingly moving portrait of a young man about to depart for war) and Noah Wyle (newly famous thanks to TV's "ER") are a group of friends who must deal with their impending separation and the changes both they and their country are experiencing. Made in 1992, *Baby* is poignant and achingly nostalgic but flawed by the familiarity of the material. ★★ $95.39

There Was a Crooked Man

(1970, 123 min, US, Joseph L. Mankiewicz) Outrageous comedy-western adventure with Kirk Douglas as a prisoner who matches wits with his incorruptible warden (Henry Fonda). Good supporting cast includes Hume Cronyn, Warren Oates, Burgess Meredith and Lee Grant. ★★★ $14.99

There's No Business Like Show Business

(1954, 117 min, US, Walter Lang) This Irving Berlin song fest is a particularly sentimental but entertaining musical about the professional and personal ups and downs of a theatrical family. Ethel Merman and Dan Dailey are the parents, with kids Donald O'Connor, Johnny Ray and Mitzi Gaynor joining the act. Marilyn Monroe also stars as an aspiring singer, and she gets to sing "Heat Wave." Sure it's sappy, but who can resist Merman and O'Connor's onstage reconciliation. ★★½ $19.99

Theremin: An Electronic Odyssey

(1995, 84 min, US, Steven M. Martin) A very interesting if incomplete documentary about the grandfather of electronic music, Russian born Leon Theremin. Theremin was an inventor and electronics mastermind who created the first all-electronic musical instrument, a wooden box with two metal probes protruding from it. This instrument, which bears his name, generates a magnetic field and is played when a person's hands interfere with the field, manipulating musical pitch. Theremin and his instrument were the toast of New York society during the '30s until an unexpected political incident completely changed his life and influence. The strength of the subject matter and the sheer weirdness of Theremin's life story fortunately compensate for the weakness of the documentary itself, which looks and feels amateurish and leaves many holes in the inventor's professional and private life. But as a good, if shallow overview of a fascinating and eccentric genius, *Theremin* is a satisfying trip. ★★★ $19.99

Therese

(1986, 90 min, France, Alain Cavalier) One of the most acclaimed films in recent years, this radiantly beautiful, impeccably crafted film recounts the life of St. Therese — the Little Flower — a teenage girl whose devotion to the Church is surpassed only by her love for Christ. Therese, who died in 1897, was canonized in 1925. Catherine Mouchet shines in the title role. Based on Therese's famous diaries. (French with English subtitles) ★★★½ $39.99

Therese and Isabelle

(1968, 102 min, France, Radley Metzger) Set in an all-girls' school, this milestone film is a tender glimpse at the erotic affair of two young women. Unlike many other works of the period, this provocative drama offers a non-exploitative picture of budding female sexuality. (French with English subtitles) ★★★ $34.99

These Three

(1936, 93 min, US, William Wyler) Lillian Hellman's controversial play, "The Children's Hour," about two women's lives torn apart by rumors of lesbianism, is toned down considerably — the play's "scandalous" relationship is now a heterosexual triangle — in this well-crafted and thoughtfully acted drama. Karen (Merle Oberon) and Martha (Miriam Hopkins) run a school for girls. Trouble begins when a student falsely accuses Martha and Joe (Joel McCrea), Karen's fiancé, of having an affair. Hellman's text is strong commentary on the destructive power of gossip and the so-called innocence of youth. Director Wyler remade the film, under the play's original title and theme, in 1962 with Shirley MacLaine and Audrey Hepburn. ★★★ $19.99

They All Laughed

(1981, 115 min, US, Peter Bogdanovich) Charming, low-key comedy about a team of detectives and their romantic adventures. Director Bogdanovich extracts pleasant performances from Audrey Hepburn, John Ritter, Ben Gazzara, Colleen Camp and (in her last film) Dorothy Stratten. ★★★ $9.99

They Call Me Mr. Tibbs

(1970, 108 min, US, Gordon Douglas) Sidney Poitier repeats his acclaimed role as Detective Virgil Tibbs from the Oscar-winning *In the Heat of the Night*. In this ordinary sequel, Tibbs has moved to San Francisco and is involved in a murder investigation in which the main suspect is local priest Martin Landau. ★★ $14.99

They Came from Within

(1975, 87 min, Canada, David Cronenberg) Cronenberg's bizarre and immensely effective horror film is about deadly parasites which infect a high-rise apartment building, causing its victims to commit exaggerated acts of sex and violence. ★★★

They Came to Cordura

(1959, 123 min, US, Robert Rossen) Gary Cooper heads a good cast in this handsomely photographed western about an Army major (Cooper) who, believing himself guilty of cowardice, is relieved of his command and assigned to locate five potential Medal of Honor candidates. In the wilds of a desert region, he finds the five heroes, a torturous struggle against the elements and Rita Hayworth. Also stars Van Heflin, Tab Hunter and Richard Conte. ★★½ $14.99

They Died with Their Boots On

(1941, 138 min, US, Raoul Walsh) Expedient adventure with Errol Flynn as a heroic General Custer. The film traces his rise in the military ranks to the legendary Battle of the Little Bighorn. What the film lacks in authenticity it makes up for in flavor and entertainment. Also with Olivia deHavilland, Arthur Kennedy and Anthony Quinn. ★★★ $19.99

They Drive by Night

(1940, 97 min, US, Raoul Walsh) Humphrey Bogart took a back seat to stars George Raft, Ann Sheridan and Ida Lupino in this riveting trucking drama — but he didn't stay there for long as *The Maltese Falcon* was released a year later. Raft plays a wildcat trucker who, with brother Bogie, unwittingly becomes involved with the mob while trying to keep his truck from repossession. A good cast in a crisp, solid 1940s entertainment. ★★★ $19.99

They Live

(1988, 87 min, US, John Carpenter) Professional wrestler Roddy "Rowdy" Piper stars in Carpenter's allegorical sci-fi action-adventure about the fateful day when we discover that aliens are among us, and they are hardly benevolent ETs. Carpenter has a great scenario but is unable to thoroughly deliver the goods. ★★½ $19.99

They Live by Night

(1949, 95 min, US, Nicholas Ray) Ray's directorial debut pairs Farley Granger and Cathy O'Donnell as young innocents who find themselves on the wrong side of the law. Howard da Silva turns in a chilling performance as their corruptor. Ray's sense of atmosphere is remarkable, and the performances and diligent screenplay elevate what should have been a "B" programmer. (Remade as *Thieves Like Us*) ★★★½

They Made Me a Criminal

(1939, 92 min, US, Busby Berkeley) Intriguing crime drama directed by Berkeley with John Garfield as a young boxer who takes refuge at a Western ranch when he thinks he's killed an opponent. Also starring Claude Rains, May Robson and The Dead End Kids. ★★★ $19.99

They Might Be Giants

(1971, 98 min, US, Anthony Harvey) Charming adaptation of James Goldman's play about a former judge who thinks he's Sherlock Holmes — and is treated by a psychiatrist named Dr. Watson. George C. Scott plays his part with great panache, and Joanne Woodward is a spirited cohort. A wonderful supporting cast populates the film, featuring a most appealing collection of eccentrics including Jack Gilford, Rue McClanahan and Oliver Clark. ★★★ $59.99

They Saved Hitler's Brain

(1963, 81 min, US, David Bradley) A fanatical band of Nazis (is there any other kind?) give life to Hitler's brain and kidnap an American scientist to help them conquer the world. Le bad cinema. ★

They Were Expendable

(1945, 135 min, US, John Ford) Rousing WWII drama about an American PT boat crew fighting in the Pacific. Robert Montgomery, John Wayne and Donna Reed star in one of the best of all the war films produced during WWII. ★★★★ $19.99

They Were Ten

(1961, 105 min, Israel, Baruch Dienar) The first feature-length film made entirely by Israelis sensitively re-creates the establishment of a 19th-century settlement in Palestine by 10 Russian Jews. These early pioneers not only undertook the tremendous task of building the land, but also had to contend with Arab resentment and the Turkish military. (Hebrew with English subtitles) ★★★ $79.99

They Won't Believe Me

(1947, 95 min, US, Irving Pichel) Startling noir thriller starring Robert Young as a man who wakes up after a car accident with a scheme for the perfect crime. He is subsequently lured by two temptresses (Susan Hayward and Jane Greer) from his wife, Rita Johnson. ★★★ $19.99

Thief

(1981, 122 min, US, Michael Mann) An extremely stylish drama from first-time director Mann (*Manhunter*), with James Caan in a splendid performance as a professional thief caught between corrupt cops and a malevolent crime boss. (Available letterboxed and pan & scan) ★★★½ $14.99

The Thief and the Cobbler

(1995, 73 min, US, Richard Williams) Miramax Films, known more for such adult releases as *Pulp Fiction* and *Trainspotting*, has their first entry into the world of animation with this take-off on the Aladdin theme. Featuring a distinctive animation style with Echer-like effects that go far beyond the typical cartoon, *The Thief and the Cobbler* follows the adventures of a hapless cobbler (nicely voiced by Matthew Broderick) who falls in love with and saves the Princess Yum-Yum (Jennifer Beals). The thief who causes all the problems for our heroes is deliciously played by Jonathan Winters, whose tongue-in-cheek humor will amuse the adults and confuse the kids. Vincent Price is perfect as the malevolent magician Zig-Zag who tries to take over the kingdom. Though the story occasionally falters, the film is of high quality and very imaginative. ★★★ $14.99

Thief of Bagdad

(1924, 138 min, US, Raoul Walsh) Classic silent film with Douglas Fairbanks, Jr. as a swashbuckling thief who falls in love with a beautiful princess. Fairbanks is at his rousing best, and the film is non-stop excitement. ★★★½ $19.99

The Thief of Bagdad

(1940, 106 min, GB, Ludwig Berger, Michael Powell & Tim Whelan) This Arabian Nights tale is classic entertainment, enhanced by gorgeous cinematography. Sabu stars as the native boy who battles an evil magician, played by Conrad Veidt. Rex Ingram makes a terrific genie. Great special effects. ★★★★ $19.99

The Thin Blue Line

(1988, 106 min, US, Errol Morris) Part documentary, part murder investigation, this highly acclaimed and original film investigates the "truth" surrounding the 1976 murder of Dallas policeman Robert Wood — who was gunned down at point blank range after stopping a car for a minor infraction. Randall Adams, the man arrested and sentenced to life in prison for the murder, claimed innocence and, indeed, through mesmerizing reconstructions of the crime from the point-of-view of investigators, witnesses, Wood's partner as well as a suspect cleared of all wrongdoing, the "facts" become all the more blurred as we begin to see that justice might well have been blind as well as perverted. ★★★★

Theremin: An Electronic Odyssey

The Thin Man Series

In the 10 years that elapsed between its first and last entries, the *Thin Man* series straddled two decades, reflecting America's mores and attitudes from her recovery from the Depression thru WWII. As personified by William Powell and Myrna Loy, Nick and Nora Charles are urbane, suave, witty and rich. They have a relationship in their marriage that most would envy today; they even raise a kid without being too damned cute about it. And they know how to handle their dog, the estimable Asta. Their friends and relatives represent a range of societal classes and reflect a diversity of lifestyles seldom found in today's homogenized entertainment. The plots are well-crafted, the wardrobe is dashing and everybody gets good lines. Other constants: He never wants the case, she always wants him to take the case and everyone else thinks he's already on the case. Nora's always assuring someone that it's all right, they're married; and their consumption of alcohol is considerable and greatly enjoyed. The supporting cast's characterizations are consistently on target, the story lines satisfyingly intricate and the black-and-white cinematography deliciously noir, especially those graced with James Wong Howe's exemplary expertise (hands off, Ted Turner!).

The Thin Man

(1934, 93 min, US, W.S. Van Dyke II) "Come on, kid. Shed the chapeau." The original, and the best. An eccentric, wealthy inventor disappears and, before too long, corpses start piling up. The inventor is actually the thin man in question, but the title became inextricably linked to Powell. Based on a Dashiell Hammett story. Costarring Maureen O'Sullivan. ★★★★ $19.99

After the Thin Man

(1936, 113 min, US, W.S. Van Dyke II) "Look at him prancing around with that clue in him." Nick's relations with Nora's (S)Nob Hill family is an element in this tale of a rich wife cheated by a gigolo husband, and a thwarted love twisted into a crime of passion. Nice touches by a young James Stewart. ★★★½ $19.99

Another Thin Man

(1939, 105 min, US, W.S. Van Dyke II) "Colonel MacFay — the swimming pool's on fire." Nick and Nora were starting on an extended trip and Nora announced her pregnancy at the end of *After the Thin Man*. *Another Thin Man* opens with their return from their travels, and with an infant. Nora's uncle is being hounded by a blackmailer with ominous dreams and a penchant for melodramatic warnings; the curmudgeon uncle seems deserving of this treatment. ★★★ $19.99

Shadow of the Thin Man

(1941, 97 min, US, W.S. Van Dyke II) "Funny how I meet you at all my homicides." A jockey is accused of throwing a race and is dead the next day, an apparent suicide. His death is convenient for the gambling syndicate, not so convenient for the crusading young reporter. Little Nicky, Jr. has his own Army uniform (he's an officer, of course) and calls his dad "Nick." There's a great restaurant fight scene, and the writing's by Dashiell Hammett. ★★★ $19.99

The Thin Man Goes Home

(1944, 100 min, US, Richard Thorpe) "You just pick out anybody at all, and I put 'em in jail for life." The effects of WWII are evidenced during Nick and Nora's train ride to Sycamore Springs, Nick's home town. Nick resolves a case of wartime industrial espionage, as well as his relationship with his father. Cinematography by Karl Freund, and another Dashiell Hammett script. ★★★ $19.99

Song of the Thin Man

(1947, 86 min, US, Edward Buzzell) "The dust don't start rising 'til deuce o' bells." Keenan Wynn is the hep cat clarinet player who gives Nick and Nora a guided tour through the netherworld of jazz musicians, high society, heavy gamblers and murderous jealousies. "And now Nick Charles is going to retire." ★★★ $19.99

The Thing

(1951, 80 min, US, Christian Nyby) Classic '50s horror film produced by Howard Hawks. An Arctic expedition is forced to fight for their lives when they dig up an alien creature frozen in the ice. The chills are rampant as the basic ingredients of sci-fi faultlessly meld with hold-your-breath terror. (Remade by John Carpenter in 1982.) ★★★★

The Thing

(1982, 108 min, US, John Carpenter) A gruesome and terrifying tale of a hideous, metamorphic monster which torments the crew of an Antarctic outpost. Carpenter's new version of the classic short story is highlighted by realistic and horrifying special effects. Stars Kurt Russell. ★★★½ $14.99

The Thing Called Love

(1993, 116 min, US, Peter Bogdanovich) Samantha Mathis stars as an East Coast gal who travels to Nashville determined to become a country music star. Upon her arrival, she immediately, and literally, bumps into a brooding, bad-boy musician (River Phoenix). A love-hate relationship ensues. Also onto the scene ambles Dermot Mulroney, a displaced Connecticut cowboy, and Sandra Bullock as a new kind of Southern belle. Though *The Thing Called Love* seems to have lost something in the editing process, its odd country-grunge quality, the interplay between the young actors and the fun they have with the music, saves this film from being a hackneyed, hayseed version of *A Star Is Born*. ★★★ $19.99

Things Change

(1988, 100 min, US, David Mamet) Don Ameche's subtle yet complex portrait of an Italian shoe repairman caught in a high stakes impersonation of a Mafia don was one of the acting highlights of 1988. Writer and director Mamet's social comedy does not deliver the visceral thrills of his previous film, *House of Games*, but nonetheless is a sly comedy which explores the honor among thieves and the deadly temptations that money and power offer. The always fascinating Joe Mantegna costars as a low level hood who is responsible for the weekend safety of Ameche. But what starts as a simple job of baby-sitting, ends in a comedy of errors as the reticent Ameche is mistaken for a Mafia kingpin. A thinking person's comedy and one that is highly recommended. ★★★½ $9.99

Things to Come

(1936, 92 min, GB, William Cameron Menzies) This stunning visualization of H.G. Wells' visionary novel features Menzies' intriguing, ultra-modern sets and a sonorous score by Arthur Bliss. Raymond Massey stars as the leader of the new world opposite Ralph Richardson as a despotic and belligerent ruler. An interesting film from a sociological standpoint as it represents the mindset of the '30s as people looked to the future. ★★★

After the Thin Man

Song of the Thin Man

Things to Do in Denver When You're Dead

(1995, 114 min, US, Gary Fleder) First-time director Fleder puts a new spin on a tried-and-true gangster formula (former hood is pulled back into the game). Andy Garcia stars as Jimmy the Saint, an ex-petty criminal who has gone legit. Soon after happening upon the woman of his dreams, Jimmy is summoned to the ghostly mansion of a quadriplegic crime lord (Christopher Walken at his creepy best), who bids him to do one more bit of service for him. Jimmy assembles the old gang one last time, and when the job is botched, the crew finds themselves on a hit list, or "buckwheats," with a master hit man (Steve Buscemi) on their trail. Distinguished particularly by its inventive dialogue (the film must break Tarantino's record for coining new phrases for a gangster pic) and excellent cast, *Things to Do...* is vastly entertaining but as a whole does not live up to its best moments. Some plot logic is sacrificed to further the style, but what style it has: the film is glossy, humorous and dark fun, and contains many a surprising twist. Jimmy's introduction is wholly original, though in portraying him, Garcia is overshadowed by the terrific ensemble, especially Treat Williams as the maniacal Critical Bill. ★★★ $19.99

3rd Degree Burn

(1989, 97 min, US, Roger Spottiswoode) Steamy made-for-cable thriller with Treat Williams as a down-and-out detective who is hired by a millionaire to watch his sexy wife. However, things get complicated when they meet, have an affair, and Williams is framed for his client's murder. ★★½ $14.99

The Third Man

(1950, 100 min, GB, Carol Reed) Based on an original screenplay by Graham Greene, this Reed classic epitomizes the aesthetics of film noir. Amid the lurid decadence of a shell-shocked, post-war Vienna, a lonely American (Joseph Cotten) searches for his maligned friend, a mysterious "third man" in a city of rampant deceit and corruption. A haunting score, shadowy cinematography and top-notch performances (notably Orson Welles as the utterly immoral Harry Lime) make this one of

the memorable tales of intrigue in film history. ★★★★ $24.99

The Third Sex/Vapors

(1958/1965, 102 min, West Germany/US, Frank Winterstein & Gerald Jackson) *The Third Sex* (1958, 77 min, Germany, Frank Winterstein) is intriguingly contemporary, especially for its time and place (West Germany in the mid-1950s). This historically important potboiler melodrama centers on a parents' efforts to make their gay son "normal." Klaus, a sleekly handsome teenager, is in a relationship with fellow classmate Manfred, an effete, pouting blond. Klaus' domineering father, aghast at his son's "sickness," goes about trying to break the two apart. And while dad's off making trouble for his son's gay friends, the alternately sympathetic but calculating mom plots to get the pretty maid into her wayward son's bed. Family troubles mount when mom is sent to jail for "procuring prostitution" (see the film!), but a jail term is a small price to pay after Klaus drops the love-lorn Manfred and aggressively (a little too much perhaps?) embraces heterosexuality. Notwithstanding the ridiculous ending, the film is quite extraordinary in its depiction of gays, society's extremist reaction to them and the clash between the old Germany and the new. *Vapors* (1965, 25 min, US, Gerald Jackson) is set in the notorious St. Mark's Bathhouse. This fascinating, stagey film deals with anonymous sexual encounters and the craving for love and intimacy. A nervous young man visits the bathhouse for the first time. There he meets an older, sexually confused married man. Instead of the standard quickie, the two engage in thoughtful conversation dealing with desire and soul searching. ★★★ $79.99

13 Ghosts

(1960, 88 min, US, William Castle) Cute ghost mystery about a family who inherit a house, complete with buried treasure and – count 'em – 13 ghosts. Starring Rosemary DeCamp, Martin Milner and Margaret Hamilton as a sinister housekeeper. ★★½ $9.99

13 Rue Madeleine

(1947, 95 min, US, Henry Hathaway) Told in an almost semidocumentary style, this absorbing spy thriller stars a rigid but forceful James Cagney as an OSS operative who trains youthful candidates. The intrigue really starts when he discovers a Nazi spy among his cadets, and is then forced to use the double agent on a dangerous mission in Germany. Perhaps too calculating in its efforts to present a realistic portrait of the spy game, the film nevertheless is gripping exactly for that reason – that and Cagney's no-nonsense portrayal. ★★★ $19.99

38: Vienna Before the Fall

(1989, 97 min, Austria, Wolfgang Gluck) Nominated for Best Foreign Film (the first such nominee from Austria), this elegant but impassioned drama is set a few months before Hitler's annexation of Austria and deals with such themes as political apathy, the roots of anti-Semitism and the Holocaust. Set against the deceptively beautiful backdrop of pre-war Vienna, the drama centers around two lovers, a Jewish playwright and a popular Aryan

actress, who are blissfully blind to the escalating inhumanity which surrounds them. A powerful film experience. (German with English subtitles) ★★★½

35 Up

(1990, 127 min, GB, Michael Apted) Director Apted continues his seven-year study of a group of British children from childhood through adulthood, which he began with *7 Up* and continued with *14 Up*, *21 Up* and *28 Up*. Having offered their hopes and dreams on-camera as children in the earlier films, it can be heart-wrenching to see adults rationalizing why they haven't realized their dreams, and mystifying to listen to a seven-year-old plot out his/her life and then watch it unfold exactly as planned. The most striking story is that of Neil, who at seven was a happy-go-lucky child skipping down the lane and at 35 is obviously mentally ill and has been essentially homeless for most of his adult life. Though *35 Up* suffers from the fact that the changes that occur between 28 and 35 are less perceptive than the dramatic swings between the other earlier ages, this series remains one of the most revealing looks at life and the aging process ever to be captured on film. ★★★½ $29.99

Thirty Is a Dangerous Age, Cynthia

(1968, 85 min, GB, Joseph McGrath) This eccentric comedy stars Dudley Moore as a nightclub pianist fast approaching his 30th birthday. Overwrought by the angst of reaching this milestone without having ever married or produced a hit song, he sets out to achieve both these goals in a six-week period. Moore cowrote the script and scores high marks with this offbeat comedy which casts a jaundiced eye at the absurdities of sex and marriage. ★★★ $59.99

The 39 Steps

(1935, 89 min, GB, Alfred Hitchcock) Robert Donat stars as an innocent man on the lam, handcuffed to Madeleine Carroll, linked with a spy ring, pursued by a villain with a severed finger and chased through the Scottish highlands. A vintage thriller which is thick with intrigue and colored with Hitchcock's droll humor. ★★★★ $24.99

Thirty Seconds over Tokyo

(1944, 138 min, US, Mervyn LeRoy) One of the top box-office hits of the 1940s, this exciting WWII drama details the first aerial attack on mainland Japan by American forces. The solid cast includes Spencer Tracy, Van Johnson, Robert Walker, Robert Mitchum and Phyllis Thaxter. A good companion piece is *Destination Tokyo*, the 1943 Cary Grant drama which tells the same story from the point of view of the submarine crew which made the air strike possible. ★★★ $19.99

36 Fillette

(1988, 88 min, France, Catherine Breillat) Heralded by many as a refreshing tale of a precocious girl's rite of sexual passage told from a woman's point of view and reviled by others for its wanton depiction of a manipulating, selfish brat, this saucy Gallic comedy will leave few viewers without a strong opinion. Lili, a pouty, sexy 14-year-old who is literally bursting out of her children's sizes, decides to lose her virginity while on vacation with her family. Her first choice for the despoiler is Maurice, a middle-aged playboy and musician, but our heroine soon finds that losing her viriginity is not such an easy decision. Promoted as a "French Lolita," this journey toward sexual awakening features Jean-Pierre Léaud. (French with English subtitles) ★★½ $19.99

32 Short Films about Glenn Gould

(1994, 94 min, Canada, Francois Girard) Director Girard has constructed a kaleidoscopic exploration of the eccentric life of world-renowned concert pianist Glenn Gould, engagingly portrayed by Colm Feore. Gould left the concert stage at age 32 at the height of his career. Searching for an ideal performance arena, he intended to communicate with the audience solely through media. Passionately obsessed with music, this justifiably egomaniacal perfectionist lived in sound, cadence and tone in a consuming vortex of self-absorbed creativity. The 32 short films include interviews with family, friends and other artists; selected performances of his compositions and radio programs; and dramatized biographical episodes. By the end of the film, this man's life assumes an almost mythic quality, as though it harkens back to a time before our memory — assuming the feeling regarding Bobby Fisher in *Searching for Bobby Fisher*. See this film. ★★★½ $19.99

This Boy's Life

(1993, 115 min, US, Michael Caton-Jones) Based on the autobiography of writer Tobias Wolff, this intensely moving and powerful coming-of-age drama is a courageous tale examining the hopes and desperation of an unsettled youth. In a passionate performance, Leonardo DiCaprio plays a troubled teen who, with his newly married mother (the first-rate Ellen Barkin), moves to a small town in Washington state to live with her new stepfather (Robert De Niro in a volatile performance). But what had promised to be a fresh start — an emotional rebirth for mother and son — quickly degenerates into an oppressive and claustrophobic lifestyle neither is able to protest or divorce. The acting from the three leads is exemplary, and in support, special mention goes to Jonah Blechman as DiCaprio's gay friend. Wolff's illuminating process of self-discovery and self-determination raises *This Boy's Life* well above the pack of a crowded genre. ★★★★ $14.99

This Could Be the Night

(1957, 105 min, US, Robert Wise) Jean Simmons shines as a schoolteacher who takes a part-time job at a New York nightclub, thus furthering her own education in matters romantic. Playboy Anthony Franciosa and lovably gruff Paul Douglas are her bosses, who both fall under the spell of Simmons' naive charm. But the comedy cuts deeper than this suggests; in fact, many a laugh is obtained at the expense of Simmons' virginity, and without resorting to the cruel and exploitative. This risque, colorful comedy features splashy musical numbers, and extracts cheerful performances from its entire cast. In addition to Douglas' knockout turn, solid support comes from Julie Wilson as a sexy singer, Neile

Alan Ladd and Veronica Lake in *This Gun for Hire*

Adams as a dancer who'd rather be a cook, Joan Blondell as her stage mother, and Rafael Campos as a busboy. ★★★ $19.99

This Gun for Hire

(1942, 80 min, US, Frank Tuttle) Taken from a Graham Greene novel, this gripping crime drama stars Alan Ladd as Raven, a tight-lipped paid assassin who, after he is double-crossed by an "employer," seeks revenge. The alluring Veronica Lake is a sultry "singing magician" who gets innocently involved and good guy Robert Preston is the detective on the trail. Above-average thriller with wonderfully complex twists and chance encounters. With an oil company as the real bad guy, the film was ahead of its time. ★★★½ $14.99

This Happy Breed

(1944, 114 min, GB, David Lean) Noël Coward's keen adaptation of his own hit play about the affairs of a lower middle-class family was immensely popular in its day. Set between the two World Wars, the film delves into the petty bickerings and small triumphs of the Gibbons clan as they grapple with the difficulties of a world ravaged by social strife and war. Director Lean makes excellent use of Ronald Neame's penetrating camerawork. ★★★½ $39.99

This Is My Life

(1992, 94 min, US, Nora Ephron) After contributing to the success of such films as *Silkwood* and *When Harry Met Sally*, writer Nora Ephron makes her directorial debut with this lightweight comedy-drama not without a certain charm. In her first big-screen starring role, Julie Kavner gives an enchanting performance as a single mother who tries to make it big in show biz. As her star slowly but assuredly ascends, it is her two daughters who are most affected by their mother's newfound success as it demands more and more of her time. Samantha Mathis and little Gaby Hoffman are her daughters, and both ably express the frustration of no longer being the sole reason for their mother's life. Though Ephron doesn't fully explore many of the scenarios she intro-

duces, she manages to infuse in the film a fair amount of good humor. ★★½ $19.99

This Is Spinal Tap

(1984, 82 min, US, Rob Reiner) Reiner's riotous, razor-sharp satire is a pseudo-rockumentary on Britain's loudest band, Spinal Tap. Captured during a swan-song U.S. tour, these over-the-hill, heavy metal moptops offer their sentiments on life in the fast lane, the merits of their "Smell the Glove" LP and the mysterious deaths of their past 35 drummers. ★★★★

This Island Earth

(1954, 86 min, US, Joseph Newman) A group of scientists are kidnapped by aliens, who need them to help defend their planet. This clever outer space tale is one of the most popular of the '50s sci-fi films. Features good special effects. (The film used for the theatrical debut for *Mystery Science Theatre 3000*.) ★★½ $9.99

This Man Must Die

(1969, 115 min, France/Italy, Claude Chabrol) One of Chabrol's finest films, this first-rate thriller concerns the father of a boy who was a hit-and-run victim and his obsessive and unrelenting need to track down his son's killer and extract his vengeance. This Hitchcockian tale has plot twists that will keep you guessing until the startling conclusion. (Dubbed) ★★★½ $59.99

This Property Is Condemned

(1966, 110 min, US, Sydney Pollack) This reworking of the Tennessee Williams tragedy stars Natalie Wood as a Southern belle who longs for out-of-towner Robert Redford to sweep her away to the big city and help her escape the family boarding house. Pollack directs and Francis Ford Coppola helped write the screenplay. Also starring Charles Bronson, Kate Reid and Dabney Coleman. ★★ $19.99

This Special Friendship

(1964, 99 min, France, Jean Delannoy) Set in a Catholic boarding school in France, this love story smolders with the youthful homoerotic bonds between several boys in the school. Their love and friendship is touching and beautifully handled by director Delannoy. (French with English subtitles) ★★★ $49.99

This Sporting Life

(1963, 129 min, GB, Lindsay Anderson) Richard Harris gives a career performance as Frank Machin, a Yorkshire lad who tries to escape the restrictions of his working-class background and his personal limitations by becoming a star on the city rugby team. Gritty and stark, peopled with great performances, among them Rachel Roberts, Alan Badel, Colin Blakely and Arthur Lowe. Screenplay by David Storey based on his book; produced by Karel Reisz and perceptively directed by Anderson. ★★★½

This Sweet Sickness

(1977, 105 min, France, Claude Miller) Forget *Boxing Helena*: For this thriller, based on the novel by Patricia Highsmith ("Strangers on a Train") and directed by Miller (*The Little Thief*), is perhaps the most realistic and chilling portrait of obsessive love ever put to the screen. Gérard Depardieu gives a compelling performance as David, a man so obsessed with his former lover, Lise, that his life becomes one of deceit and delusion. And David isn't dissuaded in his obsession by the fact that Lise is now remarried and that his neighbor (Miou Miou) has fallen in love with him. Tension builds as the characters' lives become further entangled, ultimately resulting in tragedy. Watch carefully for the wonderfully inventive ending. (French with English subtitles) ★★★★ $24.99

The Thomas Crown Affair

(1968, 102 min, US, Norman Jewison) A solid heist adventure with the ever-cool Steve McQueen masterminding an ingenious bank robbery and becoming involved with equally cool insurance investigator Faye Dunaway. Also with Jack Weston, Paul Burke and Yaphet Kotto. ★★★ $19.99

Thoroughly Modern Millie

(1967, 138 min, US, George Roy Hill) Delightfully entertaining musical spoof with Julie Andrews as the title character, a husband-hunting secretary during the Roaring '20s. Mary Tyler Moore also stars as an orphaned ingenue who comes to the big city and is befriended by Millie. Carol Channing received an Oscar nomination for her spirited performance as a daffy and lovable socialite ("Raspberries!"). Memorable Oscar-winning score by Elmer Bernstein and Andre Previn. ★★★ $14.99

A Thousand Clowns

(1965, 118 min, US, Fred Coe) Terrific screen version of Herb Gardner's Broadway comedy with Jason Robards in great form as a non-conformist who may have to change his ways when social workers look lightly at the way he's been raising his nephew. An exceptional cast includes Barbara Harris, Martin Balsam (who won an Oscar as Robards' exasperated brother), William Daniels and young Barry Gordon. ★★★½ $19.99

The Thousand Eyes of Dr. Mabuse

(1960, 103 min, West Germany, Fritz Lang) He's back! The arch super villain who foreshadowed Hitler's Germany returns from beyond the grave – now a scientist whose headquarters is a large hotel full of secret panels, peep holes and dungeons. The Mabuse series was a clear inspiration for the James Bond movies, and this one – Lang's last film – even stars Gert Fröbe who went on to play the title role of "Goldfinger" a few years later. ★★ $39.99

Thousand Pieces of Gold

(1991, 105 min, US, Nancy Kelly) A startlingly good independent film, this impressive historical and individual drama centers on the harsh life of a fiercely defiant woman thrown into the rough-and-tumble world of Gold Rush fever in the 1880s-American West. Lalu, a tall Chinese woman in her twenties, is sold by her famine-stricken father and eventually brought to San Francisco, where she is auctioned off to an obnoxious saloon keeper in a dismal Idaho town. Refusing to succumb to forced prostitution and virtual slavehood, Lalu, now renamed China Polly, must overcome insurmountable odds in preserving her dignity and gaining independence. Based on a true story, this western epic is filmed in a simple, straightforward fashion by Nancy Kelly, wonderfully recounting one woman's triumph over male betrayal and domination. Rosalind Chao is unforgettable as the determined Lalu. (English and Cantonese with English subtitles) ★★★½ $14.99

Threads

(1985, 110 min, GB, Mick Jackson) One of the best of the "day after" nuclear dramas, this powerful, uncompromising BBC production examines the devastating aftermath of global nuclear war on present-day London. Presented in pseudo-documentary style, the film is uncomfortably realistic in its portrayal of a nuclear nightmare. ★★★½

Three Ages/The Goat/My Wife's Relations

(1921/22, 111 min, US, Buster Keaton & Eddie Cline/Mal St. Clair) A collection of three Buster Keaton comedies. *Three Ages* (1923, 63 min) pokes fun at Griffith's *Intolerance*, telling three stories from different ages – The Stone Age, the Roman Empire and "Modern Times." In all three, Keaton plays the lovable schnook in love with Margaret Leahy – but Wallace Beery stands in his way. Keaton's knock-about comedy is well-played, and the story occasionally gives him material to rise to. Highlights include a funny chariot race and a wedding ceremony which looks to be the precursor to *The Graduate*. (★★★) *The Goat* (1921, 23 min) is the highly amusing story of Keaton being mistaken for a notorious gangster. The short features inventive visuals and a hilarious, prolonged chase scene. (★★★½) *My Wife's Relations* (1922, 25 min) has Keaton mistakenly married and moving in with ne'er-do-well relations. Keaton's tomfoolery makes this of interest. (★★½) $29.99

Three Amigos!

(1986, 105 min, US, John Landis) Occasionally amusing spoof of westerns and *The Magnificent Seven* in particular. Steve Martin, Chevy Chase and Martin Short play unemployed silent western stars who, thought to be real cowboys, are summoned to save a small Mexican town terrorized by desperadoes. ★★ $14.99

Three Brothers

(1980, 111 min, Italy, Francesco Rossi) Rosi (*Bizet's Carmen, Christ Stopped at Eboli*) directed this vivid and affecting portrait of three very different brothers who return to the village of their youth for their mother's funeral. Political and social concerns as well as their strained relationships are probed in this extraordinary film. (Italian with English subtitles) ★★★½

Three Came Home

(1950, 106 min, US, Jean Negulesco) A superlative performance by Claudette Colbert highlights this absorbing and powerful drama based on Agnes Keith's novel detailing her experiences in a Japanese internment camp in Borneo. Separated from their husbands, American Colbert and a group of British women endure the hardships of imprisonment and the cruelties of their captors. Sessue Hayakawa is impressive as the civilized commander who "befriends" Colbert. ★★★½ $9.99

Three Cases of Murder

(1954, 99 min, GB, David Eady, Wendy Toye & George O'Ferrall) The title says it all with this nicely executed trilogy of murder and the supernatural. The first short, *In the Picture*, is an effectively eerie chiller – which could have been penned by Oscar Wilde – about a deceased artist who comes back to life to perfect his masterpiece. The second, *You Killed Elizabeth*, is the least successful of the three. It's the story of a ménage à trois which ends in murder – but whodunit? The last piece, *Lord Mountdrago*, features an extraordinary Orson Welles as an ambitious, callous Foreign Secretary serving in Parliament who is haunted by the man who he has ruined. Based on a short story of W. Somerset Maugham, it's a fascinating, humorous tale. Alan Badel appears in all three episodes. ★★★ $39.99

Three Comrades

(1938, 98 min, US, Frank Borzage) Coscripted by F. Scott Fitzgerald and based on an Erich Maria Remarque novel, this tender, lushly romantic tearjerker gives the beguiling Margaret Sullavan the opportunity to offer her best performance, a timeless portrait of love and sacrifice. Set in post-WWI Germany, the story follows the close relationship of three soldiers (Robert Taylor, Franchot Tone and Robert Young in splendid portrayals), and their devotion to ailing, former aristocrat Sullavan after she and Taylor wed. The rise of Fascism in Germany is its backdrop, and the film effortlessly extracts the best of Fitzgerald and Remarque in the marriage of love story and political study. ★★★½ $19.99

Three Days of the Condor

(1975, 117 min, US, Sydney Pollack) Pollack's exciting espionage thriller stars Robert Redford as a CIA researcher working in a Manhattan think tank. When all of his co-workers are brutally assassinated, he suddenly finds himself on the run and not knowing whom to trust. Good performances come from Faye Dunaway, as a civilian who is kidnapped by Redford and coerced to help him, as well as Cliff Robertson, Max von Sydow and John Houseman. ★★★½ $14.99

The Three Faces of Eve

(1957, 91 min, US, **Nunnally Johnson**) Joanne Woodward won a deserved Academy Award for her stunning schizophrenic performance as a woman with a multiple personality disorder. Told in an almost documentary style (complete with narration from Alistair Cooke), the film begins as dreary Georgia housewife Eve White visits a psychiatrist (Lee J. Cobb) because of headaches and blackouts. It's soon discovered, however, she is harboring a second and third personality: Eve Black, a sexy flirt, and a sensible "normal" Jane who may be Eve's real identity. David Wayne is good in the thankless supporting role of Eve's non-supportive husband, and Cobb is especially sincere as her doctor. Based on an actual case. ★★★ $19.99

Three Fugitives

(1989, 93 min, US, **Francis Veber**) Disarming remake of the French comedy *Les Fugitifs*, with Nick Nolte as a paroled bankrobber who is taken hostage by inept Martin Short, who's committing his first hold-up. Some good slapstick in an otherwise sentimental comic tale. ★★ $9.99

3 Godfathers

(1948, 105 min, US, **John Ford**) Director Ford is in a sentimental mood with this glossy remake of Peter B. Kyne's popular story about three outlaws who find a baby while crossing the desert and take charge of it. Wonderful cinematography highlights this John Wayne tale, costarring Pedro Armendariz, Harry Carey, Jr. and Ward Bond. Filmed five times before this one (two versions with Carey, Sr.), and since then as a Jack Palance TV movie. ★★★ $19.99

317th Platoon

(1965, 94 min, France, **Pierre Schoendoerffer**) Capturing both the horrors of battle and the anguish and solitude each soldier endures, this realistic war drama describes, with wrenching clarity, the final bloody days of an army platoon. Set in 1954 during the last days of the French involvement in Southeast Asia (and filmed entirely in the jungles of Cambodia), the story follows the frantic retreat from the front lines of the 317th platoon, made up of 41 Laotians and four Frenchmen. Eschewing the simple Hollywood theme of heroism during wartime, the director and cinematographer Raoul Coutard (both veterans of the French Vietnam war) focus intimately on these ordinary young men as they, through enemy ambushes, disease and fatigue, are slowly annihilated. (French with English subtitles) ★★★½ $59.99

Three in the Attic

(1968, 92 min, US, **Richard Wilson**) Christopher Jones stars in this playful if silly 1960s sex comedy as a college student whose three girlfriends give him a lesson in fidelity when they kidnap him, lock him in an attic and literally try to fuck him to death. ★★

Three Little Words

(1950, 102 min, US, **Richard Thorpe**) Fred Astaire and Red Skelton make a nice team in this appealing, Hollywoodized biography of songwriters Bert Kalmer and Harry Ruby, whose songs include "I Wanna Be Loved by You," "Who's Sorry Now" and the title tune. ★★★ $19.99

Three Men and a Baby

(1987, 102 min, US, **Leonard Nimoy**) A box-office smash, this amiable and sometimes funny remake of the French hit *Three Men and a Cradle* stars Tom Selleck, Ted Danson and Steve Guttenberg as three bachelor roommates who find themselves playing daddy to an adorable baby when the infant's mother drops the child on their doorsteps. The sight of Selleck offering $1,000 to change a diaper should send any knowing parent into semi-hysterics. Followed by an inferior sequel. ★★½ $9.99

Three Men and a Cradle

(1985, 100 min, France, **Coline Serreau**) This farce attracted and delighted large crowds of American filmgoers. Similar to American "concept" pictures, the story line is simple: Three swinging bachelors wake up one morning and suddenly find a baby at their door, none of them the father. The antics of the novice fathers as they tend the child are predictable but also hilariously funny. The basis for the American box-office smash, *Three Men and a Baby*. (French with English subtitles) ★★★ $19.99

Three Men and a Little Lady

(1990, 100 min, US, **Emile Ardolino**) While mildly entertaining, this sugar-coated sequel fails to live up to the original (what else is new?) and is badly hampered by its utterly predictable ending. Ted Danson, Steve Guttenberg and Tom Selleck all return from the original for this thin story about Selleck's snail-paced realization that he loves the little lady's mother, Sylvia (Nancy Travis). The one shining star in the cast is Fiona Shaw, who portrays her minor character with considerable aplomb and originality. This is more aptly titled *Three Men and a Lot of Hokum*. ★½ $9.99

Three Men on a Horse

(1936, 87 min, US, **Mervyn LeRoy**) There's a Damon Runyon flavor to this zesty film adaptation of George Abbott's stage comedy. Character actor Frank McHugh probably had his finest hour as the hen-pecked greeting card writer who becomes involved with small-time gambler Sam Levene and his gang — Joan Blondell, Allen Jenkins and Teddy Hart. It seems McHugh can accurately predict the ponies, which makes him very popular with Levene and friends. There's quite an abundance of wonderfully funny lines, and silliness is the order of the day. Special mention goes to Hart for his priceless turn as a bug-eyed, gravel-mouthed stooge: he's Eddie Cantor run amock with just a dash of Joe Pesci. *Three Men on a Horse* is one of the better kept secrets of 1930s comedies. ★★★ $19.99

The Three Musketeers

(1949, 125 min, US, **George Sidney**) One of the ten screen versions of the Alexander Dumas classic. This is a colorful swashbuckler, with a mostly appealing cast (Gene Kelly, Lana Turner, Angela Lansbury, Frank Morgan and Vincent Price, among others), but it's not quite up to par with Richard Lester's wonderful 1974 romp. ★★½ $19.99

The Three Musketeers

(1974, 105 min, GB, **Richard Lester**) From the director of *A Hard Day's Night* comes this delightful tongue-in-cheek version of the Dumas classic. Michael York is at his best as the young D'Artagnan in this artful mix of swashbuckling adventure, romance and uproarious slapstick comedy. Raquel Welch (in her finest hour), Oliver Reed, Richard Chamberlain, Charlton Heston and Faye Dunaway round out the all-star cast. Followed by *The Four Musketeers*. ★★★½

The Three Musketeers

(1993, 105 min, US, **Stephen Herek**) It would take a lot of panache to equal Richard Lester's classic 1974 treatment of the Dumas novel. Unfortunately, neither director Herek (*The Mighty Ducks*) nor his Frat Pack cast are up to the challenge — the result being an enjoyable if inconsequential retelling. Charlie Sheen, Kiefer Sutherland and Oliver Platt are the wise-cracking incarnations of Athos, Aramis and Porthos. They are joined by Chris O'Donnell as D'Artagnan, a lively Tim Curry as Cardinal Richelieu, and Rebecca DeMornay as Milady. The duel scenes have a certain verve, and the costumes are splashy, but most of the sets look like throwaways from "The Pirates of the Caribbean." ★★½ $14.99

3 Ninjas

(1992, 81 min, US, **Jon Turtletaub**) *The Karate Kid* meets the Three Stooges in this obvious yet surprisingly entertaining attempt to capitalize on kids' fascination with the martial arts, à la *Teenage Mutant Ninja Turtles*. Three blond-haired, blue-eyed Asian-American (!) brothers receive martial arts training from their sensei grandfather, once a powerful ninja. When their FBI-agent dad gets on the wrong side of a ruthless international arms merchant, the kids get their chance to prove their mettle. Yes, it's hokey and totally Hollywood formula filmmaking; and yet, there are enough laughs to keep things rolling, which includes some good spoofing of the kung fu genre. One parental warning: the film trivializes violence in a big way. ★★½ $19.99

3 Nuts in Search of a Bolt

(1964, 78 min, US, **Tommy Noonan**) Three madcap loonies (Paul Gilbert, John Cronin and Mamie Van Doren), each too poor to seek help on their own, pool their funds and their neuroses to send an unemployed actor to a world-famous psychiatrist hoping to receive a cure. The results? Blackmail, movie offers, big money and Mamie Van Doren in a bathtub full of beer! ★

Three O'Clock High

(1987, 101 min, US, **Phil Joanou**) Thanks to an engaging cast and some remarkable cinematography, this teenage comedy manages to rise above the norm of the genre. Casey Siemaszko is quite appealing as a student

T

bookstore manager who accidentally "touches" the school bully. This sends the youth into a day-long hysteria when the antisocial thug (Richard Tyson) challenges him to a fight after school. ★★★ $79.99

Three of a Kind

(1984, 84 min, GB, Roger Brunskill) Before Tracy Ullman came to the U.S., she made a name for herself in England as a member of the trio (along with Lenny Henry and David Copperfield) that made up "Three of a Kind," a hit BBC comedy series. This compilation of some of the show's more hilarious sketches includes one of Ullman doing her outrageous character, Moira McBitch. ★★★ $14.99

Three of Hearts

(1993, 101 min, US, Yurek Bogayevicz) Supposedly touted upon its release as a breakthrough Hollywood film towards lesbianism, this charming romantic comedy is more notable for its lighthearted, humorous moments and believable characters than for pushing the envelope of lesbian cinema. Stung by her sudden breakup with Ellen (Sherilyn Fenn), the love-lorn Connie (Kelly Lynch) concocts a wild plan to get revenge by hiring a male hustler (William Baldwin) to trap her ex into falling in love with him, only to have him break her heart which in turn would hopefully have Ellen running back to her loving embrace. But the plan backfires when Joey, the streetwise prostitute with a heart of gold and now a roommate and friend of Connie, inadvertently falls in love with the charming university teacher. The scenes between Joey and Ellen are tender and romantic and the developing friendship between Connie, a gay woman, and Joey, a straight man, are touchingly real. ★★★ $14.99

Three Songs of Lenin

(1934, 62 min, USSR, Dziga Vertov) In this, his last feature, legendary filmmaker Vertov (*Man with a Movie Camera*) paid homage to Russia's great leader with three heartfelt examinations of life in the Soviet Union. *In a Black Prison Was My Face, We Loved Him,* and *In the Great City of Stone* all explore the life of Lenin and show the effect he had on the Soviet people and their destiny. (Silent with orchestral accompaniment) ★★★ $29.99

Three Strange Loves

(1949, 88 min, Sweden, Ingmar Bergman) This early Bergman psychological drama is set on a train trip from Germany to Sweden during which the lives of a dry scholar, his wife and his former wife all reach an impasse. (Swedish with English subtitles) ★★½

3:10 to Yuma

(1957, 92 min, US, Delmer Daves) Very suspenseful western with farmer Van Heflin agreeing to guard prisoner Glenn Ford, but losing a battle of wits while waiting for the train to take him away. A classic western adventure, one of the best of the genre. ★★★½ $9.99

Three Tenors: Encore

(1992, 57 min, Mario Dradi) How do you follow up one of the most famous live concert performances ever produced for television? With an engaging behind-the-scenes look at what goes into the preparation for such an event. A rare glimpse of the legendary tenors Domingo, Pavarotti and Carreras at work. ★★★ $19.99

Three the Hard Way

(1974, 93 min, US, Gordon Parks, Jr.) Three superstars of blaxploitation — Jim Brown, Fred Williamson and Jim Kelly — team up in this pulsating, yet unusually nonviolent thriller about a white supremacist who plans to inject a deadly serum — which kills off blacks but is harmless to whites — into the water supply. ★★½

3X3 Eyes, Pts. 1 & 2

(1991, 30 ea min, Japan, Daisuke Nishio, Carl Macek [English version]) Based on a popular Japanese comic, this is an exciting animated action-packed visit into the dark world of the occult. It begins with Pai, the last of a race of immortals, who seeks an ancient supernatural artifact needed to change her into a human being. Filled with gun battles, grotesque creatures and jolts aplenty, these two tapes are a welcome surprise for anime fans who are looking for something different. ★★★ $14.99

The Threepenny Opera

(1931, 114 min, Germany, G.W. Pabst) Pabst's wild and eerie adaptation of the Bertolt Brecht/Kurt Weill "beggar's opera" captures the play's marvelous milieu of 19th-century underworld and features the magical performances of Lotte Lenya as Jenny and Rudolph Forster as the infamous Mack the Knife. (German with English subtitles) ★★★ $19.99

Threesome

(1994, 93 min, US, Andrew Fleming) This often perceptive and funny story revolves around the friendship and evolving sexual relations between three college students sharing the same dorm. Stephen Baldwin is Stuart, a droopy-eyed, sex-obsessed jock. Eddy (Josh Charles) is the "sexually ambivalent" (read: gay) narrator/roommate, and Alex (Lara Flynn Boyle) is the sexually aggressive woman mistakenly assigned to their room. Complications arise when lust rears its ugly head: Alex has the hots for Eddy who has his eyes on the well-formed butt of Stuart, who wants to jump the bones of the disinterested Alex. Sure it's "high concept," but what saves the film from being tiresome and predictable (no surprises, though) is the witty script which is crammed with hilariously accurate thoughts on gays, straights and today's college life. Of minor complaint is the handling of Eddy's character: He's a non-threatening gay virgin who only has sex with women and violently rejects the advances of another male student. ★★★ $19.99

The Thrill of It All

(1963, 108 min, US, Norman Jewison) This delightful spoof is very typical of the good-natured, family-oriented comedies Doris Day and Universal were releasing at the time. Day stars as a housewife who becomes a celebrity spokesperson, much to the dismay of husband James Garner. Though at times the film seems to advocate feminist principles, in the end Doris' place is in the home (evidently in 1963 she couldn't have it all). ★★★ $14.99

Throne of Blood

(1957, 110 min, Japan, Akira Kurosawa) Shakespeare's "Macbeth" is superbly adapted to the screen in this gripping tragedy of a samurai warrior who is spurred by his ambitious wife and an old witch to kill his lord. Amidst an atmosphere of obsessive madness, and utilizing aspects of Noh theatre, Kurosawa concludes his film with an unforgettable and graphic depiction of Toshiro Mifune's bloody death by arrows. (Japanese with English subtitles) ★★★½ $39.99

Through a Glass Darkly

(1961, 91 min, Sweden, Ingmar Bergman) Harriet Andersson is mesmerizing as a recently released mental patient who, while vacationing on a remote island with her husband, brother and father, relapses into schizophrenia. This Oscar winner is one of Bergman's most intense and riveting films. Also starring Max von Sydow. (Swedish with English subtitles) ★★★½ $29.99

The Threepenny Opera

Throw Momma from the Train

(1987, 88 min, US, Danny DeVito) A hilariously dark black comedy, with its inspiration coming from Hitchcock's classic *Strangers on a Train*. Billy Crystal stars as a teacher who gets mixed-up with one of his students, Danny DeVito, who is determined to get rid of his overbearing, mean-spirited mother. Anne Ramsey steals the film with an over-the-top, one-of-a-kind portrayal of DeVito's wicked Mom. ★★★ $9.99

Thumbelina

(1994, 84 min, US) While the animation isn't quite up to Disney standards, the characters are charming and witty and will appeal to some adults along with the kids. Don Bluth can count this as a worthy addition to his impressive body of animation. While staying true to the basic story line, he has created two wonderful additions. Gilbert Gottfried is hilarious as a cloying, low-life beetle who kidnaps Thumbelina to the "Beetle Ballroom" to make her his star performer. However, Charo steals the show as the evil Frog's mother with her Latino song-and-dance routine about making Thumbelina a "star." ★★★ $19.99

Thunder Road

(1958, 92 min, US, Arthur Ripley) The ideal picture to watch while passing around a jug of White Lightning. This lively potboiler has interesting behind-the-scenes glimpses of Kentucky moonshiners and a fun backwoods milieu. When a big-city operation tries to muscle in, bootlegger Robert Mitchum vows to stop them while at the same time attempting to elude the ceaseless pursuit of government agents. ★★★ $19.99

Thunderball

(1965, 132 min, GB, Terence Young) Sean Connery has tongue firmly in cheek in this fourth James Bond outing. 007 is up against Emilio Largo (Adolfo Celi), who has masterminded the greatest nuclear hijacking of all time. Excellent underwater photography highlights this glorious Bond adventure, which won an Oscar for Best Special Effects. (Available letterboxed and pan & scan) ★★★ $14.99

Thunderbolt and Lightfoot

(1974, 115 min, US, Michael Cimino) Clint Eastwood stars as a master thief who teams up with a wise-cracking drifter (Jeff Bridges) to search for stolen money from a previous robbery. Bridges received an Oscar nomination for his spirited performance (not to mention his drag routine). ★★★ $14.99

Thunderheart

(1992, 118 min, US, Michael Apted) Val Kilmer stars in this fictionalized look at the conflict between members of the American Indian Movement and the Bureau of Indian Affairs on the Sioux reservation in South Dakota. Kilmer plays a half-native FBI agent who is sent to sort things out. He takes the assignment reluctantly at first, as he really has no connection with his Indian roots; but as he gets to know life on the reservation, he finds that perhaps he is on the wrong side. Apted, who also directed the excellent companion piece to this film, *Incident at Oglala*, lets the

action loose at the appropriate moments, but doesn't hesitate to meditate on the mystical ways of his Native American subjects. Graham Greene co-stars as the reservation's sherrif and Sam Shepard appears as a slick, corrupt federal agent. ★★★ $19.99

THX-1138

(1971, 88 min, US, George Lucas) Before he revitalized the sci-fi genre with *Star Wars*, Lucas directed this chilling tale set in a 1984-like society where computers regulate the subterranean populace with mind-controlling drugs. This is a feature-length version of his award-winning short film. Starring Robert Duvall and Donald Pleasence. ★★★ $14.99

Ticket to Heaven

(1981, 107 min, Canada, Ralph L. Thomas) Made a year before the equally riveting, similarly themed *Split Image*, this psychological drama stars Nick Mancuso as a teacher who comes under the influence of a religious cult, robbing the educator of his will and spirit. When friends and family finally locate him, it's a desperate struggle to "deprogram" him to the way he was. Meg Foster and Saul Rubinek offer good support. ★★★

Tie Me Up! Tie Me Down!

(1990, 101 min, Spain, Pedro Almodóvar) This Almodóvar comedy may not satisfy those people who were won over by *Women on the Verge...*, but for lovers of Pedro and his outrageous style, this will be pure delight. A released mental patient (Antonio Banderas) kidnaps a heroin addicted pornstar (Victoria Abril) and professes his love for her. Surprisingly sentimental for Almodóvar, this is an often hilarious tale of love and bondage which features a truly steamy sex scene and a water toy with a penchant for swimming into the nether regions of the female anatomy. (Spanish with English subtitles) (Available letterboxed and pan & scan) ★★★ $14.99

The Tie That Binds

(1995, 98 min, US, Wesley Strick) Combining the worst elements of the competent but none-too-original thrillers *Kalifornia* and *The Hand That Rocks the Cradle*, this worthless wreck of a movie attempts to make a statement about contemporary child-rearing but succeeds only in being a lesson in how to make a terrible film. Vincent Spano and Moira Kelly do their best to maintain straight faces as a sympathetic yuppie couple who adopt a mysterious little girl, Janie, from the state orphanage. When Janie keeps a knife under the pillow to kill the tooth fairy, they decide to check into her birth parents' background. They discover Keith Carradine and Daryl Hannah, a part-time serial killer and his psychotic white-trash/hymn-singing wife, who've decided to retrieve Janie. The plot rehashes every "psychotic (nanny-policeman-tenant) from hell" movie, with a bit of the "white-trash lovers/killers on the run" genre for extra measure. With ludicrous dialogue and a by-the-numbers story, the only tie that binds here is the one needed to keep any viewer in their seat. ★ $99.99

Tie-Dyed

(1995, 88 min, US, Andrew Behar) Behar spent a summer on the road with the world's

most fanatic fans, the Grateful Dead followers. For some of them, it's a way of life; for others, extended weekends several times a year (the reservists?). Parking lots are transformed into small mobile communities, an extended gypsy family espousing anti-materialism, environmental consciousness and a tribal spirituality — the outside world is Babylon. Yet this small town on wheels also constitutes a microcosm of the larger culture it inhabits, reflecting the animosities and conflicts which exist in any population. This is especially true during the last decade of the phenomenon's 30-year run. The film successfully captures the unique nature of this three-decades-old road trip, allowing the viewer to participate in the magic without ignoring the down side. *Tie-Dyed* is a sometimes fascinating look at a quintessentially American subculture, made accessible to even the non-fan civilian. ★★★ $19.99

Tiger Bay

(1959, 105 min, GB, J. Lee Thompson) This morality play disguised as a suspense thriller stars Hayley Mills (in her debut) as a friendless girl who witnesses a murder, then shelters the murderer (Horst Buchholz) from the investigating detective (John Mills, Hayley's father). A sensitive study of the power of loneliness, desperation and the need to be loved, which makes this not just another "cops & robbers" story. The scenes between young Hayley and Buchholz are unforgettable. ★★★

A Tiger's Tale

(1987, 97 min, US, Peter Douglas) Pleasant but aimless comedy about a high school senior (C. Thomas Howell) who becomes romantically involved with his girlfriend's mother (Ann-Margret). Charles Durning, Kelly Preston, Anne Wedgeworth and Angel Tomkins costar. Director Douglas is one of Kirk's sons. ★★

Tigers in Lipstick

(1978, 85 min, Italy, Luigi Zampa) Four of the sexiest sirens of 1970s Europe — Laura Antonelli, Monica Vitti, Urusla Andress and Sylvia Kristel — star in this tame but cute series of vignettes. Taking their inspiration from O'Henry, these humorous tales with a sexual bent all focus on the fatally seductive charms of the female sex. All feature our femme fatales as beautiful and aggressive manhandlers whose task is made all that much easier by the wide-eyed and horny complacency of their oh-so-willing victims. (Dubbed) ★★ $39.99

Tightrope

(1984, 114 min, US, Richard Tuggle) Clint Eastwood stars as a New Orleans cop who, while hunting down a vicious rapist, suffers his own descent into sexual darkness. This razor-sharp crime thriller is a gripping examination of the twisted mind of the sexual criminal. Genevieve Bujold and Dan Hedaya also star. ★★★ $19.99

Tigrero: A Film That Was Never Made

(1995, 75 min, US, Mika Kaurismäki) Forty years after his initial trip up the Amazon to scout locations for a film offered to him by producer Darryl Zanuck, the intrepid film director Samuel Fuller returns, with Jim Jarmusch in tow, to the land of the Karajá

Indian tribe. The projected film, which was to have starred John Wayne, Ava Gardner and Tyrone Power, was never made. The tribe has survived myriad incursions from the outside over the intervening years, their culture amazingly intact despite wars, power politics and that eternal nemesis, progress. Fuller and Jarmusch sometime seem like just another annoyance in the villagers' lives; but there is one scene in which Fuller holds a screening for the tribe – a screening of some of the footage which sat in his closet for those 40 years. The Karajá watch with awe and wonder and recognition, remembering friends and relatives long dead. It's a moment that speaks to the magic of the medium, the potential to heighten human awareness; a power often squandered but when used effectively is often overwhelming. ★★★ $89.99

'Til There Was You

(1997, 113 min, US, Scott Winant) There's a certain breeziness that winds its way through *'Til There Was You*, a New Age variation of *Sleepless in Seattle* about lovers who don't meet until story's end. Things casually fall out windows, trendy sculptures exhibited in trendier restaurants knock customers on the head in obvious burlesque bits, and everyone seems so attractive and successful. So why isn't anyone smiling? Jeanne Tripplehorn and Dylan McDermott are separated childhood friends and supposed soul mates. But she's forever picking the wrong guy, and he's hung up on a former TV child star (Sarah Jessica Parker giving the film's only smart performance). What it takes to bring these two together forms the core of this overly cute, minor romantic comedy-drama. Though she handles the slapstick rather well, Tripplehorn lacks the zest and appeal required for this sort of romantic fluff. The handsome McDermott seems only a degree closer to understanding the mechanics of romantic lead. ★★ $102.99

Tilaï

(1990, 81 min, Burkina Faso, Idrissa Ouedraogo) Director Ouedraogo's haunting and starkly realized tale of forbidden love and tribal law is a masterfully crafted African take on Greek tragedy. The story follows Saga, who returns to his home village after a many years' absence only to find that his father, a powerful village elder, has stolen and married *his* fiancee, Nogma. As it becomes clear that his father has taken Nogma's hand forcibly, and that the old man is completely unrepentent for such an abuse of his son's trust, Saga becomes increasingly infuriated. But his hands are tied by the strict code of law, or "Tilai," that governs the village. Ultimately, he goes into exile, but stays close enough to the village to have an illicit affair with Nogma. Ouedraogo's excellent sense of storytelling is nicely complimented by an well-honed script and exceptional performances to make this a superisingly compelling and thoughtful Oedipal spin on forbidden passion. ★★★½ $79.99

Till Marriage Do Us Part

(1976, 97 min, Italy, Luigi Comencini) Set in the early 20th century, this funny bedroom farce features Laura Antonelli as a naive and virginal beauty who, on the night of her wedding, discovers that she has married her illegitimate brother. Unable to consummate the marriage, our enterprising heroine is determined to discover and explore the "mysteries of the flesh." A delightful and bawdy romp. (Available dubbed and in Italian with English subtitles) ★★★

Till the Clouds Roll By

(1946, 137 min, US, Richard Whorf) By-the-books musical biography of songwriter Jerome Kern, with Robert Walker playing the gifted composer. An all-star cast, in supporting roles and cameos, includes Van Heflin, Judy Garland, Frank Sinatra, Cyd Charisse, Lena Horne and Angela Lansbury. ★★½ $19.99

Tillie's Punctured Romance

(1914, 73 min, US, Mack Sennett) Shot in 1914, this delightful Charlie Chaplin silent comedy was made at producer Mack Sennett's famous Keystone Pictures studio. Co-starring then-popular comedienne Mabel Normand, the film is basically a slapstick love story, replete with Chaplin's brilliant trademark physical comedy. This was the only full-length feature Chaplin made for Keystone, and was the film where Chaplin refined his character that would later become his world-famous "Little Tramp." The feature is followed by a virtually unseen Mabel Normand short. *Tillie* is a classic made by one of the most influential and brilliant entertainers of all time. ★★★★ $19.99

Tim

(1979, 108 min, Australia, Michael Pate) A sensitive and compassionate story of the developing love between a handsome, slightly retarded young man (Mel Gibson) and an older career woman (Piper Laurie). After meeting by chance, the two find themselves bound by a deep affection and a tender sensuous longing. Based on the novel by Colleen McCullough. ★★½

Time After Time

(1979, 112 min, US, Nicholas Meyer) An exhilarating sci-fi murder mystery written and directed by Meyer. In Victorian England, writer H.G. Wells (Malcolm MacDowell) learns the identity of Jack the Ripper, but the infamous murderer uses Wells' newly invented time machine to transport himself to current-day San Francisco, an environment where he's "just an amateur." Wells follows him into the future, where he is assisted by bank clerk Mary Steenburgen. David Warner makes an appropriately demented Jack. Though a bit gory, it's a thrill a minute. ★★★½ $14.99

Time Bandits

(1981, 110 min, GB, Terry Gilliam) A young boy is abducted by time-traveling midgets, who, assisted by the Supreme Being (Ralph Richardson), take him on a harrowing journey through time where they encounter Robin Hood, a giant ogre (and his lovely wife), the Titanic and much, much more. Sean Connery, Shelley Duvall and most of the Monty Python gang star in this funny and frolicking fantasy. ★★★ $14.99

Time Expired

(1992, 30 min, US, Donny Leiner) While only 30 minutes in length, this delightfully wacky love story packs both a comedic and emotional wallop, and suggests great promise for director Leiner. Winner of the Grand Prize at the USA Film Festival in 1992, the film begins with the release from prison of a butch "straight" thug from Brooklyn who is greeted by his understanding wife and mother. But this is no typical ex-con tale, as he also must contend with Ruby, his former cellmate and Puerto Rican spitfire transvestite lover who now works as a manicurist at a beauty salon and longs for a return to their affair. The character of the no-nonsense Ruby, played with compassion and verve by John Leguizamo (*To Wong Foo...*), is the real attraction of this hilarious human comedy, as she demands both respect and affection from her befuddled, loutish beau who faces the dilemma of choosing between his "normal" family life and Ruby. ★★★ $14.99

Time for Revenge

(1983, 112 min, Argentina, Adolfo Aristarain) This gripping thriller tells the story of one man's struggle against a corrupt system. In an effort to publicize the unsafe working conditions at a demolition site, our hero fakes an industrial accident in order to blackmail the ruthless company. The scam, however, backfires – resulting in the death of a co-worker. The man continues with his scheme by claiming that he was struck speechless in the explosion. The company, knowing that something is up, gets desperate in their attempt to break his silence. A compelling story of oppression and distrust which won Best Film awards at the Montreal, Cartagena and Bairritz Film Festivals. (Spanish with English subtitles) ★★★½ $24.99

Time Indefinite

(1993, 117 min, US, Ross McElwee) Self-reflexive documentarian McElwee follows up his art-house hit *Sherman's March* by going a few steps further down the road of introspection, offering this kind of cradle-to-grave examination of his own family. McElwee's wry wit and intelligent commentaries are in evidence right from the start as he narrates the opening sequence in which he and fellow documentarian Marilyn Levine film themselves announcing their engagement at his family reunion. He then wends his way through the next couple of years of his life, documenting all the joys and sorrows. *Time Indefinite* is a fascinating, revealing and highly entertaining journey that explores some of life's universal questions. ★★★½ $79.99

The Time Machine

(1960, 103 min, US, George Pal) Special effects master Pal expertly brings to the big screen another of H.G. Wells' writings (Pal did *The War of the Worlds* earlier), this time retaining the novel's Victorian setting. On his way to year 802,701, Rod Taylor witnesses our atomic Armageddon of 1966 (you remember *that* one, don't you?) and the rise of the Morlock domination of the Eloi. With Yvette Mimieux, Alan Young ("Mr. Ed") Sebastian Cabot and, of course, Whit Bissell. One of the best screen adaptations of Wells' work. ★★★½ $19.99

A Time of Destiny

(1988, 118 min, US, Gregory Nava) It should be a comfort both to William Hurt and his

A Time to Kill

fans that he'll probably never make a movie as bad as this contrived and confusing WWII drama about revenge and obsession. Timothy Hutton and Stockard Channing can probably find solace, also. ★

Time of the Gypsies

(1989, 115 min, Yugoslavia, Emir Kusturica) Sort of a Serbian version of *The Godfather II*, the story is set in a Gypsy village where a young boy, gifted with kinetic powers, grows up. His innocence and love for his mother, girlfriend and pet chicken are soon replaced by a soulless love of money, bright polyester clothing and life in the fast lane after he joins up with a gang of petty thieves. Visually hallucinatory and imbued with much humor, the director used non-professional actors and real Gypsies for most of the roles, giving the film an authentic yet eccentric feel. Winner of the Best Director Prize at Cannes in 1989. (Serbian with English subtitles) ★★★ $19.99

The Time of Their Lives

(1946, 82 min, US, Charles Barton) Extremely entertaining Abbott and Costello romp about a couple killed during Revolutionary times (Costello and Marjorie Reynolds) whose spirits reappear in the 20th century to haunt Bud, just moving into his new country home. ★★★ $14.99

Time Stands Still

(1981, 99 min, Hungary, Peter Gothar) This witty and richly composed film is a compassionate coming-of-age drama set amid the debris of post-war Hungary, with its tightening grip of repression. It follows a group of friends — two brothers abandoned by their father, an enticing nymphette and a stylish rogue — as they encounter the hardships of growing up. A brilliant, seductive film seething with sexual tension, confused violence and the foreshadow of the rock 'n' roll culture. (Hungarian with English subtitles) ★★★½

A Time to Kill

(1996, 150 min, US, Joel Schumacher) Strong performances and a particularly compelling

and textured story line combine to make this the best screen adaptation of a John Grisham novel to date. Similar in tone and theme to the classic *To Kill a Mockingbird*, *A Time to Kill* stands very much on its own as an enthralling entertainment and a powerful examination of race relations. In a star-making performance, Matthew McConaughey plays a white Southern lawyer who defends a black man (Samuel L. Jackson) on trial for murdering the men who raped his ten-year-old daughter. Unlike *Mockingbird*, the guilt of the defendant is never in question; instead the story focuses on the culpability of a prejudiced society and the morality of the crime — all under the guise of exciting and even eloquent courtroom drama. Heading a good ensemble cast, the handsome McConaughey is splendid in his first starring role, a potent combination of passion, idealism and sensitivity; and Jackson gives a finely layered portrait of rage and decency. This is very nearly great filmmaking — only director Schumacher's less-than-fluid transitions minimally mar an otherwise terrific endeavor. ★★★½ $19.99

Time without Pity

(1957, 88 min, GB, Joseph Losey) His first film made under his own name after being blacklisted during the McCarthy era, Losey's melodrama is a tense, overmannered but engaging thriller. Less of a whodunit (the murderer is revealed in the first scene) and more of a how-will-he-do-it, the film stars Michael Redgrave as the alcoholic father of a convicted murderer (Alec McCowen) sentenced to die. Having only 24 hours, Redgrave sets out to prove his son's innocence — if he can stay off the bottle. In support are Leo McKern as the real killer, Ann Todd as his wife, Peter Cushing as the defense attorney, and a young Joan Plowright as a chorus girl. Losey's anticapital punishment story is played broadly but effectively. ★★★ $39.99

Timecop

(1994, 98 min, US, Peter Hyams) Jean-Claude Van Damme is in *Terminator* territory with

this action-flavored time travel adventure which mixes predictable heroics and villainy with a few spiffy twists on time tripping. Van Damme plays a special forces cop from the future who retrieves those in the past who are changing history. He meets his match, however, in the person of ruthless presidential candidate Ron Silver, who is trying to alter the course of human events for his own political gain. Though the syndicated TV show "Time Trax" covers the same ground, *Timecop* offers neat special effects, well-placed action scenes, and an over-the-top Silver in double doses. ★★½ $14.99

The Times of Harvey Milk

(1984, 87 min, US, Robert Epstein & Richard Schmiechen) This extraordinary, compelling portrait of the slain San Francisco supervisor won a much deserved Academy Award for Best Documentary. Few films pack such a powerful wallop as it documents the true-life story of Harvey Milk, a Castro Street camera shop owner who became the country's first openly gay elected official. His rise to power and success as a leader of minorities was abruptly ended in 1978 when he and Mayor George Moscone were assassinated by Dan White, an anti-gay former colleague of Milk's on the Board of Supervisors and a former police officer. The film follows the searing episode of injustice as White is given a light sentence — using the infamous "Twinkie defense" — which sent thousands of outraged citizens into the streets of San Francisco. ★★★★

Times to Come

(1981, 98 min, Argentina, Gustavo Mosquera) This amazingly adventurous surrealist drama takes its title from the Argentinian saying, "It'll even be worse in times to come." In the ruined urban landscape of Buenos Aires, a young man is shot by a policeman during an antigovernment demonstration. He falls into a coma in the hospital but his brain is fully functioning — exploding with thoughts and feelings — all the while trapped in an unresponsive body. The policeman responsible for the shooting is an unpredictable and violent man who is in turn hounded by a mysterious caller bent on punishing him. An angry film that successfully combines political fervor with daring camera work and imaginative storytelling. A good double feature would be *The Element of Crime*. (Spanish with English subtitles) ★★★ $79.99

Tin Cup

(1996, 130 min, US, Ron Shelton) *Bull Durham* star and director reunite for this easygoing, enjoyable sports comedy set against the world of golf — and thankfully it makes the game safe for cinematic subject matter once more after the awful *Happy Gilmore*. Displaying the rustic charm he demonstrated in *Durham* (possibly his most appealing performance), Kevin Costner plays a golf pro (nicknamed "Tin Cup") relegated to giving lessons for beer money. He becomes attracted to a new student (Rene Russo), who turns out to be the girlfriend of an arrogant ex-golf partner (Don Johnson) who has hit the big time. To woo her, he readies himself for the U.S. Open — it may only happen in the movies, but here it's actually fun to watch. While lacking the red-hot

T

chemistry of *Durham*'s Costner-Sarandon coupling, *Tin Cup* is as amiable as its hapless hero: wide-eyed and determined to please in spite of itself. ★★★ $19.99

The Tin Drum

(1979, 142 min, West Germany/France, Volker Schlöndorff) This powerful adaptation of Gunter Grass' masterpiece is about a young boy, disgusted by the rising tide of Nazism, who wills himself to stop growing. A mesmerizing "realistic fantasy" with an extraordinary piece of acting by 12-year-old David Bennett as the determined dwarf. (German with English subtitles) ★★★★ $39.99

Tin Men

(1987, 112 min, US, Barry Levinson) Director Levinson is quite at home, once again, with this second entry in his "Baltimore" trilogy (*Diner, Avalon*). Richard Dreyfuss and Danny DeVito are both exceptional as feuding salesmen in early 1960s Baltimore. A small fender-bender escalates into full war, as each tries to outdo the other in retaliation, including Dreyfuss seducing DeVito's wife. Barbara Hershey is splendid as the woman innocently caught between them. An outstanding comedy-drama with an exemplary supporting cast including John Mahoney, Bruno Kirby and Michael Tucker. ★★★½ $9.99

'Tis Pity She's a Whore

(1971, 109 min, Italy, Guiseppi Patrone Griffi) Freely adapted from John Ford's Elizabethan tragedy, this surprisingly absorbing film about a scandalous, incestuous affair has the beauty of Franco Zeffirelli's *Romeo and Juliet* combined with the poetically perverse sensuality of Jean Cocteau's *Les Enfants Terribles*. Visually stunning, the film takes place in the many rooms of a spectacular castle and amidst its stark, wintry countryside. Giovanni, an intensely handsome young man, is troubled by his passionate love for his sister, Annabella (Charlotte Rampling). The two, vowing undying love and commitment towards each other, are soon torn apart by their father who forces Annabella to marry an arrogant young nobleman — all the while pregnant with Giovanni's baby. Lushly photographed with several steamy sex scenes, this absorbing drama has a shocking, overpowering finale. (Filmed in English) ★★★ $14.99

Titanic

(1953, 98 min, US, Jean Negulesco) Barbara Stanwyck and Clifton Webb offer accomplished performances in this luxuriously melodramatic retelling of the sinking of the *Titanic*. As opposed to the excellent British drama *A Night to Remember*, which tells its story via the ship's personnel, this glossy Hollywoodization is seen through the eyes of the ship's passengers, with married couple Stanwyck and Webb its main focus. And even if *Night* is more authentic, this *Titanic* is soap opera of the first order, thanks to an Academy Award-winning screenplay and a marvelous ensemble, which includes Robert Wagner, Richard Basehart and the always reliable Thelma Ritter. The story of the *Titanic* is also told in James Cameron's 1997 big-budget epic. ★★★ $19.99

To Be or Not to Be

(1942, 99 min, US, Ernst Lubitsch) With the involvement of America in WWII, most audiences didn't know what to make of Lubitsch's hilarious and biting war comedy. With the advantage of the decades, however, this black farce has taken on legendary status, and deservedly so. Carole Lombard (in her final role) and Jack Benny are a husband and wife acting team in Occupied Poland. When they cross paths with a double agent, they devise a plan — with the help of their acting troupe — to expose the spy and flee to safety. Lombard was an exceptional comedienne and farceur, and her performance is radiant; and Benny gives a truly funny performance as "...that great, great actor" Joseph Tura. An earnest though inferior remake was made by Mel Brooks in 1983. ★★★★ $14.99

To Be or Not to Be

(1983, 108 min, US, Mel Brooks) Inferior, somewhat entertaining remake of the 1942 Ernst Lubitsch classic, with Mel Brooks and Anne Bancroft as the bickering thespian couple. The film tells the story of a Polish troupe of actors who outwit the Nazis in Occupied Warsaw. Charles Durning (Oscar nominated), Tim Matheson and Jose Ferrer also star. Brooks adds a slightly misplaced but certainly well-intentioned update by introducing a gay character who also suffers under Nazi rule. ★★½ $9.99

To Catch a Killer

(1991, 95 min, Canada, Eric Till) The police investigation and arrest of serial killer John Wayne Gacy is the subject of this crime drama which has been edited from its original miniseries length. Rather than being cheap, sensationalistic exploitation, the film is actually quite suspenseful. Brian Dennehy is believable as the demented Gacy, a stocky construction contractor who was eventually sent to death row for kidnapping, sexually torturing and killing at least 33 teenage boys and then burying their bodies in the dirt basement of his Illinois home. Without the mystery of whodunit, the film instead focuses on the police's

frantic efforts in tracking him down. A determined young detective (Michael Riley) takes charge of the case, and when evidence is only circumstantial, he engages the cocky Gacy in a cat-and-mouse game as they slowly piece together the evidence needed for an arrest. Sad, creepy and riveting. ★★★ $14.99

To Catch a Thief

(1955, 97 min, US, Alfred Hitchcock) This fast-paced romantic thriller features glorious Rivera settings, sparkling comic touches and the sizzling sexual chemistry between Grace Kelly and Cary Grant. Grant plays a reformed jewel thief who may be up to his old tricks; Kelly may be his intended victim. ★★★ $14.99

To Die For

(1995, 100 min, US, Gus Van Sant) Nicole Kidman offers a tour de force performance in this stylish and hilarious social satire that attacks America's media-obsession with razor-sharp precision. Kidman is a model of icy effervescence as Suzanne Stone, a small-town New Hampshire girl who is dangerously determined to make a name in television, at any cost. After her marriage to high school sweetheart Larry Maretto (Matt Dillon), she embarks on her mission by taking a position at the local cable station. Eventually, she begins work on a video documentary about the wasted lives of three local teens, including a perfectly cast Joaquin Pheonix — whose narcoleptic performance as her unlikely paramour provides a grotesque yet riveting mirror of his brother River's performance in *My Own Private Idaho*. When her hubby Larry begins making too much racket demanding marital bliss, Suzanne, determined to stay the course, enlists the youths to help rid her of her domestic distraction. Based in part on a real incident, Buck Henry's masterful script finds itself in good hands with Van Sant. Illeana Douglas is captivating in support as Dillon's sister, who also acts to some degree as the film's Greek chorus. ★★★½ $19.99

To Forget Venice

(1979, 110 min, Italy, Franco Brusati) Brusati (*Bread and Chocolate*) has fashioned this sensi-

Carole Lombard (c.) is not one to toy with in this scene from *To Be or Not to Be*

tive and refined story of a group of people (two gay men and two lesbians) who visit together at an old country estate. The film explores the important events of their past, their first sexual encounters and their worried looks to the future. A very good film, but one in which many will debate the accuracy of the film's sexual politics (i.e., that one moment in each of their lives that made them gay). (Dubbed) ★★★

To Gillian on Her 37th Birthday

(1996, 93 min, US, Michael Pressman) Based on the off-Broadway play, this comedy-drama of a deceased wife returning from the grave and only seen by her grieving husband has a certain breeziness to it but there's nothing special to either dialogue or story line – the recent *Ghost* and *Truly, Madly, Deeply* did it better. Giving a nice, semi-romantic performance, Gallagher is a professor and father who has yet to get over the two-year death of his wife. Looking glorious (especially for a corpse), Pfeiffer plays the ghost who returns to console and romp on the beach with her husband. As his family and friends start to think him mad, they gather for a weekend of memories and therapy. Even though Gallagher and Pfeiffer work well together, and Danes is very appealing as their daughter, the film never ignites and takes off in the way it should. It also doesn't help that they changed the ending from the play. *Gillian* has its laughs, and the requisite tears, but this ghost story gets caught somewhere in limbo. ★★½ $19.99

To Have and Have Not

(1944, 101 min, US, Howard Hawks) This polished Hawks production is usually remembered more as the film in which Humphrey Bogart and Lauren Bacall first met than for any artistic accomplishment, which is a disservice to its stars, director and writers. Bogie plays a hardboiled American charter boat captain who becomes involved with French freedom fighters, Nazis and, of course, Bacall; who, among other things, teaches Bogie how to whistle. Hoagy Carmichael and a terrific Walter Brennan costar. ★★★½ $19.99

To Joy

(1950, 93 min, Sweden, Ingmar Bergman) Taking its title from Beethoven's "Ode to Joy," *To Joy* marks Bergman's creative passage from films depicting the darkness of evil forces to films that celebrate the light of affirmation. This intensely moving, sensitive film focuses on the life of a talented violinist who must come to grips with the fact that his young wife was killed. Through despair and introspection, he discovers that his love for his son and for music gives him the strength to continue. (Dubbed) ★★★

To Kill a Mockingbird

(1962, 131 min, US, Robert Mulligan) Gregory Peck won an Oscar for his brilliant performance as Southern lawyer Atticus Finch in this brilliantly realized courtroom drama and memory piece. Based on the best-selling novel by Harper Lee, the film is seen through the eyes of Finch's young daughter, Scout (Mary Badham), and recounts her days as a youth in 1930s Georgia as well as following her

father's court case in which he defends a black man accused of rape. One of the greatest of all American films. ★★★★ $14.99

To Kill a Priest

(1989, 116 min, France, Agnieszka Holland) This fictionilized account of an actual murder of a Polish priest stars Christopher Lambert as the martyred clergyman whose campaign for Solidarity disfavors him with the military authorities. Ed Harris costars as a mid-level officer with the security police who engineers, and executes, the assassination plot. Exiled Polish director Holland (*Bitter Harvest*) finds great human drama in the priest's dedication to his beliefs, but unwisely concentrates more on the dilemma of the Communist officer, whose zeal for the good of the party contradicts his own moral being. (Filmed in English) ★★½ $89.99

To Live

(1994, 135 min, China, Zhang Yimou) One might easily be predisposed to thinking that this two-hour-plus melodrama about the harrowing journey of a Chinese family (from the end of the Nationalist reign to the Cultural Revolution) is going to be a tear-jerking, ultra-sentimental mish-mash. But while *To Live* certainly does pull at the heartstrings, it revels in its visual splendor and exceptional dramatics. Ge You stars as a wealthy landlord who loses his entire estate gambling, only to be ironically spared the rod when the Reds crack down on their former oppressors. Gong Li (Zhang's perennial star) plays his strong-spirited and, at times, estranged wife. Together, with their rambunctious son and deaf daughter, they wend their way through life, suffering all of the conceivable outrages that a country at war with itself can throw their way. Not enough can possibly be said about the rapturous, easy-going performances of Ge and Gong. In the deft hands of director Zhang and with a masterful script by author Yu Hua, the two actors create characterizations that inexorably draw the viewer into the urgencies of their harrowed lives. Perhaps Zhang's best work to date. (Mandarin with English subtitles) ★★★★ $19.99

To Live and Die in L.A.

(1985, 116 min, US, William Friedkin) Gritty, fast-paced police thriller with William Petersen as a Secret Service agent who will stop at nothing to capture the counterfeiter who murdered his partner. Willem Dafoe is a particularly villainous heavy. Made at the height of TV's "Miami Vice"'s popularity, director Friedkin gives this bloody cops and robbers tale a similar, slick look. ★★★

To Play or to Die

(1990, 50 min, The Netherlands, Frank Krom) Filmed with unusual flair for a small independent film, this hyperventilating, psychosexual drama tells the story of a nerdish teenager's intense crush on a bullying but attractive classmate. With his parents away, 15-year-old Kees, fueled by a masochistic puppy love for the unresponsive and cruel Charel, finds his plans for seduction and revenge unraveling after he invites the other to his home. A simple premise, and while not at all homophobic, its theme of equating homosex-

ual desire with madness and death is a sad, frustrating one, especially problematic coming from a promising gay filmmaker. (Dutch with English subtitles) ★★½ $39.99

To Sir, with Love

(1966, 105 min, GB, James Clavell) Sidney Poitier plays an inexperienced schoolteacher, Mr. Thackeray, who's assigned a class of rowdy, headstrong and undisciplined Mods in London's East End. The students of the graduating class are determined to break Thackeray's will, but he surprises them all by giving the students respect while commanding and getting it from them. Poitier is excellent in this compelling and refreshing teacher-student drama, and he's supported by a fine group of young actors which includes Judy Geeson, Christian Roberts and Lulu (who sings the hit title song). ★★★½ $14.99

To Sleep with Anger

(1990, 95 min, US, Charles Burnett) Danny Glover put down his *Lethal Weapon* to lend his talents to this chilling independent production by maverick director Burnett. Glover plays an "old family friend" from the South who arrives at the doorstep of an upwardly mobile black family and insinuates his way into their home, wreaking havoc on the family unit by preying on their individual weaknesses. Mixing myth, metaphor and an offbeat sense of humor, director Burnett shows that progress made over shakey ground is sometimes no progress at all. Also starring Sheryl Lee Ralph, Mary Alice, Carl Lumbly and Richard Brooks. ★★★½ $14.99

To the Devil a Daughter

(1976, 95 min, GB, Peter Sykes) The legendary Hammer Studios brought forth this satanic horror story about a defrocked priest (Christopher Lee) who earmarks Nastassja Kinski for selection as the Devil's daughter on her 18th birthday. Kinski's distraught father (Denholm Elliott) enlists the aid of an expert occultist (Richard Widmark) and the fun begins. A kinky adventure into the unknown. ★★½ $9.99

To the Lighthouse

(1985, 115 min, GB, Colin Gregg) Virginia Woolf's tale of family turmoil is set in a lush Cornwall resort at the outset of WWI where the towering lighthouse comes to symbolize the spirit of reconciliation and hope for the future. Rosemary Harris, Michael Gough and Kenneth Branagh star in this touching drama. ★★★

To Wong Foo, Thanks for Everything! Julie Newmar

(1995, 108 min, US, Beeban Kidron) Destined to be forever referred to as the "American *Priscilla*," this bit of cross-dressing whimsy lacks that film's exhilaration and sharp character definition, but ultimately pleases with its good humor and spirited performances. Tough guys Patrick Swayze and Wesley Snipes get in touch with their feminine side as they don sequins and high heels as two New York drag queens who win a preliminary drag contest and ride off towards Hollywood for the finals. Along for the ride is Latina spitfire

Tokyo Story

John Leguizamo, an ill-refined drag looking to learn the ropes. En route, they run afoul of the law, and are stranded in a small Midwestern town (and befriend the locals) which provides most of the story. Though the gay characters are positively portrayed, they are virtually sexless fairy godmothers who neither love or have partners and who help the hapless heterosexuals with no fashion sense. This is so tame you can watch it with your mom. Looking like Tony Curtis in *Some Like It Hot*, Swayze seems to enjoy himself as the demure Vida; Snipes is rambunctious as the glib Noxeema; and Leguizamo steals the show as the fiery Chi Chi. ★★★ $19.99

The Todd Killings

(1971, 93 min, US, Barry Shear) Robert F. Lyons stars as a kill-for-thrills psycho in this tense and atmospheric drama. Based on real-life accounts, and pre-dating *River's Edge*, the film offers a look into the twisted mind of a killer who provides drugs and parties to a group of alienated teens who in turn protect him from the law. Barbara Bel Geddes, Ed Asner and Richard Thomas costar. ★★★ $19.99

Der Todesking

(1989, 80 min, West Germany, Jörg Buttgereit) Bathtub suicide, castration, neighbors on a killing rampage, rotting corpses and Nazi torture are just some of the "highlights" in this angst-ridden splatter film. Espousing diatribes such as "the motiveless mass murderer is the martyrdom of post-modernism," this deliberately shocking low-budgeter features a series of segments about sad, lonely, frustrated people who decide to end it all, with the finale being a cinema verité murder rampage. (German with English subtitles) ★½ $29.99

Together Alone

(1991, 87 min, US, P.J. Castellaneta) This sensual, funny and perceptive two-character drama is set entirely in a bedroom. Two men, who met anonymously at a gay bar, have just had (unsafe) sex. But instead of the usual kiss on the cheek and "I've got to go," the two begin to talk well into the night. Bryan (Todd Stites), who lives in the apartment, is an out

and outspoken gay while Brian (Terry Cury) is a married bisexual with a complicated past. The two men discuss and argue about a wide range of issues, including AIDS, sexual responsibility, dreams, betrayal and relationships. Their attempts to understand one another and reveal something of themselves is both believable and forceful. An intellectually invigorating queer drama. ★★★ $39.99

Tokyo Decadence

(1991, 112 min, Japan, Ryu Murakami) This controversial, fiercely original and visually shocking portrait of a young Japanese call girl's quest for ecstasy is adapted from director Murakami's novel "Topaz." Plunging headfirst into the steamy world of S/M, drugs and depravity, the story revolves around Ai, who as the film opens seeks beatitude through the advice of a fortune teller — whose strange prescriptions include placing a telephone book under her television and making a ring from a pink topaz. While the film bathes the viewer in a sea of heroin abuse, cocaine snorting, floggings and humiliations, these uncomfortable images are necessary to show how the successful and powerful businessmen clients seek these bizarre pleasures to further quench their thirst for power. A darkly powerful film that's clearly not for all tastes, but a challenging experience for open-minded viewers. (Available dubbed and in Japanese with English subtitles) ★★★ $29.99

Tokyo Olympiad

(1964, 170 min, Japan, Kon Ichikawa) An unlikely candidate to chronicle Japan's hosting of the 1964 Summer Olympics, Ichikawa, a celebrated director and admitted non-fan of sports, took his assignment of documenting the event seriously and produced this extraordinary celebration of the human form. Utilizing over 160 cameramen, filming in Cinemascope and intercutting slow-motion and other special effects, the film captures the visual spendor of the Olympics and is possibly the finest photographed film of athletic endeavor. Not interested in the glorification of man, as was Leni Riefenstahl's *Olympia*, Ichikawa instead focuses more on competition and the individual efforts of the athletes. When told that the Japanese committee which commissioned the work was not pleased at getting simply a newsreel accounting and suggested that they might consider reshooting, Ichikawa said, "I had to tell them that the entire cast had already left Japan." This video, the rarely seen original director's cut, will enthrall both sports fans and non-fans alike. ★★★½ $79.99

Tokyo Story

(1953, 134 min, Japan, Yasujiro Ozu) Ozu's quietly overpowering masterpiece is a deceptively simple tale about an elderly couple's visit to Tokyo and the less than enthusiastic reception they receive from their children. A master with the camera and with subtlety of statement, Ozu deftly and powerfully creates this vision of

alienation in the modern world as the "new" Japan forced the traditional values out. A true masterpiece of world cinema. (Japanese with English subtitles) ★★★★ $69.99

Tokyo-Ga

(1985, 92 min, West Germany/US, Wim Wenders) Wenders's engrossing and entertaining "filmed dairy" of his 1983 trip to Tokyo is both a fascinating glimpse of the city and a personal metaphysical search for meaning. At the start of the trip, Wenders aims to find the "pure" Japan that he knows and loves from the films of director Yasujiro Ozu. Instead of simplicity and order, however, Wenders becomes dazed by the kinetic energy of the city, as well as fascinated by the strange and, at times bizarre, lifestyles of the people. (Filmed in English) ★★★

Tom and Huck

(1995, 93 min, US, Peter Hewitt) On the heels of Disney's lively 1993 Mark Twain adaptation *The Adventures of Huck Finn*, which was directed by Stephen Sommers, comes this routine and almost lifeless adaptation of Twain's "Tom Sawyer." Though written by Sommers, neither he or director Hewitt bring much high-spiritedness to the film. TV's adolescent heartthrob Jonathan Taylor Thomas plays Sawyer, a spunky, mischievous orphan being raised by his aunt. The story concentrates on his friendship with Huck Finn (Brad Renfro), and their dilemma when they witness a murder and the wrong man is accused. The film is surprisingly tame, offers few misadventures, and has in Huck an angst-ridden 20th-century juvenile delinquent rather than a 19th-century youth bent on tomfoolery. Thomas is successful in bringing more of an innocence and playfulness to Tom Sawyer, and the young actor justifies, at least, his solo star billing. ★★ $14.99

Tom and Jerry: The Movie

(1993, 84 min, US, Phil Roman) This uneven big-screen version of everyone's favorite cat and mouse team finds them homeless and joining forces with a young girl attempting to break free of her evil guardian. The film lacks the humor (slapstick or otherwise) which made the original cartoon shorts so popular (even though many of the jokes relied on violence for their punchlines), and a newer generation of children may just be bored by it all. ★★ $14.99

Tom & Viv

(1994, 125 min, GB, Brian Gilbert) Madness and passion are equally matched in this unsettling though beautifully filmed examination of the love affair, marriage and separation of writer T.S. Eliot and his wife Vivienne. Willem Dafoe plays the American author who seems more at home in the reserved setting of the British upper crust. Miranda Richardson, in a mesmerizing, go-for-broke Oscar-nominated performance, is the aristocrat whose high-spiritedness seems the perfect tonic for the somber writer. They marry, and Eliot begins to achieve success in the field of poetry with his wife aiding him spiritually and editorially. However, as Eliot's star ascends, it soon becomes apparent that his wife is suffering from some sort of mental instability, which begins to threaten both their relationship and his career. Contrasting their deep love is the sad story of Viv's affliction and eventual, heartbreaking committal and sacrifice for her husband. It's an ending which should provoke anger as well as tears. As Viv's socially conscious but loving mother, Rosemary Harris is excellent. ★★★ $19.99

Tom, Dick and Harry

(1941, 86 min, US, Garson Kanin) Ginger Rogers sparkles in this delightful comedy with Ginger daydreaming about her three boyfriends, having to choose between them. George Murphy, Alan Marshall and Burgess Meredith are the men of her dreams. ★★★ $19.99

Tom Jones

(1963, 129 min, GB, Tony Richardson) This Academy Award Winner for Best Picture and Director richly evokes the tenor of its times — both of the setting of the novel and of the era when it was filmed. Richardson uses every cinematic trick in the book — fast motion, jump cuts, rapid editing, etc. — to capture the joie de vivre of Henry Fielding's bawdy tale of a young rake's randy adventures in 18th-century England. Albert Finney is brilliant in the lead role, and his seduction of Joyce Redman in the classic eating scene will make a gourmand out of the most abstemious. ★★★★ $19.99

tom thumb

(1958, 98 min, GB, George Pal) Winning an Oscar for Best Special Effects, this musical based on the children's fairy tale proves true the adage that good things come in small packages. "Fun for the entire family" might be a worn epithet, but this movie certainly warrants its use. Kids will enjoy the animated performance of Russ Tamblyn (West Side Story and "Twin Peaks") as he cavorts in the role of the diminutive hero. Animated also applies to Tom's toy friends, puppets brought to life by "Puppettoon" master George Pal. Adults will particularly appreciate the antics of Terry-Thomas and Peter Sellers, perfectly cast as greedy, bumbling antagonists. ★★★½ $14.99

Tombstone

(1993, 132 min, US, George P. Cosmatos) Slightly overlong and overly ambitious, Tombstone is an invigorating, extremely photogenic tale of legendary lawman Wyatt Earp's tenure in the shoot-'em-up town of Tombstone, Arizona. A slick examination of the Old West with plenty of gunplay, the film stars Kurt Russell as Wyatt, who has retired from peacekeeping and is ready to settle down. However, a notorious gang known as The Cowboys stands in his way. Of course, the film chronicles the famous gunfight at the O.K. Corral (an efficient and exciting sequence), and strives to explore Earp's personal life, as well. Though Russell firmly anchors the film with a gutsy performance, he is surrounded by an impressive gallery of supporting players; the best being Val Kilmer who gives an acerbic interpretation of the sickly Doc Holliday. ★★★ $14.99

Tommy

(1975, 110 min, GB, Ken Russell) The Who's rock opera stars Roger Daltrey as the "deaf, dumb and blind boy" who becomes a pinball wizard and New Messiah. Elton John is the dethroned champ, Eric Clapton is the preach-er and Tina Turner is the electrifying acid queen. Directed by Russell with his usual flair for the bizarre. ★★★ $14.99

Tommy Boy

(1995, 96 min, US, Peter Segal) Though it may sound suspiciously similar to Billy Madison, an awful comedy starring another "Saturday Night Live" comedian, Tommy Boy, about the moronic son of a multimillionaire, is unexpectedly funny. Chris Farley stars as the title character, a recent college grad (with a D+ average) who returns home to work for his father's automotive company. When his father dies, Tommy must not only prove himself able to take control of the company, but to save it from closing, as well. Tommy Boy is peppered with lots of amusing physical schtick, and Farley and cohort David Spade (as Tommy's caustic assistant) make an effective comedy team. They're no Hope and Crosby, but their work is infectiously appealing. In support, Bo Derek and Rob Lowe star as con artists in the film's more ordinary subplot. Tommy Boy may not be at the head of the class, but of all the "dumb" movies so far, it's one of the smartest. ★★½ $14.99

Tomorrow

(1972, 103 min, US, Joseph Anthony) A startlingly good adaptation of William Faulkner's story, featuring Robert Duvall in a tremendous performance as a workman who befriends and falls in love with a pregnant woman (Olga Bellin) deserted by her husband and family. Horton Foote (The Trip to Bountiful) wrote the screenplay. ★★★

Tomorrow Is Forever

(1946, 104 min, US, Irving Pichel) A sumptuous, moving version of "Enoch Arden," featuring a great performance by Orson Welles and a lovely portrayal by Claudette Colbert. Colbert plays a wife whose husband (Welles) dies at the end of WWI. At least that's what she thinks. She gives birth to his son, and later marries her boss. Twenty years later, her first husband, crippled and having spent those years under a new identity living in Vienna, returns to America to work for her new husband. When he meets her and the son he never knew he had, he is faced with the dilemma of whether or not to reveal his identity to them. ★★★ $19.99

Tongues Untied

(1989, 55 min, US, Marlon Riggs) This highly acclaimed film combines poetry, personal testimony, rap and performance to describe the homophobia and racism that confronts gay African-Americans. A personal and at times angry documentary that is an impassioned cry to speak out about black gay lives, the film garnered surprising controversy when some PBS stations — disturbed by its subject matter — refused to broadcast it. Two of the more memorable lines state: "Black men loving black men is the revolutionary act"; and "If in America a black is the lowest of the low, what is a gay black?" ★★★ $39.99

Toni

(1935, 90 min, France, Jean Renoir) In an attempt at film realism, Renoir left the confines of the studio and soundstage and

Tongues Untied

brought the action to the outdoors. His actors do not wear makeup, a more "natural" style of acting is used and Renoir places his camera at a distance in order for the characters and action to tell the story with the camera merely recording. The result is a wonderfully told tale of the loves and lives of four Italian immigrant miners who settle around Marseilles. (French with English subtitles) ★★★

Tonight and Every Night

(1945, 92 min, US, Victor Saville) Pleasant Rita Hayworth musical about the wartime adventures — romantic and otherwise — of a group of showgirls working in London during the blitz. Rita romances RAF pilot Lee Bowman, and must decide between love and duty when he is shipped abroad. ★★★ $19.99

Tonio Kröger

(1964, 90 min, West Germany/France, Rolf Thiele) Thomas Mann's autobiographical novella is faithfully brought to the screen in this dreamlike story of the problems encountered by a youth growing up in late 19th-century Germany. Born of a Prussian businessman and a fiery Italian woman, our hero struggles with whether he wants to belong to the bourgeois world or explore his artistic talents. This conflict between restraint and passion forces him to decide what world and lifestyle is best suited for him. (German with English subtitles) ★★

Too Beautiful for You

(1989, 91 min, France, Bertrand Blier) Gérard Depardieu stars as a wealthy businessman who has just about everything one could desire, including a dazzlingly beautiful wife (Carole Bouquet). But when he meets his new secretary, Colette, a frumpy and slightly overweight middle-aged woman, and falls deeply and passionately in love with her, he finds his material values seriously imperiled. Director Blier has taken the basic premise of farce and turned it upside down; and while the film has a gentle comic flavor throughout, it is also a serious examination of the misplaced value given to beauty. Depardieu is excellent as always and Josiane Balasko is a treat as the broodingly seductive Colette. (French with English subtitles) ★★★ $19.99

Too Hot to Handle

(1938, 105 min, US, Jack Conway) A fast-paced and extremely entertaining comedy with Clark Gable in a particularly light mood as a newsreel journalist who courts aviatrix Myrna Loy from rival reporter Walter Pidgeon. Gable and Loy, appearing together for the seventh time, are well matched in this alternately funny and action-flavored romp. Recommended, and a near-must for students of 1930s comedies. ★★★½ $19.99

Too Late the Hero

(1969, 133 min, GB, Robert Aldrich) Michael Caine and Cliff Robertson star as British and American officers in charge of a suicide mission to distract the Japanese on a small Pacific island. The two must come to grips with their cultural differences as they engage in a battle of wits with the local Japanese commander. Ian Bannen and Denholm Elliott are excellent in support. ★★★ $14.99

Too Many Girls

(1940, 85 min, US, George Abbott) One of Lucille Ball's earliest starring roles, and the sassy redhead makes the most of it. A most engaging musical comedy, the story follows the romantic adventures of college students Lucy and Eddie Bracken, Richard Carlson, Ann Miller and Desi Arnaz (this is where they met). ★★★ $19.99

Too Much Sun

(1990, 97 min, US, Robert Downey) Two pampered children of a Beverly Hills millionaire learn they will lose their deceased father's $200 million fortune unless one of them produces an heir. The problem? Sonny (Eric Idle) is gay and Bitsy (Andrea Martin) is a lesbian. The ensuing game of sexual musical chairs is further complicated by the arrival of a pair of two-bit hustlers (Robert Downey, Jr. and Ralph Macchio), who are willing to be adopted, for the right price. Howard Duff and Leo Rossi also star. From the director of *Putney Swope*. ★★½ $89.99

Too Pretty to Be Honest

(1982, 95 min, France, Richard Balducci) Four very pretty girls who share an apartment on the French Riviera witness a bank robbery on a day trip to Nice. The next day, looking through a telescope, they see the man who might be the thief so, thinking that stealing from a thief is not really stealing, they plot an elaborate scheme to lift the money. (French with English subtitles) ★★½

Too Shy to Try

(1978, 89 min, France, Pierre Richard) Richard directed and stars in this comedy about a bungling man who falls in love with a beautiful and sophisticated young woman. Unable to simply introduce himself to the young lady, our hero instead enrolls in a correspondence course in a valiant attempt to become the Casanova of his dreams. Don't expect Renoir, but fans of Richard (*Les Comperes, Tall Blond Man...*) will be entertained in this romantic comedy. (French with English subtitles) ★★½

Too Young to Die

(1990, 100 min, US, Robert Markowitz) Brad Pitt and Juliette Lewis pay a low-budget visit to *Natural Born Killers* territory with this made-for-TV movie. In The-Middle-of-Nowhere, Oklahoma, 14-year-old Amanda (Lewis) marries to escape a sexually abusive stepfather and an uncaring mother. The marriage disintegrates and Amanda is abandoned. She hits the road and is appropriated by Pitt, who delivers a dress rehearsal for his *Kalifornia* role (interestingly, someone calls him a "vampire"). *Too Young to Die's* somewhat plodding exposition is enhanced by competent performances, especially from Lewis as the tragic teen. Worth checking out if only to compare Lewis and Pitt with their more recent work. ★★½ $9.99

Tootsie

(1982, 110 min, US, Sydney Pollack) Dustin Hoffman legitimizes transvestism in this glorious comedy and slyly stirring social criticism. Forced (?) to don women's garb to propel his acting career, Dustin becomes the queen of the daytime soaps and the thwarted victim of his attraction to a female costar (Academy Award winner Jessica Lange). Sparkling support by Dabney Coleman, Charles Durning, director Pollack and the hilariously straight-faced Bill Murray. ★★★★ $14.99

Top Gun

(1986, 94 min, US, Tony Scott) Military jingoism, fine aerial photography, inane dramatics and young Tom Cruise combined to make this one of the big box-office hits of the 1980s. Story follows hotshot Navy pilot Cruise and his affair with instructor/astrophysicist (yeah, right) Kelly McGillis. (Available letterboxed and pan & scan) ★★ $14.99

Top Hat

(1935, 99 min, US, Mark Sandrich) Commonly called the "quintessential Fred Astaire-Ginger Rogers musical," *Top Hat* is a breathless combination of glorious music, marvelous dance routines which seem to float on air, captivating and sometimes silly comedy, and a cast of characters anyone would want to invite to their next soiree. Featuring a story line and displaying a look very reminiscent of *The Gay Divorcee*, the film's contrivance of a plot centers on dancer Fred falling for model Ginger (if it works once, use it again). But through a case of mistaken identity, she thinks he's married, and to a society friend she's about to meet. Edward Everett Horton is just perfect as Astaire's best friend, the one who Rogers thinks is Fred. The score is one of their best, and includes "Cheek to Cheek," "Isn't This a Lovely Day to Be Caught in the Rain" and the title tune. The dancing is pure magic. ★★★★ $19.99

Top Secret!

(1984, 90 min, US, Jim Abrahams, David & Jerry Zucker) From the team that brought us *Airplane!* and *The Naked Gun* comes this funny spoof of the espionage-thriller genre. Val Kilmer stars as an Elvis-like pop stars who travels to East Germany on a goodwill tour and gets wrapped up in the local intrigue. As in their other films, the ZAZ team throws up a relentless barrage of sight gags, pratfalls and one-liners, some of which miss their mark; but there are so many direct hits that the laughter never ceases. This is good, stupid, silly fun at its best. ★★★ $14.99

Topaz

(1969, 126 min, US, Alfred Hitchcock) When American agent John Forsythe and French counterpart Frederick Stafford uncover Russian infiltration in Cuba, a whirlwind chain of events whisks them around the globe and deep into high intrigue. Though the complex screenplay is occasionally baffling, Hitchcock sustains a tension throughout. ★★★ $14.99

Topaze

(1933, 95 min, France, Louis Gasnier) Based on the Marcel Pagnol play, this comedy of morals was a popular success on its initial release although Pagnol was disappointed with it and remade the film, directing it himself in 1936 and again in 1951. Interestingly, it was this version that has survived the test of time. Topaze (Louis Jouvet), a naive and scrupulously honest provincial schoolteacher, is unwittingly lured into a phony business scheme with a disreputable financier. About to take the fall, our hero soon realizes that doing the right thing is not always the wisest course and soon develops his own plot to not only swindle the

From left to right: Val Kilmer, Sam Elliott, Kurt Russell and Bill Paxton in *Tombstone*

swindler but to have his mistress as well. (French with English subtitles) ★★★½ $59.99

Topaze

(1933, 78 min, US, Harry D'Arrast) John Barrymore gives a sterling performance in this charming comedy based on Marcel Pagnol's play. Barrymore plays a naive college professor who is unknowingly exploited by a shady businessman – or is he? Also with Myrna Loy. ★★★ $39.99

Topkapi

(1964, 120 min, US, Jules Dassin) Dassin's often imitated gem of a movie about a gang of jewel thieves who plan an elaborate heist of the emerald encrusted dagger at the Topkapi Palace in Istanbul. Maximilian Schell and Melina Mercouri star, but it was Peter Ustinov who grabbed the Oscar for Best Supporting Actor with his inspired portrayal of their lackey. ★★★★ $19.99

Topper

(1937, 97 min, US, Norman Z. McLeod) This delightful ghost comedy stars Cary Grant and Constance Bennett as the Kirbys, who are accidentally killed in a car crash and return as spirits to haunt the ordered life of their banker, Cosmo Topper. Roland Young gives a remarkably funny performance as the harried Topper, and Billie Burke is perfect as Topper's rather scatterbrained, but lovable wife. ★★★½

Topper Returns

(1941, 88 min, US, Roy Del Ruth) More hilarity with Cosmo Topper and friends. Roland Young repeats his role for a third time as the timid banker, who here befriends ghostly Joan Blondell, helping her solve her own murder. The wonderful Billie Burke also returns as Mrs. Topper, and Eddie Anderson also stars. Though the original has more style, here the laughs are nonstop. ★★★½

Tora! Tora! Tora!

(1970, 143 min, US/Japan, Richard Fleischer, Toshio Masuda & Kinji Fukasuku) This expensive war drama is an impeccably produced re-creation of the bombing of Pearl Harbor, and the events which led to the devastating action which thrust America into WWII. Good cast includes Jason Robards, Joseph Cotten, Martin Balsam, James Whitmore and Tatsuya Mihashi. ★★★ $14.99

Torch Song

(1953, 91 min, US, Charles Walters) Music-filled melodrama about a domineering star (Joan Crawford) who finds love and learns humility in the arms of a blind pianist (Michael Wilding). With Gig Young and Marjorie Rambeau (in her Oscar-nominated performance as Crawford's mother). ★★★ $19.99

Torch Song Trilogy

(1988, 117 min, US, Paul Bogart) Harvey Fierstein's breakthrough Tony Award-winning play (which ran almost four hours on the stage) about the life and loves of the most lovable drag queen in Brooklyn reaches the screen at half the running time but with most of the play's warm humor and acute insights intact. Fierstein, in a partly autobiographical role, is both touching and hilarious as Arnold

Beckoff, whose life is presented in three non-episodic acts which examine his relationships with his bisexual boyfriend (Brian Kerwin), gay lover (Matthew Broderick), and mother (Anne Bancroft). ★★★ $19.99

Torment

(1944, 105 min, Sweden, Ingmar Bergman) Bergman's first screenplay explores the themes recurrent throughout his film career: sexual conflict, moral dilemma and the vulnerable nature of love. This gritty drama follows the love triangle between a young college student, a sadistic teacher and the girl with whom both are involved. A very young Mai Zetterling stars as the girl. (Swedish with English subtitles) ★★★ $29.99

Torn Apart

(1989, 96 min, Israel, Jack Fisher) The Romeo and Juliet story is given a new, Israeli slant in this well-intentioned story of a Jew who falls in love with an Arab. A young man, after spending six years in the United States, returns to Israel to enlist in the army and is soon reunited with his childhood friend, a lovely Arab woman. Their relationship sparks the reactions one would expect from their two families. A warm, humanist drama with convincing, heartfelt performances from the young leads. (Hebrew with English subtitles) ★★★ $19.99

Torn Curtain

(1966, 128 min, US, Alfred Hitchcock) Renowned for a brutally protracted murder sequence, this tale of Cold War espionage features Paul Newman as an atomic scientist charading as a defector in order to gain access to information on a valuable formula. Hitchcock's efficient thriller also stars Julie Andrews. ★★★ $14.99

Torrents of Spring

(1990, 102 min, France/Italy/GB, Jerzy Skolimowski) Nastassja Kinski rivals Rutger Hauer in starring in the greatest number of really bad foreign films but whose charisma and sheer force of personality gives her fans the strength to wade through the seemingly interminable cinematic muck. Skolimowski (The Lighthorsemen, Moonlighting, The Shout) directs this tepid costume drama of burning passions adapted from Ivan Turgenev's novel. Kinski stars as a wealthy married temptress who playfully teases a young aristocrat (Timothy Hutton) torn between his love for an innocent young woman and his sexual attraction to the destructive Kinski. Beautifully shot, the film goes nowhere and the only memorable moments occur when listening to Hutton's atrocious accent and stilted dialogue. ★ $9.99

The Torture Chamber of Baron Blood

(1972, 90 min, Italy, Mario Bava) Intriguing set design and unusual lighting effects highlight this story of a young man who inadvertently brings back to life the vengeful corpse of his bloodthirsty, sadistic ancestor. Joseph Cotten and Elke Sommer star. (aka: Baron Blood) ★★

The Torture Chamber of Dr. Sadism

(1967, 90 min, West Germany, Harald Reinl) This surprisingly effective bit of Grand Guignol finds Christopher Lee dismembered for killing

12 virgins. But 40 years later, when his ever-faithful batman puts him back together, Chris is out to party with virgin #13. ★★ $19.99

Tosca

(1985, 127 min, Italy, Franco Zeffirelli) Zeffirelli staged this fiery, passionate production of Puccini's classic for the Metropolitan Opera. Hildegard Behrens and Placido Domingo are commanding under the direction of conductor Giuseppe Sinopoli. (English subtitles) ★★★½ $22.99

Tosca's Kiss

(1985, 87 min, Switzerland, Daniel Schmid) The setting for this affectionate and moving documentary is Casa Verdi, a home for retired opera singers established by Guiseppi Verdi at the turn of the century. The focus is on the aging but still vibrant habitués who shamelessly preen, argue and perform for the viewer. (Italian with English subtitles) ★★★ $39.99

Total Eclipse

(1995, 111 min, GB/France, Agnieszka Holland) Pre-release publicity could not have been more promising: Europa, Europa's Holland was set to direct hot-shot American Leonardo DiCaprio, as 19th-century poet Arthur Rimbaud, and respected British actor David Thewlis, as fellow poet Verlaine, in a sexually explicit drama of their tempestuous gay relationship. The result is a laughably bad melodrama that, while delivering on the promise of an unblinking depiction of gay love, fails in just about every other aspect. Total Eclipse proves that gay-themed films can be just as bad as straight romantic dramas. The story (by Christopher Hampton) is set in France where 16-year-old Rimbaud, teen rebel and prodigiously self-assured unpublished poet, arrives in Paris to cooly make his mark on the world. His first order of business is to snag himself a sugar daddy – enter Verlaine, a 30ish sniveling, weak-willed, utterly disagreeable man who harbors the triple demons of greed, pretension and ambition. Sexual energy and narcissistic attraction fuel their ultimately tragic love-hate relationship. DiCaprio's portrayal is simply one of a sugar-cereal propelled, California teenager playing a game where only he knows the rules. ★ $19.99

Total Recall

(1990, 109 min, US, Paul Verhoeven) The elements of this production are a clear recipe for success: Dutch helmer Paul Verhoeven directing Arnold Schwarzenegger in a space sci-fi adventure based on a story by Phillip K. Dick (whose "Do Androids Dream of Electric Sheep?" inspired Blade Runner). The film's only flaw might be a few unpolished scenes and its more-than-too-much gratuitous violence. Beyond that, Verhoeven and Schwarzenegger romp through this high-speed, action-packed fugitive-on-the-run tale with a tongue-in-cheek and very playful glee. (Available letterboxed and pan & scan) ★★★ $14.99

Toto the Hero

(1991, 90 min, Belgium, Jaco Van Dormael) Stylistically inventive and delightfully off-kilter, this bittersweet tale of the joys and traumas of childhood makes for a captivating and entertaining film. Thomas is a boy absorbed in a fantasy world of secret agents and flights of adventure all in an attempt to reject his life as an ordinary boy from middle-class parents. He is also convinced that he was switched at birth with Alfred, his rich neighbor's son. That idea, carried through to old age, becomes an obsession and obstacle to growth as Alfred becomes his lifelong nemesis — a symbol of everything he is not. The film intercuts scenes from the boy's childhood with his life as a young man as well as the present, where Thomas, now an old man in a retirement home, decides to finally come to grips with his failures and lost dreams. A hard-edged comedy which captures the seemingly insignificant moments of childhood and their lasting, debilitating effect. Winner of the French César for Best Foreign Film in 1992. (French with English subtitles) ★★★★ $94.99

Touch

(1997, 97 min, US, Paul Schrader) This unfocused adaptation of Elmore Leonard's novel is never sarcastic enough to be full-fledged satire, or serious enough to make much of an impact. While this offbeat film boasts a good ensemble, Schrader, who wrote and directed, does not always know what to do with the story's strange characters. *Touch* seems to delight in poking fun at easy targets such as an airhead talk show hostess (Gina Gershon), or an extremist religious group leader (Tom Arnold). However, the film has considerably more trouble sustaining interest in its main character, Juvenal (stud of the moment Skeet Ulrich), a faith healer who is worshipped by just about everyone. Juvenal's relationships with his self-appointed "agent" (Christopher Walken in another eccentric role) and his new girlfriend (Bridget Fonda) lack urgency, and ultimately credibility. *Touch* also suffers from choppy pacing and bad editing — as many scenes ring true as fall flat. Perhaps it is damning with faint praise, but Arnold actually gives the film's best performance. ★★ $99.99

The Touch

(1971, 112 min, Sweden, Ingmar Bergman) Bergman's first English-language film certainly does not rank as one of the master's greatest works, but this sensitive and subtle story of a love triangle does have its moments. Bibi Andersson plays a "happily married" woman who, although settled and secure with doctor/husband Max von Sydow, is lured into an affair with volatile but magnetic archaeologist Elliott Gould. The human drama of the three, as they attempt to understand their actions and each other, makes this an interesting work. ★★½

A Touch of Class

(1972, 105 min, GB, Melvin Frank) Glenda Jackson won her second Oscar as the vivacious Alessio, a Londoner in the "rag trade" who falls in love with an American businessman (George Segal) who has a wife on the side. The dynamic chemistry between the two leads propels this witty, romantic and touching account of a brief love affair. ★★★½

Touch of Evil

(1958, 108 min, US, Orson Welles) Cinema's legendary bad boy, Orson Welles, directed and stars in this brooding, stylistic tour de force as a police inspector embroiled in a case on the Mexican border. A masterful exposé on moral decay, smothered in Gothic expressionism and tawdry urban landscapes. An eclectic cast includes Charlton Heston, Janet Leigh, Zsa Zsa Gabor and, in a stunning cameo performance, Marlene Dietrich. ★★★★ $14.99

Touch of Her Flesh

(1967, 78 min, US, Michael and Roberta Findlay) After catching his wife in the act of "doing the wild thang" with another guy, a hard-working businessman freaks out, ends up partially paralyzed and loses an eye after being hit by a car. Plotting his revenge on all women, he plunges full force into the sleazy world of go-go/nudie bars, complete with well-endowed femmes who parade around in some truly amazing industrial strength underwear. ★ $19.99

Tough Guys

(1986, 104 min, US, Jeff Kanew) Burt Lancaster and Kirk Douglas teamed a fifth time for this disappointing comedy which is not worthy of its two stars. The two screen legends play ex-cons, released after 30 years in prison, who find difficulty in adjusting to the 1980s lifestyle. Dana Carvey costars in a pre-"Saturday Night Live" role. ★★ $9.99

Tough Guys Don't Dance

(1987, 110 min, US, Norman Mailer) Confusing murder mystery written and directed by Mailer (from his own novel) about a writer (Ryan O'Neal) accused of murder, forced to clear his name. A real curiosity, with director Mailer echoing the atmosphere of the film noir gems of long ago, but hampered by some cheesy dialogue and bizarre plot contrivances. ★★ $14.99

Toute Une Nuit

(1982, 90 min, Belgium/France, Chantal Akerman) Abandoning standard narrative plot, Akerman's own minimalist, avant-garde story of the follies of sex and love is set on one torrid summer night in Brussels. Told in a series of amorous fragments, the film follows the various mating rites of several couples as they meet, fall in love, eat, drink and then break up. An austere yet strangely riveting experimental melodrama that is certainly not for all audiences. (French with English subtitles) ★★★ $29.99

Tower of London

(1939, 93 min, US, Rowland V. Lee) Basil Rathbone kills his way to the top as Richard III in this above-average historical thriller. Evil, conniving, back-stabbing and ruthless are some of the better adjectives one might use to describe Richard, and Rathbone has a wonderful time embodying that evil. Gleefully overacting, he leads a solid cast which also includes a young Vincent Price as a weakling Duke and Boris Karloff as Richard's medieval "campaign organizer," the clubfooted executioner Mord. Playing out his crimes on a set of dolls made to represent his contemporaries in the royal court, Rathbone slowly gets bolder and bolder until his schemes are naturally undone in the end. The real treat of this film, however, is Karloff as Mord. He manages to bring a bit of understanding and humanity to a vicious murderer, much as he did to Frankenstein's monster. A worthwhile entry in Universal's canon of "horror." Roger Corman remade it in 1962 with Price taking the role of Richard this time. ★★★ $14.99

The Towering Inferno

(1974, 165 min, US, John Guillermin) A mammoth production can't hide the loose ends to this half-baked disaster epic. An all-star cast is featured to tell the story of a skyscraper's gala opening, and the crisis which follows when the building catches fire. Paul Newman, Steve McQueen, Faye Dunaway, William Holden, Fred Astaire, Richard Chamberlain, Robert Vaughn and Jennifer Jones are some of the smoked hams who get roasted. The technical aspects of the film are very good, but it's especially mean-spirited. (Letterboxed version sells for $24.99) ★★½ $19.99

Towers Open Fire

(1962-72, 35 min, US, Antony Balch) William Burroughs is featured in two shorts in this compilation of four art films from independent filmmaker Antony Balch. *Towers Open Fire* and *The Cut-Ups* attempt to make a cinematic equivalent to Burroughs' famous "cut and paste" style of writing — in which he would write sections of a book, physically cut the story into several pages and then randomly repaste them together. As Burroughs narrates, we watch a visual collage of his writing containing many of the author's key themes. Although trying at times (watching five minutes of voice-over intoning repeatedly "yes-no" is a good test), the films are of great interest to both experimental film lovers and Burroughs fans. ★★½ $29.99

A Town Like Alice

(1980, 301 min, Australia, David Stevens) This mammoth drama of love and separation is taken from the best-selling novel by Neville Shute. Starring Bryan Brown and Helen Morse, the story is set against the brutal chaos of WWII. While in a Japanese POW camp in steamy Malaysia, an ever-cheerful Australian and an equally resilient English woman meet and fall in love. They are soon separated, but in the ensuing years meet again in the rugged outback of Australia. ★★★ $29.99

The Toxic Avenger

(1985, 100 min, US, Michael Herz & Samuel Weil) Idiotic cult comedy, though not without a few laughs, about a goofy nerd who is pushed into toxic waste and comes out a super-human crime-fighter from New Jersey. Sick humor and effects abound. ★½ $14.99

The Toxic Avenger, Part 2

(1989, 96 min, US, Michael Herz & Lloyd Kaufman) More of the gross-outs and sick humor which made *The Toxic Avenger* a sleeper hit. This time, The Toxic Avenger travels to Japan to save Tromaville. ★ $14.99

Toy Soldiers

(1991, 112 min, US, Daniel Petrie) A group of young prep school students, led by rebellious Sean Astin, band together to take back their school from gun-toting terrorists who are holding the rich kids for ransom. This is a sur-

T

557

prisingly effective suspenser, with well-done action scenes and a young cast presenting believable and likable characters. With Wil Wheaton and Keith Coogan as Astin's cohorts, and Louis Gossett, Jr. as the school's headmaster. ★★★ $9.99

Toy Story

(1995, 81 min, US, John Lasseter) With the first all-computer-animated feature film, the folks at Disney have done it again. More than just a technical marvel, *Toy Story* is an exhilarating combination of sight, sound and story which is as funny and entertaining as it is groundbreaking. Confirming every child's suspicions, *Toy Story* is set in a magical world where toys come to life – but only when humans aren't around. Six-year-old Andy's favorite toy is Woody, a pull-string talking cowboy who is leader of his fellow toy companions. That is until a new toy arrives, a state-of-the-art astronaut named Buzz Lightyear, to rival Woody for Andy's affections. It's then a game of one-upmanship as the two toys engage in a series of captivating misadventures. Featuring a marvelous screenplay with which most live-action films can't compare, part of *Toy Story's* success lies with the wonderful vocals of Tom Hanks and Tim Allen as Woody and Buzz, respectively. This is one odd couple that delivers. And this is one family film that delivers...to infinity and beyond. ★★★★ $26.99

Toys

(1992, 121 min, US, Barry Levinson) Writer-director Levinson must have dropped acid one day and walked through F.A.O. Schwartz to come up with this colorful but mind-bogglingly leaden satire. Robin Williams plays the son of a toy magnate (Donald O'Connor) who loses his inheritance of the company when his father passes away. Instead, the enterprise is given to his uncle, a nasty general (Michael Gambon) who plans to produce war toys. Eventually, militaristic Gambon and innocent Williams have a showdown, and the destructive toys go ballistic. Set in a netherworld populated by amusement park vehicles and magical machinery, the set design seems to have been inspired by the graphics of a Super Nintendo game. Williams and the ensemble (including Joan Cusack and LL Cool J) seem torpedoed by the stilted script. *Toys* should have stayed in the attic. ★½ $9.99

Toys in the Attic

(1963, 91 min, US, George Roy Hill) A good cast, including Geraldine Page, Wendy Hiller, Dean Martin and Gene Tierney, can't enliven this tedious Gothic drama based on Lillian Hellman's stage play. Martin plays the ne'er-do-well brother of spinsters Page and Hiller. With his young wife (Yvette Mimieux), he returns to his New Orleans home suspiciously boasting of new wealth. Their presence there paves the way to betrayal, recriminations, and long-hidden secrets exposed. Page and Hiller are effective, though even they can't overcome the film's contrivances. ★½ $19.99

Traces of Red

(1992, 105 min, US, Andy Wolk) Jim Belushi toplines this incredibly convoluted whodunit about a Palm Beach cop who becomes both

hunter and hunted when his bedmates start turning up dead (murder or mercy – you decide). While the film offers credible performances and a decent mystery with a good deal of twists, there are ultimately no traces of logic to be found, and only traces of dread at the too-tricky-for-its-own-good surprise ending. Also with William Russ, Tony Goldwyn as Belushi's true-blue partner, and Lorraine Bracco as a "rich bitch" femme fatale with the soul (and delivery) of a Hell's Kitchen yenta. ★½ $14.99

Track 29

(1988, 86 min, GB, Nicolas Roeg) Roeg's playfully beguiling mystery stars Theresa Russell as a bored young woman trapped in a loveless and childless marriage with model train and S/M enthusiast Christopher Lloyd. The woman's life is changed when she is (possibly) visited by a young British stranger (Gary Oldman) who claims that he is her abandoned-at-birth son. Is he a con man or prodigal son, a real person or only the figment of her rapidly deteriorating mind? Any fan of Roeg will know that the answer does not come simply in this visually exciting drama. Don't miss Sandra Bernhard's small role as the kinky dominatrix, Nurse Stein. ★★★ $14.99

Tracks

(1974, 90 min, US, Henry Jaglom) A Vietnam vet (Dennis Hopper) meets a wide array of characters while on a train. However, he is soon overtaken with war-induced paranoia. With a more traditional narrative than his other films, director Jaglom weaves a compelling and insightful tale – years before the subject matter became en vogue. Also starring Taryn Power and Dean Stockwell. ★★★ $39.99

Trading Hearts

(1987, 88 min, US, Neil Leifer) Ineffective romantic romp about an over-the-hill baseball pitcher (Raul Julia) and a minor league singer (Beverly D'Angelo) in 1957 Florida, complicated by a mischievous 11-year-old who thinks they should all live together. ★★ $14.99

Trading Places

(1983, 106 min, US, John Landis) Dan Aykroyd and Eddie Murphy are hilarious as a millionaire and street hustler, respectively, who trade places in this silly but vastly amusing comedy. The inspired casting is what raises this film above the usual "Saturday Night Live" alumnae mode of filmmaking. Ralph Bellamy and Don Ameche are great as a pair of incredibly sleazy capitalist brothers. Denholm Elliott walks away with the film as an incredulous butler. And Jamie Lee Curtis is the hooker with a heart of gold. ★★★½ $14.99

Traffic

(1971, 89 min, France, Jacques Tati) Tati stars as Monsieur Hulot, that charming and naive fool, in this hilariously chaotic comedy. Armed with youthful enthusiasm, M. Hulot attempts to transport a car from France to Holland for an auto show, and the results are side-splitting. A satire on modern living, *Traffic* takes great pleasure in dissecting the absurdity of a situation where neurosis reigns behind the wheel. There is very little dialogue, and even though there

are no subtitles, those who do not understand word one of French will be able to follow with ease this visually funny film. ★★★★ $29.99

Traffic in Souls

(1913, 88 min, US, George Loane Tucker) A docudrama decades before the coining of that dreadful term, *Traffic in Souls* dramatizes some of the more sensational aspects of the 1910 Rockefeller White Slavery Report for New York City. As the gateway for America, N.Y.C. found itself the hub of a syndicate comprised of crooked judges, cops and criminals who kidnapped immigrating women into dens of prostitution. While some of the dramaturgy may be creaky, and the interior sets decidely *trompe l'oeil*, the location shooting around the city of dirt streets and open windows give *Traffic in Souls* the feeling of an bygone era tinged with a contemporary atmosphere. So effective was the film in its day that it was shown to new female arrivals to Ellis Island as a cautionary tale – one certain to engender second thoughts to any emigré. ★★★½ $29.99

The Tragedy of a Ridiculous Man

(1981, 116 min, Italy, Bernardo Bertolucci) This psychological parable on terrorism and the clash between capitalism and leftist politics in Italy is at best a muddled exercise that seems to purposefully confuse and distance its audience. Ugo Tognazzi is a self-made man and materialistic owner of a sprawling Parma cheese factory who witnesses his left-leaning son being forcibly thrown into a car and kidnapped. But was this a real abduction or was his son in collusion with his kidnappers? Not knowing for sure, he reluctantly raises the ransom, but is undecided whether he should help his son or use the money to prop up his failing business. An admirable but unsatisfying experience. (Italian with English subtitles) ★★ $59.99

The Tragedy of Carmen

(1983, 82 min, GB, Peter Brook) Brook gives a radical new look to Bizet's classic opera. Opting to emphasize the story over the spectacle, Brook has pared down the cast to seven, reduced the size of the orchestra and gone for a completely naturalistic look as filmed by cinematographer Sven Nykvist. For fans of Brook, this is a must; but the video's one flaw is that it lacks subtitling for the libretto. ★★★

The Trail of the Pink Panther

(1982, 97 min, GB, Blake Edwards) Shortly after Peter Sellers' death, Edwards slapped together this sorry excuse for a film out of old bits and pieces of yet unseen footage from earlier *Panther* films. These out-takes are strung together with a flimsy story line about a reporter who interviews anyone he can find who knew Clouseau. Not worth the film it's printed on. ★ $14.99

The Train

(1965, 133 min, US, John Frankenheimer) A solid, rousing thriller from director Frankenheimer. Set in 1944 Occupied France, the story follows the exploits of the French Resistance and trainman Burt Lancaster who try to prevent the Nazis from shipping stolen art treasures to Germany via Burt's train. Paul

Scofield is the Nazi general assigned the task of guarding the confiscated art works. Like another actioner set almost entirely aboard a train, *The Taking of Pelham One Two Three*, from a simple plot line comes such high-powered suspense. ★★★½ $19.99

Trainspotting

(1996, 94 min, Scotland, Danny Boyle) A swaggering, highly stylized and pulsating cinematic ride, *Trainspotting* is an in-your-face adaptation of Irvine Welch's novel and play about life among a merry band of heroin addicts living it up in the lower depths of Edinburgh. Refreshingly unrepentent in tone, director Boyle's follow-up to his grisly arthouse hit *Shallow Grave* puts a fun-filled spin on the world of skag as seen through the eyes of its narrator, Renton (Ewan McGregor). He's a wiry and likable antihero, whose loquacious manner recalls another congenial film scaliwag, Alex from *A Clockwork Orange*. He takes up residence in a squalid squat with a group of fellow travellers that comprise the film's core cast of wackos. There's Spud (Ewen Bremmer), a spindly and over-the-top geek; Sick Boy (Jonny Lee Miller), a handsomish rocker type; and Begbie (Robert Carlyle), a psychopathic non-junkie whose fits of rage make the users look sane. As much as it explores the drug subculture, *Trainspotting* is also a merciless social critique that ultimately eyes the pursuit of happiness through substance as the moral equal to that of material acquisition. Sheer excitement, it's punctuated nicely by a hip, drug-inspired rock soundtrack. ★★★★ $102.99

Trancers

(1985, 76 min, US, Charles Band) Intriguing sci-fi adventure (with more than a nod to *The Terminator*) about a trooper from the year 2247 who is sent back to present-day Los Angeles to stop a mystic from murdering a future leader. (aka: *Future Cop*) ★★½ $14.99

Transmutations

(1986, 103 min, GB, George Pavlou) A sinister biochemist (Denholm Elliott) creates a subhuman species which dwells in the city's underground. Desperate for an antidote, the creatures seek out the only woman who can save them (Miranda Richardson). Penned but later disowned by horror maven Clive Barker. (aka: *Underground*) ★★ $79.99

Trapeze

(1956, 106 min, US, Carol Reed) Truly remarkable trapeze footage, and three very appealing lead performances make for a slick romantic drama set against the hurly-burly backdrop of a Parisian circus. Burt Lancaster, in splendid physical condition and doing most of his own stunts, stars as a retired trapeze artist – the only man alive who can perform a triple somersault. He is sought after by Tony Curtis, son of a high-wire aerialist, who wants Lancaster to teach him that near-impossible trick. All is well between them until beautiful and conniving Gina Lollabrigida enters the scene, tricking her way into their act and becoming involved in a romantic triangle with both men. *The Greatest Show on Earth* was never this good. ★★★ $19.99

The cast of *Trainspotting*

Trapped in Paradise

(1994, 111 min, US, George Gallo) That Jon Lovitz and Dana Carvey have been doomed in their search for adequate film material after their "Saturday Night Live" heyday is no revelation, but now they've brought Nicolas Cage along for the ride. The three stars appear as bickering brothers who hold up a bank on Christmas Eve in a Rockwell-like small town. Their problems begin when they can't get out of town and the townsfolk who they've just robbed kill them with kindness. Cage plays against type as the moral backbone of the trio, Lovitz is (surprise!) the acerbic one, and Carvey plays the slow-witted sibling with a penchant for kleptomania. The screenplay offers them numerous comic situations but rarely develops any of them, though the entire cast seems eager to please. ★★ $96.89

Trash

(1970, 110 min, US, Paul Morrissey) Holly Woodlawn is truly memorable as the trash-collecting lover of impotent drug fiend Joe Dallesandro in this wonderfully realistic slice-of-life film about New York's druggies and counterculture denizens. In this, her screen debut, Holly's character preserves her dignity and moral righteousness despite poverty, squalor and a forced-to-masturbate-with-a-beer-bottle-because-my-boyfriend-can't-get-it-up life. This is best exemplified in the exchange between her and a "with it" social worker who promises her welfare in exchange for a pair of silver platform shoes Holly found in the trash. She refuses, despite an obvious need for assistance. It is her character, and not the cute but almost catatonic Joe, which works against the film's not-so-subtle anti-drug message; an attitude which keeps with the director's moralistic and reactionary philosophy. ★★★

Trauma

(1993, 106 min, Italy, Dario Argento) A mysterious killer prowls the streets of Minneapolis. His trademark: he decapitates his victims with the Noose-O-Matic. Meanwhile, an illustrator, David (Christopher Rydell), meets Aura (Asia Argento), a disturbed youth undergoing treatment for anorexia. When her parents, including her psychic mother (Piper Laurie), fall victim to the "Headhunter Killer," Aura enlists David's help in finding their murderer. More heads roll before the two lovers discover the true identity of the assassin and the unholy secret buried within Aura's strange past. As with all his works, Argento's film operates on a pure emotional level, and is alternately gaudy, energetic, deliberately unrealistic and forceful in its style. ★★½ $14.99

Travelling North

(1987, 98 min, Australia, Carl Schultz) Charming story of a retired civil engineer (Leo McKern) who, suspecting that his days are numbered, takes off with his lady-love (Julia Blake) for a life of peaceful contentment at a cottage by the lake. McKern is at his blustery best as the Mozart-loving foreman with a talent for hurting those who love him; the entire cast contributes to making this a minor gem. ★★★

Travels with My Aunt

(1972, 109 min, GB, George Cukor) Maggie Smith received an Academy Award nomination for her delightfully eccentric performance as Aunt Augusta in this giddy and incandescent screen version of Graham Greene's novel. After the death of her estranged sister, the high-living Augusta swoops in and whisks her very unwilling nephew Henry (Alec McCowen), an affably stodgy banker, from his ordered existence and proceeds to introduce him to high adventure on the road. They set upon a worldwide quest to raise money for one of her former lovers who has been kidnapped, and as misadventures compile, Henry begins to shed his sullen exterior while learning much about his spirited, unconventional aunt. Smith's performance is pure enchantment, shading a likable and larger-than-life portrayal with whimsy, wit and wonder. McCowen is especially good as the doormat Henry who eventually learns to spread his wings. In one of his earliest roles, Lou Gossett is disarming as Smith's current lover. All this under the watchful and precise eye of director Cukor. (Letterboxed version) ★★★½ $19.99

La Traviata
(1982, 110 min, Italy, Franco Zeffirelli) Zeffirelli's lavish, powerful rendition of Verdi's opera stars Placido Domingo and Teresa Stratas in emotionally charged performances as the doomed lovers. Not just for opera fans! (Italian with English subtitles) ★★★½ $29.99

Treasure Island
(1934, 105 min, US, Victor Fleming) Flavorful adaptation of Robert Louis Stevenson's classic adventure yarn about pirates, hidden treasure, and the small boy involved with both. Jackie Cooper is the youngster who lives every small child's fantasy, and Wallace Beery is an appropriately flamboyant Long John Silver. ★★★ $19.99

The Treasure of the Sierra Madre
(1948, 124 min, US, John Huston) A taut parable on human greed and corruptibility based on the novel by the mysterious B. Traven. Humphrey Bogart gives a memorable performance as the edgy Fred C. Dobbs, whose moral bent is fractured by his discovery of gold. Tim Holt and Walter Huston (Academy Award for Best Supporting Actor) are his fellow prospectors, combating bandits, betrayal and the ill effects of the yellow dust. Huston won Best Director and Best Screenplay Oscars. ★★★★ $19.99

A Tree Grows in Brooklyn
(1945, 128 min, US, Elia Kazan) An outstanding film version of Betty Smith's novel about the hardships facing an Irish family living in a turn-of-the-century Brooklyn tenement. Dorothy McGuire is splendid as the mother, with an Oscar-winning performance by James Dunn as her alcoholic husband. Peggy Ann Garner won a special juvenile Oscar for her sensitive portrayal of a young girl looking to escape her environment, and Joan Blondell gives one of her best performances as Garner's aunt. ★★★★ $14.99

The Tree of Wooden Clogs
(1978, 186 min, Italy, Ermanno Olmi) In this deceptively simple epic, Olmi brilliantly reconstructs the peasant life in the Lombardy region of Italy at the turn-of-the-century. The director, using a non-professional cast and filming in almost documentary-like fashion, quietly explores the lives of four peasant families told through the eyes of a young boy. Long and leisurely paced, with the story told in a mosaic of small incidents, the film is not for every-

body; but for those with patience and an appreciative mind, this film will prove to be an absorbing work of art. (Italian with English subtitles) ★★★ $19.99

Trees Lounge
(1996, 94 min, US, Steve Buscemi) An impressive directorial debut for actor Buscemi, who has crafted a succulent little slice-of-life offering which is both unflinchingly perceptive and sweetly compassionate. Buscemi stars as Tommy, that guy from the neighborhood whose life seems perpetually on pause, stumbling through each day with his eyes half-closed and zero recognition of the effects of his actions. The story chronicles the events of one summer in his life as he careens amid a Runyonesque cast of characters, each sharply if briefly brought into focus by an on-target ensemble. Buscemi also wrote the wry and poignant screenplay, which spritely delineates Tommy's less-than-beneficial role on those around him. The final scene is a fitting coda, succinct in its forewarning of Tommy's future. Heavy material is delivered with a light hand, and an unerring recognition of the minute details that define and propel a person's life. ★★★½ $99.99

Tremors
(1990, 96 min, US, Ron Underwood) Taking off where the 1950s "monster-on-the-rampage" films and the Roger Corman exploitation flicks left off, this fun and funny horror film has its tongue firmly planted in its cinematic cheek. Set in a lonely, dust-covered Western town, a small group of people are invaded by mysterious underground creatures who have more than a passing resemblance to the man-eating worms from *Dune*. Kevin Bacon and Fred Ward are hilarious as two out-of-their-element handymen who must confront the shy platyhelminths as they murderously slither through the town. ★★★ $14.99

Tremors 2: Aftershocks
(1995, 100 min, US, S.S. Wilson) Fred Ward and Michael Gross return from the monstrously entertaining original film in this direct-to-video sequel made by the same production team that authored the first movie. Earl (Ward) is hired by a Mexican oil company to go "Graboid-hunting." The giant, man-eating worms have resurfaced south of the border and the oil company and Mexican army cannot stop the beasts, who have turned into a new variety of monster. While *Tremors 2* lacks the vulgar humor which made the first film feel so appealing, it retains its predecessor's redneck charm and gleeful creature-killing violence and gore. The effects are especially noteworthy, and include some very well-done computer effects of the new, above-ground monsters. Constant attention is paid to the

events of the first film, too, with references and character quirks and mannerisms being carried over. Not merely a rehash, this is a moderately original film, both funny and ★★★ $19.99

Trespass
(1992, 95 min, US, Walter Hill) Originally titled *The Looters*, this cautionary tale had its theatrical release delayed when studio executives deemed it too incendiary for an audience still recovering from the shock of the L.A. riots. Nonetheless, this urbanized retelling of the classic *Treasure of the Sierra Madre* marks a return to form for director Hill. Bill Paxton and William Sadler take the lead in this textbook "wrong place, wrong time" scenario about two "good ol' boy" firemen who go searching for buried treasure in an abandoned building just in time to witness a gangland hit by druglords Ice T and Ice Cube. Hill strikes just the right balance between well-drawn characterizations and gunplay galore to make this a welcome addition to the action genre. ★★★ $12.99

The Trial
(1963, 100 min, France/Italy/West Germany, Orson Welles) Franz Kafka's nightmarish novel of a man arrested for a crime that is never explained to him is brilliantly brought to the screen by Welles. Anthony Perkins is Joseph K, a sensitive individual pursued by a repressive bureaucracy, obsessed by an undefined guilt and bewildered by the burden of living. Welles maintained complete artistic control of the production and the result is a difficult but unforgettable expressionistic mood piece. (Filmed in English) ★★★½

The Trial
(1993, 120 min, GB, David Jones) Kyle MacLachlan stars as the archetypal victim hero, Joseph K., in this austere but oddly engrossing adaptation of Franz Kafka's novel. Waking up on the morning of his birthday, K. finds himself under arrest for no stated reason and is slowly sucked into a byzantine and murky beaurocracy. MacLachlan gives a sturdy interpretation of K., though he ill-advisedly attempts an English accent. Harold Pinter provides the screenplay, which while replete with his snappy dialogue, curiously fails to invoke any of Kafka's subversive humor. The sup-

Steve Buscemi (front) and Bronson Dudley in *Trees Lounge*

The Treasure of the Sierra Madre

porting cast is A1 with Jason Robards as K.'s phlegmatic lawyer; Michael Kitchen as the mousy Mr. Block; and Anthony Hopkins as the prison chaplin who lectures K. on the realities of "the law." Filmed on location in Prague, the production is greatly enhanced by marvelous cinematography and art design. ★★★ $19.99

Trial and Error

(1962, 78 min, GB, James Hill) Peter Sellers and Richard Attenborough play barrister and client — and several other characters — in this droll British comedy which offers only a few rewarding moments. When a rather taciturn bird seed salesman (Attenborough) murders his ebullient wife (Beryl Reid) so he can spend more quality time with his beloved budgies, his incompetent, court-appointed lawyer (Sellers) sees one last chance to finally step from the shadows. What he sees in the harsh glare of the limelight leaves him unsettled and dissolute, and finally alone. Too reverentially adapted from a minor stage play, *Trial and Error* remains as unassuming as its two protagonists. (GB title: *The Dock Brief*) ★★ $19.99

Trial by Jury

(1994, 108 min, US, Heywood Gould) Joanne Whalley-Kilmer plays a jurist who faces every jury member's nightmare: being physically coerced into finding the defendant innocent. But what's more of a nightmare is the silly scenario created by the writers as a responsible citizen faces criminals and the criminal system head-on. Sitting on the jury of a high-profile mobster (Armand Assante), Whalley-Kilmer has her and her young son's life threatened by Assante's goons. As she grapples with the moral dilemma, nearly every man in sight falls in love with her (including Assante, henchman William Hurt and fellow jurors...except the gay one). Though bordering on trashy fun, this could have been enjoyable had not Whalley-Kilmer given such a one-dimensional performance. ★★ $14.99

Les Tricheurs (The Cheats)

(1983, 95 min, France, Barbet Schroeder) Jacques Dutronc stars in this slick drama about elegantly dressed gambling addicts on the island of Madera and their attempts at pulling off an elaborate swindle. Bulle Ogier is the "lucky" stranger who becomes an unwitting accomplice in Dutronc's scheme at the roulette wheel. (French with English subtitles) ★★★ $59.99

Trick or Treat

(1986, 97 min, US, Charles Martin Smith) Imaginative horror satire about a metalhead who plays an album backwards to evoke the spirit of a dead rock star. A headbanger's delight, which unfortunately derails about halfway through. Marc Price (Skippy from TV's "Family Ties") stars, with appearances by Gene Simmons (KISS) and Ozzy Osbourne (as a TV evangelist!). Directing debut of the actor Smith. ★★½ $14.99

The Trigger Effect

(1996, 93 min, US, David Koepp) Having written the screenplays for such diverse films as *Jurassic Park* and *Apartment Zero*, writer Koepp makes a satisfying leap to director with this offbeat though uneven psychological thriller. With nods to *Miracle Mile* and "The Twilight Zone," the story focuses on man's baser instincts during time of crisis (here a power blackout) which ultimately pits neighbor against neighbor. Koepp begins the film beautifully, tracking the effect one person has on another, then that person on another and so on. The story then concentrates on the Los Angeles couple (Kyle MacLachlan and Elisabeth Shue) and their houseguest (Dermot Mulroney) as they begin to cope with an unexplained, city-wide blackout. Though Koepp's thesis of man reverting to his animal self is not new, he diffuses the obvious with inventive camerawork and a steady tension throughout the film. It's also unpredictable, which helps keep interest in a leisurely paced story centering on two disinterested characters. ★★½ $94.99

Trilogy of Terror

(1975, 78 min, US, Dan Curtis) Three eerie tales of the supernatural, with a smashing performance by Karen Black. "The Zuni Fetish Doll," the African head hunting doll from the climactic third episode, is a classic horror short. ★★★

The Trip to Bountiful

(1985, 106 min, US, Peter Masterson) Geraldine Page won a much-deserved Oscar for her lovely performance as an aging widow who literally runs away from her son's Houston apartment to return to the now-abandoned home of her youth. A fine, bittersweet comedy-drama impeccably performed by a first-rate cast. Screenplay by Horton Foote, based on his 1953 play. ★★★½ $14.99

Triple Echo

(1980, 85 min, GB, Michael Apted) Featuring understated acting and direction, this bizarre wartime drama stars Glenda Jackson as a woman living alone in a farmhouse. She meets a young soldier (Brian Deacon) who, swayed by his attraction for her, impulsively deserts his unit and hides out in Jackson's house. When investigators begin snooping around, Deacon dresses in women's clothing and masquerades as Jackson's sister. The ruse works too well when burly sergeant Oliver Reed takes a fancy to "her." ★★½

Tristina

(1970, 99 min, Spain/France/Italy, Luis Buñuel) Little of Buñuel's overt surrealist style is evident in this intriguing black comedy of corrupt morals, religious bigotry and sexual abuse. Set in provincial Toledo in the 1920s, Fernando Rey plays Don Lupe, a vain, lascivious old man with strong socialist and anti-clerical thoughts who, on the death of a friend, becomes the guardian of the young and innocent Catherine Deneuve. Lupe soon seduces/rapes his ward, but neither possesses her heart nor ignites her passions. The girl eventually flees to the arms of a handsome painter (Franco Nero), only to return a sick, emotionally cold woman intent on revenge. (Spanish with English subtitles) ★★½ $59.99

Triumph of the Spirit

(1989, 120 min, US, Robert M. Young) Based on a true story, this intense, unrelenting drama recaptures the brutal years of a Greek boxer who, as a prisoner at Auschwitz, was forced to fight "to the death" — either his or his opponent's — to the amusement of his Nazi captors. Willem Dafoe gives a powerful performance as the fighter who is sent to the death camp with his entire family — only to watch them die one by one. Filmed on location, the film is unflinchingly real in its depiction of daily existence, and there is a raw, gut-wrenching power to these scenes. As Dafoe's endearing father, Robert Loggia is outstanding; and Edward James Olmos is fine as a Gypsy kapo. ★★★ $19.99

Triumph of the Will

(1936, 120 min, Germany, Leni Riefenstahl) German director Riefenstahl's infamous propaganda documentary of Hitler's 1934 Nazi Party Congress held in Nuremberg, which helped thrust the dictator to power. Although its aim is to glorify the Nazis, it is undeniably a powerful piece of filmmaking. (German with English subtitles) ★★★½ $29.99

The Trojan Women

(1972, 105 min, Greece/US, Michael Cacoyannis) Katharine Hepburn, Irene Papas, Genevieve Bujold, Vanessa Redgrave and Patrick Magee star in this film version of the Euripides tragedy about the fall of Troy to Agamemnon's armies. Despite the somewhat listless production (Cacoyannis' work on the stage is far superior), the outstanding cast delivers a group of superlative performances, making this an emotionally charged treatise on the horrors of war. ★★½

A Troll in Central Park

(1994, 76 min, US, Don Bluth) Don Bluth continues to create a great animated alternative to Disney and this film is much more than just another walk through the park. The story follows the adventures of Stanley, a sweet-natured troll with a green thumb who can grow anything, anywhere, until he meets an evil queen who does her best to stop him. With the help of two children who befriend him, he and they learn that "if you believe in yourself, you can do anything" — always a timely lesson. Dom DeLuise does a wonderful job providing the voice of Stanley, and he is finding a whole second career in animated features. This one could easily become another classic. ★★★½ $19.99

Tron

(1982, 95 min, US, Steven Lisberger) Excellent computer graphics highlight this intriguing though lethargic sci-fi thriller about a computer programmer who is zapped into a computer and forced to live out a video arcade game. Jeff Bridges, David Warner and Bruce Boxleitner star. ★★ $14.99

Troop Beverly Hills

(1989, 105 min, US, Jeff Kanew) Shelley Long takes her snooty "Cheers" persona and transplants it to a Beverly Hills wife and mother who takes her daughter's girl scout troop on an outing. This formulaic comedy does manage a few laughs, and is a pleasant entertainment. ★★½ $14.99

Trouble Bound

(1992, 90 min, US, Jeffrey Reiner) Reiner, director of the spectacularly quirky *Blood and Concrete*, offers another serving of his specialized brand of slapstick black comedy in this entertaining road romance. Just out of jail, Harry Talbot wins a Lincoln Continental during a lucky streak at a card game and heads to Las Vegas to start a new life. His luck soon changes when Kit, a philosophical Mafia princess on the run, gets into Harry's car and demands a quick getaway from her pursuing family — then they find a body in the trunk. Rubber burns and bullets fly as Michael Madsen, as Harry, delivers an appealing variation of his stock charming rogue character and Patricia Arquette gives a spirited, if screechy, performance as Kit. The real star, however, is Reiner, who evenly blends offbeat action, comedy and romance with his own stylish way of portraying the sunsoaked asphalt wasteland of kitschy roadside Americana and the characters who call it home. ★★★ $14.99

Trouble in Mind

(1986, 111 min, US, Alan Rudolph) Rudolph weaves the themes of hope and despair, greed and jealousy, and lost and found love in this carefully spun plot starring Keith Carradine, Kris Kristofferson, Genevieve Bujold and a fine supporting role by Divine (playing a male character) as an underworld boss. Title sung by Marianne Faithfull. ★★★ $14.99

The Trouble with Angels

(1966, 112 min, US, Ida Lupino) A joyous romp set in a Catholic girls' school, this nostalgic comedy stars Hayley Mills and June Harding as two mischievous students constantly in trouble with the Sisters, and especially Mother Superior Rosalind Russell. Lots of fun. ★★★ $14.99

The Trouble with Harry

(1956, 99 min, US, Alfred Hitchcock) Shirley MacLaine and John Forsythe star in this mordant black comedy about a troublesome corpse that just won't stay buried. Hitchcock directed this offbeat gem with characteristically cheerful morbidity. ★★★ $14.99

True Believer

(1989, 103 min, US, Joseph Ruben) The spirit of the idealistic, free-spirited '60s meets the Reagan era in this suspenseful crime thriller. James Woods, in a compelling performance, stars as a Greenwich Village defense lawyer, Eddie Dodd, whose once shining star has all but faded. When he is hired to defend a convicted murderer who may have been unjustly imprisoned, Dodd, grasping at a final chance for personal and moral redemption, attacks the case with the lost vigor of his youth. Robert Downey, Jr. is fine as the novice attorney who apprentices with Dodd. ★★★ $9.99

True Colors

(1991, 111 min, US, Herbert Ross) Solid performances by John Cusack and James Spader elevate this fairly intriguing though familiar political drama about friendship and betrayal. Cusack and Spader play college chums who are working their way up the political ranks in Washington D.C.: Cusack is an opportunistic senatorial aide, and Spader is an idealistic Justice attorney. When the former runs for Congress, each must pay a high cost for his ambition/principles. Richard Widmark appears as the Senator for whom Cusack works, and Imogen Stubbs plays Widmark's daughter, once engaged to Spader and now married to her ex's best friend. ★★½ $14.99

True Confessions

(1981, 119 min, US, Ulu Grosbard) Robert De Niro and Robert Duvall give powerful performances in this gritty mystery set in 1930s Hollywood. The two acting greats are cast as brothers, one a priest and the other a police detective, who cross paths during a murder investigation. ★★★ $19.99

True Grit

(1969, 128 min, US, Henry Hathaway) John Wayne won an Oscar for his colorful portrayal of Rooster Cogburn, an aging, one-eyed marshall who helps a teenage girl (Kim Darby) track down her father's killer. A flavorful western adventure, the film is exciting, funny and atmospheric; and, in addition to offering a career role to its larger-than-life star, it's an affectionate tribute to a style of filmmaking director Hathaway and fellow compadres John Ford and Howard Hawks elevated to an art form. Wayne reprised his character in the 1975 western *Rooster Cogburn*, also starring Katharine Hepburn. ★★★ $14.99

True Identity

(1991, 93 min, US, Charles Lane) It's *Watermelon Man* for the '90s. Lane's follow-up to *Sidewalk Stories* is based on a "Saturday Night Live" sketch in which Eddie Murphy was done up in "whiteface." Black British comedian Lenny Henry plays an unfortunate passenger on what appears to be a doomed airline flight. Thinking he's about to die, the mobster sitting next to him begins confessing a lifetime of crime. When the plane fails to crash, however, poor Lenny suddenly finds himself on the wrong end of the mob. Turning to his best friend, a special effects artist, he goes "white" and the chase is on. It's an amusing premise which only delivers half

the time, but it does showcase Henry to good advantage. ★★½ $9.99

True Lies

(1994, 141 min, US, James Cameron) After the disastrous *Last Action Hero*, Arnold Schwarzenegger reteams with his *T2* director for this totally overblown action/comedy that pays tribute to the James Bond films of yore (with a dash of family values thrown in for good measure). This time out, Arnold plays a secret agent who must save the world from a wimpy villain (Art Malik) with a nuclear warhead, and keep his in-the-dark wife (Jamie Lee Curtis) from discovering his true identity. Though lacking the awe-inspiring special effects Cameron is noted for, or even a fleshed-out story line, the film features exceptional aerial stunt work and mega-hardware. Tom Arnold puts in a wonderfully comedic turn as Schwarzenegger's sidekick, and the preternaturally beautiful Tia Carrere is one of the heavies. (Letterboxed version sells for $19.99) ★★½ $14.99

True Love

(1989, 104 min, US, Nancy Savoca) The mating games and rituals of Italian-Americans in the Bronx are delightfully played out in this refreshing independent comedy-drama by newcomer and former Bronxonian Savoca. The story follows the final days leading up to the traditional wedding of Donna (Annabella Sciorra), a feisty and determined young lady, and Michael (Ron Eldard), a likable but immature deli worker. This low-budget charmer is filled with wonderfully drawn characters and presents an all-too-real glimpse into the preparations, problems and doubts leading up to the fateful day. ★★★½ $9.99

True Romance

(1993, 119 min, US, Tony Scott) What seemed like an unlikely pairing of mucho-macho auteur Quentin Tarantino and British stylist-turned-Hollywood hack Scott has paid off in spades with a hip, bullet-strewn thriller that hits you so hard it makes you laugh. This high-energy Generation X road movie stars Christian Slater as a trash culture-worshipping comic book salesman who meets happy hooker Patricia Arquette during a kung fu triple feature in Detroit. Taking inspiration from his imaginary "mentor" (the ghost of Elvis played by Val Kilmer), Slater decides to rescue his new love from her sexual servitude to a dreadlocked pimp (Gary Oldman, in a marvelously over-the-top performance). After blowing him away, Slater accidentally picks up a suitcase full of cocaine. After a quickie marriage and a visit to the tattoo parlor, Slater and Arquette hightail it out of town in a purple Cadillac. Drawing from Sam Peckinpah, Hong Kong action flicks, David Lynch (on a good day), Sergio Leone and Jim Thompson novels, *True Romance* is a gritty, high-octane mishmash that manages to solder its elements together with style and humor and features a genuinely affecting romance between Slater and Arquette. ★★★★ $14.99

True Stories

(1986, 111 min, US, David Byrne) In this slightly surreal travelogue, David Byrne takes

Juliet Stevenson is slightly shocked to see her dead lover Alan Rickman in *Truly, Madly, Deeply*

us on a few typical days in the typical lives of the typical Texan town of Virgil whose citizens are really anything but typical, or are they? The film stands as an oddly amusing vision of the mundanity of real life. ★★½ $19.99

True West

(1985, 110 min, US, Gary Sinise) The explosive performances of John Malkovich and Gary Sinise highlight this fine play-on-film adaptation of Sam Shepard's off-Broadway play about the volatile relationship between two brothers. It was this production which introduced Malkovich, as the menacing, slightly off-center thug, to a wide audience. Sinise, who plays Malkovich's educated, passive sibling, also directed the play's original run. ★★★½

La Truite

(1982, 105 min, France, Joseph Losey) Isabelle Huppert is coyly sinister in Losey's complex, funny and sensual melodrama about an innocent country girl who moves to Paris with her gay husband and vows to succeed in the business world with the aid of her feminine wiles. Jean-Pierre Cassel is a wealthy financier lured by Huppert's coquettish manner, much to the chagrin of his neglected wife (Jeanne Moreau). (French with English subtitles) ★★★ $59.99

Truly, Madly, Deeply

(1991, 107 min, GB, Anthony Minghella) Juliet Stevenson and Alan Rickman star in this highly entertaining romantic comedy with a supernatural twist. Stevenson excels as a young woman drowning in grief following the death of her lover (Alan Rickman). When he returns from the grave to soothe her sorrows, however, he turns out to be more than she can handle — especially when he and a bunch of ghostly friends take up residence in her flat, hanging about all night watching videos. Both actors give outstanding performances and first-time writer-director Minghella (who would direct *The English Patient* two pictures later) imbues the film with a bittersweet mix of hilarity and melancholy. ★★★★ $9.99

Truman Capote's A Christmas Story

(1966, 51 min, US, Frank Perry) Beginning with his cousin's observation, "Oh my, it's fruitcake weather!," this Emmy Award-winning short film, produced for ABC Stage, is a sweetly nostalgic recollection of Truman Capote's youth in the rural South during the Depression. Geraldine Page stars as his homespun "cousin" who takes care of the young Capote, with the story centering on their home life, the touching relationship between the two of them and her Christmas tradition of making over 30 fruitcakes as presents. A simple, quiet drama of love narrated by Mr. Capote himself. ★★★½ $19.99

Trust

(1990, 91 min, US, Hal Hartley) Hartley, the style-rich auteur of the MTV generation, scores with his brilliantly insightful second feature. Focusing again on young, angst-ridden suburban narcissists like those he introduced in *The Unbelievable Truth*, Hartley probes into seemingly shallow, mundane lives and comes up with funny, touching portraits of multi-dimensional charaters. Adrienne Shelley plays a pregnant cheerleader, Martin Donovan is a grenade-toting, burned-out computer whiz. Together they explore humanity, right on Long Island. ★★★½ $19.99

The Truth about Cats and Dogs

(1996, 93 min, US, Michael Lehmann) When keeping a pet is a major life decision, what hope is there for relationships between humans? Janeane Garofalo is a pleasure as a talk radio show host who helps her callers understand their verbally challenged canine and feline companions. Plump, brunette and verbally adroit, she meets her societal nemesis, a quintessential Beautiful Dumb Blonde (Uma Thurman), when she intercedes as Thurman's boyfriend manhandles her. A genuine friendship develops between this unlikely pair, and their initial stereotypes evolve into textured, believable personalities (due more to the performers than the script). A deliberate act of deception involving a too-good-to-be-true love interest (Ben Chaplin) escalates into a slapstick comedy of errors and enjoys a resolution mostly found only in the movies. The script for this gender-switched "Cyrano de Bergerac" is wildly uneven — some of the dialogue is actually painful — but it successfully depicts the everyday incivilities which define our public per-

sonas. Look for the scene which demonstrates absolutely fool-proof safe sex. ★★½ $14.99

Tucker

(1988, 120 min, US, Francis Coppola) A wonderful piece of storytelling from director Coppola. Preston Tucker was the personification of the American Dream — a man who believed anyone's dream could come true. But his Amercian Dream becomes the American Nightmare when he builds a futuristic luxury car all too well and is soon taken on by the big car manufacturers and crooked politicians, all afraid his design could set a new precedent in excellence and ruin their special interests. Based on a true story, Coppola has crafted a beautifully detailed period piece. Jeff Bridges stars in the title role, and Martin Landau, in an Oscar-nominated performance, appears as Tucker's loyal business partner and friend. ★★★½ $14.99

Tuff Turf

(1985, 113 min, US, Fritz Kiersch) A very youthful, pre-*sex, lies and videotape* James Spader stars in this satisfying teen pic as a streetwise preppy who takes on an L.A. gang and falls for the gang leader's girlfriend (Kim Richards). Not as formulaic as you'd expect, and Spader demonstrates the timing and intensity which would make him one of the movies' leading actors just a few years later. ★★½ $9.99

The Tune

(1992, 80 min, US, Bill Plympton) Plympton's highly amusing and inventive short cartoons have long become a staple of animation festivals. His unique and bizarre sense of humor, along with fantastical imagery of morphing faces and distorting body parts are near breathtaking. By these standards, *The Tune*, Plympton's first feature cartoon, is a total disappointment. The film follows a struggling songwriter who can't find the last line for his "hit" song. On the way to his boss' office, he is magically transported to the land of Flooby Nooby where he receives an education in letting his artistic talents flow. Unfortunately, most of Plympton's ingenious comedy gets eaten up by unending song-and-dance routines (it seems like every two minutes someone, or thing, is bursting into song) which mostly fizzle. Of far greater interest is the short which precedes the film, *The Draw*, in which the viewer experiences a Western shootout from the perspective of the bullet. ★½ $59.99

Tune in Tomorrow

(1990, 105 min, US, Jon Amiel) This delightfully capricious and wildly imaginative comedy stars Peter Falk as a famed radio script writer who is hired by a small station in New Orleans in the early 1950s. There he befriends adorable and painfully innocent 21-year-old Keanu Reeves, who has fallen in love with his thirtysomething, divorced aunt, Barbara Hershey. As they explore their forbidden passion, Falk surreptitiously manipulates their affair which, lo-and-behold, is echoed on his radio show. Based on a story by Peruvian author Mario Vargas Llosa, the film is filled with excursions into the absurd and surreal, especially when we are treated to brilliantly camp stagings of the daily soap episodes as Falk sees them. Though the entire cast is first-rate, the honors go to Falk, whose quips about Albanian peasantry are sidesplitting. ★★★½ $9.99

Tunes of Glory

(1960, 106 min, GB, Ronald Neame) Alec Guinness and John Mills are outstanding in this memorable character study of two rival colonels: one a careless, vicious renegade; the other a disciplined, well-mannered young officer who is slated to replace him. As the power is set to change hands at the Swiss Regiment, resentments and bitterness give rise to a violent confrontation and a shocking climax. Little known, the film features two stunning performances from Guinness and Mills. ★★★★ $29.99

The Tunnel of Love

(1958, 98 min, US, Gene Kelly) Kelly made his directorial bow with this sly, relaxed comedy based on the Broadway hit. Doris Day and Richard Widmark (in a nice change-of-pace role) play a married couple desperately trying to have a baby. Deciding to adopt, they encounter lots of red tape and counselor Gia Scala. Through some of the many misunderstandings which provide much of the film's humor, Widmark thinks, in a drug and alcohol-induced moment, that he has fathered a baby – with Scala. It's all rather tame by today's standards, but the screenplay's entendres still amuse. As Widmark's lecherous best friend, Gig Young steals the show and gets the lion's share of the best lines. ★★★ $19.99

Turbulence

(1997, 100 min, US, Robert Butler) The airline industry is in for more trouble and bad public relations with this silly action film. Lauren Holly is a stewardess (sorry... flight attendant) who puts on her best "Doris Day-Julie-I'm-gonna-save-this-plane" face (or is it "Karen Black-Airport 1975"?) when she goes up against a serial killer prisoner (Ray Liotta) who takes control of their plane. He chases her, she chases him. He rants and raves. She cries and curses a lot. Turbulence actually gets off the ground with a tense, swift scene in which the convicts escape their confinement. After that, however, the film dives out of control from the bombardment of cliché after cliché. Liotta has done this wacko role before, and is even more animated than usual. Holly, looking quite fetching, does her best to scrounge some characterization from the script. ★½ $102.99

Turkish Delight

(1974, 100 min, The Netherlands, Paul Verhoeven) Years before he burst into international stardom with the macabre and erotic The 4th Man, gifted young Dutch filmmaker Verhoeven directed this acclaimed, sexually explicit drama. This is very much a film of its period, complete with jazz soundtrack, promiscuity, a hostile "establishment" and a "youth must be served" attitude. Rutger Hauer is at first little more than a callous lothario intent on bedding a maximum number of women until he falls in love. (Dubbed) ★★★

The Turn of the Screw

(1992, 95 min, GB, Rusty Lemorande) This eerie adaptation of the Henry James ghost story is brimming with Freudian imagery and atmosphere. Patsy Kensit stars as a prim governess who is hired by a truly whacked-out Julian Sands (when is he anything else?) to tend to two small children living in a secluded English manor. Once there, of course, she is overcome by visions and other hauntings all of which seem to center around her repressed sexuality and a young boy. Stéphane Audran costars as the French cook and Marianne Faithfull plays the sole survivor of the ordeal who narrates the action. ★★½ $89.99

Turner and Hooch

(1989, 97 min, US, Roger Spottiswoode) Tom Hanks plays an officious police detective whose investigation of a murder is slightly hampered when the sole witness is a slobbering and very ugly watchdog. While most of the humor is predictable, Hanks is always a pleasure to watch and the film is at least better than the similarly themed, dog-tired K9. ★★ $9.99

The Turning Point

(1977, 119 min, US, Herbert Ross) Shirley MacLaine and Anne Bancroft give tour de force performances in this exquisite drama set in the world of ballet. Bancroft plays a star ballerina who is reunited with childhood friend MacLaine, now a housewife and dance teacher, when the latter's daughter comes to New York to study ballet. Mikhail Baryshnikov also stars as a dancer who romances the young Leslie Browne. Also with Tom Skerritt in a fine, understated performance as MacLaine's patient husband. The film features excellent ballet sequences, and can be enjoyed even by those not fond of the dance. ★★★ $19.99

Turtle Diary

(1986, 97 min, GB, John Irvin) Esteemed British playwright Harold Pinter wrote the charming adaptation of this Russell Hoban ("Ridley Walker") novel. Ben Kingsley and Glenda Jackson play a bookstore clerk and a children's writer, respectively, who conspire to set a pair of giant sea turtles loose from the London Zoo. What ensues is a gently metaphorical exploration of the meaning of liberation and rejuvenation. ★★★ $14.99

The Tuskegee Airmen

(1995, 110 min, US, Robert Markowitz) Recalling the story of the first American black pilots to serve in WWII in much the same dramatic fashion as Glory examined the first black fighting unit of the Civil War, The Tuskegee Airmen is an exhilarating, even inspiring story of courage and perseverance. Laurence Fishburne plays Hannibal Lee, a pre-med student from Iowa who is among the first cadets for pilot training. America has been at war for over a year, yet blacks were not allowed to fly planes. With politicians and military personnel against them, Lee and a small group of black enlistees must fight prejudice at home and overseas before being allowed to take on the Nazis. The film is remarkably assured in its detailing the relationships of the men, and derives its power not just from the events alone but from a thoughtful and articulate

screenplay, as well. The ensemble is uniformly good, with Fishburne anchoring the film with a nuanced portrayal of determination and loyalty. Cuba Gooding, Jr. is especially compelling as Lee's best friend "Train," and Andre Braugher brings passion (particularly to his rousing congressional speech) to the role of the group's commander. A fitting tribute to the men of the 99th and 332nd squadrons. ★★★½ $19.99

Twelfth Night: Or What You Will

(1996, 134 min, GB, Trevor Nunn) Shakespeare's ribald tale of mistaken identity and transgendered hilarity is brought to the screen with verve and vigor by stage veteran Nunn and a splendid cast. Imogen Stubbs is Viola, a young maiden who, shipwrecked and separated from her identical twin brother, takes on the appearance of a man (Cesario) in order to win favor in the court of Orsino (Toby Stephens). Orsino, it turns out, is intent on winning the love of Olivia (Helena Bonham Carter), and Cesario takes on the call of winning her over on behalf of the moody prince. But, of course, people's affections fail to land on their intended targets and before long all-out farce rules the day. To top it all off, Olivia's maid Maria (Imelda Staunton) conspires with Sir Toby Belch (Mel Smith) to humiliate the steward Malvolio (a brilliant Nigel Hawthorne) by convincing him that he is the object of Olivia's fancy. Ben Kingsley and Richard E. Grant round out the ensemble as the wandering storyteller Feste and the comic fop Sir Andrew Aguecheck, respectively. Though occasionally dragged down by some sloppy filmmaking, Nunn's experience as artistic director for the Royal Shakespeare Company pays off and he delivers an uproarious and timely comic adventure – what pleasure the bawdy Bard can be! ★★★½ $99.99

12 Angry Men

(1957, 95 min, US, Sidney Lumet) Henry Fonda heads a magnificent cast in this brilliant adaptation of Reginald Rose's gripping jury room drama. Fonda plays a juror who, uncertain of the guilt of a youth on trial for killing his father, tries to dissuade the other 11 members who are about to cast votes of guilty. The story evaluates the responsibility of the judicial and jury system, and is a bristling exposé of racial and social intolerance. The cast includes Lee J. Cobb, Ed Begley, E.G. Marshall, Jack Klugman, Jack Warden, and Martin Balsam. Notable not only for its superlative acting and direction (Lumet's film debut), but also for introducing a gallery of aspiring New York stage actors, some of whom would go on to great success in New York and Hollywood. ★★★★ $19.99

The Twelve Chairs

(1970, 94 min, US, Mel Brooks) Early Brooks always provides for solid comic entertainment, and this often-overlooked gem rates as one of his best. Ron Moody, in a hilariously manic performance, plays a Russian aristocrat who sets out on a madcap search for a dining room chair containing a fortune in jewels hidden in its upholstery. Frank Langella also stars as a transient who helps with the quest, and Dom DeLuise gives an uproarious, lunatic performance as Moody's rival for the jewels. ★★★½ $9.99

12 Monkeys

(1995, 130 min, US, Terry Gilliam) From the director of *Brazil* and *The Fisher King* comes this dark, multilayered sci-fi thriller – inspired by the obscure French short *La Jetee* – which stands firmly with Gilliam's two most accomplished efforts. Bruce Willis plays a prisoner in a futuristic underground society who becomes inextricably involved in a bureaucratic nightmare when he is forced to go back in time to track down the mythic "Army of the 12 Monkeys" and study the germ warfare holocaust that wiped out most of humanity. Overshooting the designated time period, he is thrown into an insane asylum where he must convince his shrink (Madeleine Stowe) that he is not delusional (or *is* he?). Unlike most time travel stories, this hyper-intelligent screenplay devotes proper attention to the elements of tragedy, pathos and inevitability thereby distracting from the attendant conundrums and paradoxes inherent in the genre. A masterpiece of post-apocalyptic grunge, *12 Monkeys* is replete with Gilliam's trademark set design of ductwork and steam vents. And he elicits wonderful performances – Willis proves he's more than an action star, and Brad Pitt is exceptional as an off-the-wall asylum mate who's not as crazy as he seems. (Available letterboxed and pan & scan) ★★★★ $19.99

Twelve O'Clock High

(1949, 132 min, US, Henry King) Gregory Peck gives one of his finest performances in this stirring psychological WWII drama about the pressures facing pilots and the men sending them off to die. Peck plays the newly appointed commander whose inflexibility causes resentment among his men and leads to his own breakdown. A thoroughly involving war drama, unusual for its time in that the flag waving was reduced to a minimum, with more concern for personal relationships and psychological profile. Dean Jagger, in his Oscar-winning role, stands out as the company clerk. ★★★½ $14.99

Twentieth Century

(1934, 92 min, US, Howard Hawks) Hawks' lightning-quick, hilarious adaptation of the Hecht-MacArthur play was the first popular hit of the new "screwball comedy" genre, and those unfamiliar with this comic gem will be amazed at how relentlessly funny and inventive it is. Carole Lombard and John Barrymore have an ongoing, cross-country battle-of-the-sexes aboard a train en route to her Broadway opening. The two stars are phenomenal. Barrymore brings fiendish energy to the part of a down-on-his-luck, maniacal director, and Lombard combines dazzling wit with great beauty in her role as the pampered actress. ★★★★ $19.99

Twenty Bucks

(1993, 91 min, US, Keva Rosenfeld) Based on a script that's been floating around Hollywood for over 50 years, *Twenty Bucks* has an interesting premise: Follow the life of a crisp twenty dollar bill as it passes from owner to owner, becoming limp, bloodied and torn in the process. Unfortunately, the people who come into contact with the bill, like delivery guy Brendan Fraser and homeless person/mystic Linda Hunt, aren't as engaging as the original idea. Similar in theme to the more successful *Chain of Desire*, in which the players are linked by a series of sexual rendezvous, *Twenty Bucks* attempts to uncover the brushes with fate and the unknown connections encountered in everyday life. Also starring Steve Buscemi. ★★½ $19.99

28 Up

(1985, 133 min, GB, Michael Apted) Originally made in four separate installments, Apted's fascinating documentary began with a series of interviews with English children at age seven. Over the years, he went back to follow up on their lives at ages 14, 21 and 28. The success and failure of these individuals to fulfill their dreams provide an informative and sometimes lamentable view of real life. ★★★ $19.99

25 Fireman's Street

(1973, 97 min, Hungary, István Szabó) Set in the post-war era, this evocative and haunting film explores the dreams, memories and nightmares of a group of people living in an old house on the eve of its destruction. Through the course of the film, they recall a generation of happiness and tragedy as affected by the war. (Hungarian with English subtitles) ★★★½ $69.99

Twenty-Four Eyes

(1954, 158 min, Japan, Keisuke Kinoshita) The title of this beloved Japanese classic refers to the 24 eyes of the students of an elementary class on the remote island of Shodoshima. Set in the late 1920s, the students' calm and traditional way of life is changed when a shockingly modern young teacher from Tokyo arrives. The woman, who wears a suit like a man and rides a bike to work, is slowly accepted and eventually loved by her students. Both their bright futures and the new ideas of the teacher are shattered by the impending war as well as by a rising nationalism that stifles individual growth and transforms personal ambition into unflinching devotion to the state. (Japanese with English subtitles) ★★★

29th Street

(1991, 98 min, US, George Gallo) Danny Aiello stars in this enjoyable depiction of the havoc and happiness that befalls an Italian-American family when they become winners of the New York State Lottery. Based on a true story, the film examines Frank Pesce, Jr.'s (Anthony LaPaglia) inexplicable dismay over the seemingly joyous news that he has become a multimillionaire. Aiello is solid, as always, as LaPaglia's father, Frank, Sr. and Lainie Kazan is strong in support as his wife. The real Frank Pesce, Jr. delivers a surprisingly good debut as the other son, Vito. At times funny, the film draws its strength from the heart of the Pesce family where, although they are always fighting, true bonds of love prevail. ★★★ $19.99

Twenty-One

(1990, 92 min, GB, Don Boyd) British actress Patsy Kensit (*Absolute Beginners*, *Lethal Weapon 2*) seduces her way into the hearts of viewers in this hip examination of the excesses and maladies of coming-of-age in the '90s. The film is told largely through a series of flashbacks, with Kensit delivering a series of voice-over soliloquies on her budding philosophies and unique impressions of the crazy world around her. ★★½ $89.99

26 Bathrooms

(1985, 28 min, GB, Peter Greenaway) On a short break from feature filmmaking, director Greenaway (*The Cook, the Thief, His Wife and Her Lover*) made for British TV this delightfully wacky documentary that takes an entertaining peek into the bathrooms of Great Britain. Serious in a smirking cleverish way, Greenaway's unusual travelogue visits 26 different bathrooms in and around London – all of which seek to go beyond mere functionalism and celebrate the therapeutic pleasures of the bathing ritual. And keeping with his game-playing pastime, the film is broken up into alphabetical segments running from A to Z, i.e., A is for A Bathroom, D is for Dental Hygiene, F is for Fish. ★★★½ $19.99

20,000 Leagues under the Sea

(1916, 105 min, US, Stuart Paton) This early silent version of Jules Verne's classic adventure story was one of the first films to feature innovative special effects and underwater photography. The story follows the renegade Captain Nemo who discovers a sea monster from his submarine Nautilus. Newly remastered from an archive print. ★★★ $29.99

20,000 Leagues Under the Sea

(1954, 126 min, US, Richard Fleischer) Oscar-winning special effects highlight this exciting Disney film based on Jules Verne's story of shipwrecked survivors becoming involved with the notorious Captain Nemo. Kirk Douglas, James Mason, Peter Lorre and Paul Lukas star. ★★★½ $19.99

Twice a Woman

(1985, 90 min, The Netherlands, George Sluizer) This pleasantly tender and romantic lesbian love story stars Bibi Andersson (*Wild Strawberries*, *Persona*, *Cries and Whispers*). Set in Amsterdam, the tale begins immediately with a pick-up. Laura (Andersson) is a successful 41-year-old restorer. She meets Sylvia (Sandra Dumas), a charming young girl half her age, and the two move in together. Anthony Perkins plays Laura's sleazy ex-husband who himself becomes involved with Sylvia. A tangled web of passion soon develops. ★★½

Twice in a Lifetime

(1985, 117 min, US, Bud Yorkin) Superior acting elevates this compelling family drama about a husband who leaves his wife and children for another woman. Gene Hackman gives a virtuoso performance as the working-class family man starting life anew; and terrific support comes from Ellen Burstyn, Ann-Margret, Brian Dennehy and especially Oscar-nominee Amy Madigan. Intelligent screenplay by Colin Welland. ★★★½ $79.99

Twice Upon a Time

(1983, 75 min, US, John Korty & Charles Swenson) Fun-filled animated story of an all-purpose animal named Ralph and his companion Mumford (who speaks only in sound effects), out to save the cosmos from a villain planning to unleash non-stop nightmares. Filmed with "lumage," an innovative animation technique adding depth, texture and translucency to images. George Lucas served as executive producer. ★★★ $14.99

Twilight Zone: The Movie

(1983, 102 min, US, John Landis, Steven Spielberg, Joe Dante & George Miller) Four episodes either based on teleplays from the classic TV series "Twilight Zone," or close in theme and spirit. Though the most infamous of the four (directed by Landis) is the segment starring Vic Morrow — in which the actor and two children were killed — about a bigoted man who gets his comeuppance, the best is the finale, "Nightmare at 20,000 Feet" (directed by Miller) with John Lithgow outstanding as a frightened airline passenger (based on a TV episode starring William Shatner). Other episodes include Spielberg's "Kick the Can," about a group of senior citizens who rediscover their youth; and Dante's cartoon-like story of a young boy whose magical powers don't make him very popular. ★★½ $9.99

Twin Peaks: Fire Walk with Me

(1992, 135 min, US, David Lynch) Very few contemporary filmmakers can ever be accused of originality and so it seems ironic that one of the most inventive of the lot, David Lynch, is already giving way to self-tribute. Regardless of this, however, this necessary, quasi-Gothic return to the mythical hamlet of "Twin Peaks" recycles the insightful themes introduced in the series, scaling them up to near-operatic proportions to chronicle the events leading up to the murder of Laura Palmer (it ain't over until the sad lady dies!). Sheryl Lee reprises her role as the doomed nymphet who plays out her life as if she were auditioning for "The Drew Barrymore Story" — and she's the only normal one in town! Though critically reviled by the same Cannes audience that praised his earlier works, the discerning eye will recognize this as a fitting coda to the small-town saga and the successful effort of an innovator forced to walk the tightrope which spans the chasm between cinematic genius and televised mediocrity. ★★★ $14.99

Twin Town

(1997, 99 min, Wales, Kevin Allen) The glue-sniffing, dope-smoking Lewis brothers, known as "the twins" despite three years difference in age, barter prescription drugs from senior citizens and pilfer cars for ready cash. When a local pillar of society — a club owner with police in his pocket — refuses to compensate an injury on the job sufffered by their construction worker dad, the twins embark on a path of retribution that veers from goofy prank to unexpected tragedy. The film employs a unique sensibility of earthy naturalness and heightened reality: The landscape is both pastoral and industrial wasteland, the pacing both bucolic and frenetic. A canine funeral service conducted in Welsh is hallucinogenic counterpoint to a devastating freak accident of unadorned loss. The actors are unselfconscious and direct, uniformly engaging in their portrayals of lusts and obsessions

and fragmented loyalties. Often compared to *Trainspotting*, *Twin Town* is similar in its blithe juxtaposition of the remnants of Old World charm against the harsh realities of modern day vice. Corruption and drug trafficking have become the world's common language, the common denomination that unites us all. ★★★½ $99.99

Twins

(1988, 112 min, US, Ivan Reitman) This box-office smash is basically a one-joke comedy whose punchline wears thin soon after its telling. The appealing duo of Arnold Schwarzenegger and Danny DeVito star as separated twin brothers (and scientific experiments) who are reunited when the former leaves his island paradise in search of his roots. DeVito, who can get comic mileage from a phone book, rises above the nonsensical script and direction. Yeah, it's funny Arnie and Danny are twins: for the first ten minutes that is. What about the other 102? ★★ $14.99

Twins of Evil

(1971, 85 min, GB, John Hough) This sequel to *Vampire Lovers* and *Lust for a Vampire* continues the "Carmilla" story line, this time starring *Playboy*'s first twin playmates (Madeleine and Mary Collinson). Peter Cushing returns as their puritanical adversary, appalled as much by their sexual proclivities as their dietary habits. ★★½

Twist

(1993, 78 min, US, Ron Mann) This amusing look back at the dance craze which took the early '60s by storm is peppered with delightful anecdotes and present-day interviews with some of the main players in the meteoric rise of the hip-swivelling dance. After chronicling the country's vilification of rock 'n' roll in the mid '50s, the film introduces Hank Ballard, the artist who first recorded Chubby Checker's platinum hit, "The Twist." Ballard was denied his shot at superstardom because several of his earlier songs were too risqué and he was therefore deemed unsuitable for "American Bandstand." While half-heartedly dabbling in the issue of white society appropriating African-American culture, director Mann (*Comic Book Confidential*) is happy for the most part to concentrate on the social phenomenon of the craze itself, putting together an interesting, if somewhat by-the-book, collection of talking head interviews and humorous stock footage from the era. ★★½ $19.99

Twist and Shout

(1984, 105 min, Denmark, Bille August) This harrowing, beautifully acted teenage rite-of-passage film from young Danish director August is a comedy-drama that explores a web of complex familial and romantic relationships surrounding four young friends. Never once sinking to the level of a typical American teenage "coming-of-age" film, *Twist and Shout* instead creates a kinetic excitement of youthful sexuality as director August proves himself wonderfully capable of portraying the agony and ecstacy of adolescent life. (Dubbed) ★★★½

Twister

(1988, 93 min, US, Michael Almereyda) When the production wing of Vestron Pictures went under, *Twister* was unceremoniously released on video, bypassing theatrical release. Well, the film deserved better, for it is an unqualified delight. First-time director Almereyda's innovative comedy is set in a sprawling mansion in the middle of Kansas where Harry Dean Stanton is raising a family of lunatics. Among them are newcomer Suzy Amis as his daughter who has a tenuous grasp on reality; and Crispin Glover as his abundantly confused son. Glover proves at long last that he is the James Dean (or at least the Dennis Hopper) of his generation. ★★★

Twister

(1996, 114 min, US, Jan De Bont) The director of *Speed* and Michael Crichton, the writer of *Jurassic Park* and *Congo*, unite to bring the best and worst elements of these films to one grand-slam if vacuous special effects extravaganza. Director De Bont employs the high-energy octane of his exciting bus saga with *Park*'s great F/X, and when the film allows these F/X to take center stage, *Twister* is a knock-out. But there's the matter of a story between the effects, and it's a whirlwind of mediocrity. The agreeable Helen Hunt plays a scientist who chases tornadoes. Onto the scene comes her soon-to-be ex-husband (Bill Paxton) — now there's an original concept. He was once a tornado chaser but now he's a weatherman. The two get together (with his new girlfriend Jami Gertz) and follow several tornadoes throughout the Midwest. There's a silly subplot about a rival tornado chaser (Cary Elwes) — the layperson probably never knew tornado chasing was so cutthroat. But forget about the dialogue and story — the F/X are the real interest here, and each successive twister brings on more carnage and jaw-dropping effects culminating in a smash finale. (Available letterboxed and pan & scan) ★★½ $22.99

Two Daughters

(1962, 116 min, India, Satyajit Ray) Ray's wonderful film is divided into two different stories but united in the theme of first love. The first tale, "The Postmaster," is about a young girl's growing affection for her employer; the second, "The Conclusion," is a charming parable about a girl who is forced into a loveless marriage with a bland but successful man. Her frustrations grow until she leaves him in an effort to find real love. (Hindi with English subtitles) ★★★

2 Days in the Valley

(1996, 105 min, US, John Herzfeld) Of the many post-Quentin Tarantino hipper-than-thou, comedic, violent, pulse-racing, multi-character, noir criminal saga/thrillers, the ruthlessly inventive and often extremely funny *2 Days in the Valley* is one of the most entertaining. Casting a cynical eye on a cold-blooded world and containing unpredictable twists that we've come to expect from good mysteries, the story begins as hired guns Danny Aiello and James Spader finalize a hit. Only Spader attempts to kill his partner and frame him for the murder. Barely escaping and on the run, Aiello hides out in the luxurious Valley home of pompous art dealer Greg Cruttwell. Meanwhile, Spader must return to the scene of the crime when his fee is locked away in the house, which is by now crawling with police — including Jeff Daniels and Eric Stoltz. Featuring a wild assortment of appealing characters (only Daniels' cop becomes sappy), *2 Days in the Valley* takes gleeful delight in its originality – a zestful blend of Philip Marlowe glibness and contemporary inter-genre teasing. This is two days well spent no matter which side of the gun you're on. ★★★ $19.99

Two Deaths

(1996, 102 min, GB, Nicolas Roeg) An intimate study of obsessional love related against the backdrop of the brutal absurdity of war evolves into an artfully constructed parable regarding the root causes of human self-destruction. Michael Gambon plays a well-established, extremely comfortable surgeon hosting a sumptuous dinner party for a few old college chums in an unspecified Eastern European city. The night rains random death and pointless destruction as the militia squelches a civilian uprising...or executes any unarmed travelers out after curfew — depending on your perception of the matter. Gambon's brilliant portrayal of enigmatic moral ambivalance is stark counterpoint to Sonia Braga's earthy, sensual, intelligent and focused servant; his need to dominate and possess is forcefully confronted by her willful surrender. He relates their history to the assembled guests, who, though horrified, in turn tell their own stories of loss and corruption. As political upheavel mirrors the ruin of shattered lives, they each question the moment when childhood innocence was sacrificed to adult expediency. An intricate, involving and revelatory foray into the darkest components of the human psyche. ★★★ $89.99

Two English Girls

(1971, 108 min, France, François Truffaut) A kindred companion to *Jules and Jim*, *Two English Girls* features Jean-Pierre Léaud as the pivotal figure alternately romancing two British sisters with sometimes tragic consequences. A lyrical rumination of passion's turbulent course. (French with English subtitles) ★★★ $29.99

Two Evil Eyes

(1990, 121 min, US/Italy, George Romero & Dario Argento) George Romero and Italian horror stylist Dario Argento join forces in this Poe-meets-*Creepshow* horror anthology. Romero's clever adaptation of "The Case of M. Valdemar" stars Adrienne Barbeau as a greedy wife whose hubby dies...or does he? Argento's turn is short on sense, but long on atmosphere. Harvey Keitel stars as a sadistic Weegee-style photographer who can't conceal his crimes from "The Black Cat." *Creepshow* vets E.G. Marshall and Tom Savini co-star with Kim Hunter and Martin Balsam. Music by Pino Donaggio. ★★

Two for the Road

(1967, 111 min, GB, Stanley Donen) Audrey Hepburn and Albert Finney bring sophistication and spontaneity to their roles as a married couple looking back at the many paths they've traveled during a tumultuous 12-year marriage. Through a series of flashbacks, Frederic Raphael's fresh, innovative screenplay examines several crossroads in Hepburn and Finney's lives, all while the couple are traveling on the road. It is to Raphael and director Donen's credit that the constant back-and-forth through the years — which includes their courtship, early years of marriage and current difficulties — is neither distracting nor confusing. *Two for the Road* is consistently charming, and is laced with a delightful sense of humor. In support, William Daniels and Eleanor Bron are near-perfect as "ugly American" tourists/traveling companions, and Jacqueline Bisset can be glimpsed in an early appearance. ★★★½ $19.99

Two for the Seesaw

(1962, 119 min, US, Robert Wise) Shirley MacLaine and Robert Mitchum star in this bittersweet romantic comedy based on William Gibson's acclaimed play. Mitchum plays a Midwest lawyer, about to divorce his wife of 12 years, who moves to New York City and becomes involved with "lovable crackpot waif" MacLaine. Though on stage the story is a riveting character study, director Wise is unable to overcome the talkiness of a two-character play in his screen adaptation. But this is nonetheless an involving work, and Mitchum and MacLaine offer noteworthy performances. The basis for the Broadway musical "SeeSaw." ★★★ $19.99

Two Girls and a Sailor

(1944, 125 min, US, Richard Thorpe) Two singing-and-dancing sisters (June Allyson and Gloria DeHaven) open up their dream canteen, with the help of a wily sailor (Van Johnson). Appearances made by Lena Horne, Jimmy Durante, Gracie Allen and Xavier Cugat. A cute, bright musical entertainment typical of M-G-M's 1940s song-and-dance productions. ★★★ $19.99

200 Motels

(1971, 98 min, US, Frank Zappa & Tony Palmer) Frank Zappa and The Mothers of Invention are on the road with Ringo Starr, Theodore Bikel and Keith Moon in this incredibly bizarre "surrealistic documentary." ★★★ $14.99

Two if by Sea

(1995, 95 min, US, Bill Bennett) In his stand-up and prior film appearances, comedian Denis Leary has successfully demonstrated a caustic demeanor punctuated by irreverent material and a machine-gun delivery. And while a leopard may be allowed to change its spots, Leary appears to have lost his considerable bite as star and co-author of this ordinary romantic comedy. He and Sandra Bullock appear as hired art thieves who are on the run from the law. Needing to hide out for several days before the drop-off, they find a vacant mansion (whose family is on vacation) and play house. With the police and underworld associates on their trail, they bicker, befriend a friendless teen, and attend fancy parties thrown by their handsome "neighbor" who has the hots for Bullock. The two stars try to come off as the Tracy and Hepburn of the Bonnie and Clyde set, and though they do have a charming rapport, the dialogue they are forced to recite is rarely funny or romantic, and their continual misadventures are very familiar. ★★ $19.99

Two in Twenty

(1988, 160 min, US, Laurel Chiten, Cheryl Qamar, Rachel McCollum) Originally slated to air on a public access station in Boston, *Two in Twenty* is an entertaining, amusing and ambitious lesbian soap opera. The show's five episodes (on three tapes, with outtakes on the third) are structured as an actual TV soap "aired" on WCLT, complete with humorous spoofs on commercials. The stories revolve around two lesbian households, and deal with such topics as bisexuality, promiscuity among lesbians, racial problems, lesbian child rearing and various other joys and problems that befall the many lesbian characters. The tape's finale focuses on a dramatic courtroom battle for custody of a 15-year-old girl living with her lesbian mother and lover. While not slick in production values, nor acting prowess, the show's strength is in its ability to depict — hon-

Helen Hunt (l.) and Bill Paxton in *Twister* ('96)

567

estly, directly and from a lesbian perspective — a slice of several lesbian lifestyles. ★★½ $59.99

The Two Jakes

(1990, 138 min, US, Jack Nicholson) Lacking the tension and chilling atmosphere of Roman Polanski's noirish classic *Chinatown*, this sequel directed by and starring Nicholson is fascinating and occasionally riveting. It's 1948, 11 years after the original. Private investigator Jake Gittes (Nicholson) is less ambitious, more portly, and content with mundane murder cases and rounds of golf. Problems arise when his client Jake Berman (Harvey Keitel) becomes involved in a murder. As the investigation ensues, Gittes finds himself face to face with his grisly past. A good supporting cast includes Meg Tilly, Ruben Blades and Eli Wallach; however, honors go to Harvey Keitel as Gittes' mysterious client. Nicholson demonstrates thoughtful competence as a director, but he sometimes bogs down in uninteresting side plots which lengthen the film. ★★★ $19.99

Two Moon Junction

(1988, 104 min, US, Zalman King) A bored, blonde Sherilyn Fenn dumps her privileged life and vapid beau (Martin Hewitt) and takes up with a rugged, muscle-bound carnival worker (Richard Tyson). Kristy McNichol appears as a bisexual cowgirl in this cheesy T&A tale. ★★ $14.99

The Two Mrs. Carrolls

(1947, 99 min, US, Peter Godfrey) Humphrey Bogart is an artist who killed his first wife, but not until after using her as a model for his painting "Angel of Death." It's a few years later, and now he's married to Barbara Stanwyck. And now she's starting to show signs of illness. Alexis Smith also stars as the beautiful socialite with whom he falls in love while plotting to kill the second Mrs. Carroll. This psy-

chological thriller is heavy going for the most part, and it takes its good old time building to a rather exciting climax. ★★½ $19.99

Two Mules for Sister Sara

(1970, 105 min, US, Don Siegel) Clint Eastwood and Shirley MacLaine make a good team in this entertaining comic western about drifter Eastwood coming to the aid of nun MacLaine (who sure doesn't act very religious) in the Mexican desert. ★★★ $14.99

The Two of Us

(1967, 86 min, France, Claude Berri) Michel Simon stars as an old man whose fervent anti-Semitism is challenged when he develops a close relationship with a young Jewish boy in hiding during World War II. Their growing friendship and love makes this both a charming and moving film experience. (Dubbed) ★★★

2001: A Space Odyssey

(1968, 139 min, GB, Stanley Kubrick) Both a grand hypothesis on humankind's place in the universe and a pithy examination of our efforts to control our burgeoning technology before it controls us, Kubrick's milestone sci-fi epic is nothing less than brilliant. A visual masterpiece without equal, the film was years ahead of its time with regard to special effects and Kubrick established his mastery of choreographing music with image. (Available letterboxed and pan & scan) ★★★★ $19.99

2000 Maniacs

(1964, 75 min, US, Hershell Gordon Lewis) Lewis' "masterpiece." A must see! The classic (nearing mythical) tale of Southern inhospitality given to six innocent travelers by the strange folk of Pleasant Valley. With Tom Wood and Connie Mason as two of the unfortunate passers-by. Unforgettable theme song written by HGL (with the "Pleasant Valley Boys"). ★

2010

(1984, 116 min, US, Peter Hyams) Director Hyams (*Capricorn One, Outland*) finds himself in space once again with this sequel to Stanley Kubrick's landmark *2001: A Space Odyssey*. A new space expedition locates the wrecked ship Discovery and learns the secret of its aborted mission. Though the special effects are commendable, the film doesn't share the original's narrative composition and intelligence — but then who'd actually expect it to? Starring Roy Scheider, John Lithgow, Bob Balaban, Helen Mirren and, from the original, Keir Dullea. ★★ $19.99

The 2000 Year Old Man

(1982, 25 min, US, Leo Salkin) "Who discovered women?" This and other questions for the ages are answered by the World's Oldest Know-It-All, Mel Brooks. Carl Reiner asks the questions in this animated short. ★★★ $14.99

Two Way Stretch

(1960, 87 min, GB, Robert Day) Peter Sellers stars as a prisoner who leads his fellow inmates in a scheme to break out of jail, commit a robbery and then steal back to the safety of their cells. Sly fun. ★★★

Two Women

(1960, 99 min, Italy/France, Vittorio De Sica) Sophia Loren won an Academy Award for her deeply moving, heart-wrenching portrayal of an Italian woman who, along with her daughter, is raped by soldiers during World War II. The affects of this brutalization on the woman and her relationship with her daughter are explored in this realistic and unforgettable film experience. (Italian with English subtitles) ★★★★

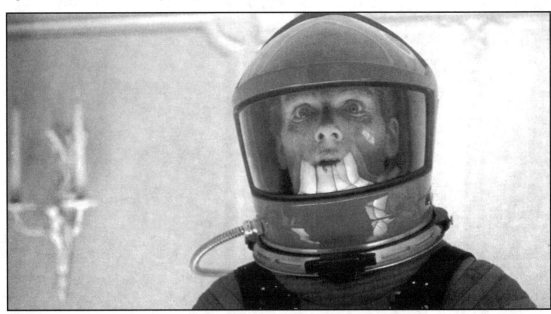

2001: A Space Odyssey

Ubu and the Grand Gidouille

(1980, 79 min, France, Jan Lenica) Freely adapted from the plays of Alfred Jarry, this fascinating animated film, made by the Polish-born Lenica, uses two-dimensional marionettes and surprisingly little action in vividly telling its violent story of greed, cowardice and tyranny. Pere Ubu is the round psycho who, with the aid of his calculating wife Mere Ubu, plots to overthrow the throne of Poland and install himself as despotic king. An intelligent, intriguing and captivating film. (French with English subtitles) ★★★½

L'Udienza

(1971, 120 min, Italy, Marco Ferreri) An all-star cast is featured in Ferreri's provocative comedy of passion and alienation set against the intrigues of the modern Vatican. It follows a peculiar young man's quixotic attempts to obtain a private audience with the Pope, in order to share ideas which he is convinced can cure the ills of society. His attempts are constantly blocked by individuals who only pretend to be sympathetic to his cause. Starring Ugo Tognazzi, Claudia Cardinale, Vittorio de Sica and Michel Piccoli. (Italian with English subtitles) ★★½

UFOria

(1980, 100 min, US, John Binder) This whacked-out comedy features a colorful assortment of oddball characters who are searching for fulfillment in a nowhere town at the edge of the Mojave Desert in a culture of revival tents and religious fanatics. Cindy Williams is a delightfully daffy, Bible-toting prophet who dreams of UFOs and a cosmic reenactment of Noah's Ark. ★★★ $59.99

The Ugly American

(1963, 120 min, US, George Englund) Marlon Brando and Eiji Okada fought together in Sarkhan against the Japanese in WWII. More than a decade later, Brando returns to Sarkhan as its American ambassador; Okada is the leader of a popular underground nationalistic movement. This well-constructed political exposé, based on the book by William J. Lederer and Eugene Burdick, plays the personal friendship against the conflicting factions vying for power in the underdeveloped Southeast Asian country. Take care to follow the convolutions of intrigue — it all leads up to a chilling final shot. ★★★ $19.99

UHF

(1989, 97 min, US, Jay Levey) By all rights, this film debut of rock spoofer "Weird Al" Yankovic should at best be a sporadically amusing, teenage, suburban mall-pleaser. But surprisingly, it is much more — a genuinely funny and fast-paced take-off on TV, movies and Americana. "Weird Al" plays a daydreaming nobody who inadvertently gets control of a near-zero rated television station. Of course, he makes the station a huge success. But hilarious take-offs in the form of commercials and strange new shows (including a gun-toting Gandhi sequel, "Conan the Librarian" and "Wheel of Fish") help you forget the pedestri-

an plot and enjoy his special (if wicked) brand of comedy. ★★½ $9.99

Ulysses

(1955, 104 min, US/Italy, Mario Camerini) Kirk Douglas brings a degree of respectability to this flavorful American-Italian coproduction about the adventures of the legendary Greek hero on his way home after the Trojan Wars, including encountering the cyclops and the sirens. ★★★

Ulysses

(1967, 140 min, US/Ireland, Joseph Strick) Adapting James Joyce's massive novel to the screen was thought to be an impossible task, but Strick for the most part succeeds in filming the unfilmable with this tale of lust and longing. The story, photographed in a style of cinematic stream of consciousness, follows a 24-hour period in the life of young poet Stephen Daedalus as his odyssey takes him through the streets and brothels of Dublin. Starring Milo O'Shea. ★★½ $29.99

Ulzana's Raid

(1972, 103 min, US, Robert Aldrich) Top-notch western adventure with Burt Lancaster as an experienced Indian scout helping new cavalry officer Bruce Davison in a counter-offensive against an Apache attack. Crisp direction from Aldrich separates this tale from other similarly themed westerns. ★★★ $14.99

Umberto D

(1955, 89 min, Italy, Vittorio De Sica) De Sica's uncompromising masterpiece is a heartrending study of a lonely old man and his struggle to survive with dignity in post-war Italy. A haunting and well-crafted film expertly told by the director. (Italian with English subtitles) ★★★★ $29.99

The Umbrellas of Cherbourg

(1964, 91 min, France, Jacques Demy) Beautifully restored version of Demy's classic, bittersweet musical of two young lovers (a luminous Catherine Deneuve and handsome Nino Castelnuovo) separated by war. Like many French New Wave films, *Umbrellas* simultaneously comments on and expands upon the conventions of an American genre. With its gorgeous pastel color scheme and attractive leads, *Umbrellas* apes the glamour of the Hollywood musical, but also undercuts this a bit with a gritty, working-class locale and everyday situations. All the dialogue is sung, and most of the music is low-key. There are no show-stopping, highly choreographed numbers; but what it lacks in bombast and spectacle it makes up for in emotional resonance. Demy perfectly captures the feel of first love — a time when emotions can be so strong that bursting into a heartfelt ditty seems the natural thing — and the myriad obstacles thrown in the face of it. A thankfully rediscovered treasure about the losses — and gains — of growing up and moving on. Michel Legrand wrote the lovely score. (Letterboxed version) (French with English subtitles) ★★★★ $79.99

The Unapproachable

(1983, 92 min, West Germany, Krystof Zanussi) A former film star, living the life of a recluse, meets a handsome young man who,

Catherine Deneuve in *The Umbrellas of Cherbourg*

under his charming veneer, is actually a scheming and ruthless opportunist. A provocative thriller that explores their developing relationship and the shifting tides of power and sexual attraction. Leslie Caron's cooly passionate performance will captivate the viewer. A probing insight into the dangerous games which men and women all-too-often play. (Dubbed) ★★★

The Unbearable Lightness of Being

(1988, 171 min, US, Philip Kaufman) An erotic, witty and intelligent film adaptation of Milan Kundera's best-selling novel. Set against the backdrop of the Prague Spring of 1968, the story follows a young, womanizing Czech doctor who finds himself caught in the turmoil of the uprising despite his aversion to politics. Daniel Day-Lewis, Juliette Binoche and Lena Olin all beautifully portray their characters' intertwined relationships against the powerfully evoked background of political upheaval and displacement. ★★★½ $19.99

The Unbelievable Truth

(1990, 90 min, US, Hal Hartley) Director Hartley throws together vivid and quirky characters in a story of a high school cynic-turned-model (Adrienne Shelley) living in a town disrupted by the return of an alleged murderer-turned-mechanic (Robert Burke). Male territorialism, miscommunication and deals fuel the dialogue-driven plot of this offbeat winner. ★★★ $9.99

Uncle Buck

(1989, 99 min, US, John Hughes) *Uncle Buck* is a pleasant and amusing comedy which offers John Candy a chance to demonstrate a heretofore unseen paternal side to his mammoth personality. Big John stars as a black-sheep uncle who tests his limits (and the limits of those around him) when he baby-sits his two nieces and nephew for a few days. Some of this may be very predictable and formulaic territory for director Hughes, but it nevertheless works. The nephew is played by Macaulay Culkin, before his *Home Alone* mugging. ★★½ $14.99

Uncommon Valor

(1983, 105 min, US, Ted Kotcheff) A father recruits his old Marine buddies to search for his son, missing in action in Laos for ten years.

The screenplay and characters are action-adventure clichés, but the cast and competent direction from Kotcheff elevate it from its formulaic roots. Starring Fred Ward, Reb Brown, Patrick Swayze, Robert Stack and Gene Hackman. ★★½ $14.99

Under Capricorn

(1949, 117 min, GB, Alfred Hitchcock) An unusual effort for Hitchcock — a period costume piece — starring Ingrid Bergman as a woman unhappily married to a respected but ruthless man. Joseph Cotten is superb as the vicious husband who drives her to alchoholism and the limits of her mental and physical endurance. Michael Wilding costars as a visitor who wreaks havoc with Cotten. Not considered one of Hitch's classics, it's worth a look nonetheless for its marvelous acting and to see the director out of his usual milieu. ★★½ $19.99

Under Fire

(1983, 128 min, US, Roger Spottiswoode) The setting is Nicaragua during the overthrow of the Somoza regime by the Sandinistas. An American journalist (Joanna Cassidy) and a hotshot photographer (Nick Nolte) find themselves caught in the cross fire of the revolution when Nolte uses a doctored photo to aid the rebel cause. A taut, engrossing drama about the moral and political issues of news reporting and the "objectivity" of the press. Costarring Gene Hackman. ★★★½

Under Milk Wood

(1973, 90 min, GB, Andrew Sinclair) Set in lush and visually stunning Wales, this production of Dylan Thomas' classic play is performed with theatrical genius by Richard Burton, Elizabeth Taylor and Peter O'Toole. Thomas' glorious poetry sparkles in this tale of a day in the life of the mythical village of Llareggub. The film has been rightly accused of over-ambitiousness and, indeed, the sense of production does weigh some of the material down. But it still offers a sterling example of ensemble acting from three great thespians. ★★½

Under Siege

(1992, 103 min, US, Andrew Davis) Action fave Steven Seagal reteams with his *Above the Law* director Davis to boldly go where Bruce Willis and Wesley Snipes have gone before: into the "one-man S.W.A.T. team" arena. In this "*Die Hard* on the high seas," Seagal has his most fulfilling effort to date, thanks mostly to Davis' slam-bang pacing. Seagal, the mumbling master, takes on the role of a military expert who just happens to be "moonlighting" as a ship's cook when high-tech pirates take over. Suspenseful action and over-the-top performances by Gary Busey and Tommy Lee Jones make this the Steven Seagal movie for people who don't like Steven Seagal. ★★★ $14.99

Under Siege 2: Dark Territory

(1995, 98 min, US, Geoff Murphy) Yet another variation of the *Die Hard* theme, this sequel welcomes back Steven Seagal as Casey Rybeck, everyone's favorite Navy SEAL-turned-cook, who must once again thwart a secret terrorist plot, kill all the bad guys, and save both a group of hostages and the world at large. This time he is pitted against an over-the-top Eric Bogosian, a nutso weapons designer whiz who hijacks a moving train and a satellite, making the deadly services of the latter available to the highest international bidder. Of course, Rybeck's on board and the only one who can stop him. While not up to the level of the exceedingly entertaining first film, *Dark Territory* still manages to be rousing if mindless fun. It has mostly everything an adventure fan could want: gruesome, creative deaths and nonstop action. Though Seagal is still one of the most wooden actors lucky enough to be receiving a paycheck, he does appear more intimidating than some of his action counterparts. ★★ $19.99

Under Suspicion

(1992, 100 min, GB, Simon Moore) The title of this old-fashioned murder mystery refers to the predicament of its two leads (Liam Neeson and Laura San Giacomo), who find themselves pointing fingers at each other over the murder

of the latter's lover. Neeson stars as a sleazy private eye (circa 1959 England) whose livelihood of faking adulteries for divorce-seekers is cut short when one of his set-ups ends in murder — with him as a prime suspect. He immediately sets out to prove his innocence by pinning the blame on San Giacomo, who is the sole beneficiary of the murdered man. This innocent-man-wrongly-accused thriller sports a wild ending twist. ★★½ $19.99

Under the Cherry Moon

(1986, 98 min, US, Prince) Prince wrote, directed and stars in this universally trashed, amateurish tale of a tormented American gigolo working in the south of France. Filmed in black and white. With Jerome Benton, Kristin Scott Thomas and Francesca Annis. ★

Under the Domim Tree

(1996, 102 min, Israel, Eli Cohen) Based on the autobiography by Gila Almagor, *Under the Domim Tree* is the poignant and very compelling story of a group of orphaned Jewish teens, all survivors of the Holocaust, who come of age and battle very real demons while living in an Israeli youth settlement. On a melancholy note, the film begins slowly and sometimes confusingly as it introduces the children and adults, setting up the story with dispassion. But as the main characters are identified and the heart of the tale unfolds, *Under the Domim Tree* discovers its voice — and a haunting one at that — and in an accomplished manner conveys in heartfelt scenes the daily lives, struggles, hopes and conflicts of these — in one way or another — tortured kids. The story is touching without being depressing, and by the sheer courage demonstrated by those who shouldn't have to have their bravery tested, it's also inspirational. (Hebrew with English subtitles) ★★★ $89.99

Under the Earth (Debajo del Mundo)

(1986, 100 min, Spain/Poland, Beda Docampo Feijoo) This forceful drama celebrating the will of the human spirit recounts the story of a Jewish family's stubborn survival in the aftermath of the Nazi Occupation of wartime Poland. Forced to flee their stable life and live underground in subhuman conditions, the family endures two years of suffering yet remains together through their faith and a hope for a better future. (Spanish with English subtitles) ★★★

Under the Roofs of Paris

(1929, 95 min, France, René Clair) The street life of Paris in the 1920s provides an exceptionally vivid backdrop to this lyrical love triangle of a street singer, his best friend, and the woman they both love. Note: This is a very early sound film, and the quality of sound is not up to par, but it is viewable. (French with English subtitles) ★★★ $14.99

Under the Sun of Satan

(1987, 98 min, France, Maurice Pialat) Pialat's stunning meditation on faith and the battle between good and evil won the Golden Palm for Best Picture at Cannes in 1987, but the controversial film was roundly booed upon that announcement. The story, told in an austere and direct style, is an adaptation of the

Albert Finney in *Under the Volcano*

Georges Bernanos 1926 novel about a tortured priest who feels unworthy of God's love until he encounters a pregnant teenager who has killed her lover. Gérard Depardieu is the village pastor who must battle Satan and Sandrine Bonnaire is the wanton girl in this demanding, intense and provocative film. (French with English subtitles) ★★★ $29.99

Under the Volcano

(1984, 109 min, US, John Huston) Huston's blistering adaptation of the Malcolm Lowry novel showcases a bravura performance by Albert Finney as a former British consul in Mexico whose mental morass prompts a tragic descent into a private hell. Jacqueline Bisset is his estranged wife whose reappearance hastens the inevitable. ★★★½ $79.99

Undercover Blues

(1993, 95 min, US, Herbert Ross) Kathleen Turner and Dennis Quaid play husband and wife espionage agents who know more about martial arts, explosives and the criminal mind than Bruce Lee, James Bond and Hannibal Lecter put together. Having taken time off to have a baby, the couple is lulled back into the realm of undercover when munitions are stolen by a Czechoslovakian sexpot. Watching *Undercover Blues* is like eating a ready-to-mix cake instead of one from scratch. Nothing in this comedic caper seems genuine: The characters, dialogue and situations are all too perfect with a highly artificial aftertaste. ★★½ $9.99

Undercurrent

(1946, 116 min, US, Vincente Minnelli) A familiar melodramatic thriller with Katharine Hepburn as a professor's daughter who marries an industrialist, only to suspect her new husband is evil. *Gaslight* and *Suspicion* did it better, though Hepburn turns in a good performance. Also starring Robert Taylor and Robert Mitchum. ★★ $19.99

The Underneath

(1995, 100 min, US, Steven Soderbergh) Peter Gallagher stars in this understated remake of the film noir classic *Criss-Cross* about a ne'er-do-well ex-con who returns home to "Smallville USA" and becomes involved with his old flame, her gangster boyfriend, and an armored car robbery. Soderbergh's complex narrative (he coauthored the screenplay pseudonymously) relies on an impressive use of color tones to delineate time periods (the stort is told on flashback and double flashback), thus giving the impression of layers being peeled away to reveal "the underneath" of his hauntingly etched characters. Also with Elisabeth Shue, Joe Don Baker, Anjanette Comer and Shelley Duvall. ★★★ $19.99

Underworld

(1997, 95 min, US, Roger Christian) Denis Leary does his best to make this Tarantino knockoff palatable, but to little avail. He plays Johnny Crown, an aging ex-con out to avenge his father's murder attempt (he was left in a coma) on one violent Father's Day night. His other agenda is the rehabilitation of a childhood friend-turned-mobster (Joe Mantegna at his most mannered and annoying). Artificial in the extreme (presumably intended to give the

film a cinematic "no specific time or place" feel but coming across like bad undergrad theatre), *Underworld* apes Tarantino to the point of embarrassment, with none of his style or wit. There's the pop culture conversations (Rodgers & Hammerstein vs. Irving Berlin!), the sudden violence and absurdist situations, '70s & '80s character actors (Larry Bishop, James Tolkan and Abe Vigoda, who is actually quite good in a small bit), and even the sentimental male-bonding ending. ★½ $99.99

Underworld U.S.A

(1961, 99 min, US, Samuel Fuller) Fuller's unrelentingly gritty murder drama stars Cliff Robertson as a young man who, as a youngster, witnessed the brutal murder of his father at the hands of an organized crime syndicate. Vowing revenge, he becomes obsessed with righting his father's death by infiltrating the mob echelon and tracking down the killers. But his plans for revenge become complicated after he finds himself caught between the villainous mob and the FBI, who want him as an informer. ★★★ $69.99

Unfaithfully Yours

(1948, 105 min, US, Preston Sturges) Through the bungling interference of his idiot brother-in-law Rudy Vallee, world-famous symphony conductor Rex Harrison is led to believe that his adoring, doe-eyed wife Linda Darnell is having an affair with his personal assistant. Contains classic sequences in which Harrison's revenge fantasies are brilliantly choreographed to various pieces of music he's conducting. Another nifty little number from Sturges. Remade in 1984 with Dudley Moore in the Harrison role. ★★★½ $59.99

Unfaithfully Yours

(1984, 96 min, US, Howard Zieff) Okay remake of the classic Preston Sturges comedy, with Dudley Moore reprising the Rex Harrison role as a conductor who believes his wife (Nastassja Kinski) guilty of adultery, and fantasizes revenge and murder. Moore is rather good as the exasperated husband, and has a particularly funny scene inside a movie theatre. ★★½ $79.99

An Unfinished Piece for the Player Piano

(1977, 105 min, USSR, Nikita Mikhalkov) Mikhalkov (*Oblomov, Slave of Love*) adapts a Chekhov play which is set in a summer dacha and features an amazing array of ensemble acting. The passions, frustrations and failings of these members of the spoiled gentry provide the nucleus for this Russian *Rules of the Game*. A sumptuous, melancholy period piece. (Russian with English subtitles) ★★★½ $29.99

Unforgettable

(1996, 111 min, US, John Dahl) Fans of Dahl's bitchy, noirish trilogy, *Kill Me Again*, *Red Rock West* and *The Last Seduction*, may find fault with this "A-budget" femme fatale-less thriller, as its roots are planted more firmly in such hallucinatory cinema as *Jacob's Ladder* and *Don't Look Now* rather than his accustomed '40s B-movie vocabulary. However, in combining both genres, Dahl has made a sometimes gripping murder mystery. Ray Liotta stars as a

Clint Eastwood in *Unforgiven*

forensics expert whose unending search for his wife's killer leads him to experiment on himself with a formula (developed by scientist Linda Fiorentino) that enables him to experience the memories of murder victims – and in some cases, to actually see who murdered them. Dahl's visual stylization of Bill Geddie's screenplay focuses on the devastating and sometimes paralyzing power of memory thereby adding an extra dimension to the story. And while Liotta's surefooted performance runs the emotional gamut, Fiorentino need no longer covet the "Helpless Female Award" as she does absolutely nothing to restore the luster of her previous teaming with Dahl in *Seduction*. ★★★ $99.99

An Unforgettable Summer

(1994, 82 min, Romania, Lucian Pintilie) Kristin Scott Thomas gives a haunting performance as the wife of a career officer (Claudiu Bleont) posted in a remote and dangerous corner of eastern Romania during the mid-1920s, a land recently controlled by either Turk, Macedonian or Bulgarian forces. When the codified cruelties of her culture begin to poison her marriage, she is forced to choose between what she knows is right and what is best for her to believe in. Like her earlier work *The Oak*, director Pintilie has fashioned a tale with few "obvious" villains and even fewer clear answers. (English, Romanian, French and Bulgarian with English subtitles) ★★★ $89.99

Unforgiven

(1992, 120 min, US, Clint Eastwood) Eastwood's lyrical, craftsmanlike direction, a brilliantly structured screenplay by David Webb Peoples, a superlative ensemble cast and superior production values all contribute to make this Oscar-winning revisionist western a modern masterpiece. Back in the saddle for the first time since 1985's *Pale Rider*, Eastwood stars as a retired gunfighter who picks up the gun for one last time when a group of prostitutes put a price on the head of a sadistic cowboy. As Clint and partner Morgan Freeman make their way, Gene Hackman's tyrannical sheriff (Hackman deservedly won an Oscar for his sensational performance as Little Bill) prepares for the expected onslaught of hired killers about to descend upon his small town.

One of the many beauties of *Unforgiven* is director Eastwood's homage to the traditional western while at the same time expanding the boundaries of the genre. Not since *Red River* has a film so successfully explored the complexities of moral ambiguity. The myth of the Old West is a bloody one and as Eastwood sees it, death is close up and not at all the stuff of lore. ★★★★ $19.99

The Unforgiven

(1960, 125 min, US, John Huston) Huston's unconventional western adventure concentrates more on racial tension between the white and Indian races than on the usual shoot-em-up hijinks. Set in 1850s Texas, the story concerns a ranching family who become at odds with both their neighbors and an Indian tribe when it is suspected that their adopted daughter is actually an Indian orphan. Gritty performances from Burt Lancaster, Audrey Hepburn and Lillian Gish. ★★★ $14.99

The Unholy

(1988, 100 min, US, Camilo Vila) Ben Cross plays a priest whose miraculous survival from a 20-story fall leads him to a New Orleans parish where demonic events have been occurring. Convoluted and not all that scary. ★½ $14.99

The Unholy Wife

(1957, 94 min, US, John Farrow) With the help of her lover, an adulterous wife (Diana Dors) plans to murder her husband (Rod Steiger). But when the plan goes awry, the pair attempt to put him behind bars instead. A mediocre tale of jealousy and revenge. ★½

Unhook the Stars

(1996, 105 min, US, Nick Cassavetes) Gena Rowlands' marvelous performance is the centerpiece of this affecting, intuitive character study cowritten and directed by her (and John Cassavetes') son Nick. He has given his mother a beautiful part. Rowlands stars as Mildred, a widowed mother of two who has seemingly lived her life for husband and kids. When her troubled daughter leaves home, and with her son married and living in another city, Mildred is reluctant to face the future alone. But her life takes an unusual turn when Monica (Marisa Tomei), her blowsy neighbor, asks Mildred to baby-sit. Thus begins a wonderful relationship between Mildred and six-year-old J.J., and a tentative one between her and Monica, who is more like the attentive daughter Mildred never had. As Mildred, Rowlands is superb in conveying the minute details of this articulate, spirited woman, whose life begins to take meaning in ways she couldn't have thought possible. Gérard Depardieu is engaging as a trucker whose romantic interest in Mildred inspires her self-realization and independence. Obviously, he knows what we know: Mildred and Gena are class acts all the way. ★★★ $102.99

The Unicorn

(1983, 29 min, GB, Carol Reed) Upon learning that unicorns have the power to grant wishes, a young boy sets out to find one. He mistakes a one-horned goat for a unicorn, but the imposter seems to fulfill everyone's wishes anyway. Adapted from "A Kid for Two Farthings," and directed by Reed, who also helmed the original, this is a sweet little tale. ★★★ $14.99

Union City

(1980, 87 min, US, Mark Reichert) Murder and paranoia are set amongst the grit of an industrial city in this convoluted though moody noir tale. A jealous accountant with a lusty wife (Deborah Harry) kills a man who has been stealing his milk bottles. Everett McGill and Pat Benatar (in her dramatic debut) also star. ★★½ $19.99

Universal Soldier

(1992, 98 min, US, Roland Emmerich) It's 'Nam, 1969. Nice Cajun boy Jean-Claude Van Damme is caught in a fight to the death with Dolph Lundgren, a psycho sergeant with a fetish for severed ears. Both die in the showdown only to reappear 25 years later when a group of sleazy Army scientists unveil a line of antiterrorist robots created through a mysterious "hyper acceleration" process using the bodies of dead U.S. soldiers. As in all such stories, science goes awry when Dolph's naturally sadistic tendencies override his programming, renewing his old rivalry with honest Van Damme and shooting up muscle enhancers. Emmerich's testosterone-driven action film is short on any technical prowess, but it certainly does qualify as good, dumb fun. (Available letterboxed and pan & scan) ★★ $14.99

Unlawful Entry

(1992, 111 min, US, Jonathan Kaplan) Affluent L.A. couple Kurt Russell and Madeleine Stowe have their home broken into. Into their lives enters friendly policeman Ray Liotta. Thus begins yet another in the continuing long line of psycho thrillers which intimate that the trusted person next to you is out to get you (*Fatal Attraction, Hand That Rocks the Cradle*, etc). While those two films had varying degrees of suspense and credibility, *Unlawful Entry* is nothing more than a first-draft throwaway which somehow bypassed rewrite and went straight to production. However, Liotta, as a menacing cop-on-the-beat who turns Russell and Stowe's lives into a living hell, brings just the right amount of intoxicating villainy and demonic glee to his character. He almost makes it worthwhile. ★½ $19.99

An Unmarried Woman

(1978, 124 min, US, Paul Mazursky) Jill Clayburgh's sensational performance is the heart of director Mazursky's penetrating drama about a dutiful wife who learns to be self-reliant after her husband leaves her for another woman. Alan Bates also stars as Clayburgh's new and sensitive paramour. One of Mazursky's most accomplished and poignant films. ★★★½ $69.99

The Unnamable

(1988, 87 min, US, Jean-Paul Ouellette) A group of college students spend the night in a haunted house to dispel rumors that a horrible creature lives there. Guess what happens. Nothing new, and not all that proficient, but there are a few scares. Based on a story by H.P. Lovecraft. ★★ $9.99

Unnatural Pursuits

(1991, 143 min, GB, Christopher Morahan) Simon Gray's West End comedy dissecting the artistic process makes for a fast and gloriously funny adaptation. In a performance reminiscent of his classic portrayal in "Butley," Alan Bates is remarkable as disheveled, acerbic playwright Hamish Partt, a chain-smoking alcoholic whose obsession to rewrite his newest play takes him from London to Los Angeles to Dallas to New York all the while experiencing a mental breakdown. In a series of escalating hallucinations, Hamish is haunted by skateboarding street people when not breaking into musical production numbers. Gray's masterful script examines Hamish's deterioration as he has thrust upon him insecure stage directors, bombastic producers, flirtatious Southern belle reporters, self-centered actors and an ogling public. Richard Wilson is splendid in support as a twit of a legendary stage director, and Bob Balaban, Deborah Rush and John Mahoney are a few of the ugly Americans Hamish meets. ★★★★ $19.99

Unsane

(1984, 92 min, Italy, Dario Argento) Originally titled *Tenebrae*, this is Argento's return to the "giallo" murder mystery genre after a brief

Unstrung Heroes

Marisa Tomei (l.) and Rosie Perez in *Untamed Heart*

foray (via *Suspiria* and *Inferno*) into a more supernatural horror. Anthony Franciosa plays Peter Neal, a popular American writer of murder mystery novels who comes to Rome for a publicity tour. He soon learns that a killer is using his book as inspiration for a series of murders. Neal and his secretary begin to help the police in their search for the killer and, like all good Argento heroes, eventually set off on their own to solve the mystery — descending into a world of madness and murder which mirrors the worst aspects of his bloody novels. *Unsane* is remarkably strong in narrative content for one of Argento's films, which usually sacrifice story for style. Its look and sound, however, do not suffer in the least, for the film is brilliantly lit and shot, including one absolutely terrifying shot at the very end as the killer is revealed. This American release is edited by 13 minutes. ★★★

The Unsinkable Molly Brown

(1964, 128 min, US, Charles Walters) Debbie Reynolds has her best film role as mountain girl-cum-society darling and *Titanic* survivor Molly Brown in this splashy screen version of Meredith Willson's (*The Music Man*) Broadway musical. Harve Presnell also stars, and songs include "I Ain't Down Yet" and "I'll Never Say No to You." ★★★ $19.99

Unstrung Heroes

(1995, 93 min, US, Diane Keaton) Young Steven Lidz (Nathan Watt) is not having a very good summer. His father (John Turturro) is a narcissistic, somewhat caustic inventor who clings with almost religous zeal to the tenants of scientific inquiry. His mother (Andie MacDowell) is slowly dying of cancer, though Steven hasn't been made privy to this fact. And their new maid, hired to pick up the duties of his ailing mom, is a bonafide bitch. Finding it all too much to take, the 12-year-old Steven runs off to live with his two uncles (Michael Richards and Maury Chaykin), a pair of paranoid schizophrenic, socialist Jews who live in an apartment piled high with decades worth of newspapers and closets full of rubber balls. Keaton's second directorial effort (her first was 1987's quasi-documentary *Heaven*) is tinged with melancholy and tempered with mirthful nostalgia and provides many a warm-

hearted moment. But ultimately the storytelling suffers at the hands of a script that, by trying to squeeze in too much, boils down to a series of loosely connected scenes that offer very little character development. Richards (who draws heavily on his Kramer persona from TV's "Seinfeld") gives a performance which, though filled with schtick, offers the only glimmer of complexity. ★★½ $19.99

Untamed Heart

(1993, 102 min, US, Tony Bill) Christian Slater gives a touching performance as a busboy whose childhood heart condition has left him emotionally and physically scarred. He's soon brought out of his silent shell by his love for a waitress (Marisa Tomei). Tomei's character is one of those women from Oprah or Geraldo "who love and give too much"; yet her distress as men walk all over her is somehow endearing and makes her attraction to Slater's speechless recluse all that more convincing. They have a real chemistry — even if Slater is more alluring before he opens his mouth and begins to pour his guts out. Though its pacing is a little off (the beginning is slow and the ending unravels too quickly), *Untamed Heart* is a sweet, warm, there's-some-one-out-there-for-everyone film that teeters quietly on the brink of being a real tearjerker. Special mention to Rosie Perez as Tomei's sidekick. ★★★ $9.99

Until the End of the World

(1991, 160 min, US, Wim Wenders) Director Wenders takes the viewer on the ultimate 'round-the-world odyssey with this futuristic "road movie," set in 1999. Filled with lots of high-tech future shock images and gadgetry, the film stars William Hurt as a man carrying a top secret device and on the run from industrial bounty hunters. He hooks up with Solveig Dommartin and together they lead their pursuers on a global chase which takes them from Paris to Berlin to Moscow to Tokyo to San Francisco and beyond. After 90 minutes of non-stop action, they wind up in the Australian Outback where the film slows to a more familiar Wenders crawl — a shift which may annoy some viewers, but will delight others. As in his other films, Wenders portrays a world in which people are desperately seeking a sense of self-understanding while craving human contact — it's a world in which, despite the explosion in global communication technology, we are more alone than ever. Max von Sydow and Jeanne Moreau costar as Hurt's mother and father. A pulsing soundtrack includes songs by The Talking Heads, U2, R.E.M., Peter Gabriel, Lou Reed and others. ★★★ $19.99

Until They Sail

(1957, 95 min, US, Robert Wise) Based on James A. Michener's wartime novel, this military drama is vintage soap opera but it's not without its compelling moments. Jean

Simmons, Joan Fontaine, Piper Laurie and Sandra Dee play sisters in WWII New Zealand. With the men of their village, including their brother and Simmons' husband, overseas, the town's women become romantic targets for the visiting American soldiers. Paul Newman is one of them. Playwright Robert Anderson ("I Never Sang for My Father") adapted the screenplay, which explores such adult themes as infidelity, wartime romance, and moral and sexual attitudes. A good double feature would be John Schlesinger's *Yanks*. ★★½ $19.99

The Untold Story

(1993, 95 min, Hong Kong, Herman Yau) Based on a true incident, this grisly tale plays like *Silence of the Lambs* with a Chinatown twist. Anthony Wong stars as a restauranteur in Macao who becomes the prime suspect in a series of murders and disappearances. The police department (led by Danny Lee) at first befriend him and sample his delicious complimentary pork buns, until they discover that they've found their missing persons — ground up within the filling of the buns! The remainder of the film shows their brutal attempts to make Wong confess to his crimes, which include having him beaten by the jailed brother of one of the people he's murdered. Wong soon becomes a victim in his own right and begins to break under the constant pressure. Wong's performance (for which he won Best Actor at the 1993 Hong Kong Film Awards) lifts the film well above its lurid subject matter; he actually manages to make the viewer care (at least a little) about this butcher's plight. Part police procedural and part serial killer horror film, *The Untold Story* is definitely meant for strong stomachs only, and will quite possibly change the way you look at dim sum. (Cantonese with English subtitles) ★★★½ $79.99

The Untouchables

(1987, 119 min, US, Brian De Palma) Director De Palma's crowning achievement is a rousing and grandly stylistic gangster movie set in crime-laden 1920s Chicago. Kevin Costner plays Eliot Ness, an idealistic government agent who goes after mob kingpin Al Capone, getting a lot of help from the cop on the beat (Sean Connery). Robert De Niro plays Capone with over-the-top abandon, and Connery is amazing in his Oscar-winning portrayal. Also with Andy Garcia and Charles Martin Smith, both first-rate, as Ness' two other "untouchables." De Palma's train station sequence, a nod to the "The Odessa Steps" sequence in *Battleship Potemkin*, is a knockout. Written by David Mamet. ★★★★ $14.99

Unzipped

(1995, 76 min, US, Douglas Keeve) This delightfully playful documentary romp through the fashion world with designer Isaac Mizrahi is a surefire crowd pleaser due in large part to his irrepressible and engaging personality. The film's action centers around the swirl of creative energy Mizrahi and staff are pumping into preparing his fall '94 collection, which is inspired by *Nanook of the North* and *Call of the Wild*. Amidst the chaos, Mizrahi (a boyishly cute, chubby Jewish queen from Brooklyn who sports a Medusa-like shock of hair) lets loose a barrage of bitchy, yet not too

573

vicious one-liners, social critiques and, of course, barbs at other designers. The film culminates with the Big Show in New York, which, in Mizrahi's case, is a brilliant piece of performance art featuring a transparent scrim that reveals the backstage chaos to the gathered celebs — it is an exquisite stroke which elevates Mizrahi's presentation to the level of guerrilla theatre. As filmed by Mizrahi's former lover Keeve, *Unzipped* is as raucous and raw as its subject — its at times annoyingly jagged camera work is saved only by masterful, zippy MTV-paced editing. The film also features the inevitable parade of super models including Cindy Crawford and Naomi Campbell, to name but a few. ★★★ $19.99

Up!

(1976, 80 min, US, Russ Meyer) Outrageously buxom women and dumb, muscular men laying their sexually aggressive prowess on the line. Narrated by a perpetually bouncing Kitten Natividad. Probably Russ' most explicit feature and definitely his most eccentric. ★★½ $79.99

Up Close and Personal

(1996, 124 min, US, Jon Avnet) Loosely based on the life of Jessica Savitch by way of *A Star Is Born*, this polished if sometimes gawky romantic drama tracing the rise of a TV newscaster doesn't have as much to say about the news industry as it pretends to, but offers especially attractive performances from its two leads. Sweet, naive but eager, Pfeiffer's aspiring newscaster lands a job on a Miami TV station. Under the tutelage of Redford, the station manager and an experienced newsman, Pfeiffer works her way up from weather girl to anchor all the while they fall in love and marry, experiencing the ups and downs inherent in a relationship marked by one spouse's sudden success. *Up Close and Personal* is punctuated by several terrific scenes which spotlight the business of news reporting, including a tense and prolonged sequence behind the walls of Philadelphia's Holmesburg Prison. But the film also gives in to clichés and coincidences, neither of which suit the talents of its two stars. ★★½ $19.99

Up in Smoke

(1978, 85 min, US, Lou Adler) Here's a film which, given the rabid antidrug hysteria of our conservative times, could never have been produced today. This first (and best) film from that doped-up comic duo, Cheech & Chong, may be dated, but it still provides kilos of laughs. All we can say is that if there are still some of you out there who enjoy the occasional mind-bender, be grateful that this testament to the halcyon days of unbridled substance abuse is still available on video. ★★★ $14.99

Up to a Certain Point

(1985, 70 min, Cuba, Tomás Gutiérrez Alea) Director Alea (*Strawberry & Chocolate*) tackles several themes, including politics, male chauvinism and marital infidelity, to bring about the tale of a writer and his attempts at writing an anti-machismo film for his actress wife. Oscar Alvarez is the screenwriter Oscar, caught between his feelings of love and the direction of his project. Mirta Ibarra shines as Lina, the independent and alluring dock work-

er who becomes the role model for his main character and the object of his affection. Interspliced with the story line are interviews with dock workers on everything from their opinions about women on the job to their labor complaints. This film is well worth the effort not only for its interesting portrayal of somewhat modern-day Cuban life but also for its honesty in the portrayal of struggles which go beyond wage earnings. (Spanish with English subtitles) ★★★ $79.99

The Uprising

(1980, 96 min, Nicaragua, Peter Lilienthal) Filmed just months after the Sandinista revolution, this raw and impassioned drama recruited the real-life peasants and soldiers of the country to authentically re-create the atmosphere of a people and of a land thrust into turbulent revolt. The story, set in the university town of León, centers on a young man, a member of Somoza's National Guard who, with the help of his father, comes to be a supporter of the rebel Sandinistas. Kind of a fictionalized documentary, this simple and direct story celebrates the solidarity and heroics of these impoverished people. (Spanish with English subtitles) ★★★ $69.99

Uptown Saturday Night

(1974, 104 min, US, Sidney Poitier) The first of three films to star Sidney Poitier and Bill Cosby. Cosby plays a man who wins a $50,000 lottery. One problem though — his wallet was taken during a holdup. Cosby and Poitier must get through a maze filled with scheming gangsters, con men and women. There are a number of great supporting characters including Richard Pryor, Flip Wilson, Roscoe Lee Browne and Harry Belafonte. A bit dated and not as good as its follow-up *Let's Do It Again*, but it certainly is fun. ★★½ $14.99

Uranus

(1991, 100 min, France, Claude Berri) This rather disappointing and convoluted drama is set in a small French village thrown into chaos immediately after WWII when it and its now-

Communist government try to come to grips with its past and attempt to sort out among themselves who were the patriots and who were the informants, Nazi sympathizers and collaborators. Gérard Depardieu steals the show as a drunken, brutish bully of a bartender with a newfound love of poetry and a nose seemingly bigger than the 14th arrondissement who is falsely implicated as an informant. Jean-Pierre Marielle is a taciturn patriot who, against his own reasoning, hides a suspected collaborator in his flat and Philippe Noiret plays a schoolteacher in a role so sickeningly sweet as to suggest a spoof. At the heart of the film is an interesting idea of a people torn apart and in near hysterics by their own actions, but the execution by director Berri is too slow and bland to create much involvement for the viewer. (French with English subtitles) ★★ $89.99

Urban Cowboy

(1980, 135 min, US, James Bridges) Cowboy John Travolta tries to lasso cowgirl Debra Winger at Gilley's Bar in Texas in this involving romantic drama. The film which created the mechanical bull stir (for awhile). ★★½

Urinal

(1991, 100 min, Canada, John Greyson) Less provocative and explicit than the title suggests, this low-budget Canadian production is a documentary-style talk fest centering on homosexual repression through the ages and, more specifically, the well-publicized entrapment cases and crackdowns in Ontario's public rest rooms by a homophobic police force. The film's premise is that several prominently rumored gays, lesbians and bisexuals from the past (Yukio Mishima, Sergei Eisenstein, Frida Kahlo, Frances Loring, Langston Hughes and Florence Whyle) are mysteriously brought together in a Toronto apartment where they hold a series of discussions on the sociology of homosexuality and how to counter gay repression. Despite its static and awkward dramatic pretensions, the film is an interesting and literate examination of gay and lesbian history as

John Travolta in his first career: *Urban Cowboy*

well as a call for action against discrimination. ★★½ $39.99

Urotsukidoji – Legend of the Overfiend

(1992, 108 min, Japan, Hideki Takayama) There's a legend which states that the Earth consists of three dimensions: The Human World, The World of Beasts and The World of Monster Demons. Every 3,000 years, the Overfiend is brought to life to unite these three dimensions into a new world of peace and happiness. Amano, from the Man-Beast World, has been on the trail of the Overfiend for over 300 years, but he now realizes that the new world that the Overfiend is supposed to create may be sickening beyond human comprehension. This vile, Grand Guignol-esque Japanimation epic not only pushes the limits of animation, but also manages to conjure images that challenge many live-action films. Not for those who are easily offended. ★★★½ $29.99

Urotsukidoji 2: Legend of the Demon Womb

(1991/1993, 88 min, Japan, Hideki Takayama) Outrageous, ultra-violent follow-up to *Urotsukidoji: Legend of the Overfiend* that picks up the story in 1944 Nazi Germany. As American bombers soar towards Berlin, a revolting Satanic ritual takes place below: Hitler and his minions are using the monstrous Nazi Death Rape Machine to rend the boundaries separating the Human World from the World of Man-Beasts and the World of Monster Demons. Intense and unbelievably adult-oriented animation at its best; not for all tastes, but more than worth a look for open-minded viewers. ★★★ $29.99

Used Cars

(1980, 111 min, US, Robert Zemeckis) It's the battle of the used car salesmen as Kurt Russell squares off against Jack Warden in a no-holds-barred customer-getting contest. An uproarious and daffy comedy written by Bob Gale and director Zemeckis. ★★★ $9.99

Used People

(1992, 116 min, US, Beeban Kidron) The comparisons of *Used People* to *Moonstruck* and *Fried Green Tomatoes* are inevitable. All share a sentimental bent without being too cute about it; wacky characters find themselves in wackier situations; and members of near-dysfunctional families endear themselves not only to the viewer but, eventually, to each other. And if *Used People* does seem very familiar at times, it's the characters' familiarity which makes this humorous and beguiling comedy-drama a welcome visitor. Heading a top-notch cast, Shirley MacLaine plays a recently widowed Jewish wife and mother from Queens. On the day of her husband's funeral, she is asked on a date by determined Italian restauranteur Marcello Mastroianni. Against her better judgment, she

The Usual Suspects

agrees. What follows is a series of disastrous family get-togethers, culture clashes and romantic pursuits as Mastroianni tries to capture the no-nonsense heart of his intended. The film is immeasurably aided by the likes of Kathy Bates, Jessica Tandy, Sylvia Sidney and Marcia Gay Harden in supporting roles. ★★★ $19.99

The Usual Suspects

(1995, 105 min, US, Bryan Singer) This witty and ingenious noir thriller is a delicious up and down ride on a twisting plotline that involves a rag-tag assemblage of small-time hoods who, having met in a lineup, join forces and commit to performing *one* job together. Predictably, this leads to further involvement that ultimately begins to get out of hand. The group's reluctant leader, Dean Keaton (Gabriel Byrne), is a former big-time grifter whose best efforts to go straight can't get him off the most-wanted list of Special Agent Kujan (Chazz Palminteri). He's joined by a couple of smaller hoodlums (Stephen Baldwin and Benicio Del Toro), a weapons expert (Kevin Pollak) and a talkative, crippled flunky known as Verbal (Kevin Spacey). Opening with a grisly massacre on a lonesome San Pedro, California, pier, the film unfolds through flashback as the tale is told by Verbal, the lone survivor, to a rapt agent Kujan. To further thicken the already Byzantine plot is the lurking presence of a mythical, almost Mephistophelian underworld figure known as Keyser Söze, who may be the mastermind behind the massacre. The film is brimming with scintillating performances, most notably from Palminteri and Byrne, but while no one delivers a dud, it is Oscar winner Spacey who walks away with the movie. His Verbal is a study in criminal paranoia accented by physi-

cal vulnerability. Director Singer and screenwriter Christopher McQuarrie (another Oscar winner) team up well with cinematographer Howard Cummings to create a brilliant and timeless crime story that's an immediate classic of the genre. (Available letterboxed and pan & scan) ★★★★ $19.99

Utu

(1983, 104 min, New Zealand, Geoff Murphy) This violent and spectacularly photographed film crosses the boundaries of both art film and action flick. Set during the Maori uprising in rural 1870s New Zealand, the story focuses on a Maori ex-army sergeant whose family and village are wiped out during a raid and who becomes the radical and vengeful leader of a group of rebellious natives intent on eradicating the white settlers by any means possible. An exciting and bloody story of the fight for survival. ★★★ $79.99

Utz

(1992, 95 min, GB/Germany/Italy, George Sluizer) From the director of the provocative *The Vanishing* comes this elegant, spare and quietly involving drama. Filmed in English, the story focuses on Baron von Utz (Armin Mueller-Stahl), a wealthy Czechoslovakian collector of German porcelain figurines. Through a series of flashbacks, we learn of the roots of his lifelong obsession with his collection as well as his mysterious life. Peter Riegert co-stars as an international antique broker who befriends him in the hope of obtaining the collection after his death, Paul Scofield is his eccentric lifelong friend and Brenda Fricker is his more-than-an-employee housekeeper. Beautiful locales in Prague provide an exotic backdrop to the gentle character study. ★★★ $29.99

V

Vagabond

(1985, 105 min, France, Agnès Varda) Sandrine Bonnaire is mesmerizing in this hauntingly nihilistic account of an aimless young woman's final days. The beginning of the film finds the girl's frozen body in a ditch. Then told in flashback by the last people to have had contact with her, the film attempts to piece together the life and values of this complex teenager. A stunning film experience and one of the most important and powerful French films of the past 20 years. (French with English subtitles) ★★★★ $24.99

Valdez Is Coming

(1971, 90 min, US, Edwin Sherin) Burt Lancaster gives a solid performance as Valdez, part-time lawman, part-time stagecoach shotgun, who is set up to kill a black man wrongly accused of murder. Realizing the mistake he has made, he attempts to accept responsibility for the dead man's pregnant Indian wife. This leads him on an odyssey through a barren, treacherous landscape populated by men without ethics or compassion. The callousness of the film's villains is in sharp contrast to Valdez's quiet dignity and a moral strength which dictates action that will not be deterred. Good ensemble acting helps overcome a somewhat pedestrian treatment of an intriguing plot line which slowly unravels just who is guilty of what. Based on a novel by Elmore Leonard. ★★½ $19.99

Valentina

(1983, 90 min, Spain, Antonio J. Betancor) Adapted from Ramon J. Sender's celebrated novel, this deeply moving film, set in a small town in northern Spain, examines a pre-adolescent boy's passionate love for the lyrical Valentina and the efforts of their families to keep them apart. Anthony Quinn is featured as the boy's understanding teacher. (Spanish with English subtitles) ★★★

Valentino

(1977, 127 min, GB, Ken Russell) Russell creates some stunning visuals but comes up short in dramatic terms in this lurid exposé on the life of silent screen star Rudolph Valentino. Opening with the frenzied scene of his funeral, the film's flashbacks attempt to chart his rise to fame as well as uncover the man behind the image. As Valentino, Rudolf Nureyev — who looks the part – is, unfortunately, wooden and uninspiring. Russell, who in the past has not side-stepped homosexual themes, curiously down-plays the Latin Lover's gayness in favor of a man constantly trying to prove his masculinity. Michelle Phillips appears as Valentino's wife/Svengali, Natasha Rambova, and Leslie Caron plays her lover, actress Nazimova. ★★ $19.99

Valley Girl

(1983, 95 min, US, Martha Coolidge) Like, can love last between a true Val (Deborah Foreman) and a punker from Hollywood (Nicolas Cage)? It's, like, a war of the cliques in this amusing little film about California culture clashes. ★★½ $9.99

The Valley (Obscured by Clouds)

(1972, 106 min, France, Barbet Schroeder) This legendary cult film is an aurally hypnotic and sensually seductive drama of the spiritual and sexual enlightenment of a group of Westerners who venture into the uncharted, mystic rainforest of New Guinea. With ravishing photography by Nestor Almendros and a spacey soundtrack by Pink Floyd, the film follows Bulle Ogier, a bored diplomat's wife who travels into the interior of a strange land searching for the feathers of a near-extinct bird for retailing in Parisian boutiques. Along the way she meets up with several hippies, dreamers and dropouts. Together, they experience a transformation of spirit when they meet the indigenous Mapuga tribesmen and travel to a secret and strangely powerful "valley of the gods." (French with English subtitles) ★★★ $59.99

Valley of the Dolls

(1967, 123 min, US, Mark Robson) Trashy, melodramatic piece of camp heaven based on Jacqueline Susann's best-selling novel that takes us on a hell-bound highway of drugs, sex, drinks and infidelity and the rise and fall of starlets in the entertainment biz. Starring Patty Duke, Sharon Tate, Susan Hayward, Lee Grant and Martin Milner, the film at times drifts into cliché-ridden waters, but is nevertheless chock full of those absolutely absurd soap opera-ish elements which make this genre so much fun. ★★★

Valmont

(1989, 137 min, GB/France, Milos Forman) Opulent settings in exotic European locales and meticulously designed period costumes can't save this uninvolving drama, based on Choderlos de Laclos' 1782 novel "Les Liaisons Dangereuses." Sadly, director Forman misses the central idea behind the story of intrigue amidst the French aristocracy by not delving into the characters' icy hearts and as a result, the film is all spectacle and no soul. Colin Firth's Valmont is, by his looks, well suited for the devilishly charming seducer, but lacks the calculating and complex personality that the

role requires. Annette Bening is sweet and pretty as the Marquise and would be the most miscast character in the film if not for Henry Thomas' somnolent role as Danceny. Stick to Stephen Frears' mesmerizing *Dangerous Liaisons*, made a year earlier, and based on the same story. ★ $14.99

Vampire in Brooklyn

(1995, 95 min, US, Wes Craven) Director Craven brings a seductive and eerie style to this shadowy vampire tale, and Eddie Murphy gives an unusually restrained and effective performance, but *Vampire in Brooklyn* ultimately succumbs to its unimaginative screenplay which is not nearly funny enough to be comedy or scary enough to be horror. Murphy stars as a vampire who comes to Brooklyn (in an impressively mounted opening) searching for a lost soul mate. He immediately finds her in the person of policewoman Angela Bassett, and begins to court her while dining on Brooklyn's not-so-finest denizens. Bassett takes a no-nothing role and brings dimension and pathos to what isn't there, giving a forceful, even inspired performance — the lady can act! Murphy abandons his usual winking at the audience, and even plays two additional characters rather well. But neither star is serviced by a thoroughly flat and undeveloped story and dialogue. ★★ $14.99

The Vampire Lovers

(1970, 89 min, GB, Roy Ward Baker) The voluptuous Ingrid Pitt stars as a lesbian vampire in this sexy but faithful redo of J. Sheridan Le Fanu's "Carmilla." Produced by Hammer Studios, the film was a groundbreaking and daring attempt to breathe new life into the horror genre by adding lesbian bloodsuckers and sexy seductions. ★★★

Vampire's Kiss

(1989, 103 min, US, Robert Biermen) If you thought Griffin Dunne had a bad night in Martin Scorsese's *After Hours*, wait till you get a load of New York's truly dark side. Nicolas Cage stars as a literary agent who unwisely picks up beautiful Jennifer Beals in a singles

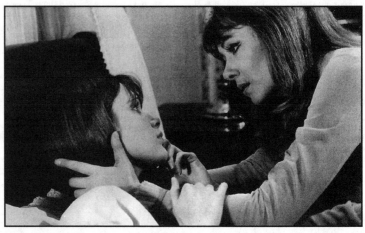

The Vampire Lovers

bar and, after a bite in the neck, becomes convinced that he's turning into a vampire. The film alternates between rip-roaring black comedy and mind-bendingly surrealistic fantasy. It is Cage's over-the-top performance which is at the heart of this sardonic work. ★★★ $9.99

Vampyr

(1931, 83 min, Germany/France, Carl Dreyer) Death and evil hover over everyone in Dreyer's psychological horror film. Dislocated shadows, eerie sounds and unexplained mysteries conspire to make *Vampyr* one of the screen's most visceral thrillers. (German with English subtitles) ★★★½ $29.99

Van Gogh

(1992, 155 min, France, Maurice Pialat) Joining the parade of recent films about Vincent van Gogh is this beautifully photographed French version starring Jacques Dutronc in the lead role. Unlike previous visions of the artist – Vincente Minnelli's *Lust for Life* starring Kirk Douglas, Robert Altman's *Vincent and Theo* starring Tim Roth or Paul Cox's documentary *Vincent* – Pialat's look at Van Gogh's last days in Auvers-Sur-Oise eschews the standard portrait of a tortured soul. Instead we see a man who lusts after women, enjoys life's pleasures and who, in the end, may have taken his own life more out of remorse over his own sensitivities than his failure to gain acceptance. Dutronc won a César Award for Best Actor for his understated portrayal. (French with English subtitles) ★★★ $19.99

Van Gogh in Arles: In Brilliant Lights

(1984, 57 min, US, Gene Searchinger) The 15 months Vincent van Gogh spent in Arles was undoubtedly the apex of his career and by far his most productive. By focusing on the works themselves and not as much on the artist's personal turmoil, *In Brilliant Lights* ends up dispelling many myths, bringing the artist as a human being into sharper focus. ★★★ $49.99

Vanina Vanini

(1969, 125 min, Italy, Roberto Rossellini) Set in 1824, this opulent political and romantic drama is a complex neorealist-influenced film that deals with political and religious corruption, social inequality, guilt and betrayal. Young Pietro, a revolutionary soldier, is sent to Rome to kill a traitor to the cause. Needing to hide from the authorities, he finds refuge in the lavish home of an aristocrat where he falls in love with the man's beautiful daughter. The two travel back north but the social differences that keep them apart soon erupt into betrayal. (Italian with English subtitles) ★★★ $59.99

The Vanishing

(1988, 105 min, The Netherlands, George Sluizer) One of the best foreign films released in the 1990s, this riveting psycho-thriller offers an unflinching look into the shadowy recesses of the human psyche. While on holiday in the South of France, a young Dutch couple stop for gas at a service station. While he fills the tank, she goes into a restaurant and mysteriously disappears without a trace. Unable to convince the police that foul play was involved, the man returns home, only to be haunted by her disappearance until he decides to retrace their steps,

hoping to entrap the possible abductor/murderer. An unrelentingly taut account that eschews the easy depiction of violence for the much more menacing idea of psychological obsession and domination. (An inferior American version was made in 1993 starring Jeff Bridges and also directed by Sluizer) (French and Dutch with English subtitles) ★★★½ $19.99

The Vanishing

(1993, 110 min, US, George Sluizer) If ever there was a film that screamed "see the original!" – this is it. Where the unique 1988 Dutch chiller was a tense, philosophical psycho-mystery which explored the tenuous relationship we all have with fate, this remake is little more than a formulaic Hollywood spine-tingler. Kiefer Sutherland stars as a young man whose life is shattered when his girlfriend (Sandra Bullock) inexplicably disappears at a road stop. He searches for her over the years until one day a slightly loony science professor (Jeff Bridges) shows up to shed some light on her fate. Director Sluizer, who also directed the original, has made a number of ill-advised changes including completely rewriting the ending which, in the first film, left the viewer with a stunned sense of helplessness. ★ $19.99

Vanya on 42nd Street

(1994, 119 min, US, Louis Malle) Malle reteams with his old *My Dinner with Andre* pals Wallace Shawn and Andre Gregory for this riveting theatrical exposition. Gregory and Shawn assembled a group of actors on a probono basis and spent four years rehearsing their bare-bones (no sets, no props, no nothin') production of David Mamet's adaptation of Chekhov's "Uncle Vanya." Entranced by their work, Malle set out to make a record and the result is invigorating. Filmed in the dilapidated New Amsterdam Theatre on 42nd Street in New York, *Vanya* is as close to true theatre on film as one will ever see. Mamet's script is 100% true to Chekhov and in the hands of stage director Gregory and his accomplished cast, his masterful examination of spiritual yearning in the face of brutal existential angst is brought vividly to life. The cast includes Shawn as Vanya; a radiant and severe Julianne Moore is Yelana, his sister-in-law and object of his desire; and Larry Pine is her other suitor, the political idealist Dr. Astrov. All are magnificent and stand up well to the scrutiny of cinematographer Declan Quinn's extreme close-ups. ★★★★ $19.99

Varietease

(1955, 75 min, US, Irving Klaw) Legendary "trailer-park Barbie" and cheesecake queen Betty Page is featured doing a torrid harem dance, along with French import Lili St. Cyr, sultry Chris LaChris, and hot transvestite Vicky Lynn in this great burlesque presentation. Outstanding color photography, campy musical numbers and zany comedy routines make this a must-see for those in search of unusual entertainment. ★★★ $24.99

Variety

(1925, 75 min, Germany, E.A. Dupont) Classic silent melodrama with Emil Jannings in fine

The Valley (Obscured by Clouds)

form as an aging circus acrobat who falls in love with a beautiful young dancer, only to become involved in murder when a handsome young man shows affection for the girl. ★★★½

Variety

(1984, 100 min, US, Bette Gordon) Christine (Sandy McLeod) works in the box office of a porno theatre in New York's squalid Times Square district. Exposed to this thick aura of sexual promise and fantasy, she becomes obsessed, not with the films, but with the endless parade of men who come to consume them. Eventually, she becomes fixated on one particular customer – a union official with ties to the mob – and she finds herself acting upon her own voyeuristic urges. This gritty, complex film about the allure and repulsion of pornography is indeed a fascinating study of the chasm between sexual desire and its gratification. ★★★

Variety Lights

(1952, 93 min, Italy, Federico Fellini & Alberto Lattuada) Codirected by Fellini and Lattuada and starring their wives (Giulietta Masina and Carla Del Poggio), *Variety Lights* explores the tawdry lifestyle of a traveling vaudeville troupe. When an ambitious young woman joins them, the group finds their lives shaken as the newcomer immediately begins an affair with the much older maestro. The blending of Lattuada's neorealist techniques with Fellini's budding imagination, as well as his interest in eccentric individuals, creates a world of alluring illusion beneath which lies the much sadder reality of everyday life. (Italian with English subtitles) ★★★ $29.99

The Velvet Touch

(1948, 97 min, US, John Gage) Rosalind Russell gives a good performance in this nifty thriller as a famous stage actress who murders her producer and becomes involved in a cat-and-mouse game with the investigating police detective. ★★★ $19.99

Vengeance Is Mine

(1979, 129 min, Japan, Shohei Imamura) This unrelenting probe of the criminal mind is powerfully brought to the screen by Imamura, director of the highly acclaimed *Ballad of Narayama* and long considered one of Japan's leading contemporary filmmakers. Structured in a documentary style, this exciting thriller stars Ken Ogata (*Mishima*) as a killer on the run. He eludes the law's net and leads the police along a bloody path paved with fraud, violence and murder. An unusual and unforgettable portrait of a "man without a heart." (Japanese with English subtitles) ★★★½ $39.99

Venus in Furs

(1970, 86 min, GB, Jess Franco) A murky drama about a jazz musician who falls for a mysterious woman who is really a recently washed ashore corpse. In the end, she turns out to be the Angel of Death come to Earth to avenge a murder by twisting and contorting a psychopathic killer's already feeble mind. Confused yet? James Darren and Klaus Kinski cannot keep this one afloat. ★½

Vera Cruz

(1954, 94 min, US, Robert Aldrich) Gary Cooper and Burt Lancaster are two adventurers involved in political intrigue in 1860s Mexico. This flavorful western also stars Denise Darcel, Cesar Romero, Ernest Borgnine and Charles Bronson. ★★★ $14.99

The Verdict

(1982, 129 min, US, Sidney Lumet) Paul Newman gives an extraordinary performance as a down-on-his-luck lawyer given a last chance at self-redemption when he is hired in a medical malpractice case. A riveting courtroom drama and character study, with a superior supporting cast including James Mason as Newman's ruthless adversary, Jack Warden, Charlotte Rampling, Milo O'Shea and Lindsay Crouse. ★★★½ $9.99

Vernon, Florida

(1987, 60 min, US, Errol Morris) Morris' wonderful, quirky look at the eccentric residents of a small backwoods town in the Florida panhandle. ★★★½ $79.99

Veronico Cruz

(1987, 106 min, Argentina/GB, Miguel Pereira) The bittersweet story about the relationship between a young boy and his schoolteacher is set against the debacle of the Malvinas/Falklands War. Perched high in the outback of the Argentinian highlands, a young boy is raised by his grandmother after his mother dies and his father abandons him. In this remote area, untouched by civilization, the boy, Veronico, grows up. His life, as well as that of the entire pueblo, is changed forever after the military junta invades their tranquil world and pits friend against friend in a relentless and senseless power struggle. A quietly moving drama of individuals caught up in the maelstrom of political zealousness. Winner of the Silver Bear – Berlin Film Festival. (Spanish with English subtitles) ★★★ $79.99

Veronika Voss

(1981, 104 min, West Germany, Rainer Werner Fassbinder) A stunning profile of a faded film star's descent into morphine addiction and emotional dependency is Fassbinder's eerie black-and-white tribute to *Sunset Boulevard*. A very un-Fassbinder-like cinematic tour de force with ceaseless camera movement and striking characterizations. The director's final film in his trilogy on the German condition during and immediately after WWII. With Rosel Zech in the title role. (German with English subtitles) ★★★½ $19.99

Vertigo

(1958, 120 min, US, Alfred Hitchcock) Perhaps the most masterful achievement in a career strewn with classics, *Vertigo* is a multilayered summary of Hitchcock's prime obsessions: the fears of physical and psychological intimacy, emotional commitment and mortality. James Stewart is superb as the detective with a debilitating case of acrophobia, which costs him not only his job but also the woman he is desperately drawn to. Kim Novak portrays the illusive heroine, a dreamlike incarnation of womanhood whose shifting identity unhinges Stewart's haunted hero. Remastered in THX. (Letterboxed version) ★★★★ $19.99

A Very Brady Sequel

(1996, 89 min, US, Arlene Sanford) After their hilarious 1995 big-screen success, the entire Brady clan – yes, those vapidly naive family values icons stuck in the loud polyester world of the '70s – returns in this equally skewering sequel. While some of the innovative satire of the first film may seem overly familiar the second time around, it should not stop anyone from enjoying this cutely funny and at times madcap spoof of the old TV sitcom. The plot revolves around the return of Carol's (Shelley Long) long-thought-dead husband (Tim Matheson), who instead of being the newest member of the blissfully content Brady world, is instead after a valuable ancient horse statue (yes, the same one that was prominently displayed in the TV show). When the rogue husband's ruse is revealed, he kidnaps the perky Mrs. Brady and takes her to Hawaii – with the loudly clothed, off-key, sing-songing Bradys in hot pursuit. Plenty of sexual innuendoes, eye-poppingly loud (but groovy) threads and shamelessly mindless fun should divert both old TV fans and newcomers alike. ★★★½ $14.99

A Very Curious Girl

(1986, 105 min, France, Nelly Kaplan) Kaplan's sexy comedy about a beautiful peasant girl who decides to sell sexual services to the men in the village. Soon, she has more power than she ever dreamed of and becomes involved in a series of hilarious events. (French with English subtitles) ★★½

A Very Natural Thing

(1973, 85 min, US, Christopher Larkin) An important film in the history of American gay filmmaking, *A Very Natural Thing* is considered the first feature film on the gay experience made by an out-of-the-closet gay director to receive a commercial distribution. The simple but insightful story involves a 26-year-old gay man who leaves the priesthood and moves to New York City in the hopes of finding a meaningful relationship. Now a schoolteacher, he soon falls in love with a handsome young advertising executive. Though the film is rather sappy and tends to preach, it is nevertheless sensitively told and refreshingly romantic. ★★★ $39.99

A Very Old Man
with Enormous Wings

(1988, 90 min, Cuba/Italy/Spain, Fernando Birri) After a violent cyclone, a poor couple discover near their desolate farmhouse a mute winged man (played by director Birri). Not understanding him, they cage him in a chicken coop where the strange old man, with supernatural physical attributes, soon becomes the area's local attraction; drawing the curious, the derisive and the devout. A bizarre fable infused with magical realism, at times cruel images and comic confusion. (Spanish with English subtitles) ★★★ $19.99

A Very Private Affair

(1962, 95 min, France/Italy, Louis Malle) This early work by Malle is a steamy examination of the trials of movie stardom and features Brigitte Bardot as a naive nymphet and newly found movie star who is constantly beset

James Stewart and Kim Novak in *Vertigo*

A Very Brady Sequel

by fans, press and photographers. The underside of stardom is pointedly looked at in this romantic melodrama. (Dubbed) ★★½

Via Appia

(1991, 90 min, Germany, Jochen Hick) When Frank, a young German flight attendant, wakes up after a one-night stand with a street hustler in Rio, he finds scrawled on the bathroom mirror, "Welcome to the AIDS club." Back in Germany with the disease beginning to take hold of him, he decides to return to Brazil (with an accompanying film crew) to find the prostitute. The grim search, all set in a film-within-a-film style, involves combing the sleazy bathhouses, back streets and even a beach known as the "AIDS Farm." He interviews various male prostitutes and lowlifes in what soon becomes, for Frank and his film crew, a meandering, existential odyssey. With time running out, the young man's longing to find the "cause" of his impending death is both gut-wrenching and disturbing. A powerful and suspenseful story filled with sexy images of an unapologetically hedonistic netherworld which continues unabated despite the looming spectre of AIDS. (In English & German and Portuguese with English subtitles) ★★★ $39.99

Vibes

(1988, 99 min, US, Ken Kwapis) A wacky comedy about two psychics (Jeff Goldblum and Cyndi Lauper) who are thrown together in a quest for a lost South American treasure, being manipulated all the way by con man Peter Falk. Lauper is appealing in her film debut in this totally silly but amiable romp. ★★½ $89.99

Vice Versa

(1988, 100 min, US, Brian Gilbert) Judge Reinhold and Fred Savage make this familiar body-switching comedy better than it really is thanks to their endearing performances. Though not as well conceived as *Big*, there's a lot to like in this tale about a department store

manager and his young son exchanging identities. ★★½ $9.99

Victim

(1961, 100 min, GB, Basil Dearden) Long considered a landmark film for its complex and sophisticated treatment of homosexuality, this exceptional thriller stars Dirk Bogarde as a married, bisexual lawyer who risks his reputation by confronting a gang of blackmailers responsible for the death of his former lover. A thoughtful and compelling piece which was instrumental in breaking new ground. ★★★½ $24.99

Victor/Victoria

(1982, 133 min, GB/US, Blake Edwards) This stylish, gender-bending, sexual/musical comedy stars Julie Andrews as a female (Victoria) who passes as a gay male female impersonator (Victor). Robert Preston offers a scintillating performance as her gay friend and mentor, Toddy. James Garner also stars as a Chicago gangster confusingly enchanted and attracted to Andrews, who he thinks is a man. Based on the 1933 German comedy, *Viktor und Viktoria*, Edwards' exuberant romp is full of snappy tunes and sophisticated hilarity. Lesley Ann Warren gives a priceless performance as Garner's dumb-blonde mistress. ★★★★ $14.99

Victory

(1981, 110 min, US, John Huston) Standard WWII prison escape adventure is heightened by an exciting finale featuring a soccer game between Allied soldiers and their German captors. With Michael Caine, Sylvester Stallone, Pele and Max von Sydow. ★★ $14.99

Videodrome

(1983, 90 min, Canada, David Cronenberg) James Woods' performance dominates this gritty horror tale from director Cronenberg. Woods plays the owner of a cable station whose programming choices begin to bring about horrifying hallucinations. Gory though spectacular special effects by Rick Baker. Not for all tastes. ★★★ $14.99

La Vie Continue

(1982, 93 min, France, Moshe Mizrahi) Annie Girardot is marvelous as a sheltered middle-class woman who, when her husband suddenly dies, is forced to make adjustments in her life. Things brighten up when she finds herself in love again. Her budding new relationship is a joy to witness as it unfolds. Remade as *Men Don't Leave*. (French with English subtitles) ★★★ $59.99

La Vie de Bohéme

(1993, 100 min, France, Aki Kaurismäki) Anyone familiar with the works of Finnish director Kaurismäki (*Leningrad Cowboys Go America*) know that his films are low-key and the comedy is usually archly subtle — he's somewhat like a Finnish Jim Jarmusch. *La Vie de Bohéme*, his first French production, proves to be no different. The story centers on the down-on-their-luck lives of three bedraggled men: Albanian painter Rodolfo, aspiring novelist Marcel, and Irish composer Schaunard. The resilient, likable trio find success, food and love always just out of their reach as they pursue their art regardless of the inevitable setbacks. There is humor in the tale but overall, the slow pacing, repetitive story line and somber look at life on the edge make this a must for Kaurismäki fans only. ★★ $19.99

Vietnam: Year of the Pig

(1968, 103 min, US, Emile de Antonio) This outstanding, Academy Award-nominated documentary offers a thought-provoking and riveting examination into America's involvement in the Vietnam War and Southeast Asia. ★★★½

A View to a Kill

(1985, 131 min, GB, John Glen) One of the weakest of the Bond films is saddled with an anemic villain played by Christopher Walken who's simply not convincingly evil. Even Grace Jones is unable to perk up the proceedings in this one. Roger Moore is simply coasting as 007. (Available letterboxed and pan & scan) ★★ $14.99

Vigil

(1984, 90 min, New Zealand, Vincent Ward) Told with strikingly stark visuals, this grim, atmospheric drama is set on a sheep farm in a desolate, darkly enchanted valley in New Zealand. The story is seen through the eyes of an 11-year-old girl, Toss. When her father dies accidentally, a mysterious stranger arrives and begins to help the family survive. Though helpful, Toss sees him as a predator; and one who must leave immediately. Director Ward spent five years making this bleak but mystical testimony to the beauty and immutability of nature and life. A startling directorial debut and a work of extraordinary beauty. ★★★½ $19.99

The Vikings

(1958, 114 min, US, Richard Fleischer) Kirk Douglas and Tony Curtis are Viking half brothers who set sail for the English coast in this fanciful tale of exploration and conquest. Also with Janet Leigh and Ernest Borgnine. ★★½ $19.99

Village of the Damned

(1960, 78 min, GB, Wolf Rilla) Classic English horror and damned scary at that! This is a low-budget shocker about a group of strange, emotionless children who attempt to take over a small village by controlling the minds of the adults. An eerie chiller of the highest order. (Remade in 1995) ★★★½ $14.99

Village of the Damned

(1995, 95 min, US, John Carpenter) Based on the semi-classic 1960 chiller, this new version from director Carpenter features updated effects and splendid cinematography, but it is not really much different than the original in plot. The inhabitants of the coastal California town of Midwich suffer a strange sleeplike trance one day but emerge seemingly unharmed – until they discover all the townswomen are pregnant. A mass birth, facilitated by local doctor Christopher Reeve and federal epidemiologist Kirstie Alley, results in a group of bizarre offspring who mature into eerie, super-intelligent adolescents. Reeve eventually discovers the alien nature of the children and their intention to enslave and destroy the world, and sets out to stop them. Carpenter, who made a terrifying update of *The Thing*, is unable to ignite the story sufficiently, though the film is still moderately scary and entertaining; but it doesn't compare favorably to many of the director's other works. ★★½ $19.99

Vincent

(1987, 105 min, Australia, Paul Cox) This thoughtful and engrossing examination into the life and art of Vincent Van Gogh takes an unconventional approach in its efforts to reveal the artist's driving creative force. More of a filmed essay than biography, the movie attempts to piece together Van Gogh's final years by the reading of the many eloquent and insightful letters he wrote to his brother, Theo (read offscreen by John Hurt); while at the same time examining the artist's work – from his earliest line drawings to his last hallucinatory portraits and landscapes. More complex and abstract than the Kirk Douglas/Vincente Minnelli *Lust For Life* or Robert Altman's *Vincent and Theo*, Cox seems more interested in revealing the intellectual and articulate Van Gogh and not the simpler image of a tortured and mad painter. ★★★ $59.99

Vincent and Theo

(1990, 138 min, US, Robert Altman) With this most accomplished work, Altman sets his sights on the lives and the delicate relationship between artist Vincent Van Gogh and his brother, Theo. In a commanding performance, Tim Roth plays the tortured genius, Vincent, who is irrevocably tied to his sibling; each in search of his own artistic identity and unable to break the confines of their bond. Paul Rhys is equally as compelling as Theo. ★★★½

Vincent, François, Paul and the Others

(1974, 118 min, France, Claude Sautet) An all-star cast of Yves Montand, Micel Piccoli, Gérard Depardieu and Stéphane Audran highlights this elegant but dolorous drama of male

Every grade schoolteacher's worst nightmare from *Village of the Damned*

mid-life crisis. Vincent, François and Paul are lifelong friends, all in their mid-fifties. The "others" are represented by a younger member of the group (Depardieu) along with their various wives and mistresses. The story follows their weekly retreat to the country where underneath the jocular drinking and eating, difficult problems of love and life confront them all. A well-acted saga which explores the problems of bourgeois life from the male perspective. (French with English subtitles) ★★★

Violence at Noon

(1966, 99 min, Japan, Nagisa Oshima) From Oshima, the director of *In the Realm of the Senses*, comes an equally disturbing and controversial examination of sensuality and passion. One of the founders of the Japanese New Wave, Oshima was strongly effected by Jean-Luc Godard, and Oshima's imagery and editing technique do not contradict this. Set in a rural Japanese commune, the story focuses on the unsettling relationship between a rapist/murderer, his wife and a woman he once raped. Protecting him from the police out of a perverted sense of loyalty, the women are strangely obedient to this man until a final confrontation. (Japanese with English subtitles) ★★★ $79.99

The Violent Years

(1956, 57 min, US, William M. Morgan) Delinquent debutantes do drugs, rob gas stations, rape rich boys, and commit murder, mayhem and assorted pajama party violence. ★ $9.99

Les Violons du Bal

(1974, 108 min, France, Michel Drach) Director Drach's remembrances of his Jewish childhood in Nazi-occupied France, as well as his attempts to get financing to make a film on the subject, are the two parallel stories in this affectionate personal drama. Using imaginative cross-cutting, Drach deftly weaves the two stories together into a perilous and deeply moving film. His son Michel charmingly plays the director as a young boy who, along with his lovely mother (played by Drach's real-life wife, Marie-José Nat) and his two siblings, attempt to stay one step ahead of the Nazis and certain

extradition to a labor camp. And while this heart-stopping drama unfolds, Drach – played by Jean-Louis Trintignant (and not the director himself, at the insistence of the overweight, cigar-chomping producer) – tries to interest people in the film project. (French with English subtitles) ★★★ $79.99

The Virgin Machine

(1988, 85 min, West Germany, Monika Treut) This thought-provoking sexual odyssey tells the story of a young West German woman and her search for "romantic love." Frustrated by the emptiness and the emotional morass of her native Hamburg, Dorothee decides to flee her home to search for her mother, who is living in San Francisco. Once arrived, however, her trek turns into a process of sexual discovery. Filmed in a steamy black and white, the film exudes a sensuality in which simple lust is transformed into glorious eroticism. While *The Virgin Machine* is clearly a feminist film about a woman's exploration of her own sexuality, its profound statement is one which applies to all. (English and German with English subtitles) ★★★ $29.99

The Virgin Queen

(1955, 92 min, US, Henry Koster) Bette Davis reprises her acclaimed role from 1939's *The Private Lives of Elizabeth and Essex* as Queen Elizabeth I, here coming in conflict with Walter Raleigh (well-played by Richard Todd). Davis, as usual, is commanding. ★★★ $19.99

The Virgin Soldiers

(1969, 96 min, GB, John Dexter) Beautiful cinematography enhances this little-known gem about the end of innocence (both sexually and otherwise) for a group of young British recruits going to battle in 1950s Singapore. A dewy-fresh Lynn Redgrave costars as the girl who escorts one of the boys (Hywell Bennet) into manhood. ★★★ $69.99

The Virgin Spring

(1960, 88 min, Sweden, Ingmar Bergman) Based on a Swedish ballad, Bergman's quietly chilling morality play brilliantly captures the quality of ancient legends – their primitive passion, human sorrow, and abrupt beauty. Set in the Swedish countryside of the 14th century, it stars Max von Sydow as the tormented father whose daughter was raped and murdered after her sister invokes a pagan curse. In the spot of her death a magical spring bursts forth. (Swedish with English subtitles) ★★★★ $29.99

Virginia City

(1940, 121 min, US, Michael Curtiz) A follow-up to his successful *Dodge City*, Errol Flynn is back in the saddle in this colorful Civil War western. There's intrigue and treachery at every turn as Union officer Flynn puts the stops on a Confederate gold shipment, and tangles with rebel officer Randolph Scott, spy Miriam Hopkins and Mexican outlaw Humphrey Bogart. The cast comes off well, except for Bogie, looking ridiculous in his Ricardo Montalban mustache. ★★★ $19.99

Viridiana

(1961, 91 min, Spain, Luis Buñuel) Buñuel's controversial and brilliant surrealistic examination of good and evil is about a young novice and her loss of innocence at her rich uncle's estate. Contains the celebrated Last Supper scene. The film which caused Buñuel to be kicked out of Spain. (Spanish with English subtitles) ★★★★ $24.99

Virtuosity

(1995, 105 min, US, Brett Leonard) With more than a little in common with the far more entertaining *Demolition Man*, this mindless, slowly paced sci-fi adventure casts Denzel Washington as a former cop who's now behind bars and is the only one who can track down the nasty bad guy. The latter would be Russell Crowe as a virtual reality villain who has come to life endowed with super powers and is killing everyone in sight. The film attempts to make a comment on violence and our appetite for it in our society, but *Virtuosity* gratuitously feeds that hunger with ridiculous plot developments, undefined characters and indiscriminate scenes of violence — *Natural Born Killers* is subtle by comparison. Lacking originality or excitement, this is by far the worst of the recent trend of cyber thrillers. ★ $14.99

A Virus Knows No Morals

(1986, 84 min, West Germnay, Rosa von Praunheim) Never one to tread softly on a controversial subject, von Praunheim tackles the issue of AIDS in this archaic black comedy. With several stories intercut throughout the film, von Praunheim's cast of weird characters includes a sex club owner who refuses to change his policies, claiming that, "I won't let them take away our freedom"; hysterical members of the press who are bent on making a story; and workers at a hospital where the deluge of AIDS patients causes them to become so bored and jaded that the night nurses roll dice to see which patient will die next. Gallows humor abounds as the director seeks to provoke, embarrass and enrage the audience into understanding the effects of the crisis. (German with English subtitles) ★★★ $39.99

Vision Quest

(1985, 107 min, US, Harold Becker) Matthew Modine and the fiery Linda Fiorentino make an attractive twosome in this compelling drama about a high school wrestler going after the state championship. Madonna sings two songs. ★★★ $14.99

Visions of 8

(1972, 110 min, Various Directors) The producer of this film had the intriguing idea to have eight different directors from around the world film various events of the 1972 Summer Olympics at Munich. Included in this menagerie of filmmakers are Kon Ichikawa, John Schlesinger, Milos Forman, Claude Lelouch and Mai Zetterling. The results are, as one would imagine, uneven. Although interesting, better examples of a filmmaker capturing the beauty and spectacle of this sporting event would be either Ichikawa's *Tokyo Olympiad* or Leni Riefenstahl's *Olympia*. ★★½

Visions of Light: The Art of Cinematography

(1993, 90 min, US, Arnold Glassman, Todd McCarthy & Stuart Samuels) Setting out to elevate cinematographers above their normal obscurity, this fascinating and entertaining documentary on the art behind making movies is a must-see for those who consider themselves film connoisseurs. The film focuses on the works of 26 of the world's greatest all-time cinematographers and points to some of their finest contributions; examining several of moviedom's most famous shots and uncovering the various methods and mistakes which went into their creation. Film buffs will find the material so absorbing that they will be wishing for more at the end of the film's breezy 90 minutes. ★★★½ $96.89

Les Visiteurs du Soir (The Devil's Envoys)

(1942, 110 min, France, Marcel Carné) This charming medieval fantasy scripted by Jacques Prévert is set in the 15th century and tells the story of two emissaries sent to earth by the Devil to corrupt two young lovers and disrupt their impending marriage. Things don't work out too well for the bad guys as the male envoy falls in love with the young princess. It takes the Devil himself to intervene by turning the couple into stone; but, much to his dismay, their pure hearts continue to beat. Made during the German Occupation, this thinly veiled allegory — of Hitler as the Devil and France the lovers — surprisingly never had problems with the authorities. Sometimes a bit stilted and forced, this visually lush fairy tale is still a fine example of the Carné/Prévert style of poetic realism. (French with English subtitles) ★★★

The Visitors

(1996, 106 min, France, Jean-Marie Poire) The French take a lot of flack here in America for their questionable taste in comedy. *The Visitors*, a huge hit in France, will not help end the Jerry Lewis jokes. Jean Reno is completely unappealing as a medieval knight who, along with his excruciating sidekick (cowriter Christian Clavier, a twisted cross between Harpo Marx and Charles Manson), is transported to modern-day France by a senile wizard. The two wacky fishes-out-of-water bumble through France, insulting, threatening or assaulting everyone they meet; all the while destroying cars, buildings and valuables in the most infantile manner possible. There's a

small amount of satire here, but like everything else in *The Visitors*, it's never developed. At least the film is fast-paced. This could've been funny. It's a dopey premise well worth exploiting (just think what the Marx Brothers did with their plots!); but as is it's laughless and just plain pointless. (French with English subtitles) ★½ $102.99

Vital Signs

(1990, 103 min, US, Marisa Silver) Routine medical drama about young med students and their professional and personal struggles. With Jimmy Smits as a caring instructor, Adrian Pasdar and Diane Lane as interns, and Norma Aleandro, who brings a heartrending dignity to her dying cancer patient. ★★½ $9.99

Vito and the Others

(1992, 90 min, Italy, Antonio Capuano) Pubescent, angel-faced boys rove the streets of a decaying Naples terrorizing all with their petty crimes, drug dealing and prostitution in this lurid *Pixote*-influenced "exposé" on urban hopelessness. Twelve-year-old Vito, living with abusive relatives after his father wipes out his family in a murderous rampage, joins up with a band of future juvenile delinquents. Sent to prison after a busted drug deal, he slips further away when he is raped by fellow prisoners and returns to the streets a hardened hooligan, indifferent to emotion and love. Violent and chilling, the film's over-the-top vision of a society submerged in poverty and numbed by senseless crime features a cast made up largely of non-professionals, infusing the film with moments of realism. But unlike *Pixote*, we never get to know much about young Vito nor are we shocked by his vicious anti-social behavior. It's too serious to be cheesy exploitation, too awkward to be effective drama. (Italian with English subtitles) ★★½ $69.99

Viva Zapata!

(1952, 113 min, US, Elia Kazan) Marlon Brando is exceptional as a Mexican peasant whose search for simple justice leads to rebellion and eventual triumph. Anthony Quinn won a Best Supporting Actor Oscar as Brando's brother. Also featuring Jean Peters and Joseph Wiseman. Kazan directed the John Steinbeck script. ★★★½

Vive L'Amour

(1996, 118 min, Taiwan, Tsai Ming-Liang) A remarkable film about passion and loneliness, *Vive L'Amour* eschews narrative convention by presenting its offbeat love story almost exclusively without dialogue. A young Taiwanese couple meet for anonymous sex in a vacant apartment. Unbeknowst to them, a sexually confused and suicidal young man is living in the abandoned space. Writer-director Ming-Liang generates tremendous drama in a series of revealing episodes that examine the sensation of communication. As the camera eavesdrops on the daily routines of its unhappy characters, the film unfolds naturally — without music — using only the noise of everyday life as it builds inexoribly to a stunning conclusion. The performances by the three leads are uniformly superb, with each actor's body language conveying their complex emotions. (In fact, two of the characters do not speak until halfway through the film.) Slowly,

Julie Delpy in *Voyager*

methodically paced and definitely not for all tastes, the fascinating and seductive *Vive L'Amour* rewards the concentration of patient viewers. (Taiwanese with English subtitles) ★★★½ $89.99

Vivre sa Vie (My Life to Live)

(1962, 85 min, France, Jean-Luc Godard) Godard's detached and at times analytical approach to his subjects continues in this richly paradoxical tale of a young shop assistant (Anna Karina) who turns to prostitution but who "gives her body to keep her soul." Set up in 12 tableaux segments, Godard has said that this film was "not a new departure, but an arrival." (French with English subtitles) ★★★ $59.99

Vixen

(1968, 70 min, US, Russ Meyer) A straightforward narrative of a bush pilot and his oversexed wife who live in the Canadian wilderness. It cost $76,000 to make and brought back over $7.5 million at the box office, bringing Meyer deserved recognition from major Hollywood studios. ★★★ $79.99

Voices of Sarafina!

(1988, 85 min, US, Nigel Noble) Interviews with cast members of the hit Broadway musical "Sarafina," with scenes from the show spliced with images of life in oppressive South African townships. A celebration of the courage and conviction of anti-Apartheid activists, set to the rhythm of Mbaganga street music (emulated on Paul Simon's "Graceland" album). ★★★ $29.99

Volcano

(1997, 102 min, US, Mick Jackson) With the sour taste of 1997's first volcano disaster film *Dante's Peak* still fresh in one's mouth, along comes Tommy Lee Jones to not only save Los Angeles but hopes for the genre as well. Sporting his customary take-control but nice-guy gruffness, Jones plays a civil supervisor

who's ready to rally the troops when L.A. is devastated by a volcano. Aided by geologist Anne Heche, the two race against time in their attempt to outwit this force of nature and save the city. All the trappings of the disaster film are here: the scientist to whom no one listens; various stereotypes coming together; children in peril; and the by-now annoying "saving of the dog." But *Volcano* has going for it an appealing ensemble (especially Don Cheadle), a quick pace, terrific effects, and a story line which won't require you to smack your head (too often) in disbelief. Despite a heavy-handed racial angle, *another* divorce brat, and a terribly clichéd ending, *Volcano* is fun to watch as it speeds down Wilshire Boulevard and amazingly levels Los Angeles — any film which does that can't be all bad. ★★½ $102.99

Volere Volare

(1993, 92 min, Italy, Maurizio Nichetti & Guido Manuli) *Volere Volare* is a kinky cartoon comedy from the director of *The Icicle Thief*. Once again, Nichetti employs surreal film techniques to portray a very comical but human love story. A sexual fantasist for hire becomes enamored with Maurizio, a cartoon sound dubber who "brings his work home with him." The slapstick fun of the film adds spice to the witty writing and stunning performances. Unlike many American romances of today, *Volere Volare* is quirky without being smutty, and romantic without being schmaltzy. ★★★ $19.99

Volpone

(1939, 95 min, France, Maurice Tourneur) Based on the classic comedy by Ben Johnson, Harry Baur stars as Volpone, a rich 16th-century Venetian merchant who pretends to be dying in order to observe how his "friends" react and jockey for his considerable inheritance and, in turn, take advantage of them. A droll satire on the ever-present human traits of power and greed. (French with English subtitles) ★★★

Volunteers

(1985, 106 min, US, Nicholas Meyer) Tom Hanks and John Candy breathe some life into this uneven comedy about a rich ne'er-do-well (Hanks) who travels to Thailand with a group of Peace Corps volunteers to escape his bookie. ★★

Von Ryan's Express

(1965, 117 min, US, Mark Robson) Frank Sinatra lends authority to this exciting WWII adventure about a daring POW escape, led by American colonel Sinatra. With Trevor Howard as a British general, at odds with the arrogant Yank. ★★★ $19.99

Voyage en Ballon

(1959, 82 min, France, Albert Lamorisse) From the director of *The Red Balloon* comes this enchanting, multi-award winning children's film. Jack Lemmon narrates this beautifully photographed tale of a young boy who stows away in a gigantic balloon that his grandfather has built. Together, the two, captain and first mate, travel across France on a wonderful, humorous and suspenseful adventure. ★★★

Voyage in Italy

(1953, 94 min, Italy, Roberto Rossellini) This third Rossellini-Ingrid Bergman collaboration (*Stromboli, Europa '51*) was panned by the critics and bombed at the box office on its initial release, but was revivified when the directors of the French New Wave hailed it as a masterpiece. Bergman and George Sanders are a bored couple who travel to Italy to inspect a villa they have inherited. Against magnificent background settings (Mt. Vesuvius, Capri, the ruins of Pompeii), their faltering marriage finally breaks up; but through a "miracle," they are reunited. With little "action," this simple film is a romantically passionate story on the renewal of life and love. (aka: *Strangers*) (Filmed in English) ★★★ $59.99

A Voyage Round My Father

(1983, 85 min, GB, Alvin Rakoff) John Mortimer's superb television adaptation of his own hit play stars Laurence Olivier and Alan Bates. Semiautobiographical in nature, this often moving and sometimes funny reminiscence centers on the occasionally tumultuous relationship between an eccentric father (Olivier) and his son (Bates). ★★★ $89.99

Voyage Surprise

(1946, 108 min, France, Pierre Prévert) This delightfully zany comedy by the Brothers Prévert (Jacques cowrote the story) tells of an old man's dream to arrange a mystery tour or "voyage surprise" on a ramshackle bus. The tourists are his family, elderly friends and various eccentrics who find themselves involved in a series of scary and comic adventures involving a wedding party, a brothel, anarchists, an evil Grand Duchess and the police. (French with English subtitles) ★★★½ $59.99

Voyage to the Bottom of the Sea

(1961, 106 min, US, Irwin Allen) The crew of an atomic submarine desperately fights to save the Earth from impending destruction. Hokey fun. Cast features Walter Pidgeon, Joan Fontaine, Barbara Eden, Peter Lorre, Michael Ansara and Frankie Avalon. Look out for the giant squid! ★★½ $14.99

Voyager

(1991, 113 min, West Germany/France, Volker Schlöndorff) Exuding existential angst like there's no tomorrow, this ruminative drama of forbidden love spans six continents in this (by European standards) big-budget production. Sam Shepard, in one of his best performances, is Walter Faber, a world-weary engineer who, because of a ruined love, retreats from the emotional world of life into the logical and predictable realm of his work. His emotional drifting ends when, after a series of improbable coincidences, he meets Sabeth, an alluring young lady (Julie Delpy) half his age. Their affair takes them from Mexico's Yucatan Peninsula through Europe until his past catches up with him with disastrous results. An engaging story similar in filming and style to Wim Wenders' *Until the End of the World*. (Filmed in English) ★★★ $19.99

The Wackiest Ship in the Army

(1960, 99 min, US, Richard Murphy) Jack Lemmon stars as a WWII naval officer saddled with a crew of butterfingered land-lubbers while trying to carry off a perilous top secret mission in the South Pacific. An entertaining mixture of wacky comedy and wartime heroics. Ricky Nelson costars. ★★★ $14.99

The Wacky World of Wills and Burke

(1985, 97 min, Australia, Bob Weis) This Monty Python-inspired spoof of the failed 1860 exploratory expedition in the Australian Outback is an outrageously satirical, light-hearted goofball of a movie. Burke, an elegantly dressed but slightly daft policeman, and the nerd astronomer Wills team up with 28 evil-smelling camels and an equally foul assortment of companions on a journey that leads them nowhere. It might be helpful for people unfamiliar with the historical event to watch the serious film *Burke and Wills* before renting this parody. ★★½

The Wages of Fear

(1953, 105 min, France, H.G. Clouzot) Four desperate men, all unscrupulous characters, are hired to transport several truckloads of nitroglycerin across the mountains and forests of South America in this compelling and suspenseful thriller. Remade as the American film *Sorcerer*. (French with English subtitles) ★★★★ $29.99

Wagner

(1983, 300 min, GB, Tony Palmer) A huge international cast fails to help this glossy and uninspiring biography of the famed composer. Richard Burton is only intermittently inspired as the lead. His costars include Vanessa Redgrave, John Gielgud, Laurence Olivier, Joan Plowright and Arthur Lowe. ★★ $29.99

Wages of Fear

Wagonmaster

(1950, 85 min, US, John Ford) Beautiful western locations highlight this Ford adventure about the perilous journey of a Morman wagon train heading west towards the Utah frontier. Ben Johnson and Ward Bond are two amblin' cowpokes who join the expedition. ★★★ $14.99

Wagons East

(1994, 100 min, US, Peter Markle) In his last film role, John Candy plays a drunken, incompetent wagonmaster who leads a group of unhappy settlers of the Old West on a journey back to a more civilized East. Unfunny to the point of embarrassment, the film goes to great lengths to set up its many *Blazing Saddles*-like jokes, but the punch lines fail to deliver. Even Richard Lewis' schtick falls flat. Among the familiar group of western characters, Ellen Greene is the hooker with a heart of gold, and Ed Lauter is a hired gunslinger. In a stereotypical portrayal, John C. McGinley plays an effeminate bookseller. His final destination — with a handsome Indian brave in tow — proves to be one of the only real laughs in this otherwise amiable bomb. ★½ $9.99

Wait Until Dark

(1967, 108 min, US, Terence Young) This intense adaptation of Frederick Knott's stage thriller stars Audrey Hepburn as a recently blinded woman who is terrorized by drug traffikers when she innocently takes possession of a doll filled with heroin. The action takes place almost entirely in her apartment, which heightens the suspense and the feeling of helplessness — it's more effective than any slasher film could hope to be. Alan Arkin is brilliant in the triple role as the head villain, and Richard Crenna also stars as a helpful detective. A pulse-pounding classic with an unforgettable finale. ★★★½ $19.99

Waiting for Godot

see: *Becket Directs*

Waiting for Guffman

(1997, 83 min, US, Christopher Guest) Proving the show must go on, *Waiting for Guffman* is an often hilarious though modest mockumentary directed and cowritten by Guest, one of the talents behind the granddaddy of the genre, *This Is Spinal Tap*. Community theatre is the target this time, and for anyone who has ever been associated with their local playhouse, much of this will seem like nirvana. The characterizations and petty politics are on-target, the tacky production values are gloriously captured, and there's enough in-jokes to make any semi-insider feel particularly in the loop. But *Guffman* is also a bit slow between the laughs. When the comedy works, this sizzles (*My Dinner with Andre* action figures!); but Guest allows some scenes to drag with no upshot. Like the film, Guest's portrayal of the untalented director — who possibly sees a ticket to Broadway with this show — has its inspired moments, but his caricature, very similar to his bisexual lover in *Beyond Therapy*, begins to wear thin. Nevertheless, the laughs are plentiful and well observed, and to anyone "in the loop," *Waiting for Guffman* is a cheerful reminder that show business is like no business you know. ★★★ $99.99

Waiting for the Light

(1990, 94 min, US, Christopher Monger) Teri Garr is ready for major life changes when she inherits a diner in a small community. She packs up the kids and Aunt Zelda (Shirley MacLaine), a woman with a decidedly unique world view, and heads out to a town about to be visited by an angel. Or so it seems. MacLaine gives another of her patented cantankerous, crotchety old lady performances, which is nonetheless endearing. A delightful cast revels in a serendipitous twist of fate in this quirky, charming film. ★★★ $14.99

Waiting for the Moon

(1987, 87 min, US, Jill Godmilow) The story of the tumultuous relationship between author Gertrude Stein and her lover/companion Alice B. Toklas. The film is minimalistic with long periods of dialogue between the women, in a style reminiscent of *My Dinner with Andre*. Upon its release, most critics disapproved of the film downplaying the women's lesbianism, opting instead for a more "matter of fact" attitude. Linda Hunt and Linda Bassett star. ★★½

Waiting to Exhale

(1995, 120 min, US, Forest Whitaker) Probably a first for a Hollywood film, *Waiting to Exhale* centers of the relationships of four African-American women. The film is occasionally appealing though sometimes static, and it is commendable for its (long overdue) subject and cast rather than for astute filmmaking or sharp insights. The story focuses less on the women's friendship (they have few scenes together) and more on their individual relationships with men, which produces a varying degree of success. In her second major film role, Whitney Houston is the catalyst of the story, moving to Phoenix to start life anew and reuniting with her longtime friends. Her romantic scenes have all the snap of a Taster's Choice commercial, though she fares better when relating to her female costars. Angela Bassett, like her character's story, has an earthiness and tenderness missing from a lot of the film, and her scenes with an uncredited Wesley Snipes are terrific. Loretta Devine gives a charming performance as an upbeat hairdresser and mother with designs on her new neighbor (Gregory Hines), and Lela Rochon, in a routine, almost incidental subplot, is a woman always meeting Mr. Wrong. ★★½ $14.99

Walk, Don't Run

(1966, 114 min, US, Charles Walters) Cary Grant's last film is not the most fitting end to a brilliant comic career, but it is nevertheless a mostly enjoyable farce. In this remake of the classic *The More the Merrier*, Grant stars as an American businessman forced to share accomodations with Samantha Eggar and Jim Hutton during the Tokyo Olympics. ★★½ $69.99

A Walk in the Clouds

(1995, 103 min, US, Alfonso Arau) An alternately awkward and magical romantic drama, *Like Water for Chocolate* director Arau's first English-language film, set in the splendrous wine country of Napa Valley, basks in the mystical glow of lovers united. Unfortunately, these tender scenes are surrounded by the

W

clichés of a contrived beginning and a predictable, abrupt ending. Keanu Reeves is a WWII vet and orphan. Traveling by train, he meets a beautiful college student (Aitana Sanchez-Gijon) returning home and agrees to pose as her husband, since she's single and pregnant and certain to feel her father's wrath. Their relationship – like the film – becomes emotionally satisfying once they arrive on the family's lush vineyards and fall in love. Sanchez-Gijon demonstrates warmth and vulnerability, and her fiery presence is a nice balance to the sullen portrayal given by Reeves – he still seems uncomfortable with period pieces. ★★½ $14.99

Walk on the Wild Side

(1962, 114 min, US, Edward Dmytryk) Inventive casting punctuates this tawdry tale of a good-natured Texan (Laurence Harvey) who travels to New Orleans to rescue his lost love (Capucine) from life in a brothel, run by a lascivious lesbian (Barbara Stanwyck). Jane Fonda tags along in yet another "sexy bad girl" role. If ever a movie deserved the tag line "good trash," this is it. ★★½ $69.99

Walkabout

(1970, 100 min, Australia, Nicolas Roeg) The long-awaited initial video release of Roeg's mesmeric journey of two young Anglos into the Australian Outback might not be quite the "classic" many had remembered and hoped for, but it is still a significant contributor to the cinematic lexicon. Jenny Agutter is undeniably fetching as the budding young woman who, with her younger brother (Lucien John), is suddenly stranded in the wilderness. With a preternatural calm (and still clad in school uniforms), they venture into the Outback searching for civilization but find instead an aboriginal teen (David Gulpilil) who's on his "walkabout" – an initiation ritual involving months of solo survival. With no common language, the threesome begin a trek that slowly breaks down their cultural barriers and sees a developing sexual tension between Agutter and Gulpilil – made all the more titillating by Roeg's soft-core treatment of Agutter swim-

ming naked in a watering hole. Pieced together in Roeg's trademark patchwork of chunks of loose narrative, and with a minimum of dialogue, *Walkabout* is at first very obtuse, but its attempt to blur the distinctions between the civilized and "primitive" worlds ultimately lacks subtlety; otherwise, maybe it would be seen as a classic. ★★★ $79.99

Walker

(1987, 95 min, US, Alex Cox) Ed Harris plays a real-life soldier of fortune who declared himself president of Nicaragua in 1855 and ruled the country for two turbulent years. Cox's anarchic sense of humor permeates this piece, so as with most of his films, expect the unexpected. With Peter Boyle, Richard Masur and Marlee Matlin. ★★ $79.99

Walking and Talking

(1996, 83 min, US, Nicole Holofcener) A sympathetic and beneficent approach and engaging portrayals elevate this regulation opus of twentysomethings struggling with faltering relationships, stress-inducing families and unfulfilling jobs. Somewhat episodic in structure, the film centers on two childhood friends (Anne Heche and Catherine Keener) as one is about to marry and the other fears she is incapable of long-term commitment. Through many layers of miscommunications, hang-ups and obsessions, the film wanders the paths of each woman's personal growth as she attempts to bring order to a chaotic and often baffling world. Developed in association with the Sundance Institute, the film's forgiving nature towards its characters' idiosyncracies encourages tolerance towards an uneven script and some awkward dialogue, ultimately resulting in an amusing and endearing examination of young adult life. And yes, it does contain the now-requisite guy-who-works-in-a-video-store character. ★★½ $102.99

The Walking Dead

(1995, 90 min, US, Preston A. Whitemore II) Cliché-ridden action at its worst, *The Walking Dead* features Joe Morton as the leader of a group of African-American marines who are sent on a rescue mission, only to discover that

they are being used as decoys. What could have been a penetrating and even insightful entertainment soon turns into a brain tumor-inducing mess, as each soldier's life is displayed in flashback telling the tragic reason why each one of them joined the service. As a wise-cracking G.I., Eddie Griffin is the saving grace of the film, bringing a degree of believability and energy to some of his scenes. This entry into the populated Vietnam War film genre plays strictly as below average made-for-cable fare. ★½ $19.99

The Wall

(1983, 117 min, Turkey, Yilmaz Guney) Guney, who directed the highly acclaimed film *Yol* from his prison cell, died of cancer soon after personally making his first and, sadly, only film after his escape from Turkish prison. *The Wall* concerns the re-creation of the revolt in a children's prison in Ankara in 1976. The harsh living conditions suffered by the children as well as their eventual uprising are brutally depicted in this searing, honest and horrifying portrait of repression. A true political statement that tears at one's conscience. (Turkish with English subtitles) ★★★½ $69.99

A Wall in Jerusalem

(1970, 91 min, Israel, Frederic Rossif) Attempting to encompass all of the important events in the history and growth of Israel into the Jewish homeland, this brilliant documentary, narrated by Richard Burton, begins with the Dreyfus Affair in 1894 and covers profiles on the leaders of early Zionism, the Balfour Declaration, the British occupation of Palestine, the Six Day War and much else. Made in 1970, the film is now a "period piece," but its ambitious scope and detail make it required viewing for those interested in Israel's history, growth and modernization, as well as the daunting problems facing this troubled land. ★★★ $59.99

Wall Street

(1987, 124 min, US, Oliver Stone) Stone's riveting, but at times heavy-handed, morality tale stars Charlie Sheen as a young stock broker who falls under the spell of Wall Street's millions and loses sight of his humanity. Michael Douglas was awarded an Oscar for his portrayal of a vicious, power hungry Donald Trump-like wheeler-dealer. Martin Sheen plays Charlie's proletariat father and Daryl Hannah appears as his love interest. ★★★ $9.99

Walpurgis Night

(1938, 75 min, Sweden, Gustaf Edgren) Set during Walpurgis, the Swedish celebration of spring, this erotic comedy stars Victor Sjostrom as a conservative newspaperman with Ingrid Bergman as his rebellious daughter. (Swedish with English subtitles) ★★★ $19.99

The Waltz of the Toreadors

(1962, 105 min, GB, John Guillermin) Peter Sellers delivers a first-rate comic performance as a licentious army colonel in this wonderful rendition of Jean Anouilh's rollicking sexual farce. ★★★ $14.99

A Waltz Through the Hills

(1988, 116 min, Australia, Frank Arnold) This coming-of-age story set in the Outback of

Walkabout

Australia follows the journey of young Andy and his little sister, Sammy. After the death of their parents and fearing they will be sent to separate orphanages, they risk traveling through the wilds to get to the coast, where they intend to take a boat to England. Their victories, hardships and courage are inspirational. ★★★ $19.99

The Wanderer (Le Gran Meaulnes)

(1987, 108 min, France, Jean-Gabriel Albiococco) An imaginative interpretation of Alain Fournier's classic novel, this visually exuberant fantasy tells the romantic story of a boy's first and true love. Set in a provincial town in turn-of-the-century France, young Augustin goes to a strange party one enchanted evening and meets the beautiful yet mysterious Yvonne (Brigitte Fossey). When Yvonne disappears, our hero desperately tries to find her. A wild and remarkable re-creation of childhood memories and youthful innocence. (French with English subtitles) ★★★

The Wanderers

(1979, 117 min, US, Philip Kaufman) Nostalgic and sometimes dark look at growing up in the Bronx in the early 1960s. Cast features Ken Wahl, John Friedrich, Linda Manz and Karen Allen. ★★★ $19.99

The Wannsee Conference

(1984, 88 min, West Germany, Heinz Schirk) A serious and startling re-creation of a meeting that occurred in a pleasant suburb on January 20, 1942. In attendance were such Nazi leaders as the Gestapo's Adolph Eichmann, Reinhard Heydrich of the Secret Police and 15 other state officials. Their mission: to decide upon and implement the so-called "final solution," sealing the fate of six million Jews. Based on the original secretary's notes, the film is presented in real time. Although concentration camps and executions were already a reality, this meeting marked the official beginning of the Third Reich's policy of mass murder and extermination. (German with English subtitles) ★★★

Wanted: Dead or Alive

(1986, 104 min, US, Gary Sherman) Rutger Hauer has a lot of fun as a modern-day bounty hunter hired to catch, preferably alive, a terrorist (Gene Simmons, of KISS). Definitely no more than your standard action-adventure film, but still entertaining. ★★ $14.99

The War

(1994, 126 min, US, Jon Avnet) As the youthful Stu, Elijah Wood is especially captivating in the strong ensemble cast which populates the small Mississippi town of Juliette. It's 1970. Stu's father, Stephen (Kevin Costner), has been an unsteady presence since his return from Vietnam, and his recent reentry into the family (Mare Winningham and Lexi Randall as mother and daughter) coincides with increased hostilities with another family's children. With a few exceptions, the dialogue rings true as the father tries to impart to the son the lessons of war. While the film suffers a muddled point-of-view, it enjoys exceptional characterizations by each cast member; all of the children are naturals, and this is

Winningham's most accomplished screen performance since *Miracle Mile*. *The War* presents people usually absent from American cinema – the rural poor – and shows them without apology or glamorization. From the director of *Fried Green Tomatoes*. ★★★ $19.99

War and Peace

(1956, 208 min, US/Italy, King Vidor) Audrey Hepburn and Henry Fonda star in this technically superior but dramatically flat version of Tolstoy's epic novel. Well-staged battle sequences. ★★★ $29.99

War and Peace

(1968, 380 min, USSR, Sergei Bondarchuk) Reportedly the most expensive Russian film ever made, with final costs exceeding $100,000,000, this Academy Award-winning epic is a dazzling and monumental portrait of Russia during the Napoleonic Wars of 1805-1812. This definitive version of Tolstoy's classic novel follows four aristocratic families and the effects of Napoleon's onslaught of Europe and Russia on their lives. The spectacular battle sequences are considered the best ever filmed, with the director using over 120,000 soldiers. An amazing film experience best suited to the big screen; but see it on video, because when was the last time *War and Peace* played your local movie house? (Dubbed) ★★★★ $99.99

The War Game

(1966, 50 min, GB, Peter Watkins) Watkins' tremendously powerful "staged" documentary about the horrors of a nuclear attack on London made its mark well before the more commercial and less stunning "The Day After." Made for BBC-TV, the film never aired because its graphic re-creation of the burns and wounds suffered by the population were considered too controversial (read: anti-war). An extremely hard-hitting piece of quasi cinema verité. ★★★½ $29.99

War in Space

(1977, 91 min, Japan, Jun Fukuda) With Tonka Toy special effects and many Godzilla-esque action sequences, this English-dubbed Japanese science fiction has that look of cheesy sci-fi flicks of the '50s and '60s but, while mildly entertaining, still begs for a Woody Allen redubbing treatment. Probably made by a Japanese equivalent of Troma, and with lines like "That's gotta be the enemy base, guys," this less-than-epic epic opens with Earth being threatened by a horde of insidious aliens intent on total destruction of the planet and galactic domination. But with Flash Gordon over-the-hill and the Enterprise and its crew tied up in syndication, the Earth's fate falls in the hands of a secret Japanese organization that sends their space battleship Gohten and its band of space warriors off to Venus for a winner-take-the-universe battle with the bad guys. Keep the popcorn coming! (Dubbed) ★★

The War of the Roses

(1989, 116 min, US, Danny DeVito) In this wicked, hilarious black comedy, Michael Douglas and Kathleen Turner portray Oliver and Barbara Rose, a married couple whose once idyllic life – complete with two children,

beautiful mansion and unlimited cash flow – has dissipated to a limb-breaking, psyche-smashing battle of the sexes. Sort of a demented '80s version of Tracy and Hepburn, Douglas and Turner – who always play well off each other – have rarely been funnier: Douglas' characteristic quirks – the "yuppie" agressiveness and his dispassionate demeanor – are well used here, and Turner is nothing short of stunning, both physically and as a comedic actress. ★★★½ $9.99

The War of the Worlds

(1953, 85 min, US, Byron Haskin) George Pal produced this classic sci-fi adventure based on the H.G. Wells novel about a Martian invasion of Earth, and the scientist (Gene Barry) out to stop them. Highlighted by terrific Academy Award-winning special effects. ★★★½ $14.99

War Party

(1988, 99 min, US, Franc Roddam) Racial tensions flair in a small Montana town on the eve of the centennial of an Indian massacre led by the U.S. Cavalry. Billy Wirth, Kevin Dillon and M. Emmett Walsh star. ★★½ $14.99

War Requiem

(1989, 90 min, GB, Derek Jarman) Jarman teamed with producer Don Boyd to create this elaborate symphony of sight and sound. Using the same non-dialogue format as Boyd's *Aria* (which featured a segment by Jarman), they have brought cinematic life to Benjamin Britten's immensely powerful "War Requiem." Written for the opening of the new Coventry Cathedral (the original was destroyed in WWII), Britten's oratorio is punctuated by the haunting poetry of Wilfred Owen – who was killed just prior to Armistice Day in 1918 at the age of 27. This exceptionally stirring piece captures Britten's theme of innocence ruined by the ravages of war. ★★★ $24.99

The War Room

(1993, 96 min, US, D.A. Pennebaker & Chris Hegedus) When filmmakers Pennebaker and Hegedus set out to document Bill Clinton's 1992 presidential campaign, they were hoping for unrestricted access to the candidate. Stonewalled by Clinton, they turned their attentions, instead, to his two top campaign managers: ragin' Cajun chief strategist James Carville, and 31-year-old upstart communications director George Stephanopoulous. And so much the better. With a snappy and aggressive verité style, the film revels in the gritty and non-stop action of behind-the-scenes politics. What gives the film its real punch, however, is Carville. This freewheeling firebrand pumps out a highly entertaining, relentless and tantalizing barrage of rhetoric and media "spin." Though certainly non-partisan, it should still provide amusement no matter what your party affiliation. ★★★ $9.99

Ward 6

(1976, 93 min, Yugoslavia, Lucian Pintilie) Yugoslavian theatre director Pintilie's adaptation of Anton Chekhov's powerful story paints the disturbing portrait of a Russian Empire in decline – moldering in moral rot. Set in a provincial town at the turn-of-the-century, a dedicated but troubled doctor oversees a

W

The Waterdance

grotesque, inhuman mental ward. Slowly numbed by the poverty and suffering, he finds solace with an inmate, the only one who seemingly comprehends the situation. A somber, claustrophobic work that uses a static camera and repetitive sounds (running water, banging machinery) to help us appreciate the suffocation of the people in this hopeless world. (Serbian with English subtitles) ★★★

Wargames

(1983, 110 min, US, John Badham) Clever computer-age adventure with young Matthew Broderick (in his first box-office hit) as a computer whiz who taps into the Defense Department's computer and nearly starts WWWIII. Also with Ally Sheedy and Dabney Coleman. ★★★ $9.99

Warhol: Portrait of an Artist

(1988, 60 min, US) The life of pop culture icon Andy Warhol, whose artistic output included painting, film, publishing, rock music and TV, is explored in this engaging documentary. Through interviews with friends, film clips and shots of his paintings and movies, we follow Warhol through his early days as a commercial artist into more heady times as a leading conceptual artist and patriarch of the avante-garde to his final days as a dazed celebrity maven. The filmmaker successfully argues that Warhol's talent and fame went far beyond simply painting Campbell soup cans and that he should be considered one of the most important artists of the 20th century. ★★★ $39.99

Warlock

(1959, 122 min, US, Edward Dmytryk) A lawman and his sidekick (Henry Fonda and Anthony Quinn) clean up a Western mining town; but another law enforcer, a reformed bandit (Richard Widmark), challenges the pair to a final showdown. An efficient western with good action and nice characterizations. ★★★ $19.99

Warlock

(1988, 102 min, US, Steve Miner) Julian Sands plays the title character, an evil witch who escapes a fiery punishment in 17th-century Massachusetts by fleeing through time to present-day Los Angeles. Once there, he plans to restore "The Grand Grimoire" (the Satanic bible said to contain the lost name of God) and unleash the power to "unmake" the universe. Though the story line maintains some interest, this is no more than a grade-B supernatural thriller. ★★½ $14.99

Warlock 2: The Armageddon

(1993, 90 min, US, Anthony Hickox) Julian Sands, an actor whose career veers from serving in heaven (*A Room with a View*) to ruling in hell (*To Kill a Vampire*) throws another log on the fire & brimstone with this stylish and surprisingly effective sequel that puts a greater emphasis on special effects and horrific visuals than its 1988 predecessor. Sands reprises his role as Satan's favorite son, hot on the trail of the seven magical jewels that can resurrect his fiery father. Only a pair of perky Druid messiahs stand in his way. Not as ridiculous as it sounds (okay, maybe it is), it's a lot of fun. ★★½ $14.99

Warm Nights on a Slow Moving Train

(1987, 91 min, Australia, Bob Ellis) "Catholic schoolteacher by day...high-class hooker by night." Yes, the concept does look like a typical exploitation flick, but appearances can deceive. For this Aussie import is a funny, erotic and wonderfully entertaining drama on the continual war between the sexes. Wendy Hughes stars as a quiet teacher who, on weekends, takes the night train from Melbourne to Sydney to visit her ailing brother. It is on the train that she dons her spiked heels, creates a new persona for the night, and becomes a classy hooker, tricking with passengers and generally using and abusing men at her will. Her cold approach to sex and relationships is challenged after she falls in love with one of her clients: a mysterious man whose interest in her might be more than just sex. Hughes' performance goes beyond the role of "the hooker with a broken heart" as she creates a memorable, believable and ultimately tragic character. ★★★

Warrior's Rest (Le Repos du Guerrier)

(1962, 98 min, France, Roger Vadim) Brigitte Bardot stars as an innocent woman who, after saving the life of a man attempting suicide, finds herself becoming more deeply involved with him. Claiming her as the keeper of his soul, this mystery man soon moves in with her. Attracted by his charms and attention, Bardot falls in love and soon abandons her previous boyfriend and lifestyle. But the tables are turned as her love turns into a one-sided affair. A fine drama of obsessive love, power and commitment. (French with English subtitles) ★★★

The Warriors

(1979, 94 min, US, Walter Hill) Controversial and violent teen pic about a New York City gang which is framed for the murder of a local

hotshot and becomes hunted by all the other gangs in the city. ★★½ $14.99

The Wash

(1988, 93 min, US, Michael Toshiyuki Uno) Set in San Fransisco, this enormously appealing and overlooked gem revolves around a recently separated husband and wife who had met at a Japanese internment camp during WWII. Mako and Nobu McCarthy give two exceptional performances as the estranged couple, whose only contact with each other is when she sees him weekly to do his wash. The film's poignant, emotional center examines the wife's (McCarthy) personal conflict when she falls in love with another man, forcing her to confront the old-world values of her heritage and the ever-changing demands of a new way of life. ★★★½

The Wasp Woman

(1960, 66 min, US, Roger Corman) Corman's knock-off of the previous year's hit, *The Fly*, finds Susan Cabot using royal jelly to stay young forever. Instead it turns her into a killer queen bee. ★ $9.99

Watch It!

(1993, 102 min, US, Tom Flynn) *Watch It!* is a supremely entertaining and bitingly accurate comedy about the way men and women relate. A lot of credit has to go to writer-director Flynn for managing to beautifully merge bitter (but witty) cynicism with sentimental (but not sickening) romance. Focusing on a group of "post-twentysomething" friends living in Chicago, *Watch It!* features a talented cast including Peter Gallagher as a non-committing drifter who shows up one morning on the doorstep of his womanizing cousin Jon Tenny. Spotlighting a few "male bonding" scenes the film also lets women in on conversations that they would never get to hear otherwise. Perhaps the only problem with *Watch It!* is that (as most films do) it spends more time with its male characters than it does with the female ones. And it's a shame, because the characters played by Suzy Amis and Lili Taylor (who is woefully underused) are as engaging and complicated as any of the male characters. ★★★ $92.99

Watch on the Rhine

(1943, 114 min, US, Herman Shumlin) Lillian Hellman's cautionary drama about the rise of Nazism in the late 1930s gets a first-rate screen treatment. Paul Lukas won an Oscar for his powerful portrayal of a German refugee, now living in Washington with his family, who is hunted by Nazi agents. Bette Davis also stars as Lukas' wife, and Lucille Watson is very good as the "Everyperson" who chooses to ignore the coming catastrophe. ★★★½ $19.99

Watcher in the Woods

(1980, 84 min, US, John Hough) Effective Disney-produced ghost story about an American family who move into Bette Davis' British country estate, where the youngest girl is haunted by visions of Davis' long-lost daughter. Also with Carroll Baker, David MacCallum and Lynn-Holly Johnson. (This is the edited version of the 108-minute theatrical release; however, the film was cut to tighten the rather

W

confusing longer version, not because of censorship or scares.) ★★½ $9.99

Water

(1985, 95 min, GB, Dick Clement) A congenial but generally inept comedy about a Caribbean British colony that is transformed by the discovery of a pure mineral water source within its tiny confines. What follows is a comedy of commercial and social exploitation with the local British Governor (Michael Caine) suddenly caught in a juggling match with greedy U.S. oil interests, an internal insurrection, and other assorted lunacies. ★★ $29.99

The Waterdance

(1992, 106 min, US, Neal Jimenez & Michael Steinberg) Superb work from an accomplished cast, which includes Eric Stoltz, Wesley Snipes and William Forsythe, does justice to a well-balanced and finely crafted script from codirector Jimenez, based on his own experiences. Stoltz is a young writer who winds up in rehabilitation after becoming paralyzed in an accident. Snipes and Forsythe are fellow paraplegics. Jimenez deftly avoids the potential heavy-handedness of his subject and instead tells his story with a wit and warmth which is unsentimental and uncompromising and invites favorable comparison to Marlon Brando's first film vehicle, *The Men.* ★★★½ $19.99

Waterfront

(1983, 284 min, Australia, Chris Thompson) Fans of five-hour spectacles should enjoy this Australian *Last Exit to Brooklyn.* Set on the turbulent waterfront of Melbourne after WWII, the drama focuses on the bitter fight between striking dock workers, a right-wing prime minister, desperate Italians hired as "scabs" and the greedy owners intent on getting the shipyard humming again. The alluring Greta Scacchi stars as an Italian immigrant reluctantly dragged into the labor battle and Jack Thompson as a union leader who falls passionately in love with her. ★★★

Waterland

(1992, 95 min, GB, Stephen Gyllenhaal) Gyllenhaal's (*Paris Trout*) moody adaptation of the Graham Swift novel stars Jeremy Irons as a high school history teacher whose past provides his jaded students with a somber lesson in history. Meanwhile, his present emulates the haunting memories of his past. Sinead Cusack is superb as Irons' wife (a role she plays in real life) as is Ethan Hawke, whose disillusioned youth serves as the catalyst for Irons' looking into his past. At times confusing and often disjointed, this film is still a challenge worth taking. ★★★ $19.99

Watermelon Man

(1970, 97 min, US, Melvin Van Peebles) Social comedy with a lot of bite about a bigoted white man who awakens one morning to discover that he has turned black. Godfrey Cambridge's broad playing helps greatly in the enjoyment of this racial parable. ★★★ $11.99

Waterworld

(1995, 135 min, US, Kevin Reynolds) Had *Waterworld* cost half its reported $175,000,000, it would have entertained the action crowd looking for a mindless, exciting summer film and probably no more word about it would have been said. However, that's not the case. Kevin Costner, in the biggest gamble of his career, stars as a half-man, half-fish — blantantly based on Mel Gibson's loner Mad Max — who becomes involved in tribal warfare on a water-logged planet, the effects of the polar icecaps melting. Dennis Hopper also stars as the nefarious head of the Smokers, a deadly group who smoke cigarettes (but it's not explained where they get them) and terrorize any and all in their path. The set design and effects of *Waterworld* are impressive, but the haunting question remains: Are they worth the sum lavished upon it? Usually films shouldn't be judged by their budgets, but occasionally you just can't ignore it. Despite the fact of the morally disgusting amount spent, *Waterworld* is a formulaic, over-produced adventure film which features spectacular production values;

it's fun for awhile but eventually its controversy sinks in and weighs it down. (Available letterboxed and pan & scan) ★★½ $19.99

Waxwork

(1988, 97 min, US, Anthony Hickox) Inventive horror film with a most unusual premise: a group of teens (that's *not* the inventive part) spend a night at a mysterious house of wax. Each visitor becomes part of the presentation by being hurled back in time and acting out the gruesome renderings. With Zack Galligan, Deborah Foreman and David Warner. ★★★ $14.99

Waxwork II: Lost in Time

(1991, 94 min, US, Anthony Hickox) Fans of 1988's ambitious *Waxwork* may appreciate this often hilarious send-up of the genre. Zach Galligan picks up where he left off as the survivor of a wax museum holocaust who is propelled into various time periods (all recognizable horror movie settings) as he tries to seal the gateway to the dark dimensions. Watch for Bruce Campbell's movie-stealing cameo. Also starring Alexander Godunov. ★★½ $14.99

Way Down East

(1920, 119 min, US, D.W. Griffith) Classic silent melodrama, with Lillian Gish as the quintessential virtuous country girl seduced by the evil city slicker. Includes the famous scene with Gish trapped and washed away on an ice floe. Also starring Richard Barthelmess and Lowell Sherman. ★★★★ $24.99

Way Out West

(1937, 66 min, US, James W. Horne) One of Laurel & Hardy's funniest films, this classic western spoof has the boys delivering the deed of a gold mine to the wrong girl. ★★★½ $19.99

The Way We Were

(1973, 118 min, US, Sydney Pollack) Compelling romantic drama with Robert Redford and Barbara Streisand meeting in college in the late 1930s and having an on-again, off-again affair over the next 15 years. Streisand plays a campus activist who is enamored by gorgeous WASP Redford, meeting years later when each has made a name for themsleves. One of the first films to explore the Hollywood blacklist of the 1950s, though it is used merely as a subplot. ★★★ $14.99

The Way West

(1967, 122 min, US, Andrew V. McLaglen) A wagon train with an aging scout (Robert Mitchum) and a ruthless U.S. Senator (Kirk Douglas) searches for the promised land of the Northwest Territories. With Richard Widmark, Stubby Kaye "and introducing Sally Field as Mercy." ★★ $14.99

Wayne's World

(1992, 95 min, US, Penelope Spheeris) Mike Meyers and Dana Carvey bring their zany, head-banging brand of seriously adolescent humor to the big screen with way cool results. Wayne and Garth must fight to save their basement cable-TV show from the clutches of unscrupulous producer Rob Lowe, and Wayne gets the hots for truly "babe-a-licious" Tia Carrere. A post-punk Spheeris directed this hilarious ode to '90s teen culture which fea-

Wayne and Garth "party on" in *Wayne's World*

tures a killer rendition of Queen's "Bohemian Rhapsody." Destined to be a cultural signpost for decades to come — NOT! ★★★ $14.99

Wayne's World 2

(1993, 94 min, US, Stephen Surjik) Their "excellencies" Wayne and Garth are back with this slightly regurgitated yet nonetheless amusing sequel. Wayne takes on the task of organizing a massive outdoor rock concert, "Waynestock," in his home town of Aurora, Illinois. This sets the stage for a '70s-inspired amalgam of loosely tied together plot contrivances which for the most part offer up winning one-liners, witticisms and spoofs. Among the film's highlights are a side-splitting tribute to the Village People; a marvelous re-creation of *The Graduate*; a dubbed chop-socky kung fu fight; and Charlton Heston. Twentysomethingers beware: Much of the film's humor seems aimed not at its target audience but Baby Boomers. ★★½ $14.99

Ways of Love (L'Amore)

(1948, 69 min, Italy, Roberto Rossellini) Two episodes, dedicated by Rossellini to "the art of Anna Magnani," comprise this indulgent drama about the illusion and pain of love. "The Miracle" stars Magnani as a slightly retarded farm girl who is seduced by a stranger (Federico Fellini) who she believes to be St. Joseph and her newborn son the child of God. "The Human Voice," based on a Jean Cocteau play, features Magnani as a woman distraught by the recent breakup with her lover. In a painfully personal monologue to her unseen and unheard lover on the telephone, she attempts to persuade him not to leave. Interestingly, the film was banned in New York for blasphemy. (Italian with English subtitles) ★★½ $59.99

We of the Never Never

(1983, 132 min, Australia, Igor Auzins) Based on the true-life experience of popular Australian novelist Jeannie Gunn, this beautifully photographed, award-winning film focuses on the first white woman to live in the vast Outback of Australia's Northern Territory. With courage and determination she faces the many hardships of this barren land and the hostility of the men in the region, while acquiring a deep compassion and respect for the Aborigines of the "never never," where one could ride all day and "never never" reach the horizon. ★★★ $59.99

We the Living

(1942, 160 min, Italy, Goffredo Alessandrini) The Russian Revolution is the fiery backdrop for this story of love's ability to endure the ravages of oppression. Based on the classic Ayn Rand novel, the film was made with great difficulty during Mussolini's reign in WWII Italy. With overtly anti-fascist themes, several of the film's key scenes were snipped for government screenings and then replaced for its world premiere at the 1942 Venice Film Festival. But the film was seized by authorities, and placed in a vault for decades until the late 1960s. Eventually, new prints were struck for this eloquent and deeply moving tale of love versus authority, and the film only in the early '90s received its first commercial screenings since

Gary Oldman (l.) and Alan Bates in *We Think the World of You*

World War II. Starring Rossano Brazzi, Alida Valli and Fosci Giachetti. (Italian with English subtitles) ★★★

We Think the World of You

(1988, 92 min, GB, Colin Gregg) This film version of J.R. Ackerley's best-selling 1961 novel about a love triangle between two men and a dog is not wholly successful and can be best described as an "interesting failure." Set in the rubble of post-WWII East-End London, Alan Bates stars as the older, set-in-his-ways part-time lover of Gary Oldman, a rougish charmer who divides his affections between his wife and child, and Bates. The situation is upset when Oldman is sent to prison for six months. The care and feeding of his beloved dog Evie, a charmer in her own right, is left to his mother. But Bates, desperate for a replacement love, begins to care for her and becomes obsessed with the dog; able to see in her qualities that his gaoled lover could never possess. Not your usual love story. ★★

We Were One Man

(1981, 105 min, France, Philippe Vallois) This touching, unusual love story chronicles the budding relationship between a wounded German soldier and the young French peasant who nurses him back to health. Excitable, dim-witted Guy's lonely existence is brightened when he comes upon Rolf in the forest. The two bask in playful, homoerotic exchanges until the war reenters their lives and tries to separate them. ★★★ $49.99

We're Back! A Dinosaur's Story

(1993, 71 min, US) A futuristic philanthropist, in order to grant the wishes of present day children, brings artificially intelligent dinosaurs to New York City. Upon their arrival, the four dinosaurs befriend a young runaway on his way to the circus, only to have to rescue him when the circus owner turns out to be an evil hypnotist. Luscious animation, a thrilling soundtrack, the voices of John Goodman, Rhea Pearlman, Martin Short and Jay Leno,

and production by Steven Spielberg all add up to a real crowd pleaser. Though the plot is somewhat thin, the visuals are exciting and the characters endearing. ★★★ $14.99

We're No Angels

(1955, 106 min, US, Michael Curtiz) Engaging comic fluff with Humphrey Bogart, Peter Ustinov and Aldo Ray as Devil's Island escapees who are taken in by a French merchant family, who are unaware of their true identity. ★★★ $14.99

We're No Angels

(1989, 108 min, US, Neil Jordan) The idea of Robert De Niro and Sean Penn costarring in a remake of the 1955 Humphrey Bogart comedy *We're No Angels*, and having it written by David Mamet, must have looked great on paper. So what happened? This is a painfully unfunny comedy with De Niro and Penn as prison escapees who masquerade as priests to elude a search party. The film captures none of the spirit of playfulness which made the original so entertaining: this version is a heavy-handed misconception and strictly for fans of the two stars. ★ $14.99

Weapons of the Spirit

(1989, 90 min, US, Pierre Sauvage) This warm and gripping documentary traces an amazing event in World War II history that occurred in the small French village of Le Chambon. As Hitler plowed and pillaged his way through Europe, fleeing Jews began to arrive in the predominantly Protestant town, where they were undeniably and even enthusiastically given refuge. Although the Nazi threat was becoming increasingly more apparent, the brave and generous townspeople continued to offer not only food and shelter, but a complete acceptance of and genuine dedication to these 5,000 Jewish inhabitants. Director Sauvage, himself born in Le Chambon, celebrates the good will and delivers what is truly a labor of love. (English and French with English subtitles) ★★★½ $59.99

The Weavers: Wasn't That a Time

(1981, 78 min, US, Jim Brown) An engaging mix of personal and concert footage from Carnegie Hall, featuring noted folk performers Pete Seeger, Lee Hays, Ronnie Gilbert and Fred Hellerman. ★★★ $19.99

Webb Wilder's Corn Flicks

(1991, 64 min, US, Stephen Mimms) This compilation of three independent shorts follows the zany antics of eccentric musician-detective Webb Wilder and his outrageous approach to life and art. The first short is most noteworthy for its trashing of cinema intellectuals and its biting one-liners. The second follows the life of 87-year-old Aunt Hallie and her paranoid campaign against discarded used condoms, which she perceives as a threat of disease. The third finds the Wilder at his cheapest and most musical. ★★½ $19.99

A Wedding

(1978, 125 min, US, Robert Altman) Altman's enjoyable follow-up to his acclaimed *Nashville* utilizes the same multicharacter collage which earmarked his classic film. Two very diverse families come together for a ritzy, upper-class wedding, revealing family skeletons and hidden passions, among other things. Carol Burnett heads a very strong ensemble cast including Mia Farrow and Lillian Gish. ★★★ $59.99

The Wedding Banquet

(1993, 111 min, Taiwan/China/US, Ang Lee) *La Cage aux Folles* Asian-American style! This wholesome gay comedy follows the family drama of Wai Tung (Winston Chao), a transplanted Taiwanese gay man and now New York real estate entrepreneur. Living with his American boyfriend, Simon (Mitchell Lichtenstein), Wai is so exasperated by his parents' persistent inquiries into his marital prospects that he arranges a marriage-of-convenience with a wacky artist from Shanghai desperate for a green card. The plan backfires, however, when his parents announce they are coming to New York to meet the bride! Frantically, the two lovers remove all vestiges of their relationship from the apartment, posing as landlord-tenant and bringing in the faux fiancée. All is well until the parents spearhead an elaborate wedding banquet that involves a night of gaudy excesses and some unwanted surprises. The delightful characters are the real attraction of this sexual and cultural comedy-of-errors which is both witty and perceptive. ★★★½ $96.89

The Wedding Gift

(1994, 87 min, GB, Richard Loncraine) Jim Broadbent and Julie Walters form the backbone of this amiable comedy-drama based on the true story of one of the early sufferers of what has come to be known as "chronic fatigue syndrome." Because of a series of unexplainable ailments, Walters becomes dependent on husband Broadbent, who becomes her devoted caretaker. Eventually, he is smitten by a nearly blind novelist (Sian Thomas), but he finds himself unable to cheat on his disabled wife. Walters, however, has another plan as she arranges for Thomas to take her place upon her death! Though this sounds like the basis for a bawdy comedy, *The*

Wedding Gift is instead a slightly somber melodrama peppered with Broadbent and Walter's witty repartee, which though pleasing to watch, is ultimately a letdown. ★★½ $19.99

Wedding in Blood

(1973, 98 min, France, Claude Chabrol) The moral degeneration of the French middle class is familiar territory for Chabrol as he continues his favorite theme in this moody drama. Stéphane Audrane and Michel Piccoli are married to each other but both are unfaithful. Each one concocts a plan to murder the other in order to free themselves. Who will get it first? A nice mystery and psychological thriller. (French with English subtitles) ★★★½ $19.99

Wedding in Galilee

(1988, 113 min, Israel, Michel Khleifi) The son of Abu Adel, an elderly patriarch, is about to be married. His father wants him to have a traditional wedding ceremony lasting well into the night. But Abu Adel and his son are Palestinians living under a dusk-to-dawn curfew imposed by the Israeli military. In order to let his son have the wedding party, the father seeks the permission of the governor to suspend the curfew for the wedding night. The governor agrees, but only under the condition that he and his entourage be allowed to attend. So begins *Wedding in Galilee*, a timely and thought-provoking examination of Palestinian-Israeli tensions from the rarely heard Palestinian point of view. (Israeli and Arabic with English subtitles) ★★★ $24.99

Wedding in White

(1972, 103 min, Canada, William Fruet) One of the most important Canadian films of the 1970s, this gritty though sensitively handled drama is set in an impoverished village during WWII. It tells the unsettling story of a young girl who is raped by her brother's army buddy and then forced to marry a middle-aged bachelor to preserve the family honor. Carol Kane is unforgettable as the young girl, and Donald Pleasence is masterful as her unyielding father. ★★★½

The Wedding March

(1928, 117 min, US, Erich von Stroheim) The only film by von Stroheim where the villain is allowed to live — only because a sequel was never completed by him! Which is a shame because part two opens with the Wedding Night (Part two was completed by someone else and released overseas as *The Honeymoon*). It's another love triangle in old Vienna with von Stroheim himself playing the prince. ★★★½ $29.99

The Wedding Party

(1969, 92 min, US, Cynthia Munroe, Brian De Palma & Wilford Leach) A groom-to-be meets his fiancée's extended family for the first time a few days before the wedding; claustrophobia and dread set in fast. Imaginative use of stop-action, fast and slow motion, non-sync sound and jump cuts enliven the screen debuts of Jill Clayburgh as the bride-to-be and Robert De Niro as a friend of the groom. Charles Pfluger is engaging (pun not intended) as the young man contemplating escape from his promise to marry. ★★

Weeds

(1987, 115 min, US, John Hancock) In this based-on-fact story, Nick Nolte gives a stirring portrayal of a convict whose plays about life behind bars lead to his parole and his works being performed both off-Broadway and in prisons around the country. ★★★ $14.99

Weekend

(1968, 103 min, France, Jean-Luc Godard) One of Godard's most successfully realized films, *Weekend* is a devastating attack on and an apocalyptic metaphor for the rapid collapse of Western capitalistic society. Beginning with a coherent plot (that soon goes astray), the story follows a bourgeois couple who travel by car from Paris to the country. The rural landscape they encounter soon becomes a nightmarish vision of chaos and destruction — with the road littered with traffic jams, burning cars, violence and death. Godard's pessimistic vision of the Left as a viable alternative is evidenced by the couple's concluding contact with a group of Maoist cannibalistic hippies. A highlight of the film is the ten-minute tracking shot of the mammoth traffic jam that encapsulates all of the anarchy of a society in decay. (French with English subtitles) ★★★½ $29.99

Weekend at Bernie's

(1989, 97 min, US, Ted Kotcheff) *Weekend at Bernie's* may be tasteless and sophomoric, but there is no denying it is funny. Andrew McCarthy and Jonathan Silverman star as young corporate go-getters who get invited to the boss' palatial oceanfront home for the weekend — to be murdered. But the tables are turned, and it is Bernie who gets his. Only problem is, the body keeps popping up everywhere and no one seems to recognize the fact that Bernie is dead. Things get even more complicated when the boys think they're next, and to save themselves, they must make it look like Bernie is really alive. "Masterpiece Theatre" it's not. It's not even *The Trouble with Harry*. But it is for undemanding comedic tastes. ★★½ $9.99

Weekend at Bernie's 2

(1993, 89 min, US, Robert Klane) The irrepressible Bernie is back in this occasionally funny but very silly follow-up to the 1989 surprise hit about the corpse that just won't stay dead. Terry Kiser reprises his role as Bernie, who this time is reanimated by a Virgin Islands voodoo priestess who's after the money he embezzled before his demise. Jonathan Silverman and Andrew McCarthy, both looking a little worn by all these shenanigans, also return as Bernie's "guardians." The humor is as macabre as in the first film, though it's really hard not to laugh at seeing Bernie dancing his way into the ocean with a harpoon through his head. Fun for the whole family — The Addams', that is. ★★ $14.99

Week-End at the Waldorf

(1945, 130 min, US, Robert Z. Leonard) This updated and Americanized version of *Grand Hotel* is a slick, surprisingly enjoyable comedy-drama. Set in New York at the Waldorf-Astoria directly at the end of WWII, the story follows the varied lives of those who have come to stay at the luxury hotel. In the Garbo role is Ginger

W

589

Welcome to the Dollhouse

Rogers, playing a famous actress who sort of wants to be alone. The ever-debonair Walter Pidgeon is the war correspondent who keeps Rogers from her solitude. This plot, which is the film's main focus, is played for laughs — of which there are quite a few. More dramatic is the subplot between injured soldier Van Johnson and gold-digging stenographer Lana Turner. Director Leonard nicely intercuts the numerous stories and elicits pleasant performances from the entire ensemble, which also includes Robert Benchley and bandleader Xavier Cugat. ★★★ $19.99

Weird Science

(1985, 94 min, US, John Hughes) A wasted comic fantasy about two high school boys (Anthony Michael Hall and Ilan Mitchell-Smith) who create their "perfect" woman from a computer. Kelly LeBrock is the dream girl. ★ $9.99

Welcome Home, Roxy Carmichael

(1990, 97 min, US, Jim Abrahams) A charming tale of an orphaned misfit who gets a new lease on life when she discovers that her mother may be a Hollywood star returning home for the first time in 15 years. Winona Ryder's penchant for eccentric characterizations (*Beetlejuice*, *Heathers*) serves her well in her portrayal of Dinky Bossetti, a misanthropic teen whose only friends are the stray animals she keeps on a makeshift ark by the lake. Jeff Daniels also stars as Denton Webb, the ex-lover who never got over losing Roxy. The overall warmth and sentimentality of the production make this an unqualified sleeper. ★★★ $14.99

Welcome to L.A.

(1977, 106 min, US, Alan Rudolph) The rock music scene in Los Angeles gets the Rudolph treatment in this world of fragile egos, quickie love affairs and broken dreams. Produced by Robert Altman and starring Keith Carradine, Sissy Spacek, Geraldine Chaplin and Harvey Keitel. ★★★

Welcome to the Dollhouse

(1996, 87 min, US, Todd Solondz) A rabid, blisteringly funny sneer at the hell of awkward adolescence, *Welcome to the Dollhouse* explores a wide range of topics from peer group terrorism, sexual identity crises, insufferable siblings, clueless parents, imprisonment in the educational system and nonspecific hysteria to the all-encompassing obsession of the first crush, the first object of desire. Heather Matarazzo is terrific as 11-year-old Dawn, who endures the unabashed cruelty of her fellow students in her nightmare junior high school and the unrelenting, alienating criticism heaped upon her at home. Dawn approaches the daily cadence of ritual ostracism, humiliation and ridicule with a weird, wired solemnity, guileless lies and the unimpeachable martyrdom of the very young. This roiling emotional morass is brought into excruciatingly sharp focus when her brother's garage band gets a new lead singer — a suburban Adonis with a rep for nailing just about any available female. Touching, raucous, hilarious, cruel and insightful by turn, *Welcome to the Dollhouse* joins the ever-growing list of films taking a contemporary look at the female coming-of-age process. ★★★½ $19.99

The Welldigger's Daughter

(1941, 142 min, France, Marcel Pagnol) The wonderful French character actor Raimu stars in this fabulous story of a simple French peasant whose humor and dignity is compromised by his daughter, who finds herself pregnant as her lover goes off to war. With this film, Pagnol continued his firm ability to take complex human predicaments and portray them for us in a rich, subtle manner. (French with English subtitles) ★★★

Werewolf of London

(1935, 75 min, US, Stuart Walker) Henry Hull plays the title creature in this early Universal horror film, made six years before Lon Chaney, Jr. immortalized himself as the more famous Wolfman. A very different werewolf tale is told here, with none of the Gypsy lore and little of the moral anguish Chaney later portrayed. Hull is an English botanist who is bitten by a werewolf on a specimen-collecting tour of Tibet. He returns to London only to realize the nature of his curse and recognizing his helplessness to stop the killing. Hull performs admirably in both human and monster roles; his werewolf is much more human than Chaney's (he even talks), and the first transformation scene is more creative than those in *The Wolfman*. The film, however, lacks the scares of Chaney's version and its protagonist is less interesting and sympathetic precisely because he is not wracked by the hand-wringing guilt for which Chaney's Larry Talbot was famous. This werewolf, unfortunately, is interesting mainly when viewed in comparison with its more famous cousin. ★★ $14.99

Wes Craven's New Nightmare

(1994, 112 min, US, Wes Craven) Craven wrote and directed this inventive movie within a dream within a movie that turns on the interesting premise that the power of the cult fol-

lowing of the previous seven *Nightmare* films has served to bring Freddy Krueger to life in the real world. Heather Langenkamp (the series' plucky ingenue) plays herself as a modern career actress whose son is being plagued by Freddy-style nightmares. When her husband and two friends are killed, she turns to fellow actors Robert Englund and John Saxon and then Craven for guidance. Scary nightmare sequences, an intelligent script and an even more menacing Freddy are put to good use, but for all this Craven cannot restore the series' original luster, and the "is it a dream, movie or real" hijinx inspire a feeling of déjà vu rather than one of dread. ★★½ $14.99

West and Soda

(1965, Italy min, 90, Bruno Bozzetto) Bozzetto's first full-length feature looks like a spaghetti western as done by Jay Ward. His clean lines and simple backgrounds perfectly mirror the moral and physical landscape inherent in these sorts of American melodramas. And it's funny, too. ★★★ $29.99

West Coast Crones

(1991, 28 min, US, Madeline Muir) The particular problems, challenges and experiences of elderly lesbians are explored in this all-too-short documentary. Proudly proclaiming themselves Old Lesbians, an articulate group of nine white, mostly middle-class women meet to discuss issues as diverse as their initial sexual experiences, coming out, their decision to have or not have children, their self-perception, friendships and relationships with other women as well as the expectancy and mental preparation for an approaching infirmity and death. A revealing glimpse into some very interesting and opinionated women. The film makes an interesting companion film with *An Empty Bed*, a film that focuses on the situation of elderly gay men. ★★½ $39.99

West Side Story

(1961, 152 min, US, Robert Wise & Jerome Robbins) Whether referring to the stage or film version, this Leonard Bernstein-Stephen Sondheim musical is one of the all-time greats. Natalie Wood and Richard Beymer are the star-crossed lovers in this updated "Romeo and Juliet" set against the backdrop of gang warfare in New York's Upper West Side. Russ Tamblyn and George Chakiris (Oscar winner) are the gang leaders, and Rita Moreno (also an Oscar winner) is Chakiris' girlfriend. Expertly directed by Wise and Robbins (who also choreographed the classic dance numbers). Winner of 11 Academy Awards, including Best Picture. (Available letterboxed and pan & scan) ★★★★ $19.99

Western Union

(1941, 94 min, US, Fritz Lang) Expansive western adventure with Robert Young and Randolph Scott about the laying of the first transcontinental Western Union wire in the mid-1800s. ★★★ $39.99

The Westerner

(1940, 100 min, US, William Wyler) Solid western adventure with Gary Cooper and Walter Brennan whooping it up in the wild, wild West. Brennan won an Oscar (his third) as

W

the infamous Judge Roy Bean, and he steals the show. With Chill Wills, Forrest Tucker and Dana Andrews. ★★★½ $19.99

Westfront 1918

(1930, 90 min, Germany, G.W. Pabst) Pabst's first sound film deals with trench warfare during the final days of World War I. Strongly antiwar, this intense drama deals with four ordinary German soldiers and the effects the war has on them. There is no glorification of battles won, but rather a meditation on the destructiveness, futility and horror of war. (German with English subtitles) ★★★

Westworld

(1973, 88 min, US, Michael Crichton) Michael Crichton made his directorial debut with this highly original sci-fi thriller about a high-tech amusement park whose mechanical robots begin to rebel. James Brolin and Richard Benjamin are the tourists caught in the melee. Yul Brynner is the gun-slinging robot ringleader. Lots of chills and much suspense. ★★★ $19.99

Wetherby

(1985, 97 min, GB, David Hare) Screenwriter-director Hare has fashioned a fascinating and thought-provoking film which tackles such uncomfortable themes as loneliness, loveless relationships and the death of innocence. Vanessa Redgrave is a quiet Yorkshire schoolteacher who, after the violent suicide of a young man who entered her life, must search her past and present in order to arrive at some understanding of her priorities. ★★★½ $79.99

The Whales of August

(1987, 90 min, US, Lindsay Anderson) Lillian Gish and Bette Davis star in Anderson's eloquent rendition of David Berry's play about two aging sisters living out their final years together. Gish plays the tenderhearted and loving caretaker who patiently looks after sister Davis — who is blind, embittered and given to

petulant outbursts. Both actresses play their parts exquisitely, each projecting a screen presence unscathed by the sands of time. In his first American production, Anderson leaves behind all the rampant political diatribe which are the hallmarks of his earlier works and concentrates on subtle human interaction — the result being a tender and heart-warming look at the delicate process of growing old. ★★★

What About Bob?

(1991, 99 min, US, Frank Oz) Bill Murray has his best role in years in this delightfully crazy comedy as a neurotic psychiatric patient who brings new meaning to the word hypochondria. Murray is passed around from doctor to doctor. His newest shrink is Richard Dreyfuss, who after one session, goes with his family on vacation in New England leaving Murray on his own in New York. What's poor multi-phobic Bob to do? Follow them, of course. Director Oz gets a lot of comic mileage from this absurd premise and the laughs are plentiful. ★★★ $9.99

What Happaned Was...

(1994, 90 min, US, Tom Noonan) A first date takes a nightmarish turn in this meandering first film from actor Noonan (probably best known as the Red Dragon serial killer in *Manhunter*). Michael (Noonan) and Jackie (Karen Sillas) are coworkers in a law firm who develop an attraction for each other. Having dinner together, the two engage in the superficial banter of first dates, then progress deeper and deeper into darker, more personal territory as the evening wears on. Each reveals closely guarded secrets to the other and becomes more frightened and uncomfortable with the person they thought they knew. Though both actors are good in their roles, the screenplay is more a compendium of urban anxieties than an exploration of the dating process. The first half of the film works fairly well, despite the characters' uncomfortable fumbling to get to know each other; but once

the bizarre second half kicks in, the viewer's trust in the film and believability is already gone. Its "Twilight Zone" antics and macabre overtones unfortunately are wasted in this ambitious but unsuccessful experiment. ★★ $96.99

What Happened to Kerouac?

(1986, 96 min, US, Richard Lerner & Lewis MacAdams) The enigmatic image of Beat novelist Jack Kerouac is put into focus in this engrossing documentary portrait of one of the most interesting American figures of the 1950s and early `60s. Once dubbed by *The New York Times* as a "Neanderthal with a typewriter," Kerouac's life and times are recounted through anecdotes from his friends and family, including William Burroughs, Allen Ginsberg, Neal Cassady, Gregory Corso and Lawrence Ferlinghetti. Included in the film are memorable appearances on Buckley's "Firing Line" and "The Steve Allen Show." A must for all Kerouac fans as well as those interested in the artist engulfed in the American culture. ★★★ $69.99

What Have I Done to Deserve This!

(1985, 100 min, Spain, Pedro Almodóvar) Almodóvar's unbelievably funny, absurdist gem lept out of the post-Franco liberalization with the velocity of a cannonball. This twisted and surreal film focuses on a modern Spanish clan which bears more than a passing resemblance to the Addams family. Mom is a frustrated No-Doze addicted housewife who lives in a tiny high-rise with her miserable cab-driving husband (who once forged Hitler's diaries) and her two sons: a 14-year-old drug dealer and a precocious 12-year-old who casually seduces his friends' fathers and is finally sold to a gay dentist. Completing this thorny nest is their batty Grandma who longs to leave Madrid and, with her pet lizard, find a place in the country. Shall we call this "Fun for the whole family?" (Spanish with English subtitles) ★★★★ $79.99

What Price Glory

(1952, 109 min, US, John Ford) Remake of the classic silent comedy-drama based on Maxwell Anderson's play about the WWI exploits of two American soldiers who fall for the same woman while stationed in France. Victor McLaglen and Edmund Lowe had better success in the original as Capt. Flagg and Sgt. Quirt than James Cagney and Dan Dailey have here. ★★½ $19.99

What Price Hollywood?

(1932, 88 min, US, George Cukor) Adela Rogers St. John's story about an alcoholic director whose career goes down as the girl he made a star eclipses him. Needless to say this was remade several times as *A Star Is Born*. Constance Bennett gives as strong performance in this suprisingly tough look at then-contemporary Hollywood. ★★★½ $19.99

What's Eating Gilbert Grape

(1993, 117 min, US, Lasse Hallström) Johnny Depp has long specialized in the alienated teen, the loner who gets by in spite of himself. In *What's Eating Gilbert Grape*, he's still a misfit, but as the title character of this offbeat

West Side Story

W

Laurence Fishburne (l.) and Angela Bassett in *What's Love Got to Do with It?*

charmer, he's probably never been so "adjusted." Living in a small Iowa town, Gilbert comes from a classic dysfunctional family: his 500-pound mother (Darlene Cates) won't move from the couch; and his younger brother (Leonardo DiCaprio) is mentally retarded and constantly climbing the water tower. Into his bored life comes a pretty drifter (Juliette Lewis) who, as it turns out, has a profound effect on all the Grape family. Funny, touching and sweet, with a dash of gentleness to its drama, the film features first-rate performances by all, including a lovely turn by newcomer Cates. But it is Oscar nominee DiCaprio who walks away with the acting honors — he gives a mesmerizing performance which never waivers in its intensity or conviction. ★★★ $14.99

What's Love Got to Do With It

(1993, 118 min, US, Brian Gibson) Angela Bassett and Laurence Fishburne both received well-earned Oscar nominations for their roles as music greats Tina and Ike Turner in this intense musical biography. Infused with the same energy director Gibson brought to the story of another musical legend in *The Josephine Baker Story*, *What's Love...* is a fascinating portrait of the professional and personal lives of the explosive couple. Based on Tina's autobiography, the story covers in varying detail Tina's childhood; her joining Ike's band and their marriage in the late 1950s: and her meteoric rise as a singer while at the same time experiencing heartbreak in her marriage. Bassett and Fishburne's performances display more soul and veracity than mere imitation, which is only one of the many strengths of the film. ★★★½ $9.99

What's New, Pussycat?

(1965, 108 min, US, Clive Donner) Woody Allen's first screenplay and first screen appearance is a comic free-for-all about a fashion editor (Peter O'Toole) and his obsession with beautiful women. Peter Sellers is hilarious as the psychiatrist who's even crazier than his patients. With Capucine, Romy Schneider, Paula Prentiss and Ursula Andress. Tom Jones sings the title tune. ★★★ $19.99

What's Up Doc

(1972, 94 min, US, Peter Bogdanovich) Bogdanovich's deliriously funny homage to screwball comedies, and *Bringing Up Baby* in particular. Barbra Streisand has rarely been funnier, and even the usually bland Ryan O'Neal is in good form, in this lunatic story of identical suitcases leading their owners on a merry chase throughout San Francisco. In her film debut as O'Neal's much-flustered fiancée, Madeline Kahn is priceless. ★★★½ $14.99

What's Up, Tiger Lily?

(1966, 80 min, US, Woody Allen) A grade-B Japanese spy-thriller is the ravaged victim of Allen's hilarious barbs as the search is on for the valuable egg salad recipe. Woody's dubbing the film in English extracts meaning from this otherwise innocuous yarn. ★★★

Whatever Happened to Baby Jane?

(1962, 132 min, US, Robert Aldrich) What more can be said about this camp favorite? Beyond the jet-black humor is a solid, well-made thriller. Bette Davis, as an aging child star, chews the scenery in one of her most memorable screen performances. Joan Crawford, as her crippled sister, is equally captivating. Sibling rivalry was never so wicked and never so much fun! ★★★★ $19.99

The Wheeler Dealers

(1963, 100 min, US, Arthur Hiller) James Garner plays a Texas wheeler dealer who sets out to New York to rope in a couple deals and make a cool million. Lee Remick is the first woman stock analyst on Wall Street who tries to lasso potential client Garner with some worthless stock. A lively if dated comedy ensues when these two players get together. The film tries to embrace a '60s feminist view, but ultimately only mocks it. With this in mind, however, there are genuine charming moments, due in large part to the gracious clowning of Garner, Remick and a seasoned supporting cast including Phil Harris, Chill Wills, Jim Backus, Louis Nye and John Astin. ★★½ $19.99

When a Man Loves a Woman

(1994, 126 min, US, Luis Mandoki) The earnest, heartfelt performances of both Andy Garcia and Meg Ryan help elevate this familiar though touching drama of a husband and wife grappling with alcohol abuse. And though a few scenes ring false, it's no fault of the two stars. Garcia and Ryan play Michael and Alice Green, a couple as ordinary as their names. When Alice's frequent drinking binges become daily occurances, much to the terror of her husband and children, her ordinary life is reshaped by hospitalizations and AA meetings. Basically a three-act drama, the story divides its time examining Alice's alcohol excesses, her drying out, and finally the healing process, which proves as difficult for Michael as it is for Alice. ★★½ $14.99

When a Stranger Calls

(1979, 97 min, US, Fred Walton) Suspenseful but ultimately unsatisfying tale of a killer who stalks a baby-sitter and her family, years after he murdered two of her charges. Carol Kane, Charles Durning, Colleen Dewhurst and Rachel Roberts star. ★★ $64.99

When Father Was Away on Business

(1985, 135 min, Yugoslavia, Emir Kusturica) Focusing on one family's life in Communist Yugoslavia in the early 1950s, this tender, Fellini-esque drama unfolds with disarmingly gentle humor and perceptive political sentiments. The story takes the point of view of Malik, a six-year-old boy whose philandering father is exposed as an "anti-Tito/Stalin Communist" by his loose-lipped lover and his Communist Party brother-in-law. He is sent to prison and his absence is explained to Malik as a "business trip," but the boy soon discovers the truth and begins to understand the compromises and lies one must make to get by. A lusty, boisterous look at life in a society repressed but undetered by the political tyranny of the times. (Serbo-Croatian with English subtitles) ★★★½ $19.99

When Harry Met Sally

(1989, 95 min, US, Rob Reiner) Billy Crystal and Meg Ryan sparkle in this enchanting comedy about the ups and downs of platonic friendship. Harry Burns (Crystal) and Sally Albright (Ryan) first meet through a rideshare in college, with Harry fetching a ride from Chicago to New York in Sally's car. Polar opposites, their relationship is doomed from the start. But over the years, things slowly warm up until eventually they are forced to confront their feelings about each other. Both actors shine and each have more than their share of truly hilarious scenes — not the least of which is Ryan's staged orgasm in a crowded New York delicatessen. Director Reiner has marched bravely into Woody Allen territory and handles the material deftly and crisply. ★★★½ $14.99

When Night Is Falling

(1994, 96 min, Canada, Patricia Rozema) From the director of *I've Heard the Mermaids Singing* comes this refreshingly liberating tale of lesbian love. Camille (Pascale Bussières) is a Christian academician romantically involved with Martin (Henry Czerny), a nice enough fel-

W

low teacher more interested in advancement than romance. Camille's repressed emotions and desire for true love come to the surface after she meets flamboyant circus performer Petra (Rachael Crawford). Despite being diametrical opposites, the two are attracted to each other. Initially denying her sexual attraction to the exotic African-Canadian Petra, Camille plays a repetitive game of "I want you, no, I don't" (see: *Claire of the Moon*). That is, until Camille finally unleashes her pent-up desires in one of the more sexually charged lesbian love scenes ever filmed. Its much appreciated romanticism and the casting of two attractive women aside, the film suffers from a symbolism-laden, seen-it-befroe screenplay and a semi-catatonic lead actress (Bussières). However, the handling of the relationship is both exciting and hopeful, conditions that are much too rare in the typical film that tackles queer love. ★★★ $99.99

When the Party's Over

(1992, 114 min, US, Matthew Irmas) Ostensibly a comedy-drama about the transition into adulthood, director Irmas' film seems aimed at (perhaps even made by) those who have not yet started the journey. In the ensemble tradition of such issue packed films as *St. Elmo's Fire*, this glossy film presents a house full of beautiful, successful young urban stereotypes trying to come to terms with adulthood and each other. The film is structured as a series of loosely connected flashbacks that lead up to a New Year's Eve crisis and the soul-searching powwow that follows. The relatively talented cast includes Rae Dawn Chong as a shallow, manipulative yuppie and Fisher Stevens as a spacey but level-headed performance artist and all get a feeble shot at trying to rise above the material. Young adulthood deserves a slightly less lamebrained rap. ★ $14.99

When the Whales Came

(1989, 100 min, GB, Clive Rees) This somber story stars Paul Scofield as a hermit who holds the secret of a mysterious island off the coast of England. Set just prior to the outbreak of WWI, the film chronicles his friendship with two young girls who break local taboo by befriending him. ★★ $14.99

When the Wind Blows

(1986, 80 min, GB, Jimmy T. Murakami) An unsettling and superior animated tale of a happily retired couple living out their golden years, until they must face living with the consequences of nuclear war. Voices of John Mills and Peggy Ashcroft. Music by David Bowie. ★★★ $79.99

When We Were Kings

(1996, 105 min, US, Leon Gast) The 1974 "Rumble in the Jungle" between Muhammad Ali and reigning heavyweight champ George Foreman is the subject of this fascinating documentary, started in '74 during the media event in Zaire, but finished 22 years later by producer Taylor Hackford. Combining talking-head interviews with comments by spectators and analysts such as George Plimpton, Norman Mailer and Spike Lee, the film introduces Ali as a successful sports figure; but through his intelligence and wit the viewer

gradually succumbs to this articulate man who became a political and moral leader. The story of how underdog Ali managed to defeat the vastly favored Foreman is fascinating enough, but when added to the events which surrounded the fight — it was Don King's first major promotion and also featured musical acts James Brown and B.B. King — it becomes the stuff of legend. More a documentary on the mesmerizing personality of Ali than a detailing of the events of the fight, *When We Were Kings* will please even a non-boxing fan. Its infectious good spirit and rousing portrait of a remarkable athlete and American hero make it well deserving of its Academy Award for Best Documentary. ★★★★ $102.99

When Worlds Collide

(1951, 81 min, US, Rudolph Maté) Good special effects highlight this sci-fi tale about the citizens of Earth preparing for the planet's destruction by an approaching meteor, and the rush to build a rocketship to send a group of selected survivors to another world. "And when worlds collide, said George Pal to his bride, I'm gonna give you a celluloid thrill." ★★★ $14.99

Where Angels Fear to Tread

(1991, 113 min, GB, Charles Sturridge) Released in the shadow of the critically acclaimed *Howards End*, this overlooked adaptation of E.M. Forster's novel is impressively produced, superbly acted and an extremely worthwhile effort. Helen Mirren stars as Lilia Harriton, a wealthy widow who enrages her stodgy in-laws when she runs off to Italy and marries a swarthy young peasant, thereby threatening the family fortune. Scandalized, their matriarch (Barbara Jefford) dispatches Mirren's brother and sister (Rupert Graves and Judy Davis) off to Italy to try and talk some sense into the merry widow. Helena Bonham Carter tops off the cast as Mirren's devoted traveling companion. All of the performances are first rate, but Davis steals the show with her truly over-the-top portrayal of the histrionic Harriet Harriton. The film sports a darker sense of humor and more tragic twists than the standard Forster fare, which makes it all-the-more entertaining and nearly as satisfying as *Howards End*. ★★★½ $14.99

Where Eagles Dare

(1968, 158 min, GB, Brian G. Hutton) Released at the height of the Tet Offensive in 1968, this underrated WWII action adventure film did not make big waves at the box office. Seems people simply weren't hungry for more war images when they could be seen on TV every night. It's kind of a shame because this is a slam-bang cliff-hanger of a tale starring Richard Burton and Clint Eastwood as two soldiers attempting to free an important officer from an escape-proof Nazi prison. Alistair MacLean adapted his own novel with great flair. ★★★½ $19.99

Where Sleeping Dogs Lie

(1991, 92 min, US, Charles Finch) Whoever thought it prudent to awaken this "sleeping dog" no doubt wished to exercise his "basic instinct" for moneymaking by cashing in on the now-bankable talents of a pre-*Basic Instinct*

Sharon Stone. But, despite her overwhelming presence on the display box, the icepick princess has less than 15 minutes of screen time as the agent (and sometimes lover) of a hapless screenwriter (Dylan McDermott) who passes off research work about a gruesome mass murder as fiction — only to have the real murderer show up on his door-step. Also with Tom Sizemore. ★½ $19.99

Where the Buffalo Roam

(1980, 100 min, US, Art Linson) Bill Murray takes on the role of American "gonzo" journalist Hunter S. Thompson, whose passion for writing was equalled only by his love of drugs, alcohol and other vices. Peter Boyle and Bruno Kirby costar. ★★ $19.99

Where the Day Takes You

(1992, 107 min, US, Marc Rocco) This film about the daily, sometimes tragic lives of teenage runaways coexisting in Los Angeles is determinedly somber — as are these kids' lives. And though the story covers little new ground of life on the street, the film possesses such grit and determination it has an immediacy which cannot be ignored. Dermot Mulroney, trading his handsome looks for that of a scraggly druggie, gives a startling performance as the leader of a small clique living by their wits, sleeping under freeway off-ramps, and scrounging for change and food. An equally impressive youthful cast including Sean Astin, Lara Flynn Boyle, Will Smith and Ricki Lake also star as other street kids. ★★½ $9.99

Where the Green Ants Dream

(1984, 100 min, West Germany/Australia, Werner Herzog) Herzog juxtaposes the mystical primitivism of the Australian Aborigine against the expansionist threats of modern industry in this voyage into a world obsessed with conquest. Set against the arid flatlands of southern Australia, the film follows a large mining corporation's effort to extract uranium deposits from the Aborigines' sacred grounds, thereby destroying the landscape and shattering the slumber of the revered "green ants," whose interrupted dreaming would signify the death of the Aboriginal culture. A visually sumptuous work that contemplates the issues of cultural relations, imperialism and the wondrous mysteries of life itself. (In English) ★★★ $24.99

Where the Heart Is

(1990, 107 min, US, John Boorman) An amiable and quirky comedy written by director Boorman and his daughter Telsche. Dabney Coleman stars as a wealthy businessman who decides to teach his three spoiled children a lesson in responsibility by forcing them out of the house and into a rundown tenement he owns. Though the story is unexceptional, the film is uplifted by winning performances all around; and by a collection of wonderful tromp l'oeil paintings. With Christopher Plummer, Crispin Glover and Joanna Cassidy. ★★½ $9.99

Where the Hot Wind Blows

(1959, 125 min, Italy/France, Jules Dassin) Although this fiery Italian soap opera has an appealing all-star cast, there is little else in this

W

tawdry melodrama to recommend. The story is about the decadence, from the peasants to the aristocracy, of a small town — sort of like an Italian *Peyton Place* (it's starting to sound better!). Stars Melina Mercouri, Gina Lollobrigida, Yves Montand and Marcello Mastroianni. (Dubbed) ★½

Where the River Runs Black

(1986, 101 min, Brazil/US, Christopher Cain) A young boy born along the banks of the Amazon River is raised by dolphins when his mother is killed by gold prospectors. When he grows up, and encounters his mother's killers, he seeks revenge. Exquisite cinematography accentuates this compelling family film. (Dubbed) ★★★

Where the Rivers Flow North

(1994, 104 min, US, Jay Craven) Rip Torn and Tantoo Cardinal star in this poignant tale of an old logger who lives on a piece of land slated to be flooded for a new dam. Torn is a man possessed as he tries to beat the corporate world with his own schemes and pipe dreams. Cardinal plays his lover/companion with eloquence and conviction. Michael J. Fox and Treat Williams make effective appearances in this labor of love — which is reminiscent in both style and story of Elia Kazan's powerful *Wild River* — that director Craven labored on for many years. The beauty of the landscape reminds one of the lost innocence of America and the power of greed. Well worth the viewing effort. ★★★½ $14.99

Where Were You When the Lights Went Out?

(1968, 94 min, US, Hy Averback) Doris Day made quite a few entertaining sex comedies in the 1960s; unfortunately, this is not one of them. Averback, a successful TV sitcom director, shows little comic flair with this farce about the goings-on on the night of the New York City 1965 blackout. Doris plays a wife who thinks her husband is cheating on her. To make him jealous, she takes up with Robert Morse...and gets caught in the blackout. Terry-Thomas, Patrick O'Neal and Steve Allen also star. ★½ $19.99

Where's Picone?

(1984, 122 min, Italy, Nanni Loy) Giancarlo Giannini is hilarious as a sleazy con man who reluctantly becomes involved with the wife of a man who inexplicably disappears while in an ambulance going to the hospital. Alternating between a love story and slapstick comedy, the film has Giannini, as a two-bit hustler living on the wrong side of respectability, discovering that the esteemed missing man had a secret life that had strayed far from the norm. A bit silly at times, this genial comedy does pack some suspense and romance in exposing the corruption and duplicitousness of Italian society and bureaucracy. (Italian with English subtitles) ★★½ $29.99

Where's Poppa?

(1970, 82 min, US, Carl Reiner) George Segal desperately tries to get rid of his senile mom (Ruth Gordon), who likes Froot Loops with Coke and has a penchant for biting his rear end.

A savagely funny cult film that pokes fun at sex, muggings and motherhood. ★★★½ $19.99

Which Way Is Up?

(1977, 94 min, US, Michael Schultz) Seriocomic look at life in central California's strife-torn farm community. Richard Pryor plays three roles — a beleaguered worker, his cranky old father, and a hypocritical preacher. An American remake of Lina Wertmüller's *The Seduction of Mimi*. ★★½ $14.99

While the City Sleeps

(1956, 100 min, US, Fritz Lang) Another Lang opus on crime in the big city, this time counterplaying the search for a psychotic serial killer against a power struggle inside a huge media conglomerate. Ably performed by Dana Andrews, Ida Lupino, Rhonda Fleming, George Sanders, Vincent Price, Howard Duff, John Drew Barrymore and Thomas Mitchell. ★★★ $29.99

While You Were Sleeping

(1995, 100 min, US, Jon Turtletaub) Sandra Bullock and Bill Pullman, both of whose stock soared in 1995, will bewitch many a heart in this beguiling romantic comedy. Essentially a Cinderella tale except for the fact that it's Prince Charming who's asleep, *While You Were Sleeping* casts Bullock as a lonely transit worker who saves the life of the handsome businessman (Peter Gallagher) whom she admires from afar. As he lies in a coma, she is mistakenly identified as his fiancée, and then welcomed with open arms into his rather daffy family. All except Gallagher's brother, played with elfin charm by Pullman. As he tries to ascertain her real identity, the two inevitably — but most endearingly — fall in love. It's a slight premise that harkens back to the 1930s and 1940s, but a most engaging cast, real chemistry between the two leads, crisp direction and a lively screenplay make this all-the-more entertaining. Bullock is simply enchanting, and Jack Warden is in good form as a family friend who encourages the charade. ★★★ $14.99

Whispers in the Dark

(1992, 103 min, US, Christopher Crowe) Annabella Sciorra continues a string of well-chosen roles (*The Hand That Rocks the Cradle*, *Jungle Fever* and *True Love*) with this sexually candid shocker. She strikes just the right balance of naiveté and intellectual savvy as a lovelorn psychiatrist who comes to suspect that her new Prince Charming (Jamey Sheridan) may be a sadomasochistic killer. Despite one major plot contrivance and a script so laden with psychobabble that Woody Allen may have penned it, the knockout performances (particularly Deborah Unger as a scene-stealing nymphomaniac) and nail-biting suspense make this an entertaining murder mystery. Also with Alan Alda, Jill Clayburgh, Anthony LaPaglia and John Leguizamo. ★★★ $19.99

The Whistle Blower

(1987, 104 min, GB, Simon Langton) Compelling political drama reminiscent of *Missing* starring Michael Caine as a father who investigates the death of his son, a translator for the British government who may have been murdered to cover up a security leak.

Caine is masterful as the tormented father determined to uncover the truth behind his son's demise. ★★★

Whistle Down the Wind

(1962, 98 min, GB, Bryan Forbes) This charming and extraordinary film is both a Christ parable and a poignant treatise on childhood innocence. Forbes, in a remarkable directorial debut, brings a deft and heart-warming touch to this story of an escaped criminal (Alan Bates) who is found by three young children in their barn and is thought by them to be Christ. ★★★½

Whistling in the Dark

(1941, 77 min, US, S. Sylvan Simon) Red Skelton lends his comic talents to this light-weight, mildly entertaining romp. Skelton is a 1940s radio personality known as The Fox, a wily sleuth who always nails the bad guy. Conrad Veidt gives a pre-Branch Davidian interpretation of a loony cult leader who kidnaps Skelton and forces him to concoct the perfect murder. Also starring Ann Rutherford, Virginia Gray and Eve Arden (in a bit role), the film was followed by two sequels, *Whistling in Brooklyn* and *Whistling in Dixie*. ★★½ $19.99

White

(1994, 93 min, France, Krzysztof Kieslowski) This, the second of Kieslowski's popular trilogy (the others being *Blue* and *Red*), is possibly the weakest of the three, although still quite good. This wry drama of obsession and revenge is played out within the symbolic battlefield of the new democratic Europe — rich Western Europe vs. the poor Eastern countries. The story centers on Karol (Zbigniew Zamahowski), a sweetly nerdish Polish hairdresser who travels to Paris and finds love in the arms of the beautiful Dominique (Julie Delpy). Karol's inability to find a job and to speak the language results in impotency and a frustrated wife. A sexually wanting Dominique divorces him, an act that forces our enterprising hero to return home and plot an elaborate, far-fetched scheme of winning her back...on his terms. Uncomfortably misogynist with an unnecessary ending, the story lacks really likable characters but entertains nonetheless. (French and Polish with English subtitles) ★★½ $19.99

The White Balloon

(1995, 85 min, Iran, Jafar Panahi) Winner of the 1995 Camera d'Or at the Cannes Film Festival, *The White Balloon* gives a quiet glimpse of a foreign land filled with familiar people, an important reminder that it is a government we hate — not a nation. The film has all the virtues of a Satyajit Ray work — most obviously *Pather Panchali* — in its simple tale of a little girl, both sweet and petulant, who loses then regains then loses again the money she has wheedled from her harried mother to buy a goldfish. If director Panahi had done no more than so perfectly captured the tenor and texture of a time, a town and a people, this film would be just as remarkable. It is only when one reflects on how casually Panahi introduces the white balloon — in the final shot! — that the film develops its subtle fla-

Julie Delpy in *White*

vors; flavors that linger long after its brief running time. (Farsi with English subtitles) ★★★★ $19.99

The White Buffalo

(1977, 97 min, US, J. Lee Thompson) Unusual western parable with Charles Bronson as Bill Hickok hunting the title bison, which represents the famous marksman's fear of death. Also with Jack Warden and Kim Novack. ★★½ $14.99

White Christmas

(1954, 120 min, US, Michael Curtiz) Bing Crosby and Danny Kaye make the most of a tuneful Irving Berlin score in this popular holiday-themed musical. Bing and Danny play entertainers who come to the rescue of their old Army superior (Dean Jagger). ★★★ $14.99

The White Dawn

(1974, 109 min, US, Philip Kaufman) A fascinating and original adventure tale about three turn-of-the-century whalers (Warren Oates, Timothy Bottoms and Louis Gossett, Jr.) who are rescued by a tribe of Eskimos when their boat capsizes. A beautifully filmed fable from the director of *The Right Stuff* and *The Unbearable Lightness of Being*. ★★★ $19.99

White Fang

(1991, 107 min, US, Randal Kleiser) Based on the novel by Jack London, this rousing Disney adventure film is good entertainment for the entire family. The story follows the twin tales of a naive young man claiming his dead father's inheritance in the Klondike, and his befriending a wolf cub raised by the Indians. Ethan Hawke and Klaus Maria Brandauer star. ★★★ $14.99

White Heat

(1949, 114 min, US, Raoul Walsh) James Cagney's intense performance highlights this classic underworld drama about ruthless killer Cody Jarrett, he with the headaches and the mother fixation; and the cop determined to put him away. "Made it, Ma. Top of the world!" ★★★★ $19.99

White Hunter, Black Heart

(1990, 112 min, US, Clint Eastwood) This fictionalized account of film director John Huston's adventures while on the set of *The African Queen* is a challenging work for director Eastwood. And as an actor, he gives a bold performance with an uncanny impersonation of the mythic Huston, though it may take some getting used to "Dirty Harry" calling everyone "kid." The story follows Huston's obsession with shooting a giant elephant, and the effect it has on himself, his film crew and his guides. A film of epic scale presented in an intimate fashion, *White Hunter, Black Heart* is a picturesque excursion into the darker regions of man's soul. ★★★ $14.99

White Lie

(1991, 93 min, US, Bill Condon) Gregory Hines gives a first-rate performance in this superior made-for-cable mystery. Hines plays a savvy New York City mayoral assistant who, upon receiving a picture of his father being lynched, returns to his Southern birthplace to uncover the truth behind the murder. There he learns his father was hung for allegedly raping a white woman. He gets unexpected assistance from the woman's daughter (Annette O'Toole), and the two begin an affair as together they attempt to unravel the mystery. One of the many interesting plot developments is having a black actor essay the role of the usually white Southern "redneck" sheriff (played with great relish by Bill Nunn). ★★★½ $89.99

White Man's Burden

(1995, 89 min, US, Desmond Nakano) Taking the thought-provoking premise of the races switched on the economic and social levels, *White Man's Burden* is an intriguing idea which is only occasionally realized. In a world parallel to 1990s America except that whites are the minority and blacks are the ruling power, John Travolta plays a hard-working family man who, after inadvertently catching a glimpse of his employer's wife in the nude, and through a possible misunderstanding by his supervisor, is fired. Unable to secure other work, thrown out of his home and at the end of his rope, Travolta's attempt to extort money from his former boss (Harry Belafonte) eventually leads to him kidnapping Belafonte. The beginning of the film is particularly good in establishing a society in which white children have no role models on TV, a little white boy prefers a black superhero doll, and privileged blacks put on charity shows for the "adorable little white kids." But once the "gimmick" has been set, and Travolta and Belafonte turn into the defiant ones, the story has trouble elaborating on its concept and a scenario of two men at odds with stereotypes rather than each other. ★★½ $19.99

White Men Can't Jump

(1992, 115 min, US, Ron Shelton) After a diverting and successful jaunt with politics in *Blaze*, writer-director Shelton (*Bull Durham*) is back in the sports arena — and this one's another winner. Wesley Snipes stars as a street-smart Venice Beach basketball hustler. He's black. Woody Harrelson also stars as a bumpkin-looking basketball hustler. He's white. A most entertaining and hip comedy emerges when these two hoop con artists team up to sucker the denizens of Southern California's hard courts. It's a great sting: Snipes gets into a game and ultimately brings in rube Harrelson. Who could resist going one-on-one with the Great White Dork? In his first two films, Shelton proved himself to be a master of romantic repartee. Here, the snap and sizzle of a verbal rebound, the volley of masculine bombastics is what distinguishes Shelton's energized film — that and some truly remarkable court footage. Rosie Perez is quite good as Harrelson's girlfriend whose dream is to be a "Jeopardy" contestant (quick, name five "Q" foods). ★★★ $14.99

White Mischief

(1988, 106 min, GB, Michael Radford) Lavishly entertaining and very sexy drama about English pleasure-seekers living in the "Happy Valley" in Kenya during WWII. Greta Scacchi is both beautiful and ideally cast as a bored wife whose affair with an English lord (Charles Dance) leads to murder. Sarah Miles and Murray Head steal the show as cynical hedonists searching for the next party. Joss Ackland gives a great performance as Scacchi's cuckold husband. ★★★

White Nights

(1957, 94 min, Italy, Luchino Visconti) Based on a Fedor Dostoevsky short story and set within a misty, dreamlike seaside city, this sad love story was a great stylistic departure from Visconti's previous, neorealist features, *Senso* and *Ossessione*. Marcello Mastroianni stars as a young man, prowling the docks for a pick-up, who meets and fatefully falls in love with a mysterious, obsessive woman (Maria Schell). In a series of brief walks, chases and attempted escapes, she reveals to him that she is waiting for her lover who, before going to sea, promised to return to her. While talking only of her long-gone lover (Jean Marais), the two develop a relationship, but one destined to end in tragedy. (Italian with English subtitles) ★★★ $59.99

W

White Nights

(1985, 135 min, US, Taylor Hackford) Probably the first musical political thriller. Mikhail Baryshnikov stars as a Russian defector whose plane crash lands him back in the USSR. Gregory Hines is an American defector who befriends him. Though far more successful in its musical moments (which feature terrific dancing by the two stars), there's enough suspense and plot twists to keep most viewers involved. ★★½ $14.99

White of the Eye

(1987, 110 min, US, Donald Cammell) What on the surface appears to be just another psycho-on-the-loose thriller is actually a visually rich and offbeat sleeper, a suspense movie that cooly seduces you and then takes you in strange, unexpected directions. Some of director Cammell's hallucinatory imagery is reminiscent of his collaborations with Nicolas Roeg in the early '70s. A rare performance by the sublime Cathy Moriarty makes this an especially rewarding film. ★★★ $14.99

White Palace

(1990, 104 min, US, Luis Mandoki) That age-old story of two unlikely people overcoming differences in age and background to find true love receives a fresh injection of star power in this touching romantic comedy. Susan Sarandon and James Spader star as, respectively, an earthy, 40-something burger joint queen and an uptight, late-20s Jewish yuppie. Though *White Palace* may be slightly sentimental and formulaic, Spader and Sarandon are as classically mismatched as any classically mismatched couple to come before them and both deliver sparkling performances: together they simply ooze sexuality. A real audience pleaser, with a few surprises and plenty of wit. ★★★ $9.99

The White Rose

(1982, 108 min, West Germany, Michael Verhoeven) This superb wartime thriller is based on the true story of a secret society of students who printed and distributed thousands of anti-Nazi leaflets under the Fuhrer's very nose, reporting the murder of 300,000 Jews and urging the citizenry to sabotage the war effort. Their ill-fated but extraordinary efforts are vividly brought to the screen by Verhoeven, director of *The Nasty Girl*. (German with English subtitles) ★★★½

White Sands

(1992, 101 min, US, Roger Donaldson) After the uneventful box office performances of *Harley Davidson and the Marlboro Man* and *Flight of the Intruder*, anyone holding a membership card to the Mickey Rourke or Willem Dafoe fan clubs would be understandably justified in burning them. But for those who believe in second chances, this exciting quasi-political thriller should restore the faith. Dafoe stars in this "Testosterone Theatre" production as a small-town sheriff who finds a body with a suitcase full of cash and decides to investigate, much to the chagrin of drugs- and arms-runner Rourke. Mary Elizabeth Mastrantonio also stars as a whiny socialite who believes that crime does pay, and Samuel L. Jackson appears as the FBI agent on the case. ★★★ $14.99

The White Sheik

(1951, 88 min, Italy, Federico Fellini) Fellini's first solo directorial effort is also his only full-fledged farce. Told with almost slapstick enthusiasm, the story follows the misadventures of a provincial couple honeymooning in Rome. The young wife wanders upon the filming of a low-brow picture and becomes infatuated with the "hero" — The White Sheik, a bungling and slightly effeminate Rudolph Valentino imitator. Passion drives her to mad pursuit of the actor while her baffled husband searches the Eternal City for his lost wife. (Italian with English subtitles) ★★★ $29.99

White Squall

(1996, 127 min, US, Ridley Scott) Though its story line is never really elevated above a "*Dead Poets Society* Go Boating" scenario, *White Squall* nevertheless manages to sustain interest thanks to some exceptional action scenes and the always reliable Jeff Bridges. Set during the early 1960s, the story centers on a group of high school teens summering on a "floating prep school" headed by Captain Jeff. The first half of the film essentially examines the varying relationships between the kids (some troubled, some naive, etc.) in very familiar fashion. However, the film's second half changes course when the titular storm, a sudden and violent torrent of water, engulfs and capsizes the ship and the crew members are left to fend for their lives. Director Scott handles the storm sequences with great assurance, and terrific cinematography and editing maximize suspense during these scenes. The director is not as fortunate, however, in creating totally believable dramatics between the young protagonists. ★★½ $19.99

White Zombie

(1932, 73 min, US, Victor Halperin) Bela Lugosi stars in this entertaining chiller as a warped magician who uses his powers to raise the dead and supply zombie laborers for a sinister plantation owner. ★★★ $19.99

Who Am I This Time?

(1982, 60 min, US, Jonathan Demme) Demme, whose films lovingly exalt more unconventional characters, is right at home with this delightfully offbeat romantic comedy based on the Kurt Vonnegut, Jr. short story. Christopher Walken plays a painfully shy clerk who only comes alive when performing at the local theatre — taking on the characteristics of the role he's playing. Susan Sarandon is a lonely newcomer who falls for the chameleon man, forcing her to use her feminine wiles, not to mention some of the theatre's great works, to keep his attention. Walken and Sarandon are remarkable; their performance of "A Streetcar Named Desire" makes you long for a full-length version. ★★★½ $24.99

Who Done It?

(1942, 75 min, US, Eric C. Kenton) An uproarious Abbott and Costello romp, with Bud and Lou as a couple of soda jerks trying to break into radio who masquerade as private detectives after an on-the-air murder. With Mary Wickes and William Bendix. ★★★ $14.99

Who Framed Roger Rabbit

(1988, 103 min, US, Robert Zemeckis) Superb animation, almost every beloved cartoon character in our movie history and state-of-the-art special effects combine to produce one of the most glorious entertainments of the decade. Bob Hoskins is a 1940s private detective hired to find out just who did frame Roger Rabbit, that successful, debonair and handsome animated cartoon hero. Christopher Lloyd and Joanna Cassidy costar in this toon-ful modern classic. ★★★★ $9.99

Who Killed Cock Robin?

(1989, 80 min, US, David Stuart) Tongue is planted firmly in cheek in this ordinary though eager-to-please gay murder comedy. Sort of a homosexual Dirty Harry, a gay cop investigates the murder of a porn star, uncovering a variety of types in and out of the industry. Most of the jokes are forced, and the humor is all camp. But it is hard to really dislike any production

White Sands

W

which has a film-quoting dowager doing his best to single-handedly bring back Gloria Swanson. Though the adult film world is the backdrop, there is neither nudity nor sex (with the exception of a simulated scene done strictly for laughs). ★★ $59.99

Who Shall Live and Who Shall Die?

(1982, 90 min, US, Lawrence Jarvick) This searing documentary utilizes previously classified information and rare newsreel footage to probe into the issue of how much the United States government knew of the Holocaust and asks the hard question, "Could the Jews of Europe have been saved?" A unique inquiry into the actions and motives of American Jewish leaders in the 1930s and '40s as well as those of the government of President Roosevelt. ★★★ $29.99

Who Slew Auntie Roo?

(1971, 90 min, US, Curtis Harrington) A kindly old widow's annual Christmas party for the local orphans takes a macabre, unexpected twist. Shelley Winters, Mark Lester, Ralph Richardson and Lionel Jeffries star in this tame though spoofy foray into '70s Gothic horror. ★★½ $69.99

Who'll Stop the Rain

(1978, 126 min, US, Karel Reisz) Nick Nolte gives a riveting performance as an ex-Marine transporting heroin from Saigon to the U.S. during the Vietnam War, finding himself set up for a drug bust. Michael Moriarty and Tuesday Weld costar. ★★★ $14.99

Who's Afraid of Opera, Vols 1-3

A wonderful introduction to opera for young and old alike. Dame Joan Sutherland and conductor Richard Bonynge entertain three puppets with some of opera's greatest arias while explaining the plots and music to the audience. Includes music from "Faust," "Rigoletto," "La Traviata," "Daughter of the Regiment," "The Barber of Seville" and "Lucia di Lammermoor." ★★★ $14.99

Who's Afraid of Virginia Woolf?

(1966, 129 min, US, Mike Nichols) Richard Burton and Elizabeth Taylor deliver career best performances as a tortured college professor and his vitriolic wife in Edward Albee's scorching domestic drama. George Segal and Sandy Dennis (at her mousiest) are the innocent young couple who spend a gut-wrenching, soul-baring evening with lush-ious Liz and down-and-out Dick. Brilliantly directed by Nichols. ★★★★ $19.99

Who's Harry Crumb?

(1989, 98 min, US, Paul Flaherty) For the answer to the question posed by the title of this film, please choose one of the following: a) Who cares b) an imbecilic moron c) a bumbling private detective assigned to a kidnapping case: only because his boss is the kidnapper and the bad guy knows Crumb is too stupid to crack the case d) a character in a film which contains no wit, predictable sight gags, and is an embarrassment to the otherwise talented John Candy e) all of the above. If you chose "e," you are correct. ★ $9.99

Who's Singing Over There

(1985, 95 min, Yugoslavia, Slobodan Sijan) Gifted young director Sijan has created this comic, poignant anti-war satire set in Yugoslavia on the eve of the Nazi invasion. He contrasts the petty squabbles of the wild, provincial characters that have boarded a Belgrade-bound bus with our awareness of the catastrophic events that are to occcur. (Yugoslavian with English subtitles) ★★★

Who's That Girl

(1987, 94 min, US, James Foley) Madonna plays a spunky parolee out to clear her name who totally changes forever the mild existence of yuppie Griffin Dunne. An awkward attempt at screwball comedy. ★ $9.99

Who's That Knocking at My Door?

(1968, 90 min, US, Martin Scorsese) Scorsese's first feature film is a fascinating and highly charged drama that is essentially a primer for his breakthrough film, *Mean Streets*. Clearly autobiographical, the story features a muscular and baby-faced Harvey Keitel in the lead as a confused young man in New York's Little Italy obsessed with the moralistic trappings of Catholicism and indecisive about committing himself to a serious relationship with his girlfriend (Zina Bethune). Scorsese's directorial talent and promise is much in evidence in this gritty and at times arty debut. ★★★ $19.99

Who's the Man

(1993, 90 min, US, Ted Demme) Yo! MTV rap hosts Doctor Dre and Ed Lover star as an inept pair of barbers who somehow become New York cops in this crazy hip-hop "Homeywood" laugher. The film focuses on the authority-questioning stars' mission to clean up their crumbling Harlem neighborhood and stop a nefarious real estate speculator's plan to gentrify the once-thriving area. A fine supporting cast (including Denis Leary), a slammin' soundtrack and over 50 cameos by rap artists (evoking images of *It's a Mad, Mad, Mad, Mad World*) combine to make this film a sure-fire choice for those in search of some witty, urban humor. Director Demme is the nephew of Jonathan Demme. ★★★ $14.99

Who's Who

(1978, 75 min, GB, Mike Leigh) In one of his earliest films, director Leigh — who has proved to be a master at letting his camera "eavesdrop" on the mundane daily lives of England's working class — sets his sights on a group of London stock traders. Though slowly paced, the film elicits some hilarious skewerings of the British caste system as he focuses on these brokerage employees: One group of over-privileged, upper-class twits who hold a dinner party, the other middle-class Thatcherites whose loyalty to Crown and country borders on the surreal. ★★★ $29.99

Whoever Says the Truth Shall Die

(1985, 60 min, The Netherlands/Italy, Philo Bregstein) Pier Paolo Pasolini, Italy's celebrated and controversial poet/novelist/filmmaker, was violently and senselessly murdered by a young male prostitute in 1975. This provocative documentary probes into Pasolini's life and work in an effort to come to some understanding of the events which led up to his death. From interviews with Bernardo Bertolucci and Alberto Moravia, clips from his many films as well as biographical backround, the film attempts to enter the private life of the director, who had a masochistic fascination with society's taboos and its unwanted denizens. Was he killed in a freakish isolated incident or was he assassinated? (Italian with English subtitles) ★★★ $59.99

Whoopee!

(1930, 93 min, US, Thornton Freeland) Eddie Cantor, re-creating his 1929 stage smash, is an absolute joy as a hypochondriac who heads West for his health and becomes involved in the locals' crazy shenanigans. Though some of the songs (those not sung by Cantor) are horribly out-of-date (fast-forward buttons will be pushed), the film does feature some interesting Busby Berkeley production numbers, as well as funny one-liners and, of course, the title tune. For those not familiar with Cantor, this is the place to start to become acquainted with the most popular comedian of his time, and one of the funniest (and unheralded) men in American film comedy (Bob Hope, Danny Kaye and even Pee-wee Herman all borrowed from him). ★★★ $19.99

Whoopi Goldberg Live

(1985, 81 min, US) Whoopi Goldberg's acclaimed one-woman show. Whoopi portrays five characters: a drug addict, a little girl, a surfer chick, a Jamaican housekeeper and a handicapped woman. Goldberg's characterizations are first-rate, and the comedy is on-target and hilarious. ★★★½

Whoops Apocalypse

(1981, 137 min, GB, John Reardon) John Cleese stars in this series of stabs at the political process as it brings us closer and closer to the moment of total annihilation. A flat and humorless piece that's not really worth the bother. ★½ $14.99

Whore

(1991, 92 min, GB/US, Ken Russell) The notorious Ken Russell, in a kind of follow-up to *Crimes of Passion*, takes a less-successful walk down those streets of despair, leaving behind his bag of psychedelic tricks. Sadly, what is intended as a searing insight into the world of prostitution completely misses the mark under Russell's histrionic mis-direction. Theresa Russell sleepwalks, er, streetwalks through this talky tale of a hooker on the run from her psychotic pimp. ★ $14.99

Whose Life Is It Anyway?

(1981, 118 min, US, John Badham) First-rate screen version of Brian Clark's award-winning play starring Richard Dreyfuss in an astonishing performance as an artist who, paralyzed from the neck down after an auto accident, petitions on the right to die. Though the subject matter sounds terribly depressing, the film is alive with a sardonic wit and features compelling performances from the supporting cast, including John Cassavetes, Christine Lahti and Kenneth McMillan. ★★★ $79.99

The Wicked City

Why Does Herr R. Run Amok?

(1970, 88 min, Germany, Rainer Werner Fassbinder) This devastating thriller on social conformity and the petit bourgeoisie stars Kurt Raab as Herr R., a successful professional who inexplicably goes berserk and takes his own life, but not before killing his wife, a neighbor and his little son. A doomed, taut polemic of failed expectations and the banality of existence. (German with English subtitles) ★★★½ $79.99

Why Me?

(1990, 87 min, US, Gene Quintano) Two mismatched jewel thieves mistakenly snatch a cursed ruby ring. Now they want to go straight, but find themselves being pursued by the cops, other thieves and religious fanatics. Christopher Lambert, Kim Greist and Christopher Lloyd star. ★★ $89.99

Why Shoot the Teacher?

(1976, 99 min, Canada, Silvio Narizzano) Bud Cort (*Harold and Maude*) stars in this amiable yet touching story of a dedicated schoolteacher who faces the grim realities of life when he is hired to teach the children of an impoverished farming town in Alberta, Canada, during the Great Depression. Initially spurned by the adults, his icy reception soon changes to acceptance as he gradually adjusts to the difficult conditions and begins to understand his pupils and their way of life. An earnest and, at times, humorous film impressively directed by Narizzano (*Georgy Girl, Loot*). ★★★

Wicked City

(1992, 95 min, Hong Kong, Mak Tai Kit) The popular Japanese adult anime is given a hyperkinetic going-over in the inimitable Hong Kong style in this very entertaining live-action version. The sex and violence of the original have been significantly toned down and the story has been vastly altered as, this time around, we follow the adventures of two agents in the Anti-Reptoid Bureau, dedicated to hunting down and destroying renegade Reptoids—other-dimensional evil beings dedicated to the destruction of humanity. A forthcoming peace conference between the Reptoid leader (played by Kurosawa favorite Tatsuya Nakadai) and a human delegation is threatened when treacherous elements in the Reptoid community plan a sabotage campaign. A wild and fun visual feast, the film sometimes sacrifices the cohesiveness of the plot in favor of a spectacular effect or action sequence. But what sequences they are. The finale, in which the two main enemies fight each other while riding astride two airborne jumbo jets, has to be seen to be believed. (In English and Mandarin with English subtitles) ★★★ $19.99

The Wicked Lady

(1945, 104 min, GB, Leslie Arliss) This period melodrama stars Margaret Lockwood as an amoral, thrill-seeking aristocrat who teams up with highwayman James Mason to embark on a life of crime. Released just after the end of WWII, the film caused a stir in its day on account of its bawdiness and perhaps the abundance of Ms. Lockwood's cleavage. ★★½

The Wicked Lady

(1983, 98 min, GB, Michael Winner) Awkward remake of the 1945 programmer, this time with Faye Dunaway camping it up as the British noblewoman by day who becomes a highway bandit by night. Featuring a triumvirate of Britain's finest (Alan Bates, John Gielgud and Denholm Elliott), the film nevertheless reflects the slipshod production usually associated with Cannon Films, and qualifies only as a guilty pleasure at best. ★½

Wicked Stepmother

(1988, 90 min, US, Larry Cohen) A witch (Bette Davis) and her daughter (Barbara Carrera) make a living at marrying rich widowers, shrinking them to shoebox size, and absconding with their money. Davis, in her last film, withdrew from this project, and a double was used in many scenes. ★ $14.99

The Wicker Man

(1973, 104 min, GB, Robin Hardy) A policeman visits a mysterious Scottish island to investigate the disappearance of a young girl. He discovers a pagan society, ruled by Christopher Lee, which has some surprises in store for him. The policeman gets a little heated up when he discovers the town's plans for a human sacrifice. This classic horror thriller in the Hammer tradition also stars the unforgettable Britt Ekland. The full-length version. ★★★ $9.99

Wide Sargasso Sea

(1993, 100 min, Australia, John Duigan) Sort of a prequel to Emily Bronte's "Jane Eyre," *Wide Sargasso Sea* reinterprets and updates the story and locates it on the steamy beaches of Jamaica. The story is told from the perspective of Rochester's (Nathaniel Parker) first wife, Antoinette (Karina Lombard), a beautiful Creole woman whose family has a foreboding history. A tale of betrayal, love, madness and power, much of the subtext is ripped from the original novel turning the first half of this film adaptation into a semi-erotic mishmash filled with shots of full frontal nudity, both male and female. Things pick up, however, in the second half when the story returns to its roots, focusing on the magical traditions of the island's people. With Michael York and Rachel Ward. ★★ $19.99

Widow Coudorc

(1974, 92 min, France, Pierre Granier-Deferre) Based on a novel by Georges Simenon, this excellent thriller features Simone Signoret as a lonely widow who falls in love with a dangerous escaped convict. Also starring Alain Delon. Similar in theme to the Catherine Deneuve drama, *Scene of the Crime*. (French with English subtitles) ★★★

Widows' Peak

(1994, 101 min, GB, John Irvin) Mia Farow's post-scandal return to the screen is this lavish romp that combines elements of Agatha Christie, *The Sting* and a little Merchant Ivory thrown in for extra measure. Joan Plowright stars as the grand dame of a small 1920s Irish village beset by scandal when the personality clash between the town spinster (Farrow) and a free-spirited, newly arrived war widow (impeccably played by Natasha Richardson) gets out of hand. Plowright, the soul of decorum, takes it upon herself to keep the peace, and the results are humorously disastrous. Sparkling performances and bitchy dialogue help make *Widows' Peak* a total delight. ★★★½ $19.99

The Wife

(1996, 90 min, US, Tom Noonan) This claustrophobic little oddity stars Julie Hagerty and Tom Noonan as a couple of New Age therapists whose Sunday evening quiet is shattered when one of their patients (Wallace Shawn) and his ex-stripper wife (Karen Young) unexpectedly show up at their door. It becomes immediately clear that Young is a bull in an emotional china shop as she peppers her hosts with embarrassing questions and makes untoward remarks about her husband. Noonan seems to take a mildly sadistic pleasure in the proceedings, while Hagerty appears on the verge of major distress over the intrusion. As the evening progresses it becomes increasingly evident that the doctors need to heal themselves and, though she's no paragon of mental health, Young is the only one at the table being honest, however inappropriate. The ensemble cast really sinks their teeth into Noonan's script and some really nice camera work and editing make *The Wife* feel more zippy than it actually is, but the film can't quite rise above its "small" premise and will ultimately only really appeal to therapy junkies and those in search of claustrophobic little oddities. ★★½ $99.99

Wife vs. Secretary

(1936, 88 min, US, Clarence Brown) Another formulaic '30s love triangle, helped immensely by three very attractive leading performances. Clark Gable stars as a successful publisher married to Myrna Loy. Jean Harlow is his devoted secretary who becomes invaluable to him on a costly and time-consuming project, prompting the titular contest. ★★½ $19.99

Wifemistress

(1977, 110 min, Italy, Marco Vicario) Laura Antonelli is a repressed, bedridden housewife until husband Marcello Mastroianni's clandestine affairs and flight from justice prod her into action. A spirited, erotic comedy-drama. (Dubbed) ★★★

W

Wigstock: The Movie

(1995, 85 min, US, Barry Shils) The boisterously extravagant, unabashedly camp, uninhibitedly costumed cross-dressing Labor Day extravaganza known as Wigstock is captured in all of its sequined and tacky glory in this spirited documentary. Recorded during the 1993 event in Tomkins Square Park and the 1994 event held on a West Village pier, we get a behind-the-scenes as well as an on-stage look at the fabulously frocked organizers, the surprisingly professional performers, and thoughts from its entranced audience. The "Lady" Bunny is the regal M.C. and performers include RuPaul, Joey Arias, Lipsinka, Mistress Formika, The Dueling Bankheads, and acting as our pseudo-tour guides, Alexis Arquette (Eva Destruction) and Jackie Beat. Director Shils' (*Vampire's Kiss*) film is more authentic than *To Wong Foo* and *Priscilla*, but less enlightening than Jennie Livingston's *Paris Is Burning*. The repeated emphasis here is fun, though the film's simplicity coupled with the lack of a structure or narrative doesn't contribute much in keeping an audience entranced for 85 minutes. ★★½ $19.99

The Wild Angels

(1966, 124 min, US, Roger Corman) Peter Fonda heads a group of fanatical motorcyclists bent on living their lives totally free of responsibility. Nancy Sinatra, Bruce Dern and Diane Ladd costar. This box-office hit started the '60s cycle film rage. ★★½ $9.99

Wild at Heart

(1990, 124 min, US, David Lynch) Lynch's dizzying, high-speed, high-energy love story follows the randy exploits of Sailor (Nicolas Cage) and Lula, aka Peanut (Laura Dern), as they wantonly cruise across the country. Cage and Dern deliver blistering performances as the loopy lovebirds. Oscar-nominee Diane Ladd, Dern's real-life mom, is superb as her screen mom, a nightmarishly alcoholic and emotionally distressed witch who tries to derail the young lovers' romance. Willem Dafoe steals the show with his portrayal of the ultimate "sleazoid," Bobby Peru. Filled with hilarious one-liners, some brutal violence and a lot of sweaty sex, *Wild at Heart* is an outrageous frolic that's "hotter than Georgia asphalt." ★★★ $14.99

Wild Bill

(1995, 98 min, US, Walter Hill) Hill's attempt to de-mythologize the legendary gunfighter and marshal is a superficial account of his last days, with a few interesting flashbacks thrown in for good measure. Jeff Bridges, though, is exceptional as the titular antihero, who comes to the town of Deadwood hoping to spend some quiet days and enjoy the status of living legend. Slowly losing his eyesight, Wild Bill is accompanied by an entourage of hangers-on, including an English intellectual played by John Hurt. Several vengeance-seeking characters have also come to Deadwood, providing the film with numerous showdowns. Saving the film from mediocrity, in addition to Bridges' excellent portrayal, is Hill's inventive visual style. Ellen Barkin is also terrific as the larger-than-life Calamity Jane who wants to rekindle a relationship with Bill. Hill seems to be trying to

attain the level of *The Shootist* in detailing the last days of a legend, or *The Man Who Shot Liberty Valance* in its deconstruction of a hero. He falls short of the mark, but does manage to present a generally tedious but somewhat entertaining character study of a character we really don't get to know. ★★ $19.99

Wild Blade

(1991, 53 min, US, David Geffner) This punky, independent film is high on style, but a bit slow going. Clark, a greasy comedian, dies while choking on a piece of meat (symbolism?). At the funeral, his wife, who's been getting a little on the side from her sexy girlfriend, is told that her husband was keeping a young male hustler on the "payroll." The rent boy, with looks that will remind one of the illegitimate son of Marsha Mason and Kevin Bacon, is an attractive deaf teen who, when not brooding intensely, is the fought-over object of desire between his abusive horse-faced pimp and the now hustler-obsessed woman. No one gets what they desire in this "interesting" effort which features a good jazz soundtrack, but is hampered by collegiate theatrical acting. ★★½ $29.99

The Wild Bunch: The Director's Cut

(1969, 144 min, US, Sam Peckinpah) Widely considered to be Peckinpah's best work, *The Wild Bunch* is a masterful piece of filmmaking, a mesmerizing treatment of contemporary American mythology utilizing to the fullest degree all aspects of the craft. The director incorporates exquisite cinematography, precision editing, arresting sound treatment and plot structure; each frame is composed with diligent care. In exploring personal rivalry within the human propensity to cling steadfastly to dying ways of life, and set within complex choreographies of violent action, Peckinpah moves from sweeping vistas to minute detail, restructuring time and place with balletic grace. This restored version runs 144 minutes, matching the European theatrical running time, an additional 10 minutes over the original U.S. running time. And this reissue is in wide screen format. This textbook example of epic American filmmaking includes the stellar cast of William Holden, Ernest Borgnine, Robert Ryan, Edmond O'Brien and Warren Oates. ★★★★ $19.99

The Wild Duck

(1983, 96 min, Australia, Henri Safran) Jeremy Irons stars in this updated adaptation of Henrik Ibsen's play about the foibles of the Ekdal (Anglicized here to "Ackland") family. The production as a whole is uneven, but Irons' performance earns the viewers' attention. Liv Ullmann costars. ★★

Wild Hearts Can't Be Broken

(1991, 89 min, US, Steve Miner) Gabrielle Anwar shines as Sonora, a teenaged orphan who follows her dream of becoming a horseback "diving girl" during the Depression. Cliff Robertson plays the traveling showman who gives her her big break and Michael Schoeffling is appealing and supportive as his son. Although it's occasionally predictable and affected, this true story is inspiring and entertaining. ★★★ $9.99

Wild Horses

(1982, 88 min, New Zealand, Derek Morton) This exciting modern-day "western" is based on a true story about an enterprising city worker who captures and sells off the wild horses in Australia's national parks. His wrangling is soon confronted by a group of people who think that the horses are a nuisance and should be killed. A nail-biting climax ends this enjoyable feature. ★★★

Wild in the Streets

(1968, 97 min, US, Barry Shear) A rock star gets the voting age lowered to 14, becomes President, and promptly has everyone over 30 carted off to internment camps. Featuring Shelley Winters, Hal Holbrook, Millie Perkins and a young Richard Pryor, who plays a militant drummer. A '60s camp classic. ★★½

The Wild One

(1954, 79 min, US, Laslo Beneder) Marlon Brando dons his leather, mounts his bike and leads his roughneck motorcycle gang into a small, staid town, wreaking havoc with every sneer and mumble. A powerful performance well complemented by Lee Marvin as an equally nasty hog rider. ★★★½ $19.99

Wild Orchid

(1990, 103 min, US, Zalman King) A match made in smarm heaven: the movie's King of Kinks, Mickey Rourke, teams with King, who wrote *9½ Weeks* and then made his debut behind the camera with Sherilyn Fenn as a belle from hell in *Two Moon Junction*. There's little in the way of intelligence on display here and the sex has moved further south — to Rio. Model Carre Otis and Jacqueline Bisset are along for the ride. Available in an unrated version. ★ $19.99

Wild Orchid II: Two Shades of Blue

(1992, 107 min, US, Zalman King) More sexual exploits, Zalman King style. The director of the original *Wild Orchid*, *9½ Weeks* and *Two Moon Junction*, does what he does...well, "best" isn't exactly the word. Not really having anything to do with the first film, the story follows the sexual exploits of a teenager (Nina Siemaszko) who, upon her father's death, is shuffled off to a posh bordello. From there it's her sexual awakening — hers and half the state's. Wendy Hughes appears as the madam: What she's doing here is anyone's guess. This is pure dribble, but for those who enjoyed Zalman's other films (c'mon, fess up), it's not a total waste of time. Unrated version. ★ $19.99

Wild Palms — The Dream Begins

(1993, 138 min, US, Peter Hewitt, Keith Gordon, Kathryn Bigelow & Phil Joanou) Oliver Stone presents a delightfully convoluted tale involving virtual reality, mind control and bald-faced deceit. James Belushi, Angie Dickinson, Ernie Hudson and Dana Delany all acquit themselves well in this poshly-produced, made-for-TV fare. However, the over-the-top, inspired mania Robert Loggia brings to the televangelical, psychotically manipulative cyberentreprenuer, whose actions are the pivot of the movie, is truly a joy to behold. In Part One, Belushi plays a TV executive who comes under the influence of nefarious senator Loggia, the megalomaniac behind a virtual reality process. As Belushi loses control of his own senses and morality, he becomes involved in murder and conspiracy. ★★★ $99.99

Wild Palms — The Dream Continues

(1993, 140 min, US, Peter Hewitt, Keith Gordon, Kathryn Bigelow & Phil Joanou) In Part Two, executive Belushi further loses his grip on reality and becomes an unwilling pawn in senator Loggia's diabolical scheme to achieve through mind control greater power and glory. In both parts, various directors helmed different segments, but lush production design and outstanding special effects aid the continuity. Given the satisfaction of its various parts, its surprising that the effort isn't completely successful — becoming unfocused two-thirds of the way through. Despite this, *Wild Palms* remains thoroughly enjoyable, and works for those seeking slick entertainment as well as those prone to political conspiracy theories. ★★★ $99.99

The Wild Party

(1975, 107 min, US, James Ivory) Veteran character actor James Coco gives a poignant performance in a rare lead role as a fading silent comic. The wild Hollywood party is supposed to harken his comeback but ends in tragedy. Raquel Welch and Perry King co-star in this early Merchant Ivory production which is loosely based on the Fatty Arbuckle scandal of the 1920s. ★★★

Wild Reeds (Les Roseaux Sauvages)

(1994, 110 min, France, André Téchiné) One of the most affecting depictions of gay first love ever committed to screen, this tender and knowing drama touchingly deals with friendship, coming out and teenage sexuality, all set against the political turmoil of the 1962 French/Algerian conflict. Made for a French TV series that was based on the early romantic remembrances of several directors, the film is set in a rural boarding school and revolves around the loves and friendships of three teenagers as well as an Algerian youth of 21. The central character is François (Gael Morel), a handsome youth (with James Dean-like looks) who falls for a fellow classmate, Serge (Stephane Rideau), a muscular student who in turn is attracted to Maite (Elodie Bouchez), Serge's best friend and a woman wise beyond her years. Entering this circle is Henri (Frédéric Gorny), a troubled nationalist Algerian. The dark-eyed and melancholy François makes for an attractive character — a young man who is open to others about his sexuality and, in a dramatic scene in front of a mirror, to himself as well. A poignant drama that captures the universal ecstasy, pain and loneliness of young love. Winner of 1995 César Awards for Best Picture, Screenplay, Actor and Female Discovery. (French with English subtitles) ★★★★ $89.99

The Wild Ride

(1960, 90 min, US, Harvey Berman) A gang of roaring hot rodders get to race in the big time in this biker/bad girl/juvenile delinquent/rebel without a cause "gem." Jack Nicholson and Georgianna Carter star. ★ $19.99

Jennifer Grey and Matthew Modine in *Wind*

Wild Rovers

(1971, 138 min, US, Blake Edwards) Released in a succession of box-office flops (*Darling Lili, The Carey Treatment*) by its director, this grandly entertaining, lighthearted western drama got lost in the theatrical shuffle. It would be a shame to miss William Holden's wonderful performance and the fine interplay between the film's characters in the story of two cowpokes who rob a bank and are chased through the countryside by a crazed posse. Even Ryan O'Neal's presence as Holden's partner-in-crime can't harm this one. ★★★ $19.99

Wild Side

(1995, 96 min, US, Franklin Brauner) The lesbian sleeper of 1995, this torrid love story is packaged in the guise of a standard straight-to-video soft-core action/thriller. Everything that *Showgirls* tried but gloriously failed to be is in this *Wild Side* — two wonderfully developed lesbian characters, several erotic episodes, and a plot so ridiculous as to keep one grinning throughout. Anne Heche is Alex Lee, a banker by day and a high-class hooker by night. Both of her careers are sent in a tailspin after a $1,500 tryst with Bruno Buckingham (Christopher Walken), a bug-eyed, high-living businessman with criminal intentions. An elegant and gorgeous Joan Chen is Virginia Chow, Bruno's wife who meets and immediately is attracted to the beautiful Alex. Before she realizes it, Alex is caught up in a plot to inject a computer virus into the national banking system, is a pawn of a sex-crazed FBI man, and in love (with Virginia) for the first time. One of the film's many strange scenes has Bruno forcing his hunky driver (Steven Bauer) to pull down his pants. In a weird act of punishment, Walken then rips off Bauer's Calvins, slaps him on the ass and then "rapes" him. Method acting never looked so kinky! ★★★ $14.99

Wild Strawberries

(1957, 93 min, Sweden, Ingmar Bergman) An elderly Stockholm professor (a brilliant Victor Sjostrom) reviews the disappointments of his life while in the company of several boisterous

youths. Effortlessly gliding through time, Bergman weaves a shimmering tapestry of memory and sensation. (Swedish with English subtitles) ★★★★ $29.99

Wild Wheels

(1993, 64 min, US, Harrold Blank) Following his father, filmmaker Les Blank (*Burden of Dreams*), in documenting the quirky, idiosyncratic characters around us, Harrold Blank has made a fascinating and at times hilarious film on customized autos and the people who make them. Blank takes us around the country where we meet an odd assortment of people who take America's obsession with cars beyond mere functionalism and into art and outrageous personal expression. Their uniquely accessorized cars are adorned with mirrors, beads, household junk, buttons, and even living grass. Taking pleasure and enjoyment in their own moving canvas of public art, the people interviewed are as interesting as their one-of-a-kind vehicles. A likably wacky and lighthearted slice of unique Americana. ★★★ $29.99

Wildcats

(1986, 107 min, US, Michael Ritchie) Goldie Hawn stars as the newly appointed football coach in a ghetto high school. There she comes in conflict with the macho head coach while slowly winning over the players. Goldie makes the best out of this harmless, clichéd comedy; and the film does produce a few laughs. ★★½ $14.99

Wilder Napalm

(1993, 109 min, US, Glenn Gordon Caron) Reluctant telekinetic pyromaniac Wilder Foudroyant (Arliss Howard) matches his incendiary abilities with his equally conflagratory brother Wallace (Dennis Quaid) to keep the hand of his fetching pyromaniac wife Vida (Debra Winger). Director Caron, creator of "Moonlighting," manages to retain the gleeful wackiness which permeated that TV show while allowing these accomplished performers sufficient latitude to uncover, layer by layer, telling moments of poignancy. An inventive, witty script and lively pacing contribute to this satisfactory examination of escalating sibling rivalry and lingering childhood guilt. Look for M. Emmet Walsh as a fireman and Jim Varney as a circus roadie. ★★★ $98.99

Wildfire

(1992, 98 min, US, Zalman King) Erotic filmmaker Zalman King, long criticized for his excessively steamy forays into female sexuality (*9½ Weeks, Wild Orchid*), finally tones down his act and the result is this castrated drama about a happily married woman (Linda Fiorentino) who must chose between the love of a good man (Will Patton) and the love of a gorgeous one (Steven Bauer). Only in the sexual safety of the '90s could this be considered a dilemma. ★½ $92.99

Wildrose

(1984, 96 min, US, John Hanson) Lisa Eichhorn's perceptive and earnest performance elevates this compassionate drama about a divorced woman who takes a job at an iron works and meets hostility from her all-male coworkers. ★★★

Will Penny

(1968, 108 min, US, Tom Gries) Charlton Heston gives one of his better performances in this exceptional western saga. Heston plays a weary, middle-aged cowboy who stays in a small town after being left in the desert for dead. He's then forced to fight the gang which left him there. Joan Hackett is splendid as the pioneer woman who rescues him. ★★★½ $14.99

Will You Dance with Me?

(1959, 89 min, France, Michel Boisrons) 1959 marked the beginning of the French New Wave and produced many classics from unheralded first time directors (Godard's *Breathless*, Truffaut's *400 Blows*, Resnais' *Hiroshima, Mon Amour*). Well, this film cannot be counted in the same league as the ones mentioned above. It is a typical, but good, lighthearted crime mystery starring Brigitte Bardot as a bewitching newlywed who becomes entangled in a web of blackmail and murder. (French with English subtitles) ★★½

Willard

(1971, 95 min, US, Daniel Mann) The story of a boy and his rat. This silly but effective horror tale stars Bruce Davison as a lonely young man who raises rats – who help him get revenge against those around him. ★★½

William Shakespeare's Romeo and Juliet

(1996, 113 min, US/GB, Baz Luhrmann) Can Shakespeare appeal to the MTV crowd? The answer is a resounding "Aye!" in this delirious amalgam of styles, colors and kinetic camera movements from the director of *Strictly Ballroom*. Using the original dialogue of the play (pared down for reasons of length), but reworking almost everything else about the scenario, Luhrmann and company have produced a work which is not only faithful to the original theme and feeling of the piece, but resonates particularly well for contemporary times (but that's the appeal of Shakespeare after all, isn't it). Set in a fictional Verona Beach, a neon-drenched cross between Miami

and Los Angeles, the story of star-crossed lovers is set between rival business families, each with their own gun-toting gang members and peculiar dysfunctions: Lady Capulet (Diane Venora) is straight out of a Tennessee Williams play and Tybalt (John Leguizamo) is a zoot-suited, two-gunned psycho. Add to this a tattooed Friar Laurence (Pete Postlethwaite) and the title characters of the story become the only "normal" people around, which makes their tragedy all the more heartbreaking: they just don't fit into this world. As Romeo and Juliet, Leonardo DiCaprio and Claire Danes perform admirably, too, never letting the Technicolor chaos which surrounds them to overshadow their fine portrayals. ★★★★ $14.99

Willy Wonka and the Chocolate Factory

(1971, 98 min, US, Mel Stuart) A strange and delightful children's musical fantasy, with Gene Wilder as an eccentric candy manufacturer who invites five contest-winning children to his mysterious factory. Songs includes "Candy Man." ★★★ $19.99

Wilson

(1944, 154 min, US, Henry King) Though acclaimed in its day, this reverent biography of America's 28th President has been long lost in the shadows of other 1940s bios praising the likes of George M. Cohan and Alvin York. Nominated for Best Picture and winner of five Academy Awards, this sincere and intelligent look at the life of Woodrow Wilson may suffer from over-glorification, but it is nevertheless a stirring examination of a political career. A history lesson told in cinematic chapters, the film traces Wilson's rise from Princeton University's president to New Jersey's governor to his two terms as Commander-in-Chief (elected in 1912 and 1916). Alexander Knox gives a solid portrayal of Wilson and he is given some inspiring speeches to recite. ★★★½ $19.99

Winchester 73

(1950, 92 min, US, Anthony Mann) Superior western adventure with James Stewart combing the wilderness for his one-of-a-kind rifle and his father's murderer. The film, which features exceptional cinematography, helped bring about the great revival of westerns in the 1950s. ★★★½ $14.99

Wind

(1992, 123 min, US, Carroll Ballard) From the director of *The Black Stallion* comes this stylishly produced, curiously enjoyable yet formulaic dramatic action story about a maverick sailor and his quest to win the America's Cup, sailing's most coveted prize. Matthew Modine and Jennifer Grey star as the two halves of a boy-and-girl sailing team. She's recently hung up her halyards, however, to pursue a career in aeronautics and he's just been offered to crew on an America's Cup yacht in Newport. Within the first 30 minutes of the film, Modine manages to lose not only his woman, but the Cup too. Can you guess where the script goes from there? Despite its complete predictability, *Wind* does manage to entertain thanks in large part to its remarkably filmed

sailing sequences which amply convey the sheer exhilaration of sailing. ★★½ $19.99

The Wind

(1928, 88 min, US, Victor Sjostrom) Sjostrom (forever identified as the old man in Ingmar Bergman's *Wild Strawberries*) was a renowned director in Sweden and made one of the greatest silent films over here. Lillian Gish gives her most riveting performance as a city-girl newlywed relocated to the desert. After she murders the man who rapes her, he comes back with the howling wind. Sjostrom makes us hear the unrelenting sand storm, the clatter of broken dishes and the footsteps on the wooden floors through brilliant editing and the use of close-ups. ★★★★ $29.99

The Wind and the Lion

(1975, 120 min, US, John Milius) Well-mounted but ultimately muddled adventure film loosely based on an actual event, with Sean Connery as a Moroccan shiek who kidnaps an American widow (Candice Bergen) and her children, setting off an international incident in which President Teddy Roosevelt (Brian Keith) himself becomes involved. ★★½ $19.99

Windom's Way

(1957, 108 min, GB, Ronald Neame) Peter Finch stars in Neame's thoughtful tale about a British doctor working in a small Malayan village who tries to rally the locals against a Communist insurgency. ★★★

The Window

(1949, 73 min, US, Ted Tetzlaff) A taut, intriguing thriller about a small boy who witnesses a murder, though no one will believe his story. With Bobby Driscoll as the youth, and also Barbara Hale and Arthur Kennedy. ★★★½ $19.99

Window Shopping

(1986, 96 min, France/Belgium, Chantal Akerman) Set within the friendly, artificial confines of a Parisian shopping mall, Akerman proves that she is not limited to producing serious, experimental studies with this delightfully witty, tongue-in-cheek musical that pays homage to Jacques Demy and M-G-M musicals. Actually nothing more than a stylish soap opera, the story follows Lili, the manager of a hair salon, and her various suitors; which includes Delphine Seyrig's love-struck son. Plot twists abound, a chorus of shampoo girls break into song and love is always around the corner in this splashy, nonsensical lark that takes delight in its own frothiness while still retaining some insight into love in the modern age. (French with English subtitles) ★★★ $29.99

Window to Paris

(1993, 101 min, Russia, Yuri Mamin) This subversively hilarious albeit uneven Russian fantasy follows a music teacher and his new flatmates through a closet door that leads from their decaying St. Petersburg apartment to the opulent streets of Paris, where the stalls are filled with fresh produce and motorcycles litter the sidewalk. The intrepid band, exhausted from eking out a mean existence in a financially depleted Russia and dealing with petty bureaucrats mired in arcane and demeaning hierarchies, fanatically embrace the opportunity to indulge in material excess. When they discover that the gateway stays open for only a certain period of time, they go for broke in their frenzy of acquisition, their physical experience of spatial refraction matched by the onset of Western ennui. Filmed with kinetic energy and a warm appreciation of human foibles. (Russian and French with English subtitles) ★★★ $96.89

Wing Chun

(1994, 93 min, Hong Kong, Yuen Woo Ping) Serious kung fu unfortunately takes a back seat to comedy in this retelling of the story of Yim Wing Chun (Michelle Yeoh), a young girl who refined the southern Chinese fighting style eventually named after her. Returning to her village, Wing Chun saves a young widow from bandits after the woman is mistaken for Wing herself. When the widow is kidnapped by the bandits, Wing Chun must refine her martial arts skills in order to defeat the gang's leader. Yuen, director of the enormously successful *Iron Monkey*, here seems a bit unfocused, alternating between blistering kung fu sequences and some typically absurd Hong Kong comedic tomfoolery. It's an awkward pairing which – while entertaining and funny in places – doesn't work to the fullest effect. However, Yeoh and Yen are terrific together, with Yeoh demonstrating the grace of a dancer and the power of a fighter. (Cantonese with English subtitles) ★★½ $79.99

Wings

(1927, 139 min, US, William A. Wellman) The first film to win the Oscar for Best Picture, this exciting silent war drama features good aerial effects to tell the story of two WWI pilots, and their love for the same girl. Starring Clara Bow, Charles "Buddy" Rogers, Richard Arlen and Gary Cooper. ★★★ $14.99

Wings of Desire

(1988, 130 min, West Germany, Wim Wenders) Director Wenders' return to Germany has spawned this deeply moving and hauntingly beautiful affirmation of the human spirit. Sumptuously photographed in both black and white and color, the film reveals the world as seen by two angels (Bruno Ganz and Otto Sander). As they hover over Berlin and listen to the lonely thoughts whispering through the minds of the disenfranchised and forgotten, we are mesmerized by their inherent compassion for humanity. Finally for Ganz's angel, this compassion turns to desire as he feels himself longing to experience the complexities of human emotions. Solveig Dommartin is stunning as the trapeze artist whose beauty inspires Ganz to yearn for an earthbound existence. (Followed by a sequel, *Faraway, So Close.*) (German with English subtitles) ★★★★ $19.99

Wings of Fame

(1990, 109 min, GB, Otakar Votocek) They say that fame is fleeting, and in this invigorating drama starring Peter O'Toole (in the familiar role of a boozy Hollywood star), fame's disappearance holds more significance than just losing a good table at Spago's. When Valentin (O'Toole) is killed by what seems like a lunatic fan (Colin Firth), who is then bumped off by a

falling spotlight, both victims find themselves in a slightly puzzling hereafter. The island paradise, which at first seems like a green version of heaven, turns out to be inhabited only by those who are dead and famous. When one's fame on Earth disappears, however, so does one's reservations at the island's swank hotel. Resting somewhere in that amorphous gap between comedy and drama, this little "slice of life" (slice of death?) offers a devilishly ponderous glimpse into the great beyond. ★★★ $89.99

Winners and Sinners

(1989, 100 min, Hong Kong, Samo Hung) A fun-filled Asian action/comedy centering around five bumbling small-time criminals who, after being arrested, form a close bond. Once they return to the outside world, they start a cleaning company and begin their search for a place in society and in the heart of a beautiful woman. After crossing paths with down-on-his-luck cop Jackie Chan during a fast-food restaurant robbery, the group becomes the unknowing target of a blood-thirsty gang of counterfeiters, having mistakenly lifted a briefcase containing the printing plates for their operation. In spite of the diminutive role Mr. Chan has in this film, fans will love the trademark stunt/action sequences and the over-the-top style that is so familiar to Chan followers. ★★★ $59.99

Winter Kills

(1979, 97 min, US, William Richert) *Winter Kills* is a rare example of a film so wild, so utterly rambunctious and so bursting with invention that it defies description. Jeff Bridges is the sole innocent searching for clues to the decade-old assassination of his half-brother, a Kennedy-esque president. What he uncovers is a murky mass of conspiracies and the mammoth excessiveness of his tyrannical father (a hilariously obscene John Huston). Don't miss this cynical swipe at the unravelling threads of the Stars and Stripes. ★★★

Winter Light

(1963, 80 min, Sweden, Ingmar Bergman) This chilling and powerful story of despair is the second of Bergman's trilogy (the others two being *The Silence* and *Through a Glass Darkly*) and for people who want to go over the edge in depression, a double feature with Bresson's *Diary of a Country Priest* should do it. The story concerns a disillusioned pastor who loses his vocation and watches as his congregation crumbles along with his faith. (Swedish with English subtitles) ★★★½ $29.99

Winter of Our Dreams

(1981, 90 min, Australia, John Duigan) A decidedly different love story which traces the roots of identity, relationships and life on the edge. Bryan Brown stars as a former activist who meets Judy Davis, a junkie hooker who becomes obsessively attached to him. Ms. Davis' incandescent performance is a tremendously moving portrait of misplaced desire and self-abuse. One of the finest films that came out of the Australian New Wave. ★★★½

Winter People

(1989, 110 min, US, Ted Kotcheff) A widower (Kurt Russell) finds himself caught between

two feuding families in the backwoods of the Carolina Mountains during the 1930s. Very little dramatic excitement. Kelly McGillis and Lloyd Bridges costar. ★★

Wisdom

(1987, 109 min, US, Emilio Estevez) Estevez wasn't too wise when he wrote, directed and starred in this mangled social fable about an unemployed man who teams with a young woman (Demi Moore) to become modern-day Robin Hoods. ★ $9.99

Wise Blood

(1979, 108 min, US, John Huston) A zealous attack against authority and the follies of faith. A soldier (Brad Dourif) returns to his Southern home town and wages a fanatical rebellion against the repressive values of his upbringing. Based on the Flannery O'Connor novel. ★★★½ $59.99

Wise Guys

(1986, 91 min, US, Brian De Palma) This annoying gangster spoof stars Danny DeVito and Joe Piscipo as low-level and bumbling hit men who pull a scam on their boss, only to be set up by him when their sting fails. ★★ $19.99

Wisecracks

(1991, 90 min, Canada, Gail Singer) The inside scoop on the world of female comedians is revealed in this alternately funny and oh-so-serious documentary. The film features a veritable "who's who" in female stand-up comedy with interviews and segments from the acts of Phyllis Diller, Whoopi Goldberg, Sandra Shamas, the Clichettes, Faking It Three, Geri Jewell, Jenny Jones, Jenny Lecoat and Paula Poundstone. Also featured are clips from comediennes of old – Lucille Ball, Eve Arnold, Carol Burnett and others. Interspersed with the routines are interviews with the funny women – frustratingly, this is the weak part of the film. For, with the exception of Diller (surprisingly informative and perceptive), the women either take their work too seriously (one even suggesting God's intervention) or are not that interesting. While not really a great or perceptive documentary, the film works best as a highlights montage of the featured comedians. ★★ $92.99

Wish You Were Here

(1987, 92 min, GB, David Leland) Emily Lloyd gives a knockout performance in this poignant and well-aimed comedy-drama set in England in the early 1950s. Lloyd perfectly plays a sassy, sexually advanced teenager whose search for fulfillment and escape from her rigid father steers her towards an ill-conceived affair with an older man, familial abandonment, and, ultimately, fervent independence. This could be – although it is not officially – the prequel to *Personal Services*, which was written by director Leland. ★★★½

Witch Hunt

(1994, 100 min, US, Paul Schrader) Joseph Dougherty, writer of HBO's highly entertaining *Cast a Deadly Spell*, teams up with director Schrader for this whimsical sequel. Set in Hollywood in the 1940s where the art of witchcraft runs rampant, the story follows the adventures of private dick H. Phillip Lovecraft

(Dennis Hopper), who is hired by a beautiful femme fatale (Penelope Ann Miller) to keep a watchful eye on her philandering husband. Lovecraft, who doesn't engage in magic himself, soon comes up against a right-wing, McCarthy-like activist (Eric Bogosian) out to destroy witches once and for all. Great special effects spice up this comical, noir-esque feature, whose sets are designed to create a dreamlike Hollywood where almost anything could happen – even the fetching of Shakespeare to write new scripts. ★★★ $19.99

Witchboard

(1986, 97 min, US, Kevin S. Tenney) An evil spirit attempts to possess a young woman (Tawny Kitaen) who has been playing with a ouija board. An occasional fright but another in a long line of schlocky horror tales. With Kathleen Wilhoite and Rose Marie. ★★½ $19.99

Witchcraft Through the Ages

(1920, 82 min, Sweden, Benjamin Christensen) An unusual semidocumentary which explores various forms and practices of Satanism and other related practices from the 15th thru 17th centuries. (Silent with English subtitles) ★★½ $39.99

The Witches

(1990, 91 min, GB, Nicolas Roeg) Roeg's collaboration with Muppets creator Jim Henson on Roald Dahl's enchanting children's story is a smashing triumph – scary fun for the kids and thoroughly enjoyable for adults. During their vacation in Cornwall, nine-year-old Luke and his witch-wise grandmother come up against a coven of witches holding their annual meeting. Learning of the witches' fiendish plot to turn all of the children in England into mice – and despite being one of the first casualties – little Luke does battle to save his young peers. The majestically camp Anjelica Huston costars as the evil and hideously ugly Grand High Witch. ★★★½ $14.99

The Witches of Eastwick

(1987, 118 min, US, George Miller) An entertaining adult fantasy, loosely based on John Updike's novel. Cher, Michelle Pfeiffer and Susan Sarandon play three dissimilar women who share a common problem: men. Together, they conjure up the "perfect" man, who arrives in the guise of Jack Nicholson, truly a devilish rogue, who promptly proceeds to manipulate the ladies' lives. Veronica Cartwright – even with this powerhouse cast – steals the film as a snoopy society matron. ★★★ $14.99

With Honors

(1994, 103 min, US, Alek Keshishian) As bland as cafeteria food, *With Honors* centers on the life of a determined-to-do-well Harvard student (Brendan Fraser) who loses his all-important term paper and must bargain with a feisty homeless man (Joe Pesci) to get it back. Of course, Pesci is not simply a homeless man, but a homeless man with all the wisdom of the ages tucked neatly beneath his tattered jacket. He imparts this wisdom not only on Fraser but his three housemates, as well, in annoyingly large

doses. Things get even worse when the roomies invite him to move in with them. ★½ $14.99

Withnail & I

(1987, 105 min, GB, Bruce Robinson) Two unemployed actors of disparate character, sharing a flat in 1969, go on holiday – subjecting themselves to each other's idiosyncracies during the rigors of ill-planned travel. Nicely drawn character studies, and a sly commentary on the temperament of the times. ★★★ $14.99

Without a Clue

(1988, 106 min, GB, Thom Eberhardt) Ben Kingsley and Michael Caine star in this delightfully zany and often very funny takeoff on the Sherlock Holmes legend. What would have happend if Dr. Watson had been the real detective, and Holmes was nothing more than a third-rate actor hired to portray the famous sleuth? Caine and Kingsley, both in fine comic form, make the most of this novel premise which finds the famous duo on the case of the missing five-pound note plates stolen from the Royal Bank of England. 106 minutes of slightly silly, laugh-out-loud tomfoolery. ★★★ $9.99

Without a Trace

(1983, 119 min, US, Stanley R. Jaffe) Kate Nelligan stars as a single mother whose young son leaves for school one morning and never returns. Judd Hirsch costars as a sympathetic detective searching for the boy. Nelligan gives a good performance as the mother who never gives up hope. Though the film sometimes gives in to melodramatics, the where-how-why of the case is suspenseful. ★★½ $59.99

Without Anesthesia

(1982, 111 min, Poland, Andrzej Wajda) From the pen of director Wajda and coauthor Agnieszka Holland (the director of *Europa, Europa* and *The Secret Garden*) comes this Communist-era story of government control and the dissolution of a marriage. This is jumpy and gritty filmmaking, and you get the feeling of being in a state controlled society where even a well-respected international journalist can be broken. Zbigbiew Zapasiewicz is convincing as a successful reporter and political analyst whose marriage falls apart, and he sets out to discover why. At the same time, he has fallen from grace with the powers that be. And making matters worse, his Kafkaesque downfall both personally and professionally is never explained. It seems to be accepted and everyone just goes with the flow of supression and inebriation. (Polish with English subtitles) ★★½ $29.99

Without Love

(1945, 111 min, US, Harold S. Bucquet) Spencer Tracy is a scientist staying at widow Katharine Hepburn's boarding house in overcrowded, wartime Washington, D.C. For convenience's sake, the two marry and, of course, eventually fall in love. A charming romantic comedy with appealing performances by Kate and Spencer. Great support from Lucille Ball and Keenan Wynn. ★★★ $19.99

Without Reservations

(1946, 101 min, US, Mervyn LeRoy) Pleasant comedy starring Claudette Colbert as a

renowned Hollywood screenwriter, searching for an unknown to star in her next movie, who meets Marine flyer John Wayne. (Wonder who gets the part?) Colbert is in good form, and Wayne – who didn't make many comedies – is actually quite funny. ★★★ $19.99

Without You I'm Nothing

(1990, 90 min, US, John Boskovich) The film version of Sandra Bernhard's audacious off-Broadway hit brims with libidinous wit and inventive characterizations. With unabashed artistic daring, Bernhard plunges into a melange of musical impersonations, poetry readings and monologues which put her on the cutting edge of standup comedy/performance art. Set in a sleepy little nightclub, Bernhard's act is played to a thinning and impassive-looking audience and culminates in a desperate and very revealing go-go dance to the tune of Prince's "Little Red Corvette." Sprinkled with moments of inspired comedic brilliance, *Without You...* establishes Bernhard as a hip, thoroughly campy urban (and urbane) satirist. ★★★½ $19.99

Witness

(1985, 112 min, US, Peter Weir) A gripping police thriller and extraordinary character study. In one of his most accomplished performances, Harrison Ford plays the odd man out on a force riddled with corruption who, in fleeing his pursuers, tumbles into the anachronistic Amish country. Kelly McGillis is very good as the Amish mother whose young son witnesses a murder. ★★★½ $14.99

The Witness

(1968, 108 min, Hungary, Pèter Bascó) After viewing this bitterly sarcastic satire of the chaotic and corrupt Communist government in Hungary, one is not only surprised that it was suppressed for 10 years, but that it was released at all during their reign. Set in 1949, the story revolves around Pelikan, a hapless party loyalist and a father of eight who is content with being a simple dike keeper. But after being caught by the authorities for illegally slaughtering a pig, he begins a series of increasingly bizarre encounters with the bumbling and secretive bureaucracy. Initially sent to prison for the pig's killing, he is immediately "rehabilitated" and promoted to jobs that he is totally unqualified for – from swimming pool manager, director of the Hungarian Orange Institute and even head of a socialist amusement park. And while making a mess of each job, he is all-the-while being quietly groomed to falsely testify against a childhood friend and recently purged government official. A subversive little gem in the tradition of *1984* and *Brazil*. (Hungarian with English subtitles) ★★★ $59.99

Witness for the Prosecution

(1957, 106 min, US, Billy Wilder) Based on the long-running Agatha Christie play, this proves to be an acting tour de force for all concerned. Marlene Dietrich is at her best as the wife of accused murderer Tyrone Power. Charles Laughton is brilliant as the defense attorney who agrees to take on the case, and Elsa Lancaster is his prohibitive nurse. To detail more of the plot would give it away.

Wittgenstein

Suffice it to say that this is one whodunit that doesn't disappoint on any level. ★★★★ $19.99

Witness to the Holocaust

(1987, 90 min, Israel, Lori Perlow) The 1961 trial of Adolf Eichmann, the SS Lieutenant-Colonel and Nazi expert of Jewish Affairs who headed the department that was responsible for the annihilation of European Jews is the subject in this penetrating documentary. Tried in Jerusalem and calling eyewitness accounts, Eichmann was found guilty of crimes against the Jewish people, crimes against humanity and of war crimes, and was executed in 1962. ★★★ $39.99

Wittgenstein

(1993, 75 min, GB, Derek Jarman) Displaying little of the queer militancy that distinguished his later-career films, and another in a series of biographies of gay historical figures (Sebastiane, Edward II, Caravaggio), Jarman's amusing, intellectual portrait of Austrian-born, British-educated philosopher Ludwig Wittgenstein is both a startling primer in low-budget filmmaking as well as a visually exuberant work. Considered one of the century's most influential philosophers, Wittgenstein's private and professional life is chronicled — from his prodigy childhood to his reluctant life as a professor at Cambridge. Jarman utilizes a pitch-black background, allowing the richly drawn, outrageously costumed characters and their witty, thought-provoking dialogue to take center stage. Karl Johnson plays the eccentric philosopher, and Tilda Swinton is lavishly campy as Lady Ottoline. Shot in less than two weeks for Channel 4, this film proves to be an invigorating, uncompromising work. ★★★ $79.99

The Wiz

(1978, 133 min, US, Sidney Lumet) A modern updating of *The Wizard of Oz*, with Diana Ross and Michael Jackson heading an all-black cast. Based on the Tony Award-winning Broadway musical, we're invited to "ease on down the road" with Dorothy (Ross), whose Oz is downtown Manhattan. There are a couple of dazzling musical sequences, but Ross' lifeless portrayal fails to excite. Also with Lena Horne,

Richard Pryor, Mabel King ("Don't You Bring Me No Bad News") and Ted Ross. ★★ $19.99

The Wizard

(1989, 100 min, US, Todd Holland) Two brothers embark on a cross-country journey to attend a national video competition. A tedious road movie for kids which is as ill-conceived as it is trite. Fred Savage, Christian Slater and Beau Bridges star. ★½ $12.99

Wizard of Gore

(1970, 70 min, US, Hershell Gordon Lewis) Ray Sager stars as Montag the Magician, a character whose monologues regarding man's fascination with the morbid seems to sum up director Lewis' own philosophies and motivations. With an incredible ending reminiscent of Buñuel. ★ $29.99

The Wizard of Loneliness

(1988, 111 min, US, Jenny Bowen) Young Lukas Haas (one of the most gifted child actors of the 1980s) is outstanding in this sensitive tale of a small boy who comes to live with his grandparents in New England during WWII. Also with Lea Thompson as his aunt, John Randolph and Anne Pitoniak. ★★½

The Wizard of Oz

(1927, 93 min, US, Larry Semon) A real treat for silent film fans or Oz fanatics! Now virtually forgotten, Larry Semon was a popular comic in his day; here he plays the Scarecrow in an adaptation that owes more to Mack Sennett than L. Frank Baum. Oliver Hardy plays the Tin Man. ★★★ $24.99

The Wizard of Oz

(1939, 101 min, US, Victor Fleming) Follow the yellow brick road to the wonderful Wizard of Oz (a wiz of a wiz, if ever a wiz there was) and join Judy Garland, Ray Bolger, Jack Haley, Bert Lahr, Frank Morgan and Margaret Hamilton in this immortal classic. ★★★★ $19.99

Wizards

(1977, 81 min, US, Ralph Bakshi) This sci-fi tale of a futuristic world mired in post-apocalyptic battles and neo-Hitlerian factions is imaginatively brought to the animated screen by Ralph Bakshi. ★★★ $19.99

Wolf

(1994, 125 min, US, Mike Nichols) *Who's Afraid of Virginia Woolf* director Nichols dances with a wolf of a different color in this mature tale of an underdog (Jack Nicholson) who finally has his day when the bite of a wolf causes him to develop distinctly lupine properties. He soon rids himself of his cheating wife (Kate Nelligan) and slimy best friend (James Spader) and begins a steamy affair with an exquisitely icy "poor little rich girl" (Michelle Pfeiffer) just as a spate of gruesome killings befalls the city. Nicholson and Pfeiffer, in their first reteaming since *The Witches of Eastwick*, wear their roles like a pair of comfortable slippers, and Spader makes full use of his stock-in-trade creepiness. However, this is not the gorefest horror fans may be anticipating, and the dime-store special effects are bound to disappoint. But Nicholson's wry, arch performance is a true

howl and a stunning return to irreverent form. ★★★ $14.99

Wolf at the Door

(1987, 90 min, France/Denmark, Henning Carlsen) Donald Sutherland is Paul Gauguin, the French painter who rejected the art world and lifestyle of France at the height of his career to live simply and paint in Tahiti. After several years on the island, he visits Paris in 1893. The film is an in-depth study of the man as he spreads the word of Tahiti's beauty and raises money for his return. Sutherland's Gauguin is complex and contradictory. He is obnoxious, a bully, a misogynist, bombastic, loving to his dark-skinned favorites but cold and callous to his Scandinavian wife; but above all, a tortured and misunderstood artist. A superlative re-creation of the artist's character. (Filmed in English) ★★★ $79.99

The Wolf Man

(1941, 70 min, US, George Waggner) Classic horror film with Lon Chaney, Jr. as the tormented Larry Talbot, man by day, but a wolf by night. More than just a damn good fright tale, *The Wolf Man* is very successful in presenting the moral conflict of a man confronted with his animal instincts. "Even the man who is pure in heart, and says his prayers by night/May become a wolf man when the wolfbane blooms, and the moon is full and bright." ★★★½ $14.99

Wolfen

(1981, 115 min, US, Michael Wadleigh) When director Wadleigh, who hadn't done much since *Woodstock*, made this updated werewolf story, he concentrated on a stylish urban atmosphere of horror over the empty thrills of special effects. New York City detective Albert Finney investigates a series of grisly and random murders being committed throughout the city. Gregory Hines is the brilliant but eccentric coroner who helps him find out who and why. Though soon to be overused by others, Wadleigh brilliantly uses the recently developed stedi-cam to simulate the running wolves in a long, sinewy take. ★★★ $14.99

A Woman at Her Window

(1977, 110 min, France, Pierre Granier-Deferre) Director Granier-Deferre collaborated with screenwriter Jorge Semprun (Z) to create this romantic drama set in the despotic era of Greece circa 1936. Romy Schneider gives an outstanding performance as an aristocratic woman who pursues affairs with various noblemen (including Philippe Noiret) while married to an Italian ambassador, who himself is involved in a series of affairs. Only when she harbors a political activist (Victor Lanoux) and helps him escape does she becomes transformed, sacrificing wealth for true love. Told in a clever use of flashbacks, *A Woman at Her Window* is a convincing, engaging and well-made film. (French with English subtitles) ★★★ $69.99

A Woman at War

(1991, 115 min, GB, Edward Bennett) Based on the autobiography "Inside the Gestapo" by Helene Moszkiewicz, this moving story of individual courage takes place in Nazi-occupied

Belgium. Martha Plimpton gives a sturdy performance as Moszkiewicz who, upon the invasion of her country, joins the underground movement, changes her name, and infiltrates the Gestapo. Eric Stoltz costars in an Oskar Schindler-like role as a Nazi profiteer who is also a member of the Resistance. Plimpton is commendable as the young Jewish woman who helps track down Jews by day and plays saboteur by night. Stoltz is merely adequate. This low-key film ably captures the dangerous tenor of the times, and manages to create a tension as to the heroine's fate even in the knowledge of the film's source. ★★★ $93.49

A Woman, Her Men and Her Futon

(1992, 90 min, US, Mussef Sibay) Jennifer Rubin (*Delusion*) stars in this low-keyed drama about the romantic exploits of a woman with two lovers too many. While not as provocative as its title implies, the film deserves kudos for its adult portrayal of a '90s woman who is sexual without being irresponsible. Also with TV heartthrob Grant Snow ("Melrose Place"). ★★ $89.99

A Woman in Flames

(1982, 106 min, West Germany, Robert van Ackeren) This volatile look at female sexuality, wish fulfillment and the obstacles hindering sexual equality became something of a *cause célèbre*. Its tone is peculiarly poised between social satire and razor-sharp melodrama. The plot reads like a supermarket tabloid, with a disgruntled bourgeois housewife who abandons her husband and studies to take up prostitution. (Dubbed) ★★★

The Woman in Red

(1984, 87 min, US, Gene Wilder) Occasionally amusing remake of the French romantic farce *Pardon Mon Affaire* with Gene Wilder as a married man who falls for "the woman in red." Also starring Gilda Radner, Kelly LeBrock, Joseph Bologna and Charles Grodin. ★★½ $9.99

Woman in the Dunes

(1964, 123 min, Japan, Hiroshi Teshigahara) Kobo Abe's allegory of a man trapped with a strange woman in a sandpit is translated into a prize-winning work of art exploring the concepts of existence, freedom and eroticism. ★★★½ $29.99

Woman in the Moon

(1929, 146 min, Germany, Fritz Lang) Lang's final silent film is a fascinating voyage of a group of people who are sent to the moon in search of gold, but find instead only greed and jealousy. The look of the rocket and other aspects of the science fiction film are amazing for the similarity to the real thing 40 years later. Not as involving as Lang's masterpiece, *Metropolis*, but nevertheless an enjoyable experience. ★★★

A Woman Is a Woman (Une Femme Est une Femme)

(1961, 80 min, France, Jean-Luc Godard) Godard's salute to the Hollywood musical is a giddy, improvisational romp up and down the boulevards of Paris. Anna Karina stars as a bubbly, high-spirited striptease artist whose only desire is to have a child. Her boyfriend (Jean-Claude Brialy), however, is preparing for an important bicycle race and doesn't wish to lose any "precious bodily fluids." So she turns to her lusting ex (Jean-Paul Belmondo) who volunteers to do whatever he can. Godard infuses the proceedings with an uncharacteristic joyful humor making this by far his most lighthearted work. (French with English subtitles) ★★★ $59.99

The Woman Next Door

(1981, 106 min, France, François Truffaut) A dark, gripping melodrama starring Gérard Depardieu and Fanny Ardant as a compulsive pair of ex-lovers, inadvertently reunited and driven to a tragic affair. (French with English subtitles) ★★★ $29.99

A Woman of Affairs

(1928, 98 min, US, Clarence Brown) Silent screen story starring a ravishing Greta Garbo as an "unlucky-in-love" woman whose free-spirited lifestyle takes its toll. After losing the man of her dreams, she marries a man who shortly thereafter takes his own life. Then, Garbo embarks on a series of foreign affairs with globetrotting dignitaries. Finally, she is reunited with her true love years later, only to learn he is engaged to another woman. With John Gilbert and Douglas Fairbanks, Jr. ★★★ $29.99

A Woman of Distinction

(1950, 85 min, US, Edward Buzzell) Campus hijinks '50s-style as professor Ray Milland and college dean Rosalind Russell are involved in a romantic scandal. The two stars are in good form and bring some spice to this pleasant comedy. ★★½ $69.99

A Woman of Paris

(1921, 78 min, US, Charles Chaplin) Chaplin proved himself a master director in this, his only serious film in which he doesn't star (he only has a bit as a porter). An innocent country girl becomes an inamorata of a rich Parisian (Adolph Menjou, in the role that made him a star). Chaplin's tight narrative structure (rare in his own films) and the use of telling detail to delineate character and relationships was a revelation that inspired such directors as von Sternberg, von Stroheim, Lubitsch and others. ★★★½

Woman of the Year

(1942, 112 min, US, George Stevens) Spencer Tracy is a sports writer and Katharine Hepburn is a highly esteemed columnist in this top-notch battle-of-the-sexes comedy. The first pairing of Hepburn and Tracy, *Woman of the Year* displays the longtime screen duo's inimitable rapport. ★★★★ $19.99

Woman Times Seven

(1967, 99 min, US/Italy, Vittorio De Sica) Shirley MacLaine mercilessly hams it up in this omnibus film which has her playing seven different, desirable women with seven different husbands and lovers in as many episodes. A light comic touch prevails throughout the film with some segments more successful than others. The international cast includes Vittorio Gassman, Alan Arkin, Michael Caine, Philippe Noiret, Peter Sellers and Anita Ekberg. (Filmed in English) ★★½

A Woman under the Influence

(1974, 147 min, US, John Cassavetes) The power of Cassavetes' films is that he strips away all the pretenses and protections we use to shield ourselves from our most frightening and shameful pain, and shoves our noses in it. Not too many actors can deliver that bare honesty; one of the few who does so without reservation is his wife Gena Rowlands. She is mesmerizing as the working-class housewife who buckles under the strain of a limited existence, a brutish husband (Peter Falk, in one of several strong collaborations with Caasavetes), insensitive relatives and an uncaring world. Rowlands is in turn heartbreaking, funny, delightful and frightening as a woman who is overwhelmed by a desperate inability to stay connected. ★★★½ $19.99

A Woman without Love

(1951, 85 min, Mexico, Luis Buñuel) Director Buñuel's filmmaking career flourished during his self-imposed exile in Mexico, although

Woman in the Dunes

most were simply potboilers for the domestic market, lacking in the director's trademark wry cinematic excesses. One of these, *A Woman without Love*, is a fiery soap opera about the barely supressed passions of hot-blooded Latins. A beautiful woman, locked in a loveless marriage with a middle-aged bourgeois, meets a handsome stranger. Their affair is short-lived but its memory is renewed 25 years later when her son receives an inheritance from a mysterious man. (Spanish with English subtitles) ★★½ $24.99

A Woman's Face

(1938, 104 min, Sweden, Gustaf Molander) Ingrid Bergman plays against type in this dark melodrama about a disfigured woman who, disturbed by the happiness she will never know, blackmails illicit lovers. (Swedish with English subtitles) ★★½ $29.99

A Woman's Face

(1941, 105 min, US, George Cukor) Joan Crawford has a juicy role as an embittered, facially scarred woman whose personality changes when she undergoes plastic surgery. An interesting melodrama with many appealing moments. ★★★ $19.99

A Woman's Revenge

(1989, 133 min, France, Jacques Doillon) A puzzling love triangle gone sour proves to be the motivating force in this elegant, if long-winded drama of passion, seduction and female retribution. Béatrice Dalle (*Betty Blue, Night on Earth*) plays Suzi, a young beauty with brooding eyes, sensuous bee-stung lips and a restless spirit who, a year after the death of her lover, meets up with his widow, Cecile (Isabelle Huppert). Bitter at her husband's death and his unfaithfulness, Cecile seeks Suzi's companionship, but is her presence an offer of forgiveness and friendship or is there a darker, possibly treacherous motive? Freely adapted from Fyodor Dostoevsky's "The Eternal Husband," the film is a bit stage-bound and incessantly talky. But for lovers of high-powered French acting, this classy though at times soap opera-ish drama is filled with layers of revealing but conflicting revelations, accusations and intrigue. (French with English subtitles) ★★½ $59.99

A Woman's Tale

(1991, 93 min, Australia, Paul Cox) This delightful tale of aging is a life-affirming, realistic and often hilarious mini-masterpiece. Filmmaker Cox tailor-made this semiautobiographical story of a spirited modern woman of almost 80 years for acclaimed actress Sheila Florance. Her character, Martha, finding the world too cynical and heartless, refuses to accept society's constraints on her lifestyle and fights the establishment with compassion and humor. Her friends include her pets, a bed-ridden neighbor and even a local prostitute. Her sexuality is still important to her, and her frank talk is revealing, touching and hilarious. Just days after winning the award for Best Actress in Australia, Florance died. *A Woman's Tale* is not only a positive portrayal of aging, it's one of the finest films of its year. ★★★★ $19.99

The Women

(1939, 133 min, US, George Cukor) Another in the long line of those great M-G-M all-star extravaganzas, this uproarious Cukor comedy (and cult favorite) more than lives up to its title: The cast is entirely female. Norma Shearer heads the once-in-a-lifetime cast as Mary, a Manhattan socialite whose storybook existence is shattered when her husband leaves her for shopgirl Joan Crawford. This puts Mary "on the road to Reno," where she meets a group of other divorce-bound women: worldly Mary Boland, showgirl Paulette Goddard, and friends Joan Fontaine and Rosalind Russell (in a smashingly funny performance). Based on Claire Boothe's Broadway hit, this is about as funny as a film can get. ★★★★ $19.99

The Women

(1965, 83 min, France, Jean Aurel) A racy, romantic comedy starring the petulant Brigitte Bardot as a very personal secretary to a handsome writer who needs some special inspiration to get his creative juices flowing. Used to women falling at his feet, he is confused and captivated by her ability to instill wanton desire in him (and she types a mean letter!), although our sexy gal friday stays aloof and keeps him guessing and panting. Silly, unimportant but fun, this look into the amorous exploits of the French should entertain BB fans who are determined to trudge through her entire videography. (Dubbed) ★★½

Women from the Lake of Scented Souls

(1993, 106 min, China, Xie Fei) In staying with the tradition of Chinese New Wave filmmakers, Xie has fashioned a film replete with stock characters and traditional story lines. History has a way of repeating itself, and so goes the plot as Xiang Ersao (Sigin Gaowa) a determined and hard-working woman, is forced into marriage as a child to a sesame oil maker who knows nothing about business. Left to keep shop while her husband gets drunk with his friends, Ersao modernizes and increases business. While this adds to their position of power in the town, their epileptic son is too old to be single. Ersao decides to continue the cycle of arranged marriages by forcing a poorer family to promise their daughter to marry for payment of their debts. Bao Xianian's camera work is nowhere near as spectacular as some of the other films to come out of China recently, but there is a gritty realism to the film and good performances on par with the soap opera plot. (Mandarin with English subtitles) ★★½ $89.99

Women in Love

(1970, 129 min, GB, Ken Russell) Russell's powerful rendition of the D.H. Lawrence classic centers on two Midlands sisters and the tempestuous relationships they form. Resolute Gudren (Glenda Jackson) becomes involved with the strong but boorish Gerald (Oliver Reed), while her romantically inclined sister Ursula (Jennie Linden) falls in love with the

The Woman Next Door

handsome but aloof Rupert (Alan Bates). A masterful examination of sexual domination and repression, brilliantly portrayed by its cast — Jackson won an Oscar and international stardom for her gutsy, complex portrayal of Gudren. ★★★★ $14.99

Women on the Verge of a Nervous Breakdown

(1988, 88 min, Spain, Pedro Almodóvar) Almodóvar's comic masterpiece is by far his most accessible film to date and is largely responsible for familiarizing many American audiences with his unique talents. Based loosely on Jean Cocteau's "The Human Voice," the story follows Pepa — brilliantly portrayed by Carmen Maura — an actress whose life crumbles around her when she comes home one day to find her lover, Ivan, has left her. The ensuing hour-and-a-half turns into a hilarious comic romp as she tries to piece her life back together. Julieta Serrano is fabulous as Ivan's insane wife and Maria Barranco is hysterical as Pepa's friend who is fleeing from Shiite terrorists. (Spanish with English subtitles) ★★★★ $19.99

Women Who Made the Movies

(1990, 50 min, US, Gwendolyn Foster-Dixon & Wheeler Dixon) This documentary, made in association with Nebraska Educational Television, chronicles the history of women directors working in an industry which barely acknowledges them. Clips from films made as early as 1904 give evidence of work as technically accomplished as any male contemporary. Subject matters range from a 1913 film on the Suffragette Movement to more traditional dramas. Interestingly, the heroines in these dramas are portrayed as unusually independent. This is a valuable compilation of an almost-lost history. The film ends with a scroll of the names of women directors; its length is most surprising. ★★★ $19.99

Wonder Man

(1945, 98 min, US, Bruce Humberstone) Danny Kaye has a field day with this bright comic romp playing twins. When one brother, an outgoing and brash entertainer, is murdered, his ghost convinces his introverted sibling to impersonate him and find out who did the dastardly deed. Kaye has some wonderful bits, and is ably supported by Virginia Mayo, Vera-Ellen and S.Z. "Cuddles" Sakall. ★★★ $19.99

The Wonderful, Horrible Life of Leni Riefenstahl

(1993, 192 min, Germany, Ray Müller) It may never be possible to judge German director Leni Riefenstahl's cinematic accomplishments without regard to their historical context. Her 1932 film, *Blue Light*, in which she produced, directed and starred, captured Hitler's attention with its Wagnerian mysticism and haunting imagery. In her early film career as an actress, she worked with Pabst and von Sternberg. She was a trailblazer, one of the few women directors of the time. In this meticulously researched biography, replete with archival footage intercut with clips from her films, Riefenstahl maintains that she was politically ignorant and unaware of Hitler's ultimate intentions. Cantankerous and forceful at 90 years of age, she fervently denies references to close personal ties to Hitler and Goebbels; refutes speculation that she staged much of the spectacle in *Triumph of the Will*; and maintains that her interest was solely in the craft of filmmaking. This documentary allows her to speak freely, alternating between words and images. A fascinating account of a wonderful, horrible life. ★★★★ $39.99

The Wonderful World of the Brothers Grimm

(1962, 129 min, US, Henry Levin & George Pal) Lavishly produced children's tale, featuring excerpts from brothers Jacob and Wilhelm Grimm's best-loved fairy tales, and taking a look at their lives. ★★★ $19.99

Wonderland

(1989, 103 min, GB, Philip Saville) This intriguing British thriller delves into an often overlooked subculture: gay youth. *Wonderland* is the story of the friendship between two gay teenagers from Liverpool, Eddie and Michael, who are forced to flee the city when they witness a gangland slaying at a local gay bar. Taking refuge at the home of a manipulative wealthy couple in Brighton, the boys' idyllic existence of freedom and safety is shattered when they meet the killers in a deadly confrontation. Both Emile Charles as the dolphin-loving, soft-hearted Eddie and Tony Forsyth as the street-wise, caring hustler Michael are excellent as the youths. (aka: *The Fruit Machine*) ★★★

Wonsan Operation

(1978, 100 min, South Korea/US, Terrence Sul) Reportedly taken from real accounts, this average action film is set during the Korean War. When rumors of bubonic plague among Red Chinese troops in enemy-held Wonsan reach the command of General MacArthur, volunteers are needed to obtain proof. This is the story of the soldiers who must infiltrate the town to find out if indeed an epidemic of the Black Death is ravishing the area. Will they be successful? Will they find an epidemic? Will they contract the horrid disease? What do you think? (Dubbed) ★★

The Wooden Gun

(1979, 91 min, Israel, Ilan Moshenson) Set in the tense atmosphere of 1950s Tel Aviv, this incisive film focuses on two rival groups of pre-teens whose behavior, motivated by their interpretations of the concepts of heroism, nationalisn and friendship, raises hard questions. Portrayed are first-generation sabras (native-born Israelis), who are separated by a tremendous psychological gap from those who came to Israel from Europe, many of them Holocaust survivors. (Hebrew with English subtitles) ★★★ $79.99

The Wooden Man's Bride

(1995, 114 min, China, Huang Jianxin) Director Huang has created an entertaining, if fallacious, parable wherein repressive tradition is bested by noble peasant "outlaws." When the arranged marriage to an aristocrat comes undone by his untimely death, a beautiful innocent (Wang Lan) is left with the prospect of an even more empty alliance: custom dictates she marry his proxy, a carved wooden effigy, and her scheming mother-in-law (Wang Yumei) is intent on upholding tradition. Only the love of her former manservant (Chang Shi) offers any chance for freedom. While *The Wooden Man's Bride* features the lush visual style of *Raise the Red Lantern* and *Shanghai Triad*, in its heart it is reactionary, its mind full of simplistic syllogisms. (Mandarin with English subtitles) ★★½ $19.99

Woodstock

(1969, 184 min, US, Michael Wadleigh) It's been nearly three decades since the monumental rock festival which served as a gleaming triumph for the counterculture, and a fitting capsulization of the spirit of a decade. An unbelievable roster of performers includes Jimi Hendrix; The Who; Crosby, Stills, Nash and Young; and The Jefferson Airplane (bless their pointed little heads). ★★★½ $29.99

Word Is Out — Stories from Some of Our Lives

(1978, 130 min, US, Peter Adair, Nancy Adair & Andrew Brown) Originally conceived as a documentary titled *Who Are We?*, this fascinating exploration of gay culture and history is made up of interviews with 26 lesbians and gay men. Ranging in age from 18 to 77, and representing many divergent types — from a beehived housewife to a sultry drag queen — the film captures their vivid experiences of growing up gay in America and at the same time, helps destroy decades of accumulated stereotypes. A moving and important gay document. ★★★ $24.99

Working Girl

(1988, 113 min, US, Mike Nichols) Melanie Griffith gives an enchanting performance in this "Cinderella" comedy set against the wheeling and dealing of Wall Street. Griffith plays a secretary who masquerades as her absentee boss (Sigourney Weaver) when her employer steals a business idea from her. Part social satire, part love story, the film traces Griffith's successful business charade and her romance with a handsome associate (a restrained Harrison Ford). ★★★ $9.99

Working Girls

(1986, 90 min, US, Lizzie Borden) In cinematic terms, the prostitute is usually portrayed either as a statuesque, high-priced call girl or as a drug-snorting, under-aged, runaway streetwalker. *Working Girls*, on the other hand, is a wryly comical and non-judgmental tale about another, less melodramatic side of the "sex-for-sale" business. Feminist filmmaker Borden tells the story of a middle-class brothel nestled in a Manhattan high-rise. Essentially, the film is a day in the life of the shrewish madam and her "girls" as seen through the eyes of Molly, a young woman who, while ambivalent about her work, is nonetheless happy not to be working 9 to 5. ★★★

The World According to Garp

(1982, 136 min, US, George Roy Hill) Robin Williams is the eponymous T.S. Garp in Hill's terrific adaptation of the wild and wooly John Irving best-seller. Glenn Close is marvelously funny as Garp's stringent celebrity mom, as is John Lithgow as the transsexual, ex-Eagles tight end. ★★★½ $14.99

World and Time Enough

(1994, 90 min, US, Eric Mueller) Mueller's directorial feature film debut is an engaging and poignant comedy-drama that has enjoyed strong popularity at gay and lesbian film festivals. The story focuses on the lives of two lovers: HIV-positive conceptual artist Mark (Matt Guidry), who is out to "save the world," and the carefree, trash-collecting Joey (Gregory G. Giles). Narrated by a dishy friend (Kraig Swartz in a cute device that tires quickly), their tender relationship unfolds as we learn about them, their friends, their frustrations and work, and the one common need that unites them: the incessant search for the father they never had. The film's strong points are the witty dialogue and the all-too-rare situation of two young men deeply in love with each other, while its weaker points lie with its increasingly maudlin story line. Marketed as a "Generation X Queer Comedy," *World and Time Enough* (filmed in Minneapolis and St. Paul) is a great example of the regional growth of gay and lesbian filmmaking. ★★½ $39.99

A World Apart

(1988, 113 min, GB, Chris Menges) Menges' emotionally charged look at Apartheid, political commitment and familial ties, as seen through the eyes of a 13-year-old white girl living in early 1960s South Africa. Jodhi May gives a truly remarkable performance as the young girl who witnesses the gradual disintegration of her family when her mother, an anti-Apartheid activist, becomes a target of the South African government. Though the events are seen through the eyes of whites and not the real victims, the blacks themselves, it does not handicap the film; either in its excellence as a production or in the emergency of its issues. As the mother whose political conviction threatens personal well-being, Barbara Hershey is outstanding; and Linda Mvusi is exceptional as the family's black maid. ★★★½

World Gone Wild

(1988, 95 min, US, Lee H. Katzin) A rag-tag band of misfits defends the last waterhole on

W

Robert Duvall and Sandra Bullock in *Wrestling Ernest Hemingway*

Earth from an evil cult leader in the post-apocalyptic future. Michael Paré, Bruce Dern, Catherine Mary Stewart and Adam Ant star. ★★ $9.99

The World of Apu

(1959, 103 min, India, Satyajit Ray) This third segment of the famed Apu Trilogy is considered the masterpiece of the series. Apu unexpectedly marries the cousin of a friend and, after a brief idyllic marriage, is thrown into great despair when his young wife dies during childbirth. A long period of spiritual regeneration is consummated when Apu is reunited with his son five years later. The Apu Trilogy is considered one of the richest humanistic statements ever committed to film. (Bengali with English subtitles) ★★★★ $19.99

The World of Henry Orient

(1964, 106 min, US, George Roy Hill) One of Peter Sellers' most hilarious performances highlights this unsung comedy gem. He's a lady-killing, playboy concert pianist whose life is made miserable by the "adoration" of two pesky teenage girls. The girls' relationship and disparate social standings are at the base of this wonderful, poignant study of adolescence. Angela Lansbury costars. ★★★½ $19.99

A World of Strangers

(1962, 89 min, Denmark, Henning Carlsen) From Nobel Prize-winning author Nadine Gordimer comes this impassioned drama that exposes the hidden face of Apartheid. Shot in deep secrecy in South Africa because of its controversial political stance, the film focuses on an open-minded young Englishman, recently transferred to Johannesburg by a publishing company, who soon makes friends with both blacks and whites. But after witnessing the everyday brutality of the whites to the black Africans, he finds himself forced to take a stand. The film conveys eloquent insights into the harsh reality of an oppressive society based on racial separation and the conclusion that no one can remain neutral. ★★★ $59.99

The World Within

(1990, 80 min, US, Suzanne Wagner) An enlightening film focusing on Carl Jung's Red Book in which he recorded images from his unconscious. There are creations, Jung comments, "which have carried me out of time into seclusion; out of the present into timelessness." A fascinating glimpse into the philosophy of C.G. Jung. ★★★ $59.99

The Worm Eaters

(1978, 75 min, US, Herb Robins) A hermit lets loose a horde of worms to infest the food supply of a small California town. Um, Um Good! ★

The Worst Boy in Town

(1989, 60 min, Mexico, Enrique Gomez Vadillo) If this film received the exploitation treatment made famous by Roger Corman, the advertising angle might be something like, "Pepe – marauding macho thug by day...coquettish transvestite whore by night!" Set in the slums of Mexico City, the film features Mexican TV star Raul Buefil as the roughish Pepe, the leader of a gang of hunky thugs who spend their days playing pool, intimidating the neighbors and harassing young girls. But there is more to Pepe than his beefy body, tight pants and macho exterior... for, after the sun sets, he dons makeup, a wig and a sexy dress and visits the local transvestite bar, and in "her" new kittenish persona, looks for a good strong man who can give him a good ....! Not to be confused with great art, this entertaining melodrama is nonetheless great fun. (Spanish with English subtitles) ★★½

Worth Winning

(1989, 103 min, US, Will MacKenzie) A handsome TV weatherman (Mark Harmon) takes a bet challenging him to get engaged to three women in three months. Lesley Ann Warren, Madeleine Stowe and Maria Holvoe are the prospective betrothed. Not very appealing, either comedically or story wise, but the cast does seem to be trying their best. ★★ $19.99

The Would-Be Gentleman

(1959, 111 min, France, Jean Meyer) The comic artistry of Jean-Baptiste Moliere is brought to the screen by Paris' renowned Comedie Francaise. Always eager to please his sovereign, Louis XIV, Moliere lamblasts the rising bourgeoisie in this hilarious drawing room farce. The script bears its teeth on an idiotic member of the nouveau riche who bumbles and fumbles his way through a series of lessons as he vainly tries to educate himself to the level of the gentry. (French with English subtitles) ★★★

Woyzeck

(1979, 80 min, West Germany, Werner Herzog) Klaus Kinski gives a harrowing and unforgettable performance as a dim-witted but well-intentioned army private who is pushed over the edge of sanity by his common-law wife (Eva Mattes) and a ruthless society. Herzog delivers a chilling and devastating parable of social repression and dormant rebellion. The film is adapted from scenes of a Georg Buchner play written in 1837, which was left unfinished after the death of the author at 23. (German with English subtitles) ★★★ $59.99

WR: Mysteries of the Organism

(1971, 86 min, Yugoslavia, Dusan Makavejev) This strikingly original film by Makavejev, the bad boy of Yugoslavian cinema, is a clever, amusing and, at times, exasperating political satire which quite seriously proposes sex as an ideological imperative for liberation: a plea for Erotic Socialism. Using a montage method of filming, Makavejev examines the theories of sexologist Wilhelm Reich and juxtaposes documentary footage of Reich's disciples with two fictional stories — scenarios that propose a link between sexual energy and political liberation and repression with Stalinism. A breakthrough film which encapsulates the political and sexual revolution of its era. (Serbo-Croatian with English subtitles) ★★★½

The Wraith

(1986, 92 min, US, Mike Marvin) Out-of-its-mind horror film about an out-of-this-world entity challenging a menacing Arizona hot rod gang to the death. With Charlie Sheen, Nick Cassavetes, Randy Quaid and, before her "Twin Peaks" fame, Sherilyn Fenn. ★

Wrangler

(1988, 93 min, Australia, Ian Berry) Just in time for the inevitable resurgence of the western as a viable moviegoing experience, as initiated by *Dances with Wolves* and perpetuated by *Unforgiven*, along comes this welcome contribution to the genre from the land of Down Under. Jeff Fahey headlines this epic adventure about the efforts of a headstrong young girl (Tushka Bergen) to protect her family estate from a greedy land baron. Featuring lush cinematography by Ross Berryman (*Dead Calm*). Fans of the "horse opera" will be well served by its release. ★★★ $14.99

The Wreck of the Mary Deare

(1959, 100 min, US/GB, Michael Anderson) There's a good amount of suspense to this straight-forward but nevertheless involving maritime adventure. Charlton Heston plays a

W

salvager who happens upon a derelict ship, the Mary Deare. However, when he boards it, he discovers it is not abandoned: Captain Gary Cooper is still on board. And he refuses to reveal the secret as to what actually happened. The film tries to maintain tension throughout as to whether Cooper is innocent or guilty of grounding the ship; it's much more successful as to why, not who. Good scenic design and special effects. ★★½ $19.99

Wrestling Ernest Hemingway

(1993, 123 min, US, Randa Haines) The teaming of Richard Harris and Robert Duvall propels this somber but involving character study which is as alluring as it is tedious. Harris plays a 70-ish old salt who when not boasting of the titular bout is drunk in self-pity. Duvall is a Cuban ex-barber, whose life seems to revolve around the crush he has on a young waitress (Sandra Bullock). The story takes off when the two men befriend each other; predictably, each brings some sort of meaning to the other's life. There are some poignant moments, but the film is sabotaged by a humorless screenplay, which only accentuates the dreariness of these men's lives. Duvall, accent and all, is fascinating to watch; Harris proves that he is 1993's real Grumpy Old Man. Shirley MacLaine also stars. ★★½ $9.99

Written on the Wind

(1956, 99 min, US, Douglas Sirk) Sirk's classic melodrama about the fall of an oil tycoon's family enjoyed a successful rerelease after a 20-year theatrical absence. Filmed in lurid color and acted in a heightened and exaggerated style, we watch the self-destructive antics of the Hadley children. The son (Robert Stack) is a lush and his sister (Dorothy Malone, in an Oscar-winning performance) is a nymphomaniac. Add "good girl" Lauren Bacall and Rock Hudson and you get a continually enjoyable potboiler in the great 1950s Hollywood tradition. "Dynasty" and "Dallas," move over! ★★★½ $14.99

The Wrong Arm of the Law

(1962, 94 min, GB, Cliff Owen) Peter Sellers excels in this comedy caper as Pearly Gates, a Cockney criminal mastermind whose recent scores are being hijacked by an Australian gang posing as cops. Also stars Lionel Jeffries, Nanette Newman and Bernard Cribbins. ★★★ $39.99

The Wrong Box

(1966, 105 min, GB, Bryan Forbes) This beguiling farce is a sterling example of the great British comedies of the `60s. Based on a story co-authored by Robert Louis Stevenson, this merry romp concerns itself with an up-for-grabs inheritance and a migratory cadaver. The comedy is utter nonsense, a precursor to Monty Python, presented with superb precision and vigor by an all-star cast: Michael Caine, John Mills, Ralph Richardson, Peter Cook, Dudley Moore, and the incomparable Peter Sellers. ★★★½ $59.99

Wrong Is Right

(1982, 117 min, US, Richard Brooks) Fans of Sean Connery should not miss this amusing, fast-paced story in which Connery plays a Scottish version of Geraldo Rivera: a superstar TV reporter whose deep involvement with his stories puts him in the middle of a violent U.S. government-hatched intrigue. The film's convoluted story, about our TV-dominated culture as well as a pre-Grenada lament on the impotency of America's strength, has some holes, but Connery is great in this breakneck action-comedy. ★★★ $79.99

The Wrong Man

(1956, 105 min, US, Alfred Hitchcock) An unusual departure for Hitchcock, this semi-documentary focuses on a New York musician (Henry Fonda) who is mistakenly arrested for a flurry of robberies. Based on a true story, this is a frightening glimpse at the rites of police and legal procedure and the ensuing dehumanization of imprisonment. Vera Miles portrays the man's wife, broken by the shattering chain of misfortune. ★★★½ $19.99

The Wrong Move

(1975, 103 min, West Germany, Wim Wenders) Wenders' most German film concerns a young writer who sets out from home to roam the country for adventure and inspiration. Along the way he meets an old singer and his mute companion, a juggler (14-year-old Nastassja Kinski) and an actress (Hanna Schygulla). They all join together in this journey through Germany. (German with English subtitles) ★★★

Wuthering Heights

(1939, 103 min, US, William Wyler) Wyler's beautiful, haunting adaptation of the Emily Brontë novel of doomed love in pre-Victorian England. Laurence Olivier is the brooding Heathcliff and Merle Oberon is his undying love, Kathy. Have extra tissues on hand for this classic tearjerker. ★★★★ $19.99

Wuthering Heights

(1953, 90 min, Mexico, Luis Buñuel) Based on the Emily Brontë classic, Buñuel's Mexican potboiler is a steamy, characteristically sinister statement on obsessive love and lethal lust. Removed from the blustery Yorkshire shores to a dusty, sunbaked landscape, the film has an even greater sense of desperation than the novel. Alejandro (the film's Heathcliff) is a coiled serpent, dashing and deadly, who returns to his childhood home determined to reclaim the affections of his longtime love, Catalina. When she remains faithful to her husband, Alejandro spitefully marries her sister. Passions flair and defenses crumble in the final confrontation at Catalina's deathbed. (Spanish with English subtitles) ★★★ $24.99

Wuthering Heights

(1970, 105 min, GB, Robert Fuest) A well-made, atmospheric version of the Emily Brontë classic of doomed love in pre-Victorian England, with a dashing Timothy Dalton as Heathcliff and Anna Calder-Marshall as Cathy. Of course it doesn't come near the 1939 Olivier-Oberon adaptation, but what could? ★★★

Wyatt Earp

(1994, 190 min, US, Lawrence Kasdan) The curious real-life relationship between no-nonsense lawman Wyatt Earp (Kevin Costner) and tubercular cardshark Doc Holliday (Dennis Quaid) translates into an engrossing cinematic experience. Quaid's performance as the morally precarious, deathly ill and completely ironic Holliday is inspired and plays perfectly against Costner's dead-pan, straightlaced Earp. Unfortunately, the Earp/Holliday relationship takes up only a quarter of the film which devotes too much time to the admittedly picturesque vistas of the American West and to Costner's steely stares. A talented roster of actors, including Gene Hackman, Michael Madsen, Tom Sizemore and Isabella Rossellini, deliver first-rate performances but none are able to sufficiently expand upon their less than delineated characters, most of whom cannot fully enliven this more than three-hour epic. (The director's cut is also available for $24.99) ★★★ $24.99

W

Wyatt Earp

X — The Unheard Music

(1986, 84 min, US, W.T. Morgan) Fascinating, technically ambitious documentary about seminal L.A. punk band X. Combining live concert footage, interviews and amazing archival clips, it manages to entertain as well as inform. Classic X songs include "Johnny Hit and Run Pauline," among many others. ★★★

Xanadu

(1980, 88 min, US, Robert Greenwald) A campy guilty pleasure, this quintessential 1980's "disco musical" was a box-office flop and despised by critics everywhere. True, the story of a muse (Olivia Newton-John) who comes to life to inspire a young artist (Michael Beck) is loaded with sappy and sometimes silly plot developments, and director Greenwald, while possessing a talent for visuals, hasn't an idea about narrative. But for those willing to bask in its unpretentious and curiously effective fantasy elements and musical numbers, *Xanadu* is a disco-thumping, roller-boogeyin' lark. The good score helps. Gene Kelly, in his final dramatic role (if you can call it dramatic), appears as sort of a wise sage who opens a dance hall and gets to perform a dance or two. ★★½ $14.99

Xica

(1976, 107 min, Brazil, Carlos Diegues) Diegues' exuberant historical comedy is based on the tale of a voluptuous black slave who single-handedly wrapped an 18th-century Brazilian village around her finger by conquering its wealthy diamond contractor with her sexual prowess. As she exploits her new-found powers, the townspeople become increasingly enraged at her extravagances and whimsical self-indulgence prompting them to call for a governmental investigator. Zeze

Xica

Motta stars as the devil-may-care Xica, whose sexual bravado and powerful flamboyance captivates men and usurps their authority. The film sparkles with humor while touching on the subject of freedom, the spirit to survive and individual revolution. (Spanish with English subtitles) ★★★ $79.99

The Yakuza

(1974, 112 min, US, Sydney Pollack) An ex-cop (Robert Mitchum) battles the Japanese mafia to rescue the kidnapped daughter of an old friend (Brian Keith). Robert Towne and Paul Schrader cowrote the script. ★★½ $14.99

Yanco

(1964, 90 min, Mexico, Servando Gonzales) A young boy in an Indian village thrives on music to escape the realities of his poverty-stricken surroundings, often running off to a secret hideout to play his homemade violin. One day, he meets an old man who is a master musician. The old man's violin becomes the instrument of their friendship as he teaches the child the wonders of music. Although in original Spanish language without subtitles, this beautifully-told tale conveys its story — whether you speak the language or not — through remarkably subtle yet overwhelming visual images. An affecting performance from Ricardo Ancona as the young boy. ★★★

Yankee Doodle Dandy

(1942, 12 min, US, MIchael Curtiz) James Cagney won an Oscar for his classic performance as the legendary song-and-dance man George M. Cohan. It is ironic that Cagney, American movies' quintessential gangster, is best remembered and had his most popular role in this entertaining musical biography. Can anyone forget Cagney's immortal interpretation of the title tune? ★★★½ $14.99

Yanks

(1979, 139 min, US, John Schlesinger) An absorbing and literate WWII drama about American G.I.s stationed in England. Richard Gere and William Devane are but two of the "Yanks" who begin relationships with British women — Gere with young Lisa Eichhorn and Devane with married Vanessa Redgrave. In support, Rachel Roberts gives a smashing performance as Eichhorn's inflexible mother. Fine direction from Schlesinger, who has a keen eye for the detail and atmosphere of the era. ★★★ $14.99

The Year My Voice Broke

(1987, 105 min, Australia, John Duigan) A better look at puberty blues than Bruce Beresford's film of that title, and as affecting and lovingly crafted as Rob Reiner's *Stand by Me*, this tale of teenage troubles is set in an Australian backwater town in the early '60s. Childhood friends Freya and Danny, along with Freya's new hoodlum boyfriend Trevor, begin the difficult transition from childhood to adolescence as well as learn of the hidden secrets of the town's older generation. Non-stereotypical characterization, disarming humor and a bittersweet conclusion that avoids simple

sentimentality save this overdone plot from being a cliché. ★★★ $89.99

The Year of Living Dangerously

(1983, 115 min, Australia, Peter Weir) Mel Gibson stars as a foreign correspondent whose attraction to a British attache (Sigourney Weaver) pits his professional instincts against his personal allegiances. Weir directs with a discerning eye this torrid account of love and betrayal amidst Indonesia's 1965 military coup. Linda Hunt won an Academy Award for her unforgettable performance as Gibson's male confidant. ★★★½ $14.99

Year of the Comet

(1992, 89 min, US, Peter Yates) The ever-perky Penelope Ann Miller stars in this text-book romantic action/comedy about the downtrodden daughter of a wine dealer who, in an attempt to prove herself to her chauvinistic father and brother, reluctantly teams up with a dashing troubleshooter (TV heartthrob Timothy Daly) to recover a stolen bottle of priceless wine. The good news is that this is acclaimed screenwriter William Goldman's first original script since *Butch Cassidy and the Sundance Kid*. The bad news is that it doesn't live up to the standards of his earlier works (including *Marathon Man* and *The Princess Bride*), nor those of director Yates (*The Dresser*, *Breaking Away*). Nevertheless, the film has a few enjoyable moments and will make a great date movie. ★★ $19.99

Year of the Dragon

(1985, 125 min, US, Michael Cimino) Controversial police thriller with Mickey Rourke as a New York City police captain assigned to the Chinatown district to keep peace among the neighboring gangs. Once there, however, he comes in conflict with a local underworld boss (John Lone). Oliver Stone wrote the screenplay which relies heavily on violence and police actioner clichés. ★★½ $14.99

Year of the Gun

(1991, 111 min, US, John Frankenheimer) After a slow start, lots of un-subtitled Italian and a less-than-compelling performance by Andrew McCarthy, this political thriller by Frankenheimer gets into gear, intensifies and delivers. Set in Rome during the late '70s, McCarthy plays a journalist writing a fictionalized account of a Red Brigade plot to kidnap Aldo Moro. Paranoia and violence quickly follow when the dangerously accurate manuscript is stolen. A good supporting cast includes John Pankow as a mysterious professor, Sharon Stone as a mysterious photojournalist and Valeria Golina as McCarthy's mysterious girlfriend. ★★½ $14.99

A Year of the Quiet Sun

(1985, 106 min, Poland/West Germany, Krzysztof Zanussi) Internationally renowned Polish filmmaker Zanussi directed this haunting and poignant love story set in a ravaged post-war Poland. An American soldier, sent to investigate war crimes, falls in love with a Polish widow. The film skillfully and sensitively captures their awkward attempts at communication, attempts that are at first hindered by the lack of a common language. A universal story about a love that is greater than the barriers of language and politics. (Polish with English subtitles) ★★★½

The Yearling

(1946, 134 min, US, Clarence Brown) Classic screen version of Marjorie Kinnan Rawling's Pulitzer Prize-winning novel about a small boy's love for a young deer. Gregory Peck and Jane Wyman are fine as the child's parents, and Claude Jarman, Jr. gives a remarkable performance as the young boy. Beautifully photographed. ★★★★ $14.99

Yellow Earth

(1984, 89 min, China, Chen Kaige) An early film collaboration of two proponents of China's New Wave of cinema, Chen and Zhang Yimou, this film revolves around a young soldier sent out to gather folk songs which will be used by the Party to rouse the patriotism of the revolutionaries. Brother Gu, as the soldier is affectionately named, is treated with great respect at a wedding and is told to stay with a sheep-herding family in the hills. The young daughter, who is a fine singer, falls for the young soldier and decides to get out of her arranged marriage in order to join him in the city. This simple tale has the same sense of unfulfilled passion of other New Wave films, but the cinematography and performances save this from being one of the usual fare. (Mandarin with English subtitles) ★★★ $19.99

Yellow Submarine

(1968, 85 min, GB, George Dunning) Fantastic animated romp with the Fab Four fighting to save Pepperland from the Blue Meanies with the message that "All You Need is Love." Other Beatles' songs include "Nowhere Man," "Lucy in the Sky with Diamonds" and "When I'm Sixty-Four." ★★★½

Yentl

(1983, 134 min, US, Barbra Streisand) Streisand shines as both star and director in this underrated, likable musical based on a story by Isaac Bashevis Singer (*Enemies: A Love Story*). Set in turn-of-the-century Russia, Streisand plays a woman who disguises herself as a boy to gain admittance to a yeshiva, an all-male school for Talmudic study. Mandy Patinkin co-stars as a fellow student who befriends "Yentl, the Yeshiva Boy," and Amy Irving nicely plays Patinkin's fiancée. ★★★ $19.99

Yesterday, Today and Tomorrow

(1964, 119 min, Italy, Vittorio De Sica) A tour de force for director De Sica as well as stars Sophia Loren and Marcello Mastroianni. This "battle-of-the-sexes" comedy is set in the framework of three episodes, each employing different stories, acting styles and locations (Rome, Milan and Naples). A delightful Academy Award-winning satire which features a striptease by Loren that still heats up the screen. (Dubbed) ★★★★ $19.99

Yiddle with a Fiddle (Yidl Mitn Fidl)

(1936, 92 min, Poland, Joseph Green) This classic Yiddish musical-comedy stars Molly Picon as a *shtetl* girl who, determined to discover a world closed off to her as a woman, disguises herself as a boy and joins up with a traveling band of musicians. Picon, luminous

Yojimbo

in the performance of her career, soon falls in love with one of her colleagues but, with delightfully humorous results, is forced to keep her identity hidden from him. Filled with Jewish songs, vaudeville skits and scenes of everyday life, this film provides a glimpse of Jewish life in Poland before it was tragically destroyed. The first international Yiddish hit, *Yiddle with a Fiddle* is considered by many to be the best Yiddish film of all time. (Yiddish with English subtitles) ★★★★ $79.99

Yojimbo

(1961, 110 min, Japan, Akira Kurosawa) In the style of an American western, *Yojimbo* matches a cynical, wandering samurai against two merchant families battling for control of a country town. Kurosawa hilariously satirizes greed, linking it to paranoia, pomposity and cowardice. (Japanese with English subtitles) ★★★★ $29.99

Yol

(1982, 111 min, Turkey/Switzerland, Serif Goren & Yilmaz Gurney) A devastating drama dealing with political, ethnic and cultural repression in contemporary Turkey. Secretly written and directed while still in prison, directors Goren and Gurney offer a harrowing vision as seen through the lives of five prisoners who are granted temporary furloughs to visit their families. (Turkish with English subtitles) ★★★½ $19.99

Yongary, Monster from the Deep

(1969, 79 min, South Korea) Monster movie madness as a 50-foot lizard menaces Seoul, South Korea. ★ $19.99

You Are Not Alone

(1981, 94 min, Denmark, Lasse Nielsen & Ernst Johansen) Unique and lyrical, this tale explores the boundaries of friendship and love between two young boys in a private boarding school in Copenhagen. The headmaster's inability to cope with the pair's mounting sexuality leads to their rebellion. (Dutch with English subtitles) ★★★ $49.99

You Can't Cheat an Honest Man

(1939, 76 min, US, George Marshall) A brisk comedy providing W.C. Fields a hilarious setting in which to flourish. As the entrepreneur of a traveling circus, Fields is adept at pulling up stakes and reaching the state line just before the law catches up with him. He also finds time to taunt children, short change his employees, and tangle with an assortment of wild animal and inanimate objects — particularly ventriloquist's dummy Charlie McCarthy. ★★★

You Can't Take It with You

(1938, 127 min, US, Frank Capra) Capra's zany and uproarious screen version of Kaufman and Hart's classic Broadway comedy. Jean Arthur stars as the daughter of an outrageously eccentric family out to win over her boyfriend's (James Stewart) conservative parents. Though there's a touch of Capra's trademark sentimentality, this doesn't detract from the total enjoyment of this Academy Award-winning Best Picture. With Lionel Barrymore, Edward Arnold, Spring Byington and Ann Miller. ★★★★ $19.99

You Only Live Once

(1937, 86 min, US, Fritz Lang) Lang directed this powerful social drama with Henry Fonda as a wrongly imprisoned ex-con who tries to go straight. Also with Sylvia Sidney as his wife. Solid performances from the two leads. Based partly on the lives of Bonnie and Clyde. ★★★

You Only Live Twice

(1967, 117 min, GB, Lewis Gilbert) SPECTRE steals both American and Soviet spacecrafts in an attempt to start WWIII. This James Bond adventure is the slightest of the Sean Connery films, beset by plot holes and stiff supporting players; it only comes alive when Donald Pleasence hits the screen as Blofeld. ★★ $14.99

You So Crazy

(1994, 86 min, US, Thomas Schlamme) Venom-tongued TV actor Martin Lawrence (Fox's "Martin") excels in this outrageous, untamed live concert performance where no

Doris Day (l.), Kirk Douglas and Lauren Bacall in *Young Man with a Horn*

stone is left unturned. Attacking everyone from Rodney King to Jeffrey Dahmer, this on-the-rise comic proves with no mercy that he is one of the funniest comedians to take the stage since Richard Pryor. Loud, rude and playfully offensive, this highly entertaining film is a must see for those in search of some trouser-wetting laughs. ★★★½ $14.99

You Were Never Lovelier

(1942, 97 min, US, Willaim A. Seiter) Fred Astaire was never debonair-er and Rita Hayworth never more breathtaking-er than in this charming tale of innocent seduction, well-intentioned meddling and haywire miscommunications. Affably zany support from Adolphe Menjou, Xavier Cugat, Larry Parks and Adele Mara. Astaire once commented that Hayworth was his favorite dancing partner. Watch this and see why. ★★★½ $19.99

You'll Never Get Rich

(1941, 88 min, US, Sidney Lanfield) Fred Astaire and Rita Hayworth make a most appealing team in this delightful musical comedy. Fred plays a Broadway hoofer and choreographer who gets drafted. He courts ravishing Rita and still manages to make the show go on. Cole Porter score includes "I Kissed My Baby Goodbye." ★★★ $19.99

You're a Big Boy Now

(1966, 96 min, US, Francis Ford Coppola) A bit of a time warp, this outrageously entertaining coming-of-age comedy stars Peter Kastner (for those old enough to remember, he was TV's "Ugliest Girl in Town") as a sheltered young man who leaves home and learns all about life, with help from dancer Elizabeth Hartman. Rip Torn and Geraldine Page also star as his parents — Page excels in what could be the most over-protective movie mom since Mrs. Bates. A real charmer. ★★★ $14.99

You've Had Worse Things in Your Mouth

(1994, 30 min, US, Allison Liddi) While little more than a polished home video, this decidedly different cooking show features 400-pound transsexual Billi Gordon (called "Oprah's evil twin" by the *National Enquirer*) as the beleaguered hostess of a cooking show from Hell. Food takes a secondary role as the surprisingly sweet Billi snaps off one-liners, listens to her nagging mother (also played by Gordon) and deals with an angry biker chick in this silly but fun party tape. ★★★ $14.99

The Young Americans

(1993, 100 min, GB, Danny Cannon) Harvey Keitel is a DEA advisor brought into a drug war investigation in London who confronts the hit man (Viggo Mortensen) he has tracked for eight years. Director Cannon delivers a well-acted, well-mounted production with a finely crafted story line and succinctly drawn characters which lift the film above its potentially derivative subject matter. Keitel's portrayal is his most modulated in recent memory, and Iain Glen (*Mountains of the Moon*) is especially affecting as a young man inadvertently drawn into the center of the investigation. This moody actioner is surprisingly effective in engaging the viewer's attention and sympathies. ★★★ $19.99

Young and Innocent

(1937, 82 min, GB, Alfred Hitchcock) Plenty of Hitchcockian touches are to be found in this charming and chilling chase drama about a young man, falsely accused of murder, who, with the help of his girlfriend, pursues the real culprit: the man with the eye twitch! ★★★ $14.99

Young Aphrodites

(1966, 87 min, Greece, Nikos Koundrouros) Filmed among the ruins of ancient Greece and using authentic shepherds and peasants, this exotic and sensual film presents the universal story of the physical longing and sexual attraction of two adolescents. This magnificently photographed film is a poetic ode to the beginning of adulthood and the loss of innocence. (Dubbed) ★★★

Young at Heart

(1954, 117 min, US, Gordon Douglas) Bright musical remake of *Four Daughters*, with Doris Day as the daughter of a small-town musician who is courted by Frank Sinatra. ★★★ $14.99

Young Catherine

(1991, 106 min, GB, Michael Anderson) Set in Russia of 1744, this period drama chronicles the power struggle between the Empress Elizabeth (Vanessa Redgrave) and her daughter-in-law, Catherine (Julia Ormond). Saddled with an impotent husband, Catherine bears a bastard child and attempts to have him installed on the throne. Christopher Plummer costars as Sir Charles, an ally to Catherine. ★★★ $89.99

Young Doctors in Love

(1982, 97 min, US, Garry Marshall) A funny farce about life in a metropolitan hospital, in the tradition of *Airplane!* and *The Naked Gun*. Cast features Michael McKean, Sean Young, Dabney Coleman and Hector Elizondo, and boasts appearances by many daytime TV soap stars. ★★★ $14.99

Young Einstein

(1989, 90 min, Australia, Yahoo Serious) Fans of *Bill and Ted's Excellent Adventure* might find humor in this minor comedy from Yahoo Serious. Once touted to be Australia's next great export, Serious directed, wrote and stars in this Albert Einstein spoof about the son of a Tazmanian farm family who knows inherently that he is destined for great things (i.e. splitting the atom to put bubbles in beer). Unfortunately, the film relies too heavily on Jeff Darling's vivid cinematography and fails to exploit the comedy of this potentially humorous premise. ★★½ $14.99

Young Frankenstein

(1974, 105 min, US, Mel Brooks) Brooks is at his best with this hilarious spoof of the *Frankenstein* films, hitting every comic mark with uncanny accuracy. Gene Wilder stars as the soon-to-be demented doc, Dr. Frankenstein ("That's Frahnken*steen*"), giving an inspired comic performance. Marty Feldman is Ygor ("That's Eye-gore"), the sardonic wit of the laboratory set, and Madeline Kahn, Cloris Leachman, Teri Garr and Peter Boyle round out an altogether winning cast. Authentic sets from the 1930s films, astounding black-and-white cinematography, and an atmospheric score by John Morris contribute to the sheer delight of this comedy classic. ★★★★ $9.99

Young Guns

(1988, 107 min, US, Christopher Cain) The Brat Pack on horses! Slick western adventure with Emilio Estevez, Kiefer Sutherland, Lou Diamond Phillips, Charlie Sheen, Casey Siemaszko and Dermot Mulroney trying to tame the wild West, and get revenge for their mentor's murder. ★★½ $14.99

Young Guns 2

(1990, 105 min, US, Geoff Murphy) Annoying sequel to the 1988 hit finds Billy the Kid (Emilio Estevez) on the run from former friend-turned-bounty hunter Pat Garrett (William Petersen). Likable cast features Kiefer Sutherland, Lou Diamond Phillips, Christian Slater, Alan Ruck and Balthazar Getty, but this one lacks the element of fun that made the first one watchable. ★½ $9.99

The Young Lions

(1958, 167 min, US, Edward Dmytryk) A somewhat overlong but nevertheless mesmerizing WWII epic, based on Irwin Shaw's novel examining the volatile relationship between two American soldiers and a Nazi officer. Montgomery Clift and Dean Martin are the former; a rather restrained Marlon Brando is the German soldier undergoing a moral edification in light of his country's actions. Maximilian Schell and Hope Lange also star. ★★★ $19.99

The Young Magician

(1986, 99 min, Waldemar Dziki) Award-winning feature about a young boy who learns he has magical powers but no way to control them. From the producers of *Bach and Broccoli*. ★★★ $14.99

Young Man with a Horn

(1950, 112 min, US, Michael Curtiz) Kirk Douglas, Lauren Bacall and Doris Day are all quite good in this romantic drama about trumpeter Douglas trying to make it in the jazz world, and torn between Bacall and Day. Based on the life of Bix Beiderbecke. ★★★ $19.99

Young Master

(1980, 105 min, Hong Kong, Jackie Chan) Made back when Jackie was beginning to exercise creative control over his own films, this amalgam of comedy and action shows Chan trying to make a movie firmly within the kung fu genre, while also developing his own unique comedic persona, as opposed to remaining the Bruce Lee clone the studio originally envisioned him as. Jackie is Ah Lung, a gifted kung fu student who is thrown out of his school in disgrace. Looking for his brother, who was also thrown out, he gets involved in a case of mistaken identity and is branded a fugitive. After clearing his name, he helps the authorities capture the real criminal. The story here is strictly by-the-numbers and the comedy touches are a bit forced, but the fighting scenes are all topnotch. The film successfully balances itself between comedy and action, too, with most of the kung fu scenes being of the funny variety, though extremely well choreographed. Two fight scenes, though, are fast, furious and played straight. The long end fight scene, in particular, stands among the best that Jackie has done. Jackie's Opera school chum Biao appears in a small, but memorable role. (Cantonese with English subtitles) ★★★ $19.99

The Young Ones: Oil, Boring and Flood

(90 min, GB) Three episodes from the BBC comedy series revolving around the antics of four university student flatmates. Quirky, original, irreverent, surreal, inventive and really funny. It's not quite clear when they attend classes, though. Starring Rik Mayall, Ade Edmondson, Nigel Planer and Christopher Ryan as the roommates; and Alexi Sayle is featured in various roles. ★★★½ $14.99

The Young Philadelphians

(1959, 136 min, US, Vincent Sherman) Paul Newman stars as a lawyer from the poor side of the tracks who works his way up the corporate and social ladders. Barbara Rush is the society woman he romances. Robert Vaughn is quite good (he received an Oscar nomination) as Newman's old Army buddy. Also with Alexis Smith, Brian Keith and Adam West. ★★★ $14.99

The Young Poisoner's Handbook

(1996, 99 min, GB, Benjamin Ross) This very entertaining black comedy tells the true story of Graham Young, a young chemistry buff who becomes obsessed with some lethal concoctions and begins testing them, in a very scientifically sound manner, mind you, and without any reservations, on other human beings. Motivated more by intellectual curiosity than hatred, he slowly poisons his mother and father in a series of carefully controlled experiments. That is, until he gets caught and sent to a psychiatric hospital. There he is taken under the wing of a doctor with a radical new method for treating psychotic misfits and Graham deludes both himself and his psychiatrist into believing that he is cured. The audience, however, knows better, and Graham reverts back to his lethally experimental ways when he is released, poisoning his whole place of employment via the afternoon tea. Reminiscent at times of *A Clockwork Orange*, the film revels in its dark comedy and its gleefully wicked re-creation/satire of England in the 1950s and '60s. This handbook will be a lot of fun for those who approve of its somewhat unconventional topic. ★★★ $99.99

Young Sherlock Holmes

(1985, 110 min, US, Barry Levinson) Steven Spielberg produced this stylish and very entertaining mystery adventure. Sherlock Holmes and Dr. Watson meet for the first time as schoolmates and investigate the apparent suicides of civic leaders. Terrific special effects include a stalking stained-glass window and pastries on parade. ★★★ $14.99

Young Winston

(1972, 157 min, GB, Richard Attenborough) Hold on to your horses. We're off on a two-and-a-half-hour essay on the youthful days of Winston Churchill. While hardly representative of Britain's finest hour, this is an interesting and entertaining account of the young Churchill's life – following him through a lonely childhood, battles in India, his exploits in the Boer Wars, and his first election to Parliament. The battle scenes are superb and the seasoned cast includes Simon Ward, Anne Bancroft, Robert Shaw, John Mills and Ian Holm. ★★★ $19.99

Youngblood

(1986, 109 min, US, Peter Markle) Tedious sports drama with Rob Lowe as a farmboy who joins a Canadian minor league hockey team, becoming involved with the coach's daughter. Patrick Swayze and Cynthia Gibb also star. ★½ $14.99

Younger & Younger

(1994, 97 min, US, Percy Adlon) Whatever happened to Percy Adlon? After making a promising start in his native Germany, he came to the States and made the wonderful *Bagdad Cafe*. But after that came dreck and more dreck. The latest dreck is *Younger & Younger*. The story (if you can call it that) concerns Jonathan Younger (Donald Sutherland) and his storage company and all the quirky people that work there and visit and all the quirky things that happen in all the quirky places in and about the company. Now there's nothing wrong with quirky – in *Bagdad Cafe* the film's quirkiness was grounded by the three-dimensional characters and inventive plot developments. But here the characters are just clichés (Jonathan is a lothario; his wife, played by Lolita Davidovich, is a frump; their son Brendan Fraser is a prig; etc.), and they add nothing to an already pointless story. ★½ $14.99

Yours, Mine and Ours

(1968, 111 min, US, Melville Shavelson) A theatrical "Brady Bunch," and not without some laughs. Henry Fonda, widowed father of ten, marries widow Lucille Ball, mother of six. All hell breaks loose when they gather the kids and move in together. An old-fashioned, sentimental comedy. ★★½ $14.99

Z

(1969, 127 min, France/Algeria, Constantin Costa-Gavras) A swiftly moving political thriller on fascist corruption in the Greek government. Costa-Gavras has delivered an exciting, even riveting exposé of social ills and the abuses of power. Starring Yves Montand, Irene Papas and Jean-Louis Trintignant. Academy Award winner for Best Foreign Film. (French with English subtitles) ★★★★ $29.99

Z.P.G.

(1972, 95 min, GB, Michael Campus) This apocalyptic vision of overpopulation is set in the 21st century where reproduction is a crime punishable by death, gas masks are the hip new fashion accessory, and state-provided robot dolls are issued to couples who want to have children. Geraldine Chaplin and Oliver Reed star as a couple who defy the government's stance of Zero Population Growth by having a real child in this grim but stylish pro-lifer's nightmare. ★★★

Zabriskie Point

(1970, 110 min, US, Michelangelo Antonioni) A political and sociological time capsule that presents a disturbing view of 1960s America – a turbulent time of political unrest and student upheaval. This rambling study by Antonioni gets a bit bogged down in polemics and the result is a film less satisfying than *Blow-Up* in documenting the social ferment in a foreign country. Nonetheless, with sweeping photography set in Death Valley, a script co-written by Sam Shepard, a cameo appearance by a young Harrison Ford and an explosive subject matter, the film is novel and compelling. (Filmed in English) ★★★ $19.99

Zardoz

(1974, 105 min, GB, John Boorman) Boorman's bizarre and overloaded science-fiction adventure is set in the year 2293 when the Eternals (a group of ageless intellectuals) live inside a dome and send orders to the Exterminator to kill the Brutals who inhabit the wasteland outside. Sean Connery plays an Exterminator with a conscience who penetrates the secrets of the dome and enters a maze of mind-boggling imagery. Boorman's imagination runs wild like it never has. ★★½ $19.99

Zatoichi

From the classic *The Life and Opinion of Masseur Ichi* springs a series of films chronicling the adventures of the blind swordsman in his travels through a rural Japan fraught with bandits, unscrupulous officials and waylaid innocents. Shintaro Katsu is engaging as the self-effacing massuese, whose sightlessness camoflages his unerring martial arts abilities. He drinks, he gambles and he kills only when necessary. He's a consistently entertaining character. First-rate production values, fine supporting casts and Katsu's endearing interpretation of his character make this series a guaranteed good time. (The inspiration for Rutger Hauer's action-adventure film *Blind Fury*.)

Zatoichi: The Life and Opinion of Masseur Ichi

(1962, 96 min, Japan, Kenji Misumi) The first entry in the *Zatoichi* series finds the blind swordsman caught between two rival war lords engaged in a bloody territorial feud. More somber in tone than the films which followed it and with slightly grainy black-and-white cinematography, but all the elements are there. Shintaro Katsu is perfection as the blind traveling masseuse whose comic bungling hides his unerring martial artistry. (Japanese with English subtitles) ★★★½ $59.99

Zatoichi: Masseur Ichi and a Chest of Gold

(1964, 83 min, Japan, Kazuo Ikehiro) Zatoichi visits the grave of a man he killed two years earlier. While he's there, the village tax payment — a chest of gold — is stolen on the way to the government office. Zatoichi is accused of the robbery and vows to find the real thieves. ★★★ $59.99

Zatoichi: The Blind Swordsman and the Chess Expert

(1965, 87 min, Japan, Kenji Misumi) Zatoichi strikes up a friendship with a Samurai chess master on an undisclosed mission, becoming involved in a convoluted web of misplaced loyalties and deceit. ★★★ $59.99

Zatoichi: The Blind Swordsman's Vengeance

(1966, 83 min, Japan, Tokuzo Tanaka) Zatoichi comes upon a man waylaid by bandits. After killing the highwaymen, he hears the last request of the dying victim: To give a full purse to someone named Taichi. He finds the intended recipient, a small boy, in a village at the mercy of a brutal overlord. You can free it from there. ★★★ $59.99

Zatoichi: The Blind Swordsman and the Fugitives

(1968, 82 min, Japan, Kimiyoshi Yasuda) Shintaro Katsu returns as Zatoichi in this entry to Japan's longest running film series. A corrupt village official, running a sweat shop with the town's young women, is blackmailed into providing refuge for a band of sadistic fugitives. While staying with the town's selfless, humanitarian doctor, Zatoichi discovers a link from the past which connects two unlikely protagonists in the ensuing conflict. Swift-moving with strong characterizations. (Japanese with English subtitles) ★★★ $59.99

Zatoichi Meets Yojimbo

(1970, 115 min, Japan, Kihachi Okamoto) Toshiro Mifune re-creates his character Yojimbo from the Akira Kurosawa classic, here teaming with blind master swordsman Zatoichi (Shintaro Katso) to eliminate the gangsters who have taken over a small village and stolen and hid a fortune in gold belonging to the government. An action-filled and fun spoof of samurai films. (Japanese with English subtitles) ★★★½ $39.99

Zazie dans le Metro

(1960, 88 min, France, Louis Malle) Nodding his appreciative head to the cinematic exuberance exhibited in Truffaut's *The 400 Blows* and Godard's *Breathless*, 28-year-old Malle joined the New Wave with this colorful, frenetic slapstick comedy. Zazie, foul-mouthed, precocious pre-teen brat, is dropped off on her uncle's (Philippe Noiret) door by her philandering mother. In the next 36 hours, Zazie, accompanied by her befuddled uncle (a female impersonator), involves herself in a series of wild, mischievous antics as she embarks on her own personalized tour of Paris. Filled with cinematic tricks, jump-cuts and references to other films, this effervescent comedy, inspired by Raymond Queneau's novel, is not Malle's masterpiece but is unabashedly great anarchistic fun. (French with English subtitles) ★★★ $29.99

Zebrahead

(1992, 100 min, US, Anthony Drazan) First-time director Drazan's masterful debut transposes "Romeo and Juliet" onto the blighted 1990s urban landscape. Set in Detroit, the story centers around Jack, a gawky, wannabe homeboy who is amongst the few white kids in his high school. Trouble comes his way when he falls hard for his best friend's cousin Nikki, a savvy young black teen who has just moved from New York. While the story is not hard to predict, the easy-going performances of Michael Rapaport and N'Bushe Wright as Zack and Nikki, along with Drazen's thoughtfully constructed script, make this an engaging and meaningful essay on race relations in the '90s. ★★★½ $9.99

A Zed and Two Naughts

(1985, 115 min, GB, Peter Greenaway) Another surrealist treat from Greenaway, the director of *The Cook, the Thief, His Wife and Her Lover*. Two ex-Siamese twins are made widowers by an auto accident and team up with the car's driver, who lost her leg in the wreck, to explore the processes of death and decay. Always one to shock his viewers, Greenaway follows their examinations with all of the visual fecundity that has become the hallmark of his filmmaking, right down to time-lapse images of decaying corpses of animals. The lush cinematography of Sacha Vierny may be lost on the small screen. ★★★

Zelig

(1983, 79 min, US, Woody Allen) The sublime story of Leonard Zelig, the outstanding chameleon-man, whose ability to alter his appearance perplexed medical experts and captivated the public's imagination. Allen's hilarious pseudo-documentary tackles the perils of conformity and the rakishness of the media. ★★★★ $14.99

Zelly and Me

(1988, 87 min, US, Tina Rathborne) A neglected rich girl is befriended by her caring governess, much to the disdain of the youngster's mean-spirited grandmother. Heavy-handed and only occasionally moving, the film suffers from a slow pace and overly mannered dramatics. With Isabella Rossellini, Glynis Johns, Alexandra Johnes, and David Lynch as Rossellini's too-good-to-be-true suitor. ★★ $79.99

Zentropa

(1991, 107 min, The Netherlands, Lars von Trier) This penetrating and mesmeric trip into the dark soul of Europe follows a young American pacifist of German descent who sojourns to post-WWII Deutschland in the belief that he can take part in the healing process of that devastated country. Once there, however, he finds himself snatched up in a nightmarish labyrinth of corruption and deceit involving American complicity in the reestablishment of the powerful industrialist families who had supplied the Nazis. Max von Sydow's haunting narration sets the tone for the naive Yankee's hypnotic entry into the bizarre purgatory of occupied Germany. Shooting mostly in shimmering black and white, von Trier uses some of the conventions established by Hans Jürgen Syberberg in *Our Hitler* and Michael Verhoeven in *The Nasty Girl*, such as spot coloring, scrims and other overtly theatrical devices. Combined with some excellent performances, these add to the film's harrowing sense of impending doom and alienation. (In English and German with English subtitles) ★★★½ $19.99

Zeram

(1991, 92 min, Japan, Keita Amemiya) Armed with a warp machine, space bazooka and a wise-cracking computer named Bob, a feisty female bounty hunter sets out to save planet Earth from Zeram, a renegade space alien with a unique taste for strange headgear. Wildly entertaining, this is wacky sci-fi action at its best, sure to appeal to fans of the classic TV shows "Space Giants" and "Ultraman." ★★★½ $19.99

Zero for Conduct (Zéro de Conduite)

(1933, 44 min, France, Jean Vigo) Vigo's first fiction film was banned for anti-French sentiment and reissued in 1945 after the liberation. It is, in part, an autobiographical account of the director's boyhood days in boarding school and, in part, a rendering of childhood fantasy. Realistic, poetic and subversive. (French with English subtitles) ★★★★ $24.99

Zero Patience

(1993, 95 min, Canada, John Greyson) From the director of the very serious *Urinal* comes this unexpectedly outrageous and satiric musical comedy about life in the age of AIDS. The story centers around "Patient Zero," Gaetan Dugas, a French-Canadian airline steward who was reported by health officials to be the man who brought AIDS to North America and helped rapidly spread it through promiscuous

XYZ

sexual activity. Gaetan returns from the dead to clear his name and solicits the help of 19th-century explorer (and now 20th-century AIDS researcher) Sir Richard Burton. Burton's development from a self-centered homophobe to an ACT-UP-styled queer is the centerpiece of this amazing story. The film also features several bizarre musical routines, inventively choreographed and sporting wittily queer lyrics. ★★★ $79.99

Ziegfeld Follies

(1946, 110 min, US, Vincente Minnelli) An all-star cast highlights this musical extravaganza, featuring the talents of Fred Astaire, Gene Kelly, Judy Garland, Red Skelton, Lena Horne, Fanny Brice and many others; with William Powell encoring his role as showman Flo Ziegfeld. ★★★ $19.99

Zig Zag Story

(1983, 100 min, France, Patrick Schulmann) More enjoyable than one would expect, given its tacky video cover box and lack of any theatrical run in the United States, this imaginative *comédie érotique* follows the madcap adventures of a lovelorn color-blind painter, his fiesty girlfriend and his sleazy partner — a sex-obsessed photographer who takes great pleasure (and pride) in wallowing in his peculiar excesses. With many genuinely funny scenes and offering plenty of full frontal nudity (mostly female), this frantic comedy is a pleasant surprise. (French with English subtitles) ★★★ $59.99

Zombie

(1979, 91 min, Italy, Lucio Fulci) In the wake of George Romero's *Dawn of the Dead* comes this graphic and quite disgusting zombie tale about a Caribbean Island with a living dead problem. (Dubbed) ★

Zombie and the Ghost Train

(1991, 88 min, Finland, Mika Kaurismäki) The so-called "slacker" culture has got nothing on the Fins — if you think Austin is bleak, wait till you get a sight of Helsinki. The Zombie of

the title is an alcoholic loser who happens to play a mean bass. The story centers on his escapades as he attempts to reconcile with his girlfriend and, possibly more importantly, join The Ghost Train (who look like Urge Overkill), the most famous band in town, although no one seems to have ever heard them play. Unfortunately, Zombie is aptly named for whenever an opportunity arises he's either too drunk or passed out somewhere. Much in the tradition of earlier Kaurismäki brothers' films (Mika is the older but unknown one compared to sibling Aki), there's not much plot but plenty of beautiful imagery and insightful moments: sometimes producing a laugh, and sometimes a lump in the throat. (Finnish with English subtitles) ★★★ $59.99

Zooman

(1994, 95 min, US, Leon Ichaso) *Sugar Hill* director Ichaso delivers another tale of life in the streets of the inner city, clean and middle-class, but still full of violence and turmoil. Based on the play "Zooman and the Sign" by Charles Fuller, this very talky, unexciting but glossy adaptation is similar in story to *Boyz n the Hood* and *Crooklyn* — and though this family drama is occasionally insightful, there's very little that hasn't been seen before. Khalil Kain is very convincing in his portrayal of Zooman, the young hood who shoots the daughter of Louis Gossett, Jr. during a rampage. In order to find the killer, Gossett enlists the local media and riles up his neighbors to face a showdown with the young killer. The music evokes some of the rage that the family feels in their grief, but the narrative is not as developed as Fuller's excellent *A Soldier's Story*. Gossett delivers a strong performance, and Charles S. Dutton is particularly intense as Gossett's brother. ★★ $9.99

Zoot Suit

(1982, 103 min, US, Luis Valdez) Adapting his own play, Valdez's determinedly theatrical film is set in 1942 Los Angeles. Based on a real incident, the story follows a violent encounter between two Chicano gangs which results in

murder, incarceration for the innocent as well as the guilty, and a bigoted justice system bent on throwing them all in prison. Narrating the proceedings and leading in wonderfully choreographed song and dance salsa is the cynical, serpentine Edward James Olmos. Unexpectedly timely in light of the recent L.A. police mugging, the film is an impassioned exposé on the prejudiced oppression of the American people and the failure of its lofty dream for the Mexican immigrants who attempt to assimilate. A serious but entertaining and lively musical. ★★★ $19.99

Zora Is My Name

(1989, 90 min, US, Neema Barnette) A funny, stirring story based on the life of Zora Neal Hurston, one of the most distinctive writers of the American South. Stars Ruby Dee, Louis Gossett, Jr., Flip Wilson and Roger Mosley. ★★★

Zorba the Greek

(1964, 146 min, US/Greece, Michael Cacoyannis) An exceptionally accomplished screen version of the acclaimed Kazantzakis novel, with Anthony Quinn giving the performance of a lifetime as the title character. Set in Crete, the story follows the adventures of the fun-loving Zorba who takes a reserved Britisher (Alan Bates) under his wing, teaching him his philosophy of life. Lila Kedrova deservedly won an Oscar as Zorba's aging mistress. Features a terrific Mikis Theodorakis score. ★★★½ $19.99

Zorro, the Gay Blade

(1981, 93 min, US, Peter Medak) After successfully spoofing the vampire movie in *Love at First Bite*, George Hamilton sets his sights on the Zorro legend, with uneven results. Hamilton plays the twin sons of Zorro, one a swashbuckler, the other a gay bon vivant. Some laughs, and to its credit, not offensive. ★★½

Zouzou

(1934, 92 min, France, Marc Allégret) A semi-autobiographical piece with Josephine Baker as a poor laundress who finds her way out of the gutter. Her first film, *Zouzou* is a little short on substantive plot, but Baker's presence nonetheless radiates and her musical numbers scintillate. (French with English subtitles) ★★½ $29.99

Zulu

(1964, 139 min, GB, Cy Endfield) An epic battle sequence highlights this exciting adventure about an undermanned British outpost in 1879 South Africa preparing to fend off an overwhelming tribe of Zulu warriors. Starring Michael Caine and Stanley Baker. ★★★ $9.99

Zulu Dawn

(1979, 121 min, US/The Netherlands, Douglas Hickox) Burt Lancaster and Peter O'Toole star in this well-made war epic about England's bullheadedness in its handling of the Zulu nation — which led to Britain's worst ever military defeat at Isandhlwana in 1879. A prequel to the 1964 film *Zulu*, this film features excellent action sequences and outstanding location shooting. ★★½

XYZ

Josephine Baker (l.) and Jean Gabin in *Zouzou*

Algeria	Jamaica
Argentina	Japan
Armenia	Korea
Australia	Luxembourg
Austria	Macedonia
Belgium	Martinique
Brazil	Mexico
Burkina Faso	The Netherlands
Canada	New Zealand
Chile	Nicaragua
China	Nigeria
Columbia	Norway
Cuba	Peru
Czechoslovokia	The Philippines
Czech Republic	Poland
Denmark	Romania
Dominican Republic	Russia/USSR
Finland	Scotland
France	South Africa
Great Britain	Spain
Germany	Sweden
Greece	Switzerland
Hong Kong	Taiwan
Hungary	Tunisia
India	Turkey
Iran	Venezuela
Ireland	Vietnam
Israel	Wales
Italy	Yugoslavia
Ivory Coast	

INDEX: COUNTRY OF ORIGIN

THE DISCERNING FILM LOVER'S GUIDE

619

THE DISCERNING FILM LOVER'S GUIDE

THE DISCERNING FILM LOVER'S GUIDE

THE DISCERNING FILM LOVER'S GUIDE

Action/Adventure
Animation
Comedy
Documentaries
Drama
Family/Kids
Film Noir
The Fine Arts
Films of Gay Male Interest
Hollywood Classics
Horror
Independents
Late-Nite Cult
Films of Lesbian Interest
Musicals
Mystery/Suspense
Sci-Fi/Fantasy
TLA Favorites
Westerns

INDEX: GENRES

Gone Fishin'
Good Morning, Vietnam
The Goodbye Girl
Goodbye, New York
The Graduate
The Great Dictator
The Great White Hype
The Green Man
Gremlins
Gremlins 2:
   The New Batch
Grief
Grosse Pointe Blank
Groundhog Day
Grumpy Old Men
Guess Who's
   Coming to Dinner
Hail the Conquering Hero
The Happiest Days
   of Your Life
Happy Gilmore
Harold and Maude
Harvey
Hear My Song
Heart and Souls
The Heartbreak Kid
Hearts of the West
Heathers
Heaven Can Wait
Heaven Help Us
Heaveyweights
Hero
High Anxiety
High Hopes
High School High
History of the World Pt. I
Hold Me, Thrill
   Me, Kiss Me
Hollywood Shuffle
Home Alone
Home for the Holidays
Honeymoon in Vegas
Hopscotch
Horse Feathers
The Hospital
Hot Shots
The Hotel New Hampshire
House of Angels
House Arrest
House Party
Household Saints
Housekeeping
Housesitter
How U Like Me Now
The Hudsucker Proxy
Husbands and Wives
I.Q.
I Love Lucy, Vols. 1-12
I Love You, Alice B. Toklas
I Love You to Death
I Wanna Hold Your Hand
If Lucy Fell
I'm All Right, Jack
I'm Gonna Git You Sucka
I've Heard the
   Mermaids Singing
The Importance of
   Being Earnest
Impure Thoughts
The In-Laws
Indian Summer
Innerspace
Is There Sex After Death?

It Could Happen to You
It Takes Two
It's a Mad, Mad,
   Mad, Mad World
Jabberwocky
Jackie Mason on Broadway
Jeffrey
The Jerk
Jingle All the Way
Johnny Stecchino
Jumpin' Jack Flash
Jungle 2 Jungle
Just Tell Me
   What You Want
Kicking and Screaming
Kids in the Hall: Brain
   Candy
Kind Hearts and Coronets
The King of Comedy
Kiss Me Stupid
L.A. Story
Larger than Life
Laserman
Late for Dinner
A League of Their Own
Lenny Bruce
   Performance Film
Leon the Pig Farmer
Let It Ride
Let's Do It Again
Letter to Brezhnev
Liar Liar
Life Is Sweet
Lily Tomlin:
   Appearing Nitely
The Linguini Incident
Little Big Man
Little Murders
Loaded Weapon 1
Local Hero
Long Gone
Look Who's Talking
Loot
Lost in America
The Lost Stooges
Love! Valour! Compassion!
Love Among the Ruins
Love and Death
Love and Other
   Catastrophes
Love at First Bite
Love Hurts
The Loved One
Lucas
Lust in the Dust
M*A*S*H
Mad Dog and Glory
Made in America
Major Barbara
Major League
Mambo Mouth
The Man in the White Suit
The Man with Two Brains
Manhattan
Manhattan Murder
   Mystery
Married to the Mob
The Mask
Mastergate
Matilda
Maverick
Max Dugan Returns
Meatballs

Medusa: Dare
   to Be Truthful
Meet Wally Sparks
Melvin and Howard
Memories of Me
Men
Mermaids
Midnight Run
A Midsummer Night's
   Sex Comedy
Mighty Aphrodite
Miss Firecracker
The Missionary
Mr. Mom
Mr. North
Mr. Wrong
Mrs. Doubtfire
Mrs. Winterbourne
Mistress
Mixed Blood
Modern Romance
Modern Times
Mon Oncle
Monkey Business
Montenegro
A Month by the Lake
Monty Python and the
   Holy Grail
Monty Python Live at the
   Hollywood Bowl
Monty Python's Flying
   Circus, Vols. 1-22
Monty Python's
   Life of Brian
Monty Python's
   The Meaning of Life
Moonstruck
Morgan!
Moscow on the Hudson
Mother
The Mouse That Roared
Movie in Your Face
Much Ado About Nothing
Multiplicity
Murder by Death
Murphy's Romance
My Best Friend's Wedding
My Dinner with Andre
My Favorite Year
My Fellow Americans
My New Gun
Mystery Science Theater
   3000
Mystic Pizza
Nadine
The Naked Gun
Naked Gun 2½:
   The Smell of Fear
Naked Gun 33⅓:
   The Final Insult
National Lampoon's
   Animal House
National Lampoon's
   Christmas Vacation
National Lampoon's
   European Vacation
National Lampoon's
   Vacation
The New Age
A New Leaf
Next Stop,
   Greenwich Village
A Night at the Opera

Night Shift
The Night They
   Raided Minsky's
9 to 5
1941
No Surrender
Noises Off!
The Norman Conquests
   I, II, & III
North Dallas Forty
Northern Exposure
Nothing in Common
The Nutty Professor
O.C. and Stiggs
The Odd Couple
On Golden Pond
Once Around
One Crazy Summer
One Fine Day
One, Two, Three
Only the Lonely
Only When I Laugh
Out Cold
The Out-of-Towners
Outrageous Fortune
Overboard
The Owl and the Pussycat
The Pallbearer
Paper Moon
Parenthood
Parting Glances
The Party
Passport to Pimlico
Pee-wee's Big Adventure
Pee-wee's Festival of Fun
Peggy Sue Got Married
Perfectly Normal
Personal Services
The Pest
Pete 'n' Tillie
Phat Beach
The Philadelphia Story
The Pink Panther
The Pink Panther
   Strikes Again
Planes, Trains
   and Automobiles
Play It Again, Sam
Playtime
Plaza Suite
The Plot Against Harry
Pocket Money
Police Academy
Polyester
Porky's
Postcards from the Edge
The President's Analyst
Pretty in Pink
The Princess Bride
The Prisoner of
   Second Avenue
Private Benjamin
Private Parts
The Producers
The Projectionist
Punchline
The Purple Rose of Cairo
Putney Swope
Quackser Fortune Has a
   Cousin in the Bronx
Quick Change
The Rachel Papers
Radio Days

A Rage in Harlem
The Rainmaker
Raising Arizona
Real Life
Reality Bites
The Ref
Repo Man
Repossessed
The Return of the
   Pink Panther
The Return of the
   Secaucus 7
Reuben, Reuben
Revenge of the Nerds
Reversal of Fortune
Richard Pryor –
   Live in Concert
Richard Pryor
   Live on Sunset Strip
Risky Business
The Ritz
Robert Townsend and His
   Partners in Crime
Robin Williams Live
Romance with
   a Double Bass
Romancing the Stone
The Romantic
   Englishwoman
A Room with a View
Romy and Michelle's High
   School·Reunion
Roxanne
Rubin and Ed
The Russians Are Coming,
   the Russians
   Are Coming!
Ruthless People
The Rutles – All
   You Need Is Cash
S.O.B.
Say Anything
Scenes from the
   Class Struggle in
   Beverly Hills
Scrooged
The Search for Signs of
   Intelligent Life in
   the Universe
The Secret of My Success
The Secret Policeman's
   Other Ball
The Secret Policeman's
   Private Parts
The Seduction of Mimi
See No Evil, Hear No Evil
Seems Like Old Times
Serial Mom
The Seven Year Itch
Sgt. Bilko
Shadow of the Thin Man
Shampoo
She Done Him Wrong
She's Gotta Have It
She's The One
She-Devil
Shirley Valentine
A Shock to the System
Short Circuit
A Shot in the Dark
Sibling Rivalry
Silent Movie
Silver Streak   (cont.)

Family/Kids (cont.)

One Magic Christmas
The Pagemaster
The Parent Trap
The Pebble and
    the Penguin
Pecos Bill: King
    of the Cowboys
Pee-wee's Big Adventure
Pee-wee's Festival of Fun
Pee-wee's Playhouse
Peep and the
    Whole Wide World
Pete's Dragon
Peter Pan (1953)
Peter Pan (1960)
The Pig's Wedding/
    The Selkie Girl
Pinocchio
Pinocchio
Pinocchio and the
    Emperor of the Night
Pocahontas
Pollyanna
Prancer
Prehysteria
The Princess and the Pea
The Princess
    Who Never Laughed
Puss in Boots
Puss in Boots
Race the Sun
Raffi on Broadway
The Railway Children
Rapunzel
The Red Balloon
The Red Shoes
The Rescuers
The Rescuers Down Under
Return from
    Witch Mountain
The Return of Jafar
Return to Oz
Return to Snowy River
Richie Rich
Rikki Tikki Tavi
Robin Hood
Rock-a-Doodle
The Rocketeer
Rosenshontz: Teddy
    Bears Jamboree
Rover Dangerfield
Rudyard Kipling's
    The Jungle Book
Rugrats: Tales
    from the Crib
Rumpelstiltskin
The Sandlot
Santa Claus – The Movie
The Santa Clause
The Second Jungle Book:
    Mowgli and Baloo
The Secret Garden (1992)
The Secret Garden (1993)
The Secret of N*I*M*H
Sesame Street: Don't
    Eat the Pictures
Sesame Street: Sing
    Along Earth Songs
Sesame Street Presents:
    Follow That Bird
Sesame Street's
    25th Birthday

The Seven Faces of Dr. Lao
Shalom Sesame Street:
    Kids Sing Israel
Sharon, Lois and
    Brams Sing A to Z
Shining Time Station
    Holiday Special:
    'Tis a Gift
Shining Time Station:
    Juke Box Puppet Band
Shipwrecked
The Silver Stallion: King
    of the Wild Brumbies
Sleeping Beauty
Sleeping Beauty
The Snow Queen (1983)
The Snow Queen (1992)
Snow White and
    the Seven Dwarfs
The Snowman
Song of Sacajawea
Spooky Tales and Tunes
Starring Bugs Bunny
Storm Boy
The Story of the Dancing
    Frog
Swiss Family Robinson
The Sword and the Rose
The Sword in the Stone
Sylvester and Tweety's
    Crazy Capers
The Tale
    of the Bunny Picnic
The Tale of
    the Frog Prince
Tall Tale: The Unbelievable
    Adventures of Pecos Bill
Teenage Mutant Ninja
    Turtles
Tex Avery's
    Screwball Classics
Tex Avery's
    Screwball Classics 2
Tex Avery's
    Screwball Classics 3
That Darn Cat
This Pretty Planet: Tom
    Chapin in Concert
The Three Little Pigs
3 Ninjas
Thumbelina
Thumbelina
Tickle Tune Typhoon:
    Let's Be Friends
Tom & Huck
Tom & Jerry's 50th
    Birthday Classics
Tom and Jerry: The Movie
tom thumb
Toy Story
A Troll in Central Park
Turbo: A Power Rangers
    Movie
Tweety & Sylvester
20,000 Leagues
    Under the Sea
The Unicorn
Voyage en Ballon
A Waltz Through the Hills
Warner Brothers Cartoons:
    A Salute to Chuck Jones
Warner Brothers Cartoons:
    A Salute to Mel Blanc

Warner Brothers Cartoons:
    Bugs Bunny
Warner Brothers Cartoons:
    Foghorn Leghorn
Warner Brothers Cartoons:
    Pepe le Pew
Warriors of Virtue
We're Back!
    A Dinosaur's Story
Wee Sing in the Marvelous
    Musical Mansion
What Every Baby Knows
What Kids Want to Know
    about Sex and
    Growing Up
Where the River
    Runs Black
White Fang
White Fang 2
Who Framed Roger Rabbit
Wild Hearts
    Can't Be Broken
Willy Wonka and the
    Chocolate Factory
Winnie the Pooh and a
    Day for Eeyore
Winnie the Pooh and
    the Blustery Day
Winnie the Pooh and
    the Honey Tree
Winnie the Pooh and
    Tigger Too
Winnie the Pooh:
    Newfound Friends
Winnie the Pooh:
    The Great Honey
    Pot Robbery
Winnie the Pooh: The
    Wishing Bear
The Witches
The Wizard of Oz
The Wonderful World of
    the Brothers Grimm
Wonderworks: The
    Canterville Ghost
Wonderworks: The
    Haunting of
    Barney Palmer
Wonderworks:
    Hector's Bunyip
Workout with
    Mommy & Me
The Yearling
The Young Magician
Young Sherlock Holmes
Zeus and Roxanne

Film Noir

After Dark, My Sweet
Against All Odds
Alphaville
The American Soldier
The Asphalt Jungle
Backfire
Beware, My Lovely
The Big Heat
The Big Sleep
The Big Steal
Blood and Wine
Blood Simple
The Blue Dahlia
Blue Velvet
Body and Soul

Body Heat
Born to Kill
Bound
Cast a Deadly Spell
Caught
China Moon
Chinatown
Choice of Arms
Confidentially Yours
Cornered
D.O.A. (1950)
The Dark Corner
Dark Passage
Dead Reckoning
Deadline at Dawn
Delusion
Desperate
Detour
Double Indemnity
Le Doulos
Fallen Angels, Vol. 1
Fallen Angels, Vol. 2
Farewell, My Lovely
Follow Me Quietly
Force of Evil
The Gangster
The Glass Key
Gods of the Plague
The Grifters
Gun Crazy (1949)
Hammett
Harper
Heaven's Prisoners
High Sierra
The Hitch-Hiker
Hot Spot
I Wake Up Screaming
In a Lonely Place
Johnny Apollo
Johnny Handsome
Key Largo
Kill Me Again
The Killer's Kiss
The Killers
The Killing
Kiss Me Deadly
Kiss of Death (1947)
Kiss of Death (1995)
Kiss Tomorrow Goodbye
The Lady in the Lake
The Last Seduction
Laura
Liebestraum
Lost Highway
Love at Large
Macao
The Maltese Falcon
The Moon in the Gutter
Moonrise
Murder, My Sweet
Naked City
The Naked Kiss
Night and the City
The Night of the Hunter
No Man of Her Own
On Dangerous Ground
One False Move
Out of the Past
Panic in the Streets
Paris Express
Pickup on South Street
The Pitfall
Point Blank

Positive I.D.
The Postman Always
    Rings Twice (1946)
The Racket
Railroaded
Red Rock West
Road House
Romeo Is Bleeding
Scarlet Street
Second Chance
The Set-Up
Shack Out on 101
Shock Corridor
Slamdance
The Strange Affair
    of Uncle Harry
Stranger on the First Floor
The Tenant
They Live by Night
They Won't Believe Me
The Third Man
This Gun for Hire
Touch of Evil
Trouble in Mind
Twin Peaks
The Two Jakes
Underworld U.S.A
Union City
While the City Sleeps
The Window

The Fine Arts

The Abduction
    from the Seraglio
Ailey Dances
La Boheme
La Boheme
Candide
Don Quixote
Godunov: The
    World to Dance In
Great Arias with
    Placido Domingo
H.M.S. Pinafore
Heifetz and Piatigorsky
High Fidelity
Horowitz in London
Horowitz in Vienna
I Am a Dancer
I Pagliacci
Idomeneo
Isaac Stern,
    Itzhak Perlman,
    Pinchas Zuckerman
Itzhak Perlman-
    Pinchas Zuckerman
Joan Sutherland
    in Concert
Julius Caesar
Kirov Ballet –
    Classic Ballet Night
Kirov Ballet in London
The Legend of Tsar Saltan
Leonard Bernstein
    Conducts
    West Side Story
Les Misérables:
    Stage by Stage
The Lovers of Teruel
Lucia di Lammermoor
The Making of
    Miss Saigon
Manon

Mystery/Suspense/Thriller (cont.)

Liebestraum
Lifeboat
The List of Adrian
    Messenger
The Little Drummer Girl
The Lodger
Lone Star
The Long Goodbye
Love at Large
Love Crimes
Magnum Force
Malice
The Maltese Falcon
The Man Inside
The Man on the
    Eiffel Tower
The Manchurian
    Candidate
Manhunter
Marathon Man
Marlowe
Marnie
Miami Blues
Mirage
The Mirror Crack'd
Missing
Mr. Arkadin
Moonrise
The Morning After
Mortal Thoughts
Mother's Boys
Mullholland Falls
Murder at 1600
Murder by Decree
Murder by Natural Causes
Murder in Texas
Murder, My Sweet
Murder on the
    Orient Express
Murder, She Said
Mute Witness
The Name of the Rose
Narrow Margin
Niagara
Nick of Time
Night Gallery
Night Moves
The Night of the Hunter
The Night Walker
Nightbreaker
Nighthawks
The Ninth Configuration
No Way Out
No Way to Treat a Lady
North by Northwest
Obsession
The Odessa File
One False Move
The Osterman Weekend
The Other
Out of the Past
Outbreak
The Package
Paint It Black
Panic in the Streets
Panique (Panic)
Paperhouse
The Parallax View
Patriot Games
The Pelican Brief

Pickup on South Street
Play Misty for Me
The Plumber
A Pocketful of Rye
Point Blank
Poison Ivy
Positive I.D.
The Postman Always
    Rings Twice
Presumed Innocent
Primal Fear
Prime Cut
The Private Life of
    Sherlock Holmes
Purple Noon
Quick
The Quiller Memorandum
Railroaded
Raising Cain
Ransom
The Raven (Le Corbeau)
Rear Window
Rebecca
Red Rock West
Relentless
Repulsion
Reservoir Dogs
The Return of Sherlock
    Holmes: The Hound
    of the Baskervilles
Rider on the Rain
Road Games
The Road Warrior
Romeo Is Bleeding
Rope
The Russia House
Sabotage
Scene of the Crime
Sea of Love
Seance on a Wet Afternoon
Second Chance
The Secret Agent
The Sender
Seven
The Seven Percent Solution
Shack Out on 101
Shadow of a Doubt
Shallow Grave
Shame
Sharky's Machine
Shattered
Sherlock Holmes:
    Adventures of the
    Master Blackmailer
Shoot to Kill
Siesta
The Silence of the Lambs
The Silent Partner
Sincerely Charlotte
Single White Female
Sisters
Slaughter of the Innocents
Sleeping with the Enemy
Sleuth
Sliver
Sneakers
Someone to Watch Over Me
Sorry, Wrong Number
Special Bulletin
Spellbound
The Spiral Staircase
The Spy Who Came in
    from the Cold

Stage Fright
Stakeout
Stand-Off
The Stepfather
Still of the Night
Stormy Monday
The Strange Affair
    of Uncle Harry
The Stranger (1946)
The Stranger (1987)
Stranger on the First Floor
Strangers on a Train
Straw Dogs
Suddenly
Suspect
Suspicion
Suture
The Taking of Pelham
    One Two Three
Tango and Cash
Target
Telefon
10 Rillington Place
The Tenant
Terror by Night
They Live by Night
Things To Do In Denver
    When You're Dead
3rd Degree Burn
The Third Man
The 39 Steps
This Gun for Hire
This Man Must Die
The Thomas Crown Affair
Three Cases of Murder
Three Days of the Condor
Tightrope
Time After Time
To Catch a Thief
To Live and Die in L.A.
The Todd Killings
Topaz
Torn Curtain
Touch of Evil
Tough Guys Don't Dance
Toy Soldiers
True Believer
True Confessions
Twin Peaks:
    Fire Walk with Me
2 Days in the Valley
The Two Jakes
Under Suspicion
Underworld U.S.A
The Untouchables
The Usual Suspects
The Vanishing
Vertigo
The Wages of Fear
Wait Until Dark
Wedding in Blood
Whatever Happened
    to Baby Jane?
Whispers in the Dark
White Lie
White Nights
White of the Eye
White Sands
Who Slew Auntie Roo?
The Window
Winter Kills
Witness
Witness for the Prosecution

Wolf
Year of the Gun
Young and Innocent
Young Sherlock Holmes

Sci-Fi/Fantasy

The Abyss
The Adventures of
    Baron Munchausen
The Adventures of
    Buckaroo Banzai
Aelita: Queen of Mars
Alien
Alien Nation
Aliens
Alien 3
Alien Resurrection
Alphaville
Altered States
Amazing Colossal Man
Android
The Andromeda Strain
The Angry Red Planet
Army of Darkness
The Arrival
Barbarella
Battle Beyond the Stars
The Beast from
    20,000 Fathoms
The Black Hole
Blade Runner
The Blob (1958)
The Blob (1988)
A Boy and His Dog
Brainstorm
Brazil
The Brother from
    Another Planet
Carnosaur
Cherry 2000
Clash of the Titans
A Clockwork Orange
Close Encounters of
    the Third Kind
Club Extinction
Cocoon
Communion
Conquest of the Planet
    of the Apes
The Curse
Cyber Ninja
Dangaio
Darkman
The Day of the Triffids
The Day the Earth
    Stood Still
Deathwatch
Demon Seed
Le Dernier Combat
    (The Last Battle)
Dr. Cyclops
Dr. Who – Pyramids
    of Mars
Donovan's Brain
Dragonheart
Dragonslayer
Dreamscape
Dune
E.T., The Extra-Terrestrial
Earth vs. the
    Flying Saucers
Edward Scissorhands

Superman and
    the Mole Men
The Empire Strikes Back
Enemy Mine
Escape from the
    Planet of the Apes
Event Horizon
Excalibur
Explorers
Fahrenheit 451
Fantastic Planet
Fantastic Voyage
The Fifth Element
The Final Countdown
Fire in the Sky
First Men in the Moon
The 5,000 Fingers
    of Dr. T.
Flash Gordon
Flash Gordon Conquers
    the Universe
Flatliners
Flight of the Navigator
The Fly
The Fly (1986)
Forbidden Planet
From the Earth
    to the Moon
Glen and Randa
Godzilla, King of Monsters
Golden Years
The Grand Tour:
    Disaster in Time
Hell Comes to Frogtown
Highlander
Highlander 2: The
    Quickening
I Come in Peace
I Married a Monster
    from Outer Space
Iceman
The Incredible
    Shrinking Man
Independence Day (1996)
Innerspace
Invaders from Mars
Invasion of the
    Body Snatchers (1956)
Invasion of the
    Body Snatchers (1978)
Invisible Adversaries
The Island of Dr. Moreau
It Came from Hollywood
Jurassic Park
Killer Klowns from
    Outer Space
Kronos
The Last Starfighter
The Lawnmower Man
Liquid Sky
Logan's Run
Looker
Lost Horizon
The Lost World: Jurassic
    Park
Man Facing Southeast
The Man Who Fell
    to Earth
Mandroid
The Manhattan Project
Marooned
Mars Attacks!

Westerns

INDEX: DIRECTORS

*Diary of a Chambermaid
(1964)
The Discreet Charm
of the Bourgeoisie
El (This Strange Passion)
The Exterminating Angel
Fever Mounts in El Pao
The Great Madcap
(El Gran Calavera)
Illusions Travel by
Streetcar
Mexican Bus Ride
(Ascent to Heaven)
The Milky Way
Nazarin
Los Olvidados (The Young
and the Damned)
The Phantom of Liberty
Simon of the Desert
Susana
That Obscure Object
of Desire
Tristina
Viridiana
A Woman without Love
Wuthering Heights (1953)*

Tim Burton

*Batman (1989)
Batman Returns
Beetlejuice
Ed Wood
Edward Scissorhands
Frankenweenie
Mars Attacks!
Pee-wee's Big Adventure
(As writer)
The Nightmare Before
Christmas*

James Cameron

*The Abyss
Aliens
Piranha 2: The Spawning
Terminator
Terminator 2:
Judgment Day
Titanic
True Lies
(As writer)
Rambo: First Blood Pt. II
Strange Days*

Jane Campion

*An Angel at My Table
Jane Campion Shorts
The Piano
The Portrait of a Lady
Sweetie*

Frank Capra

*Arsenic and Old Lace
The Bitter Tea of
General Yen
Broadway Bill
Here Comes the Groom
A Hole in the Head
It Happened One Night
It's a Wonderful Life
Lady for a Day
Lost Horizon
Meet John Doe*

*Mr. Deeds Goes to Town
Mr. Smith Goes
to Washington
The Negro Soldier
Platinum Blonde
Pocketful of Miracles
Riding High
State of the Union
You Can't Take
It With You*

Marcel Carné

*Bizarre, Bizarre
Children of Paradise (Les
Enfants du Paradis)
Le Jour Se Leve
(Daybreak)
Law Breakers (Les
Assassins de L'Ordre)
Les Visiteurs du Soir*

John Carpenter

*Assault on Precinct 13
Big Trouble in
Little China
Christine
Dark Star
Escape from L.A.
Escape from New York
The Fog
Halloween
In the Mouth of Madness
Memoirs of an
Invisible Man
Prince of Darkness
Starman
They Live!
The Thing (1982)
Village of the Damned
(1995)
(As writer)
Black Moon Rising*

John Cassavetes

*Big Trouble
A Child Is Waiting
Faces
Gloria
The Killing of a Chinese
Bookie
Love Streams
Opening Night
Shadows
A Woman Under
the Influence*

Michael Caton-Jones

*Doc Hollywood
The Jackal (1997)
Memphis Belle
Rob Roy
Scandal
This Boy's Life*

Claude Chabrol

*Bad Girls
Le Beau Serge
Betty
Les Biches
The Blood of Others
Blood Relatives
Bluebeard
Le Boucher*

*La Cérémonie
Club Extinction
Dirty Hands
L'Enfer
High Heels (1972)
Horse of Pride
Madame Bovary (1991)
Une Partie de Plaisir
(Piece of Pleasure)
The Story of Women
Ten Days Wonder
This Man Must Die
Wedding in Blood*

Charles Chaplin

*Charlie Chaplin,
the Early Years
Charlie Chaplin,
the Keystone Years
The Charlie Chaplin
Film Festival
The Circus/
A Day's Pleasure
City Lights
The Gold Rush
The Great Dictator
The Kid/The Idle Class
A King in New York
Limelight
Modern Times
Monsieur Verdoux
A Woman of Paris*

Chen Kaige

*Farewell My Concubine
Life on a String
Temptress Moon
Yellow Earth*

René Clair

*À Nous la Liberté
Beauties of the Night
Beauty and the Devil
The Crazy Ray/Entr'acte
Forever and a Day
The Ghost Goes West
I Married a Witch
The Italian Straw Hat
Le Million
Under the Roofs of Paris*

René Clément

*And Hope to Die
Forbidden Games
Gervaise
Is Paris Burning?
Joy House
Purple Noon
Rider on the Rain*

Henri-Georges Clouzot

*Le Corbeau (The Raven)
Diabolique (Les Diaboliques
[The Fiends])
The Mystery of Picasso
The Wages of Fear*

Jean Cocteau

*Beauty and the Beast
(1946)
Blood of a Poet*

*The Eagle Has Two Heads
(L'Aigle à Deux Têtes)
Orpheus
The Storm Within
(Les Parents Terribles)
The Testament of Orpheus*

Joel Coen

*Barton Fink
Blood Simple
Fargo
The Hudsucker Proxy
Miller's Crossing
Raising Arizona*

Martha Coolidge

*Angie
Crazy in Love
The Joy of Sex
Lost in Yonkers
Out to Sea
Rambling Rose
Real Genius
Three Wishes
Valley Girl*

Francis Ford Coppola

*Apocalypse Now
Bram Stoker's Dracula
The Conversation
The Cotton Club
Dementia 13
Finian's Rainbow
Gardens of Stone
The Godfather
The Godfather, Pt II
The Godfather III
The Godfather:
The Complete Epic
New York Stories
One from the Heart
The Outsiders
Peggy Sue Got Married
The Rain People
The Rainmaker
Rumble Fish
Tonight for Sure
Tucker
You're a Big Boy Now
(As writer)
The Great Gatsby (1974)
Is Paris Burning?
Patton
This Property Is
Condemned*

Roger Corman

*Bloody Mama
A Bucket of Blood
Carnival Rock
The Day the World Ended
The Fall of the House
of Usher (1960)
Frankenstein Unbound
Little Shop of Horrors
(1960)
The Masque of the
Red Death (1964)
Master of the World
The Pit and the Pendalum
(1961)*

*The Premature Burial
The Raven (1963)
The St. Valentine's
Day Massacre
Tales of Terror
The Terror
Tomb of Ligeia
Tower of London (1962)
The Trip
Wasp Woman
The Wild Trip*

Constantin Costa-Gavras

*Betrayed
Hanna K.
Missing
Music Box
The Sleeping Car Murder
State of Siege
Z*

Alex Cox

*Repo Man
Sid and Nancy
Straight to Hell
Walker
The Winner*

Paul Cox

*Cactus
Kostas
Lonelyhearts
Man of Flowers
My First Wife
Vincent
A Woman's Tale*

Wes Craven

*Deadly Blessing
Deadly Friend
The Hills Have Eyes
The Hills Have Eyes, Pt. 2
Last House on the Left
A Nightmare on Elm Street
The People Under
the Stairs
Scream
Serpent and the Rainbow
Shocker
Swamp Thing
Vampire in Brooklyn
Wes Craven's New
Nightmare*

Charles Crichton

*The Battle of the Sexes
Dead of Night
A Fish Called Wanda
The Lavender Hill Mob*

Michael Crichton

*Coma
The Great Train Robbery
Looker
Physical Evidence
Runaway
Westworld
(As writer)
The Andromeda Strain
The Carey Treatment
Congo
Disclosure* (cont.)

INDEX: DIRECTORS

Michael Crichton
(cont.)

Jurassic Park
Rising Sun
The Terminal Man

David Cronenberg
The Brood
Crash
Dead Ringers
The Dead Zone
The Fly (1986)
M. Butterfly
Naked Lunch
Rabid
Scanners
They Came from Within
Videodrome

Cameron Crowe
Jerry Maguire
Singles
Say Anything
(As writer)
Fast Times at Ridgmont High
The Wild Life

George Cukor
Adam's Rib (1949)
A Bill of Divorcement
Born Yesterday (1950)
Camille
The Corn Is Green (1979)
David Copperfield
Dinner at Eight
A Double Life
Gaslight
Holiday
It Should Happen to You
Justine
Keeper of the Flame
Les Girls
Let's Make Love
A Life of Her Own
Little Women (1933)
Love Among the Ruins
My Fair Lady
Pat and Mike
The Philadelphia Story
Rich and Famous
Romeo and Juliet (1936)
Song without End
A Star Is Born (1954)
Susan and God
Sylvia Scarlett
Two-Faced Woman
What Price Hollywood?
A Woman's Face
The Women

Michael Curtiz
The Adventures of Huckleberry Finn (1960)
The Adventures of Robin Hood
Angels with Dirty Faces
Black Fury
A Breath of Scandal
Cabin in the Cotton
Captain Blood
Captains of the Clouds
Casablanca
The Charge of the Light Brigade (1936)
Dive Bomber
Dodge City
The Egyptian
Female
Flamingo Road
Four Daughters
Kid Galahad (1937)
Life with Father
Mildred Pierce
Night and Day (1946)
Passage to Marseilles
The Private Lives of Elizabeth and Essex
Santa Fe Trail
The Sea Hawk
The Sea Wolf (1941)
This Is the Army
Virginia City
We're No Angels (1955)
White Christmas
Yankee Doodle Dandy
Young Man with a Horn

John Dahl
Kill Me Again
The Last Seduction
Red Rock West
Unforgettable

Joe Dante
Amazon Women on the Moon
The 'burbs
Explorers
Gremlins
Gremlins 2: The New Batch
The Howling
Innerspace
Matinee
Piranha
Police Squad!
Twilight Zone: The Movie

Terence Davies
Distant Voices, Still Lives
The Long Day Closes
The Neon Bible
Terence Davies Trilogy

Andrew Davis
Above the Law
Chain Reaction
Code of Silence
The Fugitive (1993)
The Package
Steal Big, Steal Little
Under Siege

Philippe de Broca
Cartouche
Dear Detective
Jupiter's Thigh
King of Hearts
Louisiana
Le Magnifique
The Oldest Profession
Practice Makes Perfect (Le Cavaleur)
That Man from Rio

Eloy de la Iglesia
Colegas
El Diputado (The Deputy)
Dulces Navajas (Navajeros)
Hidden Pleasures (Los Placeres Ocultos)
El Sacerdote (The Priest)

Brian De Palma
Blow Out
Body Double
The Bonfire of the Vanities
Carlito's Way
Carrie (1976)
Casualties of War
Dressed to Kill
The Fury
Get to Know Your Rabbit
Greetings
Hi, Mom!
Home Movies
Mission: Impossible
Obsession
The Phantom of the Paradise
Raising Cain
Scarface (1983)
Sisters
The Untouchables
The Wedding Party
Wise Guys

Vittorio De Sica
After the Fox
The Bicycle Thief
Children Are Watching Us (I Bambini Ci Guardano)
The Garden of the Finzi-Continis
The Gold of Naples
Indiscretion of an American Housewife
Miracle in Milan
The Roof
Shoeshine
Teresa Venerdi
Two Women
Umberto D
Woman Times Seven
Yesterday, Today and Tomorrow

Cecil B. DeMille
The Cheat
Cleopatra (1934)
The Crusades
The Greatest Show on Earth
The King of Kings (1927)
Madame Satan
Male and Female
Northwest Mounted Police
The Plainsman
Reap the Wild Wind
Samson and Delilah
The Sign of the Cross
The Ten Commandments (1923)
The Ten Commandments (1957)
Union Pacific

Jonathan Demme
Caged Heat
Citizen's Band
Cousin Bobby
Crazy Mama
Last Embrace
Married to the Mob
Melvin and Howard
Philadelphia
The Silence of the Lambs
Something Wild
Stop Making Sense
Swimming to Cambodia
Swing Shift
Who Am I This Time?

Carlos Diegues
Bye Bye Brazil
Quilombo
Subway to the Stars
Xica

Roger Donaldson
The Bounty
Cadillac Man
Cocktail
Dante's Peak
The Getaway (1994)
Marie
No Way Out
Sleeping Dogs
Smash Palace
Species
White Sands

Stanley Donen
Arabesque
Bedazzled
Blame It on Rio
Charade
Damn Yankees
Deep in My Heart
Funny Face
The Grass Is Greener
Indiscreet
It's Always Fair Weather
The Little Prince
Love Is Better Than Ever
Movie Movie
On the Town
The Pajama Game
Royal Wedding
Saturn 3
Seven Brides for Seven Brothers
Singin' in the Rain
Two for the Road
(As choreographer)
Cover Girl
Take Me Out to the Ball Game

Richard Donner
Assassins
Conspiracy Theory
The Goonies
Inside Moves
Ladyhawke
Lethal Weapon 1, 2, 3
Lola
Maverick
The Omen
Radio Flyer
Scrooged
Superman: The Movie

John Duigan
Far East
Flirting
The Journey of August King
Sirens
Wide Sargasso Sea
Winter of Our Dreams
The Year My Voice Broke

Clint Eastwood
Absolute Power
Bird
The Bridges of Madison County
Bronco Billy
The Eiger Sanction
Firefox
The Gauntlet
Heartbreak Ridge
High Plains Drifter
Honkytonk Man
The Outlaw Josey Wales
Pale Rider
A Perfect World
Pink Cadillac
Play Misty for Me
The Rookie
Sudden Impact
Unforgiven
White Hunter, Black Heart

Blake Edwards
Blind Date
Breakfast at Tiffany's
Curse of the Pink Panther
Darling Lili
Days of Wine and Roses
Experiment in Terror
A Fine Mess
The Great Race
The Man Who Loved Women (1983)
Micki and Maude
Operation Petticoat
The Party
The Pink Panther
The Pink Panther Strikes Again
Return of the Pink Panther
Revenge of the Pink Panther
S.O.B.
A Shot in the Dark
Skin Deep
Son of the Pink Panther
Sunset
Switch
The Tamarind Seed
10
That's Life

THE DISCERNING FILM LOVER'S GUIDE

INDEX: DIRECTORS

(cont.)

INDEX: STARS

Ingrid Bergman (cont.)

Casablanca
The Count of Old Town
Dr. Jekyll and
     Mr. Hyde (1941)
Dollar
Elena and Her Men
Fear
For Whom the Bell Tolls
Gaslight
Goodbye Again
Indiscreet
The Inn of the
     Sixth Happiness
Intermezzo (1937)
Intermezzo (1939)
Joan of Arc
June Night
A Matter of Time
Murder on the Orient
     Express
Notorious
Only One Night
Spellbound
Stromboli
Swedenhielms
Under Capricorn
Voyage in Italy (Strangers)
A Walk in the Spring
     Rain
Walpurgis Night
A Woman Called Golda
A Woman's Face

Sandra Bernhard

Heavy Petting
Hudson Hawk
Inside Monkey Zetterland
The King of Comedy
Madonna: Truth or Dare
Sesame Street Presents
     Follow That Bird
Track 29
Without You I'm Nothing

Halle Berry

Boomerang (1992)
Executive Decision
Father Hood
The Flintstones
The Last Boy Scout
Losing Isaiah
The Program
The Rich Man's Wife
Strictly Business

Michael Biehn

The Abyss
Aliens
Deadfall
Deep Red
The Fan (1981)
In a Shallow Grave
Jade
K-2
The Lords of Discipline
Navy SEALS
Rampage
The Rock
The Seventh Sign
Strapped

The Terminator
Terminator 2:
     Judgment Day
Timebomb
Tombstone

Juliette Binoche

Blue
A Couch in New York
Damage
The English Patient
Hail Mary
The Horseman on the Roof
The Unbearable Lightness
     of Being

Karen Black

Airport 1975
Auntie Lee's Meat Pies
Bound and Gagged: A
     Love Story
Burnt Offerings
Can She Bake a
     Cherry Pie?
Capricorn One
Chanel Solitaire
Come Back to the 5 &
     Dime, Jimmy Dean,
     Jimmy Dean
Crimetime
The Day of the Locust
Easy Rider
Family Plot
Five Easy Pieces
The Great Gatsby
Homer and Eddie
In Praise of Older Women
Invaders from Mars
     (1986)
It's Alive III: Island
     of the Alive
Killing Heat
Mr. Horn
Nashville
Overexposed
Portnoy's Complaint
Rubin & Ed
Tales of the City, Vols. 1-3
Trilogy of Terror
You're a Big Boy Now

Rubén Blades

Color of Night
Crazy from the Heart
Critical Condition
Crossover Dreams
Dead Man Out
The Devil's Own
Disorganized Crime
Fatal Beauty
The Josephine Baker Story
The Lemon Sisters
Life with Mikey
The Milagro Beanfield
     War
A Million to Juan
Mo' Better Blues
One Man's War
Predator 2
The Super
The Two Jakes

Dirk Bogarde

Accident
A Bridge Too Far
Daddy Nostalgia
Damn the Defiant!
The Damned
Darling
Death in Venice
Despair
Doctor in the House
The Fixer
I Could Go on Singing
Justine
Night Flight from Moscow
The Night Porter
Permission to Kill
Providence
Quartet
The Servant
The Sleeping Tiger
Song without End
A Tale of Two Cities
Victim

Humphrey Bogart

Across the Pacific
Action in the North
     Atlantic
The African Queen
All Through the Night
Angels with Dirty Faces
The Barefoot Contessa
Beat the Devil
The Big Sleep (1946)
Brother Orchid
Bullets or Ballots
The Caine Mutiny
Call It Murder
Casablanca
Chain Lightning
Conflict
Dark Passage
Dark Victory
Dead End
Dead Reckoning
Deadline USA
The Desperate
     Hours (1955)
The Enforcer (1951)
The Harder They Fall
High Sierra
In a Lonely Place
Key Largo
Kid Galahad (1937)
Knock on Any Door
The Left Hand of God
The Maltese Falcon
Marked Woman
The Oklahoma Kid
Passage to Marseille
The Petrified Forest
The Roaring Twenties
Sabrina (1954)
Sahara
Sirocco
Stand-In
Thank Your Lucky Stars
They Drive by Night
To Have and Have Not
The Treasure of the Sierra
     Madre

The Two Mrs. Carrolls
Virginia City
We're No Angels (1955)

David Bowie

Absolute Beginners
Basquiat
The Hunger
Into the Night
Just a Gigolo
Labyrinth
The Last Temptation of
     Christ
The Linguini Incident
The Man Who Fell to
     Earth
Merry Chrsitmas, Mr.
     Lawrence
Twin Peaks: Fire Walk
     with Me
Ziggy Stardust

Sonia Braga

The Burning Season
Doña Flor and Her Two
     Husbands
Gabriela
I Love You
Kiss of the Spider Woman
Lady on the Bus
The Milagro Beanfield
     War
Moon over Parador
The Rookie
Two Deaths

Kenneth Branagh

Anne Frank Remembered
Dead Again
Fortunes of War
Hamlet (1996)
Henry V (1989)
High Season
Look Back in
     Anger (1989)
Looking for Richard
Mary Shelley's
     Frankenstein
A Month in the Country
Much Ado About Nothing
Othello (1995)
Peter's Friends
Swing Kids

Klaus Maria Brandauer

Becoming Colette
Burning Secret
Colonel Redl
Hanussen
The Lightship
Mephisto
Never Say Never Again
Out of Africa
The Russia House
Streets of Gold
White Fang

Marlon Brando

Apocalypse Now
The Appaloosa
Bedtime Story

The Brave
Burn! (Queimada)
The Chase (1966)
Christopher Columbus:
     The Discovery
Desiree
Don Juan deMarco
A Dry White Season
The Formula
The Freshman
The Fugitive Kind
The Godfather
The Godfather: The
     Complete Epic
Guys and Dolls
The Island of Dr. Moreau
     (1996)
Julius Caesar (1953)
Last Tango in Paris
The Men
The Missouri Breaks
Morituri
Mutiny on the Bounty
     (1962)
The Night of the Following
     Day
The Nightcomers
On the Waterfront
One-Eyed Jacks
Reflections in a Golden
     Eye
Sayonara
A Streetcar Named Desire
Superman: The Movie
The Teahouse of the
     August Moon
The Ugly American
Viva Zapata!
The Wild One
The Young Lions
(As director)
One-Eyed Jacks

Jeff Bridges

Against All Odds
American Heart
Bad Company (1972)
Blown Away
Cutter's Way
8 Million Ways to Die
The Fabulous Baker Boys
Fat City
Fearless
The Fisher King
Hearts of the West
Heaven's Gate
Jagged Edge
King Kong (1976)
Kiss Me Goodbye
The Last American Hero
The Last Picture Show
The Mirror Has Two Faces
The Morning After
Nadine
Rancho Deluxe
See You in the Morning
Starman
Stay Hungry
Texasville
Thunderbolt and Lightfoot
Tron

Stephen Dorff (cont.)

I Shot Andy Warhol
Judgment Night
The Power of One
Reckless
Rescue Me
S.F.W.

Illeana Douglas

Cape Fear (1991)
Grace of my Heart
Picture Perfect
Search and Destroy
To Die For
Wedding Bell Blues

Kirk Douglas

Along the Great Divide
The Arrangement
The Bad and the Beautiful
The Big Sky
The Big Trees
The Brotherhood
Cast a Giant Shadow
Champion
The Devil's Disciple
Eddie Macon's Run
The Final Countdown
The Fury
Greedy
Gunfight at the O.K.
　　Corral
Home Movies
In Harm's Way
Is Paris Burning?
A Letter to Three Wives
The List of Adrian
　　Messenger
Lonely Are the Brave
Lust for Life
The Man from Snowy
　　River
Once Is Not Enough
Oscar
Out of the Past
Paths of Glory
Posse (1975)
Saturn 3
Seven Days in May
Spartacus
The Strange Love of
　　Martha Ivers
Strangers When We Meet
There Was a Crooked Man
Tough Guys
20,000 Leagues Under the
　　Sea
Ulysses
The Vikings
The Way West
Young Man with a Horn

Michael Douglas

Adam at 6 A.M.
The American President
Basic Instinct
Black Rain (1989)
The China Syndrome
A Chorus Line
Coma
Disclosure
Falling Down

Fatal Attraction
The Game
The Ghost and the
　　Darkness
Hail, Hero!
The Jewel of the Nile
Napoleon and Samantha
Romancing the Stone
Shining Through
The Star Chamber
Wall Street
The War of the Roses

Robert Downey, Jr.

Air America
Baby, It's You
Back to School
Chances Are
Chaplin
Heart and Souls
Home for the Holidays
Johnny Be Good
The Last Party
Less Than Zero
Natural Born Killers
1969
Only You
The Pick-Up Artist
Rented Lips
Restoration
Richard III (1995)
Short Cuts
Soapdish
Too Much Sun
True Believer

Richard Dreyfuss

Always (1989)
American Graffiti
The American President
Another Stakeout
The Apprenticeship of
　　Duddy Kravitz
The Big Fix
The Buddy System
Close Encounters of the
　　Third Kind
The Competition
Down and Out in Beverly
　　Hills
The Goodbye Girl
Inserts
Jaws
Let It Ride
Lost in Yonkers
Mr. Holland's Opus
Moon over Parador
Night Falls on Manhattan
Nuts
Once Around
Postcards from the Edge
Prisoner of Honor
Rosencrantz and
　　Guildenstern Are Dead
Silent Fall
Stakeout
Tin Men
Trigger Happy
What About Bob?
Whose Life Is It Anyway?

Minnie Driver

Big Night
Circle of Friends
The Flood
GoldenEye
Grosse Pointe Blank
Sleepers

Faye Dunaway

Albino Aligator
Arizona Dream
The Arrangement
Barfly
Bonnie and Clyde
Burning Secret
The Chamber
The Champ (1979)
Chinatown
Cold Sassy Tree
Don Juan deMarco
Dunston Checks In
Even Cowgirls Get
　　the Blues
Eyes of Laura Mars
The First Deadly Sin
The Four Musketeers
The Handmaid's Tale
Little Big Man
Midnight Crossing
Mommie Dearest
Network
Ordeal by Innocence
Silhouette
Supergirl
The Temp
The Thomas Crown Affair
Three Days of the Condor
The Three Musketeers
　　(1993)
Wait Until Spring,
　　Bandini
The Wicked Lady

Irene Dunne

Anna and the
　　King of Siam
The Awful Truth
Cimarron
Consolation Marriage
A Guy Named Joe
I Remember Mama
Joy of Living
Life with Father
My Favorite Wife
Penny Serenade
Roberta
Show Boat (1936)
The White Cliffs of Dover

Robert Duvall

Apocalypse Now
Badge 373
The Betsy
Breakout
Bullitt
Colors
The Conversation
Countdown
Days of Thunder
The Detective
The Eagle Has Landed

Falling Down
A Family Thing
Geronimo: An American
　　Legend
The Godfather
The Godfather, Pt II
The Great Northfield
　　Minnesota Raid
The Great Santini
The Handmaid's Tale
Hotel Colonial
Joe Kidd
The Killer Elite
Lawman
Let's Get Harry
The Lightship
Lonesome Dove
M*A*S*H
The Natural
Network
Newsies
The Outer Limits:
　　Chameleon
The Outer Limits:
　　The Inheritors
The Paper
Phenomenon
The Plague
The Pursuit of D.B.
　　Cooper
The Rain People
Rambling Rose
The Scarlet Letter (1995)
The Seven Percent
　　Solution
A Show of Force
Sling Blade
Stalin
The Stars fell on Henrietta
The Stone Boy
Tender Mercies
THX-1138
Tomorrow
True Confessions
True Grit
Wrestling Ernest
　　Hemingway
(As director)
Angelo, My Love

Clint Eastwood

Absolute Power
Any Which Way You Can
The Beguiled
The Bridges of Madison
　　County
Bronco Billy
Casper
City Heat
Coogan's Bluff
The Dead Pool
Dirty Harry
The Eiger Sanction
The Enforcer (1976)
Escape from Alcatraz
Every Which Way But
　　Loose
Firefox
A Fistful of Dollars
For a Few Dollars More
The Gauntlet

The Good, the Bad
　　and the Ugly
Hang 'em High
Heartbreak Ridge
High Plains Drifter
Honkytonk Man
In the Line of Fire
Joe Kidd
Kelly's Heroes
Magnum Force
The Outlaw Josey Wales
Paint Your Wagon
Pale Rider
A Perfect World
Pink Cadillac
Play Misty for Me
The Rookie
Sudden Impact
Tarantula
Thunderbolt and Lightfoot
Tightrope
Two Mules for Sister Sara
Unforgiven
Where Eagles Dare
White Hunter,
　　Black Heart

Anthony Edwards

The Client
Downtown
Fast Times at
　　Ridgemont High
Gotcha!
Hawks
Heart LIke a Wheel
How I Got Into College
Miracle Mile
Mr. North
Pet Sematery II
Revenge of the Nerds
Revenge of the Nerds 2
Summer Heat
The Sure Thing
Top Gun

Denholm Elliott

Alfie
The Apprenticeship of
　　Duddy Kravitz
Bleak House
Brimstone and Treacle
The Cruel Sea
Cuba
Deep Cover (1980)
Defence of the Realm
The Hound of the
　　Baskervilles
The House That
　　Dripped Blood
Indiana Jones and the
　　Last Crusade
King Rat
Madame Sin
Maurice
The Missionary
Noises Off
A Private Function
Raiders of the Lost Ark
The Razor's Edge (1984)
Robin and Marian
A Room with A View

INDEX: STARS

Hugh Grant (cont.)

Extreme Measures
Four Weddings and a
  Funeral
Impromptu
The Lair of the White
  Worm
Maurice
Night Train to Venice
Nine Months
Our Sons
The Remains of the Day
Restoration
Sense and Sensibility
  (1995)
Sirens

Pam Grier

Above the Law
The Big Doll House
Bill & Ted's Bogus
  Journey
Bucktown
Class of 1999
Coffy
Drum
Escape from L.A.
Fort Apache, The Bronx
Foxy Brown
Friday Foster
Greased Lightning
Jackie Brown
Mars Attacks!
On the Edge
Original Gangstas
The Package
Posse (1993)
Scream, Blacula, Scream
Sheba Baby
Something Wicked This
  Way Comes
The Vindicator

Melanie Griffith

Body Double
The Bonfire of the Vanities
Born Yesterday (1993)
Buffalo Girls
Cherry 2000
The Drowning Pool
Fear City
In the Spirit
The Milagro Beanfield
  War
Milk Money
Night Moves
Nobody's Fool
Now and Then
Pacific Heights
Paradise
Shining Through
Smile
Something Wild
Stormy Monday
A Stranger Among Us
Two Much
Working Girl

Alec Guinness

The Bridge on the River
  Kwai
Brother Sun, Sister Moon

The Captain's Paradise
The Comedians
Cromwell
Damn the Defiant!
The Detective (Father
  Brown)
Doctor Zhivago
The Empire Strikes Back
Fall of the Roman Empire
A Foreign Field
Great Expectations
  (1946)
A Handful of Dust
The Horse's Mouth
Hotel Paradiso
Kafka
Kind Hearts and Coronets
The Ladykillers
Last Holiday
The Lavender Hill Mob
Lawrence of Arabia
Little Dorrit – Pts. I & II
A Majority of One
The Man in the White
  Suit
Mute Witness
Oliver Twist (1948)
A Passage to India
The Promoter
The Quiller Memorandum
Scrooge
Star Wars
The Swan
Tunes of Glory

Lukas Haas

Alan and Naomi
Everyone Says I Love You
johns
Lady in White
Leap of Faith
Mars Attacks!
Music Box
Rambling Rose
See You in the Morning
Solarbabies
Testament
Warrior Spirit
Witness
The Wizard of Loneliness

Gene Hackman

Absolute Power
All Night Long
Another Woman
Bat 21
The Birdcage
Bite the Bullet
Bonnie and Clyde
A Bridge Too Far
The Chamber
Class Action
The Conversation
Crimson Tide
Downhill Racer
Eureka
Extreme Measures
The Firm
The French Connection
The French Connection II
Full Moon in Blue Water
Geronimo: An American

Legend
Get Shorty
Hawaii
Hoosiers
I Never Sang for My
  Father
Lilith
Loose Cannons
Marooned
Mississippi Burning
Narrow Margin
Night Moves
No Way Out
The Package
The Poseidon Adventure
Postcards from the Edge
Power
Prime Cut
The Quick and the Dead
Reds
Riot
Scarecrow
Split Decisions
Superman: The Movie
Superman II
Superman IV: The Quest
  for Peace
Target
Twice in a Lifetime
Two of a Kind
Uncommon Valor
Under Fire
Unforgiven
Wyatt Earp
Young Frankenstein
Zandy's Bride

Linda Hamilton

Black Moon Rising
Children of the Corn
Dante's Peak
King Kong Lives
Mr. Destiny
Silent Fall
Shadow Conspiracy
The Terminator
Terminator 2: Judgment
  Day

Tom Hanks

Apollo 13
Bachelor Party
Big
The Bonfire of the Vanities
The 'burbs
The Celluloid Closet
Dragnet (1987)
Every Time We Say
  Goodbye
Fallen Angels
Forrest Gump
He Knows You're Alone
Joe Versus the Volcano
A League of Their Own
The Man with One Red
  Shoe
The Money Pit
Nothing in Common
Philadelphia
Punchline
Radio Flyer
Sleepless in Seattle

Splash
That Thing You Do!
Toy Story
Turner and Hooch
Volunteers
  (As director)
  That Thing You Do!

Daryl Hannah

At Play in the Fields
  of the Lord
Attack of the 50-Foot
  Woman (1993)
Blade Runner
Clan of the Cave Bear
Crazy People
Grumpy Old Men
Grumpier Old Men
Hard Country
High Spirits
Legal Eagles
The Little Rascals
Memoirs of an
  Invisible Man
The Pope of
  Greenwich Village
Reckless (1984)
Roxanne
Splash
Steel Magnolias
Summer Lovers
The Tie That Binds
Wall Street

Jean Harlow

Bombshell
China Seas
Dinner at Eight
Libeled Lady
Personal Property
Platinum Blonde
Public Enemy
Reckless (1935)
Red Dust
Red-Headed Woman
RiffRaff
Saratoga
Suzy
Wife vs. Secretary

Woody Harrelson

Cool Blue
The Cowboy Way
Indecent Proposal
Kingpin
Money Train
Natural Born Killers
The People vs. Larry Flynt
Sunchaser
White Men Can't Jump
Wildcats

Ed Harris

The Abyss
Alamo Bay
Apollo 13
Borderline
China Moon
Eye for an Eye
The Firm
A Flash of Green
Glengarry Glen Ross
Jacknife

Just Cause
Knightriders
The Last Innocent Man
Milk Money
Needful Things
Nixon
Paris Trout
Places in the Heart
The Right Stuff
The Rock
Running Mates
State of Grace
Sweet Dreams
Swing Shift
To Kill a Priest
Under Fire
Walker

Richard Harris

The Bible
Camelot
The Cassandra Crossing
Cromwell
Cry, the Beloved Country
  (1995)
The Deadly Trackers
The Field
Hawaii
Juggernaut
Mack the Knife
Major Dundee
A Man Called Horse
Man in the Wilderness
Martin's Day
The Molly Maguires
Mutiny on the Bounty
  (1962)
Orca
Patriot Games
Robin and Marian
Silent Tongue
Tarzan the Ape Man
  (1980)
This Sporting Life
Unforgiven
The Wild Geese
The Wreck of the Mary
  Deare
Wrestling Ernest
  Hemingway

Rutger Hauer

Blade Runner
Blind Fury
Blind Side
The Blood of Heroes
Bloodhounds of Broadway
A Breed Apart
Buffy the Vampire Slayer
Chanel Solitaire
Cold Blood
Dandelions
Deadlock
Eureka
Fatal Error (The Outsider)
Fatherland
Flesh and Blood
Forbidden Choices
The Hitcher
Inside the Third Reich
Keetje Tippel
  (Kathi's Passion)

THE DISCERNING FILM LOVER'S GUIDE

INDEX: STARS (vertical, left margin)

(cont.)

Matthew McConaughey (cont.)

Return of the Texas Chainsaw Massacre
A Time to Kill

Frances McDormand

Beyond Rangoon
Blood Simple
The Butcher's Wife
Chattahoochee
Darkman
Fargo
Hidden Agenda
Mississippi Burning
Paradise Road
Passed Away
Primal Fear
Raising Arizona
Short Cuts
Talk of Angels

Maclolm McDowell

Blue Thunder
Bopha!
Britannia Hospital
Caligula
Cat People (1982)
Chain of Desire
Class of 1999
A Clockwork Orange
The Collection
Get Crazy
Happily Ever After
If...
Jezebel's Kiss
Long Ago Tomorrow
Look Back in Anger (1980)
Milk Money
Moon 44
Night Train to Venice
O Lucky Man!
Star Trek Generations
Sunset
Tank Girl
Time After Time
Voyage of the Damned

Ewan McGregor

Being Human
Brassed Off!
Emma
A Life Less Ordinary
Nightwatch
The Pillow Book
The Serpent's Kiss
Shallow Grave
Trainspotting

Ian McKellen

And the Band Played On
The Ballad of Little Jo
Bent
Cold Comfort Farm
The Keep
Last Action Hero
Plenty
Priest of Love
Restoration
Richard III (1995)
Scandal

The Scarlet Pimpernel (1982)
The Shadow
Six Degrees of Separation

Steve McQueen

Baby, the Rain Must Fall
The Blob (1958)
Bullitt
The Cincinnati Kid
The Getaway (1972)
The Great Escape
Hell Is for Heroes
The Honeymoon Machine
The Hunter (1980)
Junior Bonner
Love with the Proper Stranger
The Magnificent Seven
Nevada Smith
Never So Few
Papillon
The Reivers
The Sand Pebbles
Soldier in the Rain
Somebody Up There Likes Me
The Thomas Crown Affair
Tom Horn
The Towering Inferno

Bette Midler

Beaches
The Bette Midler Show
Bette Midler: Art or Bust
Big Business
Divine Madness
Down and Out in Beverly Hills
For the Boys
Get Shorty
Gypsy (1993)
Hocus Pocus
Jinxed
Outrageous Fortune
The Rose
Ruthless People
Scenes from a Mall
Stella
That Old Feeling

Toshiro Mifune

The Bad Sleep Well
The Bushido Blade
The Challenge
Drunken Angel
The Gambling Samurai
Grand Prix
Hell in the Pacific
The Hidden Fortress
High and Low
The Idiot
Life of Oharu
Love and Faith
The Lower Depths
1941
Picture Bride
Red Beard
Red Lion
Rikisha-Man
Saga of the Vagabonds
Samurai I

Samurai II
Samurai III
Samurai Saga
Sanjuro
The Seven Samurai
Shogun
Stray Dog
Sword of Doom
Throne of Blood
Winter Kills
Yojimbo
Zatoichi Meets Yojimbo

Helen Mirren

Cal
Caligula
The Collection
The Comfort of Strangers
The Cook, the Thief, His Wife & Her Lover
Dr. Bethune
Excalibur
Gospel According to Vic
The Hawk
The Long Good Friday
Losing Chase
The Madness of King George
The Mosquito Coast
O Lucky Man!
Pascali's Island
Prime Suspect
Prime Suspect 2
Prime Suspect 3
Red King, White Knight
Savage Messiah
2010
When the Whales Came
Where Angels Fear to Tread

Robert Mitchum

Anzio
The Big Sleep (1978)
The Big Steal
Blood on the Moon
Cape Fear (1962)
Cape Fear (1991)
Crossfire
El Dorado
The Enemy Below
Farewell, My Lovely
Fire Down Below
Five Card Stud
The Grass Is Greener
Holiday Affair
Home from the Hill
The Last Tycoon
The Longest Day
Macao
Maria's Lovers
Midway
Mr. North
My Forbidden Past
The Night of the Hunter
Not as a Stranger
Out of the Past
Pursued
The Racket
River of No Return
Ryan's Daughter

Scrooged
Second Chance
Secret Ceremony
The Sundowners
That Championship Season
Thirty Seconds over Tokyo
Thunder Road
Two for the Seesaw
Undercurrent
The Way West
The Yakuza

Matthew Modine

And the Band Played On
Baby, It's You
Birdy
The Blackout
The Browning Version (1994)
Bye Bye, Love
Cutthroat Island
Equinox
Fluke
Full Metal Jacket
The Gamble
Gross Anatomy
Married to the Mob
Memphis Belle
Mrs. Soffel
Orphans
Pacific Heights
Private School
Short Cuts
Streamers
Vision Quest
Wind

Marilyn Monroe

All About Eve
As Young as You Feel
The Asphalt Jungle
Bus Stop
Clash by Night
Don't Bother to Knock
Gentlemen Prefer Blondes
How to Marry a Millionaire
Ladies of the Chorus
Let's Make It Legal
Let's Make Love
Love Happy
Love Nest
The Misfits
Monkey Business (1952)
Niagara
The Prince and the Showgirl
River of No Return
The Seven Year Itch
Some Like It Hot
There's No Business Like Show Business
We're Not Married

Demi Moore

About Last Night...
Beavis and Butt-Head do America
Blame It on Rio
The Butcher's Wife
Disclosure

A Few Good Men
G.I. Jane
Ghost
The Hunchback of Notre Dame
Indecent Proposal
Mortal Thoughts
No Small Affair
Nothing But Trouble
Now and Then
One Crazy Summer
St. Elmo's Fire
The Scarlet Letter (1995)
The Seventh Sign
Striptease
We're No Angels (1989)
Wisdom

Julianne Moore

Assassins
Benny & Joon
Boogie Nights
Cast a Deadly Spell
The Fugitive
The Hand that Rocks the Cradle
The Lost World: Jurassic Park
The Myth of Fingerprints
Nine Months
Roommates
Safe
Short Cuts
Surviving Picasso
Vanya on 42nd Street

Jeanne Moreau

Alberto Express
Alex in Wonderland
The Bride Wore Black
Chimes at Midnight
Dangerous Liaisons 1960
Diary of a Chambermaid (1964)
Elevator to the Gallows
The Fire Within
A Foreign Field
Going Places
Heat of Desire
Jules and Jim
The Last Tycoon
The Little Theatre of Jean Renoir
The Lovers
Lumiere
Mademoiselle
Map of the Human Heart
Mr. Klein
Monte Walsh
Querelle
The Summer House
The Trial (1963)
Until the End of the World
Viva Maria!
A Woman Is a Woman (Une Femme Est une Femme)

Armin Mueller-Stahl

Angry Harvest
Avalon
Holy Matrimony

INDEX: STARS

Peter O'Toole (cont.)

The Stunt Man
Supergirl
Svengali
Under Milk Wood
What's New, Pussycat?
Wings of Fame
Zulu Dawn

Gary Oldman

Air Force One
Basquiat
Bram Stoker's Dracula
Chattahoochee
Criminal Law
Fallen Angels, Vol. 2
The Fifth Element
Immortal Beloved
JFK
Murder in the First
Prick Up Your Ears
The Professional
Romeo Is Bleeding
Rosencrantz and
    Guildenstern Are Dead
The Scarlett Letter (1995)
Sid and Nancy
State of Grace
Track 29
True Romance
We Think the
    World of You

Laurence Olivier

As You Like It
Battle of Britain
The Betsy
The Bounty
The Boys from Brazil
Brideshead Revisited
A Bridge Too Far
Carrie (1952)
Clash of the Titans
Clouds over Europe
The Collection
David Copperfield
The Devil's Disciple
The Divorce of Lady X
Dracula (1979)
The Ebony Tower
The Entertainer
Fire over England
The 49th Parallel
Hamlet (1948)
Henry V (1948)
The Jazz Singer (1980)
The Jig-Saw Man
Khartoum
King Lear (1984)
Lady Caroline Lamb
A Little Romance
Love Among the Ruins
Marathon Man
Nicholas and Alexandra
Pride and Prejudice
The Prince and the
    Showgirl
Rebecca
Richard III (1955)
The Seven Percent
    Solution

The Shoes of
    the Fisherman
Sleuth
Spartacus
That Hamilton Woman
A Voyage Round
    My Father
Wagner
War Requiem
Wuthering Heights
    (1939)

Edward James Olmos

American Me
The Ballad of Gregorio
    Cortez
Blade Runner
The Burning Season
A Million to Juan
My Family (Mi Familia)
Saving Grace
Selena
Stand and Deliver
Talent for the Game
Triumph of the Spirit
Wolfen
Zoot Suit

Al Pacino

...And Justice for All
Author! Author!
Bobby Deerfield
Carlito's Way
City Hall
Cruising
The Devil's Advocate
Dick Tracy
Dog Day Afternoon
Donnie Brasco
Frankie and Johnny
Glengarry Glen Ross
The Godfather
The Godfather, Pt II
The Godfather III
Heat
Looking for Richard
Revolution
Scarecrow
Scarface (1983)
Scent of a Woman
Sea of Love
Serpico
Two Bits
(As director)
Looking for Richard

Gwyneth Paltrow

Emma
Flesh and Bone
Jefferson in Paris
Malice
Mrs. Parker & the
    Vicious Circle
Moonlight and Valentino
The Pallbearer
Seven

Geraldine Page

The Beguiled
The Blue and the Gray
The Bride

Dear Heart
The Dollmaker
Harry's War
Hondo
Honky Tonk Freeway
I'm Dancing as Fast
    as I Can
Interiors
My Little Girl
Nasty Habits
Native Son
Pete 'n' Tillie
The Pope of Greenwich
    Village
Riders to the Sea
Summer and Smoke
Sweet Bird of Youth
Toys in the Attic
The Trip to Bountiful
Truman Capote's A
    Christmas Story
Walls of Glass
What Ever Happened to
    Aunt Alice
White Nights
You're a Big Boy Now

Mary-Louise Parker

Boys on the Side
Bullets over Broadway
The Client
Fried Green Tomatoes
Grand Canyon
Longtime Companion
Mr. Wonderful
Naked in New York
A Place for Annie

Mandy Patinkin

Alien Nation
Daniel
Dick Tracy
The Doctor
The House on Carroll
    Street
Impromptu
Maxie
The Music of Chance
The Princess Bride
Squanto: A Warrior's Tale
Sunday in the Park with
    George
True Colors
Yentl

Jason Patric

After Dark, My Sweet
The Beast
Denial
Frankenstein Unbound
Geronimo: An American
    Legend
Incognito
The Lost Boys
Rush
Sleepers
Solarbabies
Speed 2: Cruise Control

Bill Paxton

Aliens
Apollo 13

Boxing Helena
Brain Dead
The Dark Backward
Future Shock
Indian Summer
The Last of the Finest
The Last Supper
The Lords of Discipline
Monolith
Navy SEALS
Near Dark
Next of Kin (1989)
One False Move
Pass the Alamo
Predator 2
Slipstream
The Terminator
Titanic
Tombstone
Traveller
Trespass
True Lies
Twister (1996)
Weird Science

Gregory Peck

Amazing Grace and Chuck
Arabesque
Behold a Pale Country
The Big Country
The Blue and the Gray
The Boys from Brazil
The Bravados
Cape Fear (1962)
Cape Fear (1991)
Captain Horatio
    Hornblower
Captain Newman M.D.
David and Bathsheba
Designing Woman
Duel in the Sun
Gentleman's Agreement
The Gunfighter
The Guns of Navarone
How the West Was Won
The Keys of the Kingdom
MacArthur
Mackenna's Gold
The Man in the Gray
    Flannel Suit
Marooned
Mirage
Moby Dick
Old Gringo
The Omen
On the Beach
Only the Valiant
Other People's Money
The Paradine Case
Pork Chop Hill
The Portrait
Roman Holiday
The Scarlet and the Black
The Sea Wolves
The Snows of Kilimanjaro
Spellbound
The Stalking Moon
To Kill a Mockingbird
Twelve O'Clock High
The Yearling

Sean Penn

At Close Range
Bad Boys (1983)
Carlito's Way
Casualties of War
Colors
Crackers
Dead Man Walking
The Falcon and the
    Snowman
Fast Times at Ridgmont
    High
Judgment in Berlin
Racing with the Moon
Shanghai Surprise
She's So Lovely
State of Grace
U-Turn
We're No Angels (1989)

Rosie Perez

Criminal Justice
Do the Right Thing
Fearless
It Could Happen to You
Night on Earth
Untamed Heart
White Men Can't Jump

Anthony Perkins

The Black Hole
Catch-22
Crimes of Passion
Desire under the Elms
Edge of Sanity
Fear Strikes Out
ffolkes
The Fool Killer
Friendly Persuasion
Goodbye Again
Green Mansions
The Life and Times of
    Judge Roy Bean
The Lonely Man
Mahogany
The Matchmaker
Les Miserbables (1978)
Murder on the Orient
    Express
On the Beach
Psycho
Psycho II
Psycho III
Psycho IV: The Beginning
The Ravishing Idiot
Someone Behind the Door
Tall Story
Ten Days Wonder
The Tin Star
The Trial (1963)
Twice a Woman
Winter Kills
(As director)
Psycho III

Joe Pesci

Betsy's Wedding
A Bronx Tale
Casino
Easy Money
8 Heads in a Duffle Bag

THE DISCERNING FILM LOVER'S GUIDE

THE DISCERNING FILM LOVER'S GUIDE

INDEX: STARS

Lana Turner (cont.)

Madame X
Peyton Place
The Postman Always
  Rings Twice (1946)
The Sea Chase
Somewhere I'll Find You
The Three Musketeers
  (1948)
Who's Got the Action
Week-End at the Waldorf
Ziegfeld Girl

John Turturro

Backtrack
Barton Fink
Being Human
Box of Moonlight
Brain Donors
Clockers
The Color of Money
Desperately Seeking Susan
Do the Right Thing
Fearless
Five Corners
Hannah and Her Sisters
Girl 6
Grace of my Heart
Gung Ho
Jungle Fever
Mac
Men of Respect
Miller's Crossing
Mo' Better Blues
Off Beat
Quiz Show
Search and Destroy
The Sicilian
State of Grace
To Live & Die in L.A.
Unstrung Heroes
(As director)
Mac

Liv Tyler

Empire Records
Heavy
Inventing the Abbotts
Silent Fall
Stealing Beauty
That Thing You Do!

Cicely Tyson

The Autobiography of Miss
  Jane Pittman
Bustin' Loose
The Comedians
Fried Green Tomatoes
The Heart Is a Lonely
  Hunter
Heat Wave
A Hero Ain't Nothin' But
  a Sandwich
King
A Man Called Adam
Oldest Living Confederate
  Widow Tells All
The River Niger
Roots
Sounder
Wilma

A Woman Called Moses
The Women of Brewster
  Place

Liv Ullmann

Autumn Sonata
The Bay Boy
A Bridge Too Far
Cries and Whispers
Dangerous Moves
The Emigrants
Forty Carats
Gaby, A True Story
Hour of the Wolf
Mindwalk
The New Land
The Night Visitor
The Ox
The Passion of Anna
Persona
Richard's Things
The Rose Garden
Scenes from a Marriage
The Serpent's Egg
Shame (1968)
The Wild Duck
Zandy's Bride
(As director)
Private Confessions
Sofie

Jean-Claude Van Damme

Black Eagle
Bloodsport
Cyborg
Death Warrant
Double Impact
Double Team
Hard Target
Kickboxer
Lionheart
Maximum Risk
Monaco Forever
No Retreat, No Surrender
Nowhere to Run (1993)
The Quest
Street Fighter
Sudden Death
Timecop
Universal Soldier

Mario Van Peebles

The Cotton Club
Delivery Boys
Full Eclipse
Gunmen
Heartbreak Ridge
Highlander: The Final
  Dimension
Hot Shot
Identity Crisis
Jaws: The Revenge
Last Resort
New Jack City
Panther
Posse (1993)
Solo
(as director)
New Jack City
Panther
Posse (1993)

Jon Voight

Anaconda
Catch-22
The Champ (1979)
Coming Home
Conrack
Deliverance
Desert Bloom
Eternity
Heat
The Last of His Tribe
Lookin' to Get Out
Midnight Cowboy
Mission: Impossible
The Odessa File
Rainbow Warrior
Return to Lonesome Dove
Rosewood
Runaway Train
Table for Five

Max von Sydow

Awakenings
The Bachelor
The Best Intentions
Brass Target
Brink of Life
Citizen X
Deathwatch
Dreamscape
Duet for One
Dune
The Emigrants
The Exorcist
Exorcist II: The Heretic
Father
Flash Gordon
The Flight of the Eagle
The Greatest Story
  Ever Told
Hamson
Hannah and Her Sisters
Hawaii
Hour of the Wolf
Hurricane (1979)
Judge Dredd
A Kiss Before Dying
The Magician
Miss Julie
Needful Things
Never Say
The New Land
Never Say Never Again
The Ox
The Passion of Anna
Pelle the Conqueror
Private Confessions
The Quiller Memorandum
Red King, White Knight
The Seventh Seal
Shame (1968)
Steppenwolf
Three Days of the Condor
Through a Glass Darkly
The Touch
Until the End of the World
Victory
The Virgin Spring
Voyage of the Damned
Winter Light
Zentropa

Tom Waits

At Play in the Fields
  of the Lord
Big Time
Bram Stoker's Dracula
Candy Mountain
Cold Feet (1989)
The Cotton Club
Down by Law
Ironweed
Mystery Train
The Outsiders
Paradise Alley
Queens Logic
Rumble Fish
Short Cuts

Christopher Walken

The Addiction
The Anderson Tapes
Annie Hall
At Close Range
Basquiat
Batman Returns
Biloxi Blues
Brainstorm
A Business Affair
The Comfort of Strangers
Communion
The Dead Zone
Deadline
The Deer Hunter
The Dogs of War
Echo Park
Excess Baggage
The Funeral
Heaven's Gate
Homeboy
King of New York
Last Embrace
Last Man Standing
McBain
The Milagro
  Beanfield War
Mistress
Next Stop,
  Greenwich Village
Nick of Time
Pennies from Heaven
The Prophecy
Prophecy II
Pulp Fiction
Roseland
Sarah, Plain and Tall
Search and Destroy
The Sentinel
Things to Do in Denver
  When You're Dead
True Romance
A View to a Kill
Wayne's World 2
Who Am I This Time?

J.T. Walsh

The Big Picture
Blue Chips
Breakdown
The Client
Crazy People
Defenseless
Executive Action

A Few Good Men
Good Morning, Vietnam
The Grifters
Hoffa
Iron Maze
The Last Seduction
The Low Life
Miracle on 34th Street
  (1994)
Needful Things
Red Rock West
The Russia House
Silent Fall
Sling Blade
Sniper
True Identity
Wired

Denzel Washington

Carbon Copy
Courage Under Fire
Crimson Tide
Cry Freedom
Devil in a Blue Dress
Glory
Heart Condition
Malcolm X
The Mighty Quinn
Mo' Better Blues
Much Ado About Nothing
The Pelican Brief
Philadelphia
Power
The Preacher's Wife
Ricochet
A Soldier's Story
Virtuosity

Emily Watson

The Boxer
Breaking the Waves
The Mill on the Floss

John Wayne

The Alamo
Allegheny Uprising
Angel and the Badman
Baby Face
Back to Bataan
Big Jake
Blood Alley
Chisum
The Cowboys
El Dorado
Flame of the Barbery Coast
Flying Leathernecks
Fort Apache
The Greatest Story Ever
  Told
The Green Berets
Hatari!
The High and the Mighty
Hondo
The Horse Soldiers
How the West Was Won
In Harm's Way
A Lady Takes a Chance
The Long Voyage Home
The Longest Day
The Man Who Shot
  Liberty Valance
McLintock

INDEX: STARS

Treat Williams

Dead Heat
Deadly Hero
The Devil's Own
Echoes in the Darkness
Final Verdict
Flashpoint
Hair
Hand Gun
Heart of Dixie
Max and Helen
The Men's Club
Mullholland Falls
1941
Once upon a Time
in America
Parallel Lives
The Phantom
Prince of the City
The Pursuit of D.B.
Cooper
The Ritz
Smooth Talk
Sweet Lies
Things to Do in Denver
When You're Dead
Third Degree Burn
The Third Solution
The Water Engine
Where the River Flows
North

Elijah Wood

The Adventures of Huck
Finn (1993)
Avalon
Flipper (1996)
Forever Young
The Good Son
North
Paradise

Radio Flyer
The War

Natalie Wood

Bob & Carol &
Ted & Alice
Brainstorm
The Ghost and Mrs. Muir
The Great Race
Gypsy (1962)
Inside Daisy Clover
Kings Go Forth
The Last Married
Couple in America
Love with the
Proper Stranger
Marjorie Morningstar
Meteor
Miracle on 34th Street
(1947)
Rebel without a Cause
The Searchers
Sex and the Single Girl
The Silver Chalice
Splendor in the Grass
The Star
This Property Is
Condemned
Tomorrow Is Forever
West Side Story

Alfre Woodard

Blue Chips
Bopha!
Crooklyn
Cross Creek
Extremities
Grand Canyon
Gulliver's Travels
The Gun in Betty
Lou's Handbag

Heart and Souls
How to Make an
American Quilt
Mandela
Miss Firecracker
Passion Fish
The Piano Lesson
Primal Fear
Puss in Boots
Remember My Name
Rich in Love
Scrooged
Star Trek: First Contact
Unnatural Causes

James Woods

Against All Odds
Badge of the Assassin
Best Seller
The Boost
Casino
Cat's Eye
Chaplin
The Choirboys
Citizen Cohn
Cop
The Curse of the
Starving Class
Diggstown
Eyewitness
Fallen Angels, Vol. 1
Fast Walking
The Getaway (1994)
Ghosts of Mississippi
The Hard Way
Hercules
Immediate Family
In Love and War
Joshua Then and Now
Kicked in the Head
Killer: A Journal of

Murder
My Name Is Bill W.
Next Door
Night Moves
Nixon
Once Upon a Time in
America
The Onion Field
Salvador
The Specialist
Split Image
Straight Talk
True Believer
Videodrome
Women & Men

Joanne Woodward

The Age of Innocence
A Big Hand for
the Little Lady
Breathing Lessons
Crisis at Central
High School
The Drowning Pool
The End
A Fine Madness
Foreign Affairs
From the Terrace
The Fugitive Kind
The Glass Menagerie
Harry and Son
The Long Hot Summer
Mr. and Mrs. Bridge
A New Kind of Love
Paris Blues
Philadelphia
Rachel, Rachel
The Shadow Box
The Stripper
Summer Wishes,
Winter Dreams

Sybil
They Might Be Giants
The Three Faces of Eve
Winning

Michael York

Accident
Austin Powers:
International Man
of Mystery
Cabaret
Fedora
The Four Musketeers
The Heat of the Day
The Island of Dr. Moreau
Justine
The Last Remake
of Beau Geste
Logan's Run
Midnight Cop
Murder on the
Orient Express
The Riddle of the Sands
Romeo and Juliet (1968)
Something for Everyone
Success Is the Best Revenge
The Taming of the Shrew
The Three Musketeers
(1973)
Wide Sargasso Sea
Zeppelin

Chow Yun Fat

A Better Tomorrow
A Better Tomorrow, Part 2
Evil Cat
Full Contact
Hard-Boiled
The Killer
Once a Thief

Index: Themes, Composers & Writers

(cont.)

INDEX: THEMES

Appendix A: TLA Bests

Best Theatrical Films of 1990
1 *GoodFellas*
2 *The Grifters*
3 *The Cook, the Thief, His Wife and Her Lover*
4 *Sweetie*
5 *Dances with Wolves*
6 *Miller's Crossing*
7 *Last Exit to Brooklyn*
8 *Jesus of Montreal*
9 *Tune in Tomorrow*
10 *The Nasty Girl*

Best Director
1 **Martin Scorsese** (*GoodFellas*)
2 Stephen Frears (*The Grifters*)
3 Jane Campion (*Sweetie*)

Best Actor
1 **Jeremy Irons** (*Reversal of Fortune*)
2 Robert De Niro (*Awakenings*)
3 Gerard Depardieu (*Cyrano de Bergerac*)
   and Danny Glover (*To Sleep with Anger*)

Best Actress
1 **Anjelica Huston** (*The Grifters*)
2 Genevieve Lemon (*Sweetie*)
3 Helen Mirren (*The Cook, the Thief, His Wife and Her Lover*)

Best Supporting Actor
1 **Joe Pesci** (*GoodFellas*)
2 Bruce Davison (*Longtime Companion*)
3 John Turturro (*Miller's Crossing*)

Best Supporting Actress
1 **Jennifer Jason Leigh** (*Last Exit to Brooklyn*)
2 Whoopi Goldberg (*Ghost*)
3 Annette Bening (*The Grifters*)

Best Theatrical Films of 1991
1 *The Silence of the Lambs*
2 *Naked Lunch*
3 *My Own Private Idaho*
4 *Europa, Europa*
5 *JFK*
6 *Homicide*
7 *City of Hope*
8 *Thelma and Louise*
9 *Impromptu*
10 *Boyz n the Hood*

Best Director
1 **Jonathan Demme** (*The Silence of the Lambs*)
2 Agnieszka Holland (*Europa, Europa*)
3 David Cronenberg (*Naked Lunch*)

Best Actor
1 **Anthony Hopkins** (*The Silence of the Lambs*)
2 River Phoenix (*My Own Private Idaho*)
3 Robert De Niro (*Cape Fear*)

Best Actress
1 **Jodie Foster** (*The Silence of the Lambs*)
2 Judy Davis (*Impromptu*)
3 Susan Sarandon (*Thelma and Louise*)

Best Supporting Actor
1 **Laurence Fishburne** (*Boyz n the Hood*)
2 Michael Jeter (*The Fisher King*)
3 Robert Duvall (*Rambling Rose*)

Best Supporting Actress
1 **Mercedes Ruehl** (*The Fisher King*)
2 Juliette Lewis (*Cape Fear*)
3 Diane Ladd (*Rambling Rose*)

Best Theatrical Films of 1992
1 *The Player*
2 *The Crying Game*
3 *Howards End*
4 *Malcolm X*
5 *Reservoir Dogs*
6 *Delicatessen*
7 *Unforgiven*
8 *Aladdin*
9 *Bram Stoker's Dracula*
10 *Raise the Red Lantern*

Best Director
1 **Neil Jordan** (*The Crying Game*)
2 Robert Altman (*The Player*)
3 Tim Robbins (*Bob Roberts*)

Best Actor
1 **Denzel Washington** (*Malcolm X*)
2 Gary Oldman (*Bram Stoker's Dracula*)
3 Anthony Hopkins (*Howards End*)

Best Actress
1 **Emma Thompson** (*Howards End*)
2 Susan Sarandon (*Lorenzo's Oil*)
3 Miranda Richardson (*Enchanted April*)

Best Supporting Actor
1 **Gene Hackman** (*Unforgiven*)
2 Ned Beatty (*Hear My Song*)
3 Al Pacino (*Glengarry Glen Ross*)

Best Supporting Actress
1 **Judy Davis** (*Husbands and Wives*)
2 Vanessa Redgrave (*Howards End*)
3 Michelle Pfeiffer (*Batman Returns*)

Best Theatrical Films of 1993
1 *The Remains of the Day*
2 *Orlando*
   The Piano
4 *Schindler's List*
5 *Strictly Ballroom*
6 *Farewell My Concubine*
   Menace II Society
8 *Like Water for Chocolate*
9 *Much Ado About Nothing*
10 *The Fugitive*
   In the Name of the Father
   The Nightmare Before Christmas

Best Director
1 **James Ivory** (*The Remains of the Day*)
2 Steven Spielberg (*Schindler's List*)
3 Chen Kaige (*Farewell My Concubine*)

Best Actor
1 **Anthony Hopkins** (*The Remains of the Day*)
2 Daniel Day-Lewis (*In the Name of the Father*)
3 Jeff Bridges (*American Heart* and *Fearless*)

Best Actress
1 **Holly Hunter** (*The Piano*)
2 Emma Thompson (*The Remains of the Day*)
3 Stockard Channing (*Six Degrees of Separation*)

Best Supporting Actor
1 **Tommy Lee Jones** (*The Fugitive*)
2 Leonardo DiCaprio (*What's Eating Gilbert Grape*)
3 John Malkovich (*In the Line of Fire*)

Best Supporting Actress
1 **Anna Paquin** (*The Piano*)
2 Miriam Margolyes (*The Age of Innocence*)
3 Anjelica Huston (*Manhattan Murder Mystery*)
   and Gong Li (*Farewell My Concubine*)

Best Theatrical Films of 1994
1 *Pulp Fiction*
2 *Ed Wood*
3 *Quiz Show*
4 *Heavenly Creatures*
5 *The Last Seduction*
6 *Bullets over Broadway*
7 *To Live*
8 *Vanya on 42nd Street*
9 *The Hudsucker Proxy*
10 *The Shawshank Redemption*

Best Director
1 **Quentin Tarantino** (*Pulp Fiction*)
2 Robert Redford (*Quiz Show*)
3 Peter Jackson (*Heavenly Creatures*)

Best Actor
1 **John Travolta** (*Pulp Fiction*)
2 Ralph Fiennes (*Quiz Show*)
3 Paul Newman (*Nobody's Fool*)

Best Actress
1 **Linda Fiorentino** (*The Last Seduction*)
2 Jennifer Jason Leigh (*Mrs. Parker & the Vicious Circle* and *The Hudsucker Proxy*)
3 Jodie Foster (*Nell*)

Best Supporting Actor
1 **Martin Landau** (*Ed Wood*)
2 Samuel L. Jackson (*Pulp Fiction*)
3 Paul Scofield (*Quiz Show*)

Best Supporting Actress
1 **Dianne Wiest** (*Bullets over Broadway*)
2 Kirsten Dunst (*Interview with the Vampire*)
3 Uma Thurman (*Pulp Fiction*)

Best Theatrical Films of 1995

1 *The Usual Suspects*
2 *Leaving Las Vegas*
3 *Sense and Sensibility*
4 *Babe*
5 *Get Shorty*
6 *Apollo 13*
7 *Dead Man Walking*
8 *Nixon*
9 *Toy Story*
10 *The Postman*

Best Director

1 **Bryan Singer** (*The Usual Suspects*)
2 Mike Figgis (*Leaving Las Vegas*)
3 Chris Noonan (*Babe*)

Best Actor

1 **Nicolas Cage** (*Leaving Las Vegas*)
2 Sean Penn (*Dead Man Walking*)
3 John Travolta (*Get Shorty*)

Best Actress

1 **Elisabeth Shue** (*Leaving Las Vegas*)
2 Susan Sarandon (*Dead Man Walking*)
3 Kathy Bates (*Dolores Claiborne*)

Best Supporting Actor

1 **Kevin Spacey** (*The Usual Suspects*)
2 Don Cheadle (*Devil in a Blue Dress*)
3 Brad Pitt (*12 Monkeys*)

Best Supporting Actress

1 **Mira Sorvino** (*Mighty Aphrodite*)
2 Joan Allen (*Nixon*)
3 Illeana Douglas (*To Die For*)

Best Theatrical Films of 1996

1 *Fargo*
2 *Lone Star*
3 *Secrets & Lies*
4 *Trainspotting*
5 *The English Patient*
6 *Welcome to the Dollhouse*
7 *Bound*
8 *Shine*
9 *Flirting with Disaster*
10 *William Shakespeare's Romeo and Juliet*

Best Director

1 **Joel Coen** (*Fargo*)
2 Mike Leigh (*Secrets & Lies*)
3 John Sayles (*Lone Star*)

Best Actor

1 **Ralph Fiennes** (*The English Patient*)
2 Chris Cooper (*Lone Star*)
3 Geoffrey Rush (*Shine*)

Best Actress

1 **Frances McDormand** (*Fargo*)
2 Brenda Blethyn (*Secrets & Lies*)
3 Emily Watson (*Breaking the Waves*)

Best Supporting Actor

1 **William H. Macy** (*Fargo*)
2 Cuba Gooding, Jr. (*Jerry Maguire*)
3 Derek Jacobi (*Hamlet*)

Best Supporting Actress

1 **Courtney Love** (*The People vs. Larry Flynt*)
2 Juliette Binoche (*The English Patient*)
3 Marianne-Jean Baptiste (*Secrets & Lies*)

TLA's Film Genre Favorites

Comedy

1 Some Like It Hot
2 Young Frankenstein
3 The Producers
4 The Thin Man
5 Bringing Up Baby
6 Blazing Saddles
7 This Is Spinal Tap
8 The Philadelphia Story
9 Dr. Strangelove
10 Harold and Maude
11 Duck Soup
12 Airplane!
13 His Girl Friday
14 The Miracle of Morgan's Creek
15 Annie Hall
16 Heathers
17 Modern Times
18 Arsenic and Old Lace
19 Pee-wee's Big Adventure
20 Manhattan
21 My Favorite Year
22 The Naked Gun
23 The Lady Eve
24 The Palm Beach Story
25 Monty Python and the Holy Grail

Runners-up: Raising Arizona, Hail the Conquering Hero, Being There, 20th Century, Beyond the Valley of the Dolls, The General, Bedazzled, A Fish Called Wanda, The Court Jester, Tootsie

Hollywood Classics

1930s

1 Modern Times
2 Mr. Smith Goes to Washington
3 Duck Soup
4 Frankenstein
5 City Lights
6 Bringing Up Baby
7 Gone with the Wind
8 The Wizard of Oz
9 King Kong
10 The Thin Man
11 20th Century
12 The Awful Truth
13 All Quiet on the Western Front
14 The Adventures of Robin Hood
15 I Am A Fugitive from a Chain Gang

1940s

1 Citizen Kane
2 Casablanca
3 Double Indemnity
4 The Miracle of Morgan's Creek
5 The Treasure of the Sierre Madre
6 The Grapes of Wrath
7 His Girl Friday
8 The Maltese Falcon
9 The Philadelphia Story
10 Arsenic and Old Lace
11 Hail the Conquering Hero
12 Fantasia
13 The Lady Eve
14 It's a Wonderful Life
15 The Best Years of Our Lives

1950s

1 Some Like It Hot
2 Touch of Evil
3 The Asphalt Jungle
4 Singin' in the Rain
5 All About Eve
6 A Streetcar Named Desire
7 North by Northwest
8 Anatomy of a Murder
9 12 Angry Men
10 Rear Window
11 The Day the Earth Stood Still
12 Sunset Boulevard
13 On the Waterfront
14 The African Queen
15 Rebel without a Cause

1960s

1 The Manchurian Candidate
2 Midnight Cowboy
3 The Apartment
4 West Side Story
5 The Producers
6 2001: A Space Odyssey
7 Psycho
8 The Wild Bunch
9 Bonnie and Clyde
10 To Kill a Mockingbird
11 The Dirty Dozen
12 The Graduate
13 Goldfinger
14 Easy Rider
15 Who's Afraid of Virginia Woolf

Musicals

1 West Side Story
2 Cabaret
3 Singin' in the Rain
4 The Nightmare Before Christmas
5 The Wizard of Oz
6 An American in Paris
7 Victor/Victoria
8 Hair
9 A Hard Day's Night
10 My Fair Lady
11 Sweeney Todd
12 The Sound of Music
13 Mary Poppins
14 The Music Man
15 The King and I
16 Seven Brides for Seven Brothers
17 Guys and Dolls
18 Oliver!
19 The Rocky Horror Picture Show
20 Yankee Doodle Dandy
21 Hans Christian Andersen
22 On the Town
23 All That Jazz
24 Swing Time
25 What's Love Got to Do with It

Runners-up: Help!, A Funny Thing Happened on the Way to the Forum, Little Shop of Horrors, Top Hat, The Pajama Game, The Commitments, Fiddler on the Roof, Starstruck, Sunday in the Park with George, How To Succeed in Business without Really Trying

Horror

1 Psycho
2 Night of the Living Dead (1968)
3 The Exorcist
4 Frankenstein (1931)
5 The Bride of Frankenstein (1935)
6 Evil Dead 2
7 Dawn of the Dead
8 Carrie
9 The Evil Dead
10 The Thing (1982)
11 The Shining
12 Hellraiser
13 Nosferatu (1922)
14 The Birds
15 King Kong (1933)
16 The Haunting
17 Freaks
18 Rosemary's Baby
19 Re-Animator
20 Poltergeist
21 The Cabinet of Dr. Caligari
22 Jaws
23 An American Werewolf in London
24 Near Dark
25 Halloween

Runners-up: Nightmare on Elm Street, Dracula (1931), Suspiria, Hellraiser 2, The Thing (1951), The Dead Zone, Them!, The Fly (1956), The Texas Chainsaw Massacre, Theatre of Blood

Sci-Fi/Fantasy

1 2001: A Space Odyssey
2 Blade Runner
3 Aliens
4 Star Wars
5 A Clockwork Orange
6 Alien
7 Brazil
8 The Terminator
9 Close Encounters of the Third Kind
10 The Empire Strikes Back
11 The War of the Worlds
12 Invasion of the Body Snatchers (1956)
13 Forbidden Planet
14 Excalibur
15 Planet of the Apes
16 Return of the Jedi
17 The Time Machine
18 The Day the Earth Stood Still
19 Metropolis
20 Jurassic Park
21 Terminator 2: Judgment Day
22 The Hidden
23 Jason and the Argonauts
24 Fahrenheit 451
25 Star Trek II: The Wrath of Khan

Runners-up: Total Recall, Miracle Mile, Invasion of the Body Snatchers (1978), Fantastic Voyage, Star Trek IV: The Voyage Home, Time Bandits, E.T. The Extra-Terrestrial, Earth vs. the Flying Saucers, Solaris, Slaughterhouse-Five

Appendix B: Awards

1970

NATIONAL BOARD OF REVIEW
Film: *Patton*
Foreign Film: *The Wild Child*
Director: François Truffaut (*The Wild Child*)
Actor: George C. Scott (*Patton*)
Actress: Glenda Jackson (*Women in Love*)

NATIONAL SOCIETY OF FILM CRITICS
Film: *M*A*S*H*
Director: Ingmar Bergman (*The Passion of Anna*)
Actor: George C. Scott (*Patton*)
Actress: Glenda Jackson (*Women in Love*)

NEW YORK FILM CRITICS
Film: *Five Easy Pieces*
Director: Bob Rafelson (*Five Easy Pieces*)
Actor: George C. Scott (*Patton*)
Actress: Glenda Jackson (*Women in Love*)

ACADEMY AWARDS
Film: *Patton*
Foreign Film: *Investigation of a
    Citizen Above Suspicion*
Director: Franklin J. Schaffner (*Patton*)
Actor: George C. Scott (*Patton*)
Actress: Glenda Jackson (*Women in Love*)

1971

NATIONAL BOARD OF REVIEW
Film: *Macbeth*
Foreign Film: *Claire's Knee*
Director: Ken Russell (*The Boyfriend*
    and *The Devils*)
Actor: Gene Hackman (*The French Connection*)
Actress: Irene Papas (*The Trojan Women*)

NATIONAL SOCIETY OF FILM CRITICS
Film: *Claire's Knee*
Director: Bernardo Bertolucci (*The Conformist*)
Actor: Peter Finch (*Sunday, Bloody Sunday*)
Actress: Jane Fonda (*Klute*)

NEW YORK FILM CRITICS
Film: *A Clockwork Orange*
Director: Stanley Kubrick (*A Clockwork Orange*)
Actor: Gene Hackman (*The French Connection*)
Actress: Jane Fonda (*Klute*)

ACADEMY AWARDS
Film: *The French Connection*
Foreign Film: *The Garden of the Finzi-Continis*
Director: William Friedkin (*The French Connection*)
Actor: Gene Hackman (*The French Connection*)
Actress: Jane Fonda (*Klute*)

1972

NATIONAL BOARD OF REVIEW
Film: *Cabaret*
Foreign Film: *The Sorrow and the Pity*
Director: Bob Fosse (*Cabaret*)
Actor: Peter O'Toole
    (*Man of La Mancha* and *The Ruling Class*)
Actress: Cicely Tyson (*Sounder*)

NATIONAL SOCIETY OF FILM CRITICS
Film: *The Discreet Charm of the Bourgeoisie*
Director: Luis Buñuel
    (*The Discreet Charm of the Bourgeoisie*)
Actor: Al Pacino (*The Godfather*)
Actress: Cicely Tyson (*Sounder*)

NEW YORK FILM CRITICS
Film: *Cries and Whispers*
Director: Ingmar Bergman (*Cries and Whispers*)
Actor: Laurence Olivier (*Sleuth*)
Actress: Liv Ullmann (*Cries and Whispers*)

ACADEMY AWARDS
Film: *The Godfather*
Foreign Film: *The Discreet Charm of the Bourgeoisie*
Director: Bob Fosse (*Cabaret*)
Actor: Marlon Brando (*The Godfather*)
Actress: Liza Minnelli (*Cabaret*)

1973

NATIONAL BOARD OF REVIEW
Film: *The Sting*
Foreign Film: *Cries and Whispers*
Director: Ingmar Bergman (*Cries and Whispers*)
Actor: Al Pacino (*Serpico*) and
    Robert Ryan (*The Iceman Cometh*)
Actress: Liv Ullmann (*The New Land*)

NATIONAL SOCIETY OF FILM CRITICS
Film: *Day for Night*
Director: François Truffaut (*Day for Night*)
Actor: Marlon Brando (*Last Tango in Paris*)
Actress: Liv Ullmann (*The New Land*)

NEW YORK FILM CRITICS
Film: *Day for Night*
Director: François Truffaut (*Day for Night*)
Actor: Marlon Brando (*Last Tango in Paris*)
Actress: Joanne Woodward (*Summer Wishes,
    Winter Dreams*)

ACADEMY AWARDS
Film: *The Sting*
Foreign Film: *Day for Night*
Director: George Roy Hill (*The Sting*)
Actor: Jack Lemmon (*Save the Tiger*)
Actress: Glenda Jackson (*A Touch of Class*)

1974

NATIONAL BOARD OF REVIEW
Film: *The Conversation*
Foreign Film: *Amarcord*
Director: Francis Ford Coppola (*The Conversation*)
Actor: Gene Hackman (*The Conversation*)
Actress: Gena Rowlands
    (*A Woman under the Influence*)

NATIONAL SOCIETY OF FILM CRITICS
Film: *Scenes from a Marriage*
Director: Francis Ford Coppola (*The Conversation*
    and *The Godfather Pt. II*)
Actor: Jack Nicholson (*Chinatown* and
    The Last Detail)
Actress: Liv Ullmann (*Scenes from a Marriage*)

NEW YORK FILM CRITICS
Film: *Amarcord*
Director: Federico Fellini (*Amarcord*)
Actor: Jack Nicholson (*Chinatown* and
    The Last Detail)
Actress: Liv Ullmann (*Scenes from a Marriage*)

ACADEMY AWARDS
Film: *The Godfather Pt. II*
Foreign Film: *Amarcord*
Director: Francis Ford Coppola
    (*The Godfather Pt. II*)
Actor: Art Carney (*Harry and Tonto*)
Actress: Ellen Burstyn
    (*Alice Doesn't Live Here Anymore*)

1975

NATIONAL BOARD OF REVIEW
Film: *Barry Lyndon* and *Nashville*
Foreign Film: *The Story of Adele H.*
Director: Robert Altman (*Nashville*) and
    Stanley Kubrick (*Barry Lyndon*)
Actor: Jack Nicholson
    (*One Flew over the Cuckoo's Nest*)
Actress: Isabelle Adjani (*The Story of Adele H.*)

NATIONAL SOCIETY OF FILM CRITICS
Film: *Nashville*
Director: Robert Altman (*Nashville*)
Actor: Jack Nicholson (*...Cuckoo's Nest*)
Actress: Isabelle Adjani (*The Story of Adele H.*)

NEW YORK FILM CRITICS
Film: *Nashville*
Foreign Film: *The Story of Adele H.*
Director: Robert Altman (*Nashville*)
Actor: Jack Nicholson (*...Cuckoo's Nest*)
Actress: Isabelle Adjani (*The Story of Adele H.*)

ACADEMY AWARDS
Film: *One Flew over the Cuckoo's Nest*
Foreign Film: *Dersu Uzala*
Director: Milos Forman
    (*One Flew over the Cuckoo's Nest*)
Actor: Jack Nicholson (*...Cuckoo's Nest*)
Actress: Louise Fletcher (*...Cuckoo's Nest*)

THE DISCERNING FILM LOVER'S GUIDE

1976

LOS ANGELES FILM CRITICS
Film: *Network* and *Rocky*
Foreign Film: *Face to Face*
Director: Sidney Lumet (*Network*)
Actor: Robert De Niro (*Taxi Driver*)
Actress: Liv Ullmann (*Face to Face*)

NATIONAL BOARD OF REVIEW
Film: *All the President's Men*
Foreign Film: *The Marquis of O*
Director: Alan J. Pakula (*All the President's Men*)
Actor: David Carradine (*Bound for Glory*)
Actress: Liv Ullmann (*Face to Face*)

NATIONAL SOCIETY OF FILM CRITICS
Film: *All the President's Men*
Director: Martin Scorsese (*Taxi Driver*)
Actor: Robert De Niro (*Taxi Driver*)
Actress: Sissy Spacek (*Carrie*)

NEW YORK FILM CRITICS
Film: *All the President's Men*
Director: Alan J. Pakula (*All the President's Men*)
Actor: Robert De Niro (*Taxi Driver*)
Actress: Liv Ullmann (*Face to Face*)

ACADEMY AWARDS
Film: *Rocky*
Foreign Film: *Black and White in Color*
Director: John G. Avildsen (*Rocky*)
Actor: Peter Finch (*Network*)
Actress: Faye Dunaway (*Network*)

1977

LOS ANGELES FILM CRITICS
Film: *Star Wars*
Foreign Film: *That Obscure Object of Desire*
Director: Herbert Ross (*The Turning Point*)
Actor: Richard Dreyfuss (*The Goodbye Girl*)
Actress: Shelley Duvall (*Three Women*)

NATIONAL BOARD OF REVIEW
Film: *The Turning Point*
Foreign Film: *That Obscure Object of Desire*
Director: Luis Buñuel
  (*That Obscure Object of Desire*)
Actor: John Travolta (*Saturday Night Fever*)
Actress: Anne Bancroft (*The Turning Point*)

NATIONAL SOCIETY OF FILM CRITICS
Film: *Annie Hall*
Director: Luis Buñuel
  (*That Obscure Object of Desire*)
Actor: Art Carney (*The Late Show*)
Actress: Diane Keaton (*Annie Hall*)

NEW YORK FILM CRITICS
Film: *Annie Hall*
Director: Woody Allen (*Annie Hall*)
Actor: John Gielgud (*Providence*)
Actress: Diane Keaton (*Annie Hall*)

ACADEMY AWARDS
Film: *Annie Hall*
Foreign Film: *Madame Rosa*
Director: Woody Allen (*Annie Hall*)
Actor: Richard Dreyfuss (*The Goodbye Girl*)
Actress: Diane Keaton (*Annie Hall*)

1978

LOS ANGELES FILM CRITICS
Film: *Coming Home*
Director: Michael Cimino (*The Deer Hunter*)
Actor: Jon Voight (*Coming Home*)
Actress: Jane Fonda (*California Suite* and
  Comes a Horseman and *Coming Home*)

NATIONAL BOARD OF REVIEW
Film: *Days of Heaven*
Foreign Film: *Autumn Sonata*
Director: Ingmar Bergman (*Autumn Sonata*)
Actor: Laurence Olivier (*The Boys from Brazil*)
  and Jon Voight (*Coming Home*)
Actress: Ingrid Bergman (*Autumn Sonata*)

NATIONAL SOCIETY OF FILM CRITICS
Film: *Get Out Your Handkerchiefs*
Director: Terence Malick (*Days of Heaven*)
Actor: Gary Busey (*The Buddy Holly Story*)
Actress: Ingrid Bergman (*Autumn Sonata*)

NEW YORK FILM CRITICS
Film: *The Deer Hunter*
Foreign Film: *Bread and Chocolate*
Director: Terence Malick (*Days of Heaven*)
Actor: Jon Voight (*Coming Home*)
Actress: Ingrid Bergman (*Autumn Sonata*)

ACADEMY AWARDS
Film: *The Deer Hunter*
Foreign Film: *Get Out Your Handkerchiefs*
Director: Michael Cimino (*The Deer Hunter*)
Actor: Jon Voight (*Coming Home*)
Actress: Jane Fonda (*Coming Home*)

1979

LOS ANGELES FILM CRITICS
Film: *Kramer vs. Kramer*
Foreign Film: *Soldier of Orange*
Director: Robert Benton (*Kramer vs. Kramer*)
Actor: Dustin Hoffman (*Kramer vs. Kramer*)
Actress: Sally Field (*Norma Rae*)

NATIONAL BOARD OF REVIEW
Film: *Manhattan*
Foreign Film: *La Cage aux Folles*
Director: John Schlesinger (*Yanks*)
Actor: Peter Sellers (*Being There*)
Actress: Sally Field (*Norma Rae*)

NATIONAL SOCIETY OF FILM CRITICS
Film: *Breaking Away*
Director: Woody Allen (*Manhattan*) and
  Robert Benton (*Kramer vs. Kramer*)
Actor: Dustin Hoffman (*Kramer vs. Kramer*)
Actress: Sally Field (*Norma Rae*)

NEW YORK FILM CRITICS
Film: *Kramer vs. Kramer*
Foreign Film: *The Tree of Wooden Clogs*
Director: Woody Allen (*Manhattan*)
Actor: Dustin Hoffman (*Kramer vs. Kramer*)
Actress: Sally Field (*Norma Rae*)

ACADEMY AWARDS
Film: *Kramer vs. Kramer*
Foreign Film: *The Tin Drum*
Director: Robert Benton (*Kramer vs. Kramer*)
Actor: Dustin Hoffman (*Kramer vs. Kramer*)
Actress: Sally Field (*Norma Rae*)

1980

LOS ANGELES FILM CRITICS
Film: *Raging Bull*
Director: Roman Polanski (*Tess*)
Actor: Robert De Niro (*Raging Bull*)
Actress: Sissy Spacek (*Coal Miner's Daughter*)

NATIONAL BOARD OF REVIEW
Film: *Ordinary People*
Foreign Film: *The Tin Drum*
Director: Robert Redford (*Ordinary People*)
Actor: Robert De Niro (*Raging Bull*)
Actress: Sissy Spacek (*Coal Miner's Daughter*)

NATIONAL SOCIETY OF FILM CRITICS
Film: *Melvin and Howard*
Director: Martin Scorsese (*Ragin Bull*)
Actor: Peter O'Toole (*The Stunt Man*)
Actress: Sissy Spacek (*Coal Miner's Daughter*)

NEW YORK FILM CRITICS
Film: *Ordinary People*
Foreign Film: *Mon Oncle D'Amerique*
Director: Jonathan Demme (*Melvin and Howard*)
Actor: Robert De Niro (*Raging Bull*)
Actress: Sissy Spacek (*Coal Miner's Daughter*)

ACADEMY AWARDS
Film: *Ordinary People*
Foreign Film: *Moscow Does Not Believe in Tears*
Director: Robert Redford (*Ordinary People*)
Actor: Robert De Niro (*Raging Bull*)
Actress: Sissy Spacek (*Coal Miner's Daughter*)

1981

LOS ANGELES FILM CRITICS
Film: *Atlantic City*
Foreign Film: *Pixote*
Director: Warren Beatty (*Reds*)
Actor: Burt Lancaster (*Atlantic City*)
Actress: Meryl Streep
  (*The French Lieutenant's Woman*)

NATIONAL BOARD OF REVIEW
Film: *Red* and *Chariots of Fire*
Foreign Film: *Oblomov*
Director: Warren Beatty (*Reds*)
Actor: Henry Fonda (*On Golden Pond*)
Actress: Glenda Jackson (*Stevie*)

NATIONAL SOCIETY OF FILM CRITICS
Film: *Atlantic City*
Director: Louis Malle (*Atlantic City*)
Actor: Burt Lancaster (*Atlantic City*)
Actress: Marilla Pera (*Pixote*)

NEW YORK FILM CRITICS
Film: *Reds*
Foreign Film: *Pixote*
Director: Sidney Lumet (*Prince of the City*)
Actor: Burt Lancaster (*Atlantic City*)
Actress: Glenda Jackson (*Stevie*)

ACADEMY AWARDS
Film: *Chariots of Fire*
Foreign Film: *Mephisto*
Director: Warren Beatty (*Reds*)
Actor: Henry Fonda (*On Golden Pond*)
Actress: Katharine Hepburn (*On Golden Pond*)

1982

LOS ANGELES FILM CRITICS
Film: *E.T. The Extra-Terrestrial*
Foreign Film: *The Road Warrior*
Director: Steven Spielberg (*E.T.*)
Actor: Ben Kingsley (*Gandhi*)
Actress: Meryl Streep (*Sophie's Choice*)

NATIONAL BOARD OF REVIEW
Film: *Gandhi*
Foreign Film: *Mephisto*
Director: Sidney Lumet (*The Verdict*)
Actor: Ben Kingsley (*Gandhi*)
Actress: Meryl Streep (*Sophie's Choice*)

NATIONAL SOCIETY OF FILM CRITICS
Film: *Tootsie*
Director: Steven Spielberg (*E.T.*)
Actor: Dustin Hoffman (*Tootsie*)
Actress: Meryl Streep (*Sophie's Choice*)

NEW YORK FILM CRITICS
Film: *Gandhi*
Foreign Film: *Time Stands Still*
Director: Sydney Pollack (*Tootsie*)
Actor: Ben Kingsley (*Gandhi*)
Actress: Meryl Streep (*Sophie's Choice*)

ACADEMY AWARDS
Film: *Gandhi*
Foreign Film: *To Begin Again*
Director: Richard Attenborough (*Gandhi*)
Actor: Ben Kingsley (*Gandhi*)
Actress: Meryl Streep (*Sophie's Choice*)

1983

LOS ANGELES FILM CRITICS
Film: *Terms of Endearment*
Foreign Film: *Fanny and Alexander*
Director: James L. Brooks
　(*Terms of Endearment*)
Actor: Robert Duvall (*Tender Mercies*)
Actress: Shirley MacLaine
　(*Terms of Endearment*)

NATIONAL BOARD OF REVIEW
Film: *Betrayal* and *Terms of Endearment*
Foreign Film: *Fanny and Alexander*
Director: James L. Brooks
　(*Terms of Endearment*)
Actor: Tom Conti (*Merry Christmas Mr. Lawrence* and *Reuben, Reuben*)
Actress: Shirley MacLaine
　(*Terms of Endearment*)

NEW YORK FILM CRITICS
Film: *Terms of Endearment*
Foreign Film: *Fanny and Alexander*
Director: Ingmar Bergman
　(*Fanny and Alexander*)
Actor: Robert Duvall (*Tender Mercies*)
Actress: Shirley MacLaine
　(*Terms of Endearment*)

ACADEMY AWARDS
Film: *Terms of Endearment*
Foreign Film: *Fanny and Alexander*
Director: James L. Brooks
　(*Terms of Endearment*)
Actor: Robert Duvall (*Tender Mercies*)
Actress: Shirley MacLaine
　(*Terms of Endearment*)

1984

LOS ANGELES FILM CRITICS
Film: *Amadeus*
Foreign Film: *The Fourth Man*
Director: Milos Forman (*Amadeus*)
Actor: F. Murray Abraham (*Amadeus*) and
　Albert Finney (*Under the Volcano*)
Actress: Kathleen Turner (*Crimes of Passion* and
　Romancing the Stone)

NATIONAL BOARD OF REVIEW
Film: *A Passage to India*
Foreign Film: *Sunday in the Country*
Director: David Lean (*A Passage to India*)
Actor: Victor Banerjee (*A Passage to India*)
Actress: Peggy Ashcroft (*A Passage to India*)

NATIONAL SOCIETY OF FILM CRITICS
Film: *Stranger Than Paradise*
Director: Robert Bresson (*L'Argent*)
Actor: Steve Martin (*All of Me*)
Actress: Vanessa Redgrave (*The Bostonians*)

NEW YORK FILM CRITICS
Film: *A Passage to India*
Foreign Film: *Sunday in the Country*
Director: David Lean (*A Passage to India*)
Actor: Steve Martin (*All of Me*)
Actress: Peggy Ashcroft (*A Passage to India*)

ACADEMY AWARDS
Film: *Amadeus*
Foreign Film: *Dangerous Moves*
Director: Milos Forman (*Amadeus*)
Actor: F. Murray Abraham (*Amadeus*)
Actress: Sally Field (*Places in the Heart*)

1985

LOS ANGELES FILM CRITICS
Film: *Brazil*
Foreign Film: *The Official Story* and *Ran*
Director: Terry Gilliam (*Brazil*)
Actor: William Hurt (*Kiss of the Spider Woman*)
Actress: Meryl Streep (*Out of Africa*)

NATIONAL BOARD OF REVIEW
Film: *The Color Purple*
Foreign Film: *Ran*
Director: Akira Kurosawa (*Ran*)
Actor: William Hurt (*Kiss of the Spider Woman*)
　and Raul Julia (*Kiss of the Spider Woman*)
Actress: Whoopi Goldberg (*The Color Purple*)

NATIONAL SOCIETY OF FILM CRITICS
Film: *Ran*
Director: John Huston (*Prizzi's Honor*)
Actor: Jack Nicholson (*Prizzi's Honor*)
Actress: Vanessa Redgrave (*Wetherby*)

NEW YORK FILM CRITICS
Film: *Prizzi's Honor*
Foeign Film: *Ran*
Director: John Huston (*Prizzi's Honor*)
Actor: Jack Nicholson (*Prizzi's Honor*)
Actress: Norma Aleandro (*The Official Story*)

ACADEMY AWARDS
Film: *Out of Africa*
Foreign Film: *The Official Story*
Director: Sydney Pollack (*Out of Africa*)
Actor: William Hurt (*Kiss of the Spider Woman*)
Actress: Geraldine Page (*The Trip to Bountiful*)

1986

LOS ANGELES FILM CRITICS
Film: *Hannah and Her Sisters*
Foreign Film: *Vagabond*
Director: David Lynch (*Blue Velvet*)
Actor: Bob Hoskins (*Mona Lisa*)
Actress: Sandrine Bonnaire (*Vagabond*)

NATIONAL BOARD OF REVIEW
Film: *A Room with a View*
Foreign Film: *Otello*
Director: Woody Allen
　(*Hannah and Her Sisters*)
Actor: Paul Newman (*The Color of Money*)
Actress: Kathleen Turner
　(*Peggy Sue Got Married*)

NATIONAL SOCIETY OF FILM CRITICS
Film: *Blue Velvet*
Director: David Lynch (*Blue Velvet*)
Actor: Bob Hoskins (*Mona Lisa*)
Actress: Chloe Webb (*Sid and Nancy*)

NEW YORK FILM CRITICS
Film: *Hannah and Her Sisters*
Foreign Film: *Decline of the American Empire*
Director: Woody Allen
　(*Hannah and Her Sisters*)
Actor: Bob Hoskins (*Mona Lisa*)
Actress: Sissy Spacek (*Crimes of the Heart*)

ACADEMY AWARDS
Film: *Platoon*
Foreign Film: *The Assault*
Director: Oliver Stone (*Platoon*)
Actor: Paul Newman (*The Color of Money*)
Actress: Marlee Matlin
　(*Children of a Lesser God*)

1987

LOS ANGELES FILM CRITICS
Film: *Hope and Glory*
Foreign Film: *Au Revoir les Enfants*
Director: John Boorman (*Hope and Glory*)
Actor: Steve Martin (*Roxanne*)
Actress: Holly Hunter (*Broadcast News*)

NATIONAL BOARD OF REVIEW
Film: *Empire of the Sun*
Foreign Film: *Jean de Florette/Manon of the Spring*
Director: Steven Spielberg (*Empire of the Sun*)
Actor: Michael Douglas (*Wall Street*)
Actress: Lillian Gish (*The Whales of August*) and
　Holly Hunter (*Broadcast News*)

NATIONAL SOCIETY OF FILM CRITICS
Film: *The Dead*
Director: John Boorman (*Hope and Glory*)
Actor: Steve Martin (*Roxanne*)
Actress: Emily Lloyd (*Wish You Were Here*)

NEW YORK FILM CRITICS
Film: *Broadcast News*
Foreign Film: *My Life as a Dog*
Director: James L. Brooks (*Broadcast News*)
Actor: Jack Nicholson (*Ironweed* and
　The Witches of Eastwick)
Actress: Holly Hunter (*Broadcast News*)

THE DISCERNING FILM LOVER'S GUIDE

ACADEMY AWARDS
Film: *The Last Emperor*
Foreign Film: *Babette's Feast*
Director: Bernardo Bertolucci
   (*The Last Emperor*)
Actor: Michael Douglas (*Wall Street*)
Actress: Cher (*Moonstruck*)

1988
LOS ANGELES FILM CRITICS
Film: *Little Dorrit*
Foreign Film: *Wings of Desire*
Director: David Cronenberg (*Dead Ringers*)
Actor: Tom Hanks (*Big*)
Actress: Genevieve Bujold (*Dead Ringers* and
   The Moderns)

NATIONAL BOARD OF REVIEW
Film: *Mississippi Burning*
Foreign Film: *Women on the Verge
   of a Nervous Breakdown*
Director: Alan Parker (*Mississippi Burning*)
Actor: Gene Hackman (*Mississippi Burning*)
Actress: Jodie Foster (*The Accused*)

NATIONAL SOCIETY OF FILM CRITICS
Film: *The Unbearable Lightness of Being*
Director: Philip Kaufman
   (*The Unbearable Lightness of Being*)
Actor: Michael Keaton (*Beetlejuice* and
   Clean and Sober)
Actress: Judy Davis (*High Tide*)

NEW YORK FILM CRITICS
Film: *The Accidental Tourist*
Foreign Film: *Women on the Verge of a Nervous
   Breakdown*
Director: Chris Menges (*A World Apart*)
Actor: Jeremy Irons (*Dead Ringers*)
Actress: Meryl Streep (*A Cry in the Dark*)

ACADEMY AWARDS
Film: *Rain Man*
Foreign Film: *Pelle the Conqueror*
Director: Barry Levinson (*Rain Man*)
Actor: Dustin Hoffman (*Rain Man*)
Actress: Jodie Foster (*The Accused*)

1989
LOS ANGELES FILM CRITICS
Film: *Do the Right Thing*
Foreign Film: *Distant Voices, Still Lives* and
   Story of Women
Director: Spike Lee (*Do the Right Thing*)
Actor: Daniel Day-Lewis (*My Left Foot*)
Actress: Andie MacDowell
   (*sex, lies, and videotape*) and
   Michelle Pfeiffer
   (*The Fabulous Baker Boys*)

NATIONAL BOARD OF REVIEW
Film: *Driving Miss Daisy*
Foreign Film: *Story of Women*
Director: Kenneth Branagh (*Henry V*)
Actor: Morgan Freeman (*Driving Miss Daisy*)
Actress: Michelle Pfeiffer
   (*The Fabulous Baker Boys*)

NATIONAL SOCIETY OF FILM CRITICS
Film: *Drugstore Cowboy*
Director: Gus Van Sant (*Drugstore Cowboy*)
Actor: Daniel Day-Lewis (*My Left Foot*)
Actress: Michelle Pfeiffer
   (*The Fabulous Baker Boys*)

NEW YORK FILM CRITICS
Film: *My Left Foot*
Foreign Film: *Story of Women*
Director: Paul Mazursky
   (*Enemies, A Love Story*)
Actor: Daniel Day-Lewis (*My Left Foot*)
Actress: Michelle Pfeiffer
   (*The Fabulous Baker Boys*)

ACADEMY AWARDS
Film: *Driving Miss Daisy*
Foreign Film: *Cinema Paradiso*
Director: Oliver Stone
   (*Born on the Fourth of July*)
Actor: Daniel Day-Lewis (*My Left Foot*)
Actress: Jessica Tandy (*Driving Miss Daisy*)

1990
LOS ANGELES FILM CRITICS
Film: *GoodFellas*
Foreign Film: *Life and Nothing But*
Director: Martin Scorsese (*GoodFellas*)
Actor: Jeremy Irons (*Reversal of Fortune*)
Actress: Anjelica Huston (*The Grifters* and
   The Witches)

NATIONAL BOARD OF REVIEW
Film: *Dances with Wolves*
Foreign Film: *Cyrano de Bergerac*
Director: Kevin Costner (*Dances with Wolves*)
Actor: Robert De Niro (*Awakenings*) and
   Robin Williams (*Awakenings*)
Actress: Mia Farrow (*Alice*)

NATIONAL SOCIETY OF FILM CRITICS
Film: *GoodFellas*
Foreign Film: *Ariel*
Director: Martin Scorsese (*GoodFellas*)
Actor: Jeremy Irons (*Reversal of Fortune*)
Actress: Anjelica Huston (*The Grifters*)

NEW YORK FILM CRITICS
Film: *GoodFellas*
Foreign Film: *The Nasty Girl*
Director: Martin Scorsese (*GoodFellas*)
Actor: Robert De Niro (*Awakenings*) and
   (*GoodFellas*)
Actress: Joanne Woodward
   (*Mr. and Mrs. Bridge*)

ACADEMY AWARDS
Film: *Dances with Wolves*
Foreign Film: *Journey of Hope*
Director: Kevin Costner (*Dances with Wolves*)
Actor: Jeremy Irons (*Reversal of Fortune*)
Actress: Kathy Bates (*Misery*)

1991
LOS ANGELES FILM CRITICS
Film: *Bugsy*
Foreign Film: *La Belle Noiseuse*
Director: Barry Levinson (*Bugsy*)
Actor: Nick Nolte (*The Prince of Tides*)
Actress: Mercedes Ruehl (*The Fisher King*)

NATIONAL BOARD OF REVIEW
Film: *The Silence of the Lambs*
Foreign Film: *Europa, Europa*
Director: Jonathan Demme
   (*The Silence of the Lambs*)
Actor: Warren Beatty (*Bugsy*)
Actress: Geena Davis (*Thelma and Louise*) and
   Susan Sarandon (*Thelma and Lousie*)

NEW YORK FILM CRITICS
Film: *The Silence of the Lambs*
Foreign Film: *Europa, Europa*
Director: Jonathan Demme
   (*The Silence of the Lambs*)
Actor: Anthony Hopkins
   (*The Silence of the Lambs*)
Actress: Jodie Foster (*The Silence of the Lambs*)

ACADEMY AWARDS
Film: *The Silence of the Lambs*
Foreign Film: *Mediterraneo*
Director: Jonathan Demme
   (*The Silence of the Lambs*)
Actor: Anthony Hopkins
   (*The Silence of the Lambs*)
Actress: Jodie Foster (*The Silence of the Lambs*)

1992
LOS ANGELES FILM CRITICS
Film: *Unforgiven*
Foreign Film: *The Crying Game*
Director: Clint Eastwood (*Unforgiven*)
Actor: Clint Eastwood (*Unforgiven*)
Actress: Emma Thompson (*Howards End*)

NATIONAL BOARD OF REVIEW
Film: *Howards End*
Foreign Film: *Indochine*
Director: James Ivory (*Howards End*)
Actor: Jack Lemmon (*Glengarry Glen Ross*)
Actress: Emma Thompson (*Howards End*)

NATIONAL SOCIETY OF FILM CRITICS
Film: *Unforgiven*
Foreign Film: *Raise the Red Lantern*
Director: Clint Eastwood (*Unforgiven*)
Actor: Stephen Rea (*The Crying Game*)
Actress: Emma Thompson (*Howards End*)

NEW YORK FILM CRITICS
Film: *The Player*
Foreign Film: *Raise the Red Lantern*
Director: Robert Altman (*The Player*)
Actor: Denzel Washington (*Malcolm X*)
Actress: Emma Thompson (*Howards End*)

ACADEMY AWARDS
Film: *Unforgiven*
Foreign Film: *Indochine*
Director: Clint Eastwood (*Unforgiven*)
Actor: Al Pacino (*Scent of a Woman*)
Actress: Emma Thompson (*Howards End*)

1993

LOS ANGELES FILM CRITICS
Film: *Schindler's List*
Foreign Film: *Farewell My Concubine*
Director: Jane Campion (*The Piano*)
Actor: Anthony Hopkins (*The Remains of the Day* and *Shadowlands*)
Actress: Holly Hunter (*The Piano*)

NATIONAL BOARD OF REVIEW
Film: *Schindler's List*
Foreign Film: *Farewell My Concubine*
Director: Martin Scorsese (*The Age of Innocence*)
Actor: Anthony Hopkins (*The Remains of the Day* and *Shadowlands*)
Actress: Holly Hunter (*The Piano*)

NATIONAL SOCIETY OF FILM CRITICS
Film: *Schindler's List*
Foreign Film: *The Story of Qiu Ju*
Director: Steven Spielberg (*Schindler's List*)
Actor: David Thewlis (*Naked*)
Actress: Holly Hunter (*The Piano*)

NEW YORK FILM CRITICS
Film: *Schindler's List*
Foreign Film: *Farewell My Concubine*
Director: Jane Campion (*The Piano*)
Actor: David Thewlis (*Naked*)
Actress: Holly Hunter (*The Piano*)

ACADEMY AWARDS
Film: *Schindler's List*
Foreign Film: *Belle Epoque*
Director: Steven Spielberg (*Schindler's List*)
Actor: Tom Hanks (*Philadelphia*)
Actress: Holly Hunter (*The Piano*)

1994

LOS ANGELES FILM CRITICS
Film: *Pulp Fiction*
Foreign Film: *Red*
Director: Quentin Tarantino (*Pulp Fiction*)
Actor: John Travolta (*Pulp Fiction*)
Actress: Jessica Lange (*Blue Sky*)

NATIONAL BOARD OF REVIEW
Film: *Forrest Gump* and *Pulp Fiction*
Foreign Film: *Eat Drink Man Woman*
Director: Quentin Tarantino (*Pulp Fiction*)
Actor: Tom Hanks (*Forrest Gump*)
Actress: Miranda Richardson (*Tom & Viv*)

NATIONAL SOCIETY OF FILM CRITICS
Film: *Pulp Fiction*
Foreign Film: *Red*
Director: Quentin Tarantino (*Pulp Fiction*)
Actor: Paul Newman (*Nobody's Fool*)
Actress: Jennifer Jason Leigh (*Mrs. Parker & the Vicious Circle*)

NEW YORK FILM CRITICS
Film: *Quiz Show*
Foreign Film: *Red*
Director: Quentin Tarantino (*Pulp Fiction*)
Actor: Paul Newman (*Nobody's Fool*)
Actress: Linda Fiorentino (*The Last Seduction*)

ACADEMY AWARDS
Film: *Forrest Gump*
Foreign Film: *Burnt by the Sun*
Director: Robert Zemeckis (*Forrest Gump*)
Actor: Tom Hanks (*Forrest Gump*)
Actress: Jessica Lange (*Blue Sky*)

1995

LOS ANGELES FILM CRITICS
Film: *Leaving Las Vegas*
Foreign Film: *Wild Reeds*
Director: Mike Figgis (*Leaving Las Vegas*)
Actor: Nicolas Cage (*Leaving Las Vegas*)
Actress: Elisabeth Shue (*Leaving Las Vegas*)

NATIONAL BOARD OF REVIEW
Film: *Sense and Sensibility*
Foreign Film: *Shanghai Triad*
Director: Ang Lee (*Sense and Sensibility*)
Actor: Nicolas Cage (*Leaving Las Vegas*)
Actress: Emma Thompson (*Carrington* and *Sense and Sensibility*)

NATIONAL SOCIETY OF FILM CRITICS
Film: *Babe*
Foreign Film: *Wild Reeds*
Director: Mike Figgis (*Leaving Las Vegas*)
Actor: Nicolas Cage (*Leaving Las Vegas*)
Actress: Elisabeth Shue (*Leaving Las Vegas*)

NEW YORK FILM CRITICS
Film: *Leaving Las Vegas*
Foreign Film: *Wild Reeds*
Director: Ang Lee (*Sense and Sensibility*)
Actor: Nicolas Cage (*Leaving Las Vegas*)
Actress: Jennifer Jason Leigh (*Georgia*)

ACADEMY AWARDS
Film: *Braveheart*
Foreign Film: *Antonia's Line*
Director: Mel Gibson (*Braveheart*)
Actor: Nicolas Cage (*Leaving Las Vegas*)
Actress: Susan Sarandon (*Dead Man Walking*)

1996

LOS ANGELES FILM CRITICS
Film: *Secrets and Lies*
Foreign Film: *La Ceremonie*
Director: Mike Leigh (*Secrets and Lies*)
Actor: Geoffrey Rush (*Shine*)
Actress: Brenda Blethyn (*Secrets and Lies*)

NATIONAL BOARD OF REVIEW
Film: *Shine*
Foreign Film: *Ridicule*
Director: Joel Coen (*Fargo*)
Actor: Tom Cruise (*Jerry Maguire*)
Actress: Frances McDormand (*Fargo*)

NATIONAL SOCIETY OF FILM CRITICS
Film: *Breaking the Waves*
Director: Lars von Trier (*Breaking the Waves*)
Actor: Eddie Murphy (*The Nutty Professor*)
Actress: Emily Watson (*Breaking the Waves*)

NEW YORK FILM CRITICS
Film: *Fargo*
Foreign Film: *The White Balloon*
Director: Lars von Trier (*Breaking the Waves*)
Actor: Geoffrey Rush (*Shine*)
Actress: Emily Watson (*Breaking the Waves*)

ACADEMY AWARDS
Film: *The English Patient*
Foreign Film: *Kolya*
Director: Anthony Minghella (*The English Patient*)
Actor: Geoffrey Rush (*Shine*)
Actress: Frances McDormand (*Fargo*)

ORDER FORM

Title	Qty.	Price	Ext. Price

Subtotal	
Tax*	
Shipping	
Total	

Shipping Charges: Please include $4.00 shipping and handling for the first film and $1.50 for each additional film. **Allow 3-4 weeks for delivery.** Express UPS shipping is available for additional charge, please call for details. **Overseas Shipping:** Include $8.00 (USD) for the first film and $5.00 (USD) for each additional film.

Payment: Please send payment with order. Send Check, Money Order or Credit Card information. Check Orders please allow one extra week for delivery.

Tax: Residents of the following areas must apply local sales tax : 7% Philadelphia; 6% rest of PA.; 6% N.J.; 8¼% N.Y.C.; 4% rest of N.Y.

Name: _____

Address: _____

City: _____ State: _____ Zip: _____

Home Phone: _____ Work Phone: _____

Payment Method: ❑ Check Enclosed ❑ Money Order ❑ Visa ❑ M.C. ❑ Amex ❑ Discover

Credit Card #: _____ Exp:_____

Authorizing Signature: _____

Check here for preferred shipping ❑ UPS (No P.O. Boxes) ❑ U.S. Mail

Send this form to:
TLA Entertainment Group, Inc.
1520 Locust Street
Suite 200
Philadelphia, PA 19102
or fax it to:
215-790-1502
or call :
1-800-333-8521 or
1-215-790-1510 *(local)*

visit the tla website: www.tlavideo.com • email: sales@tlavideo.com